W9-CQU-814

The Evidence Bible

Presented to:

____

By:

____

Date:

____

The Evidence Bible

NKJV

NEW KING JAMES VERSION®

Commentary by

RAY COMFORT

Bridge-Logos

Newberry, Florida 32669

The Evidence Bible
Commentary by Ray Comfort

Published by:
Bridge-Logos, Inc.
Newberry, FL 32669, USA
www.bridgelogos.com

Edited by Lynn Copeland

Design and production by Genesis Group, Inc. (www.genesis-group.net)

Printed in India

ISBN 978-0-88270-525-5 Hardback
ISBN 978-0-88270-507-1 Duo tone brown/beige
ISBN 978-0-88270-515-6 Duo tone pink/brown

Reprinted June 2020

Please send notification of any errors to: revisions@evidencebible.com.

Contents

Springboards for Preaching and Witnessing

Principles of Growth for the New and Growing Christian

Points for Open-Air Preaching

In-depth Comments

God

Jesus Christ

The Bible

Evangelism

Evolution/Creation

Religion

Training Children

Miscellaneous

Evangelism Aids

Common Questions & Objections

God

Jesus Christ

The Bible

Sin

Heaven & Hell

Excuses

Faith

Salvation

The Ten Commandments (The Law)

Personal Witnessing

Miscellaneous

Leading Sinners to Jesus

Follow these linked verses to lead a sinner to the Savior:

Matt. 5:21,22; 5:27,28; Mark 7:20–23; 12:29–31; Psa. 51:6; Rom. 2:15,16; 1 Cor. 6:9,10; Rev. 21:8; Heb. 9:22; John 3:16,17; Rom. 10:9; 10:12

Preface

THANK YOU for picking up this Bible. If you are a Christian, there is no higher calling than to reach out to the lost. If you are not a Christian, then I'm sure you will find this publication to be very helpful when it comes to the most important of issues.

Bill Bright, founder of the international ministry Campus Crusade for Christ, said that "only two percent of believers in America regularly share their faith in Christ with others" (*The Coming Revival*, p. 65). I believe one reason for this tragedy is that the Body of Christ hasn't been suitably equipped. What soldier is going to run into the heat of battle, facing modern warfare, armed only with a feather duster?

However, a soldier who is thoroughly equipped with state-of-the-art weapons and trained in their use will find that his very weapons give him courage. *The Evidence Bible* will equip the most timid of Christ's soldiers with powerful weapons to conquer disbelief, doubt, skepticism, and fear.

As you read, you will learn that you need not feel intimidated with themes such as evolution, atheism, humanism, relativism, secular intellectualism, or any other "ism."

Much of my commentary on evangelism is drawn from my experiences open-air preaching almost daily for twelve years at "Speaker's Corner" in the city of Christchurch, in my native New Zealand. Hecklers would often ask probing questions about my faith and pose numerous objections to the gospel message I preached. During those years, I collected information that successfully rebuffed them, and wrote it in the front of my Bible. My trusty and "pregnant" Bible was the mother that gave birth to *The Evidence Bible*.

This Bible will show you that, as a Christian, you stand on intellectually solid and spiritually immovable rock. You will find in these pages quotes from many well known people, both godly and secular. The apostle Paul, when he preached to the Athenians on Mars Hill, cited secular Greek poets (Acts 17:28). Paul obviously wasn't endorsing their lifestyles or promoting their poetry. He was simply using their words, familiar to his listeners, as a springboard for the gospel. And you can learn to do the same thing.

While *The Evidence Bible* is a study Bible that can strengthen and encourage the faith of any believing Christian, it is also an evangelistic tool. And the primary purpose of this Bible is to bring the message of salvation to the unsaved.

Years ago, I had the incredible experience of floating in the Dead Sea. It is impossible to sink into its waters due to the high salt content and rich mineral deposits. The contemporary Body of Christ has become much like the Dead Sea, because there is an insufficient outflow from the Church to the world. So the Body of Christ (though rich in many ways) is evangelistically dead because it has stopped giving out what it has received.

Make sure you give out what you take in. Become familiar with the commentary and quotes included here. If possible, take this Bible with you and keep it handy so that, when you share your faith, you can open it and read portions to the unsaved.

Non-Christians often don't realize how many great men and women of history believed and loved the Word of God. They may also be ignorant of the Bible's wealth of scientific and medical knowledge. Perhaps one simple quote from a famous person of the past or present may be enough to spark a nonbeliever's interest in Holy Scripture. Perhaps God will use your words to bring the message of eternal life to those who sit in the shadow of death, unaware that eternal life is within their reach.

ABOUT THE TRANSLATION

Although *The Evidence Bible* was originally released using the King James Version, we decided to use the New King James Version. This was to broaden the readership, because as much as I love the old KJV, I have to admit that words such as "bewray," "concupiscence," "decketh," "gainsay," "haply," "howbeit," "intreaty," "waxeth," and "wot" are no longer used in contemporary language. Translating such words into contemporary English is not unlike translating the Bible into Chinese in order to distribute God's Word in a Chinese-speaking country. Would I publish a Bible in the King James English for the Chinese? No, because they don't speak that language. Would God's wrath come upon us for producing a Bible in Chinese so Chinese speakers could understand the Scriptures? I don't think so. Obviously, the Bible should be translated into the language spoken in each country; otherwise, it won't make sense to readers there.

Heaven no doubt rejoiced when the first English translation of God's Word gave light to those whom the Roman Catholic church had kept in the dark by requiring that the Bible be in Latin. I'm sure "*in principio creavit Deus caelum et terram*" makes more sense to you when you read it as "In the beginning God created the heavens and the earth."

Let's now go forward to this day and age. The King James English Bible was written for the English (another country) when they spoke another language (what we commonly call King James English). Satan didn't say, "Yea, hath God said?" (unless you think Satan and Adam and Eve spoke English). The verse was originally written in Hebrew, but was translated into English by some kind folks so that the English speakers in the 1600s could understand the Word of God.

The New King James Version does exactly the same thing today. It takes words that people don't understand and gives the contemporary equivalent. This version doesn't omit verses about the blood of Christ, repentance, or the deity of Christ; nor does it change the meaning of any verse or drop one jot or tittle from God's Word.

In closing, let me share one of the greatest encouragements in my personal life. It happened when actor Kirk Cameron called our ministry. Even though he had been a Christian for many years,

God had deeply touched his life through our book *God Has a Wonderful Plan for Your Life* (many of the principles of which are included in this commentary). So if you appreciate the principles expounded in the commentary of *The Evidence Bible* and you want more information, please go to www.livingwaters.com.

Again, may God bless you for picking up this Bible, and may He use you and this Bible to reach this dying world.

RAY COMFORT

HOW TO USE THIS BOOK

- Discover the answers to common **Questions & Objections** so you'll be ready to give a defense as you encounter these in witnessing.
- Read **in-depth articles** for a closer look at topics to help you better understand and communicate the Christian faith.
- In **Points for Open-air Preaching**, gain tips on how to draw and hold a crowd, as well as general witnessing guidelines.
- Read **Springboards for Open-air Preaching** for interesting stories that will help explain spiritual truths in both preaching and one-to-one witnessing.
- Learn **Principles of Growth for the New and Growing Christian** to aid healthy spiritual growth in the new believer's life.
- Follow **cross-references** to read more about a topic.
- Refer to the **Commentary Index** to find comments on items of interest.
- Begin by reading **"Why Christianity?"** (on page xxv) to understand why Christianity is unique among religions and why the gospel is indeed "good news."

Acknowledgments

I am very grateful to my lifelong friend Richard Gunther for his fine cartoons, and to Darin Rhue, Alex Ruiz, Joe Potter, Joel Hughs, and Scott Harvey for their quality illustrations. My gratitude also goes to my beloved wife, Sue; my sons, Daniel and Jacob; as well as to Rachel and Emeal Zwayne; Sarah and Becky Comfort; and to my good friend Mark Spence. My very special thanks to Lynn Copeland of the Genesis Group for her patience, her love of the truth, her concern for the lost, and for her wonderful editorial work. Editing this Bible was a Goliath task, but she courageously ran at this giant in the name of her God. She is the ultimate perfectionist, and it is an honor to work with someone who strives for excellence when it comes to representing the kingdom of God. I thank God for the day He brought her into my life. She made a big sow's ear into a smooth silk purse. I am also indebted to my friends at Bridge-Logos Publishers.

Preface to the New King James Version®

PURPOSE

In the preface to the 1611 edition, the translators of the Authorized Version, known popularly as the King James Bible, state that it was not their purpose "to make a new translation . . . but to make a good one better." Indebted to the earlier work of William Tyndale and others, they saw their best contribution to consist in revising and enhancing the excellence of the English versions which had sprung from the Reformation of the sixteenth century. In harmony with the purpose of the King James scholars, the translators and editors of the present work have not pursued a goal of innovation. They have perceived the Holy Bible, New King James Version, as a continuation of the labors of the earlier translators, thus unlocking for today's readers the spiritual treasures found especially in the Authorized Version of the Holy Scriptures.

A LIVING LEGACY

For nearly four hundred years, and throughout several revisions of its English form, the King James Bible has been deeply revered among the English-speaking peoples of the world. The precision of translation for which it is historically renowned, and its majesty of style, have enabled that monumental version of the word of God to become the mainspring of the religion, language, and legal foundations of our civilization.

Although the Elizabethan period and our own era share in zeal for technical advance, the former period was more aggressively devoted to classical learning. Along with this awakened concern for the classics came a flourishing companion interest in the Scriptures, an interest that was enlivened by the conviction that the manuscripts were providentially handed down and were a trustworthy record of the inspired Word of God. The King James translators were committed to producing an English Bible that would be a precise translation, and by no means a paraphrase or a broadly approximate rendering. On the one hand, the scholars were almost as familiar with the original languages of the Bible as with their native English. On the other hand, their reverence for the divine Author and His Word assured a translation of the Scriptures in which only a principle of utmost accuracy could be accepted.

In 1786 Catholic scholar Alexander Geddes said of the King James Bible, "If accuracy and strictest attention to the letter of the text be supposed to constitute an excellent version, this is of all versions the most excellent." George Bernard Shaw became a literary legend in the twentieth century because of his severe and often humorous criticisms of our most cherished values. Surprisingly, however, Shaw pays the following tribute to the scholars commissioned by King James: "The translation was extraordinarily well done because to the translators what they

were translating was not merely a curious collection of ancient books written by different authors in different stages of culture, but the Word of God divinely revealed through His chosen and expressly inspired scribes. In this conviction they carried out their work with boundless reverence and care and achieved a beautifully artistic result." History agrees with these estimates. Therefore, while seeking to unveil the excellent *form* of the traditional English Bible, special care has also been taken in the present edition to preserve the work of *precision* which is the legacy of the 1611 translators.

COMPLETE EQUIVALENCE IN TRANSLATION

Where new translation has been necessary in the New King James Version, the most complete representation of the original has been rendered by considering the history of usage and etymology of words in their contexts. This principle of complete equivalence seeks to preserve *all* of the information in the text, while presenting it in good literary form. Dynamic equivalence, a recent procedure in Bible translation, commonly results in paraphrasing where a more literal rendering is needed to reflect a specific and vital sense. For example, complete equivalence truly renders the original text in expressions such as "lifted her voice and wept" (Gen. 21:16); "I gave you cleanness of teeth" (Amos 4:6); "Jesus met them, saying, 'Rejoice!'" (Matt. 28:9); and "Woman, what does your concern have to do with Me?" (John 2:4). Complete equivalence translates fully, in order to provide an English text that is both accurate and readable.

In keeping with the principle of complete equivalence, it is the policy to translate interjections which are commonly omitted in modern language renderings of the Bible. As an example, the interjection *behold*, in the older King James editions, continues to have a place in English usage, especially in dramatically calling attention to a spectacular scene, or an event of profound importance such as the Immanuel prophecy of Isaiah 7:14. Consequently, *behold* is retained for these occasions in the present edition. However, the Hebrew and Greek originals for this word can be translated variously, depending on the circumstances in the passage. Therefore, in addition to *behold*, words such as *indeed*, *look*, *see*, and *surely* are also rendered to convey the appropriate sense suggested by the context in each case.

In faithfulness to God and to our readers, it was deemed appropriate that all participating scholars sign a statement affirming their belief in the verbal and plenary inspiration of Scripture, and in the inerrancy of the original autographs.

DEVOTIONAL QUALITY

The King James scholars readily appreciated the intrinsic beauty of divine revelation. They accordingly disciplined their talents to render well-chosen English words of their time, as well as a graceful, often musical arrangement of language, which has stirred the hearts of Bible readers through the years. The translators, the committees, and the editors of the present edition, while sensitive to the late-twentieth-century English idiom, and while adhering faithfully to the Hebrew, Aramaic, and Greek texts, have sought to maintain those lyrical and devotional qualities that are so highly regarded in the Authorized Version. This devotional quality is especially apparent in the poetic and prophetic books, although even the relatively plain style of the Gospels and Epistles cannot strictly be likened, as sometimes suggested, to modern newspaper style. The Koine Greek of the New Testament is influenced by the Hebrew background of the writers, for whom even the gospel narratives were not merely flat utterance, but often song in various degrees of rhythm.

THE STYLE

Students of the Bible applaud the timeless devotional character of our historic Bible. Yet it is also universally understood that our language, like all living languages, has undergone profound change since 1611. Subsequent revisions of the King James Bible have sought to keep abreast of changes in English speech. The present work is a further step toward this objective. Where obsolescence and other reading difficulties exist, present-day vocabulary, punctuation, and grammar have been carefully integrated. Words representing ancient objects, such as *chariot* and *phylactery*, have no modern substitutes and are therefore retained.

A special feature of the New King James Version is its conformity to the thought flow of the 1611 Bible. The reader discovers that the sequence and selection of words, phrases, and clauses of the new edition, while much clearer, are so close to the traditional that there is remarkable ease in listening to the reading of either edition while following with the other.

In the discipline of translating biblical and other ancient languages, a standard method of transliteration, that is, the English spelling of untranslated words, such as names of persons and places, has never been commonly adopted. In keeping with the design of the present work, the King James spelling of untranslated words is retained, although made uniform throughout. For example, instead of the spellings *Isaiah* and *Elijah* in the Old Testament, and *Esaias* and *Elias* in the New Testament, *Isaiah* and *Elijah* now appear in both Testaments.

King James doctrinal and theological terms, for example, *propitiation*, *justification*, and *sanctification*, are generally familiar to English-speaking peoples. Such terms have been retained except where the original language indicates need for a more precise translation.

Readers of the Authorized Version will immediately be struck by the absence of several pronouns: *thee*, *thou*, and *ye* are replaced by the simple *you*, while *your* and *yours* are substituted for *thy* and *thine* as applicable. *Thee*, *thou*, *thy* and *thine* were once forms of address to express a special relationship to human as well as divine persons. These pronouns are no longer part of our language. However, reverence for God in the present work is preserved by capitalizing pronouns, including *You*, *Your*, and *Yours*, which refer to Him. Additionally, capitalization of these pronouns benefits the reader by clearly distinguishing divine and human persons referred to in a passage. Without such capitalization the distinction is often obscure, because the antecedent of a pronoun is not always clear in the English translation.

In addition to the pronoun usages of the seventeenth century, the *-eth* and *-est* verb endings, so familiar in the earlier King James editions, are now obsolete. Unless a speaker is schooled in these verb endings, there is common difficulty in selecting the correct form to be used with a given subject of the verb in vocal prayer. That is, should we use *love*, *loveth*, or *lovest*? *do*, *doeth*, *doest*, or *dost*? *have*, *hath*, or *hast*? Because these forms are obsolete, contemporary English usage has been substituted for the previous verb endings.

In older editions of the King James Version, the frequency of the connective *and* far exceeded the limits of present English usage. Also, biblical linguists agree that the Hebrew and Greek original words for this conjunction may commonly be translated otherwise, depending on the immediate context. Therefore, instead of *and*, alternatives such as *also*, *but*, *however*, *now*, *so*, *then*, and *thus* are accordingly rendered in the present edition, when the original language permits.

The real character of the Authorized Version does not reside in its archaic pronouns or verbs or other grammatical forms of the seventeenth century, but

rather in the care taken by its scholars to impart the letter and spirit of the original text in a majestic and reverent style.

THE FORMAT

The format of the New King James Version is designed to enhance the vividness and devotional quality of the Holy Scriptures:

- Subject headings assist the reader to identify topics and transitions in the biblical content.
- Words or phrases in *italics* indicate expressions in the original language which require clarification by additional English words, as also done throughout the history of the King James Bible.
- *Oblique* type in the New Testament indicates a quotation from the Old Testament.
- Poetry is structured as contemporary verse to reflect the poetic form and beauty of the passage in the original language.
- The covenant name of God was usually translated from the Hebrew as LORD or GOD (using capital letters as shown) in the King James Old Testament. This tradition is maintained. In the present edition the name is so capitalized whenever the covenant name is quoted in the New Testament from a passage in the Old Testament.

THE OLD TESTAMENT TEXT

The Hebrew Bible has come down to us through the scrupulous care of ancient scribes who copied the original text in successive generations. By the sixth century A.D. the scribes were succeeded by a group known as the Masoretes, who continued to preserve the sacred Scriptures for another five hundred years in a form known as the Masoretic Text. Babylonia, Palestine, and Tiberias were the main centers of Masoretic activity; but by the tenth century A.D. the Masoretes of Tiberias, led by the family of ben Asher, gained the ascendancy. Through subsequent editions, the ben Asher text became in the twelfth century the only recognized form of the Hebrew Scriptures.

Daniel Bomberg printed the first Rabbinic Bible in 1516–17; that work was followed in 1524–25 by a second edition prepared by Jacob ben Chayyim and also published by Bomberg. The text of ben Chayyim was adopted in most subsequent Hebrew Bibles, including those used by the King James translators. The ben Chayyim text was also used for the first two editions of Rudolph Kittel's *Biblia Hebraica* of 1906 and 1912. In 1937 Paul Kahle published a third edition of *Biblia Hebraica*. This edition was based on the oldest dated manuscript of the ben Asher text, the Leningrad Manuscript B19a (A.D. 1008), which Kahle regarded as superior to that used by ben Chayyim.

For the New King James Version the text used was the 1967/1977 Stuttgart edition of the *Biblia Hebraica*, with frequent comparisons being made with the Bomberg edition of 1524–25. The Septuagint (Greek) Version of the Old Testament and the Latin Vulgate also were consulted. In addition to referring to a variety of ancient versions of the Hebrew Scriptures, the New King James Version draws on the resources of relevant manuscripts from the Dead Sea caves. In the few places where the Hebrew was so obscure that the 1611 King James was compelled to follow one of the versions, but where information is now available to resolve the problems, the New King James Version follows the Hebrew text. Significant variations are recorded in the New King James translators' notes.

THE NEW TESTAMENT TEXT

There is more manuscript support for the New Testament than for any other body of ancient literature. Over five thousand Greek, eight thousand Latin, and

many more manuscripts in other languages attest the integrity of the New Testament. There is only one basic New Testament used by Protestants, Roman Catholics, and Orthodox, by conservatives and liberals. Minor variations in hand copying have appeared through the centuries, before mechanical printing began about A.D. 1450.

Some variations exist in the spelling of Greek words, in word order, and in similar details. These ordinarily do not show up in translation and do not affect the sense of the text in any way.

Other manuscript differences such as omission or inclusion of a word or a clause, and two paragraphs in the Gospels, should not overshadow the overwhelming degree of *agreement* which exists among the ancient records. Bible readers may be assured that the most important differences in English New Testaments of today are due, not to manuscript divergence, but to the way in which translators view the task of translation: How literally should the text be rendered? How does the translator view the matter of biblical inspiration? Does the translator adopt a paraphrase when a literal rendering would be quite clear and more to the point? The New King James Version follows the historic precedent of the Authorized Version in maintaining a literal approach to translation, except where the idiom of the original language cannot be translated directly into our tongue.

The King James New Testament was based on the traditional text of the Greek-speaking churches, first published in 1516, and later called the Textus Receptus or Received Text. Although based on the relatively few available manuscripts, these were representative of many more which existed at the time but only became known later. In the late nineteenth century, B. Westcott and F. Hort taught that this text had been officially edited by the fourth-century church, but a total lack of historical evidence for this event has forced a revision of the theory. It is now widely held that the Byzantine Text that largely supports the Textus Receptus has as much right as the Alexandrian or any other tradition to be weighed in determining the text of the New Testament.

Since the 1880s most contemporary translations of the New Testament have relied upon a relatively few manuscripts discovered chiefly in the late nineteenth and early twentieth centuries. Such translations depend primarily on two manuscripts, Codex Vaticanus and Codex Sinaiticus, because of their greater age. The Greek text obtained by using these sources and the related papyri (our most ancient manuscripts) is known as the Alexandrian Text. However, some scholars have grounds for doubting the faithfulness of Vaticanus and Sinaiticus, since they often disagree with one another, and Sinaiticus exhibits excessive omission.

A third viewpoint of New Testament scholarship holds that the best text is based on the consensus of the majority of existing Greek manuscripts. This text is called the Majority Text. Most of these manuscripts are in substantial agreement. Even though many are late, and none is earlier than the fifth century, usually their readings are verified by papyri, ancient versions, quotations from the early church fathers, or a combination of these. The Majority Text is similar to the Textus Receptus, but it corrects those readings which have little or no support in the Greek manuscript tradition.

Today, scholars agree that the science of New Testament textual criticism is in a state of flux. Very few scholars still favor the Textus Receptus as such, and then often for its historical prestige as the text of Luther, Calvin, Tyndale, and the King James Version. For about a century most have followed a Critical Text (so called because it is edited according to specific principles of textual criticism)

which depends heavily upon the Alexandrian type of text. More recently many have abandoned this Critical Text (which is quite similar to the one edited by Westcott and Hort) for one that is more eclectic. Finally, a small but growing number of scholars prefer the Majority Text, which is close to the traditional text except in the Revelation.

In light of these facts, and also because the New King James Version is the fifth revision of a historic document translated from specific Greek texts, the editors decided to retain the traditional text in the body of the New Testament and to indicate major Critical and Majority Text variant readings in the translators' notes. Although these variations are duly indicated in the translators' notes of the present edition, it is most important to emphasize that fully eighty-five percent of the New Testament text is the same in the Textus Receptus, the Alexandrian Text, and the Majority Text.

NEW KING JAMES TRANSLATORS' NOTES

Significant textual explanations, alternate translations, and New Testament citations of Old Testament passages are supplied in the New King James translators' notes.

Important textual variants in the Old Testament are identified in a standard form.

The textual notes in the present edition of the New Testament make no evaluation of readings, but do clearly indicate the manuscript sources of readings. They objectively present the facts without such tendentious remarks as "the best manuscripts omit" or "the most reliable manuscripts read." Such notes are value judgments that differ according to varying viewpoints on the text. By giving a clearly defined set of variants the New King James Version benefits readers of all textual persuasions.

Where significant variations occur in the New Testament Greek manuscripts, textual notes are classified as follows:

NU-Text

These variations from the traditional text generally represent the Alexandrian or Egyptian type of text described previously in "The New Testament Text." They are found in the Critical Text published in the twenty-seventh edition of the Nestle-Aland Greek New Testament (N) and in the United Bible Societies' fourth edition (U), hence the acronym, "NU-Text."

M-Text

This symbol indicates points of variation in the Majority Text from the traditional text, as also previously discussed in "The New Testament Text." It should be noted that M stands for whatever reading is printed in the published *Greek New Testament According to the Majority Text*, whether supported by overwhelming, strong, or only a divided majority textual tradition.

The textual notes reflect the scholarship of the past two centuries and will assist the reader to observe the variations between the different manuscript traditions of the New Testament. Such information is generally not available in English translations of the New Testament.

Why Christianity?

Solving life's most important question

THE CHOICE

IMAGINE the excitement you would have if I offered you a choice of four gifts:

- The original Mona Lisa
- The keys to a brand new Lamborghini
- A million dollars in cash
- A parachute

You can pick only one. Which would you choose? Before you decide, here's some information that will help you to make the wisest choice: *You have to jump 10,000 feet out of an airplane.*

Does that help you to connect the dots? It should, because you *need* the parachute. It's the only one of the four gifts that will help with your dilemma. The others may have some value, but they are useless when it comes to facing the law of gravity in a 10,000-foot fall. The knowledge that you will have to jump should produce a healthy fear in you—and that kind of fear is good because it can save your life. Remember that.

Now think of the four major religions:

- Hinduism
- Buddhism
- Islam
- Christianity

Which one should you choose? Before you decide, here's some information that will help you determine which one is the wisest choice: All of humanity stands on the edge of eternity. We are *all* going to die. We will all have to pass through the door of death. It could happen to us in twenty years, or in six months, ...or today. For most of humanity, death is a huge and terrifying plummet into the unknown. So what should we do?

Do you remember how it was your knowledge of the jump that produced that healthy fear, and that fear helped you to make the right choice? You know what the law of gravity can do to you. In the same way, we are going to look at another law, and hopefully your knowledge of what it can do to you will help you make the right choice, about life's greatest issue. So, stay with me—and remember to let fear work for you.

THE LEAP

After we die we have to face what is called "the law of sin and death."[1] We know that Law as "The Ten Commandments."

So let's look at that Law and see how you will do when you face it on Judgment Day. Have you loved God above all else? Is He first in your life? He should be. He's given you your life and everything that is dear to you. Do you love Him with *all* of your heart, soul, mind, and strength? That's the requirement of the First Commandment. Or have you broken the Second Commandment by making a god in your mind that you're comfortable with—where you say, "My god is a loving and merciful god who would never send anyone to hell"? That god does not exist; he's a figment of the imagination. To create a god in your mind (your own image of God) is something the Bible calls "idolatry." Idolaters will not enter heaven.

Have you ever used God's name in vain, as a cuss word to express disgust? That's called "blasphemy," and it's very serious in God's sight. This is breaking the Third Commandment, and the Bible says God will not hold him guiltless who takes His name in vain.

Have you always honored your parents implicitly, and kept the Sabbath holy? If not, you have broken the Fourth and Fifth Commandments. Have you ever hated someone? The Bible says, "Whoever hates his brother is a murderer."[2]

The Seventh is "You shall not commit adultery," but Jesus said, "Whoever looks at a woman to lust for her has already committed adultery with her in his heart"[3] (the Seventh Commandment includes sex before marriage). Have you ever looked with lust or had sex outside of marriage? If so, you've violated that Commandment.

Have you ever lied? Ever stolen anything, regardless of value? If you have, then you're a lying thief. The Bible tells us, "Lying lips are an abomination to the Lord,"[4] because He is a God of truth and holiness. Have you coveted (jealously desired) other people's things? This is a violation of the Tenth Commandment.

LITTLE JESSICA

So that is God's moral Law that we each will face. We will be without excuse when we stand before God because He gave us our conscience to know right from wrong. Each time we lie, steal, commit adultery, murder, and so on, we know that it's wrong. So here is the crucial question. On Judgment Day, when God judges you, will you be found innocent or guilty of breaking this Law? *Think before you answer.* Will you go to heaven or hell? The Bible warns that all murderers, idolaters, liars, thieves, fornicators, and adulterers will end up in hell.[5] So where does that leave you?

Perhaps the thought of going to hell doesn't scare you, because you don't believe in it. That's like standing in the open door of a plane 10,000 feet off the ground and saying, "I don't believe there will be any consequences if I jump without a parachute."

To say that there will be no consequences for breaking God's Law is to say that God is unjust, that He is evil. This is why.

On February 24, 2005, a nine-year-old girl was reported missing from her home in Homosassa, Florida. Three weeks later, police discovered that she had been kidnapped, brutally raped, and then buried alive. Little Jessica Lunsford was found tied up, in a kneeling position, clutching a stuffed toy.

HOW DO YOU REACT?

How do you feel toward the man who murdered that helpless little girl in such an unspeakably cruel way? Are you angered? I hope so. I hope you are *outraged.* If you were completely indifferent to her fate, it would reveal something horrible about your character.

Do you think that God is indifferent to such acts of evil? You can bet your precious soul He is not. He is *outraged* by them.

The fury of Almighty God against evil is *evidence* of His goodness. If He wasn't angered, He wouldn't be good. We cannot separate God's goodness from His anger. Again, if God is good by nature, He *must* be unspeakably angry at wickedness.

But His goodness is so great that His anger isn't confined to the evils of rape and murder. Nothing is hidden from His pure and holy eyes. He is outraged by torture, terrorism, abortion, theft, lying, adultery, fornication, pedophilia, homosexuality, and blasphemy. He also sees our *thought-life*, and He will judge us for the *hidden* sins of the heart: for lust, hatred, rebellion, greed, unclean imaginations, ingratitude, selfishness, jealousy, pride, envy, deceit, etc. Jesus warned, "But I say to you that for every *idle word* men may speak, they will give account of it in the day of judgment"[6] (emphasis added).

The Bible says that God's wrath "abides"

on each of us,[7] and that every time we sin, we're storing up wrath[8] that will be revealed on Judgment Day. We are even told that we are "*by nature* children of wrath"[9] (emphasis added). Sinning against God comes naturally to us—and we naturally earn His anger by our sins.

INSTANT DEATH

Many people believe that because God is good, He will forgive everyone, and let all sinners into heaven. But they misunderstand His goodness. When Moses once asked to see God's glory, God told him that he couldn't see Him and live. Moses would instantly die if he looked upon God. Consider this:

> [God said] "*I will make all My goodness pass before you* . . . So it shall be, *while My glory passes by*, that I will put you in the cleft of the rock, and will cover you with My hand while I pass by."[10]

Notice that all of God's glory was displayed in His "goodness." The *goodness* of God would have killed Moses instantly *because of his personal sinfulness*. The fire of God's goodness would have consumed him, like a cup of water dropped onto the surface of the sun. The only way any of us can stand in the presence of God is to be pure in heart. Jesus said, "Blessed are the pure in heart, for they shall see God."[11] But as we've seen by looking at the Law, not a single one of us is "pure in heart."

These are extremely fearful thoughts, because the God we are speaking about is nothing like the commonly accepted image. He is not a benevolent Father-figure, who is happily smiling upon sinful humanity.

In the midst of these frightening thoughts, remember to let fear work for you. The fear of God is the healthiest fear you can have. The Bible calls it "the beginning of wisdom."[12]

Again, your knowledge of God's Law should help you to see that you have a life-threatening dilemma: a huge problem of God's wrath (His justifiable anger) against your personal sins. The just penalty for sin—breaking even one Law—is death, and eternity in hell. But you haven't broken just one Law. Like the rest of us, you've no doubt broken all these laws, countless times each. What kind of anger do you think a judge is justified in having toward a criminal guilty of breaking the law *thousands of times?*

LET'S SEE

Let's now look at those four major religions to see if they can help you with your predicament.

Hinduism. The religion of Hinduism says that if you've been bad, you may come back as a rat or some other animal.[13] If you've been good, you might come back as a prince. But that's like someone saying, "When you jump out of the plane, you'll get sucked back in as another passenger. If you've been bad, you go down to the Economy Class; if you've been good, you go up to First Class." It's an interesting concept, but it doesn't deal with your real problem of having sinned against God and the reality of hell.

Buddhism. Amazingly, the religion of Buddhism denies that God even exists. It teaches that life and death are sort of an illusion.[14] That's like standing at the door of the plane and saying, "I'm not really here, and there's no such thing as the law of gravity, and no ground that I'm going to hit." That may temporarily help you deal with your fears, but it doesn't square with reality. And it doesn't deal with your real problem of having sinned against God and the reality of hell.

Islam. Interestingly, Islam acknowledges the reality of sin and hell, and the justice of God, but the hope it offers is that sinners can escape God's justice if they do religious works. God will see these, *and because of them*, hopefully He will show

mercy—but they won't know for sure.[15] Each person's works will be weighed on the Day of Judgment and it will then be decided who is saved and who is not—based on whether they followed Islam, were sincere in repentance, and performed enough righteous deeds to outweigh their bad ones.

So Islam believes you can *earn* God's mercy by your own efforts. That's like jumping out of the plane, and believing that flapping your arms is going to counter the law of gravity and save you from a 10,000-foot drop.

And there's something else to consider. The Law of God shows us that the best of us is nothing but a wicked criminal, standing guilty and condemned before the throne of a perfect and holy Judge. When that is understood, then our "righteous deeds" are actually seen as an attempt to bribe the Judge of the Universe. The Bible says that *because of our guilt*, anything we offer God for our justification (our acquittal from His courtroom) is an abomination to Him,[16] and only adds to our crimes.

Islam, like the other religions, doesn't solve your problem of having sinned against God and the reality of hell.

Christianity. So why is Christianity different? Aren't all religions the same? Let's see. In Christianity, God Himself provided a "parachute" for us, and His Word says regarding the Savior, "Put on the Lord Jesus Christ."[17] Just as a parachute solved your dilemma with the law of gravity and its consequences, so the Savior perfectly solves your dilemma with the Law of God and its consequences! It is the missing puzzle-piece that you need.

How did God solve our dilemma? He satisfied His wrath by becoming a human being and taking our punishment upon Himself. The Scriptures tell us that God was in Christ, reconciling the world to Himself. Christianity provides the only parachute to save us from the consequences of the Law we have transgressed.

BACK TO THE PLANE

To illustrate this more clearly, let's go back to that plane for a moment. You are standing on the edge of a 10,000-foot drop. You have to jump. Your heart is thumping in your chest. Why? Because of fear. You know that the law of gravity will kill you when you jump.

Someone offers you the original Mona Lisa. You push it aside.

Another person passes you the keys to a brand new Lamborghini. You let them drop to the floor.

Someone else tries to put a million dollars into your hands. You push the person's hand away, and stand there in horror at your impending fate.

Suddenly, you hear a voice say, "Here's a parachute!"

Which one of those four people is going to hold the most credibility in your eyes? The one who held up the parachute! Again, it is your fear of the jump that turns you toward the good news of the parachute.

In the same way, knowledge of what God's Law will do to you produces a fear that makes the news of a Savior unspeakably good news! It solves your predicament of God's wrath. God loves you so much that He became a sinless human being in the person of Jesus of Nazareth. The Savior died an excruciating death on the cross, taking your punishment (the death penalty) upon Himself. The demands of eternal justice were satisfied the moment He cried, "It is finished!"

The lightning of God's wrath was stopped and the thunder of His indignation was silenced at Calvary's bloodied cross: "Christ has redeemed us from the curse of the law, having become a curse for us."[18] We broke the Law, but He became a man to pay our penalty in His life's blood.

Then He rose from the dead, defeating death. That means that God can now forgive every sin you have ever committed and commute your death sentence. If you repent and place your trust in Jesus, you can say with the apostle Paul:

> For the law of the Spirit of life in Christ Jesus has made me free from the law of sin and death.[19]

So you no longer need to be tormented by the fear of death, and you don't need to look any further for ways to deal with the dilemma of sin and God's wrath.[20] The Savior is God's gift to you. *The gospel is unspeakably good news for the entire, sinful human race!*

God Himself can "justify" you. He can cleanse you, and give you the "righteousness" of Christ. He can make you pure in heart by washing away your sins. He can shelter you from His fierce wrath, in the Rock of Ages that He has cleft for you.[21]

Only Jesus can save you from death and hell, something that you could never earn or deserve.[22]

DO IT TODAY

To receive the gift of eternal life, you must repent of your sins (turn from them), and put on the Lord Jesus Christ as you would put on a parachute—*trusting* in Him alone for your salvation. That means you forsake your own good works as a means of trying to please God (trying to bribe Him), and trust only in what Jesus has done for you. Simply throw yourself on the mercy of the Judge. The Bible says that He's rich in mercy to all who *call* on Him,[23] so call on Him right now. He *will* hear you if you approach Him with a humble and sorrowful heart.

Do it right now because you don't know when you will take that leap through the door of death. Confess your sins to God, put your trust in Jesus to save you, and you will pass from death to life. You have God's promise on it.[24]

Pray something like this:

> "Dear God, today I turn away from all of my sins [name them] and I put my trust in Jesus Christ alone as my Lord and Savior. Please forgive me, change my heart, and grant me Your gift of everlasting life. In Jesus' name I pray. Amen."

Now have faith in God. He is absolutely trustworthy. Never doubt His promises. He is not a man that He should lie.

The sincerity of your prayer will be evidenced by your obedience to God's will, so read His Word (the Bible) daily and obey what you read.[25] See the Matt. 6:9 comment in this Bible for principles that will help you grow in your faith. Thank you for reading this.

May God continue to bless you and yours.

NOTES

1. See Rom. 8:2.
2. 1 John 3:15.
3. Matt. 5:27,28.
4. Prov. 12:22.
5. See Rev. 21:8; 1 Cor. 6:9,10.
6. Matt. 12:36.
7. See John 3:36.
8. See Rom. 2:5.
9. See Eph. 2:3.
10. Exod. 33:19,22 (emphasis added).
11. Matt. 5:8.
12. Psa. 111:10.
13. "Is it possible for a man to be reborn as a lower animal?" Maharshi: "Yes. It is possible, as illustrated by Jada Bharata—the scriptural anecdote of a royal sage having been reborn as a deer." www.hinduism.co.za/reincarn.htm>.
14. "When you transcend your thinking mind in the realization of your own pure, timeless, ever-present awareness, then the illusion of time completely collapses, and you become utterly free of the samsaric cycle of time, change, impermanence, and suffering." <www.buddhistinformation.com>.
15. "Then those whose balance (of good deeds) is heavy, they will be successful. But those whose balance is light, will be those who have lost their souls; in hell will they abide" (Surah 23:102,103).
16. See Prov. 15:8.
17. See Rom. 13:14.
18. Gal. 3:13.
19. Rom. 8:2.
20. Beware of cults such as Jehovah's Witnesses and Mormons. They masquerade as "Christian," but they are rooted in self-righteousness (trying to do good works to earn salvation).
21. See 1 Cor. 10:4.
22. "For by grace you have been saved through faith; and that not of yourselves; it is the gift of God, not of works, lest anyone should boast" (Eph. 2:8,9).
23. "For the Scripture says, 'Whoever believes on Him will not be put to shame.' For there is no distinction between Jew and Greek, for the same Lord over all is rich to all who call upon Him. For 'whoever calls on the name of the LORD shall be saved'" (Rom. 10:11–13).
24. "Most assuredly, I say to you, he who hears My word and believes in Him who sent Me has everlasting life, and shall not come into judgment, but has passed from death into life" (John 5:24).
25. "He who has My commandments and keeps them, it is he who loves me. And he who loves Me will be loved by My Father, and I will love him and manifest Myself to him" (John 14:21).

The Old Testament

Who Can Tell Me?

By Emeal ("E.Z.") Zwayne

"Who can tell me where I came from?"
The little boy would ask.
His question was a good one,
Yet he faced a trying task.

Each man had different answers,
As he was soon to learn.
This brought him great confusion
And it caused a deep concern.

He first went to his schoolmates
And they spoke with one another.
"I know," said the brightest one,
"You came from your mother."

Now this had satisfied him,
Yet only for a time.
For as he grew, year by year,
His thoughts began to climb.

He then looked all around him
At all that he could see.
And his mind began to wonder
How it all had come to be.

He thought about the universe,
The span of outer space,
And every star and planet
That exists in every place.

He thought about the rounded Earth,
Its tilt and its rotation,
And all the seasons that occur
In yearly circulation.

He thought about the darkness
And he thought about the light.
He thought about the sun and moon
That rule the day and night.

He thought of all the creatures
Of the land and sea and skies,
Of all the different species
And their variance in size.

He thought of all the plants and trees
And all that each provides,
Each growing from a tiny seed
With roots the soil hides.

He then looked at humanity,
The sea of different faces,
Varied tongues and characters
From many distant places.

He thought of mortal bodies,
With features so profound;
And the sense of taste and touch
And smell and sight and sound.

He thought of reproduction
And the miracle of birth.
He thought of human life itself
And all that it is worth.

He then considered human will:
Both the weak and strong.
He thought about the conscience
That discerns the right from wrong.

He thought about emotions
And feelings that arise.
He thought about the love and hate
And tears that flow from eyes.

He thought about the anger
And the joy that's all around.
He thought about the happiness
And sadness that is found.

And filled with curiosity,
This boy would daily strive,
In hopeful expectation
That his answer would arrive.

He spoke with scientific men
Who claimed his question solved.
They told him of a great big bang,
That all things had evolved.

He then spoke with philosophers—
Heard some of them insist
That there's no true reality
And we do not exist.

He spoke with many people
From different groups and sects,
And heard the vast opinions
Of various intellects.

Now baffled by confusion,
A very troubled youth;
Unable to discern
What is error, what is truth.

He almost gave up looking,
But he took a second look.
And very unexpectedly
He found a special Book.

As he gazed upon the first page,
He knew his search was done.
His questions all were answered
In Genesis chapter one.

With a nod of understanding,
He smiled, so elated.
For now he surely knew—
"In the beginning God created..."

Genesis

The History of Creation

1 In the beginning God created the heavens and the earth. 2The earth was without form, and void; and darkness *was*[a] on
the face of the deep. And the Spirit of God
was hovering over the face of the waters.
3Then God said, "Let there be light";
and there was light. 4And God saw the
light, that *it was* good; and God divided
the light from the darkness. 5God called
the light Day, and the darkness He called
Night. So the evening and the morning
were the first day.
6Then God said, "Let there be a firmament in the midst of the waters, and let it
divide the waters from the waters." 7Thus
God made the firmament, and divided the
waters which *were* under the firmament
from the waters which *were* above the firmament; and it was so. 8And God called
the firmament Heaven. So the evening and
the morning were the second day.
9Then God said, "Let the waters under

1:2 [a]Words in italic type have been added for clarity. They are not found in the original Hebrew or Aramaic.

1:1 A foundational book. "Genesis is quoted from or referred to in the rest of the Bible more than any other book of the Bible. In the New Testament alone, there are at least 200 quotations from—or references to—Genesis. In fact, there are over 100 citations or direct references in the New Testament to the first eleven chapters of Genesis. And every one of those eleven chapters is referred to somewhere in the New Testament. Not only that, but each New Testament author refers somewhere in his writings to Genesis, chapters one to eleven in particular. And Jesus Himself quoted or referred to the first eleven chapters of Genesis on six different occasions.

"If Genesis isn't true, then Jesus Christ would have been lying. Also, the rest of the Bible collapses, since every biblical doctrine of theology—directly or indirectly—is founded in the book of Genesis. That's why Genesis is referred to so often throughout the Bible. Believing Genesis is the key to fully understanding God's Word." *Answers in Genesis*

For whether Christians can believe in evolution, rather than in the Genesis account of creation, see Isa. 40:28 comment.

1:1,2 These verses explain the great mystery of life's origins. We need no longer live in ignorance. The secular world is forever searching for its "genesis" (beginning). The lost have no idea of their real origins because they ignore the Book that tells us what happened and Who made it happen. However, the most effective way to convince skeptics that God is the Creator, and that Genesis tells us the genesis of life, is for them to come to know the God who gave them life. (See John 14:21; 17:3.) This happens through the new birth described in John chapter 3.

For the scientific facts contained in these verses, see Heb. 11:3 comment.

1:3 This same God who commanded light to shine in the beginning also shines the light of the glorious gospel of Christ, who is the image of the invisible God, into our dark hearts. He makes us a new creation. The moment we repent and trust in Jesus Christ, God transfers us from the kingdom of darkness into the kingdom of light. See Acts 26:18; 2 Cor. 4:6; 5:17.

For thoughts on God's voice, see Psa. 29:3–9 comment.

Questions & Objections

"How long is a 'day'?"

By Dr. Terry Mortenson, Answers in Genesis

Did God create the whole universe, including the original plants, animals, and first two people (Adam and Eve) in six literal 24-hour days? Or did creation take place over millions of years?

When we look carefully at Gen. 1, in Hebrew or even in English, it is clear that God created everything in six literal (24-hour) days. First, we are told that He created the earth in darkness and then created light (vv. 2, 3). Then He called the light "day" and He called the darkness "night" (v. 5). And then He said (in the original Hebrew) "and [there] was evening and [there] was morning, one day" (v. 5). He repeated the same statement at the end of the second day through the sixth day.

Everywhere else in the Old Testament, when the Hebrew word for "day" (*yom*) appears with "evening" or "morning" or is modified by a number (e.g., "sixth day" or "five days"), it always means a 24-hour day.

On Day Four God further showed that these were literal days by telling us the purpose for which He created the sun, moon, and stars: so we could tell time—literal years, literal seasons, and literal days.

Then in Exod. 20:8–11 God commanded the Israelites to work six literal "days" and rest on the seventh because He created in six "days" (using the same Hebrew word). Furthermore, Jesus and the New Testament apostles read Gen. 1—11 as straightforward historical narrative. There are additional good scholarly reasons for coming to that conclusion.

There is no biblical or scientific reason to be ashamed of believing in a recent six-day creation. God has spoken clearly and truthfully. Will you trust His Word over the arrogant claims of sinful men?

See also Heb. 4:4 comment.

the heavens be gathered together into one
place, and let the dry *land* appear"; and it
was so. 10And God called the dry *land*
Earth, and the gathering together of the
waters He called Seas. And God saw that
it was good.
11Then God said, "Let the earth bring
forth grass, the herb *that* yields seed, *and*
the fruit tree *that* yields fruit according to
its kind, whose seed *is* in itself, on the
earth"; and it was so. 12And the earth
brought forth grass, the herb *that* yields
seed according to its kind, and the tree
that yields fruit, whose seed *is* in itself according to its kind. And God saw that *it*
was good. 13So the evening and the morning were the third day.
14Then God said, "Let there be lights
in the firmament of the heavens to divide
the day from the night; and let them be
for signs and seasons, and for days and
years; 15and let them be for lights in the
firmament of the heavens to give light on
the earth"; and it was so. 16Then God
made two great lights: the greater light to
rule the day, and the lesser light to rule
the night. *He made* the stars also. 17God
set them in the firmament of the heavens

1:6 For thoughts on the beginning of the universe, see comments at Psa. 19:1; Isa. 34:4; and Isa. 45:18. How old is the earth? For whether scientific dating methods can be trusted, see comments at Job 20:4 and Psa. 102:25.

1:7 Do atheists believe everything came from nothing? See Psa. 121:2 comment. For additional thoughts on evolution, see Prov. 3:19 and Isa. 45:12 comments.

1:11 Did God make "grass" for smoking? See Psa. 102:3,4 comment.

1:16 Make sure you don't miss the magnitude of what God accomplished in creating the sun. Its surface temperature is about 10,000 degrees Fahrenheit, with the temperature at the core around 27 million degrees Fahrenheit. That's hot. The sun's diameter is about 870,000 miles (109 times greater than Earth), and it is 333,000 times heavier—and that is only one of over 100 billion stars that God made. The sun generates the heat and light that the Earth needs. Without it, Earth could not support life. The sun is composed of 92 percent hydrogen, 7 percent helium, and small amounts of inert gases. It burns an incredible seven million tons of natural gas every second. And Almighty God spoke it into existence.

QUESTIONS & OBJECTIONS

1:18 *"How could there be light before the sun?"*

Before God created the sun to give light to the earth (vv. 14–18), He provided a light source for the first three days. Where would the original light have come from (vv. 3–5)? The Bible tells us that God is light (1 John 1:5; Rev. 22:5), and that in the new heavens and earth there will be no need for the sun or moon, "for the glory of God illuminated it" (Rev. 21:23). Some pagan religions worship the sun, and even evolutionary theory credits the sun for the creation of life. Knowing that man is prone to worship anything but the Creator, perhaps God did it this way specifically to show that He, not the sun, is responsible for the origin of life (see Deut. 4:19; Ezek. 8:16). See also Psa. 136:7–9 comment.

"...the universe's lights, contrary to astronomers' hunches, turned on in one great burst. It was as if every chandelier in a mansion were flicked on simultaneously on a moonless night." *John Bahcall*, astrophysicist (*Newsweek*, Nov. 3, 1997)

to give light on the earth, 18and to rule
over the day and over the night, and to
divide the light from the darkness. And
God saw that *it was* good. 19So the evening
and the morning were the fourth day.
20Then God said, "Let the waters
abound with an abundance of living creatures, and let birds fly above the earth
across the face of the firmament of the
heavens." 21So God created great sea creatures and every living thing that moves,
with which the waters abounded, according to their kind, and every winged bird
according to its kind. And God saw that
it was good. 22And God blessed them, saying, "Be fruitful and multiply, and fill the
waters in the seas, and let birds multiply
on the earth." 23So the evening and the
morning were the fifth day.
24Then God said, "Let the earth bring
forth the living creature according to its
kind: cattle and creeping thing and beast
of the earth, *each* according to its kind";
and it was so. 25And God made the beast
of the earth according to its kind, cattle
according to its kind, and everything that
creeps on the earth according to its kind.
And God saw that *it was* good.
26Then God said, "Let Us make man in
Our image, according to Our likeness; let
them have dominion over the fish of the
sea, over the birds of the air, and over the
cattle, over all[a] the earth and over every
creeping thing that creeps on the earth."

1:26 [a]Syriac reads *all the wild animals of.*

1:20 How does evolution explain the origin of life? See Job 33:4 comment. For how the scientific evidence supports the Genesis creation account, see Eccles. 9:11 and 1 Cor. 15:39 comments.

1:25 For details on created "kinds," see Acts 10:12 comment.

"This notion of species as 'natural kinds' fits splendidly with creationist tenets of a pre-Darwinian age. Louis Agassiz even argued that species are God's individual thoughts, made incarnate so that we might perceive both His majesty and His message. Species, Agassiz wrote, are 'instituted by the Divine Intelligence as the categories of his mode of thinking.' But how could a division of the organic world into discrete entities be justified by an evolutionary theory that proclaimed ceaseless change as the fundamental fact of nature?" *Stephen J. Gould*, professor of geology and paleontology, Harvard University

1:26 Bible contradiction? Are there multiple "Gods" as this verse implies, or is there only one as Deut. 6:4 states: "Hear, O Israel: The LORD our God, the LORD is one"?

There is only one true God, the Creator of heaven and earth. The Bible teaches that God is Triune by nature. He exists eternally as Father, Son, and Holy Spirit—one God in three divine, co-equal Persons. For example, Scripture reveals that Jesus Christ, God the Son, was preexistent before He was manifest in human form: "In the beginning was the Word, and the Word was with God, and the Word was God... And the Word became flesh and dwelt among us" (John 1:1,2,14). Jesus said of Himself, "I and My Father are one" (John 10:30). For verses mentioning the three Persons of the Trinity, see Matt. 3:16,17; John 14:26; 15:26; 2 Cor. 13:14; Gal. 4:4–6; 1 Pet. 1:2; 1 John 5:7. For how the Trinity works in redemption, see Acts 10:38 comment.

Questions & Objections

1:31 "Can't the days of creation be long periods, since a day to the Lord is a thousand years to us?"

Read the referenced verse, 2 Pet. 3:8, in its entirety, and you will see that it says something quite different: "with the Lord one day is as a thousand years, *and a thousand years as one day*" (emphasis added). It doesn't say "one day *is* a thousand years," but that one day is "as" (like) a thousand years. Then it also says the reverse: a thousand years is "as" (like) one day. So that alone negates the idea of a different timescale. The verse is saying that both times are equivalent.

In addition, it is not comparing God's timeframe to man's. Rather, both times are from God's perspective: "*with the Lord*" these times are the same. Scripture is telling us that with God time has no meaning. Because He is eternal, outside of the dimension of time that He created, a million years, a day, and a millisecond all are the same to Him (see Psa. 90:4). He sees all of history simultaneously.

Some also misapply this verse to Adam, saying that he died "the day" he sinned because he lived less than a thousand years (see 5:5). But even if Adam had lived to 1,001 years, Gen. 2:17 would still be true: Adam *did* die the very day he chose to disobey God—he died *spiritually* that instant. See Gen. 2:17 comment for details. See also 2 Pet. 3:8 comment.

27So God created man in His *own* image;
in the image of God He created him; male
and female He created them. 28Then God
blessed them, and God said to them, "Be
fruitful and multiply; fill the earth and
subdue it; have dominion over the fish of
the sea, over the birds of the air, and over
every living thing that moves on the earth."
29And God said, "See, I have given you
every herb *that* yields seed which *is* on
the face of all the earth, and every tree
whose fruit yields seed; to you it shall be
for food. 30Also, to every beast of the earth,
to every bird of the air, and to everything
that creeps on the earth, in which *there is*
life, *I have given* every green herb for food";
and it was so. 31Then God saw everything
that He had made, and indeed *it was* very
good. So the evening and the morning
were the sixth day.

2 Thus the heavens and the earth, and
all the host of them, were finished.
2And on the seventh day God ended His
work which He had done, and He rested
on the seventh day from all His work
which He had done. 3Then God blessed
the seventh day and sanctified it, because

1:27 Mankind was created as male and female. For details, see Matt. 19:4 comment.

"Each of us has been created in the likeness of God and after His image: 'Let Us make man (male and female) in Our image, according to Our likeness.' We are three in one—spirit, soul, and body. Like God, we are immortal. The most important thing about us is our immortality—our everlasting soul. Paul said that he was called to preach the immortality that Jesus brought to light (see 2 Tim. 1:10,11). Each of us, no matter the color, shape, size, intellect or gender, are human beings (being human). But our real label is not who we are, what we do, or what we know, etc. What really matters is that we are immortal." *Garry T. Ansdell*

1:28 For the uniqueness of man and his superiority over the animal kingdom, see Psa. 8:6 and 32:9 comments.

1:30 Like man, all animals were originally created to be vegetarian. See Isa. 11:6–9; 65:25. It was not until after the Flood that God directed man to eat meat (see 9:3). See also Rev. 22:3 comment.

2:1 Scientific facts in the Bible. The original Hebrew uses the past definite tense for the verb "finished," indicating an action completed in the past, never again to occur. The creation was "finished"—once and for all. That is exactly what the First Law of Thermodynamics says. This law (often referred to as the Law of the Conservation of Energy and/or Mass) states that neither matter nor energy can be either created or destroyed. It was because of this Law that Sir Fred Hoyle's "Steady-State" (or "Continuous Creation") Theory was discarded. Hoyle stated that at points in the universe called "irtrons," matter (or energy) was constantly being created. But, the First Law states just the opposite. Indeed, there is no "creation" ongoing today. It is "finished" exactly as the Bible states.

QUESTIONS & OBJECTIONS

2:4 *"Why are there two different creation accounts in the Bible?"*

Some skeptics claim that chapters 1 and 2 are contradictory, because 1:25–27 states that God made animals and then made man, whereas 2:18,19 mentions man then says, "Out of the ground the LORD God formed every beast of the field and every bird of the air, and brought them to Adam to see what he would call them."

However, a close reading shows there is no contradiction. Genesis 1 gives the day-by-day account of the entire creation week, whereas Gen. 2 gives the details of man's creation on the sixth day. Since the creation work was finished in chapter 1 (which closes with the end of day six), Genesis 2 begins by recapping: "Thus the heavens and the earth, and all the host of them, *were finished.* And on the seventh day God ended His work which He had done, and He rested on the seventh day from all His work which He had done" (vv. 1,2). To make it even clearer, God then tells us, "*This is the history* of the heavens and the earth when they *were created*" (v. 4, emphasis added).

Obviously, the creation activity has been completed at this point, with the animals created first as Gen. 1 states. The original Hebrew used in Gen. 2 indicates that God had already (*yâtsar*) formed the animals from the earth, and then He brought them to Adam. He did not create them again. The order is this: on day six God made animals first, He made man second, He showed the animals He had already made to Adam, so Adam could see that he had no suitable mate, and then He created woman.

in it He rested from all His work which God had created and made.

4This *is* the history[a] of the heavens and the earth when they were created, in the day that the LORD God made the earth and the heavens, 5before any plant of the field was in the earth and before any herb of the field had grown. For the LORD God had not caused it to rain on the earth, and *there was* no man to till the ground; 6but a mist went up from the earth and watered the whole face of the ground.

7And the LORD God formed man *of* the dust of the ground, and breathed into his nostrils the breath of life; and man became a living being.

Life in God's Garden

8The LORD God planted a garden eastward in Eden, and there He put the man whom He had formed. 9And out of the ground the LORD God made every tree grow that is pleasant to the sight and good for food. The tree of life *was* also in the midst of the garden, and the tree of the knowledge of good and evil.

10Now a river went out of Eden to water the garden, and from there it parted and became four riverheads. 11The name of the first *is* Pishon; it *is* the one which skirts the whole land of Havilah, where *there is* gold. 12And the gold of that land *is* good. Bdellium and the onyx stone *are* there. 13The name of the second river *is* Gihon; it *is* the one which goes around the whole land of Cush. 14The name of the third river *is* Hiddekel;[a] it *is* the one which goes toward the east of Assyria. The fourth river *is* the Euphrates.

15Then the LORD God took the man and put him in the garden of Eden to tend and keep it. 16And the LORD God commanded the man, saying, "Of every tree of the garden you may freely eat; 17but of the tree of the knowledge of good and evil you shall not eat, for in the day that you eat of it you shall surely die."

18And the LORD God said, "*It is* not good

2:4 [a]Hebrew *toledoth,* literally *generations* 2:14 [a]Or *Tigris*

2:7 Were all the ingredients for life present on earth before life existed? See Job 34:14,15 comment.

"Slight variations in physical laws such as gravity or electromagnetism would make life impossible... The necessity to produce life lies at the center of the universe's whole machinery and design." *John Wheeler,* physics professor, Princeton University

QUESTIONS & OBJECTIONS

"Adam didn't die the day God said he would!"

Skeptics point to the fact that Adam lived until he was 930 years old (see Gen. 5:5) and claim that he did not die "the day" he ate the forbidden fruit. Here is another obvious "mistake"—for those who don't understand the nature of man. God created mankind with three components: body, soul, and spirit (see 1 Thess. 5:23). The body is the machine we walk around in, and our five senses enable us to be conscious of our surroundings. Our soul is our self-conscious part—the area of the emotions, will, and conscience. And our spirit is our God-conscious part, enabling us to be aware of God and relate to Him.

We have physical life when we have union with our body, and we have spiritual life when we have union with God. Just as physical death occurs when our soul separates from our body, spiritual death occurs when our soul is separated from God. Adam was unique in that when he was created, God breathed His Spirit into him, giving Adam spiritual life—so he could know and relate to His Creator. But Ezek. 18:4 tells us, "The soul who sins shall die." Because God is so holy that He cannot abide with sin (Psa. 5:4; Hab. 1:13), He withdrew His Holy Spirit from Adam when he disobeyed, and Adam died spiritually at that very moment.

The Bible says that, like Adam, we are "dead in trespasses and sins" (Eph. 2:1) until we are born again and the life of God inhabits us through the Holy Spirit. When we repent of our sins and trust in Jesus Christ, we pass "from death to life" (John 5:24; Rom. 6:13; 1 John 3:14).

See also Gen. 5:1,3 and Eph. 4:18 comments.

that man should be alone; I will make him
a helper comparable to him." 19Out of the
ground the LORD God formed every beast
of the field and every bird of the air, and
brought *them* to Adam to see what he
would call them. And whatever Adam
called each living creature, that *was* its
name. 20So Adam gave names to all cattle,
to the birds of the air, and to every beast
of the field. But for Adam there was not
found a helper comparable to him.
21And the LORD God caused a deep
sleep to fall on Adam, and he slept; and
He took one of his ribs, and closed up the
flesh in its place. 22Then the rib which the
LORD God had taken from man He made
into a woman, and He brought her to the
man.
23And Adam said:

"This *is* now bone of my bones
And flesh of my flesh;
She shall be called Woman,
Because she was taken out of Man."

24Therefore a man shall leave his father
and mother and be joined to his wife,
and they shall become one flesh.
25And they were both naked, the man
and his wife, and were not ashamed.

The Temptation and Fall of Man

3 Now the serpent was more cunning
than any beast of the field which the
LORD God had made. And he said to the
woman, "Has God indeed said, 'You shall
not eat of every tree of the garden'?"
2And the woman said to the serpent,
"We may eat the fruit of the trees of the
garden; 3but of the fruit of the tree which
is in the midst of the garden, God has
said, 'You shall not eat it, nor shall you
touch it, lest you die.' "
4Then the serpent said to the woman,
"You will not surely die. 5For God knows
that in the day you eat of it your eyes will
be opened, and you will be like God,
knowing good and evil."
6So when the woman saw that the tree
was good for food, that it *was* pleasant to
the eyes, and a tree desirable to make *one*
wise, she took of its fruit and ate. She also
gave to her husband with her, and he ate.
7Then the eyes of both of them were

3:1 How can one believe in a talking serpent? See Num. 22:28 comment.

Questions & Objections

3:5 "God wants to keep people from having knowledge!"

Some skeptics see the word "knowledge" in this verse and conclude that God wants to prohibit man from having knowledge. They claim God likes people to be ignorant and unthinking, but they fail to consider what it is a knowledge *of*. Before sin was in the world, Adam and Eve knew, and experienced, only good; in fact, God's entire creation was "very good." But their sin brought evil into the world, and once mankind knew both good and evil, he had to choose between the two. God tells us, "I have set before you today life and good, death and evil, ... therefore choose life, that both you and your descendants may live" (Deut. 30:15,19).

These same skeptics often complain about the evil they see in the world and blame it on God—yet it was because of Adam and Eve's desire to know good and evil that we now know and experience evil. However, in the new heavens and new earth, there will be no more evil, suffering, or death. God's new creation will once again be "very good." See also 2 Kings 2:1 comment.

opened, and they knew that they *were*
naked; and they sewed fig leaves together
and made themselves coverings.
8And they heard the sound of the LORD
God walking in the garden in the cool of
the day, and Adam and his wife hid themselves from the presence of the LORD God
among the trees of the garden.
9Then the LORD God called to Adam
and said to him, "Where *are* you?"
10So he said, "I heard Your voice in the
garden, and I was afraid because I was
naked; and I hid myself."
11And He said, "Who told you that
you *were* naked? Have you eaten from the
tree of which I commanded you that you
should not eat?"
12Then the man said, "The woman
whom You gave *to be* with me, she gave
me of the tree, and I ate."

3:6 A threefold temptation. Our first parents faced a threefold temptation, mentioned in 1 John 2:16: "the tree was good for food"—lust of the flesh, "it was pleasant to the eyes"—lust of the eyes, and it was "desirable to make one wise"—pride of life. These are the same three temptations that Jesus faced in the desert (see Luke 4:1–13). Where the first Adam failed, Jesus, "the second Adam," prevailed (see 1 Cor. 15:45). See also Heb. 4:15 comment.

3:7 Nakedness. The "nakedness" here is not the same as that mentioned in 2:25, where the husband and wife were naked but had nothing of which to be ashamed. As a consequence of sinning against God, they lost their covering of *righteousness*—their right standing before God, which they had at creation. God therefore had to provide a covering for them (see Isa. 61:10; Zech. 3:3,4; Rev. 3:18). See also Gen. 3:21 comment.

"The fig leaves used by Adam and Eve are called aprons, which cover only a part of the body and are not sufficient for a complete covering. The fig leaf is soft like velvet, and, under the heat of the sun, shrinks to about a quarter the size. These leaves are a type of self-righteousness. After Adam and Eve made the aprons they still hid themselves from God because they knew they were still naked in His sight. No amount of self-righteousness, or religion, or church attendance, or donations to worthy causes, or religious acts ... is sufficient to hide the sins of the heart from God's sight." *Walter Wilson*

It is the light and heat of the Law of God that withers self-righteousness and exposes the shame of our sin.

3:8 Bible contradiction? Does God have a body or is He a spirit? This verse describes Him walking in the garden, yet the Bible says that "God is Spirit" (John 4:24). It is true that God is Spirit and that "A spirit does not have flesh and bones" (Luke 24:39). The reference to God "walking" is what is known as "anthropomorphism." This is common in Scripture and attributes the characteristics of man to God, using words like "face" and "hand" to describe Him. For example, when the Bible says, "The eyes of the LORD are in every place, keeping watch on the evil and the good" (Prov. 15:3), it doesn't mean God has physical eyes that are everywhere. It simply means God is omniscient; He sees everything.

3:10 "Ah! How foolish we are! How we repeat the folly of our first parent every day when we seek to hide sin from conscience, and then think it is hidden from God." *Charles Spurgeon*

[13]And the LORD God said to the woman, "What *is* this you have done?"

The woman said, "The serpent deceived me, and I ate."

[14]So the LORD God said to the serpent:

"Because you have done this,
You *are* cursed more than all cattle,
And more than every beast of the field;
On your belly you shall go,
And you shall eat dust
All the days of your life.
[15]And I will put enmity
Between you and the woman,
And between your seed and her Seed;
He shall bruise your head,
And you shall bruise His heel."

[16]To the woman He said:

"I will greatly multiply your sorrow and your conception;
In pain you shall bring forth children;
Your desire *shall be* for your husband,
And he shall rule over you."

[17]Then to Adam He said, "Because you have heeded the voice of your wife, and have eaten from the tree of which I commanded you, saying, 'You shall not eat of it':

"Cursed *is* the ground for your sake;
In toil you shall eat *of* it
All the days of your life.
[18]Both thorns and thistles it shall bring forth for you,
And you shall eat the herb of the field.
[19]In the sweat of your face you shall eat bread
Till you return to the ground,
For out of it you were taken;
For dust you *are*,
And to dust you shall return."

[20]And Adam called his wife's name Eve, because she was the mother of all living.

[21]Also for Adam and his wife the LORD God made tunics of skin, and clothed them.

[22]Then the LORD God said, "Behold,
the man has become like one of Us, to
know good and evil. And now, lest he put
out his hand and take also of the tree of
life, and eat, and live forever"— [23]there-
fore the LORD God sent him out of the
garden of Eden to till the ground from
which he was taken. [24]So He drove out
the man; and He placed cherubim at the
east of the garden of Eden, and a flaming
sword which turned every way, to guard
the way to the tree of life.

Cain Murders Abel

4 Now Adam knew Eve his wife, and
she conceived and bore Cain, and
said, "I have acquired a man from the
LORD." [2]Then she bore again, this time
his brother Abel. Now Abel was a keeper
of sheep, but Cain was a tiller of the
ground. [3]And in the process of time it

3:17,18 The curse for man's sin falls on all of creation. See Jer. 7:20 comment.

3:21 Jesus in the Old Testament. "Before Adam and Eve sinned, they were two happy, naked vegetarians. Immediately after eating the fruit God commanded them not to eat, they were naked and ashamed. In an effort to cover their shame, they sewed fig leaves together. When God found them in the garden, He slaughtered the first animal in history to make skins to cover Adam and Eve.

"In the first sin we see man making an effort to cover his own transgression. God makes it clear that man's efforts are not sufficient to cover sin. We also see that the shedding of blood is required to forgive sins (see Heb. 9:22).

"The first animals that were ever butchered were killed by God Himself. This is our first shadowy picture of Jesus Christ, shedding His blood for the sins of mankind." *Todd Friel* (Adapted from *Don't Stub Your Toe*.)

See also Gen. 4:3–5 comment.

3:22 To prevent Adam and Eve from eating of the tree of life and remaining in their spiritually dead condition, eternally separated from God, He drove them from the garden. Those who are born again, however, will enjoy this fruit forever in the new heavens and earth. See Rev. 2:7; 22:2,14.

came to pass that Cain brought an offering of the fruit of the ground to the LORD.
[4]Abel also brought of the firstborn of his
flock and of their fat. And the LORD respected Abel and his offering, [5]but He did
not respect Cain and his offering. And
Cain was very angry, and his countenance
fell.

[6]So the LORD said to Cain, "Why are
you angry? And why has your countenance fallen? [7]If you do well, will you not
be accepted? And if you do not do well,
sin lies at the door. And its desire *is* for
you, but you should rule over it."

[8]Now Cain talked with Abel his brother;[a] and it came to pass, when they were
in the field, that Cain rose up against Abel
his brother and killed him.

[9]Then the LORD said to Cain, "Where
is Abel your brother?"

He said, "I do not know. *Am* I my
brother's keeper?"

[10]And He said, "What have you done?
The voice of your brother's blood cries
out to Me from the ground. [11]So now you
are cursed from the earth, which has
opened its mouth to receive your brother's blood from your hand. [12]When you
till the ground, it shall no longer yield its
strength to you. A fugitive and a vagabond
you shall be on the earth."

[13]And Cain said to the LORD, "My punishment *is* greater than I can bear! [14]Sure-
ly You have driven me out this day from
the face of the ground; I shall be hidden
from Your face; I shall be a fugitive and a
vagabond on the earth, and it will happen
that anyone who finds me will kill me."

[15]And the LORD said to him, "Therefore,[a] whoever kills Cain, vengeance shall
be taken on him sevenfold." And the LORD
set a mark on Cain, lest anyone finding
him should kill him.

The Family of Cain

[16]Then Cain went out from the presence of the LORD and dwelt in the land of
Nod on the east of Eden. [17]And Cain knew
his wife, and she conceived and bore
Enoch. And he built a city, and called the
name of the city after the name of his
son—Enoch. [18]To Enoch was born Irad;
and Irad begot Mehujael, and Mehujael
begot Methushael, and Methushael begot
Lamech.

4:8 [a]Samaritan Pentateuch, Septuagint, Syriac, and Vulgate add *"Let us go out to the field."* 4:15 [a]Following Masoretic Text and Targum; Septuagint, Syriac, and Vulgate read *Not so.*

4:1 The word for "knew" used here of sexual intimacy—the closest of human relationships—means "to know experientially." This pictures the intimacy and experiential knowledge that we have with God once we are born again spiritually: "And this is eternal life, that they may know You, the only true God, and Jesus Christ whom You have sent" (John 17:3). The lost think that Christians have a blind faith, but we actually know with 100 percent certainty that God exists, because we *know* Him personally. See also 1 Sam. 2:12 and Hos. 2:20 comments.

4:3–5 Jesus in the Old Testament. "Adam and Eve's first sons, Cain and Abel, made a sacrifice to God. Cain, the farmer, made a grain offering and Abel, the rancher, made a lamb sacrifice. Cain's offering was not acceptable to God and Abel's was. Why?

"Only a lamb sacrifice offered in faith was pleasing to God. Hebrews 11:4 tells us, 'By faith Abel offered to God a more excellent sacrifice than Cain, through which he obtained witness that he was righteous, God testifying of his gifts; and through it he being dead still speaks.' How does Abel still speak? He points toward a newer and better covenant. In the Old Covenant, animal blood was repeatedly offered for the covering of sins, but in the New Covenant, Jesus shed His blood once for the complete forgiveness of sins.

"This is our second shadowy picture of Jesus in the Old Testament. Hebrews 12:24 says, 'to Jesus the Mediator of the new covenant, and to the blood of sprinkling that speaks better things than that of Abel.'" *Todd Friel* (Adapted from *Don't Stub Your Toe*.)

See also Gen. 22:2 comment.

4:9 "The cool impudence of Cain is an indication of the state of heart which led up to his murdering his brother; and it was also a part of his having committed that terrible crime. He would not have proceeded to the cruel deed of bloodshed if he had not first cast off the fear of God and been ready to defy his Maker." *Charles Spurgeon*

QUESTIONS & OBJECTIONS

4:17 ***"Where did Cain get his wife?"***

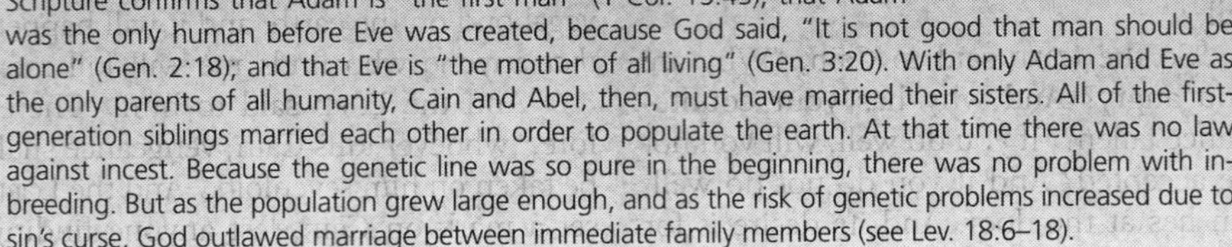

Many ask this question thinking they have found a "mistake" in the Bible—that there must have been other people besides Adam and Eve. However, Scripture confirms that Adam is "the first man" (1 Cor. 15:45); that Adam was the only human before Eve was created, because God said, "It is not good that man should be alone" (Gen. 2:18); and that Eve is "the mother of all living" (Gen. 3:20). With only Adam and Eve as the only parents of all humanity, Cain and Abel, then, must have married their sisters. All of the first-generation siblings married each other in order to populate the earth. At that time there was no law against incest. Because the genetic line was so pure in the beginning, there was no problem with inbreeding. But as the population grew large enough, and as the risk of genetic problems increased due to sin's curse, God outlawed marriage between immediate family members (see Lev. 18:6–18).

19Then Lamech took for himself two
wives: the name of one *was* Adah, and the
name of the second *was* Zillah. 20And Adah
bore Jabal. He was the father of those
who dwell in tents and have livestock.
21His brother's name *was* Jubal. He was
the father of all those who play the harp
and flute. 22And as for Zillah, she also bore
Tubal-Cain, an instructor of every craftsman in bronze and iron. And the sister of
Tubal-Cain *was* Naamah.

23Then Lamech said to his wives:

"Adah and Zillah, hear my voice;
Wives of Lamech, listen to my speech!
For I have killed a man for wounding me,
Even a young man for hurting me.
24If Cain shall be avenged sevenfold,
Then Lamech seventy-sevenfold."

A New Son

25And Adam knew his wife again, and
she bore a son and named him Seth, "For
God has appointed another seed for me
instead of Abel, whom Cain killed." 26And
as for Seth, to him also a son was born;
and he named him Enosh.[a] Then *men* began to call on the name of the LORD.

The Family of Adam

5 This is the book of the genealogy of
Adam. In the day that God created
man, He made him in the likeness of
God. 2He created them male and female,
and blessed them and called them Mankind in the day they were created. 3And
Adam lived one hundred and thirty years,
and begot *a son* in his own likeness, after
his image, and named him Seth. 4After
he begot Seth, the days of Adam were
eight hundred years; and he had sons and
daughters. 5So all the days that Adam
lived were nine hundred and thirty years;
and he died.

6Seth lived one hundred and five years,
and begot Enosh. 7After he begot Enosh,
Seth lived eight hundred and seven years,
and had sons and daughters. 8So all the
days of Seth were nine hundred and twelve
years; and he died.

9Enosh lived ninety years, and begot
Cainan.[a] 10After he begot Cainan, Enosh
lived eight hundred and fifteen years, and
had sons and daughters. 11So all the days
of Enosh were nine hundred and five
years; and he died.

4:26 [a]Greek *Enos* 5:9 [a]Hebrew *Qenan*

5:1,3 Adam was uniquely created in the "image and likeness" of God (see Gen. 1:26). But after he sinned and died spiritually (see Gen. 2:17 comment), his offspring were made in *his* fallen image. Since everything reproduces "after its own kind," all of Adam's offspring (all mankind) are born spiritually dead—separated from God. It is because we are born spiritually dead that Jesus came to give us spiritual life (John 5:40; 10:10; 14:6; etc.). This is why Jesus said that we must be born again (John 3:3).

5:27 *Ages of the Patriarchs*

By Dr. David Menton and Dr. Georgia Purdom

For 1,500 years after creation, men lived such long lives that most were either contemporaries of the first man, Adam, or personally knew someone who was! The ten patriarchs (excluding Enoch) who preceded the Great Flood lived an average of 912 years. Lamech died the youngest at the age of 777, and Methuselah lived to be the oldest at 969.

AGES OF THE PATRIARCHS FROM ADAM TO NOAH

	Patriarch	Age	Bible Reference
1	Adam	930	Genesis 5:4
2	Seth	912	Genesis 5:8
3	Enosh	905	Genesis 5:11
4	Cainan	910	Genesis 5:14
5	Mahalalel	895	Genesis 5:17
6	Jared	962	Genesis 5:20
7	Enoch	365 (translated)	Genesis 5:23
8	Methuselah	969	Genesis 5:27
9	Lamech	777	Genesis 5:31
10	Noah	950	Genesis 9:29

During the 1,000 years following the Flood, however, the Bible records a progressive decline in the life span of the patriarchs, from Noah who lived to be 950 years old until Abraham at 175. In fact, Moses was unusually old for his time (120 years) because, when he reflected on the brevity of life, he said: "The days of our lives are seventy years; and if by reason of strength they are eighty years, yet their boast is only labor and sorrow; for it is soon cut off, and we fly away" (Psa. 90:10). See also 9:28,29 comment.

[12]Cainan lived seventy years, and begot Mahalalel. [13]After he begot Mahalalel,
Cainan lived eight hundred and forty years,
and had sons and daughters. [14]So all the
days of Cainan were nine hundred and
ten years; and he died.
[15]Mahalalel lived sixty-five years, and
begot Jared. [16]After he begot Jared, Mahalalel lived eight hundred and thirty years,
and had sons and daughters. [17]So all the
days of Mahalalel were eight hundred and
ninety-five years; and he died.
[18]Jared lived one hundred and sixty-
two years, and begot Enoch. [19]After he begot Enoch, Jared lived eight hundred years,
and had sons and daughters. [20]So all the
days of Jared were nine hundred and sixty-
two years; and he died.
[21]Enoch lived sixty-five years, and begot
Methuselah. [22]After he begot Methuselah,
Enoch walked with God three hundred
years, and had sons and daughters. [23]So
all the days of Enoch were three hundred
and sixty-five years. [24]And Enoch walked
with God; and he *was* not, for God took
him.
[25]Methuselah lived one hundred and
eighty-seven years, and begot Lamech.
[26]After he begot Lamech, Methuselah lived
seven hundred and eighty-two years, and
had sons and daughters. [27]So all the days
of Methuselah were nine hundred and
sixty-nine years; and he died.
[28]Lamech lived one hundred and eighty-
two years, and had a son. [29]And he called
his name Noah, saying, "This *one* will comfort us concerning our work and the toil
of our hands, because of the ground which
the LORD has cursed." [30]After he begot
Noah, Lamech lived five hundred and
ninety-five years, and had sons and daughters. [31]So all the days of Lamech were

seven hundred and seventy-seven years;
and he died.
[32]And Noah was five hundred years old,
and Noah begot Shem, Ham, and Japheth.

The Wickedness and Judgment of Man

6 Now it came to pass, when men began to multiply on the face of the earth,
and daughters were born to them, [2]that
the sons of God saw the daughters of
men, that they *were* beautiful; and they
took wives for themselves of all whom
they chose.
[3]And the LORD said, "My Spirit shall
not strive[a] with man forever, for he *is* indeed flesh; yet his days shall be one hundred and twenty years." [4]There were giants
on the earth in those days, and also afterward, when the sons of God came in to
the daughters of men and they bore *chil-*
dren to them. Those *were* the mighty men
who *were* of old, men of renown.
[5]Then the LORD[a] saw that the wickedness of man *was* great in the earth, and
that every intent of the thoughts of his
heart *was* only evil continually. [6]And the
LORD was sorry that He had made man
on the earth, and He was grieved in His
heart. [7]So the LORD said, "I will destroy
man whom I have created from the face
of the earth, both man and beast, creeping thing and birds of the air, for I am
sorry that I have made them." [8]But Noah
found grace in the eyes of the LORD.

Noah Pleases God

[9]This is the genealogy of Noah. Noah
was a just man, perfect in his generations.
Noah walked with God. [10]And Noah begot three sons: Shem, Ham, and Japheth.
[11]The earth also was corrupt before
God, and the earth was filled with violence.
[12]So God looked upon the earth, and indeed it was corrupt; for all flesh had corrupted their way on the earth.

The Ark Prepared

[13]And God said to Noah, "The end of
all flesh has come before Me, for the earth
is filled with violence through them; and
behold, I will destroy them with the
earth. [14]Make yourself an ark of gopher-
wood; make rooms in the ark, and cover
it inside and outside with pitch. [15]And
this is how you shall make it: The length
of the ark *shall be* three hundred cubits,
its width fifty cubits, and its height thirty
cubits. [16]You shall make a window for the
ark, and you shall finish it to a cubit from
above; and set the door of the ark in its
side. You shall make it *with* lower, second, and third *decks*. [17]And behold, I Myself am bringing floodwaters on the earth,
to destroy from under heaven all flesh in
which *is* the breath of life; everything that
is on the earth shall die. [18]But I will establish My covenant with you; and you
shall go into the ark—you, your sons,
your wife, and your sons' wives with you.
[19]And of every living thing of all flesh you
shall bring two of every *sort* into the ark,
to keep *them* alive with you; they shall be

6:3 [a]Septuagint, Syriac, Targum, and Vulgate read *abide*. 6:5 [a]Following Masoretic Text and Targum; Vulgate reads *God*; Septuagint reads *LORD God*.

6:5 "Erase all thought and fear of God from a community, and selfishness and sensuality would absorb the whole man. Appetite, knowing no restraint, and suffering, having no solace or hope, would trample in scorn on the restraints of human laws. Virtue, duty, principle, would be mocked as unmeaning sounds. A sordid self-interest would supplant every feeling; and man would become, in fact, what the theory of atheism declares him to be—a companion for brutes." *McGuffey's 5th Eclectic Reader (1879)*

6:7 For evolution's "missing links," see Acts 14:15 comment.

"There are no universally accepted fossil remains which demonstrate the evolution of man." *Nature*, vol. 412, 2001, p. 131.

"Scientists concede that their most cherished theories are based on embarrassingly few fossil fragments and that huge gaps exist in the fossil record." *Time* magazine, Nov. 7, 1977

6:17 For points to ponder about the flood, see Matt. 24:38,39 and 2 Pet. 3:5,6 comments.

6:15 How Large Was Noah's Ark?

By Ken Ham and Tim Lovett, Answers in Genesis

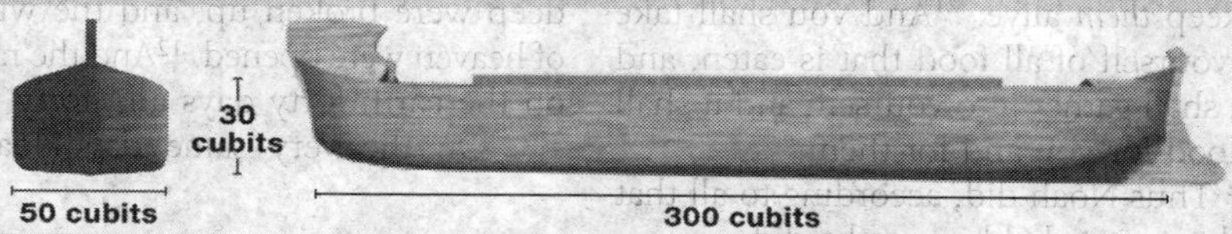

Unlike many whimsical drawings that depict the Ark as some kind of overgrown houseboat (with giraffes sticking out the top, for example), the Ark as described in the Bible was a big vessel. Not until relatively recent times (in the late 1800s) was a ship built—using steel—that far exceeded the capacity of Noah's Ark.

The dimensions of the Ark are convincing for two reasons: the proportions are like that of a modern cargo ship, and it is about as large as a wooden ship can be built. The cubit gives us a good indication of size. (The cubit was defined as the length of the forearm from elbow to fingertip. Ancient cubits vary anywhere from 17.5 inches to 22 inches, with the longer sizes dominating the major ancient constructions. Even a conservative 18-inch cubit describes a sizable vessel.)

We know the Ark must have been *at least* 450 feet long, 75 feet wide, and 45 feet high. Using a longer cubit, it would have been over 500 feet in length. In the Western world, wooden sailing ships never got much longer than about 330 feet, yet much earlier the ancient Greeks were building vessels at least this size. China built huge wooden ships in the 1400s that may have been as large as the Ark. The biblical Ark is one of the largest wooden ships of all time, a mid-sized cargo ship even by today's standards.

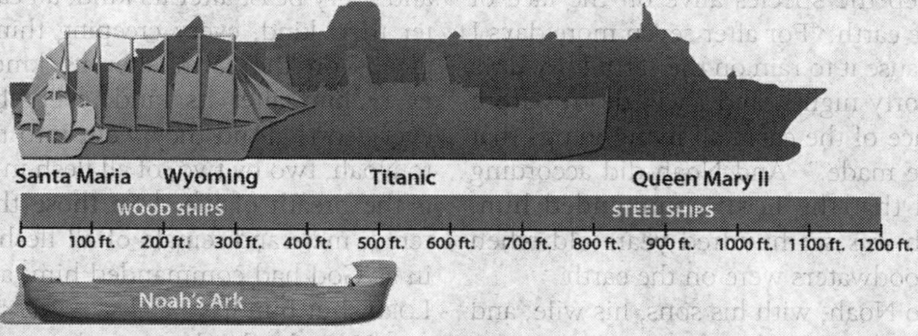

The Ark had three decks (Gen. 6:16), so this gives you an idea of its overall size. With a capacity of 1.5 million cubic feet, it would have had sufficient room for all the people, animals, and supplies. See also Matt. 24:38,39 and 2 Pet. 2:5 comments.

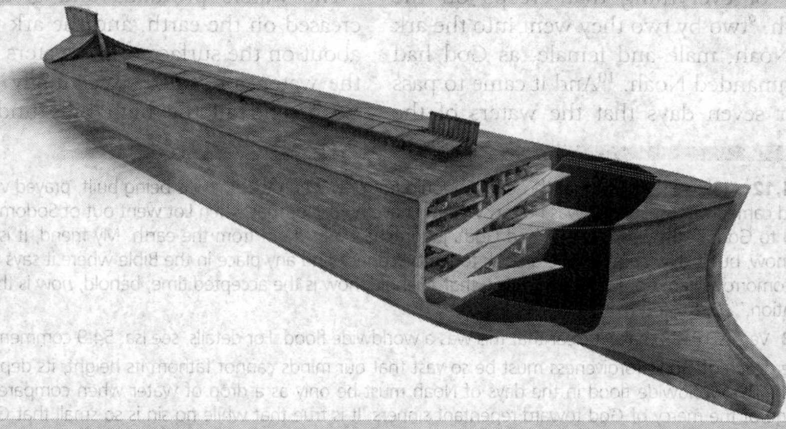

male and female. [20]Of the birds after their
kind, of animals after their kind, and of
every creeping thing of the earth after its
kind, two of every *kind* will come to you
to keep *them* alive. [21]And you shall take
for yourself of all food that is eaten, and
you shall gather *it* to yourself; and it shall
be food for you and for them."

[22]Thus Noah did; according to all that
God commanded him, so he did.

The Great Flood

7 Then the LORD said to Noah, "Come
into the ark, you and all your household, because I have seen *that* you *are*
righteous before Me in this generation.
[2]You shall take with you seven each of
every clean animal, a male and his female; two each of animals that *are* unclean, a male and his female; [3]also seven
each of birds of the air, male and female,
to keep the species alive on the face of
all the earth. [4]For after seven more days I
will cause it to rain on the earth forty days
and forty nights, and I will destroy from
the face of the earth all living things that
I have made." [5]And Noah did according
to all that the LORD commanded him.
[6]Noah *was* six hundred years old when
the floodwaters were on the earth.

[7]So Noah, with his sons, his wife, and
his sons' wives, went into the ark because
of the waters of the flood. [8]Of clean animals, of animals that *are* unclean, of birds,
and of everything that creeps on the
earth, [9]two by two they went into the ark
to Noah, male and female, as God had
commanded Noah. [10]And it came to pass
after seven days that the waters of the
flood were on the earth. [11]In the six hundredth year of Noah's life, in the second
month, the seventeenth day of the month,
on that day all the fountains of the great
deep were broken up, and the windows
of heaven were opened. [12]And the rain was
on the earth forty days and forty nights.

[13]On the very same day Noah and
Noah's sons, Shem, Ham, and Japheth, and
Noah's wife and the three wives of his
sons with them, entered the ark— [14]they
and every beast after its kind, all cattle after their kind, every creeping thing that
creeps on the earth after its kind, and
every bird after its kind, every bird of
every sort. [15]And they went into the ark
to Noah, two by two, of all flesh in which
is the breath of life. [16]So those that entered, male and female of all flesh, went
in as God had commanded him; and the
LORD shut him in.

[17]Now the flood was on the earth forty
days. The waters increased and lifted up
the ark, and it rose high above the earth.
[18]The waters prevailed and greatly increased on the earth, and the ark moved
about on the surface of the waters. [19]And
the waters prevailed exceedingly on the
earth, and all the high hills under the

> The creation-evolution debate is not about religion versus science or the Bible versus science—it's about good science versus bad science. Likewise, it's not about faith versus reason—it's about reasonable faith versus unreasonable faith.
>
> **NORMAN GEISLER**

7:11,12 "I have no doubt that those who would not pray when the ark was being built, prayed when the Flood came; but their prayer was not answered. I have no doubt that when Lot went out of Sodom, Sodom cried to God; but it was too late, and God's judgment swept them from the earth. My friend, it is not too late now, but it may be at twelve o'clock tonight. I cannot find any place in the Bible where it says you may call tomorrow. I am not justified in saying that. 'Behold, now is the accepted time; behold, *now* is the day of salvation.'" *D. L. Moody*

7:19 Verses 19–23 make it clear that this was a worldwide flood. For details, see Isa. 54:9 comment.

"The ocean of God's forgiveness must be so vast that our minds cannot fathom its height, its depth, or its width. The worldwide flood in the days of Noah must be only as a drop of water when compared to the deluge of the mercy of God toward repentant sinners. It is true that while no sin is so small that God does not see it, it is also true that there is no sin so great that God's mercy cannot wash it away." *Kirk Cameron*

QUESTIONS & OBJECTIONS

7:14,15

"How could all the animals fit on the Ark?"

By Ken Ham and Tim Lovett, Answers in Genesis

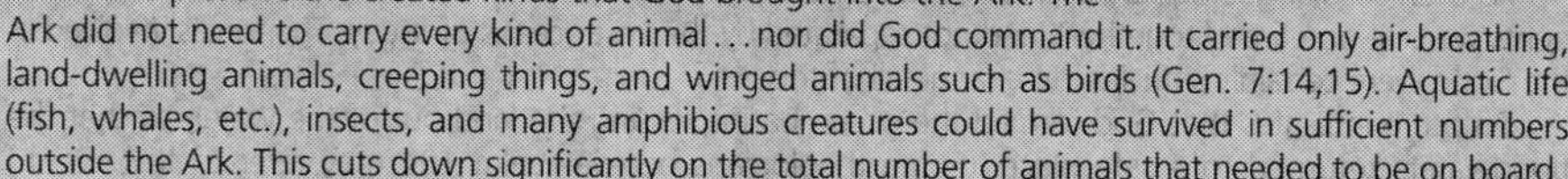

In the book *Noah's Ark: A Feasibility Study*, creationist researcher John Woodmorappe suggests that *at most* 16,000 animals were all that were needed to preserve the created kinds that God brought into the Ark. The Ark did not need to carry every kind of animal... nor did God command it. It carried only air-breathing, land-dwelling animals, creeping things, and winged animals such as birds (Gen. 7:14,15). Aquatic life (fish, whales, etc.), insects, and many amphibious creatures could have survived in sufficient numbers outside the Ark. This cuts down significantly on the total number of animals that needed to be on board.

Another factor that greatly reduces the space requirements is this: the tremendous variety in species we see today did not exist in the days of Noah. Only the parent "kinds" of these species were required to be on board in order to repopulate the earth. For example, only two dogs were needed to give rise to all the dog species that exist today. There are now more than 200 species of dogs, from the miniature poodle to the St. Bernard to various wolf species—all of which have descended from one original dog "kind." All other types of animals—cat kind, horse kind, cow kind, etc.—have similarly been naturally and selectively bred to achieve the wonderful variation in species that we have today. God "programmed" this variety into the genetic code of all animal kinds—and even human kind! God also made it impossible for the basic "kinds" of animals to breed and reproduce with each other. For example, cats and dogs cannot breed to make a new type of creature. This is by God's design, and it is one fact that makes evolution impossible.

Also, Noah wouldn't have taken the largest animals on the Ark, as there would be no reason to take "animal senior citizens" for a breeding population when the Flood was over. It is more likely that he took younger juveniles aboard the Ark, which would have required less space and less food.

Using a short cubit of 18 inches to be conservative, Woodmorappe's conclusion is that "less than half of the cumulative area of the Ark's three decks need to have been occupied by the animals and their enclosures." This meant there was plenty of room for fresh food, water, and people. See Isa. 27:1 comment.

whole heaven were covered. 20The waters
prevailed fifteen cubits upward, and the
mountains were covered. 21And all flesh
died that moved on the earth: birds and
cattle and beasts and every creeping thing
that creeps on the earth, and every man.
22All in whose nostrils *was* the breath of
the spirit[a] of life, all that *was* on the dry
land, died. 23So He destroyed all living
things which were on the face of the
ground: both man and cattle, creeping
thing and bird of the air. They were destroyed from the earth. Only Noah and
those who *were* with him in the ark remained *alive.* 24And the waters prevailed
on the earth one hundred and fifty days.

Noah's Deliverance

8 Then God remembered Noah, and
every living thing, and all the animals that *were* with him in the ark. And
God made a wind to pass over the earth,
and the waters subsided. 2The fountains
of the deep and the windows of heaven
were also stopped, and the rain from
heaven was restrained. 3And the waters
receded continually from the earth. At
the end of the hundred and fifty days the
waters decreased. 4Then the ark rested in
the seventh month, the seventeenth day
of the month, on the mountains of Ararat.
5And the waters decreased continually
until the tenth month. In the tenth *month,*
on the first *day* of the month, the tops of
the mountains were seen.

6So it came to pass, at the end of forty
days, that Noah opened the window of
the ark which he had made. 7Then he

7:22 [a]Septuagint and Vulgate omit *of the spirit.*

7:21,22 How could a flood destroy every living thing? See 2 Pet. 2:5 comment.

QUESTIONS & OBJECTIONS

8:3 *"Where did all the flood water go?"*

By Ken Ham, Answers in Genesis

Simply put, the water from the Flood is in the oceans and seas we see today. Three-quarters of the earth's surface is covered with water.

As even secular geologists observe, it does appear that the continents were at one time "together" and not separated by the vast oceans of today. The forces involved in the Flood were certainly sufficient to change all of this.

Scripture indicates that God formed the ocean basins, raising the land out of the water, so that the floodwaters returned to a safe place. (Some theologians believe Psalm 104 may refer to this event.) Some creation scientists believe this breakup of the continent was part of the mechanism that ultimately caused the Flood.

Some have speculated, because of Gen. 10:25, that the continental break occurred during the time of Peleg. However, this division is mentioned in the context of the Tower of Babel's language division of the whole earth (Gen. 10—11). So the context points to a dividing of the languages and people groups, not the land breaking apart.

If there were a massive movement of continents during the time of Peleg, there would have been another worldwide flood. The Bible indicates that the mountains of Ararat existed for the Ark to land in them (Gen. 8:4); so the Indian-Australian Plate and Eurasian Plate had to have already collided, indicating that the continents had already shifted prior to Peleg.

sent out a raven, which kept going to and fro until the waters had dried up from the earth. [8]He also sent out from himself a dove, to see if the waters had receded from the face of the ground. [9]But the dove found no resting place for the sole of her foot, and she returned into the ark to him, for the waters *were* on the face of the whole earth. So he put out his hand and took her, and drew her into the ark to himself. [10]And he waited yet another seven days, and again he sent the dove out from the ark. [11]Then the dove came to him in the evening, and behold, a freshly plucked olive leaf *was* in her mouth; and Noah knew that the waters had receded from the earth. [12]So he waited yet another seven days and sent out the dove, which did not return again to him anymore.

[13]And it came to pass in the six hundred and first year, in the first *month,* the first *day* of the month, that the waters were dried up from the earth; and Noah removed the covering of the ark and looked, and indeed the surface of the ground was dry. [14]And in the second month, on the twenty-seventh day of the month, the earth was dried.

[15]Then God spoke to Noah, saying, [16]"Go out of the ark, you and your wife, and your sons and your sons' wives with you. [17]Bring out with you every living thing of all flesh that *is* with you: birds and cattle and every creeping thing that creeps on the earth, so that they may abound on the earth, and be fruitful and multiply on the earth." [18]So Noah went out, and his sons and his wife and his sons' wives with him. [19]Every animal, every creeping thing, every bird, *and* whatever creeps on the earth, according to their families, went out of the ark.

8:20 Sacrifices. "Noah offered sacrifices of each clean animal and bird after the Flood. Assuming Gen. 7:2,3 is speaking of seven individuals (as opposed to seven pairs), this would leave six clean animals after the Flood providing a good breeding stock for Noah's three sons. Such sacrifices were imitating Abel's offering of the firstborn of his flock (Gen. 4:4), which was a reflection of what the Lord had done with the first sacrifice to cover Adam and Eve's sin (Gen. 3:21). Such sacrifices point toward Christ, the perfect 'Lamb of God who takes away the sin of the world' (John 1:29)." *Ken Ham*

God's Covenant with Creation

20 Then Noah built an altar to the LORD, and took of every clean animal and of every clean bird, and offered burnt offerings on the altar. 21 And the LORD smelled a soothing aroma. Then the LORD said in His heart, "I will never again curse the ground for man's sake, although the imagination of man's heart *is* evil from his youth; nor will I again destroy every living thing as I have done.

22 "While the earth remains,
Seedtime and harvest,
Cold and heat,
Winter and summer,
And day and night
Shall not cease."

9 So God blessed Noah and his sons, and said to them: "Be fruitful and multiply, and fill the earth.[a] 2 And the fear of you and the dread of you shall be on every beast of the earth, on every bird of the air, on all that move *on* the earth, and on all the fish of the sea. They are given into your hand. 3 Every moving thing that lives shall be food for you. I have given you all things, even as the green herbs. 4 But you shall not eat flesh with its life, *that is,* its blood. 5 Surely for your lifeblood I will demand *a reckoning;* from the hand of every beast I will require it, and from the hand of man. From the hand of every man's brother I will require the life of man.

6 "Whoever sheds man's blood,
By man his blood shall be shed;
For in the image of God
He made man.
7 And as for you, be fruitful and
multiply;
Bring forth abundantly in the earth
And multiply in it."

8 Then God spoke to Noah and to his sons with him, saying: 9 "And as for Me, behold, I establish My covenant with you and with your descendants[a] after you, 10 and with every living creature that *is* with you: the birds, the cattle, and every beast of the earth with you, of all that go out of the ark, every beast of the earth. 11 Thus I establish My covenant with you: Never again shall all flesh be cut off by the waters of the flood; never again shall there be a flood to destroy the earth."

12 And God said: "This *is* the sign of the covenant which I make between Me and you, and every living creature that *is* with you, for perpetual generations: 13 I set My rainbow in the cloud, and it shall be for the sign of the covenant between Me and the earth. 14 It shall be, when I bring a cloud over the earth, that the rainbow shall be seen in the cloud; 15 and I will remember My covenant which *is* between Me and you and every living creature of all flesh; the waters shall never again become a flood to destroy all flesh. 16 The rainbow shall be in the cloud, and I will look on it to remember the everlasting covenant between God and every living creature of all flesh that *is* on the earth."

17 And God said to Noah, "This *is* the sign of the covenant which I have established between Me and all flesh that *is* on the earth."

Noah and His Sons

18 Now the sons of Noah who went out of the ark were Shem, Ham, and Japheth. And Ham *was* the father of Canaan. 19 These three *were* the sons of Noah, and from these the whole earth was populated.

9:1 [a]Compare Genesis 1:28 9:9 [a]Literally *seed*

9:4 See Deut. 12:16 comment regarding eating meat with its blood.

9:21 Alcohol abuse has forever devastated the family unit. The Bible forbids drunkenness (see Prov. 23:20; Luke 21:34; Rom. 13:13,14; Eph. 5:18). The Levitical priesthood was not allowed to drink wine (Lev. 10:9; Ezek. 44:21) and the New Testament qualifications for eldership include the words "sober" and "not given to wine" (see 1 Tim. 3:2,3; Titus 1:7,8).

20And Noah began *to be* a farmer, and
he planted a vineyard. 21Then he drank
of the wine and was drunk, and became
uncovered in his tent. 22And Ham, the
father of Canaan, saw the nakedness of
his father, and told his two brothers outside. 23But Shem and Japheth took a garment, laid *it* on both their shoulders, and
went backward and covered the nakedness of their father. Their faces *were* turned
away, and they did not see their father's
nakedness.
24So Noah awoke from his wine, and
knew what his younger son had done to
him. 25Then he said:

"Cursed *be* Canaan;
A servant of servants
He shall be to his brethren."

26And he said:

"Blessed *be* the LORD,
The God of Shem,
And may Canaan be his servant.
27May God enlarge Japheth,
And may he dwell in the tents of Shem;
And may Canaan be his servant."

28And Noah lived after the flood three
hundred and fifty years. 29So all the days
of Noah were nine hundred and fifty years;
and he died.

Nations Descended from Noah

10 Now this *is* the genealogy of the
sons of Noah: Shem, Ham, and Japheth. And sons were born to them after
the flood.
2The sons of Japheth *were* Gomer, Magog, Madai, Javan, Tubal, Meshech, and
Tiras. 3The sons of Gomer *were* Ashkenaz, Riphath,[a] and Togarmah. 4The sons
of Javan *were* Elishah, Tarshish, Kittim,
and Dodanim.[a] 5From these the coastland
peoples of the Gentiles were separated
into their lands, everyone according to
his language, according to their families,
into their nations.
6The sons of Ham *were* Cush, Mizraim,
Put,[a] and Canaan. 7The sons of Cush
were Seba, Havilah, Sabtah, Raamah, and
Sabtechah; and the sons of Raamah *were*
Sheba and Dedan.
8Cush begot Nimrod; he began to be a
mighty one on the earth. 9He was a mighty
hunter before the LORD; therefore it is
said, "Like Nimrod the mighty hunter before the LORD." 10And the beginning of
his kingdom was Babel, Erech, Accad, and
Calneh, in the land of Shinar. 11From that
land he went to Assyria and built Nineveh, Rehoboth Ir, Calah, 12and Resen
between Nineveh and Calah (that *is* the
principal city).
13Mizraim begot Ludim, Anamim, Lehabim, Naphtuhim, 14Pathrusim, and Casluhim (from whom came the Philistines
and Caphtorim).
15Canaan begot Sidon his firstborn, and
Heth; 16the Jebusite, the Amorite, and the
Girgashite; 17the Hivite, the Arkite, and
the Sinite; 18the Arvadite, the Zemarite,
and the Hamathite. Afterward the families of the Canaanites were dispersed.
19And the border of the Canaanites was
from Sidon as you go toward Gerar, as far
as Gaza; then as you go toward Sodom,
Gomorrah, Admah, and Zeboiim, as far
as Lasha. 20These *were* the sons of Ham,
according to their families, according to
their languages, in their lands *and* in their
nations.

10:3 [a]Spelled *Diphath* in 1 Chronicles 1:6 10:4 [a]Spelled *Rodanim* in Samaritan Pentateuch and 1 Chronicles 1:7 10:6 [a]Or *Phut*

9:28,29 Long life spans. "Noah was the last recorded person in the Bible to live over 900 years. Genetic bottlenecks at the Flood and subsequently at the Tower of Babel were likely the main reasons for the decline in ages. But consider that Noah lived another 350 years after the Flood and outlived his great, great, great, grandson Peleg, who was the first recorded death (of a person) after the Flood. So it makes sense that many cultures began revering and worshiping their ancestors (e.g., the Shinto religion, Greek mythology, Egyptian mythology, Norse/Germanic mythology, and others) since they simply outlived their descendants!" *Ken Ham*

[21]And *children* were born also to Shem, the father of all the children of Eber, the brother of Japheth the elder. [22]The sons of Shem *were* Elam, Asshur, Arphaxad, Lud, and Aram. [23]The sons of Aram *were* Uz, Hul, Gether, and Mash.[a] [24]Arphaxad begot Salah,[a] and Salah begot Eber. [25]To Eber were born two sons: the name of one *was* Peleg, for in his days the earth was divided; and his brother's name *was* Joktan. [26]Joktan begot Almodad, Sheleph, Hazarmaveth, Jerah, [27]Hadoram, Uzal, Diklah, [28]Obal,[a] Abimael, Sheba, [29]Ophir, Havilah, and Jobab. All these *were* the sons of Joktan. [30]And their dwelling place was from Mesha as you go toward Sephar, the mountain of the east. [31]These *were* the sons of Shem, according to their families, according to their languages, in their lands, according to their nations.

[32]These *were* the families of the sons of Noah, according to their generations, in their nations; and from these the nations were divided on the earth after the flood.

The Tower of Babel

11 Now the whole earth had one language and one speech. [2]And it came to pass, as they journeyed from the east, that they found a plain in the land of Shinar, and they dwelt there. [3]Then they said to one another, "Come, let us make bricks and bake *them* thoroughly." They had brick for stone, and they had asphalt for mortar. [4]And they said, "Come, let us build ourselves a city, and a tower whose top *is* in the heavens; let us make a name for ourselves, lest we be scattered abroad over the face of the whole earth."

[5]But the LORD came down to see the city and the tower which the sons of men had built. [6]And the LORD said, "Indeed the people *are* one and they all have one language, and this is what they begin to do; now nothing that they propose to do will be withheld from them. [7]Come, let Us go down and there confuse their language, that they may not understand one another's speech." [8]So the LORD scattered them abroad from there over the face of all the earth, and they ceased building the city. [9]Therefore its name is called Babel, because there the LORD confused the language of all the earth; and from there the LORD scattered them abroad over the face of all the earth.

10:23 [a]Called *Meshech* in Septuagint and 1 Chronicles 1:17 10:24 [a]Following Masoretic Text, Vulgate, and Targum; Septuagint reads *Arphaxad begot Cainan, and Cainan begot Salah* (compare Luke 3:35, 36). 10:28 [a]Spelled *Ebal* in 1 Chronicles 1:22

11:9 The source of different languages. "As far as the great proliferation of different languages among men is concerned, the biblical account is the only satisfactory explanation. If all men came from one ancestral population, as most evolutionary anthropologists believe today, they originally all spoke the same language. As long as they lived together, or continued to communicate with one another, it would have been impossible for the wide differences in human languages to have evolved. Therefore, if anthropologists insist on an evolutionary explanation for the different languages, then they must likewise postulate extremely long periods of isolation and inbreeding for the different tribes, practically as long as the history of man himself. This in turn means that each of the major language groups must be identical with a major racial group. Therefore, each 'race' must have had a long evolutionary history, and it is natural to assume that some races have evolved more than others . . .

"On the other hand, it does seem obvious that all the different nations, tribes, and languages among men do have a common origin in the not-too-distant past. People of all nations are all freely interfertile and of essentially equal intelligence and potential educability. Even the 'aborigines' of Australia are quite capable of acquiring Ph.D. degrees, and some have done so. Even though their languages are widely different from each other, all can be analyzed in terms of the science of linguistics, and all can be learned by men of other languages, thus demonstrating an original common nature and origin. There is really only one kind of man—namely mankind! In actuality there is only one race among men—the human race. The source of the different languages cannot be explained in terms of evolution, though the various dialects and similar languages within the basic groups are no doubt attributable to gradual diversification from a common source tongue. But the major groups are so fundamentally different from each other as to defy explanation in any naturalistic framework. Only the Bible provides an adequate explanation." *Henry M. Morris*

Shem's Descendants

[10]This is the genealogy of Shem: Shem *was* one hundred years old, and begot Arphaxad two years after the flood. [11]After he begot Arphaxad, Shem lived five hundred years, and begot sons and daughters.

[12]Arphaxad lived thirty-five years, and begot Salah. [13]After he begot Salah, Arphaxad lived four hundred and three years, and begot sons and daughters.

[14]Salah lived thirty years, and begot Eber. [15]After he begot Eber, Salah lived four hundred and three years, and begot sons and daughters.

[16]Eber lived thirty-four years, and begot Peleg. [17]After he begot Peleg, Eber lived four hundred and thirty years, and begot sons and daughters.

[18]Peleg lived thirty years, and begot Reu. [19]After he begot Reu, Peleg lived two hundred and nine years, and begot sons and daughters.

[20]Reu lived thirty-two years, and begot Serug. [21]After he begot Serug, Reu lived two hundred and seven years, and begot sons and daughters.

[22]Serug lived thirty years, and begot Nahor. [23]After he begot Nahor, Serug lived two hundred years, and begot sons and daughters.

[24]Nahor lived twenty-nine years, and begot Terah. [25]After he begot Terah, Nahor lived one hundred and nineteen years, and begot sons and daughters.

[26]Now Terah lived seventy years, and begot Abram, Nahor, and Haran.

Terah's Descendants

[27]This *is* the genealogy of Terah: Terah begot Abram, Nahor, and Haran. Haran begot Lot. [28]And Haran died before his father Terah in his native land, in Ur of the Chaldeans. [29]Then Abram and Nahor took wives: the name of Abram's wife *was* Sarai, and the name of Nahor's wife, Milcah, the daughter of Haran the father of Milcah and the father of Iscah. [30]But Sarai was barren; she had no child.

[31]And Terah took his son Abram and his grandson Lot, the son of Haran, and his daughter-in-law Sarai, his son Abram's wife, and they went out with them from Ur of the Chaldeans to go to the land of Canaan; and they came to Haran and dwelt there. [32]So the days of Terah were two hundred and five years, and Terah died in Haran.

. . . . . .

For witnessing to those who don't speak English, see the back of this Bible for the entire gospel in picture form.

. . . . . .

Promises to Abram

12 Now the LORD had said to Abram:

"Get out of your country,
From your family
And from your father's house,
To a land that I will show you.
[2]I will make you a great nation;
I will bless you
And make your name great;
And you shall be a blessing.
[3]I will bless those who bless you,
And I will curse him who curses you;
And in you all the families of the
earth shall be blessed."

[4]So Abram departed as the LORD had spoken to him, and Lot went with him. And Abram *was* seventy-five years old

12:4 "Abraham's removal out of his country, out of Ur first and afterwards out of Haran, in compliance with the call of God: *So Abram departed*; he was not disobedient to the heavenly vision, but did as he was bidden, not conferring with flesh and blood (Gal. 1:15,16). His obedience was speedy and without delay, submissive and without dispute; for he *went out, not knowing whither he went* (Heb. 11:8), but knowing whom he followed and under whose direction he went." *Matthew Henry*

God has spoken to every Christian—to go into the entire world and preach the gospel to every creature. We must not be disobedient to the heavenly vision.

when he departed from Haran. 5Then Abram took Sarai his wife and Lot his brother's son, and all their possessions that they had gathered, and the people whom they had acquired in Haran, and they departed to go to the land of Canaan. So they came to the land of Canaan. 6Abram passed through the land to the place of Shechem, as far as the terebinth tree of Moreh.[a] And the Canaanites *were* then in the land.

7Then the LORD appeared to Abram and said, "To your descendants I will give this land." And there he built an altar to the LORD, who had appeared to him. 8And he moved from there to the mountain east of Bethel, and he pitched his tent *with* Bethel on the west and Ai on the east; there he built an altar to the LORD and called on the name of the LORD. 9So Abram journeyed, going on still toward the South.[a]

Abram in Egypt

10Now there was a famine in the land, and Abram went down to Egypt to dwell there, for the famine *was* severe in the land. 11And it came to pass, when he was close to entering Egypt, that he said to Sarai his wife, "Indeed I know that you *are* a woman of beautiful countenance. 12Therefore it will happen, when the Egyptians see you, that they will say, 'This *is* his wife'; and they will kill me, but they will let you live. 13Please say you *are* my sister, that it may be well with me for your sake, and that I[a] may live because of you."

14So it was, when Abram came into Egypt, that the Egyptians saw the woman, that she *was* very beautiful. 15The princes of Pharaoh also saw her and commended her to Pharaoh. And the woman was taken to Pharaoh's house. 16He treated Abram well for her sake. He had sheep, oxen, male donkeys, male and female servants, female donkeys, and camels.

17But the LORD plagued Pharaoh and his house with great plagues because of Sarai, Abram's wife. 18And Pharaoh called Abram and said, "What *is* this you have done to me? Why did you not tell me that she *was* your wife? 19Why did you say, 'She *is* my sister'? I might have taken her as my wife. Now therefore, here is your wife; take *her* and go your way." 20So Pharaoh commanded *his* men concerning him; and they sent him away, with his wife and all that he had.

Abram Inherits Canaan

13 Then Abram went up from Egypt, he and his wife and all that he had, and Lot with him, to the South.[a] 2Abram *was* very rich in livestock, in silver, and in gold. 3And he went on his journey from the South as far as Bethel, to the place where his tent had been at the beginning, between Bethel and Ai, 4to the place of the altar which he had made there at first. And there Abram called on the name of the LORD.

5Lot also, who went with Abram, had flocks and herds and tents. 6Now the land was not able to support them, that they might dwell together, for their possessions were so great that they could not dwell together. 7And there was strife between the herdsmen of Abram's livestock and the herdsmen of Lot's livestock. The Canaanites and the Perizzites then dwelt in the land.

8So Abram said to Lot, "Please let there be no strife between you and me, and between my herdsmen and your herdsmen; for we *are* brethren. 9*Is* not the whole land before you? Please separate from me. If *you take* the left, then I will go to the right; or, if *you go* to the right, then I will go to the left."

10And Lot lifted his eyes and saw all the plain of Jordan, that it *was* well watered everywhere (before the LORD destroyed Sodom and Gomorrah) like the garden of

12:6 [a]Hebrew *Alon Moreh* 12:9 [a]Hebrew *Negev* 12:13 [a]Literally *my soul* 13:1 [a]Hebrew *Negev*

12:13 This was a lying generation. See Psa. 116:11 comment.

the LORD, like the land of Egypt as you go toward Zoar. [11]Then Lot chose for himself all the plain of Jordan, and Lot journeyed east. And they separated from each other. [12]Abram dwelt in the land of Canaan, and Lot dwelt in the cities of the plain and pitched *his* tent even as far as Sodom. [13]But the men of Sodom *were* exceedingly wicked and sinful against the LORD.

[14]And the LORD said to Abram, after Lot had separated from him: "Lift your eyes now and look from the place where you are—northward, southward, eastward, and westward; [15]for all the land which you see I give to you and your descendants[a] forever. [16]And I will make your descendants as the dust of the earth; so that if a man could number the dust of the earth, *then* your descendants also could be numbered. [17]Arise, walk in the land through its length and its width, for I give it to you."

[18]Then Abram moved *his* tent, and went and dwelt by the terebinth trees of Mamre,[a] which *are* in Hebron, and built an altar there to the LORD.

Lot's Captivity and Rescue

14 And it came to pass in the days of Amraphel king of Shinar, Arioch king of Ellasar, Chedorlaomer king of Elam, and Tidal king of nations,[a] [2]*that* they made war with Bera king of Sodom, Birsha king of Gomorrah, Shinab king of Admah, Shemeber king of Zeboiim, and the king of Bela (that is, Zoar). [3]All these joined together in the Valley of Siddim (that is, the Salt Sea). [4]Twelve years they served Chedorlaomer, and in the thirteenth year they rebelled.

[5]In the fourteenth year Chedorlaomer and the kings that *were* with him came and attacked the Rephaim in Ashteroth Karnaim, the Zuzim in Ham, the Emim in Shaveh Kiriathaim, [6]and the Horites in their mountain of Seir, as far as El Paran, which *is* by the wilderness. [7]Then they turned back and came to En Mishpat (that is, Kadesh), and attacked all the country of the Amalekites, and also the Amorites who dwelt in Hazezon Tamar.

> When God wants to do an impossible task, He takes an impossible man, and He crushes him.
>
> **ALAN REDPATH**

[8]And the king of Sodom, the king of Gomorrah, the king of Admah, the king of Zeboiim, and the king of Bela (that *is*, Zoar) went out and joined together in battle in the Valley of Siddim [9]against Chedorlaomer king of Elam, Tidal king of nations,[a] Amraphel king of Shinar, and Arioch king of Ellasar—four kings against five. [10]Now the Valley of Siddim *was full of* asphalt pits; and the kings of Sodom and Gomorrah fled; *some* fell there, and the remainder fled to the mountains. [11]Then they took all the goods of Sodom and Gomorrah, and all their provisions, and went their way. [12]They also took Lot, Abram's

13:15 [a]Literally *seed*, and so throughout the book 13:18 [a]Hebrew *Alon Mamre* 14:1 [a]Hebrew *goyim* 14:9 [a]Hebrew *goyim*

13:13 Sin is sin. The world may soften a biblical word that describes a certain sin, but it doesn't change the fact that it is a sin. We may say that a man and woman had an "affair," but it is still adultery in God's eyes. Whether a homosexual is called a "gay" person or a "sodomite," homosexuality is a sin in God's sight. That may be politically incorrect to say, but it is the truth. So how do we convince someone who is a homosexual that his behavior is morally wrong? One key is not to get into an argument about whether or not someone is *born* a homosexual. The truth is we are *all* born with a sinful nature, and that nature may take us into the sins of lying, stealing, greed, murder, rape, fornication, adultery, or homosexuality. Instead of being sidetracked, take the sinner through the moral Law (the Ten Commandments). Show him that he is already condemned by God (see John 3:18,36) despite his sexual preference. As long as a homosexual has a proud heart, he will not listen to your reasoning, so he must be humbled by the Law. Once he has a humble heart, then he may listen as you point out 1 Cor. 6:9,10 (that homosexuals, among others, will not inherit the kingdom of God). So use the Law, because it was made for homosexuals. See 1 Tim. 1:9,10 comment.

brother's son who dwelt in Sodom, and his goods, and departed.

[13]Then one who had escaped came and told Abram the Hebrew, for he dwelt by the terebinth trees of Mamre[a] the Amorite, brother of Eshcol and brother of Aner; and they *were* allies with Abram. [14]Now when Abram heard that his brother was taken captive, he armed his three hundred and eighteen trained *servants* who were born in his own house, and went in pursuit as far as Dan. [15]He divided his forces against them by night, and he and his servants attacked them and pursued them as far as Hobah, which *is* north of Damascus. [16]So he brought back all the goods, and also brought back his brother Lot and his goods, as well as the women and the people.

[17]And the king of Sodom went out to meet him at the Valley of Shaveh (that *is*, the King's Valley), after his return from the defeat of Chedorlaomer and the kings who *were* with him.

Abram and Melchizedek

[18]Then Melchizedek king of Salem brought out bread and wine; he *was* the priest of God Most High. [19]And he blessed him and said:

"Blessed be Abram of God Most High,
Possessor of heaven and earth;
[20]And blessed be God Most High,
Who has delivered your enemies into
your hand."

And he gave him a tithe of all.

[21]Now the king of Sodom said to Abram, "Give me the persons, and take the goods for yourself."

[22]But Abram said to the king of Sodom, "I have raised my hand to the LORD, God Most High, the Possessor of heaven and earth, [23]that I *will take* nothing, from a thread to a sandal strap, and that I will not take anything that *is* yours, lest you should say, 'I have made Abram rich'— [24]except only what the young men have eaten, and the portion of the men who went with me: Aner, Eshcol, and Mamre; let them take their portion."

God's Covenant with Abram

15 After these things the word of the LORD came to Abram in a vision, saying, "Do not be afraid, Abram. I *am* your shield, your exceedingly great reward."

[2]But Abram said, "Lord GOD, what will You give me, seeing I go childless, and the heir of my house *is* Eliezer of Damascus?" [3]Then Abram said, "Look, You have given me no offspring; indeed one born in my house is my heir!"

[4]And behold, the word of the LORD *came* to him, saying, "This one shall not be your heir, but one who will come from your own body shall be your heir." [5]Then He brought him outside and said, "Look now toward heaven, and count the stars if you are able to number them." And He said to him, "So shall your descendants be."

[6]And he believed in the LORD, and He accounted it to him for righteousness.

[7]Then He said to him, "I *am* the LORD, who brought you out of Ur of the Chaldeans, to give you this land to inherit it."

[8]And he said, "Lord GOD, how shall I know that I will inherit it?"

[9]So He said to him, "Bring Me a three-year-old heifer, a three-year-old female goat, a three-year-old ram, a turtledove, and a young pigeon." [10]Then he brought all these to Him and cut them in two, down the middle, and placed each piece opposite the other; but he did not cut the birds in two. [11]And when the vultures

14:13 [a]Hebrew *Alon Mamre*

15:6 Here is the simplicity of salvation. We trust in the Savior and God imputes (freely gives) the righteousness of Christ to our account, without any works on our part. Good works issue from our faith, confirming that we truly are born of God (see Eph. 2:8,9).

came down on the carcasses, Abram drove them away.

[12]Now when the sun was going down, a deep sleep fell upon Abram; and behold, horror *and* great darkness fell upon him. [13]Then He said to Abram: "Know certainly that your descendants will be strangers in a land *that is* not theirs, and will serve them, and they will afflict them four hundred years. [14]And also the nation whom they serve I will judge; afterward they shall come out with great possessions. [15]Now as for you, you shall go to your fathers in peace; you shall be buried at a good old age. [16]But in the fourth generation they shall return here, for the iniquity of the Amorites *is* not yet complete."

[17]And it came to pass, when the sun went down and it was dark, that behold, there appeared a smoking oven and a burning torch that passed between those pieces. [18]On the same day the LORD made a covenant with Abram, saying:

"To your descendants I have given this land, from the river of Egypt to the great river, the River Euphrates— [19]the Kenites, the Kenezzites, the Kadmonites, [20]the Hittites, the Perizzites, the Rephaim, [21]the Amorites, the Canaanites, the Girgashites, and the Jebusites."

Hagar and Ishmael

16 Now Sarai, Abram's wife, had borne him no *children.* And she had an Egyptian maidservant whose name was Hagar. [2]So Sarai said to Abram, "See now, the LORD has restrained me from bearing *children.* Please, go in to my maid; perhaps I shall obtain children by her." And Abram heeded the voice of Sarai. [3]Then Sarai, Abram's wife, took Hagar her maid, the Egyptian, and gave her to her husband Abram to be his wife, after Abram had dwelt ten years in the land of Canaan. [4]So he went in to Hagar, and she conceived. And when she saw that she had conceived, her mistress became despised in her eyes.

[5]Then Sarai said to Abram, "My wrong *be* upon you! I gave my maid into your embrace; and when she saw that she had conceived, I became despised in her eyes. The LORD judge between you and me."

[6]So Abram said to Sarai, "Indeed your maid *is* in your hand; do to her as you please." And when Sarai dealt harshly with her, she fled from her presence.

[7]Now the Angel of the LORD found her by a spring of water in the wilderness, by the spring on the way to Shur. [8]And He said, "Hagar, Sarai's maid, where have you come from, and where are you going?"

She said, "I am fleeing from the presence of my mistress Sarai."

[9]The Angel of the LORD said to her, "Return to your mistress, and submit yourself under her hand." [10]Then the Angel of the LORD said to her, "I will multiply your descendants exceedingly, so that they shall not be counted for multitude." [11]And the Angel of the LORD said to her:

"Behold, you *are* with child,
And you shall bear a son.
You shall call his name Ishmael,
Because the LORD has heard your
affliction.
[12]He shall be a wild man;
His hand *shall be* against every man,
And every man's hand against him.
And he shall dwell in the presence of
all his brethren."

16:2 There may be times when you do not see any fruit for your evangelistic labors. You are planting seed in the hearts of sinners but it seems that no one is being born again. If that is the case, consider this verse: "Therefore, my beloved brethren, be steadfast, immovable, always abounding in the work of the Lord, *knowing that your labor is not in vain in the Lord*" (1 Cor. 15:58, emphasis added). Keep planting and don't be tempted to revert to using the methods of modern evangelism to get "decisions for Christ." (See 2 Cor. 2:17 comment.) That may make you rejoice because you think you are seeing fruit, but keep in mind that while we may rejoice over "decisions," Heaven reserves its rejoicing for sinners who repent (see Luke 15:7), and repentance is God-given (see 2 Tim. 2:24–26). Sow in tears, and you will reap in joy—in God's time.

[13]Then she called the name of the LORD who spoke to her, You-Are-the-God-Who-Sees; for she said, "Have I also here seen Him who sees me?" [14]Therefore the well was called Beer Lahai Roi;[a] observe, *it is* between Kadesh and Bered.

[15]So Hagar bore Abram a son; and Abram named his son, whom Hagar bore, Ishmael. [16]Abram *was* eighty-six years old when Hagar bore Ishmael to Abram.

The Sign of the Covenant

17 When Abram was ninety-nine years old, the LORD appeared to Abram and said to him, "I *am* Almighty God; walk before Me and be blameless. [2]And I will make My covenant between Me and you, and will multiply you exceedingly." [3]Then Abram fell on his face, and God talked with him, saying: [4]"As for Me, behold, My covenant is with you, and you shall be a father of many nations. [5]No longer shall your name be called Abram, but your name shall be Abraham; for I have made you a father of many nations. [6]I will make you exceedingly fruitful; and I will make nations of you, and kings shall come from you. [7]And I will establish My covenant between Me and you and your descendants after you in their generations, for an everlasting covenant, to be God to you and your descendants after you. [8]Also I give to you and your descendants after you the land in which you are a stranger, all the land of Canaan, as an everlasting possession; and I will be their God."

[9]And God said to Abraham: "As for you, you shall keep My covenant, you and your descendants after you throughout their generations. [10]This *is* My covenant which you shall keep, between Me and you and your descendants after you: Every male child among you shall be circumcised; [11]and you shall be circumcised in the flesh of your foreskins, and it shall be a sign of the covenant between Me and you. [12]He who is eight days old among you shall be circumcised, every male child in your generations, he who is born in your house or bought with money from any foreigner who is not your descendant. [13]He who is born in your house and he who is bought with your money must be circumcised, and My covenant shall be in your flesh for an everlasting covenant. [14]And the uncircumcised male child, who is not circumcised in the flesh of his foreskin, that person shall be cut off from his people; he has broken My covenant."

[15]Then God said to Abraham, "As for Sarai your wife, you shall not call her name Sarai, but Sarah *shall be* her name. [16]And I will bless her and also give you a son by her; then I will bless her, and she shall be *a mother* of nations; kings of peoples shall be from her."

[17]Then Abraham fell on his face and laughed, and said in his heart, "Shall *a child* be born to a man who is one hundred years old? And shall Sarah, who is ninety years old, bear *a child?*" [18]And Abraham said to God, "Oh, that Ishmael might live before You!"

[19]Then God said: "No, Sarah your wife shall bear you a son, and you shall call his name Isaac; I will establish My covenant with him for an everlasting covenant, *and* with his descendants after him. [20]And as for Ishmael, I have heard you. Behold, I have blessed him, and will make him fruitful, and will multiply him exceedingly. He shall beget twelve princes, and I will make him a great nation. [21]But My covenant I will establish with Isaac, whom Sarah shall bear to you at this set time next year." [22]Then He finished talking with him, and God went up from Abraham.

[23]So Abraham took Ishmael his son,

16:14 [a]Literally *Well of the One Who Lives and Sees Me*

17:10 For whether circumcision is an everlasting covenant, see Deut. 10:16 comment.
17:12 Why did God specify day eight for circumcisions? See John 20:26 comment.

all who were born in his house and all who were bought with his money, every male among the men of Abraham's house, and circumcised the flesh of their foreskins that very same day, as God had said to him. [24]Abraham *was* ninety-nine years old when he was circumcised in the flesh of his foreskin. [25]And Ishmael his son *was* thirteen years old when he was circumcised in the flesh of his foreskin. [26]That very same day Abraham was circumcised, and his son Ishmael; [27]and all the men of his house, born in the house or bought with money from a foreigner, were circumcised with him.

The Son of Promise

18 Then the LORD appeared to him by the terebinth trees of Mamre,[a] as he was sitting in the tent door in the heat of the day. [2]So he lifted his eyes and looked, and behold, three men were standing by him; and when he saw *them*, he ran from the tent door to meet them, and bowed himself to the ground, [3]and said, "My Lord, if I have now found favor in Your sight, do not pass on by Your servant. [4]Please let a little water be brought, and wash your feet, and rest yourselves under the tree. [5]And I will bring a morsel of bread, that you may refresh your hearts. After that you may pass by, inasmuch as you have come to your servant."

They said, "Do as you have said."

[6]So Abraham hurried into the tent to Sarah and said, "Quickly, make ready three measures of fine meal; knead *it* and make cakes." [7]And Abraham ran to the herd, took a tender and good calf, gave *it* to a young man, and he hastened to prepare it. [8]So he took butter and milk and the calf which he had prepared, and set *it* before them; and he stood by them under the tree as they ate.

[9]Then they said to him, "Where is Sarah your wife?"

So he said, "Here, in the tent."

[10]And He said, "I will certainly return to you according to the time of life, and behold, Sarah your wife shall have a son."

(Sarah was listening in the tent door which *was* behind him.) [11]Now Abraham and Sarah were old, well advanced in age; *and* Sarah had passed the age of childbearing.[a] [12]Therefore Sarah laughed within herself, saying, "After I have grown old, shall I have pleasure, my lord being old also?"

[13]And the LORD said to Abraham, "Why did Sarah laugh, saying, 'Shall I surely bear *a child,* since I am old?' [14]Is anything too hard for the LORD? At the appointed time I will return to you, according to the time of life, and Sarah shall have a son."

[15]But Sarah denied *it*, saying, "I did not laugh," for she was afraid.

And He said, "No, but you did laugh!"

Abraham Intercedes for Sodom

[16]Then the men rose from there and looked toward Sodom, and Abraham went with them to send them on the way. [17]And the LORD said, "Shall I hide from Abraham what I am doing, [18]since Abraham shall surely become a great and mighty nation, and all the nations of the earth shall be blessed in him? [19]For I have known him, in order that he may command his children and his household after him, that they keep the way of the LORD, to do righteousness and justice, that the LORD may bring to Abraham what He has spoken to him." [20]And the LORD said, "Because the outcry against Sodom and Gomorrah is great, and because their sin is very grave, [21]I will go down now and see whether they have done altogether according to the outcry against it that has come to Me; and if not, I will know."

18:1 [a]Hebrew *Alon Mamre* **18:11** [a]Literally *the manner of women had ceased to be with Sarah*

18:1 "Abraham knew it was the LORD, yet he also clearly saw that He had a physical body. He had both feet to wash (v. 4) and a mouth to eat (v. 8). This passage shows us the preincarnate second Person of the Trinity, our Lord Jesus Christ." *Jay Fowler*

22 Then the men turned away from there and went toward Sodom, but Abraham still stood before the LORD. 23 And Abraham came near and said, "Would You also destroy the righteous with the wicked? 24 Suppose there were fifty righteous within the city; would You also destroy the place and not spare *it* for the fifty righteous that were in it? 25 Far be it from You to do such a thing as this, to slay the righteous with the wicked, so that the righteous should be as the wicked; far be it from You! Shall not the Judge of all the earth do right?"

26 So the LORD said, "If I find in Sodom fifty righteous within the city, then I will spare all the place for their sakes."

27 Then Abraham answered and said, "Indeed now, I who *am but* dust and ashes have taken it upon myself to speak to the Lord: 28 Suppose there were five less than the fifty righteous; would You destroy all of the city for *lack of* five?"

So He said, "If I find there forty-five, I will not destroy *it*."

29 And he spoke to Him yet again and said, "Suppose there should be forty found there?"

So He said, "I will not do *it* for the sake of forty."

30 Then he said, "Let not the Lord be angry, and I will speak: Suppose thirty should be found there?"

So He said, "I will not do *it* if I find thirty there."

31 And he said, "Indeed now, I have taken it upon myself to speak to the Lord: Suppose twenty should be found there?"

So He said, "I will not destroy *it* for the sake of twenty."

32 Then he said, "Let not the Lord be angry, and I will speak but once more: Suppose ten should be found there?"

And He said, "I will not destroy *it* for the sake of ten." 33 So the LORD went His way as soon as He had finished speaking with Abraham; and Abraham returned to his place.

Sodom's Depravity

19 Now the two angels came to Sodom in the evening, and Lot was sitting in the gate of Sodom. When Lot saw *them,* he rose to meet them, and he bowed himself with his face toward the ground. 2 And he said, "Here now, my lords, please turn in to your servant's house and spend the night, and wash your feet; then you may rise early and go on your way."

And they said, "No, but we will spend the night in the open square."

3 But he insisted strongly; so they turned in to him and entered his house. Then he made them a feast, and baked unleavened bread, and they ate.

4 Now before they lay down, the men of the city, the men of Sodom, both old and young, all the people from every quarter, surrounded the house. 5 And they

18:25 It can be a difficult situation if someone you are witnessing to asks about the fate of a loved one who died and was not a Christian. Simply say, "Only God knows the eternal destiny of the person, and the Scriptures assure us that He will do what is right. So we can take consolation from that." Some may be tempted to say that the loved one went to hell, but the truth is that we don't know what happened minutes before the person's death. Remember the thief on the cross.

18:32 Abraham's grievous dilemma. "Abraham pleaded with God for his loved ones and was given a promise for ten's sake, yet not even ten righteous could be found. Lot was warned of destruction and given all his household (19:12–15), but only his wife and two daughters came out.

"How grievous and tragic the pain of these two patriarchs who had been offered what we all desire: safe passage for our loved ones. Yet those very ones refused the salvation offered.

"O what a grievous dilemma. Jesus Christ has obtained safe passage for our loved ones, yet how many will bring destruction on themselves for a lack of understanding? We must with all our heart and all our strength, by the grace of God, persuade them before destruction comes! 'Even so, come, Lord Jesus!' (Rev. 22:20)." *Stuart Scott*

This gives great hope for America and other nations. Those who trust in the righteousness of the Savior can "stand in the gap" for their nation, and God will hear their prayers.

called to Lot and said to him, "Where are
the men who came to you tonight? Bring
them out to us that we may know them
carnally."
6So Lot went out to them through the
doorway, shut the door behind him, 7and
said, "Please, my brethren, do not do so
wickedly! 8See now, I have two daughters
who have not known a man; please, let
me bring them out to you, and you may
do to them as you wish; only do nothing
to these men, since this is the reason they
have come under the shadow of my roof."
9And they said, "Stand back!" Then
they said, "This one came in to stay *here*,
and he keeps acting as a judge; now we
will deal worse with you than with them."
So they pressed hard against the man Lot,
and came near to break down the door.
10But the men reached out their hands
and pulled Lot into the house with them,
and shut the door. 11And they struck the
men who *were* at the doorway of the house
with blindness, both small and great, so
that they became weary *trying* to find the
door.

Sodom and Gomorrah Destroyed

12Then the men said to Lot, "Have you
anyone else here? Son-in-law, your sons,
your daughters, and whomever you have
in the city—take *them* out of this place!
13For we will destroy this place, because
the outcry against them has grown great
before the face of the LORD, and the LORD
has sent us to destroy it."
14So Lot went out and spoke to his sons-
in-law, who had married his daughters,
and said, "Get up, get out of this place;
for the LORD will destroy this city!" But to
his sons-in-law he seemed to be joking.
15When the morning dawned, the angels urged Lot to hurry, saying, "Arise,
take your wife and your two daughters
who are here, lest you be consumed in
the punishment of the city." 16And while
he lingered, the men took hold of his
hand, his wife's hand, and the hands of
his two daughters, the LORD being merciful to him, and they brought him out and
set him outside the city. 17So it came to
pass, when they had brought them outside, that he[a] said, "Escape for your life!
Do not look behind you nor stay anywhere in the plain. Escape to the mountains, lest you be destroyed."
18Then Lot said to them, "Please, no,
my lords! 19Indeed now, your servant has
found favor in your sight, and you have
increased your mercy which you have
shown me by saving my life; but I cannot
escape to the mountains, lest some evil
overtake me and I die. 20See now, this city
is near *enough* to flee to, and it *is* a little

19:17 [a]Septuagint, Syriac, and Vulgate read *they*.

19:8 Some skeptics point to this verse, where Lot offered two of his daughters to a pack of homosexuals who were at his door, threatening to rape Lot's two male visitors. Of course, the homosexuals did not take him up on his offer, and the visitors (angels) were very capable of protecting themselves. The Bible does not hide human stupidity; it reveals it so that we will not make the same mistakes. We are told that all of Scripture was written for our instruction (see Rom. 15:4; 2 Tim. 3:16). So, be instructed. If rapists come to your door, don't offer them your daughters. That's crazy. See also Judg. 11:39 comment.

19:11 In addition to being blinded by the god of this age (see 2 Cor. 4:4), the Bible tells us that those who give themselves to the sin of homosexuality are given over to a "debased mind" (Rom. 1:28). Those who witness regularly to homosexuals will find that they are often repentant when it comes to lying, theft, adultery, etc., but they refuse to repent of homosexuality despite the fact that the Scriptures clearly say it is sin. See 1 Cor. 6:9,10; Lev. 18:22; 20:13.

19:17 This is the message that we must preach: that all humanity flee from the wrath to come, that they are to be saved from this wicked and adulterous generation through repentance and faith in Jesus alone. Sadly, these words are rarely heard from the lips of popular preachers. Every time we enter a pulpit or open our mouths to preach in public, we should be mindful that there are more than likely unsaved people listening to our words. Their blood will be on our hands if we fail to warn them (see Ezek. 33:3–9; Acts 20:26,27).

one; please let me escape there (*is* it not a little one?) and my soul shall live."

[21]And he said to him, "See, I have favored you concerning this thing also, in that I will not overthrow this city for which you have spoken. [22]Hurry, escape there. For I cannot do anything until you arrive there."

Therefore the name of the city was called Zoar.

[23]The sun had risen upon the earth when Lot entered Zoar. [24]Then the LORD rained brimstone and fire on Sodom and Gomorrah, from the LORD out of the heavens. [25]So He overthrew those cities, all the plain, all the inhabitants of the cities, and what grew on the ground.

> A man says to me, 'Can you explain the seven trumpets of the Revelation?' No, but I can blow one in your ear, and warn you to escape from the wrath to come.
>
> **CHARLES SPURGEON**

[26]But his wife looked back behind him, and she became a pillar of salt.

[27]And Abraham went early in the morning to the place where he had stood before the LORD. [28]Then he looked toward Sodom and Gomorrah, and toward all the land of the plain; and he saw, and behold, the smoke of the land which went up like the smoke of a furnace. [29]And it came to pass, when God destroyed the cities of the plain, that God remembered Abraham, and sent Lot out of the midst of the overthrow, when He overthrew the cities in which Lot had dwelt.

The Descendants of Lot

[30]Then Lot went up out of Zoar and dwelt in the mountains, and his two daughters were with him; for he was afraid to dwell in Zoar. And he and his two daughters dwelt in a cave. [31]Now the firstborn said to the younger, "Our father *is* old, and *there is* no man on the earth to come in to us as is the custom of all the earth. [32]Come, let us make our father drink wine, and we will lie with him, that we may preserve the lineage of our father." [33]So they made their father drink wine that night. And the firstborn went in and lay with her father, and he did not know when she lay down or when she arose.

[34]It happened on the next day that the firstborn said to the younger, "Indeed I lay with my father last night; let us make him drink wine tonight also, and you go in *and* lie with him, that we may preserve the lineage of our father." [35]Then they made their father drink wine that night also. And the younger arose and lay with him, and he did not know when she lay down or when she arose.

[36]Thus both the daughters of Lot were with child by their father. [37]The firstborn bore a son and called his name Moab; he *is* the father of the Moabites to this day. [38]And the younger, she also bore a son and called his name Ben-Ammi; he is the father of the people of Ammon to this day.

Abraham and Abimelech

20 And Abraham journeyed from there to the South, and dwelt between Kadesh and Shur, and stayed in Gerar. [2]Now Abraham said of Sarah his wife, "She *is* my sister." And Abimelech king of Gerar sent and took Sarah.

[3]But God came to Abimelech in a dream by night, and said to him, "Indeed you *are* a dead man because of the woman whom you have taken, for she *is* a man's wife."

[4]But Abimelech had not come near her; and he said, "Lord, will You slay a

19:24,25 "The sin of Sodom and Gomorrah was some kind of activity—a grave, ongoing, lawless, sensuous activity—that Lot saw and heard and that tormented him as he witnessed it day after day. It was an activity in which the inhabitants indulged the flesh in corrupt desires by going after strange flesh, ultimately bringing upon them the most extensive judgment anywhere in the Bible outside of the book of Revelation." *Gregory Koukl*

righteous nation also? 5Did he not say to me, 'She *is* my sister'? And she, even she herself said, 'He *is* my brother.' In the integrity of my heart and innocence of my hands I have done this."

6And God said to him in a dream, "Yes, I know that you did this in the integrity of your heart. For I also withheld you from sinning against Me; therefore I did not let you touch her. 7Now therefore, restore the man's wife; for he *is* a prophet, and he will pray for you and you shall live. But if you do not restore *her,* know that you shall surely die, you and all who *are* yours."

8So Abimelech rose early in the morning, called all his servants, and told all these things in their hearing; and the men were very much afraid. 9And Abimelech called Abraham and said to him, "What have you done to us? How have I offended you, that you have brought on me and on my kingdom a great sin? You have done deeds to me that ought not to be done." 10Then Abimelech said to Abraham, "What did you have in view, that you have done this thing?"

11And Abraham said, "Because I thought, surely the fear of God *is* not in this place; and they will kill me on account of my wife. 12But indeed *she is* truly my sister. She *is* the daughter of my father, but not the daughter of my mother; and she became my wife. 13And it came to pass, when God caused me to wander from my father's house, that I said to her, 'This *is* your kindness that you should do for me: in every place, wherever we go, say of me, "He *is* my brother." ' "

14Then Abimelech took sheep, oxen, and male and female servants, and gave *them* to Abraham; and he restored Sarah his wife to him. 15And Abimelech said, "See, my land *is* before you; dwell where it pleases you." 16Then to Sarah he said, "Behold, I have given your brother a thousand *pieces* of silver; indeed this vindicates you[a] before all who *are* with you and before everybody." Thus she was rebuked.

17So Abraham prayed to God; and God healed Abimelech, his wife, and his female servants. Then they bore *children;* 18for the LORD had closed up all the wombs of the house of Abimelech because of Sarah, Abraham's wife.

Isaac Is Born

21 And the LORD visited Sarah as He had said, and the LORD did for Sarah as He had spoken. 2For Sarah conceived and bore Abraham a son in his old age, at the set time of which God had spoken to him. 3And Abraham called the name of his son who was born to him—whom Sarah bore to him—Isaac. 4Then Abraham circumcised his son Isaac when he was eight days old, as God had commanded him. 5Now Abraham was one hundred years old when his son Isaac was born to him. 6And Sarah said, "God has made me laugh, *and* all who hear will laugh with me." 7She also said, "Who would have said to Abraham that Sarah would nurse children? For I have borne *him* a son in his old age."

Hagar and Ishmael Depart

8So the child grew and was weaned. And Abraham made a great feast on the same day that Isaac was weaned.

9And Sarah saw the son of Hagar the Egyptian, whom she had borne to Abraham, scoffing. 10Therefore she said to Abraham, "Cast out this bondwoman and her son; for the son of this bondwoman shall

20:16 [a]Literally *it is a covering of the eyes for you*

20:11 There is no worse state for a nation or the Church to be in than to lose the fear of God. Someone once said, "I fear God, and next to God I chiefly fear him who fears Him not." Those who do not fear God will lie to you, steal from you, and even kill you if they think they can get away with it. It is the fear of the Lord that causes men to depart from evil (see Prov. 16:6). Jesus said, "Do not fear those who kill the body but cannot kill the soul. But rather fear Him who is able to destroy both soul and body in hell" (Matt. 10:28).

not be heir with my son, *namely* with Isaac." 11And the matter was very displeasing in Abraham's sight because of his son.

12But God said to Abraham, "Do not let it be displeasing in your sight because of the lad or because of your bondwoman. Whatever Sarah has said to you, listen to her voice; for in Isaac your seed shall be called. 13Yet I will also make a nation of the son of the bondwoman, because he *is* your seed."

14So Abraham rose early in the morning, and took bread and a skin of water; and putting *it* on her shoulder, he gave *it* and the boy to Hagar, and sent her away. Then she departed and wandered in the Wilderness of Beersheba. 15And the water in the skin was used up, and she placed the boy under one of the shrubs. 16Then she went and sat down across from *him* at a distance of about a bowshot; for she said to herself, "Let me not see the death of the boy." So she sat opposite *him,* and lifted her voice and wept.

17And God heard the voice of the lad. Then the angel of God called to Hagar out of heaven, and said to her, "What ails you, Hagar? Fear not, for God has heard the voice of the lad where he *is.* 18Arise, lift up the lad and hold him with your hand, for I will make him a great nation."

19Then God opened her eyes, and she saw a well of water. And she went and filled the skin with water, and gave the lad a drink. 20So God was with the lad; and he grew and dwelt in the wilderness, and became an archer. 21He dwelt in the Wilderness of Paran; and his mother took a wife for him from the land of Egypt.

A Covenant with Abimelech

22And it came to pass at that time that Abimelech and Phichol, the commander of his army, spoke to Abraham, saying, "God *is* with you in all that you do. 23Now therefore, swear to me by God that you will not deal falsely with me, with my offspring, or with my posterity; but that according to the kindness that I have done to you, you will do to me and to the land in which you have dwelt."

24And Abraham said, "I will swear."

25Then Abraham rebuked Abimelech because of a well of water which Abimelech's servants had seized. 26And Abimelech said, "I do not know who has done this thing; you did not tell me, nor had I heard *of it* until today." 27So Abraham took sheep and oxen and gave them to Abimelech, and the two of them made a covenant. 28And Abraham set seven ewe lambs of the flock by themselves.

29Then Abimelech asked Abraham, "What *is the meaning of* these seven ewe lambs which you have set by themselves?"

30And he said, "You will take *these* seven ewe lambs from my hand, that they may be my witness that I have dug this well." 31Therefore he called that place Beersheba,[a] because the two of them swore an oath there.

32Thus they made a covenant at Beersheba. So Abimelech rose with Phichol, the commander of his army, and they returned to the land of the Philistines. 33Then *Abraham* planted a tamarisk tree in Beersheba, and there called on the name of the

21:31 [a]Literally *Well of the Oath* or *Well of the Seven*

21:16–19 It was love that drove Hagar to cry out to God for the child. How can love not compel us to lift up our voices and weep, given the impending deaths of multitudes around us? God has opened our eyes to see the wells of salvation in Christ, so we must lead sinners by the hand to Him who cried, "If anyone thirsts, let him come to Me and drink" (John 7:37).

"I could abundantly justify compassion for perishing men, even on the ground of natural feelings. A mother who did not, like Hagar, weep for her dying child—call her not 'mother,' call her 'monster.' A man who passes through the scenes of misery which even this city presents in its more squalid quarters, and yet is never disturbed by them, I venture to say he is unworthy of the name of man. Even the common sorrows of our race may well suffuse our eyes with tears, but the eternal sorrow, the infinite lake of misery—he who grieves not for this, write him down a demon, though he wear the image and semblance of a man."
Charles Spurgeon

LORD, the Everlasting God. 34And Abraham stayed in the land of the Philistines many days.

Abraham's Faith Confirmed

22 Now it came to pass after these things that God tested Abraham, and said to him, "Abraham!"

And he said, "Here I am."

2Then He said, "Take now your son, your only *son* Isaac, whom you love, and go to the land of Moriah, and offer him there as a burnt offering on one of the mountains of which I shall tell you."

3So Abraham rose early in the morning and saddled his donkey, and took two of his young men with him, and Isaac his son; and he split the wood for the burnt offering, and arose and went to the place of which God had told him. 4Then on the third day Abraham lifted his eyes and saw the place afar off. 5And Abraham said to his young men, "Stay here with the donkey; the lad[a] and I will go yonder and worship, and we will come back to you."

6So Abraham took the wood of the burnt offering and laid *it* on Isaac his son; and he took the fire in his hand, and a knife, and the two of them went together. 7But Isaac spoke to Abraham his father and said, "My father!"

And he said, "Here I am, my son."

Then he said, "Look, the fire and the wood, but where *is* the lamb for a burnt offering?"

8And Abraham said, "My son, God will provide for Himself the lamb for a burnt offering." So the two of them went together.

9Then they came to the place of which God had told him. And Abraham built an altar there and placed the wood in order; and he bound Isaac his son and laid him on the altar, upon the wood. 10And Abraham stretched out his hand and took the knife to slay his son.

11But the Angel of the LORD called to him from heaven and said, "Abraham, Abraham!"

So he said, "Here I am."

12And He said, "Do not lay your hand on the lad, or do anything to him; for now I know that you fear God, since you have not withheld your son, your only *son,* from Me."

13Then Abraham lifted his eyes and looked, and there behind *him was* a ram caught in a thicket by its horns. So Abraham went and took the ram, and offered it up for a burnt offering instead of his son. 14And Abraham called the name of the place, The-LORD-Will-Provide;[a] as it is said *to* this day, "In the Mount of the LORD it shall be provided."

15Then the Angel of the LORD called to Abraham a second time out of heaven, 16and said: "By Myself I have sworn, says the LORD, because you have done this thing, and have not withheld your son, your only *son*— 17blessing I will bless you,

22:5 [a]Or *young man* **22:14** [a]Hebrew *YHWH Yireh*

22:2 Jesus in the Old Testament. "God commanded Abraham to do something that He had previously forbidden: sacrifice a human being. The location of this human sacrifice would be on a mountain of God's choosing.

"While Abraham and his soon-to-be-sacrificed son, Isaac, were walking, Isaac noticed that they did not have a lamb for a sacrifice (v. 7). And Abraham said, 'My son, God will provide for Himself the lamb for a burnt offering' (v. 8).

"We know that God stopped Abraham from sacrificing his only son on a mountain in the land of Moriah. But did God ever provide a lamb for the sacrifice? Approximately 2,000 years later, God sacrificed His only beloved Son, Jesus Christ, on a mountain in the land of Moriah (present-day Jerusalem).

"The story of Abraham and Isaac is a shadowy picture of a near-death experience of a beloved son in Jerusalem. In this story, the son was spared. The next time the sacrifice of a son was required, God did not stop. God did not spare His only beloved Son that we might have the complete forgiveness of sins. Indeed, the Lord did provide a Lamb." *Todd Friel* (Adapted from *Don't Stub Your Toe.*)

See also Exod. 11:4,5 comment.

and multiplying I will multiply your descendants as the stars of the heaven and as the sand which *is* on the seashore; and your descendants shall possess the gate of their enemies. [18]In your seed all the nations of the earth shall be blessed, because you have obeyed My voice." [19]So Abraham returned to his young men, and they rose and went together to Beersheba; and Abraham dwelt at Beersheba.

The Family of Nahor

[20]Now it came to pass after these things that it was told Abraham, saying, "Indeed Milcah also has borne children to your brother Nahor: [21]Huz his firstborn, Buz his brother, Kemuel the father of Aram, [22]Chesed, Hazo, Pildash, Jidlaph, and Bethuel." [23]And Bethuel begot Rebekah.[a] These eight Milcah bore to Nahor, Abraham's brother. [24]His concubine, whose name was Reumah, also bore Tebah, Gaham, Thahash, and Maachah.

Sarah's Death and Burial

23 Sarah lived one hundred and twenty-seven years; *these were* the years of the life of Sarah. [2]So Sarah died in Kirjath Arba (that *is,* Hebron) in the land of Canaan, and Abraham came to mourn for Sarah and to weep for her.

[3]Then Abraham stood up from before his dead, and spoke to the sons of Heth, saying, [4]"I *am* a foreigner and a visitor among you. Give me property for a burial place among you, that I may bury my dead out of my sight."

[5]And the sons of Heth answered Abraham, saying to him, [6]"Hear us, my lord: You *are* a mighty prince among us; bury your dead in the choicest of our burial places. None of us will withhold from you his burial place, that you may bury your dead."

"The cross is laid on every Christian. As we embark upon discipleship we surrender ourselves to Christ in union with his death—we give over our lives to death. When Christ calls a man, he bids him come and die."

Dietrich Bonhoeffer

[7]Then Abraham stood up and bowed himself to the people of the land, the sons of Heth. [8]And he spoke with them, saying, "If it is your wish that I bury my dead out of my sight, hear me, and meet with Ephron the son of Zohar for me, [9]that he may give me the cave of Machpelah which he has, which *is* at the end of his field. Let him give it to me at the full price, as property for a burial place among you."

[10]Now Ephron dwelt among the sons of Heth; and Ephron the Hittite answered Abraham in the presence of the sons of Heth, all who entered at the gate of his city, saying, [11]"No, my lord, hear me: I give you the field and the cave that *is* in it; I give it to you in the presence of the

22:23 [a]Spelled *Rebecca* in Romans 9:10

23:4 Abraham was a foreigner in a land in which he had the favor of the people. It is our prayer that governments give us favor for the cause of the gospel. The great missionary *Hudson Taylor* said, "When I get to China, I will have no claim on anyone for anything. My claim will be alone in God and I must learn before I leave England to move men through God by prayer alone."

sons of my people. I give it to you. Bury
your dead!"
12 Then Abraham bowed himself down
before the people of the land; 13 and he
spoke to Ephron in the hearing of the
people of the land, saying, "If you *will*
give it, please hear me. I will give you
money for the field; take *it* from me and I
will bury my dead there."
14 And Ephron answered Abraham,
saying to him, 15 "My lord, listen to me;
the land *is worth* four hundred shekels of
silver. What *is* that between you and me?
So bury your dead." 16 And Abraham listened to Ephron; and Abraham weighed
out the silver for Ephron which he had
named in the hearing of the sons of Heth,
four hundred shekels of silver, currency
of the merchants.
17 So the field of Ephron which *was* in
Machpelah, which *was* before Mamre, the
field and the cave which *was* in it, and all
the trees that *were* in the field, which *were*
within all the surrounding borders, were
deeded 18 to Abraham as a possession in
the presence of the sons of Heth, before
all who went in at the gate of his city.
19 And after this, Abraham buried Sarah
his wife in the cave of the field of Machpelah, before Mamre (that *is,* Hebron) in
the land of Canaan. 20 So the field and the
cave that *is* in it were deeded to Abraham
by the sons of Heth as property for a burial place.

A Bride for Isaac

24 Now Abraham was old, well advanced in age; and the LORD had
blessed Abraham in all things. 2 So Abraham said to the oldest servant of his house,
who ruled over all that he had, "Please,
put your hand under my thigh, 3 and I will
make you swear by the LORD, the God of
heaven and the God of the earth, that you
will not take a wife for my son from the
daughters of the Canaanites, among whom
I dwell; 4 but you shall go to my country
and to my family, and take a wife for my
son Isaac."
5 And the servant said to him, "Perhaps
the woman will not be willing to follow
me to this land. Must I take your son
back to the land from which you came?"
6 But Abraham said to him, "Beware
that you do not take my son back there.
7 The LORD God of heaven, who took me
from my father's house and from the land
of my family, and who spoke to me and
swore to me, saying, 'To your descendants[a]
I give this land,' He will send His angel
before you, and you shall take a wife for
my son from there. 8 And if the woman is
not willing to follow you, then you will
be released from this oath; only do not
take my son back there." 9 So the servant
put his hand under the thigh of Abraham
his master, and swore to him concerning
this matter.
10 Then the servant took ten of his
master's camels and departed, for all his
master's goods *were in* his hand. And he
arose and went to Mesopotamia, to the
city of Nahor. 11 And he made his camels
kneel down outside the city by a well of

24:7 [a]Literally *seed*

24:11 Ten thirsting camels. The Ten Commandments are like the ten camels that carried Abraham's servant in search of a bride for his beloved son Isaac (Gen. 24:10–20). When the servant arrived at Nahor, he had his ten camels kneel before the well at the time the women go out to draw water. He prayed that the bride-to-be would be evidenced by the fact that she would have consideration for the camels. When Rebekah saw the camels, she *ran* to the well to get water for them.

God the Father sent His Spirit to search for a bride for His only begotten Son. He has chosen the Ten Commandments to carry this special message from His Lord. While we may not be able to clearly distinguish the Bride of Christ from the rest of this world, the Holy Spirit knows that the primary reason she draws water from the Well of Salvation is to satisfy the ten thirsting camels of a holy and just Law. The true convert comes to the Savior simply to satisfy the demands of a holy Law. The espoused virgin has respect for the Commandments of God; she is not a worker of lawlessness. Like Paul, she delights in the Law, and says with the psalmist, "I will run in the way of Your commandments" (Psa. 119:32).

water at evening time, the time when women go out to draw *water.* [12]Then he said, "O LORD God of my master Abraham, please give me success this day, and show kindness to my master Abraham. [13]Behold, *here* I stand by the well of water, and the daughters of the men of the city are coming out to draw water. [14]Now let it be that the young woman to whom I say, 'Please let down your pitcher that I may drink,' and she says, 'Drink, and I will also give your camels a drink'—*let* her *be the one* You have appointed for Your servant Isaac. And by this I will know that You have shown kindness to my master."

[15]And it happened, before he had finished speaking, that behold, Rebekah, who was born to Bethuel, son of Milcah, the wife of Nahor, Abraham's brother, came out with her pitcher on her shoulder. [16]Now the young woman *was* very beautiful to behold, a virgin; no man had known her. And she went down to the well, filled her pitcher, and came up. [17]And the servant ran to meet her and said, "Please let me drink a little water from your pitcher."

[18]So she said, "Drink, my lord." Then she quickly let her pitcher down to her hand, and gave him a drink. [19]And when she had finished giving him a drink, she said, "I will draw *water* for your camels also, until they have finished drinking." [20]Then she quickly emptied her pitcher into the trough, ran back to the well to draw *water,* and drew for all his camels. [21]And the man, wondering at her, remained silent so as to know whether the LORD had made his journey prosperous or not.

[22]So it was, when the camels had finished drinking, that the man took a golden nose ring weighing half a shekel, and two bracelets for her wrists weighing ten *shekels* of gold, [23]and said, "Whose daughter *are* you? Tell me, please, is there room *in* your father's house for us to lodge?"

[24]†So she said to him, "I *am* the daughter of Bethuel, Milcah's son, whom she bore to Nahor." [25]Moreover she said to him, "We have both straw and feed enough, and room to lodge."

[26]Then the man bowed down his head and worshiped the LORD. [27]And he said, "Blessed *be* the LORD God of my master Abraham, who has not forsaken His mercy and His truth toward my master. As for me, being on the way, the LORD led me to the house of my master's brethren." [28]So the young woman ran and told her mother's household these things.

[29]Now Rebekah had a brother whose name *was* Laban, and Laban ran out to the man by the well. [30]So it came to pass, when he saw the nose ring, and the bracelets on his sister's wrists, and when he heard the words of his sister Rebekah, saying, "Thus the man spoke to me," that he went to the man. And there he stood by the camels at the well. [31]And he said, "Come in, O blessed of the LORD! Why do you stand outside? For I have prepared the house, and a place for the camels."

[32]Then the man came to the house. And he unloaded the camels, and provided straw and feed for the camels, and water to wash his feet and the feet of the men who *were* with him. [33]*Food* was set before him to eat, but he said, "I will not eat until I have told about my errand."

And he said, "Speak on."

[34]So he said, "I *am* Abraham's servant. [35]The LORD has blessed my master greatly, and he has become great; and He has given him flocks and herds, silver and gold, male and female servants, and camels and donkeys. [36]And Sarah my master's wife bore a son to my master when she was old; and to him he has given all that

24:26,27 There are times when the miraculous happens and convinces the believer that what he is experiencing could only be the hand of God. It is always a wonderful mystery as to why God would condescend to involve man in working out His great purposes. It is also a great mystery as to how He could possibly orchestrate circumstances of the future so perfectly. In such experiences words don't suffice. One can only bow in worship.

he has. 37Now my master made me swear, saying, 'You shall not take a wife for my son from the daughters of the Canaanites, in whose land I dwell; 38but you shall go to my father's house and to my family, and take a wife for my son.' 39And I said to my master, 'Perhaps the woman will not follow me.' 40But he said to me, 'The LORD, before whom I walk, will send His angel with you and prosper your way; and you shall take a wife for my son from my family and from my father's house. 41You will be clear from this oath when you arrive among my family; for if they will not give *her* to you, then you will be released from my oath.'

> Apart from the deadening effect of the Law, no one would feel the need to cast himself at the mercy of Christ.
>
> **BILL BRIGHT**

42"And this day I came to the well and said, 'O LORD God of my master Abraham, if You will now prosper the way in which I go, 43behold, I stand by the well of water; and it shall come to pass that when the virgin comes out to draw *water,* and I say to her, "Please give me a little water from your pitcher to drink," 44and she says to me, "Drink, and I will draw for your camels also,"—*let* her *be* the woman whom the LORD has appointed for my master's son.'

45"But before I had finished speaking in my heart, there was Rebekah, coming out with her pitcher on her shoulder; and she went down to the well and drew *water.* And I said to her, 'Please let me drink.' 46And she made haste and let her pitcher down from her *shoulder,* and said, 'Drink, and I will give your camels a drink also.' So I drank, and she gave the camels a drink also. 47Then I asked her, and said, 'Whose daughter *are* you?' And she said, 'The daughter of Bethuel, Nahor's son, whom Milcah bore to him.' So I put the nose ring on her nose and the bracelets on her wrists. 48And I bowed my head and worshiped the LORD, and blessed the LORD God of my master Abraham, who had led me in the way of truth to take the daughter of my master's brother for his son. 49Now if you will deal kindly and truly with my master, tell me. And if not, tell me, that I may turn to the right hand or to the left."

50Then Laban and Bethuel answered and said, "The thing comes from the LORD; we cannot speak to you either bad or good. 51Here *is* Rebekah before you; take *her* and go, and let her be your master's son's wife, as the LORD has spoken."

52And it came to pass, when Abraham's servant heard their words, that he worshiped the LORD, *bowing himself* to the earth. 53Then the servant brought out jewelry of silver, jewelry of gold, and clothing, and gave *them* to Rebekah. He also gave precious things to her brother and to her mother.

54And he and the men who *were* with him ate and drank and stayed all night. Then they arose in the morning, and he said, "Send me away to my master."

55But her brother and her mother said, "Let the young woman stay with us *a few* days, at least ten; after that she may go."

56And he said to them, "Do not hinder me, since the LORD has prospered my way; send me away so that I may go to my master."

57So they said, "We will call the young woman and ask her personally." 58Then they called Rebekah and said to her, "Will you go with this man?"

And she said, "I will go."

59So they sent away Rebekah their sister and her nurse, and Abraham's servant and his men. 60And they blessed Rebekah and said to her:

24:58 When God draws a sinner to Himself and saves him, he becomes part of the virgin Bride of Christ. The believer who has seen the love of God in Christ will take up his cross and follow Him (see Mark 8:34).

"Our sister, *may* you *become*
The mother of thousands of ten
thousands;
And may your descendants possess
The gates of those who hate them."

[61]Then Rebekah and her maids arose, and they rode on the camels and followed the man. So the servant took Rebekah and departed.

[62]Now Isaac came from the way of Beer Lahai Roi, for he dwelt in the South. [63]And Isaac went out to meditate in the field in the evening; and he lifted his eyes and looked, and there, the camels *were* coming. [64]Then Rebekah lifted her eyes, and when she saw Isaac she dismounted from her camel; [65]for she had said to the servant, "Who *is* this man walking in the field to meet us?"

The servant said, "It *is* my master." So she took a veil and covered herself.

[66]And the servant told Isaac all the things that he had done. [67]Then Isaac brought her into his mother Sarah's tent; and he took Rebekah and she became his wife, and he loved her. So Isaac was comforted after his mother's *death.*

Abraham and Keturah

25 Abraham again took a wife, and her name *was* Keturah. [2]And she bore him Zimran, Jokshan, Medan, Midian, Ishbak, and Shuah. [3]Jokshan begot Sheba and Dedan. And the sons of Dedan were Asshurim, Letushim, and Leummim. [4]And the sons of Midian *were* Ephah, Epher, Hanoch, Abidah, and Eldaah. All these *were* the children of Keturah.

[5]And Abraham gave all that he had to Isaac. [6]But Abraham gave gifts to the sons of the concubines which Abraham had; and while he was still living he sent them eastward, away from Isaac his son, to the country of the east.

Abraham's Death and Burial

[7]This *is* the sum of the years of Abraham's life which he lived: one hundred and seventy-five years. [8]Then Abraham breathed his last and died in a good old age, an old man and full *of years,* and was gathered to his people. [9]And his sons Isaac and Ishmael buried him in the cave of Machpelah, which *is* before Mamre, in the field of Ephron the son of Zohar the Hittite, [10]the field which Abraham purchased from the sons of Heth. There Abraham was buried, and Sarah his wife. [11]And it came to pass, after the death of Abraham, that God blessed his son Isaac. And Isaac dwelt at Beer Lahai Roi.

The Families of Ishmael and Isaac

[12]Now this *is* the genealogy of Ishmael, Abraham's son, whom Hagar the Egyptian, Sarah's maidservant, bore to Abraham. [13]And these *were* the names of the sons of Ishmael, by their names, according to their generations: The firstborn of Ishmael, Nebajoth; then Kedar, Adbeel, Mibsam, [14]Mishma, Dumah, Massa, [15]Hadar,[a] Tema, Jetur, Naphish, and Kedemah. [16]These *were* the sons of Ishmael and these *were* their names, by their towns and their settlements, twelve princes according to their nations. [17]These *were* the years of the life of Ishmael: one hundred and thirty-seven years; and he breathed his last and died, and was gathered to his people. [18](They dwelt from Havilah as far as Shur, which *is* east of Egypt as you go toward Assyria.) He died in the presence of all his brethren.

[19]This *is* the genealogy of Isaac, Abraham's son. Abraham begot Isaac. [20]Isaac was forty years old when he took Rebekah as wife, the daughter of Bethuel the Syrian of Padan Aram, the sister of Laban the Syrian. [21]Now Isaac pleaded with the LORD

25:15 [a]Masoretic Text reads *Hadad.*

25:8 Abraham did not die without hope. Jesus said, "Your father Abraham rejoiced to see My day, and he saw it and was glad" (John 8:56). Abraham was made righteous by grace through faith in the coming Messiah. "And the Scripture, foreseeing that God would justify the Gentiles by faith, preached the gospel to Abraham beforehand, saying, 'In you all the nations shall be blessed'" (Gal. 3:8).

for his wife, because she *was* barren; and
the LORD granted his plea, and Rebekah
his wife conceived. 22But the children struggled together within her; and she said, "If
all is well, why *am I like* this?" So she went
to inquire of the LORD.
23And the LORD said to her:

"Two nations *are* in your womb,
Two peoples shall be separated from
your body;
One people shall be stronger than the
other,
And the older shall serve the younger."

24So when her days were fulfilled *for*
her to give birth, indeed *there were* twins
in her womb. 25And the first came out
red. *He was* like a hairy garment all over;
so they called his name Esau.[a] 26After-
ward his brother came out, and his hand
took hold of Esau's heel; so his name was
called Jacob.[a] Isaac *was* sixty years old
when she bore them.
27So the boys grew. And Esau was a
skillful hunter, a man of the field; but Jacob was a mild man, dwelling in tents.
28And Isaac loved Esau because he ate *of*
his game, but Rebekah loved Jacob.

Esau Sells His Birthright

29Now Jacob cooked a stew; and Esau
came in from the field, and he *was* weary.
30And Esau said to Jacob, "Please feed me
with that same red *stew,* for I *am* weary."
Therefore his name was called Edom.[a]
31But Jacob said, "Sell me your birthright as of this day."
32And Esau said, "Look, I *am* about to
die; so what *is* this birthright to me?"
33Then Jacob said, "Swear to me as of
this day."
So he swore to him, and sold his birthright to Jacob. 34And Jacob gave Esau
bread and stew of lentils; then he ate and
drank, arose, and went his way. Thus Esau
despised *his* birthright.

Isaac and Abimelech

26 There was a famine in the land,
besides the first famine that was in
the days of Abraham. And Isaac went to
Abimelech king of the Philistines, in Gerar.
2Then the LORD appeared to him and
said: "Do not go down to Egypt; live in
the land of which I shall tell you. 3Dwell
in this land, and I will be with you and
bless you; for to you and your descendants I give all these lands, and I will perform the oath which I swore to Abraham
your father. 4And I will make your descendants multiply as the stars of heaven;
I will give to your descendants all these
lands; and in your seed all the nations of
the earth shall be blessed; 5because Abraham obeyed My voice and kept My charge,
My commandments, My statutes, and My
laws."
6So Isaac dwelt in Gerar. 7And the men
of the place asked about his wife. And he
said, "She *is* my sister"; for he was afraid
to say, "*She is* my wife," *because he thought,*
"lest the men of the place kill me for Rebekah, because she *is* beautiful to behold."
8Now it came to pass, when he had been
there a long time, that Abimelech king of
the Philistines looked through a window,
and saw, and there was Isaac, showing en-
dearment to Rebekah his wife. 9Then
Abimelech called Isaac and said, "Quite
obviously she *is* your wife; so how could

25:25 [a]Literally *Hairy* 25:26 [a]Literally *Supplanter* 25:30 [a]Literally *Red*

25:32 Esau gave up his precious birthright because of the cravings of his flesh. Those who make a profession of faith without a humble heart (which the Law produces) have the experience described in 2 Pet. 2:22: "'A dog returns to his own vomit,' and 'a sow, having washed, to her wallowing in the mire.'" This is the tragic result of casting pearls of the gospel of grace to the proud, those whom the Bible calls "dogs" and "swine." The false convert has never "crucified the flesh with its passions and desires" (Gal. 5:24). Pigs need to wallow in mire because they crave the slime to cool their flesh. So it is with the false convert. He never repented, so his flesh was not crucified with Christ. It is instead burning with unlawful desire. The heat of lust is too much for his sinful heart. He must go back to the filth.

you say, 'She *is* my sister'?"

Isaac said to him, "Because I said, 'Lest I die on account of her.' "

10And Abimelech said, "What *is* this you have done to us? One of the people might soon have lain with your wife, and you would have brought guilt on us." 11So Abimelech charged all *his* people, saying, "He who touches this man or his wife shall surely be put to death."

12Then Isaac sowed in that land, and reaped in the same year a hundredfold; and the LORD blessed him. 13The man began to prosper, and continued prospering until he became very prosperous; 14for he had possessions of flocks and possessions of herds and a great number of servants. So the Philistines envied him. 15Now the Philistines had stopped up all the wells which his father's servants had dug in the days of Abraham his father, and they had filled them with earth. 16And Abimelech said to Isaac, "Go away from us, for you are much mightier than we."

17Then Isaac departed from there and pitched his tent in the Valley of Gerar, and dwelt there. 18And Isaac dug again the wells of water which they had dug in the days of Abraham his father, for the Philistines had stopped them up after the death of Abraham. He called them by the names which his father had called them.

19Also Isaac's servants dug in the valley, and found a well of running water there. 20But the herdsmen of Gerar quarreled with Isaac's herdsmen, saying, "The water *is* ours." So he called the name of the well Esek,[a] because they quarreled with him. 21Then they dug another well, and they quarreled over that *one* also. So he called its name Sitnah.[a] 22And he moved from there and dug another well, and they did not quarrel over it. So he called its name Rehoboth,[a] because he said, "For now the LORD has made room for us, and we shall be fruitful in the land."

23Then he went up from there to Beersheba. 24And the LORD appeared to him the same night and said, "I *am* the God of your father Abraham; do not fear, for I *am* with you. I will bless you and multiply your descendants for My servant Abraham's sake." 25So he built an altar there and called on the name of the LORD, and he pitched his tent there; and there Isaac's servants dug a well.

26Then Abimelech came to him from Gerar with Ahuzzath, one of his friends, and Phichol the commander of his army. 27And Isaac said to them, "Why have you come to me, since you hate me and have sent me away from you?"

28But they said, "We have certainly seen that the LORD is with you. So we said, 'Let there now be an oath between us, between you and us; and let us make a covenant with you, 29that you will do us no harm, since we have not touched you, and since we have done nothing to you but good and have sent you away in peace. You *are* now the blessed of the LORD.' "

30So he made them a feast, and they ate and drank. 31Then they arose early in the morning and swore an oath with one another; and Isaac sent them away, and they departed from him in peace.

32It came to pass the same day that Isaac's servants came and told him about the well which they had dug, and said to him, "We have found water." 33So he called it Shebah.[a] Therefore the name of the city *is* Beersheba[b] to this day.

34When Esau was forty years old, he took as wives Judith the daughter of Beeri the Hittite, and Basemath the daughter of

26:20 [a]Literally *Quarrel* **26:21** [a]Literally *Enmity* **26:22** [a]Literally *Spaciousness* **26:33** [a]Literally *Oath* or *Seven* [b]Literally *Well of the Oath* or *Well of the Seven*

26:24 This doesn't mean that Isaac saw the essence of God. No man can see God and live (see Exod. 33:20). Isaac saw a *manifestation* of God, as did Moses and others. The only way a man or woman can stand in the presence of God without being consumed by His holiness is to be pure of heart. That can come only by God's mercy through the blood of the cross. All who are made pure in heart through faith in Jesus will see God (see Matt. 5:8).

Elon the Hittite. 35And they were a grief
of mind to Isaac and Rebekah.

Isaac Blesses Jacob

27 Now it came to pass, when Isaac
was old and his eyes were so dim
that he could not see, that he called Esau
his older son and said to him, "My son."
And he answered him, "Here I am."
2Then he said, "Behold now, I am old.
I do not know the day of my death. 3Now
therefore, please take your weapons, your
quiver and your bow, and go out to the
field and hunt game for me. 4And make
me savory food, such as I love, and bring
it to me that I may eat, that my soul may
bless you before I die."
5Now Rebekah was listening when
Isaac spoke to Esau his son. And Esau
went to the field to hunt game and to
bring *it.* 6So Rebekah spoke to Jacob her
son, saying, "Indeed I heard your father
speak to Esau your brother, saying, 7'Bring
me game and make savory food for me,
that I may eat it and bless you in the presence of the LORD before my death.' 8Now
therefore, my son, obey my voice according to what I command you. 9Go now to
the flock and bring me from there two
choice kids of the goats, and I will make
savory food from them for your father,
such as he loves. 10Then you shall take *it*
to your father, that he may eat *it,* and that
he may bless you before his death."
11And Jacob said to Rebekah his
mother, "Look, Esau my brother *is* a hairy
man, and I *am* a smooth-*skinned* man.
12Perhaps my father will feel me, and I
shall seem to be a deceiver to him; and I
shall bring a curse on myself and not a
blessing."
13But his mother said to him, "*Let* your
curse *be* on me, my son; only obey my
voice, and go, get *them* for me." 14And he
went and got *them* and brought *them* to
his mother, and his mother made savory
food, such as his father loved. 15Then Rebekah took the choice clothes of her elder
son Esau, which *were* with her in the
house, and put them on Jacob her younger son. 16And she put the skins of the
kids of the goats on his hands and on the
smooth part of his neck. 17Then she gave
the savory food and the bread, which she
had prepared, into the hand of her son
Jacob.
18So he went to his father and said,
"My father."
And he said, "Here I am. Who *are* you,
my son?"
19Jacob said to his father, "I *am* Esau
your firstborn; I have done just as you told
me; please arise, sit and eat of my game,
that your soul may bless me."
20But Isaac said to his son, "How *is it*
that you have found *it* so quickly, my son?"
And he said, "Because the LORD your
God brought *it* to me."
21Isaac said to Jacob, "Please come near,
that I may feel you, my son, whether you
are really my son Esau or not." 22So Jacob
went near to Isaac his father, and he felt
him and said, "The voice *is* Jacob's voice,
but the hands *are* the hands of Esau."
23And he did not recognize him, because
his hands were hairy like his brother
Esau's hands; so he blessed him.
24Then he said, "*Are* you really my son
Esau?"
He said, "I *am.*"
25He said, "Bring *it* near to me, and I
will eat of my son's game, so that my soul
may bless you." So he brought *it* near to
him, and he ate; and he brought him wine,
and he drank. 26Then his father Isaac said
to him, "Come near now and kiss me, my

27:8 As sons of God, we are commanded to take the gospel to the ends of the earth (see Acts 1:8).
"Ultimately, evangelistic apathy is not a methodological failure; it is spiritual disobedience. The Bible is replete with commands and admonitions to communicate passionately the Gospel with others. Our failure to do so is nothing less than sinful disobedience to the God who gave us unmerited favor through His Son, Jesus Christ." *Thom Rainer*

son." 27And he came near and kissed him;
and he smelled the smell of his clothing,
and blessed him and said:

"Surely, the smell of my son
Is like the smell of a field
Which the LORD has blessed.
28Therefore may God give you
Of the dew of heaven,
Of the fatness of the earth,
And plenty of grain and wine.
29Let peoples serve you,
And nations bow down to you.
Be master over your brethren,
And let your mother's sons bow down
to you.
Cursed *be* everyone who curses you,
And blessed *be* those who bless you!"

Esau's Lost Hope

30Now it happened, as soon as Isaac
had finished blessing Jacob, and Jacob had
scarcely gone out from the presence of
Isaac his father, that Esau his brother came
in from his hunting. 31He also had made
savory food, and brought it to his father,
and said to his father, "Let my father arise
and eat of his son's game, that your soul
may bless me."
32And his father Isaac said to him,
"Who *are* you?"
So he said, "I *am* your son, your firstborn, Esau."
33Then Isaac trembled exceedingly, and
said, "Who? Where *is* the one who hunted
game and brought *it* to me? I ate all *of it*
before you came, and I have blessed him
—*and* indeed he shall be blessed."
34When Esau heard the words of his
father, he cried with an exceedingly great
and bitter cry, and said to his father, "Bless
me—me also, O my father!"
35But he said, "Your brother came with
deceit and has taken away your blessing."
36And *Esau* said, "Is he not rightly
named Jacob? For he has supplanted me
these two times. He took away my birthright, and now look, he has taken away
my blessing!" And he said, "Have you not
reserved a blessing for me?"
37Then Isaac answered and said to Esau,
"Indeed I have made him your master,
and all his brethren I have given to him
as servants; with grain and wine I have
sustained him. What shall I do now for
you, my son?"

> Without absolutes revealed from without by God Himself, we are left rudderless in a sea of conflicting ideas about manners, justice and right and wrong, issuing from a multitude of self-opinionated thinkers.
>
> **JOHN OWEN**

38And Esau said to his father, "Have you
only one blessing, my father? Bless me—
me also, O my father!" And Esau lifted up
his voice and wept.
39Then Isaac his father answered and
said to him:

"Behold, your dwelling shall be of the
fatness of the earth,
And of the dew of heaven from above.
40By your sword you shall live,
And you shall serve your brother;
And it shall come to pass, when you
become restless,
That you shall break his yoke from
your neck."

Jacob Escapes from Esau

41So Esau hated Jacob because of the
blessing with which his father blessed him,
and Esau said in his heart, "The days of
mourning for my father are at hand; then
I will kill my brother Jacob."
42And the words of Esau her older son
were told to Rebekah. So she sent and
called Jacob her younger son, and said to
him, "Surely your brother Esau comforts
himself concerning you *by intending* to
kill you. 43Now therefore, my son, obey
my voice: arise, flee to my brother Laban
in Haran. 44And stay with him a few days,
until your brother's fury turns away, 45un-
til your brother's anger turns away from
you, and he forgets what you have done
to him; then I will send and bring you

POINTS FOR OPEN-AIR PREACHING

28:3

The Math of Open-air Preaching

To get started in open-air preaching, keep in mind that you are needed to "go into the world," so don't listen to your fears; just do it. If you have ever felt the joy of sharing the gospel with someone who is genuinely listening to every word you are saying, multiply that by 30. That's a good open-air session. There's nothing like it when you have a good heckler, and a crowd of people listening to the words of everlasting life.

If you're fearful about preaching open-air for the first time, practice at home before doing it "live." Go over the gospel in your mind until it's second nature—no, until it's first nature. When you are alone, preach it. (In the shower is a great place to preach.) Go through a few anecdotes. Get used to the sound of your own voice. Pretend to engage a heckler. Invite some friends over to role-play with you—and practice what you preach.

If you are afraid of looking foolish if you mentally draw a blank while speaking, have a backup plan. Keep a New Testament with you and if you freeze up, say, "I would just like to read something to you." Read John 3:16–18 and conclude with, "Thank you for listening." Just knowing that you have that option will dissipate the fear.

If someone asks you a question that you don't know how to answer, simply say, "I'm sorry, I don't know the answer to that, but I will try to find it for you, if you like." There's nothing wrong with a humble admission. In fact, it may speak volumes more to your hearers than an eloquent answer.

from there. Why should I be bereaved also
of you both in one day?"
46And Rebekah said to Isaac, "I am
weary of my life because of the daughters
of Heth; if Jacob takes a wife of the daughters of Heth, like these *who are* the daughters of the land, what good will my life be
to me?"

28 Then Isaac called Jacob and blessed
him, and charged him, and said
to him: "You shall not take a wife from
the daughters of Canaan. 2Arise, go to
Padan Aram, to the house of Bethuel your
mother's father; and take yourself a wife
from there of the daughters of Laban
your mother's brother.

3"May God Almighty bless you,
And make you fruitful and multiply
you,
That you may be an assembly of
peoples;
4And give you the blessing of Abraham,
To you and your descendants with you,
That you may inherit the land
In which you are a stranger,
Which God gave to Abraham."

5So Isaac sent Jacob away, and he went to
Padan Aram, to Laban the son of Bethuel
the Syrian, the brother of Rebekah, the
mother of Jacob and Esau.

Esau Marries Mahalath

6Esau saw that Isaac had blessed Jacob
and sent him away to Padan Aram to take
himself a wife from there, *and that* as he
blessed him he gave him a charge, saying,
"You shall not take a wife from the daughters of Canaan," 7and that Jacob had obeyed
his father and his mother and had gone
to Padan Aram. 8Also Esau saw that the
daughters of Canaan did not please his father Isaac. 9So Esau went to Ishmael and
took Mahalath the daughter of Ishmael,
Abraham's son, the sister of Nebajoth, to
be his wife in addition to the wives he had.

Jacob's Vow at Bethel

10Now Jacob went out from Beersheba
and went toward Haran. 11So he came to
a certain place and stayed there all night,
because the sun had set. And he took one
of the stones of that place and put it at his
head, and he lay down in that place to
sleep. 12Then he dreamed, and behold, a
ladder *was* set up on the earth, and its top
reached to heaven; and there the angels of
God were ascending and descending on it.
13And behold, the LORD stood above it
and said: "I *am* the LORD God of Abraham

your father and the God of Isaac; the land on which you lie I will give to you and your descendants. [14]Also your descendants shall be as the dust of the earth; you shall spread abroad to the west and the east, to the north and the south; and in you and in your seed all the families of the earth shall be blessed. [15]Behold, I *am* with you and will keep you wherever you go, and will bring you back to this land; for I will not leave you until I have done what I have spoken to you."

[16]Then Jacob awoke from his sleep and said, "Surely the LORD is in this place, and I did not know *it*." [17]And he was afraid and said, "How awesome *is* this place! This *is* none other than the house of God, and this *is* the gate of heaven!"

[18]Then Jacob rose early in the morning, and took the stone that he had put at his head, set it up as a pillar, and poured oil on top of it. [19]And he called the name of that place Bethel;[a] but the name of that city had been Luz previously. [20]Then Jacob made a vow, saying, "If God will be with me, and keep me in this way that I am going, and give me bread to eat and clothing to put on, [21]so that I come back to my father's house in peace, then the LORD shall be my God. [22]And this stone which I have set as a pillar shall be God's house, and of all that You give me I will surely give a tenth to You."

Jacob Meets Rachel

29 So Jacob went on his journey and came to the land of the people of the East. [2]And he looked, and saw a well in the field; and behold, there *were* three flocks of sheep lying by it; for out of that well they watered the flocks. A large stone *was* on the well's mouth. [3]Now all the flocks would be gathered there; and they would roll the stone from the well's mouth, water the sheep, and put the stone back in its place on the well's mouth.

[4]And Jacob said to them, "My brethren, where *are* you from?"

And they said, "We *are* from Haran."

[5]Then he said to them, "Do you know Laban the son of Nahor?"

And they said, "We know him."

[6]So he said to them, "Is he well?"

And they said, "*He is* well. And look, his daughter Rachel is coming with the sheep."

[7]Then he said, "Look, *it is* still high day; *it is* not time for the cattle to be gathered together. Water the sheep, and go and feed *them*."

[8]But they said, "We cannot until all the flocks are gathered together, and they have rolled the stone from the well's mouth; then we water the sheep."

[9]Now while he was still speaking with them, Rachel came with her father's sheep, for she was a shepherdess. [10]And it came to pass, when Jacob saw Rachel the daughter of Laban his mother's brother, and the sheep of Laban his mother's brother, that Jacob went near and rolled the stone from the well's mouth, and watered the flock of Laban his mother's brother. [11]Then Jacob kissed Rachel, and lifted up his voice and wept. [12]And Jacob told Rachel that he *was* her father's relative and that he *was* Rebekah's son. So she ran and told her father.

[13]Then it came to pass, when Laban heard the report about Jacob his sister's son, that he ran to meet him, and embraced him and kissed him, and brought him to his house. So he told Laban all these things. [14]And Laban said to him,

28:19 [a]Literally *House of God*

28:12 "Christ . . . is this ladder: the foot on earth is his human nature, the top in heaven is his divine nature; or, the former is his humiliation, the latter is his exaltation. All the intercourse between heaven and earth since the fall is by this ladder. Christ is the way: all God's favors come to us, and all our services come to him, by Christ. If God dwell with us, and we with him, it is by Christ: we have no way of getting to heaven but by this ladder; for the kind offices the angels do us, are all owing to Christ, who hath reconciled things on earth and things in heaven (Col. 1:20)." *John Wesley*

"Surely you *are* my bone and my flesh."
And he stayed with him for a month.

Jacob Marries Leah and Rachel

15Then Laban said to Jacob, "Because
you *are* my relative, should you therefore
serve me for nothing? Tell me, what *should*
your wages *be?*" 16Now Laban had two
daughters: the name of the elder *was* Leah,
and the name of the younger *was* Rachel.
17Leah's eyes *were* delicate, but Rachel was
beautiful of form and appearance.

18Now Jacob loved Rachel; so he said,
"I will serve you seven years for Rachel
your younger daughter."

19And Laban said, "*It is* better that I
give her to you than that I should give
her to another man. Stay with me." 20So
Jacob served seven years for Rachel, and
they seemed *only* a few days to him because of the love he had for her.

21Then Jacob said to Laban, "Give *me*
my wife, for my days are fulfilled, that I
may go in to her." 22And Laban gathered
together all the men of the place and
made a feast. 23Now it came to pass in the
evening, that he took Leah his daughter
and brought her to Jacob; and he went in
to her. 24And Laban gave his maid Zilpah
to his daughter Leah *as* a maid. 25So it
came to pass in the morning, that behold,
it *was* Leah. And he said to Laban, "What
is this you have done to me? Was it not
for Rachel that I served you? Why then
have you deceived me?"

26And Laban said, "It must not be done
so in our country, to give the younger before the firstborn. 27Fulfill her week, and
we will give you this one also for the service which you will serve with me still
another seven years."

28Then Jacob did so and fulfilled her
week. So he gave him his daughter Rachel
as wife also. 29And Laban gave his maid
Bilhah to his daughter Rachel as a maid.
30Then *Jacob* also went in to Rachel, and
he also loved Rachel more than Leah.
And he served with Laban still another
seven years.

The Children of Jacob

31When the LORD saw that Leah *was*
unloved, He opened her womb; but Rachel
was barren. 32So Leah conceived and bore
a son, and she called his name Reuben;[a]
for she said, "The LORD has surely looked
on my affliction. Now therefore, my husband will love me." 33Then she conceived
again and bore a son, and said, "Because
the LORD has heard that I *am* unloved, He
has therefore given me this *son* also." And
she called his name Simeon.[a] 34She conceived again and bore a son, and said,
"Now this time my husband will become
attached to me, because I have borne him
three sons." Therefore his name was called
Levi.[a] 35And she conceived again and bore
a son, and said, "Now I will praise the
LORD." Therefore she called his name Judah.[a] Then she stopped bearing.

30 Now when Rachel saw that she
bore Jacob no children, Rachel
envied her sister, and said to Jacob, "Give
me children, or else I die!"

29:32 [a]Literally *See, a Son* 29:33 [a]Literally *Heard* 29:34 [a]Literally *Attached* 29:35 [a]Literally *Praise*

29:20 Evangelism is an arduous task. None of us like the rejection and hatred that come from proclaiming the truth in a sin-loving world. However, in light of the love of God that was expressed toward us through the cross, the task is not burdensome (see 1 John 5:3). We delight to do His will.

30:1 "You all desire to glorify Christ by becoming soul-winners—I hope you do—and be it remembered that, other things being equal, he is the fittest in God's hand to win souls who pities souls most. I believe he preaches best who loves best, and in the Sunday-school and in private life each soul-seeker shall have the blessing very much in proportion to his yearning for it. Paul becomes a savior of many because his heart's desire and prayer to God is that they may be saved. If you can live without souls being converted, you shall live without their being converted; but if your soul breaks for the longing that it hath towards Christ's glory and the conversion of the ungodly, if like her of old you say, 'Give me children, or I die,' your insatiable hunger shall be satisfied, the craving of your spirit shall be gratified." *Charles Spurgeon*

2And Jacob's anger was aroused against Rachel, and he said, "*Am* I in the place of God, who has withheld from you the fruit of the womb?"

3So she said, "Here is my maid Bilhah; go in to her, and she will bear *a child* on my knees, that I also may have children by her." 4Then she gave him Bilhah her maid as wife, and Jacob went in to her. 5And Bilhah conceived and bore Jacob a son. 6Then Rachel said, "God has judged my case; and He has also heard my voice and given me a son." Therefore she called his name Dan.[a] 7And Rachel's maid Bilhah conceived again and bore Jacob a second son. 8Then Rachel said, "With great wrestlings I have wrestled with my sister, *and* indeed I have prevailed." So she called his name Naphtali.[a]

9When Leah saw that she had stopped bearing, she took Zilpah her maid and gave her to Jacob as wife. 10And Leah's maid Zilpah bore Jacob a son. 11Then Leah said, "A troop comes!"[a] So she called his name Gad.[b] 12And Leah's maid Zilpah bore Jacob a second son. 13Then Leah said, "I am happy, for the daughters will call me blessed." So she called his name Asher.[a]

14Now Reuben went in the days of wheat harvest and found mandrakes in the field, and brought them to his mother Leah. Then Rachel said to Leah, "Please give me *some* of your son's mandrakes."

15But she said to her, "*Is it* a small matter that you have taken away my husband? Would you take away my son's mandrakes also?"

And Rachel said, "Therefore he will lie with you tonight for your son's mandrakes."

16When Jacob came out of the field in the evening, Leah went out to meet him and said, "You must come in to me, for I have surely hired you with my son's mandrakes." And he lay with her that night.

17And God listened to Leah, and she conceived and bore Jacob a fifth son. 18Leah said, "God has given me my wages, because I have given my maid to my husband." So she called his name Issachar.[a] 19Then Leah conceived again and bore Jacob a sixth son. 20And Leah said, "God has endowed me *with* a good endowment; now my husband will dwell with me, because I have borne him six sons." So she called his name Zebulun.[a] 21Afterward she bore a daughter, and called her name Dinah.

22Then God remembered Rachel, and God listened to her and opened her womb. 23And she conceived and bore a son, and said, "God has taken away my reproach." 24So she called his name Joseph,[a] and said, "The LORD shall add to me another son."

Jacob's Agreement with Laban

25And it came to pass, when Rachel had borne Joseph, that Jacob said to Laban, "Send me away, that I may go to my own place and to my country. 26Give *me* my wives and my children for whom I have served you, and let me go; for you know my service which I have done for you."

27And Laban said to him, "Please *stay,* if I have found favor in your eyes, *for* I have learned by experience that the LORD

30:6 [a]Literally *Judge* 30:8 [a]Literally *My Wrestling* 30:11 [a]Following Qere, Syriac, and Targum; Kethib, Septuagint, and Vulgate read *in fortune*. [b]Literally *Troop* or *Fortune* 30:13 [a]Literally *Happy* 30:18 [a]Literally *Wages* 30:20 [a]Literally *Dwelling* 30:24 [a]Literally *He Will Add*

30:8 "Envy is grieving at the good of another, than which no sin is more injurious both to God, our neighbor, and ourselves. But this was not all, she said to Jacob, give me children or else I die—A child would not content her; but because Leah has more than one, she must have more too . . . Observe a difference between Rachel's asking for this mercy, and Hannah's (1 Sam 1:10, etc). Rachel envied, Hannah wept: Rachel must have children, and she died of the second; Hannah prayed for this child, and she had four more: Rachel is importunate and peremptory, Hannah is submissive and devout, If thou wilt give me a child, I will give him to the Lord. Let Hannah be imitated, and not Rachel; and let our desires be always under the conduct and check of reason and religion." *John Wesley*

has blessed me for your sake." 28Then he
said, "Name me your wages, and I will
give *it.*"
29So *Jacob* said to him, "You know how
I have served you and how your livestock
has been with me. 30For what you had before I *came was* little, and it has increased
to a great amount; the LORD has blessed
you since my coming. And now, when
shall I also provide for my own house?"
31So he said, "What shall I give you?"
And Jacob said, "You shall not give me
anything. If you will do this thing for me,
I will again feed and keep your flocks: 32Let
me pass through all your flock today, removing from there all the speckled and
spotted sheep, and all the brown ones
among the lambs, and the spotted and
speckled among the goats; and *these* shall
be my wages. 33So my righteousness will
answer for me in time to come, when the
subject of my wages comes before you:
every one that *is* not speckled and spotted among the goats, and brown among
the lambs, will be considered stolen, if *it*
is with me."
34And Laban said, "Oh, that it were according to your word!" 35So he removed
that day the male goats that were speckled and spotted, all the female goats that
were speckled and spotted, every one that
had *some* white in it, and all the brown
ones among the lambs, and gave *them* into
the hand of his sons. 36Then he put three
days' journey between himself and Jacob,
and Jacob fed the rest of Laban's flocks.
37Now Jacob took for himself rods of
green poplar and of the almond and chestnut trees, peeled white strips in them, and
exposed the white which *was* in the rods.
38And the rods which he had peeled, he
set before the flocks in the gutters, in the
watering troughs where the flocks came
to drink, so that they should conceive
when they came to drink. 39So the flocks
conceived before the rods, and the flocks
brought forth streaked, speckled, and spotted. 40Then Jacob separated the lambs, and
made the flocks face toward the streaked
and all the brown in the flock of Laban;
but he put his own flocks by themselves
and did not put them with Laban's flock.
41And it came to pass, whenever the
stronger livestock conceived, that Jacob
placed the rods before the eyes of the livestock in the gutters, that they might conceive among the rods. 42But when the
flocks were feeble, he did not put *them* in;
so the feebler were Laban's and the stronger Jacob's. 43Thus the man became exceedingly prosperous, and had large flocks, female and male servants, and camels and
donkeys.

. . . . . .

Does the Bible mention dinosaurs?
See Job 40:15–24 comment.

. . . . . .

Jacob Flees from Laban

31 Now *Jacob* heard the words of Laban's sons, saying, "Jacob has
taken away all that was our father's, and
from what was our father's he has acquired all this wealth." 2And Jacob saw
the countenance of Laban, and indeed it
was not *favorable* toward him as before.
3Then the LORD said to Jacob, "Return to
the land of your fathers and to your family, and I will be with you."
4So Jacob sent and called Rachel and
Leah to the field, to his flock, 5and said to
them, "I see your father's countenance,
that it *is* not *favorable* toward me as before; but the God of my father has been
with me. 6And you know that with all my
might I have served your father. 7Yet your
father has deceived me and changed my
wages ten times, but God did not allow
him to hurt me. 8If he said thus: 'The
speckled shall be your wages,' then all
the flocks bore speckled. And if he said
thus: 'The streaked shall be your wages,'
then all the flocks bore streaked. 9So God
has taken away the livestock of your father and given *them* to me.
10"And it happened, at the time when
the flocks conceived, that I lifted my eyes
and saw in a dream, and behold, the

rams which leaped upon the flocks *were* streaked, speckled, and gray-spotted. [11]Then the Angel of God spoke to me in a dream, saying, 'Jacob.' And I said, 'Here I am.' [12]And He said, 'Lift your eyes now and see, all the rams which leap on the flocks *are* streaked, speckled, and gray-spotted; for I have seen all that Laban is doing to you. [13]I *am* the God of Bethel, where you anointed the pillar *and* where you made a vow to Me. Now arise, get out of this land, and return to the land of your family.' "

[14]Then Rachel and Leah answered and said to him, "Is there still any portion or inheritance for us in our father's house? [15]Are we not considered strangers by him? For he has sold us, and also completely consumed our money. [16]For all these riches which God has taken from our father are *really* ours and our children's; now then, whatever God has said to you, do it."

[17]Then Jacob rose and set his sons and his wives on camels. [18]And he carried away all his livestock and all his possessions which he had gained, his acquired livestock which he had gained in Padan Aram, to go to his father Isaac in the land of Canaan. [19]Now Laban had gone to shear his sheep, and Rachel had stolen the household idols that were her father's. [20]And Jacob stole away, unknown to Laban the Syrian, in that he did not tell him that he intended to flee. [21]So he fled with all that he had. He arose and crossed the river, and headed toward the mountains of Gilead.

Laban Pursues Jacob

[22]And Laban was told on the third day that Jacob had fled. [23]Then he took his brethren with him and pursued him for seven days' journey, and he overtook him in the mountains of Gilead. [24]But God had come to Laban the Syrian in a dream by night, and said to him, "Be careful that you speak to Jacob neither good nor bad."

[25]So Laban overtook Jacob. Now Jacob had pitched his tent in the mountains, and Laban with his brethren pitched in the mountains of Gilead.

[26]And Laban said to Jacob: "What have you done, that you have stolen away unknown to me, and carried away my daughters like captives *taken* with the sword? [27]Why did you flee away secretly, and steal away from me, and not tell me; for I might have sent you away with joy and songs, with timbrel and harp? [28]And you did not allow me to kiss my sons and my daughters. Now you have done foolishly in *so* doing. [29]It is in my power to do you harm, but the God of your father spoke to me last night, saying, 'Be careful that you speak to Jacob neither good nor bad.' [30]And now you have surely gone because you greatly long for your father's house, *but* why did you steal my gods?"

[31]Then Jacob answered and said to Laban, "Because I was afraid, for I said, 'Perhaps you would take your daughters from me by force.' [32]With whomever you find your gods, do not let him live. In the presence of our brethren, identify what I have of yours and take *it* with you." For Jacob did not know that Rachel had stolen them.

[33]And Laban went into Jacob's tent, into Leah's tent, and into the two maids' tents, but he did not find *them.* Then he went out of Leah's tent and entered Rachel's tent. [34]Now Rachel had taken the household idols, put them in the camel's saddle, and sat on them. And Laban searched all about the tent but did not find *them.* [35]And she said to her father, "Let it not displease my lord that I cannot rise before you, for the manner of women *is* with me." And he searched but did not find the household idols.

[36]Then Jacob was angry and rebuked Laban, and Jacob answered and said to Laban: "What *is* my trespass? What *is* my sin, that you have so hotly pursued me? [37]Although you have searched all my things, what part of your household things have you found? Set *it* here before my brethren and your brethren, that they may judge between us both! [38]These twenty years I *have been* with you; your ewes and your female goats have not miscarried

their young, and I have not eaten the rams
of your flock. [39]That which was torn *by*
beasts I did not bring to you; I bore the
loss of it. You required it from my hand,
whether stolen by day or stolen by night.
[40]*There* I was! In the day the drought consumed me, and the frost by night, and
my sleep departed from my eyes. [41]Thus
I have been in your house twenty years; I
served you fourteen years for your two
daughters, and six years for your flock, and
you have changed my wages ten times.
[42]Unless the God of my father, the God of
Abraham and the Fear of Isaac, had been
with me, surely now you would have sent
me away empty-handed. God has seen
my affliction and the labor of my hands,
and rebuked *you* last night."

Laban's Covenant with Jacob

[43]And Laban answered and said to Jacob, "*These* daughters *are* my daughters,
and *these* children *are* my children, and
this flock *is* my flock; all that you see *is*
mine. But what can I do this day to these
my daughters or to their children whom
they have borne? [44]Now therefore, come,
let us make a covenant, you and I, and let
it be a witness between you and me."

[45]So Jacob took a stone and set it up *as*
a pillar. [46]Then Jacob said to his brethren,
"Gather stones." And they took stones and
made a heap, and they ate there on the
heap. [47]Laban called it Jegar Sahadutha,[a]
but Jacob called it Galeed.[b] [48]And Laban
said, "This heap *is* a witness between you
and me this day." Therefore its name was
called Galeed, [49]also Mizpah,[a] because he
said, "May the LORD watch between you
and me when we are absent one from another. [50]If you afflict my daughters, or if
you take *other* wives besides my daughters, *although* no man *is* with us—see,
God *is* witness between you and me!"

[51]Then Laban said to Jacob, "Here is
this heap and here is *this* pillar, which I
have placed between you and me. [52]This
heap *is* a witness, and *this* pillar *is* a witness, that I will not pass beyond this heap
to you, and you will not pass beyond this
heap and this pillar to me, for harm. [53]The
God of Abraham, the God of Nahor, and
the God of their father judge between us."
And Jacob swore by the Fear of his father
Isaac. [54]Then Jacob offered a sacrifice on
the mountain, and called his brethren to
eat bread. And they ate bread and stayed
all night on the mountain. [55]And early in
the morning Laban arose, and kissed his
sons and daughters and blessed them.
Then Laban departed and returned to his
place.

Esau Comes to Meet Jacob

32 So Jacob went on his way, and the
angels of God met him. [2]When
Jacob saw them, he said, "This *is* God's
camp." And he called the name of that
place Mahanaim.[a]

[3]Then Jacob sent messengers before
him to Esau his brother in the land of
Seir, the country of Edom. [4]And he commanded them, saying, "Speak thus to my
lord Esau, 'Thus your servant Jacob says:
"I have dwelt with Laban and stayed there
until now. [5]I have oxen, donkeys, flocks,
and male and female servants; and I have
sent to tell my lord, that I may find favor
in your sight." ' "

[6]Then the messengers returned to Jacob, saying, "We came to your brother
Esau, and he also is coming to meet you,
and four hundred men *are* with him." [7]So
Jacob was greatly afraid and distressed;
and he divided the people that *were* with
him, and the flocks and herds and camels,
into two companies. [8]And he said, "If

31:47 [a]Literally, in Aramaic, *Heap of Witness* [b]Literally, in Hebrew, *Heap of Witness* 31:49 [a]Literally *Watch* 32:2 [a]Literally *Double Camp*

31:50 The words "God is witness between you and me" should not be taken lightly. God is the omniscient witness. He is ever-present and sees all—all thoughts, all actions, all intent, and all desire. Even the darkness is pure light to Him. Nothing is hidden from His holy eyes, and we should therefore live in the light of such a fearful truth.

Esau comes to the one company and attacks it, then the other company which is
left will escape."
[9]Then Jacob said, "O God of my father
Abraham and God of my father Isaac, the
LORD who said to me, 'Return to your
country and to your family, and I will
deal well with you': [10]I am not worthy of
the least of all the mercies and of all the
truth which You have shown Your servant; for I crossed over this Jordan with
my staff, and now I have become two
companies. [11]Deliver me, I pray, from the
hand of my brother, from the hand of
Esau; for I fear him, lest he come and attack me *and* the mother with the children. [12]For You said, 'I will surely treat
you well, and make your descendants as
the sand of the sea, which cannot be
numbered for multitude.' "
[13]So he lodged there that same night,
and took what came to his hand as a present for Esau his brother: [14]two hundred
female goats and twenty male goats, two
hundred ewes and twenty rams, [15]thirty
milk camels with their colts, forty cows
and ten bulls, twenty female donkeys and
ten foals. [16]Then he delivered *them* to the
hand of his servants, every drove by itself,
and said to his servants, "Pass over before
me, and put some distance between successive droves." [17]And he commanded the
first one, saying, "When Esau my brother
meets you and asks you, saying, 'To whom
do you belong, and where are you going?
Whose *are* these in front of you?' [18]then
you shall say, 'They *are* your servant Jacob's.
It *is* a present sent to my lord Esau; and
behold, he also *is* behind us.' " [19]So he
commanded the second, the third, and
all who followed the droves, saying, "In
this manner you shall speak to Esau when
you find him; [20]and also say, 'Behold, your
servant Jacob *is* behind us.' " For he said,
"I will appease him with the present that
goes before me, and afterward I will see
his face; perhaps he will accept me." [21]So
the present went on over before him, but
he himself lodged that night in the camp.

Wrestling with God

[22]And he arose that night and took his
two wives, his two female servants, and
his eleven sons, and crossed over the ford
of Jabbok. [23]He took them, sent them over
the brook, and sent over what he had.
[24]Then Jacob was left alone; and a Man
wrestled with him until the breaking of
day. [25]Now when He saw that He did not
prevail against him, He touched the socket
of his hip; and the socket of Jacob's hip
was out of joint as He wrestled with him.

32:24 Wrestling with God. It has been said that Jacob was as twisted as a corkscrew, and it took an act of God to straighten him out. Jacob, by an act of deceit, had robbed his older brother, Esau, of their father's blessing. It was fear that his vengeful brother would kill him that drove Jacob to seek God's favor.

It is legitimate to come to the Savior in fear. We have greatly wronged the One who gave us life by violating His Law, and His wrath abides upon us. If we do not repent and trust in the Savior, we will reap the terrifying fruit of our actions: death and everlasting hell. What a fearful thing it is to fall into the hands of the living God (Heb. 10:31)! *R. C. Sproul* rightly said that Jesus doesn't save us *to* God, He saves us *from* God.

Those who have had an encounter with God will, like Jacob, thereafter walk with a limp. Whereas we once had a haughty look and proud heart, we now bow in quiet humility and walk in lowliness of mind. And like Jacob was given a new name, when we meet the Lord we, too, become new creatures (2 Cor. 5:17). We are born again, with a new heart and with new desires.

And just as Jacob wrestled alone with God, each of us must make our own peace with God; no one else can do it for us. Notice that Jacob said he would not let God go until He blessed him. God honors persistence. Seek God's blessing until you know that you have peace with Him. Call on the name of the Lord. Be like the blind man Bartimaeus, who in desperation called to Jesus, despite the rebuke of those around him (Mark 10:48). Do not give up until you have made your own call and election sure (2 Pet. 1:10).

After you encounter God, be earnest always to keep His smile on your life. Jacob asked God for His name and then rejoiced that his life had been preserved (v. 30). Once you have come to know Him who suffered for you, you will rejoice with joy unspeakable and never forget the name of the One whose blood preserved you for His everlasting kingdom.

26 And He said, "Let Me go, for the day breaks."

But he said, "I will not let You go unless You bless me!"

27 So He said to him, "What is your name?"

He said, "Jacob."

28 And He said, "Your name shall no longer be called Jacob, but Israel;[a] for you have struggled with God and with men, and have prevailed."

29 Then Jacob asked, saying, "Tell *me* Your name, I pray."

And He said, "Why *is* it *that* you ask about My name?" And He blessed him there.

30 So Jacob called the name of the place Peniel:[a] "For I have seen God face to face, and my life is preserved." 31 Just as he crossed over Penuel[a] the sun rose on him, and he limped on his hip. 32 Therefore to this day the children of Israel do not eat the muscle that shrank, which *is* on the hip socket, because He touched the socket of Jacob's hip in the muscle that shrank.

Jacob and Esau Meet

33 Now Jacob lifted his eyes and looked, and there, Esau was coming, and with him were four hundred men. So he divided the children among Leah, Rachel, and the two maidservants. 2 And he put the maidservants and their children in front, Leah and her children behind, and Rachel and Joseph last. 3 Then he crossed over before them and bowed himself to the ground seven times, until he came near to his brother.

4 But Esau ran to meet him, and embraced him, and fell on his neck and kissed him, and they wept. 5 And he lifted his eyes and saw the women and children, and said, "Who *are* these with you?"

So he said, "The children whom God has graciously given your servant." 6 Then the maidservants came near, they and their children, and bowed down. 7 And Leah also came near with her children, and they bowed down. Afterward Joseph and Rachel came near, and they bowed down.

8 Then Esau said, "What *do* you *mean by* all this company which I met?"

And he said, "*These are* to find favor in the sight of my lord."

9 But Esau said, "I have enough, my brother; keep what you have for yourself."

10 And Jacob said, "No, please, if I have now found favor in your sight, then receive my present from my hand, inasmuch as I have seen your face as though I had seen the face of God, and you were pleased with me. 11 Please, take my blessing that is brought to you, because God has dealt graciously with me, and because I have enough." So he urged him, and he took *it*.

12 Then Esau said, "Let us take our journey; let us go, and I will go before you."

13 But Jacob said to him, "My lord knows that the children *are* weak, and the flocks and herds which are nursing *are* with me. And if the men should drive them hard one day, all the flock will die. 14 Please let my lord go on ahead before his servant. I will lead on slowly at a pace which the livestock that go before me, and the children, are able to endure, until I come to my lord in Seir."

15 And Esau said, "Now let me leave with you *some* of the people who *are* with me."

But he said, "What need is there? Let me find favor in the sight of my lord." 16 So Esau returned that day on his way to Seir. 17 And Jacob journeyed to Succoth, built himself a house, and made booths for his livestock. Therefore the name of the place is called Succoth.[a]

Jacob Comes to Canaan

18 Then Jacob came safely to the city of Shechem, which *is* in the land of Canaan,

32:28 [a]Literally *Prince with God* 32:30 [a]Literally *Face of God* 32:31 [a]Same as *Peniel*, verse 30 33:17 [a]Literally *Booths*

32:31 "Whom God would use greatly He will hurt deeply." *A. W. Tozer*

when he came from Padan Aram; and he pitched his tent before the city. 19And he bought the parcel of land, where he had pitched his tent, from the children of Hamor, Shechem's father, for one hundred pieces of money. 20Then he erected an altar there and called it El Elohe Israel.[a]

The Dinah Incident

34 Now Dinah the daughter of Leah, whom she had borne to Jacob, went out to see the daughters of the land. 2And when Shechem the son of Hamor the Hivite, prince of the country, saw her, he took her and lay with her, and violated her. 3His soul was strongly attracted to Dinah the daughter of Jacob, and he loved the young woman and spoke kindly to the young woman. 4So Shechem spoke to his father Hamor, saying, "Get me this young woman as a wife."

5And Jacob heard that he had defiled Dinah his daughter. Now his sons were with his livestock in the field; so Jacob held his peace until they came. 6Then Hamor the father of Shechem went out to Jacob to speak with him. 7And the sons of Jacob came in from the field when they heard *it;* and the men were grieved and very angry, because he had done a disgraceful thing in Israel by lying with Jacob's daughter, a thing which ought not to be done. 8But Hamor spoke with them, saying, "The soul of my son Shechem longs for your daughter. Please give her to him as a wife. 9And make marriages with us; give your daughters to us, and take our daughters to yourselves. 10So you shall dwell with us, and the land shall be before you. Dwell and trade in it, and acquire possessions for yourselves in it."

11Then Shechem said to her father and her brothers, "Let me find favor in your eyes, and whatever you say to me I will give. 12Ask me ever so much dowry and gift, and I will give according to what you say to me; but give me the young woman as a wife."

13But the sons of Jacob answered Shechem and Hamor his father, and spoke deceitfully, because he had defiled Dinah their sister. 14And they said to them, "We cannot do this thing, to give our sister to one who is uncircumcised, for that *would be* a reproach to us. 15But on this *condition* we will consent to you: If you will become as we *are,* if every male of you is circumcised, 16then we will give our daughters to you, and we will take your daughters to us; and we will dwell with you, and we will become one people. 17But if you will not heed us and be circumcised, then we will take our daughter and be gone."

18And their words pleased Hamor and Shechem, Hamor's son. 19So the young man did not delay to do the thing, because he delighted in Jacob's daughter. He *was* more honorable than all the household of his father.

20And Hamor and Shechem his son came to the gate of their city, and spoke with the men of their city, saying: 21"These men *are* at peace with us. Therefore let them dwell in the land and trade in it. For indeed the land *is* large enough for them. Let us take their daughters to us as wives, and let us give them our daugh-

33:20 [a]Literally *God, the God of Israel*

34:1,2 "Young persons, especially females, are never so safe and well off as under the care of pious parents. Their own ignorance, and the flattery and artifices of designing, wicked people, who are ever laying snares for them, expose them to great danger. They are their own enemies if they desire to go abroad, especially alone, among strangers to true religion. Those parents are very wrong who do not hinder their children from needlessly exposing themselves to danger. Indulged children, like Dinah, often become a grief and shame to their families. Her pretence was, to see the daughters of the land, to see how they dressed, and how they danced, and what was fashionable among them; she went to see, yet that was not all, she went to be seen too. She went to get acquaintance with the Canaanites, and to learn their ways. See what came of Dinah's gadding. The beginning of sin is as the letting forth of water. How great a matter does a little fire kindle! We should carefully avoid all occasions of sin and approaches to it." *Matthew Henry*

ters. 22Only on this *condition* will the men
consent to dwell with us, to be one people: if every male among us is circumcised
as they *are* circumcised. 23*Will* not their
livestock, their property, and every animal of theirs *be* ours? Only let us consent
to them, and they will dwell with us."
24And all who went out of the gate of his
city heeded Hamor and Shechem his son;
every male was circumcised, all who
went out of the gate of his city.

25Now it came to pass on the third day,
when they were in pain, that two of the
sons of Jacob, Simeon and Levi, Dinah's
brothers, each took his sword and came
boldly upon the city and killed all the
males. 26And they killed Hamor and Shechem his son with the edge of the sword,
and took Dinah from Shechem's house,
and went out. 27The sons of Jacob came
upon the slain, and plundered the city,
because their sister had been defiled.
28They took their sheep, their oxen, and
their donkeys, what *was* in the city and
what *was* in the field, 29and all their wealth.
All their little ones and their wives they
took captive; and they plundered even all
that *was* in the houses.

30Then Jacob said to Simeon and Levi,
"You have troubled me by making me ob-
noxious among the inhabitants of the land,
among the Canaanites and the Perizzites;
and since I *am* few in number, they will
gather themselves together against me and
kill me. I shall be destroyed, my household and I."

31But they said, "Should he treat our
sister like a harlot?"

Jacob's Return to Bethel

35 Then God said to Jacob, "Arise,
go up to Bethel and dwell there;
and make an altar there to God, who appeared to you when you fled from the
face of Esau your brother."

2And Jacob said to his household and
to all who *were* with him, "Put away the
foreign gods that *are* among you, purify
yourselves, and change your garments.
3Then let us arise and go up to Bethel;
and I will make an altar there to God,
who answered me in the day of my distress and has been with me in the way
which I have gone." 4So they gave Jacob
all the foreign gods which *were* in their
hands, and the earrings which *were* in
their ears; and Jacob hid them under the
terebinth tree which *was* by Shechem.
5And they journeyed, and the terror of
God was upon the cities that *were* all
around them, and they did not pursue
the sons of Jacob. 6So Jacob came to Luz
(that *is*, Bethel), which *is* in the land of
Canaan, he and all the people who *were*
with him. 7And he built an altar there
and called the place El Bethel,[a] because
there God appeared to him when he fled
from the face of his brother.

> As Christians we accept one foundational truth—God—and everything else makes sense. An atheist denies God and has to accept incredible explanations for everything else. It takes more faith to deny God than to believe in Him.
>
> **JOHN MACARTHUR**

8Now Deborah, Rebekah's nurse, died,
and she was buried below Bethel under
the terebinth tree. So the name of it was
called Allon Bachuth.[a]

9Then God appeared to Jacob again,
when he came from Padan Aram, and
blessed him. 10And God said to him,
"Your name *is* Jacob; your name shall not
be called Jacob anymore, but Israel shall

35:7 [a]Literally *God of the House of God* 35:8 [a]Literally *Terebinth of Weeping*

35:5 The world has a bias toward idolatry. The lost would never begin to believe that God could or would terrify. However, a little honest reading of Scripture will convince them that God is to be greatly feared. The apostle Paul said that it is knowledge of the terror of the Lord that should cause the Christian to persuade men and woman to flee to the Savior (see 2 Cor. 5:11).

be your name." So He called his name Israel. 11Also God said to him: "I *am* God Almighty. Be fruitful and multiply; a nation and a company of nations shall proceed from you, and kings shall come from your body. 12The land which I gave Abraham and Isaac I give to you; and to your descendants after you I give this land." 13Then God went up from him in the place where He talked with him. 14So Jacob set up a pillar in the place where He talked with him, a pillar of stone; and he poured a drink offering on it, and he poured oil on it. 15And Jacob called the name of the place where God spoke with him, Bethel.

Death of Rachel

16Then they journeyed from Bethel. And when there was but a little distance to go to Ephrath, Rachel labored *in childbirth,* and she had hard labor. 17Now it came to pass, when she was in hard labor, that the midwife said to her, "Do not fear; you will have this son also." 18And so it was, as her soul was departing (for she died), that she called his name Ben-Oni;[a] but his father called him Benjamin.[b] 19So Rachel died and was buried on the way to Ephrath (that *is,* Bethlehem). 20And Jacob set a pillar on her grave, which *is* the pillar of Rachel's grave to this day.

21Then Israel journeyed and pitched his tent beyond the tower of Eder. 22And it happened, when Israel dwelt in that land, that Reuben went and lay with Bilhah his father's concubine; and Israel heard *about it.*

Jacob's Twelve Sons

Now the sons of Jacob were twelve: 23the sons of Leah *were* Reuben, Jacob's firstborn, and Simeon, Levi, Judah, Issachar, and Zebulun; 24the sons of Rachel *were* Joseph and Benjamin; 25the sons of Bilhah, Rachel's maidservant, *were* Dan and Naphtali; 26and the sons of Zilpah, Leah's maidservant, *were* Gad and Asher. These *were* the sons of Jacob who were born to him in Padan Aram.

Death of Isaac

27Then Jacob came to his father Isaac at Mamre, or Kirjath Arba[a] (that *is,* Hebron), where Abraham and Isaac had dwelt. 28Now the days of Isaac were one hundred and eighty years. 29So Isaac breathed his last and died, and was gathered to his people, *being* old and full of days. And his sons Esau and Jacob buried him.

The Family of Esau

36 Now this *is* the genealogy of Esau, who is Edom. 2Esau took his wives from the daughters of Canaan: Adah the daughter of Elon the Hittite; Aholibamah the daughter of Anah, the daughter of Zibeon the Hivite; 3and Basemath, Ishmael's daughter, sister of Nebajoth. 4Now Adah bore Eliphaz to Esau, and Basemath bore Reuel. 5And Aholibamah bore Jeush, Jaalam, and Korah. These *were* the sons of Esau who were born to him in the land of Canaan.

6Then Esau took his wives, his sons, his daughters, and all the persons of his household, his cattle and all his animals, and all his goods which he had gained in the land of Canaan, and went to a country away from the presence of his brother Jacob. 7For their possessions were too great for them to dwell together, and the land where they were strangers could not support them because of their livestock.

35:18 [a]Literally *Son of My Sorrow* [b]Literally *Son of the Right Hand* 35:27 [a]Literally *Town of Arba*

36:1 The Bible is careful to list genealogies to show the faithfulness of God regarding His promises. The New Testament also lists names (often at the end of epistles) of some who have been faithful to God. There you will find names of those who "labored" with Paul, were called his "fellow workers," and "a faithful and beloved brother." May God be able to count on each of us as His faithful laborers, and fellow workers in the gospel.

8So Esau dwelt in Mount Seir. Esau *is*
Edom.
9And this *is* the genealogy of Esau the
father of the Edomites in Mount Seir.
10These *were* the names of Esau's sons:
Eliphaz the son of Adah the wife of Esau,
and Reuel the son of Basemath the wife of
Esau. 11And the sons of Eliphaz were Teman, Omar, Zepho,[a] Gatam, and Kenaz.
12Now Timna was the concubine of
Eliphaz, Esau's son, and she bore Amalek
to Eliphaz. These *were* the sons of Adah,
Esau's wife.

Can Christians believe in evolution? See Isa. 40:28 comment.

13These *were* the sons of Reuel: Nahath,
Zerah, Shammah, and Mizzah. These were
the sons of Basemath, Esau's wife.
14These were the sons of Aholibamah,
Esau's wife, the daughter of Anah, the
daughter of Zibeon. And she bore to Esau:
Jeush, Jaalam, and Korah.

The Chiefs of Edom

15These *were* the chiefs of the sons of
Esau. The sons of Eliphaz, the firstborn
son of Esau, were Chief Teman, Chief
Omar, Chief Zepho, Chief Kenaz, 16Chief
Korah,[a] Chief Gatam, *and* Chief Amalek.
These *were* the chiefs of Eliphaz in the
land of Edom. They *were* the sons of Adah.
17These *were* the sons of Reuel, Esau's
son: Chief Nahath, Chief Zerah, Chief
Shammah, and Chief Mizzah. These *were*
the chiefs of Reuel in the land of Edom.
These *were* the sons of Basemath, Esau's
wife.
18And these *were* the sons of Aholibamah, Esau's wife: Chief Jeush, Chief
Jaalam, and Chief Korah. These *were* the
chiefs *who descended* from Aholibamah,
Esau's wife, the daughter of Anah. 19These
were the sons of Esau, who is Edom, and
these *were* their chiefs.

The Sons of Seir

20These *were* the sons of Seir the
Horite who inhabited the land: Lotan,
Shobal, Zibeon, Anah, 21Dishon, Ezer, and
Dishan. These *were* the chiefs of the Horites, the sons of Seir, in the land of Edom.
22And the sons of Lotan were Hori and
Hemam.[a] Lotan's sister *was* Timna.
23These *were* the sons of Shobal: Alvan,[a] Manahath, Ebal, Shepho,[b] and Onam.
24These *were* the sons of Zibeon: both
Ajah and Anah. This *was the* Anah who
found the water[a] in the wilderness as he
pastured the donkeys of his father Zibeon. 25These *were* the children of Anah:
Dishon and Aholibamah the daughter of
Anah.
26These *were* the sons of Dishon:[a] Hemdan,[b] Eshban, Ithran, and Cheran. 27These
were the sons of Ezer: Bilhan, Zaavan,
and Akan.[a] 28These *were* the sons of Dishan: Uz and Aran.
29These *were* the chiefs of the Horites:
Chief Lotan, Chief Shobal, Chief Zibeon,
Chief Anah, 30Chief Dishon, Chief Ezer,
and Chief Dishan. These *were* the chiefs
of the Horites, according to their chiefs in
the land of Seir.

The Kings of Edom

31Now these *were* the kings who reigned
in the land of Edom before any king
reigned over the children of Israel: 32Bela

36:11 [a]Spelled *Zephi* in 1 Chronicles 1:36 **36:16** [a]Samaritan Pentateuch omits *Chief Korah.* **36:22** [a]Spelled *Homam* in 1 Chronicles 1:39 **36:23** [a]Spelled *Alian* in 1 Chronicles 1:40 [b]Spelled *Shephi* in 1 Chronicles 1:40 **36:24** [a]Following Masoretic Text and Vulgate (*hot springs*); Septuagint reads *Jamin;* Targum reads *mighty men;* Talmud interprets as *mules.* **36:26** [a]Hebrew *Dishan* [b]Spelled *Hamran* in 1 Chronicles 1:41 **36:27** [a]Spelled *Jaakan* in 1 Chronicles 1:42

the son of Beor reigned in Edom, and the
name of his city *was* Dinhabah. 33 And
when Bela died, Jobab the son of Zerah of
Bozrah reigned in his place. 34 When Jobab
died, Husham of the land of the Temanites reigned in his place. 35 And when Husham died, Hadad the son of Bedad, who
attacked Midian in the field of Moab,
reigned in his place. And the name of his
city *was* Avith. 36 When Hadad died, Samlah of Masrekah reigned in his place. 37 And
when Samlah died, Saul of Rehoboth-*by*-
the-River reigned in his place. 38 When
Saul died, Baal-Hanan the son of Achbor
reigned in his place. 39 And when Baal-
Hanan the son of Achbor died, Hadar[a]
reigned in his place; and the name of his
city *was* Pau.[b] His wife's name *was* Mehetabel, the daughter of Matred, the daughter of Mezahab.

The Chiefs of Esau

40 And these *were* the names of the
chiefs of Esau, according to their families
and their places, by their names: Chief
Timnah, Chief Alvah,[a] Chief Jetheth,
41 Chief Aholibamah, Chief Elah, Chief
Pinon, 42 Chief Kenaz, Chief Teman, Chief
Mibzar, 43 Chief Magdiel, and Chief Iram.
These *were* the chiefs of Edom, according
to their dwelling places in the land of
their possession. Esau *was* the father of
the Edomites.

Joseph Dreams of Greatness

37 Now Jacob dwelt in the land where
his father was a stranger, in the
land of Canaan. 2 This *is* the history of
Jacob.

Joseph, *being* seventeen years old, was
feeding the flock with his brothers. And
the lad *was* with the sons of Bilhah and
the sons of Zilpah, his father's wives; and
Joseph brought a bad report of them to
his father.

3 Now Israel loved Joseph more than
all his children, because he *was* the son of
his old age. Also he made him a tunic of
many colors. 4 But when his brothers saw
that their father loved him more than all
his brothers, they hated him and could
not speak peaceably to him.

5 Now Joseph had a dream, and he told
it to his brothers; and they hated him
even more. 6 So he said to them, "Please
hear this dream which I have dreamed:
7 There we were, binding sheaves in the
field. Then behold, my sheaf arose and also
stood upright; and indeed your sheaves
stood all around and bowed down to my
sheaf."

8 And his brothers said to him, "Shall
you indeed reign over us? Or shall you
indeed have dominion over us?" So they
hated him even more for his dreams and
for his words.

9 Then he dreamed still another dream
and told it to his brothers, and said, "Look,
I have dreamed another dream. And this
time, the sun, the moon, and the eleven
stars bowed down to me."

36:39 [a]Spelled *Hadad* in Samaritan Pentateuch, Syriac, and 1 Chronicles 1:50 [b]Spelled *Pai* in 1 Chronicles 1:50 36:40 [a]Spelled *Aliah* in 1 Chronicles 1:51

37:2 Joseph foreshadows the Savior. The history of Joseph, who saved his family and all of Egypt from death due to starvation, foreshadows the Messiah to come, who has the power to save us, whether Jew or Gentile, from eternal damnation.

Joseph was greatly favored by his father, Israel (v. 3). Israel sent Joseph into the fields to find his brothers (vv. 13,14). Joseph sought his brothers and found them (vv. 15–17). But when Joseph's brothers saw him coming, they conspired to kill him (vv. 18–20). They stripped his coat off of him (v. 23) and sold him into slavery for 20 pieces of silver (v. 28).

Jesus, too, was favored by His heavenly Father (Matt. 3:17; Mark 1:11), who sent Jesus into the world in search of us, His brothers and sisters (Rom. 8:17; Gal. 4:7; Matt. 12:50; 25:40).

But when Jesus "came to His own... His own did not receive Him" (John 1:11). Those of the same bloodline as Jesus (Matt. 1:1–17) demanded that He be crucified (John 19:6,15). Jesus was eventually stripped and beaten (Matt. 27:26,28) and, through an exchange of silver, Jesus was betrayed by His own disciple (Matt. 26:15; 27:9).

10So he told *it* to his father and his
brothers; and his father rebuked him and
said to him, "What is this dream that you
have dreamed? Shall your mother and I
and your brothers indeed come to bow
down to the earth before you?" 11And his
brothers envied him, but his father kept
the matter *in mind.*

Joseph Sold by His Brothers

12Then his brothers went to feed their
father's flock in Shechem. 13And Israel said
to Joseph, "Are not your brothers feeding
the flock in Shechem? Come, I will send
you to them."

So he said to him, "Here I am."

14Then he said to him, "Please go and
see if it is well with your brothers and
well with the flocks, and bring back word
to me." So he sent him out of the Valley
of Hebron, and he went to Shechem.

15Now a certain man found him, and
there he was, wandering in the field. And
the man asked him, saying, "What are you
seeking?"

16So he said, "I am seeking my brothers. Please tell me where they are feeding
their flocks."

17And the man said, "They have departed from here, for I heard them say, 'Let
us go to Dothan.' " So Joseph went after
his brothers and found them in Dothan.

18Now when they saw him afar off,
even before he came near them, they conspired against him to kill him. 19Then they
said to one another, "Look, this dreamer
is coming! 20Come therefore, let us now
kill him and cast him into some pit; and
we shall say, 'Some wild beast has devoured him.' We shall see what will become of his dreams!"

21But Reuben heard *it,* and he delivered
him out of their hands, and said, "Let us
not kill him." 22And Reuben said to them,
"Shed no blood, *but* cast him into this pit
which *is* in the wilderness, and do not lay
a hand on him"—that he might deliver
him out of their hands, and bring him
back to his father.

23So it came to pass, when Joseph had
come to his brothers, that they stripped
Joseph *of* his tunic, the tunic of *many* colors that *was* on him. 24Then they took
him and cast him into a pit. And the pit
was empty; *there was* no water in it.

25And they sat down to eat a meal.
Then they lifted their eyes and looked,
and there was a company of Ishmaelites,
coming from Gilead with their camels,
bearing spices, balm, and myrrh, on their
way to carry *them* down to Egypt. 26So
Judah said to his brothers, "What profit *is*
there if we kill our brother and conceal
his blood? 27Come and let us sell him to
the Ishmaelites, and let not our hand be
upon him, for he *is* our brother *and* our
flesh." And his brothers listened. 28Then
Midianite traders passed by; so *the broth-*
ers pulled Joseph up and lifted him out of
the pit, and sold him to the Ishmaelites
for twenty *shekels* of silver. And they took
Joseph to Egypt.

29Then Reuben returned to the pit, and
indeed Joseph *was* not in the pit; and he
tore his clothes. 30And he returned to his
brothers and said, "The lad *is* no *more;* and
I, where shall I go?"

31So they took Joseph's tunic, killed a
kid of the goats, and dipped the tunic in
the blood. 32Then they sent the tunic of
many colors, and they brought *it* to their
father and said, "We have found this. Do
you know whether it *is* your son's tunic
or not?"

33And he recognized it and said, "*It is*
my son's tunic. A wild beast has devoured
him. Without doubt Joseph is torn to
pieces." 34Then Jacob tore his clothes, put

37:11 Fortify yourself with the love of God. It will be a shield against the sin of jealousy. When a brother or sister is praised and we are neglected, love will not notice. It is blind to the shallowness of the praise of man. If King Saul had loved David, he would have rejoiced when David was praised for his endeavors of war (see 1 Sam. 18:6–8). Instead, Saul allowed the cancer of jealousy to eat away at his soul. Hatred and murder were its bitter bedfellows.

sackcloth on his waist, and mourned for his son many days. [35]And all his sons and all his daughters arose to comfort him; but he refused to be comforted, and he said, "For I shall go down into the grave to my son in mourning." Thus his father wept for him.

[36]Now the Midianites[a] had sold him in Egypt to Potiphar, an officer of Pharaoh *and* captain of the guard.

Judah and Tamar

38 It came to pass at that time that Judah departed from his brothers, and visited a certain Adullamite whose name *was* Hirah. [2]And Judah saw there a daughter of a certain Canaanite whose name *was* Shua, and he married her and went in to her. [3]So she conceived and bore a son, and he called his name Er. [4]She conceived again and bore a son, and she called his name Onan. [5]And she conceived yet again and bore a son, and called his name Shelah. He was at Chezib when she bore him.

[6]Then Judah took a wife for Er his firstborn, and her name *was* Tamar. [7]But Er, Judah's firstborn, was wicked in the sight of the LORD, and the LORD killed him. [8]And Judah said to Onan, "Go in to your brother's wife and marry her, and raise up an heir to your brother." [9]But Onan knew that the heir would not be his; and it came to pass, when he went in to his brother's wife, that he emitted on the ground, lest he should give an heir to his brother. [10]And the thing which he did displeased the LORD; therefore He killed him also.

[11]Then Judah said to Tamar his daughter-in-law, "Remain a widow in your father's house till my son Shelah is grown." For he said, "Lest he also die like his brothers." And Tamar went and dwelt in her father's house.

[12]Now in the process of time the daughter of Shua, Judah's wife, died; and Judah was comforted, and went up to his sheepshearers at Timnah, he and his friend Hirah the Adullamite. [13]And it was told Tamar, saying, "Look, your father-in-law is going up to Timnah to shear his sheep." [14]So she took off her widow's garments, covered *herself* with a veil and wrapped herself, and sat in an open place which *was* on the way to Timnah; for she saw that Shelah was grown, and she was not given to him as a wife. [15]When Judah saw her, he thought she *was* a harlot, because she had covered her face. [16]Then he turned to her by the way, and said, "Please let me come in to you"; for he did not know that she *was* his daughter-in-law.

So she said, "What will you give me, that you may come in to me?"

[17]And he said, "I will send a young goat from the flock."

So she said, "Will you give *me* a pledge till you send *it?*"

[18]Then he said, "What pledge shall I give you?"

So she said, "Your signet and cord, and your staff that *is* in your hand." Then he gave *them* to her, and went in to her, and she conceived by him. [19]So she arose and went away, and laid aside her veil and put on the garments of her widowhood.

[20]And Judah sent the young goat by the hand of his friend the Adullamite, to receive *his* pledge from the woman's hand, but he did not find her. [21]Then he asked the men of that place, saying, "Where is the harlot who *was* openly by the roadside?"

And they said, "There was no harlot in this *place.*"

37:36 [a]Masoretic Text reads *Medanites.*

38:7 This is a powerful evangelistic verse to use when preaching or witnessing to the complacent unsaved. Most sinners believe that God's patience is inexhaustible. This verse shows that is not true. God lost patience with a rich man who said that he would build bigger barns and take life easy. He told the man that he was a fool and He took his life that night (see Luke 12:19–21). He also lost patience with a man and his wife when they told one lie, and killed them (see Acts 5:1–11). Such verses have a way of sobering us and bringing to us the most necessary virtues—the fear of the Lord.

22So he returned to Judah and said, "I cannot find her. Also, the men of the place said there was no harlot in this *place.*" 23Then Judah said, "Let her take *them* for herself, lest we be shamed; for I sent this young goat and you have not found her."

24And it came to pass, about three months after, that Judah was told, saying, "Tamar your daughter-in-law has played the harlot; furthermore she *is* with child by harlotry."

So Judah said, "Bring her out and let her be burned!"

25When she *was* brought out, she sent to her father-in-law, saying, "By the man to whom these belong, I *am* with child." And she said, "Please determine whose these *are*—the signet and cord, and staff."

26So Judah acknowledged *them* and said, "She has been more righteous than I, because I did not give her to Shelah my son." And he never knew her again.

27Now it came to pass, at the time for giving birth, that behold, twins *were* in her womb. 28And so it was, when she was giving birth, that *the one* put out *his* hand; and the midwife took a scarlet *thread* and bound it on his hand, saying, "This one came out first." 29Then it happened, as he drew back his hand, that his brother came out unexpectedly; and she said, "How did you break through? *This* breach *be* upon you!" Therefore his name was called Perez.[a] 30Afterward his brother came out who had the scarlet *thread* on his hand. And his name was called Zerah.

Joseph a Slave in Egypt

39 Now Joseph had been taken down to Egypt. And Potiphar, an officer of Pharaoh, captain of the guard, an Egyptian, bought him from the Ishmaelites who had taken him down there. 2The LORD was with Joseph, and he was a successful man; and he was in the house of his master the Egyptian. 3And his master saw that the LORD *was* with him and that the LORD made all he did to prosper in his hand. 4So Joseph found favor in his sight, and served him. Then he made him overseer of his house, and all *that* he had he put under his authority. 5So it was, from the time *that* he had made him overseer of his house and all that he had, that the LORD blessed the Egyptian's house for Joseph's sake; and the blessing of the LORD was on all that he had in the house and in the field. 6Thus he left all that he had in Joseph's hand, and he did not know what he had except for the bread which he ate.

Now Joseph was handsome in form and appearance.

7And it came to pass after these things that his master's wife cast longing eyes on Joseph, and she said, "Lie with me."

8But he refused and said to his master's wife, "Look, my master does not know what *is* with me in the house, and he has committed all that he has to my hand. 9*There is* no one greater in this house than I, nor has he kept back anything from me but you, because you *are* his wife. How then can I do this great wickedness, and sin against God?"

10So it was, as she spoke to Joseph day by day, that he did not heed her, to lie with her *or* to be with her.

11But it happened about this time, when Joseph went into the house to do his work, and none of the men of the house *was* inside, 12that she caught him by his garment, saying, "Lie with me." But he left his garment in her hand, and fled and ran outside. 13And so it was, when she saw that he had left his garment in her

38:29 [a]Literally *Breach* or *Breakthrough*

39:7 Potiphar's wife is still around. Her name is "Lust," and she incessantly calls to every man to spend time with her. (First and Second Peter often speak of the sin of lust.) When she calls, do what Joseph wisely did: run (see v. 12). Flee fornication. Guard your eyes. It would be better to be blind than to let your eyes offend you. Guard your heart. Keep lust from entering your mind. How easy it would have been for Joseph to yield to temptation, but his salvation was the fear of the Lord (see v. 9).

hand and fled outside, 14that she called to
the men of her house and spoke to them,
saying, "See, he has brought in to us a
Hebrew to mock us. He came in to me to
lie with me, and I cried out with a loud
voice. 15And it happened, when he heard
that I lifted my voice and cried out, that
he left his garment with me, and fled and
went outside."

16So she kept his garment with her until his master came home. 17Then she
spoke to him with words like these, saying, "The Hebrew servant whom you
brought to us came in to me to mock me;
18so it happened, as I lifted my voice and
cried out, that he left his garment with
me and fled outside."

19So it was, when his master heard the
words which his wife spoke to him, saying, "Your servant did to me after this
manner," that his anger was aroused.
20Then Joseph's master took him and put
him into the prison, a place where the
king's prisoners *were* confined. And he
was there in the prison. 21But the LORD
was with Joseph and showed him mercy,
and He gave him favor in the sight of the
keeper of the prison. 22And the keeper of
the prison committed to Joseph's hand all
the prisoners who *were* in the prison;
whatever they did there, it was his doing.
23The keeper of the prison did not look
into anything *that was* under *Joseph's* authority,[a] because the LORD was with him;
and whatever he did, the LORD made *it*
prosper.

The Prisoners' Dreams

40 It came to pass after these things
that the butler and the baker of
the king of Egypt offended their lord, the
king of Egypt. 2And Pharaoh was angry
with his two officers, the chief butler and
the chief baker. 3So he put them in custody in the house of the captain of the
guard, in the prison, the place where Joseph *was* confined. 4And the captain of
the guard charged Joseph with them, and
he served them; so they were in custody
for a while.

5Then the butler and the baker of the
king of Egypt, who *were* confined in the
prison, had a dream, both of them, each
man's dream in one night *and* each man's
dream with its *own* interpretation. 6And
Joseph came in to them in the morning
and looked at them, and saw that they
were sad. 7So he asked Pharaoh's officers
who *were* with him in the custody of his
lord's house, saying, "Why do you look *so*
sad today?"

8And they said to him, "We each have
had a dream, and *there is* no interpreter of
it."

So Joseph said to them, "Do not interpretations belong to God? Tell *them* to me,
please."

> The modern world detests authority but worships relevance. Our Christian conviction is that the Bible has both authority and relevance, and that the secret of both is Jesus Christ.
>
> **JOHN R. W. STOTT**

9Then the chief butler told his dream to
Joseph, and said to him, "Behold, in my
dream a vine *was* before me, 10and in the
vine *were* three branches; it *was* as though
it budded, its blossoms shot forth, and its
clusters brought forth ripe grapes. 11Then
Pharaoh's cup *was* in my hand; and I took
the grapes and pressed them into Pharaoh's cup, and placed the cup in Pharaoh's
hand."

12And Joseph said to him, "This *is* the
interpretation of it: The three branches
are three days. 13Now within three days
Pharaoh will lift up your head and restore
you to your place, and you will put Pharaoh's cup in his hand according to the
former manner, when you were his butler.
14But remember me when it is well with
you, and please show kindness to me;
make mention of me to Pharaoh, and get
me out of this house. 15For indeed I was
stolen away from the land of the Hebrews;

39:23 [a]Literally *his hand*

and also I have done nothing here that they should put me into the dungeon."

16When the chief baker saw that the interpretation was good, he said to Joseph, "I also *was* in my dream, and there *were* three white baskets on my head. 17In the uppermost basket *were* all kinds of baked goods for Pharaoh, and the birds ate them out of the basket on my head."

18So Joseph answered and said, "This *is* the interpretation of it: The three baskets *are* three days. 19Within three days Pharaoh will lift off your head from you and hang you on a tree; and the birds will eat your flesh from you."

20Now it came to pass on the third day, *which was* Pharaoh's birthday, that he made a feast for all his servants; and he lifted up the head of the chief butler and of the chief baker among his servants. 21Then he restored the chief butler to his butlership again, and he placed the cup in Pharaoh's hand. 22But he hanged the chief baker, as Joseph had interpreted to them. 23Yet the chief butler did not remember Joseph, but forgot him.

Pharaoh's Dreams

41 Then it came to pass, at the end of two full years, that Pharaoh had a dream; and behold, he stood by the river. 2Suddenly there came up out of the river seven cows, fine looking and fat; and they fed in the meadow. 3Then behold, seven other cows came up after them out of the river, ugly and gaunt, and stood by the *other* cows on the bank of the river. 4And the ugly and gaunt cows ate up the seven fine looking and fat cows. So Pharaoh awoke. 5He slept and dreamed a second time; and suddenly seven heads of grain came up on one stalk, plump and good. 6Then behold, seven thin heads, blighted by the east wind, sprang up after them. 7And the seven thin heads devoured the seven plump and full heads. So Pharaoh awoke, and indeed, *it was* a dream. 8Now it came to pass in the morning that his spirit was troubled, and he sent and called for all the magicians of Egypt and all its wise men. And Pharaoh told them his dreams, but *there was* no one who could interpret them for Pharaoh.

9Then the chief butler spoke to Pharaoh, saying: "I remember my faults this day. 10When Pharaoh was angry with his servants, and put me in custody in the house of the captain of the guard, *both* me and the chief baker, 11we each had a dream in one night, he and I. Each of us dreamed according to the interpretation of his *own* dream. 12Now there *was* a young Hebrew man with us there, a servant of the captain of the guard. And we told him, and he interpreted our dreams for us; to each man he interpreted according to his *own* dream. 13And it came to pass, just as he interpreted for us, so it happened. He restored me to my office, and he hanged him."

14Then Pharaoh sent and called Joseph, and they brought him quickly out of the dungeon; and he shaved, changed his clothing, and came to Pharaoh. 15And Pharaoh said to Joseph, "I have had a dream, and *there is* no one who can interpret it. But I have heard it said of you *that* you can understand a dream, to interpret it."

16So Joseph answered Pharaoh, saying, "*It is* not in me; God will give Pharaoh an answer of peace."

17Then Pharaoh said to Joseph: "Behold, in my dream I stood on the bank of the river. 18Suddenly seven cows came up out of the river, fine looking and fat; and they fed in the meadow. 19Then behold, seven other cows came up after them, poor and very ugly and gaunt, such ugliness as I have never seen in all the land of Egypt. 20And the gaunt and ugly cows ate

41:12 We know what the future holds for this sinful world. God has given the believer an understanding of the times in which we live. We know of the terrible fate of the ungodly, and we long for this people (this Egypt in which we live) to listen to us and to believe the words we speak. They are not our personal interpretation, but are the words of the Living God, directly from the Word of God.

up the first seven, the fat cows. [21]When
they had eaten them up, no one would
have known that they had eaten them,
for they *were* just as ugly as at the beginning. So I awoke. [22]Also I saw in my
dream, and suddenly seven heads came
up on one stalk, full and good. [23]Then
behold, seven heads, withered, thin, *and*
blighted by the east wind, sprang up after them. [24]And the thin heads devoured
the seven good heads. So I told *this* to the
magicians, but *there was* no one who could
explain *it* to me."

[25]Then Joseph said to Pharaoh, "The
dreams of Pharaoh *are* one; God has shown
Pharaoh what He *is* about to do: [26]The
seven good cows *are* seven years, and the
seven good heads *are* seven years; the
dreams *are* one. [27]And the seven thin and
ugly cows which came up after them *are*
seven years, and the seven empty heads
blighted by the east wind are seven years
of famine. [28]This *is* the thing which I have
spoken to Pharaoh. God has shown Pharaoh what He *is* about to do. [29]Indeed seven
years of great plenty will come throughout all the land of Egypt; [30]but after them
seven years of famine will arise, and all
the plenty will be forgotten in the land of
Egypt; and the famine will deplete the
land. [31]So the plenty will not be known
in the land because of the famine following, for it *will be* very severe. [32]And the
dream was repeated to Pharaoh twice because the thing *is* established by God,
and God will shortly bring it to pass.

[33]"Now therefore, let Pharaoh select a
discerning and wise man, and set him over
the land of Egypt. [34]Let Pharaoh do *this,*
and let him appoint officers over the land,
to collect one-fifth *of the produce* of the
land of Egypt in the seven plentiful years.
[35]And let them gather all the food of those
good years that are coming, and store up
grain under the authority of Pharaoh, and
let them keep food in the cities. [36]Then
that food shall be as a reserve for the land
for the seven years of famine which shall
be in the land of Egypt, that the land may
not perish during the famine."

Joseph's Rise to Power

[37]So the advice was good in the eyes of
Pharaoh and in the eyes of all his servants. [38]And Pharaoh said to his servants,
"Can we find *such a one* as this, a man in
whom *is* the Spirit of God?"

[39]Then Pharaoh said to Joseph, "Inasmuch as God has shown you all this,
there is no one as discerning and wise as
you. [40]You shall be over my house, and
all my people shall be ruled according to
your word; only in regard to the throne
will I be greater than you." [41]And Pharaoh said to Joseph, "See, I have set you
over all the land of Egypt."

[42]Then Pharaoh took his signet ring
off his hand and put it on Joseph's hand;

41:30 Egypt's deliverance depended upon their faith. Had they not believed Joseph, they would not have bothered to store up for the future during the times of plenty. Our salvation rests on faith in Jesus and God's Word. If we did not believe that there is a coming Judgment Day, we would not trust in the righteousness of Christ. We would instead gorge ourselves during the times of plenty—in the pleasurable sins of this world.

41:38 Joseph foreshadows the Savior. After a lengthy imprisonment for a crime he did not commit, Joseph was called to serve Pharaoh. Pleased with Joseph's service, Pharaoh exalted him to a high position of authority. When Joseph's brothers later come to him for help, Joseph forgave them for their betrayal of him and saved their lives by providing the food they needed.

In these details, Joseph continues to foreshadow the Savior to come, who took the form of a slave, was crucified as a sacrifice for sins He did not commit, and was then raised from death. God the Father was "well pleased" with Jesus (see Matt. 3:17) and exalted Him to the highest position of authority.

Compare the account of Pharaoh's exalting Joseph in Gen. 41:40–44 with descriptions of Jesus in Eph. 1:19–22; Matt. 28:18; Phil. 2:7–10. And compare the risen Christ in John 17:2, "You have given Him authority over all flesh, that He should give eternal life to as many as You have given Him" with Joseph's statement to his brothers in Gen. 45:7, "And God sent me before you . . . to save your lives by a great deliverance."

and he clothed him in garments of fine linen and put a gold chain around his neck. 43And he had him ride in the second chariot which he had; and they cried out before him, "Bow the knee!" So he set him over all the land of Egypt. 44Pharaoh also said to Joseph, "I *am* Pharaoh, and without your consent no man may lift his hand or foot in all the land of Egypt." 45And Pharaoh called Joseph's name Zaphnath-Paaneah. And he gave him as a wife Asenath, the daughter of Poti-Pherah priest of On. So Joseph went out over *all* the land of Egypt.

46Joseph was thirty years old when he stood before Pharaoh king of Egypt. And Joseph went out from the presence of Pharaoh, and went throughout all the land of Egypt. 47Now in the seven plentiful years the ground brought forth abundantly. 48So he gathered up all the food of the seven years which were in the land of Egypt, and laid up the food in the cities; he laid up in every city the food of the fields which surrounded them. 49Joseph gathered very much grain, as the sand of the sea, until he stopped counting, for *it was* immeasurable.

50And to Joseph were born two sons before the years of famine came, whom Asenath, the daughter of Poti-Pherah priest of On, bore to him. 51Joseph called the name of the firstborn Manasseh:[a] "For God has made me forget all my toil and all my father's house." 52And the name of the second he called Ephraim:[a] "For God has caused me to be fruitful in the land of my affliction."

53Then the seven years of plenty which were in the land of Egypt ended, 54and the seven years of famine began to come, as Joseph had said. The famine was in all lands, but in all the land of Egypt there was bread. 55So when all the land of Egypt was famished, the people cried to Pharaoh for bread. Then Pharaoh said to all the Egyptians, "Go to Joseph; whatever he says to you, do." 56The famine was over all the face of the earth, and Joseph opened all the storehouses[a] and sold to the Egyptians. And the famine became severe in the land of Egypt. 57So all countries came to Joseph in Egypt to buy *grain*, because the famine was severe in all lands.

Joseph's Brothers Go to Egypt

42 When Jacob saw that there was grain in Egypt, Jacob said to his sons, "Why do you look at one another?" 2And he said, "Indeed I have heard that there is grain in Egypt; go down to that place and buy for us there, that we may live and not die."

3So Joseph's ten brothers went down to buy grain in Egypt. 4But Jacob did not send Joseph's brother Benjamin with his brothers, for he said, "Lest some calamity befall him." 5And the sons of Israel went to buy *grain* among those who journeyed, for the famine was in the land of Canaan.

6Now Joseph *was* governor over the land; and it was he who sold to all the people of the land. And Joseph's brothers came and bowed down before him with *their* faces to the earth. 7Joseph saw his brothers and recognized them, but he acted as a stranger to them and spoke roughly to them. Then he said to them, "Where do you come from?"

And they said, "From the land of Canaan to buy food."

8So Joseph recognized his brothers, but they did not recognize him. 9Then Joseph remembered the dreams which he had dreamed about them, and said to them,

41:51 [a]Literally *Making Forgetful* 41:52 [a]Literally *Fruitfulness* 41:56 [a]Literally *all that was in them*

42:6 Joseph foreshadows the Savior. This is the fulfillment of the dream Joseph had in Gen. 37:7: "Then behold, my sheaf arose and also stood upright; and indeed your sheaves stood all around and bowed down to my sheaf." Pharaoh had set Joseph over all the land of Egypt and all the people bowed the knee before him (see 41:43). God has given Jesus Christ a name that is above every name, and the day will come when all humanity will bow the knee to Jesus Christ (see Phil. 2:10).

"You *are* spies! You have come to see the nakedness of the land!"

10And they said to him, "No, my lord, but your servants have come to buy food. 11We *are* all one man's sons; we *are* honest *men;* your servants are not spies."

12But he said to them, "No, but you have come to see the nakedness of the land."

13And they said, "Your servants *are* twelve brothers, the sons of one man in the land of Canaan; and in fact, the youngest *is* with our father today, and one *is* no more."

14But Joseph said to them, "It *is* as I spoke to you, saying, 'You *are* spies!' 15In this *manner* you shall be tested: By the life of Pharaoh, you shall not leave this place unless your youngest brother comes here. 16Send one of you, and let him bring your brother; and you shall be kept in prison, that your words may be tested to see whether *there is* any truth in you; or else, by the life of Pharaoh, surely you *are* spies!" 17So he put them all together in prison three days.

18Then Joseph said to them the third day, "Do this and live, *for* I fear God: 19If you *are* honest *men,* let one of your brothers be confined to your prison house; but you, go and carry grain for the famine of your houses. 20And bring your youngest brother to me; so your words will be verified, and you shall not die."

And they did so. 21Then they said to one another, "We *are* truly guilty concerning our brother, for we saw the anguish of his soul when he pleaded with us, and we would not hear; therefore this distress has come upon us."

22And Reuben answered them, saying, "Did I not speak to you, saying, 'Do not sin against the boy'; and you would not listen? Therefore behold, his blood is now required of us." 23But they did not know that Joseph understood *them,* for he spoke to them through an interpreter. 24And he turned himself away from them and wept. Then he returned to them again, and talked with them. And he took Simeon from them and bound him before their eyes.

The Brothers Return to Canaan

25Then Joseph gave a command to fill their sacks with grain, to restore every man's money to his sack, and to give them provisions for the journey. Thus he did for them. 26So they loaded their donkeys with the grain and departed from there. 27But as one *of them* opened his sack to give his donkey feed at the encampment, he saw his money; and there it was, in the mouth of his sack. 28So he said to his brothers, "My money has been restored, and there it is, in my sack!" Then their hearts failed *them* and they were afraid, saying to one another, "What *is* this *that* God has done to us?"

29Then they went to Jacob their father in the land of Canaan and told him all that had happened to them, saying: 30"The man *who is* lord of the land spoke roughly to us, and took us for spies of the country. 31But we said to him, 'We *are* honest *men;* we are not spies. 32We *are* twelve brothers, sons of our father; one *is* no *more,* and the youngest *is* with our father this day in the land of Canaan.' 33Then the man, the lord of the country, said to us, 'By this I will know that you *are* hon-

42:21–24 It seems that it took all this time for them to honestly acknowledge what a wicked thing they had done, not only to their brother, but to their father. Jacob was in anguish for all those years because of their deceit. *Matthew Henry* said, "The office of conscience is to bring to mind things long since said and done. When the guilt of this sin of Joseph's brethren was fresh, they made light of it, and sat down to eat bread; but now, long afterward, their consciences accused them of it. See the good of afflictions; they often prove the happy means of awakening conscience, and bringing sin to our remembrance." There is a way to awaken the conscience without having to wait for life's afflictions to humble sinners. Afflict them with God's Law. Remind them of their sins by doing what Jesus did, and going through the Ten Commandments. *Charles Spurgeon* said, "They must be slain by the Law before they can be made alive by the gospel."

est *men:* Leave one of your brothers *here* with me, take *food for* the famine of your households, and be gone. 34And bring your youngest brother to me; so I shall know that you *are* not spies, but *that* you *are* honest *men.* I will grant your brother to you, and you may trade in the land.' "

35Then it happened as they emptied their sacks, that surprisingly each man's bundle of money *was* in his sack; and when they and their father saw the bundles of money, they were afraid. 36And Jacob their father said to them, "You have bereaved me: Joseph is no *more,* Simeon is no *more,* and you want to take Benjamin. All these things are against me."

37Then Reuben spoke to his father, saying, "Kill my two sons if I do not bring him *back* to you; put him in my hands, and I will bring him back to you."

38But he said, "My son shall not go down with you, for his brother is dead, and he is left alone. If any calamity should befall him along the way in which you go, then you would bring down my gray hair with sorrow to the grave."

Joseph's Brothers Return with Benjamin

43 Now the famine *was* severe in the land. 2And it came to pass, when they had eaten up the grain which they had brought from Egypt, that their father said to them, "Go back, buy us a little food."

3But Judah spoke to him, saying, "The man solemnly warned us, saying, 'You shall not see my face unless your brother *is* with you.' 4If you send our brother with us, we will go down and buy you food. 5But if you will not send *him,* we will not go down; for the man said to us, 'You shall not see my face unless your brother *is* with you.' "

6And Israel said, "Why did you deal *so* wrongfully with me *as* to tell the man whether you had still *another* brother?"

7But they said, "The man asked us pointedly about ourselves and our family, saying, '*Is* your father still alive? Have you *another* brother?' And we told him according to these words. Could we possibly have known that he would say, 'Bring your brother down'?"

8Then Judah said to Israel his father, "Send the lad with me, and we will arise and go, that we may live and not die, both we and you *and* also our little ones. 9I myself will be surety for him; from my hand you shall require him. If I do not bring him *back* to you and set him before you, then let me bear the blame forever. 10For if we had not lingered, surely by now we would have returned this second time."

11And their father Israel said to them, "If *it must be* so, then do this: Take some of the best fruits of the land in your vessels and carry down a present for the man —a little balm and a little honey, spices and myrrh, pistachio nuts and almonds. 12Take double money in your hand, and take back in your hand the money that was returned in the mouth of your sacks; perhaps it was an oversight. 13Take your brother also, and arise, go back to the man. 14And may God Almighty give you mercy before the man, that he may release your other brother and Benjamin. If I am bereaved, I am bereaved!"

15So the men took that present and Benjamin, and they took double money in their hand, and arose and went down to Egypt; and they stood before Joseph. 16When Joseph saw Benjamin with them, he said to the steward of his house, "Take *these* men to my home, and slaughter an animal and make ready; for *these* men will dine with me at noon." 17Then the man did as Joseph ordered, and the man brought the men into Joseph's house.

18Now the men were afraid because

42:37 Be careful of what you vow. Sometimes life can create circumstances that make it impossible to fulfill what we rashly promise. Only God can make a promise that is utterly immutable. See also Judg. 11:39 comment.

they were brought into Joseph's house; and they said, "*It is* because of the money, which was returned in our sacks the first time, that we are brought in, so that he may make a case against us and seize us, to take us as slaves with our donkeys."

[19]When they drew near to the steward of Joseph's house, they talked with him at the door of the house, [20]and said, "O sir, we indeed came down the first time to buy food; [21]but it happened, when we came to the encampment, that we opened our sacks, and there, *each* man's money *was* in the mouth of his sack, our money in full weight; so we have brought it back in our hand. [22]And we have brought down other money in our hands to buy food. We do not know who put our money in our sacks."

[23]But he said, "Peace *be* with you, do not be afraid. Your God and the God of your father has given you treasure in your sacks; I had your money." Then he brought Simeon out to them.

[24]So the man brought the men into Joseph's house and gave *them* water, and they washed their feet; and he gave their donkeys feed. [25]Then they made the present ready for Joseph's coming at noon, for they heard that they would eat bread there.

[26]And when Joseph came home, they brought him the present which *was* in their hand into the house, and bowed down before him to the earth. [27]Then he asked them about *their* well-being, and said, "*Is* your father well, the old man of whom you spoke? *Is* he still alive?"

[28]And they answered, "Your servant our father *is* in good health; he *is* still alive." And they bowed their heads down and prostrated themselves.

[29]Then he lifted his eyes and saw his brother Benjamin, his mother's son, and said, "*Is* this your younger brother of whom you spoke to me?" And he said, "God be gracious to you, my son." [30]Now his heart yearned for his brother; so Joseph made haste and sought *somewhere* to weep. And he went into *his* chamber and wept there. [31]Then he washed his face and came out; and he restrained himself, and said, "Serve the bread."

[32]So they set him a place by himself, and them by themselves, and the Egyptians who ate with him by themselves; because the Egyptians could not eat food with the Hebrews, for that *is* an abomination to the Egyptians. [33]And they sat before him, the firstborn according to his birthright and the youngest according to his youth; and the men looked in astonishment at one another. [34]Then he took servings to them from before him, but Benjamin's serving was five times as much as any of theirs. So they drank and were merry with him.

Joseph's Cup

44 And he commanded the steward of his house, saying, "Fill the men's sacks with food, as much as they can carry, and put each man's money in the mouth of his sack. [2]Also put my cup, the silver cup, in the mouth of the sack of the youngest, and his grain money." So he did

43:32 Do not be surprised if the world does not want to dine with you. Keep in mind the promise of Luke 6:22: "Blessed are you when men hate you, and when they exclude you, and revile you, and cast out your name as evil, for the Son of Man's sake." However, we are to love them, daily pray for them, and reach out to them in the hope that they will listen and turn to the Savior.

Charles Spurgeon said, "Michaelangelo, when painting an altar-piece in the conventional church, in Florence, in order that the figures might be as death-like as possible, obtained permission of the prior to have the coffins of the newly-buried opened and placed beside him during the night; an appalling expedient, but successful in enabling him to reproduce with terrible effect, not the mortal pallor only, but the very anatomy of death. If we would preach well to the souls of men we must acquaint ourselves with their ruined state, must have their case always on our hearts both night and day, must know the terrors of the Lord, and the value of the soul, and feel a sacred sympathy with perishing sinners. There is no masterly, prevailing preaching without this."

according to the word that Joseph had spoken. 3As soon as the morning dawned, the men were sent away, they and their donkeys. 4When they had gone out of the city, *and* were not *yet* far off, Joseph said to his steward, "Get up, follow the men; and when you overtake them, say to them, 'Why have you repaid evil for good? 5*Is* not this *the one* from which my lord drinks, and with which he indeed practices divination? You have done evil in so doing.' "

6So he overtook them, and he spoke to them these same words. 7And they said to him, "Why does my lord say these words? Far be it from us that your servants should do such a thing. 8Look, we brought back to you from the land of Canaan the money which we found in the mouth of our sacks. How then could we steal silver or gold from your lord's house? 9With whomever of your servants it is found, let him die, and we also will be my lord's slaves."

10And he said, "Now also *let* it *be* according to your words; he with whom it is found shall be my slave, and you shall be blameless." 11Then each man speedily let down his sack to the ground, and each opened his sack. 12So he searched. He began with the oldest and left off with the youngest; and the cup was found in Benjamin's sack. 13Then they tore their clothes, and each man loaded his donkey and returned to the city.

14So Judah and his brothers came to Joseph's house, and he *was* still there; and they fell before him on the ground. 15And Joseph said to them, "What deed *is* this you have done? Did you not know that such a man as I can certainly practice divination?"

16Then Judah said, "What shall we say to my lord? What shall we speak? Or how shall we clear ourselves? God has found out the iniquity of your servants; here we are, my lord's slaves, both we and *he* also with whom the cup was found."

17But he said, "Far be it from me that I should do so; the man in whose hand the cup was found, he shall be my slave. And as for you, go up in peace to your father."

Judah Intercedes for Benjamin

18Then Judah came near to him and said: "O my lord, please let your servant speak a word in my lord's hearing, and do not let your anger burn against your servant; for you *are* even like Pharaoh. 19My lord asked his servants, saying, 'Have you a father or a brother?' 20And we said to my lord, 'We have a father, an old man, and a child of *his* old age, *who is* young; his brother is dead, and he alone is left of his mother's children, and his father loves him.' 21Then you said to your servants, 'Bring him down to me, that I may set my eyes on him.' 22And we said to my lord, 'The lad cannot leave his father, for *if* he should leave his father, *his father* would die.' 23But you said to your servants, 'Unless your youngest brother comes down with you, you shall see my face no more.'

24"So it was, when we went up to your servant my father, that we told him the words of my lord. 25And our father said, 'Go back *and* buy us a little food.' 26But we said, 'We cannot go down; if our youngest brother is with us, then we will go down; for we may not see the man's face unless our youngest brother *is* with us.' 27Then your servant my father said to us, 'You know that my wife bore me two sons;

44:16 "God hath found out the iniquity of thy servants—Referring to the injury they had formerly done to Joseph, for which they thought God was now reckoning with them. Even in those afflictions wherein we apprehend ourselves wronged by men, yet we must own that God is righteous, and finds out our iniquity. We cannot judge what men are, by what they have been formerly, not what they will do, by what they have done. Age and experience may make men wiser and better. They that had sold Joseph, yet would not abandon Benjamin." *John Wesley*

In one sense, God does not "find out" our iniquity. That insinuates that at one point our sins were hidden from Him. Rather, we find out that He knows our most secret sins.

28and the one went out from me, and I said, "Surely he is torn to pieces"; and I have not seen him since. 29But if you take this one also from me, and calamity befalls him, you shall bring down my gray hair with sorrow to the grave.'

30"Now therefore, when I come to your servant my father, and the lad *is* not with us, since his life is bound up in the lad's life, 31it will happen, when he sees that the lad *is* not *with us,* that he will die. So your servants will bring down the gray hair of your servant our father with sorrow to the grave. 32For your servant became surety for the lad to my father, saying, 'If I do not bring him *back* to you, then I shall bear the blame before my father forever.' 33Now therefore, please let your servant remain instead of the lad as a slave to my lord, and let the lad go up with his brothers. 34For how shall I go up to my father if the lad *is* not with me, lest perhaps I see the evil that would come upon my father?"

Joseph Revealed to His Brothers

45 Then Joseph could not restrain himself before all those who stood by him, and he cried out, "Make everyone go out from me!" So no one stood with him while Joseph made himself known to his brothers. 2And he wept aloud, and the Egyptians and the house of Pharaoh heard *it.*

3Then Joseph said to his brothers, "I *am* Joseph; does my father still live?" But his brothers could not answer him, for they were dismayed in his presence. 4And Joseph said to his brothers, "Please come near to me." So they came near. Then he said: "I *am* Joseph your brother, whom you sold into Egypt. 5But now, do not therefore be grieved or angry with yourselves because you sold me here; for God sent me before you to preserve life. 6For these two years the famine *has been* in the land, and *there are* still five years in which *there will be* neither plowing nor harvesting. 7And God sent me before you to preserve a posterity for you in the earth, and to save your lives by a great deliverance. 8So now *it was* not you *who* sent me here, but God; and He has made me a father to Pharaoh, and lord of all his house, and a ruler throughout all the land of Egypt.

9"Hurry and go up to my father, and say to him, 'Thus says your son Joseph: "God has made me lord of all Egypt; come down to me, do not tarry. 10You shall dwell in the land of Goshen, and you shall be near to me, you and your children, your children's children, your flocks and your herds, and all that you have. 11There I will provide for you, lest you and your household, and all that you have, come to poverty; for *there are* still five years of famine." '

12"And behold, your eyes and the eyes of my brother Benjamin see that *it is* my mouth that speaks to you. 13So you shall tell my father of all my glory in Egypt, and of all that you have seen; and you shall hurry and bring my father down here."

14Then he fell on his brother Benjamin's neck and wept, and Benjamin wept on his neck. 15Moreover he kissed all his brothers and wept over them, and after that his brothers talked with him.

16Now the report of it was heard in Pharaoh's house, saying, "Joseph's brothers have come." So it pleased Pharaoh and his servants well. 17And Pharaoh said to Joseph, "Say to your brothers, 'Do this: Load your animals and depart; go to the land of Canaan. 18Bring your father and your households and come to me; I will give you the best of the land of Egypt, and you will eat the fat of the land. 19Now

---

45:5 Joseph foreshadows the Savior. Joseph forgave his brothers, the sons of Israel, explaining that God used their act of betrayal to bring him to Egypt, so he could save their lives (v. 5).

Jesus, during the trial before His crucifixion, told Pilate that his authority to sentence Him to death was due only to God's will: "You could have no power at all against Me unless it had been given you from above" (John 19:11). Jesus, too, forgave those who crucified Him (Luke 23:34).

you are commanded—do this: Take carts out of the land of Egypt for your little ones and your wives; bring your father and come. 20Also do not be concerned about your goods, for the best of all the land of Egypt *is* yours.' "

21Then the sons of Israel did so; and Joseph gave them carts, according to the command of Pharaoh, and he gave them provisions for the journey. 22He gave to all of them, to each man, changes of garments; but to Benjamin he gave three hundred *pieces* of silver and five changes of garments. 23And he sent to his father these *things:* ten donkeys loaded with the good things of Egypt, and ten female donkeys loaded with grain, bread, and food for his father for the journey. 24So he sent his brothers away, and they departed; and he said to them, "See that you do not become troubled along the way."

25Then they went up out of Egypt, and came to the land of Canaan to Jacob their father. 26And they told him, saying, "Joseph *is* still alive, and he *is* governor over all the land of Egypt." And Jacob's heart stood still, because he did not believe them. 27But when they told him all the words which Joseph had said to them, and when he saw the carts which Joseph had sent to carry him, the spirit of Jacob their father revived. 28Then Israel said, "*It is* enough. Joseph my son *is* still alive. I will go and see him before I die."

Jacob's Journey to Egypt

46 So Israel took his journey with all that he had, and came to Beersheba, and offered sacrifices to the God of his father Isaac. 2Then God spoke to Israel in the visions of the night, and said, "Jacob, Jacob!"

And he said, "Here I am."

3So He said, "I *am* God, the God of your father; do not fear to go down to Egypt, for I will make of you a great nation there. 4I will go down with you to Egypt, and I will also surely bring you up *again;* and Joseph will put his hand on your eyes."

5Then Jacob arose from Beersheba; and the sons of Israel carried their father Jacob, their little ones, and their wives, in the carts which Pharaoh had sent to carry him. 6So they took their livestock and their goods, which they had acquired in the land of Canaan, and went to Egypt, Jacob and all his descendants with him. 7His sons and his sons' sons, his daughters and his sons' daughters, and all his descendants he brought with him to Egypt.

8Now these *were* the names of the children of Israel, Jacob and his sons, who went to Egypt: Reuben *was* Jacob's firstborn. 9The sons of Reuben *were* Hanoch, Pallu, Hezron, and Carmi. 10The sons of Simeon *were* Jemuel,[a] Jamin, Ohad, Jachin,[b] Zohar,[c] and Shaul, the son of a Canaanite woman. 11The sons of Levi *were* Gershon, Kohath, and Merari. 12The sons of Judah *were* Er, Onan, Shelah, Perez, and Zerah (but Er and Onan died in the land of Canaan). The sons of Perez were Hezron and Hamul. 13The sons of Issachar *were* Tola, Puvah,[a] Job,[b] and Shimron. 14The sons of Zebulun *were* Sered, Elon, and Jahleel. 15These *were* the sons of Leah, whom she bore to Jacob in Padan Aram, with his daughter Dinah. All the

46:10 [a]Spelled *Nemuel* in 1 Chronicles 4:24 [b]Called *Jarib* in 1 Chronicles 4:24 [c]Called *Zerah* in 1 Chronicles 4:24 46:13 [a]Spelled *Puah* in 1 Chronicles 7:1 [b]Same as *Jashub* in Numbers 26:24 and 1 Chronicles 7:1

46:3,4 We should never fear to go into the world, because God is with us. We are to be *in the midst* of a crooked and perverse nation, *among whom* we shine of lights *in the world*.

"Even as to those events and undertakings which appear most joyful, we should seek counsel, assistance, and a blessing from the Lord. Attending on his ordinances, and receiving the pledges of his covenant love, we expect his presence, and that peace which it confers. In all removals we should be reminded of our removal out of this world. Nothing can encourage us to fear no evil when passing through the valley of the shadow of death, but the presence of Christ." *Matthew Henry*

persons, his sons and his daughters, *were* thirty-three.

16The sons of Gad *were* Ziphion,[a] Haggi, Shuni, Ezbon,[b] Eri, Arodi,[c] and Areli. 17The sons of Asher *were* Jimnah, Ishuah, Isui, Beriah, and Serah, their sister. And the sons of Beriah *were* Heber and Malchiel. 18These *were* the sons of Zilpah, whom Laban gave to Leah his daughter; and these she bore to Jacob: sixteen persons.

19The sons of Rachel, Jacob's wife, *were* Joseph and Benjamin. 20And to Joseph in the land of Egypt were born Manasseh and Ephraim, whom Asenath, the daughter of Poti-Pherah priest of On, bore to him. 21The sons of Benjamin *were* Belah, Becher, Ashbel, Gera, Naaman, Ehi, Rosh, Muppim, Huppim,[a] and Ard. 22These *were* the sons of Rachel, who were born to Jacob: fourteen persons in all.

23The son of Dan *was* Hushim.[a] 24The sons of Naphtali *were* Jahzeel,[a] Guni, Jezer, and Shillem.[b] 25These *were* the sons of Bilhah, whom Laban gave to Rachel his daughter, and she bore these to Jacob: seven persons in all.

26All the persons who went with Jacob to Egypt, who came from his body, besides Jacob's sons' wives, *were* sixty-six persons in all. 27And the sons of Joseph who were born to him in Egypt *were* two persons. All the persons of the house of Jacob who went to Egypt were seventy.

Jacob Settles in Goshen

28Then he sent Judah before him to Joseph, to point out before him *the way* to Goshen. And they came to the land of Goshen. 29So Joseph made ready his chariot and went up to Goshen to meet his father Israel; and he presented himself to him, and fell on his neck and wept on his neck a good while.

30And Israel said to Joseph, "Now let me die, since I have seen your face, because you *are* still alive."

31Then Joseph said to his brothers and to his father's household, "I will go up and tell Pharaoh, and say to him, 'My brothers and those of my father's house, who *were* in the land of Canaan, have come to me. 32And the men *are* shepherds, for their occupation has been to feed livestock; and they have brought their flocks, their herds, and all that they have.' 33So it shall be, when Pharaoh calls you and says, 'What is your occupation?' 34that you shall say, 'Your servants' occupation has been with livestock from our youth even till now, both we *and* also our fathers,' that you may dwell in the land of Goshen; for every shepherd *is* an abomination to the Egyptians."

47 Then Joseph went and told Pharaoh, and said, "My father and my brothers, their flocks and their herds and all that they possess, have come from the land of Canaan; and indeed they *are* in the land of Goshen." 2And he took five men from among his brothers and presented them to Pharaoh. 3Then Pharaoh said to his brothers, "What *is* your occupation?"

And they said to Pharaoh, "Your servants *are* shepherds, both we *and* also our fathers." 4And they said to Pharaoh, "We have come to dwell in the land, because your servants have no pasture for their

46:16 [a]Spelled *Zephon* in Samaritan Pentateuch, Septuagint, and Numbers 26:15 [b]Called *Ozni* in Numbers 26:16 [c]Spelled *Arod* in Numbers 26:17 46:21 [a]Called *Hupham* in Numbers 26:39 46:23 [a]Called *Shuham* in Numbers 26:42 46:24 [a]Spelled *Jahziel* in 1 Chronicles 7:13 [b]Spelled *Shallum* in 1 Chronicles 7:13

47:3 We are seeking lost sheep to bring to the Good Shepherd. See John 10:1–16.

"Though Joseph was a great man, especially in Egypt, yet he owned his brethren. Let the rich and great in the world not overlook or despise poor relations. Our Lord Jesus is not ashamed to call us brethren. In answer to Pharaoh's inquiry, What is your calling? they told him that they were shepherds, adding that they were come to sojourn in the land for a time, while the famine prevailed in Canaan. Pharaoh offered to employ them as shepherds, provided they were active men. Whatever our business or employment is, we should aim to excel in it, and to prove ourselves clever and industrious." *Matthew Henry*

flocks, for the famine *is* severe in the land of Canaan. Now therefore, please let your servants dwell in the land of Goshen."

[5]Then Pharaoh spoke to Joseph, saying, "Your father and your brothers have come to you. [6]The land of Egypt *is* before you. Have your father and brothers dwell in the best of the land; let them dwell in the land of Goshen. And if you know *any* competent men among them, then make them chief herdsmen over my livestock."

[7]Then Joseph brought in his father Jacob and set him before Pharaoh; and Jacob blessed Pharaoh. [8]Pharaoh said to Jacob, "How old *are* you?"

[9]And Jacob said to Pharaoh, "The days of the years of my pilgrimage *are* one hundred and thirty years; few and evil have been the days of the years of my life, and they have not attained to the days of the years of the life of my fathers in the days of their pilgrimage." [10]So Jacob blessed Pharaoh, and went out from before Pharaoh.

[11]And Joseph situated his father and his brothers, and gave them a possession in the land of Egypt, in the best of the land, in the land of Rameses, as Pharaoh had commanded. [12]Then Joseph provided his father, his brothers, and all his father's household with bread, according to the number in *their* families.

Joseph Deals with the Famine

[13]Now *there was* no bread in all the land; for the famine *was* very severe, so that the land of Egypt and the land of Canaan languished because of the famine. [14]And Joseph gathered up all the money that was found in the land of Egypt and in the land of Canaan, for the grain which they bought; and Joseph brought the money into Pharaoh's house.

[15]So when the money failed in the land of Egypt and in the land of Canaan, all the Egyptians came to Joseph and said, "Give us bread, for why should we die in your presence? For the money has failed."

[16]Then Joseph said, "Give your livestock, and I will give you *bread* for your livestock, if the money is gone." [17]So they brought their livestock to Joseph, and Joseph gave them bread *in exchange* for the horses, the flocks, the cattle of the herds, and for the donkeys. Thus he fed them with bread *in exchange* for all their livestock that year.

[18]When that year had ended, they came to him the next year and said to him, "We will not hide from my lord that our money is gone; my lord also has our herds of livestock. There is nothing left in the sight of my lord but our bodies and our lands. [19]Why should we die before your eyes, both we and our land? Buy us and our land for bread, and we and our land will be servants of Pharaoh; give *us* seed, that we may live and not die, that the land may not be desolate."

Can a mortal ask questions which God finds unanswerable? Quite easily, I should think. All nonsense questions are unanswerable.

C. S. LEWIS

[20]Then Joseph bought all the land of Egypt for Pharaoh; for every man of the Egyptians sold his field, because the famine was severe upon them. So the land became Pharaoh's. [21]And as for the people, he moved them into the cities,[a] from *one* end of the borders of Egypt to the *other* end. [22]Only the land of the priests he did not buy; for the priests had rations *allotted to them* by Pharaoh, and they ate their rations which Pharaoh gave them; therefore they did not sell their lands.

[23]Then Joseph said to the people, "Indeed I have bought you and your land this day for Pharaoh. Look, *here is* seed for you, and you shall sow the land. [24]And it shall come to pass in the harvest that you shall give one-fifth to Pharaoh. Four-fifths shall be your own, as seed for the field and for your food, for those of

47:21 [a]Following Masoretic Text and Targum; Samaritan Pentateuch, Septuagint, and Vulgate read *made the people virtual slaves.*

your households and as food for your little ones."

[25]So they said, "You have saved our lives; let us find favor in the sight of my lord, and we will be Pharaoh's servants." [26]And Joseph made it a law over the land of Egypt to this day, *that* Pharaoh should have one-fifth, except for the land of the priests only, *which* did not become Pharaoh's.

Joseph's Vow to Jacob

[27]So Israel dwelt in the land of Egypt, in the country of Goshen; and they had possessions there and grew and multiplied exceedingly. [28]And Jacob lived in the land of Egypt seventeen years. So the length of Jacob's life was one hundred and forty-seven years. [29]When the time drew near that Israel must die, he called his son Joseph and said to him, "Now if I have found favor in your sight, please put your hand under my thigh, and deal kindly and truly with me. Please do not bury me in Egypt, [30]but let me lie with my fathers; you shall carry me out of Egypt and bury me in their burial place."

And he said, "I will do as you have said."

[31]Then he said, "Swear to me." And he swore to him. So Israel bowed himself on the head of the bed.

Jacob Blesses Joseph's Sons

48 Now it came to pass after these things that Joseph was told, "Indeed your father *is* sick"; and he took with him his two sons, Manasseh and Ephraim. [2]And Jacob was told, "Look, your son Joseph is coming to you"; and Israel strengthened himself and sat up on the bed. [3]Then Jacob said to Joseph: "God Almighty appeared to me at Luz in the land of Canaan and blessed me, [4]and said to me, 'Behold, I will make you fruitful and multiply you, and I will make of you a multitude of people, and give this land to your descendants after you *as* an everlasting possession.' [5]And now your two sons, Ephraim and Manasseh, who were born to you in the land of Egypt before I came to you in Egypt, *are* mine; as Reuben and Simeon, they shall be mine. [6]Your offspring whom you beget after them shall be yours; they will be called by the name of their brothers in their inheritance. [7]But as for me, when I came from Padan, Rachel died beside me in the land of Canaan on the way, when *there was* but a little distance to go to Ephrath; and I buried her there on the way to Ephrath (that is, Bethlehem)."

[8]Then Israel saw Joseph's sons, and said, "Who *are* these?"

[9]Joseph said to his father, "They *are* my sons, whom God has given me in this *place*."

And he said, "Please bring them to me, and I will bless them." [10]Now the eyes of Israel were dim with age, *so that* he could not see. Then Joseph brought them near him, and he kissed them and embraced them. [11]And Israel said to Joseph, "I had not thought to see your face; but in fact, God has also shown me your offspring!"

[12]So Joseph brought them from beside his knees, and he bowed down with his face to the earth. [13]And Joseph took them both, Ephraim with his right hand toward Israel's left hand, and Manasseh with his left hand toward Israel's right hand, and brought *them* near him. [14]Then Israel stretched out his right hand and laid *it* on Ephraim's head, who *was* the younger, and his left hand on Manasseh's head, guiding his hands knowingly, for Manasseh *was* the firstborn. [15]And he blessed Joseph, and said:

"God, before whom my fathers
Abraham and Isaac walked,

48:11 Never be discouraged when it comes to sharing your faith. Biblical evangelism is simply planting the seed of God's Word in the soil of sinners' hearts. God makes the seed grow. The day will come, either in this life or in the next, when you will see your spiritual "offspring"—those who have been born again through your faithfulness.

The God who has fed me all my life
long to this day,
[16]The Angel who has redeemed me
from all evil,
Bless the lads;
Let my name be named upon them,
And the name of my fathers Abraham
and Isaac;
And let them grow into a multitude in
the midst of the earth."

[17]Now when Joseph saw that his father
laid his right hand on the head of Ephraim, it displeased him; so he took hold
of his father's hand to remove it from
Ephraim's head to Manasseh's head. [18]And
Joseph said to his father, "Not so, my father, for this *one is* the firstborn; put your
right hand on his head."
[19]But his father refused and said, "I
know, my son, I know. He also shall become a people, and he also shall be great;
but truly his younger brother shall be
greater than he, and his descendants shall
become a multitude of nations."
[20]So he blessed them that day, saying,
"By you Israel will bless, saying, 'May God
make you as Ephraim and as Manasseh!' "
And thus he set Ephraim before Manasseh.
[21]Then Israel said to Joseph, "Behold,
I am dying, but God will be with you and
bring you back to the land of your fathers. [22]Moreover I have given to you one
portion above your brothers, which I
took from the hand of the Amorite with
my sword and my bow."

Jacob's Last Words to His Sons

49 And Jacob called his sons and said,
"Gather together, that I may tell
you what shall befall you in the last days:

[2]"Gather together and hear, you sons of
Jacob,
And listen to Israel your father.

[3]"Reuben, you are my firstborn,
My might and the beginning of my
strength,
The excellency of dignity and the
excellency of power.
[4]Unstable as water, you shall not excel,
Because you went up to your father's
bed;
Then you defiled *it*—
He went up to my couch.

[5]"Simeon and Levi *are* brothers;
Instruments of cruelty *are in* their
dwelling place.
[6]Let not my soul enter their council;
Let not my honor be united to their
assembly;
For in their anger they slew a man,
And in their self-will they hamstrung
an ox.
[7]Cursed *be* their anger, for *it is* fierce;
And their wrath, for it is cruel!
I will divide them in Jacob
And scatter them in Israel.

[8]"Judah, you *are he* whom your
brothers shall praise;
Your hand *shall be* on the neck of
your enemies;
Your father's children shall bow
down before you.
[9]Judah *is* a lion's whelp;
From the prey, my son, you have
gone up.
He bows down, he lies down as a lion;
And as a lion, who shall rouse him?
[10]The scepter shall not depart from
Judah,
Nor a lawgiver from between his feet,
Until Shiloh comes;
And to Him *shall be* the obedience of
the people.
[11]Binding his donkey to the vine,
And his donkey's colt to the choice
vine,
He washed his garments in wine,
And his clothes in the blood of grapes.
[12]His eyes *are* darker than wine,

49:10 This is a direct reference to Jesus of Nazareth. See also Num. 24:17; Matt. 2:2; Rev. 22:16.

And his teeth whiter than milk.

[13]"Zebulun shall dwell by the haven of
the sea;
He *shall become* a haven for ships,
And his border shall adjoin Sidon.

[14]"Issachar is a strong donkey,
Lying down between two burdens;
[15]He saw that rest *was* good,
And that the land *was* pleasant;
He bowed his shoulder to bear *a burden,*
And became a band of slaves.

[16]"Dan shall judge his people
As one of the tribes of Israel.
[17]Dan shall be a serpent by the way,
A viper by the path,
That bites the horse's heels
So that its rider shall fall backward.
[18]I have waited for your salvation, O
LORD!

[19]"Gad, a troop shall tramp upon him,
But he shall triumph at last.

[20]"Bread from Asher *shall be* rich,
And he shall yield royal dainties.

[21]"Naphtali *is* a deer let loose;
He uses beautiful words.

[22]"Joseph *is* a fruitful bough,
A fruitful bough by a well;
His branches run over the wall.
[23]The archers have bitterly grieved him,
Shot *at him* and hated him.
[24]But his bow remained in strength,
And the arms of his hands were made
strong
By the hands of the Mighty *God* of Jacob
(From there *is* the Shepherd, the
Stone of Israel),
[25]By the God of your father who will
help you,
And by the Almighty who will bless you
With blessings of heaven above,
Blessings of the deep that lies beneath,
Blessings of the breasts and of the
womb.
[26]The blessings of your father
Have excelled the blessings of my
ancestors,
Up to the utmost bound of the
everlasting hills.
They shall be on the head of Joseph,
And on the crown of the head of him
who was separate from his
brothers.

[27]"Benjamin is a ravenous wolf;
In the morning he shall devour the
prey,
And at night he shall divide the spoil."

[28]All these *are* the twelve tribes of Israel, and this *is* what their father spoke to
them. And he blessed them; he blessed
each one according to his own blessing.

Jacob's Death and Burial

[29]Then he charged them and said to
them: "I am to be gathered to my people;
bury me with my fathers in the cave that
is in the field of Ephron the Hittite, [30]in
the cave that *is* in the field of Machpelah,
which *is* before Mamre in the land of Canaan, which Abraham bought with the
field of Ephron the Hittite as a possession
for a burial place. [31]There they buried
Abraham and Sarah his wife, there they
buried Isaac and Rebekah his wife, and
there I buried Leah. [32]The field and the
cave that *is* there *were* purchased from the
sons of Heth." [33]And when Jacob had finished commanding his sons, he drew his
feet up into the bed and breathed his last,
and was gathered to his people.

50 Then Joseph fell on his father's face
and wept over him, and kissed him.
[2]And Joseph commanded his servants the
physicians to embalm his father. So the
physicians embalmed Israel. [3]Forty days
were required for him, for such are the days
required for those who are embalmed;
and the Egyptians mourned for him seventy days.

[4]Now when the days of his mourning
were past, Joseph spoke to the household

of Pharaoh, saying, "If now I have found favor in your eyes, please speak in the hearing of Pharaoh, saying, [5]'My father made me swear, saying, "Behold, I am dying; in my grave which I dug for myself in the land of Canaan, there you shall bury me." Now therefore, please let me go up and bury my father, and I will come back.' "

[6]And Pharaoh said, "Go up and bury your father, as he made you swear."

[7]So Joseph went up to bury his father; and with him went up all the servants of Pharaoh, the elders of his house, and all the elders of the land of Egypt, [8]as well as all the house of Joseph, his brothers, and his father's house. Only their little ones, their flocks, and their herds they left in the land of Goshen. [9]And there went up with him both chariots and horsemen, and it was a very great gathering.

[10]Then they came to the threshing floor of Atad, which *is* beyond the Jordan, and they mourned there with a great and very solemn lamentation. He observed seven days of mourning for his father. [11]And when the inhabitants of the land, the Canaanites, saw the mourning at the threshing floor of Atad, they said, "This *is* a deep mourning of the Egyptians." Therefore its name was called Abel Mizraim,[a] which *is* beyond the Jordan. [12]So his sons did for him just as he had commanded them. [13]For his sons carried him to the land of Canaan, and buried him in the cave of the field of Machpelah, before Mamre, which Abraham bought with the field from Ephron the Hittite as property for a burial place. [14]And after he had buried his father, Joseph returned to Egypt, he and his brothers and all who went up with him to bury his father.

Joseph Reassures His Brothers

[15]When Joseph's brothers saw that their father was dead, they said, "Perhaps Joseph will hate us, and may actually repay us for all the evil which we did to him." [16]So they sent *messengers* to Joseph, saying, "Before your father died he commanded, saying, [17]'Thus you shall say to Joseph: "I beg you, please forgive the trespass of your brothers and their sin; for they did evil to you." ' Now, please, forgive the trespass of the servants of the God of your father." And Joseph wept when they spoke to him.

[18]Then his brothers also went and fell down before his face, and they said, "Behold, we *are* your servants."

[19]Joseph said to them, "Do not be afraid, for *am* I in the place of God? [20]But as for you, you meant evil against me; *but* God meant it for good, in order to bring it about as *it is* this day, to save many people alive. [21]Now therefore, do not be afraid; I will provide for you and your little ones." And he comforted them and spoke kindly to them.

Death of Joseph

[22]So Joseph dwelt in Egypt, he and his father's household. And Joseph lived one hundred and ten years. [23]Joseph saw Ephraim's children to the third *generation.* The children of Machir, the son of Manasseh, were also brought up on Joseph's knees.

[24]And Joseph said to his brethren, "I am dying; but God will surely visit you, and bring you out of this land to the land of which He swore to Abraham, to Isaac, and to Jacob." [25]Then Joseph took an oath from the children of Israel, saying, "God will surely visit you, and you shall carry up my bones from here." [26]So Joseph died, *being* one hundred and ten years old; and they embalmed him, and he was put in a coffin in Egypt.

50:11 [a]Literally *Mourning of Egypt*

50:19 It is God's prerogative to punish for sin. We are to forgive. Never let bitterness for being wronged cling to you. Give it to the Lord and, with His help, forget it. Sinners are going to hell and you have been commanded to preach to them. Unforgiveness is one of the enemy's most subtle devices to hinder you from such an important task.

Exodus

Israel's Suffering in Egypt

1 Now these *are* the names of the children of Israel who came to Egypt; each man and his household came with Jacob: 2Reuben, Simeon, Levi, and Judah; 3Issachar, Zebulun, and Benjamin; 4Dan, Naphtali, Gad, and Asher. 5All those who were descendants[a] of Jacob were seventy[b] persons (for Joseph was in Egypt *already*). 6And Joseph died, all his brothers, and all that generation. 7But the children of Israel were fruitful and increased abundantly, multiplied and grew exceedingly mighty; and the land was filled with them.

8Now there arose a new king over Egypt, who did not know Joseph. 9And he said to his people, "Look, the people of the children of Israel *are* more and mightier than we; 10come, let us deal shrewdly with them, lest they multiply, and it happen, in the event of war, that they also join our enemies and fight against us, and *so* go up out of the land." 11Therefore they set taskmasters over them to afflict them with their burdens. And they built for Pharaoh supply cities, Pithom and Raamses. 12But the more they afflicted them, the more they multiplied and grew. And they were in dread of the children of Israel. 13So the Egyptians made the children of Israel serve with rigor. 14And they made their lives bitter with hard bondage—in mortar, in brick, and in all manner of service in the field. All their service in which they made them serve *was* with rigor.

15Then the king of Egypt spoke to the Hebrew midwives, of whom the name of one *was* Shiphrah and the name of the other Puah; 16and he said, "When you do the duties of a midwife for the Hebrew women, and see *them* on the birthstools, if it *is* a son, then you shall kill him; but if it *is* a daughter, then she shall live." 17But the midwives feared God, and did not do as the king of Egypt commanded them, but saved the male children alive. 18So the king of Egypt called for the midwives and said to them, "Why have you done this thing, and saved the male children alive?"

19And the midwives said to Pharaoh, "Because the Hebrew women *are* not like the Egyptian women; for they *are* lively and give birth before the midwives come to them."

1:5 [a]Literally *who came from the loins of* [b]Dead Sea Scrolls and Septuagint read *seventy-five* (compare Acts 7:14).

1:17 It is due to a lack of fear of God that millions of unborn children have been murdered through abortion. "The care of human life and happiness, and not their destruction, is the sole legitimate object of good government." *Thomas Jefferson*

1:19–21 For whether lying is ever permissible, see Josh. 2:4,5 comment.

[20]Therefore God dealt well with the midwives, and the people multiplied and grew very mighty. [21]And so it was, because the midwives feared God, that He provided households for them. [22]So Pharaoh commanded all his people, saying, "Every son who is born[a] you shall cast into the river, and every daughter you shall save alive."

Moses Is Born

2 And a man of the house of Levi went and took *as wife* a daughter of Levi. [2]So the woman conceived and bore a son. And when she saw that he *was* a beautiful *child,* she hid him three months. [3]But when she could no longer hide him, she took an ark of bulrushes for him, daubed it with asphalt and pitch, put the child in it, and laid *it* in the reeds by the river's bank. [4]And his sister stood afar off, to know what would be done to him.

[5]Then the daughter of Pharaoh came down to bathe at the river. And her maidens walked along the riverside; and when she saw the ark among the reeds, she sent her maid to get it. [6]And when she opened *it,* she saw the child, and behold, the baby wept. So she had compassion on him, and said, "This is one of the Hebrews' children."

[7]Then his sister said to Pharaoh's daughter, "Shall I go and call a nurse for you from the Hebrew women, that she may nurse the child for you?"

[8]And Pharaoh's daughter said to her, "Go." So the maiden went and called the child's mother. [9]Then Pharaoh's daughter said to her, "Take this child away and nurse him for me, and I will give *you* your wages." So the woman took the child and nursed him. [10]And the child grew, and she brought him to Pharaoh's daughter, and he became her son. So she called his name Moses,[a] saying, "Because I drew him out of the water."

Moses Flees to Midian

[11]Now it came to pass in those days, when Moses was grown, that he went out to his brethren and looked at their burdens. And he saw an Egyptian beating a Hebrew, one of his brethren. [12]So he looked this way and that way, and when he saw no one, he killed the Egyptian and hid him in the sand. [13]And when he went out the second day, behold, two Hebrew men were fighting, and he said to the one who did the wrong, "Why are you striking your companion?"

[14]Then he said, "Who made you a prince and a judge over us? Do you intend to kill me as you killed the Egyptian?"

So Moses feared and said, "Surely this thing is known!" [15]When Pharaoh heard of this matter, he sought to kill Moses. But Moses fled from the face of Pharaoh and dwelt in the land of Midian; and he sat down by a well.

[16]Now the priest of Midian had seven daughters. And they came and drew water, and they filled the troughs to water their father's flock. [17]Then the shepherds came and drove them away; but Moses stood up and helped them, and watered their flock.

[18]When they came to Reuel their father, he said, "How *is it that* you have come so soon today?"

[19]And they said, "An Egyptian delivered us from the hand of the shepherds, and he also drew enough water for us and watered the flock."

[20]So he said to his daughters, "And where *is* he? Why *is* it *that* you have left the man? Call him, that he may eat bread."

[21]Then Moses was content to live with the man, and he gave Zipporah his daughter to Moses. [22]And she bore *him* a son. He called his name Gershom,[a] for he said, "I have been a stranger in a foreign land."

[23]Now it happened in the process of time that the king of Egypt died. Then

1:22 [a]Samaritan Pentateuch, Septuagint, and Targum add *to the Hebrews.* 2:10 [a]Literally *Drawn Out* 2:22 [a]Literally *Stranger There*

2:1–8 God is able to take the most tragic of situations and work them for His own purposes. See Rom. 8:28 for the Christian's great consolation in trials.

the children of Israel groaned because of the bondage, and they cried out; and their cry came up to God because of the bondage. [24]So God heard their groaning, and God remembered His covenant with Abraham, with Isaac, and with Jacob. [25]And God looked upon the children of Israel, and God acknowledged *them.*

Moses at the Burning Bush

3 Now Moses was tending the flock of Jethro his father-in-law, the priest of Midian. And he led the flock to the back of the desert, and came to Horeb, the mountain of God. [2]And the Angel of the LORD appeared to him in a flame of fire from the midst of a bush. So he looked, and behold, the bush was burning with fire, but the bush *was* not consumed. [3]Then Moses said, "I will now turn aside and see this great sight, why the bush does not burn."

[4]So when the LORD saw that he turned aside to look, God called to him from the midst of the bush and said, "Moses, Moses!"

And he said, "Here I am."

[5]Then He said, "Do not draw near this place. Take your sandals off your feet, for the place where you stand *is* holy ground." [6]Moreover He said, "I *am* the God of your father—the God of Abraham, the God of Isaac, and the God of Jacob." And Moses hid his face, for he was afraid to look upon God.

[7]And the LORD said: "I have surely seen the oppression of My people who *are* in Egypt, and have heard their cry because of their taskmasters, for I know their sorrows. [8]So I have come down to deliver them out of the hand of the Egyptians, and to bring them up from that land to a good and large land, to a land flowing with milk and honey, to the place of the Canaanites and the Hittites and the Amorites and the Perizzites and the Hivites and the Jebusites. [9]Now therefore, behold, the cry of the children of Israel has come to Me, and I have also seen the oppression with which the Egyptians oppress them. [10]Come now, therefore, and I will send you to Pharaoh that you may bring My people, the children of Israel, out of Egypt."

[11]But Moses said to God, "Who *am* I that I should go to Pharaoh, and that I should bring the children of Israel out of Egypt?"

[12]So He said, "I will certainly be with you. And this *shall be* a sign to you that I have sent you: When you have brought the people out of Egypt, you shall serve God on this mountain."

[13]Then Moses said to God, "Indeed, *when* I come to the children of Israel and say to them, 'The God of your fathers has sent me to you,' and they say to me, 'What *is* His name?' what shall I say to them?"

[14]And God said to Moses, "I AM WHO I AM." And He said, "Thus you shall say to the children of Israel, 'I AM has sent me to you.' " [15]Moreover God said to Moses, "Thus you shall say to the children of Israel: 'The LORD God of your fathers, the God of Abraham, the God of Isaac, and the God of Jacob, has sent me to you. This *is* My name forever, and this *is* My memorial to all generations.' [16]Go and gather the elders of Israel together, and say to them, 'The LORD God of your fathers, the God of Abraham, of Isaac, and of Jacob, appeared to me, saying, "I have surely visited you and *seen* what is done to you in Egypt; [17]and I have said I will bring you up out of the affliction of Egypt to the land of the Canaanites and the Hittites and the Amorites and the Perizzites and the Hivites and the Jebusites, to a land flowing with milk and honey." ' [18]Then they will heed your voice; and you shall come, you and the elders of Israel, to the king of Egypt; and you shall

3:5 God has made us holy in Christ. We have our "beautiful" feet shod with the preparation of the gospel of peace, so that we can take the message of salvation to those who stand on unholy ground (see Rom. 10:15; Eph. 6:15).

say to him, 'The LORD God of the Hebrews has met with us; and now, please, let us go three days' journey into the wilderness, that we may sacrifice to the LORD our God.' 19But I am sure that the king of Egypt will not let you go, no, not even by a mighty hand. 20So I will stretch out My hand and strike Egypt with all My wonders which I will do in its midst; and after that he will let you go. 21And I will give this people favor in the sight of the Egyptians; and it shall be, when you go, that you shall not go empty-handed. 22But every woman shall ask of her neighbor, namely, of her who dwells near her house, articles of silver, articles of gold, and clothing; and you shall put *them* on your sons and on your daughters. So you shall plunder the Egyptians."

Miraculous Signs for Pharaoh

4 Then Moses answered and said, "But suppose they will not believe me or listen to my voice; suppose they say, 'The LORD has not appeared to you.' "

2So the LORD said to him, "What *is* that in your hand?"

He said, "A rod."

3And He said, "Cast it on the ground." So he cast it on the ground, and it became a serpent; and Moses fled from it. 4Then the LORD said to Moses, "Reach out your hand and take *it* by the tail" (and he reached out his hand and caught it, and it became a rod in his hand), 5"that they may believe that the LORD God of their fathers, the God of Abraham, the God of Isaac, and the God of Jacob, has appeared to you."

6Furthermore the LORD said to him, "Now put your hand in your bosom." And he put his hand in his bosom, and when he took it out, behold, his hand *was* leprous, like snow. 7And He said, "Put your hand in your bosom again." So he put his hand in his bosom again, and drew it out of his bosom, and behold, it was restored like his *other* flesh. 8"Then it will be, if they do not believe you, nor heed the message of the first sign, that they may believe the message of the latter sign. 9And it shall be, if they do not believe even these two signs, or listen to your voice, that you shall take water from the river[a] and pour *it* on the dry *land.* The water which you take from the river will become blood on the dry *land.*"

10Then Moses said to the LORD, "O my Lord, I *am* not eloquent, neither before nor since You have spoken to Your servant; but I *am* slow of speech and slow of tongue."

11So the LORD said to him, "Who has made man's mouth? Or who makes the mute, the deaf, the seeing, or the blind? *Have* not I, the LORD? 12Now therefore, go, and I will be with your mouth and teach you what you shall say."

13But he said, "O my Lord, please send by the hand of whomever *else* You may send."

14So the anger of the LORD was kindled against Moses, and He said: "Is not Aaron the Levite your brother? I know that he can speak well. And look, he is also coming out to meet you. When he sees you, he will be glad in his heart. 15Now you shall speak to him and put the words in his mouth. And I will be with your mouth and with his mouth, and I will teach you what you shall do. 16So he shall be your spokesman to the people. And he himself shall be as a mouth for you, and you shall be to him as God. 17And you shall take this rod in your hand, with which you shall do the signs."

Moses Goes to Egypt

18So Moses went and returned to Jethro his father-in-law, and said to him,

4:9 [a]That is, the Nile

4:10,11 Moses said that he wasn't eloquent. But God assured him that He would be with Moses and would give him the words to say (v. 12). This is the same promise God gave to Jeremiah when he argued that he couldn't speak (see Jer. 1:8,9). You have the same assurance from God today.

4:1,2 *What Is That in Your Hand?*

It is easy to understand why Moses reacted as he did. When we speak to the lost, we want more than "God sent me to tell you something." The world is full of people who say that they were sent by God. Jehovah's Witnesses say that only they are His representatives on earth, that I AM sent them. So do Mormons. They claim that they alone represent God. Muslims say a similar thing; and there are myriad cults, strange sects, and weirdos who say that they are speaking for God.

So, God asked Moses, "What is that in your hand?" (v. 2). It was a rod that Moses held in his hand. Perhaps you did not realize that you also have the rod of Moses in your hand. You do *hold* to the Law, don't you? Do you think that it is good? Is it right for the Law to forbid murder, stealing, lying, and adultery? Of course, you hold to it. We cannot fault the moral Law. As the Bible says, it is perfect, holy, just, and good (see Psa. 19:7; Rom. 7:12). Perhaps you have never thought much about the Law (the Ten Commandments) or that you could do anything evangelistic with it. You have simply used the Commandments to steady yourself morally in your Christian walk, and to fend off the enemy's attacks. You know that to transgress any of the Law's precepts—to lie, covet, steal, commit adultery, and so on—is to "give place to the devil" (Eph. 4:27).

But, as you study Scripture, you will see that the Law can be turned into something radically different. It can be used to bring to this world "the knowledge of sin" (Rom. 3:20). It can be used as a "tutor" to bring sinners to Christ (see Gal. 3:24). Jesus, Paul, and others cast it down as a serpent to guilty sinners—to be a convincing sign that God had sent them.

So, do what Moses did. Simply cast it before the feet of a sinful world and watch what it does. In this case, seeing *is* believing. The Law bites into the human conscience. It has power to bring death, as it did for Paul in his own life. In Rom. 7 he explained how the Law showed him the true nature of sin—that it was "exceedingly sinful." It produced evidence of his guilt and then passed its terrible sentence. The Law condemned him to death. With Paul, the serpent had a fatal bite:

> I was alive once without the law, but when the commandment came, sin revived and I died. And the commandment, which was to bring life, I found to bring death. (Rom. 7:9,10)

The Law of God plagues a guilty sinner in the same way civil law plagues a guilty criminal. A murderer has little concern if he thinks he has outwitted the law. But the moment it puts steel handcuffs on his wrists, it produces a justifiable fear. It arrests him and forces him to face the just consequences of his crime.

That is why we must not allow sinners to think for a moment that they have outwitted God's Law. They must be made to understand that the Judge of the universe will bring every work to judgment, including every secret thing, whether it is good or evil (see Eccles. 12:14). And the way to convince them that what you are saying is true is to simply cast the rod at their feet. God will do the rest. He will do a miracle by turning the dead, inanimate rod of the Law into a living and fiery serpent (see John 16:8).

The rod of Moses gave him courage. It was the sign that "I AM" was with him. What more could we want than to have God work through us to reach the lost? So take what is in your hand, and with the help of God, labor in the gospel while there is still time. See also 7:9–12 comment.

For how to battle the fear of man, see 2 Chron. 20:15 comment.

"All men are under the Law by nature, and consequently they are condemned by it because they have broken its commands; and apart from our Lord Jesus men are only reprieved criminals, respited from day to day, but still under sentence and waiting for the appointed hour when the warrant shall be solemnly executed upon them." *Charles Spurgeon*

"Please let me go and return to my brethren who *are* in Egypt, and see whether they are still alive."

And Jethro said to Moses, "Go in peace."

[19]Now the LORD said to Moses in Midian, "Go, return to Egypt; for all the men who sought your life are dead." [20]Then Moses took his wife and his sons and set them on a donkey, and he returned to the land of Egypt. And Moses took the rod of God in his hand.

[21]And the LORD said to Moses, "When you go back to Egypt, see that you do all those wonders before Pharaoh which I have put in your hand. But I will harden his heart, so that he will not let the people go. [22]Then you shall say to Pharaoh, 'Thus says the LORD: "Israel is My son, My firstborn. [23]So I say to you, let My son go

that he may serve Me. But if you refuse to let him go, indeed I will kill your son, your firstborn." ' "

[24]And it came to pass on the way, at the encampment, that the LORD met him and sought to kill him. [25]Then Zipporah took a sharp stone and cut off the foreskin of her son and cast *it* at *Moses'*[a] feet, and said, "Surely you *are* a husband of blood to me!" [26]So He let him go. Then she said, "*You are* a husband of blood!"—because of the circumcision.

[27]And the LORD said to Aaron, "Go into the wilderness to meet Moses." So he went and met him on the mountain of God, and kissed him. [28]So Moses told Aaron all the words of the LORD who had sent him, and all the signs which He had commanded him. [29]Then Moses and Aaron went and gathered together all the elders of the children of Israel. [30]And Aaron spoke all the words which the LORD had spoken to Moses. Then he did the signs in the sight of the people. [31]So the people believed; and when they heard that the LORD had visited the children of Israel and that He had looked on their affliction, then they bowed their heads and worshiped.

First Encounter with Pharaoh

5 Afterward Moses and Aaron went in and told Pharaoh, "Thus says the LORD God of Israel: 'Let My people go, that they may hold a feast to Me in the wilderness.' "

[2]And Pharaoh said, "Who *is* the LORD, that I should obey His voice to let Israel go? I do not know the LORD, nor will I let Israel go."

[3]So they said, "The God of the Hebrews has met with us. Please, let us go three days' journey into the desert and sacrifice to the LORD our God, lest He fall upon us with pestilence or with the sword."

[4]Then the king of Egypt said to them, "Moses and Aaron, why do you take the people from their work? Get *back* to your labor." [5]And Pharaoh said, "Look, the people of the land *are* many now, and you make them rest from their labor!"

[6]So the same day Pharaoh commanded the taskmasters of the people and their officers, saying, [7]"You shall no longer give the people straw to make brick as before. Let them go and gather straw for themselves. [8]And you shall lay on them the quota of bricks which they made before. You shall not reduce it. For they are idle; therefore they cry out, saying, 'Let us go *and* sacrifice to our God.' [9]Let more work be laid on the men, that they may labor in it, and let them not regard false words."

> He is not seeking a powerful people to represent Him. Rather, He looks for all those who are weak, foolish, despised, and written off: and He inhabits them with His own strength.
>
> **GRAHAM COOKE**

[10]And the taskmasters of the people and their officers went out and spoke to the people, saying, "Thus says Pharaoh: 'I will not give you straw. [11]Go, get yourselves straw where you can find it; yet none of your work will be reduced.' " [12]So the people were scattered abroad throughout all the land of Egypt to gather stubble instead of straw. [13]And the taskmasters forced *them* to hurry, saying, "Fulfill your work, *your* daily quota, as when there was straw." [14]Also the officers of the children of Israel, whom Pharaoh's taskmasters had set over them, were beaten *and* were asked, "Why have you not fulfilled your task in making brick both yesterday and today, as before?"

[15]Then the officers of the children of Israel came and cried out to Pharaoh, saying, "Why are you dealing thus with your servants? [16]There is no straw given to your servants, and they say to us, 'Make brick!' And indeed your servants *are* beaten, but the fault *is* in your *own* people."

[17]But he said, "You *are* idle! Idle! Therefore you say, 'Let us go *and* sacrifice to the

4:25 [a]Literally *his*

LORD.' 18 Therefore go now *and* work; for
no straw shall be given you, yet you shall
deliver the quota of bricks." 19 And the officers of the children of Israel saw *that*
they *were* in trouble after it was said, "You
shall not reduce *any* bricks from your daily
quota."

20 Then, as they came out from Pharaoh,
they met Moses and Aaron who stood
there to meet them. 21 And they said to
them, "Let the LORD look on you and
judge, because you have made us abhor-
rent in the sight of Pharaoh and in the
sight of his servants, to put a sword in
their hand to kill us."

Israel's Deliverance Assured

22 So Moses returned to the LORD and
said, "Lord, why have You brought trouble on this people? Why *is* it You have
sent me? 23 For since I came to Pharaoh to
speak in Your name, he has done evil to
this people; neither have You delivered
Your people at all."

6 Then the LORD said to Moses, "Now
you shall see what I will do to Pharaoh. For with a strong hand he will let
them go, and with a strong hand he will
drive them out of his land."

2 And God spoke to Moses and said to
him: "I *am* the LORD. 3 I appeared to Abraham, to Isaac, and to Jacob, as God
Almighty, but *by* My name LORD[a] I was
not known to them. 4 I have also established My covenant with them, to give
them the land of Canaan, the land of their
pilgrimage, in which they were strangers.
5 And I have also heard the groaning of
the children of Israel whom the Egyptians keep in bondage, and I have remembered My covenant. 6 Therefore say
to the children of Israel: 'I *am* the LORD; I
will bring you out from under the burdens of the Egyptians, I will rescue you
from their bondage, and I will redeem
you with an outstretched arm and with
great judgments. 7 I will take you as My
people, and I will be your God. Then you
shall know that I *am* the LORD your God
who brings you out from under the burdens of the Egyptians. 8 And I will bring
you into the land which I swore to give to
Abraham, Isaac, and Jacob; and I will
give it to you *as* a heritage: I *am* the
LORD.' " 9 So Moses spoke thus to the children of Israel; but they did not heed
Moses, because of anguish of spirit and
cruel bondage.

10 And the LORD spoke to Moses, saying, 11 "Go in, tell Pharaoh king of Egypt
to let the children of Israel go out of his
land."

12 And Moses spoke before the LORD,
saying, "The children of Israel have not
heeded me. How then shall Pharaoh heed

6:3 [a] Hebrew *YHWH*, traditionally *Jehovah*

5:22,23 A trouble-free life? The contemporary Church promises a wonderful new life for the sinner, if he will just "give his heart to Jesus." This is not only unbiblical, it is untrue. Things do not always go better with Christ. More often than not they go worse. Ask Stephen about the "wonderful" new life as his body was being pummeled by great stones, or ask Paul as he was being beaten and whipped for his faith, or ask the martyrs as their flesh burned at the stake. The true convert, who has been enjoying the pleasures of sin for a season, upon conversion, is suddenly thrown into the heat of a terrible battle. It is a battle against the world, the flesh, and the devil (see 2 Cor. 4:4 comment). The flesh continually tries to pull him back to sin. The devil tempts and taunts, afflicts and accuses him. The world, with its many sinful pleasures, tries to allure him back to its warm embrace. Former friends and even his family may hate him and even have him put to death, thinking they are doing God a favor (see John 16:2). However, when a genuine convert finds himself in a fearful lion's den, he will not shake his fist at God. He will drop to his knees. To understand the principles of biblical evangelism, see 2 Cor. 2:17 comment.

"Few things do so much harm in religion as exaggerated expectations. People look for a degree of worldly comfort in Christ's service which they have no right to expect, and not finding what they look for, are tempted to give up religion in disgust. Happy is he who thoroughly understands, that though Christianity holds out a crown in the end, it brings also a cross in the way." *J. C. Ryle*

me, for I *am* of uncircumcised lips?"

[13]Then the LORD spoke to Moses and Aaron, and gave them a command for the children of Israel and for Pharaoh king of Egypt, to bring the children of Israel out of the land of Egypt.

The Family of Moses and Aaron

[14]These *are* the heads of their fathers' houses: The sons of Reuben, the firstborn of Israel, *were* Hanoch, Pallu, Hezron, and Carmi. These are the families of Reuben. [15]And the sons of Simeon *were* Jemuel,[a] Jamin, Ohad, Jachin, Zohar, and Shaul the son of a Canaanite woman. These *are* the families of Simeon. [16]These *are* the names of the sons of Levi according to their generations: Gershon, Kohath, and Merari. And the years of the life of Levi *were* one hundred and thirty-seven. [17]The sons of Gershon *were* Libni and Shimi according to their families. [18]And the sons of Kohath *were* Amram, Izhar, Hebron, and Uzziel. And the years of the life of Kohath *were* one hundred and thirty-three. [19]The sons of Merari *were* Mahli and Mushi. These *are* the families of Levi according to their generations.

[20]Now Amram took for himself Jochebed, his father's sister, as wife; and she bore him Aaron and Moses. And the years of the life of Amram *were* one hundred and thirty-seven. [21]The sons of Izhar *were* Korah, Nepheg, and Zichri. [22]And the sons of Uzziel *were* Mishael, Elzaphan, and Zithri. [23]Aaron took to himself Elisheba, daughter of Amminadab, sister of Nahshon, as wife; and she bore him Nadab, Abihu, Elemazar, and Ithamar. [24]And the sons of Korah *were* Assir, Elkanah, and Abiasaph. These are the families of the Korahites. [25]Eleazar, Aaron's son, took for himself one of the daughters of Putiel as wife; and she bore him Phinehas. These *are* the heads of the fathers' houses of the Levites according to their families.

[26]These *are the same* Aaron and Moses to whom the LORD said, "Bring out the children of Israel from the land of Egypt according to their armies." [27]These *are* the ones who spoke to Pharaoh king of Egypt, to bring out the children of Israel from Egypt. These *are the same* Moses and Aaron.

Aaron Is Moses' Spokesman

[28]And it came to pass, on the day the LORD spoke to Moses in the land of Egypt, [29]that the LORD spoke to Moses, saying, "I *am* the LORD. Speak to Pharaoh king of Egypt all that I say to you."

[30]But Moses said before the LORD, "Behold, I *am* of uncircumcised lips, and how shall Pharaoh heed me?"

7 So the LORD said to Moses: "See, I have made you *as* God to Pharaoh, and Aaron your brother shall be your prophet. [2]You shall speak all that I command you. And Aaron your brother shall tell Pharaoh to send the children of Israel out of his land. [3]And I will harden Pharaoh's heart, and multiply My signs and My wonders in the land of Egypt. [4]But Pharaoh will not heed you, so that I may lay My hand on Egypt and bring My armies *and* My people, the children of Israel, out of the land of Egypt by great judgments. [5]And the Egyptians shall know that I *am* the LORD, when I stretch out My hand on Egypt and bring out the children of Israel from among them."

[6]Then Moses and Aaron did *so;* just as the LORD commanded them, so they did. [7]And Moses *was* eighty years old and

6:15 [a]Spelled *Nemuel* in Numbers 26:12

6:30 An awareness of a lack of eloquence is a virtue in the kingdom of God. Those who are conscious of their own inability are the ones who will pray that God helps them. They will rely on the Lord rather than on their own talents.

7:7 "Joseph, who was to be only a servant to Pharaoh, was preferred at thirty years old; but Moses, who was to be a god to Pharaoh, was not so dignified till he was eighty years old. It is fit he should long wait for such an honor, and be long in preparing for such a service." *John Wesley*

SPRINGBOARDS FOR PREACHING AND WITNESSING

Who Is Winding Your Clock?

7:16 Who are you serving? The Bible says that it is either God or the devil. If it is God, you will believe there is a devil, and if it is the devil, you won't believe there is a God. Or at least not the God of the Bible. You will either deny God's existence or you will make up your own image of a god.

If you are serving the devil, you will live for yourself. If you are serving God, you will live for the One who gave you life, and you will care about those who live for the devil. You will plead with them, pray for them, and hopefully weep for them. Whatever their fate, one day they will understand why. They are blinded by the devil, and as the Bible says, he has taken them captive to do his will. And his will they gladly do.

If he is winding your clock, your time is running out. You will soon be in eternity. If you are serving sin, you are serving the devil, and his wages are really bad. Physical death is the first down-payment for the wages of sin. After death, there is hell to pay. I strongly suggest—no, I *plead* with you—quit before payday.

Aaron eighty-three years old when they
spoke to Pharaoh.

Aaron's Miraculous Rod

8Then the LORD spoke to Moses and
Aaron, saying, 9"When Pharaoh speaks to
you, saying, 'Show a miracle for yourselves,' then you shall say to Aaron, 'Take
your rod and cast *it* before Pharaoh, *and*
let it become a serpent.' " 10So Moses and
Aaron went in to Pharaoh, and they did
so, just as the LORD commanded. And
Aaron cast down his rod before Pharaoh
and before his servants, and it became a
serpent.
11But Pharaoh also called the wise men
and the sorcerers; so the magicians of
Egypt, they also did in like manner with
their enchantments. 12For every man threw
down his rod, and they became serpents.
But Aaron's rod swallowed up their rods.
13And Pharaoh's heart grew hard, and he
did not heed them, as the LORD had said.

The First Plague: Waters Become Blood

14So the LORD said to Moses: "Pharaoh's heart *is* hard; he refuses to let the
people go. 15Go to Pharaoh in the morning, when he goes out to the water, and
you shall stand by the river's bank to
meet him; and the rod which was turned
to a serpent you shall take in your hand.
16And you shall say to him, 'The LORD
God of the Hebrews has sent me to you,
saying, "Let My people go, that they may
serve Me in the wilderness"; but indeed,
until now you would not hear! 17Thus
says the LORD: "By this you shall know
that I *am* the LORD. Behold, I will strike
the waters which *are* in the river with the
rod that is in my hand, and they shall be

7:9–12 Cast down the Law. As a Christian, you need not dread the Law. If you are in Christ, the Law will not bite you (see Rom. 8:1). So take hold of it and do what Jesus did in Mark 10:17. Let the world know that lust is adultery in God's sight (see Matt. 5:27,28), and that a holy God considers hatred to be murder (see 1 John 3:15). Use the Ten Commandments as Paul did when he personalized them for his hearers: "You who preach that a man should not steal, do *you* steal? You who say, 'Do not commit adultery,' do *you* commit adultery? You who abhor idols, do *you* rob temples?" (Rom. 2:21,22, emphasis added).

When we cast down the rod of the Law, it helps to convince the lost that the gospel of salvation is from God. Once they are "convicted by the law as transgressors" (James 2:9), they are ready for the good news of the gospel—that they can be saved from its bite because the rod has already struck the Savior for our justification. The Law's holy demands have been satisfied in Christ. In Exod. 17:5, when Moses used his rod to strike a rock, water gushed out. The New Testament tells us that "that rock was Christ" (1 Cor. 10:4). Jesus had to be struck by Moses before we could freely drink of the water of life (see John 7:37,38).

For more details on using the Law in evangelism, see John 4:7 and 2 Sam. 12:1–14 comments.

"The true function of the Law is to accuse and to kill; but the function of the gospel is to make alive." *Martin Luther*

turned to blood. 18And the fish that *are* in the river shall die, the river shall stink, and the Egyptians will loathe to drink the water of the river." ' "

19Then the LORD spoke to Moses, "Say to Aaron, 'Take your rod and stretch out your hand over the waters of Egypt, over their streams, over their rivers, over their ponds, and over all their pools of water, that they may become blood. And there shall be blood throughout all the land of Egypt, both in *buckets of* wood and *pitchers of* stone.' " 20And Moses and Aaron did so, just as the LORD commanded. So he lifted up the rod and struck the waters that *were* in the river, in the sight of Pharaoh and in the sight of his servants. And all the waters that *were* in the river were turned to blood. 21The fish that *were* in the river died, the river stank, and the Egyptians could not drink the water of the river. So there was blood throughout all the land of Egypt.

22Then the magicians of Egypt did so with their enchantments; and Pharaoh's heart grew hard, and he did not heed them, as the LORD had said. 23And Pharaoh turned and went into his house. Neither was his heart moved by this. 24So all the Egyptians dug all around the river for water to drink, because they could not drink the water of the river. 25And seven days passed after the LORD had struck the river.

The Second Plague: Frogs

8 And the LORD spoke to Moses, "Go to Pharaoh and say to him, 'Thus says the LORD: "Let My people go, that they may serve Me. 2But if you refuse to let *them* go, behold, I will smite all your territory with frogs. 3So the river shall bring forth frogs abundantly, which shall go up and come into your house, into your bedroom, on your bed, into the houses of your servants, on your people, into your ovens, and into your kneading bowls. 4And the frogs shall come up on you, on your people, and on all your servants." ' "

5Then the LORD spoke to Moses, "Say to Aaron, 'Stretch out your hand with your rod over the streams, over the rivers, and over the ponds, and cause frogs to come up on the land of Egypt.' " 6So Aaron stretched out his hand over the waters of Egypt, and the frogs came up and covered the land of Egypt. 7And the magicians did so with their enchantments, and brought up frogs on the land of Egypt.

8Then Pharaoh called for Moses and Aaron, and said, "Entreat the LORD that He may take away the frogs from me and from my people; and I will let the people go, that they may sacrifice to the LORD."

9And Moses said to Pharaoh, "Accept the honor of saying when I shall intercede for you, for your servants, and for your people, to destroy the frogs from you and your houses, *that* they may remain in the river only."

10So he said, "Tomorrow." And he said, "*Let it be* according to your word, that you may know that *there is* no one like the LORD our God. 11And the frogs shall depart from you, from your houses, from your servants, and from your people. They shall remain in the river only."

12Then Moses and Aaron went out from Pharaoh. And Moses cried out to the LORD concerning the frogs which He had brought against Pharaoh. 13So the LORD did according to the word of Moses. And the frogs died out of the houses, out of the courtyards, and out of the fields. 14They gathered them together in heaps, and the land stank. 15But when Pharaoh saw that there was relief, he hardened his heart and did not heed them, as the LORD had said.

8:1–15 "Pharaoh gave way under this plague. He promises that he will let the people go. Those who bid defiance to God and prayer, first or last, will be made to see their need of both. But when Pharaoh saw there was respite, he hardened his heart. Till the heart is renewed by the grace of God, the thoughts made by affliction do not abide; the convictions wear off, and the promises that were given are forgotten. Till the state of the air is changed, what thaws in the sun will freeze again in the shade." *Matthew Henry*

The Third Plague: Lice

16So the LORD said to Moses, "Say to
Aaron, 'Stretch out your rod, and strike
the dust of the land, so that it may become lice throughout all the land of
Egypt.' " 17And they did so. For Aaron
stretched out his hand with his rod and
struck the dust of the earth, and it became lice on man and beast. All the dust
of the land became lice throughout all the
land of Egypt.

18Now the magicians so worked with
their enchantments to bring forth lice,
but they could not. So there were lice on
man and beast. 19Then the magicians said
to Pharaoh, "This *is* the finger of God."
But Pharaoh's heart grew hard, and he did
not heed them, just as the LORD had said.

The Fourth Plague: Flies

20And the LORD said to Moses, "Rise
early in the morning and stand before
Pharaoh as he comes out to the water.
Then say to him, 'Thus says the LORD: "Let
My people go, that they may serve Me.
21Or else, if you will not let My people
go, behold, I will send swarms *of flies* on
you and your servants, on your people
and into your houses. The houses of the
Egyptians shall be full of swarms *of flies,*
and also the ground on which they *stand.*
22And in that day I will set apart the land
of Goshen, in which My people dwell,
that no swarms *of flies* shall be there, in
order that you may know that I *am* the
LORD in the midst of the land. 23I will
make a difference[a] between My people
and your people. Tomorrow this sign
shall be." ' " 24And the LORD did so. Thick
swarms *of flies* came into the house of
Pharaoh, *into* his servants' houses, and
into all the land of Egypt. The land was
corrupted because of the swarms *of flies.*

25Then Pharaoh called for Moses and
Aaron, and said, "Go, sacrifice to your
God in the land."

26And Moses said, "It is not right to do
so, for we would be sacrificing the abomination of the Egyptians to the LORD our
God. If we sacrifice the abomination of
the Egyptians before their eyes, then will
they not stone us? 27We will go three days'
journey into the wilderness and sacrifice
to the LORD our God as He will command
us."

28So Pharaoh said, "I will let you go,
that you may sacrifice to the LORD your
God in the wilderness; only you shall not
go very far away. Intercede for me."

29Then Moses said, "Indeed I am going
out from you, and I will entreat the LORD,
that the swarms *of flies* may depart tomorrow from Pharaoh, from his servants,
and from his people. But let Pharaoh not
deal deceitfully anymore in not letting
the people go to sacrifice to the LORD."

30So Moses went out from Pharaoh
and entreated the LORD. 31And the LORD
did according to the word of Moses; He
removed the swarms *of flies* from Pharaoh, from his servants, and from his people. Not one remained. 32But Pharaoh
hardened his heart at this time also; neither would he let the people go.

The Fifth Plague: Livestock Diseased

9 Then the Lord said to Moses, "Go in
to Pharaoh and tell him, 'Thus says
the LORD God of the Hebrews: "Let My
people go, that they may serve Me. 2For
if you refuse to let *them* go, and still hold
them, 3behold, the hand of the LORD will
be on your cattle in the field, on the
horses, on the donkeys, on the camels,
on the oxen, and on the sheep—a very
severe pestilence. 4And the LORD will
make a difference between the livestock
of Israel and the livestock of Egypt. So
nothing shall die of all *that* belongs to
the children of Israel." ' " 5Then the LORD
appointed a set time, saying, "Tomorrow
the LORD will do this thing in the land."

6So the LORD did this thing on the next
day, and all the livestock of Egypt died;
but of the livestock of the children of Israel, not one died. 7Then Pharaoh sent,
and indeed, not even one of the livestock
of the Israelites was dead. But the heart of

8:23 [a]Literally *set a ransom* (compare Exodus 9:4 and 11:7)

Pharaoh became hard, and he did not let the people go.

The Sixth Plague: Boils

8So the LORD said to Moses and Aaron, "Take for yourselves handfuls of ashes from a furnace, and let Moses scatter it toward the heavens in the sight of Pharaoh. 9And it will become fine dust in all the land of Egypt, and it will cause boils that break out in sores on man and beast throughout all the land of Egypt." 10Then they took ashes from the furnace and stood before Pharaoh, and Moses scattered *them* toward heaven. And *they* caused boils that break out in sores on man and beast. 11And the magicians could not stand before Moses because of the boils, for the boils were on the magicians and on all the Egyptians. 12But the LORD hardened the heart of Pharaoh; and he did not heed them, just as the LORD had spoken to Moses.

The Seventh Plague: Hail

13Then the LORD said to Moses, "Rise early in the morning and stand before Pharaoh, and say to him, 'Thus says the LORD God of the Hebrews: "Let My people go, that they may serve Me, 14for at this time I will send all My plagues to your very heart, and on your servants and on your people, that you may know that *there is* none like Me in all the earth. 15Now if I had stretched out My hand and struck you and your people with pestilence, then you would have been cut off from the earth. 16But indeed for this *purpose* I have raised you up, that I may show My power *in* you, and that My name may be declared in all the earth. 17As yet you exalt yourself against My people in that you will not let them go. 18Behold, tomorrow about this time I will cause very heavy hail to rain down, such as has not been in Egypt since its founding until now. 19Therefore send now *and* gather your livestock and all that you have in the field, for the hail shall come down on every man and every animal which is found in the field and is not brought home; and they shall die." ' "

20He who feared the word of the LORD among the servants of Pharaoh made his servants and his livestock flee to the houses. 21But he who did not regard the word of the LORD left his servants and his livestock in the field.

> People who don't believe in missions have not read the New Testament. Right from the beginning Jesus said the field is the world. The early church took Him at His word and went East, West, North and South.
>
> **J. HOWARD EDINGTON**

22Then the LORD said to Moses, "Stretch out your hand toward heaven, that there may be hail in all the land of Egypt—on man, on beast, and on every herb of the field, throughout the land of Egypt." 23And Moses stretched out his rod toward heaven; and the LORD sent thunder and hail, and fire darted to the ground. And the LORD rained hail on the land of Egypt. 24So there was hail, and fire mingled with the hail, so very heavy that there was none like it in all the land of Egypt since it became a nation. 25And the hail struck throughout the whole land of Egypt, all that *was* in the field, both man and beast; and the hail struck every herb of the field and broke every tree of the field. 26Only in the land of Goshen, where the children of Israel *were*, there was no hail.

27And Pharaoh sent and called for Moses and Aaron, and said to them, "I have sinned this time. The LORD *is* righteous, and my

9:20 Those who come to Christ in genuine repentance are those who fear the word of the Lord. Those who don't fear God may enter the house of God as false converts, but their hearts are still in the field of the world.

QUESTIONS & OBJECTIONS

"Nature reveals cruelty, not the hand of God."

Atheist George Carlin (who passed into eternity in 2008) said, "But I want you to know something, this is sincere, I want you to know, when it comes to believing in God, I really tried. I really, really tried. I tried to believe that there is a God, who created each of us in His own image and likeness, loves us very much, and keeps a close eye on things. I really tried to believe that, but I gotta tell you, the longer you live, the more you look around, the more you realize, something is . . . wrong here. War, disease, death, destruction, hunger, filth, poverty, torture, crime, corruption . . . Something is definitely wrong. This is not good work. If this is the best God can do, I am not impressed."

When an atheist rejects Genesis 1 (about creation), he automatically rejects Genesis 3 (about the Fall of mankind). God created all things perfect, but when Adam sinned against God, it brought God's curse on all of creation. Thus, disease, suffering, pain, and death are ultimately the fault of man, not God. Reject that explanation and you end up with a philosophy similar to George Carlin. The sufferings of this world shouldn't be used as an excuse to reject the Scriptures, but should be seen as very real evidence that what the Bible says is true.

people and I *are* wicked. 28Entreat the
LORD, that there may be no *more* mighty
thundering and hail, for *it is* enough. I will
let you go, and you shall stay no longer."
29So Moses said to him, "As soon as I
have gone out of the city, I will spread out
my hands to the LORD; the thunder will
cease, and there will be no more hail, that
you may know that the earth *is* the LORD's.
30But as for you and your servants, I know
that you will not yet fear the LORD God."
31Now the flax and the barley were
struck, for the barley *was* in the head and
the flax *was* in bud. 32But the wheat and
the spelt were not struck, for they *are* late
crops.
33So Moses went out of the city from
Pharaoh and spread out his hands to the
LORD; then the thunder and the hail
ceased, and the rain was not poured on
the earth. 34And when Pharaoh saw that
the rain, the hail, and the thunder had
ceased, he sinned yet more; and he hardened his heart, he and his servants. 35So
the heart of Pharaoh was hard; neither
would he let the children of Israel go, as
the LORD had spoken by Moses.

The Eighth Plague: Locusts

10 Now the LORD said to Moses, "Go
in to Pharaoh; for I have hardened
his heart and the hearts of his servants,
that I may show these signs of Mine before him, 2and that you may tell in the
hearing of your son and your son's son
the mighty things I have done in Egypt,
and My signs which I have done among
them, that you may know that I *am* the
LORD."
3So Moses and Aaron came in to
Pharaoh and said to him, "Thus says the
LORD God of the Hebrews: 'How long will
you refuse to humble yourself before Me?
Let My people go, that they may serve
Me. 4Or else, if you refuse to let My people go, behold, tomorrow I will bring locusts into your territory. 5And they shall
cover the face of the earth, so that no one
will be able to see the earth; and they
shall eat the residue of what is left, which
remains to you from the hail, and they
shall eat every tree which grows up for
you out of the field. 6They shall fill your
houses, the houses of all your servants,
and the houses of all the Egyptians—
which neither your fathers nor your fathers' fathers have seen, since the day that
they were on the earth to this day.' " And
he turned and went out from Pharaoh.
7Then Pharaoh's servants said to him,
"How long shall this man be a snare to
us? Let the men go, that they may serve
the LORD their God. Do you not yet know
that Egypt is destroyed?"
8So Moses and Aaron were brought
again to Pharaoh, and he said to them,

"Go, serve the LORD your God. Who *are*
the ones that are going?"
9And Moses said, "We will go with our
young and our old; with our sons and
our daughters, with our flocks and our
herds we will go, for we must hold a feast
to the LORD."
10Then he said to them, "The LORD
had better be with you when I let you
and your little ones go! Beware, for evil is
ahead of you. 11Not so! Go now, you *who
are* men, and serve the LORD, for that is
what you desired." And they were driven
out from Pharaoh's presence.
12Then the LORD said to Moses, "Stretch
out your hand over the land of Egypt for
the locusts, that they may come upon the
land of Egypt, and eat every herb of the
land—all that the hail has left." 13So
Moses stretched out his rod over the land
of Egypt, and the LORD brought an east
wind on the land all that day and all *that*
night. When it was morning, the east wind
brought the locusts. 14And the locusts
went up over all the land of Egypt and
rested on all the territory of Egypt. *They
were* very severe; previously there had
been no such locusts as they, nor shall
there be such after them. 15For they covered the face of the whole earth, so that
the land was darkened; and they ate
every herb of the land and all the fruit of
the trees which the hail had left. So there
remained nothing green on the trees or
on the plants of the field throughout all
the land of Egypt.
16Then Pharaoh called for Moses and
Aaron in haste, and said, "I have sinned
against the LORD your God and against
you. 17Now therefore, please forgive my
sin only this once, and entreat the LORD
your God, that He may take away from
me this death only." 18So he went out
from Pharaoh and entreated the LORD.
19And the LORD turned a very strong west
wind, which took the locusts away and
blew them into the Red Sea. There remained not one locust in all the territory
of Egypt. 20But the LORD hardened Pharaoh's heart, and he did not let the children of Israel go.

The Ninth Plague: Darkness

21Then the LORD said to Moses, "Stretch
out your hand toward heaven, that there
may be darkness over the land of Egypt,
darkness *which* may even be felt." 22So
Moses stretched out his hand toward heav-
en, and there was thick darkness in all the
land of Egypt three days. 23They did not
see one another; nor did anyone rise from
his place for three days. But all the children of Israel had light in their dwellings.
24Then Pharaoh called to Moses and
said, "Go, serve the LORD; only let your
flocks and your herds be kept back. Let
your little ones also go with you."
25But Moses said, "You must also give
us sacrifices and burnt offerings, that we
may sacrifice to the LORD our God. 26Our
livestock also shall go with us; not a hoof
shall be left behind. For we must take
some of them to serve the LORD our God,
and even we do not know with what we
must serve the LORD until we arrive there."
27But the LORD hardened Pharaoh's
heart, and he would not let them go.
28Then Pharaoh said to him, "Get away
from me! Take heed to yourself and see
my face no more! For in the day you see
my face you shall die!"
29So Moses said, "You have spoken well.
I will never see your face again."

Death of the Firstborn Announced

11 And the LORD said to Moses, "I will
bring one more plague on Pharaoh and on Egypt. Afterward he will let

10:16,17 As with Pharaoh, the "repentance" of many today is superficial. They turn to God for a Band-Aid to cover life's plagues and pains. We should instead flee to the Savior because we have sinned against God. Read Psa. 51 for the motive for mercy from God. See also 2 Cor. 2:17 comment.

10:27 The same sunlight that melts wax hardens clay. The heart of the sinner determines his response to the Word of God.

you go from here. When he lets *you* go, he will surely drive you out of here altogether. 2Speak now in the hearing of the people, and let every man ask from his neighbor and every woman from her neighbor, articles of silver and articles of gold." 3And the LORD gave the people favor in the sight of the Egyptians. Moreover the man Moses *was* very great in the land of Egypt, in the sight of Pharaoh's servants and in the sight of the people.

4Then Moses said, "Thus says the LORD: 'About midnight I will go out into the midst of Egypt; 5and all the firstborn in the land of Egypt shall die, from the firstborn of Pharaoh who sits on his throne, even to the firstborn of the female servant who *is* behind the handmill, and all the firstborn of the animals. 6Then there shall be a great cry throughout all the land of Egypt, such as was not like it *before,* nor shall be like it again. 7But against none of the children of Israel shall a dog move its tongue, against man or beast, that you may know that the LORD does make a difference between the Egyptians and Israel.' 8And all these your servants shall come down to me and bow down to me, saying, 'Get out, and all the people who follow you!' After that I will go out." Then he went out from Pharaoh in great anger.

9But the LORD said to Moses, "Pharaoh will not heed you, so that My wonders may be multiplied in the land of Egypt." 10So Moses and Aaron did all these wonders before Pharaoh; and the LORD hardened Pharaoh's heart, and he did not let the children of Israel go out of his land.

The Passover Instituted

12 Now the LORD spoke to Moses and Aaron in the land of Egypt, saying, 2"This month *shall be* your beginning of months; it *shall be* the first month of the year to you. 3Speak to all the congregation of Israel, saying: 'On the tenth of this month every man shall take for himself a lamb, according to the house of *his* father, a lamb for a household. 4And if the household is too small for the lamb, let him and his neighbor next to his house take *it* according to the number of the persons; according to each man's need you shall make your count for the lamb. 5Your lamb shall be without blemish, a male of the first year. You may take *it* from the sheep or from the goats. 6Now you shall keep it until the fourteenth day of the same month. Then the whole assembly of the congregation of Israel shall kill it at twilight. 7And they shall take *some* of the blood and put *it* on the two doorposts and on the lintel of the houses where they eat it. 8Then they shall eat the flesh on that night; roasted in fire, with unleavened bread *and* with bitter *herbs* they shall eat it. 9Do not eat it raw, nor boiled at all with water, but roasted in fire—its head with its legs and its entrails. 10You shall let none of it remain until morning,

---

11:4,5 Jesus in the Old Testament. "The Jews are now in Egypt working as slaves. God decided to rescue them by sending ten plagues to Pharaoh. The first nine plagues failed to soften Pharaoh's heart, so God warned Pharaoh, 'If you don't let My people go, I will kill every firstborn child' (Exod. 11:4,5). However, God provided a way for the Israelites to escape the death of their firstborn children.

"In Exod. 12 we learn that each Israelite family was to select a spotless, male lamb to dwell with them for a short time and then kill the lamb without breaking any of its bones. The blood of the lamb, applied to their doorposts, would cause the angel of death to pass over those who put their trust in God.

"God commanded the Jews to commemorate this event annually with a Passover celebration that included the sacrifice of an unblemished lamb. It was during this celebration that Jesus, our Passover Lamb, who dwelt with His people for a short time, was killed without a single bone being broken.

"Because of His perfect sacrifice, death has no more sting and will pass over those who are His." *Todd Friel* (Adapted from *Don't Stub Your Toe.*) See Lev. 16:15 comment.

12:7–13 Here is the truth of the gospel of salvation. God's wrath will pass over all who apply the blood of the Savior to the doorposts of their lives. All those who obeyed Moses had to exercise humility of heart and faith in his words. He told them to do something that seemed foolish. Such is the way of the gospel; it is foolishness to those who are perishing (see 1 Cor. 1:18).

and what remains of it until morning you
shall burn with fire. 11And thus you shall
eat it: *with* a belt on your waist, your sandals on your feet, and your staff in your
hand. So you shall eat it in haste. It *is* the
LORD's Passover.

12'For I will pass through the land of
Egypt on that night, and will strike all the
firstborn in the land of Egypt, both man
and beast; and against all the gods of Egypt
I will execute judgment: I *am* the LORD.
13Now the blood shall be a sign for you
on the houses where you *are*. And when
I see the blood, I will pass over you; and
the plague shall not be on you to destroy
you when I strike the land of Egypt.

14'So this day shall be to you a memorial; and you shall keep it as a feast to the
LORD throughout your generations. You
shall keep it as a feast by an everlasting
ordinance. 15Seven days you shall eat unleavened bread. On the first day you shall
remove leaven from your houses. For whoever eats leavened bread from the first
day until the seventh day, that person
shall be cut off from Israel. 16On the first
day *there shall be* a holy convocation, and
on the seventh day there shall be a holy
convocation for you. No manner of work
shall be done on them; but *that* which
everyone must eat—that only may be
prepared by you. 17So you shall observe
the Feast of Unleavened Bread, for on this
same day I will have brought your armies
out of the land of Egypt. Therefore you
shall observe this day throughout your
generations as an everlasting ordinance.
18In the first *month*, on the fourteenth day
of the month at evening, you shall eat unleavened bread, until the twenty-first day
of the month at evening. 19For seven days
no leaven shall be found in your houses,
since whoever eats what is leavened, that
same person shall be cut off from the congregation of Israel, whether *he is* a stranger
or a native of the land. 20You shall eat
nothing leavened; in all your dwellings
you shall eat unleavened bread.' "

21Then Moses called for all the elders
of Israel and said to them, "Pick out and
take lambs for yourselves according to
your families, and kill the Passover *lamb*.
22And you shall take a bunch of hyssop,
dip *it* in the blood that is in the basin, and
strike the lintel and the two doorposts
with the blood that is in the basin. And
none of you shall go out of the door of his
house until morning. 23For the LORD will
pass through to strike the Egyptians; and
when He sees the blood on the lintel and
on the two doorposts, the LORD will pass
over the door and not allow the destroyer
to come into your houses to strike *you*.
24And you shall observe this thing as an
ordinance for you and your sons forever.
25It will come to pass when you come to
the land which the LORD will give you,
just as He promised, that you shall keep
this service. 26And it shall be, when your
children say to you, 'What do you mean
by this service?' 27that you shall say, 'It *is*
the Passover sacrifice of the LORD, who
passed over the houses of the children of
Israel in Egypt when He struck the Egyptians and delivered our households.' " So
the people bowed their heads and worshiped. 28Then the children of Israel went
away and did *so*; just as the LORD had
commanded Moses and Aaron, so they
did.

The Tenth Plague: Death of the Firstborn

29And it came to pass at midnight that
the LORD struck all the firstborn in the
land of Egypt, from the firstborn of Pharaoh who sat on his throne to the firstborn
of the captive who *was* in the dungeon,
and all the firstborn of livestock. 30So
Pharaoh rose in the night, he, all his servants, and all the Egyptians; and there
was a great cry in Egypt, for *there was* not
a house where *there was* not one dead.

The Exodus

31Then he called for Moses and Aaron
by night, and said, "Rise, go out from
among my people, both you and the children of Israel. And go, serve the LORD as
you have said. 32Also take your flocks and

12:26 *Take the Lead in Training Your Children*

Among the many topics you talk about with your children, the most important one is God. Too many parents consider the church to have the primary responsibility for spiritually training their kids. But the responsibility lies on your shoulders. If you are a father, take the lead in teaching your children about the things of the Lord; don't leave it up to your wife. Consider the command of Scripture: "And, you, fathers, do not provoke your children to wrath, but bring them up in the training and admonition of the Lord" (Eph. 6:4).

Perhaps you feel inadequate to lead. If so, be aware that pride will often masquerade as a feeling of inadequacy. Humble yourself. Forget what your wife thinks. Forget what your kids think. Forget what you think about your inabilities. Your only concern should be what God thinks. If you are a single parent, step into the role of the leader.

It is interesting to note that when the Bible tells fathers to bring their children up "in the training and admonition of the Lord," it doesn't give detailed instructions. It just says to do it.

Think about your instincts as a parent. Did anyone have to tell you how to raise your children? There were certain things that you knew instinctively to do. You must feed, clothe, house, and educate your kids. You don't want to leave them cold, hungry, destitute, and illiterate. You taught them that fire burns, water drowns, and if they climb they may fall. What you learned by experience and what you possessed by instinct, you intuitively passed on to those you love.

The same applies spiritually. If you love your children, feed them spiritually. Clothe them in righteousness. Teach them the importance of clothing themselves in humility. Educate them about what will harm them in this life and in the next. What you have learned by experience about spiritual things, deliberately pass on to your children. If you are shallow spiritually, then your instruction to your children will be shallow, so deepen your own walk with the Lord. Be sensitive to what pleases God. Have your senses *exercised* to discern both good and evil (see Heb. 5:14). Whatever your conscience instinctively tells you about moral issues, pass on to those you love. One of the best ways to do this and build godly principles into the lives of your children is through an intentional time dedicated to that goal—a daily family devotional time. See Mal. 2:15 comment.

(Adapted from *How to Bring Your Children to Christ… & Keep Them There.*)

your herds, as you have said, and be gone;
and bless me also."
33And the Egyptians urged the people,
that they might send them out of the land
in haste. For they said, "We *shall* all *be*
dead." 34So the people took their dough
before it was leavened, having their kneading bowls bound up in their clothes on
their shoulders. 35Now the children of Israel had done according to the word of
Moses, and they had asked from the Egyptians articles of silver, articles of gold, and
clothing. 36And the LORD had given the
people favor in the sight of the Egyptians,
so that they granted them *what they requested.* Thus they plundered the Egyptians.
37Then the children of Israel journeyed
from Rameses to Succoth, about six hundred thousand men on foot, besides children. 38A mixed multitude went up with
them also, and flocks and herds—a great
deal of livestock. 39And they baked unleavened cakes of the dough which they
had brought out of Egypt; for it was not
leavened, because they were driven out
of Egypt and could not wait, nor had they
prepared provisions for themselves.
40Now the sojourn of the children of
Israel who lived in Egypt[a] *was* four hundred and thirty years. 41And it came to
pass at the end of the four hundred and
thirty years—on that very same day—it
came to pass that all the armies of the
LORD went out from the land of Egypt.
42It *is* a night of solemn observance to the
LORD for bringing them out of the land of
Egypt. This *is* that night of the LORD, a
solemn observance for all the children of
Israel throughout their generations.

Passover Regulations

43And the LORD said to Moses and
Aaron, "This *is* the ordinance of the Passover: No foreigner shall eat it. 44But every
man's servant who is bought for money,

12:40 [a]Samaritan Pentateuch and Septuagint read *Egypt and Canaan.*

when you have circumcised him, then he may eat it. 45A sojourner and a hired servant shall not eat it. 46In one house it shall be eaten; you shall not carry any of the flesh outside the house, nor shall you break one of its bones. 47All the congregation of Israel shall keep it. 48And when a stranger dwells with you *and wants* to keep the Passover to the LORD, let all his males be circumcised, and then let him come near and keep it; and he shall be as a native of the land. For no uncircumcised person shall eat it. 49One law shall be for the native-born and for the stranger who dwells among you."

50Thus all the children of Israel did; as the LORD commanded Moses and Aaron, so they did. 51And it came to pass, on that very same day, that the LORD brought the children of Israel out of the land of Egypt according to their armies.

The Firstborn Consecrated

13 Then the LORD spoke to Moses, saying, 2"Consecrate to Me all the firstborn, whatever opens the womb among the children of Israel, *both* of man and beast; it is Mine."

The Feast of Unleavened Bread

3And Moses said to the people: "Remember this day in which you went out of Egypt, out of the house of bondage; for by strength of hand the LORD brought you out of this *place*. No leavened bread shall be eaten. 4On this day you are going out, in the month Abib. 5And it shall be, when the LORD brings you into the land of the Canaanites and the Hittites and the Amorites and the Hivites and the Jebusites, which He swore to your fathers to give you, a land flowing with milk and honey, that you shall keep this service in this month. 6Seven days you shall eat unleavened bread, and on the seventh day *there shall be* a feast to the LORD. 7Unleavened bread shall be eaten seven days. And no leavened bread shall be seen among you, nor shall leaven be seen among you in all your quarters. 8And you shall tell your son in that day, saying, '*This is done* because of what the LORD did for me when I came up from Egypt.' 9It shall be as a sign to you on your hand and as a memorial between your eyes, that the LORD's law may be in your mouth; for with a strong hand the LORD has brought you out of Egypt. 10You shall therefore keep this ordinance in its season from year to year.

. . . . . .

Are we all children of God?
See Mal. 2:10 comment.

. . . . . .

The Law of the Firstborn

11"And it shall be, when the LORD brings you into the land of the Canaanites, as He swore to you and your fathers, and gives it to you, 12that you shall set apart to the LORD all that open the womb, that is, every firstborn that comes from an animal which you have; the males *shall be* the LORD's. 13But every firstborn of a donkey you shall redeem with a lamb; and if you will not redeem *it,* then you shall break its neck. And all the firstborn of man among your sons you shall redeem. 14So it shall be, when your son asks you in time to come, saying, 'What *is* this?' that you shall say to him, 'By strength of hand the LORD brought us out of Egypt, out of the house of bondage. 15And it came to pass, when Pharaoh was stubborn about letting us go, that the LORD killed all the firstborn in the land of Egypt, both the

---

12:46 None of the Passover lamb's bones were to be broken. Just so, while the others crucified with Jesus had their legs broken by soldiers to hasten their death, Jesus' bones were not broken (see John 19:33,36).

13:9 Moses told Israel of God's plan for them, that He wanted to put His Law in their mouth. In the new covenant, God puts His Law into our hearts and causes us to walk in His statutes. See Ezek. 36:26,27 and Jer. 31:32,33 for more details.

firstborn of man and the firstborn of
beast. Therefore I sacrifice to the LORD all
males that open the womb, but all the
firstborn of my sons I redeem.' 16It shall
be as a sign on your hand and as frontlets
between your eyes, for by strength of
hand the LORD brought us out of Egypt."

The Wilderness Way

17Then it came to pass, when Pharaoh
had let the people go, that God did not lead
them *by* way of the land of the Philistines,
although that *was* near; for God said,
"Lest perhaps the people change their
minds when they see war, and return to
Egypt." 18So God led the people around
by way of the wilderness of the Red Sea.
And the children of Israel went up in orderly ranks out of the land of Egypt.
19And Moses took the bones of Joseph
with him, for he had placed the children
of Israel under solemn oath, saying, "God
will surely visit you, and you shall carry
up my bones from here with you."[a]
20So they took their journey from Succoth and camped in Etham at the edge of
the wilderness. 21And the LORD went before them by day in a pillar of cloud to
lead the way, and by night in a pillar of
fire to give them light, so as to go by day
and night. 22He did not take away the pillar of cloud by day or the pillar of fire by
night *from* before the people.

The Red Sea Crossing

14 Now the LORD spoke to Moses,
saying: 2"Speak to the children of
Israel, that they turn and camp before Pi
Hahiroth, between Migdol and the sea,
opposite Baal Zemphon; you shall camp
before it by the sea. 3For Pharaoh will say
of the children of Israel, 'They *are* bewildered by the land; the wilderness has
closed them in.' 4Then I will harden Pharaoh's heart, so that he will pursue them;
and I will gain honor over Pharaoh and
over all his army, that the Egyptians may
know that I *am* the LORD." And they did
so.
5Now it was told the king of Egypt
that the people had fled, and the heart of
Pharaoh and his servants was turned
against the people; and they said, "Why
have we done this, that we have let Israel
go from serving us?" 6So he made ready
his chariot and took his people with him.
7Also, he took six hundred choice chariots, and all the chariots of Egypt with captains over every one of them. 8And the
LORD hardened the heart of Pharaoh king
of Egypt, and he pursued the children of
Israel; and the children of Israel went out
with boldness. 9So the Egyptians pursued
them, all the horses *and* chariots of Pharaoh, his horsemen and his army, and overtook them camping by the sea beside Pi
Hahiroth, before Baal Zephon.
10And when Pharaoh drew near, the
children of Israel lifted their eyes, and behold, the Egyptians marched after them.
So they were very afraid, and the children
of Israel cried out to the LORD. 11Then
they said to Moses, "Because *there were* no
graves in Egypt, have you taken us away
to die in the wilderness? Why have you
so dealt with us, to bring us up out of
Egypt? 12*Is* this not the word that we told
you in Egypt, saying, 'Let us alone that
we may serve the Egyptians'? For *it would
have been* better for us to serve the Egyptians than that we should die in the
wilderness."
13And Moses said to the people, "Do
not be afraid. Stand still, and see the salvation of the LORD, which He will accomplish for you today. For the Egyptians
whom you see today, you shall see again
no more forever. 14The LORD will fight for
you, and you shall hold your peace."
15And the LORD said to Moses, "Why
do you cry to Me? Tell the children of Israel to go forward. 16But lift up your rod,

13:19 [a]Genesis 50:25

14:13 All we ask is for those in the world to stand still and see the salvation of God. We want them to stop their arguments, set aside their prejudices, and look to the cross of Jesus Christ.

and stretch out your hand over the sea and divide it. And the children of Israel shall go on dry *ground* through the midst of the sea. 17And I indeed will harden the hearts of the Egyptians, and they shall follow them. So I will gain honor over Pharaoh and over all his army, his chariots, and his horsemen. 18Then the Egyptians shall know that I *am* the LORD, when I have gained honor for Myself over Pharaoh, his chariots, and his horsemen."

19And the Angel of God, who went before the camp of Israel, moved and went behind them; and the pillar of cloud went from before them and stood behind them. 20So it came between the camp of the Egyptians and the camp of Israel. Thus it was a cloud and darkness *to the one,* and it gave light by night *to the other,* so that the one did not come near the other all that night.

21Then Moses stretched out his hand over the sea; and the LORD caused the sea to go *back* by a strong east wind all that night, and made the sea into dry *land,* and the waters were divided. 22So the children of Israel went into the midst of the sea on the dry *ground,* and the waters *were* a wall to them on their right hand and on their left. 23And the Egyptians pursued and went after them into the midst of the sea, all Pharaoh's horses, his chariots, and his horsemen.

24Now it came to pass, in the morning watch, that the LORD looked down upon the army of the Egyptians through the pillar of fire and cloud, and He troubled the army of the Egyptians. 25And He took off[a] their chariot wheels, so that they drove them with difficulty; and the Egyptians said, "Let us flee from the face of Israel, for the LORD fights for them against the Egyptians."

26Then the LORD said to Moses, "Stretch out your hand over the sea, that the waters may come back upon the Egyptians, on their chariots, and on their horsemen." 27And Moses stretched out his hand over the sea; and when the morning appeared, the sea returned to its full depth, while the Egyptians were fleeing into it. So the LORD overthrew the Egyptians in the midst of the sea. 28Then the waters returned and covered the chariots, the horsemen, *and* all the army of Pharaoh that came into the sea after them. Not so much as one of them remained. 29But the children of Israel had walked on dry *land* in the midst of the sea, and the waters *were* a wall to them on their right hand and on their left.

30So the LORD saved Israel that day out of the hand of the Egyptians, and Israel saw the Egyptians dead on the seashore. 31Thus Israel saw the great work which the LORD had done in Egypt; so the people feared the LORD, and believed the LORD and His servant Moses.

The Song of Moses

15 Then Moses and the children of Israel sang this song to the LORD, and spoke, saying:

"I will sing to the LORD,
For He has triumphed gloriously!
The horse and its rider
He has thrown into the sea!
2The LORD is my strength and song,
And He has become my salvation;
He *is* my God, and I will praise Him;
My father's God, and I will exalt Him.
3The LORD is a man of war;
The LORD is His name.
4Pharaoh's chariots and his army He
has cast into the sea;
His chosen captains also are drowned
in the Red Sea.
5The depths have covered them;

14:25 [a]Samaritan Pentateuch, Septuagint, and Syriac read *bound.*

14:16 The Law is the rod of God in the hand of Moses. It will open up the Red Sea and bring deliverance of those who have been "taken captive" by the devil (see 2 Tim. 2:26). It is a "tutor to bring us to Christ" (Gal. 3:24).

QUESTIONS & OBJECTIONS

15:4 "God violates the laws of nature and of logic."

God can and does defy human "logic." His very omniscience is illogical. How can He be aware of every thought of every human heart at one time (see Psa. 139:1–10)? That makes no sense. We struggle to entertain two thoughts at once. Try it (not while you are driving). Opening the Red Sea is not logical. How did the water stand upright on each side of the Hebrews as they walked through on dry land? Where was gravity when this went on? It is not logical to feed 5,000 people with five loaves and two fish. How were the fish multiplied? Did new fish appear, or did the two miraculously divide into thousands of pieces?

Then again, invisible television waves making live news anchors appear in my home does not make sense either. Neither is it logical that old movies invisibly and instantly (in full color) speed through the air and manifest themselves on my TV screen. Nor does it make sense that a 747 jet floats through the sky, packed with hundreds of people. Instant communication via email with my family in New Zealand (7,000 miles away) does not seem logical. How can I email digital photos to them? Photography, both still and video, makes no sense. Imagine trying to explain the concept to Galileo; he would think you are crazy.

So many natural things that we now take for granted defy the logic of earlier days. So it is not logical to reject the idea that the Creator of this universe—the One who created the laws of nature—could turn water into wine, still storms, curse a fig tree, and raise the dead. God made the sea; He can part it if He so desires. He can also walk on it. Since He created the human body, He can fix it without medicine. He can create pillars of salt, pillars of fire, and pillars of goose feathers, if He wants. Virgin birth? No problem. Resurrection—easy (see Acts 26:8). If I acknowledge that a supernatural Creator exists, everything becomes possible.

They sank to the bottom like a stone.

6"Your right hand, O LORD, has become
glorious in power;
Your right hand, O LORD, has dashed
the enemy in pieces.
7And in the greatness of Your
excellence
You have overthrown those who rose
against You;
You sent forth Your wrath;
It consumed them like stubble.
8And with the blast of Your nostrils
The waters were gathered together;
The floods stood upright like a heap;
The depths congealed in the heart of
the sea.
9The enemy said, 'I will pursue,
I will overtake,
I will divide the spoil;
My desire shall be satisfied on them.
I will draw my sword,
My hand shall destroy them.'
10You blew with Your wind,
The sea covered them;
They sank like lead in the mighty
waters.

11"Who *is* like You, O LORD, among the
gods?
Who *is* like You, glorious in holiness,
Fearful in praises, doing wonders?
12You stretched out Your right hand;
The earth swallowed them.
13You in Your mercy have led forth
The people whom You have redeemed;
You have guided *them* in Your strength
To Your holy habitation.
14"The people will hear *and* be afraid;
Sorrow will take hold of the
inhabitants of Philistia.
15Then the chiefs of Edom will be
dismayed;
The mighty men of Moab,

15:3 Bible contradiction? Skeptics claim that this verse contradicts numerous others that call God "the God of peace" (e.g., Rom. 15:33). The Bible tells us that God fought many wars for Israel to destroy wicked nations, and that He promises "the peace of God, which surpasses all understanding" (Phil. 4:7) to all who repent and trust the Savior. It is clear that Exod. 15:3 is a reference to war, while Rom. 15:33 simply refers to peace of mind.

Trembling will take hold of them;
All the inhabitants of Canaan will
melt away.
16Fear and dread will fall on them;
By the greatness of Your arm
They will be *as* still as a stone,
Till Your people pass over, O LORD,
Till the people pass over
Whom You have purchased.
17You will bring them in and plant them
In the mountain of Your inheritance,
In the place, O LORD, *which* You have
made
For Your own dwelling,
The sanctuary, O Lord, *which* Your
hands have established.

18"The LORD shall reign forever and ever."

19For the horses of Pharaoh went with
his chariots and his horsemen into the
sea, and the LORD brought back the waters of the sea upon them. But the children of Israel went on dry *land* in the
midst of the sea.

The Song of Miriam

20Then Miriam the prophetess, the sister of Aaron, took the timbrel in her
hand; and all the women went out after
her with timbrels and with dances. 21And
Miriam answered them:

"Sing to the LORD,
For He has triumphed gloriously!
The horse and its rider
He has thrown into the sea!"

Bitter Waters Made Sweet

22So Moses brought Israel from the
Red Sea; then they went out into the Wilderness of Shur. And they went three
days in the wilderness and found no water. 23Now when they came to Marah,
they could not drink the waters of Marah,
for they *were* bitter. Therefore the name
of it was called Marah.[a] 24And the people
complained against Moses, saying, "What
shall we drink?" 25So he cried out to the
LORD, and the LORD showed him a tree.
When he cast *it* into the waters, the waters were made sweet.

There He made a statute and an ordinance for them, and there He tested them,
26and said, "If you diligently heed the
voice of the LORD your God and do what
is right in His sight, give ear to His commandments and keep all His statutes, I
will put none of the diseases on you which
I have brought on the Egyptians. For I *am*
the LORD who heals you."

27Then they came to Elim, where there
were twelve wells of water and seventy
palm trees; so they camped there by the
waters.

Bread from Heaven

16 And they journeyed from Elim, and
all the congregation of the children of Israel came to the Wilderness of
Sin, which is between Elim and Sinai, on
the fifteenth day of the second month after they departed from the land of Egypt.
2Then the whole congregation of the children of Israel complained against Moses
and Aaron in the wilderness. 3And the
children of Israel said to them, "Oh, that
we had died by the hand of the LORD in
the land of Egypt, when we sat by the
pots of meat *and* when we ate bread to
the full! For you have brought us out into
this wilderness to kill this whole assembly with hunger."

4Then the LORD said to Moses, "Behold, I will rain bread from heaven for
you. And the people shall go out and
gather a certain quota every day, that I

15:23 [a]Literally *Bitter*

15:25 It was the "tree" on which Jesus hung (see Acts 5:30) that made it possible for us to freely drink from the waters of eternal life. See John 4:14 to see what Jesus said about this.

15:26 To learn about the healing power of Jesus' sacrifice, see Isa. 53:5 and 1 Pet. 2:24.

may test them, whether they will walk in My law or not. 5And it shall be on the sixth day that they shall prepare what they bring in, and it shall be twice as much as they gather daily."

6Then Moses and Aaron said to all the children of Israel, "At evening you shall know that the LORD has brought you out of the land of Egypt. 7And in the morning you shall see the glory of the LORD; for He hears your complaints against the LORD. But what *are* we, that you complain against us?" 8Also Moses said, "*This shall be seen* when the LORD gives you meat to eat in the evening, and in the morning bread to the full; for the LORD hears your complaints which you make against Him. And what *are* we? Your complaints *are* not against us but against the LORD."

If you teach men that God is the source of their pleasure and sin is the source of their pain, they will run to God and away from sin.

JACQUELYN K. HEASLEY

9Then Moses spoke to Aaron, "Say to all the congregation of the children of Israel, 'Come near before the LORD, for He has heard your complaints.' " 10Now it came to pass, as Aaron spoke to the whole congregation of the children of Israel, that they looked toward the wilderness, and behold, the glory of the LORD appeared in the cloud.

11And the LORD spoke to Moses, saying, 12"I have heard the complaints of the children of Israel. Speak to them, saying, 'At twilight you shall eat meat, and in the morning you shall be filled with bread. And you shall know that I *am* the LORD your God.' "

13So it was that quails came up at evening and covered the camp, and in the morning the dew lay all around the camp. 14And when the layer of dew lifted, there, on the surface of the wilderness, was a small round substance, *as* fine as frost on the ground. 15So when the children of Israel saw *it*, they said to one another, "What is it?" For they did not know what it *was*.

And Moses said to them, "This *is* the bread which the LORD has given you to eat. 16This is the thing which the LORD has commanded: 'Let every man gather it according to each one's need, one omer for each person, *according to the* number of persons; let every man take for *those* who *are* in his tent.' "

17Then the children of Israel did so and gathered, some more, some less. 18So when they measured *it* by omers, he who gathered much had nothing left over, and he who gathered little had no lack. Every man had gathered according to each one's need. 19And Moses said, "Let no one leave any of it till morning." 20Notwithstanding they did not heed Moses. But some of them left part of it until morning, and it bred worms and stank. And Moses was angry with them. 21So they gathered it every morning, every man according to his need. And when the sun became hot, it melted.

22And so it was, on the sixth day, *that* they gathered twice as much bread, two omers for each one. And all the rulers of the congregation came and told Moses. 23Then he said to them, "This *is what* the LORD has said: 'Tomorrow *is* a Sabbath rest, a holy Sabbath to the LORD. Bake what you will bake *today*, and boil what you will boil; and lay up for yourselves all that remains, to be kept until morning.' " 24So they laid it up till morning, as Moses commanded; and it did not stink, nor were

16:12 For thoughts on vegetarianism, see Psa. 66:15 comment.

16:14–20 Make sure you daily gather sustenance from God's Word. If you suspect that someone is a false convert, ask when he last read the Bible. His response will indicate whether he is close to or distant from the Lord. False converts, who let sin into their hearts, will often still pray to their concept of God but will stop reading God's Word. It becomes odious to them because of their sin.

there any worms in it. 25 Then Moses said, "Eat that today, for today *is* a Sabbath to the LORD; today you will not find it in the field. 26 Six days you shall gather it, but on the seventh day, the Sabbath, there will be none."

27 Now it happened *that some* of the people went out on the seventh day to gather, but they found none. 28 And the LORD said to Moses, "How long do you refuse to keep My commandments and My laws? 29 See! For the LORD has given you the Sabbath; therefore He gives you on the sixth day bread for two days. Let every man remain in his place; let no man go out of his place on the seventh day." 30 So the people rested on the seventh day.

31 And the house of Israel called its name Manna.[a] And it *was* like white coriander seed, and the taste of it *was* like wafers *made* with honey.

32 Then Moses said, "This *is* the thing which the LORD has commanded: 'Fill an omer with it, to be kept for your generations, that they may see the bread with which I fed you in the wilderness, when I brought you out of the land of Egypt.' " 33 And Moses said to Aaron, "Take a pot and put an omer of manna in it, and lay it up before the LORD, to be kept for your generations." 34 As the LORD commanded Moses, so Aaron laid it up before the Testimony, to be kept. 35 And the children of Israel ate manna forty years, until they came to an inhabited land; they ate manna until they came to the border of the land of Canaan. 36 Now an omer *is* one-tenth of an ephah.

Water from the Rock

17 Then all the congregation of the children of Israel set out on their journey from the Wilderness of Sin, according to the commandment of the LORD, and camped in Rephidim; but *there was* no water for the people to drink. 2 Therefore the people contended with Moses, and said, "Give us water, that we may drink."

So Moses said to them, "Why do you contend with me? Why do you tempt the LORD?"

3 And the people thirsted there for water, and the people complained against Moses, and said, "Why *is* it you have brought us up out of Egypt, to kill us and our children and our livestock with thirst?"

4 So Moses cried out to the LORD, saying, "What shall I do with this people? They are almost ready to stone me!"

5 And the LORD said to Moses, "Go on before the people, and take with you some of the elders of Israel. Also take in your hand your rod with which you struck the river, and go. 6 Behold, I will stand before you there on the rock in Horeb; and you shall strike the rock, and water will come out of it, that the people may drink."

And Moses did so in the sight of the elders of Israel. 7 So he called the name of the place Massah[a] and Meribah,[b] because of the contention of the children of Israel, and because they tempted the LORD, saying, "Is the LORD among us or not?"

Victory over the Amalekites

8 Now Amalek came and fought with Israel in Rephidim. 9 And Moses said to Joshua, "Choose us some men and go out, fight with Amalek. Tomorrow I will stand on the top of the hill with the rod of God in my hand." 10 So Joshua did as

16:31 [a]Literally *What?* (compare Exodus 16:15)

17:6 "The apostle says that Rock was Christ, 1Co 10:4, it was a type of him. While the curse of God might justly have been executed upon our guilty souls, behold the Son of God is smitten for us. Let us ask and receive. There was a constant, abundant supply of this water. Numerous as believers are, the supply of the Spirit of Christ is enough for all. The water flowed from the rock in streams to refresh the wilderness, and attended them on their way towards Canaan; and this water flows from Christ, through the ordinances, in the barren wilderness of this world, to refresh our souls, until we come to glory." *Matthew Henry*

QUESTIONS & OBJECTIONS

17:14

"God said He would blot out all remembrance of Amalek. The Bible itself disproves this by mentioning Amalek to this day."

God told Moses to "write this for a memorial in the book," and God preserved the Book for 5,000 years so skeptics would know that God keeps every promise He makes. The phrase "I will utterly blot out the remembrance of Amalek from under heaven" means that He will blot them out as a nation from the earth. There are no descendants of the Amalekites on the earth. They don't exist.

Moses said to him, and fought with Amalek. And Moses, Aaron, and Hur went up
to the top of the hill. 11And so it was,
when Moses held up his hand, that Israel
prevailed; and when he let down his hand,
Amalek prevailed. 12But Moses' hands *became* heavy; so they took a stone and put
it under him, and he sat on it. And Aaron
and Hur supported his hands, one on one
side, and the other on the other side; and
his hands were steady until the going down
of the sun. 13So Joshua defeated Amalek
and his people with the edge of the sword.
14Then the LORD said to Moses, "Write
this *for* a memorial in the book and recount *it* in the hearing of Joshua, that I
will utterly blot out the remembrance of
Amalek from under heaven." 15And Moses
built an altar and called its name, The-
LORD-Is-My-Banner;[a] 16for he said, "Because the LORD has sworn: the LORD *will
have* war with Amalek from generation to
generation."

Jethro's Advice

18 And Jethro, the priest of Midian,
Moses' father-in-law, heard of all
that God had done for Moses and for Israel
His people—that the LORD had brought
Israel out of Egypt. 2Then Jethro, Moses'
father-in-law, took Zipporah, Moses' wife,
after he had sent her back, 3with her two
sons, of whom the name of one *was* Gershom (for he said, "I have been a stranger
in a foreign land")[a] 4and the name of the
other *was* Eliezer[a] (for *he said,* "The God
of my father *was* my help, and delivered
me from the sword of Pharaoh"); 5and
Jethro, Moses' father-in-law, came with his
sons and his wife to Moses in the wilderness, where he was encamped at the mountain of God. 6Now he had said to Moses,
"I, your father-in-law Jethro, am coming
to you with your wife and her two sons
with her."
7So Moses went out to meet his father-
in-law, bowed down, and kissed him. And
they asked each other about *their* well-
being, and they went into the tent. 8And
Moses told his father-in-law all that the
LORD had done to Pharaoh and to the
Egyptians for Israel's sake, all the hardship that had come upon them on the
way, and *how* the LORD had delivered
them. 9Then Jethro rejoiced for all the
good which the LORD had done for Israel,
whom He had delivered out of the hand
of the Egyptians. 10And Jethro said,
"Blessed *be* the LORD, who has delivered

17:7 [a]Literally *Tempted* [b]Literally *Contention* 17:15 [a]Hebrew *YHWH Nissi* 18:3 [a]Compare Exodus 2:22 18:4 [a]Literally *My God Is Help*

17:9 We hear sermons about Aaron and Hur holding up the hands of Moses, as Joshua led Israel in a battle against Amalek, as examples of intercessory prayer. As long as Moses' hands were held up, Joshua prevailed. But notice what Moses was holding: "the rod of God" (v. 9).

When we lift up the rod of the Law in the battle for souls, we will prevail. Scripture and church history testify to that. The enemy hates the use of the Law in witnessing, because he knows that if our evangelistic efforts (with the help of God) produce genuine converts, they will in turn reproduce their own kind, set our churches on fire and bring revival to this dying world. See Luke 11:52 comment.

you out of the hand of the Egyptians and
out of the hand of Pharaoh, *and* who has
delivered the people from under the hand
of the Egyptians. 11Now I know that the
LORD *is* greater than all the gods; for in
the very thing in which they behaved
proudly, *He was* above them." 12Then
Jethro, Moses' father-in-law, took[a] a burnt
offering and *other* sacrifices *to offer* to
God. And Aaron came with all the elders
of Israel to eat bread with Moses' father-
in-law before God.

13And so it was, on the next day, that
Moses sat to judge the people; and the
people stood before Moses from morning
until evening. 14So when Moses' father-
in-law saw all that he did for the people,
he said, "What *is* this thing that you are
doing for the people? Why do you alone
sit, and all the people stand before you
from morning until evening?"

15And Moses said to his father-in-law,
"Because the people come to me to inquire of God. 16When they have a difficulty, they come to me, and I judge between one and another; and I make
known the statutes of God and His laws."

17So Moses' father-in-law said to him,
"The thing that you do is not good. 18Both
you and these people who *are* with you
will surely wear yourselves out. For this
thing *is* too much for you; you are not
able to perform it by yourself. 19Listen
now to my voice; I will give you counsel,
and God will be with you: Stand before
God for the people, so that you may bring
the difficulties to God. 20And you shall
teach them the statutes and the laws, and
show them the way in which they must
walk and the work they must do. 21More-
over you shall select from all the people
able men, such as fear God, men of truth,
hating covetousness; and place *such* over
them *to be* rulers of thousands, rulers of
hundreds, rulers of fifties, and rulers of
tens. 22And let them judge the people at
all times. Then it will be *that* every great
matter they shall bring to you, but every
small matter they themselves shall judge.
So it will be easier for you, for they will
bear *the burden* with you. 23If you do this
thing, and God *so* commands you, then
you will be able to endure, and all this
people will also go to their place in peace."

24So Moses heeded the voice of his father-in-law and did all that he had said.
25And Moses chose able men out of all Israel, and made them heads over the people: rulers of thousands, rulers of hundreds, rulers of fifties, and rulers of tens.
26So they judged the people at all times;
the hard cases they brought to Moses, but
they judged every small case themselves.

27Then Moses let his father-in-law depart, and he went his way to his own land.

Israel at Mount Sinai

19 In the third month after the children of Israel had gone out of the
land of Egypt, on the same day, they came
to the Wilderness of Sinai. 2For they had
departed from Rephidim, had come *to* the
Wilderness of Sinai, and camped in the
wilderness. So Israel camped there before
the mountain.

3And Moses went up to God, and the
LORD called to him from the mountain,
saying, "Thus you shall say to the house
of Jacob, and tell the children of Israel:
4'You have seen what I did to the Egyptians, and *how* I bore you on eagles' wings
and brought you to Myself. 5Now therefore, if you will indeed obey My voice
and keep My covenant, then you shall be
a special treasure to Me above all people;

18:12 [a]Following Masoretic Text and Septuagint; Syriac, Targum, and Vulgate read *offered.*

18:18 It is often said that we should "come apart" before we come apart. We should make sure we take the time to rest. If you are overwhelmed with your work for God, delegate, but don't just do nothing while sinners sink into Hell. It is far better to burn out than to rust out. Pray always. Preach the word, in season and out of season . . . always laboring in the Lord, knowing that your labor is not in vain. We will have eternity to rest.

for all the earth *is* Mine. 6And you shall be to Me a kingdom of priests and a holy nation.' These *are* the words which you shall speak to the children of Israel."

7So Moses came and called for the elders of the people, and laid before them all these words which the LORD commanded him. 8Then all the people answered together and said, "All that the LORD has spoken we will do." So Moses brought back the words of the people to the LORD. 9And the LORD said to Moses, "Behold, I come to you in the thick cloud, that the people may hear when I speak with you, and believe you forever."

So Moses told the words of the people to the LORD.

10Then the LORD said to Moses, "Go to the people and consecrate them today and tomorrow, and let them wash their clothes. 11And let them be ready for the third day. For on the third day the LORD will come down upon Mount Sinai in the sight of all the people. 12You shall set bounds for the people all around, saying, 'Take heed to yourselves *that* you do *not* go up to the mountain or touch its base. Whoever touches the mountain shall surely be put to death. 13Not a hand shall touch him, but he shall surely be stoned or shot *with an arrow;* whether man or beast, he shall not live.' When the trumpet sounds long, they shall come near the mountain."

14So Moses went down from the mountain to the people and sanctified the people, and they washed their clothes. 15And he said to the people, "Be ready for the third day; do not come near *your* wives."

16Then it came to pass on the third day, in the morning, that there were thunderings and lightnings, and a thick cloud on the mountain; and the sound of the trumpet was very loud, so that all the people who *were* in the camp trembled. 17And Moses brought the people out of the camp to meet with God, and they stood at the foot of the mountain. 18Now Mount Sinai *was* completely in smoke, because the LORD descended upon it in fire. Its smoke ascended like the smoke of a furnace, and the whole mountain[a] quaked greatly. 19And when the blast of the trumpet sounded long and became louder and louder, Moses spoke, and God answered him by voice. 20Then the LORD came down upon Mount Sinai, on the top of the mountain. And the LORD called Moses to the top of the mountain, and Moses went up.

21And the LORD said to Moses, "Go down and warn the people, lest they break through to gaze at the LORD, and many of them perish. 22Also let the priests who come near the LORD consecrate themselves, lest the LORD break out against them."

23But Moses said to the LORD, "The people cannot come up to Mount Sinai; for You warned us, saying, 'Set bounds around the mountain and consecrate it.' "

24Then the LORD said to him, "Away! Get down and then come up, you and Aaron with you. But do not let the priests and the people break through to come up to the LORD, lest He break out against

19:18 [a]Septuagint reads *all the people.*

19:12 What a fearful thing it was when God gave His Law. And this was when He came in peace. He was not manifesting His terrible wrath, but simply giving His Law to Israel through Moses, yet it was an unspeakably fearful sight. A number of times in this chapter God warned Israel to be careful not to approach the mountain, "lest the LORD break out against them" (v. 22). The holiness of God would fall upon sinful man quicker than a massive bolt of lightning would consume a dead ant. Think of an unrepentant murderer, who has raped innocent young girls then callously cut their throats, standing before a judge. As the good judge looks upon the devious criminal, he is filled with anger as he brings down his gavel and passes the death sentence. Desire for justice fuels his wrath. How much more will a perfect and holy God be wrath-filled and break out on sinful humanity for our wickedness! No man can stand in God's presence and live. His holiness demands our death. The only way we can live is to be sheltered in Jesus Christ.

19:20 If the sinner will humble himself before God, God will draw near to the sinner: "Humble yourselves in the sight of the Lord, and He will lift you up" (James 4:8–10).

them." [25]So Moses went down to the people and spoke to them.

The Ten Commandments

20 And God spoke all these words, saying:
[2]"I *am* the LORD your God, who brought you out of the land of Egypt, out of the house of bondage.
[3]"You shall have no other gods before Me.
[4]"You shall not make for yourself a carved image—any likeness *of anything* that *is* in heaven above, or that *is* in the earth beneath, or that *is* in the water under the earth; [5]you shall not bow down to them nor serve them. For I, the LORD your God, *am* a jealous God, visiting the iniquity of the fathers upon the children to the third and fourth *generations* of those who hate Me, [6]but showing mercy to thousands, to those who love Me and keep My commandments.
[7]"You shall not take the name of the LORD your God in vain, for the LORD will not hold *him* guiltless who takes His name in vain.
[8]"Remember the Sabbath day, to keep it holy. [9]Six days you shall labor and do all your work, [10]but the seventh day *is* the Sabbath of the LORD your God. *In it* you shall do no work: you, nor your son, nor your daughter, nor your male servant, nor your female servant, nor your cattle, nor your stranger who *is* within your gates. [11]For *in* six days the LORD made the heavens and the earth, the sea, and all that *is* in them, and rested the seventh day. Therefore the LORD blessed the Sabbath day and hallowed it.
[12]"Honor your father and your mother, that your days may be long upon the land which the LORD your God is giving you.
[13]"You shall not murder.
[14]"You shall not commit adultery.
[15]"You shall not steal.
[16]"You shall not bear false witness against your neighbor.
[17]"You shall not covet your neighbor's house; you shall not covet your neighbor's wife, nor his male servant, nor his female servant, nor his ox, nor his donkey, nor anything that *is* your neighbor's."

The People Afraid of God's Presence

[18]Now all the people witnessed the thunderings, the lightning flashes, the sound of the trumpet, and the mountain smoking; and when the people saw *it*, they trembled and stood afar off. [19]Then they said to Moses, "You speak with us, and we will hear; but let not God speak with us, lest we die."

20:3 Memorize God's Law for the purpose of sharing your faith (see page 652). Learn to use the Commandments to speak directly to the conscience and bring the knowledge of sin, as Jesus did (see Mark 10:17–21) and as Paul did (see Rom. 2:21–24). See John 4:7 comment.

20:14 Adultery. Don't rely solely on your conscience to save you from sin. Our love for sin can overwhelm the still, small voice of conscience.

A woman in her early forties committed adultery and was so weighed down with a sense of guilt that she cried off and on for three months. In an effort to be free from guilt, she finally confessed her sin to her husband, who forgave her immediately. However, the woman still found no relief from her guilt, sinking deeper and deeper into depression. She would often sleep downstairs in their two-story home, wrapped in a blanket, weeping and praying.

One night, her loving husband crept downstairs and was relieved to see her wrapped in a blanket, soundly sleeping. In the morning, he went outside and picked a rose. He then wrote her a love note and left it on the table for her to find. After some time, he went into the room and was horrified to find that she had committed suicide during the night. We need more than our conscience to keep us from sin; we need a healthy fear of God. See Prov. 2:1–5 comment.

For some repercussions of adultery, see Psa. 107:17 comment.

QUESTIONS & OBJECTIONS

20:17 ***"In the Tenth Commandment, why are wives listed with houses, oxen, and donkeys, which are property?"***

You seem to have Christianity confused with other religions, such as Hinduism, that treat wives as mere property. The Tenth Commandment prohibits coveting (covetousness is an unlawful desire), and lists some of the items we are not to lust after. I'm sure you would agree that men tend to lust after women. So, women are included in the list. The association with other things we covet has nothing to do with their worth.

Christianity treats women with the utmost respect. In the Old Testament they were entrusted with high political offices, and Prov. 31 shows they were given great dignity and worth. When it was considered disreputable and undignified for a man to speak to a woman in public, Jesus spoke to the woman at the well. When women were not considered reliable witnesses, Jesus chose a woman to be the first person to see Him after His resurrection. A woman was privileged to be the first to share the good news that Jesus rose from the dead. Jesus had many women followers, whom He treated with respect and compassion. While some religions don't want women to be educated, they listened to His teaching and were valuable coworkers in the Church.

The New Testament instructs husbands to love their wives sacrificially, "just as Christ also loved the church and gave Himself for her" (Eph. 5:25). You cannot honor someone more than that. So your inference that Christianity endorses treating women as property is unfounded. See also Prov. 31:10 comment.

[20]And Moses said to the people, "Do
not fear; for God has come to test you, and
that His fear may be before you, so that
you may not sin." [21]So the people stood
afar off, but Moses drew near the thick
darkness where God *was.*

The Law of the Altar

[22]Then the LORD said to Moses, "Thus
you shall say to the children of Israel: 'You
have seen that I have talked with you
from heaven. [23]You shall not make *anything to be* with Me—gods of silver or gods
of gold you shall not make for yourselves.
[24]An altar of earth you shall make for Me,
and you shall sacrifice on it your burnt
offerings and your peace offerings, your
sheep and your oxen. In every place where
I record My name I will come to you, and
I will bless you. [25]And if you make Me an
altar of stone, you shall not build it of
hewn stone; for if you use your tool on it,
you have profaned it. [26]Nor shall you go
up by steps to My altar, that your nakedness may not be exposed on it.'

The Law Concerning Servants

21 "Now these *are* the judgments
which you shall set before them:
[2]If you buy a Hebrew servant, he shall
serve six years; and in the seventh he
shall go out free and pay nothing. [3]If he
comes in by himself, he shall go out by
himself; if he *comes in* married, then his
wife shall go out with him. [4]If his master
has given him a wife, and she has borne
him sons or daughters, the wife and her
children shall be her master's, and he
shall go out by himself. [5]But if the servant
plainly says, 'I love my master, my wife,
and my children; I will not go out free,'
[6]then his master shall bring him to the
judges. He shall also bring him to the
door, or to the doorpost, and his master

20:18 "If the giving of the Law, while it was yet unbroken, was attended with such a display of awe-inspiring power, what will that day be when the Lord shall, with flaming fire, take vengeance on those who have willfully broken that Law?" *Charles Spurgeon*

"Secure sinners must hear the thundering of Mount Sinai before we bring them to Mount Zion. Every minister should be a Boanerges, a son of thunder, as well as Barnabas, a son of consolation." *George Whitefield*

"No man knows the brightness of the gospel till he understands the blackness of those clouds which surround the Law of the Lord." *Charles Spurgeon*

20:19 See Heb. 12:25 comment regarding God speaking to humanity.

shall pierce his ear with an awl; and he
shall serve him forever.
7“And if a man sells his daughter to be
a female slave, she shall not go out as the
male slaves do. 8If she does not please her
master, who has betrothed her to himself,
then he shall let her be redeemed. He
shall have no right to sell her to a foreign
people, since he has dealt deceitfully with
her. 9And if he has betrothed her to his
son, he shall deal with her according to
the custom of daughters. 10If he takes another *wife,* he shall not diminish her food,
her clothing, and her marriage rights.
11And if he does not do these three for
her, then she shall go out free, without
paying money.

The Law Concerning Violence

12“He who strikes a man so that he
dies shall surely be put to death. 13How-
ever, if he did not lie in wait, but God delivered *him* into his hand, then I will appoint for you a place where he may flee.
14“But if a man acts with premedita-
tion against his neighbor, to kill him by
treachery, you shall take him from My altar, that he may die.
15“And he who strikes his father or his
mother shall surely be put to death.
16“He who kidnaps a man and sells
him, or if he is found in his hand, shall
surely be put to death.
17“And he who curses his father or his
mother shall surely be put to death.
18“If men contend with each other, and
one strikes the other with a stone or with
his fist, and he does not die but is confined to *his* bed, 19if he rises again and
walks about outside with his staff, then
he who struck *him* shall be acquitted. He
shall only pay *for* the loss of his time, and
shall provide *for him* to be thoroughly
healed.
20“And if a man beats his male or female servant with a rod, so that he dies
under his hand, he shall surely be punished. 21Notwithstanding, if he remains
alive a day or two, he shall not be punished; for he *is* his property.

> So pure, so just, so uncompromising is the Law of God, that when it is really understood, it makes us quail, and brings us to our knees.
>
> **CHARLES SPURGEON**

22“If men fight, and hurt a woman with
child, so that she gives birth prematurely,
yet no harm follows, he shall surely be
punished accordingly as the woman's husband imposes on him; and he shall pay as
the judges *determine.* 23But if *any* harm
follows, then you shall give life for life,
24eye for eye, tooth for tooth, hand for
hand, foot for foot, 25burn for burn, wound
for wound, stripe for stripe.
26“If a man strikes the eye of his male
or female servant, and destroys it, he shall
let him go free for the sake of his eye.
27And if he knocks out the tooth of his
male or female servant, he shall let him
go free for the sake of his tooth.

21:5,6 The sinner, upon conversion, becomes a servant of Jesus Christ. He presents his body as a living sacrifice, and his ear is forever open to the voice of His Master (John 10:3). See also Deut. 23:15,16 comment.

"The slavery which existed among the ancient Jews was a very different thing from that which has disgraced humanity in modern times... [The slave then] was quite free to leave his master's house and go whither he pleased. But it seems that the servitude was so exceedingly light, and, indeed, was so much for the benefit of the person in it, that frequently he would not go free. They preferred to continue as they were, servants to their masters." *Charles Spurgeon*

21:15,17 The death sentence is given for violation of the Fifth Commandment. See also Lev. 20:9 and Matt. 15:4.

21:22 Notice that the phrase is "a woman with child," not "a woman with a blob of cells." A child's life begins at the moment of conception, and is to be protected. See Psa 127:3 comment.

21:23–25 The world often misinterprets "an eye for an eye" to mean that we can take vengeance on those who wrong us. For the real meaning, see Matt. 5:38 comment.

Animal Control Laws

28“If an ox gores a man or a woman to
death, then the ox shall surely be stoned,
and its flesh shall not be eaten; but the
owner of the ox *shall be* acquitted. 29But if
the ox tended to thrust with its horn in
times past, and it has been made known
to his owner, and he has not kept it confined, so that it has killed a man or a woman, the ox shall be stoned and its owner
also shall be put to death. 30If there is imposed on him a sum of money, then he
shall pay to redeem his life, whatever is
imposed on him. 31Whether it has gored
a son or gored a daughter, according to
this judgment it shall be done to him. 32If
the ox gores a male or female servant, he
shall give to their master thirty shekels of
silver, and the ox shall be stoned.
33“And if a man opens a pit, or if a
man digs a pit and does not cover it, and
an ox or a donkey falls in it, 34the owner
of the pit shall make *it* good; he shall give
money to their owner, but the dead *animal* shall be his.
35“If one man's ox hurts another's, so
that it dies, then they shall sell the live ox
and divide the money from it; and the
dead *ox* they shall also divide. 36Or if it
was known that the ox tended to thrust
in time past, and its owner has not kept
it confined, he shall surely pay ox for ox,
and the dead animal shall be his own.

Responsibility for Property

22 “If a man steals an ox or a sheep,
and slaughters it or sells it, he shall
restore five oxen for an ox and four sheep
for a sheep. 2If the thief is found breaking
in, and he is struck so that he dies, *there
shall be* no guilt for his bloodshed. 3If the
sun has risen on him, *there shall be* guilt
for his bloodshed. He should make full
restitution; if he has nothing, then he
shall be sold for his theft. 4If the theft is
certainly found alive in his hand, whether it is an ox or donkey or sheep, he shall
restore double.
5“If a man causes a field or vineyard to
be grazed, and lets loose his animal, and
it feeds in another man's field, he shall
make restitution from the best of his own
field and the best of his own vineyard.
6“If fire breaks out and catches in thorns,
so that stacked grain, standing grain, or
the field is consumed, he who kindled
the fire shall surely make restitution.
7“If a man delivers to his neighbor
money or articles to keep, and it is stolen
out of the man's house, if the thief is
found, he shall pay double. 8If the thief is
not found, then the master of the house
shall be brought to the judges *to see*
whether he has put his hand into his
neighbor's goods.
9“For any kind of trespass, *whether it
concerns* an ox, a donkey, a sheep, or clothing, *or* for any kind of lost thing which
another claims to be his, the cause of both
parties shall come before the judges; *and*
whomever the judges condemn shall pay
double to his neighbor. 10If a man delivers
to his neighbor a donkey, an ox, a sheep,
or any animal to keep, and it dies, is hurt,
or driven away, no one seeing *it,* 11*then* an
oath of the LORD shall be between them
both, that he has not put his hand into
his neighbor's goods; and the owner of it
shall accept *that,* and he shall not make *it*
good. 12But if, in fact, it is stolen from him,
he shall make restitution to the owner of
it. 13If it is torn to pieces *by a beast, then*
he shall bring it as evidence, *and* he shall
not make good what was torn.
14“And if a man borrows *anything* from
his neighbor, and it becomes injured or
dies, the owner of it not *being* with it, he
shall surely make *it* good. 15If its owner
was with it, he shall not make *it* good; if
it *was* hired, it came for its hire.

Moral and Ceremonial Principles

16“If a man entices a virgin who is not
betrothed, and lies with her, he shall sure-

21:32 Judas considered Jesus' worth to be the same as that of an ox. See Matt. 26:15.

ly pay the bride-price for her *to be* his wife. 17If her father utterly refuses to give her to him, he shall pay money according to the bride-price of virgins.

18“You shall not permit a sorceress to live.

19“Whoever lies with an animal shall surely be put to death.

20“He who sacrifices to *any* god, except to the LORD only, he shall be utterly destroyed.

21“You shall neither mistreat a stranger nor oppress him, for you were strangers in the land of Egypt.

22“You shall not afflict any widow or fatherless child. 23If you afflict them in any way, *and* they cry at all to Me, I will surely hear their cry; 24and My wrath will become hot, and I will kill you with the sword; your wives shall be widows, and your children fatherless.

25“If you lend money to *any of* My people *who are* poor among you, you shall not be like a moneylender to him; you shall not charge him interest. 26If you ever take your neighbor's garment as a pledge, you shall return it to him before the sun goes down. 27For that *is* his only covering, it *is* his garment for his skin. What will he sleep in? And it will be that when he cries to Me, I will hear, for I *am* gracious.

28“You shall not revile God, nor curse a ruler of your people.

29“You shall not delay *to offer* the first of your ripe produce and your juices. The firstborn of your sons you shall give to Me. 30Likewise you shall do with your oxen *and* your sheep. It shall be with its mother seven days; on the eighth day you shall give it to Me.

31“And you shall be holy men to Me: you shall not eat meat torn *by beasts* in the field; you shall throw it to the dogs.

Justice for All

23 “You shall not circulate a false report. Do not put your hand with the wicked to be an unrighteous witness. 2You shall not follow a crowd to do evil; nor shall you testify in a dispute so as to turn aside after many to pervert *justice*. 3You shall not show partiality to a poor man in his dispute.

4“If you meet your enemy's ox or his donkey going astray, you shall surely bring it back to him again. 5If you see the donkey of one who hates you lying under its burden, and you would refrain from helping it, you shall surely help him with it.

6“You shall not pervert the judgment of your poor in his dispute. 7Keep yourself far from a false matter; do not kill the innocent and righteous. For I will not justify the wicked. 8And you shall take no bribe, for a bribe blinds the discerning and perverts the words of the righteous.

9“Also you shall not oppress a stranger, for you know the heart of a stranger, because you were strangers in the land of Egypt.

The Law of Sabbaths

10“Six years you shall sow your land and gather in its produce, 11but the seventh *year* you shall let it rest and lie fallow, that the poor of your people may eat;

23:4,5 Israelites were commanded to love their enemies (see Matt. 5:44).

23:10,11 How modern Jews get around this law. “This year, 5768 by the Jewish calendar, is a *shmita*, or sabbatical year. Jewish-owned land is to be left fallow, whatever grows there is to be free and at year's end, all personal debts are to be forgiven. *Shmita* occurs every seventh year, as a kind of sabbatical for the land, and it is mandated in the Torah. In Exodus 23:10,11, for instance, *shmita* precedes the injunction for individuals to rest on the seventh day...

“That presumably worked fine in a primitive economy before decent fertilizer, but *shmita* presented problems for the new Jewish state. Zionism was founded on the notion of a return to the land, but a modern country cannot live on what falls to the ground. So respected rabbis from both the Ashkenazic and the Sephardic communities compromised. Charged with interpreting religious law, or *halacha*, they devised the ‘heter mechira,’ or sale permit, which allows Jews to temporarily ‘sell’ their land to non-Jews for the *shmita* year, so the land may be cultivated.” *Steven Erlanger* (*New York Times*, Oct. 8, 2007)

and what they leave, the beasts of the field may eat. In like manner you shall do with your vineyard *and* your olive grove. [12]Six days you shall do your work, and on the seventh day you shall rest, that your ox and your donkey may rest, and the son of your female servant and the stranger may be refreshed.

[13]"And in all that I have said to you, be circumspect and make no mention of the name of other gods, nor let it be heard from your mouth.

Three Annual Feasts

[14]"Three times you shall keep a feast to Me in the year: [15]You shall keep the Feast of Unleavened Bread (you shall eat unleavened bread seven days, as I commanded you, at the time appointed in the month of Abib, for in it you came out of Egypt; none shall appear before Me empty); [16]and the Feast of Harvest, the firstfruits of your labors which you have sown in the field; and the Feast of Ingathering at the end of the year, when you have gathered in *the fruit of* your labors from the field.

[17]"Three times in the year all your males shall appear before the Lord GOD.[a]

[18]"You shall not offer the blood of My sacrifice with leavened bread; nor shall the fat of My sacrifice remain until morning. [19]The first of the firstfruits of your land you shall bring into the house of the LORD your God. You shall not boil a young goat in its mother's milk.

The Angel and the Promises

[20]"Behold, I send an Angel before you to keep you in the way and to bring you into the place which I have prepared. [21]Beware of Him and obey His voice; do not provoke Him, for He will not pardon your transgressions; for My name *is* in Him. [22]But if you indeed obey His voice and do all that I speak, then I will be an enemy to your enemies and an adversary to your adversaries. [23]For My Angel will go before you and bring you in to the Amorites and the Hittites and the Perizzites and the Canaanites and the Hivites and the Jebusites; and I will cut them off. [24]You shall not bow down to their gods, nor serve them, nor do according to their works; but you shall utterly overthrow them and completely break down their *sacred* pillars.

[25]"So you shall serve the LORD your God, and He will bless your bread and your water. And I will take sickness away from the midst of you. [26]No one shall suffer miscarriage or be barren in your land; I will fulfill the number of your days.

[27]"I will send My fear before you, I will cause confusion among all the people to whom you come, and will make all your enemies turn *their* backs to you. [28]And I

23:17 [a]Hebrew *YHWH*, usually translated LORD

23:16 Laborers in the harvest. Once someone becomes a genuine convert, he learns he has tremendous evangelistic responsibility. He begins to see derivatives of the word "laborer" throughout Scripture. Jesus spoke of His disciples reaping where they "have not labored" (John 4:37,38) and of others who "labored in the Lord" (Rom. 16:12). We are told that our "labor is not in vain in the Lord" (1 Cor. 15:58). In 1 Thess. 2:9 Paul said, "For you remember, brethren, our labor and toil; for laboring night and day, ... we preached to you the gospel of God."

A "laborer" is one who goes into the harvest fields and suffers the heat of the noonday sun. He is prepared to sweat for the Lord. It is someone who is willing to apply himself to the irksome task of evangelism, of which Jesus said there is a shortage.

There are two major reasons for this shortage of laborers. First, we have neglected Jesus' command to pray for laborers (see Luke 10:2). But if we are not actively involved in evangelism ourselves, we are not going to pray for laborers—our conscience would condemn us. How could we ask God to raise up people to do the job we are refusing to do? So the enemy gets a double victory. Not only do we not labor for the gospel, but we don't even pray for others to become laborers.

The second reason for the lack of laborers is that we fear the reproach of the gospel. We desire the praise of men more than the praise of God, so we busy ourselves in anything but reaching out to the lost.

23:25–27 Look at these incredible promises of blessing for Israel if they served God.

will send hornets before you, which shall drive out the Hivite, the Canaanite, and the Hittite from before you. 29I will not drive them out from before you in one year, lest the land become desolate and the beasts of the field become too numerous for you. 30Little by little I will drive them out from before you, until you have increased, and you inherit the land. 31And I will set your bounds from the Red Sea to the sea, Philistia, and from the desert to the River.[a] For I will deliver the inhabitants of the land into your hand, and you shall drive them out before you. 32You shall make no covenant with them, nor with their gods. 33They shall not dwell in your land, lest they make you sin against Me. For *if* you serve their gods, it will surely be a snare to you."

Israel Affirms the Covenant

24 Now He said to Moses, "Come up to the LORD, you and Aaron, Nadab and Abihu, and seventy of the elders of Israel, and worship from afar. 2And Moses alone shall come near the LORD, but they shall not come near; nor shall the people go up with him."

3So Moses came and told the people all the words of the LORD and all the judgments. And all the people answered with one voice and said, "All the words which the LORD has said we will do." 4And Moses wrote all the words of the LORD. And he rose early in the morning, and built an altar at the foot of the mountain, and twelve pillars according to the twelve tribes of Israel. 5Then he sent young men of the children of Israel, who offered burnt offerings and sacrificed peace offerings of oxen to the LORD. 6And Moses took half the blood and put *it* in basins, and half the blood he sprinkled on the altar. 7Then he took the Book of the Covenant and read in the hearing of the people. And they said, "All that the LORD has said we will do, and be obedient." 8And Moses took the blood, sprinkled *it* on the people, and said, "This is the blood of the covenant which the LORD has made with you according to all these words."

On the Mountain with God

9Then Moses went up, also Aaron, Nadab, and Abihu, and seventy of the elders of Israel, 10and they saw the God of Israel. And *there was* under His feet as it were a paved work of sapphire stone, and it was like the very heavens in *its* clarity. 11But on the nobles of the children of Israel He did not lay His hand. So they saw God, and they ate and drank.

12Then the LORD said to Moses, "Come up to Me on the mountain and be there; and I will give you tablets of stone, and the law and commandments which I have written, that you may teach them."

13So Moses arose with his assistant Joshua, and Moses went up to the mountain of God. 14And he said to the elders, "Wait here for us until we come back to you. Indeed, Aaron and Hur *are* with you. If any man has a difficulty, let him go to them." 15Then Moses went up into the mountain, and a cloud covered the mountain.

16Now the glory of the LORD rested on Mount Sinai, and the cloud covered it six days. And on the seventh day He called to Moses out of the midst of the cloud. 17The sight of the glory of the LORD *was* like a consuming fire on the top of the mountain in the eyes of the children of Israel. 18So Moses went into the midst of the cloud and went up into the mountain. And Moses was on the mountain forty days and forty nights.

Offerings for the Sanctuary

25 Then the LORD spoke to Moses, saying: 2"Speak to the children of Israel, that they bring Me an offering. From everyone who gives it willingly with his heart you shall take My offering. 3And this *is* the offering which you shall take from them: gold, silver, and bronze; 4blue, purple, and scarlet *thread,* fine linen, and goats' *hair;* 5ram skins dyed red, badger skins, and acacia wood; 6oil for the light,

23:31 [a]Hebrew *Nahar,* the Euphrates

25:10,11 *The Ark of the Covenant as a Prophetic Type*

By Dr. David R. Reagan
Not only is the Bible resplendent with prophetic verses, it is also full of prophetic types. "Prophecy in type" is symbolic prophecy. Think of it as prophecy that has come alive, embodied in the life of a person, ceremony or thing.

Everything about the Ark of the Covenant was symbolic of the Messiah. It was made of wood, indicating the Messiah would be a human. It was overlaid with gold, signifying the Messiah would be divine.

The Ark contained three objects: the tablets of stone, a pot of manna, and Aaron's rod that budded. The tablets signified that the Messiah would have the Law of God in His heart. The manna meant the Messiah would be the Bread of Life. The rod with blossoms was a prophecy that the Messiah would arise from the dead.

The lid of the Ark was called the Mercy Seat. Once a year the High Priest sprinkled blood on the Mercy Seat to atone for the sins of Israel. The Mercy Seat pointed to the fact that through the work of the Messiah the mercy of God would cover the Law. The blood foreshadowed the fact that the Messiah would have to shed His own blood to atone for our sins.

Jesus fulfilled every prophetic type of the Ark. He was God in the flesh (John 10:30). He had the Law in His heart (Matt. 5:17). He declared Himself to be the "Bread of Life" (John 6:35). And He shed His blood on the Cross, atoning for our sins and covering the Law with Grace (Rom. 3:21–26).

and spices for the anointing oil and for
the sweet incense; 7onyx stones, and stones
to be set in the ephod and in the breastplate. 8And let them make Me a sanctuary,
that I may dwell among them. 9According
to all that I show you, *that is,* the pattern
of the tabernacle and the pattern of all its
furnishings, just so you shall make *it.*

The Ark of the Testimony

10"And they shall make an ark of acacia wood; two and a half cubits *shall be* its
length, a cubit and a half its width, and a
cubit and a half its height. 11And you shall
overlay it with pure gold, inside and out
you shall overlay it, and shall make on it
a molding of gold all around. 12You shall
cast four rings of gold for it, and put *them*
in its four corners; two rings *shall be* on
one side, and two rings on the other side.
13And you shall make poles *of* acacia wood,
and overlay them with gold. 14You shall
put the poles into the rings on the sides
of the ark, that the ark may be carried by
them. 15The poles shall be in the rings of
the ark; they shall not be taken from it.
16And you shall put into the ark the Testimony which I will give you.
17"You shall make a mercy seat of pure
gold; two and a half cubits *shall be* its
length and a cubit and a half its width.
18And you shall make two cherubim of
gold; of hammered work you shall make
them at the two ends of the mercy seat.
19Make one cherub at one end, and the
other cherub at the other end; you shall
make the cherubim at the two ends of it
of one piece with the mercy seat. 20And the
cherubim shall stretch out *their* wings
above, covering the mercy seat with their
wings, and they shall face one another;
the faces of the cherubim *shall be* toward
the mercy seat. 21You shall put the mercy
seat on top of the ark, and in the ark you
shall put the Testimony that I will give
you. 22And there I will meet with you,
and I will speak with you from above the
mercy seat, from between the two cherubim which *are* on the ark of the Testimony, about everything which I will give
you in commandment to the children of
Israel.

25:2 Then, as now, God loves a cheerful giver, and each is to give "as he purposes in his heart" (2 Cor. 9:7). "This offering was to be given willingly, and with the heart. It was not prescribed to them what or how much they must give, but it was left to their generosity, that they might show their good-will to the house of God, and the offices thereof." *John Wesley*

The Table for the Showbread

23“You shall also make a table of acacia wood; two cubits *shall be* its length, a cubit its width, and a cubit and a half its height. 24And you shall overlay it with pure gold, and make a molding of gold all around. 25You shall make for it a frame of a handbreadth all around, and you shall make a gold molding for the frame all around. 26And you shall make for it four rings of gold, and put the rings on the four corners that *are* at its four legs. 27The rings shall be close to the frame, as holders for the poles to bear the table. 28And you shall make the poles of acacia wood, and overlay them with gold, that the table may be carried with them. 29You shall make its dishes, its pans, its pitchers, and its bowls for pouring. You shall make them of pure gold. 30And you shall set the showbread on the table before Me always.

. . . . . .

Will the Ten Commandments be God's standard of judgment? See Ezek. 44:24 comment.

. . . . . .

The Gold Lampstand

31“You shall also make a lampstand of pure gold; the lampstand shall be of hammered work. Its shaft, its branches, its bowls, its *ornamental* knobs, and flowers shall be *of one piece.* 32And six branches shall come out of its sides: three branches of the lampstand out of one side, and three branches of the lampstand out of the other side. 33Three bowls *shall be* made like almond *blossoms* on one branch, *with* an *ornamental* knob and a flower, and three bowls made like almond *blossoms* on the other branch, *with* an *ornamental* knob and a flower—and so for the six branches that come out of the lampstand. 34On the lampstand itself four bowls *shall be* made like almond *blossoms, each with* its *ornamental* knob and flower. 35And *there shall be* a knob under the *first* two branches of the same, a knob under the *second* two branches of the same, and a knob under the *third* two branches of the same, according to the six branches that extend from the lampstand. 36Their knobs and their branches *shall be of one piece;* all of it *shall be* one hammered piece of pure gold. 37You shall make seven lamps for it, and they shall arrange its lamps so that they give light in front of it. 38And its wick-trimmers and their trays *shall be* of pure gold. 39It shall be made of a talent of pure gold, with all these utensils. 40And see to it that you make *them* according to the pattern which was shown you on the mountain.

The Tabernacle

26 “Moreover you shall make the tabernacle *with* ten curtains *of* fine woven linen and blue, purple, and scarlet *thread;* with artistic designs of cherubim you shall weave them. 2The length of each curtain *shall be* twenty-eight cubits, and the width of each curtain four cubits. And every one of the curtains shall have the same measurements. 3Five curtains shall be coupled to one another, and *the other* five curtains *shall be* coupled to one another. 4And you shall make loops of blue *yarn* on the edge of the curtain on the selvedge of *one* set, and likewise you shall do on the outer edge of *the other* curtain of the second set. 5Fifty loops you shall make in the one curtain, and fifty loops you shall make on the edge of the curtain that *is* on the end of the second set, that the loops may be clasped to one another. 6And you shall make fifty clasps of gold, and couple the curtains together with the clasps, so that it may be one tabernacle.

7“You shall also make curtains of goats' *hair,* to be a tent over the tabernacle. You shall make eleven curtains. 8The length of each curtain *shall be* thirty cubits, and the width of each curtain four cubits; and the eleven curtains shall all have the same measurements. 9And you shall couple five curtains by themselves and six curtains by themselves, and you shall double

over the sixth curtain at the forefront of
the tent. [10]You shall make fifty loops on
the edge of the curtain that is outermost
in *one* set, and fifty loops on the edge of
the curtain of the second set. [11]And you
shall make fifty bronze clasps, put the
clasps into the loops, and couple the tent
together, that it may be one. [12]The remnant that remains of the curtains of the
tent, the half curtain that remains, shall
hang over the back of the tabernacle.
[13]And a cubit on one side and a cubit on
the other side, of what remains of the
length of the curtains of the tent, shall
hang over the sides of the tabernacle, on
this side and on that side, to cover it.

[14]"You shall also make a covering of
ram skins dyed red for the tent, and a
covering of badger skins above that.

[15]"And for the tabernacle you shall
make the boards of acacia wood, standing
upright. [16]Ten cubits *shall be* the length of
a board, and a cubit and a half *shall be* the
width of each board. [17]Two tenons *shall
be* in each board for binding one to another. Thus you shall make for all the
boards of the tabernacle. [18]And you shall
make the boards for the tabernacle,
twenty boards for the south side. [19]You
shall make forty sockets of silver under
the twenty boards: two sockets under
each of the boards for its two tenons.
[20]And for the second side of the tabernacle, the north side, *there shall be* twenty
boards [21]and their forty sockets of silver:
two sockets under each of the boards.
[22]For the far side of the tabernacle, westward, you shall make six boards. [23]And
you shall also make two boards for the two
back corners of the tabernacle. [24]They
shall be coupled together at the bottom
and they shall be coupled together at the
top by one ring. Thus it shall be for both
of them. They shall be for the two corners. [25]So there shall be eight boards with
their sockets of silver—sixteen sockets—
two sockets under each of the boards.

[26]"And you shall make bars of acacia
wood: five for the boards on one side of
the tabernacle, [27]five bars for the boards
on the other side of the tabernacle, and
five bars for the boards of the side of the
tabernacle, for the far side westward.
[28]The middle bar shall pass through the
midst of the boards from end to end.
[29]You shall overlay the boards with gold,
make their rings of gold *as* holders for the
bars, and overlay the bars with gold. [30]And
you shall raise up the tabernacle according to its pattern which you were shown
on the mountain.

[31]"You shall make a veil woven of
blue, purple, and scarlet *thread,* and fine
woven linen. It shall be woven with an
artistic design of cherubim. [32]You shall
hang it upon the four pillars of acacia *wood*
overlaid with gold. Their hooks *shall be*
gold, upon four sockets of silver. [33]And
you shall hang the veil from the clasps.
Then you shall bring the ark of the Testimony in there, behind the veil. The veil
shall be a divider for you between the
holy *place* and the Most Holy. [34]You shall
put the mercy seat upon the ark of the
Testimony in the Most Holy. [35]You shall
set the table outside the veil, and the
lampstand across from the table on the
side of the tabernacle toward the south;
and you shall put the table on the north
side.

[36]"You shall make a screen for the door
of the tabernacle, *woven of* blue, purple,

26:10 Notice how God expects Israel to be careful with details when building the tabernacle. How much more should we be careful as we help to build the Church, the temple of the living God (2 Cor. 6:16)? The modern Church prides itself in being free from the traditions that held the blind Pharisees, yet the average altar call is soaked in manmade traditions: "with every eye closed, while the music is playing, while counselors are coming, no one is watching you ... won't you come and invite Jesus into your heart?" Such traditions are not based in Holy Scripture, are filling our churches with false converts, and are creating those we erroneously call "backsliders." In reaching the lost, it is essential that we follow the pattern given in Scripture. For details, see Luke 11:52 comment.

and scarlet *thread,* and fine woven linen,
made by a weaver. 37And you shall make
for the screen five pillars of acacia *wood,*
and overlay them with gold; their hooks
shall be gold, and you shall cast five sockets of bronze for them.

The Altar of Burnt Offering

27 "You shall make an altar of acacia
wood, five cubits long and five
cubits wide—the altar shall be square—
and its height *shall be* three cubits. 2You
shall make its horns on its four corners;
its horns shall be of one piece with it.
And you shall overlay it with bronze. 3Also
you shall make its pans to receive its
ashes, and its shovels and its basins and
its forks and its firepans; you shall make
all its utensils of bronze. 4You shall make
a grate for it, a network of bronze; and on
the network you shall make four bronze
rings at its four corners. 5You shall put it
under the rim of the altar beneath, that
the network may be midway up the altar.
6And you shall make poles for the altar,
poles of acacia wood, and overlay them
with bronze. 7The poles shall be put in
the rings, and the poles shall be on the
two sides of the altar to bear it. 8You shall
make it hollow with boards; as it was
shown you on the mountain, so shall they
make *it.*

The Court of the Tabernacle

9"You shall also make the court of the
tabernacle. For the south side *there shall
be* hangings for the court *made of* fine woven linen, one hundred cubits long for
one side. 10And its twenty pillars and their
twenty sockets *shall be* bronze. The hooks
of the pillars and their bands *shall be* silver. 11Likewise along the length of the
north side *there shall be* hangings one
hundred *cubits* long, with its twenty pillars and their twenty sockets of bronze,
and the hooks of the pillars and their
bands of silver.

12"And along the width of the court on
the west side *shall be* hangings of fifty cubits, with their ten pillars and their ten
sockets. 13The width of the court on the
east side *shall be* fifty cubits. 14The hangings on *one* side *of the gate shall be* fifteen
cubits, *with* their three pillars and their
three sockets. 15And on the other side
shall be hangings of fifteen *cubits, with*
their three pillars and their three sockets.

> I have but one passion: It is He, it is He alone. The world is the field and the field is the world; and henceforth that country shall be my home where I can be most used in winning souls for Christ.
>
> **COUNT NICOLAUS ZINZENDORF**

16"For the gate of the court *there shall
be* a screen twenty cubits long, *woven of*
blue, purple, and scarlet *thread,* and fine
woven linen, made by a weaver. It *shall
have* four pillars and four sockets. 17All
the pillars around the court shall have
bands of silver; their hooks *shall be* of silver and their sockets of bronze. 18The
length of the court *shall be* one hundred
cubits, the width fifty throughout, and
the height five cubits, *made of* fine woven
linen, and its sockets of bronze. 19All the
utensils of the tabernacle for all its service, all its pegs, and all the pegs of the
court, *shall be* of bronze.

The Care of the Lampstand

20"And you shall command the children
of Israel that they bring you pure oil of
pressed olives for the light, to cause the
lamp to burn continually. 21In the tabernacle of meeting, outside the veil which *is*
before the Testimony, Aaron and his sons
shall tend it from evening until morning
before the LORD. *It shall be* a statute forever to their generations on behalf of the
children of Israel.

27:21 The tabernacle is often called the tabernacle of witness (see Num. 17:7,8; Acts 7:44). The Church is the tabernacle of witness in the wilderness of this world.

Garments for the Priesthood

28 "Now take Aaron your brother, and his sons with him, from among the children of Israel, that he may minister to Me as priest, Aaron *and* Aaron's sons: Nadab, Abihu, Eleazar, and Ithamar. [2]And you shall make holy garments for Aaron your brother, for glory and for beauty. [3]So you shall speak to all *who are* gifted artisans, whom I have filled with the spirit of wisdom, that they may make Aaron's garments, to consecrate him, that he may minister to Me as priest. [4]And these *are* the garments which they shall make: a breastplate, an ephod,[a] a robe, a skillfully woven tunic, a turban, and a sash. So they shall make holy garments for Aaron your brother and his sons, that he may minister to Me as priest.

The Ephod

[5]"They shall take the gold, blue, purple, and scarlet *thread,* and the fine linen, [6]and they shall make the ephod of gold, blue, purple, *and* scarlet *thread,* and fine woven linen, artistically worked. [7]It shall have two shoulder straps joined at its two edges, and *so* it shall be joined together. [8]And the intricately woven band of the ephod, which *is* on it, shall be of the same workmanship, *made of* gold, blue, purple, and scarlet *thread,* and fine woven linen.

[9]"Then you shall take two onyx stones and engrave on them the names of the sons of Israel: [10]six of their names on one stone and six names on the other stone, in order of their birth. [11]With the work of an engraver in stone, *like* the engravings of a signet, you shall engrave the two stones with the names of the sons of Israel. You shall set them in settings of gold. [12]And you shall put the two stones on the shoulders of the ephod *as* memorial stones for the sons of Israel. So Aaron shall bear their names before the LORD on his two shoulders as a memorial. [13]You shall also make settings of gold, [14]and you shall make two chains of pure gold like braided cords, and fasten the braided chains to the settings.

The Breastplate

[15]"You shall make the breastplate of judgment. Artistically woven according to the workmanship of the ephod you shall make it: of gold, blue, purple, and scarlet *thread,* and fine woven linen, you shall make it. [16]It shall be doubled into a square: a span *shall be* its length, and a span *shall be* its width. [17]And you shall put settings of stones in it, four rows of stones: *The first* row *shall be* a sardius, a topaz, and an emerald; *this shall be* the first row; [18]the second row *shall be* a turquoise, a sapphire, and a diamond; [19]the third row, a jacinth, an agate, and an amethyst; [20]and the fourth row, a beryl, an onyx, and a jasper. They shall be set in gold settings. [21]And the stones shall have the names of the sons of Israel, twelve according to their names, *like* the engravings of a signet, each one with its own name; they shall be according to the twelve tribes.

[22]"You shall make chains for the breastplate at the end, like braided cords of pure gold. [23]And you shall make two rings of gold for the breastplate, and put the two rings on the two ends of the breastplate. [24]Then you shall put the two braided *chains* of gold in the two rings which are on the ends of the breastplate; [25]and the *other* two ends of the two braided *chains* you shall fasten to the two settings, and put them on the shoulder straps of the ephod in the front.

[26]"You shall make two rings of gold, and put them on the two ends of the breastplate, on the edge of it, which is on the inner side of the ephod. [27]And two *other* rings of gold you shall make, and put them on the two shoulder straps, underneath the ephod toward its front, right at the seam above the intricately woven band of the ephod. [28]They shall bind the breastplate by means of its rings to the rings of the ephod, using a blue cord, so that it is above the intricately woven band of the ephod, and so that the breastplate

28:4 [a]That is, an ornamented vest

does not come loose from the ephod.

29"So Aaron shall bear the names of the sons of Israel on the breastplate of judgment over his heart, when he goes into the holy *place,* as a memorial before the LORD continually. 30And you shall put in the breastplate of judgment the Urim and the Thummim,[a] and they shall be over Aaron's heart when he goes in before the LORD. So Aaron shall bear the judgment of the children of Israel over his heart before the LORD continually.

Other Priestly Garments

31"You shall make the robe of the ephod all of blue. 32There shall be an opening for his head in the middle of it; it shall have a woven binding all around its opening, like the opening in a coat of mail, so that it does not tear. 33And upon its hem you shall make pomegranates of blue, purple, and scarlet, all around its hem, and bells of gold between them all around: 34a golden bell and a pomegranate, a golden bell and a pomegranate, upon the hem of the robe all around. 35And it shall be upon Aaron when he ministers, and its sound will be heard when he goes into the holy *place* before the LORD and when he comes out, that he may not die.

36"You shall also make a plate of pure gold and engrave on it, *like* the engraving of a signet:

HOLINESS TO THE LORD.

37And you shall put it on a blue cord, that it may be on the turban; it shall be on the front of the turban. 38So it shall be on Aaron's forehead, that Aaron may bear the iniquity of the holy things which the children of Israel hallow in all their holy gifts; and it shall always be on his forehead, that they may be accepted before the LORD.

39"You shall skillfully weave the tunic of fine linen *thread,* you shall make the turban of fine linen, and you shall make the sash of woven work.

40"For Aaron's sons you shall make tunics, and you shall make sashes for them. And you shall make hats for them, for glory and beauty. 41So you shall put them on Aaron your brother and on his sons with him. You shall anoint them, consecrate them, and sanctify them, that they may minister to Me as priests. 42And you shall make for them linen trousers to cover their nakedness; they shall reach from the waist to the thighs. 43They shall be on Aaron and on his sons when they come into the tabernacle of meeting, or when they come near the altar to minister in the holy *place,* that they do not incur iniquity and die. *It shall be* a statute forever to him and his descendants after him.

Aaron and His Sons Consecrated

29 "And this is what you shall do to them to hallow them for ministering to Me as priests: Take one young bull and two rams without blemish, 2and unleavened bread, unleavened cakes mixed with oil, and unleavened wafers anointed with oil (you shall make them of wheat flour). 3You shall put them in one basket and bring them in the basket, with the bull and the two rams.

4"And Aaron and his sons you shall bring to the door of the tabernacle of meeting, and you shall wash them with water. 5Then you shall take the garments, put the tunic on Aaron, and the robe of the ephod, the ephod, and the breastplate, and gird him with the intricately woven band of the ephod. 6You shall put the turban on his head, and put the holy crown on the turban. 7And you shall take the anointing oil, pour *it* on his head, and anoint him. 8Then you shall bring his sons

28:30 [a]Literally *the Lights and the Perfections* (compare Leviticus 8:8)

28:38 Jesus bore our iniquities once and for all, so that we could be acceptable before God (see 1 Pet. 2:24).

and put tunics on them. [9]And you shall
gird them with sashes, Aaron and his sons,
and put the hats on them. The priesthood
shall be theirs for a perpetual statute. So
you shall consecrate Aaron and his sons.
[10]"You shall also have the bull brought
before the tabernacle of meeting, and Aaron
and his sons shall put their hands on the
head of the bull. [11]Then you shall kill the
bull before the LORD, *by* the door of the
tabernacle of meeting. [12]You shall take
some of the blood of the bull and put *it* on
the horns of the altar with your finger,
and pour all the blood beside the base of
the altar. [13]And you shall take all the fat
that covers the entrails, the fatty lobe *attached* to the liver, and the two kidneys
and the fat that *is* on them, and burn
them on the altar. [14]But the flesh of the
bull, with its skin and its offal, you shall
burn with fire outside the camp. It *is* a sin
offering.
[15]"You shall also take one ram, and
Aaron and his sons shall put their hands
on the head of the ram; [16]and you shall
kill the ram, and you shall take its blood
and sprinkle *it* all around on the altar.
[17]Then you shall cut the ram in pieces,
wash its entrails and its legs, and put *them*
with its pieces and with its head. [18]And
you shall burn the whole ram on the altar. It *is* a burnt offering to the LORD; it *is*
a sweet aroma, an offering made by fire to
the LORD.
[19]"You shall also take the other ram,
and Aaron and his sons shall put their
hands on the head of the ram. [20]Then you
shall kill the ram, and take some of its
blood and put *it* on the tip of the right ear
of Aaron and on the tip of the right ear of
his sons, on the thumb of their right hand
and on the big toe of their right foot, and
sprinkle the blood all around on the altar.
[21]And you shall take some of the blood
that is on the altar, and some of the anointing oil, and sprinkle *it* on Aaron and on
his garments, on his sons and on the gar-

"Prayer is the language of the poor. The self-sufficient don't need to pray. The self-satisfied don't want to pray. The self-righteous can't pray. The only ones who can pray are those who realize that we need a power outside of ourselves."

Leonard Ravenhill

ments of his sons with him; and he and
his garments shall be hallowed, and his
sons and his sons' garments with him.
[22]"Also you shall take the fat of the
ram, the fat tail, the fat that covers the entrails, the fatty lobe *attached to* the liver,
the two kidneys and the fat on them, the
right thigh (for it *is* a ram of consecration), [23]one loaf of bread, one cake *made
with* oil, and one wafer from the basket of
the unleavened bread that *is* before the
LORD; [24]and you shall put all these in the
hands of Aaron and in the hands of his
sons, and you shall wave them *as* a wave
offering before the LORD. [25]You shall receive them back from their hands and
burn *them* on the altar as a burnt offering,
as a sweet aroma before the LORD. It *is* an
offering made by fire to the LORD.
[26]"Then you shall take the breast of
the ram of Aaron's consecration and wave
it *as* a wave offering before the LORD; and
it shall be your portion. [27]And from the

29:20 See Lev. 8:23 comment.

ram of the consecration you shall consecrate the breast of the wave offering which is waved, and the thigh of the heave offering which is raised, of *that* which is for Aaron and of *that* which is for his sons. [28]It shall be from the children of Israel *for* Aaron and his sons by a statute forever. For it is a heave offering; it shall be a heave offering from the children of Israel from the sacrifices of their peace offerings, *that is,* their heave offering to the LORD.

[29]"And the holy garments of Aaron shall be his sons' after him, to be anointed in them and to be consecrated in them. [30]That son who becomes priest in his place shall put them on for seven days, when he enters the tabernacle of meeting to minister in the holy *place.*

[31]"And you shall take the ram of the consecration and boil its flesh in the holy place. [32]Then Aaron and his sons shall eat the flesh of the ram, and the bread that *is* in the basket, *by* the door of the tabernacle of meeting. [33]They shall eat those things with which the atonement was made, to consecrate *and* to sanctify them; but an outsider shall not eat *them,* because they *are* holy. [34]And if any of the flesh of the consecration offerings, or of the bread, remains until the morning, then you shall burn the remainder with fire. It shall not be eaten, because it *is* holy.

[35]"Thus you shall do to Aaron and his sons, according to all that I have commanded you. Seven days you shall consecrate them. [36]And you shall offer a bull every day *as* a sin offering for atonement. You shall cleanse the altar when you make atonement for it, and you shall anoint it to sanctify it. [37]Seven days you shall make atonement for the altar and sanctify it. And the altar shall be most holy. Whatever touches the altar must be holy.[a]

The Daily Offerings

[38]"Now this *is* what you shall offer on the altar: two lambs of the first year, day by day continually. [39]One lamb you shall offer in the morning, and the other lamb you shall offer at twilight. [40]With the one lamb shall be one-tenth *of an ephah* of flour mixed with one-fourth of a hin of pressed oil, and one-fourth of a hin of wine *as* a drink offering. [41]And the other lamb you shall offer at twilight; and you shall offer with it the grain offering and the drink offering, as in the morning, for a sweet aroma, an offering made by fire to the LORD. [42]*This shall be* a continual burnt offering throughout your generations *at* the door of the tabernacle of meeting before the LORD, where I will meet you to speak with you. [43]And there I will meet with the children of Israel, and *the tabernacle* shall be sanctified by My glory. [44]So I will consecrate the tabernacle of meeting and the altar. I will also consecrate both Aaron and his sons to minister to Me as priests. [45]I will dwell among the children of Israel and will be their God. [46]And they shall know that I *am* the LORD their God, who brought them up out of the land of Egypt, that I may dwell among them. I *am* the LORD their God.

The Altar of Incense

30 "You shall make an altar to burn incense on; you shall make it of acacia wood. [2]A cubit *shall be* its length and a cubit its width—it shall be square—and two cubits *shall be* its height. Its horns *shall be* of one piece with it. [3]And you shall overlay its top, its sides all around, and its horns with pure gold; and you shall make for it a molding of gold all around. [4]Two gold rings you shall make for it, under the molding on both its sides. You shall place *them* on its two sides, and they will be holders for the poles with which to bear it. [5]You shall

29:37 [a]Compare Numbers 4:15 and Haggai 2:11–13

29:42 How wonderful that we no longer need to go through such a meticulous process to have fellowship with a holy God. By the one sacrifice of the Lamb of God, we are forever made acceptable to Him (see Heb. 10:11,12).

make the poles of acacia wood, and overlay them with gold. [6]And you shall put it before the veil that *is* before the ark of the Testimony, before the mercy seat that *is* over the Testimony, where I will meet with you.

[7]"Aaron shall burn on it sweet incense every morning; when he tends the lamps, he shall burn incense on it. [8]And when Aaron lights the lamps at twilight, he shall burn incense on it, a perpetual incense before the LORD throughout your generations. [9]You shall not offer strange incense on it, or a burnt offering, or a grain offering; nor shall you pour a drink offering on it. [10]And Aaron shall make atonement upon its horns once a year with the blood of the sin offering of atonement; once a year he shall make atonement upon it throughout your generations. It *is* most holy to the LORD."

· · · · · ·

For how to have a "family altar," see Josh. 4:21,22 comment.

· · · · · ·

The Ransom Money

[11]Then the LORD spoke to Moses, saying: [12]"When you take the census of the children of Israel for their number, then every man shall give a ransom for himself to the LORD, when you number them, that there may be no plague among them when *you* number them. [13]This is what everyone among those who are numbered shall give: half a shekel according to the shekel of the sanctuary (a shekel *is* twenty gerahs). The half-shekel *shall be* an offering to the LORD. [14]Everyone included among those who are numbered, from twenty years old and above, shall give an offering to the LORD. [15]The rich shall not give more and the poor shall not give less than half a shekel, when *you* give an offering to the LORD, to make atonement for yourselves. [16]And you shall take the atonement money of the children of Israel, and shall appoint it for the service of the tabernacle of meeting, that it may be a memorial for the children of Israel before the LORD, to make atonement for yourselves."

The Bronze Laver

[17]Then the LORD spoke to Moses, saying: [18]"You shall also make a laver of bronze, with its base also of bronze, for washing. You shall put it between the tabernacle of meeting and the altar. And you shall put water in it, [19]for Aaron and his sons shall wash their hands and their feet in water from it. [20]When they go into the tabernacle of meeting, or when they come near the altar to minister, to burn an offering made by fire to the LORD, they shall wash with water, lest they die. [21]So they shall wash their hands and their feet, lest they die. And it shall be a statute forever to them—to him and his descendants throughout their generations."

The Holy Anointing Oil

[22]Moreover the LORD spoke to Moses, saying: [23]"Also take for yourself quality spices—five hundred *shekels* of liquid myrrh, half as much sweet-smelling cinnamon (two hundred and fifty *shekels*), two hundred and fifty *shekels* of sweet-smelling cane, [24]five hundred *shekels* of cassia, according to the shekel of the sanctuary, and a hin of olive oil. [25]And you shall make from these a holy anointing oil, an ointment compounded according to the art of the perfumer. It shall be a holy anointing oil. [26]With it you shall anoint the tabernacle of meeting and the ark of the Testimony; [27]the table and all its utensils, the lampstand and its utensils, and the altar of incense; [28]the altar of burnt offering with all its utensils, and the laver and its base. [29]You shall conse-

30:6 Notice that the ark is called the "ark of the Testimony." It contained the Law that testified against us, and we are to take that same testimony to this sinful world. Without it the lost have no knowledge of sin or of the manifold mercies of God. Read Rom. 7:7–13 to see what the Law did for the apostle Paul.

crate them, that they may be most holy; whatever touches them must be holy.[a] [30]And you shall anoint Aaron and his sons, and consecrate them, that *they* may minister to Me as priests.

[31]"And you shall speak to the children of Israel, saying: 'This shall be a holy anointing oil to Me throughout your generations. [32]It shall not be poured on man's flesh; nor shall you make *any other* like it, according to its composition. It *is* holy, *and* it shall be holy to you. [33]Whoever compounds *any* like it, or whoever puts *any* of it on an outsider, shall be cut off from his people.' "

The Incense

[34]And the LORD said to Moses: "Take sweet spices, stacte and onycha and galbanum, and pure frankincense with *these* sweet spices; there shall be equal amounts of each. [35]You shall make of these an incense, a compound according to the art of the perfumer, salted, pure, *and* holy. [36]And you shall beat *some* of it very fine, and put some of it before the Testimony in the tabernacle of meeting where I will meet with you. It shall be most holy to you. [37]But *as for* the incense which you shall make, you shall not make any for yourselves, according to its composition. It shall be to you holy for the LORD. [38]Whoever makes *any* like it, to smell it, he shall be cut off from his people."

Artisans for Building the Tabernacle

31 Then the LORD spoke to Moses, saying: [2]"See, I have called by name Bezalel the son of Uri, the son of Hur, of the tribe of Judah. [3]And I have filled him with the Spirit of God, in wisdom, in understanding, in knowledge, and in all *manner of* workmanship, [4]to design artistic works, to work in gold, in silver, in bronze, [5]in cutting jewels for setting, in carving wood, and to work in all *manner of* workmanship.

[6]"And I, indeed I, have appointed with him Aholiab the son of Ahisamach, of the tribe of Dan; and I have put wisdom in the hearts of all the gifted artisans, that they may make all that I have commanded you: [7]the tabernacle of meeting, the ark of the Testimony and the mercy seat that *is* on it, and all the furniture of the tabernacle—[8]the table and its utensils, the pure *gold* lampstand with all its utensils, the altar of incense, [9]the altar of burnt offering with all its utensils, and the laver and its base—[10]the garments of ministry,[a] the holy garments for Aaron the priest and the garments of his sons, to minister as priests, [11]and the anointing oil and sweet incense for the holy *place*. According to all that I have commanded you they shall do."

The Sabbath Law

[12]And the LORD spoke to Moses, saying, [13]"Speak also to the children of Israel, saying: 'Surely My Sabbaths you shall keep, for it *is* a sign between Me and you throughout your generations, that *you* may know that I *am* the LORD who sanctifies you. [14]You shall keep the Sabbath, therefore, for *it is* holy to you. Everyone who profanes it shall surely be put to death; for whoever does *any* work on it, that person shall be cut off from among his people. [15]Work shall be done for six days, but the seventh *is* the Sabbath of rest, holy to the LORD. Whoever does *any* work on the Sabbath day, he shall surely be put to death. [16]Therefore the children of Israel shall keep the Sabbath, to observe the Sabbath throughout their generations *as* a perpetual covenant. [17]It *is* a sign between Me and the children of Is-

30:29 [a]Compare Numbers 4:15 and Haggai 2:11–13

31:2,3 Plead with God to do the same to you, for the sake of the lost—that you would be a workman who does not need to be ashamed (see 2 Tim. 2:15).

31:14 For freedom from Sabbath-keeping, see Col. 2:16 comment.

rael forever; for *in* six days the LORD made
the heavens and the earth, and on the
seventh day He rested and was refreshed.' "
[18]And when He had made an end of
speaking with him on Mount Sinai, He
gave Moses two tablets of the Testimony,
tablets of stone, written with the finger of
God.

The Gold Calf

32 Now when the people saw that
Moses delayed coming down from
the mountain, the people gathered together to Aaron, and said to him, "Come,
make us gods that shall go before us; for
as for this Moses, the man who brought
us up out of the land of Egypt, we do not
know what has become of him."
[2]And Aaron said to them, "Break off
the golden earrings which *are* in the ears
of your wives, your sons, and your daughters, and bring *them* to me." [3]So all the
people broke off the golden earrings which
were in their ears, and brought *them* to
Aaron. [4]And he received *the gold* from
their hand, and he fashioned it with an
engraving tool, and made a molded calf.
Then they said, "This *is* your god, O
Israel, that brought you out of the land of
Egypt!"
[5]So when Aaron saw *it,* he built an altar before it. And Aaron made a proclamation and said, "Tomorrow *is* a feast to the
LORD." [6]Then they rose early on the next
day, offered burnt offerings, and brought
peace offerings; and the people sat down
to eat and drink, and rose up to play.
[7]And the LORD said to Moses, "Go, get
down! For your people whom you brought
out of the land of Egypt have corrupted
themselves. [8]They have turned aside quickly out of the way which I commanded
them. They have made themselves a molded calf, and worshiped it and sacrificed to
it, and said, 'This *is* your god, O Israel, that
brought you out of the land of Egypt!' "
[9]And the LORD said to Moses, "I have seen
this people, and indeed it *is* a stiff-necked
people! [10]Now therefore, let Me alone,
that My wrath may burn hot against them
and I may consume them. And I will make
of you a great nation."
[11]Then Moses pleaded with the LORD
his God, and said: "LORD, why does Your
wrath burn hot against Your people whom
You have brought out of the land of Egypt
with great power and with a mighty hand?
[12]Why should the Egyptians speak, and

31:10 [a]Or *woven garments*

31:17 Creation in six days. Why would an omnipotent God, who could speak creation into existence, take a whole six days to do so? Some of the early church fathers therefore believed that God created everything in only one day, or in an instant. To counter this teaching, *Martin Luther* wrote: "When Moses writes that God created heaven and earth and whatever is in them in six days, then let this period continue to have been six days, and do not venture to devise any comment according to which six days were one day. But, if you cannot understand how this could have been done in six days, then grant the Holy Spirit the honor of being more learned than you are. For you are to deal with Scripture in such a way that you bear in mind that God Himself says what is written. But since God is speaking, it is not fitting for you to wantonly turn His Word in the direction you wish it to go." See also Gen. 1:5 and Heb. 4:4 comments.

"So far as I know, there is no professor of Hebrew or Old Testament at any world-class university who does not believe that the writer(s) of Genesis 1–11 intended to convey to their readers the idea that (a) creation took place in a series of six days which were the same as the days of 24 hours we now experience; (b) the figures contained in the Genesis genealogies provided by simple addition a chronology from the beginning of the world up to later stages in the biblical story; (c) Noah's Flood was understood to be worldwide and extinguish all human and animal life except for those in the ark." *Dr. James Barr*, professor of Hebrew, Oxford University

31:18 This was God's signature. The moral Law was *personally* handwritten by the Creator of the universe. This is why we must preach the Law to a lawless and hellbound world. This was God's mind and will for humanity. He wrote the work of the Law on the heart of Adam and his descendants, and He wrote the Law in stone with His finger, to confirm that this was His character and unchanging nature. For a comparison of the Ten Commandments and God's character, see page 280.

say, 'He brought them out to harm them, to kill them in the mountains, and to consume them from the face of the earth'? Turn from Your fierce wrath, and relent from this harm to Your people. 13Remember Abraham, Isaac, and Israel, Your servants, to whom You swore by Your own self, and said to them, 'I will multiply your descendants as the stars of heaven; and all this land that I have spoken of I give to your descendants, and they shall inherit *it* forever.' "[a] 14So the LORD relented from the harm which He said He would do to His people.

15And Moses turned and went down from the mountain, and the two tablets of the Testimony *were* in his hand. The tablets *were* written on both sides; on the one *side* and on the other they were written. 16Now the tablets *were* the work of God, and the writing *was* the writing of God engraved on the tablets.

17And when Joshua heard the noise of the people as they shouted, he said to Moses, "*There is* a noise of war in the camp."

18But he said:

"*It is* not the noise of the shout of
victory,
Nor the noise of the cry of defeat,
But the sound of singing I hear."

19So it was, as soon as he came near the camp, that he saw the calf *and* the dancing. So Moses' anger became hot, and he cast the tablets out of his hands and broke them at the foot of the mountain. 20Then he took the calf which they had made, burned *it* in the fire, and ground *it* to powder; and he scattered *it* on the water and made the children of Israel drink *it*. 21And Moses said to Aaron, "What did this people do to you that you have brought *so* great a sin upon them?"

22So Aaron said, "Do not let the anger of my lord become hot. You know the people, that they *are set* on evil. 23For they said to me, 'Make us gods that shall

32:13 [a]Genesis 13:15 and 22:17

32:1 Fear and trembling. The Bible tells us that the fear of the Lord is the beginning of wisdom. We are often admonished to "fear God," and to work out our salvation with "fear and trembling." How do we obtain the commanded virtue of the fear of God?

One great key is to look at Israel. They lost sight of Moses, so they created their own image of god (the golden calf). Suddenly Moses appeared in wrath, threw the Ten Commandments at their feet, and cried, "Who is on the Lord's side?" The people decided whether they wanted to serve sin or God. Those who refused to stand with Moses came under the sword. That undoubtedly produced the fear of the Lord.

We live in an age where many have lost sight of Moses. The moral Law has been removed from the marketplace, from schools, and even from many churches. As a result, America has made her own image of god. Our commission is to cry to the world, "Who is on the Lord's side?" We are to proclaim the gospel of peace. Those who refuse to make peace with God through the blood of the cross will be cut down by the wrath of the Law. That should put the fear of God into any of us.

But there is another key to help us fear God. First Peter says to "conduct yourselves throughout the time of your stay here in fear" (1:17). Why should we do that? The following verse tells us: "knowing that you were not redeemed with corruptible things, like silver or gold,... but with the precious blood of Christ, as of a lamb without blemish and without spot" (1 Pet. 1:18,19). If anything should produce the fear of God in our hearts, it is the cost that God went to so that we could be forgiven. If I deliberately violated civil law and it cost my father every penny he owned to pay my fine, what sort of heartless ingrate would I be to go back to crime? Rather, in light of his incredible sacrifice, I should be humbled and filled with gratitude at such an expression of his love.

God did not pay our fine with mere silver or gold. He redeemed us with the precious blood of Jesus of Nazareth. Golgotha was not only a display of love, but a display of how much God cares about justice. The cross of Calvary was an expression of His just wrath against sin, and if we understand that, we will rightly fear the Lord.

32:6 For those who worship idols, the idols' silence gives them the illusion of permission to sin, to rise up early and embrace the pleasures of sin.

"Whatever we make the most of is our God." *Martin Luther*

go before us; *as for* this Moses, the man who brought us out of the land of Egypt, we do not know what has become of him.’ 24And I said to them, ‘Whoever has any gold, let them break *it* off.’ So they gave *it* to me, and I cast it into the fire, and this calf came out.”

25Now when Moses saw that the people *were* unrestrained (for Aaron had not restrained them, to *their* shame among their enemies), 26then Moses stood in the entrance of the camp, and said, “Whoever *is* on the LORD’s side—*come* to me!” And all the sons of Levi gathered themselves together to him. 27And he said to them, “Thus says the LORD God of Israel: ‘Let every man put his sword on his side, and go in and out from entrance to entrance throughout the camp, and let every man kill his brother, every man his companion, and every man his neighbor.’ ” 28So the sons of Levi did according to the word of Moses. And about three thousand men of the people fell that day. 29Then Moses said, “Consecrate yourselves today to the LORD, that He may bestow on you a blessing this day, for every man has opposed his son and his brother.”

30Now it came to pass on the next day that Moses said to the people, “You have committed a great sin. So now I will go up to the LORD; perhaps I can make atonement for your sin.” 31Then Moses returned to the LORD and said, “Oh, these people have committed a great sin, and have made for themselves a god of gold! 32Yet now, if You will forgive their sin—but if not, I pray, blot me out of Your book which You have written.”

33And the LORD said to Moses, “Whoever has sinned against Me, I will blot him out of My book. 34Now therefore, go, lead the people to *the place* of which I have spoken to you. Behold, My Angel shall go before you. Nevertheless, in the day when I visit for punishment, I will visit punishment upon them for their sin.”

35So the LORD plagued the people because of what they did with the calf which Aaron made.

The Command to Leave Sinai

33 Then the LORD said to Moses, “Depart *and* go up from here, you and the people whom you have brought out of the land of Egypt, to the land of which I swore to Abraham, Isaac, and Jacob, saying, ‘To your descendants I will give it.’ 2And I will send *My* Angel before you, and I will drive out the Canaanite and the Amorite and the Hittite and the Perizzite and the Hivite and the Jebusite. 3*Go up* to a land flowing with milk and honey; for I will not go up in your midst, lest I consume you on the way, for you *are* a stiff-necked people.”

4And when the people heard this bad news, they mourned, and no one put on his ornaments. 5For the LORD had said to Moses, “Say to the children of Israel, ‘You *are* a stiff-necked people. I could come up into your midst in one moment and consume you. Now therefore, take off your ornaments, that I may know what to do to you.’ ” 6So the children of Israel stripped themselves of their ornaments by Mount Horeb.

Moses Meets with the Lord

7Moses took his tent and pitched it outside the camp, far from the camp, and called it the tabernacle of meeting. And it

32:28 Because of their sin, 3,000 died that day. On the day of Pentecost, Peter preached and 3,000 found life (see Acts 2:41). The Law brings death and the gospel brings life.

32:32 “Evangelism is the sob of God. It is the anguished cry of Jesus as He weeps over a doomed city. It is the cry of Paul, ‘I could wish that myself were accursed from Christ for my brethren, my kinsmen according to the flesh.’ Evangelism is the heart-winning plea of Moses. ‘Oh this people have sinned. Yet now, if thou wilt, forgive their sin; if not, blot me, I pray thee, out of the book which thou hast written.’ It is the cry of John Knox, ‘Give me Scotland or I die.’ It is the declaration of John Wesley, ‘The world is my parish.’ It is the sob of parents in the night, weeping over a prodigal child. The key to evangelism is a burden for the lost.” *Jonathan McLeod*

came to pass *that* everyone who sought the LORD went out to the tabernacle of meeting which *was* outside the camp. 8So it was, whenever Moses went out to the tabernacle, *that* all the people rose, and each man stood *at* his tent door and watched Moses until he had gone into the tabernacle. 9And it came to pass, when Moses entered the tabernacle, that the pillar of cloud descended and stood *at* the door of the tabernacle, and *the* LORD talked with Moses. 10All the people saw the pillar of cloud standing *at* the tabernacle door, and all the people rose and worshiped, each man *in* his tent door. 11So the LORD spoke to Moses face to face, as a man speaks to his friend. And he would return to the camp, but his servant Joshua the son of Nun, a young man, did not depart from the tabernacle.

The Promise of God's Presence

12Then Moses said to the LORD, "See, You say to me, 'Bring up this people.' But You have not let me know whom You will send with me. Yet You have said, 'I know you by name, and you have also found grace in My sight.' 13Now therefore, I pray, if I have found grace in Your sight, show me now Your way, that I may know You and that I may find grace in Your sight. And consider that this nation *is* Your people."

14And He said, "My Presence will go *with you,* and I will give you rest."

15Then he said to Him, "If Your Presence does not go *with us,* do not bring us up from here. 16For how then will it be known that Your people and I have found grace in Your sight, except You go with us? So we shall be separate, Your people and I, from all the people who *are* upon the face of the earth."

17So the LORD said to Moses, "I will also do this thing that you have spoken; for you have found grace in My sight, and I know you by name."

18And he said, "Please, show me Your glory."

19Then He said, "I will make all My goodness pass before you, and I will proclaim the name of the LORD before you. I will be gracious to whom I will be gracious, and I will have compassion on whom I will have compassion." 20But He said, "You cannot see My face; for no man shall see Me, and live." 21And the LORD said, "Here is a place by Me, and you shall stand on the rock. 22So it shall be, while My glory passes by, that I will put you in the cleft of the rock, and will cover you with My hand while I pass by. 23Then I will take away My hand, and you shall see My back; but My face shall not be seen."

> If I cannot see Thy face and live, then let me see Thy face and die.
>
> **JOHN WESLEY**

Moses Makes New Tablets

34 And the LORD said to Moses, "Cut two tablets of stone like the first *ones,* and I will write on *these* tablets the words that were on the first tablets which you broke. 2So be ready in the morning, and come up in the morning to Mount Sinai, and present yourself to Me there on the top of the mountain. 3And no man shall come up with you, and let no man be seen throughout all the mountain; let neither flocks nor herds feed before that mountain."

4So he cut two tablets of stone like the first *ones.* Then Moses rose early in the morning and went up Mount Sinai, as the LORD had commanded him; and he took in his hand the two tablets of stone.

5Now the LORD descended in the cloud and stood with him there, and proclaimed the name of the LORD. 6And the LORD passed before him and proclaimed, "The LORD, the LORD God, merciful and gracious, longsuffering, and abounding in goodness and truth, 7keeping mercy for thousands, forgiving iniquity and transgression and sin, by no means clearing *the guilty,* visiting the iniquity of the fathers upon the children and the chil-

dren's children to the third and the fourth generation."

8So Moses made haste and bowed his head toward the earth, and worshiped. 9Then he said, "If now I have found grace in Your sight, O Lord, let my Lord, I pray, go among us, even though we *are* a stiff-necked people; and pardon our iniquity and our sin, and take us as Your inheritance."

The Covenant Renewed

10And He said: "Behold, I make a covenant. Before all your people I will do marvels such as have not been done in all the earth, nor in any nation; and all the people among whom you *are* shall see the work of the LORD. For it *is* an awesome thing that I will do with you. 11Observe what I command you this day. Behold, I am driving out from before you the Amorite and the Canaanite and the Hittite and the Perizzite and the Hivite and the Jebusite. 12Take heed to yourself, lest you make a covenant with the inhabitants of the land where you are going, lest it be a snare in your midst. 13But you shall destroy their altars, break their *sacred* pillars, and cut down their wooden images 14(for you shall worship no other god, for the LORD, whose name *is* Jealous, *is* a jealous God), 15lest you make a covenant with the inhabitants of the land, and they play the harlot with their gods and make sacrifice to their gods, and *one of them* invites you and you eat of his sacrifice, 16and you take of his daughters for your sons, and his daughters play the harlot with their gods and make your sons play the harlot with their gods.

17"You shall make no molded gods for yourselves.

18"The Feast of Unleavened Bread you shall keep. Seven days you shall eat unleavened bread, as I commanded you, in the appointed time of the month of Abib; for in the month of Abib you came out from Egypt.

19"All that open the womb *are* Mine, and every male firstborn among your livestock, *whether* ox or sheep. 20But the firstborn of a donkey you shall redeem with a lamb. And if you will not redeem *him*, then you shall break his neck. All the firstborn of your sons you shall redeem.

"And none shall appear before Me empty-handed.

21"Six days you shall work, but on the seventh day you shall rest; in plowing time and in harvest you shall rest.

22"And you shall observe the Feast of Weeks, of the firstfruits of wheat harvest, and the Feast of Ingathering at the year's end.

23"Three times in the year all your men shall appear before the Lord, the LORD God of Israel. 24For I will cast out the nations before you and enlarge your borders; neither will any man covet your land when you go up to appear before the LORD your God three times in the year.

25"You shall not offer the blood of My sacrifice with leaven, nor shall the sacrifice of the Feast of the Passover be left until morning.

26"The first of the firstfruits of your land you shall bring to the house of the LORD your God. You shall not boil a young goat in its mother's milk."

27Then the LORD said to Moses, "Write these words, for according to the tenor of these words I have made a covenant with you and with Israel." 28So he was there with the LORD forty days and forty nights; he neither ate bread nor drank water.

34:6–9 Those who say that the God of the Old Testament is "vindictive" should also know that the Lord is merciful, gracious, longsuffering, abounding in goodness and truth. He will forgive sin, but those who refuse His mercy offered in the gospel will reap His judgment. He will by no means clear the guilty. Without His intervention through conversion, the sins of the fathers (immorality, drunkenness, physical abuse, divorce, anger, racial prejudice, blasphemy, etc.) are often passed to the next generation.

34:14 The jealousy of God is without sin, as is His wrath. See Ezek. 5:15 comment. See also Deut. 4:24.

THE FUNCTION OF THE LAW

34:29,30 None of us can steadfastly look into the face of the Law. Its light shines rays of Eternal Justice into the very depths of our soul. See Psa. 19:7–11 for some of the functions of the Law.

"When the glory and holiness of Christ, revealed through the preaching of the Gospel, is rightly perceived then the glory of the Law—which is but a feeble and transitory glory—is seen to be not really glorious. It is mere dark clouds in contrast to the light of Christ shining to lead us out of sin, death and hell unto God and eternal life." *Martin Luther*

And He wrote on the tablets the words of
the covenant, the Ten Commandments.[a]

The Shining Face of Moses

29Now it was so, when Moses came
down from Mount Sinai (and the two tablets of the Testimony *were* in Moses' hand
when he came down from the mountain),
that Moses did not know that the skin of
his face shone while he talked with Him.
30So when Aaron and all the children of
Israel saw Moses, behold, the skin of his
face shone, and they were afraid to come
near him. 31Then Moses called to them,
and Aaron and all the rulers of the congregation returned to him; and Moses
talked with them. 32Afterward all the
children of Israel came near, and he gave
them as commandments all that the LORD
had spoken with him on Mount Sinai.
33And when Moses had finished speaking
with them, he put a veil on his face. 34But
whenever Moses went in before the LORD
to speak with Him, he would take the veil
off until he came out; and he would come
out and speak to the children of Israel
whatever he had been commanded. 35And
whenever the children of Israel saw the
face of Moses, that the skin of Moses' face
shone, then Moses would put the veil on
his face again, until he went in to speak
with Him.

Sabbath Regulations

35 Then Moses gathered all the congregation of the children of Israel
together, and said to them, "These *are* the
words which the LORD has commanded
you to do: 2Work shall be done for six
days, but the seventh day shall be a holy
day for you, a Sabbath of rest to the LORD.
Whoever does any work on it shall be put
to death. 3You shall kindle no fire throughout your dwellings on the Sabbath day."

Offerings for the Tabernacle

4And Moses spoke to all the congregation of the children of Israel, saying, "This
is the thing which the LORD commanded,
saying: 5'Take from among you an offering to the LORD. Whoever *is* of a willing
heart, let him bring it as an offering to the
LORD: gold, silver, and bronze; 6blue,
purple, and scarlet *thread*, fine linen, and

34:28 [a]Literally *Ten Words*

35:1–3 Bible contradiction? Skeptics argue that these verses contradict Paul's later statements that the Sabbath commandment was temporary and believers could decide for themselves regarding its observance (Rom. 14:5; Col. 2:14–16).

Scripture makes it clear that no one can be justified (made right with God) by keeping the Sabbath holy, or by keeping any other Commandment. All the Law does is bring the knowledge of sin to show us that we need a Savior. Jesus fulfilled the demands of the Law, which means we can be made right with God through faith in Him alone (see Eph. 2:8,9). Believers now serve in the spirit, not the letter of the law, and the principle behind the Sabbath is this: Just as God created for six days then rested on the seventh, man is to work for six days and rest on the seventh—to cease working. Those who trust in Christ's finished work on the cross have ceased trying to be justified through their own efforts and instead find their rest in Him. (See Heb. 4:3,10.) That is why keeping the Sabbath is a non-issue for Christians when it comes to eternal salvation. It is simply a matter of conscience. Christians have incredible liberty—no one can tell us what we must eat or drink, or what days we must observe. See also Col. 2:16 comment.

"The spiritual rest which God especially intends in this commandment is that we not only cease from our labor and trade but much more—that we let God alone work in us, and that in all our powers we do nothing of our own." *Martin Luther*

goats' *hair;* [7]ram skins dyed red, badger skins, and acacia wood; [8]oil for the light, and spices for the anointing oil and for the sweet incense; [9]onyx stones, and stones to be set in the ephod and in the breastplate.

Articles of the Tabernacle

[10]'All *who are* gifted artisans among you shall come and make all that the LORD has commanded: [11]the tabernacle, its tent, its covering, its clasps, its boards, its bars, its pillars, and its sockets; [12]the ark and its poles, *with* the mercy seat, and the veil of the covering; [13]the table and its poles, all its utensils, and the showbread; [14]also the lampstand for the light, its utensils, its lamps, and the oil for the light; [15]the incense altar, its poles, the anointing oil, the sweet incense, and the screen for the door at the entrance of the tabernacle; [16]the altar of burnt offering with its bronze grating, its poles, all its utensils, *and* the laver and its base; [17]the hangings of the court, its pillars, their sockets, and the screen for the gate of the court; [18]the pegs of the tabernacle, the pegs of the court, and their cords; [19]the garments of ministry,[a] for ministering in the holy *place*—the holy garments for Aaron the priest and the garments of his sons, to minister as priests.' "

The Tabernacle Offerings Presented

[20]And all the congregation of the children of Israel departed from the presence of Moses. [21]Then everyone came whose heart was stirred, and everyone whose spirit was willing, *and* they brought the LORD's offering for the work of the tabernacle of meeting, for all its service, and for the holy garments. [22]They came, both men and women, as many as had a willing heart, *and* brought earrings and nose rings, rings and necklaces, all jewelry of gold, that is, every man who *made* an offering of gold to the LORD. [23]And every man, with whom was found blue, purple, and scarlet *thread*, fine linen, goats' *hair,* red skins of rams, and badger skins, brought *them.* [24]Everyone who offered an offering of silver or bronze brought the LORD's offering. And everyone with whom was found acacia wood for any work of the service, brought *it.* [25]All the women *who were* gifted artisans spun yarn with their hands, and brought what they had spun, of blue, purple, *and* scarlet, and fine linen. [26]And all the women whose hearts stirred with wisdom spun yarn of goats' *hair.* [27]The rulers brought onyx stones, and the stones to be set in the ephod and in the breastplate, [28]and spices and oil for the light, for the anointing oil, and for the sweet incense. [29]The children of Israel brought a freewill offering to the LORD, all the men and women whose hearts were willing to bring *material* for all kinds of work which the LORD, by the hand of Moses, had commanded to be done.

The Artisans Called by God

[30]And Moses said to the children of Israel, "See, the LORD has called by name Bezalel the son of Uri, the son of Hur, of the tribe of Judah; [31]and He has filled him with the Spirit of God, in wisdom and understanding, in knowledge and all manner of workmanship, [32]to design artistic works, to work in gold and silver and bronze, [33]in cutting jewels for setting, in carving wood, and to work in all manner of artistic workmanship.

[34]"And He has put in his heart the ability to teach, *in* him and Aholiab the son of Ahisamach, of the tribe of Dan. [35]He has filled them with skill to do all manner of work of the engraver and the designer and the tapestry maker, in blue, purple, and scarlet *thread,* and fine linen,

35:19 [a]Or *woven garments*

35:30–34 If God has blessed you with wisdom and understanding, teach others. See 2 Tim. 2:2 for God's admonition to you.

and of the weaver—those who do every
work and those who design artistic works.

36 "And Bezalel and Aholiab, and
every gifted artisan in whom the
LORD has put wisdom and understanding, to know how to do all manner of
work for the service of the sanctuary,
shall do according to all that the LORD has
commanded."

The People Give More than Enough

2Then Moses called Bezalel and Aholiab, and every gifted artisan in whose
heart the LORD had put wisdom, everyone whose heart was stirred, to come and
do the work. 3And they received from
Moses all the offering which the children
of Israel had brought for the work of the
service of making the sanctuary. So they
continued bringing to him freewill offerings every morning. 4Then all the craftsmen who were doing all the work of the
sanctuary came, each from the work he
was doing, 5and they spoke to Moses, saying, "The people bring much more than
enough for the service of the work which
the LORD commanded *us* to do."

6So Moses gave a commandment, and
they caused it to be proclaimed throughout the camp, saying, "Let neither man
nor woman do any more work for the offering of the sanctuary." And the people
were restrained from bringing, 7for the
material they had was sufficient for all the
work to be done—indeed too much.

Building the Tabernacle

8Then all the gifted artisans among
them who worked on the tabernacle made
ten curtains woven of fine linen, and of
blue, purple, and scarlet *thread; with* artistic designs of cherubim they made them.
9The length of each curtain *was* twenty-
eight cubits, and the width of each curtain four cubits; the curtains *were* all the
same size. 10And he coupled five curtains
to one another, and *the other* five curtains
he coupled to one another. 11He made
loops of blue *yarn* on the edge of the curtain on the selvedge of one set; likewise
he did on the outer edge of *the other* curtain of the second set. 12Fifty loops he made
on one curtain, and fifty loops he made
on the edge of the curtain on the end of
the second set; the loops held one *curtain*
to another. 13And he made fifty clasps of
gold, and coupled the curtains to one another with the clasps, that it might be one
tabernacle.

14He made curtains of goats' *hair* for the
tent over the tabernacle; he made eleven
curtains. 15The length of each curtain *was*
thirty cubits, and the width of each curtain four cubits; the eleven curtains *were*
the same size. 16He coupled five curtains
by themselves and six curtains by themselves. 17And he made fifty loops on the
edge of the curtain that is outermost in
one set, and fifty loops he made on the
edge of the curtain of the second set. 18He
also made fifty bronze clasps to couple
the tent together, that it might be one.
19Then he made a covering for the tent of
ram skins dyed red, and a covering of
badger skins above *that*.

20For the tabernacle he made boards
of acacia wood, standing upright. 21The
length of each board *was* ten cubits, and
the width of each board a cubit and a
half. 22Each board had two tenons for
binding one to another. Thus he made for
all the boards of the tabernacle. 23And he
made boards for the tabernacle, twenty
boards for the south side. 24Forty sockets
of silver he made to go under the twenty
boards: two sockets under each of the
boards for its two tenons. 25And for the
other side of the tabernacle, the north
side, he made twenty boards 26and their

36:8 Those who were gifted built the tabernacle in the wilderness with the ten curtains of God's Commandments. We must use our gifts to build the Church using the ten curtains of the Law, as a tutor to bring sinners to Christ (see Gal. 3:24). The demands of a holy Law bring us to the foot of the cross and keep us there, trusting only in the grace of God.

forty sockets of silver: two sockets under each of the boards. [27]For the west side of the tabernacle he made six boards. [28]He also made two boards for the two back corners of the tabernacle. [29]And they were coupled at the bottom and coupled together at the top by one ring. Thus he made both of them for the two corners. [30]So there were eight boards and their sockets—sixteen sockets of silver—two sockets under each of the boards.

[31]And he made bars of acacia wood: five for the boards on one side of the tabernacle, [32]five bars for the boards on the other side of the tabernacle, and five bars for the boards of the tabernacle on the far side westward. [33]And he made the middle bar to pass through the boards from one end to the other. [34]He overlaid the boards with gold, made their rings of gold *to be* holders for the bars, and overlaid the bars with gold.

[35]And he made a veil of blue, purple, and scarlet *thread,* and fine woven linen; it was worked *with* an artistic design of cherubim. [36]He made for it four pillars of acacia *wood,* and overlaid them with gold, with their hooks of gold; and he cast four sockets of silver for them.

[37]He also made a screen for the tabernacle door, of blue, purple, and scarlet *thread,* and fine woven linen, made by a weaver, [38]and its five pillars with their hooks. And he overlaid their capitals and their rings with gold, but their five sockets *were* bronze.

Making the Ark of the Testimony

37 Then Bezalel made the ark of acacia wood; two and a half cubits *was* its length, a cubit and a half its width, and a cubit and a half its height. [2]He overlaid it with pure gold inside and outside, and made a molding of gold all around it. [3]And he cast for it four rings of gold *to be set* in its four corners: two rings on one side, and two rings on the other side of it. [4]He made poles of acacia wood, and overlaid them with gold. [5]And he put the poles into the rings at the sides of the ark, to bear the ark. [6]He also made the mercy seat of pure gold; two and a half cubits *was* its length and a cubit and a half its width. [7]He made two cherubim of beaten gold; he made them of one piece at the two ends of the mercy seat: [8]one cherub at one end on this side, and the other cherub at the *other* end on that side. He made the cherubim at the two ends *of one piece* with the mercy seat. [9]The cherubim spread out *their* wings above, *and* covered the mercy seat with their wings. They faced one another; the faces of the cherubim were toward the mercy seat.

Making the Table for the Showbread

[10]He made the table of acacia wood; two cubits *was* its length, a cubit its width, and a cubit and a half its height. [11]And he overlaid it with pure gold, and made a molding of gold all around it. [12]Also he made a frame of a handbreadth all around it, and made a molding of gold for the frame all around it. [13]And he cast for it four rings of gold, and put the rings on the four corners that *were* at its four legs. [14]The rings were close to the frame, as holders for the poles to bear the table. [15]And he made the poles of acacia wood to bear the table, and overlaid them with gold. [16]He made of pure gold the utensils which were on the table: its dishes, its cups, its bowls, and its pitchers for pouring.

Making the Gold Lampstand

[17]He also made the lampstand of pure gold; of hammered work he made the lampstand. Its shaft, its branches, its bowls, its *ornamental* knobs, and its flowers were of the same piece. [18]And six branches came out of its sides: three branches of the lampstand out of one side, and three branches

37:1–5 Bezalel had the privilege of creating the ark of God. His name means "in the shadow (protection) of God." The Law drives us to the shadow of the cross, where we find God-given protection from the wrath of a holy Creator.

of the lampstand out of the other side. 19There were three bowls made like almond *blossoms* on one branch, with an *ornamental* knob and a flower, and three bowls made like almond *blossoms* on the other branch, with an *ornamental* knob and a flower—and so for the six branches coming out of the lampstand. 20And on the lampstand itself *were* four bowls made like almond *blossoms, each with* its *ornamental* knob and flower. 21*There was* a knob under the *first* two branches of the same, a knob under the *second* two branches of the same, and a knob under the *third* two branches of the same, according to the six branches extending from it. 22Their knobs and their branches were of one piece; all of it *was* one hammered piece of pure gold. 23And he made its seven lamps, its wick-trimmers, and its trays of pure gold. 24Of a talent of pure gold he made it, with all its utensils.

Making the Altar of Incense

25He made the incense altar of acacia wood. Its length *was* a cubit and its width a cubit—*it was* square—and two cubits *was* its height. Its horns were *of one piece* with it. 26And he overlaid it with pure gold: its top, its sides all around, and its horns. He also made for it a molding of gold all around it. 27He made two rings of gold for it under its molding, by its two corners on both sides, as holders for the poles with which to bear it. 28And he made the poles of acacia wood, and overlaid them with gold.

Making the Anointing Oil and the Incense

29He also made the holy anointing oil and the pure incense of sweet spices, according to the work of the perfumer.

Making the Altar of Burnt Offering

38 He made the altar of burnt offering of acacia wood; five cubits *was* its length and five cubits its width—*it was* square—and its height *was* three cubits. 2He made its horns on its four corners; the horns were *of one piece* with it. And he overlaid it with bronze. 3He made all the utensils for the altar: the pans, the shovels, the basins, the forks, and the firepans; all its utensils he made of bronze. 4And he made a grate of bronze network for the altar, under its rim, midway from the bottom. 5He cast four rings for the four corners of the bronze grating, *as* holders for the poles. 6And he made the poles of acacia wood, and overlaid them with bronze. 7Then he put the poles into the rings on the sides of the altar, with which to bear it. He made the altar hollow with boards.

Making the Bronze Laver

8He made the laver of bronze and its base of bronze, from the bronze mirrors of the serving women who assembled at the door of the tabernacle of meeting.

Making the Court of the Tabernacle

9Then he made the court on the south side; the hangings of the court *were of* fine woven linen, one hundred cubits long. 10There *were* twenty pillars for them, with twenty bronze sockets. The hooks of the pillars and their bands *were* silver. 11On the north side *the hangings were* one hundred cubits *long*, with twenty pillars and their twenty bronze sockets. The hooks of the pillars and their bands *were* silver. 12And on the west side *there were* hangings of fifty cubits, with ten pillars and their ten sockets. The hooks of the pillars and their bands *were* silver. 13For the east side *the hangings were* fifty cubits. 14The hangings of one side *of the gate were* fifteen cubits *long, with* their three pillars and their three sockets, 15and the same for the other side of the court gate; on this side and that *were* hangings of fifteen cubits, *with* their three pillars and their three sockets. 16All the hangings of the court all around *were of* fine woven linen. 17The sockets for the pillars *were* bronze, the hooks of the pillars and their bands *were* silver, and the overlay of their capitals *was* silver; and all the pillars of the court had bands of silver. 18The screen for

the gate of the court *was* woven of blue,
purple, and scarlet *thread,* and of fine woven linen. The length *was* twenty cubits,
and the height along its width *was* five
cubits, corresponding to the hangings of
the court. [19]And *there were* four pillars
with their four sockets of bronze; their
hooks *were* silver, and the overlay of their
capitals and their bands *was* silver. [20]All
the pegs of the tabernacle, and of the
court all around, *were* bronze.

Materials of the Tabernacle

[21]This is the inventory of the tabernacle, the tabernacle of the Testimony, which
was counted according to the commandment of Moses, for the service of the
Levites, by the hand of Ithamar, son of
Aaron the priest.
[22]Bezalel the son of Uri, the son of
Hur, of the tribe of Judah, made all that
the LORD had commanded Moses. [23]And
with him *was* Aholiab the son of Ahisamach, of the tribe of Dan, an engraver
and designer, a weaver of blue, purple, and
scarlet *thread,* and of fine linen.

> We Christians are debtors to all men at all times in all places, but we are so smug to the lostness of men. We've been 'living in Laodicea,' lax, loose, lustful, and lazy. Why is there this criminal indifference to the lostness of men?
>
> **LEONARD RAVENHILL**

[24]All the gold that was used in all the
work of the holy *place,* that is, the gold of
the offering, was twenty-nine talents and
seven hundred and thirty shekels, according to the shekel of the sanctuary.
[25]And the silver from those who were
numbered of the congregation *was* one
hundred talents and one thousand seven
hundred and seventy-five shekels, according to the shekel of the sanctuary: [26]a
bekah for each man (*that is,* half a shekel,
according to the shekel of the sanctuary),
for everyone included in the numbering
from twenty years old and above, for six
hundred and three thousand, five hundred and fifty *men.* [27]And from the hundred talents of silver were cast the sockets of the sanctuary and the bases of the
veil: one hundred sockets from the hundred talents, one talent for each socket.
[28]Then from the one thousand seven hundred and seventy-five *shekels* he made
hooks for the pillars, overlaid their capitals, and made bands for them.
[29]The offering of bronze *was* seventy
talents and two thousand four hundred
shekels. [30]And with it he made the sockets for the door of the tabernacle of meeting, the bronze altar, the bronze grating
for it, and all the utensils for the altar,
[31]the sockets for the court all around, the
bases for the court gate, all the pegs for
the tabernacle, and all the pegs for the
court all around.

Making the Garments of the Priesthood

39 Of the blue, purple, and scarlet
thread they made garments of ministry,[a] for ministering in the holy *place,*
and made the holy garments for Aaron, as
the LORD had commanded Moses.

Making the Ephod

[2]He made the ephod of gold, blue,
purple, and scarlet *thread,* and of fine woven linen. [3]And they beat the gold into
thin sheets and cut *it into* threads, to
work *it* in *with* the blue, purple, and scarlet *thread,* and the fine linen, *into* artistic
designs. [4]They made shoulder straps for
it to couple *it* together; it was coupled together at its two edges. [5]And the intricately woven band of his ephod that *was*
on it *was* of the same workmanship,
woven of gold, blue, purple, and scarlet
thread, and of fine woven linen, as the
LORD had commanded Moses.
[6]And they set onyx stones, enclosed in
settings of gold; they were engraved, as
signets are engraved, with the names of
the sons of Israel. [7]He put them on the

39:1 [a]Or *woven garments*

shoulders of the ephod *as* memorial stones for the sons of Israel, as the LORD had commanded Moses.

Making the Breastplate

8And he made the breastplate, artistically woven like the workmanship of the ephod, of gold, blue, purple, and scarlet *thread,* and of fine woven linen. 9They made the breastplate square by doubling it; a span *was* its length and a span its width when doubled. 10And they set in it four rows of stones: a row with a sardius, a topaz, and an emerald was the first row; 11the second row, a turquoise, a sapphire, and a diamond; 12the third row, a jacinth, an agate, and an amethyst; 13the fourth row, a beryl, an onyx, and a jasper. *They were* enclosed in settings of gold in their mountings. 14*There were* twelve stones according to the names of the sons of Israel: according to their names, *engraved like* a signet, each one with its own name according to the twelve tribes. 15And they made chains for the breastplate at the ends, like braided cords of pure gold. 16They also made two settings of gold and two gold rings, and put the two rings on the two ends of the breastplate. 17And they put the two braided *chains* of gold in the two rings on the ends of the breastplate. 18The two ends of the two braided *chains* they fastened in the two settings, and put them on the shoulder straps of the ephod in the front. 19And they made two rings of gold and put *them* on the two ends of the breastplate, on the edge of it, which *was* on the inward side of the ephod. 20They made two *other* gold rings and put them on the two shoulder straps, underneath the ephod toward its front, right at the seam above the intricately woven band of the ephod. 21And they bound the breastplate by means of its rings to the rings of the ephod with a blue cord, so that it would be above the intricately woven band

"Lord, make me a crisis man. Let me not be a mile-post on a single road, but make me a fork that men must turn one way or another in facing Christ in me."

Jim Elliot

of the ephod, and that the breastplate would not come loose from the ephod, as the LORD had commanded Moses.

Making the Other Priestly Garments

22He made the robe of the ephod of woven work, all of blue. 23And *there was* an opening in the middle of the robe, like the opening in a coat of mail, *with* a woven binding all around the opening, so that it would not tear. 24They made on the hem of the robe pomegranates of blue, purple, and scarlet, and of fine woven *linen.* 25And they made bells of pure gold, and put the bells between the pomegranates on the hem of the robe all around between the pomegranates: 26a bell and a pomegranate, a bell and a pomegranate, all around the hem of the robe to minister in, as the LORD had commanded Moses.

27They made tunics, artistically woven of fine linen, for Aaron and his sons, 28a turban of fine linen, exquisite hats of fine

39:27 The fine linen is the righteousness of the saints (see Rev. 19:8). God has given us robes of righteousness in Christ. See Isa. 61:10 for why the Christian should greatly rejoice.

linen, short trousers of fine woven linen, [29]and a sash of fine woven linen with blue, purple, and scarlet *thread,* made by a weaver, as the LORD had commanded Moses.

[30]Then they made the plate of the holy crown of pure gold, and wrote on it an inscription *like* the engraving of a signet:

HOLINESS TO THE LORD.

[31]And they tied to it a blue cord, to fasten *it* above on the turban, as the LORD had commanded Moses.

The Work Completed

[32]Thus all the work of the tabernacle of the tent of meeting was finished. And the children of Israel did according to all that the LORD had commanded Moses; so they did. [33]And they brought the tabernacle to Moses, the tent and all its furnishings: its clasps, its boards, its bars, its pillars, and its sockets; [34]the covering of ram skins dyed red, the covering of badger skins, and the veil of the covering; [35]the ark of the Testimony with its poles, and the mercy seat; [36]the table, all its utensils, and the showbread; [37]the pure *gold* lampstand with its lamps (the lamps set in order), all its utensils, and the oil for light; [38]the gold altar, the anointing oil, and the sweet incense; the screen for the tabernacle door; [39]the bronze altar, its grate of bronze, its poles, and all its utensils; the laver with its base; [40]the hangings of the court, its pillars and its sockets, the screen for the court gate, its cords, and its pegs; all the utensils for the service of the tabernacle, for the tent of meeting; [41]and the garments of ministry,[a] to minister in the holy *place:* the holy garments for Aaron the priest, and his sons' garments, to minister as priests.

[42]According to all that the LORD had commanded Moses, so the children of Israel did all the work. [43]Then Moses looked over all the work, and indeed they had done it; as the LORD had commanded, just so they had done it. And Moses blessed them.

The Tabernacle Erected and Arranged

40 Then the LORD spoke to Moses, saying: [2]"On the first day of the first month you shall set up the tabernacle of the tent of meeting. [3]You shall put in it the ark of the Testimony, and partition off the ark with the veil. [4]You shall bring in the table and arrange the things that are to be set in order on it; and you shall bring in the lampstand and light its lamps. [5]You shall also set the altar of gold for the incense before the ark of the Testimony, and put up the screen for the door of the tabernacle. [6]Then you shall set the altar of the burnt offering before the door of the tabernacle of the tent of meeting. [7]And you shall set the laver between the tabernacle of meeting and the altar, and put water in it. [8]You shall set up the court all around, and hang up the screen at the court gate.

> Every true friend, if you could get his advice, would tell you to be saved now.
>
> **D. L. MOODY**

[9]"And you shall take the anointing oil, and anoint the tabernacle and all that *is* in it; and you shall hallow it and all its utensils, and it shall be holy. [10]You shall anoint the altar of the burnt offering and all its utensils, and consecrate the altar. The altar shall be most holy. [11]And you shall anoint the laver and its base, and consecrate it.

[12]"Then you shall bring Aaron and his sons to the door of the tabernacle of meeting and wash them with water. [13]You shall put the holy garments on Aaron, and anoint him and consecrate him, that

39:41 [a]Or *woven garments*

40:13 As believers, we have been made holy, anointed, and sanctified in Christ.

he may minister to Me as priest. 14And
you shall bring his sons and clothe them
with tunics. 15You shall anoint them, as
you anointed their father, that they may
minister to Me as priests; for their anointing shall surely be an everlasting priesthood throughout their generations."
16Thus Moses did; according to all that
the LORD had commanded him, so he did.
17And it came to pass in the first month
of the second year, on the first *day* of the
month, *that* the tabernacle was raised up.
18So Moses raised up the tabernacle, fastened its sockets, set up its boards, put in
its bars, and raised up its pillars. 19And
he spread out the tent over the tabernacle
and put the covering of the tent on top of
it, as the LORD had commanded Moses.

> The unattended garden will soon be overrun with weeds; the heart that fails to cultivate truth and root out error will shortly be a theological wilderness.
>
> **A. W. TOZER**

20He took the Testimony and put *it* into
the ark, inserted the poles through the
rings of the ark, and put the mercy seat
on top of the ark. 21And he brought the
ark into the tabernacle, hung up the veil
of the covering, and partitioned off the
ark of the Testimony, as the LORD had
commanded Moses.
22He put the table in the tabernacle of
meeting, on the north side of the tabernacle, outside the veil; 23and he set the
bread in order upon it before the LORD, as
the LORD had commanded Moses. 24He
put the lampstand in the tabernacle of
meeting, across from the table, on the
south side of the tabernacle; 25and he lit
the lamps before the LORD, as the LORD
had commanded Moses. 26He put the gold
altar in the tabernacle of meeting in front
of the veil; 27and he burned sweet incense on it, as the LORD had commanded
Moses. 28He hung up the screen *at* the
door of the tabernacle. 29And he put the
altar of burnt offering *before* the door of
the tabernacle of the tent of meeting, and
offered upon it the burnt offering and the
grain offering, as the LORD had commanded Moses. 30He set the laver between the
tabernacle of meeting and the altar, and
put water there for washing; 31and Moses,
Aaron, and his sons would wash their
hands and their feet *with water* from it.
32Whenever they went into the tabernacle of meeting, and when they came near
the altar, they washed, as the LORD had
commanded Moses. 33And he raised up
the court all around the tabernacle and
the altar, and hung up the screen of the
court gate. So Moses finished the work.

The Cloud and the Glory

34Then the cloud covered the tabernacle of meeting, and the glory of the LORD
filled the tabernacle. 35And Moses was
not able to enter the tabernacle of meeting, because the cloud rested above it,
and the glory of the LORD filled the tabernacle. 36Whenever the cloud was taken
up from above the tabernacle, the children of Israel would go onward in all
their journeys. 37But if the cloud was not
taken up, then they did not journey till
the day that it was taken up. 38For the
cloud of the LORD *was* above the tabernacle by day, and fire was over it by night,
in the sight of all the house of Israel,
throughout all their journeys.

> *"Could a mariner sit idle if he heard the drowning cry?*
> *Could a doctor sit in comfort and just let his patients die?*
> *Could a fireman sit idle, let men burn and give no hand?*
> *Can you sit at ease in Zion with the world around you damned?"*
>
> **LEONARD RAVENHILL**

Leviticus

The Burnt Offering

1 Now the LORD called to Moses, and
spoke to him from the tabernacle of
meeting, saying, 2“Speak to the children
of Israel, and say to them: ‘When any
one of you brings an offering to the LORD,
you shall bring your offering of the livestock—of the herd and of the flock.
3‘If his offering *is* a burnt sacrifice of the
herd, let him offer a male without blemish; he shall offer it of his own free will at
the door of the tabernacle of meeting before the LORD. 4Then he shall put his hand
on the head of the burnt offering, and it
will be accepted on his behalf to make
atonement for him. 5He shall kill the bull
before the LORD; and the priests, Aaron’s
sons, shall bring the blood and sprinkle
the blood all around on the altar that *is by*
the door of the tabernacle of meeting. 6And
he shall skin the burnt offering and cut it
into its pieces. 7The sons of Aaron the
priest shall put fire on the altar, and lay
the wood in order on the fire. 8Then the
priests, Aaron’s sons, shall lay the parts,
the head, and the fat in order on the wood
that *is* on the fire upon the altar; 9but he
shall wash its entrails and its legs with
water. And the priest shall burn all on the
altar as a burnt sacrifice, an offering made
by fire, a sweet aroma to the LORD.
10‘If his offering *is* of the flocks—of the
sheep or of the goats—as a burnt sacrifice, he shall bring a male without blemish. 11He shall kill it on the north side of
the altar before the LORD; and the priests,
Aaron’s sons, shall sprinkle its blood all
around on the altar. 12And he shall cut it
into its pieces, with its head and its fat;
and the priest shall lay them in order on
the wood that *is* on the fire upon the altar; 13but he shall wash the entrails and
the legs with water. Then the priest shall
bring *it* all and burn *it* on the altar; it *is* a
burnt sacrifice, an offering made by fire,
a sweet aroma to the LORD.
14‘And if the burnt sacrifice of his offering to the LORD *is* of birds, then he
shall bring his offering of turtledoves or
young pigeons. 15The priest shall bring it
to the altar, wring off its head, and burn
it on the altar; its blood shall be drained
out at the side of the altar. 16And he shall
remove its crop with its feathers and cast
it beside the altar on the east side, into
the place for ashes. 17Then he shall split
it at its wings, *but* shall not divide *it* completely; and the priest shall burn it on the
altar, on the wood that *is* on the fire. It *is*
a burnt sacrifice, an offering made by fire,
a sweet aroma to the LORD.

1:1–4 It is no wonder that modern-day Jews gravitate toward their own traditions rather than to the Word of God. Because of sin, the demands of the Law meant a continual need for a bloody sacrifice. For how Jewish people atone for their sins today, see Lev. 16:30–34 comment.

The Grain Offering

2 'When anyone offers a grain offering
to the LORD, his offering shall be *of*
fine flour. And he shall pour oil on it, and
put frankincense on it. 2He shall bring it
to Aaron's sons, the priests, one of whom
shall take from it his handful of fine flour
and oil with all the frankincense. And the
priest shall burn *it as* a memorial on the
altar, an offering made by fire, a sweet
aroma to the LORD. 3The rest of the grain
offering *shall be* Aaron's and his sons'. *It
is* most holy of the offerings to the LORD
made by fire.
4'And if you bring as an offering a
grain offering baked in the oven, *it shall
be* unleavened cakes of fine flour mixed
with oil, or unleavened wafers anointed
with oil. 5But if your offering *is* a grain offering *baked* in a pan, *it shall be of* fine
flour, unleavened, mixed with oil. 6You
shall break it in pieces and pour oil on it;
it *is* a grain offering.
7'If your offering *is* a grain offering
baked in a covered pan, it shall be made
of fine flour with oil. 8You shall bring the
grain offering that is made of these things
to the LORD. And when it is presented to
the priest, he shall bring it to the altar.
9Then the priest shall take from the grain
offering a memorial portion, and burn *it*
on the altar. *It is* an offering made by fire,
a sweet aroma to the LORD. 10And what is
left of the grain offering *shall be* Aaron's
and his sons'. *It is* most holy of the offerings to the LORD made by fire.
11'No grain offering which you bring
to the LORD shall be made with leaven,
for you shall burn no leaven nor any
honey in any offering to the LORD made
by fire. 12As for the offering of the firstfruits, you shall offer them to the LORD,
but they shall not be burned on the altar
for a sweet aroma. 13And every offering of
your grain offering you shall season with
salt; you shall not allow the salt of the
covenant of your God to be lacking from
your grain offering. With all your offerings you shall offer salt.
14'If you offer a grain offering of your
firstfruits to the LORD, you shall offer for
the grain offering of your firstfruits green
heads of grain roasted on the fire, grain
beaten from full heads. 15And you shall
put oil on it, and lay frankincense on it.
It *is* a grain offering. 16Then the priest
shall burn the memorial portion: *part* of
its beaten grain and *part* of its oil, with all
the frankincense, as an offering made by
fire to the LORD.

The Peace Offering

3 'When his offering *is* a sacrifice of a
peace offering, if he offers *it* of the
herd, whether male or female, he shall
offer it without blemish before the LORD.
2And he shall lay his hand on the head
of his offering, and kill it *at* the door of
the tabernacle of meeting; and Aaron's
sons, the priests, shall sprinkle the blood
all around on the altar. 3Then he shall
offer from the sacrifice of the peace offering an offering made by fire to the LORD.
The fat that covers the entrails and all
the fat that *is* on the entrails, 4the two
kidneys and the fat that *is* on them by
the flanks, and the fatty lobe *attached* to
the liver above the kidneys, he shall re-

2:1–11 The grain offering. "Meat [grain] offerings may typify Christ, as presented to God for us, and as being the Bread of life to our souls; but they rather seem to denote our obligation to God for the blessings of providence, and those good works which are acceptable to God. The term meat was, and still is, properly given to any kind of provision, and the greater part of this offering was to be eaten for food, not burned. These meat offerings are mentioned after the burnt offerings: without an interest in the sacrifice of Christ, and devotedness of heart to God, such services cannot be accepted. Leaven is the emblem of pride, malice, and hypocrisy, and honey of sensual pleasure. The former are directly opposed to the graces of humility, love, and sincerity, which God approves; the latter takes men from the exercises of devotion, and the practice of good works. Christ, in his character and sacrifice, was wholly free from the things denoted by leaven; and his suffering life and agonizing death were the very opposites to worldly pleasure. His people are called to follow, and to be like him." *Matthew Henry*

move; [5]and Aaron's sons shall burn it on the altar upon the burnt sacrifice, which *is* on the wood that *is* on the fire, *as* an offering made by fire, a sweet aroma to the LORD.

[6]'If his offering as a sacrifice of a peace offering to the LORD *is* of the flock, *whether* male or female, he shall offer it without blemish. [7]If he offers a lamb as his offering, then he shall offer it before the LORD. [8]And he shall lay his hand on the head of his offering, and kill it before the tabernacle of meeting; and Aaron's sons shall sprinkle its blood all around on the altar.

[9]'Then he shall offer from the sacrifice of the peace offering, as an offering made by fire to the LORD, its fat *and* the whole fat tail which he shall remove close to the backbone. And the fat that covers the entrails and all the fat that *is* on the entrails, [10]the two kidneys and the fat that *is* on them by the flanks, and the fatty lobe *attached* to the liver above the kidneys, he shall remove; [11]and the priest shall burn *them* on the altar *as* food, an offering made by fire to the LORD.

[12]'And if his offering *is* a goat, then he shall offer it before the LORD. [13]He shall lay his hand on its head and kill it before the tabernacle of meeting; and the sons of Aaron shall sprinkle its blood all around on the altar. [14]Then he shall offer from it his offering, as an offering made by fire to the LORD. The fat that covers the entrails and all the fat that *is* on the entrails, [15]the two kidneys and the fat that *is* on them by the flanks, and the fatty lobe *attached* to the liver above the kidneys, he shall remove; [16]and the priest shall burn them on the altar *as* food, an offering made by fire for a sweet aroma; all the fat *is* the LORD's.

[17]'*This shall be* a perpetual statute throughout your generations in all your dwellings: you shall eat neither fat nor blood.' "

The Sin Offering

4 Now the LORD spoke to Moses, saying, [2]"Speak to the children of Israel, saying: 'If a person sins unintentionally against any of the commandments of the LORD *in anything* which ought not to be done, and does any of them, [3]if the anointed priest sins, bringing guilt on the people, then let him offer to the LORD for his sin which he has sinned a young bull without blemish as a sin offering. [4]He shall bring the bull to the door of the tabernacle of meeting before the LORD, lay his hand on the bull's head, and kill the bull before the LORD. [5]Then the anointed priest shall take some of the bull's blood and bring it to the tabernacle of meeting. [6]The priest shall dip his finger in the blood and sprinkle some of the blood seven times before the LORD, in front of the veil of the sanctuary. [7]And the priest shall put some of the blood on the horns of the altar of sweet incense before the LORD, which is in the tabernacle of meeting; and he shall pour the remaining blood of the bull at the base of the altar of the burnt offering, which is

---

4:2 Breaking the Commandments. Since the greatest Commandment is to love God with all of our heart (see Matt. 22:36,37), it is reasonable to say that the greatest sin is a failure to do so. The Bible tells us that no one seeks after God (see Rom. 3:11), so all of humanity is guilty of this sin of omission. Occasionally individuals will deliberately lie as you take them through the Ten Commandments, by claiming that they have never lied, stolen, blasphemed, or looked with lust. When that happens, ask if they have kept the first of the Ten Commandments. They will almost certainly say that they have.

To help them see their sin, you can explain it this way: "The Word of God says no one has kept that Commandment, so one of you is lying—and it is impossible for God to lie. So you have just lied to me and have broken not only the First Commandment, but also the Ninth. Now that we have established that you are a liar, I can't believe what you've just told me about stealing, blasphemy, and lust. It's obvious that your problem is one of idolatry—you have a wrong image of God, which means that you have also broken the Second Commandment." For details on how to use the Law in evangelism, see Psa. 51:6 and John 4:7 comments.

at the door of the tabernacle of meeting.
8He shall take from it all the fat of the
bull as the sin offering. The fat that covers the entrails and all the fat which *is* on
the entrails, 9the two kidneys and the fat
that *is* on them by the flanks, and the
fatty lobe *attached* to the liver above the
kidneys, he shall remove, 10as it was
taken from the bull of the sacrifice of the
peace offering; and the priest shall burn
them on the altar of the burnt offering.
11But the bull's hide and all its flesh, with
its head and legs, its entrails and offal—
12the whole bull he shall carry outside
the camp to a clean place, where the ashes
are poured out, and burn it on wood with
fire; where the ashes are poured out it
shall be burned.

> Simple assent to the gospel, divorced from a transforming commitment to the living Christ, is by biblical standards less than faith, and less than saving, and to elicit only assent of this kind would be to secure only false conversions.
>
> **J. I. PACKER**

13'Now if the whole congregation of
Israel sins unintentionally, and the thing
is hidden from the eyes of the assembly,
and they have done *something against* any
of the commandments of the LORD *in anything* which should not be done, and are
guilty; 14when the sin which they have
committed becomes known, then the assembly shall offer a young bull for the
sin, and bring it before the tabernacle of
meeting. 15And the elders of the congregation shall lay their hands on the head
of the bull before the LORD. Then the bull
shall be killed before the LORD. 16The
anointed priest shall bring some of the
bull's blood to the tabernacle of meeting.
17Then the priest shall dip his finger in
the blood and sprinkle *it* seven times before the LORD, in front of the veil. 18And
he shall put *some* of the blood on the horns
of the altar which *is* before the LORD,
which *is* in the tabernacle of meeting; and
he shall pour the remaining blood at the
base of the altar of burnt offering, which
is at the door of the tabernacle of meeting. 19He shall take all the fat from it and
burn *it* on the altar. 20And he shall do
with the bull as he did with the bull as a
sin offering; thus he shall do with it. So
the priest shall make atonement for
them, and it shall be forgiven them.
21Then he shall carry the bull outside the
camp, and burn it as he burned the first
bull. It *is* a sin offering for the assembly.

22'When a ruler has sinned, and done
something unintentionally *against* any of
the commandments of the LORD his God
in anything which should not be done,
and is guilty, 23or if his sin which he has
committed comes to his knowledge, he
shall bring as his offering a kid of the
goats, a male without blemish. 24And he
shall lay his hand on the head of the goat,
and kill it at the place where they kill the
burnt offering before the LORD. It *is* a sin
offering. 25The priest shall take some of
the blood of the sin offering with his finger, put *it* on the horns of the altar of
burnt offering, and pour its blood at the
base of the altar of burnt offering. 26And
he shall burn all its fat on the altar, like
the fat of the sacrifice of the peace offering. So the priest shall make atonement
for him concerning his sin, and it shall be
forgiven him.

27'If anyone of the common people sins
unintentionally by doing *something against*
any of the commandments of the LORD *in
anything* which ought not to be done, and
is guilty, 28or if his sin which he has committed comes to his knowledge, then he
shall bring as his offering a kid of the

4:27,28 Just as in our society, ignorance of the Law is no excuse. Even if someone breaks a law unintentionally and is not aware that he is in transgression, he is still guilty of the offense. God has written His Law on our heart and our conscience bears witness (see Rom. 2:15), so none of us can legitimately claim that we didn't know it was wrong when we transgressed it. See also 5:17; Ezek. 45:20 comment.

goats, a female without blemish, for his sin which he has committed. 29And he shall lay his hand on the head of the sin offering, and kill the sin offering at the place of the burnt offering. 30Then the priest shall take *some* of its blood with his finger, put *it* on the horns of the altar of burnt offering, and pour all *the remaining* blood at the base of the altar. 31He shall remove all its fat, as fat is removed from the sacrifice of the peace offering; and the priest shall burn it on the altar for a sweet aroma to the LORD. So the priest shall make atonement for him, and it shall be forgiven him.

32'If he brings a lamb as his sin offering, he shall bring a female without blemish. 33Then he shall lay his hand on the head of the sin offering, and kill it as a sin offering at the place where they kill the burnt offering. 34The priest shall take *some* of the blood of the sin offering with his finger, put *it* on the horns of the altar of burnt offering, and pour all *the remaining* blood at the base of the altar. 35He shall remove all its fat, as the fat of the lamb is removed from the sacrifice of the peace offering. Then the priest shall burn it on the altar, according to the offerings made by fire to the LORD. So the priest shall make atonement for his sin that he has committed, and it shall be forgiven him.

The Trespass Offering

5 'If a person sins in hearing the utterance of an oath, and *is* a witness, whether he has seen or known *of the matter*—if he does not tell *it,* he bears guilt.

2'Or if a person touches any unclean thing, whether *it is* the carcass of an unclean beast, or the carcass of unclean livestock, or the carcass of unclean creeping things, and he is unaware of it, he also shall be unclean and guilty. 3Or if he touches human uncleanness—whatever uncleanness with which a man may be defiled, and he is unaware of it—when he realizes *it,* then he shall be guilty.

4'Or if a person swears, speaking thoughtlessly with *his* lips to do evil or to do good, whatever *it is* that a man may pronounce by an oath, and he is unaware of it—when he realizes *it,* then he shall be guilty in any of these *matters.*

5'And it shall be, when he is guilty in any of these *matters,* that he shall confess that he has sinned in that *thing;* 6and he shall bring his trespass offering to the LORD for his sin which he has committed, a female from the flock, a lamb or a kid of the goats as a sin offering. So the priest shall make atonement for him concerning his sin.

7'If he is not able to bring a lamb, then he shall bring to the LORD, for his trespass which he has committed, two turtledoves or two young pigeons: one as a sin offering and the other as a burnt offering. 8And he shall bring them to the priest, who shall offer *that* which *is* for the sin offering first, and wring off its head from its neck, but shall not divide *it* completely. 9Then he shall sprinkle *some* of the blood of the sin offering on the side of the altar, and the rest of the blood shall be drained out at the base of the altar. It *is* a sin offering. 10And he shall offer the second *as* a burnt offering according to the prescribed manner. So the priest shall make atonement on his behalf for his sin which he has committed, and it shall be forgiven him.

11'But if he is not able to bring two turtledoves or two young pigeons, then he who sinned shall bring for his offering one-tenth of an ephah of fine flour as a sin offering. He shall put no oil on it, nor shall he put frankincense on it, for it *is* a sin offering. 12Then he shall bring it to the priest, and the priest shall take his handful of it as a memorial portion, and burn *it* on the altar according to the offerings made by fire to the LORD. It *is* a sin

5:5 Those who say that Christianity is a "guilt trip" are correct. It's a guilt trip to the foot of a blood-stained cross, where the guilt is removed.

offering. 13The priest shall make atonement for him, for his sin that he has committed in any of these matters; and it shall be forgiven him. *The rest* shall be the priest's as a grain offering.' "

Offerings with Restitution

14Then the LORD spoke to Moses, saying: 15"If a person commits a trespass, and sins unintentionally in regard to the holy things of the LORD, then he shall bring to the LORD as his trespass offering a ram without blemish from the flocks, with your valuation in shekels of silver according to the shekel of the sanctuary, as a trespass offering. 16And he shall make restitution for the harm that he has done in regard to the holy thing, and shall add one-fifth to it and give it to the priest. So the priest shall make atonement for him with the ram of the trespass offering, and it shall be forgiven him.

17"If a person sins, and commits any of these things which are forbidden to be done by the commandments of the LORD, though he does not know *it,* yet he is guilty and shall bear his iniquity. 18And he shall bring to the priest a ram without blemish from the flock, with your valuation, as a trespass offering. So the priest shall make atonement for him regarding his ignorance in which he erred and did not know *it,* and it shall be forgiven him. 19It is a trespass offering; he has certainly trespassed against the LORD."

6 And the LORD spoke to Moses, saying: 2"If a person sins and commits a trespass against the LORD by lying to his neighbor about what was delivered to him for safekeeping, or about a pledge, or about a robbery, or if he has extorted from his neighbor, 3or if he has found what was lost and lies concerning it, and swears falsely—in any one of these things that a man may do in which he sins: 4then it shall be, because he has sinned and is guilty, that he shall restore what he has stolen, or the thing which he has extorted, or what was delivered to him for safekeeping, or the lost thing which he found, 5or all that about which he has sworn falsely. He shall restore its full value, add one-fifth more to it, *and* give it to whomever it belongs, on the day of his trespass offering. 6And he shall bring his trespass offering to the LORD, a ram without blemish from the flock, with your valuation, as a trespass offering, to the priest. 7So the priest shall make atonement for him before the LORD, and he shall be forgiven for any one of these things that he may have done in which he trespasses."

· · · · · ·

For how to witness to Mormons,
see Mark 11:25 comment.

· · · · · ·

The Law of the Burnt Offering

8Then the LORD spoke to Moses, saying, 9"Command Aaron and his sons, saying, 'This *is* the law of the burnt offering: The burnt offering *shall be* on the hearth upon the altar all night until morning, and the fire of the altar shall be kept burning on it. 10And the priest shall put on his linen garment, and his linen trousers he shall put on his body, and take up the ashes of the burnt offering which the fire has consumed on the altar, and he shall put them beside the altar. 11Then he shall take off his garments, put on other garments, and carry the ashes outside the camp to a clean place. 12And the fire on the altar shall be kept burning on it; it shall not be put out. And the priest shall burn wood on it every morning, and lay the burnt offering in or-

6:2 All sin is against God. Most of this world doesn't understand that fact. When we sin we violate God's Law, for "sin is lawlessness" (1 John 3:4). Notice to whom David directed his repentance after Nathan rebuked him for violating the Commandments. He said, "Against You, You only, have I sinned, and done this evil in Your sight" (Psa. 51:4). See also 2 Sam. 12:1–14 comment.

der on it; and he shall burn on it the fat of the peace offerings. 13 A fire shall always be burning on the altar; it shall never go out.

The Law of the Grain Offering

14 "This *is* the law of the grain offering: The sons of Aaron shall offer it on the altar before the LORD. 15 He shall take from it his handful of the fine flour of the grain offering, with its oil, and all the frankincense which *is* on the grain offering, and shall burn *it* on the altar *for* a sweet aroma, as a memorial to the LORD. 16 And the remainder of it Aaron and his sons shall eat; with unleavened bread it shall be eaten in a holy place; in the court of the tabernacle of meeting they shall eat it. 17 It shall not be baked with leaven. I have given it *as* their portion of My offerings made by fire; it *is* most holy, like the sin offering and the trespass offering. 18 All the males among the children of Aaron may eat it. *It shall be* a statute forever in your generations concerning the offerings made by fire to the LORD. Everyone who touches them must be holy.' "[a]

19 And the LORD spoke to Moses, saying, 20 "This *is* the offering of Aaron and his sons, which they shall offer to the LORD, *beginning* on the day when he is anointed: one-tenth of an ephah of fine flour as a daily grain offering, half of it in the morning and half of it at night. 21 It shall be made in a pan with oil. *When it is* mixed, you shall bring it in. The baked pieces of the grain offering you shall offer *for* a sweet aroma to the LORD. 22 The priest from among his sons, who is anointed in his place, shall offer it. *It is* a statute forever to the LORD. It shall be wholly burned. 23 For every grain offering for the priest shall be wholly burned. It shall not be eaten."

The Law of the Sin Offering

24 Also the LORD spoke to Moses, saying, 25 "Speak to Aaron and to his sons, saying, 'This *is* the law of the sin offering: In the place where the burnt offering is killed, the sin offering shall be killed before the LORD. It *is* most holy. 26 The priest who offers it for sin shall eat it. In a holy place it shall be eaten, in the court of the tabernacle of meeting. 27 Everyone who touches its flesh must be holy.[a] And when its blood is sprinkled on any garment, you shall wash that on which it was sprinkled, in a holy place. 28 But the earthen vessel in which it is boiled shall be broken. And if it is boiled in a bronze pot, it shall be both scoured and rinsed in water. 29 All the males among the priests may eat it. It *is* most holy. 30 But no sin offering from which *any* of the blood is brought into the tabernacle of meeting, to make atonement in the holy *place*,[a] shall be eaten. It shall be burned in the fire.

The Law of the Trespass Offering

7 'Likewise this *is* the law of the trespass offering (it *is* most holy): 2 In the place where they kill the burnt offering they shall kill the trespass offering. And its blood he shall sprinkle all around on the altar. 3 And he shall offer from it all its fat. The fat tail and the fat that covers the entrails, 4 the two kidneys and the fat that *is* on them by the flanks, and the fatty lobe *attached* to the liver above the kidneys, he shall remove; 5 and the priest shall burn them on the altar *as* an offering made by fire to the LORD. It *is* a trespass offering. 6 Every male among the priests may eat it. It shall be eaten in a

6:18 [a]Compare Numbers 4:15 and Haggai 2:11–13 6:27 [a]Compare Numbers 4:15 and Haggai 2:11–13 6:30 [a]The Most Holy Place when capitalized

6:13 "People talk about our being earnest and fanatical—about our being on fire. Would to God the church were on fire! This world would soon shake to its foundation. May God wake up a slumbering church! What we want you to do is not to shout 'amen' and clap your hands. The deepest and quietest waters very often run swiftest. We want you to go right to work; there will be a chance for you to shout by and by. Go and speak to your neighbor and tell him of Christ and heaven. You need not go far before you will find someone passing down to the darkness of eternal death. Haste to his rescue!" *D. L. Moody*

holy place. It *is* most holy. 7The trespass offering *is* like the sin offering; *there is* one law for them both: the priest who makes atonement with it shall have *it.* 8And the priest who offers anyone's burnt offering, that priest shall have for himself the skin of the burnt offering which he has offered. 9Also every grain offering that is baked in the oven and all that is prepared in the covered pan, or in a pan, shall be the priest's who offers it. 10Every grain offering, *whether* mixed with oil or dry, shall belong to all the sons of Aaron, to one *as much* as the other.

The Law of Peace Offerings

11'This *is* the law of the sacrifice of peace offerings which he shall offer to the LORD: 12If he offers it for a thanksgiving, then he shall offer, with the sacrifice of thanksgiving, unleavened cakes mixed with oil, unleavened wafers anointed with oil, or cakes of blended flour mixed with oil. 13Besides the cakes, *as* his offering he shall offer leavened bread with the sacrifice of thanksgiving of his peace offering. 14And from it he shall offer one cake from each offering *as* a heave offering to the LORD. It shall belong to the priest who sprinkles the blood of the peace offering. 15'The flesh of the sacrifice of his peace offering for thanksgiving shall be eaten the same day it is offered. He shall not leave any of it until morning. 16But if the sacrifice of his offering *is* a vow or a voluntary offering, it shall be eaten the same day that he offers his sacrifice; but on the next day the remainder of it also may be eaten; 17the remainder of the flesh of the sacrifice on the third day must be burned with fire. 18And if *any* of the flesh of the sacrifice of his peace offering is eaten at all on the third day, it shall not be accepted, nor shall it be imputed to him; it shall be an abomination *to* him who offers it, and the person who eats of it shall bear guilt.

19'The flesh that touches any unclean thing shall not be eaten. It shall be burned with fire. And as for the *clean* flesh, all who are clean may eat of it. 20But the person who eats the flesh of the sacrifice of the peace offering that *belongs* to the LORD, while he is unclean, that person shall be cut off from his people. 21Moreover the person who touches any unclean thing, *such as* human uncleanness, *an* unclean animal, or any abominable unclean thing,[a] and who eats the flesh of the sacrifice of the peace offering that *belongs* to the LORD, that person shall be cut off from his people.' "

Fat and Blood May Not Be Eaten

22And the LORD spoke to Moses, saying, 23"Speak to the children of Israel, saying: 'You shall not eat any fat, of ox or sheep or goat. 24And the fat of an animal that dies *naturally,* and the fat of what is torn by wild beasts, may be used in any other way; but you shall by no means eat it. 25For whoever eats the fat of the animal of which men offer an offering made by fire to the LORD, the person who eats *it* shall be cut off from his people. 26Moreover you shall not eat any blood in any of your dwellings, *whether* of bird or beast. 27Whoever eats any blood, that person shall be cut off from his people.' "

The Portion of Aaron and His Sons

28Then the LORD spoke to Moses, saying, 29"Speak to the children of Israel, saying: 'He who offers the sacrifice of his peace offering to the LORD shall bring his offering to the LORD from the sacrifice of his peace offering. 30His own hands shall bring the offerings made by fire to the LORD. The fat with the breast he shall bring, that the breast may be waved *as* a wave offering before the LORD. 31And the priest shall burn the fat on the altar, but the breast shall be Aaron's and his sons'. 32Also the right thigh you shall give to the priest *as* a heave offering from the sacrifices of your peace offerings. 33He among the sons of Aaron, who offers the blood

7:21 [a]Following Masoretic Text, Septuagint, and Vulgate; Samaritan Pentateuch, Syriac, and Targum read *swarming thing* (compare 5:2).

of the peace offering and the fat, shall have the right thigh for *his* part. [34]For the breast of the wave offering and the thigh of the heave offering I have taken from the children of Israel, from the sacrifices of their peace offerings, and I have given them to Aaron the priest and to his sons from the children of Israel by a statute forever.' "

[35]This *is* the consecrated portion for Aaron and his sons, from the offerings made by fire to the LORD, on the day when *Moses* presented them to minister to the LORD as priests. [36]The LORD commanded this to be given to them by the children of Israel, on the day that He anointed them, *by* a statute forever throughout their generations.

[37]This *is* the law of the burnt offering, the grain offering, the sin offering, the trespass offering, the consecrations, and the sacrifice of the peace offering, [38]which the LORD commanded Moses on Mount Sinai, on the day when He commanded the children of Israel to offer their offerings to the LORD in the Wilderness of Sinai.

Aaron and His Sons Consecrated

8 And the LORD spoke to Moses, saying: [2]"Take Aaron and his sons with him, and the garments, the anointing oil, a bull as the sin offering, two rams, and a basket of unleavened bread; [3]and gather all the congregation together at the door of the tabernacle of meeting."

[4]So Moses did as the LORD commanded him. And the congregation was gathered together at the door of the tabernacle of meeting. [5]And Moses said to the congregation, "This *is* what the LORD commanded to be done."

[6]Then Moses brought Aaron and his sons and washed them with water. [7]And he put the tunic on him, girded him with the sash, clothed him with the robe, and put the ephod on him; and he girded him with the intricately woven band of the ephod, and with it tied *the ephod* on him. [8]Then he put the breastplate on him, and he put the Urim and the Thummim[a] in the breastplate. [9]And he put the turban on his head. Also on the turban, on its front, he put the golden plate, the holy crown, as the LORD had commanded Moses.

[10]Also Moses took the anointing oil, and anointed the tabernacle and all that *was* in it, and consecrated them. [11]He sprinkled some of it on the altar seven times, anointed the altar and all its utensils, and the laver and its base, to consecrate them. [12]And he poured some of the anointing oil on Aaron's head and anointed him, to consecrate him.

[13]Then Moses brought Aaron's sons and put tunics on them, girded them with sashes, and put hats on them, as the LORD had commanded Moses.

[14]And he brought the bull for the sin offering. Then Aaron and his sons laid their hands on the head of the bull for the sin offering, [15]and Moses killed *it*. Then he took the blood, and put *some* on the horns of the altar all around with his finger, and purified the altar. And he poured the blood at the base of the altar, and consecrated it, to make atonement for it. [16]Then he took all the fat that *was* on the entrails, the fatty lobe *attached to* the liver, and the two kidneys with their fat, and Moses burned *them* on the altar. [17]But the bull, its hide, its flesh, and its offal, he burned with fire outside the camp, as the LORD had commanded Moses.

[18]Then he brought the ram as the burnt offering. And Aaron and his sons laid their hands on the head of the ram, [19]and Moses killed *it*. Then he sprinkled the blood all around on the altar. [20]And he cut the ram into pieces; and Moses burned the head, the pieces, and the fat. [21]Then he washed the entrails and the legs in water. And Moses burned the whole ram on the altar. It *was* a burnt sacrifice for a sweet aroma, an offering made by fire to the LORD, as the LORD had commanded Moses.

8:8 [a]Literally *the Lights and the Perfections* (compare Exodus 28:30)

22And he brought the second ram, the ram of consecration. Then Aaron and his sons laid their hands on the head of the ram, 23and Moses killed *it.* Also he took *some* of its blood and put it on the tip of Aaron's right ear, on the thumb of his right hand, and on the big toe of his right foot. 24Then he brought Aaron's sons. And Moses put *some* of the blood on the tips of their right ears, on the thumbs of their right hands, and on the big toes of their right feet. And Moses sprinkled the blood all around on the altar. 25Then he took the fat and the fat tail, all the fat that *was* on the entrails, the fatty lobe *attached to* the liver, the two kidneys and their fat, and the right thigh; 26and from the basket of unleavened bread that was before the LORD he took one unleavened cake, a cake of bread *anointed with* oil, and one wafer, and put *them* on the fat and on the right thigh; 27and he put all *these* in Aaron's hands and in his sons' hands, and waved them *as* a wave offering before the LORD. 28Then Moses took them from their hands and burned *them* on the altar, on the burnt offering. They *were* consecration offerings for a sweet aroma. That *was* an offering made by fire to the LORD. 29And Moses took the breast and waved it *as* a wave offering before the LORD. It was Moses' part of the ram of consecration, as the LORD had commanded Moses.

30Then Moses took some of the anointing oil and some of the blood which *was* on the altar, and sprinkled *it* on Aaron, on his garments, on his sons, and on the garments of his sons with him; and he consecrated Aaron, his garments, his sons, and the garments of his sons with him.

31And Moses said to Aaron and his sons, "Boil the flesh *at* the door of the tabernacle of meeting, and eat it there with the bread that *is* in the basket of consecration offerings, as I commanded, saying, 'Aaron and his sons shall eat it.' 32What remains of the flesh and of the bread you shall burn with fire. 33And you shall not go outside the door of the tabernacle of meeting *for* seven days, until the days of your consecration are ended. For seven days he shall consecrate you. 34As he has done this day, *so* the LORD has commanded to do, to make atonement for you. 35Therefore you shall stay *at* the door of the tabernacle of meeting day and night for seven days, and keep the charge of the LORD, so that you may not die; for so I have been commanded." 36So Aaron and his sons did all the things that the LORD had commanded by the hand of Moses.

The Priestly Ministry Begins

9 It came to pass on the eighth day that Moses called Aaron and his sons and the elders of Israel. 2And he said to Aaron, "Take for yourself a young bull as a sin offering and a ram as a burnt offering, without blemish, and offer *them* before the LORD. 3And to the children of Israel you shall speak, saying, 'Take a kid of the goats as a sin offering, and a calf and a lamb, *both* of the first year, without blemish, as a burnt offering, 4also a bull and a ram as peace offerings, to sacrifice before the LORD, and a grain offering mixed with oil; for today the LORD will appear to you.' "

5So they brought what Moses commanded before the tabernacle of meeting. And all the congregation drew near and stood before the LORD. 6Then Moses said, "This *is* the thing which the LORD commanded you to do, and the glory of the LORD will appear to you." 7And Moses said to Aaron, "Go to the altar, offer your sin offering and your burnt offering, and make atonement for yourself and for the people. Offer the offering of the people, and make atonement for them, as the LORD commanded."

8:23 When the blood of Christ is applied to the sinner, it opens his ear to the voice of the Lord, which guides what he puts his hand to and the places where he goes. He is no longer his own. He is bought with a price and now he does everything with respect to God and His will (see 1 Cor. 6:19,20).

[8]Aaron therefore went to the altar and
killed the calf of the sin offering, which
was for himself. [9]Then the sons of Aaron
brought the blood to him. And he dipped
his finger in the blood, put *it* on the horns
of the altar, and poured the blood at the
base of the altar. [10]But the fat, the kidneys, and the fatty lobe from the liver of
the sin offering he burned on the altar, as
the LORD had commanded Moses. [11]The
flesh and the hide he burned with fire
outside the camp.

[12]And he killed the burnt offering; and
Aaron's sons presented to him the blood,
which he sprinkled all around on the altar. [13]Then they presented the burnt offering to him, with its pieces and head,
and he burned *them* on the altar. [14]And
he washed the entrails and the legs, and
burned *them* with the burnt offering on
the altar.

[15]Then he brought the people's offering, and took the goat, which *was* the sin
offering for the people, and killed it and
offered it for sin, like the first one. [16]And
he brought the burnt offering and offered
it according to the prescribed manner.
[17]Then he brought the grain offering,
took a handful of it, and burned *it* on the
altar, besides the burnt sacrifice of the
morning.

[18]He also killed the bull and the ram
as sacrifices of peace offerings, which *were*
for the people. And Aaron's sons presented to him the blood, which he sprinkled all around on the altar, [19]and the fat
from the bull and the ram—the fatty tail,
what covers *the entrails* and the kidneys,
and the fatty lobe *attached to* the liver;
[20]and they put the fat on the breasts.
Then he burned the fat on the altar; [21]but
the breasts and the right thigh Aaron
waved *as* a wave offering before the LORD,
as Moses had commanded.

[22]Then Aaron lifted his hand toward
the people, blessed them, and came down
from offering the sin offering, the burnt
offering, and peace offerings. [23]And Moses
and Aaron went into the tabernacle of
meeting, and came out and blessed the
people. Then the glory of the LORD appeared to all the people, [24]and fire came
out from before the LORD and consumed
the burnt offering and the fat on the altar.
When all the people saw *it*, they shouted
and fell on their faces.

The Profane Fire of Nadab and Abihu

10 Then Nadab and Abihu, the sons
of Aaron, each took his censer and
put fire in it, put incense on it, and offered profane fire before the LORD, which
He had not commanded them. [2]So fire
went out from the LORD and devoured
them, and they died before the LORD. [3]And
Moses said to Aaron, "This is what the
LORD spoke, saying:

'By those who come near Me
I must be regarded as holy;
And before all the people
I must be glorified.' "

So Aaron held his peace.

[4]Then Moses called Mishael and Elzaphan, the sons of Uzziel the uncle of Aaron,
and said to them, "Come near, carry your
brethren from before the sanctuary out of

9:7 "If men do not understand the Law, they will not feel that they are sinners. And if they are not consciously sinners, they will never value the sin offering. There is no healing a man till the Law has wounded him, no making him alive till the Law has slain him." *Charles Spurgeon*

10:1–3 Unauthorized fire. These men, who were to approach God on behalf of the children of Israel, were to come on His terms. He killed them because they neglected to do as they were instructed. They were supposed to get the fire for their censers from the brazen altar, where the sacrifices or "sin offerings" were made. Any sinner wanting to approach God must do so on His terms—through repentance and faith in Jesus. Those who refuse to obey God will be destroyed by fire: "when the Lord Jesus is revealed from heaven with His mighty angels, in flaming fire taking vengeance on those who do not know God, and on those who do not obey the gospel of our Lord Jesus Christ. These shall be punished with everlasting destruction from the presence of the Lord and from the glory of His power" (2 Thess. 1:7–9).

the camp." 5So they went near and carried them by their tunics out of the camp, as Moses had said.

6And Moses said to Aaron, and to Eleazar and Ithamar, his sons, "Do not uncover your heads nor tear your clothes, lest you die, and wrath come upon all the people. But let your brethren, the whole house of Israel, bewail the burning which the LORD has kindled. 7You shall not go out from the door of the tabernacle of meeting, lest you die, for the anointing oil of the LORD *is* upon you." And they did according to the word of Moses.

Conduct Prescribed for Priests

8Then the LORD spoke to Aaron, saying: 9"Do not drink wine or intoxicating drink, you, nor your sons with you, when you go into the tabernacle of meeting, lest you die. *It shall be* a statute forever throughout your generations, 10that you may distinguish between holy and unholy, and between unclean and clean, 11and that you may teach the children of Israel all the statutes which the LORD has spoken to them by the hand of Moses."

12And Moses spoke to Aaron, and to Eleazar and Ithamar, his sons who were left: "Take the grain offering that remains of the offerings made by fire to the LORD, and eat it without leaven beside the altar; for it *is* most holy. 13You shall eat it in a holy place, because it *is* your due and your sons' due, of the sacrifices made by fire to the LORD; for so I have been commanded. 14The breast of the wave offering and the thigh of the heave offering you shall eat in a clean place, you, your sons, and your daughters with you; for *they are* your due and your sons' due, *which* are given from the sacrifices of peace offerings of the children of Israel. 15The thigh of the heave offering and the breast of the wave offering they shall bring with the offerings of fat made by fire, to offer *as* a wave offering before the LORD. And it shall be yours and your sons' with you, by a statute forever, as the LORD has commanded."

16Then Moses made careful inquiry about the goat of the sin offering, and there it was—burned up. And he was angry with Eleazar and Ithamar, the sons of Aaron *who were* left, saying, 17"Why have you not eaten the sin offering in a holy place, since it *is* most holy, and *God* has given it to you to bear the guilt of the congregation, to make atonement for them before the LORD? 18See! Its blood was not brought inside the holy *place;*[a] indeed you should have eaten it in a holy *place,* as I commanded."

19And Aaron said to Moses, "Look, this day they have offered their sin offering and their burnt offering before the LORD, and such things have befallen me! *If* I had eaten the sin offering today, would it have been accepted in the sight of the LORD?" 20So when Moses heard *that,* he was content.

Foods Permitted and Forbidden

11 Now the LORD spoke to Moses and Aaron, saying to them, 2"Speak to the children of Israel, saying, 'These *are* the animals which you may eat among all the animals that *are* on the earth: 3Among the animals, whatever divides the hoof, having cloven hooves *and* chewing the cud—that you may eat. 4Nevertheless these you shall not eat among those that chew the cud or those that have cloven hooves: the camel, because it chews the cud but does not have cloven hooves, is unclean to you; 5the rock hyrax, because it chews the cud but does not have cloven hooves, *is* unclean to you; 6the hare, because it chews the cud but does not have cloven hooves, *is* unclean to you; 7and the swine, though it divides the hoof, having cloven hooves, yet does not chew the cud, *is* unclean to you. 8Their flesh you shall not eat, and their carcasses you shall not touch. They *are* unclean to you.

9'These you may eat of all that *are* in the water: whatever in the water has fins and scales, whether in the seas or in the

10:18 [a]The Most Holy Place when capitalized

POINTS FOR OPEN-AIR PREACHING

11:16

Look for the Seagulls

There is a difference between messages preached in the open air and those preached in a building where people are sitting and attentive. People in a church building are there willingly and are a captive audience. In the open air, if people don't like what you are saying or think you are boring, they leave. Therefore, you need to learn the skills of open-air preaching. The analogy of "fishing" for men is so applicable. A good fisherman is a skilled fisherman, and his skill comes by experience. Knowing that seagulls gather where the fish are, he learns to go where the fish gather. He knows that certain seaweeds attract certain fish, how to bait a hook so that it is disguised, when to reel in the fish, etc. These skills come by experience, but to hasten that experience see Jer. 19:2 comment for suggestions on choosing a suitable "fishing hole," and Acts 2:14 comment for how to draw a crowd.

One way to attract "fish" is to use any type of entertainment, such as playing a guitar and singing. If it would help me pull in a crowd, I would sing, if I could. If I could dance or juggle or smash wood with my fist, I would use that skill for the glory of God. If you have a talent of any sort, give serious consideration to using it to reach the lost. Some Christians have a great talent but set it aside, thinking that it was just part of their old, sinful life. Then resurrect it for the sake of the unsaved. If you can do sleight-of-hand (magic), do it. Rekindle the skill.

However, make sure that any entertainment is used to attract people to the message, rather than distract them from it. If it continues while you're witnessing, people won't be listening to your words. So once you have their attention, stop the entertainment, but keep it handy, and do something else for your listeners when you have finished speaking to leave them with a positive note.

rivers—that you may eat. 10But all in the
seas or in the rivers that do not have fins
and scales, all that move in the water or
any living thing which *is* in the water,
they *are* an abomination to you. 11They
shall be an abomination to you; you shall
not eat their flesh, but you shall regard
their carcasses as an abomination. 12What-
ever in the water does not have fins or
scales—that *shall be* an abomination to you.
13'And these you shall regard as an
abomination among the birds; they shall
not be eaten, they *are* an abomination:
the eagle, the vulture, the buzzard, 14the
kite, and the falcon after its kind; 15every
raven after its kind, 16the ostrich, the short-
eared owl, the sea gull, and the hawk after its kind; 17the little owl, the fisher owl,
and the screech owl; 18the white owl, the
jackdaw, and the carrion vulture; 19the
stork, the heron after its kind, the hoopoe,
and the bat.

20'All flying insects that creep on *all*
fours *shall be* an abomination to you. 21Yet
these you may eat of every flying insect
that creeps on *all* fours: those which have
jointed legs above their feet with which
to leap on the earth. 22These you may eat:
the locust after its kind, the destroying
locust after its kind, the cricket after its
kind, and the grasshopper after its kind.
23But all *other* flying insects which have
four feet *shall be* an abomination to you.

Unclean Animals

24'By these you shall become unclean;
whoever touches the carcass of any of
them shall be unclean until evening;
25whoever carries part of the carcass of
any of them shall wash his clothes and be
unclean until evening: 26*The carcass* of
any animal which divides the foot, but is
not cloven-hoofed or does not chew the
cud, *is* unclean to you. Everyone who

11:10,11 Skeptics mockingly point to the food laws in the Book of Leviticus. While there were undoubtedly some health issues involved with eating the scavengers (trash collectors) of the sea, God's primary purpose was for Israel to be a distinct people, separated from the customs of their idolatrous neighbors. This is also the reason they were prohibited from wearing garments made with wool and linen woven together (Deut. 22:11), which was a superstitious custom of the pagans. Many similar regulations were symbolic to keep Israel pure and unmixed with the surrounding nations.

touches it shall be unclean. 27And whatever goes on its paws, among all kinds of
animals that go on *all* fours, those *are* unclean to you. Whoever touches any such
carcass shall be unclean until evening.
28Whoever carries *any such* carcass shall
wash his clothes and be unclean until
evening. It *is* unclean to you.

29'These also *shall be* unclean to you
among the creeping things that creep on
the earth: the mole, the mouse, and the
large lizard after its kind; 30the gecko, the
monitor lizard, the sand reptile, the sand
lizard, and the chameleon. 31These *are* unclean to you among all that creep. Whoever touches them when they are dead
shall be unclean until evening. 32Any-
thing on which *any* of them falls, when
they are dead shall be unclean, whether *it*
is any item of wood or clothing or skin or
sack, whatever item *it is,* in which *any*
work is done, it must be put in water. And
it shall be unclean until evening; then it
shall be clean. 33Any earthen vessel into
which *any* of them falls you shall break;
and whatever *is* in it shall be unclean: 34in
such a vessel, any edible food upon which
water falls becomes unclean, and any
drink that may be drunk from it becomes
unclean. 35And everything on which *a part*
of *any such* carcass falls shall be unclean;
whether it is an oven or cooking stove, it
shall be broken down; *for* they *are* unclean, and shall be unclean to you. 36Nev-
ertheless a spring or a cistern, *in which*
there is plenty of water, shall be clean, but
whatever touches any such carcass becomes unclean. 37And if a part of *any such*
carcass falls on any planting seed which
is to be sown, it *remains* clean. 38But if
water is put on the seed, and if *a part* of
any such carcass falls on it, it *becomes* unclean to you.

39'And if any animal which you may
eat dies, he who touches its carcass shall
be unclean until evening. 40He who eats
of its carcass shall wash his clothes and
be unclean until evening. He also who
carries its carcass shall wash his clothes
and be unclean until evening.

41'And every creeping thing that creeps
on the earth *shall be* an abomination. It
shall not be eaten. 42Whatever crawls on
its belly, whatever goes on *all* fours, or
whatever has many feet among all creeping things that creep on the earth—these
you shall not eat, for they *are* an abomination. 43You shall not make yourselves
abominable with any creeping thing that
creeps; nor shall you make yourselves
unclean with them, lest you be defiled by
them. 44For I *am* the LORD your God. You
shall therefore consecrate yourselves, and
you shall be holy; for I *am* holy. Neither
shall you defile yourselves with any creeping thing that creeps on the earth. 45For I

11:44 The different laws of God. If we don't "rightly divide the word of truth," we will be confused as to what God requires in His Law. There are three categories into which the Old Testament Law may be divided: the Moral Law, the Ceremonial Law, and the Civil (judicial) Law. The Moral Law, summarized in the Ten Commandments, represents God's own moral character. (For a chart comparing God's character and the Ten Commandments, see page 280.) These are forever binding, in both old and new covenants. God will judge humanity by the standard of His moral Law (see Rom. 2:12; James 2:12). The Law brings the knowledge of sin, so that we see our need of the Savior. It acts as a mirror to show us ourselves in truth.

The second is the Ceremonial Law. These are types, shadows, and figures of the coming Christ. This is the sacrificial system of the old covenant, and also includes the whole cleanliness code including restrictions on food, etc. Hebrews 10:1 says that the law is only "a shadow of the good things to come, and not the very image of the things."

The third category is the Civil (or judicial) Law. These are the laws for the nation of Israel that represented the criminal code, with all its procedures and punishments, as well as many other regulations and restrictions.

As for which Law to use in the gospel presentation, look to the example of Scripture. For instance, Paul (Rom. 2:21–24), James (James 2:10,11), and Jesus (Luke 18:18–20) each used the moral Law, the Ten Commandments, to bring the knowledge of sin. It is only the moral Law that is written on the hearts of all men (see Rom. 2:15). The conscience speaks to the sins of lust, hatred, lying, theft, adultery, etc., not to whether or not we should eat snails or a fish with scales.

am the LORD who brings you up out of
the land of Egypt, to be your God. You
shall therefore be holy, for I *am* holy.
46'This *is* the law of the animals and
the birds and every living creature that
moves in the waters, and of every creature that creeps on the earth, 47to distinguish between the unclean and the clean,
and between the animal that may be eaten
and the animal that may not be eaten.' "

The Ritual After Childbirth

12 Then the LORD spoke to Moses,
saying, 2"Speak to the children of
Israel, saying: 'If a woman has conceived,
and borne a male child, then she shall be
unclean seven days; as in the days of her
customary impurity she shall be unclean.
3And on the eighth day the flesh of his
foreskin shall be circumcised. 4She shall
then continue in the blood of *her* purification thirty-three days. She shall not
touch any hallowed thing, nor come into
the sanctuary until the days of her purification are fulfilled.
5'But if she bears a female child, then
she shall be unclean two weeks, as in her
customary impurity, and she shall continue in the blood of *her* purification sixty-
six days.
6'When the days of her purification are
fulfilled, whether for a son or a daughter,
she shall bring to the priest a lamb of the
first year as a burnt offering, and a young
pigeon or a turtledove as a sin offering, to
the door of the tabernacle of meeting.
7Then he shall offer it before the LORD,
and make atonement for her. And she
shall be clean from the flow of her blood.
This *is* the law for her who has borne a
male or a female.
8'And if she is not able to bring a lamb,
then she may bring two turtledoves or
two young pigeons—one as a burnt offering and the other as a sin offering. So
the priest shall make atonement for her,
and she will be clean.' "

The Law Concerning Leprosy

13 And the LORD spoke to Moses and
Aaron, saying: 2"When a man has
on the skin of his body a swelling, a scab,
or a bright spot, and it becomes on the
skin of his body *like* a leprous[a] sore, then
he shall be brought to Aaron the priest or
to one of his sons the priests. 3The priest
shall examine the sore on the skin of the
body; and if the hair on the sore has
turned white, and the sore appears *to be*
deeper than the skin of his body, it *is* a
leprous sore. Then the priest shall examine him, and pronounce him unclean.
4But if the bright spot *is* white on the skin
of his body, and does not appear *to be*
deeper than the skin, and its hair has not
turned white, then the priest shall isolate
the one who has the sore seven days. 5And
the priest shall examine him on the seventh day; and indeed *if* the sore appears
to be as it was, *and* the sore has not spread
on the skin, then the priest shall isolate
him another seven days. 6Then the priest
shall examine him again on the seventh
day; and indeed *if* the sore has faded, *and*
the sore has not spread on the skin, then
the priest shall pronounce him clean; it *is*
only a scab, and he shall wash his clothes
and be clean. 7But if the scab should at all
spread over the skin, after he has been
seen by the priest for his cleansing, he
shall be seen by the priest again. 8And *if*
the priest sees that the scab has indeed
spread on the skin, then the priest shall
pronounce him unclean. It *is* leprosy.
9"When the leprous sore is on a per-

13:2 [a]Hebrew *saraath,* disfiguring skin diseases, including leprosy, and so in verses 2–46 and 14:1–32

12:6–8 The New Testament says of Mary, "Now when the days of her purification according to the law of Moses were completed, they brought Him to Jerusalem to present Him to the Lord (as it is written in the law of the Lord, 'Every male who opens the womb shall be called holy to the LORD'), and to offer a sacrifice according to what is said in the law of the Lord, 'A pair of turtledoves or two young pigeons'" (Luke 2:22–25).

13:5 For fascinating facts in the Bible, see Psa. 38:11 comment.

son, then he shall be brought to the priest.
10And the priest shall examine *him;* and
indeed *if* the swelling on the skin *is* white,
and it has turned the hair white, and
there is a spot of raw flesh in the swelling,
11it *is* an old leprosy on the skin of his
body. The priest shall pronounce him unclean, and shall not isolate him, for he *is*
unclean.

12"And if leprosy breaks out all over
the skin, and the leprosy covers all the
skin of *the one who has* the sore, from his
head to his foot, wherever the priest looks,
13then the priest shall consider; and indeed *if* the leprosy has covered all his
body, he shall pronounce *him* clean *who
has* the sore. It has all turned white. He *is*
clean. 14But when raw flesh appears on
him, he shall be unclean. 15And the priest
shall examine the raw flesh and pronounce him to be unclean; *for* the raw
flesh *is* unclean. It *is* leprosy. 16Or if the
raw flesh changes and turns white again,
he shall come to the priest. 17And the
priest shall examine him; and indeed *if*
the sore has turned white, then the priest
shall pronounce *him* clean *who has* the
sore. He *is* clean.

18"If the body develops a boil in the
skin, and it is healed, 19and in the place
of the boil there comes a white swelling
or a bright spot, reddish-white, then it
shall be shown to the priest; 20and *if,*
when the priest sees it, it indeed appears
deeper than the skin, and its hair has
turned white, the priest shall pronounce
him unclean. It *is* a leprous sore which
has broken out of the boil. 21But if the
priest examines it, and indeed *there are*
no white hairs in it, and it is not deeper
than the skin, but has faded, then the
priest shall isolate him seven days; 22and
if it should at all spread over the skin,
then the priest shall pronounce him unclean. It *is* a leprous sore. 23But if the
bright spot stays in one place, *and* has not
spread, it *is* the scar of the boil; and the
priest shall pronounce him clean.

24"Or if the body receives a burn on its
skin by fire, and the raw *flesh* of the burn
becomes a bright spot, reddish-white or
white, 25then the priest shall examine it;
and indeed *if* the hair of the bright spot
has turned white, and it appears deeper
than the skin, it *is* leprosy broken out in
the burn. Therefore the priest shall pronounce him unclean. It *is* a leprous sore.
26But if the priest examines it, and indeed
there are no white hairs in the bright spot,
and it *is* not deeper than the skin, but has
faded, then the priest shall isolate him
seven days. 27And the priest shall examine him on the seventh day. If it has at all
spread over the skin, then the priest shall
pronounce him unclean. It *is* a leprous
sore. 28But if the bright spot stays in one
place, *and* has not spread on the skin, but
has faded, it *is* a swelling from the burn.
The priest shall pronounce him clean, for
it *is* the scar from the burn.

29"If a man or woman has a sore on the
head or the beard, 30then the priest shall
examine the sore; and indeed if it appears
deeper than the skin, *and there is* in it thin
yellow hair, then the priest shall pronounce him unclean. It *is* a scaly leprosy
of the head or beard. 31But if the priest
examines the scaly sore, and indeed it
does not appear deeper than the skin,
and *there is* no black hair in it, then the
priest shall isolate *the one who has* the
scale seven days. 32And on the seventh

13:9–15 Declaring sinners unclean. As priests of the Lord (see 1 Pet. 2:5; Rev. 1:6) we are to pronounce the sinner as unclean. How can we do that without appearing judgmental? Simply by doing what Jesus did and pointing to the Ten Commandments (see Mark 10:17–22). Consider how Paul did this in Rom. 2:21–23: "You, therefore, who teach another, do you not teach yourself? You who preach that a man should not steal, do you steal? You who say, 'Do not commit adultery,' do you commit adultery? You who abhor idols, do you rob temples? You who make your boast in the law, do you dishonor God through breaking the law?" Notice that he asks questions of his hearers. Do the same. Ask, "Have you ever told a lie? Have you ever stolen something, used God's name in vain (etc.)?" For details, see Psa. 51:6 comment.

day the priest shall examine the sore; and indeed *if* the scale has not spread, and there is no yellow hair in it, and the scale does not appear deeper than the skin, 33he shall shave himself, but the scale he shall not shave. And the priest shall isolate *the one who has* the scale another seven days. 34On the seventh day the priest shall examine the scale; and indeed *if* the scale has not spread over the skin, and does not appear deeper than the skin, then the priest shall pronounce him clean. He shall wash his clothes and be clean. 35But if the scale should at all spread over the skin after his cleansing, 36then the priest shall examine him; and indeed *if* the scale has spread over the skin, the priest need not seek for yellow hair. He *is* unclean. 37But if the scale appears to be at a standstill, and there is black hair grown up in it, the scale has healed. He *is* clean, and the priest shall pronounce him clean.

38"If a man or a woman has bright spots on the skin of the body, *specifically* white bright spots, 39then the priest shall look; and indeed *if* the bright spots on the skin of the body *are* dull white, it *is* a white spot *that* grows on the skin. He *is* clean.

40"As for the man whose hair has fallen from his head, he *is* bald, *but* he *is* clean. 41He whose hair has fallen from his forehead, he *is* bald on the forehead, *but* he *is* clean. 42And if there is on the bald head or bald forehead a reddish-white sore, it *is* leprosy breaking out on his bald head or his bald forehead. 43Then the priest shall examine it; and indeed *if* the swelling of the sore *is* reddish-white on his bald head or on his bald forehead, as the appearance of leprosy on the skin of the body, 44he is a leprous man. He *is* unclean. The priest shall surely pronounce him unclean; his sore *is* on his head.

45"Now the leper on whom the sore *is*, his clothes shall be torn and his head bare; and he shall cover his mustache, and cry, 'Unclean! Unclean!' 46He shall be unclean. All the days he has the sore he shall be unclean. He *is* unclean, and he shall dwell alone; his dwelling *shall be* outside the camp.

The Law Concerning Leprous Garments

47"Also, if a garment has a leprous plague[a] in it, *whether it is* a woolen garment or a linen garment, 48whether *it is* in the warp or woof of linen or wool, whether in leather or in anything made of leather, 49and if the plague is greenish or reddish in the garment or in the leather, whether in the warp or in the woof, or in anything made of leather, it *is* a leprous plague and shall be shown to the priest. 50The priest shall examine the plague and isolate *that which has* the plague seven days. 51And he shall examine the plague on the seventh day. If the plague has spread in the garment, either in the warp or in the woof, in the leather *or* in anything made of leather, the plague *is* an active leprosy. It *is* unclean. 52He shall therefore burn that garment in which is the plague, whether warp or woof, in wool or in linen, or anything of leather, for it *is* an active leprosy; *the garment* shall be burned in the fire.

53"But if the priest examines *it*, and indeed the plague has not spread in the garment, either in the warp or in the woof, or in anything made of leather, 54then the priest shall command that they wash *the thing* in which *is* the plague; and he shall

13:47 [a]A mold, fungus, or similar infestation, and so in verses 47–59

13:52 Leprosy is like sin, in that the sufferer feels no pain and is therefore unaware that his flesh is rotting on his body. In the same way, a sinner is unaware that sin is eating at his flesh and will bring about his death and damnation. This is why, as faithful priests of the Lord, we are to diagnose his disease and pronounce that he is unclean in the sight of God. "And on some have compassion, making a distinction; but others save with fear, pulling them out of the fire, hating even the garment defiled by the flesh" (Jude 22,23).

isolate it another seven days. 55Then the priest shall examine the plague after it has been washed; and indeed *if* the plague has not changed its color, though the plague has not spread, it *is* unclean, and you shall burn it in the fire; it continues eating away, *whether* the damage *is* outside or inside. 56If the priest examines *it,* and indeed the plague has faded after washing it, then he shall tear it out of the garment, whether out of the warp or out of the woof, or out of the leather. 57But if it appears again in the garment, either in the warp or in the woof, or in anything made of leather, it *is* a spreading *plague;* you shall burn with fire that in which is the plague. 58And if you wash the garment, either warp or woof, or whatever is made of leather, if the plague has disappeared from it, then it shall be washed a second time, and shall be clean.

59"This *is* the law of the leprous plague in a garment of wool or linen, either in the warp or woof, or in anything made of leather, to pronounce it clean or to pronounce it unclean."

The Ritual for Cleansing Healed Lepers

14 Then the LORD spoke to Moses, saying, 2"This shall be the law of the leper for the day of his cleansing: He shall be brought to the priest. 3And the priest shall go out of the camp, and the priest shall examine *him;* and indeed, *if* the leprosy is healed in the leper, 4then the priest shall command to take for him who is to be cleansed two living *and* clean birds, cedar wood, scarlet, and hyssop. 5And the priest shall command that one of the birds be killed in an earthen vessel over running water. 6As for the living bird, he shall take it, the cedar wood and the scarlet and the hyssop, and dip them and the living bird in the blood of the bird *that was* killed over the running water. 7And he shall sprinkle it seven times on him who is to be cleansed from the leprosy, and shall pronounce him clean, and shall let the living bird loose in the open field. 8He who is to be cleansed shall wash his clothes, shave off all his hair, and wash himself in water, that he may be clean. After that he shall come into the camp, and shall stay outside his tent seven days. 9But on the seventh day he shall shave all the hair off his head and his beard and his eyebrows—all his hair he shall shave off. He shall wash his clothes and wash his body in water, and he shall be clean.

10"And on the eighth day he shall take two male lambs without blemish, one ewe lamb of the first year without blemish, three-tenths *of an ephah* of fine flour mixed with oil as a grain offering, and one log of oil. 11Then the priest who makes *him* clean shall present the man who is to be made clean, and those things, before the LORD, *at* the door of the tabernacle of meeting. 12And the priest shall take one male lamb and offer it as a trespass offering, and the log of oil, and wave them *as* a wave offering before the LORD. 13Then he shall kill the lamb in the place where he kills the sin offering and the burnt offering, in a holy place; for as the sin offering *is* the priest's, so *is* the trespass offering. It *is* most holy. 14The priest shall take *some* of the blood of the trespass offering, and the priest shall put *it* on the tip of the right ear of him who is to be cleansed, on the thumb of his right hand, and on the big toe of his right foot. 15And the priest shall take *some* of the log of oil, and pour *it* into the palm of his own left hand. 16Then the priest shall dip his right finger in the oil that *is* in his left hand, and shall sprinkle some of the oil with his finger seven times before the LORD. 17And of the rest of the oil in his hand, the priest shall put *some* on the tip of the right ear of him who is to be cleansed, on the thumb of his right hand, and on the big toe of his right foot, on the blood of the trespass offering. 18The rest of the oil that *is* in the priest's hand he shall put on the head of him who is to be cleansed. So the priest shall make atonement for him before the LORD.

19“Then the priest shall offer the sin offering, and make atonement for him who is to be cleansed from his uncleanness. Afterward he shall kill the burnt offering. 20And the priest shall offer the burnt offering and the grain offering on the altar. So the priest shall make atonement for him, and he shall be clean.

21“But if he *is* poor and cannot afford it, then he shall take one male lamb *as* a trespass offering to be waved, to make atonement for him, one-tenth *of an ephah* of fine flour mixed with oil as a grain offering, a log of oil, 22and two turtledoves or two young pigeons, such as he is able to afford: one shall be a sin offering and the other a burnt offering. 23He shall bring them to the priest on the eighth day for his cleansing, to the door of the tabernacle of meeting, before the LORD. 24And the priest shall take the lamb of the trespass offering and the log of oil, and the priest shall wave them *as* a wave offering before the LORD. 25Then he shall kill the lamb of the trespass offering, and the priest shall take *some* of the blood of the trespass offering and put *it* on the tip of the right ear of him who is to be cleansed, on the thumb of his right hand, and on the big toe of his right foot. 26And the priest shall pour some of the oil into the palm of his own left hand. 27Then the priest shall sprinkle with his right finger *some* of the oil that *is* in his left hand seven times before the LORD. 28And the priest shall put *some* of the oil that *is* in his hand on the tip of the right ear of him who is to be cleansed, on the thumb of the right hand, and on the big toe of his right foot, on the place of the blood of the trespass offering. 29The rest of the oil that *is* in the priest’s hand he shall put on the head of him who is to be cleansed, to make atonement for him before the LORD. 30And he shall offer one of the turtledoves or young pigeons, such as he can afford— 31such as he is able to afford, the one *as* a sin offering and the other *as* a burnt offering, with the grain offering. So the priest shall make atonement for him who is to be cleansed before the LORD. 32This *is* the law *for one* who had a leprous sore, who cannot afford the usual cleansing.”

The Law Concerning Leprous Houses

33And the LORD spoke to Moses and Aaron, saying: 34“When you have come into the land of Canaan, which I give you as a possession, and I put the leprous plague[a] in a house in the land of your possession, 35and he who owns the house comes and tells the priest, saying, ‘It seems to me that *there is* some plague in the house,’ 36then the priest shall command that they empty the house, before the priest goes *into it* to examine the plague, that all that *is* in the house may not be made unclean; and afterward the priest shall go in to examine the house. 37And he shall examine the plague; and indeed *if* the plague *is* on the walls of the house with ingrained streaks, greenish or reddish, which appear to be deep in the wall, 38then the priest shall go out of the house, to the door of the house, and shut up the house seven days. 39And the priest shall come again on the seventh day and look; and indeed *if* the plague has spread on the walls of the house, 40then the priest shall command that they take away the stones in which *is* the plague, and they shall cast them into an unclean place outside the city. 41And he shall cause the house to be scraped inside, all around, and the dust that they scrape off they shall pour out in an unclean place outside the city. 42Then they shall take other stones and put *them* in the place of *those* stones, and he shall take other mortar and plaster the house.

43“Now if the plague comes back and breaks out in the house, after he has taken away the stones, after he has scraped the house, and after it is plastered, 44then the priest shall come and look; and indeed *if* the plague has spread in the house, it *is* an active leprosy in the house. It *is* unclean. 45And he shall break down the house, its

14:34 [a]Decomposition by mildew, mold, dry rot, etc., and so in verses 34–53

stones, its timber, and all the plaster of
the house, and he shall carry *them* outside the city to an unclean place. 46More-
over he who goes into the house at all
while it is shut up shall be unclean until
evening. 47And he who lies down in the
house shall wash his clothes, and he who
eats in the house shall wash his clothes.

48"But if the priest comes in and examines *it,* and indeed the plague has not
spread in the house after the house was
plastered, then the priest shall pronounce
the house clean, because the plague is
healed. 49And he shall take, to cleanse the
house, two birds, cedar wood, scarlet, and
hyssop. 50Then he shall kill one of the
birds in an earthen vessel over running
water; 51and he shall take the cedar wood,
the hyssop, the scarlet, and the living bird,
and dip them in the blood of the slain
bird and in the running water, and sprinkle the house seven times. 52And he shall
cleanse the house with the blood of the
bird and the running water and the living
bird, with the cedar wood, the hyssop,
and the scarlet. 53Then he shall let the living bird loose outside the city in the open
field, and make atonement for the house,
and it shall be clean.

54"This *is* the law for any leprous sore
and scale, 55for the leprosy of a garment
and of a house, 56for a swelling and a scab
and a bright spot, 57to teach when *it is* unclean and when *it is* clean. This *is* the law
of leprosy."

The Law Concerning Bodily Discharges

15 And the LORD spoke to Moses and
Aaron, saying, 2"Speak to the children of Israel, and say to them: 'When
any man has a discharge from his body,
his discharge *is* unclean. 3And this shall
be his uncleanness in regard to his discharge—whether his body runs with his
discharge, or his body is stopped up by
his discharge, it *is* his uncleanness. 4Every
bed is unclean on which he who has the
discharge lies, and everything on which
he sits shall be unclean. 5And whoever
touches his bed shall wash his clothes and
bathe in water, and be unclean until evening. 6He who sits on anything on which
he who has the discharge sat shall wash
his clothes and bathe in water, and be unclean until evening. 7And he who touches
the body of him who has the discharge
shall wash his clothes and bathe in water,
and be unclean until evening. 8If he who
has the discharge spits on him who is
clean, then he shall wash his clothes and
bathe in water, and be unclean until evening. 9Any saddle on which he who has the
discharge rides shall be unclean. 10Who-
ever touches anything that was under
him shall be unclean until evening. He
who carries *any of* those things shall wash
his clothes and bathe in water, and be unclean until evening. 11And whomever the
one who has the discharge touches, and
has not rinsed his hands in water, he shall
wash his clothes and bathe in water, and
be unclean until evening. 12The vessel of
earth that he who has the discharge
touches shall be broken, and every vessel
of wood shall be rinsed in water.

The early disciples were fishers of men—while modern disciples are often little more than aquarium keepers.

UNKNOWN

13'And when he who has a discharge is
cleansed of his discharge, then he shall
count for himself seven days for his cleansing, wash his clothes, and bathe his body
in running water; then he shall be clean.
14On the eighth day he shall take for himself two turtledoves or two young pigeons, and come before the LORD, to the
door of the tabernacle of meeting, and give
them to the priest. 15Then the priest shall
offer them, the one *as* a sin offering and
the other *as* a burnt offering. So the priest
shall make atonement for him before the
LORD because of his discharge.

16'If any man has an emission of semen,
then he shall wash all his body in water,
and be unclean until evening. 17And any

garment and any leather on which there
is semen, it shall be washed with water,
and be unclean until evening. 18Also, when
a woman lies with a man, and *there is* an
emission of semen, they shall bathe in
water, and be unclean until evening.

19'If a woman has a discharge, *and* the
discharge from her body is blood, she shall
be set apart seven days; and whoever
touches her shall be unclean until evening. 20Everything that she lies on during
her impurity shall be unclean; also everything that she sits on shall be unclean.
21Whoever touches her bed shall wash
his clothes and bathe in water, and be unclean until evening. 22And whoever touches
anything that she sat on shall wash his
clothes and bathe in water, and be unclean until evening. 23If *anything* is on *her*
bed or on anything on which she sits,
when he touches it, he shall be unclean
until evening. 24And if any man lies with
her at all, so that her impurity is on him,
he shall be unclean seven days; and every
bed on which he lies shall be unclean.

25'If a woman has a discharge of blood
for many days, other than at the time of
her *customary* impurity, or if it runs beyond her *usual time of* impurity, all the
days of her unclean discharge shall be as
the days of her *customary* impurity. She
shall be unclean. 26Every bed on which
she lies all the days of her discharge shall
be to her as the bed of her impurity; and
whatever she sits on shall be unclean, as
the uncleanness of her impurity. 27Who-
ever touches those things shall be unclean; he shall wash his clothes and bathe
in water, and be unclean until evening.

28'But if she is cleansed of her discharge,
then she shall count for herself seven
days, and after that she shall be clean.
29And on the eighth day she shall take for
herself two turtledoves or two young pigeons, and bring them to the priest, to
the door of the tabernacle of meeting.
30Then the priest shall offer the one *as* a
sin offering and the other *as* a burnt offering, and the priest shall make atonement for her before the LORD for the discharge of her uncleanness.

31'Thus you shall separate the children
of Israel from their uncleanness, lest they
die in their uncleanness when they defile
My tabernacle that *is* among them. 32This
is the law for one who has a discharge,
and *for him* who emits semen and is unclean thereby, 33and for her who is indis-
posed because of her *customary* impurity,
and for one who has a discharge, either
man or woman, and for him who lies
with her who is unclean.' "

The Day of Atonement

16 Now the LORD spoke to Moses after the death of the two sons of
Aaron, when they offered *profane fire* before the LORD, and died; 2and the LORD
said to Moses: "Tell Aaron your brother
not to come at *just* any time into the Holy
Place inside the veil, before the mercy
seat which *is* on the ark, lest he die; for I
will appear in the cloud above the mercy
seat.

3"Thus Aaron shall come into the Holy
Place: with *the blood of* a young bull as a
sin offering, and *of* a ram as a burnt offering. 4He shall put the holy linen tunic
and the linen trousers on his body; he
shall be girded with a linen sash, and
with the linen turban he shall be attired.
These *are* holy garments. Therefore he
shall wash his body in water, and put
them on. 5And he shall take from the
congregation of the children of Israel two
kids of the goats as a sin offering, and one
ram as a burnt offering.

6"Aaron shall offer the bull as a sin offering, which *is* for himself, and make
atonement for himself and for his house.
7He shall take the two goats and present
them before the LORD *at* the door of the
tabernacle of meeting. 8Then Aaron shall
cast lots for the two goats: one lot for the
LORD and the other lot for the scapegoat.
9And Aaron shall bring the goat on which
the LORD's lot fell, and offer it *as* a sin offering. 10But the goat on which the lot fell
to be the scapegoat shall be presented
alive before the LORD, to make atonement

upon it, *and* to let it go as the scapegoat
into the wilderness.
11"And Aaron shall bring the bull of
the sin offering, which is for himself, and
make atonement for himself and for his
house, and shall kill the bull as the sin offering which *is* for himself. 12Then he
shall take a censer full of burning coals of
fire from the altar before the LORD, with
his hands full of sweet incense beaten fine,
and bring *it* inside the veil. 13And he shall
put the incense on the fire before the LORD,
that the cloud of incense may cover the
mercy seat that *is* on the Testimony, lest
he die. 14He shall take some of the blood
of the bull and sprinkle *it* with his finger
on the mercy seat on the east *side;* and before the mercy seat he shall sprinkle some
of the blood with his finger seven times.
15"Then he shall kill the goat of the sin
offering, which *is* for the people, bring its
blood inside the veil, do with that blood
as he did with the blood of the bull, and
sprinkle it on the mercy seat and before
the mercy seat. 16So he shall make atonement for the Holy *Place,* because of the
uncleanness of the children of Israel, and
because of their transgressions, for all their
sins; and so he shall do for the tabernacle
of meeting which remains among them in
the midst of their uncleanness. 17There
shall be no man in the tabernacle of
meeting when he goes in to make atonement in the Holy *Place,* until he comes
out, that he may make atonement for himself, for his household, and for all the assembly of Israel. 18And he shall go out to
the altar that *is* before the LORD, and
make atonement for it, and shall take
some of the blood of the bull and some of
the blood of the goat, and put it on the
horns of the altar all around. 19Then he
shall sprinkle some of the blood on it
with his finger seven times, cleanse it,
and consecrate it from the uncleanness of
the children of Israel.
20"And when he has made an end of
atoning for the Holy *Place,* the tabernacle
of meeting, and the altar, he shall bring
the live goat. 21Aaron shall lay both his
hands on the head of the live goat, confess
over it all the iniquities of the children of
Israel, and all their transgressions, concerning all their sins, putting them on the
head of the goat, and shall send *it* away
into the wilderness by the hand of a suitable man. 22The goat shall bear on itself
all their iniquities to an uninhabited land;

16:12,13 Burning coals. We are told in Prov. 25:21,22, "If your enemy is hungry, give him bread to eat; and if he is thirsty, give him water to drink; for so you will heap coals of fire on his head, and the LORD will reward you." This shouldn't be interpreted as paying someone back with a good deed so we can heap condemnation on him. The high priest would fill his censer on the Day of Atonement with "coals of fire" from the altar of burnt offering, and then put incense on the coals to create a pleasing, sweet-smelling fragrance. The cloud or smoke of the incense would then cover the mercy seat and was acceptable to God for atonement. When we show genuine love to our enemies, it is pleasing in the sight of God. Jesus said to love our enemies and do good to those who spitefully use us. By following the example He so vividly gave us on the cross, may our good works serve as burning coals of conviction to bring the lost to Christ (see Matt. 5:16).

16:15 Jesus in the Old Testament. "The Jews have escaped Egypt and are now at the foot of Mount Sinai. God provided a long list of rules for His people to follow, including instructions for the priests to make an annual sacrifice for the covering of people's sins. This was the Day of Atonement (Yom Kippur). On this day, a priest would lay his hands on the head of an unblemished lamb, signifying the transfer of sins from the people to the lamb. The priest would then slit the throat of the lamb and it would bleed to death for the *covering* of their sins.

"Why was this necessary? Leviticus 17:11 tells us that 'it is the blood that makes atonement for the soul.' Imagine the amount of blood that was shed over the centuries. This was a constant reminder to the Jewish people that blood was required for the covering of sins. Unfortunately for them, a lamb could not *forgive* sins. This was merely a picture of a greater sacrifice that was needed.

"Who was the Lamb who could provide complete forgiveness of sins? Only Jesus Christ, about whom John the Baptist proclaimed, 'Behold! The Lamb of God who takes away the sin of the world!' (John 1:29)."
Todd Friel (Adapted from *Don't Stub Your Toe.*)

See Jer. 31:34 comment.

and he shall release the goat in the wilderness.

23“Then Aaron shall come into the tabernacle of meeting, shall take off the linen garments which he put on when he went into the Holy *Place,* and shall leave them there. 24And he shall wash his body with water in a holy place, put on his garments, come out and offer his burnt offering and the burnt offering of the people, and make atonement for himself and for the people. 25The fat of the sin offering he shall burn on the altar. 26And he who released the goat as the scapegoat shall wash his clothes and bathe his body in water, and afterward he may come into the camp. 27The bull *for* the sin offering and the goat *for* the sin offering, whose blood was brought in to make atonement in the Holy *Place,* shall be carried outside the camp. And they shall burn in the fire their skins, their flesh, and their offal. 28Then he who burns them shall wash his clothes and bathe his body in water, and afterward he may come into the camp.

29“*This* shall be a statute forever for you: In the seventh month, on the tenth *day* of the month, you shall afflict your souls, and do no work at all, *whether* a native of your own country or a stranger who dwells among you. 30For on that day *the priest* shall make atonement for you, to cleanse you, *that* you may be clean from all your sins before the LORD. 31It *is* a sabbath of solemn rest for you, and you shall afflict your souls. *It is* a statute forever. 32And the priest, who is anointed and consecrated to minister as priest in his father's place, shall make atonement, and put on the linen clothes, the holy garments; 33then he shall make atonement for the Holy Sanctuary,[a] and he shall make atonement for the tabernacle of meeting and for the altar, and he shall make atonement for the priests and for all the people of the assembly. 34This shall be an everlasting statute for you, to make atonement for the children of Israel, for all their sins, once a year.” And he did as the LORD commanded Moses.

The Sanctity of Blood

17 And the LORD spoke to Moses, saying, 2“Speak to Aaron, to his sons, and to all the children of Israel, and say to them, ‘This *is* the thing which the LORD has commanded, saying: 3“Whatever man of the house of Israel who kills an ox or lamb or goat in the camp, or who kills *it* outside the camp, 4and does not bring it to the door of the tabernacle of meeting to offer an offering to the LORD before the tabernacle of the LORD, the guilt of bloodshed shall be imputed to that man. He has shed blood; and that man shall be cut off from among his people, 5to the end that the children of Israel may bring their sacrifices which they offer in the open field, that they may bring them to the LORD at the door of the tabernacle of meeting, to the priest, and offer them *as* peace offerings to the LORD. 6And the priest shall sprinkle the blood on the altar of the LORD *at* the door of the taber-

16:33 [a]That is, the Most Holy Place

16:30–34 Jewish atonement today. Modern Jews have abandoned blood sacrifice, and instead observe one day each year of self-examination and affliction of the soul, to atone for the sins of the past year: “Yom Kippur atones only for sins between man and G-d, not for sins against another person. To atone for sins against another person, you must first seek reconciliation with that person, righting the wrongs you committed against them if possible. That must all be done before Yom Kippur. Yom Kippur is a complete Sabbath; no work can be performed on that day. It is well-known that you are supposed to refrain from eating and drinking (even water) on Yom Kippur. It is a complete, 25-hour fast beginning before sunset on the evening before Yom Kippur and ending after nightfall on the day of Yom Kippur. The Talmud also specifies additional restrictions that are less well-known: washing and bathing, anointing one's body (with cosmetics, deodorants, etc.), wearing leather shoes (Orthodox Jews routinely wear canvas sneakers under their dress clothes on Yom Kippur), and engaging in sexual relations are all prohibited on Yom Kippur.” *“Yom Kippur,” Jewish Virtual Library*

THE FUNCTION OF THE LAW

18:5 "Now, my friend, are you ready to be weighed by this Law of God? A great many people say that if they keep the Commandments they do not need to be forgiven and saved through Christ. But have you kept them? I will admit that if you perfectly keep the Commandments, you do not need to be saved by Christ; but is there a man in the wide world who can truly say that he has done this? Young lady, can you say: 'I am ready to be weighed by the Law?' Can you, young man? Will you step into the scales and be weighed one by one by the Ten Commandments? Now face these Ten Commandments honestly and prayerfully. See if your life is right, and if you are treating God fairly. God's statutes are just, are they not? If they are right, let us see if we are right. Let us get alone with God and read His Law—read it carefully and prayerfully, and ask Him to forgive us our sin and what He would have us to do." *D. L. Moody*

nacle of meeting, and burn the fat for a sweet aroma to the LORD. 7They shall no more offer their sacrifices to demons, after whom they have played the harlot. This shall be a statute forever for them throughout their generations." '

8"Also you shall say to them: 'Whatever man of the house of Israel, or of the strangers who dwell among you, who offers a burnt offering or sacrifice, 9and does not bring it to the door of the tabernacle of meeting, to offer it to the LORD, that man shall be cut off from among his people.

10'And whatever man of the house of Israel, or of the strangers who dwell among you, who eats any blood, I will set My face against that person who eats blood, and will cut him off from among his people. 11For the life of the flesh *is* in the blood, and I have given it to you upon the altar to make atonement for your souls; for it *is* the blood *that* makes atonement for the soul.' 12Therefore I said to the children of Israel, 'No one among you shall eat blood, nor shall any stranger who dwells among you eat blood.'

13"Whatever man of the children of Israel, or of the strangers who dwell among you, who hunts and catches any animal or bird that may be eaten, he shall pour out its blood and cover it with dust; 14for *it is* the life of all flesh. Its blood sustains its life. Therefore I said to the children of Israel, 'You shall not eat the blood of any flesh, for the life of all flesh is its blood. Whoever eats it shall be cut off.'

15"And every person who eats what died *naturally* or what was torn *by beasts, whether he is* a native of your own country or a stranger, he shall both wash his clothes and bathe in water, and be unclean until evening. Then he shall be clean. 16But if he does not wash *them* or bathe his body, then he shall bear his guilt."

Laws of Sexual Morality

18 Then the LORD spoke to Moses, saying, 2"Speak to the children of Israel, and say to them: 'I am the LORD your God. 3According to the doings of the land of Egypt, where you dwelt, you shall not do; and according to the doings of the land of Canaan, where I am bringing you, you shall not do; nor shall you walk in their ordinances. 4You shall observe My judgments and keep My ordinances, to walk in them: I *am* the LORD your God. 5You shall therefore keep My statutes and My judgments, which if a man does, he shall live by them: I *am* the LORD.

6'None of you shall approach anyone who is near of kin to him, to uncover his nakedness: I *am* the LORD. 7The nakedness of your father or the nakedness of

17:7 Gentile religions are delving into a spirituality that is not from God. Believers in these religions open themselves to the demonic realm: "the things which the Gentiles sacrifice they sacrifice to demons and not to God, and I do not want you to have fellowship with demons" (1 Cor. 10:20).

17:11 It is only the shed blood of a perfect sacrifice that can atone for sin (see Heb. 9:22). This is why Jesus, the sinless Son of God, shed His blood on the cross for us. To see how the "scarlet thread" of redemption is woven throughout Scripture, see Gen. 3:21 comment.

your mother you shall not uncover. She is your mother; you shall not uncover her nakedness. [8]The nakedness of your father's wife you shall not uncover; it *is* your father's nakedness. [9]The nakedness of your sister, the daughter of your father, or the daughter of your mother, *whether* born at home or elsewhere, their nakedness you shall not uncover. [10]The nakedness of your son's daughter or your daughter's daughter, their nakedness you shall not uncover; for theirs *is* your own nakedness. [11]The nakedness of your father's wife's daughter, begotten by your father—she *is* your sister—you shall not uncover her nakedness. [12]You shall not uncover the nakedness of your father's sister; she *is* near of kin to your father. [13]You shall not uncover the nakedness of your mother's sister, for she *is* near of kin to your mother. [14]You shall not uncover the nakedness of your father's brother. You shall not approach his wife; she *is* your aunt. [15]You shall not uncover the nakedness of your daughter-in-law—she *is* your son's wife—you shall not uncover her nakedness. [16]You shall not uncover the nakedness of your brother's wife; it *is* your brother's nakedness. [17]You shall not uncover the nakedness of a woman and her daughter, nor shall you take her son's daughter or her daughter's daughter, to uncover her nakedness. They *are* near of kin to her. It *is* wickedness. [18]Nor shall you take a woman as a rival to her sister, to uncover her nakedness while the other is alive.

[19]'Also you shall not approach a woman to uncover her nakedness as long as she is in her *customary* impurity. [20]Moreover you shall not lie carnally with your neighbor's wife, to defile yourself with her. [21]And you shall not let any of your descendants pass through *the fire* to Molech, nor shall you profane the name of your God: I *am* the LORD. [22]You shall not lie with a male as with a woman. It *is* an abomination. [23]Nor shall you mate with any animal, to defile yourself with it. Nor shall any woman stand before an animal to mate with it. It *is* perversion.

[24]'Do not defile yourselves with any of these things; for by all these the nations are defiled, which I am casting out before you. [25]For the land is defiled; therefore I visit the punishment of its iniquity upon it, and the land vomits out its inhabitants. [26]You shall therefore keep My statutes and My judgments, and shall not commit *any* of these abominations, *either* any of your own nation or any stranger who dwells among you [27](for all these abominations the men of the land have done, who *were* before you, and thus the land is defiled), [28]lest the land vomit you out also when you defile it, as it vomited out the nations that *were* before you. [29]For whoever commits any of these abominations, the persons who commit *them* shall be cut off from among their people.

[30]'Therefore you shall keep My ordinance, so that *you* do not commit *any* of these abominable customs which were committed before you, and that you do not defile yourselves by them: I *am* the LORD your God.' "

Moral and Ceremonial Laws

19 And the LORD spoke to Moses, saying, [2]"Speak to all the congregation of the children of Israel, and say to them: 'You shall be holy, for I the LORD your God *am* holy.

[3]'Every one of you shall revere his mother and his father, and keep My Sabbaths: I *am* the LORD your God.

[4]'Do not turn to idols, nor make for

18:22–24 Once people reject the biblical view of sexuality—that sexual activity of any kind is restricted to one man and one woman in the confines of marriage—the floodgates are open for every man and woman to do what is right in their own eyes. Who is to say that sex between any two (or more) consenting adults is wrong—or sex with underage children, between siblings, or between parents and children? In our society today, some have sex with infants and even with animals. Man's depravity knows no depths. Regarding homosexuality, see Lev. 20:13 comment. For thoughts on biblical sexuality, see also 1 Cor. 7:2–5 comment.

QUESTIONS & OBJECTIONS

19:11

"Aren't there some circumstances when violating God's Law is justified?"

Let's say a man's wife will die if she doesn't receive medicine immediately. The nearest hospital is hours away, but the medicine is available at a nearby store. However, the store is currently closed, and the man doesn't have enough money to buy the medicine even if the store were open. So he breaks in that night, steals the medicine (and doesn't touch anything else), and saves his wife's life. Is this morally wrong? Is it a sin?

The Bible says, "People do not despise a thief if he steals to satisfy himself when he is starving. Yet when he is found, he must restore sevenfold; he may have to give up all the substance of his house" (Prov. 6:30,31). If a man steals to save the life of his wife, he is still a thief and is therefore guilty of breaking both man's law and God's Law. However, any reasonable judge would take the motive for his transgression into account and be merciful. No doubt God will do the same on Judgment Day with those who have found themselves in such a predicament. God will do what is right. However, if you dig a little into the motive of the person asking this question, you will more than likely find that neither he nor his loved one is in a life-or-death predicament; he is merely creating imaginary scenarios to try to justify his sin.

yourselves molded gods: I *am* the LORD
your God.
5'And if you offer a sacrifice of a peace
offering to the LORD, you shall offer it of
your own free will. 6It shall be eaten the
same day you offer *it,* and on the next
day. And if any remains until the third
day, it shall be burned in the fire. 7And if
it is eaten at all on the third day, it *is* an
abomination. It shall not be accepted.
8Therefore *everyone* who eats it shall bear
his iniquity, because he has profaned the
hallowed *offering* of the LORD; and that
person shall be cut off from his people.
9'When you reap the harvest of your
land, you shall not wholly reap the corners of your field, nor shall you gather
the gleanings of your harvest. 10And you
shall not glean your vineyard, nor shall
you gather *every* grape of your vineyard;
you shall leave them for the poor and the
stranger: I *am* the LORD your God.
11'You shall not steal, nor deal falsely,
nor lie to one another. 12And you shall not
swear by My name falsely, nor shall you
profane the name of your God: I *am* the
LORD.
13'You shall not cheat your neighbor,
nor rob *him.* The wages of him who is
hired shall not remain with you all night
until morning. 14You shall not curse the
deaf, nor put a stumbling block before
the blind, but shall fear your God: I *am*
the LORD.

19:4 How Jewish people view Christianity. Many Jews understandably equate Christianity with Roman Catholicism. When they watch the news at Christmas or Easter, they see people kneeling and kissing the hand of a man in a white robe with a big white hat and a golden scepter—the pope. Then they see people bowing down to graven images of saints and praying to and worshiping Mary. To the Jews, Christianity is therefore a false religion because it directly violates the First and Second Commandments.

Many Jews even equate Christianity with Adolf Hitler—despite the fact that biblical Christianity is soaked in love of humanity, while Hitler's philosophy was saturated in the blood of pure hatred. Hitler infiltrated the church by installing his own leaders and Nazi "pastors," then used the church structure to mock the Bible and teach that Jews were "children of the devil." The Nazi army even had belt buckles engraved with "*Gott mit uns*" ("God with us"). So in the eyes of many Jews, the evil of Nazism came directly through the Christian church. That is why, when we approach a Jewish person with a New Testament in our hand or a cross around our neck, and sweetly say, "I would like to talk with you about Jesus," to them we might as well be saying, "Hi, I represent an institution that is filled with pedophiles, bows down to idols, worships false gods, and was responsible for the murder of six million of your Jewish brothers and sisters." No wonder they are reluctant to talk with us. That is why it is important to learn to go through Moses to get to Jesus. Take Jewish people (as you should anyone who is self-righteous) through the Law before you tell them about grace. For more on Judaism, see page 1782. For Roman Catholicism, see page 1810.

POINTS FOR OPEN-AIR PREACHING

19:18

Let Love Be Your Motive

Continually check the spirit in which you preach. Be careful of sarcasm, condescension, or a self-righteous spirit. It's easy to react in a sinful manner when people call you names, cuss at you, say things that aren't true, talk over you, and twist your words. The key is to always let love be your motivation. We don't like rejection or humiliation, and it's only the love of God in us that can give us the grace to handle such things.

It is a sad testimony to our lack of love that we had to be *commanded* to preach the gospel to every creature (see Mark 16:15). It reveals something about our sinful character. When we are held captive to our fears it reveals our lack of love. What would you think of a doctor who had a cure to cancer in his hand, and had to be *commanded* to take it to his dying patients? Imagine if you asked him why he was hesitating and he said, "I'm afraid they will laugh at me" or, "It's not my gifting to take it to them," or, "I don't know what to say to them." As *Charles Spurgeon* said, "We must be ashamed at the mere suspicion of unconcern." So if we lack enough love to preach or we lack love when preaching, we need to get on our knees and ask afresh for the help of God.

"If we are devoted to the cause of humanity, we shall soon be crushed and brokenhearted, for we shall often meet with more ingratitude from men than we would from a dog; but if our motive is love to God, no ingratitude can hinder us from serving our fellow men." *Oswald Chambers*

15'You shall do no injustice in judgment. You shall not be partial to the poor,
nor honor the person of the mighty. In
righteousness you shall judge your neighbor. 16You shall not go about *as* a talebearer among your people; nor shall you
take a stand against the life of your neighbor: I *am* the LORD.

17'You shall not hate your brother in
your heart. You shall surely rebuke your
neighbor, and not bear sin because of
him. 18You shall not take vengeance, nor
bear any grudge against the children of
your people, but you shall love your neighbor as yourself: I *am* the LORD.

19'You shall keep My statutes. You shall
not let your livestock breed with another
kind. You shall not sow your field with
mixed seed. Nor shall a garment of mixed
linen and wool come upon you.

20'Whoever lies carnally with a woman
who *is* betrothed to a man as a concubine, and who has not at all been redeemed nor given her freedom, for this
there shall be scourging; *but* they shall
not be put to death, because she was not
free. 21And he shall bring his trespass offering to the LORD, to the door of the
tabernacle of meeting, a ram as a trespass
offering. 22The priest shall make atonement for him with the ram of the trespass
offering before the LORD for his sin which
he has committed. And the sin which he
has committed shall be forgiven him.

23'When you come into the land, and
have planted all kinds of trees for food,
then you shall count their fruit as uncircumcised. Three years it shall be as uncircumcised to you. *It* shall not be eaten.
24But in the fourth year all its fruit shall
be holy, a praise to the LORD. 25And in the
fifth year you may eat its fruit, that it may
yield to you its increase: I *am* the LORD
your God.

26'You shall not eat *anything* with the
blood, nor shall you practice divination or
soothsaying. 27You shall not shave around
the sides of your head, nor shall you disfigure the edges of your beard. 28You shall
not make any cuttings in your flesh for
the dead, nor tattoo any marks on you: I
am the LORD.

29'Do not prostitute your daughter, to
cause her to be a harlot, lest the land fall
into harlotry, and the land become full of
wickedness.

30'You shall keep My Sabbaths and
reverence My sanctuary: I *am* the LORD.

31'Give no regard to mediums and familiar spirits; do not seek after them, to
be defiled by them: I *am* the LORD your
God.

32'You shall rise before the gray headed and honor the presence of an old man, and fear your God: I *am* the LORD.

33'And if a stranger dwells with you in your land, you shall not mistreat him. 34The stranger who dwells among you shall be to you as one born among you, and you shall love him as yourself; for you were strangers in the land of Egypt: I *am* the LORD your God.

35'You shall do no injustice in judgment, in measurement of length, weight, or volume. 36You shall have honest scales, honest weights, an honest ephah, and an honest hin: I *am* the LORD your God, who brought you out of the land of Egypt.

37'Therefore you shall observe all My statutes and all My judgments, and perform them: I *am* the LORD.' "

Penalties for Breaking the Law

20 Then the LORD spoke to Moses, saying, 2"Again, you shall say to the children of Israel: 'Whoever of the children of Israel, or of the strangers who dwell in Israel, who gives *any* of his descendants to Molech, he shall surely be put to death. The people of the land shall stone him with stones. 3I will set My face against that man, and will cut him off from his people, because he has given *some* of his descendants to Molech, to defile My sanctuary and profane My holy name. 4And if the people of the land should in any way hide their eyes from the man, when he gives *some* of his descendants to Molech, and they do not kill him, 5then I will set My face against that man and against his family; and I will cut him off from his people, and all who prostitute themselves with him to commit harlotry with Molech.

6'And the person who turns to mediums and familiar spirits, to prostitute himself with them, I will set My face against that person and cut him off from his people. 7Consecrate yourselves therefore, and be holy, for I *am* the LORD your God. 8And you shall keep My statutes, and perform them: I *am* the LORD who sanctifies you.

9'For everyone who curses his father or his mother shall surely be put to death. He has cursed his father or his mother. His blood *shall be* upon him.

10'The man who commits adultery with *another* man's wife, *he* who commits adultery with his neighbor's wife, the adulterer and the adulteress, shall surely be put to death. 11The man who lies with his father's wife has uncovered his father's nakedness; both of them shall surely be put to death. Their blood *shall be* upon them. 12If a man lies with his daughter-

19:31 Familiar spirits. Many people don't understand the demonic realm. They believe there are good and bad spirits and that we can tap into the supernatural realm and not be burned. The Word of God forbids any contact with "familiar spirits." A "spirit guide" website describes them as benevolent: "Spirit guides are literally spirits who choose you before you are born and agree to guide you. It does not matter that you may not be consciously aware of them; they are still there for you. Everyone has at least one guide but often there are more... [Channeling] is meant to help you talk to spirits in the light. It means that they will address things with you in a way that you understand—and is in your best interests based on your soul needs." In truth, these "spirit guides" are nothing but demonic and seek to harm whoever is foolish enough to invite their presence. See also 1 Chron. 10:13,14 comment.

20:1–9 Sacrificing children. "Are we shocked at the unnatural cruelty of the ancient idolaters in sacrificing their children? We may justly be so. But are there not very many parents, who, by bad teaching and wicked examples, and by the mysteries of iniquity which they show their children, devote them to the service of Satan, and forward their everlasting ruin, in a manner even more to be lamented? What an account must such parents render to God, and what a meeting will they have with their children at the day of judgment! On the other hand, let children remember that he who cursed father or mother was surely put to death. This law Christ confirmed. Laws which were made before are repeated, and penalties annexed to them. If men will not avoid evil practices, because the law has made these practices sin, and it is right that we go on that principle, surely they should avoid them when the law has made them death, from a principle of self-preservation." *Matthew Henry*

in-law, both of them shall surely be put to death. They have committed perversion. Their blood *shall be* upon them. [13]If a man lies with a male as he lies with a woman, both of them have committed an abomination. They shall surely be put to death. Their blood *shall be* upon them. [14]If a man marries a woman and her mother, it *is* wickedness. They shall be burned with fire, both he and they, that there may be no wickedness among you. [15]If a man mates with an animal, he shall surely be put to death, and you shall kill the animal. [16]If a woman approaches any animal and mates with it, you shall kill the woman and the animal. They shall surely be put to death. Their blood *is* upon them.

[17]'If a man takes his sister, his father's daughter or his mother's daughter, and sees her nakedness and she sees his nakedness, it *is* a wicked thing. And they shall be cut off in the sight of their people. He has uncovered his sister's nakedness. He shall bear his guilt. [18]If a man lies with a woman during her sickness and uncovers her nakedness, he has exposed her flow, and she has uncovered the flow of her blood. Both of them shall be cut off from their people.

[19]'You shall not uncover the nakedness of your mother's sister nor of your father's sister, for that would uncover his near of kin. They shall bear their guilt. [20]If a man lies with his uncle's wife, he has uncovered his uncle's nakedness. They shall bear their sin; they shall die childless. [21]If a man takes his brother's wife, it *is* an unclean thing. He has uncovered his brother's nakedness. They shall be childless.

[22]'You shall therefore keep all My statutes and all My judgments, and perform them, that the land where I am bringing you to dwell may not vomit you out. [23]And you shall not walk in the statutes of the nation which I am casting out before you; for they commit all these things, and therefore I abhor them. [24]But I have said to you, "You shall inherit their land, and I will give it to you to possess, a land flowing with milk and honey." I *am* the LORD your God, who has separated you from the peoples. [25]You shall therefore distinguish between clean animals and unclean, between unclean birds and clean, and you shall not make yourselves abominable by beast or by bird, or by any kind of living thing that creeps on the ground, which I have separated from you as unclean. [26]And you shall be holy to Me, for I the LORD *am* holy, and have separated you from the peoples, that you should be Mine.

[27]'A man or a woman who is a medium, or who has familiar spirits, shall surely be put to death; they shall stone them with stones. Their blood *shall be* upon them.' "

Regulations for Conduct of Priests

21 And the LORD said to Moses, "Speak to the priests, the sons of Aaron, and say to them: 'None shall defile himself for the dead among his people, [2]except for his relatives who are nearest to him: his mother, his father, his son, his daughter, and his brother; [3]also his virgin sister who is near to him, who has had no husband, for her he may defile himself. [4]*Otherwise* he shall not defile himself, *being* a chief man among his people, to profane himself.

[5]'They shall not make any bald *place* on their heads, nor shall they shave the edges of their beards nor make any cuttings in their flesh. [6]They shall be holy to their God and not profane the name of their God, for they offer the offerings of

20:13 In the light of this clear verse, there is no justification for the sin of homosexuality (see also Lev. 18:22 and Rom. 1:26,27). When homosexuals claim that they are "born that way," simply agree with them. We are all born with sinful tendencies, and that's why we must be born again to enter the kingdom of heaven (see John 3:3). For how to witness to homosexuals, see comments at 1 Tim. 1:9,10; 2 Pet. 2:6–8; and Jude 7.

the LORD made by fire, *and* the bread of their God; therefore they shall be holy. 7They shall not take a wife *who is* a harlot or a defiled woman, nor shall they take a woman divorced from her husband; for *the priest*[a] is holy to his God. 8Therefore you shall consecrate him, for he offers the bread of your God. He shall be holy to you, for I the LORD, who sanctify you, *am* holy. 9The daughter of any priest, if she profanes herself by playing the harlot, she profanes her father. She shall be burned with fire.

10'*He who is* the high priest among his brethren, on whose head the anointing oil was poured and who is consecrated to wear the garments, shall not uncover his head nor tear his clothes; 11nor shall he go near any dead body, nor defile himself for his father or his mother; 12nor shall he go out of the sanctuary, nor profane the sanctuary of his God; for the consecration of the anointing oil of his God is upon him: I *am* the LORD. 13And he shall take a wife in her virginity. 14A widow or a divorced woman or a defiled woman *or* a harlot—these he shall not marry; but he shall take a virgin of his own people as wife. 15Nor shall he profane his posterity among his people, for I the LORD sanctify him.' "

16And the LORD spoke to Moses, saying, 17"Speak to Aaron, saying: 'No man of your descendants in *succeeding* generations, who has *any* defect, may approach to offer the bread of his God. 18For any man who has a defect shall not approach: a man blind or lame, who has a marred *face* or any *limb* too long, 19a man who has a broken foot or broken hand, 20or is a hunchback or a dwarf, or *a man* who has a defect in his eye, or eczema or scab, or is a eunuch. 21No man of the descendants of Aaron the priest, who has a defect, shall come near to offer the offerings made by fire to the LORD. He has a defect; he shall not come near to offer the bread of his God. 22He may eat the bread of his God, *both* the most holy and the holy; 23only he shall not go near the veil or approach the altar, because he has a defect, lest he profane My sanctuaries; for I the LORD sanctify them.' "

24And Moses told *it* to Aaron and his sons, and to all the children of Israel.

22 Then the LORD spoke to Moses, saying, 2"Speak to Aaron and his sons, that they separate themselves from the holy things of the children of Israel, and that they do not profane My holy name *by* what they dedicate to Me: I *am* the LORD. 3Say to them: 'Whoever of all your descendants throughout your generations, who goes near the holy things which the children of Israel dedicate to the LORD, while he has uncleanness upon him, that person shall be cut off from My presence: I *am* the LORD.

4'Whatever man of the descendants of Aaron, who *is* a leper or has a discharge, shall not eat the holy offerings until he is clean. And whoever touches anything made unclean *by* a corpse, or a man who has had an emission of semen, 5or whoever touches any creeping thing by which he would be made unclean, or any person by whom he would become unclean, whatever his uncleanness may be— 6the person who has touched any such thing shall be unclean until evening, and shall not eat the holy *offerings* unless he washes his body with water. 7And when the sun goes down he shall be clean; and afterward he may eat the holy *offerings*, because it *is* his food. 8Whatever dies *naturally* or

21:7 [a]Literally *he*

21:16–23 This prohibition may seem harsh and exclusive, but this same God is rich in mercy and has opened the kingdom of God so that "whoever believes in Him should not perish" (see John 3:16; Rom. 10:9–13). In Christ, we are cleansed by God's grace from every spot and blemish. We are made perfect by His perfect righteousness. However, those who refuse to repent and trust the Savior will be excluded from the kingdom of God. Nothing defiled shall enter.

is torn *by beasts* he shall not eat, to defile himself with it: I *am* the LORD.

9'They shall therefore keep My ordinance, lest they bear sin for it and die thereby, if they profane it: I the LORD sanctify them.

10'No outsider shall eat the holy *offering;* one who dwells with the priest, or a hired servant, shall not eat the holy thing. 11But if the priest buys a person with his money, he may eat it; and one who is born in his house may eat his food. 12If the priest's daughter is married to an outsider, she may not eat of the holy offerings. 13But if the priest's daughter is a widow or divorced, and has no child, and has returned to her father's house as in her youth, she may eat her father's food; but no outsider shall eat it.

14'And if a man eats the holy *offering* unintentionally, then he shall restore a holy *offering* to the priest, and add one-fifth to it. 15They shall not profane the holy *offerings* of the children of Israel, which they offer to the LORD, 16or allow them to bear the guilt of trespass when they eat their holy *offerings;* for I the LORD sanctify them.' "

Offerings Accepted and Not Accepted

17And the LORD spoke to Moses, saying, 18"Speak to Aaron and his sons, and to all the children of Israel, and say to them: 'Whatever man of the house of Israel, or of the strangers in Israel, who offers his sacrifice for any of his vows or for any of his freewill offerings, which they offer to the LORD as a burnt offering— 19*you shall offer* of your own free will a male without blemish from the cattle, from the sheep, or from the goats. 20Whatever has a defect, you shall not offer, for it shall not be acceptable on your behalf. 21And whoever offers a sacrifice of a peace offering to the LORD, to fulfill *his* vow, or a freewill offering from the cattle or the sheep, it must be perfect to be accepted; there shall be no defect in it. 22Those *that are* blind or broken or maimed, or have an ulcer or eczema or scabs, you shall not offer to the LORD, nor make an offering by fire of them on the altar to the LORD. 23Either a bull or a lamb that has any limb too long or too short you may offer *as* a freewill offering, but for a vow it shall not be accepted.

I have read Plato and Cicero sayings that are very wise and beautiful; but I never read in either of them: 'Come unto me all ye that labor and are heavy laden and I will give thee rest.'

AUGUSTINE

24'You shall not offer to the LORD what is bruised or crushed, or torn or cut; nor shall you make *any offering of them* in your land. 25Nor from a foreigner's hand shall you offer any of these as the bread of your God, because their corruption *is* in them, *and* defects *are* in them. They shall not be accepted on your behalf.' "

26And the LORD spoke to Moses, saying: 27"When a bull or a sheep or a goat is born, it shall be seven days with its mother; and from the eighth day and thereafter it shall be accepted as an offering made by fire to the LORD. 28*Whether it is* a cow or ewe, do not kill both her and her young on the same day. 29And when you offer a sacrifice of thanksgiving to the LORD, offer *it* of your own free will. 30On the same day it shall be eaten; you shall leave none of it until morning: I *am* the LORD.

31"Therefore you shall keep My commandments, and perform them: I *am* the LORD. 32You shall not profane My holy name, but I will be hallowed among the children of Israel. I *am* the LORD who sanctifies you, 33who brought you out of

22:20,21 The blood of Christ has cleansed the believer from the defilement of sin. Now he can offer himself as a living sacrifice, and because of grace, he is holy and acceptable to God (see Rom. 12:1).

the land of Egypt, to be your God: I *am*
the LORD."

Feasts of the Lord

23 And the LORD spoke to Moses,
saying, 2"Speak to the children of
Israel, and say to them: 'The feasts of the
LORD, which you shall proclaim *to be* holy
convocations, these *are* My feasts.

The Sabbath

3'Six days shall work be done, but the
seventh day *is* a Sabbath of solemn rest, a
holy convocation. You shall do no work
on it; it is the Sabbath of the LORD in all
your dwellings.

· · · · · ·

Does the Bible endorse baptism for the dead? See 1 Cor. 15:29 comment.

· · · · · ·

The Passover and Unleavened Bread

4'These *are* the feasts of the LORD, holy
convocations which you shall proclaim at
their appointed times. 5On the fourteenth
day of the first month at twilight *is* the
LORD's Passover. 6And on the fifteenth day
of the same month *is* the Feast of Unleavened Bread to the LORD; seven days you
must eat unleavened bread. 7On the first
day you shall have a holy convocation;
you shall do no customary work on it.
8But you shall offer an offering made by
fire to the LORD for seven days. The seventh day *shall be* a holy convocation; you
shall do no customary work *on it.*' "

The Feast of Firstfruits

9And the LORD spoke to Moses, saying,
10"Speak to the children of Israel, and say
to them: 'When you come into the land
which I give to you, and reap its harvest,
then you shall bring a sheaf of the firstfruits of your harvest to the priest. 11He
shall wave the sheaf before the LORD, to
be accepted on your behalf; on the day
after the Sabbath the priest shall wave it.
12And you shall offer on that day, when
you wave the sheaf, a male lamb of the
first year, without blemish, as a burnt offering to the LORD. 13Its grain offering
shall be two-tenths *of an ephah* of fine
flour mixed with oil, an offering made by
fire to the LORD, for a sweet aroma; and
its drink offering *shall be* of wine, one-
fourth of a hin. 14You shall eat neither
bread nor parched grain nor fresh grain
until the same day that you have brought
an offering to your God; *it shall be* a
statute forever throughout your generations in all your dwellings.

The Feast of Weeks

15'And you shall count for yourselves
from the day after the Sabbath, from the
day that you brought the sheaf of the wave
offering: seven Sabbaths shall be completed. 16Count fifty days to the day after
the seventh Sabbath; then you shall offer
a new grain offering to the LORD. 17You
shall bring from your dwellings two wave
loaves of two-tenths *of an ephah.* They
shall be of fine flour; they shall be baked
with leaven. *They are* the firstfruits to the
LORD. 18And you shall offer with the
bread seven lambs of the first year, without blemish, one young bull, and two
rams. They shall be *as* a burnt offering to
the LORD, with their grain offering and
their drink offerings, an offering made by
fire for a sweet aroma to the LORD. 19Then
you shall sacrifice one kid of the goats as
a sin offering, and two male lambs of the
first year as a sacrifice of a peace offering.
20The priest shall wave them with the
bread of the firstfruits *as* a wave offering
before the LORD, with the two lambs.
They shall be holy to the LORD for the
priest. 21And you shall proclaim on the
same day *that* it is a holy convocation to
you. You shall do no customary work *on
it. It shall be* a statute forever in all your
dwellings throughout your generations.
22'When you reap the harvest of your
land, you shall not wholly reap the corners of your field when you reap, nor
shall you gather any gleaning from your
harvest. You shall leave them for the poor

and for the stranger: I *am* the LORD your God.' "

The Feast of Trumpets

23Then the LORD spoke to Moses, saying, 24"Speak to the children of Israel, saying: 'In the seventh month, on the first *day* of the month, you shall have a sabbath-*rest,* a memorial of blowing of trumpets, a holy convocation. 25You shall do no customary work *on it;* and you shall offer an offering made by fire to the LORD.' "

The Day of Atonement

26And the LORD spoke to Moses, saying: 27"Also the tenth *day* of this seventh month *shall be* the Day of Atonement. It shall be a holy convocation for you; you shall afflict your souls, and offer an offering made by fire to the LORD. 28And you shall do no work on that same day, for it *is* the Day of Atonement, to make atonement for you before the LORD your God. 29For any person who is not afflicted *in soul* on that same day shall be cut off from his people. 30And any person who does any work on that same day, that person I will destroy from among his people. 31You shall do no manner of work; *it shall be* a statute forever throughout your generations in all your dwellings. 32It *shall be* to you a sabbath of *solemn* rest, and you shall afflict your souls; on the ninth *day* of the month at evening, from evening to evening, you shall celebrate your sabbath."

The Feast of Tabernacles

33Then the LORD spoke to Moses, saying, 34"Speak to the children of Israel, saying: 'The fifteenth day of this seventh month *shall be* the Feast of Tabernacles *for* seven days to the LORD. 35On the first day *there shall be* a holy convocation. You shall do no customary work *on it.* 36*For* seven days you shall offer an offering made by fire to the LORD. On the eighth day you shall have a holy convocation, and you shall offer an offering made by fire to the LORD. It *is* a sacred assembly, *and* you shall do no customary work *on it.*

37'These *are* the feasts of the LORD which you shall proclaim *to be* holy convocations, to offer an offering made by fire to the LORD, a burnt offering and a grain offering, a sacrifice and drink offerings, everything on its day— 38besides the Sabbaths of the LORD, besides your gifts, besides all your vows, and besides all your freewill offerings which you give to the LORD.

39'Also on the fifteenth day of the seventh month, when you have gathered in the fruit of the land, you shall keep the feast of the LORD *for* seven days; on the first day *there shall be* a sabbath-*rest,* and on the eighth day a sabbath-*rest.* 40And you shall take for yourselves on the first day the fruit of beautiful trees, branches of palm trees, the boughs of leafy trees, and willows of the brook; and you shall rejoice before the LORD your God for seven days. 41You shall keep it as a feast to the LORD for seven days in the year. *It shall be* a statute forever in your generations. You shall celebrate it in the seventh month. 42You shall dwell in booths for seven days. All who are native Israelites shall dwell in booths, 43that your generations may know that I made the children of Israel dwell in booths when I brought them out of the land of Egypt: I *am* the LORD your God.' "

44So Moses declared to the children of Israel the feasts of the LORD.

Care of the Tabernacle Lamps

24 Then the LORD spoke to Moses, saying: 2"Command the children of Israel that they bring to you pure oil of pressed olives for the light, to make the lamps burn continually. 3Outside the veil of the Testimony, in the tabernacle of meeting, Aaron shall be in charge of it from evening until morning before the LORD continually; *it shall be* a statute forever in your generations. 4He shall be in charge of the lamps on the pure *gold* lampstand before the LORD continually.

The Bread of the Tabernacle

5"And you shall take fine flour and

bake twelve cakes with it. Two-tenths *of an ephah* shall be in each cake. [6]You shall set them in two rows, six in a row, on the pure *gold* table before the LORD. [7]And you shall put pure frankincense on *each* row, that it may be on the bread for a memorial, an offering made by fire to the LORD. [8]Every Sabbath he shall set it in order before the LORD continually, *being taken* from the children of Israel by an everlasting covenant. [9]And it shall be for Aaron and his sons, and they shall eat it in a holy place; for it *is* most holy to him from the offerings of the LORD made by fire, by a perpetual statute."

The Penalty for Blasphemy

[10]Now the son of an Israelite woman, whose father *was* an Egyptian, went out among the children of Israel; and this Israelite *woman's* son and a man of Israel fought each other in the camp. [11]And the Israelite woman's son blasphemed the name *of the LORD* and cursed; and so they brought him to Moses. (His mother's name *was* Shelomith the daughter of Dibri, of the tribe of Dan.) [12]Then they put him in custody, that the mind of the LORD might be shown to them.

[13]And the LORD spoke to Moses, saying, [14]"Take outside the camp him who has cursed; then let all who heard *him* lay their hands on his head, and let all the congregation stone him.

[15]"Then you shall speak to the children of Israel, saying: 'Whoever curses his God shall bear his sin. [16]And whoever blasphemes the name of the LORD shall surely be put to death. All the congregation shall certainly stone him, the stranger as well as him who is born in the land. When he blasphemes the name *of the LORD*, he shall be put to death.

[17]'Whoever kills any man shall surely be put to death. [18]Whoever kills an animal shall make it good, animal for animal.

[19]'If a man causes disfigurement of his neighbor, as he has done, so shall it be done to him— [20]fracture for fracture, eye for eye, tooth for tooth; as he has caused disfigurement of a man, so shall it be done to him. [21]And whoever kills an animal shall restore it; but whoever kills a man shall be put to death. [22]You shall have the same law for the stranger and for one from your own country; for I *am* the LORD your God.' "

[23]Then Moses spoke to the children of Israel; and they took outside the camp him who had cursed, and stoned him with stones. So the children of Israel did as the LORD commanded Moses.

The Sabbath of the Seventh Year

25 And the LORD spoke to Moses on Mount Sinai, saying, [2]"Speak to the children of Israel, and say to them: 'When you come into the land which I give you, then the land shall keep a sabbath to the LORD. [3]Six years you shall sow your field, and six years you shall prune your vineyard, and gather its fruit; [4]but in the seventh year there shall be a sabbath of solemn rest for the land, a sabbath to the LORD. You shall neither sow your field nor prune your vineyard. [5]What grows of its own accord of your harvest you shall not reap, nor gather the grapes of your untended vine, *for* it is a year of rest for the land. [6]And the sabbath *produce* of the

---

24:16 We live in blasphemous times, when God's holy name isn't honored and is even used as a cuss word. Biblical scribes so honored His name that they would wash their hands before and after they wrote Scripture, yet today it is so despised. Sinners try to justify blasphemy by saying that God's name is "just a word" that they don't even think about when they use. Their own mouth condemns them. His precious name rolls off their sinful tongue without a second thought, as though He didn't exist. By giving it no honor, they certainly use His name "in vain." Humanity may take the sin of blasphemy lightly, but God doesn't. He gives it the death sentence. (See www.HollywoodandGod.com.)

24:20 See Matt. 5:38 comment.

25:3,4 This practice, in modern Judaism, is called *Shmita*. For details, see Exod. 23:10,11 comment.

land shall be food for you: for you, your
male and female servants, your hired man,
and the stranger who dwells with you,
7for your livestock and the beasts that *are*
in your land—all its produce shall be for
food.

The Year of Jubilee

8'And you shall count seven sabbaths
of years for yourself, seven times seven
years; and the time of the seven sabbaths
of years shall be to you forty-nine years.
9Then you shall cause the trumpet of the
Jubilee to sound on the tenth *day* of the
seventh month; on the Day of Atonement
you shall make the trumpet to sound
throughout all your land. 10And you shall
consecrate the fiftieth year, and proclaim
liberty throughout *all* the land to all its
inhabitants. It shall be a Jubilee for you;
and each of you shall return to his possession, and each of you shall return to
his family. 11That fiftieth year shall be a
Jubilee to you; in it you shall neither sow
nor reap what grows of its own accord,
nor gather *the grapes* of your untended
vine. 12For it *is* the Jubilee; it shall be holy
to you; you shall eat its produce from the
field.

13'In this Year of Jubilee, each of you
shall return to his possession. 14And if
you sell anything to your neighbor or buy
from your neighbor's hand, you shall not
oppress one another. 15According to the
number of years after the Jubilee you shall
buy from your neighbor, and according to
the number of years of crops he shall sell
to you. 16According to the multitude of
years you shall increase its price, and according to the fewer number of years you
shall diminish its price; for he sells to you
according to the number *of the years* of the
crops. 17Therefore you shall not oppress
one another, but you shall fear your God;
for I *am* the LORD your God.

Provisions for the Seventh Year

18'So you shall observe My statutes and
keep My judgments, and perform them;
and you will dwell in the land in safety.
19Then the land will yield its fruit, and
you will eat your fill, and dwell there in
safety.

20'And if you say, "What shall we eat in
the seventh year, since we shall not sow
nor gather in our produce?" 21Then I will
command My blessing on you in the
sixth year, and it will bring forth produce
enough for three years. 22And you shall
sow in the eighth year, and eat old produce until the ninth year; until its produce comes in, you shall eat *of* the old
harvest.

Redemption of Property

23'The land shall not be sold permanently, for the land *is* Mine; for you *are*
strangers and sojourners with Me. 24And
in all the land of your possession you
shall grant redemption of the land.

25'If one of your brethren becomes
poor, and has sold *some* of his possession,
and if his redeeming relative comes to redeem it, then he may redeem what his
brother sold. 26Or if the man has no one
to redeem it, but he himself becomes able
to redeem it, 27then let him count the years
since its sale, and restore the remainder
to the man to whom he sold it, that he may
return to his possession. 28But if he is not
able to have *it* restored to himself, then
what was sold shall remain in the hand of
him who bought it until the Year of Jubilee;
and in the Jubilee it shall be released, and
he shall return to his possession.

29'If a man sells a house in a walled
city, then he may redeem it within a whole
year after it is sold; *within* a full year he
may redeem it. 30But if it is not redeemed
within the space of a full year, then the
house in the walled city shall belong permanently to him who bought it, throughout his generations. It shall not be released in the Jubilee. 31However the houses
of villages which have no wall around
them shall be counted as the fields of the
country. They may be redeemed, and they
shall be released in the Jubilee. 32Never-
theless the cities of the Levites, *and* the
houses in the cities of their possession,

the Levites may redeem at any time.
[33]And if a man purchases a house from the Levites, then the house that was sold in the city of his possession shall be released in the Jubilee; for the houses in the cities of the Levites *are* their possession among the children of Israel.
[34]But the field of the common-land of their cities may not be sold, for it *is* their perpetual possession.

Lending to the Poor

[35]'If one of your brethren becomes poor, and falls into poverty among you, then you shall help him, like a stranger or a sojourner, that he may live with you.
[36]Take no usury or interest from him; but fear your God, that your brother may live with you.
[37]You shall not lend him your money for usury, nor lend him your food at a profit.
[38]I *am* the LORD your God, who brought you out of the land of Egypt, to give you the land of Canaan *and* to be your God.

The Law Concerning Slavery

[39]'And if *one of* your brethren *who dwells* by you becomes poor, and sells himself to you, you shall not compel him to serve as a slave.
[40]As a hired servant *and* a sojourner he shall be with you, *and* shall serve you until the Year of Jubilee.
[41]And *then* he shall depart from you—he and his children with him—and shall return to his own family. He shall return to the possession of his fathers.
[42]For they *are* My servants, whom I brought out of the land of Egypt; they shall not be sold as slaves.
[43]You shall not rule over him with rigor, but you shall fear your God.
[44]And as for your male and female slaves whom you may have—from the nations that are around you, from them you may buy male and female slaves.
[45]Moreover you may buy the children of the strangers who dwell among you, and their families who are with you, which they beget in your land; and they shall become your property.
[46]And you may take them as an inheritance for your children after you, to

"The Great Commission is not an option to be considered; it is a command to be obeyed."

Hudson Taylor

inherit *them as* a possession; they shall be your permanent slaves. But regarding your brethren, the children of Israel, you shall not rule over one another with rigor.
[47]'Now if a sojourner or stranger close to you becomes rich, and *one of* your brethren *who dwells* by him becomes poor, and sells himself to the stranger *or* sojourner close to you, or to a member of the stranger's family,
[48]after he is sold he may be redeemed again. One of his brothers may redeem him;
[49]or his uncle or his uncle's son may redeem him; or *anyone* who is near of kin to him in his family may redeem him; or if he is able he may redeem himself.
[50]Thus he shall reckon with him who bought him: The price of his release shall be according to the number of years, from the year that he was sold to him until the Year of Jubilee; *it shall be* according to the time of a hired servant for him.
[51]If *there are* still many years *remaining*, according to them he shall repay the price of his redemption from the money with which he was bought.
[52]And if there remain but a few years until the Year of Jubilee, then he shall reckon with him, *and* according to his years he shall repay him

the price of his redemption. [53]He shall be
with him as a yearly hired servant, and he
shall not rule with rigor over him in your
sight. [54]And if he is not redeemed in these
years, then he shall be released in the Year
of Jubilee—he and his children with him.
[55]For the children of Israel *are* servants to
Me; they *are* My servants whom I brought
out of the land of Egypt: I *am* the LORD
your God.

Promise of Blessing and Retribution

26 'You shall not make idols for yourselves;
neither a carved image nor a *sacred* pillar shall you rear up for Yourselves;
nor shall you set up an engraved stone in your land, to bow down to it;
for I *am* the LORD your God.
[2]You shall keep My Sabbaths and reverence My sanctuary:
I *am* the LORD.

[3]'If you walk in My statutes and keep My commandments, and perform them,
[4]then I will give you rain in its season, the land shall yield its produce, and the trees of the field shall yield their fruit.
[5]Your threshing shall last till the time of vintage, and the vintage shall last till the time of sowing;
you shall eat your bread to the full, and dwell in your land safely.
[6]I will give peace in the land, and you shall lie down, and none will make *you* afraid;
I will rid the land of evil beasts,
and the sword will not go through your land.
[7]You will chase your enemies, and they shall fall by the sword before you.
[8]Five of you shall chase a hundred, and a hundred of you shall put ten thousand to flight;
your enemies shall fall by the sword before you.
[9]'For I will look on you favorably and make you fruitful, multiply you and confirm My covenant with you.
[10]You shall eat the old harvest, and clear out the old because of the new.
[11]I will set My tabernacle among you, and My soul shall not abhor you.
[12]I will walk among you and be your God, and you shall be My people.
[13]I *am* the LORD your God, who brought you out of the land of Egypt, that *you* should not be their slaves;
I have broken the bands of your yoke and made you walk upright.

[14]'But if you do not obey Me, and do not observe all these commandments,
[15]and if you despise My statutes, or if your soul abhors My judgments, so that you do not perform all My commandments, *but* break My covenant,
[16]I also will do this to you:
I will even appoint terror over you, wasting disease and fever which shall consume the eyes and cause sorrow of heart.
And you shall sow your seed in vain, for your enemies shall eat it.
[17]I will set My face against you, and you shall be defeated by your enemies.
Those who hate you shall reign over you, and you shall flee when no one pursues you.

26:3,4 In this passage (vv. 1–13), notice these wonderful blessings that God promised to Israel if they would obey Him. The rain would come in due season. The land would yield its harvest and the trees their fruit. Their food would satisfy them. They would have peace in the land, and no wild beasts would devour them. Truly blessed is the nation whose God is the LORD (Psa. 33:12).

Notice also the fearful curses that come with disobedience, which is so evident in our sinful nation: we are plagued with cancer and terrible diseases, violence, earthquakes, droughts, fires, tornadoes, killer bees, hurricanes, and floods.

[18]'And after all this, if you do not obey
Me, then I will punish you seven
times more for your sins.
[19]I will break the pride of your power;
I will make your heavens like iron
and your earth like bronze.
[20]And your strength shall be spent in
vain;
for your land shall not yield its
produce, nor shall the trees of the
land yield their fruit.
[21]'Then, if you walk contrary to Me, and
are not willing to obey Me, I will
bring on you seven times more
plagues, according to your sins.
[22]I will also send wild beasts among
you, which shall rob you of your
children, destroy your livestock,
and make you few in number;
and your highways shall be desolate.

[23]'And if by these things you are not
reformed by Me, but walk
contrary to Me,
[24]then I also will walk contrary to you,
and I will punish you yet seven
times for your sins.
[25]And I will bring a sword against you
that will execute the vengeance
of the covenant;
when you are gathered together within
your cities I will send pestilence
among you;
and you shall be delivered into the
hand of the enemy.
[26]When I have cut off your supply of
bread, ten women shall bake
your bread in one oven, and they
shall bring back your bread by
weight, and you shall eat and not
be satisfied.

[27]'And after all this, if you do not obey
Me, but walk contrary to Me,
[28]then I also will walk contrary to you
in fury;
and I, even I, will chastise you seven
times for your sins.
[29]You shall eat the flesh of your sons,
and you shall eat the flesh of
your daughters.
[30]I will destroy your high places, cut
down your incense altars, and
cast your carcasses on the lifeless
forms of your idols;
and My soul shall abhor you.
[31]I will lay your cities waste and bring
your sanctuaries to desolation,
and I will not smell the fragrance
of your sweet aromas.
[32]I will bring the land to desolation,
and your enemies who dwell in it
shall be astonished at it.
[33]I will scatter you among the nations
and draw out a sword after you;
your land shall be desolate and your
cities waste.
[34]Then the land shall enjoy its sabbaths
as long as it lies desolate and you
are in your enemies' land;
then the land shall rest and enjoy its
sabbaths.
[35]As long as *it* lies desolate it shall
rest—
for the time it did not rest on your
sabbaths when you dwelt in it.

[36]'And as for those of you who are left,
I will send faintness into their
hearts in the lands of their
enemies;
the sound of a shaken leaf shall cause
them to flee;
they shall flee as though fleeing from
a sword, and they shall fall when
no one pursues.
[37]They shall stumble over one another,
as it were before a sword, when
no one pursues;
and you shall have no *power* to stand
before your enemies.
[38]You shall perish among the nations,
and the land of your enemies
shall eat you up.
[39]And those of you who are left shall
waste away in their iniquity in
your enemies' lands;
also in their fathers' iniquities, which
are with them, they shall waste
away.

SPRINGBOARDS FOR PREACHING AND WITNESSING

Fools Mock at Sin

26:40,41

A woman in Florida was in court for running over a bike rider with her car. As she was in prison awaiting her sentence (which was predicted to be one to four years), she was allowed to take a phone call from a friend, and laughed as he made jokes about the victim's death. When the judge heard the recorded phone call, he threw the book at her, and gave her the maximum sentence of more than ten years. Why did he do that? Because her laughter revealed that she had no contrition (true sorrow). She didn't see the seriousness of her crime.

What is it that will bring swift mercy from the Judge of the Universe? What is it that will open the door of the grace of God to guilty sinners? It is what the Bible calls "godly sorrow." It is only when we see the seriousness of our transgressions against God that we will have godly sorrow, and it is godly sorrow that produces repentance (2 Cor. 7:10). Each of us has a choice. We can be a fool and mock at sin, or we can see sin as being "exceedingly sinful" (Rom. 7:13). You have God's Word on it: He will throw the Book at the proud and impenitent, but He will give grace to the humble. So humble yourself today, acknowledge your sins, and as you trust in the Savior, you will taste of the grace of God.

40'*But* if they confess their iniquity and
the iniquity of their fathers, with
their unfaithfulness in which
they were unfaithful to Me, and
that they also have walked
contrary to Me,
41and *that* I also have walked contrary
to them and have brought them
into the land of their enemies;
if their uncircumcised hearts are
humbled, and they accept their
guilt—
42then I will remember My covenant
with Jacob, and My covenant
with Isaac and My covenant with
Abraham I will remember;
I will remember the land.
43The land also shall be left empty by
them, and will enjoy its sabbaths
while it lies desolate without them;
they will accept their guilt, because
they despised My judgments and
because their soul abhorred My
statutes.
44Yet for all that, when they are in the
land of their enemies, I will not
cast them away, nor shall I abhor
them, to utterly destroy them and
break My covenant with them;
for I *am* the LORD their God.
45But for their sake I will remember the
covenant of their ancestors, whom
I brought out of the land of
Egypt in the sight of the nations,
that I might be their God:
I *am* the LORD.' "

46These *are* the statutes and judgments
and laws which the LORD made between
Himself and the children of Israel on
Mount Sinai by the hand of Moses.

Redeeming Persons and Property Dedicated to God

27 Now the LORD spoke to Moses,
saying, 2"Speak to the children of
Israel, and say to them: 'When a man consecrates by a vow certain persons to the
LORD, according to your valuation, 3if
your valuation is of a male from twenty
years old up to sixty years old, then your
valuation shall be fifty shekels of silver,
according to the shekel of the sanctuary.
4If it *is* a female, then your valuation shall
be thirty shekels; 5and if from five years
old up to twenty years old, then your valuation for a male shall be twenty shekels,
and for a female ten shekels; 6and if from
a month old up to five years old, then your
valuation for a male shall be five shekels
of silver, and for a female your valuation
shall be three shekels of silver; 7and if
from sixty years old and above, if *it is* a
male, then your valuation shall be fifteen
shekels, and for a female ten shekels.

8'But if he is too poor to pay your valuation, then he shall present himself before the priest, and the priest shall set a

value for him; according to the ability of him who vowed, the priest shall value him.

9'If *it is* an animal that men may bring as an offering to the LORD, all that *anyone* gives to the LORD shall be holy. 10He shall not substitute it or exchange it, good for bad or bad for good; and if he at all exchanges animal for animal, then both it and the one exchanged for it shall be holy. 11If *it is* an unclean animal which they do not offer as a sacrifice to the LORD, then he shall present the animal before the priest; 12and the priest shall set a value for it, whether it is good or bad; as you, the priest, value it, so it shall be. 13But if he *wants* at all *to* redeem it, then he must add one-fifth to your valuation.

14'And when a man dedicates his house *to be* holy to the LORD, then the priest shall set a value for it, whether it is good or bad; as the priest values it, so it shall stand. 15If he who dedicated it *wants to* redeem his house, then he must add one-fifth of the money of your valuation to it, and it shall be his.

16'If a man dedicates to the LORD *part* of a field of his possession, then your valuation shall be according to the seed for it. A homer of barley seed *shall be valued* at fifty shekels of silver. 17If he dedicates his field from the Year of Jubilee, according to your valuation it shall stand. 18But if he dedicates his field after the Jubilee, then the priest shall reckon to him the money due according to the years that remain till the Year of Jubilee, and it shall be deducted from your valuation. 19And if he who dedicates the field ever wishes to redeem it, then he must add one-fifth of the money of your valuation to it, and it shall belong to him. 20But if he does not want to redeem the field, or if he has sold the field to another man, it shall not be redeemed anymore; 21but the field, when it is released in the Jubilee, shall be holy to the LORD, as a devoted field; it shall be the possession of the priest.

22'And if a man dedicates to the LORD a field which he has bought, which is not the field of his possession, 23then the priest shall reckon to him the worth of your valuation, up to the Year of Jubilee, and he shall give your valuation on that day *as* a holy *offering* to the LORD. 24In the Year of Jubilee the field shall return to him from whom it was bought, to the one who *owned* the land as a possession. 25And all your valuations shall be according to the shekel of the sanctuary: twenty gerahs to the shekel.

26'But the firstborn of the animals, which should be the LORD's firstborn, no man shall dedicate; whether *it is* an ox or sheep, it *is* the LORD's. 27And if *it is* an unclean animal, then he shall redeem *it* according to your valuation, and shall add one-fifth to it; or if it is not redeemed, then it shall be sold according to your valuation.

28'Nevertheless no devoted *offering* that a man may devote to the LORD of all that he has, *both* man and beast, or the field of his possession, shall be sold or redeemed; every devoted *offering is* most holy to the LORD. 29No person under the ban, who may become doomed to destruction among men, shall be redeemed, *but* shall surely be put to death. 30And all the tithe of the land, *whether* of the seed of the land *or* of the fruit of the tree, *is* the LORD's. It *is* holy to the LORD. 31If a man wants at all to redeem *any* of his tithes, he shall add one-fifth to it. 32And concerning the tithe of the herd or the flock, of whatever passes under the rod, the tenth one shall be holy to the LORD. 33He shall not inquire whether it is good or bad, nor shall he exchange it; and if he exchanges it at all, then both it and the one exchanged for it shall be holy; it shall not be redeemed.' "

34These *are* the commandments which the LORD commanded Moses for the children of Israel on Mount Sinai.

Numbers

The First Census of Israel

1 Now the LORD spoke to Moses in the Wilderness of Sinai, in the tabernacle of meeting, on the first *day* of the second month, in the second year after they had come out of the land of Egypt, saying: 2"Take a census of all the congregation of the children of Israel, by their families, by their fathers' houses, according to the number of names, every male individually, 3from twenty years old and above—all who *are able to* go to war in Israel. You and Aaron shall number them by their armies. 4And with you there shall be a man from every tribe, each one the head of his father's house.

5"These are the names of the men who shall stand with you: from Reuben, Elizur the son of Shedeur; 6from Simeon, Shelumiel the son of Zurishaddai; 7from Judah, Nahshon the son of Amminadab; 8from Issachar, Nethanel the son of Zuar; 9from Zebulun, Eliab the son of Helon; 10from the sons of Joseph: from Ephraim, Elishama the son of Ammihud; from Manasseh, Gamaliel the son of Pedahzur; 11from Benjamin, Abidan the son of Gideoni; 12from Dan, Ahiezer the son of Ammishaddai; 13from Asher, Pagiel the son of Ocran; 14from Gad, Eliasaph the son of Deuel;[a] 15from Naphtali, Ahira the son of Enan." 16These *were* chosen from the congregation, leaders of their fathers' tribes, heads of the divisions in Israel.

17Then Moses and Aaron took these men who had been mentioned by name, 18and they assembled all the congregation together on the first *day* of the second month; and they recited their ancestry by families, by their fathers' houses, according to the number of names, from twenty years old and above, each one individually. 19As the LORD commanded Moses, so he numbered them in the Wilderness of Sinai.

20Now the children of Reuben, Israel's oldest son, their genealogies by their families, by their fathers' house, according to the number of names, every male individually, from twenty years old and above, all who *were able to* go to war: 21those who were numbered of the tribe of Reuben

1:14 [a]Spelled *Reuel* in 2:14

1:2 We may wonder why God directed Moses to take a census, while David was punished for taking a census of his people. David's reason for doing so was not because God had instructed him to. Rather, it was Satan who tempted him to do so: "Now Satan stood up against Israel, and moved David to number Israel" (1 Chron. 21:1). David was putting more confidence in the strength of his army than in the living God.

1:5 Though these men are memorialized by having their names listed in Holy Scripture, there is only one place where having our names really matters—the Book of Life: "There shall by no means enter it anything that defiles, or causes an abomination or a lie, but only those who are written in the Lamb's Book of Life" (Rev. 21:27).

were forty-six thousand five hundred.
22From the children of Simeon, their
genealogies by their families, by their fathers' house, of those who were numbered,
according to the number of names, every
male individually, from twenty years old
and above, all who *were able to* go to war:
23those who were numbered of the tribe
of Simeon *were* fifty-nine thousand three
hundred.
24From the children of Gad, their genealogies by their families, by their fathers'
house, according to the number of names,
from twenty years old and above, all who
were able to go to war: 25those who were
numbered of the tribe of Gad *were* forty-
five thousand six hundred and fifty.

> The American church has lost its wonder of prayer because we have departed from teaching the Law and using it in evangelism. The lack of reverence for the Law causes a low view of sin, which causes a low view of God, which causes a low view of prayer.
>
> **MATTHEW S. JOHNSON**

26From the children of Judah, their genealogies by their families, by their fathers' house, according to the number of
names, from twenty years old and above,
all who *were able to* go to war: 27those
who were numbered of the tribe of Judah
were seventy-four thousand six hundred.
28From the children of Issachar, their
genealogies by their families, by their fathers' house, according to the number of
names, from twenty years old and above,
all who *were able to* go to war: 29those who
were numbered of the tribe of Issachar *were*
fifty-four thousand four hundred.
30From the children of Zebulun, their
genealogies by their families, by their fathers' house, according to the number of
names, from twenty years old and above,
all who *were able to* go to war: 31those who
were numbered of the tribe of Zebulun
were fifty-seven thousand four hundred.
32From the sons of Joseph, the children of Ephraim, their genealogies by
their families, by their fathers' house, according to the number of names, from
twenty years old and above, all who *were*
able to go to war: 33those who were numbered of the tribe of Ephraim *were* forty
thousand five hundred.
34From the children of Manasseh, their
genealogies by their families, by their fathers' house, according to the number of
names, from twenty years old and above,
all who *were able to* go to war: 35those who
were numbered of the tribe of Manasseh
were thirty-two thousand two hundred.
36From the children of Benjamin, their
genealogies by their families, by their fathers' house, according to the number of
names, from twenty years old and above,
all who *were able to* go to war: 37those who
were numbered of the tribe of Benjamin
were thirty-five thousand four hundred.
38From the children of Dan, their genealogies by their families, by their fathers'
house, according to the number of names,
from twenty years old and above, all who
were able to go to war: 39those who were
numbered of the tribe of Dan *were* sixty-
two thousand seven hundred.
40From the children of Asher, their genealogies by their families, by their fathers' house, according to the number of
names, from twenty years old and above,
all who *were able to* go to war: 41those
who were numbered of the tribe of Asher
were forty-one thousand five hundred.
42From the children of Naphtali, their
genealogies by their families, by their fathers' house, according to the number of
names, from twenty years old and above,
all who *were able to* go to war: 43those who
were numbered of the tribe of Naphtali
were fifty-three thousand four hundred.
44These are the ones who were numbered, whom Moses and Aaron numbered,
with the leaders of Israel, twelve men,
each one representing his father's house.
45So all who were numbered of the children of Israel, by their fathers' houses,
from twenty years old and above, all who

were able to go to war in Israel— 46all who
were numbered were six hundred and
three thousand five hundred and fifty.
47But the Levites were not numbered
among them by their fathers' tribe; 48for
the LORD had spoken to Moses, saying:
49"Only the tribe of Levi you shall not
number, nor take a census of them among
the children of Israel; 50but you shall appoint the Levites over the tabernacle of
the Testimony, over all its furnishings,
and over all things that belong to it; they
shall carry the tabernacle and all its furnishings; they shall attend to it and camp
around the tabernacle. 51And when the
tabernacle is to go forward, the Levites
shall take it down; and when the tabernacle is to be set up, the Levites shall set
it up. The outsider who comes near shall
be put to death. 52The children of Israel
shall pitch their tents, everyone by his
own camp, everyone by his own standard, according to their armies; 53but the
Levites shall camp around the tabernacle
of the Testimony, that there may be no
wrath on the congregation of the children
of Israel; and the Levites shall keep charge
of the tabernacle of the Testimony."
54Thus the children of Israel did; according to all that the LORD commanded
Moses, so they did.

The Tribes and Leaders by Armies

2 And the LORD spoke to Moses and
Aaron, saying: 2"Everyone of the children of Israel shall camp by his own standard, beside the emblems of his father's
house; they shall camp some distance from
the tabernacle of meeting. 3On the east
side, toward the rising of the sun, those
of the standard of the forces with Judah
shall camp according to their armies; and
Nahshon the son of Amminadab *shall be*
the leader of the children of Judah." 4And
his army was numbered at seventy-four
thousand six hundred.
5"Those who camp next to him *shall be*
the tribe of Issachar, and Nethanel the
son of Zuar *shall be* the leader of the children of Issachar." 6And his army was numbered at fifty-four thousand four hundred.
7"Then *comes* the tribe of Zebulun, and
Eliab the son of Helon *shall be* the leader
of the children of Zebulun." 8And his army
was numbered at fifty-seven thousand four
hundred. 9"All who were numbered according to their armies of the forces with
Judah, one hundred and eighty-six thousand four hundred—these shall break
camp first.
10"On the south side *shall be* the standard of the forces with Reuben according
to their armies, and the leader of the children of Reuben *shall be* Elizur the son of
Shedeur." 11And his army was numbered
at forty-six thousand five hundred.
12"Those who camp next to him *shall
be* the tribe of Simeon, and the leader of
the children of Simeon *shall be* Shelumiel
the son of Zurishaddai." 13And his army
was numbered at fifty-nine thousand three
hundred.
14"Then *comes* the tribe of Gad, and
the leader of the children of Gad *shall be*
Eliasaph the son of Reuel."[a] 15And his army
was numbered at forty-five thousand six
hundred and fifty. 16"All who were numbered according to their armies of the forces
with Reuben, one hundred and fifty-one
thousand four hundred and fifty—they
shall be the second to break camp.
17"And the tabernacle of meeting shall
move out with the camp of the Levites in
the middle of the camps; as they camp,
so they shall move out, everyone in his
place, by their standards.
18"On the west side *shall be* the standard of the forces with Ephraim according to their armies, and the leader of the
children of Ephraim *shall be* Elishama the
son of Ammihud." 19And his army was
numbered at forty thousand five hundred.
20"Next to him *comes* the tribe of Manasseh, and the leader of the children of
Manasseh *shall be* Gamaliel the son of
Pedahzur." 21And his army was numbered
at thirty-two thousand two hundred.
22"Then *comes* the tribe of Benjamin,

2:14 [a]Spelled *Deuel* in 1:14 and 7:42

and the leader of the children of Benjamin *shall be* Abidan the son of Gideoni." [23]And his army was numbered at thirty-five thousand four hundred. [24]"All who were numbered according to their armies of the forces with Ephraim, one hundred and eight thousand one hundred—they shall be the third to break camp.

[25]"The standard of the forces with Dan *shall be* on the north side according to their armies, and the leader of the children of Dan *shall be* Ahiezer the son of Ammishaddai." [26]And his army was numbered at sixty-two thousand seven hundred.

[27]"Those who camp next to him *shall be* the tribe of Asher, and the leader of the children of Asher *shall be* Pagiel the son of Ocran." [28]And his army was numbered at forty-one thousand five hundred.

[29]"Then *comes* the tribe of Naphtali, and the leader of the children of Naphtali *shall be* Ahira the son of Enan." [30]And his army was numbered at fifty-three thousand four hundred. [31]"All who were numbered of the forces with Dan, one hundred and fifty-seven thousand six hundred—they shall break camp last, with their standards."

[32]These *are* the ones who were numbered of the children of Israel by their fathers' houses. All who were numbered according to their armies of the forces *were* six hundred and three thousand five hundred and fifty. [33]But the Levites were not numbered among the children of Israel, just as the LORD commanded Moses.

[34]Thus the children of Israel did according to all that the LORD commanded Moses; so they camped by their standards and so they broke camp, each one by his family, according to their fathers' houses.

The Sons of Aaron

3 Now these *are* the records of Aaron and Moses when the LORD spoke with Moses on Mount Sinai. [2]And these *are* the names of the sons of Aaron: Nadab, the firstborn, and Abihu, Eleazar, and Ithamar. [3]These *are* the names of the sons of Aaron, the anointed priests, whom he consecrated to minister as priests. [4]Nadab and Abihu had died before the LORD when they offered profane fire before the LORD in the Wilderness of Sinai; and they had no children. So Eleazar and Ithamar ministered as priests in the presence of Aaron their father.

The Levites Serve in the Tabernacle

[5]And the LORD spoke to Moses, saying: [6]"Bring the tribe of Levi near, and present them before Aaron the priest, that they may serve him. [7]And they shall attend to his needs and the needs of the whole congregation before the tabernacle of meeting, to do the work of the tabernacle. [8]Also they shall attend to all the furnishings of the tabernacle of meeting, and to the needs of the children of Israel, to do the work of the tabernacle. [9]And you shall give the Levites to Aaron and his sons; they *are* given entirely to him[a] from among the children of Israel. [10]So you shall appoint Aaron and his sons, and they shall attend to their priesthood; but the outsider who comes near shall be put to death."

[11]Then the LORD spoke to Moses, saying: [12]"Now behold, I Myself have taken the Levites from among the children of Israel instead of every firstborn who opens the womb among the children of Israel. Therefore the Levites shall be Mine, [13]because all the firstborn *are* Mine. On the day that I struck all the firstborn in the land of Egypt, I sanctified to Myself all the firstborn in Israel, both man and beast. They shall be Mine: I *am* the LORD."

Census of the Levites Commanded

[14]Then the LORD spoke to Moses in the Wilderness of Sinai, saying: [15]"Number the children of Levi by their fathers' houses, by their families; you shall number every male from a month old and above."

[16]So Moses numbered them according to the word of the LORD, as he was commanded. [17]These were the sons of Levi by their names: Gershon, Kohath, and Merari.

3:9 [a]Samaritan Pentateuch and Septuagint read *Me*.

ari. [18]And these *are* the names of the sons of Gershon by their families: Libni and Shimei. [19]And the sons of Kohath by their families: Amram, Izehar, Hebron, and Uzziel. [20]And the sons of Merari by their families: Mahli and Mushi. These *are* the families of the Levites by their fathers' houses.

[21]From Gershon *came* the family of the Libnites and the family of the Shimites; these *were* the families of the Gershonites. [22]Those who were numbered, according to the number of all the males from a month old and above—of those who were numbered *there were* seven thousand five hundred. [23]The families of the Gershonites were to camp behind the tabernacle westward. [24]And the leader of the father's house of the Gershonites *was* Eliasaph the son of Lael. [25]The duties of the children of Gershon in the tabernacle of meeting *included* the tabernacle, the tent with its covering, the screen for the door of the tabernacle of meeting, [26]the screen for the door of the court, the hangings of the court which *are* around the tabernacle and the altar, and their cords, according to all the work relating to them.

[27]From Kohath *came* the family of the Amramites, the family of the Izharites, the family of the Hebronites, and the family of the Uzzielites; these *were* the families of the Kohathites. [28]According to the number of all the males, from a month old and above, *there were* eight thousand six[a] hundred keeping charge of the sanctuary. [29]The families of the children of Kohath were to camp on the south side of the tabernacle. [30]And the leader of the fathers' house of the families of the Kohathites *was* Elizaphan the son of Uzziel. [31]Their duty *included* the ark, the table, the lampstand, the altars, the utensils of the sanctuary with which they ministered, the screen, and all the work relating to them.

[32]And Eleazar the son of Aaron the priest *was to be* chief over the leaders of the Levites, *with* oversight of those who kept charge of the sanctuary.

[33]From Merari *came* the family of the Mahlites and the family of the Mushites; these *were* the families of Merari. [34]And those who were numbered, according to the number of all the males from a month old and above, *were* six thousand two hundred. [35]The leader of the fathers' house of the families of Merari *was* Zuriel the son of Abihail. These *were* to camp on the north side of the tabernacle. [36]And the appointed duty of the children of Merari *included* the boards of the tabernacle, its bars, its pillars, its sockets, its utensils, all the work relating to them, [37]and the pillars of the court all around, with their sockets, their pegs, and their cords.

[38]Moreover those who were to camp before the tabernacle on the east, before the tabernacle of meeting, *were* Moses, Aaron, and his sons, keeping charge of the sanctuary, to meet the needs of the children of Israel; but the outsider who came near was to be put to death. [39]All who were numbered of the Levites, whom Moses and Aaron numbered at the commandment of the LORD, by their families, all the males from a month old and above, *were* twenty-two thousand.

Levites Dedicated Instead of the Firstborn

[40]Then the LORD said to Moses: "Number all the firstborn males of the children of Israel from a month old and above, and take the number of their names. [41]And you shall take the Levites for Me—I *am* the LORD—instead of all the firstborn among the children of Israel, and the livestock of the Levites instead of all the firstborn among the livestock of the children of Israel." [42]So Moses numbered all the firstborn among the children of Israel, as the LORD commanded him. [43]And all the firstborn males, according to the number of names from a month old and above, of those who were numbered of them, were twenty-two thousand two hundred and seventy-three.

[44]Then the LORD spoke to Moses, say-

3:28 [a]Some manuscripts of the Septuagint read *three*.

ing: 45"Take the Levites instead of all the firstborn among the children of Israel, and the livestock of the Levites instead of their livestock. The Levites shall be Mine: I *am* the LORD. 46And for the redemption of the two hundred and seventy-three of the firstborn of the children of Israel, who are more than the number of the Levites, 47you shall take five shekels for each one individually; you shall take *them* in the currency of the shekel of the sanctuary, the shekel of twenty gerahs. 48And you shall give the money, with which the excess number of them is redeemed, to Aaron and his sons."

49So Moses took the redemption money from those who were over and above those who were redeemed by the Levites. 50From the firstborn of the children of Israel he took the money, one thousand three hundred and sixty-five *shekels,* according to the shekel of the sanctuary. 51And Moses gave their redemption money to Aaron and his sons, according to the word of the LORD, as the LORD commanded Moses.

Duties of the Sons of Kohath

4 Then the LORD spoke to Moses and Aaron, saying: 2"Take a census of the sons of Kohath from among the children of Levi, by their families, by their fathers' house, 3from thirty years old and above, even to fifty years old, all who enter the service to do the work in the tabernacle of meeting.

4"This *is* the service of the sons of Kohath in the tabernacle of meeting, *relating to* the most holy things: 5When the camp prepares to journey, Aaron and his sons shall come, and they shall take down the covering veil and cover the ark of the Testimony with it. 6Then they shall put on it a covering of badger skins, and spread over *that* a cloth entirely of blue; and they shall insert its poles.

7"On the table of showbread they shall spread a blue cloth, and put on it the dishes, the pans, the bowls, and the pitchers for pouring; and the showbread[a] shall be on it. 8They shall spread over them a scarlet cloth, and cover the same with a covering of badger skins; and they shall insert its poles. 9And they shall take a blue cloth and cover the lampstand of the light, with its lamps, its wick-trimmers, its trays, and all its oil vessels, with which they service it. 10Then they shall put it with all its utensils in a covering of badger skins, and put *it* on a carrying beam.

11"Over the golden altar they shall spread a blue cloth, and cover it with a covering of badger skins; and they shall insert its poles. 12Then they shall take all the utensils of service with which they minister in the sanctuary, put *them* in a blue cloth, cover them with a covering of badger skins, and put *them* on a carrying beam. 13Also they shall take away the ashes from the altar, and spread a purple cloth over it. 14They shall put on it all its implements with which they minister there—the firepans, the forks, the shovels, the basins, and all the utensils of the altar—and they shall spread on it a covering of badger skins, and insert its poles. 15And when Aaron and his sons have finished covering the sanctuary and all the furnishings of the sanctuary, when the camp is set to go, then the sons of Kohath shall come to carry *them;* but they shall not touch any holy thing, lest they die.

"These *are* the things in the tabernacle of meeting which the sons of Kohath are to carry.

16"The appointed duty of Eleazar the son of Aaron the priest *is* the oil for the light, the sweet incense, the daily grain offering, the anointing oil, the oversight of all the tabernacle, of all that *is* in it, with the sanctuary and its furnishings."

17Then the LORD spoke to Moses and Aaron, saying: 18"Do not cut off the tribe

4:7 [a]Literally *the continual bread*

4:15 See 1 Chron. 13:7–10 comment.

of the families of the Kohathites from among the Levites; [19]but do this in regard to them, that they may live and not die when they approach the most holy things: Aaron and his sons shall go in and appoint each of them to his service and his task. [20]But they shall not go in to watch while the holy things are being covered, lest they die."

Duties of the Sons of Gershon

[21]Then the LORD spoke to Moses, saying: [22]"Also take a census of the sons of Gershon, by their fathers' house, by their families. [23]From thirty years old and above, even to fifty years old, you shall number them, all who enter to perform the service, to do the work in the tabernacle of meeting. [24]This *is* the service of the families of the Gershonites, in serving and carrying: [25]They shall carry the curtains of the tabernacle and the tabernacle of meeting *with* its covering, the covering of badger skins that *is* on it, the screen for the door of the tabernacle of meeting, [26]the screen for the door of the gate of the court, the hangings of the court which *are* around the tabernacle and altar, and their cords, all the furnishings for their service and all that is made for these things: so shall they serve.

[27]"Aaron and his sons shall assign all the service of the sons of the Gershonites, all their tasks and all their service. And you shall appoint to them all their tasks as their duty. [28]This *is* the service of the families of the sons of Gershon in the tabernacle of meeting. And their duties *shall be* under the authority[a] of Ithamar the son of Aaron the priest.

Duties of the Sons of Merari

[29]"*As for* the sons of Merari, you shall number them by their families and by their fathers' house. [30]From thirty years old and above, even to fifty years old, you shall number them, everyone who enters the service to do the work of the tabernacle of meeting. [31]And this *is* what they must carry as all their service for the tabernacle of meeting: the boards of the tabernacle, its bars, its pillars, its sockets, [32]and the pillars around the court with their sockets, pegs, and cords, with all their furnishings and all their service; and you shall assign *to each man* by name the items he must carry. [33]This *is* the service of the families of the sons of Merari, as all their service for the tabernacle of meeting, under the authority[a] of Ithamar the son of Aaron the priest."

Census of the Levites

[34]And Moses, Aaron, and the leaders of the congregation numbered the sons of the Kohathites by their families and by their fathers' house, [35]from thirty years old and above, even to fifty years old, everyone who entered the service for work in the tabernacle of meeting; [36]and those who were numbered by their families were two thousand seven hundred and fifty. [37]These *were* the ones who were numbered of the families of the Kohathites, all who might serve in the tabernacle of meeting, whom Moses and Aaron numbered according to the commandment of the LORD by the hand of Moses.

[38]And those who were numbered of the sons of Gershon, by their families and by their fathers' house, [39]from thirty years old and above, even to fifty years old, everyone who entered the service for work in the tabernacle of meeting— [40]those who were numbered by their families, by their fathers' house, were two thousand six hundred and thirty. [41]These *are* the ones who were numbered of the families of the sons of Gershon, of all who might serve in the tabernacle of meeting, whom Moses and Aaron numbered according to the commandment of the LORD.

[42]Those of the families of the sons of Merari who were numbered, by their families, by their fathers' house, [43]from thirty years old and above, even to fifty years old, everyone who entered the service for work in the tabernacle of meet-

4:28, 33 [a]Literally *hand*

ing— [44]those who were numbered by their families were three thousand two hundred. [45]These *are* the ones who were numbered of the families of the sons of Merari, whom Moses and Aaron numbered according to the word of the LORD by the hand of Moses.

[46]All who were numbered of the Levites, whom Moses, Aaron, and the leaders of Israel numbered, by their families and by their fathers' houses, [47]from thirty years old and above, even to fifty years old, everyone who came to do the work of service and the work of bearing burdens in the tabernacle of meeting— [48]those who were numbered were eight thousand five hundred and eighty.

[49]According to the commandment of the LORD they were numbered by the hand of Moses, each according to his service and according to his task; thus were they numbered by him, as the LORD commanded Moses.

Ceremonially Unclean Persons Isolated

5 And the LORD spoke to Moses, saying: [2]"Command the children of Israel that they put out of the camp every leper, everyone who has a discharge, and whoever becomes defiled by a corpse. [3]You shall put out both male and female; you shall put them outside the camp, that they may not defile their camps in the midst of which I dwell." [4]And the children of Israel did so, and put them outside the camp; as the LORD spoke to Moses, so the children of Israel did.

Confession and Restitution

[5]Then the LORD spoke to Moses, saying, [6]"Speak to the children of Israel: 'When a man or woman commits any sin that men commit in unfaithfulness against the LORD, and that person is guilty, [7]then he shall confess the sin which he has committed. He shall make restitution for his trespass in full, plus one-fifth of it, and give *it* to the one he has wronged. [8]But if the man has no relative to whom restitution may be made for the wrong, the restitution for the wrong *must go* to the LORD for the priest, in addition to the ram of the atonement with which atonement is made for him. [9]Every offering of all the holy things of the children of Israel, which they bring to the priest, shall be his. [10]And every man's holy things shall be his; whatever any man gives the priest shall be his.' "

Concerning Unfaithful Wives

[11]And the LORD spoke to Moses, saying, [12]"Speak to the children of Israel, and say to them: 'If any man's wife goes astray and behaves unfaithfully toward him, [13]and a man lies with her carnally, and it is hidden from the eyes of her husband, and it is concealed that she has defiled herself, and *there was* no witness against her, nor was she caught— [14]if the spirit of jealousy comes upon him and he becomes jealous of his wife, who has defiled herself; or if the spirit of jealousy comes upon him and he becomes jealous of his wife, although she has not defiled herself— [15]then the man shall bring his wife to the priest. He shall bring the offering required for her, one-tenth of an ephah of barley meal; he shall pour no oil on it and put no frankincense on it, because it *is* a grain offering of jealousy, an offering for remembering, for bringing iniquity to remembrance.

[16]'And the priest shall bring her near, and set her before the LORD. [17]The priest shall take holy water in an earthen vessel, and take some of the dust that is on the floor of the tabernacle and put *it* into the water. [18]Then the priest shall stand the woman before the LORD, uncover the woman's head, and put the offering for remembering in her hands, which *is* the grain offering of jealousy. And the priest shall have in his hand the bitter water that brings a curse. [19]And the priest shall put her under oath, and say to the woman, "If no man has lain with you, and if you have not gone astray to uncleanness *while* under your husband's *authority,* be

free from this bitter water that brings a curse. [20]But if you have gone astray *while* under your husband's *authority,* and if you have defiled yourself and some man other than your husband has lain with you"— [21]then the priest shall put the woman under the oath of the curse, and he shall say to the woman—"the LORD make you a curse and an oath among your people, when the LORD makes your thigh rot and your belly swell; [22]and may this water that causes the curse go into your stomach, and make *your* belly swell and *your* thigh rot."

'Then the woman shall say, "Amen, so be it."

. . . . . .

For the immense complexity of our DNA code, see Isa. 42:5 comment.

. . . . . .

[23]'Then the priest shall write these curses in a book, and he shall scrape *them* off into the bitter water. [24]And he shall make the woman drink the bitter water that brings a curse, and the water that brings the curse shall enter her *to become* bitter. [25]Then the priest shall take the grain offering of jealousy from the woman's hand, shall wave the offering before the LORD, and bring it to the altar; [26]and the priest shall take a handful of the offering, as its memorial portion, burn *it* on the altar, and afterward make the woman drink the water. [27]When he has made her drink the water, then it shall be, if she has defiled herself and behaved unfaithfully toward her husband, that the water that brings a curse will enter her *and become* bitter, and her belly will swell, her thigh will rot, and the woman will become a curse among her people. [28]But if the woman has not defiled herself, and is clean, then she shall be free and may conceive children.

[29]'This *is* the law of jealousy, when a wife, *while* under her husband's *authority,* goes astray and defiles herself, [30]or when the spirit of jealousy comes upon a man, and he becomes jealous of his wife; then he shall stand the woman before the LORD, and the priest shall execute all this law upon her. [31]Then the man shall be free from iniquity, but that woman shall bear her guilt.' "

The Law of the Nazirite

6 Then the LORD spoke to Moses, saying, [2]"Speak to the children of Israel, and say to them: 'When either a man or woman consecrates an offering to take the vow of a Nazirite, to separate himself to the LORD, [3]he shall separate himself from wine and *similar* drink; he shall drink neither vinegar made from wine nor vinegar made from *similar* drink; neither shall he drink any grape juice, nor eat fresh grapes or raisins. [4]All the days of his separation he shall eat nothing that is produced by the grapevine, from seed to skin.

[5]'All the days of the vow of his separation no razor shall come upon his head; until the days are fulfilled for which he separated himself to the LORD, he shall be holy. *Then* he shall let the locks of the hair of his head grow. [6]All the days that he separates himself to the LORD he shall not go near a dead body. [7]He shall not make himself unclean even for his father or his mother, for his brother or his sister, when they die, because his separation to God *is* on his head. [8]All the days of his separation he shall be holy to the LORD.

[9]'And if anyone dies very suddenly beside him, and he defiles his consecrated head, then he shall shave his head on the day of his cleansing; on the seventh day he shall shave it. [10]Then on the eighth day he shall bring two turtledoves or two young pigeons to the priest, to the door of the tabernacle of meeting; [11]and the priest shall offer one as a sin offering and *the* other as a burnt offering, and make atonement for him, because he sinned in regard to the corpse; and he shall sanctify his head that same day. [12]He shall consecrate to the LORD the days of his separation, and bring a male lamb in its first

year as a trespass offering; but the former days shall be lost, because his separation was defiled.

13‘Now this *is* the law of the Nazirite: When the days of his separation are fulfilled, he shall be brought to the door of the tabernacle of meeting. 14And he shall present his offering to the LORD: one male lamb in its first year without blemish as a burnt offering, one ewe lamb in its first year without blemish as a sin offering, one ram without blemish as a peace offering, 15a basket of unleavened bread, cakes of fine flour mixed with oil, unleavened wafers anointed with oil, and their grain offering with their drink offerings.

16‘Then the priest shall bring *them* before the LORD and offer his sin offering and his burnt offering; 17and he shall offer the ram as a sacrifice of a peace offering to the LORD, with the basket of unleavened bread; the priest shall also offer its grain offering and its drink offering. 18Then the Nazirite shall shave his consecrated head *at* the door of the tabernacle of meeting, and shall take the hair from his consecrated head and put *it* on the fire which is under the sacrifice of the peace offering.

19‘And the priest shall take the boiled shoulder of the ram, one unleavened cake from the basket, and one unleavened wafer, and put *them* upon the hands of the Nazirite after he has shaved his consecrated *hair,* 20and the priest shall wave them as a wave offering before the LORD; they *are* holy for the priest, together with the breast of the wave offering and the thigh of the heave offering. After that the Nazirite may drink wine.’

21“This is the law of the Nazirite who vows to the LORD the offering for his separation, and besides that, whatever else his hand is able to provide; according to the vow which he takes, so he must do according to the law of his separation.”

The Priestly Blessing

22And the LORD spoke to Moses, saying: 23“Speak to Aaron and his sons, saying, ‘This is the way you shall bless the children of Israel. Say to them:

24“The LORD bless you and keep you;
25The LORD make His face shine upon
  you,
And be gracious to you;
26The LORD lift up His countenance
  upon you,
And give you peace.” ’

27“So they shall put My name on the children of Israel, and I will bless them.”

Offerings of the Leaders

7 Now it came to pass, when Moses had finished setting up the tabernacle, that he anointed it and consecrated it and all its furnishings, and the altar and all its utensils; so he anointed them and consecrated them. 2Then the leaders of Israel, the heads of their fathers’ houses, who *were* the leaders of the tribes and over those who were numbered, made an offering. 3And they brought their offering before the LORD, six covered carts and twelve oxen, a cart for *every* two of the leaders, and for each one an ox; and they presented them before the tabernacle.

4Then the LORD spoke to Moses, saying, 5“Accept *these* from them, that they may be used in doing the work of the tabernacle of meeting; and you shall give them to the Levites, *to* every man according to his service.” 6So Moses took the carts and the oxen, and gave them to the Levites. 7Two carts and four oxen he gave to the sons of Gershon, according to their service; 8and four carts and eight oxen he gave to the sons of Merari, according to their service, under the authority[a] of Ith-

7:8 [a]Literally *hand*

6:24–27 There is no greater blessing in this life than to have the blessing of Almighty God, to have His face shine on you. If you have His favor, it is because He has been gracious to you.

amar the son of Aaron the priest. 9But to the sons of Kohath he gave none, because theirs *was* the service of the holy things, *which* they carried on their shoulders.

10Now the leaders offered the dedication *offering* for the altar when it was anointed; so the leaders offered their offering before the altar. 11For the LORD said to Moses, "They shall offer their offering, one leader each day, for the dedication of the altar."

12And the one who offered his offering on the first day *was* Nahshon the son of Amminadab, from the tribe of Judah. 13His offering *was* one silver platter, the weight of which *was* one hundred and thirty *shekels,* and one silver bowl of seventy shekels, according to the shekel of the sanctuary, both of them full of fine flour mixed with oil as a grain offering; 14one gold pan of ten *shekels,* full of incense; 15one young bull, one ram, and one male lamb in its first year, as a burnt offering; 6one kid of the goats as a sin offering; 17and for the sacrifice of peace offerings: two oxen, five rams, five male goats, and five male lambs in their first year. This *was* the offering of Nahshon the son of Amminadab.

18On the second day Nethanel the son of Zuar, leader of Issachar, presented *an offering.* 19*For* his offering he offered one silver platter, the weight of which *was* one hundred and thirty *shekels,* and one silver bowl of seventy shekels, according to the shekel of the sanctuary, both of them full of fine flour mixed with oil as a grain offering; 20one gold pan of ten *shekels,* full of incense; 21one young bull, one ram, and one male lamb in its first year, as a burnt offering; 22one kid of the goats as a sin offering; 23and as the sacrifice of peace offerings: two oxen, five rams, five male goats, and five male lambs in their first year. This *was* the offering of Nethanel the son of Zuar.

24On the third day Eliab the son of Helon, leader of the children of Zebulun, *presented an offering.* 25His offering *was* one silver platter, the weight of which *was* one hundred and thirty *shekels,* and one silver bowl of seventy shekels, according to the shekel of the sanctuary, both of them full of fine flour mixed with oil as a grain offering; 26one gold pan of ten *shekels,* full of incense; 27one young bull, one ram, and one male lamb in its first year, as a burnt offering; 28one kid of the goats as a sin offering; 29and for the sacrifice of peace offerings: two oxen, five rams, five male goats, and five male lambs in their first year. This *was* the offering of Eliab the son of Helon.

> The tragedy of disbelieving in God is not that a man ends up believing in nothing. Alas, it is much worse, that person may end up believing in anything.
>
> **G. K. CHESTERTON**

30On the fourth day Elizur the son of Shedeur, leader of the children of Reuben, *presented an offering.* 31His offering *was* one silver platter, the weight of which *was* one hundred and thirty *shekels,* and one silver bowl of seventy shekels, according to the shekel of the sanctuary, both of them full of fine flour mixed with oil as a grain offering; 32one gold pan of ten *shekels,* full of incense; 33one young bull, one ram, and one male lamb in its first year, as a burnt offering; 34one kid of the goats as a sin offering; 35and as the sacrifice of peace offerings: two oxen, five rams, five male goats, and five male lambs in their first year. This *was* the offering of Elizur the son of Shedeur.

36On the fifth day Shelumiel the son of Zurishaddai, leader of the children of Simeon, *presented an offering.* 37His offering *was* one silver platter, the weight of which *was* one hundred and thirty *shekels,* and one silver bowl of seventy shekels, according to the shekel of the sanctuary, both of them full of fine flour mixed with oil as a grain offering; 38one gold pan of ten *shekels,* full of incense; 39one young bull, one ram, and one male lamb in its first year, as a burnt offering; 40one kid of

the goats as a sin offering; [41]and as the sacrifice of peace offerings: two oxen, five rams, five male goats, and five male lambs in their first year. This *was* the offering of Shelumiel the son of Zurishaddai.

[42]On the sixth day Eliasaph the son of Deuel,[a] leader of the children of Gad, *presented an offering.* [43]His offering *was* one silver platter, the weight of which *was* one hundred and thirty *shekels,* and one silver bowl of seventy shekels, according to the shekel of the sanctuary, both of them full of fine flour mixed with oil as a grain offering; [44]one gold pan of ten *shekels,* full of incense; [45]one young bull, one ram, and one male lamb in its first year, as a burnt offering; [46]one kid of the goats as a sin offering; [47]and as the sacrifice of peace offerings: two oxen, five rams, five male goats, and five male lambs in their first year. This *was* the offering of Eliasaph the son of Deuel.

[48]On the seventh day Elishama the son of Ammihud, leader of the children of Ephraim, *presented an offering.* [49]His offering *was* one silver platter, the weight of which *was* one hundred and thirty *shekels,* and one silver bowl of seventy shekels, according to the shekel of the sanctuary, both of them full of fine flour mixed with oil as a grain offering; [50]one gold pan of ten *shekels,* full of incense; [51]one young bull, one ram, and one male lamb in its first year, as a burnt offering; [52]one kid of the goats as a sin offering; [53]and as the sacrifice of peace offerings: two oxen, five rams, five male goats, and five male lambs in their first year. This *was* the offering of Elishama the son of Ammihud.

[54]On the eighth day Gamaliel the son of Pedahzur, leader of the children of Manasseh, *presented an offering.* [55]His offering *was* one silver platter, the weight of which *was* one hundred and thirty *shekels,* and one silver bowl of seventy shekels, according to the shekel of the sanctuary, both of them full of fine flour mixed with oil as a grain offering; [56]one gold pan of ten *shekels,* full of incense; [57]one young bull, one ram, and one male lamb in its first year, as a burnt offering; [58]one kid of the goats as a sin offering; [59]and as the sacrifice of peace offerings: two oxen, five rams, five male goats, and five male lambs in their first year. This *was* the offering of Gamaliel the son of Pedahzur.

[60]On the ninth day Abidan the son of Gideoni, leader of the children of Benjamin, *presented an offering.* [61]His offering *was* one silver platter, the weight of which *was* one hundred and thirty *shekels,* and one silver bowl of seventy shekels, according to the shekel of the sanctuary, both of them full of fine flour mixed with oil as a grain offering; [62]one gold pan of ten *shekels,* full of incense; [63]one young bull, one ram, and one male lamb in its first year, as a burnt offering; [64]one kid of the goats as a sin offering; [65]and as the sacrifice of peace offerings: two oxen, five rams, five male goats, and five male lambs in their first year. This *was* the offering of Abidan the son of Gideoni.

[66]On the tenth day Ahiezer the son of Ammishaddai, leader of the children of Dan, *presented an offering.* [67]His offering *was* one silver platter, the weight of which *was* one hundred and thirty *shekels,* and one silver bowl of seventy shekels, according to the shekel of the sanctuary, both of them full of fine flour mixed with oil as a grain offering; [68]one gold pan of ten *shekels,* full of incense; [69]one young bull, one ram, and one male lamb in its

7:42 [a]Spelled *Reuel* in 2:14

7:38 "I wonder in my heart, were Jesus Christ to come to much of the professing church today, throughout the world and say, 'I want to prove whether or not you have an act of faith. I want you now to lay down all your plans. I want you to lay down all your ambitions, and all your dreams. I want you now to begin to journey with Me, trusting that if I choose to I can even raise the things that are dear to your heart from the dead, but still first you've got to give them to Me. You've got to lay it out, you've got to put in on an altar.'" *Paris Reidhead*

first year, as a burnt offering; 70 one kid of
the goats as a sin offering; 71 and as the
sacrifice of peace offerings: two oxen, five
rams, five male goats, and five male lambs
in their first year. This *was* the offering of
Ahiezer the son of Ammishaddai.

72 On the eleventh day Pagiel the son
of Ocran, leader of the children of Asher,
presented an offering. 73 His offering *was*
one silver platter, the weight of which *was*
one hundred and thirty *shekels,* and one
silver bowl of seventy shekels, according
to the shekel of the sanctuary, both of
them full of fine flour mixed with oil as a
grain offering; 74 one gold pan of ten
shekels, full of incense; 75 one young bull,
one ram, and one male lamb in its first
year, as a burnt offering; 76 one kid of the
goats as a sin offering; 77 and as the sacrifice of peace offerings: two oxen, five rams,
five male goats, and five male lambs in
their first year. This *was* the offering of
Pagiel the son of Ocran.

78 On the twelfth day Ahira the son of
Enan, leader of the children of Naphtali,
presented an offering. 79 His offering *was*
one silver platter, the weight of which *was*
one hundred and thirty *shekels,* and one
silver bowl of seventy shekels, according
to the shekel of the sanctuary, both of
them full of fine flour mixed with oil as a
grain offering; 80 one gold pan of ten *shekels,*
full of incense; 81 one young bull, one
ram, and one male lamb in its first year,
as a burnt offering; 82 one kid of the goats
as a sin offering; 83 and as the sacrifice of
peace offerings: two oxen, five rams, five
male goats, and five male lambs in their
first year. This *was* the offering of Ahira
the son of Enan.

84 This *was* the dedication *offering* for
the altar from the leaders of Israel, when
it was anointed: twelve silver platters,
twelve silver bowls, and twelve gold pans.
85 Each silver platter *weighed* one hundred
and thirty *shekels* and each bowl seventy
shekels. All the silver of the vessels *weighed*
two thousand four hundred *shekels,* according to the shekel of the sanctuary.
86 The twelve gold pans full of incense
weighed ten *shekels* apiece, according to
the shekel of the sanctuary; all the gold of
the pans *weighed* one hundred and twenty
shekels. 87 All the oxen for the burnt offering *were* twelve young bulls, the rams
twelve, the male lambs in their first year
twelve, with their grain offering, and the
kids of the goats as a sin offering twelve.
88 And all the oxen for the sacrifice of
peace offerings were twenty-four bulls, the
rams sixty, the male goats sixty, and the
lambs in their first year sixty. This *was* the
dedication *offering* for the altar after it
was anointed.

89 Now when Moses went into the
tabernacle of meeting to speak with Him,
he heard the voice of One speaking to
him from above the mercy seat that *was*
on the ark of the Testimony, from between the two cherubim; thus He spoke
to him.

Arrangement of the Lamps

8 And the LORD spoke to Moses, saying:
2 "Speak to Aaron, and say to him,
'When you arrange the lamps, the seven
lamps shall give light in front of the lampstand.' " 3 And Aaron did so; he arranged
the lamps to face toward the front of the
lampstand, as the LORD commanded
Moses. 4 Now this workmanship of the
lampstand *was* hammered gold; from its
shaft to its flowers it *was* hammered work.
According to the pattern which the LORD
had shown Moses, so he made the lampstand.

Cleansing and Dedication of the Levites

5 Then the LORD spoke to Moses, saying: 6 "Take the Levites from among the
children of Israel and cleanse them *cere-
monially.* 7 Thus you shall do to them to
cleanse them: Sprinkle water of purification on them, and let them shave all their
body, and let them wash their clothes,
and *so* make themselves clean. 8 Then let
them take a young bull with its grain offering of fine flour mixed with oil, and
you shall take another young bull as a sin

offering. [9]And you shall bring the Levites before the tabernacle of meeting, and you shall gather together the whole congregation of the children of Israel. [10]So you shall bring the Levites before the LORD, and the children of Israel shall lay their hands on the Levites; [11]and Aaron shall offer the Levites before the LORD *like* a wave offering from the children of Israel, that they may perform the work of the LORD. [12]Then the Levites shall lay their hands on the heads of the young bulls, and you shall offer one as a sin offering and the other as a burnt offering to the LORD, to make atonement for the Levites.

[13]"And you shall stand the Levites before Aaron and his sons, and then offer them *like* a wave offering to the LORD. [14]Thus you shall separate the Levites from among the children of Israel, and the Levites shall be Mine. [15]After that the Levites shall go in to service the tabernacle of meeting. So you shall cleanse them and offer them *like* a wave offering. [16]For they *are* wholly given to Me from among the children of Israel; I have taken them for Myself instead of all who open the womb, the firstborn of all the children of Israel. [17]For all the firstborn among the children of Israel *are* Mine, *both* man and beast; on the day that I struck all the firstborn in the land of Egypt I sanctified them to Myself. [18]I have taken the Levites instead of all the firstborn of the children of Israel. [19]And I have given the Levites as a gift to Aaron and his sons from among the children of Israel, to do the work for the children of Israel in the tabernacle of meeting, and to make atonement for the children of Israel, that there be no plague among the children of Israel when the children of Israel come near the sanctuary."

[20]Thus Moses and Aaron and all the congregation of the children of Israel did to the Levites; according to all that the LORD commanded Moses concerning the Levites, so the children of Israel did to them. [21]And the Levites purified themselves and washed their clothes; then Aaron presented them *like* a wave offering before the LORD, and Aaron made atonement for them to cleanse them. [22]After that the Levites went in to do their work in the tabernacle of meeting before Aaron and his sons; as the LORD commanded Moses concerning the Levites, so they did to them.

[23]Then the LORD spoke to Moses, saying, [24]"This *is* what *pertains* to the Levites: From twenty-five years old and above one may enter to perform service in the work of the tabernacle of meeting; [25]and at the age of fifty years they must cease performing this work, and shall work no more. [26]They may minister with their brethren in the tabernacle of meeting, to attend to needs, but they *themselves* shall do no work. Thus you shall do to the Levites regarding their duties."

The Second Passover

9 Now the LORD spoke to Moses in the Wilderness of Sinai, in the first month of the second year after they had come out of the land of Egypt, saying: [2]"Let the children of Israel keep the Passover at its appointed time. [3]On the fourteenth day of this month, at twilight, you shall keep it at its appointed time. According to all its rites and ceremonies you shall keep it." [4]So Moses told the children of Israel that they should keep the Passover. [5]And they kept the Passover on the fourteenth day of the first month, at twilight, in the Wilderness of Sinai; according to all that the LORD commanded Moses, so the children of Israel did.

[6]Now there were *certain* men who were defiled by a human corpse, so that they could not keep the Passover on that

---

9:1 God will often speak to our hearts in the "wilderness." There are times when we find ourselves in the heat of burning tribulation, and times when God comforts our hearts and His grace becomes sufficient for us.

day; and they came before Moses and Aaron that day. 7And those men said to him, "We *became* defiled by a human corpse. Why are we kept from presenting the offering of the LORD at its appointed time among the children of Israel?"

8And Moses said to them, "Stand still, that I may hear what the LORD will command concerning you."

9Then the LORD spoke to Moses, saying, 10"Speak to the children of Israel, saying: 'If anyone of you or your posterity is unclean because of a corpse, or *is* far away on a journey, he may still keep the LORD's Passover. 11On the fourteenth day of the second month, at twilight, they may keep it. They shall eat it with unleavened bread and bitter herbs. 12They shall leave none of it until morning, nor break one of its bones. According to all the ordinances of the Passover they shall keep it. 13But the man who *is* clean and is not on a journey, and ceases to keep the Passover, that same person shall be cut off from among his people, because he did not bring the offering of the LORD at its appointed time; that man shall bear his sin.

14'And if a stranger dwells among you, and would keep the LORD's Passover, he must do so according to the rite of the Passover and according to its ceremony; you shall have one ordinance, both for the stranger and the native of the land.' "

The Cloud and the Fire

15Now on the day that the tabernacle was raised up, the cloud covered the tabernacle, the tent of the Testimony; from evening until morning it was above the tabernacle like the appearance of fire. 16So it was always: the cloud covered it *by day,* and the appearance of fire by night. 17Whenever the cloud was taken up from above the tabernacle, after that the children of Israel would journey; and in the place where the cloud settled, there the children of Israel would pitch their tents. 18At the command of the LORD the children of Israel would journey, and at the command of the LORD they would camp; as long as the cloud stayed above the tabernacle they remained encamped. 19Even when the cloud continued long, many days above the tabernacle, the children of Israel kept the charge of the LORD and did not journey. 20So it was, when the cloud was above the tabernacle a few days: according to the command of the LORD they would remain encamped, and according to the command of the LORD they would journey. 21So it was, when the cloud remained only from evening until morning: when the cloud was taken up in the morning, then they would journey; whether by day or by night, whenever the cloud was taken up, they would journey. 22*Whether it was* two days, a month, or a year that the cloud remained above the tabernacle, the children of Israel would remain encamped and not journey; but when it was taken up, they would journey. 23At the command of the LORD they remained encamped, and at the command of the LORD they journeyed; they kept the charge of the LORD, at the command of the LORD by the hand of Moses.

Two Silver Trumpets

10 And the LORD spoke to Moses, saying: 2"Make two silver trumpets for yourself; you shall make them of hammered work; you shall use them for calling the congregation and for directing the movement of the camps. 3When they blow both of them, all the congregation shall gather before you at the door of the tabernacle of meeting. 4But if they blow *only* one, then the leaders, the heads of the divisions of Israel, shall gather to you. 5When you sound the advance, the camps that lie on the east side shall then begin their journey. 6When you sound the advance the second time, then the camps that lie on the south side shall begin their journey; they shall sound the call for them to begin their journeys. 7And when the assembly is to be gathered together, you shall blow, but not sound the advance. 8The sons of Aaron, the priests, shall

blow the trumpets; and these shall be to
you as an ordinance forever throughout
your generations.
9“When you go to war in your land
against the enemy who oppresses you,
then you shall sound an alarm with the
trumpets, and you will be remembered
before the LORD your God, and you will
be saved from your enemies. 10Also in the
day of your gladness, in your appointed
feasts, and at the beginning of your months,
you shall blow the trumpets over your
burnt offerings and over the sacrifices of
your peace offerings; and they shall be a
memorial for you before your God: I *am*
the LORD your God.”

Departure from Sinai

11Now it came to pass on the twentieth
day of the second month, in the second
year, that the cloud was taken up from
above the tabernacle of the Testimony.
12And the children of Israel set out from
the Wilderness of Sinai on their journeys;
then the cloud settled down in the Wilderness of Paran. 13So they started out for
the first time according to the command
of the LORD by the hand of Moses.
14The standard of the camp of the children of Judah set out first according to
their armies; over their army was Nahshon the son of Amminadab. 15Over the
army of the tribe of the children of Issachar *was* Nethanel the son of Zuar. 16And
over the army of the tribe of the children
of Zebulun *was* Eliab the son of Helon.
17Then the tabernacle was taken down;
and the sons of Gershon and the sons of
Merari set out, carrying the tabernacle.
18And the standard of the camp of
Reuben set out according to their armies;
over their army *was* Elizur the son of Shedeur. 19Over the army of the tribe of the
children of Simeon *was* Shelumiel the son
of Zurishaddai. 20And over the army of
the tribe of the children of Gad *was* Eliasaph the son of Deuel.
21Then the Kohathites set out, carrying
the holy things. (The tabernacle would be
prepared for their arrival.)
22And the standard of the camp of the
children of Ephraim set out according to
their armies; over their army *was* Elishama
the son of Ammihud. 23Over the army of
the tribe of the children of Manasseh *was*
Gamaliel the son of Pedahzur. 24And over
the army of the tribe of the children of
Benjamin *was* Abidan the son of Gideoni.
25Then the standard of the camp of the
children of Dan (the rear guard of all the
camps) set out according to their armies;
over their army *was* Ahiezer the son of
Ammishaddai. 26Over the army of the
tribe of the children of Asher *was* Pagiel
the son of Ocran. 27And over the army of
the tribe of the children of Naphtali *was*
Ahira the son of Enan.
28Thus *was* the order of march of the
children of Israel, according to their
armies, when they began their journey.
29Now Moses said to Hobab the son of
Reuel[a] the Midianite, Moses’ father-in-law,
“We are setting out for the place of which
the LORD said, ‘I will give it to you.’ Come
with us, and we will treat you well; for
the LORD has promised good things to
Israel.”
30And he said to him, “I will not go, but
I will depart to my *own* land and to my
relatives.”
31So *Moses* said, “Please do not leave,
inasmuch as you know how we are to
camp in the wilderness, and you can be
our eyes. 32And it shall be, if you go with
us—indeed it shall be—that whatever
good the LORD will do to us, the same we
will do to you.”
33So they departed from the mountain
of the LORD on a journey of three days;
and the ark of the covenant of the LORD

10:29 [a]Septuagint reads *Raguel* (compare Exodus 2:18).

10:9 “Let us not glide through this world and then slip quietly into heaven, without having blown the trumpet loud and long for our Redeemer, Jesus Christ. Let us see to it that the devil will hold a thanksgiving service in hell, when he gets the news of our departure from the field of battle.” *C. T. Studd*

went before them for the three days' journey, to search out a resting place for them.
34And the cloud of the LORD *was* above
them by day when they went out from
the camp.
35So it was, whenever the ark set out,
that Moses said:

"Rise up, O LORD!
Let Your enemies be scattered,
And let those who hate You flee
before You."

36And when it rested, he said:

"Return, O LORD,
To the many thousands of Israel."

The People Complain

11 Now *when* the people complained,
it displeased the LORD; for the LORD
heard *it,* and His anger was aroused. So
the fire of the LORD burned among them,
and consumed *some* in the outskirts of
the camp. 2Then the people cried out to
Moses, and when Moses prayed to the
LORD, the fire was quenched. 3So he called
the name of the place Taberah,[a] because
the fire of the LORD had burned among
them.
4Now the mixed multitude who were
among them yielded to intense craving;
so the children of Israel also wept again
and said: "Who will give us meat to eat?
5We remember the fish which we ate
freely in Egypt, the cucumbers, the mel-
ons, the leeks, the onions, and the garlic;
6but now our whole being *is* dried up;
there is nothing at all except this manna
before our eyes!"
7Now the manna *was* like coriander
seed, and its color like the color of bdellium. 8The people went about and gathered *it,* ground *it* on millstones or beat *it*
in the mortar, cooked *it* in pans, and
made cakes of it; and its taste was like the
taste of pastry prepared with oil. 9And
when the dew fell on the camp in the
night, the manna fell on it.
10Then Moses heard the people weeping throughout their families, everyone at
the door of his tent; and the anger of the
LORD was greatly aroused; Moses also was
displeased. 11So Moses said to the LORD,
"Why have You afflicted Your servant?
And why have I not found favor in Your
sight, that You have laid the burden of all
these people on me? 12Did I conceive all
these people? Did I beget them, that You
should say to me, 'Carry them in your
bosom, as a guardian carries a nursing
child,' to the land which You swore to
their fathers? 13Where am I to get meat to
give to all these people? For they weep all
over me, saying, 'Give us meat, that we
may eat.' 14I am not able to bear all these
people alone, because the burden *is* too
heavy for me. 15If You treat me like this,
please kill me here and now—if I have
found favor in Your sight—and do not let
me see my wretchedness!"

The Seventy Elders

16So the LORD said to Moses: "Gather
to Me seventy men of the elders of Israel,
whom you know to be the elders of the
people and officers over them; bring
them to the tabernacle of meeting, that
they may stand there with you. 17Then I
will come down and talk with you there.
I will take of the Spirit that *is* upon you
and will put *the same* upon them; and
they shall bear the burden of the people
with you, that you may not bear *it* yourself alone. 18Then you shall say to the
people, 'Consecrate yourselves for tomorrow, and you shall eat meat; for you have
wept in the hearing of the LORD, saying,
"Who will give us meat to eat? For *it was*
well with us in Egypt." Therefore the LORD

11:3 [a]Literally *Burning*

11:4–6 "The true believer is the one who lays everything down. That's as simple as it can get. The one who is counterfeit holds on to the world, his habits, his career. He wants to hold it. And that's when Jesus says, "No, you can't be my believer. Let go, let go." *Paris Reidhead*

will give you meat, and you shall eat. [19]You shall eat, not one day, nor two days, nor five days, nor ten days, nor twenty days, [20]but *for* a whole month, until it comes out of your nostrils and becomes loathsome to you, because you have despised the LORD who is among you, and have wept before Him, saying, "Why did we ever come up out of Egypt?" ' "

[21]And Moses said, "The people whom I *am* among *are* six hundred thousand men on foot; yet You have said, 'I will give them meat, that they may eat *for* a whole month.' [22]Shall flocks and herds be slaughtered for them, to provide enough for them? Or shall all the fish of the sea be gathered together for them, to provide enough for them?"

[23]And the LORD said to Moses, "Has the LORD's arm been shortened? Now you shall see whether what I say will happen to you or not."

[24]So Moses went out and told the people the words of the LORD, and he gathered the seventy men of the elders of the people and placed them around the tabernacle. [25]Then the LORD came down in the cloud, and spoke to him, and took of the Spirit that *was* upon him, and placed *the same* upon the seventy elders; and it happened, when the Spirit rested upon them, that they prophesied, although they never did *so* again.[a]

[26]But two men had remained in the camp: the name of one *was* Eldad, and the name of the other Medad. And the Spirit rested upon them. Now they *were* among those listed, but who had not gone out to the tabernacle; yet they prophesied in the camp. [27]And a young man ran and told Moses, and said, "Eldad and Medad are prophesying in the camp."

[28]So Joshua the son of Nun, Moses' assistant, *one* of his choice men, answered and said, "Moses my lord, forbid them!"

[29]Then Moses said to him, "Are you zealous for my sake? Oh, that all the LORD's people were prophets *and* that the LORD would put His Spirit upon them!" [30]And Moses returned to the camp, he and the elders of Israel.

The Lord Sends Quail

[31]Now a wind went out from the LORD, and it brought quail from the sea and left *them* fluttering near the camp, about a day's journey on this side and about a day's journey on the other side, all around the camp, and about two cubits above the surface of the ground. [32]And the people stayed up all that day, all night, and all the next day, and gathered the quail (he who gathered least gathered ten homers); and they spread *them* out for themselves all around the camp. [33]But while the meat *was* still between their teeth, before it was chewed, the wrath of the LORD was aroused against the people, and the LORD struck the people with a very great plague. [34]So he called the name of that place Kibroth Hattaavah,[a] because there they buried the people who had yielded to craving.

[35]From Kibroth Hattaavah the people moved to Hazeroth, and camped at Hazeroth.

Dissension of Aaron and Miriam

12 Then Miriam and Aaron spoke against Moses because of the Ethiopian woman whom he had married; for

11:25 [a]Targum and Vulgate read *did not cease.* 11:34 [a]Literally *Graves of Craving*

11:18–20 Be careful what you ask for; you may get it. God sometimes gives us the desires of our heart—to our detriment (see v. 33). We should be content with God's provision. See also Psa. 78:29–31; 106:15.

11:25 When God comes down to earth, it's for a reason. In the incarnation, Jesus came to earth so that dying sinners might have everlasting life. If God gave you His Holy Spirit, it was for a reason—so that you could preach the gospel with power (see Acts 1:8). Never cease to do so.

11:34 We all have cravings of various kinds, but we can choose whether to act on them. See Jude 7 comment.

he had married an Ethiopian woman. 2So they said, "Has the LORD indeed spoken only through Moses? Has He not spoken through us also?" And the LORD heard *it*. 3(Now the man Moses *was* very humble, more than all men who *were* on the face of the earth.)

4Suddenly the LORD said to Moses, Aaron, and Miriam, "Come out, you three, to the tabernacle of meeting!" So the three came out. 5Then the LORD came down in the pillar of cloud and stood *in* the door of the tabernacle, and called Aaron and Miriam. And they both went forward. 6Then He said,

"Hear now My words:
If there is a prophet among you,
I, the LORD, make Myself known to
him in a vision;
I speak to him in a dream.
7Not so with My servant Moses;
He *is* faithful in all My house.
8I speak with him face to face,
Even plainly, and not in dark sayings;
And he sees the form of the LORD.
Why then were you not afraid
To speak against My servant Moses?"

9So the anger of the LORD was aroused against them, and He departed. 10And when the cloud departed from above the tabernacle, suddenly Miriam *became* leprous, as *white as* snow. Then Aaron turned toward Miriam, and there she was, a leper. 11So Aaron said to Moses, "Oh, my lord! Please do not lay *this* sin on us, in which we have done foolishly and in which we have sinned. 12Please do not let her be as one dead, whose flesh is half consumed when he comes out of his mother's womb!"

13So Moses cried out to the LORD, saying, "Please heal her, O God, I pray!"

14Then the LORD said to Moses, "If her father had but spit in her face, would she not be shamed seven days? Let her be shut out of the camp seven days, and afterward she may be received *again*." 15So Miriam was shut out of the camp seven days, and the people did not journey till Miriam was brought in *again*. 16And afterward the people moved from Hazeroth and camped in the Wilderness of Paran.

Spies Sent into Canaan

13 And the LORD spoke to Moses, saying, 2"Send men to spy out the land of Canaan, which I am giving to the children of Israel; from each tribe of their fathers you shall send a man, every one a leader among them."

3So Moses sent them from the Wilderness of Paran according to the command of the LORD, all of them men who *were* heads of the children of Israel. 4Now these *were* their names: from the tribe of Reuben, Shammua the son of Zaccur; 5from the tribe of Simeon, Shaphat the son of Hori; 6from the tribe of Judah, Caleb the son of Jephunneh; 7from the tribe of Issachar, Igal the son of Joseph; 8from the tribe of Ephraim, Hoshea[a] the son of Nun; 9from the tribe of Benjamin, Palti the son of Raphu; 10from the tribe of Zebulun, Gaddiel the son of Sodi; 11from the tribe of Joseph, *that is*, from the tribe of Manasseh, Gaddi the son of Susi; 12from the tribe of Dan, Ammiel the son of Gemalli; 13from the tribe of Asher, Sethur the son of Michael; 14from the tribe of Naphtali, Nahbi the son of Vophsi; 15from the tribe of Gad, Geuel the son of Machi.

16These *are* the names of the men whom Moses sent to spy out the land. And Moses called Hoshea[a] the son of Nun, Joshua.

17Then Moses sent them to spy out the land of Canaan, and said to them, "Go up

13:8 [a]Septuagint and Vulgate read *Oshea*. 13:16 [a]Septuagint and Vulgate read *Oshea*.

12:7 God Himself said that Moses was His "faithful servant." What an unspeakably high honor—to be called a faithful servant. These are the words that we should all live to hear on the day we stand before the Lord: "Well done, good and faithful servant" (Matt. 25:23). See also Dan. 7:9,10 comment.

this *way* into the South, and go up to the
mountains, 18and see what the land is like:
whether the people who dwell in it *are*
strong or weak, few or many; 19whether
the land they dwell in *is* good or bad;
whether the cities they inhabit *are* like
camps or strongholds; 20whether the land
is rich or poor; and whether there are forests there or not. Be of good courage. And
bring some of the fruit of the land." Now
the time *was* the season of the first ripe
grapes.

21So they went up and spied out the
land from the Wilderness of Zin as far as
Rehob, near the entrance of Hamath.
22And they went up through the South
and came to Hebron; Ahiman, Sheshai,
and Talmai, the descendants of Anak,
were there. (Now Hebron was built seven
years before Zoan in Egypt.) 23Then they
came to the Valley of Eshcol, and there
cut down a branch with one cluster of
grapes; they carried it between two of
them on a pole. *They* also *brought* some of
the pomegranates and figs. 24The place
was called the Valley of Eshcol,[a] because
of the cluster which the men of Israel cut
down there. 25And they returned from
spying out the land after forty days.

26Now they departed and came back
to Moses and Aaron and all the congregation of the children of Israel in the Wilderness of Paran, at Kadesh; they brought
back word to them and to all the congregation, and showed them the fruit of the
land. 27Then they told him, and said: "We
went to the land where you sent us. It
truly flows with milk and honey, and this
is its fruit. 28Nevertheless the people who
dwell in the land *are* strong; the cities *are*
fortified *and* very large; moreover we saw
the descendants of Anak there. 29The
Amalekites dwell in the land of the South;
the Hittites, the Jebusites, and the Amorites
dwell in the mountains; and the Canaanites dwell by the sea and along the banks
of the Jordan."

30Then Caleb quieted the people before
Moses, and said, "Let us go up at once
and take possession, for we are well able
to overcome it."

31But the men who had gone up with
him said, "We are not able to go up against
the people, for they *are* stronger than we."
32And they gave the children of Israel a
bad report of the land which they had
spied out, saying, "The land through which
we have gone as spies *is* a land that devours its inhabitants, and all the people
whom we saw in it *are* men of *great* stature.
33There we saw the giants[a] (the descendants of Anak came from the giants); and
we were like grasshoppers in our own
sight, and so we were in their sight."

Israel Refuses to Enter Canaan

14 So all the congregation lifted up
their voices and cried, and the people wept that night. 2And all the children
of Israel complained against Moses and
Aaron, and the whole congregation said
to them, "If only we had died in the land
of Egypt! Or if only we had died in this
wilderness! 3Why has the LORD brought
us to this land to fall by the sword, that
our wives and children should become

13:24 [a]Literally *Cluster* 13:33 [a]Hebrew *nephilim*

13:31–33 Giants in our sight. Sinners will often seem like formidable giants when we are planning to witness to them. The key is to realize that you are made strong in your weakness. Your fear will cause you to pray, and will then become your strength. So use fear to drive you to your knees. Another key is to remember the fate of the sinner if he dies in his sins. If God gives him justice he will end up in hell. Take courage, let love swallow your fears, and make your approach. Be like David—he ran toward Goliath (see 1 Sam. 17:48). You will learn that, with few exceptions, your fears will not be realized.

Matthew Henry said, "Difficulties that are in the way of salvation dwindle and vanish before a lively, active faith in the power and promise of God. All things are possible, if they are promised, to him that believes; but carnal sense and carnal professors are not to be trusted. Unbelief overlooks the promises and power of God, magnifies every danger and difficulty, and fills the heart with discouragement. May the Lord help us to believe! We shall then find all things possible."

victims? Would it not be better for us to
return to Egypt?" [4]So they said to one another, "Let us select a leader and return to
Egypt."
[5]Then Moses and Aaron fell on their
faces before all the assembly of the congregation of the children of Israel.
[6]But Joshua the son of Nun and Caleb
the son of Jephunneh, *who were* among
those who had spied out the land, tore
their clothes; [7]and they spoke to all the
congregation of the children of Israel,
saying: "The land we passed through to
spy out *is* an exceedingly good land. [8]If
the LORD delights in us, then He will
bring us into this land and give it to us, 'a
land which flows with milk and honey.'[a]
[9]Only do not rebel against the LORD, nor
fear the people of the land, for they *are*
our bread; their protection has departed
from them, and the LORD *is* with us. Do
not fear them."
[10]And all the congregation said to
stone them with stones. Now the glory of
the LORD appeared in the tabernacle of
meeting before all the children of Israel.

Moses Intercedes for the People

[11]Then the LORD said to Moses: "How
long will these people reject Me? And how
long will they not believe Me, with all the
signs which I have performed among
them? [12]I will strike them with the pestilence and disinherit them, and I will make
of you a nation greater and mightier than
they."
[13]And Moses said to the LORD: "Then
the Egyptians will hear *it,* for by Your
might You brought these people up from
among them, [14]and they will tell *it* to the
inhabitants of this land. They have heard
that You, LORD, *are* among these people;
that You, LORD, are seen face to face and
Your cloud stands above them, and You
go before them in a pillar of cloud by day
and in a pillar of fire by night. [15]Now *if*
You kill these people as one man, then
the nations which have heard of Your fame
will speak, saying, [16]'Because the LORD
was not able to bring this people to the
land which He swore to give them, therefore He killed them in the wilderness.'
[17]And now, I pray, let the power of my
Lord be great, just as You have spoken,
saying, [18]'The LORD is longsuffering and
abundant in mercy, forgiving iniquity and
transgression; but He by no means clears
the guilty, visiting the iniquity of the fathers on the children to the third and
fourth *generation.*'[a] [19]Pardon the iniquity
of this people, I pray, according to the
greatness of Your mercy, just as You have
forgiven this people, from Egypt even until now."
[20]Then the LORD said: "I have pardoned,
according to your word; [21]but truly, as I
live, all the earth shall be filled with the
glory of the LORD— [22]because all these
men who have seen My glory and the signs
which I did in Egypt and in the wilderness, and have put Me to the test now
these ten times, and have not heeded My
voice, [23]they certainly shall not see the
land of which I swore to their fathers, nor
shall any of those who rejected Me see it.
[24]But My servant Caleb, because he has a

14:8 [a]Exodus 3:8 14:18 [a]Exodus 34:6, 7

14:11 Christianity is not a blind faith. God gives us all the signs and evidences we need to not only know that He exists, but to know that we can trust Him with our lives. See Acts 1:3 comment.

"Biblical faith does not call people to crucify their intellect or take irrational leaps of faith into the darkness with the hope that Christ will catch us. Rather we are called to leap out of the darkness and into the light... True faith involves trusting in the evidence that God has amply provided in and through His Word."
R. C. Sproul

14:18 Here is a revelation of God's true character. He is amazingly patient and incredibly merciful and forgiving, but a sinner who refuses to repent will be given justice. God will by no means clear the guilty. (See Nah. 1:3; Job 10:14.) The great truth of our justification in Christ is that our very guilt is removed. We are not simply forgiven guilty sinners, but we have been given the righteousness of Christ. The grace of God justifies us so that it is as though we never sinned in the first place.

different spirit in him and has followed
Me fully, I will bring into the land where
he went, and his descendants shall inherit it. [25]Now the Amalekites and the
Canaanites dwell in the valley; tomorrow
turn and move out into the wilderness by
the Way of the Red Sea."

Death Sentence on the Rebels

[26]And the LORD spoke to Moses and
Aaron, saying, [27]"How long *shall I bear
with* this evil congregation who complain
against Me? I have heard the complaints
which the children of Israel make against
Me. [28]Say to them, 'As I live,' says the
LORD, 'just as you have spoken in My hearing, so I will do to you: [29]The carcasses of
you who have complained against Me
shall fall in this wilderness, all of you
who were numbered, according to your
entire number, from twenty years old and
above. [30]Except for Caleb the son of Jephunneh and Joshua the son of Nun, you
shall by no means enter the land which I
swore I would make you dwell in. [31]But
your little ones, whom you said would be
victims, I will bring in, and they shall
know the land which you have despised.
[32]But *as for* you, your carcasses shall fall
in this wilderness. [33]And your sons shall
be shepherds in the wilderness forty years,
and bear the brunt of your infidelity, until your carcasses are consumed in the
wilderness. [34]According to the number of
the days in which you spied out the land,
forty days, for each day you shall bear
your guilt one year, *namely* forty years,
and you shall know My rejection. [35]I the
LORD have spoken this. I will surely do so
to all this evil congregation who are gathered together against Me. In this wilderness they shall be consumed, and there
they shall die.' "

[36]Now the men whom Moses sent to
spy out the land, who returned and made
all the congregation complain against
him by bringing a bad report of the land,
[37]those very men who brought the evil
report about the land, died by the plague
before the LORD. [38]But Joshua the son of
Nun and Caleb the son of Jephunneh remained alive, of the men who went to spy
out the land.

A Futile Invasion Attempt

[39]Then Moses told these words to all
the children of Israel, and the people
mourned greatly. [40]And they rose early in
the morning and went up to the top of
the mountain, saying, "Here we are, and
we will go up to the place which the LORD
has promised, for we have sinned!"

> God will not compromise His moral Law. He is the same yesterday, today, and forever. God will judge humanity with His law, written in stone and written upon every man's heart.
>
> **JAY FOWLER**

[41]And Moses said, "Now why do you
transgress the command of the LORD? For
this will not succeed. [42]Do not go up, lest
you be defeated by your enemies, for the
LORD *is* not among you. [43]For the Amalekites and the Canaanites *are* there before
you, and you shall fall by the sword; because you have turned away from the
LORD, the LORD will not be with you."

[44]But they presumed to go up to the
mountaintop. Nevertheless, neither the
ark of the covenant of the LORD nor Moses
departed from the camp. [45]Then the Amalekites and the Canaanites who dwelt in that
mountain came down and attacked them,
and drove them back as far as Hormah.

Laws of Grain and Drink Offerings

15 And the LORD spoke to Moses,
saying, [2]"Speak to the children of
Israel, and say to them: 'When you have
come into the land you are to inhabit,
which I am giving to you, [3]and you make
an offering by fire to the LORD, a burnt offering or a sacrifice, to fulfill a vow or as
a freewill offering or in your appointed
feasts, to make a sweet aroma to the
LORD, from the herd or the flock, [4]then he
who presents his offering to the LORD

shall bring a grain offering of one-tenth *of an ephah* of fine flour mixed with one-fourth of a hin of oil; [5]and one-fourth of a hin of wine as a drink offering you shall prepare with the burnt offering or the sacrifice, for each lamb. [6]Or for a ram you shall prepare as a grain offering two-tenths *of an ephah* of fine flour mixed with one-third of a hin of oil; [7]and as a drink offering you shall offer one-third of a hin of wine as a sweet aroma to the LORD. [8]And when you prepare a young bull as a burnt offering, or as a sacrifice to fulfill a vow, or as a peace offering to the LORD, [9]then shall be offered with the young bull a grain offering of three-tenths *of an ephah* of fine flour mixed with half a hin of oil; [10]and you shall bring as the drink offering half a hin of wine as an offering made by fire, a sweet aroma to the LORD.

[11]'Thus it shall be done for each young bull, for each ram, or for each lamb or young goat. [12]According to the number that you prepare, so you shall do with everyone according to their number. [13]All who are native-born shall do these things in this manner, in presenting an offering made by fire, a sweet aroma to the LORD. [14]And if a stranger dwells with you, or whoever *is* among you throughout your generations, and would present an offering made by fire, a sweet aroma to the LORD, just as you do, so shall he do. [15]One ordinance *shall be* for you of the assembly and for the stranger who dwells *with you*, an ordinance forever throughout your generations; as you are, so shall the stranger be before the LORD. [16]One law and one custom shall be for you and for the stranger who dwells with you.' "[a]

[17]Again the LORD spoke to Moses, saying, [18]"Speak to the children of Israel, and say to them: 'When you come into the land to which I bring you, [19]then it will be, when you eat of the bread of the land, that you shall offer up a heave offering to the LORD. [20]You shall offer up a cake of the first of your ground meal *as* a heave offering; as a heave offering of the threshing floor, so shall you offer it up. [21]Of the first of your ground meal you shall give to the LORD a heave offering throughout your generations.

Laws Concerning Unintentional Sin

[22]'If you sin unintentionally, and do not observe all these commandments which the LORD has spoken to Moses— [23]all that the LORD has commanded you by the hand of Moses, from the day the LORD gave commandment and onward throughout your generations— [24]then it will be, if it is unintentionally committed, without the knowledge of the congregation, that the whole congregation shall offer one young bull as a burnt offering, as a sweet aroma to the LORD, with its grain offering and its drink offering, according to the ordinance, and one kid of the goats as a sin offering. [25]So the priest shall make atonement for the whole congregation of the children of Israel, and it shall be forgiven them, for it was unintentional; they shall bring their offering, an offering made by fire to the LORD, and their sin offering before the LORD, for their

15:16 [a]Compare Exodus 12:49

15:22 Regarding sin that is committed unintentionally, see Lev. 4:27,28 comment.

15:24–28 Bible contradiction? To skeptics, these verses seem to say that sacrifices can, in at least some cases, take away sin, which contradicts Heb. 10:11: "sacrifices . . . can never take away sins." Scripture states that the Old Testament sacrifices could never make the person offering them "perfect" (see Heb. 7:19). Each time Israel sinned, they would have to make further atonement (see Heb. 9:9). However, when God provided His own sacrificial Lamb (Jesus of Nazareth), Jesus' death on the cross accomplished what the sacrificial system could not do. It made the believer perfect in the sight of God. (See Heb. 10:9–14.)

The Numbers passage does not say that sacrifices can "take away sin," just that God offered temporary forgiveness through the sacrificial system. Humanity's sin debt wasn't "paid in full" until Jesus shed His blood in payment. It's like the difference between accepting a check as payment, and actually cashing the check and receiving the funds. There is no contradiction in these passages.

THE FUNCTION OF THE LAW

15:31 "The Law is the Word in which God teaches and tells us what we are to do and not to do, as in the Ten Commandments. Now wherever human nature is alone, without the grace of God, the Law cannot be kept, because since Adam's fall in paradise man is corrupt and has nothing but a wicked desire to sin and in his heart cannot be favorably disposed toward the Law, as we know by our own experience. For there is no one who would not rather have no Law at all, and everyone finds and feels within himself that while it is difficult to be pious and do good, it is easy to be wicked and to do evil. And this difficulty or this unwillingness to do what is good prevents us from keeping God's Law; for what is kept with dislike, difficulty, and unwillingness, rates before God as not having been kept at all. And so the Law of God convinces us by our experience that we are naturally wicked, disobedient, lovers of sin, and enemies of God's commandments." *Martin Luther*

unintended sin. [26]It shall be forgiven the
whole congregation of the children of Israel and the stranger who dwells among
them, because all the people *did it* unintentionally.

[27]'And if a person sins unintentionally,
then he shall bring a female goat in its
first year as a sin offering. [28]So the priest
shall make atonement for the person who
sins unintentionally, when he sins unintentionally before the LORD, to make atonement for him; and it shall be forgiven him.
[29]You shall have one law for him who sins
unintentionally, *for* him who is native-born among the children of Israel and for
the stranger who dwells among them.

Law Concerning Presumptuous Sin

[30]'But the person who does *anything*
presumptuously, *whether he is* native-born
or a stranger, that one brings reproach on
the LORD, and he shall be cut off from
among his people. [31]Because he has despised the word of the LORD, and has broken His commandment, that person shall
be completely cut off; his guilt *shall be*
upon him.' "

Penalty for Violating the Sabbath

[32]Now while the children of Israel
were in the wilderness, they found a man
gathering sticks on the Sabbath day. [33]And
those who found him gathering sticks
brought him to Moses and Aaron, and to
all the congregation. [34]They put him under guard, because it had not been explained what should be done to him.

[35]Then the LORD said to Moses, "The
man must surely be put to death; all the
congregation shall stone him with stones
outside the camp." [36]So, as the LORD commanded Moses, all the congregation
brought him outside the camp and stoned
him with stones, and he died.

Tassels on Garments

[37]Again the LORD spoke to Moses, saying, [38]"Speak to the children of Israel: Tell
them to make tassels on the corners of
their garments throughout their generations, and to put a blue thread in the tassels of the corners. [39]And you shall have
the tassel, that you may look upon it and
remember all the commandments of the
LORD and do them, and that you *may* not
follow the harlotry to which your own
heart and your own eyes are inclined,
[40]and that you may remember and do all
My commandments, and be holy for your
God. [41]I *am* the LORD your God, who
brought you out of the land of Egypt, to
be your God: I *am* the LORD your God."

Rebellion Against Moses and Aaron

16 Now Korah the son of Izhar, the
son of Kohath, the son of Levi, with
Dathan and Abiram the sons of Eliab, and
On the son of Peleth, sons of Reuben,

15:32–36 These verses show how God's Law is without mercy. Those who object to the harshness of this Law should realize that it is this same Law that will judge them on Judgment Day. Such thoughts should make us flee evil and cleave to the Savior.

took *men;* 2and they rose up before Moses
with some of the children of Israel, two
hundred and fifty leaders of the congregation, representatives of the congregation, men of renown. 3They gathered together against Moses and Aaron, and said
to them, "*You take* too much upon yourselves, for all the congregation *is* holy,
every one of them, and the LORD *is* among
them. Why then do you exalt yourselves
above the assembly of the LORD?"
4So when Moses heard *it,* he fell on his
face; 5and he spoke to Korah and all his
company, saying, "Tomorrow morning the
LORD will show who *is* His and *who is*
holy, and will cause *him* to come near to
Him. That one whom He chooses He will
cause to come near to Him. 6Do this:
Take censers, Korah and all your company; 7put fire in them and put incense in
them before the LORD tomorrow, and it
shall be *that* the man whom the LORD
chooses *is* the holy one. *You take* too
much upon yourselves, you sons of Levi!"
8Then Moses said to Korah, "Hear
now, you sons of Levi: 9*Is it* a small thing
to you that the God of Israel has separated you from the congregation of Israel,
to bring you near to Himself, to do the
work of the tabernacle of the LORD, and
to stand before the congregation to serve
them; 10and that He has brought you near
to Himself, you and all your brethren, the
sons of Levi, with you? And are you seeking the priesthood also? 11Therefore you
and all your company *are* gathered together against the LORD. And what *is* Aaron
that you complain against him?"
12And Moses sent to call Dathan and
Abiram the sons of Eliab, but they said,
"We will not come up! 13*Is it* a small thing
that you have brought us up out of a land
flowing with milk and honey, to kill us in
the wilderness, that you should keep acting like a prince over us? 14Moreover you
have not brought us into a land flowing
with milk and honey, nor given us inheritance of fields and vineyards. Will you
put out the eyes of these men? We will
not come up!"
15Then Moses was very angry, and said
to the LORD, "Do not respect their offering.
I have not taken one donkey from them,
nor have I hurt one of them."
16And Moses said to Korah, "Tomorrow,
you and all your company be present before the LORD—you and they, as well as
Aaron. 17Let each take his censer and put
incense in it, and each of you bring his
censer before the LORD, two hundred and
fifty censers; both you and Aaron, each
with his censer." 18So every man took his
censer, put fire in it, laid incense on it,
and stood at the door of the tabernacle of
meeting with Moses and Aaron. 19And
Korah gathered all the congregation against
them at the door of the tabernacle of
meeting. Then the glory of the LORD appeared to all the congregation.
20And the LORD spoke to Moses and
Aaron, saying, 21"Separate yourselves from
among this congregation, that I may consume them in a moment."

> There are only two kinds of people in the end: those who say to God, 'Thy will be done,' and those to whom God says, in the end, 'Thy will be done.' All that are in hell, choose it. Without that self-choice there could be no hell.
>
> **C. S. LEWIS**

22Then they fell on their faces, and said,
"O God, the God of the spirits of all flesh,
shall one man sin, and You be angry with
all the congregation?"
23So the LORD spoke to Moses, saying,
24"Speak to the congregation, saying, 'Get
away from the tents of Korah, Dathan,
and Abiram.' "
25Then Moses rose and went to Dathan
and Abiram, and the elders of Israel followed him. 26And he spoke to the congregation, saying, "Depart now from the
tents of these wicked men! Touch nothing of theirs, lest you be consumed in all
their sins." 27So they got away from around
the tents of Korah, Dathan, and Abiram;
and Dathan and Abiram came out and

stood at the door of their tents, with their wives, their sons, and their little children.

28 And Moses said: "By this you shall know that the LORD has sent me to do all these works, for *I have* not *done them* of my own will. 29 If these men die naturally like all men, or if they are visited by the common fate of all men, *then* the LORD has not sent me. 30 But if the LORD creates a new thing, and the earth opens its mouth and swallows them up with all that belongs to them, and they go down alive into the pit, then you will understand that these men have rejected the LORD."

31 Now it came to pass, as he finished speaking all these words, that the ground split apart under them, 32 and the earth opened its mouth and swallowed them up, with their households and all the men with Korah, with all *their* goods. 33 So they and all those with them went down alive into the pit; the earth closed over them, and they perished from among the assembly. 34 Then all Israel who *were* around them fled at their cry, for they said, "Lest the earth swallow us up *also!*"

35 And a fire came out from the LORD and consumed the two hundred and fifty men who were offering incense.

36 Then the LORD spoke to Moses, saying: 37 "Tell Eleazar, the son of Aaron the priest, to pick up the censers out of the blaze, for they are holy, and scatter the fire some distance away. 38 The censers of these men who sinned against their own souls, let them be made into hammered plates as a covering for the altar. Because they presented them before the LORD, therefore they are holy; and they shall be a sign to the children of Israel." 39 So Eleazar the priest took the bronze censers, which those who were burned up had presented, and they were hammered out as a covering on the altar, 40 *to be* a memorial to the children of Israel that no outsider, who *is* not a descendant of Aaron, should come near to offer incense before the LORD, that he might not become like Korah and his companions, just as the LORD had said to him through Moses.

Complaints of the People

41 On the next day all the congregation of the children of Israel complained against Moses and Aaron, saying, "You have killed the people of the LORD." 42 Now it happened, when the congregation had gathered against Moses and Aaron, that they turned toward the tabernacle of meeting; and suddenly the cloud covered it, and the glory of the LORD appeared. 43 Then Moses and Aaron came before the tabernacle of meeting.

44 And the LORD spoke to Moses, saying, 45 "Get away from among this congregation, that I may consume them in a moment."

And they fell on their faces.

46 So Moses said to Aaron, "Take a censer and put fire in it from the altar, put incense *on it,* and take it quickly to the congregation and make atonement for them; for wrath has gone out from the LORD. The plague has begun." 47 Then Aaron took *it* as Moses commanded, and ran into the midst of the assembly; and already the plague had begun among the people. So he put in the incense and made atonement for the people. 48 And he stood between the dead and the living; so the plague was stopped. 49 Now those who died in the plague were fourteen thousand seven hundred, besides those who died in the Korah incident. 50 So Aaron returned to Moses at the door of the tabernacle of meeting, for the plague had stopped.

16:46 "Wrath, the Bible tells us, is an attribute of God. The modern habit throughout the Christian church is to play this subject down. Those who still believe in the wrath of God (not all do) say little about it; perhaps they do not think much about it. To an age which has unashamedly sold itself to the gods of greed, pride, sex, and self-will, the church mumbles on about God's kindness, but says virtually nothing about His judgment . . . The fact is that the subject of divine wrath has become taboo in modern society, and Christians by and large have accepted the taboo and conditioned themselves never to raise the subject." *J. I. Packer*

The Budding of Aaron's Rod

17 And the LORD spoke to Moses,
saying: 2"Speak to the children of
Israel, and get from them a rod from each
father's house, all their leaders according
to their fathers' houses—twelve rods.
Write each man's name on his rod. 3And
you shall write Aaron's name on the rod
of Levi. For there shall be one rod for the
head of *each* father's house. 4Then you
shall place them in the tabernacle of
meeting before the Testimony, where I
meet with you. 5And it shall be *that* the
rod of the man whom I choose will blossom; thus I will rid Myself of the complaints of the children of Israel, which
they make against you."

6So Moses spoke to the children of Israel, and each of their leaders gave him a
rod apiece, for each leader according to
their fathers' houses, twelve rods; and the
rod of Aaron *was* among their rods. 7And
Moses placed the rods before the LORD in
the tabernacle of witness.

8Now it came to pass on the next day
that Moses went into the tabernacle of
witness, and behold, the rod of Aaron, of
the house of Levi, had sprouted and put
forth buds, had produced blossoms and
yielded ripe almonds. 9Then Moses
brought out all the rods from before the
LORD to all the children of Israel; and
they looked, and each man took his rod.

10And the LORD said to Moses, "Bring
Aaron's rod back before the Testimony, to
be kept as a sign against the rebels, that
you may put their complaints away from
Me, lest they die." 11Thus did Moses; just
as the LORD had commanded him, so he
did.

12So the children of Israel spoke to
Moses, saying, "Surely we die, we perish,
we all perish! 13Whoever even comes near
the tabernacle of the LORD must die. Shall
we all utterly die?"

Duties of Priests and Levites

18 Then the LORD said to Aaron: "You
and your sons and your father's
house with you shall bear the iniquity *related to* the sanctuary, and you and your
sons with you shall bear the iniquity *associated with* your priesthood. 2Also bring
with you your brethren of the tribe of
Levi, the tribe of your father, that they
may be joined with you and serve you
while you and your sons *are* with you before the tabernacle of witness. 3They shall
attend to your needs and all the needs of
the tabernacle; but they shall not come
near the articles of the sanctuary and the
altar, lest they die—they and you also.
4They shall be joined with you and attend to the needs of the tabernacle of
meeting, for all the work of the tabernacle; but an outsider shall not come near
you. 5And you shall attend to the duties
of the sanctuary and the duties of the altar, that there *may* be no more wrath on
the children of Israel. 6Behold, I Myself
have taken your brethren the Levites
from among the children of Israel; *they
are* a gift to you, given by the LORD, to do
the work of the tabernacle of meeting.
7Therefore you and your sons with you
shall attend to your priesthood for everything at the altar and behind the veil; and
you shall serve. I give your priesthood *to
you* as a gift for service, but the outsider
who comes near shall be put to death."

Offerings for Support of the Priests

8And the LORD spoke to Aaron: "Here,
I Myself have also given you charge of My
heave offerings, all the holy gifts of the
children of Israel; I have given them as a
portion to you and your sons, as an ordinance forever. 9This shall be yours of the
most holy things *reserved* from the fire:
every offering of theirs, every grain offering and every sin offering and every trespass offering which they render to Me,
shall be most holy for you and your sons.
10In a most holy *place* you shall eat it;
every male shall eat it. It shall be holy to
you.

11"This also *is* yours: the heave offering
of their gift, with all the wave offerings of
the children of Israel; I have given them
to you, and your sons and daughters with

you, as an ordinance forever. Everyone who is clean in your house may eat it.

[12]"All the best of the oil, all the best of the new wine and the grain, their firstfruits which they offer to the LORD, I have given them to you. [13]Whatever first ripe fruit is in their land, which they bring to the LORD, shall be yours. Everyone who is clean in your house may eat it.

[14]"Every devoted thing in Israel shall be yours.

[15]"Everything that first opens the womb of all flesh, which they bring to the LORD, whether man or beast, shall be yours; nevertheless the firstborn of man you shall surely redeem, and the firstborn of unclean animals you shall redeem. [16]And those redeemed of the devoted things you shall redeem when one month old, according to your valuation, for five shekels of silver, according to the shekel of the sanctuary, which *is* twenty gerahs. [17]But the firstborn of a cow, the firstborn of a sheep, or the firstborn of a goat you shall not redeem; they *are* holy. You shall sprinkle their blood on the altar, and burn their fat *as* an offering made by fire for a sweet aroma to the LORD. [18]And their flesh shall be yours, just as the wave breast and the right thigh are yours.

[19]"All the heave offerings of the holy things, which the children of Israel offer to the LORD, I have given to you and your sons and daughters with you as an ordinance forever; it *is* a covenant of salt forever before the LORD with you and your descendants with you."

[20]Then the LORD said to Aaron: "You shall have no inheritance in their land, nor shall you have any portion among them; I *am* your portion and your inheritance among the children of Israel.

Tithes for Support of the Levites

[21]"Behold, I have given the children of Levi all the tithes in Israel as an inheritance in return for the work which they perform, the work of the tabernacle of meeting. [22]Hereafter the children of Israel shall not come near the tabernacle of meeting, lest they bear sin and die. [23]But the Levites shall perform the work of the tabernacle of meeting, and they shall bear their iniquity; *it shall be* a statute forever, throughout your generations, that among the children of Israel they shall have no inheritance. [24]For the tithes of the children of Israel, which they offer up *as* a heave offering to the LORD, I have given to the Levites as an inheritance; therefore I have said to them, 'Among the children of Israel they shall have no inheritance.' "

The Tithe of the Levites

[25]Then the LORD spoke to Moses, saying, [26]"Speak thus to the Levites, and say to them: 'When you take from the children of Israel the tithes which I have given you from them as your inheritance, then you shall offer up a heave offering of it to the LORD, a tenth of the tithe. [27]And your heave offering shall be reckoned to you as though *it were* the grain of the threshing floor and as the fullness of the winepress. [28]Thus you shall also offer a heave offering to the LORD from all your tithes which you receive from the children of Israel, and you shall give the LORD's heave offering from it to Aaron the priest. [29]Of all your gifts you shall offer up every heave offering due to the LORD, from all the best of them, the consecrated part of them.' [30]Therefore you shall say to them: 'When you have lifted up the best of it, then *the rest* shall be accounted to the Levites as the produce of the threshing floor and as the produce of the winepress. [31]You may eat it in any place, you and your households, for it *is* your reward for your work in the tabernacle of meeting. [32]And you shall bear no sin because of it, when you have lifted up the best of it. But you shall not profane the holy gifts of the children of Israel, lest you die.' "

Laws of Purification

19 Now the LORD spoke to Moses and Aaron, saying, [2]"This *is* the ordinance of the law which the LORD has commanded, saying: 'Speak to the chil-

dren of Israel, that they bring you a red heifer without blemish, in which there *is* no defect *and* on which a yoke has never come. 3You shall give it to Eleazar the priest, that he may take it outside the camp, and it shall be slaughtered before him; 4and Eleazar the priest shall take some of its blood with his finger, and sprinkle some of its blood seven times directly in front of the tabernacle of meeting. 5Then the heifer shall be burned in his sight: its hide, its flesh, its blood, and its offal shall be burned. 6And the priest shall take cedar wood and hyssop and scarlet, and cast *them* into the midst of the fire burning the heifer. 7Then the priest shall wash his clothes, he shall bathe in water, and afterward he shall come into the camp; the priest shall be unclean until evening. 8And the one who burns it shall wash his clothes in water, bathe in water, and shall be unclean until evening. 9Then a man *who is* clean shall gather up the ashes of the heifer, and store *them* outside the camp in a clean place; and they shall be kept for the congregation of the children of Israel for the water of purification;[a] it *is* for purifying from sin. 10And the one who gathers the ashes of the heifer shall wash his clothes, and be unclean until evening. It shall be a statute forever to the children of Israel and to the stranger who dwells among them.

11‘He who touches the dead body of anyone shall be unclean seven days. 12He shall purify himself with the water on the third day and on the seventh day; *then* he will be clean. But if he does not purify himself on the third day and on the seventh day, he will not be clean. 13Whoever touches the body of anyone who has died, and does not purify himself, defiles the tabernacle of the LORD. That person shall be cut off from Israel. He shall be unclean, because the water of purification was not sprinkled on him; his uncleanness *is* still on him.

14‘This *is* the law when a man dies in a tent: All who come into the tent and all who *are* in the tent shall be unclean seven days; 15and every open vessel, which has no cover fastened on it, *is* unclean. 16Whoever in the open field touches one who is slain by a sword or who has died, or a bone of a man, or a grave, shall be unclean seven days.

17‘And for an unclean *person* they shall take some of the ashes of the heifer burnt for purification from sin, and running water shall be put on them in a vessel. 18A clean person shall take hyssop and dip *it* in the water, sprinkle *it* on the tent, on all the vessels, on the persons who were there, or on the one who touched a bone, the slain, the dead, or a grave. 19The clean *person* shall sprinkle the unclean on the third day and on the seventh day; and on the seventh day he shall purify himself, wash his clothes, and bathe in water; and at evening he shall be clean.

20‘But the man who is unclean and does not purify himself, that person shall be cut off from among the assembly, because he has defiled the sanctuary of the LORD. The water of purification has not been sprinkled on him; he *is* unclean. 21It shall be a perpetual statute for them. He who sprinkles the water of purification shall wash his clothes; and he who touches the water of purification shall be unclean until evening. 22Whatever the unclean *person* touches shall be unclean; and the person who touches *it* shall be unclean until evening.’ ”

19:9 [a]Literally *impurity*

19:1–10 "The heifer was to be wholly burned. This typified the painful sufferings of our Lord Jesus, both in soul and body, as a sacrifice made by fire, to satisfy God's justice for man's sin. These ashes are said to be laid up as a purification for sin, because, though they were only to purify from ceremonial uncleanness, yet they were a type of that purification for sin which our Lord Jesus made by his death. The blood of Christ is laid up for us in the word and sacraments, as a fountain of merit, to which by faith we may have constant recourse, for cleansing our consciences." *Matthew Henry*

Moses' Error at Kadesh

20 Then the children of Israel, the whole congregation, came into the Wilderness of Zin in the first month, and the people stayed in Kadesh; and Miriam died there and was buried there.

2Now there was no water for the congregation; so they gathered together against Moses and Aaron. 3And the people contended with Moses and spoke, saying: "If only we had died when our brethren died before the LORD! 4Why have you brought up the assembly of the LORD into this wilderness, that we and our animals should die here? 5And why have you made us come up out of Egypt, to bring us to this evil place? It *is* not a place of grain or figs or vines or pomegranates; nor *is* there any water to drink." 6So Moses and Aaron went from the presence of the assembly to the door of the tabernacle of meeting, and they fell on their faces. And the glory of the LORD appeared to them.

7Then the LORD spoke to Moses, saying, 8"Take the rod; you and your brother Aaron gather the congregation together. Speak to the rock before their eyes, and it will yield its water; thus you shall bring water for them out of the rock, and give drink to the congregation and their animals." 9So Moses took the rod from before the LORD as He commanded him.

10And Moses and Aaron gathered the assembly together before the rock; and he said to them, "Hear now, you rebels! Must we bring water for you out of this rock?" 11Then Moses lifted his hand and struck the rock twice with his rod; and water came out abundantly, and the congregation and their animals drank.

12Then the LORD spoke to Moses and Aaron, "Because you did not believe Me, to hallow Me in the eyes of the children of Israel, therefore you shall not bring this assembly into the land which I have given them."

13This *was* the water of Meribah,[a] because the children of Israel contended with the LORD, and He was hallowed among them.

Passage Through Edom Refused

14Now Moses sent messengers from Kadesh to the king of Edom. "Thus says your brother Israel: 'You know all the hardship that has befallen us, 15how our fathers went down to Egypt, and we dwelt in Egypt a long time, and the Egyptians afflicted us and our fathers. 16When we cried out to the LORD, He heard our voice and sent the Angel and brought us up out of Egypt; now here we are in Kadesh, a city on the edge of your border. 17Please let us pass through your country. We will not pass through fields or vineyards, nor will we drink water from wells; we will go along the King's Highway; we will not turn aside to the right hand or to the left until we have passed through your territory.' "

18Then Edom said to him, "You shall not pass through my *land,* lest I come out against you with the sword."

19So the children of Israel said to him, "We will go by the Highway, and if I or my livestock drink any of your water, then I will pay for it; let me only pass through on foot, nothing *more.*"

20Then he said, "You shall not pass through." So Edom came out against them with many men and with a strong hand. 21Thus Edom refused to give Israel passage through his territory; so Israel turned away from him.

Death of Aaron

22Now the children of Israel, the whole congregation, journeyed from Kadesh and came to Mount Hor. 23And the LORD spoke to Moses and Aaron in Mount Hor

20:13 [a]Literally *Contention*

20:7–12 It is vital that we learn this lesson from the Scriptures, which were written for our instruction. God requires that we follow His instructions precisely. This is particularly true when it comes to evangelism.

by the border of the land of Edom, saying: [24]"Aaron shall be gathered to his people, for he shall not enter the land which I have given to the children of Israel, because you rebelled against My word at the water of Meribah. [25]Take Aaron and Eleazar his son, and bring them up to Mount Hor; [26]and strip Aaron of his garments and put them on Eleazar his son; for Aaron shall be gathered *to his people* and die there." [27]So Moses did just as the LORD commanded, and they went up to Mount Hor in the sight of all the congregation. [28]Moses stripped Aaron of his garments and put them on Eleazar his son; and Aaron died there on the top of the mountain. Then Moses and Eleazar came down from the mountain. [29]Now when all the congregation saw that Aaron was dead, all the house of Israel mourned for Aaron thirty days.

Canaanites Defeated at Hormah

21 The king of Arad, the Canaanite, who dwelt in the South, heard that Israel was coming on the road to Atharim. Then he fought against Israel and took *some* of them prisoners. [2]So Israel made a vow to the LORD, and said, "If You will indeed deliver this people into my hand, then I will utterly destroy their cities." [3]And the LORD listened to the voice of Israel and delivered up the Canaanites, and they utterly destroyed them and their cities. So the name of that place was called Hormah.[a]

The Bronze Serpent

[4]Then they journeyed from Mount Hor by the Way of the Red Sea, to go around the land of Edom; and the soul of the people became very discouraged on the way. [5]And the people spoke against God and against Moses: "Why have you brought us up out of Egypt to die in the wilderness? For *there is* no food and no water, and our soul loathes this worthless bread." [6]So the LORD sent fiery serpents among the people, and they bit the people; and many of the people of Israel died.

[7]Therefore the people came to Moses, and said, "We have sinned, for we have spoken against the LORD and against you; pray to the LORD that He take away the serpents from us." So Moses prayed for the people.

[8]Then the LORD said to Moses, "Make a fiery *serpent,* and set it on a pole; and it shall be that everyone who is bitten, when he looks at it, shall live." [9]So Moses made a bronze serpent, and put it on a pole; and so it was, if a serpent had bitten anyone, when he looked at the bronze serpent, he lived.

From Mount Hor to Moab

[10]Now the children of Israel moved on and camped in Oboth. [11]And they journeyed from Oboth and camped at Ije Abarim, in the wilderness which *is* east of Moab, toward the sunrise. [12]From there they moved and camped in the Valley of Zered. [13]From there they moved and camped on the other side of the Arnon, which *is* in the wilderness that extends from the border of the Amorites; for the Arnon *is* the border of Moab, between Moab and the Amorites. [14]Therefore it is

21:3 [a]Literally *Utter Destruction*

21:6–9 Fiery serpents. When fiery serpents were sent among Israel, their deadly bite caused the Israelites to admit that they had sinned. However, God also sent a cure for the serpent bite; He told Moses to make a bronze serpent and place it on a pole. Those who had been bitten and were doomed to die could look at the bronze serpent and be saved from death. Jesus later cited this passage in reference to salvation from sin (see John 3:14,15).

The Ten Commandments are like ten biting serpents that carry with them the venomous curse of God's Law. This Law convicts us of our sin and drives us to look to the One lifted up on a cross, the Messiah, who saves us from the fatal sting of the Law (see 1 Cor. 15:56). It was the Law of Moses that put Jesus on the cross. The Messiah became a curse for us, and redeemed us from the curse of the Law (see Gal. 3:13).

said in the Book of the Wars of the LORD:

> "Waheb in Suphah,[a]
> The brooks of the Arnon,
> 15And the slope of the brooks
> That reaches to the dwelling of Ar,
> And lies on the border of Moab."

16From there *they went* to Beer, which *is* the well where the LORD said to Moses, "Gather the people together, and I will give them water." 17Then Israel sang this song:

> "Spring up, O well!
> All of you sing to it—
> 18The well the leaders sank,
> Dug by the nation's nobles,
> By the lawgiver, with their staves."

And from the wilderness *they went* to Mattanah, 19from Mattanah to Nahaliel, from Nahaliel to Bamoth, 20and from Bamoth, *in* the valley that *is* in the country of Moab, to the top of Pisgah which looks down on the wasteland.[a]

King Sihon Defeated

21Then Israel sent messengers to Sihon king of the Amorites, saying, 22"Let me pass through your land. We will not turn aside into fields or vineyards; we will not drink water from wells. We will go by the King's Highway until we have passed through your territory." 23But Sihon would not allow Israel to pass through his territory. So Sihon gathered all his people together and went out against Israel in the wilderness, and he came to Jahaz and fought against Israel. 24Then Israel defeated him with the edge of the sword, and took possession of his land from the Arnon to the Jabbok, as far as the people of Ammon; for the border of the people of Ammon *was* fortified. 25So Israel took all these cities, and Israel dwelt in all the cities of the Amorites, in Heshbon and in all its villages. 26For Heshbon *was* the city of Sihon king of the Amorites, who had fought against the former king of Moab, and had taken all his land from his hand as far as the Arnon. 27Therefore those who speak in proverbs say:

> "Come to Heshbon, let it be built;
> Let the city of Sihon be repaired.
>
> 28"For fire went out from Heshbon,
> A flame from the city of Sihon;
> It consumed Ar of Moab,
> The lords of the heights of the Arnon.
> 29Woe to you, Moab!
> You have perished, O people of
> Chemosh!
> He has given his sons as fugitives,
> And his daughters into captivity,
> To Sihon king of the Amorites.
>
> 30"But we have shot at them;
> Heshbon has perished as far as Dibon.
> Then we laid waste as far as Nophah,
> Which *reaches* to Medeba."

31Thus Israel dwelt in the land of the Amorites. 32Then Moses sent to spy out Jazer; and they took its villages and drove out the Amorites who *were* there.

King Og Defeated

33And they turned and went up by the way to Bashan. So Og king of Bashan went out against them, he and all his people, to battle at Edrei. 34Then the LORD said to Moses, "Do not fear him, for I have delivered him into your hand, with all his people and his land; and you shall do to him as you did to Sihon king of the Amorites, who dwelt at Heshbon." 35So they defeated him, his sons, and all his people, until there was no survivor left him; and they took possession of his land.

Balak Sends for Balaam

22 Then the children of Israel moved, and camped in the plains of Moab on the side of the Jordan *across from* Jericho.

2Now Balak the son of Zippor saw all that Israel had done to the Amorites.

21:14 [a]Ancient unknown places; Vulgate reads *What He did in the Red Sea.* **21:20** [a]Hebrew *Jeshimon*

3And Moab was exceedingly afraid of the people because they *were* many, and Moab was sick with dread because of the children of Israel. 4So Moab said to the elders of Midian, "Now this company will lick up everything around us, as an ox licks up the grass of the field." And Balak the son of Zippor *was* king of the Moabites at that time. 5Then he sent messengers to Balaam the son of Beor at Pethor, which *is* near the River[a] in the land of the sons of his people,[b] to call him, saying: "Look, a people has come from Egypt. See, they cover the face of the earth, and are settling next to me! 6Therefore please come at once, curse this people for me, for they *are* too mighty for me. Perhaps I shall be able to defeat them and drive them out of the land, for I know that he whom you bless *is* blessed, and he whom you curse is cursed."

7So the elders of Moab and the elders of Midian departed with the diviner's fee in their hand, and they came to Balaam and spoke to him the words of Balak. 8And he said to them, "Lodge here tonight, and I will bring back word to you, as the LORD speaks to me." So the princes of Moab stayed with Balaam.

9Then God came to Balaam and said, "Who *are* these men with you?"

10So Balaam said to God, "Balak the son of Zippor, king of Moab, has sent to me, *saying,* 11'Look, a people has come out of Egypt, and they cover the face of the earth. Come now, curse them for me; perhaps I shall be able to overpower them and drive them out.' "

12And God said to Balaam, "You shall not go with them; you shall not curse the people, for they *are* blessed."

13So Balaam rose in the morning and said to the princes of Balak, "Go back to your land, for the LORD has refused to give me permission to go with you."

14And the princes of Moab rose and went to Balak, and said, "Balaam refuses to come with us."

15Then Balak again sent princes, more numerous and more honorable than they. 16And they came to Balaam and said to him, "Thus says Balak the son of Zippor: 'Please let nothing hinder you from coming to me; 17for I will certainly honor you greatly, and I will do whatever you say to me. Therefore please come, curse this people for me.' "

18Then Balaam answered and said to the servants of Balak, "Though Balak were to give me his house full of silver and gold, I could not go beyond the word of the LORD my God, to do less or more. 19Now therefore, please, you also stay here tonight, that I may know what more the LORD will say to me."

20And God came to Balaam at night and said to him, "If the men come to call you, rise *and* go with them; but only the word which I speak to you—that you shall do." 21So Balaam rose in the morning, saddled his donkey, and went with the princes of Moab.

Balaam, the Donkey, and the Angel

22Then God's anger was aroused because he went, and the Angel of the LORD took His stand in the way as an adversary against him. And he was riding on his donkey, and his two servants *were* with him. 23Now the donkey saw the Angel of the LORD standing in the way with His drawn sword in His hand, and the donkey

22:5 [a]That is, the Euphrates [b]Or *the people of Amau*

22:1–14 "Balaam was no stranger to Israel's cause; so that he ought to have answered the messengers at once, that he would never curse a people whom God had blessed; but he takes a night's time to consider what he should do. When we parley with temptations, we are in great danger of being overcome. Balaam was not faithful in returning God's answer to the messengers. Those are a fair mark for Satan's temptation, who lessen Divine restraints; as if to go against God's law were only to go without his leave. The messengers also are not faithful in returning Balaam's answer to Balak. Thus many are abused by the flatteries of those about them, and are prevented from seeing their own faults and follies." *Matthew Henry*

QUESTIONS & OBJECTIONS

22:28

"How can you believe in a talking snake, etc.?"

I am sure a talking parrot, three hundred people flying through the sky in a big tin can called a jumbo jet, a human being growing inside another person, and men walking on the moon don't sound logical to the uninformed. However, science and technology have given the word "logical" a completely different meaning than it had one hundred years ago.

Some people are limited by the confines of what they see as logic. However, when we are born again, the Supernatural takes logic into a new realm. When we discover that the Supernatural is a reality, our mind is suddenly expanded.

Animals could easily talk—if the Supernatural is involved. A man could easily live in the stomach of a "great fish" if it was "prepared" by the God who made it, as the Bible says it was. A virgin could easily become pregnant if the One who made the virgin was involved. And walking on water is a breeze . . . when God is manifest in human form.

turned aside out of the way and went into
the field. So Balaam struck the donkey to
turn her back onto the road. 24Then the
Angel of the LORD stood in a narrow path
between the vineyards, *with* a wall on this
side and a wall on that side. 25And when
the donkey saw the Angel of the LORD,
she pushed herself against the wall and
crushed Balaam's foot against the wall; so
he struck her again. 26Then the Angel of
the LORD went further, and stood in a
narrow place where there *was* no way to
turn either to the right hand or to the left.
27And when the donkey saw the Angel of
the LORD, she lay down under Balaam; so
Balaam's anger was aroused, and he
struck the donkey with his staff.

28Then the LORD opened the mouth of
the donkey, and she said to Balaam, "What
have I done to you, that you have struck
me these three times?"

29And Balaam said to the donkey, "Because you have abused me. I wish there
were a sword in my hand, for now I would
kill you!"

30So the donkey said to Balaam, "*Am* I
not your donkey on which you have ridden, ever since *I became* yours, to this day?
Was I ever disposed to do this to you?"

And he said, "No."

31Then the LORD opened Balaam's eyes,
and he saw the Angel of the LORD standing in the way with His drawn sword in
His hand; and he bowed his head and fell
flat on his face. 32And the Angel of the
LORD said to him, "Why have you struck
your donkey these three times? Behold, I
have come out to stand against you, because *your* way is perverse before Me.
33The donkey saw Me and turned aside
from Me these three times. If she had not
turned aside from Me, surely I would also
have killed you by now, and let her live."

34And Balaam said to the Angel of the
LORD, "I have sinned, for I did not know
You stood in the way against me. Now
therefore, if it displeases You, I will turn
back."

35Then the Angel of the LORD said to
Balaam, "Go with the men, but only the
word that I speak to you, that you shall
speak." So Balaam went with the princes
of Balak.

36Now when Balak heard that Balaam
was coming, he went out to meet him at
the city of Moab, which *is* on the border
at the Arnon, the boundary of the territory. 37Then Balak said to Balaam, "Did I
not earnestly send to you, calling for you?
Why did you not come to me? Am I not
able to honor you?"

38And Balaam said to Balak, "Look, I

22:31 May God open our eyes to the terrible plight of the lost, and may He also open the eyes of the lost to the truth of the gospel.

have come to you! Now, have I any power at all to say anything? The word that God puts in my mouth, that I must speak." [39]So Balaam went with Balak, and they came to Kirjath Huzoth. [40]Then Balak offered oxen and sheep, and he sent *some* to Balaam and to the princes who *were* with him.

Balaam's First Prophecy

[41]So it was, the next day, that Balak took Balaam and brought him up to the high places of Baal, that from there he might observe the extent of the people.

23 Then Balaam said to Balak, "Build seven altars for me here, and prepare for me here seven bulls and seven rams."

[2]And Balak did just as Balaam had spoken, and Balak and Balaam offered a bull and a ram on *each* altar. [3]Then Balaam said to Balak, "Stand by your burnt offering, and I will go; perhaps the LORD will come to meet me, and whatever He shows me I will tell you." So he went to a desolate height. [4]And God met Balaam, and he said to Him, "I have prepared the seven altars, and I have offered on *each* altar a bull and a ram."

[5]Then the LORD put a word in Balaam's mouth, and said, "Return to Balak, and thus you shall speak." [6]So he returned to him, and there he was, standing by his burnt offering, he and all the princes of Moab.

[7]And he took up his oracle and said:

"Balak the king of Moab has brought
me from Aram,
From the mountains of the east.
'Come, curse Jacob for me,
And come, denounce Israel!'

[8]"How shall I curse whom God has not
cursed?
And how shall I denounce *whom* the
LORD has not denounced?
[9]For from the top of the rocks I see him,
And from the hills I behold him;
There! A people dwelling alone,
Not reckoning itself among the nations.

[10]"Who can count the dust[a] of Jacob,
Or number one-fourth of Israel?
Let me die the death of the righteous,
And let my end be like his!"

[11]Then Balak said to Balaam, "What have you done to me? I took you to curse my enemies, and look, you have blessed *them* bountifully!"

[12]So he answered and said, "Must I not take heed to speak what the LORD has put in my mouth?"

Balaam's Second Prophecy

[13]Then Balak said to him, "Please come with me to another place from which you may see them; you shall see only the outer part of them, and shall not see them all; curse them for me from there." [14]So he brought him to the field of Zophim, to the top of Pisgah, and built seven altars, and offered a bull and a ram on *each* altar.

[15]And he said to Balak, "Stand here by your burnt offering while I meet[a] *the LORD* over there."

[16]Then the LORD met Balaam, and put a word in his mouth, and said, "Go back to Balak, and thus you shall speak." [17]So he came to him, and there he was, standing by his burnt offering, and the princes of Moab were with him. And Balak said to him, "What has the LORD spoken?"

[18]Then he took up his oracle and said:

"Rise up, Balak, and hear!
Listen to me, son of Zippor!

[19]"God *is* not a man, that He should lie,
Nor a son of man, that He should
repent.
Has He said, and will He not do?
Or has He spoken, and will He not
make it good?
[20]Behold, I have received *a command* to
bless;

23:10 [a]Or *dust cloud* **23:15** [a]Following Masoretic Text, Targum, and Vulgate; Syriac reads *call*; Septuagint reads *go and ask God*.

He has blessed, and I cannot reverse it.

21"He has not observed iniquity in Jacob,
Nor has He seen wickedness in Israel.
The LORD his God *is* with him,
And the shout of a King *is* among them.
22God brings them out of Egypt;
He has strength like a wild ox.

23"For *there is* no sorcery against Jacob,
Nor any divination against Israel.
It now must be said of Jacob
And of Israel, 'Oh, what God has done!'
24Look, a people rises like a lioness,
And lifts itself up like a lion;
It shall not lie down until it devours
the prey,
And drinks the blood of the slain."

25Then Balak said to Balaam, "Neither
curse them at all, nor bless them at all!"
26So Balaam answered and said to
Balak, "Did I not tell you, saying, 'All that
the LORD speaks, that I must do'?"

Balaam's Third Prophecy

27Then Balak said to Balaam, "Please
come, I will take you to another place;
perhaps it will please God that you may
curse them for me from there." 28So Balak
took Balaam to the top of Peor, that overlooks the wasteland.[a] 29Then Balaam said
to Balak, "Build for me here seven altars,
and prepare for me here seven bulls and
seven rams." 30And Balak did as Balaam
had said, and offered a bull and a ram on
every altar.

24 Now when Balaam saw that it
pleased the LORD to bless Israel, he
did not go as at other times, to seek to use
sorcery, but he set his face toward the wilderness. 2And Balaam raised his eyes, and
saw Israel encamped according to their
tribes; and the Spirit of God came upon
him.

3Then he took up his oracle and said:

"The utterance of Balaam the son of
Beor,
The utterance of the man whose eyes
are opened,
4The utterance of him who hears the
words of God,
Who sees the vision of the Almighty,
Who falls down, with eyes wide open:

5"How lovely are your tents, O Jacob!
Your dwellings, O Israel!
6Like valleys that stretch out,
Like gardens by the riverside,
Like aloes planted by the LORD,
Like cedars beside the waters.
7He shall pour water from his buckets,
And his seed *shall be* in many waters.

"His king shall be higher than Agag,
And his kingdom shall be exalted.

8"God brings him out of Egypt;
He has strength like a wild ox;
He shall consume the nations, his
enemies;
He shall break their bones
And pierce *them* with his arrows.
9'He bows down, he lies down as a lion;
And as a lion, who shall rouse him?'[a]

"Blessed *is* he who blesses you,
And cursed *is* he who curses you."

10Then Balak's anger was aroused against
Balaam, and he struck his hands together; and Balak said to Balaam, "I called
you to curse my enemies, and look, you
have bountifully blessed *them* these three
times! 11Now therefore, flee to your place.
I said I would greatly honor you, but in fact,
the LORD has kept you back from honor."
12So Balaam said to Balak, "Did I not

23:28 [a]Hebrew *Jeshimon* 24:9 [a]Genesis 49:9

23:19 Mormons believe the oldest lie in the Book: that man can be like God. To them, God is just a flesh-and-bones man who was exalted to godhood: "As man is, God once was. As God is, man may become." For details, see page 1684. For whether God "repents," see Jer. 18:8 comment.

also speak to your messengers whom you sent to me, saying, [13]'If Balak were to give me his house full of silver and gold, I could not go beyond the word of the LORD, to do good or bad of my own will. What the LORD says, that I must speak'? [14]And now, indeed, I am going to my people. Come, I will advise you what this people will do to your people in the latter days."

Balaam's Fourth Prophecy

[15]So he took up his oracle and said:

"The utterance of Balaam the son of
Beor,
And the utterance of the man whose
eyes are opened;
[16]The utterance of him who hears the
words of God,
And has the knowledge of the Most
High,
Who sees the vision of the Almighty,
Who falls down, with eyes wide open:

[17]"I see Him, but not now;
I behold Him, but not near;
A Star shall come out of Jacob;
A Scepter shall rise out of Israel,
And batter the brow of Moab,
And destroy all the sons of tumult.[a]

[18]"And Edom shall be a possession;
Seir also, his enemies, shall be a
possession,
While Israel does valiantly.
[19]Out of Jacob One shall have dominion,
And destroy the remains of the city."

[20]Then he looked on Amalek, and he took up his oracle and said:

"Amalek *was* first among the nations,
But *shall be* last until he perishes."

[21]Then he looked on the Kenites, and he took up his oracle and said:

"Firm is your dwelling place,
And your nest is set in the rock;
[22]Nevertheless Kain shall be burned.
How long until Asshur carries you
away captive?"

[23]Then he took up his oracle and said:

"Alas! Who shall live when God does
this?
[24]But ships *shall come* from the coasts of
Cyprus,[a]
And they shall afflict Asshur and
afflict Eber,
And so shall *Amalek*,[b] until he
perishes."

[25]So Balaam rose and departed and returned to his place; Balak also went his way.

Israel's Harlotry in Moab

25 Now Israel remained in Acacia Grove,[a] and the people began to commit harlotry with the women of Moab. [2]They invited the people to the sacrifices

24:17 [a]Hebrew *Sheth* (compare Jeremiah 48:45) 24:24 [a]Hebrew *Kittim* [b]Literally *he* or *that one* 25:1 [a]Hebrew *Shittim*

24:15,16 Eyes wide open. When we come to Jesus Christ, the Light of the World, we no longer walk in darkness. Non-Christians are like someone who is driving directly toward the sun, low on the horizon. It is very difficult to see clearly. But it is so different when driving with a low sun behind you—*everything* can be seen clearly. To those who have never repented and trusted in Jesus Christ, nothing will be clear. They search outer space to try to find their origins, because they don't know where they came from. Neither do they know why they are here, or where they are heading. However, repentance is a complete change of direction. When we repent and trust in Jesus, all things become clear. Our eyes are opened to the truth, and we hear the words of the Lord. We come to *know* Him and why we are here. We are not an accident, but were made by God for God. That is the purpose of our existence: to enjoy Him and His creation forever.

25:1,2 "The invasion of the Church by the world is a menace to the extension of Christ's kingdom. In all ages conformity to the world by Christians has resulted in lack of spiritual life and a consequent lack of spiritual vision and enterprise. A secularized or self-centered Church can never evangelize the world." *John R. Mott*

of their gods, and the people ate and bowed down to their gods. 3So Israel was joined to Baal of Peor, and the anger of the LORD was aroused against Israel.

4Then the LORD said to Moses, "Take all the leaders of the people and hang the offenders before the LORD, out in the sun, that the fierce anger of the LORD may turn away from Israel."

5So Moses said to the judges of Israel, "Every one of you kill his men who were joined to Baal of Peor."

6And indeed, one of the children of Israel came and presented to his brethren a Midianite woman in the sight of Moses and in the sight of all the congregation of the children of Israel, who *were* weeping at the door of the tabernacle of meeting. 7Now when Phinehas the son of Eleazar, the son of Aaron the priest, saw *it,* he rose from among the congregation and took a javelin in his hand; 8and he went after the man of Israel into the tent and thrust both of them through, the man of Israel, and the woman through her body. So the plague was stopped among the children of Israel. 9And those who died in the plague were twenty-four thousand.

10Then the LORD spoke to Moses, saying: 11"Phinehas the son of Eleazar, the son of Aaron the priest, has turned back My wrath from the children of Israel, because he was zealous with My zeal among them, so that I did not consume the children of Israel in My zeal. 12Therefore say, 'Behold, I give to him My covenant of peace; 13and it shall be to him and his descendants after him a covenant of an everlasting priesthood, because he was zealous for his God, and made atonement for the children of Israel.' "

14Now the name of the Israelite who was killed, who was killed with the Midianite woman, *was* Zimri the son of Salu, a leader of a father's house among the Simeonites. 15And the name of the Midianite woman who was killed *was* Cozbi the daughter of Zur; he *was* head of the people of a father's house in Midian.

16Then the LORD spoke to Moses, saying: 17"Harass the Midianites, and attack them; 18for they harassed you with their schemes by which they seduced you in the matter of Peor and in the matter of Cozbi, the daughter of a leader of Midian, their sister, who was killed in the day of the plague because of Peor."

The Second Census of Israel

26 And it came to pass, after the plague, that the LORD spoke to Moses and Eleazar the son of Aaron the priest, saying: 2"Take a census of all the congregation of the children of Israel from twenty years old and above, by their fathers' houses, all who are able to go to war in Israel." 3So Moses and Eleazar the priest spoke with them in the plains of Moab by the Jordan, *across from* Jericho, saying: 4"*Take a census of the people* from twenty years old and above, just as the LORD commanded Moses and the children of Israel who came out of the land of Egypt."

5Reuben *was* the firstborn of Israel. The children of Reuben *were: of* Hanoch, the family of the Hanochites; *of* Pallu, the family of the Palluites; 6*of* Hezron, the family of the Hezronites; *of* Carmi, the family of the Carmites. 7These *are* the families of the Reubenites: those who were numbered of them were forty-three thousand seven hundred and thirty. 8And the son of Pallu *was* Eliab. 9The sons of Eliab *were* Nemuel, Dathan, and Abiram. These *are* the Dathan and Abiram, representatives of the congregation, who contended against Moses and Aaron in the company of Korah, when they contended against the LORD; 10and the earth opened its mouth

---

26:2 "We are not called to proclaim philosophy and metaphysics, but the simple gospel. Man's fall, his need of a new birth, forgiveness through atonement, and salvation as the result of faith, these are our battle-ax and weapons of war." *Charles Spurgeon*

and swallowed them up together with Korah when that company died, when the fire devoured two hundred and fifty men; and they became a sign. 11Nevertheless the children of Korah did not die.

12The sons of Simeon according to their families *were: of* Nemuel,[a] the family of the Nemuelites; *of* Jamin, the family of the Jaminites; *of* Jachin,[b] the family of the Jachinites; 13*of* Zerah,[a] the family of the Zarhites; *of* Shaul, the family of the Shaulites. 14These *are* the families of the Simeonites: twenty-two thousand two hundred.

15The sons of Gad according to their families *were: of* Zephon,[a] the family of the Zephonites; *of* Haggi, the family of the Haggites; *of* Shuni, the family of the Shunites; 16*of* Ozni,[a] the family of the Oznites; *of* Eri, the family of the Erites; 17*of* Arod,[a] the family of the Arodites; *of* Areli, the family of the Arelites. 18These *are* the families of the sons of Gad according to those who were numbered of them: forty thousand five hundred.

19The sons of Judah *were* Er and Onan; and Er and Onan died in the land of Canaan. 20And the sons of Judah according to their families were: *of* Shelah, the family of the Shelanites; *of* Perez, the family of the Parzites; *of* Zerah, the family of the Zarhites. 21And the sons of Perez were: *of* Hezron, the family of the Hezronites; *of* Hamul, the family of the Hamulites. 22These *are* the families of Judah according to those who were numbered of them: seventy-six thousand five hundred.

23The sons of Issachar according to their families *were: of* Tola, the family of the Tolaites; of Puah,[a] the family of the Punites;[b] 24of Jashub, the family of the Jashubites; of Shimron, the family of the Shimronites. 25These *are* the families of Issachar according to those who were numbered of them: sixty-four thousand three hundred.

26The sons of Zebulun according to their families *were:* of Sered, the family of the Sardites; of Elon, the family of the Elonites; of Jahleel, the family of the Jahleelites. 27These *are* the families of the Zebulunites according to those who were numbered of them: sixty thousand five hundred.

28The sons of Joseph according to their families, by Manasseh and Ephraim, *were:* 29The sons of Manasseh: of Machir, the family of the Machirites; and Machir begot Gilead; of Gilead, the family of the Gileadites. 30These *are* the sons of Gilead: *of* Jeezer,[a] the family of the Jeezerites; of Helek, the family of the Helekites; 31*of* Asriel, the family of the Asrielites; *of* Shechem, the family of the Shechemites; 32*of* Shemida, the family of the Shemidaites; *of* Hepher, the family of the Hepherites. 33Now Zelophehad the son of Hepher had no sons, but daughters; and the names of the daughters of Zelophehad *were* Mahlah, Noah, Hoglah, Milcah, and Tirzah. 34These *are* the families of Manasseh; and those who were numbered of them *were* fifty-two thousand seven hundred.

35These *are* the sons of Ephraim according to their families: of Shuthelah, the family of the Shuthalhites; of Becher,[a] the family of the Bachrites; of Tahan, the family of the Tahanites. 36And these *are* the sons of Shuthelah: of Eran, the family of the Eranites. 37These *are* the families of the sons of Ephraim according to those who were numbered of them: thirty-two thousand five hundred.

These *are* the sons of Joseph according to their families.

38The sons of Benjamin according to their families were: of Bela, the family of the Belaites; of Ashbel, the family of the Ashbelites; of Ahiram, the family of the Ahiramites; 39of Shupham,[a] the family of the Shuphamites; of Hupham,[b] the family of the Huphamites. 40And the sons of

26:12 [a]Spelled *Jemuel* in Genesis 46:10 and Exodus 6:15 [b]Called *Jarib* in 1 Chronicles 4:24 **26:13** [a]Called *Zohar* in Genesis 46:10 **26:15** [a]Called *Ziphion* in Genesis 46:16 **26:16** [a]Called *Ezbon* in Genesis 46:16 **26:17** [a]Spelled *Arodi* in Samaritan Pentateuch, Syriac, and Genesis 46:16 **26:23** [a]Hebrew *Puvah* (compare Genesis 46:13 and 1 Chronicles 7:1); Samaritan Pentateuch, Septuagint, Syriac, and Vulgate read *Puah.* [b]Samaritan Pentateuch, Septuagint, Syriac, and Vulgate read *Puaites.* **26:30** [a]Called *Abiezer* in Joshua 17:2 **26:35** [a]Called *Bered* in 1 Chronicles 7:20 **26:39** [a]Masoretic Text reads *Shephupham,* spelled *Shephuphan* in 1 Chronicles 8:5. [b]Called *Huppim* in Genesis 46:21

Bela were Ard[a] and Naaman: *of Ard,* the
family of the Ardites; of Naaman, the family of the Naamites. 41These *are* the sons
of Benjamin according to their families;
and those who were numbered of them
were forty-five thousand six hundred.
42These *are* the sons of Dan according
to their families: of Shuham,[a] the family
of the Shuhamites. These *are* the families
of Dan according to their families. 43All
the families of the Shuhamites, according
to those who were numbered of them,
were sixty-four thousand four hundred.
44The sons of Asher according to their
families *were:* of Jimna, the family of the
Jimnites; of Jesui, the family of the Je-
suites; of Beriah, the family of the Beri-
ites. 45Of the sons of Beriah: of Heber, the
family of the Heberites; of Malchiel, the
family of the Malchielites. 46And the name
of the daughter of Asher *was* Serah. 47These
are the families of the sons of Asher according to those who were numbered of
them: fifty-three thousand four hundred.
48The sons of Naphtali according to
their families *were:* of Jahzeel,[a] the family
of the Jahzeelites; of Guni, the family of
the Gunites; 49of Jezer, the family of the
Jezerites; of Shillem, the family of the Shil-
lemites. 50These *are* the families of Naphtali according to their families; and those
who were numbered of them *were* forty-
five thousand four hundred.
51These *are* those who were numbered
of the children of Israel: six hundred and
one thousand seven hundred and thirty.
52Then the LORD spoke to Moses, saying: 53"To these the land shall be divided
as an inheritance, according to the number of names. 54To a large *tribe* you shall
give a larger inheritance, and to a small
tribe you shall give a smaller inheritance.
Each shall be given its inheritance according to those who were numbered of
them. 55But the land shall be divided by
lot; they shall inherit according to the
names of the tribes of their fathers. 56Ac-
cording to the lot their inheritance shall
be divided between the larger and the
smaller."
57And these *are* those who were numbered of the Levites according to their
families: of Gershon, the family of the
Gershonites; of Kohath, the family of the
Kohathites; of Merari, the family of the
Merarites. 58These *are* the families of the
Levites: the family of the Libnites, the
family of the Hebronites, the family of the
Mahlites, the family of the Mushites, and
the family of the Korathites. And Kohath
begot Amram. 59The name of Amram's
wife *was* Jochebed the daughter of Levi,
who was born to Levi in Egypt; and to
Amram she bore Aaron and Moses and
their sister Miriam. 60To Aaron were born
Nadab and Abihu, Eleazar and Ithamar.
61And Nadab and Abihu died when they
offered profane fire before the LORD.
62Now those who were numbered of
them were twenty-three thousand, every
male from a month old and above; for
they were not numbered among the other
children of Israel, because there was no
inheritance given to them among the
children of Israel.
63These *are* those who were numbered
by Moses and Eleazar the priest, who
numbered the children of Israel in the
plains of Moab by the Jordan, *across from*
Jericho. 64But among these there was not
a man of those who were numbered by
Moses and Aaron the priest when they
numbered the children of Israel in the
Wilderness of Sinai. 65For the LORD had
said of them, "They shall surely die in the
wilderness." So there was not left a man
of them, except Caleb the son of Jephunneh and Joshua the son of Nun.

Inheritance Laws

27 Then came the daughters of Zelophehad the son of Hepher, the
son of Gilead, the son of Machir, the son
of Manasseh, from the families of Manasseh the son of Joseph; and these *were* the
names of his daughters: Mahlah, Noah,
Hoglah, Milcah, and Tirzah. 2And they

26:40 [a]Called *Addar* in 1 Chronicles 8:3 26:42 [a]Called *Hushim* in Genesis 46:23 26:48 [a]Spelled *Jahziel* in 1 Chronicles 7:13

stood before Moses, before Eleazar the priest, and before the leaders and all the congregation, *by* the doorway of the tabernacle of meeting, saying: 3"Our father died in the wilderness; but he was not in the company of those who gathered together against the LORD, in company with Korah, but he died in his own sin; and he had no sons. 4Why should the name of our father be removed from among his family because he had no son? Give us a possession among our father's brothers."

5So Moses brought their case before the LORD.

6And the LORD spoke to Moses, saying: 7"The daughters of Zelophehad speak *what is* right; you shall surely give them a possession of inheritance among their father's brothers, and cause the inheritance of their father to pass to them. 8And you shall speak to the children of Israel, saying: 'If a man dies and has no son, then you shall cause his inheritance to pass to his daughter. 9If he has no daughter, then you shall give his inheritance to his brothers. 10If he has no brothers, then you shall give his inheritance to his father's brothers. 11And if his father has no brothers, then you shall give his inheritance to the relative closest to him in his family, and he shall possess it.' " And it shall be to the children of Israel a statute of judgment, just as the LORD commanded Moses.

Joshua the Next Leader of Israel

12Now the LORD said to Moses: "Go up into this Mount Abarim, and see the land which I have given to the children of Israel. 13And when you have seen it, you also shall be gathered to your people, as Aaron your brother was gathered. 14For in the Wilderness of Zin, during the strife of the congregation, you rebelled against My command to hallow Me at the waters before their eyes." (These *are* the waters of Meribah, at Kadesh in the Wilderness of Zin.)

15Then Moses spoke to the LORD, saying: 16"Let the LORD, the God of the spirits of all flesh, set a man over the congregation, 17who may go out before them and go in before them, who may lead them out and bring them in, that the congregation of the LORD may not be like sheep which have no shepherd."

18And the LORD said to Moses: "Take Joshua the son of Nun with you, a man in whom *is* the Spirit, and lay your hand on him; 19set him before Eleazar the priest and before all the congregation, and inaugurate him in their sight. 20And you shall give *some* of your authority to him, that all the congregation of the children of Israel may be obedient. 21He shall stand before Eleazar the priest, who shall inquire before the LORD for him by the judgment of the Urim. At his word they shall go out, and at his word they shall come in, he and all the children of Israel with him—all the congregation."

22So Moses did as the LORD commanded him. He took Joshua and set him before Eleazar the priest and before all the congregation. 23And he laid his hands on him and inaugurated him, just as the LORD commanded by the hand of Moses.

. . . . . .

For how to use the Law in evangelism, see Matt. 19:17–22 comment.

. . . . . .

Daily Offerings

28 Now the LORD spoke to Moses, saying, 2"Command the children of Israel, and say to them, 'My offering, My food for My offerings made by fire as a sweet aroma to Me, you shall be careful to offer to Me at their appointed time.'

3"And you shall say to them, 'This *is* the offering made by fire which you shall offer to the LORD: two male lambs in their first year without blemish, day by day, as a regular burnt offering. 4The one lamb you shall offer in the morning, the other lamb you shall offer in the evening, 5and one-tenth of an ephah of fine flour as a grain offering mixed with one-fourth of a

hin of pressed oil. 6*It is* a regular burnt offering which was ordained at Mount Sinai for a sweet aroma, an offering made by fire to the LORD. 7And its drink offering *shall be* one-fourth of a hin for each lamb; in a holy *place* you shall pour out the drink to the LORD as an offering. 8The other lamb you shall offer in the evening; as the morning grain offering and its drink offering, you shall offer *it* as an offering made by fire, a sweet aroma to the LORD.

Sabbath Offerings

9'And on the Sabbath day two lambs in their first year, without blemish, and two-tenths *of an ephah* of fine flour as a grain offering, mixed with oil, with its drink offering— 10*this is* the burnt offering for every Sabbath, besides the regular burnt offering with its drink offering.

Monthly Offerings

11'At the beginnings of your months you shall present a burnt offering to the LORD: two young bulls, one ram, and seven lambs in their first year, without blemish; 12three-tenths *of an ephah* of fine flour as a grain offering, mixed with oil, for each bull; two-tenths *of an ephah* of fine flour as a grain offering, mixed with oil, for the one ram; 13and one-tenth *of an ephah* of fine flour, mixed with oil, as a grain offering for each lamb, as a burnt offering of sweet aroma, an offering made by fire to the LORD. 14Their drink offering shall be half a hin of wine for a bull, one-third of a hin for a ram, and one-fourth of a hin for a lamb; this *is* the burnt offering for each month throughout the months of the year. 15Also one kid of the goats as a sin offering to the LORD shall be offered, besides the regular burnt offering and its drink offering.

Offerings at Passover

16'On the fourteenth day of the first month *is* the Passover of the LORD. 17And on the fifteenth day of this month *is* the feast; unleavened bread shall be eaten for seven days. 18On the first day *you shall have* a holy convocation. You shall do no customary work. 19And you shall present an offering made by fire as a burnt offering to the LORD: two young bulls, one ram, and seven lambs in their first year. Be sure they are without blemish. 20Their grain offering shall be of fine flour mixed with oil: three-tenths *of an ephah* you shall offer for a bull, and two-tenths for a ram; 21you shall offer one-tenth *of an ephah* for each of the seven lambs; 22also one goat *as* a sin offering, to make atonement for you. 23You shall offer these besides the burnt offering of the morning, which *is* for a regular burnt offering. 24In this manner you shall offer the food of the offering made by fire daily for seven days, as a sweet aroma to the LORD; it shall be offered besides the regular burnt offering and its drink offering. 25And on the seventh day you shall have a holy convocation. You shall do no customary work.

Offerings at the Feast of Weeks

26'Also on the day of the firstfruits, when you bring a new grain offering to the LORD at your *Feast of* Weeks, you shall have a holy convocation. You shall do no customary work. 27You shall present a burnt offering as a sweet aroma to the LORD: two young bulls, one ram, and seven lambs in their first year, 28with their grain offering of fine flour mixed with oil: three-tenths *of an ephah* for each bull, two-tenths for the one ram, 29and one-tenth for each of the seven lambs; 30*also* one kid of the goats, to make atonement for you. 31Be sure they are without blemish. You shall present *them* with their drink offerings, besides the regular burnt offering with its grain offering.

Offerings at the Feast of Trumpets

29 'And in the seventh month, on the first *day* of the month, you shall have a holy convocation. You shall do no customary work. For you it is a day of blowing the trumpets. 2You shall offer a burnt offering as a sweet aroma to the

LORD: one young bull, one ram, *and* seven
lambs in their first year, without blemish.
3Their grain offering *shall be* fine flour
mixed with oil: three-tenths *of an ephah*
for the bull, two-tenths for the ram, 4and
one-tenth for each of the seven lambs;
5also one kid of the goats *as* a sin offering,
to make atonement for you; 6besides the
burnt offering with its grain offering for
the New Moon, the regular burnt offering
with its grain offering, and their drink offerings, according to their ordinance, as a
sweet aroma, an offering made by fire to
the LORD.

Offerings on the Day of Atonement

7'On the tenth *day* of this seventh
month you shall have a holy convocation.
You shall afflict your souls; you shall not
do any work. 8You shall present a burnt
offering to the LORD *as* a sweet aroma:
one young bull, one ram, *and* seven
lambs in their first year. Be sure they are
without blemish. 9Their grain offering
shall be of fine flour mixed with oil: three-
tenths *of an ephah* for the bull, two-tenths
for the one ram, 10and one-tenth for each
of the seven lambs; 11also one kid of the
goats *as* a sin offering, besides the sin offering for atonement, the regular burnt
offering with its grain offering, and their
drink offerings.

Offerings at the Feast of Tabernacles

12'On the fifteenth day of the seventh
month you shall have a holy convocation.
You shall do no customary work, and you
shall keep a feast to the LORD seven days.
13You shall present a burnt offering, an
offering made by fire as a sweet aroma to
the LORD: thirteen young bulls, two rams,
and fourteen lambs in their first year.
They shall be without blemish. 14Their
grain offering *shall be of* fine flour mixed
with oil: three-tenths *of an ephah* for each
of the thirteen bulls, two-tenths for each
of the two rams, 15and one-tenth for each
of the fourteen lambs; 16also one kid of
the goats *as* a sin offering, besides the
regular burnt offering, its grain offering,
and its drink offering.

17'On the second day *present* twelve
young bulls, two rams, fourteen lambs in
their first year without blemish, 18and
their grain offering and their drink offerings for the bulls, for the rams, and for
the lambs, by their number, according to
the ordinance; 19also one kid of the goats
as a sin offering, besides the regular burnt
offering with its grain offering, and their
drink offerings.

20'On the third day *present* eleven bulls,
two rams, fourteen lambs in their first
year without blemish, 21and their grain
offering and their drink offerings for the
bulls, for the rams, and for the lambs, by
their number, according to the ordinance;
22also one goat *as* a sin offering, besides
the regular burnt offering, its grain offering, and its drink offering.

23'On the fourth day *present* ten bulls,
two rams, *and* fourteen lambs in their first
year, without blemish, 24and their grain
offering and their drink offerings for the
bulls, for the rams, and for the lambs, by
their number, according to the ordinance;
25also one kid of the goats *as* a sin offering, besides the regular burnt offering, its
grain offering, and its drink offering.

26'On the fifth day *present* nine bulls,
two rams, *and* fourteen lambs in their first
year without blemish, 27and their grain
offering and their drink offerings for the
bulls, for the rams, and for the lambs, by
their number, according to the ordinance;
28also one goat *as* a sin offering, besides
the regular burnt offering, its grain offering, and its drink offering.

29'On the sixth day *present* eight bulls,
two rams, *and* fourteen lambs in their

29:1–12 "There were more sacred solemnities in the seventh month than in any other. It was the space between harvest and seed-time. The more leisure we have from the pressing occupations of this life, the more time we should spend in the immediate service of God." *Matthew Henry*

first year without blemish, 30and their grain offering and their drink offerings for the bulls, for the rams, and for the lambs, by their number, according to the ordinance; 31also one goat *as* a sin offering, besides the regular burnt offering, its grain offering, and its drink offering.

32'On the seventh day *present* seven bulls, two rams, *and* fourteen lambs in their first year without blemish, 33and their grain offering and their drink offerings for the bulls, for the rams, and for the lambs, by their number, according to the ordinance; 34also one goat *as* a sin offering, besides the regular burnt offering, its grain offering, and its drink offering.

35'On the eighth day you shall have a sacred assembly. You shall do no customary work. 36You shall present a burnt offering, an offering made by fire as a sweet aroma to the LORD: one bull, one ram, seven lambs in their first year without blemish, 37and their grain offering and their drink offerings for the bull, for the ram, and for the lambs, by their number, according to the ordinance; 38also one goat *as* a sin offering, besides the regular burnt offering, its grain offering, and its drink offering.

39'These you shall present to the LORD at your appointed feasts (besides your vowed offerings and your freewill offerings) as your burnt offerings and your grain offerings, as your drink offerings and your peace offerings.' "

40So Moses told the children of Israel everything, just as the LORD commanded Moses.

The Law Concerning Vows

30 Then Moses spoke to the heads of the tribes concerning the children of Israel, saying, "This *is* the thing which the LORD has commanded: 2If a man makes a vow to the LORD, or swears an oath to bind himself by some agreement, he shall not break his word; he shall do according to all that proceeds out of his mouth.

3"Or if a woman makes a vow to the LORD, and binds *herself* by some agreement while in her father's house in her youth, 4and her father hears her vow and the agreement by which she has bound herself, and her father holds his peace, then all her vows shall stand, and every agreement with which she has bound herself shall stand. 5But if her father overrules her on the day that he hears, then none of her vows nor her agreements by which she has bound herself shall stand; and the LORD will release her, because her father overruled her.

6"If indeed she takes a husband, while bound by her vows or by a rash utterance from her lips by which she bound herself, 7and her husband hears *it,* and makes no response to her on the day that he hears, then her vows shall stand, and her agreements by which she bound herself shall stand. 8But if her husband overrules her on the day that he hears *it,* he shall make void her vow which she took and what she uttered with her lips, by which she bound herself, and the LORD will release her.

9"Also any vow of a widow or a divorced woman, by which she has bound herself, shall stand against her.

10"If she vowed in her husband's house, or bound herself by an agreement with an oath, 11and her husband heard *it,* and made no response to her *and* did not overrule her, then all her vows shall stand, and every agreement by which she bound herself shall stand. 12But if her husband truly made them void on the day he heard *them,* then whatever proceeded from her lips concerning her vows or concerning the agreement binding her, it shall not stand; her husband has made them void, and the LORD will release her. 13Every vow and every binding oath to afflict her soul, her husband may confirm it, or her husband may make it void. 14Now if her husband makes no response whatever to her from day to day, then he confirms all her vows or all the agreements that bind her; he confirms them, because he made no response to her on

the day that he heard *them.* 15But if he does make them void after he has heard *them,* then he shall bear her guilt."

16These *are* the statutes which the LORD commanded Moses, between a man and his wife, and between a father and his daughter in her youth in her father's house.

Vengeance on the Midianites

31 And the LORD spoke to Moses, saying: 2"Take vengeance on the Midianites for the children of Israel. Afterward you shall be gathered to your people."

3So Moses spoke to the people, saying, "Arm some of yourselves for war, and let them go against the Midianites to take vengeance for the LORD on Midian. 4A thousand from each tribe of all the tribes of Israel you shall send to the war."

5So there were recruited from the divisions of Israel one thousand from *each* tribe, twelve thousand armed for war. 6Then Moses sent them to the war, one thousand from *each* tribe; he sent them to the war with Phinehas the son of Eleazar the priest, with the holy articles and the signal trumpets in his hand. 7And they warred against the Midianites, just as the LORD commanded Moses, and they killed all the males. 8They killed the kings of Midian with *the rest of* those who were killed—Evi, Rekem, Zur, Hur, and Reba, the five kings of Midian. Balaam the son of Beor they also killed with the sword.

9And the children of Israel took the women of Midian captive, with their little ones, and took as spoil all their cattle, all their flocks, and all their goods. 10They also burned with fire all the cities where they dwelt, and all their forts. 11And they took all the spoil and all the booty—of man and beast.

Return from the War

12Then they brought the captives, the booty, and the spoil to Moses, to Eleazar the priest, and to the congregation of the children of Israel, to the camp in the plains of Moab by the Jordan, *across from* Jericho. 13And Moses, Eleazar the priest, and all the leaders of the congregation, went to meet them outside the camp. 14But Moses was angry with the officers of the army, *with* the captains over thousands and captains over hundreds, who had come from the battle.

15And Moses said to them: "Have you kept all the women alive? 16Look, these *women* caused the children of Israel, through the counsel of Balaam, to trespass against the LORD in the incident of Peor, and there was a plague among the congregation of the LORD. 17Now therefore, kill every male among the little ones, and kill every woman who has known a man intimately. 18But keep alive for yourselves all the young girls who have not known a man intimately. 19And as for you, remain outside the camp seven days; whoever has killed any person, and whoever has touched any slain, purify yourselves and your captives on the third day and on the seventh day. 20Purify every garment, everything made of leather, everything woven of goats' *hair,* and everything made of wood."

21Then Eleazar the priest said to the men of war who had gone to the battle, "This *is* the ordinance of the law which the LORD commanded Moses: 22"Only the gold, the silver, the bronze, the iron, the tin, and the lead, 23everything that can endure fire, you shall put through the fire, and it shall be clean; and it shall be purified with the water of purification. But all that cannot endure fire you shall put through water. 24And you shall wash your clothes on the seventh day and be clean, and afterward you may come into the camp."

31:8 "If preaching could save a man, Judas would not have been damned. If prophesying could save a man, Balaam would not have been a castaway. We may preach with the tongues of men and of angels, yet, if we have not love, it profits us nothing. We may be even leaders of the Church in the noblest and, highest enterprises and yet, for all that, Christ may say to us, at the last, 'I never knew you.'" *Charles Spurgeon*

Division of the Plunder

25Now the LORD spoke to Moses, saying: 26"Count up the plunder that was
taken—of man and beast—you and
Eleazar the priest and the chief fathers of
the congregation; 27and divide the plunder into two parts, between those who
took part in the war, who went out to
battle, and all the congregation. 28And
levy a tribute for the LORD on the men of
war who went out to battle: one of every
five hundred of the persons, the cattle,
the donkeys, and the sheep; 29take *it* from
their half, and give *it* to Eleazar the priest
as a heave offering to the LORD. 30And
from the children of Israel's half you shall
take one of every fifty, drawn from the
persons, the cattle, the donkeys, and the
sheep, from all the livestock, and give
them to the Levites who keep charge of
the tabernacle of the LORD." 31So Moses
and Eleazar the priest did as the LORD
commanded Moses.

32The booty remaining from the plunder, which the men of war had taken, was
six hundred and seventy-five thousand
sheep, 33seventy-two thousand cattle,
34sixty-one thousand donkeys, 35and thirty-
two thousand persons in all, of women
who had not known a man intimately.
36And the half, the portion for those who
had gone out to war, was in number three
hundred and thirty-seven thousand five
hundred sheep; 37and the LORD's tribute
of the sheep was six hundred and seventy-
five. 38The cattle *were* thirty-six thousand,
of which the LORD's tribute *was* seventy-
two. 39The donkeys *were* thirty thousand
five hundred, of which the LORD's tribute
was sixty-one. 40The persons *were* sixteen
thousand, of which the LORD's tribute *was*
thirty-two persons. 41So Moses gave the
tribute *which was* the LORD's heave offering to Eleazar the priest, as the LORD
commanded Moses.

42And from the children of Israel's half,
which Moses separated from the men who
fought— 43now the half belonging to the
congregation was three hundred and thirty-
seven thousand five hundred sheep,
44thirty-six thousand cattle, 45thirty thousand five hundred donkeys, 46and sixteen
thousand persons— 47and from the children of Israel's half Moses took one of
every fifty, drawn from man and beast,
and gave them to the Levites, who kept
charge of the tabernacle of the LORD, as
the LORD commanded Moses.

48Then the officers who *were* over thousands of the army, the captains of thousands and captains of hundreds, came
near to Moses; 49and they said to Moses,
"Your servants have taken a count of the
men of war who *are* under our command,
and not a man of us is missing. 50There-
fore we have brought an offering for the
LORD, what every man found of ornaments of gold: armlets and bracelets and
signet rings and earrings and necklaces,
to make atonement for ourselves before
the LORD." 51So Moses and Eleazar the
priest received the gold from them, all the
fashioned ornaments. 52And all the gold
of the offering that they offered to the
LORD, from the captains of thousands and
captains of hundreds, was sixteen thousand seven hundred and fifty shekels.
53(The men of war had taken spoil, every
man for himself.) 54And Moses and
Eleazar the priest received the gold from
the captains of thousands and of hundreds, and brought it into the tabernacle
of meeting as a memorial for the children
of Israel before the LORD.

The Tribes Settling East of the Jordan

32 Now the children of Reuben and
the children of Gad had a very
great multitude of livestock; and when
they saw the land of Jazer and the land of
Gilead, that indeed the region *was* a place
for livestock, 2the children of Gad and
the children of Reuben came and spoke
to Moses, to Eleazar the priest, and to the
leaders of the congregation, saying, 3"Ataroth, Dibon, Jazer, Nimrah, Heshbon,
Elealeh, Shebam, Nebo, and Beon, 4the
country which the LORD defeated before
the congregation of Israel, *is* a land for
livestock, and your servants have live-

stock." 5Therefore they said, "If we have
found favor in your sight, let this land be
given to your servants as a possession. Do
not take us over the Jordan."

6And Moses said to the children of
Gad and to the children of Reuben: "Shall
your brethren go to war while you sit
here? 7Now why will you discourage the
heart of the children of Israel from going
over into the land which the LORD has
given them? 8Thus your fathers did when
I sent them away from Kadesh Barnea to
see the land. 9For when they went up to
the Valley of Eshcol and saw the land,
they discouraged the heart of the children of Israel, so that they did not go into
the land which the LORD had given them.
10So the LORD's anger was aroused on that
day, and He swore an oath, saying,
11'Surely none of the men who came up
from Egypt, from twenty years old and
above, shall see the land of which I swore
to Abraham, Isaac, and Jacob, because
they have not wholly followed Me, 12ex-
cept Caleb the son of Jephunneh, the
Kenizzite, and Joshua the son of Nun, for
they have wholly followed the LORD.' 13So
the LORD's anger was aroused against Israel, and He made them wander in the
wilderness forty years, until all the generation that had done evil in the sight of the
LORD was gone. 14And look! You have risen
in your fathers' place, a brood of sinful
men, to increase still more the fierce anger
of the LORD against Israel. 15For if you
turn away from following Him, He will
once again leave them in the wilderness,
and you will destroy all these people."

16Then they came near to him and
said: "We will build sheepfolds here for
our livestock, and cities for our little
ones, 17but we ourselves will be armed,
ready *to go* before the children of Israel
until we have brought them to their
place; and our little ones will dwell in the
fortified cities because of the inhabitants
of the land. 18We will not return to our
homes until every one of the children of
Israel has received his inheritance. 19For
we will not inherit with them on the
other side of the Jordan and beyond, because our inheritance has fallen to us on
this eastern side of the Jordan."

20Then Moses said to them: "If you do
this thing, if you arm yourselves before
the LORD for the war, 21and all your armed
men cross over the Jordan before the
LORD until He has driven out His enemies
from before Him, 22and the land is subdued before the LORD, then afterward you
may return and be blameless before the
LORD and before Israel; and this land
shall be your possession before the LORD.
23But if you do not do so, then take note,
you have sinned against the LORD; and be
sure your sin will find you out. 24Build
cities for your little ones and folds for
your sheep, and do what has proceeded
out of your mouth."

> I believe in Christianity as I believe that the sun has risen: not only because I see it, but because by it I see everything else.
>
> **C. S. LEWIS**

25And the children of Gad and the
children of Reuben spoke to Moses, saying: "Your servants will do as my lord
commands. 26Our little ones, our wives,
our flocks, and all our livestock will be
there in the cities of Gilead; 27but your
servants will cross over, every man armed
for war, before the LORD to battle, just as
my lord says."

28So Moses gave command concerning
them to Eleazar the priest, to Joshua the
son of Nun, and to the chief fathers of the
tribes of the children of Israel. 29And
Moses said to them: "If the children of
Gad and the children of Reuben cross over
the Jordan with you, every man armed
for battle before the LORD, and the land is

32:23 Sin will always find us out. It attracts the wrath of the Law of God, like a tornado to a trailer park.

subdued before you, then you shall give them the land of Gilead as a possession. [30]But if they do not cross over armed with you, they shall have possessions among you in the land of Canaan."

[31]Then the children of Gad and the children of Reuben answered, saying: "As the LORD has said to your servants, so we will do. [32]We will cross over armed before the LORD into the land of Canaan, but the possession of our inheritance *shall remain* with us on this side of the Jordan."

[33]So Moses gave to the children of Gad, to the children of Reuben, and to half the tribe of Manasseh the son of Joseph, the kingdom of Sihon king of the Amorites and the kingdom of Og king of Bashan, the land with its cities within the borders, the cities of the surrounding country. [34]And the children of Gad built Dibon and Ataroth and Aroer, [35]Atroth and Shophan and Jazer and Jogbehah, [36]Beth Nimrah and Beth Haran, fortified cities, and folds for sheep. [37]And the children of Reuben built Heshbon and Elealeh and Kirjathaim, [38]Nebo and Baal Meon (*their* names being changed) and Shibmah; and they gave *other* names to the cities which they built.

[39]And the children of Machir the son of Manasseh went to Gilead and took it, and dispossessed the Amorites who *were* in it. [40]So Moses gave Gilead to Machir the son of Manasseh, and he dwelt in it. [41]Also Jair the son of Manasseh went and took its small towns, and called them Havoth Jair.[a] [42]Then Nobah went and took Kenath and its villages, and he called it Nobah, after his own name.

Israel's Journey from Egypt Reviewed

33 These *are* the journeys of the children of Israel, who went out of the land of Egypt by their armies under the hand of Moses and Aaron. [2]Now Moses wrote down the starting points of their journeys at the command of the LORD. And these *are* their journeys according to their starting points:

[3]They departed from Rameses in the first month, on the fifteenth day of the first month; on the day after the Passover the children of Israel went out with boldness in the sight of all the Egyptians. [4]For the Egyptians were burying all *their* firstborn, whom the LORD had killed among them. Also on their gods the LORD had executed judgments.

[5]Then the children of Israel moved from Rameses and camped at Succoth. [6]They departed from Succoth and camped at Etham, which *is* on the edge of the wilderness. [7]They moved from Etham and turned back to Pi Hahiroth, which *is* east of Baal Zephon; and they camped near Migdol. [8]They departed from before Hahiroth[a] and passed through the midst of the sea into the wilderness, went three days' journey in the Wilderness of Etham, and camped at Marah. [9]They moved from Marah and came to Elim. At Elim *were* twelve springs of water and seventy palm trees; so they camped there.

[10]They moved from Elim and camped by the Red Sea. [11]They moved from the Red Sea and camped in the Wilderness of Sin. [12]They journeyed from the Wilderness of Sin and camped at Dophkah. [13]They departed from Dophkah and camped at Alush. [14]They moved from Alush and camped at Rephidim, where there was no water for the people to drink.

[15]They departed from Rephidim and camped in the Wilderness of Sinai. [16]They moved from the Wilderness of Sinai and camped at Kibroth Hattaavah. [17]They departed from Kibroth Hattaavah and camped at Hazeroth. [18]They departed from Hazeroth and camped at Rithmah. [19]They departed from Rithmah and camped at Rimmon Perez. [20]They departed from Rimmon Perez and camped at Libnah. [21]They moved from Libnah and camped at Rissah. [22]They journeyed from Rissah and camped at Kehelathah. [23]They went from Kehelathah and camped at Mount Shepher. [24]They moved from Mount Shepher

32:41 [a]Literally *Towns of Jair* **33:8** [a]Many Hebrew manuscripts, Samaritan Pentateuch, Syriac, Targum, and Vulgate read *from Pi Hahiroth* (compare verse 7).

and camped at Haradah. 25They moved
from Haradah and camped at Makheloth.
26They moved from Makheloth and
camped at Tahath. 27They departed from
Tahath and camped at Terah. 28They moved
from Terah and camped at Mithkah. 29They
went from Mithkah and camped at Hash-
monah. 30They departed from Hashmo-
nah and camped at Moseroth. 31They departed from Moseroth and camped at Bene
Jaakan. 32They moved from Bene Jaakan
and camped at Hor Hagidgad. 33They went
from Hor Hagidgad and camped at Jotbathah. 34They moved from Jotbathah
and camped at Abronah. 35They departed
from Abronah and camped at Ezion Geber.
36They moved from Ezion Geber and
camped in the Wilderness of Zin, which
is Kadesh. 37They moved from Kadesh and
camped at Mount Hor, on the boundary
of the land of Edom.

38Then Aaron the priest went up to
Mount Hor at the command of the LORD,
and died there in the fortieth year after
the children of Israel had come out of the
land of Egypt, on the first *day* of the fifth
month. 39Aaron *was* one hundred and
twenty-three years old when he died on
Mount Hor.

40Now the king of Arad, the Canaanite, who dwelt in the South in the land of
Canaan, heard of the coming of the children of Israel.

41So they departed from Mount Hor
and camped at Zalmonah. 42They departed
from Zalmonah and camped at Punon.
43They departed from Punon and camped
at Oboth. 44They departed from Oboth
and camped at Ije Abarim, at the border
of Moab. 45They departed from Ijim[a] and
camped at Dibon Gad. 46They moved from
Dibon Gad and camped at Almon Diblathaim. 47They moved from Almon Diblathaim and camped in the mountains of Abarim, before Nebo. 48They departed from
the mountains of Abarim and camped in
the plains of Moab by the Jordan, *across
from* Jericho. 49They camped by the Jordan, from Beth Jesimoth as far as the Abel
Acacia Grove[a] in the plains of Moab.

Instructions for the Conquest of Canaan

50Now the LORD spoke to Moses in the
plains of Moab by the Jordan, *across from*
Jericho, saying, 51"Speak to the children
of Israel, and say to them: 'When you have
crossed the Jordan into the land of Canaan, 52then you shall drive out all the inhabitants of the land from before you, destroy all their engraved stones, destroy all
their molded images, and demolish all their
high places; 53you shall dispossess *the inhabitants of* the land and dwell in it, for I
have given you the land to possess. 54And
you shall divide the land by lot as an inheritance among your families; to the
larger you shall give a larger inheritance,
and to the smaller you shall give a smaller
inheritance; there everyone's *inheritance*
shall be whatever falls to him by lot. You
shall inherit according to the tribes of
your fathers. 55But if you do not drive out
the inhabitants of the land from before
you, then it shall be that those whom you
let remain *shall be* irritants in your eyes
and thorns in your sides, and they shall

33:45 [a]Same as *Ije Abarim*, verse 44 33:49 [a]Hebrew *Abel Shittim*

33:51–55 "All who, without commission from God, dare to execute private revenge, and who, from ambition, covetousness, or resentment, wage war and desolate kingdoms, must one day answer for it. But if God, instead of sending an earthquake, a pestilence, or a famine, be pleased to authorize and command any people to avenge his cause, such a commission surely is just and right. The Israelites could show such a commission, though no persons now can do so. Their wars were begun and carried on expressly by Divine direction, and they were enabled to conquer by miracles. Unless it can be proved that the wicked Canaanites did not deserve their doom, objectors only prove their dislike to God, and their love to his enemies. Man makes light of the evil of sin, but God abhors it. This explains the terrible executions of the nations which had filled the measure of their sins." *Matthew Henry*

harass you in the land where you dwell. [56]Moreover it shall be *that* I will do to you as I thought to do to them.' "

The Appointed Boundaries of Canaan

34 Then the LORD spoke to Moses, saying, [2]"Command the children of Israel, and say to them: 'When you come into the land of Canaan, this *is* the land that shall fall to you as an inheritance—the land of Canaan to its boundaries. [3]Your southern border shall be from the Wilderness of Zin along the border of Edom; then your southern border shall extend eastward to the end of the Salt Sea; [4]your border shall turn from the southern side of the Ascent of Akrabbim, continue to Zin, and be on the south of Kadesh Barnea; then it shall go on to Hazar Addar, and continue to Azmon; [5]the border shall turn from Azmon to the Brook of Egypt, and it shall end at the Sea.

[6]'As for the western border, you shall have the Great Sea for a border; this shall be your western border.

[7]'And this shall be your northern border: From the Great Sea you shall mark out your *border* line to Mount Hor; [8]from Mount Hor you shall mark out *your border* to the entrance of Hamath; then the direction of the border shall be toward Zedad; [9]the border shall proceed to Ziphron, and it shall end at Hazar Enan. This shall be your northern border.

[10]'You shall mark out your eastern border from Hazar Enan to Shepham; [11]the border shall go down from Shepham to Riblah on the east side of Ain; the border shall go down and reach to the eastern side of the Sea of Chinnereth; [12]the border shall go down along the Jordan, and it shall end at the Salt Sea. This shall be your land with its surrounding boundaries.' "

[13]Then Moses commanded the children of Israel, saying: "This *is* the land which you shall inherit by lot, which the LORD has commanded to give to the nine tribes and to the half-tribe. [14]For the tribe of the children of Reuben according to the house of their fathers, and the tribe of the children of Gad according to the house of their fathers, have received *their inheritance;* and the half-tribe of Manasseh has received its inheritance. [15]The two tribes and the half-tribe have received their inheritance on this side of the Jordan, *across from* Jericho eastward, toward the sunrise."

The Leaders Appointed to Divide the Land

[16]And the LORD spoke to Moses, saying, [17]"These *are* the names of the men who shall divide the land among you as an inheritance: Eleazar the priest and Joshua the son of Nun. [18]And you shall take one leader of every tribe to divide the land for the inheritance. [19]These *are* the names of the men: from the tribe of Judah, Caleb the son of Jephunneh; [20]from the tribe of the children of Simeon, Shemuel the son of Ammihud; [21]from the tribe of Benjamin, Elidad the son of Chislon; [22]a leader from the tribe of the children of Dan, Bukki the son of Jogli; [23]from the sons of Joseph: a leader from the tribe of the children of Manasseh, Hanniel the son of Ephod, [24]and a leader from the tribe of the children of Ephraim, Kemuel the son of Shiphtan; [25]a leader from the tribe of the children of Zebulun, Elizaphan the son of Parnach; [26]a leader from the tribe of the children of Issachar, Paltiel the son of Azzan; [27]a leader from the tribe of the children of Asher, Ahihud the son of Shelomi; [28]and a leader from the tribe of the children of Naphtali, Pedahel the son of Ammihud."

[29]These *are* the ones the LORD commanded to divide the inheritance among the children of Israel in the land of Canaan.

Cities for the Levites

35 And the LORD spoke to Moses in the plains of Moab by the Jordan *across from* Jericho, saying: [2]"Command the children of Israel that they give the Levites cities to dwell in from the inheri-

tance of their possession, and you shall *also* give the Levites common-land around the cities. 3They shall have the cities to dwell in; and their common-land shall be for their cattle, for their herds, and for all their animals. 4The common-land of the cities which you will give the Levites *shall extend* from the wall of the city outward a thousand cubits all around. 5And you shall measure outside the city on the east side two thousand cubits, on the south side two thousand cubits, on the west side two thousand cubits, and on the north side two thousand cubits. The city *shall be* in the middle. This shall belong to them as common-land for the cities.

6"Now among the cities which you will give to the Levites *you shall appoint* six cities of refuge, to which a manslayer may flee. And to these you shall add forty-two cities. 7So all the cities you will give to the Levites *shall be* forty-eight; these *you shall give* with their common-land. 8And the cities which you will give *shall be* from the possession of the children of Israel; from the larger *tribe* you shall give many, from the smaller you shall give few. Each shall give some of its cities to the Levites, in proportion to the inheritance that each receives."

Cities of Refuge

9Then the LORD spoke to Moses, saying, 10"Speak to the children of Israel, and say to them: 'When you cross the Jordan into the land of Canaan, 11then you shall appoint cities to be cities of refuge for you, that the manslayer who kills any person accidentally may flee there. 12They shall be cities of refuge for you from the avenger, that the manslayer may not die until he stands before the congregation in judgment. 13And of the cities which you give, you shall have six cities of refuge. 14You shall appoint three cities on this side of the Jordan, and three cities you shall appoint in the land of Canaan, *which* will be cities of refuge. 15These six cities shall be for refuge for the children of Israel, for the stranger, and for the sojourner among them, that anyone who kills a person accidentally may flee there.

16'But if he strikes him with an iron implement, so that he dies, he *is* a murderer; the murderer shall surely be put to death. 17And if he strikes him with a stone in the hand, by which one could die, and he does die, he *is* a murderer; the murderer shall surely be put to death. 18Or *if* he strikes him with a wooden hand weapon, by which one could die, and he does die, he *is* a murderer; the murderer shall surely be put to death. 19The avenger of blood himself shall put the murderer to death; when he meets him, he shall put him to death. 20If he pushes him out of hatred or, while lying in wait, hurls something at him so that he dies, 21or in enmity he strikes him with his hand so that he dies, the one who struck *him* shall surely be put to death. He *is* a murderer. The avenger of blood shall put the murderer to death when he meets him.

22'However, if he pushes him suddenly without enmity, or throws anything at him without lying in wait, 23or uses a stone, by which a man could die, throwing *it* at him without seeing *him*, so that he dies, while he was not his enemy or seeking his harm, 24then the congregation shall judge between the manslayer and the avenger of blood according to these judgments. 25So the congregation shall deliver the manslayer from the hand of the avenger of blood, and the congregation shall return him to the city of refuge where he had fled, and he shall remain there until the death of the high priest who was anointed with the holy oil. 26But if the manslayer at any time goes outside the limits of the city of refuge where he fled, 27and the avenger of blood finds him outside the limits of his city of refuge, and the avenger of blood kills the manslayer, he shall not be guilty of blood, 28because he should have remained in his city of refuge until the death of the high priest. But after the death of the high priest the manslayer may return to the land of

his possession.

29'And these *things* shall be a statute of judgment to you throughout your generations in all your dwellings. 30Whoever kills a person, the murderer shall be put to death on the testimony of witnesses; but one witness is not *sufficient* testimony against a person for the death *penalty*. 31Moreover you shall take no ransom for the life of a murderer who *is* guilty of death, but he shall surely be put to death. 32And you shall take no ransom for him who has fled to his city of refuge, that he may return to dwell in the land before the death of the priest. 33So you shall not pollute the land where you *are;* for blood defiles the land, and no atonement can be made for the land, for the blood that is shed on it, except by the blood of him who shed it. 34Therefore do not defile the land which you inhabit, in the midst of which I dwell; for I the LORD dwell among the children of Israel.' "

Marriage of Female Heirs

36 Now the chief fathers of the families of the children of Gilead the son of Machir, the son of Manasseh, of the families of the sons of Joseph, came near and spoke before Moses and before the leaders, the chief fathers of the children of Israel. 2And they said: "The LORD commanded my lord *Moses* to give the land as an inheritance by lot to the children of Israel, and my lord was commanded by the LORD to give the inheritance of our brother Zelophehad to his daughters. 3Now if they are married to any of the sons of the *other* tribes of the children of Israel, then their inheritance will be taken from the inheritance of our fathers, and it will be added to the inheritance of the tribe into which they marry; so it will be taken from the lot of our inheritance. 4And when the Jubilee of the children of Israel comes, then their inheritance will be added to the inheritance of the tribe into which they marry; so their inheritance will be taken away from the inheritance of the tribe of our fathers."

5Then Moses commanded the children of Israel according to the word of the LORD, saying: "What the tribe of the sons of Joseph speaks is right. 6This *is* what the LORD commands concerning the daughters of Zelophehad, saying, 'Let them marry whom they think best, but they may marry only within the family of their father's tribe.' 7So the inheritance of the children of Israel shall not change hands from tribe to tribe, for every one of the children of Israel shall keep the inheritance of the tribe of his fathers. 8And every daughter who possesses an inheritance in any tribe of the children of Israel shall be the wife of one of the family of her father's tribe, so that the children of Israel each may possess the inheritance of his fathers. 9Thus no inheritance shall change hands from *one* tribe to another, but every tribe of the children of Israel shall keep its own inheritance."

10Just as the LORD commanded Moses, so did the daughters of Zelophehad; 11for Mahlah, Tirzah, Hoglah, Milcah, and Noah, the daughters of Zelophehad, were married to the sons of their father's brothers. 12They were married into the families of the children of Manasseh the son of Joseph, and their inheritance remained in the tribe of their father's family.

13These *are* the commandments and the judgments which the LORD commanded the children of Israel by the hand of Moses in the plains of Moab by the Jordan, *across from* Jericho.

35:27 "He who does not take the step of faith, and so enter upon the road to heaven, will perish. It will be an awful thing to die just outside the gate of life. Almost saved, but altogether lost! This is the most terrible of positions. A man just outside Noah's ark would have been drowned; a manslayer close to the wall of the city of refuge, but yet outside of it, would be slain; and the man who is within a yard of Christ, and yet has not trusted him, will be lost." *Charles Spurgeon*

Deuteronomy

The Previous Command to Enter Canaan

1 These *are* the words which Moses
spoke to all Israel on this side of the
Jordan in the wilderness, in the plain[a]
opposite Suph,[b] between Paran, Tophel,
Laban, Hazeroth, and Dizahab. 2*It is* eleven
days' *journey* from Horeb by way of Mount
Seir to Kadesh Barnea. 3Now it came to
pass in the fortieth year, in the eleventh
month, on the first *day* of the month,
that Moses spoke to the children of Israel
according to all that the LORD had given
him as commandments to them, 4after
he had killed Sihon king of the Amorites,
who dwelt in Heshbon, and Og king of
Bashan, who dwelt at Ashtaroth in[a] Edrei.
5On this side of the Jordan in the land
of Moab, Moses began to explain this law,
saying, 6"The LORD our God spoke to us
in Horeb, saying: 'You have dwelt long
enough at this mountain. 7Turn and take
your journey, and go to the mountains of
the Amorites, to all the neighboring *places*
in the plain,[a] in the mountains and in the
lowland, in the South and on the seacoast, to the land of the Canaanites and
to Lebanon, as far as the great river, the
River Euphrates. 8See, I have set the land
before you; go in and possess the land
which the LORD swore to your fathers—
to Abraham, Isaac, and Jacob—to give to
them and their descendants after them.'

Tribal Leaders Appointed

9"And I spoke to you at that time, saying: 'I alone am not able to bear you.
10The LORD your God has multiplied you,
and here you *are* today, as the stars of
heaven in multitude. 11May the LORD God
of your fathers make you a thousand times
more numerous than you are, and bless
you as He has promised you! 12How can
I alone bear your problems and your burdens and your complaints? 13Choose wise,
understanding, and knowledgeable men
from among your tribes, and I will make
them heads over you.' 14And you answered
me and said, 'The thing which you have
told *us* to do *is* good.' 15So I took the heads
of your tribes, wise and knowledgeable
men, and made them heads over you,
leaders of thousands, leaders of hundreds,
leaders of fifties, leaders of tens, and officers for your tribes.
16"Then I commanded your judges at
that time, saying, 'Hear *the cases* between

1:1 [a]Hebrew *arabah* [b]One manuscript of the Septuagint, also Targum and Vulgate, read *Red Sea.* 1:4 [a]Septuagint, Syriac, and Vulgate read *and* (compare Joshua 12:4). 1:7 [a]Hebrew *arabah*

1:1–8 We also have a land that God has set before us. It is the promised land of the kingdom of God. We are to contend for the faith and compel sinners to come in. If you have never shared your faith, take courage, and do it. Ask someone what he thinks happens after we die, and let him do the talking. Just hearing people share their thoughts on the subject will help you to deal with your own fears. For more encouragement, see Prov. 29:25 comment.

your brethren, and judge righteously between a man and his brother or the stranger who is with him. 17You shall not show partiality in judgment; you shall hear the small as well as the great; you shall not be afraid in any man's presence, for the judgment *is* God's. The case that is too hard for you, bring to me, and I will hear it.' 18And I commanded you at that time all the things which you should do.

Israel's Refusal to Enter the Land

19"So we departed from Horeb, and went through all that great and terrible wilderness which you saw on the way to the mountains of the Amorites, as the LORD our God had commanded us. Then we came to Kadesh Barnea. 20And I said to you, 'You have come to the mountains of the Amorites, which the LORD our God is giving us. 21Look, the LORD your God has set the land before you; go up *and* possess *it,* as the LORD God of your fathers has spoken to you; do not fear or be discouraged.'

22"And every one of you came near to me and said, 'Let us send men before us, and let them search out the land for us, and bring back word to us of the way by which we should go up, and of the cities into which we shall come.'

23"The plan pleased me well; so I took twelve of your men, one man from *each* tribe. 24And they departed and went up into the mountains, and came to the Valley of Eshcol, and spied it out. 25They also took *some* of the fruit of the land in their hands and brought *it* down to us; and they brought back word to us, saying, '*It is* a good land which the LORD our God is giving us.'

26"Nevertheless you would not go up, but rebelled against the command of the LORD your God; 27and you complained in your tents, and said, 'Because the LORD hates us, He has brought us out of the land of Egypt to deliver us into the hand of the Amorites, to destroy us. 28Where can we go up? Our brethren have discouraged our hearts, saying, "The people *are* greater and taller than we; the cities *are* great and fortified up to heaven; moreover we have seen the sons of the Anakim there." '

29"Then I said to you, 'Do not be terrified, or afraid of them. 30The LORD your God, who goes before you, He will fight for you, according to all He did for you in Egypt before your eyes, 31and in the wilderness where you saw how the LORD your God carried you, as a man carries his son, in all the way that you went until you came to this place.' 32Yet, for all that, you did not believe the LORD your God, 33who went in the way before you to search out a place for you to pitch your tents, to show you the way you should go, in the fire by night and in the cloud by day.

The Penalty for Israel's Rebellion

34"And the LORD heard the sound of your words, and was angry, and took an oath, saying, 35'Surely not one of these men of this evil generation shall see that good land of which I swore to give to your fa-

---

1:19 "Moses reminds the Israelites of their march from Horeb to Kadesh-barnea, through that great and terrible wilderness. He shows how near they were to a happy settlement in Canaan. It will aggravate the eternal ruin of hypocrites, that they were not far from the kingdom of God. As if it were not enough that they were sure of their God before them, they would send men before them. Never any looked into the Holy Land, but they must own it to be a good land. And was there any cause to distrust this God? An unbelieving heart was at the bottom of all this. All disobedience to God's laws, and distrust of his power and goodness, flow from disbelief of his word, as all true obedience springs from faith.

"It is profitable for us to divide our past lives into distinct periods; to give thanks to God for the mercies we have received in each, to confess and seek the forgiveness of all the sins we can remember; and thus to renew our acceptance of God's salvation, and our surrender of ourselves to his service. Our own plans seldom avail to good purpose; while courage in the exercise of faith, and in the path of duty, enables the believer to follow the Lord fully, to disregard all that opposes, to triumph over all opposition, and to take firm hold upon the promised blessings." *Matthew Henry*

thers, [36]except Caleb the son of Jephunneh; he shall see it, and to him and his children I am giving the land on which he walked, because he wholly followed the LORD.' [37]The LORD was also angry with me for your sakes, saying, 'Even you shall not go in there. [38]Joshua the son of Nun, who stands before you, he shall go in there. Encourage him, for he shall cause Israel to inherit it.

[39]'Moreover your little ones and your children, who you say will be victims, who today have no knowledge of good and evil, they shall go in there; to them I will give it, and they shall possess it. [40]But *as for* you, turn and take your journey into the wilderness by the Way of the Red Sea.'

[41]"Then you answered and said to me, 'We have sinned against the LORD; we will go up and fight, just as the LORD our God commanded us.' And when everyone of you had girded on his weapons of war, you were ready to go up into the mountain. [42]"And the LORD said to me, 'Tell them, "Do not go up nor fight, for I *am* not among you; lest you be defeated before your enemies." ' [43]So I spoke to you; yet you would not listen, but rebelled against the command of the LORD, and presumptuously went up into the mountain. [44]And the Amorites who dwelt in that mountain came out against you and chased you as bees do, and drove you back from Seir to Hormah. [45]Then you returned and wept before the LORD, but the LORD would not listen to your voice nor give ear to you.

[46]"So you remained in Kadesh many days, according to the days that you spent *there.*

The Desert Years

2 "Then we turned and journeyed into the wilderness of the Way of the Red Sea, as the LORD spoke to me, and we skirted Mount Seir for many days.

[2]"And the LORD spoke to me, saying: [3]'You have skirted this mountain long enough; turn northward. [4]And command the people, saying, "You *are about to* pass through the territory of your brethren, the descendants of Esau, who live in Seir; and they will be afraid of you. Therefore watch yourselves carefully. [5]Do not meddle with them, for I will not give you *any* of their land, no, not so much as one footstep, because I have given Mount Seir to Esau *as* a possession. [6]You shall buy food from them with money, that you may eat; and you shall also buy water from them with money, that you may drink.

[7]"For the LORD your God has blessed you in all the work of your hand. He knows your trudging through this great wilderness. These forty years the LORD your God *has been* with you; you have lacked nothing." '

[8]"And when we passed beyond our brethren, the descendants of Esau who dwell in Seir, away from the road of the plain, away from Elath and Ezion Geber, we turned and passed by way of the Wilderness of Moab. [9]Then the LORD said to me, 'Do not harass Moab, nor contend with them in battle, for I will not give you *any* of their land *as* a possession, because I have given Ar to the descendants of Lot *as* a possession.' "

[10](The Emim had dwelt there in times past, a people as great and numerous and tall as the Anakim. [11]They were also regarded as giants,[a] like the Anakim, but the Moabites call them Emim. [12]The Horites formerly dwelt in Seir, but the descendants of Esau dispossessed them and

2:11 [a]Hebrew *rephaim*

1:43 Never be concerned that taking the initiative in reaching out to the lost is "presumption." To have presumption is to have "an arrogant taking for granted." If you fear God you will never have that attitude. Preach the Word "in season and out of season," using any means to save some (see 1 Cor. 9:19–22).

2:9 The Holy Spirit forbade the disciples to take the gospel to Asia (see Acts 16:6). Obviously, God has His perfect timing and purposes. So don't feel bad if you can't seem to get through to some people. Simply back off and pray for them.

destroyed them from before them, and
dwelt in their place, just as Israel did to
the land of their possession which the
LORD gave them.)
13“ ‘Now rise and cross over the Valley
of the Zered.’ So we crossed over the Valley of the Zered. 14And the time we took to
come from Kadesh Barnea until we crossed
over the Valley of the Zered *was* thirty-
eight years, until all the generation of the
men of war was consumed from the midst
of the camp, just as the LORD had sworn
to them. 15For indeed the hand of the
LORD was against them, to destroy them
from the midst of the camp until they
were consumed.

> I hate to hear the terrors of the Lord proclaimed by men whose hard visages, harsh tones, and unfeeling spirit betray a sort of doctrinal desiccation: all the milk of human kindness is dried out of them.
>
> **CHARLES SPURGEON**

16“So it was, when all the men of war
had finally perished from among the people, 17that the LORD spoke to me, saying:
18‘This day you are to cross over at Ar, the
boundary of Moab. 19And *when* you come
near the people of Ammon, do not harass
them or meddle with them, for I will not
give you *any* of the land of the people of
Ammon *as* a possession, because I have
given it to the descendants of Lot *as* a
possession.’ ”
20(That was also regarded as a land of
giants;[a] giants formerly dwelt there. But
the Ammonites call them Zamzummim,
21a people as great and numerous and tall
as the Anakim. But the LORD destroyed
them before them, and they dispossessed
them and dwelt in their place, 22just as
He had done for the descendants of Esau,
who dwelt in Seir, when He destroyed
the Horites from before them. They dispossessed them and dwelt in their place,
even to this day. 23And the Avim, who
dwelt in villages as far as Gaza—the
Caphtorim, who came from Caphtor, destroyed them and dwelt in their place.)
24“ ‘Rise, take your journey, and cross
over the River Arnon. Look, I have given
into your hand Sihon the Amorite, king
of Heshbon, and his land. Begin to possess *it*, and engage him in battle. 25This
day I will begin to put the dread and fear
of you upon the nations under the whole
heaven, who shall hear the report of you,
and shall tremble and be in anguish because of you.’

King Sihon Defeated

26“And I sent messengers from the
Wilderness of Kedemoth to Sihon king of
Heshbon, with words of peace, saying,
27‘Let me pass through your land; I will
keep strictly to the road, and I will turn
neither to the right nor to the left. 28You
shall sell me food for money, that I may
eat, and give me water for money, that I
may drink; only let me pass through on
foot, 29just as the descendants of Esau
who dwell in Seir and the Moabites who
dwell in Ar did for me, until I cross the
Jordan to the land which the LORD our
God is giving us.’
30“But Sihon king of Heshbon would
not let us pass through, for the LORD your
God hardened his spirit and made his heart
obstinate, that He might deliver him into
your hand, as *it is* this day.
31“And the LORD said to me, ‘See, I have
begun to give Sihon and his land over to
you. Begin to possess *it*, that you may inherit his land.’ 32Then Sihon and all his
people came out against us to fight at Jahaz. 33And the LORD our God delivered
him over to us; so we defeated him, his
sons, and all his people. 34We took all his
cities at that time, and we utterly destroyed the men, women, and little ones
of every city; we left none remaining.
35We took only the livestock as plunder
for ourselves, with the spoil of the cities
which we took. 36From Aroer, which *is*
on the bank of the River Arnon, and *from*
the city that *is* in the ravine, as far as

2:20 [a]Hebrew *rephaim*

QUESTIONS & OBJECTIONS

3:6

"What kind of God would sanction the killing of women and children?"

Let me tell you about my father. When I was young, he regularly left my mother and us three kids to fend for ourselves. I was there when he killed a helpless animal with his bare hands. Not only that, but he hit me (often). Based on this information, you could be justified in believing that my father was a tyrant. However, there is some missing information. The reason he left us each day was to work to earn money to provide food, clothing, and shelter for us. He killed the animal because it had been hit by a car and was in agony. He put it out of its misery, and it grieved him to do so. He regularly chastened me because he loved me enough to teach me right from wrong (I was a brat).

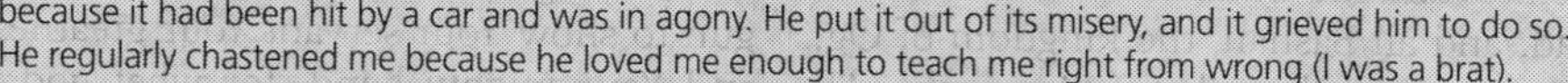

So, now you have a balanced view of my dad. He was a loving father and a very compassionate man.

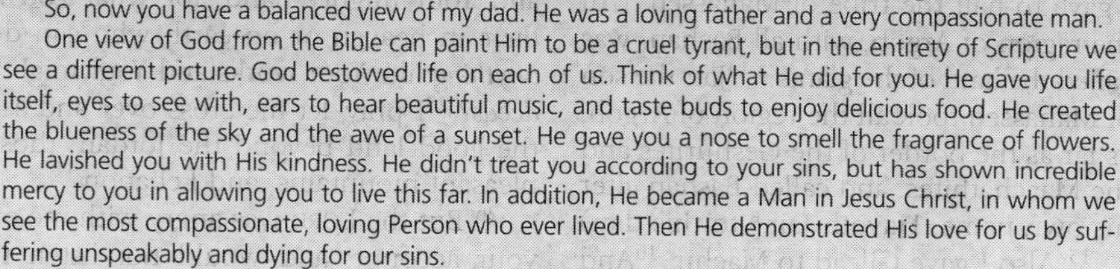

One view of God from the Bible can paint Him to be a cruel tyrant, but in the entirety of Scripture we see a different picture. God bestowed life on each of us. Think of what He did for you. He gave you life itself, eyes to see with, ears to hear beautiful music, and taste buds to enjoy delicious food. He created the blueness of the sky and the awe of a sunset. He gave you a nose to smell the fragrance of flowers. He lavished you with His kindness. He didn't treat you according to your sins, but has shown incredible mercy to you in allowing you to live this far. In addition, He became a Man in Jesus Christ, in whom we see the most compassionate, loving Person who ever lived. Then He demonstrated His love for us by suffering unspeakably and dying for our sins.

With that extra knowledge, it's easy for me to look at anything God did and say, "All His judgments are true and righteous altogether" (Psa. 19:9). Some will say, "But He instigated the deaths of men, women, and children!" Yes, and He did that with the whole of humanity. The Judge of the universe said, "The soul who sins shall die" (Ezek. 18:4). God proclaimed the death sentence on every man, woman, and child. But this same God of justice is rich in mercy and will grant everlasting life to every man, woman, and child who will humble themselves, repent of their sin, and trust in Jesus Christ.

Gilead, there was not one city too strong
for us; the LORD our God delivered all to
us. 37Only you did not go near the land
of the people of Ammon—anywhere
along the River Jabbok, or to the cities of
the mountains, or wherever the LORD our
God had forbidden us.

King Og Defeated

3 "Then we turned and went up the
road to Bashan; and Og king of Bashan
came out against us, he and all his people,
to battle at Edrei. 2And the LORD said to
me, 'Do not fear him, for I have delivered
him and all his people and his land into
your hand; you shall do to him as you
did to Sihon king of the Amorites, who
dwelt at Heshbon.'

3"So the LORD our God also delivered
into our hands Og king of Bashan, with
all his people, and we attacked him until
he had no survivors remaining. 4And we
took all his cities at that time; there was
not a city which we did not take from
them: sixty cities, all the region of Argob,
the kingdom of Og in Bashan. 5All these
cities *were* fortified with high walls, gates,
and bars, besides a great many rural towns.
6And we utterly destroyed them, as we
did to Sihon king of Heshbon, utterly destroying
the men, women, and children
of every city. 7But all the livestock and the
spoil of the cities we took as booty for
ourselves.

8"And at that time we took the land
from the hand of the two kings of the
Amorites who *were* on this side of the Jordan,
from the River Arnon to Mount Hermon
9(the Sidonians call Hermon Sirion,
and the Amorites call it Senir), 10all the
cities of the plain, all Gilead, and all
Bashan, as far as Salcah and Edrei, cities
of the kingdom of Og in Bashan.

11"For only Og king of Bashan remained
of the remnant of the giants.[a] Indeed his
bedstead *was* an iron bedstead. (*Is* it not

3:11 [a]Hebrew *rephaim*

in Rabbah of the people of Ammon?) Nine cubits *is* its length and four cubits its width, according to the standard cubit.

The Land East of the Jordan Divided

12"And this land, *which* we possessed at that time, from Aroer, which *is* by the River Arnon, and half the mountains of Gilead and its cities, I gave to the Reubenites and the Gadites. 13The rest of Gilead, and all Bashan, the kingdom of Og, I gave to half the tribe of Manasseh. (All the region of Argob, with all Bashan, was called the land of the giants.[a] 14Jair the son of Manasseh took all the region of Argob, as far as the border of the Geshurites and the Maachathites, and called Bashan after his own name, Havoth Jair,[a] to this day.)

15"Also I gave Gilead to Machir. 16And to the Reubenites and the Gadites I gave from Gilead as far as the River Arnon, the middle of the river as *the* border, as far as the River Jabbok, the border of the people of Ammon; 17the plain also, with the Jordan as *the* border, from Chinnereth as far as the east side of the Sea of the Arabah (the Salt Sea), below the slopes of Pisgah.

18"Then I commanded you at that time, saying: 'The LORD your God has given you this land to possess. All you men of valor shall cross over armed before your brethren, the children of Israel. 19But your wives, your little ones, and your livestock (I know that you have much livestock) shall stay in your cities which I have given you, 20until the LORD has given rest to your brethren as to you, and they also possess the land which the LORD your God is giving them beyond the Jordan. Then each of you may return to his possession which I have given you.'

21"And I commanded Joshua at that time, saying, 'Your eyes have seen all that the LORD your God has done to these two kings; so will the LORD do to all the kingdoms through which you pass. 22You must not fear them, for the LORD your God Himself fights for you.'

Moses Forbidden to Enter the Land

23"Then I pleaded with the LORD at that time, saying: 24'O Lord GOD, You have begun to show Your servant Your greatness and Your mighty hand, for what god *is there* in heaven or on earth who can do *anything* like Your works and Your mighty *deeds*? 25I pray, let me cross over and see the good land beyond the Jordan, those pleasant mountains, and Lebanon.'

26"But the LORD was angry with me on your account, and would not listen to me. So the LORD said to me: 'Enough of that! Speak no more to Me of this matter. 27Go up to the top of Pisgah, and lift your eyes toward the west, the north, the south, and the east; behold *it* with your eyes, for you shall not cross over this Jordan. 28But command Joshua, and encourage him and strengthen him; for he shall go over before this people, and he shall cause them to inherit the land which you will see.'

29"So we stayed in the valley opposite Beth Peor.

Moses Commands Obedience

4 "Now, O Israel, listen to the statutes and the judgments which I teach you to observe, that you may live, and go in and possess the land which the LORD God of your fathers is giving you. 2You shall not add to the word which I command you, nor take from it, that you may keep the commandments of the LORD

3:13 [a]Hebrew *rephaim* 3:14 [a]Literally *Towns of Jair*

3:24 We haven't even begun to see the greatness of Almighty God.

"Pray that God might raise up men who would see the beauty of the Lord our God and would begin to preach it and hold it out to people, instead of offering peace of mind, deliverance from cigarettes, a better job and nicer cottage... What good is all our busy religion if God isn't in it? What good is it if we've lost majesty, reverence, worship—an awareness of the divine?" *A. W. Tozer*

The Function of the Law

4:1 "The Law of the Lord is perfect, converting the soul: the testimony of the Lord is sure, making wise the simple: the statutes of the Lord are right, rejoicing the heart: the commandment of the Lord is pure, enlightening the eyes (Psa. 19:7,8). Now the question for you and me is—are we keeping these Commandments? Have we fulfilled all the requirements of the Law? If God made us, as we know He did, He had a right to make that Law; and if we don't use it aright it would have been better for us if we had never had it, for it will condemn us. We shall be found wanting. The Law is all right, but are we right?" *D. L. Moody*

your God which I command you. 3Your
eyes have seen what the LORD did at Baal
Peor; for the LORD your God has destroyed
from among you all the men who followed Baal of Peor. 4But you who held
fast to the LORD your God *are* alive today,
every one of you.

5"Surely I have taught you statutes and
judgments, just as the LORD my God
commanded me, that you should act according *to them* in the land which you go
to possess. 6Therefore be careful to observe *them;* for this *is* your wisdom and
your understanding in the sight of the
peoples who will hear all these statutes,
and say, 'Surely this great nation *is* a wise
and understanding people.'

7"For what great nation *is there* that
has God *so* near to it, as the LORD our
God *is* to us, for whatever *reason* we may
call upon Him? 8And what great nation *is*
there that has *such* statutes and righteous
judgments as are in all this law which I
set before you this day? 9Only take heed
to yourself, and diligently keep yourself,
lest you forget the things your eyes have
seen, and lest they depart from your heart
all the days of your life. And teach them
to your children and your grandchildren,
10*especially concerning* the day you stood
before the LORD your God in Horeb,
when the LORD said to me, 'Gather the
people to Me, and I will let them hear My
words, that they may learn to fear Me all
the days they live on the earth, and *that*
they may teach their children.'

11"Then you came near and stood at
the foot of the mountain, and the mountain burned with fire to the midst of
heaven, with darkness, cloud, and thick
darkness. 12And the LORD spoke to you
out of the midst of the fire. You heard the
sound of the words, but saw no form; *you*
only *heard* a voice. 13So He declared to you
His covenant which He commanded you
to perform, the Ten Commandments; and
He wrote them on two tablets of stone.
14And the LORD commanded me at that
time to teach you statutes and judgments,
that you might observe them in the land
which you cross over to possess.

Beware of Idolatry

15"Take careful heed to yourselves, for
you saw no form when the LORD spoke to
you at Horeb out of the midst of the fire,
16lest you act corruptly and make for
yourselves a carved image in the form of
any figure: the likeness of male or female,
17the likeness of any animal that *is* on the
earth or the likeness of any winged bird
that flies in the air, 18the likeness of anything that creeps on the ground or the
likeness of any fish that *is* in the water beneath the earth. 19And *take heed,* lest you
lift your eyes to heaven, and *when* you see
the sun, the moon, and the stars, all the
host of heaven, you feel driven to worship
them and serve them, which the LORD

4:9,10 Parents who don't make time for family devotions should not be mystified when their children turn from the things of God in their teenage years. If you love your children enough to be concerned for their eternal welfare, be sure to build a solid spiritual foundation for them during their impressionable years (see Psa. 78:4,5). For how to have a "family altar," see Josh. 4:21,22 comment.

4:13 No other nation had this great advantage. No race of people had the Creator actually speak to them and show them the holy standard that He required. The Law's perfection drove them to trust in His mercy and seek justification by faith alone. See Rom. 3:1,2 and Heb. 11:20–31.

Springboards for Preaching and Witnessing

A Consuming Fire

4:24 If you were to place a dried leaf into the presence of fire, you would notice that the fire would not hesitate to consume the leaf in a matter of seconds. The fire must consume the leaf because of its very nature. Even if the fire didn't want to dispose of the leaf, it wouldn't matter; it still must consume it because their natures are diametrically opposed to one other.

Our God is a consuming fire. By His very nature, God must consume anything and everything that opposes His nature. We must put on the Lord Jesus Christ, or we will be consumed by the ever-pure, burning holiness of the King of kings. In a fire, the only safe place is where it has already burned. On Judgment Day, the only place of safety is where God's wrath has already been—Christ.

your God has given to all the peoples under the whole heaven as a heritage. 20But
the LORD has taken you and brought you
out of the iron furnace, out of Egypt, to
be His people, an inheritance, as you are
this day. 21Furthermore the LORD was angry with me for your sakes, and swore
that I would not cross over the Jordan,
and that I would not enter the good land
which the LORD your God is giving you as
an inheritance. 22But I must die in this
land, I must not cross over the Jordan;
but you shall cross over and possess that
good land. 23Take heed to yourselves, lest
you forget the covenant of the LORD your
God which He made with you, and make
for yourselves a carved image in the form
of anything which the LORD your God has
forbidden you. 24For the LORD your God is
a consuming fire, a jealous God.
25"When you beget children and grandchildren and have grown old in the land,
and act corruptly and make a carved image in the form of anything, and do evil
in the sight of the LORD your God to provoke Him to anger, 26I call heaven and
earth to witness against you this day, that
you will soon utterly perish from the land
which you cross over the Jordan to possess; you will not prolong *your* days in it,
but will be utterly destroyed. 27And the
LORD will scatter you among the peoples,
and you will be left few in number among
the nations where the LORD will drive
you. 28And there you will serve gods, the
work of men's hands, wood and stone,
which neither see nor hear nor eat nor
smell. 29But from there you will seek the
LORD your God, and you will find *Him* if
you seek Him with all your heart and
with all your soul. 30When you are in distress, and all these things come upon you
in the latter days, when you turn to the
LORD your God and obey His voice 31(for
the LORD your God *is* a merciful God), He
will not forsake you nor destroy you, nor
forget the covenant of your fathers which
He swore to them.
32"For ask now concerning the days
that are past, which were before you, since
the day that God created man on the
earth, and *ask* from one end of heaven to
the other, whether *any* great *thing* like
this has happened, or *anything* like it has
been heard. 33Did *any* people *ever* hear
the voice of God speaking out of the midst
of the fire, as you have heard, and live?
34Or did God *ever* try to go *and* take for
Himself a nation from the midst of *another* nation, by trials, by signs, by wonders, by war, by a mighty hand and an
outstretched arm, and by great terrors,

4:29 "I believe the reason why so few find Christ is that they do not search for Him with all their hearts; they are not terribly in earnest about their souls' salvation." *D. L. Moody*

4:30,31 This verse is applicable to contemporary Israel. Most present-day Jews are secular and give little attention to the Scriptures. With the buildup of nuclear arms, and the deep-rooted hatred of Israel in the surrounding Arab nations, it is only a matter of time until "tribulation" comes to the tiny nation. However, they have the promise that if they turn to the Lord, He will be faithful and deliver them from their enemies.

4:32 *Evolution: Happy Coincidence*

Notice how awkwardly physicist Freeman J. Dyson of Princeton's Institute for Advanced Study tries to explain the design of the universe without God:

> As we look out into the universe and identify *the many accidents* of physics and astronomy that have worked to our benefit, it almost seems as if the universe must in some sense have known that we were coming.

Physicist and Nobel laureate Arno Penzias, in contemplating this amazing design in our universe, came to a similar conclusion:

> Astronomy leads us to a unique event, a universe that was created out of nothing and delicately balanced to provide exactly the conditions required to support life. In the absence of an *absurdly improbable accident*, the observations of modern science seem to suggest an underlying, one might say, supernatural plan.

Speaking of the "absurdly improbable," Harvard paleontologist Stephen Jay Gould described humans as "a glorious accident" of evolution which required *60 trillion contingent events*. With cosmologists estimating the Earth to be 4.55 billion years old, to accomplish those 60 trillion events would require more than 36 necessary events per day, each day for 4.55 billion years—just to get *Homo sapiens*. And conveniently, each of these 36 daily new events just happened to occur in the right place at the right time in the right sequence. And this doesn't take into account the astronomical number of "accidents" necessary to form the tens, perhaps hundreds of thousands of separate ecosystems.

One individual put it this way: The odds would be better of getting hit by lightning at the moment you won the Powerball lottery while dying in the crash of a plane that got struck by a meteor. But then, such things don't happen every day.

In 1950, in his book *The Nature of the Universe*, astronomer Sir Fred Hoyle also argued for accidental coincidence to explain the many unique but necessary properties of the universe and of our own planet. But the discoveries of the following thirty years dramatically changed his mind, as described in his book *The Intelligent Universe*. In 1983 he wrote, "Such properties seem to run through the fabric of the natural world like a thread of *happy coincidences*. But there are so many *odd coincidences* essential to life that some explanation seems required to account for them."

It is easy to understand why many scientists like Hoyle have changed their minds in recent years. It doesn't take a rocket scientist to figure out that this amazing universe cannot be explained as a series of happy coincidental accidents, the result of a thinking universe that "knew we were coming." This is why Frederic B. Burnham, a well-known historian of science, declared, "The scientific community is prepared to consider the idea that God created the universe a more respectable hypothesis today than at any time in the last 100 years."

Michael Ruse, a preeminent evolutionist, wrote in *New Scientist*: "An increasing number of scientists, most particularly a growing number of evolutionists . . . argue that Darwinian evolutionary theory is no genuine scientific theory at all . . . Many of the critics have the highest intellectual credentials." (Adapted from *How to Know God Exists*.)

"It would be very difficult to explain why the universe should have begun in just this way, except as the act of a God who intended to create beings like us." *Stephen Hawking*

"We are, by astronomical standards, a pampered, cosseted, cherished group of creatures . . . If the Universe had not been made with the most exacting precision we could never have come into existence. It is my view that these circumstances indicate the universe was created for man to live in." *John O'Keefe*, NASA astronomer

according to all that the LORD your God
did for you in Egypt before your eyes?
35 To you it was shown, that you might
know that the LORD Himself *is* God; *there*
is none other besides Him. 36 Out of heav-
en He let you hear His voice, that He might
instruct you; on earth He showed you
His great fire, and you heard His words
out of the midst of the fire. 37 And because
He loved your fathers, therefore He chose
their descendants after them; and He
brought you out of Egypt with His Presence, with His mighty power, 38 driving
out from before you nations greater and
mightier than you, to bring you in, to give
you their land *as* an inheritance, as *it is*
this day. 39 Therefore know this day, and
consider *it* in your heart, that the LORD
Himself *is* God in heaven above and on
the earth beneath; *there is* no other. 40 You

shall therefore keep His statutes and His
commandments which I command you
today, that it may go well with you and
with your children after you, and that
you may prolong *your* days in the land
which the LORD your God is giving you
for all time."

Cities of Refuge East of the Jordan

41Then Moses set apart three cities on
this side of the Jordan, toward the rising
of the sun, 42that the manslayer might flee
there, who kills his neighbor unintentionally, without having hated him in time
past, and that by fleeing to one of these
cities he might live: 43Bezer in the wilderness on the plateau for the Reubenites,
Ramoth in Gilead for the Gadites, and
Golan in Bashan for the Manassites.

Introduction to God's Law

44Now this *is* the law which Moses set
before the children of Israel. 45These *are*
the testimonies, the statutes, and the judgments which Moses spoke to the children
of Israel after they came out of Egypt,
46on this side of the Jordan, in the valley
opposite Beth Peor, in the land of Sihon
king of the Amorites, who dwelt at Heshbon, whom Moses and the children of Israel defeated after they came out of Egypt.
47And they took possession of his land
and the land of Og king of Bashan, two
kings of the Amorites, who *were* on this
side of the Jordan, toward the rising of
the sun, 48from Aroer, which *is* on the bank
of the River Arnon, even to Mount Sion[a]
(that is, Hermon), 49and all the plain on
the east side of the Jordan as far as the Sea
of the Arabah, below the slopes of Pisgah.

The Ten Commandments Reviewed

5 And Moses called all Israel, and said
to them: "Hear, O Israel, the statutes
and judgments which I speak in your
hearing today, that you may learn them
and be careful to observe them. 2The LORD
our God made a covenant with us in
Horeb. 3The LORD did not make this covenant with our fathers, but with us, those
who *are* here today, all of us who *are*
alive. 4The LORD talked with you face to
face on the mountain from the midst of
the fire. 5I stood between the LORD and
you at that time, to declare to you the
word of the LORD; for you were afraid because of the fire, and you did not go up
the mountain. *He* said:

6'I *am* the LORD your God who brought
you out of the land of Egypt, out
of the house of bondage.
7'You shall have no other gods before
Me.
8'You shall not make for yourself a
carved image—any likeness *of*
anything that *is* in heaven above,
or that *is* in the earth beneath, or
that *is* in the water under the
earth; 9you shall not bow down
to them nor serve them. For I,
the LORD your God, *am* a jealous
God, visiting the iniquity of the
fathers upon the children to the
third and fourth *generations* of
those who hate Me, 10but
showing mercy to thousands, to
those who love Me and keep My
commandments.
11'You shall not take the name of the
LORD your God in vain, for the
LORD will not hold *him* guiltless
who takes His name in vain.
12'Observe the Sabbath day, to keep it
holy, as the LORD your God
commanded you. 13Six days you
shall labor and do all your work,
14but the seventh day *is* the
Sabbath of the LORD your God. *In*
it you shall do no work: you, nor

4:48 [a]Syriac reads *Sirion* (compare 3:9).

5:8,9 The Catholic Catechism, the official teachings of the Roman Catholic church, omits the Second Commandment about idols. For details on Roman Catholicism, see page 1810. See also Mic. 5:13 comment.

your son, nor your daughter, nor
your male servant, nor your
female servant, nor your ox, nor
your donkey, nor any of your
cattle, nor your stranger who *is*
within your gates, that your male
servant and your female servant
may rest as well as you. [15]And
remember that you were a slave
in the land of Egypt, and the
LORD your God brought you out
from there by a mighty hand and
by an outstretched arm; therefore
the LORD your God commanded
you to keep the Sabbath day.

[16]'Honor your father and your mother,
as the LORD your God has
commanded you, that your days
may be long, and that it may be
well with you in the land which
the LORD your God is giving you.

[17]'You shall not murder.

[18]'You shall not commit adultery.

[19]'You shall not steal.

[20]'You shall not bear false witness
against your neighbor.

[21]'You shall not covet your neighbor's
wife; and you shall not desire
your neighbor's house, his field,
his male servant, his female
servant, his ox, his donkey, or
anything that *is* your neighbor's.'

[22]"These words the Lord spoke to all
your assembly, in the mountain
from the midst of the fire, the
cloud, and the thick darkness,
with a loud voice; and He added
no more. And He wrote them on
two tablets of stone and gave
them to me.

The People Afraid of God's Presence

[23]"So it was, when you heard the voice
from the midst of the darkness, while the
mountain was burning with fire, that you
came near to me, all the heads of your
tribes and your elders. [24]And you said:
'Surely the LORD our God has shown us
His glory and His greatness, and we have
heard His voice from the midst of the fire.
We have seen this day that God speaks
with man; yet he *still* lives. [25]Now therefore, why should we die? For this great
fire will consume us; if we hear the voice
of the LORD our God anymore, then we
shall die. [26]For who *is there* of all flesh
who has heard the voice of the living God
speaking from the midst of the fire, as we
have, and lived? [27]You go near and hear
all that the LORD our God may say, and
tell us all that the LORD our God says to
you, and we will hear and do *it.*'

[28]"Then the LORD heard the voice of
your words when you spoke to me, and
the LORD said to me: 'I have heard the
voice of the words of this people which
they have spoken to you. They are right
in all that they have spoken. [29]Oh, that
they had such a heart in them that they
would fear Me and always keep all My
commandments, that it might be well with
them and with their children forever! [30]Go
and say to them, "Return to your tents."
[31]But as for you, stand here by Me, and I
will speak to you all the commandments,
the statutes, and the judgments which
you shall teach them, that they may observe *them* in the land which I am giving
them to possess.'

[32]"Therefore you shall be careful to do
as the LORD your God has commanded
you; you shall not turn aside to the right
hand or to the left. [33]You shall walk in all
the ways which the LORD your God has
commanded you, that you may live and
that it may be well with you, and *that* you
may prolong *your* days in the land which
you shall possess.

The Greatest Commandment

6 "Now this *is* the commandment, *and*
these are the statutes and judgments

5:29 This is the cry of the very heart of God—that we would fear Him and keep His Commandments, and all would be well with us forever.

which the LORD your God has commanded to teach you, that you may observe *them* in the land which you are crossing over to possess, 2that you may fear the LORD your God, to keep all His statutes and His commandments which I command you, you and your son and your grandson, all the days of your life, and that your days may be prolonged. 3Therefore hear, O Israel, and be careful to observe *it,* that it may be well with you, and that you may multiply greatly as the LORD God of your fathers has promised you—'a land flowing with milk and honey.'[a]

4"Hear, O Israel: The LORD our God, the LORD *is* one![a] 5You shall love the LORD your God with all your heart, with all your soul, and with all your strength.

6"And these words which I command you today shall be in your heart. 7You shall teach them diligently to your children, and shall talk of them when you sit in your house, when you walk by the way, when you lie down, and when you rise up. 8You shall bind them as a sign on your hand, and they shall be as frontlets between your eyes. 9You shall write them on the doorposts of your house and on your gates.

Caution Against Disobedience

10"So it shall be, when the LORD your God brings you into the land of which He swore to your fathers, to Abraham, Isaac, and Jacob, to give you large and beautiful cities which you did not build, 11houses full of all good things, which you did not fill, hewn-out wells which you did not dig, vineyards and olive trees which you did not plant—when you have eaten and are full— 12*then* beware, lest you forget the LORD who brought you out of the land of Egypt, from the house of bondage. 13You shall fear the LORD your God and serve Him, and shall take oaths in His name. 14You shall not go after other gods, the gods of the peoples who *are* all around you 15(for the LORD your God *is* a jealous God among you), lest the anger of the LORD your God be aroused against you and destroy you from the face of the earth.

16"You shall not tempt the LORD your God as you tempted *Him* in Massah. 17You shall diligently keep the commandments of the LORD your God, His testimonies, and His statutes which He has commanded you. 18And you shall do *what is* right and good in the sight of the LORD, that it may be well with you, and that you may go in and possess the good land of which the LORD swore to your fathers, 19to cast out all your enemies from before you, as the LORD has spoken.

20"When your son asks you in time to come, saying, 'What *is the meaning of* the testimonies, the statutes, and the judgments which the LORD our God has commanded you?' 21then you shall say to your son: 'We were slaves of Pharaoh in Egypt, and the LORD brought us out of Egypt with a mighty hand; 22and the LORD showed signs and wonders before our eyes, great and severe, against Egypt, Pharaoh, and all his household. 23Then He brought us out from there, that He might bring us in, to give us the land of which He swore to our fathers. 24And the LORD commanded

6:3 [a]Exodus 3:8 **6:4** [a]Or *The LORD is our God, the LORD alone* (that is, the only one)

6:4 Jewish people refer to this verse as the *Shema*. For details on Jewish beliefs and how to reach Jews with the gospel, see page 1782.

6:5–9 This is a direct reference to the Ten Commandments (see 5:6–21). Teach your children the moral Law—not to improve their memory or to help them win an Awana contest, but to awaken their conscience and prepare the soil of their hearts for the life-giving seed of the gospel. Do it throughout your day, from the time you get up to the time you go to bed. This will instill in your children the knowledge of sin (see Rom. 3:19,20; 7:7,13), teaching them that it is wrong to disobey, lie, steal, covet, etc. The purpose of God's Law is to teach them the holiness of God, to show them their need for the Savior and bring them to the foot of a blood-stained cross (see Gal. 3:24). No wonder the enemy hates God's Law. See Prov. 22:6 comment.

QUESTIONS & OBJECTIONS

"Is there a difference in attending a wedding for a gay couple and one for a couple that is living together? What about if the bride is pregnant?"

The moral Law is spiritual, so anyone who has as much as looked with lust has committed adultery in the heart (see Matt. 5:27,28). It is therefore not unreasonable to conclude that in some way *every* couple has sinned sexually in God's eyes—whether they are physical adulterers, adulterers-at-heart, or fornicators, pregnant or not. However, by getting legally married they are fulfilling God's plan for a man and a woman, because He is the One who sanctioned the institution of marriage (see Gen. 2:24, Matt. 19:5,6). Every wedding I have attended falls into this category.

"Marriage" between homosexuals, on the other hand, has never been sanctioned by God. Marriage is God's institution and He said it is between a man and a woman. Two men or two women *cannot* be married. So when gays are "joined together in holy matrimony," it is as meaningless as a man being married to his dog or cat, hoping for God's blessing on bestiality. God has never authorized such a union, nor such behavior. God's Word says, "If a man lies with a male as he lies with a woman, both of them have committed an abomination" (Lev. 20:13). For more on marriage, see Deut. 22:13–21 comment.

us to observe all these statutes, to fear the
LORD our God, for our good always, that
He might preserve us alive, as *it is* this day.
[25]Then it will be righteousness for us, if
we are careful to observe all these commandments before the LORD our God, as
He has commanded us.'

A Chosen People

7 "When the LORD your God brings you
into the land which you go to possess, and has cast out many nations before
you, the Hittites and the Girgashites and
the Amorites and the Canaanites and the
Perizzites and the Hivites and the Jebusites, seven nations greater and mightier
than you, [2]and when the LORD your God
delivers them over to you, you shall conquer them *and* utterly destroy them. You
shall make no covenant with them nor
show mercy to them. [3]Nor shall you make
marriages with them. You shall not give
your daughter to their son, nor take their
daughter for your son. [4]For they will turn
your sons away from following Me, to
serve other gods; so the anger of the
LORD will be aroused against you and destroy you suddenly. [5]But thus you shall
deal with them: you shall destroy their altars, and break down their *sacred* pillars,
and cut down their wooden images,[a] and
burn their carved images with fire.
[6]"For you *are* a holy people to the LORD
your God; the LORD your God has chosen
you to be a people for Himself, a special
treasure above all the peoples on the face
of the earth. [7]The LORD did not set His love
on you nor choose you because you were
more in number than any other people,
for you were the least of all peoples; [8]but
because the LORD loves you, and because
He would keep the oath which He swore
to your fathers, the LORD has brought you
out with a mighty hand, and redeemed
you from the house of bondage, from the
hand of Pharaoh king of Egypt.
[9]"Therefore know that the LORD your
God, He *is* God, the faithful God who
keeps covenant and mercy for a thousand
generations with those who love Him and
keep His commandments; [10]and He repays
those who hate Him to their face, to destroy them. He will not be slack with him
who hates Him; He will repay him to his
face. [11]Therefore you shall keep the commandment, the statutes, and the judgments
which I command you today, to observe
them.

Blessings of Obedience

[12]"Then it shall come to pass, because
you listen to these judgments, and keep
and do them, that the LORD your God will
keep with you the covenant and the mercy

7:5 [a]Hebrew *Asherim*, Canaanite deities

which He swore to your fathers. 13And
He will love you and bless you and multiply you; He will also bless the fruit of
your womb and the fruit of your land,
your grain and your new wine and your
oil, the increase of your cattle and the offspring of your flock, in the land of which
He swore to your fathers to give you.
14You shall be blessed above all peoples;
there shall not be a male or female barren
among you or among your livestock.
15And the LORD will take away from you
all sickness, and will afflict you with none
of the terrible diseases of Egypt which you
have known, but will lay *them* on all those
who hate you. 16Also you shall destroy all
the peoples whom the LORD your God
delivers over to you; your eye shall have
no pity on them; nor shall you serve their
gods, for that *will be* a snare to you.
17"If you should say in your heart,
'These nations are greater than I; how can
I dispossess them?'— 18you shall not be
afraid of them, *but* you shall remember
well what the LORD your God did to
Pharaoh and to all Egypt: 19the great trials which your eyes saw, the signs and the
wonders, the mighty hand and the outstretched arm, by which the LORD your
God brought you out. So shall the LORD
your God do to all the peoples of whom
you are afraid. 20Moreover the LORD your
God will send the hornet among them
until those who are left, who hide themselves from you, are destroyed. 21You shall
not be terrified of them; for the LORD
your God, the great and awesome God, *is*
among you. 22And the LORD your God
will drive out those nations before you
little by little; you will be unable to destroy them at once, lest the beasts of the
field become *too* numerous for you. 23But
the LORD your God will deliver them over
to you, and will inflict defeat upon them
until they are destroyed. 24And He will
deliver their kings into your hand, and
you will destroy their name from under
heaven; no one shall be able to stand
against you until you have destroyed
them. 25You shall burn the carved images
of their gods with fire; you shall not covet
the silver or gold *that is* on them, nor take
it for yourselves, lest you be snared by it;
for it *is* an abomination to the LORD your
God. 26Nor shall you bring an abomination into your house, lest you be doomed
to destruction like it. You shall utterly detest it and utterly abhor it, for it *is* an accursed thing.

Remember the Lord Your God

8 "Every commandment which I command you today you must be careful
to observe, that you may live and multiply, and go in and possess the land of
which the LORD swore to your fathers.
2And you shall remember that the LORD
your God led you all the way these forty
years in the wilderness, to humble you
and test you, to know what *was* in your
heart, whether you would keep His commandments or not. 3So He humbled you,
allowed you to hunger, and fed you with
manna which you did not know nor did
your fathers know, that He might make
you know that man shall not live by
bread alone; but man lives by every *word*
that proceeds from the mouth of the LORD.
4Your garments did not wear out on you,
nor did your foot swell these forty years.
5You should know in your heart that as a
man chastens his son, *so* the LORD your
God chastens you.
6"Therefore you shall keep the commandments of the LORD your God, to
walk in His ways and to fear Him. 7For
the LORD your God is bringing you into a
good land, a land of brooks of water, of
fountains and springs, that flow out of
valleys and hills; 8a land of wheat and

7:25,26 Be sure you don't allow any idols in your home, even if they are souvenirs from an overseas trip. Don't sell or donate them, enabling them to influence others. Instead, follow the example of the new believers in Ephesus who burned their magic books (see Acts 19:19).

barley, of vines and fig trees and pomegranates, a land of olive oil and honey; [9]a
land in which you will eat bread without
scarcity, in which you will lack nothing; a
land whose stones *are* iron and out of
whose hills you can dig copper. [10]When
you have eaten and are full, then you shall
bless the LORD your God for the good
land which He has given you.
[11]"Beware that you do not forget the
LORD your God by not keeping His commandments, His judgments, and His statutes which I command you today, [12]lest
—*when* you have eaten and are full, and
have built beautiful houses and dwell *in*
them; [13]and *when* your herds and your
flocks multiply, and your silver and your
gold are multiplied, and all that you have
is multiplied; [14]when your heart is lifted
up, and you forget the LORD your God
who brought you out of the land of Egypt,
from the house of bondage; [15]who led
you through that great and terrible wilderness, *in which were* fiery serpents and
scorpions and thirsty land where there
was no water; who brought water for you
out of the flinty rock; [16]who fed you in
the wilderness with manna, which your
fathers did not know, that He might
humble you and that He might test you,
to do you good in the end— [17]then you say
in your heart, 'My power and the might
of my hand have gained me this wealth.'
[18]"And you shall remember the LORD
your God, for *it is* He who gives you
power to get wealth, that He may establish
His covenant which He swore to your fathers, as *it is* this day. [19]Then it shall be, if
you by any means forget the LORD your
God, and follow other gods, and serve
them and worship them, I testify against
you this day that you shall surely perish.
[20]As the nations which the LORD destroys
before you, so you shall perish, because
you would not be obedient to the voice of
the LORD your God.

Israel's Rebellions Reviewed

9 "Hear, O Israel: You *are* to cross over
the Jordan today, and go in to dispossess nations greater and mightier than
yourself, cities great and fortified up to
heaven, [2]a people great and tall, the descendants of the Anakim, whom you
know, and *of whom* you heard *it said,* 'Who
can stand before the descendants of
Anak?' [3]Therefore understand today that
the LORD your God *is* He who goes over
before you *as* a consuming fire. He will
destroy them and bring them down before you; so you shall drive them out and
destroy them quickly, as the LORD has said
to you.
[4]"Do not think in your heart, after the
LORD your God has cast them out before
you, saying, 'Because of my righteousness
the LORD has brought me in to possess
this land'; but *it is* because of the wickedness of these nations *that* the LORD is driving them out from before you. [5]*It is* not
because of your righteousness or the uprightness of your heart *that* you go in to
possess their land, but because of the
wickedness of these nations *that* the LORD
your God drives them out from before
you, and that He may fulfill the word
which the LORD swore to your fathers, to
Abraham, Isaac, and Jacob. [6]Therefore
understand that the LORD your God is not
giving you this good land to possess because of your righteousness, for you *are* a
stiff-necked people.
[7]"Remember! Do not forget how you
provoked the LORD your God to wrath in

8:11–14 Discipline yourself to read the Bible daily (v. 3). Let it search out your sin and remind you where you would be heading without the cross. If you forget the Word, you may just forget the cross, and get caught up in the things of this sinful world. For the importance of feeding on God's Word, see 1 Pet. 2:2 comment.

9:7 Partake regularly in communion, and as you eat the bread and drink of the cup, remember your past sins. God has forgotten them, but it is good for us to remember them for a moment to recall that we were once children of wrath wandering in the wilderness of sin. Such thoughts keep us at the foot of the cross, crying, "Grace alone!"

the wilderness. From the day that you departed from the land of Egypt until you came to this place, you have been rebellious against the LORD. [8]Also in Horeb you provoked the LORD to wrath, so that the LORD was angry *enough* with you to have destroyed you. [9]When I went up into the mountain to receive the tablets of stone, the tablets of the covenant which the LORD made with you, then I stayed on the mountain forty days and forty nights. I neither ate bread nor drank water. [10]Then the LORD delivered to me two tablets of stone written with the finger of God, and on them *were* all the words which the LORD had spoken to you on the mountain from the midst of the fire in the day of the assembly. [11]And it came to pass, at the end of forty days and forty nights, *that* the LORD gave me the two tablets of stone, the tablets of the covenant.

> I'd rather have people hate me with the knowledge that I tried to save them.
>
> **KEITH GREEN**

[12]"Then the LORD said to me, 'Arise, go down quickly from here, for your people whom you brought out of Egypt have acted corruptly; they have quickly turned aside from the way which I commanded them; they have made themselves a molded image.'

[13]"Furthermore the LORD spoke to me, saying, 'I have seen this people, and indeed they are a stiff-necked people. [14]Let Me alone, that I may destroy them and blot out their name from under heaven; and I will make of you a nation mightier and greater than they.'

[15]"So I turned and came down from the mountain, and the mountain burned with fire; and the two tablets of the covenant *were* in my two hands. [16]And I looked, and behold, you had sinned against the LORD your God—had made for yourselves a molded calf! You had turned aside quickly from the way which the LORD had commanded you. [17]Then I took the two tablets and threw them out of my two hands and broke them before your eyes. [18]And I fell down before the LORD, as at the first, forty days and forty nights; I neither ate bread nor drank water, because of all your sin which you committed in doing wickedly in the sight of the LORD, to provoke Him to anger. [19]For I was afraid of the anger and hot displeasure with which the LORD was angry with you, to destroy you. But the LORD listened to me at that time also. [20]And the LORD was very angry with Aaron *and* would have destroyed him; so I prayed for Aaron also at the same time. [21]Then I took your sin, the calf which you had made, and burned it with fire and crushed it *and* ground *it* very small, until it was as fine as dust; and I threw its dust into the brook that descended from the mountain.

[22]"Also at Taberah and Massah and Kibroth Hattaavah you provoked the LORD to wrath. [23]Likewise, when the LORD sent you from Kadesh Barnea, saying, 'Go up and possess the land which I have given you,' then you rebelled against the commandment of the LORD your God, and you did not believe Him nor obey His voice. [24]You have been rebellious against the LORD from the day that I knew you.

[25]"Thus I prostrated myself before the LORD; forty days and forty nights I kept prostrating myself, because the LORD had said He would destroy you. [26]Therefore I prayed to the LORD, and said: 'O Lord GOD, do not destroy Your people and Your inheritance whom You have redeemed through Your greatness, whom You have brought out of Egypt with a mighty hand. [27]Remember Your servants, Abraham, Isaac, and Jacob; do not look on the stubbornness of this people, or on their wickedness or their sin, [28]lest the land from which You brought us should say, "Because the LORD was not able to bring them to the land which He promised them, and because He hated them, He has brought them out to kill them in the wilderness." [29]Yet they *are* Your people and Your inheritance, whom You brought out by Your

POINTS FOR OPEN-AIR PREACHING

10:4

Ten for Ten

Offer $1 to anyone who can name ten beers. If someone names only five, give him a dollar "as a consolation prize." This creates good will with the crowd. Keep asking for other volunteers who can name ten. After that, offer $10 to anyone who can name all of the Ten Commandments, in order (very few can). That will get several people quoting the Commandments, making it easy for you to ask who has kept each one.

Then offer $20 to anyone who *proves* to be a good person. When taking someone through the Ten Commandments, appoint six people in the crowd to act as a jury (people are usually quick to judge the sins of others). That will help to engage the crowd, and it will take the heat off you. After giving the gospel it's good to say, "Thanks for being a good sport. You didn't prove to be a good person, so you don't get the $20. But I have something else for you. Here's $5 as a gift. You didn't earn it, but I'm giving it to you because I care for you. That's called 'grace.' God offers everlasting life as a gift to sinners, not because we earned it, but simply because of His amazing grace." Have the person come forward to receive the $5, then explain that it wasn't his until he received it. So it is with the gift of God.

mighty power and by Your outstretched arm.'

The Second Pair of Tablets

10 "At that time the LORD said to me, 'Hew for yourself two tablets of stone like the first, and come up to Me on the mountain and make yourself an ark of wood. 2And I will write on the tablets the words that were on the first tablets, which you broke; and you shall put them in the ark.'

3"So I made an ark of acacia wood, hewed two tablets of stone like the first, and went up the mountain, having the two tablets in my hand. 4And He wrote on the tablets according to the first writing, the Ten Commandments, which the LORD had spoken to you in the mountain from the midst of the fire in the day of the assembly; and the LORD gave them to me. 5Then I turned and came down from the mountain, and put the tablets in the ark which I had made; and there they are, just as the LORD commanded me."

6(Now the children of Israel journeyed from the wells of Bene Jaakan to Moserah, where Aaron died, and where he was buried; and Eleazar his son ministered as priest in his stead. 7From there they journeyed to Gudgodah, and from Gudgodah to Jotbathah, a land of rivers of water. 8At that time the LORD separated the tribe of Levi to bear the ark of the covenant of the LORD, to stand before the LORD to minister to Him and to bless in His name, to this day. 9Therefore Levi has no portion nor inheritance with his brethren; the LORD *is* his inheritance, just as the LORD your God promised him.)

10"As at the first time, I stayed in the mountain forty days and forty nights; the LORD also heard me at that time, *and* the LORD chose not to destroy you. 11Then the LORD said to me, 'Arise, begin *your* journey before the people, that they may go in and possess the land which I swore to their fathers to give them.'

The Essence of the Law

12"And now, Israel, what does the LORD your God require of you, but to fear the LORD your God, to walk in all His ways and to love Him, to serve the LORD your God with all your heart and with all your soul, 13*and* to keep the commandments of the LORD and His statutes which I command you today for your good? 14Indeed heaven and the highest heavens belong to the LORD your God, *also* the earth with all that *is* in it. 15The LORD delighted only in your fathers, to love them; and He chose their descendants after them, you above all peoples, as *it is* this day. 16Therefore circumcise the foreskin of your heart, and be stiff-necked no longer. 17For the LORD your God *is* God of gods and Lord of lords, the great God, mighty and awesome, who

Questions & Objections

10:12,13 ***"If we tell people to trust in Jesus to go to heaven and avoid hell, won't that motive create false converts?"***

Think of the story Jesus told of the prodigal son (see Luke 15:11–32). The father had great pleasure when the son came into a *right relationship* with him. The son cried, "Father, I have sinned against heaven and before you, and I am no longer worthy to be called your son" (vv. 18,19). Obviously, his father would not have rejoiced in the same way if a happy but impenitent son had returned with a prostitute on each arm. Obviously, it was the son's humble turning from his sinful lifestyle that pleased the father. The son's happiness was irrelevant; *righteousness* was the issue. The world has no concern for righteousness. Its chief goal is the prodigal's happiness, whether he is in or out of the pigsty.

Christianity's goal is absolute righteousness, which we are told in Scripture will ultimately result in the glory of God and the pleasure of man (see Psa. 16:11). That is why we must always focus on man's depravity (revealed by the moral Law) and God's righteousness (revealed in His Law and in the cross; see Rom. 1:16,17). The gap between depravity and holiness will reveal the need for righteousness. Happiness is irrelevant to the gospel proclamation, even though (because of God's kindness) it is ultimately the end result.

However, we need never feel any sense of guilt because someone responded to the gospel with a desire to live. It was self-preservation that motivated the prodigal to get up out of that pigsty ("I perish with hunger!"; Luke 15:17), and every sane human being likewise has been given an instinct for self-preservation. We have been endowed by our Creator with the good sense to know that life is better than death, and that heaven is better than hell. We came to Christ because of a hunger and a thirst for righteousness, and the ultimate end of righteousness will be "pleasures forevermore," to the glory of God. See also Ruth 2:12 comment.

shows no partiality nor takes a bribe.
18He administers justice for the fatherless
and the widow, and loves the stranger,
giving him food and clothing. 19Therefore
love the stranger, for you were strangers
in the land of Egypt. 20You shall fear the
LORD your God; you shall serve Him, and
to Him you shall hold fast, and take oaths
in His name. 21He *is* your praise, and He
is your God, who has done for you these
great and awesome things which your
eyes have seen. 22Your fathers went down
to Egypt with seventy persons, and now
the LORD your God has made you as the
stars of heaven in multitude.

Love and Obedience Rewarded

11 "Therefore you shall love the LORD
your God, and keep His charge,
His statutes, His judgments, and His commandments always. 2Know today that *I*
do not *speak* with your children, who
have not known and who have not seen
the chastening of the LORD your God, His
greatness and His mighty hand and His
outstretched arm— 3His signs and His
acts which He did in the midst of Egypt,
to Pharaoh king of Egypt, and to all his
land; 4what He did to the army of Egypt,
to their horses and their chariots: how He
made the waters of the Red Sea overflow

10:16 Bible contradiction? Skeptics argue that the Bible's statement that the covenant of circumcision is to be everlasting (Gen. 17:7,10–11) contradicts verses saying that the circumcision is of no consequence (Gal. 6:15).

The means by which a man is justified in God's sight isn't through circumcision or any external observance, but only through faith in Jesus Christ. In Gal. 6:13, Paul points out that "not even those who are circumcised keep the law." The outward symbolism is worthless for their salvation if their heart is not right with God: "For he is not a Jew who is one outwardly, nor is circumcision that which is outward in the flesh; but he is a Jew who is one inwardly; and circumcision is that of the heart, in the Spirit, not in the letter; whose praise is not from men but from God" (Rom. 2:28,29).

The "circumcision" that God desires is that of the heart, which occurs when a person is born again and receives a new heart and new spirit. That's why Paul writes, "For in Christ Jesus neither circumcision nor uncircumcision avails anything, but a new creation" (Gal. 6:15). See also Deut. 30:6.

them as they pursued you, and *how* the LORD has destroyed them to this day; 5what He did for you in the wilderness until you came to this place; 6and what He did to Dathan and Abiram the sons of Eliab, the son of Reuben: how the earth opened its mouth and swallowed them up, their households, their tents, and all the substance that *was* in their possession, in the midst of all Israel— 7but your eyes have seen every great act of the LORD which He did.

8"Therefore you shall keep every commandment which I command you today, that you may be strong, and go in and possess the land which you cross over to possess, 9and that you may prolong *your* days in the land which the LORD swore to give your fathers, to them and their descendants, 'a land flowing with milk and honey.'[a] 10For the land which you go to possess *is* not like the land of Egypt from which you have come, where you sowed your seed and watered *it* by foot, as a vegetable garden; 11but the land which you cross over to possess *is* a land of hills and valleys, which drinks water from the rain of heaven, 12a land for which the LORD your God cares; the eyes of the LORD your God *are* always on it, from the beginning of the year to the very end of the year.

13'And it shall be that if you earnestly obey My commandments which I command you today, to love the LORD your God and serve Him with all your heart and with all your soul, 14then I[a] will give *you* the rain for your land in its season, the early rain and the latter rain, that you may gather in your grain, your new wine, and your oil. 15And I will send grass in your fields for your livestock, that you may eat and be filled.' 16Take heed to yourselves, lest your heart be deceived, and you turn aside and serve other gods and worship them, 17lest the LORD's anger be aroused against you, and He shut up the heavens so that there be no rain, and the land yield no produce, and you perish quickly from the good land which the LORD is giving you.

18"Therefore you shall lay up these words of mine in your heart and in your soul, and bind them as a sign on your hand, and they shall be as frontlets between your eyes. 19You shall teach them to your children, speaking of them when you sit in your house, when you walk by the way, when you lie down, and when you rise up. 20And you shall write them on the doorposts of your house and on your gates, 21that your days and the days of your children may be multiplied in the land of which the LORD swore to your fathers to give them, like the days of the heavens above the earth.

22"For if you carefully keep all these commandments which I command you to do—to love the LORD your God, to walk in all His ways, and to hold fast to Him— 23then the LORD will drive out all these nations from before you, and you will dispossess greater and mightier nations than yourselves. 24Every place on which the sole of your foot treads shall be yours: from the wilderness and Lebanon, from the river, the River Euphrates, even to the Western Sea,[a] shall be your territory. 25No man shall be able to stand against you; the LORD your God will put the dread of you and the fear of you upon all the land where you tread, just as He has said to you.

26"Behold, I set before you today a blessing and a curse: 27the blessing, if you obey the commandments of the LORD your God which I command you today; 28and the curse, if you do not obey the commandments of the LORD your God, but turn aside from the way which I com-

11:9 [a]Exodus 3:8 **11:14** [a]Following Masoretic Text and Targum; Samaritan Pentateuch, Septuagint, and Vulgate read *He.* **11:24** [a]That is, the Mediterranean

11:14 May God send the rains of revival—and may we have the full grain of His Word, the wine of His Spirit, and the oil of joy.

11:19 *How to Bring Your Children to Christ*

Scripture tells us that God is "not willing that any should perish but that all should come to repentance" (2 Pet. 3:9). The words "any" and "all" include your children. Scripture also says that God wants *all* to be saved and to come to the knowledge of the truth (1 Tim. 2:4). So when we ask for what is in accordance with His will (1 John 5:14,15), we can confidently trust God to be at work in the lives of our children, drawing them toward the Savior.

Think of the process like a healthy pregnancy. The seed is planted in the womb, then God causes the miracle of gestation. During the growth period, all that is needed is for the mother to provide the proper nutrients for her developing child and to keep away from poisons such as drugs, alcohol, and cigarettes. When the baby is ready, the birth will happen at the right time.

Jesus said that one must be born again in order to see the kingdom of God (John 3:3). So in this spiritual pregnancy, for your children to be born again, you must plant the good seed of the pure Word of God (1 Pet. 1:23). You also need to ensure that you avoid toxins that will cause a stillbirth.

It is essential that you be aware of the biblical reality of true and false conversion. Do not assume that everyone who names the name of Christ is genuinely saved. Children are particularly vulnerable when it comes to false conversions. This is because parents and children's workers, rightly concerned for the children's eternal welfare, want them to be converted at an early age. However, it is often a "zeal without knowledge" if they are unaware of such as thing as spurious (false) conversion.

"Decisions for Christ" are easy to get from kids. Simply ask a group of children, "Kids, how do you live forever?" "By giving your heart to Jesus!" "Who wants to give their heart to Jesus?" A sea of hands wave—fifty decisions. All this accomplishes is giving the children, and ourselves, a false sense of assurance. Countless grieved parents say their children were "converted" at a very young age, but have since strayed into drugs, alcohol, sex, etc., usually in their teenage years. It is likely that these children had false conversions, a fact made evident when temptation came their way. A plant may seem healthy, but a burning hot sun will cause it to whither and die if it has a faulty root system or is in shallow soil. In addressing parents, Dr. Robert A. Morey says,

> While the desire to see your children saved is proper and necessary, some parents become so desperate to believe that their children are saved that they will grasp at anything. Even when their son or daughter openly denies the faith and engages in gross wickedness, they will still comfort themselves by saying, "Well, at least my son is saved. He may not act like it now but I know he is saved because he accepted Jesus when he was five years old. He doesn't go to church anymore and married [someone from a different religion] but I still say he is saved."
>
> Instead of facing the reality that their child is on his way to hell, some parents will cling to false hopes so they can sleep at night. But instead of seeking their own psychological comfort, they should seek the conversion of their child by telling him the truth.

The truth is that, for any child (or adult) to be saved, there must be an understanding of the nature of sin. He must turn from his sin and trust in Jesus to save him. Eternal life comes not from saying a prayer or making a decision, but from exercising "repentance toward God and faith toward our Lord Jesus Christ" (Acts 20:21). Leading a child in what is commonly called a "sinner's prayer," when there is no understanding of the true nature of sin, can do great damage. When these false converts fall away, they become bitter, and their latter end becomes worse than the first (see 2 Pet. 2:20) because they are inoculated against the truth. They think they "tried Jesus" when they were kids and it didn't work.

Genuine salvation must be a work of God. We can have as much a part in the spiritual birth of our children as we have in the planting of a tree. We can prepare the soil and water the seed, but it will grow only as God sees fit to cause it to do so. All we can do is make ready the soil of the child's heart, plant the pure seed of the Word of God, keep away harmful influences, and faithfully water it with believing prayer.

See also Exod. 12:26 comment.

(Adapted from *How to Bring Your Children to Christ...& Keep Them There.*)

mand you today, to go after other gods
which you have not known. 29Now it
shall be, when the LORD your God has
brought you into the land which you go
to possess, that you shall put the blessing
on Mount Gerizim and the curse on Mount
Ebal. 30*Are* they not on the other side of
the Jordan, toward the setting sun, in the

Questions & Objections

"We should do what's right just because it's right, not because of fear of punishment or promise of reward."

There are some who think their worldview is superior to Christianity, because they don't need to be threatened with punishment in order to do the right thing. However, such idealism is unrealistic—as our overflowing jails attest. Sin-laden sinners, with desperately wicked hearts, are incapable of such noble motives. That's why we have court systems that threaten punishment to lawbreakers. If we violate traffic rules we are punished by a ticket or even imprisonment. God has "wired" fallen sinners to respond to rewards and punishments. From the moment we are born, we have the ability to respond positively to a smile and negatively to a frown. We respond positively to incentives. We work toward a wage, run to win the medal, and climb to reach the highest peak. We also avoid certain behaviors because they come with a threat of punishment. Without fear of punishment, every man would do what is right in his own eyes. If you take a sinner through the Commandments, you will find that he does *not* do what's right.

"A man's ethical behavior should be based effectually on sympathy, education, and social ties; no religious basis is necessary. Man would indeed be in a poor way if he had to be restrained by fear of punishment and hope of reward after death." *Albert Einstein*

Jeffrey Dahmer, an infamous serial killer and atheist sentenced to 900 years in prison, said, "If a person doesn't think that there is a God to be accountable to, then what's the point of trying to modify your behavior to keep it within acceptable ranges?"

land of the Canaanites who dwell in the
plain opposite Gilgal, beside the terebinth
trees of Moreh? 31For you will cross over
the Jordan and go in to possess the land
which the LORD your God is giving you,
and you will possess it and dwell in it.
32And you shall be careful to observe all
the statutes and judgments which I set before you today.

A Prescribed Place of Worship

12 "These *are* the statutes and judgments which you shall be careful
to observe in the land which the LORD
God of your fathers is giving you to possess, all the days that you live on the
earth. 2You shall utterly destroy all the
places where the nations which you shall
dispossess served their gods, on the high
mountains and on the hills and under
every green tree. 3And you shall destroy
their altars, break their *sacred* pillars, and
burn their wooden images with fire; you
shall cut down the carved images of their
gods and destroy their names from that
place. 4You shall not worship the LORD
your God *with* such *things*.
5"But you shall seek the place where
the LORD your God chooses, out of all your
tribes, to put His name for His dwelling
place; and there you shall go. 6There you
shall take your burnt offerings, your sacrifices, your tithes, the heave offerings of
your hand, your vowed offerings, your
freewill offerings, and the firstborn of your
herds and flocks. 7And there you shall eat
before the LORD your God, and you shall
rejoice in all to which you have put your
hand, you and your households, in which
the LORD your God has blessed you.
8"You shall not at all do as we are doing here today—every man doing whatever *is* right in his own eyes— 9for as yet
you have not come to the rest and the inheritance which the LORD your God is
giving you. 10But *when* you cross over the
Jordan and dwell in the land which the
LORD your God is giving you to inherit,
and He gives you rest from all your enemies round about, so that you dwell in
safety, 11then there will be the place where
the LORD your God chooses to make His
name abide. There you shall bring all that
I command you: your burnt offerings,
your sacrifices, your tithes, the heave offerings of your hand, and all your choice
offerings which you vow to the LORD.
12And you shall rejoice before the LORD
your God, you and your sons and your
daughters, your male and female ser-

vants, and the Levite who *is* within your gates, since he has no portion nor inheritance with you. [13]Take heed to yourself that you do not offer your burnt offerings in every place that you see; [14]but in the place which the LORD chooses, in one of your tribes, there you shall offer your burnt offerings, and there you shall do all that I command you.

[15]"However, you may slaughter and eat meat within all your gates, whatever your heart desires, according to the blessing of the LORD your God which He has given you; the unclean and the clean may eat of it, of the gazelle and the deer alike. [16]Only you shall not eat the blood; you shall pour it on the earth like water. [17]You may not eat within your gates the tithe of your grain or your new wine or your oil, of the firstborn of your herd or your flock, of any of your offerings which you vow, of your freewill offerings, or of the heave offering of your hand. [18]But you must eat them before the LORD your God in the place which the LORD your God chooses, you and your son and your daughter, your male servant and your female servant, and the Levite who *is* within your gates; and you shall rejoice before the LORD your God in all to which you put your hands. [19]Take heed to yourself that you do not forsake the Levite as long as you live in your land.

[20]"When the LORD your God enlarges your border as He has promised you, and you say, 'Let me eat meat,' because you long to eat meat, you may eat as much meat as your heart desires. [21]If the place where the LORD your God chooses to put His name is too far from you, then you may slaughter from your herd and from your flock which the LORD has given you, just as I have commanded you, and you may eat within your gates as much as your heart desires. [22]Just as the gazelle and the deer are eaten, so you may eat them; the unclean and the clean alike may eat them. [23]Only be sure that you do not eat the blood, for the blood *is* the life; you may not eat the life with the meat. [24]You shall not eat it; you shall pour it on the earth like water. [25]You shall not eat it, that it may go well with you and your children after you, when you do *what is* right in the sight of the LORD. [26]Only the holy things which you have, and your vowed offerings, you shall take and go to the place which the LORD chooses. [27]And you shall offer your burnt offerings, the meat and the blood, on the altar of the LORD your God; and the blood of your sacrifices shall be poured out on the altar of the LORD your God, and you shall eat the meat. [28]Observe and obey all these words which I command you, that it may go well with you and your children after you forever, when you do *what is* good and right in the sight of the LORD your God.

. . . . . .

For how to teach your children the Ten Commandments, see Prov. 22:6 comment.

. . . . . .

Beware of False Gods

[29]"When the LORD your God cuts off from before you the nations which you go to dispossess, and you displace them and dwell in their land, [30]take heed to yourself that you are not ensnared to follow them, after they are destroyed from before you, and that you do not inquire after their gods, saying, 'How did these nations serve their gods? I also will do likewise.' [31]You shall not worship the LORD your God in that way; for every abomination to the LORD which He hates they have done to their gods; for they burn even their sons and daughters in the fire to their gods.

[32]"Whatever I command you, be care-

12:16 It seems that as we have become more godless as a nation, it has become popular to eat meat that barely touches the frying pan and is dripping with blood.

ful to observe it; you shall not add to it
nor take away from it.

Punishment of Apostates

13 "If there arises among you a prophet or a dreamer of dreams, and he
gives you a sign or a wonder, 2and the
sign or the wonder comes to pass, of which
he spoke to you, saying, 'Let us go after
other gods'—which you have not known
—'and let us serve them,' 3you shall not
listen to the words of that prophet or that
dreamer of dreams, for the LORD your God
is testing you to know whether you love
the LORD your God with all your heart
and with all your soul. 4You shall walk after the LORD your God and fear Him, and
keep His commandments and obey His
voice; you shall serve Him and hold fast
to Him. 5But that prophet or that dreamer
of dreams shall be put to death, because
he has spoken in order to turn *you* away
from the LORD your God, who brought
you out of the land of Egypt and redeemed
you from the house of bondage, to entice
you from the way in which the LORD your
God commanded you to walk. So you
shall put away the evil from your midst.
6"If your brother, the son of your
mother, your son or your daughter, the
wife of your bosom, or your friend who is
as your own soul, secretly entices you,
saying, 'Let us go and serve other gods,'
which you have not known, neither you
nor your fathers, 7of the gods of the people which *are* all around you, near to you
or far off from you, from *one* end of the
earth to the *other* end of the earth, 8you
shall not consent to him or listen to him,
nor shall your eye pity him, nor shall you
spare him or conceal him; 9but you shall
surely kill him; your hand shall be first
against him to put him to death, and afterward the hand of all the people. 10And
you shall stone him with stones until he
dies, because he sought to entice you away
from the LORD your God, who brought
you out of the land of Egypt, from the
house of bondage. 11So all Israel shall hear
and fear, and not again do such wickedness as this among you.
12"If you hear someone in one of your
cities, which the LORD your God gives
you to dwell in, saying, 13'Corrupt men
have gone out from among you and enticed the inhabitants of their city, saying,
"Let us go and serve other gods" '—
which you have not known— 14then you
shall inquire, search out, and ask diligently. And *if it is* indeed true *and* certain
that such an abomination was committed
among you, 15you shall surely strike the
inhabitants of that city with the edge of
the sword, utterly destroying it, all that is
in it and its livestock—with the edge of
the sword. 16And you shall gather all its
plunder into the middle of the street, and
completely burn with fire the city and all
its plunder, for the LORD your God. It
shall be a heap forever; it shall not be built
again. 17So none of the accursed things
shall remain in your hand, that the LORD
may turn from the fierceness of His anger
and show you mercy, have compassion
on you and multiply you, just as He swore
to your fathers, 18because you have listened to the voice of the LORD your God,
to keep all His commandments which I
command you today, to do *what is* right
in the eyes of the LORD your God.

Improper Mourning

14 "You *are* the children of the LORD
your God; you shall not cut yourselves nor shave the front of your head
for the dead. 2For you *are* a holy people
to the LORD your God, and the LORD has
chosen you to be a people for Himself, a
special treasure above all the peoples
who *are* on the face of the earth.

Clean and Unclean Meat

3"You shall not eat any detestable thing.
4These *are* the animals which you may

13:1–5 Such warnings should motivate us to make sure the image of God that we preach is biblical.

eat: the ox, the sheep, the goat, 5the deer, the gazelle, the roe deer, the wild goat, the mountain goat,[a] the antelope, and the mountain sheep. 6And you may eat every animal with cloven hooves, having the hoof split into two parts, *and that* chews the cud, among the animals. 7Nevertheless, of those that chew the cud or have cloven hooves, you shall not eat, *such as* these: the camel, the hare, and the rock hyrax; for they chew the cud but do not have cloven hooves; they *are* unclean for you. 8Also the swine is unclean for you, because it has cloven hooves, yet *does* not *chew* the cud; you shall not eat their flesh or touch their dead carcasses.

9"These you may eat of all that *are* in the waters: you may eat all that have fins and scales. 10And whatever does not have fins and scales you shall not eat; it *is* unclean for you.

11"All clean birds you may eat. 12But these you shall not eat: the eagle, the vulture, the buzzard, 13the red kite, the falcon, and the kite after their kinds; 14every raven after its kind; 15the ostrich, the short-eared owl, the sea gull, and the hawk after their kinds; 16the little owl, the screech owl, the white owl, 17the jackdaw, the carrion vulture, the fisher owl, 18the stork, the heron after its kind, and the hoopoe and the bat.

19"Also every creeping thing that flies is unclean for you; they shall not be eaten.

20"You may eat all clean birds.

21"You shall not eat anything that dies *of itself;* you may give it to the alien who *is* within your gates, that he may eat it, or you may sell it to a foreigner; for you *are* a holy people to the LORD your God.

"You shall not boil a young goat in its mother's milk.

Tithing Principles

22"You shall truly tithe all the increase of your grain that the field produces year by year. 23And you shall eat before the LORD your God, in the place where He chooses to make His name abide, the tithe of your grain and your new wine and your oil, of the firstborn of your herds and your flocks, that you may learn to fear the LORD your God always. 24But if the journey is too long for you, so that you are not able to carry *the tithe, or* if the place where the LORD your God chooses to put His name is too far from you, when the LORD your God has blessed you, 25then you shall exchange *it* for money, take the money in your hand, and go to the place which the LORD your God chooses. 26And you shall spend that money for whatever your heart desires: for oxen or sheep, for wine or similar drink, for whatever your heart desires; you shall eat there before the LORD your God, and you shall rejoice, you and your household. 27You shall not forsake the Levite who *is* within your gates, for he has no part nor inheritance with you.

28"At the end of *every* third year you shall bring out the tithe of your produce of that year and store *it* up within your gates. 29And the Levite, because he has no portion nor inheritance with you, and the stranger and the fatherless and the

14:5 [a]Or *addax*

14:22–29 Tithes. "A second portion from the produce of their land was required. The whole appointment evidently was against the covetousness, distrust, and selfishness of the human heart. It promoted friendliness, liberality, and cheerfulness, and raised a fund for the relief of the poor. They were taught that their worldly portion was most comfortably enjoyed, when shared with their brethren who were in want. If we thus serve God, and do good with what we have, it is promised that the Lord our God will bless us in all the works of our land. The blessing of God is all to our outward prosperity; and without that blessing, the work of our hands will bring nothing to pass. The blessing descends upon the working hand. Expect not that God should bless thee in thy idleness and love of ease. And it descends upon the giving hand. He who thus scatters, certainly increases; and to be free and generous in the support of religion, and any good work, is the surest and safest way of thriving." *Matthew Henry*

SPRINGBOARDS FOR PREACHING AND WITNESSING

15:11

Atheist Missions

There are tens of thousands of Christian missions around the world that feed the hungry, shelter the homeless, and take care of the poor. So I wondered how many atheist missions I could find on the Internet. I typed in "Atheist Missions," and guess how many came up? Zip. I tried the search words "atheists feed the poor." None. "Atheists helping the homeless." No results. I got more results from typing in "hen's teeth." So, if the economy turns sour and leaves you homeless, thank God that there are Christian missions out there that will feed you, clothe you, and give you and your children somewhere to sleep. If you find yourself in a disaster, thank God for the Salvation Army and the Red Cross, or if you are taken to a hospital because of a serious illness, you may end up in a Saint John's, a Saint Jude's, or some other hospital whose name reminds us of its roots.

One more thought. If you find yourself in a lifeboat with no food and a group of very hungry people who are checking you out for lunch (it has happened), who would you rather be sharing the lifeboat with: a group of starving evolutionists who believe in "survival of the fittest" and have no moral absolutes, or a group of Christians who love their neighbor as themselves and fear God?

widow who *are* within your gates, may
come and eat and be satisfied, that the
LORD your God may bless you in all the
work of your hand which you do.

Debts Canceled Every Seven Years

15 "At the end of *every* seven years
you shall grant a release *of debts.*
2And this *is* the form of the release: Every
creditor who has lent *anything* to his
neighbor shall release *it;* he shall not require *it* of his neighbor or his brother, because it is called the LORD's release. 3Of a
foreigner you may require *it;* but you shall
give up your claim to what is owed by
your brother, 4except when there may be
no poor among you; for the LORD will
greatly bless you in the land which the
LORD your God is giving you to possess *as*
an inheritance— 5only if you carefully
obey the voice of the LORD your God, to
observe with care all these commandments which I command you today. 6For
the LORD your God will bless you just as
He promised you; you shall lend to many
nations, but you shall not borrow; you
shall reign over many nations, but they
shall not reign over you.

Generosity to the Poor

7"If there is among you a poor man of
your brethren, within any of the gates in
your land which the LORD your God is
giving you, you shall not harden your
heart nor shut your hand from your poor
brother, 8but you shall open your hand
wide to him and willingly lend him sufficient for his need, whatever he needs.
9Beware lest there be a wicked thought in
your heart, saying, 'The seventh year, the
year of release, is at hand,' and your eye
be evil against your poor brother and you
give him nothing, and he cry out to the
LORD against you, and it become sin
among you. 10You shall surely give to him,
and your heart should not be grieved
when you give to him, because for this
thing the LORD your God will bless you in
all your works and in all to which you
put your hand. 11For the poor will never
cease from the land; therefore I command
you, saying, 'You shall open your hand
wide to your brother, to your poor and
your needy, in your land.'

The Law Concerning Bondservants

12"If your brother, a Hebrew man, or a
Hebrew woman, is sold to you and serves
you six years, then in the seventh year
you shall let him go free from you. 13And
when you send him away free from you,
you shall not let him go away empty-

15:6 As America turned its back on God, it went trillions of dollars into debt. See Deut. 28:15 comment.

handed; [14]you shall supply him liberally
from your flock, from your threshing floor,
and from your winepress. *From what* the
LORD your God has blessed you with, you
shall give to him. [15]You shall remember
that you were a slave in the land of Egypt,
and the LORD your God redeemed you;
therefore I command you this thing today.
[16]And if it happens that he says to you, 'I
will not go away from you,' because he
loves you and your house, since he prospers with you, [17]then you shall take an awl
and thrust *it* through his ear to the door,
and he shall be your servant forever. Also
to your female servant you shall do likewise. [18]It shall not seem hard to you when
you send him away free from you; for he
has been worth a double hired servant in
serving you six years. Then the LORD your
God will bless you in all that you do.

The Law Concerning Firstborn Animals

[19]"All the firstborn males that come
from your herd and your flock you shall
sanctify to the LORD your God; you shall
do no work with the firstborn of your
herd, nor shear the firstborn of your flock.
[20]You and your household shall eat *it* before the LORD your God year by year in
the place which the LORD chooses. [21]But
if there is a defect in it, *if it is* lame or
blind *or has* any serious defect, you shall
not sacrifice it to the LORD your God. [22]You
may eat it within your gates; the unclean
and the clean *person* alike *may eat it,* as *if it
were* a gazelle or a deer. [23]Only you shall
not eat its blood; you shall pour it on the
ground like water.

The Passover Reviewed

16 "Observe the month of Abib, and
keep the Passover to the LORD
your God, for in the month of Abib the
LORD your God brought you out of Egypt
by night. [2]Therefore you shall sacrifice
the Passover to the LORD your God, from
the flock and the herd, in the place where
the LORD chooses to put His name. [3]You
shall eat no leavened bread with it; seven
days you shall eat unleavened bread with
it, *that is,* the bread of affliction (for you
came out of the land of Egypt in haste),
that you may remember the day in which
you came out of the land of Egypt all the
days of your life. [4]And no leaven shall be
seen among you in all your territory for
seven days, nor shall *any* of the meat which
you sacrifice the first day at twilight remain overnight until morning.

[5]"You may not sacrifice the Passover
within any of your gates which the LORD
your God gives you; [6]but at the place where
the LORD your God chooses to make His
name abide, there you shall sacrifice the
Passover at twilight, at the going down of
the sun, at the time you came out of Egypt.
[7]And you shall roast and eat *it* in the place
which the LORD your God chooses, and in
the morning you shall turn and go to your
tents. [8]Six days you shall eat unleavened
bread, and on the seventh day there *shall
be* a sacred assembly to the LORD your
God. You shall do no work *on it.*

The Feast of Weeks Reviewed

[9]"You shall count seven weeks for yourself; begin to count the seven weeks from
the time you begin *to put* the sickle to the
grain. [10]Then you shall keep the Feast of
Weeks to the LORD your God with the
tribute of a freewill offering from your
hand, which you shall give as the LORD
your God blesses you. [11]You shall rejoice
before the LORD your God, you and your
son and your daughter, your male servant
and your female servant, the Levite who
is within your gates, the stranger and the

15:16,17 It is said that when Abraham Lincoln told a young slave girl he had just purchased that he was setting her free, she asked, "To go anywhere I want to go?" Lincoln said, "Yes." The girl replied, "Then I'm going with you!" Such is our attitude toward Christ. We were slaves of sin until we surrendered to Jesus Christ; now we are slaves of righteousness (see Rom. 6:19). With grateful hearts, we love our Master and delight to do His will.

fatherless and the widow who *are* among you, at the place where the LORD your God chooses to make His name abide. 12And you shall remember that you were a slave in Egypt, and you shall be careful to observe these statutes.

The Feast of Tabernacles Reviewed

13"You shall observe the Feast of Tabernacles seven days, when you have gathered from your threshing floor and from your winepress. 14And you shall rejoice in your feast, you and your son and your daughter, your male servant and your female servant and the Levite, the stranger and the fatherless and the widow, who *are* within your gates. 15Seven days you shall keep a sacred feast to the LORD your God in the place which the LORD chooses, because the LORD your God will bless you in all your produce and in all the work of your hands, so that you surely rejoice.

16"Three times a year all your males shall appear before the LORD your God in the place which He chooses: at the Feast of Unleavened Bread, at the Feast of Weeks, and at the Feast of Tabernacles; and they shall not appear before the LORD empty-handed. 17Every man *shall give* as he is able, according to the blessing of the LORD your God which He has given you.

Justice Must Be Administered

18"You shall appoint judges and officers in all your gates, which the LORD your God gives you, according to your tribes, and they shall judge the people with just judgment. 19You shall not pervert justice; you shall not show partiality, nor take a bribe, for a bribe blinds the eyes of the wise and twists the words of the righteous. 20You shall follow what is altogether just, that you may live and inherit the land which the LORD your God is giving you.

21"You shall not plant for yourself any tree, as a wooden image, near the altar which you build for yourself to the LORD your God. 22You shall not set up a sacred pillar, which the LORD your God hates.

17

"You shall not sacrifice to the LORD your God a bull or sheep which has any blemish *or* defect, for that *is* an abomination to the LORD your God.

2"If there is found among you, within any of your gates which the LORD your God gives you, a man or a woman who has been wicked in the sight of the LORD your God, in transgressing His covenant, 3who has gone and served other gods and worshiped them, either the sun or moon or any of the host of heaven, which I have not commanded, 4and it is told you, and you hear *of it,* then you shall inquire diligently. And if *it is* indeed true *and* certain that such an abomination has been committed in Israel, 5then you shall bring out to your gates that man or woman who has committed that wicked thing, and shall stone to death that man or woman with stones. 6Whoever is deserving of death shall be put to death on the testimony of two or three witnesses; he shall not be put to death on the testimony of one witness. 7The hands of the witnesses shall be the first against him to put him to death, and afterward the hands of all the people. So you shall put away the evil from among you.

8"If a matter arises which is too hard for you to judge, between degrees of guilt for bloodshed, between one judgment or another, or between one punishment or another, matters of controversy within your gates, then you shall arise and go up to the place which the LORD your God

---

16:16 In Christ there is neither male nor female. We are all told to present our bodies as living sacrifices to God (see Rom. 12:1). Never let anyone convince you that women shouldn't be actively involved in the Great Commission. When we each appear before the Lord, none of us want to be empty-handed; we want to bring as many people as possible into the kingdom.

17:2–5 Idolatry is punishable by death under God's Law. The Law's wrath will be manifest on Judgment Day.

chooses. 9And you shall come to the priests, the Levites, and to the judge *there* in those days, and inquire *of them;* they shall pronounce upon you the sentence of judgment. 10You shall do according to the sentence which they pronounce upon you in that place which the LORD chooses. And you shall be careful to do according to all that they order you. 11According to the sentence of the law in which they instruct you, according to the judgment which they tell you, you shall do; you shall not turn aside *to* the right hand or *to* the left from the sentence which they pronounce upon you. 12Now the man who acts presumptuously and will not heed the priest who stands to minister there before the LORD your God, or the judge, that man shall die. So you shall put away the evil from Israel. 13And all the people shall hear and fear, and no longer act presumptuously.

Principles Governing Kings

14"When you come to the land which the LORD your God is giving you, and possess it and dwell in it, and say, 'I will set a king over me like all the nations that *are* around me,' 15you shall surely set a king over you whom the LORD your God chooses; *one* from among your brethren you shall set as king over you; you may not set a foreigner over you, who *is* not your brother. 16But he shall not multiply horses for himself, nor cause the people to return to Egypt to multiply horses, for the LORD has said to you, 'You shall not return that way again.' 17Neither shall he multiply wives for himself, lest his heart turn away; nor shall he greatly multiply silver and gold for himself.

18"Also it shall be, when he sits on the throne of his kingdom, that he shall write for himself a copy of this law in a book, from *the one* before the priests, the Levites. 19And it shall be with him, and he shall read it all the days of his life, that he may learn to fear the LORD his God and be careful to observe all the words of this law and these statutes, 20that his heart may not be lifted above his brethren, that he may not turn aside from the commandment *to* the right hand or *to* the left, and that he may prolong *his* days in his kingdom, he and his children in the midst of Israel.

The Portion of the Priests and Levites

18 "The priests, the Levites—all the tribe of Levi—shall have no part nor inheritance with Israel; they shall eat the offerings of the LORD made by fire, and His portion. 2Therefore they shall have no inheritance among their brethren; the LORD is their inheritance, as He said to them.

3"And this shall be the priest's due from the people, from those who offer a sacrifice, whether *it is* bull or sheep: they shall give to the priest the shoulder, the cheeks, and the stomach. 4The firstfruits of your grain and your new wine and your oil, and the first of the fleece of your sheep, you shall give him. 5For the LORD your God has chosen him out of all your tribes to stand to minister in the name of the LORD, him and his sons forever.

> Though God's attributes are equal, yet His mercy is more attractive and pleasing in our eyes than His justice.
>
> **MIGUEL DE CERVANTES**

6"So if a Levite comes from any of your gates, from where he dwells among all Israel, and comes with all the desire of his mind to the place which the LORD chooses, 7then he may serve in the name of the LORD his God as all his brethren the Levites *do,* who stand there before the LORD. 8They shall have equal portions to eat, besides what comes from the sale of his inheritance.

Avoid Wicked Customs

9"When you come into the land which the LORD your God is giving you, you shall not learn to follow the abominations of those nations. 10There shall not be

found among you *anyone* who makes his
son or his daughter pass through the fire,
or one who practices witchcraft, *or* a soothsayer, or one who interprets omens, or a
sorcerer, 11or one who conjures spells, or
a medium, or a spiritist, or one who calls
up the dead. 12For all who do these things
are an abomination to the LORD, and because of these abominations the LORD
your God drives them out from before
you. 13You shall be blameless before the
LORD your God. 14For these nations which
you will dispossess listened to soothsayers and diviners; but as for you, the LORD
your God has not appointed such for you.

A New Prophet Like Moses

15"The LORD your God will raise up for
you a Prophet like me from your midst,
from your brethren. Him you shall hear,
16according to all you desired of the LORD
your God in Horeb in the day of the assembly, saying, 'Let me not hear again the
voice of the LORD my God, nor let me see
this great fire anymore, lest I die.'

17"And the LORD said to me: 'What
they have spoken is good. 18I will raise up
for them a Prophet like you from among
their brethren, and will put My words in
His mouth, and He shall speak to them
all that I command Him. 19And it shall be
that whoever will not hear My words,
which He speaks in My name, I will require *it* of him. 20But the prophet who
presumes to speak a word in My name,
which I have not commanded him to
speak, or who speaks in the name of other
gods, that prophet shall die.' 21And if you
say in your heart, 'How shall we know
the word which the LORD has not spoken?'— 22when a prophet speaks in the
name of the LORD, if the thing does not
happen or come to pass, that *is* the thing
which the LORD has not spoken; the
prophet has spoken it presumptuously;
you shall not be afraid of him.

Three Cities of Refuge

19 "When the LORD your God has cut
off the nations whose land the
LORD your God is giving you, and you
dispossess them and dwell in their cities
and in their houses, 2you shall separate
three cities for yourself in the midst of
your land which the LORD your God is
giving you to possess. 3You shall prepare
roads for yourself, and divide into three
parts the territory of your land which the
LORD your God is giving you to inherit,
that any manslayer may flee there.

4"And this *is* the case of the manslayer
who flees there, that he may live: Whoever kills his neighbor unintentionally,
not having hated him in time past— 5as
when *a man* goes to the woods with his
neighbor to cut timber, and his hand
swings a stroke with the ax to cut down
the tree, and the head slips from the handle and strikes his neighbor so that he
dies—he shall flee to one of these cities
and live; 6lest the avenger of blood, while
his anger is hot, pursue the manslayer and
overtake him, because the way is long,
and kill him, though he *was* not deserving
of death, since he had not hated the victim in time past. 7Therefore I command
you, saying, 'You shall separate three cities
for yourself.'

8"Now if the LORD your God enlarges
your territory, as He swore to your fathers,
and gives you the land which He promised to give to your fathers, 9and if you
keep all these commandments and do
them, which I command you today, to love
the LORD your God and to walk always in
His ways, then you shall add three more

18:9–12 We sacrifice four million children annually through abortion. Our movies, television programs, magazines, books, and newspapers are permeated with things that are abominations to God, and interest in the occult is increasing each year. For how we are invoking God's wrath, see Deut. 28:15 comment.

Note also that God's condemnation is directed not toward the activity itself, but toward the person committing it (v. 12). See 1 Tim. 1:9,10 comment.

18:18,19 This messianic prophecy was fulfilled in John 12:48,49 and Acts 3:22,23.

QUESTIONS & OBJECTIONS

18:20–22 ***"Bible predictions are vague, like those of Nostradamus."***

I once believed Nostradamus was able to somewhat predict the future. However, after closely studying him I found that he stole many of his "prophecies" from the Bible (which he read in secret), revised them, and claimed them as his own. For example, like the Bible, he made continual references to wars, earthquakes, famines, pestilences, and plagues; he speaks of the King of kings, "a kingdom divided," and "the blood of innocents." His predictions contain phrases such as "milk and honey," "tribulation," "God loosed Satan," "anti-Christ," "latter days," "Gog and Magog," "the sea shall be red," etc. Today, as in his day, anyone who is ignorant of the Bible's prophecies will be impressed with the writings of Nostradamus. His "predictions," though, are incredibly generic (just as horoscopes and tarot cards are), and people can read into them any meaning they desire.

That is not the case with biblical prophecies, which are extremely detailed and precise. Unlike other religious books, the Bible offers a multitude of specific predictions—some thousands of years in advance—that either have been literally fulfilled or point to a definite future time when they will come true. No other religion has specific, repeated, and unfailing fulfillment of predictions many years in advance of events over which the predictor had no control. The sacred writings of Buddhism, Islam, Confucius, etc., are all missing the element of proven prophecy. These kinds of predictions are unique to the Bible.

Only one who is omniscient can accurately predict details of events thousands of years in the future. Limited human beings know the future only if it is told to them by an omniscient Being. God provided this evidence for us so we would know that the Scriptures have a divine Author: "For I am God, and there is no other; I am God, and there is none like Me, declaring the end from the beginning, and from ancient times things that are not yet done" (Isa. 46:9,10).

In addition, the Bible declares that prophets must be 100 percent accurate—no exceptions. If anyone claimed to be speaking for God and the prophesied event didn't come to pass, he was proven to be a liar. The writings of Mormons and Jehovah's Witnesses are littered with false prophecies, so we can know whether they are written by men or by God.

The Bible's sixty-six books, written between 1400 B.C. and A.D. 90, contain approximately 3,856 verses concerned with prophecy. Even more important are the many prophecies of a coming Messiah. God said He would send someone to redeem mankind from sin, and He wanted there to be no mistake about who that Person would be. In all, there are over three hundred prophecies that tell of the ancestry, birth, life, ministry, death, resurrection, and ascension of Jesus of Nazareth. All have been literally fulfilled to the smallest detail. For details of fulfilled prophecies, see Matt. 4:4 comment.

A fact often overlooked by critics is that, even if most biblical predictions could be explained naturally, the existence of just one real case of fulfilled prophecy is sufficient to establish the Bible's supernatural origin. Over 25 percent of the entire Bible contains specific predictive prophecies that have been literally fulfilled. This is true of no other book in the world. And it is a sure sign of its divine origin.

(Adapted from *How to Know God Exists.*)

cities for yourself besides these three, [10]lest
innocent blood be shed in the midst of
your land which the LORD your God is
giving you *as* an inheritance, and *thus*
guilt of bloodshed be upon you.

[11]"But if anyone hates his neighbor,
lies in wait for him, rises against him and
strikes him mortally, so that he dies, and
he flees to one of these cities, [12]then the
elders of his city shall send and bring him
from there, and deliver him over to the
hand of the avenger of blood, that he may
die. [13]Your eye shall not pity him, but you
shall put away *the guilt of* innocent blood
from Israel, that it may go well with you.

Property Boundaries

[14]"You shall not remove your neighbor's landmark, which the men of old
have set, in your inheritance which you
will inherit in the land that the LORD your
God is giving you to possess.

19:11,12 The Law differentiates between manslaughter (vv. 4–6) and premeditated murder. The death sentence is an effective deterrent; the murderer will not murder again.

The Law Concerning Witnesses

15"One witness shall not rise against a man concerning any iniquity or any sin that he commits; by the mouth of two or three witnesses the matter shall be established. 16If a false witness rises against any man to testify against him of wrongdoing, 17then both men in the controversy shall stand before the LORD, before the priests and the judges who serve in those days. 18And the judges shall make careful inquiry, and indeed, *if* the witness *is* a false witness, who has testified falsely against his brother, 19then you shall do to him as he thought to have done to his brother; so you shall put away the evil from among you. 20And those who remain shall hear and fear, and hereafter they shall not again commit such evil among you. 21Your eye shall not pity: life *shall be* for life, eye for eye, tooth for tooth, hand for hand, foot for foot.

Principles Governing Warfare

20 "When you go out to battle against your enemies, and see horses and chariots *and* people more numerous than you, do not be afraid of them; for the LORD your God *is* with you, who brought you up from the land of Egypt. 2So it shall be, when you are on the verge of battle, that the priest shall approach and speak to the people. 3And he shall say to them, 'Hear, O Israel: Today you are on the verge of battle with your enemies. Do not let your heart faint, do not be afraid, and do not tremble or be terrified because of them; 4for the LORD your God is He who goes with you, to fight for you against your enemies, to save you.'

5"Then the officers shall speak to the people, saying: 'What man *is there* who has built a new house and has not dedicated it? Let him go and return to his house, lest he die in the battle and another man dedicate it. 6Also what man *is there* who has planted a vineyard and has not eaten of it? Let him go and return to his house, lest he die in the battle and another man eat of it. 7And what man *is there* who is betrothed to a woman and has not married her? Let him go and return to his house, lest he die in the battle and another man marry her.'

8"The officers shall speak further to the people, and say, 'What man *is there who is* fearful and fainthearted? Let him go and return to his house, lest the heart of his brethren faint[a] like his heart.' 9And so it shall be, when the officers have finished speaking to the people, that they shall make captains of the armies to lead the people.

10"When you go near a city to fight against it, then proclaim an offer of peace to it. 11And it shall be that if they accept your offer of peace, and open to you, then all the people *who are* found in it shall be placed under tribute to you, and serve you. 12Now if *the city* will not make peace with you, but war against you, then you shall besiege it. 13And when the LORD your God delivers it into your hands, you shall strike every male in it with the edge of the sword. 14But the women, the little ones, the livestock, and all that is in the city, all its spoil, you shall plunder for yourself; and you shall eat the enemies' plunder which the LORD your God gives you. 15Thus you shall do to all the cities *which are* very far from you, which *are* not of the cities of these nations.

16"But of the cities of these peoples which the LORD your God gives you *as* an inheritance, you shall let nothing that breathes remain alive, 17but you shall utterly destroy them: the Hittite and the

20:8 [a]Following Masoretic Text and Targum; Samaritan Pentateuch, Septuagint, Syriac, and Vulgate read *lest he make his brother's heart faint.*

20:1–4 Never listen to your fears when approaching the unsaved. The fear will always be there whispering its poison, but faith in God deafens its pathetic voice. The amount of fear we have reveals the amount of faith we have. The disciples were fearful in a storm because they had "little faith" (see Matt. 8:26). Always remember that the LORD your God goes with you.

Amorite and the Canaanite and the Perizzite and the Hivite and the Jebusite, just
as the LORD your God has commanded
you, [18]lest they teach you to do according
to all their abominations which they have
done for their gods, and you sin against
the LORD your God.

[19]"When you besiege a city for a long
time, while making war against it to take
it, you shall not destroy its trees by wield-
ing an ax against them; if you can eat of
them, do not cut them down to use in the
siege, for the tree of the field *is* man's *food.*
[20]Only the trees which you know *are* not
trees for food you may destroy and cut
down, to build siegeworks against the
city that makes war with you, until it is
subdued.

The Law Concerning Unsolved Murder

21 "If *anyone* is found slain, lying in
the field in the land which the
LORD your God is giving you to possess,
and it is not known who killed him, [2]then
your elders and your judges shall go out
and measure *the distance* from the slain
man to the surrounding cities. [3]And it
shall be *that* the elders of the city nearest
to the slain man will take a heifer which
has not been worked *and* which has not
pulled with a yoke. [4]The elders of that
city shall bring the heifer down to a valley with flowing water, which is neither
plowed nor sown, and they shall break
the heifer's neck there in the valley. [5]Then
the priests, the sons of Levi, shall come
near, for the LORD your God has chosen
them to minister to Him and to bless in
the name of the LORD; by their word
every controversy and every assault shall
be *settled.* [6]And all the elders of that city
nearest to the slain *man* shall wash their
hands over the heifer whose neck was
broken in the valley. [7]Then they shall answer and say, 'Our hands have not shed
this blood, nor have our eyes seen *it.*
[8]Provide atonement, O LORD, for Your
people Israel, whom You have redeemed,
and do not lay innocent blood to the
charge of Your people Israel.' And atonement shall be provided on their behalf for
the blood. [9]So you shall put away the
guilt of innocent blood from among you
when you do *what is* right in the sight of
the LORD.

Female Captives

[10]"When you go out to war against
your enemies, and the LORD your God
delivers them into your hand, and you
take them captive, [11]and you see among
the captives a beautiful woman, and desire her and would take her for your wife,
[12]then you shall bring her home to your
house, and she shall shave her head and
trim her nails. [13]She shall put off the
clothes of her captivity, remain in your
house, and mourn her father and her
mother a full month; after that you may
go in to her and be her husband, and she
shall be your wife. [14]And it shall be, if
you have no delight in her, then you shall
set her free, but you certainly shall not
sell her for money; you shall not treat her
brutally, because you have humbled her.

Firstborn Inheritance Rights

[15]"If a man has two wives, one loved
and the other unloved, and they have borne
him children, *both* the loved and the
unloved, and *if* the firstborn son is of her
who is unloved, [16]then it shall be, on the
day he bequeaths his possessions to his
sons, *that* he must not bestow firstborn
status on the son of the loved wife in
preference to the son of the unloved, the
true firstborn. [17]But he shall acknowledge
the son of the unloved wife *as* the firstborn by giving him a double portion of
all that he has, for he *is* the beginning of
his strength; the right of the firstborn *is*
his.

The Rebellious Son

[18]"If a man has a stubborn and rebellious son who will not obey the voice of
his father or the voice of his mother, and
who, when they have chastened him, will
not heed them, [19]then his father and his

QUESTIONS & OBJECTIONS

21:18–21 ***"The Bible says that children were to be stoned to death."***

This refers not to a young child but to a *youth* who was a continual drunkard and was persistently rebellious, stubborn, gluttonous, and disobedient (which describes many contemporary teenagers). If a son consistently refused to abide by his parents' authority, the men of the city were to enforce swift capital punishment.

However, there is no record in Scripture of even one rebellious youth in Israel being put to death by stoning. The Law of Moses was read to all of Israel, so no doubt all children were made aware of this law's terrifying threat before they reached their teenage years. (That it was an effective deterrent shows God's wisdom in setting such a harsh penalty.) In contrast, each year in the U.S. thousands of youths die through drunk driving, violence, alcohol poisoning, drug abuse, etc., as a tragic result of their rebellious lifestyles.

That same merciless Law of Moses will judge all of humanity on the Day of Judgment. However, Jesus took our capital punishment upon Himself so that we could leave the courtroom without suffering the consequences of our sins. All that God requires of us is that we repent of our stubborn, rebellious, and disobedient lifestyle and trust in the Savior before the great stone of God's Law falls on us and grinds us "to powder" (see Luke 20:18).

mother shall take hold of him and bring
him out to the elders of his city, to the
gate of his city. 20And they shall say to the
elders of his city, 'This son of ours is stubborn and rebellious; he will not obey our
voice; he is a glutton and a drunkard.'
21Then all the men of his city shall stone
him to death with stones; so you shall
put away the evil from among you, and
all Israel shall hear and fear.

Miscellaneous Laws

22"If a man has committed a sin deserving of death, and he is put to death,
and you hang him on a tree, 23his body
shall not remain overnight on the tree,
but you shall surely bury him that day, so
that you do not defile the land which the
LORD your God is giving you *as* an inheritance; for he who is hanged *is* accursed
of God.

22 "You shall not see your brother's
ox or his sheep going astray, and
hide yourself from them; you shall certainly bring them back to your brother.
2And if your brother *is* not near you, or if
you do not know him, then you shall
bring it to your own house, and it shall
remain with you until your brother seeks
it; then you shall restore it to him. 3You
shall do the same with his donkey, and so
shall you do with his garment; with any
lost thing of your brother's, which he has
lost and you have found, you shall do
likewise; you must not hide yourself.
4"You shall not see your brother's donkey or his ox fall down along the road,
and hide yourself from them; you shall
surely help him lift *them* up again.
5"A woman shall not wear anything
that pertains to a man, nor shall a man
put on a woman's garment, for all who do
so *are* an abomination to the LORD your
God.
6"If a bird's nest happens to be before
you along the way, in any tree or on the
ground, with young ones or eggs, with
the mother sitting on the young or on the
eggs, you shall not take the mother with
the young; 7you shall surely let the mother go, and take the young for yourself,
that it may be well with you and *that* you
may prolong *your* days.
8"When you build a new house, then
you shall make a parapet for your roof,
that you may not bring guilt of bloodshed on your household if anyone falls
from it.
9"You shall not sow your vineyard
with different kinds of seed, lest the yield
of the seed which you have sown and the

QUESTIONS & OBJECTIONS

22:13–21 ***"Why does the Bible call for the stoning of non-virgins?"***

The Law of God did call for the stoning of non-virgin brides, as well as rebellious, drunken youths (see 21:18–21), with the purpose that "all Israel shall hear and fear." However, there is no recorded incident in Scripture of either happening. It seems that the Law was feared in those days. That same Law will judge all humanity (see Rom. 2:12; James 2:12), and we would be wise to heed its fearful warning.

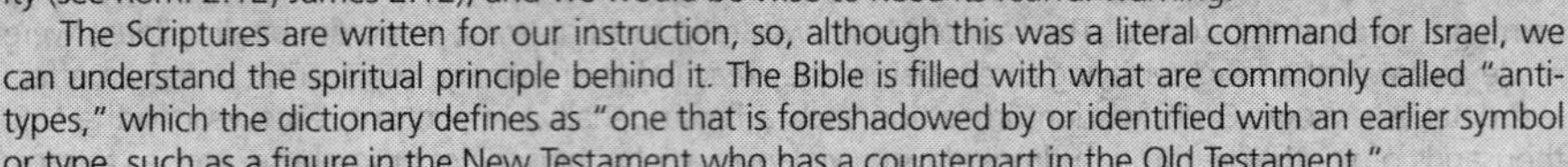

The Scriptures are written for our instruction, so, although this was a literal command for Israel, we can understand the spiritual principle behind it. The Bible is filled with what are commonly called "antitypes," which the dictionary defines as "one that is foreshadowed by or identified with an earlier symbol or type, such as a figure in the New Testament who has a counterpart in the Old Testament."

Christians are what the Bible calls "chaste virgins" (2 Cor. 11:2). As the Bride of Christ (Eph. 5:25–32), we are waiting for the Bridegroom, the Lord Jesus Christ, to come for us. (Every human marriage is a "type" of Christ and His Church.) However, those who are hypocrites—who profess to be chaste virgins but in truth are committing spiritual adultery by loving this sinful world—will face the severe judgment of God.

fruit of your vineyard be defiled.
10"You shall not plow with an ox and a
donkey together.
11"You shall not wear a garment of different sorts, *such as* wool and linen mixed
together.
12"You shall make tassels on the four
corners of the clothing with which you
cover *yourself*.

Laws of Sexual Morality

13"If any man takes a wife, and goes in
to her, and detests her, 14and charges her
with shameful conduct, and brings a bad
name on her, and says, 'I took this woman, and when I came to her I found she
was not a virgin,' 15then the father and
mother of the young woman shall take
and bring out *the evidence of* the young
woman's virginity to the elders of the city
at the gate. 16And the young woman's father shall say to the elders, 'I gave my
daughter to this man as wife, and he detests her. 17Now he has charged her with
shameful conduct, saying, "I found your
daughter *was* not a virgin," and yet these
are the evidences of my daughter's virginity.' And they shall spread the cloth before the elders of the city. 18Then the elders of that city shall take that man and
punish him; 19and they shall fine him one
hundred *shekels* of silver and give *them* to
the father of the young woman, because
he has brought a bad name on a virgin of
Israel. And she shall be his wife; he cannot divorce her all his days.
20"But if the thing is true, *and evidences
of* virginity are not found for the young
woman, 21then they shall bring out the
young woman to the door of her father's
house, and the men of her city shall stone
her to death with stones, because she has
done a disgraceful thing in Israel, to play
the harlot in her father's house. So you
shall put away the evil from among you.
22"If a man is found lying with a woman married to a husband, then both of
them shall die—the man that lay with the
woman, and the woman; so you shall put
away the evil from Israel.
23"If a young woman *who is* a virgin is
betrothed to a husband, and a man finds

22:9 We must be careful to sow the pure seed of the gospel, lest we reap false converts.

22:11 Skeptics often mock this verse without understanding its symbolism. See Lev. 11:10,11 comment.

22:12 The tassels were to remind them of the Ten Commandments so they would obey them (see Num. 15:38–40).

her in the city and lies with her, [24]then you shall bring them both out to the gate of that city, and you shall stone them to death with stones, the young woman because she did not cry out in the city, and the man because he humbled his neighbor's wife; so you shall put away the evil from among you.

[25]"But if a man finds a betrothed young woman in the countryside, and the man forces her and lies with her, then only the man who lay with her shall die. [26]But you shall do nothing to the young woman; *there is* in the young woman no sin *deserving* of death, for just as when a man rises against his neighbor and kills him, even so *is* this matter. [27]For he found her in the countryside, *and* the betrothed young woman cried out, but *there was* no one to save her.

[28]"If a man finds a young woman *who is* a virgin, who is not betrothed, and he seizes her and lies with her, and they are found out, [29]then the man who lay with her shall give to the young woman's father fifty *shekels* of silver, and she shall be his wife because he has humbled her; he shall not be permitted to divorce her all his days.

[30]"A man shall not take his father's wife, nor uncover his father's bed.

Those Excluded from the Congregation

23 "He who is emasculated by crushing or mutilation shall not enter the assembly of the LORD.

[2]"One of illegitimate birth shall not enter the assembly of the LORD; even to the tenth generation none of his *descendants* shall enter the assembly of the LORD.

[3]"An Ammonite or Moabite shall not enter the assembly of the LORD; even to the tenth generation none of his *descendants* shall enter the assembly of the LORD forever, [4]because they did not meet you with bread and water on the road when you came out of Egypt, and because they hired against you Balaam the son of Beor from Pethor of Mesopotamia,[a] to curse you. [5]Nevertheless the LORD your God would not listen to Balaam, but the LORD your God turned the curse into a blessing for you, because the LORD your God loves you. [6]You shall not seek their peace nor their prosperity all your days forever.

[7]"You shall not abhor an Edomite, for he *is* your brother. You shall not abhor an Egyptian, because you were an alien in his land. [8]The children of the third generation born to them may enter the assembly of the LORD.

Cleanliness of the Campsite

[9]"When the army goes out against your enemies, then keep yourself from every wicked thing. [10]If there is any man among you who becomes unclean by some occurrence in the night, then he shall go outside the camp; he shall not come inside the camp. [11]But it shall be, when evening comes, that he shall wash with water; and when the sun sets, he may come into the camp.

23:4 [a]Hebrew *Aram Naharaim*

23:5 "God loves you." Should we tell sinners that God loves them? For the biblical presentation of God's love, see Matt. 10:22 comment.

"Every time I hear a preacher tell his people that God loves them unconditionally, I want to ask that the man be defrocked for such a violation of the Word of God. What pagan does not hear in that statement that he has no need of repentance, so he can continue in sin without fear, knowing that it's all taken care of? . . . Just because a man is ordained is no guarantee that he is in the kingdom of God. The odds are astronomical that many are still under the curse of God. There are ordained men who have not yet fled to the cross, who are still counting on the nebulous idea of the unconditional love of God to get them through, or even worse, still thinking that they can get into the kingdom of God through their good works. They don't understand that unless they perfectly obey the law of God, which they have not done for five minutes since they were born, they are under the curse of God. That is the reality we must make clear to our people—either they will bear the curse of God themselves or they will flee to the One who took it for them." *R. C. Sproul*

QUESTIONS & OBJECTIONS

23:15,16 ***"How can you worship a God who encourages the cruelty of slavery?"***

The Bible does acknowledge the reality of slavery in those times. A person could be taken as a slave if he was a prisoner of war, if he couldn't pay a debt, if he stole something that he couldn't repay, etc. However, there were laws governing how slaves could be treated and also ways they could gain their freedom. It's important to realize that we view the subject through the lens of American slavery, with its incredible cruelty. To be a slave in Bible times was more like being a modern-day servant. In fact, the Bible uses the word "bondservant" when referring to slaves, and instructs masters to treat them kindly (Eph. 6:5–9). The apostle Paul speaks of Christians as being "slaves" of God and of Jesus Christ (Rom. 6:22; 1 Cor. 7:22). See also Exod. 21:5,6 comment.

12"Also you shall have a place outside the camp, where you may go out; 13and you shall have an implement among your equipment, and when you sit down outside, you shall dig with it and turn and cover your refuse. 14For the LORD your God walks in the midst of your camp, to deliver you and give your enemies over to you; therefore your camp shall be holy, that He may see no unclean thing among you, and turn away from you.

Miscellaneous Laws

15"You shall not give back to his master the slave who has escaped from his master to you. 16He may dwell with you in your midst, in the place which he chooses within one of your gates, where it seems best to him; you shall not oppress him.

17"There shall be no *ritual* harlot[a] of the daughters of Israel, or a perverted[b] one of the sons of Israel. 18You shall not bring the wages of a harlot or the price of a dog to the house of the LORD your God for any vowed offering, for both of these *are* an abomination to the LORD your God.

19"You shall not charge interest to your brother—interest on money *or* food *or* anything that is lent out at interest. 20To a foreigner you may charge interest, but to your brother you shall not charge interest, that the LORD your God may bless you in all to which you set your hand in the land which you are entering to possess.

21"When you make a vow to the LORD your God, you shall not delay to pay it; for the LORD your God will surely require it of you, and it would be sin to you. 22But if you abstain from vowing, it shall not be sin to you. 23That which has gone from your lips you shall keep and perform, for you voluntarily vowed to the LORD your God what you have promised with your mouth.

24"When you come into your neighbor's vineyard, you may eat your fill of grapes at your pleasure, but you shall not put *any* in your container. 25When you come into your neighbor's standing grain, you may pluck the heads with your hand, but you shall not use a sickle on your neighbor's standing grain.

Law Concerning Divorce

24 "When a man takes a wife and marries her, and it happens that she finds no favor in his eyes because he has found some uncleanness in her, and he writes her a certificate of divorce, puts

23:17 [a]Hebrew *qedeshah*, feminine of *qadesh* (see note *b*) [b]Hebrew *qadesh*, that is, one practicing sodomy and prostitution in religious rituals

23:17,18 No defiled person will enter the kingdom of God (see also Rev. 21:27). After listing all those who will not enter the kingdom, Paul says, "And such were some of you. But you were washed, but you were sanctified, but you were justified in the name of the Lord Jesus and by the Spirit of our God" (1 Cor. 6:9–11).

it in her hand, and sends her out of his
house, 2when she has departed from his
house, and goes and becomes another
man's *wife,* 3*if* the latter husband detests
her and writes her a certificate of divorce,
puts *it* in her hand, and sends her out of
his house, or if the latter husband dies
who took her as his wife, 4*then* her former
husband who divorced her must not take
her back to be his wife after she has been
defiled; for that *is* an abomination before
the LORD, and you shall not bring sin on
the land which the LORD your God is giving you *as* an inheritance.

. . . . . .

For how Jesus is pictured in the Tabernacle, see Heb. 9:2 comment.

. . . . . .

Miscellaneous Laws

5"When a man has taken a new wife,
he shall not go out to war or be charged
with any business; he shall be free at
home one year, and bring happiness to
his wife whom he has taken.
6"No man shall take the lower or the
upper millstone in pledge, for he takes
one's living in pledge.
7"If a man is found kidnapping any of
his brethren of the children of Israel, and
mistreats him or sells him, then that kid-
napper shall die; and you shall put away
the evil from among you.
8"Take heed in an outbreak of leprosy,
that you carefully observe and do according to all that the priests, the Levites, shall
teach you; just as I commanded them, *so*
you shall be careful to do. 9Remember
what the LORD your God did to Miriam
on the way when you came out of Egypt!
10"When you lend your brother anything, you shall not go into his house to
get his pledge. 11You shall stand outside,
and the man to whom you lend shall bring
the pledge out to you. 12And if the man *is*
poor, you shall not keep his pledge overnight. 13You shall in any case return the
pledge to him again when the sun goes
down, that he may sleep in his own garment and bless you; and it shall be righteousness to you before the LORD your God.
14"You shall not oppress a hired servant *who is* poor and needy, *whether* one
of your brethren or one of the aliens who
is in your land within your gates. 15Each
day you shall give *him* his wages, and not
let the sun go down on it, for he *is* poor
and has set his heart on it; lest he cry out
against you to the LORD, and it be sin to
you.
16"Fathers shall not be put to death for
their children, nor shall children be put
to death for *their* fathers; a person shall
be put to death for his own sin.
17"You shall not pervert justice due the
stranger or the fatherless, nor take a widow's garment as a pledge. 18But you shall
remember that you were a slave in Egypt,
and the LORD your God redeemed you
from there; therefore I command you to
do this thing.
19"When you reap your harvest in
your field, and forget a sheaf in the field,
you shall not go back to get it; it shall be
for the stranger, the fatherless, and the
widow, that the LORD your God may bless
you in all the work of your hands. 20When
you beat your olive trees, you shall not go
over the boughs again; it shall be for the
stranger, the fatherless, and the widow.
21When you gather the grapes of your
vineyard, you shall not glean *it* afterward;
it shall be for the stranger, the fatherless,
and the widow. 22And you shall remember that you were a slave in the land of
Egypt; therefore I command you to do
this thing.

25 "If there is a dispute between
men, and they come to court, that
the judges may judge them, and they justify the righteous and condemn the wicked,
2then it shall be, if the wicked man deserves to be beaten, that the judge will
cause him to lie down and be beaten in
his presence, according to his guilt, with
a certain number of blows. 3Forty blows he
may give him *and* no more, lest he should

exceed this and beat him with many blows
above these, and your brother be humiliated in your sight.
4“You shall not muzzle an ox while it
treads out *the grain.*

Marriage Duty of the Surviving Brother

5“If brothers dwell together, and one
of them dies and has no son, the widow
of the dead man shall not be *married* to a
stranger outside *the family;* her husband's
brother shall go in to her, take her as his
wife, and perform the duty of a husband's
brother to her. 6And it shall be *that* the
firstborn son which she bears will succeed to the name of his dead brother, that
his name may not be blotted out of Israel.
7But if the man does not want to take his
brother's wife, then let his brother's wife
go up to the gate to the elders, and say,
‘My husband's brother refuses to raise up
a name to his brother in Israel; he will not
perform the duty of my husband's brother.’
8Then the elders of his city shall call him
and speak to him. But *if* he stands firm
and says, ‘I do not want to take her,’ 9then
his brother's wife shall come to him in the
presence of the elders, remove his sandal
from his foot, spit in his face, and answer
and say, ‘So shall it be done to the man
who will not build up his brother's house.’
10And his name shall be called in Israel,
‘The house of him who had his sandal removed.’

Miscellaneous Laws

11“If *two* men fight together, and the
wife of one draws near to rescue her husband from the hand of the one attacking
him, and puts out her hand and seizes
him by the genitals, 12then you shall cut
off her hand; your eye shall not pity *her.*
13“You shall not have in your bag differing weights, a heavy and a light. 14You
shall not have in your house differing
measures, a large and a small. 15You shall
have a perfect and just weight, a perfect
and just measure, that your days may be
lengthened in the land which the LORD
your God is giving you. 16For all who do
such things, all who behave unright-
eously, *are* an abomination to the LORD
your God.

Destroy the Amalekites

17“Remember what Amalek did to you
on the way as you were coming out of
Egypt, 18how he met you on the way and
attacked your rear ranks, all the stragglers
at your rear, when you *were* tired and
weary; and he did not fear God. 19There-
fore it shall be, when the LORD your God
has given you rest from your enemies all
around, in the land which the LORD your
God is giving you to possess *as* an inheritance, *that* you will blot out the remembrance of Amalek from under heaven.
You shall not forget.

Offerings of Firstfruits and Tithes

26 “And it shall be, when you come
into the land which the LORD your
God is giving you *as* an inheritance, and
you possess it and dwell in it, 2that you
shall take some of the first of all the produce of the ground, which you shall
bring from your land that the LORD your
God is giving you, and put *it* in a basket
and go to the place where the LORD your
God chooses to make His name abide.
3And you shall go to the one who is priest
in those days, and say to him, ‘I declare
today to the LORD your[a] God that I have

26:3 [a]Septuagint reads *my.*

25:4 “This is a charge to husbandmen. It teaches us to make much of the animals that serve us. But we must learn, not only to be just, but kind to all who are employed for the good of our better part, our souls, 1Co 9:9.” *Matthew Henry*

In 1 Cor. 9, Paul speaks of allowing oxen to eat while treading out grain, to make a point about taking care of those who labor in the gospel, but we are also reminded to show kindness to animals (see Prov. 12:10).

25:19 For what happened to the Amalekites, see Exod. 17:14 comment.

come to the country which the LORD swore to our fathers to give us.'

4"Then the priest shall take the basket out of your hand and set it down before the altar of the LORD your God. 5And you shall answer and say before the LORD your God: 'My father *was* a Syrian,[a] about to perish, and he went down to Egypt and dwelt there, few in number; and there he became a nation, great, mighty, and populous. 6But the Egyptians mistreated us, afflicted us, and laid hard bondage on us. 7Then we cried out to the LORD God of our fathers, and the LORD heard our voice and looked on our affliction and our labor and our oppression. 8So the LORD brought us out of Egypt with a mighty hand and with an outstretched arm, with great terror and with signs and wonders. 9He has brought us to this place and has given us this land, "a land flowing with milk and honey";[a] 10and now, behold, I have brought the firstfruits of the land which you, O LORD, have given me.'

"Then you shall set it before the LORD your God, and worship before the LORD your God. 11So you shall rejoice in every good *thing* which the LORD your God has given to you and your house, you and the Levite and the stranger who *is* among you.

12"When you have finished laying aside all the tithe of your increase in the third year—the year of tithing—and have given *it* to the Levite, the stranger, the fatherless, and the widow, so that they may eat within your gates and be filled, 13then you shall say before the LORD your God: 'I have removed the holy *tithe* from *my* house, and also have given them to the Levite, the stranger, the fatherless, and the widow, according to all Your commandments which You have commanded me; I have not transgressed Your commandments, nor have I forgotten *them*. 14I have not eaten any of it when in mourning, nor have I removed *any* of it for an unclean *use*, nor given *any* of it for the dead. I have obeyed the voice of the LORD my God, and have done according to all that You have commanded me. 15Look down from Your holy habitation, from heaven, and bless Your people Israel and the land which You have given us, just as You swore to our fathers, "a land flowing with milk and honey." '[a]

A Special People of God

16"This day the LORD your God commands you to observe these statutes and judgments; therefore you shall be careful to observe them with all your heart and with all your soul. 17Today you have proclaimed the LORD to be your God, and that you will walk in His ways and keep His statutes, His commandments, and His judgments, and that you will obey His voice. 18Also today the LORD has proclaimed you to be His special people, just as He promised you, that *you* should keep all His commandments, 19and that He will set you high above all nations which He has made, in praise, in name, and in honor, and that you may be a holy people to the LORD your God, just as He has spoken."

The Law Inscribed on Stones

27 Now Moses, with the elders of Israel, commanded the people, saying: "Keep all the commandments which I command you today. 2And it shall be, on the day when you cross over the Jordan to the land which the LORD your God is giving you, that you shall set up for yourselves large stones, and whitewash them with lime. 3You shall write on them all the words of this law, when you have crossed over, that you may enter the land which the LORD your God is giving you,

26:5 [a]Or *Aramean* 26:9 [a]Exodus 3:8 26:15 [a]Exodus 3:8

26:18,19 How different would the history of Israel have been if they'd had a heart to keep God's Commandments.

'a land flowing with milk and honey,'[a] just
as the LORD God of your fathers promised
you. 4Therefore it shall be, when you have
crossed over the Jordan, *that* on Mount
Ebal you shall set up these stones, which
I command you today, and you shall whitewash them with lime. 5And there you
shall build an altar to the LORD your God,
an altar of stones; you shall not use an
iron *tool* on them. 6You shall build with
whole stones the altar of the LORD your
God, and offer burnt offerings on it to the
LORD your God. 7You shall offer peace offerings, and shall eat there, and rejoice
before the LORD your God. 8And you
shall write very plainly on the stones all
the words of this law."

9Then Moses and the priests, the Levites, spoke to all Israel, saying, "Take heed
and listen, O Israel: This day you have
become the people of the LORD your God.
10Therefore you shall obey the voice of the
LORD your God, and observe His commandments and His statutes which I command you today."

Curses Pronounced from Mount Ebal

11And Moses commanded the people
on the same day, saying, 12"These shall
stand on Mount Gerizim to bless the people, when you have crossed over the Jordan: Simeon, Levi, Judah, Issachar, Joseph,
and Benjamin; 13and these shall stand on
Mount Ebal to curse: Reuben, Gad, Asher,
Zebulun, Dan, and Naphtali.

14"And the Levites shall speak with a
loud voice and say to all the men of Israel: 15'Cursed *is* the one who makes a
carved or molded image, an abomination
to the LORD, the work of the hands of the
craftsman, and sets *it* up in secret.'

"And all the people shall answer and
say, 'Amen!'

16'Cursed *is* the one who treats his father or his mother with contempt.'

"And all the people shall say, 'Amen!'

17'Cursed *is* the one who moves his
neighbor's landmark.'

"And all the people shall say, 'Amen!'

18'Cursed *is* the one who makes the
blind to wander off the road.'

"And all the people shall say, 'Amen!'

19'Cursed *is* the one who perverts the
justice due the stranger, the fatherless,
and widow.'

"And all the people shall say, 'Amen!'

20'Cursed *is* the one who lies with his
father's wife, because he has uncovered
his father's bed.'

"And all the people shall say, 'Amen!'

21'Cursed *is* the one who lies with any
kind of animal.'

"And all the people shall say, 'Amen!'

22'Cursed *is* the one who lies with his
sister, the daughter of his father or the
daughter of his mother.'

"And all the people shall say, 'Amen!'

23'Cursed *is* the one who lies with his
mother-in-law.'

"And all the people shall say, 'Amen!'

24'Cursed *is* the one who attacks his
neighbor secretly.'

"And all the people shall say, 'Amen!'

25'Cursed *is* the one who takes a bribe
to slay an innocent person.'

"And all the people shall say, 'Amen!'

26'Cursed *is* the one who does not confirm *all* the words of this law by observing them.'

"And all the people shall say, 'Amen!' "

27:3 [a]Exodus 3:8

27:26 If a man is hanging on for dear life to a chain, if it breaks in just one link he will still plummet to his death. Breaking even one law, one time, is enough to condemn us. See James 2:10 comment.

"Without the atoning blood of Christ, sinners can neither have communion with a holy God, nor do any thing acceptable to him; his righteous law condemns every one who, at any time, or in any thing, transgresses it. Under its awful curse we remain as transgressors, until the redemption of Christ is applied to our hearts. Wherever the grace of God brings salvation, it teaches the believer to deny ungodliness and worldly lusts, to live soberly, righteously, and godly in this present world, consenting to, and delighting in the words of God's law, after the inward man. In this holy walk, true peace and solid joy are to be found." *Matthew Henry*

Blessings on Obedience

28 "Now it shall come to pass, if you diligently obey the voice of the LORD your God, to observe carefully all His commandments which I command you today, that the LORD your God will set you high above all nations of the earth. 2And all these blessings shall come upon you and overtake you, because you obey the voice of the LORD your God:

3"Blessed *shall* you *be* in the city, and blessed *shall* you *be* in the country.

4"Blessed *shall be* the fruit of your body, the produce of your ground and the increase of your herds, the increase of your cattle and the offspring of your flocks.

5"Blessed *shall be* your basket and your kneading bowl.

6"Blessed *shall* you *be* when you come in, and blessed *shall* you *be* when you go out.

7"The LORD will cause your enemies who rise against you to be defeated before your face; they shall come out against you one way and flee before you seven ways.

8"The LORD will command the blessing on you in your storehouses and in all to which you set your hand, and He will bless you in the land which the LORD your God is giving you.

9"The LORD will establish you as a holy people to Himself, just as He has sworn to you, if you keep the commandments of the LORD your God and walk in His ways. 10Then all peoples of the earth shall see that you are called by the name of the LORD, and they shall be afraid of you. 11And the LORD will grant you plenty of goods, in the fruit of your body, in the increase of your livestock, and in the produce of your ground, in the land of which the LORD swore to your fathers to give you. 12The LORD will open to you His good treasure, the heavens, to give the rain to your land in its season, and to bless all the work of your hand. You shall lend to many nations, but you shall not borrow. 13And the LORD will make you the head and not the tail; you shall be above only, and not be beneath, if you heed the commandments of the LORD your God, which I command you today, and are careful to observe *them*. 14So you shall not turn aside from any of the words which I command you this day, *to* the right or the left, to go after other gods to serve them.

Curses on Disobedience

15"But it shall come to pass, if you do not obey the voice of the LORD your God,

28:15 The divine butler. As of 2010, America was over $13 trillion in debt (a trillion is a thousand billion). That is no small change. Ironically, hundreds of billions of that debt was to Arab nations, $900 billion to China, and $128 billion to Russia.

Over 2.8 million homes were in foreclosure, with 4 million foreclosures estimated by year end. A gallon of milk cost as much as a gallon of gas, and a gallon of gas cost an arm and a leg. Add to that the bad news that over 2.3 million Americans were diagnosed with cancer that year, many of whom were children.

ABC News reported that more than 60 percent of the U.S. was in a drought. We became used to seeing onslaughts of floods, hurricanes lining up on our coasts, and killer tornadoes by the dozens ripping up the nation like there is no tomorrow. And, of course, we were in a war on terror that it seemed we couldn't win.

The above are all signs of God's dealings with a sinful nation. If you find that hard to believe, read Deut. 28 and see what God warned would happen to Israel if they forsook His Law and turned their backs on Him. Underline places where Scripture warns that they will get into financial debt to other nations and become the tail, not the head. Think about those nations to whom we are in debt. Underline where God says that aliens will flood the country, that their enemies will overcome them, and that disease will plague them.

As you hold your pen also hold on to your theology, because this chapter will destroy any image of God as a celestial Santa Claus or a divine butler. He is a God of justice and wrath as much as He is of love and mercy. To form an image of God with only one or two of His virtues, and to leave out the others, is to create an idol in your mind.

We are no different from ancient Israel. These sufferings have come to us because we have not been thankful to God, but instead have forsaken His Law. If we heeded the Ten Commandments, they would show us our sinful state and drive us to the cleansing blood of the Savior. Hearts and minds that are responsive to God, and not political change, is the key to healing for our land.

to observe carefully all His commandments and His statutes which I command
you today, that all these curses will come
upon you and overtake you:
16“Cursed *shall* you *be* in the city, and
cursed *shall* you *be* in the country.
17“Cursed *shall be* your basket and
your kneading bowl.
18“Cursed *shall be* the fruit of your body
and the produce of your land, the increase
of your cattle and the offspring of your
flocks.
19“Cursed *shall* you *be* when you come
in, and cursed *shall* you *be* when you go
out.

> The missionary church is a praying church. The history of missions is a history of prayer. Everything vital to the success of the world's evangelization hinges on prayer. Are thousands of missionaries and tens of thousands of native workers needed? 'Pray ye therefore the Lord of the harvest, that He send forth laborers into His harvest.'
>
> **JOHN R. MOTT**

20“The LORD will send on you cursing,
confusion, and rebuke in all that you set
your hand to do, until you are destroyed
and until you perish quickly, because of
the wickedness of your doings in which
you have forsaken Me. 21The LORD will
make the plague cling to you until He has
consumed you from the land which you
are going to possess. 22The LORD will strike
you with consumption, with fever, with
inflammation, with severe burning fever,
with the sword, with scorching, and with
mildew; they shall pursue you until you
perish. 23And your heavens which *are*
over your head shall be bronze, and the
earth which is under you *shall be* iron.
24The LORD will change the rain of your
land to powder and dust; from the heaven
it shall come down on you until you are
destroyed.
25“The LORD will cause you to be defeated before your enemies; you shall go
out one way against them and flee seven
ways before them; and you shall become
troublesome to all the kingdoms of the
earth. 26Your carcasses shall be food for
all the birds of the air and the beasts of
the earth, and no one shall frighten *them*
away. 27The LORD will strike you with the
boils of Egypt, with tumors, with the
scab, and with the itch, from which you
cannot be healed. 28The LORD will strike
you with madness and blindness and confusion of heart. 29And you shall grope at
noonday, as a blind man gropes in darkness; you shall not prosper in your ways;
you shall be only oppressed and plundered
continually, and no one shall save *you.*
30“You shall betroth a wife, but another man shall lie with her; you shall
build a house, but you shall not dwell in
it; you shall plant a vineyard, but shall
not gather its grapes. 31Your ox *shall be*
slaughtered before your eyes, but you
shall not eat of it; your donkey *shall be* violently taken away from before you, and
shall not be restored to you; your sheep
shall be given to your enemies, and you
shall have no one to rescue *them.* 32Your
sons and your daughters *shall be* given to
another people, and your eyes shall look
and fail *with longing* for them all day long;
and *there shall be* no strength in your
hand. 33A nation whom you have not
known shall eat the fruit of your land and
the produce of your labor, and you shall
be only oppressed and crushed continually. 34So you shall be driven mad because
of the sight which your eyes see. 35The
LORD will strike you in the knees and on
the legs with severe boils which cannot
be healed, and from the sole of your foot
to the top of your head.
36“The LORD will bring you and the
king whom you set over you to a nation
which neither you nor your fathers have
known, and there you shall serve other
gods—wood and stone. 37And you shall
become an astonishment, a proverb, and
a byword among all nations where the
LORD will drive you.
38“You shall carry much seed out to
the field but gather little in, for the locust
shall consume it. 39You shall plant vine-

yards and tend *them,* but you shall neither drink *of* the wine nor gather the *grapes;* for the worms shall eat them. 40You shall have olive trees throughout all your territory, but you shall not anoint *yourself* with the oil; for your olives shall drop off. 41You shall beget sons and daughters, but they shall not be yours; for they shall go into captivity. 42Locusts shall consume all your trees and the produce of your land.

43"The alien who *is* among you shall rise higher and higher above you, and you shall come down lower and lower. 44He shall lend to you, but you shall not lend to him; he shall be the head, and you shall be the tail.

45"Moreover all these curses shall come upon you and pursue and overtake you, until you are destroyed, because you did not obey the voice of the LORD your God, to keep His commandments and His statutes which He commanded you. 46And they shall be upon you for a sign and a wonder, and on your descendants forever.

47"Because you did not serve the LORD your God with joy and gladness of heart, for the abundance of everything, 48therefore you shall serve your enemies, whom the LORD will send against you, in hunger, in thirst, in nakedness, and in need of everything; and He will put a yoke of iron on your neck until He has destroyed you. 49The LORD will bring a nation against you from afar, from the end of the earth, *as swift* as the eagle flies, a nation whose language you will not understand, 50a nation of fierce countenance, which does not respect the elderly nor show favor to the young. 51And they shall eat the increase of your livestock and the produce of your land, until you are destroyed; they shall not leave you grain or new wine or oil, *or* the increase of your cattle or the offspring of your flocks, until they have destroyed you.

52"They shall besiege you at all your gates until your high and fortified walls, in which you trust, come down throughout all your land; and they shall besiege you at all your gates throughout all your land which the LORD your God has given you. 53You shall eat the fruit of your own body, the flesh of your sons and your daughters whom the LORD your God has given you, in the siege and desperate straits in which your enemy shall distress you. 54The sensitive and very refined man among you will be hostile toward his brother, toward the wife of his bosom, and toward the rest of his children whom he leaves behind, 55so that he will not give any of them the flesh of his children whom he will eat, because he has nothing left in the siege and desperate straits in which your enemy shall distress you at all your gates. 56The tender and delicate woman among you, who would not venture to set the sole of her foot on the ground because of her delicateness and sensitivity, will refuse[a] to the husband of her bosom, and to her son and her daughter, 57her placenta which comes out from between her feet and her children whom she bears; for she will eat them secretly for lack of everything in the siege and desperate straits in which your enemy shall distress you at all your gates.

58"If you do not carefully observe all the words of this law that are written in this book, that you may fear this glorious and awesome name, THE LORD YOUR GOD, 59then the LORD will bring upon you and your descendants extraordinary plagues—great and prolonged plagues—

28:56 [a]Literally *her eye shall be evil toward*

28:58 See Lev. 24:16 comment regarding honoring God's holy name.

"Does it grieve you, my friends, that the name of God is being taken in vain and desecrated? Does it grieve you that we are living in a godless age? ... But we are living in such an age and the main reason we should be praying about revival is that we are anxious to see God's name vindicated and His glory manifested. We should be anxious to see something happening that will arrest the nations, all the peoples, and cause them to stop and to think again." *Martyn Lloyd-Jones*

and serious and prolonged sicknesses. 60 Moreover He will bring back on you all the diseases of Egypt, of which you were afraid, and they shall cling to you. 61 Also every sickness and every plague, which *is* not written in this Book of the Law, will the LORD bring upon you until you are destroyed. 62 You shall be left few in number, whereas you were as the stars of heaven in multitude, because you would not obey the voice of the LORD your God. 63 And it shall be, *that* just as the LORD rejoiced over you to do you good and multiply you, so the LORD will rejoice over you to destroy you and bring you to nothing; and you shall be plucked from off the land which you go to possess.

64 "Then the LORD will scatter you among all peoples, from one end of the earth to the other, and there you shall serve other gods, which neither you nor your fathers have known—wood and stone. 65 And among those nations you shall find no rest, nor shall the sole of your foot have a resting place; but there the LORD will give you a trembling heart, failing eyes, and anguish of soul. 66 Your life shall hang in doubt before you; you shall fear day and night, and have no assurance of life. 67 In the morning you shall say, 'Oh, that it were evening!' And at evening you shall say, 'Oh, that it were morning!' because of the fear which terrifies your heart, and because of the sight which your eyes see.

68 "And the LORD will take you back to Egypt in ships, by the way of which I said to you, 'You shall never see it again.' And there you shall be offered for sale to your enemies as male and female slaves, but no one will buy *you*."

The Covenant Renewed in Moab

29 These *are* the words of the covenant which the LORD commanded Moses to make with the children of Israel in the land of Moab, besides the covenant which He made with them in Horeb.

2 Now Moses called all Israel and said to them: "You have seen all that the LORD did before your eyes in the land of Egypt, to Pharaoh and to all his servants and to all his land— 3 the great trials which your eyes have seen, the signs, and those great wonders. 4 Yet the LORD has not given you a heart to perceive and eyes to see and ears to hear, to this *very* day. 5 And I have led you forty years in the wilderness. Your clothes have not worn out on you, and your sandals have not worn out on your feet. 6 You have not eaten bread, nor have you drunk wine or *similar* drink, that you may know that I *am* the LORD your God. 7 And when you came to this place, Sihon king of Heshbon and Og king of Bashan came out against us to battle, and we conquered them. 8 We took their land and gave it as an inheritance to the Reubenites, to the Gadites, and to half the tribe of Manasseh. 9 Therefore keep the words of this covenant, and do them, that you may prosper in all that you do.

10 "All of you stand today before the LORD your God: your leaders and your tribes and your elders and your officers, all the men of Israel, 11 your little ones and your wives—also the stranger who *is* in your camp, from the one who cuts your wood to the one who draws your water— 12 that you may enter into covenant with the LORD your God, and into His oath, which the LORD your God makes with you today, 13 that He may establish you today as a people for Himself, and *that* He may be God to you, just as He has spoken to you, and just as He has sworn to your fathers, to Abraham, Isaac, and Jacob.

14 "I make this covenant and this oath, not with you alone, 15 but with *him* who stands here with us today before the LORD our God, as well as with *him* who *is* not here with us today 16 (for you know that we dwelt in the land of Egypt and that we came through the nations which you passed by, 17 and you saw their abominations and their idols which *were* among them—wood and stone and silver and gold); 18 so that there may not be among you man or woman or family or tribe, whose heart turns away today from the

LORD our God, to go *and* serve the gods of these nations, and that there may not be among you a root bearing bitterness or wormwood; [19]and so it may not happen, when he hears the words of this curse, that he blesses himself in his heart, saying, 'I shall have peace, even though I follow the dictates[a] of my heart'—as though the drunkard could be included with the sober.

[20]"The LORD would not spare him; for then the anger of the LORD and His jealousy would burn against that man, and every curse that is written in this book would settle on him, and the LORD would blot out his name from under heaven. [21]And the LORD would separate him from all the tribes of Israel for adversity, according to all the curses of the covenant that are written in this Book of the Law, [22]so that the coming generation of your children who rise up after you, and the foreigner who comes from a far land, would say, when they see the plagues of that land and the sicknesses which the LORD has laid on it:

[23]'The whole land *is* brimstone, salt, and burning; it is not sown, nor does it bear, nor does any grass grow there, like the overthrow of Sodom and Gomorrah, Admah, and Zeboiim, which the LORD overthrew in His anger and His wrath.' [24]All nations would say, 'Why has the LORD done so to this land? What does the heat of this great anger mean?' [25]Then *people* would say: 'Because they have forsaken the covenant of the LORD God of their fathers, which He made with them when He brought them out of the land of Egypt; [26]for they went and served other gods and worshiped them, gods that they did not know and that He had not given to them. [27]Then the anger of the LORD was aroused against this land, to bring on it every curse that is written in this book. [28]And the LORD uprooted them from their land in anger, in wrath, and in great indignation, and cast them into another land, as *it is* this day.'

[29]"The secret *things belong* to the LORD our God, but those *things which are* revealed *belong* to us and to our children forever, that *we* may do all the words of this law.

The Blessing of Returning to God

30 "Now it shall come to pass, when all these things come upon you, the blessing and the curse which I have set before you, and you call *them* to mind among all the nations where the LORD your God drives you, [2]and you return to the LORD your God and obey His voice, according to all that I command you today, you and your children, with all your heart and with all your soul, [3]that the LORD your God will bring you back from captivity, and have compassion on you, and gather you again from all the nations where the LORD your God has scattered you. [4]If *any* of you are driven out to the farthest *parts* under heaven, from there the LORD your God will gather you, and from there He will bring you. [5]Then the LORD your God will bring you to the land which your fathers possessed, and you shall possess it. He will prosper you and multiply you more than your fathers. [6]And the LORD your God will circumcise your heart and the heart of your descendants, to love the LORD your God with all your heart and with all your soul, that you may live.

[7]"Also the LORD your God will put all these curses on your enemies and on those who hate you, who persecuted you. [8]And you will again obey the voice of the LORD and do all His commandments which I command you today. [9]The LORD your God will make you abound in all the work of

29:19 [a]Or *stubbornness*

29:19,20 The ungodly don't know that God sees the imaginations of the heart. This is a primary reason why God sent the flood in Noah's day—because every intent of the thoughts of men's hearts was continually evil (see Gen. 6:5).

THE FUNCTION OF THE LAW

30:10 "The First Commandment, 'Thou shalt have no other gods before Me': My friend, are you ready to be weighed against this Commandment? Have you fulfilled, or are you willing to fulfill all the requirements of this Law? Put it into one of the scales, and step into the other. Is your heart set upon God alone? Have you no other God? Do you love Him above father or mother, the wife of your bosom, your children, home or land, wealth or pleasure? If men were true to this commandment, obedience to the remaining nine would follow naturally. It is because they are unsound in this that they break the others." *D. L. Moody*

your hand, in the fruit of your body, in the increase of your livestock, and in the produce of your land for good. For the LORD will again rejoice over you for good as He rejoiced over your fathers, 10if you obey the voice of the LORD your God, to keep His commandments and His statutes which are written in this Book of the Law, *and* if you turn to the LORD your God with all your heart and with all your soul.

The Choice of Life or Death

11"For this commandment which I command you today *is* not *too* mysterious for you, nor is it far off. 12It *is* not in heaven, that you should say, 'Who will ascend into heaven for us and bring it to us, that we may hear it and do it?' 13Nor *is* it beyond the sea, that you should say, 'Who will go over the sea for us and bring it to us, that we may hear it and do it?' 14But the word *is* very near you, in your mouth and in your heart, that you may do it.

15"See, I have set before you today life and good, death and evil, 16in that I command you today to love the LORD your God, to walk in His ways, and to keep His commandments, His statutes, and His judgments, that you may live and multiply; and the LORD your God will bless you in the land which you go to possess. 17But if your heart turns away so that you do not hear, and are drawn away, and worship other gods and serve them, 18I announce to you today that you shall surely perish; you shall not prolong *your* days in the land which you cross over the Jordan to go in and possess. 19I call heaven and earth as witnesses today against you, *that* I have set before you life and death, blessing and cursing; therefore choose life, that both you and your descendants may live; 20that you may love the LORD your God, that you may obey His voice, and that you may cling to Him, for He *is* your life and the length of your days; and that you may dwell in the land which the LORD swore to your fathers, to Abraham, Isaac, and Jacob, to give them."

Joshua the New Leader of Israel

31 Then Moses went and spoke these words to all Israel. 2And he said to them: "I *am* one hundred and twenty years old today. I can no longer go out and come in. Also the LORD has said to me, 'You shall not cross over this Jordan.' 3The LORD your God Himself crosses over before you; He will destroy these nations from before you, and you shall dispossess them. Joshua himself crosses over before you, just as the LORD has said. 4And the LORD will do to them as He did to Sihon and Og, the kings of the Amorites and their land, when He destroyed them. 5The LORD will give them over to you, that you may do to them according to every commandment which I have commanded you. 6Be strong and of good courage, do not fear nor be afraid of them; for the LORD your

30:15 Once Adam and Eve ate of the tree of the knowledge of good and evil (see Gen. 2:17), mankind has known both good and evil and has had to choose between the two. See Gen. 3:5 comment.

30:19,20 This is the essence of the gospel that we preach to unbelievers. Set before them are the way of life and the way of death, the way of blessing and the way of cursing. If they reject Jesus Christ, and the love He demonstrated on the cross, they reject the One who is Life itself (see John 1:4; 14:6; 1 John 5:11,12).

God, He *is* the One who goes with you. He will not leave you nor forsake you."

[7]Then Moses called Joshua and said to him in the sight of all Israel, "Be strong and of good courage, for you must go with this people to the land which the LORD has sworn to their fathers to give them, and you shall cause them to inherit
it. [8]And the LORD, He *is* the One who goes before you. He will be with you, He will not leave you nor forsake you; do not fear nor be dismayed."

The Law to Be Read Every Seven Years

[9]So Moses wrote this law and delivered it to the priests, the sons of Levi, who bore the ark of the covenant of the LORD,
and to all the elders of Israel. [10]And Moses
commanded them, saying: "At the end of *every* seven years, at the appointed time in the year of release, at the Feast of
Tabernacles, [11]when all Israel comes to
appear before the LORD your God in the place which He chooses, you shall read this law before all Israel in their hearing.
[12]Gather the people together, men and women and little ones, and the stranger who *is* within your gates, that they may hear and that they may learn to fear the LORD your God and carefully observe all
the words of this law, [13]and *that* their
children, who have not known it, may hear and learn to fear the LORD your God as long as you live in the land which you cross the Jordan to possess."

Prediction of Israel's Rebellion

[14]Then the LORD said to Moses, "Behold, the days approach when you must die; call Joshua, and present yourselves in the tabernacle of meeting, that I may inaugurate him."

So Moses and Joshua went and presented themselves in the tabernacle of
meeting. [15]Now the LORD appeared at the
tabernacle in a pillar of cloud, and the pillar of cloud stood above the door of the tabernacle.

[16]And the LORD said to Moses: "Behold, you will rest with your fathers; and this people will rise and play the harlot with the gods of the foreigners of the land, where they go *to be* among them, and they will forsake Me and break My covenant which I have made with them.
[17]Then My anger shall be aroused against
them in that day, and I will forsake them, and I will hide My face from them, and they shall be devoured. And many evils and troubles shall befall them, so that they will say in that day, 'Have not these evils come upon us because our God *is*
not among us?' [18]And I will surely hide
My face in that day because of all the evil which they have done, in that they have turned to other gods.

> The law is like a moral mirror. It shuts our mouths and opens our eyes. It condemns but does not convert. It challenges but does not change. It points the finger but can't give mercy. And it drives us to Jesus, who has the answer we are looking for.
>
> **GREG LAURIE**

[19]"Now therefore, write down this song for yourselves, and teach it to the children of Israel; put it in their mouths, that this song may be a witness for Me
against the children of Israel. [20]When I
have brought them to the land flowing with milk and honey, of which I swore to their fathers, and they have eaten and filled themselves and grown fat, then they will turn to other gods and serve them; and they will provoke Me and break My
covenant. [21]Then it shall be, when many
evils and troubles have come upon them, that this song will testify against them as

31:6 Because all the promises of God in Christ are "Yes" and "Amen" (see 2 Cor. 1:20), you can personalize this promise if you are in Christ.

a witness; for it will not be forgotten in
the mouths of their descendants, for I
know the inclination of their behavior today, even before I have brought them to
the land of which I swore *to give them.*"
22Therefore Moses wrote this song the
same day, and taught it to the children of
Israel. 23Then He inaugurated Joshua the
son of Nun, and said, "Be strong and of
good courage; for you shall bring the
children of Israel into the land of which I
swore to them, and I will be with you."
24So it was, when Moses had completed writing the words of this law in a
book, when they were finished, 25that
Moses commanded the Levites, who bore
the ark of the covenant of the LORD, saying: 26"Take this Book of the Law, and put
it beside the ark of the covenant of the
LORD your God, that it may be there as a
witness against you; 27for I know your rebellion and your stiff neck. *If* today, while
I am yet alive with you, you have been rebellious against the LORD, then how much
more after my death? 28Gather to me all
the elders of your tribes, and your officers,
that I may speak these words in their
hearing and call heaven and earth to witness against them. 29For I know that after
my death you will become utterly corrupt,
and turn aside from the way which I have
commanded you. And evil will befall you
in the latter days, because you will do evil
in the sight of the LORD, to provoke Him
to anger through the work of your hands."

The Song of Moses

30Then Moses spoke in the hearing of
all the assembly of Israel the words of this
song until they were ended:

32 "Give ear, O heavens, and I will speak;
And hear, O earth, the words of my mouth.
2Let my teaching drop as the rain,
My speech distill as the dew,
As raindrops on the tender herb,
And as showers on the grass.
3For I proclaim the name of the LORD:
Ascribe greatness to our God.
4*He is* the Rock, His work *is* perfect;
For all His ways *are* justice,
A God of truth and without injustice;
Righteous and upright *is* He.

5"They have corrupted themselves;
They are not His children,
Because of their blemish:
A perverse and crooked generation.
6Do you thus deal with the LORD,
O foolish and unwise people?
Is He not your Father, *who* bought you?
Has He not made you and established you?

7"Remember the days of old,
Consider the years of many generations.
Ask your father, and he will show you;
Your elders, and they will tell you:
8When the Most High divided their inheritance to the nations,
When He separated the sons of Adam,
He set the boundaries of the peoples
According to the number of the children of Israel.
9For the LORD's portion *is* His people;
Jacob *is* the place of His inheritance.

10"He found him in a desert land
And in the wasteland, a howling wilderness;
He encircled him, He instructed him,
He kept him as the apple of His eye.
11As an eagle stirs up its nest,
Hovers over its young,
Spreading out its wings, taking them up,
Carrying them on its wings,
12*So* the LORD alone led him,
And *there was* no foreign god with him.

13"He made him ride in the heights of the earth,
That he might eat the produce of the fields;
He made him draw honey from the rock,
And oil from the flinty rock;

QUESTIONS & OBJECTIONS

"If hell exists, where in the universe is this huge place?"

Do you know where the city of Invercargill is located? More than likely you don't (it is at the bottom of the South Island of New Zealand). So, does the city not exist because you cannot identify where it is? We know hell exists because we have the greatest authority on this earth stating that it does—the Word of God. We also have reason on our side. If God is good, He will see to it that murderers and rapists get justice. However, He will be so thorough in His justice, He will see that thieves, liars, adulterers, fornicators, etc., are punished, and God's "prison" is a place called hell. While the Bible says that heaven is "up" and hell is "down," I don't need to know any more than that to know I don't want to go to a horrible place of eternal torment. See also Rev. 1:18 comment.

"Hell is a reflection of the holiness of God. Hell is as bad as God is good. The severity of hell shows you how good God must be. Because if the punishment for sinning against Him is that severe, He must be awfully good." *Bob Glenn*

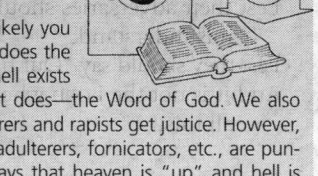

14Curds from the cattle, and milk of the flock,
With fat of lambs;
And rams of the breed of Bashan, and goats,
With the choicest wheat;
And you drank wine, the blood of the grapes.

15"But Jeshurun grew fat and kicked;
You grew fat, you grew thick,
You are obese!
Then he forsook God *who* made him,
And scornfully esteemed the Rock of his salvation.
16They provoked Him to jealousy with foreign *gods;*
With abominations they provoked Him to anger.
17They sacrificed to demons, not to God,
To gods they did not know,
To new *gods,* new arrivals
That your fathers did not fear.
18Of the Rock *who* begot you, you are unmindful,
And have forgotten the God who fathered you.

19"And when the LORD saw *it,* He spurned *them,*
Because of the provocation of His sons and His daughters.
20And He said: 'I will hide My face from them,
I will see what their end *will be,*
For they *are* a perverse generation,
Children in whom *is* no faith.
21They have provoked Me to jealousy by *what* is not God;
They have moved Me to anger by their foolish idols.
But I will provoke them to jealousy by *those who are* not a nation;
I will move them to anger by a foolish nation.
22For a fire is kindled in My anger,
And shall burn to the lowest hell;
It shall consume the earth with her increase,
And set on fire the foundations of the mountains.

23'I will heap disasters on them;
I will spend My arrows on them.
24*They shall be* wasted with hunger,
Devoured by pestilence and bitter destruction;
I will also send against them the teeth of beasts,
With the poison of serpents of the dust.
25The sword shall destroy outside;
There shall be terror within
For the young man and virgin,
The nursing child with the man of gray hairs.
26I would have said, "I will dash them in pieces,

I will make the memory of them to
cease from among men,"
27Had I not feared the wrath of the
enemy,
Lest their adversaries should
misunderstand,
Lest they should say, "Our hand *is* high;
And it is not the LORD who has done
all this." '

28"For they *are* a nation void of counsel,
Nor *is there any* understanding in them.
29Oh, that they were wise, *that* they
understood this,
That they would consider their latter
end!
30How could one chase a thousand,
And two put ten thousand to flight,
Unless their Rock had sold them,
And the LORD had surrendered them?
31For their rock *is* not like our Rock,
Even our enemies themselves *being*
judges.
32For their vine *is* of the vine of Sodom
And of the fields of Gomorrah;
Their grapes *are* grapes of gall,
Their clusters *are* bitter.
33Their wine *is* the poison of serpents,
And the cruel venom of cobras.

34'*Is* this not laid up in store with Me,
Sealed up among My treasures?
35Vengeance is Mine, and recompense;
Their foot shall slip in *due* time;
For the day of their calamity *is* at hand,
And the things to come hasten upon
them.'

36"For the LORD will judge His people
And have compassion on His servants,
When He sees that *their* power is gone,
And *there is* no one *remaining*, bond
or free.
37He will say: 'Where *are* their gods,
The rock in which they sought refuge?
38Who ate the fat of their sacrifices,
And drank the wine of their drink
offering?
Let them rise and help you,
And be your refuge.

39'Now see that I, *even* I, *am* He,
And *there is* no God besides Me;
I kill and I make alive;
I wound and I heal;
Nor *is there any* who can deliver from
My hand.
40For I raise My hand to heaven,
And say, "*As* I live forever,
41If I whet My glittering sword,
And My hand takes hold on judgment,
I will render vengeance to My enemies,
And repay those who hate Me.
42I will make My arrows drunk with
blood,
And My sword shall devour flesh,
With the blood of the slain and the
captives,
From the heads of the leaders of the
enemy." '

43"Rejoice, O Gentiles, *with* His people;[a]
For He will avenge the blood of His
servants,
And render vengeance to His
adversaries;
He will provide atonement for His
land *and* His people."

32:43 [a]A Dead Sea Scroll fragment adds *And let all the gods (angels) worship Him* (compare Septuagint and Hebrews 1:6).

32:29 Few really consider their latter end. Death is something that happens to other people. We therefore need to learn how to confront the lost and make them face their mortality. They must think about their eternity—and the way to help them do that is to use the Law to bring about the knowledge of sin and its consequences. For details, see 2 Sam. 12:1–14 and James 4:14 comments.

32:39–41 We need not hide verses that speak of God killing whom He will. All of His judgments are true and righteous altogether, and the One who gave us life has the right to take it from all who sin (see 1 Sam. 2:6; Job 12:10). If God were to give humanity absolute justice, we all would be struck down the moment we sinned. However, He has extended His mercy toward us and let us live, giving us opportunity to repent (see 2 Pet. 3:9). See also Deut. 3:6 and 1 Sam. 15:3 comments.

[44]So Moses came with Joshua[a] the son of Nun and spoke all the words of this song in the hearing of the people.
[45]Moses finished speaking all these words to all Israel, [46]and he said to them: "Set your hearts on all the words which I testify among you today, which you shall command your children to be careful to observe—all the words of this law. [47]For it *is* not a futile thing for you, because it *is* your life, and by this word you shall prolong *your* days in the land which you cross over the Jordan to possess."

Moses to Die on Mount Nebo

[48]Then the LORD spoke to Moses that very same day, saying: [49]"Go up this mountain of the Abarim, Mount Nebo, which *is* in the land of Moab, across from Jericho; view the land of Canaan, which I give to the children of Israel as a possession;
[50]and die on the mountain which you ascend, and be gathered to your people, just as Aaron your brother died on Mount Hor and was gathered to his people; [51]because you trespassed against Me among the children of Israel at the waters of Meribah Kadesh, in the Wilderness of Zin, because you did not hallow Me in the midst of the children of Israel. [52]Yet you shall see the land before *you,* though you shall not go there, into the land which I am giving to the children of Israel."

Moses' Final Blessing on Israel

33 Now this *is* the blessing with which Moses the man of God blessed the children of Israel before his death. [2]And he said:

"The LORD came from Sinai,
And dawned on them from Seir;
He shone forth from Mount Paran,
And He came with ten thousands of saints;
From His right hand
Came a fiery law for them.
[3]Yes, He loves the people;
All His saints *are* in Your hand;
They sit down at Your feet;
Everyone receives Your words.
[4]Moses commanded a law for us,
A heritage of the congregation of Jacob.
[5]And He was King in Jeshurun,
When the leaders of the people were gathered,
All the tribes of Israel together.

[6]"Let Reuben live, and not die,
Nor let his men be few."

[7]And this he said of Judah:

"Hear, LORD, the voice of Judah,
And bring him to his people;
Let his hands be sufficient for him,
And may You be a help against his enemies."

[8]And of Levi he said:

"*Let* Your Thummim and Your Urim *be* with Your holy one,
Whom You tested at Massah,
And with whom You contended at the waters of Meribah,
[9]Who says of his father and mother,
'I have not seen them';
Nor did he acknowledge his brothers,
Or know his own children;
For they have observed Your word
And kept Your covenant.
[10]They shall teach Jacob Your judgments,
And Israel Your law.

32:44 [a]Hebrew *Hoshea* (compare Numbers 13:8, 16)

33:3 It was love that brought Jesus to this earth and drove Him to the cross. Those who return that love will sit at His feet and learn from Him (see Luke 10:39–44). They will hear His words and put them into practice. See Matt. 7:26,27.

33:9 Though Jesus was a Son, the Scriptures tell us that He learned obedience by the things that He suffered (see Heb. 5:8). Obedience is evidence of love for God.

"We make a living by what we get, but we make a life by what we give."

Winston Churchill

They shall put incense before You,
And a whole burnt sacrifice on Your
altar.
11Bless his substance, LORD,
And accept the work of his hands;
Strike the loins of those who rise
against him,
And of those who hate him, that they
rise not again."

12Of Benjamin he said:

"The beloved of the LORD shall dwell
in safety by Him,
Who shelters him all the day long;
And he shall dwell between His
shoulders."

13And of Joseph he said:

"Blessed of the LORD *is* his land,
With the precious things of heaven,
with the dew,
And the deep lying beneath,
14With the precious fruits of the sun,
With the precious produce of the
months,
15With the best things of the ancient
mountains,
With the precious things of the
everlasting hills,
16With the precious things of the earth
and its fullness,
And the favor of Him who dwelt in
the bush.
Let *the blessing* come 'on the head of
Joseph,
And on the crown of the head of him
who was separate from his
brothers.'[a]
17His glory *is like* a firstborn bull,
And his horns *like* the horns of the
wild ox;
Together with them
He shall push the peoples
To the ends of the earth;
They *are* the ten thousands of Ephraim,
And they *are* the thousands of
Manasseh."

18And of Zebulun he said:

"Rejoice, Zebulun, in your going out,
And Issachar in your tents!
19They shall call the peoples *to* the
mountain;
There they shall offer sacrifices of
righteousness;
For they shall partake *of* the
abundance of the seas
And *of* treasures hidden in the sand."

20And of Gad he said:

"Blessed *is* he who enlarges Gad;
He dwells as a lion,
And tears the arm and the crown of
his head.
21He provided the first *part* for himself,
Because a lawgiver's portion was
reserved there.
He came *with* the heads of the people;
He administered the justice of the
LORD,
And His judgments with Israel."

22And of Dan he said:

33:16 [a]Genesis 49:26

"Dan *is* a lion's whelp;
He shall leap from Bashan."

23And of Naphtali he said:

"O Naphtali, satisfied with favor,
And full of the blessing of the LORD,
Possess the west and the south."

24And of Asher he said:

"Asher *is* most blessed of sons;
Let him be favored by his brothers,
And let him dip his foot in oil.
25Your sandals *shall be* iron and bronze;
As your days, *so shall* your strength *be*.

26"*There is* no one like the God of
Jeshurun,
Who rides the heavens to help you,
And in His excellency on the clouds.
27The eternal God *is your* refuge,
And underneath *are* the everlasting
arms;
He will thrust out the enemy from
before you,
And will say, 'Destroy!'
28Then Israel shall dwell in safety,
The fountain of Jacob alone,
In a land of grain and new wine;
His heavens shall also drop dew.
29Happy *are* you, O Israel!
Who *is* like you, a people saved by
the LORD,
The shield of your help
And the sword of your majesty!
Your enemies shall submit to you,
And you shall tread down their high
places."

Moses Dies on Mount Nebo

34 Then Moses went up from the
plains of Moab to Mount Nebo, to
the top of Pisgah, which is across from
Jericho. And the LORD showed him all the
land of Gilead as far as Dan, 2all Naphtali
and the land of Ephraim and Manasseh,
all the land of Judah as far as the Western
Sea,[a] 3the South, and the plain of the Valley of Jericho, the city of palm trees, as far
as Zoar. 4Then the LORD said to him,
"This *is* the land of which I swore to give
Abraham, Isaac, and Jacob, saying, 'I will
give it to your descendants.' I have caused
you to see *it* with your eyes, but you shall
not cross over there."

> Men are pretty near the kingdom of God when they do not see anything good in themselves.
>
> **D. L. MOODY**

5So Moses the servant of the LORD died
there in the land of Moab, according to
the word of the LORD. 6And He buried
him in a valley in the land of Moab, opposite Beth Peor; but no one knows his
grave to this day. 7Moses *was* one hundred and twenty years old when he died.
His eyes were not dim nor his natural
vigor diminished. 8And the children of
Israel wept for Moses in the plains of
Moab thirty days. So the days of weeping
and mourning for Moses ended.
9Now Joshua the son of Nun was full
of the spirit of wisdom, for Moses had
laid his hands on him; so the children of
Israel heeded him, and did as the LORD
had commanded Moses.
10But since then there has not arisen in
Israel a prophet like Moses, whom the
LORD knew face to face, 11in all the signs
and wonders which the LORD sent him to
do in the land of Egypt, before Pharaoh,
before all his servants, and in all his land,
12and by all that mighty power and all the
great terror which Moses performed in
the sight of all Israel.

34:2 [a]That is, the Mediterranean

34:4 Moses could not enter the Promised Land. The Law can do nothing but point us to Christ, that we may enter in by faith. See Gal. 3:24.

The Ten Commandments Compared to God's Character

The Ten Commandments are a reflection of God's nature in that they contain universal and unchanging principles of morality and describe our relationship to God and our fellow human beings. The reason God cannot tolerate sin is that it is a defilement of His very own character.

ATTRIBUTE	GOD'S CHARACTER	TEN COMMANDMENTS
Love	1 John 4:8; 1 John 4:16	Rom. 13:8–10; Gal. 5:14
Perfect	Matt. 5:48	James 1:25; Psa. 19:7
Holy	1 Pet. 1:15; Psa. 99:9	Rom. 7:12; 2 Pet. 2:21
Eternal	Rom. 16:26; Deut. 33:27	Psa. 111:7,8; Luke 16:17
Truth	Deut. 32:4; John 14:6	Psa. 119:142,151
Pure	1 John 3:3; Job 4:17	Psa. 19:7,8
Good	Nah. 1:7; Luke 18:19	Rom. 7:12,16; 1 Tim. 1:8
Spiritual	John 4:24	Rom. 7:14
Just	Isa. 45:21; Rom. 3:26	Rom. 7:12
Faithful	1 Cor. 1:9; 2 Thess. 3:3	Psa. 119:86
Light	1 John 1:5	Prov. 6:23
Life	John 14:6; Psa. 36:9	Matt. 19:17; Prov. 3:1,2
Righteous	Psa. 145:17; Jer. 23:6	Rom. 9:31; Psa. 119:172
True	John 3:33; 1 John 5:20	Neh. 9:13
Peace	Rom. 15:33; Heb. 13:20	Psa. 119:165
Honorable	Isa. 58:13	Isa. 42:21
Great	Psa. 48:1	Hos. 8:12
Wonderful	Isa. 9:6	Psa. 119:18
The Way	John 14:6	Psa. 119:30–32
Sure	2 Tim. 2:19	Psa. 19:7; 111:7
Unchanging	Mal. 3:6; Heb. 13:8	Matt. 5:18; Psa. 111:7,8
Wise	Dan. 2:20; Job 36:5; Jude 1:25	Psa. 119:98; 19:7
Enlightenment	Psa. 18:28	Psa. 19:8
Blessed	1 Tim. 1:11; Psa. 28:6	Rev. 22:14; Exod. 20:11
Happiness	Psa. 146:5	Prov. 29:18
Merciful	2 Cor. 1:3; Exod. 34:6	Matt. 23:23; Neh. 1:5
Understanding	Psa. 147:5	Psa. 119:73; 119:99
Delight	Psa. 37:4	Psa. 1:2
Liberty	2 Cor. 3:17	James 1:25; Psa. 119:45
Knowledge	Isa. 11:2	Rom. 3:20
Hope	Psa. 71:5; Rom. 15:13	Psa. 119:43
Our Meditation	Psa. 63:6	Psa. 1:2

Joshua

God's Commission to Joshua

1 After the death of Moses the servant of the LORD, it came to pass that the LORD spoke to Joshua the son of Nun, Moses' assistant, saying: 2"Moses My servant is dead. Now therefore, arise, go over this Jordan, you and all this people, to the land which I am giving to them—the children of Israel. 3Every place that the sole of your foot will tread upon I have given you, as I said to Moses. 4From the wilderness and this Lebanon as far as the great river, the River Euphrates, all the land of the Hittites, and to the Great Sea toward the going down of the sun, shall be your territory. 5No man shall *be able to* stand before you all the days of your life; as I was with Moses, *so* I will be with you. I will not leave you nor forsake you. 6Be strong and of good courage, for to this people you shall divide as an inheritance the land which I swore to their fathers to give them. 7Only be strong and very courageous, that you may observe to do according to all the law which Moses My servant commanded you; do not turn from it to the right hand or to the left, that you may prosper wherever you go. 8This Book of the Law shall not depart from your mouth, but you shall meditate in it day and night, that you may observe to do according to all that is written in it. For then you will make your way prosperous, and then you will have good success. 9Have I not commanded you? Be strong and of good courage; do not be afraid, nor be dismayed, for the LORD your God *is* with you wherever you go."

The Order to Cross the Jordan

10Then Joshua commanded the officers of the people, saying, 11"Pass through the camp and command the people, saying, 'Prepare provisions for yourselves, for within three days you will cross over this Jordan, to go in to possess the land which the LORD your God is giving you to possess.'"

12And to the Reubenites, the Gadites, and half the tribe of Manasseh Joshua spoke, saying, 13"Remember the word which Moses the servant of the LORD commanded you, saying, 'The LORD your God is giving you rest and is giving you this land.' 14Your wives, your little ones, and your livestock shall remain in the land

1:2 Moses can't take us into the Promised Land; only Jesus can (see John 14:6). The Law can only take us to the foot of a blood-stained cross. It is a tutor to bring us to Christ. See Rom. 3:19,20; 7:7; and Gal. 3:24 for its function.

1:6–9 The key to biblical "good success" is obedience. Notice that this is called "the Book of the Law." The moral Law is the essence of the books of Moses. God cannot be separated from His Law because it is a reflection of His character. Both God and His Law are perfect, holy, just, and good. For a comparison of God's character and the Ten Commandments, see page 280.

QUESTIONS & OBJECTIONS

"Are there times when lying is acceptable?"

This is a contentious issue. Most husbands would lie if an armed intruder asked if his wife was hiding in the house. If he said, "Yes, she's under the bed," then he would be enabling her murder. What would he say if he's forced at gunpoint to watch while the gunman rapes his wife before murdering her: "Sorry, honey; I didn't want to tell a lie"? These scenarios are often brought up by the unsaved to justify lying. But God knows the difference between incidents like these to protect the life of innocent victims, the use of "discretion" to protect someone's feelings, and bold, deceitful lies to protect ourselves.

which Moses gave you on this side of the Jordan. But you shall pass before your brethren armed, all your mighty men of valor, and help them, [15]until the LORD has given your brethren rest, as He *gave* you, and they also have taken possession of the land which the LORD your God is giving them. Then you shall return to the land of your possession and enjoy it, which Moses the LORD's servant gave you on this side of the Jordan toward the sunrise."

[16]So they answered Joshua, saying, "All that you command us we will do, and wherever you send us we will go. [17]Just as we heeded Moses in all things, so we will heed you. Only the LORD your God be with you, as He was with Moses. [18]Whoever rebels against your command and does not heed your words, in all that you command him, shall be put to death. Only be strong and of good courage."

Rahab Hides the Spies

2 Now Joshua the son of Nun sent out two men from Acacia Grove[a] to spy secretly, saying, "Go, view the land, especially Jericho."

So they went, and came to the house of a harlot named Rahab, and lodged there. [2]And it was told the king of Jericho, saying, "Behold, men have come here tonight from the children of Israel to search out the country."

[3]So the king of Jericho sent to Rahab, saying, "Bring out the men who have come to you, who have entered your house, for they have come to search out all the country."

[4]Then the woman took the two men and hid them. So she said, "Yes, the men came to me, but I did not know where they *were* from. [5]And it happened as the gate was being shut, when it was dark, that the men went out. Where the men went I do not know; pursue them quickly, for you may overtake them." [6](But she had brought them up to the roof and hidden them with the stalks of flax, which she had laid in order on the roof.) [7]Then the men pursued them by the road to the Jordan, to the fords. And as soon as those who pursued them had gone out, they shut the gate.

[8]Now before they lay down, she came up to them on the roof, [9]and said to the men: "I know that the LORD has given you the land, that the terror of you has fallen on us, and that all the inhabitants of the land are fainthearted because of you. [10]For we have heard how the LORD dried up the water of the Red Sea for you when you came out of Egypt, and what you did to the two kings of the Amorites who *were* on the other side of the Jordan, Sihon and Og, whom you utterly destroyed. [11]And as soon as we heard *these things,* our hearts melted; neither did there remain any more courage in anyone because of you, for the LORD your God, He *is* God in heaven above and on earth beneath. [12]Now therefore, I beg you, swear to me by the LORD, since I have shown you kindness, that you also will show kindness to my father's house, and give

2:1 [a]Hebrew *Shittim*

me a true token, [13]and spare my father,
my mother, my brothers, my sisters, and
all that they have, and deliver our lives
from death."
[14]So the men answered her, "Our lives
for yours, if none of you tell this business
of ours. And it shall be, when the LORD
has given us the land, that we will deal
kindly and truly with you."
[15]Then she let them down by a rope
through the window, for her house *was*
on the city wall; she dwelt on the wall.
[16]And she said to them, "Get to the mountain, lest the pursuers meet you. Hide there
three days, until the pursuers have returned. Afterward you may go your way."
[17]So the men said to her: "We *will be*
blameless of this oath of yours which you
have made us swear, [18]unless, *when* we
come into the land, you bind this line of
scarlet cord in the window through which
you let us down, and unless you bring
your father, your mother, your brothers,
and all your father's household to your
own home. [19]So it shall be *that* whoever
goes outside the doors of your house into
the street, his blood *shall be* on his own
head, and we *will be* guiltless. And whoever is with you in the house, his blood
shall be on our head if a hand is laid on
him. [20]And if you tell this business of
ours, then we will be free from your oath
which you made us swear."
[21]Then she said, "According to your
words, so *be* it." And she sent them away,
and they departed. And she bound the
scarlet cord in the window.
[22]They departed and went to the mountain, and stayed there three days until the
pursuers returned. The pursuers sought
them all along the way, but did not find
them. [23]So the two men returned, descended from the mountain, and crossed over;
and they came to Joshua the son of Nun,
and told him all that had befallen them.
[24]And they said to Joshua, "Truly the LORD
has delivered all the land into our hands,
for indeed all the inhabitants of the country are fainthearted because of us."

Israel Crosses the Jordan

3 Then Joshua rose early in the morning; and they set out from Acacia
Grove[a] and came to the Jordan, he and
all the children of Israel, and lodged there
before they crossed over. [2]So it was, after
three days, that the officers went through
the camp; [3]and they commanded the
people, saying, "When you see the ark of
the covenant of the LORD your God, and
the priests, the Levites, bearing it, then
you shall set out from your place and go
after it. [4]Yet there shall be a space between you and it, about two thousand
cubits by measure. Do not come near it,
that you may know the way by which
you must go, for you have not passed *this*
way before."
[5]And Joshua said to the people, "Sanctify yourselves, for tomorrow the LORD will
do wonders among you." [6]Then Joshua
spoke to the priests, saying, "Take up the
ark of the covenant and cross over before
the people."
So they took up the ark of the covenant and went before the people.
[7]And the LORD said to Joshua, "This
day I will begin to exalt you in the sight
of all Israel, that they may know that, as
I was with Moses, *so* I will be with you.
[8]You shall command the priests who bear
the ark of the covenant, saying, 'When you
have come to the edge of the water of the
Jordan, you shall stand in the Jordan.' "
[9]So Joshua said to the children of Israel, "Come here, and hear the words of
the LORD your God." [10]And Joshua said,
"By this you shall know that the living

3:1 [a]Hebrew *Shittim*

2:18,19 It is the scarlet thread of the blood of Christ that protects us from the wrath of the Law. All who are sheltered in Christ are protected from eternal justice. For how this "scarlet thread" of redemption is woven throughout Scripture, see Gen. 3:21 comment.

The Function of the Law

3:17 "It is worthy of grateful note that this gospel blessing reaches down to the exact spot where the law leaves us when it has done for us the very best within its power or design. The utmost the law can accomplish for our fallen humanity is to lay bare our spiritual poverty, and convince us of it. It cannot by any possibility enrich a man: its greatest service is to tear away from him his fancied wealth of self-righteousness, show him his overwhelming indebtedness to God, and bow him to the earth in self-despair.

"Like Moses, it leads away from Goshen, conducts into the wilderness, and brings to the verge of an impassable stream, but it can do no more; Joshua Jesus is needed to divide the Jordan, and conduct into the promised land. The law rends the goodly Babylonish garment of our imaginary merits into ten pieces, and proves our wedge of gold to be mere dross, and thus it leaves us, 'naked, and poor, and miserable.' To this point Jesus descends; his full line of blessing comes up to the verge of destruction, rescues the lost, and enriches the poor. The gospel is as full as it is free." *Charles Spurgeon*

God is among you, and *that* He will without fail drive out from before you the Canaanites and the Hittites and the Hivites and the Perizzites and the Girgashites and the Amorites and the Jebusites: [11]Behold, the ark of the covenant of the Lord of all the earth is crossing over before you into the Jordan. [12]Now therefore, take for yourselves twelve men from the tribes of Israel, one man from every tribe. [13]And it shall come to pass, as soon as the soles of the feet of the priests who bear the ark of the LORD, the Lord of all the earth, shall rest in the waters of the Jordan, *that* the waters of the Jordan shall be cut off, the waters that come down from upstream, and they shall stand as a heap."

[14]So it was, when the people set out from their camp to cross over the Jordan, with the priests bearing the ark of the covenant before the people, [15]and as those who bore the ark came to the Jordan, and the feet of the priests who bore the ark dipped in the edge of the water (for the Jordan overflows all its banks during the whole time of harvest), [16]that the waters which came down from upstream stood *still, and* rose in a heap very far away at Adam, the city that *is* beside Zaretan. So the waters that went down into the Sea of the Arabah, the Salt Sea, failed, *and* were cut off; and the people crossed over opposite Jericho. [17]Then the priests who bore the ark of the covenant of the LORD stood firm on dry ground in the midst of the Jordan; and all Israel crossed over on dry ground, until all the people had crossed completely over the Jordan.

The Memorial Stones

4 And it came to pass, when all the people had completely crossed over the Jordan, that the LORD spoke to Joshua, saying: [2]"Take for yourselves twelve men from the people, one man from every tribe, [3]and command them, saying, 'Take for yourselves twelve stones from here, out of the midst of the Jordan, from the place where the priests' feet stood firm. You shall carry them over with you and leave them in the lodging place where you lodge tonight.' "

[4]Then Joshua called the twelve men whom he had appointed from the children of Israel, one man from every tribe; [5]and Joshua said to them: "Cross over before the ark of the LORD your God into the midst of the Jordan, and each one of you take up a stone on his shoulder, according to the number of the tribes of the children of Israel, [6]that this may be a sign among you when your children ask in time to come, saying, 'What do these stones *mean* to you?' [7]Then you shall answer them that the waters of the Jordan were cut off before the ark of the covenant of the LORD; when it crossed over the

3:14–16 The flow of death was cut off from Adam's race through the gospel (see 2 Tim. 1:10).

4:4–7 Just as the twelve stones were placed as immovable witnesses, the church, too, was established with twelve witnesses (see Acts 1:21–26).

Jordan, the waters of the Jordan were cut
off. And these stones shall be for a memorial to the children of Israel forever."
8And the children of Israel did so, just
as Joshua commanded, and took up twelve
stones from the midst of the Jordan, as
the LORD had spoken to Joshua, according to the number of the tribes of the
children of Israel, and carried them over
with them to the place where they lodged,
and laid them down there. 9Then Joshua
set up twelve stones in the midst of the
Jordan, in the place where the feet of the
priests who bore the ark of the covenant
stood; and they are there to this day.
10So the priests who bore the ark
stood in the midst of the Jordan until
everything was finished that the LORD
had commanded Joshua to speak to the
people, according to all that Moses had
commanded Joshua; and the people hurried and crossed over. 11Then it came to
pass, when all the people had completely
crossed over, that the ark of the LORD and
the priests crossed over in the presence of
the people. 12And the men of Reuben, the
men of Gad, and half the tribe of Manasseh crossed over armed before the children of Israel, as Moses had spoken to
them. 13About forty thousand prepared
for war crossed over before the LORD for
battle, to the plains of Jericho. 14On that
day the LORD exalted Joshua in the sight
of all Israel; and they feared him, as they
had feared Moses, all the days of his life.
15Then the LORD spoke to Joshua, saying, 16"Command the priests who bear the
ark of the Testimony to come up from the
Jordan." 17Joshua therefore commanded
the priests, saying, "Come up from the
Jordan." 18And it came to pass, when the
priests who bore the ark of the covenant
of the LORD had come from the midst of
the Jordan, *and* the soles of the priests'
feet touched the dry land, that the waters
of the Jordan returned to their place and
overflowed all its banks as before.
19Now the people came up from the
Jordan on the tenth *day* of the first month,
and they camped in Gilgal on the east
border of Jericho. 20And those twelve
stones which they took out of the Jordan,
Joshua set up in Gilgal. 21Then he spoke
to the children of Israel, saying: "When

4:21,22 *The Family Altar*

In Old Testament times, people built altars to God to commemorate something He had done. Altars served as a memorial to teach succeeding generations about God and His character. Gathering for a family "altar" or a devotional time is a good way to teach your children about God and His ways. Here are some practical points to consider when establishing your family altar.

Open in prayer. Begin devotions by thanking God for your family and prayerfully asking Him, "Open my eyes, that I may see wondrous things from Your Law" (Psa. 119:18). The Law reveals God's holiness, His righteousness, His justice and truth, and is the very instrument that the Holy Spirit uses to convert the soul (Psa. 19:7). If we want our children to be truly converted, we must first know the wondrous things from His Law, and that comes only by prayer and revelation of the Holy Spirit.

As time goes by, ask your children to open in prayer to build their confidence about "public" praying. They could start with a simple, "Dear Lord, please help us learn. Amen." Keep it brief. A short, stumbling but sincere prayer of a child is infinitely better in God's sight than long-winded Pharisaical and empty eloquence.

Read the Bible out loud. The Bible says, "A servant of the Lord must…be able to teach" (2 Tim. 2:24). So if you are worried about a lack of teaching ability, don't say, "I can't teach"; say, "Success comes in cans." Memorize this promise from Scripture: "I can do all things through Christ who strengthens me" (Phil. 4:13).

Simply start by reading five verses from one of the Gospels. Then have each family member read five verses; this will help them gain confidence in reading aloud and keep them attentive. Pause occasionally to ask what they think a particular verse means. Be ready for (and don't be discouraged by) a regular "I dunno." Tell your children what you think the verse means, and continue reading, making use of any Bible cross-references. If you have young children, start with a "picture" Bible.

(continued)

(4:21,22 continued)

Forget your inhibitions. This is not a time to worry about your dignity. Role-play with your kids when they are small. Be Goliath, and give each of them a turn at being David. Have them throw a pillow or other object at you, then fall down when you get hit. Act out Daniel in the lion's den. Be a lion and roar. Play out Bible stories with your children whenever you can. It will help them retain the principles behind the story.

If I remember correctly, when kids hear something, they retain 10 percent of what's heard. If they hear and see something, they retain about 40 percent. But if they actually *experience* something (see, hear, and participate in), they retain approximately 80 percent. (I can't remember the exact statistics, because I only heard them.)

Use the time when they are young and impressionable to impress upon them eternal biblical truths.

Keep it short...and sweet. So that the devotional time doesn't seem like a drag, keep it to 10–15, perhaps 20 minutes. In fact, if you stop devotions when the kids are having fun, they will look forward to the next time.

From the Scripture passage you read, select a memory verse and have your kids repeat it together six times. Perhaps they could write memory verses in a special book and review them regularly. Repeat the verse each night, and if they remember it at the end of the week, give them a reward. The reward is important. We all need incentives in life, and candy is a good one for kids. It can be small, such as a few jelly beans. If you are worried about rotting their teeth, have them brush afterwards. (Or perhaps you could substitute a healthy treat or small monetary reward as an incentive.)

Use anecdotes and humor. To keep the attention of your children, thoroughly flavor the reading with anecdotes. It is said of the Messiah, "I will open my mouth in a parable" (Psa. 78:2). Jesus often used parables—stories that carried a deeper meaning. Follow in the steps of the greatest Teacher, and open your mouth in a parable. They will make your teaching more palatable. Make them short, and preferably humorous.

Some people argue that Jesus didn't tell jokes, so we shouldn't either. But as Charles Spurgeon said, the use of humor in a sermon is like a flash of lightning on a dark night: it makes people sit up and wait for the next flash. Using humor keeps the attention of your children so you can convey timeless truths.

Close in prayer. End your family devotions in prayer, asking God to help you and your family to remember—and act upon—the lessons you have learned. Consider having each person say a brief prayer.

Now, commit yourself to having a family altar with your children. Do it as "a living sacrifice, holy, acceptable to God, which is your reasonable service" (Rom. 12:1). See also Prov. 22:6 comment.

(Adapted from *How to Bring Your Children to Christ…& Keep Them There*.)

your children ask their fathers in time to
come, saying, 'What *are* these stones?'
[22]then you shall let your children know,
saying, 'Israel crossed over this Jordan on
dry land'; [23]for the LORD your God dried
up the waters of the Jordan before you
until you had crossed over, as the LORD
your God did to the Red Sea, which He
dried up before us until we had crossed
over, [24]that all the peoples of the earth
may know the hand of the LORD, that it *is*
mighty, that you may fear the LORD your
God forever."

The Second Generation Circumcised

5 So it was, when all the kings of the
Amorites who *were* on the west side
of the Jordan, and all the kings of the
Canaanites who *were* by the sea, heard
that the LORD had dried up the waters of
the Jordan from before the children of
Israel until we[a] had crossed over, that their
heart melted; and there was no spirit in
them any longer because of the children
of Israel.

[2]At that time the LORD said to Joshua,
"Make flint knives for yourself, and circumcise
the sons of Israel again the second
time." [3]So Joshua made flint knives
for himself, and circumcised the sons of
Israel at the hill of the foreskins.[a] [4]And

5:1 [a]Following Kethib; Qere, some Hebrew manuscripts and editions, Septuagint, Syriac, Targum, and Vulgate read *they.*
5:3 [a]Hebrew *Gibeath Haaraloth*

4:24 God chose Israel, not so that they alone would be His people, but so that through them His glory would be displayed to all nations. Likewise, our purpose is to reveal God's glory to the world so that all would come to the Savior. See Eph. 3:8–11.

this *is* the reason why Joshua circumcised them: All the people who came out of Egypt *who were* males, all the men of war, had died in the wilderness on the way, after they had come out of Egypt. [5]For all the people who came out had been circumcised, but all the people born in the wilderness, on the way as they came out of Egypt, had not been circumcised. [6]For the children of Israel walked forty years in the wilderness, till all the people *who were* men of war, who came out of Egypt, were consumed, because they did not obey the voice of the LORD—to whom the LORD swore that He would not show them the land which the LORD had sworn to their fathers that He would give us, "a land flowing with milk and honey."[a] [7]Then Joshua circumcised their sons *whom* He raised up in their place; for they were uncircumcised, because they had not been circumcised on the way.

> Everywhere a greater joy is preceded by a greater suffering.
>
> **AUGUSTINE**

[8]So it was, when they had finished circumcising all the people, that they stayed in their places in the camp till they were healed. [9]Then the LORD said to Joshua, "This day I have rolled away the reproach of Egypt from you." Therefore the name of the place is called Gilgal[a] to this day.

[10]Now the children of Israel camped in Gilgal, and kept the Passover on the fourteenth day of the month at twilight on the plains of Jericho. [11]And they ate of the produce of the land on the day after the Passover, unleavened bread and parched grain, on the very same day. [12]Then the manna ceased on the day after they had eaten the produce of the land; and the children of Israel no longer had manna, but they ate the food of the land of Canaan that year.

The Commander of the Army of the Lord

[13]And it came to pass, when Joshua was by Jericho, that he lifted his eyes and looked, and behold, a Man stood opposite him with His sword drawn in His hand. And Joshua went to Him and said to Him, "*Are* You for us or for our adversaries?"

[14]So He said, "No, but *as* Commander of the army of the LORD I have now come."

And Joshua fell on his face to the earth and worshiped, and said to Him, "What does my Lord say to His servant?"

[15]Then the Commander of the LORD's army said to Joshua, "Take your sandal off your foot, for the place where you stand *is* holy." And Joshua did so.

The Destruction of Jericho

6 Now Jericho was securely shut up because of the children of Israel; none went out, and none came in. [2]And the LORD said to Joshua: "See! I have given Jericho into your hand, its king, *and* the mighty men of valor. [3]You shall march around the city, all *you* men of war; you shall go all around the city once. This you shall do six days. [4]And seven priests shall bear seven trumpets of rams' horns before the ark. But the seventh day you shall march around the city seven times, and the priests shall blow the trumpets. [5]It shall come to pass, when they make a long *blast* with the ram's horn, *and* when you hear the sound of the trumpet, that

5:6 [a]Exodus 3:8 5:9 [a]Literally *Rolling*

5:7–9 We are circumcised into the Body of Christ and separated from this sinful world. See Col. 2:11 for details.

6:4,5 In this incident, when Joshua seizes the city of Jericho, notice the emphasis on the presence of the ark of the Lord, which contained the tablets of God's Law. The ark is mentioned ten times in this chapter before the city walls fall down. If we want to see the downfall of the enemy, the presentation of the Ten Commandments must precede the victorious shout of the gospel.

all the people shall shout with a great shout; then the wall of the city will fall down flat. And the people shall go up every man straight before him."

[6]Then Joshua the son of Nun called the priests and said to them, "Take up the ark of the covenant, and let seven priests bear seven trumpets of rams' horns before the ark of the LORD." [7]And he said to the people, "Proceed, and march around the city, and let him who is armed advance before the ark of the LORD."

[8]So it was, when Joshua had spoken to the people, that the seven priests bearing the seven trumpets of rams' horns before the LORD advanced and blew the trumpets, and the ark of the covenant of the LORD followed them. [9]The armed men went before the priests who blew the trumpets, and the rear guard came after the ark, while *the priests* continued blowing the trumpets. [10]Now Joshua had commanded the people, saying, "You shall not shout or make any noise with your voice, nor shall a word proceed out of your mouth, until the day I say to you, 'Shout!' Then you shall shout." [11]So he had the ark of the LORD circle the city, going around *it* once. Then they came into the camp and lodged in the camp.

[12]And Joshua rose early in the morning, and the priests took up the ark of the LORD. [13]Then seven priests bearing seven trumpets of rams' horns before the ark of the LORD went on continually and blew with the trumpets. And the armed men went before them. But the rear guard came after the ark of the LORD, while *the priests* continued blowing the trumpets. [14]And the second day they marched around the city once and returned to the camp. So they did six days.

[15]But it came to pass on the seventh day that they rose early, about the dawning of the day, and marched around the city seven times in the same manner. On that day only they marched around the city seven times. [16]And the seventh time it happened, when the priests blew the trumpets, that Joshua said to the people: "Shout, for the LORD has given you the city! [17]Now the city shall be doomed by the LORD to destruction, it and all who *are* in it. Only Rahab the harlot shall live, she and all who *are* with her in the house, because she hid the messengers that we sent. [18]And you, by all means abstain from the accursed things, lest you become accursed when you take of the accursed things, and make the camp of Israel a curse, and trouble it. [19]But all the silver and gold, and vessels of bronze and iron, *are* consecrated to the LORD; they shall come into the treasury of the LORD."

[20]So the people shouted when *the priests* blew the trumpets. And it happened when the people heard the sound of the trumpet, and the people shouted with a great shout, that the wall fell down flat. Then the people went up into the city, every man straight before him, and they took the city. [21]And they utterly destroyed all that *was* in the city, both man and woman, young and old, ox and sheep and donkey, with the edge of the sword.

[22]But Joshua had said to the two men who had spied out the country, "Go into the harlot's house, and from there bring out the woman and all that she has, as you swore to her." [23]And the young men who had been spies went in and brought out Rahab, her father, her mother, her brothers, and all that she had. So they brought out all her relatives and left them outside the camp of Israel. [24]But they burned the city and all that *was* in it with fire. Only the silver and gold, and the vessels of bronze and iron, they put into the treasury of the house of the LORD. [25]And Joshua spared Rahab the harlot, her father's household, and all that she had. So she dwells in Israel to this day,

---

6:17 All who abide in Christ will be saved. Outside of Christ, all will be lost. (See John 15:5,6; Rom. 8:1.) See also John 14:6 and Acts 4:12 for the exclusive nature of salvation.

because she hid the messengers whom Joshua sent to spy out Jericho.

26Then Joshua charged *them* at that time, saying, "Cursed *be* the man before the LORD who rises up and builds this city Jericho; he shall lay its foundation with his firstborn, and with his youngest he shall set up its gates."

27So the LORD was with Joshua, and his fame spread throughout all the country.

Defeat at Ai

7 But the children of Israel committed a trespass regarding the accursed things, for Achan the son of Carmi, the son of Zabdi,[a] the son of Zerah, of the tribe of Judah, took of the accursed things; so the anger of the LORD burned against the children of Israel.

2Now Joshua sent men from Jericho to Ai, which *is* beside Beth Aven, on the east side of Bethel, and spoke to them, saying, "Go up and spy out the country." So the men went up and spied out Ai. 3And they returned to Joshua and said to him, "Do not let all the people go up, but let about two or three thousand men go up and attack Ai. Do not weary all the people there, for *the people of Ai are* few." 4So about three thousand men went up there from the people, but they fled before the men of Ai. 5And the men of Ai struck down about thirty-six men, for they chased them *from* before the gate as far as Shebarim, and struck them down on the descent; therefore the hearts of the people melted and became like water.

6Then Joshua tore his clothes, and fell to the earth on his face before the ark of the LORD until evening, he and the elders of Israel; and they put dust on their heads. 7And Joshua said, "Alas, Lord GOD, why have You brought this people over the Jordan at all—to deliver us into the hand of the Amorites, to destroy us? Oh, that we had been content, and dwelt on the other side of the Jordan! 8O Lord, what shall I say when Israel turns its back before its enemies? 9For the Canaanites and all the inhabitants of the land will hear *it,* and surround us, and cut off our name from the earth. Then what will You do for Your great name?"

The Sin of Achan

10So the LORD said to Joshua: "Get up! Why do you lie thus on your face? 11Israel has sinned, and they have also transgressed My covenant which I commanded them. For they have even taken some of the accursed things, and have both stolen and deceived; and they have also put *it* among their own stuff. 12Therefore the children of Israel could not stand before their enemies, *but* turned *their* backs before their enemies, because they have become doomed to destruction. Neither will I be with you anymore, unless you destroy the accursed from among you. 13Get up, sanctify the people, and say, 'Sanctify yourselves for tomorrow, because thus says the LORD God of Israel: "*There is* an accursed thing in your midst, O Israel; you cannot stand before your enemies until you take away the accursed thing from among you." 14In the morning therefore you shall be brought according to your tribes. And it shall be *that* the tribe which

7:1 [a]Called *Zimri* in 1 Chronicles 2:6

7:1 This chapter should instantly make us fear God. Achan gave himself to covetousness and theft (see v. 21). His sin brought trouble to Israel and, even though he eventually confessed (vv. 20,21), it had terrible repercussions on his family. Sin often not only destroys us, but those we love the most. The Bible tells us that Old Testament examples were written for our admonition, "to the intent that we should not lust after evil things as they also lusted" (1 Cor. 10:6–11).

The root of Achan's problem was idolatry. If he'd had a right image of God, he would have known that nothing can be hidden from the ever-present eye of a holy God, who will bring every work to judgment, including every secret thing. See Eccles. 12:13,14 for instructions for the godly.

7:10,11 We cannot be the power-filled Church so evidently seen in the Book of Acts as long as we compromise with sin. Prayer is no substitute for obedience.

the LORD takes shall come according to families; and the family which the LORD takes shall come by households; and the household which the LORD takes shall come man by man. 15Then it shall be *that* he who is taken with the accursed thing shall be burned with fire, he and all that he has, because he has transgressed the covenant of the LORD, and because he has done a disgraceful thing in Israel.' "

16So Joshua rose early in the morning and brought Israel by their tribes, and the tribe of Judah was taken. 17He brought the clan of Judah, and he took the family of the Zarhites; and he brought the family of the Zarhites man by man, and Zabdi was taken. 18Then he brought his household man by man, and Achan the son of Carmi, the son of Zabdi, the son of Zerah, of the tribe of Judah, was taken.

19Now Joshua said to Achan, "My son, I beg you, give glory to the LORD God of Israel, and make confession to Him, and tell me now what you have done; do not hide *it* from me."

20And Achan answered Joshua and said, "Indeed I have sinned against the LORD God of Israel, and this is what I have done: 21When I saw among the spoils a beautiful Babylonian garment, two hundred shekels of silver, and a wedge of gold weighing fifty shekels, I coveted them and took them. And there they are, hidden in the earth in the midst of my tent, with the silver under it."

22So Joshua sent messengers, and they ran to the tent; and there it was, hidden in his tent, with the silver under it. 23And they took them from the midst of the tent, brought them to Joshua and to all the children of Israel, and laid them out before the LORD. 24Then Joshua, and all Israel with him, took Achan the son of Zerah, the silver, the garment, the wedge of gold, his sons, his daughters, his oxen, his donkeys, his sheep, his tent, and all that he had, and they brought them to the Valley of Achor. 25And Joshua said, "Why have you troubled us? The LORD will trouble you this day." So all Israel stoned him with stones; and they burned them with fire after they had stoned them with stones.

26Then they raised over him a great heap of stones, still there to this day. So the LORD turned from the fierceness of His anger. Therefore the name of that place has been called the Valley of Achor[a] to this day.

The Fall of Ai

8 Now the LORD said to Joshua: "Do not be afraid, nor be dismayed; take all the people of war with you, and arise, go up to Ai. See, I have given into your hand the king of Ai, his people, his city, and his land. 2And you shall do to Ai and its king as you did to Jericho and its king. Only its spoil and its cattle you shall take as booty for yourselves. Lay an ambush for the city behind it."

3So Joshua arose, and all the people of war, to go up against Ai; and Joshua chose thirty thousand mighty men of valor and sent them away by night. 4And he commanded them, saying: "Behold, you shall lie in ambush against the city, behind the city. Do not go very far from the city, but all of you be ready. 5Then I and all the people who *are* with me will approach the city; and it will come about, when they come out against us as at the first, that we shall flee before them. 6For they will come out after us till we have drawn them from the city, for they will say, '*They are* fleeing before us as at the first.' Therefore we will flee before them. 7Then you shall rise from the ambush and seize the city, for the LORD your God will deliver it into your hand. 8And it will be, when you have taken the city, *that* you shall set the city on fire. According to the commandment of the LORD you shall do. See, I have commanded you."

9Joshua therefore sent them out; and they went to lie in ambush, and stayed between Bethel and Ai, on the west side of Ai; but Joshua lodged that night among the people. 10Then Joshua rose up early in

7:26 [a]**Literally *Trouble***

the morning and mustered the people, and went up, he and the elders of Israel, before the people to Ai. 11And all the people of war who *were* with him went up and drew near; and they came before the city and camped on the north side of Ai. Now a valley *lay* between them and Ai. 12So he took about five thousand men and set them in ambush between Bethel and Ai, on the west side of the city. 13And when they had set the people, all the army that *was* on the north of the city, and its rear guard on the west of the city, Joshua went that night into the midst of the valley.

14Now it happened, when the king of Ai saw *it,* that the men of the city hurried and rose early and went out against Israel to battle, he and all his people, at an appointed place before the plain. But he did not know that *there was* an ambush against him behind the city. 15And Joshua and all Israel made as if they were beaten before them, and fled by the way of the wilderness. 16So all the people who *were* in Ai were called together to pursue them. And they pursued Joshua and were drawn away from the city. 17There was not a man left in Ai or Bethel who did not go out after Israel. So they left the city open and pursued Israel.

18Then the LORD said to Joshua, "Stretch out the spear that *is* in your hand toward Ai, for I will give it into your hand." And Joshua stretched out the spear that *was* in his hand toward the city. 19So *those in* ambush arose quickly out of their place; they ran as soon as he had stretched out his hand, and they entered the city and took it, and hurried to set the city on fire. 20And when the men of Ai looked behind them, they saw, and behold, the smoke of the city ascended to heaven. So they had no power to flee this way or that way, and the people who had fled to the wilderness turned back on the pursuers.

21Now when Joshua and all Israel saw that the ambush had taken the city and that the smoke of the city ascended, they turned back and struck down the men of Ai. 22Then the others came out of the city against them; so they were *caught* in the midst of Israel, some on this side and some on that side. And they struck them down, so that they let none of them remain or escape. 23But the king of Ai they took alive, and brought him to Joshua.

24And it came to pass when Israel had made an end of slaying all the inhabitants of Ai in the field, in the wilderness where they pursued them, and when they all had fallen by the edge of the sword until they were consumed, that all the Israelites returned to Ai and struck it with the edge of the sword. 25So it was *that* all who fell that day, both men and women, *were* twelve thousand—all the people of Ai. 26For Joshua did not draw back his hand, with which he stretched out the spear, until he had utterly destroyed all the inhabitants of Ai. 27Only the livestock and the spoil of that city Israel took as booty for themselves, according to the word of the LORD which He had commanded Joshua. 28So Joshua burned Ai and made it a heap forever, a desolation to this day. 29And the king of Ai he hanged on a tree until evening. And as soon as the sun was down, Joshua commanded that they should take his corpse down from the tree, cast it at the entrance of the gate of the city, and raise over it a great heap of stones *that remains* to this day.

Joshua Renews the Covenant

30Now Joshua built an altar to the LORD God of Israel in Mount Ebal, 31as Moses the servant of the LORD had commanded the children of Israel, as it is written in the Book of the Law of Moses: "an altar of whole stones over which no man has wielded an iron *tool.*"[a] And they offered on it burnt offerings to the LORD, and sac-

8:31 [a]Deuteronomy 27:5, 6

8:31 We are not made acceptable to God by any of the works of our hands, but by grace through faith alone in the offering that God Himself provided.

THE FUNCTION OF THE LAW

8:32 "We call it the 'Mosaic' Law, but it has been well said that the Commandments did not originate with Moses, nor were they done away with when the Mosaic Law was fulfilled in Christ, and many of its ceremonies and regulations abolished. We can find no trace of the existence of any law-making body in those early times, no parliament, or congress that built up a system of laws. It has come down to us complete and finished, and the only satisfactory account is that which tells us that God Himself wrote the Commandments on tables of stone." *D. L. Moody*

rificed peace offerings. [32]And there, in the
presence of the children of Israel, he wrote
on the stones a copy of the law of Moses,
which he had written. [33]Then all Israel,
with their elders and officers and judges,
stood on either side of the ark before the
priests, the Levites, who bore the ark of
the covenant of the LORD, the stranger as
well as he who was born among them.
Half of them *were* in front of Mount Gerizim and half of them in front of Mount
Ebal, as Moses the servant of the LORD
had commanded before, that they should
bless the people of Israel. [34]And afterward he read all the words of the law, the
blessings and the cursings, according to
all that is written in the Book of the Law.
[35]There was not a word of all that Moses
had commanded which Joshua did not
read before all the assembly of Israel,
with the women, the little ones, and the
strangers who were living among them.

The Treaty with the Gibeonites

9 And it came to pass when all the kings
who *were* on this side of the Jordan,
in the hills and in the lowland and in all
the coasts of the Great Sea toward Lebanon
—the Hittite, the Amorite, the Canaanite,
the Perizzite, the Hivite, and the Jebusite
—heard *about it,* [2]that they gathered together to fight with Joshua and Israel with
one accord.
[3]But when the inhabitants of Gibeon
heard what Joshua had done to Jericho and
Ai, [4]they worked craftily, and went and
pretended to be ambassadors. And they
took old sacks on their donkeys, old wineskins torn and mended, [5]old and patched
sandals on their feet, and old garments on
themselves; and all the bread of their provision was dry *and* moldy. [6]And they went
to Joshua, to the camp at Gilgal, and said
to him and to the men of Israel, "We have
come from a far country; now therefore,
make a covenant with us."
[7]Then the men of Israel said to the
Hivites, "Perhaps you dwell among us; so
how can we make a covenant with you?"
[8]But they said to Joshua, "We *are* your
servants."

> Run, John, run, the law commands,
> But gives me neither feet nor hands;
> Far better news the gospel brings:
> It bids me fly and gives me wings.
>
> **JOHN BUNYAN**

And Joshua said to them, "Who *are*
you, and where do you come from?"
[9]So they said to him: "From a very far
country your servants have come, because
of the name of the LORD your God; for we
have heard of His fame, and all that He
did in Egypt, [10]and all that He did to the
two kings of the Amorites who *were* beyond the Jordan—to Sihon king of Heshbon, and Og king of Bashan, who was at
Ashtaroth. [11]Therefore our elders and all
the inhabitants of our country spoke to us,
saying, 'Take provisions with you for the
journey, and go to meet them, and say to
them, "We *are* your servants; now therefore, make a covenant with us." ' [12]This

8:35 "It is a common temptation of Satan to make us give up the reading of the Word and prayer when our enjoyment is gone; as if it were of no use to read the Scriptures when we do not enjoy them, and as if it were no use to pray when we have no spirit of prayer. The truth is that in order to enjoy the Word, we ought to continue to read it, and the way to obtain a spirit of prayer is to continue praying. The less we read the Word of God, the less we desire to read it, and the less we pray, the less we desire to pray." *George Mueller*

bread of ours we took hot *for* our provision from our houses on the day we departed to come to you. But now look, it is dry and moldy. [13]And these wineskins which we filled *were* new, and see, they are torn; and these our garments and our sandals have become old because of the very long journey."

[14]Then the men of Israel took some of their provisions; but they did not ask counsel of the LORD. [15]So Joshua made peace with them, and made a covenant with them to let them live; and the rulers of the congregation swore to them.

[16]And it happened at the end of three days, after they had made a covenant with them, that they heard that they *were* their neighbors who dwelt near them. [17]Then the children of Israel journeyed and came to their cities on the third day. Now their cities *were* Gibeon, Chephirah, Beeroth, and Kirjath Jearim. [18]But the children of Israel did not attack them, because the rulers of the congregation had sworn to them by the LORD God of Israel. And all the congregation complained against the rulers.

[19]Then all the rulers said to all the congregation, "We have sworn to them by the LORD God of Israel; now therefore, we may not touch them. [20]This we will do to them: We will let them live, lest wrath be upon us because of the oath which we swore to them." [21]And the rulers said to them, "Let them live, but let them be woodcutters and water carriers for all the congregation, as the rulers had promised them."

[22]Then Joshua called for them, and he spoke to them, saying, "Why have you deceived us, saying, 'We *are* very far from you,' when you dwell near us? [23]Now therefore, you *are* cursed, and none of you shall be freed from being slaves—woodcutters and water carriers for the house of my God."

[24]So they answered Joshua and said, "Because your servants were clearly told that the LORD your God commanded His servant Moses to give you all the land, and to destroy all the inhabitants of the land from before you; therefore we were very much afraid for our lives because of you, and have done this thing. [25]And now, here we are, in your hands; do with us as it seems good and right to do to us." [26]So he did to them, and delivered them out of the hand of the children of Israel, so that they did not kill them. [27]And that day Joshua made them woodcutters and water carriers for the congregation and for the altar of the LORD, in the place which He would choose, even to this day.

The Sun Stands Still

10 Now it came to pass when Adoni-Zedek king of Jerusalem heard how Joshua had taken Ai and had utterly destroyed it—as he had done to Jericho and its king, so he had done to Ai and its king—and how the inhabitants of Gibeon had made peace with Israel and were among them, [2]that they feared greatly, because Gibeon *was* a great city, like one of the royal cities, and because it *was* greater than Ai, and all its men *were* mighty. [3]Therefore Adoni-Zedek king of Jerusalem sent to Hoham king of Hebron, Piram king of Jarmuth, Japhia king of Lachish, and Debir king of Eglon, saying, [4]"Come up to me and help me, that we may attack Gibeon, for it has made peace with Joshua and with the children of Israel." [5]Therefore the five kings of the Amorites, the king of Jerusalem, the king of Hebron, the king of Jarmuth, the king of Lachish, *and* the king of Eglon, gathered together and went up, they and all their armies, and camped before Gibeon and made war against it.

9:14 "Listen to no man who fails to listen to God. No man has any right to counsel others who is not ready to hear and follow the counsel of the Lord. True moral wisdom must always be an echo of God's voice. The only safe light for our path is the light which is reflected from Christ, the Light of the World." *A. W. Tozer*

9:19 If you are going to give your word, keep your word. See Psa. 15 for a description of godly character.

6And the men of Gibeon sent to Joshua
at the camp at Gilgal, saying, "Do not forsake your servants; come up to us quickly,
save us and help us, for all the kings of
the Amorites who dwell in the mountains
have gathered together against us."
7So Joshua ascended from Gilgal, he
and all the people of war with him, and
all the mighty men of valor. 8And the
LORD said to Joshua, "Do not fear them,
for I have delivered them into your hand;
not a man of them shall stand before
you." 9Joshua therefore came upon them
suddenly, having marched all night from
Gilgal. 10So the LORD routed them before
Israel, killed them with a great slaughter
at Gibeon, chased them along the road
that goes to Beth Horon, and struck them
down as far as Azekah and Makkedah.
11And it happened, as they fled before
Israel *and* were on the descent of Beth
Horon, that the LORD cast down large
hailstones from heaven on them as far as
Azekah, and they died. *There were* more
who died from the hailstones than the
children of Israel killed with the sword.
12Then Joshua spoke to the LORD in
the day when the LORD delivered up the
Amorites before the children of Israel, and
he said in the sight of Israel:

"Sun, stand still over Gibeon;
And Moon, in the Valley of Aijalon."
13So the sun stood still,
And the moon stopped,
Till the people had revenge
Upon their enemies.

Is this not written in the Book of Jasher?
So the sun stood still in the midst of
heaven, and did not hasten to go *down*
for about a whole day. 14And there has
been no day like that, before it or after it,
that the LORD heeded the voice of a man;
for the LORD fought for Israel.
15Then Joshua returned, and all Israel
with him, to the camp at Gilgal.

The Amorite Kings Executed

16But these five kings had fled and hidden themselves in a cave at Makkedah.
17And it was told Joshua, saying, "The five
kings have been found hidden in the cave
at Makkedah."
18So Joshua said, "Roll large stones
against the mouth of the cave, and set men
by it to guard them. 19And do not stay
there yourselves, *but* pursue your enemies,
and attack their rear *guard*. Do not allow
them to enter their cities, for the LORD
your God has delivered them into your
hand." 20Then it happened, while Joshua
and the children of Israel made an end of
slaying them with a very great slaughter,
till they had finished, that those who escaped entered fortified cities. 21And all the
people returned to the camp, to Joshua at
Makkedah, in peace.
No one moved his tongue against any
of the children of Israel.
22Then Joshua said, "Open the mouth
of the cave, and bring out those five kings
to me from the cave." 23And they did so,
and brought out those five kings to him
from the cave: the king of Jerusalem, the
king of Hebron, the king of Jarmuth, the
king of Lachish, *and* the king of Eglon.
24So it was, when they brought out
those kings to Joshua, that Joshua called
for all the men of Israel, and said to the
captains of the men of war who went
with him, "Come near, put your feet on
the necks of these kings." And they drew
near and put their feet on their necks.
25Then Joshua said to them, "Do not be
afraid, nor be dismayed; be strong and of
good courage, for thus the LORD will do
to all your enemies against whom you
fight." 26And afterward Joshua struck
them and killed them, and hanged them
on five trees; and they were hanging on
the trees until evening. 27So it was at the

10:12–14 With God, nothing is impossible. See Matt. 21:21 for what Jesus said about faith and the power of God.

time of the going down of the sun *that* Joshua commanded, and they took them down from the trees, cast them into the cave where they had been hidden, and laid large stones against the cave's mouth, *which remain* until this very day.

Conquest of the Southland

28 On that day Joshua took Makkedah, and struck it and its king with the edge of the sword. He utterly destroyed them[a]—all the people who *were* in it. He let none remain. He also did to the king of Makkedah as he had done to the king of Jericho.

29 Then Joshua passed from Makkedah, and all Israel with him, to Libnah; and they fought against Libnah. 30 And the LORD also delivered it and its king into the hand of Israel; he struck it and all the people who *were* in it with the edge of the sword. He let none remain in it, but did to its king as he had done to the king of Jericho.

31 Then Joshua passed from Libnah, and all Israel with him, to Lachish; and they encamped against it and fought against it. 32 And the LORD delivered Lachish into the hand of Israel, who took it on the second day, and struck it and all the people who *were* in it with the edge of the sword, according to all that he had done to Libnah. 33 Then Horam king of Gezer came up to help Lachish; and Joshua struck him and his people, until he left him none remaining.

34 From Lachish Joshua passed to Eglon, and all Israel with him; and they encamped against it and fought against it. 35 They took it on that day and struck it with the edge of the sword; all the people who *were* in it he utterly destroyed that day, according to all that he had done to Lachish.

36 So Joshua went up from Eglon, and all Israel with him, to Hebron; and they fought against it. 37 And they took it and struck it with the edge of the sword—its king, all its cities, and all the people who *were* in it; he left none remaining, according to all that he had done to Eglon, but utterly destroyed it and all the people who *were* in it.

38 Then Joshua returned, and all Israel with him, to Debir; and they fought against it. 39 And he took it and its king and all its cities; they struck them with the edge of the sword and utterly destroyed all the people who *were* in it. He left none remaining; as he had done to Hebron, so he did to Debir and its king, as he had done also to Libnah and its king.

> While women weep, as they do now, I'll fight; while children go hungry as they do now, I'll fight; while men go to prison, in and out, in and out, as they do now, I'll fight; while there is a drunkard left, while there is a poor lost girl upon the streets, while there remains one dark soul without the light of God, I'll fight; I'll fight to the very end!
>
> **WILLIAM BOOTH**

40 So Joshua conquered all the land: the mountain country and the South[a] and the lowland and the wilderness slopes, and all their kings; he left none remaining, but utterly destroyed all that breathed, as the LORD God of Israel had commanded. 41 And Joshua conquered them from Kadesh Barnea as far as Gaza, and all the country of Goshen, even as far as Gibeon. 42 All these kings and their land Joshua took at one time, because the LORD God of Israel fought for Israel. 43 Then Joshua returned, and all Israel with him, to the camp at Gilgal.

The Northern Conquest

11 And it came to pass, when Jabin king of Hazor heard *these things,* that he sent to Jobab king of Madon, to the king of Shimron, to the king of Achshaph, 2 and to the kings who *were* from the north, in the mountains, in the plain

10:28 [a]Following Masoretic Text and most authorities; many Hebrew manuscripts, some manuscripts of the Septuagint, and some manuscripts of the Targum read *it.* 10:40 [a]Hebrew *Negev,* and so throughout this book

south of Chinneroth, in the lowland, and in the heights of Dor on the west, 3to the Canaanites in the east and in the west, the Amorite, the Hittite, the Perizzite, the Jebusite in the mountains, and the Hivite below Hermon in the land of Mizpah. 4So they went out, they and all their armies with them, *as* many people *as* the sand that *is* on the seashore in multitude, with very many horses and chariots. 5And when all these kings had met together, they came and camped together at the waters of Merom to fight against Israel.

6But the LORD said to Joshua, "Do not be afraid because of them, for tomorrow about this time I will deliver all of them slain before Israel. You shall hamstring their horses and burn their chariots with fire." 7So Joshua and all the people of war with him came against them suddenly by the waters of Merom, and they attacked them. 8And the LORD delivered them into the hand of Israel, who defeated them and chased them to Greater Sidon, to the Brook Misrephoth,[a] and to the Valley of Mizpah eastward; they attacked them until they left none of them remaining. 9So Joshua did to them as the LORD had told him: he hamstrung their horses and burned their chariots with fire.

10Joshua turned back at that time and took Hazor, and struck its king with the sword; for Hazor was formerly the head of all those kingdoms. 11And they struck all the people who *were* in it with the edge of the sword, utterly destroying *them.* There was none left breathing. Then he burned Hazor with fire.

12So all the cities of those kings, and all their kings, Joshua took and struck with the edge of the sword. He utterly destroyed them, as Moses the servant of the LORD had commanded. 13But *as for* the cities that stood on their mounds,[a] Israel burned none of them, except Hazor only, *which* Joshua burned. 14And all the spoil of these cities and the livestock, the children of Israel took as booty for themselves; but they struck every man with the edge of the sword until they had destroyed them, and they left none breathing. 15As the LORD had commanded Moses his servant, so Moses commanded Joshua, and so Joshua did. He left nothing undone of all that the LORD had commanded Moses.

Summary of Joshua's Conquests

16Thus Joshua took all this land: the mountain country, all the South, all the land of Goshen, the lowland, and the Jordan plain[a]—the mountains of Israel and its lowlands, 17from Mount Halak and the ascent to Seir, even as far as Baal Gad in the Valley of Lebanon below Mount Hermon. He captured all their kings, and struck them down and killed them. 18Joshua made war a long time with all those kings. 19There was not a city that made peace with the children of Israel, except the Hivites, the inhabitants of Gibeon. All *the others* they took in battle. 20For it was of the LORD to harden their hearts, that they should come against Israel in battle, that He might utterly destroy them, *and* that they might receive no mercy, but that He might destroy them, as the LORD had commanded Moses.

21And at that time Joshua came and cut off the Anakim from the mountains: from Hebron, from Debir, from Anab, from all the mountains of Judah, and from all the mountains of Israel; Joshua utterly

11:8 [a]Hebrew *Misrephoth Maim* **11:13** [a]Hebrew *tel,* a heap of successive city ruins **11:16** [a]Hebrew *arabah*

11:18–20 There can be no compromise in the war with this sinful world. The only option for sinners is to surrender to God. See also Dan. 10:12,13 comment.

"Just as rebellion leads to war, so surrender results in peace . . . The choice is ours—a virtual war with God or a peaceful surrender. Whichever we choose, we will find that God is more stubborn, more fierce, and more loving than we could possibly imagine. His call for us to surrender is unconditional, for the battle over our souls is intense. This is one war where victory would annihilate us and only surrender can save us." *Gary Thomas*

destroyed them with their cities. [22]None of the Anakim were left in the land of the children of Israel; they remained only in Gaza, in Gath, and in Ashdod.

[23]So Joshua took the whole land, according to all that the LORD had said to Moses; and Joshua gave it as an inheritance to Israel according to their divisions by their tribes. Then the land rested from war.

The Kings Conquered by Moses

12 These *are* the kings of the land whom the children of Israel defeated, and whose land they possessed on the other side of the Jordan toward the rising of the sun, from the River Arnon to Mount Hermon, and all the eastern Jordan plain: [2]*One king was* Sihon king of the Amorites, who dwelt in Heshbon *and* ruled half of Gilead, from Aroer, which is on the bank of the River Arnon, from the middle of that river, even as far as the River Jabbok, *which is* the border of the Ammonites, [3]and the eastern Jordan plain from the Sea of Chinneroth as far as the Sea of the Arabah (the Salt Sea), the road to Beth Jeshimoth, and southward below the slopes of Pisgah. [4]*The other king was* Og king of Bashan and his territory, *who was* of the remnant of the giants, who dwelt at Ashtaroth and at Edrei, [5]and reigned over Mount Hermon, over Salcah, over all Bashan, as far as the border of the Geshurites and the Maachathites, and over half of Gilead *to* the border of Sihon king of Heshbon.

[6]These Moses the servant of the LORD and the children of Israel had conquered; and Moses the servant of the LORD had given it *as* a possession to the Reubenites, the Gadites, and half the tribe of Manasseh.

The Kings Conquered by Joshua

[7]And these *are* the kings of the country which Joshua and the children of Israel conquered on this side of the Jordan, on the west, from Baal Gad in the Valley of Lebanon as far as Mount Halak and the ascent to Seir, which Joshua gave to the tribes of Israel *as* a possession according to their divisions, [8]in the mountain country, in the lowlands, in the *Jordan* plain, in the slopes, in the wilderness, and in the South—the Hittites, the Amorites, the Canaanites, the Perizzites, the Hivites, and the Jebusites: [9]the king of Jericho, one; the king of Ai, which *is* beside Bethel, one; [10]the king of Jerusalem, one; the king of Hebron, one; [11]the king of Jarmuth, one; the king of Lachish, one; [12]the king of Eglon, one; the king of Gezer, one; [13]the king of Debir, one; the king of Geder, one; [14]the king of Hormah, one; the king of Arad, one; [15]the king of Libnah, one; the king of Adullam, one; [16]the king of Makkedah, one; the king of Bethel, one; [17]the king of Tappuah, one; the king of Hepher, one; [18]the king of Aphek, one; the king of Lasharon, one; [19]the king of Madon, one; the king of Hazor, one; [20]the king of Shimron Meron, one; the king of Achshaph, one; [21]the king of Taanach, one; the king of Megiddo, one; [22]the king of Kedesh, one; the king of Jokneam in Carmel, one; [23]the king of Dor in the heights of Dor, one; the king of the people of Gilgal, one; [24]the king of Tirzah, one—all the kings, thirty-one.

Remaining Land to Be Conquered

13 Now Joshua was old, advanced in years. And the LORD said to him: "You are old, advanced in years, and there remains very much land yet to be possessed. [2]This is the land that yet remains:

12:3 The Salt Sea (now known as the Dead Sea) reaches a depth of 1,200 feet. The salt content of the Dead Sea is over eight times that of the oceans. The high salinity is the reason that very little life is found in the waters—it truly is a dead sea. The Jordan River is the main source of water for the Dead Sea, with a few smaller rivers also emptying into it. The problem is that there is a constant inflow, but it has no outlet. This is what happens to the Church when it fails to have an outlet to the lost—it becomes a dead sea of humanity. We need to be a conduit of Living Water to those who desperately need it.

all the territory of the Philistines and all *that of* the Geshurites, 3from Sihor, which *is* east of Egypt, as far as the border of Ekron northward (*which* is counted as Canaanite); the five lords of the Philistines—the Gazites, the Ashdodites, the Ashkelonites, the Gittites, and the Ekronites; also the Avites; 4from the south, all the land of the Canaanites, and Mearah that belongs to the Sidonians as far as Aphek, to the border of the Amorites; 5the land of the Gebalites,[a] and all Lebanon, toward the sunrise, from Baal Gad below Mount Hermon as far as the entrance to Hamath; 6all the inhabitants of the mountains from Lebanon as far as the Brook Misrephoth,[a] *and* all the Sidonians—them I will drive out from before the children of Israel; only divide it by lot to Israel as an inheritance, as I have commanded you. 7Now therefore, divide this land as an inheritance to the nine tribes and half the tribe of Manasseh."

The Land Divided East of the Jordan

8With the other half-tribe the Reubenites and the Gadites received their inheritance, which Moses had given them, beyond the Jordan eastward, as Moses the servant of the LORD had given them: 9from Aroer which *is* on the bank of the River Arnon, and the town that *is* in the midst of the ravine, and all the plain of Medeba as far as Dibon; 10all the cities of Sihon king of the Amorites, who reigned in Heshbon, as far as the border of the children of Ammon; 11Gilead, and the border of the Geshurites and Maachathites, all Mount Hermon, and all Bashan as far as Salcah; 12all the kingdom of Og in Bashan, who reigned in Ashtaroth and Edrei, who remained of the remnant of the giants; for Moses had defeated and cast out these.

13Nevertheless the children of Israel did not drive out the Geshurites or the Maachathites, but the Geshurites and the Maachathites dwell among the Israelites until this day.

14Only to the tribe of Levi he had given no inheritance; the sacrifices of the LORD God of Israel made by fire *are* their inheritance, as He said to them.

The Land of Reuben

15And Moses had given to the tribe of the children of Reuben *an inheritance* according to their families. 16Their territory was from Aroer, which *is* on the bank of the River Arnon, and the city that *is* in the midst of the ravine, and all the plain by Medeba; 17Heshbon and all its cities that *are* in the plain: Dibon, Bamoth Baal, Beth Baal Meon, 18Jahaza, Kedemoth, Mephaath, 19Kirjathaim, Sibmah, Zereth Shahar on the mountain of the valley, 20Beth Peor, the slopes of Pisgah, and Beth Jeshimoth— 21all the cities of the plain and all the kingdom of Sihon king of the Amorites, who reigned in Heshbon, whom Moses had struck with the princes of Midian: Evi, Rekem, Zur, Hur, and Reba, who *were* princes of Sihon dwelling in the country. 22The children of Israel also killed with the sword Balaam the son of Beor, the soothsayer, among those who were killed by them. 23And the border of the children of Reuben was the bank of the Jordan. This *was* the inheritance of the children of Reuben according to their families, the cities and their villages.

The Land of Gad

24Moses also had given *an inheritance* to the tribe of Gad, to the children of Gad according to their families. 25Their territory was Jazer, and all the cities of Gilead, and half the land of the Ammonites as far

13:5 [a]Or *Giblites* 13:6 [a]Hebrew *Misrephoth Maim*

13:14,15 We await our inheritance in Christ, "an inheritance incorruptible and undefiled and that does not fade away, reserved in heaven for you, who are kept by the power of God through faith for salvation ready to be revealed in the last time" (1 Pet. 1:3–5).

as Aroer, which *is* before Rabbah, [26]and from Heshbon to Ramath Mizpah and Betonim, and from Mahanaim to the border of Debir, [27]and in the valley Beth Haram, Beth Nimrah, Succoth, and Zaphon, the rest of the kingdom of Sihon king of Heshbon, with the Jordan as *its* border, as far as the edge of the Sea of Chinnereth, on the other side of the Jordan eastward. [28]This *is* the inheritance of the children of Gad according to their families, the cities and their villages.

Half the Tribe of Manasseh (East)

[29]Moses also had given *an inheritance* to half the tribe of Manasseh; it was for half the tribe of the children of Manasseh according to their families: [30]Their territory was from Mahanaim, all Bashan, all the kingdom of Og king of Bashan, and all the towns of Jair which are in Bashan, sixty cities; [31]half of Gilead, and Ashtaroth and Edrei, cities of the kingdom of Og in Bashan, *were* for the children of Machir the son of Manasseh, for half of the children of Machir according to their families.

[32]These *are the areas* which Moses had distributed as an inheritance in the plains of Moab on the other side of the Jordan, by Jericho eastward. [33]But to the tribe of Levi Moses had given no inheritance; the LORD God of Israel *was* their inheritance, as He had said to them.

The Land Divided West of the Jordan

14 These *are the areas* which the children of Israel inherited in the land of Canaan, which Eleazar the priest, Joshua the son of Nun, and the heads of the fathers of the tribes of the children of Israel distributed as an inheritance to them. [2]Their inheritance *was* by lot, as the LORD had commanded by the hand of Moses, for the nine tribes and the half-tribe. [3]For Moses had given the inheritance of the two tribes and the half-tribe on the other side of the Jordan; but to the Levites he had given no inheritance among them. [4]For the children of Joseph were two tribes: Manasseh and Ephraim. And they gave no part to the Levites in the land, except cities to dwell *in*, with their common-lands for their livestock and their property. [5]As the LORD had commanded Moses, so the children of Israel did; and they divided the land.

· · · · · · ·

What should the motive be when witnessing? See Phil. 1:18 comment.

· · · · · · ·

Caleb Inherits Hebron

[6]Then the children of Judah came to Joshua in Gilgal. And Caleb the son of Jephunneh the Kenizzite said to him: "You know the word which the LORD said to Moses the man of God concerning you and me in Kadesh Barnea. [7]I *was* forty years old when Moses the servant of the LORD sent me from Kadesh Barnea to spy out the land, and I brought back word to him as *it was* in my heart. [8]Nevertheless my brethren who went up with me made the heart of the people melt, but I wholly followed the LORD my God. [9]So Moses swore on that day, saying, 'Surely the land where your foot has trodden shall be your inheritance and your children's forever, because you have wholly followed the LORD my God.' [10]And now, behold, the LORD has kept me alive, as He said, these forty-five years, ever since the LORD spoke this word to Moses while Israel wandered in the wilderness; and now, here I am this day, eighty-five years old. [11]As yet I *am as* strong this day as on the day that Moses sent me; just as my strength *was* then, so now *is* my strength for war, both for going out and for coming in. [12]Now therefore, give me this mountain of which the LORD spoke in that day; for

14:10,11 May God do this for every Christian who is active in sharing the gospel.

you heard in that day how the Anakim *were* there, and *that* the cities *were* great *and* fortified. It may be that the LORD *will be* with me, and I shall be able to drive them out as the LORD said."

[13]And Joshua blessed him, and gave Hebron to Caleb the son of Jephunneh as an inheritance. [14]Hebron therefore became the inheritance of Caleb the son of Jephunneh the Kenizzite to this day, because he wholly followed the LORD God of Israel. [15]And the name of Hebron formerly was Kirjath Arba (*Arba was* the greatest man among the Anakim).

Then the land had rest from war.

The Land of Judah

15 So *this* was the lot of the tribe of the children of Judah according to their families:

The border of Edom at the Wilderness of Zin southward *was* the extreme southern boundary. [2]And their southern border began at the shore of the Salt Sea, from the bay that faces southward. [3]Then it went out to the southern side of the Ascent of Akrabbim, passed along to Zin, ascended on the south side of Kadesh Barnea, passed along to Hezron, went up to Adar, and went around to Karkaa. [4]*From there* it passed toward Azmon and went out to the Brook of Egypt; and the border ended at the sea. This shall be your southern border.

[5]The east border *was* the Salt Sea as far as the mouth of the Jordan.

And the border on the northern quarter *began* at the bay of the sea at the mouth of the Jordan. [6]The border went up to Beth Hoglah and passed north of Beth Arabah; and the border went up to the stone of Bohan the son of Reuben. [7]Then the border went up toward Debir from the Valley of Achor, and it turned northward toward Gilgal, which *is* before the Ascent of Adummim, which *is* on the south side of the valley. The border continued toward the waters of En Shemesh and ended at En Rogel. [8]And the border went up by the Valley of the Son of Hinnom to the southern slope of the Jebusite *city* (which *is* Jerusalem). The border went up to the top of the mountain that *lies* before the Valley of Hinnom westward, which *is* at the end of the Valley of Rephaim[a] northward. [9]Then the border went around from the top of the hill to the fountain of the water of Nephtoah, and extended to the cities of Mount Ephron. And the border went around to Baalah (which *is* Kirjath Jearim). [10]Then the border turned westward from Baalah to Mount Seir, passed along to the side of Mount Jearim on the north (which *is* Chesalon), went down to Beth Shemesh, and passed on to Timnah. [11]And the border went out to the side of Ekron northward. Then the border went around to Shicron, passed along to Mount Baalah, and extended to Jabneel; and the border ended at the sea.

[12]The west border *was* the coastline of the Great Sea. This *is* the boundary of the children of Judah all around according to their families.

Caleb Occupies Hebron and Debir

[13]Now to Caleb the son of Jephunneh he gave a share among the children of Judah, according to the commandment of the LORD to Joshua, *namely,* Kirjath Arba, which *is* Hebron (*Arba was* the father of Anak). [14]Caleb drove out the three sons of Anak from there: Sheshai, Ahiman, and Talmai, the children of Anak. [15]Then he went up from there to the inhabitants of Debir (formerly the name of Debir *was* Kirjath Sepher).

[16]And Caleb said, "He who attacks Kirjath Sepher and takes it, to him I will give Achsah my daughter as wife." [17]So Othniel the son of Kenaz, the brother of Caleb, took it; and he gave him Achsah his daughter as wife. [18]Now it was so, when she came *to him,* that she persuaded him to ask her father for a field. So she dismounted from *her* donkey, and Caleb said to her, "What do you wish?" [19]She

15:8 [a]Literally *Giants*

answered, "Give me a blessing; since you have given me land in the South, give me also springs of water." So he gave her the upper springs and the lower springs.

The Cities of Judah

[20]This *was* the inheritance of the tribe of the children of Judah according to their families:

[21]The cities at the limits of the tribe of the children of Judah, toward the border of Edom in the South, were Kabzeel, Eder, Jagur, [22]Kinah, Dimonah, Adadah, [23]Kedesh, Hazor, Ithnan, [24]Ziph, Telem, Bealoth, [25]Hazor, Hadattah, Kerioth, Hezron (which *is* Hazor), [26]Amam, Shema, Moladah, [27]Hazar Gaddah, Heshmon, Beth Pelet, [28]Hazar Shual, Beersheba, Bizjothjah, [29]Baalah, Ijim, Ezem, [30]Eltolad, Chesil, Hormah, [31]Ziklag, Madmannah, Sansannah, [32]Lebaoth, Shilhim, Ain, and Rimmon: all the cities *are* twenty-nine, with their villages.

[33]In the lowland: Eshtaol, Zorah, Ashnah, [34]Zanoah, En Gannim, Tappuah, Enam, [35]Jarmuth, Adullam, Socoh, Azekah, [36]Sharaim, Adithaim, Gederah, and Gederothaim: fourteen cities with their villages; [37]Zenan, Hadashah, Migdal Gad, [38]Dilean, Mizpah, Joktheel, [39]Lachish, Bozkath, Eglon, [40]Cabbon, Lahmas,[a] Kithlish, [41]Gederoth, Beth Dagon, Naamah, and Makkedah: sixteen cities with their villages; [42]Libnah, Ether, Ashan, [43]Jiphtah, Ashnah, Nezib, [44]Keilah, Achzib, and Mareshah: nine cities with their villages; [45]Ekron, with its towns and villages; [46]from Ekron to the sea, all that *lay* near Ashdod, with their villages; [47]Ashdod with its towns and villages, Gaza with its towns and villages—as far as the Brook of Egypt and the Great Sea with *its* coastline.

[48]And in the mountain country: Shamir, Jattir, Sochoh, [49]Dannah, Kirjath Sannah (which *is* Debir), [50]Anab, Eshtemoh, Anim, [51]Goshen, Holon, and Giloh: eleven cities with their villages; [52]Arab, Dumah, Eshean, [53]Janum, Beth Tappuah, Aphekah, [54]Humtah, Kirjath Arba (which *is* Hebron), and Zior: nine cities with their villages; [55]Maon, Carmel, Ziph, Juttah, [56]Jezreel, Jokdeam, Zanoah, [57]Kain, Gibeah, and Timnah: ten cities with their villages; [58]Halhul, Beth Zur, Gedor, [59]Maarath, Beth Anoth, and Eltekon: six cities with their villages; [60]Kirjath Baal (which *is* Kirjath Jearim) and Rabbah: two cities with their villages.

[61]In the wilderness: Beth Arabah, Middin, Secacah, [62]Nibshan, the City of Salt, and En Gedi: six cities with their villages.

[63]As for the Jebusites, the inhabitants of Jerusalem, the children of Judah could not drive them out; but the Jebusites dwell with the children of Judah at Jerusalem to this day.

Ephraim and West Manasseh

16 The lot fell to the children of Joseph from the Jordan, by Jericho, to the waters of Jericho on the east, to the wilderness that goes up from Jericho through the mountains to Bethel, [2]then went out from Bethel to Luz,[a] passed along to the border of the Archites at Ataroth, [3]and went down westward to the boundary of the Japhletites, as far as the boundary of Lower Beth Horon to Gezer; and it ended at the sea.

[4]So the children of Joseph, Manasseh and Ephraim, took their inheritance.

The Land of Ephraim

[5]The border of the children of Ephraim, according to their families, was *thus:* The border of their inheritance on the east side was Ataroth Addar as far as Up-

15:40 [a]Or *Lahmam* **16:2** [a]Septuagint reads *Bethel* (that is, Luz).

15:17–19 She asked her father for a field, and he gave it to her. God the Father told the Son to ask Him for the field of the world: "Ask of Me, and I will give You the nations for Your inheritance, and the ends of the earth for Your possession" (Psa. 2:8). Jesus said that all things we ask in prayer believing, we shall receive. If you are born again (see John 3:3–6), God is your Father, so be bold in your prayers for the lost.

per Beth Horon.

6And the border went out toward the sea on the north side of Michmethath; then the border went around eastward to Taanath Shiloh, and passed by it on the east of Janohah. 7Then it went down from Janohah to Ataroth and Naarah,[a] reached to Jericho, and came out at the Jordan.

8The border went out from Tappuah westward to the Brook Kanah, and it ended at the sea. This *was* the inheritance of the tribe of the children of Ephraim according to their families. 9The separate cities for the children of Ephraim *were* among the inheritance of the children of Manasseh, all the cities with their villages.

10And they did not drive out the Canaanites who dwelt in Gezer; but the Canaanites dwell among the Ephraimites to this day and have become forced laborers.

The Other Half-Tribe of Manasseh (West)

17 There was also a lot for the tribe of Manasseh, for he *was* the firstborn of Joseph: *namely* for Machir the firstborn of Manasseh, the father of Gilead, because he was a man of war; therefore he was given Gilead and Bashan. 2And there was *a lot* for the rest of the children of Manasseh according to their families: for the children of Abiezer,[a] the children of Helek, the children of Asriel, the children of Shechem, the children of Hepher, and the children of Shemida; these *were* the male children of Manasseh the son of Joseph according to their families.

3But Zelophehad the son of Hepher, the son of Gilead, the son of Machir, the son of Manasseh, had no sons, but only daughters. And these *are* the names of his daughters: Mahlah, Noah, Hoglah, Milcah, and Tirzah. 4And they came near before Eleazar the priest, before Joshua the son of Nun, and before the rulers, saying, "The LORD commanded Moses to give us an inheritance among our brothers." Therefore, according to the commandment of the LORD, he gave them an inheritance among their father's brothers. 5Ten shares fell to Manasseh, besides the land of Gilead and Bashan, which *were* on the other side of the Jordan, 6because the daughters of Manasseh received an inheritance among his sons; and the rest of Manasseh's sons had the land of Gilead.

7And the territory of Manasseh was from Asher to Michmethath, that *lies* east of Shechem; and the border went along south to the inhabitants of En Tappuah. 8Manasseh had the land of Tappuah, but Tappuah on the border of Manasseh *belonged* to the children of Ephraim. 9And the border descended to the Brook Kanah, southward to the brook. These cities of Ephraim *are* among the cities of Manasseh. The border of Manasseh *was* on the north side of the brook; and it ended at the sea.

10Southward *it was* Ephraim's, northward *it was* Manasseh's, and the sea was its border. Manasseh's territory was adjoining Asher on the north and Issachar on the east. 11And in Issachar and in Asher, Manasseh had Beth Shean and its towns, Ibleam and its towns, the inhabitants of Dor and its towns, the inhabitants of En Dor and its towns, the inhabitants of Taanach and its towns, and the inhabitants of Megiddo and its towns—three hilly regions. 12Yet the children of Manasseh could not drive out *the inhabitants of* those cities, but the Canaanites were determined to dwell in that land. 13And it happened, when the children of Israel grew strong, that they put the

16:7 [a]Or *Naaran* (compare 1 Chronicles 7:28) 17:2 [a]Called *Jeezer* in Numbers 26:30

16:10 God instructed Israel to put these people to death (see Deut. 20:16–18). Skeptics often accuse God of sanctioning genocide. However, if God treated any of us according to our sins, we would not only be put to death (see Rom. 6:23), we would be justly condemned to hell. All of God's judgments are true and righteous (see Psa. 19:9). None of them are unjust, including this instruction to Israel. See 1 Sam. 15:3 comment.

Canaanites to forced labor, but did not
utterly drive them out.

More Land for Ephraim and Manasseh

14Then the children of Joseph spoke to
Joshua, saying, "Why have you given us
only one lot and one share to inherit, since
we *are* a great people, inasmuch as the
LORD has blessed us until now?"

15So Joshua answered them, "If you
are a great people, *then* go up to the forest *country* and clear a place for yourself
there in the land of the Perizzites and the
giants, since the mountains of Ephraim
are too confined for you."

16But the children of Joseph said, "The
mountain country is not enough for us;
and all the Canaanites who dwell in the
land of the valley have chariots of iron,
both those who *are* of Beth Shean and its
towns and *those* who *are* of the Valley of
Jezreel."

17And Joshua spoke to the house of
Joseph—to Ephraim and Manasseh—saying, "You *are* a great people and have great
power; you shall not have *only* one lot,
18but the mountain country shall be yours.
Although it *is* wooded, you shall cut it
down, and its farthest extent shall be
yours; for you shall drive out the Canaanites, though they have iron chariots *and*
are strong."

The Remainder of the Land Divided

18 Now the whole congregation of
the children of Israel assembled
together at Shiloh, and set up the tabernacle of meeting there. And the land was
subdued before them. 2But there remained
among the children of Israel seven tribes
which had not yet received their inheritance.

3Then Joshua said to the children of
Israel: "How long will you neglect to go
and possess the land which the LORD God
of your fathers has given you? 4Pick out
from among you three men for *each* tribe,
and I will send them; they shall rise and
go through the land, survey it according
to their inheritance, and come *back* to
me. 5And they shall divide it into seven
parts. Judah shall remain in their territory on the south, and the house of
Joseph shall remain in their territory on
the north. 6You shall therefore survey the
land in seven parts and bring *the survey*
here to me, that I may cast lots for you
here before the LORD our God. 7But the
Levites have no part among you, for the
priesthood of the LORD *is* their inheritance. And Gad, Reuben, and half the tribe
of Manasseh have received their inheritance beyond the Jordan on the east, which
Moses the servant of the LORD gave them."

> Everything is safe which we commit to Him, and nothing is really safe which is not so committed.
>
> **A. W. TOZER**

8Then the men arose to go away; and
Joshua charged those who went to survey
the land, saying, "Go, walk through the
land, survey it, and come back to me,
that I may cast lots for you here before
the LORD in Shiloh." 9So the men went,
passed through the land, and wrote the
survey in a book in seven parts by cities;
and they came to Joshua at the camp in
Shiloh. 10Then Joshua cast lots for them
in Shiloh before the LORD, and there
Joshua divided the land to the children of
Israel according to their divisions.

The Land of Benjamin

11Now the lot of the tribe of the children of Benjamin came up according to
their families, and the territory of their lot
came out between the children of Judah
and the children of Joseph. 12Their border on the north side began at the Jordan,
and the border went up to the side of Jericho on the north, and went up through the
mountains westward; it ended at the Wilderness of Beth Aven. 13The border went
over from there toward Luz, to the side of
Luz (which *is* Bethel) southward; and the
border descended to Ataroth Addar, near

the hill that *lies* on the south side of Lower Beth Horon.

[14]Then the border extended around the west side to the south, from the hill that *lies* before Beth Horon southward; and it ended at Kirjath Baal (which *is* Kirjath Jearim), a city of the children of Judah. This *was* the west side.

[15]The south side *began* at the end of Kirjath Jearim, and the border extended on the west and went out to the spring of the waters of Nephtoah. [16]Then the border came down to the end of the mountain that *lies* before the Valley of the Son of Hinnom, which *is* in the Valley of the Rephaim[a] on the north, descended to the Valley of Hinnom, to the side of the Jebusite *city* on the south, and descended to En Rogel. [17]And it went around from the north, went out to En Shemesh, and extended toward Geliloth, which is before the Ascent of Adummim, and descended to the stone of Bohan the son of Reuben. [18]Then it passed along toward the north side of Arabah,[a] and went down to Arabah. [19]And the border passed along to the north side of Beth Hoglah; then the border ended at the north bay at the Salt Sea, at the south end of the Jordan. This *was* the southern boundary.

[20]The Jordan was its border on the east side. This *was* the inheritance of the children of Benjamin, according to its boundaries all around, according to their families.

[21]Now the cities of the tribe of the children of Benjamin, according to their families, were Jericho, Beth Hoglah, Emek Keziz, [22]Beth Arabah, Zemaraim, Bethel, [23]Avim, Parah, Ophrah, [24]Chephar Haammoni, Ophni, and Gaba: twelve cities with their villages; [25]Gibeon, Ramah, Beeroth, [26]Mizpah, Chephirah, Mozah, [27]Rekem, Irpeel, Taralah, [28]Zelah, Eleph, Jebus (which *is* Jerusalem), Gibeath, *and* Kirjath: fourteen cities with their villages. This was the inheritance of the children of Benjamin according to their families.

Simeon's Inheritance with Judah

19 The second lot came out for Simeon, for the tribe of the children of Simeon according to their families. And their inheritance was within the inheritance of the children of Judah. [2]They had in their inheritance Beersheba (Sheba), Moladah, [3]Hazar Shual, Balah, Ezem, [4]Eltolad, Bethul, Hormah, [5]Ziklag, Beth Marcaboth, Hazar Susah, [6]Beth Lebaoth, and Sharuhen: thirteen cities and their villages; [7]Ain, Rimmon, Ether, and Ashan: four cities and their villages; [8]and all the villages that *were* all around these cities as far as Baalath Beer, Ramah of the South. This *was* the inheritance of the tribe of the children of Simeon according to their families.

[9]The inheritance of the children of Simeon *was included* in the share of the children of Judah, for the share of the children of Judah was too much for them. Therefore the children of Simeon had *their* inheritance within the inheritance of that people.

The Land of Zebulun

[10]The third lot came out for the children of Zebulun according to their families, and the border of their inheritance was as far as Sarid. [11]Their border went toward the west and to Maralah, went to Dabbasheth, and extended along the brook that is east of Jokneam. [12]Then from Sarid it went eastward toward the sunrise along the border of Chisloth Tabor, and went out toward Daberath, bypassing Japhia. [13]And from there it passed along

18:16 [a]Literally *Giants* **18:18** [a]Or *Beth Arabah* (compare 15:6 and 18:22)

18:16 The Valley of Hinnom was a place where the pagan worshipers burned children alive as sacrifices to the false gods Moloch and Baal. One part of the valley was called Tophet ("fire-stove"), where the children were slaughtered (see Jer. 7:30–32).

on the east of Gath Hepher, toward Eth Kazin, and extended to Rimmon, which borders on Neah. [14]Then the border went around it on the north side of Hannathon, and it ended in the Valley of Jiphthah El. [15]Included were Kattath, Nahallal, Shimron, Idalah, and Bethlehem: twelve cities with their villages. [16]This *was* the inheritance of the children of Zebulun according to their families, these cities with their villages.

The Land of Issachar

[17]The fourth lot came out to Issachar, for the children of Issachar according to their families. [18]And their territory went to Jezreel, and *included* Chesulloth, Shunem, [19]Haphraim, Shion, Anaharath, [20]Rabbith, Kishion, Abez, [21]Remeth, En Gannim, En Haddah, and Beth Pazzez. [22]And the border reached to Tabor, Shahazimah, and Beth Shemesh; their border ended at the Jordan: sixteen cities with their villages. [23]This *was* the inheritance of the tribe of the children of Issachar according to their families, the cities and their villages.

The Land of Asher

[24]The fifth lot came out for the tribe of the children of Asher according to their families. [25]And their territory included Helkath, Hali, Beten, Achshaph, [26]Alammelech, Amad, and Mishal; it reached to Mount Carmel westward, along *the Brook* Shihor Libnath. [27]It turned toward the sunrise to Beth Dagon; and it reached to Zebulun and to the Valley of Jiphthah El, then northward beyond Beth Emek and Neiel, bypassing Cabul *which was* on the left, [28]including Ebron,[a] Rehob, Hammon, and Kanah, as far as Greater Sidon. [29]And the border turned to Ramah and to the fortified city of Tyre; then the border turned to Hosah, and ended at the sea by the region of Achzib. [30]Also Ummah, Aphek, and Rehob *were included:* twenty-two cities with their villages. [31]This *was* the inheritance of the tribe of the children of Asher according to their families, these cities with their villages.

The Land of Naphtali

[32]The sixth lot came out to the children of Naphtali, for the children of Naphtali according to their families. [33]And their border began at Heleph, enclosing the territory from the terebinth tree in Zaanannim, Adami Nekeb, and Jabneel, as far as Lakkum; it ended at the Jordan. [34]From Heleph the border extended westward to Aznoth Tabor, and went out from there toward Hukkok; it adjoined Zebulun on the south side and Asher on the west side, and ended at Judah by the Jordan toward the sunrise. [35]And the fortified cities *are* Ziddim, Zer, Hammath, Rakkath, Chinnereth, [36]Adamah, Ramah, Hazor, [37]Kedesh, Edrei, En Hazor, [38]Iron, Migdal El, Horem, Beth Anath, and Beth Shemesh: nineteen cities with their villages. [39]This *was* the inheritance of the tribe of the children of Naphtali according to their families, the cities and their villages.

The Land of Dan

[40]The seventh lot came out for the tribe of the children of Dan according to their families. [41]And the territory of their inheritance was Zorah, Eshtaol, Ir Shemesh, [42]Shaalabbin, Aijalon, Jethlah, [43]Elon, Timnah, Ekron, [44]Eltekeh, Gibbethon, Baalath, [45]Jehud, Bene Berak, Gath Rimmon, [46]Me Jarkon, and Rakkon, with the region near Joppa. [47]And the border of the children of Dan went beyond these, because the children of Dan went up to fight against Leshem and took it; and they struck it with the edge of the sword, took possession of it, and dwelt in it. They called Leshem, Dan, after the name of Dan their father. [48]This *is* the inheritance of the tribe of the children of Dan according to their families, these cities with their villages.

Joshua's Inheritance

[49]When they had made an end of di-

19:28 [a]Following Masoretic Text, Targum, and Vulgate; a few Hebrew manuscripts read *Abdon* (compare 21:30 and 1 Chronicles 6:74).

viding the land as an inheritance according to their borders, the children of Israel gave an inheritance among them to Joshua the son of Nun. [50]According to the word of the LORD they gave him the city which he asked for, Timnath Serah in the mountains of Ephraim; and he built the city and dwelt in it.

[51]These *were* the inheritances which Eleazar the priest, Joshua the son of Nun, and the heads of the fathers of the tribes of the children of Israel divided as an inheritance by lot in Shiloh before the LORD, at the door of the tabernacle of meeting. So they made an end of dividing the country.

The Cities of Refuge

20 The LORD also spoke to Joshua, saying, [2]"Speak to the children of Israel, saying: 'Appoint for yourselves cities of refuge, of which I spoke to you through Moses, [3]that the slayer who kills a person accidentally *or* unintentionally may flee there; and they shall be your refuge from the avenger of blood. [4]And when he flees to one of those cities, and stands at the entrance of the gate of the city, and declares his case in the hearing of the elders of that city, they shall take him into the city as one of them, and give him a place, that he may dwell among them. [5]Then if the avenger of blood pursues him, they shall not deliver the slayer into his hand, because he struck his neighbor unintentionally, but did not hate him beforehand. [6]And he shall dwell in that city until he stands before the congregation for judgment, *and* until the death of the one who is high priest in those days. Then the slayer may return and come to his own city and his own house, to the city from which he fled.' "

[7]So they appointed Kedesh in Galilee, in the mountains of Naphtali, Shechem in the mountains of Ephraim, and Kirjath Arba (which *is* Hebron) in the mountains of Judah. [8]And on the other side of the Jordan, by Jericho eastward, they assigned Bezer in the wilderness on the plain, from the tribe of Reuben, Ramoth in Gilead, from the tribe of Gad, and Golan in Bashan, from the tribe of Manasseh. [9]These were the cities appointed for all the children of Israel and for the stranger who dwelt among them, that whoever killed a person accidentally might flee there, and not die by the hand of the avenger of blood until he stood before the congregation.

Cities of the Levites

21 Then the heads of the fathers' *houses* of the Levites came near to Eleazar the priest, to Joshua the son of Nun, and to the heads of the fathers' *houses* of the tribes of the children of Israel. [2]And they spoke to them at Shiloh in the land of Canaan, saying, "The LORD commanded through Moses to give us cities to dwell in, with their common-lands for our livestock." [3]So the children of Israel gave to the Levites from their inheritance, at the commandment of the LORD, these cities and their common-lands:

19:49,50 After his conquests, Joshua was given a city to dwell in. While we wage the good warfare, we wait "for the city which has foundations, whose builder and maker is God" (Heb. 11:10). See John 14:1–3 and Rev. 21:10 for further details.

20:9 Avenger of blood. "It was the avenger's right and duty to slay the murderer (2 Sam. 14:7,11) if he found him outside of a city of refuge. In order that this law might be guarded against abuse, Moses appointed six cities of refuge (Ex. 21:13; Num. 35:13; Deut. 19:1,9). These were in different parts of the country, and every facility was afforded the manslayer that he might flee to the city that lay nearest him for safety.

"The avenger was forbidden to follow him into the city of refuge. This arrangement applied only to cases where the death was not premeditated. The case had to be investigated by the authorities of the city, and the willful murderer was on no account to be spared. He was regarded as an impure and polluted person, and was delivered up to the [avenger] (Deut. 19:11–13)." *Christiananswers.net*

God is the ultimate Avenger of blood. He will see to it that every transgression against the moral Law will find just retribution. See Eccles. 12:14.

[4]Now the lot came out for the families of the Kohathites. And the children of Aaron the priest, *who were* of the Levites, had thirteen cities by lot from the tribe of Judah, from the tribe of Simeon, and from the tribe of Benjamin. [5]The rest of the children of Kohath had ten cities by lot from the families of the tribe of Ephraim, from the tribe of Dan, and from the half-tribe of Manasseh.

[6]And the children of Gershon had thirteen cities by lot from the families of the tribe of Issachar, from the tribe of Asher, from the tribe of Naphtali, and from the half-tribe of Manasseh in Bashan.

[7]The children of Merari according to their families had twelve cities from the tribe of Reuben, from the tribe of Gad, and from the tribe of Zebulun.

[8]And the children of Israel gave these cities with their common-lands by lot to the Levites, as the LORD had commanded by the hand of Moses.

[9]So they gave from the tribe of the children of Judah and from the tribe of the children of Simeon these cities which are designated by name, [10]which were for the children of Aaron, one of the families of the Kohathites, *who were* of the children of Levi; for the lot was theirs first. [11]And they gave them Kirjath Arba (*Arba was* the father of Anak), which *is* Hebron, in the mountains of Judah, with the common-land surrounding it. [12]But the fields of the city and its villages they gave to Caleb the son of Jephunneh as his possession.

[13]Thus to the children of Aaron the priest they gave Hebron with its common-land (a city of refuge for the slayer), Libnah with its common-land, [14]Jattir with its common-land, Eshtemoa with its common-land, [15]Holon with its common-land, Debir with its common-land, [16]Ain with its common-land, Juttah with its common-land, and Beth Shemesh with its common-land: nine cities from those two tribes; [17]and from the tribe of Benjamin, Gibeon with its common-land, Geba with its common-land, [18]Anathoth with

"We cannot read the history of our rise and development as a nation, without reckoning with the place the Bible has occupied in shaping the advances of the Republic... Where we have been the truest and most consistent in obeying its precepts, we have attained the greatest measure of contentment and prosperity."

Franklin Roosevelt

its common-land, and Almon with its common-land: four cities. [19]All the cities of the children of Aaron, the priests, *were* thirteen cities with their common-lands.

[20]And the families of the children of Kohath, the Levites, the rest of the children of Kohath, even they had the cities of their lot from the tribe of Ephraim. [21]For they gave them Shechem with its common-land in the mountains of Ephraim (a city of refuge for the slayer), Gezer with its common-land, [22]Kibzaim with its common-land, and Beth Horon with its common-land: four cities; [23]and from the tribe of Dan, Eltekeh with its common-land, Gibbethon with its common-land, [24]Aijalon with its common-land, *and* Gath Rimmon with its common-land: four cities; [25]and from the half-tribe of Manasseh, Tanach with its common-land and Gath Rimmon with its common-land: two cities. [26]All the ten cities with their common-lands were for the rest of the families of the children of Kohath.

27Also to the children of Gershon, of the families of the Levites, from the *other* half-tribe of Manasseh, *they gave* Golan in Bashan with its common-land (a city of refuge for the slayer), and Be Eshterah with its common-land: two cities; 28and from the tribe of Issachar, Kishion with its common-land, Daberath with its common-land, 29Jarmuth with its common-land, *and* En Gannim with its common-land: four cities; 30and from the tribe of Asher, Mishal with its common-land, Abdon with its common-land, 31Helkath with its common-land, and Rehob with its common-land: four cities; 32and from the tribe of Naphtali, Kedesh in Galilee with its common-land (a city of refuge for the slayer), Hammoth Dor with its common-land, and Kartan with its common-land: three cities. 33All the cities of the Gershonites according to their families *were* thirteen cities with their common-lands.

34And to the families of the children of Merari, the rest of the Levites, from the tribe of Zebulun, Jokneam with its common-land, Kartah with its common-land, 35Dimnah with its common-land, *and* Nahalal with its common-land: four cities; 36and from the tribe of Reuben, Bezer with its common-land, Jahaz with its common-land, 37Kedemoth with its common-land, and Mephaath with its common-land: four cities;[a] 38and from the tribe of Gad, Ramoth in Gilead with its common-land (a city of refuge for the slayer), Mahanaim with its common-land, 39Heshbon with its common-land, *and* Jazer with its common-land: four cities in all. 40So all the cities for the children of Merari according to their families, the rest of the families of the Levites, were *by* their lot twelve cities.

41All the cities of the Levites within the possession of the children of Israel *were* forty-eight cities with their common-lands. 42Every one of these cities had its common-land surrounding it; thus *were* all these cities.

The Promise Fulfilled

43So the LORD gave to Israel all the land of which He had sworn to give to their fathers, and they took possession of it and dwelt in it. 44The LORD gave them rest all around, according to all that He had sworn to their fathers. And not a man of all their enemies stood against them; the LORD delivered all their enemies into their hand. 45Not a word failed of any good thing which the LORD had spoken to the house of Israel. All came to pass.

Eastern Tribes Return to Their Lands

22 Then Joshua called the Reubenites, the Gadites, and half the tribe of Manasseh, 2and said to them: "You have kept all that Moses the servant of the LORD commanded you, and have obeyed my voice in all that I commanded you. 3You have not left your brethren these many days, up to this day, but have kept the charge of the commandment of the LORD your God. 4And now the LORD your God has given rest to your brethren, as He promised them; now therefore, return and go to your tents *and* to the land of your possession, which Moses the servant of the LORD gave you on the other side of the Jordan. 5But take careful heed to do the commandment and the law which Moses the servant of the LORD commanded you, to love the LORD your God, to walk in all His ways, to keep His commandments, to hold fast to Him, and to serve Him with all your heart and with all your soul." 6So Joshua blessed them and sent them away, and they went to their tents.

7Now to half the tribe of Manasseh Moses had given a possession in Bashan, but to the *other* half of it Joshua gave *a possession* among their brethren on this side of the Jordan, westward. And indeed,

21:37 [a]Following Septuagint and Vulgate (compare 1 Chronicles 6:78, 79); Masoretic Text, Bomberg, and Targum omit verses 36 and 37.

21:43–45 We can trust God to keep every promise He makes. It is impossible for Him to lie. See Titus 1:2.

THE FUNCTION OF THE LAW

22:5 The essence of God's Law is to love Him with all of our heart and soul. However, there is a big problem—not with the Law, but with us. We cannot walk in His ways, keep His commandments, hold fast to Him, and serve Him with all of our heart and soul because there is another law at work in our members: the law of sin (see Rom. 7:5). We love to sin, hold fast to it, and serve it with heart and soul, as Paul found in his own experience (Rom. 7). The function of the Law is to bring the knowledge that we fall short of its perfect demands, and therefore desperately need a Savior.

The Heidelberg Disputation (1518) said, "The Law brings the wrath of God, kills, reviles, accuses, judges, and condemns everything that is not in Christ."

when Joshua sent them away to their
tents, he blessed them, 8and spoke to
them, saying, "Return with much riches
to your tents, with very much livestock,
with silver, with gold, with bronze, with
iron, and with very much clothing. Divide the spoil of your enemies with your
brethren."
9So the children of Reuben, the children of Gad, and half the tribe of Manasseh returned, and departed from the
children of Israel at Shiloh, which *is* in
the land of Canaan, to go to the country
of Gilead, to the land of their possession,
which they had obtained according to the
word of the LORD by the hand of Moses.

An Altar by the Jordan

10And when they came to the region of
the Jordan which *is* in the land of Canaan, the children of Reuben, the children
of Gad, and half the tribe of Manasseh
built an altar there by the Jordan—a great,
impressive altar. 11Now the children of
Israel heard *someone* say, "Behold, the
children of Reuben, the children of Gad,
and half the tribe of Manasseh have built
an altar on the frontier of the land of
Canaan, in the region of the Jordan—on
the children of Israel's side." 12And when
the children of Israel heard *of it,* the whole
congregation of the children of Israel
gathered together at Shiloh to go to war
against them.
13Then the children of Israel sent
Phinehas the son of Eleazar the priest to
the children of Reuben, to the children of
Gad, and to half the tribe of Manasseh,
into the land of Gilead, 14and with him
ten rulers, one ruler each from the chief
house of every tribe of Israel; and each
one *was* the head of the house of his father among the divisions[a] of Israel. 15Then
they came to the children of Reuben, to
the children of Gad, and to half the tribe
of Manasseh, to the land of Gilead, and
they spoke with them, saying, 16"Thus
says the whole congregation of the LORD:
'What treachery *is* this that you have
committed against the God of Israel, to
turn away this day from following the
LORD, in that you have built for yourselves an altar, that you might rebel this
day against the LORD? 17*Is* the iniquity of
Peor not enough for us, from which we
are not cleansed till this day, although
there was a plague in the congregation of
the LORD, 18but that you must turn away
this day from following the LORD? And it
shall be, if you rebel today against the
LORD, that tomorrow He will be angry
with the whole congregation of Israel.
19Nevertheless, if the land of your possession *is* unclean, *then* cross over to the
land of the possession of the LORD, where
the LORD's tabernacle stands, and take
possession among us; but do not rebel
against the LORD, nor rebel against us, by
building yourselves an altar besides the
altar of the LORD our God. 20Did not
Achan the son of Zerah commit a trespass
in the accursed thing, and wrath fell on
all the congregation of Israel? And that
man did not perish alone in his iniquity.' "
21Then the children of Reuben, the
children of Gad, and half the tribe of Manasseh answered and said to the heads of
the divisions[a] of Israel: 22"The LORD God
of gods, the LORD God of gods, He
knows, and let Israel itself know—if *it is*
in rebellion, or if in treachery against the

22:14 [a]Literally *thousands* **22:21** [a]Literally *thousands*

LORD, do not save us this day. [23]If we have built ourselves an altar to turn from following the LORD, or if to offer on it burnt offerings or grain offerings, or if to offer peace offerings on it, let the LORD Himself require *an account.* [24]But in fact we have done it for fear, for a reason, saying, 'In time to come your descendants may speak to our descendants, saying, "What have you to do with the LORD God of Israel? [25]For the LORD has made the Jordan a border between you and us, *you* children of Reuben and children of Gad. You have no part in the LORD." So your descendants would make our descendants cease fearing the LORD.' [26]Therefore we said, 'Let us now prepare to build ourselves an altar, not for burnt offering nor for sacrifice, [27]but *that* it *may be* a witness between you and us and our generations after us, that we may perform the service of the LORD before Him with our burnt offerings, with our sacrifices, and with our peace offerings; that your descendants may not say to our descendants in time to come, "You have no part in the LORD." ' [28]Therefore we said that it will be, when they say *this* to us or to our generations in time to come, that we may say, 'Here is the replica of the altar of the LORD which our fathers made, though not for burnt offerings nor for sacrifices; but it *is* a witness between you and us.' [29]Far be it from us that we should rebel against the LORD, and turn from following the LORD this day, to build an altar for burnt offerings, for grain offerings, or for sacrifices, besides the altar of the LORD our God which *is* before His tabernacle."

[30]Now when Phinehas the priest and the rulers of the congregation, the heads of the divisions[a] of Israel who *were* with him, heard the words that the children of Reuben, the children of Gad, and the children of Manasseh spoke, it pleased them. [31]Then Phinehas the son of Eleazar the priest said to the children of Reuben, the children of Gad, and the children of Manasseh, "This day we perceive that the LORD *is* among us, because you have not committed this treachery against the LORD. Now you have delivered the children of Israel out of the hand of the LORD."

[32]And Phinehas the son of Eleazar the priest, and the rulers, returned from the children of Reuben and the children of Gad, from the land of Gilead to the land of Canaan, to the children of Israel, and brought back word to them. [33]So the thing pleased the children of Israel, and the children of Israel blessed God; they spoke no more of going against them in battle, to destroy the land where the children of Reuben and Gad dwelt.

[34]The children of Reuben and the children of Gad[a] called the altar, *Witness,* "For *it is* a witness between us that the LORD *is* God."

Joshua's Farewell Address

23 Now it came to pass, a long time after the LORD had given rest to Israel from all their enemies round about, that Joshua was old, advanced in age. [2]And Joshua called for all Israel, for their elders, for their heads, for their judges, and for their officers, and said to them:

"I am old, advanced in age. [3]You have seen all that the LORD your God has done to all these nations because of you, for the LORD your God *is* He who has fought for you. [4]See, I have divided to you by lot these nations that remain, to be an inheritance for your tribes, from the Jordan, with all the nations that I have cut off, as far as the Great Sea westward. [5]And the LORD your God will expel them from before you and drive them out of your sight. So you shall possess their land, as

22:30 [a]Literally *thousands* 22:34 [a]Septuagint adds *and half the tribe of Manasseh.*

22:22 There is only one Creator—the God of gods—but there are many false gods (idols). Satan is called the god of this age (see 2 Cor. 4:4).

QUESTIONS & OBJECTIONS

23:7 ***"Which 'god' are you talking about: Thor, Zeus, etc.?"***

The inference in this question is, "These were mythical gods, and so is yours." Atheists are correct about these gods being myths. Man gravitates toward idolatry (making up false gods) as a moth does to a flame. There are millions of false gods—Hinduism alone has 330 million—but there is only one Creator. That is the God who revealed Himself to Moses and gave us His moral Law. And that is the God you and I will have to face on Judgment Day.

Another argument atheists use is that they cannot prove that God doesn't exist, just as you and I cannot prove that the tooth fairy doesn't exist. This is a demeaning way of equating belief in God with belief in the tooth fairy. It is true that we cannot disprove the existence of either the tooth fairy or God. However, belief in the existence of the tooth fairy is inconsequential. Belief in and therefore obedience to the one true God has eternal consequences.

the LORD your God promised you. 6There-
fore be very courageous to keep and to
do all that is written in the Book of the
Law of Moses, lest you turn aside from it
to the right hand or to the left, 7*and* lest
you go among these nations, these who
remain among you. You shall not make
mention of the name of their gods, nor
cause *anyone* to swear *by them;* you shall
not serve them nor bow down to them,
8but you shall hold fast to the LORD your
God, as you have done to this day. 9For
the LORD has driven out from before you
great and strong nations; but *as for* you,
no one has been able to stand against you
to this day. 10One man of you shall chase
a thousand, for the LORD your God *is* He
who fights for you, as He promised you.
11Therefore take careful heed to yourselves, that you love the LORD your God.
12Or else, if indeed you do go back, and
cling to the remnant of these nations—
these that remain among you—and make
marriages with them, and go in to them
and they to you, 13know for certain that
the LORD your God will no longer drive
out these nations from before you. But
they shall be snares and traps to you, and
scourges on your sides and thorns in your
eyes, until you perish from this good land
which the LORD your God has given you.
14"Behold, this day I *am* going the way
of all the earth. And you know in all your
hearts and in all your souls that not one
thing has failed of all the good things
which the LORD your God spoke concerning you. All have come to pass for you;
not one word of them has failed. 15There-
fore it shall come to pass, that as all the
good things have come upon you which
the LORD your God promised you, so the
LORD will bring upon you all harmful
things, until He has destroyed you from
this good land which the LORD your God
has given you. 16When you have transgressed the covenant of the LORD your
God, which He commanded you, and have
gone and served other gods, and bowed
down to them, then the anger of the LORD
will burn against you, and you shall per-

23:7 Idolatry is at the root of every sin. A man will blaspheme, lie, steal, commit adultery, and murder because he has no fear of God. He has no fear of God because he has no understanding of the true nature of his Creator. Cultivate a biblical understanding of God, and keep yourself from idolatry (see 1 John 5:20,21).

23:14 "It seems perfectly reasonable that God should have given us a glimpse of the future, for we are constantly losing some of our friends by death, and the first thought that comes to us is, 'where have they gone?' When a loved one is taken away from us, how that thought comes up before us! How we wonder if we will ever see them again, and where and when it will be! Then it is that we turn to this blessed Book, for there is no other book in all the world that can give us the slightest comfort; no other book that can tell us where the loved ones have gone." *D. L. Moody*

ish quickly from the good land which He has given you."

The Covenant at Shechem

24 Then Joshua gathered all the tribes of Israel to Shechem and called for the elders of Israel, for their heads, for their judges, and for their officers; and they presented themselves before God. 2And Joshua said to all the people, "Thus says the LORD God of Israel: 'Your fathers, *including* Terah, the father of Abraham and the father of Nahor, dwelt on the other side of the River[a] in old times; and they served other gods. 3Then I took your father Abraham from the other side of the River, led him throughout all the land of Canaan, and multiplied his descendants and gave him Isaac. 4To Isaac I gave Jacob and Esau. To Esau I gave the mountains of Seir to possess, but Jacob and his children went down to Egypt. 5Also I sent Moses and Aaron, and I plagued Egypt, according to what I did among them. Afterward I brought you out.

6'Then I brought your fathers out of Egypt, and you came to the sea; and the Egyptians pursued your fathers with chariots and horsemen to the Red Sea. 7So they cried out to the LORD; and He put darkness between you and the Egyptians, brought the sea upon them, and covered them. And your eyes saw what I did in Egypt. Then you dwelt in the wilderness a long time. 8And I brought you into the land of the Amorites, who dwelt on the other side of the Jordan, and they fought with you. But I gave them into your hand, that you might possess their land, and I destroyed them from before you. 9Then Balak the son of Zippor, king of Moab, arose to make war against Israel, and sent and called Balaam the son of Beor to curse you. 10But I would not listen to Balaam; therefore he continued to bless you. So I delivered you out of his hand. 11Then you went over the Jordan and came to Jericho. And the men of Jericho fought against you—*also* the Amorites, the Perizzites, the Canaanites, the Hittites, the Girgashites, the Hivites, and the Jebusites. But I delivered them into your hand. 12I sent the hornet before you which drove them out from before you, *also* the two kings of the Amorites, *but* not with your sword or with your bow. 13I have given you a land for which you did not labor, and cities which you did not build, and you dwell in them; you eat of the vineyards and olive groves which you did not plant.'

14"Now therefore, fear the LORD, serve Him in sincerity and in truth, and put away the gods which your fathers served on the other side of the River and in Egypt. Serve the LORD! 15And if it seems evil to you to serve the LORD, choose for yourselves this day whom you will serve, whether the gods which your fathers served that *were* on the other side of the River, or the gods of the Amorites, in whose

24:2 [a]Hebrew *Nahar,* the Euphrates, and so in verses 3, 14, and 15

24:14 Sincerity must be coupled with truth. A man may sincerely believe that he is on a plane heading for New York, but if the plane is heading for Australia, his sincerity means nothing. All who worship false gods, however sincerely, are still in grave error. We must worship God in *truth* (see John 4:23,24). See also 1 Cor. 5:8 comment.

"The first duty of a man is the seeking after and the investigation of truth." *Cicero*

24:15 It is simple common sense to repent and trust the Savior. It's a choice between life and death. But if sinners insist on serving the devil, God allows them to, but with the knowledge that such service will lead to death and hell (see Rom. 1:32). He gives them over to a debased mind (see Rom. 1:28). For the choice between God and the devil, life and death, see also 1 Kings 18:21; Ezek. 20:39; Rev. 3:15,16.

"In the moral conflict now raging around us, whoever is on God's side is on the winning side and cannot lose; whoever is on the other side is on the losing side and cannot win. Here there is no chance, no gamble. There is freedom to choose which side we shall be on, but no freedom to negotiate the results of the choice once it is made." *A. W. Tozer*

land you dwell. But as for me and my house, we will serve the LORD."

16So the people answered and said: "Far be it from us that we should forsake the LORD to serve other gods; 17for the LORD our God *is* He who brought us and our fathers up out of the land of Egypt, from the house of bondage, who did those great signs in our sight, and preserved us in all the way that we went and among all the people through whom we passed. 18And the LORD drove out from before us all the people, including the Amorites who dwelt in the land. We also will serve the LORD, for He *is* our God."

19But Joshua said to the people, "You cannot serve the LORD, for He *is* a holy God. He *is* a jealous God; He will not forgive your transgressions nor your sins. 20If you forsake the LORD and serve foreign gods, then He will turn and do you harm and consume you, after He has done you good."

21And the people said to Joshua, "No, but we will serve the LORD!"

22So Joshua said to the people, "You *are* witnesses against yourselves that you have chosen the LORD for yourselves, to serve Him."

And they said, "*We are* witnesses!"

23"Now therefore," *he said,* "put away the foreign gods which *are* among you, and incline your heart to the LORD God of Israel."

24And the people said to Joshua, "The LORD our God we will serve, and His voice we will obey!"

25So Joshua made a covenant with the people that day, and made for them a statute and an ordinance in Shechem.

26Then Joshua wrote these words in the Book of the Law of God. And he took a large stone, and set it up there under the oak that *was* by the sanctuary of the LORD. 27And Joshua said to all the people, "Behold, this stone shall be a witness to us, for it has heard all the words of the LORD which He spoke to us. It shall therefore be a witness to you, lest you deny your God." 28So Joshua let the people depart, each to his own inheritance.

Death of Joshua and Eleazar

29Now it came to pass after these things that Joshua the son of Nun, the servant of the LORD, died, *being* one hundred and ten years old. 30And they buried him within the border of his inheritance at Timnath Serah, which *is* in the mountains of Ephraim, on the north side of Mount Gaash.

31Israel served the LORD all the days of Joshua, and all the days of the elders who outlived Joshua, who had known all the works of the LORD which He had done for Israel.

32The bones of Joseph, which the children of Israel had brought up out of Egypt, they buried at Shechem, in the plot of ground which Jacob had bought from the sons of Hamor the father of Shechem for one hundred pieces of silver, and which had become an inheritance of the children of Joseph.

33And Eleazar the son of Aaron died. They buried him in a hill *belonging to* Phinehas his son, which was given to him in the mountains of Ephraim.

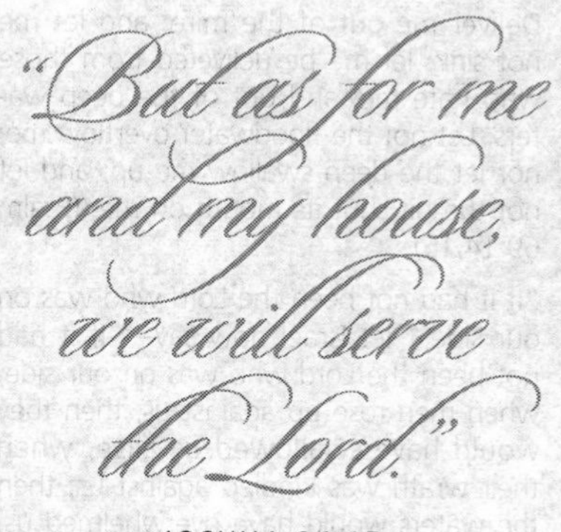

JOSHUA 24:15

24:29 "God has removed the sting of death for each believer. I should save my sorrow for those without Christ and seek to win them." *Larry Clark*

Joshua's "Underwater Memorial"

By Carl Kerby

Remember that throughout the Old Testament, God provided signs to His people to reveal Himself, His plans, and especially the promise of a coming Messiah. The book of Joshua begins with the people preparing to enter the Promised Land, their God-given inheritance. They are not led by Moses, who represents the Law, but by Joshua, an Old Testament picture and foreshadow of our Savior, who is the only way to our inheritance.

We read in Joshua 3:17 that the ark stood firm on dry ground in the middle of the Jordan while the people passed through untouched by the waters of the Jordan. Often in the Bible we see where water serves as a symbol of the wrath or judgment of God: the Flood (Genesis 6:17; Hebrews 11:7); the Red Sea drowning of the Egyptians (Exodus 14:28; Hebrews 11:29); Jonah going under the waters (Jonah 1; 2:3). Even the word "Jordan" implies judgment. A. W. Pink breaks the word into two Hebrew roots: *jor* or *yar*, which is literally "spread," and *dan*, which means "judging" (Genesis 30:6). Others define it as *yar-dane*, meaning "descender." Baptism, where the person is immersed in water and risen to new life by the power of Christ, is also a picture of the old man being judged by God, dying to self, and being saved by Christ. Jesus' followers are commissioned to be "fishers of men" (Matthew 4:19; Mark 1:17), and the Psalms confirm our being taken out from the waters:

> He sent from above, He took me; He drew me out of many waters. (Psalm 18:16)
>
> Deliver me out of the mire, and let me not sink; let me be delivered from those who hate me, and out of the deep waters. Let not the floodwater overflow me, nor let the deep swallow me up; and let not the pit shut its mouth on me. (Psalm 69:14,15)
>
> "If it had not been the Lord who was on our side," let Israel now say—"If it had not been the Lord who was on our side, when men rose up against us, then they would have swallowed us alive, when their wrath was kindled against us; then the waters would have overwhelmed us, the stream would have gone over our soul; then the swollen waters would have gone over our soul." (Psalm 124:1–5)
>
> "I will pour out My wrath on them like water." (Hosea 5:10)

In Joshua 4, God instructed the twelve men (one from each tribe) to take a stone from the middle of the dry riverbed to build a memorial on the west bank of the Jordan. These stones came from the place that pictures death, the miry bottom of a riverbed. They had been buried beneath the waters, the picture of wrath and judgment. The "ark of the LORD," which is a picture of Christ (in both construction and in being the place where God dwelled among His people) stood in the midst of the Jordan, allowing these stones to be brought up out of the waters (death) to create a memorial of deliverance (redemption). Remember, this was done "that this may be a sign among you . . ." (Joshua 4:6).

We read in Joshua 4:9 that it was Joshua, not the twelve, who was told to "set up twelve stones in the midst of the Jordan, in the place where the feet of the priests who bore the ark of the covenant stood; and they are there to this day." This is a picture of the unredeemed, those who die in their sin, who are buried in death by the righteous judgment of God—"and they are there to this day" (Joshua 4:9). What a frightening thought and a reminder to all of us to be bold in sharing the saving grace of the gospel.

The twelve stones taken out from the Jordan depths and placed on dry ground "where they lodged" (Joshua 4:8) symbolize those who were redeemed by Christ (the ark) and came out from under the judgment of God (the waters) to new life in the Promised Land (inheritance of life in Christ). And remember that the people crossed over the Jordan at the time of Passover! This was at the "time of harvest" (Joshua 3:15), "on the tenth day of the first month" (Joshua 4:19). This is a beautiful picture of the saving grace of Jesus Christ.

The Joshua 4 memorial also reminds us of a future promise given in Isaiah 43:2, where God says, "When you pass through the waters, I will be with you; and through the rivers, they shall not overflow you." Notice that promise says "when," not "if." We all know that in this life trials will come our way, and we must always remember that He promises to be with us, to deliver us, to set our feet on solid ground. Keep in mind this verse:

> He also brought me up out of a horrible pit, out of the miry clay, and set my feet upon a rock, and established my steps. (Psalm 40:2)

(Reprinted from *Reasons for Hope in the Mosaic of Your Life*.)

Judges

The Continuing Conquest of Canaan

1 Now after the death of Joshua it came
to pass that the children of Israel asked
the LORD, saying, "Who shall be first to
go up for us against the Canaanites to
fight against them?"
[2]And the LORD said, "Judah shall go
up. Indeed I have delivered the land into
his hand."
[3]So Judah said to Simeon his brother,
"Come up with me to my allotted territory, that we may fight against the Canaanites; and I will likewise go with you
to your allotted territory." And Simeon
went with him. [4]Then Judah went up,
and the LORD delivered the Canaanites
and the Perizzites into their hand; and
they killed ten thousand men at Bezek.
[5]And they found Adoni-Bezek in Bezek,
and fought against him; and they defeated the Canaanites and the Perizzites.
[6]Then Adoni-Bezek fled, and they pursued him and caught him and cut off his
thumbs and big toes. [7]And Adoni-Bezek
said, "Seventy kings with their thumbs
and big toes cut off used to gather *scraps*
under my table; as I have done, so God
has repaid me." Then they brought him
to Jerusalem, and there he died.
[8]Now the children of Judah fought
against Jerusalem and took it; they struck
it with the edge of the sword and set the
city on fire. [9]And afterward the children
of Judah went down to fight against the
Canaanites who dwelt in the mountains,
in the South,[a] and in the lowland. [10]Then
Judah went against the Canaanites who
dwelt in Hebron. (Now the name of Hebron *was* formerly Kirjath Arba.) And they
killed Sheshai, Ahiman, and Talmai.
[11]From there they went against the inhabitants of Debir. (The name of Debir
was formerly Kirjath Sepher.)
[12]Then Caleb said, "Whoever attacks
Kirjath Sepher and takes it, to him I will
give my daughter Achsah as wife." [13]And
Othniel the son of Kenaz, Caleb's younger brother, took it; so he gave him his
daughter Achsah as wife. [14]Now it happened, when she came *to him,* that she
urged him[a] to ask her father for a field.
And she dismounted from *her* donkey, and
Caleb said to her, "What do you wish?"
[15]So she said to him, "Give me a blessing;
since you have given me land in the South,
give me also springs of water."
And Caleb gave her the upper springs
and the lower springs.
[16]Now the children of the Kenite,
Moses' father-in-law, went up from the
City of Palms with the children of Judah
into the Wilderness of Judah, which *lies*
in the South *near* Arad; and they went
and dwelt among the people. [17]And Judah
went with his brother Simeon, and they
attacked the Canaanites who inhabited
Zephath, and utterly destroyed it. So the
name of the city was called Hormah.
[18]Also Judah took Gaza with its territory,

1:9 [a]Hebrew *Negev,* and so throughout this book 1:14 [a]Septuagint and Vulgate read *he urged her.*

Ashkelon with its territory, and Ekron with its territory. 19So the LORD was with Judah. And they drove out the mountaineers, but they could not drive out the inhabitants of the lowland, because they had chariots of iron. 20And they gave Hebron to Caleb, as Moses had said. Then he expelled from there the three sons of Anak. 21But the children of Benjamin did not drive out the Jebusites who inhabited Jerusalem; so the Jebusites dwell with the children of Benjamin in Jerusalem to this day.

22And the house of Joseph also went up against Bethel, and the LORD *was* with them. 23So the house of Joseph sent men to spy out Bethel. (The name of the city *was* formerly Luz.) 24And when the spies saw a man coming out of the city, they said to him, "Please show us the entrance to the city, and we will show you mercy." 25So he showed them the entrance to the city, and they struck the city with the edge of the sword; but they let the man and all his family go. 26And the man went to the land of the Hittites, built a city, and called its name Luz, which *is* its name to this day.

Incomplete Conquest of the Land

27However, Manasseh did not drive out *the inhabitants of* Beth Shean and its villages, or Taanach and its villages, or the inhabitants of Dor and its villages, or the inhabitants of Ibleam and its villages, or the inhabitants of Megiddo and its villages; for the Canaanites were determined to dwell in that land. 28And it came to pass, when Israel was strong, that they put the Canaanites under tribute, but did not completely drive them out.

29Nor did Ephraim drive out the Canaanites who dwelt in Gezer; so the Canaanites dwelt in Gezer among them.

30Nor did Zebulun drive out the inhabitants of Kitron or the inhabitants of Nahalol; so the Canaanites dwelt among them, and were put under tribute.

31Nor did Asher drive out the inhabitants of Acco or the inhabitants of Sidon, or of Ahlab, Achzib, Helbah, Aphik, or Rehob. 32So the Asherites dwelt among the Canaanites, the inhabitants of the land; for they did not drive them out.

33Nor did Naphtali drive out the inhabitants of Beth Shemesh or the inhabitants of Beth Anath; but they dwelt among the Canaanites, the inhabitants of the land. Nevertheless the inhabitants of Beth Shemesh and Beth Anath were put under tribute to them.

34And the Amorites forced the children of Dan into the mountains, for they would not allow them to come down to the valley; 35and the Amorites were determined to dwell in Mount Heres, in Aijalon, and in Shaalbim;[a] yet when the strength of the house of Joseph became greater, they were put under tribute.

36Now the boundary of the Amorites *was* from the Ascent of Akrabbim, from Sela, and upward.

Israel's Disobedience

2 Then the Angel of the LORD came up from Gilgal to Bochim, and said: "I led you up from Egypt and brought you to the land of which I swore to your fathers; and I said, 'I will never break My covenant with you. 2And you shall make no covenant with the inhabitants of this

1:35 [a]Spelled *Shaalabbin* in Joshua 19:42

1:19 Bible contradiction? Some skeptics think this verse contradicts Luke 1:37, "For with God nothing will be impossible." It was Judah, not God, who could not drive out the inhabitants of the valley. The assumption is that because God was with Judah, they were therefore promised victory over their enemies. This is clearly a faulty deduction. It is true that nothing is impossible with God and that He was with Judah, but the problem was their disobedience. Even though they had earlier been assured of victory against their enemies with iron chariots (Josh. 17:18), they apparently became fearful and failed to trust God to give them victory. God is with the believer; nothing is impossible for Him to accomplish through those who obey Him. There is no contradiction in these passages.

land; you shall tear down their altars.' But you have not obeyed My voice. Why have you done this? 3Therefore I also said, 'I will not drive them out before you; but they shall be *thorns* in your side,[a] and their gods shall be a snare to you.' " 4So it was, when the Angel of the LORD spoke these words to all the children of Israel, that the people lifted up their voices and wept.

5Then they called the name of that place Bochim;[a] and they sacrificed there to the LORD. 6And when Joshua had dismissed the people, the children of Israel went each to his own inheritance to possess the land.

Death of Joshua

7So the people served the LORD all the days of Joshua, and all the days of the elders who outlived Joshua, who had seen all the great works of the LORD which He had done for Israel. 8Now Joshua the son of Nun, the servant of the LORD, died *when he was* one hundred and ten years old. 9And they buried him within the border of his inheritance at Timnath Heres, in the mountains of Ephraim, on the north side of Mount Gaash. 10When all that generation had been gathered to their fathers, another generation arose after them who did not know the LORD nor the work which He had done for Israel.

Israel's Unfaithfulness

11Then the children of Israel did evil in the sight of the LORD, and served the Baals; 12and they forsook the LORD God of their fathers, who had brought them out of the land of Egypt; and they followed other gods from *among* the gods of the people who *were* all around them, and they bowed down to them; and they provoked the LORD to anger. 13They forsook the LORD and served Baal and the Ashtoreths.[a] 14And the anger of the LORD was hot against Israel. So He delivered them into the hands of plunderers who despoiled them; and He sold them into the hands of their enemies all around, so that they could no longer stand before their enemies. 15Wherever they went out, the hand of the LORD was against them for calamity, as the LORD had said, and as the LORD had sworn to them. And they were greatly distressed.

16Nevertheless, the LORD raised up judges who delivered them out of the hand of those who plundered them. 17Yet they would not listen to their judges, but they played the harlot with other gods, and bowed down to them. They turned quickly from the way in which their fathers walked, in obeying the commandments of the LORD; they did not do so. 18And when the LORD raised up judges for them, the LORD was with the judge and delivered them out of the hand of their enemies all the days of the judge; for the LORD was moved to pity by their groaning because of those who oppressed them and harassed them. 19And it came to pass, when the judge was dead, that

2:3 [a]Septuagint, Targum, and Vulgate read *enemies to you.*
2:5 [a]Literally *Weeping* **2:13** [a]Canaanite goddesses

2:1 "I shall need, too, the favor of that Being in whose hands we are, who led our fathers, as Israel of old, from their native land and planted them in a country flowing with all the necessaries and comforts of life; who has covered our infancy with His providence and our riper years with His wisdom and power, and to whose goodness I ask you to join in supplications with me that He will so enlighten the minds of your servants, guide their councils, and prosper their measures that whatsoever they do shall result in your good, and shall secure to you the peace, friendship, and approbation of all nations." *Thomas Jefferson*

2:10 The biblical challenge to an unsaved person is, "Do you know the Lord?" If someone is a "backslider" (a false convert), ask him, "Did you know the Lord?" That puts him between a rock and a hard place. If he says he did, then he is admitting that God is real and that he is in rebellion to Him. If he says that he *didn't* know Him, he is admitting that he was never a Christian. He had a false conversion, as so clearly taught in the Parable of the Sower (Mark 4). See John 17:3 for the definition of a Christian.

Questions & Objections

3:4

"How can God be omniscient if He didn't know what Israel would do?"

God "tests" us, not for *His* sake, but for *ours*. For example, Eccles. 3:18 tells us, "God tests them, *that they may see* that they themselves are like animals" (emphasis added). In school, students are given periodic tests to show them their current progress—what they think they know but don't, where they are wrong and need to relearn—so they can have a "course correction" before it is too late. After seeing God's miraculous provision, both Abraham and the children of Israel were "tested" to see if they had learned the lesson that they could trust God (Gen. 22:1; Exod. 15:25). God brings tests and trials to those He loves, to cause them to mature and develop godly character. Tribulation, temptation, and persecution "establish, strengthen, and settle" the godly (see 1 Pet. 5:10). See also Psa. 66:10–12.

they reverted and behaved more corruptly
than their fathers, by following other
gods, to serve them and bow down to
them. They did not cease from their own
doings nor from their stubborn way.
20Then the anger of the LORD was hot
against Israel; and He said, "Because this
nation has transgressed My covenant
which I commanded their fathers, and
has not heeded My voice, 21I also will no
longer drive out before them any of the
nations which Joshua left when he died,
22so that through them I may test Israel,
whether they will keep the ways of the
LORD, to walk in them as their fathers
kept *them*, or not." 23Therefore the LORD
left those nations, without driving them
out immediately; nor did He deliver them
into the hand of Joshua.

The Nations Remaining in the Land

3 Now these *are* the nations which the
LORD left, that He might test Israel by
them, *that is*, all who had not known any
of the wars in Canaan 2(*this was* only so
that the generations of the children of
Israel might be taught to know war, at
least those who had not formerly known
it), 3*namely*, five lords of the Philistines,
all the Canaanites, the Sidonians, and the
Hivites who dwelt in Mount Lebanon,
from Mount Baal Hermon to the entrance
of Hamath. 4And they were *left, that He
might* test Israel by them, to know whether
they would obey the commandments of
the LORD, which He had commanded
their fathers by the hand of Moses.
5Thus the children of Israel dwelt
among the Canaanites, the Hittites, the
Amorites, the Perizzites, the Hivites, and
the Jebusites. 6And they took their daughters
to be their wives, and gave their
daughters to their sons; and they served
their gods.

Othniel

7So the children of Israel did evil in the
sight of the LORD. They forgot the LORD
their God, and served the Baals and Asherahs.[a] 8Therefore the anger of the LORD
was hot against Israel, and He sold them
into the hand of Cushan-Rishathaim king
of Mesopotamia; and the children of Israel
served Cushan-Rishathaim eight years.
9When the children of Israel cried out to
the LORD, the LORD raised up a deliverer
for the children of Israel, who delivered
them: Othniel the son of Kenaz, Caleb's
younger brother. 10The Spirit of the LORD
came upon him, and he judged Israel. He

3:7 [a]Name or symbol for Canaanite goddesses

3:10 In the Old Testament the Holy Spirit often came upon and temporarily indwelt the godly to fulfill certain purposes. King David, for example, spoke of having fellowship with the Holy Spirit; see Psa. 51:11. First Peter 1:11 says the prophets received revelations of the salvation to come by "the Spirit of Christ who was in them." After the giving of the Holy Spirit at Pentecost, however, the believer has the assurance that He will never leave us. See John 14:16,17; 2 Cor. 1:22; Eph. 1:13.

went out to war, and the LORD delivered Cushan-Rishathaim king of Mesopotamia into his hand; and his hand prevailed over Cushan-Rishathaim. [11]So the land had rest for forty years. Then Othniel the son of Kenaz died.

Ehud

[12]And the children of Israel again did evil in the sight of the LORD. So the LORD strengthened Eglon king of Moab against Israel, because they had done evil in the sight of the LORD. [13]Then he gathered to himself the people of Ammon and Amalek, went and defeated Israel, and took possession of the City of Palms. [14]So the children of Israel served Eglon king of Moab eighteen years.

> Whatever is only almost true is quite false, and among the most dangerous of errors, because being so near truth, it is the more likely to lead astray.
>
> **HENRY WARD BEECHER**

[15]But when the children of Israel cried out to the LORD, the LORD raised up a deliverer for them: Ehud the son of Gera, the Benjamite, a left-handed man. By him the children of Israel sent tribute to Eglon king of Moab. [16]Now Ehud made himself a dagger (it was double-edged and a cubit in length) and fastened it under his clothes on his right thigh. [17]So he brought the tribute to Eglon king of Moab. (Now Eglon *was* a very fat man.) [18]And when he had finished presenting the tribute, he sent away the people who had carried the tribute. [19]But he himself turned back from the stone images that *were* at Gilgal, and said, "I have a secret message for you, O king."

He said, "Keep silence!" And all who attended him went out from him.

[20]So Ehud came to him (now he was sitting upstairs in his cool private chamber). Then Ehud said, "I have a message from God for you." So he arose from *his* seat. [21]Then Ehud reached with his left hand, took the dagger from his right thigh, and thrust it into his belly. [22]Even the hilt went in after the blade, and the fat closed over the blade, for he did not draw the dagger out of his belly; and his entrails came out. [23]Then Ehud went out through the porch and shut the doors of the upper room behind him and locked them. [24]When he had gone out, *Eglon's*[a] servants came to look, and *to their* surprise, the doors of the upper room were locked. So they said, "He is probably attending to his needs in the cool chamber." [25]So they waited till they were embarrassed, and still he had not opened the doors of the upper room. Therefore they took the key and opened *them*. And there was their master, fallen dead on the floor.

[26]But Ehud had escaped while they delayed, and passed beyond the stone images and escaped to Seirah. [27]And it happened, when he arrived, that he blew the trumpet in the mountains of Ephraim, and the children of Israel went down with him from the mountains; and he led them. [28]Then he said to them, "Follow *me*, for the LORD has delivered your enemies the Moabites into your hand." So they went down after him, seized the fords of the Jordan leading to Moab, and did not allow anyone to cross over. [29]And at that time they killed about ten thousand men of Moab, all stout men of valor; not a man escaped. [30]So Moab was subdued that day under the hand of Israel. And the land had rest for eighty years.

Shamgar

[31]After him was Shamgar the son of Anath, who killed six hundred men of the Philistines with an ox goad; and he also delivered Israel.

Deborah

4 When Ehud was dead, the children of Israel again did evil in the sight of the LORD. [2]So the LORD sold them into the hand of Jabin king of Canaan, who reigned in Hazor. The commander of his

3:24 [a]Literally *his*

army *was* Sisera, who dwelt in Harosheth Hagoyim. 3And the children of Israel cried out to the LORD; for Jabin had nine hundred chariots of iron, and for twenty years he had harshly oppressed the children of Israel.

4Now Deborah, a prophetess, the wife of Lapidoth, was judging Israel at that time. 5And she would sit under the palm tree of Deborah between Ramah and Bethel in the mountains of Ephraim. And the children of Israel came up to her for judgment. 6Then she sent and called for Barak the son of Abinoam from Kedesh in Naphtali, and said to him, "Has not the LORD God of Israel commanded, 'Go and deploy *troops* at Mount Tabor; take with you ten thousand men of the sons of Naphtali and of the sons of Zebulun; 7and against you I will deploy Sisera, the commander of Jabin's army, with his chariots and his multitude at the River Kishon; and I will deliver him into your hand'?"

8And Barak said to her, "If you will go with me, then I will go; but if you will not go with me, I will not go!"

9So she said, "I will surely go with you; nevertheless there will be no glory for you in the journey you are taking, for the LORD will sell Sisera into the hand of a woman." Then Deborah arose and went with Barak to Kedesh. 10And Barak called Zebulun and Naphtali to Kedesh; he went up with ten thousand men under his command,[a] and Deborah went up with him.

11Now Heber the Kenite, of the children of Hobab the father-in-law of Moses, had separated himself from the Kenites and pitched his tent near the terebinth tree at Zaanaim, which *is* beside Kedesh.

12And they reported to Sisera that Barak the son of Abinoam had gone up to Mount Tabor. 13So Sisera gathered together all his chariots, nine hundred chariots of iron, and all the people who *were* with him, from Harosheth Hagoyim to the River Kishon.

14Then Deborah said to Barak, "Up! For this *is* the day in which the LORD has delivered Sisera into your hand. Has not the LORD gone out before you?" So Barak went down from Mount Tabor with ten thousand men following him. 15And the LORD routed Sisera and all *his* chariots and all *his* army with the edge of the sword before Barak; and Sisera alighted from *his* chariot and fled away on foot. 16But Barak pursued the chariots and the army as far as Harosheth Hagoyim, and all the army of Sisera fell by the edge of the sword; not a man was left.

17However, Sisera had fled away on foot to the tent of Jael, the wife of Heber the Kenite; for *there was* peace between Jabin king of Hazor and the house of Heber the Kenite. 18And Jael went out to meet Sisera, and said to him, "Turn aside, my lord, turn aside to me; do not fear." And when he had turned aside with her into the tent, she covered him with a blanket.

19Then he said to her, "Please give me a little water to drink, for I am thirsty." So she opened a jug of milk, gave him a drink, and covered him. 20And he said to her, "Stand at the door of the tent, and if any man comes and inquires of you, and says, 'Is there any man here?' you shall say, 'No.' "

21Then Jael, Heber's wife, took a tent peg and took a hammer in her hand, and went softly to him and drove the peg into his temple, and it went down into the ground; for he was fast asleep and weary. So he died. 22And then, as Barak pursued Sisera, Jael came out to meet him, and said

4:10 [a]Literally *at his feet*

4:17–24 "Sisera's chariots had been his pride and his confidence. Thus are those disappointed who rest on the creature; like a broken reed, it not only breaks under them, but pierces them with many sorrows. The idol may quickly become a burden, Isa 46:1; what we were sick for, God can make us sick of. It is probable that Jael really intended kindness to Sisera; but by a Divine impulse she was afterwards led to consider him as the determined enemy of the Lord and of his people, and to destroy him." *Matthew Henry*

to him, "Come, I will show you the man whom you seek." And when he went into her *tent,* there lay Sisera, dead with the peg in his temple.

23So on that day God subdued Jabin king of Canaan in the presence of the children of Israel. 24And the hand of the children of Israel grew stronger and stronger against Jabin king of Canaan, until they had destroyed Jabin king of Canaan.

The Song of Deborah

5 Then Deborah and Barak the son of Abinoam sang on that day, saying:

2"When leaders lead in Israel,
When the people willingly offer
themselves,
Bless the LORD!

3"Hear, O kings! Give ear, O princes!
I, *even* I, will sing to the LORD;
I will sing praise to the LORD God of
Israel.

4"LORD, when You went out from Seir,
When You marched from the field of
Edom,
The earth trembled and the heavens
poured,
The clouds also poured water;
5The mountains gushed before the
LORD,
This Sinai, before the LORD God of
Israel.

6"In the days of Shamgar, son of Anath,
In the days of Jael,
The highways were deserted,
And the travelers walked along the
byways.
7Village life ceased, it ceased in Israel,
Until I, Deborah, arose,
Arose a mother in Israel.
8They chose new gods;
Then *there was* war in the gates;
Not a shield or spear was seen among
forty thousand in Israel.
9My heart *is* with the rulers of Israel
Who offered themselves willingly
with the people.
Bless the LORD!

10"Speak, you who ride on white donkeys,
Who sit in judges' attire,
And who walk along the road.
11Far from the noise of the archers,
among the watering places,
There they shall recount the righteous
acts of the LORD,
The righteous acts *for* His villagers in
Israel;
Then the people of the LORD shall go
down to the gates.

12"Awake, awake, Deborah!
Awake, awake, sing a song!
Arise, Barak, and lead your captives
away,
O son of Abinoam!

13"Then the survivors came down, the
people against the nobles;
The LORD came down for me against
the mighty.
14From Ephraim *were* those whose
roots were in Amalek.
After you, Benjamin, with your
peoples,
From Machir rulers came down,
And from Zebulun those who bear
the recruiter's staff.
15And the princes of Issachar[a] *were*
with Deborah;
As Issachar, so *was* Barak
Sent into the valley under his
command;[b]

5:15 [a]Following Septuagint, Syriac, Targum, and Vulgate; Masoretic Text reads *And my princes in Issachar.* [b]Literally *at his feet*

5:5 This was when God gave His Law to Moses. See Heb. 12:18–28 for details.

"The fundamental basis of this nation's law was given to Moses on the Mount. The fundamental basis of our Bill of Rights comes from the teaching we get from Exodus and St. Matthew, from Isaiah and St. Paul." *Harry S. Truman*

Among the divisions of Reuben
There were great resolves of heart.
16Why did you sit among the sheepfolds,
To hear the pipings for the flocks?
The divisions of Reuben have great
searchings of heart.
17Gilead stayed beyond the Jordan,
And why did Dan remain on ships?[a]
Asher continued at the seashore,
And stayed by his inlets.
18Zebulun *is* a people *who* jeopardized
their lives to the point of death,
Naphtali also, on the heights of the
battlefield.

19"The kings came *and* fought,
Then the kings of Canaan fought
In Taanach, by the waters of Megiddo;
They took no spoils of silver.
20They fought from the heavens;
The stars from their courses fought
against Sisera.
21The torrent of Kishon swept them
away,
That ancient torrent, the torrent of
Kishon.
O my soul, march on in strength!
22Then the horses' hooves pounded,
The galloping, galloping of his steeds.
23'Curse Meroz,' said the angel[a] of the
LORD,
'Curse its inhabitants bitterly,
Because they did not come to the
help of the LORD,
To the help of the LORD against the
mighty.'

24"Most blessed among women is Jael,
The wife of Heber the Kenite;
Blessed is she among women in tents.
25He asked for water, she gave milk;
She brought out cream in a lordly
bowl.
26She stretched her hand to the tent peg,
Her right hand to the workmen's
hammer;
She pounded Sisera, she pierced his
head,
She split and struck through his
temple.
27At her feet he sank, he fell, he lay still;
At her feet he sank, he fell;
Where he sank, there he fell dead.

28"The mother of Sisera looked through
the window,
And cried out through the lattice,
'Why is his chariot *so* long in coming?
Why tarries the clatter of his chariots?'
29Her wisest ladies answered her,
Yes, she answered herself,
30'Are they not finding and dividing the
spoil:
To every man a girl *or* two;
For Sisera, plunder of dyed garments,
Plunder of garments embroidered and
dyed,
Two pieces of dyed embroidery for
the neck of the looter?'

31"Thus let all Your enemies perish, O
LORD!
But *let* those who love Him *be* like the
sun
When it comes out in full strength."

So the land had rest for forty years.

Midianites Oppress Israel

6 Then the children of Israel did evil in
the sight of the LORD. So the LORD
delivered them into the hand of Midian
for seven years, 2and the hand of Midian
prevailed against Israel. Because of the

5:17 [a]Or *at ease* 5:23 [a]Or *Angel*

5:24–27 The Bible is filled with incredible violence—from the first murder, to the drowning of almost the entire human race, to the death of Jezebel (and her aftermath), to the stomach-turning death of Eglon (see 3:21–24) and the hammering of a tent-peg through the head of a sleeping man. Babies are cut from wombs, people are eaten, beheaded, burned alive, and cut in half. The Bible doesn't hide the bloody history of mankind. It reveals it, and then offers the solution to the wicked and violent heart of man—the gospel of peace.

Midianites, the children of Israel made
for themselves the dens, the caves, and the
strongholds which *are* in the mountains.
3So it was, whenever Israel had sown, Midianites would come up; also Amalekites
and the people of the East would come
up against them. 4Then they would encamp against them and destroy the produce of the earth as far as Gaza, and leave
no sustenance for Israel, neither sheep
nor ox nor donkey. 5For they would
come up with their livestock and their
tents, coming in as numerous as locusts;
both they and their camels were without
number; and they would enter the land
to destroy it. 6So Israel was greatly impoverished because of the Midianites,
and the children of Israel cried out to the
LORD.

7And it came to pass, when the children of Israel cried out to the LORD because of the Midianites, 8that the LORD
sent a prophet to the children of Israel,
who said to them, "Thus says the LORD
God of Israel: 'I brought you up from
Egypt and brought you out of the house
of bondage; 9and I delivered you out of
the hand of the Egyptians and out of the
hand of all who oppressed you, and drove
them out before you and gave you their
land. 10Also I said to you, "I *am* the LORD
your God; do not fear the gods of the
Amorites, in whose land you dwell." But
you have not obeyed My voice.' "

Gideon

11Now the Angel of the LORD came and
sat under the terebinth tree which *was* in
Ophrah, which *belonged* to Joash the Abiez-
rite, while his son Gideon threshed wheat
in the winepress, in order to hide *it* from
the Midianites. 12And the Angel of the
LORD appeared to him, and said to him,
"The LORD *is* with you, you mighty man
of valor!"

13Gideon said to Him, "O my lord,[a] if
the LORD is with us, why then has all this
happened to us? And where *are* all His
miracles which our fathers told us about,
saying, 'Did not the LORD bring us up
from Egypt?' But now the LORD has forsaken us and delivered us into the hands
of the Midianites."

14Then the LORD turned to him and
said, "Go in this might of yours, and you
shall save Israel from the hand of the
Midianites. Have I not sent you?"

15So he said to Him, "O my Lord,[a]
how can I save Israel? Indeed my clan *is*
the weakest in Manasseh, and I *am* the
least in my father's house."

16And the LORD said to him, "Surely I
will be with you, and you shall defeat the
Midianites as one man."

17Then he said to Him, "If now I have
found favor in Your sight, then show me
a sign that it is You who talk with me.
18Do not depart from here, I pray, until I
come to You and bring out my offering
and set *it* before You."

And He said, "I will wait until you
come back."

19So Gideon went in and prepared a
young goat, and unleavened bread from
an ephah of flour. The meat he put in a

6:13 [a]Hebrew *adoni*, used of man 6:15 [a]Hebrew *Adonai*, used of God

6:12 As a Christian, you may feel inadequate for the task of reaching out to the lost, but you too are a mighty man or woman of valor because the Lord is with you. See Matt. 28:20; Rom. 8:31.

6:13 Trials are not necessarily a sign that God has forsaken you. The Christian life is filled with lion's dens and Red Seas. Trust God to shut the mouths of lions and open Red Seas. However, even if He doesn't see fit to do the things for which you are hoping, joyfully trust Him anyway, because whatever you are going through will be worked out for your good (see Rom. 8:28). Follow the example of Shadrach and his friends, who would not bow to an idol. They told the king, "Our God whom we serve is able to deliver us from the burning fiery furnace, and He will deliver us from your hand, O king. *But if not*, let it be known to you, O king, that we do not serve your gods, nor will we worship the gold image which you have set up" (Dan. 3:17,18, emphasis added).

basket, and he put the broth in a pot; and he brought *them* out to Him under the terebinth tree and presented *them*. 20 The Angel of God said to him, "Take the meat and the unleavened bread and lay *them* on this rock, and pour out the broth." And he did so.

21 Then the Angel of the LORD put out the end of the staff that *was* in His hand, and touched the meat and the unleavened bread; and fire rose out of the rock and consumed the meat and the unleavened bread. And the Angel of the LORD departed out of his sight.

22 Now Gideon perceived that He *was* the Angel of the LORD. So Gideon said, "Alas, O Lord GOD! For I have seen the Angel of the LORD face to face."

23 Then the LORD said to him, "Peace *be* with you; do not fear, you shall not die." 24 So Gideon built an altar there to the LORD, and called it The-LORD-*Is*-Peace.[a] To this day it *is* still in Ophrah of the Abiezrites.

> World peace will come only when all mankind turns wholeheartedly to God in complete humility and voluntary unconditional surrender. Until human nature is changed, we'll have war.
>
> **ROBERT PAGE**

25 Now it came to pass the same night that the LORD said to him, "Take your father's young bull, the second bull of seven years old, and tear down the altar of Baal that your father has, and cut down the wooden image[a] that *is* beside it; 26 and build an altar to the LORD your God on top of this rock in the proper arrangement, and take the second bull and offer a burnt sacrifice with the wood of the image which you shall cut down." 27 So Gideon took ten men from among his servants and did as the LORD had said to him. But because he feared his father's household and the men of the city too much to do *it* by day, he did *it* by night.

Gideon Destroys the Altar of Baal

28 And when the men of the city arose early in the morning, there was the altar of Baal, torn down; and the wooden image that *was* beside it was cut down, and the second bull was being offered on the altar *which had been* built. 29 So they said to one another, "Who has done this thing?" And when they had inquired and asked, they said, "Gideon the son of Joash has done this thing." 30 Then the men of the city said to Joash, "Bring out your son, that he may die, because he has torn down the altar of Baal, and because he has cut down the wooden image that *was* beside it."

31 But Joash said to all who stood against him, "Would you plead for Baal? Would you save him? Let the one who would plead for him be put to death by morning! If he *is* a god, let him plead for himself, because his altar has been torn down!" 32 Therefore on that day he called him Jerubbaal,[a] saying, "Let Baal plead against him, because he has torn down his altar."

33 Then all the Midianites and Amalekites, the people of the East, gathered together; and they crossed over and encamped in the Valley of Jezreel. 34 But the

6:24 [a]Hebrew *YHWH Shalom* 6:25 [a]Hebrew *Asherah*, a Canaanite goddess 6:32 [a]Literally *Let Baal Plead*

6:27 There is no denying that when God asks us to reach out to the unsaved, we often battle fear. Gideon also had a battle with fear, but he did not let it paralyze him. Notice that what he was afraid to do during the day he did at night—but he did it. One great key was that he took "ten men from among his servants and did as the Lord had said to him." Do the same. Take the Ten Commandments and use them as servants to do what God has said (see Mark 16:15). (Follow the example of Jesus in Mark 10:17–22.) If you cannot open-air preach, then witness one-to-one. If you cannot do that, then give out tracts. If you cannot do that, then discreetly leave a tract somewhere. Whatever you do, don't let fear paralyze you into doing nothing. If you cannot evangelize in the sight of men, then evangelize when no one is looking.

Spirit of the LORD came upon Gideon; then
he blew the trumpet, and the Abiezrites
gathered behind him. 35And he sent messengers throughout all Manasseh, who also
gathered behind him. He also sent messengers to Asher, Zebulun, and Naphtali;
and they came up to meet them.

The Sign of the Fleece

36So Gideon said to God, "If You will
save Israel by my hand as You have
said— 37look, I shall put a fleece of wool
on the threshing floor; if there is dew on
the fleece only, and *it is* dry on all the
ground, then I shall know that You will
save Israel by my hand, as You have said."
38And it was so. When he rose early the
next morning and squeezed the fleece together, he wrung the dew out of the
fleece, a bowlful of water. 39Then Gideon
said to God, "Do not be angry with me,
but let me speak just once more: Let me
test, I pray, just once more with the fleece;
let it now be dry only on the fleece, but
on all the ground let there be dew." 40And
God did so that night. It was dry on the
fleece only, but there was dew on all the
ground.

Gideon's Valiant Three Hundred

7 Then Jerubbaal (that *is,* Gideon) and
all the people who *were* with him
rose early and encamped beside the well
of Harod, so that the camp of the Midianites was on the north side of them by
the hill of Moreh in the valley.
2And the LORD said to Gideon, "The
people who *are* with you *are* too many for
Me to give the Midianites into their hands,
lest Israel claim glory for itself against
Me, saying, 'My own hand has saved me.'
3Now therefore, proclaim in the hearing
of the people, saying, 'Whoever *is* fearful
and afraid, let him turn and depart at
once from Mount Gilead.' " And twenty-
two thousand of the people returned,
and ten thousand remained.
4But the LORD said to Gideon, "The
people *are* still *too* many; bring them
down to the water, and I will test them
for you there. Then it will be, *that* of whom
I say to you, 'This one shall go with you,'
the same shall go with you; and of whomever I say to you, 'This one shall not go
with you,' the same shall not go." 5So he
brought the people down to the water.
And the LORD said to Gideon, "Everyone
who laps from the water with his tongue,
as a dog laps, you shall set apart by himself; likewise everyone who gets down on
his knees to drink." 6And the number of
those who lapped, *putting* their hand to
their mouth, was three hundred men; but
all the rest of the people got down on
their knees to drink water. 7Then the LORD
said to Gideon, "By the three hundred
men who lapped I will save you, and deliver the Midianites into your hand. Let
all the *other* people go, every man to his
place." 8So the people took provisions
and their trumpets in their hands. And he
sent away all *the rest of* Israel, every man
to his tent, and retained those three hundred men. Now the camp of Midian was

---

6:36–40 "The purport of this is, *Lord, I believe, help thou my unbelief*. He found his own faith weak and wavering, and therefore begged of God by this sign to perfect what was lacking in it. We may suppose that God, who intended to give him these signs, for the glorifying of his own power and goodness, put it into his heart to ask them." *Matthew Henry*

7:3–7 Do not be surprised if, in a church of 22,000, you can only find 300 who are prepared to reach out to the lost. Sadly, most Christians are afraid to share their faith with nonbelievers and would rather stay home than tell others how to find eternal life. Such reluctance among professed Christians is a tragedy, but it will leave you with an army (small though it may be) of soldiers who keep their eyes peeled for opportunities to present the gospel message to the unsaved.

These soldiers know that the fear they battle isn't from God. They are aware that "we do not wrestle against flesh and blood, but against principalities, against powers, against the rulers of the darkness of this age, against spiritual hosts of wickedness in the heavenly places" (Eph. 6:12), and they are the ones God will use for His purposes.

below him in the valley.

9It happened on the same night that the LORD said to him, "Arise, go down against the camp, for I have delivered it into your hand. 10But if you are afraid to go down, go down to the camp with Purah your servant, 11and you shall hear what they say; and afterward your hands shall be strengthened to go down against the camp." Then he went down with Purah his servant to the outpost of the armed men who *were* in the camp. 12Now the Midianites and Amalekites, all the people of the East, were lying in the valley as numerous as locusts; and their camels *were* without number, as the sand by the seashore in multitude.

13And when Gideon had come, there was a man telling a dream to his companion. He said, "I have had a dream: *To my* surprise, a loaf of barley bread tumbled into the camp of Midian; it came to a tent and struck it so that it fell and overturned, and the tent collapsed."

14Then his companion answered and said, "This *is* nothing else but the sword of Gideon the son of Joash, a man of Israel! Into his hand God has delivered Midian and the whole camp."

15And so it was, when Gideon heard the telling of the dream and its interpretation, that he worshiped. He returned to the camp of Israel, and said, "Arise, for the LORD has delivered the camp of Midian into your hand." 16Then he divided the three hundred men *into* three companies, and he put a trumpet into every man's hand, with empty pitchers, and torches inside the pitchers. 17And he said to them, "Look at me and do likewise; watch, and when I come to the edge of the camp you shall do as I do: 18When I blow the trumpet, I and all who *are* with me, then you also blow the trumpets on every side of the whole camp, and say, '*The sword of* the LORD and of Gideon!' "

19So Gideon and the hundred men who *were* with him came to the outpost of the camp at the beginning of the middle watch, just as they had posted the watch; and they blew the trumpets and broke the pitchers that *were* in their hands. 20Then the three companies blew the trumpets and broke the pitchers—they held the torches in their left hands and the trumpets in their right hands for blowing—and they cried, "The sword of the LORD and of Gideon!" 21And every man stood in his place all around the camp; and the whole army ran and cried out and fled. 22When the three hundred blew the trumpets, the LORD set every man's sword against his companion throughout the whole camp; and the army fled to Beth Acacia,[a] toward Zererah, as far as the border of Abel Meholah, by Tabbath.

23And the men of Israel gathered together from Naphtali, Asher, and all Manasseh, and pursued the Midianites.

24Then Gideon sent messengers throughout all the mountains of Ephraim, saying, "Come down against the Midianites, and seize from them the watering places as far as Beth Barah and the Jordan." Then all the men of Ephraim gathered together and seized the watering places as far as Beth Barah and the Jordan. 25And they captured two princes of the Midianites, Oreb and Zeeb. They killed Oreb at the rock of Oreb, and Zeeb they killed at the winepress of Zeeb. They pursued Midian and brought the heads of Oreb and Zeeb to Gideon on the other side of the Jordan.

7:22 [a]Hebrew *Beth Shittah*

7:15–19 God desires broken vessels who will let their light shine before men. (See Matt. 5:14–16 and Phil. 2:15 for what Jesus said about shining as lights in this dark world.) He wants soldiers of Christ who will take up the two-edged sword of the Word of God and boldly lift up their voice as a trumpet and show people their transgression (see Isa. 58:1).

"I have but one candle of life to burn, and I would rather burn it out in a land filled with darkness than in a land flooded with light." *John Keith Falconer*

Gideon Subdues the Midianites

8 Now the men of Ephraim said to him,
"Why have you done this to us by not
calling us when you went to fight with
the Midianites?" And they reprimanded
him sharply.
2So he said to them, "What have I
done now in comparison with you? *Is* not
the gleaning *of the grapes* of Ephraim better than the vintage of Abiezer? 3God has
delivered into your hands the princes of
Midian, Oreb and Zeeb. And what was I
able to do in comparison with you?"
Then their anger toward him subsided
when he said that.
4When Gideon came to the Jordan, he
and the three hundred men who *were*
with him crossed over, exhausted but still
in pursuit. 5Then he said to the men of
Succoth, "Please give loaves of bread to
the people who follow me, for they are
exhausted, and I am pursuing Zebah and
Zalmunna, kings of Midian."
6And the leaders of Succoth said, "*Are*
the hands of Zebah and Zalmunna now
in your hand, that we should give bread
to your army?"
7So Gideon said, "For this cause, when
the LORD has delivered Zebah and Zalmunna into my hand, then I will tear
your flesh with the thorns of the wilderness and with briers!" 8Then he went up
from there to Penuel and spoke to them
in the same way. And the men of Penuel
answered him as the men of Succoth had
answered. 9So he also spoke to the men
of Penuel, saying, "When I come back in
peace, I will tear down this tower!"
10Now Zebah and Zalmunna *were* at
Karkor, and their armies with them, about
fifteen thousand, all who were left of all
the army of the people of the East; for
one hundred and twenty thousand men
who drew the sword had fallen. 11Then
Gideon went up by the road of those who
dwell in tents on the east of Nobah and
Jogbehah; and he attacked the army while
the camp felt secure. 12When Zebah and
Zalmunna fled, he pursued them; and he
took the two kings of Midian, Zebah and

"The spirit of Christ is the spirit of missions. The nearer we get to Him, the more intensely missionary we become."

Henry Martyn

Zalmunna, and routed the whole army.
13Then Gideon the son of Joash returned from battle, from the Ascent of
Heres. 14And he caught a young man of
the men of Succoth and interrogated him;
and he wrote down for him the leaders of
Succoth and its elders, seventy-seven
men. 15Then he came to the men of Succoth and said, "Here are Zebah and Zalmunna, about whom you ridiculed me,
saying, '*Are* the hands of Zebah and Zalmunna now in your hand, that we should
give bread to your weary men?' " 16And
he took the elders of the city, and thorns
of the wilderness and briers, and with them
he taught the men of Succoth. 17Then he
tore down the tower of Penuel and killed
the men of the city.
18And he said to Zebah and Zalmunna,
"What kind of men *were they* whom you
killed at Tabor?"
So they answered, "As you *are,* so *were*
they; each one resembled the son of a king."
19Then he said, "They *were* my brothers, the sons of my mother. As the LORD
lives, if you had let them live, I would not
kill you." 20And he said to Jether his first-

born, "Rise, kill them!" But the youth
would not draw his sword; for he was
afraid, because he *was* still a youth.
21So Zebah and Zalmunna said, "Rise
yourself, and kill us; for as a man *is, so is*
his strength." So Gideon arose and killed
Zebah and Zalmunna, and took the crescent ornaments that *were* on their camels'
necks.

Gideon's Ephod

22Then the men of Israel said to Gideon, "Rule over us, both you and your son,
and your grandson also; for you have delivered us from the hand of Midian."
23But Gideon said to them, "I will not
rule over you, nor shall my son rule over
you; the LORD shall rule over you." 24Then
Gideon said to them, "I would like to
make a request of you, that each of you
would give me the earrings from his
plunder." For they had golden earrings,
because they *were* Ishmaelites.
25So they answered, "We will gladly
give *them*." And they spread out a garment, and each man threw into it the earrings from his plunder. 26Now the weight
of the gold earrings that he requested was
one thousand seven hundred *shekels* of
gold, besides the crescent ornaments, pendants, and purple robes which *were* on
the kings of Midian, and besides the chains
that *were* around their camels' necks.
27Then Gideon made it into an ephod and
set it up in his city, Ophrah. And all Israel
played the harlot with it there. It became
a snare to Gideon and to his house.
28Thus Midian was subdued before the
children of Israel, so that they lifted their
heads no more. And the country was quiet
for forty years in the days of Gideon.

Death of Gideon

29Then Jerubbaal the son of Joash went
and dwelt in his own house. 30Gideon
had seventy sons who were his own offspring, for he had many wives. 31And his
concubine who *was* in Shechem also bore
him a son, whose name he called Abimelech. 32Now Gideon the son of Joash
died at a good old age, and was buried in
the tomb of Joash his father, in Ophrah of
the Abiezrites.
33So it was, as soon as Gideon was dead,
that the children of Israel again played
the harlot with the Baals, and made Baal-
Berith their god. 34Thus the children of
Israel did not remember the LORD their
God, who had delivered them from the
hands of all their enemies on every side;
35nor did they show kindness to the house
of Jerubbaal (Gideon) in accordance with
the good he had done for Israel.

Abimelech's Conspiracy

9 Then Abimelech the son of Jerubbaal
went to Shechem, to his mother's
brothers, and spoke with them and with
all the family of the house of his mother's
father, saying, 2"Please speak in the hearing of all the men of Shechem: 'Which is
better for you, that all seventy of the
sons of Jerubbaal reign over you, or that
one reign over you?' Remember that I *am*
your own flesh and bone."

> The God of this world is riches, pleasure and pride.
>
> **MARTIN LUTHER**

3And his mother's brothers spoke all
these words concerning him in the hearing of all the men of Shechem; and their
heart was inclined to follow Abimelech,
for they said, "He is our brother." 4So they
gave him seventy *shekels* of silver from
the temple of Baal-Berith, with which
Abimelech hired worthless and reckless
men; and they followed him. 5Then he
went to his father's house at Ophrah and
killed his brothers, the seventy sons of
Jerubbaal, on one stone. But Jotham the
youngest son of Jerubbaal was left, because he hid himself. 6And all the men of
Shechem gathered together, all of Beth
Millo, and they went and made Abimelech king beside the terebinth tree at the
pillar that *was* in Shechem.

The Parable of the Trees

[7]Now when they told Jotham, he went and stood on top of Mount Gerizim, and lifted his voice and cried out. And he said to them:

"Listen to me, you men of Shechem,
That God may listen to you!

[8]"The trees once went forth to anoint a king over them.
And they said to the olive tree,
'Reign over us!'
[9]But the olive tree said to them,
'Should I cease giving my oil,
With which they honor God and men,
And go to sway over trees?'

[10]"Then the trees said to the fig tree,
'You come *and* reign over us!'
[11]But the fig tree said to them,
'Should I cease my sweetness and my good fruit,
And go to sway over trees?'

[12]"Then the trees said to the vine,
'You come *and* reign over us!'
[13]But the vine said to them,
'Should I cease my new wine,
Which cheers *both* God and men,
And go to sway over trees?'

[14]"Then all the trees said to the bramble,
'You come *and* reign over us!'
[15]And the bramble said to the trees,
'If in truth you anoint me as king over you,
Then come *and* take shelter in my shade;
But if not, let fire come out of the bramble
And devour the cedars of Lebanon!'

[16]"Now therefore, if you have acted in truth and sincerity in making Abimelech king, and if you have dealt well with Jerubbaal and his house, and have done to him as he deserves— [17]for my father fought for you, risked his life, and delivered you out of the hand of Midian; [18]but you have risen up against my father's house this day, and killed his seventy sons on one stone, and made Abimelech, the son of his female servant, king over the men of Shechem, because he is your brother— [19]if then you have acted in truth and sincerity with Jerubbaal and with his house this day, *then* rejoice in Abimelech, and let him also rejoice in you. [20]But if not, let fire come from Abimelech and devour the men of Shechem and Beth Millo; and let fire come from the men of Shechem and from Beth Millo and devour Abimelech!" [21]And Jotham ran away and fled; and he went to Beer and dwelt there, for fear of Abimelech his brother.

Downfall of Abimelech

[22]After Abimelech had reigned over Israel three years, [23]God sent a spirit of ill will between Abimelech and the men of Shechem; and the men of Shechem dealt treacherously with Abimelech, [24]that the crime *done* to the seventy sons of Jerubbaal might be settled and their blood be laid on Abimelech their brother, who killed them, and on the men of Shechem, who aided him in the killing of his brothers. [25]And the men of Shechem set men in ambush against him on the tops of the mountains, and they robbed all who passed by them along that way; and it was told Abimelech.

[26]Now Gaal the son of Ebed came with his brothers and went over to Shechem; and the men of Shechem put their confidence in him. [27]So they went out into the fields, and gathered *grapes* from their vineyards and trod *them*, and made merry. And they went into the house of their god, and ate and drank, and cursed Abimelech. [28]Then Gaal the son of Ebed said,

9:23 Some may accuse God of sin because He sent an evil spirit. But He had His own perfectly righteous purposes in doing so (see v. 24).

"Who *is* Abimelech, and who *is* Shechem,
that we should serve him? *Is he* not the
son of Jerubbaal, and *is not* Zebul his officer? Serve the men of Hamor the father
of Shechem; but why should we serve
him? 29If only this people were under my
authority![a] Then I would remove Abimelech." So he[b] said to Abimelech, "Increase your army and come out!"

30When Zebul, the ruler of the city,
heard the words of Gaal the son of Ebed,
his anger was aroused. 31And he sent messengers to Abimelech secretly, saying,
"Take note! Gaal the son of Ebed and his
brothers have come to Shechem; and here
they are, fortifying the city against you.
32Now therefore, get up by night, you
and the people who *are* with you, and lie
in wait in the field. 33And it shall be, as
soon as the sun is up in the morning, *that*
you shall rise early and rush upon the
city; and *when* he and the people who are
with him come out against you, you may
then do to them as you find opportunity."

34So Abimelech and all the people who
were with him rose by night, and lay in
wait against Shechem in four companies.
35When Gaal the son of Ebed went out
and stood in the entrance to the city gate,
Abimelech and the people who *were* with
him rose from lying in wait. 36And when
Gaal saw the people, he said to Zebul,
"Look, people are coming down from the
tops of the mountains!"

But Zebul said to him, "You see the
shadows of the mountains as *if they were*
men."

37So Gaal spoke again and said, "See,
people are coming down from the center
of the land, and another company is coming from the Diviners'[a] Terebinth Tree."

38Then Zebul said to him, "Where indeed *is* your mouth now, with which you
said, 'Who is Abimelech, that we should
serve him?' *Are* not these the people
whom you despised? Go out, if you will,
and fight with them now."

39So Gaal went out, leading the men of
Shechem, and fought with Abimelech.
40And Abimelech chased him, and he fled
from him; and many fell wounded, to the
very entrance of the gate. 41Then Abimelech dwelt at Arumah, and Zebul drove
out Gaal and his brothers, so that they
would not dwell in Shechem.

42And it came about on the next day
that the people went out into the field,
and they told Abimelech. 43So he took his
people, divided them into three companies, and lay in wait in the field. And he
looked, and there were the people, coming out of the city; and he rose against
them and attacked them. 44Then Abimelech and the company that *was* with him
rushed forward and stood at the entrance
of the gate of the city; and the *other* two
companies rushed upon all who *were* in
the fields and killed them. 45So Abimelech fought against the city all that day;
he took the city and killed the people
who *were* in it; and he demolished the
city and sowed it with salt.

46Now when all the men of the tower
of Shechem had heard *that,* they entered
the stronghold of the temple of the god
Berith. 47And it was told Abimelech that
all the men of the tower of Shechem were
gathered together. 48Then Abimelech
went up to Mount Zalmon, he and all the
people who *were* with him. And Abimelech took an ax in his hand and cut down
a bough from the trees, and took it and
laid *it* on his shoulder; then he said to the
people who were with him, "What you
have seen me do, make haste *and* do as I
have done." 49So each of the people likewise cut down his own bough and followed Abimelech, put *them* against the
stronghold, and set the stronghold on fire
above them, so that all the people of the
tower of Shechem died, about a thousand
men and women.

50Then Abimelech went to Thebez, and
he encamped against Thebez and took it.
51But there was a strong tower in the city,
and all the men and women—all the people of the city—fled there and shut them-

9:29 [a]Literally *hand* [b]Following Masoretic Text and Targum; Dead Sea Scrolls read *they;* Septuagint reads *I.* 9:37 [a]Hebrew *Meonenim*

selves in; then they went up to the top of the tower. [52]So Abimelech came as far as the tower and fought against it; and he drew near the door of the tower to burn it with fire. [53]But a certain woman dropped an upper millstone on Abimelech's head and crushed his skull. [54]Then he called quickly to the young man, his armorbearer, and said to him, "Draw your sword and kill me, lest men say of me, 'A woman killed him.' " So his young man thrust him through, and he died. [55]And when the men of Israel saw that Abimelech was dead, they departed, every man to his place.

[56]Thus God repaid the wickedness of Abimelech, which he had done to his father by killing his seventy brothers. [57]And all the evil of the men of Shechem God returned on their own heads, and on them came the curse of Jotham the son of Jerubbaal.

Tola

10 After Abimelech there arose to save Israel Tola the son of Puah, the son of Dodo, a man of Issachar; and he dwelt in Shamir in the mountains of Ephraim. [2]He judged Israel twenty-three years; and he died and was buried in Shamir.

Jair

[3]After him arose Jair, a Gileadite; and he judged Israel twenty-two years. [4]Now he had thirty sons who rode on thirty donkeys; they also had thirty towns, which are called "Havoth Jair"[a] to this day, which *are* in the land of Gilead. [5]And Jair died and was buried in Camon.

Israel Oppressed Again

[6]Then the children of Israel again did evil in the sight of the LORD, and served the Baals and the Ashtoreths, the gods of Syria, the gods of Sidon, the gods of Moab, the gods of the people of Ammon, and the gods of the Philistines; and they forsook the LORD and did not serve Him. [7]So the anger of the LORD was hot against Israel; and He sold them into the hands of the Philistines and into the hands of the people of Ammon. [8]From that year they harassed and oppressed the children of Israel for eighteen years—all the children of Israel who *were* on the other side of the Jordan in the land of the Amorites, in Gilead. [9]Moreover the people of Ammon crossed over the Jordan to fight against Judah also, against Benjamin, and against the house of Ephraim, so that Israel was severely distressed.

[10]And the children of Israel cried out to the LORD, saying, "We have sinned against You, because we have both forsaken our God and served the Baals!"

[11]So the LORD said to the children of Israel, "*Did I* not *deliver you* from the Egyptians and from the Amorites and from the people of Ammon and from the Philistines? [12]Also the Sidonians and Amalekites and Maonites[a] oppressed you; and you cried out to Me, and I delivered you from their hand. [13]Yet you have forsaken Me and served other gods. Therefore I will deliver you no more. [14]Go and cry out to the gods which you have chosen; let them deliver you in your time of distress."

[15]And the children of Israel said to the LORD, "We have sinned! Do to us whatever seems best to You; only deliver us this day, we pray." [16]So they put away the foreign gods from among them and served the LORD. And His soul could no longer endure the misery of Israel.

[17]Then the people of Ammon gathered together and encamped in Gilead. And

10:4 [a]Literally *Towns of Jair* (compare Numbers 32:41 and Deuteronomy 3:14) **10:12** [a]Some Septuagint manuscripts read *Midianites.*

10:11–14 Forgetting what they had been delivered from led Israel to forsake the One who had delivered them. Understanding the spiritual nature of the Law from which we have been delivered will keep us close to the foot of the cross in heartfelt gratitude.

10:15 *Spurgeon and the "Sinner's Prayer"*

People often wonder if it is legitimate to use a "sinner's prayer" to lead someone to Christ, since the practice is not found in Scripture. Let the person pray, if he wants to, because it is not the words that matter, but the person's heart. God knows if he is truly sorry and repentant. (See John 1:13 comment.)

Even so, some of our gospel tracts end with what is commonly called a "sinner's prayer," preceded by the words "Pray something like this." Some have criticized the practice, but Charles Spurgeon did a similar thing in suggesting what the sinner might say to God. At the conclusion of his sermon "A Call to the Unconverted," he addressed this to the lost:

> Oh, can you say, "I believe this Word—it is true—blessed be His dear name; it is true to me, for whatever I may not be, I know that I am a sinner; the sermon of this night convinces me of that, if there were nothing else; and, good Lord, you know when I say I am a sinner, I do not mean what I used to mean by that word. I mean that I am a real sinner. I mean that if you should damn me, I deserve it; if you should cast me from thy presence forever, it is only what I have merited richly. O my Lord I am a sinner; I am a hopeless sinner, unless you save me; I am a helpless sinner, unless you deliver me. I have no hope in my self-righteousness; and Lord, I bless your name, there is one thing else, I am a sorrowful sinner, for sin grieves me; I can not rest, I am troubled. Oh, if I could get rid of sin, I would be holy, even as God is holy. Lord, I believe . . . O Lord, it is all true what that man said; I am condemned, and Lord, I deserve it. O Lord, I have tried to be better, and have done nothing with it all, but have only grown worse. O Lord, I have slighted your grace, I have despised your gospel: I wonder [that] you have not damned me years ago; Lord, I marvel at myself; that you allowed such a base wretch as I am to live at all. I have despised a mother's teaching, I have forgotten a father's prayers. Lord, I have forgotten you; I have broken your Sabbath, taken your name in vain. I have done everything that is wrong; and if you do condemn me, what can I say? Lord, I am dumb before your presence. I have nothing to plead. But Lord; I come to tell you to-night, you have said in the Word of God, 'Him that comes to me, I will in no wise cast out.' Lord, I come: my only plea is that you have said, 'This is a faithful saying, and worthy of all acceptation, that Jesus Christ came into the world to save sinners.' Lord, I am a sinner; he came to save me; I trust in it—sink or swim—Lord, this is my only hope: I cast away every other, and hate myself to think I ever should have had any other. Lord, I rely on Jesus only. Do but save me, and though I can not hope by my future life to blot out my past sin, O Lord, I will ask of thee to give me a new heart and a right spirit, that from this time forth even for ever I may run in the way of your commandments: for, Lord, I desire nothing so much as to be your child. You know, O Lord, I would give all, if you would but love me; and I am encouraged to think that you do love me; for my heart feels so. I am guilty, but I should never have known that I was guilty if you had not taught it to me. I am vile, but I never should have known my vileness, unless you had revealed it. Surely, you will not destroy me, O God, after having taught me this. If you do, you are just, but, 'Save a trembling sinner, Lord, whose hopes still hovering round your Word, would light on some sweet promise there; some sure support against despair.'"

Then, with perhaps a smile, the Prince of Preachers said, "If you cannot pray such a long prayer as that, I [will] tell you what to go home and say. Say this: 'Lord Jesus, I know I am nothing at all; be my precious all in all.'"

the children of Israel assembled together
and encamped in Mizpah. 18And the people, the leaders of Gilead, said to one another, "Who *is* the man who will begin
the fight against the people of Ammon?
He shall be head over all the inhabitants
of Gilead."

Jephthah

11 Now Jephthah the Gileadite was a
mighty man of valor, but he *was*
the son of a harlot; and Gilead begot
Jephthah. 2Gilead's wife bore sons; and
when his wife's sons grew up, they drove
Jephthah out, and said to him, "You shall

have no inheritance in our father's house,
for you *are* the son of another woman."
[3]Then Jephthah fled from his brothers
and dwelt in the land of Tob; and worthless men banded together with Jephthah
and went out *raiding* with him.
[4]It came to pass after a time that the
people of Ammon made war against Israel. [5]And so it was, when the people of
Ammon made war against Israel, that the
elders of Gilead went to get Jephthah from
the land of Tob. [6]Then they said to Jephthah, "Come and be our commander, that
we may fight against the people of Ammon."
[7]So Jephthah said to the elders of Gilead, "Did you not hate me, and expel me
from my father's house? Why have you
come to me now when you are in distress?"
[8]And the elders of Gilead said to Jephthah, "That is why we have turned again
to you now, that you may go with us and
fight against the people of Ammon, and
be our head over all the inhabitants of
Gilead."
[9]So Jephthah said to the elders of
Gilead, "If you take me back home to
fight against the people of Ammon, and
the LORD delivers them to me, shall I be
your head?"
[10]And the elders of Gilead said to
Jephthah, "The LORD will be a witness between us, if we do not do according to
your words." [11]Then Jephthah went with
the elders of Gilead, and the people made
him head and commander over them;
and Jephthah spoke all his words before
the LORD in Mizpah.
[12]Now Jephthah sent messengers to
the king of the people of Ammon, saying,
"What do you have against me, that you
have come to fight against me in my land?"
[13]And the king of the people of Ammon answered the messengers of Jephthah, "Because Israel took away my land
when they came up out of Egypt, from
the Arnon as far as the Jabbok, and to the
Jordan. Now therefore, restore those
lands peaceably."
[14]So Jephthah again sent messengers
to the king of the people of Ammon,
[15]and said to him, "Thus says Jephthah:
'Israel did not take away the land of
Moab, nor the land of the people of Ammon; [16]for when Israel came up from
Egypt, they walked through the wilderness as far as the Red Sea and came to
Kadesh. [17]Then Israel sent messengers to
the king of Edom, saying, "Please let me
pass through your land." But the king of
Edom would not heed. And in like manner they sent to the king of Moab, but he
would not *consent*. So Israel remained in
Kadesh. [18]And they went along through
the wilderness and bypassed the land of
Edom and the land of Moab, came to the
east side of the land of Moab, and encamped on the other side of the Arnon.
But they did not enter the border of Moab,
for the Arnon *was* the border of Moab.
[19]Then Israel sent messengers to Sihon
king of the Amorites, king of Heshbon;
and Israel said to him, "Please let us pass
through your land into our place." [20]But
Sihon did not trust Israel to pass through
his territory. So Sihon gathered all his
people together, encamped in Jahaz, and
fought against Israel. [21]And the LORD God
of Israel delivered Sihon and all his people into the hand of Israel, and they defeated them. Thus Israel gained possession of all the land of the Amorites, who
inhabited that country. [22]They took possession of all the territory of the Amorites, from the Arnon to the Jabbok and
from the wilderness to the Jordan.
[23]'And now the LORD God of Israel has
dispossessed the Amorites from before
His people Israel; should you then possess it? [24]Will you not possess whatever
Chemosh your god gives you to possess?
So whatever the LORD our God takes pos-

11:3–10 Millions of professing Christians want Jesus to ease their distress, but their lifestyles reveal that they refuse to submit to Him as Lord. See Matt. 7:21–23 for their terrible fate.

session of before us, we will possess.
[25]And now, *are* you any better than Balak
the son of Zippor, king of Moab? Did he
ever strive against Israel? Did he ever
fight against them? [26]While Israel dwelt
in Heshbon and its villages, in Aroer and
its villages, and in all the cities along the
banks of the Arnon, for three hundred
years, why did you not recover *them*
within that time? [27]Therefore I have not
sinned against you, but you wronged me
by fighting against me. May the LORD, the
Judge, render judgment this day between
the children of Israel and the people of
Ammon.' " [28]However, the king of the
people of Ammon did not heed the words
which Jephthah sent him.

Jephthah's Vow and Victory

[29]Then the Spirit of the LORD came
upon Jephthah, and he passed through
Gilead and Manasseh, and passed through
Mizpah of Gilead; and from Mizpah of
Gilead he advanced *toward* the people of
Ammon. [30]And Jephthah made a vow to
the LORD, and said, "If You will indeed
deliver the people of Ammon into my
hands, [31]then it will be that whatever
comes out of the doors of my house to
meet me, when I return in peace from the
people of Ammon, shall surely be the
LORD's, and I will offer it up as a burnt
offering."

[32]So Jephthah advanced toward the
people of Ammon to fight against them,
and the LORD delivered them into his
hands. [33]And he defeated them from Aroer
as far as Minnith—twenty cities—and to
Abel Keramim,[a] with a very great slaughter. Thus the people of Ammon were subdued before the children of Israel.

Jephthah's Daughter

[34]When Jephthah came to his house at
Mizpah, there was his daughter, coming
out to meet him with timbrels and dancing; and she *was his* only child. Besides
her he had neither son nor daughter.
[35]And it came to pass, when he saw her,
that he tore his clothes, and said, "Alas,
my daughter! You have brought me very
low! You are among those who trouble
me! For I have given my word to the
LORD, and I cannot go back on it."

> How shall I feel at the judgment, if multitudes of missed opportunities pass before me in full review, and all my excuses prove to be disguises of my cowardice and pride?
>
> **W. E. SANGSTER**

[36]So she said to him, "My father, *if* you
have given your word to the LORD, do to
me according to what has gone out of your
mouth, because the LORD has avenged you
of your enemies, the people of Ammon."
[37]Then she said to her father, "Let this
thing be done for me: let me alone for
two months, that I may go and wander
on the mountains and bewail my virginity, my friends and I."

[38]So he said, "Go." And he sent her
away *for* two months; and she went with
her friends, and bewailed her virginity on
the mountains. [39]And it was so at the end
of two months that she returned to her
father, and he carried out his vow with her
which he had vowed. She knew no man.

11:33 [a]Literally *Plain of Vineyards*

11:39 Jephthah sacrifices his daughter. Some believe that, because the Bible related the incident, it was somehow condoning it, and that the action pleased God. However, God clearly condemns this detestable pagan practice as an "abomination" (see Jer. 7:31; 32:35). The Scriptures are given to us for our instruction. We can learn life-lessons from all the stupid things that men and women did in the Bible. Noah became drunk and shamed himself. Saul became jealous and destroyed his life. Judas was a hypocrite and ended up killing himself. Peter slept when he should have been in prayer, and denied his Lord. David let lust into his heart, and committed adultery and murder. These incidents were written for our admonition, and we can either humbly learn from them or proudly walk down the same tragic path. The choice is ours. See also Judg. 19:23–30 comment.

And it became a custom in Israel 40*that* the daughters of Israel went four days each year to lament the daughter of Jephthah the Gileadite.

Jephthah's Conflict with Ephraim

12 Then the men of Ephraim gathered together, crossed over toward Zaphon, and said to Jephthah, "Why did you cross over to fight against the people of Ammon, and did not call us to go with you? We will burn your house down on you with fire!"

2And Jephthah said to them, "My people and I were in a great struggle with the people of Ammon; and when I called you, you did not deliver me out of their hands. 3So when I saw that you would not deliver *me,* I took my life in my hands and crossed over against the people of Ammon; and the LORD delivered them into my hand. Why then have you come up to me this day to fight against me?" 4Now Jephthah gathered together all the men of Gilead and fought against Ephraim. And the men of Gilead defeated Ephraim, because they said, "You Gileadites *are* fugitives of Ephraim among the Ephraimites *and* among the Manassites." 5The Gileadites seized the fords of the Jordan before the Ephraimites *arrived.* And when *any* Ephraimite who escaped said, "Let me cross over," the men of Gilead would say to him, "*Are* you an Ephraimite?" If he said, "No," 6then they would say to him, "Then say, 'Shibboleth'!" And he would say, "Sibboleth," for he could not pronounce *it* right. Then they would take him and kill him at the fords of the Jordan. There fell at that time forty-two thousand Ephraimites.

7And Jephthah judged Israel six years. Then Jephthah the Gileadite died and was buried among the cities of Gilead.

Ibzan, Elon, and Abdon

8After him, Ibzan of Bethlehem judged Israel. 9He had thirty sons. And he gave away thirty daughters in marriage, and brought in thirty daughters from elsewhere for his sons. He judged Israel seven years. 10Then Ibzan died and was buried at Bethlehem.

11After him, Elon the Zebulunite judged Israel. He judged Israel ten years. 12And Elon the Zebulunite died and was buried at Aijalon in the country of Zebulun.

13After him, Abdon the son of Hillel the Pirathonite judged Israel. 14He had forty sons and thirty grandsons, who rode on seventy young donkeys. He judged Israel eight years. 15Then Abdon the son of Hillel the Pirathonite died and was buried in Pirathon in the land of Ephraim, in the mountains of the Amalekites.

The Birth of Samson

13 Again the children of Israel did evil in the sight of the LORD, and the LORD delivered them into the hand of the Philistines for forty years.

2Now there was a certain man from Zorah, of the family of the Danites, whose name *was* Manoah; and his wife *was* barren and had no children. 3And the Angel of the LORD appeared to the woman and said to her, "Indeed now, you are barren and have borne no children, but you shall conceive and bear a son. 4Now therefore, please be careful not to drink wine or *similar* drink, and not to eat anything unclean. 5For behold, you shall conceive and bear a son. And no razor shall come upon his head, for the child shall be a Nazirite to God from the womb; and he shall begin to deliver Israel out of the hand of the Philistines."

6So the woman came and told her husband, saying, "A Man of God came to me, and His countenance *was* like the countenance of the Angel of God, very awesome; but I did not ask Him where He *was* from, and He did not tell me His name. 7And He said to me, 'Behold, you

---

12:6 In World War II, New Zealanders used the word "Blenheim" as a password. Germans could not pronounce it accurately.

shall conceive and bear a son. Now drink no wine or *similar* drink, nor eat anything unclean, for the child shall be a Nazirite to God from the womb to the day of his death.' "

[8]Then Manoah prayed to the LORD, and said, "O my Lord, please let the Man of God whom You sent come to us again and teach us what we shall do for the child who will be born."

[9]And God listened to the voice of Manoah, and the Angel of God came to the woman again as she was sitting in the field; but Manoah her husband *was* not
with her. [10]Then the woman ran in haste and told her husband, and said to him, "Look, the Man who came to me the *other* day has just now appeared to me!"

[11]So Manoah arose and followed his wife. When he came to the Man, he said to Him, "Are You the Man who spoke to this woman?"

And He said, "I *am*."

[12]Manoah said, "Now let Your words come *to pass!* What will be the boy's rule of life, and his work?"

[13]So the Angel of the LORD said to Manoah, "Of all that I said to the woman
let her be careful. [14]She may not eat anything that comes from the vine, nor may she drink wine or *similar* drink, nor eat anything unclean. All that I commanded her let her observe."

[15]Then Manoah said to the Angel of the LORD, "Please let us detain You, and we will prepare a young goat for You."

[16]And the Angel of the LORD said to Manoah, "Though you detain Me, I will not eat your food. But if you offer a burnt offering, you must offer it to the LORD." (For Manoah did not know He *was* the Angel of the LORD.)

[17]Then Manoah said to the Angel of the LORD, "What *is* Your name, that when Your words come *to pass* we may honor You?"

[18]And the Angel of the LORD said to him, "Why do you ask My name, seeing it *is* wonderful?"

[19]So Manoah took the young goat with the grain offering, and offered it upon the rock to the LORD. And He did a wondrous thing while Manoah and his wife looked
on— [20]it happened as the flame went up toward heaven from the altar—the Angel of the LORD ascended in the flame of the altar! When Manoah and his wife saw *this,* they fell on their faces to the ground.
[21]When the Angel of the LORD appeared no more to Manoah and his wife, then Manoah knew that He *was* the Angel of the LORD.

[22]And Manoah said to his wife, "We shall surely die, because we have seen God!"

[23]But his wife said to him, "If the LORD had desired to kill us, He would not have accepted a burnt offering and a grain offering from our hands, nor would He have shown us all these *things,* nor would He have told us *such things* as these at this time."

[24]So the woman bore a son and called his name Samson; and the child grew, and
the LORD blessed him. [25]And the Spirit of the LORD began to move upon him at Mahaneh Dan[a] between Zorah and Eshtaol.

Samson's Philistine Wife

14 Now Samson went down to Timnah, and saw a woman in Timnah of the daughters of the Philistines.
[2]So he went up and told his father and mother, saying, "I have seen a woman in Timnah of the daughters of the Philistines; now therefore, get her for me as a wife."

[3]Then his father and mother said to him, "*Is there* no woman among the daughters of your brethren, or among all my people, that you must go and get a

13:25 [a]Literally *Camp of Dan* (compare 18:12)

13:22 Manoah was mistaken; he saw only a *manifestation* of God. No man can see God and live (see Exod. 33:20).

POINTS FOR OPEN-AIR PREACHING

14:12

Trivia Pursuit

One very effective way to gather a crowd is to ask trivia questions and give dollar bills to those who answer correctly. Have the crowd applaud enthusiastically when answers are given—even if they are incorrect. Say, "That was wrong, but it was a good try. Let's give him a hand!" Loud, enthusiastic applause draws more people to the crowd, so the more people clapping the better. Considering having a friend step forward at appropriate times with an "Applause!" sign and encourage everyone to clap.

As an alternative to real money, you might want to give Million Dollar Bill tracts as consolation prizes to those who get the answer wrong, and give Giant Money tracts to those who get them right. (God is good to both the just and the unjust.) That way you can get gospel tracts into more hands.

Here are some suggested trivia questions:

1. What was Elvis Presley's first record label? *(Sun Records)*
2. What are Latter-Day Saints otherwise known as? *(Mormons)*
3. What do you call a puppet controlled by strings? *(Marionette)*
4. Astraphobia is a fear of what? *(Lightning)*
5. What presidents' faces are sculpted on Mount Rushmore? *(Washington, Jefferson, Roosevelt, and Lincoln)*
6. Where in the human body is the thyroid gland? *(Neck)*
7. What insect lives in a formicary? *(Ant)*
8. What is John F. Kennedy's middle name? *(Fitzgerald)*
9. Which U.S. city has the largest population? *(New York)*
10. What is the common name for nitrous oxide? *(Laughing gas)*
11. What type of domestic cat has no tail? *(Manx)*
12. What is the world's longest river? *(The Nile)*

wife from the uncircumcised Philistines?"

And Samson said to his father, "Get her for me, for she pleases me well."

4But his father and mother did not know that it was of the LORD—that He was seeking an occasion to move against the Philistines. For at that time the Philistines had dominion over Israel.

5So Samson went down to Timnah with his father and mother, and came to the vineyards of Timnah.

Now *to his* surprise, a young lion *came* roaring against him. 6And the Spirit of the LORD came mightily upon him, and he tore the lion apart as one would have torn apart a young goat, though *he had* nothing in his hand. But he did not tell his father or his mother what he had done.

7Then he went down and talked with the woman; and she pleased Samson well. 8After some time, when he returned to get her, he turned aside to see the carcass of the lion. And behold, a swarm of bees and honey *were* in the carcass of the lion. 9He took some of it in his hands and went along, eating. When he came to his father and mother, he gave *some* to them, and they also ate. But he did not tell them that he had taken the honey out of the carcass of the lion.

10So his father went down to the woman. And Samson gave a feast there, for young men used to do so. 11And it happened, when they saw him, that they brought thirty companions to be with him.

12Then Samson said to them, "Let me pose a riddle to you. If you can correctly solve and explain it to me within the seven days of the feast, then I will give you thirty linen garments and thirty changes of clothing. 13But if you cannot explain *it* to me, then you shall give me thirty linen garments and thirty changes of clothing."

And they said to him, "Pose your riddle, that we may hear it."

14So he said to them:

"Out of the eater came something to eat,
And out of the strong came
something sweet."

Now for three days they could not ex-

plain the riddle.
[15]But it came to pass on the seventh[a]
day that they said to Samson's wife, "Entice your husband, that he may explain
the riddle to us, or else we will burn you
and your father's house with fire. Have
you invited us in order to take what is
ours? *Is that* not *so*?"
[16]Then Samson's wife wept on him,
and said, "You only hate me! You do not
love me! You have posed a riddle to the
sons of my people, but you have not explained *it* to me."
And he said to her, "Look, I have not
explained *it* to my father or my mother;
so should I explain *it* to you?" [17]Now she
had wept on him the seven days while
their feast lasted. And it happened on the
seventh day that he told her, because she
pressed him so much. Then she explained
the riddle to the sons of her people. [18]So
the men of the city said to him on the
seventh day before the sun went down:

"What *is* sweeter than honey?
And what *is* stronger than a lion?"

And he said to them:

"If you had not plowed with my heifer,
You would not have solved my riddle!"

[19]Then the Spirit of the LORD came
upon him mightily, and he went down to
Ashkelon and killed thirty of their men,
took their apparel, and gave the changes
of clothing to those who had explained the
riddle. So his anger was aroused, and he
went back up to his father's house. [20]And
Samson's wife was *given* to his companion, who had been his best man.

Samson Defeats the Philistines

15 After a while, in the time of wheat
harvest, it happened that Samson
visited his wife with a young goat. And
he said, "Let me go in to my wife, into *her*
room." But her father would not permit
him to go in.
[2]Her father said, "I really thought that
you thoroughly hated her; therefore I gave
her to your companion. *Is* not her younger sister better than she? Please, take her
instead."
[3]And Samson said to them, "This time
I shall be blameless regarding the Philistines if I harm them!" [4]Then Samson
went and caught three hundred foxes;
and he took torches, turned *the foxes* tail
to tail, and put a torch between each pair
of tails. [5]When he had set the torches on
fire, he let *the foxes* go into the standing
grain of the Philistines, and burned up
both the shocks and the standing grain,
as well as the vineyards *and* olive groves.
[6]Then the Philistines said, "Who has
done this?"
And they answered, "Samson, the son-
in-law of the Timnite, because he has
taken his wife and given her to his companion." So the Philistines came up and
burned her and her father with fire.
[7]Samson said to them, "Since you
would do a thing like this, I will surely
take revenge on you, and after that I will
cease." [8]So he attacked them hip and
thigh with a great slaughter; then he went
down and dwelt in the cleft of the rock of
Etam.
[9]Now the Philistines went up, encamped in Judah, and deployed themselves against Lehi. [10]And the men of Judah
said, "Why have you come up against us?"
So they answered, "We have come up
to arrest Samson, to do to him as he has
done to us."
[11]Then three thousand men of Judah
went down to the cleft of the rock of Etam,
and said to Samson, "Do you not know
that the Philistines rule over us? What *is*
this you have done to us?"

14:15 [a]Following Masoretic Text, Targum, and Vulgate; Septuagint and Syriac read *fourth.*

14:18 Jesus, the Lion of Judah, brought the sweetness of eternal salvation out of death itself.

And he said to them, "As they did to me, so I have done to them."

[12]But they said to him, "We have come down to arrest you, that we may deliver you into the hand of the Philistines."

Then Samson said to them, "Swear to me that you will not kill me yourselves."

[13]So they spoke to him, saying, "No, but we will tie you securely and deliver you into their hand; but we will surely not kill you." And they bound him with two new ropes and brought him up from the rock.

. . . . . .

For some of the many names of Jesus, see Eph. 1:21 comment.

. . . . . .

[14]When he came to Lehi, the Philistines came shouting against him. Then the Spirit of the LORD came mightily upon him; and the ropes that *were* on his arms became like flax that is burned with fire, and his bonds broke loose from his hands. [15]He found a fresh jawbone of a donkey, reached out his hand and took it, and killed a thousand men with it. [16]Then Samson said:

"With the jawbone of a donkey,
Heaps upon heaps,
With the jawbone of a donkey
I have slain a thousand men!"

[17]And so it was, when he had finished speaking, that he threw the jawbone from his hand, and called that place Ramath Lehi.[a]

[18]Then he became very thirsty; so he cried out to the LORD and said, "You have given this great deliverance by the hand of Your servant; and now shall I die of thirst and fall into the hand of the uncircumcised?" [19]So God split the hollow place that *is* in Lehi,[a] and water came out, and he drank; and his spirit returned, and he revived. Therefore he called its name En Hakkore,[b] which is in Lehi to this day. [20]And he judged Israel twenty years in the days of the Philistines.

Samson and Delilah

16 Now Samson went to Gaza and saw a harlot there, and went in to her. [2]*When* the Gazites *were told,* "Samson has come here!" they surrounded *the place* and lay in wait for him all night at the gate of the city. They were quiet all night, saying, "In the morning, when it is daylight, we will kill him." [3]And Samson lay *low* till midnight; then he arose at midnight, took hold of the doors of the gate of the city and the two gateposts, pulled them up, bar and all, put *them* on his shoulders, and carried them to the top of the hill that faces Hebron.

[4]Afterward it happened that he loved a woman in the Valley of Sorek, whose name *was* Delilah. [5]And the lords of the Philistines came up to her and said to her, "Entice him, and find out where his great strength *lies,* and by what *means* we may overpower him, that we may bind him to afflict him; and every one of us will give you eleven hundred *pieces* of silver."

[6]So Delilah said to Samson, "Please tell me where your great strength *lies,* and with what you may be bound to afflict you."

[7]And Samson said to her, "If they bind me with seven fresh bowstrings, not yet dried, then I shall become weak, and be like any *other* man."

15:17 [a]Literally *Jawbone Height* 15:19 [a]Literally *Jawbone* (compare verse 14) [b]Literally *Spring of the Caller*

15:15 God is searching for "jawbones of donkeys" (lowly and stubborn creatures) who, in His hand, will faithfully preach the everlasting gospel to this dying generation.

16:1 Samson "saw" a harlot. Lust begins with the eyes. He should have done as Job did (see Job 31:1). Read and memorize what Jesus said in Matt. 5:27–29 about our eyes causing us to sin. See also v. 21.

Springboards for Preaching and Witnessing

Weak-minded Christians

16:7 I have lost count of how many times I have heard that Christianity is a crutch for weak-minded people who cannot make it in life without faith. That may be, but we are not the only ones who need to lean on something. Do you know how many people use alcohol or drugs as a "crutch" to get them through life, or how many cannot walk into a room without clutching onto a cigarette? According to the Substance Abuse and Mental Health Services Administration, over 22 million Americans are addicted to drug abuse and alcohol. Those sorts of crutches tend to snap and leave the patient in a worse state.

Faith in God is not like that. He will never let you down, in this short life or in the life to come. You can lean on Him. I don't have to be concerned with the troubles of the future, because the future is in His hands. He is already there, so nothing takes Him by surprise. A "crutch" is a poor metaphor for the Savior. It is more accurate to say that faith in Jesus is a like a "parachute," and that death is a fearful jump into eternity. The Bible tells us to "put on the Lord Jesus Christ" (Rom. 13:14). You may believe that a parachute is a crutch, used by weak-minded people who cannot handle the jump by themselves. If that is the case, then I am weak-minded. I need a Savior.

8So the lords of the Philistines brought
up to her seven fresh bowstrings, not yet
dried, and she bound him with them.
9Now *men were* lying in wait, staying with
her in the room. And she said to him,
"The Philistines *are* upon you, Samson!"
But he broke the bowstrings as a strand
of yarn breaks when it touches fire. So
the secret of his strength was not known.
10Then Delilah said to Samson, "Look,
you have mocked me and told me lies.
Now, please tell me what you may be
bound with."
11So he said to her, "If they bind me
securely with new ropes that have never
been used, then I shall become weak, and
be like any *other* man."
12Therefore Delilah took new ropes
and bound him with them, and said to
him, "The Philistines *are* upon you, Samson!"
And *men were* lying in wait, staying
in the room. But he broke them off his
arms like a thread.
13Delilah said to Samson, "Until now
you have mocked me and told me lies.
Tell me what you may be bound with."
And he said to her, "If you weave the
seven locks of my head into the web of
the loom"—
14So she wove *it* tightly with the batten
of the loom, and said to him, "The Philistines
are upon you, Samson!" But he
awoke from his sleep, and pulled out the
batten and the web from the loom.
15Then she said to him, "How can you
say, 'I love you,' when your heart *is* not
with me? You have mocked me these
three times, and have not told me where
your great strength *lies*." 16And it came to
pass, when she pestered him daily with
her words and pressed him, *so* that his
soul was vexed to death, 17that he told
her all his heart, and said to her, "No razor
has ever come upon my head, for I
have been a Nazirite to God from my
mother's womb. If I am shaven, then my
strength will leave me, and I shall become
weak, and be like any *other* man."
18When Delilah saw that he had told
her all his heart, she sent and called for
the lords of the Philistines, saying, "Come
up once more, for he has told me all his
heart." So the lords of the Philistines
came up to her and brought the money in
their hand. 19Then she lulled him to sleep
on her knees, and called for a man and
had him shave off the seven locks of his
head. Then she began to torment him,[a]
and his strength left him. 20And she said,
"The Philistines *are* upon you, Samson!"
So he awoke from his sleep, and said, "I
will go out as before, at other times, and
shake myself free!" But he did not know

16:19 [a]Following Masoretic Text, Targum, and Vulgate; Septuagint reads *he began to be weak*.

that the LORD had departed from him. 21Then the Philistines took him and put out his eyes, and brought him down to Gaza. They bound him with bronze fetters, and he became a grinder in the prison. 22However, the hair of his head began to grow again after it had been shaven.

Samson Dies with the Philistines

23Now the lords of the Philistines gathered together to offer a great sacrifice to Dagon their god, and to rejoice. And they said:

"Our god has delivered into our hands
Samson our enemy!"

24When the people saw him, they praised their god; for they said:

"Our god has delivered into our hands
our enemy,
The destroyer of our land,
And the one who multiplied our dead."

25So it happened, when their hearts were merry, that they said, "Call for Samson, that he may perform for us." So they called for Samson from the prison, and he performed for them. And they stationed him between the pillars. 26Then Samson said to the lad who held him by the hand, "Let me feel the pillars which support the temple, so that I can lean on them." 27Now the temple was full of men and women. All the lords of the Philistines *were* there—about three thousand men and women on the roof watching while Samson performed.

28Then Samson called to the LORD, saying, "O Lord GOD, remember me, I pray! Strengthen me, I pray, just this once, O God, that I may with one *blow* take vengeance on the Philistines for my two eyes!" 29And Samson took hold of the two middle pillars which supported the temple, and he braced himself against them, one on his right and the other on his left. 30Then Samson said, "Let me die with the Philistines!" And he pushed with *all his* might, and the temple fell on the lords and all the people who *were* in it. So the dead that he killed at his death were more than he had killed in his life.

31And his brothers and all his father's household came down and took him, and brought *him* up and buried him between Zorah and Eshtaol in the tomb of his father Manoah. He had judged Israel twenty years.

Micah's Idolatry

17 Now there was a man from the mountains of Ephraim, whose name *was* Micah. 2And he said to his mother, "The eleven hundred *shekels* of silver that were taken from you, and on which you put a curse, even saying it in my ears—here *is* the silver with me; I took it."

And his mother said, "*May you be* blessed by the LORD, my son!" 3So when he had returned the eleven hundred *shekels* of silver to his mother, his mother said, "I had wholly dedicated the silver from my hand to the LORD for my son, to make a carved image and a molded image; now therefore, I will return it to you." 4Thus he returned the silver to his mother. Then his mother took two hundred *shekels* of silver and gave them to the silversmith, and he made it into a carved image and a molded image; and they were in the house of Micah.

5The man Micah had a shrine, and made an ephod and household idols;[a] and he consecrated one of his sons, who became his priest. 6In those days *there*

17:5 [a]Hebrew *teraphim*

16:25–30 The enemy has blinded the Church about the use of God's Law in evangelism. Be the lad who takes the hands of the blinded Church and places them on the pillars of God's Law. Then we will see a revival of the power of the Church. See Luke 11:52 comment.

was no king in Israel; everyone did *what was* right in his own eyes.

7Now there was a young man from Bethlehem in Judah, of the family of Judah; he *was* a Levite, and was staying there. 8The man departed from the city of Bethlehem in Judah to stay wherever he could find *a place.* Then he came to the mountains of Ephraim, to the house of Micah, as he journeyed. 9And Micah said to him, "Where do you come from?"

So he said to him, "I *am* a Levite from Bethlehem in Judah, and I am on my way to find *a place* to stay."

10Micah said to him, "Dwell with me, and be a father and a priest to me, and I will give you ten *shekels* of silver per year, a suit of clothes, and your sustenance." So the Levite went in. 11Then the Levite was content to dwell with the man; and the young man became like one of his sons to him. 12So Micah consecrated the Levite, and the young man became his priest, and lived in the house of Micah. 13Then Micah said, "Now I know that the LORD will be good to me, since I have a Levite as priest!"

The Danites Adopt Micah's Idolatry

18 In those days *there was* no king in Israel. And in those days the tribe of the Danites was seeking an inheritance for itself to dwell in; for until that day *their* inheritance among the tribes of Israel had not fallen to them. 2So the children of Dan sent five men of their family from their territory, men of valor from Zorah and Eshtaol, to spy out the land and search it. They said to them, "Go, search the land." So they went to the mountains of Ephraim, to the house of Micah, and lodged there. 3While they *were* at the house of Micah, they recognized the voice of the young Levite. They turned aside and said to him, "Who brought you here? What are you doing in this *place?* What do you have here?"

4He said to them, "Thus and so Micah did for me. He has hired me, and I have become his priest."

5So they said to him, "Please inquire of God, that we may know whether the journey on which we go will be prosperous."

6And the priest said to them, "Go in peace. The presence of the LORD *be* with you on your way."

7So the five men departed and went to Laish. They saw the people who *were* there, how they dwelt safely, in the manner of the Sidonians, quiet and secure. *There were* no rulers in the land who might put *them* to shame for anything. They *were* far from the Sidonians, and they had no ties with anyone.[a]

8Then *the spies* came back to their brethren at Zorah and Eshtaol, and their brethren said to them, "What *is* your *report?*"

9So they said, "Arise, let us go up against them. For we have seen the land, and indeed it *is* very good. *Would* you *do* nothing? Do not hesitate to go, *and* enter to possess the land. 10When you go, you will come to a secure people and a large land. For God has given it into your hands, a place where *there is* no lack of anything that *is* on the earth."

11And six hundred men of the family of the Danites went from there, from Zo-

18:7 [a]Following Masoretic Text, Targum, and Vulgate; Septuagint reads *with Syria.*

17:6 This is the result of a nation that forsakes God's Law. Morality becomes subjective. The only answer is the power of the gospel changing the heart of the sinner so that he will want to do what is right in God's eyes. See also Judg. 21:25 comment.

"How did the evangelical movement get so far off track? I wouldn't suggest that evangelicalism's recent obsession with political activism is the only factor, but I do think it's a *major* one. If the same energies and resources that were poured into failed political efforts had been channeled into evangelism instead, I'm convinced that would have been instrumental in producing more spiritual good and hindering more of society's evils than all our lobbying, demonstrating, and voting combined." *Phil Johnson*

rah and Eshtaol, armed with weapons of war. [12]Then they went up and encamped in Kirjath Jearim in Judah. (Therefore they call that place Mahaneh Dan[a] to this day. There *it is,* west of Kirjath Jearim.) [13]And they passed from there to the mountains of Ephraim, and came to the house of Micah.

[14]Then the five men who had gone to spy out the country of Laish answered and said to their brethren, "Do you know that there are in these houses an ephod, household idols, a carved image, and a molded image? Now therefore, consider what you should do." [15]So they turned aside there, and came to the house of the young Levite man—to the house of Micah—and greeted him. [16]The six hundred men armed with their weapons of war, who *were* of the children of Dan, stood by the entrance of the gate. [17]Then the five men who had gone to spy out the land went up. Entering there, they took the carved image, the ephod, the household idols, and the molded image. The priest stood at the entrance of the gate with the six hundred men *who were* armed with weapons of war.

[18]When these went into Micah's house and took the carved image, the ephod, the household idols, and the molded image, the priest said to them, "What are you doing?"

[19]And they said to him, "Be quiet, put your hand over your mouth, and come with us; be a father and a priest to us. *Is it* better for you to be a priest to the household of one man, or that you be a priest to a tribe and a family in Israel?" [20]So the priest's heart was glad; and he took the ephod, the household idols, and the carved image, and took his place among the people.

[21]Then they turned and departed, and put the little ones, the livestock, and the goods in front of them. [22]When they were a good way from the house of Micah, the men who *were* in the houses near Micah's house gathered together and overtook the children of Dan. [23]And they called out to the children of Dan. So they turned around and said to Micah, "What ails you, that you have gathered such a company?"

[24]So he said, "You have taken away my gods which I made, and the priest, and you have gone away. Now what more do I have? How can you say to me, 'What ails you?' "

[25]And the children of Dan said to him, "Do not let your voice be heard among us, lest angry men fall upon you, and you lose your life, with the lives of your household!" [26]Then the children of Dan went their way. And when Micah saw that they *were* too strong for him, he turned and went back to his house.

Danites Settle in Laish

[27]So they took *the things* Micah had made, and the priest who had belonged to him, and went to Laish, to a people quiet and secure; and they struck them with the edge of the sword and burned the city with fire. [28]*There was* no deliverer, because it *was* far from Sidon, and they had no ties with anyone. It was in the valley that belongs to Beth Rehob. So they rebuilt the city and dwelt there. [29]And they called the name of the city Dan, after the name of Dan their father, who was born to Israel. However, the name of the city formerly *was* Laish.

[30]Then the children of Dan set up for themselves the carved image; and Jonathan the son of Gershom, the son of Manasseh,[a] and his sons were priests to the tribe of Dan until the day of the captivity of the land. [31]So they set up for themselves Micah's carved image which he

18:12 [a]Literally *Camp of Dan* 18:30 [a]Septuagint and Vulgate read *Moses.*

18:14–26 "So far they were in the right, that it was desirable to have God's presence with them, but wretchedly mistaken when they took these images (which were fitter to be used in a puppet-play than in acts of devotion) for tokens of God's presence." *Matthew Henry*

made, all the time that the house of God was in Shiloh.

The Levite's Concubine

19 And it came to pass in those days, when *there was* no king in Israel, that there was a certain Levite staying in the remote mountains of Ephraim. He took for himself a concubine from Bethlehem in Judah. 2But his concubine played the harlot against him, and went away from him to her father's house at Bethlehem in Judah, and was there four whole months. 3Then her husband arose and went after her, to speak kindly to her *and* bring her back, having his servant and a couple of donkeys with him. So she brought him into her father's house; and when the father of the young woman saw him, he was glad to meet him. 4Now his father-in-law, the young woman's father, detained him; and he stayed with him three days. So they ate and drank and lodged there.

5Then it came to pass on the fourth day that they arose early in the morning, and he stood to depart; but the young woman's father said to his son-in-law, "Refresh your heart with a morsel of bread, and afterward go your way."

6So they sat down, and the two of them ate and drank together. Then the young woman's father said to the man, "Please be content to stay all night, and let your heart be merry." 7And when the man stood to depart, his father-in-law urged him; so he lodged there again. 8Then he arose early in the morning on the fifth day to depart, but the young woman's father said, "Please refresh your heart." So they delayed until afternoon; and both of them ate.

9And when the man stood to depart—he and his concubine and his servant—his father-in-law, the young woman's father, said to him, "Look, the day is now drawing toward evening; please spend the night. See, the day is coming to an end; lodge here, that your heart may be merry. Tomorrow go your way early, so that you may get home."

10However, the man was not willing to spend that night; so he rose and departed, and came opposite Jebus (that is, Jerusalem). With him were the two saddled donkeys; his concubine *was* also with him. 11They *were* near Jebus, and the day was far spent; and the servant said to his master, "Come, please, and let us turn aside into this city of the Jebusites and lodge in it."

12But his master said to him, "We will not turn aside here into a city of foreigners, who *are* not of the children of Israel; we will go on to Gibeah." 13So he said to his servant, "Come, let us draw near to one of these places, and spend the night in Gibeah or in Ramah." 14And they passed by and went their way; and the sun went down on them near Gibeah, which belongs to Benjamin. 15They turned aside there to go in to lodge in Gibeah. And when he went in, he sat down in the open square of the city, for no one would take them into *his* house to spend the night.

Without God there is for mankind no purpose, no goal, no hope, only a wavering future, an eternal dread of every darkness.

JEAN PAUL

16Just then an old man came in from his work in the field at evening, who also *was* from the mountains of Ephraim; he was staying in Gibeah, whereas the men of the place *were* Benjamites. 17And when he raised his eyes, he saw the traveler in the open square of the city; and the old man said, "Where are you going, and where do you come from?"

18So he said to him, "We *are* passing from Bethlehem in Judah toward the remote mountains of Ephraim; I *am* from there. I went to Bethlehem in Judah; *now* I am going to the house of the LORD. But there *is* no one who will take me into his house, 19although we have both straw and fodder for our donkeys, and bread

and wine for myself, for your female servant, and for the young man *who is* with your servant; *there is* no lack of anything."

20And the old man said, "Peace *be* with you! However, *let* all your needs *be* my responsibility; only do not spend the night in the open square." 21So he brought him into his house, and gave fodder to the donkeys. And they washed their feet, and ate and drank.

Gibeah's Crime

22As they were enjoying themselves, suddenly certain men of the city, perverted men,[a] surrounded the house *and* beat on the door. They spoke to the master of the house, the old man, saying, "Bring out the man who came to your house, that we may know him *carnally!*"

23But the man, the master of the house, went out to them and said to them, "No, my brethren! I beg you, do not act *so* wickedly! Seeing this man has come into my house, do not commit this outrage. 24Look, *here is* my virgin daughter and *the man's*[a] concubine; let me bring them out now. Humble them, and do with them as you please; but to this man do not do such a vile thing!" 25But the men would not heed him. So the man took his concubine and brought *her* out to them. And they knew her and abused her all night until morning; and when the day began to break, they let her go.

26Then the woman came as the day was dawning, and fell down at the door of the man's house where her master *was,* till it was light.

27When her master arose in the morning, and opened the doors of the house and went out to go his way, there was his concubine, fallen *at* the door of the house with her hands on the threshold. 28And he said to her, "Get up and let us be going." But there was no answer. So the man lifted her onto the donkey; and the man got up and went to his place.

29When he entered his house he took a knife, laid hold of his concubine, and divided her into twelve pieces, limb by limb,[a] and sent her throughout all the territory of Israel. 30And so it was that all who saw it said, "No such deed has been done or seen from the day that the children of Israel came up from the land of Egypt until this day. Consider it, confer, and speak up!"

Israel's War with the Benjamites

20 So all the children of Israel came out, from Dan to Beersheba, as well as from the land of Gilead, and the congregation gathered together as one man before the LORD at Mizpah. 2And the leaders of all the people, all the tribes of Israel, presented themselves in the assembly of the people of God, four hundred thousand foot soldiers who drew the sword. 3(Now the children of Benjamin heard that the children of Israel had gone up to Mizpah.)

Then the children of Israel said, "Tell *us,* how did this wicked deed happen?"

4So the Levite, the husband of the woman who was murdered, answered and said, "My concubine and I went into Gibeah, which belongs to Benjamin, to spend the night. 5And the men of Gibeah rose against me, and surrounded the house at night because of me. They intended to kill me, but instead they ravished my concubine so that she died. 6So I took hold of my concubine, cut her in pieces, and sent her throughout all the territory of the inheritance of Israel, because they

19:22 [a]Literally *sons of Belial* 19:24 [a]Literally *his* 19:29 [a]Literally *with her bones*

19:23–30 Skeptics often point to this passage and accuse God of wrongdoing. However, God didn't sanction this incident. The Bible is filled with strange, foolish, and wicked acts of men: Lot foolishly offering his daughters to homosexuals, Jephthah's rash vow (see 11:30–34), and many others. These incidents were not instigated by God, but were recorded for our instruction (see 1 Cor. 10:11; 2 Tim. 3:16), so that we would not make the same foolish mistakes.

committed lewdness and outrage in Israel. [7]Look! All of you *are* children of Israel; give your advice and counsel here
and now!"
[8]So all the people arose as one man,
saying, "None *of us* will go to his tent, nor
will any turn back to his house; [9]but now
this *is* the thing which we will do to
Gibeah: *We will go up* against it by lot.
[10]We will take ten men out of *every* hundred throughout all the tribes of Israel, a
hundred out of *every* thousand, and a
thousand out of *every* ten thousand, to
make provisions for the people, that when
they come to Gibeah in Benjamin, they
may repay all the vileness that they have
done in Israel." [11]So all the men of Israel
were gathered against the city, united together as one man.

· · · · · ·

Where did the conscience come from?
See 1 Cor. 8:10 comment.

· · · · · ·

[12]Then the tribes of Israel sent men
through all the tribe of Benjamin, saying,
"What *is* this wickedness that has occurred among you? [13]Now therefore, deliver up the men, the perverted men[a] who
are in Gibeah, that we may put them to
death and remove the evil from Israel!"
But the children of Benjamin would not
listen to the voice of their brethren, the
children of Israel. [14]Instead, the children
of Benjamin gathered together from their
cities to Gibeah, to go to battle against
the children of Israel. [15]And from their
cities at that time the children of Benjamin numbered twenty-six thousand men
who drew the sword, besides the inhabitants of Gibeah, who numbered seven
hundred select men. [16]Among all this people *were* seven hundred select men *who*
were left-handed; every one could sling a
stone at a hair's *breadth* and not miss.
[17]Now besides Benjamin, the men of Israel numbered four hundred thousand
men who drew the sword; all of these
were men of war.
[18]Then the children of Israel arose and
went up to the house of God[a] to inquire
of God. They said, "Which of us shall go
up first to battle against the children of
Benjamin?"
The LORD said, "Judah first!"
[19]So the children of Israel rose in the
morning and encamped against Gibeah.
[20]And the men of Israel went out to battle against Benjamin, and the men of Israel put themselves in battle array to fight
against them at Gibeah. [21]Then the children of Benjamin came out of Gibeah,
and on that day cut down to the ground
twenty-two thousand men of the Israelites. [22]And the people, that is, the men of
Israel, encouraged themselves and again
formed the battle line at the place where
they had put themselves in array on the
first day. [23]Then the children of Israel went
up and wept before the LORD until evening,
and asked counsel of the LORD, saying,
"Shall I again draw near for battle against
the children of my brother Benjamin?"
And the LORD said, "Go up against him."
[24]So the children of Israel approached
the children of Benjamin on the second
day. [25]And Benjamin went out against

20:13 [a]Literally *sons of Belial* 20:18 [a]Or *Bethel* 20:26 [a]Or *Bethel*

20:12–17 "They desire them to consider how great the wickedness was that was committed (v. 12), and that it was done among them: and how necessary it was therefore that they should either punish the malefactors with death themselves, according to the law of Moses, or deliver them up to the general assembly, to be so much the more publicly and solemnly punished, that evil might be put away from Israel, the national guilt removed, the infection stopped by cutting off the gangrened part, and national judgments prevented; for the sin was so very like that of the Sodomites that they might justly fear, if they did not punish it, God would rain hail from heaven upon them, as he did, not only upon Sodom, but the neighboring cities." *Matthew Henry*

them from Gibeah on the second day, and cut down to the ground eighteen thousand more of the children of Israel; all these drew the sword.

[26]Then all the children of Israel, that is, all the people, went up and came to the house of God[a] and wept. They sat there before the LORD and fasted that day until evening; and they offered burnt offerings and peace offerings before the LORD. [27]So the children of Israel inquired of the LORD (the ark of the covenant of God *was* there in those days, [28]and Phinehas the son of Eleazar, the son of Aaron, stood before it in those days), saying, "Shall I yet again go out to battle against the children of my brother Benjamin, or shall I cease?"

And the LORD said, "Go up, for tomorrow I will deliver them into your hand."

[29]Then Israel set men in ambush all around Gibeah. [30]And the children of Israel went up against the children of Benjamin on the third day, and put themselves in battle array against Gibeah as at the other times. [31]So the children of Benjamin went out against the people, *and* were drawn away from the city. They began to strike down *and* kill some of the people, as at the other times, in the highways (one of which goes up to Bethel and the other to Gibeah) and in the field, about thirty men of Israel. [32]And the children of Benjamin said, "They *are* defeated before us, as at first."

But the children of Israel said, "Let us flee and draw them away from the city to the highways." [33]So all the men of Israel rose from their place and put themselves in battle array at Baal Tamar. Then Israel's men in ambush burst forth from their position in the plain of Geba. [34]And ten thousand select men from all Israel came against Gibeah, and the battle was fierce. But *the Benjamites*[a] did not know that disaster *was* upon them. [35]The LORD defeated Benjamin before Israel. And the children of Israel destroyed that day twenty-five thousand one hundred Benjamites; all these drew the sword.

[36]So the children of Benjamin saw that they were defeated. The men of Israel had given ground to the Benjamites, because they relied on the men in ambush whom they had set against Gibeah. [37]And the men in ambush quickly rushed upon Gibeah; the men in ambush spread out and struck the whole city with the edge of the sword. [38]Now the appointed signal between the men of Israel and the men in ambush was that they would make a great cloud of smoke rise up from the city, [39]whereupon the men of Israel would turn in battle.

> Never before has the world been so desperately asking for answers to crucial questions, and never before has the world been so frantically committed to the idea that no answers are possible.
>
> **EDMUND CLOWNEY**

Now Benjamin had begun to strike *and* kill about thirty of the men of Israel. For they said, "Surely they are defeated before us, as *in* the first battle." [40]But when the cloud began to rise from the city in a column of smoke, the Benjamites looked behind them, and there was the whole city going up *in smoke* to heaven. [41]And when the men of Israel turned back, the men of Benjamin panicked, for they saw that disaster had come upon them. [42]Therefore they turned *their backs* before the men of Israel in the direction of the wilderness; but the battle overtook them, and whoever *came* out of the cities they destroyed in their midst. [43]They surrounded the Benjamites, chased them, *and* easily trampled them down as far as the front of Gibeah toward the east. [44]And eighteen thousand men of Benjamin fell; all these *were* men of valor. [45]Then they[a] turned and fled toward the wilderness to the rock of Rimmon; and they cut down five thousand of them on the highways. Then they pursued them relentlessly up to Gidom, and killed two thousand of them. [46]So all who fell of Benjamin that day were twenty-

20:34 [a]Literally *they* **20:45** [a]Septuagint reads *the rest.*

five thousand men who drew the sword; all these *were* men of valor.

[47]But six hundred men turned and fled toward the wilderness to the rock of Rimmon, and they stayed at the rock of Rimmon for four months. [48]And the men of Israel turned back against the children of Benjamin, and struck them down with the edge of the sword—from *every* city, men and beasts, all who were found. They also set fire to all the cities they came to.

Wives Provided for the Benjamites

21 Now the men of Israel had sworn an oath at Mizpah, saying, "None of us shall give his daughter to Benjamin as a wife." [2]Then the people came to the house of God,[a] and remained there before God till evening. They lifted up their voices and wept bitterly, [3]and said, "O LORD God of Israel, why has this come to pass in Israel, that today there should be one tribe *missing* in Israel?"

[4]So it was, on the next morning, that the people rose early and built an altar there, and offered burnt offerings and peace offerings. [5]The children of Israel said, "Who *is there* among all the tribes of Israel who did not come up with the assembly to the LORD?" For they had made a great oath concerning anyone who had not come up to the LORD at Mizpah, saying, "He shall surely be put to death." [6]And the children of Israel grieved for Benjamin their brother, and said, "One tribe is cut off from Israel today. [7]What shall we do for wives for those who remain, seeing we have sworn by the LORD that we will not give them our daughters as wives?"

[8]And they said, "What one *is there* from the tribes of Israel who did not come up to Mizpah to the LORD?" And, in fact, no one had come to the camp from Jabesh Gilead to the assembly. [9]For when the people were counted, indeed, not one of the inhabitants of Jabesh Gilead *was* there. [10]So the congregation sent out there twelve thousand of their most valiant men, and commanded them, saying, "Go and strike the inhabitants of Jabesh Gilead with the edge of the sword, including the women and children. [11]And this *is* the thing that you shall do: You shall utterly destroy every male, and every woman who has known a man intimately." [12]So they found among the inhabitants of Jabesh Gilead four hundred young virgins who had not known a man intimately; and they brought them to the camp at Shiloh, which is in the land of Canaan.

[13]Then the whole congregation sent *word* to the children of Benjamin who *were* at the rock of Rimmon, and announced peace to them. [14]So Benjamin came back at that time, and they gave them the women whom they had saved alive of the women of Jabesh Gilead; and yet they had not found enough for them.

[15]And the people grieved for Benjamin, because the LORD had made a void in the tribes of Israel.

Mormon teaching humanizes God and deifies man.
For details, see page 1684.

[16]Then the elders of the congregation said, "What shall we do for wives for those who remain, since the women of Benjamin have been destroyed?" [17]And they said, "*There must be* an inheritance for the survivors of Benjamin, that a tribe may not be destroyed from Israel. [18]However, we cannot give them wives from our daughters, for the children of Israel have sworn an oath, saying, 'Cursed *be* the one who gives a wife to Benjamin.' " [19]Then they said, "In fact, *there is* a yearly feast of the LORD in Shiloh, which *is* north of Bethel, on the east side of the highway that goes up from Bethel to Shechem, and south of Lebonah."

[20]Therefore they instructed the children of Benjamin, saying, "Go, lie in wait in the vineyards, [21]and watch; and just

21:2 [a]Or *Bethel*

21:25 Relativism

By Mark Spence

Relativism is the philosophical position that all points of view are equally valid, and that all truth is left up to the individual to define. This means that all moral positions, all religious systems, all political movements, are *truths* that are relative to the individual. In other words, there are no right or wrong answers . . . to anything!

It's easy to recognize relativism because most of its statements sound intellectual but they are simply ridiculous and self-refuting. They go something like this:

"You can't know anything for sure."
"You shouldn't judge."
"Nobody's right."
"You can't know anything."
"What is true for you is not true for me."

The easiest way to refute statements like these is to simply turn them back around.

- "You can't know anything for *sure*."
  Are you *sure* of that? Are you *sure* you can't know anything for sure?
- "You shouldn't *judge*."
  Is that your *judgment*? And if you shouldn't *judge*, then why are you *judging* my *judgment*?
- *"Nobody's* right."
  Are you *right*? Are you right that *nobody's* right? And if you are *right* then you're *wrong* about *nobody* being right.
- "You can't *know* anything."
  Do you *know* that? Do you *know* that you can't *know* anything?
- "What is *true* for you is not *true* for me."
  Well, that's true. And what is *true* for me is that you are wrong.

So, the next time you're confronted with that relativity nonsense, just turn it around to question the person's logic and help him realize that his point of view is just plain silly.

See also 1 Thess. 2:13 comment on absolute truth.

when the daughters of Shiloh come out to perform their dances, then come out from the vineyards, and every man catch a wife for himself from the daughters of Shiloh; then go to the land of Benjamin.
[22]Then it shall be, when their fathers or their brothers come to us to complain, that we will say to them, 'Be kind to them for our sakes, because we did not take a wife for any of them in the war; for *it is* not *as though* you have given the *women* to them at this time, making yourselves guilty of your oath.' "

[23]And the children of Benjamin did so; they took enough wives for their number from those who danced, whom they caught. Then they went and returned to their inheritance, and they rebuilt the cities and dwelt in them. [24]So the children of Israel departed from there at that time, every man to his tribe and family; they went out from there, every man to his inheritance.

[25]In those days *there was* no king in Israel; everyone did *what was* right in his own eyes.

"We face a humanity that is too precious to neglect.
We know a remedy for the ills of the world too wonderful to withhold.
We have a Christ too glorious to hide.
We have an adventure that is too thrilling to miss."

THEODORE WILLIAMS

Legal Rights in Public Speaking

Police and city officials understand their obligation to protect the free speech rights of citizens.

Public streets and parks are considered to be "traditional public forums." This is the classic place where citizens have always been permitted to share their beliefs and ideas with one another either verbally or through the distribution of literature.

In the case of *Hague v. C.I.O.*, 307 U.S. 496 (1939), the United States Supreme Court held that citizens have a "guaranteed access" to streets, parks, and other "traditional public forum." The privilege to use the streets and parks for communication of views may be regulated in the best interests of all, but it must not, under the guise of regulation, be abridged or denied. Mere inconvenience to the government will not outweigh free speech interests.

The "traditional public forum" is the most protected place for Christian witnessing, street preaching, and tract distribution. All citizens have an absolute right to share their faith in the "traditional public forum" of streets and parks. This absolute right is subject only to limited controls in the interest of public safety and order; e.g., two parades cannot march down the same street at the same time so parade permits, if constitutionally granted, are permissible.

- It is important to note that controls for public safety and order may not be imposed for reasons such as potential littering, potential offense to other citizens, or attempts to silence some citizens while continuing to permit others to speak in the forum.
- In the case of *Schneider v. State*, 308 U.S. 147 (1939), the United States Supreme Court did not permit cities to forbid leaflet distribution in order to prevent littering. The objective of keeping the streets clean does not outweigh the right to distribute literature in public.

Amplification may be regulated by ordinances setting noise decibel levels under *Kovacs v. Cooper*, 335 U.S. 77 (1949):

> Christians are free to witness and distribute Gospel tracts in public streets and parks. Christians are also free to preach, sing, or present dramatizations, which might collect a crowd as long as that crowd will not block pedestrian or vehicular traffic. Permits may sometimes be required for formal crowd generating activities but they must be available on a neutral basis to all who request them and must allow real communication to take place. In the case of *Freedman v. Maryland*, 380 U.S. 51 (1965), the United States Supreme Court held that public officials may not be given overly broad discretion to grant or deny permits or licenses.

First Amendment law also does not allow city police or officials to interfere with a citizen's right of freedom of speech simply because that speech might offend a listener. These cases are particularly important:

- In the case of *Cantwell v. Connecticut*, 310 U.S. 296 (1940), the United States Supreme Court held that speech may not be prohibited merely because it offends some listeners.
- Several other Supreme Court cases have also dealt with this issue of giving offense to other citizens, which is sometimes called the "Heckler's Veto" and is not permitted.
- In the case of *Cox v. Louisiana*, 379 U.S. 536 (1965), the United States Supreme Court held that hecklers may not be allowed to veto a speaker's right of free speech. Police must control a crowd rather than arrest the speaker in order to maintain order.
- A similar ruling that offensiveness is not a reason to limit free speech rights was made by the Supreme Court in the case of *Cohen v. California*, 403 U.S. 15 (1971).

In America, citizens, police, and city officials are still held to the legal rights of free speech simply stated in the maxim: "I may not agree with what you say, but I will defend to the death your right to say it." That is still the law in these United States. It is also true that we may be offended by what others say but we must protect their constitutional right to say it.

Witnessing, "street preaching," and distribution of free literature are constitutionally protected activities because they are the ways in which citizens have always exercised their rights of free speech.

Important Note: *This summary does not constitute the giving of legal advice. For more information, contact: Christian Law Association (727-399-8300) and American Center for Law & Justice (800-296-4529).*

Ruth

Elimelech's Family Goes to Moab

1 Now it came to pass, in the days when
the judges ruled, that there was a
famine in the land. And a certain man of
Bethlehem, Judah, went to dwell in the
country of Moab, he and his wife and his
two sons. 2The name of the man *was*
Elimelech, the name of his wife *was*
Naomi, and the names of his two sons
were Mahlon and Chilion—Ephrathites
of Bethlehem, Judah. And they went to
the country of Moab and remained there.
3Then Elimelech, Naomi's husband, died;
and she was left, and her two sons. 4Now
they took wives of the women of Moab:
the name of the one *was* Orpah, and the
name of the other Ruth. And they dwelt
there about ten years. 5Then both Mahlon and Chilion also died; so the woman
survived her two sons and her husband.

Naomi Returns with Ruth

6Then she arose with her daughters-
in-law that she might return from the
country of Moab, for she had heard in the
country of Moab that the LORD had visited His people by giving them bread.
7Therefore she went out from the place
where she was, and her two daughters-
in-law with her; and they went on the
way to return to the land of Judah. 8And
Naomi said to her two daughters-in-law,
"Go, return each to her mother's house.
The LORD deal kindly with you, as you
have dealt with the dead and with me.
9The LORD grant that you may find rest,
each in the house of her husband."
So she kissed them, and they lifted up
their voices and wept. 10And they said to
her, "Surely we will return with you to
your people."
11But Naomi said, "Turn back, my
daughters; why will you go with me? *Are*
there still sons in my womb, that they
may be your husbands? 12Turn back, my
daughters, go—for I am too old to have a
husband. If I should say I have hope, *if* I
should have a husband tonight and should
also bear sons, 13would you wait for them
till they were grown? Would you restrain
yourselves from having husbands? No,
my daughters; for it grieves me very much
for your sakes that the hand of the LORD
has gone out against me!"
14Then they lifted up their voices and
wept again; and Orpah kissed her mother-
in-law, but Ruth clung to her.
15And she said, "Look, your sister-in-
law has gone back to her people and to
her gods; return after your sister-in-law."
16But Ruth said:

"Entreat me not to leave you,
Or to turn back from following after
you;
For wherever you go, I will go;
And wherever you lodge, I will lodge;
Your people *shall be* my people,
And your God, my God.
17Where you die, I will die,
And there will I be buried.
The LORD do so to me, and more also,

If *anything but* death parts you and me."

[18]When she saw that she was determined to go with her, she stopped speaking to her.

[19]Now the two of them went until they came to Bethlehem. And it happened, when they had come to Bethlehem, that all the city was excited because of them; and the women said, "*Is* this Naomi?"

[20]But she said to them, "Do not call me Naomi;[a] call me Mara,[b] for the Almighty has dealt very bitterly with me. [21]I went out full, and the LORD has brought me home again empty. Why do you call me Naomi, since the LORD has testified against me, and the Almighty has afflicted me?"

[22]So Naomi returned, and Ruth the Moabitess her daughter-in-law with her, who returned from the country of Moab. Now they came to Bethlehem at the beginning of barley harvest.

Ruth Meets Boaz

2 There was a relative of Naomi's husband, a man of great wealth, of the family of Elimelech. His name *was* Boaz.
[2]So Ruth the Moabitess said to Naomi, "Please let me go to the field, and glean heads of grain after *him* in whose sight I may find favor."

And she said to her, "Go, my daughter."
[3]Then she left, and went and gleaned in the field after the reapers. And she happened to come to the part of the field *belonging* to Boaz, who *was* of the family of Elimelech.

[4]Now behold, Boaz came from Bethlehem, and said to the reapers, "The LORD *be* with you!"

And they answered him, "The LORD bless you!"

[5]Then Boaz said to his servant who was in charge of the reapers, "Whose young woman *is* this?"

[6]So the servant who was in charge of the reapers answered and said, "It *is* the young Moabite woman who came back with Naomi from the country of Moab.
[7]And she said, 'Please let me glean and gather after the reapers among the sheaves.' So she came and has continued from morning until now, though she rested a little in the house."

[8]Then Boaz said to Ruth, "You will listen, my daughter, will you not? Do not go to glean in another field, nor go from here, but stay close by my young women.
[9]*Let* your eyes *be* on the field which they reap, and go after them. Have I not commanded the young men not to touch you? And when you are thirsty, go to the vessels and drink from what the young men have drawn."

> I believe God is managing affairs and that He doesn't need any advice from me. With God in charge, I believe everything will work out for the best in the end. So what is there to worry about?
>
> **HENRY FORD**

[10]So she fell on her face, bowed down to the ground, and said to him, "Why have I found favor in your eyes, that you should take notice of me, since I *am* a foreigner?"

[11]And Boaz answered and said to her, "It has been fully reported to me, all that you have done for your mother-in-law since the death of your husband, and *how* you have left your father and your mother and the land of your birth, and have come to a people whom you did not know before.
[12]The LORD repay your work, and a full reward be given you by the LORD God of Israel, under whose wings you have come for refuge."

[13]Then she said, "Let me find favor in

1:20 [a]Literally *Pleasant* [b]Literally *Bitter*

1:20,21 Tragedy can either drive us closer to the Lord or make us bitter. Soak yourself regularly in Rom. 8:28. Faith in that wonderful promise is the antidote to a lifetime of self-destructive bitterness.

your sight, my lord; for you have comforted me, and have spoken kindly to your maidservant, though I am not like one of your maidservants."

14Now Boaz said to her at mealtime, "Come here, and eat of the bread, and dip your piece of bread in the vinegar." So she sat beside the reapers, and he passed parched *grain* to her; and she ate and was satisfied, and kept some back. 15And when she rose up to glean, Boaz commanded his young men, saying, "Let her glean even among the sheaves, and do not reproach her. 16Also let *grain* from the bundles fall purposely for her; leave *it* that she may glean, and do not rebuke her."

17So she gleaned in the field until evening, and beat out what she had gleaned, and it was about an ephah of barley. 18Then she took *it* up and went into the city, and her mother-in-law saw what she had gleaned. So she brought out and gave to her what she had kept back after she had been satisfied.

19And her mother-in-law said to her, "Where have you gleaned today? And where did you work? Blessed be the one who took notice of you."

So she told her mother-in-law with whom she had worked, and said, "The man's name with whom I worked today *is* Boaz."

20Then Naomi said to her daughter-in-law, "Blessed *be* he of the LORD, who has not forsaken His kindness to the living and the dead!" And Naomi said to her, "This man *is* a relation of ours, one of our close relatives."

21Ruth the Moabitess said, "He also said to me, 'You shall stay close by my young men until they have finished all my harvest.' "

22And Naomi said to Ruth her daughter-in-law, "*It is* good, my daughter, that you go out with his young women, and that people do not meet you in any other field." 23So she stayed close by the young women of Boaz, to glean until the end of barley harvest and wheat harvest; and she dwelt with her mother-in-law.

Ruth's Redemption Assured

3 Then Naomi her mother-in-law said to her, "My daughter, shall I not seek security for you, that it may be well with you? 2Now Boaz, whose young women you were with, *is he* not our relative? In fact, he is winnowing barley tonight at the threshing floor. 3Therefore wash yourself and anoint yourself, put on your *best* garment and go down to the threshing floor; *but* do not make yourself known to the man until he has finished eating and drinking. 4Then it shall be, when he lies down, that you shall notice the place where he lies; and you shall go in, uncover his feet, and lie down; and he will tell you what you should do."

5And she said to her, "All that you say to me I will do."

6So she went down to the threshing floor and did according to all that her mother-in-law instructed her. 7And after Boaz had eaten and drunk, and his heart was cheerful, he went to lie down at the

2:12 The Christian's works follow him. God doesn't forget your labor of love and work of faith, and He will reward you. See also Deut. 10:12,13 comment.

"The New Testament has lots to say about self-denial, but not about self-denial as an end in itself. We are told to deny ourselves and to take up our crosses in order that we may follow Christ; and nearly every description of what we shall ultimately find if we do so contains an appeal to desire.

"If there lurks in most modern minds the notion that to desire our own good and earnestly to hope for the enjoyment of it is a bad thing, I submit that this notion has crept in from Kant and the Stoics and is no part of the Christian faith. Indeed, if we consider the unblushing promises of reward and the staggering nature of the rewards promised in the Gospels, it would seem that our Lord finds our desires not too strong, but too weak. We are half-hearted creatures, fooling about with drink and sex and ambition when infinite joy is offered us, like an ignorant child who wants to go on making mud pies in a slum because he cannot imagine what is meant by the offer of a holiday at the sea. We are far too easily pleased." *C. S. Lewis*

"Faith sees the invisible, believes the unbelievable, and receives the impossible."

Corrie ten Boom

end of the heap of grain; and she came
softly, uncovered his feet, and lay down.
8Now it happened at midnight that
the man was startled, and turned himself;
and there, a woman was lying at his feet.
9And he said, "Who *are* you?"

So she answered, "I *am* Ruth, your maidservant. Take your maidservant under your wing,[a] for you are a close relative."

10Then he said, "Blessed *are* you of the
LORD, my daughter! For you have shown more kindness at the end than at the beginning, in that you did not go after
young men, whether poor or rich. 11And
now, my daughter, do not fear. I will do for you all that you request, for all the people of my town know that you *are* a
virtuous woman. 12Now it is true that I
am a close relative; however, there is a
relative closer than I. 13Stay this night,
and in the morning it shall be *that* if he will perform the duty of a close relative for you—good; let him do it. But if he does not want to perform the duty for you, then I will perform the duty for you, *as* the LORD lives! Lie down until morning."
14So she lay at his feet until morning,
and she arose before one could recognize another. Then he said, "Do not let it be known that the woman came to the threshing floor." 15Also he said, "Bring the shawl
that *is* on you and hold it." And when she held it, he measured six *ephahs* of barley, and laid *it* on her. Then she[a] went into the city.

16When she came to her mother-in-law, she said, "*Is* that you, my daughter?"

Then she told her all that the man had
done for her. 17And she said, "These six
ephahs of barley he gave me; for he said to me, 'Do not go empty-handed to your mother-in-law.' "

18Then she said, "Sit still, my daughter, until you know how the matter will turn out; for the man will not rest until he has concluded the matter this day."

Boaz Redeems Ruth

4 Now Boaz went up to the gate and sat down there; and behold, the close relative of whom Boaz had spoken came by. So Boaz said, "Come aside, friend,[a] sit down here." So he came aside and sat
down. 2And he took ten men of the elders
of the city, and said, "Sit down here." So
they sat down. 3Then he said to the close
relative, "Naomi, who has come back from the country of Moab, sold the piece of land which *belonged* to our brother
Elimelech. 4And I thought to inform you, saying, 'Buy *it* back in the presence of the inhabitants and the elders of my people. If you will redeem *it*, redeem *it;* but if you[a] will not redeem *it, then* tell me, that I may know; for *there is* no one but you to redeem *it,* and I *am* next after you.' "

3:9 [a]Or *Spread the corner of your garment over your maidservant* 3:15 [a]Many Hebrew manuscripts, Syriac, and Vulgate read *she;* Masoretic Text, Septuagint, and Targum read *he.* 4:1 [a]Hebrew *peloni almoni;* literally *so and so* 4:4 [a]Following many Hebrew manuscripts, Septuagint, Syriac, Targum, and Vulgate; Masoretic Text reads *he.*

3:8,9 The Church lies as a freed slave, a servant at the feet of her Redeemer.

And he said, "I will redeem *it*."
5Then Boaz said, "On the day you buy
the field from the hand of Naomi, you
must also buy *it* from Ruth the Moabitess,
the wife of the dead, to perpetuate[a] the
name of the dead through his inheritance."
6And the close relative said, "I cannot
redeem *it* for myself, lest I ruin my own
inheritance. You redeem my right of redemption for yourself, for I cannot redeem
it."
7Now this *was the custom* in former
times in Israel concerning redeeming and
exchanging, to confirm anything: one man
took off his sandal and gave *it* to the other,
and this *was* a confirmation in Israel.

> God's holiness demands consequences for sin. We have broken His standard of holiness, and His holiness demands that He judge sin, not ignore or excuse it.
>
> **BILL BRIGHT**

8Therefore the close relative said to
Boaz, "Buy *it* for yourself." So he took off
his sandal. 9And Boaz said to the elders
and all the people, "You *are* witnesses this
day that I have bought all that was Elimelech's, and all that *was* Chilion's and
Mahlon's, from the hand of Naomi. 10More-
over, Ruth the Moabitess, the widow of
Mahlon, I have acquired as my wife, to
perpetuate the name of the dead through
his inheritance, that the name of the dead
may not be cut off from among his
brethren and from his position at the
gate.[a] You *are* witnesses this day."
11And all the people who *were* at the
gate, and the elders, said, "*We are* witnesses. The LORD make the woman who
is coming to your house like Rachel and
Leah, the two who built the house of Israel; and may you prosper in Ephrathah
and be famous in Bethlehem. 12May your
house be like the house of Perez, whom
Tamar bore to Judah, because of the offspring which the LORD will give you from
this young woman."

Descendants of Boaz and Ruth

13So Boaz took Ruth and she became
his wife; and when he went in to her, the
LORD gave her conception, and she bore a
son. 14Then the women said to Naomi,
"Blessed *be* the LORD, who has not left you
this day without a close relative; and may
his name be famous in Israel! 15And may
he be to you a restorer of life and a nour-
isher of your old age; for your daughter-
in-law, who loves you, who is better to
you than seven sons, has borne him."
16Then Naomi took the child and laid
him on her bosom, and became a nurse
to him. 17Also the neighbor women gave
him a name, saying, "There is a son born
to Naomi." And they called his name
Obed. He *is* the father of Jesse, the father
of David.
18Now this *is* the genealogy of Perez:
Perez begot Hezron; 19Hezron begot Ram,
and Ram begot Amminadab; 20Ammi-
nadab begot Nahshon, and Nahshon begot Salmon;[a] 21Salmon begot Boaz, and
Boaz begot Obed; 22Obed begot Jesse,
and Jesse begot David.

4:5 [a]Literally *raise up* 4:10 [a]Probably his civic office 4:20 [a]Hebrew *Salmah*

4:1–12 "This kinsman, when he heard the conditions of the bargain, refused it. In like manner many are shy of the great redemption; they are not willing to espouse religion; they have heard well of it, and have nothing to say against it; they will give it their good word, but they are willing to part with it, and cannot be bound to it, for fear of marring their own inheritance in this world. The right was resigned to Boaz." *Matthew Henry*

The Love Test

With an honest heart, contemplate these statements.

1. The thought of sharing my faith:
a. Terrifies me
b. Embarrasses me
c. Excites me
d. Bores me

2. I believe the person with whom I share my faith would probably:
a. Thank me
b. Physically attack me
c. Think I'm a fanatic
d. It doesn't matter what they do to me

3. A person who is not born again will:
a. Be eternally happy
b. Die unfulfilled
c. Still go to heaven
d. Spend eternity in hell

4. The fact that anyone could suffer in hell forever:
a. Doesn't worry me
b. Concerns me
c. Horrifies me
d. Isn't my problem

5. I could conquer my fears about sharing my faith if each time I tried I was given:
a. $20
b. $100
c. $1,000
d. A promise that God would be with me

6. According to Colossians 1:28, we are told that we should be warning:
a. All Jews
b. Our relatives
c. Every person
d. Every Christian

7. In light of that command, I have been:
a. Disobedient
b. Faithful
c. Unaware of my responsibility
d. Complacent

8. I am:
a. An on-fire Christian who will use any means to reach the lost with the gospel
b. Neither hot nor cold, but lukewarm (see Revelation 3:16)
c. Not sure if my love for Christ is strong enough (see John 14:15)

9. If I saw a blind man walking toward a 1,000 foot cliff, I would immediately:
a. Offer him my favorite Christian CD
b. Invite him to my house for a non-confrontational BBQ the following weekend
c. Suggest a more fulfilling place to walk
d. Warn him about the cliff

10. When Paul pleaded with the people on Mars Hill (Acts 17), he demonstrated his concern for them by:
a. Inviting them to a worship service in the upper room
b. Smiling and hoping they noticed the peace in his eyes
c. Saying something to make them feel good about themselves
d. Telling them about the coming Day of Judgment and what they must do to be saved

11. If we know someone who is not born again, we should do all we can to:
a. Spend months building their trust and hope they ask us what makes us different (assuming they don't die first . . . which we can't assume)
b. Invite them to church and hope they want to come back
c. Wear a cross around our neck so they'll know we're sold out for Jesus
d. Learn to go to them in love and compassion, speaking the truth, leading them to the Savior

12. In light of the fact that 150,000 people die every day, and I know how to cure death, what would I like to do now?
a. Pray about it
b. Think about something else
c. Begin to learn how to share my faith, effectively, biblically—the way Jesus did—and reach the lost with the gospel

1 Samuel

The Family of Elkanah

1 Now there was a certain man of
Ramathaim Zophim, of the mountains of Ephraim, and his name *was*
Elkanah the son of Jeroham, the son of
Elihu,[a] the son of Tohu,[b] the son of Zuph,
an Ephraimite. 2And he had two wives:
the name of one *was* Hannah, and the
name of the other Peninnah. Peninnah
had children, but Hannah had no children. 3This man went up from his city
yearly to worship and sacrifice to the LORD
of hosts in Shiloh. Also the two sons of
Eli, Hophni and Phinehas, the priests of
the LORD, *were* there. 4And whenever the
time came for Elkanah to make an offering, he would give portions to Peninnah
his wife and to all her sons and daughters. 5But to Hannah he would give a
double portion, for he loved Hannah, although the LORD had closed her womb.
6And her rival also provoked her severely, to make her miserable, because the
LORD had closed her womb. 7So it was,
year by year, when she went up to the
house of the LORD, that she provoked
her; therefore she wept and did not eat.

Hannah's Vow

8Then Elkanah her husband said to
her, "Hannah, why do you weep? Why do
you not eat? And why is your heart grieved?
Am I not better to you than ten sons?"
9So Hannah arose after they had finished eating and drinking in Shiloh. Now
Eli the priest was sitting on the seat by
the doorpost of the tabernacle[a] of the
LORD. 10And she *was* in bitterness of soul,
and prayed to the LORD and wept in anguish. 11Then she made a vow and said,
"O LORD of hosts, if You will indeed look
on the affliction of Your maidservant and
remember me, and not forget Your maidservant, but will give Your maidservant a
male child, then I will give him to the
LORD all the days of his life, and no razor
shall come upon his head."
12And it happened, as she continued
praying before the LORD, that Eli watched
her mouth. 13Now Hannah spoke in her
heart; only her lips moved, but her voice
was not heard. Therefore Eli thought she
was drunk. 14So Eli said to her, "How long
will you be drunk? Put your wine away
from you!"
15But Hannah answered and said, "No,
my lord, I *am* a woman of sorrowful spirit.
I have drunk neither wine nor intoxicating drink, but have poured out my soul
before the LORD. 16Do not consider your
maidservant a wicked woman,[a] for out of

1:1 [a]Spelled *Eliel* in 1 Chronicles 6:34 [b]Spelled *Toah* in 1 Chronicles 6:34 1:9 [a]Hebrew *heykal,* palace or temple 1:16 [a]Literally *daughter of Belial*

1:9–11 This is the spirit in which we should pray for the lost. A majority in the Church have a barren womb and are not spiritually reproducing; there are relatively few live births. Up to 90 percent of those who profess to be born again at large crusades and in local churches prove to be stillborn. See also 2 Cor. 2:17 comment.

the abundance of my complaint and grief
I have spoken until now."
[17]Then Eli answered and said, "Go in
peace, and the God of Israel grant your
petition which you have asked of Him."
[18]And she said, "Let your maidservant
find favor in your sight." So the woman
went her way and ate, and her face was
no longer *sad.*

Samuel Is Born and Dedicated

[19]Then they rose early in the morning
and worshiped before the LORD, and returned and came to their house at Ramah.
And Elkanah knew Hannah his wife, and
the LORD remembered her. [20]So it came to
pass in the process of time that Hannah
conceived and bore a son, and called his
name Samuel,[a] *saying,* "Because I have
asked for him from the LORD."
[21]Now the man Elkanah and all his
house went up to offer to the LORD the
yearly sacrifice and his vow. [22]But Hannah
did not go up, for she said to her husband, "*Not* until the child is weaned; then
I will take him, that he may appear before
the LORD and remain there forever."
[23]So Elkanah her husband said to her,
"Do what seems best to you; wait until
you have weaned him. Only let the LORD
establish His[a] word." Then the woman
stayed and nursed her son until she had
weaned him.
[24]Now when she had weaned him, she
took him up with her, with three bulls,[a]
one ephah of flour, and a skin of wine,
and brought him to the house of the
LORD in Shiloh. And the child *was* young.
[25]Then they slaughtered a bull, and
brought the child to Eli. [26]And she said,
"O my lord! As your soul lives, my lord, I
am the woman who stood by you here,
praying to the LORD. [27]For this child I
prayed, and the LORD has granted me my
petition which I asked of Him. [28]There-
fore I also have lent him to the LORD; as
long as he lives he shall be lent to the
LORD." So they worshiped the LORD there.

Hannah's Prayer

2 And Hannah prayed and said:

"My heart rejoices in the LORD;
My horn[a] is exalted in the LORD.
I smile at my enemies,
Because I rejoice in Your salvation.

[2]"No one is holy like the LORD,
For *there is* none besides You,
Nor *is there* any rock like our God.

[3]"Talk no more so very proudly;
Let no arrogance come from your
mouth,
For the LORD *is* the God of
knowledge;
And by Him actions are weighed.

[4]"The bows of the mighty men *are*
broken,
And those who stumbled are girded
with strength.
[5]*Those who were* full have hired
themselves out for bread,
And the hungry have ceased *to hunger.*
Even the barren has borne seven,
And she who has many children has
become feeble.
[6]"The LORD kills and makes alive;
He brings down to the grave and
brings up.
[7]The LORD makes poor and makes
rich;
He brings low and lifts up.
[8]He raises the poor from the dust
And lifts the beggar from the ash
heap,
To set *them* among princes

1:20 [a]Literally *Heard by God* 1:23 [a]Following Masoretic Text, Targum, and Vulgate; Dead Sea Scrolls, Septuagint, and Syriac read *your.* 1:24 [a]Dead Sea Scrolls, Septuagint, and Syriac read *a three-year-old bull.* 2:1 [a]That is, strength

1:18 This is evidence of her faith (see Luke 1:45).

2:1–10 See Luke 1:46–55 for the similarity between Hannah's and Mary's prayers.

QUESTIONS & OBJECTIONS

2:12 "What does it means to 'know the Lord'? How can someone know the Lord the way you do?"

This is a great question. Let me first explain why I use the phrase "know the Lord." This is the biblical definition of a Christian. It is used many times in Scripture, but it is particularly used in reference to the gospel, in Jer. 31:34: "No more shall every man teach his neighbor, and every man his brother, saying, 'Know the LORD,' for they all shall know Me, from the least of them to the greatest of them, says the LORD. For I will forgive their iniquity, and their sin I will remember no more."

It is because Jesus took our sin upon Himself that we can be forgiven. That means instead of being separated from God (having no real consciousness of His presence or reality), we can have fellowship with Him. Jesus said, "And this is eternal life, that they may know You, the only true God, and Jesus Christ whom You have sent" (John 17:3).

I often say that there's no such thing as an atheist who is an "ex-Christian." This is because there are only two alternatives that the "ex-Christian" can choose. If he knew the Lord, then he is admitting that God exists and he therefore cannot be an atheist. Or if he simply *thought* he knew the Lord but actually didn't, he was therefore a false convert (a hypocrite). Some in this category fall away from the faith, but many stay within the Church as "goats" among the sheep and will be sorted out on Judgment Day. Notice Scripture's wording in reference to that Day:

> "Not everyone who says to Me, 'Lord, Lord,' shall enter the kingdom of heaven, but he who does the will of My Father in heaven. Many will say to Me in that day, 'Lord, Lord, have we not prophesied in Your name, cast out demons in Your name, and done many wonders in Your name?' And then I will declare to them, *'I never knew you*; depart from Me, you who practice lawlessness!'" (Matt. 7:21–24, emphasis added)

False converts don't "know the Lord." He "never knew" them. There was no intimate relationship with them because they were still in their sins (playing the hypocrite).

Now to the essence of your question: What does it mean to know the Lord? Probably the best way to explain it is to say that it is very similar to me knowing my wife. We are best friends. She is forever in my thoughts. When we are not in the same room, our different locations don't change the fact of our relationship. I still know her, love her, and trust her implicitly.

The moment I repented and put my trust in Jesus, I began a relationship with God that is more real than my relationship with my wife. Though it has the same feelings, it is not contingent upon feelings but rather on trust (as are all relationships). While I don't "see" God, I still have a relationship with Him, as with the relationship with my wife even though we are apart. The Bible puts it this way:

> Without having seen Him, you love Him; though you do not [even] now see Him, you believe in Him and exult and thrill with inexpressible and glorious (triumphant, heavenly) joy. [At the same time] you receive the result (outcome, consummation) of your faith, the salvation of your souls (1 Pet. 1:8,9, *Amplified* Bible).

To know the Lord, simply humble yourself, and with a tender conscience look at the Ten Commandments. Have you ever lied, stolen, blasphemed, looked with lust (adultery of the heart), etc.? Honestly judge yourself: are you innocent or guilty? Would you go to heaven or hell? Then look to the cross—God in the person of Jesus Christ took your punishment upon Himself, paying your fine so that you could leave the courtroom. Through His death and resurrection, you can have everlasting life, if you will repent (turn from your sins—something the hypocrite fails to do) and trust the Savior. The minute you do so, you will come to know the Lord (see John 14:21 for details). See also Hos. 2:20 comment.

And make them inherit the throne of
glory.

"For the pillars of the earth *are* the
LORD's,
And He has set the world upon them.
9He will guard the feet of His saints,
But the wicked shall be silent in
darkness.

"For by strength no man shall prevail.
10The adversaries of the LORD shall be
broken in pieces;
From heaven He will thunder against
them.
The LORD will judge the ends of the
earth.

"He will give strength to His king,

And exalt the horn of His anointed."

[11]Then Elkanah went to his house at
Ramah. But the child ministered to the
LORD before Eli the priest.

The Wicked Sons of Eli

[12]Now the sons of Eli *were* corrupt;[a]
they did not know the LORD. [13]And the
priests' custom with the people *was that*
when any man offered a sacrifice, the
priest's servant would come with a three-
pronged fleshhook in his hand while the
meat was boiling. [14]Then he would thrust
it into the pan, or kettle, or caldron, or
pot; and the priest would take for himself
all that the fleshhook brought up. So they
did in Shiloh to all the Israelites who came
there. [15]Also, before they burned the fat,
the priest's servant would come and say
to the man who sacrificed, "Give meat for
roasting to the priest, for he will not take
boiled meat from you, but raw."
[16]And *if* the man said to him, "They
should really burn the fat first; *then* you
may take *as much* as your heart desires,"
he would then answer him, "*No,* but you
must give *it* now; and if not, I will take *it*
by force."
[17]Therefore the sin of the young men
was very great before the LORD, for men
abhorred the offering of the LORD.

Samuel's Childhood Ministry

[18]But Samuel ministered before the
LORD, *even as* a child, wearing a linen
ephod. [19]Moreover his mother used to
make him a little robe, and bring *it* to him
year by year when she came up with her
husband to offer the yearly sacrifice.
[20]And Eli would bless Elkanah and his
wife, and say, "The LORD give you descendants from this woman for the loan
that was given to the LORD." Then they
would go to their own home.
[21]And the LORD visited Hannah, so
that she conceived and bore three sons
and two daughters. Meanwhile the child
Samuel grew before the LORD.

Prophecy Against Eli's Household

[22]Now Eli was very old; and he heard
everything his sons did to all Israel,[a] and
how they lay with the women who assembled at the door of the tabernacle of
meeting. [23]So he said to them, "Why do
you do such things? For I hear of your
evil dealings from all the people. [24]No,
my sons! For *it is* not a good report that I
hear. You make the LORD's people transgress. [25]If one man sins against another,
God will judge him. But if a man sins
against the LORD, who will intercede for
him?" Nevertheless they did not heed the
voice of their father, because the LORD desired to kill them.
[26]And the child Samuel grew in stature, and in favor both with the LORD and
men.
[27]Then a man of God came to Eli and
said to him, "Thus says the LORD: 'Did I
not clearly reveal Myself to the house of
your father when they were in Egypt in
Pharaoh's house? [28]Did I not choose him
out of all the tribes of Israel *to be* My
priest, to offer upon My altar, to burn incense, and to wear an ephod before Me?
And did I not give to the house of your
father all the offerings of the children of
Israel made by fire? [29]Why do you kick at
My sacrifice and My offering which I
have commanded *in My* dwelling place,
and honor your sons more than Me, to
make yourselves fat with the best of all
the offerings of Israel My people?' [30]There-
fore the LORD God of Israel says: 'I said
indeed *that* your house and the house of

2:12 [a]Literally *sons of Belial* 2:22 [a]Following Masoretic Text, Targum, and Vulgate; Dead Sea Scrolls and Septuagint omit the rest of this verse.

2:29 Parents have a responsibility to train their children in the way they should go. Eli knew of his son's sins (vv. 22–24), but by doing nothing to restrain them his inaction dishonored God. In putting his sons before the Lord, he was in violation of the First Commandment. (See also Matt. 10:37.)

your father would walk before Me forever.' But now the LORD says: 'Far be it from Me; for those who honor Me I will honor, and those who despise Me shall be lightly esteemed. [31]Behold, the days are coming that I will cut off your arm and the arm of your father's house, so that there will not be an old man in your house. [32]And you will see an enemy *in My* dwelling place, *despite* all the good which God does for Israel. And there shall not be an old man in your house forever. [33]But any of your men *whom* I do not cut off from My altar shall consume your eyes and grieve your heart. And all the descendants of your house shall die in the flower of their age. [34]Now this *shall be* a sign to you that will come upon your two sons, on Hophni and Phinehas: in one day they shall die, both of them. [35]Then I will raise up for Myself a faithful priest *who* shall do according to what *is* in My heart and in My mind. I will build him a sure house, and he shall walk before My anointed forever. [36]And it shall come to pass that everyone who is left in your house will come *and* bow down to him for a piece of silver and a morsel of bread, and say, "Please, put me in one of the priestly positions, that I may eat a piece of bread." ' "

Samuel's First Prophecy

3 Now the boy Samuel ministered to the LORD before Eli. And the word of the LORD was rare in those days; *there was* no widespread revelation. [2]And it came to pass at that time, while Eli *was* lying down in his place, and when his eyes had begun to grow so dim that he could not see, [3]and before the lamp of God went out in the tabernacle[a] of the LORD where the ark of God *was,* and while Samuel was lying down, [4]that the LORD called Samuel. And he answered, "Here I am!" [5]So he ran to Eli and said, "Here I am, for you called me."

And he said, "I did not call; lie down again." And he went and lay down.

[6]Then the LORD called yet again, "Samuel!"

So Samuel arose and went to Eli, and said, "Here I am, for you called me." He answered, "I did not call, my son; lie down again." [7](Now Samuel did not yet know the LORD, nor was the word of the LORD yet revealed to him.)

[8]And the LORD called Samuel again the third time. So he arose and went to Eli, and said, "Here I am, for you did call me."

Then Eli perceived that the LORD had called the boy. [9]Therefore Eli said to Samuel, "Go, lie down; and it shall be, if He calls you, that you must say, 'Speak, LORD, for Your servant hears.' " So Samuel went and lay down in his place.

[10]Now the LORD came and stood and called as at other times, "Samuel! Samuel!"

And Samuel answered, "Speak, for Your servant hears."

[11]Then the LORD said to Samuel: "Behold, I will do something in Israel at which both ears of everyone who hears it will tingle. [12]In that day I will perform against Eli all that I have spoken concerning his house, from beginning to end. [13]For I have told him that I will judge his house forever for the iniquity which he knows, because his sons made themselves vile, and he did not restrain them. [14]And therefore I have sworn to the house of Eli that the iniquity of Eli's house shall not be atoned for by sacrifice or offering forever."

[15]So Samuel lay down until morning,[a] and opened the doors of the house of the

3:3 [a]Hebrew *heykal,* palace or temple 3:15 [a]Following Masoretic Text, Targum, and Vulgate; Septuagint adds *and he arose in the morning.*

3:1 We are privileged to have the "word of the Lord" in the Scriptures, and have been given a revelation of sinners going to hell. That vision should be ever before us. We have no excuse for inactivity. To the Lord's call for laborers, we should answer, "Here I am!"

LORD. And Samuel was afraid to tell Eli the vision. [16]Then Eli called Samuel and said, "Samuel, my son!"

He answered, "Here I am."

[17]And he said, "What *is* the word that *the* LORD spoke to you? Please do not hide *it* from me. God do so to you, and more also, if you hide anything from me of all the things that He said to you." [18]Then Samuel told him everything, and hid nothing from him. And he said, "It *is* the LORD. Let Him do what seems good to Him."

[19]So Samuel grew, and the LORD was with him and let none of his words fall to the ground. [20]And all Israel from Dan to Beersheba knew that Samuel *had been* established as a prophet of the LORD. [21]Then the LORD appeared again in Shiloh. For the LORD revealed Himself to Samuel in Shiloh by the word of the LORD.

. . . . . .

To learn the damage of gossip, see Prov. 11:13 comment.

. . . . . .

4 And the word of Samuel came to all Israel.[a]

The Ark of God Captured

Now Israel went out to battle against the Philistines, and encamped beside Ebenezer; and the Philistines encamped in Aphek. [2]Then the Philistines put themselves in battle array against Israel. And when they joined battle, Israel was defeated by the Philistines, who killed about four thousand men of the army in the field. [3]And when the people had come into the camp, the elders of Israel said, "Why has the LORD defeated us today before the Philistines? Let us bring the ark of the covenant of the LORD from Shiloh to us, that when it comes among us it may save us from the hand of our enemies." [4]So the people sent to Shiloh, that they might bring from there the ark of the covenant of the LORD of hosts, who dwells *between* the cherubim. And the two sons of Eli, Hophni and Phinehas, *were* there with the ark of the covenant of God.

[5]And when the ark of the covenant of the LORD came into the camp, all Israel shouted so loudly that the earth shook. [6]Now when the Philistines heard the noise of the shout, they said, "What *does* the sound of this great shout in the camp of the Hebrews *mean?*" Then they understood that the ark of the LORD had come into the camp. [7]So the Philistines were afraid, for they said, "God has come into the camp!" And they said, "Woe to us! For such a thing has never happened before. [8]Woe to us! Who will deliver us from the hand of these mighty gods? These *are* the gods who struck the Egyptians with all the plagues in the wilderness. [9]Be strong and conduct yourselves like men, you Philistines, that you do not become servants of the Hebrews, as they have been to you. Conduct yourselves like men, and fight!"

[10]So the Philistines fought, and Israel was defeated, and every man fled to his tent. There was a very great slaughter, and there fell of Israel thirty thousand foot soldiers. [11]Also the ark of God was captured; and the two sons of Eli, Hophni and Phinehas, died.

Death of Eli

[12]Then a man of Benjamin ran from the battle line the same day, and came to Shiloh with his clothes torn and dirt on his head. [13]Now when he came, there was Eli, sitting on a seat by the wayside watching,[a] for his heart trembled for the ark of God. And when the man came into the city and told *it*, all the city cried out. [14]When Eli heard the noise of the outcry, he said, "What *does* the sound of this tumult *mean?*" And the man came quickly and told Eli. [15]Eli was ninety-eight years old, and his eyes were so dim that he

4:1 [a]Following Masoretic Text and Targum; Septuagint and Vulgate add *And it came to pass in those days that the Philistines gathered themselves together to fight;* Septuagint adds further *against Israel.* **4:13** [a]Following Masoretic Text and Vulgate; Septuagint reads *beside the gate watching the road.*

could not see.

16 Then the man said to Eli, "I *am* he who came from the battle. And I fled today from the battle line."

And he said, "What happened, my son?"

17 So the messenger answered and said, "Israel has fled before the Philistines, and there has been a great slaughter among the people. Also your two sons, Hophni and Phinehas, are dead; and the ark of God has been captured."

18 Then it happened, when he made mention of the ark of God, that Eli fell off the seat backward by the side of the gate; and his neck was broken and he died, for the man was old and heavy. And he had judged Israel forty years.

Ichabod

19 Now his daughter-in-law, Phinehas' wife, was with child, *due* to be delivered; and when she heard the news that the ark of God was captured, and that her father-in-law and her husband were dead, she bowed herself and gave birth, for her labor pains came upon her. 20 And about the time of her death the women who stood by her said to her, "Do not fear, for you have borne a son." But she did not answer, nor did she regard *it.* 21 Then she named the child Ichabod,[a] saying, "The glory has departed from Israel!" because the ark of God had been captured and because of her father-in-law and her husband. 22 And she said, "The glory has departed from Israel, for the ark of God has been captured."

The Philistines and the Ark

5 Then the Philistines took the ark of God and brought it from Ebenezer to Ashdod. 2 When the Philistines took the ark of God, they brought it into the house of Dagon[a] and set it by Dagon. 3 And when the people of Ashdod arose early in the morning, there was Dagon, fallen on its face to the earth before the ark of the LORD. So they took Dagon and set it in its place again. 4 And when they arose early the next morning, there was Dagon, fallen on its face to the ground before the ark of the LORD. The head of Dagon and both the palms of its hands *were* broken off on the threshold; only Dagon's *torso*[a] was left of it. 5 Therefore neither the priests of Dagon nor any who come into Dagon's house tread on the threshold of Dagon in Ashdod to this day.

6 But the hand of the LORD was heavy on the people of Ashdod, and He ravaged them and struck them with tumors,[a] *both* Ashdod and its territory. 7 And when the men of Ashdod saw how *it was,* they said, "The ark of the God of Israel must not remain with us, for His hand is harsh toward us and Dagon our god." 8 Therefore they sent and gathered to themselves all the lords of the Philistines, and said, "What shall we do with the ark of the God of Israel?"

And they answered, "Let the ark of the God of Israel be carried away to Gath." So they carried the ark of the God of Israel away. 9 So it was, after they had carried it away, that the hand of the LORD was against the city with a very great destruction; and He struck the men of the city, both small and great, and tumors broke out on them.

10 Therefore they sent the ark of God to Ekron. So it was, as the ark of God came

4:21 [a]Literally *Inglorious* 5:2 [a]A Philistine idol 5:4 [a]Following Septuagint, Syriac, Targum, and Vulgate; Masoretic Text reads *Dagon.* 5:6 [a]Probably bubonic plague. Septuagint and Vulgate add here *And in the midst of their land rats sprang up, and there was a great death panic in the city.*

4:18 We tend to value the ark and forget that it contained the precious tablets of the Law of God. David cried, "Oh, how I love Your law!" (Psa. 119:97). He didn't say how he loved the ark. It was simply the golden container for the perfect, holy, just, and good Law of God.

5:1–4 Man's idols cannot stand before the powerful Law of Almighty God. When the Law is preached, it throws dumb idols into the dirt and destroys their reach of spiritual influence. See 1 Chron. 16:25,26 to see David's attitude toward idolatry.

to Ekron, that the Ekronites cried out, saying, "They have brought the ark of the God of Israel to us, to kill us and our people!" 11So they sent and gathered together all the lords of the Philistines, and said, "Send away the ark of the God of Israel, and let it go back to its own place, so that it does not kill us and our people." For there was a deadly destruction throughout all the city; the hand of God was very heavy there. 12And the men who did not die were stricken with the tumors, and the cry of the city went up to heaven.

The Ark Returned to Israel

6 Now the ark of the LORD was in the country of the Philistines seven months. 2And the Philistines called for the priests and the diviners, saying, "What shall we do with the ark of the LORD? Tell us how we should send it to its place."

3So they said, "If you send away the ark of the God of Israel, do not send it empty; but by all means return *it* to Him *with* a trespass offering. Then you will be healed, and it will be known to you why His hand is not removed from you."

4Then they said, "What *is* the trespass offering which we shall return to Him?"

They answered, "Five golden tumors and five golden rats, *according to* the number of the lords of the Philistines. For the same plague *was* on all of you and on your lords. 5Therefore you shall make images of your tumors and images of your rats that ravage the land, and you shall give glory to the God of Israel; perhaps He will lighten His hand from you, from your gods, and from your land. 6Why then do you harden your hearts as the Egyptians and Pharaoh hardened their hearts? When He did mighty things among them, did they not let the people go, that they might depart? 7Now therefore, make a new cart, take two milk cows which have never been yoked, and hitch the cows to the cart; and take their calves home, away from them. 8Then take the ark of the LORD and set it on the cart; and put the articles of gold which you are returning to Him *as* a trespass offering in a chest by its side. Then send it away, and let it go. 9And watch: if it goes up the road to its own territory, to Beth Shemesh, *then* He has done us this great evil. But if not, then we shall know that *it is* not His hand *that* struck us—it happened to us by chance."

10Then the men did so; they took two milk cows and hitched them to the cart, and shut up their calves at home. 11And they set the ark of the LORD on the cart, and the chest with the gold rats and the images of their tumors. 12Then the cows headed straight for the road to Beth Shemesh, *and* went along the highway, lowing as they went, and did not turn aside to the right hand or the left. And the lords of the Philistines went after them to the border of Beth Shemesh.

> Obedience is the greatest commentary upon the Bible—Do, and thou shalt know.
>
> **THEODDORE MONOD**

13Now *the people of* Beth Shemesh *were* reaping their wheat harvest in the valley; and they lifted their eyes and saw the ark, and rejoiced to see *it*. 14Then the cart came into the field of Joshua of Beth Shemesh, and stood there; a large stone *was* there. So they split the wood of the cart and offered the cows as a burnt offering to the LORD. 15The Levites took down the ark of the LORD and the chest that *was* with it, in which *were* the articles of gold, and put *them* on the large stone. Then the men of Beth Shemesh offered burnt offerings and made sacrifices the same day to the LORD. 16So when the five lords of the Philistines had seen *it*, they returned to Ekron the same day.

17These *are* the golden tumors which the Philistines returned *as* a trespass offering to the LORD: one for Ashdod, one for Gaza, one for Ashkelon, one for Gath, one for Ekron; 18and the golden rats, *according to* the number of all the cities of

the Philistines *belonging* to the five lords, *both* fortified cities and country villages, even as far as the large *stone of* Abel on which they set the ark of the LORD, *which stone remains* to this day in the field of Joshua of Beth Shemesh.

19 Then He struck the men of Beth Shemesh, because they had looked into the ark of the LORD. He struck fifty thousand and seventy men[a] of the people, and the people lamented because the LORD had struck the people with a great slaughter.

The Ark at Kirjath Jearim

20 And the men of Beth Shemesh said, "Who is able to stand before this holy LORD God? And to whom shall it go up from us?" 21 So they sent messengers to the inhabitants of Kirjath Jearim, saying, "The Philistines have brought back the ark of the LORD; come down *and* take it up with you."

7

Then the men of Kirjath Jearim came and took the ark of the LORD, and brought it into the house of Abinadab on the hill, and consecrated Eleazar his son to keep the ark of the LORD.

Samuel Judges Israel

2 So it was that the ark remained in Kirjath Jearim a long time; it was there twenty years. And all the house of Israel lamented after the LORD.

3 Then Samuel spoke to all the house of Israel, saying, "If you return to the LORD with all your hearts, *then* put away the foreign gods and the Ashtoreths[a] from among you, and prepare your hearts for the LORD, and serve Him only; and He will deliver you from the hand of the Philistines." 4 So the children of Israel put away the Baals and the Ashtoreths,[a] and served the LORD only.

5 And Samuel said, "Gather all Israel to Mizpah, and I will pray to the LORD for you." 6 So they gathered together at Mizpah, drew water, and poured *it* out before the LORD. And they fasted that day, and said there, "We have sinned against the LORD." And Samuel judged the children of Israel at Mizpah.

7 Now when the Philistines heard that the children of Israel had gathered together at Mizpah, the lords of the Philistines went up against Israel. And when the children of Israel heard *of it*, they were afraid of the Philistines. 8 So the children of Israel said to Samuel, "Do not cease to cry out to the LORD our God for us, that He may save us from the hand of the Philistines."

9 And Samuel took a suckling lamb and offered *it as* a whole burnt offering to the LORD. Then Samuel cried out to the LORD for Israel, and the LORD answered him. 10 Now as Samuel was offering up the burnt offering, the Philistines drew near to battle against Israel. But the LORD thundered with a loud thunder upon the Philistines that day, and so confused them that they were overcome before Israel. 11 And the men of Israel went out of Mizpah and pursued the Philistines, and drove them back as far as below Beth Car. 12 Then Samuel took a stone and set *it* up between Mizpah and Shen, and called its name Ebenezer,[a] saying, "Thus far the LORD has helped us."

13 So the Philistines were subdued, and

6:19 [a]Or *He struck seventy men of the people and fifty oxen of a man* 7:3 [a]Canaanite goddesses 7:4 [a]Canaanite goddesses 7:12 [a]Literally *Stone of Help*

6:19 The Law executes fearful justice. No one can look upon the Law without having a Savior to blot their sins from its vengeance, and that is the message of the gospel. The Law will be the terrifying and perfect standard of judgment on Judgment Day (see Ezek. 44:24 comment).

7:3 True repentance surrenders all to God. It doesn't keep secret sins. It means that we rid ourselves of all "idols"—not just graven images of foreign gods or statues that are bowed to, but also the idolatry of loving our family, work, or possessions more than we love God. It means forsaking "covetousness, which is idolatry" (Col. 3:5).

they did not come anymore into the territory of Israel. And the hand of the LORD
was against the Philistines all the days of
Samuel. [14]Then the cities which the Philistines had taken from Israel were restored to Israel, from Ekron to Gath; and
Israel recovered its territory from the hands
of the Philistines. Also there was peace
between Israel and the Amorites.

[15]And Samuel judged Israel all the days
of his life. [16]He went from year to year on
a circuit to Bethel, Gilgal, and Mizpah,
and judged Israel in all those places. [17]But
he always returned to Ramah, for his home
was there. There he judged Israel, and
there he built an altar to the LORD.

Israel Demands a King

8 Now it came to pass when Samuel
was old that he made his sons judges
over Israel. [2]The name of his firstborn
was Joel, and the name of his second,
Abijah; *they were* judges in Beersheba.
[3]But his sons did not walk in his ways;
they turned aside after dishonest gain,
took bribes, and perverted justice.

[4]Then all the elders of Israel gathered
together and came to Samuel at Ramah,
[5]and said to him, "Look, you are old, and
your sons do not walk in your ways. Now
make us a king to judge us like all the
nations."

[6]But the thing displeased Samuel when
they said, "Give us a king to judge us." So
Samuel prayed to the LORD. [7]And the
LORD said to Samuel, "Heed the voice of
the people in all that they say to you; for
they have not rejected you, but they have
rejected Me, that I should not reign over
them. [8]According to all the works which
they have done since the day that I brought
them up out of Egypt, even to this day—
with which they have forsaken Me and
served other gods—so they are doing to
you also. [9]Now therefore, heed their voice.
However, you shall solemnly forewarn
them, and show them the behavior of the
king who will reign over them."

[10]So Samuel told all the words of the
LORD to the people who asked him for a
king. [11]And he said, "This will be the behavior of the king who will reign over
you: He will take your sons and appoint
them for his own chariots and *to be* his
horsemen, and *some* will run before his
chariots. [12]He will appoint captains over
his thousands and captains over his
fifties, *will set some* to plow his ground
and reap his harvest, and *some* to make
his weapons of war and equipment for
his chariots. [13]He will take your daughters *to be* perfumers, cooks, and bakers.
[14]And he will take the best of your fields,
your vineyards, and your olive groves,
and give *them* to his servants. [15]He will
take a tenth of your grain and your vintage, and give it to his officers and servants. [16]And he will take your male servants, your female servants, your finest
young men,[a] and your donkeys, and put
them to his work. [17]He will take a tenth of
your sheep. And you will be his servants.
[18]And you will cry out in that day because of your king whom you have chosen for yourselves, and the LORD will not
hear you in that day."

[19]Nevertheless the people refused to
obey the voice of Samuel; and they said,
"No, but we will have a king over us,
[20]that we also may be like all the nations,
and that our king may judge us and go
out before us and fight our battles."

[21]And Samuel heard all the words of
the people, and he repeated them in the
hearing of the LORD. [22]So the LORD said to
Samuel, "Heed their voice, and make them
a king."

And Samuel said to the men of Israel,

8:16 [a]Septuagint reads *cattle.*

8:1–3 This is both strange and tragic—that Samuel's sons followed in the footsteps of Eli's sons (see 1 Sam. 2:17). Never allow your ministry to cause you to neglect your family's spiritual growth. Your faith is worth nothing if you do not provide for your own in the area that is most important. For how to raise godly offspring, see Deut. 11:19 comment. See 1 Tim. 3:4,5 for the priorities of godly leaders.

"Every man go to his city."

Saul Chosen to Be King

9 There was a man of Benjamin whose
name *was* Kish the son of Abiel, the
son of Zeror, the son of Bechorath, the
son of Aphiah, a Benjamite, a mighty
man of power. 2 And he had a choice and
handsome son whose name *was* Saul.
There was not a more handsome person
than he among the children of Israel.
From his shoulders upward *he was* taller
than any of the people.

3 Now the donkeys of Kish, Saul's father, were lost. And Kish said to his son
Saul, "Please take one of the servants with
you, and arise, go and look for the donkeys." 4 So he passed through the mountains of Ephraim and through the land of
Shalisha, but they did not find *them.*
Then they passed through the land of
Shaalim, and *they were* not *there.* Then he
passed through the land of the Benjamites, but they did not find *them.*

5 When they had come to the land of
Zuph, Saul said to his servant who *was*
with him, "Come, let us return, lest my
father cease *caring* about the donkeys and
become worried about us."

6 And he said to him, "Look now, *there
is* in this city a man of God, and *he is* an
honorable man; all that he says surely
comes to pass. So let us go there; perhaps
he can show us the way that we should
go."

7 Then Saul said to his servant, "But
look, *if* we go, what shall we bring the
man? For the bread in our vessels is all
gone, and *there is* no present to bring to
the man of God. What do we have?"

8 And the servant answered Saul again
and said, "Look, I have here at hand one-
fourth of a shekel of silver. I will give *that*
to the man of God, to tell us our way."
9 (Formerly in Israel, when a man went to
inquire of God, he spoke thus: "Come, let
us go to the seer"; for *he who is* now *called*
a prophet was formerly called a seer.)

10 Then Saul said to his servant, "Well
said; come, let us go." So they went to the
city where the man of God *was.*

11 As they went up the hill to the city,
they met some young women going out
to draw water, and said to them, "Is the
seer here?"

12 And they answered them and said,
"Yes, there he is, just ahead of you. Hurry
now; for today he came to this city, because there is a sacrifice of the people today on the high place. 13 As soon as you
come into the city, you will surely find
him before he goes up to the high place
to eat. For the people will not eat until he
comes, because he must bless the sacrifice; afterward those who are invited will
eat. Now therefore, go up, for about this
time you will find him." 14 So they went
up to the city. As they were coming into
the city, there was Samuel, coming out
toward them on his way up to the high
place.

15 Now the LORD had told Samuel in
his ear the day before Saul came, saying,
16 "Tomorrow about this time I will send
you a man from the land of Benjamin,
and you shall anoint him commander
over My people Israel, that he may save
My people from the hand of the Philistines; for I have looked upon My people, because their cry has come to Me."

17 So when Samuel saw Saul, the LORD
said to him, "There he is, the man of whom
I spoke to you. This one shall reign over
My people." 18 Then Saul drew near to
Samuel in the gate, and said, "Please tell
me, where *is* the seer's house?"

9:6 Can God say that about us? Can He have sinners cross our paths knowing that we will speak the truth and show them the way to the Savior?

"Every man is a missionary, now and forever, for good or for evil, whether he intends or designs it or not. He may be a blot radiating his dark influence outward to the very circumference of society, or he may be a blessing spreading benediction over the length and breadth of the world. But a blank he cannot be: there are no moral blanks; there are no neutral characters." *Thomas Chalmers*

19Samuel answered Saul and said, "I
am the seer. Go up before me to the high
place, for you shall eat with me today;
and tomorrow I will let you go and will
tell you all that *is* in your heart. 20But as
for your donkeys that were lost three
days ago, do not be anxious about them,
for they have been found. And on whom
is all the desire of Israel? *Is it* not on you
and on all your father's house?"
21And Saul answered and said, "*Am* I
not a Benjamite, of the smallest of the
tribes of Israel, and my family the least of
all the families of the tribe[a] of Benjamin?
Why then do you speak like this to me?"
22Now Samuel took Saul and his servant and brought them into the hall, and
had them sit in the place of honor among
those who were invited; there *were* about
thirty persons. 23And Samuel said to the
cook, "Bring the portion which I gave
you, of which I said to you, 'Set it apart.' "
24So the cook took up the thigh with its
upper part and set *it* before Saul. And
Samuel said, "Here it is, what was kept
back. *It* was set apart for you. Eat; for until this time it has been kept for you,
since I said I invited the people." So Saul
ate with Samuel that day.
25When they had come down from the
high place into the city, *Samuel* spoke
with Saul on the top of the house.[a] 26They
arose early; and it was about the dawning
of the day that Samuel called to Saul on
the top of the house, saying, "Get up, that
I may send you on your way." And Saul
arose, and both of them went outside, he
and Samuel.

Saul Anointed King

27As they were going down to the outskirts of the city, Samuel said to Saul, "Tell
the servant to go on ahead of us." And he
went on. "But you stand here awhile, that
I may announce to you the word of God."

10 Then Samuel took a flask of oil and
poured *it* on his head, and kissed
him and said: "*Is it* not because the LORD
has anointed you commander over His
inheritance?[a] 2When you have departed
from me today, you will find two men by
Rachel's tomb in the territory of Benjamin
at Zelzah; and they will say to you, 'The
donkeys which you went to look for have
been found. And now your father has
ceased caring about the donkeys and is
worrying about you, saying, "What shall
I do about my son?" ' 3Then you shall go
on forward from there and come to the
terebinth tree of Tabor. There three men
going up to God at Bethel will meet you,
one carrying three young goats, another
carrying three loaves of bread, and another carrying a skin of wine. 4And they
will greet you and give you two *loaves* of
bread, which you shall receive from their
hands. 5After that you shall come to the
hill of God where the Philistine garrison
is. And it will happen, when you have
come there to the city, that you will meet
a group of prophets coming down from
the high place with a stringed instrument, a tambourine, a flute, and a harp
before them; and they will be prophesying. 6Then the Spirit of the LORD will
come upon you, and you will prophesy
with them and be turned into another man.
7And let it be, when these signs come to
you, *that* you do as the occasion demands;
for God *is* with you. 8You shall go down
before me to Gilgal; and surely I will come
down to you to offer burnt offerings *and*
make sacrifices of peace offerings. Seven

9:21 [a]Literally *tribes* 9:25 [a]Following Masoretic Text and Targum; Septuagint omits *He spoke with Saul on the top of the house;* Septuagint and Vulgate add *And he prepared a bed for Saul on the top of the house, and he slept.* 10:1 [a]Following Masoretic Text, Targum, and Vulgate; Septuagint reads *His people Israel; and you shall rule the people of the Lord;* Septuagint and Vulgate add *And you shall deliver His people from the hands of their enemies all around them. And this shall be a sign to you, that God has anointed you to be a prince.*

10:6 This is what we can assure every sinner. If he will repent and trust Jesus Christ for his eternal salvation, he will become a completely different person (see 2 Cor. 5:17). God will give him a new heart (v. 9) and a new spirit. See also Ezek. 11:19 comment.

days you shall wait, till I come to you and
show you what you should do."
[9]So it was, when he had turned his
back to go from Samuel, that God gave
him another heart; and all those signs
came to pass that day. [10]When they came
there to the hill, there was a group of
prophets to meet him; then the Spirit of
God came upon him, and he prophesied
among them. [11]And it happened, when
all who knew him formerly saw that he
indeed prophesied among the prophets,
that the people said to one another,
"What *is* this *that* has come upon the son
of Kish? *Is* Saul also among the prophets?" [12]Then a man from there answered
and said, "But who *is* their father?" Therefore it became a proverb: "*Is* Saul also
among the prophets?" [13]And when he had
finished prophesying, he went to the high
place.
[14]Then Saul's uncle said to him and his
servant, "Where did you go?"

So he said, "To look for the donkeys. When we saw that *they were* nowhere *to be found,* we went to Samuel."

[15]And Saul's uncle said, "Tell me, please,
what Samuel said to you."
[16]So Saul said to his uncle, "He told us
plainly that the donkeys had been found."
But about the matter of the kingdom, he
did not tell him what Samuel had said.

Saul Proclaimed King

[17]Then Samuel called the people together to the LORD at Mizpah, [18]and said
to the children of Israel, "Thus says the
LORD God of Israel: 'I brought up Israel
out of Egypt, and delivered you from the
hand of the Egyptians *and* from the hand
of all kingdoms and from those who oppressed you.' [19]But you have today rejected your God, who Himself saved you
from all your adversities and your tribulations; and you have said to Him, 'No,
set a king over us!' Now therefore, present yourselves before the LORD by your
tribes and by your clans."[a]
[20]And when Samuel had caused all the
tribes of Israel to come near, the tribe of

"I would rather win souls than be the greatest king or emperor on earth; I would rather win souls than be the greatest general that ever commanded an army... My one ambition in life is to win as many as possible. Oh, it is the only thing worth doing; to save souls, and, men and women, we can all do it."

R. A. Torrey

Benjamin was chosen. [21]When he had
caused the tribe of Benjamin to come
near by their families, the family of Matri
was chosen. And Saul the son of Kish was
chosen. But when they sought him, he
could not be found. [22]Therefore they inquired of the LORD further, "Has the man
come here yet?"

And the LORD answered, "There he is, hidden among the equipment."

[23]So they ran and brought him from
there; and when he stood among the people, he was taller than any of the people
from his shoulders upward. [24]And Samuel
said to all the people, "Do you see him
whom the LORD has chosen, that *there is*
no one like him among all the people?"

So all the people shouted and said, "Long live the king!"

[25]Then Samuel explained to the people the behavior of royalty, and wrote *it* in
a book and laid *it* up before the LORD.
And Samuel sent all the people away,

10:19 [a]Literally *thousands*

every man to his house. 26And Saul also went home to Gibeah; and valiant *men* went with him, whose hearts God had touched. 27But some rebels said, "How can this man save us?" So they despised him, and brought him no presents. But he held his peace.

Saul Saves Jabesh Gilead

11 Then Nahash the Ammonite came up and encamped against Jabesh Gilead; and all the men of Jabesh said to Nahash, "Make a covenant with us, and we will serve you."

2And Nahash the Ammonite answered them, "On this *condition* I will make *a covenant* with you, that I may put out all your right eyes, and bring reproach on all Israel."

3Then the elders of Jabesh said to him, "Hold off for seven days, that we may send messengers to all the territory of Israel. And then, if *there is* no one to save us, we will come out to you."

4So the messengers came to Gibeah of Saul and told the news in the hearing of the people. And all the people lifted up their voices and wept. 5Now there was Saul, coming behind the herd from the field; and Saul said, "What *troubles* the people, that they weep?" And they told him the words of the men of Jabesh. 6Then the Spirit of God came upon Saul when he heard this news, and his anger was greatly aroused. 7So he took a yoke of oxen and cut them in pieces, and sent *them* throughout all the territory of Israel by the hands of messengers, saying, "Whoever does not go out with Saul and Samuel to battle, so it shall be done to his oxen."

And the fear of the LORD fell on the people, and they came out with one consent. 8When he numbered them in Bezek, the children of Israel were three hundred thousand, and the men of Judah thirty thousand. 9And they said to the messengers who came, "Thus you shall say to the men of Jabesh Gilead: 'Tomorrow, by *the time* the sun is hot, you shall have help.'" Then the messengers came and reported *it* to the men of Jabesh, and they were glad. 10Therefore the men of Jabesh said, "Tomorrow we will come out to you, and you may do with us whatever seems good to you."

11So it was, on the next day, that Saul put the people in three companies; and they came into the midst of the camp in the morning watch, and killed Ammonites until the heat of the day. And it happened that those who survived were scattered, so that no two of them were left together.

12Then the people said to Samuel, "Who *is* he who said, 'Shall Saul reign over us?' Bring the men, that we may put them to death."

13But Saul said, "Not a man shall be put to death this day, for today the LORD has accomplished salvation in Israel."

14Then Samuel said to the people, "Come, let us go to Gilgal and renew the kingdom there." 15So all the people went to Gilgal, and there they made Saul king before the LORD in Gilgal. There they made sacrifices of peace offerings before the LORD, and there Saul and all the men of Israel rejoiced greatly.

Samuel's Address at Saul's Coronation

12 Now Samuel said to all Israel: "Indeed I have heeded your voice in all that you said to me, and have made a king over you. 2And now here is the king, walking before you; and I am old and grayheaded, and look, my sons *are* with you. I have walked before you from my childhood to this day. 3Here I am. Witness against me before the LORD and before His anointed: Whose ox have I taken, or whose donkey have I taken, or whom have I cheated? Whom have I oppressed,

11:2 The enemy wanted to destroy their ability to fight. It was because they covered their left side with a shield that their right eye was essential for fighting.

or from whose hand have I received *any* bribe with which to blind my eyes? I will restore *it* to you."

[4]And they said, "You have not cheated us or oppressed us, nor have you taken anything from any man's hand."

[5]Then he said to them, "The LORD *is* witness against you, and His anointed *is* witness this day, that you have not found anything in my hand."

And they answered, "*He is* witness."

[6]Then Samuel said to the people, "*It is* the LORD who raised up Moses and Aaron, and who brought your fathers up from the land of Egypt. [7]Now therefore, stand still, that I may reason with you before the LORD concerning all the righteous acts of the LORD which He did to you and your fathers: [8]When Jacob had gone into Egypt,[a] and your fathers cried out to the LORD, then the LORD sent Moses and Aaron, who brought your fathers out of Egypt and made them dwell in this place. [9]And when they forgot the LORD their God, He sold them into the hand of Sisera, commander of the army of Hazor, into the hand of the Philistines, and into the hand of the king of Moab; and they fought against them. [10]Then they cried out to the LORD, and said, 'We have sinned, because we have forsaken the LORD and served the Baals and Ashtoreths;[a] but now deliver us from the hand of our enemies, and we will serve You.' [11]And the LORD sent Jerubbaal,[a] Bedan,[b] Jephthah, and Samuel,[c] and delivered you out of the hand of your enemies on every side; and you dwelt in safety. [12]And when you saw that Nahash king of the Ammonites came against you, you said to me, 'No, but a king shall reign over us,' when the LORD your God *was* your king.

[13]"Now therefore, here is the king whom you have chosen *and* whom you have desired. And take note, the LORD has set a king over you. [14]If you fear the LORD and serve Him and obey His voice, and do not rebel against the commandment of the LORD, then both you and the king who reigns over you will continue following the LORD your God. [15]However, if you do not obey the voice of the LORD, but rebel against the commandment of the LORD, then the hand of the LORD will be against you, as *it was* against your fathers.

[16]"Now therefore, stand and see this great thing which the LORD will do before your eyes: [17]*Is* today not the wheat harvest? I will call to the LORD, and He will send thunder and rain, that you may perceive and see that your wickedness *is* great, which you have done in the sight of the LORD, in asking a king for yourselves."

[18]So Samuel called to the LORD, and the LORD sent thunder and rain that day; and all the people greatly feared the LORD and Samuel.

[19]And all the people said to Samuel, "Pray for your servants to the LORD your God, that we may not die; for we have added to all our sins the evil of asking a king for ourselves."

[20]Then Samuel said to the people, "Do not fear. You have done all this wickedness; yet do not turn aside from following the LORD, but serve the LORD with all your heart. [21]And do not turn aside; for *then you would go* after empty things which cannot profit or deliver, for they *are* nothing. [22]For the LORD will not forsake His people, for His great name's sake, because it has pleased the LORD to make you His people. [23]Moreover, as for me, far be it from me that I should sin against the LORD in ceasing to pray for you; but I will teach you the good and the right way. [24]Only fear the LORD, and serve Him in truth with all your heart; for consider what great things He has done for you. [25]But if you still do wickedly, you shall be swept away, both you and your king."

Saul's Unlawful Sacrifice

13 Saul reigned one year; and when he had reigned two years over Is-

12:8 [a]Following Masoretic Text, Targum, and Vulgate; Septuagint adds *and the Egyptians afflicted them.* 12:10 [a]Canaanite goddesses 12:11 [a]Syriac reads *Deborah;* Targum reads *Gideon.* [b]Septuagint and Syriac read *Barak;* Targum reads *Simson.* [c]Syriac reads *Simson.*

rael,[a] [2]Saul chose for himself three thousand *men* of Israel. Two thousand were with Saul in Michmash and in the mountains of Bethel, and a thousand were with Jonathan in Gibeah of Benjamin. The rest of the people he sent away, every man to his tent.

[3]And Jonathan attacked the garrison of the Philistines that *was* in Geba, and the Philistines heard *of it.* Then Saul blew the trumpet throughout all the land, saying, "Let the Hebrews hear!" [4]Now all Israel heard it said *that* Saul had attacked a garrison of the Philistines, and *that* Israel had also become an abomination to the Philistines. And the people were called together to Saul at Gilgal.

[5]Then the Philistines gathered together to fight with Israel, thirty[a] thousand chariots and six thousand horsemen, and people as the sand which is on the seashore in multitude. And they came up and encamped in Michmash, to the east of Beth Aven. [6]When the men of Israel saw that they were in danger (for the people were distressed), then the people hid in caves, in thickets, in rocks, in holes, and in pits. [7]And *some of* the Hebrews crossed over the Jordan to the land of Gad and Gilead.

As for Saul, he *was* still in Gilgal, and all the people followed him trembling. [8]Then he waited seven days, according to the time set by Samuel. But Samuel did not come to Gilgal; and the people were scattered from him. [9]So Saul said, "Bring a burnt offering and peace offerings here to me." And he offered the burnt offering. [10]Now it happened, as soon as he had finished presenting the burnt offering, that Samuel came; and Saul went out to meet him, that he might greet him.

[11]And Samuel said, "What have you done?"

Saul said, "When I saw that the people were scattered from me, and *that* you did not come within the days appointed, and *that* the Philistines gathered together at Michmash, [12]then I said, 'The Philistines will now come down on me at Gilgal, and I have not made supplication to the LORD.' Therefore I felt compelled, and offered a burnt offering."

[13]And Samuel said to Saul, "You have done foolishly. You have not kept the commandment of the LORD your God, which He commanded you. For now the LORD would have established your kingdom over Israel forever. [14]But now your kingdom shall not continue. The LORD has sought for Himself a man after His own heart, and the LORD has commanded him *to be* commander over His people, because you have not kept what the LORD commanded you."

[15]Then Samuel arose and went up from Gilgal to Gibeah of Benjamin.[a] And Saul numbered the people present with him, about six hundred men.

No Weapons for the Army

[16]Saul, Jonathan his son, and the peo-

13:1 [a]The Hebrew is difficult (compare 2 Samuel 5:4; 2 Kings 14:2; see also 2 Samuel 2:10; Acts 13:21). 13:5 [a]Following Masoretic Text, Septuagint, Targum, and Vulgate; Syriac and some manuscripts of the Septuagint read *three.* 13:15 [a]Following Masoretic Text and Targum; Septuagint and Vulgate add *And the rest of the people went up after Saul to meet the people who fought against them, going from Gilgal to Gibeah in the hill of Benjamin.*

12:23,24 Make it a habit to pray without ceasing—to commit all things to God. Pray for the lost, for wisdom, for direction, compassion, understanding, etc., always considering what an unspeakably great thing He did for us at the cross.

"I commend intercessory prayer, because it opens man's soul, gives a healthy play to his sympathies, constrains him to feel that he is not everybody, and that this wide world and this great universe were not after all made that he might be its petty lord, that everything might bend to his will, and all creatures crouch at his feet." *Charles Spurgeon*

13:12 It is a true test of conversion when the professing Christian has the choice of feeling "compelled" to do something that is in direct contradiction to God's Word. Are we willing to compromise the truth based on our circumstances? See Psa. 15 for the mindset and the reward of the godly.

ple present with them remained in Gibeah of Benjamin. But the Philistines encamped in Michmash. [17]Then raiders came out of the camp of the Philistines in three companies. One company turned onto the road to Ophrah, to the land of Shual, [18]another company turned to the road *to* Beth Horon, and another company turned *to* the road of the border that overlooks the Valley of Zeboim toward the wilderness.

[19]Now there was no blacksmith to be found throughout all the land of Israel, for the Philistines said, "Lest the Hebrews make swords or spears." [20]But all the Israelites would go down to the Philistines to sharpen each man's plowshare, his mattock, his ax, and his sickle; [21]and the charge for a sharpening was a pim[a] for the plowshares, the mattocks, the forks, and the axes, and to set the points of the goads. [22]So it came about, on the day of battle, that there was neither sword nor spear found in the hand of any of the people who *were* with Saul and Jonathan. But they were found with Saul and Jonathan his son.

[23]And the garrison of the Philistines went out to the pass of Michmash.

Jonathan Defeats the Philistines

14 Now it happened one day that Jonathan the son of Saul said to the young man who bore his armor, "Come, let us go over to the Philistines' garrison that is on the other side." But he did not tell his father. [2]And Saul was sitting in the outskirts of Gibeah under a pomegranate tree which is in Migron. The people who *were* with him *were* about six hundred men. [3]Ahijah the son of Ahitub, Ichabod's brother, the son of Phinehas, the son of Eli, the LORD's priest in Shiloh, was wearing an ephod. But the people did not know that Jonathan had gone.

[4]Between the passes, by which Jonathan sought to go over to the Philistines' garrison, *there was* a sharp rock on one side and a sharp rock on the other side. And the name of one *was* Bozez, and the name of the other Seneh. [5]The front of one faced northward opposite Michmash, and the other southward opposite Gibeah.

[6]Then Jonathan said to the young man who bore his armor, "Come, let us go over to the garrison of these uncircumcised; it may be that the LORD will work for us. For nothing restrains the LORD from saving by many or by few."

[7]So his armorbearer said to him, "Do all that is in your heart. Go then; here I am with you, according to your heart."

[8]Then Jonathan said, "Very well, let us cross over to *these* men, and we will show ourselves to them. [9]If they say thus to us, 'Wait until we come to you,' then we will stand still in our place and not go up to them. [10]But if they say thus, 'Come up to us,' then we will go up. For the LORD has delivered them into our hand, and this *will be* a sign to us."

[11]So both of them showed themselves to the garrison of the Philistines. And the Philistines said, "Look, the Hebrews are coming out of the holes where they have hidden." [12]Then the men of the garrison called to Jonathan and his armorbearer, and said, "Come up to us, and we will show you something."

Jonathan said to his armorbearer, "Come up after me, for the LORD has delivered them into the hand of Israel." [13]And Jonathan climbed up on his hands and knees with his armorbearer after him; and they fell before Jonathan. And as he came after him, his armorbearer killed them. [14]That first slaughter which Jonathan and his armorbearer made was

13:21 [a]About two-thirds shekel weight

13:19–22 The evangelist has been given to the Church to equip it for ministry (see Eph. 4:11,12). Sadly, this is a ministry that the enemy has almost done away with. So many money-hungry "evangelists" have fleeced the flock that the local shepherd is now hesitant to trust them with his sheep. However, the true evangelist is a blacksmith who sharpens the weapons of the soldier of Christ.

about twenty men within about half an acre of land.[a]

[15]And there was trembling in the camp, in the field, and among all the people. The garrison and the raiders also trembled; and the earth quaked, so that it was a very great trembling. [16]Now the watchmen of Saul in Gibeah of Benjamin looked, and *there* was the multitude, melting away; and they went here and there. [17]Then Saul said to the people who *were* with him, "Now call the roll and see who has gone from us." And when they had called the roll, surprisingly, Jonathan and his armorbearer *were* not *there.* [18]And Saul said to Ahijah, "Bring the ark[a] of God here" (for at that time the ark[b] of God was with the children of Israel). [19]Now it happened, while Saul talked to the priest, that the noise which *was* in the camp of the Philistines continued to increase; so Saul said to the priest, "Withdraw your hand." [20]Then Saul and all the people who *were* with him assembled, and they went to the battle; and indeed every man's sword was against his neighbor, *and there was* very great confusion. [21]Moreover the Hebrews *who* were with the Philistines before that time, who went up with them into the camp *from the* surrounding *country,* they also joined the Israelites who *were* with Saul and Jonathan. [22]Likewise all the men of Israel who had hidden in the mountains of Ephraim, *when* they heard that the Philistines fled, they also followed hard after them in the battle. [23]So the LORD saved Israel that day, and the battle shifted to Beth Aven.

Saul's Rash Oath

[24]And the men of Israel were distressed that day, for Saul had placed the people under oath, saying, "Cursed *is* the man who eats *any* food until evening, before I have taken vengeance on my enemies." So none of the people tasted food. [25]Now all *the people* of the land came to a forest; and there was honey on the ground. [26]And when the people had come into the woods, there was the honey, dripping; but no one put his hand to his mouth, for the people feared the oath. [27]But Jonathan had not heard his father charge the people with the oath; therefore he stretched out the end of the rod that *was* in his hand and dipped it in a honeycomb, and put his hand to his mouth; and his countenance brightened. [28]Then one of the people said, "Your father strictly charged the people with an oath, saying, 'Cursed *is* the man who eats food this day.' " And the people were faint.

[29]But Jonathan said, "My father has troubled the land. Look now, how my countenance has brightened because I tasted a little of this honey. [30]How much better if the people had eaten freely today of the spoil of their enemies which they found! For now would there not have been a much greater slaughter among the Philistines?"

[31]Now they had driven back the Philistines that day from Michmash to Aijalon. So the people were very faint. [32]And the people rushed on the spoil, and took sheep, oxen, and calves, and slaughtered *them* on the ground; and the people ate *them* with the blood. [33]Then they told Saul, saying, "Look, the people are sinning against the LORD by eating with the blood!"

So he said, "You have dealt treacherously; roll a large stone to me this day." [34]Then Saul said, "Disperse yourselves among the people, and say to them, 'Bring me here every man's ox and every man's sheep, slaughter *them* here, and eat; and do not sin against the LORD by eating with the blood.' " So every one of the people

14:14 [a]Literally *half the area plowed by a yoke* (of oxen in a day) **14:18** [a]Following Masoretic Text, Targum, and Vulgate; Septuagint reads *ephod.* [b]Following Masoretic Text, Targum, and Vulgate; Septuagint reads *ephod.*

14:27 The rod of the Law dips into the sweet honey of the gospel and enlightens the eyes. "The commandment of the LORD is pure, enlightening the eyes" (Psa. 19:8). See Eph. 1:18 for the result of enlightened eyes.

brought his ox with him that night, and
slaughtered *it* there. 35Then Saul built an
altar to the LORD. This was the first altar
that he built to the LORD.
36Now Saul said, "Let us go down after the Philistines by night, and plunder
them until the morning light; and let us
not leave a man of them."
And they said, "Do whatever seems
good to you."
Then the priest said, "Let us draw near
to God here."
37So Saul asked counsel of God, "Shall
I go down after the Philistines? Will You
deliver them into the hand of Israel?" But
He did not answer him that day. 38And
Saul said, "Come over here, all you chiefs
of the people, and know and see what
this sin was today. 39For *as* the LORD lives,
who saves Israel, though it be in Jonathan
my son, he shall surely die." But not a
man among all the people answered him.
40Then he said to all Israel, "You be on
one side, and my son Jonathan and I will
be on the other side."
And the people said to Saul, "Do what
seems good to you."
41Therefore Saul said to the LORD God
of Israel, "Give a perfect *lot*."[a] So Saul and
Jonathan were taken, but the people escaped. 42And Saul said, "Cast *lots* between
my son Jonathan and me." So Jonathan
was taken. 43Then Saul said to Jonathan,
"Tell me what you have done."
And Jonathan told him, and said, "I
only tasted a little honey with the end of
the rod that *was* in my hand. So now I
must die!"
44Saul answered, "God do so and more
also; for you shall surely die, Jonathan."
45But the people said to Saul, "Shall
Jonathan die, who has accomplished this
great deliverance in Israel? Certainly not!
As the LORD lives, not one hair of his head
shall fall to the ground, for he has
worked with God this day." So the people
rescued Jonathan, and he did not die.
46Then Saul returned from pursuing
the Philistines, and the Philistines went
to their own place.

Saul's Continuing Wars

47So Saul established his sovereignty
over Israel, and fought against all his enemies on every side, against Moab, against
the people of Ammon, against Edom,
against the kings of Zobah, and against
the Philistines. Wherever he turned, he
harassed *them*.[a] 48And he gathered an army
and attacked the Amalekites, and delivered Israel from the hands of those who
plundered them.
49The sons of Saul were Jonathan,
Jishui,[a] and Malchishua. And the names
of his two daughters *were these*: the name
of the firstborn Merab, and the name of
the younger Michal. 50The name of Saul's
wife *was* Ahinoam the daughter of Ahimaaz. And the name of the commander
of his army *was* Abner the son of Ner,
Saul's uncle. 51Kish *was* the father of Saul,
and Ner the father of Abner *was* the son
of Abiel.
52Now there was fierce war with the
Philistines all the days of Saul. And when
Saul saw any strong man or any valiant
man, he took him for himself.

Saul Spares King Agag

15 Samuel also said to Saul, "The
LORD sent me to anoint you king
over His people, over Israel. Now therefore, heed the voice of the words of the
LORD. 2Thus says the LORD of hosts: 'I will
punish Amalek *for* what he did to Israel,
how he ambushed him on the way when
he came up from Egypt. 3Now go and attack Amalek, and utterly destroy all that
they have, and do not spare them. But
kill both man and woman, infant and
nursing child, ox and sheep, camel and
donkey.'"
4So Saul gathered the people together
and numbered them in Telaim, two hundred thousand foot soldiers and ten thousand men of Judah. 5And Saul came to a

14:41 [a]Following Masoretic Text and Targum; Septuagint and Vulgate read *Why do You not answer Your servant today? If the injustice is with me or Jonathan my son, O LORD God of Israel, give proof; and if You say it is with Your people Israel, give holiness.* **14:47** [a]Septuagint and Vulgate read *prospered*. **14:49** [a]Called *Abinadab* in 1 Chronicles 8:33 and 9:39

QUESTIONS & OBJECTIONS

15:3

"Why did God order the killing of an entire people group? That's genocide."

By Mark Spence

The reason we can so quickly fault God for wiping out multitudes of people is that we have a subjective definition of what is "good."

For example, we define "good" perhaps as helping some old lady across the street. Someone watching us do such a task is impressed with our servanthood and gives us kudos. However, we don't see the big picture. If we knew that sweet old lady whom we just helped was crossing that street to slip cyanide in everyone's cups at the corner coffee shop, we hopefully would not have helped her carry out the task.

Or we may think it is a good task to give money to someone on the street. While that may seem noble, what if you discovered that the person was going to use it to purchase drugs? It would not be such a good thing after all, would it?

Or we may think it is good to give a stranger a ride to the grocery store. While that act may seem noble, what if you discovered that the person was going there to rob the place? Would you still think it is a good thing to do?

Therefore, who among you is able to define "good"? What gives you the right to say whether what God does is right or wrong? If goodness is subjective, then there is no right or wrong. Rather, you could only say that what God did is not your preference. However, even then, how can you make that statement since you are not omniscient to know whether destroying a certain people group was the correct action based on all the information?

Therefore, God alone has the right to define what is good. With God seeing the whole picture, He never makes a mistake. There is no hindsight with God. Everything God does is motivated by His nature: His goodness, His justice, His holiness. And that is why God can kill an individual or a group of people, like the Amalekites, and it can be a good thing. In fact, it can be considered the best thing.

Rather than standing in judgment over God, when we have all the information, we discover that God is justified in killing not only the Amalekites, but all of us. We all are sentenced to die because we have broken His holy Law a multitude of times. But God, in His love, paid the penalty for our sin so we wouldn't have to die. See also Num. 33:51–55 comment.

city of Amalek, and lay in wait in the valley.
[6]Then Saul said to the Kenites, "Go,
depart, get down from among the Amalekites, lest I destroy you with them. For
you showed kindness to all the children
of Israel when they came up out of Egypt."
So the Kenites departed from among the
Amalekites. [7]And Saul attacked the Amalekites, from Havilah all the way to Shur,
which is east of Egypt. [8]He also took
Agag king of the Amalekites alive, and utterly destroyed all the people with the
edge of the sword. [9]But Saul and the people spared Agag and the best of the sheep,
the oxen, the fatlings, the lambs, and all
that was good, and were unwilling to utterly destroy them. But everything despised and worthless, that they utterly
destroyed.

Saul Rejected as King

[10]Now the word of the LORD came to
Samuel, saying, [11]"I greatly regret that I
have set up Saul *as* king, for he has
turned back from following Me, and has
not performed My commandments." And
it grieved Samuel, and he cried out to the
LORD all night. [12]So when Samuel rose
early in the morning to meet Saul, it was
told Samuel, saying, "Saul went to Carmel,
and indeed, he set up a monument for
himself; and he has gone on around,

15:11 Scripture may give the impression that some things take God by surprise, that He isn't omniscient. However, we are told that *nothing* is hidden from His eyes. All things lie naked and open before Him (see Heb. 4:13). Words that give such an impression simply tell us of God's emotions rather than His ignorance. See also Psa. 135:14 comment.

passed by, and gone down to Gilgal." 13Then Samuel went to Saul, and Saul said to him, "Blessed *are* you of the LORD! I have performed the commandment of the LORD."

14But Samuel said, "What then *is* this bleating of the sheep in my ears, and the lowing of the oxen which I hear?"

15And Saul said, "They have brought them from the Amalekites; for the people spared the best of the sheep and the oxen, to sacrifice to the LORD your God; and the rest we have utterly destroyed."

16Then Samuel said to Saul, "Be quiet! And I will tell you what the LORD said to me last night."

And he said to him, "Speak on."

17So Samuel said, "When you *were* little in your own eyes, *were* you not head of the tribes of Israel? And did not the LORD anoint you king over Israel? 18Now the LORD sent you on a mission, and said, 'Go, and utterly destroy the sinners, the Amalekites, and fight against them until they are consumed.' 19Why then did you not obey the voice of the LORD? Why did you swoop down on the spoil, and do evil in the sight of the LORD?"

20And Saul said to Samuel, "But I have obeyed the voice of the LORD, and gone on the mission on which the LORD sent me, and brought back Agag king of Amalek; I have utterly destroyed the Amalekites. 21But the people took of the plunder, sheep and oxen, the best of the things which should have been utterly destroyed, to sacrifice to the LORD your God in Gilgal."

22So Samuel said:

"Has the LORD *as great* delight in burnt
offerings and sacrifices,
As in obeying the voice of the LORD?
Behold, to obey is better than
sacrifice,
And to heed than the fat of rams.
23For rebellion *is as* the sin of witchcraft,
And stubbornness *is as* iniquity and
idolatry.
Because you have rejected the word of
the LORD,
He also has rejected you from *being*
king."

24Then Saul said to Samuel, "I have sinned, for I have transgressed the commandment of the LORD and your words, because I feared the people and obeyed their voice. 25Now therefore, please pardon my sin, and return with me, that I may worship the LORD."

26But Samuel said to Saul, "I will not return with you, for you have rejected the word of the LORD, and the LORD has re-

15:15 True repentance never tries to justify itself. The mouth of the true penitent is stopped (see Rom. 3:19). Here Saul reveals his sinful heart by blaming others for his own sins. He was truly the offspring of Adam, who blamed God and Eve, rather than himself for his transgression. Listen closely to the mouth of sinners as you use the Law to bring the knowledge of sin. If you ask, "How many lies have you told in your life?" you will hear, "Everyone lies," or, "They are only little white lies." Sinners, like Saul, want to spread the blame to others or trivialize their transgressions. Saul says that "*we*... destroyed," but then he blames "the people" for what "they" did wrong. The root cause of his problem is revealed when he refers to "*your* God"—not his own. Idolatry, having our own concept of the nature of God, is at the root of most sins. See 1 Cor. 10:1–14 for an example.

15:22 Obedience is better than sacrifice. Multitudes will end up damned because they misunderstand this crucial point. Like Saul, they do what they think is right, rather than what God requires. They observe religious ordinances, fasting, prayers, good works, etc., thinking that these commend them to God and earn them everlasting life. How could God not be pleased with such sacrifice? Without the revealing light of God's Law, religious works seem to be a legitimate way to please God. However, when the Law enters, it shows that the sinner is a "criminal" in God's eyes, guilty of a multitude of heinous crimes before a holy Judge. The religious "works" that he offers are not acceptable in the slightest, but are seen for what they are—despicable attempts to bribe the Judge of the universe. Good works, prayers, fasting, etc., issue from a *justified* sinner—one whose case has been dismissed by the Judge, and therefore they become acceptable in the sight of God. See Hos. 6:6; Isa. 1:11–17.

jected you from being king over Israel."

27And as Samuel turned around to go away, *Saul* seized the edge of his robe, and it tore. 28So Samuel said to him, "The LORD has torn the kingdom of Israel from you today, and has given it to a neighbor of yours, *who is* better than you. 29And also the Strength of Israel will not lie nor relent. For He *is* not a man, that He should relent."

30Then he said, "I have sinned; *yet* honor me now, please, before the elders of my people and before Israel, and return with me, that I may worship the LORD your God." 31So Samuel turned back after Saul, and Saul worshiped the LORD.

32Then Samuel said, "Bring Agag king of the Amalekites here to me." So Agag came to him cautiously.

And Agag said, "Surely the bitterness of death is past."

33But Samuel said, "As your sword has made women childless, so shall your mother be childless among women." And Samuel hacked Agag in pieces before the LORD in Gilgal.

34Then Samuel went to Ramah, and Saul went up to his house at Gibeah of Saul. 35And Samuel went no more to see Saul until the day of his death. Nevertheless Samuel mourned for Saul, and the LORD regretted that He had made Saul king over Israel.

David Anointed King

16 Now the LORD said to Samuel, "How long will you mourn for Saul, seeing I have rejected him from reigning over Israel? Fill your horn with oil, and go; I am sending you to Jesse the Bethlehemite. For I have provided Myself a king among his sons."

2And Samuel said, "How can I go? If Saul hears *it,* he will kill me."

But the LORD said, "Take a heifer with you, and say, 'I have come to sacrifice to the LORD.' 3Then invite Jesse to the sacrifice, and I will show you what you shall do; you shall anoint for Me the one I name to you."

4So Samuel did what the LORD said, and went to Bethlehem. And the elders of the town trembled at his coming, and said, "Do you come peaceably?"

5And he said, "Peaceably; I have come to sacrifice to the LORD. Sanctify yourselves, and come with me to the sacrifice." Then he consecrated Jesse and his sons, and invited them to the sacrifice.

6So it was, when they came, that he looked at Eliab and said, "Surely the LORD's anointed *is* before Him!"

7But the LORD said to Samuel, "Do not look at his appearance or at his physical stature, because I have refused him. For *the LORD does* not *see* as man sees;[a] for man looks at the outward appearance, but the LORD looks at the heart."

8So Jesse called Abinadab, and made him pass before Samuel. And he said, "Neither has the LORD chosen this one." 9Then Jesse made Shammah pass by. And he said, "Neither has the LORD chosen this one." 10Thus Jesse made seven of his sons pass before Samuel. And Samuel said to Jesse, "The LORD has not chosen these." 11And Samuel said to Jesse, "Are all the young men here?" Then he said, "There remains yet the youngest, and there he is, keeping the sheep."

And Samuel said to Jesse, "Send and bring him. For we will not sit down[a] till he comes here." 12So he sent and brought him in. Now he *was* ruddy, with bright

16:7 [a]Septuagint reads *For God does not see as man sees;* Targum reads *It is not by the appearance of a man;* Vulgate reads *Nor do I judge according to the looks of a man.* **16:11** [a]Following Septuagint and Vulgate; Masoretic Text reads *turn around;* Targum and Syriac read *turn away.*

16:7 We tend to be flippant about the omniscience of God, and yet it is something that should put us in absolute awe. How can God look into our heart? How can He see the invisible soul, the spirit, the mind, the hidden emotions, and the deepest secret thoughts? The fact that He sees the inward parts of every human being on the earth, all at once, is incredible. God is to be utterly feared and held in the utmost awe for who He is and what He can do. See also 1 Kings 8:39.

eyes, and good-looking. And the LORD
said, "Arise, anoint him; for this *is* the
one!" 13Then Samuel took the horn of oil
and anointed him in the midst of his
brothers; and the Spirit of the LORD came
upon David from that day forward. So
Samuel arose and went to Ramah.

A Distressing Spirit Troubles Saul

14But the Spirit of the LORD departed
from Saul, and a distressing spirit from
the LORD troubled him. 15And Saul's servants said to him, "Surely, a distressing
spirit from God is troubling you. 16Let
our master now command your servants,
who are before you, to seek out a man *who*
is a skillful player on the harp. And it
shall be that he will play it with his hand
when the distressing spirit from God is
upon you, and you shall be well."

17So Saul said to his servants, "Provide
me now a man who can play well, and
bring *him* to me."

18Then one of the servants answered
and said, "Look, I have seen a son of Jesse
the Bethlehemite, *who is* skillful in playing, a mighty man of valor, a man of war,
prudent in speech, and a handsome person; and the LORD *is* with him."

19Therefore Saul sent messengers to
Jesse, and said, "Send me your son David,
who *is* with the sheep." 20And Jesse took
a donkey *loaded with* bread, a skin of
wine, and a young goat, and sent *them* by
his son David to Saul. 21So David came to
Saul and stood before him. And he loved
him greatly, and he became his armorbearer. 22Then Saul sent to Jesse, saying,
"Please let David stand before me, for he
has found favor in my sight." 23And so it
was, whenever the spirit from God was
upon Saul, that David would take a harp
and play *it* with his hand. Then Saul would
become refreshed and well, and the distressing spirit would depart from him.

David and Goliath

17 Now the Philistines gathered their
armies together to battle, and were
gathered at Sochoh, which *belongs* to Judah; they encamped between Sochoh and
Azekah, in Ephes Dammim. 2And Saul
and the men of Israel were gathered together, and they encamped in the Valley
of Elah, and drew up in battle array against
the Philistines. 3The Philistines stood on
a mountain on one side, and Israel stood
on a mountain on the other side, with a
valley between them.

4And a champion went out from the
camp of the Philistines, named Goliath,
from Gath, whose height *was* six cubits
and a span. 5*He had* a bronze helmet on
his head, and he *was* armed with a coat of
mail, and the weight of the coat *was* five
thousand shekels of bronze. 6And *he had*
bronze armor on his legs and a bronze
javelin between his shoulders. 7Now the
staff of his spear *was* like a weaver's beam,
and his iron spearhead *weighed* six hundred shekels; and a shield-bearer went
before him. 8Then he stood and cried out
to the armies of Israel, and said to them,
"Why have you come out to line up for
battle? *Am* I not a Philistine, and you the
servants of Saul? Choose a man for yourselves, and let him come down to me. 9If
he is able to fight with me and kill me,
then we will be your servants. But if I
prevail against him and kill him, then you
shall be our servants and serve us." 10And
the Philistine said, "I defy the armies of
Israel this day; give me a man, that we
may fight together." 11When Saul and all
Israel heard these words of the Philistine,
they were dismayed and greatly afraid.

12Now David *was* the son of that
Ephrathite of Bethlehem Judah, whose
name *was* Jesse, and who had eight sons.
And the man was old, advanced *in years,*
in the days of Saul. 13The three oldest
sons of Jesse had gone to follow Saul to
the battle. The names of his three sons
who went to the battle *were* Eliab the
firstborn, next to him Abinadab, and the
third Shammah. 14David *was* the youngest. And the three oldest followed Saul.
15But David occasionally went and returned from Saul to feed his father's sheep
at Bethlehem.

16And the Philistine drew near and
presented himself forty days, morning and
evening.
17Then Jesse said to his son David,
"Take now for your brothers an ephah of
this dried *grain* and these ten loaves, and
run to your brothers at the camp. 18And
carry these ten cheeses to the captain of
their thousand, and see how your brothers fare, and bring back news of them."
19Now Saul and they and all the men of
Israel *were* in the Valley of Elah, fighting
with the Philistines.
20So David rose early in the morning,
left the sheep with a keeper, and took *the
things* and went as Jesse had commanded
him. And he came to the camp as the
army was going out to the fight and
shouting for the battle. 21For Israel and
the Philistines had drawn up in battle array, army against army. 22And David left
his supplies in the hand of the supply
keeper, ran to the army, and came and
greeted his brothers. 23Then as he talked
with them, there was the champion, the
Philistine of Gath, Goliath by name, coming up from the armies of the Philistines;
and he spoke according to the same
words. So David heard *them*. 24And all the
men of Israel, when they saw the man,
fled from him and were dreadfully afraid.
25So the men of Israel said, "Have you
seen this man who has come up? Surely
he has come up to defy Israel; and it shall
be *that* the man who kills him the king
will enrich with great riches, will give
him his daughter, and give his father's
house exemption *from taxes* in Israel."
26Then David spoke to the men who
stood by him, saying, "What shall be
done for the man who kills this Philistine
and takes away the reproach from Israel?
For who *is* this uncircumcised Philistine,
that he should defy the armies of the living God?"
27And the people answered him in this
manner, saying, "So shall it be done for
the man who kills him."
28Now Eliab his oldest brother heard
when he spoke to the men; and Eliab's
anger was aroused against David, and he
said, "Why did you come down here?
And with whom have you left those few
sheep in the wilderness? I know your
pride and the insolence of your heart, for
you have come down to see the battle."
29And David said, "What have I done
now? *Is there* not a cause?" 30Then he
turned from him toward another and said
the same thing; and these people answered him as the first ones *did*.
31Now when the words which David
spoke were heard, they reported *them* to
Saul; and he sent for him. 32Then David
said to Saul, "Let no man's heart fail because of him; your servant will go and
fight with this Philistine."
33And Saul said to David, "You are not
able to go against this Philistine to fight
with him; for you *are* a youth, and he a
man of war from his youth."
34But David said to Saul, "Your servant
used to keep his father's sheep, and when
a lion or a bear came and took a lamb out
of the flock, 35I went out after it and
struck it, and delivered *the lamb* from its
mouth; and when it arose against me, I
caught *it* by its beard, and struck and
killed it. 36Your servant has killed both
lion and bear; and this uncircumcised Philistine will be like one of them, seeing he
has defied the armies of the living God."
37Moreover David said, "The LORD, who
delivered me from the paw of the lion
and from the paw of the bear, He will deliver me from the hand of this Philistine."
And Saul said to David, "Go, and the
LORD be with you!"
38So Saul clothed David with his armor, and he put a bronze helmet on his

---

17:28 If you desire to live for God and for His glory, especially in the area of evangelism, expect discouragement from the most unexpected of places. Don't be surprised at baseless accusations, often from those closest to you.

head; he also clothed him with a coat of
mail. 39David fastened his sword to his
armor and tried to walk, for he had not
tested *them*. And David said to Saul, "I
cannot walk with these, for I have not
tested *them*." So David took them off.
40Then he took his staff in his hand;
and he chose for himself five smooth
stones from the brook, and put them in a
shepherd's bag, in a pouch which he had,
and his sling was in his hand. And he
drew near to the Philistine. 41So the Philistine came, and began drawing near to
David, and the man who bore the shield
went before him. 42And when the Philistine looked about and saw David, he disdained him; for he was *only* a youth,
ruddy and good-looking. 43So the Philistine said to David, "*Am* I a dog, that you
come to me with sticks?" And the Philistine cursed David by his gods. 44And the
Philistine said to David, "Come to me,
and I will give your flesh to the birds of
the air and the beasts of the field!"
45Then David said to the Philistine,
"You come to me with a sword, with a
spear, and with a javelin. But I come to
you in the name of the LORD of hosts, the
God of the armies of Israel, whom you
have defied. 46This day the LORD will deliver you into my hand, and I will strike
you and take your head from you. And
this day I will give the carcasses of the
camp of the Philistines to the birds of the
air and the wild beasts of the earth, that
all the earth may know that there is a
God in Israel. 47Then all this assembly
shall know that the LORD does not save
with sword and spear; for the battle *is* the
LORD's, and He will give you into our
hands."
48So it was, when the Philistine arose
and came and drew near to meet David,
that David hurried and ran toward the
army to meet the Philistine. 49Then David
put his hand in his bag and took out a
stone; and he slung *it* and struck the Philistine in his forehead, so that the stone
sank into his forehead, and he fell on his
face to the earth. 50So David prevailed
over the Philistine with a sling and a
stone, and struck the Philistine and killed
him. But *there was* no sword in the hand
of David. 51Therefore David ran and stood
over the Philistine, took his sword and
drew it out of its sheath and killed him,
and cut off his head with it.
And when the Philistines saw that
their champion was dead, they fled. 52Now
the men of Israel and Judah arose and
shouted, and pursued the Philistines as
far as the entrance of the valley[a] and to
the gates of Ekron. And the wounded of
the Philistines fell along the road to Shaaraim, even as far as Gath and Ekron.
53Then the children of Israel returned
from chasing the Philistines, and they
plundered their tents. 54And David took
the head of the Philistine and brought it
to Jerusalem, but he put his armor in his
tent.
55When Saul saw David going out
against the Philistine, he said to Abner,

17:52 [a]Following Masoretic Text, Syriac, Targum, and Vulgate; Septuagint reads *Gath*.

17:40 David took five smooth stones, but four remained in the bag. Only one was used to defeat the enemy. The Church has five "stones"—a fivefold office for ministry: apostles, prophets, evangelists, pastors and teachers (see Eph. 4:11). But only one stone goes *outside* of the Church to face the enemy: the evangelist and those he has equipped to do the work of ministry. Be a lively stone.

17:48 If you feel fearful when witnessing, think of how David *ran toward* Goliath. He ran because God was with him, and you have the same God with you. So do not be intimidated by the Goliath of the fear of man. Faith in God will dwarf him before your eyes. Run toward the lost and do what you know you should. See Isa. 35:4 comment for encouragement.

17:50 God's Law is the sling that gives the stone of the gospel its thrust to conquer the enemy. Without God's Law, the gospel does not penetrate the mind of the sinner. Why should he repent and trust in the Savior if he has no understanding of the true nature of sin? That understanding is something only the Law can give (see Rom. 7:7).

the commander of the army, "Abner, whose son *is* this youth?"

And Abner said, "As your soul lives, O king, I do not know."

56So the king said, "Inquire whose son this young man is."

57Then, as David returned from the slaughter of the Philistine, Abner took him and brought him before Saul with the head of the Philistine in his hand. 58And Saul said to him, "Whose son *are* you, young man?"

So David answered, "*I am* the son of your servant Jesse the Bethlehemite."

Saul Resents David

18 Now when he had finished speaking to Saul, the soul of Jonathan was knit to the soul of David, and Jonathan loved him as his own soul. 2Saul took him that day, and would not let him go home to his father's house anymore. 3Then Jonathan and David made a covenant, because he loved him as his own soul. 4And Jonathan took off the robe that *was* on him and gave it to David, with his armor, even to his sword and his bow and his belt.

5So David went out wherever Saul sent him, *and* behaved wisely. And Saul set him over the men of war, and he was accepted in the sight of all the people and also in the sight of Saul's servants. 6Now it had happened as they were coming *home*, when David was returning from the slaughter of the Philistine, that the women had come out of all the cities of Israel, singing and dancing, to meet King Saul, with tambourines, with joy, and with musical instruments. 7So the women sang as they danced, and said:

"Saul has slain his thousands,
And David his ten thousands."

8Then Saul was very angry, and the saying displeased him; and he said, "They have ascribed to David ten thousands, and to me they have ascribed only thousands. Now what more can he have but the kingdom?" 9So Saul eyed David from that day forward.

10And it happened on the next day that the distressing spirit from God came upon Saul, and he prophesied inside the house. So David played *music* with his hand, as at other times; but *there was* a spear in Saul's hand. 11And Saul cast the spear, for he said, "I will pin David to the wall!" But David escaped his presence twice.

12Now Saul was afraid of David, because the LORD was with him, but had departed from Saul. 13Therefore Saul removed him from his presence, and made him his captain over a thousand; and he went out and came in before the people. 14And David behaved wisely in all his ways, and the LORD *was* with him. 15Therefore, when Saul saw that he behaved very wisely, he was afraid of him. 16But all Israel and Judah loved David, because he went out and came in before them.

David Marries Michal

17Then Saul said to David, "Here is my older daughter Merab; I will give her to you as a wife. Only be valiant for me, and fight the LORD's battles." For Saul thought, "Let my hand not be against him, but let the hand of the Philistines be against him."

18So David said to Saul, "Who *am* I, and what *is* my life *or* my father's family in Israel, that I should be son-in-law to the king?" 19But it happened at the time when Merab, Saul's daughter, should have been given to David, that she was given to Adriel the Meholathite as a wife.

18:1–3 May God knit together the hearts of all true believers, that we may honor one another and prefer one another above ourselves. We are commanded in dozens of verses to love one another, as Christ has loved us, fervently with a pure heart (see John 15:12; 1 Pet. 1:22). It is not optional, and is how the world knows that we are His disciples.

18:8–11 Beware of the whisperings of pride. It is the root of many sins.

[20]Now Michal, Saul's daughter, loved
David. And they told Saul, and the thing
pleased him. [21]So Saul said, "I will give her
to him, that she may be a snare to him,
and that the hand of the Philistines may
be against him." Therefore Saul said to
David a second time, "You shall be my
son-in-law today."

[22]And Saul commanded his servants,
"Communicate with David secretly, and
say, 'Look, the king has delight in you,
and all his servants love you. Now therefore, become the king's son-in-law.' "

[23]So Saul's servants spoke those words
in the hearing of David. And David said,
"Does it seem to you *a* light *thing* to be a
king's son-in-law, seeing I *am* a poor and
lightly esteemed man?" [24]And the servants
of Saul told him, saying, "In this manner
David spoke."

· · · · · · ·

Read how Charles Spurgeon used the Law.
See Gal. 3:19 comment.

· · · · · · ·

[25]Then Saul said, "Thus you shall say
to David: 'The king does not desire any
dowry but one hundred foreskins of the
Philistines, to take vengeance on the king's
enemies.' " But Saul thought to make
David fall by the hand of the Philistines.
[26]So when his servants told David these
words, it pleased David well to become
the king's son-in-law. Now the days had
not expired; [27]therefore David arose and
went, he and his men, and killed two hundred men of the Philistines. And David
brought their foreskins, and they gave
them in full count to the king, that he
might become the king's son-in-law. Then
Saul gave him Michal his daughter as a
wife.

[28]Thus Saul saw and knew that the
LORD *was* with David, and *that* Michal,
Saul's daughter, loved him; [29]and Saul was
still more afraid of David. So Saul became
David's enemy continually. [30]Then the
princes of the Philistines went out *to war.*
And so it was, whenever they went out,
that David behaved more wisely than all
the servants of Saul, so that his name became highly esteemed.

Saul Persecutes David

19 Now Saul spoke to Jonathan his
son and to all his servants, that
they should kill David; but Jonathan, Saul's
son, delighted greatly in David. [2]So Jonathan told David, saying, "My father Saul
seeks to kill you. Therefore please be on
your guard until morning, and stay in a
secret *place* and hide. [3]And I will go out
and stand beside my father in the field
where you *are,* and I will speak with my
father about you. Then what I observe, I
will tell you."

[4]Thus Jonathan spoke well of David to
Saul his father, and said to him, "Let not
the king sin against his servant, against
David, because he has not sinned against
you, and because his works *have been*
very good toward you. [5]For he took his
life in his hands and killed the Philistine,
and the LORD brought about a great deliverance for all Israel. You saw *it* and rejoiced. Why then will you sin against innocent blood, to kill David without a cause?"

[6]So Saul heeded the voice of Jonathan,
and Saul swore, "*As* the LORD lives, he
shall not be killed." [7]Then Jonathan called
David, and Jonathan told him all these
things. So Jonathan brought David to Saul,
and he was in his presence as in times past.

[8]And there was war again; and David
went out and fought with the Philistines,
and struck them with a mighty blow, and
they fled from him.

[9]Now the distressing spirit from the
LORD came upon Saul as he sat in his house

19:9,10 This is the third time Saul attempted to murder David. And it was all because Saul allowed the seed of jealousy to find root in the dirty soil of his sinful heart (see 18:8). Love rejoices at another's success, while jealousy invites the spirit of hatred to enter and take up residence. Be so filled with the love of God that there is no room for *any* subtle sin. See Rom. 13:8–10 for how the Law and love are synonymous.

with his spear in his hand. And David was playing *music* with *his* hand. [10]Then Saul sought to pin David to the wall with the spear, but he slipped away from Saul's presence; and he drove the spear into the wall. So David fled and escaped that night.

[11]Saul also sent messengers to David's house to watch him and to kill him in the morning. And Michal, David's wife, told him, saying, "If you do not save your life tonight, tomorrow you will be killed." [12]So Michal let David down through a window. And he went and fled and escaped. [13]And Michal took an image and laid *it* in the bed, put a cover of goats' *hair* for his head, and covered *it* with clothes. [14]So when Saul sent messengers to take David, she said, "He *is* sick."

[15]Then Saul sent the messengers *back* to see David, saying, "Bring him up to me in the bed, that I may kill him." [16]And when the messengers had come in, there was the image in the bed, with a cover of goats' *hair* for his head. [17]Then Saul said to Michal, "Why have you deceived me like this, and sent my enemy away, so that he has escaped?"

And Michal answered Saul, "He said to me, 'Let me go! Why should I kill you?' "

[18]So David fled and escaped, and went to Samuel at Ramah, and told him all that Saul had done to him. And he and Samuel went and stayed in Naioth. [19]Now it was told Saul, saying, "Take note, David *is* at Naioth in Ramah!" [20]Then Saul sent messengers to take David. And when they saw the group of prophets prophesying, and Samuel standing *as* leader over them, the Spirit of God came upon the messengers of Saul, and they also prophesied. [21]And when Saul was told, he sent other messengers, and they prophesied likewise. Then Saul sent messengers again the third time, and they prophesied also. [22]Then he also went to Ramah, and came to the great well that *is* at Sechu. So he asked, and said, "Where *are* Samuel and David?"

And *someone* said, "Indeed *they are* at Naioth in Ramah." [23]So he went there to Naioth in Ramah. Then the Spirit of God was upon him also, and he went on and prophesied until he came to Naioth in Ramah. [24]And he also stripped off his clothes and prophesied before Samuel in like manner, and lay down naked all that day and all that night. Therefore they say, "*Is* Saul also among the prophets?"[a]

Jonathan's Loyalty to David

20 Then David fled from Naioth in Ramah, and went and said to Jonathan, "What have I done? What *is* my iniquity, and what *is* my sin before your father, that he seeks my life?"

[2]So Jonathan said to him, "By no means! You shall not die! Indeed, my father will do nothing either great or small without first telling me. And why should my father hide this thing from me? It *is* not *so!*"

[3]Then David took an oath again, and said, "Your father certainly knows that I have found favor in your eyes, and he has said, 'Do not let Jonathan know this, lest he be grieved.' But truly, *as* the LORD lives and *as* your soul lives, *there is* but a step between me and death."

[4]So Jonathan said to David, "Whatever you yourself desire, I will do *it* for you."

[5]And David said to Jonathan, "Indeed tomorrow *is* the New Moon, and I should not fail to sit with the king to eat. But let me go, that I may hide in the field until the third *day* at evening. [6]If your father misses me at all, then say, 'David earnestly asked *permission* of me that he might run over to Bethlehem, his city, for *there is* a yearly sacrifice there for all the family.' [7]If he says thus: '*It is* well,' your servant will be safe. But if he is very angry, be sure that evil is determined by him. [8]Therefore you shall deal kindly with your servant, for you have brought your servant into a covenant of the LORD with you. Nevertheless, if there is iniquity in me, kill me yourself, for why should you bring me to your father?"

19:24 [a]Compare 1 Samuel 10:12

9But Jonathan said, "Far be it from you!
For if I knew certainly that evil was determined by my father to come upon
you, then would I not tell you?"
10Then David said to Jonathan, "Who
will tell me, or what *if* your father answers you roughly?"
11And Jonathan said to David, "Come,
let us go out into the field." So both of
them went out into the field. 12Then
Jonathan said to David: "The LORD God
of Israel *is witness!* When I have sounded
out my father sometime tomorrow, *or* the
third *day,* and indeed *there is* good toward
David, and I do not send to you and tell
you, 13may the LORD do so and much
more to Jonathan. But if it pleases my father *to do* you evil, then I will report it to
you and send you away, that you may go
in safety. And the LORD be with you as He
has been with my father. 14And you shall
not only show me the kindness of the
LORD while I still live, that I may not die;
15but you shall not cut off your kindness
from my house forever, no, not when the
LORD has cut off every one of the enemies
of David from the face of the earth." 16So
Jonathan made *a covenant* with the house
of David, *saying,* "Let the LORD require *it*
at the hand of David's enemies."
17Now Jonathan again caused David to
vow, because he loved him; for he loved
him as he loved his own soul. 18Then
Jonathan said to David, "Tomorrow *is* the
New Moon; and you will be missed, because your seat will be empty. 19And *when*
you have stayed three days, go down
quickly and come to the place where you
hid on the day of the deed; and remain
by the stone Ezel. 20Then I will shoot
three arrows to the side, as though I shot
at a target; 21and there I will send a lad,
saying, 'Go, find the arrows.' If I expressly
say to the lad, 'Look, the arrows *are* on
this side of you; get them and come'—
then, as the LORD lives, *there is* safety for
you and no harm. 22But if I say thus to
the young man, 'Look, the arrows *are* beyond you'—go your way, for the LORD has
sent you away. 23And as for the matter
which you and I have spoken of, indeed
the LORD *be* between you and me forever."
24Then David hid in the field. And
when the New Moon had come, the king
sat down to eat the feast. 25Now the king
sat on his seat, as at other times, on a seat
by the wall. And Jonathan arose,[a] and
Abner sat by Saul's side, but David's place
was empty. 26Nevertheless Saul did not
say anything that day, for he thought,
"Something has happened to him; he *is*
unclean, surely he *is* unclean." 27And it
happened the next day, the second *day* of
the month, that David's place was empty.
And Saul said to Jonathan his son, "Why
has the son of Jesse not come to eat, either
yesterday or today?"

> God loves you; therefore love and obey him. Christ died for you; therefore die to sin. Christ is risen; therefore rise in the image of God. Christ liveth ever more; therefore live to God till you live with him in glory.
>
> **JOHN WESLEY**

28So Jonathan answered Saul, "David
earnestly asked *permission* of me *to go* to
Bethlehem. 29And he said, 'Please let me
go, for our family has a sacrifice in the
city, and my brother has commanded me
to be there. And now, if I have found favor
in your eyes, please let me get away and
see my brothers.' Therefore he has not
come to the king's table."
30Then Saul's anger was aroused against
Jonathan, and he said to him, "You son of
a perverse, rebellious *woman!* Do I not
know that you have chosen the son of
Jesse to your own shame and to the

20:25 [a]Following Masoretic Text, Syriac, Targum, and Vulgate; Septuagint reads *he sat across from Jonathan.*

20:17 God is the lover of your soul, proven through the blood of the cross (see Rom. 5:8).

shame of your mother's nakedness? 31For as long as the son of Jesse lives on the earth, you shall not be established, nor your kingdom. Now therefore, send and bring him to me, for he shall surely die."

32And Jonathan answered Saul his father, and said to him, "Why should he be killed? What has he done?" 33Then Saul cast a spear at him to kill him, by which Jonathan knew that it was determined by his father to kill David.

34So Jonathan arose from the table in fierce anger, and ate no food the second day of the month, for he was grieved for David, because his father had treated him shamefully.

35And so it was, in the morning, that Jonathan went out into the field at the time appointed with David, and a little lad *was* with him. 36Then he said to his lad, "Now run, find the arrows which I shoot." As the lad ran, he shot an arrow beyond him. 37When the lad had come to the place where the arrow was which Jonathan had shot, Jonathan cried out after the lad and said, "*Is* not the arrow beyond you?" 38And Jonathan cried out after the lad, "Make haste, hurry, do not delay!" So Jonathan's lad gathered up the arrows and came back to his master. 39But the lad did not know anything. Only Jonathan and David knew of the matter. 40Then Jonathan gave his weapons to his lad, and said to him, "Go, carry *them* to the city."

41As soon as the lad had gone, David arose from *a place* toward the south, fell on his face to the ground, and bowed down three times. And they kissed one another; and they wept together, but David more so. 42Then Jonathan said to David, "Go in peace, since we have both sworn in the name of the LORD, saying, 'May the LORD be between you and me, and between your descendants and my descendants, forever.' " So he arose and departed, and Jonathan went into the city.

David and the Holy Bread

21 Now David came to Nob, to Ahimelech the priest. And Ahimelech was afraid when he met David, and said to him, "Why *are* you alone, and no one is with you?"

2So David said to Ahimelech the priest, "The king has ordered me on some business, and said to me, 'Do not let anyone know anything about the business on which I send you, or what I have commanded you.' And I have directed *my* young men to such and such a place. 3Now therefore, what have you on hand? Give *me* five *loaves of* bread in my hand, or whatever can be found."

4And the priest answered David and said, "*There is* no common bread on hand; but there is holy bread, if the young men have at least kept themselves from women."

5Then David answered the priest, and said to him, "Truly, women *have been* kept from us about three days since I came out. And the vessels of the young men are holy, and *the bread is* in effect common, even though it was consecrated in the vessel this day."

6So the priest gave him holy *bread;* for there was no bread there but the showbread which had been taken from before the LORD, in order to put hot bread *in its place* on the day when it was taken away.

7Now a certain man of the servants of Saul *was* there that day, detained before the LORD. And his name *was* Doeg, an Edomite, the chief of the herdsmen who *belonged* to Saul.

8And David said to Ahimelech, "Is there not here on hand a spear or a sword? For I have brought neither my sword nor my weapons with me, because the king's business required haste."

9So the priest said, "The sword of Goliath the Philistine, whom you killed in the Valley of Elah, there it is, wrapped in a cloth behind the ephod. If you will take

21:7 Doeg was a Judas, betraying David's whereabouts (see 22:9–18). Be careful who you trust. If David had been more discreet, eighty-five innocent priests may not have been murdered. See 22:18,22.

that, take *it*. For *there is* no other except that one here."

And David said, "*There is* none like it; give it to me."

David Flees to Gath

10Then David arose and fled that day from before Saul, and went to Achish the king of Gath. 11And the servants of Achish said to him, "*Is* this not David the king of the land? Did they not sing of him to one another in dances, saying:

'Saul has slain his thousands,
And David his ten thousands'?"[a]

12Now David took these words to heart, and was very much afraid of Achish the king of Gath. 13So he changed his behavior before them, pretended madness in their hands, scratched on the doors of the gate, and let his saliva fall down on his beard. 14Then Achish said to his servants, "Look, you see the man is insane. Why have you brought him to me? 15Have I need of madmen, that you have brought this *fellow* to play the madman in my presence? Shall this *fellow* come into my house?"

David's Four Hundred Men

22 David therefore departed from there and escaped to the cave of Adullam. So when his brothers and all his father's house heard *it*, they went down there to him. 2And everyone *who was* in distress, everyone who *was* in debt, and everyone *who was* discontented gathered to him. So he became captain over them. And there were about four hundred men with him.

3Then David went from there to Mizpah of Moab; and he said to the king of Moab, "Please let my father and mother come here with you, till I know what God will do for me." 4So he brought them before the king of Moab, and they dwelt with him all the time that David was in the stronghold.

5Now the prophet Gad said to David, "Do not stay in the stronghold; depart, and go to the land of Judah." So David departed and went into the forest of Hereth.

Saul Murders the Priests

6When Saul heard that David and the men who *were* with him had been discovered—now Saul was staying in Gibeah under a tamarisk tree in Ramah, with his spear in his hand, and all his servants standing about him— 7then Saul said to his servants who stood about him, "Hear now, you Benjamites! Will the son of Jesse give every one of you fields and vineyards, *and* make you all captains of thousands and captains of hundreds? 8All of you have conspired against me, and *there is* no one who reveals to me that my son has made a covenant with the son of Jesse; and *there is* not one of you who is sorry for me or reveals to me that my son has stirred up my servant against me, to lie in wait, as *it is* this day."

9Then answered Doeg the Edomite, who was set over the servants of Saul, and said, "I saw the son of Jesse going to Nob, to Ahimelech the son of Ahitub. 10And he inquired of the LORD for him, gave him provisions, and gave him the sword of Goliath the Philistine."

11So the king sent to call Ahimelech the priest, the son of Ahitub, and all his father's house, the priests who *were* in Nob. And they all came to the king. 12And Saul said, "Hear now, son of Ahitub!"

He answered, "Here I am, my lord."

13Then Saul said to him, "Why have you conspired against me, you and the son of Jesse, in that you have given him bread and a sword, and have inquired of God for him, that he should rise against me, to lie in wait, as it is this day?"

14So Ahimelech answered the king and said, "And who among all your servants *is as* faithful as David, who is the king's son-in-law, who goes at your bidding, and is honorable in your house? 15Did I then begin to inquire of God for

21:11 [a]Compare 1 Samuel 18:7

him? Far be it from me! Let not the king impute anything to his servant, *or* to any in the house of my father. For your servant knew nothing of all this, little or much."

[16]And the king said, "You shall surely die, Ahimelech, you and all your father's house!" [17]Then the king said to the guards who stood about him, "Turn and kill the priests of the LORD, because their hand also *is* with David, and because they knew when he fled and did not tell it to me." But the servants of the king would not lift their hands to strike the priests of the LORD. [18]And the king said to Doeg, "You turn and kill the priests!" So Doeg the Edomite turned and struck the priests, and killed on that day eighty-five men who wore a linen ephod. [19]Also Nob, the city of the priests, he struck with the edge of the sword, both men and women, children and nursing infants, oxen and donkeys and sheep—with the edge of the sword.

[20]Now one of the sons of Ahimelech the son of Ahitub, named Abiathar, escaped and fled after David. [21]And Abiathar told David that Saul had killed the LORD's priests. [22]So David said to Abiathar, "I knew that day, when Doeg the Edomite *was* there, that he would surely tell Saul. I have caused *the death* of all the persons of your father's house. [23]Stay with me; do not fear. For he who seeks my life seeks your life, but with me you *shall be* safe."

David Saves the City of Keilah

23 Then they told David, saying, "Look, the Philistines are fighting against Keilah, and they are robbing the threshing floors."

[2]Therefore David inquired of the LORD, saying, "Shall I go and attack these Philistines?"

And the LORD said to David, "Go and attack the Philistines, and save Keilah."

[3]But David's men said to him, "Look, we are afraid here in Judah. How much more then if we go to Keilah against the armies of the Philistines?" [4]Then David inquired of the LORD once again.

And the LORD answered him and said, "Arise, go down to Keilah. For I will deliver the Philistines into your hand." [5]And David and his men went to Keilah and fought with the Philistines, struck them with a mighty blow, and took away their livestock. So David saved the inhabitants of Keilah.

[6]Now it happened, when Abiathar the son of Ahimelech fled to David at Keilah, *that* he went down *with* an ephod in his hand.

[7]And Saul was told that David had gone to Keilah. So Saul said, "God has delivered him into my hand, for he has shut himself in by entering a town that has gates and bars." [8]Then Saul called all the people together for war, to go down to Keilah to besiege David and his men.

[9]When David knew that Saul plotted evil against him, he said to Abiathar the priest, "Bring the ephod here." [10]Then David said, "O LORD God of Israel, Your servant has certainly heard that Saul seeks to come to Keilah to destroy the city for my sake. [11]Will the men of Keilah deliver me into his hand? Will Saul come down, as Your servant has heard? O LORD God of Israel, I pray, tell Your servant."

And the LORD said, "He will come down."

[12]Then David said, "Will the men of Keilah deliver me and my men into the hand of Saul?"

And the LORD said, "They will deliver *you.*"

[13]So David and his men, about six hun-

22:14 This testimony of David's character was true, and yet one spark of jealousy had enflamed Saul's imagination to an inferno of hatred.

23:2 David took the time to inquire of the Lord. Make sure you do not run ahead of Him and *presume* that He will bless an endeavor simply because it seems like the right thing to do. Acknowledge Him in all of your ways and He will direct your paths (see Prov. 3:6).

dred, arose and departed from Keilah and went wherever they could go. Then it was told Saul that David had escaped from Keilah; so he halted the expedition.

David in Wilderness Strongholds

[14]And David stayed in strongholds in the wilderness, and remained in the mountains in the Wilderness of Ziph. Saul sought him every day, but God did not deliver him into his hand. [15]So David saw that Saul had come out to seek his life. And David *was* in the Wilderness of Ziph in a forest.[a] [16]Then Jonathan, Saul's son, arose and went to David in the woods and strengthened his hand in God. [17]And he said to him, "Do not fear, for the hand of Saul my father shall not find you. You shall be king over Israel, and I shall be next to you. Even my father Saul knows that." [18]So the two of them made a covenant before the LORD. And David stayed in the woods, and Jonathan went to his own house.

> He who prays as he ought will endeavor to live as he prays.
>
> **JOHN OWEN**

[19]Then the Ziphites came up to Saul at Gibeah, saying, "Is David not hiding with us in strongholds in the woods, in the hill of Hachilah, which *is* on the south of Jeshimon? [20]Now therefore, O king, come down according to all the desire of your soul to come down; and our part *shall be* to deliver him into the king's hand."

[21]And Saul said, "Blessed *are* you of the LORD, for you have compassion on me. [22]Please go and find out for sure, and see the place where his hideout is, *and* who has seen him there. For I am told he is very crafty. [23]See therefore, and take knowledge of all the lurking places where he hides; and come back to me with certainty, and I will go with you. And it shall be, if he is in the land, that I will search for him throughout all the clans[a] of Judah."

[24]So they arose and went to Ziph before Saul. But David and his men *were* in the Wilderness of Maon, in the plain on the south of Jeshimon. [25]When Saul and his men went to seek *him,* they told David. Therefore he went down to the rock, and stayed in the Wilderness of Maon. And when Saul heard *that,* he pursued David in the Wilderness of Maon. [26]Then Saul went on one side of the mountain, and David and his men on the other side of the mountain. So David made haste to get away from Saul, for Saul and his men were encircling David and his men to take them.

[27]But a messenger came to Saul, saying, "Hurry and come, for the Philistines have invaded the land!" [28]Therefore Saul returned from pursuing David, and went against the Philistines; so they called that place the Rock of Escape.[a] [29]Then David went up from there and dwelt in strongholds at En Gedi.

David Spares Saul

24 Now it happened, when Saul had returned from following the Philistines, that it was told him, saying, "Take note! David *is* in the Wilderness of En Gedi." [2]Then Saul took three thousand chosen men from all Israel, and went to seek David and his men on the Rocks of the Wild Goats. [3]So he came to the sheepfolds by the road, where there *was* a cave; and Saul went in to attend to his needs. (David and his men were staying in the recesses of the cave.) [4]Then the men of David said to him, "This is the day of which the LORD said to you, 'Behold, I will deliver your enemy into your hand, that you may do to him as it seems good to you.' " And David arose and secretly cut off a corner of Saul's robe. [5]Now it happened afterward that David's heart troubled him because he had cut Saul's *robe.* [6]And he said to his men, "The LORD forbid that I should do this thing to my master, the LORD's anointed, to stretch

23:15 [a]Or *in Horesh* 23:23 [a]Literally *thousands* 23:28 [a]Hebrew *Sela Hammahlekoth*

out my hand against him, seeing he is the anointed of the LORD." 7So David restrained his servants with *these* words, and did not allow them to rise against Saul. And Saul got up from the cave and went on *his* way.

8David also arose afterward, went out of the cave, and called out to Saul, saying, "My lord the king!" And when Saul looked behind him, David stooped with his face to the earth, and bowed down. 9And David said to Saul: "Why do you listen to the words of men who say, 'Indeed David seeks your harm'? 10Look, this day your eyes have seen that the LORD delivered you today into my hand in the cave, and *someone* urged *me* to kill you. But *my eye* spared you, and I said, 'I will not stretch out my hand against my lord, for he *is* the LORD's anointed.' 11Moreover, my father, see! Yes, see the corner of your robe in my hand! For in that I cut off the corner of your robe, and did not kill you, know and see that *there is* neither evil nor rebellion in my hand, and I have not sinned against you. Yet you hunt my life to take it. 12Let the LORD judge between you and me, and let the LORD avenge me on you. But my hand shall not be against you. 13As the proverb of the ancients says, 'Wickedness proceeds from the wicked.' But my hand shall not be against you. 14After whom has the king of Israel come out? Whom do you pursue? A dead dog? A flea? 15Therefore let the LORD be judge, and judge between you and me, and see and plead my case, and deliver me out of your hand."

16So it was, when David had finished speaking these words to Saul, that Saul said, "*Is* this your voice, my son David?" And Saul lifted up his voice and wept. 17Then he said to David: "You *are* more righteous than I; for you have rewarded me with good, whereas I have rewarded you with evil. 18And you have shown this day how you have dealt well with me; for when the LORD delivered me into your hand, you did not kill me. 19For if a man finds his enemy, will he let him get away safely? Therefore may the LORD reward you with good for what you have done to me this day. 20And now I know indeed that you shall surely be king, and that the kingdom of Israel shall be established in your hand. 21Therefore swear now to me by the LORD that you will not cut off my descendants after me, and that you will not destroy my name from my father's house."

22So David swore to Saul. And Saul went home, but David and his men went up to the stronghold.

Death of Samuel

25 Then Samuel died; and the Israelites gathered together and lamented for him, and buried him at his home in Ramah. And David arose and went down to the Wilderness of Paran.[a]

David and the Wife of Nabal

2Now *there was* a man in Maon whose business *was* in Carmel, and the man *was* very rich. He had three thousand sheep and a thousand goats. And he was shearing his sheep in Carmel. 3The name of the man *was* Nabal, and the name of his wife Abigail. And *she was* a woman of good understanding and beautiful appearance; but the man *was* harsh and evil in *his* doings. He *was of the house of* Caleb.

4When David heard in the wilderness that Nabal was shearing his sheep, 5David sent ten young men; and David said to the young men, "Go up to Carmel, go to Nabal, and greet him in my name.

25:1 [a]Following Masoretic Text, Syriac, Targum, and Vulgate; Septuagint reads *Maon*.

24:5 It is a pity that David's conscience was not as tender once he became king. Its voice seemed to be completely muffled when he committed adultery and murder (see 2 Sam. 11). Men, be careful of lust. That was David's weakness, as it is every man's. Women, be careful of lighting the fuse of lust; be modest in your dress.

6And thus you shall say to him who lives
in prosperity: 'Peace *be* to you, peace to
your house, and peace to all that you
have! 7Now I have heard that you have
shearers. Your shepherds were with us,
and we did not hurt them, nor was there
anything missing from them all the while
they were in Carmel. 8Ask your young
men, and they will tell you. Therefore let
my young men find favor in your eyes,
for we come on a feast day. Please give
whatever comes to your hand to your servants and to your son David.' "

9So when David's young men came,
they spoke to Nabal according to all these
words in the name of David, and waited.

10Then Nabal answered David's servants, and said, "Who *is* David, and who
is the son of Jesse? There are many servants nowadays who break away each
one from his master. 11Shall I then take
my bread and my water and my meat that
I have killed for my shearers, and give *it*
to men when I do not know where they
are from?"

12So David's young men turned on
their heels and went back; and they came
and told him all these words. 13Then
David said to his men, "Every man gird on
his sword." So every man girded on his
sword, and David also girded on his sword.
And about four hundred men went with
David, and two hundred stayed with the
supplies.

14Now one of the young men told Abigail, Nabal's wife, saying, "Look, David
sent messengers from the wilderness to
greet our master; and he reviled them.
15But the men *were* very good to us, and
we were not hurt, nor did we miss anything as long as we accompanied them,
when we were in the fields. 16They were
a wall to us both by night and day, all the
time we were with them keeping the
sheep. 17Now therefore, know and consider what you will do, for harm is determined against our master and against all
his household. For he *is such* a scoundrel[a]
that *one* cannot speak to him."

18Then Abigail made haste and took
two hundred *loaves* of bread, two skins of
wine, five sheep already dressed, five
seahs of roasted *grain,* one hundred clusters of raisins, and two hundred cakes of
figs, and loaded *them* on donkeys. 19And
she said to her servants, "Go on before
me; see, I am coming after you." But she
did not tell her husband Nabal.

20So it was, *as* she rode on the donkey,
that she went down under cover of the
hill; and there were David and his men,
coming down toward her, and she met
them. 21Now David had said, "Surely in
vain I have protected all that this *fellow*
has in the wilderness, so that nothing was
missed of all that *belongs* to him. And he
has repaid me evil for good. 22May God
do so, and more also, to the enemies of
David, if I leave one male of all who *belong* to him by morning light."

23Now when Abigail saw David, she
dismounted quickly from the donkey, fell
on her face before David, and bowed
down to the ground. 24So she fell at his
feet and said: "On me, my lord, *on* me *let*
this iniquity *be!* And please let your
maidservant speak in your ears, and hear
the words of your maidservant. 25Please,
let not my lord regard this scoundrel Nabal. For as his name *is,* so *is* he: Nabal[a] *is*
his name, and folly *is* with him! But I,
your maidservant, did not see the young
men of my lord whom you sent. 26Now
therefore, my lord, *as* the LORD lives and
as your soul lives, since the LORD has held
you back from coming to bloodshed and
from avenging yourself with your own
hand, now then, let your enemies and
those who seek harm for my lord be as
Nabal. 27And now this present which your

25:17 [a]Literally *son of Belial* **25:25** [a]Literally *Fool*

25:11 Notice the use of personal pronouns by Nabal: three times he said "I" and four times "my." Read vv. 37,38 to see how much of his material wealth he took with him when God required his soul.

maidservant has brought to my lord, let it be given to the young men who follow my lord. 28Please forgive the trespass of your maidservant. For the LORD will certainly make for my lord an enduring house, because my lord fights the battles of the LORD, and evil is not found in you throughout your days. 29Yet a man has risen to pursue you and seek your life, but the life of my lord shall be bound in the bundle of the living with the LORD your God; and the lives of your enemies He shall sling out, *as from* the pocket of a sling. 30And it shall come to pass, when the LORD has done for my lord according to all the good that He has spoken concerning you, and has appointed you ruler over Israel, 31that this will be no grief to you, nor offense of heart to my lord, either that you have shed blood without cause, or that my lord has avenged himself. But when the LORD has dealt well with my lord, then remember your maidservant."

32Then David said to Abigail: "Blessed *is* the LORD God of Israel, who sent you this day to meet me! 33And blessed *is* your advice and blessed *are* you, because you have kept me this day from coming to bloodshed and from avenging myself with my own hand. 34For indeed, *as* the LORD God of Israel lives, who has kept me back from hurting you, unless you had hurried and come to meet me, surely by morning light no males would have been left to Nabal!" 35So David received from her hand what she had brought him, and said to her, "Go up in peace to your house. See, I have heeded your voice and respected your person."

36Now Abigail went to Nabal, and there he was, holding a feast in his house, like the feast of a king. And Nabal's heart *was* merry within him, for he *was* very drunk; therefore she told him nothing, little or much, until morning light. 37So it was, in the morning, when the wine had gone from Nabal, and his wife had told him these things, that his heart died within him, and he became *like* a stone. 38Then it happened, *after* about ten days, that the LORD struck Nabal, and he died.

39So when David heard that Nabal was dead, he said, "Blessed *be* the LORD, who has pleaded the cause of my reproach from the hand of Nabal, and has kept His servant from evil! For the LORD has returned the wickedness of Nabal on his own head."

And David sent and proposed to Abigail, to take her as his wife. 40When the servants of David had come to Abigail at Carmel, they spoke to her saying, "David sent us to you, to ask you to become his wife."

41Then she arose, bowed her face to the earth, and said, "Here is your maidservant, a servant to wash the feet of the servants of my lord." 42So Abigail rose in haste and rode on a donkey, attended by five of her maidens; and she followed the messengers of David, and became his wife. 43David also took Ahinoam of Jezreel, and so both of them were his wives.

44But Saul had given Michal his daughter, David's wife, to Palti[a] the son of Laish, who *was* from Gallim.

David Spares Saul a Second Time

26 Now the Ziphites came to Saul at Gibeah, saying, "Is David not hiding in the hill of Hachilah, opposite Jeshimon?" 2Then Saul arose and went down to the Wilderness of Ziph, having three thousand chosen men of Israel with him, to seek David in the Wilderness of Ziph. 3And Saul encamped in the hill of Hachilah, which *is* opposite Jeshimon, by the road. But David stayed in the wilderness, and he saw that Saul came after him into the wilderness. 4David therefore sent out spies, and understood that Saul had indeed come.

5So David arose and came to the place where Saul had encamped. And David saw the place where Saul lay, and Abner the son of Ner, the commander of his army. Now Saul lay within the camp, with the people

25:44 [a]Spelled *Paltiel* in 2 Samuel 3:15

encamped all around him. [6]Then David
answered, and said to Ahimelech the Hittite and to Abishai the son of Zeruiah,
brother of Joab, saying, "Who will go down
with me to Saul in the camp?"

And Abishai said, "I will go down with
you."

[7]So David and Abishai came to the
people by night; and there Saul lay sleeping within the camp, with his spear stuck
in the ground by his head. And Abner
and the people lay all around him. [8]Then
Abishai said to David, "God has delivered
your enemy into your hand this day. Now
therefore, please, let me strike him at once
with the spear, right to the earth; and I
will not *have to strike* him a second time!"

[9]But David said to Abishai, "Do not
destroy him; for who can stretch out his
hand against the LORD's anointed, and be
guiltless?" [10]David said furthermore, "*As*
the LORD lives, the LORD shall strike him,
or his day shall come to die, or he shall
go out to battle and perish. [11]The LORD
forbid that I should stretch out my hand
against the LORD's anointed. But please,
take now the spear and the jug of water
that *are* by his head, and let us go." [12]So
David took the spear and the jug of water
by Saul's head, and they got away; and no
man saw or knew *it* or awoke. For they
were all asleep, because a deep sleep from
the LORD had fallen on them.

[13]Now David went over to the other
side, and stood on the top of a hill afar
off, a great distance *being* between them.
[14]And David called out to the people and
to Abner the son of Ner, saying, "Do you
not answer, Abner?"

Then Abner answered and said, "Who
are you, calling out to the king?"

[15]So David said to Abner, "*Are* you not
a man? And who *is* like you in Israel?
Why then have you not guarded your
lord the king? For one of the people came
in to destroy your lord the king. [16]This
thing that you have done *is* not good. *As*
the LORD lives, you deserve to die, because you have not guarded your master,
the LORD's anointed. And now see where
the king's spear *is,* and the jug of water that
was by his head."

[17]Then Saul knew David's voice, and
said, "*Is* that your voice, my son David?"

David said, "*It is* my voice, my lord, O
king." [18]And he said, "Why does my lord
thus pursue his servant? For what have I
done, or what evil *is* in my hand? [19]Now
therefore, please, let my lord the king hear
the words of his servant: If the LORD has
stirred you up against me, let Him accept
an offering. But if *it is* the children of men,
may they *be* cursed before the LORD, for
they have driven me out this day from
sharing in the inheritance of the LORD,
saying, 'Go, serve other gods.' [20]So now,
do not let my blood fall to the earth before the face of the LORD. For the king of
Israel has come out to seek a flea, as when
one hunts a partridge in the mountains."

[21]Then Saul said, "I have sinned. Return, my son David. For I will harm you
no more, because my life was precious in
your eyes this day. Indeed I have played
the fool and erred exceedingly."

[22]And David answered and said, "Here
is the king's spear. Let one of the young
men come over and get it. [23]May the LORD
repay every man *for* his righteousness
and his faithfulness; for the LORD delivered you into *my* hand today, but I would
not stretch out my hand against the LORD's
anointed. [24]And indeed, as your life was
valued much this day in my eyes, so let
my life be valued much in the eyes of the
LORD, and let Him deliver me out of all
tribulation."

[25]Then Saul said to David, "*May* you
be blessed, my son David! You shall both
do great things and also still prevail."

26:8–12 David was a man of great mercy and forgiveness, with a deep trust that God was sovereign and would work out His will in His timing. Perhaps that is why God called him "a man after My own heart" (Acts 13:22).

So David went on his way, and Saul returned to his place.

David Allied with the Philistines

27 And David said in his heart, "Now I shall perish someday by the hand of Saul. *There is* nothing better for me than that I should speedily escape to the land of the Philistines; and Saul will despair of me, to seek me anymore in any part of Israel. So I shall escape out of his hand." 2Then David arose and went over with the six hundred men who *were* with him to Achish the son of Maoch, king of Gath. 3So David dwelt with Achish at Gath, he and his men, each man with his household, *and* David with his two wives, Ahinoam the Jezreelitess, and Abigail the Carmelitess, Nabal's widow. 4And it was told Saul that David had fled to Gath; so he sought him no more.

5Then David said to Achish, "If I have now found favor in your eyes, let them give me a place in some town in the country, that I may dwell there. For why should your servant dwell in the royal city with you?" 6So Achish gave him Ziklag that day. Therefore Ziklag has belonged to the kings of Judah to this day. 7Now the time that David dwelt in the country of the Philistines was one full year and four months.

8And David and his men went up and raided the Geshurites, the Girzites,[a] and the Amalekites. For those *nations* were the inhabitants of the land from of old, as you go to Shur, even as far as the land of Egypt. 9Whenever David attacked the land, he left neither man nor woman alive, but took away the sheep, the oxen, the donkeys, the camels, and the apparel, and returned and came to Achish. 10Then Achish would say, "Where have you made a raid today?" And David would say, "Against the southern *area* of Judah, or against the southern *area* of the Jerahmeelites, or against the southern *area* of the Kenites." 11David would save neither man nor woman alive, to bring *news* to Gath, saying, "Lest they should inform on us, saying, 'Thus David did.' " And thus *was* his behavior all the time he dwelt in the country of the Philistines. 12So Achish believed David, saying, "He has made his people Israel utterly abhor him; therefore he will be my servant forever."

28 Now it happened in those days that the Philistines gathered their armies together for war, to fight with Israel. And Achish said to David, "You assuredly know that you will go out with me to battle, you and your men."

2So David said to Achish, "Surely you know what your servant can do."

And Achish said to David, "Therefore I will make you one of my chief guardians forever."

Saul Consults a Medium

3Now Samuel had died, and all Israel had lamented for him and buried him in Ramah, in his own city. And Saul had put the mediums and the spiritists out of the land.

4Then the Philistines gathered together, and came and encamped at Shunem. So Saul gathered all Israel together, and they encamped at Gilboa. 5When Saul saw the army of the Philistines, he was afraid, and his heart trembled greatly. 6And when Saul inquired of the LORD, the LORD did not answer him, either by dreams or by Urim or by the prophets.

7Then Saul said to his servants, "Find me a woman who is a medium, that I may go to her and inquire of her."

And his servants said to him, "In fact,

27:8 [a]Or *Gezrites*

27:9 Here is something that is hard to reconcile with David's heart of mercy. God Himself rebuked David because he had been "a man of war and [had] shed blood" (1 Chron. 28:3).

28:7 Saul did what was forbidden by God. (See Lev. 19:31; 20:6,7,27; Deut. 18:9,10.) We have a little of Saul in each of us. May our "Saul" fall on the sword of the Word of God and be put to death (see 31:4).

there is a woman who is a medium at En Dor."

8So Saul disguised himself and put on other clothes, and he went, and two men with him; and they came to the woman by night. And he said, "Please conduct a séance for me, and bring up for me the one I shall name to you."

9Then the woman said to him, "Look, you know what Saul has done, how he has cut off the mediums and the spiritists from the land. Why then do you lay a snare for my life, to cause me to die?"

10And Saul swore to her by the LORD, saying, "*As* the LORD lives, no punishment shall come upon you for this thing."

11Then the woman said, "Whom shall I bring up for you?"

And he said, "Bring up Samuel for me."

12When the woman saw Samuel, she cried out with a loud voice. And the woman spoke to Saul, saying, "Why have you deceived me? For you *are* Saul!"

13And the king said to her, "Do not be afraid. What did you see?"

And the woman said to Saul, "I saw a spirit[a] ascending out of the earth."

14So he said to her, "What *is* his form?"

And she said, "An old man is coming up, and he *is* covered with a mantle." And Saul perceived that it *was* Samuel, and he stooped with *his* face to the ground and bowed down.

15Now Samuel said to Saul, "Why have you disturbed me by bringing me up?"

And Saul answered, "I am deeply distressed; for the Philistines make war against me, and God has departed from me and does not answer me anymore, neither by prophets nor by dreams. Therefore I have called you, that you may reveal to me what I should do."

16Then Samuel said: "So why do you ask me, seeing the LORD has departed from you and has become your enemy? 17And the LORD has done for Himself[a] as He spoke by me. For the LORD has torn the kingdom out of your hand and given it to your neighbor, David. 18Because you did not obey the voice of the LORD nor execute His fierce wrath upon Amalek, therefore the LORD has done this thing to you this day. 19Moreover the LORD will also deliver Israel with you into the hand of the Philistines. And tomorrow you and your sons *will be* with me. The LORD will also deliver the army of Israel into the hand of the Philistines."

20Immediately Saul fell full length on the ground, and was dreadfully afraid because of the words of Samuel. And there was no strength in him, for he had eaten no food all day or all night.

21And the woman came to Saul and saw that he was severely troubled, and said to him, "Look, your maidservant has obeyed your voice, and I have put my life in my hands and heeded the words which you spoke to me. 22Now therefore, please, heed also the voice of your maidservant, and let me set a piece of bread before you; and eat, that you may have strength when you go on *your* way."

23But he refused and said, "I will not eat."

So his servants, together with the woman, urged him; and he heeded their voice. Then he arose from the ground and sat on the bed. 24Now the woman had a fatted calf in the house, and she hastened to kill it. And she took flour and kneaded *it*, and baked unleavened bread from it. 25So she brought *it* before Saul and his servants, and they ate. Then they rose and went away that night.

The Philistines Reject David

29 Then the Philistines gathered together all their armies at Aphek, and the Israelites encamped by a fountain which *is* in Jezreel. 2And the lords of the Philistines passed in review by hundreds and by thousands, but David and his men passed in review at the rear with Achish. 3Then the princes of the Philistines said, "What *are* these Hebrews *doing here?*"

And Achish said to the princes of the

28:13 [a]Hebrew *elohim* **28:17** [a]Or *him*, that is, David

Philistines, "*Is* this not David, the servant of Saul king of Israel, who has been with me these days, or these years? And to this day I have found no fault in him since he defected *to me.*"

4But the princes of the Philistines were angry with him; so the princes of the Philistines said to him, "Make this fellow return, that he may go back to the place which you have appointed for him, and do not let him go down with us to battle, lest in the battle he become our adversary. For with what could he reconcile himself to his master, if not with the heads of these men? 5*Is* this not David, of whom they sang to one another in dances, saying:

'Saul has slain his thousands,
And David his ten thousands'?"[a]

6Then Achish called David and said to him, "Surely, *as* the LORD lives, you have been upright, and your going out and your coming in with me in the army *is* good in my sight. For to this day I have not found evil in you since the day of your coming to me. Nevertheless the lords do not favor you. 7Therefore return now, and go in peace, that you may not displease the lords of the Philistines."

8So David said to Achish, "But what have I done? And to this day what have you found in your servant as long as I have been with you, that I may not go and fight against the enemies of my lord the king?"

9Then Achish answered and said to David, "I know that you *are* as good in my sight as an angel of God; nevertheless the princes of the Philistines have said, 'He shall not go up with us to the battle.' 10Now therefore, rise early in the morning with your master's servants who have come with you.[a] And as soon as you are up early in the morning and have light, depart."

11So David and his men rose early to depart in the morning, to return to the land of the Philistines. And the Philistines went up to Jezreel.

David's Conflict with the Amalekites

30 Now it happened, when David and his men came to Ziklag, on the third day, that the Amalekites had invaded the South and Ziklag, attacked Ziklag and burned it with fire, 2and had taken captive the women and those who *were* there, from small to great; they did not kill anyone, but carried *them* away and went their way. 3So David and his men came to the city, and there it was, burned with fire; and their wives, their sons, and their daughters had been taken captive. 4Then David and the people who *were* with him lifted up their voices and wept, until they had no more power to weep. 5And David's two wives, Ahinoam the Jezreelitess, and Abigail the widow of Nabal the Carmelite, had been taken captive. 6Now David was greatly distressed, for the people spoke of stoning him, because the soul of all the people was grieved, every man for his sons and his daughters. But David strengthened himself in the LORD his God.

7Then David said to Abiathar the priest, Ahimelech's son, "Please bring the ephod here to me." And Abiathar brought the ephod to David. 8So David inquired of the LORD, saying, "Shall I pursue this troop? Shall I overtake them?"

And He answered him, "Pursue, for you shall surely overtake *them* and without fail recover *all.*"

9So David went, he and the six hun-

29:5 [a]Compare 1 Samuel 18:7 29:10 [a]Following Masoretic Text, Targum, and Vulgate; Septuagint adds *and go to the place which I have selected for you there; and set no bothersome word in your heart, for you are good before me. And rise on your way.*

29:5 Make it your goal to have a reputation for bringing sinners to the life of God in Christ.

30:3 We have an enemy that came to steal, kill, and destroy (see John 10:10). We have been given the same promise of victory as David was in v. 8.

dred men who *were* with him, and came
to the Brook Besor, where those stayed
who were left behind. [10]But David pursued, he and four hundred men; for two
hundred stayed *behind,* who were so weary
that they could not cross the Brook Besor.
[11]Then they found an Egyptian in the
field, and brought him to David; and they
gave him bread and he ate, and they let
him drink water. [12]And they gave him a
piece of a cake of figs and two clusters of
raisins. So when he had eaten, his strength
came back to him; for he had eaten no
bread nor drunk water for three days and
three nights. [13]Then David said to him,
"To whom do you *belong,* and where *are*
you from?"

And he said, "I *am* a young man from Egypt, servant of an Amalekite; and my master left me behind, because three days
ago I fell sick. [14]We made an invasion of
the southern *area* of the Cherethites, in the *territory* which *belongs* to Judah, and of the southern *area* of Caleb; and we burned Ziklag with fire."

[15]And David said to him, "Can you take me down to this troop?"

So he said, "Swear to me by God that you will neither kill me nor deliver me into the hands of my master, and I will take you down to this troop."

[16]And when he had brought him down,
there they were, spread out over all the
land, eating and drinking and dancing,
because of all the great spoil which they
had taken from the land of the Philistines
and from the land of Judah. [17]Then David
attacked them from twilight until the
evening of the next day. Not a man of them
escaped, except four hundred young men
who rode on camels and fled. [18]So David
recovered all that the Amalekites had carried away, and David rescued his two
wives. [19]And nothing of theirs was lacking, either small or great, sons or daughters, spoil or anything which they had
taken from them; David recovered all.
[20]Then David took all the flocks and
herds they had driven before those *other*
livestock, and said, "This *is* David's spoil."

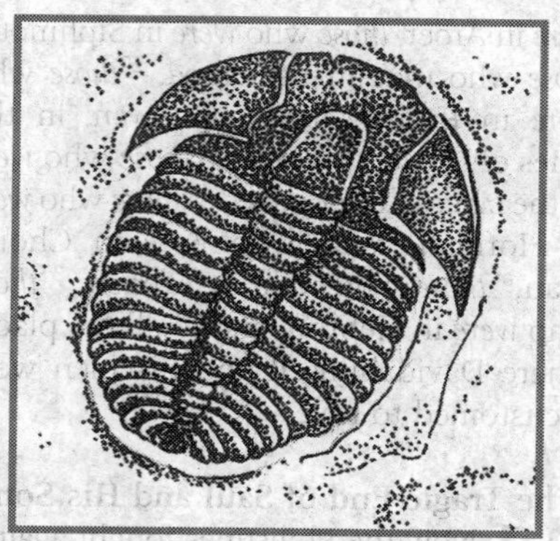
For what the fossil evidence really shows, see Jer. 27:5 comment.

[21]Now David came to the two hun-
dred men who had been so weary that they could not follow David, whom they also had made to stay at the Brook Besor. So they went out to meet David and to meet the people who *were* with him. And when David came near the people, he
greeted them. [22]Then all the wicked and
worthless men[a] of those who went with David answered and said, "Because they did not go with us, we will not give them *any* of the spoil that we have recovered, except for every man's wife and children, that they may lead *them* away and depart."
[23]But David said, "My brethren, you
shall not do so with what the LORD has given us, who has preserved us and delivered into our hand the troop that came
against us. [24]For who will heed you in
this matter? But as his part *is* who goes down to the battle, so *shall* his part *be* who stays by the supplies; they shall
share alike." [25]So it was, from that day
forward; he made it a statute and an ordinance for Israel to this day.
[26]Now when David came to Ziklag, he
sent *some* of the spoil to the elders of Judah, to his friends, saying, "Here is a present for you from the spoil of the enemies
of the LORD"— [27]to *those* who *were* in
Bethel, *those* who *were* in Ramoth of the
South, *those* who *were* in Jattir, [28]*those* who

30:22 [a]**Literally** ***men of Belial***

were in Aroer, *those* who *were* in Siphmoth, *those* who *were* in Eshtemoa, [29]*those* who *were* in Rachal, *those* who *were* in the cities of the Jerahmeelites, *those* who *were* in the cities of the Kenites, [30]*those* who *were* in Hormah, *those* who *were* in Chorashan,[a] *those* who *were* in Athach, [31]*those* who *were* in Hebron, and to all the places where David himself and his men were accustomed to rove.

The Tragic End of Saul and His Sons

31 Now the Philistines fought against Israel; and the men of Israel fled from before the Philistines, and fell slain on Mount Gilboa. [2]Then the Philistines followed hard after Saul and his sons. And the Philistines killed Jonathan, Abinadab, and Malchishua, Saul's sons. [3]The battle became fierce against Saul. The archers hit him, and he was severely wounded by the archers.

[4]Then Saul said to his armorbearer, "Draw your sword, and thrust me through with it, lest these uncircumcised men come and thrust me through and abuse me."

But his armorbearer would not, for he was greatly afraid. Therefore Saul took a sword and fell on it. [5]And when his armorbearer saw that Saul was dead, he also fell on his sword, and died with him. [6]So Saul, his three sons, his armorbearer, and all his men died together that same day.

> Die, *v.*: To stop sinning suddenly.
>
> **ELBERT HUBBARD**

[7]And when the men of Israel who *were* on the other side of the valley, and *those* who *were* on the other side of the Jordan, saw that the men of Israel had fled and that Saul and his sons were dead, they forsook the cities and fled; and the Philistines came and dwelt in them. [8]So it happened the next day, when the Philistines came to strip the slain, that they found Saul and his three sons fallen on Mount Gilboa. [9]And they cut off his head and stripped off his armor, and sent *word* throughout the land of the Philistines, to proclaim *it in* the temple of their idols and among the people. [10]Then they put his armor in the temple of the Ashtoreths, and they fastened his body to the wall of Beth Shan.[a]

"Do I not destroy my enemies when I make them my friends?"

Abraham Lincoln

[11]Now when the inhabitants of Jabesh Gilead heard what the Philistines had done to Saul, [12]all the valiant men arose and traveled all night, and took the body of Saul and the bodies of his sons from the wall of Beth Shan; and they came to Jabesh and burned them there. [13]Then they took their bones and buried *them* under the tamarisk tree at Jabesh, and fasted seven days.

30:30 [a]Or *Borashan* **31:10** [a]Spelled *Beth Shean* in Joshua 17:11 and elsewhere

31:4 Some believe that all who commit suicide will go to hell. However, the Bible is silent on the matter of the eternal destiny of those who tragically take their own lives. We should imitate it. See 1 Cor. 3:17 comment.

2 Samuel

The Report of Saul's Death

1 Now it came to pass after the death of
Saul, when David had returned from
the slaughter of the Amalekites, and
David had stayed two days in Ziklag, 2on
the third day, behold, it happened that a
man came from Saul's camp with his
clothes torn and dust on his head. So it
was, when he came to David, that he fell
to the ground and prostrated himself.

3And David said to him, "Where have
you come from?"

So he said to him, "I have escaped
from the camp of Israel."

4Then David said to him, "How did
the matter go? Please tell me."

And he answered, "The people have
fled from the battle, many of the people
are fallen and dead, and Saul and Jonathan his son are dead also."

5So David said to the young man who
told him, "How do you know that Saul
and Jonathan his son are dead?"

6Then the young man who told him
said, "As I happened by chance *to be* on
Mount Gilboa, there was Saul, leaning on
his spear; and indeed the chariots and
horsemen followed hard after him. 7Now
when he looked behind him, he saw me
and called to me. And I answered, 'Here
I am.' 8And he said to me, 'Who *are* you?'
So I answered him, 'I *am* an Amalekite.'
9He said to me again, 'Please stand over
me and kill me, for anguish has come
upon me, but my life still *remains* in me.'
10So I stood over him and killed him, because I was sure that he could not live after he had fallen. And I took the crown
that *was* on his head and the bracelet that
was on his arm, and have brought them
here to my lord."

11Therefore David took hold of his
own clothes and tore them, and *so did* all
the men who *were* with him. 12And they
mourned and wept and fasted until evening for Saul and for Jonathan his son,
for the people of the LORD and for the
house of Israel, because they had fallen
by the sword.

13Then David said to the young man
who told him, "Where *are* you from?"

And he answered, "I *am* the son of an
alien, an Amalekite."

14So David said to him, "How was it
you were not afraid to put forth your
hand to destroy the LORD's anointed?"
15Then David called one of the young
men and said, "Go near, *and* execute him!"
And he struck him so that he died. 16So
David said to him, "Your blood *is* on your
own head, for your own mouth has testified against you, saying, 'I have killed the
LORD's anointed.' "

1:10 Obviously, the Amalekite was lying (see 1 Sam. 31:3–5). It is likely that, after encountering Saul's body, he decided to brag to the new king to gain his favor. He did not anticipate how his "little white lie" could hurt himself.

The Song of the Bow

[17]Then David lamented with this lamentation over Saul and over Jonathan his son, [18]and he told *them* to teach the children of Judah *the Song of* the Bow; indeed *it is* written in the Book of Jasher:

[19]"The beauty of Israel is slain on your
high places!
How the mighty have fallen!
[20]Tell *it* not in Gath,
Proclaim *it* not in the streets of
Ashkelon—
Lest the daughters of the Philistines
rejoice,
Lest the daughters of the
uncircumcised triumph.

[21]"O mountains of Gilboa,
Let there be no dew nor rain upon you,
Nor fields of offerings.
For the shield of the mighty is cast
away there!
The shield of Saul, not anointed with
oil.
[22]From the blood of the slain,
From the fat of the mighty,
The bow of Jonathan did not turn
back,
And the sword of Saul did not return
empty.

[23]"Saul and Jonathan *were* beloved and
pleasant in their lives,
And in their death they were not
divided;
They were swifter than eagles,
They were stronger than lions.

[24]"O daughters of Israel, weep over Saul,
Who clothed you in scarlet, with
luxury;
Who put ornaments of gold on your
apparel.

[25]"How the mighty have fallen in the
midst of the battle!
Jonathan *was* slain in your high places.
[26]I am distressed for you, my brother
Jonathan;
You have been very pleasant to me;
Your love to me was wonderful,
Surpassing the love of women.

[27]"How the mighty have fallen,
And the weapons of war perished!"

David Anointed King of Judah

2 It happened after this that David inquired of the LORD, saying, "Shall I go up to any of the cities of Judah?"

And the LORD said to him, "Go up."

David said, "Where shall I go up?"

And He said, "To Hebron."

[2]So David went up there, and his two
wives also, Ahinoam the Jezreelitess, and
Abigail the widow of Nabal the Carmelite. [3]And David brought up the men who
were with him, every man with his household. So they dwelt in the cities of Hebron.
[4]Then the men of Judah came, and
there they anointed David king over the
house of Judah. And they told David,
saying, "The men of Jabesh Gilead *were
the ones* who buried Saul." [5]So David sent
messengers to the men of Jabesh Gilead,
and said to them, "You *are* blessed of the
LORD, for you have shown this kindness
to your lord, to Saul, and have buried
him. [6]And now may the LORD show kindness and truth to you. I also will repay
you this kindness, because you have
done this thing. [7]Now therefore, let your
hands be strengthened, and be valiant;
for your master Saul is dead, and also the
house of Judah has anointed me king over
them."

Ishbosheth Made King of Israel

[8]But Abner the son of Ner, commander of Saul's army, took Ishbosheth[a] the
son of Saul and brought him over to Mahanaim; [9]and he made him king over
Gilead, over the Ashurites, over Jezreel,
over Ephraim, over Benjamin, and over all
Israel. [10]Ishbosheth, Saul's son, *was* forty
years old when he began to reign over Israel, and he reigned two years. Only the

2:8 [a]Called *Esh-Baal* in 1 Chronicles 8:33 and 9:39

house of Judah followed David. 11And the time that David was king in Hebron over the house of Judah was seven years and six months.

Israel and Judah at War

12Now Abner the son of Ner, and the servants of Ishbosheth the son of Saul, went out from Mahanaim to Gibeon. 13And Joab the son of Zeruiah, and the servants of David, went out and met them by the pool of Gibeon. So they sat down, one on one side of the pool and the other on the other side of the pool. 14Then Abner said to Joab, "Let the young men now arise and compete before us."

And Joab said, "Let them arise."

15So they arose and went over by number, twelve from Benjamin, *followers* of Ishbosheth the son of Saul, and twelve from the servants of David. 16And each one grasped his opponent by the head and *thrust* his sword in his opponent's side; so they fell down together. Therefore that place was called the Field of Sharp Swords,[a] which *is* in Gibeon. 17So there was a very fierce battle that day, and Abner and the men of Israel were beaten before the servants of David.

18Now the three sons of Zeruiah were there: Joab and Abishai and Asahel. And Asahel *was as* fleet of foot as a wild gazelle. 19So Asahel pursued Abner, and in going he did not turn to the right hand or to the left from following Abner.

20Then Abner looked behind him and said, "*Are* you Asahel?"

He answered, "I *am*."

21And Abner said to him, "Turn aside to your right hand or to your left, and lay hold on one of the young men and take his armor for yourself." But Asahel would not turn aside from following him. 22So Abner said again to Asahel, "Turn aside from following me. Why should I strike you to the ground? How then could I face your brother Joab?" 23However, he refused to turn aside. Therefore Abner struck him in the stomach with the blunt end of the spear, so that the spear came out of his back; and he fell down there and died on the spot. So it was *that* as many as came to the place where Asahel fell down and died, stood still.

24Joab and Abishai also pursued Abner. And the sun was going down when they came to the hill of Ammah, which *is* before Giah by the road to the Wilderness of Gibeon. 25Now the children of Benjamin gathered together behind Abner and became a unit, and took their stand on top of a hill. 26Then Abner called to Joab and said, "Shall the sword devour forever? Do you not know that it will be bitter in the latter end? How long will it be then until you tell the people to return from pursuing their brethren?"

27And Joab said, "*As* God lives, unless you had spoken, surely then by morning all the people would have given up pursuing their brethren." 28So Joab blew a trumpet; and all the people stood still and did not pursue Israel anymore, nor did they fight anymore. 29Then Abner and his men went on all that night through the plain, crossed over the Jordan, and went through all Bithron; and they came to Mahanaim.

30So Joab returned from pursuing Abner. And when he had gathered all the people together, there were missing of David's servants nineteen men and Asahel. 31But the servants of David had struck down, of Benjamin and Abner's men, three hundred and sixty men who died. 32Then they took up Asahel and buried him in his father's tomb, which *was in* Bethlehem. And Joab and his men went all night, and they came to Hebron at daybreak.

2:16 [a]Hebrew *Helkath Hazzurim*

2:20–23 Asahel is like the sinner chasing hard after sin. It will be the death of him, if he refuses to turn from it.

3 Now there was a long war between the house of Saul and the house of David. But David grew stronger and stronger, and the house of Saul grew weaker and weaker.

Sons of David

2Sons were born to David in Hebron: His firstborn was Amnon by Ahinoam the Jezreelitess; 3his second, Chileab, by Abigail the widow of Nabal the Carmelite; the third, Absalom the son of Maacah, the daughter of Talmai, king of Geshur; 4the fourth, Adonijah the son of Haggith; the fifth, Shephatiah the son of Abital; 5and the sixth, Ithream, by David's wife Eglah. These were born to David in Hebron.

Abner Joins Forces with David

6Now it was so, while there was war between the house of Saul and the house of David, that Abner was strengthening *his hold* on the house of Saul.

7And Saul had a concubine, whose name *was* Rizpah, the daughter of Aiah. So *Ishbosheth* said to Abner, "Why have you gone in to my father's concubine?"

8Then Abner became very angry at the words of Ishbosheth, and said, "*Am* I a dog's head that belongs to Judah? Today I show loyalty to the house of Saul your father, to his brothers, and to his friends, and have not delivered you into the hand of David; and you charge me today with a fault concerning this woman? 9May God do so to Abner, and more also, if I do not do for David as the LORD has sworn to him— 10to transfer the kingdom from the house of Saul, and set up the throne of David over Israel and over Judah, from Dan to Beersheba." 11And he could not answer Abner another word, because he feared him.

12Then Abner sent messengers on his behalf to David, saying, "Whose *is* the land?" saying *also,* "Make your covenant with me, and indeed my hand *shall be* with you to bring all Israel to you."

13And *David* said, "Good, I will make a covenant with you. But one thing I require of you: you shall not see my face unless you first bring Michal, Saul's daughter, when you come to see my face." 14So David sent messengers to Ishbosheth, Saul's son, saying, "Give *me* my wife Michal, whom I betrothed to myself for a hundred foreskins of the Philistines." 15And Ishbosheth sent and took her from *her* husband, from Paltiel[a] the son of Laish. 16Then her husband went along with her to Bahurim, weeping behind her. So Abner said to him, "Go, return!" And he returned.

17Now Abner had communicated with the elders of Israel, saying, "In time past you were seeking for David *to be* king over you. 18Now then, do *it!* For the LORD has spoken of David, saying, 'By the hand of My servant David, I[a] will save My people Israel from the hand of the Philistines and the hand of all their enemies.' " 19And Abner also spoke in the hearing of Benjamin. Then Abner also went to speak in the hearing of David in Hebron all that seemed good to Israel and the whole house of Benjamin.

20So Abner and twenty men with him came to David at Hebron. And David made a feast for Abner and the men who *were* with him. 21Then Abner said to David, "I will arise and go, and gather all Israel to my lord the king, that they may make a covenant with you, and that you may reign over all that your heart desires." So David sent Abner away, and he went in peace.

Joab Murders Abner

22At that moment the servants of David and Joab came from a raid and brought much spoil with them. But Abner *was* not

3:15 [a]Spelled *Palti* in 1 Samuel 25:44 3:18 [a]Following many Hebrew manuscripts, Septuagint, Syriac, and Targum; Masoretic Text reads *he.*

3:1 Every soul that is added to the Church is a soul from the camp of the enemy.

with David in Hebron, for he had sent
him away, and he had gone in peace.
23When Joab and all the troops that *were*
with him had come, they told Joab, saying, "Abner the son of Ner came to the
king, and he sent him away, and he has
gone in peace." 24Then Joab came to the
king and said, "What have you done?
Look, Abner came to you; why *is* it *that*
you sent him away, and he has already
gone? 25Surely you realize that Abner the
son of Ner came to deceive you, to know
your going out and your coming in, and
to know all that you are doing."

26And when Joab had gone from
David's presence, he sent messengers after Abner, who brought him back from
the well of Sirah. But David did not know
it. 27Now when Abner had returned to
Hebron, Joab took him aside in the gate
to speak with him privately, and there
stabbed him in the stomach, so that he
died for the blood of Asahel his brother.

28Afterward, when David heard *it,* he
said, "My kingdom and I *are* guiltless before the LORD forever of the blood of Abner the son of Ner. 29Let it rest on the
head of Joab and on all his father's house;
and let there never fail to be in the house
of Joab one who has a discharge or is a
leper, who leans on a staff or falls by the
sword, or who lacks bread." 30So Joab
and Abishai his brother killed Abner, because he had killed their brother Asahel
at Gibeon in the battle.

David's Mourning for Abner

31Then David said to Joab and to all
the people who were with him, "Tear your
clothes, gird yourselves with sackcloth,
and mourn for Abner." And King David
followed the coffin. 32So they buried Abner in Hebron; and the king lifted up his
voice and wept at the grave of Abner, and
all the people wept. 33And the king sang
a lament over Abner and said:

"Should Abner die as a fool dies?
34Your hands were not bound
Nor your feet put into fetters;
As a man falls before wicked men, *so*
you fell."

Then all the people wept over him again.

35And when all the people came to
persuade David to eat food while it was
still day, David took an oath, saying, "God
do so to me, and more also, if I taste bread
or anything else till the sun goes down!"
36Now all the people took note *of it,* and
it pleased them, since whatever the king
did pleased all the people. 37For all the
people and all Israel understood that day
that it had not been the king's *intent* to
kill Abner the son of Ner. 38Then the king
said to his servants, "Do you not know
that a prince and a great man has fallen
this day in Israel? 39And I *am* weak today,
though anointed king; and these men,
the sons of Zeruiah, *are* too harsh for me.
The LORD shall repay the evildoer according to his wickedness."

. . . . . .

*For questions to ask evolutionists,
see Prov. 3:19 comment.*

. . . . . .

Ishbosheth Is Murdered

4 When Saul's son[a] heard that Abner
had died in Hebron, he lost heart, and
all Israel was troubled. 2Now Saul's son
had two men *who were* captains of troops.
The name of one *was* Baanah and the
name of the other Rechab, the sons of
Rimmon the Beerothite, of the children
of Benjamin. (For Beeroth also was *part*
of Benjamin, 3because the Beerothites fled
to Gittaim and have been sojourners
there until this day.)

4Jonathan, Saul's son, had a son *who
was* lame in *his* feet. He was five years old
when the news about Saul and Jonathan
came from Jezreel; and his nurse took
him up and fled. And it happened, as she
made haste to flee, that he fell and became
lame. His name *was* Mephibosheth.[a]

4:1 [a]That is, Ishbosheth **4:4** [a]Called *Merib-Baal* in 1 Chronicles 8:34 and 9:40

5Then the sons of Rimmon the Beerothite, Rechab and Baanah, set out and came at about the heat of the day to the house of Ishbosheth, who was lying on his bed at noon. 6And they came there, all the way into the house, *as though* to get wheat, and they stabbed him in the stomach. Then Rechab and Baanah his brother escaped. 7For when they came into the house, he was lying on his bed in his bedroom; then they struck him and killed him, beheaded him and took his head, and were all night escaping through the plain. 8And they brought the head of Ishbosheth to David at Hebron, and said to the king, "Here is the head of Ishbosheth, the son of Saul your enemy, who sought your life; and the LORD has avenged my lord the king this day of Saul and his descendants."

9But David answered Rechab and Baanah his brother, the sons of Rimmon the Beerothite, and said to them, "*As the* LORD lives, who has redeemed my life from all adversity, 10when someone told me, saying, 'Look, Saul is dead,' thinking to have brought good news, I arrested him and had him executed in Ziklag—the one who *thought* I would give him a reward for *his* news. 11How much more, when wicked men have killed a righteous person in his own house on his bed? Therefore, shall I not now require his blood at your hand and remove you from the earth?" 12So David commanded his young men, and they executed them, cut off their hands and feet, and hanged *them* by the pool in Hebron. But they took the head of Ishbosheth and buried *it* in the tomb of Abner in Hebron.

David Reigns over All Israel

5 Then all the tribes of Israel came to David at Hebron and spoke, saying, "Indeed we *are* your bone and your flesh. 2Also, in time past, when Saul was king over us, you were the one who led Israel out and brought them in; and the LORD said to you, 'You shall shepherd My people Israel, and be ruler over Israel.' " 3Therefore all the elders of Israel came to the king at Hebron, and King David made a covenant with them at Hebron before the LORD. And they anointed David king over Israel. 4David *was* thirty years old when he began to reign, *and* he reigned forty years. 5In Hebron he reigned over Judah seven years and six months, and in Jerusalem he reigned thirty-three years over all Israel and Judah.

The Conquest of Jerusalem

6And the king and his men went to Jerusalem against the Jebusites, the inhabitants of the land, who spoke to David, saying, "You shall not come in here; but the blind and the lame will repel you," thinking, "David cannot come in here." 7Nevertheless David took the stronghold of Zion (that *is*, the City of David).

8Now David said on that day, "Whoever climbs up by way of the water shaft and defeats the Jebusites (the lame and the blind, *who are* hated by David's soul), *he shall be chief and captain.*"[a] Therefore they say, "The blind and the lame shall not come into the house."

9Then David dwelt in the stronghold, and called it the City of David. And David built all around from the Millo[a] and inward. 10So David went on and became great, and the LORD God of hosts *was* with him.

11Then Hiram king of Tyre sent messengers to David, and cedar trees, and carpenters and masons. And they built

5:8 [a]Compare 1 Chronicles 11:6 5:9 [a]Literally *The Landfill*

4:5–12 How many are there who hate Christians, and have even killed them thinking that they are pleasing God? Saul of Tarsus was one who, when he heard the voice from heaven, was no doubt expecting a commendation, but instead received condemnation.

5:4 Jesus was thirty years old when He began His ministry, and He will reign forever.

David a house. 12So David knew that the LORD had established him as king over Israel, and that He had exalted His kingdom for the sake of His people Israel.

13And David took more concubines and wives from Jerusalem, after he had come from Hebron. Also more sons and daughters were born to David. 14Now these *are* the names of those who were born to him in Jerusalem: Shammua,[a] Shobab, Nathan, Solomon, 15Ibhar, Elishua,[a] Nepheg, Japhia, 16Elishama, Eliada, and Eliphelet.

The Philistines Defeated

17Now when the Philistines heard that they had anointed David king over Israel, all the Philistines went up to search for David. And David heard *of it* and went down to the stronghold. 18The Philistines also went and deployed themselves in the Valley of Rephaim. 19So David inquired of the LORD, saying, "Shall I go up against the Philistines? Will You deliver them into my hand?"

And the LORD said to David, "Go up, for I will doubtless deliver the Philistines into your hand."

20So David went to Baal Perazim, and David defeated them there; and he said, "The LORD has broken through my enemies before me, like a breakthrough of water." Therefore he called the name of that place Baal Perazim.[a] 21And they left their images there, and David and his men carried them away.

22Then the Philistines went up once again and deployed themselves in the Valley of Rephaim. 23Therefore David inquired of the LORD, and He said, "You shall not go up; circle around behind them, and come upon them in front of the mulberry trees. 24And it shall be, when you hear the sound of marching in the tops of the mulberry trees, then you shall advance quickly. For then the LORD will go out before you to strike the camp of the Philistines." 25And David did so, as the LORD commanded him; and he drove back the Philistines from Geba[a] as far as Gezer.

The Ark Brought to Jerusalem

6 Again David gathered all *the* choice *men* of Israel, thirty thousand. 2And David arose and went with all the people who *were* with him from Baale Judah to bring up from there the ark of God, whose name is called by the Name,[a] the LORD of Hosts, who dwells *between* the cherubim. 3So they set the ark of God on a new cart, and brought it out of the house of Abinadab, which *was* on the hill; and Uzzah and Ahio, the sons of Abinadab, drove the new cart.[a] 4And they brought it out of the house of Abinadab, which *was* on the hill, accompanying the ark of God; and Ahio went before the ark. 5Then David and all the house of Israel played *music* before the LORD on all kinds of *instruments of* fir wood, on harps, on stringed instruments, on tambourines, on sistrums, and on cymbals.

6And when they came to Nachon's

5:14 [a]Spelled *Shimea* in 1 Chronicles 3:5 5:15 [a]Spelled *Elishama* in 1 Chronicles 3:6 5:20 [a]Literally *Master of Breakthroughs* 5:25 [a]Following Masoretic Text, Targum, and Vulgate; Septuagint reads *Gibeon.* 6:2 [a]Septuagint, Targum, and Vulgate omit *by the Name;* many Hebrew manuscripts and Syriac read *there.* 6:3 [a]Septuagint adds *with the ark.*

6:1–11 David presumed that all God required was sincerity, despite the fact that only the sons of Kohath were supposed to carry the ark and that anyone who touched it would die (see Num. 4:1–15). Remember that the ark contained the Law of God. The ark was holy only because the Law is holy. The lesson is that it does matter how we "carry" the gospel into this world. It exists only because of the Law. It was the Law of Moses that put Jesus on the cross. Had there been no perfect righteousness demanded by the Law, Jesus would not have had to suffer for our sins. If God is so serious about how the Law is physically carried, how much more should we fear if we neglect it—and even despise it—when proclaiming the gospel? All the song and dance in the world doesn't please God, if we don't do things according to the pattern laid out so clearly in Holy Scripture.

threshing floor, Uzzah put out *his hand* to the ark of God and took hold of it, for the oxen stumbled. [7]Then the anger of the LORD was aroused against Uzzah, and God struck him there for *his* error; and he died there by the ark of God. [8]And David became angry because of the LORD's outbreak against Uzzah; and he called the name of the place Perez Uzzah[a] to this day.

[9]David was afraid of the LORD that day; and he said, "How can the ark of the LORD come to me?" [10]So David would not move the ark of the LORD with him into the City of David; but David took it aside into the house of Obed-Edom the Gittite. [11]The ark of the LORD remained in the house of Obed-Edom the Gittite three months. And the LORD blessed Obed-Edom and all his household.

[12]Now it was told King David, saying, "The LORD has blessed the house of Obed-Edom and all that *belongs* to him, because of the ark of God." So David went and brought up the ark of God from the house of Obed-Edom to the City of David with gladness. [13]And so it was, when those bearing the ark of the LORD had gone six paces, that he sacrificed oxen and fatted sheep. [14]Then David danced before the LORD with all *his* might; and David *was* wearing a linen ephod. [15]So David and all the house of Israel brought up the ark of the LORD with shouting and with the sound of the trumpet.

[16]Now as the ark of the LORD came into the City of David, Michal, Saul's daughter, looked through a window and saw King David leaping and whirling before the LORD; and she despised him in her heart. [17]So they brought the ark of the LORD, and set it in its place in the midst of the tabernacle that David had erected for it. Then David offered burnt offerings and peace offerings before the LORD. [18]And when David had finished offering burnt offerings and peace offerings, he blessed the people in the name of the LORD of hosts. [19]Then he distributed among all the people, among the whole multitude of Israel, both the women and the men, to everyone a loaf of bread, a piece *of meat,* and a cake of raisins. So all the people departed, everyone to his house.

[20]Then David returned to bless his household. And Michal the daughter of Saul came out to meet David, and said, "How glorious was the king of Israel today, uncovering himself today in the eyes of the maids of his servants, as one of the base fellows shamelessly uncovers himself!"

[21]So David said to Michal, "*It was* before the LORD, who chose me instead of your father and all his house, to appoint me ruler over the people of the LORD, over Israel. Therefore I will play *music* before the LORD. [22]And I will be even more undignified than this, and will be humble in my own sight. But as for the maidservants of whom you have spoken, by them I will be held in honor."

[23]Therefore Michal the daughter of Saul had no children to the day of her death.

God's Covenant with David

7 Now it came to pass when the king was dwelling in his house, and the LORD had given him rest from all his enemies all around, [2]that the king said to Nathan the prophet, "See now, I dwell in a house of cedar, but the ark of God dwells inside tent curtains."

[3]Then Nathan said to the king, "Go, do all that *is* in your heart, for the LORD *is* with you."

[4]But it happened that night that the word of the LORD came to Nathan, saying, [5]"Go and tell My servant David, 'Thus says

6:8 [a]Literally *Outburst Against Uzzah*

7:5 The Scriptures say that God does not dwell in temples made with hands (see Acts 17:24). He is omnipresent. God dwells by His Spirit within all who are born again, and they compose the "temple of the living God" (2 Cor. 6:16). The ungodly seem to think that God is confined to a building that they erroneously call a "church."

the LORD: "Would you build a house for Me to dwell in? [6]For I have not dwelt in a house since the time that I brought the children of Israel up from Egypt, even to this day, but have moved about in a tent and in a tabernacle. [7]Wherever I have moved about with all the children of Israel, have I ever spoken a word to anyone from the tribes of Israel, whom I commanded to shepherd My people Israel, saying, 'Why have you not built Me a house of cedar?' " ' [8]Now therefore, thus shall you say to My servant David, 'Thus says the LORD of hosts: "I took you from the sheepfold, from following the sheep, to be ruler over My people, over Israel. [9]And I have been with you wherever you have gone, and have cut off all your enemies from before you, and have made you a great name, like the name of the great men who *are* on the earth. [10]Moreover I will appoint a place for My people Israel, and will plant them, that they may dwell in a place of their own and move no more; nor shall the sons of wickedness oppress them anymore, as previously, [11]since the time that I commanded judges *to be* over My people Israel, and have caused you to rest from all your enemies. Also the LORD tells you that He will make you a house.[a]

[12]"When your days are fulfilled and you rest with your fathers, I will set up your seed after you, who will come from your body, and I will establish his kingdom. [13]He shall build a house for My name, and I will establish the throne of his kingdom forever. [14]I will be his Father, and he shall be My son. If he commits iniquity, I will chasten him with the rod of men and with the blows of the sons of men. [15]But My mercy shall not depart from him, as I took *it* from Saul, whom I removed from before you. [16]And your house and your kingdom shall be established forever before you.[a] Your throne shall be established forever." ' "

[17]According to all these words and according to all this vision, so Nathan spoke to David.

David's Thanksgiving to God

[18]Then King David went in and sat before the LORD; and he said: "Who *am* I, O Lord GOD? And what is my house, that You have brought me this far? [19]And yet this was a small thing in Your sight, O Lord GOD; and You have also spoken of Your servant's house for a great while to come. *Is* this the manner of man, O Lord GOD? [20]Now what more can David say to You? For You, Lord GOD, know Your servant. [21]For Your word's sake, and according to Your own heart, You have done all these great things, to make Your servant know *them.* [22]Therefore You are great, O Lord GOD.[a] For *there is* none like You, nor *is there any* God besides You, according to all that we have heard with our ears.

> I have a fundamental belief in the Bible as the Word of God, written by men who were inspired. I study the Bible daily. Opposition to godliness is atheism in profession and idolatry in practice. Atheism is so senseless and odious to mankind that it never had many professors.
>
> **SIR ISAAC NEWTON**

[23]And who *is* like Your people, like Israel, the one nation on the earth whom God went to redeem for Himself as a people, to make for Himself a name—and to do for Yourself great and awesome deeds for Your land—before Your people whom You redeemed for Yourself from Egypt, the nations, and their gods? [24]For You have made Your people Israel Your very own people forever; and You, LORD, have become their God.

[25]"Now, O LORD God, the word which You have spoken concerning Your servant and concerning his house, establish *it* forever and do as You have said. [26]So let Your name be magnified forever, saying, 'The LORD of hosts *is* the God over Israel.'

7:11 [a]That is, a royal dynasty 7:16 [a]Septuagint reads *Me.* 7:22 [a]Targum and Syriac read *O LORD God.*

And let the house of Your servant David be established before You. 27For You, O LORD of hosts, God of Israel, have revealed *this* to Your servant, saying, 'I will build you a house.' Therefore Your servant has found it in his heart to pray this prayer to You.

28"And now, O Lord GOD, You are God, and Your words are true, and You have promised this goodness to Your servant. 29Now therefore, let it please You to bless the house of Your servant, that it may continue before You forever; for You, O Lord GOD, have spoken *it,* and with Your blessing let the house of Your servant be blessed forever."

David's Further Conquests

8 After this it came to pass that David attacked the Philistines and subdued them. And David took Metheg Ammah from the hand of the Philistines.

2Then he defeated Moab. Forcing them down to the ground, he measured them off with a line. With two lines he measured off those to be put to death, and with one full line those to be kept alive. So the Moabites became David's servants, *and* brought tribute.

3David also defeated Hadadezer the son of Rehob, king of Zobah, as he went to recover his territory at the River Euphrates. 4David took from him one thousand *chariots,* seven hundred[a] horsemen, and twenty thousand foot soldiers. Also David hamstrung all the chariot horses, except that he spared *enough* of them for one hundred chariots.

5When the Syrians of Damascus came to help Hadadezer king of Zobah, David killed twenty-two thousand of the Syrians. 6Then David put garrisons in Syria of Damascus; and the Syrians became David's servants, *and* brought tribute. So the LORD preserved David wherever he went. 7And David took the shields of gold that had belonged to the servants of Hadadezer, and brought them to Jerusalem. 8Also from Betah[a] and from Berothai, cities of Hadadezer, King David took a large amount of bronze.

9When Toi[a] king of Hamath heard that David had defeated all the army of Hadadezer, 10then Toi sent Joram[a] his son to King David, to greet him and bless him, because he had fought against Hadadezer and defeated him (for Hadadezer had been at war with Toi); and *Joram* brought with him articles of silver, articles of gold, and articles of bronze. 11King David also dedicated these to the LORD, along with the silver and gold that he had dedicated from all the nations which he had subdued— 12from Syria,[a] from Moab, from the people of Ammon, from the Philistines, from Amalek, and from the spoil of Hadadezer the son of Rehob, king of Zobah.

13And David made *himself* a name when he returned from killing eighteen thousand Syrians[a] in the Valley of Salt. 14He also put garrisons in Edom; throughout all Edom he put garrisons, and all the Edomites became David's servants. And the LORD preserved David wherever he went.

David's Administration

15So David reigned over all Israel; and David administered judgment and justice to all his people. 16Joab the son of Zeruiah *was* over the army; Jehoshaphat the son of Ahilud *was* recorder; 17Zadok the son of Ahitub and Ahimelech the son of Abiathar *were* the priests; Seraiah[a] *was* the scribe; 18Benaiah the son of Jehoiada *was over* both the Cherethites and the Pelethites; and David's sons were chief ministers.

8:4 [a]Or *seven thousand* (compare 1 Chronicles 18:4) 8:8 [a]Spelled *Tibhath* in 1 Chronicles 18:8 8:9 [a]Spelled *Tou* in 1 Chronicles 18:9 8:10 [a]Spelled *Hadoram* in 1 Chronicles 18:10 8:12 [a]Septuagint, Syriac, and some Hebrew manuscripts read *Edom.* 8:13 [a]Septuagint, Syriac, and some Hebrew manuscripts read *Edomites* (compare 1 Chronicles 18:12). 8:17 [a]Spelled *Shavsha* in 1 Chronicles 18:16

8:6,14 Christians are forever "preserved" in Jesus Christ (see Jude 1:1).

David's Kindness to Mephibosheth

9 Now David said, "Is there still anyone who is left of the house of Saul, that I may show him kindness for Jonathan's sake?"

[2]And *there was* a servant of the house of Saul whose name *was* Ziba. So when they had called him to David, the king said to him, "*Are* you Ziba?"

He said, "At your service!"

[3]Then the king said, "*Is* there not still someone of the house of Saul, to whom I may show the kindness of God?"

And Ziba said to the king, "There is still a son of Jonathan *who is* lame in *his* feet."

[4]So the king said to him, "Where *is* he?"

And Ziba said to the king, "Indeed he *is* in the house of Machir the son of Ammiel, in Lo Debar."

[5]Then King David sent and brought him out of the house of Machir the son of Ammiel, from Lo Debar.

[6]Now when Mephibosheth the son of Jonathan, the son of Saul, had come to David, he fell on his face and prostrated himself. Then David said, "Mephibosheth?"

And he answered, "Here is your servant!"

[7]So David said to him, "Do not fear, for I will surely show you kindness for Jonathan your father's sake, and will restore to you all the land of Saul your grandfather; and you shall eat bread at my table continually."

[8]Then he bowed himself, and said, "What *is* your servant, that you should look upon such a dead dog as I?"

[9]And the king called to Ziba, Saul's servant, and said to him, "I have given to your master's son all that belonged to Saul and to all his house. [10]You therefore, and your sons and your servants, shall work the land for him, and you shall bring in *the harvest,* that your master's son may have food to eat. But Mephibosheth your master's son shall eat bread at my table always." Now Ziba had fifteen sons and twenty servants.

[11]Then Ziba said to the king, "According to all that my lord the king has commanded his servant, so will your servant do."

"As for Mephibosheth," *said the king,* "he shall eat at my table[a] like one of the king's sons." [12]Mephibosheth had a young son whose name *was* Micha. And all who dwelt in the house of Ziba *were* servants of Mephibosheth. [13]So Mephibosheth dwelt in Jerusalem, for he ate continually at the king's table. And he was lame in both his feet.

The Ammonites and Syrians Defeated

10 It happened after this that the king of the people of Ammon died, and Hanun his son reigned in his place. [2]Then David said, "I will show kindness to Hanun the son of Nahash, as his father showed kindness to me."

So David sent by the hand of his servants to comfort him concerning his father. And David's servants came into the land of the people of Ammon. [3]And the princes of the people of Ammon said to Hanun their lord, "Do you think that David really honors your father because he has sent comforters to you? Has David not *rather* sent his servants to you to search the city, to spy it out, and to overthrow it?"

[4]Therefore Hanun took David's servants, shaved off half of their beards, cut off their garments in the middle, at their buttocks, and sent them away. [5]When

9:11 [a]Septuagint reads *David's table.*

9:5–13 We come to God as helpless beggars, lame in our feet, and He shows us great kindness and mercy for Christ's sake, inviting us to dine in His presence eternally.

10:2 How sad that this fighting came out of unjustified suspicion. Misunderstanding is fertile ground for the enemy to sow seeds of discord. Endeavor always to have humble, open, and honest communication.

they told David, he sent to meet them, because the men were greatly ashamed. And the king said, "Wait at Jericho until your beards have grown, and *then* return."

6When the people of Ammon saw that they had made themselves repulsive to David, the people of Ammon sent and hired the Syrians of Beth Rehob and the Syrians of Zoba, twenty thousand foot soldiers; and from the king of Maacah one thousand men, and from Ish-Tob twelve thousand men. 7Now when David heard *of it,* he sent Joab and all the army of the mighty men. 8Then the people of Ammon came out and put themselves in battle array at the entrance of the gate. And the Syrians of Zoba, Beth Rehob, Ish-Tob, and Maacah *were* by themselves in the field.

9When Joab saw that the battle line was against him before and behind, he chose some of Israel's best and put *them* in battle array against the Syrians. 10And the rest of the people he put under the command of Abishai his brother, that he might set *them* in battle array against the people of Ammon. 11Then he said, "If the Syrians are too strong for me, then you shall help me; but if the people of Ammon are too strong for you, then I will come and help you. 12Be of good courage, and let us be strong for our people and for the cities of our God. And may the LORD do *what is* good in His sight."

13So Joab and the people who *were* with him drew near for the battle against the Syrians, and they fled before him. 14When the people of Ammon saw that the Syrians were fleeing, they also fled before Abishai, and entered the city. So Joab returned from the people of Ammon and went to Jerusalem.

15When the Syrians saw that they had been defeated by Israel, they gathered together. 16Then Hadadezer[a] sent and brought out the Syrians who *were* beyond the River,[b] and they came to Helam. And Shobach the commander of Hadadezer's army *went* before them. 17When it was told David, he gathered all Israel, crossed over the Jordan, and came to Helam. And the Syrians set themselves in battle array against David and fought with him. 18Then the Syrians fled before Israel; and David killed seven hundred charioteers and forty thousand horsemen of the Syrians, and struck Shobach the commander of their army, who died there. 19And when all the kings *who were* servants to Hadadezer[a] saw that they were defeated by Israel, they made peace with Israel and served them. So the Syrians were afraid to help the people of Ammon anymore.

. . . . . .

Are dinosaurs mentioned in the Bible? See Isa. 27:1 comment.

. . . . . .

David, Bathsheba, and Uriah

11 It happened in the spring of the year, at the time when kings go out *to battle,* that David sent Joab and his servants with him, and all Israel; and they destroyed the people of Ammon and besieged Rabbah. But David remained at Jerusalem.

2Then it happened one evening that David arose from his bed and walked on the roof of the king's house. And from the roof he saw a woman bathing, and the woman *was* very beautiful to behold. 3So David sent and inquired about the woman. And *someone* said, "*Is* this not Bath-

10:16 [a]Hebrew *Hadarezer* [b]That is, the Euphrates 10:19 [a]Hebrew *Hadarezer*

11:1–5 Keep yourself busy warring against the world, the flesh, and the devil. You cannot let down your guard for a moment. Protect your thoughts, and keep your heart free from sin. Don't let your mind wander into lust. The Scriptures warn that lust brings forth sin, and sin when it is full grown brings forth death (see James 1:14,15). The enemy knows your Achilles heel. If you are a male with red blood in your veins, you will have a battle with lust, but you are not alone in your fight. To gain victory in this area, see Gal. 5:16 comment.

sheba, the daughter of Eliam, the wife of Uriah the Hittite?" [4]Then David sent messengers, and took her; and she came to him, and he lay with her, for she was cleansed from her impurity; and she returned to her house. [5]And the woman conceived; so she sent and told David, and said, "I *am* with child."

[6]Then David sent to Joab, *saying,* "Send me Uriah the Hittite." And Joab sent Uriah to David. [7]When Uriah had come to him, David asked how Joab was doing, and how the people were doing, and how the war prospered. [8]And David said to Uriah, "Go down to your house and wash your feet." So Uriah departed from the king's house, and a gift *of food* from the king followed him. [9]But Uriah slept at the door of the king's house with all the servants of his lord, and did not go down to his house. [10]So when they told David, saying, "Uriah did not go down to his house," David said to Uriah, "Did you not come from a journey? Why did you not go down to your house?"

[11]And Uriah said to David, "The ark and Israel and Judah are dwelling in tents, and my lord Joab and the servants of my lord are encamped in the open fields. Shall I then go to my house to eat and drink, and to lie with my wife? *As* you live, and *as* your soul lives, I will not do this thing."

[12]Then David said to Uriah, "Wait here today also, and tomorrow I will let you depart." So Uriah remained in Jerusalem that day and the next. [13]Now when David called him, he ate and drank before him; and he made him drunk. And at evening he went out to lie on his bed with the servants of his lord, but he did not go down to his house.

[14]In the morning it happened that David wrote a letter to Joab and sent *it* by the hand of Uriah. [15]And he wrote in the letter, saying, "Set Uriah in the forefront of the hottest battle, and retreat from him, that he may be struck down and die." [16]So it was, while Joab besieged the city, that he assigned Uriah to a place where he knew there *were* valiant men. [17]Then the men of the city came out and fought with Joab. And *some* of the people of the servants of David fell; and Uriah the Hittite died also.

[18]Then Joab sent and told David all the things concerning the war, [19]and charged the messenger, saying, "When you have finished telling the matters of the war to the king, [20]if it happens that the king's wrath rises, and he says to you: 'Why did you approach so near to the city when you fought? Did you not know that they would shoot from the wall? [21]Who struck Abimelech the son of Jerubbesheth?[a] Was it not a woman who cast a piece of a millstone on him from the wall, so that he died in Thebez? Why did you go near the wall?'—then you shall say, 'Your servant Uriah the Hittite is dead also.' "

[22]So the messenger went, and came and told David all that Joab had sent by him. [23]And the messenger said to David, "Surely the men prevailed against us and came out to us in the field; then we drove them back as far as the entrance of the gate. [24]The archers shot from the wall at your servants; and *some* of the king's servants are dead, and your servant Uriah the Hittite is dead also."

[25]Then David said to the messenger, "Thus you shall say to Joab: 'Do not let this thing displease you, for the sword devours one as well as another. Strengthen your attack against the city, and overthrow it.' So encourage him."

[26]When the wife of Uriah heard that Uriah her husband was dead, she mourned for her husband. [27]And when her mourn-

11:21 [a]Same as *Jerubbaal* (Gideon), Judges 6:32ff

11:27 David swept his sin under the carpet of discretion, but Scripture had ten damning words: "But the thing that David had done displeased the LORD." The world sweeps sin under the carpet of discretion, but God has given us the Ten Commandments to expose their sins and point them to the Savior.

ing was over, David sent and brought her
to his house, and she became his wife
and bore him a son. But the thing that
David had done displeased the LORD.

Nathan's Parable and David's Confession

12 Then the LORD sent Nathan to
David. And he came to him, and
said to him: "There were two men in one
city, one rich and the other poor. 2The
rich *man* had exceedingly many flocks
and herds. 3But the poor *man* had nothing, except one little ewe lamb which he
had bought and nourished; and it grew
up together with him and with his children. It ate of his own food and drank
from his own cup and lay in his bosom;
and it was like a daughter to him. 4And a
traveler came to the rich man, who refused to take from his own flock and
from his own herd to prepare one for the
wayfaring man who had come to him;
but he took the poor man's lamb and prepared it for the man who had come to
him."
5So David's anger was greatly aroused
against the man, and he said to Nathan,
"*As* the LORD lives, the man who has done
this shall surely die! 6And he shall restore
fourfold for the lamb, because he did this
thing and because he had no pity."
7Then Nathan said to David, "You *are*
the man! Thus says the LORD God of Israel: 'I anointed you king over Israel, and
I delivered you from the hand of Saul. 8I
gave you your master's house and your
master's wives into your keeping, and
gave you the house of Israel and Judah.
And if *that had been* too little, I also would
have given you much more! 9Why have
you despised the commandment of the

12:1–14 *How to Confront Sinners*

While the world would say that David was an unfortunate victim of his own moral weaknesses, the truth is that he was a covetous man. He was a devious liar, a thief, an adulterer, and a murderer. He dishonored his parents and he caused the name of the Lord to be blasphemed by the enemies of the God who had lavished His goodness on him. So Nathan was commissioned by God to reprove the king.

There is great significance in the order in which the reproof came. Did Nathan begin by saying, "There is a God-shaped hole in your heart"? Of course not. What would that have to do with anything? David was a criminal who had violated God's Law. It is easy to see sin in others, but not in ourselves. There was a huge log of sin in David's eye so that he couldn't see clearly. So Nathan gave David (the shepherd of Israel) a parable about something that David could understand—sheep. He began with the natural realm, rather than immediately exposing the king's sin. He told a story about a rich man who, instead of taking a sheep from his own flock, killed a poor man's pet lamb to feed a stranger.

David was indignant, and sat up on his high throne of self-righteousness. In v. 6, he revealed his knowledge of the Law (see Exod. 22:1) by declaring that the guilty party must restore fourfold and must die for his crime. The work of the Law is written on the heart of every sinner (see Rom. 2:15), so we must therefore use the Law to bring the knowledge of sin.

When going through the Ten Commandments with sinners, you will find the same thing—they will not look at themselves with the same moral measure with which they look at others. For years I had a hurdle I couldn't seem to get over. I would ask people, "Do you think you are a good person?" "Yes." I would then say, "Well, let's look at the Ten Commandments to see if that's true. Have you ever told a lie?" "Yes." Then I would try to personalize it by saying, "What does that make you?" and I would frequently hear, "Well, it doesn't make me a liar." So I would say, "What would you call *me* if I told lies?" and they would quickly concede, "A liar." However, I've found a better way. Instead of asking, "Have you ever told a lie?" I now ask, "So, how many lies do you think you have told in your life?" People would immediately say, "Many." That made it so much easier to get them to concede that a person who has told lies is a liar.

Notice how Nathan *personalized* David's sin. He didn't dilute the king's guilt by saying, "*All* have sinned and fall short of the glory of God." He didn't generalize his transgression. He knew David must be made to know that *his* sin had an-

(continued)

LORD, to do evil in His sight? You have
killed Uriah the Hittite with the sword;
you have taken his wife *to be* your wife,
and have killed him with the sword of the
people of Ammon. [10]Now therefore, the
sword shall never depart from your house,
because you have despised Me, and have
taken the wife of Uriah the Hittite to be
your wife.' [11]Thus says the LORD: 'Behold,
I will raise up adversity against you from
your own house; and I will take your
wives before your eyes and give *them* to
your neighbor, and he shall lie with your
wives in the sight of this sun. [12]For you
did *it* secretly, but I will do this thing before all Israel, before the sun.' "

[13]So David said to Nathan, "I have
sinned against the LORD."

And Nathan said to David, "The LORD
also has put away your sin; you shall not
die. [14]However, because by this deed you
have given great occasion to the enemies
of the LORD to blaspheme, the child also
who is born to you shall surely die."
[15]Then Nathan departed to his house.

The Death of David's Son

And the LORD struck the child that
Uriah's wife bore to David, and it became
ill. [16]David therefore pleaded with God
for the child, and David fasted and went
in and lay all night on the ground. [17]So
the elders of his house arose *and went* to
him, to raise him up from the ground.
But he would not, nor did he eat food with
them. [18]Then on the seventh day it came
to pass that the child died. And the servants of David were afraid to tell him that
the child was dead. For they said, "Indeed, while the child was alive, we spoke
to him, and he would not heed our voice.
How can we tell him that the child is

(12:1–14 continued)
gered God. David had *despised* "the commandment of the LORD." Nathan exposed the king's sin of taking another man's "lamb," saying, "*You* are the man!...Why have you despised the commandment of the Lord, to do evil in his sight?"

Consider how Paul similarly personalized the Law: "You, therefore, who teach another, do you not teach yourself? You who preach that a man should not steal, do you steal? You who say, 'Do not commit adultery,' do you commit adultery? You who abhor idols, do you rob temples? You who make your boast in the law, do you dishonor God through breaking the law?" (Rom. 2:21–23).

Imagine if Nathan, fearful of rejection, glossed over the personal nature of David's sin, and instead told David, "God loves you and has a wonderful plan for your life. However, there is something that is keeping you from enjoying this wonderful plan; it is called 'sin.'" David's reaction may have been, "What sin are you talking about?" rather than to admit his terrible transgression. Think of it—why should he cry, "I have sinned against the Lord" at the sound of that message? Instead, he may have, in a sincere desire to experience this "wonderful plan," admitted that he, like all men, had sinned and fallen short of the glory of God.

If David had not been made to tremble under the wrath of the Law, the prophet would have removed the very means of producing godly sorrow, which was so necessary for David's repentance. It is "godly sorrow" that produces repentance (2 Cor. 7:10). It was the weight of David's guilt that caused him to cry out, "I have sinned against the Lord." The Law caused him to labor and become heavy laden; it made him hunger and thirst for righteousness. It enlightened him as to the serious nature of sin as far as God was concerned.

Only *after* David acknowledged his personal transgression did Nathan give him the "gospel" (the good news). When David admitted he had sinned against God, the prophet then gave him grace and said, "The Lord also has put away your sin; you shall not die." The Law should always precede mercy, because it is the Law that *necessitates* mercy. In David's wonderful prayer of contrition in Psalm 51, notice how the Commandments made sin personal (note how many times David says "I," "me," and "my"): "Have mercy upon *me*, O God, according to Your lovingkindness; according to the multitude of Your tender mercies, blot out *my* transgressions. Wash *me* thoroughly from *my* iniquity, and cleanse *me* from *my* sin. For I acknowledge *my* transgressions, and *my* sin is always before *me*. Against You, You only, have I sinned, and done this evil in Your sight—that You may be found just when You speak, and blameless when You judge."

We are called to walk in the steps of Nathan—to preach the Word, to convince, rebuke, exhort, with all longsuffering and teaching (see 2 Tim. 4:2). Preach Law before grace and you will see similar results.

dead? He may do some harm!"

19When David saw that his servants were whispering, David perceived that the child was dead. Therefore David said to his servants, "Is the child dead?"

And they said, "He is dead."

20So David arose from the ground, washed and anointed himself, and changed his clothes; and he went into the house of the LORD and worshiped. Then he went to his own house; and when he requested, they set food before him, and he ate. 21Then his servants said to him, "What *is* this that you have done? You fasted and wept for the child *while he was* alive, but when the child died, you arose and ate food."

22And he said, "While the child was alive, I fasted and wept; for I said, 'Who can tell *whether* the LORD[a] will be gracious to me, that the child may live?' 23But now he is dead; why should I fast? Can I bring him back again? I shall go to him, but he shall not return to me."

Solomon Is Born

24Then David comforted Bathsheba his wife, and went in to her and lay with her. So she bore a son, and he[a] called his name Solomon. Now the LORD loved him, 25and He sent *word* by the hand of Nathan the prophet: So he[a] called his name Jedidiah,[b] because of the LORD.

Rabbah Is Captured

26Now Joab fought against Rabbah of the people of Ammon, and took the royal city. 27And Joab sent messengers to David, and said, "I have fought against Rabbah, and I have taken the city's water *supply.* 28Now therefore, gather the rest of the people together and encamp against the city and take it, lest I take the city and it be called after my name." 29So David gathered all the people together and went to Rabbah, fought against it, and took it. 30Then he took their king's crown from his head. Its weight *was* a talent of gold, with precious stones. And it was *set* on David's head. Also he brought out the spoil of the city in great abundance. 31And he brought out the people who *were* in it, and put *them to work* with saws and iron picks and iron axes, and made them cross over to the brick works. So he did to all the cities of the people of Ammon. Then David and all the people returned to Jerusalem.

Amnon and Tamar

13 After this Absalom the son of David had a lovely sister, whose name *was* Tamar; and Amnon the son of David loved her. 2Amnon was so distressed over his sister Tamar that he became sick; for she *was* a virgin. And it was improper for Amnon to do anything to her. 3But Amnon had a friend whose name *was* Jonadab the son of Shimeah, David's brother. Now Jonadab *was* a very crafty man. 4And he said to him, "Why *are* you, the king's son, becoming thinner day after day? Will you not tell me?"

Amnon said to him, "I love Tamar, my brother Absalom's sister."

5So Jonadab said to him, "Lie down on your bed and pretend to be ill. And when your father comes to see you, say to him, 'Please let my sister Tamar come and give me food, and prepare the food in my sight, that I may see *it* and eat it from her hand.'" 6Then Amnon lay down and pretended to be ill; and when the king came to see him, Amnon said to the king, "Please let Tamar my sister come and make a couple of cakes for me in my sight, that I may eat from her hand."

7And David sent home to Tamar, saying, "Now go to your brother Amnon's house, and prepare food for him." 8So Tamar went to her brother Amnon's house; and he was lying down. Then she took flour and kneaded *it,* made cakes in his sight, and baked the cakes. 9And she took the pan and placed *them* out before

12:22 [a]A few Hebrew manuscripts and Syriac read *God.*
12:24 [a]Following Kethib, Septuagint, and Vulgate; Qere, a few Hebrew manuscripts, Syriac, and Targum read *she.*
12:25 [a]Qere, some Hebrew manuscripts, Syriac, and Targum read *she.* [b]Literally *Beloved of the LORD*

QUESTIONS & OBJECTIONS

13:1,2

"Why did God give us sexual desire (lust) if it's bad?"

There is a difference between lust and sexual desire. God did give us sexual desire and it is not a bad thing. In fact it is a good thing. How else would we be attracted to a prospective spouse, and why would we even procreate if there was no "desire"?

So what is the difference between sexual attraction and lust? One dictionary says that "lust" is "uncontrolled or *illicit* sexual desire or appetite; lecherousness." Or to put it another way, lust is pornography of the mind.

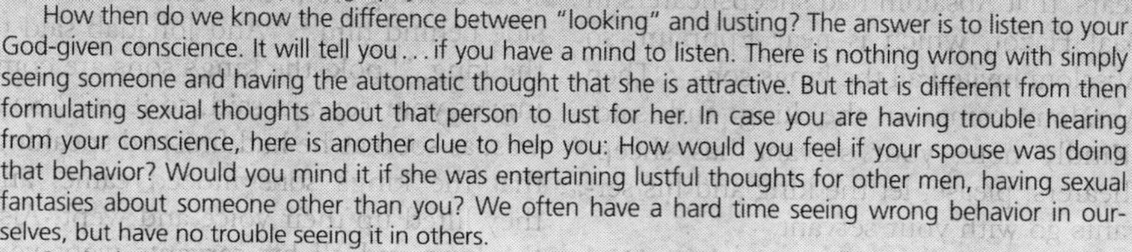

How then do we know the difference between "looking" and lusting? The answer is to listen to your God-given conscience. It will tell you . . . if you have a mind to listen. There is nothing wrong with simply seeing someone and having the automatic thought that she is attractive. But that is different from then formulating sexual thoughts about that person to lust for her. In case you are having trouble hearing from your conscience, here is another clue to help you: How would you feel if your spouse was doing that behavior? Would you mind it if she was entertaining lustful thoughts for other men, having sexual fantasies about someone other than you? We often have a hard time seeing wrong behavior in ourselves, but have no trouble seeing it in others.

So God cannot be blamed for "setting us up to fail." To believe that would be like a criminal saying during his trial, "Judge, I raped that woman, but it really isn't my fault. God made me with sexual desire so it's His fault." If that will not hold water in a court of law, it is not going to be a valid defense on Judgment Day.

him, but he refused to eat. Then Amnon
said, "Have everyone go out from me."
And they all went out from him. 10Then
Amnon said to Tamar, "Bring the food
into the bedroom, that I may eat from your
hand." And Tamar took the cakes which
she had made, and brought *them* to Amnon her brother in the bedroom. 11Now
when she had brought *them* to him to eat,
he took hold of her and said to her,
"Come, lie with me, my sister."

12But she answered him, "No, my
brother, do not force me, for no such
thing should be done in Israel. Do not do
this disgraceful thing! 13And I, where
could I take my shame? And as for you,
you would be like one of the fools in Israel. Now therefore, please speak to the
king; for he will not withhold me from
you." 14However, he would not heed her
voice; and being stronger than she, he
forced her and lay with her.

15Then Amnon hated her exceedingly,
so that the hatred with which he hated
her *was* greater than the love with which
he had loved her. And Amnon said to her,
"Arise, be gone!"

16So she said to him, "No, indeed! This
evil of sending me away *is* worse than the
other that you did to me."

But he would not listen to her. 17Then
he called his servant who attended him,
and said, "Here! Put this *woman* out, away
from me, and bolt the door behind her."
18Now she had on a robe of many colors,
for the king's virgin daughters wore such
apparel. And his servant put her out and
bolted the door behind her.

19Then Tamar put ashes on her head,
and tore her robe of many colors that *was*
on her, and laid her hand on her head and
went away crying bitterly. 20And Absalom
her brother said to her, "Has Amnon your
brother been with you? But now hold
your peace, my sister. He *is* your brother;
do not take this thing to heart." So Tamar
remained desolate in her brother Absalom's house.

13:15 Human love is often selfish and shallow. It is common to hear of a man "loving" a woman, but killing her because of jealousy—if he can't have her, nobody can. What a contrast to the love of God expressed on the cross!

21But when King David heard of all
these things, he was very angry. 22And
Absalom spoke to his brother Amnon
neither good nor bad. For Absalom hated
Amnon, because he had forced his sister
Tamar.

Absalom Murders Amnon

23And it came to pass, after two full
years, that Absalom had sheepshearers in
Baal Hazor, which *is* near Ephraim; so
Absalom invited all the king's sons. 24Then
Absalom came to the king and said,
"Kindly note, your servant has sheep-
shearers; please, let the king and his ser-
vants go with your servant."

25But the king said to Absalom, "No,
my son, let us not all go now, lest we be
a burden to you." Then he urged him, but
he would not go; and he blessed him.

26Then Absalom said, "If not, please
let my brother Amnon go with us."

And the king said to him, "Why should
he go with you?" 27But Absalom urged
him; so he let Amnon and all the king's
sons go with him.

28Now Absalom had commanded his
servants, saying, "Watch now, when Amnon's heart is merry with wine, and when
I say to you, 'Strike Amnon!' then kill him.
Do not be afraid. Have I not commanded
you? Be courageous and valiant." 29So the
servants of Absalom did to Amnon as Absalom had commanded. Then all the
king's sons arose, and each one got on his
mule and fled.

30And it came to pass, while they were
on the way, that news came to David, saying, "Absalom has killed all the king's
sons, and not one of them is left!" 31So
the king arose and tore his garments and
lay on the ground, and all his servants
stood by with their clothes torn. 32Then
Jonadab the son of Shimeah, David's
brother, answered and said, "Let not my
lord suppose they have killed all the young
men, the king's sons, for only Amnon is
dead. For by the command of Absalom
this has been determined from the day
that he forced his sister Tamar. 33Now
therefore, let not my lord the king take
the thing to his heart, to think that all the
king's sons are dead. For only Amnon is
dead."

Absalom Flees to Geshur

34Then Absalom fled. And the young
man who was keeping watch lifted his
eyes and looked, and there, many people
were coming from the road on the hillside behind him.[a] 35And Jonadab said to
the king, "Look, the king's sons are coming; as your servant said, so it is." 36So it
was, as soon as he had finished speaking,
that the king's sons indeed came, and
they lifted up their voice and wept. Also
the king and all his servants wept very
bitterly.

37But Absalom fled and went to Talmai
the son of Ammihud, king of Geshur.
And *David* mourned for his son every day.
38So Absalom fled and went to Geshur,
and was there three years. 39And King
David[a] longed to go to[b] Absalom. For he
had been comforted concerning Amnon,
because he was dead.

Absalom Returns to Jerusalem

14 So Joab the son of Zeruiah perceived that the king's heart *was*
concerned about Absalom. 2And Joab sent
to Tekoa and brought from there a wise
woman, and said to her, "Please pretend
to be a mourner, and put on mourning
apparel; do not anoint yourself with oil,
but act like a woman who has been
mourning a long time for the dead. 3Go
to the king and speak to him in this
manner." So Joab put the words in her
mouth.

4And when the woman of Tekoa
spoke[a] to the king, she fell on her face to
the ground and prostrated herself, and

13:34 [a]Septuagint adds *And the watchman went and told the king, and said, "I see men from the way of Horonaim, from the regions of the mountains."* **13:39** [a]Following Masoretic Text, Syriac, and Vulgate; Septuagint reads *the spirit of the king;* Targum reads *the soul of King David.* [b]Following Masoretic Text and Targum; Septuagint and Vulgate read *ceased to pursue after.* **14:4** [a]Many Hebrew manuscripts, Septuagint, Syriac, and Vulgate read *came.*

said, "Help, O king!"
5Then the king said to her, "What
troubles you?"
And she answered, "Indeed I *am* a
widow, my husband is dead. 6Now your
maidservant had two sons; and the two
fought with each other in the field, and
there was no one to part them, but the
one struck the other and killed him.
7And now the whole family has risen up
against your maidservant, and they said,
'Deliver him who struck his brother, that
we may execute him for the life of his
brother whom he killed; and we will destroy the heir also.' So they would extinguish my ember that is left, and leave to
my husband *neither* name nor remnant
on the earth."
8Then the king said to the woman,
"Go to your house, and I will give orders
concerning you."
9And the woman of Tekoa said to the
king, "My lord, O king, *let* the iniquity *be*
on me and on my father's house, and the
king and his throne *be* guiltless."
10So the king said, "Whoever says *anything* to you, bring him to me, and he
shall not touch you anymore."
11Then she said, "Please let the king
remember the LORD your God, and do not
permit the avenger of blood to destroy
anymore, lest they destroy my son."
And he said, "*As* the LORD lives, not
one hair of your son shall fall to the
ground."
12Therefore the woman said, "Please,
let your maidservant speak *another* word
to my lord the king."
And he said, "Say on."
13So the woman said: "Why then have
you schemed such a thing against the
people of God? For the king speaks this
thing as one who is guilty, *in that* the king
does not bring his banished one home
again. 14For we will surely die and *become*
like water spilled on the ground, which
cannot be gathered up again. Yet God
does not take away a life; but He devises
means, so that His banished ones are not
expelled from Him. 15Now therefore, I
have come to speak of this thing to my
lord the king because the people have
made me afraid. And your maidservant
said, 'I will now speak to the king; it may
be that the king will perform the request
of his maidservant. 16For the king will
hear and deliver his maidservant from
the hand of the man *who would* destroy
me and my son together from the inheritance of God.' 17Your maidservant said,
'The word of my lord the king will now
be comforting; for as the angel of God, so
is my lord the king in discerning good
and evil. And may the LORD your God be
with you.' "
18Then the king answered and said to
the woman, "Please do not hide from me
anything that I ask you."
And the woman said, "Please, let my
lord the king speak."
19So the king said, "*Is* the hand of Joab
with you in all this?" And the woman answered and said, "*As* you live, my lord the
king, no one can turn to the right hand or
to the left from anything that my lord the
king has spoken. For your servant Joab
commanded me, and he put all these
words in the mouth of your maidservant.
20To bring about this change of affairs
your servant Joab has done this thing;
but my lord *is* wise, according to the wisdom of the angel of God, to know everything that *is* in the earth."
21And the king said to Joab, "All right,

14:14 This woman was wise (see v. 2), and it is wise for anyone to see that life without Jesus Christ is empty futility. Without Him our lives are being poured out like water onto dry sand. It is good to help the ungodly see this by reminding them that death is waiting for them, and that it is just a matter of time until they are taken into eternity. Never underestimate the power of an unsaved person's will to live. Such reasoning can often find a willing ear. How wonderful that, although sin banished the Adamic race from God's presence, He made a way for sinners to be reconciled to Him through the cross: "God was in Christ reconciling the world to Himself" (2 Cor. 5:19). See James 4:14 comment.

I have granted this thing. Go therefore, bring back the young man Absalom."

22 Then Joab fell to the ground on his face and bowed himself, and thanked the king. And Joab said, "Today your servant knows that I have found favor in your sight, my lord, O king, in that the king has fulfilled the request of his servant." 23 So Joab arose and went to Geshur, and brought Absalom to Jerusalem. 24 And the king said, "Let him return to his own house, but do not let him see my face." So Absalom returned to his own house, but did not see the king's face.

David Forgives Absalom

25 Now in all Israel there was no one who was praised as much as Absalom for his good looks. From the sole of his foot to the crown of his head there was no blemish in him. 26 And when he cut the hair of his head—at the end of every year he cut *it* because it was heavy on him—when he cut it, he weighed the hair of his head at two hundred shekels according to the king's standard. 27 To Absalom were born three sons, and one daughter whose name *was* Tamar. She was a woman of beautiful appearance.

28 And Absalom dwelt two full years in Jerusalem, but did not see the king's face. 29 Therefore Absalom sent for Joab, to send him to the king, but he would not come to him. And when he sent again the second time, he would not come. 30 So he said to his servants, "See, Joab's field is near mine, and he has barley there; go and set it on fire." And Absalom's servants set the field on fire.

31 Then Joab arose and came to Absalom's house, and said to him, "Why have your servants set my field on fire?"

32 And Absalom answered Joab, "Look, I sent to you, saying, 'Come here, so that I may send you to the king, to say, "Why have I come from Geshur? *It would be* better for me *to be* there still." ' Now therefore, let me see the king's face; but if there is iniquity in me, let him execute me."

33 So Joab went to the king and told him. And when he had called for Absalom, he came to the king and bowed himself on his face to the ground before the king. Then the king kissed Absalom.

Absalom's Treason

15 After this it happened that Absalom provided himself with chariots and horses, and fifty men to run before him. 2 Now Absalom would rise early and stand beside the way to the gate. *So* it was, whenever anyone who had a lawsuit came to the king for a decision, that Absalom would call to him and say, "What city *are* you from?" And he would say, "Your servant *is* from such and such a tribe of Israel." 3 Then Absalom would say to him, "Look, your case is good and

---

14:21 "How is God going to forgive a sinner, if he won't repent? If he was allowing an unrepentant sinner into his kingdom, there would be war in heaven in twenty-four hours... Look at King David with his son Absalom. After he had been sent away, he gets his friends to intercede for him, to get him back to Jerusalem. They succeeded in getting him back to the city; but someone told the king that he hadn't repented, and his father would not see him. After he had been in Jerusalem some time, trying his best to get into favor and position again without repentance, he sent a friend, Joab, to the king, and told him to say to his father: 'Examine me, and if you find no iniquity in me, take me in.' He was forgiven; but the most foolish thing King David ever did was to forgive that young prince. What was the result? He drove him from the throne. That's what the sinner would do, if he got into heaven unrepentant. He would just drive God from the throne—tear the crown from him. No unrepentant sinner can get into the kingdom of heaven." *D. L. Moody*

14:32 Until the Law is applied to the conscience, the ungodly convince themselves that they are without iniquity. However, only the pure in heart will see the King.

15:1–6 Never cause division in your local church. It is easy to do. Just take people aside and say, "If I were the pastor, I would do it this way..." If something your pastor says or does upsets you, make it a matter of prayer. Prayer moves mountains. Whispering destroys churches.

right; but *there is* no deputy of the king to hear you." [4]Moreover Absalom would say, "Oh, that I were made judge in the land, and everyone who has any suit or cause would come to me; then I would give him justice." [5]And *so* it was, whenever anyone came near to bow down to him, that he would put out his hand and take him and kiss him. [6]In this manner Absalom acted toward all Israel who came to the king for judgment. So Absalom stole the hearts of the men of Israel.

[7]Now it came to pass after forty[a] years that Absalom said to the king, "Please, let me go to Hebron and pay the vow which I made to the LORD. [8]For your servant took a vow while I dwelt at Geshur in Syria, saying, 'If the LORD indeed brings me back to Jerusalem, then I will serve the LORD.' "

[9]And the king said to him, "Go in peace." So he arose and went to Hebron.

[10]Then Absalom sent spies throughout all the tribes of Israel, saying, "As soon as you hear the sound of the trumpet, then you shall say, 'Absalom reigns in Hebron!' " [11]And with Absalom went two hundred men invited from Jerusalem, and they went along innocently and did not know anything. [12]Then Absalom sent for Ahithophel the Gilonite, David's counselor, from his city—from Giloh—while he offered sacrifices. And the conspiracy grew strong, for the people with Absalom continually increased in number.

David Escapes from Jerusalem

[13]Now a messenger came to David, saying, "The hearts of the men of Israel are with Absalom."

[14]So David said to all his servants who *were* with him at Jerusalem, "Arise, and let us flee, or we shall not escape from Absalom. Make haste to depart, lest he overtake us suddenly and bring disaster upon us, and strike the city with the edge of the sword."

[15]And the king's servants said to the king, "We *are* your servants, *ready to do* whatever my lord the king commands." [16]Then the king went out with all his household after him. But the king left ten women, concubines, to keep the house. [17]And the king went out with all the people after him, and stopped at the outskirts. [18]Then all his servants passed before him; and all the Cherethites, all the Pelethites, and all the Gittites, six hundred men who had followed him from Gath, passed before the king.

[19]Then the king said to Ittai the Gittite, "Why are you also going with us? Return and remain with the king. For you *are* a foreigner and also an exile from your own place. [20]In fact, you came *only* yesterday. Should I make you wander up and down with us today, since I go I know not where? Return, and take your brethren back. Mercy and truth *be* with you."

To be a Christian means to forgive the inexcusable, because God has forgiven the inexcusable in you.

C. S. LEWIS

[21]But Ittai answered the king and said, "*As* the LORD lives, and *as* my lord the king lives, surely in whatever place my lord the king shall be, whether in death or life, even there also your servant will be."

[22]So David said to Ittai, "Go, and cross over." Then Ittai the Gittite and all his men and all the little ones who *were* with him crossed over. [23]And all the country wept with a loud voice, and all the people crossed over. The king himself also crossed over the Brook Kidron, and all the people crossed over toward the way of the wilderness.

[24]There was Zadok also, and all the Levites with him, bearing the ark of the covenant of God. And they set down the ark of God, and Abiathar went up until all the people had finished crossing over from the city. [25]Then the king said to

15:7 [a]Septuagint manuscripts, Syriac, and Josephus read *four.*

Zadok, "Carry the ark of God back into the city. If I find favor in the eyes of the LORD, He will bring me back and show me *both* it and His dwelling place. [26]But if He says thus: 'I have no delight in you,' here I am, let Him do to me as seems good to Him." [27]The king also said to Zadok the priest, "*Are* you *not* a seer? Return to the city in peace, and your two sons with you, Ahimaaz your son, and Jonathan the son of Abiathar. [28]See, I will wait in the plains of the wilderness until word comes from you to inform me." [29]Therefore Zadok and Abiathar carried the ark of God back to Jerusalem. And they remained there.

[30]So David went up by the Ascent of the *Mount of* Olives, and wept as he went up; and he had his head covered and went barefoot. And all the people who *were* with him covered their heads and went up, weeping as they went up. [31]Then *someone* told David, saying, "Ahithophel *is* among the conspirators with Absalom." And David said, "O LORD, I pray, turn the counsel of Ahithophel into foolishness!"

[32]Now it happened when David had come to the top *of the mountain,* where he worshiped God—there was Hushai the Archite coming to meet him with his robe torn and dust on his head. [33]David said to him, "If you go on with me, then you will become a burden to me. [34]But if you return to the city, and say to Absalom, 'I will be your servant, O king; *as* I *was* your father's servant previously, so I *will* now also *be* your servant,' then you may defeat the counsel of Ahithophel for me. [35]And *do* you not *have* Zadok and Abiathar the priests with you there? Therefore it will be *that* whatever you hear from the king's house, you shall tell to Zadok and Abiathar the priests. [36]Indeed *they have* there with them their two sons, Ahimaaz, Zadok's *son,* and Jonathan, Abiathar's *son;* and by them you shall send me everything you hear."

[37]So Hushai, David's friend, went into the city. And Absalom came into Jerusalem.

Mephibosheth's Servant

16 When David was a little past the top *of the mountain,* there was Ziba the servant of Mephibosheth, who met him with a couple of saddled donkeys, and on them two hundred *loaves* of bread, one hundred clusters of raisins, one hundred summer fruits, and a skin of wine. [2]And the king said to Ziba, "What do you mean to do with these?"

So Ziba said, "The donkeys *are* for the king's household to ride on, the bread and summer fruit for the young men to eat, and the wine for those who are faint in the wilderness to drink."

[3]Then the king said, "And where *is* your master's son?"

And Ziba said to the king, "Indeed he is staying in Jerusalem, for he said, 'Today the house of Israel will restore the kingdom of my father to me.' "

[4]So the king said to Ziba, "Here, all that *belongs* to Mephibosheth *is* yours."

And Ziba said, "I humbly bow before you, *that* I may find favor in your sight, my lord, O king!"

Shimei Curses David

[5]Now when King David came to Bahurim, there was a man from the family of the house of Saul, whose name *was* Shimei the son of Gera, coming from there. He came out, cursing continuously as he came. [6]And he threw stones at David and at all the servants of King David. And all the people and all the mighty men *were* on his right hand and on his left. [7]Also Shimei said thus when he cursed: "Come out! Come out! You bloodthirsty man, you rogue! [8]The LORD has brought upon you all the blood of the

16:5–8 Do not take accusations to heart. Instead, take them to the Lord, and then forget about them. Commit yourself to Him who judges righteously. There will be retribution, if God sees fit. David need not have concerned himself, because Shimei was the one in deception (see 19:16–20).

house of Saul, in whose place you have reigned; and the LORD has delivered the kingdom into the hand of Absalom your son. So now you *are caught* in your own evil, because you are a bloodthirsty man!"

[9]Then Abishai the son of Zeruiah said to the king, "Why should this dead dog curse my lord the king? Please, let me go over and take off his head!"

[10]But the king said, "What have I to do with you, you sons of Zeruiah? So let him curse, because the LORD has said to him, 'Curse David.' Who then shall say, 'Why have you done so?' "

[11]And David said to Abishai and all his servants, "See how my son who came from my own body seeks my life. How much more now *may this* Benjamite? Let him alone, and let him curse; for so the LORD has ordered him. [12]It may be that the LORD will look on my affliction,[a] and that the LORD will repay me with good for his cursing this day." [13]And as David and his men went along the road, Shimei went along the hillside opposite him and cursed as he went, threw stones at him and kicked up dust. [14]Now the king and all the people who *were* with him became weary; so they refreshed themselves there.

The Advice of Ahithophel

[15]Meanwhile Absalom and all the people, the men of Israel, came to Jerusalem; and Ahithophel *was* with him. [16]And so it was, when Hushai the Archite, David's friend, came to Absalom, that Hushai said to Absalom, "*Long* live the king! *Long* live the king!"

[17]So Absalom said to Hushai, "*Is* this your loyalty to your friend? Why did you not go with your friend?"

[18]And Hushai said to Absalom, "No, but whom the LORD and this people and all the men of Israel choose, his I will be, and with him I will remain. [19]"Furthermore, whom should I serve? *Should I* not *serve* in the presence of his son? As I have served in your father's presence, so will I be in your presence."

[20]Then Absalom said to Ahithophel, "Give advice as to what we should do."

[21]And Ahithophel said to Absalom, "Go in to your father's concubines, whom he has left to keep the house; and all Israel will hear that you are abhorred by your father. Then the hands of all who are with you will be strong." [22]So they pitched a tent for Absalom on the top of the house, and Absalom went in to his father's concubines in the sight of all Israel.

[23]Now the advice of Ahithophel, which he gave in those days, *was* as if one had inquired at the oracle of God. So *was* all the advice of Ahithophel both with David and with Absalom.

17 Moreover Ahithophel said to Absalom, "Now let me choose twelve thousand men, and I will arise and pursue David tonight. [2]I will come upon him while he *is* weary and weak, and make him afraid. And all the people who *are* with him will flee, and I will strike only the king. [3]Then I will bring back all the people to you. When all return except the man whom you seek, all the people will be at peace." [4]And the saying pleased Absalom and all the elders of Israel.

The Advice of Hushai

[5]Then Absalom said, "Now call Hushai the Archite also, and let us hear what he says too." [6]And when Hushai came to Absalom, Absalom spoke to him, saying, "Ahithophel has spoken in this manner. Shall we do as he says? If not, speak up."

[7]So Hushai said to Absalom: "The advice that Ahithophel has given *is* not good at this time. [8]For," said Hushai, "you know your father and his men, that they *are* mighty men, and they *are* enraged in their minds, like a bear robbed of her cubs in the field; and your father *is* a man of war, and will not camp with the people. [9]Surely by now he is hidden in some pit, or in some *other* place. And it will be, when some of them are overthrown at the

16:12 [a]Following Kethib, Septuagint, Syriac, and Vulgate; Qere reads *my eyes*; Targum reads *tears of my eyes*.

first, that whoever hears *it* will say, 'There is a slaughter among the people who follow Absalom.' 10And even he *who is* valiant, whose heart *is* like the heart of a lion, will melt completely. For all Israel knows that your father *is* a mighty man, and *those* who *are* with him *are* valiant men. 11Therefore I advise that all Israel be fully gathered to you, from Dan to Beersheba, like the sand that *is* by the sea for multitude, and that you go to battle in person. 12So we will come upon him in some place where he may be found, and we will fall on him as the dew falls on the ground. And of him and all the men who *are* with him there shall not be left so much as one. 13Moreover, if he has withdrawn into a city, then all Israel shall bring ropes to that city; and we will pull it into the river, until there is not one small stone found there."

14So Absalom and all the men of Israel said, "The advice of Hushai the Archite *is* better than the advice of Ahithophel." For the LORD had purposed to defeat the good advice of Ahithophel, to the intent that the LORD might bring disaster on Absalom.

Hushai Warns David to Escape

15Then Hushai said to Zadok and Abiathar the priests, "Thus and so Ahithophel advised Absalom and the elders of Israel, and thus and so I have advised. 16Now therefore, send quickly and tell David, saying, 'Do not spend this night in the plains of the wilderness, but speedily cross over, lest the king and all the people who *are* with him be swallowed up.' " 17Now Jonathan and Ahimaaz stayed at En Rogel, for they dared not be seen coming into the city; so a female servant would come and tell them, and they would go and tell King David. 18Nevertheless a lad saw them, and told Absalom. But both of them went away quickly and came to a man's house in Bahurim, who had a well in his court; and they went down into it. 19Then the woman took and spread a covering over the well's mouth, and spread ground grain on it; and the thing was not known. 20And when Absalom's servants came to the woman at the house, they said, "Where *are* Ahimaaz and Jonathan?"

So the woman said to them, "They have gone over the water brook."

And when they had searched and could not find *them*, they returned to Jerusalem. 21Now it came to pass, after they had departed, that they came up out of the well and went and told King David, and said to David, "Arise and cross over the water quickly. For thus has Ahithophel advised against you." 22So David and all the people who *were* with him arose and crossed over the Jordan. By morning light not one of them was left who had not gone over the Jordan.

23Now when Ahithophel saw that his advice was not followed, he saddled a donkey, and arose and went home to his house, to his city. Then he put his household in order, and hanged himself, and died; and he was buried in his father's tomb.

24Then David went to Mahanaim. And Absalom crossed over the Jordan, he and all the men of Israel with him. 25And Absalom made Amasa captain of the army instead of Joab. This Amasa *was* the son of a man whose name *was* Jithra,[a] an Israelite,[b] who had gone in to Abigail the daughter of Nahash, sister of Zeruiah, Joab's mother. 26So Israel and Absalom encamped in the land of Gilead.

17:25 [a]Spelled *Jether* in 1 Chronicles 2:17 and elsewhere [b]Following Masoretic Text, some manuscripts of the Septuagint, and Targum; some manuscripts of the Septuagint read *Ishmaelite* (compare 1 Chronicles 2:17); Vulgate reads *of Jezrael.*

17:23 *Ahithophel* means "brother of foolishness." Rejection has a predictable and slippery downward path. First we feel "hurt" by something someone said or did. Then we feel rejected, followed by a justifiable self-pity, resentment that turns into anger, hatred, bitterness, and then suicidal tendencies. It is very predictable. So do yourself a big favor—cut it off at the "hurt" by forgiving (from the heart) and forgetting.

27Now it happened, when David had
come to Mahanaim, that Shobi the son of
Nahash from Rabbah of the people of
Ammon, Machir the son of Ammiel from
Lo Debar, and Barzillai the Gileadite from
Rogelim, 28brought beds and basins,
earthen vessels and wheat, barley and
flour, parched *grain* and beans, lentils and
parched *seeds,* 29honey and curds, sheep
and cheese of the herd, for David and the
people who *were* with him to eat. For
they said, "The people are hungry and
weary and thirsty in the wilderness."

Absalom's Defeat and Death

18 And David numbered the people
who *were* with him, and set captains of thousands and captains of hundreds over them. 2Then David sent out
one third of the people under the hand of
Joab, one third under the hand of Abishai
the son of Zeruiah, Joab's brother, and
one third under the hand of Ittai the Gittite. And the king said to the people, "I
also will surely go out with you myself."
3But the people answered, "You shall
not go out! For if we flee away, they will
not care about us; nor if half of us die,
will they care about us. But *you are* worth
ten thousand of us now. For you are now
more help to us in the city."
4Then the king said to them, "Whatever seems best to you I will do." So the
king stood beside the gate, and all the
people went out by hundreds and by
thousands. 5Now the king had commanded Joab, Abishai, and Ittai, saying,
"*Deal* gently for my sake with the young
man Absalom." And all the people heard
when the king gave all the captains orders concerning Absalom.
6So the people went out into the field
of battle against Israel. And the battle was
in the woods of Ephraim. 7The people of
Israel were overthrown there before the
servants of David, and a great slaughter
of twenty thousand took place there that
day. 8For the battle there was scattered
over the face of the whole countryside,
and the woods devoured more people that
day than the sword devoured.
9Then Absalom met the servants of
David. Absalom rode on a mule. The mule
went under the thick boughs of a great
terebinth tree, and his head caught in the
terebinth; so he was left hanging between
heaven and earth. And the mule which
was under him went on. 10Now a certain
man saw *it* and told Joab, and said, "I just
saw Absalom hanging in a terebinth tree!"
11So Joab said to the man who told
him, "You just saw *him!* And why did you
not strike him there to the ground? I
would have given you ten *shekels* of silver
and a belt."
12But the man said to Joab, "Though I
were to receive a thousand *shekels* of silver in my hand, I would not raise my
hand against the king's son. For in our
hearing the king commanded you and
Abishai and Ittai, saying, 'Beware lest
anyone *touch* the young man Absalom!'[a]
13Otherwise I would have dealt falsely
against my own life. For there is nothing
hidden from the king, and you yourself
would have set yourself against *me*."
14Then Joab said, "I cannot linger with
you." And he took three spears in his
hand and thrust them through Absalom's
heart, while he was *still* alive in the midst
of the terebinth tree. 15And ten young
men who bore Joab's armor surrounded
Absalom, and struck and killed him.
16So Joab blew the trumpet, and the
people returned from pursuing Israel. For

18:12 [a]The ancient versions read *'Protect the young man Absalom for me!'*

18:14–16 We are to reckon the sinful nature dead to our threefold enemy (the world, the flesh, and the devil) as it hangs with Christ on the cross of Calvary. However, to effectively do this, we need the assistance of the Ten Commandments to kill our sinful nature (see Rom. 7:10,11). The Law sends us to the cross and keeps us there. "You shall not commit adultery" keeps our heart from lust. "You shall not covet" keeps our eyes off this attractive world, etc. See Rom. 13:8–10 for what the Commandments do for the godly.

Joab held back the people. 17And they
took Absalom and cast him into a large
pit in the woods, and laid a very large
heap of stones over him. Then all Israel
fled, everyone to his tent.
18Now Absalom in his lifetime had
taken and set up a pillar for himself, which
is in the King's Valley. For he said, "I have
no son to keep my name in remem-
brance." He called the pillar after his own
name. And to this day it is called Absalom's Monument.

David Hears of Absalom's Death

19Then Ahimaaz the son of Zadok
said, "Let me run now and take the news
to the king, how the LORD has avenged
him of his enemies."
20And Joab said to him, "You shall not
take the news this day, for you shall take
the news another day. But today you shall
take no news, because the king's son is
dead." 21Then Joab said to the Cushite,
"Go, tell the king what you have seen." So
the Cushite bowed himself to Joab and
ran.
22And Ahimaaz the son of Zadok said
again to Joab, "But whatever happens,
please let me also run after the Cushite."
So Joab said, "Why will you run, my
son, since you have no news ready?"
23"But whatever happens," *he said,* "let
me run."
So he said to him, "Run." Then Ahimaaz ran by way of the plain, and outran
the Cushite.
24Now David was sitting between the
two gates. And the watchman went up to
the roof over the gate, to the wall, lifted
his eyes and looked, and there was a man,
running alone. 25Then the watchman
cried out and told the king. And the king
said, "If he *is* alone, *there is* news in his
mouth." And he came rapidly and drew
near.
26Then the watchman saw *another*
man running, and the watchman called
to the gatekeeper and said, "There is *another* man, running alone!"
And the king said, "He also brings
news."
27So the watchman said, "I think the
running of the first is like the running of
Ahimaaz the son of Zadok."
And the king said, "He *is* a good man,
and comes with good news."
28So Ahimaaz called out and said to
the king, "All is well!" Then he bowed
down with his face to the earth before the
king, and said, "Blessed *be* the LORD your
God, who has delivered up the men who
raised their hand against my lord the king!"
29The king said, "Is the young man
Absalom safe?"
Ahimaaz answered, "When Joab sent
the king's servant and *me* your servant, I
saw a great tumult, but I did not know
what *it was about.*"
30And the king said, "Turn aside *and*
stand here." So he turned aside and stood
still.
31Just then the Cushite came, and the
Cushite said, "There is good news, my
lord the king! For the LORD has avenged
you this day of all those who rose against
you."
32And the king said to the Cushite, "Is
the young man Absalom safe?"
So the Cushite answered, "May the enemies of my lord the king, and all who
rise against you to do harm, be like *that*
young man!"

David's Mourning for Absalom

33Then the king was deeply moved,
and went up to the chamber over the
gate, and wept. And as he went, he said
thus: "O my son Absalom—my son, my
son Absalom—if only I had died in your
place! O Absalom my son, my son!"

19 And Joab was told, "Behold, the
king is weeping and mourning for
Absalom." 2So the victory that day was
turned into mourning for all the people.
For the people heard it said that day, "The
king is grieved for his son." 3And the people stole back into the city that day, as
people who are ashamed steal away when
they flee in battle. 4But the king covered

his face, and the king cried out with a loud voice, "O my son Absalom! O Absalom, my son, my son!"

5Then Joab came into the house to the king, and said, "Today you have disgraced all your servants who today have saved your life, the lives of your sons and daughters, the lives of your wives and the lives of your concubines, 6in that you love your enemies and hate your friends. For you have declared today that you regard neither princes nor servants; for today I perceive that if Absalom had lived and all of us had died today, then it would have pleased you well. 7Now therefore, arise, go out and speak comfort to your servants. For I swear by the LORD, if you do not go out, not one will stay with you this night. And that will be worse for you than all the evil that has befallen you from your youth until now." 8Then the king arose and sat in the gate. And they told all the people, saying, "There is the king, sitting in the gate." So all the people came before the king.

For everyone of Israel had fled to his tent.

David Returns to Jerusalem

9Now all the people were in a dispute throughout all the tribes of Israel, saying, "The king saved us from the hand of our enemies, he delivered us from the hand of the Philistines, and now he has fled from the land because of Absalom. 10But Absalom, whom we anointed over us, has died in battle. Now therefore, why do you say nothing about bringing back the king?"

11So King David sent to Zadok and Abiathar the priests, saying, "Speak to the elders of Judah, saying, 'Why are you the last to bring the king back to his house, since the words of all Israel have come to the king, to his *very* house? 12You *are* my brethren, you *are* my bone and my flesh. Why then are you the last to bring back the king?' 13And say to Amasa, '*Are* you not my bone and my flesh? God do so to me, and more also, if you are not commander of the army before me continually in place of Joab.' " 14So he swayed the hearts of all the men of Judah, just as *the heart of* one man, so that they sent *this word* to the king: "Return, you and all your servants!"

15Then the king returned and came to the Jordan. And Judah came to Gilgal, to go to meet the king, to escort the king across the Jordan. 16And Shimei the son of Gera, a Benjamite, who *was* from Bahurim, hurried and came down with the men of Judah to meet King David.

> The ultimate proof of the sinner is that he doesn't know his own sin. Our job is to make him see it.
>
> **MARTIN LUTHER**

17*There were* a thousand men of Benjamin with him, and Ziba the servant of the house of Saul, and his fifteen sons and his twenty servants with him; and they went over the Jordan before the king. 18Then a ferryboat went across to carry over the king's household, and to do what he thought good.

David's Mercy to Shimei

Now Shimei the son of Gera fell down before the king when he had crossed the Jordan. 19Then he said to the king, "Do not let my lord impute iniquity to me, or remember what wrong your servant did on the day that my lord the king left Jerusalem, that the king should take *it* to heart. 20For I, your servant, know that I have sinned. Therefore here I am, the first to come today of all the house of Joseph to go down to meet my lord the king."

21But Abishai the son of Zeruiah answered and said, "Shall not Shimei be put to death for this, because he cursed the LORD's anointed?"

22And David said, "What have I to do with you, you sons of Zeruiah, that you should be adversaries to me today? Shall any man be put to death today in Israel?

For do I not know that today I *am* king over Israel?" 23Therefore the king said to Shimei, "You shall not die." And the king swore to him.

David and Mephibosheth Meet

24Now Mephibosheth the son of Saul came down to meet the king. And he had not cared for his feet, nor trimmed his mustache, nor washed his clothes, from the day the king departed until the day he returned in peace. 25So it was, when he had come to Jerusalem to meet the king, that the king said to him, "Why did you not go with me, Mephibosheth?"

26And he answered, "My lord, O king, my servant deceived me. For your servant said, 'I will saddle a donkey for myself, that I may ride on it and go to the king,' because your servant *is* lame. 27And he has slandered your servant to my lord the king, but my lord the king *is* like the angel of God. Therefore do *what is* good in your eyes. 28For all my father's house were but dead men before my lord the king. Yet you set your servant among those who eat at your own table. Therefore what right have I still to cry out anymore to the king?"

29So the king said to him, "Why do you speak anymore of your matters? I have said, 'You and Ziba divide the land.' "

30Then Mephibosheth said to the king, "Rather, let him take it all, inasmuch as my lord the king has come back in peace to his own house."

David's Kindness to Barzillai

31And Barzillai the Gileadite came down from Rogelim and went across the Jordan with the king, to escort him across the Jordan. 32Now Barzillai was a very aged man, eighty years old. And he had provided the king with supplies while he stayed at Mahanaim, for he *was* a very rich man. 33And the king said to Barzillai, "Come across with me, and I will provide for you while you are with me in Jerusalem."

34But Barzillai said to the king, "How long have I to live, that I should go up with the king to Jerusalem? 35I *am* today eighty years old. Can I discern between the good and bad? Can your servant taste what I eat or what I drink? Can I hear any longer the voice of singing men and singing women? Why then should your servant be a further burden to my lord the king? 36Your servant will go a little way across the Jordan with the king. And why should the king repay me *with* such a reward? 37Please let your servant turn back again, that I may die in my own city, near the grave of my father and mother. But here is your servant Chimham; let him cross over with my lord the king, and do for him what seems good to you."

38And the king answered, "Chimham shall cross over with me, and I will do for him what seems good to you. Now whatever you request of me, I will do for you." 39Then all the people went over the Jordan. And when the king had crossed over, the king kissed Barzillai and blessed him, and he returned to his own place.

The Quarrel About the King

40Now the king went on to Gilgal, and Chimham[a] went on with him. And all the people of Judah escorted the king, and also half the people of Israel. 41Just then all the men of Israel came to the king, and said to the king, "Why have our brethren, the men of Judah, stolen you away and brought the king, his household, and all David's men with him across the Jordan?"

42So all the men of Judah answered the men of Israel, "Because the king *is* a close relative of ours. Why then are you angry over this matter? Have we ever eaten

19:40 [a]Masoretic Text reads *Chimhan*.

19:24 This world is vanity; it is all transient. All of our lusts and possessions are temporal. We await the return of the King.

at the king's *expense*? Or has he given us any gift?"

43 And the men of Israel answered the men of Judah, and said, "We have ten shares in the king; therefore we also have more *right* to David than you. Why then do you despise us—were we not the first to advise bringing back our king?"

Yet the words of the men of Judah were fiercer than the words of the men of Israel.

The Rebellion of Sheba

20 And there happened to be there a rebel,[a] whose name *was* Sheba the son of Bichri, a Benjamite. And he blew a trumpet, and said:

"We have no share in David,
Nor do we have inheritance in the
son of Jesse;
Every man to his tents, O Israel!"

2 So every man of Israel deserted David, *and* followed Sheba the son of Bichri. But the men of Judah, from the Jordan as far as Jerusalem, remained loyal to their king.

3 Now David came to his house at Jerusalem. And the king took the ten women, his concubines whom he had left to keep the house, and put them in seclusion and supported them, but did not go in to them. So they were shut up to the day of their death, living in widowhood.

4 And the king said to Amasa, "Assemble the men of Judah for me within three days, and be present here yourself." 5 So Amasa went to assemble *the men of* Judah. But he delayed longer than the set time which David had appointed him. 6 And David said to Abishai, "Now Sheba the son of Bichri will do us more harm than Absalom. Take your lord's servants and pursue him, lest he find for himself fortified cities, and escape us." 7 So Joab's men, with the Cherethites, the Pelethites, and all the mighty men, went out after him. And they went out of Jerusalem to pursue Sheba the son of Bichri. 8 When they *were* at the large stone which *is* in Gibeon, Amasa came before them. Now Joab was dressed in battle armor; on it was a belt *with* a sword fastened in its sheath at his hips; and as he was going forward, it fell out. 9 Then Joab said to Amasa, "*Are* you in health, my brother?" And Joab took Amasa by the beard with his right hand to kiss him. 10 But Amasa did not notice the sword that *was* in Joab's hand. And he struck him with it in the stomach, and his entrails poured out on the ground; and he did not *strike* him again. Thus he died.

Then Joab and Abishai his brother pursued Sheba the son of Bichri. 11 Meanwhile one of Joab's men stood near Amasa, and said, "Whoever favors Joab and whoever *is* for David—follow Joab!" 12 But Amasa wallowed in *his* blood in the middle of the highway. And when the man saw that all the people stood still, he moved Amasa from the highway to the field and threw a garment over him, when he saw that everyone who came upon him halted. 13 When he was removed from the highway, all the people went on after Joab to pursue Sheba the son of Bichri.

14 And he went through all the tribes of Israel to Abel and Beth Maachah and all the Berites. So they were gathered together and also went after *Sheba*.[a] 15 Then they came and besieged him in Abel of Beth Maachah; and they cast up a siege

20:1 [a]Literally *man of Belial* **20:14** [a]Literally *him*

20:3 This is what much of the Church has done with the Ten Commandments. They set the Law aside and fail to honor it; some even despise it. But the Scriptures tell us that the Law is perfect, holy, just, and good (see Rom. 7:12; James 1:25). David said that he *loved* the Law. Paul "delighted" in it. Sure, it has been abused by others who have used it illegitimately (seeking to be justified by the Law, promoting legalism), but that is no reason to neglect its God-given function to convert the soul and bring about the new birth through the gospel. See Psa. 19:7 for one function of the Law.

mound against the city, and it stood by the rampart. And all the people who *were* with Joab battered the wall to throw it down.

[16]Then a wise woman cried out from the city, "Hear, hear! Please say to Joab, 'Come nearby, that I may speak with you.' " [17]When he had come near to her, the woman said, "*Are* you Joab?"

He answered, "I *am*."

Then she said to him, "Hear the words of your maidservant."

And he answered, "I am listening."

[18]So she spoke, saying, "They used to talk in former times, saying, 'They shall surely seek *guidance* at Abel,' and so they would end *disputes*. [19]I *am among the* peaceable *and* faithful in Israel. You seek to destroy a city and a mother in Israel. Why would you swallow up the inheritance of the LORD?"

[20]And Joab answered and said, "Far be it, far be it from me, that I should swallow up or destroy! [21]That *is* not so. But a man from the mountains of Ephraim, Sheba the son of Bichri by name, has raised his hand against the king, against David. Deliver him only, and I will depart from the city."

So the woman said to Joab, "Watch, his head will be thrown to you over the wall." [22]Then the woman in her wisdom went to all the people. And they cut off the head of Sheba the son of Bichri, and threw *it* out to Joab. Then he blew a trumpet, and they withdrew from the city, every man to his tent. So Joab returned to the king at Jerusalem.

David's Government Officers

[23]And Joab *was* over all the army of Israel; Benaiah the son of Jehoiada *was* over the Cherethites and the Pelethites; [24]Adoram *was* in charge of revenue; Jehoshaphat the son of Ahilud *was* recorder; [25]Sheva *was* scribe; Zadok and Abiathar *were* the priests; [26]and Ira the Jairite was a chief minister under David.

David Avenges the Gibeonites

21 Now there was a famine in the days of David for three years, year after year; and David inquired of the LORD. And the LORD answered, "*It* is because of Saul and *his* bloodthirsty house, because he killed the Gibeonites." [2]So the king called the Gibeonites and spoke to them. Now the Gibeonites *were* not of the children of Israel, but of the remnant of the Amorites; the children of Israel had sworn protection to them, but Saul had sought to kill them in his zeal for the children of Israel and Judah.

[3]Therefore David said to the Gibeonites, "What shall I do for you? And with what shall I make atonement, that you may bless the inheritance of the LORD?"

[4]And the Gibeonites said to him, "We will have no silver or gold from Saul or from his house, nor shall you kill any man in Israel for us."

So he said, "Whatever you say, I will do for you."

[5]Then they answered the king, "As for the man who consumed us and plotted against us, *that* we should be destroyed from remaining in any of the territories of Israel, [6]let seven men of his descendants be delivered to us, and we will hang them before the LORD in Gibeah of Saul, *whom* the LORD chose."

And the king said, "I will give *them*."

[7]But the king spared Mephibosheth the son of Jonathan, the son of Saul, because of the LORD's oath that *was* between them, between David and Jonathan the son of Saul. [8]So the king took Armoni and Mephibosheth, the two sons of Rizpah

---

21:6–11 The name Rizpah means "live coal." She was broken beyond words that her beloved sons were hanged on a tree, so she camped out on a rock to keep scavengers away and didn't rest until the harvest rains came. If God has touched our lips with live coals from the altar of sacrifice, we will be broken beyond words at the thought of His beloved Son on the cross. As we encamp upon the Rock of Ages, may we not rest until God gives us the rains of revival.

the daughter of Aiah, whom she bore to Saul, and the five sons of Michal[a] the daughter of Saul, whom she brought up for Adriel the son of Barzillai the Meholathite; 9and he delivered them into the hands of the Gibeonites, and they hanged them on the hill before the LORD. So they fell, *all* seven together, and were put to death in the days of harvest, in the first *days,* in the beginning of barley harvest.

10Now Rizpah the daughter of Aiah took sackcloth and spread it for herself on the rock, from the beginning of harvest until the late rains poured on them from heaven. And she did not allow the birds of the air to rest on them by day nor the beasts of the field by night.

11And David was told what Rizpah the daughter of Aiah, the concubine of Saul, had done. 12Then David went and took the bones of Saul, and the bones of Jonathan his son, from the men of Jabesh Gilead who had stolen them from the street of Beth Shan,[a] where the Philistines had hung them up, after the Philistines had struck down Saul in Gilboa. 13So he brought up the bones of Saul and the bones of Jonathan his son from there; and they gathered the bones of those who had been hanged. 14They buried the bones of Saul and Jonathan his son in the country of Benjamin in Zelah, in the tomb of Kish his father. So they performed all that the king commanded. And after that God heeded the prayer for the land.

Philistine Giants Destroyed

15When the Philistines were at war again with Israel, David and his servants with him went down and fought against the Philistines; and David grew faint. 16Then Ishbi-Benob, who *was* one of the sons of the giant, the weight of whose bronze spear *was* three hundred *shekels,* who was bearing a new *sword,* thought he could kill David. 17But Abishai the son of Zeruiah came to his aid, and struck the Philistine and killed him. Then the men of David swore to him, saying, "You shall go out no more with us to battle, lest you quench the lamp of Israel."

18Now it happened afterward that there was again a battle with the Philistines at Gob. Then Sibbechai the Hushathite killed Saph,[a] who *was* one of the sons of the giant. 19Again there was war at Gob with the Philistines, where Elhanan the son of Jaare-Oregim[a] the Bethlehemite killed *the brother of* Goliath the Gittite, the shaft of whose spear *was* like a weaver's beam.

20Yet again there was war at Gath, where there was a man of *great* stature, who had six fingers on each hand and six toes on each foot, twenty-four in number; and he also was born to the giant. 21So when he defied Israel, Jonathan the son of Shimea,[a] David's brother, killed him.

22These four were born to the giant in Gath, and fell by the hand of David and by the hand of his servants.

· · · · · ·

How long was Jesus in the tomb?
For an answer, see Matt. 12:40 comment.

· · · · · ·

Praise for God's Deliverance

22 Then David spoke to the LORD the words of this song, on the day when the LORD had delivered him from the hand of all his enemies, and from the hand of Saul. 2And he said:[a]

"The LORD *is* my rock and my fortress
and my deliverer;
3The God of my strength, in whom I
will trust;
My shield and the horn of my
salvation,
My stronghold and my refuge;
My Savior, You save me from violence.
4I will call upon the LORD, *who is worthy*
to be praised;

21:8 [a]Or *Merab* (compare 1 Samuel 18:19 and 25:44; 2 Samuel 3:14 and 6:23) 21:12 [a]Spelled *Beth Shean* in Joshua 17:11 and elsewhere 21:18 [a]Spelled *Sippai* in 1 Chronicles 20:4 21:19 [a]Spelled *Jair* in 1 Chronicles 20:5 21:21 [a]Spelled *Shammah* in 1 Samuel 16:9 and elsewhere 22:2 [a]Compare Psalm 18

So shall I be saved from my enemies.

5"When the waves of death surrounded
me,
The floods of ungodliness made me
afraid.
6The sorrows of Sheol surrounded me;
The snares of death confronted me.
7In my distress I called upon the LORD,
And cried out to my God;
He heard my voice from His temple,
And my cry *entered* His ears.

8"Then the earth shook and trembled;
The foundations of heaven[a] quaked
and were shaken,
Because He was angry.
9Smoke went up from His nostrils,
And devouring fire from His mouth;
Coals were kindled by it.
10He bowed the heavens also, and came
down
With darkness under His feet.
11He rode upon a cherub, and flew;
And He was seen[a] upon the wings of
the wind.
12He made darkness canopies around
Him,
Dark waters *and* thick clouds of the
skies.
13From the brightness before Him
Coals of fire were kindled.

14"The LORD thundered from heaven,
And the Most High uttered His voice.
15He sent out arrows and scattered
them;
Lightning bolts, and He vanquished
them.
16Then the channels of the sea were seen,
The foundations of the world were
uncovered,
At the rebuke of the LORD,
At the blast of the breath of His
nostrils.

17"He sent from above, He took me,
He drew me out of many waters.
18He delivered me from my strong
enemy,
From those who hated me;
For they were too strong for me.
19They confronted me in the day of my
calamity,
But the LORD was my support.
20He also brought me out into a broad
place;
He delivered me because He
delighted in me.

21"The LORD rewarded me according to
my righteousness;
According to the cleanness of my
hands
He has recompensed me.
22For I have kept the ways of the LORD,
And have not wickedly departed from
my God.
23For all His judgments *were* before me;
And *as for* His statutes, I did not
depart from them.
24I was also blameless before Him,
And I kept myself from my iniquity.
25Therefore the LORD has recompensed
me according to my
righteousness,
According to my cleanness in His
eyes.[a]

26"With the merciful You will show
Yourself merciful;
With a blameless man You will show
Yourself blameless;
27With the pure You will show Yourself
pure;
And with the devious You will show
Yourself shrewd.
28You will save the humble people;
But Your eyes *are* on the haughty, *that*
You may bring *them* down.

29"For You *are* my lamp, O LORD;
The LORD shall enlighten my darkness.

22:8 [a]Following Masoretic Text, Septuagint, and Targum; Syriac and Vulgate read *hills* (compare Psalm 18:7). **22:11** [a]Following Masoretic Text and Septuagint; many Hebrew manuscripts, Syriac, and Vulgate read *He flew* (compare Psalm 18:10); Targum reads *He spoke with power.* **22:25** [a]Septuagint, Syriac, and Vulgate read *the cleanness of my hands in His sight* (compare Psalm 18:24); Targum reads *my cleanness before His word.*

[30]For by You I can run against a troop;
By my God I can leap over a wall.
[31]*As for* God, His way *is* perfect;
The word of the LORD *is* proven;
He *is* a shield to all who trust in Him.

[32]"For who *is* God, except the LORD?
And who *is* a rock, except our God?
[33]God *is* my strength *and* power,[a]
And He makes my[b] way perfect.
[34]He makes my[a] feet like the *feet* of deer,
And sets me on my high places.
[35]He teaches my hands to make war,
So that my arms can bend a bow of
bronze.

[36]"You have also given me the shield of
Your salvation;
Your gentleness has made me great.
[37]You enlarged my path under me;
So my feet did not slip.

[38]"I have pursued my enemies and
destroyed them;
Neither did I turn back again till they
were destroyed.
[39]And I have destroyed them and
wounded them,
So that they could not rise;
They have fallen under my feet.
[40]For You have armed me with strength
for the battle;
You have subdued under me those
who rose against me.
[41]You have also given me the necks of
my enemies,
So that I destroyed those who hated me.
[42]They looked, but *there was* none to
save;
Even to the LORD, but He did not
answer them.
[43]Then I beat them as fine as the dust
of the earth;
I trod them like dirt in the streets,
And I spread them out.

[44]"You have also delivered me from the
strivings of my people;
You have kept me as the head of the
nations.
A people I have not known shall serve
me.
[45]The foreigners submit to me;
As soon as they hear, they obey me.
[46]The foreigners fade away,
And come frightened[a] from their
hideouts.

[47]"The LORD lives!
Blessed *be* my Rock!
Let God be exalted,
The Rock of my salvation!
[48]*It is* God who avenges me,
And subdues the peoples under me;
[49]He delivers me from my enemies.
You also lift me up above those who
rise against me;
You have delivered me from the
violent man.
[50]Therefore I will give thanks to You, O
LORD, among the Gentiles,
And sing praises to Your name.

[51]*He is* the tower of salvation to His
king,
And shows mercy to His anointed,
To David and his descendants
forevermore."

David's Last Words

23 Now these *are* the last words of
David.
Thus says David the son of Jesse;

22:33 [a]Dead Sea Scrolls, Septuagint, Syriac, and Vulgate read *It is God who arms me with strength* (compare Psalm 18:32); Targum reads *It is God who sustains me with strength.* [b]Following Qere, Septuagint, Syriac, Targum, and Vulgate (compare Psalm 18:32); Kethib reads *His.* 22:34 [a]Following Qere, Septuagint, Syriac, Targum, and Vulgate (compare Psalm 18:33); Kethib reads *His.* 22:46 [a]Following Septuagint, Targum, and Vulgate (compare Psalm 18:45); Masoretic Text reads *gird themselves.*

22:29–31 Jesus is the light of the world. We follow Him, and we walk in the light as He is in the light. He is our strength, and a shield to all who trust in Him. His way is perfect, His Law is perfect, and through the cross we are presented perfect in His sight so that when we face that Law, we are free from its wrath.

SPRINGBOARDS FOR PREACHING AND WITNESSING

Common Courtesy

22:50

Have you ever had the experience of showing someone "road courtesy" and they don't bother to acknowledge it? I have to admit, those who don't show appreciation make me mad. I immediately wish I hadn't bothered to be nice. However, if I slow down to let someone merge in front of me, and they give a small wave or a nod of appreciation, it makes me feel good. I don't think many of us like ingratitude. We feel upset if we give a child a piece of candy, and he snatches it, stuffs it into his mouth, and runs off without so much as a "Thank you."

But that was me for 22 years. I was an ungrateful brat, who never once thanked God for His incredible kindness. I never showed an ounce of gratitude for having eyes to see this incredible creation. I never thanked Him for ears to enjoy good music, or taste buds to enjoy good food. Not once did I ever humbly bow my head before a meal and thank God for my food. Ingratitude is a horrible sin.

Then again, gratitude without obedience to God is nothing but empty hypocrisy. True appreciation for His goodness will also bow to His will. Those who don't do God's will lose their most precious possession. If death seizes them while they are still in their sins, they will never again see God's gift of light, of color, beauty, love, and laughter. They will never again hear a kind word, or feel the warmth of human comfort. They weren't thankful, so they will be damned from all of God's goodness. Forever. Imagine that—never seeing beauty ever again. Never hearing laughter ever again. Never satisfying the craving of unspeakable thirst. Ever. All because of sin.

Thus says the man raised up on high,
The anointed of the God of Jacob,
And the sweet psalmist of Israel:

2"The Spirit of the LORD spoke by me,
And His word *was* on my tongue.
3The God of Israel said,
The Rock of Israel spoke to me:
'He who rules over men *must be* just,
Ruling in the fear of God.
4And *he shall be* like the light of the morning *when* the sun rises,
A morning without clouds,
Like the tender grass *springing* out of the earth,
By clear shining after rain.'

5"Although my house *is* not so with God,
Yet He has made with me an everlasting covenant,
Ordered in all *things* and secure.
For *this is* all my salvation and all *my* desire;
Will He not make *it* increase?
6But *the sons* of rebellion *shall* all *be* as thorns thrust away,
Because they cannot be taken with hands.
7But the man *who* touches them
Must be armed with iron and the shaft of a spear,
And they shall be utterly burned with fire in *their* place."

David's Mighty Men

8These *are* the names of the mighty men
whom David had: Josheb-Basshebeth[a]
the Tachmonite, chief among the captains.[b] He was called Adino the Eznite,
because he had killed eight hundred men
at one time. 9And after him *was* Eleazar
the son of Dodo,[a] the Ahohite, *one* of the
three mighty men with David when they
defied the Philistines *who* were gathered
there for battle, and the men of Israel had
retreated. 10He arose and attacked the
Philistines until his hand was weary, and
his hand stuck to the sword. The LORD
brought about a great victory that day;
and the people returned after him only to
plunder. 11And after him *was* Shammah
the son of Agee the Hararite. The Philistines had gathered together into a troop
where there was a piece of ground full of
lentils. So the people fled from the Philistines. 12But he stationed himself in the
middle of the field, defended it, and killed
the Philistines. So the LORD brought about

23:8 [a]Literally *One Who Sits in the Seat* (compare 1 Chronicles 11:11) [b]Following Masoretic Text and Targum; Septuagint and Vulgate read *the three.* 23:9 [a]Spelled *Dodai* in 1 Chronicles 27:4

a great victory.

[13]Then three of the thirty chief men went down at harvest time and came to David at the cave of Adullam. And the troop of Philistines encamped in the Valley of Rephaim. [14]David *was* then in the stronghold, and the garrison of the Philistines *was* then *in* Bethlehem. [15]And David said with longing, "Oh, that someone would give me a drink of the water from the well of Bethlehem, which *is* by the gate!" [16]So the three mighty men broke through the camp of the Philistines, drew water from the well of Bethlehem that *was* by the gate, and took it and brought *it* to David. Nevertheless he would not drink it, but poured it out to the LORD. [17]And he said, "Far be it from me, O LORD, that I should do this! Is *this not* the blood of the men who went in *jeopardy of* their lives?" Therefore he would not drink it.

These things were done by the three mighty men.

[18]Now Abishai the brother of Joab, the son of Zeruiah, was chief of *another* three.[a] He lifted his spear against three hundred *men,* killed *them,* and won a name among *these* three. [19]Was he not the most honored of three? Therefore he became their captain. However, he did not attain to the *first* three.

[20]Benaiah *was* the son of Jehoiada, the son of a valiant man from Kabzeel, who had done many deeds. He had killed two lion-like heroes of Moab. He also had gone down and killed a lion in the midst of a pit on a snowy day. [21]And he killed an Egyptian, a spectacular man. The Egyptian *had* a spear in his hand; so he went down to him with a staff, wrested the spear out of the Egyptian's hand, and killed him with his own spear. [22]These *things* Benaiah the son of Jehoiada did, and won a name among three mighty men. [23]He was more honored than the thirty, but he did not attain to the *first* three. And David appointed him over his guard.

[24]Asahel the brother of Joab *was* one of the thirty; Elhanan the son of Dodo of Bethlehem, [25]Shammah the Harodite, Elika the Harodite, [26]Helez the Paltite, Ira the son of Ikkesh the Tekoite, [27]Abiezer the Anathothite, Mebunnai the Hushathite, [28]Zalmon the Ahohite, Maharai the Netophathite, [29]Heleb the son of Baanah (the Netophathite), Ittai the son of Ribai from Gibeah of the children of Benjamin, [30]Benaiah a Pirathonite, Hiddai from the brooks of Gaash, [31]Abi-Albon the Arbathite, Azmaveth the Barhumite, [32]Eliahba the Shaalbonite (of the sons of Jashen), Jonathan, [33]Shammah the Hararite, Ahiam the son of Sharar the Hararite, [34]Eliphelet the son of Ahasbai, the son of the Maachathite, Eliam the son of Ahithophel the Gilonite, [35]Hezrai[a] the Carmelite, Paarai the Arbite, [36]Igal the son of Nathan of Zobah, Bani the Gadite, [37]Zelek the Ammonite, Naharai the Beerothite (armorbearer of Joab the son of Zeruiah), [38]Ira the Ithrite, Gareb the Ithrite, [39]*and* Uriah the Hittite: thirty-seven in all.

David's Census of Israel and Judah

24 Again the anger of the LORD was aroused against Israel, and He moved David against them to say, "Go, number Israel and Judah."

23:18 [a]Following Masoretic Text, Septuagint, and Vulgate; some Hebrew manuscripts and Syriac read *thirty*; Targum reads *the mighty men.* 23:35 [a]Spelled *Hezro* in 1 Chronicles 11:37

23:13–17 A drink offering. The mighty three had a love for David that was more than lip service, demonstrated by risking their lives merely to get a drink of water for their beloved leader. Yet, David's reaction to their display of love was to pour the water out on the ground as a drink offering to the Lord. Some may be tempted to say, "Surely, if those men went to such effort to get the water, at least David could have drunk it!" But we have here something far deeper than mere human gratitude. *David's conscience would not allow him to indulge in self-gratification*. He said, "Is this not the blood of the men who went in jeopardy of their lives?" *How could he drink it?* It was more than just a cup of water. It was an evident token, proof of their love and devotion to him. The cost was too great. His only course of action was to give it to God, to pour that precious water out as a drink offering to the Lord.

2 So the king said to Joab the commander of the army who *was* with him, "Now go throughout all the tribes of Israel, from Dan to Beersheba, and count the people, that I may know the number of the people."

3 And Joab said to the king, "Now may the LORD your God add to the people a hundred times more than there are, and may the eyes of my lord the king see *it.* But why does my lord the king desire this thing?" 4 Nevertheless the king's word prevailed against Joab and against the captains of the army. Therefore Joab and the captains of the army went out from the presence of the king to count the people of Israel.

5 And they crossed over the Jordan and camped in Aroer, on the right side of the town which *is* in the midst of the ravine of Gad, and toward Jazer. 6 Then they came to Gilead and to the land of Tahtim Hodshi; they came to Dan Jaan and around to Sidon; 7 and they came to the stronghold of Tyre and to all the cities of the Hivites and the Canaanites. Then they went out to South Judah *as far as* Beersheba. 8 So when they had gone through all the land, they came to Jerusalem at the end of nine months and twenty days. 9 Then Joab gave the sum of the number of the people to the king. And there were in Israel eight hundred thousand valiant men who drew the sword, and the men of Judah were five hundred thousand men.

The Judgment on David's Sin

10 And David's heart condemned him after he had numbered the people. So David said to the LORD, "I have sinned greatly in what I have done; but now, I pray, O LORD, take away the iniquity of Your servant, for I have done very foolishly."

11 Now when David arose in the morning, the word of the LORD came to the prophet Gad, David's seer, saying, 12 "Go and tell David, 'Thus says the LORD: "I offer you three *things;* choose one of them for yourself, that I may do *it* to you." ' " 13 So Gad came to David and told him; and he said to him, "Shall seven[a] years of famine come to you in your land? Or shall you flee three months before your enemies, while they pursue you? Or shall there be three days' plague in your land? Now consider and see what answer I should take back to Him who sent me."

14 And David said to Gad, "I am in great distress. Please let us fall into the hand of the LORD, for His mercies *are* great; but do not let me fall into the hand of man."

15 So the LORD sent a plague upon Israel from the morning till the appointed time. From Dan to Beersheba seventy thousand men of the people died. 16 And when the angel[a] stretched out His hand over Jerusalem to destroy it, the LORD relented from the destruction, and said to the angel who was destroying the people, "It is enough; now restrain your hand." And the angel of the LORD was by the threshing floor of Araunah[b] the Jebusite.

17 Then David spoke to the LORD when he saw the angel who was striking the people, and said, "Surely I have sinned, and I have done wickedly; but these sheep, what have they done? Let Your hand, I pray, be against me and against my father's house."

24:13 [a]Following Masoretic Text, Syriac, Targum, and Vulgate; Septuagint reads *three* (compare 1 Chronicles 21:12).
24:16 [a]Or *Angel* [b]Spelled *Ornan* in 1 Chronicles 21:15

24:9 Are you one who "draws the sword"? Do you use the Word of God in prayer, in preaching, and in witnessing? See Eph. 6:17 and Heb. 4:12 for insight into the power of the Word.

24:10 "We won't need any one to condemn us at the bar of God; it will be our own conscience that will come up as a witness against us. God won't condemn us at his bar; we shall condemn ourselves. Memory is God's officer, and when He shall touch these secret springs and say, 'Son, daughter, remember'—then tramp, tramp, tramp will come before us, in a long procession, all the sins we have ever committed." *D. L. Moody*

The Altar on the Threshing Floor

18And Gad came that day to David and
said to him, "Go up, erect an altar to the
LORD on the threshing floor of Araunah the
Jebusite." 19So David, according to the
word of Gad, went up as the LORD commanded. 20Now Araunah looked, and saw
the king and his servants coming toward
him. So Araunah went out and bowed before the king with his face to the ground.
21Then Araunah said, "Why has my
lord the king come to his servant?"

And David said, "To buy the threshing
floor from you, to build an altar to the
LORD, that the plague may be withdrawn
from the people."

22Now Araunah said to David, "Let my
lord the king take and offer up whatever
seems good to him. Look, *here are* oxen
for burnt sacrifice, and threshing implements and the yokes of the oxen for wood.
23All these, O king, Araunah has given to
the king."

And Araunah said to the king, "May
the LORD your God accept you."

24Then the king said to Araunah, "No,
but I will surely buy *it* from you for a
price; nor will I offer burnt offerings to
the LORD my God with that which costs
me nothing." So David bought the threshing floor and the oxen for fifty shekels of
silver. 25And David built there an altar to
the LORD, and offered burnt offerings and
peace offerings. So the LORD heeded the
prayers for the land, and the plague was
withdrawn from Israel.

Persecution in the Book of Acts

By Glenn M. Penner, The Voice of the Martyrs

In surveying the Book of Acts, we can see some common themes regarding persecution.

1. Persecution is part of the plan of God. The persecution of the disciples fulfills the predictions of Jesus. Just as He predicted, Stephen is martyred by those who obviously believed that they were doing a service to God (Luke 21:16; John 16:2–4). Paul appears before "kings and governors for my [Jesus'] name's sake" (Luke 21:12; Acts 26:30). Paul sees his suffering as something that must take place in the plan of God (Acts 20:22–24).

2. Persecution is the rejection of God's agents. Often in Acts the most intense persecution comes from the religious leaders of the Jews, by those who are supposed to be God's people. This rejection of God's messengers is the main thrust of Stephen's sermon. In killing Jesus and Stephen, the Jews continue to walk in the footprints of their fathers (7:51). Paul's parting words to the Jews in 28:26–28 are virtually identical to Stephen's words —God's people keep resisting His messengers.

3. The persecuted stand in continuity with God's prophets. Persecution authenticates that the apostles and others who proclaim the gospel are God's messengers. In killing Stephen, the Sanhedrin confirms the very point of Stephen's sermon, that he is in line with the rest of Israel's prophets.

4. Persecution is an integral consequence of following Jesus. Like in his Gospel, Luke commonly links the persecution of the disciples to their identification with Jesus through the use of the expression "my name." The disciples proclaim the "name" of Jesus, baptize "in his name," and do miracles "in his name," and so it is only proper that the expression should be used to indicate the reason for their persecution. They are persecuted because of their association with Jesus.

5. Persecution is the occasion of divine triumph. In an expression of divine irony and sovereignty, we witness in Luke's account that Christ's Church not only grows in spite of persecution, it even spreads because of it. The persecution of the church in Jerusalem results in the disciples being scattered, and as they go out, they share the gospel. Paul's imprisonment and illegal beating in Philippi leads to the jailer and his family coming to faith. Paul's persecution often leads to his going somewhere else to proclaim the good news of Jesus. As when he goes to Rome, it is not as a missionary as he had hoped (Rom. 15:23), but as a prisoner. The Word of God is spread through his "providential failure."

God's victory is also seen in His keeping power of the disciples in the midst of their affliction, and in their ability to rejoice and remain obedient even in the midst of unchanging situations.

(See the chart on the following page, listing just a few incidents of persecution in Acts.)

(continued)

Persecution in the Book of Acts (continued)

PASSAGE	NATURE OF PERSECUTION	RESULT
Acts 4	Threats	Prayer (v. 24), filling with the Spirit (v. 31), unity (v. 32), witness (v. 33)
Acts 5	Beatings	Rejoicing (v. 41), witness (v. 42)
Acts 7	Killing of an individual	Saul witnesses Stephen's death
Acts 8	Widespread persecution, arrests	Spreading of the gospel (8:1,4), conversion of Saul (chapter 9)
Acts 9	Plot to kill Paul	Unity (vv. 26,27), witness (v. 28), more persecution (v. 29)
Acts 12	James killed, Peter arrested	Prayer (v. 5), answered prayer
Acts 13	Paul reviled (v. 36), mob incited violence, driven from the city (v. 50)	Gospel goes to the Gentiles
Acts 14:1–7	Plot to harm Paul and Barnabas (v. 5)	Left and preached the gospel (v. 7)
Acts 14:8–22	Paul stoned and left for dead (v. 19)	Believers strengthened and taught to continue in faith, to enter the kingdom of God through many tribulations (v. 22)
Acts 16	Paul imprisoned and beaten (vv. 23,24)	Praised God (v. 25), jailer and family come to Christ (vv. 32–34), their Roman rights were upheld (vv. 35–39)
Acts 17:1–12	Mob riot (v. 5)	Paul sent to Berea (v. 10), many received the message (v. 11)
Acts 17:13–34	Opposition incited by Jews from Thessalonica (v. 13)	Paul sent to Athens (v. 14), some believed (v. 34)
Acts 18	Persecutors become abusive (v. 6)	Paul takes the message to the Gentiles, many believe (vv. 6–8)
Acts 19	Mob action (vv. 23,34)	Paul advised by church to stay away from the crowd; situation settles down, church protected by authorities (v. 37)
Acts 21—23	Paul attacked by Jews and arrested by Romans in the temple	Paul appeals for his legal rights as a Roman; sent to Rome to testify for Christ (23:11); witnesses to political leaders (chap. 24), Festus (25:1–12), Herod Agrippa (25:23—26:32); preaches and teaches in Rome (28:31)

(Adapted from *In the Shadow of the Cross*, Living Sacrifice Books, www.persecution.com.)

1 Kings

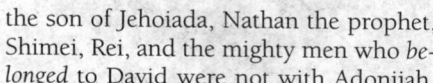

Adonijah Presumes to Be King

1 Now King David was old, advanced in years; and they put covers on him, but he could not get warm. 2Therefore his servants said to him, "Let a young woman, a virgin, be sought for our lord the king, and let her stand before the king, and let her care for him; and let her lie in your bosom, that our lord the king may be warm." 3So they sought for a lovely young woman throughout all the territory of Israel, and found Abishag the Shunammite, and brought her to the king. 4The young woman *was* very lovely; and she cared for the king, and served him; but the king did not know her.

5Then Adonijah the son of Haggith exalted himself, saying, "I will be king"; and he prepared for himself chariots and horsemen, and fifty men to run before him. 6(And his father had not rebuked him at any time by saying, "Why have you done so?" He *was* also very good-looking. *His mother* had borne him after Absalom.) 7Then he conferred with Joab the son of Zeruiah and with Abiathar the priest, and they followed and helped Adonijah. 8But Zadok the priest, Benaiah the son of Jehoiada, Nathan the prophet, Shimei, Rei, and the mighty men who *belonged* to David were not with Adonijah.

9And Adonijah sacrificed sheep and oxen and fattened cattle by the stone of Zoheleth, which *is* by En Rogel; he also invited all his brothers, the king's sons, and all the men of Judah, the king's servants. 10But he did not invite Nathan the prophet, Benaiah, the mighty men, or Solomon his brother.

11So Nathan spoke to Bathsheba the mother of Solomon, saying, "Have you not heard that Adonijah the son of Haggith has become king, and David our lord does not know *it?* 12Come, please, let me now give you advice, that you may save your own life and the life of your son Solomon. 13Go immediately to King David and say to him, 'Did you not, my lord, O king, swear to your maidservant, saying, "Assuredly your son Solomon shall reign after me, and he shall sit on my throne"? Why then has Adonijah become king?' 14Then, while you are still talking there with the king, I also will come in after you and confirm your words."

15So Bathsheba went into the chamber

1:1 This was David, the strong and agile youth who *ran* toward Goliath. The only difference between the young and the elderly is time. If you have the strength and vitality of youth, don't waste them by spending them on yourself. Invest them in the kingdom of God. In a church service years ago an elderly man trembled with age as he looked at the congregation, and with all earnestness said, "When I was a young man I gave myself to sport!" He added that it was a waste of time, and pleaded with those who were young to serve the Lord. Listen to such wisdom. Pray, "Teach me to number my days, that I may gain a heart of wisdom" (see Psa. 90:12) and realize that the wisest thing you can do with your life is to seek and save what is lost. He who wins souls is wise (see Prov. 11:30).

"I care not where I go, or how I live, or what I endure so that I may save souls. When I sleep I dream of them; when I awake they are first in my thoughts."

David Brainerd

to the king. (Now the king was very old,
and Abishag the Shunammite was serving the king.) 16And Bathsheba bowed
and did homage to the king. Then the
king said, "What is your wish?"
17Then she said to him, "My lord, you
swore by the LORD your God to your
maidservant, *saying,* 'Assuredly Solomon
your son shall reign after me, and he shall
sit on my throne.' 18So now, look! Adonijah has become king; and now, my lord
the king, you do not know about *it.* 19He
has sacrificed oxen and fattened cattle
and sheep in abundance, and has invited
all the sons of the king, Abiathar the
priest, and Joab the commander of the
army; but Solomon your servant he has
not invited. 20And as for you, my lord, O
king, the eyes of all Israel *are* on you, that
you should tell them who will sit on the
throne of my lord the king after him.
21Otherwise it will happen, when my
lord the king rests with his fathers, that I
and my son Solomon will be counted as
offenders."
22And just then, while she was still
talking with the king, Nathan the prophet
also came in. 23So they told the king, saying, "Here is Nathan the prophet." And
when he came in before the king, he
bowed down before the king with his face
to the ground. 24And Nathan said, "My
lord, O king, have you said, 'Adonijah
shall reign after me, and he shall sit on
my throne'? 25For he has gone down today, and has sacrificed oxen and fattened
cattle and sheep in abundance, and has
invited all the king's sons, and the commanders of the army, and Abiathar the
priest; and look! They are eating and
drinking before him; and they say, '*Long*
live King Adonijah!' 26But he has not invited me—me your servant—nor Zadok
the priest, nor Benaiah the son of Jehoiada, nor your servant Solomon. 27Has this
thing been done by my lord the king, and
you have not told your servant who
should sit on the throne of my lord the
king after him?"

David Proclaims Solomon King

28Then King David answered and said,
"Call Bathsheba to me." So she came into
the king's presence and stood before the
king. 29And the king took an oath and
said, "*As* the LORD lives, who has redeemed my life from every distress, 30just
as I swore to you by the LORD God of Israel, saying, 'Assuredly Solomon your
son shall be king after me, and he shall sit
on my throne in my place,' so I certainly
will do this day."
31Then Bathsheba bowed with *her* face
to the earth, and paid homage to the king,
and said, "Let my lord King David live
forever!"
32And King David said, "Call to me
Zadok the priest, Nathan the prophet,
and Benaiah the son of Jehoiada." So they
came before the king. 33The king also said
to them, "Take with you the servants of
your lord, and have Solomon my son ride
on my own mule, and take him down to
Gihon. 34There let Zadok the priest and
Nathan the prophet anoint him king over
Israel; and blow the horn, and say, '*Long*
live King Solomon!' 35Then you shall come

up after him, and he shall come and sit on my throne, and he shall be king in my place. For I have appointed him to be ruler over Israel and Judah."

36Benaiah the son of Jehoiada answered the king and said, "Amen! May the LORD God of my lord the king say so *too.* 37As the LORD has been with my lord the king, even so may He be with Solomon, and make his throne greater than the throne of my lord King David."

38So Zadok the priest, Nathan the prophet, Benaiah the son of Jehoiada, the Cherethites, and the Pelethites went down and had Solomon ride on King David's mule, and took him to Gihon. 39Then Zadok the priest took a horn of oil from the tabernacle and anointed Solomon. And they blew the horn, and all the people said, "*Long* live King Solomon!" 40And all the people went up after him; and the people played the flutes and rejoiced with great joy, so that the earth *seemed to* split with their sound.

41Now Adonijah and all the guests who *were* with him heard *it* as they finished eating. And when Joab heard the sound of the horn, he said, "Why *is* the city in such a noisy uproar?" 42While he was still speaking, there came Jonathan, the son of Abiathar the priest. And Adonijah said to him, "Come in, for you *are* a prominent man, and bring good news."

43Then Jonathan answered and said to Adonijah, "No! Our lord King David has made Solomon king. 44The king has sent with him Zadok the priest, Nathan the prophet, Benaiah the son of Jehoiada, the Cherethites, and the Pelethites; and they have made him ride on the king's mule. 45So Zadok the priest and Nathan the prophet have anointed him king at Gihon; and they have gone up from there rejoicing, so that the city is in an uproar. This *is* the noise that you have heard. 46Also Solomon sits on the throne of the kingdom. 47And moreover the king's servants have gone to bless our lord King David, saying, 'May God make the name of Solomon better than your name, and may He make his throne greater than your throne.' Then the king bowed himself on the bed. 48Also the king said thus, 'Blessed *be* the LORD God of Israel, who has given *one* to sit on my throne this day, while my eyes see *it!*' "

49So all the guests who were with Adonijah were afraid, and arose, and each one went his way.

50Now Adonijah was afraid of Solomon; so he arose, and went and took hold of the horns of the altar. 51And it was told Solomon, saying, "Indeed Adonijah is afraid of King Solomon; for look, he has taken hold of the horns of the altar, saying, 'Let King Solomon swear to me today that he will not put his servant to death with the sword.' "

52Then Solomon said, "If he proves himself a worthy man, not one hair of him shall fall to the earth; but if wickedness is found in him, he shall die." 53So King Solomon sent them to bring him down from the altar. And he came and fell down before King Solomon; and Solomon said to him, "Go to your house."

1:50,51 Horns of the altar. The horns of the altar were the place of mercy: "The laying hold upon the literal horns of an altar, which can be handled, availed not Joab. There are many—oh, how many still!—that are hoping to be saved, because they lay hold, as they think, upon the horns of the *sacraments*. Men of unhallowed life, nevertheless, come to the sacramental table, looking for a blessing. Do they not know that they pollute it? Do they not know that they are committing a high sin, and a great misdemeanor against God, by coming amongst his people, where they have no right to be? And yet they think that by committing this atrocity they are securing to themselves safety. How common it is to find in this city, when an irreligious man is dying, that someone will say, 'Oh, he is all right; for a clergyman has been, and given him the sacrament.' I often marvel how men calling themselves the servants of God can dare thus to profane the ordinance of the Lord. Did he ever intend the blessed memorial of the Lord's supper to be a kind of superstitious *vialicum*, something upon which ungodly men may depend in their last hour, as if it could put away sin?" *Charles Spurgeon*

David's Instructions to Solomon

2 Now the days of David drew near that he should die, and he charged Solomon his son, saying: 2"I go the way of all the earth; be strong, therefore, and prove yourself a man. 3And keep the charge of the LORD your God: to walk in His ways, to keep His statutes, His commandments, His judgments, and His testimonies, as it is written in the Law of Moses, that you may prosper in all that you do and wherever you turn; 4that the LORD may fulfill His word which He spoke concerning me, saying, 'If your sons take heed to their way, to walk before Me in truth with all their heart and with all their soul,' He said, 'you shall not lack a man on the throne of Israel.'

5"Moreover you know also what Joab the son of Zeruiah did to me, *and* what he did to the two commanders of the armies of Israel, to Abner the son of Ner and Amasa the son of Jether, whom he killed. And he shed the blood of war in peacetime, and put the blood of war on his belt that *was* around his waist, and on his sandals that *were* on his feet. 6Therefore do according to your wisdom, and do not let his gray hair go down to the grave in peace.

7"But show kindness to the sons of Barzillai the Gileadite, and let them be among those who eat at your table, for so they came to me when I fled from Absalom your brother.

8"And see, *you have* with you Shimei the son of Gera, a Benjamite from Bahurim, who cursed me with a malicious curse in the day when I went to Mahanaim. But he came down to meet me at the Jordan, and I swore to him by the LORD, saying, 'I will not put you to death with the sword.' 9Now therefore, do not hold him guiltless, for you *are* a wise man and know what you ought to do to him; but bring his gray hair down to the grave with blood."

Death of David

10So David rested with his fathers, and was buried in the City of David. 11The period that David reigned over Israel *was* forty years; seven years he reigned in Hebron, and in Jerusalem he reigned thirty-three years. 12Then Solomon sat on the throne of his father David; and his kingdom was firmly established.

Solomon Executes Adonijah

13Now Adonijah the son of Haggith came to Bathsheba the mother of Solomon. So she said, "Do you come peaceably?"

And he said, "Peaceably." 14Moreover he said, "I have something *to say* to you."

And she said, "Say it."

15Then he said, "You know that the kingdom was mine, and all Israel had set their expectations on me, that I should reign. However, the kingdom has been turned over, and has become my brother's; for it was his from the LORD. 16Now I ask one petition of you; do not deny me."

And she said to him, "Say it."

17Then he said, "Please speak to King Solomon, for he will not refuse you, that he may give me Abishag the Shunammite as wife."

18So Bathsheba said, "Very well, I will speak for you to the king."

19Bathsheba therefore went to King Solomon, to speak to him for Adonijah. And the king rose up to meet her and bowed down to her, and sat down on his throne and had a throne set for the king's mother; so she sat at his right hand. 20Then she said, "I desire one small petition of you; do not refuse me."

And the king said to her, "Ask it, my mother, for I will not refuse you."

21So she said, "Let Abishag the Shunammite be given to Adonijah your brother

---

2:1–4 What would your last words be to your loved ones? It is good to think about such things, and to say them now to those you love. You may not have the luxury of a deathbed, or have the time or the mind to say any last words. See 1 Cor. 15:55 comment for the last words of famous people.

as wife."

[22]And King Solomon answered and said to his mother, "Now why do you ask Abishag the Shunammite for Adonijah? Ask for him the kingdom also—for he *is* my older brother—for him, and for Abiathar the priest, and for Joab the son of Zeruiah." [23]Then King Solomon swore by the LORD, saying, "May God do so to me, and more also, if Adonijah has not spoken this word against his own life! [24]Now therefore, *as* the LORD lives, who has confirmed me and set me on the throne of David my father, and who has established a house[a] for me, as He promised, Adonijah shall be put to death today!"

[25]So King Solomon sent by the hand of Benaiah the son of Jehoiada; and he struck him down, and he died.

Abiathar Exiled, Joab Executed

[26]And to Abiathar the priest the king said, "Go to Anathoth, to your own fields, for you *are* deserving of death; but I will not put you to death at this time, because you carried the ark of the Lord GOD before my father David, and because you were afflicted every time my father was afflicted." [27]So Solomon removed Abiathar from being priest to the LORD, that he might fulfill the word of the LORD which He spoke concerning the house of Eli at Shiloh.

[28]Then news came to Joab, for Joab had defected to Adonijah, though he had not defected to Absalom. So Joab fled to the tabernacle of the LORD, and took hold of the horns of the altar. [29]And King Solomon was told, "Joab has fled to the tabernacle of the LORD; there *he is,* by the altar." Then Solomon sent Benaiah the son of Jehoiada, saying, "Go, strike him down." [30]So Benaiah went to the tabernacle of the LORD, and said to him, "Thus says the king, 'Come out!' "

And he said, "No, but I will die here." And Benaiah brought back word to the king, saying, "Thus said Joab, and thus he answered me."

[31]Then the king said to him, "Do as he has said, and strike him down and bury him, that you may take away from me and from the house of my father the innocent blood which Joab shed. [32]So the LORD will return his blood on his head, because he struck down two men more righteous and better than he, and killed them with the sword—Abner the son of Ner, the commander of the army of Israel, and Amasa the son of Jether, the commander of the army of Judah—though my father David did not know *it.* [33]Their blood shall therefore return upon the head of Joab and upon the head of his descendants forever. But upon David and his descendants, upon his house and his throne, there shall be peace forever from the LORD."

[34]So Benaiah the son of Jehoiada went up and struck and killed him; and he was buried in his own house in the wilderness. [35]The king put Benaiah the son of Jehoiada in his place over the army, and the king put Zadok the priest in the place of Abiathar.

Shimei Executed

[36]Then the king sent and called for Shimei, and said to him, "Build yourself a house in Jerusalem and dwell there, and do not go out from there anywhere. [37]For it shall be, on the day you go out and cross the Brook Kidron, know for certain you shall surely die; your blood shall be on your own head."

[38]And Shimei said to the king, "The saying *is* good. As my lord the king has said, so your servant will do." So Shimei dwelt in Jerusalem many days.

[39]Now it happened at the end of three years, that two slaves of Shimei ran away to Achish the son of Maachah, king of Gath. And they told Shimei, saying, "Look, your slaves *are* in Gath!" [40]So Shimei arose, saddled his donkey, and went to Achish at Gath to seek his slaves. And Shimei went and brought his slaves from Gath. [41]And Solomon was told that Shimei

2:24 [a]That is, a royal dynasty

had gone from Jerusalem to Gath and had come back. 42Then the king sent and called for Shimei, and said to him, "Did I not make you swear by the LORD, and warn you, saying, 'Know for certain that on the day you go out and travel anywhere, you shall surely die'? And you said to me, 'The word I have heard *is* good.' 43Why then have you not kept the oath of the LORD and the commandment that I gave you?" 44The king said moreover to Shimei, "You know, as your heart acknowledges, all the wickedness that you did to my father David; therefore the LORD will return your wickedness on your own head. 45But King Solomon *shall be* blessed, and the throne of David shall be established before the LORD forever."

46So the king commanded Benaiah the son of Jehoiada; and he went out and struck him down, and he died. Thus the kingdom was established in the hand of Solomon.

Solomon Requests Wisdom

3 Now Solomon made a treaty with Pharaoh king of Egypt, and married Pharaoh's daughter; then he brought her to the City of David until he had finished building his own house, and the house of the LORD, and the wall all around Jerusalem. 2Meanwhile the people sacrificed at the high places, because there was no house built for the name of the LORD until those days. 3And Solomon loved the LORD, walking in the statutes of his father David, except that he sacrificed and burned incense at the high places.

4Now the king went to Gibeon to sacrifice there, for that *was* the great high place: Solomon offered a thousand burnt offerings on that altar. 5At Gibeon the LORD appeared to Solomon in a dream by night; and God said, "Ask! What shall I give you?"

6And Solomon said: "You have shown great mercy to Your servant David my father, because he walked before You in truth, in righteousness, and in uprightness of heart with You; You have continued this great kindness for him, and You have given him a son to sit on his throne, as *it is* this day. 7Now, O LORD my God, You have made Your servant king instead of my father David, but I *am* a little child; I do not know *how* to go out or come in. 8And Your servant *is* in the midst of Your people whom You have chosen, a great people, too numerous to be numbered or counted. 9Therefore give to Your servant an understanding heart to judge Your people, that I may discern between good and evil. For who is able to judge this great people of Yours?"

10The speech pleased the LORD, that Solomon had asked this thing. 11Then God said to him: "Because you have asked this thing, and have not asked long life for yourself, nor have asked riches for yourself, nor have asked the life of your enemies, but have asked for yourself understanding to discern justice, 12behold, I have done according to your words; see, I have given you a wise and understanding heart, so that there has not been anyone like you before you, nor shall any like you arise after you. 13And I have also given you what you have not asked: both riches and honor, so that there shall not be anyone like you among the kings all your days. 14So if you walk in My ways, to keep My statutes and My commandments, as your father David walked, then I will lengthen your days."

15Then Solomon awoke; and indeed it had been a dream. And he came to Jerusalem and stood before the ark of the covenant of the LORD, offered up burnt offerings, offered peace offerings, and made a feast for all his servants.

3:9 How wise of Solomon to ask for wisdom and understanding. You have an open invitation from God to do the same (see James 1:5–8). Make sure you also soak your soul in the Book of Proverbs. Such wisdom can save you a lot of pain. See John 14:14 comment.

THE FUNCTION OF THE LAW

3:16–28 God's Law prepares the heart of the sinner for the good news of the gospel. Without this preparatory work, his heart is hardened and he therefore becomes a candidate for a false conversion. Now and then we can catch a glimpse of the difference between the true and false converts. Here we read the famous narrative of two women, both claiming to be the mother of one child. Solomon, in his wisdom, commanded that the baby be cut in half and thus revealed the true mother.

Both of these women dwelt in the same house. The true and false converts dwell together in the house of the Lord. Each of the women called Solomon "lord." Both the true and false convert call Jesus "Lord," and it therefore takes the wisdom of Solomon to discern between the true and false. What was it that showed Solomon the real mother? It was that the true mother revealed genuine love. She would rather lose her child than see him cut in two with a sword.

Here is how to tell the true convert from the false. The spurious convert will reveal himself by dividing the Body of Christ in two with some pet doctrine, rather than backing down in humility. He will cut a body of believers in half because of a particular interpretation of Scripture regarding a non-essential. He lacks the wisdom that is peaceable and open to reason. In contrast, the true convert will strive to keep the unity of the body. He will not even put meat to his mouth if it causes his brother to stumble, let alone push a personal interpretation and cause division.

Solomon's Wise Judgment

16Now two women *who were* harlots
came to the king, and stood before him.
17And one woman said, "O my lord, this
woman and I dwell in the same house;
and I gave birth while she *was* in the
house. 18Then it happened, the third day
after I had given birth, that this woman
also gave birth. And we *were* together; no
one *was* with us in the house, except the
two of us in the house. 19And this woman's son died in the night, because she
lay on him. 20So she arose in the middle
of the night and took my son from my
side, while your maidservant slept, and
laid him in her bosom, and laid her dead
child in my bosom. 21And when I rose in
the morning to nurse my son, there he
was, dead. But when I had examined him
in the morning, indeed, he was not my
son whom I had borne."

22Then the other woman said, "No!
But the living one *is* my son, and the dead
one *is* your son."

And the first woman said, "No! But
the dead one *is* your son, and the living
one *is* my son."

Thus they spoke before the king.
23And the king said, "The one says,
'This *is* my son, who lives, and your son
is the dead one'; and the other says, 'No!
But your son *is* the dead one, and my son
is the living one.' " 24Then the king said,
"Bring me a sword." So they brought a
sword before the king. 25And the king
said, "Divide the living child in two, and
give half to one, and half to the other."
26Then the woman whose son *was* living spoke to the king, for she yearned
with compassion for her son; and she
said, "O my lord, give her the living child,
and by no means kill him!"

But the other said, "Let him be neither
mine nor yours, *but* divide *him*."
27So the king answered and said,
"Give the first woman the living child,
and by no means kill him; she *is* his
mother."

28And all Israel heard of the judgment
which the king had rendered; and they
feared the king, for they saw that the
wisdom of God *was* in him to administer
justice.

Solomon's Administration

4 So King Solomon was king over all
Israel. 2And these *were* his officials:
Azariah the son of Zadok, the priest;
3Elihoreph and Ahijah, the sons of Shisha,
scribes; Jehoshaphat the son of Ahilud,
the recorder; 4Benaiah the son of Jehoiada,
over the army; Zadok and Abiathar, the
priests; 5Azariah the son of Nathan, over
the officers; Zabud the son of Nathan, a
priest *and* the king's friend; 6Ahishar,
over the household; and Adoniram the
son of Abda, over the labor force.
7And Solomon had twelve governors

over all Israel, who provided food for the
king and his household; each one made
provision for one month of the year.
8These *are* their names: Ben-Hur,[a] in the
mountains of Ephraim; 9Ben-Deker,[a] in
Makaz, Shaalbim, Beth Shemesh, and
Elon Beth Hanan; 10Ben-Hesed,[a] in Arub-
both; to him *belonged* Sochoh and all the
land of Hepher; 11Ben-Abinadab,[a] *in* all
the regions of Dor; he had Taphath the
daughter of Solomon as wife; 12Baana the
son of Ahilud, *in* Taanach, Megiddo, and
all Beth Shean, which *is* beside Zaretan
below Jezreel, from Beth Shean to Abel
Meholah, as far as the other side of
Jokneam; 13Ben-Geber,[a] in Ramoth Gilead;
to him *belonged* the towns of Jair the son
of Manasseh, in Gilead; to him *also belonged* the region of Argob in Bashan—
sixty large cities with walls and bronze
gate-bars; 14Ahinadab the son of Iddo, *in*
Mahanaim; 15Ahimaaz, in Naphtali; he
also took Basemath the daughter of Solomon as wife; 16Baanah the son of Hushai,
in Asher and Aloth; 17Jehoshaphat the
son of Paruah, in Issachar; 18Shimei the
son of Elah, in Benjamin; 19Geber the son
of Uri, in the land of Gilead, *in* the country of Sihon king of the Amorites, and of
Og king of Bashan. *He was* the only governor who *was* in the land.

Prosperity and Wisdom of Solomon's Reign

20Judah and Israel *were* as numerous
as the sand by the sea in multitude, eating and drinking and rejoicing. 21So Solomon reigned over all kingdoms from the
River[a] *to* the land of the Philistines, as far
as the border of Egypt. *They* brought tribute and served Solomon all the days of
his life.

22Now Solomon's provision for one
day was thirty kors of fine flour, sixty
kors of meal, 23ten fatted oxen, twenty
oxen from the pastures, and one hundred
sheep, besides deer, gazelles, roebucks,
and fatted fowl.

24For he had dominion over all *the region* on this side of the River[a] from Tiphsah even to Gaza, namely over all the
kings on this side of the River; and he
had peace on every side all around him.
25And Judah and Israel dwelt safely, each
man under his vine and his fig tree, from
Dan as far as Beersheba, all the days of
Solomon.

26Solomon had forty[a] thousand stalls
of horses for his chariots, and twelve
thousand horsemen. 27And these governors, each man in his month, provided
food for King Solomon and for all who
came to King Solomon's table. There was
no lack in their supply. 28They also
brought barley and straw to the proper
place, for the horses and steeds, each
man according to his charge.

29And God gave Solomon wisdom and
exceedingly great understanding, and
largeness of heart like the sand on the
seashore. 30Thus Solomon's wisdom excelled the wisdom of all the men of the
East and all the wisdom of Egypt. 31For
he was wiser than all men—than Ethan
the Ezrahite, and Heman, Chalcol, and
Darda, the sons of Mahol; and his fame
was in all the surrounding nations. 32He
spoke three thousand proverbs, and his
songs were one thousand and five. 33Also
he spoke of trees, from the cedar tree of
Lebanon even to the hyssop that springs
out of the wall; he spoke also of animals,
of birds, of creeping things, and of fish.
34And men of all nations, from all the
kings of the earth who had heard of his
wisdom, came to hear the wisdom of
Solomon.

4:8 [a]Literally *Son of Hur* 4:9 [a]Literally *Son of Deker* 4:10 [a]Literally *Son of Hesed* 4:11 [a]Literally *Son of Abinadab* 4:13 [a]Literally *Son of Geber* 4:21 [a]That is, the Euphrates 4:24 [a]That is, the Euphrates 4:26 [a]Following Masoretic Text and most other authorities; some manuscripts of the Septuagint read *four* (compare 2 Chronicles 9:25).

4:29 You will experience this in a comparatively small way when you share your faith. The Holy Spirit will give you wisdom and guidance and will deepen your compassion for the lost as you witness.

4:33 *Evolution's Difficult Questions*

Many have zealously embraced Darwinian evolution without question, as if it were the gospel truth. But can evolution stand the test of close examination?

Zoologists have recorded an amazing 20,000 species of fish. Each of these species has a two-chambered heart that pumps cold blood throughout its cold body.

There are 6,000 species of reptiles. They also have cold blood, but theirs is a three-chambered heart (except for the crocodile, which has four). The 1,000 or so different amphibians (frogs, toads, and newts) have cold blood and a three-chambered heart.

There are over 9,000 species of birds. From the massive Andean condor with its wingspan of 12 feet, to the tiny hummingbird whose heart beats 1,400 times a minute, each of those 9,000 species has a four-chambered heart (left and right atrium, left and right ventricle)—just like humans.

Of course, the 15,000 species of mammals also have a four-chambered heart, which faithfully pumps blood throughout a series of intricate blood vessels to the rest of the body.

Here are some interesting questions for the thinking evolutionist. Can you explain which came first—the blood or the heart—and why? Did the heart in all these different species of fish, reptiles, birds, and mammals evolve before there were blood vessels throughout their bodies? When did the blood evolve? Was it before the vessels evolved or after they evolved?

If it was before, what was it that carried the blood to the heart, if there were no vessels? Did the heart beat before the blood evolved? Why was it beating if there was no blood to pump? If it wasn't beating, why did it start when it didn't know anything about blood?

If the blood vessels evolved before there was blood, why did they evolve if there was no such thing as blood? And if the blood evolved before the heart evolved, what was it that kept it circulating around the body?

The only reasonable answer to these questions is that God made the human body (and the bodies of all the other creatures) with a heart, lungs (to oxygenate the blood), kidneys (to filter wastes from the blood), blood vessels, arteries, blood, skin (to hold it all in), etc., at one moment in time, as the Bible states. Scientist Brad Harrub sums it up well:

> The final hurdle that evolutionists have not (and cannot) overcome involves the co-dependence of the respiratory system and the circulatory system. The heart muscle requires oxygenated blood to remain alive. The respiratory system depends on the circulating blood to deliver oxygen and remove carbon dioxide. So which came first, and how was it able to function properly without the other? Yet, another chicken-egg problem for Darwinians! Evolution may continue to be taught as a "fact" in the classroom, but it has yet to answer such basic life-dependency questions as these.

(Adapted from *How to Know God Exists*.)

Solomon Prepares to Build the Temple

5 Now Hiram king of Tyre sent his servants to Solomon, because he heard that they had anointed him king in place of his father, for Hiram had always loved David. [2]Then Solomon sent to Hiram, saying:

[3]You know how my father David could not build a house for the name of the LORD his God because of the wars which were fought against him on every side, until the LORD put *his foes*[a] under the soles of his feet.
[4]But now the LORD my God has given me rest on every side; *there is* neither adversary nor evil occurrence.
[5]And behold, I propose to build a house for the name of the LORD my God, as the LORD spoke to my father David, saying, "Your son, whom I will set on your throne in your place, he shall build the house for My name."
[6]Now therefore, command that they cut down cedars for me from Lebanon; and my servants will be with your servants, and I will pay you wages for your servants according to whatever you say. For you know *there is* none among us who has skill to cut timber like the Sidonians.

5:3 [a]Literally *them*

7 So it was, when Hiram heard the
words of Solomon, that he rejoiced greatly
and said,

> Blessed *be* the LORD this day, for He
> has given David a wise son over this
> great people!

8 Then Hiram sent to Solomon, saying:

> I have considered *the message* which
> you sent me, *and* I will do all you
> desire concerning the cedar and
> cypress logs.
> 9 My servants shall bring *them* down
> from Lebanon to the sea; I will float
> them in rafts by sea to the place you
> indicate to me, and will have them
> broken apart there; then you can take
> *them* away. And you shall fulfill my
> desire by giving food for my
> household.

10 Then Hiram gave Solomon cedar
and cypress logs *according to* all his desire. 11 And Solomon gave Hiram twenty
thousand kors of wheat *as* food for his
household, and twenty[a] kors of pressed
oil. Thus Solomon gave to Hiram year by
year.
12 So the LORD gave Solomon wisdom,
as He had promised him; and there was
peace between Hiram and Solomon, and
the two of them made a treaty together.
13 Then King Solomon raised up a labor force out of all Israel; and the labor
force was thirty thousand men. 14 And he
sent them to Lebanon, ten thousand a
month in shifts: they were one month in
Lebanon *and* two months at home;
Adoniram *was* in charge of the labor
force. 15 Solomon had seventy thousand
who carried burdens, and eighty thousand who quarried *stone* in the mountains,
16 besides three thousand three hundred[a]
from the chiefs of Solomon's deputies,
who supervised the people who labored
in the work. 17 And the king commanded
them to quarry large stones, costly stones,
and hewn stones, to lay the foundation of
the temple.[a] 18 So Solomon's builders, Hiram's builders, and the Gebalites quarried
them; and they prepared timber and stones
to build the temple.

Solomon Builds the Temple

6 And it came to pass in the four hundred and eightieth[a] year after the
children of Israel had come out of the
land of Egypt, in the fourth year of Solomon's reign over Israel, in the month of
Ziv, which *is* the second month, that he
began to build the house of the LORD.
2 Now the house which King Solomon
built for the LORD, its length *was* sixty
cubits, its width twenty, and its height
thirty cubits. 3 The vestibule in front of
the sanctuary[a] of the house *was* twenty
cubits long across the width of the house,
and the width of *the vestibule*[b] *extended*

5:11 [a]Following Masoretic Text, Targum, and Vulgate; Septuagint and Syriac read *twenty thousand.* 5:16 [a]Following Masoretic Text, Targum, and Vulgate; Septuagint reads *three thousand six hundred.* 5:17 [a]Literally *house,* and so frequently throughout this book 6:1 [a]Following Masoretic Text, Targum, and Vulgate; Septuagint reads *fortieth.* 6:3 [a]Hebrew *heykal;* here the main room of the temple, elsewhere called the holy place (compare Exodus 26:33 and Ezekiel 41:1) [b]Literally *it*

5:13–18 We are laboring together with God to build the everlasting house of the Lord, made up of the living stones of believers. Do you carry a burden for the lost? We should spare no expense of time, effort, or money when it comes to reaching even one soul for Christ.

"One single soul saved shall outlive and outweigh all the kingdoms of the world." *J. C. Ryle*

6:1 "Allowing forty years to Moses, seventeen to Joshua, two hundred ninety-nine to the Judges, forty to Eli, forty to Samuel and Saul, forty to David, and four to Solomon before he began the work, we have just the sum of four hundred and eighty. So long it was before that holy house was built, which in less than four hundred and thirty years was burnt by Nebuchadnezzar. It was thus deferred, because Israel had by their sins, made themselves unworthy of this honor: and because God would show how little he values external pomp and splendor in his service. And God ordered it now, chiefly to be a shadow of good things to come." *John Wesley*

ten cubits from the front of the house. 4And he made for the house windows with beveled frames.

5Against the wall of the temple he built chambers all around, *against* the walls of the temple, all around the sanctuary and the inner sanctuary.[a] Thus he made side chambers all around it. 6The lowest chamber *was* five cubits wide, the middle *was* six cubits wide, and the third *was* seven cubits wide; for he made narrow ledges around the outside of the temple, so that *the support beams* would not be fastened into the walls of the temple. 7And the temple, when it was being built, was built with stone finished at the quarry, so that no hammer or chisel *or* any iron tool was heard in the temple while it was being built. 8The doorway for the middle story[a] *was* on the right side of the temple. They went up by stairs to the middle *story*, and from the middle to the third.

9So he built the temple and finished it, and he paneled the temple with beams and boards of cedar. 10And he built side chambers against the entire temple, each five cubits high; they were attached to the temple with cedar beams.

11Then the word of the LORD came to Solomon, saying: 12"*Concerning* this temple which you are building, if you walk in My statutes, execute My judgments, keep all My commandments, and walk in them, then I will perform My word with you, which I spoke to your father David. 13And I will dwell among the children of Israel, and will not forsake My people Israel."

14So Solomon built the temple and finished it. 15And he built the inside walls of the temple with cedar boards; from the floor of the temple to the ceiling he paneled the inside with wood; and he covered the floor of the temple with planks of cypress. 16Then he built the twenty-cubit room at the rear of the temple, from floor to ceiling, with cedar boards; he built *it* inside as the inner sanctuary, as the Most Holy *Place*. 17And in front of it the temple sanctuary was forty cubits *long*. 18The inside of the temple was cedar, carved with ornamental buds and open flowers. All *was* cedar; there was no stone *to be* seen.

19And he prepared the inner sanctuary inside the temple, to set the ark of the covenant of the LORD there. 20The inner sanctuary *was* twenty cubits long, twenty cubits wide, and twenty cubits high. He overlaid it with pure gold, and overlaid the altar of cedar. 21So Solomon overlaid the inside of the temple with pure gold. He stretched gold chains across the front of the inner sanctuary, and overlaid it with gold. 22The whole temple he overlaid with gold, until he had finished all the temple; also he overlaid with gold the entire altar that *was* by the inner sanctuary.

23Inside the inner sanctuary he made two cherubim *of* olive wood, *each* ten cubits high. 24One wing of the cherub *was* five cubits, and the other wing of the cherub five cubits: ten cubits from the tip of one wing to the tip of the other. 25And the other cherub *was* ten cubits; both cherubim *were* of the same size and shape. 26The height of one cherub *was* ten cubits, and so *was* the other cherub. 27Then he set the cherubim inside the inner room;[a] and they stretched out the wings of the cherubim so that the wing of the one touched *one* wall, and the wing of the other cherub touched the other wall. And their wings touched each other in the middle of the room. 28Also he overlaid the cherubim with gold.

29Then he carved all the walls of the temple all around, both the inner and outer *sanctuaries*, with carved figures of cherubim, palm trees, and open flowers. 30And the floor of the temple he overlaid with gold, both the inner and outer *sanctuaries*.

31For the entrance of the inner sanctuary he made doors *of* olive wood; the lintel *and* doorposts *were* one-fifth *of the*

6:5 [a]Hebrew *debir*; here the inner room of the temple, elsewhere called the Most Holy Place (compare verse 16) 6:8 [a]Following Masoretic Text and Vulgate; Septuagint reads *upper story*; Targum reads *ground story*. 6:27 [a]Literally *house*

wall. 32 The two doors *were of* olive wood; and he carved on them figures of cherubim, palm trees, and open flowers, and overlaid *them* with gold; and he spread gold on the cherubim and on the palm trees. 33 So for the door of the sanctuary he also made doorposts *of* olive wood, one-fourth *of the wall.* 34 And the two doors *were of* cypress wood; two panels *comprised* one folding door, and two panels *comprised* the other folding door. 35 Then he carved cherubim, palm trees, and open flowers *on them,* and overlaid *them* with gold applied evenly on the carved work.

36 And he built the inner court with three rows of hewn stone and a row of cedar beams.

37 In the fourth year the foundation of the house of the LORD was laid, in the month of Ziv. 38 And in the eleventh year, in the month of Bul, which is the eighth month, the house was finished in all its details and according to all its plans. So he was seven years in building it.

Solomon's Other Buildings

7 But Solomon took thirteen years to build his own house; so he finished all his house.

2 He also built the House of the Forest of Lebanon; its length *was* one hundred cubits, its width fifty cubits, and its height thirty cubits, with four rows of cedar pillars, and cedar beams on the pillars. 3 And *it was* paneled with cedar above the beams that *were* on forty-five pillars, fifteen *to* a row. 4 *There were* windows *with beveled frames in* three rows, and window *was* opposite window *in* three tiers. 5 And all the doorways and doorposts *had* rectangular frames; and window *was* opposite window *in* three tiers.

6 He also made the Hall of Pillars: its length *was* fifty cubits, and its width thirty cubits; and in front of them *was* a portico with pillars, and a canopy *was* in front of them.

7 Then he made a hall for the throne, the Hall of Judgment, where he might judge; and *it was* paneled with cedar from floor to ceiling.[a]

8 And the house where he dwelt *had* another court inside the hall, of like workmanship. Solomon also made a house like this hall for Pharaoh's daughter, whom he had taken *as wife.*

9 All these *were of* costly stones cut to size, trimmed with saws, inside and out, from the foundation to the eaves, and also on the outside to the great court. 10 The foundation *was of* costly stones, large stones, some ten cubits and some eight cubits. 11 And above *were* costly stones, hewn to size, and cedar wood. 12 The great court *was* enclosed with three rows of hewn stones and a row of cedar beams. So were the inner court of the house of the LORD and the vestibule of the temple.

Hiram the Craftsman

13 Now King Solomon sent and brought Huram[a] from Tyre. 14 He *was* the son of a widow from the tribe of Naphtali, and his father *was* a man of Tyre, a bronze worker; he was filled with wisdom and understanding and skill in working with all kinds of bronze work. So he came to King Solomon and did all his work.

The Bronze Pillars for the Temple

15 And he cast two pillars of bronze, each one eighteen cubits high, and a line of twelve cubits measured the circumference of each. 16 Then he made two capitals *of* cast bronze, to set on the tops of the pillars. The height of one capital *was* five cubits, and the height of the other capital *was* five cubits. 17 *He made* a lattice network, with wreaths of chainwork, for the capitals which *were* on top of the pillars: seven chains for one capital and seven for the other capital. 18 So he made the pillars, and two rows of pomegranates above the network all around to cover the capitals that *were* on top; and

7:7 [a]Literally *floor,* that is, of the upper level 7:13 [a]Hebrew *Hiram* (compare 2 Chronicles 2:13, 14)

thus he did for the other capital.

19The capitals which *were* on top of the pillars in the hall *were* in the shape of lilies, four cubits. 20The capitals on the two pillars also *had pomegranates* above, by the convex surface which *was* next to the network; and there *were* two hundred such pomegranates in rows on each of the capitals all around.

21Then he set up the pillars by the vestibule of the temple; he set up the pillar on the right and called its name Jachin, and he set up the pillar on the left and called its name Boaz. 22The tops of the pillars were in the shape of lilies. So the work of the pillars was finished.

· · · · · ·

What does science say about the origin of life? See Job 33:4 comment.

· · · · · ·

The Sea and the Oxen

23And he made the Sea of cast bronze, ten cubits from one brim to the other; *it was* completely round. Its height *was* five cubits, and a line of thirty cubits measured its circumference.

24Below its brim *were* ornamental buds encircling it all around, ten to a cubit, all the way around the Sea. The ornamental buds *were* cast in two rows when it was cast. 25It stood on twelve oxen: three looking toward the north, three looking toward the west, three looking toward the south, and three looking toward the east; the Sea *was set* upon them, and all their back parts *pointed* inward. 26It *was* a handbreadth thick; and its brim was shaped like the brim of a cup, *like* a lily blossom. It contained two thousand[a] baths.

The Carts and the Lavers

27He also made ten carts of bronze; four cubits *was* the length of each cart, four cubits its width, and three cubits its height. 28And this *was* the design of the carts: They had panels, and the panels *were* between frames; 29on the panels that *were* between the frames *were* lions, oxen, and cherubim. And on the frames *was* a pedestal on top. Below the lions and oxen *were* wreaths of plaited work. 30Every cart had four bronze wheels and axles of bronze, and its four feet had supports. Under the laver *were* supports of cast *bronze* beside each wreath. 31Its opening inside the crown at the top *was* one cubit in diameter; and the opening *was* round, shaped *like* a pedestal, one and a half cubits in outside diameter; and also on the opening *were* engravings, but the panels were square, not round. 32Under the panels *were* the four wheels, and the axles of the wheels *were joined* to the cart. The height of a wheel *was* one and a half cubits. 33The workmanship of the wheels *was* like the workmanship of a chariot wheel; their axle pins, their rims, their spokes, and their hubs *were* all of cast *bronze*. 34And *there were* four supports at the four corners of each cart; its supports *were* part of the cart itself. 35On the top of the cart, at the height of half a cubit, *it was* perfectly round. And on the top of the cart, its flanges and its panels *were* of the same casting. 36On the plates of its flanges and on its panels he engraved cherubim, lions, and palm trees, wherever there was a clear space on each, with wreaths all around. 37Thus he made the ten carts. All of them were of the same mold, one measure, *and* one shape.

38Then he made ten lavers of bronze; each laver contained forty baths, *and* each laver *was* four cubits. On each of the ten carts *was* a laver. 39And he put five carts on the right side of the house, and five on the left side of the house. He set the Sea on the right side of the house, toward the southeast.

Furnishings of the Temple

40Huram[a] made the lavers and the shovels and the bowls. So Huram fin-

7:26 [a]Or *three thousand* (compare 2 Chronicles 4:5) 7:40 [a]Hebrew *Hiram* (compare 2 Chronicles 2:13, 14)

ished doing all the work that he was to do for King Solomon *for* the house of the LORD: 41the two pillars, the *two* bowl-shaped capitals that *were* on top of the two pillars; the two networks covering the two bowl-shaped capitals which *were* on top of the pillars; 42four hundred pomegranates for the two networks (two rows of pomegranates for each network, to cover the two bowl-shaped capitals that *were* on top of the pillars); 43the ten carts, and ten lavers on the carts; 44one Sea, and twelve oxen under the Sea; 45the pots, the shovels, and the bowls.

All these articles which Huram[a] made for King Solomon *for* the house of the LORD *were of* burnished bronze. 46In the plain of Jordan the king had them cast in clay molds, between Succoth and Zaretan. 47And Solomon did not weigh all the articles, because *there were* so many; the weight of the bronze was not determined.

48Thus Solomon had all the furnishings made for the house of the LORD: the altar of gold, and the table of gold on which *was* the showbread; 49the lampstands of pure gold, five on the right *side* and five on the left in front of the inner sanctuary, with the flowers and the lamps and the wick-trimmers of gold; 50the basins, the trimmers, the bowls, the ladles, and the censers of pure gold; and the hinges of gold, *both* for the doors of the inner room (the Most Holy *Place*) *and* for the doors of the main hall of the temple.

51So all the work that King Solomon had done for the house of the LORD was finished; and Solomon brought in the things which his father David had dedicated: the silver and the gold and the furnishings. He put them in the treasuries of the house of the LORD.

The Ark Brought into the Temple

8 Now Solomon assembled the elders of Israel and all the heads of the tribes, the chief fathers of the children of Israel, to King Solomon in Jerusalem, that they might bring up the ark of the covenant of the LORD from the City of David, which *is* Zion. 2Therefore all the men of Israel assembled with King Solomon at the feast in the month of Ethanim, which *is* the seventh month. 3So all the elders of Israel came, and the priests took up the ark. 4Then they brought up the ark of the LORD, the tabernacle of meeting, and all the holy furnishings that *were* in the tabernacle. The priests and the Levites brought them up. 5Also King Solomon, and all the congregation of Israel who were assembled with him, *were* with him before the ark, sacrificing sheep and oxen that could not be counted or numbered for multitude. 6Then the priests brought in the ark of the covenant of the LORD to its place, into the inner sanctuary of the temple, to the Most Holy *Place,* under the wings of the cherubim. 7For the cherubim spread *their* two wings over the place of the ark, and the cherubim overshadowed the ark and its poles.

> Here is a test to find whether your mission on earth is finished: If you are alive, it isn't.
>
> **RICHARD BACH**

8The poles extended so that the ends of the poles could be seen from the holy *place,* in front of the inner sanctuary; but they could not be seen from outside. And they are there to this day. 9Nothing *was* in the ark except the two tablets of stone which Moses put there at Horeb, when the LORD made *a covenant* with the children of Israel, when they came out of the land of Egypt.

10And it came to pass, when the priests came out of the holy *place,* that the cloud filled the house of the LORD, 11so that the priests could not continue ministering because of the cloud; for the glory of the LORD filled the house of the LORD.

12Then Solomon spoke:

7:45 [a]Hebrew *Hiram* (compare 2 Chronicles 2:13, 14)

"The LORD said He would dwell in the
dark cloud.
13I have surely built You an exalted
house,
And a place for You to dwell in
forever."

Solomon's Speech at Completion of the Work

14Then the king turned around and
blessed the whole assembly of Israel, while
all the assembly of Israel was standing.
15And he said: "Blessed *be* the LORD God
of Israel, who spoke with His mouth to
my father David, and with His hand has
fulfilled *it,* saying, 16'Since the day that I
brought My people Israel out of Egypt, I
have chosen no city from any tribe of Israel *in which* to build a house, that My
name might be there; but I chose David
to be over My people Israel.' 17Now it was
in the heart of my father David to build a
temple[a] for the name of the LORD God of
Israel. 18But the LORD said to my father
David, 'Whereas it was in your heart to
build a temple for My name, you did well
that it was in your heart. 19Nevertheless
you shall not build the temple, but your
son who will come from your body, he
shall build the temple for My name.' 20So
the LORD has fulfilled His word which He
spoke; and I have filled the position of
my father David, and sit on the throne of
Israel, as the LORD promised; and I have
built a temple for the name of the LORD
God of Israel. 21And there I have made a
place for the ark, in which *is* the covenant
of the LORD which He made with our fathers, when He brought them out of the
land of Egypt."

Solomon's Prayer of Dedication

22Then Solomon stood before the altar
of the LORD in the presence of all the assembly of Israel, and spread out his hands
toward heaven; 23and he said: "LORD God
of Israel, *there is* no God in heaven above
or on earth below like You, who keep
Your covenant and mercy with Your servants who walk before You with all their
hearts. 24You have kept what You promised Your servant David my father; You
have both spoken with Your mouth and
fulfilled *it* with Your hand, as *it is* this day.
25Therefore, LORD God of Israel, now keep
what You promised Your servant David
my father, saying, 'You shall not fail to
have a man sit before Me on the throne of
Israel, only if your sons take heed to their
way, that they walk before Me as you
have walked before Me.' 26And now I
pray, O God of Israel, let Your word come
true, which You have spoken to Your servant David my father.

27"But will God indeed dwell on the
earth? Behold, heaven and the heaven of
heavens cannot contain You. How much
less this temple which I have built! 28Yet
regard the prayer of Your servant and his
supplication, O LORD my God, and listen
to the cry and the prayer which Your servant is praying before You today: 29that
Your eyes may be open toward this temple night and day, toward the place of
which You said, 'My name shall be there,'
that You may hear the prayer which Your
servant makes toward this place. 30And
may You hear the supplication of Your
servant and of Your people Israel, when
they pray toward this place. Hear in heav-
en Your dwelling place; and when You
hear, forgive.

31"When anyone sins against his
neighbor, and is forced to take an oath,

8:17 [a]Literally *house*, and so in verses 18–20

8:9–11 Notice that the ark was the centerpiece: they "assembled . . . before the ark," they "brought in the ark," etc. Also notice that there was nothing in the ark but the Ten Commandments. God loves His Law (the reason for the cross), and He cannot be separated from it. Scripture calls Him the "habitation of justice" (see Jer. 50:7). We are told that God is perfect, holy, just, and good, and that His Law—the very essence of His character—is also perfect, holy, just, and good (see Psa. 19:7; Rom. 7:12). This is why God came down in such glory. May the Church honor and uphold His Law and have the same experience. See also page 280.

QUESTIONS & OBJECTIONS

"How can we witness to people cross-culturally?"

While we must be culturally sensitive in foreign countries, we need not do what most missionaries have done in the past—spend years learning the culture and the language of the nation before sharing the gospel.

The biblical gospel message is applicable to all people everywhere—whether they are in the U.S. or overseas, in a high-rise or a lowly hut, rich or poor, happy or hurting, regardless of their beliefs or their lifestyles. We do not need to tailor specific outreaches to each individual group, because the disease of sin and the cure of the Savior apply to all humanity. God has given light to every man, and the universal moral Law is written on the heart of all people in all cultures.

In every nation people have a God-given conscience and a will to live. To be effective (with God's help), all we need is a good translator and the knowledge of how to tap into the will to live and the human conscience using the Law. For details, see James 4:14 and Psa. 51:6 comments.

and comes *and* takes an oath before Your
altar in this temple, 32then hear in heaven,
and act, and judge Your servants, condemning the wicked, bringing his way on
his head, and justifying the righteous by
giving him according to his righteousness.
33"When Your people Israel are defeated before an enemy because they
have sinned against You, and when they
turn back to You and confess Your name,
and pray and make supplication to You
in this temple, 34then hear in heaven, and
forgive the sin of Your people Israel, and
bring them back to the land which You
gave to their fathers.
35"When the heavens are shut up and
there is no rain because they have sinned
against You, when they pray toward this
place and confess Your name, and turn
from their sin because You afflict them,
36then hear in heaven, and forgive the sin
of Your servants, Your people Israel, that
You may teach them the good way in
which they should walk; and send rain
on Your land which You have given to
Your people as an inheritance.
37"When there is famine in the land,
pestilence *or* blight *or* mildew, locusts *or*
grasshoppers; when their enemy besieges
them in the land of their cities; whatever
plague or whatever sickness *there is;*
38whatever prayer, whatever supplication
is made by anyone, *or* by all Your people
Israel, when each one knows the plague
of his own heart, and spreads out his hands
toward this temple: 39then hear in heaven
Your dwelling place, and forgive, and act,
and give to everyone according to all his
ways, whose heart You know (for You
alone know the hearts of all the sons of
men), 40that they may fear You all the
days that they live in the land which You
gave to our fathers.
41"Moreover, concerning a foreigner,
who *is* not of Your people Israel, but has
come from a far country for Your name's
sake 42(for they will hear of Your great
name and Your strong hand and Your outstretched arm), when he comes and prays
toward this temple, 43hear in heaven Your
dwelling place, and do according to all
for which the foreigner calls to You, that
all peoples of the earth may know Your
name and fear You, as *do* Your people Israel, and that they may know that this
temple which I have built is called by
Your name.
44"When Your people go out to battle
against their enemy, wherever You send
them, and when they pray to the LORD
toward the city which You have chosen

8:39 True repentance requires an understanding that God sees our heart and our thought-life. He requires truth in the "inward parts" (Psa. 51:6).

and the temple which I have built for
Your name, [45]then hear in heaven their
prayer and their supplication, and maintain their cause.
[46]"When they sin against You (for *there
is* no one who does not sin), and You become angry with them and deliver them
to the enemy, and they take them captive
to the land of the enemy, far or near; [47]*yet*
when they come to themselves in the
land where they were carried captive, and
repent, and make supplication to You in
the land of those who took them captive,
saying, 'We have sinned and done wrong,
we have committed wickedness'; [48]and
when they return to You with all their
heart and with all their soul in the land of
their enemies who led them away captive, and pray to You toward their land
which You gave to their fathers, the city
which You have chosen and the temple
which I have built for Your name: [49]then
hear in heaven Your dwelling place their
prayer and their supplication, and maintain their cause, [50]and forgive Your people who have sinned against You, and all
their transgressions which they have
transgressed against You; and grant them
compassion before those who took them
captive, that they may have compassion
on them [51](for they *are* Your people and
Your inheritance, whom You brought out
of Egypt, out of the iron furnace), [52]that
Your eyes may be open to the supplication of Your servant and the supplication
of Your people Israel, to listen to them
whenever they call to You. [53]For You separated them from among all the peoples
of the earth *to be* Your inheritance, as You
spoke by Your servant Moses, when You
brought our fathers out of Egypt, O Lord
GOD."

Solomon Blesses the Assembly

[54]And so it was, when Solomon had
finished praying all this prayer and supplication to the LORD, that he arose from
before the altar of the LORD, from kneeling on his knees with his hands spread
up to heaven. [55]Then he stood and blessed
all the assembly of Israel with a loud
voice, saying: [56]"Blessed *be* the LORD, who
has given rest to His people Israel, according to all that He promised. There
has not failed one word of all His good
promise, which He promised through His
servant Moses. [57]May the LORD our God
be with us, as He was with our fathers.
May He not leave us nor forsake us,
[58]that He may incline our hearts to Himself, to walk in all His ways, and to keep
His commandments and His statutes and
His judgments, which He commanded
our fathers. [59]And may these words of
mine, with which I have made supplication before the LORD, be near the LORD
our God day and night, that He may
maintain the cause of His servant and the
cause of His people Israel, as each day
may require, [60]that all the peoples of the
earth may know that the LORD *is* God;
there is no other. [61]Let your heart therefore be loyal to the LORD our God, to walk
in His statutes and keep His commandments, as at this day."

Solomon Dedicates the Temple

[62]Then the king and all Israel with him
offered sacrifices before the LORD. [63]And
Solomon offered a sacrifice of peace offerings, which he offered to the LORD,
twenty-two thousand bulls and one hundred and twenty thousand sheep. So the
king and all the children of Israel dedicated the house of the LORD. [64]On the

8:47,48 See 2 Chron. 6:37,38 comment.

8:54 Prayer. "All hell is vanquished when the believer bows his knee in importunate supplication. Beloved brethren, let us pray. We cannot all argue, but we can all pray; we cannot all be leaders, but we can all be pleaders; we cannot all be mighty in rhetoric, but we can all be prevalent in prayer. I would sooner see you eloquent with God than with men. Prayer links us with the Eternal, the Omnipotent, the Infinite, and hence it is our chief resort...Be sure that you are with God, and then you may be sure that God is with you." *Charles Spurgeon*

same day the king consecrated the middle of the court that *was* in front of the house of the LORD; for there he offered burnt offerings, grain offerings, and the fat of the peace offerings, because the bronze altar that *was* before the LORD *was* too small to receive the burnt offerings, the grain offerings, and the fat of the peace offerings.

65 At that time Solomon held a feast, and all Israel with him, a great assembly from the entrance of Hamath to the Brook of Egypt, before the LORD our God, seven days and seven *more* days—fourteen days. 66 On the eighth day he sent the people away; and they blessed the king, and went to their tents joyful and glad of heart for all the good that the LORD had done for His servant David, and for Israel His people.

God's Second Appearance to Solomon

9 And it came to pass, when Solomon had finished building the house of the LORD and the king's house, and all Solomon's desire which he wanted to do, 2 that the LORD appeared to Solomon the second time, as He had appeared to him at Gibeon. 3 And the LORD said to him: "I have heard your prayer and your supplication that you have made before Me; I have consecrated this house which you have built to put My name there forever, and My eyes and My heart will be there perpetually. 4 Now if you walk before Me as your father David walked, in integrity of heart and in uprightness, to do according to all that I have commanded you, *and* if you keep My statutes and My judgments, 5 then I will establish the throne of your kingdom over Israel forever, as I promised David your father, saying, 'You shall not fail to have a man on the throne of Israel.' 6 *But* if you or your sons at all turn from following Me, and do not keep My commandments *and* My statutes which I have set before you, but go and serve other gods and worship them, 7 then I will cut off Israel from the land which I have given them; and this house which I have consecrated for My name I will cast out of My sight. Israel will be a proverb and a byword among all peoples. 8 And *as for* this house, *which* is exalted, everyone who passes by it will be astonished and will hiss, and say, 'Why has the LORD done thus to this land and to this house?' 9 Then they will answer, 'Because they forsook the LORD their God, who brought their fathers out of the land of Egypt, and have embraced other gods, and worshiped them and served them; therefore the LORD has brought all this calamity on them.' "

Solomon and Hiram Exchange Gifts

10 Now it happened at the end of twenty years, when Solomon had built the two houses, the house of the LORD and the king's house 11 (Hiram the king of Tyre had supplied Solomon with cedar and cypress and gold, as much as he desired), *that* King Solomon then gave Hiram twenty cities in the land of Galilee. 12 Then Hiram went from Tyre to see the cities which Solomon had given him, but they did not please him. 13 So he said, "What *kind of* cities *are* these which you have given me, my brother?" And he called them the land of Cabul,[a] as they are to this day. 14 Then Hiram sent the king one hundred and twenty talents of gold.

Solomon's Additional Achievements

15 And this *is* the reason for the labor force which King Solomon raised: to build the house of the LORD, his own house, the Millo,[a] the wall of Jerusalem, Hazor, Megid-

9:13 [a]Literally *Good for Nothing* 9:15 [a]Literally *The Landfill*

9:7 We should never disregard the warnings of Holy Scripture. The Bible is God's Word and His will for sinful humanity. If we refuse to take note, we will suffer terrible consequences. God warned His people that if they refused to walk in obedience, He would severely punish them as a nation. Had they taken heed they would have enjoyed great blessings, rather than endure great suffering.

do, and Gezer. 16(Pharaoh king of Egypt had gone up and taken Gezer and burned it with fire, had killed the Canaanites who dwelt in the city, and had given it *as* a dowry to his daughter, Solomon's wife.) 17And Solomon built Gezer, Lower Beth Horon, 18Baalath, and Tadmor in the wilderness, in the land *of Judah,* 19all the storage cities that Solomon had, cities for his chariots and cities for his cavalry, and whatever Solomon desired to build in Jerusalem, in Lebanon, and in all the land of his dominion.

20All the people *who were* left of the Amorites, Hittites, Perizzites, Hivites, and Jebusites, who *were* not of the children of Israel— 21that is, their descendants who were left in the land after them, whom the children of Israel had not been able to destroy completely—from these Solomon raised forced labor, as it is to this day. 22But of the children of Israel Solomon made no forced laborers, because they *were* men of war and his servants: his officers, his captains, commanders of his chariots, and his cavalry.

23Others *were* chiefs of the officials who *were* over Solomon's work: five hundred and fifty, who ruled over the people who did the work.

24But Pharaoh's daughter came up from the City of David to her house which *Solomon*[a] had built for her. Then he built the Millo.

25Now three times a year Solomon offered burnt offerings and peace offerings on the altar which he had built for the LORD, and he burned incense with them *on the altar* that *was* before the LORD. So he finished the temple.

26King Solomon also built a fleet of ships at Ezion Geber, which *is* near Elath[a] on the shore of the Red Sea, in the land of Edom. 27Then Hiram sent his servants with the fleet, seamen who knew the sea, to work with the servants of Solomon. 28And they went to Ophir, and acquired four hundred and twenty talents of gold from there, and brought *it* to King Solomon.

The Queen of Sheba's Praise of Solomon

10 Now when the queen of Sheba heard of the fame of Solomon concerning the name of the LORD, she came to test him with hard questions. 2She came to Jerusalem with a very great retinue, with camels that bore spices, very much gold, and precious stones; and when she came to Solomon, she spoke with him about all that was in her heart. 3So Solomon answered all her questions; there was nothing so difficult for the king that he could not explain *it* to her. 4And when the queen of Sheba had seen all the wisdom of Solomon, the house that he had built, 5the food on his table, the seating of his servants, the service of his waiters and their apparel, his cupbearers, and his entryway by which he went up to the house of the LORD, there was no more spirit in her. 6Then she said to the king: "It was a true report which I heard in my own land about your words and your wisdom. 7However I did not believe the words until I came and saw with my own eyes; and indeed the half was not told me. Your wisdom and prosperity exceed the fame of which I heard. 8Happy *are* your men and happy *are* these your servants, who stand continually before you *and* hear your wisdom! 9Blessed be the LORD your God, who delighted in you, setting you on the throne of Israel! Because the LORD has loved Israel forever, therefore He made you king, to do justice and righteousness."

10Then she gave the king one hundred and twenty talents of gold, spices in great quantity, and precious stones. There never

9:24 [a]Literally *he* (compare 2 Chronicles 8:11) **9:26** [a]Hebrew *Eloth* (compare 2 Kings 14:22)

10:7,8 This is how a sinner feels in the first days of his conversion. We had no idea of the unspeakable riches that were hidden in Christ. (See Col. 1:27; 2:2,3; Eph. 3:8.)

again came such abundance of spices as
the queen of Sheba gave to King Solomon. [11]Also, the ships of Hiram, which
brought gold from Ophir, brought great
quantities of almug[a] wood and precious
stones from Ophir. [12]And the king made
steps of the almug wood for the house of
the LORD and for the king's house, also
harps and stringed instruments for singers.
There never again came such almug
wood, nor has the like been seen to this
day.

[13]Now King Solomon gave the queen
of Sheba all she desired, whatever she
asked, besides what Solomon had given
her according to the royal generosity. So
she turned and went to her own country,
she and her servants.

Solomon's Great Wealth

[14]The weight of gold that came to Solomon yearly was six hundred and sixty-six
talents of gold, [15]besides *that* from the
traveling merchants, from the income of
traders, from all the kings of Arabia, and
from the governors of the country.

[16]And King Solomon made two hundred large shields *of* hammered gold; six
hundred *shekels* of gold went into each
shield. [17]He also *made* three hundred
shields *of* hammered gold; three minas of
gold went into each shield. The king put
them in the House of the Forest of
Lebanon.

[18]Moreover the king made a great
throne of ivory, and overlaid it with pure
gold. [19]The throne had six steps, and the
top of the throne *was* round at the back;
there were armrests on either side of the
place of the seat, and two lions stood beside the armrests. [20]Twelve lions stood
there, one on each side of the six steps;
nothing like *this* had been made for any
other kingdom.

[21]All King Solomon's drinking vessels
were gold, and all the vessels of the House
of the Forest of Lebanon *were* pure gold.
Not *one was* silver, for this was accounted
as nothing in the days of Solomon. [22]For
the king had merchant ships[a] at sea with
the fleet of Hiram. Once every three years
the merchant ships came bringing gold,
silver, ivory, apes, and monkeys.[b] [23]So
King Solomon surpassed all the kings of
the earth in riches and wisdom.

[24]Now all the earth sought the presence of Solomon to hear his wisdom,
which God had put in his heart. [25]Each
man brought his present: articles of silver
and gold, garments, armor, spices, horses,
and mules, at a set rate year by year.

[26]And Solomon gathered chariots and
horsemen; he had one thousand four
hundred chariots and twelve thousand
horsemen, whom he stationed[a] in the
chariot cities and with the king at Jerusalem. [27]The king made silver *as common*
in Jerusalem as stones, and he made cedar
trees as abundant as the sycamores which
are in the lowland.

[28]Also Solomon had horses imported
from Egypt and Keveh; the king's merchants bought them in Keveh at the *current* price. [29]Now a chariot that was imported from Egypt cost six hundred *shekels*
of silver, and a horse one hundred and
fifty; and thus, through their agents,[a] they
exported *them* to all the kings of the Hittites and the kings of Syria.

Solomon's Heart Turns from the Lord

11 But King Solomon loved many foreign women, as well as the daughter of Pharaoh: women of the Moabites,
Ammonites, Edomites, Sidonians, *and* Hit-

10:11 [a]Or *algum* (compare 2 Chronicles 9:10, 11) **10:22** [a]Literally *ships of Tarshish*, deep-sea vessels [b]Or *peacocks* **10:26** [a]Following Septuagint, Syriac, Targum, and Vulgate (compare 2 Chronicles 9:25); Masoretic Text reads *led*. **10:29** [a]Literally *by their hands*

11:1–4,9 Solomon had incredible wisdom and yet lust turned his head from God to women, and then (predictably) to idolatry to accommodate his sin. Christians, however, have the Holy Spirit living within us to help us overcome sin, and the Word of God warning us to flee from sexual sin and to keep our hearts free from idols.

tites— 2from the nations of whom the
LORD had said to the children of Israel,
"You shall not intermarry with them, nor
they with you. Surely they will turn away
your hearts after their gods." Solomon
clung to these in love. 3And he had seven
hundred wives, princesses, and three hundred concubines; and his wives turned
away his heart. 4For it was so, when Solomon was old, that his wives turned his
heart after other gods; and his heart was
not loyal to the LORD his God, as *was* the
heart of his father David. 5For Solomon
went after Ashtoreth the goddess of the
Sidonians, and after Milcom the abomination of the Ammonites. 6Solomon did
evil in the sight of the LORD, and did not
fully follow the LORD, as *did* his father
David. 7Then Solomon built a high place
for Chemosh the abomination of Moab,
on the hill that *is* east of Jerusalem, and
for Molech the abomination of the people
of Ammon. 8And he did likewise for all
his foreign wives, who burned incense and
sacrificed to their gods.

9So the LORD became angry with Solomon, because his heart had turned from
the LORD God of Israel, who had appeared
to him twice, 10and had commanded him
concerning this thing, that he should not
go after other gods; but he did not keep
what the LORD had commanded. 11There-
fore the LORD said to Solomon, "Because
you have done this, and have not kept
My covenant and My statutes, which I
have commanded you, I will surely tear
the kingdom away from you and give it
to your servant. 12Nevertheless I will not
do it in your days, for the sake of your father David; I will tear it out of the hand
of your son. 13However I will not tear
away the whole kingdom; I will give one
tribe to your son for the sake of My servant David, and for the sake of Jerusalem
which I have chosen."

Adversaries of Solomon

14Now the LORD raised up an adversary against Solomon, Hadad the Edomite; he *was* a descendant of the king in
Edom. 15For it happened, when David was
in Edom, and Joab the commander of the
army had gone up to bury the slain, after
he had killed every male in Edom 16(because for six months Joab remained there
with all Israel, until he had cut down
every male in Edom), 17that Hadad fled
to go to Egypt, he and certain Edomites
of his father's servants with him. Hadad
was still a little child. 18Then they arose
from Midian and came to Paran; and they
took men with them from Paran and
came to Egypt, to Pharaoh king of Egypt,
who gave him a house, apportioned food
for him, and gave him land. 19And Hadad
found great favor in the sight of Pharaoh,
so that he gave him as wife the sister of
his own wife, that is, the sister of Queen
Tahpenes. 20Then the sister of Tahpenes
bore him Genubath his son, whom Tahpenes weaned in Pharaoh's house. And
Genubath was in Pharaoh's household
among the sons of Pharaoh.

To offer a sinner the gift of salvation based upon the work of Christ, while at the same time allowing him to retain the idea that the gift carries with it no moral implications, is to do him untold injury where it hurts him worst.

A. W. TOZER

21So when Hadad heard in Egypt that
David rested with his fathers, and that
Joab the commander of the army was
dead, Hadad said to Pharaoh, "Let me depart, that I may go to my own country."

22Then Pharaoh said to him, "But what
have you lacked with me, that suddenly
you seek to go to your own country?"

So he answered, "Nothing, but do let
me go anyway."

23And God raised up *another* adversary
against him, Rezon the son of Eliadah, who
had fled from his lord, Hadadezer king of
Zobah. 24So he gathered men to him and
became captain over a band *of raiders*,
when David killed those *of Zobah*. And
they went to Damascus and dwelt there,

and reigned in Damascus. 25He was an adversary of Israel all the days of Solomon (besides the trouble that Hadad *caused*); and he abhorred Israel, and reigned over Syria.

Jeroboam's Rebellion

26Then Solomon's servant, Jeroboam the son of Nebat, an Ephraimite from Zereda, whose mother's name *was* Zeruah, a widow, also rebelled against the king.

27And this *is* what caused him to rebel against the king: Solomon had built the Millo *and* repaired the damages to the City of David his father. 28The man Jeroboam *was* a mighty man of valor; and Solomon, seeing that the young man was industrious, made him the officer over all the labor force of the house of Joseph.

29Now it happened at that time, when Jeroboam went out of Jerusalem, that the prophet Ahijah the Shilonite met him on the way; and he had clothed himself with a new garment, and the two *were* alone in the field. 30Then Ahijah took hold of the new garment that *was* on him, and tore it *into* twelve pieces. 31And he said to Jeroboam, "Take for yourself ten pieces, for thus says the LORD, the God of Israel: 'Behold, I will tear the kingdom out of the hand of Solomon and will give ten tribes to you 32(but he shall have one tribe for the sake of My servant David, and for the sake of Jerusalem, the city which I have chosen out of all the tribes of Israel), 33because they have[a] forsaken Me, and worshiped Ashtoreth the goddess of the Sidonians, Chemosh the god of the Moabites, and Milcom the god of the people of Ammon, and have not walked in My ways to do *what is* right in My eyes and *keep* My statutes and My judgments, as *did* his father David. 34However I will not take the whole kingdom out of his hand, because I have made him ruler all the days of his life for the sake of My servant David, whom I chose because he kept My commandments and My statutes. 35But I will take the kingdom out of his son's hand and give it to you—ten tribes. 36And to his son I will give one tribe, that My servant David may always have a lamp before Me in Jerusalem, the city which I have chosen for Myself, to put My name there. 37So I will take you, and you shall reign over all your heart desires, and you shall be king over Israel. 38Then it shall be, if you heed all that I command you, walk in My ways, and do *what is* right in My sight, to keep My statutes and My commandments, as My servant David did, then I will be with you and build for you an enduring house, as I built for David, and will give Israel to you. 39And I will afflict the descendants of David because of this, but not forever.' "

40Solomon therefore sought to kill Jeroboam. But Jeroboam arose and fled to Egypt, to Shishak king of Egypt, and was in Egypt until the death of Solomon.

Death of Solomon

41Now the rest of the acts of Solomon, all that he did, and his wisdom, *are* they not written in the book of the acts of Solomon? 42And the period that Solomon reigned in Jerusalem over all Israel *was* forty years. 43Then Solomon rested with his fathers, and was buried in the City of David his father. And Rehoboam his son reigned in his place.

The Revolt Against Rehoboam

12 And Rehoboam went to Shechem, for all Israel had gone to Shechem to make him king. 2So it happened, when Jeroboam the son of Nebat heard *it* (he was still in Egypt, for he had fled from the presence of King Solomon and had been dwelling in Egypt), 3that they sent and called him. Then Jeroboam and the whole assembly of Israel came and spoke to Rehoboam, saying, 4"Your father made our yoke heavy; now therefore, lighten the burdensome service of your father, and his heavy yoke which he put on us, and we will serve you."

11:33 [a]Following Masoretic Text and Targum; Septuagint, Syriac, and Vulgate read *he has*.

5So he said to them, "Depart *for* three days, then come back to me." And the people departed.

6Then King Rehoboam consulted the elders who stood before his father Solomon while he still lived, and he said, "How do you advise *me* to answer these people?"

7And they spoke to him, saying, "If you will be a servant to these people today, and serve them, and answer them, and speak good words to them, then they will be your servants forever."

8But he rejected the advice which the elders had given him, and consulted the young men who had grown up with him, who stood before him. 9And he said to them, "What advice do you give? How should we answer this people who have spoken to me, saying, 'Lighten the yoke which your father put on us'?"

10Then the young men who had grown up with him spoke to him, saying, "Thus you should speak to this people who have spoken to you, saying, 'Your father made our yoke heavy, but you make *it* lighter on us'—thus you shall say to them: 'My little *finger* shall be thicker than my father's waist! 11And now, whereas my father put a heavy yoke on you, I will add to your yoke; my father chastised you with whips, but I will chastise you with scourges!' "[a]

12So Jeroboam and all the people came to Rehoboam the third day, as the king had directed, saying, "Come back to me the third day." 13Then the king answered the people roughly, and rejected the advice which the elders had given him; 14and he spoke to them according to the advice of the young men, saying, "My father made your yoke heavy, but I will add to your yoke; my father chastised you with whips, but I will chastise you with scourges!"[a] 15So the king did not listen to the people; for the turn *of events* was from the LORD, that He might fulfill His word, which the LORD had spoken by Ahijah the Shilonite to Jeroboam the son of Nebat.

16Now when all Israel saw that the king did not listen to them, the people answered the king, saying:

"What share have we in David?
We have no inheritance in the son of
Jesse.
To your tents, O Israel!
Now, see to your own house, O David!"

So Israel departed to their tents. 17But Rehoboam reigned over the children of Israel who dwelt in the cities of Judah.

18Then King Rehoboam sent Adoram, who *was* in charge of the revenue; but all Israel stoned him with stones, and he died. Therefore King Rehoboam mounted his chariot in haste to flee to Jerusalem. 19So Israel has been in rebellion against the house of David to this day.

20Now it came to pass when all Israel heard that Jeroboam had come back, they sent for him and called him to the congregation, and made him king over all Israel. There was none who followed the house of David, but the tribe of Judah only.

21And when Rehoboam came to Jerusalem, he assembled all the house of Judah with the tribe of Benjamin, one hundred and eighty thousand chosen *men* who were warriors, to fight against the house of Israel, that he might restore the kingdom to Rehoboam the son of Solomon. 22But the word of God came to Shemaiah the man of God, saying, 23"Speak to Rehoboam the son of Solomon, king of Judah, to all the house of Judah and Benjamin, and to the rest of the people, saying, 24'Thus says the LORD: "You shall not go up nor fight against your brethren the children of Israel. Let every man return to his house, for this thing is from Me." ' " Therefore they obeyed the word of the LORD, and turned back, according to the word of the LORD.

Jeroboam's Gold Calves

25Then Jeroboam built Shechem in the

12:11 [a]Literally *scorpions* 12:14 [a]Literally *scorpions*

mountains of Ephraim, and dwelt there. Also he went out from there and built Penuel. [26]And Jeroboam said in his heart, "Now the kingdom may return to the house of David: [27]If these people go up to offer sacrifices in the house of the LORD at Jerusalem, then the heart of this people will turn back to their lord, Rehoboam king of Judah, and they will kill me and go back to Rehoboam king of Judah."

[28]Therefore the king asked advice, made two calves of gold, and said to the people, "It is too much for you to go up to Jerusalem. Here are your gods, O Israel, which brought you up from the land of Egypt!" [29]And he set up one in Bethel, and the other he put in Dan. [30]Now this thing became a sin, for the people went *to worship* before the one as far as Dan. [31]He made shrines[a] on the high places, and made priests from every class of people, who were not of the sons of Levi.

[32]Jeroboam ordained a feast on the fifteenth day of the eighth month, like the feast that *was* in Judah, and offered sacrifices on the altar. So he did at Bethel, sacrificing to the calves that he had made. And at Bethel he installed the priests of the high places which he had made. [33]So he made offerings on the altar which he had made at Bethel on the fifteenth day of the eighth month, in the month which he had devised in his own heart. And he ordained a feast for the children of Israel, and offered sacrifices on the altar and burned incense.

The Message of the Man of God

13 And behold, a man of God went from Judah to Bethel by the word of the LORD, and Jeroboam stood by the altar to burn incense. [2]Then he cried out against the altar by the word of the LORD, and said, "O altar, altar! Thus says the LORD: 'Behold, a child, Josiah by name, shall be born to the house of David; and on you he shall sacrifice the priests of the high places who burn incense on you, and men's bones shall be burned on you.' " [3]And he gave a sign the same day, saying, "This *is* the sign which the LORD has spoken: Surely the altar shall split apart, and the ashes on it shall be poured out."

[4]So it came to pass when King Jeroboam heard the saying of the man of God, who cried out against the altar in Bethel, that he stretched out his hand from the altar, saying, "Arrest him!" Then his hand, which he stretched out toward him, withered, so that he could not pull it back to himself. [5]The altar also was split apart, and the ashes poured out from the altar, according to the sign which the man of God had given by the word of the LORD. [6]Then the king answered and said to the man of God, "Please entreat the favor of the LORD your God, and pray for me, that my hand may be restored to me."

So the man of God entreated the LORD, and the king's hand was restored to him, and became as before. [7]Then the king said to the man of God, "Come home with me and refresh yourself, and I will give you a reward."

[8]But the man of God said to the king, "If you were to give me half your house, I would not go in with you; nor would I eat bread nor drink water in this place. [9]For so it was commanded me by the word of the LORD, saying, 'You shall not eat bread, nor drink water, nor return by the same way you came.' " [10]So he went another way and did not return by the way he came to Bethel.

12:31 [a]Literally *a house*

12:24 "This breaking up of the kingdom of Solomon into two parts was the result of Solomon's sin and Rehoboam's folly; yet God was in it: 'This thing is from me, saith the Lord.' God had nothing to do with the sin or the folly, but in some way which we can never explain, in a mysterious way in which we are to believe without hesitation, God was in it all. The most notable instance of this truth is the death of our Lord Jesus Christ; that was the greatest of human crimes, yet it was foreordained and predetermined of the Most High, to whom there can be no such thing as crime, nor any sort of compact with sin." *Charles Spurgeon*

Death of the Man of God

[11]Now an old prophet dwelt in Bethel, and his sons came and told him all the works that the man of God had done that day in Bethel; they also told their father the words which he had spoken to the king. [12]And their father said to them, "Which way did he go?" For his sons had seen[a] which way the man of God went who came from Judah. [13]Then he said to his sons, "Saddle the donkey for me." So they saddled the donkey for him; and he rode on it, [14]and went after the man of God, and found him sitting under an oak. Then he said to him, "*Are* you the man of God who came from Judah?"

And he said, "I *am*."

[15]Then he said to him, "Come home with me and eat bread."

[16]And he said, "I cannot return with you nor go in with you; neither can I eat bread nor drink water with you in this place. [17]For I have been told by the word of the LORD, 'You shall not eat bread nor drink water there, nor return by going the way you came.' "

[18]He said to him, "I too *am* a prophet as you *are,* and an angel spoke to me by the word of the LORD, saying, 'Bring him back with you to your house, that he may eat bread and drink water.' " (He was lying to him.)

[19]So he went back with him, and ate bread in his house, and drank water.

[20]Now it happened, as they sat at the table, that the word of the LORD came to the prophet who had brought him back; [21]and he cried out to the man of God who came from Judah, saying, "Thus says the LORD: 'Because you have disobeyed the word of the LORD, and have not kept the commandment which the LORD your God commanded you, [22]but you came back, ate bread, and drank water in the place of which *the* LORD said to you, "Eat no bread and drink no water," your corpse shall not come to the tomb of your fathers.' "

[23]So it was, after he had eaten bread and after he had drunk, that he saddled the donkey for him, the prophet whom he had brought back. [24]When he was gone, a lion met him on the road and killed him. And his corpse was thrown on the road, and the donkey stood by it. The lion also stood by the corpse. [25]And there, men passed by and saw the corpse thrown on the road, and the lion standing by the corpse. Then they went and told *it* in the city where the old prophet dwelt.

[26]Now when the prophet who had brought him back from the way heard *it,* he said, "It *is* the man of God who was disobedient to the word of the LORD. Therefore the LORD has delivered him to the lion, which has torn him and killed him, according to the word of the LORD which He spoke to him." [27]And he spoke to his sons, saying, "Saddle the donkey for me." So they saddled *it.* [28]Then he went and found his corpse thrown on the road, and the donkey and the lion standing by the corpse. The lion had not eaten the corpse nor torn the donkey. [29]And the prophet took up the corpse of the man of God, laid it on the donkey, and brought it back. So the old prophet came to the city to mourn, and to bury him. [30]Then he laid the corpse in his own tomb; and they mourned over him, *saying,* "Alas, my

13:12 [a]Septuagint, Syriac, Targum, and Vulgate read *showed him.*

13:24 The faithful and surrendered soul will always justify God in any of His actions: "But why doth God punish a good man so severely for so small an offence? His sin was not small, for it was a gross disobedience to a positive command. And it cannot seem strange if God should bring his deserved death upon him in this manner, for the accomplishment of his own glorious designs, to vindicate his own justice from the imputation of partiality; to assure the truth of his predictions, and thereby provoke Jeroboam and his idolatrous followers to repentance; and to justify himself in all his dreadful judgments which he intended to inflict upon Jeroboam's house, and the whole kingdom of Israel." *John Wesley*

brother!" [31]So it was, after he had buried him, that he spoke to his sons, saying, "When I am dead, then bury me in the tomb where the man of God *is* buried; lay my bones beside his bones. [32]For the saying which he cried out by the word of the LORD against the altar in Bethel, and against all the shrines[a] on the high places which *are* in the cities of Samaria, will surely come to pass."

[33]After this event Jeroboam did not turn from his evil way, but again he made priests from every class of people for the high places; whoever wished, he consecrated him, and he became *one* of the priests of the high places. [34]And this thing was the sin of the house of Jeroboam, so as to exterminate and destroy *it* from the face of the earth.

Judgment on the House of Jeroboam

14 At that time Abijah the son of Jeroboam became sick. [2]And Jeroboam said to his wife, "Please arise, and disguise yourself, that they may not recognize you as the wife of Jeroboam, and go to Shiloh. Indeed, Ahijah the prophet *is* there, who told me that *I would be* king over this people. [3]Also take with you ten loaves, *some* cakes, and a jar of honey, and go to him; he will tell you what will become of the child." [4]And Jeroboam's wife did so; she arose and went to Shiloh, and came to the house of Ahijah. But Ahijah could not see, for his eyes were glazed by reason of his age.

[5]Now the LORD had said to Ahijah, "Here is the wife of Jeroboam, coming to ask you something about her son, for he *is* sick. Thus and thus you shall say to her; for it will be, when she comes in, that she will pretend *to be* another *woman*."

[6]And so it was, when Ahijah heard the sound of her footsteps as she came through the door, he said, "Come in, wife of Jeroboam. Why do you pretend *to be* another *person*? For I *have been* sent to you *with* bad *news*. [7]Go, tell Jeroboam, 'Thus says the LORD God of Israel: "Because I exalted you from among the people, and made you ruler over My people Israel, [8]and tore the kingdom away from the house of David, and gave it to you; and *yet* you have not been as My servant David, who kept My commandments and who followed Me with all his heart, to do only *what was* right in My eyes; [9]but you have done more evil than all who were before you, for you have gone and made for yourself other gods and molded images to provoke Me to anger, and have cast Me behind your back— [10]therefore behold! I will bring disaster on the house of Jeroboam, and will cut off from Jeroboam every male in Israel, bond and free; I will take away the remnant of the house of Jeroboam, as one takes away refuse until it is all gone. [11]The dogs shall eat whoever belongs to Jeroboam and dies in the city, and the birds of the air shall eat whoever dies in the field; for the LORD has spoken!" ' [12]Arise therefore, go to your own house. When your feet enter the city, the child shall die. [13]And all Israel shall mourn for him and bury him, for he is the only one of Jeroboam who shall come to the grave, because in him there is found something good toward

13:32 [a]Literally *houses*

14:13 "In what an unhappy condition is that person who cannot derive comfort from the salvation of his own child! Yet there are many men and women in such a state. They care nothing for the souls of their own offspring. It would bring no joy to them if they saw all their children walking in the truth nor does it cause them any concern to see them otherwise. To see them sharp in business, or fair in countenance, is their main ambition; but to have them beloved of the Lord is no matter of desire. Poor souls, their own carnality overflows and saturates their family! To some it would even cause anger and wrath to see their children turning to the Lord; they so despise true religion that, if their sons and daughters were converted, they would rather hate them than love them the more. Such is the alienation which sin works in the human mind, that it will in some instances curdle human affection into enmity, at the sight of the grace of God." *Charles Spurgeon*

the LORD God of Israel in the house of Jeroboam.

14“Moreover the LORD will raise up for Himself a king over Israel who shall cut off the house of Jeroboam; this is the day. What? Even now! 15For the LORD will strike Israel, as a reed is shaken in the water. He will uproot Israel from this good land which He gave to their fathers, and will scatter them beyond the River,[a] because they have made their wooden images,[b] provoking the LORD to anger. 16And He will give Israel up because of the sins of Jeroboam, who sinned and who made Israel sin.”

17Then Jeroboam’s wife arose and departed, and came to Tirzah. When she came to the threshold of the house, the child died. 18And they buried him; and all Israel mourned for him, according to the word of the LORD which He spoke through His servant Ahijah the prophet.

. . . . . .

Is evolution a proven fact?
See Job 35:16 comment.

. . . . . .

Death of Jeroboam

19Now the rest of the acts of Jeroboam, how he made war and how he reigned, indeed they *are* written in the book of the chronicles of the kings of Israel. 20The period that Jeroboam reigned *was* twenty-two years. So he rested with his fathers. Then Nadab his son reigned in his place.

Rehoboam Reigns in Judah

21And Rehoboam the son of Solomon reigned in Judah. Rehoboam *was* forty-one years old when he became king. He reigned seventeen years in Jerusalem, the city which the LORD had chosen out of all the tribes of Israel, to put His name there. His mother’s name *was* Naamah, an Ammonitess. 22Now Judah did evil in the sight of the LORD, and they provoked Him to jealousy with their sins which they committed, more than all that their fathers had done. 23For they also built for themselves high places, *sacred* pillars, and wooden images on every high hill and under every green tree. 24And there were also perverted persons[a] in the land. They did according to all the abominations of the nations which the LORD had cast out before the children of Israel.

25It happened in the fifth year of King Rehoboam *that* Shishak king of Egypt came up against Jerusalem. 26And he took away the treasures of the house of the LORD and the treasures of the king’s house; he took away everything. He also took away all the gold shields which Solomon had made. 27Then King Rehoboam made bronze shields in their place, and committed *them* to the hands of the captains of the guard, who guarded the doorway of the king’s house. 28And whenever the king entered the house of the LORD, the guards carried them, then brought them back into the guardroom.

29Now the rest of the acts of Rehoboam, and all that he did, *are* they not written in the book of the chronicles of the kings of Judah? 30And there was war between Rehoboam and Jeroboam all *their* days. 31So Rehoboam rested with his fathers, and was buried with his fathers in the City of David. His mother’s name *was* Naamah, an Ammonitess. Then Abijam[a] his son reigned in his place.

Abijam Reigns in Judah

15 In the eighteenth year of King Jeroboam the son of Nebat, Abijam became king over Judah. 2He reigned three years in Jerusalem. His mother’s name *was*

14:15 [a]That is, the Euphrates [b]Hebrew *Asherim,* Canaanite deities 14:24 [a]Hebrew *qadesh,* that is, one practicing sodomy and prostitution in religious rituals 14:31 [a]Spelled *Abijah* in 2 Chronicles 12:16ff

14:24 They were in direct violation of Deut. 23:17 by imitating the sinful nations that surrounded them. We must take care not to imitate this sinful world and be drawn into things that are offensive to God.

Maachah the granddaughter of Abishalom. 3And he walked in all the sins of his father, which he had done before him; his heart was not loyal to the LORD his God, as was the heart of his father David. 4Nevertheless for David's sake the LORD his God gave him a lamp in Jerusalem, by setting up his son after him and by establishing Jerusalem; 5because David did *what was* right in the eyes of the LORD, and had not turned aside from anything that He commanded him all the days of his life, except in the matter of Uriah the Hittite. 6And there was war between Rehoboam[a] and Jeroboam all the days of his life. 7Now the rest of the acts of Abijam, and all that he did, *are* they not written in the book of the chronicles of the kings of Judah? And there was war between Abijam and Jeroboam.

8So Abijam rested with his fathers, and they buried him in the City of David. Then Asa his son reigned in his place.

Asa Reigns in Judah

9In the twentieth year of Jeroboam king of Israel, Asa became king over Judah. 10And he reigned forty-one years in Jerusalem. His grandmother's name *was* Maachah the granddaughter of Abishalom. 11Asa did *what was* right in the eyes of the LORD, as *did* his father David. 12And he banished the perverted persons[a] from the land, and removed all the idols that his fathers had made. 13Also he removed Maachah his grandmother from *being* queen mother, because she had made an obscene image of Asherah.[a] And Asa cut down her obscene image and burned *it* by the Brook Kidron. 14But the high places were not removed. Nevertheless Asa's heart was loyal to the LORD all his days. 15He also brought into the house of the LORD the things which his father had dedicated, and the things which he himself had dedicated: silver and gold and utensils.

16Now there was war between Asa and Baasha king of Israel all their days. 17And Baasha king of Israel came up against Judah, and built Ramah, that he might let none go out or come in to Asa king of Judah. 18Then Asa took all the silver and gold *that was* left in the treasuries of the house of the LORD and the treasuries of the king's house, and delivered them into the hand of his servants. And King Asa sent them to Ben-Hadad the son of Tabrimmon, the son of Hezion, king of Syria, who dwelt in Damascus, saying, 19"*Let there be* a treaty between you and me, as there was between my father and your father. See, I have sent you a present of silver and gold. Come and break your treaty with Baasha king of Israel, so that he will withdraw from me."

20So Ben-Hadad heeded King Asa, and sent the captains of his armies against the cities of Israel. He attacked Ijon, Dan, Abel Beth Maachah, and all Chinneroth, with all the land of Naphtali. 21Now it happened, when Baasha heard *it,* that he stopped building Ramah, and remained in Tirzah.

22Then King Asa made a proclamation throughout all Judah; none *was* exempted. And they took away the stones and timber of Ramah, which Baasha had used for building; and with them King Asa built Geba of Benjamin, and Mizpah.

23The rest of all the acts of Asa, all his might, all that he did, and the cities which he built, *are* they not written in the book of the chronicles of the kings of Judah? But in the time of his old age he was diseased in his feet. 24So Asa rested with his fathers, and was buried with his fathers in the City of David his father. Then Jehoshaphat his son reigned in his place.

Nadab Reigns in Israel

25Now Nadab the son of Jeroboam became king over Israel in the second year of Asa king of Judah, and he reigned over Israel two years. 26And he did evil in the

15:6 [a]Following Masoretic Text, Septuagint, Targum, and Vulgate; some Hebrew manuscripts and Syriac read *Abijam.* **15:12** [a]Hebrew *qedeshim,* that is, those practicing sodomy and prostitution in religious rituals **15:13** [a]A Canaanite goddess

sight of the LORD, and walked in the way of his father, and in his sin by which he had made Israel sin.

[27]Then Baasha the son of Ahijah, of the house of Issachar, conspired against him. And Baasha killed him at Gibbethon, which *belonged* to the Philistines, while Nadab and all Israel laid siege to Gibbethon. [28]Baasha killed him in the third year of Asa king of Judah, and reigned in his place. [29]And it was so, when he became king, *that* he killed all the house of Jeroboam. He did not leave to Jeroboam anyone that breathed, until he had destroyed him, according to the word of the LORD which He had spoken by His servant Ahijah the Shilonite, [30]because of the sins of Jeroboam, which he had sinned and by which he had made Israel sin, because of his provocation with which he had provoked the LORD God of Israel to anger.

[31]Now the rest of the acts of Nadab, and all that he did, *are* they not written in the book of the chronicles of the kings of Israel? [32]And there was war between Asa and Baasha king of Israel all their days.

Baasha Reigns in Israel

[33]In the third year of Asa king of Judah, Baasha the son of Ahijah became king over all Israel in Tirzah, and *reigned* twenty-four years. [34]He did evil in the sight of the LORD, and walked in the way of Jeroboam, and in his sin by which he had made Israel sin.

16 Then the word of the LORD came to Jehu the son of Hanani, against Baasha, saying: [2]"Inasmuch as I lifted you out of the dust and made you ruler over My people Israel, and you have walked in the way of Jeroboam, and have made My people Israel sin, to provoke Me to anger with their sins, [3]surely I will take away the posterity of Baasha and the posterity of his house, and I will make your house like the house of Jeroboam the son of Nebat. [4]The dogs shall eat whoever belongs to Baasha and dies in the city, and the birds of the air shall eat whoever dies in the fields."

[5]Now the rest of the acts of Baasha, what he did, and his might, *are* they not written in the book of the chronicles of the kings of Israel? [6]So Baasha rested with his fathers and was buried in Tirzah. Then Elah his son reigned in his place.

[7]And also the word of the LORD came by the prophet Jehu the son of Hanani against Baasha and his house, because of all the evil that he did in the sight of the LORD in provoking Him to anger with the work of his hands, in being like the house of Jeroboam, and because he killed them.

Elah Reigns in Israel

[8]In the twenty-sixth year of Asa king of Judah, Elah the son of Baasha became king over Israel, *and reigned* two years in Tirzah. [9]Now his servant Zimri, commander of half *his* chariots, conspired against him as he was in Tirzah drinking himself drunk in the house of Arza, steward of *his* house in Tirzah. [10]And Zimri went in and struck him and killed him in the twenty-seventh year of Asa king of Judah, and reigned in his place.

[11]Then it came to pass, when he began to reign, as soon as he was seated on his throne, *that* he killed all the household of Baasha; he did not leave him one male, neither of his relatives nor of his friends. [12]Thus Zimri destroyed all the household of Baasha, according to the word of the

16:1,2 When God chastened individuals, He often began by reminding them of all the good He had done for them and the great kindness He had shown. Is it too much to ask that, out of gratitude for His incredible mercies, they obey Him? To whom much is given, much is required.

"That we, when we desire to receive any mercy from him, should humbly supplicate the Divine Being for the bestowment of that mercy, is but a suitable acknowledgment of our dependence on the power and mercy of God for that which we need, and but a suitable honor paid to the great Author and Fountain of all good." *Jonathan Edwards*

LORD, which He spoke against Baasha by
Jehu the prophet, 13for all the sins of
Baasha and the sins of Elah his son, by
which they had sinned and by which
they had made Israel sin, in provoking
the LORD God of Israel to anger with their
idols.
14Now the rest of the acts of Elah, and
all that he did, *are* they not written in the
book of the chronicles of the kings of
Israel?

Zimri Reigns in Israel

15In the twenty-seventh year of Asa
king of Judah, Zimri had reigned in Tirzah
seven days. And the people *were* encamped
against Gibbethon, which *belonged* to the
Philistines. 16Now the people *who were*
encamped heard it said, "Zimri has conspired and also has killed the king." So all
Israel made Omri, the commander of the
army, king over Israel that day in the
camp. 17Then Omri and all Israel with
him went up from Gibbethon, and they
besieged Tirzah. 18And it happened,
when Zimri saw that the city was taken,
that he went into the citadel of the king's
house and burned the king's house down
upon himself with fire, and died, 19be-
cause of the sins which he had committed in doing evil in the sight of the LORD,
in walking in the way of Jeroboam, and
in his sin which he had committed to
make Israel sin.
20Now the rest of the acts of Zimri,
and the treason he committed, *are* they
not written in the book of the chronicles
of the kings of Israel?

Omri Reigns in Israel

21Then the people of Israel were divided into two parts: half of the people
followed Tibni the son of Ginath, to make
him king, and half followed Omri. 22But
the people who followed Omri prevailed
over the people who followed Tibni the
son of Ginath. So Tibni died and Omri
reigned. 23In the thirty-first year of Asa
king of Judah, Omri became king over Israel, *and reigned* twelve years. Six years he
reigned in Tirzah. 24And he bought the
hill of Samaria from Shemer for two talents of silver; then he built on the hill,
and called the name of the city which he
built, Samaria, after the name of Shemer,
owner of the hill. 25Omri did evil in the
eyes of the LORD, and did worse than all
who *were* before him. 26For he walked in
all the ways of Jeroboam the son of
Nebat, and in his sin by which he had
made Israel sin, provoking the LORD God
of Israel to anger with their idols.

The old cross slew men; the new cross entertains them. The old cross condemned; the new cross amuses. The old cross destroyed confidence in the flesh; the new cross encourages it. We must get back to the preaching of the cross as the central message of Christianity.

A. W. TOZER

27Now the rest of the acts of Omri
which he did, and the might that he
showed, *are* they not written in the book
of the chronicles of the kings of Israel?
28So Omri rested with his fathers and
was buried in Samaria. Then Ahab his
son reigned in his place.

Ahab Reigns in Israel

29In the thirty-eighth year of Asa king
of Judah, Ahab the son of Omri became
king over Israel; and Ahab the son of Omri
reigned over Israel in Samaria twenty-two
years. 30Now Ahab the son of Omri did
evil in the sight of the LORD, more than all
who *were* before him. 31And it came to
pass, as though it had been a trivial thing
for him to walk in the sins of Jeroboam
the son of Nebat, that he took as wife
Jezebel the daughter of Ethbaal, king of
the Sidonians; and he went and served
Baal and worshiped him. 32Then he set
up an altar for Baal in the temple of Baal,
which he had built in Samaria. 33And
Ahab made a wooden image.[a] Ahab did

16:33 [a]Hebrew *Asherah*, a Canaanite goddess

more to provoke the LORD God of Israel to anger than all the kings of Israel who were before him. 34In his days Hiel of Bethel built Jericho. He laid its foundation with Abiram his firstborn, and with his youngest *son* Segub he set up its gates, according to the word of the LORD, which He had spoken through Joshua the son of Nun.[a]

Elijah Proclaims a Drought

17 And Elijah the Tishbite, of the inhabitants of Gilead, said to Ahab, "*As* the LORD God of Israel lives, before whom I stand, there shall not be dew nor rain these years, except at my word."

2Then the word of the LORD came to him, saying, 3"Get away from here and turn eastward, and hide by the Brook Cherith, which flows into the Jordan. 4And it will be *that* you shall drink from the brook, and I have commanded the ravens to feed you there."

5So he went and did according to the word of the LORD, for he went and stayed by the Brook Cherith, which flows into the Jordan. 6The ravens brought him bread and meat in the morning, and bread and meat in the evening; and he drank from the brook. 7And it happened after a while that the brook dried up, because there had been no rain in the land.

Elijah and the Widow

8Then the word of the LORD came to him, saying, 9"Arise, go to Zarephath, which *belongs* to Sidon, and dwell there. See, I have commanded a widow there to provide for you." 10So he arose and went to Zarephath. And when he came to the gate of the city, indeed a widow *was* there gathering sticks. And he called to her and said, "Please bring me a little water in a cup, that I may drink." 11And as she was going to get *it*, he called to her and said, "Please bring me a morsel of bread in your hand."

12So she said, "As the LORD your God lives, I do not have bread, only a handful of flour in a bin, and a little oil in a jar; and see, I *am* gathering a couple of sticks that I may go in and prepare it for myself and my son, that we may eat it, and die."

13And Elijah said to her, "Do not fear; go *and* do as you have said, but make me a small cake from it first, and bring *it* to me; and afterward make *some* for yourself and your son. 14For thus says the LORD God of Israel: 'The bin of flour shall not be used up, nor shall the jar of oil run dry, until the day the LORD sends rain on the earth.' "

15So she went away and did according to the word of Elijah; and she and he and her household ate for *many* days. 16The bin of flour was not used up, nor did the jar of oil run dry, according to the word of the LORD which He spoke by Elijah.

Elijah Revives the Widow's Son

17Now it happened after these things *that* the son of the woman who owned the house became sick. And his sickness was so serious that there was no breath left in him. 18So she said to Elijah, "What have I to do with you, O man of God? Have you come to me to bring my sin to remembrance, and to kill my son?"

19And he said to her, "Give me your son." So he took him out of her arms and carried him to the upper room where he was staying, and laid him on his own bed. 20Then he cried out to the LORD and said, "O LORD my God, have You also brought tragedy on the widow with whom I lodge, by killing her son?" 21And he stretched himself out on the child three times, and cried out to the LORD and said,

16:34 [a]Compare Joshua 6:26

17:16 "So long as we have a full barrel of our own merits, God will have nothing to do with us. So long as the cruse of oil is full to overflowing, we shall never taste the mercy of God. For God will not fill us until we are emptied of self." *Charles Spurgeon*

"O LORD my God, I pray, let this child's soul come back to him." [22]Then the LORD heard the voice of Elijah; and the soul of the child came back to him, and he revived.

[23]And Elijah took the child and brought him down from the upper room into the house, and gave him to his mother. And Elijah said, "See, your son lives!"

[24]Then the woman said to Elijah, "Now by this I know that you *are* a man of God, *and* that the word of the LORD in your mouth *is* the truth."

Elijah's Message to Ahab

18 And it came to pass *after* many days that the word of the LORD came to Elijah, in the third year, saying, "Go, present yourself to Ahab, and I will send rain on the earth."

[2]So Elijah went to present himself to Ahab; and *there was* a severe famine in Samaria. [3]And Ahab had called Obadiah, who *was* in charge of *his* house. (Now Obadiah feared the LORD greatly. [4]For so it was, while Jezebel massacred the prophets of the LORD, that Obadiah had taken one hundred prophets and hidden them, fifty to a cave, and had fed them with bread and water.) [5]And Ahab had said to Obadiah, "Go into the land to all the springs of water and to all the brooks; perhaps we may find grass to keep the horses and mules alive, so that we will not have to kill any livestock." [6]So they divided the land between them to explore it; Ahab went one way by himself, and Obadiah went another way by himself.

[7]Now as Obadiah was on his way, suddenly Elijah met him; and he recognized him, and fell on his face, and said, "*Is* that you, my lord Elijah?"

[8]And he answered him, "*It is* I. Go, tell your master, 'Elijah *is here.*' "

[9]So he said, "How have I sinned, that you are delivering your servant into the hand of Ahab, to kill me? [10]*As* the LORD your God lives, there is no nation or kingdom where my master has not sent someone to hunt for you; and when they said, '*He is* not *here,*' he took an oath from the kingdom or nation that they could not find you. [11]And now you say, 'Go, tell your master, "Elijah *is here*" '! [12]And it shall come to pass, *as soon as* I am gone from you, that the Spirit of the LORD will carry you to a place I do not know; so when I go and tell Ahab, and he cannot find you, he will kill me. But I your servant have feared the LORD from my youth. [13]Was it not reported to my lord what I did when Jezebel killed the prophets of the LORD, how I hid one hundred men of the LORD's prophets, fifty to a cave, and fed them with bread and water? [14]And now you say, 'Go, tell your master, "Elijah *is here.*" ' He will kill me!"

[15]Then Elijah said, "*As* the LORD of hosts lives, before whom I stand, I will surely present myself to him today."

[16]So Obadiah went to meet Ahab, and told him; and Ahab went to meet Elijah.

[17]Then it happened, when Ahab saw Elijah, that Ahab said to him, "*Is that* you, O troubler of Israel?"

[18]And he answered, "I have not troubled Israel, but you and your father's house *have,* in that you have forsaken the commandments of the LORD and have followed the Baals. [19]Now therefore, send *and* gather all Israel to me on Mount Carmel, the four hundred and fifty prophets of Baal, and the four hundred prophets of Asherah,[a] who eat at Jezebel's table."

Elijah's Mount Carmel Victory

[20]So Ahab sent for all the children of

18:19 [a]A Canaanite goddess

17:21,22 Some don't believe that we have a soul that continues on after death. This verse clearly shows that physical death occurs when the soul separates from the body (in the same way that spiritual death is separation from God). See also Gen. 2:17 comment.

18:17 Those who stand for righteousness will be considered "trouble" in the world's eyes. See Acts 24:5 comment.

Israel, and gathered the prophets together on Mount Carmel. 21And Elijah came to all the people, and said, "How long will you falter between two opinions? If the LORD *is* God, follow Him; but if Baal, follow him." But the people answered him not a word. 22Then Elijah said to the people, "I alone am left a prophet of the LORD; but Baal's prophets *are* four hundred and fifty men. 23Therefore let them give us two bulls; and let them choose one bull for themselves, cut it in pieces, and lay *it* on the wood, but put no fire *under it;* and I will prepare the other bull, and lay *it* on the wood, but put no fire *under it.* 24Then you call on the name of your gods, and I will call on the name of the LORD; and the God who answers by fire, He is God."

> Christianity, if false, is of no importance, and if true, of infinite importance. The only thing it cannot be is moderately important.
>
> **C. S. LEWIS**

So all the people answered and said, "It is well spoken."

25Now Elijah said to the prophets of Baal, "Choose one bull for yourselves and prepare *it* first, for you *are* many; and call on the name of your god, but put no fire *under it.*"

26So they took the bull which was given them, and they prepared *it,* and called on the name of Baal from morning even till noon, saying, "O Baal, hear us!" But *there was* no voice; no one answered. Then they leaped about the altar which they had made.

27And so it was, at noon, that Elijah mocked them and said, "Cry aloud, for he *is* a god; either he is meditating, or he is busy, or he is on a journey, *or* perhaps he is sleeping and must be awakened." 28So they cried aloud, and cut themselves, as was their custom, with knives and lances, until the blood gushed out on them. 29And when midday was past, they prophesied until the *time* of the offering of the *evening* sacrifice. But *there was* no voice; no one answered, no one paid attention.

30Then Elijah said to all the people, "Come near to me." So all the people came near to him. And he repaired the altar of the LORD *that was* broken down. 31And Elijah took twelve stones, according to the number of the tribes of the sons of Jacob, to whom the word of the LORD had come, saying, "Israel shall be your name."[a] 32Then with the stones he built an altar in the name of the LORD; and he made a trench around the altar large enough to hold two seahs of seed. 33And he put the wood in order, cut the bull in pieces, and laid *it* on the wood, and said, "Fill four waterpots with water, and pour *it* on the burnt sacrifice and on the wood." 34Then he said, "Do *it* a second time," and they did *it* a second time;

18:31 [a]Genesis 32:28

18:21 Indecision is a deep valley that will take multitudes to hell. Think of the millions who have a form of knowledge about God, but they have never seen the real issues that are at stake. If our Creator is the God of the Bible, then hell is a reality for those who transgress His perfect Law. But through the gospel, God sets before humanity the way of salvation. All we need do to find everlasting life is repent and trust in Jesus Christ, and yet millions have never resolved to do that. They "believe" but do not obey. If the gospel is true, then we should run at it with all of our strength and embrace it with absolute resolution. If it is not true, then we should run at this world with all of its sinful pleasures, eat, drink, and be merry, for tomorrow we die.

Charles Spurgeon said, "If God be God, *follow him;* if Baal, *follow* him. You are not decided in practice. Men's opinions are not such things as we imagine. It is generally said now-a-days, that all opinions are right, and if a man shall honestly hold his convictions, he is, without doubt, right. Not so; truth is not changed by our opinions; a thing is either true or false of itself, and it is neither made true nor false by our views of it." See Josh. 24:15 comment.

and he said, "Do *it* a third time," and they
did *it* a third time. 35So the water ran all
around the altar; and he also filled the
trench with water.
36And it came to pass, at *the time of* the
offering of the *evening* sacrifice, that Elijah the prophet came near and said,
"LORD God of Abraham, Isaac, and Israel,
let it be known this day that You *are* God
in Israel and I *am* Your servant, and *that* I
have done all these things at Your word.
37Hear me, O LORD, hear me, that this
people may know that You *are* the LORD
God, and *that* You have turned their
hearts back *to You* again."
38Then the fire of the LORD fell and
consumed the burnt sacrifice, and the
wood and the stones and the dust, and it
licked up the water that *was* in the
trench. 39Now when all the people saw *it,*
they fell on their faces; and they said, "The
LORD, He *is* God! The LORD, He *is* God!"
40And Elijah said to them, "Seize the
prophets of Baal! Do not let one of them
escape!" So they seized them; and Elijah
brought them down to the Brook Kishon
and executed them there.

The Drought Ends

41Then Elijah said to Ahab, "Go up,
eat and drink; for *there is* the sound of
abundance of rain." 42So Ahab went up to
eat and drink. And Elijah went up to the
top of Carmel; then he bowed down on
the ground, and put his face between his
knees, 43and said to his servant, "Go up
now, look toward the sea."

So he went up and looked, and said,
"*There is* nothing." And seven times he
said, "Go again."
44Then it came to pass the seventh
time, that he said, "There is a cloud, as
small as a man's hand, rising out of the
sea!" So he said, "Go up, say to Ahab,
'Prepare *your chariot,* and go down before
the rain stops you.' "
45Now it happened in the meantime
that the sky became black with clouds
and wind, and there was a heavy rain. So
Ahab rode away and went to Jezreel.
46Then the hand of the LORD came upon
Elijah; and he girded up his loins and ran
ahead of Ahab to the entrance of Jezreel.

Elijah Escapes from Jezebel

19 And Ahab told Jezebel all that Elijah had done, also how he had executed all the prophets with the sword.
2Then Jezebel sent a messenger to Elijah,
saying, "So let the gods do *to me,* and
more also, if I do not make your life as
the life of one of them by tomorrow
about this time." 3And when he saw *that,*
he arose and ran for his life, and went to
Beersheba, which *belongs* to Judah, and
left his servant there.
4But he himself went a day's journey
into the wilderness, and came and sat
down under a broom tree. And he prayed
that he might die, and said, "It is enough!
Now, LORD, take my life, for I *am* no better than my fathers!"
5Then as he lay and slept under a
broom tree, suddenly an angel[a] touched
him, and said to him, "Arise *and* eat."
6Then he looked, and there by his head
was a cake baked on coals, and a jar of
water. So he ate and drank, and lay down
again. 7And the angel[a] of the LORD came
back the second time, and touched him,
and said, "Arise *and* eat, because the journey *is* too great for you." 8So he arose,
and ate and drank; and he went in the
strength of that food forty days and forty
nights as far as Horeb, the mountain of
God.

19:5 [a]Or *Angel* 19:7 [a]Or *Angel*

19:1–3 Joseph had Potiphar's wife to plague him. John the Baptist had Herod's conniving mistress. Paul had a persistent demon-possessed woman follow him for "many days." So, beware of your Jezebel. She may come to you with fluttering eyes and a promise of pleasure, but her agenda is your downfall. Her soft, inviting bed leads to hell. If you can't resist her, run as Joseph ran. *Flee* fornication. King David could have saved himself and others much pain if he had heeded such advice.

9And there he went into a cave, and
spent the night in that place; and behold,
the word of the LORD *came* to him, and
He said to him, "What are you doing
here, Elijah?"
10So he said, "I have been very zealous
for the LORD God of hosts; for the children of Israel have forsaken Your covenant, torn down Your altars, and killed
Your prophets with the sword. I alone am
left; and they seek to take my life."

God's Revelation to Elijah

11Then He said, "Go out, and stand on
the mountain before the LORD." And behold, the LORD passed by, and a great and
strong wind tore into the mountains and
broke the rocks in pieces before the LORD,
but the LORD *was* not in the wind; and after the wind an earthquake, *but* the LORD
was not in the earthquake; 12and after the
earthquake a fire, *but* the LORD *was* not in
the fire; and after the fire a still small voice.
13So it was, when Elijah heard *it,* that
he wrapped his face in his mantle and
went out and stood in the entrance of the
cave. Suddenly a voice *came* to him, and
said, "What are you doing here, Elijah?"
14And he said, "I have been very zealous for the LORD God of hosts; because
the children of Israel have forsaken Your
covenant, torn down Your altars, and
killed Your prophets with the sword. I
alone am left; and they seek to take my
life."
15Then the LORD said to him: "Go, return on your way to the Wilderness of
Damascus; and when you arrive, anoint
Hazael *as* king over Syria. 16Also you
shall anoint Jehu the son of Nimshi *as*
king over Israel. And Elisha the son of
Shaphat of Abel Meholah you shall
anoint *as* prophet in your place. 17It shall
be *that* whoever escapes the sword of
Hazael, Jehu will kill; and whoever escapes the sword of Jehu, Elisha will kill.
18Yet I have reserved seven thousand in
Israel, all whose knees have not bowed to
Baal, and every mouth that has not kissed
him."

Elisha Follows Elijah

19So he departed from there, and
found Elisha the son of Shaphat, who *was*
plowing *with* twelve yoke *of oxen* before
him, and he was with the twelfth. Then
Elijah passed by him and threw his mantle on him. 20And he left the oxen and ran
after Elijah, and said, "Please let me kiss
my father and my mother, and *then* I will
follow you."
And he said to him, "Go back again,
for what have I done to you?"
21So *Elisha* turned back from him, and
took a yoke of oxen and slaughtered them
and boiled their flesh, using the oxen's
equipment, and gave it to the people, and
they ate. Then he arose and followed Elijah, and became his servant.

Ahab Defeats the Syrians

20 Now Ben-Hadad the king of Syria
gathered all his forces together;
thirty-two kings *were* with him, with
horses and chariots. And he went up and
besieged Samaria, and made war against
it. 2Then he sent messengers into the city
to Ahab king of Israel, and said to him,
"Thus says Ben-Hadad: 3'Your silver and
your gold *are* mine; your loveliest wives
and children are mine.' "
4And the king of Israel answered and
said, "My lord, O king, just as you say, I
and all that I have *are* yours."
5Then the messengers came back and
said, "Thus speaks Ben-Hadad, saying,
'Indeed I have sent to you, saying, "You
shall deliver to me your silver and your
gold, your wives and your children"; 6but
I will send my servants to you tomorrow
about this time, and they shall search
your house and the houses of your servants. And it shall be, *that* whatever is
pleasant in your eyes, they will put *it* in

19:10 See Acts 18:10 comment.

their hands and take *it.*' "

[7]So the king of Israel called all the elders of the land, and said, "Notice, please, and see how this *man* seeks trouble, for he sent to me for my wives, my children, my silver, and my gold; and I did not deny him."

[8]And all the elders and all the people said to him, "Do not listen or consent."

[9]Therefore he said to the messengers of Ben-Hadad, "Tell my lord the king, 'All that you sent for to your servant the first time I will do, but this thing I cannot do.' "

And the messengers departed and brought back word to him.

[10]Then Ben-Hadad sent to him and said, "The gods do so to me, and more also, if enough dust is left of Samaria for a handful for each of the people who follow me."

[11]So the king of Israel answered and said, "Tell *him,* 'Let not the one who puts on *his armor* boast like the one who takes *it off.*' "

[12]And it happened when *Ben-Hadad* heard this message, as he and the kings *were* drinking at the command post, that he said to his servants, "Get ready." And they got ready to attack the city.

[13]Suddenly a prophet approached Ahab king of Israel, saying, "Thus says the LORD: 'Have you seen all this great multitude? Behold, I will deliver it into your hand today, and you shall know that I *am* the LORD.' "

[14]So Ahab said, "By whom?"

And he said, "Thus says the LORD: 'By the young leaders of the provinces.' "

Then he said, "Who will set the battle in order?"

And he answered, "You."

[15]Then he mustered the young leaders of the provinces, and there were two hundred and thirty-two; and after them he mustered all the people, all the children of Israel—seven thousand.

[16]So they went out at noon. Meanwhile Ben-Hadad and the thirty-two kings helping him were getting drunk at the command post. [17]The young leaders of the provinces went out first. And Ben-Hadad sent out *a patrol,* and they told him, saying, "Men are coming out of Samaria!" [18]So he said, "If they have come out for peace, take them alive; and if they have come out for war, take them alive."

[19]Then these young leaders of the provinces went out of the city with the army which followed them. [20]And each one killed his man; so the Syrians fled, and Israel pursued them; and Ben-Hadad the king of Syria escaped on a horse with the cavalry. [21]Then the king of Israel went out and attacked the horses and chariots, and killed the Syrians with a great slaughter.

[22]And the prophet came to the king of Israel and said to him, "Go, strengthen yourself; take note, and see what you should do, for in the spring of the year the king of Syria will come up against you."

The Syrians Again Defeated

[23]Then the servants of the king of Syria said to him, "Their gods *are* gods of the hills. Therefore they were stronger than we; but if we fight against them in the plain, surely we will be stronger than they. [24]So do this thing: Dismiss the kings, each from his position, and put captains in their places; [25]and you shall muster an army like the army that you have lost, horse for horse and chariot for chariot. Then we will fight against them in the plain; surely we will be stronger than they."

And he listened to their voice and did so.

[26]So it was, in the spring of the year, that Ben-Hadad mustered the Syrians and went up to Aphek to fight against Israel. [27]And the children of Israel were mustered and given provisions, and they went against them. Now the children of Israel encamped before them like two little flocks of goats, while the Syrians filled the countryside.

[28]Then a man of God came and spoke to the king of Israel, and said, "Thus says the LORD: 'Because the Syrians have said,

"The LORD *is* God of the hills, but He *is*
not God of the valleys," therefore I will
deliver all this great multitude into your
hand, and you shall know that I *am* the
LORD.' " [29]And they encamped opposite
each other for seven days. So it was that
on the seventh day the battle was joined;
and the children of Israel killed one hundred thousand foot soldiers *of* the Syrians
in one day. [30]But the rest fled to Aphek,
into the city; then a wall fell on twenty-
seven thousand of the men *who were* left.

And Ben-Hadad fled and went into the
city, into an inner chamber.

Ahab's Treaty with Ben-Hadad

[31]Then his servants said to him, "Look
now, we have heard that the kings of the
house of Israel *are* merciful kings. Please,
let us put sackcloth around our waists
and ropes around our heads, and go out
to the king of Israel; perhaps he will spare
your life." [32]So they wore sackcloth
around their waists and *put* ropes around
their heads, and came to the king of Israel and said, "Your servant Ben-Hadad
says, 'Please let me live.' "

And he said, "*Is* he still alive? He *is* my
brother."

[33]Now the men were watching closely
to see whether *any sign of mercy would
come* from him; and they quickly grasped
at this word and said, "Your brother Ben-
Hadad."

So he said, "Go, bring him." Then
Ben-Hadad came out to him; and he had
him come up into the chariot.

[34]So *Ben-Hadad* said to him, "The
cities which my father took from your father I will restore; and you may set up
marketplaces for yourself in Damascus,
as my father did in Samaria."

Then *Ahab said*, "I will send you away
with this treaty." So he made a treaty with
him and sent him away.

Ahab Condemned

[35]Now a certain man of the sons of the
prophets said to his neighbor by the
word of the LORD, "Strike me, please." And
the man refused to strike him. [36]Then he
said to him, "Because you have not obeyed
the voice of the LORD, surely, as soon as
you depart from me, a lion shall kill you."
And as soon as he left him, a lion found
him and killed him.

[37]And he found another man, and
said, "Strike me, please." So the man struck
him, inflicting a wound. [38]Then the
prophet departed and waited for the king
by the road, and disguised himself with a
bandage over his eyes. [39]Now as the king
passed by, he cried out to the king and
said, "Your servant went out into the midst
of the battle; and there, a man came over
and brought a man to me, and said,
'Guard this man; if by any means he is
missing, your life shall be for his life, or
else you shall pay a talent of silver.'
[40]While your servant was busy here and
there, he was gone."

Then the king of Israel said to him,
"So *shall* your judgment *be;* you yourself
have decided *it.*"

[41]And he hastened to take the bandage
away from his eyes; and the king of Israel
recognized him as one of the prophets.
[42]Then he said to him, "Thus says the
LORD: 'Because you have let slip out of
your hand a man whom I appointed to

20:31–33 "You have never failed in business; you have brought up your children well; you never swear; you were never a drunkard; midnight orgies never saw you mixed up in them; this is well, but I pray thee, put not on this as thy proper dress: the proper dress for a sinner to go to Christ in, is sackcloth and the rope. 'Well,' says one, 'I never will acknowledge that I deserve to be damned!' Then you never will be saved. 'Well,' says another, 'I never will take the language of a great sinner upon my lips.' Then you shall never be saved; for unless you are willing to confess that God may justly damn you, God will never save you; but if you feel in your heart to-night, that if he sends your soul to hell, his righteous law approves it well; if you wonder how it is that you are not in the pit, and marvel why such mercy should have been shown to you, come, brother, come; come as you are, for you wear the true court-dress of a sinner." *Charles Spurgeon*

utter destruction, therefore your life shall
go for his life, and your people for his
people.' "
43So the king of Israel went to his
house sullen and displeased, and came to
Samaria.

Naboth Is Murdered for His Vineyard

21 And it came to pass after these
things *that* Naboth the Jezreelite
had a vineyard which *was* in Jezreel, next
to the palace of Ahab king of Samaria. 2So
Ahab spoke to Naboth, saying, "Give me
your vineyard, that I may have it for a
vegetable garden, because it *is* near, next
to my house; and for it I will give you a
vineyard better than it. *Or,* if it seems good
to you, I will give you its worth in money."
3But Naboth said to Ahab, "The LORD
forbid that I should give the inheritance
of my fathers to you!"
4So Ahab went into his house sullen
and displeased because of the word
which Naboth the Jezreelite had spoken
to him; for he had said, "I will not give
you the inheritance of my fathers." And
he lay down on his bed, and turned away
his face, and would eat no food. 5But
Jezebel his wife came to him, and said to
him, "Why is your spirit so sullen that
you eat no food?"
6He said to her, "Because I spoke to
Naboth the Jezreelite, and said to him,
'Give me your vineyard for money; or
else, if it pleases you, I will give you *an-*
other vineyard for it.' And he answered, 'I
will not give you my vineyard.' "
7Then Jezebel his wife said to him,
"You now exercise authority over Israel!
Arise, eat food, and let your heart be
cheerful; I will give you the vineyard of
Naboth the Jezreelite."
8And she wrote letters in Ahab's name,
sealed *them* with his seal, and sent the letters to the elders and the nobles who *were*
dwelling in the city with Naboth. 9She
wrote in the letters, saying,

Proclaim a fast, and seat Naboth with
high honor among the people; 10and
seat two men, scoundrels, before him
to bear witness against him, saying,
"You have blasphemed God and the
king." *Then* take him out, and stone
him, that he may die.

11So the men of his city, the elders and
nobles who were inhabitants of his city,
did as Jezebel had sent to them, as it *was*
written in the letters which she had sent
to them. 12They proclaimed a fast, and
seated Naboth with high honor among
the people. 13And two men, scoundrels,
came in and sat before him; and the
scoundrels witnessed against him, against
Naboth, in the presence of the people,
saying, "Naboth has blasphemed God
and the king!" Then they took him outside the city and stoned him with stones,
so that he died. 14Then they sent to Jezebel,
saying, "Naboth has been stoned and is
dead."
15And it came to pass, when Jezebel
heard that Naboth had been stoned and
was dead, that Jezebel said to Ahab,
"Arise, take possession of the vineyard of
Naboth the Jezreelite, which he refused
to give you for money; for Naboth is not
alive, but dead." 16So it was, when Ahab
heard that Naboth was dead, that Ahab
got up and went down to take possession
of the vineyard of Naboth the Jezreelite.

The Lord Condemns Ahab

17Then the word of the LORD came to
Elijah the Tishbite, saying, 18"Arise, go
down to meet Ahab king of Israel, who
lives in Samaria. There *he is,* in the vineyard of Naboth, where he has gone down
to take possession of it. 19You shall speak
to him, saying, 'Thus says the LORD:
"Have you murdered and also taken pos-

21:4 Ahab was a spoiled brat. Such is human nature left to itself. However, God showed him mercy, as He does to all who seek Him in a spirit of humility, repentance, and trust in Christ (see v. 29).

session?" ' And you shall speak to him, saying, 'Thus says the LORD: "In the place where dogs licked the blood of Naboth, dogs shall lick your blood, even yours." ' "

20So Ahab said to Elijah, "Have you found me, O my enemy?"

And he answered, "I have found *you,* because you have sold yourself to do evil in the sight of the LORD: 21'Behold, I will bring calamity on you. I will take away your posterity, and will cut off from Ahab every male in Israel, both bond and free. 22I will make your house like the house of Jeroboam the son of Nebat, and like the house of Baasha the son of Ahijah, because of the provocation with which you have provoked *Me* to anger, and made Israel sin.' 23And concerning Jezebel the LORD also spoke, saying, 'The dogs shall eat Jezebel by the wall[a] of Jezreel.' 24The dogs shall eat whoever belongs to Ahab and dies in the city, and the birds of the air shall eat whoever dies in the field."

25But there was no one like Ahab who sold himself to do wickedness in the sight of the LORD, because Jezebel his wife stirred him up. 26And he behaved very abominably in following idols, according to all *that* the Amorites had done, whom the LORD had cast out before the children of Israel.

> That there is a devil is a thing doubted by none but such as are under the influence of the devil!
>
> **COTTON MATHER**

27So it was, when Ahab heard those words, that he tore his clothes and put sackcloth on his body, and fasted and lay in sackcloth, and went about mourning.

28And the word of the LORD came to Elijah the Tishbite, saying, 29"See how Ahab has humbled himself before Me? Because he has humbled himself before Me, I will not bring the calamity in his days. In the days of his son I will bring the calamity on his house."

Micaiah Warns Ahab

22 Now three years passed without war between Syria and Israel. 2Then it came to pass, in the third year, that Jehoshaphat the king of Judah went down to *visit* the king of Israel.

3And the king of Israel said to his servants, "Do you know that Ramoth in Gilead *is* ours, but we hesitate to take it out of the hand of the king of Syria?" 4So he said to Jehoshaphat, "Will you go with me to fight at Ramoth Gilead?"

Jehoshaphat said to the king of Israel, "I *am* as you *are,* my people as your people, my horses as your horses." 5Also Jehoshaphat said to the king of Israel, "Please inquire for the word of the LORD today."

6Then the king of Israel gathered the prophets together, about four hundred men, and said to them, "Shall I go against Ramoth Gilead to fight, or shall I refrain?"

So they said, "Go up, for the Lord will deliver *it* into the hand of the king."

7And Jehoshaphat said, "*Is there* not still a prophet of the LORD here, that we may inquire of Him?"[a]

8So the king of Israel said to Jehoshaphat, "*There is* still one man, Micaiah the son of Imlah, by whom we may inquire of the LORD; but I hate him, because he does not prophesy good concerning me, but evil."

And Jehoshaphat said, "Let not the king say such things!"

9Then the king of Israel called an officer and said, "Bring Micaiah the son of Imlah quickly!"

10The king of Israel and Jehoshaphat the king of Judah, having put on *their* robes, sat each on his throne, at a threshing floor at the entrance of the gate of Samaria; and all the prophets prophesied before them. 11Now Zedekiah the son of Chenaanah had made horns of iron for himself; and he said, "Thus says the LORD: 'With these you shall gore the Syrians until they are destroyed.' " 12And all the

21:23 [a]Following Masoretic Text and Septuagint; some Hebrew manuscripts, Syriac, Targum, and Vulgate read *plot of ground* (compare 2 Kings 9:36). **22:7** [a]Or *him*

prophets prophesied so, saying, "Go up
to Ramoth Gilead and prosper, for the
LORD will deliver *it* into the king's hand."
13Then the messenger who had gone
to call Micaiah spoke to him, saying, "Now
listen, the words of the prophets with one
accord encourage the king. Please, let your
word be like the word of one of them,
and speak encouragement."
14And Micaiah said, "*As* the LORD lives,
whatever the LORD says to me, that I will
speak."
15Then he came to the king; and the
king said to him, "Micaiah, shall we go to
war against Ramoth Gilead, or shall we
refrain?"
And he answered him, "Go and prosper, for the LORD will deliver *it* into the
hand of the king!"
16So the king said to him, "How many
times shall I make you swear that you tell
me nothing but the truth in the name of
the LORD?"
17Then he said, "I saw all Israel scattered on the mountains, as sheep that
have no shepherd. And the LORD said,
'These have no master. Let each return to
his house in peace.' "
18And the king of Israel said to Jehoshaphat, "Did I not tell you he would
not prophesy good concerning me, but
evil?"
19Then *Micaiah* said, "Therefore hear
the word of the LORD: I saw the LORD sitting on His throne, and all the host of
heaven standing by, on His right hand
and on His left. 20And the LORD said,
'Who will persuade Ahab to go up, that
he may fall at Ramoth Gilead?' So one
spoke in this manner, and another spoke
in that manner. 21Then a spirit came forward and stood before the LORD, and
said, 'I will persuade him.' 22The LORD
said to him, 'In what way?' So he said, 'I
will go out and be a lying spirit in the
mouth of all his prophets.' And the LORD
said, 'You shall persuade *him,* and also
prevail. Go out and do so.' 23Therefore
look! The LORD has put a lying spirit in
the mouth of all these prophets of yours,
and the LORD has declared disaster
against you."
24Now Zedekiah the son of Chenaanah went near and struck Micaiah on
the cheek, and said, "Which way did the
spirit from the LORD go from me to speak
to you?"
25And Micaiah said, "Indeed, you shall
see on that day when you go into an inner
chamber to hide!"
26So the king of Israel said, "Take Micaiah, and return him to Amon the governor of the city and to Joash the king's
son; 27and say, 'Thus says the king: "Put
this *fellow* in prison, and feed him with
bread of affliction and water of affliction,
until I come in peace." ' "
28But Micaiah said, "If you ever return
in peace, the LORD has not spoken by me."
And he said, "Take heed, all you people!"

Ahab Dies in Battle

29So the king of Israel and Jehoshaphat the king of Judah went up to
Ramoth Gilead. 30And the king of Israel
said to Jehoshaphat, "I will disguise myself and go into battle; but you put on
your robes." So the king of Israel disguised himself and went into battle.
31Now the king of Syria had com-

22:16 Before witnesses give testimony in our contemporary courts, they must take an oath: "Do you swear to tell the truth, the whole truth, and nothing but the truth, so help you God?" As Paul gave testimony to the Jews and Greeks, he "kept back nothing that was helpful," but proclaimed the whole truth: "repentance toward God and faith toward our Lord Jesus Christ" (Acts 20:20,21). As you witness, with God's help, be sure you tell the whole truth—that God commands all men everywhere to repent and trust in Jesus.

22:23 This is a favorite verse of skeptics and atheists. In the ultimate delusion of grandeur, they stand in moral judgment over Almighty God. They dare accuse Him of sin. But all of God's judgments are true and righteous altogether (see Psa. 19:9). He is without sin. They, however, are not, and would be wise to lay their judgmental hand over their sinful mouth, and repent and trust the Savior while they still have time. See 2 Chron. 18:19–21 comment.

"There is a dreadful hell, and everlasting pains; where sinners must with devils dwell, in darkness, fire, and chains."

Isaac Watts

manded the thirty-two captains of his
chariots, saying, "Fight with no one small
or great, but only with the king of Israel."
32So it was, when the captains of the
chariots saw Jehoshaphat, that they said,
"Surely it *is* the king of Israel!" Therefore
they turned aside to fight against him,
and Jehoshaphat cried out. 33And it happened, when the captains of the chariots
saw that it *was* not the king of Israel, that
they turned back from pursuing him.
34Now a *certain* man drew a bow at random, and struck the king of Israel between the joints of his armor. So he said
to the driver of his chariot, "Turn around
and take me out of the battle, for I am
wounded."

35The battle increased that day; and
the king was propped up in his chariot,
facing the Syrians, and died at evening.
The blood ran out from the wound onto
the floor of the chariot. 36Then, as the sun
was going down, a shout went throughout the army, saying, "Every man to his
city, and every man to his own country!"
37So the king died, and was brought to
Samaria. And they buried the king in
Samaria. 38Then *someone* washed the
chariot at a pool in Samaria, and the dogs
licked up his blood while the harlots
bathed,[a] according to the word of the
LORD which He had spoken.
39Now the rest of the acts of Ahab, and
all that he did, the ivory house which he
built and all the cities that he built, *are*
they not written in the book of the chronicles of the kings of Israel? 40So Ahab
rested with his fathers. Then Ahaziah his
son reigned in his place.

Jehoshaphat Reigns in Judah

41Jehoshaphat the son of Asa had become king over Judah in the fourth year
of Ahab king of Israel. 42Jehoshaphat *was*
thirty-five years old when he became
king, and he reigned twenty-five years in
Jerusalem. His mother's name *was* Azubah the daughter of Shilhi. 43And he
walked in all the ways of his father Asa.
He did not turn aside from them, doing
what was right in the eyes of the LORD.
Nevertheless the high places were not
taken away, *for* the people offered sacrifices and burned incense on the high

22:38 [a]Syriac and Targum read *they washed his armor.*

22:34 What are the odds? "On Sept. 11, 2001, as soon as that second plane hit the World Trade Center, we *knew* it wasn't an accident. Something was radically wrong. Two planes flying into buildings accidentally on the same day? No way! Yet in order for the first living cell, with the ability to reproduce, to have come into existence by chance, it would have required an uncountable number of accidents to have occurred all at the same time! If we don't believe two jetliners would crash into two buildings on the same day by accident, then why would anyone rational ever believe the most sophisticated, complex mechanism known to man could have happened by accident? The answer is given by zoologist D. M. S. Watson. Writing in the journal *Nature*, he speaks of "the theory of evolution itself, a theory universally accepted not because it can be proved by logically coherent evidence to be true but because the only alternative, special creation, is clearly incredible." *Stuart Scott*

See also Heb. 1:10 and Rev. 14:7 comments.

places. 44 Also Jehoshaphat made peace
with the king of Israel.
45 Now the rest of the acts of Jehoshaphat, the might that he showed, and how
he made war, *are* they not written in the
book of the chronicles of the kings of Judah? 46 And the rest of the perverted persons,[a] who remained in the days of his
father Asa, he banished from the land.
47 *There was* then no king in Edom, only a
deputy of the king.
48 Jehoshaphat made merchant ships[a]
to go to Ophir for gold; but they never
sailed, for the ships were wrecked at Ezion
Geber. 49 Then Ahaziah the son of Ahab
said to Jehoshaphat, "Let my servants go
with your servants in the ships." But Jehoshaphat would not.
50 And Jehoshaphat rested with his fathers, and was buried with his fathers in
the City of David his father. Then Jehoram his son reigned in his place.

Ahaziah Reigns in Israel

51 Ahaziah the son of Ahab became
king over Israel in Samaria in the seventeenth year of Jehoshaphat king of Judah,
and reigned two years over Israel. 52 He
did evil in the sight of the LORD, and
walked in the way of his father and in the
way of his mother and in the way of Jeroboam the son of Nebat, who had made
Israel sin; 53 for he served Baal and worshiped him, and provoked the LORD God
of Israel to anger, according to all that his
father had done.

22:46 [a]Hebrew *qadesh,* that is, one practicing sodomy and prostitution in religious rituals 22:48 [a]Or *ships of Tarshish*

Buddhism

With about 375 million adherents, Buddhism is the fourth-largest religion in the world behind Christianity, Islam, and Hinduism. There are only about 1.5 million Buddhists living in the U.S., so their beliefs may not be very familiar. It is the dominant religion of the Far East and is becoming increasingly popular in the West, especially among movie stars. Many of us associate Buddhism with celebrities like Richard Gere, monks dressed in orange, and, of course, the most famous of all Buddhists, the Dalai Lama.

Buddhism appeals to many people because it promotes non-violence and tolerance, and offers a moral life of peace, tranquility, and enlightenment —all without any accountability or obligation to a God. It may sound odd, but God has as much place in Buddhism as in atheism—yet both belief systems are considered religions. The Buddhist's view of God is explained in *A Basic Buddhism Guide*:

> There is no almighty God in Buddhism. There is no one to hand out rewards or punishments on a supposed Judgment Day. Buddhism is strictly not a religion *in the context of being a faith and worship owing allegiance to a supernatural being.*

Over its long history Buddhism has developed into a wide variety of forms, ranging from an emphasis on religious rituals and worship of deities to a complete rejection of both rituals and deities in favor of pure meditation. But all share in common a great respect for the teachings of the Buddha, "The Enlightened One."

BACKGROUND

Buddhism was founded around the 5th century B.C. by an Indian prince named Siddhartha Gautama. According to tradition, the young prince lived an affluent and sheltered life until a journey during which he saw an old man, a sick man, a poor man, and a corpse. What he observed was that nothing lasted—people desired to hold on to life, health, possessions, and each other. But all these things pass away, which causes suffering.

Troubled by these scenes of human pain and suffering, on his 29th birthday Gautama left his wife and infant son on a search for truth and the meaning of life. After wandering for six years, and experimenting with yoga, asceticism, and near starvation, Gautama sat beneath a tree and vowed not to move until he had attained enlightenment.

Days later, the 35-year-old prince felt he attained understanding and arose as the Buddha—the "Enlightened One." He spent the remaining 45

(continued)

years of his life teaching the path to liberation from suffering (the *dharma*) and establishing a community of monks (the *sangha*).

In the 2,500 years since the Buddha's "enlightenment," Buddhism has spread over many countries, split into numerous sects, and adopted a wide variety of beliefs, practices, rituals, and customs. It has evolved into three main philosophies, or schools:

- *Theravada* (the "Doctrine of the Elders") represents approximately 38 percent of the Buddhist population. Theravada is the closest to the original atheistic philosophy.
- *Mahayana* (the "Greater Vehicle") represents approximately 56 percent of Buddhists. Over the years, Mahayana has accommodated many different Asian beliefs and now worships Buddha as a god.
- *Vajrayana* (also known as Lamaism or Tantrism) represents the remaining 6 percent of Buddhists. Vajrayana has added elements of shamanism and the occult.

Some groups may involve more animistic superstitions than others. Many participate in idol worship, the veneration of the spirits of dead ancestors, and ceremonial rituals to appease evil spirits. The beliefs, practices, rites and ceremonies, customs and habits of Buddhists can vary in different countries, making them especially difficult to define. Following is just a sampling of some of their views on the important topics of God, the afterlife, and salvation.

SCRIPTURES

There are a large number of religious texts and scriptures in Buddhism. The *Sutras* are considered to be the actual sayings of Buddha. The *Tripitaka* is one of the earliest compilations of Buddhist teachings. Over the years, many new observations were added until today it consists of up to 50 volumes—and it is over 10 times larger than the Bible. The collection is also known as the Pali Canon and is considered sacred by some.

Other texts consist of observations on the Sutras, compilations of quotes, histories, grammars, etc.

WHO IS GOD?

One doctrine agreed upon by all branches of modern Buddhism is: "This world is not created and ruled by a God." The idea of a personal, loving Creator who interacts with people is foreign to Buddhists. It is thought that Siddhartha Gautama rejected theistic beliefs because he had difficulty reconciling the reality of suffering, judgment, and evil with the existence of a good and holy God.

Although Buddhism does not concern itself with God and the afterlife, some say Buddha (Gautama) did not rule out the existence of a God or gods altogether. So as Buddhism grew and spread, local deities and religious practices were included in it. Today, Tibetan Buddhists believe in a large number of "divine beings."

Gautama never taught that he was a god or that he should be worshiped as a god, but the Mahayana sect believes Buddha became a *Bodhisattva*, a savior-like god, and can be called upon for help. The Mahayana believe numerous celestial Buddhas and Bodhisattvas occupy the universe as gods and goddesses that assist and inspire the Buddhist practitioner, while the Theravada sect of Buddhism does not believe in the existence of deities.

WHO IS JESUS?

Most Buddhists would probably consider Jesus to be an Enlightened Master, though definitely not the Son of God. The Dalai Lama believes that Jesus is "a fully enlightened being." In an article in *Christianity Today*, the interviewer challenged the Dalai Lama with this thought:

> If Jesus is fully enlightened, wouldn't he be teaching the truth about himself? Therefore, if he is teaching the truth, then he is the Son of God, and there is a God, and Jesus is the Savior. If he is fully enlightened, he should teach the truth. If he is not teaching the truth, he is not that enlightened.

The Dalai Lama stated that Jesus had lived previous lives and that His purpose was to teach a message of tolerance and compassion, to help us become better human beings.

HEAVEN AND HELL

Buddhism does not teach eternal life spent in either a heaven or hell after death. They may consider it "hell" to have to endure the untold sufferings of many lifetimes on earth, but they don't believe in any place of eternal punishment. There also is no place of eternal reward in heaven. Instead, their goal in life is to reach Nirvana, or Enlightenment—a state of mind that is free from desire.

SIN AND SALVATION

The idea of original sin, or of sin at all, has no place in Buddhism, so there is no need for salvation from sin and its consequences. In fact, Buddhists believe that people do not have individual souls. Instead, they are composed of five elements (physical form, feelings, ideations, mental developments, and awareness) that combine to form a human being at the time of birth. Although there is no eternal soul to continue on after death, Buddhism still believes in karma and reincarnation (rebirth). Their view differs from the Hindu view, however.

In Hinduism, the same individual is reincarnated into another body through numerous lives, as he continually tries to work out his karma. In Buddhism, a person who dies is reborn as someone else. Still, because Buddhists believe in karma, they contend that the person's achievements in life will continue on into their next bodily form. The way they explain it is that "the consciousness of a person remains even after he is no more. It even manifests in his future life." So the person continues, but

(continued)

Buddhism (continued)

there is no soul. As one Buddhist website admits, "One finds a little contradiction here."

Because karma, the Buddhist law of moral cause and effect, is completely rigid and impersonal, life for a Buddhist is very oppressive. Under karma, there can be no appeal, no mercy, and no escape except through unceasing effort at self-perfection. Through numerous lifetimes, Buddhists endure an endless cycle of continuous suffering, and their goal is to break out of this cycle by finally extinguishing the flame of life and entering a permanent state of pure nonexistence (Nirvana). The ultimate goal of the Buddhist is not life, but death (extinction) by releasing their attachment to desire and the self. The reward for all their ceaseless labor is therefore to cease to exist. In this way they hope to achieve liberation and freedom ("salvation") from suffering.

BUDDHIST CUSTOMS

The basics of the Buddhist belief system are contained in the Four Noble Truths, the Noble Eightfold Path, and the Five Precepts.

The Four Noble Truths assert that:

1. Life is full of suffering (*dukkha*).
2. Suffering is caused by craving (*samudaya*).
3. Suffering will cease only when craving ceases (*nirodha*).
4. Suffering can be eliminated by following the Noble Eightfold Path.

The Noble Eightfold Path supposedly is the way to the cessation of suffering. It includes the following:

1. Right Understanding—Understanding reality as it is, not just as it appears to be.
2. Right Thought—Change in the pattern of thinking.
3. Right Speech—One speaks in a non-hurtful, not exaggerated, truthful way.
4. Right Action—Wholesome action, avoiding action that would do harm.
5. Right Livelihood—One's way of livelihood does not harm in any way oneself or others, directly or indirectly.
6. Right Effort—One makes an effort to improve.
7. Right Mindfulness—Mental ability to see things for what they are with clear consciousness.
8. Right Concentration—Being aware of the present reality within oneself, without any craving or aversion (involves deep meditation).

The Noble Eightfold Path is seen as a practical guideline for ethical and mental development to free the individual from "attachments and delusions" (things that cause suffering). Buddhists believe that following it will lead to understanding the truth about all things. They emphasize the practical aspect, because it is only through practice that they can hope to attain a higher level of existence and finally reach Nirvana. The eight aspects of the path are not a sequence of steps, but are attitudes and actions that can be developed simultaneously.

The Five Precepts are the basis of Buddhist morality. They are not in the form of commands such as "You shall not...," but are rules to live a better life in which one is happy, worry-free, and can meditate well. The Five Precepts include:

1. Abstain from harming living beings (non-violence toward sentient life forms). This includes human beings, animals and insects. However, Buddhists can eat meat, if the animal has not been killed for them specifically.
2. Abstain from stealing, which means not taking what is not given.
3. Abstain from sexual misconduct. This includes unfaithfulness to one's partner, involvement with prostitution or pornography, immoral thoughts, etc.
4. Abstain from false speech, which includes lying, gossiping, etc. This means speaking the truth always.
5. Abstain from intoxicating drinks and drugs (which lead to loss of mindfulness), except those taken for medicinal purposes.

HOW TO REACH A BUDDHIST

It is clear from the teachings of Buddhism that this is another works-righteousness religion, with a fear that if righteousness is not attained, there will be another rebirth into this world of suffering.

Hollywood has made reincarnation look like an intriguing alternative to heaven. Many people have latched onto the belief that they may have lived another life in the past and will return after death in another life. But a little probing shows that they haven't given much thought about their belief: Who is in charge of giving out bodies? What is the criteria God (or whoever is in charge) uses for doing so? If people are hoping to come back as royalty or a great stallion, what do they have to do in this life to merit such a reward? Or what does one have to do to end up coming back as a cockroach? What were they in past lives, and what did they do to merit the life they have now? Asking some of these questions may help them see that their belief is illogical, and has no proof.

Then share with them the Good News, that if they want to go where there is no more suffering, there is only one Way for that to happen—and it is a belief that can be backed up by verifiable evidence.

As in other religions, Buddhism uses some of the same words as Christianity, but with entirely different meanings. For example, to avoid confusion, don't tell a Buddhist that he must be "born again." Since the Buddhist's goal is to avoid being reborn, that phrase indicates failure and gives a negative view of what becoming a Christian means. Instead, explain to him that he can be born as a new person spiritually and be saved eternally.

(Adapted from *World Religions in a Nutshell*.)

2 Kings

God Judges Ahaziah

1 Moab rebelled against Israel after the death of Ahab.

[2]Now Ahaziah fell through the lattice
of his upper room in Samaria, and was
injured; so he sent messengers and said
to them, "Go, inquire of Baal-Zebub, the
god of Ekron, whether I shall recover
from this injury." [3]But the angel[a] of the
LORD said to Elijah the Tishbite, "Arise,
go up to meet the messengers of the king
of Samaria, and say to them, '*Is it* because
there is no God in Israel *that* you are going to inquire of Baal-Zebub, the god of
Ekron?' [4]Now therefore, thus says the
LORD: 'You shall not come down from the
bed to which you have gone up, but you
shall surely die.' " So Elijah departed.

[5]And when the messengers returned
to him, he said to them, "Why have you
come back?"

[6]So they said to him, "A man came up
to meet us, and said to us, 'Go, return to
the king who sent you, and say to him,
"Thus says the LORD: '*Is it* because *there is*
no God in Israel *that* you are sending to
inquire of Baal-Zebub, the god of Ekron?
Therefore you shall not come down from
the bed to which you have gone up, but
you shall surely die.' " ' "

[7]Then he said to them, "What kind of
man *was it* who came up to meet you and
told you these words?"

[8]So they answered him, "A hairy man
wearing a leather belt around his waist."

And he said, "It *is* Elijah the Tishbite."

[9]Then the king sent to him a captain
of fifty with his fifty men. So he went up
to him; and there he was, sitting on the
top of a hill. And he spoke to him: "Man
of God, the king has said, 'Come down!' "

[10]So Elijah answered and said to the
captain of fifty, "If I *am* a man of God,
then let fire come down from heaven and
consume you and your fifty men." And
fire came down from heaven and consumed him and his fifty. [11]Then he sent
to him another captain of fifty with his
fifty men.

And he answered and said to him:
"Man of God, thus has the king said,
'Come down quickly!' "

[12]So Elijah answered and said to them,
"If I *am* a man of God, let fire come down
from heaven and consume you and your
fifty men." And the fire of God came

1:3 [a]Or *Angel*

1:9–15 This scenario happened three times. However, only the last third were saved from the consuming fire because they came in humility (see v. 13). A total of 153 men were involved. Compare this to the 153 fish Peter caught in his net (see John 21:11 and Matt. 13:47–50 comment). Jesus will come in flaming fire and consume those who refuse to humble themselves and obey the gospel (see 2 Thess. 1:7,8). Our churches are full of those who profess to be saved, but are strangers to genuine repentance. Could it be that down through the ages only one-third of the professed Church will be saved?

down from heaven and consumed him and his fifty.

13Again, he sent a third captain of fifty with his fifty men. And the third captain of fifty went up, and came and fell on his knees before Elijah, and pleaded with him, and said to him: "Man of God, please let my life and the life of these fifty servants of yours be precious in your sight. 14Look, fire has come down from heaven and burned up the first two captains of fifties with their fifties. But let my life now be precious in your sight."

15And the angel[a] of the LORD said to Elijah, "Go down with him; do not be afraid of him." So he arose and went down with him to the king. 16Then he said to him, "Thus says the LORD: 'Because you have sent messengers to inquire of Baal-Zebub, the god of Ekron, *is it* because *there is* no God in Israel to inquire of His word? Therefore you shall not come down from the bed to which you have gone up, but you shall surely die.' "

17So *Ahaziah* died according to the word of the LORD which Elijah had spoken. Because he had no son, Jehoram[a] became king in his place, in the second year of Jehoram the son of Jehoshaphat, king of Judah.

18Now the rest of the acts of Ahaziah which he did, *are* they not written in the book of the chronicles of the kings of Israel?

Elijah Ascends to Heaven

2 And it came to pass, when the LORD was about to take up Elijah into heaven by a whirlwind, that Elijah went with Elisha from Gilgal. 2Then Elijah said to Elisha, "Stay here, please, for the LORD has sent me on to Bethel."

But Elisha said, "*As* the LORD lives, and *as* your soul lives, I will not leave you!" So they went down to Bethel.

3Now the sons of the prophets who *were* at Bethel came out to Elisha, and said to him, "Do you know that the LORD will take away your master from over you today?"

And he said, "Yes, I know; keep silent!"

4Then Elijah said to him, "Elisha, stay here, please, for the LORD has sent me on to Jericho."

But he said, "*As* the LORD lives, and *as* your soul lives, I will not leave you!" So they came to Jericho.

5Now the sons of the prophets who *were* at Jericho came to Elisha and said to him, "Do you know that the LORD will take away your master from over you today?"

So he answered, "Yes, I know; keep silent!"

6Then Elijah said to him, "Stay here, please, for the LORD has sent me on to the Jordan."

But he said, "*As* the LORD lives, and *as* your soul lives, I will not leave you!" So the two of them went on. 7And fifty men of the sons of the prophets went and stood facing *them* at a distance, while the two of them stood by the Jordan. 8Now Elijah took his mantle, rolled *it* up, and struck the water; and it was divided this way and that, so that the two of them crossed over on dry ground.

9And so it was, when they had crossed over, that Elijah said to Elisha, "Ask! What may I do for you, before I am taken away from you?"

Elisha said, "Please let a double portion of your spirit be upon me."

10So he said, "You have asked a hard thing. *Nevertheless,* if you see me *when I am* taken from you, it shall be so for you; but if not, it shall not be *so.*" 11Then it happened, as they continued on and

1:15 [a]Or *Angel* 1:17 [a]The son of Ahab king of Israel (compare 3:1)

2:9 God gives all believers the gift of the Holy Spirit, making each of us fit for His service (see Acts 1:8; 2:38).

QUESTIONS & OBJECTIONS

2:1 *"Where is heaven, and what is it like?"*

The location of heaven doesn't concern me. Just because I couldn't tell you the exact location of the country of Mauritania doesn't mean it doesn't exist. All we can say for certain is that it is "up" (see Deut. 30:12; Amos 9:2; John 3:13).

Most people don't realize the Bible teaches that heaven is coming down to earth. We are waiting for a new heavens and a new earth in which God will make all things new (see Isa. 65:17; 2 Pet. 3:13). Completely. When God sets up His kingdom on this earth, He is going to remove the Genesis curse; that means there will be no more floods, tornadoes, hurricanes, droughts, earthquakes, disease, weeds, pain, suffering, or death. It is then that "the wolf and the lamb shall feed together" (Isa. 65:25), and creation will stop devouring itself (see Rom. 8:18–25). Those who trust in Jesus Christ will be given brand new bodies that will be like the resurrected body of Jesus—bodies that can eat, touch, feel, etc., but will never age or feel pain or sorrow. All this all sounds too good to be true, but it can be a proven reality for those who obey the gospel.

Think of it—eternal life, on this wonderful earth restored to when it was like the Garden of Eden. A place where there are no rapists, no murderers, no pedophiles, no hypocrites, liars, blasphemers, or thieves. A place of perfect fruit, incredible animals, unimaginable color, massive waterfalls, amazing plants, more beautiful birds, bigger fish, grander canyons. We are also told that God will remove the sea (Rev. 21:1), which will give us a little more room.

But best of all, the Creator of the universe, Almighty God, will be there. Scripture tells us a number of times that "God is light." So there will no longer be a need for the sun, because He Himself will radiate in all of His unspeakable glory (see Rev. 21:23). Two thousand years ago He was manifest in human form to save us from death. However, Jesus of Nazareth is no longer the Man who was limited to time and space. He has ascended into heaven and is "glorified"—in the state He was in before He came to this earth. He dwells in "unapproachable light" and shines "brighter than the sun" (1 Tim. 6:16; Acts 26:13).

Mere words could never express my infinite gratitude to Him for giving me life, and then for saving me from being justly damned in hell for my sins. But I will have eternity to love and worship Him at whose right hand are "pleasures forevermore" (Psa. 16:11). No enjoyment on this sad, old earth has come even close to the unending pleasures that God has prepared "for those who love Him" (1 Cor. 2:9). What a tragedy for people to miss out, simply because they refuse to repent and trust the Savior.

talked, that suddenly a chariot of fire *appeared* with horses of fire, and separated the two of them; and Elijah went up by a whirlwind into heaven.
12And Elisha saw *it*, and he cried out, "My father, my father, the chariot of Israel and its horsemen!" So he saw him no more. And he took hold of his own clothes
and tore them into two pieces. 13He also
took up the mantle of Elijah that had fallen from him, and went back and
stood by the bank of the Jordan. 14Then
he took the mantle of Elijah that had fallen from him, and struck the water, and said, "Where *is* the LORD God of Elijah?" And when he also had struck the water, it was divided this way and that; and Elisha crossed over.
15Now when the sons of the prophets
who *were* from Jericho saw him, they said, "The spirit of Elijah rests on Elisha." And they came to meet him, and bowed
to the ground before him. 16Then they
said to him, "Look now, there are fifty strong men with your servants. Please let them go and search for your master, lest perhaps the Spirit of the LORD has taken him up and cast him upon some mountain or into some valley."

And he said, "You shall not send anyone."
17But when they urged him till he was ashamed, he said, "Send *them!*" Therefore they sent fifty men, and they searched for
three days but did not find him. 18And
when they came back to him, for he had stayed in Jericho, he said to them, "Did I not say to you, 'Do not go'?"

Elisha Performs Miracles

19Then the men of the city said to Elisha, "Please notice, the situation of this city *is* pleasant, as my lord sees; but the water *is* bad, and the ground barren."

20And he said, "Bring me a new bowl, and put salt in it." So they brought *it* to him. 21Then he went out to the source of the water, and cast in the salt there, and said, "Thus says the LORD: 'I have healed this water; from it there shall be no more death or barrenness.' " 22So the water remains healed to this day, according to the word of Elisha which he spoke.

23Then he went up from there to Bethel; and as he was going up the road, some youths came from the city and mocked him, and said to him, "Go up, you baldhead! Go up, you baldhead!"

24So he turned around and looked at them, and pronounced a curse on them in the name of the LORD. And two female bears came out of the woods and mauled forty-two of the youths.

25Then he went from there to Mount Carmel, and from there he returned to Samaria.

Moab Rebels Against Israel

3 Now Jehoram the son of Ahab became king over Israel at Samaria in the eighteenth year of Jehoshaphat king of Judah, and reigned twelve years. 2And he did evil in the sight of the LORD, but not like his father and mother; for he put away the *sacred* pillar of Baal that his father had made. 3Nevertheless he persisted in the sins of Jeroboam the son of Nebat, who had made Israel sin; he did not depart from them.

4Now Mesha king of Moab was a sheepbreeder, and he regularly paid the king of Israel one hundred thousand lambs and the wool of one hundred thousand rams. 5But it happened, when Ahab died, that the king of Moab rebelled against the king of Israel.

6So King Jehoram went out of Samaria at that time and mustered all Israel. 7Then he went and sent to Jehoshaphat

"Jesus Christ is still working in the world through the transformation of the human heart... If you know Him and are making Him known to others, then you are a part of the most exciting phenonemon on Planet Earth: the advancement of the kingdom of God!"

D. James Kennedy

king of Judah, saying, "The king of Moab has rebelled against me. Will you go with me to fight against Moab?"

And he said, "I will go up; I *am* as you *are,* my people as your people, my horses as your horses." 8Then he said, "Which way shall we go up?"

And he answered, "By way of the Wilderness of Edom."

9So the king of Israel went with the king of Judah and the king of Edom, and they marched on that roundabout route seven days; and there was no water for the army, nor for the animals that followed them. 10And the king of Israel said, "Alas! For the LORD has called these three kings together to deliver them into the hand of Moab."

11But Jehoshaphat said, "*Is there* no prophet of the LORD here, that we may inquire of the LORD by him?"

So one of the servants of the king of Israel answered and said, "Elisha the son of Shaphat *is* here, who poured water on the hands of Elijah."

12And Jehoshaphat said, "The word of
the LORD is with him." So the king of
Israel and Jehoshaphat and the king of
Edom went down to him.

13Then Elisha said to the king of Israel,
"What have I to do with you? Go to the
prophets of your father and the prophets
of your mother."

But the king of Israel said to him, "No,
for the LORD has called these three kings
together to deliver them into the hand of
Moab."

14And Elisha said, "*As* the LORD of
hosts lives, before whom I stand, surely
were it not that I regard the presence of
Jehoshaphat king of Judah, I would not
look at you, nor see you. 15But now bring
me a musician."

Then it happened, when the musician
played, that the hand of the LORD came
upon him. 16And he said, "Thus says the
LORD: 'Make this valley full of ditches.'
17For thus says the LORD: 'You shall not
see wind, nor shall you see rain; yet that
valley shall be filled with water, so that
you, your cattle, and your animals may
drink.' 18And this is a simple matter in
the sight of the LORD; He will also deliver
the Moabites into your hand. 19Also you
shall attack every fortified city and every
choice city, and shall cut down every
good tree, and stop up every spring of
water, and ruin every good piece of land
with stones."

20Now it happened in the morning,
when the grain offering was offered, that
suddenly water came by way of Edom,
and the land was filled with water.

21And when all the Moabites heard
that the kings had come up to fight against
them, all who were able to bear arms and
older were gathered; and they stood at
the border. 22Then they rose up early in
the morning, and the sun was shining on
the water; and the Moabites saw the water
on the other side *as* red as blood. 23And
they said, "This is blood; the kings have
surely struck swords and have killed one
another; now therefore, Moab, to the spoil!"

24So when they came to the camp of
Israel, Israel rose up and attacked the
Moabites, so that they fled before them;
and they entered *their* land, killing the
Moabites. 25Then they destroyed the cities,
and each man threw a stone on every
good piece of land and filled it; and they
stopped up all the springs of water and
cut down all the good trees. But they left
the stones of Kir Haraseth *intact*. However the slingers surrounded and attacked
it.

26And when the king of Moab saw that
the battle was too fierce for him, he took
with him seven hundred men who drew
swords, to break through to the king of
Edom, but they could not. 27Then he took
his eldest son who would have reigned in
his place, and offered him *as* a burnt offering upon the wall; and there was great
indignation against Israel. So they departed from him and returned to *their
own* land.

Elisha and the Widow's Oil

4 A certain woman of the wives of the
sons of the prophets cried out to
Elisha, saying, "Your servant my husband is dead, and you know that your
servant feared the LORD. And the creditor
is coming to take my two sons to be his

3:27 *Matthew Henry* said, "...he took his own son, his eldest son, that was to succeed him, than whom nothing could be more dear to himself and his people, and *offered him for a burnt-offering upon the wall,* 2 Kings 3:27. He designed by this, (1.) To obtain the favour of Chemosh his god, which, being a devil, delighted in blood and murder, and the destruction of mankind."

Skeptics often say, "What sort of father would kill his own son? And yet that's what God did to Jesus!" However, although Jesus is called the Son of God, and the Father refers to Him as His Son, there is far more to this than meets the unregenerate eye. The Bible tells us that God was in Christ, reconciling Himself to the world (see 2 Cor. 5:19). God was manifest in human form; He created a body and filled that body as a hand fills a glove (see 1 Tim. 3:16; Col. 1:15–20). So it was not a matter of an aloof God punishing an innocent person for the sin of the world, but rather, He took the sin of the world upon Himself, in Christ.

slaves."
[2]So Elisha said to her, "What shall I do
for you? Tell me, what do you have in the
house?" And she said, "Your maidservant
has nothing in the house but a jar of oil."
[3]Then he said, "Go, borrow vessels
from everywhere, from all your neighbors—empty vessels; do not gather just a
few. [4]And when you have come in, you
shall shut the door behind you and your
sons; then pour it into all those vessels,
and set aside the full ones."
[5]So she went from him and shut the
door behind her and her sons, who
brought *the vessels* to her; and she poured
it out. [6]Now it came to pass, when the
vessels were full, that she said to her son,
"Bring me another vessel."
And he said to her, "*There is* not another vessel." So the oil ceased. [7]Then she
came and told the man of God. And he
said, "Go, sell the oil and pay your debt;
and you *and* your sons live on the rest."

Elisha Raises the Shunammite's Son

[8]Now it happened one day that Elisha
went to Shunem, where there *was* a notable woman, and she persuaded him to
eat some food. So it was, as often as he
passed by, he would turn in there to eat
some food. [9]And she said to her husband,
"Look now, I know that this *is* a holy man
of God, who passes by us regularly.
[10]Please, let us make a small upper room
on the wall; and let us put a bed for him
there, and a table and a chair and a lampstand; so it will be, whenever he comes to
us, he can turn in there."
[11]And it happened one day that he
came there, and he turned in to the upper room and lay down there. [12]Then he
said to Gehazi his servant, "Call this Shunammite woman." When he had called
her, she stood before him. [13]And he said
to him, "Say now to her, 'Look, you have
been concerned for us with all this care.
What *can I* do for you? Do you want me
to speak on your behalf to the king or to
the commander of the army?' "
She answered, "I dwell among my own
people."
[14]So he said, "What then *is* to be done
for her?"
And Gehazi answered, "Actually, she
has no son, and her husband is old."
[15]So he said, "Call her." When he had
called her, she stood in the doorway.
[16]Then he said, "About this time next year
you shall embrace a son."
And she said, "No, my lord. Man of
God, do not lie to your maidservant!"

Faith is to believe what we do not see, and the reward of this faith is to see what we believe.

AUGUSTINE

[17]But the woman conceived, and bore
a son when the appointed time had come,
of which Elisha had told her.
[18]And the child grew. Now it happened
one day that he went out to his father, to
the reapers. [19]And he said to his father,
"My head, my head!"
So he said to a servant, "Carry him to
his mother." [20]When he had taken him
and brought him to his mother, he sat on
her knees till noon, and *then* died. [21]And
she went up and laid him on the bed of
the man of God, shut *the door* upon him,
and went out. [22]Then she called to her
husband, and said, "Please send me one
of the young men and one of the donkeys, that I may run to the man of God
and come back."
[23]So he said, "Why are you going to
him today? *It is* neither the New Moon

4:10 As a man or woman of God, do you have a "closet" in which you pray, and do you plead with God to raise up laborers as you have been commanded to do (see Luke 10:2)? This is perhaps the most neglected command in Scripture. If we do not seek the lost, the last thing we are going to pray for is for someone else to do it. So the enemy gets a double victory. Not only is there a shortage of laborers, but there is also a shortage of people praying for laborers.

nor the Sabbath."
And she said, "*It is* well." 24Then she
saddled a donkey, and said to her servant,
"Drive, and go forward; do not slacken
the pace for me unless I tell you." 25And
so she departed, and went to the man of
God at Mount Carmel.
So it was, when the man of God saw
her afar off, that he said to his servant Gehazi, "Look, the Shunammite woman!
26Please run now to meet her, and say to
her, '*Is it* well with you? *Is it* well with
your husband? *Is it* well with the child?' "
And she answered, "*It is* well." 27Now
when she came to the man of God at the
hill, she caught him by the feet, but Gehazi came near to push her away. But the
man of God said, "Let her alone; for her
soul *is* in deep distress, and the LORD has
hidden *it* from me, and has not told me."
28So she said, "Did I ask a son of my
lord? Did I not say, 'Do not deceive me'?"
29Then he said to Gehazi, "Get yourself ready, and take my staff in your hand,
and be on your way. If you meet anyone,
do not greet him; and if anyone greets
you, do not answer him; but lay my staff
on the face of the child."
30And the mother of the child said, "*As*
the LORD lives, and *as* your soul lives, I
will not leave you." So he arose and followed her. 31Now Gehazi went on ahead
of them, and laid the staff on the face of
the child; but *there was* neither voice nor
hearing. Therefore he went back to meet
him, and told him, saying, "The child has
not awakened."
32When Elisha came into the house,
there was the child, lying dead on his
bed. 33He went in therefore, shut the
door behind the two of them, and prayed
to the LORD. 34And he went up and lay on
the child, and put his mouth on his
mouth, his eyes on his eyes, and his hands
on his hands; and he stretched himself
out on the child, and the flesh of the
child became warm. 35He returned and
walked back and forth in the house, and
again went up and stretched himself out
on him; then the child sneezed seven
times, and the child opened his eyes.
36And he called Gehazi and said, "Call
this Shunammite woman." So he called
her. And when she came in to him, he
said, "Pick up your son." 37So she went in,
fell at his feet, and bowed to the ground;
then she picked up her son and went out.

Elisha Purifies the Pot of Stew

38And Elisha returned to Gilgal, and
there was a famine in the land. Now the
sons of the prophets *were* sitting before
him; and he said to his servant, "Put on
the large pot, and boil stew for the sons
of the prophets." 39So one went out into
the field to gather herbs, and found a
wild vine, and gathered from it a lapful of
wild gourds, and came and sliced *them*
into the pot of stew, though they did not
know *what they were.* 40Then they served
it to the men to eat. Now it happened, as
they were eating the stew, that they cried
out and said, "Man of God, *there is* death
in the pot!" And they could not eat *it.*
41So he said, "Then bring some flour."
And he put *it* into the pot, and said, "Serve
it to the people, that they may eat." And
there was nothing harmful in the pot.

Elisha Feeds One Hundred Men

42Then a man came from Baal Shalisha, and brought the man of God bread
of the firstfruits, twenty loaves of barley
bread, and newly ripened grain in his
knapsack. And he said, "Give *it* to the
people, that they may eat."
43But his servant said, "What? Shall I
set this before one hundred men?"
He said again, "Give it to the people,
that they may eat; for thus says the LORD:
'They shall eat and have *some* left over.' "
44So he set *it* before them; and they ate

4:44 Compare this incident with Jesus' feeding of the 5,000 men plus women and children. In both instances, there was enough bread for all to eat and some left over (see Matt. 14:17–20). We have eaten of the Bread of Life, and now we must take that Bread to a starving world.

and had *some* left over, according to the
word of the LORD.

Naaman's Leprosy Healed

5 Now Naaman, commander of the
army of the king of Syria, was a great
and honorable man in the eyes of his
master, because by him the LORD had
given victory to Syria. He was also a
mighty man of valor, *but* a leper. 2And
the Syrians had gone out on raids, and
had brought back captive a young girl
from the land of Israel. She waited on
Naaman's wife. 3Then she said to her mistress, "If only my master *were* with the
prophet who *is* in Samaria! For he would
heal him of his leprosy." 4And *Naaman*
went in and told his master, saying, "Thus
and thus said the girl who is from the
land of Israel."

5Then the king of Syria said, "Go now,
and I will send a letter to the king of Israel."

So he departed and took with him ten
talents of silver, six thousand *shekels* of
gold, and ten changes of clothing. 6Then
he brought the letter to the king of Israel,
which said,

> Now be advised, when this letter
> comes to you, that I have sent Naaman
> my servant to you, that you may heal
> him of his leprosy.

7And it happened, when the king of Israel
read the letter, that he tore his clothes
and said, "*Am* I God, to kill and make
alive, that this man sends a man to me to
heal him of his leprosy? Therefore please
consider, and see how he seeks a quarrel
with me."

8So it was, when Elisha the man of
God heard that the king of Israel had torn
his clothes, that he sent to the king, saying, "Why have you torn your clothes?
Please let him come to me, and he shall
know that there is a prophet in Israel."

9Then Naaman went with his horses
and chariot, and he stood at the door of
Elisha's house. 10And Elisha sent a messenger to him, saying, "Go and wash in
the Jordan seven times, and your flesh
shall be restored to you, and *you shall* be
clean." 11But Naaman became furious, and
went away and said, "Indeed, I said to
myself, 'He will surely come out *to me,*
and stand and call on the name of the
LORD his God, and wave his hand over
the place, and heal the leprosy.' 12*Are* not
the Abanah[a] and the Pharpar, the rivers
of Damascus, better than all the waters of
Israel? Could I not wash in them and be
clean?" So he turned and went away in a
rage. 13And his servants came near and
spoke to him, and said, "My father, *if* the
prophet had told you *to do* something
great, would you not have done *it*? How
much more then, when he says to you,
'Wash, and be clean'?" 14So he went down
and dipped seven times in the Jordan, according to the saying of the man of God;
and his flesh was restored like the flesh of
a little child, and he was clean.

> Humility is the illusive and most difficult of all human graces.
>
> **BRUCE GARNER**

15And he returned to the man of God,
he and all his aides, and came and stood

5:12 [a]Following Kethib, Septuagint, and Vulgate; Qere, Syriac, and Targum read *Amanah*.

5:1 The story of Naaman is a wonderful example of true salvation. All humanity has the leprous disease of sin. To be cleansed we have to humble ourselves. Pride keeps so many from coming to Christ because of the seemingly foolish way of salvation.

"Humility pleases God wherever it is found, and the humble person will have God for his or her friend and helper always. Only the humble are completely sane, for they are the only ones who see clearly their own size and limitations. Egotists see things out of focus. To themselves they are large and God is correspondingly small, and that is a kind of moral insanity." *A. W. Tozer*

before him; and he said, "Indeed, now I know that *there is* no God in all the earth, except in Israel; now therefore, please take a gift from your servant."

16But he said, "*As* the LORD lives, before whom I stand, I will receive nothing." And he urged him to take *it,* but he refused.

17So Naaman said, "Then, if not, please let your servant be given two mule-loads of earth; for your servant will no longer offer either burnt offering or sacrifice to other gods, but to the LORD. 18Yet in this thing may the LORD pardon your servant: when my master goes into the temple of Rimmon to worship there, and he leans on my hand, and I bow down in the temple of Rimmon—when I bow down in the temple of Rimmon, may the LORD please pardon your servant in this thing."

19Then he said to him, "Go in peace." So he departed from him a short distance.

Gehazi's Greed

20But Gehazi, the servant of Elisha the man of God, said, "Look, my master has spared Naaman this Syrian, while not receiving from his hands what he brought; but *as* the LORD lives, I will run after him and take something from him." 21So Gehazi pursued Naaman. When Naaman saw *him* running after him, he got down from the chariot to meet him, and said, "*Is* all well?"

22And he said, "All *is* well. My master has sent me, saying, 'Indeed, just now two young men of the sons of the prophets have come to me from the mountains of Ephraim. Please give them a talent of silver and two changes of garments.' "

23So Naaman said, "Please, take two talents." And he urged him, and bound two talents of silver in two bags, with two changes of garments, and handed *them* to two of his servants; and they carried *them* on ahead of him. 24When he came to the citadel, he took *them* from their hand, and stored *them* away in the house; then he let the men go, and they departed. 25Now he went in and stood before his master. Elisha said to him, "Where *did you go,* Gehazi?"

And he said, "Your servant did not go anywhere."

26Then he said to him, "Did not my heart go *with you* when the man turned back from his chariot to meet you? *Is it* time to receive money and to receive clothing, olive groves and vineyards, sheep and oxen, male and female servants? 27Therefore the leprosy of Naaman shall cling to you and your descendants forever." And he went out from his presence leprous, *as white* as snow.

The Floating Ax Head

6 And the sons of the prophets said to Elisha, "See now, the place where we dwell with you is too small for us. 2Please, let us go to the Jordan, and let every man take a beam from there, and let us make there a place where we may dwell."

So he answered, "Go."

3Then one said, "Please consent to go with your servants."

And he answered, "I will go." 4So he went with them. And when they came to the Jordan, they cut down trees. 5But as one was cutting down a tree, the iron *ax head* fell into the water; and he cried out and said, "Alas, master! For it was borrowed."

6So the man of God said, "Where did it fall?" And he showed him the place. So he cut off a stick, and threw *it* in there; and he made the iron float. 7Therefore he said, "Pick *it* up for yourself." So he reached out his hand and took it.

6:4–7 The axe of the Law has been lost from the hand of the Church for many years. Take it firmly in your hand and lay it at the root of the tree of sin. Never be afraid to lift its sharp blade and threaten the sinner with its holy precepts. Its purpose is to bring him to the foot of the cross. Paul called it a "tutor to bring us to Christ" (see Gal. 3:24).

The Blinded Syrians Captured

8 Now the king of Syria was making war against Israel; and he consulted with his servants, saying, "My camp *will be* in such and such a place." 9 And the man of God sent to the king of Israel, saying, "Beware that you do not pass this place, for the Syrians are coming down there." 10 Then the king of Israel sent *someone* to the place of which the man of God had told him. Thus he warned him, and he was watchful there, not just once or twice.

11 Therefore the heart of the king of Syria was greatly troubled by this thing; and he called his servants and said to them, "Will you not show me which of us *is* for the king of Israel?"

12 And one of his servants said, "None, my lord, O king; but Elisha, the prophet who *is* in Israel, tells the king of Israel the words that you speak in your bedroom."

13 So he said, "Go and see where he *is*, that I may send and get him."

And it was told him, saying, "Surely *he is* in Dothan."

14 Therefore he sent horses and chariots and a great army there, and they came by night and surrounded the city. 15 And when the servant of the man of God arose early and went out, there was an army, surrounding the city with horses and chariots. And his servant said to him, "Alas, my master! What shall we do?"

16 So he answered, "Do not fear, for those who *are* with us *are* more than those who *are* with them." 17 And Elisha prayed, and said, "LORD, I pray, open his eyes that he may see." Then the LORD opened the eyes of the young man, and he saw. And behold, the mountain *was* full of horses and chariots of fire all around Elisha. 18 So when *the Syrians* came down to him, Elisha prayed to the LORD, and said, "Strike this people, I pray, with blindness." And He struck them with blindness according to the word of Elisha.

19 Now Elisha said to them, "This *is* not the way, nor *is* this the city. Follow me, and I will bring you to the man whom you seek." But he led them to Samaria.

20 So it was, when they had come to Samaria, that Elisha said, "LORD, open the eyes of these *men*, that they may see." And the LORD opened their eyes, and they saw; and there *they were*, inside Samaria!

21 Now when the king of Israel saw them, he said to Elisha, "My father, shall I kill *them*? Shall I kill *them*?"

22 But he answered, "You shall not kill *them*. Would you kill those whom you have taken captive with your sword and your bow? Set food and water before them, that they may eat and drink and go to their master." 23 Then he prepared a great feast for them; and after they ate and drank, he sent them away and they went to their master. So the bands of Syrian *raiders* came no more into the land of Israel.

Syria Besieges Samaria in Famine

24 And it happened after this that Ben-Hadad king of Syria gathered all his army, and went up and besieged Samaria. 25 And there was a great famine in Samaria; and indeed they besieged it until a donkey's head was *sold* for eighty *shekels* of silver, and one-fourth of a kab of dove droppings for five *shekels* of silver.

26 Then, as the king of Israel was passing by on the wall, a woman cried out to him, saying, "Help, my lord, O king!"

27 And he said, "If the LORD does not help you, where can I find help for you? From the threshing floor or from the winepress?" 28 Then the king said to her, "What is troubling you?"

And she answered, "This woman said to me, 'Give your son, that we may eat him today, and we will eat my son tomorrow.' 29 So we boiled my son, and ate him. And I said to her on the next day, 'Give your son, that we may eat him'; but she has hidden her son."

6:17 Through the eye of faith we know that we are not alone in our battle to reach the lost.

30 Now it happened, when the king
heard the words of the woman, that he
tore his clothes; and as he passed by on
the wall, the people looked, and there
underneath *he had* sackcloth on his body.
31 Then he said, "God do so to me and
more also, if the head of Elisha the son of
Shaphat remains on him today!"
32 But Elisha was sitting in his house,
and the elders were sitting with him. And
the king sent a man ahead of him, but before the messenger came to him, he said
to the elders, "Do you see how this son of
a murderer has sent someone to take
away my head? Look, when the messenger comes, shut the door, and hold him
fast at the door. *Is* not the sound of his
master's feet behind him?" 33 And while
he was still talking with them, there was
the messenger, coming down to him; and
then *the king* said, "Surely this calamity *is*
from the LORD; why should I wait for the
LORD any longer?"

7 Then Elisha said, "Hear the word of
the LORD. Thus says the LORD: 'Tomorrow about this time a seah of fine
flour *shall be sold* for a shekel, and two
seahs of barley for a shekel, at the gate of
Samaria.' "
2 So an officer on whose hand the king
leaned answered the man of God and
said, "Look, *if* the LORD would make windows in heaven, could this thing be?"
And he said, "In fact, you shall see *it*
with your eyes, but you shall not eat of it."

The Syrians Flee

3 Now there were four leprous men at
the entrance of the gate; and they said to
one another, "Why are we sitting here
until we die? 4 If we say, 'We will enter the
city,' the famine *is* in the city, and we shall
die there. And if we sit here, we die also.
Now therefore, come, let us surrender to
the army of the Syrians. If they keep us
alive, we shall live; and if they kill us, we
shall only die." 5 And they rose at twilight
to go to the camp of the Syrians; and
when they had come to the outskirts of
the Syrian camp, to their surprise no one
was there. 6 For the LORD had caused the
army of the Syrians to hear the noise of
chariots and the noise of horses—the
noise of a great army; so they said to one
another, "Look, the king of Israel has
hired against us the kings of the Hittites
and the kings of the Egyptians to attack
us!" 7 Therefore they arose and fled at twilight, and left the camp intact—their
tents, their horses, and their donkeys—
and they fled for their lives. 8 And when
these lepers came to the outskirts of the
camp, they went into one tent and ate
and drank, and carried from it silver and
gold and clothing, and went and hid
them; then they came back and entered
another tent, and carried *some* from there
also, and went and hid *it.*

As long as there are millions destitute of the Word of God and knowledge of Jesus Christ, it will be impossible for me to devote time and energy to those who have both.

J. L. EWEN

9 Then they said to one another, "We
are not doing right. This day *is* a day of
good news, and we remain silent. If we
wait until morning light, some punishment will come upon us. Now therefore,
come, let us go and tell the king's household." 10 So they went and called to the
gatekeepers of the city, and told them,

7:8,9 How could these lepers keep this good news to themselves? Their conscience spoke to them of their moral obligations. How much more should we feel an obligation to take the ultimate good tidings of everlasting life to a dying world? We have been cleansed from the leprosy of sin and have found the Bread of Life. We therefore cannot be silent; we must speak the things which we have seen and heard (see Acts 4:20).

"If you have no wish to bring others to heaven, you are not going there yourself." *Charles Spurgeon*

saying, "We went to the Syrian camp, and surprisingly no one *was* there, not a human sound—only horses and donkeys tied, and the tents intact." 11And the gatekeepers called out, and they told *it* to the king's household inside.

12So the king arose in the night and said to his servants, "Let me now tell you what the Syrians have done to us. They know that we *are* hungry; therefore they have gone out of the camp to hide themselves in the field, saying, 'When they come out of the city, we shall catch them alive, and get into the city.' "

13And one of his servants answered and said, "Please, let several *men* take five of the remaining horses which are left in the city. Look, they *may either become* like all the multitude of Israel that are left in it; or indeed, *I say,* they *may become* like all the multitude of Israel left from those who are consumed; so let us send them and see." 14Therefore they took two chariots with horses; and the king sent them in the direction of the Syrian army, saying, "Go and see." 15And they went after them to the Jordan; and indeed all the road *was* full of garments and weapons which the Syrians had thrown away in their haste. So the messengers returned and told the king. 16Then the people went out and plundered the tents of the Syrians. So a seah of fine flour was *sold* for a shekel, and two seahs of barley for a shekel, according to the word of the LORD.

17Now the king had appointed the officer on whose hand he leaned to have charge of the gate. But the people trampled him in the gate, and he died, just as the man of God had said, who spoke when the king came down to him. 18So it happened just as the man of God had spoken to the king, saying, "Two seahs of barley for a shekel, and a seah of fine flour for a shekel, shall be *sold* tomorrow about this time in the gate of Samaria."

19Then that officer had answered the man of God, and said, "Now look, *if* the LORD would make windows in heaven, could such a thing be?"

And he had said, "In fact, you shall see *it* with your eyes, but you shall not eat of it." 20And so it happened to him, for the people trampled him in the gate, and he died.

The King Restores the Shunammite's Land

8 Then Elisha spoke to the woman whose son he had restored to life, saying, "Arise and go, you and your household, and stay wherever you can; for the LORD has called for a famine, and furthermore, it will come upon the land for seven years." 2So the woman arose and did according to the saying of the man of God, and she went with her household and dwelt in the land of the Philistines seven years.

3It came to pass, at the end of seven years, that the woman returned from the land of the Philistines; and she went to make an appeal to the king for her house and for her land. 4Then the king talked with Gehazi, the servant of the man of God, saying, "Tell me, please, all the great things Elisha has done." 5Now it happened, as he was telling the king how he had restored the dead to life, that there was the woman whose son he had restored to life, appealing to the king for her house and for her land. And Gehazi said, "My lord, O king, this is the woman, and this is her son whom Elisha restored to life." 6And when the king asked the woman, she told him.

So the king appointed a certain officer for her, saying, "Restore all that *was* hers, and all the proceeds of the field from the day that she left the land until now."

Death of Ben-Hadad

7Then Elisha went to Damascus, and Ben-Hadad king of Syria was sick; and it was told him, saying, "The man of God has come here." 8And the king said to Hazael, "Take a present in your hand, and go to meet the man of God, and inquire of the LORD by him, saying, 'Shall I recover from this disease?' " 9So Hazael went

to meet him and took a present with him, of every good thing of Damascus, forty camel-loads; and he came and stood before him, and said, "Your son Ben-Hadad king of Syria has sent me to you, saying, 'Shall I recover from this disease?' "

10And Elisha said to him, "Go, say to him, 'You shall certainly recover.' However the LORD has shown me that he will really die." 11Then he set his countenance in a stare until he was ashamed; and the man of God wept. 12And Hazael said, "Why is my lord weeping?"

He answered, "Because I know the evil that you will do to the children of Israel: Their strongholds you will set on fire, and their young men you will kill with the sword; and you will dash their children, and rip open their women with child."

13So Hazael said, "But what *is* your servant—a dog, that he should do this gross thing?"

And Elisha answered, "The LORD has shown me that you *will become* king over Syria."

14Then he departed from Elisha, and came to his master, who said to him, "What did Elisha say to you?" And he answered, "He told me you would surely recover." 15But it happened on the next day that he took a thick cloth and dipped *it* in water, and spread *it* over his face so that he died; and Hazael reigned in his place.

Jehoram Reigns in Judah

16Now in the fifth year of Joram the son of Ahab, king of Israel, Jehoshaphat *having been* king of Judah, Jehoram the son of Jehoshaphat began to reign as king of Judah. 17He was thirty-two years old when he became king, and he reigned eight years in Jerusalem. 18And he walked in the way of the kings of Israel, just as the house of Ahab had done, for the daughter of Ahab was his wife; and he did evil in the sight of the LORD. 19Yet the LORD would not destroy Judah, for the sake of His servant David, as He promised him to give a lamp to him *and* his sons forever.

20In his days Edom revolted against Judah's authority, and made a king over themselves. 21So Joram[a] went to Zair, and all his chariots with him. Then he rose by night and attacked the Edomites who had surrounded him and the captains of the chariots; and the troops fled to their tents. 22Thus Edom has been in revolt against Judah's authority to this day. And Libnah revolted at that time.

23Now the rest of the acts of Joram, and all that he did, *are* they not written in the book of the chronicles of the kings of Judah? 24So Joram rested with his fathers, and was buried with his fathers in the City of David. Then Ahaziah his son reigned in his place.

8:21 [a]Spelled *Jehoram* in verse 16

8:8 Prime-evil Tribe. I dreamed I was a doctor. I was stationed in the darkest of places, fighting a deadly disease among a very primitive tribe. This tribal group was particularly vicious by nature, and what is more, they did not like me at all.

Their primitive beliefs were certainly strange. They were utterly convinced that they were related to gorillas, and that they originally came from a puddle of water.

In the dream, I wanted to run from their delusions, but I couldn't because I knew that they needed to be inoculated or they would all die. My job was to convince them that they were in serious danger and that they needed to hold still while I plunged a needle into their tender flesh—a difficult task indeed.

It was hard because these tribal people were particularly proud, and thought that they needed nothing and knew everything. They were so primitive in their thinking that they only believed in what they could see. They were especially resistant to the idea that there were unseen microorganisms, and that the deadly disease that was killing them was being promoted by their filthy lifestyle.

Then I awoke to the fact that it was not a dream at all, and that I have a difficult task ahead of me, but one from which I will not run.

8:12 It is a mystery why God allows extremely evil people to live. However, we can rest assured that all of His judgments are just. If He killed evil people in their youth, none of us would be left on earth. See also 1 Pet. 3:12 comment.

Ahaziah Reigns in Judah

25In the twelfth year of Joram the son of Ahab, king of Israel, Ahaziah the son of Jehoram, king of Judah, began to reign. 26Ahaziah *was* twenty-two years old when he became king, and he reigned one year in Jerusalem. His mother's name *was* Athaliah the granddaughter of Omri, king of Israel. 27And he walked in the way of the house of Ahab, and did evil in the sight of the LORD, like the house of Ahab, for he *was* the son-in-law of the house of Ahab.

28Now he went with Joram the son of Ahab to war against Hazael king of Syria at Ramoth Gilead; and the Syrians wounded Joram. 29Then King Joram went back to Jezreel to recover from the wounds which the Syrians had inflicted on him at Ramah, when he fought against Hazael king of Syria. And Ahaziah the son of Jehoram, king of Judah, went down to see Joram the son of Ahab in Jezreel, because he was sick.

Jehu Anointed King of Israel

9 And Elisha the prophet called one of the sons of the prophets, and said to him, "Get yourself ready, take this flask of oil in your hand, and go to Ramoth Gilead. 2Now when you arrive at that place, look there for Jehu the son of Jehoshaphat, the son of Nimshi, and go in and make him rise up from among his associates, and take him to an inner room. 3Then take the flask of oil, and pour *it* on his head, and say, 'Thus says the LORD: "I have anointed you king over Israel." ' Then open the door and flee, and do not delay."

4So the young man, the servant of the prophet, went to Ramoth Gilead. 5And when he arrived, there *were* the captains of the army sitting; and he said, "I have a message for you, Commander."

Jehu said, "For which *one* of us?"

And he said, "For you, Commander." 6Then he arose and went into the house. And he poured the oil on his head, and said to him, "Thus says the LORD God of Israel: 'I have anointed you king over the people of the LORD, over Israel. 7You shall strike down the house of Ahab your master, that I may avenge the blood of My servants the prophets, and the blood of all the servants of the LORD, at the hand of Jezebel. 8For the whole house of Ahab shall perish; and I will cut off from Ahab all the males in Israel, both bond and free. 9So I will make the house of Ahab like the house of Jeroboam the son of Nebat, and like the house of Baasha the son of Ahijah. 10The dogs shall eat Jezebel on the plot *of ground* at Jezreel, and *there shall be* none to bury *her.*' " And he opened the door and fled.

11Then Jehu came out to the servants of his master, and *one* said to him, "*Is* all well? Why did this madman come to you?"

And he said to them, "You know the man and his babble."

12And they said, "A lie! Tell us now."

So he said, "Thus and thus he spoke to me, saying, 'Thus says the LORD: "I have anointed you king over Israel." ' "

13Then each man hastened to take his garment and put *it* under him on the top of the steps; and they blew trumpets, saying, "Jehu is king!"

· · · · · ·

For where Cain got his wife, see Gen. 4:17 comment.

· · · · · ·

Joram of Israel Killed

14So Jehu the son of Jehoshaphat, the son of Nimshi, conspired against Joram. (Now Joram had been defending Ramoth Gilead, he and all Israel, against Hazael king of Syria. 15But King Joram had returned to Jezreel to recover from the wounds which the Syrians had inflicted on him when he fought with Hazael king of Syria.) And Jehu said, "If you are so minded, let no one leave *or* escape from the city to go and tell *it* in Jezreel." 16So Jehu rode in a chariot and went to Jezreel, for Joram was laid up there; and

Ahaziah king of Judah had come down to
see Joram.
[17]Now a watchman stood on the tower
in Jezreel, and he saw the company of
Jehu as he came, and said, "I see a company of men."
And Joram said, "Get a horseman and
send him to meet them, and let him say,
'*Is it* peace?' "
[18]So the horseman went to meet him,
and said, "Thus says the king: '*Is it* peace?' "
And Jehu said, "What have you to do
with peace? Turn around and follow me."
So the watchman reported, saying,
"The messenger went to them, but is not
coming back."
[19]Then he sent out a second horseman
who came to them, and said, "Thus says
the king: '*Is it* peace?' "
And Jehu answered, "What have you
to do with peace? Turn around and follow me."
[20]So the watchman reported, saying,
"He went up to them and is not coming
back; and the driving *is* like the driving of
Jehu the son of Nimshi, for he drives
furiously!"
[21]Then Joram said, "Make ready." And
his chariot was made ready. Then Joram
king of Israel and Ahaziah king of Judah
went out, each in his chariot; and they
went out to meet Jehu, and met him on
the property of Naboth the Jezreelite.
[22]Now it happened, when Joram saw Jehu,
that he said, "*Is it* peace, Jehu?"
So he answered, "What peace, as long
as the harlotries of your mother Jezebel
and her witchcraft *are so* many?"
[23]Then Joram turned around and fled,
and said to Ahaziah, "Treachery, Ahaziah!"
[24]Now Jehu drew his bow with full
strength and shot Jehoram between his
arms; and the arrow came out at his
heart, and he sank down in his chariot.
[25]Then *Jehu* said to Bidkar his captain,
"Pick *him* up, *and* throw him into the
tract of the field of Naboth the Jezreelite;
for remember, when you and I were riding together behind Ahab his father, that
the LORD laid this burden upon him:
[26]'Surely I saw yesterday the blood of
Naboth and the blood of his sons,' says
the LORD, 'and I will repay you in this
plot,' says the LORD. Now therefore, take
and throw him on the plot *of ground,* according to the word of the LORD."

Ahaziah of Judah Killed

[27]But when Ahaziah king of Judah saw
this, he fled by the road to Beth Haggan.[a]
So Jehu pursued him, and said, "Shoot
him also in the chariot." *And they shot him*
at the Ascent of Gur, which is by Ibleam.
Then he fled to Megiddo, and died there.
[28]And his servants carried him in the
chariot to Jerusalem, and buried him in
his tomb with his fathers in the City of
David. [29]In the eleventh year of Joram the
son of Ahab, Ahaziah had become king
over Judah.

Jezebel's Violent Death

[30]Now when Jehu had come to Jezreel,
Jezebel heard *of it;* and she put paint on
her eyes and adorned her head, and
looked through a window. [31]Then, as Jehu
entered at the gate, she said, "*Is it* peace,
Zimri, murderer of your master?"
[32]And he looked up at the window,
and said, "Who *is* on my side? Who?" So
two *or* three eunuchs looked out at him.
[33]Then he said, "Throw her down." So
they threw her down, and *some* of her
blood spattered on the wall and on the
horses; and he trampled her underfoot.
[34]And when he had gone in, he ate and
drank. Then he said, "Go now, see to this
accursed *woman,* and bury her, for she
was a king's daughter." [35]So they went to
bury her, but they found no more of her
than the skull and the feet and the palms
of *her* hands. [36]Therefore they came back

9:27 [a]Literally *The Garden House*

9:33–37 The wicked will get what is coming to them, either in this life or in the next.

and told him. And he said, "This *is* the
word of the LORD, which He spoke by His
servant Elijah the Tishbite, saying, 'On
the plot *of ground* at Jezreel dogs shall eat
the flesh of Jezebel;[a] 37and the corpse of
Jezebel shall be as refuse on the surface of
the field, in the plot at Jezreel, so that
they shall not say, "Here *lies* Jezebel." ' "

Ahab's Seventy Sons Killed

10 Now Ahab had seventy sons in
Samaria. And Jehu wrote and sent
letters to Samaria, to the rulers of Jezreel,[a] to the elders, and to those who
reared Ahab's *sons,* saying:

> 2Now as soon as this letter comes to
> you, since your master's sons *are* with
> you, and you have chariots and
> horses, a fortified city also, and
> weapons, 3choose the best qualified of
> your master's sons, set *him* on his
> father's throne, and fight for your
> master's house.

4But they were exceedingly afraid, and
said, "Look, two kings could not stand
up to him; how then can we stand?" 5And
he who *was* in charge of the house, and
he who *was* in charge of the city, the elders also, and those who reared *the sons,*
sent to Jehu, saying, "We *are* your servants, we will do all you tell us; but we
will not make anyone king. Do *what is*
good in your sight." 6Then he wrote a
second letter to them, saying:

> If you *are* for me and will obey my
> voice, take the heads of the men,
> your master's sons, and come to me
> at Jezreel by this time tomorrow.

Now the king's sons, seventy persons,
were with the great men of the city, *who*
were rearing them. 7So it was, when the
letter came to them, that they took the
king's sons and slaughtered seventy persons, put their heads in baskets and sent
them to him at Jezreel.

8Then a messenger came and told him,
saying, "They have brought the heads of
the king's sons."

And he said, "Lay them in two heaps
at the entrance of the gate until morning."

9So it was, in the morning, that he
went out and stood, and said to all the
people, "You *are* righteous. Indeed I conspired against my master and killed him;
but who killed all these? 10Know now
that nothing shall fall to the earth of the
word of the LORD which the LORD spoke
concerning the house of Ahab; for the
LORD has done what He spoke by His servant Elijah." 11So Jehu killed all who remained of the house of Ahab in Jezreel,
and all his great men and his close acquaintances and his priests, until he left
him none remaining.

Ahaziah's Forty-two Brothers Killed

12And he arose and departed and went
to Samaria. On the way, at Beth Eked[a] of
the Shepherds, 13Jehu met with the brothers of Ahaziah king of Judah, and said,
"Who *are* you?"

So they answered, "We *are* the brothers of Ahaziah; we have come down to
greet the sons of the king and the sons of
the queen mother."

14And he said, "Take them alive!" So
they took them alive, and killed them at
the well of Beth Eked, forty-two men;
and he left none of them.

The Rest of Ahab's Family Killed

15Now when he departed from there,
he met Jehonadab the son of Rechab,
coming to meet him; and he greeted him
and said to him, "Is your heart right, as
my heart *is* toward your heart?"

And Jehonadab answered, "It is."

Jehu said, "If it is, give *me* your hand."
So he gave *him* his hand, and he took him
up to him into the chariot. 16Then he
said, "Come with me, and see my zeal for
the LORD." So they had him ride in his
chariot. 17And when he came to Samaria,

9:36 [a]1 Kings 21:23 10:1 [a]Following Masoretic Text, Syriac, and Targum; Septuagint reads *Samaria;* Vulgate reads *city.*
10:12 [a]Or *The Shearing House*

10:16 *What Produces Zeal for the Lost?*

I was in Israel, traveling by bus on the mountainous road from Jericho to Jerusalem. From my seat at the front right, I was enjoying a view of the mountain across the valley, deep in thought about the story Jesus told of the Good Samaritan. As we approached a sharp left turn, to get around the corner our driver swung the bus as far to the right as possible and then made the turn.

This had the effect of suddenly hanging me over the edge of a 3,000-foot cliff. I was so deep in thought that I wasn't even aware we were turning. *All I knew was that I was a dead man!* I cannot express the horror of that instant. I was certain I was about to die a terrible death.

Just as suddenly as I went over the cliff edge, the bus turned the corner and we were merrily driving along the roadway. No one on the bus knew what I had just been through. I was dead, and suddenly I was alive again. I cannot express the appreciation I had for the fact that I wasn't going to die. Tears of gratitude filled my eyes.

At the age of 22 I had the revelation that I was part of the ultimate statistic: ten out of ten die. *I was going to die and there was nothing I could do about it.* It was just a matter of time. I cannot express the horror of that revelation.

Then, suddenly, on the night of my conversion, my life radically turned a corner and I was sent on the straight and narrow. Jesus Christ, my precious Lord and Savior, saved me from the valley of the shadow of death. He saved me from being damned in hell. *I cannot express the unspeakable gratitude I have for the gift of everlasting life.* But what I cannot put into words, I put into works. I delight to do the will of God—to obey the Great Commission. There is an unending fire of gratitude burning in my soul for the cross of Calvary.

If you lack zeal for the lost, it may be that you have never seen that your own sin makes you worthy of death and damnation. We have been *justly* hung over the valley of the shadow of death, with no hope outside of the mercy of God. This is why it is so beneficial to go through the Ten Commandments. Study their spiritual nature (see Matt. 5:1 comment), and then plead with God for an understanding of what you look like to Him in light of that Law.

See also 2 Chron. 20:15 comment.

he killed all who remained to Ahab in Samaria, till he had destroyed them, according to the word of the LORD which He spoke to Elijah.

Worshipers of Baal Killed

18Then Jehu gathered all the people together, and said to them, "Ahab served Baal a little, Jehu will serve him much.
19Now therefore, call to me all the prophets of Baal, all his servants, and all his priests. Let no one be missing, for I have a great sacrifice for Baal. Whoever is missing shall not live." But Jehu acted deceptively, with the intent of destroying the worshipers of Baal.
20And Jehu said, "Proclaim a solemn assembly for Baal." So they proclaimed *it.*
21Then Jehu sent throughout all Israel; and all the worshipers of Baal came, so that there was not a man left who did not come. So they came into the temple[a] of Baal, and the temple of Baal was full from one end to the other.
22And he said to the one in charge of the wardrobe, "Bring out vestments for all the worshipers of Baal." So he brought out vestments for them.
23Then Jehu and Jehonadab the son of Rechab went into the temple of Baal, and said to the worshipers of Baal, "Search and see that no servants of the LORD are here with you, but only the worshipers of Baal."
24So they went in to offer sacrifices and burnt offerings. Now Jehu had appointed for himself eighty men on the outside, and had said, "*If* any of the men whom I have brought into your hands escapes, *whoever lets him escape, it shall be* his life for the life of the other."

25Now it happened, as soon as he had made an end of offering the burnt offering, that Jehu said to the guard and to the captains, "Go in *and* kill them; let no one come out!" And they killed them with the edge of the sword; then the guards and the officers threw *them* out, and went into the inner room of the temple of Baal.
26And they brought the *sacred* pillars out

10:21 [a]Literally *house,* and so elsewhere in this chapter

of the temple of Baal and burned them.
[27]Then they broke down the *sacred* pillar
of Baal, and tore down the temple of Baal
and made it a refuse dump to this day.
[28]Thus Jehu destroyed Baal from Israel.
[29]However Jehu did not turn away from
the sins of Jeroboam the son of Nebat,
who had made Israel sin, *that is*, from the
golden calves that *were* at Bethel and
Dan. [30]And the LORD said to Jehu, "Because you have done well in doing *what is*
right in My sight, *and* have done to the
house of Ahab all that *was* in My heart,
your sons shall sit on the throne of Israel
to the fourth *generation*." [31]But Jehu took
no heed to walk in the law of the LORD
God of Israel with all his heart; for he did
not depart from the sins of Jeroboam,
who had made Israel sin.

Death of Jehu

[32]In those days the LORD began to cut
off *parts* of Israel; and Hazael conquered
them in all the territory of Israel [33]from
the Jordan eastward: all the land of
Gilead—Gad, Reuben, and Manasseh—
from Aroer, which is by the River Arnon,
including Gilead and Bashan.
[34]Now the rest of the acts of Jehu, all
that he did, and all his might, *are* they
not written in the book of the chronicles
of the kings of Israel? [35]So Jehu rested
with his fathers, and they buried him in
Samaria. Then Jehoahaz his son reigned
in his place. [36]And the period that Jehu
reigned over Israel in Samaria *was* twenty-
eight years.

Athaliah Reigns in Judah

11 When Athaliah the mother of
Ahaziah saw that her son was
dead, she arose and destroyed all the
royal heirs. [2]But Jehosheba, the daughter
of King Joram, sister of Ahaziah, took
Joash the son of Ahaziah, and stole him

THE FUNCTION OF THE LAW

10:31 The unsaved, in their ignorance, think that they can keep God's Law. The Ten Commandments give a sense of comfort to him, until each one is seen in truth. Each Commandment comes as a sharp axe and one by one cuts down the tree of self-righteousness and destroys false hope. (See Mark 10:17.)

"For it is impossible to keep the Law without Christ, though man may, for the sake of honor or property, or from fear of punishment, feign outward holiness. The heart which does not discern God's grace in Christ cannot turn to God nor trust in him; it cannot love his Commandments and delight in them, but rather resists them." *Martin Luther*

away from among the king's sons *who*
were being murdered; and they hid him
and his nurse in the bedroom, from
Athaliah, so that he was not killed. [3]So he
was hidden with her in the house of the
LORD for six years, while Athaliah reigned
over the land.

Joash Crowned King of Judah

[4]In the seventh year Jehoiada sent and
brought the captains of hundreds—of the
bodyguards and the escorts—and brought
them into the house of the LORD to him.
And he made a covenant with them and
took an oath from them in the house of
the LORD, and showed them the king's
son. [5]Then he commanded them, saying,
"This *is* what you shall do: One-third of
you who come on duty on the Sabbath
shall be keeping watch over the king's
house, [6]one-third *shall be* at the gate of
Sur, and one-third at the gate behind the
escorts. You shall keep the watch of the
house, lest it be broken down. [7]The two
contingents of you who go off duty on
the Sabbath shall keep the watch of the
house of the LORD for the king. [8]But you
shall surround the king on all sides, every

10:29 There are certain sins that are darling to us. We must put them to death before they put us to death.

"There are only two kinds of persons: those dead in sin and those dead to sin." *Leonard Ravenhill*

man with his weapons in his hand; and whoever comes within range, let him be put to death. You are to be with the king as he goes out and as he comes in."

[9]So the captains of the hundreds did according to all that Jehoiada the priest commanded. Each of them took his men who were to be on duty on the Sabbath, with those who were going off duty on the Sabbath, and came to Jehoiada the priest. [10]And the priest gave the captains of hundreds the spears and shields which *had belonged* to King David, that were in the temple of the LORD. [11]Then the escorts stood, every man with his weapons in his hand, all around the king, from the right side of the temple to the left side of the temple, by the altar and the house. [12]And he brought out the king's son, put the crown on him, and *gave him* the Testimony;[a] they made him king and anointed him, and they clapped their hands and said, "Long live the king!"

Death of Athaliah

[13]Now when Athaliah heard the noise of the escorts *and* the people, she came to the people *in* the temple of the LORD. [14]When she looked, there was the king standing by a pillar according to custom; and the leaders and the trumpeters were by the king. All the people of the land were rejoicing and blowing trumpets. So Athaliah tore her clothes and cried out, "Treason! Treason!"

[15]And Jehoiada the priest commanded the captains of the hundreds, the officers of the army, and said to them, "Take her outside under guard, and slay with the sword whoever follows her." For the priest had said, "Do not let her be killed in the house of the LORD." [16]So they seized her; and she went by way of the horses' entrance *into* the king's house, and there she was killed.

[17]Then Jehoiada made a covenant between the LORD, the king, and the people, that they should be the LORD's people, and *also* between the king and the people. [18]And all the people of the land went to the temple of Baal, and tore it down. They thoroughly broke in pieces its altars and images, and killed Mattan the priest of Baal before the altars. And the priest appointed officers over the house of the LORD. [19]Then he took the captains of hundreds, the bodyguards, the escorts, and all the people of the land; and they brought the king down from the house of the LORD, and went by way of the gate of the escorts to the king's house. Then he sat on the throne of the kings. [20]So all the people of the land rejoiced; and the city was quiet, for they had slain Athaliah with the sword *in* the king's house. [21]Jehoash *was* seven years old when he became king.

Jehoash Repairs the Temple

12 In the seventh year of Jehu, Jehoash[a] became king, and he reigned forty years in Jerusalem. His mother's name *was* Zibiah of Beersheba. [2]Jehoash did *what was* right in the sight of the LORD all the days in which Jehoiada the priest instructed him. [3]But the high places were not taken away; the people still sacrificed and burned incense on the high places.

[4]And Jehoash said to the priests, "All the money of the dedicated gifts that are brought into the house of the LORD—each man's census money, each man's assessment money[a]—*and* all the money that a man purposes in his heart to bring into the house of the LORD, [5]let the priests take *it* themselves, each from his constituency; and let them repair the damages of the temple, wherever any dilapidation is found."

[6]Now it was so, by the twenty-third

11:12 [a]That is, the Law (compare Exodus 25:16, 21 and Deuteronomy 31:9) **12:1** [a]Spelled *Joash* in 11:2ff **12:4** [a]Compare Leviticus 27:2ff

11:18 Make it your aim to destroy idols. Never be deceived into believing that God is anything other than the One who is revealed in Holy Scripture.

year of King Jehoash, *that* the priests had
not repaired the damages of the temple.
7So King Jehoash called Jehoiada the
priest and the *other* priests, and said to
them, "Why have you not repaired the
damages of the temple? Now therefore,
do not take *more* money from your constituency, but deliver it for repairing the
damages of the temple." 8And the priests
agreed that they would neither receive
more money from the people, nor repair
the damages of the temple.

9Then Jehoiada the priest took a chest,
bored a hole in its lid, and set it beside
the altar, on the right side as one comes
into the house of the LORD; and the
priests who kept the door put there all
the money brought into the house of the
LORD. 10So it was, whenever they saw that
there was much money in the chest, that
the king's scribe and the high priest came
up and put it in bags, and counted the
money that was found in the house of the
LORD. 11Then they gave the money, which
had been apportioned, into the hands of
those who did the work, who had the
oversight of the house of the LORD; and
they paid it out to the carpenters and
builders who worked on the house of the
LORD, 12and to masons and stonecutters,
and for buying timber and hewn stone, to
repair the damage of the house of the
LORD, and for all that was paid out to repair the temple. 13However there were
not made for the house of the LORD basins
of silver, trimmers, sprinkling-bowls,
trumpets, any articles of gold or articles
of silver, from the money brought into
the house of the LORD. 14But they gave
that to the workmen, and they repaired
the house of the LORD with it. 15Moreover
they did not require an account from the
men into whose hand they delivered the
money to be paid to workmen, for they
dealt faithfully. 16The money from the
trespass offerings and the money from
the sin offerings was not brought into the
house of the LORD. It belonged to the
priests.

Hazael Threatens Jerusalem

17Hazael king of Syria went up and
fought against Gath, and took it; then
Hazael set his face to go up to Jerusalem.
18And Jehoash king of Judah took all the
sacred things that his fathers, Jehoshaphat and Jehoram and Ahaziah, kings of
Judah, had dedicated, and his own sacred
things, and all the gold found in the treasuries of the house of the LORD and in the
king's house, and sent *them* to Hazael
king of Syria. Then he went away from
Jerusalem.

Death of Joash

19Now the rest of the acts of Joash,[a]
and all that he did, *are* they not written in
the book of the chronicles of the kings of
Judah?

20And his servants arose and formed a
conspiracy, and killed Joash in the house
of the Millo,[a] which goes down to Silla.
21For Jozachar[a] the son of Shimeath and
Jehozabad the son of Shomer,[b] his servants, struck him. So he died, and they
buried him with his fathers in the City of
David. Then Amaziah his son reigned in
his place.

Jehoahaz Reigns in Israel

13 In the twenty-third year of Joash[a]
the son of Ahaziah, king of Judah,
Jehoahaz the son of Jehu became king
over Israel in Samaria, *and reigned* seventeen years. 2And he did evil in the sight of

12:19 [a]Spelled *Jehoash* in 12:1ff 12:20 [a]Literally *The Landfill*
12:21 [a]Called *Zabad* in 2 Chronicles 24:26 [b]Called *Shimrith* in
2 Chronicles 24:26 13:1 [a]Spelled *Jehoash* in 12:1ff

12:5 Perhaps the greatest breach in the contemporary Church is the preaching of a gospel that has allowed multitudes to enter the church building, but not to enter the Body of Christ. Multitudes have "asked Jesus into their heart," and have been assured that they have passed from death to life, when in truth they are strangers to genuine repentance. Repair the breach by restoring the use of the Law of God to bring the knowledge of sin. Preach the narrow gate and the difficult way (see Matt. 7:13,14).

the LORD, and followed the sins of Jeroboam the son of Nebat, who had made Israel sin. He did not depart from them.
[3]Then the anger of the LORD was aroused against Israel, and He delivered them into the hand of Hazael king of Syria, and into the hand of Ben-Hadad the son of Hazael, all *their* days. [4]So Jehoahaz pleaded with the LORD, and the LORD listened to him; for He saw the oppression of Israel, because the king of Syria oppressed them. [5]Then the LORD gave Israel a deliverer, so that they escaped from under the hand of the Syrians; and the children of Israel dwelt in their tents as before. [6]Nevertheless they did not depart from the sins of the house of Jeroboam, who had made Israel sin, *but* walked in them; and the wooden image[a] also remained in Samaria. [7]For He left of the army of Jehoahaz only fifty horsemen, ten chariots, and ten thousand foot soldiers; for the king of Syria had destroyed them and made them like the dust at threshing.
[8]Now the rest of the acts of Jehoahaz, all that he did, and his might, *are* they not written in the book of the chronicles of the kings of Israel? [9]So Jehoahaz rested with his fathers, and they buried him in Samaria. Then Joash his son reigned in his place.

Jehoash Reigns in Israel

[10]In the thirty-seventh year of Joash king of Judah, Jehoash[a] the son of Jehoahaz became king over Israel in Samaria, *and reigned* sixteen years. [11]And he did evil in the sight of the LORD. He did not depart from all the sins of Jeroboam the son of Nebat, who made Israel sin, *but* walked in them.
[12]Now the rest of the acts of Joash, all that he did, and his might with which he fought against Amaziah king of Judah, *are* they not written in the book of the chronicles of the kings of Israel? [13]So Joash rested with his fathers. Then Jeroboam sat on his throne. And Joash was buried in Samaria with the kings of Israel.

Death of Elisha

[14]Elisha had become sick with the illness of which he would die. Then Joash the king of Israel came down to him, and wept over his face, and said, "O my father, my father, the chariots of Israel and their horsemen!"
[15]And Elisha said to him, "Take a bow and some arrows." So he took himself a bow and some arrows. [16]Then he said to the king of Israel, "Put your hand on the bow." So he put his hand *on it,* and Elisha put his hands on the king's hands. [17]And he said, "Open the east window"; and he opened *it.* Then Elisha said, "Shoot"; and he shot. And he said, "The arrow of the LORD's deliverance and the arrow of deliverance from Syria; for you must strike the Syrians at Aphek till you have destroyed *them.*" [18]Then he said, "Take the arrows"; so he took *them.* And he said to the king of Israel, "Strike the ground"; so he struck three times, and stopped. [19]And the man of God was angry with him, and said, "You should have struck five or six times; then you would have struck Syria till you had destroyed *it!* But now you will strike Syria *only* three times."

13:6 [a]Hebrew *Asherah,* a Canaanite goddess 13:10 [a]Spelled *Joash* in verse 9

13:2 Jeroboam made two golden calves in direct violation of God's Law, and told the people to worship them (see 1 Kings 12:25–33). *John Wesley* spoke of this sin as "an occasion of great wickedness, not only of idolatry, which is called sin by way of eminency; nor only of the worship of the calves, wherein they pretended to worship the true God; but also of the worship of Baal, and of the utter desertion of the true God; and of all sorts of impiety."

13:11 Notice how the sin of Jeroboam (see v. 2) led to the downfall of many kings. Idolatry is a curse that is passed from generation to generation. Flee from any manmade concept of God. (See also 2 Kings 14:24; 15:9,18,24,28.)

[20]Then Elisha died, and they buried him. And the *raiding* bands from Moab invaded the land in the spring of the year. [21]So it was, as they were burying a man, that suddenly they spied a band *of raiders;* and they put the man in the tomb of Elisha; and when the man was let down and touched the bones of Elisha, he revived and stood on his feet.

Israel Recaptures Cities from Syria

[22]And Hazael king of Syria oppressed Israel all the days of Jehoahaz. [23]But the LORD was gracious to them, had compassion on them, and regarded them, because of His covenant with Abraham, Isaac, and Jacob, and would not yet destroy them or cast them from His presence.

[24]Now Hazael king of Syria died. Then Ben-Hadad his son reigned in his place. [25]And Jehoash[a] the son of Jehoahaz recaptured from the hand of Ben-Hadad, the son of Hazael, the cities which he had taken out of the hand of Jehoahaz his father by war. Three times Joash defeated him and recaptured the cities of Israel.

Amaziah Reigns in Judah

14 In the second year of Joash the son of Jehoahaz, king of Israel, Amaziah the son of Joash, king of Judah, became king. [2]He was twenty-five years old when he became king, and he reigned twenty-nine years in Jerusalem. His mother's name was Jehoaddan of Jerusalem. [3]And he did *what was* right in the sight of the LORD, yet not like his father David; he did everything as his father Joash had done. [4]However the high places were not taken away, and the people still sacrificed and burned incense on the high places.

[5]Now it happened, as soon as the kingdom was established in his hand, that he executed his servants who had murdered his father the king. [6]But the children of the murderers he did not execute, according to what is written in the Book of the Law of Moses, in which the LORD commanded, saying, "Fathers shall not be put to death for their children, nor shall children be put to death for their fathers; but a person shall be put to death for his own sin."[a]

[7]He killed ten thousand Edomites in the Valley of Salt, and took Sela by war, and called its name Joktheel to this day.

[8]Then Amaziah sent messengers to Jehoash[a] the son of Jehoahaz, the son of Jehu, king of Israel, saying, "Come, let us face one another *in battle.*" [9]And Jehoash king of Israel sent to Amaziah king of Judah, saying, "The thistle that *was* in Lebanon sent to the cedar that *was* in Lebanon, saying, 'Give your daughter to my son as wife'; and a wild beast that *was* in Lebanon passed by and trampled the thistle. [10]You have indeed defeated Edom, and your heart has lifted you up. Glory *in that,* and stay at home; for why should you meddle with trouble so that you fall—you and Judah with you?"

[11]But Amaziah would not heed. Therefore Jehoash king of Israel went out; so he and Amaziah king of Judah faced one another at Beth Shemesh, which *belongs* to Judah. [12]And Judah was defeated by Israel, and every man fled to his tent. [13]Then Jehoash king of Israel captured Amaziah king of Judah, the son of Jehoash, the son of Ahaziah, at Beth Shemesh; and he went to Jerusalem, and broke down the wall of Jerusalem from the Gate of Ephraim to the Corner Gate—four hundred cubits. [14]And he took all the gold and silver, all the articles

13:25 [a]Spelled *Joash* in verses 12–14, 25 14:6 [a]Deuteronomy 24:16 14:8 [a]Spelled *Joash* in 13:12ff and 2 Chronicles 25:17ff

13:21 May our lives still be instrumental in reaching those who are spiritually dead, even after we go to be with the Lord. We can do this by living a godly life, by kind words and deeds, by a verbal witness of the gospel, and by that which we put in writing. These are testimonies that can be remembered by others for many years.

that were found in the house of the LORD and in the treasuries of the king's house, and hostages, and returned to Samaria.

[15]Now the rest of the acts of Jehoash which he did—his might, and how he fought with Amaziah king of Judah—*are* they not written in the book of the chronicles of the kings of Israel? [16]So Jehoash rested with his fathers, and was buried in Samaria with the kings of Israel. Then Jeroboam his son reigned in his place.

[17]Amaziah the son of Joash, king of Judah, lived fifteen years after the death of Jehoash the son of Jehoahaz, king of Israel. [18]Now the rest of the acts of Amaziah, *are* they not written in the book of the chronicles of the kings of Judah? [19]And they formed a conspiracy against him in Jerusalem, and he fled to Lachish; but they sent after him to Lachish and killed him there. [20]Then they brought him on horses, and he was buried at Jerusalem with his fathers in the City of David.

[21]And all the people of Judah took Azariah,[a] who *was* sixteen years old, and made him king instead of his father Amaziah. [22]He built Elath and restored it to Judah, after the king rested with his fathers.

Jeroboam II Reigns in Israel

[23]In the fifteenth year of Amaziah the son of Joash, king of Judah, Jeroboam the son of Joash, king of Israel, became king in Samaria, *and reigned* forty-one years. [24]And he did evil in the sight of the LORD; he did not depart from all the sins of Jeroboam the son of Nebat, who had made Israel sin. [25]He restored the territory of Israel from the entrance of Hamath to the Sea of the Arabah, according to the word of the LORD God of Israel, which He had spoken through His servant Jonah the son of Amittai, the prophet who *was* from Gath Hepher. [26]For the LORD saw *that* the affliction of Israel *was* very bitter; and whether bond or free, there was no helper for Israel. [27]And the LORD did not say that He would blot out the name of Israel from under heaven; but He saved them by the hand of Jeroboam the son of Joash.

[28]Now the rest of the acts of Jeroboam, and all that he did—his might, how he made war, and how he recaptured for Israel, from Damascus and Hamath, *what had belonged* to Judah—*are* they not written in the book of the chronicles of the kings of Israel? [29]So Jeroboam rested with his fathers, the kings of Israel. Then Zechariah his son reigned in his place.

Azariah Reigns in Judah

15 In the twenty-seventh year of Jeroboam king of Israel, Azariah the son of Amaziah, king of Judah, became king. [2]He was sixteen years old when he became king, and he reigned fifty-two years in Jerusalem. His mother's name *was* Jecholiah of Jerusalem. [3]And he did *what was* right in the sight of the LORD, according to all that his father Amaziah had done, [4]except that the high places were not removed; the people still sacrificed and burned incense on the high places. [5]Then the LORD struck the king, so that he was a leper until the day of his death; so he dwelt in an isolated house. And Jotham the king's son *was* over the *royal* house, judging the people of the land.

[6]Now the rest of the acts of Azariah, and all that he did, *are* they not written in the book of the chronicles of the kings of Judah? [7]So Azariah rested with his fathers, and they buried him with his fathers in the City of David. Then Jotham his son reigned in his place.

Zechariah Reigns in Israel

[8]In the thirty-eighth year of Azariah king of Judah, Zechariah the son of Jeroboam reigned over Israel in Samaria six months. [9]And he did evil in the sight of the LORD, as his fathers had done; he did not depart from the sins of Jeroboam the son of Nebat, who had made Israel sin. [10]Then Shallum the son of Jabesh conspired against him, and struck and killed him in front of the people; and he reigned in his place.

14:21 [a]Called *Uzziah* in 2 Chronicles 26:1ff, Isaiah 6:1, and elsewhere

"Being filled with the Spirit is simply this—having my whole personality yielded to His power. When the whole soul is yielded to the Holy Spirit, God Himself will fill it."

Andrew Murray

11Now the rest of the acts of Zechariah, indeed they *are* written in the book
of the chronicles of the kings of Israel.
12This *was* the word of the LORD which
He spoke to Jehu, saying, "Your sons shall
sit on the throne of Israel to the fourth
generation."[a] And so it was.

Shallum Reigns in Israel

13Shallum the son of Jabesh became
king in the thirty-ninth year of Uzziah[a]
king of Judah; and he reigned a full month
in Samaria. 14For Menahem the son of
Gadi went up from Tirzah, came to
Samaria, and struck Shallum the son of
Jabesh in Samaria and killed him; and he
reigned in his place.
15Now the rest of the acts of Shallum,
and the conspiracy which he led, indeed
they *are* written in the book of the chronicles of the kings of Israel. 16Then from
Tirzah, Menahem attacked Tiphsah, all
who *were* there, and its territory. Because
they did not surrender, therefore he attacked *it.* All the women there who were
with child he ripped open.

Menahem Reigns in Israel

17In the thirty-ninth year of Azariah
king of Judah, Menahem the son of Gadi
became king over Israel, *and reigned* ten
years in Samaria. 18And he did evil in the
sight of the LORD; he did not depart all
his days from the sins of Jeroboam the
son of Nebat, who had made Israel sin.
19Pul[a] king of Assyria came against the
land; and Menahem gave Pul a thousand
talents of silver, that his hand might be
with him to strengthen the kingdom under his control. 20And Menahem exacted
the money from Israel, from all the very
wealthy, from each man fifty shekels of
silver, to give to the king of Assyria. So
the king of Assyria turned back, and did
not stay there in the land.
21Now the rest of the acts of Menahem, and all that he did, *are* they not
written in the book of the chronicles of
the kings of Israel? 22So Menahem rested
with his fathers. Then Pekahiah his son
reigned in his place.

Pekahiah Reigns in Israel

23In the fiftieth year of Azariah king of
Judah, Pekahiah the son of Menahem became king over Israel in Samaria, *and
reigned* two years. 24And he did evil in the
sight of the LORD; he did not depart from
the sins of Jeroboam the son of Nebat,
who had made Israel sin. 25Then Pekah
the son of Remaliah, an officer of his,
conspired against him and killed him in
Samaria, in the citadel of the king's
house, along with Argob and Arieh; and
with him were fifty men of Gilead. He
killed him and reigned in his place.
26Now the rest of the acts of Pekahiah,
and all that he did, indeed they *are* written in the book of the chronicles of the
kings of Israel.

Pekah Reigns in Israel

27In the fifty-second year of Azariah
king of Judah, Pekah the son of Remaliah

15:12 [a]2 Kings 10:30 15:13 [a]Called *Azariah* in 14:21ff and 15:1ff 15:19 [a]That is, Tiglath-Pileser III (compare verse 29)

became king over Israel in Samaria, *and reigned* twenty years. 28And he did evil in the sight of the LORD; he did not depart from the sins of Jeroboam the son of Nebat, who had made Israel sin. 29In the days of Pekah king of Israel, Tiglath-Pileser king of Assyria came and took Ijon, Abel Beth Maachah, Janoah, Kedesh, Hazor, Gilead, and Galilee, all the land of Naphtali; and he carried them captive to Assyria. 30Then Hoshea the son of Elah led a conspiracy against Pekah the son of Remaliah, and struck and killed him; so he reigned in his place in the twentieth year of Jotham the son of Uzziah.

31Now the rest of the acts of Pekah, and all that he did, indeed they *are* written in the book of the chronicles of the kings of Israel.

Jotham Reigns in Judah

32In the second year of Pekah the son of Remaliah, king of Israel, Jotham the son of Uzziah, king of Judah, began to reign. 33He was twenty-five years old when he became king, and he reigned sixteen years in Jerusalem. His mother's name *was* Jerusha[a] the daughter of Zadok. 34And he did *what was* right in the sight of the LORD; he did according to all that his father Uzziah had done. 35However the high places were not removed; the people still sacrificed and burned incense on the high places. He built the Upper Gate of the house of the LORD.

36Now the rest of the acts of Jotham, and all that he did, *are* they not written in the book of the chronicles of the kings of Judah? 37In those days the LORD began to send Rezin king of Syria and Pekah the son of Remaliah against Judah. 38So Jotham rested with his fathers, and was buried with his fathers in the City of David his father. Then Ahaz his son reigned in his place.

Ahaz Reigns in Judah

16 In the seventeenth year of Pekah the son of Remaliah, Ahaz the son of Jotham, king of Judah, began to reign. 2Ahaz *was* twenty years old when he became king, and he reigned sixteen years in Jerusalem; and he did not do *what was* right in the sight of the LORD his God, as his father David *had done.* 3But he walked in the way of the kings of Israel; indeed he made his son pass through the fire, according to the abominations of the nations whom the LORD had cast out from before the children of Israel. 4And he sacrificed and burned incense on the high places, on the hills, and under every green tree.

5Then Rezin king of Syria and Pekah the son of Remaliah, king of Israel, came up to Jerusalem to *make* war; and they besieged Ahaz but could not overcome *him.* 6At that time Rezin king of Syria captured Elath for Syria, and drove the men of Judah from Elath. Then the Edomites[a] went to Elath, and dwell there to this day.

7So Ahaz sent messengers to Tiglath-Pileser king of Assyria, saying, "I *am* your servant and your son. Come up and save me from the hand of the king of Syria and from the hand of the king of Israel, who rise up against me." 8And Ahaz took the silver and gold that was found in the house of the LORD, and in the treasuries of the king's house, and sent *it as* a present to the king of Assyria. 9So the king of Assyria heeded him; for the king of Assyria went up against Damascus and took it, carried *its people* captive to Kir, and killed Rezin.

10Now King Ahaz went to Damascus to meet Tiglath-Pileser king of Assyria, and saw an altar that *was* at Damascus; and King Ahaz sent to Urijah the priest the design of the altar and its pattern, according to all its workmanship. 11Then Urijah the priest built an altar according to all that King Ahaz had sent from Damascus. So Urijah the priest made *it* before King Ahaz came back from Damascus. 12And when the king came back from Damascus, the king saw the altar; and the

15:33 [a]Spelled *Jerushah* in 2 Chronicles 27:1 16:6 [a]Some ancient authorities read *Syrians.*

king approached the altar and made offerings on it. 13So he burned his burnt offering and his grain offering; and he
poured his drink offering and sprinkled
the blood of his peace offerings on the altar. 14He also brought the bronze altar
which *was* before the LORD, from the
front of the temple—from between the
new altar and the house of the LORD—and
put it on the north side of the *new* altar.
15Then King Ahaz commanded Urijah
the priest, saying, "On the great *new* altar
burn the morning burnt offering, the
evening grain offering, the king's burnt
sacrifice, and his grain offering, with the
burnt offering of all the people of the
land, their grain offering, and their drink
offerings; and sprinkle on it all the blood
of the burnt offering and all the blood of
the sacrifice. And the bronze altar shall
be for me to inquire *by.*" 16Thus did Urijah
the priest, according to all that King Ahaz
commanded.

17And King Ahaz cut off the panels of
the carts, and removed the lavers from
them; and he took down the Sea from the
bronze oxen that *were* under it, and put it
on a pavement of stones. 18Also he removed the Sabbath pavilion which they
had built in the temple, and he removed
the king's outer entrance from the house of
the LORD, on account of the king of Assyria.

19Now the rest of the acts of Ahaz which
he did, *are* they not written in the book
of the chronicles of the kings of Judah?
20So Ahaz rested with his fathers, and
was buried with his fathers in the City of
David. Then Hezekiah his son reigned in
his place.

Hoshea Reigns in Israel

17 In the twelfth year of Ahaz king of
Judah, Hoshea the son of Elah became king of Israel in Samaria, *and he
reigned* nine years. 2And he did evil in the
sight of the LORD, but not as the kings of
Israel who were before him. 3Shalman-
eser king of Assyria came up against him;
and Hoshea became his vassal, and paid
him tribute money. 4And the king of Assyria uncovered a conspiracy by Hoshea;
for he had sent messengers to So, king of
Egypt, and brought no tribute to the king
of Assyria, as *he had done* year by year.
Therefore the king of Assyria shut him
up, and bound him in prison.

Israel Carried Captive to Assyria

5Now the king of Assyria went throughout all the land, and went up to Samaria
and besieged it for three years. 6In the
ninth year of Hoshea, the king of Assyria
took Samaria and carried Israel away to
Assyria, and placed them in Halah and by
the Habor, the River of Gozan, and in the
cities of the Medes.

Every truth leads towards holiness; every error of doctrine, directly or indirectly, leads to sin.

CHARLES SPURGEON

7For so it was that the children of Israel had sinned against the LORD their
God, who had brought them up out of
the land of Egypt, from under the hand of
Pharaoh king of Egypt; and they had
feared other gods, 8and had walked in the
statutes of the nations whom the LORD
had cast out from before the children of
Israel, and of the kings of Israel, which
they had made. 9Also the children of Israel secretly did against the LORD their
God things that *were* not right, and they
built for themselves high places in all
their cities, from watchtower to fortified
city. 10They set up for themselves *sacred*
pillars and wooden images[a] on every high
hill and under every green tree. 11There
they burned incense on all the high
places, like the nations whom the LORD
had carried away before them; and they
did wicked things to provoke the LORD to
anger, 12for they served idols, of which
the LORD had said to them, "You shall not
do this thing."

13Yet the LORD testified against Israel

17:10 [a]Hebrew *Asherim,* Canaanite deities

and against Judah, by all of His prophets,
every seer, saying, "Turn from your evil
ways, and keep My commandments *and*
My statutes, according to all the law
which I commanded your fathers, and
which I sent to you by My servants the
prophets." 14Nevertheless they would not
hear, but stiffened their necks, like the
necks of their fathers, who did not believe in the LORD their God. 15And they
rejected His statutes and His covenant
that He had made with their fathers, and
His testimonies which He had testified
against them; they followed idols, became idolaters, and *went* after the nations
who *were* all around them, *concerning*
whom the LORD had charged them that
they should not do like them. 16So they
left all the commandments of the LORD
their God, made for themselves a molded
image *and* two calves, made a wooden
image and worshiped all the host of heav-
en, and served Baal. 17And they caused
their sons and daughters to pass through
the fire, practiced witchcraft and soothsaying, and sold themselves to do evil in
the sight of the LORD, to provoke Him to
anger. 18Therefore the LORD was very angry
with Israel, and removed them from His
sight; there was none left but the tribe of
Judah alone.

19Also Judah did not keep the commandments of the LORD their God, but
walked in the statutes of Israel which
they made. 20And the LORD rejected all
the descendants of Israel, afflicted them,
and delivered them into the hand of
plunderers, until He had cast them from
His sight. 21For He tore Israel from the
house of David, and they made Jeroboam
the son of Nebat king. Then Jeroboam
drove Israel from following the LORD, and
made them commit a great sin. 22For the
children of Israel walked in all the sins of
Jeroboam which he did; they did not depart from them, 23until the LORD removed
Israel out of His sight, as He had said by
all His servants the prophets. So Israel was
carried away from their own land to Assyria, *as it is* to this day.

Assyria Resettles Samaria

24Then the king of Assyria brought
people from Babylon, Cuthah, Ava, Hamath, and from Sepharvaim, and placed
them in the cities of Samaria instead of
the children of Israel; and they took possession of Samaria and dwelt in its cities.
25And it was so, at the beginning of their
dwelling there, *that* they did not fear the
LORD; therefore the LORD sent lions among
them, which killed *some* of them. 26So
they spoke to the king of Assyria, saying,
"The nations whom you have removed
and placed in the cities of Samaria do not
know the rituals of the God of the land;
therefore He has sent lions among them,
and indeed, they are killing them because
they do not know the rituals of the God
of the land." 27Then the king of Assyria
commanded, saying, "Send there one of
the priests whom you brought from there;
let him go and dwell there, and let him
teach them the rituals of the God of the
land." 28Then one of the priests whom
they had carried away from Samaria came
and dwelt in Bethel, and taught them
how they should fear the LORD.

29However every nation continued to
make gods of its own, and put *them* in the
shrines on the high places which the
Samaritans had made, *every* nation in the
cities where they dwelt. 30The men of
Babylon made Succoth Benoth, the men
of Cuth made Nergal, the men of Hamath
made Ashima, 31and the Avites made
Nibhaz and Tartak; and the Sepharvites
burned their children in fire to Adrammelech and Anammelech, the gods of
Sepharvaim. 32So they feared the LORD,
and from every class they appointed for
themselves priests of the high places,
who sacrificed for them in the shrines of
the high places. 33They feared the LORD,
yet served their own gods—according to
the rituals of the nations from among
whom they were carried away.

34To this day they continue practicing
the former rituals; they do not fear the
LORD, nor do they follow their statutes or
their ordinances, or the law and com-

mandment which the LORD had commanded the children of Jacob, whom He named Israel, [35]with whom the LORD had made a covenant and charged them, saying: "You shall not fear other gods, nor bow down to them nor serve them nor sacrifice to them; [36]but the LORD, who brought you up from the land of Egypt with great power and an outstretched arm, Him you shall fear, Him you shall worship, and to Him you shall offer sacrifice. [37]And the statutes, the ordinances, the law, and the commandment which He wrote for you, you shall be careful to observe forever; you shall not fear other gods. [38]And the covenant that I have made with you, you shall not forget, nor shall you fear other gods. [39]But the LORD your God you shall fear; and He will deliver you from the hand of all your enemies." [40]However they did not obey, but they followed their former rituals. [41]So these nations feared the LORD, yet served their carved images; also their children and their children's children have continued doing as their fathers did, even to this day.

Hezekiah Reigns in Judah

18 Now it came to pass in the third year of Hoshea the son of Elah, king of Israel, *that* Hezekiah the son of Ahaz, king of Judah, began to reign. [2]He was twenty-five years old when he became king, and he reigned twenty-nine years in Jerusalem. His mother's name *was* Abi[a] the daughter of Zechariah. [3]And he did *what was* right in the sight of the LORD, according to all that his father David had done.

[4]He removed the high places and broke the *sacred* pillars, cut down the wooden image[a] and broke in pieces the bronze serpent that Moses had made; for until those days the children of Israel burned incense to it, and called it Nehushtan.[b] [5]He trusted in the LORD God of Israel, so that after him was none like him among all the kings of Judah, nor who were before him. [6]For he held fast to the LORD; he did not depart from following Him, but kept His commandments, which the LORD had commanded Moses. [7]The LORD was with him; he prospered wherever he went. And he rebelled against the king of Assyria and did not serve him. [8]He subdued the Philistines, as far as Gaza and its territory, from watchtower to fortified city.

[9]Now it came to pass in the fourth year of King Hezekiah, which *was* the seventh year of Hoshea the son of Elah, king of Israel, *that* Shalmaneser king of Assyria came up against Samaria and besieged it. [10]And at the end of three years they took it. In the sixth year of Hezekiah, that *is,* the ninth year of Hoshea king of Israel, Samaria was taken. [11]Then the king of Assyria carried Israel away captive to Assyria, and put them in Halah and by the Habor, the River of Gozan, and in the cities of the Medes, [12]because they did not obey the voice of the LORD their God, but transgressed His covenant *and* all that Moses the servant of the LORD had commanded; and they would neither hear nor do *them.*

18:2 [a]Called *Abijah* in 2 Chronicles 29:1ff 18:4 [a]Hebrew *Asherah,* a Canaanite goddess [b]Literally *Bronze Thing*

17:41 "Though these strangers feared Jehovah, and were willing to learn the way of his worship, yet *they stuck to their old gods*. 'Ah,' said the Babylonian, 'I listen respectfully to what you have to say of this God, of the land; but Succoth-benoth for me; when I go home I shall offer sacrifice to him.' The men of Cuthah said, 'Verily this is good doctrine concerning the God of Israel; but the god of our fathers was Nergal, and to him will we cleave'; and the Sepharvites, though they wished to hear of the pure and holy Jehovah, and therefore learned from his law the command, 'Thou shalt not kill,' yet still they passed their children through the fire to Moloch, and did not cease from that most cruel of all religious rites. Thus you see that this mingle-mangle religion left the people practically where they were: whatever their fear might be, their customs and practices remained the same." *Charles Spurgeon*

18:5–7 Trust in the Lord with all of your heart so that your evangelistic endeavors will prosper.

13And in the fourteenth year of King
Hezekiah, Sennacherib king of Assyria
came up against all the fortified cities of
Judah and took them. 14Then Hezekiah
king of Judah sent to the king of Assyria
at Lachish, saying, "I have done wrong;
turn away from me; whatever you impose
on me I will pay." And the king of Assyria
assessed Hezekiah king of Judah three
hundred talents of silver and thirty talents of gold. 15So Hezekiah gave *him* all
the silver that was found in the house of
the LORD and in the treasuries of the
king's house. 16At that time Hezekiah
stripped *the gold from* the doors of the
temple of the LORD, and *from* the pillars
which Hezekiah king of Judah had overlaid, and gave it to the king of Assyria.

Sennacherib Boasts Against the Lord

17Then the king of Assyria sent *the*
Tartan,[a] *the* Rabsaris,[b] *and the* Rabshakeh[c]
from Lachish, with a great army against
Jerusalem, to King Hezekiah. And they
went up and came to Jerusalem. When
they had come up, they went and stood
by the aqueduct from the upper pool,
which *was* on the highway to the Fuller's
Field. 18And when they had called to the
king, Eliakim the son of Hilkiah, who *was*
over the household, Shebna the scribe,
and Joah the son of Asaph, the recorder,
came out to them. 19Then *the* Rabshakeh
said to them, "Say now to Hezekiah, 'Thus
says the great king, the king of Assyria:
"What confidence *is* this in which you
trust? 20You speak of *having* plans and
power for war; but *they are* mere words.
And in whom do you trust, that you rebel
against me? 21Now look! You are trusting
in the staff of this broken reed, Egypt, on
which if a man leans, it will go into his
hand and pierce it. So *is* Pharaoh king of
Egypt to all who trust in him. 22But if you
say to me, 'We trust in the LORD our God,'
is it not He whose high places and whose
altars Hezekiah has taken away, and said
to Judah and Jerusalem, 'You shall worship before this altar in Jerusalem'?" '
23Now therefore, I urge you, give a pledge
to my master the king of Assyria, and I
will give you two thousand horses—if
you are able on your part to put riders on
them! 24How then will you repel one captain of the least of my master's servants,
and put your trust in Egypt for chariots
and horsemen? 25Have I now come up
without the LORD against this place to destroy it? The LORD said to me, 'Go up
against this land, and destroy it.' "

26Then Eliakim the son of Hilkiah,
Shebna, and Joah said to *the* Rabshakeh,
"Please speak to your servants in Aramaic, for we understand *it;* and do not
speak to us in Hebrew[a] in the hearing of
the people who *are* on the wall."

27But *the* Rabshakeh said to them,
"Has my master sent me to your master
and to you to speak these words, and not
to the men who sit on the wall, who will
eat and drink their own waste with you?"

28Then *the* Rabshakeh stood and
called out with a loud voice in Hebrew,
and spoke, saying, "Hear the word of the
great king, the king of Assyria! 29Thus
says the king: 'Do not let Hezekiah deceive you, for he shall not be able to deliver you from his hand; 30nor let Hezekiah make you trust in the LORD, saying,
"The LORD will surely deliver us; this city
shall not be given into the hand of the
king of Assyria." ' 31Do not listen to Hezekiah; for thus says the king of Assyria:
'Make *peace* with me by a present and
come out to me; and every one of you eat
from his own vine and every one from his
own fig tree, and every one of you drink
the waters of his own cistern; 32until I
come and take you away to a land like

18:17 [a]A title, probably *Commander in Chief* [b]A title, probably *Chief Officer* [c]A title, probably *Chief of Staff* or *Governor*
18:26 [a]Literally *Judean*

18:19–36 Here is insight into the wiles of the devil. See Eph. 6:11–18 for information on how to overcome him who seeks to undermine our faith in God.

your own land, a land of grain and new
wine, a land of bread and vineyards, a
land of olive groves and honey, that you
may live and not die. But do not listen to
Hezekiah, lest he persuade you, saying,
"The LORD will deliver us." 33Has any of
the gods of the nations at all delivered its
land from the hand of the king of Assyria? 34Where *are* the gods of Hamath
and Arpad? Where *are* the gods of Sepharvaim and Hena and Ivah? Indeed, have
they delivered Samaria from my hand?
35Who among all the gods of the lands
have delivered their countries from my
hand, that the LORD should deliver Jerusalem from my hand?' "

36But the people held their peace and
answered him not a word; for the king's
commandment was, "Do not answer him."
37Then Eliakim the son of Hilkiah, who
was over the household, Shebna the scribe,
and Joah the son of Asaph, the recorder,
came to Hezekiah with *their* clothes torn,
and told him the words of *the* Rabshakeh.

Isaiah Assures Deliverance

19 And so it was, when King Hezekiah heard *it,* that he tore his
clothes, covered himself with sackcloth,
and went into the house of the LORD.
2Then he sent Eliakim, who *was* over the
household, Shebna the scribe, and the elders of the priests, covered with sackcloth, to Isaiah the prophet, the son of
Amoz. 3And they said to him, "Thus says
Hezekiah: 'This day *is* a day of trouble,
and rebuke, and blasphemy; for the children have come to birth, but *there is* no
strength to bring them forth. 4It may be
that the LORD your God will hear all the
words of *the* Rabshakeh, whom his master the king of Assyria has sent to reproach the living God, and will rebuke
the words which the LORD your God has
heard. Therefore lift up *your* prayer for
the remnant that is left.' "

5So the servants of King Hezekiah
came to Isaiah. 6And Isaiah said to them,
"Thus you shall say to your master, 'Thus
says the LORD: "Do not be afraid of the
words which you have heard, with which
the servants of the king of Assyria have
blasphemed Me. 7Surely I will send a
spirit upon him, and he shall hear a rumor and return to his own land; and I
will cause him to fall by the sword in his
own land." ' "

Sennacherib's Threat and Hezekiah's Prayer

8Then *the* Rabshakeh returned and
found the king of Assyria warring against
Libnah, for he heard that he had departed
from Lachish. 9And the king heard concerning Tirhakah king of Ethiopia, "Look,
he has come out to make war with you."
So he again sent messengers to Hezekiah,
saying, 10"Thus you shall speak to Hezekiah king of Judah, saying: 'Do not let
your God in whom you trust deceive
you, saying, "Jerusalem shall not be given
into the hand of the king of Assyria."

> Solid, lasting missionary work is done on our knees.
>
> J. O. FRASER

11Look! You have heard what the kings of
Assyria have done to all lands by utterly
destroying them; and shall you be delivered? 12Have the gods of the nations delivered those whom my fathers have destroyed, Gozan and Haran and Rezeph,
and the people of Eden who *were* in
Telassar? 13Where *is* the king of Hamath,
the king of Arpad, and the king of the
city of Sepharvaim, Hena, and Ivah?' "

19:1 When trials come our way, we do not need to rip our clothes, cover ourselves with sackcloth, and go to the temple of the Lord. We instead rend our hearts not our garments, humble ourselves, and speak directly to the Lord, because He has made the believer His dwelling place.

19:7 God turns the hearts of kings any way He wishes (see Prov. 21:1).

[14]And Hezekiah received the letter
from the hand of the messengers, and
read it; and Hezekiah went up to the
house of the LORD, and spread it before
the LORD. [15]Then Hezekiah prayed before
the LORD, and said: "O LORD God of Israel, *the One* who dwells *between* the
cherubim, You are God, You alone, of all
the kingdoms of the earth. You have made
heaven and earth. [16]Incline Your ear, O
LORD, and hear; open Your eyes, O LORD,
and see; and hear the words of Sennacherib, which he has sent to reproach
the living God. [17]Truly, LORD, the kings of
Assyria have laid waste the nations and
their lands, [18]and have cast their gods
into the fire; for they *were* not gods, but
the work of men's hands—wood and
stone. Therefore they destroyed them.
[19]Now therefore, O LORD our God, I pray,
save us from his hand, that all the kingdoms of the earth may know that You *are*
the LORD God, You alone."

The Word of the Lord Concerning Sennacherib

[20]Then Isaiah the son of Amoz sent to
Hezekiah, saying, "Thus says the LORD
God of Israel: 'Because you have prayed to
Me against Sennacherib king of Assyria, I
have heard.' [21]This *is* the word which the
LORD has spoken concerning him:

'The virgin, the daughter of Zion,
Has despised you, laughed you to
scorn;
The daughter of Jerusalem
Has shaken *her* head behind your
back!

[22]'Whom have you reproached and
blasphemed?
Against whom have you raised *your*
voice,
And lifted up your eyes on high?
Against the Holy *One* of Israel.
[23]By your messengers you have
reproached the Lord,
And said: "By the multitude of my
chariots
I have come up to the height of the
mountains,
To the limits of Lebanon;
I will cut down its tall cedars
And its choice cypress trees;
I will enter the extremity of its
borders,
To its fruitful forest.
[24]I have dug and drunk strange water,
And with the soles of my feet I have
dried up
All the brooks of defense."

[25]'Did you not hear long ago
How I made it,
From ancient times that I formed it?
Now I have brought it to pass,
That you should be
For crushing fortified cities *into* heaps
of ruins.
[26]Therefore their inhabitants had little
power;
They were dismayed and
confounded;
They were *as* the grass of the field
And the green herb,
As the grass on the housetops
And *grain* blighted before it is grown.

[27]'But I know your dwelling place,
Your going out and your coming in,
And your rage against Me.

19:15 Always look to the greatness of God rather than the greatness of your problem.

"Many Christians estimate difficulties in the light of their own resources, and thus attempt little and often fail in the little they attempt. All God's giants have been weak men who did great things for God because they reckoned on His power and presence with them." *Hudson Taylor*

"It is not your goodness that will ensure an answer to your prayer—it is the greatness of your need. Even if you have sunk very low in your own esteem, till not a ray of hope seems left to you and you are shut up in the blackest darkness of despair, that is the very time for you to pray, even as the Psalmist said, 'Out of the depths I have cried unto You, O Lord.'" *Charles Spurgeon*

28Because your rage against Me and
your tumult
Have come up to My ears,
Therefore I will put My hook in your
nose
And My bridle in your lips,
And I will turn you back
By the way which you came.

29'This *shall be* a sign to you:

You shall eat this year such as grows
of itself,
And in the second year what springs
from the same;
Also in the third year sow and reap,
Plant vineyards and eat the fruit of
them.
30And the remnant who have escaped
of the house of Judah
Shall again take root downward,
And bear fruit upward.
31For out of Jerusalem shall go a
remnant,
And those who escape from Mount
Zion.
The zeal of the LORD of hosts[a] will do
this.'

32"Therefore thus says the LORD concerning the king of Assyria:

'He shall not come into this city,
Nor shoot an arrow there,
Nor come before it with shield,
Nor build a siege mound against it.
33By the way that he came,
By the same shall he return;
And he shall not come into this city,'
Says the LORD.
34'For I will defend this city, to save it
For My own sake and for My servant
David's sake.' "

Sennacherib's Defeat and Death

35And it came to pass on a certain
night that the angel[a] of the LORD went
out, and killed in the camp of the Assyrians one hundred and eighty-five thousand; and when *people* arose early in the
morning, there were the corpses—all
dead. 36So Sennacherib king of Assyria
departed and went away, returned *home*,
and remained at Nineveh. 37Now it came
to pass, as he was worshiping in the temple of Nisroch his god, that his sons Adrammelech and Sharezer struck him down with the sword; and they escaped into the land of Ararat. Then Esarhaddon his son reigned in his place.

Hezekiah's Life Extended

20 In those days Hezekiah was sick and near death. And Isaiah the prophet, the son of Amoz, went to him and said to him, "Thus says the LORD: 'Set your house in order, for you shall die, and not live.' "

2Then he turned his face toward the
wall, and prayed to the LORD, saying,
3"Remember now, O LORD, I pray, how I
have walked before You in truth and with a loyal heart, and have done *what was* good in Your sight." And Hezekiah wept bitterly.

4And it happened, before Isaiah had gone out into the middle court, that the word of the LORD came to him, saying,
5"Return and tell Hezekiah the leader of
My people, 'Thus says the LORD, the God of David your father: "I have heard your prayer, I have seen your tears; surely I will heal you. On the third day you shall
go up to the house of the LORD. 6And I
will add to your days fifteen years. I will deliver you and this city from the hand of the king of Assyria; and I will defend this city for My own sake, and for the sake of My servant David." ' "

19:31 [a]Following many Hebrew manuscripts and ancient versions (compare Isaiah 37:32); Masoretic Text omits *of hosts.* **19:35** [a]Or *Angel*

20:6 God holds the days of our lives in the palm of His hand. This is a great comfort for those who have peace with Him and a dread for those who don't.

7Then Isaiah said, "Take a lump of figs." So they took and laid *it* on the boil, and he recovered.

8And Hezekiah said to Isaiah, "What *is* the sign that the LORD will heal me, and that I shall go up to the house of the LORD the third day?"

9Then Isaiah said, "This is the sign to you from the LORD, that the LORD will do the thing which He has spoken: *shall* the shadow go forward ten degrees or go backward ten degrees?"

10And Hezekiah answered, "It is an easy thing for the shadow to go down ten degrees; no, but let the shadow go backward ten degrees."

11So Isaiah the prophet cried out to the LORD, and He brought the shadow ten degrees backward, by which it had gone down on the sundial of Ahaz.

The Babylonian Envoys

12At that time Berodach-Baladan[a] the son of Baladan, king of Babylon, sent letters and a present to Hezekiah, for he heard that Hezekiah had been sick. 13And Hezekiah was attentive to them, and showed them all the house of his treasures—the silver and gold, the spices and precious ointment, and all[a] his armory—all that was found among his treasures. There was nothing in his house or in all his dominion that Hezekiah did not show them.

14Then Isaiah the prophet went to King Hezekiah, and said to him, "What did these men say, and from where did they come to you?"

So Hezekiah said, "They came from a far country, from Babylon."

15And he said, "What have they seen in your house?"

So Hezekiah answered, "They have seen all that *is* in my house; there is nothing among my treasures that I have not shown them."

16Then Isaiah said to Hezekiah, "Hear the word of the LORD: 17'Behold, the days are coming when all that *is* in your house, and what your fathers have accumulated until this day, shall be carried to Babylon; nothing shall be left,' says the LORD. 18'And they shall take away some of your sons who will descend from you, whom you will beget; and they shall be eunuchs in the palace of the king of Babylon.' "

19So Hezekiah said to Isaiah, "The word of the LORD which you have spoken *is* good!" For he said, "Will there not be peace and truth at least in my days?"

Death of Hezekiah

20Now the rest of the acts of Hezekiah—all his might, and how he made a pool and a tunnel and brought water into the city—*are* they not written in the book of the chronicles of the kings of Judah? 21So Hezekiah rested with his fathers. Then Manasseh his son reigned in his place.

Manasseh Reigns in Judah

21 Manasseh *was* twelve years old when he became king, and he reigned fifty-five years in Jerusalem. His mother's name *was* Hephzibah. 2And he did evil in the sight of the LORD, according to the abominations of the nations whom the LORD had cast out before the children of Israel. 3For he rebuilt the high places which Hezekiah his father had destroyed; he raised up altars for Baal, and made a wooden image,[a] as Ahab king of Israel had done; and he worshiped all the host of heaven[b] and served them. 4He also built altars in the house of the LORD, of which the LORD had said, "In Jerusalem I will put My name." 5And he built altars for all the host of heaven in the two courts of the house of the LORD. 6Also he made his son pass through the fire, practiced soothsaying, used witchcraft, and consulted spiritists and mediums. He did much evil in the sight of the LORD, to provoke *Him* to anger. 7He even set a carved image of Asherah[a] that he had made, in

20:12 [a]Spelled *Merodach-Baladan* in Isaiah 39:1 **20:13** [a]Following many Hebrew manuscripts, Syriac, and Targum; Masoretic Text omits *all*. **21:3** [a]Hebrew *Asherah*, a Canaanite goddess [b]The gods of the Assryians **21:7** [a]A Canaanite goddess

the house of which the LORD had said to
David and to Solomon his son, "In this
house and in Jerusalem, which I have
chosen out of all the tribes of Israel, I will
put My name forever; 8and I will not
make the feet of Israel wander anymore
from the land which I gave their fathers
—only if they are careful to do according
to all that I have commanded them, and
according to all the law that My servant
Moses commanded them." 9But they paid
no attention, and Manasseh seduced
them to do more evil than the nations
whom the LORD had destroyed before the
children of Israel.

10And the LORD spoke by His servants
the prophets, saying, 11"Because Manasseh
king of Judah has done these abominations (he has acted more wickedly than
all the Amorites who *were* before him,
and has also made Judah sin with his
idols), 12therefore thus says the LORD God
of Israel: 'Behold, *I* am bringing *such*
calamity upon Jerusalem and Judah, that
whoever hears of it, both his ears will tingle. 13And I will stretch over Jerusalem
the measuring line of Samaria and the
plummet of the house of Ahab; I will
wipe Jerusalem as *one* wipes a dish, wiping *it* and turning *it* upside down. 14So I
will forsake the remnant of My inheritance and deliver them into the hand of
their enemies; and they shall become victims of plunder to all their enemies, 15be-
cause they have done evil in My sight,
and have provoked Me to anger since the
day their fathers came out of Egypt, even
to this day.' "

16Moreover Manasseh shed very much
innocent blood, till he had filled Jerusalem from one end to another, besides his
sin by which he made Judah sin, in doing
evil in the sight of the LORD.

17Now the rest of the acts of Manasseh—all that he did, and the sin that he
committed—*are* they not written in the
book of the chronicles of the kings of Judah? 18So Manasseh rested with his fathers, and was buried in the garden of his
own house, in the garden of Uzza. Then
his son Amon reigned in his place.

Amon's Reign and Death

19Amon *was* twenty-two years old
when he became king, and he reigned
two years in Jerusalem. His mother's name
was Meshullemeth the daughter of Haruz
of Jotbah. 20And he did evil in the sight of
the LORD, as his father Manasseh had
done. 21So he walked in all the ways that
his father had walked; and he served the
idols that his father had served, and worshiped them. 22He forsook the LORD God
of his fathers, and did not walk in the
way of the LORD.

23Then the servants of Amon conspired against him, and killed the king in
his own house. 24But the people of the
land executed all those who had conspired against King Amon. Then the people of the land made his son Josiah king
in his place.

25Now the rest of the acts of Amon
which he did, *are* they not written in the
book of the chronicles of the kings of Judah? 26And he was buried in his tomb in
the garden of Uzza. Then Josiah his son
reigned in his place.

Josiah Reigns in Judah

22 Josiah *was* eight years old when
he became king, and he reigned
thirty-one years in Jerusalem. His mother's
name *was* Jedidah the daughter of Adaiah
of Bozkath. 2And he did *what was* right in
the sight of the LORD, and walked in all
the ways of his father David; he did not
turn aside to the right hand or to the left.

Hilkiah Finds the Book of the Law

3Now it came to pass, in the eighteenth year of King Josiah, *that* the king
sent Shaphan the scribe, the son of Aza-
liah, the son of Meshullam, to the house

22:3–7 How good it is to have trustworthy laborers in the gospel.

of the LORD, saying: [4]"Go up to Hilkiah the high priest, that he may count the money which has been brought into the house of the LORD, which the doorkeepers have gathered from the people. [5]And let them deliver it into the hand of those doing the work, who are the overseers in the house of the LORD; let them give it to those who *are* in the house of the LORD doing the work, to repair the damages of the house— [6]to carpenters and builders and masons—and to buy timber and hewn stone to repair the house. [7]However there need be no accounting made with them of the money delivered into their hand, because they deal faithfully."

[8]Then Hilkiah the high priest said to Shaphan the scribe, "I have found the Book of the Law in the house of the LORD." And Hilkiah gave the book to Shaphan, and he read it. [9]So Shaphan the scribe went to the king, bringing the king word, saying, "Your servants have gathered the money that was found in the house, and have delivered it into the hand of those who do the work, who oversee the house of the LORD." [10]Then Shaphan the scribe showed the king, saying, "Hilkiah the priest has given me a book." And Shaphan read it before the king.

The Scriptures were not given to increase our knowledge but to change our lives.

D. L. MOODY

[11]Now it happened, when the king heard the words of the Book of the Law, that he tore his clothes. [12]Then the king commanded Hilkiah the priest, Ahikam the son of Shaphan, Achbor[a] the son of Michaiah, Shaphan the scribe, and Asaiah a servant of the king, saying, [13]"Go, inquire of the LORD for me, for the people and for all Judah, concerning the words of this book that has been found; for great *is* the wrath of the LORD that is aroused against us, because our fathers have not obeyed the words of this book,

THE FUNCTION OF THE LAW

22:11–13 This is the work of the Law: it brings about the wrath of God (see Rom. 4:15).

"When God means to save a man, He usually begins by making him sorrow on account of his evil ways. It is the sharp steel needle of the Law of God that goes through the convicted heart and draws the silken thread of comfort and salvation after it!" *Charles Spurgeon*

"The gospel is to be preached as well as the Law, and the Law is to be preached only to make way for the gospel, and in order that it may be preached more effectually." *Jonathan Edwards*

to do according to all that is written concerning us."

[14]So Hilkiah the priest, Ahikam, Achbor, Shaphan, and Asaiah went to Huldah the prophetess, the wife of Shallum the son of Tikvah, the son of Harhas, keeper of the wardrobe. (She dwelt in Jerusalem in the Second Quarter.) And they spoke with her. [15]Then she said to them, "Thus says the LORD God of Israel, 'Tell the man who sent you to Me, [16]"Thus says the LORD: 'Behold, I will bring calamity on this place and on its inhabitants—all the words of the book which the king of Judah has read— [17]because they have forsaken Me and burned incense to other gods, that they might provoke Me to anger with all the works of their hands. Therefore My wrath shall be aroused against this place and shall not be quenched.' " ' [18]But as for the king of Judah, who sent you to inquire of the LORD, in this manner you shall speak to him, 'Thus says the LORD God of Israel: "*Concerning* the words which you have heard— [19]because your heart was tender, and you humbled yourself before the LORD when you heard what I spoke against this place and against its inhabitants, that they would become a desolation and a curse, and you tore your clothes and wept before Me, I also have heard *you*," says the LORD. [20]"Surely, therefore, I will

22:12 [a]*Abdon the son of Micah* in 2 Chronicles 34:20

gather you to your fathers, and you shall be gathered to your grave in peace; and your eyes shall not see all the calamity which I will bring on this place." ' " So they brought back word to the king.

Josiah Restores True Worship

23 Now the king sent them to gather all the elders of Judah and Jerusalem to him. 2The king went up to the house of the LORD with all the men of Judah, and with him all the inhabitants of Jerusalem—the priests and the prophets and all the people, both small and great. And he read in their hearing all the words of the Book of the Covenant which had been found in the house of the LORD.

3Then the king stood by a pillar and made a covenant before the LORD, to follow the LORD and to keep His commandments and His testimonies and His statutes, with all *his* heart and all *his* soul, to perform the words of this covenant that were written in this book. And all the people took a stand for the covenant. 4And the king commanded Hilkiah the high priest, the priests of the second order, and the doorkeepers, to bring out of the temple of the LORD all the articles that were made for Baal, for Asherah,[a] and for all the host of heaven;[b] and he burned them outside Jerusalem in the fields of Kidron, and carried their ashes to Bethel. 5Then he removed the idolatrous priests whom the kings of Judah had ordained to burn incense on the high places in the cities of Judah and in the places all around Jerusalem, and those who burned incense to Baal, to the sun, to the moon, to the constellations, and to all the host of heaven. 6And he brought out the wooden image[a] from the house of the LORD, to the Brook Kidron outside Jerusalem, burned it at the Brook Kidron and ground *it* to ashes, and threw its ashes on the graves of the common people. 7Then he tore down the *ritual* booths of the perverted persons[a] that *were* in the house of the LORD, where the women wove hangings for the wooden image. 8And he brought all the priests from the cities of Judah, and defiled the high places where the priests had burned incense, from Geba to Beersheba; also he broke down the high places at the gates which *were* at the entrance of the Gate of Joshua the governor of the city, which *were* to the left of the city gate. 9Nevertheless the priests of the high places did not come up to the altar of the LORD in Jerusalem, but they ate unleavened bread among their brethren.

10And he defiled Topheth, which *is* in the Valley of the Son[a] of Hinnom, that no man might make his son or his daughter pass through the fire to Molech. 11Then he removed the horses that the kings of Judah had dedicated to the sun, at the entrance to the house of the LORD, by the chamber of Nathan-Melech, the officer who *was* in the court; and he burned the chariots of the sun with fire. 12The altars that *were* on the roof, the upper chamber of Ahaz, which the kings of Judah had made, and the altars which Manasseh had made in the two courts of the house of the LORD, the king broke down and pulverized there, and threw their dust into the Brook Kidron. 13Then the king defiled the high places that *were* east of Jerusalem, which *were* on the south of the Mount of Corruption, which Solomon king of Israel had built for Ashtoreth the abomination of the Sidonians, for Chemosh the abomination of the Moabites, and for Milcom

23:4 [a]A Canaanite goddess [b]The gods of the Assyrians 23:6 [a]Hebrew *Asherah*, a Canaanite goddess 23:7 [a]Hebrew *qedeshim*, that is, those practicing sodomy and prostitution in religious rituals 23:10 [a]Kethib reads *Sons*.

23:1–15: How we need the truth of the moral Law. It opens blind eyes to the evil of the sin of idolatry. It gives us a zeal to destroy every remnant of idolatry in the land. We live in an age of idolatry, where professed intelligent people believe that God is whatever they perceive Him to be. He is not. He is an unchanging God of holiness, righteousness, justice, and truth, and no amount of fertile human imagination can change the fact that we must face Him on Judgment Day.

the abomination of the people of Ammon.
[14]And he broke in pieces the *sacred* pillars
and cut down the wooden images, and
filled their places with the bones of men.

[15]Moreover the altar that *was* at Bethel,
and the high place which Jeroboam the
son of Nebat, who made Israel sin, had
made, both that altar and the high place
he broke down; and he burned the high
place *and* crushed *it* to powder, and
burned the wooden image. [16]As Josiah
turned, he saw the tombs that *were* there
on the mountain. And he sent and took
the bones out of the tombs and burned
them on the altar, and defiled it according
to the word of the LORD which the man of
God proclaimed, who proclaimed these
words. [17]Then he said, "What gravestone
is this that I see?"

So the men of the city told him, "*It is*
the tomb of the man of God who came
from Judah and proclaimed these things
which you have done against the altar of
Bethel."

[18]And he said, "Let him alone; let no
one move his bones." So they let his bones
alone, with the bones of the prophet who
came from Samaria.

[19]Now Josiah also took away all the
shrines of the high places that *were* in the
cities of Samaria, which the kings of Israel had made to provoke the LORD[a] to
anger; and he did to them according to
all the deeds he had done in Bethel. [20]He
executed all the priests of the high places
who *were* there, on the altars, and burned
men's bones on them; and he returned to
Jerusalem.

[21]Then the king commanded all the
people, saying, "Keep the Passover to the
LORD your God, as *it is* written in this Book
of the Covenant." [22]Such a Passover surely
had never been held since the days of the
judges who judged Israel, nor in all the
days of the kings of Israel and the kings
of Judah. [23]But in the eighteenth year of
King Josiah this Passover was held before
the LORD in Jerusalem. [24]Moreover Josiah
put away those who consulted mediums
and spiritists, the household gods and
idols, all the abominations that were seen
in the land of Judah and in Jerusalem,
that he might perform the words of the
law which were written in the book that
Hilkiah the priest found in the house of
the LORD. [25]Now before him there was no
king like him, who turned to the LORD
with all his heart, with all his soul, and
with all his might, according to all the
Law of Moses; nor after him did *any* arise
like him.

Impending Judgment on Judah

[26]Nevertheless the LORD did not turn
from the fierceness of His great wrath, with
which His anger was aroused against Judah, because of all the provocations with
which Manasseh had provoked Him.
[27]And the LORD said, "I will also remove
Judah from My sight, as I have removed
Israel, and will cast off this city Jerusalem
which I have chosen, and the house of
which I said, 'My name shall be there.' "[a]

Josiah Dies in Battle

[28]Now the rest of the acts of Josiah,
and all that he did, *are* they not written in
the book of the chronicles of the kings of
Judah? [29]In his days Pharaoh Necho king
of Egypt went to the aid of the king of Assyria, to the River Euphrates; and King
Josiah went against him. And *Pharaoh Necho* killed him at Megiddo when he confronted him. [30]Then his servants moved
his body in a chariot from Megiddo,
brought him to Jerusalem, and buried
him in his own tomb. And the people of
the land took Jehoahaz the son of Josiah,
anointed him, and made him king in his
father's place.

The Reign and Captivity of Jehoahaz

[31]Jehoahaz *was* twenty-three years old
when he became king, and he reigned
three months in Jerusalem. His mother's
name *was* Hamutal the daughter of Jeremiah of Libnah. [32]And he did evil in the
sight of the LORD, according to all that his

23:19 [a]Following Septuagint, Syriac, and Vulgate; Masoretic Text and Targum omit *the LORD*. **23:27** [a]1 Kings 8:29

fathers had done. 33Now Pharaoh Necho put him in prison at Riblah in the land of Hamath, that he might not reign in Jerusalem; and he imposed on the land a tribute of one hundred talents of silver and a talent of gold. 34Then Pharaoh Necho made Eliakim the son of Josiah king in place of his father Josiah, and changed his name to Jehoiakim. And *Pharaoh* took Jehoahaz and went to Egypt, and he[a] died there.

Jehoiakim Reigns in Judah

35So Jehoiakim gave the silver and gold to Pharaoh; but he taxed the land to give money according to the command of Pharaoh; he exacted the silver and gold from the people of the land, from every one according to his assessment, to give *it* to Pharaoh Necho. 36Jehoiakim *was* twenty-five years old when he became king, and he reigned eleven years in Jerusalem. His mother's name *was* Zebudah the daughter of Pedaiah of Rumah. 37And he did evil in the sight of the LORD, according to all that his fathers had done.

. . . . . .

For how to bring your children to Christ, see Deut. 11:19 comment.

. . . . . .

Judah Overrun by Enemies

24 In his days Nebuchadnezzar king of Babylon came up, and Jehoiakim became his vassal *for* three years. Then he turned and rebelled against him. 2And the LORD sent against him *raiding* bands of Chaldeans, bands of Syrians, bands of Moabites, and bands of the people of Ammon; He sent them against Judah to destroy it, according to the word of the LORD which He had spoken by His servants the prophets. 3Surely at the commandment of the LORD *this* came upon Judah, to remove *them* from His sight because of the sins of Manasseh, according to all that he had done, 4and also because of the innocent blood that he had shed; for he had filled Jerusalem with innocent blood, which the LORD would not pardon.

5Now the rest of the acts of Jehoiakim, and all that he did, *are* they not written in the book of the chronicles of the kings of Judah? 6So Jehoiakim rested with his fathers. Then Jehoiachin his son reigned in his place.

7And the king of Egypt did not come out of his land anymore, for the king of Babylon had taken all that belonged to the king of Egypt from the Brook of Egypt to the River Euphrates.

The Reign and Captivity of Jehoiachin

8Jehoiachin *was* eighteen years old when he became king, and he reigned in Jerusalem three months. His mother's name *was* Nehushta the daughter of Elnathan of Jerusalem. 9And he did evil in the sight of the LORD, according to all that his father had done.

10At that time the servants of Nebuchadnezzar king of Babylon came up against Jerusalem, and the city was besieged. 11And Nebuchadnezzar king of Babylon came against the city, as his ser-

23:34 [a]That is, Jehoahaz

24:4 A pardon must be accepted. In 1830, a man named George Wilson robbed the U.S. mail and assaulted a government employee who caught him in the act. He was tried and sentenced to be hanged. However, President Andrew Jackson sent him a pardon. But strangely, Wilson refused to accept the pardon, and no one knew what to do. So the case went to the Supreme Court. Chief Justice Marshall, who wrote the court's opinion, said, "A pardon is a deed, to the validity of which delivery is essential, and delivery is not complete without acceptance. It may then be rejected by the person to whom it is tendered, and if it be rejected, we have discovered no power in a court to force it on him." And so George Wilson was hanged.

Tragically, many sinners refuse to humble themselves and accept the pardon that God offers. Some refuse because they love their sin. Others refuse to believe that God offers everlasting life. To say that they will regret their foolish refusal the moment they stand guilty before a holy God is the understatement of eternity. The Bible warns, "How shall we escape if we neglect so great a salvation . . . ?" (Heb. 2:3).

vants were besieging it. [12]Then Jehoiachin king of Judah, his mother, his servants, his princes, and his officers went out to the king of Babylon; and the king of Babylon, in the eighth year of his reign, took him prisoner.

The Captivity of Jerusalem

[13]And he carried out from there all the treasures of the house of the LORD and the treasures of the king's house, and he cut in pieces all the articles of gold which Solomon king of Israel had made in the temple of the LORD, as the LORD had said. [14]Also he carried into captivity all Jerusalem: all the captains and all the mighty men of valor, ten thousand captives, and all the craftsmen and smiths. None remained except the poorest people of the land. [15]And he carried Jehoiachin captive to Babylon. The king's mother, the king's wives, his officers, and the mighty of the land he carried into captivity from Jerusalem to Babylon. [16]All the valiant men, seven thousand, and craftsmen and smiths, one thousand, all *who were* strong *and* fit for war, these the king of Babylon brought captive to Babylon.

Zedekiah Reigns in Judah

[17]Then the king of Babylon made Mattaniah, *Jehoiachin's*[a] uncle, king in his place, and changed his name to Zedekiah.

[18]Zedekiah *was* twenty-one years old when he became king, and he reigned eleven years in Jerusalem. His mother's name *was* Hamutal the daughter of Jeremiah of Libnah. [19]He also did evil in the sight of the LORD, according to all that Jehoiakim had done. [20]For because of the anger of the LORD *this* happened in Jerusalem and Judah, that He finally cast them out from His presence. Then Zedekiah rebelled against the king of Babylon.

The Fall and Captivity of Judah

25 Now it came to pass in the ninth year of his reign, in the tenth month, on the tenth *day* of the month, *that* Nebuchadnezzar king of Babylon and all his army came against Jerusalem and encamped against it; and they built a siege wall against it all around. [2]So the city was besieged until the eleventh year of King Zedekiah. [3]By the ninth *day* of the *fourth* month the famine had become so severe in the city that there was no food for the people of the land.

[4]Then the city wall was broken through, and all the men of war *fled* at night by way of the gate between two walls, which was by the king's garden, even though the Chaldeans *were* still encamped all around against the city. And *the king*[a] went by way of the plain.[b] [5]But the army of the Chaldeans pursued the king, and they overtook him in the plains of Jericho. All his army was scattered from him. [6]So they took the king and brought him up to the king of Babylon at Riblah, and they pronounced judgment on him. [7]Then they killed the sons of Zedekiah before his eyes, put out the eyes of Zedekiah, bound him with bronze fetters, and took him to Babylon.

[8]And in the fifth month, on the seventh *day* of the month (which *was* the nineteenth year of King Nebuchadnezzar king of Babylon), Nebuzaradan the captain of the guard, a servant of the king of Babylon, came to Jerusalem. [9]He burned the house of the LORD and the king's house; all the houses of Jerusalem, that is,

24:17 [a]Literally *his* 25:4 [a]Literally *he* [b]Or *Arabah,* that is, the Jordan Valley

24:18–20 Zedekiah held the fate of his people in his unbelieving hands. How different things might have been if he had been a king who feared the Lord.

25:7 How tragic for any parents to see their sons slaughtered before their eyes. Yet, that happens so often with the ungodly in contemporary society. They don't fear the Lord, and so their children grow up like their parents, become involved in a violent lifestyle of drugs or alcohol, and die young. The thief does not come except to steal, to kill, and to destroy (see John 10:10).

all the houses of the great, he burned with fire. 10And all the army of the Chaldeans who *were with* the captain of the guard broke down the walls of Jerusalem all around.

11Then Nebuzaradan the captain of the guard carried away captive the rest of the people *who* remained in the city and the defectors who had deserted to the king of Babylon, with the rest of the multitude. 12But the captain of the guard left *some* of the poor of the land as vinedressers and farmers. 13The bronze pillars that *were* in the house of the LORD, and the carts and the bronze Sea that *were* in the house of the LORD, the Chaldeans broke in pieces, and carried their bronze to Babylon. 14They also took away the pots, the shovels, the trimmers, the spoons, and all the bronze utensils with which the priests ministered. 15The firepans and the basins, the things of solid gold and solid silver, the captain of the guard took away. 16The two pillars, one Sea, and the carts, which Solomon had made for the house of the LORD, the bronze of all these articles was beyond measure. 17The height of one pillar *was* eighteen cubits, and the capital on it *was* of bronze. The height of the capital was three cubits, and the network and pomegranates all around the capital were all of bronze. The second pillar was the same, with a network.

18And the captain of the guard took Seraiah the chief priest, Zephaniah the second priest, and the three doorkeepers. 19He also took out of the city an officer who had charge of the men of war, five men of the king's close associates who were found in the city, the chief recruiting officer of the army, who mustered the people of the land, and sixty men of the people of the land *who were* found in the city. 20So Nebuzaradan, captain of the guard, took these and brought them to the king of Babylon at Riblah. 21Then the king of Babylon struck them and put them to death at Riblah in the land of Hamath. Thus Judah was carried away captive from its own land.

Gedaliah Made Governor of Judah

22Then he made Gedaliah the son of Ahikam, the son of Shaphan, governor over the people who remained in the land of Judah, whom Nebuchadnezzar king of Babylon had left. 23Now when all the captains of the armies, they and *their* men, heard that the king of Babylon had made Gedaliah governor, they came to Gedaliah at Mizpah—Ishmael the son of Nethaniah, Johanan the son of Careah, Seraiah the son of Tanhumeth the Netophathite, and Jaazaniah[a] the son of a Maachathite, they and their men. 24And Gedaliah took an oath before them and their men, and said to them, "Do not be afraid of the servants of the Chaldeans. Dwell in the land and serve the king of Babylon, and it shall be well with you."

25But it happened in the seventh month that Ishmael the son of Nethaniah, the son of Elishama, of the royal family, came with ten men and struck and killed Gedaliah, the Jews, as well as the Chaldeans who were with him at Mizpah. 26And all the people, small and great, and the captains of the armies, arose and went to Egypt; for they were afraid of the Chaldeans.

Jehoiachin Released from Prison

27Now it came to pass in the thirty-seventh year of the captivity of Jehoiachin king of Judah, in the twelfth month, on the twenty-seventh *day* of the month, *that* Evil-Merodach[a] king of Babylon, in the year that he began to reign, released Jehoiachin king of Judah from prison. 28He spoke kindly to him, and gave him a more prominent seat than those of the kings who *were* with him in Babylon. 29So Jehoiachin changed from his prison garments, and he ate bread regularly before the king all the days of his life. 30And as for his provisions, *there was* a regular ration given him by the king, a portion for each day, all the days of his life.

25:23 [a]Spelled *Jezaniah* in Jeremiah 40:8 **25:27** [a]Literally *Man of Marduk*

1 Chronicles

The Family of Adam—Seth to Abraham

1 Adam, Seth, Enosh, [2]Cainan,[a] Mahalalel, Jared, [3]Enoch, Methuselah, Lamech, [4]Noah,[a] Shem, Ham, and Japheth.

[5]The sons of Japheth *were* Gomer, Magog, Madai, Javan, Tubal, Meshech, and Tiras. [6]The sons of Gomer *were* Ashkenaz, Diphath,[a] and Togarmah. [7]The sons of Javan *were* Elishah, Tarshishah,[a] Kittim, and Rodanim.[b]

[8]The sons of Ham *were* Cush, Mizraim, Put, and Canaan. [9]The sons of Cush *were* Seba, Havilah, Sabta,[a] Raama,[b] and Sabtecha. The sons of Raama *were* Sheba and Dedan. [10]Cush begot Nimrod; he began to be a mighty one on the earth. [11]Mizraim begot Ludim, Anamim, Lehabim, Naphtuhim, [12]Pathrusim, Casluhim (from whom came the Philistines and the Caphtorim). [13]Canaan begot Sidon, his firstborn, and Heth; [14]the Jebusite, the Amorite, and the Girgashite; [15]the Hivite, the Arkite, and the Sinite; [16]the Arvadite, the Zemarite, and the Hamathite.

[17]The sons of Shem *were* Elam, Asshur, Arphaxad, Lud, Aram, Uz, Hul, Gether, and Meshech.[a] [18]Arphaxad begot Shelah, and Shelah begot Eber. [19]To Eber were born two sons: the name of one *was* Peleg,[a] for in his days the earth was divided; and his brother's name *was* Joktan. [20]Joktan begot Almodad, Sheleph, Hazarmaveth, Jerah, [21]Hadoram, Uzal, Diklah, [22]Ebal,[a] Abimael, Sheba, [23]Ophir, Havilah, and Jobab. All these *were* the sons of Joktan.

[24]Shem, Arphaxad, Shelah, [25]Eber, Peleg, Reu, [26]Serug, Nahor, Terah, [27]and Abram, who is Abraham. [28]The sons of Abraham *were* Isaac and Ishmael.

The Family of Ishmael

[29]These *are* their genealogies: The firstborn of Ishmael *was* Nebajoth; then Kedar, Adbeel, Mibsam, [30]Mishma, Dumah, Massa, Hadad,[a] Tema, [31]Jetur, Naphish, and Kedemah. These *were* the sons of Ishmael.

The Family of Keturah

[32]Now the sons born to Keturah, Abraham's concubine, *were* Zimran, Jokshan, Medan, Midian, Ishbak, and Shuah. The sons of Jokshan *were* Sheba and Dedan. [33]The sons of Midian *were* Ephah, Epher, Hanoch, Abida, and Eldaah. All these were the children of Keturah.

The Family of Isaac

[34]And Abraham begot Isaac. The sons

1:2 [a]Hebrew *Qenan* 1:4 [a]Following Masoretic Text and Vulgate; Septuagint adds *of Noah.* 1:6 [a]Spelled *Riphath* in Genesis 10:3 1:7 [a]Spelled *Tarshish* in Genesis 10:4 [b]Spelled *Dodanim* in Genesis 10:4 1:9 [a]Spelled *Sabtah* in Genesis 10:7 [b]Spelled *Raamah* in Genesis 10:7 1:17 [a]Spelled *Mash* in Genesis 10:23 1:19 [a]Literally *Division* 1:22 [a]Spelled *Obal* in Genesis 10:28 1:30 [a]Spelled *Hadar* in Genesis 25:15

1:1 Adam was not just a mythical figure in the creation story, but was a literal person, with literal descendents. See 1 Cor. 15:45 comment.

of Isaac *were* Esau and Israel. 35The sons of
Esau *were* Eliphaz, Reuel, Jeush, Jaalam,
and Korah. 36And the sons of Eliphaz
were Teman, Omar, Zephi,[a] Gatam, *and*
Kenaz; and *by* Timna,[b] Amalek. 37The
sons of Reuel *were* Nahath, Zerah, Shammah, and Mizzah.

The Family of Seir

38The sons of Seir *were* Lotan, Shobal,
Zibeon, Anah, Dishon, Ezer, and Dishan.
39And the sons of Lotan *were* Hori and
Homam; Lotan's sister *was* Timna. 40The
sons of Shobal *were* Alian,[a] Manahath,
Ebal, Shephi,[b] and Onam. The sons of
Zibeon *were* Ajah and Anah. 41The son of
Anah *was* Dishon. The sons of Dishon *were*
Hamran,[a] Eshban, Ithran, and Cheran.
42The sons of Ezer *were* Bilhan, Zaavan,
and Jaakan.[a] The sons of Dishan *were* Uz
and Aran.

The Kings of Edom

43Now these *were* the kings who
reigned in the land of Edom before a king
reigned over the children of Israel: Bela
the son of Beor, and the name of his city
was Dinhabah. 44And when Bela died,
Jobab the son of Zerah of Bozrah reigned
in his place. 45When Jobab died, Husham
of the land of the Temanites reigned in
his place. 46And when Husham died,
Hadad the son of Bedad, who attacked
Midian in the field of Moab, reigned in
his place. The name of his city *was* Avith.
47When Hadad died, Samlah of Masrekah
reigned in his place. 48And when Samlah
died, Saul of Rehoboth-by-the-River
reigned in his place. 49When Saul died,
Baal-Hanan the son of Achbor reigned in
his place. 50And when Baal-Hanan died,
Hadad[a] reigned in his place; and the name
of his city was Pai.[b] His wife's name was
Mehetabel the daughter of Matred, the
daughter of Mezahab. 51Hadad died also.
And the chiefs of Edom were Chief Timnah, Chief Aliah,[a] Chief Jetheth, 52Chief
Aholibamah, Chief Elah, Chief Pinon,
53Chief Kenaz, Chief Teman, Chief Mibzar,
54Chief Magdiel, and Chief Iram. These
were the chiefs of Edom.

The Family of Israel

2 These *were* the sons of Israel: Reuben,
Simeon, Levi, Judah, Issachar, Zebu-
lun, 2Dan, Joseph, Benjamin, Naphtali,
Gad, and Asher.

From Judah to David

3The sons of Judah *were* Er, Onan, and
Shelah. *These* three were born to him by
the daughter of Shua, the Canaanitess.
Er, the firstborn of Judah, was wicked in
the sight of the LORD; so He killed him.
4And Tamar, his daughter-in-law, bore
him Perez and Zerah. All the sons of Judah
were five.

5The sons of Perez *were* Hezron and
Hamul. 6The sons of Zerah *were* Zimri,
Ethan, Heman, Calcol, and Dara—five of
them in all.

7The son of Carmi *was* Achar,[a] the
troubler of Israel, who transgressed in the
accursed thing.

8The son of Ethan *was* Azariah.

9Also the sons of Hezron who were
born to him *were* Jerahmeel, Ram, and
Chelubai.[a] 10Ram begot Amminadab, and
Amminadab begot Nahshon, leader of
the children of Judah; 11Nahshon begot
Salma,[a] and Salma begot Boaz; 12Boaz begot Obed, and Obed begot Jesse; 13Jesse
begot Eliab his firstborn, Abinadab the

1:36 [a]Spelled *Zepho* in Genesis 36:11 [b]Compare Genesis 36:12 1:40 [a]Spelled *Alvan* in Genesis 36:23 [b]Spelled *Shepho* in Genesis 36:23 1:41 [a]Spelled *Hemdan* in Genesis 36:26 1:42 [a]Spelled *Akan* in Genesis 36:27 1:50 [a]Spelled *Hadar* in Genesis 36:39 [b]Spelled *Pau* in Genesis 36:39 1:51 [a]Spelled *Alvah* in Genesis 36:40 2:7 [a]Spelled *Achan* in Joshua 7:1 and elsewhere 2:9 [a]Spelled *Caleb* in 2:18, 42 2:11 [a]Spelled *Salmon* in Ruth 4:21 and Luke 3:32 2:13 [a]Spelled *Shammah* in 1 Samuel 16:9 and elsewhere

2:3 This incident is mentioned in Gen. 38:7, but we are not given details of what he did that was so wicked. There are a number of cases in Scripture where God lost patience with certain people, and took their lives. See Gen. 38:10 for another such incident involving Er's brother, Onan. God also killed a husband and wife because they told one lie (see Acts 5:1–10 for details).

second, Shimea[a] the third, [14]Nethanel the fourth, Raddai the fifth, [15]Ozem the sixth, *and* David the seventh.

[16]Now their sisters *were* Zeruiah and Abigail. And the sons of Zeruiah *were* Abishai, Joab, and Asahel—three. [17]Abigail bore Amasa; and the father of Amasa *was* Jether the Ishmaelite.[a]

The Family of Hezron

[18]Caleb the son of Hezron had children by Azubah, *his* wife, and by Jerioth. Now these were her sons: Jesher, Shobab, and Ardon. [19]When Azubah died, Caleb took Ephrath[a] as his wife, who bore him Hur. [20]And Hur begot Uri, and Uri begot Bezalel.

[21]Now afterward Hezron went in to the daughter of Machir the father of Gilead, whom he married when he *was* sixty years old; and she bore him Segub. [22]Segub begot Jair, who had twenty-three cities in the land of Gilead. [23](Geshur and Syria took from them the towns of Jair, with Kenath and its towns—sixty towns.) All these *belonged to* the sons of Machir the father of Gilead. [24]After Hezron died in Caleb Ephrathah, Hezron's wife Abijah bore him Ashhur the father of Tekoa.

The Family of Jerahmeel

[25]The sons of Jerahmeel, the firstborn of Hezron, *were* Ram, the firstborn, and Bunah, Oren, Ozem, *and* Ahijah. [26]Jerahmeel had another wife, whose name was Atarah; she was the mother of Onam. [27]The sons of Ram, the firstborn of Jerahmeel, were Maaz, Jamin, and Eker. [28]The sons of Onam were Shammai and Jada. The sons of Shammai *were* Nadab and Abishur.

[29]And the name of the wife of Abishur *was* Abihail, and she bore him Ahban and Molid. [30]The sons of Nadab *were* Seled and Appaim; Seled died without children. [31]The son of Appaim *was* Ishi, the son of Ishi *was* Sheshan, and Sheshan's son *was* Ahlai. [32]The sons of Jada, the brother of Shammai, *were* Jether and Jonathan; Jether died without children. [33]The sons of Jonathan *were* Peleth and Zaza. These were the sons of Jerahmeel.

[34]Now Sheshan had no sons, only daughters. And Sheshan had an Egyptian servant whose name *was* Jarha. [35]Sheshan gave his daughter to Jarha his servant as wife, and she bore him Attai. [36]Attai begot Nathan, and Nathan begot Zabad; [37]Zabad begot Ephlal, and Ephlal begot Obed; [38]Obed begot Jehu, and Jehu begot Azariah; [39]Azariah begot Helez, and Helez begot Eleasah; [40]Eleasah begot Sismai, and Sismai begot Shallum; [41]Shallum begot Jekamiah, and Jekamiah begot Elishama.

The Family of Caleb

[42]The descendants of Caleb the brother of Jerahmeel *were* Mesha, his firstborn, who was the father of Ziph, and the sons of Mareshah the father of Hebron. [43]The sons of Hebron *were* Korah, Tappuah, Rekem, and Shema. [44]Shema begot Raham the father of Jorkoam, and Rekem begot Shammai. [45]And the son of Shammai *was* Maon, and Maon *was* the father of Beth Zur.

[46]Ephah, Caleb's concubine, bore Haran, Moza, and Gazez; and Haran begot Gazez. [47]And the sons of Jahdai *were* Regem, Jotham, Geshan, Pelet, Ephah, and Shaaph.

[48]Maachah, Caleb's concubine, bore Sheber and Tirhanah. [49]She also bore Shaaph the father of Madmannah, Sheva the father of Machbenah and the father of Gibea. And the daughter of Caleb *was* Achsah.

[50]These were the descendants of Caleb: The sons of Hur, the firstborn of Ephrathah, *were* Shobal the father of Kirjath Jearim, [51]Salma the father of Bethlehem, *and* Hareph the father of Beth Gader.

[52]And Shobal the father of Kirjath Jearim had descendants: Haroeh, *and* half of the *families of* Manuhoth.[a] [53]The families of Kirjath Jearim *were* the Ithrites, the Puthites, the Shumathites, and the Mish-

2:17 [a]Compare 2 Samuel 17:25 2:19 [a]Spelled *Ephrathah* elsewhere 2:52 [a]Same as *the Manahethites,* verse 54

raites. From these came the Zorathites and the Eshtaolites.

54The sons of Salma *were* Bethlehem, the Netophathites, Atroth Beth Joab, half of the Manahethites, and the Zorites.

55And the families of the scribes who dwelt at Jabez *were* the Tirathites, the Shimeathites, *and* the Suchathites. These *were* the Kenites who came from Hammath, the father of the house of Rechab.

The Family of David

3 Now these were the sons of David who were born to him in Hebron: The firstborn *was* Amnon, by Ahinoam the Jezreelitess; the second, Daniel,[a] by Abigail the Carmelitess; 2the third, Absalom the son of Maacah, the daughter of Talmai, king of Geshur; the fourth, Adonijah the son of Haggith; 3the fifth, Shephatiah, by Abital; the sixth, Ithream, by his wife Eglah.

4*These* six were born to him in Hebron. There he reigned seven years and six months, and in Jerusalem he reigned thirty-three years. 5And these were born to him in Jerusalem: Shimea,[a] Shobab, Nathan, and Solomon—four by Bathshua[b] the daughter of Ammiel.[c] 6Also *there* were Ibhar, Elishama,[a] Eliphelet,[b] 7Nogah, Nepheg, Japhia, 8Elishama, Eliada,[a] and Eliphelet—nine *in all.* 9*These were* all the sons of David, besides the sons of the concubines, and Tamar their sister.

The Family of Solomon

10Solomon's son *was* Rehoboam; Abijah[a] *was* his son, Asa his son, Jehoshaphat his son, 11Joram[a] his son, Ahaziah his son, Joash[b] his son, 12Amaziah his son, Azariah[a] his son, Jotham his son, 13Ahaz his son, Hezekiah his son, Manasseh his son, 14Amon his son, *and* Josiah his son. 15The sons of Josiah *were* Johanan the firstborn, the second Jehoiakim, the third Zedekiah, and the fourth Shallum.[a] 16The sons of Jehoiakim *were* Jeconiah his son *and* Zedekiah[a] his son.

The Family of Jeconiah

17And the sons of Jeconiah[a] *were* Assir,[b] Shealtiel his son, 18*and* Malchiram, Pedaiah, Shenazzar, Jecamiah, Hoshama, and Nedabiah. 19The sons of Pedaiah *were* Zerubbabel and Shimei. The sons of Zerubbabel *were* Meshullam, Hananiah, Shelomith their sister, 20and Hashubah, Ohel, Berechiah, Hasadiah, and Jushab-Hesed—five *in all.*

21The sons of Hananiah *were* Pelatiah and Jeshaiah, the sons of Rephaiah, the sons of Arnan, the sons of Obadiah, and the sons of Shechaniah. 22The son of Shechaniah was Shemaiah. The sons of Shemaiah *were* Hattush, Igal, Bariah, Neariah, and Shaphat—six *in all.* 23The sons of Neariah *were* Elioenai, Hezekiah, and Azrikam—three *in all.* 24The sons of Elioenai *were* Hodaviah, Eliashib, Pelaiah, Akkub, Johanan, Delaiah, and Anani—seven *in all.*

The Family of Judah

4 The sons of Judah *were* Perez, Hezron, Carmi, Hur, and Shobal. 2And Reaiah

3:1 [a]Called *Chileab* in 2 Samuel 3:3 3:5 [a]Spelled *Shammua* in 14:4 and 2 Samuel 5:14 [b]Spelled *Bathsheba* in 2 Samuel 11:3 [c]Called *Eliam* in 2 Samuel 11:3 3:6 [a]Spelled *Elishua* in 14:5 and 2 Samuel 5:15 [b]Spelled *Elpelet* in 14:5 3:8 [a]Spelled *Beeliada* in 14:7 3:10 [a]Spelled *Abijam* in 1 Kings 15:1 3:11 [a]Spelled *Jehoram* in 2 Kings 1:17 and 8:16 [b]Spelled *Jehoash* in 2 Kings 12:1 3:12 [a]Called *Uzziah* in Isaiah 6:1 3:15 [a]Called *Jehoahaz* in 2 Kings 23:31 3:16 [a]Compare 2 Kings 24:17 3:17 [a]Also called *Coniah* in Jeremiah 22:24 and *Jehoiachin* in 2 Kings 24:8 [b]Or *Jeconiah the captive were*

3:9 "Concubinage was practiced in many ancient cultures, especially in Mesopotamia . . . where a private citizen might have one or two concubines in addition to his primary wife . . . A concubine was often a slave or part of the booty of war (Judg. 5:30). A man might have a concubine simply as an economical form of marriage, since no dowry or bride-price was required. A concubine could add to a man's prestige by giving him two wives and thus an increased capacity for children. Such offspring were normally delivered onto the knees of the legal wife, thus establishing their legitimacy as family members. The concubine was also another servant to add to his work force." *Baker Encyclopedia of the Bible*

the son of Shobal begot Jahath, and Jahath begot Ahumai and Lahad. These *were* the families of the Zorathites. 3These *were* the sons *of the father* of Etam: Jezreel, Ishma, and Idbash; and the name of their sister *was* Hazelelponi; 4and Penuel *was* the father of Gedor, and Ezer *was the* father of Hushah.

These *were* the sons of Hur, the firstborn of Ephrathah the father of Bethlehem.

5And Ashhur the father of Tekoa had two wives, Helah and Naarah. 6Naarah bore him Ahuzzam, Hepher, Temeni, and Haahashtari. These *were* the sons of Naarah. 7The sons of Helah *were* Zereth, Zohar, and Ethnan; 8and Koz begot Anub, Zobebah, and the families of Aharhel the son of Harum.

9Now Jabez was more honorable than his brothers, and his mother called his name Jabez,[a] saying, "Because I bore *him* in pain." 10And Jabez called on the God of Israel saying, "Oh, that You would bless me indeed, and enlarge my territory, that Your hand would be with me, and that You would keep *me* from evil, that I may not cause pain!" So God granted him what he requested.

11Chelub the brother of Shuhah begot Mehir, who *was* the father of Eshton. 12And Eshton begot Beth-Rapha, Paseah, and Tehinnah the father of Ir-Nahash. These *were* the men of Rechah.

13The sons of Kenaz *were* Othniel and Seraiah. The sons of Othniel *were* Hathath,[a] 14and Meonothai *who* begot Ophrah. Seraiah begot Joab the father of Ge Harashim,[a] for they were craftsmen. 15The sons of Caleb the son of Jephunneh *were* Iru, Elah, and Naam. The son of Elah *was* Kenaz. 16The sons of Jehallelel *were* Ziph, Ziphah, Tiria, and Asarel. 17The sons of Ezrah *were* Jether, Mered, Epher, and Jalon. And *Mered's wife*[a] bore Miriam, Shammai, and Ishbah the father of Eshtemoa. 18(His wife Jehudijah[a] bore Jered the father of Gedor, Heber the father of Sochoh, and Jekuthiel the father of Zanoah.) And these were the sons of Bithiah the daughter of Pharaoh, whom Mered took.

19The sons of Hodiah's wife, the sister of Naham, *were* the fathers of Keilah the Garmite and of Eshtemoa the Maachathite. 20And the sons of Shimon *were* Amnon, Rinnah, Ben-Hanan, and Tilon. And the sons of Ishi *were* Zoheth and Ben-Zoheth.

21The sons of Shelah the son of Judah *were* Er the father of Lecah, Laadah the father of Mareshah, and the families of the house of the linen workers of the house of Ashbea; 22also Jokim, the men of Chozeba, and Joash; Saraph, who ruled in Moab, and Jashubi-Lehem. Now the records are ancient. 23These *were* the potters and those who dwell at Netaim[a] and Gederah;[b] there they dwelt with the king for his work.

The Family of Simeon

24The sons of Simeon *were* Nemuel, Jamin, Jarib,[a] Zerah,[b] *and* Shaul, 25Shallum his son, Mibsam his son, and Mishma his son. 26And the sons of Mishma *were* Hamuel his son, Zacchur his son, and Shimei his son. 27Shimei had sixteen sons and six daughters; but his brothers did not have many children, nor did any of their families multiply as much as the children of Judah.

28They dwelt at Beersheba, Moladah, Hazar Shual, 29Bilhah, Ezem, Tolad, 30Bethuel, Hormah, Ziklag, 31Beth Marcaboth, Hazar Susim, Beth Biri, and at Shaaraim. These *were* their cities until the reign of David. 32And their villages *were*

4:9 [a]Literally *He Will Cause Pain* 4:13 [a]Septuagint and Vulgate add *and Meonothai.* 4:14 [a]Literally *Valley of Craftsmen* 4:17 [a]Literally *she* 4:18 [a]Or *His Judean wife* 4:23 [a]Literally *Plants* [b]Literally *Hedges* 4:24 [a]Called *Jachin* in Genesis 46:10 [b]Called *Zohar* in Genesis 46:10

4:10 God honored the request of Jabez. How much more will He honor us if we plead with Him to use us to reach the lost—to enlarge *His* kingdom?

Etam, Ain, Rimmon, Tochen, and Ashan —five cities— 33and all the villages that *were* around these cities as far as Baal.[a] These *were* their dwelling places, and they maintained their genealogy: 34Meshobab, Jamlech, and Joshah the son of Amaziah; 35Joel, and Jehu the son of Joshibiah, the son of Seraiah, the son of Asiel; 36Elioenai, Jaakobah, Jeshohaiah, Asaiah, Adiel, Jesimiel, and Benaiah; 37Ziza the son of Shiphi, the son of Allon, the son of Jedaiah, the son of Shimri, the son of Shemaiah— 38these mentioned by name *were* leaders in their families, and their father's house increased greatly.

39So they went to the entrance of Gedor, as far as the east side of the valley, to seek pasture for their flocks. 40And they found rich, good pasture, and the land *was* broad, quiet, and peaceful; for some Hamites formerly lived there.

41These recorded by name came in the days of Hezekiah king of Judah; and they attacked their tents and the Meunites who were found there, and utterly destroyed them, as it is to this day. So they dwelt in their place, because *there was* pasture for their flocks there. 42Now *some* of them, five hundred men of the sons of Simeon, went to Mount Seir, having as their captains Pelatiah, Neariah, Rephaiah, and Uzziel, the sons of Ishi. 43And they defeated the rest of the Amalekites who had escaped. They have dwelt there to this day.

The Family of Reuben

5 Now the sons of Reuben the firstborn of Israel—he *was* indeed the firstborn, but because he defiled his father's bed, his birthright was given to the sons of Joseph, the son of Israel, so that the genealogy is not listed according to the birthright; 2yet Judah prevailed over his brothers, and from him *came* a ruler, although the birthright was Joseph's— 3the sons of Reuben the firstborn of Israel were Hanoch, Pallu, Hezron, and Carmi.

4The sons of Joel *were* Shemaiah his son, Gog his son, Shimei his son, 5Micah his son, Reaiah his son, Baal his son, 6and Beerah his son, whom Tiglath-Pileser[a] king of Assyria carried into captivity. He *was* leader of the Reubenites. 7And his brethren by their families, when the genealogy of their generations was registered: the chief, Jeiel, and Zechariah, 8and Bela the son of Azaz, the son of Shema, the son of Joel, who dwelt in Aroer, as far as Nebo and Baal Meon. 9Eastward they settled as far as the entrance of the wilderness this side of the River Euphrates, because their cattle had multiplied in the land of Gilead.

10Now in the days of Saul they made war with the Hagrites, who fell by their hand; and they dwelt in their tents throughout the entire *area* east of Gilead.

The Family of Gad

11And the children of Gad dwelt next to them in the land of Bashan as far as Salcah: 12Joel *was* the chief, Shapham the next, then Jaanai and Shaphat in Bashan, 13and their brethren of their father's house: Michael, Meshullam, Sheba, Jorai, Jachan, Zia, and Eber—seven *in all.* 14These *were* the children of Abihail the son of Huri, the son of Jaroah, the son of Gilead, the son of Michael, the son of Jeshishai, the son of Jahdo, the son of Buz; 15Ahi the son of Abdiel, the son of Guni, *was* chief of their father's house. 16And *the Gadites* dwelt in Gilead, in Bashan and in its villages, and in all the common-lands of Sharon within their borders. 17All these were registered by genealogies in the days of Jotham king of Judah, and in the days of Jeroboam king of Israel.

18The sons of Reuben, the Gadites, and half the tribe of Manasseh *had* forty-four thousand seven hundred and sixty valiant men, men able to bear shield and sword, to shoot with the bow, and skillful in war, who went to war. 19They made war with the Hagrites, Jetur, Naphish,

4:33 [a]Or *Baalath Beer* (compare Joshua 19:8) 5:6 [a]Hebrew *Tilgath-Pilneser*

and Nodab. 20And they were helped against them, and the Hagrites were delivered into their hand, and all who *were* with them, for they cried out to God in the battle. He heeded their prayer, because they put their trust in Him. 21Then they took away their livestock—fifty thousand of their camels, two hundred and fifty thousand of their sheep, and two thousand of their donkeys—also one hundred thousand of their men; 22for many fell dead, because the war *was* God's. And they dwelt in their place until the captivity.

The Family of Manasseh (East)

23So the children of the half-tribe of Manasseh dwelt in the land. Their *numbers* increased from Bashan to Baal Hermon, that is, to Senir, or Mount Hermon. 24These *were* the heads of their fathers' houses: Epher, Ishi, Eliel, Azriel, Jeremiah, Hodaviah, and Jahdiel. They were mighty men of valor, famous men, *and* heads of their fathers' houses.

25And they were unfaithful to the God of their fathers, and played the harlot after the gods of the peoples of the land, whom God had destroyed before them. 26So the God of Israel stirred up the spirit of Pul king of Assyria, that is, Tiglath-Pileser[a] king of Assyria. He carried the Reubenites, the Gadites, and the half-tribe of Manasseh into captivity. He took them to Halah, Habor, Hara, and the river of Gozan to this day.

The Family of Levi

6 The sons of Levi *were* Gershon, Kohath, and Merari. 2The sons of Kohath *were* Amram, Izhar, Hebron, and Uzziel. 3The children of Amram *were* Aaron, Moses, and Miriam. And the sons of Aaron *were* Nadab, Abihu, Eleazar, and Ithamar. 4Eleazar begot Phinehas, *and* Phinehas begot Abishua; 5Abishua begot Bukki, and Bukki begot Uzzi; 6Uzzi begot Zerahiah, and Zerahiah begot Meraioth; 7Meraioth begot Amariah, and Amariah begot Ahitub; 8Ahitub begot Zadok, and Zadok begot Ahimaaz; 9Ahimaaz begot Azariah, and Azariah begot Johanan; 10Johanan begot Azariah (it was he who ministered as priest in the temple that Solomon built in Jerusalem); 11Azariah begot Amariah, and Amariah begot Ahitub; 12Ahitub begot Zadok, and Zadok begot Shallum; 13Shallum begot Hilkiah, and Hilkiah begot Azariah; 14Azariah begot Seraiah, and Seraiah begot Jehozadak. 15Jehozadak went *into captivity* when the LORD carried Judah and Jerusalem into captivity by the hand of Nebuchadnezzar.

16The sons of Levi *were* Gershon,[a] Kohath, and Merari. 17These are the names of the sons of Gershon: Libni and Shimei. 18The sons of Kohath *were* Amram, Izhar, Hebron, and Uzziel. 19The sons of Merari *were* Mahli and Mushi. Now these *are* the families of the Levites according to their fathers: 20Of Gershon *were* Libni his son, Jahath his son, Zimmah his son, 21Joah his son, Iddo his son, Zerah his son, *and* Jeatherai his son. 22The sons of Kohath *were* Amminadab his son, Korah his son, Assir his son, 23Elkanah his son, Ebiasaph his son, Assir his son, 24Tahath his son,

5:26 [a]Hebrew *Tilgath-Pilneser* 6:16 [a]Hebrew *Gershom* (alternate spelling of *Gershon,* as in verses 1, 17, 20, 43, 62, and 71)

5:18–20 "Valiant" soldiers of Christ are those who bear the shield of faith and carry the sword of the Word of God. They are able to "shoot with the bow" of God's Law, giving the arrow of the gospel its power. This is what makes them skillful in the battle for souls. They have success, not because they trust in themselves, but because they trust in God and cry out to Him in battle. Their strength is in the Lord.

"Brethren, do something; do something, do something! While societies and unions make constitutions, let us win souls. I pray you, be men of action all of you. Get to work and quit yourselves like men. Old Suvarov's idea of war is mine: 'Forward and strike! No theory! Attack! Form a column! Charge bayonets! Plunge into the center of the enemy! Our one aim is to win souls; and this we are not to talk about, but do in the power of God!'" *Charles Spurgeon*

Uriel his son, Uzziah his son, and Shaul his son. 25The sons of Elkanah *were* Amasai and Ahimoth. 26*As for* Elkanah,[a] the sons of Elkanah *were* Zophai[b] his son, Nahath[c] his son, 27Eliab[a] his son, Jeroham his son, *and* Elkanah his son. 28The sons of Samuel *were Joel*[a] the firstborn, and Abijah the second.[b] 29The sons of Merari *were* Mahli, Libni his son, Shimei his son, Uzzah his son, 30Shimea his son, Haggiah his son, *and* Asaiah his son.

Musicians in the House of the Lord

31Now these are the men whom David appointed over the service of song in the house of the LORD, after the ark came to rest. 32They were ministering with music before the dwelling place of the tabernacle of meeting, until Solomon had built the house of the LORD in Jerusalem, and they served in their office according to their order.

33And these *are* the ones who ministered with their sons: Of the sons of the Kohathites *were* Heman the singer, the son of Joel, the son of Samuel, 34the son of Elkanah, the son of Jeroham, the son of Eliel,[a] the son of Toah,[b] 35the son of Zuph, the son of Elkanah, the son of Mahath, the son of Amasai, 36the son of Elkanah, the son of Joel, the son of Azariah, the son of Zephaniah, 37the son of Tahath, the son of Assir, the son of Ebiasaph, the son of Korah, 38the son of Izhar, the son of Kohath, the son of Levi, the son of Israel. 39And his brother Asaph, who stood at his right hand, *was* Asaph the son of Berachiah, the son of Shimea, 40the son of Michael, the son of Baaseiah, the son of Malchijah, 41the son of Ethni, the son of Zerah, the son of Adaiah, 42the son of Ethan, the son of Zimmah, the son of Shimei, 43the son of Jahath, the son of Gershon, the son of Levi.

44Their brethren, the sons of Merari, on the left hand, *were* Ethan the son of Kishi, the son of Abdi, the son of Malluch, 45the son of Hashabiah, the son of Amaziah, the son of Hilkiah, 46the son of Amzi, the son of Bani, the son of Shamer, 47the son of Mahli, the son of Mushi, the son of Merari, the son of Levi.

48And their brethren, the Levites, *were* appointed to every kind of service of the tabernacle of the house of God.

The Family of Aaron

49But Aaron and his sons offered sacrifices on the altar of burnt offering and on the altar of incense, for all the work of the Most Holy *Place*, and to make atonement for Israel, according to all that Moses the servant of God had commanded. 50Now these *are* the sons of Aaron: Eleazar his son, Phinehas his son, Abishua his son, 51Bukki his son, Uzzi his son, Zerahiah his son, 52Meraioth his son, Amariah his son, Ahitub his son, 53Zadok his son, *and* Ahimaaz his son.

Dwelling Places of the Levites

54Now these *are* their dwelling places throughout their settlements in their territory, for they were *given* by lot to the sons of Aaron, of the family of the Kohathites: 55They gave them Hebron in the land of Judah, with its surrounding common-lands. 56But the fields of the city and its villages they gave to Caleb the son of Jephunneh. 57And to the sons of Aaron they gave *one of* the cities of refuge,

6:26 [a]Compare verse 35 [b]Spelled *Zuph* in verse 35 and 1 Samuel 1:1 [c]Compare verse 34 6:27 [a]Compare verse 34 6:28 [a]Following Septuagint, Syriac, and Arabic (compare verse 33 and 1 Samuel 8:2) [b]Hebrew *Vasheni* 6:34 [a]Spelled *Elihu* in 1 Samuel 1:1 [b]Spelled *Tohu* in 1 Samuel 1:1

6:57 America was founded as "a city of refuge" against religious persecution: "Many of the British North American colonies that eventually formed the United States of America were settled in the seventeenth century by men and women, who, in the face of European persecution, refused to compromise passionately held religious convictions and fled Europe. The New England colonies, New Jersey, Pennsylvania, and Maryland were conceived and established 'as plantations of religion.'" *Library of Congress*

Hebron; also Libnah with its common-
lands, Jattir, Eshtemoa with its common-
lands, 58 Hilen[a] with its common-lands,
Debir with its common-lands, 59 Ashan[a]
with its common-lands, and Beth Shemesh
with its common-lands. 60 And from the
tribe of Benjamin: Geba with its common-
lands, Alemeth[a] with its common-lands,
and Anathoth with its common-lands. All
their cities among their families *were*
thirteen.

> The truths that I know best I have learned on my knees. I never know a thing well, till it is burned into my heart by prayer.
>
> **JOHN BUNYAN**

61 To the rest of the family of the tribe
of the Kohathites *they gave* by lot ten
cities from half the tribe of Manasseh.
62 And to the sons of Gershon, throughout
their families, *they gave* thirteen cities from
the tribe of Issachar, from the tribe of
Asher, from the tribe of Naphtali, and
from the tribe of Manasseh in Bashan.
63 To the sons of Merari, throughout their
families, *they gave* twelve cities from the
tribe of Reuben, from the tribe of Gad,
and from the tribe of Zebulun. 64 So the
children of Israel gave *these* cities with their
common-lands to the Levites. 65 And they
gave by lot from the tribe of the children
of Judah, from the tribe of the children of
Simeon, and from the tribe of the children of Benjamin these cities which are
called by *their* names.

66 Now some of the families of the sons
of Kohath *were given* cities as their territory from the tribe of Ephraim. 67 And
they gave them *one of* the cities of refuge,
Shechem with its common-lands, in the
mountains of Ephraim, also Gezer with
its common-lands, 68 Jokmeam with its
common-lands, Beth Horon with its
common-lands, 69 Aijalon with its common-
lands, and Gath Rimmon with its common-
lands. 70 And from the half-tribe of Manasseh: Aner with its common-lands and
Bileam with its common-lands, for the
rest of the family of the sons of Kohath.

71 From the family of the half-tribe of
Manasseh the sons of Gershon *were given*
Golan in Bashan with its common-lands
and Ashtaroth with its common-lands.
72 And from the tribe of Issachar: Kedesh
with its common-lands, Daberath with its
common-lands, 73 Ramoth with its common-lands, and Anem with its common-
lands. 74 And from the tribe of Asher:
Mashal with its common-lands, Abdon
with its common-lands, 75 Hukok with its
common-lands, and Rehob with its
common-lands. 76 And from the tribe of
Naphtali: Kedesh in Galilee with its common-lands, Hammon with its common-
lands, and Kirjathaim with its common-
lands.

77 From the tribe of Zebulun the rest of
the children of Merari *were given* Rimmon[a] with its common-lands and Tabor
with its common-lands. 78 And on the
other side of the Jordan, across from Jericho, on the east side of the Jordan, *they
were given* from the tribe of Reuben: Bezer
in the wilderness with its common-lands,
Jahzah with its common-lands, 79 Kedemoth with its common-lands, and Mephaath with its common-lands. 80 And
from the tribe of Gad: Ramoth in Gilead
with its common-lands, Mahanaim with
its common-lands, 81 Heshbon with its
common-lands, and Jazer with its common-lands.

The Family of Issachar

7 The sons of Issachar *were* Tola, Puah,[a]
Jashub, and Shimron—four *in all.*
2 The sons of Tola *were* Uzzi, Rephaiah,
Jeriel, Jahmai, Jibsam, and Shemuel, heads
of their father's house. *The sons* of Tola
were mighty men of valor in their generations; their number in the days of David
was twenty-two thousand six hundred.

6:58 [a]Spelled *Holon* in Joshua 21:15 6:59 [a]Spelled *Ain* in Joshua 21:16 6:60 [a]Spelled *Almon* in Joshua 21:18 6:77 [a]Hebrew *Rimmono,* alternate spelling of *Rimmon;* see 4:32 7:1 [a]Spelled *Puvah* in Genesis 46:13

3The son of Uzzi *was* Izrahiah, and the sons of Izrahiah *were* Michael, Obadiah, Joel, and Ishiah. All five of them *were* chief men. 4And with them, by their generations, according to their fathers' houses, *were* thirty-six thousand troops ready for war; for they had many wives and sons.

5Now their brethren among all the families of Issachar *were* mighty men of valor, listed by their genealogies, eighty-seven thousand in all.

The Family of Benjamin

6*The sons* of Benjamin *were* Bela, Becher, and Jediael—three *in all.* 7The sons of Bela were Ezbon, Uzzi, Uzziel, Jerimoth, and Iri—five *in all.* They *were* heads of *their* fathers' houses, and they were listed by their genealogies, twenty-two thousand and thirty-four mighty men of valor. 8The sons of Becher *were* Zemirah, Joash, Eliezer, Elioenai, Omri, Jerimoth, Abijah, Anathoth, and Alemeth. All these *are* the sons of Becher. 9And they were recorded by genealogy according to their generations, heads of their fathers' houses, twenty thousand two hundred mighty men of valor. 10The son of Jediael *was* Bilhan, and the sons of Bilhan *were* Jeush, Benjamin, Ehud, Chenaanah, Zethan, Tharshish, and Ahishahar.

11All these sons of Jediael *were* heads of their fathers' houses; *there were* seventeen thousand two hundred mighty men of valor fit to go out for war *and* battle. 12Shuppim and Huppim[a] *were* the sons of Ir, *and* Hushim *was* the son of Aher.

The Family of Naphtali

13The sons of Naphtali *were* Jahziel,[a] Guni, Jezer, and Shallum,[b] the sons of Bilhah.

The Family of Manasseh (West)

14The descendants of Manasseh: his Syrian concubine bore him Machir the father of Gilead, the father of Asriel.[a] 15Machir took as his wife *the sister* of Huppim and Shuppim,[a] whose name *was* Maachah. The name of *Gilead's* grandson[b] *was* Zelophehad,[c] but Zelophehad begot only daughters. 16(Maachah the wife of Machir bore a son, and she called his name Peresh. The name of his brother *was* Sheresh, and his sons *were* Ulam and Rakem. 17The son of Ulam *was* Bedan.) These *were* the descendants of Gilead the son of Machir, the son of Manasseh.

18His sister Hammoleketh bore Ishhod, Abiezer, and Mahlah.

19And the sons of Shemida were Ahian, Shechem, Likhi, and Aniam.

The Family of Ephraim

20The sons of Ephraim *were* Shuthelah, Bered his son, Tahath his son, Eladah his son, Tahath his son, 21Zabad his son, Shuthelah his son, and Ezer and Elead. The men of Gath who were born in *that* land killed *them* because they came down to take away their cattle. 22Then Ephraim their father mourned many days, and his brethren came to comfort him.

23And when he went in to his wife, she conceived and bore a son; and he called his name Beriah,[a] because tragedy had come upon his house. 24Now his daughter *was* Sheerah, who built Lower and Upper Beth Horon and Uzzen Sheerah; 25and Rephah *was* his son, *as well* as Resheph, and Telah his son, Tahan his

7:12 [a]Called *Hupham* in Numbers 26:39 7:13 [a]Spelled *Jahzeel* in Genesis 46:24 [b]Spelled *Shillem* in Genesis 46:24 7:14 [a]The son of Gilead (compare Numbers 26:30, 31) 7:15 [a]Compare verse 12 [b]Literally *the second* [c]Compare Numbers 26:30–33 7:23 [a]Literally *In Tragedy*

7:11 As soldiers of Christ we must always be "fit" to go to war and to do battle. We should *always* be prepared to share our faith (1 Pet. 3:15). So, practice what you preach. Practice how to answer everyone—atheist, agnostic, Mormon, Jehovah's Witness, etc.—with the reason for the hope that is within you.

"We are not called to proclaim philosophy and metaphysics, but the simple gospel. Man's fall, his need of a new birth, forgiveness through atonement, and salvation as the result of faith, these are our battle-ax and weapons of war." *Charles Spurgeon*

son, [26]Laadan his son, Ammihud his son, Elishama his son, [27]Nun[a] his son, and Joshua his son.

[28]Now their possessions and dwelling places *were* Bethel and its towns: to the east Naaran, to the west Gezer and its towns, and Shechem and its towns, as far as Ayyah[a] and its towns; [29]and by the borders of the children of Manasseh *were* Beth Shean and its towns, Taanach and its towns, Megiddo and its towns, Dor and its towns. In these dwelt the children of Joseph, the son of Israel.

The Family of Asher

[30]The sons of Asher *were* Imnah, Ishvah, Ishvi, Beriah, and their sister Serah. [31]The sons of Beriah *were* Heber and Malchiel, who was the father of Birzaith.[a] [32]And Heber begot Japhlet, Shomer,[a] Hotham,[b] and their sister Shua. [33]The sons of Japhlet *were* Pasach, Bimhal, and Ashvath. These *were* the children of Japhlet. [34]The sons of Shemer *were* Ahi, Rohgah, Jehubbah, and Aram. [35]And the sons of his brother Helem *were* Zophah, Imna, Shelesh, and Amal. [36]The sons of Zophah *were* Suah, Harnepher, Shual, Beri, Imrah, [37]Bezer, Hod, Shamma, Shilshah, Jithran,[a] and Beera. [38]The sons of Jether *were* Jephunneh, Pispah, and Ara. [39]The sons of Ulla *were* Arah, Haniel, and Rizia.

[40]All these *were* the children of Asher, heads of *their* fathers' houses, choice men, mighty men of valor, chief leaders. And they were recorded by genealogies among the army fit for battle; their number *was* twenty-six thousand.

The Family Tree of King Saul of Benjamin

8 Now Benjamin begot Bela his firstborn, Ashbel the second, Aharah[a] the third, [2]Nohah the fourth, and Rapha the fifth. [3]The sons of Bela *were* Addar,[a] Gera, Abihud, [4]Abishua, Naaman, Ahoah, [5]Gera, Shephuphan, and Huram.

[6]These *are* the sons of Ehud, who were the heads of the fathers' *houses* of the inhabitants of Geba, and who forced them to move to Manahath: [7]Naaman, Ahijah, and Gera who forced them to move. He begot Uzza and Ahihud.

[8]Also Shaharaim had children in the country of Moab, after he had sent away Hushim and Baara his wives. [9]By Hodesh his wife he begot Jobab, Zibia, Mesha, Malcam, [10]Jeuz, Sachiah, and Mirmah. These *were* his sons, heads of their fathers' *houses.*

[11]And by Hushim he begot Abitub and Elpaal. [12]The sons of Elpaal *were* Eber, Misham, and Shemed, who built Ono and Lod with its towns; [13]and Beriah and Shema, who *were* heads of their fathers' *houses* of the inhabitants of Aijalon, who drove out the inhabitants of Gath. [14]Ahio, Shashak, Jeremoth, [15]Zebadiah, Arad, Eder, [16]Michael, Ispah, and Joha *were* the sons of Beriah. [17]Zebadiah, Meshullam, Hizki, Heber, [18]Ishmerai, Jizliah, and Jobab *were* the sons of Elpaal. [19]Jakim, Zichri, Zabdi, [20]Elienai, Zillethai, Eliel, [21]Adaiah, Beraiah, and Shimrath *were* the sons of Shimei. [22]Ishpan, Eber, Eliel, [23]Abdon, Zichri, Hanan, [24]Hananiah, Elam, Antothijah, [25]Iphdeiah, and Penuel *were* the sons of Shashak. [26]Shamsherai, Shehariah, Athaliah, [27]Jaareshiah, Elijah, and Zichri *were* the sons of Jeroham.

[28]These *were* heads of the fathers' *houses* by their generations, chief men. These dwelt in Jerusalem.

[29]Now the father of Gibeon, whose wife's name *was* Maacah, dwelt at Gibeon. [30]And his firstborn son *was* Abdon, then Zur, Kish, Baal, Nadab, [31]Gedor, Ahio, Zecher, [32]and Mikloth, *who* begot Shimeah.[a] They also dwelt alongside their relatives in Jerusalem, with their brethren. [33]Ner[a] begot Kish, Kish begot Saul, and Saul begot Jonathan, Malchishua, Abinadab,[b] and Esh-Baal.[c] [34]The son of

7:27 [a]Hebrew *Non* 7:28 [a]Many Hebrew manuscripts, Bomberg, Septuagint, Targum, and Vulgate read *Gazza.* 7:31 [a]Or *Birzavith* or *Birzoth* 7:32 [a]Spelled *Shemer* in verse 34 [b]Spelled *Helem* in verse 35 7:37 [a]Spelled *Jether* in verse 38 8:1 [a]Spelled *Ahiram* in Numbers 26:38 8:3 [a]Called *Ard* in Numbers 26:40 8:32 [a]Spelled *Shimeam* in 9:38 8:33 [a]Also the son of Gibeon (compare 9:36, 39) [b]Called *Jishui* in 1 Samuel 14:49 [c]Called *Ishbosheth* in 2 Samuel 2:8 and elsewhere

Jonathan *was* Merib-Baal,[a] and Merib-Baal begot Micah. 35The sons of Micah *were* Pithon, Melech, Tarea, and Ahaz. 36And Ahaz begot Jehoaddah;[a] Jehoaddah begot Alemeth, Azmaveth, and Zimri; and Zimri begot Moza. 37Moza begot Binea, Raphah[a] his son, Eleasah his son, *and* Azel his son.

38Azel had six sons whose names *were* these: Azrikam, Bocheru, Ishmael, Sheariah, Obadiah, and Hanan. All these *were* the sons of Azel. 39And the sons of Eshek his brother *were* Ulam his firstborn, Jeush the second, and Eliphelet the third.

40The sons of Ulam were mighty men of valor—archers. *They* had many sons and grandsons, one hundred and fifty *in all*. These *were* all sons of Benjamin.

9 So all Israel was recorded by genealogies, and indeed, they *were* inscribed in the book of the kings of Israel. But Judah was carried away captive to Babylon because of their unfaithfulness. 2And the first inhabitants who *dwelt* in their possessions in their cities *were* Israelites, priests, Levites, and the Nethinim.

Dwellers in Jerusalem

3Now in Jerusalem the children of Judah dwelt, and some of the children of Benjamin, and of the children of Ephraim and Manasseh: 4Uthai the son of Ammihud, the son of Omri, the son of Imri, the son of Bani, of the descendants of Perez, the son of Judah. 5Of the Shilonites: Asaiah the firstborn and his sons. 6Of the sons of Zerah: Jeuel, and their brethren—six hundred and ninety. 7Of the sons of Benjamin: Sallu the son of Meshullam, the son of Hodaviah, the son of Hassenuah; 8Ibneiah the son of Jeroham; Elah the son of Uzzi, the son of Michri; Meshullam the son of Shephatiah, the son of Reuel, the son of Ibnijah; 9and their brethren, according to their generations—nine hundred and fifty-six. All these men *were* heads of a father's *house* in their fathers' houses.

The Priests at Jerusalem

10Of the priests: Jedaiah, Jehoiarib, and Jachin; 11Azariah the son of Hilkiah, the son of Meshullam, the son of Zadok, the son of Meraioth, the son of Ahitub, the officer over the house of God; 12Adaiah the son of Jeroham, the son of Pashur, the son of Malchijah; Maasai the son of Adiel, the son of Jahzerah, the son of Meshullam, the son of Meshillemith, the son of Immer; 13and their brethren, heads of their fathers' houses—one thousand seven hundred and sixty. *They were* very able men for the work of the service of the house of God.

The Levites at Jerusalem

14Of the Levites: Shemaiah the son of Hasshub, the son of Azrikam, the son of Hashabiah, of the sons of Merari; 15Bakbakkar, Heresh, Galal, and Mattaniah the son of Micah, the son of Zichri, the son of Asaph; 16Obadiah the son of Shemaiah, the son of Galal, the son of Jeduthun; and Berechiah the son of Asa, the son of Elkanah, who lived in the villages of the Netophathites.

The Levite Gatekeepers

17And the gatekeepers *were* Shallum, Akkub, Talmon, Ahiman, and their brethren. Shallum *was* the chief. 18Until then *they had been* gatekeepers for the camps

8:34 [a]Called *Mephibosheth* in 2 Samuel 4:4 8:36 [a]Spelled *Jarah* in 9:42 8:37 [a]Spelled *Rephaiah* in 9:43

8:40 Archers needed to be strong to bend the bow. God's Law is the bow that gives the arrow of the gospel its thrust. Be strong in the Lord and never hesitate to pull back the bow of the Law, as Jesus did. See Mark 10:17–19 for Jesus' answer on how to gain eternal life.

9:19 The Korahites (sons of Korah) were Levites, and were singers along with the Kohathites (see 2 Chron. 20:19). Eleven psalms are dedicated to the sons of Korah. Notice that they were "gatekeepers." Never forget when you worship God that we are commanded to worship and serve Him (see Luke 4:8). It's easy to get so caught up in the clouds of worship that we lose sight of the fact that we are "keepers" of the narrow gate—we have been entrusted with evangelistic responsibility.

of the children of Levi at the King's Gate on the east.

19Shallum the son of Kore, the son of Ebiasaph, the son of Korah, and his brethren, from his father's house, the Korahites, *were* in charge of the work of the service, gatekeepers of the tabernacle. Their fathers had been keepers of the entrance to the camp of the LORD. 20And Phinehas the son of Eleazar had been the officer over them in time past; the LORD *was* with him. 21Zechariah the son of Meshelemiah *was* keeper of the door of the tabernacle of meeting.

22All those chosen as gatekeepers *were* two hundred and twelve. They were recorded by their genealogy, in their villages. David and Samuel the seer had appointed them to their trusted office. 23So they and their children *were* in charge of the gates of the house of the LORD, the house of the tabernacle, by assignment. 24The gatekeepers were assigned to the four directions: the east, west, north, and south. 25And their brethren in their villages *had* to come with them from time to time for seven days. 26For in this trusted office *were* four chief gatekeepers; they were Levites. And they had charge over the chambers and treasuries of the house of God. 27And they lodged *all* around the house of God because they *had* the responsibility, and they *were* in charge of opening *it* every morning.

Other Levite Responsibilities

28Now *some* of them were in charge of the serving vessels, for they brought them in and took them out by count. 29*Some* of them *were* appointed over the furnishings and over all the implements of the sanctuary, and over the fine flour and the wine and the oil and the incense and the spices. 30And *some* of the sons of the priests made the ointment of the spices.

31Mattithiah of the Levites, the firstborn of Shallum the Korahite, had the trusted office over the things that were baked in the pans. 32And some of their brethren of the sons of the Kohathites *were* in charge of preparing the showbread for every Sabbath.

33These are the singers, heads of the fathers' *houses* of the Levites, *who lodged* in the chambers, *and were* free *from other duties;* for they were employed in *that* work day and night. 34These heads of the fathers' *houses* of the Levites *were* heads throughout their generations. They dwelt at Jerusalem.

The Family of King Saul

35Jeiel the father of Gibeon, whose wife's name *was* Maacah, dwelt at Gibeon. 36His firstborn son *was* Abdon, then Zur, Kish, Baal, Ner, Nadab, 37Gedor, Ahio, Zechariah,[a] and Mikloth. 38And Mikloth begot Shimeam.[a] They also dwelt alongside their relatives in Jerusalem, with their brethren. 39Ner begot Kish, Kish begot Saul, and Saul begot Jonathan, Malchishua, Abinadab, and Esh-Baal. 40The son of Jonathan *was* Merib-Baal, and Merib-Baal begot Micah. 41The sons of Micah *were* Pithon, Melech, Tahrea,[a] and Ahaz.[b] 42And Ahaz begot Jarah;[a] Jarah begot Alemeth, Azmaveth, and Zimri; and Zimri begot Moza; 43Moza begot Binea, Rephaiah[a] his son, Eleasah his son, and Azel his son. 44And Azel had six sons whose names *were* these: Azrikam, Bocheru, Ishmael, Sheariah, Obadiah, and Hanan; these *were* the sons of Azel.

Tragic End of Saul and His Sons

10 Now the Philistines fought against Israel; and the men of Israel fled from before the Philistines, and fell slain on Mount Gilboa. 2Then the Philistines followed hard after Saul and his sons. And the Philistines killed Jonathan, Abinadab, and Malchishua, Saul's sons. 3The battle became fierce against Saul. The archers hit him, and he was wounded by the archers. 4Then Saul said to his armor-

9:37 [a]Called *Zecher* in 8:31 9:38 [a]Spelled *Shimeah* in 8:32 9:41 [a]Spelled *Tarea* in 8:35 [b]Following Arabic, Syriac, Targum, and Vulgate (compare 8:35); Masoretic Text and Septuagint omit *and Ahaz*. 9:42 [a]Spelled *Jehoaddah* in 8:36 9:43 [a]Spelled *Raphah* in 8:37

QUESTIONS & OBJECTIONS

10:13,14 "Is it wrong to 'speak to the dead'?"

Those who attempt to speak to the dead are dabbling with the demonic realm, a forbidden occult practice that is punishable by stoning: "A man or a woman who is a medium, or who has familiar spirits, shall surely be put to death; they shall stone them with stones" (Lev. 20:27).

Unger's Bible Dictionary tells us: "[A] familiar spirit is a divining demon present in the physical body of the conjurer…The term 'familiar' is used to describe the foreboding demon because it was regarded by the English translators as a secret (*famulus*), belonging to the family (*familiaris*), who was on intimate terms with and might be readily summoned by the one possessing it." God prohibits "one who practices witchcraft, or a soothsayer, or one who interprets omens, or a sorcerer, or one who conjures spells, or a medium, or a spiritist, or one who calls up the dead. For all who do these things are an abomination to the LORD" (Deut. 18:10–12). God killed King Saul after he sought guidance through a familiar spirit, rather than through the Lord (see 1 Sam. 28:7). Those who desire the supernatural should seek God through prayer and through His Word. See also Lev. 19:31 comment and Isa. 8:19.

bearer, "Draw your sword, and thrust me
through with it, lest these uncircumcised
men come and abuse me." But his armorbearer would not, for he was greatly
afraid. Therefore Saul took a sword and
fell on it. 5And when his armorbearer
saw that Saul was dead, he also fell on his
sword and died. 6So Saul and his three
sons died, and all his house died together.
7And when all the men of Israel who
were in the valley saw that they had fled
and that Saul and his sons were dead,
they forsook their cities and fled; then
the Philistines came and dwelt in them.
8So it happened the next day, when
the Philistines came to strip the slain, that
they found Saul and his sons fallen on
Mount Gilboa. 9And they stripped him
and took his head and his armor, and sent
word throughout the land of the Philistines to proclaim the news *in the temple* of
their idols and among the people. 10Then
they put his armor in the temple of their
gods, and fastened his head in the temple
of Dagon.
11And when all Jabesh Gilead heard all
that the Philistines had done to Saul, 12all
the valiant men arose and took the body
of Saul and the bodies of his sons; and
they brought them to Jabesh, and buried
their bones under the tamarisk tree at
Jabesh, and fasted seven days.
13So Saul died for his unfaithfulness
which he had committed against the
LORD, because he did not keep the word
of the LORD, and also because he consulted a medium for guidance. 14But *he*
did not inquire of the LORD; therefore He
killed him, and turned the kingdom over
to David the son of Jesse.

David Made King over All Israel

11 Then all Israel came together to
David at Hebron, saying, "Indeed
we *are* your bone and your flesh. 2Also,
in time past, even when Saul was king,
you *were* the one who led Israel out and
brought them in; and the LORD your God
said to you, 'You shall shepherd My people Israel, and be ruler over My people Israel.' " 3Therefore all the elders of Israel
came to the king at Hebron, and David
made a covenant with them at Hebron
before the LORD. And they anointed David
king over Israel, according to the word of
the LORD by Samuel.

The City of David

4And David and all Israel went to Jerusalem, which is Jebus, where the Jebusites

10:3–6 Who killed King Saul? Was it the Philistines, or did he commit suicide? The answer is that God killed him. He guided the arrow that pierced the king. See vv. 13,14.

were, the inhabitants of the land. [5]But the inhabitants of Jebus said to David, "You shall not come in here!" Nevertheless David took the stronghold of Zion (that is, the City of David). [6]Now David said, "Whoever attacks the Jebusites first shall be chief and captain." And Joab the son of Zeruiah went up first, and became chief. [7]Then David dwelt in the stronghold; therefore they called it the City of David. [8]And he built the city around it, from the Millo[a] to the surrounding area. Joab repaired the rest of the city. [9]So David went on and became great, and the LORD of hosts *was* with him.

The Mighty Men of David

[10]Now these *were* the heads of the mighty men whom David had, who strengthened themselves with him in his kingdom, with all Israel, to make him king, according to the word of the LORD concerning Israel.

[11]And this is the number of the mighty men whom David had: Jashobeam the son of a Hachmonite, chief of the captains;[a] he had lifted up his spear against three hundred, killed *by him* at one time.

[12]After him *was* Eleazar the son of Dodo, the Ahohite, who *was one* of the three mighty men. [13]He was with David at Pasdammim. Now there the Philistines were gathered for battle, and there was a piece of ground full of barley. So the people fled from the Philistines. [14]But they stationed themselves in the middle of *that* field, defended it, and killed the Philistines. So the LORD brought about a great victory.

[15]Now three of the thirty chief men went down to the rock to David, into the cave of Adullam; and the army of the Philistines encamped in the Valley of Rephaim. [16]David *was* then in the stronghold, and the garrison of the Philistines *was* then in Bethlehem. [17]And David said with longing, "Oh, that someone would give me a drink of water from the well of Bethlehem, which is by the gate!" [18]So the three broke through the camp of the Philistines, drew water from the well of Bethlehem that *was* by the gate, and took *it* and brought *it* to David. Nevertheless David would not drink it, but poured it out to the LORD. [19]And he said, "Far be it from me, O my God, that I should do this! Shall I drink the blood of these men *who have put* their lives *in jeopardy?* For at the risk of their lives they brought it." Therefore he would not drink it. These things were done by the three mighty men.

[20]Abishai the brother of Joab was chief of *another* three.[a] He had lifted up his spear against three hundred *men,* killed *them,* and won a name among *these* three. [21]Of the three he was more honored than the other two men. Therefore he became their captain. However he did not attain to the *first* three.

[22]Benaiah was the son of Jehoiada, the son of a valiant man from Kabzeel, who had done many deeds. He had killed two lion-like heroes of Moab. He also had gone down and killed a lion in the midst of a pit on a snowy day. [23]And he killed an Egyptian, a man of *great* height, five cubits tall. In the Egyptian's hand *there was* a spear like a weaver's beam; and he went down to him with a staff, wrested the spear out of the Egyptian's hand, and killed him with his own spear. [24]These *things* Benaiah the son of Jehoiada did, and won a name among three mighty men. [25]Indeed he was more honored than

11:8 [a]Literally *The Landfill* 11:11 [a]Following Qere; Kethib, Septuagint, and Vulgate read *the thirty* (compare 2 Samuel 23:8). 11:20 [a]Following Masoretic Text, Septuagint, and Vulgate; Syriac reads *thirty.*

11:17–19 The true convert holds the Cup of Salvation in his trembling hands. He has seen the cost of his redemption. He sees that he was not redeemed with silver or gold, but with the precious blood of Christ. Like David, he cannot drink of that cup in a spirit of self-indulgence. Rather than drink in the pleasures and comforts of the Christian life, his reasonable service is to present himself as a living sacrifice, holy and acceptable, and pour his life out as a drink offering to the Lord. See also 2 Sam. 23:13–17 comment.

the thirty, but he did not attain to the *first* three. And David appointed him over his guard.

[26]Also the mighty warriors *were* Asahel the brother of Joab, Elhanan the son of Dodo of Bethlehem, [27]Shammoth the Harorite,[a] Helez the Pelonite,[b] [28]Ira the son of Ikkesh the Tekoite, Abiezer the Anathothite, [29]Sibbechai the Hushathite, Ilai the Ahohite, [30]Maharai the Netophathite, Heled[a] the son of Baanah the Netophathite, [31]Ithai[a] the son of Ribai of Gibeah, of the sons of Benjamin, Benaiah the Pirathonite, [32]Hurai[a] of the brooks of Gaash, Abiel[b] the Arbathite, [33]Azmaveth the Baharumite,[a] Eliahba the Shaalbonite, [34]the sons of Hashem the Gizonite, Jonathan the son of Shageh the Hararite, [35]Ahiam the son of Sacar the Hararite, Eliphal the son of Ur, [36]Hepher the Mecherathite, Ahijah the Pelonite, [37]Hezro the Carmelite, Naarai the son of Ezbai, [38]Joel the brother of Nathan, Mibhar the son of Hagri, [39]Zelek the Ammonite, Naharai the Berothite[a] (the armorbearer of Joab the son of Zeruiah), [40]Ira the Ithrite, Gareb the Ithrite, [41]Uriah the Hittite, Zabad the son of Ahlai, [42]Adina the son of Shiza the Reubenite (a chief of the Reubenites) and thirty with him, [43]Hanan the son of Maachah, Joshaphat the Mithnite, [44]Uzzia the Ashterathite, Shama and Jeiel the sons of Hotham the Aroerite, [45]Jediael the son of Shimri, and Joha his brother, the Tizite, [46]Eliel the Mahavite, Jeribai and Joshaviah the sons of Elnaam, Ithmah the Moabite, [47]Eliel, Obed, and Jaasiel the Mezobaite.

The Growth of David's Army

12 Now these *were* the men who came to David at Ziklag while he was still a fugitive from Saul the son of Kish; and they *were* among the mighty men, helpers in the war, [2]armed with bows, using both the right hand and the left in *hurling* stones and *shooting* arrows with the bow. *They were* of Benjamin, Saul's brethren.

[3]The chief *was* Ahiezer, then Joash, the sons of Shemaah the Gibeathite; Jeziel and Pelet the sons of Azmaveth; Berachah, and Jehu the Anathothite; [4]Ishmaiah the Gibeonite, a mighty man among the thirty, and over the thirty; Jeremiah, Jahaziel, Johanan, and Jozabad the Gederathite; [5]Eluzai, Jerimoth, Bealiah, Shemariah, and Shephatiah the Haruphite; [6]Elkanah, Jisshiah, Azarel, Joezer, and Jashobeam, the Korahites; [7]and Joelah and Zebadiah the sons of Jeroham of Gedor.

[8]*Some* Gadites joined David at the stronghold in the wilderness, mighty men of valor, men trained for battle, who could handle shield and spear, whose faces *were like* the faces of lions, and *were* as swift as gazelles on the mountains: [9]Ezer the first, Obadiah the second, Eliab the third, [10]Mishmannah the fourth, Jeremiah the fifth, [11]Attai the sixth, Eliel the seventh, [12]Johanan the eighth, Elzabad the ninth, [13]Jeremiah the tenth, and Machbanai the eleventh. [14]These *were* from the sons of Gad, captains of the army; the least was over a hundred, and the greatest was over a thousand. [15]These *are* the ones who crossed the Jordan in the first month, when it had overflowed all its banks; and they put to flight all *those* in the valleys, to the east and to the west.

[16]Then some of the sons of Benjamin and Judah came to David at the stronghold. [17]And David went out to meet them, and answered and said to them, "If you have come peaceably to me to help me, my heart will be united with you; but if to betray me to my enemies, since *there is*

11:27 [a]Spelled *Harodite* in 2 Samuel 23:25 [b]Called *Paltite* in 2 Samuel 23:26 11:30 [a]Spelled *Heleb* in 2 Samuel 23:29 and *Heldai* in 1 Chronicles 27:15 11:31 [a]Spelled *Ittai* in 2 Samuel 23:29 11:32 [a]Spelled *Hiddai* in 2 Samuel 23:30 [b]Spelled *Abi-Albon* in 2 Samuel 23:31 11:33 [a]Spelled *Barhumite* in 2 Samuel 23:31 11:39 [a]Spelled *Beerothite* in 2 Samuel 23:37

12:8 A lion fears nothing. It is called "the king of the beasts." Never let fear hinder you from doing the will of God. See Rom. 8:35–39 to see why you have nothing to fear but God.

no wrong in my hands, may the God of our fathers look and bring judgment." [18]Then the Spirit came upon Amasai, chief of the captains, *and he said:*

"We *are* yours, O David;
We *are* on your side, O son of Jesse!
Peace, peace to you,
And peace to your helpers!
For your God helps you."

So David received them, and made them captains of the troop.

[19]And *some* from Manasseh defected to David when he was going with the Philistines to battle against Saul; but they did not help them, for the lords of the Philistines sent him away by agreement, saying, "He may defect to his master Saul *and endanger* our heads." [20]When he went to Ziklag, those of Manasseh who defected to him were Adnah, Jozabad, Jediael, Michael, Jozabad, Elihu, and Zillethai, captains of the thousands who *were* from Manasseh. [21]And they helped David against the bands *of raiders,* for they *were* all mighty men of valor, and they were captains in the army. [22]For at *that* time they came to David day by day to help him, until *it was* a great army, like the army of God.

David's Army at Hebron

[23]Now these *were* the numbers of the divisions *that were* equipped for war, *and* came to David at Hebron to turn *over* the kingdom of Saul to him, according to the word of the LORD: [24]of the sons of Judah bearing shield and spear, six thousand eight hundred armed for war; [25]of the sons of Simeon, mighty men of valor fit for war, seven thousand one hundred; [26]of the sons of Levi four thousand six hundred; [27]Jehoiada, the leader of the Aaronites, and with him three thousand seven hundred; [28]Zadok, a young man, a valiant warrior, and from his father's house twenty-two captains; [29]of the sons of Benjamin, relatives of Saul, three thousand (until then the greatest part of them had remained loyal to the house of Saul); [30]of the sons of Ephraim twenty thousand eight hundred, mighty men of valor, famous men throughout their father's house; [31]of the half-tribe of Manasseh eighteen thousand, who were designated by name to come and make David king; [32]of the sons of Issachar who had understanding of the times, to know what Israel ought to do, their chiefs were two hundred; and all their brethren were at their command; [33]of Zebulun there were fifty thousand who went out to battle, expert in war with all weapons of war, stouthearted men who could keep ranks; [34]of Naphtali one thousand captains, and with them thirty-seven thousand with shield and spear; [35]of the Danites who could keep battle formation, twenty-eight thousand six hundred; [36]of Asher, those who could go out to war, able to keep battle formation, forty thousand; [37]of the Reubenites and the Gadites and the half-tribe of Manasseh, from the other side of the Jordan, one hundred and twenty thousand armed for battle with every *kind* of weapon of war.

[38]All these men of war, who could keep ranks, came to Hebron with a loyal heart, to make David king over all Israel; and all the rest of Israel *were* of one mind to make David king. [39]And they were there with David three days, eating and drinking, for their brethren had prepared for them. [40]Moreover those who were near to them, from as far away as Issachar and Zebulun and Naphtali, were bringing food on donkeys and camels, on mules and oxen—provisions of flour and cakes of figs and cakes of raisins, wine and oil and oxen and sheep abundantly, for *there was* joy in Israel.

The Ark Brought from Kirjath Jearim

13 Then David consulted with the captains of thousands and hundreds, *and* with every leader. [2]And David said to all the assembly of Israel, "If *it seems* good to you, and if it is of the LORD our God, let us send out to our brethren

everywhere *who are* left in all the land of Israel, and with them to the priests and Levites *who are* in their cities *and* their common-lands, that they may gather together to us; 3and let us bring the ark of our God back to us, for we have not inquired at it since the days of Saul." 4Then all the assembly said that they would do so, for the thing was right in the eyes of all the people.

5So David gathered all Israel together, from Shihor in Egypt to as far as the entrance of Hamath, to bring the ark of God from Kirjath Jearim. 6And David and all Israel went up to Baalah,[a] to Kirjath Jearim, which belonged to Judah, to bring up from there the ark of God the LORD, who dwells *between* the cherubim, where *His* name is proclaimed. 7So they carried the ark of God on a new cart from the house of Abinadab, and Uzza and Ahio drove the cart. 8Then David and all Israel played *music* before God with all *their* might, with singing, on harps, on stringed instruments, on tambourines, on cymbals, and with trumpets.

9And when they came to Chidon's[a] threshing floor, Uzza put out his hand to hold the ark, for the oxen stumbled. 10Then the anger of the LORD was aroused against Uzza, and He struck him because he put his hand to the ark; and he died there before God. 11And David became angry because of the LORD's outbreak against Uzza; therefore that place is called Perez Uzza[a] to this day. 12David was afraid of God that day, saying, "How can I bring the ark of God to me?"

13So David would not move the ark with him into the City of David, but took it aside into the house of Obed-Edom the Gittite. 14The ark of God remained with the family of Obed-Edom in his house three months. And the LORD blessed the house of Obed-Edom and all that he had.

David Established at Jerusalem

14 Now Hiram king of Tyre sent messengers to David, and cedar trees, with masons and carpenters, to build him a house. 2So David knew that the LORD had established him as king over Israel, for his kingdom was highly exalted for the sake of His people Israel.

3Then David took more wives in Jerusalem, and David begot more sons and daughters. 4And these are the names of his children whom he had in Jerusalem: Shammua,[a] Shobab, Nathan, Solomon, 5Ibhar, Elishua,[a] Elpelet,[b] 6Nogah, Nepheg, Japhia, 7Elishama, Beeliada,[a] and Eliphelet.

The Philistines Defeated

8Now when the Philistines heard that David had been anointed king over all Israel, all the Philistines went up to search for David. And David heard *of it* and went out against them. 9Then the Philistines went and made a raid on the Valley of Rephaim. 10And David inquired of God, saying, "Shall I go up against the Philistines? Will You deliver them into my hand?"

The LORD said to him, "Go up, for I will deliver them into your hand."

11So they went up to Baal Perazim, and David defeated them there. Then David said, "God has broken through my

13:6 [a]Called *Baale Judah* in 2 Samuel 6:2 13:9 [a]Called *Nachon* in 2 Samuel 6:6 13:11 [a]Literally *Outburst Against Uzza* 14:4 [a]Spelled *Shimea* in 3:5 14:5 [a]Spelled *Elishama* in 3:6 [b]Spelled *Eliphelet* in 3:6 14:7 [a]Spelled *Eliada* in 3:8

13:7–10 Someone once said that when Uzza attempted to keep the ark from falling to the ground, he was concerned that the ark not touch the dirt. He thought that his own hand was cleaner than the dirt under his feet. The ark was holy because it contained the Law that is holy. David didn't follow the instructions on how to handle the ark. Instead, he presumed that all God required was sincerity, rather than obedience. See Num. 4:15 and 1 Chron. 15:15 for the instructions on how to carry the ark.

14:10 All David needed to do was to "go," as he had been told. God would look after the results. The same applies with the Great Commission. We have been told to "Go into all the world . . ." (Mark 16:15). God will look after the results.

enemies by my hand like a breakthrough of water." Therefore they called the name of that place Baal Perazim.[a] 12And when they left their gods there, David gave a commandment, and they were burned with fire.

13Then the Philistines once again made a raid on the valley. 14Therefore David inquired again of God, and God said to him, "You shall not go up after them; circle around them, and come upon them in front of the mulberry trees. 15And it shall be, when you hear a sound of marching in the tops of the mulberry trees, then you shall go out to battle, for God has gone out before you to strike the camp of the Philistines." 16So David did as God commanded him, and they drove back the army of the Philistines from Gibeon as far as Gezer. 17Then the fame of David went out into all lands, and the LORD brought the fear of him upon all nations.

The Ark Brought to Jerusalem

15 *David* built houses for himself in the City of David; and he prepared a place for the ark of God, and pitched a tent for it. 2Then David said, "No one may carry the ark of God but the Levites, for the LORD has chosen them to carry the ark of God and to minister before Him forever." 3And David gathered all Israel together at Jerusalem, to bring up the ark of the LORD to its place, which he had prepared for it. 4Then David assembled the children of Aaron and the Levites: 5of the sons of Kohath, Uriel the chief, and one hundred and twenty of his brethren; 6of the sons of Merari, Asaiah the chief, and two hundred and twenty of his brethren; 7of the sons of Gershom, Joel the chief, and one hundred and thirty of his brethren; 8of the sons of Elizaphan, Shemaiah the chief, and two hundred of his brethren; 9of the sons of Hebron, Eliel the chief, and eighty of his brethren; 10of the sons of Uzziel, Amminadab the chief, and one hundred and twelve of his brethren.

11And David called for Zadok and Abiathar the priests, and for the Levites: for Uriel, Asaiah, Joel, Shemaiah, Eliel, and Amminadab. 12He said to them, "You *are* the heads of the fathers' *houses* of the Levites; sanctify yourselves, you and your brethren, that you may bring up the ark of the LORD God of Israel to *the place* I have prepared for it. 13For because you *did* not *do it* the first *time,* the LORD our God broke out against us, because we did not consult Him about the proper order."

> A person fully confident that he is able to do God's work is often the one that fails to submit to God. It is the humble servant, fully dependent upon God, who succeeds.
>
> **CHARLES F. STANLEY**

14So the priests and the Levites sanctified themselves to bring up the ark of the LORD God of Israel. 15And the children of the Levites bore the ark of God on their shoulders, by its poles, as Moses had commanded according to the word of the LORD.

16Then David spoke to the leaders of the Levites to appoint their brethren *to be* the singers accompanied by instruments of music, stringed instruments, harps, and cymbals, by raising the voice with resounding joy. 17So the Levites appointed Heman the son of Joel; and of his brethren, Asaph the son of Berechiah; and of their brethren, the sons of Merari, Ethan the son of Kushaiah; 18and with them their brethren of the second *rank:* Zechariah, Ben,[a] Jaaziel, Shemiramoth, Jehiel,

14:11 [a]Literally *Master of Breakthroughs* **15:18** [a]Following Masoretic Text and Vulgate; Septuagint omits *Ben.*

15:2,3 We should let our mistakes be our teachers. David made a terrible mistake (see 13:8–10), but he didn't let that experience discourage him from eventually doing the right thing. See vv. 12–15.

Unni, Eliab, Benaiah, Maaseiah, Mattithiah, Elipheleh, Mikneiah, Obed-Edom, and Jeiel, the gatekeepers; [19]the singers, Heman, Asaph, and Ethan, *were* to sound the cymbals of bronze; [20]Zechariah, Aziel, Shemiramoth, Jehiel, Unni, Eliab, Maaseiah, and Benaiah, with strings according to Alamoth; [21]Mattithiah, Elipheleh, Mikneiah, Obed-Edom, Jeiel, and Azaziah, to direct with harps on the Sheminith; [22]Chenaniah, leader of the Levites, was instructor *in charge of* the music, because he *was* skillful; [23]Berechiah and Elkanah *were* doorkeepers for the ark; [24]Shebaniah, Joshaphat, Nethanel, Amasai, Zechariah, Benaiah, and Eliezer, the priests, were to blow the trumpets before the ark of God; and Obed-Edom and Jehiah, doorkeepers for the ark.

[25]So David, the elders of Israel, and the captains over thousands went to bring up the ark of the covenant of the LORD from the house of Obed-Edom with joy. [26]And so it was, when God helped the Levites who bore the ark of the covenant of the LORD, that they offered seven bulls and seven rams. [27]David was clothed with a robe of fine linen, as were all the Levites who bore the ark, the singers, and Chenaniah the music master *with* the singers. David also wore a linen ephod. [28]Thus all Israel brought up the ark of the covenant of the LORD with shouting and with the sound of the horn, with trumpets and with cymbals, making music with stringed instruments and harps.

[29]And it happened, *as* the ark of the covenant of the LORD came to the City of David, that Michal, Saul's daughter, looked through a window and saw King David whirling and playing music; and she despised him in her heart.

The Ark Placed in the Tabernacle

16 So they brought the ark of God, and set it in the midst of the tabernacle that David had erected for it. Then they offered burnt offerings and peace offerings before God. [2]And when David had finished offering the burnt offerings and the peace offerings, he blessed the people in the name of the LORD. [3]Then he distributed to everyone of Israel, both man and woman, to everyone a loaf of bread, a piece *of meat,* and a cake of raisins.

[4]And he appointed some of the Levites to minister before the ark of the LORD, to commemorate, to thank, and to praise the LORD God of Israel: [5]Asaph the chief, and next to him Zechariah, *then* Jeiel, Shemiramoth, Jehiel, Mattithiah, Eliab, Benaiah, and Obed-Edom: Jeiel with stringed instruments and harps, but Asaph made music with cymbals; [6]Benaiah and Jahaziel the priests regularly *blew* the trumpets before the ark of the covenant of God.

David's Song of Thanksgiving

[7]On that day David first delivered *this psalm* into the hand of Asaph and his brethren, to thank the LORD:

[8]Oh, give thanks to the LORD!
Call upon His name;
Make known His deeds among the
peoples!
[9]Sing to Him, sing psalms to Him;
Talk of all His wondrous works!
[10]Glory in His holy name;
Let the hearts of those rejoice who
seek the LORD!
[11]Seek the LORD and His strength;
Seek His face evermore!
[12]Remember His marvelous works
which He has done,
His wonders, and the judgments of
His mouth,
[13]O seed of Israel His servant,
You children of Jacob, His chosen ones!

[14]He *is* the LORD our God;

16:8 The best way to show our thankfulness to the Lord is to let His deeds be known among those who need to hear it. Tell others what Jesus did for them on the cross so that they too can call upon His name and be saved.

His judgments *are* in all the earth.
15Remember His covenant forever,
The word which He commanded, for
a thousand generations,
16*The covenant which* He made with
Abraham,
And His oath to Isaac,
17And confirmed it to Jacob for a
statute,
To Israel *for* an everlasting covenant,
18Saying, "To you I will give the land of
Canaan
As the allotment of your inheritance,"
19When you were few in number,
Indeed very few, and strangers in it.

20When they went from one nation to
another,
And from *one* kingdom to another
people,
21He permitted no man to do them
wrong;
Yes, He rebuked kings for their sakes,
22*Saying,* "Do not touch My anointed
ones,
And do My prophets no harm."[a]

23Sing to the LORD, all the earth;
Proclaim the good news of His
salvation from day to day.
24Declare His glory among the nations,
His wonders among all peoples.

25For the LORD *is* great and greatly to be
praised;
He *is* also to be feared above all gods.
26For all the gods of the peoples *are*
idols,
But the LORD made the heavens.
27Honor and majesty *are* before Him;
Strength and gladness are in His
place.

28Give to the LORD, O families of the
peoples,
Give to the LORD glory and strength.
29Give to the LORD the glory *due* His
name;
Bring an offering, and come before
Him.
Oh, worship the LORD in the beauty
of holiness!
30Tremble before Him, all the earth.
The world also is firmly established,
It shall not be moved.

31Let the heavens rejoice, and let the
earth be glad;
And let them say among the nations,
"The LORD reigns."
32Let the sea roar, and all its fullness;
Let the field rejoice, and all that *is* in it.
33Then the trees of the woods shall
rejoice before the LORD,
For He is coming to judge the earth.[a]

34Oh, give thanks to the LORD, for *He is*
good!
For His mercy *endures* forever.[a]
35And say, "Save us, O God of our
salvation;
Gather us together, and deliver us
from the Gentiles,
To give thanks to Your holy name,
To triumph in Your praise."

36Blessed *be* the LORD God of Israel
From everlasting to everlasting![a]

And all the people said, "Amen!" and
praised the LORD.

Regular Worship Maintained

37So he left Asaph and his brothers
there before the ark of the covenant of
the LORD to minister before the ark regularly, as every day's work required; 38and
Obed-Edom with his sixty-eight brethren,
including Obed-Edom the son of Jeduthun, and Hosah, *to be* gatekeepers; 39and
Zadok the priest and his brethren the
priests, before the tabernacle of the LORD
at the high place that *was* at Gibeon, 40to
offer burnt offerings to the LORD on the
altar of burnt offering regularly morning
and evening, and *to do* according to all

16:22 [a]Compare verses 8–22 with Psalm 105:1–15 16:33 [a]Compare verses 23–33 with Psalm 96:1–13 16:34 [a]Compare verse 34 with Psalm 106:1 16:36 [a]Compare verses 35, 36 with Psalm 106:47, 48

Springboards for Preaching and Witnessing

16:34

American Pie

How music savvy are you? Do you know the words to the famous song "American Pie"? Sing along: "Did you write the Book of Love? Do you have faith in God above?... Do you believe in rock and roll? Can music save your mortal soul?"

Interesting words. One of the virtues of being made in God's image is that, unlike animals, we can appreciate good music. No doubt you enjoy listening to a catchy tune, but have you ever taken the time to thank God for the fact that you are not deaf? To be able to hear is a tremendous blessing.

Do you love the vivid colors of flowers and birds on this amazing planet on which we live? Then thank God that you can feast your eyes on all this spectacular color. Count your blessings. Thank Him that you are not blind. If you suddenly go blind, science cannot do a thing for you. It hasn't a clue how to even begin to make an eye. Where do you start? What would you use? Where do you gather the 137 million light-sensitive cells? How do you make focusing muscles that move 100,000 times a day?

Do you enjoy good food? Then thank God that you are not starving to death in some impoverished country, lying on the ground with flies crawling across your face. God has been good to you. He hasn't treated you according to your sins. We can read, think, feel, and love, and it is a sad fact of human nature that familiarity does breed contempt. We don't know what we've got until it's gone. The truth is, most of us have been given a generous slice of the American pie.

Do you love life? Then thank God that you haven't yet died in your sins and been damned from all of His future goodness. It is not too late for you to repent and trust the Savior. And make sure you don't fall into the trap of superficial thanksgiving. Thanksgiving without obedience to God is nothing but empty hypocrisy. Prove that you are genuine in your appreciation of His goodness by obedience to His Word (see John 14:21 for further details).

Now, sing along: "This could be the day that I die; this could be the day that I die..."

that is written in the Law of the LORD which He commanded Israel; 41 and with them Heman and Jeduthun and the rest who were chosen, who were designated by name, to give thanks to the LORD, because His mercy *endures* forever; 42 and with them Heman and Jeduthun, to sound aloud with trumpets and cymbals and the musical instruments of God. Now the sons of Jeduthun *were* gatekeepers.

43 Then all the people departed, every man to his house; and David returned to bless his house.

God's Covenant with David

17 Now it came to pass, when David was dwelling in his house, that David said to Nathan the prophet, "See now, I dwell in a house of cedar, but the ark of the covenant of the LORD *is* under tent curtains."

2 Then Nathan said to David, "Do all that *is* in your heart, for God *is* with you."

3 But it happened that night that the word of God came to Nathan, saying, 4 "Go and tell My servant David, 'Thus says the LORD: "You shall not build Me a house to dwell in. 5 For I have not dwelt in a house since the time that I brought up Israel, even to this day, but have gone from tent to tent, and from *one* tabernacle *to another.* 6 Wherever I have moved about with all Israel, have I ever spoken a word to any of the judges of Israel, whom I commanded to shepherd My people, saying, 'Why have you not built Me a house of cedar?' " ' 7 Now therefore, thus shall you say to My servant David, 'Thus says the LORD of hosts: "I took you from the sheepfold, from following the sheep, to be ruler over My people Israel. 8 And I have been with you wherever you have gone, and have cut off all your enemies from before you, and have made you a name like the name of the great men who *are* on the earth. 9 Moreover I will appoint a place for My people Israel, and will plant them, that they may dwell in a place of their own and move no more; nor shall the sons of wickedness oppress them anymore, as previously, 10 since the time that I commanded judges *to be* over

My people Israel. Also I will subdue all your enemies. Furthermore I tell you that the LORD will build you a house.[a] 11And it shall be, when your days are fulfilled, when you must go *to be* with your fathers, that I will set up your seed after you, who will be of your sons; and I will establish his kingdom. 12He shall build Me a house, and I will establish his throne forever. 13I will be his Father, and he shall be My son; and I will not take My mercy away from him, as I took *it* from *him* who was before you. 14And I will establish him in My house and in My kingdom forever; and his throne shall be established forever." ' "

15According to all these words and according to all this vision, so Nathan spoke to David.

16Then King David went in and sat before the LORD; and he said: "Who *am* I, O LORD God? And what is my house, that You have brought me this far? 17And *yet* this was a small thing in Your sight, O God; and You have *also* spoken of Your servant's house for a great while to come, and have regarded me according to the rank of a man of high degree, O LORD God. 18What more can David *say* to You for the honor of Your servant? For You know Your servant. 19O LORD, for Your servant's sake, and according to Your own heart, You have done all this greatness, in making known all these great things. 20O LORD, *there is* none like You, nor *is there any* God besides You, according to all that we have heard with our ears. 21And who *is* like Your people Israel, the one nation on the earth whom God went to redeem for Himself *as* a people—to make for Yourself a name by great and awesome deeds, by driving out nations from before Your people whom You redeemed from Egypt? 22For You have made Your people Israel Your very own people forever; and You, LORD, have become their God.

23"And now, O LORD, the word which You have spoken concerning Your servant and concerning his house, *let it* be established forever, and do as You have said. 24So let it be established, that Your name may be magnified forever, saying, 'The LORD of hosts, the God of Israel, *is* Israel's God.' And let the house of Your servant David be established before You. 25For You, O my God, have revealed to Your servant that You will build him a house. Therefore Your servant has found it *in his heart* to pray before You. 26And now, LORD, You are God, and have promised this goodness to Your servant. 27Now You have been pleased to bless the house of Your servant, that it may continue before You forever; for You have blessed it, O LORD, and *it shall be* blessed forever."

David's Further Conquests

18 After this it came to pass that David attacked the Philistines, subdued them, and took Gath and its towns from the hand of the Philistines. 2Then he defeated Moab, and the Moabites became David's servants, *and* brought tribute.

3And David defeated Hadadezer[a] king of Zobah *as far as* Hamath, as he went to establish his power by the River Euphrates. 4David took from him one thousand chariots, seven thousand[a] horsemen, and twenty thousand foot soldiers. Also David hamstrung all the chariot

17:10 [a]That is, a royal dynasty 18:3 [a]Hebrew *Hadarezer,* and so throughout chapters 18 and 19 18:4 [a]Or *seven hundred* (compare 2 Samuel 8:4)

17:11 If Jesus tarries, the day will come when we must go to be with our fathers. So make the best use of every precious moment of time. As a Christian, you are more important than the most skilled of surgeons. Surgeons merely prolong death. God has chosen you to proclaim the message of everlasting life to dying humanity. Share the gospel whenever and wherever you can. Always carry gospel tracts, and when you can't stop to talk with people, slip one into their hands and pray that God speaks to them through it.

"Some men's passion is for gold. Some men's passion is for art. Some men's passion is for fame. My passion is for souls." *William Booth*

horses, except that he spared enough of them for one hundred chariots.

5When the Syrians of Damascus came to help Hadadezer king of Zobah, David killed twenty-two thousand of the Syrians. 6Then David put *garrisons* in Syria of Damascus; and the Syrians became David's servants, *and* brought tribute. So the LORD preserved David wherever he went. 7And David took the shields of gold that were on the servants of Hadadezer, and brought them to Jerusalem. 8Also from Tibhath[a] and from Chun, cities of Hadadezer, David brought a large amount of bronze, with which Solomon made the bronze Sea, the pillars, and the articles of bronze.

9Now when Tou[a] king of Hamath heard that David had defeated all the army of Hadadezer king of Zobah, 10he sent Hadoram[a] his son to King David, to greet him and bless him, because he had fought against Hadadezer and defeated him (for Hadadezer had been at war with Tou); and *Hadoram brought with him* all kinds of articles of gold, silver, and bronze. 11King David also dedicated these to the LORD, along with the silver and gold that he had brought from all *these* nations—from Edom, from Moab, from the people of Ammon, from the Philistines, and from Amalek.

12Moreover Abishai the son of Zeruiah killed eighteen thousand Edomites[a] in the Valley of Salt. 13He also put garrisons in Edom, and all the Edomites became David's servants. And the LORD preserved David wherever he went.

David's Administration

14So David reigned over all Israel, and administered judgment and justice to all his people. 15Joab the son of Zeruiah *was* over the army; Jehoshaphat the son of Ahilud *was* recorder; 16Zadok the son of Ahitub and Abimelech the son of Abiathar *were* the priests; Shavsha[a] *was* the scribe; 17Benaiah the son of Jehoiada *was* over the Cherethites and the Pelethites; and David's sons *were* chief ministers at the king's side.

The Ammonites and Syrians Defeated

19 It happened after this that Nahash the king of the people of Ammon died, and his son reigned in his place. 2Then David said, "I will show kindness to Hanun the son of Nahash, because his father showed kindness to me." So David sent messengers to comfort him concerning his father. And David's servants came to Hanun in the land of the people of Ammon to comfort him.

3And the princes of the people of Ammon said to Hanun, "Do you think that David really honors your father because he has sent comforters to you? Did his servants not come to you to search and to overthrow and to spy out the land?"

4Therefore Hanun took David's servants, shaved them, and cut off their garments in the middle, at their buttocks, and sent them away. 5Then *some* went and told David about the men; and he sent to meet them, because the men were greatly ashamed. And the king said, "Wait at Jericho until your beards have grown, and *then* return."

6When the people of Ammon saw that they had made themselves repulsive to David, Hanun and the people of Ammon sent a thousand talents of silver to hire

18:8 [a]Spelled *Betah* in 2 Samuel 8:8 18:9 [a]Spelled *Toi* in 2 Samuel 8:9, 10 18:10 [a]Spelled *Joram* in 2 Samuel 8:10 18:12 [a]Or *Syrians* (compare 2 Samuel 8:13) 18:16 [a]Spelled *Seraiah* in 2 Samuel 8:17

18:14 There is much speculation about why God called David "a man after My own heart" (1 Sam. 13:14; Acts 13:22). This seems strange given his sin with Bathsheba and the fact that God said he was a "man of war" who has shed much blood (1 Chron. 22:8; 28:3). Perhaps it was because David was a king who executed judgment and justice over all his people (see Isa. 56:1; Prov. 21:3), and yet he knew how to show mercy, as he did with King Saul when it seems he could have justifiably killed him.

for themselves chariots and horsemen from Mesopotamia,[a] from Syrian Maacah, and from Zobah.[b] 7So they hired for themselves thirty-two thousand chariots, with the king of Maacah and his people, who came and encamped before Medeba. Also the people of Ammon gathered together from their cities, and came to battle.

8Now when David heard *of it,* he sent Joab and all the army of the mighty men. 9Then the people of Ammon came out and put themselves in battle array before the gate of the city, and the kings who had come *were* by themselves in the field.

10When Joab saw that the battle line was against him before and behind, he chose some of Israel's best, and put *them* in battle array against the Syrians. 11And the rest of the people he put under the command of Abishai his brother, and they set *themselves* in battle array against the people of Ammon. 12Then he said, "If the Syrians are too strong for me, then you shall help me; but if the people of Ammon are too strong for you, then I will help you. 13Be of good courage, and let us be strong for our people and for the cities of our God. And may the LORD do *what is* good in His sight."

14So Joab and the people who *were* with him drew near for the battle against the Syrians, and they fled before him. 15When the people of Ammon saw that the Syrians were fleeing, they also fled before Abishai his brother, and entered the city. So Joab went to Jerusalem.

16Now when the Syrians saw that they had been defeated by Israel, they sent messengers and brought the Syrians who were beyond the River,[a] and Shophach[b] the commander of Hadadezer's army *went* before them. 17When it was told David, he gathered all Israel, crossed over the Jordan and came upon them, and set up in *battle* array against them. So when David had set up in battle array against the Syrians, they fought with him. 18Then the Syrians fled before Israel; and David killed seven thousand[a] charioteers and forty thousand foot soldiers[b] of the Syrians, and killed Shophach the commander of the army. 19And when the servants of Hadadezer saw that they were defeated by Israel, they made peace with David and became his servants. So the Syrians were not willing to help the people of Ammon anymore.

Rabbah Is Conquered

20 It happened in the spring of the year, at the time kings go out *to battle,* that Joab led out the armed forces and ravaged the country of the people of Ammon, and came and besieged Rabbah. But David stayed at Jerusalem. And Joab defeated Rabbah and overthrew it. 2Then David took their king's crown from his head, and found it to weigh a talent of gold, and *there were* precious stones in it. And it was set on David's head. Also he brought out the spoil of the city in great abundance. 3And he brought out the people who *were* in it, and put *them* to work[a] with saws, with iron picks, and with axes. So David did to all the cities of the people of Ammon. Then David and all the people returned *to* Jerusalem.

Philistine Giants Destroyed

4Now it happened afterward that war broke out at Gezer with the Philistines, at which time Sibbechai the Hushathite killed Sippai,[a] *who was one* of the sons of the giant. And they were subdued.

5Again there was war with the Philistines, and Elhanan the son of Jair[a] killed

19:6 [a]Hebrew *Aram Naharaim* [b]Spelled *Zoba* in 2 Samuel 10:6 19:16 [a]That is, the Euphrates [b]Spelled *Shobach* in 2 Samuel 10:16 19:18 [a]Or *seven hundred* (compare 2 Samuel 10:18) [b]Or *horsemen* (compare 2 Samuel 10:18) 20:3 [a]Septuagint reads *cut them.* 20:4 [a]Spelled *Saph* in 2 Samuel 21:18 20:5 [a]Spelled *Jaare-Oregim* in 2 Samuel 21:19

19:19 A sinner who understands that he is an enemy of Almighty God is wise to surrender and become a servant. See Luke 14:31,32 for what Jesus had to say about the subject.

Lahmi the brother of Goliath the Gittite, the shaft of whose spear *was* like a weaver's beam.

6Yet again there was war at Gath, where there was a man of *great* stature, with twenty-four fingers and toes, six *on each hand* and six *on each foot;* and he also was born to the giant. 7So when he defied Israel, Jonathan the son of Shimea,[a] David's brother, killed him.

8These were born to the giant in Gath, and they fell by the hand of David and by the hand of his servants.

The Census of Israel and Judah

21 Now Satan stood up against Israel, and moved David to number Israel. 2So David said to Joab and to the leaders of the people, "Go, number Israel from Beersheba to Dan, and bring the number of them to me that I may know *it.*"

3And Joab answered, "May the LORD make His people a hundred times more than they are. But, my lord the king, *are* they not all my lord's servants? Why then does my lord require this thing? Why should he be a cause of guilt in Israel?"

4Nevertheless the king's word prevailed against Joab. Therefore Joab departed and went throughout all Israel and came to Jerusalem. 5Then Joab gave the sum of the number of the people to David. All Israel *had* one million one hundred thousand men who drew the sword, and Judah *had* four hundred and seventy thousand men who drew the sword. 6But he did not count Levi and Benjamin among them, for the king's word was abominable to Joab.

7And God was displeased with this thing; therefore He struck Israel. 8So David said to God, "I have sinned greatly, because I have done this thing; but now, I pray, take away the iniquity of Your servant, for I have done very foolishly."

9Then the LORD spoke to Gad, David's seer, saying, 10"Go and tell David, saying, 'Thus says the LORD: "I offer you three *things;* choose one of them for yourself, that I may do *it* to you." ' "

11So Gad came to David and said to him, "Thus says the LORD: 'Choose for yourself, 12either three[a] years of famine, or three months to be defeated by your foes with the sword of your enemies overtaking *you,* or else for three days the sword of the LORD—the plague in the land, with the angel[b] of the LORD destroying throughout all the territory of Israel.' Now consider what answer I should take back to Him who sent me."

13And David said to Gad, "I am in great distress. Please let me fall into the hand of the LORD, for His mercies *are* very great; but do not let me fall into the hand of man."

14So the LORD sent a plague upon Israel, and seventy thousand men of Israel fell. 15And God sent an angel to Jerusalem to destroy it. As he[a] was destroying, the LORD looked and relented of the dis-

20:7 [a]Spelled *Shimeah* in 2 Samuel 21:21 and *Shammah* in 1 Samuel 16:9 **21:12** [a]Or *seven* (compare 2 Samuel 24:13) [b]Or *Angel*, and so elsewhere in this chapter **21:15** [a]Or *He* [b]Or *Your* [c]Spelled *Araunah* in 2 Samuel 24:16

20:6,7 No doubt Jonathan was spurred on by David's courage against Goliath, as we are inspired by the example of those who have so courageously gone before us. See Heb. 11 for a list of godly heroes.

21:1 Should we try to number converts? There is always a temptation to track numbers when it comes to evangelism. It is wise not to do so, because only God knows those who are truly repentant. It is amazing how many evangelists and preachers seem to have access to the Book of Life by citing salvation statistics, but such numbering reveals a lack of understanding of the nature of true and false conversion. Making a "decision," walking an aisle, or raising a hand do not indicate whether someone truly repents and trusts in the Savior. The fact that we have planted the good seed of the Word of God is evangelistic "success." The rest is up to God.

Regarding keeping tabs of "decisions for Christ," *D. L. Moody* stated: "'Is it well to number converts?' [David] got into trouble by trying to number Israel. It is best to let the Lord keep the record. It makes me creep all over to hear a man tell how many he has converted."

aster, and said to the angel who was destroying, "It is enough; now restrain your[b] hand." And the angel of the LORD stood by the threshing floor of Ornan[c] the Jebusite.

16Then David lifted his eyes and saw the angel of the LORD standing between earth and heaven, having in his hand a drawn sword stretched out over Jerusalem. So David and the elders, clothed in sackcloth, fell on their faces. 17And David said to God, "Was it not I who commanded the people to be numbered? I am the one who has sinned and done evil indeed; but these sheep, what have they done? Let Your hand, I pray, O LORD my God, be against me and my father's house, but not against Your people that they should be plagued."

18Therefore, the angel of the LORD commanded Gad to say to David that David should go and erect an altar to the LORD on the threshing floor of Ornan the Jebusite. 19So David went up at the word of Gad, which he had spoken in the name of the LORD. 20Now Ornan turned and saw the angel; and his four sons *who were* with him hid themselves, but Ornan continued threshing wheat. 21So David came to Ornan, and Ornan looked and saw David. And he went out from the threshing floor, and bowed before David with *his* face to the ground. 22Then David said to Ornan, "Grant me the place of *this* threshing floor, that I may build an altar on it to the LORD. You shall grant it to me at the full price, that the plague may be withdrawn from the people."

23But Ornan said to David, "Take *it* to yourself, and let my lord the king do *what is* good in his eyes. Look, I *also* give *you* the oxen for burnt offerings, the threshing implements for wood, and the wheat for the grain offering; I give *it* all."

24Then King David said to Ornan, "No, but I will surely buy *it* for the full price, for I will not take what is yours for the LORD, nor offer burnt offerings with *that which* costs *me* nothing." 25So David gave Ornan six hundred shekels of gold by weight for the place. 26And David built there an altar to the LORD, and offered burnt offerings and peace offerings, and called on the LORD; and He answered him from heaven by fire on the altar of burnt offering.

27So the LORD commanded the angel, and he returned his sword to its sheath.

28At that time, when David saw that the LORD had answered him on the threshing floor of Ornan the Jebusite, he sacrificed there. 29For the tabernacle of the LORD and the altar of the burnt offering, which Moses had made in the wilderness, *were* at that time at the high place in Gibeon. 30But David could not go before it to inquire of God, for he was afraid of the sword of the angel of the LORD.

David Prepares to Build the Temple

22 Then David said, "This *is* the house of the LORD God, and this *is* the altar of burnt offering for Israel." 2So David commanded to gather the aliens who *were* in the land of Israel; and he appointed masons to cut hewn stones to build the house of God. 3And David prepared iron in abundance for the nails of the doors of the gates and for the joints, and bronze in abundance beyond measure, 4and cedar trees in abundance; for the Sidonians and those from Tyre brought much cedar wood to David.

5Now David said, "Solomon my son *is* young and inexperienced, and the house to be built for the LORD *must be* exceedingly magnificent, famous and glorious throughout all countries. I will now make preparation for it." So David made abundant preparations before his death.

6Then he called for his son Solomon, and charged him to build a house for the LORD God of Israel. 7And David said to Solomon: "My son, as for me, it was in my mind to build a house to the name of the LORD my God; 8but the word of the LORD came to me, saying, 'You have shed much blood and have made great wars; you shall not build a house for My name, because you have shed much blood on

the earth in My sight. 9Behold, a son shall be born to you, who shall be a man of rest; and I will give him rest from all his enemies all around. His name shall be Solomon,[a] for I will give peace and quietness to Israel in his days. 10He shall build a house for My name, and he shall be My son, and I *will be* his Father; and I will establish the throne of his kingdom over Israel forever.' 11Now, my son, may the LORD be with you; and may you prosper, and build the house of the LORD your God, as He has said to you. 12Only may the LORD give you wisdom and understanding, and give you charge concerning Israel, that you may keep the law of the LORD your God. 13Then you will prosper, if you take care to fulfill the statutes and judgments with which the LORD charged Moses concerning Israel. Be strong and of good courage; do not fear nor be dismayed. 14Indeed I have taken much trouble to prepare for the house of the LORD one hundred thousand talents of gold and one million talents of silver, and bronze and iron beyond measure, for it is so abundant. I have prepared timber and stone also, and you may add to them. 15Moreover *there are* workmen with you in abundance: woodsmen and stonecutters, and all types of skillful men for every kind of work. 16Of gold and silver and bronze and iron *there is* no limit. Arise and begin working, and the LORD be with you."

17David also commanded all the leaders of Israel to help Solomon his son, *saying*, 18"Is not the LORD your God with you? And has He *not* given you rest on every side? For He has given the inhabitants of the land into my hand, and the land is subdued before the LORD and before His people. 19Now set your heart and your soul to seek the LORD your God. Therefore arise and build the sanctuary of the LORD God, to bring the ark of the covenant of the LORD and the holy articles of God into the house that is to be built for the name of the LORD."

The Divisions of the Levites

23 So when David was old and full of days, he made his son Solomon king over Israel.

2And he gathered together all the leaders of Israel, with the priests and the Levites. 3Now the Levites were numbered from the age of thirty years and above; and the number of individual males was thirty-eight thousand. 4Of these, twenty-four thousand *were* to look after the work of the house of the LORD, six thousand *were* officers and judges, 5four thousand *were* gatekeepers, and four thousand praised the LORD with *musical* instruments, "which I made," *said David,* "for giving praise."

6Also David separated them into divisions among the sons of Levi: Gershon, Kohath, and Merari.

7Of the Gershonites: Laadan[a] and Shimei. 8The sons of Laadan: the first Jehiel, then Zetham and Joel—three *in all.* 9The sons of Shimei: Shelomith, Haziel, and Haran—three *in all.* These were the heads of the fathers' *houses* of Laadan. 10And the sons of Shimei: Jahath, Zina,[a] Jeush, and Beriah. These *were* the four sons of Shimei. 11Jahath was the first and Zizah the second. But Jeush and Beriah did not have many sons; therefore they were assigned as one father's house.

12The sons of Kohath: Amram, Izhar, Hebron, and Uzziel—four *in all.* 13The sons of Amram: Aaron and Moses; and Aaron was set apart, he and his sons forever, that he should sanctify the most holy things, to burn incense before the LORD, to minister to Him, and to give the

22:9 [a]Literally *Peaceful* 23:7 [a]Spelled *Libni* in Exodus 6:17 23:10 [a]Septuagint and Vulgate read *Zizah* (compare verse 11).

22:11 There is no greater truth than to know that God is with you. The word "good-bye" comes from the old English phrase "God be with ye." See Rom. 8:31–39 to see how much God is "with" those who love His Son.

blessing in His name forever. [14]Now the
sons of Moses the man of God were reckoned to the tribe of Levi. [15]The sons of
Moses *were* Gershon[a] and Eliezer. [16]Of the
sons of Gershon, Shebuel[a] *was* the first.
[17]Of the descendants of Eliezer, Rehabiah
was the first. And Eliezer had no other
sons, but the sons of Rehabiah were very
many. [18]Of the sons of Izhar, Shelomith
was the first. [19]Of the sons of Hebron, Jeriah *was* the first, Amariah the second, Jahaziel the third, and Jekameam the
fourth. [20]Of the sons of Uzziel, Michah
was the first and Jesshiah the second.

[21]The sons of Merari *were* Mahli and
Mushi. The sons of Mahli *were* Eleazar
and Kish. [22]And Eleazar died, and had no
sons, but only daughters; and their brethren, the sons of Kish, took them *as wives.*
[23]The sons of Mushi *were* Mahli, Eder,
and Jeremoth—three *in all.*

[24]These *were* the sons of Levi by their
fathers' houses—the heads of the fathers'
houses as they were counted individually
by the number of their names, who did
the work for the service of the house of
the LORD, from the age of twenty years
and above.

[25]For David said, "The LORD God of Israel has given rest to His people, that
they may dwell in Jerusalem forever";
[26]and also to the Levites, "They shall no
longer carry the tabernacle, or any of the
articles for its service." [27]For by the last
words of David the Levites *were* numbered from twenty years old and above;
[28]because their duty *was* to help the sons
of Aaron in the service of the house of the
LORD, in the courts and in the chambers,
in the purifying of all holy things and the
work of the service of the house of God,
[29]both with the showbread and the fine
flour for the grain offering, with the unleavened cakes and *what is baked in* the
pan, with what is mixed and with all
kinds of measures and sizes; [30]to stand
every morning to thank and praise the
LORD, and likewise at evening; [31]and at
every presentation of a burnt offering to
the LORD on the Sabbaths and on the
New Moons and on the set feasts, by
number according to the ordinance governing them, regularly before the LORD;
[32]and that they should attend to the
needs of the tabernacle of meeting, the
needs of the holy *place,* and the needs of
the sons of Aaron their brethren in the
work of the house of the LORD.

The Divisions of the Priests

24 Now *these are* the divisions of the
sons of Aaron. The sons of Aaron
were Nadab, Abihu, Eleazar, and Ithamar.
[2]And Nadab and Abihu died before their
father, and had no children; therefore
Eleazar and Ithamar ministered as priests.
[3]Then David with Zadok of the sons of
Eleazar, and Ahimelech of the sons of
Ithamar, divided them according to the
schedule of their service.

[4]There were more leaders found of the
sons of Eleazar than of the sons of Ithamar, and *thus* they were divided. Among
the sons of Eleazar *were* sixteen heads of
their fathers' houses, and eight heads of
their fathers' houses among the sons of
Ithamar. [5]Thus they were divided by lot,
one group as another, for there were officials of the sanctuary and officials *of the
house* of God, from the sons of Eleazar
and from the sons of Ithamar. [6]And the
scribe, Shemaiah the son of Nethanel, *one
of* the Levites, wrote them down before
the king, the leaders, Zadok the priest,
Ahimelech the son of Abiathar, and the
heads of the fathers' *houses* of the priests

23:15 [a]Hebrew *Gershom* (compare 6:16) 23:16 [a]Spelled *Shubael* in 24:20

23:30 It is easy to praise God, in light of the cross. See Gal. 6:14 for Paul's attitude toward Calvary.

24:2 It is tragic when the Church is barren. Too much of what is called "church growth" is nothing but Christians playing musical pews. There must be a passion for the lost for there to be new life within the Church.

and Levites, one father's house taken for Eleazar and *one* for Ithamar.

[7]Now the first lot fell to Jehoiarib, the second to Jedaiah, [8]the third to Harim, the fourth to Seorim, [9]the fifth to Malchijah, the sixth to Mijamin, [10]the seventh to Hakkoz, the eighth to Abijah, [11]the ninth to Jeshua, the tenth to Shecaniah, [12]the eleventh to Eliashib, the twelfth to Jakim, [13]the thirteenth to Huppah, the fourteenth to Jeshebeab, [14]the fifteenth to Bilgah, the sixteenth to Immer, [15]the seventeenth to Hezir, the eighteenth to Happizzez,[a] [16]the nineteenth to Pethahiah, the twentieth to Jehezekel,[a] [17]the twenty-first to Jachin, the twenty-second to Gamul, [18]the twenty-third to Delaiah, the twenty-fourth to Maaziah.

[19]This *was* the schedule of their service for coming into the house of the LORD according to their ordinance by the hand of Aaron their father, as the LORD God of Israel had commanded him.

Other Levites

[20]And the rest of the sons of Levi: of the sons of Amram, Shubael;[a] of the sons of Shubael, Jehdeiah. [21]Concerning Rehabiah, of the sons of Rehabiah, the first *was* Isshiah. [22]Of the Izharites, Shelomoth;[a] of the sons of Shelomoth, Jahath. [23]Of the sons *of Hebron,*[a] Jeriah *was the first,*[b] Amariah the second, Jahaziel the third, *and* Jekameam the fourth. [24]*Of* the sons of Uzziel, Michah; of the sons of Michah, Shamir. [25]The brother of Michah, Isshiah; of the sons of Isshiah, Zechariah. [26]The sons of Merari *were* Mahli and Mushi; the son of Jaaziah, Beno. [27]The sons of Merari by Jaaziah *were* Beno, Shoham, Zaccur, and Ibri. [28]Of Mahli: Eleazar, who had no sons. [29]Of Kish: the son of Kish, Jerahmeel.

[30]Also the sons of Mushi *were* Mahli, Eder, and Jerimoth. These *were* the sons of the Levites according to their fathers' houses.

[31]These also cast lots just as their brothers the sons of Aaron did, in the presence of King David, Zadok, Ahimelech, and the heads of the fathers' *houses* of the priests and Levites. The chief fathers *did* just as their younger brethren.

The Musicians

25 Moreover David and the captains of the army separated for the service *some* of the sons of Asaph, of Heman, and of Jeduthun, who *should* prophesy with harps, stringed instruments, and cymbals. And the number of the skilled men performing their service was: [2]Of the sons of Asaph: Zaccur, Joseph, Nethaniah, and Asharelah;[a] the sons of Asaph *were* under the direction of Asaph, who prophesied according to the order of the king. [3]Of Jeduthun, the sons of Jeduthun: Gedaliah, Zeri,[a] Jeshaiah, Shimei, Hashabiah, and Mattithiah, six,[b] under the direction of their father Jeduthun, who prophesied with a harp to give thanks and to praise the LORD. [4]Of Heman, the sons of Heman: Bukkiah, Mattaniah, Uzziel,[a] Shebuel,[b] Jerimoth,[c] Hananiah, Hanani, Eliathah, Giddalti, Romamti-Ezer, Joshbekashah, Mallothi, Hothir, *and* Mahazioth. [5]All these *were* the sons of Heman the king's seer in the words of God, to exalt his horn.[a] For God gave Heman fourteen sons and three daughters.

[6]All these *were* under the direction of their father for the music *in* the house of the LORD, with cymbals, stringed instruments, and harps, for the service of the house of God. Asaph, Jeduthun, and Heman *were* under the authority of the king. [7]So the number of them, with their brethren who were instructed in the songs of the LORD, all who were skillful, *was* two hundred and eighty-eight.

[8]And they cast lots for their duty, the

24:15 [a]Septuagint and Vulgate read *Aphses.* 24:16 [a]Masoretic Text reads *Jehezkel.* 24:20 [a]Spelled *Shebuel* in 23:16 24:22 [a]Spelled *Shelomith* in 23:18 24:23 [a]Supplied from 23:19 (following some Hebrew manuscripts and Septuagint manuscripts) [b]Supplied from 23:19 (following some Hebrew manuscripts and Septuagint manuscripts) 25:2 [a]Spelled *Jesharelah* in verse 14 25:3 [a]Spelled *Jizri* in verse 11 [b]*Shimei,* appearing in one Hebrew and several Septuagint manuscripts, completes the total of six sons (compare verse 17). 25:4 [a]Spelled *Azarel* in verse 18 [b]Spelled *Shubael* in verse 20 [c]Spelled *Jeremoth* in verse 22 25:5 [a]That is, to increase his power or influence

small as well as the great, the teacher
with the student.
9Now the first lot for Asaph came out
for Joseph; the second for Gedaliah, him
with his brethren and sons, twelve; 10the
third for Zaccur, his sons and his brethren, twelve; 11the fourth for Jizri,[a] his
sons and his brethren, twelve; 12the fifth
for Nethaniah, his sons and his brethren,
twelve; 13the sixth for Bukkiah, his sons
and his brethren, twelve; 14the seventh
for Jesharelah,[a] his sons and his brethren,
twelve; 15the eighth for Jeshaiah, his sons
and his brethren, twelve; 16the ninth for
Mattaniah, his sons and his brethren,
twelve; 17the tenth for Shimei, his sons
and his brethren, twelve; 18the eleventh
for Azarel,[a] his sons and his brethren,
twelve; 19the twelfth for Hashabiah, his
sons and his brethren, twelve; 20the thirteenth for Shubael,[a] his sons and his brethren, twelve; 21the fourteenth for Mattithiah, his sons and his brethren, twelve;
22the fifteenth for Jeremoth,[a] his sons and
his brethren, twelve; 23the sixteenth for
Hananiah, his sons and his brethren,
twelve; 24the seventeenth for Joshbekashah, his sons and his brethren, twelve;
25the eighteenth for Hanani, his sons and
his brethren, twelve; 26the nineteenth for
Mallothi, his sons and his brethren,
twelve; 27the twentieth for Eliathah, his
sons and his brethren, twelve; 28the
twenty-first for Hothir, his sons and his
brethren, twelve; 29the twenty-second for
Giddalti, his sons and his brethren, twelve;
30the twenty-third for Mahazioth, his sons
and his brethren, twelve; 31the twenty-
fourth for Romamti-Ezer, his sons and his
brethren, twelve.

The Gatekeepers

26 Concerning the divisions of the
gatekeepers: of the Korahites,
Meshelemiah the son of Kore, of the sons
of Asaph. 2And the sons of Meshelemiah
were Zechariah the firstborn, Jediael the
second, Zebadiah the third, Jathniel the
fourth, 3Elam the fifth, Jehohanan the
sixth, Eliehoenai the seventh.
4Moreover the sons of Obed-Edom *were*
Shemaiah the firstborn, Jehozabad the
second, Joah the third, Sacar the fourth,
Nethanel the fifth, 5Ammiel the sixth, Issachar the seventh, Peulthai the eighth;
for God blessed him.
6Also to Shemaiah his son were sons
born who governed their fathers' houses,
because they *were* men of great ability.
7The sons of Shemaiah *were* Othni,
Rephael, Obed, and Elzabad, whose brothers Elihu and Semachiah *were* able men.
8All these *were* of the sons of Obed-
Edom, they and their sons and their brethren, able men with strength for the work:
sixty-two of Obed-Edom.
9And Meshelemiah had sons and
brethren, eighteen able men.
10Also Hosah, of the children of Merari, had sons: Shimri the first (for *though*
he was not the firstborn, his father made
him the first), 11Hilkiah the second, Teba-
liah the third, Zechariah the fourth; all the
sons and brethren of Hosah *were* thirteen.
12Among these *were* the divisions of
the gatekeepers, among the chief men,
having duties just like their brethren, to
serve in the house of the LORD. 13And
they cast lots for each gate, the small as
well as the great, according to their father's house. 14The lot for the East *Gate*
fell to Shelemiah. Then they cast lots *for*
his son Zechariah, a wise counselor, and
his lot came out for the North Gate; 15to
Obed-Edom the South Gate, and to his
sons the storehouse.[a] 16To Shuppim and
Hosah *the lot came out* for the West Gate,
with the Shallecheth Gate on the ascending highway—watchman opposite watchman. 17On the east *were* six Levites, on
the north four each day, on the south four
each day, and for the storehouse[a] two by
two. 18As for the Parbar[a] on the west,
there were four on the highway *and* two at
the Parbar. 19These were the divisions of

25:11 [a]Spelled *Zeri* in verse 3 25:14 [a]Spelled *Asharelah* in verse 2 25:18 [a]Spelled *Uzziel* in verse 4 25:20 [a]Spelled *Shebuel* in verse 4 25:22 [a]Spelled *Jerimoth* in verse 4 26:15 [a]Hebrew *asuppim* 26:17 [a]Hebrew *asuppim* 26:18 [a]Probably a court or colonnade extending west of the temple

the gatekeepers among the sons of Korah and among the sons of Merari.

The Treasuries and Other Duties

20Of the Levites, Ahijah *was* over the treasuries of the house of God and over the treasuries of the dedicated things. 21The sons of Laadan, the descendants of the Gershonites of Laadan, heads of their fathers' *houses*, of Laadan the Gershonite: Jehieli. 22The sons of Jehieli, Zetham and Joel his brother, *were* over the treasuries of the house of the LORD. 23Of the Amramites, the Izharites, the Hebronites, and the Uzzielites: 24Shebuel the son of Gershom, the son of Moses, *was* overseer of the treasuries. 25And his brethren by Eliezer *were* Rehabiah his son, Jeshaiah his son, Joram his son, Zichri his son, and Shelomith his son.

26This Shelomith and his brethren *were* over all the treasuries of the dedicated things which King David and the heads of fathers' *houses*, the captains over thousands and hundreds, and the captains of the army, had dedicated. 27Some of the spoils won in battles they dedicated to maintain the house of the LORD. 28And all that Samuel the seer, Saul the son of Kish, Abner the son of Ner, and Joab the son of Zeruiah had dedicated, every dedicated *thing*, was under the hand of Shelomith and his brethren.

29Of the Izharites, Chenaniah and his sons *performed* duties as officials and judges over Israel outside Jerusalem.

30Of the Hebronites, Hashabiah and his brethren, one thousand seven hundred able men, had the oversight of Israel on the west side of the Jordan for all the business of the LORD, and in the service of the king. 31Among the Hebronites, Jerijah *was* head of the Hebronites according to his genealogy of the fathers. In the fortieth year of the reign of David they were sought, and there were found among them capable men at Jazer of Gilead. 32And his brethren *were* two thousand seven hundred able men, heads of fathers' *houses*, whom King David made officials over the Reubenites, the Gadites, and the half-tribe of Manasseh, for every matter pertaining to God and the affairs of the king.

The Military Divisions

27 And the children of Israel, according to their number, the heads of fathers' *houses*, the captains of thousands and hundreds and their officers, served the king in every matter of the *military* divisions. *These divisions* came in and went out month by month throughout all the months of the year, each division *having* twenty-four thousand.

2Over the first division for the first month *was* Jashobeam the son of Zabdiel, and in his division *were* twenty-four thousand; 3*he was* of the children of Perez, and the chief of all the captains of the army for the first month. 4Over the division of the second month *was* Dodai[a] an Ahohite, and of his division Mikloth also *was* the leader; in his division *were* twenty-four thousand. 5The third captain of the army for the third month *was* Benaiah, the son of Jehoiada the priest, who was chief; in his division *were* twenty-four thousand. 6This was the Benaiah *who was* mighty *among* the thirty, and was over the thirty; in his division *was* Ammizabad his son. 7The fourth *captain* for the fourth month *was* Asahel the brother of Joab, and Zebadiah his son after him; in his division *were* twenty-four thousand. 8The fifth captain for the fifth month *was* Shamhuth[a] the Izrahite; in his division were twenty-four thousand. 9The sixth

27:4 [a]Hebrew *Dodai*, usually spelled *Dodo* (compare 2 Samuel 23:9) 27:8 [a]Spelled *Shammoth* in 11:27 and *Shammah* in 2 Samuel 23:11

27:6 See 2 Sam. 8:18 and 23:20–23 for further references to this mighty warrior. You have the mind of Christ. You have access to the power of prayer and the armor of God. The Lord is with you, and He gave you His Holy Spirit as a helper. You have been entrusted with the everlasting gospel in the last days. Believe what you are in Christ, and use the valor and might that you have in Him to reach this sinful world.

captain for the sixth month *was* Ira the
son of Ikkesh the Tekoite; in his division
were twenty-four thousand. 10The seventh
captain for the seventh month *was* Helez
the Pelonite, of the children of Ephraim;
in his division *were* twenty-four thousand.
11The eighth *captain* for the eighth month
was Sibbechai the Hushathite, of the Zarhites; in his division *were* twenty-four
thousand. 12The ninth *captain* for the
ninth month *was* Abiezer the Anathothite, of the Benjamites; in his division *were*
twenty-four thousand. 13The tenth *captain*
for the tenth month *was* Maharai the Netophathite, of the Zarhites; in his division
were twenty-four thousand. 14The eleventh *captain* for the eleventh month *was*
Benaiah the Pirathonite, of the children
of Ephraim; in his division *were* twenty-
four thousand. 15The twelfth *captain* for
the twelfth month *was* Heldai[a] the Netophathite, of Othniel; in his division *were*
twenty-four thousand.

Leaders of Tribes

16Furthermore, over the tribes of Israel: the officer over the Reubenites *was*
Eliezer the son of Zichri; over the Simeonites, Shephatiah the son of Maachah;
17*over* the Levites, Hashabiah the son of
Kemuel; over the Aaronites, Zadok; 18*over*
Judah, Elihu, *one* of David's brothers; *over*
Issachar, Omri the son of Michael; 19*over*
Zebulun, Ishmaiah the son of Obadiah;
over Naphtali, Jerimoth the son of Azriel;
20*over* the children of Ephraim, Hoshea
the son of Azaziah; *over* the half-tribe of
Manasseh, Joel the son of Pedaiah; 21*over*
the half-*tribe* of Manasseh in Gilead, Iddo
the son of Zechariah; *over* Benjamin, Jaasiel
the son of Abner; 22*over* Dan, Azarel the
son of Jeroham. These *were* the leaders of
the tribes of Israel.

23But David did not take the number
of those twenty years old and under, because the LORD had said He would multiply Israel like the stars of the heavens.
24Joab the son of Zeruiah began a census,
but he did not finish, for wrath came
upon Israel because of this census; nor
was the number recorded in the account
of the chronicles of King David.

Other State Officials

25And Azmaveth the son of Adiel *was*
over the king's treasuries; and Jehonathan
the son of Uzziah was over the storehouses in the field, in the cities, in the
villages, and in the fortresses. 26Ezri the
son of Chelub was over those who did
the work of the field for tilling the
ground. 27And Shimei the Ramathite *was*
over the vineyards, and Zabdi the Shiph-
mite was over the produce of the vineyards for the supply of wine. 28Baal-Hanan
the Gederite was over the olive trees and
the sycamore trees that *were* in the lowlands, and Joash *was* over the store of oil.
29And Shitrai the Sharonite *was* over the
herds that fed in Sharon, and Shaphat the
son of Adlai was over the herds *that were*
in the valleys. 30Obil the Ishmaelite *was*
over the camels, Jehdeiah the Meronothite *was* over the donkeys, 31and Jaziz the
Hagrite *was* over the flocks. All these *were*
the officials over King David's property.

32Also Jehonathan, David's uncle, *was*
a counselor, a wise man, and a scribe;
and Jehiel the son of Hachmoni *was* with
the king's sons. 33Ahithophel *was* the king's
counselor, and Hushai the Archite *was*
the king's companion. 34After Ahithophel
was Jehoiada the son of Benaiah, then
Abiathar. And the general of the king's
army *was* Joab.

Solomon Instructed to Build the Temple

28 Now David assembled at Jerusalem all the leaders of Israel: the
officers of the tribes and the captains of
the divisions who served the king, the
captains over thousands and captains
over hundreds, and the stewards over all
the substance and possessions of the king
and of his sons, with the officials, the
valiant men, and all the mighty men of
valor.

27:15 [a]Spelled *Heled* in 11:30 and *Heleb* in 2 Samuel 23:29

QUESTIONS & OBJECTIONS

"You believe Christianity only because you were raised in a Christian culture."

It is true that children do tend to adopt the religion they learned about from their parents. In all other religions, one automatically becomes a follower by birth, by being baptized as an infant, or by observing certain religious practices. For example, a child is a Jew if born to a Jewish mother, or is considered a Mormon or Muslim if born into a Mormon or Muslim family. But one becomes a Christian only by personally repenting of his sins and placing his trust in Jesus Christ alone for his salvation. It is an individual decision, regardless of the religion practiced by the parents. Many people raised in other cultures decide to leave their religion and become Christians. God knows those whose hearts are truly seeking Him, and He ensures that they hear the gospel no matter where they are located. He can reveal Himself to people even in the midst of Hindu, Muslim, or animist cultures, so that they can put their trust in the Savior.

Also, keep in mind that believing something doesn't necessarily make it true. Other religions are not equally true just because people were raised to believe them. Only Christianity is backed up by objective, historical, archaeological, and experiential evidence to verify that it is true.

2Then King David rose to his feet and
said, "Hear me, my brethren and my people: I *had* it in my heart to build a house
of rest for the ark of the covenant of the
LORD, and for the footstool of our God,
and had made preparations to build it.
3But God said to me, 'You shall not build
a house for My name, because you *have
been* a man of war and have shed blood.'
4However the LORD God of Israel chose
me above all the house of my father to be
king over Israel forever, for He has chosen Judah *to be* the ruler. And of the
house of Judah, the house of my father,
and among the sons of my father, He was
pleased with me to make *me* king over all
Israel. 5And of all my sons (for the LORD
has given me many sons) He has chosen
my son Solomon to sit on the throne of
the kingdom of the LORD over Israel.
6Now He said to me, 'It is your son Solomon *who* shall build My house and My
courts; for I have chosen him *to be* My
son, and I will be his Father. 7Moreover I
will establish his kingdom forever, if he is
steadfast to observe My commandments
and My judgments, as it is this day.' 8Now
therefore, in the sight of all Israel, the assembly of the LORD, and in the hearing of
our God, be careful to seek out all the
commandments of the LORD your God,
that you may possess this good land, and
leave *it* as an inheritance for your children after you forever.

9"As for you, my son Solomon, know
the God of your father, and serve Him
with a loyal heart and with a willing
mind; for the LORD searches all hearts and
understands all the intent of the thoughts.
If you seek Him, He will be found by
you; but if you forsake Him, He will cast
you off forever. 10Consider now, for the
LORD has chosen you to build a house for
the sanctuary; be strong, and do it."

11Then David gave his son Solomon
the plans for the vestibule, its houses, its
treasuries, its upper chambers, its inner
chambers, and the place of the mercy
seat; 12and the plans for all that he had by
the Spirit, of the courts of the house of
the LORD, of all the chambers all around,
of the treasuries of the house of God, and
of the treasuries for the dedicated things;
13also for the division of the priests and
the Levites, for all the work of the service
of the house of the LORD, and for all the
articles of service in the house of the
LORD. 14*He gave* gold by weight for *things*
of gold, for all articles used in every kind
of service; also *silver* for all articles of silver by weight, for all articles used in
every kind of service; 15the weight for the
lampstands of gold, and their lamps of
gold, by weight for each lampstand and
its lamps; for the lampstands of silver by
weight, for the lampstand and its lamps,

according to the use of each lampstand. [16]And by weight *he gave* gold for the tables of the showbread, for each table, and silver for the tables of silver; [17]also pure gold for the forks, the basins, the pitchers of pure gold, and the golden bowls—*he gave gold* by weight for every bowl; and for the silver bowls, *silver* by weight for every bowl; [18]and refined gold by weight for the altar of incense, and for the construction of the chariot, that is, the gold cherubim that spread *their wings* and overshadowed the ark of the covenant of the LORD. [19]"All *this,*" *said David,* "the LORD made me understand in writing, by *His* hand upon me, all the works of these plans."

[20]And David said to his son Solomon, "Be strong and of good courage, and do *it;* do not fear nor be dismayed, for the LORD God—my God—*will be* with you. He will not leave you nor forsake you, until you have finished all the work for the service of the house of the LORD. [21]*Here are* the divisions of the priests and the Levites for all the service of the house of God; and every willing craftsman *will be* with you for all manner of workmanship, for every kind of service; also the leaders and all the people *will be* completely at your command."

Offerings for Building the Temple

29 Furthermore King David said to all the assembly: "My son Solomon, whom alone God has chosen, *is* young and inexperienced; and the work is great, because the temple[a] *is* not for man but for the LORD God. [2]Now for the house of my God I have prepared with all my might: gold for *things to be made of* gold, silver for *things of* silver, bronze for *things of* bronze, iron for *things of* iron, wood for *things of* wood, onyx stones, *stones* to be set, glistening stones of various colors, all kinds of precious stones, and marble slabs in abundance. [3]Moreover, because I have set my affection on the house of my God, I have given to the house of my God, over and above all that I have prepared for the holy house, my own special treasure of gold and silver: [4]three thousand talents of gold, of the gold of Ophir, and seven thousand talents of refined silver, to overlay the walls of the houses; [5]the gold for *things of* gold and the silver for *things of* silver, and for all kinds of work *to be done* by the hands of craftsmen. Who *then* is willing to consecrate himself this day to the LORD?"

> If dependence is God's agenda, then weakness is actually our advantage.
>
> **ALISTAIR BEGG**

[6]Then the leaders of the fathers' *houses,* leaders of the tribes of Israel, the captains of thousands and of hundreds, with the officers over the king's work, offered willingly. [7]They gave for the work of the house of God five thousand talents and ten thousand darics of gold, ten thousand talents of silver, eighteen thousand talents of bronze, and one hundred thousand talents of iron. [8]And whoever had *precious* stones gave *them* to the treasury of the house of the LORD, into the hand of Jehiel[a] the Gershonite. [9]Then the people rejoiced, for they had offered willingly, because with a loyal heart they had offered willingly to the LORD; and King David also rejoiced greatly.

David's Praise to God

[10]Therefore David blessed the LORD before all the assembly; and David said:

"Blessed are You, LORD God of Israel,
our Father, forever and ever.
[11]Yours, O LORD, is the greatness,
The power and the glory,
The victory and the majesty;
For all *that is* in heaven and in earth *is*
Yours;
Yours *is* the kingdom, O LORD,
And You are exalted as head over all.

29:1 [a]Literally *palace* 29:8 [a]Possibly the same as *Jehieli* (compare 26:21, 22)

12 Both riches and honor *come* from You,
And You reign over all.
In Your hand *is* power and might;
In Your hand *it is* to make great
And to give strength to all.

13 "Now therefore, our God,
We thank You
And praise Your glorious name.
14 But who *am* I, and who *are* my people,
That we should be able to offer so
willingly as this?
For all things *come* from You,
And of Your own we have given You.
15 For we *are* aliens and pilgrims before
You,
As *were* all our fathers;
Our days on earth *are* as a shadow,
And without hope.

Only by imitating the spirit and manner of the Lord Jesus shall we become wise to win souls.

CHARLES SPURGEON

16 "O LORD our God, all this abundance
that we have prepared to build You a
house for Your holy name is from Your
hand, and *is* all Your own. 17 I know also,
my God, that You test the heart and have
pleasure in uprightness. As for me, in the
uprightness of my heart I have willingly
offered all these *things;* and now with joy
I have seen Your people, who are present
here to offer willingly to You. 18 O LORD
God of Abraham, Isaac, and Israel, our
fathers, keep this forever in the intent of
the thoughts of the heart of Your people,
and fix their heart toward You. 19 And give
my son Solomon a loyal heart to keep
Your commandments and Your testimonies and Your statutes, to do all *these*
things, and to build the temple[a] for which
I have made provision."

20 Then David said to all the assembly,
"Now bless the LORD your God." So all
the assembly blessed the LORD God of their fathers, and bowed their heads and prostrated themselves before the LORD and the king.

Solomon Anointed King

21 And they made sacrifices to the LORD
and offered burnt offerings to the LORD on the next day: a thousand bulls, a thousand rams, a thousand lambs, with their drink offerings, and sacrifices in abundance for all Israel. 22 So they ate and
drank before the LORD with great gladness on that day. And they made Solomon the son of David king the second time, and anointed *him* before the LORD *to be* the leader, and Zadok *to be* priest.
23 Then Solomon sat on the throne of the
LORD as king instead of David his father, and prospered; and all Israel obeyed him.
24 All the leaders and the mighty men, and
also all the sons of King David, submitted
themselves to King Solomon. 25 So the
LORD exalted Solomon exceedingly in the sight of all Israel, and bestowed on him *such* royal majesty as had not been on any king before him in Israel.

The Close of David's Reign

26 Thus David the son of Jesse reigned
over all Israel. 27 And the period that he
reigned over Israel *was* forty years; seven years he reigned in Hebron, and thirty-
three *years* he reigned in Jerusalem. 28 So
he died in a good old age, full of days and riches and honor; and Solomon his son
reigned in his place. 29 Now the acts of
King David, first and last, indeed they *are* written in the book of Samuel the seer, in the book of Nathan the prophet, and in
the book of Gad the seer, 30 with all his
reign and his might, and the events that happened to him, to Israel, and to all the kingdoms of the lands.

29:19 [a]Literally *palace*

29:10–12 It seems that almost everything Jesus said had it roots in the Old Testament. These verses sound like the essence of what is commonly called "The Lord's Prayer" (see Matt. 6:9–13).

2 Chronicles

Solomon Requests Wisdom

1 Now Solomon the son of David was strengthened in his kingdom, and the LORD his God *was* with him and exalted him exceedingly.

[2]And Solomon spoke to all Israel, to the captains of thousands and of hundreds, to the judges, and to every leader in all Israel, the heads of the fathers' *houses.* [3]Then Solomon, and all the assembly with him, went to the high place that *was* at Gibeon; for the tabernacle of meeting with God was there, which Moses the servant of the LORD had made in the wilderness. [4]But David had brought up the ark of God from Kirjath Jearim to *the place* David had prepared for it, for he had pitched a tent for it at Jerusalem. [5]Now the bronze altar that Bezalel the son of Uri, the son of Hur, had made, he put[a] before the tabernacle of the LORD; Solomon and the assembly sought Him *there.* [6]And Solomon went up there to the bronze altar before the LORD, which *was* at the tabernacle of meeting, and offered a thousand burnt offerings on it.

[7]On that night God appeared to Solomon, and said to him, "Ask! What shall I give you?"

[8]And Solomon said to God: "You have shown great mercy to David my father, and have made me king in his place. [9]Now, O LORD God, let Your promise to David my father be established, for You have made me king over a people like the dust of the earth in multitude. [10]Now give me wisdom and knowledge, that I may go out and come in before this people; for who can judge this great people of Yours?"

[11]Then God said to Solomon: "Because this was in your heart, and you have not asked riches or wealth or honor or the life of your enemies, nor have you asked long life—but have asked wisdom and knowledge for yourself, that you may judge My people over whom I have made you king— [12]wisdom and knowledge *are* granted to you; and I will give you riches and wealth and honor, such as none of the kings have had who *were* before you, nor shall any after you have the like."

Solomon's Military and Economic Power

[13]So Solomon came to Jerusalem from the high place that *was* at Gibeon, from

1:5 [a]Some authorities read *it was there.*

1:6 Notice that God didn't rebuke Solomon for killing a thousand animals. See 7:5 comment.

1:7–12 How it pleased God that Solomon asked for wisdom and knowledge. Wisdom helps us think right, do right, and speak right. You too can please God if you ask Him for wisdom to reach the lost. Glean it from the Bible and pray that God gives you the wisdom to make good use of your time, to make right decisions, and to say the right things to those who are sitting in the shadow of death. See James 1:5–8 for the conditions needed to receive anything from the Lord.

before the tabernacle of meeting, and
reigned over Israel. 14And Solomon gathered chariots and horsemen; he had one
thousand four hundred chariots and twelve
thousand horsemen, whom he stationed
in the chariot cities and with the king in
Jerusalem. 15Also the king made silver and
gold as common in Jerusalem as stones,
and he made cedars as abundant as the
sycamores which *are* in the lowland. 16And
Solomon had horses imported from Egypt
and Keveh; the king's merchants bought
them in Keveh at the *current* price. 17They
also acquired and imported from Egypt a
chariot for six hundred *shekels* of silver,
and a horse for one hundred and fifty;
thus, through their agents,[a] they exported
them to all the kings of the Hittites and
the kings of Syria.

Solomon Prepares to Build the Temple

2 Then Solomon determined to build a
temple for the name of the LORD, and
a royal house for himself. 2Solomon selected seventy thousand men to bear burdens, eighty thousand to quarry *stone* in
the mountains, and three thousand six
hundred to oversee them.
3Then Solomon sent to Hiram[a] king of
Tyre, saying:

As you have dealt with David my
father, and sent him cedars to build
himself a house to dwell in, *so deal
with me.* 4Behold, I am building a
temple for the name of the LORD my
God, to dedicate *it* to Him, to burn
before Him sweet incense, for the
continual showbread, for the burnt
offerings morning and evening, on
the Sabbaths, on the New Moons, and
on the set feasts of the LORD our God.
This *is an ordinance* forever to Israel.

5And the temple which I build *will be*
great, for our God is greater than all
gods. 6But who is able to build Him a
temple, since heaven and the heaven
of heavens cannot contain Him? Who
am I then, that I should build Him a
temple, except to burn sacrifice
before Him?

7Therefore send me at once a man
skillful to work in gold and silver, in
bronze and iron, in purple and
crimson and blue, who has skill to
engrave with the skillful men who are
with me in Judah and Jerusalem,
whom David my father provided.
8Also send me cedar and cypress and
algum logs from Lebanon, for I know
that your servants have skill to cut
timber in Lebanon; and indeed my
servants *will be* with your servants, 9to
prepare timber for me in abundance,
for the temple which I am about to
build *shall be* great and wonderful.

10And indeed I will give to your servants,
the woodsmen who cut timber, twenty
thousand kors of ground wheat,
twenty thousand kors of barley,
twenty thousand baths of wine, and
twenty thousand baths of oil.

11Then Hiram king of Tyre answered
in writing, which he sent to Solomon:

Because the LORD loves His people,
He has made you king over them.

12Hiram[a] also said:

Blessed *be* the LORD God of Israel,
who made heaven and earth, for He
has given King David a wise son,
endowed with prudence and
understanding, who will build a
temple for the LORD and a royal
house for himself!

1:17 [a]Literally *by their hands* 2:3 [a]Hebrew *Huram* (compare 1 Kings 5:1) 2:12 [a]Hebrew *Huram* (compare 1 Kings 5:1)

2:5 Are there multiple gods? See Psa. 115:4–9 comment.

[13]And now I have sent a skillful man,
endowed with understanding,
Huram[a] my master[b] *craftsman* [14](the
son of a woman of the daughters of
Dan, and his father was a man of
Tyre), skilled to work in gold and
silver, bronze and iron, stone and
wood, purple and blue, fine linen and
crimson, and to make any engraving
and to accomplish any plan which
may be given to him, with your
skillful men and with the skillful men
of my lord David your father.

[15]Now therefore, the wheat, the barley,
the oil, and the wine which my lord
has spoken of, let him send to his
servants. [16]And we will cut wood from
Lebanon, as much as you need; we will
bring it to you in rafts by sea to Joppa,
and you will carry it up to Jerusalem.

[17]Then Solomon numbered all the aliens who *were* in the land of Israel, after the census in which David his father had numbered them; and there were found to be one hundred and fifty-three thousand six hundred. [18]And he made seventy thousand of them bearers of burdens, eighty thousand stonecutters in the mountain, and three thousand six hundred overseers to make the people work.

Solomon Builds the Temple

3 Now Solomon began to build the house of the LORD at Jerusalem on Mount Moriah, where *the LORD*[a] had appeared to his father David, at the place that David had prepared on the threshing floor of Ornan[b] the Jebusite. [2]And he began to build on the second *day* of the second month in the fourth year of his reign.

[3]This is the foundation which Solomon laid for building the house of God: The length *was* sixty cubits (by cubits according to the former measure) and the width twenty cubits. [4]And the vestibule that *was* in front *of the sanctuary*[a] was twenty cubits long across the width of the house, and the height *was* one hundred and[b] twenty. He overlaid the inside with pure gold. [5]The larger room[a] he paneled with cypress which he overlaid with fine gold, and he carved palm trees and chainwork on it. [6]And he decorated the house with precious stones for beauty, and the gold *was* gold from Parvaim. [7]He also overlaid the house—the beams and doorposts, its walls and doors—with gold; and he carved cherubim on the walls.

[8]And he made the Most Holy Place. Its length was according to the width of the house, twenty cubits, and its width twenty cubits. He overlaid it with six hundred talents of fine gold. [9]The weight of the nails *was* fifty shekels of gold; and he overlaid the upper area with gold. [10]In the Most Holy Place he made two cherubim, fashioned by carving, and overlaid them with gold. [11]The wings of the cherubim *were* twenty cubits in *overall* length: one wing *of the one cherub was* five cubits, touching the wall of the room, and the other wing *was* five cubits, touching the wing of the other cherub; [12]*one* wing of the other cherub *was* five cubits, touching the wall of the room, and the other wing *also was* five cubits, touching the wing of the other cherub. [13]The wings of these cherubim spanned twenty cubits overall. They stood on their feet, and they faced inward. [14]And he made the veil of blue, purple, crimson, and fine linen, and wove cherubim into it.

[15]Also he made in front of the temple[a] two pillars thirty-five[b] cubits high, and the capital that *was* on the top of each of *them* was five cubits. [16]He made wreaths of chainwork, as in the inner sanctuary, and put *them* on top of the pillars; and he made one hundred pomegranates, and put *them* on the wreaths of chainwork.

2:13 [a]Spelled *Hiram* in 1 Kings 7:13 [b]Literally *father* (compare 1 Kings 7:13, 14) 3:1 [a]Literally *He*, following Masoretic Text and Vulgate; Septuagint reads *the LORD;* Targum reads *the Angel of the LORD.* [b]Spelled *Araunah* in 2 Samuel 24:16ff 3:4 [a]The main room of the temple; elsewhere called the holy place (compare 1 Kings 6:3) [b]Following Masoretic Text, Septuagint, and Vulgate; Arabic, some manuscripts of the Septuagint, and Syriac omit *one hundred and.* 3:5 [a]Literally *house* 3:15 [a]Literally *house* [b]Or *eighteen* (compare 1 Kings 7:15; 2 Kings 25:17; and Jeremiah 52:21)

17Then he set up the pillars before the
temple, one on the right hand and the
other on the left; he called the name of
the one on the right hand Jachin, and the
name of the one on the left Boaz.

Furnishings of the Temple

4 Moreover he made a bronze altar:
twenty cubits was its length, twenty
cubits its width, and ten cubits its height.
2Then he made the Sea of cast *bronze,*
ten cubits from one brim to the other; *it*
was completely round. Its height *was* five
cubits, and a line of thirty cubits measured
its circumference. 3And under it *was* the
likeness of oxen encircling it all around,
ten to a cubit, all the way around the Sea.
The oxen *were* cast in two rows, when it
was cast. 4It stood on twelve oxen: three
looking toward the north, three looking
toward the west, three looking toward the
south, and three looking toward the east;
the Sea *was set* upon them, and all their
back parts *pointed* inward. 5It *was* a handbreadth thick; and its brim was shaped
like the brim of a cup, *like* a lily blossom.
It contained three thousand[a] baths.
6He also made ten lavers, and put five
on the right side and five on the left, to
wash in them; such things as they offered
for the burnt offering they would wash in
them, but the Sea *was* for the priests to
wash in. 7And he made ten lampstands of
gold according to their design, and set
them in the temple, five on the right side
and five on the left. 8He also made ten tables, and placed *them* in the temple, five
on the right side and five on the left. And
he made one hundred bowls of gold.
9Furthermore he made the court of
the priests, and the great court and doors
for the court; and he overlaid these doors
with bronze. 10He set the Sea on the right
side, toward the southeast.
11Then Huram made the pots and the
shovels and the bowls. So Huram finished
doing the work that he was to do for King
Solomon for the house of God: 12the two
pillars and the bowl-shaped capitals *that*
were on top of the two pillars; the two
networks covering the two bowl-shaped
capitals which *were* on top of the pillars;
13four hundred pomegranates for the two
networks (two rows of pomegranates for
each network, to cover the two bowl-
shaped capitals that *were* on the pillars);
14he also made carts and the lavers on the
carts; 15one Sea and twelve oxen under it;
16also the pots, the shovels, the forks—
and all their articles Huram his master[a]
craftsman made of burnished bronze for
King Solomon for the house of the LORD.
17In the plain of Jordan the king had
them cast in clay molds, between Succoth and Zeredah.[a] 18And Solomon had
all these articles made in such great
abundance that the weight of the bronze
was not determined.

19Thus Solomon had all the furnishings made for the house of God: the altar
of gold and the tables on which *was* the

4:5 [a]Or *two thousand* (compare 1 Kings 7:26) 4:16 [a]Literally *father* 4:17 [a]Spelled *Zaretan* in 1 Kings 7:46

3:14 So much of Scripture has hidden "types" and wonderful analogies that we often overlook. Purple is the color of royalty, and "fine linen" is "the righteous acts of the saints" (Rev. 19:8). In Luke 16:19 Jesus spoke of a rich man who "was clothed in purple and fine linen and fared sumptuously every day." It appears the rich man is a "type" of the self-indulgent Laodicean church that lets the sinner starve at his gate without offering the Bread of Life. It says that it's rich, but it is wretched, miserable, poor, blind, and naked.

4:4 As laborers, we are sent to the four corners of the earth. The vast sea of lost humanity weighs heavy upon us.

"Look! Don't be deceived by appearances—men and things are not what they seem. All who are not on the rock are in the sea! Look at them from the standpoint of the great White Throne, and what a sight you have! Jesus Christ, the Son of God is, through His Spirit, in the midst of this dying multitude, struggling to save them. And He is calling on you to jump into the sea—to go right away to His side and help Him in the holy strife. Will you jump? That is, will you go to His feet and place yourself absolutely at His disposal?"
William Booth

showbread; [20]the lampstands with their lamps of pure gold, to burn in the prescribed manner in front of the inner sanctuary, [21]with the flowers and the lamps and the wick-trimmers of gold, of purest gold; [22]the trimmers, the bowls, the ladles, and the censers of pure gold. As for the entry of the sanctuary, its inner doors to the Most Holy *Place*, and the doors of the main hall of the temple, *were* gold.

5 So all the work that Solomon had done for the house of the LORD was finished; and Solomon brought in the things which his father David had dedicated: the silver and the gold and all the furnishings. And he put *them* in the treasuries of the house of God.

The Ark Brought into the Temple

[2]Now Solomon assembled the elders of Israel and all the heads of the tribes, the chief fathers of the children of Israel, in Jerusalem, that they might bring the ark of the covenant of the LORD up from the City of David, which *is* Zion. [3]Therefore all the men of Israel assembled with the king at the feast, which *was* in the seventh month. [4]So all the elders of Israel came, and the Levites took up the ark. [5]Then they brought up the ark, the tabernacle of meeting, and all the holy furnishings that *were* in the tabernacle. The priests and the Levites brought them up. [6]Also King Solomon, and all the congregation of Israel who were assembled with him before the ark, were sacrificing sheep and oxen that could not be counted or numbered for multitude. [7]Then the priests brought in the ark of the covenant of the LORD to its place, into the inner sanctuary of the temple,[a] to the Most Holy *Place*, under the wings of the cherubim. [8]For the cherubim spread *their* wings over the place of the ark, and the cherubim overshadowed the ark and its poles. [9]The poles extended so that the ends of the poles of the ark could be seen from *the holy place*, in front of the inner sanctuary; but they could not be seen from outside. And they are there to this day. [10]Nothing was in the ark except the two tablets which Moses put *there* at Horeb, when the LORD made *a covenant* with the children of Israel, when they had come out of Egypt.

[11]And it came to pass when the priests came out of the *Most* Holy *Place* (for all the priests who *were* present had sanctified themselves, without keeping to their divisions), [12]and the Levites *who were* the singers, all those of Asaph and Heman and Jeduthun, with their sons and their brethren, stood at the east end of the altar, clothed in white linen, having cymbals, stringed instruments and harps, and with them one hundred and twenty priests sounding with trumpets— [13]indeed it came to pass, when the trumpeters and singers *were* as one, to make one sound to be heard in praising and thanking the LORD, and when they lifted up their voice with the trumpets and cymbals and instruments of music, and praised the LORD, *saying:*

> "*For He is* good,
> For His mercy *endures* forever,"[a]

that the house, the house of the LORD, was filled with a cloud, [14]so that the priests could not continue ministering because of the cloud; for the glory of the LORD filled the house of God.

THE FUNCTION OF THE LAW

5:10 "Some people seem to think we have got beyond the commandments. What did Christ say? 'Think not that I am come to destroy the law and the prophets; I am not come to destroy but to fulfill. For verily I say unto you, Till heaven and earth pass away, one jot or one tittle shall in no wise pass from the law, till all be fulfilled.' The commandments of God given to Moses in the Mount at Horeb are as binding today as ever they have been since the time they were proclaimed in the hearing of the people. The Jews said the law was not given in Palestine (which belonged to Israel), but in the wilderness, because the law was for all nations." *D. L. Moody*

5:7 [a]Literally *house* 5:13 [a]Compare Psalm 106:1

6 Then Solomon spoke:

"The LORD said He would dwell in the
dark cloud.
2I have surely built You an exalted
house,
And a place for You to dwell in forever."

Solomon's Speech upon Completion of the Work

3Then the king turned around and blessed the whole assembly of Israel, while all the assembly of Israel was standing. 4And he said: "Blessed *be* the LORD God of Israel, who has fulfilled with His hands *what* He spoke with His mouth to my father David, saying, 5'Since the day that I brought My people out of the land of Egypt, I have chosen no city from any tribe of Israel *in which* to build a house, that My name might be there, nor did I choose any man to be a ruler over My people Israel. 6Yet I have chosen Jerusalem, that My name may be there, and I have chosen David to be over My people Israel.' 7Now it was in the heart of my father David to build a temple[a] for the name of the LORD God of Israel. 8But the LORD said to my father David, 'Whereas it was in your heart to build a temple for My name, you did well in that it was in your heart. 9Nevertheless you shall not build the temple, but your son who will come from your body, he shall build the temple for My name.' 10So the LORD has fulfilled His word which He spoke, and I have filled the position of my father David, and sit on the throne of Israel, as the LORD promised; and I have built the temple for the name of the LORD God of Israel. 11And there I have put the ark, in which *is* the covenant of the LORD which He made with the children of Israel."

Solomon's Prayer of Dedication

12Then *Solomon*[a] stood before the altar of the LORD in the presence of all the assembly of Israel, and spread out his hands 13(for Solomon had made a bronze platform five cubits long, five cubits wide, and three cubits high, and had set it in the midst of the court; and he stood on it, knelt down on his knees before all the assembly of Israel, and spread out his hands toward heaven); 14and he said: "LORD God of Israel, *there is* no God in heaven or on earth like You, who keep *Your* covenant and mercy with Your servants who walk before You with all their hearts. 15You have kept what You promised Your servant David my father; You have both spoken with Your mouth and fulfilled *it* with Your hand, as *it is* this day. 16Therefore, LORD God of Israel, now keep what You promised Your servant David my father, saying, 'You shall not fail to have a man sit before Me on the throne of Israel, only if your sons take heed to their way, that they walk in My law as you have walked before Me.' 17And now, O LORD God of Israel, let Your word come true, which You have spoken to Your servant David.

18"But will God indeed dwell with men on the earth? Behold, heaven and the heaven of heavens cannot contain You. How much less this temple[a] which I have built! 19Yet regard the prayer of Your servant and his supplication, O LORD my God, and listen to the cry and the prayer which Your servant is praying before You: 20that Your eyes may be open toward this temple day and night, toward the place where *You* said *You would* put Your name, that You may hear the prayer which Your servant makes toward this place. 21And may You hear the supplications of Your servant and of Your people Israel, when they pray toward this place. Hear from heaven Your dwelling place, and when You hear, forgive.

22"If anyone sins against his neighbor,

6:7 [a]Literally *house,* and so in verses 8–10 6:12 [a]Literally *he* (compare 1 Kings 8:22) 6:18 [a]Literally *house*

6:11 The reason Solomon built the temple was to house the ark. See 1 Kings 8:9–11 comment.

and is forced to take an oath, and comes *and* takes an oath before Your altar in this temple, [23]then hear from heaven, and act, and judge Your servants, bringing retribution on the wicked by bringing his way on his own head, and justifying the righteous by giving him according to his righteousness.

[24]"Or if Your people Israel are defeated before an enemy because they have sinned against You, and return and confess Your name, and pray and make supplication before You in this temple, [25]then hear from heaven and forgive the sin of Your people Israel, and bring them back to the land which You gave to them and their fathers.

[26]"When the heavens are shut up and there is no rain because they have sinned against You, when they pray toward this place and confess Your name, and turn from their sin because You afflict them, [27]then hear *in* heaven, and forgive the sin of Your servants, Your people Israel, that You may teach them the good way in which they should walk; and send rain on Your land which You have given to Your people as an inheritance.

[28]"When there is famine in the land, pestilence or blight or mildew, locusts or grasshoppers; when their enemies besiege them in the land of their cities; whatever plague or whatever sickness *there is;* [29]whatever prayer, whatever supplication is *made* by anyone, or by all Your people Israel, when each one knows his own burden and his own grief, and spreads out his hands to this temple: [30]then hear from heaven Your dwelling place, and forgive, and give to everyone according to all his ways, whose heart You know (for You alone know the hearts of the sons of men), [31]that they may fear You, to walk in Your ways as long as they live in the land which You gave to our fathers.

[32]"Moreover, concerning a foreigner, who is not of Your people Israel, but has come from a far country for the sake of Your great name and Your mighty hand and Your outstretched arm, when they come and pray in this temple; [33]then hear from heaven Your dwelling place, and do according to all for which the foreigner calls to You, that all peoples of the earth may know Your name and fear You, as *do* Your people Israel, and that they may know that this temple which I have built is called by Your name.

[34]"When Your people go out to battle against their enemies, wherever You send them, and when they pray to You toward this city which You have chosen and the temple which I have built for Your name, [35]then hear from heaven their prayer and their supplication, and maintain their cause.

[36]"When they sin against You (for *there is* no one who does not sin), and You become angry with them and deliver them to the enemy, and they take them captive to a land far or near; [37]*yet* when they come to themselves in the land where they were carried captive, and repent, and make supplication to You in the land of their captivity, saying, 'We have sinned, we have done wrong, and have committed wickedness'; [38]and *when* they return to You with all their heart and with all their soul in the land of their captivity, where they have been carried captive, and pray toward their land which You gave to their fathers, the city which You have chosen, and toward the temple which I have built for Your name: [39]then hear from heaven Your dwelling place their prayer and their supplications, and

6:30,31 There is hope for sinful nations, if they seek God and appropriate the everlasting gospel. But how will they hear without a preacher? See Rom. 10:13–15 for details.

6:37,38 The ungodly are not in their right mind. Like the prodigal son who "came to himself" (Luke 15:17), it is only when we realize our appetites are unclean that we come to our senses, confess our sins, and repent. When we turn to Christ we receive "a sound mind" (see 2 Tim. 1:7). See Luke 15:17 comment.

maintain their cause, and forgive Your people who have sinned against You. 40Now, my God, I pray, let Your eyes be open and *let* Your ears *be* attentive to the prayer *made* in this place.

41"Now therefore,
Arise, O LORD God, to Your resting
place,
You and the ark of Your strength.
Let Your priests, O LORD God, be
clothed with salvation,
And let Your saints rejoice in goodness.

42"O LORD God, do not turn away the
face of Your Anointed;
Remember the mercies of Your
servant David."[a]

Solomon Dedicates the Temple

7 When Solomon had finished praying, fire came down from heaven and consumed the burnt offering and the sacrifices; and the glory of the LORD filled the temple.[a] 2And the priests could not enter the house of the LORD, because the glory of the LORD had filled the LORD's house. 3When all the children of Israel saw how the fire came down, and the glory of the LORD on the temple, they bowed their faces to the ground on the pavement, and worshiped and praised the LORD, *saying:*

"For *He is* good,
For His mercy *endures* forever."[a]

4Then the king and all the people offered sacrifices before the LORD. 5King Solomon offered a sacrifice of twenty-two thousand bulls and one hundred and twenty thousand sheep. So the king and all the people dedicated the house of God. 6And the priests attended to their services; the Levites also with instruments of the music of the LORD, which King David had made to praise the LORD, saying, "For His mercy *endures* forever,"[a] whenever David offered praise by their ministry. The priests sounded trumpets opposite them, while all Israel stood.

7Furthermore Solomon consecrated the middle of the court that *was* in front of the house of the LORD; for there he offered burnt offerings and the fat of the peace offerings, because the bronze altar which Solomon had made was not able to receive the burnt offerings, the grain offerings, and the fat.

8At that time Solomon kept the feast seven days, and all Israel with him, a very great assembly from the entrance of Hamath to the Brook of Egypt.[a] 9And on the eighth day they held a sacred assembly, for they observed the dedication of the altar seven days, and the feast seven days. 10On the twenty-third day of the seventh month he sent the people away to their tents, joyful and glad of heart for the good that the LORD had done for David, for Solomon, and for His people Israel. 11Thus Solomon finished the house of the LORD and the king's house; and Solomon successfully accomplished all that came into his heart to make in the house of the LORD and in his own house.

God's Second Appearance to Solomon

12Then the LORD appeared to Solomon by night, and said to him: "I have heard your prayer, and have chosen this place for Myself as a house of sacrifice. 13When I shut up heaven and there is no rain, or command the locusts to devour the land, or send pestilence among My people, 14if

6:42 [a]Compare Psalm 132:8–10 7:1 [a]Literally *house* 7:3 [a]Compare Psalm 106:1 7:6 [a]Compare Psalm 106:1 7:8 [a]That is, the Shihor (compare 1 Chronicles 13:5)

7:1–3 It is because God's mercy endures forever that we have immortality in Christ.

7:5 Animal-rights advocates who insist that "meat is murder" are misguided. God didn't chide the king for his sacrificial worship. The slaying of 22,000 bulls and 120,000 sheep as part of a religious rite would today be an animal-rights nightmare.

My people who are called by My name
will humble themselves, and pray and
seek My face, and turn from their wicked
ways, then I will hear from heaven, and
will forgive their sin and heal their land.
15Now My eyes will be open and My ears
attentive to prayer *made* in this place.
16For now I have chosen and sanctified
this house, that My name may be there
forever; and My eyes and My heart will
be there perpetually. 17As for you, if you
walk before Me as your father David
walked, and do according to all that I have
commanded you, and if you keep My
statutes and My judgments, 18then I will
establish the throne of your kingdom, as
I covenanted with David your father, saying, 'You shall not fail *to have* a man as
ruler in Israel.'

19"But if you turn away and forsake
My statutes and My commandments
which I have set before you, and go and
serve other gods, and worship them,
20then I will uproot them from My land
which I have given them; and this house
which I have sanctified for My name I
will cast out of My sight, and will make it a
proverb and a byword among all peoples.
21"And *as for* this house, which is exalted, everyone who passes by it will be
astonished and say, 'Why has the LORD
done thus to this land and this house?'
22Then they will answer, 'Because they
forsook the LORD God of their fathers,
who brought them out of the land of
Egypt, and embraced other gods, and
worshiped them and served them; therefore He has brought all this calamity on
them.' "

Solomon's Additional Achievements

8 It came to pass at the end of twenty
years, when Solomon had built the
house of the LORD and his own house,
2that the cities which Hiram[a] had given
to Solomon, Solomon built them; and he
settled the children of Israel there. 3And
Solomon went to Hamath Zobah and
seized it. 4He also built Tadmor in the
wilderness, and all the storage cities which
he built in Hamath. 5He built Upper
Beth Horon and Lower Beth Horon, fortified cities *with* walls, gates, and bars,
6also Baalath and all the storage cities
that Solomon had, and all the chariot
cities and the cities of the cavalry, and all
that Solomon desired to build in Jerusalem, in Lebanon, and in all the land of
his dominion.

7All the people *who were* left of the
Hittites, Amorites, Perizzites, Hivites, and
Jebusites, who *were* not of Israel— 8that
is, their descendants who were left in the
land after them, whom the children of Israel did not destroy—from these Solomon raised forced labor, as it is to this day.
9But Solomon did not make the children
of Israel servants for his work. Some *were*
men of war, captains of his officers, captains of his chariots, and his cavalry.
10And others *were* chiefs of the officials of
King Solomon: two hundred and fifty,
who ruled over the people.

11Now Solomon brought the daughter
of Pharaoh up from the City of David to
the house he had built for her, for he
said, "My wife shall not dwell in the
house of David king of Israel, because *the
places* to which the ark of the LORD has
come are holy."

12Then Solomon offered burnt offerings to the LORD on the altar of the LORD
which he had built before the vestibule,
13according to the daily rate, offering according to the commandment of Moses,
for the Sabbaths, the New Moons, and

8:2 [a]Hebrew *Huram* (compare 2 Chronicles 2:3)

7:14 Seek His face. "What God in His sovereignty may yet do on a worldscale I do not claim to know. But what He will do for the plain man or woman who seeks His face I believe I do know and can tell others. Let any man turn to God in earnest, let him begin to exercise himself unto godliness, let him seek to develop his powers of spiritual receptivity by trust and obedience and humility, and the results will exceed anything he may have hoped in his leaner and weaker days." *A. W. Tozer*

the three appointed yearly feasts—the Feast of Unleavened Bread, the Feast of Weeks, and the Feast of Tabernacles. [14]And, according to the order of David his father, he appointed the divisions of the priests for their service, the Levites for their duties (to praise and serve before the priests) as the duty of each day required, and the gatekeepers by their divisions at each gate; for so David the man of God had commanded. [15]They did not depart from the command of the king to the priests and Levites concerning any matter or concerning the treasuries.

[16]Now all the work of Solomon was well-ordered from[a] the day of the foundation of the house of the LORD until it was finished. So the house of the LORD was completed.

[17]Then Solomon went to Ezion Geber and Elath[a] on the seacoast, in the land of Edom. [18]And Hiram sent him ships by the hand of his servants, and servants who knew the sea. They went with the servants of Solomon to Ophir, and acquired four hundred and fifty talents of gold from there, and brought it to King Solomon.

The Queen of Sheba's Praise of Solomon

9 Now when the queen of Sheba heard of the fame of Solomon, she came to Jerusalem to test Solomon with hard questions, *having* a very great retinue, camels that bore spices, gold in abundance, and precious stones; and when she came to Solomon, she spoke with him about all that was in her heart. [2]So Solomon answered all her questions; there was nothing so difficult for Solomon that he could not explain it to her. [3]And when the queen of Sheba had seen the wisdom of Solomon, the house that he had built, [4]the food on his table, the seating of his servants, the service of his waiters and their apparel, his cupbearers and their apparel, and his entryway by which he went up to the house of the LORD, there was no more spirit in her.

[5]Then she said to the king: "*It was* a true report which I heard in my own land about your words and your wisdom. [6]However I did not believe their words until I came and saw with my own eyes; and indeed the half of the greatness of your wisdom was not told me. You exceed the fame of which I heard. [7]Happy *are* your men and happy *are* these your servants, who stand continually before you and hear your wisdom! [8]Blessed be the LORD your God, who delighted in you, setting you on His throne *to be* king for the LORD your God! Because your God has loved Israel, to establish them forever, therefore He made you king over them, to do justice and righteousness."

[9]And she gave the king one hundred and twenty talents of gold, spices in great abundance, and precious stones; there never were any spices such as those the queen of Sheba gave to King Solomon.

[10]Also, the servants of Hiram and the servants of Solomon, who brought gold from Ophir, brought algum[a] wood and precious stones. [11]And the king made walkways *of* the algum[a] wood for the house of the LORD and for the king's house, also harps and stringed instruments for singers; and there were none such *as these* seen before in the land of Judah.

[12]Now King Solomon gave to the queen of Sheba all she desired, whatever

8:16 [a]Following Septuagint, Syriac, and Vulgate; Masoretic Text reads *as far as*. 8:17 [a]Hebrew *Eloth* (compare 2 Kings 14:22) 9:10 [a]Or *almug* (compare 1 Kings 10:11, 12) 9:11 [a]Or *almug* (compare 1 Kings 10:11, 12)

8:16 We are never to be discouraged from our labors, because we are building with God and His work will be completed. See 1 Cor. 15:58 for encouragement.

9:5–8 The queen of Sheba's words are dwarfed by what we found when we came to Christ. We came to Him as criminals and He made us kings and priests. We came to have our sins forgiven and He will give us pleasures forevermore. We will have eternity to gaze with awe on the wonderful works of God.

she asked, *much more* than she had brought to the king. So she turned and went to her own country, she and her servants.

Solomon's Great Wealth

[13]The weight of gold that came to Solomon yearly was six hundred and sixty-six talents of gold, [14]besides *what* the traveling merchants and traders brought. And all the kings of Arabia and governors of the country brought gold and silver to Solomon. [15]And King Solomon made two hundred large shields of hammered gold; six hundred *shekels* of hammered gold went into each shield. [16]*He* also *made* three hundred shields of hammered gold; three hundred *shekels*[a] of gold went into each shield. The king put them in the House of the Forest of Lebanon.

[17]Moreover the king made a great throne of ivory, and overlaid it with pure gold. [18]The throne *had* six steps, with a footstool of gold, *which were* fastened to the throne; there were armrests on either side of the place of the seat, and two lions stood beside the armrests. [19]Twelve lions stood there, one on each side of the six steps; nothing like *this* had been made for any *other* kingdom.

[20]All King Solomon's drinking vessels *were* gold, and all the vessels of the House of the Forest of Lebanon *were* pure gold. Not *one was* silver, for this was accounted as nothing in the days of Solomon. [21]For the king's ships went to Tarshish with the servants of Hiram.[a] Once every three years the merchant ships[b] came, bringing gold, silver, ivory, apes, and monkeys.[c]

· · · · · ·

Does DNA prove men are related to monkeys? See Job 17:14 comment.

· · · · · ·

[22]So King Solomon surpassed all the kings of the earth in riches and wisdom. [23]And all the kings of the earth sought the presence of Solomon to hear his wisdom, which God had put in his heart. [24]Each man brought his present: articles of silver and gold, garments, armor, spices, horses, and mules, at a set rate year by year.

[25]Solomon had four thousand stalls for horses and chariots, and twelve thousand horsemen whom he stationed in the chariot cities and with the king at Jerusalem.

When men seek Christ as they do wealth, they will soon find Him.

D. L. MOODY

[26]So he reigned over all the kings from the River[a] to the land of the Philistines, as far as the border of Egypt. [27]The king made silver *as common* in Jerusalem as stones, and he made cedar trees as abundant as the sycamores which *are* in the lowland. [28]And they brought horses to Solomon from Egypt and from all lands.

Death of Solomon

[29]Now the rest of the acts of Solomon, first and last, *are* they not written in the book of Nathan the prophet, in the prophecy of Ahijah the Shilonite, and in the visions of Iddo the seer concerning Jeroboam the son of Nebat? [30]Solomon reigned in Jerusalem over all Israel forty years. [31]Then Solomon rested with his fathers, and was buried in the City of David his father. And Rehoboam his son reigned in his place.

The Revolt Against Rehoboam

10 And Rehoboam went to Shechem, for all Israel had gone to Shechem to make him king. [2]So it happened, when Jeroboam the son of Nebat heard *it* (he was in Egypt, where he had fled from the presence of King Solomon), that Jeroboam returned from Egypt. [3]Then they sent for him and called him. And Jeroboam and all Israel came and spoke to

9:16 [a]Or *three minas* (compare 1 Kings 10:17) 9:21 [a]Hebrew *Huram* (compare 1 Kings 10:22) [b]Literally *ships of Tarshish* (deep-sea vessels) [c]Or *peacocks* 9:26 [a]That is, the Euphrates

Rehoboam, saying, 4"Your father made our yoke heavy; now therefore, lighten the burdensome service of your father and his heavy yoke which he put on us, and we will serve you."

5So he said to them, "Come back to me after three days." And the people departed.

6Then King Rehoboam consulted the elders who stood before his father Solomon while he still lived, saying, "How do you advise *me* to answer these people?"

7And they spoke to him, saying, "If you are kind to these people, and please them, and speak good words to them, they will be your servants forever."

8But he rejected the advice which the elders had given him, and consulted the young men who had grown up with him, who stood before him. 9And he said to them, "What advice do you give? How should we answer this people who have spoken to me, saying, 'Lighten the yoke which your father put on us'?"

10Then the young men who had grown up with him spoke to him, saying, "Thus you should speak to the people who have spoken to you, saying, 'Your father made our yoke heavy, but you make *it* lighter on us'—thus you shall say to them: 'My little *finger* shall be thicker than my father's waist! 11And now, whereas my father put a heavy yoke on you, I will add to your yoke; my father chastised you with whips, but I *will chastise you* with scourges!' "[a]

12So Jeroboam and all the people came to Rehoboam on the third day, as the king had directed, saying, "Come back to me the third day." 13Then the king answered them roughly. King Rehoboam rejected the advice of the elders, 14and he spoke to them according to the advice of the young men, saying, "My father[a] made your yoke heavy, but I will add to it; my father chastised you with whips, but I *will chastise you* with scourges!"[b] 15So the king did not listen to the people; for the turn *of events* was from God, that the LORD might fulfill His word, which He had spoken by the hand of Ahijah the Shilonite to Jeroboam the son of Nebat.

16Now when all Israel *saw* that the king did not listen to them, the people answered the king, saying:

"What share have we in David?
We have no inheritance in the son of
Jesse.
Every man to your tents, O Israel!
Now see to your own house, O David!"

So all Israel departed to their tents. 17But Rehoboam reigned over the children of Israel who dwelt in the cities of Judah.

18Then King Rehoboam sent Hadoram, who *was* in charge of revenue; but the children of Israel stoned him with stones, and he died. Therefore King Rehoboam mounted *his* chariot in haste to flee to Jerusalem. 19So Israel has been in rebellion against the house of David to this day.

11 Now when Rehoboam came to Jerusalem, he assembled from the house of Judah and Benjamin one hundred and eighty thousand chosen *men* who were warriors, to fight against Israel, that he might restore the kingdom to Rehoboam.

2But the word of the LORD came to

10:11 [a]Literally *scorpions* 10:14 [a]Following many Hebrew manuscripts, Septuagint, Syriac, and Vulgate (compare verse 10 and 1 Kings 12:14); Masoretic Text reads *I.* [b]Literally *scorpions*

10:8 Wisdom is so often forged in the sufferings of experience. Youth forget that the aged were once young and impetuous, and formed much of their life's philosophies from their mistakes. A wise man said that parents should never worry if teenagers don't seem to listen to their advice because, in time, those teenagers will become parents and then will give the same advice to their kids. Seek counsel from the experienced—and heed it. Yet, as vv. 13–15 show, despite the unwise counsel the king received, God was working to fulfill His purposes.

Shemaiah the man of God, saying, 3“Speak
to Rehoboam the son of Solomon, king of
Judah, and to all Israel in Judah and Benjamin, saying, 4‘Thus says the LORD: “You
shall not go up or fight against your
brethren! Let every man return to his
house, for this thing is from Me.” ’ ”
Therefore they obeyed the words of the
LORD, and turned back from attacking
Jeroboam.

Rehoboam Fortifies the Cities

5So Rehoboam dwelt in Jerusalem, and
built cities for defense in Judah. 6And he
built Bethlehem, Etam, Tekoa, 7Beth Zur,
Sochoh, Adullam, 8Gath, Mareshah, Ziph,
9Adoraim, Lachish, Azekah, 10Zorah, Aijalon, and Hebron, which are in Judah and
Benjamin, fortified cities. 11And he fortified the strongholds, and put captains in
them, and stores of food, oil, and wine.
12Also in every city *he put* shields and
spears, and made them very strong, having Judah and Benjamin on his side.

Priests and Levites Move to Judah

13And from all their territories the
priests and the Levites who *were* in all Israel took their stand with him. 14For the
Levites left their common-lands and their
possessions and came to Judah and
Jerusalem, for Jeroboam and his sons had
rejected them from serving as priests to
the LORD. 15Then he appointed for himself priests for the high places, for the
demons, and the calf idols which he had
made. 16And after *the Levites left,*[a] those
from all the tribes of Israel, such as set
their heart to seek the LORD God of Israel,
came to Jerusalem to sacrifice to the LORD
God of their fathers. 17So they strengthened the kingdom of Judah, and made
Rehoboam the son of Solomon strong for
three years, because they walked in the
way of David and Solomon for three years.

The Family of Rehoboam

18Then Rehoboam took for himself as
wife Mahalath the daughter of Jerimoth
the son of David, *and of* Abihail the
daughter of Eliah the son of Jesse. 19And
she bore him children: Jeush, Shamariah,
and Zaham. 20After her he took Maachah
the granddaughter[a] of Absalom; and she
bore him Abijah, Attai, Ziza, and Shelomith. 21Now Rehoboam loved Maachah
the granddaughter of Absalom more than
all his wives and his concubines; for he
took eighteen wives and sixty concubines,
and begot twenty-eight sons and sixty
daughters. 22And Rehoboam appointed
Abijah the son of Maachah as chief, *to be*
leader among his brothers; for he *intended*
to make him king. 23He dealt wisely, and
dispersed some of his sons throughout all
the territories of Judah and Benjamin, to
every fortified city; and he gave them
provisions in abundance. He also sought
many wives *for them.*

Egypt Attacks Judah

12 Now it came to pass, when Rehoboam had established the kingdom and had strengthened himself, that
he forsook the law of the LORD, and all Israel along with him. 2And it happened in
the fifth year of King Rehoboam *that*
Shishak king of Egypt came up against
Jerusalem, because they had transgressed
against the LORD, 3with twelve hundred
chariots, sixty thousand horsemen, and
people without number who came with
him out of Egypt—the Lubim and the
Sukkiim and the Ethiopians. 4And he took
the fortified cities of Judah and came to
Jerusalem.

5Then Shemaiah the prophet came to
Rehoboam and the leaders of Judah, who

11:16 [a]Literally *after them* **11:20** [a]Literally *daughter,* but in the broader sense of granddaughter (compare 2 Chronicles 13:2)

11:16 The essence of being a Christian (a disciple of Christ) is to be disciplined to set our hearts to seek the Lord. That means to daily take up the cross and to deny ourselves.

12:1 When a nation forsakes the Law of God, it forsakes God Himself. See v. 5.

QUESTIONS & OBJECTIONS

12:12

"The lost should want to serve God not to avoid hell, but because the Lord is worthy of all glory."

The unregenerate human heart is so desperately wicked, the motive for fleeing from wrath should be honorable, but it's not. How could it be? The wicked criminal comes to be "saved" because he is wicked. How can a vile sinner suddenly become virtuous in motive? It would be admirable for one to hear about the terrors of hell and not be fearful, and instead come to Christ because God is worthy of glory, but from where would a blind and lost sinner have found such theology? The truth is that there is nothing good in his own unregenerate and evil heart.

That is the reason we preach the Law—to show the sinner the magnitude of his crimes. Recognizing that he rightly deserves hell—but is offered mercy instead—is what makes him respond in gratitude for all that Christ has done for him. Sinai produces fear of God, because of His wrath. Calvary produces love for God, because of His mercy. See also Deut. 12:8 comment.

were gathered together in Jerusalem because of Shishak, and said to them, "Thus says the LORD: 'You have forsaken Me, and therefore I also have left you in the hand of Shishak.' "

[6]So the leaders of Israel and the king humbled themselves; and they said, "The LORD *is* righteous."

[7]Now when the LORD saw that they humbled themselves, the word of the LORD came to Shemaiah, saying, "They have humbled themselves; *therefore* I will not destroy them, but I will grant them some deliverance. My wrath shall not be poured out on Jerusalem by the hand of
Shishak. [8]Nevertheless they will be his servants, that they may distinguish My service from the service of the kingdoms of the nations."

[9]So Shishak king of Egypt came up against Jerusalem, and took away the treasures of the house of the LORD and the treasures of the king's house; he took everything. He also carried away the gold
shields which Solomon had made. [10]Then King Rehoboam made bronze shields in their place, and committed *them* to the hands of the captains of the guard, who guarded the doorway of the king's house.
[11]And whenever the king entered the house of the LORD, the guard would go and bring them out; then they would take them back into the guardroom. [12]When
he humbled himself, the wrath of the LORD turned from him, so as not to destroy *him* completely; and things also went well in Judah.

The End of Rehoboam's Reign

[13]Thus King Rehoboam strengthened himself in Jerusalem and reigned. Now Rehoboam *was* forty-one years old when he became king; and he reigned seventeen years in Jerusalem, the city which the LORD had chosen out of all the tribes of Israel, to put His name there. His mother's name *was* Naamah, an Ammonitess. [14]And he did evil, because he did not prepare his heart to seek the LORD.

[15]The acts of Rehoboam, first and last, *are* they not written in the book of Shemaiah the prophet, and of Iddo the seer concerning genealogies? And *there were* wars between Rehoboam and Jeroboam all their days. [16]So Rehoboam rested with
his fathers, and was buried in the City of David. Then Abijah[a] his son reigned in his place.

Abijah Reigns in Judah

13 In the eighteenth year of King Jeroboam, Abijah became king over

12:16 [a]Spelled *Abijam* in 1 Kings 14:31

12:6 Repentance follows naturally from the humble acknowledgment that God is righteous. See Psa. 51:4.

Judah. [2]He reigned three years in Jerusalem. His mother's name *was* Michaiah[a] the daughter of Uriel of Gibeah.

And there was war between Abijah and Jeroboam. [3]Abijah set the battle in order with an army of valiant warriors, four hundred thousand choice men. Jeroboam also drew up in battle formation against him with eight hundred thousand choice men, mighty men of valor.

[4]Then Abijah stood on Mount Zemaraim, which *is* in the mountains of Ephraim, and said, "Hear me, Jeroboam and all Israel: [5]Should you not know that the LORD God of Israel gave the dominion over Israel to David forever, to him and his sons, by a covenant of salt? [6]Yet Jeroboam the son of Nebat, the servant of Solomon the son of David, rose up and rebelled against his lord. [7]Then worthless rogues gathered to him, and strengthened themselves against Rehoboam the son of Solomon, when Rehoboam was young and inexperienced and could not withstand them. [8]And now you think to withstand the kingdom of the LORD, which is in the hand of the sons of David; and you *are* a great multitude, and with you are the gold calves which Jeroboam made for you as gods. [9]Have you not cast out the priests of the LORD, the sons of Aaron, and the Levites, and made for yourselves priests, like the peoples of *other* lands, so that whoever comes to consecrate himself with a young bull and seven rams may be a priest of *things that are* not gods? [10]But as for us, the LORD is our God, and we have not forsaken Him; and the priests who minister to the LORD *are* the sons of Aaron, and the Levites *attend* to *their* duties. [11]And they burn to the LORD every morning and every evening burnt sacrifices and sweet incense; *they* also *set* the showbread *in order on* the pure *gold* table, and the lampstand of gold with its lamps to burn every evening; for we keep the command of the LORD our God, but you have forsaken Him. [12]Now look, God Himself is with us as *our* head, and His priests with sounding trumpets to sound the alarm against you. O children of Israel, do not fight against the LORD God of your fathers, for you shall not prosper!"

> The only saving faith is that which casts itself on God for life or death.
>
> **MARTIN LUTHER**

[13]But Jeroboam caused an ambush to go around behind them; so they were in front of Judah, and the ambush *was* behind them. [14]And when Judah looked around, to their surprise the battle line *was* at both front and rear; and they cried out to the LORD, and the priests sounded the trumpets. [15]Then the men of Judah gave a shout; and as the men of Judah shouted, it happened that God struck Jeroboam and all Israel before Abijah and Judah. [16]And the children of Israel fled before Judah, and God delivered them into their hand. [17]Then Abijah and his people struck them with a great slaughter; so five hundred thousand choice men of Israel fell slain. [18]Thus the children of Israel were subdued at that time; and the children of Judah prevailed, because they relied on the LORD God of their fathers.

[19]And Abijah pursued Jeroboam and took cities from him: Bethel with its villages, Jeshanah with its villages, and Ephrain[a] with its villages. [20]So Jeroboam did not recover strength again in the days of Abijah; and the LORD struck him, and he died.

13:2 [a]Spelled *Maachah* in 11:20, 21 and 1 Kings 15:2 13:19 [a]Or *Ephron*

13:21 It might seem that in the Old Testament God sanctioned polygamy. Not so. Jesus said that in the beginning "the two shall become one flesh" (Matt. 19:4,5). He did not say "the fifteen shall become one flesh." God gave Israel kings, but that was His *permissive* will, not His *perfect* will. Polygamy is in the same category.

21But Abijah grew mighty, married fourteen wives, and begot twenty-two sons and sixteen daughters. 22Now the rest of the acts of Abijah, his ways, and his sayings *are* written in the annals of the prophet Iddo.

14 So Abijah rested with his fathers, and they buried him in the City of David. Then Asa his son reigned in his place. In his days the land was quiet for ten years.

Asa Reigns in Judah

2Asa did *what was* good and right in the eyes of the LORD his God, 3for he removed the altars of the foreign *gods* and the high places, and broke down the *sacred* pillars and cut down the wooden images. 4He commanded Judah to seek the LORD God of their fathers, and to observe the law and the commandment. 5He also removed the high places and the incense altars from all the cities of Judah, and the kingdom was quiet under him. 6And he built fortified cities in Judah, for the land had rest; he had no war in those years, because the LORD had given him rest. 7Therefore he said to Judah, "Let us build these cities and make walls around *them,* and towers, gates, and bars, *while* the land *is* yet before us, because we have sought the LORD our God; we have sought *Him,* and He has given us rest on every side." So they built and prospered. 8And Asa had an army of three hundred thousand from Judah who carried shields and spears, and from Benjamin two hundred and eighty thousand men who carried shields and drew bows; all these *were* mighty men of valor.

9Then Zerah the Ethiopian came out against them with an army of a million men and three hundred chariots, and he came to Mareshah. 10So Asa went out against him, and they set the troops in battle array in the Valley of Zephathah at Mareshah. 11And Asa cried out to the LORD his God, and said, "LORD, *it is* nothing for You to help, whether with many or with those who have no power; help us, O LORD our God, for we rest on You, and in Your name we go against this multitude. O LORD, You *are* our God; do not let man prevail against You!"

12So the LORD struck the Ethiopians before Asa and Judah, and the Ethiopians fled. 13And Asa and the people who *were* with him pursued them to Gerar. So the Ethiopians were overthrown, and they could not recover, for they were broken before the LORD and His army. And they carried away very much spoil. 14Then they defeated all the cities around Gerar, for the fear of the LORD came upon them; and they plundered all the cities, for there was exceedingly much spoil in them. 15They also attacked the livestock enclosures, and carried off sheep and camels in abundance, and returned to Jerusalem.

The Reforms of Asa

15 Now the Spirit of God came upon Azariah the son of Oded. 2And he went out to meet Asa, and said to him:

14:7 It is God who gives peace to a nation, something for which we are exhorted to pray (see 1 Tim. 2:1–3).

15:1,2 See James 4:8 for a confirmation of this promise.

"You may be now saved—completely saved, and live in the full enjoyment of that knowledge. 'If thou seek him, he will be found of thee.' The notion is that there are a great many very mysterious preliminaries, a great deal to do, and a great deal to be, and all quite beyond our power. It is not so, but seek him. We will tell you what that means, and he that seeks him finds him. 'If thou seek him, he will be found of thee'" It has been supposed that we should want a good deal of help in seeking after salvation. Certain persons who step in to be absolutely necessary priests between us and God. A great delusion, but there be thousands who believe it and who fancy that God won't hear them if they pray, except they have some respect for these human mediators. Away with the whole, away with any pretence for anyone to stand between the soul and God, save Jesus Christ. 'If thou seek him, he will be found of thee.'" *Charles Spurgeon*

"Hear me, Asa, and all Judah and Benjamin. The LORD *is* with you while you are with Him. If you seek Him, He will be found by you; but if you forsake Him, He will forsake you. [3]For a long time Israel *has been* without the true God, without a teaching priest, and without law; [4]but when in their trouble they turned to the LORD God of Israel, and sought Him, He was found by them. [5]And in those times *there was* no peace to the one who went out, nor to the one who came in, but great turmoil *was* on all the inhabitants of the lands. [6]So nation was destroyed by nation, and city by city, for God troubled them with every adversity. [7]But you, be strong and do not let your hands be weak, for your work shall be rewarded!"

[8]And when Asa heard these words and the prophecy of Oded[a] the prophet, he took courage, and removed the abominable idols from all the land of Judah and Benjamin and from the cities which he had taken in the mountains of Ephraim; and he restored the altar of the LORD that *was* before the vestibule of the LORD. [9]Then he gathered all Judah and Benjamin, and those who dwelt with them from Ephraim, Manasseh, and Simeon, for they came over to him in great numbers from Israel when they saw that the LORD his God was with him.

[10]So they gathered together at Jerusalem in the third month, in the fifteenth year of the reign of Asa. [11]And they offered to the LORD at that time seven hundred bulls and seven thousand sheep from the spoil they had brought. [12]Then they entered into a covenant to seek the LORD God of their fathers with all their heart and with all their soul; [13]and whoever would not seek the LORD God of Israel was to be put to death, whether small or great, whether man or woman. [14]Then they took an oath before the LORD with a loud voice, with shouting and trumpets and rams' horns. [15]And all Judah rejoiced at the oath, for they had sworn with all their heart and sought Him with all their soul; and He was found by them, and the LORD gave them rest all around.

[16]Also he removed Maachah, the mother of Asa the king, from *being* queen mother, because she had made an obscene image of Asherah;[a] and Asa cut down her obscene image, then crushed and burned *it* by the Brook Kidron. [17]But the high places were not removed from Israel. Nevertheless the heart of Asa was loyal all his days.

[18]He also brought into the house of God the things that his father had dedicated and that he himself had dedicated: silver and gold and utensils. [19]And there was no war until the thirty-fifth year of the reign of Asa.

Asa's Treaty with Syria

16 In the thirty-sixth year of the reign of Asa, Baasha king of Israel came up against Judah and built Ramah, that he might let none go out or come in to Asa king of Judah. [2]Then Asa brought silver and gold from the treasuries of the house of the LORD and of the king's house, and sent to Ben-Hadad king of Syria, who dwelt in Damascus, saying, [3]"*Let there be* a treaty between you and me, as there was between my father and your father. See, I have sent you silver and gold; come, break your treaty with Baasha king of Israel, so that he will withdraw from me."

[4]So Ben-Hadad heeded King Asa, and sent the captains of his armies against the cities of Israel. They attacked Ijon, Dan, Abel Maim, and all the storage cities of Naphtali. [5]Now it happened, when Baasha heard *it*, that he stopped building Ramah and ceased his work. [6]Then King Asa took

15:8 [a]Following Masoretic Text and Septuagint; Syriac and Vulgate read *Azariah the son of Oded* (compare verse 1).
15:16 [a]A Canaanite deity

15:4 Sadly, tribulation doesn't always turn sinners toward heaven. Some harden their hearts and become bitter at God.

15:15 *Atheist's Test*

When an atheist approached me recently and said, "I have three tests for you," I knew what the "tests" were before he asked them. The first two were, would I take poison (based on the promise Jesus gave in Mark 16:18) and would I jump off a high cliff? I told my atheist friend that if I were to deliberately take poison or jump off a high cliff, I would be tempting God, something the Bible says not to do (see Matt. 4:7). I'm not into snake handling either. Of course, that answer never satisfies atheists, and so their tests remain powerful proofs (in their minds) that God doesn't exist.

The third test was, can I move mountains? Jesus said that the Christian can move them (see Matt. 17:20), so if we can't, then God doesn't exist.

When Jesus talked about swallowing camels, or of Him being the "door," or the necessity of eating His flesh and drinking His blood to be saved, or moving mountains, these weren't literal statements. They were symbolic. How do we know the difference between literal and symbolic? Context and common sense.

Other supposed powerful arguments that the Bible isn't true (and therefore God doesn't exist) are: bats aren't birds, there seem to be two accounts of creation, God can't make a rock that He can't lift, the Catholic church and their crusades—their terrible Inquisition and their imprisonment of Galileo. Also, Cain married a sister, the way Judas died, and of course the powerful "proof" of the theory of evolution. If evolution is true, then in the mind of the atheist, God doesn't exist.

The essence of the evolution argument is: Did God make man in His image with moral responsibility, or did man evolve without a Maker and he therefore has no moral accountability? If it's the former, the atheist is in big trouble. It means that he is a wicked sinner in the eyes of a perfect and holy God, and that hell is a reality. If it's the latter, then all is well with him, because there is no such thing as sin, no moral accountability, and therefore no hell.

So what is the ultimate solution to this continual standoff? It would be for the atheist to simply seek God for himself. He has creation and his conscience as evidence for starters, but if he came to actually know God, that would forever settle the issue for him. So, here's a promise from God that is not symbolic but is literal: "And you will seek Me and find Me, when you search for Me with *all your heart*" (Jer. 29:13, emphasis added). I did that on April 25, 1972, and I "found" Him at 1:30 in the morning. Countless millions of others have likewise found God, when they sought Him with genuine sincerity. Why should the atheist seek Him like that? Because God is the essence of life itself, and the atheist's time is running out... with his every heartbeat.

all Judah, and they carried away the stones
and timber of Ramah, which Baasha had
used for building; and with them he built
Geba and Mizpah.

Hanani's Message to Asa

7And at that time Hanani the seer came
to Asa king of Judah, and said to him:
"Because you have relied on the king of
Syria, and have not relied on the LORD
your God, therefore the army of the king
of Syria has escaped from your hand.
8Were the Ethiopians and the Lubim not
a huge army with very many chariots and
horsemen? Yet, because you relied on the
LORD, He delivered them into your hand.
9For the eyes of the LORD run to and fro
throughout the whole earth, to show
Himself strong on behalf of *those* whose
heart *is* loyal to Him. In this you have
done foolishly; therefore from now on you
shall have wars." 10Then Asa was angry
with the seer, and put him in prison, for
he was enraged at him because of this.
And Asa oppressed *some* of the people at
that time.

Illness and Death of Asa

11Note that the acts of Asa, first and
last, are indeed written in the book of the
kings of Judah and Israel. 12And in the
thirty-ninth year of his reign, Asa became
diseased in his feet, and his malady was
severe; yet in his disease he did not seek

16:9 God is looking for those who have presented themselves as living sacrifices, for His glory. Have you obeyed Rom. 12:1,2?

the LORD, but the physicians.
13So Asa rested with his fathers; he
died in the forty-first year of his reign.
14They buried him in his own tomb, which
he had made for himself in the City of
David; and they laid him in the bed
which was filled with spices and various
ingredients prepared in a mixture of ointments. They made a very great burning
for him.

Jehoshaphat Reigns in Judah

17 Then Jehoshaphat his son reigned
in his place, and strengthened himself against Israel. 2And he placed troops
in all the fortified cities of Judah, and set
garrisons in the land of Judah and in the
cities of Ephraim which Asa his father
had taken. 3Now the LORD was with Jehoshaphat, because he walked in the former ways of his father David; he did not
seek the Baals, 4but sought the God[a] of
his father, and walked in His commandments and not according to the acts of Israel. 5Therefore the LORD established the
kingdom in his hand; and all Judah gave
presents to Jehoshaphat, and he had
riches and honor in abundance. 6And his
heart took delight in the ways of the LORD;
moreover he removed the high places
and wooden images from Judah.
7Also in the third year of his reign he
sent his leaders, Ben-Hail, Obadiah, Zechariah, Nethanel, and Michaiah, to teach
in the cities of Judah. 8And with them *he
sent* Levites: Shemaiah, Nethaniah, Zebadiah, Asahel, Shemiramoth, Jehonathan,
Adonijah, Tobijah, and Tobadonijah—
the Levites; and with them Elishama and
Jehoram, the priests. 9So they taught in
Judah, and *had* the Book of the Law of
the LORD with them; they went throughout all the cities of Judah and taught the
people.
10And the fear of the LORD fell on all
the kingdoms of the lands that *were* around
Judah, so that they did not make war
against Jehoshaphat. 11Also *some* of the
Philistines brought Jehoshaphat presents
and silver as tribute; and the Arabians

THE FUNCTION OF THE LAW

17:9,10 Understanding the truth of the Law produces the fear of the Lord. See Rom. 2:17–24 for how Paul used the moral Law to bring the knowledge of sin. Seeing sin in its true light makes us rightly fear God, which causes us to depart from sin.

"When man, conscious of his failure to keep God's command, is constantly urged by the Law to make payment of his debt and confronted with nothing but the terrible wrath of God and eternal condemnation, he cannot but sink into despair over his sins. Such is the inevitable consequence where the Law alone is taught with a view to attaining heaven thereby." *Martin Luther*

brought him flocks, seven thousand seven
hundred rams and seven thousand seven
hundred male goats.
12So Jehoshaphat became increasingly
powerful, and he built fortresses and
storage cities in Judah. 13He had much
property in the cities of Judah; and the
men of war, mighty men of valor, *were* in
Jerusalem.
14These *are* their numbers, according
to their fathers' houses. Of Judah, the
captains of thousands: Adnah the captain, and with him three hundred thousand mighty men of valor; 15and next to
him *was* Jehohanan the captain, and with
him two hundred and eighty thousand;
16and next to him *was* Amasiah the son of
Zichri, who willingly offered himself to
the LORD, and with him two hundred
thousand mighty men of valor. 17Of Benjamin: Eliada a mighty man of valor, and
with him two hundred thousand men
armed with bow and shield; 18and next to
him *was* Jehozabad, and with him one
hundred and eighty thousand prepared
for war. 19These served the king, besides
those the king put in the fortified cities
throughout all Judah.

Micaiah Warns Ahab

18 Jehoshaphat had riches and honor
in abundance; and by marriage he
allied himself with Ahab. 2After some years

17:4 [a]Septuagint reads *LORD God*.

he went down to *visit* Ahab in Samaria;
and Ahab killed sheep and oxen in abundance for him and the people who were
with him, and persuaded him to go up
with him to Ramoth Gilead. [3]So Ahab
king of Israel said to Jehoshaphat king of
Judah, "Will you go with me *against*
Ramoth Gilead?"

And he answered him, "I *am* as you *are,* and my people as your people; *we will be* with you in the war."

[4]Also Jehoshaphat said to the king of Israel, "Please inquire for the word of the LORD today."

[5]Then the king of Israel gathered the prophets together, four hundred men, and said to them, "Shall we go to war against Ramoth Gilead, or shall I refrain?"

So they said, "Go up, for God will deliver it into the king's hand."

[6]But Jehoshaphat said, "*Is there* not still a prophet of the LORD here, that we may inquire of Him?"[a]

[7]So the king of Israel said to Jehoshaphat, "*There is* still one man by whom we may inquire of the LORD; but I hate him, because he never prophesies good concerning me, but always evil. He *is* Micaiah the son of Imla."

And Jehoshaphat said, "Let not the king say such things!"

[8]Then the king of Israel called one *of his* officers and said, "Bring Micaiah the son of Imla quickly!"

[9]The king of Israel and Jehoshaphat
king of Judah, clothed in *their* robes, sat
each on his throne; and they sat at a
threshing floor at the entrance of the gate
of Samaria; and all the prophets prophesied before them. [10]Now Zedekiah the
son of Chenaanah had made horns of
iron for himself; and he said, "Thus says
the LORD: 'With these you shall gore the
Syrians until they are destroyed.' "

[11]And all the prophets prophesied so, saying, "Go up to Ramoth Gilead and prosper, for the LORD will deliver *it* into the king's hand."

[12]Then the messenger who had gone to call Micaiah spoke to him, saying, "Now listen, the words of the prophets with one accord encourage the king. Therefore please let your word be like *the word of* one of them, and speak encouragement."

> Are you without a character, with nobody to say a good word for you? I bring you good news. Call on the Son of God, and He will hear you.
>
> **D. L. MOODY**

[13]And Micaiah said, "*As* the LORD lives, whatever my God says, that I will speak."

[14]Then he came to the king; and the king said to him, "Micaiah, shall we go to war against Ramoth Gilead, or shall I refrain?"

And he said, "Go and prosper, and they shall be delivered into your hand!"

[15]So the king said to him, "How many times shall I make you swear that you tell me nothing but the truth in the name of the LORD?"

[16]Then he said, "I saw all Israel scattered on the mountains, as sheep that have no shepherd. And the LORD said, 'These have no master. Let each return to his house in peace.' "

[17]And the king of Israel said to Jehoshaphat, "Did I not tell you he would not prophesy good concerning me, but evil?"

[18]Then *Micaiah* said, "Therefore hear

18:6 [a]Or *him*

18:7 Perhaps if Ahab had lived a more virtuous life, the prophet may have had something good to tell him. Regardless, it is infinitely better to speak the truth and have the frown of the world than to withhold the truth and have the frown of God. Jesus promised that the world would hate us because it hates Him, so don't expect otherwise.

18:15 See 1 Kings 22:16 comment.

18:16 See Matt. 9:36.

the word of the LORD: I saw the LORD sitting on His throne, and all the host of heaven standing on His right hand and His left. [19]And the LORD said, 'Who will persuade Ahab king of Israel to go up, that he may fall at Ramoth Gilead?' So one spoke in this manner, and another spoke in that manner. [20]Then a spirit came forward and stood before the LORD, and said, 'I will persuade him.' The LORD said to him, 'In what way?' [21]So he said, 'I will go out and be a lying spirit in the mouth of all his prophets.' And *the LORD* said, 'You shall persuade *him* and also prevail; go out and do so.' [22]Therefore look! The LORD has put a lying spirit in the mouth of these prophets of yours, and the LORD has declared disaster against you."

[23]Then Zedekiah the son of Chenaanah went near and struck Micaiah on the cheek, and said, "Which way did the spirit from the LORD go from me to speak to you?"

[24]And Micaiah said, "Indeed you shall see on that day when you go into an inner chamber to hide!"

[25]Then the king of Israel said, "Take Micaiah, and return him to Amon the governor of the city and to Joash the king's son; [26]and say, 'Thus says the king: "Put this *fellow* in prison, and feed him with bread of affliction and water of affliction, until I return in peace." ' "

[27]But Micaiah said, "If you ever return in peace, the LORD has not spoken by me." And he said, "Take heed, all you people!"

Ahab Dies in Battle

[28]So the king of Israel and Jehoshaphat the king of Judah went up to Ramoth Gilead. [29]And the king of Israel said to Jehoshaphat, "I will disguise myself and go into battle; but you put on your robes." So the king of Israel disguised himself, and they went into battle.

[30]Now the king of Syria had commanded the captains of the chariots who *were* with him, saying, "Fight with no one small or great, but only with the king of Israel."

[31]So it was, when the captains of the chariots saw Jehoshaphat, that they said, "It *is* the king of Israel!" Therefore they surrounded him to attack; but Jehoshaphat cried out, and the LORD helped him, and God diverted them from him. [32]For so it was, when the captains of the chariots saw that it was not the king of Israel, that they turned back from pursuing him. [33]Now a certain man drew a bow at random, and struck the king of Israel between the joints of his armor. So he said to the driver of his chariot, "Turn around and take me out of the battle, for I am wounded." [34]The battle increased that day, and the king of Israel propped *himself* up in *his* chariot facing the Syrians until evening; and about the time of sunset he died.

19 Then Jehoshaphat the king of Judah returned safely to his house in Jerusalem. [2]And Jehu the son of Hanani the seer went out to meet him, and said

18:19–21 Lying spirits. There are some who stand in moral judgment over God and accuse Him of sin, because He sent lying spirits to Ahab. But this incident is consistent with other similar occurrences in Scripture (see Ezek. 14:9; 2 Thess. 2:11). Those who don't have the wisdom to fear God will point a holier-than-thou finger at the heavens and accuse God of sin. But those who fear Him will say, "The judgments of the LORD are true and righteous altogether" (Psa. 19:9). The Bible teaches that sinners "give place to the devil" (Eph. 4:27), and warns that Satan "walks about like a roaring lion, seeking whom he *may* devour" (1 Pet. 5:8, emphasis added). If the Father of Lies deceives sinners and blinds their minds, it is because they are willingly *serving* him as their spiritual father (see John 8:44). They are children of disobedience (see Eph. 2:2; 5:6). This is all done under the *permissive* will of God. In His perfect righteousness, He *allows* Satan to steal, kill, and destroy, as evident in the case of Job. In this passage, Micaiah informed Ahab that his prophets were all deceived by a lie, and that God was going to bring disaster on him—but still Ahab refused to believe the word spoken by the prophet. Sinners so often do the same when they hear the truth of the gospel. They willingly serve the devil and spurn the truth, ignoring the warning to flee to Christ.

Questions & Objections

"I thought God was supposed to be our friend, not our enemy."

Most people are shocked to learn that the Bible doesn't paint God as a friend of humanity. That picture doesn't go with their image of God. But the Bible makes it clear that our sins alienate us from Him, and paints a picture of a wicked and guilty criminal before a good Judge. Colossians 1:21 describes the lost as "alienated and enemies in your mind by wicked works." Romans 8:7 says that "the carnal mind is enmity [in a state of hostility] against God; for it is not subject to the law of God, nor indeed can be." The unregenerate mind spits blasphemy out of an unclean mouth. We are filled with rebellion toward God, and specifically His moral Law.

Jesus said, "You are My friends *if you do whatever I command you*" (John 15:14, emphasis added). It is essential to note the second part of the verse. We are enemies of God as long as we are friends with this sinful world (see James 4:4,5).

to King Jehoshaphat, "Should you help the wicked and love those who hate the LORD? Therefore the wrath of the LORD *is* upon you. 3Nevertheless good things are found in you, in that you have removed the wooden images from the land, and have prepared your heart to seek God."

The Reforms of Jehoshaphat

4So Jehoshaphat dwelt at Jerusalem; and he went out again among the people from Beersheba to the mountains of Ephraim, and brought them back to the LORD God of their fathers. 5Then he set judges in the land throughout all the fortified cities of Judah, city by city, 6and said to the judges, "Take heed to what you are doing, for you do not judge for man but for the LORD, who *is* with you in the judgment. 7Now therefore, let the fear of the LORD be upon you; take care and do *it,* for *there is* no iniquity with the LORD our God, no partiality, nor taking of bribes."

8Moreover in Jerusalem, for the judgment of the LORD and for controversies, Jehoshaphat appointed some of the Levites and priests, and some of the chief fathers of Israel, when they returned to Jerusalem.[a] 9And he commanded them, saying, "Thus you shall act in the fear of the LORD, faithfully and with a loyal heart: 10Whatever case comes to you from your brethren who dwell in their cities, whether of bloodshed or offenses against law or commandment, against statutes or ordinances, you shall warn them, lest they trespass against the LORD and wrath come upon you and your brethren. Do this, and you will not be guilty. 11And take notice: Amariah the chief priest *is* over you in all matters of the LORD; and Zebadiah the son of Ishmael, the ruler of the house of Judah, for all the king's matters; also the Levites *will be* officials before you. Behave courageously, and the LORD will be with the good."

Ammon, Moab, and Mount Seir Defeated

20 It happened after this *that* the people of Moab with the people of Ammon, and *others* with them besides the Ammonites,[a] came to battle against Jehoshaphat. 2Then some came and told

19:8 [a]Septuagint and Vulgate read *for the inhabitants of Jerusalem.* 20:1 [a]Following Masoretic Text and Vulgate; Septuagint reads *Meunites* (compare 26:7).

19:7 The judge we must face on Judgment Day is perfect, holy, and righteous. He is without iniquity and He will not be bribed. Celebrities, famous politicians, the rich, and our adored sporting figures don't impress God as they impress humanity. God shows no partiality, as Peter affirms in Acts 10:33–35.

20:2,3 Trials tend to bring us to the safety of our knees. See 1 Pet. 1:6,7 to see the fruit of tribulation for the true convert.

QUESTIONS & OBJECTIONS

20:15 ***"How can we overcome our fear of evangelizing?"***

We overcome our fears through love. The Bible says that perfect love casts out all fear. Think of a firefighter. He's up a sixty-foot ladder. In front of him are a mother and two children, clinging to each other in a window on the fourth floor of a burning building. Flames are licking at the terrified family. If he doesn't rescue them, they will certainly die. Would he rather be home spending time with his wife and kids? Of course he would. But he ignores his fears and he denies himself his own legitimate pleasures *because he is thinking of that family's terrible fate*. Love consumes his fears.

The Bible likens Christians to firefighters: "On some have compassion, making a distinction; but others save with fear, pulling them out of the fire, hating even the garment defiled by the flesh" (Jude 22,23).

"I care not where I go, or how I live, or what I endure so that I may save souls. When I sleep I dream of them; when I awake they are first in my thoughts...no amount of scholastic attainment, of able and profound exposition of brilliant and stirring eloquence can atone for the absence of a deep impassioned sympathetic love for human souls." *David Brainerd*

Jehoshaphat, saying, "A great multitude
is coming against you from beyond the
sea, from Syria;[a] and they are in Hazazon
Tamar" (which *is* En Gedi). 3And Jehoshaphat feared, and set himself to seek the
LORD, and proclaimed a fast throughout
all Judah. 4So Judah gathered together to
ask *help* from the LORD; and from all the
cities of Judah they came to seek the
LORD.

5Then Jehoshaphat stood in the assembly of Judah and Jerusalem, in the
house of the LORD, before the new court,
6and said: "O LORD God of our fathers,
are You not God in heaven, and do You
not rule over all the kingdoms of the nations, and in Your hand *is there not* power
and might, so that no one is able to withstand You? 7*Are* You not our God, *who*
drove out the inhabitants of this land before Your people Israel, and gave it to the
descendants of Abraham Your friend forever? 8And they dwell in it, and have
built You a sanctuary in it for Your name,
saying, 9'If disaster comes upon us—
sword, judgment, pestilence, or famine—
we will stand before this temple and in
Your presence (for Your name *is* in this
temple), and cry out to You in our affliction, and You will hear and save.' 10And
now, here are the people of Ammon,
Moab, and Mount Seir—whom You
would not let Israel invade when they
came out of the land of Egypt, but they
turned from them and did not destroy
them— 11here they are, rewarding us by
coming to throw us out of Your possession which You have given us to inherit.
12O our God, will You not judge them?
For we have no power against this great
multitude that is coming against us; nor
do we know what to do, but our eyes *are*
upon You."

13Now all Judah, with their little ones,
their wives, and their children, stood before the LORD.

14Then the Spirit of the LORD came
upon Jahaziel the son of Zechariah, the
son of Benaiah, the son of Jeiel, the son of
Mattaniah, a Levite of the sons of Asaph,
in the midst of the assembly. 15And he
said, "Listen, all you of Judah and you inhabitants of Jerusalem, and you, King Jehoshaphat! Thus says the LORD to you:
'Do not be afraid nor dismayed because
of this great multitude, for the battle *is*
not yours, but God's. 16Tomorrow go down
against them. They will surely come up
by the Ascent of Ziz, and you will find
them at the end of the brook before the
Wilderness of Jeruel. 17You will not *need*
to fight in this *battle*. Position yourselves,
stand still and see the salvation of the

20:2 [a]Following Masoretic Text, Septuagint, and Vulgate; some Hebrew manuscripts and Old Latin read *Edom*.

LORD, who is with you, O Judah and Jerusalem!' Do not fear or be dismayed; tomorrow go out against them, for the LORD *is* with you."

18 And Jehoshaphat bowed his head with *his* face to the ground, and all Judah and the inhabitants of Jerusalem bowed before the LORD, worshiping the LORD. 19 Then the Levites of the children of the Kohathites and of the children of the Korahites stood up to praise the LORD God of Israel with voices loud and high.

20 So they rose early in the morning and went out into the Wilderness of Tekoa; and as they went out, Jehoshaphat stood and said, "Hear me, O Judah and you inhabitants of Jerusalem: Believe in the LORD your God, and you shall be established; believe His prophets, and you shall prosper." 21 And when he had consulted with the people, he appointed those who should sing to the LORD, and who should praise the beauty of holiness, as they went out before the army and were saying:

"Praise the LORD,
For His mercy *endures* forever."[a]

22 Now when they began to sing and to praise, the LORD set ambushes against the people of Ammon, Moab, and Mount Seir, who had come against Judah; and they were defeated. 23 For the people of Ammon and Moab stood up against the inhabitants of Mount Seir to utterly kill and destroy *them.* And when they had made an end of the inhabitants of Seir, they helped to destroy one another.

24 So when Judah came to a place overlooking the wilderness, they looked toward the multitude; and there *were* their dead bodies, fallen on the earth. No one had escaped.

25 When Jehoshaphat and his people came to take away their spoil, they found among them an abundance of valuables on the dead bodies,[a] and precious jewelry, which they stripped off for themselves, more than they could carry away; and they were three days gathering the spoil because there was so much. 26 And on the fourth day they assembled in the Valley of Berachah, for there they blessed the LORD; therefore the name of that place was called The Valley of Berachah[a] until this day. 27 Then they returned, every man of Judah and Jerusalem, with Jehoshaphat in front of them, to go back to Jerusalem with joy, for the LORD had made them rejoice over their enemies. 28 So they came to Jerusalem, with stringed instruments and harps and trumpets, to the house of the LORD. 29 And the fear of God was on all the kingdoms of *those* countries when they heard that the LORD had fought against the enemies of Israel. 30 Then the realm of Jehoshaphat was quiet, for his God gave him rest all around.

The End of Jehoshaphat's Reign

31 So Jehoshaphat was king over Judah. *He was* thirty-five years old when he became king, and he reigned twenty-five years in Jerusalem. His mother's name *was* Azubah the daughter of Shilhi. 32 And he walked in the way of his father Asa, and did not turn aside from it, doing *what was* right in the sight of the LORD. 33 Nevertheless the high places were not taken away, for as yet the people had not directed their hearts to the God of their fathers.

34 Now the rest of the acts of Jehoshaphat, first and last, indeed they *are* written in the book of Jehu the son of Hanani, which *is* mentioned in the book of the kings of Israel.

35 After this Jehoshaphat king of Judah allied himself with Ahaziah king of Israel, who acted very wickedly. 36 And he allied himself with him to make ships to go to Tarshish, and they made the ships in Ezion Geber. 37 But Eliezer the son of Dodavah of Mareshah prophesied against Jehoshaphat, saying, "Because you have allied yourself with Ahaziah, the LORD has

20:21 [a]Compare Psalm 106:1 **20:25** [a]A few Hebrew manuscripts, Old Latin, and Vulgate read *garments*; Septuagint reads *armor.* **20:26** [a]Literally *Blessing*

destroyed your works." Then the ships were wrecked, so that they were not able to go to Tarshish.

Jehoram Reigns in Judah

21 And Jehoshaphat rested with his fathers, and was buried with his fathers in the City of David. Then Jehoram his son reigned in his place. 2He had brothers, the sons of Jehoshaphat: Azariah, Jehiel, Zechariah, Azaryahu, Michael, and Shephatiah; all these *were* the sons of Jehoshaphat king of Israel. 3Their father gave them great gifts of silver and gold and precious things, with fortified cities in Judah; but he gave the kingdom to Jehoram, because he *was* the firstborn.

4Now when Jehoram was established over the kingdom of his father, he strengthened himself and killed all his brothers with the sword, and also *others* of the princes of Israel.

5Jehoram *was* thirty-two years old when he became king, and he reigned eight years in Jerusalem. 6And he walked in the way of the kings of Israel, just as the house of Ahab had done, for he had the daughter of Ahab as a wife; and he did evil in the sight of the LORD. 7Yet the LORD would not destroy the house of David, because of the covenant that He had made with David, and since He had promised to give a lamp to him and to his sons forever.

8In his days Edom revolted against Judah's authority, and made a king over themselves. 9So Jehoram went out with his officers, and all his chariots with him. And he rose by night and attacked the Edomites who had surrounded him and the captains of the chariots. 10Thus Edom has been in revolt against Judah's authority to this day. At that time Libnah revolted against his rule, because he had forsaken the LORD God of his fathers. 11Moreover he made high places in the mountains of Judah, and caused the inhabitants of Jerusalem to commit harlotry, and led Judah astray.

12And a letter came to him from Elijah the prophet, saying,

> Thus says the LORD God of your
> father David:
> Because you have not walked in the
> ways of Jehoshaphat your father, or
> in the ways of Asa king of Judah,
> 13but have walked in the way of the
> kings of Israel, and have made Judah
> and the inhabitants of Jerusalem to
> play the harlot like the harlotry of the
> house of Ahab, and also have killed
> your brothers, those of your father's
> household, *who were* better than
> yourself, 14behold, the LORD will
> strike your people with a serious
> affliction—your children, your wives,
> and all your possessions; 15and you
> *will become* very sick with a disease of
> your intestines, until your intestines
> come out by reason of the sickness,
> day by day.

16Moreover the LORD stirred up against Jehoram the spirit of the Philistines and the Arabians who *were* near the Ethiopians. 17And they came up into Judah and invaded it, and carried away all the possessions that were found in the king's house, and also his sons and his wives, so that there was not a son left to him except Jehoahaz,[a] the youngest of his sons.

18After all this the LORD struck him in his intestines with an incurable disease. 19Then it happened in the course of time, after the end of two years, that his intestines came out because of his sickness; so he died in severe pain. And his people made no burning for him, like the burning for his fathers.

20He was thirty-two years old when he

21:17 [a]Elsewhere called *Ahaziah* (compare 2 Chronicles 22:1)

21:7 The Messiah, "the light of the world" (John 8:12), came from the house of David.

became king. He reigned in Jerusalem eight years and, to no one's sorrow, departed. However they buried him in the City of David, but not in the tombs of the kings.

Ahaziah Reigns in Judah

22 Then the inhabitants of Jerusalem made Ahaziah his youngest son king in his place, for the raiders who came with the Arabians into the camp had killed all the older *sons*. So Ahaziah the son of Jehoram, king of Judah, reigned. [2]Ahaziah *was* forty-two[a] years old when he became king, and he reigned one year in Jerusalem. His mother's name *was* Athaliah the granddaughter of Omri. [3]He also walked in the ways of the house of Ahab, for his mother advised him to do wickedly. [4]Therefore he did evil in the sight of the LORD, like the house of Ahab; for they were his counselors after the death of his father, to his destruction. [5]He also followed their advice, and went with Jehoram[a] the son of Ahab king of Israel to war against Hazael king of Syria at Ramoth Gilead; and the Syrians wounded Joram. [6]Then he returned to Jezreel to recover from the wounds which he had received at Ramah, when he fought against Hazael king of Syria. And Azariah[a] the son of Jehoram, king of Judah, went down to see Jehoram the son of Ahab in Jezreel, because he was sick.

[7]His going to Joram was God's occasion for Ahaziah's downfall; for when he arrived, he went out with Jehoram against Jehu the son of Nimshi, whom the LORD had anointed to cut off the house of Ahab. [8]And it happened, when Jehu was executing judgment on the house of Ahab, and found the princes of Judah and the sons of Ahaziah's brothers who served Ahaziah, that he killed them. [9]Then he searched for Ahaziah; and they caught him (he was hiding in Samaria), and brought him to Jehu. When they had killed him, they buried him, "because," they said, "he is the son of Jehoshaphat, who sought the LORD with all his heart."

So the house of Ahaziah had no one to assume power over the kingdom.

Athaliah Reigns in Judah

[10]Now when Athaliah the mother of Ahaziah saw that her son was dead, she arose and destroyed all the royal heirs of the house of Judah. [11]But Jehoshabeath,[a] the daughter of the king, took Joash the son of Ahaziah, and stole him away from among the king's sons who were being murdered, and put him and his nurse in a bedroom. So Jehoshabeath, the daughter of King Jehoram, the wife of Jehoiada the priest (for she was the sister of Ahaziah), hid him from Athaliah so that she did not kill him. [12]And he was hidden with them in the house of God for six years, while Athaliah reigned over the land.

Joash Crowned King of Judah

23 In the seventh year Jehoiada strengthened himself, *and made a* covenant with the captains of hundreds: Azariah the son of Jeroham, Ishmael the son of Jehohanan, Azariah the son of Obed, Maaseiah the son of Adaiah, and Elishaphat the son of Zichri. [2]And they went throughout Judah and gathered the Levites from all the cities of Judah, and the chief fathers of Israel, and they came to Jerusalem.

[3]Then all the assembly made a covenant with the king in the house of God. And he said to them, "Behold, the king's son shall reign, as the LORD has said of the sons of David. [4]This *is* what you shall

22:2 [a]Or *twenty-two* (compare 2 Kings 8:26) 22:5 [a]Also spelled *Joram* (compare verses 5 and 7; 2 Kings 8:28; and elsewhere) 22:6 [a]Some Hebrew manuscripts, Septuagint, Syriac, Vulgate, and 2 Kings 8:29 read *Ahaziah*. 22:11 [a]Spelled *Jehosheba* in 2 Kings 11:2

22:10,11 Jesus was stolen away into Egypt to avoid being murdered by Herod. See Matt. 2:13,14 for the details.

do: One-third of you entering on the Sabbath, of the priests and the Levites, *shall be* keeping watch over the doors; 5one-third *shall be* at the king's house; and one-third at the Gate of the Foundation. All the people *shall be* in the courts of the house of the LORD. 6But let no one come into the house of the LORD except the priests and those of the Levites who serve. They may go in, for they *are* holy; but all the people shall keep the watch of the LORD. 7And the Levites shall surround the king on all sides, every man with his weapons in his hand; and whoever comes into the house, let him be put to death. You are to be with the king when he comes in and when he goes out."

8So the Levites and all Judah did according to all that Jehoiada the priest commanded. And each man took his men who were to be on duty on the Sabbath, with those who were going *off duty* on the Sabbath; for Jehoiada the priest had not dismissed the divisions. 9And Jehoiada the priest gave to the captains of hundreds the spears and the large and small shields which *had belonged* to King David, that *were* in the temple of God. 10Then he set all the people, every man with his weapon in his hand, from the right side of the temple to the left side of the temple, along by the altar and by the temple, all around the king. 11And they brought out the king's son, put the crown on him, *gave him* the Testimony,[a] and made him king. Then Jehoiada and his sons anointed him, and said, "*Long* live the king!"

Death of Athaliah

12Now when Athaliah heard the noise of the people running and praising the king, she came to the people *in* the temple of the LORD. 13*When* she looked, there was the king standing by his pillar at the entrance; and the leaders and the trumpeters *were* by the king. All the people of the land were rejoicing and blowing trumpets, also the singers with musical instruments, and those who led in praise. So Athaliah tore her clothes and said, "Treason! Treason!"

14And Jehoiada the priest brought out the captains of hundreds who were set over the army, and said to them, "Take her outside under guard, and slay with the sword whoever follows her." For the priest had said, "Do not kill her in the house of the LORD."

15So they seized her; and she went by way of the entrance of the Horse Gate *into* the king's house, and they killed her there.

> Only a true gospel, preached and demonstrated by God's people, can overcome the moral corruption in our country. Study! Pray! Live!
>
> **PAUL WASHER**

16Then Jehoiada made a covenant between himself, the people, and the king, that they should be the LORD's people. 17And all the people went to the temple[a] of Baal, and tore it down. They broke in pieces its altars and images, and killed Mattan the priest of Baal before the altars. 18Also Jehoiada appointed the oversight of the house of the LORD to the hand of the priests, the Levites, whom David had assigned in the house of the LORD, to offer the burnt offerings of the LORD, as *it is* written in the Law of Moses, with rejoicing and with singing, *as it was established* by David. 19And he set the gatekeepers at the gates of the house of the LORD, so that no one *who was* in any way unclean should enter.

20Then he took the captains of hundreds, the nobles, the governors of the people, and all the people of the land,

23:11 [a]That is, the Law (compare Exodus 25:16, 21; 31:18)
23:17 [a]Literally *house*

23:19 Nothing unclean will enter the New Jerusalem (see Rev. 21:27).

and brought the king down from the house of the LORD; and they went through the Upper Gate to the king's house, and set the king on the throne of the kingdom. [21]So all the people of the land rejoiced; and the city was quiet, for they had slain Athaliah with the sword.

Joash Repairs the Temple

24 Joash *was* seven years old when he became king, and he reigned forty years in Jerusalem. His mother's name *was* Zibiah of Beersheba. [2]Joash did *what was* right in the sight of the LORD all the days of Jehoiada the priest. [3]And Jehoiada took two wives for him, and he had sons and daughters.

[4]Now it happened after this *that* Joash set his heart on repairing the house of the LORD. [5]Then he gathered the priests and the Levites, and said to them, "Go out to the cities of Judah, and gather from all Israel money to repair the house of your God from year to year, and see that you do it quickly."

However the Levites did not do it quickly. [6]So the king called Jehoiada the chief *priest,* and said to him, "Why have you not required the Levites to bring in from Judah and from Jerusalem the collection, *according to the commandment* of Moses the servant of the LORD and of the assembly of Israel, for the tabernacle of witness?" [7]For the sons of Athaliah, that wicked woman, had broken into the house of God, and had also presented all the dedicated things of the house of the LORD to the Baals.

[8]Then at the king's command they made a chest, and set it outside at the gate of the house of the LORD. [9]And they made a proclamation throughout Judah and Jerusalem to bring to the LORD the collection *that* Moses the servant of God *had imposed* on Israel in the wilderness. [10]Then all the leaders and all the people rejoiced, brought their contributions, and put *them* into the chest until all had given. [11]So it was, at that time, when the chest was brought to the king's official by the hand of the Levites, and when they saw that *there was* much money, that the king's scribe and the high priest's officer came and emptied the chest, and took it and returned it to its place. Thus they did day by day, and gathered money in abundance.

[12]The king and Jehoiada gave it to those who did the work of the service of the house of the LORD; and they hired masons and carpenters to repair the house of the LORD, and also those who worked in iron and bronze to restore the house of the LORD. [13]So the workmen labored, and the work was completed by them; they restored the house of God to its original condition and reinforced it. [14]When they had finished, they brought the rest of the money before the king and Jehoiada; they made from it articles for the house of the LORD, articles for serving and offering, spoons and vessels of gold and silver. And they offered burnt offerings in the house of the LORD continually all the days of Jehoiada.

Apostasy of Joash

[15]But Jehoiada grew old and was full of days, and he died; *he was* one hundred and thirty years old when he died. [16]And they buried him in the City of David among the kings, because he had done good in Israel, both toward God and His house.

[17]Now after the death of Jehoiada the leaders of Judah came and bowed down to the king. And the king listened to them. [18]Therefore they left the house of the LORD God of their fathers, and served wooden images and idols; and wrath came upon Judah and Jerusalem because of their trespass. [19]Yet He sent prophets to them, to bring them back to the LORD; and they testified against them, but they would not listen.

24:15,16 May this be said of every Christian—that we live a long life pleasing to both God and His people.

20Then the Spirit of God came upon Zechariah the son of Jehoiada the priest, who stood above the people, and said to them, "Thus says God: 'Why do you transgress the commandments of the LORD, so that you cannot prosper? Because you have forsaken the LORD, He also has forsaken you.' " 21So they conspired against him, and at the command of the king they stoned him with stones in the court of the house of the LORD. 22Thus Joash the king did not remember the kindness which Jehoiada his father had done to him, but killed his son; and as he died, he said, "The LORD look on *it,* and repay!"

· · · · · ·

For last words of famous people, see 1 Cor. 15:55 comment.

· · · · · ·

Death of Joash

23So it happened in the spring of the year *that* the army of Syria came up against him; and they came to Judah and Jerusalem, and destroyed all the leaders of the people from among the people, and sent all their spoil to the king of Damascus. 24For the army of the Syrians came with a small company of men; but the LORD delivered a very great army into their hand, because they had forsaken the LORD God of their fathers. So they executed judgment against Joash. 25And when they had withdrawn from him (for they left him severely wounded), his own servants conspired against him because of the blood of the sons[a] of Jehoiada the priest, and killed him on his bed. So he died. And they buried him in the City of David, but they did not bury him in the tombs of the kings.

26These are the ones who conspired against him: Zabad[a] the son of Shimeath the Ammonitess, and Jehozabad the son of Shimrith[b] the Moabitess. 27Now *concerning* his sons, and the many oracles about him, and the repairing of the house of God, indeed they *are* written in the annals of the book of the kings. Then Amaziah his son reigned in his place.

Amaziah Reigns in Judah

25 Amaziah *was* twenty-five years old *when* he became king, and he reigned twenty-nine years in Jerusalem. His mother's name *was* Jehoaddan of Jerusalem. 2And he did *what was* right in the sight of the LORD, but not with a loyal heart.

3Now it happened, as soon as the kingdom was established for him, that he executed his servants who had murdered his father the king. 4However he did not execute their children, but *did* as *it is* written in the Law in the Book of Moses, where the LORD commanded, saying, "The fathers shall not be put to death for their children, nor shall the children be put to death for their fathers; but a person shall die for his own sin."[a]

The War Against Edom

5Moreover Amaziah gathered Judah together and set over them captains of thousands and captains of hundreds, according to *their* fathers' houses, throughout all Judah and Benjamin; and he numbered them from twenty years old and above, and found them to be three hundred thousand choice *men, able* to go to war, who could handle spear and shield. 6He also hired one hundred thousand mighty men of valor from Israel for one hundred talents of silver. 7But a man of God came to him, saying, "O king, do not let the army of Israel go with you, for the LORD *is* not with Israel—*not with* any of the children of Ephraim. 8But if you go, be gone! Be strong in battle! *Even so,* God

24:25 [a]Septuagint and Vulgate read *son* (compare verses 20–22). 24:26 [a]Or *Jozachar* (compare 2 Kings 12:21) [b]Or *Shomer* (compare 2 Kings 12:21) 25:4 [a]Deuteronomy 24:16

25:2 We can do the right thing without a wholeheartedness. See Phil. 1:18 comment and Col. 3:23.

shall make you fall before the enemy; for
God has power to help and to overthrow."
9Then Amaziah said to the man of
God, "But what *shall we* do about the
hundred talents which I have given to the
troops of Israel?"

And the man of God answered, "The
LORD is able to give you much more than
this." 10So Amaziah discharged the troops
that had come to him from Ephraim, to
go back home. Therefore their anger was
greatly aroused against Judah, and they
returned home in great anger.
11Then Amaziah strengthened himself,
and leading his people, he went to the
Valley of Salt and killed ten thousand of
the people of Seir. 12Also the children of
Judah took captive ten thousand alive,
brought them to the top of the rock, and
cast them down from the top of the rock,
so that they all were dashed in pieces.
13But as for the soldiers of the army
which Amaziah had discharged, so that
they would not go with him to battle,
they raided the cities of Judah from
Samaria to Beth Horon, killed three thousand in them, and took much spoil.
14Now it was so, after Amaziah came
from the slaughter of the Edomites, that
he brought the gods of the people of Seir,
set them up *to be* his gods, and bowed
down before them and burned incense to
them. 15Therefore the anger of the LORD
was aroused against Amaziah, and He sent
him a prophet who said to him, "Why
have you sought the gods of the people,
which could not rescue their own people
from your hand?"
16So it was, as he talked with him, that
the king said to him, "Have we made you
the king's counselor? Cease! Why should
you be killed?"

Then the prophet ceased, and said, "I
know that God has determined to destroy
you, because you have done this and
have not heeded my advice."

Israel Defeats Judah

17Now Amaziah king of Judah asked
advice and sent to Joash[a] the son of Jehoahaz, the son of Jehu, king of Israel, saying,
"Come, let us face one another *in battle*."
18And Joash king of Israel sent to Amaziah king of Judah, saying, "The thistle that
was in Lebanon sent to the cedar that was
in Lebanon, saying, 'Give your daughter
to my son as wife'; and a wild beast that
was in Lebanon passed by and trampled
the thistle. 19Indeed you say that you have
defeated the Edomites, and your heart is
lifted up to boast. Stay at home now; why
should you meddle with trouble, that you
should fall—you and Judah with you?"
20But Amaziah would not heed, for it
came from God, that He might give them
into the hand *of their enemies*, because
they sought the gods of Edom. 21So Joash
king of Israel went out; and he and
Amaziah king of Judah faced one another
at Beth Shemesh, which *belongs* to Judah.
22And Judah was defeated by Israel, and
every man fled to his tent. 23Then Joash
the king of Israel captured Amaziah king
of Judah, the son of Joash, the son of Jehoahaz, at Beth Shemesh; and he brought

"The real attitude of sin in the heart towards God is that of being without God; it is pride, the worship of myself, that is the great atheistic fact in human life."

Oswald Chambers

25:17 [a]Spelled *Jehoash* in 2 Kings 14:8ff

him to Jerusalem, and broke down the wall of Jerusalem from the Gate of Ephraim to the Corner Gate—four hundred cubits. [24]And *he took* all the gold and silver, all the articles that were found in the house of God with Obed-Edom, the treasures of the king's house, and hostages, and returned to Samaria.

Death of Amaziah

[25]Amaziah the son of Joash, king of Judah, lived fifteen years after the death of Joash the son of Jehoahaz, king of Israel. [26]Now the rest of the acts of Amaziah, from first to last, indeed *are* they not written in the book of the kings of Judah and Israel? [27]After the time that Amaziah turned away from following the LORD, they made a conspiracy against him in Jerusalem, and he fled to Lachish; but they sent after him to Lachish and killed him there. [28]Then they brought him on horses and buried him with his fathers in the City of Judah.

Uzziah Reigns in Judah

26 Now all the people of Judah took Uzziah,[a] who *was* sixteen years old, and made him king instead of his father Amaziah. [2]He built Elath[a] and restored it to Judah, after the king rested with his fathers.

[3]Uzziah *was* sixteen years old when he became king, and he reigned fifty-two years in Jerusalem. His mother's name was Jecholiah of Jerusalem. [4]And he did *what was* right in the sight of the LORD, according to all that his father Amaziah had done. [5]He sought God in the days of Zechariah, who had understanding in the visions[a] of God; and as long as he sought the LORD, God made him prosper.

[6]Now he went out and made war against the Philistines, and broke down the wall of Gath, the wall of Jabneh, and the wall of Ashdod; and he built cities *around* Ashdod and among the Philistines. [7]God helped him against the Philistines, against the Arabians who lived in Gur Baal, and against the Meunites. [8]Also the Ammonites brought tribute to Uzziah. His fame spread as far as the entrance of Egypt, for he became exceedingly strong.

[9]And Uzziah built towers in Jerusalem at the Corner Gate, at the Valley Gate, and at the corner buttress of the wall; then he fortified them. [10]Also he built towers in the desert. He dug many wells, for he had much livestock, both in the lowlands and in the plains; *he also had* farmers and vinedressers in the mountains and in Carmel, for he loved the soil.

[11]Moreover Uzziah had an army of fighting men who went out to war by companies, according to the number on their roll as prepared by Jeiel the scribe and Maaseiah the officer, under the hand of Hananiah, *one* of the king's captains. [12]The total number of chief officers[a] of the mighty men of valor *was* two thousand six hundred. [13]And under their authority *was* an army of three hundred and seven thousand five hundred, that made war with mighty power, to help the king against the enemy. [14]Then Uzziah prepared for them, for the entire army, shields, spears, helmets, body armor, bows, and slings *to cast* stones. [15]And he made devices in Jerusalem, invented by skillful men, to be on the towers and the corners, to shoot arrows and large stones. So his fame spread far and wide, for he was marvelously helped till he became strong.

The Penalty for Uzziah's Pride

[16]But when he was strong his heart

26:1 [a]Called *Azariah* in 2 Kings 14:21ff 26:2 [a]Hebrew *Eloth* 26:5 [a]Several Hebrew manuscripts, Septuagint, Syriac, Targum, and Arabic read *fear.* 26:12 [a]Literally *chief fathers*

26:16 What a tragedy it is when a man or woman of God falls into sin. It all starts in the secret chamber of the heart. Be careful of entertaining sinful thoughts. Never welcome pride, lust, conceit, jealousy, unforgiveness, anger, covetousness, etc., because they will manifest sin in your life, and will cause your downfall. Walk in the fear of the Lord, and cultivate a tender conscience before Him. See vv. 19–21 for the terrible result of sin in the heart.

was lifted up, to *his* destruction, for he transgressed against the LORD his God by entering the temple of the LORD to burn incense on the altar of incense. 17So Azariah the priest went in after him, and with him were eighty priests of the LORD —valiant men. 18And they withstood King Uzziah, and said to him, "*It is* not for you, Uzziah, to burn incense to the LORD, but for the priests, the sons of Aaron, who are consecrated to burn incense. Get out of the sanctuary, for you have trespassed! You *shall have* no honor from the LORD God."

> The more I study religions the more I am convinced that man never worshiped anything but himself.
>
> **RICHARD BURTON**

19Then Uzziah became furious; and he *had* a censer in his hand to burn incense. And while he was angry with the priests, leprosy broke out on his forehead, before the priests in the house of the LORD, beside the incense altar. 20And Azariah the chief priest and all the priests looked at him, and there, on his forehead, he *was* leprous; so they thrust him out of that place. Indeed he also hurried to get out, because the LORD had struck him.

21King Uzziah was a leper until the day of his death. He dwelt in an isolated house, because he was a leper; for he was cut off from the house of the LORD. Then Jotham his son *was* over the king's house, judging the people of the land.

22Now the rest of the acts of Uzziah, from first to last, the prophet Isaiah the son of Amoz wrote. 23So Uzziah rested with his fathers, and they buried him with his fathers in the field of burial which *belonged* to the kings, for they said, "He is a leper." Then Jotham his son reigned in his place.

Jotham Reigns in Judah

27 Jotham *was* twenty-five years old when he became king, and he reigned sixteen years in Jerusalem. His mother's name *was* Jerushah[a] the daughter of Zadok. 2And he did *what was* right in the sight of the LORD, according to all that his father Uzziah had done (although he did not enter the temple of the LORD). But still the people acted corruptly.

3He built the Upper Gate of the house of the LORD, and he built extensively on the wall of Ophel. 4Moreover he built cities in the mountains of Judah, and in the forests he built fortresses and towers. 5He also fought with the king of the Ammonites and defeated them. And the people of Ammon gave him in that year one hundred talents of silver, ten thousand kors of wheat, and ten thousand of barley. The people of Ammon paid this to him in the second and third years also. 6So Jotham became mighty, because he prepared his ways before the LORD his God.

7Now the rest of the acts of Jotham, and all his wars and his ways, indeed they *are* written in the book of the kings of Israel and Judah. 8He was twenty-five years old when he became king, and he reigned sixteen years in Jerusalem. 9So Jotham rested with his fathers, and they buried him in the City of David. Then Ahaz his son reigned in his place.

27:1 [a]Spelled *Jerusha* in 2 Kings 15:33

27:6 He became mighty because he prepared his ways before the Lord his God. Do the same. Set aside a daily quiet time with the Lord. Search your heart, confess your sins, feed on the Word, and pray that God uses you that day to reach the lost and glorify His name. *Charles Spurgeon* said, "Evangelists, go on preaching at the street corner—you that visit the low lodging-houses, go on. Get into the room and talk of Jesus Christ there as you have done. You that go into the country towns on the Sabbath and speak on the village-greens of Christ, go on with it. I am glad to see you, but I am glad to miss you when I know you are about the Master's work. We don't want to keep the salt in the box: let it be rubbed into the putrid mass to stay the putrification. We don't want the seed forever in the corn-bin: let it be scattered and it will give us more."

Ahaz Reigns in Judah

28 Ahaz *was* twenty years old when
he became king, and he reigned
sixteen years in Jerusalem; and he did not
do *what was* right in the sight of the LORD,
as his father David *had done*. [2]For he
walked in the ways of the kings of Israel,
and made molded images for the Baals.
[3]He burned incense in the Valley of the
Son of Hinnom, and burned his children
in the fire, according to the abominations
of the nations whom the LORD had cast
out before the children of Israel. [4]And he
sacrificed and burned incense on the
high places, on the hills, and under every
green tree.

Syria and Israel Defeat Judah

[5]Therefore the LORD his God delivered
him into the hand of the king of Syria.
They defeated him, and carried away a
great multitude of them as captives, and
brought *them* to Damascus. Then he was
also delivered into the hand of the king of
Israel, who defeated him with a great
slaughter. [6]For Pekah the son of Remaliah
killed one hundred and twenty thousand
in Judah in one day, all valiant men, because they had forsaken the LORD God of
their fathers. [7]Zichri, a mighty man of
Ephraim, killed Maaseiah the king's son,
Azrikam the officer over the house, and
Elkanah *who was* second to the king.
[8]And the children of Israel carried away
captive of their brethren two hundred
thousand women, sons, and daughters;
and they also took away much spoil from
them, and brought the spoil to Samaria.

Israel Returns the Captives

[9]But a prophet of the LORD was there,
whose name *was* Oded; and he went out
before the army that came to Samaria, and
said to them: "Look, because the LORD
God of your fathers was angry with Judah,
He has delivered them into your hand;
but you have killed them in a rage *that*
reaches up to heaven. [10]And now you propose to force the children of Judah and
Jerusalem to be your male and female
slaves; *but are* you not also guilty before
the LORD your God? [11]Now hear me, therefore, and return the captives, whom you
have taken captive from your brethren, for
the fierce wrath of the LORD *is* upon you."
[12]Then some of the heads of the children of Ephraim, Azariah the son of
Johanan, Berechiah the son of Meshillemoth, Jehizkiah the son of Shallum, and
Amasa the son of Hadlai, stood up against
those who came from the war, [13]and said
to them, "You shall not bring the captives
here, for we *already* have offended the
LORD. You intend to add to our sins and
to our guilt; for our guilt is great, and
there is fierce wrath against Israel." [14]So
the armed men left the captives and the
spoil before the leaders and all the assembly. [15]Then the men who were designated by name rose up and took the captives, and from the spoil they clothed all
who were naked among them, dressed
them and gave them sandals, gave them
food and drink, and anointed them; and
they let all the feeble ones ride on donkeys. So they brought them to their brethren at Jericho, the city of palm trees.
Then they returned to Samaria.

Assyria Refuses to Help Judah

[16]At the same time King Ahaz sent to
the kings[a] of Assyria to help him. [17]For
again the Edomites had come, attacked
Judah, and carried away captives. [18]The
Philistines also had invaded the cities of
the lowland and of the South of Judah,
and had taken Beth Shemesh, Aijalon,
Gederoth, Sochoh with its villages, Timnah with its villages, and Gimzo with its
villages; and they dwelt there. [19]For the
LORD brought Judah low because of Ahaz
king of Israel, for he had encouraged
moral decline in Judah and had been
continually unfaithful to the LORD. [20]Also
Tiglath-Pileser[a] king of Assyria came to
him and distressed him, and did not assist him. [21]For Ahaz took part *of the trea-*

28:16 [a]Septuagint, Syriac, and Vulgate read *king* (compare verse 20). 28:20 [a]Hebrew *Tilgath-Pilneser*

sures from the house of the LORD, from the house of the king, and from the leaders, and he gave *it* to the king of Assyria; but he did not help him.

Apostasy and Death of Ahaz

22Now in the time of his distress King Ahaz became increasingly unfaithful to the LORD. This *is that* King Ahaz. 23For he sacrificed to the gods of Damascus which had defeated him, saying, "Because the gods of the kings of Syria help them, I will sacrifice to them that they may help me." But they were the ruin of him and of all Israel. 24So Ahaz gathered the articles of the house of God, cut in pieces the articles of the house of God, shut up the doors of the house of the LORD, and made for himself altars in every corner of Jerusalem. 25And in every single city of Judah he made high places to burn incense to other gods, and provoked to anger the LORD God of his fathers.

26Now the rest of his acts and all his ways, from first to last, indeed they *are* written in the book of the kings of Judah and Israel. 27So Ahaz rested with his fathers, and they buried him in the city, in Jerusalem; but they did not bring him into the tombs of the kings of Israel. Then Hezekiah his son reigned in his place.

Hezekiah Reigns in Judah

29 Hezekiah became king *when he was* twenty-five years old, and he reigned twenty-nine years in Jerusalem. His mother's name *was* Abijah[a] the daughter of Zechariah. 2And he did *what was* right in the sight of the LORD, according to all that his father David had done.

Hezekiah Cleanses the Temple

3In the first year of his reign, in the first month, he opened the doors of the house of the LORD and repaired them. 4Then he brought in the priests and the Levites, and gathered them in the East Square, 5and said to them: "Hear me, Levites! Now sanctify yourselves, sanctify the house of the LORD God of your fathers, and carry out the rubbish from the holy *place*. 6For our fathers have trespassed and done evil in the eyes of the LORD our God; they have forsaken Him, have turned their faces away from the dwelling place of the LORD, and turned *their* backs *on Him*. 7They have also shut up the doors of the vestibule, put out the lamps, and have not burned incense or offered burnt offerings in the holy *place* to the God of Israel. 8Therefore the wrath of the LORD fell upon Judah and Jerusalem, and He has given them up to trouble, to desolation, and to jeering, as you see with your eyes. 9For indeed, because of this our fathers have fallen by the sword; and our sons, our daughters, and our wives *are* in captivity.

10"Now *it is* in my heart to make a covenant with the LORD God of Israel, that His fierce wrath may turn away from us. 11My sons, do not be negligent now, for the LORD has chosen you to stand before Him, to serve Him, and that you should minister to Him and burn incense."

12Then these Levites arose: Mahath the son of Amasai and Joel the son of Azariah, of the sons of the Kohathites; of the sons of Merari, Kish the son of Abdi and Azariah the son of Jehallelel; of the Gershonites, Joah the son of Zimmah and Eden the son of Joah; 13of the sons of Elizaphan, Shimri and Jeiel; of the sons of Asaph, Zechariah and Mattaniah; 14of the sons of Heman, Jehiel and Shimei; and of the sons of Jeduthun, Shemaiah and Uzziel.

29:1 [a]Spelled *Abi* in 2 Kings 18:2

28:22,23 Times of distress drive a true convert closer to God, not further away. Make sure that the soil of your heart is free from sin, so that the storms of this life will send the roots of God's Word deep into the soil.

29:6–9 We tend to inherit the spirituality of the preceding generation. The key to healing is in v. 5. To help the next generation follow God, see Deut. 11:19 comment on how to lead your kids to Christ.

15 And they gathered their brethren, sanctified themselves, and went according to the commandment of the king, at the words of the LORD, to cleanse the house of the LORD. 16 Then the priests went into the inner part of the house of the LORD to cleanse *it,* and brought out all the debris that they found in the temple of the LORD to the court of the house of the LORD. And the Levites took *it* out and carried *it* to the Brook Kidron.

17 Now they began to sanctify on the first *day* of the first month, and on the eighth day of the month they came to the vestibule of the LORD. So they sanctified the house of the LORD in eight days, and on the sixteenth day of the first month they finished.

18 Then they went in to King Hezekiah and said, "We have cleansed all the house of the LORD, the altar of burnt offerings with all its articles, and the table of the showbread with all its articles. 19 Moreover all the articles which King Ahaz in his reign had cast aside in his transgression we have prepared and sanctified; and there they *are,* before the altar of the LORD."

Hezekiah Restores Temple Worship

20 Then King Hezekiah rose early, gathered the rulers of the city, and went up to the house of the LORD. 21 And they brought seven bulls, seven rams, seven lambs, and seven male goats for a sin offering for the kingdom, for the sanctuary, and for Judah. Then he commanded the priests, the sons of Aaron, to offer *them* on the altar of the LORD. 22 So they killed the bulls, and the priests received the blood and sprinkled *it* on the altar. Likewise they killed the rams and sprinkled the blood on the altar. They also killed the lambs and sprinkled the blood on the altar. 23 Then they brought out the male goats *for* the sin offering before the king and the assembly, and they laid their hands on them. 24 And the priests killed them; and they presented their blood on the altar as a sin offering to make an atonement for all Israel, for the king commanded *that* the burnt offering and the sin offering *be made* for all Israel.

25 And he stationed the Levites in the house of the LORD with cymbals, with stringed instruments, and with harps, according to the commandment of David, of Gad the king's seer, and of Nathan the prophet; for thus *was* the commandment of the LORD by His prophets. 26 The Levites stood with the instruments of David, and the priests with the trumpets. 27 Then Hezekiah commanded *them* to offer the burnt offering on the altar. And when the burnt offering began, the song of the LORD *also* began, with the trumpets and with the instruments of David king of Israel. 28 So all the assembly worshiped, the singers sang, and the trumpeters sounded; all *this continued* until the burnt offering was finished. 29 And when they had finished offering, the king and all who were present with him bowed and worshiped. 30 Moreover King Hezekiah and the leaders commanded the Levites to sing

---

29:30,31 Worship requires obedience. At a Christian event 100,000 believers gathered to pray for revival and worship God. They were dismissed, not with a challenge to share the gospel, but with a challenge to worship the Lord wherever they went. What an unspeakable tragedy! Soldiers were told to feast in the barracks when they have been enlisted to fight on the front-lines of the battlefield. We are not short of worshipers; we are dreadfully short of those who will go into the world and preach the gospel to those headed for hell. What a tragedy that so many are not exhorted by their leaders to do what God has told us to do: to preach the gospel to every creature. Obeying Him by doing what He commanded is true worship in action.

"Have you noticed how much praying for revival has been going on of late and how little revival has resulted? I believe the problem is that we have been trying to substitute praying for obeying, and it simply will not work. To pray for revival while ignoring the plain precept laid down in Scripture is to waste a lot of words and get nothing for our trouble. Prayer will become effective when we stop using it as a substitute for obedience." *A. W. Tozer*

praise to the LORD with the words of
David and of Asaph the seer. So they sang
praises with gladness, and they bowed
their heads and worshiped.
[31]Then Hezekiah answered and said,
"Now *that* you have consecrated yourselves to the LORD, come near, and bring
sacrifices and thank offerings into the
house of the LORD." So the assembly
brought in sacrifices and thank offerings,
and as many as were of a willing heart
brought burnt offerings. [32]And the number of the burnt offerings which the assembly brought was seventy bulls, one
hundred rams, *and* two hundred lambs;
all these *were* for a burnt offering to the
LORD. [33]The consecrated things *were* six
hundred bulls and three thousand sheep.

> We shall have all eternity in which to celebrate our victories, but we have only one swift hour before the sunset in which to win them.
>
> **ROBERT MOFFATT**

[34]But the priests were too few, so that
they could not skin all the burnt offerings; therefore their brethren the Levites
helped them until the work was ended
and until the *other* priests had sanctified
themselves, for the Levites were more
diligent in sanctifying themselves than
the priests. [35]Also the burnt offerings
were in abundance, with the fat of the
peace offerings and *with* the drink offerings for *every* burnt offering.
So the service of the house of the LORD
was set in order. [36]Then Hezekiah and all
the people rejoiced that God had prepared the people, since the events took
place so suddenly.

Hezekiah Keeps the Passover

30 And Hezekiah sent to all Israel
and Judah, and also wrote letters
to Ephraim and Manasseh, that they
should come to the house of the LORD at
Jerusalem, to keep the Passover to the
LORD God of Israel. [2]For the king and his
leaders and all the assembly in Jerusalem
had agreed to keep the Passover in the
second month. [3]For they could not keep
it at the regular time,[a] because a sufficient
number of priests had not consecrated
themselves, nor had the people gathered
together at Jerusalem. [4]And the matter
pleased the king and all the assembly. [5]So
they resolved to make a proclamation
throughout all Israel, from Beersheba to
Dan, that they should come to keep the
Passover to the LORD God of Israel at
Jerusalem, since they had not done *it* for
a long *time* in the *prescribed* manner.
[6]Then the runners went throughout
all Israel and Judah with the letters from
the king and his leaders, and spoke according to the command of the king:
"Children of Israel, return to the LORD
God of Abraham, Isaac, and Israel; then
He will return to the remnant of you who
have escaped from the hand of the kings
of Assyria. [7]And do not be like your fathers and your brethren, who trespassed
against the LORD God of their fathers, so
that He gave them up to desolation, as
you see. [8]Now do not be stiff-necked, as
your fathers *were, but* yield yourselves to
the LORD; and enter His sanctuary, which
He has sanctified forever, and serve the
LORD your God, that the fierceness of His
wrath may turn away from you. [9]For if
you return to the LORD, your brethren
and your children *will be treated* with
compassion by those who lead them captive, so that they may come back to this
land; for the LORD your God is gracious
and merciful, and will not turn *His* face
from you if you return to Him."

30:3 [a]That is, the first month (compare Leviticus 23:5); literally *at that time*

30:8 It is in human nature to be stiff-necked and to have a stubborn resolve against God, as Rom. 8:7 confirms.

10So the runners passed from city to
city through the country of Ephraim and
Manasseh, as far as Zebulun; but they
laughed at them and mocked them.
11Nevertheless some from Asher, Manasseh, and Zebulun humbled themselves
and came to Jerusalem. 12Also the hand
of God was on Judah to give them single-
ness of heart to obey the command of the
king and the leaders, at the word of the
LORD.

13Now many people, a very great assembly, gathered at Jerusalem to keep the
Feast of Unleavened Bread in the second
month. 14They arose and took away the
altars that *were* in Jerusalem, and they
took away all the incense altars and cast
them into the Brook Kidron. 15Then they
slaughtered the Passover *lambs* on the
fourteenth *day* of the second month. The
priests and the Levites were ashamed,
and sanctified themselves, and brought
the burnt offerings to the house of the
LORD. 16They stood in their place according to their custom, according to the Law
of Moses the man of God; the priests
sprinkled the blood *received* from the
hand of the Levites. 17For *there were* many
in the assembly who had not sanctified
themselves; therefore the Levites had
charge of the slaughter of the Passover
lambs for everyone *who was* not clean, to
sanctify *them* to the LORD. 18For a multitude of the people, many from Ephraim,
Manasseh, Issachar, and Zebulun, had
not cleansed themselves, yet they ate the
Passover contrary to what was written.
But Hezekiah prayed for them, saying,
"May the good LORD provide atonement
for everyone 19*who* prepares his heart to
seek God, the LORD God of his fathers,
though *he is* not *cleansed* according to the
purification of the sanctuary." 20And the
LORD listened to Hezekiah and healed the
people.

21So the children of Israel who were
present at Jerusalem kept the Feast of
Unleavened Bread seven days with great
gladness; and the Levites and the priests
praised the LORD day by day, *singing* to
the LORD, accompanied by loud instruments. 22And Hezekiah gave encouragement to all the Levites who taught the
good knowledge of the LORD; and they
ate throughout the feast seven days, offering peace offerings and making confession to the LORD God of their fathers.

23Then the whole assembly agreed to
keep *the feast* another seven days, and
they kept it *another* seven days with gladness. 24For Hezekiah king of Judah gave
to the assembly a thousand bulls and
seven thousand sheep, and the leaders
gave to the assembly a thousand bulls
and ten thousand sheep; and a great
number of priests sanctified themselves.
25The whole assembly of Judah rejoiced,
also the priests and Levites, all the assembly that came from Israel, the sojourners
who came from the land of Israel, and
those who dwelt in Judah. 26So there was
great joy in Jerusalem, for since the time
of Solomon the son of David, king of Israel, *there had* been nothing like this in
Jerusalem. 27Then the priests, the Levites,
arose and blessed the people, and their
voice was heard; and their prayer came
up to His holy dwelling place, to heaven.

The Reforms of Hezekiah

31 Now when all this was finished,
all Israel who were present went
out to the cities of Judah and broke the
sacred pillars in pieces, cut down the
wooden images, and threw down the
high places and the altars—from all Judah, Benjamin, Ephraim, and Manasseh—until they had utterly destroyed
them all. Then all the children of Israel
returned to their own cities, every man to
his possession.

2And Hezekiah appointed the divisions
of the priests and the Levites according to
their divisions, each man according to his
service, the priests and Levites for burnt
offerings and peace offerings, to serve, to
give thanks, and to praise in the gates of
the camp[a] of the LORD. 3The king also *ap-*

31:2 [a]That is, the temple

pointed a portion of his possessions for
the burnt offerings: for the morning and
evening burnt offerings, the burnt offerings for the Sabbaths and the New Moons
and the set feasts, as *it is* written in the
Law of the LORD.

[4]Moreover he commanded the people
who dwelt in Jerusalem to contribute
support for the priests and the Levites,
that they might devote themselves to the
Law of the LORD.

[5]As soon as the commandment was
circulated, the children of Israel brought
in abundance the firstfruits of grain and
wine, oil and honey, and of all the produce of the field; and they brought in
abundantly the tithe of everything. [6]And
the children of Israel and Judah, who
dwelt in the cities of Judah, brought the
tithe of oxen and sheep; also the tithe of
holy things which were consecrated to
the LORD their God they laid in heaps.

[7]In the third month they began laying
them in heaps, and they finished in the
seventh month. [8]And when Hezekiah and
the leaders came and saw the heaps, they
blessed the LORD and His people Israel.
[9]Then Hezekiah questioned the priests
and the Levites concerning the heaps.
[10]And Azariah the chief priest, from the
house of Zadok, answered him and said,
"Since *the people* began to bring the offerings into the house of the LORD, we have
had enough to eat and have plenty left,
for the LORD has blessed His people; and
what is left *is* this great abundance."

[11]Now Hezekiah commanded *them* to
prepare rooms in the house of the LORD,
and they prepared them. [12]Then they
faithfully brought in the offerings, the
tithes, and the dedicated things; Cononiah the Levite had charge of them, and
Shimei his brother *was* the next. [13]Jehiel,
Azaziah, Nahath, Asahel, Jerimoth, Jozabad, Eliel, Ismachiah, Mahath, and Benaiah *were* overseers under the hand of
Cononiah and Shimei his brother, at the
commandment of Hezekiah the king and
Azariah the ruler of the house of God.
[14]Kore the son of Imnah the Levite, the
keeper of the East Gate, *was* over the
freewill offerings to God, to distribute the
offerings of the LORD and the most holy
things. [15]And under him *were* Eden,
Miniamin, Jeshua, Shemaiah, Amariah,
and Shecaniah, *his* faithful assistants in
the cities of the priests, to distribute al-
lotments to their brethren by divisions, to
the great as well as the small.

[16]Besides those males from three years
old and up who were written in the genealogy, they distributed to everyone
who entered the house of the LORD his
daily portion for the work of his service,
by his division, [17]and to the priests who
were written in the genealogy according
to their father's house, and to the Levites
from twenty years old and up according
to their work, by their divisions, [18]and to
all who were written in the genealogy—
their little ones and their wives, their
sons and daughters, the whole company
of them—for in their faithfulness they
sanctified themselves in holiness.

[19]Also for the sons of Aaron the
priests, *who were* in the fields of the common-lands of their cities, in every single
city, *there were* men who were designated
by name to distribute portions to all the
males among the priests and to all who
were listed by genealogies among the
Levites.

[20]Thus Hezekiah did throughout all
Judah, and he did what *was* good and
right and true before the LORD his God.
[21]And in every work that he began in the
service of the house of God, in the law
and in the commandment, to seek his
God, he did *it* with all his heart. So he
prospered.

31:20,21 Consider this wonderful testimony of Hezekiah. He did what was good, right, and true before the Lord. He exalted God's Law and did everything with all of his heart, and as a result, he prospered. See Psa. 1 for how you can prosper in your marriage, your vocation, and your evangelistic endeavors.

Sennacherib Boasts Against the Lord

32 After these deeds of faithfulness,
Sennacherib king of Assyria came
and entered Judah; he encamped against
the fortified cities, thinking to win them
over to himself. 2And when Hezekiah
saw that Sennacherib had come, and that
his purpose was to make war against
Jerusalem, 3he consulted with his leaders
and commanders[a] to stop the water from
the springs which *were* outside the city;
and they helped him. 4Thus many people
gathered together who stopped all the
springs and the brook that ran through
the land, saying, "Why should the kings[a]
of Assyria come and find much water?"
5And he strengthened himself, built up
all the wall that was broken, raised *it* up
to the towers, and *built* another wall outside; also he repaired the Millo[a] *in* the
City of David, and made weapons and
shields in abundance. 6Then he set military captains over the people, gathered
them together to him in the open square
of the city gate, and gave them encouragement, saying, 7"Be strong and courageous; do not be afraid nor dismayed before the king of Assyria, nor before all the
multitude that *is* with him; for *there are*
more with us than with him. 8With him
is an arm of flesh; but with us *is* the LORD
our God, to help us and to fight our battles." And the people were strengthened
by the words of Hezekiah king of Judah.
9After this Sennacherib king of Assyria
sent his servants to Jerusalem (but he and
all the forces with him *laid siege* against
Lachish), to Hezekiah king of Judah, and
to all Judah who *were* in Jerusalem, saying, 10"Thus says Sennacherib king of Assyria: 'In what do you trust, that you remain under siege in Jerusalem? 11Does
not Hezekiah persuade you to give yourselves over to die by famine and by thirst,
saying, "The LORD our God will deliver us
from the hand of the king of Assyria"?
12Has not the same Hezekiah taken away
His high places and His altars, and commanded Judah and Jerusalem, saying, "You
shall worship before one altar and burn
incense on it"? 13Do you not know what I
and my fathers have done to all the peoples of *other* lands? Were the gods of the
nations of those lands in any way able to
deliver their lands out of my hand? 14Who
was there among all the gods of those nations that my fathers utterly destroyed
that could deliver his people from my
hand, that your God should be able to
deliver you from my hand? 15Now therefore, do not let Hezekiah deceive you or
persuade you like this, and do not believe
him; for no god of any nation or kingdom
was able to deliver his people from my
hand or the hand of my fathers. How
much less will your God deliver you from
my hand?' "
16Furthermore, his servants spoke
against the LORD God and against His servant Hezekiah.
17He also wrote letters to revile the
LORD God of Israel, and to speak against
Him, saying, "As the gods of the nations
of *other* lands have not delivered their
people from my hand, so the God of Hezekiah will not deliver His people from my
hand." 18Then they called out with a loud
voice in Hebrew[a] to the people of Jerusalem who *were* on the wall, to frighten
them and trouble them, that they might
take the city. 19And they spoke against
the God of Jerusalem, as against the gods
of the people of the earth—the work of
men's hands.

32:3 [a]Literally *mighty men* 32:4 [a]Following Masoretic Text and Vulgate; Arabic, Septuagint, and Syriac read *king*. 32:5 [a]Literally *The Landfill*
32:18 [a]Literally *Judean*

32:7,8 Faith in God is the key to fighting fear. Hezekiah was simply speaking the truth, and the people believed and were strengthened by his words. See v. 21 for how God was faithful.

"I have found that there are three stages in every great work of God: first it is impossible, then it is difficult, then it is done." *Hudson Taylor*

SPRINGBOARDS FOR PREACHING AND WITNESSING

The Elephant in the Room

32:24 The reason why people look to the heavens is a mystery until we think seriously about life for a moment. There is a huge elephant in the room called "death," and it will eventually stomp on all of us. When we realize this, it makes sense for us to see if there is any way we can avoid being stomped on. That is why many people become interested in God, the Giver of life. Some are slower than others to give it serious thought, but as those around them die, it dawns on them that they too have a problem. A big one. It is an issue everyone with a brain thinks about, but few people talk about.

The most sobering time for many of us is when we are on our deathbed. It is in those last moments that we tend to open our hearts and expose our fears. Consider these fearful last words of some famous people: Queen Elizabeth the First of England whispered, "All my possessions for one moment of time." The famous composer Ludwig van Beethoven cried, "Too bad, too bad! It's too late!" Thomas Hobbs (famous 17th century English philosopher) said, "I am about to take my last voyage, a great leap in the dark." Socrates, the classical Greek philosopher, said, "All of the wisdom of this world is but a tiny raft upon which we must set sail when we leave this earth. If only there was a firmer foundation upon which to sail, perhaps some divine word."

There is a "firm foundation"; there is a "divine word." It is the Bible, but so few listen to and obey its divine instructions. The famous humanist Aldous Huxley said, "It is a bit embarrassing to have been concerned with the human problem all one's life and find at the end that one has no more to offer by way of advice than 'Try to be a little kinder.'"

Listen to the last words of Napoleon. He said, "I marvel that where the ambitious dreams of myself and of Alexander and of Caesar should have vanished into thin air, a Judean peasant—Jesus—should be able to stretch his hands across the centuries, and control the destinies of men and nations." He also lamented, "I die before my time, and my body will be given back to the earth. Such is the fate of him who has been called the great Napoleon. What an abyss between my deep misery and the eternal kingdom of Christ!"

That "abyss" is the separation made by sin. The moment you repent and trust Jesus Christ, it will disappear, and you will come to know the One whom the Bible says is "life eternal."

Sennacherib's Defeat and Death

[20]Now because of this King Hezekiah and the prophet Isaiah, the son of Amoz, prayed and cried out to heaven. [21]Then the LORD sent an angel who cut down every mighty man of valor, leader, and captain in the camp of the king of Assyria. So he returned shamefaced to his own land. And when he had gone into the temple of his god, some of his own offspring struck him down with the sword there.

[22]Thus the LORD saved Hezekiah and the inhabitants of Jerusalem from the hand of Sennacherib the king of Assyria, and from the hand of all *others,* and guided them[a] on every side. [23]And many brought gifts to the LORD at Jerusalem, and presents to Hezekiah king of Judah, so that he was exalted in the sight of all nations thereafter.

Hezekiah Humbles Himself

[24]In those days Hezekiah was sick and near death, and he prayed to the LORD; and He spoke to him and gave him a sign. [25]But Hezekiah did not repay according to the favor *shown* him, for his heart was lifted up; therefore wrath was looming over him and over Judah and Jerusalem. [26]Then Hezekiah humbled himself for the pride of his heart, he and the inhabitants of Jerusalem, so that the wrath of the LORD did not come upon them in the days of Hezekiah.

Hezekiah's Wealth and Honor

[27]Hezekiah had very great riches and honor. And he made himself treasuries for silver, for gold, for precious stones, for spices, for shields, and for all kinds of desirable items; [28]storehouses for the harvest of grain, wine, and oil; and stalls for all kinds of livestock, and folds for flocks.[a] [29]Moreover he provided cities for himself, and possessions of flocks and

---

32:22 [a]Septuagint reads *gave them rest;* Vulgate reads *gave them treasures.*

herds in abundance; for God had given him very much property. [30]This same Hezekiah also stopped the water outlet of Upper Gihon, and brought the water by tunnel[a] to the west side of the City of David. Hezekiah prospered in all his works.

[31]However, *regarding* the ambassadors of the princes of Babylon, whom they sent to him to inquire about the wonder that was *done* in the land, God withdrew from him, in order to test him, that He might know all *that was* in his heart.

Death of Hezekiah

[32]Now the rest of the acts of Hezekiah, and his goodness, indeed they *are* written in the vision of Isaiah the prophet, the son of Amoz, *and* in the book of the kings of Judah and Israel. [33]So Hezekiah rested with his fathers, and they buried him in the upper tombs of the sons of David; and all Judah and the inhabitants of Jerusalem honored him at his death. Then Manasseh his son reigned in his place.

Manasseh Reigns in Judah

33 Manasseh *was* twelve years old when he became king, and he reigned fifty-five years in Jerusalem. [2]But he did evil in the sight of the LORD, according to the abominations of the nations whom the LORD had cast out before the children of Israel. [3]For he rebuilt the high places which Hezekiah his father had broken down; he raised up altars for the Baals, and made wooden images; and he worshiped all the host of heaven[a] and served them. [4]He also built altars in the house of the LORD, of which the LORD had said, "In Jerusalem shall My name be forever." [5]And he built altars for all the host of heaven in the two courts of the house of the LORD. [6]Also he caused his sons to pass through the fire in the Valley of the Son of Hinnom; he practiced soothsaying, used witchcraft and sorcery, and consulted mediums and spiritists. He did much evil in the sight of the LORD, to provoke Him to anger. [7]He even set a carved image, the idol which he had made, in the house of God, of which God had said to David and to Solomon his son, "In this house and in Jerusalem, which I have chosen out of all the tribes of Israel, I will put My name forever; [8]and I will not again remove the foot of Israel from the land which I have appointed for your fathers—only if they are careful to do all that I have commanded them, according to the whole law and the statutes and the ordinances by the hand of Moses." [9]So Manasseh seduced Judah and the inhabitants of Jerusalem to do more evil than the nations whom the LORD had destroyed before the children of Israel.

Manasseh Restored After Repentance

[10]And the LORD spoke to Manasseh and his people, but they would not listen. [11]Therefore the LORD brought upon them the captains of the army of the king of Assyria, who took Manasseh with hooks,[a] bound him with bronze *fetters,* and carried him off to Babylon. [12]Now when he was in affliction, he implored the LORD his God, and humbled himself greatly before the God of his fathers, [13]and prayed to Him; and He received his entreaty,

32:28 [a]Following Septuagint and Vulgate; Arabic and Syriac omit *folds for flocks;* Masoretic Text reads *flocks for sheepfolds.* 32:30 [a]Literally *brought it straight* (compare 2 Kings 20:20) 33:3 [a]The gods of the Assyrians 33:11 [a]That is, nose hooks (compare 2 Kings 19:28)

33:10,11 Never stop pleading with those who are not receptive to the gospel. That seemingly hardhearted person may be thinking about every word you speak. We tend to overlook the fact that Jesus rebuked the hardhearted Pharisees and other religious leaders, because He cared enough about them to speak the truth. We do not know how many of them were in that great crowd on the Day of Pentecost and ended up being part of the Church, because of His love.

"If you are walking with Jesus, in the Spirit, you need not fear going too far. No believer has gone as far as God wants him to go." *A. A. Allen*

heard his supplication, and brought him
back to Jerusalem into his kingdom.
Then Manasseh knew that the LORD *was*
God.
14After this he built a wall outside the
City of David on the west side of Gihon,
in the valley, as far as the entrance of the
Fish Gate; and *it* enclosed Ophel, and he
raised it to a very great height. Then he
put military captains in all the fortified
cities of Judah. 15He took away the foreign gods and the idol from the house of
the LORD, and all the altars that he had
built in the mount of the house of the
LORD and in Jerusalem; and he cast *them*
out of the city. 16He also repaired the altar of the LORD, sacrificed peace offerings
and thank offerings on it, and commanded Judah to serve the LORD God of
Israel. 17Nevertheless the people still sacrificed on the high places, *but* only to the
LORD their God.

Death of Manasseh

18Now the rest of the acts of Manasseh, his prayer to his God, and the
words of the seers who spoke to him in
the name of the LORD God of Israel, indeed they *are written* in the book[a] of the
kings of Israel. 19Also his prayer and *how*
God received his entreaty, and all his sin
and trespass, and the sites where he built
high places and set up wooden images
and carved images, before he was humbled, indeed they *are* written among the
sayings of Hozai.[a] 20So Manasseh rested
with his fathers, and they buried him in
his own house. Then his son Amon
reigned in his place.

Amon's Reign and Death

21Amon *was* twenty-two years old
when he became king, and he reigned
two years in Jerusalem. 22But he did evil
in the sight of the LORD, as his father
Manasseh had done; for Amon sacrificed
to all the carved images which his father
Manasseh had made, and served them.
23And he did not humble himself before
the LORD, as his father Manasseh had
humbled himself; but Amon trespassed
more and more.
24Then his servants conspired against
him, and killed him in his own house.
25But the people of the land executed all
those who had conspired against King
Amon. Then the people of the land made
his son Josiah king in his place.

Josiah Reigns in Judah

34 Josiah *was* eight years old when
he became king, and he reigned
thirty-one years in Jerusalem. 2And he
did *what was* right in the sight of the
LORD, and walked in the ways of his father David; *he* did *not* turn aside to the
right hand or to the left.
3For in the eighth year of his reign,
while he was still young, he began to seek
the God of his father David; and in the
twelfth year he began to purge Judah and
Jerusalem of the high places, the wooden
images, the carved images, and the
molded images. 4They broke down the
altars of the Baals in his presence, and the
incense altars which *were* above them he
cut down; and the wooden images, the
carved images, and the molded images he
broke in pieces, and made dust of them
and scattered *it* on the graves of those
who had sacrificed to them. 5He also
burned the bones of the priests on their
altars, and cleansed Judah and Jerusalem.
6And *so he did* in the cities of Manasseh,
Ephraim, and Simeon, as far as Naphtali
and all around, with axes.[a] 7When he had
broken down the altars and the wooden
images, had beaten the carved images
into powder, and cut down all the incense altars throughout all the land of Israel, he returned to Jerusalem.

Hilkiah Finds the Book of the Law

8In the eighteenth year of his reign,
when he had purged the land and the
temple,[a] he sent Shaphan the son of Aza-
liah, Maaseiah the governor of the city,

33:18 [a]Literally *words* 33:19 [a]Septuagint reads *the seers.*
34:6 [a]Literally *swords* 34:8 [a]Literally *house*

and Joah the son of Joahaz the recorder,
to repair the house of the LORD his God.
9When they came to Hilkiah the high
priest, they delivered the money that was
brought into the house of God, which the
Levites who kept the doors had gathered
from the hand of Manasseh and Ephraim,
from all the remnant of Israel, from all Judah and Benjamin, and *which* they had
brought back to Jerusalem. 10Then they
put *it* in the hand of the foremen who
had the oversight of the house of the
LORD; and they gave it to the workmen
who worked in the house of the LORD, to
repair and restore the house. 11They gave
it to the craftsmen and builders to buy
hewn stone and timber for beams, and to
floor the houses which the kings of Judah
had destroyed. 12And the men did the
work faithfully. Their overseers *were* Jahath and Obadiah the Levites, of the sons
of Merari, and Zechariah and Meshullam,
of the sons of the Kohathites, to super-
vise. *Others of* the Levites, all of whom
were skillful with instruments of music,
13*were* over the burden bearers and *were*
overseers of all who did work in any kind
of service. And *some* of the Levites *were*
scribes, officers, and gatekeepers.
14Now when they brought out the
money that was brought into the house of
the LORD, Hilkiah the priest found the
Book of the Law of the LORD *given* by
Moses. 15Then Hilkiah answered and said
to Shaphan the scribe, "I have found the
Book of the Law in the house of the
LORD." And Hilkiah gave the book to
Shaphan. 16So Shaphan carried the book
to the king, bringing the king word, saying, "All that was committed to your servants they are doing. 17And they have
gathered the money that was found in the
house of the LORD, and have delivered it
into the hand of the overseers and the
workmen." 18Then Shaphan the scribe
told the king, saying, "Hilkiah the priest
has given me a book." And Shaphan read
it before the king.
19Thus it happened, when the king
heard the words of the Law, that he tore

THE FUNCTION OF THE LAW

34:19–21 This is the effect of the Law: it brings the knowledge of sin, convicts the conscience, and makes the wrath of God understandable as the just consequence of sin. Use the Law to reach the lost as Jesus did. (See Mark 10:17 for an example of Jesus using the Law.)

"When the sinner sees the awful consequences of breaking the Law of God—that he cannot escape the certainty of judgment—he will see his need to put on the Lord Jesus Christ. When we preach future punishment by the Law, the sinner comes to Christ solely to flee from 'the wrath to come.'" *Charles Spurgeon*

his clothes. 20Then the king commanded
Hilkiah, Ahikam the son of Shaphan, Abdon[a] the son of Micah, Shaphan the
scribe, and Asaiah a servant of the king,
saying, 21"Go, inquire of the LORD for me,
and for those who are left in Israel and
Judah, concerning the words of the book
that is found; for great *is* the wrath of the
LORD that is poured out on us, because
our fathers have not kept the word of the
LORD, to do according to all that is written in this book."
22So Hilkiah and those the king *had
appointed* went to Huldah the prophetess,
the wife of Shallum the son of Tokhath,[a]
the son of Hasrah,[b] keeper of the wardrobe. (She dwelt in Jerusalem in the Second Quarter.) And they spoke to her to
that *effect*.
23Then she answered them, "Thus says
the LORD God of Israel, 'Tell the man who
sent you to Me, 24"Thus says the LORD:
'Behold, I will bring calamity on this
place and on its inhabitants, all the curses
that are written in the book which they
have read before the king of Judah, 25be-
cause they have forsaken Me and burned
incense to other gods, that they might
provoke Me to anger with all the works of
their hands. Therefore My wrath will be
poured out on this place, and not be
quenched.' " ' 26But as for the king of Ju-

34:20 [a]*Achbor the son of Michaiah* in 2 Kings 22:12 34:22 [a]Spelled *Tikvah* in 2 Kings 22:14 [b]Spelled *Harhas* in 2 Kings 22:14

dah, who sent you to inquire of the LORD,
in this manner you shall speak to him,
'Thus says the LORD God of Israel: "*Concerning* the words which you have
heard— 27because your heart was tender,
and you humbled yourself before God
when you heard His words against this
place and against its inhabitants, and you
humbled yourself before Me, and you
tore your clothes and wept before Me, I
also have heard *you*," says the LORD.
28"Surely I will gather you to your fathers,
and you shall be gathered to your grave
in peace; and your eyes shall not see all
the calamity which I will bring on this
place and its inhabitants." ' " So they
brought back word to the king.

Josiah Restores True Worship

29Then the king sent and gathered all
the elders of Judah and Jerusalem. 30The
king went up to the house of the LORD,
with all the men of Judah and the inhabitants of Jerusalem—the priests and the
Levites, and all the people, great and
small. And he read in their hearing all the
words of the Book of the Covenant which
had been found in the house of the LORD.

> God is not moved or impressed with our worship until our hearts are moved and impressed by Him.
>
> **KELLY SPARKS**

31Then the king stood in his place and
made a covenant before the LORD, to follow the LORD, and to keep His commandments and His testimonies and His
statutes with all his heart and all his soul,
to perform the words of the covenant that
were written in this book. 32And he made
all who were present in Jerusalem and
Benjamin take a stand. So the inhabitants
of Jerusalem did according to the covenant of God, the God of their fathers.
33Thus Josiah removed all the abominations from all the country that *belonged* to
the children of Israel, and made all who
were present in Israel diligently serve the
LORD their God. All his days they did not
depart from following the LORD God of
their fathers.

Josiah Keeps the Passover

35 Now Josiah kept a Passover to the
LORD in Jerusalem, and they
slaughtered the Passover *lambs* on the
fourteenth *day* of the first month. 2And
he set the priests in their duties and encouraged them for the service of the
house of the LORD. 3Then he said to the
Levites who taught all Israel, who were
holy to the LORD: "Put the holy ark in the
house which Solomon the son of David,
king of Israel, built. *It shall* no longer *be* a
burden on *your* shoulders. Now serve the
LORD your God and His people Israel.
4Prepare *yourselves* according to your fathers' houses, according to your divisions, following the written instruction of
David king of Israel and the written instruction of Solomon his son. 5And stand
in the holy *place* according to the divisions of the fathers' houses of your
brethren the *lay* people, and *according to*
the division of the father's house of the
Levites. 6So slaughter the Passover *offerings*, consecrate yourselves, and prepare
them for your brethren, that *they* may do
according to the word of the LORD by the
hand of Moses."
7Then Josiah gave the *lay* people
lambs and young goats from the flock, all
for Passover *offerings* for all who were
present, to the number of thirty thousand, as well as three thousand cattle;
these *were* from the king's possessions.
8And his leaders gave willingly to the
people, to the priests, and to the Levites.
Hilkiah, Zechariah, and Jehiel, rulers
of the house of God, gave to the priests

35:3 The Law was never designed to sit on our shoulders and be a burden to God's people. Its purpose is to drive us to the cross, where we find rest from its heavy demands. See Acts 15:10 for the Church's attitude toward the Law.

for the Passover *offerings* two thousand
six hundred *from the flock,* and three hundred cattle. 9Also Conaniah, his brothers
Shemaiah and Nethanel, and Hashabiah
and Jeiel and Jozabad, chief of the Levites, gave to the Levites for Passover *of-*
ferings five thousand *from the flock* and
five hundred cattle.

10So the service was prepared, and the
priests stood in their places, and the
Levites in their divisions, according to
the king's command. 11And they slaughtered the Passover *offerings;* and the
priests sprinkled *the blood* with their
hands, while the Levites skinned *the ani-*
mals. 12Then they removed the burnt offerings that *they* might give them to the
divisions of the fathers' houses of the *lay*
people, to offer to the LORD, as *it is* written in the Book of Moses. And so *they did*
with the cattle. 13Also they roasted the
Passover *offerings* with fire according to
the ordinance; but the *other* holy *offerings*
they boiled in pots, in caldrons, and in
pans, and divided *them* quickly among all
the *lay* people. 14Then afterward they
prepared portions for themselves and for
the priests, because the priests, the sons
of Aaron, *were busy* in offering burnt offerings and fat until night; therefore the
Levites prepared portions for themselves
and for the priests, the sons of Aaron.
15And the singers, the sons of Asaph, *were*
in their places, according to the command
of David, Asaph, Heman, and Jeduthun
the king's seer. Also the gatekeepers were
at each gate; they did not have to leave
their position, because their brethren the
Levites prepared portions for them.

16So all the service of the LORD was
prepared the same day, to keep the
Passover and to offer burnt offerings on
the altar of the LORD, according to the
command of King Josiah. 17And the children of Israel who were present kept the
Passover at that time, and the Feast of
Unleavened Bread for seven days. 18There
had been no Passover kept in Israel like
that since the days of Samuel the prophet;
and none of the kings of Israel had kept
such a Passover as Josiah kept, with the
priests and the Levites, all Judah and Israel who were present, and the inhabitants
of Jerusalem. 19In the eighteenth year of
the reign of Josiah this Passover was kept.

Josiah Dies in Battle

20After all this, when Josiah had prepared the temple, Necho king of Egypt
came up to fight against Carchemish by
the Euphrates; and Josiah went out against
him. 21But he sent messengers to him,
saying, "What have I to do with you, king
of Judah? *I have* not *come* against you this
day, but against the house with which I
have war; for God commanded me to
make haste. Refrain *from meddling with*
God, who *is* with me, lest He destroy
you." 22Nevertheless Josiah would not turn
his face from him, but disguised himself
so that he might fight with him, and did
not heed the words of Necho from the
mouth of God. So he came to fight in the
Valley of Megiddo.

23And the archers shot King Josiah;
and the king said to his servants, "Take
me away, for I am severely wounded."
24His servants therefore took him out of
that chariot and put him in the second
chariot that he had, and they brought
him to Jerusalem. So he died, and was
buried in *one of* the tombs of his fathers.
And all Judah and Jerusalem mourned
for Josiah.

25Jeremiah also lamented for Josiah.
And to this day all the singing men and
the singing women speak of Josiah in
their lamentations. They made it a custom in Israel; and indeed they *are* written
in the Laments.

26Now the rest of the acts of Josiah and
his goodness, according to *what was* written in the Law of the LORD, 27and his
deeds from first to last, indeed they *are*
written in the book of the kings of Israel
and Judah.

The Reign and Captivity of Jehoahaz

36 Then the people of the land took
Jehoahaz the son of Josiah, and

made him king in his father's place in Jerusalem. 2Jehoahaz[a] *was* twenty-three years old when he became king, and he reigned three months in Jerusalem. 3Now the king of Egypt deposed him at Jerusalem; and he imposed on the land a tribute of one hundred talents of silver and a talent of gold. 4Then the king of Egypt made *Jehoahaz's*[a] brother Eliakim king over Judah and Jerusalem, and changed his name to Jehoiakim. And Necho took Jehoahaz[b] his brother and carried him off to Egypt.

The Reign and Captivity of Jehoiakim

5Jehoiakim *was* twenty-five years old when he became king, and he reigned eleven years in Jerusalem. And he did evil in the sight of the LORD his God. 6Nebuchadnezzar king of Babylon came up against him, and bound him in bronze *fetters* to carry him off to Babylon. 7Nebuchadnezzar also carried off *some* of the articles from the house of the LORD to Babylon, and put them in his temple at Babylon. 8Now the rest of the acts of Jehoiakim, the abominations which he did, and what was found against him, indeed they *are* written in the book of the kings of Israel and Judah. Then Jehoiachin his son reigned in his place.

The Reign and Captivity of Jehoiachin

9Jehoiachin *was* eight[a] years old when he became king, and he reigned in Jerusalem three months and ten days. And he did evil in the sight of the LORD. 10At the turn of the year King Nebuchadnezzar summoned *him* and took him to Babylon, with the costly articles from the house of the LORD, and made Zedekiah, *Jehoiakim's*[a] brother, king over Judah and Jerusalem.

Zedekiah Reigns in Judah

11Zedekiah *was* twenty-one years old when he became king, and he reigned eleven years in Jerusalem. 12He did evil in the sight of the LORD his God, *and* did not humble himself before Jeremiah the prophet, *who spoke* from the mouth of the LORD. 13And he also rebelled against King Nebuchadnezzar, who had made him swear *an oath* by God; but he stiffened his neck and hardened his heart against turning to the LORD God of Israel. 14Moreover all the leaders of the priests and the people transgressed more and more, *according* to all the abominations of the nations, and defiled the house of the LORD which He had consecrated in Jerusalem.

The Fall of Jerusalem

15And the LORD God of their fathers sent *warnings* to them by His messengers, rising up early and sending *them*, because He had compassion on His people and on His dwelling place. 16But they mocked the messengers of God, despised His words, and scoffed at His prophets, until the wrath of the LORD arose against His people, till *there was* no remedy.

17Therefore He brought against them the king of the Chaldeans, who killed their young men with the sword in the house of their sanctuary, and had no compassion on young man or virgin, on the aged or the weak; He gave *them* all into his hand. 18And all the articles from the house of God, great and small, the treasures of the house of the LORD, and the treasures of the king and of his leaders, all *these* he took to Babylon. 19Then they burned the house of God, broke down the wall of Jerusalem, burned all its palaces with fire, and destroyed all its precious possessions. 20And those who

36:2 [a]Masoretic Text reads *Joahaz*. 36:4 [a]Literally *his* [b]Masoretic Text reads *Joahaz*. 36:9 [a]Some Hebrew manuscripts, Septuagint, Syriac, and 2 Kings 24:8 read *eighteen*. 36:10 [a]Literally *his* (compare 2 Kings 24:17)

36:11–16 The ungodly are like Zedekiah. They do what is evil in God's eyes, then add to their sin with their pride, mockery, and stubborn rebellion. Read and memorize Matt. 5:10–12 so that you will have consolation when you are persecuted for the cause of the gospel.

escaped from the sword he carried away to Babylon, where they became servants to him and his sons until the rule of the kingdom of Persia, [21]to fulfill the word of the LORD by the mouth of Jeremiah, until the land had enjoyed her Sabbaths. As long as she lay desolate she kept Sabbath, to fulfill seventy years.

The Proclamation of Cyrus

[22]Now in the first year of Cyrus king of Persia, that the word of the LORD by the mouth of Jeremiah might be fulfilled, the LORD stirred up the spirit of Cyrus king of Persia, so that he made a proclamation throughout all his kingdom, and also *put it* in writing, saying,

[23]Thus says Cyrus king of Persia:
All the kingdoms of the earth the
LORD God of heaven has given me.
And He has commanded me to build
Him a house at Jerusalem which is in
Judah. Who *is* among you of all His
people? May the LORD his God *be*
with him, and let him go up!

Hinduism

ORIGIN: India, about 1500 B.C. to 2500 B.C.

FOUNDER: No single person

ADHERENTS: 1998 worldwide: 825–850 million; India 780 million; Bangladesh 20 million; Nepal 20 million; Indonesia 7 million; Sri Lanka 3 million; Pakistan 2 million. In Fiji, Guyana, Mauritius, Surinam, and Trinidad and Tobago, over 20 percent of their people practice Hinduism. A considerable number of Hindus live in Africa, Myanmar, and the United Kingdom. U.S.: Estimated 1.5 to 2 million.

SCRIPTURES: *Vedas*, *Upanishads*, *epics*, *Puranas*, and the *Bhagavad Gita* explain the essence of Hinduism. Hinduism is the world's oldest surviving organized religion. It is a complex family of sects whose copious scriptures, written over a period of almost 2,000 years (1500 B.C.–A.D. 250), allow a diverse belief system. Hinduism has no single creed and recognizes no final truth. At its core, Hinduism has a pagan background in which the forces of nature and human heroes are personified as gods and goddesses. They are worshiped with prayers and offerings. Hinduism can be divided into Popular Hinduism, characterized by the worship of gods through offerings, rituals, and prayers; and Philosophical Hinduism, the complex belief system understood by those who can study ancient texts, meditate, and practice yoga.

GOD: God (*Brahman*) is the one impersonal, ultimate, but unknowable, spiritual Reality. Sectarian Hinduism personalizes Brahman as *Brahma* (Creator, with four heads symbolizing creative energy), *Vishnu* (Preserver, the god of stability and control), and *Shiva* (Destroyer, god of endings). Most Hindus worship two of Vishnu's 10 mythical incarnations: Krishna and Rama. On special occasions, Hindus may worship other gods, as well as family and individual deities. Hindus claim that there are 330 million gods. In Hinduism, belief in astrology, evil spirits, and curses also prevails.

Christian Response: If God (Ultimate Reality) is impersonal, then the impersonal must be greater than the personal. Our life experiences reveal that the personal is of more value than the impersonal. Even Hindus treat their children as having more value than a rock in a field.

The Bible teaches that God is personal and describes Him as having personal attributes. The Bible regularly describes God in ways used to describe human personality. God talks, rebukes, feels, becomes angry, is jealous, laughs, loves, and even has a personal name (Gen. 1:3; 6:6, 12; Ex. 3:15; 16:12; 20:5; Lev. 20:23; Deut. 5:9; 1 Sam. 26:19; Ps. 2:4; 59:9; Hos. 1:8–9; Amos 9:4; Zeph. 3:17). The Bible also warns Christians to avoid all forms of idolatry (Gen. 35:2; Ex. 23:13; Josh. 23:7; Ezek. 20:7; 1 Cor. 10:20). No idol or pagan deity is a representation of the true God. They are all false deities and must be rejected.

CREATION: Hindus accept various forms of pantheism and reject the Christian doctrine of creation. According to Hinduism, Brahman alone exists; everything is ultimately an illusion (*maya*). God emanated itself to cause the illusion of creation. There is no beginning or conclusion to creation, only endless repetitions or cycles of creation and destruction. History has little value since it is based on an illusion.

(continued)

Hinduism (continued)

Christian Response: Christianity affirms the reality of the material world and the genuineness of God's creation. The Bible declares that all is not God. God is present in His creation but He is not to be confused with it. The Bible teaches that in the beginning God created that which was not God (Gen. 1:1ff; Heb 11:3). The Bible contradicts pantheism by teaching creation rather than pantheistic emanation. The Bible issues strong warnings to those who confuse God with His creation (Rom. 1:22–23). God created the world at a definite time and will consummate His creation (2 Pet. 2:12–13). Christianity is founded upon the historical event of God's incarnation in Jesus Christ (John 1:1–14).

MAN: The eternal soul (*atman*) of man is a manifestation or "spark" of Brahman mysteriously trapped in the physical body. *Samsara*, repeated lives or reincarnations, are required before the soul can be liberated (*moksha*) from the body. An individual's present life is determined by the law of *karma* (actions, words, and thoughts in previous lifetimes). The physical body is ultimately an illusion (*maya*) with little inherent or permanent worth. Bodies generally are cremated, and the eternal soul goes to an intermediate state of punishment or reward before rebirth in another body. Rebirths are experienced until karma has been removed to allow the soul's re-absorption into Brahman.

Christian Response: People are created in God's image (Gen. 1:27). The body's physical resurrection and eternal worth are emphasized in John 2:18–22 and 1 Corinthians 15. The Bible declares, "And as it is appointed unto men once to die, but after this the judgment: so Christ was once offered to bear the sins of many" (Heb. 9:27–28, KJV). Since we die only once, reincarnation cannot be true. Instead of reincarnation, the Bible teaches resurrection (John 5:25). At death, Christians enjoy a state of conscious fellowship with Christ (Matt. 22:32; 2 Cor. 5:8; Phil. 1:23) to await the resurrection and heavenly reward. A person's eternal destiny is determined by his or her acceptance or rejection of Jesus Christ as Savior and Lord (John 3:36; Rom. 10:9–10).

SIN: Hindus have no concept of rebellion against a holy God. Ignorance of unity with Brahman, desire, and violation of *dharma* (one's social duty) are humanity's problems.

Christian Response: Sin is not ignorance of unity with Brahman, but is rather a willful act of rebellion against God and His commandments (Eccl. 7:20; Rom. 1:28–32; 2:1–16; 3:9,19; 11:32; Gal. 3:22; 1 John 1:8–10). The Bible declares, "All have sinned and fall short of the glory of God" (Rom. 3:23, NIV).

SALVATION: There is no clear concept of salvation in Hinduism. *Moksha* (freedom from infinite being and self-hood and final self-realization of the truth) is the goal of existence. *Yoga* and meditation (especially *raja-yoga*) taught by a *guru* (religious teacher) is one way to attain *moksha*. The other valid paths for *moksha* are: the way of works (*karma marga*), the way of knowledge (*jnana marga*), and the way of love and devotion (*bhakti marga*). Hindus hope to eventually get off the cycle of reincarnation. They believe the illusion of personal existence will end and they will become one with the impersonal God.

Christian Response: Salvation is a gift from God through faith in Jesus Christ (Eph. 2:8–10). Belief in reincarnation opposes the teaching of the Bible (Heb. 9:27). The Christian hope of eternal life means that all true believers in Christ will not only have personal existence but personal fellowship with God. It is impossible to earn one's salvation by good works (Titus 3:1–7). Religious deeds and exercises cannot save (Matt. 7:22–23; Rom 9:32; Gal. 2:16; Eph. 2:8–9).

WORSHIP: Hindu worship has an almost endless variety with color symbolism, offerings, fasting, and dance as integral parts. Most Hindus daily worship an image of their chosen deity, with chants (*mantras*), flowers, and incense. Worship, whether in a home or temple, is primarily individualistic rather than congregational.

HINDUS IN THE UNITED STATES

- Traditional movements include the Ramakrishna Mission and Vedanta Societies, Sri Aurobindo Society, Satya Sai Baba Movement, Self-Realization Fellowship, and International Sivananda Yoga Society.
- Hindu-based sects include the International Society for Krishna Consciousness (Hare Krishna), Transcendental Meditation, Vedanta Society, Self-Realization Fellowship, Theosophy, and Eckankar.
- Sects that have "Americanized" Hindu concepts include Church of Christ, Scientists (Christian Science); Unity School of Christianity; and several groups within the New Age Movement.

WITNESSING TO HINDUS

- Pray and trust the Holy Spirit to use the gospel message to reach the heart and mind of your Hindu friend.
- Share your personal faith in Jesus Christ as your Lord and Savior. Keep your testimony short.
- Stress the uniqueness of Jesus Christ as God's revelation of Himself.
- Stress the necessity of following Jesus to the exclusion of all other deities.
- Keep the gospel presentation Christ-centered.
- Share the assurance of salvation that God's grace gives you and about your hope in the resurrection. Make sure you communicate that your assurance is derived from God's grace and not from your good works or your ability to be spiritual (1 John 5:13).
- Give a copy of the New Testament. If a Hindu desires to study the Bible, begin with the Gospel of John. Point out passages that explain salvation.

Ezra

End of the Babylonian Captivity

1 Now in the first year of Cyrus king of Persia, that the word of the LORD by the mouth of Jeremiah might be fulfilled, the LORD stirred up the spirit of Cyrus king of Persia, so that he made a proclamation throughout all his kingdom, and also *put it* in writing, saying,

> [2]Thus says Cyrus king of Persia:
> All the kingdoms of the earth the
> LORD God of heaven has given me.
> And He has commanded me to build
> Him a house at Jerusalem which *is* in
> Judah. [3]Who *is* among you of all His
> people? May his God be with him,
> and let him go up to Jerusalem which
> *is* in Judah, and build the house of
> the LORD God of Israel (He *is* God),
> which *is* in Jerusalem. [4]And whoever
> is left in any place where he dwells,
> let the men of his place help him
> with silver and gold, with goods and
> livestock, besides the freewill offerings
> for the house of God which *is* in
> Jerusalem.

[5]Then the heads of the fathers' *houses* of Judah and Benjamin, and the priests and the Levites, with all whose spirits God had moved, arose to go up and build the house of the LORD which *is* in Jerusalem. [6]And all those who *were* around them encouraged them with articles of silver and gold, with goods and livestock, and with precious things, besides all *that* was willingly offered.

[7]King Cyrus also brought out the articles of the house of the LORD, which Nebuchadnezzar had taken from Jerusalem and put in the temple of his gods; [8]and Cyrus king of Persia brought them out by the hand of Mithredath the treasurer, and counted them out to Sheshbazzar the prince of Judah. [9]This *is* the number of them: thirty gold platters, one thousand silver platters, twenty-nine knives, [10]thirty gold basins, four hundred and ten silver basins of a similar *kind, and* one thousand other articles. [11]All the articles of gold and silver *were* five thousand four hundred. All *these* Sheshbazzar took with the captives who were brought from Babylon to Jerusalem.

The Captives Who Returned to Jerusalem

2 Now[a] these *are* the people of the province who came back from the captivity, of those who had been carried away, whom Nebuchadnezzar the king of Babylon had carried away to Babylon, and

2:1 [a]Compare this chapter with Nehemiah 7:6–73.

1:3 The God of Israel is the one true God. Was the universe created by the gods of Eastern religions? Or by Baal or Dagon? No, the Creator of all things is the One who revealed Himself to Israel. He gave His perfect Law to Moses to show humanity that He is perfect, holy, just, and good (see Rom. 3:19,20).

who returned to Jerusalem and Judah,
everyone to his *own* city.

2*Those* who came with Zerubbabel *were*
Jeshua, Nehemiah, Seraiah, Reelaiah, Mordecai, Bilshan, Mispar,[a] Bigvai, Rehum,[b]
and Baanah. The number of the men of the
people of Israel: 3the people of Parosh, two
thousand one hundred and seventy-two;
4the people of Shephatiah, three hundred
and seventy-two; 5the people of Arah,
seven hundred and seventy-five; 6the people of Pahath-Moab, of the people of Jeshua
and Joab, two thousand eight hundred
and twelve; 7the people of Elam, one thousand two hundred and fifty-four; 8the people of Zattu, nine hundred and forty-five;
9the people of Zaccai, seven hundred and
sixty; 10the people of Bani,[a] six hundred
and forty-two; 11the people of Bebai, six
hundred and twenty-three; 12the people of
Azgad, one thousand two hundred and
twenty-two; 13the people of Adonikam, six
hundred and sixty-six; 14the people of Bigvai, two thousand and fifty-six; 15the people of Adin, four hundred and fifty-four;
16the people of Ater of Hezekiah, ninety-
eight; 17the people of Bezai, three hundred
and twenty-three; 18the people of Jorah,[a]
one hundred and twelve; 19the people of
Hashum, two hundred and twenty-three;
20the people of Gibbar,[a] ninety-five; 21the
people of Bethlehem, one hundred and
twenty-three; 22the men of Netophah,
fifty-six; 23the men of Anathoth, one hundred and twenty-eight; 24the people of Azmaveth,[a] forty-two; 25the people of Kirjath
Arim,[a] Chephirah, and Beeroth, seven
hundred and forty-three; 26the people of
Ramah and Geba, six hundred and
twenty-one; 27the men of Michmas, one
hundred and twenty-two; 28the men of
Bethel and Ai, two hundred and twenty-
three; 29the people of Nebo, fifty-two;
30the people of Magbish, one hundred and
fifty-six; 31the people of the other Elam,
one thousand two hundred and fifty-four;
32the people of Harim, three hundred and
twenty; 33the people of Lod, Hadid, and
Ono, seven hundred and twenty-five;
34the people of Jericho, three hundred and
forty-five; 35the people of Senaah, three
thousand six hundred and thirty.

36The priests: the sons of Jedaiah, of
the house of Jeshua, nine hundred and
seventy-three; 37the sons of Immer, one
thousand and fifty-two; 38the sons of
Pashhur, one thousand two hundred and
forty-seven; 39the sons of Harim, one
thousand and seventeen.

40The Levites: the sons of Jeshua and
Kadmiel, of the sons of Hodaviah,[a]
seventy-four.

41The singers: the sons of Asaph, one
hundred and twenty-eight.

42The sons of the gatekeepers: the sons
of Shallum, the sons of Ater, the sons of
Talmon, the sons of Akkub, the sons of
Hatita, and the sons of Shobai, one hundred and thirty-nine *in* all.

43The Nethinim: the sons of Ziha, the
sons of Hasupha, the sons of Tabbaoth,
44the sons of Keros, the sons of Siaha,[a]
the sons of Padon, 45the sons of Lebanah,
the sons of Hagabah, the sons of Akkub,
46the sons of Hagab, the sons of Shalmai,
the sons of Hanan, 47the sons of Giddel,
the sons of Gahar, the sons of Reaiah,
48the sons of Rezin, the sons of Nekoda,
the sons of Gazzam, 49the sons of Uzza,
the sons of Paseah, the sons of Besai,
50the sons of Asnah, the sons of Meunim,
the sons of Nephusim,[a] 51the sons of Bakbuk, the sons of Hakupha, the sons of
Harhur, 52the sons of Bazluth,[a] the sons
of Mehida, the sons of Harsha, 53the sons
of Barkos, the sons of Sisera, the sons of
Tamah, 54the sons of Neziah, and the
sons of Hatipha.

55The sons of Solomon's servants: the
sons of Sotai, the sons of Sophereth, the
sons of Peruda,[a] 56the sons of Jaala, the
sons of Darkon, the sons of Giddel, 57the
sons of Shephatiah, the sons of Hattil, the

2:2 [a]Spelled *Mispereth* in Nehemiah 7:7 [b]Spelled *Nehum* in Nehemiah 7:7 2:10 [a]Spelled *Binnui* in Nehemiah 7:15 2:18 [a]Called *Hariph* in Nehemiah 7:24 2:20 [a]Called *Gibeon* in Nehemiah 7:25 2:24 [a]Called *Beth Azmaveth* in Nehemiah 7:28 2:25 [a]Called *Kirjath Jearim* in Nehemiah 7:29 2:40 [a]Spelled *Hodevah* in Nehemiah 7:43 2:44 [a]Spelled *Sia* in Nehemiah 7:47 2:50 [a]Spelled *Nephishesim* in Nehemiah 7:52 2:52 [a]Spelled *Bazlith* in Nehemiah 7:54 2:55 [a]Spelled *Perida* in Nehemiah 7:57

sons of Pochereth of Zebaim, and the sons of Ami.[a] 58All the Nethinim and the children of Solomon's servants were three hundred and ninety-two.

59And these *were* the ones who came up from Tel Melah, Tel Harsha, Cherub, Addan,[a] and Immer; but they could not identify their father's house or their genealogy,[b] whether they *were* of Israel: 60the sons of Delaiah, the sons of Tobiah, and the sons of Nekoda, six hundred and fifty-two; 61and of the sons of the priests: the sons of Habaiah, the sons of Koz,[a] and the sons of Barzillai, who took a wife of the daughters of Barzillai the Gileadite, and was called by their name. 62These sought their listing *among* those who were registered by genealogy, but they were not found; therefore they *were excluded* from the priesthood as defiled. 63And the governor[a] said to them that they should not eat of the most holy things till a priest could consult with the Urim and Thummim.

64The whole assembly together *was* forty-two thousand three hundred *and* sixty, 65besides their male and female servants, of whom *there were* seven thousand three hundred and thirty-seven; and they had two hundred men and women singers. 66Their horses *were* seven hundred and thirty-six, their mules two hundred and forty-five, 67their camels four hundred and thirty-five, and *their* donkeys six thousand seven hundred and twenty.

68*Some* of the heads of the fathers' *houses,* when they came to the house of the LORD which *is* in Jerusalem, offered freely for the house of God, to erect it in its place: 69According to their ability, they gave to the treasury for the work sixty-one thousand gold drachmas, five thousand minas of silver, and one hundred priestly garments.

THE FUNCTION OF THE LAW

3:2 "I have been thinking. Where did Moses get that Law? I have read history. The Egyptians and the adjacent nations were idolaters; so were the Greeks and Romans; and the wisest or best Greeks or Romans never gave a code of morals like this. Where did Moses obtain that Law, which surpasses the wisdom and philosophy of the most enlightened ages? He lived at a period comparatively barbarous; but he has given a Law in which the learning and sagacity of all subsequent time can detect no flaw. Where did he obtain it? He could not have soared so far above his age as to have devised it himself. I am satisfied where he obtained it. It came down from heaven. It has convinced me of the truth of the religion of the Bible." *D. L. Moody*

70So the priests and the Levites, *some* of the people, the singers, the gatekeepers, and the Nethinim, dwelt in their cities, and all Israel in their cities.

Worship Restored at Jerusalem

3 And when the seventh month had come, and the children of Israel *were* in the cities, the people gathered together as one man to Jerusalem. 2Then Jeshua the son of Jozadak[a] and his brethren the priests, and Zerubbabel the son of Shealtiel and his brethren, arose and built the altar of the God of Israel, to offer burnt offerings on it, as *it is* written in the Law of Moses the man of God. 3Though fear *had come* upon them because of the people of those countries, they set the altar

2:57 [a]Spelled *Amon* in Nehemiah 7:59 2:59 [a]Spelled *Addon* in Nehemiah 7:61 [b]Literally *seed* 2:61 [a]Or *Hakkoz* 2:63 [a]Hebrew *Tirshatha* 3:2 [a]Spelled *Jehozadak* in 1 Chronicles 6:14

2:62 It is a tragic day when unsaved men and women (those whom the Bible calls "false brethren"—see 2 Cor. 11:26; Gal. 2:4) find their way into places of leadership within the Church.

"The Jews were generally very exact in their genealogies from their own choice and interest, that they might preserve the distinctions of the several tribes and families, which was necessary both to make out their titles to offices or inheritances, and to govern themselves thereby in the matter of marriages, and from the special providence of God, that so it might be certainly known of what tribe and family the Messiah was born." *John Wesley*

on its bases; and they offered burnt offerings on it to the LORD, *both* the morning and evening burnt offerings. 4They also kept the Feast of Tabernacles, as *it is* written, and *offered* the daily burnt offerings in the number required by ordinance for each day. 5Afterwards *they offered* the regular burnt offering, and *those* for New Moons and for all the appointed feasts of the LORD that were consecrated, and *those* of everyone who willingly offered a freewill offering to the LORD. 6From the first day of the seventh month they began to offer burnt offerings to the LORD, although the foundation of the temple of the LORD had not been laid. 7They also gave money to the masons and the carpenters, and food, drink, and oil to the people of Sidon and Tyre to bring cedar logs from Lebanon to the sea, to Joppa, according to the permission which they had from Cyrus king of Persia.

Restoration of the Temple Begins

8Now in the second month of the second year of their coming to the house of God at Jerusalem, Zerubbabel the son of Shealtiel, Jeshua the son of Jozadak,[a] and the rest of their brethren the priests and the Levites, and all those who had come out of the captivity to Jerusalem, began *work* and appointed the Levites from twenty years old and above to oversee the work of the house of the LORD. 9Then Jeshua *with* his sons and brothers, Kadmiel *with* his sons, and the sons of Judah,[a] arose as one to oversee those working on the house of God: the sons of Henadad *with* their sons and their brethren the Levites.

10When the builders laid the foundation of the temple of the LORD, the priests stood[a] in their apparel with trumpets, and the Levites, the sons of Asaph, with cymbals, to praise the LORD, according to the ordinance of David king of Israel. 11And they sang responsively, praising and giving thanks to the LORD:

"For *He is* good,
For His mercy *endures* forever toward
Israel."[a]

Then all the people shouted with a great shout, when they praised the LORD, because the foundation of the house of the LORD was laid.

12But many of the priests and Levites and heads of the fathers' *houses,* old men who had seen the first temple, wept with a loud voice when the foundation of this temple was laid before their eyes. Yet many shouted aloud for joy, 13so that the people could not discern the noise of the shout of joy from the noise of the weeping of the people, for the people shouted with a loud shout, and the sound was heard afar off.

Resistance to Rebuilding the Temple

4 Now when the adversaries of Judah and Benjamin heard that the descendants of the captivity were building the temple of the LORD God of Israel, 2they came to Zerubbabel and the heads of the fathers' *houses,* and said to them, "Let us build with you, for we seek your God as you *do;* and we have sacrificed to Him since the days of Esarhaddon king of Assyria, who brought us here." 3But Zerubbabel and Jeshua and the rest of the heads of the fathers' *houses* of Israel said to them, "You may do nothing with us to build a house for our God; but we alone will build to the LORD God of Israel, as King Cyrus the king of Persia has com-

3:8 [a]Spelled *Jehozadak* in 1 Chronicles 6:14 **3:9** [a]Or *Hodaviah* (compare 2:40) **3:10** [a]Following Septuagint, Syriac, and Vulgate; Masoretic Text reads *they stationed the priests.* **3:11** [a]Compare Psalm 136:1

3:11 Every human being is morally obligated to thank and praise God for the precious gift of life. So often we treat Him as we would the "sound man" at church, giving Him no thought until something goes wrong. As Christians, we should also be bursting with worship, praise, and thanksgiving to God for laying the foundation of our eternal salvation—Jesus, the chief cornerstone (1 Pet. 2:7). See also Psa. 136:1; Rom. 1:20,21.

manded us." 4Then the people of the land tried to discourage the people of Judah. They troubled them in building, 5and hired counselors against them to frustrate their purpose all the days of Cyrus king of Persia, even until the reign of Darius king of Persia.

Rebuilding of Jerusalem Opposed

6In the reign of Ahasuerus, in the beginning of his reign, they wrote an accusation against the inhabitants of Judah and Jerusalem.

7In the days of Artaxerxes also, Bishlam, Mithredath, Tabel, and the rest of their companions wrote to Artaxerxes king of Persia; and the letter *was* written in Aramaic script, and translated into the Aramaic language. 8Rehum[a] the commander and Shimshai the scribe wrote a letter against Jerusalem to King Artaxerxes in this fashion:

9From[a] Rehum the commander, Shimshai the scribe, and the rest of their companions—*representatives* of the Dinaites, the Apharsathchites, the Tarpelites, the people of Persia and Erech and Babylon and Shushan,[b] the Dehavites, the Elamites, 10and the rest of the nations whom the great and noble Osnapper took captive and settled in the cities of Samaria and the remainder beyond the River[a]—and so forth.[b]

11(This *is* a copy of the letter that they sent him)

To King Artaxerxes from your servants, the men *of the region* beyond the River, and so forth:[a]

12Let it be known to the king that the Jews who came up from you have come to us at Jerusalem, and are building the rebellious and evil city, and are finishing *its* walls and repairing the foundations. 13Let it now be known to the king that, if this city is built and the walls completed, they will not pay tax, tribute, or custom, and the king's treasury will be diminished. 14Now because we receive support from the palace, it was not proper for us to see the king's dishonor; therefore we have sent and informed the king, 15that search may be made in the book of the records of your fathers. And you will find in the book of the records and know that this city *is* a rebellious city, harmful to kings and provinces, and that they have incited sedition within the city in former times, for which cause this city was destroyed.

16We inform the king that if this city is rebuilt and its walls are completed, the result will be that you will have no dominion beyond the River.

17The king sent an answer:

To Rehum the commander, *to* Shimshai the scribe, *to* the rest of their companions who dwell in Samaria, and *to* the remainder beyond the River:

Peace, and so forth.[a]

18The letter which you sent to us has been clearly read before me. 19And I gave the command, and a search has been made, and it was found that

4:8 [a]The original language of Ezra 4:8 through 6:18 is Aramaic. 4:9 [a]Literally *Then* [b]Or *Susa* 4:10 [a]That is, the Euphrates [b]Literally *and now* 4:11 [a]Literally *and now* 4:17 [a]Literally *and now*

4:3–5 The believer has become the temple of God (1 Cor. 3:16,17). The adversary wants to discourage us and frustrate our purposes, so we must pray that God strengthens our hands and encourages our evangelistic efforts. When the enemies of the Lord are quick to give you lessons on what you should and shouldn't talk about when sharing your faith, show them love and kindness, and ignore their counsel (see Psa. 1:1).

this city in former times has revolted
against kings, and rebellion and
sedition have been fostered in it.
20There have also been mighty kings
over Jerusalem, who have ruled over
all *the region* beyond the River; and
tax, tribute, and custom were paid to
them. 21Now give the command to
make these men cease, that this city
may not be built until the command
is given by me.

22Take heed now that you do not fail
to do this. Why should damage
increase to the hurt of the kings?

23Now when the copy of King Artaxerxes' letter *was* read before Rehum, Shimshai the scribe, and their companions,
they went up in haste to Jerusalem against
the Jews, and by force of arms made them
cease. 24Thus the work of the house of God
which *is* at Jerusalem ceased, and it was
discontinued until the second year of the
reign of Darius king of Persia.

Restoration of the Temple Resumed

5 Then the prophet Haggai and Zechariah the son of Iddo, prophets, prophesied to the Jews who *were* in Judah and
Jerusalem, in the name of the God of
Israel, *who was* over them. 2So Zerubbabel the son of Shealtiel and Jeshua the
son of Jozadak[a] rose up and began to
build the house of God which *is* in Jerusalem; and the prophets of God *were* with
them, helping them.
3At the same time Tattenai the governor of *the region* beyond the River[a] and
Shethar-Boznai and their companions
came to them and spoke thus to them:
"Who has commanded you to build this
temple and finish this wall?" 4Then, accordingly, we told them the names of the
men who were constructing this building.
5But the eye of their God was upon the
elders of the Jews, so that they could not
make them cease till a report could go to
Darius. Then a written answer was returned concerning this *matter.* 6This is a
copy of the letter that Tattenai sent:

The governor of *the region* beyond the
River, and Shethar-Boznai, and his
companions, the Persians who *were in
the region* beyond the River, to Darius
the king.

7(They sent a letter to him, in which was
written thus)

To Darius the king:

All peace.

8Let it be known to the king that we
went into the province of Judea, to
the temple of the great God, which is
being built with heavy stones, and
timber is being laid in the walls; and
this work goes on diligently and
prospers in their hands.

9Then we asked those elders, *and* spoke
thus to them: "Who commanded you
to build this temple and to finish
these walls?" 10We also asked them
their names to inform you, that we
might write the names of the men
who *were* chief among them.

11And thus they returned us an answer,
saying: "We are the servants of the
God of heaven and earth, and we are
rebuilding the temple that was built
many years ago, which a great king of
Israel built and completed. 12But

5:2 [a]Spelled *Jehozadak* in 1 Chronicles 6:14 5:3 [a]That is, the Euphrates

5:3–5 Be humbly *stubborn* about evangelism. Do not let man or demon keep you from the Great Commission (Mark 16:15) because if you are walking in holiness, you have more than God's eye watching you. You have Him working with you. See Rom. 8:31–39 for encouragement.

because our fathers provoked the God
of heaven to wrath, He gave them
into the hand of Nebuchadnezzar
king of Babylon, the Chaldean, *who*
destroyed this temple and carried the
people away to Babylon. 13However,
in the first year of Cyrus king of
Babylon, King Cyrus issued a decree
to build this house of God. 14Also,
the gold and silver articles of the
house of God, which Nebuchadnezzar
had taken from the temple that *was*
in Jerusalem and carried into the
temple of Babylon—those King Cyrus
took from the temple of Babylon, and
they were given to one named Sheshbazzar, whom he had made governor.
15And he said to him, 'Take these
articles; go, carry them to the temple
site that *is* in Jerusalem, and let the
house of God be rebuilt on its former
site.' 16Then the same Sheshbazzar
came *and* laid the foundation of the
house of God which *is* in Jerusalem;
but from that time even until now it
has been under construction, and it
is not finished."

17Now therefore, if *it seems* good to the
king, let a search be made in the
king's treasure house, which *is* there
in Babylon, whether it is *so* that a
decree was issued by King Cyrus to
build this house of God at Jerusalem,
and let the king send us his pleasure
concerning this *matter.*

The Decree of Darius

6 Then King Darius issued a decree,
and a search was made in the ar-
chives,[a] where the treasures were stored
in Babylon. 2And at Achmetha,[a] in the
palace that *is* in the province of Media, a
scroll was found, and in it a record *was*
written thus:

3In the first year of King Cyrus, King
Cyrus issued a decree *concerning* the
house of God at Jerusalem: "Let the
house be rebuilt, the place where they
offered sacrifices; and let the foundations of it be firmly laid, its height
sixty cubits *and* its width sixty cubits,
4*with* three rows of heavy stones and
one row of new timber. Let the
expenses be paid from the king's
treasury. 5Also let the gold and silver
articles of the house of God, which
Nebuchadnezzar took from the
temple which *is* in Jerusalem and
brought to Babylon, be restored and
taken back to the temple which *is* in
Jerusalem, *each* to its place; and
deposit *them* in the house of God"—

6Now *therefore,* Tattenai, governor of
the region beyond the River, and
Shethar-Boznai, and your companions
the Persians who *are* beyond the
River, keep yourselves far from there.
7Let the work of this house of God
alone; let the governor of the Jews
and the elders of the Jews build this
house of God on its site.

8Moreover I issue a decree *as to* what
you shall do for the elders of these
Jews, for the building of this house of
God: Let the cost be paid at the king's
expense from taxes *on the region*
beyond the River; this is to be given
immediately to these men, so that
they are not hindered. 9And whatever
they need—young bulls, rams, and
lambs for the burnt offerings of the
God of heaven, wheat, salt, wine, and
oil, according to the request of the
priests who *are* in Jerusalem—let it be
given them day by day without fail,
10that they may offer sacrifices of
sweet aroma to the God of heaven,

6:1 [a]Literally *house of the scrolls* 6:2 [a]Probably *Ecbatana,* the ancient capital of Media

5:12 Sin is a lightning rod for eternal justice.

and pray for the life of the king and
his sons.

11Also I issue a decree that whoever
alters this edict, let a timber be pulled
from his house and erected, and let
him be hanged on it; and let his house
be made a refuse heap because of
this. 12And may the God who causes
His name to dwell there destroy any
king or people who put their hand to
alter it, or to destroy this house of God
which is in Jerusalem. I Darius issue
a decree; let it be done diligently.

The Temple Completed and Dedicated

13Then Tattenai, governor of *the region*
beyond the River, Shethar-Boznai, and
their companions diligently did according
to what King Darius had sent. 14So the elders of the Jews built, and they prospered
through the prophesying of Haggai the
prophet and Zechariah the son of Iddo.
And they built and finished *it*, according
to the commandment of the God of Israel, and according to the command of
Cyrus, Darius, and Artaxerxes king of
Persia. 15Now the temple was finished on
the third day of the month of Adar, which
was in the sixth year of the reign of King
Darius. 16Then the children of Israel, the
priests and the Levites and the rest of the
descendants of the captivity, celebrated
the dedication of this house of God with
joy. 17And they offered sacrifices at the
dedication of this house of God, one
hundred bulls, two hundred rams, four
hundred lambs, and as a sin offering for
all Israel twelve male goats, according to
the number of the tribes of Israel. 18They
assigned the priests to their divisions and
the Levites to their divisions, over the
service of God in Jerusalem, as it is written in the Book of Moses.

The Passover Celebrated

19And the descendants of the captivity
kept the Passover on the fourteenth *day*
of the first month. 20For the priests and
the Levites had purified themselves; all of
them *were ritually* clean. And they slaughtered the Passover *lambs* for all the descendants of the captivity, for their brethren the priests, and for themselves. 21Then
the children of Israel who had returned
from the captivity ate together with all
who had separated themselves from the
filth of the nations of the land in order to
seek the LORD God of Israel. 22And they
kept the Feast of Unleavened Bread seven
days with joy; for the LORD made them
joyful, and turned the heart of the king of
Assyria toward them, to strengthen their
hands in the work of the house of God,
the God of Israel.

The Arrival of Ezra

7 Now after these things, in the reign
of Artaxerxes king of Persia, Ezra the
son of Seraiah, the son of Azariah, the
son of Hilkiah, 2the son of Shallum, the
son of Zadok, the son of Ahitub, 3the
son of Amariah, the son of Azariah, the
son of Meraioth, 4the son of Zerahiah,
the son of Uzzi, the son of Bukki, 5the
son of Abishua, the son of Phinehas, the
son of Eleazar, the son of Aaron the chief
priest— 6this Ezra came up from Babylon; and he *was* a skilled scribe in the
Law of Moses, which the LORD God of
Israel had given. The king granted him
all his request, according to the hand of
the LORD his God upon him. 7*Some* of
the children of Israel, the priests, the
Levites, the singers, the gatekeepers, and
the Nethinim came up to Jerusalem in
the seventh year of King Artaxerxes. 8And
Ezra came to Jerusalem in the fifth month,
which *was* in the seventh year of the
king. 9On the first *day* of the first month

6:22 The joy of the Lord is your strength, and your joy comes from trusting the promises of God. Never doubt them for a moment. Believe them with all of your heart and soul, and you will have joy in the lion's den, at the Red Sea, and in the fiery furnace. See Rom. 8:28 to remember why you can have joy in the midst of tribulation.

he began *his* journey from Babylon, and
on the first *day* of the fifth month he
came to Jerusalem, according to the good
hand of his God upon him. [10]For Ezra
had prepared his heart to seek the Law
of the LORD, and to do *it*, and to teach
statutes and ordinances in Israel.

The Letter of Artaxerxes to Ezra

[11]This *is* a copy of the letter that King
Artaxerxes gave Ezra the priest, the scribe,
expert in the words of the commandments
of the LORD, and of His statutes to Israel:

[12]Artaxerxes,[a] king of kings,

To Ezra the priest, a scribe of the Law
of the God of heaven:

Perfect *peace*, and so forth.[b]

[13]I issue a decree that all those of the
people of Israel and the priests and
Levites in my realm, who volunteer
to go up to Jerusalem, may go with
you. [14]And whereas you are being
sent by the king and his seven
counselors to inquire concerning
Judah and Jerusalem, with regard to
the Law of your God which *is* in your
hand; [15]and *whereas you are* to carry
the silver and gold which the king
and his counselors have freely offered
to the God of Israel, whose dwelling
is in Jerusalem; [16]and *whereas* all the
silver and gold that you may find in
all the province of Babylon, along
with the freewill offering of the
people and the priests, *are to be* freely
offered for the house of their God in
Jerusalem— [17]now therefore, be
careful to buy with this money bulls,
rams, and lambs, with their grain
offerings and their drink offerings,
and offer them on the altar of the
house of your God in Jerusalem.

[18]And whatever seems good to you and
your brethren to do with the rest of
the silver and the gold, do it
according to the will of your God.
[19]Also the articles that are given to
you for the service of the house of
your God, deliver in full before the
God of Jerusalem. [20]And whatever
more may be needed for the house of
your God, which you may have
occasion to provide, pay *for it* from
the king's treasury.

The way to stimulate and provoke others unto good works is to strive to outrun them in the race. The way to rebuke the cold and indifferent is to be always full of zeal and 'abounding in the work of the Lord' yourself. Men will be much more ready to answer a call to come up to your level, than a command to advance beyond you.

RECORD OF CHRISTIAN WORK

[21]And I, *even* I, Artaxerxes the king,
issue a decree to all the treasurers
who *are in the region* beyond the
River, that whatever Ezra the priest,
the scribe of the Law of the God of
heaven, may require of you, let it be
done diligently, [22]up to one hundred
talents of silver, one hundred kors of
wheat, one hundred baths of wine,
one hundred baths of oil, and salt
without prescribed limit. [23]Whatever
is commanded by the God of heaven,
let it diligently be done for the house
of the God of heaven. For why
should there be wrath against the
realm of the king and his sons?

[24]Also we inform you that it shall not
be lawful to impose tax, tribute, or
custom *on* any of the priests, Levites,
singers, gatekeepers, Nethinim, or
servants of this house of God. [25]And
you, Ezra, according to your God-
given wisdom, set magistrates and

7:12 [a]The original language of Ezra 7:12–26 is Aramaic. [b]Literally *and now*

judges who may judge all the people who *are in the region* beyond the River, all such as know the laws of your God; and teach those who do not know *them.* [26]Whoever will not observe the law of your God and the law of the king, let judgment be executed speedily on him, whether *it be* death, or banishment, or confiscation of goods, or imprisonment.

[27]Blessed *be* the LORD God of our fathers, who has put *such a thing* as this in the king's heart, to beautify the house of the LORD which *is* in Jerusalem, [28]and has extended mercy to me before the king and his counselors, and before all the king's mighty princes.

So I was encouraged, as the hand of the LORD my God *was* upon me; and I gathered leading men of Israel to go up with me.

Heads of Families Who Returned with Ezra

8 These *are* the heads of their fathers' *houses,* and *this is* the genealogy of those who went up with me from Babylon, in the reign of King Artaxerxes: [2]of the sons of Phinehas, Gershom; of the sons of Ithamar, Daniel; of the sons of David, Hattush; [3]of the sons of Shecaniah, of the sons of Parosh, Zechariah; and registered with him *were* one hundred and fifty males; [4]of the sons of Pahath-Moab, Eliehoenai the son of Zerahiah, and with him two hundred males; [5]of the sons of Shechaniah,[a] Ben-Jahaziel, and with him three hundred males; [6]of the sons of Adin, Ebed the son of Jonathan, and with him fifty males; [7]of the sons of Elam, Jeshaiah the son of Athaliah, and with him seventy males; [8]of the sons of Shephatiah, Zebadiah the son of Michael, and with him eighty males; [9]of the sons of Joab, Obadiah the son of Jehiel, and with him two hundred and eighteen males; [10]of the sons of Shelomith,[a] Ben-Josiphiah, and with him one hundred and sixty males; [11]of the sons of Bebai, Zechariah the son of Bebai, and with him twenty-eight males; [12]of the sons of Azgad, Johanan the son of Hakkatan, and with him one hundred and ten males; [13]of the last sons of Adonikam, whose names *are* these—Eliphelet, Jeiel, and Shemaiah—and with them sixty males; [14]also of the sons of Bigvai, Uthai and Zabbud, and with them seventy males.

Servants for the Temple

[15]Now I gathered them by the river that flows to Ahava, and we camped there three days. And I looked among the people and the priests, and found none of the sons of Levi there. [16]Then I sent for Eliezer, Ariel, Shemaiah, Elnathan, Jarib, Elnathan, Nathan, Zechariah, and Meshullam, leaders; also for Joiarib and Elnathan, men of understanding. [17]And I gave them a command for Iddo the chief man at the place Casiphia, and I told them what they should say to Iddo *and* his brethren[a] the Nethinim at the place Casiphia—that they should bring us servants for the house of our God. [18]Then, by the good hand of our God upon us, they brought us a man of understanding, of the sons of Mahli the son of Levi, the son of Israel, namely Sherebiah, with his sons and brothers, eighteen men; [19]and

8:5 [a]Following Masoretic Text and Vulgate; Septuagint reads *the sons of Zatho, Shechaniah.* 8:10 [a]Following Masoretic Text and Vulgate; Septuagint reads *the sons of Banni, Shelomith.* 8:17 [a]Following Vulgate; Masoretic Text reads *to Iddo his brother;* Septuagint reads *to their brethren.*

7:25,26 Our civil law has its roots in divine Law. If any country fully obeyed the Ten Commandments, it would not need any other laws on its books. See Rom. 13:8–10 for why. See also Psa. 22:28 and 33:12 comments.

"Human law must rest its authority ultimately upon the authority of that law which is divine." *James Wilson* (signer of the Declaration of Independence and U.S. Constitution)

Hashabiah, and with him Jeshaiah of the sons of Merari, his brothers and their sons, twenty men; [20]also of the Nethinim, whom David and the leaders had appointed for the service of the Levites, two hundred and twenty Nethinim. All of them were designated by name.

Fasting and Prayer for Protection

[21]Then I proclaimed a fast there at the river of Ahava, that we might humble ourselves before our God, to seek from Him the right way for us and our little ones and all our possessions. [22]For I was ashamed to request of the king an escort of soldiers and horsemen to help us against the enemy on the road, because we had spoken to the king, saying, "The hand of our God *is* upon all those for good who seek Him, but His power and His wrath *are* against all those who forsake Him." [23]So we fasted and entreated our God for this, and He answered our prayer.

Gifts for the Temple

[24]And I separated twelve of the leaders of the priests—Sherebiah, Hashabiah, and ten of their brethren with them—[25]and weighed out to them the silver, the gold, and the articles, the offering for the house of our God which the king and his counselors and his princes, and all Israel *who were* present, had offered. [26]I weighed into their hand six hundred and fifty talents of silver, silver articles *weighing* one hundred talents, one hundred talents of gold, [27]twenty gold basins *worth* a thousand drachmas, and two vessels of fine polished bronze, precious as gold. [28]And I said to them, "You *are* holy to the LORD; the articles *are* holy also; and the silver and the gold *are* a freewill offering to the LORD God of your fathers. [29]Watch and keep *them* until you weigh *them* before the leaders of the priests and the Levites and heads of the fathers' *houses* of Israel in Jerusalem, *in* the chambers of the house of the LORD." [30]So the priests and the Levites received the silver and the gold and the articles by weight, to bring *them* to Jerusalem to the house of our God.

The Return to Jerusalem

[31]Then we departed from the river of Ahava on the twelfth *day* of the first month, to go to Jerusalem. And the hand of our God was upon us, and He delivered us from the hand of the enemy and from ambush along the road. [32]So we came to Jerusalem, and stayed there three days.

[33]Now on the fourth day the silver and the gold and the articles were weighed in the house of our God by the hand of Meremoth the son of Uriah the priest, and with him *was* Eleazar the son of Phinehas; with them *were* the Levites, Jozabad the son of Jeshua and Noadiah the son of Binnui, [34]with the number *and* weight of everything. All the weight was written down at that time.

[35]The children of those who had been carried away captive, who had come from the captivity, offered burnt offerings to the God of Israel: twelve bulls for all Israel, ninety-six rams, seventy-seven lambs, and twelve male goats *as* a sin offering. All *this was* a burnt offering to the LORD.

[36]And they delivered the king's orders to the king's satraps and the governors *in the region* beyond the River. So they gave support to the people and the house of God.

Intermarriage with Pagans

9 When these things were done, the leaders came to me, saying, "The people of Israel and the priests and the Levites have not separated themselves from the peoples of the lands, with respect to the abominations of the Canaanites, the

---

8:22 Behold the goodness and the severity of God. See Psa. 2:12; John 3:36; Rom. 1:18; 2:8; and Eph. 5:6 for details.

9:1,2 We are called to live in holiness—to be free from any love for this sinful world, and to be in the world but not of it. Whoever is a friend of this world is an enemy of God. See 1 John 2:15; James 4:4 for details.

Hittites, the Perizzites, the Jebusites, the Ammonites, the Moabites, the Egyptians, and the Amorites. 2For they have taken some of their daughters *as wives* for themselves and their sons, so that the holy seed is mixed with the peoples of *those* lands. Indeed, the hand of the leaders and rulers has been foremost in this trespass." 3So when I heard this thing, I tore my garment and my robe, and plucked out some of the hair of my head and beard, and sat down astonished. 4Then everyone who trembled at the words of the God of Israel assembled to me, because of the transgression of those who had been carried away captive, and I sat astonished until the evening sacrifice.

5At the evening sacrifice I arose from my fasting; and having torn my garment and my robe, I fell on my knees and spread out my hands to the LORD my God. 6And I said: "O my God, I am too ashamed and humiliated to lift up my face to You, my God; for our iniquities have risen higher than *our* heads, and our guilt has grown up to the heavens. 7Since the days of our fathers to this day we *have been* very guilty, and for our iniquities we, our kings, *and* our priests have been delivered into the hand of the kings of the lands, to the sword, to captivity, to plunder, and to humiliation, as *it is* this day. 8And now for a little while grace has been *shown* from the LORD our God, to leave us a remnant to escape, and to give us a peg in His holy place, that our God may enlighten our eyes and give us a measure of revival in our bondage. 9For we *were* slaves. Yet our God did not forsake us in our bondage; but He extended mercy to us in the sight of the kings of Persia, to revive us, to repair the house of our God, to rebuild its ruins, and to give us a wall in Judah and Jerusalem. 10And now, O our God, what shall we say after this? For we have forsaken Your commandments, 11which You commanded by Your servants the prophets, saying, 'The land which you are entering to possess is an unclean land, with the uncleanness of the peoples of the lands, with their abominations which have filled it from one end to another with their impurity. 12Now therefore, do not give your daughters as wives for their sons, nor take their daughters to your sons; and never seek their peace or prosperity, that you may be strong and eat the good of the land, and leave *it* as an inheritance to your children forever.' 13And after all that has come upon us for our evil deeds and for our great guilt, since You our God have punished us less than our iniquities *deserve,* and have given us *such*

THE FUNCTION OF THE LAW

9:13 "Do you realize, dear Hearers, you who are now hearing the Gospel, but have not received it, that God's threats take effect at once? 'No,' you say, 'He has not dealt with us after our sins, nor rewarded us according to our iniquities.' That is most true, yet there is a sense in which His sentence takes effect at once. For instance, 'He that believes not is condemned already, because he has not believed in the name of the only begotten Son of God.' If you have heard the Gospel—and some of you have heard it many, many years—and yet have not heeded it, you will not be condemned for the first time at the Last Great Day, you are condemned even now!" *Charles Spurgeon*

"It is God's manner to show men the plague of their own hearts by some means or other, before he reveals his redeeming love to their souls. While sinners are unconvinced, sin lies hid. They take no notice of it. But God makes the law effectual to bring men's own sins of heart and life to be reflected on, and observed." *Jonathan Edwards*

9:6 Ezra was burdened and ashamed to face his Creator because of the compromise of God's people. Compromise in the Christian takes away his confidence before God.

"Ah, what misery does conviction of sin cause in the breast of the sinner. I have known some so wretched, that all the torments of the inquisition could not equal their agony. If tyrants could invent the knife, the hot irons, the spear, splinters put beneath the nails, and the like, yet could not they equal the torment which some men have felt when under conviction of sin." *Charles Spurgeon*

deliverance as this, [14]should we again break Your commandments, and join in marriage with the people *committing* these abominations? Would You not be angry with us until You had consumed *us,* so that *there would be* no remnant or survivor? [15]O LORD God of Israel, You *are* righteous, for we are left as a remnant, as *it is* this day. Here we *are* before You, in our guilt, though no one can stand before You because of this!"

Confession of Improper Marriages

10 Now while Ezra was praying, and while he was confessing, weeping, and bowing down before the house of God, a very large assembly of men, women, and children gathered to him from Israel; for the people wept very bitterly. [2]And Shechaniah the son of Jehiel, *one* of the sons of Elam, spoke up and said to Ezra, "We have trespassed against our God, and have taken pagan wives from the peoples of the land; yet now there is hope in Israel in spite of this. [3]Now therefore, let us make a covenant with our God to put away all these wives and those who have been born to them, according to the advice of my master and of those who tremble at the commandment of our God; and let it be done according to the law. [4]Arise, for *this* matter *is your responsibility.* We also *are* with you. Be of good courage, and do *it.*"

[5]Then Ezra arose, and made the leaders of the priests, the Levites, and all Israel swear an oath that they would do according to this word. So they swore an oath. [6]Then Ezra rose up from before the house of God, and went into the chamber of Jehohanan the son of Eliashib; and *when* he came there, he ate no bread and drank no water, for he mourned because of the guilt of those from the captivity.

[7]And they issued a proclamation throughout Judah and Jerusalem to all the descendants of the captivity, that they must gather at Jerusalem, [8]and that whoever would not come within three days, according to the instructions of the leaders and elders, all his property would be confiscated, and he himself would be separated from the assembly of those from the captivity.

> To obey Christ in one or two or ten instances and then in fear of consequences to back away and refuse to obey in another is to cloud our life with the suspicion that we are only fair-weather followers and not true believers at all. To obey when it costs us nothing and refuse when the results are costly is to convict ourselves of moral trifling and gross insincerity.
>
> **A. W. TOZER**

[9]So all the men of Judah and Benjamin gathered at Jerusalem within three days. It *was* the ninth month, on the twentieth of the month; and all the people sat in the open square of the house of God, trembling because of *this* matter and because of heavy rain. [10]Then Ezra the priest stood up and said to them, "You have transgressed and have taken pagan wives, add-

---

10:1–4 Ezra was grieved over the sins of the people, but repentance is more than a feeling of grief and confession of sin. Genuine repentance must have "fruit." There are millions who regularly confess their sins to God and grieve over their sinful condition and even the wickedness that surrounds them. But they must be told to repent and trust in Jesus alone for their salvation, and then to produce fruit that is evidence of their repentance.

10:10 Why God did command divorce? Intermarrying with pagan nations often led to the downfall of God's people. Some may question why God would require families to separate, but even Solomon, the wisest man who ever lived, was lured away from God by his many pagan wives to worship worthless idols (see 1 Kings 11:1–8 and Neh.13:26 for details). God wants His people to be faithful to Him and not be enticed to commit spiritual adultery. James 4:4 warns us, "Adulterers and adulteresses! Do you not know that friendship with the world is enmity with God? Whoever therefore wants to be a friend of the world makes himself an enemy of God."

ing to the guilt of Israel. 11Now therefore,
make confession to the LORD God of your
fathers, and do His will; separate yourselves from the peoples of the land, and
from the pagan wives."

12Then all the assembly answered and
said with a loud voice, "Yes! As you have
said, so we must do. 13But *there are* many
people; *it is* the season for heavy rain, and
we are not able to stand outside. Nor *is*
this the work of one or two days, for *there*
are many of us who have transgressed in
this matter. 14Please, let the leaders of our
entire assembly stand; and let all those in
our cities who have taken pagan wives
come at appointed times, together with
the elders and judges of their cities, until
the fierce wrath of our God is turned away
from us in this matter." 15Only Jonathan
the son of Asahel and Jahaziah the son of
Tikvah opposed this, and Meshullam and
Shabbethai the Levite gave them support.

16Then the descendants of the captivity did so. And Ezra the priest, *with* certain heads of the fathers' *households,* were
set apart by the fathers' *households,* each
of them by name; and they sat down on
the first day of the tenth month to examine the matter. 17By the first day of the
first month they finished *questioning* all
the men who had taken pagan wives.

. . . . . .

Does God really expect us to be perfect? See Matt. 5:48 comment.

. . . . . .

Pagan Wives Put Away

18And among the sons of the priests
who had taken pagan wives *the following*
were found of the sons of Jeshua the son
of Jozadak,[a] and his brothers: Maaseiah,
Eliezer, Jarib, and Gedaliah. 19And they
gave their promise that they would put
away their wives; and *being* guilty, *they*
presented a ram of the flock as their trespass offering.

20Also of the sons of Immer: Hanani
and Zebadiah; 21of the sons of Harim:
Maaseiah, Elijah, Shemaiah, Jehiel, and
Uzziah; 22of the sons of Pashhur: Elioenai,
Maaseiah, Ishmael, Nethanel, Jozabad,
and Elasah.

23Also of the Levites: Jozabad, Shimei,
Kelaiah (the same *is* Kelita), Pethahiah,
Judah, and Eliezer.

24Also of the singers: Eliashib; and of
the gatekeepers: Shallum, Telem, and Uri.

25And others of Israel: of the sons of
Parosh: Ramiah, Jeziah, Malchiah, Mijamin, Eleazar, Malchijah, and Benaiah;
26of the sons of Elam: Mattaniah, Zechariah, Jehiel, Abdi, Jeremoth, and Eliah;
27of the sons of Zattu: Elioenai, Eliashib,
Mattaniah, Jeremoth, Zabad, and Aziza;
28of the sons of Bebai: Jehohanan, Hananiah, Zabbai, *and* Athlai; 29of the sons of
Bani: Meshullam, Malluch, Adaiah, Jashub,
Sheal, *and* Ramoth;[a] 30of the sons of Pahath-Moab: Adna, Chelal, Benaiah, Maaseiah, Mattaniah, Bezalel, Binnui, and
Manasseh; 31*of* the sons of Harim: Eliezer,
Ishijah, Malchijah, Shemaiah, Shimeon,
32Benjamin, Malluch, *and* Shemariah; 33of
the sons of Hashum: Mattenai, Mattattah,
Zabad, Eliphelet, Jeremai, Manasseh, *and*
Shimei; 34of the sons of Bani: Maadai,
Amram, Uel, 35Benaiah, Bedeiah, Cheluh,[a]
36Vaniah, Meremoth, Eliashib, 37Mattaniah,
Mattenai, Jaasai,[a] 38Bani, Binnui, Shimei,
39Shelemiah, Nathan, Adaiah, 40Machna-
debai, Shashai, Sharai, 41Azarel, Shelemiah, Shemariah, 42Shallum, Amariah,
and Joseph; 43of the sons of Nebo: Jeiel,
Mattithiah, Zabad, Zebina, Jaddai,[a] Joel,
and Benaiah.

44All these had taken pagan wives, and
some of them had wives *by whom* they
had children.

10:18 [a]Spelled *Jehozadak* in 1 Chronicles 6:14 10:29 [a]Or *Jeremoth* 10:35 [a]Or *Cheluhi,* or *Cheluhu* 10:37 [a]Or *Jaasu* 10:43 [a]Or *Jaddu*

Nehemiah

Nehemiah Prays for His People

1 The words of Nehemiah the son of
Hachaliah.
It came to pass in the month of
Chislev, *in* the twentieth year, as I was in
Shushan[a] the citadel, 2that Hanani one of
my brethren came with men from Judah;
and I asked them concerning the Jews
who had escaped, who had survived the
captivity, and concerning Jerusalem.
3And they said to me, "The survivors who
are left from the captivity in the province
are there in great distress and reproach.
The wall of Jerusalem *is* also broken down,
and its gates are burned with fire."
4So it was, when I heard these words,
that I sat down and wept, and mourned
for many days; I was fasting and praying
before the God of heaven.
5And I said: "I pray, LORD God of
heaven, O great and awesome God, *You*
who keep *Your* covenant and mercy with
those who love You[a] and observe Your[b]
commandments, 6please let Your ear be
attentive and Your eyes open, that You may
hear the prayer of Your servant which I
pray before You now, day and night, for
the children of Israel Your servants, and
confess the sins of the children of Israel
which we have sinned against You. Both
my father's house and I have sinned. 7We
have acted very corruptly against You,
and have not kept the commandments,
the statutes, nor the ordinances which
You commanded Your servant Moses.
8Remember, I pray, the word that You
commanded Your servant Moses, saying,
'*If* you are unfaithful, I will scatter you
among the nations;[a] 9but *if* you return to
Me, and keep My commandments and do
them, though some of you were cast out
to the farthest part of the heavens, *yet* I
will gather them from there, and bring

1:1 [a]Or *Susa* 1:5 [a]Literally *Him* [b]Literally *His* 1:8 [a]Leviticus 26:33 1:9 [a]Deuteronomy 30:2–5

1:4 In this book, Nehemiah seeks God in prayer eleven times. John of Antioch, also called *Chrysostom* ("golden-mouthed"), extolled the benefits of prayer: "The potency of prayer has subdued the strength of fire; it has bridled the rage of lions, hushed anarchy to rest, extinguished wars, appeased the elements, expelled demons, burst the chains of death, expanded the fates of heaven, assuaged diseases, repelled frauds, rescued cities from destruction, stayed the sun in its course, and arrested the progress of the thunderbolt. Prayer is an all-sufficient panoply, a treasure undiminished, a mine which is never exhausted, a sky unobscured by clouds, a heaven unruffled by the storm. It is the root, the fountain, the mother of a thousand blessings."

1:8,9 Often the godly remind the Lord of His promises, as an act of faith on their part rather than forgetfulness by God. The only thing He truly forgets are the sins that are covered by the blood of Christ. According to Scripture, He has cast them as far as the east is from the west (see Psa. 103:12). We can locate "north" on the earth, and say that it is a certain distance from "south" (there are approximately 22,000 miles between the two poles). However, we can't locate "east" or "west" and define how far they are from each other. East is an infinite distance from west.

them to the place which I have chosen as
a dwelling for My name.'[a] 10Now these *are*
Your servants and Your people, whom
You have redeemed by Your great power,
and by Your strong hand. 11O Lord, I pray,
please let Your ear be attentive to the
prayer of Your servant, and to the prayer
of Your servants who desire to fear Your
name; and let Your servant prosper this
day, I pray, and grant him mercy in the
sight of this man."

For I was the king's cupbearer.

Nehemiah Sent to Judah

2 And it came to pass in the month of
Nisan, in the twentieth year of King
Artaxerxes, *when* wine *was* before him,
that I took the wine and gave it to the
king. Now I had never been sad in his
presence before. 2Therefore the king said
to me, "Why *is* your face sad, since you
are not sick? This *is* nothing but sorrow
of heart."

So I became dreadfully afraid, 3and said
to the king, "May the king live forever!
Why should my face not be sad, when
the city, the place of my fathers' tombs,
lies waste, and its gates are burned with
fire?"

4Then the king said to me, "What do
you request?"

So I prayed to the God of heaven.
5And I said to the king, "If it pleases the
king, and if your servant has found favor
in your sight, I ask that you send me to
Judah, to the city of my fathers' tombs,
that I may rebuild it."

6Then the king said to me (the queen
also sitting beside him), "How long will
your journey be? And when will you return?" So it pleased the king to send me;
and I set him a time.

7Furthermore I said to the king, "If it
pleases the king, let letters be given to me
for the governors *of the region* beyond the
River,[a] that they must permit me to pass
through till I come to Judah, 8and a letter
to Asaph the keeper of the king's forest,
that he must give me timber to make
beams for the gates of the citadel which
pertains to the temple,[a] for the city wall,
and for the house that I will occupy." And
the king granted *them* to me according to
the good hand of my God upon me.

9Then I went to the governors *in the
region* beyond the River, and gave them
the king's letters. Now the king had sent
captains of the army and horsemen with
me. 10When Sanballat the Horonite and
Tobiah the Ammonite official[a] heard *of it,*
they were deeply disturbed that a man
had come to seek the well-being of the
children of Israel.

Nehemiah Views the Wall of Jerusalem

11So I came to Jerusalem and was there
three days. 12Then I arose in the night, I
and a few men with me; I told no one
what my God had put in my heart to do
at Jerusalem; nor was there any animal
with me, except the one on which I rode.
13And I went out by night through the
Valley Gate to the Serpent Well and the
Refuse Gate, and viewed the walls of
Jerusalem which were broken down and
its gates which were burned with fire.
14Then I went on to the Fountain Gate
and to the King's Pool, but *there was* no
room for the animal under me to pass.
15So I went up in the night by the valley,
and viewed the wall; then I turned back
and entered by the Valley Gate, and so re-

2:7 [a]That is, the Euphrates, and so elsewhere in this book
2:8 [a]Literally *house* 2:10 [a]Literally *servant*, and so elsewhere in this book

1:11 The key to being heard by God is to be a servant who delights in the fear of the Lord. Jesus was heard in that He feared: "who, in the days of His flesh, when He had offered up prayers and supplications, with vehement cries and tears to Him who was able to save Him from death, and was heard because of His godly fear" (Heb. 5:7).

2:8,9 We have not only been given authority from the King to build the kingdom of God, we are also co-laborers with the Captain of our salvation and the hosts of heaven (see Heb. 1:13,14).

turned. 16And the officials did not know where I had gone or what I had done; I had not yet told the Jews, the priests, the nobles, the officials, or the others who did the work.

17Then I said to them, "You see the distress that we *are* in, how Jerusalem *lies* waste, and its gates are burned with fire. Come and let us build the wall of Jerusalem, that we may no longer be a reproach." 18And I told them of the hand of my God which had been good upon me, and also of the king's words that he had spoken to me.

So they said, "Let us rise up and build." Then they set their hands to *this* good *work.*

19But when Sanballat the Horonite, Tobiah the Ammonite official, and Geshem the Arab heard *of it,* they laughed at us and despised us, and said, "What *is* this thing that you are doing? Will you rebel against the king?"

20So I answered them, and said to them, "The God of heaven Himself will prosper us; therefore we His servants will arise and build, but you have no heritage or right or memorial in Jerusalem."

Rebuilding the Wall

3 Then Eliashib the high priest rose up with his brethren the priests and built the Sheep Gate; they consecrated it and hung its doors. They built as far as the Tower of the Hundred,[a] *and* consecrated it, then as far as the Tower of Hananel. 2Next to *Eliashib*[a] the men of Jericho built. And next to them Zaccur the son of Imri built.

3Also the sons of Hassenaah built the Fish Gate; they laid its beams and hung its doors with its bolts and bars. 4And next to them Meremoth the son of Urijah, the son of Koz,[a] made repairs. Next to them Meshullam the son of Berechiah, the son of Meshezabel, made repairs. Next to them Zadok the son of Baana made repairs. 5Next to them the Tekoites made repairs; but their nobles did not put their shoulders[a] to the work of their Lord.

6Moreover Jehoiada the son of Paseah and Meshullam the son of Besodeiah repaired the Old Gate; they laid its beams and hung its doors, with its bolts and bars. 7And next to them Melatiah the Gibeonite, Jadon the Meronothite, the men of Gibeon and Mizpah, repaired the residence[a] of the governor *of the region* beyond the River. 8Next to him Uzziel the son of Harhaiah, one of the goldsmiths, made repairs. Also next to him Hananiah, one[a] of the perfumers, made repairs; and they fortified Jerusalem as far as the Broad Wall. 9And next to them Rephaiah the son of Hur, leader of half the district of Jerusalem, made repairs. 10Next to them Jedaiah the son of Harumaph made repairs in front of his house. And next to him Hattush the son of Hashabniah made repairs.

11Malchijah the son of Harim and Hashub the son of Pahath-Moab repaired another section, as well as the Tower of the Ovens. 12And next to him was Shallum the son of Hallohesh, leader of half the district of Jerusalem; he and his daughters made repairs.

13Hanun and the inhabitants of Zanoah repaired the Valley Gate. They built it, hung its doors with its bolts and bars, and *repaired* a thousand cubits of the wall as far as the Refuse Gate.

14Malchijah the son of Rechab, leader of the district of Beth Haccerem, repaired the Refuse Gate; he built it and hung its doors with its bolts and bars.

15Shallun the son of Col-Hozeh, leader

3:1 [a]Hebrew *Hammeah,* also at 12:39 3:2 [a]Literally *On his hand* 3:4 [a]Or *Hakkoz* 3:5 [a]Literally *necks* 3:7 [a]Literally *throne* 3:8 [a]Literally *the son*

2:18 We must strengthen our hands for the "good work" of evangelism. See 2 Tim. 2:21; 4:2.

3:1–3 Every church needs to build the Sheep Gate and the Fish Gate. We are followers of the Good Shepherd and we are fishers of men. See Matt. 7:13 to learn what Jesus said about gates.

of the district of Mizpah, repaired the Fountain Gate; he built it, covered it, hung its doors with its bolts and bars, and repaired the wall of the Pool of Shelah by the King's Garden, as far as the stairs that go down from the City of David. 16After him Nehemiah the son of Azbuk, leader of half the district of Beth Zur, made repairs as far as *the place* in front of the tombs[a] of David, to the man-made pool, and as far as the House of the Mighty.

17After him the Levites, *under* Rehum the son of Bani, made repairs. Next to him Hashabiah, leader of half the district of Keilah, made repairs for his district. 18After him their brethren, *under* Bavai[a] the son of Henadad, leader of the *other* half of the district of Keilah, made repairs. 19And next to him Ezer the son of Jeshua, the leader of Mizpah, repaired another section in front of the Ascent to the Armory at the buttress. 20After him Baruch the son of Zabbai[a] carefully repaired the other section, from the buttress to the door of the house of Eliashib the high priest. 21After him Meremoth the son of Urijah, the son of Koz,[a] repaired another section, from the door of the house of Eliashib to the end of the house of Eliashib.

22And after him the priests, the men of the plain, made repairs. 23After him Benjamin and Hasshub made repairs opposite their house. After them Azariah the son of Maaseiah, the son of Ananiah, made repairs by his house. 24After him Binnui the son of Henadad repaired another section, from the house of Azariah to the buttress, even as far as the corner. 25Palal the son of Uzai *made repairs* opposite the buttress, and on the tower which projects from the king's upper house that *was* by the court of the prison. After him Pedaiah the son of Parosh *made repairs.*

26Moreover the Nethinim who dwelt in Ophel *made repairs* as far as *the place* in front of the Water Gate toward the east, and on the projecting tower. 27After them the Tekoites repaired another section, next to the great projecting tower, and as far as the wall of Ophel.

28Beyond the Horse Gate the priests made repairs, each in front of his *own* house. 29After them Zadok the son of Immer made repairs in front of his *own* house. After him Shemaiah the son of Shechaniah, the keeper of the East Gate, made repairs. 30After him Hananiah the son of Shelemiah, and Hanun, the sixth son of Zalaph, repaired another section. After him Meshullam the son of Berechiah made repairs in front of his dwelling. 31After him Malchijah, one of the goldsmiths, made repairs as far as the house of the Nethinim and of the merchants, in front of the Miphkad[a] Gate, and as far as the upper room at the corner. 32And between the upper room at the corner, as far as the Sheep Gate, the goldsmiths and the merchants made repairs.

The Wall Defended Against Enemies

4 But it so happened, when Sanballat heard that we were rebuilding the wall, that he was furious and very indignant, and mocked the Jews. 2And he spoke before his brethren and the army of Samaria, and said, "What are these feeble Jews doing? Will they fortify themselves? Will they offer sacrifices? Will they complete it in a day? Will they revive the stones from the heaps of rubbish—*stones* that are burned?"

3:16 [a]Septuagint, Syriac, and Vulgate read *tomb.* 3:18 [a]Following Masoretic Text and Vulgate; some Hebrew manuscripts, Septuagint, and Syriac read *Binnui* (compare verse 24). 3:20 [a]A few Hebrew manuscripts, Syriac, and Vulgate read *Zaccai.* 3:21 [a]Or *Hakkoz* 3:31 [a]Literally *Inspection* or *Recruiting*

4:1–6 In the world's incongruent attitude toward the Church, Christians are, on the one hand, considered to be a feeble folk engaged in a futile work. At the same time, non-Christians are often greatly threatened by the Church and will work hard to hamper its work, often through ridicule. No one likes to be mocked. But those of us who labor for the King give ourselves to prayer and have a mind to work. See Phil. 1:27,28 for encouragement to stand firm.

[3]Now Tobiah the Ammonite *was* beside him, and he said, "Whatever they build, if even a fox goes up *on it,* he will break down their stone wall."

[4]Hear, O our God, for we are despised; turn their reproach on their own heads, and give them as plunder to a land of captivity! [5]Do not cover their iniquity, and do not let their sin be blotted out from before You; for they have provoked *You* to anger before the builders.

[6]So we built the wall, and the entire wall was joined together up to half its *height,* for the people had a mind to work.

[7]Now it happened, when Sanballat, Tobiah, the Arabs, the Ammonites, and the Ashdodites heard that the walls of Jerusalem were being restored and the gaps were beginning to be closed, that they became very angry, [8]and all of them conspired together to come *and* attack Jerusalem and create confusion. [9]Nevertheless we made our prayer to our God, and because of them we set a watch against them day and night.

[10]Then Judah said, "The strength of the laborers is failing, and *there is* so much rubbish that we are not able to build the wall."

[11]And our adversaries said, "They will neither know nor see anything, till we come into their midst and kill them and cause the work to cease."

[12]So it was, when the Jews who dwelt near them came, that they told us ten times, "From whatever place you turn, *they will be* upon us."

[13]Therefore I positioned *men* behind the lower parts of the wall, at the openings; and I set the people according to their families, with their swords, their spears, and their bows. [14]And I looked, and arose and said to the nobles, to the leaders, and to the rest of the people, "Do not be afraid of them. Remember the Lord, great and awesome, and fight for your brethren, your sons, your daughters, your wives, and your houses."

[15]And it happened, when our enemies heard that it was known to us, and *that* God had brought their plot to nothing, that all of us returned to the wall, everyone to his work. [16]So it was, from that time on, *that* half of my servants worked at construction, while the other half held the spears, the shields, the bows, and *wore* armor; and the leaders *were* behind all the house of Judah. [17]Those who built on the wall, and those who carried burdens, loaded themselves so that with one hand they worked at construction, and with the other held a weapon. [18]Every one of the builders had his sword girded at his side as he built. And the one who sounded the trumpet *was* beside me.

[19]Then I said to the nobles, the rulers, and the rest of the people, "The work *is* great and extensive, and we are separated far from one another on the wall. [20]Wherever you hear the sound of the trumpet, rally to us there. Our God will fight for us."

4:11 Be on the watch for "false brethren" in our midst. See Gal. 2:3–5 for details. Also see Matt. 5:11,12 and 1 Pet. 2:21–24 for how we should respond.

"The invasion of the Church by the world is a menace to the extension of Christ's kingdom. In all ages conformity to the world by Christians has resulted in lack of spiritual life and a consequent lack of spiritual vision and enterprise. A secularized or self-centered Church can never evangelize the world." *John R. Mott*

4:17–20 As we work to build the Lord's kingdom on earth, we may sometimes be separated as Christians far from one another. Even so, each of us must not only keep our spiritual weapons ready at our sides, we must also keep listening for the trumpet of God and the voice of the archangel (see 1 Thess. 4:16).

It is then that the Lord Jesus will be "revealed from heaven with His mighty angels, in flaming fire taking vengeance on those who do not know God, and on those who do not obey the gospel of our Lord Jesus Christ. These shall be punished with everlasting destruction from the presence of the Lord and from the glory of His power" (2 Thess. 1:7–9).

Our unified efforts will keep our mind working while it is yet day. For the night is coming when no one can work (see John 9:4).

[21]So we labored in the work, and half of *the men*[a] held the spears from daybreak until the stars appeared. [22]At the same time I also said to the people, "Let each man and his servant stay at night in Jerusalem, that they may be our guard by night and a working party by day." [23]So neither I, my brethren, my servants, nor the men of the guard who followed me took off our clothes, *except* that everyone took them off for washing.

Nehemiah Deals with Oppression

5 And there was a great outcry of the people and their wives against their Jewish brethren. [2]For there were those who said, "We, our sons, and our daughters *are* many; therefore let us get grain, that we may eat and live."

[3]There were also *some* who said, "We have mortgaged our lands and vineyards and houses, that we might buy grain because of the famine."

[4]There were also those who said, "We have borrowed money for the king's tax *on* our lands and vineyards. [5]Yet now our flesh *is* as the flesh of our brethren, our children as their children; and indeed we are forcing our sons and our daughters to be slaves, and *some* of our daughters have been brought into slavery. *It is* not in our power *to redeem them,* for other men have our lands and vineyards."

[6]And I became very angry when I heard their outcry and these words. [7]After serious thought, I rebuked the nobles and rulers, and said to them, "Each of you is exacting usury from his brother." So I called a great assembly against them. [8]And I said to them, "According to our ability we have redeemed our Jewish brethren who were sold to the nations. Now indeed, will you even sell your brethren? Or should they be sold to us?" Then they were silenced and found nothing *to say.* [9]Then I said, "What you are doing *is* not good. Should you not walk in the fear of our God because of the reproach of the nations, our enemies? [10]I also, *with* my brethren and my servants, am lending them money and grain. Please, let us stop this usury! [11]Restore now to them, even this day, their lands, their vineyards, their olive groves, and their houses, also a hundredth of the money and the grain, the new wine and the oil, that you have charged them."

[12]So they said, "We will restore *it,* and will require nothing from them; we will do as you say."

Then I called the priests, and required an oath from them that they would do according to this promise. [13]Then I shook out the fold of my garment[a] and said, "So may God shake out each man from his house, and from his property, who does not perform this promise. Even thus may he be shaken out and emptied."

And all the assembly said, "Amen!" and praised the LORD. Then the people did according to this promise.

The Generosity of Nehemiah

[14]Moreover, from the time that I was appointed to be their governor in the land of Judah, from the twentieth year until the thirty-second year of King Artaxerxes, twelve years, neither I nor my brothers ate the governor's provisions. [15]But the former governors who *were* before me laid burdens on the people, and took from them bread and wine, besides forty shekels of silver. Yes, even their servants bore rule over the people, but I did not do so, because of the fear of God. [16]Indeed, I also continued the work on

4:21 [a]Literally *them* 5:13 [a]Literally *my lap*

5:8 It is a good thing to be able to stop the mouth of sinners, to lay a case before them that they cannot refute. God has given us His Law for this very purpose—it stops the mouth of justification (see Rom. 3:19).

5:16 Every leader should set an example in doing the work of evangelism. The apostle Paul had the highest calling and yet pleaded for prayer that he would open his mouth and speak the mystery of the gospel boldly, "as I ought to speak" (Eph. 6:20).

this wall, and we[a] did not buy any land.
All my servants *were* gathered there for
the work.
17And at my table *were* one hundred
and fifty Jews and rulers, besides those
who came to us from the nations around
us. 18Now *that* which was prepared daily
was one ox *and* six choice sheep. Also fowl
were prepared for me, and once every ten
days an abundance of all kinds of wine.
Yet in spite of this I did not demand the
governor's provisions, because the bondage was heavy on this people.
19Remember me, my God, for good,
according to all that I have done for this
people.

Conspiracy Against Nehemiah

6 Now it happened when Sanballat,
Tobiah, Geshem the Arab, and the
rest of our enemies heard that I had rebuilt the wall, and *that* there were no
breaks left in it (though at that time I had
not hung the doors in the gates), 2that
Sanballat and Geshem sent to me, saying, "Come, let us meet together among
the villages in the plain of Ono." But
they thought to do me harm.
3So I sent messengers to them, saying,
"I *am* doing a great work, so that I cannot
come down. Why should the work cease
while I leave it and go down to you?"
4But they sent me this message four
times, and I answered them in the same
manner.
5Then Sanballat sent his servant to me
as before, the fifth time, with an open letter in his hand. 6In it *was* written:

It is reported among the nations, and
Geshem[a] says, *that* you and the Jews
plan to rebel; therefore, according to
these rumors, you are rebuilding the
wall, that you may be their king.
7And you have also appointed
prophets to proclaim concerning you
at Jerusalem, saying, "*There is* a king
in Judah!" Now these matters will be
reported to the king. So come,
therefore, and let us consult together.

8Then I sent to him, saying, "No such
things as you say are being done, but you
invent them in your own heart."
9For they all *were trying to* make us
afraid, saying, "Their hands will be weakened in the work, and it will not be done."
Now therefore, *O God,* strengthen my
hands.

> I am ready to burn out for God. I am ready to endure any hardship, if by any means I might save some. The longing of my heart is to make known my glorious Redeemer to those who have never heard.
>
> **WILLIAM BURNS**

10Afterward I came to the house of
Shemaiah the son of Delaiah, the son of
Mehetabel, who *was* a secret informer;
and he said, "Let us meet together in the
house of God, within the temple, and let
us close the doors of the temple, for they

5:16 [a]Following Masoretic Text; Septuagint, Syriac, and Vulgate read *I.* 6:6 [a]Hebrew *Gashmu*

6:3 The enemy's aim is to have the Church cease from the work of evangelism. But we know that we are doing the greatest of all works that man can be involved in on earth. We will not cease. We cannot cease (see 1 Cor. 15:58).

6:8,9 If the enemy cannot use apathy to cause us to cease from our labors on behalf of the gospel, he will use intimidation. Fear is his poison, but faith is the antidote.

"Let those who are tempted to idle merry meetings by vain companions, thus answer the temptation, We have work to do, and must not neglect it. We must never suffer ourselves to be overcome, by repeated urgency, to do anything sinful or imprudent; but when attacked with the same temptation, must resist it with the same reason and resolution . . . Nehemiah lifted up his heart to heaven in a short prayer. When, in our Christian work and warfare, we enter upon any service or conflict, this is a good prayer, I have such a duty to do, such a temptation to grapple with; now, therefore, O God, strengthen my hands. Every temptation to draw us from duty, should quicken us the more to duty." *Matthew Henry*

are coming to kill you; indeed, at night they will come to kill you."

11And I said, "Should such a man as I flee? And who *is there* such as I who would go into the temple to save his life? I will not go in!" 12Then I perceived that God had not sent him at all, but that he pronounced *this* prophecy against me because Tobiah and Sanballat had hired him. 13For this reason he *was* hired, that I should be afraid and act that way and sin, so *that* they might have *cause* for an evil report, that they might reproach me.

14My God, remember Tobiah and Sanballat, according to these their works, and the prophetess Noadiah and the rest of the prophets who would have made me afraid.

The Wall Completed

15So the wall was finished on the twenty-fifth *day* of Elul, in fifty-two days. 16And it happened, when all our enemies heard *of it,* and all the nations around us saw *these things,* that they were very disheartened in their own eyes; for they perceived that this work was done by our God.

17Also in those days the nobles of Judah sent many letters to Tobiah, and *the letters of* Tobiah came to them. 18For many in Judah were pledged to him, because he was the son-in-law of Shechaniah the son of Arah, and his son Jehohanan had married the daughter of Meshullam the son of Berechiah. 19Also they reported his good deeds before me, and reported my words to him. Tobiah sent letters to frighten me.

7 Then it was, when the wall was built and I had hung the doors, when the gatekeepers, the singers, and the Levites had been appointed, 2that I gave the charge of Jerusalem to my brother Hanani, and Hananiah the leader of the citadel, for he *was* a faithful man and feared God more than many.

3And I said to them, "Do not let the gates of Jerusalem be opened until the sun is hot; and while they stand *guard,* let them shut and bar the doors; and appoint guards from among the inhabitants of Jerusalem, one at his watch station and another in front of his own house."

The Captives Who Returned to Jerusalem

4Now the city *was* large and spacious, but the people in it *were* few, and the houses *were* not rebuilt. 5Then my God put it into my heart to gather the nobles, the rulers, and the people, that they might be registered by genealogy. And I found a register of the genealogy of those who

7:2 How to "abound" with blessings. The Bible asks the rhetorical question: "Most men will proclaim each his own goodness, but who can find a faithful man?" (Prov. 20:6). These hard-to-find "faithful" people often have unique and much appreciated characteristics:

1. When asked to do something, they will almost always write it down. This shows that they consider the request to be of importance and don't want it to slip their mind. This also reveals a humble heart, because it shows they are aware of their weaknesses. God didn't just speak the Ten Commandments. He wrote them down so that we would remember them (see Deut. 9:10).
2. They will never complain when asked to do something, even though they may be extremely busy. It has been well said that if you want something done, give it to the busiest person you know. He will do it, and do it quickly (see Prov. 25:13).
3. They will keep their word, even if it hurts them (see Psa. 15:4).
4. They enthusiastically appreciate their job, and take pride in their appearance and their workplace (Col. 3:23).
5. Proverbs 25:19 says, "Confidence in an unfaithful man in time of trouble is like a bad tooth and a foot out of joint." A bad tooth and a foot out of joint produce pain when pressure is applied. It is during the times of pressure that a faithful person is most appreciated.
6. The basis of all these things is that they love and fear God, and do all things as unto Him (see Psa. 101:6; Col. 3:23).
7. God's hand is evident upon them: "A faithful man shall abound with blessings" (Prov. 28:20).

had come up in the first *return,* and found
written in it:

[6]These[a] *are* the people of the province
who came back from the captivity, of
those who had been carried away,
whom Nebuchadnezzar the king of
Babylon had carried away, and who
returned to Jerusalem and Judah,
everyone to his city.

[7]Those who came with Zerubbabel
were Jeshua, Nehemiah, Azariah,
Raamiah, Nahamani, Mordecai,
Bilshan, Mispereth,[a] Bigvai, Nehum,
and Baanah.

The number of the men of the people
of Israel: [8]the sons of Parosh, two
thousand one hundred and seventy-
two;
[9]the sons of Shephatiah, three
hundred and seventy-two;
[10]the sons of Arah, six hundred and
fifty-two;
[11]the sons of Pahath-Moab, of the
sons of Jeshua and Joab, two thousand eight hundred and eighteen;
[12]the sons of Elam, one thousand two
hundred and fifty-four;
[13]the sons of Zattu, eight hundred
and forty-five;
[14]the sons of Zaccai, seven hundred
and sixty;
[15]the sons of Binnui,[a] six hundred
and forty-eight;
[16]the sons of Bebai, six hundred and
twenty-eight;
[17]the sons of Azgad, two thousand
three hundred and twenty-two;
[18]the sons of Adonikam, six hundred
and sixty-seven;
[19]the sons of Bigvai, two thousand
and sixty-seven;
[20]the sons of Adin, six hundred and
fifty-five;
[21]the sons of Ater of Hezekiah,
ninety-eight;
[22]the sons of Hashum, three hundred
and twenty-eight;
[23]the sons of Bezai, three hundred
and twenty-four;
[24]the sons of Hariph,[a] one hundred
and twelve;
[25]the sons of Gibeon,[a] ninety-five;
[26]the men of Bethlehem and Netophah, one hundred and eighty-eight;
[27]the men of Anathoth, one hundred
and twenty-eight;
[28]the men of Beth Azmaveth,[a] forty-
two;
[29]the men of Kirjath Jearim,
Chephirah, and Beeroth, seven
hundred and forty-three;
[30]the men of Ramah and Geba, six
hundred and twenty-one;
[31]the men of Michmas, one hundred
and twenty-two;
[32]the men of Bethel and Ai, one
hundred and twenty-three;
[33]the men of the other Nebo, fifty-two;
[34]the sons of the other Elam, one
thousand two hundred and fifty-four;
[35]the sons of Harim, three hundred
and twenty;
[36]the sons of Jericho, three hundred
and forty-five;
[37]the sons of Lod, Hadid, and Ono,
seven hundred and twenty-one;
[38]the sons of Senaah, three thousand
nine hundred and thirty.

[39]The priests: the sons of Jedaiah, of
the house of Jeshua, nine hundred
and seventy-three;
[40]the sons of Immer, one thousand
and fifty-two;
[41]the sons of Pashhur, one thousand
two hundred and forty-seven;
[42]the sons of Harim, one thousand
and seventeen.

[43]The Levites: the sons of Jeshua, of
Kadmiel,
and of the sons of Hodevah,[a] seventy-
four.

7:6 [a]Compare verses 6–72 with Ezra 2:1–70 7:7 [a]Spelled *Mispar* in Ezra 2:2 7:15 [a]Spelled *Bani* in Ezra 2:10 7:24 [a]Called *Jorah* in Ezra 2:18 7:25 [a]Called *Gibbar* in Ezra 2:20 7:28 [a]Called *Azmaveth* in Ezra 2:24 7:43 [a]Spelled *Hodaviah* in Ezra 2:40

44 The singers: the sons of Asaph, one
hundred and forty-eight.

45 The gatekeepers: the sons of Shallum,
the sons of Ater,
the sons of Talmon,
the sons of Akkub,
the sons of Hatita,
the sons of Shobai, one hundred and
thirty-eight.

46 The Nethinim: the sons of Ziha,
the sons of Hasupha,
the sons of Tabbaoth,
47 the sons of Keros,
the sons of Sia,[a]
the sons of Padon,
48 the sons of Lebana,[a]
the sons of Hagaba,[b]
the sons of Salmai,[c]
49 the sons of Hanan,
the sons of Giddel,
the sons of Gahar,
50 the sons of Reaiah,
the sons of Rezin,
the sons of Nekoda,
51 the sons of Gazzam,
the sons of Uzza,
the sons of Paseah,
52 the sons of Besai,
the sons of Meunim,
the sons of Nephishesim,[a]
53 the sons of Bakbuk,
the sons of Hakupha,
the sons of Harhur,
54 the sons of Bazlith,[a]
the sons of Mehida,
the sons of Harsha,
55 the sons of Barkos,
the sons of Sisera,
the sons of Tamah,
56 the sons of Neziah,
and the sons of Hatipha.

57 The sons of Solomon's servants: the
sons of Sotai,
the sons of Sophereth,
the sons of Perida,[a]
58 the sons of Jaala,
the sons of Darkon,
the sons of Giddel,
59 the sons of Shephatiah,
the sons of Hattil,
the sons of Pochereth of Zebaim,
and the sons of Amon.[a]
60 All the Nethinim, and the sons of
Solomon's servants, *were* three
hundred and ninety-two.

61 And these *were* the ones who came
up from Tel Melah, Tel Harsha,
Cherub, Addon,[a] and Immer, but
they could not identify their father's
house nor their lineage, whether they
were of Israel: 62 the sons of Delaiah,
the sons of Tobiah,
the sons of Nekoda, six hundred and
forty-two;
63 and of the priests: the sons of
Habaiah,
the sons of Koz,[a]
the sons of Barzillai, who took a wife
of the daughters of Barzillai the
Gileadite, and was called by their
name.
64 These sought their listing *among*
those who were registered by
genealogy, but it was not found;
therefore they were excluded from
the priesthood as defiled. 65 And the
governor[a] said to them that they
should not eat of the most holy
things till a priest could consult with
the Urim and Thummim.

66 Altogether the whole assembly *was*
forty-two thousand three hundred
and sixty, 67 besides their male and
female servants, of whom *there were*
seven thousand three hundred and
thirty-seven; and they had two
hundred and forty-five men and
women singers. 68 Their horses were
seven hundred and thirty-six, their
mules two hundred and forty-five,

7:47 [a]Spelled *Siaha* in Ezra 2:44 7:48 [a]Masoretic Text reads *Lebanah.* [b]Masoretic Text reads *Hogabah.* [c]Or *Shalmai*, or *Shamlai* 7:52 [a]Spelled *Nephusim* in Ezra 2:50 7:54 [a]Spelled *Bazluth* in Ezra 2:52 7:57 [a]Spelled *Peruda* in Ezra 2:55 7:59 [a]Spelled *Ami* in Ezra 2:57 7:61 [a]Spelled *Addan* in Ezra 2:59 7:63 [a]Or *Hakkoz* 7:65 [a]Hebrew *Tirshatha*

POINTS FOR OPEN-AIR PREACHING

8:1

A Place of Influence

College campuses are wonderful places to witness because there are often large groups of students sitting between classes or gathering in common areas for lunch. Young people are often more open to discuss the things of God than those who have become hardened in their philosophies. Also keep in mind that you will be speaking to future doctors, lawyers, and politicians—society leaders, those who could greatly influence the future. Just one word from you that God uses could change many lives. If you don't bother to reach out to them, they will become steeped in the errors of humanism, atheism, and evolution. So take courage—call or visit your local college or university, tell them you'd like to come and speak, and ask for their requirements. They may let you speak with or without amplification. You may need some sort of insurance, or they may want to restrict you to a certain area. If a Christian organization on campus invites you, that usually gets around any red tape.

Get a lightweight easel, and print a poster-sized picture of Einstein to help attract listeners (see "Free Downloads" on www.livingwaters.com). Ask trivia questions, give dollar bills to those who answer, then ask what they think happens after death. You can do this! Don't listen to your fears or discouraging thoughts. The time will come when your spirit will be willing but your flesh will be weak because you are old and feeble. Imagine sitting in a convalescent home, thinking about how you wasted your youth pursuing your own pleasures when people were going to hell. We often apply the verse "Remember now your Creator in the days of your youth" (Eccles. 12:1) to the ungodly, when we should apply it to ourselves.

69*their* camels four hundred and
thirty-five, *and* donkeys six thousand
seven hundred and twenty.

70And some of the heads of the fathers'
houses gave to the work. The governor[a]
gave to the treasury one thousand
gold drachmas, fifty basins, and five
hundred and thirty priestly garments.
71Some of the heads of the fathers'
houses gave to the treasury of the work
twenty thousand gold drachmas, and
two thousand two hundred silver
minas. 72And that which the rest of
the people gave *was* twenty thousand
gold drachmas, two thousand silver
minas, and sixty-seven priestly
garments.

73So the priests, the Levites, the gatekeepers, the singers, *some* of the people, the
Nethinim, and all Israel dwelt in their cities.

Ezra Reads the Law

When the seventh month came, the children of Israel *were* in their cities.

8 Now all the people gathered together
as one man in the open square that
was in front of the Water Gate; and they
told Ezra the scribe to bring the Book of
the Law of Moses, which the LORD had
commanded Israel. 2So Ezra the priest
brought the Law before the assembly of
men and women and all who *could* hear
with understanding on the first day of
the seventh month. 3Then he read from
it in the open square that *was* in front of
the Water Gate from morning until midday, before the men and women and
those who could understand; and the
ears of all the people *were attentive* to the
Book of the Law.

4So Ezra the scribe stood on a platform of wood which they had made for
the purpose; and beside him, at his right
hand, stood Mattithiah, Shema, Anaiah,
Urijah, Hilkiah, and Maaseiah; and at his
left hand Pedaiah, Mishael, Malchijah,
Hashum, Hashbadana, Zechariah, *and*
Meshullam. 5And Ezra opened the book

7:70 [a]Hebrew *Tirshatha*

8:3 We must bring God's Law to the people; they will not come to it. Men love darkness rather than light, and they will not come to the light lest their deeds be exposed (see John 3:19–21). It is the light of this Law that exposes sin (see Rom. 7:7). The Law faces the Water Gate; it causes those who hear with understanding to thirst for the righteousness that can be found only in Jesus Christ.

THE FUNCTION OF THE LAW

8:9 Ezra and the Levites caused the people to understand the Law by presenting it distinctly, giving its sense, and helping them comprehend its meaning. We do the same by opening up the spirituality of the Ten Commandments. We tell our hearers that God sees their thoughts, and that He requires truth in the inward parts. We make clear that God considers lust to be adultery and hatred to be murder, etc. We explain that God's holy, perfect, just, and good Law is the measure against which they will be judged. Those who hear and understand will find a place of contrition before God (v. 9) and at that point will be receptive to the gospel of grace.

"How the people were wounded with the words of the Law that were read to them. The Law works death and speaks terror; shows men their sins and their misery and danger because of sin, and it thunders a curse against every one that continues not in every pact of his duty.

"Therefore, when they heard it they all wept. It was a good sign that their hearts were tender, like Josiah's when he heard the words of the Law. They wept to think how they had offended God and exposed themselves, by their many violations of the Law; when some wept, all wept, for they all saw themselves guilty before God." *Matthew Henry*

in the sight of all the people, for he was *standing* above all the people; and when he opened it, all the people stood up. 6And Ezra blessed the LORD, the great God.

Then all the people answered, "Amen, Amen!" while lifting up their hands. And they bowed their heads and worshiped the LORD with *their* faces to the ground.

7Also Jeshua, Bani, Sherebiah, Jamin, Akkub, Shabbethai, Hodijah, Maaseiah, Kelita, Azariah, Jozabad, Hanan, Pelaiah, and the Levites, helped the people to understand the Law; and the people *stood* in their place. 8So they read distinctly from the book, in the Law of God; and they gave the sense, and helped *them* to understand the reading.

9And Nehemiah, who *was* the governor,[a] Ezra the priest *and* scribe, and the Levites who taught the people said to all the people, "This day *is* holy to the LORD your God; do not mourn nor weep." For all the people wept, when they heard the words of the Law.

10Then he said to them, "Go your way, eat the fat, drink the sweet, and send portions to those for whom nothing is prepared; for *this* day *is* holy to our Lord. Do not sorrow, for the joy of the LORD is your strength."

11So the Levites quieted all the people, saying, "Be still, for the day *is* holy; do not be grieved." 12And all the people went their way to eat and drink, to send portions and rejoice greatly, because they understood the words that were declared to them.

The Feast of Tabernacles

13Now on the second day the heads of the fathers' *houses* of all the people, with the priests and Levites, were gathered to Ezra the scribe, in order to understand the words of the Law. 14And they found written in the Law, which the LORD had commanded by Moses, that the children of Israel should dwell in booths during the feast of the seventh month, 15and that they should announce and proclaim in all their cities and in Jerusalem, saying, "Go out to the mountain, and bring olive branches, branches of oil trees, myrtle branches, palm branches, and branches of leafy trees, to make booths, as *it is* written."

16Then the people went out and brought *them* and made themselves booths, each one on the roof of his house,

8:9 [a]Hebrew *Tirshatha*

8:10 "As the beast in the meadow knows not the far-reaching thoughts of him who reads the stars and threads the spheres, so neither can the carnal man make so much as a guess of what are the joys which God hath prepared for them that love him, which any day and every day, when our hearts seek it, he reveals to us by his Spirit. This is 'the joy of the Lord,' fellowship with the Father and with his Son Jesus Christ. Beloved, if we reach this point, we must labor to maintain our standing, for our Lord saith to us 'abide in me.' The habit of communion is the life of happiness." *Charles Spurgeon*

or in their courtyards or the courts of the
house of God, and in the open square of
the Water Gate and in the open square of
the Gate of Ephraim. [17]So the whole assembly of those who had returned from
the captivity made booths and sat under
the booths; for since the days of Joshua
the son of Nun until that day the children
of Israel had not done so. And there was
very great gladness. [18]Also day by day, from
the first day until the last day, he read
from the Book of the Law of God. And
they kept the feast seven days; and on the
eighth day *there was* a sacred assembly,
according to the *prescribed* manner.

The People Confess Their Sins

9 Now on the twenty-fourth day of this
month the children of Israel were assembled with fasting, in sackcloth, and
with dust on their heads.[a] [2]Then those of
Israelite lineage separated themselves
from all foreigners; and they stood and
confessed their sins and the iniquities of
their fathers. [3]And they stood up in their
place and read from the Book of the Law
of the LORD their God *for one*-fourth of
the day; and *for another* fourth they confessed and worshiped the LORD their God.
[4]Then Jeshua, Bani, Kadmiel, Shebaniah, Bunni, Sherebiah, Bani, *and* Chenani
stood on the stairs of the Levites and cried
out with a loud voice to the LORD their
God. [5]And the Levites, Jeshua, Kadmiel,
Bani, Hashabniah, Sherebiah, Hodijah,
Shebaniah, *and* Pethahiah, said:

"Stand up and bless the LORD your God
Forever and ever!

"Blessed be Your glorious name,
Which is exalted above all blessing
and praise!
[6]You alone *are* the LORD;
You have made heaven,
The heaven of heavens, with all their
host,
The earth and everything on it,
The seas and all that is in them,
And You preserve them all.
The host of heaven worships You.

[7]"You *are* the LORD God,
Who chose Abram,
And brought him out of Ur of the
Chaldeans,
And gave him the name Abraham;
[8]You found his heart faithful before You,
And made a covenant with him
To give the land of the Canaanites,
The Hittites, the Amorites,
The Perizzites, the Jebusites,
And the Girgashites—
To give *it* to his descendants.
You have performed Your words,
For You *are* righteous.

[9]"You saw the affliction of our fathers
in Egypt,
And heard their cry by the Red Sea.
[10]You showed signs and wonders
against Pharaoh,
Against all his servants,
And against all the people of his land.
For You knew that they acted proudly
against them.
So You made a name for Yourself, as *it*
is this day.
[11]And You divided the sea before them,
So that they went through the midst
of the sea on the dry land;
And their persecutors You threw into
the deep,
As a stone into the mighty waters.
[12]Moreover You led them by day with a
cloudy pillar,
And by night with a pillar of fire,
To give them light on the road

9:1 [a]Literally *earth on them*

9:6 God made the heavens with "all" their host. He made the earth and "all" things on it. He made the seas and "all" that are in them. There is no room for theories that anything evolved of its own accord.

9:7,8 See Rom. 4:17–21 for details on Abraham's attitude toward the promise of God.

Which they should travel.

[13]"You came down also on Mount Sinai,
And spoke with them from heaven,
And gave them just ordinances and true laws,
Good statutes and commandments.
[14]You made known to them Your holy Sabbath,
And commanded them precepts, statutes and laws,
By the hand of Moses Your servant.
[15]You gave them bread from heaven for their hunger,
And brought them water out of the rock for their thirst,
And told them to go in to possess the land
Which You had sworn to give them.

[16]"But they and our fathers acted proudly,
Hardened their necks,
And did not heed Your commandments.
[17]They refused to obey,
And they were not mindful of Your wonders
That You did among them.
But they hardened their necks,
And in their rebellion[a]
They appointed a leader
To return to their bondage.
But You *are* God,
Ready to pardon,
Gracious and merciful,
Slow to anger,
Abundant in kindness,
And did not forsake them.

[18]"Even when they made a molded calf for themselves,
And said, 'This *is* your god
That brought you up out of Egypt,'
And worked great provocations,
[19]Yet in Your manifold mercies
You did not forsake them in the wilderness.
The pillar of the cloud did not depart from them by day,
To lead them on the road;
Nor the pillar of fire by night,
To show them light,
And the way they should go.
[20]You also gave Your good Spirit to instruct them,
And did not withhold Your manna from their mouth,
And gave them water for their thirst.
[21]Forty years You sustained them in the wilderness;
They lacked nothing;
Their clothes did not wear out[a]
And their feet did not swell.

[22]"Moreover You gave them kingdoms and nations,
And divided them into districts.[a]
So they took possession of the land of Sihon,
The land of[b] the king of Heshbon,
And the land of Og king of Bashan.
[23]You also multiplied their children as the stars of heaven,
And brought them into the land
Which You had told their fathers
To go in and possess.
[24]So the people went in
And possessed the land;
You subdued before them the inhabitants of the land,
The Canaanites,
And gave them into their hands,
With their kings
And the people of the land,
That they might do with them as they wished.

9:17 [a]Following Masoretic Text and Vulgate; Septuagint reads *in Egypt*. 9:21 [a]Compare Deuteronomy 29:5 9:22 [a]Literally *corners* [b]Following Masoretic Text and Vulgate; Septuagint omits *The land of*.

9:15 Jesus is the bread from heaven (see John 6:33–35). He is also the Rock from which flows the water of life (see 1 Cor. 10:4).

9:17 God has not changed. He is still patiently waiting, not willing that any perish, but that all come to repentance (2 Pet. 3:9).

25And they took strong cities and a rich land,
And possessed houses full of all goods,
Cisterns *already* dug, vineyards, olive groves,
And fruit trees in abundance.
So they ate and were filled and grew fat,
And delighted themselves in Your great goodness.

26"Nevertheless they were disobedient
And rebelled against You,
Cast Your law behind their backs
And killed Your prophets, who testified against them
To turn them to Yourself;
And they worked great provocations.
27Therefore You delivered them into the hand of their enemies,
Who oppressed them;
And in the time of their trouble,
When they cried to You,
You heard from heaven;
And according to Your abundant mercies
You gave them deliverers who saved them
From the hand of their enemies.

28"But after they had rest,
They again did evil before You.
Therefore You left them in the hand of their enemies,
So that they had dominion over them;
Yet when they returned and cried out to You,
You heard from heaven;
And many times You delivered them according to Your mercies,
29And testified against them,
That You might bring them back to Your law.
Yet they acted proudly,
And did not heed Your commandments,
But sinned against Your judgments,
'Which if a man does, he shall live by them.'[a]
And they shrugged their shoulders,
Stiffened their necks,
And would not hear.
30Yet for many years You had patience with them,
And testified against them by Your Spirit in Your prophets.
Yet they would not listen;
Therefore You gave them into the hand of the peoples of the lands.
31Nevertheless in Your great mercy
You did not utterly consume them nor forsake them;
For You *are* God, gracious and merciful.

32"Now therefore, our God,
The great, the mighty, and awesome God,
Who keeps covenant and mercy:
Do not let all the trouble seem small before You
That has come upon us,
Our kings and our princes,
Our priests and our prophets,
Our fathers and on all Your people,
From the days of the kings of Assyria until this day.
33However You *are* just in all that has befallen us;
For You have dealt faithfully,
But we have done wickedly.
34Neither our kings nor our princes,
Our priests nor our fathers,
Have kept Your law,
Nor heeded Your commandments and Your testimonies,

9:29 [a]Leviticus 18:5

9:26 The disobedient and rebellious hate God's Law. They think that their moral dilemma will be solved and they can sin with guilt-free abandonment if they expel the Ten Commandments and those who preach God's Law. However, God wrote His Law in stone with His own finger, and He engraved its work on the tablets of their heart (see Rom. 2:15). They will still have to face Him and His Law on the Day of Wrath.

9:29 See Zech. 7:11,12 comment.

With which You testified against them.
[35]For they have not served You in their
kingdom,
Or in the many good *things* that You
gave them,
Or in the large and rich land which
You set before them;
Nor did they turn from their wicked
works.

[36]"Here we *are,* servants today!
And the land that You gave to our
fathers,
To eat its fruit and its bounty,
Here we *are,* servants in it!
[37]And it yields much increase to the
kings
You have set over us,
Because of our sins;
Also they have dominion over our
bodies and our cattle
At their pleasure;
And we *are* in great distress.

[38]" And because of all this,
We make a sure *covenant* and write *it;*
Our leaders, our Levites, *and* our
priests seal *it.*"

The People Who Sealed the Covenant

10 Now those who placed *their* seal on *the document were:*
Nehemiah the governor, the son of
Hacaliah, and Zedekiah, [2]Seraiah,
Azariah, Jeremiah, [3]Pashhur,
Amariah, Malchijah, [4]Hattush,
Shebaniah, Malluch, [5]Harim,
Meremoth, Obadiah, [6]Daniel,
Ginnethon, Baruch, [7]Meshullam,
Abijah, Mijamin, [8]Maaziah, Bilgai, *and*
Shemaiah. These *were* the priests.

[9]The Levites: Jeshua the son of
Azaniah, Binnui of the sons of
Henadad, *and* Kadmiel.
[10]Their brethren: Shebaniah, Hodijah,
Kelita, Pelaiah, Hanan, [11]Micha, Rehob,
Hashabiah, [12]Zaccur, Sherebiah, Sheb-
aniah, [13]Hodijah, Bani, *and* Beninu.

[14]The leaders of the people: Parosh,
Pahath-Moab, Elam, Zattu, Bani,
[15]Bunni, Azgad, Bebai, [16]Adonijah,
Bigvai, Adin, [17]Ater, Hezekiah, Azzur,
[18]Hodijah, Hashum, Bezai, [19]Hariph,
Anathoth, Nebai, [20]Magpiash,
Meshullam, Hezir, [21]Meshezabel,
Zadok, Jaddua, [22]Pelatiah, Hanan,
Anaiah, [23]Hoshea, Hananiah,
Hasshub, [24]Hallohesh, Pilha, Shobek,
[25]Rehum, Hashabnah, Maaseiah,
[26]Ahijah, Hanan, Anan, [27]Malluch,
Harim, *and* Baanah.

The Covenant That Was Sealed

[28]Now the rest of the people—the
priests, the Levites, the gatekeepers, the
singers, the Nethinim, and all those who
had separated themselves from the peoples of the lands to the Law of God, their
wives, their sons, and their daughters,
everyone who had knowledge and understanding— [29]these joined with their
brethren, their nobles, and entered into a
curse and an oath to walk in God's Law,
which was given by Moses the servant of
God, and to observe and do all the commandments of the LORD our Lord, and
His ordinances and His statutes: [30]We
would not give our daughters as wives to
the peoples of the land, nor take their
daughters for our sons; [31]*if* the peoples of
the land brought wares or any grain to
sell on the Sabbath day, we would not
buy it from them on the Sabbath, or on a
holy day; and we would forego the seventh year's *produce* and the exacting of
every debt.
[32]Also we made ordinances for ourselves, to exact from ourselves yearly one-

10:28 Holiness is not cutting ourselves off from this sinful world. It means to separate ourselves from their sinful works. We are to live in this world with the purpose of reaching out to the unsaved. See Jude 22,23 for details.

10:29 For the spiritual nature of God's Law, see Matt. 15:19 comment.

"The purpose of a devout and united people was set forth in the pages of the Bible... 1) to live in freedom, 2) to work in a prosperous land,... and 3) to obey the Commandments of God."

Dwight Eisenhower

third of a shekel for the service of the
house of our God: 33for the showbread,
for the regular grain offering, for the regular burnt offering of the Sabbaths, the
New Moons, and the set feasts; for the
holy things, for the sin offerings to make
atonement for Israel, and all the work of
the house of our God. 34We cast lots
among the priests, the Levites, and the
people, for *bringing* the wood offering
into the house of our God, according to
our fathers' houses, at the appointed times
year by year, to burn on the altar of the
LORD our God as *it is* written in the Law.

35And *we made ordinances* to bring the
firstfruits of our ground and the firstfruits
of all fruit of all trees, year by year, to the
house of the LORD; 36to bring the firstborn of our sons and our cattle, as *it is*
written in the Law, and the firstborn of
our herds and our flocks, to the house of
our God, to the priests who minister in
the house of our God; 37to bring the firstfruits of our dough, our offerings, the
fruit from all kinds of trees, *the* new wine
and oil, to the priests, to the storerooms
of the house of our God; and to bring the
tithes of our land to the Levites, for the
Levites should receive the tithes in all our
farming communities. 38And the priest,
the descendant of Aaron, shall be with
the Levites when the Levites receive tithes;
and the Levites shall bring up a tenth of
the tithes to the house of our God, to the
rooms of the storehouse.

39For the children of Israel and the
children of Levi shall bring the offering of
the grain, of the new wine and the oil, to
the storerooms where the articles of the
sanctuary *are, where* the priests who minister and the gatekeepers and the singers
are; and we will not neglect the house of
our God.

The People Dwelling in Jerusalem

11 Now the leaders of the people
dwelt at Jerusalem; the rest of the
people cast lots to bring one out of ten to
dwell in Jerusalem, the holy city, and
nine-tenths *were to dwell* in *other* cities.
2And the people blessed all the men who
willingly offered themselves to dwell at
Jerusalem.

3These *are* the heads of the province
who dwelt in Jerusalem. (But in the cities
of Judah everyone dwelt in his own possession in their cities—Israelites, priests,

11:1,2 "In all ages, men have preferred their own ease and advantage to the public good. Even the professors of religion too commonly seek their own, and not the things of Christ. Few have had such attachment to holy things and holy places, as to renounce pleasure for their sake. Yet surely, our souls should delight to dwell where holy persons and opportunities of spiritual improvement most abound. If we have not this love to the city of our God, and to every thing that assists our communion with the Savior, how shall we be willing to depart hence; to be absent from the body, that we may be present with the Lord? To the carnal-minded, the perfect holiness of the New Jerusalem would be still harder to bear than the holiness of God's church on earth. Let us seek first the favour of God, and his glory; let us study to be patient, contented, and useful in our several stations, and wait, with cheerful hope, for admission into the holy city of God." *Matthew Henry*

Levites, Nethinim, and descendants of
Solomon's servants.) [4]Also in Jerusalem
dwelt *some* of the children of Judah and
of the children of Benjamin.

The children of Judah: Athaiah the
son of Uzziah, the son of Zechariah, the
son of Amariah, the son of Shephatiah,
the son of Mahalalel, of the children of
Perez; [5]and Maaseiah the son of Baruch,
the son of Col-Hozeh, the son of Haza-
iah, the son of Adaiah, the son of Joiarib,
the son of Zechariah, the son of Shiloni.
[6]All the sons of Perez who dwelt at Jerusalem *were* four hundred and sixty-eight
valiant men.

[7]And these are the sons of Benjamin:
Sallu the son of Meshullam, the son of
Joed, the son of Pedaiah, the son of Kolaiah, the son of Maaseiah, the son of Ithiel,
the son of Jeshaiah; [8]and after him Gab-
bai *and* Sallai, nine hundred and twenty-
eight. [9]Joel the son of Zichri *was* their
overseer, and Judah the son of Senuah[a]
was second over the city.

[10]Of the priests: Jedaiah the son of
Joiarib, and Jachin; [11]Seraiah the son of
Hilkiah, the son of Meshullam, the son of
Zadok, the son of Meraioth, the son of
Ahitub, *was* the leader of the house of
God. [12]Their brethren who did the work
of the house *were* eight hundred and
twenty-two; and Adaiah the son of Jeroham, the son of Pelaliah, the son of Amzi,
the son of Zechariah, the son of Pashhur,
the son of Malchijah, [13]and his brethren,
heads of the fathers' *houses, were* two
hundred and forty-two; and Amashai the
son of Azarel, the son of Ahzai, the son of
Meshillemoth, the son of Immer, [14]and
their brethren, mighty men of valor, *were*
one hundred and twenty-eight. Their
overseer *was* Zabdiel the son of *one of* the
great men.[a]

[15]Also of the Levites: Shemaiah the
son of Hasshub, the son of Azrikam, the
son of Hashabiah, the son of Bunni;
[16]Shabbethai and Jozabad, of the heads of
the Levites, *had* the oversight of the business outside of the house of God; [17]Mat-
taniah the son of Micha,[a] the son of
Zabdi, the son of Asaph, the leader *who*
began the thanksgiving with prayer; Bakbukiah, the second among his brethren;
and Abda the son of Shammua, the son of
Galal, the son of Jeduthun. [18]All the
Levites in the holy city *were* two hundred
and eighty-four.

[19]Moreover the gatekeepers, Akkub,
Talmon, and their brethren who kept the
gates, *were* one hundred and seventy-two.

[20]And the rest of Israel, of the priests
and Levites, *were* in all the cities of Judah,
everyone in his inheritance. [21]But the
Nethinim dwelt in Ophel. And Ziha and
Gishpa *were* over the Nethinim.

[22]Also the overseer of the Levites at
Jerusalem *was* Uzzi the son of Bani, the
son of Hashabiah, the son of Mattaniah,
the son of Micha, of the sons of Asaph,
the singers in charge of the service of the
house of God. [23]For *it was* the king's command concerning them that a certain
portion should be for the singers, a quota
day by day. [24]Pethahiah the son of
Meshezabel, of the children of Zerah the
son of Judah, *was* the king's deputy[a] in all
matters concerning the people.

The People Dwelling Outside Jerusalem

[25]And as for the villages with their
fields, *some* of the children of Judah dwelt
in Kirjath Arba and its villages, Dibon
and its villages, Jekabzeel and its villages;
[26]in Jeshua, Moladah, Beth Pelet, [27]Hazar
Shual, and Beersheba and its villages; [28]in
Ziklag and Meconah and its villages; [29]in
En Rimmon, Zorah, Jarmuth, [30]Zanoah,
Adullam, and their villages; in Lachish
and its fields; in Azekah and its villages.
They dwelt from Beersheba to the Valley
of Hinnom.

[31]Also the children of Benjamin from
Geba *dwelt* in Michmash, Aija, and Bethel,
and their villages; [32]in Anathoth, Nob,
Ananiah; [33]in Hazor, Ramah, Gittaim;
[34]in Hadid, Zeboim, Neballat; [35]in Lod,

11:9 [a]Or *Hassenuah* **11:14** [a]Or *the son of Haggedolim*
11:17 [a]Or *Michah* **11:24** [a]Literally *at the king's hand*

Ono, *and* the Valley of Craftsmen. [36]Some of the Judean divisions of Levites *were* in Benjamin.

The Priests and Levites

12 Now these *are* the priests and the Levites who came up with Zerubbabel the son of Shealtiel, and Jeshua: Seraiah, Jeremiah, Ezra, [2]Amariah, Malluch, Hattush, [3]Shechaniah, Rehum, Meremoth, [4]Iddo, Ginnethoi,[a] Abijah, [5]Mijamin, Maadiah, Bilgah, [6]Shemaiah, Joiarib, Jedaiah, [7]Sallu, Amok, Hilkiah, *and* Jedaiah.

These *were* the heads of the priests and their brethren in the days of Jeshua.

[8]Moreover the Levites *were* Jeshua, Binnui, Kadmiel, Sherebiah, Judah, *and* Mattaniah *who led* the thanksgiving *psalms*, he and his brethren. [9]Also Bakbukiah and Unni, their brethren, *stood* across from them in *their* duties.

[10]Jeshua begot Joiakim, Joiakim begot Eliashib, Eliashib begot Joiada, [11]Joiada begot Jonathan, and Jonathan begot Jaddua.

[12]Now in the days of Joiakim, the priests, the heads of the fathers' *houses were:* of Seraiah, Meraiah; of Jeremiah, Hananiah; [13]of Ezra, Meshullam; of Amariah, Jehohanan; [14]of Melichu,[a] Jonathan; of Shebaniah,[b] Joseph; [15]of Harim,[a] Adna; of Meraioth,[b] Helkai; [16]of Iddo, Zechariah; of Ginnethon, Meshullam; [17]of Abijah, Zichri; *the son* of Minjamin;[a] of Moadiah,[b] Piltai; [18]of Bilgah, Shammua; of Shemaiah, Jehonathan; [19]of Joiarib, Mattenai; of Jedaiah, Uzzi; [20]of Sallai,[a] Kallai; of Amok, Eber; [21]of Hilkiah, Hashabiah; *and* of Jedaiah, Nethanel.

[22]During the reign of Darius the Persian, a record *was also kept* of the Levites and priests *who had been* heads of their fathers' *houses* in the days of Eliashib, Joiada, Johanan, and Jaddua. [23]The sons of Levi, the heads of the fathers' *houses* until the days of Johanan the son of Eliashib, *were* written in the book of the chronicles.

[24]And the heads of the Levites *were* Hashabiah, Sherebiah, and Jeshua the son of Kadmiel, with their brothers across from them, to praise *and* give thanks, group alternating with group, according to the command of David the man of God. [25]Mattaniah, Bakbukiah, Obadiah, Meshullam, Talmon, and Akkub *were* gatekeepers keeping the watch at the storerooms of the gates. [26]These *lived* in the days of Joiakim the son of Jeshua, the son of Jozadak,[a] and in the days of Nehemiah the governor, and of Ezra the priest, the scribe.

Nehemiah Dedicates the Wall

[27]Now at the dedication of the wall of Jerusalem they sought out the Levites in all their places, to bring them to Jerusalem to celebrate the dedication with gladness, both with thanksgivings and singing, *with* cymbals and stringed instruments and harps. [28]And the sons of the singers gathered together from the countryside around Jerusalem, from the villages of the Netophathites, [29]from the house of Gilgal, and from the fields of Geba and Azmaveth; for the singers had built themselves villages all around Jerusalem. [30]Then the priests and Levites purified themselves, and purified the people, the gates, and the wall.

[31]So I brought the leaders of Judah up on the wall, and appointed two large thanksgiving choirs. *One* went to the right hand on the wall toward the Refuse Gate. [32]After them went Hoshaiah and half of the leaders of Judah, [33]and Azariah, Ezra, Meshullam, [34]Judah, Benjamin, Shemaiah, Jeremiah, [35]and some of the priests' sons with trumpets—Zechariah the son of Jonathan, the son of Shemaiah, the son of Mattaniah, the son of Michaiah, the son of Zaccur, the son of Asaph, [36]and his brethren, Shemaiah, Azarel, Milalai, Gilalai, Maai, Nethanel, Judah, *and* Hanani, with the musical instruments of

12:4 [a]Or *Ginnethon* (compare verse 16) 12:14 [a]Or *Malluch* (compare verse 2) [b]Or *Shechaniah* (compare verse 3) 12:15 [a]Or *Rehum* (compare verse 3) [b]Or *Meremoth* (compare verse 3) 12:17 [a]Or *Mijamin* (compare verse 5) [b]Or *Maadiah* (compare verse 5) 12:20 [a]Or *Sallu* (compare verse 7) 12:26 [a]Spelled *Jehozadak* in 1 Chronicles 6:14

David the man of God. And Ezra the scribe *went* before them. [37]By the Fountain Gate, in front of them, they went up the stairs of the City of David, on the stairway of the wall, beyond the house of David, as far as the Water Gate eastward.

[38]The other thanksgiving choir went the opposite *way,* and I *was* behind them with half of the people on the wall, going past the Tower of the Ovens as far as the Broad Wall, [39]and above the Gate of Ephraim, above the Old Gate, above the Fish Gate, the Tower of Hananel, the Tower of the Hundred, as far as the Sheep Gate; and they stopped by the Gate of the Prison.

[40]So the two thanksgiving choirs stood in the house of God, likewise I and the half of the rulers with me; [41]and the priests, Eliakim, Maaseiah, Minjamin,[a] Michaiah, Elioenai, Zechariah, *and* Hananiah, with trumpets; [42]also Maaseiah, Shemaiah, Eleazar, Uzzi, Jehohanan, Malchijah, Elam, and Ezer. The singers sang loudly with Jezrahiah the director.

[43]Also that day they offered great sacrifices, and rejoiced, for God had made them rejoice with great joy; the women and the children also rejoiced, so that the joy of Jerusalem was heard afar off.

Temple Responsibilities

[44]And at the same time some were appointed over the rooms of the storehouse for the offerings, the firstfruits, and the tithes, to gather into them from the fields of the cities the portions specified by the Law for the priests and Levites; for Judah rejoiced over the priests and Levites who ministered. [45]Both the singers and the gatekeepers kept the charge of their God and the charge of the purification, according to the command of David *and* Solomon his son. [46]For in the days of David and Asaph of old *there were* chiefs of the singers, and songs of praise and thanksgiving to God. [47]In the days of Zerubbabel and in the days of Nehemiah all Israel gave the portions for the singers and the gatekeepers, a portion for each day. They also consecrated *holy things* for the Levites, and the Levites consecrated *them* for the children of Aaron.

Principles of Separation

13 On that day they read from the Book of Moses in the hearing of the people, and in it was found written that no Ammonite or Moabite should ever come into the assembly of God, [2]because they had not met the children of Israel with bread and water, but hired Balaam against them to curse them. However, our God turned the curse into a blessing. [3]So it was, when they had heard the Law, that they separated all the mixed multitude from Israel.

The Reforms of Nehemiah

[4]Now before this, Eliashib the priest, having authority over the storerooms of the house of our God, *was* allied with Tobiah. [5]And he had prepared for him a large room, where previously they had stored the grain offerings, the frankincense, the articles, the tithes of grain, the new wine and oil, which were commanded *to be given* to the Levites and singers and gatekeepers, and the offerings for the priests. [6]But during all this I was not in Jerusalem, for in the thirty-second year of Artaxerxes king of Babylon I had returned to the king. Then after certain days I obtained leave from the king, [7]and I came to Jerusalem and discovered the evil that Eliashib had done for Tobiah, in

12:41 [a]Or *Mijamin* (compare verse 5)

12:43 "The children rejoiced—and their hosannas were not despised, but are recorded to their praise. All that share in public mercies, ought to join in public thanksgivings." *John Wesley*

13:1–3 The Church needs to thunder God's Law from its pulpits. It will not only awaken the sinner in the pew, but it will separate those who are tares among the wheat. God's Law will arouse the false convert to his true condition before a holy God.

POINTS FOR OPEN-AIR PREACHING

13:17

Contending or Contentious?

As you are contending for the faith, of course you want to always make sure you are respectful, congenial, and uncompromising. But people won't stay and listen to boring preaching, so you have to be a bit "on the edge." Christians sometimes think that it's unloving to speak in such a way, but it is necessary if you want to hold your hearers. When I share the gospel with one or two people, there is an obvious gentleness in my tone. However, if you heard me preach in the open air, it may seem provocative or contentious. This is because if I preached the same way I speak, I would never hold a crowd. It is important in both cases that I am motivated by love, but if I don't keep the preaching "on the edge," I will lose my hearers in minutes (if not seconds).

John Wesley put it this way: "In the streets a man must from beginning to end be intense, and for that very reason he must be condensed and concentrated in his thought and utterance." This "intense" preaching may be misunderstood by those who don't know why it's there. The problem is that when we read the Gospels, we don't see the passion involved in its discourses. When Jesus spoke, there were those in the crowd who hated Him and wanted to kill Him. People undoubtedly called out, accusing Him of blasphemy, or challenging Him with questions. The atmosphere likely would have been electric. That's the atmosphere that holds a crowd's attention. To become passive in the name of love and gentleness will pull the plug out and the electricity will immediately leave. (See Spurgeon's thoughts on page 1743.)

So be ready, because you may be accused of preaching without love. The accusations almost always come from those brethren who have never preached in the open air. When speaking of open-air preaching, *R. A. Torrey* said, "Don't be soft. One of these nice, namby-pamby, sentimental sort of fellows in an open-air meeting, the crowd cannot and will not stand. The temptation to throw a brick or a rotten apple at him is perfectly irresistible, and one can hardly blame the crowd."

preparing a room for him in the courts of
the house of God. 8And it grieved me bitterly; therefore I threw all the household
goods of Tobiah out of the room. 9Then I
commanded them to cleanse the rooms;
and I brought back into them the articles
of the house of God, with the grain offering and the frankincense.

10I also realized that the portions for
the Levites had not been given *them;* for
each of the Levites and the singers who
did the work had gone back to his field.
11So I contended with the rulers, and
said, "Why is the house of God forsaken?"
And I gathered them together and set
them in their place. 12Then all Judah
brought the tithe of the grain and the
new wine and the oil to the storehouse.
13And I appointed as treasurers over the
storehouse Shelemiah the priest and
Zadok the scribe, and of the Levites,
Pedaiah; and next to them *was* Hanan the
son of Zaccur, the son of Mattaniah; for
they were considered faithful, and their
task *was* to distribute to their brethren.

14Remember me, O my God, concerning this, and do not wipe out my good
deeds that I have done for the house of
my God, and for its services!

15In those days I saw *people* in Judah
treading wine presses on the Sabbath,
and bringing in sheaves, and loading donkeys with wine, grapes, figs, and all *kinds
of* burdens, which they brought into Jerusalem on the Sabbath day. And I warned
them about the day on which they were
selling provisions. 16Men of Tyre dwelt
there also, who brought in fish and all
kinds of goods, and sold *them* on the Sabbath to the children of Judah, and in
Jerusalem.

17Then I contended with the nobles of
Judah, and said to them, "What evil thing
is this that you do, by which you profane
the Sabbath day? 18Did not your fathers
do thus, and did not our God bring all
this disaster on us and on this city? Yet
you bring added wrath on Israel by profaning the Sabbath."

19So it was, at the gates of Jerusalem,
as it began to be dark before the Sabbath,
that I commanded the gates to be shut,
and charged that they must not be opened
till after the Sabbath. Then I posted *some*

"The Christian ideal has not been tried and found wanting. It has been found difficult and left untried."

G. K. Chesterton

of my servants at the gates, *so that* no burdens would be brought in on the Sabbath day. [20]Now the merchants and sellers of all kinds of wares lodged outside Jerusalem once or twice.

[21]Then I warned them, and said to them, "Why do you spend the night around the wall? If you do *so* again, I will lay hands on you!" From that time on they came no *more* on the Sabbath. [22]And I commanded the Levites that they should cleanse themselves, and that they should go and guard the gates, to sanctify the Sabbath day.

Remember me, O my God, *concerning* this also, and spare me according to the greatness of Your mercy!

[23]In those days I also saw Jews *who* had married women of Ashdod, Ammon, *and* Moab. [24]And half of their children spoke the language of Ashdod, and could not speak the language of Judah, but spoke according to the language of one or the other people.

[25]So I contended with them and cursed them, struck some of them and pulled out their hair, and made them swear by God, *saying,* "You shall not give your daughters as wives to their sons, nor take their daughters for your sons or yourselves. [26]Did not Solomon king of Israel sin by these things? Yet among many nations there was no king like him, who was beloved of his God; and God made him king over all Israel. Nevertheless pagan women caused even him to sin. [27]Should we then hear of your doing all this great evil, transgressing against our God by marrying pagan women?"

A religion which costs nothing is worth nothing. Awake before it is too late. Awake and repent. Awake and be converted. Awake and believe. Awake and pray. Rest not till you give a satisfactory answer to my question, 'What does it cost?'

J. C. RYLE

[28]And *one* of the sons of Joiada, the son of Eliashib the high priest, *was* a son-in-law of Sanballat the Horonite; therefore I drove him from me.

[29]Remember them, O my God, because they have defiled the priesthood and the covenant of the priesthood and the Levites.

[30]Thus I cleansed them of everything pagan. I also assigned duties to the priests and the Levites, each to his service, [31]and *to bringing* the wood offering and the firstfruits at appointed times.

Remember me, O my God, for good!

Esther

The King Dethrones Queen Vashti

1 Now it came to pass in the days of
Ahasuerus[a] (this *was* the Ahasuerus
who reigned over one hundred and
twenty-seven provinces, from India to
Ethiopia), 2in those days when King
Ahasuerus sat on the throne of his kingdom, which *was* in Shushan[a] the citadel,
3*that* in the third year of his reign he
made a feast for all his officials and servants—the powers of Persia and Media,
the nobles, and the princes of the provinces *being* before him— 4when he showed
the riches of his glorious kingdom and
the splendor of his excellent majesty for
many days, one hundred and eighty days
in all.

5And when these days were completed, the king made a feast lasting
seven days for all the people who were
present in Shushan the citadel, from great
to small, in the court of the garden of the
king's palace. 6*There were* white and blue
linen *curtains* fastened with cords of fine
linen and purple on silver rods and marble pillars; *and the* couches *were* of gold
and silver on a *mosaic* pavement of alabaster, turquoise, and white and black
marble. 7And they served drinks in golden
vessels, each vessel being different from
the other, with royal wine in abundance,
according to the generosity of the king.
8In accordance with the law, the drinking
was not compulsory; for so the king had
ordered all the officers of his household,
that they should do according to each
man's pleasure.

9Queen Vashti also made a feast for
the women *in* the royal palace which *belonged* to King Ahasuerus.

10On the seventh day, when the heart
of the king was merry with wine, he commanded Mehuman, Biztha, Harbona,
Bigtha, Abagtha, Zethar, and Carcas, seven
eunuchs who served in the presence of
King Ahasuerus, 11to bring Queen Vashti
before the king, *wearing* her royal crown,
in order to show her beauty to the people
and the officials, for she *was* beautiful to
behold. 12But Queen Vashti refused to
come at the king's command *brought* by
his eunuchs; therefore the king was furious, and his anger burned within him.

13Then the king said to the wise men
who understood the times (for this *was*
the king's manner toward all who knew
law and justice, 14those closest to him *being* Carshena, Shethar, Admatha, Tarshish,
Meres, Marsena, and Memucan, the seven
princes of Persia and Media, who had access to the king's presence, *and* who ranked
highest in the kingdom): 15"What *shall we*
do to Queen Vashti, according to law, because she did not obey the command of
King Ahasuerus *brought to her* by the
eunuchs?"

16And Memucan answered before the
king and the princes: "Queen Vashti has
not only wronged the king, but also all

1:1 [a]Generally identified with Xerxes I (485–464 B.C.) **1:2** [a]Or *Susa*, and so throughout this book

the princes, and all the people who *are* in
all the provinces of King Ahasuerus.
17For the queen's behavior will become
known to all women, so that they will despise their husbands in their eyes, when
they report, 'King Ahasuerus commanded
Queen Vashti to be brought in before
him, but she did not come.' 18This very
day the *noble* ladies of Persia and Media
will say to all the king's officials that they
have heard of the behavior of the queen.
Thus *there will be* excessive contempt and
wrath. 19If it pleases the king, let a royal
decree go out from him, and let it be recorded in the laws of the Persians and the
Medes, so that it will not be altered, that
Vashti shall come no more before King
Ahasuerus; and let the king give her royal
position to another who is better than
she. 20When the king's decree which he
will make is proclaimed throughout all
his empire (for it is great), all wives will
honor their husbands, both great and
small."

21And the reply pleased the king and
the princes, and the king did according
to the word of Memucan. 22Then he sent
letters to all the king's provinces, to each
province in its own script, and to every
people in their own language, that each
man should be master in his own house,
and speak in the language of his own
people.

Esther Becomes Queen

2 After these things, when the wrath of
King Ahasuerus subsided, he remembered Vashti, what she had done, and
what had been decreed against her. 2Then
the king's servants who attended him
said: "Let beautiful young virgins be
sought for the king; 3and let the king appoint officers in all the provinces of his
kingdom, that they may gather all the
beautiful young virgins to Shushan the
citadel, into the women's quarters, under
the custody of Hegai[a] the king's eunuch,
custodian of the women. And let beauty
preparations be given *them.* 4Then let the
young woman who pleases the king be
queen instead of Vashti."

This thing pleased the king, and he
did so.

5In Shushan the citadel there was a
certain Jew whose name *was* Mordecai the
son of Jair, the son of Shimei, the son of
Kish, a Benjamite. 6*Kish*[a] had been carried
away from Jerusalem with the captives
who had been captured with Jeconiah[b]
king of Judah, whom Nebuchadnezzar
the king of Babylon had carried away.
7And *Mordecai* had brought up Hadassah,
that *is,* Esther, his uncle's daughter, for
she had neither father nor mother. The
young woman *was* lovely and beautiful.
When her father and mother died,
Mordecai took her as his own daughter.

8So it was, when the king's command
and decree were heard, and when many
young women were gathered at Shushan
the citadel, *under* the custody of Hegai,
that Esther also was taken to the king's
palace, into the care of Hegai the custodian of the women. 9Now the young woman pleased him, and she obtained his
favor; so he readily gave beauty preparations to her, besides her allowance. Then
seven choice maidservants were provided
for her from the king's palace, and he
moved her and her maidservants to the
best *place* in the house of the women.

10Esther had not revealed her people
or family, for Mordecai had charged her
not to reveal *it.* 11And every day Mordecai
paced in front of the court of the women's
quarters, to learn of Esther's welfare and
what was happening to her.

12Each young woman's turn came to
go in to King Ahasuerus after she had

2:3 [a]Hebrew *Hege* 2:6 [a]Literally *Who* [b]Same as *Jehoiachin,* 2 Kings 24:6 and elsewhere

1:17 Some say that the queen had good reason to refuse. God forbid that we should ever refuse to be seen as the Bride of Christ and dishonor our Bridegroom (see 2 Cor. 11:2). By our boldness we encourage others to be bold in their faith. See Phil. 1:14.

completed twelve months' preparation, according to the regulations for the women,
for thus were the days of their preparation apportioned: six months with oil of
myrrh, and six months with perfumes
and preparations for beautifying women.
[13]Thus *prepared, each* young woman went
to the king, and she was given whatever
she desired to take with her from the women's quarters to the king's palace. [14]In
the evening she went, and in the morning
she returned to the second house of the
women, to the custody of Shaashgaz, the
king's eunuch who kept the concubines.
She would not go in to the king again unless the king delighted in her and called
for her by name.

[15]Now when the turn came for Esther
the daughter of Abihail the uncle of Mordecai, who had taken her as his daughter,
to go in to the king, she requested nothing but what Hegai the king's eunuch, the
custodian of the women, advised. And
Esther obtained favor in the sight of all
who saw her. [16]So Esther was taken to
King Ahasuerus, into his royal palace, in
the tenth month, which *is* the month of
Tebeth, in the seventh year of his reign.
[17]The king loved Esther more than all the
other women, and she obtained grace and
favor in his sight more than all the virgins; so he set the royal crown upon her
head and made her queen instead of Vashti.
[18]Then the king made a great feast, the
Feast of Esther, for all his officials and
servants; and he proclaimed a holiday in
the provinces and gave gifts according to
the generosity of a king.

Mordecai Discovers a Plot

[19]When virgins were gathered together a second time, Mordecai sat within
the king's gate. [20]*Now* Esther had not revealed her family and her people, just as
Mordecai had charged her, for Esther
obeyed the command of Mordecai as when
she was brought up by him.

[21]In those days, while Mordecai sat
within the king's gate, two of the king's
eunuchs, Bigthan and Teresh, doorkeepers, became furious and sought to lay
hands on King Ahasuerus. [22]So the matter became known to Mordecai, who told
Queen Esther, and Esther informed the
king in Mordecai's name. [23]And when an
inquiry was made into the matter, it was
confirmed, and both were hanged on a
gallows; and it was written in the book of
the chronicles in the presence of the king.

Haman's Conspiracy Against the Jews

3 After these things King Ahasuerus
promoted Haman, the son of Hammedatha the Agagite, and advanced him
and set his seat above all the princes who
were with him. [2]And all the king's servants who *were* within the king's gate
bowed and paid homage to Haman, for
so the king had commanded concerning
him. But Mordecai would not bow or
pay homage. [3]Then the king's servants
who *were* within the king's gate said to
Mordecai, "Why do you transgress the
king's command?" [4]Now it happened,
when they spoke to him daily and he
would not listen to them, that they told
it to Haman, to see whether Mordecai's
words would stand; for *Mordecai* had told
them that he *was* a Jew. [5]When Haman
saw that Mordecai did not bow or pay
him homage, Haman was filled with
wrath. [6]But he disdained to lay hands on
Mordecai alone, for they had told him of
the people of Mordecai. Instead, Haman
sought to destroy all the Jews who *were*
throughout the whole kingdom of Ahasuerus—the people of Mordecai.

[7]In the first month, which is the

2:17 We obtain grace and favor from our King and are given the crown of life (James 1:12), but not because of our beauty. There is nothing in us that draws out the love of God. God loves us because He is love itself (1 John 4:8).

3:5 Jesus was invited to pay the devil homage, but He did not bow to the god of this age. See Luke 4:6–8 for His response when He was tempted to become a Satan worshiper.

3:12,13 *Displaying God's Justice and Mercy*

Esther is one of only two books in the Bible in which God is not mentioned directly (the other is Song of Songs). Though He is not identified by name in this small book, He reveals an important spiritual truth in its few pages. The story of Haman and King Xerxes is a redemption story displaying both God's justice and His mercy.

Haman is a picture of Satan, and he is called "the enemy of the Jews" (3:10; cf. Matthew 10:39). His aim is "to destroy, to kill, and to annihilate" (3:13; cf. John 10:10), and he is "the adversary and the enemy" of God's people (7:6; cf. 1 Peter 5:8). Prideful Haman was infuriated when Mordecai refused to bow to him, just as Satan desires to show himself equal to God and receive mans' worship (Matt. 4:9).

Through Haman's influence, the king has issued a death warrant against the Jews because "they do not keep the king's laws" (3:8). Once a decree is signed by the king, it is irrevocable. Because he is a righteous and just king, he cannot go back on his declared word. His law is immutable and His death decree must remain in place.

However, the king has a plan to render the effects of this death sentence null and void, to save the citizens in his kingdom. He issues a second decree allowing the Jews to defend themselves—giving them a way to counter the enemy's intent and preserve their lives.

In the same way, due to Satan's influence in leading Adam and Eve to sin, God has issued the death penalty against all mankind—because we do not keep the King's Laws. This decree is irrevocable. Because He is righteous and just, He cannot overlook it and just change His mind. Lawbreakers must be punished, and the sentence of death must remain in place. However, God has also made a way for us to avoid the death penalty. He Himself has provided our only defense against death—Christ's blood shed on the cross for our sins.

Note that although the king provided the way of escape, the people had to choose to take that way, or they would perish. He did not just automatically spare them all; they had to respond. If they had decided not to act on the opportunity they were given, they would have died. We too must choose to accept the way of deliverance that God has provided. If we do not, we will perish. As with the gospel message, the king's decree was "published for all people" (8:13) and as a result many Gentiles were converted (8:17).

It's also interesting that the people didn't react by blaming the king for issuing the death decree in the first place, and then refuse to accept the solution. Instead, they took the solution that was offered, and rejoiced at the life they gained with the second decree. How many unbelievers complain about God taking human life and especially about His decreeing eternal death and hell. Yet they stubbornly refuse to accept the solution He graciously offers to save them from destruction!

month of Nisan, in the twelfth year of
King Ahasuerus, they cast Pur (that *is*, the
lot), before Haman to determine the day
and the month,[a] until *it fell on the* twelfth
month,[b] which *is* the month of Adar.
8Then Haman said to King Ahasuerus,
"There is a certain people scattered and
dispersed among the people in all the
provinces of your kingdom; their laws *are*
different from all *other* people's, and they
do not keep the king's laws. Therefore it
is not fitting for the king to let them remain. 9If it pleases the king, let *a decree*
be written that they be destroyed, and I
will pay ten thousand talents of silver
into the hands of those who do the work,
to bring *it* into the king's treasuries."
10So the king took his signet ring from
his hand and gave it to Haman, the son of
Hammedatha the Agagite, the enemy of
the Jews. 11And the king said to Haman,
"The money and the people *are* given to
you, to do with them as seems good to
you."
12Then the king's scribes were called
on the thirteenth day of the first month,
and *a decree* was written according to all
that Haman commanded—to the king's
satraps, to the governors who *were* over
each province, to the officials of all people, to every province according to its
script, and to every people in their language. In the name of King Ahasuerus it
was written, and sealed with the king's
signet ring. 13And the letters were sent by
couriers into all the king's provinces, to

3:7 [a]Septuagint adds *to destroy the people of Mordecai in one day*; Vulgate adds *the nation of the Jews should be destroyed*. [b]Following Masoretic Text and Vulgate; Septuagint reads *and the lot fell on the fourteenth of the month*.

destroy, to kill, and to annihilate all the Jews, both young and old, little children and women, in one day, on the thirteenth *day* of the twelfth *month,* which *is* the month of Adar, and to plunder their possessions.[a] [14]A copy of the document was to be issued as law in every province, being published for all people, that they should be ready for that day. [15]The couriers went out, hastened by the king's command; and the decree was proclaimed in Shushan the citadel. So the king and Haman sat down to drink, but the city of Shushan was perplexed.

Esther Agrees to Help the Jews

4

When Mordecai learned all that had happened, he tore his clothes and put on sackcloth and ashes, and went out into the midst of the city. He cried out with a loud and bitter cry. [2]He went as far as the front of the king's gate, for no one *might* enter the king's gate clothed with sackcloth. [3]And in every province where the king's command and decree arrived, *there was* great mourning among the Jews, with fasting, weeping, and wailing; and many lay in sackcloth and ashes.

[4]So Esther's maids and eunuchs came and told her, and the queen was deeply distressed. Then she sent garments to clothe Mordecai and take his sackcloth away from him, but he would not accept *them.* [5]Then Esther called Hathach, *one* of the king's eunuchs whom he had appointed to attend her, and she gave him a command concerning Mordecai, to learn what and why this *was.* [6]So Hathach went out to Mordecai in the city square that *was* in front of the king's gate. [7]And Mordecai told him all that had happened to him, and the sum of money that Haman had promised to pay into the king's treasuries to destroy the Jews. [8]He also gave him a copy of the written decree for their destruction, which was given at Shushan, that he might show it to Esther and explain it to her, and that he might command her to go in to the king to make supplication to him and plead before him for her people. [9]So Hathach returned and told Esther the words of Mordecai.

[10]Then Esther spoke to Hathach, and gave him a command for Mordecai: [11]"All the king's servants and the people of the king's provinces know that any man or woman who goes into the inner court to the king, who has not been called, *he has* but one law: put *all* to death, except the one to whom the king holds out the golden scepter, that he may live. Yet I myself have not been called to go in to the king these thirty days." [12]So they told Mordecai Esther's words.

[13]And Mordecai told *them* to answer Esther: "Do not think in your heart that you will escape in the king's palace any more than all the other Jews. [14]For if you remain completely silent at this time, relief and deliverance will arise for the Jews from another place, but you and your father's house will perish. Yet who knows whether you have come to the kingdom for *such* a time as this?"

[15]Then Esther told *them* to reply to Mordecai: [16]"Go, gather all the Jews who are present in Shushan, and fast for me; neither eat nor drink for three days, night or day. My maids and I will fast likewise. And so I will go to the king, which *is*

3:13 [a]Septuagint adds the text of the letter here.

4:14 God created you for this particular time in history. You weren't born in the Dark Ages, or in the eighteenth century. Your time is at hand. Today, seek and save that which is lost. Go into all the world and preach the gospel to every creature. Hand out a tract. Ask God for a divine encounter—a woman at the well (see John 4), someone He has prepared to receive the Word. You were born for such a time as this.

4:16 This is the attitude of one who has already died to self—the same attitude that should be shared by all who have been crucified with Christ (see Gal. 2:20). See Acts 21:13 for Paul's resolve.

"Jesus called people to follow Him—and there was only one place He was going: a cross. The true nature of spiritual living involves sacrifice, duty, and commitment." *James Emery White*

against the law; and if I perish, I perish!"
17So Mordecai went his way and did
according to all that Esther commanded
him.[a]

Esther's Banquet

5 Now it happened on the third day
that Esther put on *her* royal *robes* and
stood in the inner court of the king's
palace, across from the king's house,
while the king sat on his royal throne in
the royal house, facing the entrance of
the house.[a] 2So it was, when the king saw
Queen Esther standing in the court, *that*
she found favor in his sight, and the king
held out to Esther the golden scepter
that *was* in his hand. Then Esther went
near and touched the top of the scepter.
3And the king said to her, "What do
you wish, Queen Esther? What *is* your request? It shall be given to you—up to half
the kingdom!"

4So Esther answered, "If it pleases the
king, let the king and Haman come today
to the banquet that I have prepared for
him."

5Then the king said, "Bring Haman
quickly, that he may do as Esther has
said." So the king and Haman went to the
banquet that Esther had prepared.

6At the banquet of wine the king said
to Esther, "What *is* your petition? It shall
be granted you. What *is* your request, up
to half the kingdom? It shall be done!"
7Then Esther answered and said, "My
petition and request *is this:* 8If I have
found favor in the sight of the king, and
if it pleases the king to grant my petition
and fulfill my request, then let the king
and Haman come to the banquet which I
will prepare for them, and tomorrow I
will do as the king has said."

Haman's Plot Against Mordecai

9So Haman went out that day joyful
and with a glad heart; but when Haman
saw Mordecai in the king's gate, and that
he did not stand or tremble before him,
he was filled with indignation against Mordecai. 10Nevertheless Haman restrained
himself and went home, and he sent and
called for his friends and his wife Zeresh.
11Then Haman told them of his great
riches, the multitude of his children,
everything in which the king had promoted him, and how he had advanced
him above the officials and servants of
the king.

12Moreover Haman said, "Besides,
Queen Esther invited no one but me to
come in with the king to the banquet that
she prepared; and tomorrow I am again
invited by her, along with the king. 13Yet
all this avails me nothing, so long as I see
Mordecai the Jew sitting at the king's gate."

14Then his wife Zeresh and all his
friends said to him, "Let a gallows be made,
fifty cubits high, and in the morning suggest to the king that Mordecai be hanged
on it; then go merrily with the king to the
banquet."

And the thing pleased Haman; so he
had the gallows made.

4:17 [a]Septuagint adds a prayer of Mordecai here. 5:1 [a]Sep-
tuagint adds many extra details in verses 1 and 2.

5:2,3 God extends favor toward us as we stand before Him clothed in the righteousness of Christ. We can boldly draw near the throne of grace, having obtained redemption in Christ (see Heb. 4:16). It is now the Father's good pleasure to give us the kingdom (Luke 12:32).

5:9,13 When pride rears its ugly head, it robs us of our joy. The human ego hankers for the empty praise of men. May we live only for the praise of God.

"How much eager-beaver religious work is done out of a carnal desire to make good… The true Christian should turn away from all this. Especially should ministers of the gospel search their own hearts and look deep into their inner motives. No man is worthy to succeed until he is willing to fail. No man is morally worthy of success in religious activities until he is willing that the honor of succeeding should go to another if God so wills." *A. W. Tozer*

5:14 This gallows was 75 feet in height and is believed to be for impaling rather than for conventional hanging.

SPRINGBOARDS FOR PREACHING AND WITNESSING

Some Personal Questions

6:1 Do you like to snuggle up in a warm bed on a cold night? Do you have a favorite position for going to sleep? Have you ever woken up from a nightmare, and taken several minutes to shake off a feeling of terror?

Has your whole body suddenly "jumped" because you thought you were taking a step, just before you dropped off to sleep?

Do you get annoyed when someone asks you personal questions, or do you feel a sense of identification, because you've had these same experiences?

I hope you do identify with me. This is because it is the knowledge that you and I are similar that drives me to try to reach you with the gospel.

We have many of the same loves, fears, desires, and concerns. You, like me, want to enjoy the pleasures of this life. No one in his right mind wants to be unhappy, and you therefore instinctively don't want to die. Everything within you recoils at the thought of death. It is the ultimate root-canal for which there is no painkiller outside of conversion to Jesus Christ.

So, if you don't know the Lord, ask yourself some personal questions about me. What is my motive for pleading with you like this? I don't get paid for doing this. I am not asking for your money, nor am I trying to get you to join a church. It is simply out of a deep concern for your eternal welfare. Please, repent and trust the Savior before death seizes on you and it is too late.

The King Honors Mordecai

6 That night the king could not sleep.
So one was commanded to bring the
book of the records of the chronicles; and
they were read before the king. 2And it
was found written that Mordecai had told
of Bigthana and Teresh, two of the king's
eunuchs, the doorkeepers who had sought
to lay hands on King Ahasuerus. 3Then
the king said, "What honor or dignity
has been bestowed on Mordecai for this?"

And the king's servants who attended
him said, "Nothing has been done for
him."

4So the king said, "Who *is* in the
court?" Now Haman had *just* entered the
outer court of the king's palace to suggest
that the king hang Mordecai on the gallows
that he had prepared for him.

5The king's servants said to him,
"Haman is there, standing in the court."

And the king said, "Let him come in."

6So Haman came in, and the king
asked him, "What shall be done for the
man whom the king delights to honor?"

Now Haman thought in his heart,
"Whom would the king delight to honor
more than me?" 7And Haman answered
the king, "*For* the man whom the king
delights to honor, 8let a royal robe be
brought which the king has worn, and a
horse on which the king has ridden,
which has a royal crest placed on its
head. 9Then let this robe and horse be
delivered to the hand of one of the king's
most noble princes, that he may array the
man whom the king delights to honor.
Then parade him on horseback through
the city square, and proclaim before him:
'Thus shall it be done to the man whom
the king delights to honor!' "

10Then the king said to Haman,
"Hurry, take the robe and the horse, as
you have suggested, and do so for Mordecai
the Jew who sits within the king's
gate! Leave nothing undone of all that
you have spoken."

11So Haman took the robe and the
horse, arrayed Mordecai and led him on
horseback through the city square, and
proclaimed before him, "Thus shall it be
done to the man whom the king delights
to honor!"

12Afterward Mordecai went back to
the king's gate. But Haman hurried to his
house, mourning and with his head cov-

6:2,3 Though the world may not acknowledge our good deeds, God never forgets. In Christ, our works follow us (see Rev. 14:13).

ered. [13]When Haman told his wife Zeresh and all his friends everything that had happened to him, his wise men and his wife Zeresh said to him, "If Mordecai, before whom you have begun to fall, is of Jewish descent, you will not prevail against him but will surely fall before him."

[14]While they *were* still talking with him, the king's eunuchs came, and hastened to bring Haman to the banquet which Esther had prepared.

Haman Hanged Instead of Mordecai

7 So the king and Haman went to dine with Queen Esther. [2]And on the second day, at the banquet of wine, the king again said to Esther, "What *is* your petition, Queen Esther? It shall be granted you. And what *is* your request, up to half the kingdom? It shall be done!"

[3]Then Queen Esther answered and said, "If I have found favor in your sight, O king, and if it pleases the king, let my life be given me at my petition, and my people at my request. [4]For we have been sold, my people and I, to be destroyed, to be killed, and to be annihilated. Had we been sold as male and female slaves, I would have held my tongue, although the enemy could never compensate for the king's loss."

[5]So King Ahasuerus answered and said to Queen Esther, "Who is he, and where is he, who would dare presume in his heart to do such a thing?"

[6]And Esther said, "The adversary and enemy *is* this wicked Haman!"

So Haman was terrified before the king and queen.

[7]Then the king arose in his wrath from the banquet of wine *and went* into the palace garden; but Haman stood before Queen Esther, pleading for his life, for he saw that evil was determined against him by the king. [8]When the king returned from the palace garden to the place of the banquet of wine, Haman had fallen across the couch where Esther *was.* Then the king said, "Will he also assault the queen while I *am* in the house?"

As the word left the king's mouth, they covered Haman's face. [9]Now Harbonah, one of the eunuchs, said to the king, "Look! The gallows, fifty cubits high, which Haman made for Mordecai, who spoke good on the king's behalf, is standing at the house of Haman."

Then the king said, "Hang him on it!"

[10]So they hanged Haman on the gallows that he had prepared for Mordecai. Then the king's wrath subsided.

Esther Saves the Jews

8 On that day King Ahasuerus gave Queen Esther the house of Haman, the enemy of the Jews. And Mordecai came before the king, for Esther had told how he *was related* to her. [2]So the king took off his signet ring, which he had taken from Haman, and gave it to Mordecai; and Esther appointed Mordecai over the house of Haman.

[3]Now Esther spoke again to the king, fell down at his feet, and implored him with tears to counteract the evil of Haman the Agagite, and the scheme which he had devised against the Jews. [4]And the king held out the golden scepter toward Esther. So Esther arose and stood before the king, [5]and said, "If it pleases the king, and if I have found favor in his sight and the thing *seems* right to the king and I am

---

7:6 We have an adversary, Satan, who roams about as a roaring lion seeking whom he may devour (see 1 Pet. 5:8). Unrepentant sin gives the enemy permission to destroy.

7:9,10 The proud who erect gallows with the intention of destroying God's witnesses, the loyal servants of the King, have strung just enough rope to hang themselves. See Rom. 2:3. In the same way, the cross was Satan's defeat. His evil plot was turned into our victory.

8:4 "Last of all, let each child of God rejoice that *we have a guardian so near the throne*. Every Jew in Shushan must have felt hope when he remembered that the queen was a Jewess. To-day let us be glad that Jesus is exalted." *Charles Spurgeon*

pleasing in his eyes, let it be written to revoke the letters devised by Haman, the son of Hammedatha the Agagite, which he wrote to annihilate the Jews who *are* in all the king's provinces. 6For how can I endure to see the evil that will come to my people? Or how can I endure to see the destruction of my countrymen?"

7Then King Ahasuerus said to Queen Esther and Mordecai the Jew, "Indeed, I have given Esther the house of Haman, and they have hanged him on the gallows because he *tried to* lay his hand on the Jews. 8You yourselves write *a decree* concerning the Jews, as you please, in the king's name, and seal *it* with the king's signet ring; for whatever is written in the king's name and sealed with the king's signet ring no one can revoke."

9So the king's scribes were called at that time, in the third month, which *is* the month of Sivan, on the twenty-third *day;* and it was written, according to all that Mordecai commanded, to the Jews, the satraps, the governors, and the princes of the provinces from India to Ethiopia, one hundred and twenty-seven provinces *in all,* to every province in its own script, to every people in their own language, and to the Jews in their own script and language. 10And he wrote in the name of King Ahasuerus, sealed *it* with the king's signet ring, and sent letters by couriers on horseback, riding on royal horses bred from swift steeds.[a]

11By these letters the king permitted the Jews who *were* in every city to gather together and protect their lives—to destroy, kill, and annihilate all the forces of any people or province that would assault them, *both* little children and women, and to plunder their possessions, 12on one day in all the provinces of King Ahasuerus, on the thirteenth *day* of the twelfth month, which *is* the month of Adar.[a] 13A copy of the document was to be issued as a decree in every province and published for all people, so that the Jews would be ready on that day to avenge themselves on their enemies. 14The couriers who rode on royal horses went out, hastened and pressed on by the king's command. And the decree was issued in Shushan the citadel.

15So Mordecai went out from the presence of the king in royal apparel of blue and white, with a great crown of gold and a garment of fine linen and purple; and the city of Shushan rejoiced and was glad. 16The Jews had light and gladness, joy and honor. 17And in every province and city, wherever the king's command and decree came, the Jews had joy and gladness, a feast and a holiday. Then many of the people of the land became Jews, because fear of the Jews fell upon them.

Learn how to prove God's existence. See Rom. 1:20 comment.

The Jews Destroy Their Tormentors

9 Now in the twelfth month, that *is,* the month of Adar, on the thirteenth day, *the time* came for the king's command and his decree to be executed. On the day that the enemies of the Jews had hoped to overpower them, the opposite occurred, in that the Jews themselves overpowered those who hated them. 2The Jews gathered together in their cities throughout all the provinces of King Ahasuerus to lay hands on those who sought their harm. And no one could withstand them, because fear of them fell upon all people. 3And all the officials of the provinces, the satraps, the governors,

8:10 [a]Literally *sons of the swift horses* 8:12 [a]Septuagint adds the text of the letter here.

8:8 If the king's decree could be immutable, how much more is the decree of God? See His marvelous decree in Psa. 2:7,8.

and all those doing the king's work,
helped the Jews, because the fear of Mordecai fell upon them. 4For Mordecai *was*
great in the king's palace, and his fame
spread throughout all the provinces; for
this man Mordecai became increasingly
prominent. 5Thus the Jews defeated all
their enemies with the stroke of the sword,
with slaughter and destruction, and did
what they pleased with those who hated
them.

6And in Shushan the citadel the Jews
killed and destroyed five hundred men.
7Also Parshandatha, Dalphon, Aspatha,
8Poratha, Adalia, Aridatha, 9Parmashta,
Arisai, Aridai, and Vajezatha— 10the ten
sons of Haman the son of Hammedatha,
the enemy of the Jews—they killed; but
they did not lay a hand on the plunder.

11On that day the number of those who
were killed in Shushan the citadel was
brought to the king. 12And the king said
to Queen Esther, "The Jews have killed and
destroyed five hundred men in Shushan
the citadel, and the ten sons of Haman.
What have they done in the rest of the
king's provinces? Now what is your petition? It shall be granted to you. Or what
is your further request? It shall be done."

13Then Esther said, "If it pleases the
king, let it be granted to the Jews who *are*
in Shushan to do again tomorrow according to today's decree, and let Haman's ten
sons be hanged on the gallows."

14So the king commanded this to be
done; the decree was issued in Shushan,
and they hanged Haman's ten sons.

15And the Jews who *were* in Shushan
gathered together again on the fourteenth
day of the month of Adar and killed three
hundred men at Shushan; but they did
not lay a hand on the plunder.

16The remainder of the Jews in the
king's provinces gathered together and
protected their lives, had rest from their
enemies, and killed seventy-five thousand
of their enemies; but they did not lay a
hand on the plunder. 17*This was* on the
thirteenth day of the month of Adar. And
on the fourteenth of *the month*[a] they rested
and made it a day of feasting and gladness.

The Feast of Purim

18But the Jews who *were* at Shushan
assembled together on the thirteenth *day,*
as well as on the fourteenth; and on the
fifteenth of *the month*[a] they rested, and
made it a day of feasting and gladness.
19Therefore the Jews of the villages who
dwelt in the unwalled towns celebrated
the fourteenth day of the month of Adar
with gladness and feasting, as a holiday,
and for sending presents to one another.

We are to bear with those we cannot amend, and to be content with offering them to God. This is true resignation. And since He has borne our infirmities, we may well bear those of each other for His sake.

JOHN WESLEY

20And Mordecai wrote these things and
sent letters to all the Jews, near and far,
who *were* in all the provinces of King
Ahasuerus, 21to establish among them that
they should celebrate yearly the fourteenth and fifteenth days of the month of
Adar, 22as the days on which the Jews had
rest from their enemies, as the month
which was turned from sorrow to joy for
them, and from mourning to a holiday;

9:17 [a]Literally *it* 9:18 [a]Literally *it*

9:13 Esther had the ten sons of Haman hanged. This is a picture of "repentance toward God," when we rid ourselves of the enemy by putting to death the works of the flesh—the nature received from our father, the devil (see John 8:44; Eph. 2:2).

The works of the flesh are traced to transgression of the Ten Commandments (see 1 John 3:4). The ten sons of Haman (the ten sins of humanity) are rebellion against God, idolatry, blasphemy, Sabbath breaking, dishonoring parents, murder, adultery, theft, lying, and covetousness.

"Ignorance of the nature and design of the Law is at the bottom of most religious mistakes."

John Newton

that they should make them days of feasting and joy, of sending presents to one
another and gifts to the poor. 23So the
Jews accepted the custom which they had
begun, as Mordecai had written to them,
24because Haman, the son of Hammedatha the Agagite, the enemy of all the
Jews, had plotted against the Jews to annihilate them, and had cast Pur (that *is,*
the lot), to consume them and destroy
them; 25but when *Esther*[a] came before the
king, he commanded by letter that this[b]
wicked plot which *Haman* had devised
against the Jews should return on his own
head, and that he and his sons should be
hanged on the gallows.

26So they called these days Purim, after the name Pur. Therefore, because of
all the words of this letter, what they had
seen concerning this matter, and what
had happened to them, 27the Jews established and imposed it upon themselves
and their descendants and all who would
join them, that without fail they should
celebrate these two days every year, according to the written *instructions* and according to the *prescribed* time, 28*that* these
days *should be* remembered and kept
throughout every generation, every family, every province, and every city, that
these days of Purim should not fail *to be
observed* among the Jews, and *that* the
memory of them should not perish among
their descendants.

29Then Queen Esther, the daughter of
Abihail, with Mordecai the Jew, wrote with
full authority to confirm this second letter
about Purim. 30And *Mordecai* sent letters
to all the Jews, to the one hundred and
twenty-seven provinces of the kingdom of
Ahasuerus, *with* words of peace and truth,
31to confirm these days of Purim at their
appointed time, as Mordecai the Jew and
Queen Esther had prescribed for them,
and as they had decreed for themselves
and their descendants concerning matters
of their fasting and lamenting. 32So the
decree of Esther confirmed these matters
of Purim, and it was written in the book.

Mordecai's Advancement

10 And King Ahasuerus imposed
tribute on the land and *on* the islands of the sea. 2Now all the acts of his
power and his might, and the account of
the greatness of Mordecai, to which the
king advanced him, *are* they not written
in the book of the chronicles of the kings
of Media and Persia? 3For Mordecai the
Jew *was* second to King Ahasuerus, and
was great among the Jews and well received by the multitude of his brethren,
seeking the good of his people and speaking peace to all his countrymen.[a]

9:25 [a]Literally *she* or *it* [b]Literally *his* 10:3 [a]Literally *seed.* Septuagint and Vulgate add a dream of Mordecai here; Vulgate adds six more chapters.

9:27,28 Purim is celebrated annually on the 14th day of the Hebrew month of Adar, the day following the victory of the Jews over their enemies. As with all Jewish holidays, Purim begins at sundown on the previous day.

Memorize the Ten Commandments

Memorize the Ten Commandments using these special picture figures. Then test your memory, and grade yourself. Put each picture in your mind, and it will remind you of each commandment.

1. "You shall have no other gods before Me"
(God should be Number One)

2. "You shall not make for yourself a carved image"
(Don't bow down to anything but God)

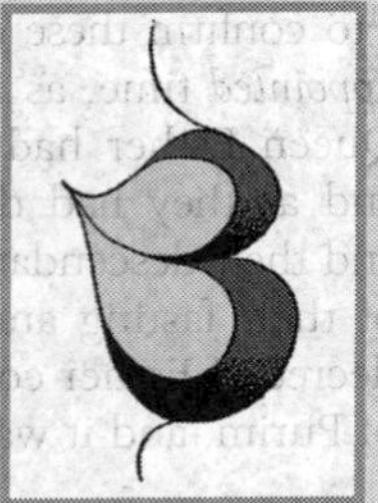

3. "You shall not take the name of the Lord your God in vain"
(Don't use your lips to dishonor God)

4. "Remember the Sabbath day, to keep it holy"
(Don't neglect the things of God)

5. "Honor your father and your mother"

6. "You shall not murder"

7. "You shall not commit adultery"
(Adultery leaves a heart broken)

8. "You shall not steal"

9. "You shall not lie"
(a "lying" nine)

10. "You shall not covet"
(want what others have)

Job

Job and His Family in Uz

1 There was a man in the land of Uz, whose name *was* Job; and that man was blameless and upright, and one who feared God and shunned evil. 2 And seven sons and three daughters were born to him. 3 Also, his possessions were seven thousand sheep, three thousand camels, five hundred yoke of oxen, five hundred female donkeys, and a very large household, so that this man was the greatest of all the people of the East.

4 And his sons would go and feast *in their* houses, each on his *appointed* day, and would send and invite their three sisters to eat and drink with them. 5 So it was, when the days of feasting had run their course, that Job would send and sanctify them, and he would rise early in the morning and offer burnt offerings *according to* the number of them all. For Job said, "It may be that my sons have sinned and cursed[a] God in their hearts." Thus Job did regularly.

Satan Attacks Job's Character

6 Now there was a day when the sons of God came to present themselves before the LORD, and Satan[a] also came among them. 7 And the LORD said to Satan, "From where do you come?"

So Satan answered the LORD and said, "From going to and fro on the earth, and from walking back and forth on it."

8 Then the LORD said to Satan, "Have you considered My servant Job, that *there is* none like him on the earth, a blameless and upright man, one who fears God and shuns evil?"

9 So Satan answered the LORD and said, "Does Job fear God for nothing? 10 Have You not made a hedge around him, around his household, and around all that he has on every side? You have blessed the work of his hands, and his possessions have increased in the land. 11 But now, stretch out Your hand and touch all that he has, and he will surely curse You to Your face!"

12 And the LORD said to Satan, "Behold, all that he has *is* in your power; only do not lay a hand on his *person*."

So Satan went out from the presence of the LORD.

Job Loses His Property and Children

13 Now there was a day when his sons and daughters *were* eating and drinking

1:5 [a]Literally *blessed,* but used here in the evil sense, and so in verse 11 and 2:5, 9 1:6 [a]Literally *the Adversary,* and so throughout this book

1:6 Satan is the accuser of the brethren. See Zech. 3:1; Rev. 12:10.

1:7 Never forget that you have an adversary who "walks about like a roaring lion, seeking whom he may devour" (1 Pet. 5:8). Notice the word "may." It is a word of permission. If you are in sin (his territory), he has permission to devour you. But you must "flee these things and pursue righteousness, godliness, faith, love, patience, gentleness. Fight the good fight of faith, lay hold on eternal life, to which you were also called and have confessed the good confession in the presence of many witnesses" (1 Tim. 6:11,12).

wine in their oldest brother's house; 14and
a messenger came to Job and said, "The
oxen were plowing and the donkeys feeding beside them, 15when the Sabeans[a]
raided *them* and took them away—indeed they have killed the servants with
the edge of the sword; and I alone have
escaped to tell you!"
16While he *was* still speaking, another
also came and said, "The fire of God fell
from heaven and burned up the sheep
and the servants, and consumed them;
and I alone have escaped to tell you!"
17While he *was* still speaking, another
also came and said, "The Chaldeans formed
three bands, raided the camels and took
them away, yes, and killed the servants
with the edge of the sword; and I alone
have escaped to tell you!"
18While he *was* still speaking, another
also came and said, "Your sons and daughters *were* eating and drinking wine in
their oldest brother's house, 19and suddenly a great wind came from across[a] the
wilderness and struck the four corners of
the house, and it fell on the young people, and they are dead; and I alone have
escaped to tell you!"
20Then Job arose, tore his robe, and
shaved his head; and he fell to the ground
and worshiped. 21And he said:

"Naked I came from my mother's womb,
And naked shall I return there.
The LORD gave, and the LORD has
taken away;
Blessed be the name of the LORD."

22In all this Job did not sin nor charge
God with wrong.

Satan Attacks Job's Health

2 Again there was a day when the sons
of God came to present themselves
before the LORD, and Satan came also
among them to present himself before
the LORD. 2And the LORD said to Satan,
"From where do you come?"
Satan answered the LORD and said,
"From going to and fro on the earth, and
from walking back and forth on it."
3Then the LORD said to Satan, "Have
you considered My servant Job, that *there*
is none like him on the earth, a blameless
and upright man, one who fears God and
shuns evil? And still he holds fast to his
integrity, although you incited Me against
him, to destroy him without cause."
4So Satan answered the LORD and said,
"Skin for skin! Yes, all that a man has he
will give for his life. 5But stretch out Your
hand now, and touch his bone and his
flesh, and he will surely curse You to Your
face!"
6And the LORD said to Satan, "Behold,
he is in your hand, but spare his life."
7So Satan went out from the presence
of the LORD, and struck Job with painful
boils from the sole of his foot to the crown
of his head. 8And he took for himself a
potsherd with which to scrape himself
while he sat in the midst of the ashes.
9Then his wife said to him, "Do you
still hold fast to your integrity? Curse God
and die!"
10But he said to her, "You speak as one
of the foolish women speaks. Shall we indeed accept good from God, and shall we

1:15 [a]Literally *Sheba* (compare 6:19) 1:19 [a]Septuagint omits *across.*

1:21 Job took the good with the bad, and gave God thanks. He knew that everything that comes to us comes by the will of God. There is His *permissive* will, and His *perfect* will. God obviously *allows* certain seemingly bad events to come to us, and we have His promise that whatever life throws at us is only for our good (Rom. 8:28).

2:9 "Friendly fire" can be as deadly as an enemy bullet. Always be mindful that attacks can come from the closest of friends and family. They are the ones who can hurt if you let your guard down and forget that you are not wrestling against flesh and blood (see Eph. 6:12–20). It was Peter who attempted to discourage Jesus from going to the cross. But Jesus knew the source of the attack and said, "Get behind me, Satan" (Matt. 16:23). Do the same in your heart when attacked in such a way. Keep your shield of faith held high.

not accept adversity?" In all this Job did
not sin with his lips.

Job's Three Friends

[11]Now when Job's three friends heard
of all this adversity that had come upon
him, each one came from his own
place—Eliphaz the Temanite, Bildad the
Shuhite, and Zophar the Naamathite. For
they had made an appointment together
to come and mourn with him, and to
comfort him. [12]And when they raised their
eyes from afar, and did not recognize
him, they lifted their voices and wept;
and each one tore his robe and sprinkled
dust on his head toward heaven. [13]So they
sat down with him on the ground seven
days and seven nights, and no one spoke
a word to him, for they saw that *his* grief
was very great.

Job Deplores His Birth

3 After this Job opened his mouth and
cursed the day of his *birth.* [2]And Job
spoke, and said:

[3]"May the day perish on which I was
born,
And the night *in which* it was said,
'A male child is conceived.'
[4]May that day be darkness;
May God above not seek it,
Nor the light shine upon it.
[5]May darkness and the shadow of
death claim it;
May a cloud settle on it;
May the blackness of the day terrify it.
[6]*As for* that night, may darkness seize it;
May it not rejoice[a] among the days of
the year,
May it not come into the number of
the months.
[7]Oh, may that night be barren!
May no joyful shout come into it!
[8]May those curse it who curse the day,
Those who are ready to arouse
Leviathan.
[9]May the stars of its morning be dark;
May it look for light, but *have* none,
And not see the dawning of the day;
[10]Because it did not shut up the doors
of my *mother's* womb,
Nor hide sorrow from my eyes.

[11]"Why did I not die at birth?
Why did I *not* perish when I came
from the womb?
[12]Why did the knees receive me?
Or why the breasts, that I should
nurse?
[13]For now I would have lain still and
been quiet,
I would have been asleep;
Then I would have been at rest
[14]With kings and counselors of the earth,
Who built ruins for themselves,
[15]Or with princes who had gold,
Who filled their houses *with* silver;
[16]Or *why* was I not hidden like a
stillborn child,
Like infants who never saw light?
[17]There the wicked cease *from*
troubling,
And there the weary are at rest.
[18]*There* the prisoners rest together;
They do not hear the voice of the
oppressor.
[19]The small and great are there,
And the servant *is* free from his master.

[20]"Why is light given to him who is in
misery,
And life to the bitter of soul,
[21]Who long for death, but it does not
come,
And search for it more than hidden
treasures;
[22]Who rejoice exceedingly,
And are glad when they can find the
grave?
[23]*Why is light given* to a man whose way
is hidden,
And whom God has hedged in?
[24]For my sighing comes before I eat,[a]
And my groanings pour out like
water.
[25]For the thing I greatly feared has

3:6 [a]Septuagint, Syriac, Targum, and Vulgate read *be joined.*
3:24 [a]Literally *my bread*

come upon me,
And what I dreaded has happened to
me.
26I am not at ease, nor am I quiet;
I have no rest, for trouble comes."

Eliphaz: Job Has Sinned

4 Then Eliphaz the Temanite answered
and said:
2"If one attempts a word with you, will
you become weary?
But who can withhold himself from
speaking?
3Surely you have instructed many,
And you have strengthened weak
hands.

Bear up the hands that hang down, by faith and prayer; support the tottering knees. Have you any days of fasting and prayer? Storm the throne of grace and persevere therein, and mercy will come down.

JOHN WESLEY

4Your words have upheld him who
was stumbling,
And you have strengthened the feeble
knees;
5But now it comes upon you, and you
are weary;
It touches you, and you are troubled.
6*Is* not your reverence your confidence?
And the integrity of your ways your
hope?

7"Remember now, who *ever* perished
being innocent?
Or where were the upright *ever* cut off?
8Even as I have seen,
Those who plow iniquity
And sow trouble reap the same.
9By the blast of God they perish,
And by the breath of His anger they
are consumed.
10The roaring of the lion,
The voice of the fierce lion,
And the teeth of the young lions are
broken.
11The old lion perishes for lack of prey,
And the cubs of the lioness are
scattered.

12"Now a word was secretly brought to
me,
And my ear received a whisper of it.
13In disquieting thoughts from the
visions of the night,
When deep sleep falls on men,
14Fear came upon me, and trembling,
Which made all my bones shake.
15Then a spirit passed before my face;
The hair on my body stood up.
16It stood still,
But I could not discern its

3:25 Christians have nothing to fear but God. Romans 8:28 is our wonderful safety net.

4:4 Irreducible complexity. In his book *Darwin's Black Box*, biochemistry professor *Michael J. Behe*, an evolutionist, acknowledges a "powerful challenge to Darwinian evolution"—something he calls "irreducible complexity." This refers to a system with interacting parts, which is so complex it could not have come together piece by piece and still function. He gives a simple example: the humble mousetrap. The mousetrap has five major components that make it functional. If any one of these components is missing, it will not function. It is worthless as a mousetrap until all the components are in place.

He explains that an irreducibly complex system cannot be produced by slight, successive modifications, "because any precursor to an irreducibly complex system that is missing a part is by definition nonfunctional ... Since natural selection can only choose systems that are already working, then if a biological system cannot be produced gradually it would have to arise as an integrated unit, in one fell swoop, for natural selection to have anything to act on."

One example in the human body is the knee joint, which contains at least 16 essential components. Since it is irreducibly complex, the knee could not have evolved gradually but must have been created all at once as a whole, fully functioning joint.

Charles Darwin admitted, "If it could be demonstrated that any complex organ existed which could not possibly have been formed by numerous, successive, slight modifications, my theory would absolutely break down" (*The Origin of Species*). For more on evolution, see Job 33:4 comment.

appearance.
A form *was* before my eyes;
There was silence;
Then I heard a voice *saying:*
[17]'Can a mortal be more righteous than
God?
Can a man be more pure than his
Maker?
[18]If He puts no trust in His servants,
If He charges His angels with error,
[19]How much more those who dwell in
houses of clay,
Whose foundation is in the dust,
Who are crushed before a moth?
[20]They are broken in pieces from
morning till evening;
They perish forever, with no one
regarding.
[21]Does not their own excellence go away?
They die, even without wisdom.'

Eliphaz: Job Is Chastened by God

5 "Call out now;
Is there anyone who will answer you?
And to which of the holy ones will
you turn?
[2]For wrath kills a foolish man,
And envy slays a simple one.
[3]I have seen the foolish taking root,
But suddenly I cursed his dwelling
place.
[4]His sons are far from safety,
They are crushed in the gate,
And *there is* no deliverer.
[5]Because the hungry eat up his
harvest,
Taking it even from the thorns,[a]
And a snare snatches their substance.[b]
[6]For affliction does not come from the
dust,
Nor does trouble spring from the
ground;
[7]Yet man is born to trouble,
As the sparks fly upward.

[8]"But as for me, I would seek God,
And to God I would commit my
cause—
[9]Who does great things, and
unsearchable,
Marvelous things without number.
[10]He gives rain on the earth,
And sends waters on the fields.
[11]He sets on high those who are lowly,
And those who mourn are lifted to
safety.
[12]He frustrates the devices of the crafty,
So that their hands cannot carry out
their plans.
[13]He catches the wise in their own
craftiness,
And the counsel of the cunning
comes quickly upon them.
[14]They meet with darkness in the
daytime,
And grope at noontime as in the night.
[15]But He saves the needy from the sword,
From the mouth of the mighty,
And from their hand.
[16]So the poor have hope,
And injustice shuts her mouth.

[17]"Behold, happy *is* the man whom God
corrects;
Therefore do not despise the
chastening of the Almighty.
[18]For He bruises, but He binds up;
He wounds, but His hands make
whole.
[19]He shall deliver you in six troubles,

5:5 [a]Septuagint reads *They shall not be taken from evil men;* Vulgate reads *And the armed man shall take him by violence.* [b]Septuagint reads *The might shall draw them off;* Vulgate reads *And the thirsty shall drink up their riches.*

4:17 Many people think so. There is a "generation that is pure in its own eyes, yet is not washed from its filthiness" (Prov. 30:12). They need the Law to show them that their heart is deceitfully wicked and their sin is exceedingly sinful. See how the Law works: Rom. 3:19,20; 7:7,13.

5:18 God's Law wounds us, so that the gospel can heal us and make us whole.

"If men do not understand the Law, they will not feel that they are sinners. And if they are not consciously sinners, they will never value the sin offering. There is no healing a man till the Law has wounded him, no making him alive till the Law has slain him." *Charles Spurgeon*

Yes, in seven no evil shall touch you.
20In famine He shall redeem you from death,
And in war from the power of the sword.
21You shall be hidden from the scourge of the tongue,
And you shall not be afraid of destruction when it comes.
22You shall laugh at destruction and famine,
And you shall not be afraid of the beasts of the earth.
23For you shall have a covenant with the stones of the field,
And the beasts of the field shall be at peace with you.
24You shall know that your tent *is* in peace;
You shall visit your dwelling and find nothing amiss.
25You shall also know that your descendants *shall be* many,
And your offspring like the grass of the earth.
26You shall come to the grave at a full age,
As a sheaf of grain ripens in its season.
27Behold, this we have searched out;
It *is* true.
Hear it, and know for yourself."

Job: My Complaint Is Just

6 Then Job answered and said:
2"Oh, that my grief were fully weighed,
And my calamity laid with it on the scales!
3For then it would be heavier than the sand of the sea—
Therefore my words have been rash.
4For the arrows of the Almighty *are* within me;
My spirit drinks in their poison;
The terrors of God are arrayed against me.
5Does the wild donkey bray when it has grass,
Or does the ox low over its fodder?
6Can flavorless food be eaten without salt?
Or is there *any* taste in the white of an egg?
7My soul refuses to touch them;
They *are* as loathsome food to me.

8"Oh, that I might have my request,
That God would grant *me* the thing that I long for!
9That it would please God to crush me,
That He would loose His hand and cut me off!
10Then I would still have comfort;
Though in anguish I would exult,
He will not spare;
For I have not concealed the words of the Holy One.

11"What strength do I have, that I should hope?
And what *is* my end, that I should prolong my life?
12*Is* my strength the strength of stones?
Or is my flesh bronze?
13*Is* my help not within me?
And is success driven from me?

14"To him who is afflicted, kindness *should be shown* by his friend,
Even though he forsakes the fear of the Almighty.
15My brothers have dealt deceitfully like a brook,
Like the streams of the brooks that pass away,
16Which are dark because of the ice,
And into which the snow vanishes.

6:2,3 If we go through fiery trials, it is only because God sees fit to put us through them for our good. First Pet. 1:6–9 confirms this.

6:6 Job liked salt on his eggs. Jesus said that salt is good (see Mark 9:50), and that eggs are "good" things to give to children (see Luke 11:12,13). When the world's experts say that certain God-given foods are bad, take what they say with a grain of salt.

SPRINGBOARDS FOR PREACHING AND WITNESSING

6:11

Hang in There

There was once a daring escape from a Nazi war prison. The inmates had dug a tunnel, but it surfaced twenty feet short of the cover of a wooded area. So they waited until a moonless night and sent one man into the woods to watch for the time when the guard turned his back. The prisoner was to pull on a piece of string that ran from the woods down into the tunnel, letting the next prisoner know it was safe for him to emerge. One by one, the men felt the tug of the string and surfaced, running into the safety of the dark woods. Unfortunately the guard heard a sound and walked over to near where the hole was located. He didn't see the opening but stood by it for some time, looking suspiciously around the area. Time seemed to stand still for the next prisoner who was waiting underground for the tug on the string.

Suddenly, the man lost his patience. He could stand it no longer. He moved forward, then up and out of the hole in the dark. It was the last thing he did. The guard swung around and fired on him with his machine gun, filling him full of lead.

We can learn from that man's fatal mistake. His error was threefold. He lacked patience, faith, and obedience. If only he had trusted the one on the other end. If only he had obeyed the instructions given to him, he would have found his freedom. Instead, he lost his very life.

The Bible tells us that we inherit the promises of God through "faith and patience" (Heb. 6:12). There are times when a Christian asks God for something, and there is a delay. But he doesn't lose patience. He hangs in there. The One holding onto the string can see things he can't, and He knows what is best for him. The Bible says, "Trust in the LORD with all your heart, and lean not on your own understanding" (Prov. 3:5).

17When it is warm, they cease to flow;
When it is hot, they vanish from their place.
18The paths of their way turn aside,
They go nowhere and perish.
19The caravans of Tema look,
The travelers of Sheba hope for them.
20They are disappointed because they were confident;
They come there and are confused.
21For now you are nothing,
You see terror and are afraid.
22Did I ever say, 'Bring *something* to me'?
Or, 'Offer a bribe for me from your wealth'?
23Or, 'Deliver me from the enemy's hand'?
Or, 'Redeem me from the hand of oppressors'?

24"Teach me, and I will hold my tongue;
Cause me to understand wherein I have erred.
25How forceful are right words!
But what does your arguing prove?
26Do you intend to rebuke *my* words,
And the speeches of a desperate one, *which are* as wind?
27Yes, you overwhelm the fatherless,
And you undermine your friend.
28Now therefore, be pleased to look at me;
For I would never lie to your face.
29Yield now, let there be no injustice!
Yes, concede, my righteousness still stands!
30Is there injustice on my tongue?
Cannot my taste discern the unsavory?

Job: My Suffering Is Comfortless

7 "*Is there* not a time of hard service for man
on earth?
Are not his days also like the days of a hired man?
2Like a servant who earnestly desires the shade,
And like a hired man who eagerly looks for his wages,
3So I have been allotted months of futility,
And wearisome nights have been appointed to me.
4When I lie down, I say, 'When shall I arise,

And the night be ended?'
For I have had my fill of tossing till
dawn.
5My flesh is caked with worms and
dust,
My skin is cracked and breaks out
afresh.

6"My days are swifter than a weaver's
shuttle,
And are spent without hope.
7Oh, remember that my life *is* a breath!
My eye will never again see good.
8The eye of him who sees me will see
me no *more;*
While your *eyes* are upon me, I shall
no longer *be.*
9*As* the cloud disappears and vanishes
away,
So he who goes down to the grave
does not come up.
10He shall never return to his house,
Nor shall his place know him anymore.

> No one ever dies an atheist . . .
> **PLATO**

11"Therefore I will not restrain my
mouth;
I will speak in the anguish of my spirit;
I will complain in the bitterness of my
soul.
12*Am* I a sea, or a sea serpent,
That You set a guard over me?
13When I say, 'My bed will comfort me,
My couch will ease my complaint,'
14Then You scare me with dreams
And terrify me with visions,
15So that my soul chooses strangling
And death rather than my body.[a]
16I loathe *my life;*
I would not live forever.
Let me alone,
For my days *are but* a breath.

17"What *is* man, that You should exalt
him,
That You should set Your heart on him,
18That You should visit him every
morning,
And test him every moment?
19How long?
Will You not look away from me,
And let me alone till I swallow my
saliva?
20Have I sinned?
What have I done to You, O watcher
of men?
Why have You set me as Your target,
So that I am a burden to myself?[a]
21Why then do You not pardon my
transgression,
And take away my iniquity?
For now I will lie down in the dust,
And You will seek me diligently,
But I *will* no longer *be.*"

Bildad: Job Should Repent

8 Then Bildad the Shuhite answered
and said:
2"How long will you speak these *things,*
And the words of your mouth *be like*
a strong wind?
3Does God subvert judgment?
Or does the Almighty pervert justice?
4If your sons have sinned against Him,
He has cast them away for their
transgression.
5If you would earnestly seek God

7:15 [a]Literally *my bones* 7:20 [a]Following Masoretic Text, Targum, and Vulgate; Septuagint and Jewish tradition read *to You.*

7:6,7 Life is like a mist that disappears quickly (see Psa. 78:39). Use your time wisely by reaching out to the lost. The unsaved live in futility, and are held captive to the fear of death (see Heb. 2:14,15). It is legitimate to confront them with their mortality, to awaken them to their plight before death seizes them. To do this, explain that they are swiftly being drawn toward death because they have transgressed the Law of God. For how to tap into their will to live, see James 4:14 comment.

7:9 For whether we return from the grave through reincarnation, see Job 10:21; 16:22; and Heb. 9:27 comment.

And make your supplication to the
Almighty,
6If you *were* pure and upright,
Surely now He would awake for you,
And prosper your rightful dwelling
place.
7Though your beginning was small,
Yet your latter end would increase
abundantly.

8"For inquire, please, of the former age,
And consider the things discovered
by their fathers;
9For we *were born* yesterday, and know
nothing,
Because our days on earth *are* a shadow.
10Will they not teach you and tell you,
And utter words from their heart?

11"Can the papyrus grow up without a
marsh?
Can the reeds flourish without water?
12While it *is* yet green *and* not cut down,
It withers before any *other* plant.
13So *are* the paths of all who forget God;
And the hope of the hypocrite shall
perish,
14Whose confidence shall be cut off,
And whose trust *is* a spider's web.
15He leans on his house, but it does
not stand.
He holds it fast, but it does not endure.
16He grows green in the sun,
And his branches spread out in his
garden.
17His roots wrap around the rock heap,
And look for a place in the stones.
18If he is destroyed from his place,
Then *it* will deny him, *saying,* 'I have
not seen you.'

19"Behold, this is the joy of His way,
And out of the earth others will grow.
20Behold, God will not cast away the
blameless,
Nor will He uphold the evildoers.
21He will yet fill your mouth with
laughing,
And your lips with rejoicing.
22Those who hate you will be clothed
with shame,
And the dwelling place of the wicked
will come to nothing."[a]

Job: There Is No Mediator

9 Then Job answered and said:

2"Truly I know *it is* so,

8:22 [a]Literally *will not be*

8:3 Justice will be done. If there were no hell, and no ultimate justice, then the Almighty would be guilty of perverting justice.

There were approximately 200,000 homicides committed during the 1990s, only half of which were solved. That means more than 100,000 murderers were never brought to justice from 1990–2000. Think of it. In one decade over 100,000 people were stabbed, shot, strangled, poisoned, had their throats cut, etc., and the murderers got away free. If God is not going to punish the perpetrators for such terrible crimes, then He is unjust.

However, the opposite is the case. God will bring to justice every secret thing, whether it is good or evil (see Eccles. 12:14). He will be so thorough, so sweeping in His justice that He will consider hatred to be murder (see 1 John 3:15) and will judge humanity right down to the thoughts and intents of the heart.

In 2001, a man in the U.S. was sentenced to twelve years in prison for conspiring to kill his wife. She was planning to take everything he had through a bitter divorce, and he decided that murdering her would solve his problem. He was caught because his hateful thoughts were made known to a hit man, who recorded them on video. True hatred conspires to murder (within the mind) and as God has access to human thought, He considers the person guilty even if he hasn't physically carried out the crime.

8:5 "At Dublin a young man found Christ. He went home and lived so godly and so Christlike a life that two of his brothers could not understand what had wrought the change in him. They left Dublin and followed us to Sheffield, and there found Christ. They were in earnest. But, thanks be to God, Christ can be found now. I firmly believe every reader can find Christ now, if you will seek for Him with all your heart. He says, 'Call upon me.'" *D. L. Moody*

8:6,7 Beware of those who believe that God prospers us according to our righteousness. Most billionaires aren't the slightest bit godly.

But how can a man be righteous
before God?
[3]If one wished to contend with Him,
He could not answer Him one time
out of a thousand.
[4]*God is* wise in heart and mighty in
strength.
Who has hardened *himself* against
Him and prospered?
[5]He removes the mountains, and they
do not know
When He overturns them in His anger;
[6]He shakes the earth out of its place,
And its pillars tremble;
[7]He commands the sun, and it does
not rise;
He seals off the stars;
[8]He alone spreads out the heavens,
And treads on the waves of the sea;
[9]He made the Bear, Orion, and the
Pleiades,
And the chambers of the south;
[10]He does great things past finding out,
Yes, wonders without number.
[11]If He goes by me, I do not see *Him;*
If He moves past, I do not perceive
Him;
[12]If He takes away, who can hinder Him?
Who can say to Him, 'What are You
doing?'
[13]God will not withdraw His anger,
The allies of the proud[a] lie prostrate
beneath Him.

[14]"How then can I answer Him,
And choose my words *to reason* with
Him?
[15]For though I were righteous, I could
not answer Him;
I would beg mercy of my Judge.
[16]If I called and He answered me,
I would not believe that He was
listening to my voice.
[17]For He crushes me with a tempest,
And multiplies my wounds without
cause.
[18]He will not allow me to catch my
breath,
But fills me with bitterness.
[19]If *it is a matter* of strength, indeed *He*
is strong;
And if of justice, who will appoint my
day *in court?*
[20]Though I were righteous, my own
mouth would condemn me;
Though I *were* blameless, it would
prove me perverse.

[21]"I am blameless, yet I do not know
myself;
I despise my life.
[22]It *is* all one *thing;*
Therefore I say, 'He destroys the
blameless and the wicked.'
[23]If the scourge slays suddenly,
He laughs at the plight of the innocent.
[24]The earth is given into the hand of
the wicked.
He covers the faces of its judges.
If it is not *He,* who else could it be?

[25]"Now my days are swifter than a
runner;
They flee away, they see no good.
[26]They pass by like swift ships,
Like an eagle swooping on its prey.
[27]If I say, 'I will forget my complaint,
I will put off my sad face and wear a

9:13 [a]Hebrew *rahab*

9:2 The answer to such a profound question is that a man can be made righteous only by grace, through faith (see Eph. 2:8,9). It is the moral Law in the hand of the Spirit of God that makes a man thirst for righteousness. It is not in himself to do so. Without God's influence he thirsts only for iniquity, which he drinks like water (see Job 15:16). So use the Law to make men and women see their danger, and begin to ask what they should do to make things right between them and God. Shake their world so that they will cry like the Philippian jailer, "What must I do to be saved?" (Acts 16:30).

9:8 Only God, our omnipotent Creator, could tread on the sea. See Matt. 14:26; Mark 6:48; John 6:19 for where Jesus did this, showing that He is God.

9:10–12 The immortal, invisible Creator does what He wants when He wants. See Rom. 11:33.

smile,'
[28]I am afraid of all my sufferings;
I know that You will not hold me
innocent.
[29]*If* I am condemned,
Why then do I labor in vain?
[30]If I wash myself with snow water,
And cleanse my hands with soap,
[31]Yet You will plunge me into the pit,
And my own clothes will abhor me.

[32]"For *He* is not a man, as I *am,*
That I may answer Him,
And that we should go to court
together.
[33]Nor is there any mediator between us,
Who may lay his hand on us both.
[34]Let Him take His rod away from me,
And do not let dread of Him terrify me.
[35]*Then* I would speak and not fear Him,
But it is not so with me.

Job: I Would Plead with God

10 "My soul loathes my life;
I will give free course to my
complaint,
I will speak in the bitterness of my
soul.
[2]I will say to God, 'Do not condemn
me;
Show me why You contend with me.
[3]*Does it* seem good to You that You
should oppress,
That You should despise the work of
Your hands,
And smile on the counsel of the
wicked?
[4]Do You have eyes of flesh?
Or do You see as man sees?
[5]*Are* Your days like the days of a
mortal man?
Are Your years like the days of a
mighty man,
[6]That You should seek for my iniquity
And search out my sin,
[7]Although You know that I am not
wicked,
And *there is* no one who can deliver
from Your hand?

[8]'Your hands have made me and
fashioned me,
An intricate unity;
Yet You would destroy me.
[9]Remember, I pray, that You have
made me like clay.
And will You turn me into dust again?
[10]Did You not pour me out like milk,
And curdle me like cheese,
[11]Clothe me with skin and flesh,
And knit me together with bones and
sinews?
[12]You have granted me life and favor,
And Your care has preserved my spirit.

[13]'And these *things* You have hidden in
Your heart;
I know that this *was* with You:
[14]If I sin, then You mark me,
And will not acquit me of my iniquity.
[15]If I am wicked, woe to me;
Even *if* I am righteous, I cannot lift up
my head.
I am full of disgrace;
See my misery!
[16]If *my head* is exalted,
You hunt me like a fierce lion,
And again You show Yourself
awesome against me.
[17]You renew Your witnesses against me,

9:33 Job longed for a mediator to state his case in court before the Judge. God would later send one for humanity: "There is one God and one Mediator between God and men, the Man Christ Jesus" (see 1 Tim. 2:5,6). See also 33:23–28 comment.

10:4 Little did Job realize that one day this would happen: God would become flesh and dwell among us. See 1 Tim. 3:16.

10:7 No one likes to admit that his heart is wicked. This is because we are ignorant of God's righteousness until the Law is applied to the conscience.

10:14 God will not at all acquit the wicked (see Nah. 1:3). He will ensure that justice is served. See also 8:3 comment.

And increase Your indignation toward
me;
Changes and war are *ever* with me.
[18]"Why then have You brought me out
of the womb?
Oh, that I had perished and no eye
had seen me!
[19]I would have been as though I had
not been.
I would have been carried from the
womb to the grave.
[20]Are not my days few?
Cease! Leave me alone, that I may
take a little comfort,
[21]Before I go *to the place from which* I
shall not return,
To the land of darkness and the
shadow of death,
[22]A land as dark as darkness *itself*,
As the shadow of death, without any
order,
Where even the light *is* like darkness.' "

Zophar Urges Job to Repent

11 Then Zophar the Naamathite answered and said:
[2]"Should not the multitude of words be
answered?
And should a man full of talk be
vindicated?
[3]Should your empty talk make men
hold their peace?
And when you mock, should no one
rebuke you?
[4]For you have said,
"My doctrine *is* pure,
And I am clean in your eyes.'
[5]But oh, that God would speak,
And open His lips against you,
[6]That He would show you the secrets
of wisdom!
For *they would* double *your* prudence.
Know therefore that God exacts from
you
Less than your iniquity *deserves*.
[7]"Can you search out the deep things
of God?
Can you find out the limits of the
Almighty?
[8]*They are* higher than heaven— what
can you do?
Deeper than Sheol— what can you
know?
[9]Their measure *is* longer than the earth
And broader than the sea.

[10]"If He passes by, imprisons, and
gathers *to judgment*,
Then who can hinder Him?
[11]For He knows deceitful men;
He sees wickedness also.
Will He not then consider *it*?
[12]For an empty-headed man will be
wise,
When a wild donkey's colt is born a
man.

[13]"If you would prepare your heart,
And stretch out your hands toward
Him;
[14]If iniquity *were* in your hand, *and you*
put it far away,
And would not let wickedness dwell
in your tents;
[15]Then surely you could lift up your
face without spot;
Yes, you could be steadfast, and not
fear;
[16]Because you would forget *your*
misery,
And remember *it* as waters *that have*
passed away,
[17]And *your* life would be brighter than
noonday.
Though you were dark, you would be
like the morning.

11:7,8 We have so very little understanding of the nature of God. Scripture puts us in the shallowest of shores on the very edge of the deepest of oceans. It will take all of eternity for us to explore our Creator's amazing attributes.

"If God were small enough to be understood, He would not be big enough to be worshiped." *Evelyn Underhill*

18And you would be secure, because
there is hope;
Yes, you would dig *around you, and*
take your rest in safety.
19You would also lie down, and no one
would make *you* afraid;
Yes, many would court your favor.
20But the eyes of the wicked will fail,
And they shall not escape,
And their hope—loss of life!"

Job Answers His Critics

12 Then Job answered and said:

2"No doubt you *are* the people,
And wisdom will die with you!
3But I have understanding as well as
you;
I *am* not inferior to you.
Indeed, who does not *know* such
things as these?

4"I am one mocked by his friends,
Who called on God, and He answered
him,
The just and blameless *who is* ridiculed.
5A lamp[a] is despised in the thought of
one who is at ease;
It is made ready for those whose feet
slip.
6The tents of robbers prosper,
And those who provoke God are
secure—
In what God provides by His hand.

7"But now ask the beasts, and they will
teach you;
And the birds of the air, and they will
tell you;
8Or speak to the earth, and it will
teach you;
And the fish of the sea will explain to
you.
9Who among all these does not know
That the hand of the LORD has done
this,
10In whose hand *is* the life of every
living thing,
And the breath of all mankind?
11Does not the ear test words
And the mouth taste its food?
12Wisdom *is* with aged men,
And with length of days,
understanding.

. . . . . .

For the differences between humans and animals, see Psa 32:9 comment.

. . . . . .

13"With Him *are* wisdom and strength,
He has counsel and understanding.
14If He breaks *a thing* down, it cannot
be rebuilt;
If He imprisons a man, there can be
no release.
15If He withholds the waters, they dry
up;
If He sends them out, they
overwhelm the earth.
16With Him *are* strength and prudence.
The deceived and the deceiver *are* His.

12:5 [a]Or *disaster*

12:6 The ungodly see that they live as well as, if not better than, those who refrain from sin (see Matt. 5:45). Instead of being humbled by God's goodness, they see Heaven's silence as approval.

12:7–9 Don't believe that atheists exist. The definition of an atheist is "one who denies the existence of God." Those who deny the inner light that God has given to every man are nothing less than fools, who so love their sin that they deny God-given reason—thinking that gives them license to indulge in sin (see Psa. 14:1). Since God has given mankind sufficient proof so that we are all without excuse, an atheist is a person who *pretends* there is no God.

"It amazes me to find an intelligent person who fights against something which he does not at all believe exists." *Gandhi*

12:10 Every breath we breathe comes by the permission of God. The only thing we can guarantee is the air going into our lungs at the present moment. We cannot guarantee another; that comes only by the mercy of God. If He says, "Tonight your soul is required of you," we breathe no more. This is why, when someone murders another person, they primarily sin against the One who owns that life. See 14:5 comment.

[17]He leads counselors away plundered,
And makes fools of the judges.
[18]He loosens the bonds of kings,
And binds their waist with a belt.
[19]He leads princes[a] away plundered,
And overthrows the mighty.
[20]He deprives the trusted ones of speech,
And takes away the discernment of
the elders.
[21]He pours contempt on princes,
And disarms the mighty.
[22]He uncovers deep things out of
darkness,
And brings the shadow of death to
light.
[23]He makes nations great, and destroys
them;
He enlarges nations, and guides them.
[24]He takes away the understanding[a] of
the chiefs of the people of the
earth,
And makes them wander in a pathless
wilderness.
[25]They grope in the dark without light,
And He makes them stagger like a
drunken *man.*

13 "Behold, my eye has seen all *this,*
My ear has heard and understood
it.
[2]What you know, I also know;
I *am* not inferior to you.
[3]But I would speak to the Almighty,
And I desire to reason with God.
[4]But you forgers of lies,
You *are* all worthless physicians.
[5]Oh, that you would be silent,
And it would be your wisdom!
[6]Now hear my reasoning,
And heed the pleadings of my lips.
[7]Will you speak wickedly for God,
And talk deceitfully for Him?
[8]Will you show partiality for Him?
Will you contend for God?
[9]Will it be well when He searches you
out?
Or can you mock Him as one mocks
a man?
[10]He will surely rebuke you
If you secretly show partiality.
[11]Will not His excellence make you
afraid,
And the dread of Him fall upon you?
[12]Your platitudes *are* proverbs of ashes,
Your defenses are defenses of clay.

[13]"Hold your peace with me, and let me
speak,
Then let come on me what *may!*
[14]Why do I take my flesh in my teeth,
And put my life in my hands?
[15]Though He slay me, yet will I trust
Him.
Even so, I will defend my own ways
before Him.
[16]He also *shall* be my salvation,
For a hypocrite could not come
before Him.
[17]Listen carefully to my speech,
And to my declaration with your ears.
[18]See now, I have prepared *my* case,
I know that I shall be vindicated.
[19]Who is he *who* will contend with me?
If now I hold my tongue, I perish.

Job's Despondent Prayer

[20]"Only two *things* do not do to me,
Then I will not hide myself from You:
[21]Withdraw Your hand far from me,
And let not the dread of You make me
afraid.
[22]Then call, and I will answer;
Or let me speak, then You respond to
me.
[23]How many *are* my iniquities and sins?

12:19 [a]Literally *priests,* but not in a technical sense **12:24** [a]Literally *heart*

12:22 This is what Jesus did. See Luke 1:79.

13:15 Despite his misery and pain, Job did trust God's judgments. This kind of faith is a wonderful light in the midst of terrible darkness. Spurgeon said that faith may swim, where reason may only paddle. If you are going through a dark time of testing, let faith lift your head above the waves. Hold onto His mighty hand and thank Him that He is working all this out for your eternal good (see Rom. 8:28).

Make me know my transgression and
my sin.
24Why do You hide Your face,
And regard me as Your enemy?
25Will You frighten a leaf driven to and
fro?
And will You pursue dry stubble?
26For You write bitter things against me,
And make me inherit the iniquities of
my youth.
27You put my feet in the stocks,
And watch closely all my paths.
You set a limit[a] for the soles of my feet.

28"*Man*[a] decays like a rotten thing,
Like a garment that is moth-eaten.

14 "Man *who is* born of woman
Is of few days and full of trouble.
2He comes forth like a flower and
fades away;
He flees like a shadow and does not
continue.
3And do You open Your eyes on such a
one,
And bring me[a] to judgment with
Yourself?
4Who can bring a clean *thing* out of an
unclean?
No one!
5Since his days *are* determined,
The number of his months *is* with
You;
You have appointed his limits, so that
he cannot pass.
6Look away from him that he may rest,
Till like a hired man he finishes his
day.

7"For there is hope for a tree,
If it is cut down, that it will sprout
again,
And that its tender shoots will not
cease.
8Though its root may grow old in the
earth,
And its stump may die in the ground,
9*Yet* at the scent of water it will bud
And bring forth branches like a plant.
10But man dies and is laid away;
Indeed he breathes his last
And where *is* he?
11*As* water disappears from the sea,
And a river becomes parched and
dries up,
12So man lies down and does not rise.
Till the heavens *are* no more,
They will not awake
Nor be roused from their sleep.

13"Oh, that You would hide me in the
grave,
That You would conceal me until

13:27 [a]Literally *inscribe a print* 13:28 [a]Literally *He* 14:3 [a]Septuagint, Syriac, and Vulgate read *him*.

14:1 See Isa. 40:6.

14:4 When we are in Christ, God does not make a clean thing out of an unclean thing. Instead, He makes us new creatures (see 2 Cor. 5:17).

14:5 "My religious beliefs teach me to feel as safe in battle as in bed. God has fixed the time of my death. I do not concern myself with that, but to be always ready whenever it may overtake me. That is the way all men should live, and all men would be equally brave." *Stonewall Jackson*

14:10 Near-death experiences. *Omni* magazine (March 1985) reported a study by *Dr. Maurice Rawlings* (at the time a devout atheist), cardiologist and professor of medicine at the University of Tennessee College of Medicine in Chattanooga and author of the book *To Hell and Back*. He and his emergency room colleagues are constantly treating such cases. It is now standard that those who have near-death experiences later speak of having experiences of light, lush green meadows, rows of smiling relatives, and tremendous peace. However, in his study (also reported in his book *Beyond Death's Door*), Dr. Rawlings obtained new information by interviewing patients immediately after resuscitation while they are still too shaken to deny where they have been. Nearly 50 percent of the group of 300 interviewed reported lakes of fire and brimstone, devil-like figures, and other sights hailing from the darkness of hell. He says they later change their story because most people are simply ashamed to admit they have been to hell; they won't even admit it to their families. Concludes Dr. Rawlings, "Just listening to these patients has changed my whole life. There's a life after death, and if I don't know where I'm going, it's not safe to die."

Your wrath is past,
That You would appoint me a set
time, and remember me!
14If a man dies, shall he live *again*?
All the days of my hard service I will
wait,
Till my change comes.
15You shall call, and I will answer You;
You shall desire the work of Your
hands.
16For now You number my steps,
But do not watch over my sin.
17My transgression *is* sealed up in a bag,
And You cover[a] my iniquity.

18"But *as* a mountain falls *and* crumbles
away,
And *as* a rock is moved from its place;
19*As* water wears away stones,
And as torrents wash away the soil of
the earth;
So You destroy the hope of man.
20You prevail forever against him, and
he passes on;
You change his countenance and send
him away.
21His sons come to honor, and he does
not know *it*;
They are brought low, and he does
not perceive *it*.
22But his flesh will be in pain over it,
And his soul will mourn over it."

Eliphaz Accuses Job of Folly

15 Then Eliphaz the Temanite answered and said:
2"Should a wise man answer with
empty knowledge,
And fill himself with the east wind?
3Should he reason with unprofitable
talk,
Or by speeches with which he can do
no good?
4Yes, you cast off fear,
And restrain prayer before God.
5For your iniquity teaches your mouth,
And you choose the tongue of the
crafty.
6Your own mouth condemns you, and
not I;
Yes, your own lips testify against you.

7"*Are* you the first man *who* was born?
Or were you made before the hills?
8Have you heard the counsel of God?
Do you limit wisdom to yourself?
9What do you know that we do not
know?
What do you understand that *is* not in
us?
10Both the gray-haired and the aged *are*
among us,
Much older than your father.
11*Are* the consolations of God too small
for you,
And the word *spoken* gently[a] with you?
12Why does your heart carry you away,
And what do your eyes wink at,
13That you turn your spirit against God,
And let *such* words go out of your
mouth?

14"What *is* man, that he could be pure?
And *he who is* born of a woman, that
he could be righteous?
15If *God* puts no trust in His saints,
And the heavens are not pure in His
sight,

14:17 [a]Literally *plaster over* 15:11 [a]Septuagint reads *a secret thing.*

14:14 Every person who dies will stand before God in judgment. It has been well said, "Death is not the termination of existence; but the entrance into an eternal and unchanging state."

"Once you will read in the newspapers that Dwight Moody of East Northfield has died. Don't believe it. Then I will be more alive than now. What is born of the flesh can die, but what is born of the Spirit will live eternally." *D. L Moody*

15:6 See Luke 19:22. When we take a sinner though the Ten Commandments and ask if he has violated them, his own mouth condemns him. See how Paul does this in Rom. 2:21–24.

15:15,16 One doesn't have to look far to see the truth of this; just visit a secular video store or a magazine rack and see what the unsaved thirst for (see Psa. 14:3).

[16]How much less man, *who is*
abominable and filthy,
Who drinks iniquity like water!

[17]"I will tell you, hear me;
What I have seen I will declare,
[18]What wise men have told,
Not hiding *anything received* from
their fathers,
[19]To whom alone the land was given,
And no alien passed among them:
[20]The wicked man writhes with pain all
his days,
And the number of years is hidden
from the oppressor.
[21]Dreadful sounds *are* in his ears;
In prosperity the destroyer comes
upon him.
[22]He does not believe that he will
return from darkness,
For a sword is waiting for him.
[23]He wanders about for bread, *saying,*
'Where *is it?*'
He knows that a day of darkness is
ready at his hand.
[24]Trouble and anguish make him afraid;
They overpower him, like a king
ready for battle.
[25]For he stretches out his hand against
God,
And acts defiantly against the
Almighty,
[26]Running stubbornly against Him
With his strong, embossed shield.

> Atheism is a crutch for those who cannot bear the reality of God.
>
> **TOM STOPPARD**

[27]"Though he has covered his face with
his fatness,
And made *his* waist heavy with fat,
[28]He dwells in desolate cities,
In houses which no one inhabits,
Which are destined to become ruins.
[29]He will not be rich,
Nor will his wealth continue,
Nor will his possessions overspread
the earth.
[30]He will not depart from darkness;
The flame will dry out his branches,
And by the breath of His mouth he
will go away.
[31]Let him not trust in futile *things,*
deceiving himself,
For futility will be his reward.
[32]It will be accomplished before his
time,
And his branch will not be green.
[33]He will shake off his unripe grape
like a vine,
And cast off his blossom like an olive
tree.
[34]For the company of hypocrites *will be*
barren,
And fire will consume the tents of
bribery.
[35]They conceive trouble and bring forth
futility;
Their womb prepares deceit."

Job Reproaches His Pitiless Friends

16 Then Job answered and said:

[2]"I have heard many such things;
Miserable comforters *are* you all!
[3]Shall words of wind have an end?
Or what provokes you that you
answer?
[4]I also could speak as you *do,*
If your soul were in my soul's place.
I could heap up words against you,
And shake my head at you;
[5]*But* I would strengthen you with my
mouth,
And the comfort of my lips would
relieve *your grief.*

[6]"Though I speak, my grief is not
relieved;
And *if* I remain silent, how am I eased?
[7]But now He has worn me out;
You have made desolate all my
company.
[8]You have shriveled me up,
And it is a witness *against me;*
My leanness rises up against me
And bears witness to my face.

[9]He tears *me* in His wrath, and hates me;
He gnashes at me with His teeth;
My adversary sharpens His gaze on me.
[10]They gape at me with their mouth,
They strike me reproachfully on the cheek,
They gather together against me.
[11]God has delivered me to the ungodly,
And turned me over to the hands of the wicked.
[12]I was at ease, but He has shattered me;
He also has taken *me* by my neck, and shaken me to pieces;
He has set me up for His target,
[13]His archers surround me.
He pierces my heart[a] and does not pity;
He pours out my gall on the ground.
[14]He breaks me with wound upon wound;
He runs at me like a warrior.[a]

[15]"I have sewn sackcloth over my skin,
And laid my head[a] in the dust.
[16]My face is flushed from weeping,
And on my eyelids *is* the shadow of death;
[17]Although no violence *is* in my hands,
And my prayer *is* pure.

[18]"O earth, do not cover my blood,
And let my cry have no *resting* place!
[19]Surely even now my witness *is* in heaven,
And my evidence *is* on high.
[20]My friends scorn me;
My eyes pour out *tears* to God.
[21]Oh, that one might plead for a man with God,
As a man *pleads* for his neighbor!
[22]For when a few years are finished,
I shall go the way of no return.

Job Prays for Relief

17 "My spirit is broken,
My days are extinguished,
The grave *is ready* for me.
[2]*Are* not mockers with me?
And does not my eye dwell on their provocation?

[3]"Now put down a pledge for me with Yourself.
Who *is* he *who* will shake hands with me?
[4]For You have hidden their heart from understanding;
Therefore You will not exalt *them.*
[5]He who speaks flattery to *his* friends,
Even the eyes of his children will fail.

[6]"But He has made me a byword of the people,
And I have become one in whose face men spit.
[7]My eye has also grown dim because of sorrow,
And all my members *are* like shadows.
[8]Upright *men* are astonished at this,
And the innocent stirs himself up against the hypocrite.
[9]Yet the righteous will hold to his way,
And he who has clean hands will be stronger and stronger.

[10]"But please, come back again, all of you,[a]
For I shall not find *one* wise *man* among you.
[11]My days are past,
My purposes are broken off,
Even the thoughts of my heart.
[12]They change the night into day;
'The light *is* near,' *they say,* in the face of darkness.
[13]If I wait *for* the grave *as* my house,

16:13 [a]Literally *kidneys* 16:14 [a]Vulgate reads *giant.* 16:15 [a]Literally *horn* 17:10 [a]Following some Hebrew manuscripts, Septuagint, Syriac, and Vulgate; Masoretic Text and Targum read *all of them.*

16:10 Psalm 22:13 applies this same phrase to the Messiah as He hung on the cross.

16:21 We have an Advocate, one to plead for us in the presence of God, Jesus Christ the righteous (see 1 John 2:1,2).

17:14 *DNA Similarities*

One typical "proof" evolutionists give for ape-to-man evolution is that chimpanzees and humans have very similar DNA. In previous DNA studies, based on only portions of the chimp genome, scientists announced that humans and chimps were 98–99 percent identical, depending on what was counted. After completing the mapping of the chimp genome in 2005, evolutionists are now hailing the result as "the most dramatic confirmation yet" that chimps and humans have common ancestry. Their overwhelming "proof" is the finding that the genetic difference is 4 percent—which is interesting proof, because it's actually twice the amount that they've been claiming for years.

In addition, even if the difference is only 4 percent of the 3 billion base pairs of DNA in every cell, that represents 120,000,000 entries in the DNA code that are different! In our DNA instruction book (see Isa. 42:5 comment), that's equivalent to about 12 million words—so that seemingly small percentage has a tremendous impact. Men and monkeys also have another fundamental difference: humans have 23 pairs of chromosomes while chimps have 24, so the DNA isn't as similar as you've been led to believe.

More importantly, this claim of evolutionists makes a huge assumption. What is the scientific basis for assuming that similar DNA means a common ancestor? When you see a biplane and a jet—which share common features of wings, body, tires, engine, controls, etc.—do you assume that one must have evolved from the other naturally, without a maker? That's illogical. It's more reasonable to conclude that similar design indicates a common, intelligent designer. An architect typically uses the same building materials for numerous buildings, and a car manufacturer commonly uses the same parts in various models. So if we have a common Designer, we would expect to find that a similar "blueprint" was used in many different creatures.

After all, DNA is the coding for the way our bodies look and operate, so creatures with similar features or body functions (eyes for vision, enzymes for digestion, etc.) would have similar coding for these things in their DNA. Because human cells have the same biochemical functions as many different animals and even plants, we share some of the same genes. The more we have in common, the more we find similar coding in the blueprints. This is just simple reasoning—not proof of common ancestry!

So, even though we share 96 percent of our genetic make-up with chimps, that does not mean we are 96 percent chimp. Be careful you don't fall for the illogic of this "evolutionary proof," or scientists will not only make a monkey out of you, they'll make a banana out of you! According to evolutionist Steven Jones, a renowned British geneticist, "We also share about 50% of our DNA with bananas and that doesn't make us half bananas..." See also Jer. 27:5 comment.

(Adapted from *How to Know God Exists.*)

If I make my bed in the darkness,
14If I say to corruption, 'You *are* my
father,'
And to the worm, 'You *are* my mother
and my sister,'
15Where then *is* my hope?
As for my hope, who can see it?
16*Will* they go down to the gates of Sheol?
Shall *we have* rest together in the dust?"

Bildad: The Wicked Are Punished

18 Then Bildad the Shuhite answered
and said:
2"How long *till* you put an end to words?
Gain understanding, and afterward
we will speak.
3Why are we counted as beasts,
And regarded as stupid in your sight?

We admit that we are like apes, but we seldom realize that we are apes.

RICHARD DAWKINS

4You who tear yourself in anger,
Shall the earth be forsaken for you?
Or shall the rock be removed from its
place?

17:15 Without Jesus of Nazareth, none of us have any hope. If He was not who He said He was, we are still in our sins and hell awaits us. Never doubt the promises of God, even for a moment. He who does so cuts gaping holes in his own parachute.

[5]"The light of the wicked indeed goes out,
And the flame of his fire does not shine.
[6]The light is dark in his tent,
And his lamp beside him is put out.
[7]The steps of his strength are shortened,
And his own counsel casts him down.
[8]For he is cast into a net by his own feet,
And he walks into a snare.
[9]The net takes *him* by the heel,
And a snare lays hold of him.
[10]A noose *is* hidden for him on the ground,
And a trap for him in the road.
[11]Terrors frighten him on every side,
And drive him to his feet.
[12]His strength is starved,
And destruction *is* ready at his side.
[13]It devours patches of his skin;
The firstborn of death devours his limbs.
[14]He is uprooted from the shelter of his tent,
And they parade him before the king of terrors.
[15]They dwell in his tent *who are* none of his;
Brimstone is scattered on his dwelling.
[16]His roots are dried out below,
And his branch withers above.
[17]The memory of him perishes from the earth,
And he has no name among the renowned.[a]
[18]He is driven from light into darkness,
And chased out of the world.
[19]He has neither son nor posterity among his people,
Nor any remaining in his dwellings.
[20]Those in the west are astonished at his day,
As those in the east are frightened.
[21]Surely such *are* the dwellings of the wicked,
And this *is* the place *of him who* does not know God."

Job Trusts in His Redeemer

19 Then Job answered and said:

[2]"How long will you torment my soul,
And break me in pieces with words?
[3]These ten times you have reproached me;
You are not ashamed *that* you have wronged me.[a]
[4]And if indeed I have erred,
My error remains with me.
[5]If indeed you exalt *yourselves* against me,
And plead my disgrace against me,
[6]Know then that God has wronged me,
And has surrounded me with His net.

[7]"If I cry out concerning wrong, I am not heard.
If I cry aloud, *there is* no justice.
[8]He has fenced up my way, so that I cannot pass;
And He has set darkness in my paths.
[9]He has stripped me of my glory,
And taken the crown *from* my head.
[10]He breaks me down on every side,
And I am gone;
My hope He has uprooted like a tree.
[11]He has also kindled His wrath against me,
And He counts me as *one of* His enemies.
[12]His troops come together
And build up their road against me;
They encamp all around my tent.

[13]"He has removed my brothers far from me,
And my acquaintances are completely

18:17 [a]Literally *before the outside,* meaning distinguished, famous 19:3 [a]A Jewish tradition reads *make yourselves strange to me.*

18:2 It would be easy to counsel Daniel from the top of the lion's den. Such speech was rebuked by God Himself. See Job 42:7.

estranged from me.
[14]My relatives have failed,
And my close friends have forgotten me.
[15]Those who dwell in my house, and my maidservants,
Count me as a stranger;
I am an alien in their sight.
[16]I call my servant, but he gives no answer;
I beg him with my mouth.
[17]My breath is offensive to my wife,
And I am repulsive to the children of my own body.
[18]Even young children despise me;
I arise, and they speak against me.
[19]All my close friends abhor me,
And those whom I love have turned against me.
[20]My bone clings to my skin and to my flesh,
And I have escaped by the skin of my teeth.

[21]"Have pity on me, have pity on me, O you my friends,
For the hand of God has struck me!
[22]Why do you persecute me as God *does*,
And are not satisfied with my flesh?

[23]"Oh, that my words were written!
Oh, that they were inscribed in a book!
[24]That they were engraved on a rock
With an iron pen and lead, forever!
[25]For I know *that* my Redeemer lives,
And He shall stand at last on the earth;
[26]And after my skin is destroyed, this *I know,*
That in my flesh I shall see God,
[27]Whom I shall see for myself,
And my eyes shall behold, and not another.
How my heart yearns within me!
[28]If you should say, 'How shall we persecute him?'—
Since the root of the matter is found in me,
[29]Be afraid of the sword for yourselves;
For wrath *brings* the punishment of the sword,
That you may know *there is* a judgment."

Zophar's Sermon on the Wicked Man

20 Then Zophar the Naamathite answered and said:

[2]"Therefore my anxious thoughts make me answer,
Because of the turmoil within me.
[3]I have heard the rebuke that reproaches me,
And the spirit of my understanding causes me to answer.

[4]"Do you *not* know this of old,
Since man was placed on earth,
[5]That the triumphing of the wicked is short,
And the joy of the hypocrite is *but* for a moment?
[6]Though his haughtiness mounts up to the heavens,

19:17 Job is not alone. Make sure you understand the great truth that when Adam fell, so did his breath. Use mints when sharing the gospel so the only thing offensive is your message.

19:25,26 Job, who existed thousands of years before the coming of the Messiah, had faith that God would deliver him from death. Along with Abraham, he rejoiced to see the day of Jesus Christ (see John 8:56; Heb. 11:32–40). Their salvation would come by grace through their faith in the coming Redeemer (see Eph. 2:8,9).

20:5 The world often complains about the hypocrites they think are "in the Church." Yet hypocrites (pretenders) are not part of the Church, which is made up of true believers. Hypocrites merely dwell as goats among the Lord's sheep, bad fish among the good, tares among wheat until the day God separates them. This verse confirms that sin can bring joy—but only temporarily (see Jer. 12:1; Heb. 11:24,25; also Job 27:8,9). See Matt. 25:12 comment.

"As much as we need to convert the lost to Christianity, more and more we need to convert the Christians to Christianity." *G. K. Chesterton*

20:4 Can Radiometric Dating Be Trusted?

By Bodie Hodge, Answers in Genesis

Radiometric dating was the culminating factor that led to the belief in *billions* of years for earth history. Radiometric dating is one form of dating based on uniformitarianism—the idea that all processes happen at a constant rate, past or future. But did you know that the results from some radiometric dating methods completely undermine those from other radiometric methods? One example is carbon-14 dating. As long as an organism is alive it takes in carbon-14; however, when it dies, the carbon intake stops. Since carbon-14 is radioactive (decays into nitrogen), the amount present in a dead organism decreases over time. (Carbon-14 is called the parent element and the nitrogen-14 it decays into is called the daughter element.) The amount of carbon-14 remaining can be used to date samples which were once alive, such as wood or bone.

Carbon-14 has a half-life of 5,730 years, so any carbon-14 in organic material supposedly 100,000 years old should all have decayed into nitrogen. Some things, such as wood trapped in lava flows, said to be millions of years old by other radiometric dating methods still contain carbon-14. If the items were really millions of years old, then they should not have any traces of carbon-14 left.

Coal and diamonds, which are found in or sandwiched between rock layers allegedly millions or billions of years old, have been shown to have carbon-14 ages of only tens of thousands of years. So which date, if any, is correct? The diamonds or coal cannot be millions of years old if they have any traces of carbon-14 still in them.

Many who put their faith in radiometric dating methods are not aware of the assumptions the methods are founded in:

- What were the initial amounts of parent and daughter?
- Was any parent or daughter added over time?
- Was any parent or daughter removed over time?
- Has the rate of decay always been constant?

The carbon-14 results show that these dating methods are completely unreliable and that the assumptions they are based on are erroneous.

Similar kinds of problems are seen in the case of potassium-argon dating, which has been considered one of the most reliable methods. Dr. Andrew Snelling, a geologist, points out several of these problems with potassium-argon dating, as seen below.

POTASSIUM-ARGON (K-AR) DATES IN ERROR

Volcanic eruption	When the rock formed	Date by (K-Ar) radiometric dating
Mt. Etna basalt, Sicily	122 B.C.	170,000–330,000 years old
Mt. Etna basalt, Sicily	A.D. 1972	210,000–490,000 years old
Mt. St. Helens, Washington	A.D. 1986	Up to 2.8 million years old
Hualalai basalt, Hawaii	A.D. 1800–1801	1.32–1.76 million years old
Mt. Ngauruhoe, New Zealand	A.D. 1954	Up to 3.5 million years old
Kilauea Iki basalt, Hawaii	A.D. 1959	1.7–15.3 million years old

These and other examples raise a critical question. If radiometric dating fails to get an accurate date on something of which we do know the true age, then how can it be trusted to give us the correct age for rocks that had no human observers to record when they formed? If the methods don't work on rocks of known age, it is most unreasonable to trust that they work on rocks of unknown age. It is far more rational to trust the Word of the God who created the world, knows its history perfectly, and has revealed sufficient information in the Bible for us to understand that history and the age of the creation. See also Psa. 102:25 comment.

And his head reaches to the clouds,
7 *Yet* he will perish forever like his own
refuse;
Those who have seen him will say,
'Where is he?'
8 He will fly away like a dream, and
not be found;
Yes, he will be chased away like a

vision of the night.
9The eye *that* saw him will *see him* no more,
Nor will his place behold him anymore.
10His children will seek the favor of the poor,
And his hands will restore his wealth.
11His bones are full of his youthful vigor,
But it will lie down with him in the dust.

12"Though evil is sweet in his mouth,
And he hides it under his tongue,
13*Though* he spares it and does not forsake it,
But still keeps it in his mouth,
14*Yet* his food in his stomach turns sour;
It becomes cobra venom within him.
15He swallows down riches
And vomits them up again;
God casts them out of his belly.
16He will suck the poison of cobras;
The viper's tongue will slay him.
17He will not see the streams,
The rivers flowing with honey and cream.
18He will restore that for which he labored,
And will not swallow *it* down;
From the proceeds of business
He will get no enjoyment.
19For he has oppressed *and* forsaken the poor,
He has violently seized a house which he did not build.

20"Because he knows no quietness in his heart,[a]
He will not save anything he desires.
21Nothing is left for him to eat;
Therefore his well-being will not last.
22In his self-sufficiency he will be in distress;
Every hand of misery will come against him.
23*When* he is about to fill his stomach,
God will cast on him the fury of His wrath,
And will rain *it* on him while he is eating.
24He will flee from the iron weapon;
A bronze bow will pierce him through.
25It is drawn, and comes out of the body;
Yes, the glittering *point comes* out of his gall.
Terrors *come* upon him;
26Total darkness *is* reserved for his treasures.
An unfanned fire will consume him;
It shall go ill with him who is left in his tent.
27The heavens will reveal his iniquity,
And the earth will rise up against him.
28The increase of his house will depart,
And his goods will flow away in the day of His wrath.
29This *is* the portion from God for a wicked man,
The heritage appointed to him by God."

Job's Discourse on the Wicked

21 Then Job answered and said:

2"Listen carefully to my speech,
And let this be your consolation.
3Bear with me that I may speak,
And after I have spoken, keep mocking.

4"As for me, *is* my complaint against man?
And if *it were,* why should I not be impatient?
5Look at me and be astonished;
Put *your* hand over *your* mouth.
6Even when I remember I am terrified,
And trembling takes hold of my flesh.
7Why do the wicked live *and* become old,
Yes, become mighty in power?
8Their descendants are established with them in their sight,
And their offspring before their eyes.
9Their houses *are* safe from fear,
Neither *is* the rod of God upon them.
10Their bull breeds without failure;
Their cow calves without miscarriage.
11They send forth their little ones like a flock,

20:20 [a]Literally *belly*

And their children dance.
[12]They sing to the tambourine and harp,
And rejoice to the sound of the flute.
[13]They spend their days in wealth,
And in a moment go down to the grave.[a]
[14]Yet they say to God, 'Depart from us,
For we do not desire the knowledge of Your ways.
[15]Who *is* the Almighty, that we should serve Him?
And what profit do we have if we pray to Him?'
[16]Indeed their prosperity *is* not in their hand;
The counsel of the wicked is far from me.

[17]"How often is the lamp of the wicked put out?
How often does their destruction come upon them,
The sorrows *God* distributes in His anger?
[18]They are like straw before the wind,
And like chaff that a storm carries away.
[19]*They say,* 'God lays up one's[a] iniquity for his children';
Let Him recompense him, that he may know *it.*
[20]Let his eyes see his destruction,
And let him drink of the wrath of the Almighty.
[21]For what does he care about his household after him,
When the number of his months is cut in half?

[22]"Can *anyone* teach God knowledge,
Since He judges those on high?
[23]One dies in his full strength,
Being wholly at ease and secure;
[24]His pails[a] are full of milk,
And the marrow of his bones is moist.
[25]Another man dies in the bitterness of his soul,
Never having eaten with pleasure.
[26]They lie down alike in the dust,
And worms cover them.

[27]"Look, I know your thoughts,
And the schemes *with which* you would wrong me.
[28]For you say,
'Where *is* the house of the prince?
And where *is* the tent,[a]
The dwelling place of the wicked?'
[29]Have you not asked those who travel the road?
And do you not know their signs?
[30]For the wicked are reserved for the day of doom;
They shall be brought out on the day of wrath.
[31]Who condemns his way to his face?
And who repays him *for what* he has done?
[32]Yet he shall be brought to the grave,
And a vigil kept over the tomb.
[33]The clods of the valley shall be sweet to him;
Everyone shall follow him,
As countless *have gone* before him.
[34]How then can you comfort me with empty words,
Since falsehood remains in your answers?"

Eliphaz Accuses Job of Wickedness

22 Then Eliphaz the Temanite answered and said:

[2]"Can a man be profitable to God,
Though he who is wise may be profitable to himself?
[3]*Is it* any pleasure to the Almighty that

21:13 [a]Or *Sheol* 21:19 [a]Literally *his* 21:24 [a]Septuagint and Vulgate read *bowels;* Syriac reads *sides;* Targum reads *breasts.* 21:28 [a]Vulgate omits *the tent.*

21:7–13 One of the great mysteries of life is that God allows wicked men to live, let alone prosper. Why did God let Herod do what he did (see Matt. 2:16–19)? Couldn't He have struck him dead before he slaughtered all the male children under age two? For the answer, see Isa. 55:9.

POINTS FOR OPEN-AIR PREACHING

22:2

Seeing Stars

Search the Internet for pictures of celebrities who have died. Print a large copy of each and staple the top left corner. Go through them one at a time, asking the crowd who they are and why they are famous (their most notable movie, etc.). Then ask what they all have in common.

As people call out their answers, watch for someone who is confident and loud. Ask for his name as you ask why the celebrity was famous, etc. Be sure you deliberately log his name into your memory. Call on him a couple of times and ask him for the identity of the next celebrity. In doing so you are building a relationship so that you can come back to him (or a couple of other people you have befriended) and ask, "Bill, tell me—what are your thoughts on what happens after someone dies? Is there a heaven? Is the person reincarnated? Do you think there is a hell?" Then take him through the Commandments (see Psa. 51:6 and John 4:7 comments).

Even if you don't sense a conviction of sin from the individual you're addressing, when open-air preaching it's wise to go ahead and explain the gospel. It may seem like a contentious crowd, but there could be one or more individuals who are listening.

you are righteous?
Or *is it* gain *to Him* that you make
your ways blameless?

4"Is it because of your fear of Him that
He corrects you,
And enters into judgment with you?
5*Is* not your wickedness great,
And your iniquity without end?
6For you have taken pledges from
your brother for no reason,
And stripped the naked of their
clothing.
7You have not given the weary water
to drink,
And you have withheld bread from
the hungry.
8But the mighty man possessed the land,
And the honorable man dwelt in it.
9You have sent widows away empty,
And the strength of the fatherless was
crushed.
10Therefore snares *are* all around you,
And sudden fear troubles you,
11Or darkness *so that* you cannot see;
And an abundance of water covers you.

12"Is not God in the height of heaven?
And see the highest stars, how lofty
they are!
13And you say, 'What does God know?
Can He judge through the deep
darkness?
14Thick clouds cover Him, so that He
cannot see,
And He walks above the circle of
heaven.'
15Will you keep to the old way
Which wicked men have trod,
16Who were cut down before their time,
Whose foundations were swept away
by a flood?
17They said to God, 'Depart from us!
What can the Almighty do to them?'[a]
18Yet He filled their houses with good
things;
But the counsel of the wicked is far
from me.

19"The righteous see *it* and are glad,
And the innocent laugh at them:
20'Surely our adversaries[a] are cut down,
And the fire consumes their remnant.'

21"Now acquaint yourself with Him, and
be at peace;
Thereby good will come to you.

22:17 [a]Septuagint and Syriac read *us*. 22:20 [a]Septuagint reads *substance*.

22:21 We are born not acquainted with God; neither are we at peace with Him. It is the Law that acquaints us with God's character and brings us to the foot of the cross (see Gal. 3:24).

[22]Receive, please, instruction from His
mouth,
And lay up His words in your heart.
[23]If you return to the Almighty, you
will be built up;
You will remove iniquity far from
your tents.
[24]Then you will lay your gold in the
dust,
And the *gold* of Ophir among the
stones of the brooks.
[25]Yes, the Almighty will be your gold[a]
And your precious silver;
[26]For then you will have your delight
in the Almighty,
And lift up your face to God.
[27]You will make your prayer to Him,
He will hear you,
And you will pay your vows.
[28]You will also declare a thing,
And it will be established for you;
So light will shine on your ways.
[29]When they cast *you* down, and you
say, 'Exaltation *will come!*'
Then He will save the humble *person*.
[30]He will *even* deliver one who is not
innocent;
Yes, he will be delivered by the purity
of your hands."

Job Proclaims God's Righteous Judgments

23 Then Job answered and said:

[2]"Even today my complaint is bitter;
My[a] hand is listless because of my
groaning.
[3]Oh, that I knew where I might find
Him,
That I might come to His seat!
[4]I would present *my* case before Him,
And fill my mouth with arguments.
[5]I would know the words *which* He
would answer me,
And understand what He would say
to me.
[6]Would He contend with me in His
great power?
No! But He would take *note* of me.
[7]There the upright could reason with
Him,
And I would be delivered forever
from my Judge.

[8]"Look, I go forward, but He is not
there,
And backward, but I cannot perceive
Him;
[9]When He works on the left hand, I
cannot behold *Him;*
When He turns to the right hand, I
cannot see *Him.*
[10]But He knows the way that I take;
When He has tested me, I shall come
forth as gold.
[11]My foot has held fast to His steps;
I have kept His way and not turned
aside.
[12]I have not departed from the
commandment of His lips;
I have treasured the words of His
mouth
More than my necessary *food.*

22:25 [a]The ancient versions suggest *defense;* Hebrew reads *gold* as in verse 24. **23:2** [a]Following Masoretic Text, Targum, and Vulgate; Septuagint and Syriac read *His.*

22:22 Memorize Scriptures. Lay them up in your heart (see Psa. 119:11). To do this, see page 1259.

"The Bible . . . is the one supreme source of revelation of the meaning of life, the nature of God and spiritual nature and needs of men. It is the only guide of life which really leads the spirit in the way of peace and salvation." *Woodrow Wilson*

22:26 What a blessing to be able to lift up our face to God! All our sins are washed away through the blood of the cross (see Rev. 1:5). We no longer need to hide our face in shame.

23:12 Do you love God's Word? Do you read it daily without fail? If not, let me ask you: Do you feed your stomach daily to nourish your body? Treasure His Word more than your necessary food. That means feeding on it daily to nourish your spirit. The prophet Jeremiah said, "Your words were found, and I ate them, and Your word was to me the joy and rejoicing of my heart" (Jer. 15:16). See the conditions and the wonderful promises of Psa. 1.

[13]"But He *is* unique, and who can make
Him change?
And *whatever* His soul desires, *that* He
does.
[14]For He performs *what is* appointed
for me,
And many such *things are* with Him.
[15]Therefore I am terrified at His
presence;
When I consider *this,* I am afraid of
Him.
[16]For God made my heart weak,
And the Almighty terrifies me;
[17]Because I was not cut off from the
presence of darkness,
And He did *not* hide deep darkness
from my face.

Job Complains of Violence on the Earth

24 "*Since* times are not hidden from
the Almighty,
Why do those who know Him see not
His days?

[2]"*Some* remove landmarks;
They seize flocks violently and feed
on them;
[3]They drive away the donkey of the
fatherless;
They take the widow's ox as a pledge.
[4]They push the needy off the road;
All the poor of the land are forced to
hide.
[5]Indeed, *like* wild donkeys in the desert,
They go out to their work, searching
for food.
The wilderness *yields* food for them
and for *their* children.
[6]They gather their fodder in the field
And glean in the vineyard of the
wicked.
[7]They spend the night naked, without
clothing,
And have no covering in the cold.
[8]They are wet with the showers of the
mountains,
And huddle around the rock for want
of shelter.

[9]"*Some* snatch the fatherless from the
breast,
And take a pledge from the poor.
[10]They cause *the poor* to go naked,
without clothing;
And they take away the sheaves from
the hungry.
[11]They press out oil within their walls,
And tread winepresses, yet suffer thirst.
[12]The dying groan in the city,
And the souls of the wounded cry out;
Yet God does not charge *them* with
wrong.

[13]"There are those who rebel against the
light;
They do not know its ways
Nor abide in its paths.
[14]The murderer rises with the light;
He kills the poor and needy;
And in the night he is like a thief.
[15]The eye of the adulterer waits for the
twilight,
Saying, 'No eye will see me';
And he disguises *his* face.
[16]In the dark they break into houses
Which they marked for themselves in
the daytime;
They do not know the light.
[17]For the morning is the same to them
as the shadow of death;
If *someone* recognizes *them,*
They are in the terrors of the shadow
of death.

24:13 God has given light to every man (see Job 25:3; John 1:9), but many refuse to be "enlightened with the light of life" (see Job 33:30; John 3:19,20).

"There is enough light for those who desire only to see, and enough darkness for those of a contrary disposition." *Blaise Pascal*

24:15 Some primitive tribes paint their faces so that their gods cannot recognize them when they kill. We may smile at such absurdity, but modern man is no different. He thinks that God, who made his eyes, cannot see his sin. But it is the sinner, not God, who is blind. See Psa. 94:7–11.

QUESTIONS & OBJECTIONS

"Why would the Bible compare us to a worm?"

Perhaps it is because, compared to the greatness of Almighty God, we are small, insignificant, and helpless. A lowly, crawling worm epitomizes blind helplessness. If you wanted to stomp on a worm crawling across your driveway, it could offer no resistance. It has no legs to be able to run; no claws to fend you off; no hiss, growl, or bite to scare you. It just lies there awaiting the fate of your big foot. Squish, and it is gone.

That is how we are when it comes to death. It hovers over us like a huge foot. It is so close that the Bible says we live "in the shadow of death," and we are helpless to change it.

However, when Jesus was born, we are told that upon those who sat "in the shadow of death, light has dawned" (Matt. 4:16). The Light of the World, Jesus Christ, has abolished death through His suffering death and resurrection.

So any who recognize that they are small, insignificant, and helpless can call upon Him in repentance and faith today, and He will rescue them from their greatest enemy. He did it for small, insignificant, and helpless me.

18"They *should be* swift on the face of
the waters,
Their portion *should be* cursed in the
earth,
So that no *one would* turn into the way
of their vineyards.
19As drought and heat consume the
snow waters,
So the grave[a] *consumes those who* have
sinned.
20The womb *should* forget him,
The worm *should* feed sweetly on him;
He *should* be remembered no more,
And wickedness *should* be broken like
a tree.
21For he preys on the barren *who* do
not bear,
And does no good for the widow.

22"But *God* draws the mighty away with
His power;
He rises up, but no *man* is sure of life.
23He gives them security, and they rely
on it;
Yet His eyes *are* on their ways.
24They are exalted for a little while,
Then they are gone.
They are brought low;
They are taken out of the way like all
others;
They dry out like the heads of grain.

25"Now if *it is* not *so,* who will prove me
a liar,
And make my speech worth nothing?"

Bildad: How Can Man Be Righteous?

25 Then Bildad the Shuhite answered
and said:
2"Dominion and fear *belong* to Him;
He makes peace in His high places.
3Is there any number to His armies?
Upon whom does His light not rise?
4How then can man be righteous
before God?
Or how can he be pure *who is* born of
a woman?
5If even the moon does not shine,
And the stars are not pure in His sight,
6How much less man, *who is* a maggot,
And a son of man, *who is* a worm?"

Job: Man's Frailty and God's Majesty

26 But Job answered and said:

2"How have you helped *him who is*
without power?
How have you saved the arm *that has*

24:19 [a]Or *Sheol*

25:4 Looking back on the cross, we can see how God intervened and can make us righteous before Him. In His eyes, the believer in Jesus is pure and blameless (see Col. 1:21,22).

no strength?
[3]How have you counseled *one who has* no wisdom?
And *how* have you declared sound advice to many?
[4]To whom have you uttered words?
And whose spirit came from you?

[5]"The dead tremble,
Those under the waters and those inhabiting them.
[6]Sheol *is* naked before Him,
And Destruction has no covering.
[7]He stretches out the north over empty space;
He hangs the earth on nothing.
[8]He binds up the water in His thick clouds,
Yet the clouds are not broken under it.
[9]He covers the face of *His* throne,
And spreads His cloud over it.
[10]He drew a circular horizon on the face of the waters,
At the boundary of light and darkness.
[11]The pillars of heaven tremble,
And are astonished at His rebuke.
[12]He stirs up the sea with His power,
And by His understanding He breaks up the storm.
[13]By His Spirit He adorned the heavens;
His hand pierced the fleeing serpent.
[14]Indeed these *are* the mere edges of His ways,
And how small a whisper we hear of Him!
But the thunder of His power who can understand?"

Job Maintains His Integrity

27 Moreover Job continued his discourse, and said:
[2]"*As* God lives, *who* has taken away my justice,
And the Almighty, *who* has made my soul bitter,
[3]As long as my breath *is* in me,
And the breath of God in my nostrils,
[4]My lips will not speak wickedness,
Nor my tongue utter deceit.
[5]Far be it from me
That I should say you are right;
Till I die I will not put away my integrity from me.
[6]My righteousness I hold fast, and will not let it go;
My heart shall not reproach *me* as long as I live.

[7]"May my enemy be like the wicked,
And he who rises up against me like the unrighteous.
[8]For what is the hope of the hypocrite,
Though he may gain *much*,
If God takes away his life?
[9]Will God hear his cry
When trouble comes upon him?
[10]Will he delight himself in the Almighty?
Will he always call on God?

[11]"I will teach you about the hand of God;
What *is* with the Almighty I will not conceal.
[12]Surely all of you have seen *it*;

26:6 Is hell "separation from God"? See Psa. 139:7,8 comment.

26:7 Although the Bible is not a scientific book, it contains scientific truths that were not discovered by science until thousands of years after they were written. Scripture has the indelible fingerprint of God all over it. See Heb. 11:3 comment.

26:14 In the city of Christchurch, New Zealand, the first part of this verse is carved into stone above the doorway of the city's museum. How few gaze at the marvels of God's creation and see the unspeakable genius of His incredible creative hand. They admire the painting and ignore the Painter (see Rom. 1:25).

27:6 Without an understanding of the spiritual nature of the moral Law, sinners will affirm their own righteousness. The Law convinces them that their "righteous" deeds are as filthy rags (see Isa. 64:6).

"We study the law of God because the law reveals to us not only the righteousness of God and His holiness, but by contrast it stands as a mirror. I look in the mirror of God's law and I realize my utter helplessness in and of myself." *R. C. Sproul*

Why then do you behave with
complete nonsense?

13"This is the portion of a wicked man
with God,
And the heritage of oppressors,
received from the Almighty:
14If his children are multiplied, *it is* for
the sword;
And his offspring shall not be
satisfied with bread.
15Those who survive him shall be
buried in death,
And their[a] widows shall not weep,
16Though he heaps up silver like dust,
And piles up clothing like clay—
17He may pile *it* up, but the just will
wear *it*,
And the innocent will divide the silver.
18He builds his house like a moth,[a]
Like a booth *which* a watchman makes.
19The rich man will lie down,
But not be gathered *up*;[a]
He opens his eyes,
And he *is* no more.
20Terrors overtake him like a flood;
A tempest steals him away in the night.
21The east wind carries him away, and
he is gone;
It sweeps him out of his place.
22It hurls against him and does not
spare;
He flees desperately from its power.
23*Men* shall clap their hands at him,
And shall hiss him out of his place.

Job's Discourse on Wisdom

28 "Surely there is a mine for silver,
And a place *where* gold is refined.
2Iron is taken from the earth,
And copper *is* smelted *from* ore.
3*Man* puts an end to darkness,
And searches every recess
For ore in the darkness and the
shadow of death.
4He breaks open a shaft away from
people;
In places forgotten by feet
They hang far away from men;
They swing to and fro.
5*As for* the earth, from it comes bread,
But underneath it is turned up as by
fire;
6Its stones *are* the source of sapphires,
And it contains gold dust.
7*That* path no bird knows,
Nor has the falcon's eye seen it.
8The proud lions[a] have not trodden it,
Nor has the fierce lion passed over it.
9He puts his hand on the flint;
He overturns the mountains at the
roots.
10He cuts out channels in the rocks,
And his eye sees every precious thing.
11He dams up the streams from trickling;
What is hidden he brings forth to light.

I do not feel obliged to believe that same God who endowed us with sense, reason, and intellect had intended for us to forgo their use.

GALILEO

12"But where can wisdom be found?
And where *is* the place of
understanding?
13Man does not know its value,
Nor is it found in the land of the living.
14The deep says, '*It is* not in me';
And the sea says, '*It is* not with me.'
15It cannot be purchased for gold,
Nor can silver be weighed *for* its price.
16It cannot be valued in the gold of
Ophir,
In precious onyx or sapphire.
17Neither gold nor crystal can equal it,

27:15 [a]Literally *his* 27:18 [a]Following Masoretic Text and Vulgate; Septuagint and Syriac read *spider* (compare 8:14); Targum reads *decay*. 27:19 [a]Following Masoretic Text and Targum; Septuagint and Syriac read *But shall not add* (that is, do it again); Vulgate reads *But take away nothing*. 28:8 [a]Literally *sons of pride*, figurative of the great lions

28:12 See vv. 18 and 28. Wisdom and understanding come from God alone, and we have access to them through the name of Jesus. See James 1:5,6 for God's promise of wisdom to all who ask it of Him.

Nor can it be exchanged for jewelry
of fine gold.
18No mention shall be made of coral or
quartz,
For the price of wisdom *is* above rubies.
19The topaz of Ethiopia cannot equal it,
Nor can it be valued in pure gold.

20"From where then does wisdom come?
And where *is* the place of
understanding?
21It is hidden from the eyes of all living,
And concealed from the birds of the
air.
22Destruction and Death say,
'We have heard a report about it with
our ears.'
23God understands its way,
And He knows its place.
24For He looks to the ends of the earth,
And sees under the whole heavens,
25To establish a weight for the wind,
And apportion the waters by measure.
26When He made a law for the rain,
And a path for the thunderbolt,
27Then He saw *wisdom*[a] and declared it;
He prepared it, indeed, He searched it
out.
28And to man He said,
'Behold, the fear of the Lord, that *is*
wisdom,
And to depart from evil *is*
understanding.' "

Job's Summary Defense

29 Job further continued his discourse,
and said:
2"Oh, that I were as *in* months past,
As *in* the days *when* God watched
over me;
3When His lamp shone upon my head,
And when by His light I walked
through darkness;
4Just as I was in the days of my prime,
When the friendly counsel of God
was over my tent;
5When the Almighty *was* yet with me,
When my children *were* around me;
6When my steps were bathed with
cream,[a]
And the rock poured out rivers of oil
for me!

7"When I went out to the gate by the
city,
When I took my seat in the open
square,
8The young men saw me and hid,
And the aged arose *and* stood;
9The princes refrained from talking,
And put *their* hand on their mouth;
10The voice of nobles was hushed,
And their tongue stuck to the roof of
their mouth.
11When the ear heard, then it blessed me,
And when the eye saw, then it
approved me;
12Because I delivered the poor who
cried out,
The fatherless and *the one who* had no
helper.
13The blessing of a perishing *man* came
upon me,
And I caused the widow's heart to
sing for joy.
14I put on righteousness, and it clothed
me;
My justice *was* like a robe and a turban.
15I *was* eyes to the blind,
And I *was* feet to the lame.
16I *was* a father to the poor,

28:27 [a]Literally *it* 29:6 [a]Masoretic Text reads *wrath;* ancient versions and some Hebrew manuscripts read *cream* (compare 20:17).

28:26 Scientific facts in the Bible. Centuries after Job wrote this, scientists began to discern the "law for the rain." Rainfall is part of a process called the "hydrologic cycle." The sun evaporates water from the ocean. The water vapor then rises and becomes clouds. This water in the clouds falls back to earth as rain, and collects in streams and rivers, then makes its way back to the ocean. That process repeats itself again and again. Scientists discovered this cycle in the seventeenth century, but amazingly the Scriptures described it centuries before. The prophet Amos (9:6) wrote that God "calls for the waters of the sea, and pours them out upon the face of the earth." Scientists are just beginning to fully understand God's "laws for the rain."

And I searched out the case *that* I did
not know.
17I broke the fangs of the wicked,
And plucked the victim from his teeth.

18"Then I said, 'I shall die in my nest,
And multiply *my* days as the sand.
19My root *is* spread out to the waters,
And the dew lies all night on my
branch.
20My glory *is* fresh within me,
And my bow is renewed in my hand.'

21"*Men* listened to me and waited,
And kept silence for my counsel.
22After my words they did not speak
again,
And my speech settled on them *as dew.*
23They waited for me *as* for the rain,
And they opened their mouth wide *as*
for the spring rain.
24*If* I mocked at them, they did not
believe *it,*
And the light of my countenance they
did not cast down.
25I chose the way for them, and sat as
chief;
So I dwelt as a king in the army,
As one *who* comforts mourners.

30 "But now they mock at me, *men*
younger than I,
Whose fathers I disdained to put
with the dogs of my flock.
2Indeed, what *profit* is the strength of
their hands to me?
Their vigor has perished.
3*They are* gaunt from want and famine,
Fleeing late to the wilderness,
desolate and waste,
4Who pluck mallow by the bushes,
And broom tree roots *for* their food.
5They were driven out from among
men,
They shouted at them as *at* a thief.
6*They had* to live in the clefts of the
valleys,
In caves of the earth and the rocks.
7Among the bushes they brayed,
Under the nettles they nestled.
8*They were* sons of fools,
Yes, sons of vile men;
They were scourged from the land.

9" And now I am their taunting song;
Yes, I am their byword.
10They abhor me, they keep far from me;
They do not hesitate to spit in my face.
11Because He has loosed my[a] bowstring
and afflicted me,
They have cast off restraint before me.
12At *my* right *hand* the rabble arises;
They push away my feet,
And they raise against me their ways
of destruction.
13They break up my path,
They promote my calamity;
They have no helper.
14They come as broad breakers;
Under the ruinous storm they roll
along.
15Terrors are turned upon me;
They pursue my honor as the wind,
And my prosperity has passed like a
cloud.

16" And now my soul is poured out
because of my *plight;*
The days of affliction take hold of me.
17My bones are pierced in me at night,
And my gnawing pains take no rest.
18By great force my garment is
disfigured;
It binds me about as the collar of my
coat.
19He has cast me into the mire,
And I have become like dust and ashes.

20"I cry out to You, but You do not
answer me;
I stand up, and You regard me.
21*But* You have become cruel to me;
With the strength of Your hand You
oppose me.
22You lift me up to the wind and cause
me to ride *on it;*
You spoil my success.

30:11 [a]Following Masoretic Text, Syriac, and Targum; Septuagint and Vulgate read *His.*

23For I know *that* You will bring me *to*
death,
And *to* the house appointed for all
living.

24"Surely He would not stretch out *His*
hand against a heap of ruins,
If they cry out when He destroys *it*.
25Have I not wept for him who was in
trouble?
Has *not* my soul grieved for the poor?
26But when I looked for good, evil
came *to me;*
And when I waited for light, then
came darkness.
27My heart is in turmoil and cannot rest;
Days of affliction confront me.
28I go about mourning, but not in the
sun;
I stand up in the assembly *and* cry out
for help.
29I am a brother of jackals,
And a companion of ostriches.
30My skin grows black and falls from me;
My bones burn with fever.
31My harp is *turned* to mourning,
And my flute to the voice of those
who weep.

31 "I have made a covenant with my
eyes;
Why then should I look upon a
young woman?
2For what *is* the allotment of God from
above,
And the inheritance of the Almighty
from on high?
3*Is* it not destruction for the wicked,
And disaster for the workers of
iniquity?
4Does He not see my ways,
And count all my steps?

5"If I have walked with falsehood,
Or if my foot has hastened to deceit,
6Let me be weighed on honest scales,
That God may know my integrity.
7If my step has turned from the way,
Or my heart walked after my eyes,
Or if any spot adheres to my hands,
8*Then* let me sow, and another eat;
Yes, let my harvest be rooted out.

9"If my heart has been enticed by a
woman,
Or *if* I have lurked at my neighbor's
door,
10*Then* let my wife grind for another,
And let others bow down over her.
11For that *would be* wickedness;
Yes, it *would be* iniquity *deserving of*
judgment.
12For that *would be* a fire *that* consumes
to destruction,
And would root out all my increase.

13"If I have despised the cause of my
male or female servant
When they complained against me,
14What then shall I do when God rises
up?
When He punishes, how shall I
answer Him?
15Did not He who made me in the
womb make them?
Did not the same One fashion us in
the womb?

16"If I have kept the poor from *their*
desire,

30:23 See Heb. 9:27 on why we die. Death is an appointment we all must keep. For whether death is the end, see Rev. 20:14 comment.

"There is no question of death or life for any of us, only a question of this death or of that—of a machine gun bullet now or a cancer forty years later. What does war do to death? It certainly does not make it more frequent; 100 percent of us die, and the percentage cannot be increased." *C. S. Lewis*

31:1 Lust is an attractive flame to the moth of a sinful heart. If lust is not put to death, it will put us to death. Whoever commits adultery "destroys his own soul" (Prov. 6:32). Read what Jesus said about lust in Matt. 5:27–29. See also Phil. 4:8; James 1:14,15. To guard yourself against the temptation of pornography, see Gal. 5:16 comment.

Or caused the eyes of the widow to
fail,
17Or eaten my morsel by myself,
So that the fatherless could not eat of it
18(But from my youth I reared him as a
father,
And from my mother's womb I
guided *the widow*[a]);
19If I have seen anyone perish for lack
of clothing,
Or any poor *man* without covering;
20If his heart[a] has not blessed me,
And *if* he was *not* warmed with the
fleece of my sheep;
21If I have raised my hand against the
fatherless,
When I saw I had help in the gate;
22*Then* let my arm fall from my
shoulder,
Let my arm be torn from the socket.
23For destruction *from* God *is* a terror
to me,
And because of His magnificence I
cannot endure.

One of the most striking things about the Bible is the vigor with which both Testaments emphasize the reality and terror of God's wrath.

J. I. PACKER

24"If I have made gold my hope,
Or said to fine gold, '*You are* my
confidence';
25If I have rejoiced because my wealth
was great,
And because my hand had gained
much;
26If I have observed the sun[a] when it
shines,
Or the moon moving *in* brightness,
27So that my heart has been secretly
enticed,
And my mouth has kissed my hand;
28This also *would be* an iniquity
deserving of judgment,
For I would have denied God *who is*
above.

29"If I have rejoiced at the destruction of
him who hated me,
Or lifted myself up when evil found
him
30(Indeed I have not allowed my mouth
to sin
By asking for a curse on his soul);
31If the men of my tent have not said,
'Who is there that has not been
satisfied with his meat?'
32(*But* no sojourner had to lodge in the
street,
For I have opened my doors to the
traveler[a]);
33If I have covered my transgressions as
Adam,
By hiding my iniquity in my bosom,
34Because I feared the great multitude,
And dreaded the contempt of
families,
So that I kept silence
And did not go out of the door—
35Oh, that I had one to hear me!
Here is my mark.
Oh, that the Almighty would answer
me,
That my Prosecutor had written a book!
36Surely I would carry it on my
shoulder,
And bind it on me *like* a crown;
37I would declare to Him the number
of my steps;
Like a prince I would approach Him.

38"If my land cries out against me,
And its furrows weep together;
39If I have eaten its fruit[a] without money,
Or caused its owners to lose their lives;
40*Then* let thistles grow instead of wheat,
And weeds instead of barley."

The words of Job are ended.

Elihu Contradicts Job's Friends

32 So these three men ceased answering Job, because he *was* right-

31:18 [a]Literally *her* (compare verse 16) 31:20 [a]Literally *loins* 31:26 [a]Literally *light* 31:32 [a]Following Septuagint, Syriac, Targum, and Vulgate; Masoretic Text reads *road.* 31:39 [a]Literally *its strength*

eous in his own eyes. [2]Then the wrath of
Elihu, the son of Barachel the Buzite, of
the family of Ram, was aroused against
Job; his wrath was aroused because he
justified himself rather than God. [3]Also
against his three friends his wrath was
aroused, because they had found no answer, and *yet* had condemned Job.
[4]Now because they *were* years older
than he, Elihu had waited to speak to
Job.[a] [5]When Elihu saw that *there was* no
answer in the mouth of these three men,
his wrath was aroused.
[6]So Elihu, the son of Barachel the
Buzite, answered and said:

"I *am* young in years, and you *are* very old;
Therefore I was afraid,
And dared not declare my opinion to you.
[7]I said, 'Age[a] should speak,
And multitude of years should teach wisdom.'
[8]But *there is* a spirit in man,
And the breath of the Almighty gives him understanding.
[9]Great men[a] are not *always* wise,
Nor do the aged *always* understand justice.

[10]"Therefore I say, 'Listen to me,
I also will declare my opinion.'
[11]Indeed I waited for your words,
I listened to your reasonings, while you searched out what to say.
[12]I paid close attention to you;
And surely not one of you convinced Job,
Or answered his words—
[13]Lest you say,
'We have found wisdom';
God will vanquish him, not man.
[14]Now he has not directed *his* words against me;
So I will not answer him with your words.

[15]"They are dismayed and answer no more;
Words escape them.
[16]And I have waited, because they did not speak,
Because they stood still *and* answered no more.
[17]I also will answer my part,
I too will declare my opinion.
[18]For I am full of words;
The spirit within me compels me.
[19]Indeed my belly *is* like wine *that* has no vent;
It is ready to burst like new wineskins.
[20]I will speak, that I may find relief;
I must open my lips and answer.
[21]Let me not, I pray, show partiality to anyone;
Nor let me flatter any man.
[22]For I do not know how to flatter,
Else my Maker would soon take me away.

Elihu Contradicts Job

33 "But please, Job, hear my speech,
And listen to all my words.
[2]Now, I open my mouth;
My tongue speaks in my mouth.
[3]My words *come* from my upright heart;
My lips utter pure knowledge.

32:4 [a]Vulgate reads *till Job had spoken.* 32:7 [a]Literally *Days,* that is, years 32:9 [a]Or *Men of many years*

32:1,2 Elihu was angry because Job was righteous in his own eyes and tried to justify himself rather than justify God. This is so often what sinners do. Instead of blaming themselves for sin, they blame God: "He made me like this!"

Likewise, when a natural tragedy happens, the world calls it "an act of God." Instead of understanding that we live in a fallen creation and that suffering and tragedies are a result of man's sin, they blame God. The godly, however, would rather justify a holy God than sinful man.

32:18 The Job of this old world is covered in sour boils. The Christian is like Elihu. The spirit of Christ compels him to speak. He is full of new wine and is ready to burst with the truth of the gospel.

33:4 The Origin of Life

The theory of biological evolution requires that nonliving chemicals somehow developed completely by chance into highly complex, living organisms. However, nonliving things coming to life is the stuff of science fiction, not science. Louis Pasteur's famous and repeatable experiments have demonstrated the Law of Biogenesis: that "spontaneous generation" is impossible and that life can arise only from other life.

Scientists have spent decades trying to create life in the laboratory in carefully controlled experiments, and have repeatedly failed. If highly intelligent scientists using all the latest, most sophisticated equipment available cannot create a living cell—even with the code and materials of life available to them—how could molecules possibly assemble themselves into living cells through only mindless, undirected random chance?

The famous astronomer and mathematician Sir Frederick Hoyle calculated the probability of the spontaneous generation of life:

> No matter how large the environment one considers, life cannot have had a random beginning. Troops of monkeys thundering away at random on typewriters could not produce the works of Shakespeare, for the practical reason that the whole observable universe is not large enough to contain the necessary monkey hordes, the necessary typewriters, and certainly not the waste paper baskets required for the deposition of wrong attempts. The same is true for living material.
>
> The likelihood of the spontaneous formation of life from inanimate matter is one to a number with 40,000 noughts after it...It is big enough to bury Darwin and the whole theory of evolution. There was no primeval soup, neither on this planet nor on any other, and if the beginnings of life were not random, they must therefore have been the product of purposeful intelligence.

In Darwin's time, it was assumed that "simple" cells were just primitive blobs of protoplasm, so it wasn't too hard for scientists to envision them assembling by random chance. Because cells cannot be seen with the naked eye, scientists mistakenly thought that the chemistry of life was simple. But with today's sophisticated microscopes, molecular biology has shown how vastly complex even a "simple" cell actually is.

Molecular biologist Michael Denton, an evolutionist, acknowledges:

> Although the tiniest bacterial cells are incredibly small, weighing less than 10^{-12} grams, each is in effect a veritable micro-miniaturized factory containing thousands of exquisitely designed pieces of intricate molecular machinery, made up altogether of one hundred thousand million atoms, far more complicated than any machinery built by man and absolutely without parallel in the non-living world.

Not only are there no experiments demonstrating how life could have come into being, but the more scientists search for answers the more they are astounded at the complexity they find—and the more the evidence confirms that life could not have arisen purely by chance. Geochemist Jeffrey Bada, from the San Diego Scripps Institute, points out the evolutionists' ongoing dilemma concerning this question:

> Today as we leave the twentieth century, we still face the biggest unsolved problem that we had when we entered the twentieth century: How did life originate on Earth?

In 2001, PBS aired the TV series "Evolution," in which they put together all the best information they could find to demonstrate the case for evolution. In a *Washington Post* online forum, producer Richard Hutton was asked, "What are some of the larger questions which are still unanswered by evolutionary theory?" He named several items in his response, but the item topping his list is very telling:

> The origin of life. There is no consensus at all here—lots of theories, little science. That's one of the reasons we didn't cover it in the series. The evidence wasn't very good.

We can appreciate his honest admission that all they have is theories—no scientific proof. If they had any evidence at all, they would have presented it. Of course, there is no evidence supporting the claim that life arose by natural causes—because life has a Supernatural Cause.

(Adapted from *How to Know God Exists.*)

"There is not a shred of objective evidence to support the hypothesis that life began in an organic soup here on the earth...So why do biologists indulge in unsubstantiated fantasies in order to deny what is so patently obvious, that the 200,000 amino acid chains, and hence life, did not appear by chance?" *Frederick Hoyle*

[4]The Spirit of God has made me,
And the breath of the Almighty gives me life.
[5]If you can answer me,
Set *your words* in order before me;
Take your stand.
[6]Truly I *am* as your spokesman[a] before God;
I also have been formed out of clay.
[7]Surely no fear of me will terrify you,
Nor will my hand be heavy on you.

[8]"Surely you have spoken in my hearing,
And I have heard the sound of *your* words, *saying,*
[9]'I *am* pure, without transgression;
I *am* innocent, and *there is* no iniquity in me.
[10]Yet He finds occasions against me,
He counts me as His enemy;
[11]He puts my feet in the stocks,
He watches all my paths.'

[12]"Look, *in* this you are not righteous.
I will answer you,
For God is greater than man.
[13]Why do you contend with Him?
For He does not give an accounting of any of His words.
[14]For God may speak in one way, or in another,
Yet man does not perceive it.
[15]In a dream, in a vision of the night,
When deep sleep falls upon men,
While slumbering on their beds,
[16]Then He opens the ears of men,
And seals their instruction.
[17]In order to turn man *from his* deed,
And conceal pride from man,
[18]He keeps back his soul from the Pit,
And his life from perishing by the sword.

[19]"*Man* is also chastened with pain on his bed,
And with strong *pain* in many of his bones,
[20]So that his life abhors bread,
And his soul succulent food.
[21]His flesh wastes away from sight,
And his bones stick out *which once* were not seen.
[22]Yes, his soul draws near the Pit,
And his life to the executioners.

[23]"If there is a messenger for him,
A mediator, one among a thousand,
To show man His uprightness,
[24]Then He is gracious to him, and says,
"Deliver him from going down to the Pit;
I have found a ransom';
[25]His flesh shall be young like a child's,
He shall return to the days of his youth.
[26]He shall pray to God, and He will delight in him,
He shall see His face with joy,
For He restores to man His righteousness.
[27]Then he looks at men and says,
"I have sinned, and perverted *what was* right,
And it did not profit me.'
[28]He will redeem his[a] soul from going down to the Pit,
And his[b] life shall see the light.

[29]"Behold, God works all these *things,*
Twice, *in fact,* three *times* with a man,
[30]To bring back his soul from the Pit,
That he may be enlightened with the light of life.

[31]"Give ear, Job, listen to me;
Hold your peace, and I will speak.
[32]If you have anything to say, answer me;
Speak, for I desire to justify you.

33:6 [a]Literally *as your mouth* 33:28 [a]Or *my* (Kethib) [b]Or *my* (Kethib)

33:23–28 Here is the plan of salvation. God provided a Mediator to show man God's uprightness, to provide a ransom, to redeem our souls and save us from hell. See also Job 9:33 comment.

QUESTIONS & OBJECTIONS

Q 34:14,15

"Were all the ingredients to produce life present on earth before life existed?"

Definitely not. Dirt is just dirt; it has no life at all. The life came from the source of all life, God: "The LORD God formed man of the dust of the ground, and breathed into his nostrils the breath of life; and man became a living being" (Gen. 2:7).

You are a living being. Your life (your soul) is invisible. When that soul leaves the body in which it lives, no one will see it leave. A doctor may pronounce you dead because your life has left your body, but he won't see your life pass into eternity. Again, God is the source of that life. When someone becomes a Christian he is "born" spiritually (see John 3:3–5). The Holy Spirit abides in him; he receives the life of God, and that spiritual life is eternal.

If you carefully study the words of Jesus, you will notice that He continually made the incredible claim that He was the very source of life: "I am the way, the truth, and the life," "I am the resurrection and the life," "I have come that they might have life," etc. The Bible says of Jesus, "In Him was life," "Christ, who is our life," and "He who has the Son has life."

So those who reject Jesus Christ reject the most valuable thing in the universe: eternal life. See also Gen. 3:19; Psa. 104:29; Eccles. 12:7. For the origin of life, see 33:4 comment.

33If not, listen to me;
Hold your peace, and I will teach you wisdom."

Elihu Proclaims God's Justice

34 Elihu further answered and said:

2"Hear my words, you wise *men;*
Give ear to me, you who have knowledge.
3For the ear tests words
As the palate tastes food.
4Let us choose justice for ourselves;
Let us know among ourselves what *is* good.

5"For Job has said, 'I am righteous,
But God has taken away my justice;
6Should I lie concerning my right?
My wound *is* incurable, *though I am* without transgression.'
7What man *is* like Job,
Who drinks scorn like water,
8Who goes in company with the workers of iniquity,
And walks with wicked men?
9For he has said, 'It profits a man nothing
That he should delight in God.'

10"Therefore listen to me, you men of understanding:
Far be it from God *to do* wickedness,
And *from* the Almighty to *commit* iniquity.
11For He repays man *according to* his work,
And makes man to find a reward according to *his* way.
12Surely God will never do wickedly,
Nor will the Almighty pervert justice.
13Who gave Him charge over the earth?
Or who appointed *Him over* the whole world?
14If He should set His heart on it,
If He should gather to Himself His Spirit and His breath,
15All flesh would perish together,
And man would return to dust.

16"If *you have* understanding, hear this;
Listen to the sound of my words:
17Should one who hates justice govern?
Will you condemn *Him who is* most just?
18*Is it fitting* to say to a king, '*You are*

34:10–12 We need never question the integrity of God. He is without sin. If He gave us our just reward according to our sins, we would be in hell in an instant. See vv. 14,15.

worthless,'
And to nobles, '*You are* wicked'?
19Yet He is not partial to princes,
Nor does He regard the rich more than the poor;
For they *are* all the work of His hands.
20In a moment they die, in the middle of the night;
The people are shaken and pass away;
The mighty are taken away without a hand.

21"For His eyes *are* on the ways of man,
And He sees all his steps.
22There is no darkness nor shadow of death
Where the workers of iniquity may hide themselves.
23For He need not further consider a man,
That he should go before God in judgment.
24He breaks in pieces mighty men without inquiry,
And sets others in their place.
25Therefore He knows their works;
He overthrows *them* in the night,
And they are crushed.
26He strikes them as wicked *men*
In the open sight of others,
27Because they turned back from Him,
And would not consider any of His ways,
28So that they caused the cry of the poor to come to Him;
For He hears the cry of the afflicted.
29When He gives quietness, who then can make trouble?
And when He hides *His* face, who then can see Him,
Whether *it is* against a nation or a man alone?—
30That the hypocrite should not reign,
Lest the people be ensnared.
31"For has *anyone* said to God,
'I have borne *chastening;*
I will offend no more;
32Teach me *what* I do not see;
If I have done iniquity, I will do no more'?
33Should He repay *it* according to your *terms,*
Just because you disavow it?
You must choose, and not I;
Therefore speak what you know.

34"Men of understanding say to me,
Wise men who listen to me:
35'Job speaks without knowledge,
His words *are* without wisdom.'
36Oh, that Job were tried to the utmost,
Because *his* answers *are like* those of wicked men!
37For he adds rebellion to his sin;
He claps *his hands* among us,
And multiplies his words against God."

Elihu Condemns Self-Righteousness

35 Moreover Elihu answered and said:
2"Do you think this is right?
Do you say,
'My righteousness is more than God's'?
3For you say,
'What advantage will it be to You?
What profit shall I have, more than *if* I had sinned?'

4"I will answer you,
And your companions with you.
5Look to the heavens and see;
And behold the clouds—
They are higher than you.

34:21 Even the grave will not hide sinful man from the justice of Almighty God. See also Amos 9:2 comment.

34:34–37 Job was convinced that he was a righteous man (see 31:5–8; 32:1). This was because he lacked knowledge, and therefore his words were spoken without wisdom. This is why the Law must be used to reach the lost. They are convinced that they are righteous, and they need the Law to bring the knowledge of sin (see Rom. 3:19,20). This "key of knowledge" opens the sinner's heart to the gospel, but read Luke 11:52 to learn what the teachers of the Law did with it in the time of Christ.

QUESTIONS & OBJECTIONS

35:16 "Evolution is a proven fact."

At one time scientists didn't know that the surface of the Earth was spinning at over 1,000 miles per hour, that the continents move, and that bowling balls don't fall faster than marbles. No doubt many things science teaches as truth today will be laughed at in one hundred years. (See Eph. 3:9 comment.) Regardless, many people have been led to believe that science deals in certainties and provides us with facts and proofs that we can place our trust in. But the field of science actually cannot give us any *knowledge* at all. Despite the fact that the very meaning of the word "science" is "knowledge," science can never truly *know* anything definitively, as Bertrand Russell explains:

> A religious creed differs from a scientific theory in claiming to embody eternal and absolutely certain truth, whereas science is always tentative, expecting that modification in its present theories will sooner or later be found necessary, and aware that its method is one which is logically incapable of arriving at a complete and final demonstration.

Richard Phillips Feynman, an accomplished American physicist, stated, "If you thought that science was certain—well, that is just an error on your part." Since all scientific statements are open to reevaluation as new data is acquired, the reality is that science can never establish anything as "truth" or "fact." No scientific statement is ever formally beyond question. So whenever "proof" is mentioned in a scientific context, it is inaccurate.

Why then would evolutionists falsely claim that evolution "is a fact and we don't need to prove it anymore"? Perhaps they try to convince people that evolution has already been conclusively proven . . . because they have no actual proof to offer. There is no concrete evidence for the theory of evolution. *There isn't any*. It is simply an idea that cannot be backed up with evidence. How then can anyone think that the theory of evolution is scientific? Information theorist Hubert Yockey rightly observed:

> One must conclude that, contrary to the established and current wisdom, a scenario describing the genesis of life on earth by chance and natural causes which can be accepted on the basis of *fact and not faith* has not yet been written.

(Adapted from *How to Know God Exists*.)

6If you sin, what do you accomplish
against Him?
Or, *if* your transgressions are
multiplied, what do you do to
Him?
7If you are righteous, what do you give
Him?
Or what does He receive from your
hand?
8Your wickedness affects a man such
as you,
And your righteousness a son of man.

9"Because of the multitude of
oppressions they cry out;
They cry out for help because of the
arm of the mighty.
10But no one says, 'Where *is* God my
Maker,
Who gives songs in the night,
11Who teaches us more than the beasts
of the earth,
And makes us wiser than the birds of
heaven?'
12There they cry out, but He does not
answer,
Because of the pride of evil men.
13Surely God will not listen to empty *talk,*

35:10–12 We are not just a higher form of animal, but have been made in the image of God. He has given us the ability to understand, to reason, to create. We are moral beings. See Psa. 32:9 comment.

However, blinding pride stops so many from giving God thanks for His wonderful blessings. Pride is such a wicked thing. It tears apart families when proud husbands and wives will not humble themselves and apologize. They would rather destroy their marriage, leave their family in ruin, and keep their cursed pride. The Bible says, "Everyone proud in heart is an abomination to the LORD" (Prov. 16:5.) God resists the proud and gives grace to the humble (see 1 Pet. 5:5).

Nor will the Almighty regard it.
[14]Although you say you do not see Him,
Yet justice *is* before Him, and you
must wait for Him.
[15]And now, because He has not
punished in His anger,
Nor taken much notice of folly,
[16]Therefore Job opens his mouth in vain;
He multiplies words without
knowledge."

Elihu Proclaims God's Goodness

36 Elihu also proceeded and said:
[2]"Bear with me a little, and I will show
you
That *there are* yet words to speak on
God's behalf.
[3]I will fetch my knowledge from afar;
I will ascribe righteousness to my
Maker.
[4]For truly my words *are* not false;
One who is perfect in knowledge *is*
with you.

[5]"Behold, God *is* mighty, but despises
no one;
He is mighty in strength of
understanding.
[6]He does not preserve the life of the
wicked,
But gives justice to the oppressed.
[7]He does not withdraw His eyes from
the righteous;
But *they are* on the throne with kings,
For He has seated them forever,
And they are exalted.
[8]And if *they are* bound in fetters,
Held in the cords of affliction,
[9]Then He tells them their work and
their transgressions—
That they have acted defiantly.
[10]He also opens their ear to instruction,
And commands that they turn from
iniquity.
[11]If they obey and serve *Him,*
They shall spend their days in
prosperity,
And their years in pleasures.
[12]But if they do not obey,
They shall perish by the sword,
And they shall die without knowledge.[a]

[13]"But the hypocrites in heart store up
wrath;
They do not cry for help when He
binds them.
[14]They die in youth,
And their life *ends* among the
perverted persons.[a]
[15]He delivers the poor in their affliction,
And opens their ears in oppression.

[16]"Indeed He would have brought you
out of dire distress,
Into a broad place where *there is* no
restraint;
And what is set on your table *would*
be full of richness.
[17]But you are filled with the judgment
due the wicked;
Judgment and justice take hold *of you.*
[18]Because *there is* wrath, *beware* lest He
take you away with *one* blow;
For a large ransom would not help
you avoid *it.*
[19]Will your riches,
Or all the mighty forces,
Keep you from distress?
[20]Do not desire the night,
When people are cut off in their place.
[21]Take heed, do not turn to iniquity,
For you have chosen this rather than
affliction.

[22]"Behold, God is exalted by His power;
Who teaches like Him?

36:12 [a]Masoretic Text reads *as one without knowledge.* 36:14 [a]Hebrew *qedeshim,* that is, those practicing sodomy and prostitution in religious rituals

36:13 See Rom. 2:5 to see what is in store for the ungodly.

36:18 The Law reveals to the sinner the reality of God's wrath and his utter helplessness to save himself from God's justice (see John 3:36; Rom. 4:15). See also Psa. 49:6,7 and Prov. 11:4 comments.

[23]Who has assigned Him His way,
Or who has said, 'You have done wrong'?

Elihu Proclaims God's Majesty

[24]"Remember to magnify His work,
Of which men have sung.
[25]Everyone has seen it;
Man looks on *it* from afar.

[26]"Behold, God *is* great, and we do not know *Him;*
Nor can the number of His years *be* discovered.
[27]For He draws up drops of water,
Which distill as rain from the mist,
[28]Which the clouds drop down
And pour abundantly on man.
[29]Indeed, can *anyone* understand the spreading of clouds,
The thunder from His canopy?
[30]Look, He scatters His light upon it,
And covers the depths of the sea.
[31]For by these He judges the peoples;
He gives food in abundance.
[32]He covers *His* hands with lightning,
And commands it to strike.
[33]His thunder declares it,
The cattle also, concerning the rising *storm.*

37 "At this also my heart trembles,
And leaps from its place.
[2]Hear attentively the thunder of His voice,
And the rumbling *that* comes from His mouth.
[3]He sends it forth under the whole heaven,
His lightning to the ends of the earth.
[4]After it a voice roars;
He thunders with His majestic voice,
And He does not restrain them when His voice is heard.
[5]God thunders marvelously with His voice;
He does great things which we cannot comprehend.
[6]For He says to the snow, 'Fall *on* the earth';
Likewise to the gentle rain and the heavy rain of His strength.
[7]He seals the hand of every man,
That all men may know His work.
[8]The beasts go into dens,
And remain in their lairs.
[9]From the chamber *of the south* comes the whirlwind,
And cold from the scattering winds *of the north.*
[10]By the breath of God ice is given,
And the broad waters are frozen.
[11]Also with moisture He saturates the thick clouds;
He scatters His bright clouds.
[12]And they swirl about, being turned by His guidance,
That they may do whatever He commands them
On the face of the whole earth.[a]
[13]He causes it to come,
Whether for correction,
Or for His land,
Or for mercy.

[14]"Listen to this, O Job;
Stand still and consider the wondrous works of God.
[15]Do you know when God dispatches them,
And causes the light of His cloud to shine?
[16]Do you know how the clouds are balanced,

37:12 [a]Literally *the world of the earth*

37:14 We are often too busy to consider the amazing creation in which we live. See Psa. 111:2–6 for why God's marvelous works should be studied. When we ponder the clouds, the stars, the birds, the trees, the flowers, the animals, the vast array of foods, the marvels of the human body, etc., all in light of God's creative hand, audible praise is not enough to express the incredible greatness of our God. We instead bow our heads and remain still in worshipful adoration of this Creator who gave us life and redeemed us by His blood.

Those wondrous works of Him who
is perfect in knowledge?
17Why *are* your garments hot,
When He quiets the earth by the
south *wind?*
18With Him, have you spread out the
skies,
Strong as a cast metal mirror?

19"Teach us what we should say to Him,
For we can prepare nothing because
of the darkness.
20Should He be told that I *wish to* speak?
If a man were to speak, surely he
would be swallowed up.
21Even now *men* cannot look at the
light *when it is* bright in the skies,
When the wind has passed and
cleared them.

When you speak of God or His attributes, let it be seriously and with reverence.

GEORGE WASHINGTON

22He comes from the north *as* golden
splendor;
With God *is* awesome majesty.
23*As for* the Almighty, we cannot find
Him;
He is excellent in power,
In judgment and abundant justice;
He does not oppress.
24Therefore men fear Him;
He shows no partiality to any *who are*
wise of heart."

The Lord Reveals His Omnipotence to Job

38 Then the LORD answered Job out
of the whirlwind, and said:

2"Who *is* this who darkens counsel
By words without knowledge?
3Now prepare yourself like a man;
I will question you, and you shall
answer Me.

4"Where were you when I laid the
foundations of the earth?
Tell *Me,* if you have understanding.
5Who determined its measurements?
Surely you know!
Or who stretched the line upon it?
6To what were its foundations fastened?
Or who laid its cornerstone,
7When the morning stars sang
together,
And all the sons of God shouted for
joy?

8"Or *who* shut in the sea with doors,
When it burst forth *and* issued from
the womb;

38:1,2 The heavens break their silence and Almighty God speaks to a mortal man. How incredible that He inspired the Bible's authors to record His words.

Spoken out of a whirlwind, His words in these verses also apply to contemporary evangelism. Many sincere people preach the gospel but fail to precede it with God's moral Law. Such preachers ignore the fact that the Law brings the knowledge of sin (Rom. 3:20), and thus the counsel of the gospel remains darkened "words without knowledge" to lost sinners.

The preaching of the cross will be foolishness to the world as long as we fail to walk in the footsteps of Jesus and open up the divine Law before we preach the gospel (see Mark 10:17–21; Luke 10:25–37; 18:18–22). For details, see 2 Sam. 12:1–14 and John 4:7 comments.

38:3 Job was reproved by God Himself. God now asks Job seventy questions that left him with his hand upon his ignorant mouth (see 40:4). The next four chapters of this book contain scientifically accurate truths rehearsing the wonders of creation.

38:4–6 If it was not God who set in motion the laws that govern the earth, who was it? Whoever it was revealed His absolute genius through His unspeakably creative hand, and deserves our total gratitude and absolute obedience.

"Everyone who is seriously involved in the pursuit of science becomes convinced that a spirit is manifest in the laws of the Universe—a spirit vastly superior to that of man, and one in the face of which we with our modest powers must feel humble." *Albert Einstein*

[9]When I made the clouds its garment,
And thick darkness its swaddling band;
[10]When I fixed My limit for it,
And set bars and doors;
[11]When I said,
'This far you may come, but no farther,
And here your proud waves must stop!'

[12]"Have you commanded the morning since your days *began*,
And caused the dawn to know its place,
[13]That it might take hold of the ends of the earth,
And the wicked be shaken out of it?
[14]It takes on form like clay *under* a seal,
And stands out like a garment.
[15]From the wicked their light is withheld,
And the upraised arm is broken.

[16]"Have you entered the springs of the sea?
Or have you walked in search of the depths?
[17]Have the gates of death been revealed to you?
Or have you seen the doors of the shadow of death?
[18]Have you comprehended the breadth of the earth?
Tell *Me*, if you know all this.

[19]"Where *is* the way *to* the dwelling of light?
And darkness, where *is* its place,
[20]That you may take it to its territory,
That you may know the paths *to* its home?
[21]Do you know *it*, because you were born then,
Or *because* the number of your days *is* great?

[22]"Have you entered the treasury of snow,
Or have you seen the treasury of hail,
[23]Which I have reserved for the time of trouble,
For the day of battle and war?
[24]By what way is light diffused,
Or the east wind scattered over the earth?

[25]"Who has divided a channel for the overflowing *water*,
Or a path for the thunderbolt,
[26]To cause it to rain on a land *where there is* no one,
A wilderness in which *there is* no man;
[27]To satisfy the desolate waste,
And cause to spring forth the growth of tender grass?
[28]Has the rain a father?
Or who has begotten the drops of dew?
[29]From whose womb comes the ice?
And the frost of heaven, who gives it birth?
[30]The waters harden like stone,
And the surface of the deep is frozen.

[31]"Can you bind the cluster of the Pleiades,
Or loose the belt of Orion?
[32]Can you bring out Mazzaroth[a] in its season?
Or can you guide the Great Bear with

38:32 [a]Literally *Constellations*

38:16 Springs of the sea. "Modern deep-sea-diving cameras have discovered amazing hot-water vents on the floor of the oceans. These thermal vents release huge amounts of mineral-rich, super-heated water springs in the darkness." *Richard Gunther*

"There are four main points in this matter that the Old Testament affirms. First, the Old Testament asserts positively that springs do exist in the ocean [Job 38:16]. The source of this knowledge claims omniscience and is allowing that omniscience to be tested by scientific investigation of the ocean floor. Second, the undersea springs are said to have been established at the earth's creation [Psa. 33:6,7]. Third, the Flood of Noah is claimed to have been caused, at least in part, by an unusual activity of ocean floor springs [Gen. 7:11]. Finally, springs are mentioned so we can marvel at the wisdom and power of God [Prov. 8:22,28]." *Steven A. Austin, Ph.D.*

38:17 Jesus holds the keys to this gate (see Rev. 1:18).

its cubs?
33Do you know the ordinances of the
heavens?
Can you set their dominion over the
earth?

34"Can you lift up your voice to the
clouds,
That an abundance of water may
cover you?
35Can you send out lightnings, that
they may go,
And say to you, 'Here we *are!*'?
36Who has put wisdom in the mind?[a]
Or who has given understanding to
the heart?
37Who can number the clouds by
wisdom?
Or who can pour out the bottles of
heaven,
38When the dust hardens in clumps,
And the clods cling together?

39"Can you hunt the prey for the lion,
Or satisfy the appetite of the young
lions,
40When they crouch in *their* dens,
Or lurk in their lairs to lie in wait?
41Who provides food for the raven,
When its young ones cry to God,
And wander about for lack of food?

39

"Do you know the time when the
wild mountain goats bear young?
Or can you mark when the deer gives
birth?
2Can you number the months *that*
they fulfill?
Or do you know the time when they
bear young?
3They bow down,
They bring forth their young,
They deliver their offspring.[a]
4Their young ones are healthy,
They grow strong with grain;
They depart and do not return to them.

5"Who set the wild donkey free?
Who loosed the bonds of the onager,
6Whose home I have made the
wilderness,
And the barren land his dwelling?
7He scorns the tumult of the city;
He does not heed the shouts of the
driver.
8The range of the mountains *is* his
pasture,
And he searches after every green
thing.

. . . . . .

What does science say about the origin of the universe? See Isa. 45:18 comment.

. . . . . .

9"Will the wild ox be willing to serve
you?
Will he bed by your manger?
10Can you bind the wild ox in the
furrow with ropes?
Or will he plow the valleys behind you?
11Will you trust him because his
strength *is* great?
Or will you leave your labor to him?
12Will you trust him to bring home
your grain,
And gather it to your threshing floor?

13"The wings of the ostrich wave proudly,

38:36 [a]Literally *inward parts* 39:3 [a]Literally *pangs*, figurative of offspring

38:35 For the Bible's scientific facts, see Heb. 11:3 comment.

38:36 God is the source of all wisdom and understanding (see Prov. 2:6). To the animals He has given instinct (see 39:16), but with mankind He grants wisdom to those who fear the Lord and understanding to those who obey His commandments (see Psa. 111:10).

39:1,2 Outside of the creative hand of God there is no logical explanation for the instincts of the animal kingdom. To credit evolution with the marvels of creation is to pay homage to a non-existent idol (see Rom. 1:18–23).

39:9–12 God has created certain animals to willingly serve man. See Psa. 8:6 comment.

But are her wings and pinions *like the*
kindly stork's?
[14]For she leaves her eggs on the ground,
And warms them in the dust;
[15]She forgets that a foot may crush them,
Or that a wild beast may break them.
[16]She treats her young harshly, as
though *they were* not hers;
Her labor is in vain, without concern,
[17]Because God deprived her of wisdom,
And did not endow her with
understanding.
[18]When she lifts herself on high,
She scorns the horse and its rider.

[19]"Have you given the horse strength?
Have you clothed his neck with
thunder?[a]
[20]Can you frighten him like a locust?
His majestic snorting strikes terror.
[21]He paws in the valley, and rejoices in
his strength;
He gallops into the clash of arms.
[22]He mocks at fear, and is not frightened;
Nor does he turn back from the sword.
[23]The quiver rattles against him,
The glittering spear and javelin.
[24]He devours the distance with
fierceness and rage;
Nor does he come to a halt because
the trumpet *has* sounded.
[25]At *the blast of* the trumpet he says,
'Aha!'
He smells the battle from afar,
The thunder of captains and shouting.

[26]"Does the hawk fly by your wisdom,
And spread its wings toward the
south?
[27]Does the eagle mount up at your
command,
And make its nest on high?
[28]On the rock it dwells and resides,
On the crag of the rock and the
stronghold.
[29]From there it spies out the prey;
Its eyes observe from afar.
[30]Its young ones suck up blood;
And where the slain *are*, there it *is*."

40 Moreover the LORD answered Job,
and said:

[2]"Shall the one who contends with the
Almighty correct *Him?*
He who rebukes God, let him answer
it."

Job's Response to God

[3]Then Job answered the LORD and said:

39:19 [a]Or *a mane*

39:19–25 A broken spirit. God made the horse like no other animal. It is clothed with a courageous "thunder"—an incredibly brave spirit, an amazing energy that can be harnessed by man and taken into the very heat of battle unafraid. After David sinned with Bathsheba, he cried, "The sacrifices of God are a broken spirit, a broken and a contrite heart—these, O God, You will not despise" (Psa. 51:17). To understand what is meant by "a broken spirit," think of a wild horse. Although beautiful, it is useless to man. So man takes that wild animal and "breaks" its spirit. He does not take away its beauty or its character; he just harnesses its incredible energy so he can turn the animal any way he wishes. James spoke of this: "Indeed, we put bits in horses' mouths that they may obey us, and we turn their whole body" (James 3:3).

That is what God wants from you and me. He wants to "break" our wild, rebellious spirit so He can take us into the heat of battle, and trust us to turn any way He wishes. You have never been more needed in the battle to reach the lost. Have you surrendered the reigns of your life to God? Do you have a "broken spirit"? Can He trust you to rush into the heat of the battle and share the gospel with those headed to hell? If not, why not?

39:27–29 One marvels at the incredible intricacies of the human eye, but man's eye is but a Brownie box camera compared to the incredible eye of the eagle. When we think we have caught a glimpse of the genius of God, He outdoes our estimation of His greatness. Yet, in this creation we have not begun to see what God can do (see 1 Cor. 2:9). See also Psa. 139:14 and Prov. 20:12 comments.

40:2 Some proud people do attempt to contend with God. They put themselves on the throne of righteousness, and put God on the stand as a criminal (see v. 8). They have the ultimate delusions of grandeur and need the moral Law to put them in their place.

QUESTIONS & OBJECTIONS

"How can you justify God killing everyone in a flood?"

Whether it is the deaths of individuals, children, people groups, or the entire world, God is justified in demanding the death of sinners. As the Giver of life, He has the right to take it away at any time: "The soul who sins shall die" (Ezek. 18:4). The difference between the godly and ungodly is that the godly (those who have been regenerated by the Holy Spirit) will always justify God; the ungodly will try to justify man.

So let's demonstrate the truth of the above statement. I am convinced from Scripture and from experience that mankind is intrinsically evil. For evidence, just watch the TV news tonight. He is born with a sinful nature and goes astray from the moment he takes his first step (no parent has to restrain a child from being virtuous, but rather the opposite). Children instinctively know how to be selfish, to lie, to be rebellious, etc. We have to *teach* them to share, to speak the truth, and to be obedient.

God, however, is perfect. He is without sin. He is absolute purity of holiness. He cannot have an evil thought or make an evil decision. The Bible tells us that all of His judgments are true and righteous altogether (Psa. 19:9).

You will now likely attempt to justify man, by saying that he is basically good and that God is the One who is evil. You therefore choose not to worship and serve a God whom you consider to be a tyrant. That is your choice, but know for certain that you will one day meet your "tyrant" Maker, stand before His absolute holiness, and be judged for the sins you have committed. If you refuse the incredible mercy that He offers in Christ, you will be justly damned in hell for eternity.

God, however, will not condemn you. Your sins will do that, in the same way that it is not the judge who sends the wicked criminal to prison; his crimes send him there. See also 1 Sam. 15:3 comment.

4"Behold, I am vile;
What shall I answer You?
I lay my hand over my mouth.
5Once I have spoken, but I will not answer;
Yes, twice, but I will proceed no further."

God's Challenge to Job

6Then the LORD answered Job out of the whirlwind, and said:

7"Now prepare yourself like a man;
I will question you, and you shall answer Me:

8"Would you indeed annul My judgment?
Would you condemn Me that you may be justified?
9Have you an arm like God?
Or can you thunder with a voice like His?
10Then adorn yourself *with* majesty and splendor,
And array yourself with glory and beauty.
11Disperse the rage of your wrath;
Look on everyone *who is* proud, and humble him.
12Look on everyone *who is* proud, *and* bring him low;
Tread down the wicked in their place.
13Hide them in the dust together,
Bind their faces in hidden *darkness*.
14Then I will also confess to you
That your own right hand can save you.
15"Look now at the behemoth,[a] which I made *along* with you;

40:15 [a]A large animal, exact identity unknown

40:4 This is what God's Law does to the receptive sinner. He sees his own desperately wicked heart revealed under the brilliant light of the Ten Commandments. And he suddenly sees sin as being "exceedingly sinful" (Rom. 7:13). He has a straightedge so that he can recognize how crooked he is. It halts the mouth of justification. That is what God's Law does: it "stops every mouth and leaves the whole world guilty before God" (Rom. 3:19). See Job 42:5,6.

QUESTIONS & OBJECTIONS

40:15–24

"Were there dinosaurs in the Bible?"

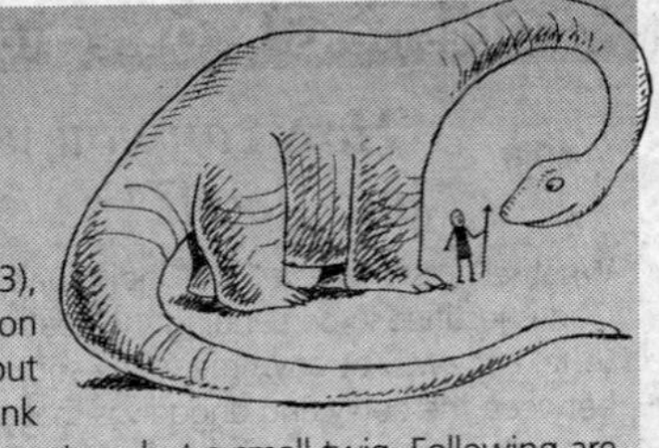

The Bible tells us that all things were made by God (see John 1:3), including dinosaurs. All land animals and humans were created on Day 6 (see v. 15; Gen. 1:24–31). In this passage, God speaks about a great creature called the *behemoth*. Some commentators think this was a hippopotamus. However, the hippo's tail isn't like a large tree, but a small twig. Following are the characteristics of this huge creature: It was the largest of all the land animals God made, was plant-eating (herbivorous), had great strength in its hips and thighs, and had a tail like a cedar. It had very strong bones, lived among the trees, drank massive amounts of water, and was not disturbed by a raging river. Such a powerful creature appears impervious to attack and unable to be snared—an apt description of a large dinosaur. For more on dinosaurs, see Isa. 27:1 comment.

He eats grass like an ox.
16See now, his strength *is* in his hips,
And his power *is* in his stomach muscles.
17He moves his tail like a cedar;
The sinews of his thighs are tightly knit.
18His bones *are like* beams of bronze,
His ribs like bars of iron.
19He *is* the first of the ways of God;
Only He who made him can bring near His sword.
20Surely the mountains yield food for him,
And all the beasts of the field play there.
21He lies under the lotus trees,
In a covert of reeds and marsh.
22The lotus trees cover him *with* their shade;
The willows by the brook surround him.
23Indeed the river may rage,
Yet he is not disturbed;
He is confident, though the Jordan gushes into his mouth,
24*Though* he takes it in his eyes,
Or one pierces *his* nose with a snare.

41

"Can you draw out Leviathan[a] with a hook,
Or *snare* his tongue with a line *which* you lower?
2Can you put a reed through his nose,
Or pierce his jaw with a hook?
3Will he make many supplications to you?
Will he speak softly to you?
4Will he make a covenant with you?
Will you take him as a servant forever?

> We are intelligent beings, and intelligent beings could not have been formed by a blind, brute, insensible thing.
>
> **VOLTAIRE**

5Will you play with him as *with* a bird,
Or will you leash him for your maidens?
6Will *your* companions make a banquet[a] of him?
Will they apportion him among the merchants?
7Can you fill his skin with harpoons,
Or his head with fishing spears?
8Lay your hand on him;
Remember the battle—
Never do it again!
9Indeed, *any* hope of *overcoming* him is false;

41:1 [a]A large sea creature, exact identity unknown 41:6 [a]Or *bargain over him*

41:1 Some believe that the Leviathan may have been some variety of massive dinosaur, now extinct. This is not a mere crocodile, shark, or whale. The description of this sea creature sounds more like a great sea serpent or dragon. With so many dragon legends from around the world matching these characteristics, it is likely that they were based on encounters with actual dinosaurs.

Shall *one not* be overwhelmed at the
sight of him?
10No one *is so* fierce that he would dare
stir him up.
Who then is able to stand against Me?
11Who has preceded Me, that I should
pay *him?*
Everything under heaven is Mine.

12"I will not conceal[a] his limbs,
His mighty power, or his graceful
proportions.
13Who can remove his outer coat?
Who can approach *him* with a double
bridle?
14Who can open the doors of his face,
With his terrible teeth all around?
15*His* rows of scales are *his* pride,
Shut up tightly *as with* a seal;
16One is so near another
That no air can come between them;
17They are joined one to another,
They stick together and cannot be
parted.
18His sneezings flash forth light,
And his eyes *are* like the eyelids of the
morning.
19Out of his mouth go burning lights;
Sparks of fire shoot out.
20Smoke goes out of his nostrils,
As *from* a boiling pot and burning
rushes.
21His breath kindles coals,
And a flame goes out of his mouth.
22Strength dwells in his neck,
And sorrow dances before him.
23The folds of his flesh are joined
together;
They are firm on him and cannot be
moved.
24His heart is as hard as stone,
Even as hard as the lower *millstone*.
25When he raises himself up, the
mighty are afraid;
Because of his crashings they are
beside[a] themselves.
26*Though* the sword reaches him, it
cannot avail;
Nor does spear, dart, or javelin.
27He regards iron as straw,
And bronze as rotten wood.
28The arrow cannot make him flee;
Slingstones become like stubble to him.
29Darts are regarded as straw;
He laughs at the threat of javelins.
30His undersides *are* like sharp
potsherds;
He spreads pointed *marks* in the mire.
31He makes the deep boil like a pot;
He makes the sea like a pot of
ointment.
32He leaves a shining wake behind him;
One would think the deep had white
hair.
33On earth there is nothing like him,
Which is made without fear.
34He beholds every high *thing;*
He *is* king over all the children of
pride."

· · · · · ·

To learn how the "Cambrian Explosion" explodes the theory of evolution, see 1 Cor. 15:39 comment.

· · · · · ·

Job's Repentance and Restoration

42 Then Job answered the LORD and
said:
2"I know that You can do everything,
And that no purpose *of Yours* can be
withheld from You.
3*You asked,* 'Who is this who hides
counsel without knowledge?'
Therefore I have uttered what I did

41:12 [a]Literally *keep silent about* **41:25** [a]Or *purify themselves*

42:1–6 Never hesitate to use the Law of God as a great fire from heaven, as a terrible whirlwind (see 38:1,2), to show the sinner that though he may consider himself to be rich in this world, he has nothing. Time will strip him of everything he holds dear. The Law lets him hear God's voice out of the whirlwind, and the wonderful result will be that he will repent in dust and ashes. From there he will catch a glimpse of God's incredible mercy toward vile sinners, expressed so amazingly on Calvary's cross.

"I had the intention of becoming a theologian . . . but now I see how God is, by my endeavours, also glorified in astronomy, for 'the heavens declare the glory of God.'"

Johann Kepler

not understand,
Things too wonderful for me, which I did not know.
4Listen, please, and let me speak;
You said, 'I will question you, and you shall answer Me.'

5"I have heard of You by the hearing of the ear,
But now my eye sees You.
6Therefore I abhor *myself,*
And repent in dust and ashes."

7And so it was, after the LORD had spoken these words to Job, that the LORD
said to Eliphaz the Temanite, "My wrath
is aroused against you and your two
friends, for you have not spoken of Me
what is right, as My servant Job *has.* 8Now
therefore, take for yourselves seven bulls
and seven rams, go to My servant Job,
and offer up for yourselves a burnt offering; and My servant Job shall pray for
you. For I will accept him, lest I deal with
you *according to your* folly; because you
have not spoken of Me *what is* right, as
My servant Job *has.*"

9So Eliphaz the Temanite and Bildad
the Shuhite *and* Zophar the Naamathite
went and did as the LORD commanded
them; for the LORD had accepted Job.
10And the LORD restored Job's losses[a] when
he prayed for his friends. Indeed the
LORD gave Job twice as much as he had
before. 11Then all his brothers, all his sisters, and all those who had been his acquaintances before, came to him and ate
food with him in his house; and they
consoled him and comforted him for all
the adversity that the LORD had brought
upon him. Each one gave him a piece of
silver and each a ring of gold.

12Now the LORD blessed the latter *days*
of Job more than his beginning; for he had
fourteen thousand sheep, six thousand
camels, one thousand yoke of oxen, and
one thousand female donkeys. 13He also
had seven sons and three daughters. 14And
he called the name of the first Jemimah,
the name of the second Keziah, and the
name of the third Keren-Happuch. 15In
all the land were found no women *so*
beautiful as the daughters of Job; and their
father gave them an inheritance among
their brothers.

16After this Job lived one hundred and
forty years, and saw his children and
grandchildren *for* four generations. 17So
Job died, old and full of days.

42:10 [a]Literally *Job's captivity,* that is, what was captured from Job

42:7 "Job's friends chose the right time to visit him, but took not the right course of improving their visit; had they spent the time in praying for him which they did in hot disputes with him, they would have profited him; and pleased God more." *William Gurnall*

Psalms

Book One: Psalms 1—41

PSALM 1

The Way of the Righteous and the End of the Ungodly

[1]Blessed *is* the man
Who walks not in the counsel of the ungodly,
Nor stands in the path of sinners,
Nor sits in the seat of the scornful;
[2]But his delight *is* in the law of the LORD,
And in His law he meditates day and night.
[3]He shall be like a tree
Planted by the rivers of water,
That brings forth its fruit in its season,
Whose leaf also shall not wither;
And whatever he does shall prosper.

[4]The ungodly *are* not so,
But *are* like the chaff which the wind drives away.
[5]Therefore the ungodly shall not stand in the judgment,
Nor sinners in the congregation of the righteous.
[6]For the LORD knows the way of the righteous,
But the way of the ungodly shall perish.

PSALM 2

The Messiah's Triumph and Kingdom

[1]Why do the nations rage,
And the people plot a vain thing?
[2]The kings of the earth set themselves,
And the rulers take counsel together,
Against the LORD and against His Anointed, *saying,*
[3]"Let us break Their bonds in pieces
And cast away Their cords from us."

[4]He who sits in the heavens shall laugh;
The Lord shall hold them in derision.
[5]Then He shall speak to them in His wrath,
And distress them in His deep displeasure:
[6]"Yet I have set My King
On My holy hill of Zion."

[7]"I will declare the decree:
The LORD has said to Me,

1:1–3 Here is the biblical formula for success. The key to fruitfulness as a Christian is to meditate on God's Word every day, without fail. Have you ever gone one day when you have been too busy or have forgotten to read the Bible? Have you ever gone one day when you have been too busy or have forgotten to feed your stomach? Which comes first, your Bible or your belly? Be like Job, who "treasured the words of His mouth more than [his] necessary food" (Job 23:12). Then whatever we do "shall prosper" (v. 3), including our evangelistic endeavors.

1:5 If the fate of the ungodly is our continual meditation, concern for their salvation will be our continual motivation.

QUESTIONS & OBJECTIONS

1:6 ### "Why are there so many denominations?"

In the early 1500s, a German monk named Martin Luther was so conscious of his sins that he spent up to six hours in the confessional. Through study of the Scriptures he found that salvation didn't come through anything he did, but simply through trusting in the finished work of the cross of Jesus Christ. He listed the contradictions between what the Scriptures said and what his church taught, and nailed his "95 Theses" to the church door in Wittenberg, Germany.

Martin Luther became the first to "protest" against the Roman Catholic church, and thus he became the father of the Protestant church. Since that split, there have been many disagreements about how much water one should baptize with, how to sing what and why, who should govern who, etc., causing thousands of splinter groups. Many of these groups are convinced that they alone are right. These have become known as Protestant "denominations." Despite the confusion, these churches subscribe to certain foundational beliefs such as the deity, death, burial, and resurrection of Jesus Christ. Jesus says, "My sheep hear My voice, and I know them, and they follow Me" (John 10:27). All true believers follow Him and obey His Word (John 14:23).

Thomas Jefferson once wrote about a preacher, *Richard Mote*, who "exclaimed aloud to his congregation that he did not believe there was a Quaker, Presbyterian, Methodist, or Baptist in heaven, having paused to give his hearers time to stare and to wonder. He added that, in heaven, God knew no distinctions."

'You *are* My Son,
Today I have begotten You.
8 Ask of Me, and I will give *You*
The nations *for* Your inheritance,
And the ends of the earth *for* Your
possession.
9 You shall break[a] them with a rod of
iron;
You shall dash them to pieces like a
potter's vessel.' "

10 Now therefore, be wise, O kings;
Be instructed, you judges of the earth.
11 Serve the LORD with fear,
And rejoice with trembling.
12 Kiss the Son,[a] lest He[b] be angry,
And you perish *in* the way,
When His wrath is kindled but a
little.
Blessed *are* all those who put their
trust in Him.

PSALM 3

The Lord Helps His Troubled People

A Psalm of David when he fled from Absalom his son.

1 LORD, how they have increased who
trouble me!
Many *are* they who rise up against me.
2 Many *are* they who say of me,
"*There is* no help for him in God." *Selah*

3 But You, O LORD, *are* a shield for me,
My glory and the One who lifts up
my head.
4 I cried to the LORD with my voice,
And He heard me from His holy hill.
Selah

2:9 [a]Following Masoretic Text and Targum; Septuagint, Syriac, and Vulgate read *rule* (compare Revelation 2:27). 2:12 [a]Septuagint and Vulgate read *Embrace discipline*; Targum reads *Receive instruction*. [b]Septuagint reads *the* LORD.

2:12 The warning of God's wrath. In 1969, twenty-four people decided to ignore warnings that Hurricane Camille was heading for Mississippi. They instead made up their minds that they were going to ride it out. Twenty-three of them died in the hurricane.

The cross is a warning of the fierce hurricane of God's wrath, which no one will "ride out" on Judgment Day. The only way to flee the coming wrath is to "kiss the Son"—to yield to the Lordship of the Savior, Jesus Christ. Those who put their trust in Him are blessed with forgiveness and eternal life.

[5]I lay down and slept;
I awoke, for the LORD sustained me.
[6]I will not be afraid of ten thousands of people
Who have set *themselves* against me all around.

[7]Arise, O LORD;
Save me, O my God!
For You have struck all my enemies on the cheekbone;
You have broken the teeth of the ungodly.
[8]Salvation *belongs* to the LORD.
Your blessing *is* upon Your people. *Selah*

PSALM 4

The Safety of the Faithful

To the Chief Musician. With stringed instruments. A Psalm of David.

[1]Hear me when I call, O God of my righteousness!
You have relieved me in *my* distress;
Have mercy on me, and hear my prayer.

[2]How long, O you sons of men,
Will you turn my glory to shame?
How long will you love worthlessness
And seek falsehood? *Selah*
[3]But know that the LORD has set apart[a] for Himself him who is godly;
The LORD will hear when I call to Him.

[4]Be angry, and do not sin.
Meditate within your heart on your bed, and be still. *Selah*
[5]Offer the sacrifices of righteousness,
And put your trust in the LORD.

[6]*There are* many who say,
"Who will show us *any* good?"
LORD, lift up the light of Your countenance upon us.
[7]You have put gladness in my heart,
More than in the season that their grain and wine increased.
[8]I will both lie down in peace, and sleep;
For You alone, O LORD, make me dwell in safety.

PSALM 5

A Prayer for Guidance

To the Chief Musician. With flutes.[a] A Psalm of David.

[1]Give ear to my words, O LORD,
Consider my meditation.
[2]Give heed to the voice of my cry,
My King and my God,
For to You I will pray.
[3]My voice You shall hear in the morning, O LORD;
In the morning I will direct *it* to You,
And I will look up.

[4]For You *are* not a God who takes pleasure in wickedness,
Nor shall evil dwell with You.
[5]The boastful shall not stand in Your sight;
You hate all workers of iniquity.

THE FUNCTION OF THE LAW

5:5 "This Law, then, should be arrayed in all its majesty against selfishness and enmity of the sinner. All men know that they have sinned, but all are not convicted of the guilt and ill dessert of sin. But without this they cannot understand or appreciate the gospel method of salvation. Away with this milk-and-water preaching of a love of Christ that has no holiness or moral discrimination in it. Away with preaching a love of God that is not angry with sinners every day." *Charles Finney*

4:3 [a]Many Hebrew manuscripts, Septuagint, Targum, and Vulgate read *made wonderful*. **5:title** [a]Hebrew *nehiloth*

3:8 Salvation belongs to the Lord. Scripture tells us that there are none who seek after God, and that no man can come to the Son unless the Father draws him (see John 6:44). We have as much to do with our salvation as Lazarus had to do with his own raising from the dead. It is the Lord who speaks life to us—we respond to His voice, repent, and are born again.

5:5 In the Strongest Terms

By Stuart Scott

Men love to hear about the lovingkindness of God, but rarely acknowledge His abhorrence (hatred) of evildoers. Although it is only natural to want to hear the pleasant and avoid the offensive, Scripture does not give us that option. Being made to realize our guilt is very uncomfortable, but is necessary for repentance and the ultimate comfort of salvation.

The truth is that while God is love, He is also just and holy. Love and holiness, by their nature, are the opposites of evil. It makes sense then that by His nature, God hates evil. Since evil is what men do, and you cannot separate evil from the doer (see 1 Tim. 1:9,10 comment), we must conclude that God hates all those who do evil. As the following Scriptures bear out, God, in the strongest terms, "is angry with the wicked every day" (Psa. 7:11). God hates the following:

- All workers of iniquity: Psa. 5:5
- The wicked and the violent: Psa. 11:5
- A proud look: Prov. 6:17
- A lying tongue: Prov. 6:17
- Hands that shed innocent blood (abortion?): Prov. 6:17
- Hearts that devise wicked plans: Prov. 6:18
- Feet that run to evil: Prov. 6:18
- A false witness who lies: Prov. 6:19
- Those who sow discord among brethren: Prov. 6:19
- Pride and arrogance: Prov. 8:13
- The evil way: Prov. 8:13
- A perverse mouth: Prov. 8:13
- Those who commit idolatry by worshiping and serving other gods: Jer. 44:3,4
- His own people the Israelites (spoken of as His own sons and daughters) because of their evil deeds: Hos. 9:15
- Those who think evil in their heart: Zech. 8:17
- Those who make false promises: Zech. 8:17
- Divorce: Mal. 2:16
- The deeds and doctrines of the Nicolaitans: Rev. 2:6,15

God abhors those who do these things:

- Sacrifice their children to idols: Lev. 20:2 (also Deut. 12:31)
- Stand by and turn a blind eye to evildoers: Lev. 20:4,5
- Turn to mediums and familiar spirits: Lev. 20:6
- Curse their father or mother: Lev. 20:9
- Commit sexual sins (adultery, incest, homosexuality, bestiality): Lev. 20:10–21

God instructs us to hate the evil and cling to the good:

- The fear of the Lord is to hate evil (Prov. 8:13).
- Hate the evil, and love the good (Amos 5:15).
- Abhor what is evil, cling to what is good (Rom. 12:9).
- God anointed Jesus because He loved righteousness and hated lawlessness (Heb. 1:9).

6You shall destroy those who speak
falsehood;
The LORD abhors the bloodthirsty and
deceitful man.

7But as for me, I will come into Your
house in the multitude of Your
mercy;
In fear of You I will worship toward
Your holy temple.

8Lead me, O LORD, in Your righteousness because of my enemies;
Make Your way straight before my
face.

9For *there is* no faithfulness in their
mouth;
Their inward part is destruction;
Their throat *is* an open tomb;
They flatter with their tongue.

5:5 Does God hate sinners? How can God hate sinners when John 3:16 says that He loves the world? *Norman Geisler* and *Thomas Howe* write, "There is no contradiction in these statements. The difficulty arises when we wrongly assume that God hates in the same way men hate. Hatred in human beings is generally thought of in terms of strong emotional distaste or dislike for someone or something. However, in God, hate is a judicial act on the part of the righteous judge who separates the sinner from Himself" *(When Critics Ask)*. See Psa. 7:11–13 comment.

5:9 Sinful man speaks from the abundance of his depraved heart. See Jer. 17:9; Mark 7:21–23; Rom. 3:10–18.

[10]Pronounce them guilty, O God!
Let them fall by their own counsels;
Cast them out in the multitude of
their transgressions,
For they have rebelled against You.

[11]But let all those rejoice who put their
trust in You;
Let them ever shout for joy, because
You defend them;
Let those also who love Your name
Be joyful in You.
[12]For You, O LORD, will bless the
righteous;
With favor You will surround him as
with a shield.

PSALM 6

A Prayer of Faith in Time of Distress

To the Chief Musician. With stringed instruments.
On an eight-stringed harp.[a] A Psalm of David.

[1]O LORD, do not rebuke me in Your
anger,
Nor chasten me in Your hot
displeasure.
[2]Have mercy on me, O LORD, for I *am*
weak;
O LORD, heal me, for my bones are
troubled.
[3]My soul also is greatly troubled;
But You, O LORD—how long?

[4]Return, O LORD, deliver me!
Oh, save me for Your mercies' sake!
[5]For in death *there is* no remembrance
of You;
In the grave who will give You thanks?

[6]I am weary with my groaning;
All night I make my bed swim;
I drench my couch with my tears.
[7]My eye wastes away because of grief;
It grows old because of all my enemies.

[8]Depart from me, all you workers of
iniquity;
For the LORD has heard the voice of
my weeping.
[9]The LORD has heard my supplication;
The LORD will receive my prayer.
[10]Let all my enemies be ashamed and
greatly troubled;
Let them turn back *and* be ashamed
suddenly.

PSALM 7

Prayer and Praise for Deliverance from Enemies

A Meditation[a] of David, which he sang to the LORD
concerning the words of Cush, a Benjamite.

[1]O LORD my God, in You I put my trust;
Save me from all those who persecute
me;
And deliver me,
[2]Lest they tear me like a lion,
Rending *me* in pieces, while *there is*
none to deliver.

[3]O LORD my God, if I have done this:
If there is iniquity in my hands,
[4]If I have repaid evil to him who was
at peace with me,
Or have plundered my enemy
without cause,
[5]Let the enemy pursue me and
overtake *me;*
Yes, let him trample my life to the
earth,
And lay my honor in the dust. *Selah*

[6]Arise, O LORD, in Your anger;
Lift Yourself up because of the rage of
my enemies;
Rise up for me[a] *to* the judgment You
have commanded!
[7]So the congregation of the peoples
shall surround You;
For their sakes, therefore, return on
high.
[8]The LORD shall judge the peoples;
Judge me, O LORD, according to my
righteousness,
And according to my integrity within
me.

6:title [a]Hebrew *sheminith* 7:title [a]Hebrew *Shiggaion* 7:6 [a]Following Masoretic Text, Targum, and Vulgate; Septuagint reads *O LORD my God.*

[9]Oh, let the wickedness of the wicked
come to an end,
But establish the just;
For the righteous God tests the hearts
and minds.
[10]My defense *is* of God,
Who saves the upright in heart.

[11]God *is* a just judge,
And God is angry *with the wicked*
every day.
[12]If he does not turn back,
He will sharpen His sword;
He bends His bow and makes it ready.
[13]He also prepares for Himself
instruments of death;
He makes His arrows into fiery shafts.

[14]Behold, *the wicked* brings forth iniquity;
Yes, he conceives trouble and brings
forth falsehood.
[15]He made a pit and dug it out,
And has fallen into the ditch *which* he
made.
[16]His trouble shall return upon his own
head,
And his violent dealing shall come
down on his own crown.

[17]I will praise the LORD according to
His righteousness,
And will sing praise to the name of
the LORD Most High.

PSALM 8

The Glory of the Lord in Creation

To the Chief Musician. On the instrument of Gath.[a]
A Psalm of David.

[1]O LORD, our Lord,
How excellent *is* Your name in all the
earth,
Who have set Your glory above the
heavens!

[2]Out of the mouth of babes and
nursing infants
You have ordained strength,
Because of Your enemies,
That You may silence the enemy and
the avenger.

[3]When I consider Your heavens, the
work of Your fingers,
The moon and the stars, which You
have ordained,
[4]What is man that You are mindful of
him,
And the son of man that You visit him?
[5]For You have made him a little lower
than the angels,[a]
And You have crowned him with
glory and honor.

[6]You have made him to have dominion

8:title [a]Hebrew *Al Gittith* 8:5 [a]Hebrew *Elohim, God;* Septuagint, Syriac, Targum, and Jewish tradition translate as *angels.*

7:11–13 This is the message we must bring to a sinful world. God is angry with the wicked every day. His wrath abides on them (John 3:36). Every time they sin, they are storing up for themselves wrath that will be revealed on the Day of Judgment (Rom. 2:5). Unless they are convinced that there is wrath to come, they will not flee to the One who can deliver them from that wrath (1 Thess.1:10). See 1 Tim. 1:9,10 comment.

8:5 "See what wickedness there is in the nature of man. How much are we beholden to the restraining grace of God! For, were it not for this, man, who was made but a little lower than angels, would make himself a great deal lower than the devils." *Matthew Henry*

8:6 Man's dominion. Man is not just an animal on the evolutionary food chain. God has given him dominion (authority) over all the animals (Gen. 1:28). Man is intellectually superior to them and has *priority* over them —every animal is "under his feet" and may be brought into submission by him (James 3:7). Birds (parrots) can be taught to speak. With a crack of a whip lions will do what he says. Even killer whales obey his voice.

Man's dominion is obvious. Cows yield milk for his cereal, cheese for his hamburger, butter for his bread, yogurt to keep him healthy, and ice cream to delight his taste buds on hot days. The same cow gives him meat to keep him strong and leather to keep him warm. Sheep and goats also yield many of these same products. Chickens make eggs for his breakfast and provide finger-licking meat for his dinner. The oceans overflow with an incredible variety of seafood for him to catch and eat. Dogs protect his property and herd his sheep. Elephants lift great weights for him. Camels carry him across deserts. The horse is perfectly designed to be ridden by him. See also Matt. 6:26 comment.

8:3 Evolution: Follow the Evidence

In 2004, the atheist world was shocked when famed British atheist Antony Flew announced that he believed in the existence of God. For decades he had heralded the cause of atheism. It was the incredible complexity of DNA that opened his eyes:

> In a recent interview, Flew stated, "It now seems to me that the findings of more than fifty years of DNA research have provided materials for a new and enormously powerful argument to design." Flew also renounced naturalistic theories of evolution: "It has become inordinately difficult even to begin to think about constructing a naturalistic theory of the evolution of that first reproducing organism."
>
> In Flew's own words, he simply "had to go where the evidence leads." According to Flew, "It seems to me that the case for an Aristotelian God who has the characteristics of power and also intelligence, is now much stronger than it ever was before."

DNA is an incredibly detailed language, revealing vast amounts of information encoded in each and every living cell—which could not have arisen by accidental, mindless chance. Information requires intelligence and design requires a designer. Janet Folger reasons: "There is a mountain in South Dakota that proves what evolutionists have been saying all along: if you just have enough time, wind, rain, erosion, and pure chance, you can get a mountain with the faces of four U.S. presidents on it! If we can all admit that the faces of Mt. Rushmore didn't just accidentally appear, how much more complex are the people standing behind the podiums who want to be president? . . . Which is more complex: a) The faces of Mt. Rushmore; b) a 747; c) your cell phone; d) a worm. If you guessed 'worm,' you are right. The DNA structures, digestive system, and reproductive system are far more complex than those other things that obviously had a designer. Maybe, just maybe, someone designed that worm, too."

(Adapted from *How to Know God Exists*.)

over the works of Your hands;
You have put all *things* under his feet,
7 All sheep and oxen—
Even the beasts of the field,
8 The birds of the air,
And the fish of the sea
That pass through the paths of the seas.

9 O LORD, our Lord,
How excellent is Your name in all the earth!

PSALM 9

Prayer and Thanksgiving for the Lord's Righteous Judgments

To the Chief Musician. To *the tune of* "Death of the Son."[a] A Psalm of David.

1 I will praise *You,* O LORD, with my whole heart;
I will tell of all Your marvelous works.
2 I will be glad and rejoice in You;
I will sing praise to Your name, O Most High.

3 When my enemies turn back,
They shall fall and perish at Your presence.
4 For You have maintained my right and my cause;
You sat on the throne judging in righteousness.
5 You have rebuked the nations,
You have destroyed the wicked;
You have blotted out their name

9:title [a]Hebrew *Muth Labben*

8:8 Scientific facts in the Bible. What does the Bible mean by "paths of the seas"? Man discovered the existence of ocean currents in the 1850s, but the Bible declared the science of oceanography 2,800 years ago. *Matthew Maury* (1806–1873), considered the father of oceanography, noticed the expression "paths of the sea" in Psa. 8:8. "If God said there are paths in the sea," Maury said, "I am going to find them." Maury took God at His word and went looking for these paths. We are indebted to his discovery of the warm and cold continental currents. His book on oceanography remains a basic text on the subject and is still used in universities. Maury used the Bible as a guide to a scientific discovery; if only more would use the Bible as a guide in their personal lives.

forever and ever.

6O enemy, destructions are finished
forever!
And you have destroyed cities;
Even their memory has perished.
7But the LORD shall endure forever;
He has prepared His throne for
judgment.
8He shall judge the world in
righteousness,
And He shall administer judgment for
the peoples in uprightness.

All men who are eminently useful are made to feel their weakness in a supreme degree.

CHARLES SPURGEON

9The LORD also will be a refuge for the
oppressed,
A refuge in times of trouble.
10And those who know Your name will
put their trust in You;
For You, LORD, have not forsaken
those who seek You.

11Sing praises to the LORD, who dwells
in Zion!
Declare His deeds among the people.
12When He avenges blood, He
remembers them;
He does not forget the cry of the
humble.

13Have mercy on me, O LORD!
Consider my trouble from those who
hate me,
You who lift me up from the gates of
death,
14That I may tell of all Your praise
In the gates of the daughter of Zion.
I will rejoice in Your salvation.

15The nations have sunk down in the
pit *which* they made;
In the net which they hid, their own
foot is caught.
16The LORD is known *by* the judgment
He executes;
The wicked is snared in the work of
his own hands.
Meditation.[a] *Selah*

17The wicked shall be turned into hell,
And all the nations that forget God.
18For the needy shall not always be
forgotten;
The expectation of the poor shall *not*
perish forever.

19Arise, O LORD,
Do not let man prevail;
Let the nations be judged in Your sight.
20Put them in fear, O LORD,
That the nations may know
themselves *to be but* men. *Selah*

PSALM 10

A Song of Confidence in God's Triumph over Evil

1Why do You stand afar off, O LORD?
Why do You hide in times of trouble?
2The wicked in *his* pride persecutes
the poor;
Let them be caught in the plots which
they have devised.

3For the wicked boasts of his heart's
desire;
He blesses the greedy *and* renounces
the LORD.
4The wicked in his proud countenance
does not seek *God;*
God *is* in none of his thoughts.

9:16 [a]Hebrew *Higgaion*

9:8 See Acts 17:31.

9:17 How wrong it is for us to forget the One who gave us life. When nations, like individuals, forget God, they therefore die in their sins and reap His great wrath. See 1 John 1:9 comment.

[5]His ways are always prospering;
Your judgments *are* far above, out of his sight;
As for all his enemies, he sneers at them.
[6]He has said in his heart, "I shall not be moved;
I shall never be in adversity."
[7]His mouth is full of cursing and deceit and oppression;
Under his tongue *is* trouble and iniquity.

[8]He sits in the lurking places of the villages;
In the secret places he murders the innocent;
His eyes are secretly fixed on the helpless.
[9]He lies in wait secretly, as a lion in his den;
He lies in wait to catch the poor;
He catches the poor when he draws him into his net.
[10]So he crouches, he lies low,
That the helpless may fall by his strength.
[11]He has said in his heart,
"God has forgotten;
He hides His face;
He will never see."

[12]Arise, O LORD!
O God, lift up Your hand!
Do not forget the humble.
[13]Why do the wicked renounce God?
He has said in his heart,
"You will not require *an account.*"

[14]But You have seen, for You observe trouble and grief,
To repay *it* by Your hand.
The helpless commits himself to You;
You are the helper of the fatherless.
[15]Break the arm of the wicked and the evil *man;*
Seek out his wickedness *until* You find none.

[16]The LORD *is* King forever and ever;
The nations have perished out of His land.
[17]LORD, You have heard the desire of the humble;
You will prepare their heart;
You will cause Your ear to hear,
[18]To do justice to the fatherless and the oppressed,
That the man of the earth may oppress no more.

PSALM 11

Faith in the Lord's Righteousness

To the Chief Musician. *A Psalm* of David.

[1]In the LORD I put my trust;
How can you say to my soul,
"Flee *as* a bird to your mountain"?
[2]For look! The wicked bend *their* bow,
They make ready their arrow on the string,
That they may shoot secretly at the upright in heart.
[3]If the foundations are destroyed,
What can the righteous do?

[4]The LORD *is* in His holy temple,
The LORD's throne *is* in heaven;
His eyes behold,
His eyelids test the sons of men.
[5]The LORD tests the righteous,
But the wicked and the one who loves violence His soul hates.

10:4 The thoughts of sinners. In vv. 4–13, Scripture gives us insight into the thoughts of the unsaved: 1) His pride keeps him from seeking God. Any admittance of guilt is a blow to the pride of the human heart. 2) Because he's self-centered and self-sufficient, he feels no need to even consider God. 3) He thinks that he is in control of his life and that adversity will never come to him. 4) His willful ignorance leaves him without understanding of God's righteous judgments. 5) He believes that either God is blinded to his sinful lifestyle, or He has no sense of justice and will therefore not require any account for his lawlessness.

The reason the proud don't seek after God is that they don't want to—they *will* not seek after God because they don't want to leave their sins. It is not that they cannot find Him, but that they *will* not.

6Upon the wicked He will rain coals;
Fire and brimstone and a burning wind
Shall be the portion of their cup.

7For the LORD *is* righteous,
He loves righteousness;
His countenance beholds the upright.[a]

PSALM 12

Man's Treachery and God's Constancy

To the Chief Musician. On an eight-stringed harp.[a] A Psalm of David.

1Help, LORD, for the godly man ceases!
For the faithful disappear from among the sons of men.
2They speak idly everyone with his neighbor;
With flattering lips *and* a double heart they speak.

3May the LORD cut off all flattering lips,
And the tongue that speaks proud things,
4Who have said,
"With our tongue we will prevail;
Our lips *are* our own;
Who *is* lord over us?"

5"For the oppression of the poor, for the sighing of the needy,
Now I will arise," says the LORD;
"I will set *him* in the safety for which he yearns."

6The words of the LORD *are* pure words,
Like silver tried in a furnace of earth,
Purified seven times.
7You shall keep them, O LORD,
You shall preserve them from this generation forever.

8The wicked prowl on every side,
When vileness is exalted among the sons of men.

PSALM 13

Trust in the Salvation of the Lord

To the Chief Musician. A Psalm of David.

1How long, O LORD? Will You forget me forever?
How long will You hide Your face from me?
2How long shall I take counsel in my soul,
Having sorrow in my heart daily?
How long will my enemy be exalted over me?

3Consider *and* hear me, O LORD my God;
Enlighten my eyes,
Lest I sleep the *sleep of* death;
4Lest my enemy say,
"I have prevailed against him";
Lest those who trouble me rejoice when I am moved.

5But I have trusted in Your mercy;
My heart shall rejoice in Your salvation.
6I will sing to the LORD,
Because He has dealt bountifully with me.

PSALM 14

Folly of the Godless, and God's Final Triumph

To the Chief Musician. *A Psalm* of David.

1The fool has said in his heart,
"*There is* no God."
They are corrupt,
They have done abominable works,
There is none who does good.

2The LORD looks down from heaven upon the children of men,

11:7 [a]Or *The upright beholds His countenance* 12:title [a]Hebrew *sheminith*

12:6,7 Men may list what they consider to be mistakes in the Bible. However, all Scripture is given by inspiration of God (2 Tim. 3:16); every word of the Lord is pure. Any seeming "mistakes" are there because God has put them there, and they are therefore not mistakes. In time, we will find that the "mistakes" are actually ours. See Mark 15:26 comment.

To see if there are any who
understand, who seek God.
3They have all turned aside,
They have together become corrupt;
There is none who does good,
No, not one.

4Have all the workers of iniquity no
knowledge,
Who eat up my people *as* they eat
bread,
And do not call on the LORD?
5There they are in great fear,
For God *is* with the generation of the
righteous.
6You shame the counsel of the poor,
But the LORD *is* his refuge.

7Oh, that the salvation of Israel *would
come* out of Zion!
When the LORD brings back the
captivity of His people,
Let Jacob rejoice *and* Israel be glad.

PSALM 15

The Character of Those Who May Dwell with the Lord

A Psalm of David.

1LORD, who may abide in Your
tabernacle?
Who may dwell in Your holy hill?

2He who walks uprightly,
And works righteousness,
And speaks the truth in his heart;
3He *who* does not backbite with his
tongue,
Nor does evil to his neighbor,
Nor does he take up a reproach
against his friend;
4In whose eyes a vile person is despised,
But he honors those who fear the
LORD;
He *who* swears to his own hurt and
does not change;
5He *who* does not put out his money at
usury,
Nor does he take a bribe against the
innocent.

He who does these *things* shall never
be moved.

PSALM 16

The Hope of the Faithful, and the Messiah's Victory

A Michtam of David.

1Preserve me, O God, for in You I put
my trust.

2*O my soul,* you have said to the LORD,
"You *are* my Lord,
My goodness is nothing apart from
You."
3As for the saints who *are* on the earth,
"They are the excellent ones, in whom
is all my delight."

4Their sorrows shall be multiplied
who hasten *after* another *god;*
Their drink offerings of blood I will
not offer,
Nor take up their names on my lips.

5O LORD, *You are* the portion of my
inheritance and my cup;

14:1 There is no such thing as an "atheist." He is a "fool." See Psa. 53:1 comment.

14:3 Who is "good"? As far as the world is concerned, there are many people who do good. However, here is God's view of humanity: 1) All people are corrupt and do abominable things. 2) No one understands or seeks God. 3) All have turned away from God. 4) They have together become filthy. 5) There is no one who does good, not even one.

The world may consider it a good deed when a celebrity gives millions to charity. God, however, sees the motive for the act, which may be guilt for a past adulterous lifestyle. As long as the world is ignorant of God's Law (which Rom. 7:12 says is "good"), it will have no idea of what "good" is.

15:1–5 This is the standard by which the Christian should live. We must walk in righteousness, speak the truth, keep our heart free from sin, keep our word, and be free from any corruption and covetousness. Those who fear God and want to be effective in their witness will gladly conform.

You maintain my lot.
6The lines have fallen to me in
pleasant *places;*
Yes, I have a good inheritance.

7I will bless the LORD who has given
me counsel;
My heart also instructs me in the
night seasons.
8I have set the LORD always before me;
Because *He is* at my right hand I shall
not be moved.

9Therefore my heart is glad, and my
glory rejoices;
My flesh also will rest in hope.
10For You will not leave my soul in Sheol,
Nor will You allow Your Holy One to
see corruption.
11You will show me the path of life;
In Your presence *is* fullness of joy;
At Your right hand *are* pleasures
forevermore.

PSALM 17

Prayer with Confidence in Final Salvation

A Prayer of David.

1Hear a just cause, O LORD,
Attend to my cry;
Give ear to my prayer *which is* not
from deceitful lips.
2Let my vindication come from Your
presence;
Let Your eyes look on the things that
are upright.

3You have tested my heart;
You have visited *me* in the night;
You have tried me and have found
nothing;
I have purposed that my mouth shall
not transgress.
4Concerning the works of men,
By the word of Your lips,
I have kept away from the paths of
the destroyer.
5Uphold my steps in Your paths,
That my footsteps may not slip.

6I have called upon You, for You will
hear me, O God;
Incline Your ear to me, *and* hear my
speech.
7Show Your marvelous lovingkindness
by Your right hand,
O You who save those who trust *in You*
From those who rise up *against them.*
8Keep me as the apple of Your eye;
Hide me under the shadow of Your
wings,
9From the wicked who oppress me,
From my deadly enemies who
surround me.

10They have closed up their fat *hearts;*
With their mouths they speak proudly.
11They have now surrounded us in our
steps;
They have set their eyes, crouching
down to the earth,
12As a lion is eager to tear his prey,
And like a young lion lurking in
secret places.

13Arise, O LORD,
Confront him, cast him down;
Deliver my life from the wicked with
Your sword,
14With Your hand from men, O LORD,
From men of the world *who have* their
portion in *this* life,
And whose belly You fill with Your
hidden treasure.
They are satisfied with children,
And leave the rest of their *possession*
for their babes.

16:7 It is most profitable to arise from bed, pray, then be still and allow your heart to speak to you in the still of the night season. See Psa. 119:62.

16:10 Messianic prophecy: This was fulfilled in Acts 2:31.

16:11 "Joy is not the absence of suffering, but the presence of God." *Elisabeth Elliot*

[15]As for me, I will see Your face in
righteousness;
I shall be satisfied when I awake in
Your likeness.

PSALM 18

God the Sovereign Savior

To the Chief Musician. *A Psalm* of David the servant of the LORD, who spoke to the LORD the words of this song on the day that the LORD delivered him from the hand of all his enemies and from the hand of Saul. And he said:

[1]I will love You, O LORD, my strength.
[2]The LORD is my rock and my fortress
and my deliverer;
My God, my strength, in whom I will
trust;
My shield and the horn of my
salvation, my stronghold.
[3]I will call upon the LORD, *who is
worthy* to be praised;
So shall I be saved from my enemies.

[4]The pangs of death surrounded me,
And the floods of ungodliness made
me afraid.
[5]The sorrows of Sheol surrounded me;
The snares of death confronted me.
[6]In my distress I called upon the LORD,
And cried out to my God;
He heard my voice from His temple,
And my cry came before Him, *even* to
His ears.

[7]Then the earth shook and trembled;
The foundations of the hills also
quaked and were shaken,
Because He was angry.
[8]Smoke went up from His nostrils,
And devouring fire from His mouth;
Coals were kindled by it.
[9]He bowed the heavens also, and came
down
With darkness under His feet.
[10]And He rode upon a cherub, and
flew;
He flew upon the wings of the wind.
[11]He made darkness His secret place;
His canopy around Him *was* dark
waters
And thick clouds of the skies.
[12]From the brightness before Him,
His thick clouds passed with
hailstones and coals of fire.

[13]The LORD thundered from heaven,
And the Most High uttered His voice,
Hailstones and coals of fire.[a]
[14]He sent out His arrows and scattered
the foe,
Lightnings in abundance, and He
vanquished them.
[15]Then the channels of the sea were
seen,
The foundations of the world were
uncovered
At Your rebuke, O LORD,
At the blast of the breath of Your
nostrils.

[16]He sent from above, He took me;
He drew me out of many waters.
[17]He delivered me from my strong
enemy,
From those who hated me,
For they were too strong for me.
[18]They confronted me in the day of my
calamity,
But the LORD was my support.
[19]He also brought me out into a broad
place;
He delivered me because He
delighted in me.

[20]The LORD rewarded me according to
my righteousness;
According to the cleanness of my
hands
He has recompensed me.
[21]For I have kept the ways of the LORD,
And have not wickedly departed from
my God.
[22]For all His judgments *were* before me,
And I did not put away His statutes
from me.
[23]I was also blameless before Him,
And I kept myself from my iniquity.

18:13 [a]**Following Masoretic Text, Targum, and Vulgate; a few Hebrew manuscripts and Septuagint omit** ***Hailstones and coals of fire.***

24 Therefore the LORD has recompensed
me according to my righteousness,
According to the cleanness of my
hands in His sight.

25 With the merciful You will show
Yourself merciful;
With a blameless man You will show
Yourself blameless;
26 With the pure You will show Yourself
pure;
And with the devious You will show
Yourself shrewd.
27 For You will save the humble people,
But will bring down haughty looks.

28 For You will light my lamp;
The LORD my God will enlighten my
darkness.
29 For by You I can run against a troop,
By my God I can leap over a wall.
30 *As for* God, His way *is* perfect;
The word of the LORD is proven;
He *is* a shield to all who trust in Him.

31 For who *is* God, except the LORD?
And who *is* a rock, except our God?
32 *It is* God who arms me with strength,
And makes my way perfect.
33 He makes my feet like the *feet of* deer,
And sets me on my high places.
34 He teaches my hands to make war,
So that my arms can bend a bow of
bronze.

35 You have also given me the shield of
Your salvation;
Your right hand has held me up,
Your gentleness has made me great.
36 You enlarged my path under me,
So my feet did not slip.

37 I have pursued my enemies and
overtaken them;
Neither did I turn back again till they
were destroyed.
38 I have wounded them,
So that they could not rise;
They have fallen under my feet.
39 For You have armed me with strength
for the battle;
You have subdued under me those
who rose up against me.
40 You have also given me the necks of
my enemies,
So that I destroyed those who hated
me.
41 They cried out, but *there was* none to
save;
Even to the LORD, but He did not
answer them.
42 Then I beat them as fine as the dust
before the wind;
I cast them out like dirt in the streets.

43 You have delivered me from the
strivings of the people;
You have made me the head of the
nations;
A people I have not known shall serve
me.
44 As soon as they hear of me they obey
me;
The foreigners submit to me.
45 The foreigners fade away,
And come frightened from their
hideouts.

46 The LORD lives!
Blessed *be* my Rock!
Let the God of my salvation be exalted.
47 *It is* God who avenges me,
And subdues the peoples under me;
48 He delivers me from my enemies.
You also lift me up above those who
rise against me;

18:30 A perfect God gave a perfect Law (see 19:7) that demands that we live up to its perfection. He makes us perfect in Christ (Col. 1:28). See v. 32.

18:39 We must run to the battle for the souls of men. Our aim is not to kill, but to make alive. Men have rushed into battle merely to obtain dirt. Many have given their lives to get back a hill in Vietnam, Korea, or Israel—a hill that may be returned to the enemy through peace negotiations twenty years later. Their costly efforts proved to be futile. Our labor, however, is not in vain (1 Cor. 15:58).

Questions & Objections

"Doesn't the Big Bang theory disprove the Genesis account of creation?"

Try to think of any explosion that has produced order. Does a terrorist bomb create harmony? Big bangs cause chaos. How could a Big Bang produce roses, apple trees, fish, sunsets, the seasons, hummingbirds, polar bears—thousands of birds and animals, each with its own eyes, nose, and mouth? A *child* can see that there is "grand design" in creation.

Try this interesting experiment: Empty your garage of every piece of metal, wood, paint, rubber, and plastic. *Make sure there is nothing there.* Nothing. Then wait for ten years and see if a Mercedes evolves. Try it. If it doesn't appear, leave it for 20 years. If that doesn't work, try it for 100 years. Then try leaving it for 10,000 years.

Here's what will produce the necessary blind faith to make the evolutionary process believable: leave it for 250 million years. See also Isa. 34:4 and 45:18 comments on the origin of the universe.

"New scientific revelations about supernovas, black holes, quarks, and the big bang even suggest to some scientists that there is a 'grand design' in the universe." (*U.S. News & World Report*)

"The universe suddenly exploded into being... The big bang bears an uncanny resemblance to the Genesis command." *Jim Holt*, science writer, *Wall Street Journal*

You have delivered me from the
violent man.
49 Therefore I will give thanks to You, O
LORD, among the Gentiles,
And sing praises to Your name.

50 Great deliverance He gives to His king,
And shows mercy to His anointed,
To David and his descendants
forevermore.

PSALM 19

The Perfect Revelation of the Lord

To the Chief Musician. A Psalm of David.

1 The heavens declare the glory of God;
And the firmament shows His
handiwork.
2 Day unto day utters speech,
And night unto night reveals
knowledge.
3 *There is* no speech nor language
Where their voice is not heard.
4 Their line[a] has gone out through all
the earth,
And their words to the end of the
world.

In them He has set a tabernacle for
the sun,
5 Which *is* like a bridegroom coming
out of his chamber,
And rejoices like a strong man to run
its race.
6 Its rising *is* from one end of heaven,
And its circuit to the other end;
And there is nothing hidden from its
heat.

19:4 [a]Septuagint, Syriac, and Vulgate read *sound;* Targum reads *business.*

19:1–4 Creation reveals the genius of God's creative hand. Men are without excuse when it comes to believing in God's existence. See Psa. 33:8 comment and Rom. 1:20.

19:4–6 Scientific facts in the Bible. In speaking of the sun, the psalmist says that "its rising is from one end of heaven, and its circuit to the other end." For many years critics scoffed at these verses, claiming that they taught the old false doctrine of geocentricity (i.e., the sun revolves around the earth). Scientists thought the sun was stationary. Then it was discovered in recent years that the sun is in fact moving through space at approximately 600,000 miles per hour. It is traveling through the heavens and has a "circuit" just as the Bible says. Its circuit is so large that it would take approximately 200 million years to complete one orbit.

THE FUNCTION OF THE LAW

19:7–11 God's Law is perfect. It is His tool to convert the soul. When a sinner is confronted with God's holy Law, his conscience affirms its truth. The Law makes wise the simple by giving understanding to the unregenerate mind. It reveals God's true and righteous judgments and therefore produces the fear of God, leading to repentance. It is of great worth. It is sweet to the converted soul. Its function is to warn sinners of the wrath to come and lead them to shelter in the Savior.

"The law of the Lord . . . is of use to convert the soul, to bring us back to ourselves, to our God, to our duty; for it shows us our sinfulness and misery in our departures from God and the indispensable necessity of our return to Him.

"Those who would know sin must get the knowledge of the Law in its strictness, extent, and spiritual nature." *Matthew Henry*

7The law of the LORD *is* perfect,
converting the soul;
The testimony of the LORD *is* sure,
making wise the simple;
8The statutes of the LORD *are* right,
rejoicing the heart;
The commandment of the LORD *is*
pure, enlightening the eyes;
9The fear of the LORD *is* clean,
enduring forever;
The judgments of the LORD *are* true
and righteous altogether.
10More to be desired *are they* than gold,
Yea, than much fine gold;
Sweeter also than honey and the
honeycomb.
11Moreover by them Your servant is
warned,
And in keeping them *there* is great
reward.

12Who can understand *his* errors?
Cleanse me from secret *faults.*
13Keep back Your servant also from
presumptuous *sins;*
Let them not have dominion over me.
Then I shall be blameless,
And I shall be innocent of great
transgression.

14Let the words of my mouth and the
meditation of my heart
Be acceptable in Your sight,
O LORD, my strength and my Redeemer.

PSALM 20

The Assurance of God's Saving Work

To the Chief Musician. A Psalm of David.

1May the LORD answer you in the day
of trouble;
May the name of the God of Jacob
defend you;
2May He send you help from the
sanctuary,
And strengthen you out of Zion;
3May He remember all your offerings,
And accept your burnt sacrifice. *Selah*

4May He grant you according to your
heart's *desire,*
And fulfill all your purpose.
5We will rejoice in your salvation,
And in the name of our God we will
set up *our* banners!
May the LORD fulfill all your petitions.

6Now I know that the LORD saves His
anointed;
He will answer him from His holy
heaven
With the saving strength of His right
hand.

7Some *trust* in chariots, and some in
horses;
But we will remember the name of
the LORD our God.
8They have bowed down and fallen;
But we have risen and stand upright.

9Save, LORD!
May the King answer us when we call.

19:6 God's Law is like the sun. On Judgment Day it will arise with its burning heat and shine the brilliant light of eternal justice on the dark corners of the human heart. Nothing will be hidden from its consuming heat.

QUESTIONS & OBJECTIONS

"On the cross, Jesus said God forsook Him. This proves He was a fake."

Jesus' words recorded in Matt. 27:46 and Mark 15:34 were the fulfillment of David's prophecy in Psa. 22:1. Verse 3 of this psalm then gives us insight into why God forsook Jesus as He hung on the cross: "But You are holy..." A holy Creator cannot have fellowship with sin. When Jesus was on the cross, the sin of the entire world was laid upon Him (Isa. 53:6; 2 Cor. 5:21), but Scripture says God is "of purer eyes than to behold evil, and cannot look on wickedness" (Hab. 1:13). Jesus *had* to tread the winepress alone (Isa. 63:3), but He had the consolation that God would highly exalt Him and give Him back the glory He had before the incarnation.

PSALM 21

Joy in the Salvation of the Lord

To the Chief Musician. A Psalm of David.

1 The king shall have joy in Your strength, O LORD;
And in Your salvation how greatly shall he rejoice!
2 You have given him his heart's desire,
And have not withheld the request of his lips. *Selah*
3 For You meet him with the blessings of goodness;
You set a crown of pure gold upon his head.
4 He asked life from You, *and* You gave *it* to him—
Length of days forever and ever.
5 His glory is great in Your salvation;
Honor and majesty You have placed upon him.
6 For You have made him most blessed forever;
You have made him exceedingly glad with Your presence.
7 For the king trusts in the LORD,
And through the mercy of the Most High he shall not be moved.

8 Your hand will find all Your enemies;
Your right hand will find those who hate You.
9 You shall make them as a fiery oven in the time of Your anger;
The LORD shall swallow them up in His wrath,
And the fire shall devour them.
10 Their offspring You shall destroy from the earth,
And their descendants from among the sons of men.
11 For they intended evil against You;
They devised a plot *which* they are not able *to perform.*
12 Therefore You will make them turn their back;
You will make ready *Your arrows* on Your string toward their faces.

13 Be exalted, O LORD, in Your own strength!
We will sing and praise Your power.

PSALM 22

The Suffering, Praise, and Posterity of the Messiah

To the Chief Musician. Set to "The Deer of the Dawn."[a] A Psalm of David.

1 My God, My God, why have You forsaken Me?
Why are You so far from helping Me,
And from the words of My groaning?

22:title [a]Hebrew *Aijeleth Hashahar*

21:1 "I sometimes wonder whether all pleasures are not substitutes for joy." *C. S. Lewis*

21:9 "There's probably no concept in theology more repugnant to modern America than the idea of divine wrath." *R. C. Sproul*

[2]O My God, I cry in the daytime, but
You do not hear;
And in the night season, and am not
silent.

[3]But You *are* holy,
Enthroned in the praises of Israel.
[4]Our fathers trusted in You;
They trusted, and You delivered them.
[5]They cried to You, and were delivered;
They trusted in You, and were not
ashamed.

[6]But I *am* a worm, and no man;
A reproach of men, and despised by
the people.
[7]All those who see Me ridicule Me;
They shoot out the lip, they shake the
head, *saying,*
[8]"He trusted[a] in the LORD, let Him
rescue Him;
Let Him deliver Him, since He
delights in Him!"

[9]But You *are* He who took Me out of
the womb;
You made Me trust *while* on My
mother's breasts.
[10]I was cast upon You from birth.
From My mother's womb
You *have been* My God.
[11]Be not far from Me,
For trouble *is* near;
For *there is* none to help.

[12]Many bulls have surrounded Me;
Strong *bulls* of Bashan have encircled
Me.
[13]They gape at Me *with* their mouths,
Like a raging and roaring lion.

[14]I am poured out like water,
And all My bones are out of joint;
My heart is like wax;
It has melted within Me.
[15]My strength is dried up like a
potsherd,

22:8 [a]Septuagint, Syriac, and Vulgate read *hoped;* Targum reads *praised.*

22:6–8 Christ's suffering on the cross. "Man, at the best, is a worm; but he [Jesus] became a worm, and no man. If he had not made himself a worm, he could not have been trampled upon as he was. The word signifies such a worm as was used in dyeing scarlet or purple, whence some make it an allusion to his bloody sufferings. See what abuses were put upon him. He was ridiculed as a foolish man, and one that not only deceived others, but himself too. Those that saw him hanging on the cross laughed him to scorn. So far were they from pitying him, or concerning themselves for him, that they added to his afflictions, with all the gestures and expressions of insolence upbraiding him with his fall. They make mouths at him, make merry over him, and make a jest of his sufferings: 'They shoot out the lip, they shake their head, saying, "This was he that said he trusted God would deliver him; now let him deliver him."'

"David was sometimes taunted for his confidence in God; but in the sufferings of Christ this was literally and exactly fulfilled. Those very gestures were used by those that reviled him (Matt. 27:39); they wagged their heads, nay, and so far did their malice make them forget themselves that they used the very words (v. 43), 'He trusted in God; let him deliver him.' Our Lord Jesus, having undertaken to satisfy for the dishonor we had done to God by our sins, did it by submitting to the lowest possible instance of ignominy and disgrace." *Matthew Henry, Commentary on the Whole Bible*

22:12–18 Messianic prophecy: This was clearly fulfilled in the crucifixion of Jesus of Nazareth. See John 19:28,37; Luke 23:35; and Matt. 27:35. Here is a graphic description of the Messiah on the cross: He was aware of their ridicule (vv. 7); He could hear the mocking words (v. 8); He was praying (vv. 9–13); the strain of crucifixion pulled His bones out of joint (v. 14); loss of blood made His heart feel as though it were melting (v. 14); His strength completely left Him (v. 15); thirst caused His tongue to adhere to His mouth (v. 15); they pierced His hands and feet (v. 16); and He could see them gambling for His clothes (v. 18).

22:14 "The placing of the cross in its socket had shaken Him with great violence, had strained all the ligaments, pained every nerve, and more or less dislocated all His bones. Burdened with His own weight, the august sufferer felt the strain increasing every moment of those six long hours. His sense of faintness and general weakness were overpowering; while to His own consciousness He became nothing but a mass of misery and swooning sickness...To us, sensations such as our Lord endured would have been insupportable, and kind unconsciousness would have come to our rescue; but in His case, He was wounded and *felt* the sword; He drained the cup and *tasted* every drop." *Charles Spurgeon*

And My tongue clings to My jaws;
You have brought Me to the dust of
death.

16For dogs have surrounded Me;
The congregation of the wicked has
enclosed Me.
They pierced[a] My hands and My feet;
17I can count all My bones.
They look *and* stare at Me.
18They divide My garments among them,
And for My clothing they cast lots.

19But You, O LORD, do not be far from
Me;
O My Strength, hasten to help Me!
20Deliver Me from the sword,
My precious *life* from the power of
the dog.
21Save Me from the lion's mouth
And from the horns of the wild oxen!

You have answered Me.

22I will declare Your name to My
brethren;
In the midst of the assembly I will
praise You.
23You who fear the LORD, praise Him!
All you descendants of Jacob, glorify
Him,
And fear Him, all you offspring of
Israel!
24For He has not despised nor abhorred
the affliction of the afflicted;
Nor has He hidden His face from Him;
But when He cried to Him, He heard.

25My praise *shall be* of You in the great
assembly;
I will pay My vows before those who
fear Him.
26The poor shall eat and be satisfied;
Those who seek Him will praise the
LORD.
Let your heart live forever!

27All the ends of the world
Shall remember and turn to the LORD,
And all the families of the nations
Shall worship before You.[a]
28For the kingdom *is* the LORD's,
And He rules over the nations.

You do not really preach the gospel if you leave Christ out—if He is omitted, it is not the gospel! You may invite men to listen to your message, but you are only inviting them to gaze upon an empty table unless Christ is the very center and substance of all that you set before them!

CHARLES SPURGEON

29All the prosperous of the earth
Shall eat and worship;
All those who go down to the dust
Shall bow before Him,
Even he who cannot keep himself
alive.

22:16 [a]Following some Hebrew manuscripts, Septuagint, Syriac, Vulgate; Masoretic Text reads *Like a lion*. 22:27 [a]Following Masoretic Text, Septuagint, and Targum; Arabic, Syriac, and Vulgate read *Him*.

22:16 Messianic prophecy: This was fulfilled in Luke 24:39.

22:18 *Matthew Henry* wrote, "The shame of nakedness was the immediate consequence of sin [Gen. 3:7], and therefore our Lord Jesus was stripped of His clothes, when He was crucified, that the shame of our nakedness might not appear." See Rev. 3:17,18; 16:15.

22:18 Messianic prophecy: This was fulfilled in Mark 15:24.

22:28 "Men, in a word, must necessarily be controlled, either by a power within them, or by a power without them; either by the word of God, or by the strong arm of man; either by the Bible, or by the bayonet." *Robert Winthrop*

"We staked the whole future of American civilization, not upon the power of government, far from it. We have staked the future of all our political institutions upon the capacity of mankind for self-government; upon the capacity of each and all of us to govern ourselves, to control ourselves according to the Commandments of God." *James Madison*

"Those who will not be governed by God will be ruled by tyrants."

William Penn

[30]A posterity shall serve Him.
It will be recounted of the Lord to the *next* generation,
[31]They will come and declare His righteousness to a people who will be born,
That He has done *this.*

PSALM 23

The Lord the Shepherd of His People

A Psalm of David.

[1]The LORD *is* my shepherd;
I shall not want.
[2]He makes me to lie down in green pastures;
He leads me beside the still waters.
[3]He restores my soul;
He leads me in the paths of righteousness
For His name's sake.
[4]Yea, though I walk through the valley of the shadow of death,
I will fear no evil;
For You *are* with me;
Your rod and Your staff, they comfort me.

[5]You prepare a table before me in the presence of my enemies;
You anoint my head with oil;
My cup runs over.
[6]Surely goodness and mercy shall follow me
All the days of my life;
And I will dwell[a] in the house of the LORD
Forever.

PSALM 24

The King of Glory and His Kingdom

A Psalm of David.

[1]The earth *is* the LORD's, and all its fullness,
The world and those who dwell therein.
[2]For He has founded it upon the seas,
And established it upon the waters.

[3]Who may ascend into the hill of the LORD?
Or who may stand in His holy place?
[4]He who has clean hands and a pure heart,
Who has not lifted up his soul to an idol,
Nor sworn deceitfully.

23:6 [a]Following Septuagint, Syriac, Targum, and Vulgate; Masoretic Text reads *return.*

23:1 See John 10:11 comment.

23:4 This life is the valley of the shadow of death. The Scriptures describe all of humanity as sitting in darkness and the shadow of death, because they rebelled against the words of God (Psa. 107:10,11). The birth of the Savior gives "light to those who sit in darkness and the shadow of death" (Luke 1:79). The light of the gospel not only banishes the shadow of death, but the believer fears no evil because God is now for him, rather than against him.

24:1 No one truly "owns" anything. We are merely temporary custodians of that which God has entrusted to us. The entire earth and all who dwell in it belong to the Lord.

[5]He shall receive blessing from the LORD,
And righteousness from the God of
his salvation.
[6]This *is* Jacob, the generation of those
who seek Him,
Who seek Your face. *Selah*

[7]Lift up your heads, O you gates!
And be lifted up, you everlasting doors!
And the King of glory shall come in.
[8]Who *is* this King of glory?
The LORD strong and mighty,
The LORD mighty in battle.
[9]Lift up your heads, O you gates!
Lift up, you everlasting doors!
And the King of glory shall come in.
[10]Who is this King of glory?
The LORD of hosts,
He is the King of glory. *Selah*

PSALM 25
A Plea for Deliverance and Forgiveness

A Psalm of David.

[1]To You, O LORD, I lift up my soul.
[2]O my God, I trust in You;
Let me not be ashamed;
Let not my enemies triumph over me.
[3]Indeed, let no one who waits on You
be ashamed;
Let those be ashamed who deal
treacherously without cause.

[4]Show me Your ways, O LORD;
Teach me Your paths.
[5]Lead me in Your truth and teach me,
For You *are* the God of my salvation;
On You I wait all the day.

[6]Remember, O LORD, Your tender
mercies and Your
lovingkindnesses,
For they *are* from of old.
[7]Do not remember the sins of my
youth, nor my transgressions;
According to Your mercy remember
me,
For Your goodness' sake, O LORD.

[8]Good and upright *is* the LORD;
Therefore He teaches sinners in the way.
[9]The humble He guides in justice,
And the humble He teaches His way.
[10]All the paths of the LORD *are* mercy
and truth,
To such as keep His covenant and His
testimonies.
[11]For Your name's sake, O LORD,
Pardon my iniquity, for it *is* great.

[12]Who *is* the man that fears the LORD?
Him shall He[a] teach in the way He[b]
chooses.
[13]He himself shall dwell in prosperity,
And his descendants shall inherit the
earth.
[14]The secret of the LORD *is* with those
who fear Him,
And He will show them His covenant.

25:12 [a]Or *he* [b]Or *he*

25:12–14 Look at what wonderful fruit comes from the fear of the Lord: God Himself will teach us. We will dwell in prosperity. Our descendants will be blessed, and we will be partakers of His incredible covenant.

25:14 *Samuel Morse*, famous for his invention of the telegraph, gave God the glory for his inventions. It is fitting that the first message he ever sent over the wire was taken from Scripture: "What hath God wrought!" (Num. 23:23). Morse, who graduated from Yale in 1810, wrote these words four years before he died: "The nearer I approach the end of my pilgrimage, the clearer is the evidence of the divine origin of the Bible. The grandeur and sublimity of God's remedy for fallen man are more appreciated and the future is illuminated with hope and joy."

Scientists who believe. "Most of the great scientists of the past who founded and developed the key disciplines of science were creationists. Note the following sampling:

Physics: Newton, Faraday, Maxwell, Kelvin
Chemistry: Boyle, Dalton, Pascal, Ramsay
Biology: Ray, Linnaeus, Mendel, Pasteur
Geology: Steno, Woodward, Brewster, Agassiz
Astronomy: Kepler, Galileo, Herschel, Maunder

(continued)

15 My eyes *are* ever toward the LORD,
For He shall pluck my feet out of the net.

16 Turn Yourself to me, and have mercy on me,
For I *am* desolate and afflicted.
17 The troubles of my heart have enlarged;
Bring me out of my distresses!
18 Look on my affliction and my pain,
And forgive all my sins.
19 Consider my enemies, for they are many;
And they hate me with cruel hatred.
20 Keep my soul, and deliver me;
Let me not be ashamed, for I put my trust in You.
21 Let integrity and uprightness preserve me,
For I wait for You.

22 Redeem Israel, O God,
Out of all their troubles!

PSALM 26

A Prayer for Divine Scrutiny and Redemption

A Psalm of David.

1 Vindicate me, O LORD,
For I have walked in my integrity.
I have also trusted in the LORD;
I shall not slip.
2 Examine me, O LORD, and prove me;
Try my mind and my heart.
3 For Your lovingkindness *is* before my eyes,
And I have walked in Your truth.
4 I have not sat with idolatrous mortals,
Nor will I go in with hypocrites.
5 I have hated the assembly of evildoers,
And will not sit with the wicked.

6 I will wash my hands in innocence;

(25:14 continued)

"These men, as well as scores of others who could be mentioned, were creationists, not evolutionists, and their names are practically synonymous with the rise of modern science. To them, the scientific enterprise was a high calling, one dedicated to 'thinking God's thoughts after Him.'" *Henry M. Morris* and *Gary E. Parker*

"Science is the glimpse of God's purpose in nature. The very existence of the amazing world of the atom and radiation points to a purposeful creation, to the idea that there is a God and an intelligent purpose back of everything . . . An orderly universe testifies to the greatest statement ever uttered: 'In the beginning, God . . .'" *Arthur H. Compton*, winner of Nobel Prize in Physics

"The chief aim of all investigation of the external world should be to discover the rational order and harmony which has been imposed on it by God." *Johann Kepler*

"Overwhelmingly strong proofs of intelligent and benevolent design lie around us . . . the atheistic idea is so nonsensical that I cannot put it into words." *Lord Kelvin*

"All material things seem to have been composed of the hard and solid particles abovementioned, variously associated in the first creation by the counsel of an intelligent Agent. For it became Him who created them to set them in order. And if He did so, it's unphilosophical to seek for any other origin of the world, or to pretend that it might arise out of a chaos by the mere laws of nature." *Sir Isaac Newton*

"It is evident that an acquaintance with natural laws means no less than an acquaintance with the mind of God therein expressed." *James Prescott Joule*

See also Psa. 33:8 comment.

26:4 Hypocrites. "Many people have forsaken the church, complaining that there is too much hypocrisy in it. Business is full of hypocrites, too, but no one stops making money because of that. The relationship between sexes, generations, and nations is full of hypocrisy. Notwithstanding, people fall in love, cohabit with children and parents. Nations coexist. How many remain bachelors and spinsters because married life is full of hypocrites?

"One place is surely full of hypocrites. It is hell. Instead of not going to church because you cannot suffer those who only pretend to be religious, you had better beware that you don't go to hell which is full of men with false hearts. In church you are with the hypocrites for only an hour; in hell for eternity. If you loathe hypocrisy, then take decided steps to get to heaven, the only place where full sincerity reigns." *Richard Wurmbrand*

So I will go about Your altar, O LORD,
7That I may proclaim with the voice of thanksgiving,
And tell of all Your wondrous works.
8LORD, I have loved the habitation of Your house,
And the place where Your glory dwells.

9Do not gather my soul with sinners,
Nor my life with bloodthirsty men,
10In whose hands *is* a sinister scheme,
And whose right hand is full of bribes.

11But as for me, I will walk in my integrity;
Redeem me and be merciful to me.
12My foot stands in an even place;
In the congregations I will bless the LORD.

PSALM 27

An Exuberant Declaration of Faith

A Psalm of David.

1The LORD *is* my light and my salvation;
Whom shall I fear?
The LORD *is* the strength of my life;
Of whom shall I be afraid?
2When the wicked came against me
To eat up my flesh,
My enemies and foes,
They stumbled and fell.
3Though an army may encamp against me,
My heart shall not fear;
Though war may rise against me,
In this I *will be* confident.

4One *thing* I have desired of the LORD,
That will I seek:
That I may dwell in the house of the LORD
All the days of my life,
To behold the beauty of the LORD,
And to inquire in His temple.
5For in the time of trouble
He shall hide me in His pavilion;
In the secret place of His tabernacle
He shall hide me;
He shall set me high upon a rock.

6And now my head shall be lifted up above my enemies all around me;
Therefore I will offer sacrifices of joy in His tabernacle;
I will sing, yes, I will sing praises to the LORD.

7Hear, O LORD, *when* I cry with my voice!
Have mercy also upon me, and answer me.
8*When You said,* "Seek My face,"
My heart said to You, "Your face, LORD, I will seek."
9Do not hide Your face from me;
Do not turn Your servant away in anger;
You have been my help;
Do not leave me nor forsake me,
O God of my salvation.
10When my father and my mother forsake me,
Then the LORD will take care of me.

11Teach me Your way, O LORD,
And lead me in a smooth path, because of my enemies.
12Do not deliver me to the will of my adversaries;
For false witnesses have risen against me,
And such as breathe out violence.
13*I would have lost heart,* unless I had believed
That I would see the goodness of the LORD
In the land of the living.

14Wait on the LORD;
Be of good courage,
And He shall strengthen your heart;
Wait, I say, on the LORD!

27:12 Messianic prophecy: This was fulfilled in Matt. 26:60.

PSALM 28

Rejoicing in Answered Prayer

A Psalm of David.

[1]To You I will cry, O LORD my Rock:
Do not be silent to me,
Lest, if You *are* silent to me,
I become like those who go down to the pit.
[2]Hear the voice of my supplications
When I cry to You,
When I lift up my hands toward Your holy sanctuary.

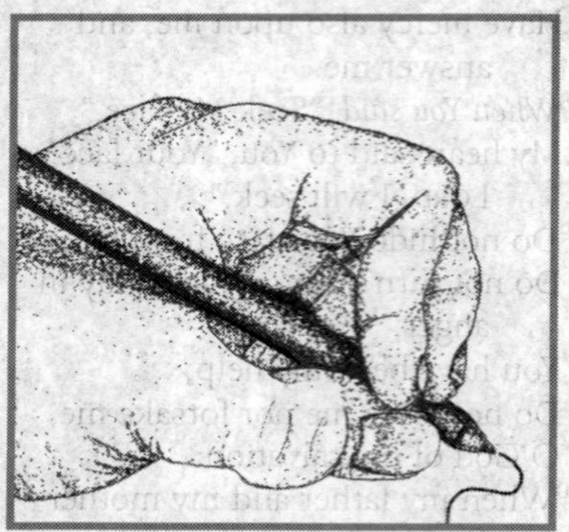

Who wrote the Bible—God or men? See 2 Pet. 1:21 comment.

[3]Do not take me away with the wicked
And with the workers of iniquity,
Who speak peace to their neighbors,
But evil *is* in their hearts.
[4]Give them according to their deeds,
And according to the wickedness of their endeavors;
Give them according to the work of their hands;
Render to them what they deserve.
[5]Because they do not regard the works of the LORD,
Nor the operation of His hands,
He shall destroy them
And not build them up.

[6]Blessed *be* the LORD,
Because He has heard the voice of my supplications!
[7]The LORD *is* my strength and my shield;
My heart trusted in Him, and I am helped;
Therefore my heart greatly rejoices,
And with my song I will praise Him.

[8]The LORD *is* their strength,[a]
And He *is* the saving refuge of His anointed.
[9]Save Your people,
And bless Your inheritance;
Shepherd them also,
And bear them up forever.

PSALM 29

Praise to God in His Holiness and Majesty

A Psalm of David.

[1]Give unto the LORD, O you mighty ones,
Give unto the LORD glory and strength.
[2]Give unto the LORD the glory due to His name;
Worship the LORD in the beauty of holiness.

[3]The voice of the LORD *is* over the waters;
The God of glory thunders;
The LORD *is* over many waters.
[4]The voice of the LORD *is* powerful;
The voice of the LORD *is* full of majesty.

[5]The voice of the LORD breaks the cedars,
Yes, the LORD splinters the cedars of Lebanon.
[6]He makes them also skip like a calf,
Lebanon and Sirion like a young wild ox.
[7]The voice of the LORD divides the flames of fire.

28:8 [a]Following Masoretic Text and Targum; Septuagint, Syriac, and Vulgate read *the strength of His people*.

28:4,5 It is a fearful thing for sinners to be given exactly what they deserve.

8 The voice of the LORD shakes the wilderness;
The LORD shakes the Wilderness of Kadesh.
9 The voice of the LORD makes the deer give birth,
And strips the forests bare;
And in His temple everyone says, "Glory!"

10 The LORD sat *enthroned* at the Flood,
And the LORD sits as King forever.
11 The LORD will give strength to His people;
The LORD will bless His people with peace.

PSALM 30

The Blessedness of Answered Prayer

A Psalm. A Song at the dedication of the house of David.

1 I will extol You, O LORD, for You have lifted me up,
And have not let my foes rejoice over me.
2 O LORD my God, I cried out to You,
And You healed me.
3 O LORD, You brought my soul up from the grave;
You have kept me alive, that I should not go down to the pit.[a]

4 Sing praise to the LORD, you saints of His,
And give thanks at the remembrance of His holy name.[a]
5 For His anger *is but for* a moment,
His favor *is for* life;
Weeping may endure for a night,
But joy *comes* in the morning.
6 Now in my prosperity I said,
"I shall never be moved."
7 LORD, by Your favor You have made my mountain stand strong;
You hid Your face, *and* I was troubled.

8 I cried out to You, O LORD;
And to the LORD I made supplication:
9 "What profit *is there* in my blood,
When I go down to the pit?
Will the dust praise You?
Will it declare Your truth?
10 Hear, O LORD, and have mercy on me;
LORD, be my helper!"

11 You have turned for me my mourning into dancing;
You have put off my sackcloth and clothed me with gladness,
12 To the end that *my* glory may sing praise to You and not be silent.
O LORD my God, I will give thanks to You forever.

PSALM 31

The Lord a Fortress in Adversity

To the Chief Musician. A Psalm of David.

1 In You, O LORD, I put my trust;
Let me never be ashamed;
Deliver me in Your righteousness.
2 Bow down Your ear to me,
Deliver me speedily;
Be my rock of refuge,
A fortress of defense to save me.

30:3 [a]Following Qere and Targum; Kethib, Septuagint, Syriac, and Vulgate read *from those who descend to the pit.*
30:4 [a]Or *His holiness*

29:3–9 The voice of the Lord. It was the "voice of the LORD" (His Word) that brought creation into existence (see Gen. 1:3; John 1:1–3). God's voice then became flesh in the person of Jesus of Nazareth (John 1:14; 1 John 1:1–3). That's why Jesus said strange things about His voice: "Do not marvel at this; for the hour is coming in which all who are in the graves will hear [My] voice" (John 5:28). He said, "The words that I speak to you are spirit, and they are life" (John 6:63). It was the voice of the Savior that brought Lazarus back to life (John 11:43), and it is His voice that will bring the dead out of their graves at the final resurrection (John 5:28,29). His voice brings life.

This is just one example of a wonderfully unique aspect of the Bible. One can study a multitude of subjects in its different books, and find incredible continuity, despite the fact that the books were written thousands of years apart.

[3]For You *are* my rock and my fortress;
Therefore, for Your name's sake,
Lead me and guide me.
[4]Pull me out of the net which they
have secretly laid for me,
For You *are* my strength.
[5]Into Your hand I commit my spirit;
You have redeemed me, O LORD God
of truth.

[6]I have hated those who regard useless
idols;
But I trust in the LORD.
[7]I will be glad and rejoice in Your mercy,
For You have considered my trouble;
You have known my soul in
adversities,
[8]And have not shut me up into the
hand of the enemy;
You have set my feet in a wide place.

[9]Have mercy on me, O LORD, for I am
in trouble;
My eye wastes away with grief,
Yes, my soul and my body!
[10]For my life is spent with grief,
And my years with sighing;
My strength fails because of my
iniquity,
And my bones waste away.
[11]I am a reproach among all my enemies,
But especially among my neighbors,
And *am* repulsive to my acquaintances;
Those who see me outside flee from
me.
[12]I am forgotten like a dead man, out of
mind;
I am like a broken vessel.
[13]For I hear the slander of many;
Fear *is* on every side;
While they take counsel together
against me,
They scheme to take away my life.

[14]But as for me, I trust in You, O LORD;
I say, "You *are* my God."
[15]My times *are* in Your hand;
Deliver me from the hand of my
enemies,
And from those who persecute me.
[16]Make Your face shine upon Your
servant;
Save me for Your mercies' sake.
[17]Do not let me be ashamed, O LORD,
for I have called upon You;
Let the wicked be ashamed;
Let them be silent in the grave.
[18]Let the lying lips be put to silence,
Which speak insolent things proudly
and contemptuously against the
righteous.

[19]Oh, how great *is* Your goodness,
Which You have laid up for those
who fear You,
Which You have prepared for those
who trust in You
In the presence of the sons of men!
[20]You shall hide them in the secret
place of Your presence
From the plots of man;
You shall keep them secretly in a
pavilion
From the strife of tongues.

[21]Blessed *be* the LORD,
For He has shown me His marvelous
kindness in a strong city!
[22]For I said in my haste,
"I am cut off from before Your eyes";
Nevertheless You heard the voice of
my supplications
When I cried out to You.

[23]Oh, love the LORD, all you His saints!
For the LORD preserves the faithful,
And fully repays the proud person.
[24]Be of good courage,
And He shall strengthen your heart,
All you who hope in the LORD.

31:18 The ungodly try to justify themselves by saying that a "fib" or "white lie" never hurts anybody. Sin offends a holy God who demands retribution. See Prov. 13:5.

31:19 Here is an amazing promise to those who are not ashamed to bear the reproach of the gospel.

QUESTIONS & OBJECTIONS

"What if someone says, 'I've broken every one of the Ten Commandments'?"

Do not take this statement to mean that the person has seen the gravity of his sinful state before God. He may say something like, "I'm a really *bad* person!" It is often used as a way of shrugging off conviction. Say to him, "Well, let's take the time to go through them one by one and see if you have." As he is confronted with the righteous standard of God's moral Law, pray that the Holy Spirit brings conviction of sin (John 16:8). For how to do this, see 2 Sam. 12:1–14 and Psa. 51:6 comments.

PSALM 32

The Joy of Forgiveness

A Psalm of David. A Contemplation.[a]

1 Blessed *is he whose* transgression *is*
forgiven,
Whose sin *is* covered.
2 Blessed *is* the man to whom the LORD
does not impute iniquity,
And in whose spirit *there is* no deceit.

3 When I kept silent, my bones grew
old
Through my groaning all the day
long.
4 For day and night Your hand was
heavy upon me;
My vitality was turned into the
drought of summer. *Selah*
5 I acknowledged my sin to You,
And my iniquity I have not hidden.
I said, "I will confess my
transgressions to the LORD,"
And You forgave the iniquity of my
sin. *Selah*

6 For this cause everyone who is godly
shall pray to You
In a time when You may be found;
Surely in a flood of great waters
They shall not come near him.
7 You *are* my hiding place;
You shall preserve me from trouble;
You shall surround me with songs of
deliverance. *Selah*

8 I will instruct you and teach you in
the way you should go;
I will guide you with My eye.
9 Do not be like the horse *or* like the
mule,
Which have no understanding,
Which must be harnessed with bit
and bridle,

32:title [a]Hebrew *Maschil*

32:1,2 *Transgression* is violation of the Law. *Sin* is falling short of the Law's standard. *Iniquity* is lawlessness.

32:5 Contrition does not save us. Its outworking can be seen in these verses: we acknowledge our sin to God rather than justifying ourselves. No longer do we try to hide anything from God, but we confess our transgressions to Him.

32:9 Differences between men and animals. The Bible tells us that animals are created "without understanding." Human beings are different from animals. We are made in God's "image." As human beings, we are aware of our "being." God is "I AM," and we know that "we are." We have understanding that we exist.

Among other unique characteristics, we have an innate ability to appreciate God's creation. What animal gazes with awe at a sunset, or at the magnificence of the Grand Canyon? What animal obtains joy from the sounds of music or takes the time to form an orchestra to create music? We are also moral beings. What animal among the beasts sets up court systems and apportions justice to its fellow creatures?

While birds and other creatures have instincts to create (nests, etc.), we have the ability to uncover the hidden laws of electricity. We can utilize the law of aerodynamics to transport ourselves around the globe. We also have the God-given ability to appreciate the value of creation. We unearth the hidden treasures of gold, silver, diamonds, and oil and make use of them for our own benefit. Only humans have the unique ability to appreciate God for this incredible creation and to respond to His love.

Else they will not come near you.

[10]Many sorrows *shall be* to the wicked;
But he who trusts in the LORD, mercy
shall surround him.
[11]Be glad in the LORD and rejoice, you
righteous;
And shout for joy, all *you* upright in
heart!

PSALM 33

The Sovereignty of the Lord in Creation and History

[1]Rejoice in the LORD, O you righteous!
For praise from the upright is beautiful.
[2]Praise the LORD with the harp;
Make melody to Him with an
instrument of ten strings.
[3]Sing to Him a new song;
Play skillfully with a shout of joy.

[4]For the word of the LORD *is* right,
And all His work *is done* in truth.
[5]He loves righteousness and justice;
The earth is full of the goodness of
the LORD.

[6]By the word of the LORD the heavens
were made,
And all the host of them by the breath
of His mouth.
[7]He gathers the waters of the sea
together as a heap;[a]
He lays up the deep in storehouses.

[8]Let all the earth fear the LORD;
Let all the inhabitants of the world
stand in awe of Him.
[9]For He spoke, and it was *done;*
He commanded, and it stood fast.

[10]The LORD brings the counsel of the
nations to nothing;
He makes the plans of the peoples of
no effect.
[11]The counsel of the LORD stands forever,
The plans of His heart to all
generations.
[12]Blessed *is* the nation whose God *is* the
LORD,
The people He has chosen as His own
inheritance.

[13]The LORD looks from heaven;
He sees all the sons of men.
[14]From the place of His dwelling He
looks
On all the inhabitants of the earth;
[15]He fashions their hearts individually;
He considers all their works.

[16]No king *is* saved by the multitude of

33:7 [a]Septuagint, Targum, and Vulgate read *in a vessel.*

33:8 Awe for the Creator. "Science can only be created by those who are thoroughly imbued with the aspiration toward truth and understanding. This source of feeling, however, springs from the sphere of religion. To this there also belongs the faith in the possibility that the regulations valid for the world of existence are rational, that is, comprehensible to reason. I cannot conceive of a genuine scientist without that profound faith." *Albert Einstein*

Sir John Frederick Herschel, an English astronomer who discovered over 500 stars, stated: "All human discoveries seem to be made only for the purpose of confirming more and more strongly the truths that come from on high and are contained in the Sacred Writings." His father, *Sir William Herschel*, also a renowned astronomer, insisted, "The undevout astronomer must be mad." See also Psa. 25:14 comment.

"In antiquity and in what is called the Dark Ages, men did not know what they now know about humanity and the cosmos. They did not know the lock but they possessed the key, which is God. Now many have excellent descriptions of the lock, but they have lost the key. The proper solution is union between religion and science. We should be owners of the lock *and* the key. The fact is that as science advances, it discovers what was said thousands of years ago in the Bible." *Richard Wurmbrand*

"Calvin said that the Bible—God's special revelation—was spectacles that we must put on if we are to correctly read the book of nature—God's revelation in creation. Unfortunately, between the beginning of science and our day, many scientists have discarded these glasses, and many distortions have followed." *D. James Kennedy* and *Jerry Newcombe*

an army;
A mighty man is not delivered by
great strength.
17A horse *is* a vain hope for safety;
Neither shall it deliver *any* by its great
strength.

18Behold, the eye of the LORD *is* on
those who fear Him,
On those who hope in His mercy,
19To deliver their soul from death,
And to keep them alive in famine.

20Our soul waits for the LORD;
He *is* our help and our shield.
21For our heart shall rejoice in Him,
Because we have trusted in His holy
name.
22Let Your mercy, O LORD, be upon us,
Just as we hope in You.

PSALM 34

The Happiness of Those Who Trust in God

A Psalm of David when he pretended madness before Abimelech, who drove him away, and he departed.

1I will bless the LORD at all times;
His praise *shall* continually *be* in my
mouth.
2My soul shall make its boast in the
LORD;
The humble shall hear *of it* and be glad.
3Oh, magnify the LORD with me,
And let us exalt His name together.

4I sought the LORD, and He heard me,
And delivered me from all my fears.
5They looked to Him and were radiant,
And their faces were not ashamed.
6This poor man cried out, and the
LORD heard *him,*
And saved him out of all his troubles.
7The angel[a] of the LORD encamps all
around those who fear Him,
And delivers them.

I remember two things: I am a great sinner and I have a great Savior; and I don't suppose an old slave trader needs to remember much more than that.

JOHN NEWTON

8Oh, taste and see that the LORD *is* good;
Blessed *is* the man *who* trusts in Him!
9Oh, fear the LORD, you His saints!
There is no want to those who fear Him.
10The young lions lack and suffer
hunger;
But those who seek the LORD shall not
lack any good *thing.*

34:7 [a]Or *Angel*

33:12 The source of a nation's blessings. In Lev. 26:1–13, God promises Israel many wonderful blessings if they would simply obey Him: The rain would come in due season; the land would yield its harvest and the trees would yield their fruit; their food would satisfy them; they would have peace and safety in the land (no violence); and they would prevail over their enemies. Truly, blessed is the nation whose God is the Lord.

"Suppose a nation in some distant region should take the Bible for their only law book, and every member should regulate his conduct by the precepts there exhibited! Every member would be obliged in conscience, to temperance, frugality, and industry; to justice, kindness, and charity towards his fellow men; and to piety, love, and reverence toward Almighty God... What a Utopia, what a Paradise would this region be." *John Adams*

"If we abide by the principles taught in the Bible, our country will go on prospering and to prosper; but if we and our posterity neglect its instructions and authority, no man can tell how sudden a catastrophe may overwhelm us and bury all our glory in profound obscurity." *Daniel Webster*

34:2 The proud are not glad to hear a soul boast in the Lord. Try telling a proud unsaved person about an obvious answer to prayer, and watch him try to explain it away as coincidence. It is a humble heart that can hear a boast about God.

34:8,9 The goodness of God cannot be separated from the fear of the Lord. Those who maintain that it is "the goodness of God" that leads to repentance, and therefore we need only speak of His goodness, need to study the context of Rom. 2:3–11.

QUESTIONS & OBJECTIONS

34:11 *"The threat of hell is psychologically damaging to children."*

The existence of hell is a legitimate reason to come to the Savior, and it is perhaps why so many profess faith in Christ. Though there are undoubtedly some who, in the name of Christianity, have hung its threat over the masses to keep them and their children in line, the biblical threat of hell is real and fearful. However, God's offer of heaven is just as real and unspeakably wonderful. The threat without the offer is a horrid thing.

None of the children I know have been psychologically damaged by the fear of hell. In fact, it is just the opposite. They don't fear hell at all, because they know that they have escaped it through faith in Jesus Christ.

However, I know that many children have been psychologically damaged because of the fear of *death*. That is another legitimate fear—death is a reality all of us must face. As an atheist, what do you tell your beloved children when they, with fear in their eyes, say, "Daddy, I don't want to die!"? Do you tell them that it is nature's way, and that they just have to deal with it? Or do you tell them that they shouldn't think of negative things and to concentrate on life?

Christians don't need to cop out when that question is asked. We can tell our children how we were created, why we were created, why we are all going to die, what happens after death, and what we can do about it.

Our society is filled with adults with psychological problems due to a fear of death. It terrorizes them every minute of every day. Millions live in quiet futility as they wait to die, and are driven to drugs, to the psychiatrist's couch, to alcohol, and to suicide, solely because they fear death.

The tragedy is, that fear could instantly leave them if they repent and place their faith in the One who came to "release those who through fear of death were all their lifetime subject to bondage" (Heb. 2:15).

11Come, you children, listen to me;
I will teach you the fear of the LORD.
12Who *is* the man *who* desires life,
And loves *many* days, that he may see good?
13Keep your tongue from evil,
And your lips from speaking deceit.
14Depart from evil and do good;
Seek peace and pursue it.

15The eyes of the LORD *are* on the righteous,
And His ears *are open* to their cry.
16The face of the LORD *is* against those who do evil,
To cut off the remembrance of them from the earth.

17*The righteous* cry out, and the LORD hears,
And delivers them out of all their troubles.
18The LORD *is* near to those who have a broken heart,
And saves such as have a contrite spirit.

19Many *are* the afflictions of the righteous,
But the LORD delivers him out of them all.
20He guards all his bones;
Not one of them is broken.
21Evil shall slay the wicked,
And those who hate the righteous shall be condemned.
22The LORD redeems the soul of His servants,
And none of those who trust in Him shall be condemned.

PSALM 35

The Lord the Avenger of His People

A Psalm of David.

1Plead *my cause,* O LORD, with those who strive with me;
Fight against those who fight against me.

34:20 Messianic prophecy: This was fulfilled in John 19:33.

[2]Take hold of shield and buckler,
And stand up for my help.
[3]Also draw out the spear,
And stop those who pursue me.
Say to my soul,
"I *am* your salvation."

[4]Let those be put to shame and brought to dishonor
Who seek after my life;
Let those be turned back and brought to confusion
Who plot my hurt.
[5]Let them be like chaff before the wind,
And let the angel[a] of the LORD chase *them.*
[6]Let their way be dark and slippery,
And let the angel of the LORD pursue them.
[7]For without cause they have hidden their net for me *in* a pit,
Which they have dug without cause for my life.
[8]Let destruction come upon him unexpectedly,
And let his net that he has hidden catch himself;
Into that very destruction let him fall.

[9]And my soul shall be joyful in the LORD;
It shall rejoice in His salvation.
[10]All my bones shall say,
"LORD, who *is* like You,
Delivering the poor from him who is too strong for him,
Yes, the poor and the needy from him who plunders him?"

[11]Fierce witnesses rise up;
They ask me *things* that I do not know.
[12]They reward me evil for good,
To the sorrow of my soul.
[13]But as for me, when they were sick,
My clothing *was* sackcloth;
I humbled myself with fasting;
And my prayer would return to my own heart.
[14]I paced about as though *he were* my friend *or* brother;
I bowed down heavily, as one who mourns *for his* mother.

[15]But in my adversity they rejoiced
And gathered together;
Attackers gathered against me,
And I did not know *it;*
They tore *at me* and did not cease;
[16]With ungodly mockers at feasts
They gnashed at me with their teeth.

. . . . . .

To learn the damage of gossip, see Prov. 11:13 comment.

. . . . . .

[17]Lord, how long will You look on?
Rescue me from their destructions,
My precious *life* from the lions.
[18]I will give You thanks in the great assembly;
I will praise You among many people.

[19]Let them not rejoice over me who are wrongfully my enemies;
Nor let them wink with the eye who hate me without a cause.
[20]For they do not speak peace,
But they devise deceitful matters
Against *the* quiet ones in the land.
[21]They also opened their mouth wide against me,
And said, "Aha, aha!
Our eyes have seen *it.*"

[22]*This* You have seen, O LORD;
Do not keep silence.
O Lord, do not be far from me.
[23]Stir up Yourself, and awake to my vindication,
To my cause, my God and my Lord.

35:5 [a]Or *Angel*

35:13 It is wise to make fasting a way of life. Missing a meal on a regular basis will help you to keep your appetite in check. It will also put a joyful thanksgiving in your heart every time you sit down to a meal.

[24]Vindicate me, O LORD my God,
according to Your righteousness;
And let them not rejoice over me.
[25]Let them not say in their hearts, "Ah,
so we would have it!"
Let them not say, "We have swallowed
him up."

[26]Let them be ashamed and brought to
mutual confusion
Who rejoice at my hurt;
Let them be clothed with shame and
dishonor
Who exalt themselves against me.

[27]Let them shout for joy and be glad,
Who favor my righteous cause;
And let them say continually,
"Let the LORD be magnified,
Who has pleasure in the prosperity of
His servant."
[28]And my tongue shall speak of Your
righteousness
And of Your praise all the day long.

PSALM 36

Man's Wickedness and God's Perfections

To the Chief Musician. *A Psalm* of David the servant of the LORD.

[1]An oracle within my heart concerning
the transgression of the wicked:
There is no fear of God before his eyes.
[2]For he flatters himself in his own eyes,
When he finds out his iniquity *and*
when he hates.
[3]The words of his mouth *are*
wickedness and deceit;
He has ceased to be wise *and* to do
good.
[4]He devises wickedness on his bed;
He sets himself in a way *that is* not
good;
He does not abhor evil.

[5]Your mercy, O LORD, *is* in the heavens;
Your faithfulness *reaches* to the clouds.
[6]Your righteousness *is* like the great
mountains;
Your judgments *are* a great deep;
O LORD, You preserve man and beast.

[7]How precious *is* Your lovingkindness,
O God!
Therefore the children of men put
their trust under the shadow of
Your wings.
[8]They are abundantly satisfied with
the fullness of Your house,
And You give them drink from the
river of Your pleasures.
[9]For with You *is* the fountain of life;
In Your light we see light.

[10]Oh, continue Your lovingkindness to
those who know You,
And Your righteousness to the upright
in heart.
[11]Let not the foot of pride come against
me,
And let not the hand of the wicked
drive me away.
[12]There the workers of iniquity have
fallen;
They have been cast down and are
not able to rise.

PSALM 37

The Heritage of the Righteous and the Calamity of the Wicked

A Psalm of David.

[1]Do not fret because of evildoers,
Nor be envious of the workers of
iniquity.
[2]For they shall soon be cut down like
the grass,
And wither as the green herb.

[3]Trust in the LORD, and do good;
Dwell in the land, and feed on His
faithfulness.
[4]Delight yourself also in the LORD,

36:2 "The greatest fault is to be conscious of none." *Thomas Carlyle*

36:6 *Mutating Theory*

Many people have been led to believe that organisms develop favorable mutations based on their environments. For example, it is often thought that bacteria can become resistant to antibiotics, thus proving that they evolve. But the website "Understanding Evolution" (co-produced by the National Center for Science Education) explains how mutations work:

> Mutations do not "try" to supply what the organism "needs."...For example, exposure to harmful chemicals may increase the mutation rate, but will not cause more mutations that make the organism resistant to those chemicals. In this respect, mutations are random—whether a particular mutation happens or not is unrelated to how useful that mutation would be.

To illustrate, they explain that where people have access to shampoos with chemicals that kill lice, there are a lot of lice that are resistant to those chemicals. So either: 1) resistant strains of lice were always there—and are just more frequent now because all the non-resistant lice died; or 2) exposure to lice shampoo actually caused mutations that provide resistance to the shampoo. Based on their scientific experiments, they conclude that "the first explanation is the right one and that directed mutations, the second possible explanation relying on non-random mutation, is not correct."

After numerous experiments, researchers have found that none unambiguously support directed mutation. In the case of bacteria, scientific experiments have demonstrated that "the penicillin-resistant bacteria were there in the population before they encountered penicillin. They did not evolve resistance in response to exposure to the antibiotic."

Therefore, mutations are not logical adaptations that make a creature better suited for its environment. They are completely random—the result of mindless, undirected chance.

Even if random mutations *could* happen to cause a lump of a wing to begin to form, how would that help the creature to survive? In evolutionary theory, natural selection will enable the survival of creatures that develop some sort of beneficial trait. But until it becomes a fully formed wing, any stub would be more of a detriment than a benefit. Consider the following observations from noted evolutionists:

> The reasons for rejecting Darwin's proposal were many, but first of all that many innovations cannot possibly come into existence through accumulation of many small steps, and even if they can, natural selection cannot accomplish it, because incipient and intermediate stages are not advantageous.
>
> —Embryologist Soren Lovtrup

> But how do you get from nothing to such an elaborate something if evolution must proceed through a long sequence of intermediate stages, each favored by natural selection? You can't fly with 2 percent of a wing...
>
> —Paleontologist Stephen Jay Gould

> Darwinism is claiming that all the adaptive structures in nature, all the organisms which have existed throughout history were generated by the accumulation of entirely undirected mutations. That is an *entirely unsubstantiated belief* for which there is not the slightest evidence whatsoever.
>
> —Molecular biologist Michael Denton

Mutations do not work as a mechanism to fuel the evolutionary process. They are random instead of purposeful, and they only modify or remove information, but never add it—a requirement of the theory (see Isa. 45:12 comment). Any mutation that supposedly creates a "transitional form" would be far more likely to doom the poor creature than to help it up the evolutionary chain. But don't just take my word for it. About 150 of the world's leading evolutionary theorists gathered at a Macroevolution Conference in Chicago to consider the question, "Are mutation and natural selection enough?" Evolutionist Roger Lewin sums up the conclusion of the conference:

> The central question of the Chicago conference was whether the mechanisms underlying *micro*evolution can be extrapolated to explain the phenomena of *macro*evolution. At the risk of doing violence to the positions of some of the people at the meeting, the answer can be given as a clear, *No*.

Consider this response from evolutionist Michael Denton, author of *Evolution: A Theory in Crisis*. Asked in an interview if Darwinian theory adequately explained what we see in nature, he very honestly admitted its weaknesses:

> The basic pattern it fails to explain is the apparent uniqueness and isolation of major types of organisms...It strikes me as being a flagrant denial of common sense to swallow that all these things were built up

(continued)

(36:6 continued)

by accumulative small random changes. This is simply a nonsensical claim, especially for the great majority of cases, where nobody can think of any credible explanation of how it came about. And this is a very profound question which everybody skirts, everybody brushes over, everybody tries to sweep under the carpet.

The fact is that the majority of these complex adaptations in nature cannot be adequately explained by a series of intermediate forms. And this is a fundamental problem. Common sense tells me there must be something wrong.

Evolutionary theory is a "nonsensical claim" that is a "flagrant denial of common sense," yet this is the story that we're told repeatedly is a proven fact. There *is* something wrong.

The truth is that mutations cannot create any new features, or new creatures, which explains why the transitional forms that evolution requires just aren't there. See also 2 Tim. 4:9 comment.

(Adapted from *How to Know God Exists*.)

And He shall give you the desires of
your heart.

5Commit your way to the LORD,
Trust also in Him,
And He shall bring *it* to pass.
6He shall bring forth your
righteousness as the light,
And your justice as the noonday.

7Rest in the LORD, and wait patiently
for Him;
Do not fret because of him who
prospers in his way,
Because of the man who brings
wicked schemes to pass.
8Cease from anger, and forsake wrath;
Do not fret—*it* only *causes* harm.

9For evildoers shall be cut off;
But those who wait on the LORD,
They shall inherit the earth.
10For yet a little while and the wicked
shall be no *more;*
Indeed, you will look carefully for his
place,
But it *shall be* no *more.*

11But the meek shall inherit the earth,
And shall delight themselves in the
abundance of peace.

12The wicked plots against the just,
And gnashes at him with his teeth.
13The Lord laughs at him,
For He sees that his day is coming.
14The wicked have drawn the sword
And have bent their bow,
To cast down the poor and needy,
To slay those who are of upright
conduct.
15Their sword shall enter their own
heart,
And their bows shall be broken.

16A little that a righteous man has
Is better than the riches of many
wicked.
17For the arms of the wicked shall be
broken,
But the LORD upholds the righteous.

18The LORD knows the days of the
upright,
And their inheritance shall be forever.

37:4 Desires of the heart. What are our desires? What do we want most in life? Do we desire above all things to have a better paying job, a bigger house, thicker carpet, a superior car, and more money? Are we controlled by the lust of the flesh, the lust of the eyes, and the pride of life? Or have we been transformed from the way of this world by "the renewing of [our] mind" (Rom. 12:2), that we may prove what is that good, and acceptable, and perfect will of God? Are our desires now in line with God's desires? Are we above all things "not willing that any should perish but that all should come to repentance" (2 Pet. 3:9)? If we delight ourselves in the Lord, the desires of our heart will match His—and those are the desires He will grant.

37:9 Does the reference to the wicked being "cut off" mean that they are annihilated? "If it did, then the Messiah would have been annihilated when He died, since the same word (*karath*) is used of the death of the Messiah (in Dan. 9:26)." *Norman Geisler* and *Thomas Howe*

Springboards for Preaching and Witnessing

Rusty Harp

37:11 Some people have the idea that Christians will spend eternity sitting on clouds playing rusty harps. If that's all I hoped for, I wouldn't be a Christian. The hope I have is not nebulous; it is concrete. It is an "anchor of the soul," and is both sure and steadfast. Here is my hope. Consider the beauty of this massive earth. Think of a majestic snowcapped mountain, a clear babbling brook, or a beautiful beach with clean white sand and turquoise waters filled with an amazing array of brightly colored fish. The pristine waters reflect a clear blue sky, and the beach is surrounded with tall, lush palm trees. Think of majestic California redwoods or of the incredible assortment of tasty fruit trees, or the breathtaking beauty of a sunset, or the magnificence of the Grand Canyon or Niagara Falls. Got it in mind?

Now consider this. All who repent and trust in Jesus Christ, whether Jew or Gentile, black or white, male or female, rich or poor, will "inherit the earth." God has given it to us, and it will be ours for eternity. God's spiritual kingdom came to this earth on the day of Pentecost, and the time will come when the literal kingdom will come to this earth. God will replace this cursed and fallen creation with a new heavens and a new earth, and God's will, will be done on earth as it is in heaven. We not only escape hell, but, by God's grace, we get heaven on earth. What an unspeakably incredible future we have! We are going to see God and fellowship with Him *forever*, in a "world without end," where we will have "pleasures forevermore." If you are not saved, please think about your sins, and then think about the Savior. Think about what He did for you on the cross, because if you die in your sins, you will not only miss out on the pleasures of heaven on earth, but you will have to endure an everlasting hell, and that would be an unspeakable tragedy.

19 They shall not be ashamed in the evil time,
And in the days of famine they shall be satisfied.
20 But the wicked shall perish;
And the enemies of the LORD,
Like the splendor of the meadows, shall vanish.
Into smoke they shall vanish away.

21 The wicked borrows and does not repay,
But the righteous shows mercy and gives.
22 For *those* blessed by Him shall inherit the earth,
But *those* cursed by Him shall be cut off.

23 The steps of a *good* man are ordered by the LORD,
And He delights in his way.
24 Though he fall, he shall not be utterly cast down;
For the LORD upholds *him with* His hand.

25 I have been young, and *now* am old;
Yet I have not seen the righteous forsaken,
Nor his descendants begging bread.
26 *He is* ever merciful, and lends;
And his descendants *are* blessed.

27 Depart from evil, and do good;
And dwell forevermore.
28 For the LORD loves justice,
And does not forsake His saints;
They are preserved forever,
But the descendants of the wicked shall be cut off.
29 The righteous shall inherit the land,
And dwell in it forever.

30 The mouth of the righteous speaks wisdom,
And his tongue talks of justice.
31 The law of his God *is* in his heart;
None of his steps shall slide.

32 The wicked watches the righteous,
And seeks to slay him.
33 The LORD will not leave him in his

37:30,31 When we share the gospel, we speak the wisdom of God in Christ and of the justice of a holy God, revealed in a perfect Law.

QUESTIONS & OBJECTIONS

38:4

"Could God create a boulder so heavy that He cannot lift it?"

There are many things God cannot do—things related to His character rather than His ability. The Bible makes it clear that God cannot lie. (See Heb. 6:18 comment.) He cannot sin. He also cannot let injustice go unpunished. As for whether God can create a rock that He cannot lift, when it comes to the ability of God, nothing is impossible.

However, this question reveals a lack of common sense. The questioner thinks that if God couldn't create a rock too big for Him to lift then He is not omnipotent. Then again, we could ask if God could make a square peg and put it into a round hole, and make it fit perfectly. Or, could God make an egg that is not an egg?

These questions are asked to divert attention away from the real issue. But it seems that God had the atheist pegged thousands of years ago when He said, "Do not answer a fool according to his folly, lest you also be like him" (Prov. 26:4).

Here is one more "nonsensical" question that may make sense: Could God take a man who is a fool but thinks that he's wise, and make him see that he is a fool, so that he will be wise? The answer is in 1 Cor. 3:18.

hand,
Nor condemn him when he is judged.

34Wait on the LORD,
And keep His way,
And He shall exalt you to inherit the land;
When the wicked are cut off, you shall see *it*.
35I have seen the wicked in great power,
And spreading himself like a native green tree.
36Yet he passed away,[a] and behold, he *was* no *more;*
Indeed I sought him, but he could not be found.

37Mark the blameless *man,* and observe the upright;
For the future of *that* man *is* peace.
38But the transgressors shall be destroyed together;
The future of the wicked shall be cut off.

39But the salvation of the righteous *is* from the LORD;
He is their strength in the time of trouble.
40And the LORD shall help them and deliver them;
He shall deliver them from the wicked,
And save them,
Because they trust in Him.

PSALM 38

Prayer in Time of Chastening

A Psalm of David. To bring to remembrance.

1O LORD, do not rebuke me in Your wrath,
Nor chasten me in Your hot displeasure!
2For Your arrows pierce me deeply,
And Your hand presses me down.

3*There is* no soundness in my flesh
Because of Your anger,
Nor *any* health in my bones
Because of my sin.
4For my iniquities have gone over my head;
Like a heavy burden they are too heavy for me.
5My wounds are foul *and* festering
Because of my foolishness.

6I am troubled, I am bowed down greatly;
I go mourning all the day long.
7For my loins are full of inflammation,

37:36 [a]Following Masoretic Text, Septuagint, and Targum; Syriac and Vulgate read *I passed by*.

And *there is* no soundness in my flesh.
8I am feeble and severely broken;
I groan because of the turmoil of my heart.

9Lord, all my desire *is* before You;
And my sighing is not hidden from You.
10My heart pants, my strength fails me;
As for the light of my eyes, it also has gone from me.

11My loved ones and my friends stand aloof from my plague,
And my relatives stand afar off.
12Those also who seek my life lay snares *for me;*
Those who seek my hurt speak of destruction,
And plan deception all the day long.

13But I, like a deaf *man,* do not hear;
And *I am* like a mute *who* does not open his mouth.
14Thus I am like a man who does not hear,
And in whose mouth *is* no response.

15For in You, O LORD, I hope;
You will hear, O Lord my God.
16For I said, "*Hear me,* lest they rejoice over me,
Lest, when my foot slips, they exalt *themselves* against me."

17For I *am* ready to fall,
And my sorrow *is* continually before me.
18For I will declare my iniquity;
I will be in anguish over my sin.
19But my enemies *are* vigorous, *and* they are strong;
And those who hate me wrongfully have multiplied.
20Those also who render evil for good,
They are my adversaries, because I follow *what is* good.

21Do not forsake me, O LORD;
O my God, be not far from me!
22Make haste to help me,
O Lord, my salvation!

PSALM 39

Prayer for Wisdom and Forgiveness

To the Chief Musician. To Jeduthun.
A Psalm of David.

1I said, "I will guard my ways,
Lest I sin with my tongue;
I will restrain my mouth with a muzzle,
While the wicked are before me."
2I was mute with silence,
I held my peace *even* from good;
And my sorrow was stirred up.
3My heart was hot within me;
While I was musing, the fire burned.
Then I spoke with my tongue:

4"LORD, make me to know my end,
And what *is* the measure of my days,
That I may know how frail I *am.*
5Indeed, You have made my days *as* handbreadths,
And my age *is* as nothing before You;
Certainly every man at his best state *is* but vapor. *Selah*

38:11 The Bible's fascinating facts. If, down through the ages, scriptural principles had been applied during epidemics such as the Black Plague, millions of lives would have been saved. Long before man understood the principles of quarantine, the Bible spoke of the importance of isolating those who had a contagious disease and of disinfecting their houses. See Lev. 13 and 14.

39:3 "Oh! I would to God there should come upon us a divine hunger which cannot stay itself except men yield themselves to Jesus; an intense, earnest, longing, panting desire that men should submit themselves to the gospel of Jesus. This will teach you better than the best college training how to deal with human hearts. This will give the stammering tongue the ready word; the hot heart shall burn the cords which held fast the tongue. You shall become wise to win souls, even though you never exhibit the brilliance of eloquence or the force of logic." *Charles Spurgeon*

[6]Surely every man walks about like a
shadow;
Surely they busy themselves in vain;
He heaps up *riches,*
And does not know who will gather
them.

[7]"And now, Lord, what do I wait for?
My hope *is* in You.
[8]Deliver me from all my transgressions;
Do not make me the reproach of the
foolish.
[9]I was mute, I did not open my mouth,
Because it was You who did *it.*
[10]Remove Your plague from me;
I am consumed by the blow of Your
hand.
[11]When with rebukes You correct man
for iniquity,
You make his beauty melt away like a
moth;
Surely every man *is* vapor. *Selah*

[12]"Hear my prayer, O LORD,
And give ear to my cry;
Do not be silent at my tears;
For I *am* a stranger with You,
A sojourner, as all my fathers *were.*
[13]Remove Your gaze from me, that I
may regain strength,
Before I go away and am no more."

PSALM 40

Faith Persevering in Trial

To the Chief Musician. A Psalm of David.

[1]I waited patiently for the LORD;
And He inclined to me,
And heard my cry.
[2]He also brought me up out of a
horrible pit,
Out of the miry clay,
And set my feet upon a rock,
And established my steps.
[3]He has put a new song in my mouth—
Praise to our God;
Many will see *it* and fear,
And will trust in the LORD.

[4]Blessed *is* that man who makes the
LORD his trust,
And does not respect the proud, nor
such as turn aside to lies.
[5]Many, O LORD my God, *are* Your
wonderful works
Which You have done;
And Your thoughts toward us
Cannot be recounted to You in order;
If I would declare and speak *of them,*
They are more than can be numbered.

[6]Sacrifice and offering You did not
desire;
My ears You have opened.
Burnt offering and sin offering You
did not require.
[7]Then I said, "Behold, I come;
In the scroll of the book *it is* written
of me.
[8]I delight to do Your will, O my God,
And Your law *is* within my heart."

[9]I have proclaimed the good news of
righteousness
In the great assembly;
Indeed, I do not restrain my lips,
O LORD, You Yourself know.
[10]I have not hidden Your righteousness
within my heart;
I have declared Your faithfulness and
Your salvation;
I have not concealed Your
lovingkindness and Your truth
From the great assembly.

[11]Do not withhold Your tender mercies
from me, O LORD;
Let Your lovingkindness and Your

40:7–9 This is a direct reference to the Messiah (see Heb. 10:7). Jesus preached righteousness because God's Law was within His heart. When God's Law is written in our hearts, we delight to do His will and proclaim the good news of righteousness. We do this by preaching "the righteousness which is of the Law" (Rom. 10:5). This shows men that they have sinned, and therefore need a Savior. See Rom. 3:19,20.

truth continually preserve me.
[12]For innumerable evils have surrounded me;
My iniquities have overtaken me, so that I am not able to look up;
They are more than the hairs of my head;
Therefore my heart fails me.

[13]Be pleased, O LORD, to deliver me;
O LORD, make haste to help me!
[14]Let them be ashamed and brought to mutual confusion
Who seek to destroy my life;
Let them be driven backward and brought to dishonor
Who wish me evil.
[15]Let them be confounded because of their shame,
Who say to me, "Aha, aha!"

[16]Let all those who seek You rejoice and be glad in You;
Let such as love Your salvation say continually,
"The LORD be magnified!"
[17]But I *am* poor and needy;
Yet the LORD thinks upon me.
You *are* my help and my deliverer;
Do not delay, O my God.

PSALM 41

The Blessing and Suffering of the Godly

To the Chief Musician. A Psalm of David.

[1]Blessed *is* he who considers the poor;
The LORD will deliver him in time of trouble.
[2]The LORD will preserve him and keep him alive,
And he will be blessed on the earth;
You will not deliver him to the will of his enemies.
[3]The LORD will strengthen him on his bed of illness;
You will sustain him on his sickbed.

[4]I said, "LORD, be merciful to me;
Heal my soul, for I have sinned against You."
[5]My enemies speak evil of me:
"When will he die, and his name perish?"
[6]And if he comes to see *me,* he speaks lies;
His heart gathers iniquity to itself;
When he goes out, he tells *it.*

[7]All who hate me whisper together against me;
Against me they devise my hurt.
[8]"An evil disease," *they say,* "clings to him.
And *now* that he lies down, he will rise up no more."
[9]Even my own familiar friend in whom I trusted,
Who ate my bread,
Has lifted up *his* heel against me.

[10]But You, O LORD, be merciful to me, and raise me up,
That I may repay them.
[11]By this I know that You are well pleased with me,
Because my enemy does not triumph over me.
[12]As for me, You uphold me in my integrity,
And set me before Your face forever.

[13]Blessed *be* the LORD God of Israel
From everlasting to everlasting!
Amen and Amen.

40:17 King David had great wealth and had his every need met, so he is speaking here in a spiritual sense. Describing himself as "poor and needy" shows he recognized his moral poverty and desperate need for God. See Luke 4:18 comment.

41:4 For how to confront sinners, see 2 Sam. 12:1–14 comment.

41:9 **Messianic prophecy:** This was fulfilled in Mark 14:10.

Book Two: Psalms 42—72

PSALM 42

Yearning for God in the Midst of Distresses

To the Chief Musician. A Contemplation[a] of the sons of Korah.

1As the deer pants for the water brooks,
So pants my soul for You, O God.
2My soul thirsts for God, for the living God.
When shall I come and appear before God?[a]
3My tears have been my food day and night,
While they continually say to me,
"Where *is* your God?"

4When I remember these *things,*
I pour out my soul within me.
For I used to go with the multitude;
I went with them to the house of God,
With the voice of joy and praise,
With a multitude that kept a pilgrim feast.

5Why are you cast down, O my soul?
And *why* are you disquieted within me?
Hope in God, for I shall yet praise Him
For the help of His countenance.[a]

6O my God,[a] my soul is cast down within me;
Therefore I will remember You from the land of the Jordan,
And from the heights of Hermon,
From the Hill Mizar.
7Deep calls unto deep at the noise of Your waterfalls;
All Your waves and billows have gone over me.
8The LORD will command His lovingkindness in the daytime,
And in the night His song *shall be* with me—
A prayer to the God of my life.

9I will say to God my Rock,
"Why have You forgotten me?
Why do I go mourning because of the oppression of the enemy?"
10*As* with a breaking of my bones,
My enemies reproach me,
While they say to me all day long,
"Where *is* your God?"

11Why are you cast down, O my soul?
And why are you disquieted within me?
Hope in God;
For I shall yet praise Him,
The help of my countenance and my God.

PSALM 43

Prayer to God in Time of Trouble

1Vindicate me, O God,
And plead my cause against an ungodly nation;
Oh, deliver me from the deceitful and unjust man!
2For You *are* the God of my strength;
Why do You cast me off?
Why do I go mourning because of the oppression of the enemy?

3Oh, send out Your light and Your truth!
Let them lead me;
Let them bring me to Your holy hill
And to Your tabernacle.
4Then I will go to the altar of God,
To God my exceeding joy;
And on the harp I will praise You,
O God, my God.

5Why are you cast down, O my soul?
And why are you disquieted within me?
Hope in God;
For I shall yet praise Him,
The help of my countenance and my God.

42:title [a]Hebrew *Maschil* **42:2** [a]Following Masoretic Text and Vulgate; some Hebrew manuscripts, Septuagint, Syriac, and Targum read *I see the face of God.* **42:5** [a]Following Masoretic Text and Targum; a few Hebrew manuscripts, Septuagint, Syriac, and Vulgate read *The help of my countenance, my God.* **42:6** [a]Following Masoretic Text and Targum; a few Hebrew manuscripts, Septuagint, Syriac, and Vulgate put *my God* at the end of verse 5.

PSALM 44

Redemption Remembered in Present Dishonor

To the Chief Musician. A Contemplation[a] of the sons of Korah.

[1]We have heard with our ears, O God,
Our fathers have told us,
The deeds You did in their days,
In days of old:
[2]You drove out the nations with Your hand,
But them You planted;
You afflicted the peoples, and cast them out.
[3]For they did not gain possession of the land by their own sword,
Nor did their own arm save them;
But it was Your right hand, Your arm, and the light of Your countenance,
Because You favored them.

[4]You are my King, O God;[a]
Command[b] victories for Jacob.
[5]Through You we will push down our enemies;
Through Your name we will trample those who rise up against us.
[6]For I will not trust in my bow,
Nor shall my sword save me.
[7]But You have saved us from our enemies,
And have put to shame those who hated us.
[8]In God we boast all day long,
And praise Your name forever. *Selah*

[9]But You have cast *us* off and put us to shame,
And You do not go out with our armies.
[10]You make us turn back from the enemy,
And those who hate us have taken spoil for themselves.
[11]You have given us up like sheep *intended* for food,
And have scattered us among the nations.
[12]You sell Your people for *next to* nothing,
And are not enriched by selling them.

[13]You make us a reproach to our neighbors,
A scorn and a derision to those all around us.
[14]You make us a byword among the nations,
A shaking of the head among the peoples.
[15]My dishonor *is* continually before me,
And the shame of my face has covered me,
[16]Because of the voice of him who reproaches and reviles,
Because of the enemy and the avenger.

[17]All this has come upon us;
But we have not forgotten You,
Nor have we dealt falsely with Your covenant.
[18]Our heart has not turned back,
Nor have our steps departed from Your way;
[19]But You have severely broken us in the place of jackals,
And covered us with the shadow of death.

[20]If we had forgotten the name of our God,
Or stretched out our hands to a foreign god,
[21]Would not God search this out?
For He knows the secrets of the heart.

44:title [a]Hebrew *Maschil* **44:4** [a]Following Masoretic Text and Targum; Septuagint and Vulgate read *and my God.* [b]Following Masoretic Text and Targum; Septuagint, Syriac, and Vulgate read *Who commands.*

44:21 It is so easy to say, "God sees the heart." Think for a moment how incredible God must be to be able to search the thoughts of even one person. He sees the motives, the desires, and the deepest secrets. Sometimes our thoughts are so numerous that even we have trouble tracking them. Yet God sees the thoughts of every living person on this earth. This can either be a great comfort or a great terror, depending on whether or not our sins are forgiven.

[22]Yet for Your sake we are killed all day
long;
We are accounted as sheep for the
slaughter.

[23]Awake! Why do You sleep, O Lord?
Arise! Do not cast *us* off forever.
[24]Why do You hide Your face,
And forget our affliction and our
oppression?
[25]For our soul is bowed down to the
dust;
Our body clings to the ground.
[26]Arise for our help,
And redeem us for Your mercies' sake.

PSALM 45

The Glories of the Messiah and His Bride

To the Chief Musician. Set to "The Lilies."[a]
A Contemplation[b] of the sons of Korah.
A Song of Love.

[1]My heart is overflowing with a good
theme;
I recite my composition concerning
the King;
My tongue *is* the pen of a ready writer.

[2]You are fairer than the sons of men;
Grace is poured upon Your lips;
Therefore God has blessed You forever.
[3]Gird Your sword upon *Your* thigh, O
Mighty One,
With Your glory and Your majesty.
[4]And in Your majesty ride
prosperously because of truth,
humility, *and* righteousness;
And Your right hand shall teach You
awesome things.
[5]Your arrows *are* sharp in the heart of
the King's enemies;
The peoples fall under You.

[6]Your throne, O God, *is* forever and
ever;
A scepter of righteousness *is* the
scepter of Your kingdom.
[7]You love righteousness and hate
wickedness;
Therefore God, Your God, has
anointed You
With the oil of gladness more than
Your companions.
[8]All Your garments *are scented* with
myrrh and aloes *and* cassia,
Out of the ivory palaces, by which
they have made You glad.
[9]Kings' daughters *are* among Your
honorable women;
At Your right hand stands the queen
in gold from Ophir.

[10]Listen, O daughter,
Consider and incline your ear;
Forget your own people also, and
your father's house;
[11]So the King will greatly desire your
beauty;
Because He *is* your Lord, worship Him.
[12]And the daughter of Tyre *will come*
with a gift;
The rich among the people will seek
your favor.

> Time, whose tooth gnaws away at everything else, is powerless against the truth.
>
> **THOMAS HUXLEY**

[13]The royal daughter *is* all glorious
within *the palace;*
Her clothing *is* woven with gold.
[14]She shall be brought to the King in
robes of many colors;
The virgins, her companions who
follow her, shall be brought to You.
[15]With gladness and rejoicing they
shall be brought;
They shall enter the King's palace.

[16]Instead of Your fathers shall be Your
sons,
Whom You shall make princes in all
the earth.
[17]I will make Your name to be
remembered in all generations;

45:title [a]Hebrew *Shoshannim* [b]Hebrew *Maschil*

"Worshipping God and the Lamb in the temple: God, for his benefaction in creating all things, and the Lamb, for his benefaction in redeeming us with his blood."

Isaac Newton

Therefore the people shall praise You
forever and ever.

PSALM 46

God the Refuge of His People and Conqueror of the Nations

To the Chief Musician. *A Psalm* of the sons of Korah. A Song for Alamoth.

1God *is* our refuge and strength,
A very present help in trouble.
2Therefore we will not fear,
Even though the earth be removed,
And though the mountains be carried
into the midst of the sea;
3*Though* its waters roar *and* be troubled,
Though the mountains shake with its
swelling. *Selah*

4*There is* a river whose streams shall
make glad the city of God,
The holy *place* of the tabernacle of the
Most High.
5God *is* in the midst of her, she shall
not be moved;
God shall help her, just at the break
of dawn.
6The nations raged, the kingdoms
were moved;
He uttered His voice, the earth melted.

7The LORD of hosts *is* with us;
The God of Jacob *is* our refuge. *Selah*

8Come, behold the works of the LORD,
Who has made desolations in the
earth.
9He makes wars cease to the end of
the earth;
He breaks the bow and cuts the spear
in two;
He burns the chariot in the fire.

10Be still, and know that I *am* God;
I will be exalted among the nations,
I will be exalted in the earth!

11The LORD of hosts *is* with us;
The God of Jacob *is* our refuge. *Selah*

PSALM 47

Praise to God, the Ruler of the Earth

To the Chief Musician.
A Psalm of the sons of Korah.

1Oh, clap your hands, all you peoples!
Shout to God with the voice of
triumph!
2For the LORD Most High *is* awesome;
He is a great King over all the earth.
3He will subdue the peoples under us,
And the nations under our feet.
4He will choose our inheritance for us,
The excellence of Jacob whom He
loves. *Selah*

5God has gone up with a shout,
The LORD with the sound of a
trumpet.
6Sing praises to God, sing praises!
Sing praises to our King, sing praises!
7For God *is* the King of all the earth;
Sing praises with understanding.

8God reigns over the nations;
God sits on His holy throne.
9The princes of the people have

gathered together,
The people of the God of Abraham.
For the shields of the earth *belong* to God;
He is greatly exalted.

PSALM 48

The Glory of God in Zion

A Song. A Psalm of the sons of Korah.

1 Great *is* the LORD, and greatly to be praised
In the city of our God,
In His holy mountain.
2 Beautiful in elevation,
The joy of the whole earth,
Is Mount Zion *on* the sides of the north,
The city of the great King.
3 God *is* in her palaces;
He is known as her refuge.

A man can no more possess a private religion than he can possess a private sun and moon.

G. K. CHESTERTON

4 For behold, the kings assembled,
They passed by together.
5 They saw *it, and* so they marveled;
They were troubled, they hastened away.
6 Fear took hold of them there,
And pain, as of a woman in birth pangs,
7 *As when* You break the ships of Tarshish
With an east wind.

8 As we have heard,
So we have seen
In the city of the LORD of hosts,
In the city of our God:
God will establish it forever. *Selah*

9 We have thought, O God, on Your lovingkindness,
In the midst of Your temple.
10 According to Your name, O God,
So *is* Your praise to the ends of the earth;
Your right hand is full of righteousness.
11 Let Mount Zion rejoice,
Let the daughters of Judah be glad,
Because of Your judgments.

12 Walk about Zion,
And go all around her.
Count her towers;
13 Mark well her bulwarks;
Consider her palaces;
That you may tell *it* to the generation following.
14 For this *is* God,
Our God forever and ever;
He will be our guide
Even to death.[a]

PSALM 49

The Confidence of the Foolish

To the Chief Musician. A Psalm of the sons of Korah.

1 Hear this, all peoples;
Give ear, all inhabitants of the world,
2 Both low and high,
Rich and poor together.
3 My mouth shall speak wisdom,
And the meditation of my heart *shall give* understanding.
4 I will incline my ear to a proverb;
I will disclose my dark saying on the harp.

5 Why should I fear in the days of evil,
When the iniquity at my heels surrounds me?
6 Those who trust in their wealth
And boast in the multitude of their riches,
7 None *of them* can by any means redeem *his* brother,
Nor give to God a ransom for him—
8 For the redemption of their souls *is* costly,
And it shall cease forever—
9 That he should continue to live eternally,

48:14 [a]Following Masoretic Text and Syriac; Septuagint and Vulgate read *Forever*.

QUESTIONS & OBJECTIONS

49:15 ***"When you're dead, you're dead."***

What if you are wrong? What if God, Jesus, the prophets, the Jews, and Christians are right and you are wrong? If there is no afterlife, no Judgment Day, no heaven, and no hell, then God is unjust and each of the above is guilty of being a false witness. It means that Almighty God couldn't care less about the fact that a man rapes a woman, then slits her throat and is never brought to justice. If you are right, and there is no ultimate justice, you won't even have the satisfaction of saying, "I told you so." However, if you are wrong, you will lose your soul and end up eternally damned. You are playing Russian roulette with a fully loaded gun.

See also Heb. 9:27 comment.

And not see the Pit.

[10]For he sees wise men die;
Likewise the fool and the senseless
person perish,
And leave their wealth to others.
[11]Their inner thought *is that* their
houses *will last* forever,[a]
Their dwelling places to all generations;
They call *their* lands after their own
names.
[12]Nevertheless man, *though* in honor,
does not remain;[a]
He is like the beasts *that* perish.

[13]This is the way of those who *are*
foolish,
And of their posterity who approve
their sayings. *Selah*
[14]Like sheep they are laid in the grave;
Death shall feed on them;
The upright shall have dominion over
them in the morning;
And their beauty shall be consumed
in the grave, far from their
dwelling.
[15]But God will redeem my soul from
the power of the grave,
For He shall receive me. *Selah*

[16]Do not be afraid when one becomes
rich,
When the glory of his house is
increased;
[17]For when he dies he shall carry
nothing away;
His glory shall not descend after him.
[18]Though while he lives he blesses
himself
(For *men* will praise you when you do

49:11 [a]Septuagint, Syriac, Targum, and Vulgate read *Their graves shall be their houses forever.* **49:12** [a]Following Masoretic Text and Targum; Septuagint, Syriac, and Vulgate read *understand* (compare verse 20).

49:7 Grief for the lost. Many of us have felt sorrow and grief over loved ones who don't know the salvation of God. If there was something we could do to save them, we would gladly do it. But often there is nothing we can do but pray—none of us can by any means redeem his brother or give God a ransom for him. We can however, trust God in the fact that One has already become a curse for Israel and for our loved ones. One has already provided the necessary redemption—He has paid the ransom for them. We inherit the promises of God through faith and patience, and therefore rest in the knowledge that God will answer our prayers for our loved ones' salvation.

But our zeal for the salvation of sinners shouldn't be limited to our loved ones. Salvation in the heart of the Christian should cause him to love his neighbor as he loves himself.

49:7,8 The blood of Jesus Christ was the precious cost of our redemption, something that humanity could not provide. See 1 Pet. 1:18,19.

Roman Catholics, however, believe it is possible for them to "ransom" someone out of "purgatory." See page 1810 for details.

49:17 "When we die we leave behind all that we have, and take with us all that we are." *Chapel of the Air*

well for yourself),
[19]He shall go to the generation of his
fathers;
They shall never see light.
[20]A man *who is* in honor, yet does not
understand,
Is like the beasts *that* perish.

PSALM 50

God the Righteous Judge

A Psalm of Asaph.

[1]The Mighty One, God the LORD,
Has spoken and called the earth
From the rising of the sun to its going
down.
[2]Out of Zion, the perfection of beauty,
God will shine forth.
[3]Our God shall come, and shall not
keep silent;
A fire shall devour before Him,
And it shall be very tempestuous all
around Him.

[4]He shall call to the heavens from
above,
And to the earth, that He may judge
His people:
[5]"Gather My saints together to Me,
Those who have made a covenant
with Me by sacrifice."
[6]Let the heavens declare His
righteousness,
For God Himself *is* Judge. *Selah*

[7]"Hear, O My people, and I will speak,
O Israel, and I will testify against you;
I *am* God, your God!
[8]I will not rebuke you for your sacrifices
Or your burnt offerings,
Which are continually before Me.
[9]I will not take a bull from your house,
Nor goats out of your folds.
[10]For every beast of the forest *is* Mine,
And the cattle on a thousand hills.
[11]I know all the birds of the mountains,
And the wild beasts of the field *are*
Mine.

[12]"If I were hungry, I would not tell you;
For the world *is* Mine, and all its
fullness.
[13]Will I eat the flesh of bulls,
Or drink the blood of goats?
[14]Offer to God thanksgiving,
And pay your vows to the Most High.
[15]Call upon Me in the day of trouble;
I will deliver you, and you shall
glorify Me."

[16]But to the wicked God says:
"What *right* have you to declare My
statutes,
Or take My covenant in your mouth,
[17]Seeing you hate instruction
And cast My words behind you?
[18]When you saw a thief, you
consented[a] with him,
And have been a partaker with
adulterers.
[19]You give your mouth to evil,
And your tongue frames deceit.
[20]You sit *and* speak against your
brother;
You slander your own mother's son.
[21]These *things* you have done, and I
kept silent;
You thought that I was altogether like
you;
But I will rebuke you,
And set *them* in order before your eyes.

[22]"Now consider this, you who forget
God,
Lest I tear *you* in pieces,
And *there be* none to deliver:
[23]Whoever offers praise glorifies Me;
And to him who orders *his* conduct

50:18 [a]Septuagint, Syriac, Targum, and Vulgate read *ran.*

50:16 Verses 16–23 contain a fearful word for a godless world that delights in entertainment glorifying theft, violence, adultery, and hatred. They assume that heaven's silence is heaven's sanction. God threatens fearful wrath, then offers salvation to those who will listen. This is the biblical order of gospel proclamation: Law before grace. See 2 Sam. 12:1–14 comment.

51:6 How to Use the Ten Commandments in Witnessing

This should be done in a spirit of love and gentleness:

"Do you think you have kept the Ten Commandments? Have you ever told a lie (including 'white lies,' half-truths, exaggerations, etc.)? If you have, then you are a 'liar,' and you cannot enter the kingdom of God. Have you ever stolen anything? (The value is irrelevant.) Then you are a thief. Jesus said that if you look with lust, you have committed adultery in your heart. If you hate someone, then you have committed murder in your heart. God requires truth 'in the inward parts'—He sees even the thought-life.

"Have you loved God above all else? Has He always been first in your affections? Have you made a 'god' to suit yourself (having your own beliefs about God)? That is called idolatry, and the Bible warns that no idolater will enter the kingdom of God. Have you ever used God's holy name to curse, or been greedy? Have you kept the Sabbath holy? Have you always implicitly honored your parents? Have you broken any of the Ten Commandments?

"Knowing that God has seen your thought-life and every deed done in darkness, will you be innocent or guilty on Judgment Day? You know you will be guilty. So, will you end up in heaven or hell?"

The Law brings individuals to a point of seeing that they have sinned against God—that His wrath abides on them. It causes them to see that their own "goodness" can't save them. It stops their mouth of justification (Rom. 3:19), and prepares the heart for the good news of the gospel:

"The only thing you can do to be saved from His wrath is to repent and put your faith in the Savior, Jesus Christ. When He died on the cross, He took the punishment for our sins. He, once and for all, stepped into the Courtroom and completely paid the fine for us. Then He rose from the dead, defeating death. If you want to be saved from God's wrath, confess and forsake your sins, put your faith in Jesus for your eternal salvation, and you will pass from death into life. Then read the Bible daily and obey what you read (see John 14:21). God will never let you down."

For leading sinners to Jesus, see Rom. 2:15,16 comment.

aright
I will show the salvation of God."

PSALM 51

A Prayer of Repentance

To the Chief Musician. A Psalm of David when Nathan the prophet went to him, after he had gone in to Bathsheba.

1 Have mercy upon me, O God,
According to Your lovingkindness;
According to the multitude of Your
tender mercies,
Blot out my transgressions.
2 Wash me thoroughly from my iniquity,
And cleanse me from my sin.

3 For I acknowledge my transgressions,
And my sin *is* always before me.
4 Against You, You only, have I sinned,
And done *this* evil in Your sight—
That You may be found just when
You speak,[a]
And blameless when You judge.

5 Behold, I was brought forth in iniquity,
And in sin my mother conceived me.
6 Behold, You desire truth in the
inward parts,
And in the hidden *part* You will make
me to know wisdom.

51:4 [a]Septuagint, Targum, and Vulgate read *in Your words*.

51:1–4 When a sinner is ready for salvation, he exhibits personal responsibility for his sins. In these four verses David uses the words *me*, *my*, and *I* ten times in reference to his sins. See also Luke 15:21 comment.

51:6 Civil law can search your house. It can search your car and even your person, but it cannot search the heart. Civil law cannot see human thoughts. God's Law, however, searches the inward parts. Like ten hungry bloodhounds, it chases the scent of injustice. It will pursue the guilty criminal until he is brought to justice. There is only one way for the ten ravenous hounds to leave the trail: sinners must cross over a "river." There is a river of blood that flows from Calvary's cross. Only the blood of Jesus Christ satisfies the Law's insatiable appetite for righteousness. See Heb. 9:22.

[7]Purge me with hyssop, and I shall be clean;
Wash me, and I shall be whiter than snow.
[8]Make me hear joy and gladness,
That the bones You have broken may rejoice.
[9]Hide Your face from my sins,
And blot out all my iniquities.

[10]Create in me a clean heart, O God,
And renew a steadfast spirit within me.
[11]Do not cast me away from Your presence,
And do not take Your Holy Spirit from me.

The root of joy is gratefulness... It is not joy that makes us grateful; it is gratitude that makes us joyful.

DAVID STEINDL-RAST

[12]Restore to me the joy of Your salvation,
And uphold me *by Your* generous Spirit.
[13]*Then* I will teach transgressors Your ways,
And sinners shall be converted to You.

[14]Deliver me from the guilt of bloodshed, O God,
The God of my salvation,
And my tongue shall sing aloud of Your righteousness.
[15]O Lord, open my lips,
And my mouth shall show forth Your praise.
[16]For You do not desire sacrifice, or else I would give *it;*
You do not delight in burnt offering.
[17]The sacrifices of God *are* a broken spirit,
A broken and a contrite heart—
These, O God, You will not despise.

[18]Do good in Your good pleasure to Zion;
Build the walls of Jerusalem.
[19]Then You shall be pleased with the sacrifices of righteousness,
With burnt offering and whole burnt offering;
Then they shall offer bulls on Your altar.

PSALM 52

The End of the Wicked and the Peace of the Godly

To the Chief Musician. A Contemplation[a] of David when Doeg the Edomite went and told Saul, and said to him, "David has gone to the house of Ahimelech."

[1]Why do you boast in evil, O mighty man?
The goodness of God *endures* continually.
[2]Your tongue devises destruction,
Like a sharp razor, working deceitfully.
[3]You love evil more than good,
Lying rather than speaking righteousness. *Selah*
[4]You love all devouring words,
You deceitful tongue.

[5]God shall likewise destroy you forever;
He shall take you away, and pluck you out of *your* dwelling place,

52:title [a]Hebrew *Maschil*

51:7 "Direct my thoughts, words, and work. Wash away my sins in the immaculate Blood of the Lamb, and purge my heart by Thy Holy Spirit... Daily frame me more and more into the likeness of Thy Son Jesus Christ." *George Washington*, in his prayer book

51:10 Those who confess and forsake their sins are given a clean heart and a new spirit in Christ, and the fruit of genuine salvation is a concern for the lost. See v. 13. See also Ezek. 11:19 comment.

51:13–17 "Transgressors" are those who have transgressed the moral Law. The Law is the "tutor" that teaches them that they are sinners in the eyes of God (Gal. 3:24; Rom. 3:19,20). It is the Law that sings aloud of God's righteousness, breaks the human spirit, and gives the sinner reason to be contrite over sins in which he previously delighted. See Rom. 7:13,24,25.

And uproot you from the land of the
living. *Selah*
[6]The righteous also shall see and fear,
And shall laugh at him, *saying,*
[7]"Here is the man *who* did not make
God his strength,
But trusted in the abundance of his
riches,
And strengthened himself in his
wickedness."

[8]But I *am* like a green olive tree in the
house of God;
I trust in the mercy of God forever
and ever.
[9]I will praise You forever,
Because You have done *it;*
And in the presence of Your saints
I will wait on Your name, for *it is* good.

PSALM 53

Folly of the Godless, and the Restoration of Israel

To the Chief Musician. Set to "Mahalath." A Contemplation[a] of David.

[1]The fool has said in his heart,
"*There is* no God."
They are corrupt, and have done
abominable iniquity;
There is none who does good.

[2]God looks down from heaven upon
the children of men,
To see if there are *any* who
understand, who seek God.
[3]Every one of them has turned aside;
They have together become corrupt;
There is none who does good,
No, not one.

[4]Have the workers of iniquity no
knowledge,
Who eat up my people *as* they eat
bread,
And do not call upon God?
[5]There they are in great fear
Where no fear was,
For God has scattered the bones of
him who encamps against you;
You have put *them* to shame,
Because God has despised them.

[6]Oh, that the salvation of Israel would
come out of Zion!
When God brings back the captivity
of His people,
Let Jacob rejoice *and* Israel be glad.

PSALM 54

Answered Prayer for Deliverance from Adversaries

To the Chief Musician. With stringed instruments.[a] A Contemplation[b] of David when the Ziphites went and said to Saul, "Is David not hiding with us?"

[1]Save me, O God, by Your name,
And vindicate me by Your strength.
[2]Hear my prayer, O God;
Give ear to the words of my mouth.
[3]For strangers have risen up against me,
And oppressors have sought after my
life;
They have not set God before them.
Selah

53:title [a]Hebrew *Maschil* 54:title [a]Hebrew *neginoth* [b]Hebrew *Maschil*

52:7 The New Testament reminds us of this truth: We cannot love God *and* mammon (Luke 16:13).

53:1 The fact that there is a God is axiomatic (self-evident). The Bible does not enter into the case for God's existence. It simply begins by stating, "In the beginning God..." (Gen. 1:1). See Psa. 90:2 comment.

"It takes no brains to be an atheist. Any stupid person can deny the existence of a supernatural power because man's physical senses cannot detect it. But there cannot be ignored the influence of conscience, the respect we feel for the moral Law, the mystery of first life...or the marvelous order in which the universe moves about us on this earth. All these evidence the handiwork of the beneficent Deity...That Deity is the God of the Bible and Jesus Christ, His Son." *Dwight Eisenhower*

53:1–3 There are many "good" people from man's viewpoint. However, here is *God's* point of view. These verses leave no room for the self-righteous. See also Mark 10:17 comment.

[4]Behold, God *is* my helper;
The Lord *is* with those who uphold my life.
[5]He will repay my enemies for their evil.
Cut them off in Your truth.

[6]I will freely sacrifice to You;
I will praise Your name, O LORD, for *it is* good.
[7]For He has delivered me out of all trouble;
And my eye has seen *its desire* upon my enemies.

PSALM 55

Trust in God Concerning the Treachery of Friends

To the Chief Musician. With stringed instruments.[a] A Contemplation[b] of David.

[1]Give ear to my prayer, O God,
And do not hide Yourself from my supplication.
[2]Attend to me, and hear me;
I am restless in my complaint, and moan noisily,
[3]Because of the voice of the enemy,
Because of the oppression of the wicked;
For they bring down trouble upon me,
And in wrath they hate me.

[4]My heart is severely pained within me,
And the terrors of death have fallen upon me.
[5]Fearfulness and trembling have come upon me,
And horror has overwhelmed me.
[6]So I said, "Oh, that I had wings like a dove!
I would fly away and be at rest.
[7]Indeed, I would wander far off,
And remain in the wilderness. *Selah*
[8]I would hasten my escape
From the windy storm *and* tempest."

[9]Destroy, O Lord, *and* divide their tongues,
For I have seen violence and strife in the city.
[10]Day and night they go around it on its walls;
Iniquity and trouble *are* also in the midst of it.
[11]Destruction *is* in its midst;
Oppression and deceit do not depart from its streets.

[12]For *it is* not an enemy *who* reproaches me;
Then I could bear *it*.
Nor *is it* one *who* hates me who has exalted *himself* against me;
Then I could hide from him.
[13]But *it was* you, a man my equal,
My companion and my acquaintance.
[14]We took sweet counsel together,
And walked to the house of God in the throng.

[15]Let death seize them;
Let them go down alive into hell,
For wickedness *is* in their dwellings *and* among them.

[16]As for me, I will call upon God,
And the LORD shall save me.
[17]Evening and morning and at noon
I will pray, and cry aloud,
And He shall hear my voice.
[18]He has redeemed my soul in peace from the battle *that was* against me,
For there were many against me.
[19]God will hear, and afflict them,
Even He who abides from of old. *Selah*
Because they do not change,
Therefore they do not fear God.

[20]He has put forth his hands against those who were at peace with him;
He has broken his covenant.
[21]*The words* of his mouth were smoother than butter,
But war *was* in his heart;
His words were softer than oil,
Yet they *were* drawn swords.

[22]Cast your burden on the LORD,

55:title [a]Hebrew *neginoth* [b]Hebrew *Maschil*

QUESTIONS & OBJECTIONS

55:15

"I don't mind going to hell. All my friends will be there."

Obviously, those who flippantly say such things don't believe in the biblical concept of hell. Their understanding of the nature of God is erroneous. The slow-witted criminal thinks that the electric chair is a place to put up his feet for a while and relax.

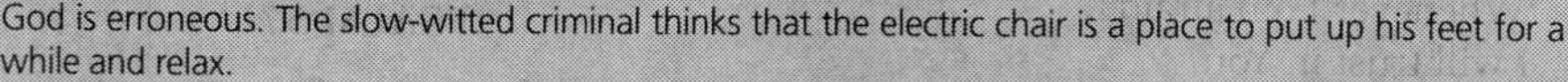

It may be wise therefore to speak with him for a few moments about the *reasonableness* of a place called hell. Reason with him by saying, "If a judge turns a blind eye to the unlawful dealings of the Mafia, if he sees their murderous acts and deliberately turns the other way, is he a good or bad judge? He is obviously corrupt, and should be brought to justice himself. If he is a good judge, he will do everything within his power to bring those murderers to justice. He should make sure that they are justly punished.

"If Almighty God sees a man rape and strangle to death your sister or mother, do you think He should look the other way, or bring that murderer to justice? If He looks the other way, He's corrupt and should be brought to justice Himself. It makes sense then, that if God is good, He will do everything in His power to ensure justice is done. The Bible tells us that He *will* punish murderers, and the place of punishment—the prison God will send them to—is a place called hell.

"God should punish murderers and rapists. However, God is so good, he will also punish thieves, liars, adulterers, fornicators, and blasphemers. He will even punish those who *desired* to murder and rape but never took the opportunity. He warns that if we hate someone, we commit murder in our hearts. If we lust, we commit adultery in the heart, etc."

Then take the time to tell him of the *reality* of hell. Sinners like to picture hell as a fun, hedonistic, pleasure-filled place where they can relish in all the sensual sins that the Bible forbids. But Jesus said that it is a place of torment, where the worm never dies and the fire is never quenched (Mark 9:43,44). We tend to forget what pain is like when we don't have it. Can you begin to imagine how terrible it would be to be in agony, with no hope of relief?

Many human beings go insane if they are simply isolated for a long time from other people. Imagine how terrible it would be if God simply withdrew all the things we hold so dear—friendship, love, color, light, peace, joy, laughter, and security. Hell isn't just a place with an absence of God's blessings, it is punishment for sin. It is literal torment, forever. That's why the Bible warns that it is a fearful thing to fall into the hands of the living God (Heb. 10:31).

God has given His Law to convince men of their sins, and unless a sinner is convinced that he has sinned against God, he won't see that hell is his eternal destiny. He may consider it a fit place for others, but not for himself. That's why we mustn't hesitate to open up the Law and show that each individual is personally responsible for sin, and that God's wrath abides on him because of it (John 3:36).

Ask him to consider why you would say such a thing to him if it wasn't true. Tell him to examine your motives. You are so concerned for his eternal welfare that you are prepared to risk offending him.

Then ask him if he would sell an eye for a million dollars. Would he sell *both* for ten million? No one in his right mind would. Our eyes are precious to us. How much more then is our eternal soul worth? (For a biblical description of hell, see Rev. 1:18 comment.)

And He shall sustain you;
He shall never permit the righteous to
be moved.

[23]But You, O God, shall bring them
down to the pit of destruction;
Bloodthirsty and deceitful men shall
not live out half their days;
But I will trust in You.

PSALM 56

Prayer for Relief from Tormentors

To the Chief Musician. Set to "The Silent Dove in Distant Lands."[a] A Michtam of David when the Philistines captured him in Gath.

[1]Be merciful to me, O God, for man

56:title [a]Hebrew *Jonath Elem Rechokim*

55:22 What an incredible promise—we have an anchor for the soul. See Matt. 6:25–34 for some of the ways the Lord sustains us.

would swallow me up;
Fighting all day he oppresses me.
2My enemies would hound *me* all day,
For *there are* many who fight against
me, O Most High.

3Whenever I am afraid,
I will trust in You.
4In God (I will praise His word),
In God I have put my trust;
I will not fear.
What can flesh do to me?

5All day they twist my words;
All their thoughts *are* against me for
evil.
6They gather together,
They hide, they mark my steps,
When they lie in wait for my life.
7Shall they escape by iniquity?
In anger cast down the peoples, O
God!

Holy practice is the most decisive evidence of the reality of our repentance.

JONATHAN EDWARDS

8You number my wanderings;
Put my tears into Your bottle;
Are they not in Your book?
9When I cry out *to You,*
Then my enemies will turn back;
This I know, because God *is* for me.
10In God (I will praise *His* word),
In the LORD (I will praise *His* word),
11In God I have put my trust;
I will not be afraid.
What can man do to me?

12Vows *made* to You *are binding* upon
me, O God;
I will render praises to You,
13For You have delivered my soul from
death.
Have You not *kept* my feet from falling,
That I may walk before God
In the light of the living?

PSALM 57

Prayer for Safety from Enemies

To the Chief Musician. Set to "Do Not Destroy."[a] A Michtam of David when he fled from Saul into the cave.

1Be merciful to me, O God, be
merciful to me!
For my soul trusts in You;
And in the shadow of Your wings I
will make my refuge,
Until *these* calamities have passed by.

2I will cry out to God Most High,
To God who performs *all things* for me.
3He shall send from heaven and save
me;
He reproaches the one who would
swallow me up. *Selah*
God shall send forth His mercy and
His truth.

4My soul *is* among lions;
I lie *among* the sons of men
Who are set on fire,
Whose teeth *are* spears and arrows,
And their tongue a sharp sword.
5Be exalted, O God, above the heavens;
Let Your glory *be* above all the earth.

6They have prepared a net for my steps;
My soul is bowed down;
They have dug a pit before me;
Into the midst of it they *themselves*
have fallen. *Selah*

57:title [a]Hebrew *Al Tashcheth*

56:11 The fear of man is the devil's paralyzing poison. Faith in God is the antidote. When the enemy feeds you the lie that you cannot share your faith, answer him with "I can do all things through Christ who strengthens me" (Phil. 4:13). Then put works with your faith—follow your convictions.

"Stop caring about what people think; begin to think about caring for people." *Emeal Zwayne*

[7]My heart is steadfast, O God, my
heart is steadfast;
I will sing and give praise.
[8]Awake, my glory!
Awake, lute and harp!
I will awaken the dawn.

[9]I will praise You, O Lord, among the
peoples;
I will sing to You among the nations.
[10]For Your mercy reaches unto the
heavens,
And Your truth unto the clouds.

[11]Be exalted, O God, above the heavens;
Let Your glory *be* above all the earth.

PSALM 58

The Just Judgment of the Wicked

To the Chief Musician. Set to "Do Not Destroy."[a]
A Michtam of David.

[1]Do you indeed speak righteousness,
you silent ones?
Do you judge uprightly, you sons of
men?
[2]No, in heart you work wickedness;
You weigh out the violence of your
hands in the earth.

[3]The wicked are estranged from the
womb;
They go astray as soon as they are
born, speaking lies.
[4]Their poison *is* like the poison of a
serpent;
They are like the deaf cobra *that* stops
its ear,
[5]Which will not heed the voice of
charmers,
Charming ever so skillfully.

[6]Break their teeth in their mouth, O
God!
Break out the fangs of the young
lions, O LORD!
[7]Let them flow away as waters *which*
run continually;
When he bends *his bow,*
Let his arrows be as if cut in pieces.
[8]*Let them be* like a snail which melts
away as it goes,
Like a stillborn child of a woman, that
they may not see the sun.

[9]Before your pots can feel *the burning*
thorns,
He shall take them away as with a
whirlwind,
As in His living and burning wrath.
[10]The righteous shall rejoice when he
sees the vengeance;
He shall wash his feet in the blood of
the wicked,
[11]So that men will say,
"Surely *there is* a reward for the
righteous;
Surely He is God who judges in the
earth."

PSALM 59

The Assured Judgment of the Wicked

To the Chief Musician. Set to "Do Not Destroy."[a]
A Michtam of David when Saul sent men, and
they watched the house in order to kill him.

[1]Deliver me from my enemies, O my
God;
Defend me from those who rise up
against me.
[2]Deliver me from the workers of

58:title [a]Hebrew *Al Tashcheth* **59:title** [a]Hebrew *Al Tashcheth*

58:6 Some have wondered how David could possibly be "a man after [God's] own heart" (Acts 13:22) when he exhibited such a vindictive attitude. However, he was merely pouring out his anger in prayer. Let it be a lesson to those of us who would like to seek vengeance—take it to God in prayer. Those who learn that secret prayer is the place to leave grievances will find that like David, they can then show mercy to those who have wronged them (see 1 Sam. 26:1–12).

58:10,11 Bible contradiction? Skeptics argue that these verses contradict Prov. 24:16–18: "Do not rejoice when your enemy falls . . . " The context of these verses is God's judgment of the wicked. There is a big difference between rejoicing when misfortune comes and when justice is eventually done.

iniquity,
And save me from bloodthirsty men.

3For look, they lie in wait for my life;
The mighty gather against me,
Not *for* my transgression nor *for* my sin, O LORD.
4They run and prepare themselves through no fault *of mine.*

Awake to help me, and behold!
5You therefore, O LORD God of hosts, the God of Israel,
Awake to punish all the nations;
Do not be merciful to any wicked transgressors. *Selah*

To learn the beliefs of Hindus and how to witness to them, see page 1263.

6At evening they return,
They growl like a dog,
And go all around the city.
7Indeed, they belch with their mouth;
Swords *are* in their lips;
For *they say,* "Who hears?"

8But You, O LORD, shall laugh at them;
You shall have all the nations in derision.
9I will wait for You, O You his Strength;[a]
For God *is* my defense.
10My God of mercy[a] shall come to meet me;
God shall let me see *my desire* on my enemies.

11Do not slay them, lest my people forget;
Scatter them by Your power,
And bring them down,
O Lord our shield.
12*For* the sin of their mouth *and* the words of their lips,
Let them even be taken in their pride,
And for the cursing and lying *which* they speak.
13Consume *them* in wrath, consume *them,*
That they *may* not *be;*
And let them know that God rules in Jacob
To the ends of the earth. *Selah*

14And at evening they return,
They growl like a dog,
And go all around the city.
15They wander up and down for food,
And howl[a] if they are not satisfied.

16But I will sing of Your power;
Yes, I will sing aloud of Your mercy in the morning;
For You have been my defense
And refuge in the day of my trouble.
17To You, O my Strength, I will sing praises;
For God is my defense,
My God of mercy.

PSALM 60

Urgent Prayer for the Restored Favor of God

To the Chief Musician. Set to "Lily of the Testimony."[a] A Michtam of David. For teaching. When he fought against Mesopotamia and Syria of Zobah, and Joab returned and killed twelve thousand Edomites in the Valley of Salt.

1O God, You have cast us off;
You have broken us down;
You have been displeased;

59:9 [a]Following Masoretic Text and Syriac; some Hebrew manuscripts, Septuagint, Targum, and Vulgate read *my Strength.* **59:10** [a]Following Qere; some Hebrew manuscripts, Septuagint, and Vulgate read *My God, His mercy;* Kethib, some Hebrew manuscripts and Targum read *O God, my mercy;* Syriac reads *O God, Your mercy.* **59:15** [a]Following Septuagint and Vulgate; Masoretic Text, Syriac, and Targum read *spend the night.* **60:title** [a]Hebrew *Shushan Eduth*

Oh, restore us again!
[2]You have made the earth tremble;
You have broken it;
Heal its breaches, for it is shaking.
[3]You have shown Your people hard things;
You have made us drink the wine of confusion.

[4]You have given a banner to those who fear You,
That it may be displayed because of the truth. *Selah*
[5]That Your beloved may be delivered,
Save *with* Your right hand, and hear me.

[6]God has spoken in His holiness:
"I will rejoice;
I will divide Shechem
And measure out the Valley of Succoth.
[7]Gilead *is* Mine, and Manasseh *is* Mine;
Ephraim also *is* the helmet for My head;
Judah *is* My lawgiver.
[8]Moab *is* My washpot;
Over Edom I will cast My shoe;
Philistia, shout in triumph because of Me."

[9]Who will bring me *to* the strong city?
Who will lead me to Edom?
[10]*Is it* not You, O God, *who* cast us off?
And You, O God, *who* did not go out with our armies?
[11]Give us help from trouble,
For the help of man *is* useless.
[12]Through God we will do valiantly,
For *it is* He *who* shall tread down our enemies.[a]

PSALM 61

Assurance of God's Eternal Protection

To the Chief Musician. On a stringed instrument.[a] *A Psalm* of David.

[1]Hear my cry, O God;
Attend to my prayer.
[2]From the end of the earth I will cry to You,
When my heart is overwhelmed;
Lead me to the rock that is higher than I.

[3]For You have been a shelter for me,
A strong tower from the enemy.
[4]I will abide in Your tabernacle forever;
I will trust in the shelter of Your wings. *Selah*

[5]For You, O God, have heard my vows;
You have given *me* the heritage of those who fear Your name.
[6]You will prolong the king's life,
His years as many generations.
[7]He shall abide before God forever.
Oh, prepare mercy and truth, *which* may preserve him!

[8]So I will sing praise to Your name forever,
That I may daily perform my vows.

PSALM 62

A Calm Resolve to Wait for the Salvation of God

To the Chief Musician. To Jeduthun. A Psalm of David.

[1]Truly my soul silently *waits* for God;
From Him *comes* my salvation.
[2]He only *is* my rock and my salvation;
He is my defense;
I shall not be greatly moved.

[3]How long will you attack a man?
You shall be slain, all of you,
Like a leaning wall and a tottering fence.
[4]They only consult to cast *him* down from his high position;
They delight in lies;
They bless with their mouth,
But they curse inwardly. *Selah*

[5]My soul, wait silently for God alone,

60:12 [a]Compare verses 5–12 with 108:6–13 **61:title** [a]Hebrew *neginah*

For my expectation *is* from Him.
6He only *is* my rock and my salvation;
He is my defense;
I shall not be moved.
7In God *is* my salvation and my glory;
The rock of my strength,
And my refuge, *is* in God.

8Trust in Him at all times, you people;
Pour out your heart before Him;
God *is* a refuge for us. *Selah*

9Surely men of low degree *are* a vapor,
Men of high degree *are* a lie;
If they are weighed on the scales,
They *are* altogether *lighter* than vapor.
10Do not trust in oppression,
Nor vainly hope in robbery;
If riches increase,
Do not set *your* heart *on them.*

11God has spoken once,
Twice I have heard this:
That power *belongs* to God.
12Also to You, O Lord, *belongs* mercy;
For You render to each one according to his work.

PSALM 63

Joy in the Fellowship of God

A Psalm of David when he was in the wilderness of Judah.

1O God, You *are* my God;
Early will I seek You;
My soul thirsts for You;
My flesh longs for You
In a dry and thirsty land
Where there is no water.
2So I have looked for You in the sanctuary,
To see Your power and Your glory.

3Because Your lovingkindness *is* better than life,
My lips shall praise You.
4Thus I will bless You while I live;
I will lift up my hands in Your name.
5My soul shall be satisfied as with marrow and fatness,
And my mouth shall praise You with joyful lips.

6When I remember You on my bed,
I meditate on You in the *night* watches.
7Because You have been my help,
Therefore in the shadow of Your wings I will rejoice.
8My soul follows close behind You;
Your right hand upholds me.

9But those *who* seek my life, to destroy *it,*
Shall go into the lower parts of the earth.
10They shall fall by the sword;
They shall be a portion for jackals.

11But the king shall rejoice in God;
Everyone who swears by Him shall glory;
But the mouth of those who speak lies shall be stopped.

PSALM 64

Oppressed by the Wicked but Rejoicing in the Lord

To the Chief Musician. A Psalm of David.

1Hear my voice, O God, in my meditation;
Preserve my life from fear of the enemy.
2Hide me from the secret plots of the wicked,
From the rebellion of the workers of iniquity,
3Who sharpen their tongue like a sword,
And bend *their bows to shoot* their arrows—bitter words,
4That they may shoot in secret at the blameless;
Suddenly they shoot at him and do not fear.

5They encourage themselves *in* an evil matter;
They talk of laying snares secretly;
They say, “Who will see them?”
6They devise iniquities:
“We have perfected a shrewd scheme.”

63:1 *Why Do People Believe in God?*

Here is a dilemma for the staunch atheist who embraces evolution. The theory of evolution asserts that everything evolved for a reason. We supposedly evolved thumbs because they provided an advantage. We evolved the skull, the eyes, nose, mouth, and ears because they served some purpose. We evolved the urge to sleep to rest us, an appetite to drive us to food, and thirst to drive us to water. Even within the human psyche we have evolved the emotion of fear to protect us, love to help us bond to the opposite sex for raising offspring, etc. All of these happened for our benefit, and so nothing evolved without a good reason.

So why then do the vast majority of human beings have an innate belief in the existence of God? Robin Marantz Henig, in an article in the *New York Times* titled "Darwin's God," offers "a scientific exploration of how we have come to believe in God." Henig says that "there seems an inherent human drive to believe in something transcendent, unfathomable and otherworldly, something beyond the reach or understanding of science." But where would such a belief come from? She reasons:

> Which is the better biological explanation for a belief in God—evolutionary adaptation or neurological accident? Is there something about the cognitive functioning of humans that makes us receptive to belief in a supernatural deity? And if scientists are able to explain God, what then? Is explaining religion the same thing as explaining it away? Are the nonbelievers right, and is religion at its core an empty undertaking, a misdirection, a vestigial artifact of a primitive mind? Or are the believers right, and does the fact that we have the mental capacities for discerning God suggest that it was God who put them there?
>
> In short, are we hard-wired to believe in God? And if we are, how and why did that happen?

Charles Darwin also noted the tendency to believe in the supernatural in *The Descent of Man*. "A belief in all-pervading spiritual agencies," he wrote, "seems to be universal." Henig reports that, according to anthropologists, religions that share certain supernatural beliefs—belief in an immaterial God or gods, in the afterlife, and in the power of prayer—are found in virtually every culture on earth.

This universality certainly is true in the U.S. where 91 percent of adults say they believe in God. Out of 6.5 billion people worldwide, only 2.36 percent are atheists. But that's not surprising. Since God created us to be in relationship with Him, He would naturally have designed us so that we could believe in Him. We have hunger that can be satisfied with food; we have thirst that can be satisfied with water; we have desires for companionship, for love, for sexual intimacy, etc., because things exist that can satisfy these desires (not that we always get them, but they do exist). Likewise, we have a desire for God, because He exists to satisfy that desire. This "yearning for the supernatural" is given by God so that we might seek Him. (Adapted from *How to Know God Exists*.)

"If I find in myself desires which nothing in this world can satisfy, the only logical explanation is that I was made for another world." *C. S. Lewis*

Both the inward thought and the
heart of man are deep.

7But God shall shoot at them *with* an
arrow;
Suddenly they shall be wounded.
8So He will make them stumble over
their own tongue;
All who see them shall flee away.
9All men shall fear,
And shall declare the work of God;
For they shall wisely consider His
doing.

10The righteous shall be glad in the
LORD, and trust in Him.
And all the upright in heart shall glory.

PSALM 65

Praise to God for His Salvation and Providence

To the Chief Musician. A Psalm of David. A Song.

1Praise is awaiting You, O God, in Zion;
And to You the vow shall be performed.
2O You who hear prayer,
To You all flesh will come.
3Iniquities prevail against me;
As for our transgressions,
You will provide atonement for them.

Springboards for Preaching and Witnessing

Big News

64:6 A man in Connecticut just wanted to jot down a phone number when he picked up what he thought was litter on a sidewalk. But what he found was an envelope containing a check for $185,000. Guess what he did? The man, who receives food stamps and works at McDonald's, said he didn't think twice about trying to cash it. Instead, the 47-year-old took a bus to a bank and returned the check to the landlord to whom the check was written. That made national news, and so it should. It is big news when a human being does what is right in the face of such temptation. However, the fact that doing the right thing is so unusual as to be newsworthy simply verifies the truth of Scripture—that the heart of man is not good; it is "desperately wicked."

4Blessed *is the man* You choose,
And cause to approach *You*,
That he may dwell in Your courts.
We shall be satisfied with the goodness of Your house,
Of Your holy temple.

5*By* awesome deeds in righteousness You will answer us,
O God of our salvation,
You who are the confidence of all the ends of the earth,
And of the far-off seas;
6Who established the mountains by His strength,
Being clothed with power;
7You who still the noise of the seas,
The noise of their waves,
And the tumult of the peoples.
8They also who dwell in the farthest parts are afraid of Your signs;
You make the outgoings of the morning and evening rejoice.

9You visit the earth and water it,
You greatly enrich it;
The river of God is full of water;
You provide their grain,
For so You have prepared it.
10You water its ridges abundantly,
You settle its furrows;
You make it soft with showers,
You bless its growth.

11You crown the year with Your goodness,
And Your paths drip *with* abundance.
12They drop *on* the pastures of the wilderness,
And the little hills rejoice on every side.
13The pastures are clothed with flocks;
The valleys also are covered with grain;
They shout for joy, they also sing.

PSALM 66

Praise to God for His Awesome Works

To the Chief Musician. A Song. A Psalm.

1Make a joyful shout to God, all the earth!
2Sing out the honor of His name;
Make His praise glorious.
3Say to God,
"How awesome are Your works!
Through the greatness of Your power
Your enemies shall submit themselves to You.
4All the earth shall worship You
And sing praises to You;
They shall sing praises *to* Your name."
Selah

5Come and see the works of God;
He is awesome *in His* doing toward the sons of men.
6He turned the sea into dry *land;*
They went through the river on foot.
There we will rejoice in Him.
7He rules by His power forever;
His eyes observe the nations;
Do not let the rebellious exalt themselves. *Selah*

8Oh, bless our God, you peoples!
And make the voice of His praise to be heard,

[9]Who keeps our soul among the living,
And does not allow our feet to be
moved.
[10]For You, O God, have tested us;
You have refined us as silver is refined.
[11]You brought us into the net;
You laid affliction on our backs.
[12]You have caused men to ride over our
heads;
We went through fire and through
water;
But You brought us out to rich
fulfillment.

[13]I will go into Your house with burnt
offerings;
I will pay You my vows,
[14]Which my lips have uttered
And my mouth has spoken when I
was in trouble.
[15]I will offer You burnt sacrifices of fat
animals,
With the sweet aroma of rams;
I will offer bulls with goats. *Selah*

[16]Come *and* hear, all you who fear God,
And I will declare what He has done
for my soul.
[17]I cried to Him with my mouth,
And He was extolled with my tongue.
[18]If I regard iniquity in my heart,
The Lord will not hear.
[19]*But* certainly God has heard *me;*
He has attended to the voice of my
prayer.

[20]Blessed *be* God,
Who has not turned away my prayer,
Nor His mercy from me!

PSALM 67

An Invocation and a Doxology

To the Chief Musician. On stringed instruments.[a]
A Psalm. A Song.

[1]God be merciful to us and bless us,
And cause His face to shine upon us,
Selah
[2]That Your way may be known on
earth,
Your salvation among all nations.

[3]Let the peoples praise You, O God;
Let all the peoples praise You.
[4]Oh, let the nations be glad and sing
for joy!
For You shall judge the people
righteously,
And govern the nations on earth. *Selah*

[5]Let the peoples praise You, O God;
Let all the peoples praise You.
[6]*Then* the earth shall yield her
increase;

67:title [a]Hebrew *neginoth*

66:10–12 We often blame tribulation on the enemy when God uses this very instrument to fulfill His will for our lives. God takes us through the fire, not to burn us, but to purify us. He takes us through the water, not to drown us, but to wash us. Understanding that the Lord chastens those He loves enables us to endure trials. The psalmist wrote, "It is good for me that I have been afflicted; that I may learn Your statutes" (119:71). See also Heb. 12:10–13.

66:15 Animal rights advocates who insist that "meat is murder" are misguided. God was the first to kill an animal (Gen. 3:21). In Exod. 12:5–8 God told Israel to kill and eat lambs. King Solomon sacrificed 22,000 oxen and 120,000 sheep when he dedicated the temple to God (1 Kings 8:63). When three angels appeared to Abraham, he killed a "tender and good" calf for them to eat (Gen. 18:7,8). In Gen. 27:7 we are told that Jacob ate venison (deer meat), which was his favorite food. Jesus ate the Passover lamb (Mark 14:12,18). In the parable of the prodigal son, the father rejoiced at his son's return by killing the fatted calf and eating it (Luke 15:23). See 1 Tim. 4:3,4 comment.

67:4 "It is the duty of all nations to acknowledge the Providence of Almighty God, to obey His will, to be grateful for His benefits, and humbly to implore His protection and favor." *George Washington*

"The foundations of our society and our government rest so much on the teachings of the Bible that it would be difficult to support them if faith in these teachings would cease to be practically universal in our country." *Calvin Coolidge*

66:18 *The Problem of Unanswered Prayer*

Many think God doesn't exist because their prayers weren't answered. Yet, we are warned in Scripture that if we have sin in our hearts, God will not hear our prayers (see Psa. 66:18; John 9:31; see also Prov. 28:9; Isa. 1:15). So rather than being disillusioned and thinking that God didn't exist, they should have repented and trusted the Savior, and their prayers would have then been answered.

My prayers are always answered. Sometimes I know that God has said "Yes," because He grants me my requests. Sometimes I know that He has said "No" because He doesn't grant them. However, when I don't get an immediate response, I console myself with the thought that He may be saying, "Wait a moment." The Bible tells us that we inherit the promises of God through faith and patience. That doesn't come easy to the "give it to me now" generation that we have become. So "Yes," "No," and "Wait a minute" are all answers to prayer. They just may not be the answers we wanted.

In reality, the atheist has a problem with both unanswered and answered prayer. Here's a scenario that no doubt happens daily somewhere in the world. A young boy becomes deathly ill. The entire family gathers for prayer. However, despite earnest and sincere prayer, the child tragically dies. Their explanation for the death is that God took him to heaven because He wanted the child there. That's seen by the atheist as "unanswered prayer." Or the child miraculously makes a recovery, which the family hails as an evident miracle. God obviously answered the family's prayers by saving the child from death. The atheist maintains that it wasn't answered prayer but that the child recovered because his body healed itself.

Was the recovery a miracle? Perhaps. Then again, perhaps it wasn't. Only God knows. The fact is that we have no idea what happened. However, one thing we do know is that answered or unanswered prayer has nothing to do with God's existence. Let me explain. My wife has a Dodge Caravan. Let's say it has a problem. What would be my intellectual capacity if I concluded that it had no manufacturer simply because I couldn't contact them about the dilemma? The fact of their existence has nothing to do with whether or not they return my calls.

Neither does God's existence have anything to do with the fact that there are those who have experienced miracles, seen visions, or supposedly heard His voice. The sun doesn't exist because we see its light, or because we feel its warmth. Its existence has nothing to do with any human testimony. Nor does it cease to exist because a blind man is unaware of its reality, or because it becomes cloudy, or the night falls. The sun exists, period.

God's existence is not dependent on the Bible or its authenticity, the existence of the Church, the prophets, or even creation. God existed before the Scriptures were penned, before creation came into being. Even if the Bible was proved to be fraudulent, God would still exist.

Adamant atheist April Pedersen writes, "The human trait of seeking comfort through prayer is a strong one." This is true. However, April fails to see that human nature itself is very predictable. If men will not embrace the biblical revelation of God, their nature is to delve into idolatry. "Idolatry" is the act of creating a god in our image, whether it is shaped with the human hands (a physical idol), or shaped in the human mind through the imagination. Those who create their own god then use it as a "good-luck charm" to do their bidding. The idolater uses his god for his own ends. He calls on his god to win a football game, a boxing match, the lottery, or a war. Idolatry is as predictable as it is illogical.

God, our own God, shall bless us.
7God shall bless us,
And all the ends of the earth shall fear
Him.

PSALM 68
The Glory of God in His Goodness to Israel

To the Chief Musician. A Psalm of David. A Song.

1Let God arise,
Let His enemies be scattered;
Let those also who hate Him flee
before Him.
2As smoke is driven away,
So drive *them* away;
As wax melts before the fire,
So let the wicked perish at the
presence of God.
3But let the righteous be glad;
Let them rejoice before God;
Yes, let them rejoice exceedingly.

4Sing to God, sing praises to His name;
Extol Him who rides on the clouds,[a]

68:4 [a]Masoretic Text reads *deserts*; Targum reads *heavens* (compare verse 34 and Isaiah 19:1).

By His name YAH,
And rejoice before Him.

[5]A father of the fatherless, a defender of widows,
Is God in His holy habitation.
[6]God sets the solitary in families;
He brings out those who are bound into prosperity;
But the rebellious dwell in a dry *land*.

[7]O God, when You went out before Your people,
When You marched through the wilderness, *Selah*
[8]The earth shook;
The heavens also dropped *rain* at the presence of God;
Sinai itself *was moved* at the presence of God, the God of Israel.
[9]You, O God, sent a plentiful rain,
Whereby You confirmed Your inheritance,
When it was weary.
[10]Your congregation dwelt in it;
You, O God, provided from Your goodness for the poor.

[11]The Lord gave the word;
Great *was* the company of those who proclaimed *it*:
[12]"Kings of armies flee, they flee,
And she who remains at home divides the spoil.
[13]Though you lie down among the sheepfolds,
You will be like the wings of a dove covered with silver,
And her feathers with yellow gold."
[14]When the Almighty scattered kings in it,
It was *white* as snow in Zalmon.

[15]A mountain of God *is* the mountain of Bashan;
A mountain *of many* peaks *is* the mountain of Bashan.
[16]Why do you fume with envy, you mountains of *many* peaks?
This is the mountain *which* God desires to dwell in;
Yes, the LORD will dwell *in it* forever.

[17]The chariots of God *are* twenty thousand,
Even thousands of thousands;
The Lord is among them *as in* Sinai, in the Holy *Place*.
[18]You have ascended on high,
You have led captivity captive;
You have received gifts among men,
Even *from* the rebellious,
That the LORD God might dwell *there*.

[19]Blessed *be* the Lord,
Who daily loads us *with benefits*,
The God of our salvation! *Selah*
[20]Our God *is* the God of salvation;
And to GOD the Lord *belong* escapes from death.

[21]But God will wound the head of His enemies,
The hairy scalp of the one who still goes on in his trespasses.
[22]The Lord said, "I will bring back from Bashan,
I will bring *them* back from the depths of the sea,
[23]That your foot may crush *them*[a] in blood,
And the tongues of your dogs *may have* their portion from *your* enemies."

[24]They have seen Your procession, O God,
The procession of my God, my King, into the sanctuary.
[25]The singers went before, the players on instruments *followed* after;
Among *them were* the maidens playing timbrels.
[26]Bless God in the congregations,
The Lord, from the fountain of Israel.
[27]There *is* little Benjamin, their leader,
The princes of Judah *and* their company,

68:23 [a]Septuagint, Syriac, Targum, and Vulgate read *you may dip your foot*.

The princes of Zebulun *and* the
princes of Naphtali.

28 Your God has commanded[a] your
strength;
Strengthen, O God, what You have
done for us.
29 Because of Your temple at Jerusalem,
Kings will bring presents to You.
30 Rebuke the beasts of the reeds,
The herd of bulls with the calves of
the peoples,
Till everyone submits himself with
pieces of silver.
Scatter the peoples *who* delight in war.
31 Envoys will come out of Egypt;
Ethiopia will quickly stretch out her
hands to God.

32 Sing to God, you kingdoms of the
earth;
Oh, sing praises to the Lord, *Selah*
33 To Him who rides on the heaven of
heavens, *which were* of old!
Indeed, He sends out His voice, a
mighty voice.
34 Ascribe strength to God;
His excellence *is* over Israel,
And His strength *is* in the clouds.
35 O God, *You are* more awesome than
Your holy places.
The God of Israel *is* He who gives
strength and power to *His* people.

Blessed *be* God!

PSALM 69
An Urgent Plea for Help in Trouble

To the Chief Musician. Set to "The Lilies."[a]
A Psalm of David.

1 Save me, O God!
For the waters have come up to *my*
neck.
2 I sink in deep mire,
Where *there is* no standing;
I have come into deep waters,
Where the floods overflow me.
3 I am weary with my crying;
My throat is dry;
My eyes fail while I wait for my God.

4 Those who hate me without a cause
Are more than the hairs of my head;
They are mighty who would destroy
me,
Being my enemies wrongfully;
Though I have stolen nothing,
I *still* must restore *it.*

5 O God, You know my foolishness;
And my sins are not hidden from You.
6 Let not those who wait for You, O
Lord GOD of hosts, be ashamed
because of me;
Let not those who seek You be
confounded because of me, O
God of Israel.
7 Because for Your sake I have borne
reproach;
Shame has covered my face.
8 I have become a stranger to my
brothers,
And an alien to my mother's children;
9 Because zeal for Your house has eaten
me up,
And the reproaches of those who
reproach You have fallen on me.
10 When I wept *and chastened* my soul
with fasting,
That became my reproach.
11 I also made sackcloth my garment;
I became a byword to them.
12 Those who sit in the gate speak
against me,
And I *am* the song of the drunkards.

13 But as for me, my prayer *is* to You,
O LORD, *in* the acceptable time;
O God, in the multitude of Your mercy,
Hear me in the truth of Your salvation.

68:28 [a]Septuagint, Syriac, Targum, and Vulgate read *Command, O God.* 69:title [a]Hebrew *Shoshannim*

69:9 This is a direct reference to the Messiah. See John 2:17.

14Deliver me out of the mire,
And let me not sink;
Let me be delivered from those who hate me,
And out of the deep waters.
15Let not the floodwater overflow me,
Nor let the deep swallow me up;
And let not the pit shut its mouth on me.

16Hear me, O LORD, for Your lovingkindness *is* good;
Turn to me according to the multitude of Your tender mercies.
17And do not hide Your face from Your servant,
For I am in trouble;
Hear me speedily.
18Draw near to my soul, *and* redeem it;
Deliver me because of my enemies.

19You know my reproach, my shame, and my dishonor;
My adversaries *are* all before You.
20Reproach has broken my heart,
And I am full of heaviness;
I looked *for someone* to take pity, but *there was* none;
And for comforters, but I found none.
21They also gave me gall for my food,
And for my thirst they gave me vinegar to drink.

22Let their table become a snare before them,
And their well-being a trap.
23Let their eyes be darkened, so that they do not see;
And make their loins shake continually.
24Pour out Your indignation upon them,
And let Your wrathful anger take hold of them.
25Let their dwelling place be desolate;
Let no one live in their tents.
26For they persecute the *ones* You have struck,
And talk of the grief of those You have wounded.
27Add iniquity to their iniquity,
And let them not come into Your righteousness.
28Let them be blotted out of the book of the living,
And not be written with the righteous.

29But I *am* poor and sorrowful;
Let Your salvation, O God, set me up on high.
30I will praise the name of God with a song,
And will magnify Him with thanksgiving.
31*This* also shall please the LORD better than an ox *or* bull,
Which has horns and hooves.
32The humble shall see *this and* be glad;
And you who seek God, your hearts shall live.
33For the LORD hears the poor,
And does not despise His prisoners.

34Let heaven and earth praise Him,
The seas and everything that moves in them.
35For God will save Zion
And build the cities of Judah,
That they may dwell there and possess it.
36Also, the descendants of His servants shall inherit it,
And those who love His name shall dwell in it.

PSALM 70

Prayer for Relief from Adversaries

To the Chief Musician. *A Psalm* of David. To bring to remembrance.

1*Make haste,* O God, to deliver me!
Make haste to help me, O LORD!

2Let them be ashamed and confounded
Who seek my life;

69:21 Messianic prophecy: This was fulfilled in John 19:29.

Let them be turned back[a] and confused
Who desire my hurt.
3Let them be turned back because of
their shame,
Who say, "Aha, aha!"

4Let all those who seek You rejoice
and be glad in You;
And let those who love Your salvation
say continually,
"Let God be magnified!"

5But I *am* poor and needy;
Make haste to me, O God!
You *are* my help and my deliverer;
O LORD, do not delay.

PSALM 71

God the Rock of Salvation

1In You, O LORD, I put my trust;
Let me never be put to shame.
2Deliver me in Your righteousness,
and cause me to escape;
Incline Your ear to me, and save me.
3Be my strong refuge,
To which I may resort continually;
You have given the commandment to
save me,
For You *are* my rock and my fortress.

4Deliver me, O my God, out of the
hand of the wicked,
Out of the hand of the unrighteous
and cruel man.
5For You are my hope, O Lord GOD;
You are my trust from my youth.
6By You I have been upheld from birth;
You are He who took me out of my
mother's womb.
My praise *shall be* continually of You.

7I have become as a wonder to many,
But You *are* my strong refuge.
8Let my mouth be filled *with* Your
praise
And with Your glory all the day.

9Do not cast me off in the time of old
age;
Do not forsake me when my strength
fails.
10For my enemies speak against me;
And those who lie in wait for my life
take counsel together,
11Saying, "God has forsaken him;
Pursue and take him, for *there is* none
to deliver *him*."

12O God, do not be far from me;
O my God, make haste to help me!
13Let them be confounded *and* consumed
Who are adversaries of my life;
Let them be covered *with* reproach
and dishonor
Who seek my hurt.

Beloved, we must win souls; we cannot live and see men damned.

CHARLES SPURGEON

14But I will hope continually,
And will praise You yet more and more.
15My mouth shall tell of Your
righteousness
And Your salvation all the day,
For I do not know *their* limits.
16I will go in the strength of the Lord
GOD;
I will make mention of Your
righteousness, of Yours only.

17O God, You have taught me from my
youth;
And to this *day* I declare Your
wondrous works.

70:2 [a]Following Masoretic Text, Septuagint, Targum, and Vulgate; some Hebrew manuscripts and Syriac read *be appalled* (compare 40:15).

70:3 An accusing world is quick to point out the slightest weakness in the Christian. If we become impatient, they say, "Aha... you're supposed to be a Christian." They are unaware that they will be judged by the same measure by which they judge. See Rom. 2:1,3.

[18]Now also when *I am* old and
grayheaded,
O God, do not forsake me,
Until I declare Your strength to *this*
generation,
Your power to everyone *who* is to
come.

[19]Also Your righteousness, O God, *is*
very high,
You who have done great things;
O God, who *is* like You?
[20]*You*, who have shown me great and
severe troubles,
Shall revive me again,
And bring me up again from the
depths of the earth.
[21]You shall increase my greatness,
And comfort me on every side.

[22]Also with the lute I will praise You—
And Your faithfulness, O my God!
To You I will sing with the harp,
O Holy One of Israel.
[23]My lips shall greatly rejoice when I
sing to You,
And my soul, which You have
redeemed.
[24]My tongue also shall talk of Your
righteousness all the day long;
For they are confounded,
For they are brought to shame
Who seek my hurt.

PSALM 72

Glory and Universality of the Messiah's Reign

A Psalm of Solomon.

[1]Give the king Your judgments, O God,
And Your righteousness to the king's
Son.
[2]He will judge Your people with
righteousness,
And Your poor with justice.
[3]The mountains will bring peace to
the people,
And the little hills, by righteousness.
[4]He will bring justice to the poor of
the people;
He will save the children of the needy,
And will break in pieces the oppressor.

[5]They shall fear You[a]
As long as the sun and moon endure,
Throughout all generations.
[6]He shall come down like rain upon
the grass before mowing,
Like showers *that* water the earth.
[7]In His days the righteous shall flourish,
And abundance of peace,
Until the moon is no more.

[8]He shall have dominion also from sea
to sea,

72:5 [a]Following Masoretic Text and Targum; Septuagint and Vulgate read *They shall continue*.

72:2 The Bible's inspiration. To any reasonable person, the Bible can easily be shown to be inspired by God. It was written over a period of around 1,600 years, by around 40 authors from all walks of life, and yet there is a wonderful continuity of thought running throughout its pages. For example, consider the subject of "righteousness," a word that is used 301 times in the NKJV translation. Jesus died on the cross because God demanded perfect justice to satisfy His perfect righteousness. Look at the amazing continuity of Scripture. Psalm 9:8 (written around 800 B.C.) warned that God "shall judge the world in righteousness." Proverbs 11:4 warns again, "Riches do not profit in the day of wrath, but righteousness delivers from death." So, how can guilty sinners become righteous in the sight of a holy God? Hosea 10:12 tells us, "For it is time to seek the LORD, till He comes and rains righteousness on you." It was on the Day of Pentecost that righteousness rained down from heaven. Now God commands all men everywhere to repent. Why? "Because He has appointed a day on which He will judge the world in righteousness" (Acts 17:30,31).

As the apostle Paul was about to die he said, "Finally, there is laid up for me the crown of righteousness, which the Lord, the righteous Judge, will give to me on that Day, and not to me only but also to all who have loved His appearing" (2 Tim. 4:8). In the meanwhile, you and I wait for a new heavens and new earth "in which righteousness dwells" (2 Pet. 3:13). So, what should we be doing as Christians while we wait? Daniel 12:3 tells us: "Those who are wise shall shine like the brightness of the firmament, and those who turn many to righteousness like the stars forever and ever."

"No educated man can afford to be ignorant of the Bible."

Theodore Roosevelt

And from the River to the ends of the
earth.
9Those who dwell in the wilderness
will bow before Him,
And His enemies will lick the dust.
10The kings of Tarshish and of the isles
Will bring presents;
The kings of Sheba and Seba
Will offer gifts.
11Yes, all kings shall fall down before
Him;
All nations shall serve Him.

12For He will deliver the needy when
he cries,
The poor also, and *him* who has no
helper.
13He will spare the poor and needy,
And will save the souls of the needy.
14He will redeem their life from
oppression and violence;
And precious shall be their blood in
His sight.

15And He shall live;
And the gold of Sheba will be given
to Him;
Prayer also will be made for Him
continually,
And daily He shall be praised.

16There will be an abundance of grain
in the earth,
On the top of the mountains;
Its fruit shall wave like Lebanon;
And *those* of the city shall flourish like
grass of the earth.

17His name shall endure forever;
His name shall continue as long as
the sun.
And *men* shall be blessed in Him;
All nations shall call Him blessed.

18Blessed *be* the LORD God, the God of
Israel,
Who only does wondrous things!
19And blessed *be* His glorious name
forever!
And let the whole earth be filled *with*
His glory.
Amen and Amen.

20The prayers of David the son of Jesse
are ended.

Book Three: Psalms 73—89

PSALM 73

The Tragedy of the Wicked, and the Blessedness of Trust in God

A Psalm of Asaph.

1Truly God *is* good to Israel,
To such as are pure in heart.
2But as for me, my feet had almost
stumbled;
My steps had nearly slipped.
3For I *was* envious of the boastful,
When I saw the prosperity of the
wicked.

4For *there are* no pangs in their death,
But their strength *is* firm.
5They *are* not in trouble *as other* men,
Nor are they plagued like *other* men.
6Therefore pride serves as their
necklace;

Violence covers them *like* a garment.
7Their eyes bulge[a] with abundance;
They have more than heart could wish.
8They scoff and speak wickedly
concerning oppression;
They speak loftily.
9They set their mouth against the
heavens,
And their tongue walks through the
earth.

10Therefore his people return here,
And waters of a full *cup* are drained
by them.
11And they say, "How does God know?
And is there knowledge in the Most
High?"
12Behold, these *are* the ungodly,
Who are always at ease;
They increase *in* riches.
13Surely I have cleansed my heart *in* vain,
And washed my hands in innocence.
14For all day long I have been plagued,
And chastened every morning.

15If I had said, "I will speak thus,"
Behold, I would have been untrue to
the generation of Your children.
16When I thought *how* to understand
this,
It *was* too painful for me—
17Until I went into the sanctuary of God;
Then I understood their end.

18Surely You set them in slippery places;
You cast them down to destruction.
19Oh, how they are *brought* to
desolation, as in a moment!
They are utterly consumed with terrors.
20As a dream when *one* awakes,
So, Lord, when You awake,
You shall despise their image.

21Thus my heart was grieved,
And I was vexed in my mind.
22I *was* so foolish and ignorant;
I was *like* a beast before You.
23Nevertheless I *am* continually with You;
You hold *me* by my right hand.
24You will guide me with Your counsel,
And afterward receive me *to* glory.

25Whom have I in heaven *but You?*
And *there is* none upon earth *that* I
desire besides You.
26My flesh and my heart fail;
But God *is* the strength of my heart
and my portion forever.

27For indeed, those who are far from
You shall perish;
You have destroyed all those who
desert You for harlotry.
28But *it is* good for me to draw near to
God;
I have put my trust in the Lord GOD,
That I may declare all Your works.

PSALM 74

A Plea for Relief from Oppressors

A Contemplation[a] of Asaph.

1O God, why have You cast *us* off
forever?
Why does Your anger smoke against
the sheep of Your pasture?
2Remember Your congregation, *which*
You have purchased of old,
The tribe of Your inheritance, *which*
You have redeemed—
This Mount Zion where You have
dwelt.
3Lift up Your feet to the perpetual
desolations.
The enemy has damaged everything
in the sanctuary.
4Your enemies roar in the midst of
Your meeting place;

73:7 [a]Targum reads *face bulges;* Septuagint, Syriac, and Vulgate read *iniquity bulges.* 74:title [a]Hebrew *Maschil*

73:22 "It is amazing how many intellectuals call themselves 'agnostics,' not realizing that this is the Greek word for 'ignorant.' To be ignorant is a shame when one has the possibility of acquiring knowledge. The Christian religion gives satisfactory answers to the ultimate problems of life." *Richard Wurmbrand*

They set up their banners *for* signs.
[5]They seem like men who lift up
Axes among the thick trees.
[6]And now they break down its carved
work, all at once,
With axes and hammers.
[7]They have set fire to Your sanctuary;
They have defiled the dwelling place
of Your name to the ground.
[8]They said in their hearts,
"Let us destroy them altogether."
They have burned up all the meeting
places of God in the land.

[9]We do not see our signs;
There is no longer any prophet;
Nor *is there* any among us who knows
how long.
[10]O God, how long will the adversary
reproach?
Will the enemy blaspheme Your name
forever?
[11]Why do You withdraw Your hand,
even Your right hand?
Take it out of Your bosom and destroy
them.
[12]For God *is* my King from of old,
Working salvation in the midst of the
earth.
[13]You divided the sea by Your strength;
You broke the heads of the sea
serpents in the waters.
[14]You broke the heads of Leviathan in
pieces,
And gave him *as* food to the people
inhabiting the wilderness.
[15]You broke open the fountain and the
flood;
You dried up mighty rivers.
[16]The day *is* Yours, the night also *is* Yours;
You have prepared the light and the
sun.
[17]You have set all the borders of the earth;
You have made summer and winter.

[18]Remember this, *that* the enemy has
reproached, O LORD,
And *that* a foolish people has
blasphemed Your name.
[19]Oh, do not deliver the life of Your
turtledove to the wild beast!
Do not forget the life of Your poor
forever.
[20]Have respect to the covenant;
For the dark places of the earth are
full of the haunts of cruelty.
[21]Oh, do not let the oppressed return
ashamed!
Let the poor and needy praise Your
name.

[22]Arise, O God, plead Your own cause;
Remember how the foolish man
reproaches You daily.
[23]Do not forget the voice of Your
enemies;
The tumult of those who rise up
against You increases continually.

PSALM 75

Thanksgiving for God's Righteous Judgment

To the Chief Musician. Set to "Do Not Destroy."[a] A Psalm of Asaph. A Song.

[1]We give thanks to You, O God, we
give thanks!
For Your wondrous works declare
that Your name is near.

[2]"When I choose the proper time,
I will judge uprightly.
[3]The earth and all its inhabitants are
dissolved;
I set up its pillars firmly. *Selah*

[4]"I said to the boastful, 'Do not deal
boastfully,'
And to the wicked, 'Do not lift up the
horn.

75:title [a]Hebrew *Al Tashcheth*

75:1 "It is a terrible thing, I found, to be grateful and have no one to thank, to be awed and have no one to worship." *Philip Yancey*

[5]Do not lift up your horn on high;
Do *not* speak with a stiff neck.' "

[6]For exaltation *comes* neither from the east
Nor from the west nor from the south.
[7]But God *is* the Judge:
He puts down one,
And exalts another.
[8]For in the hand of the LORD *there is* a cup,
And the wine is red;
It is fully mixed, and He pours it out;
Surely its dregs shall all the wicked of the earth
Drain *and* drink down.

[9]But I will declare forever,
I will sing praises to the God of Jacob.

[10]"All the horns of the wicked I will also cut off,
But the horns of the righteous shall be exalted."

PSALM 76

The Majesty of God in Judgment

To the Chief Musician. On stringed instruments.[a]
A Psalm of Asaph. A Song.

[1]In Judah God *is* known;
His name *is* great in Israel.
[2]In Salem[a] also is His tabernacle,
And His dwelling place in Zion.
[3]There He broke the arrows of the bow,
The shield and sword of battle. *Selah*

[4]You *are* more glorious and excellent
Than the mountains of prey.
[5]The stouthearted were plundered;
They have sunk into their sleep;
And none of the mighty men have found the use of their hands.
[6]At Your rebuke, O God of Jacob,
Both the chariot and horse were cast into a dead sleep.

[7]You, Yourself, *are* to be feared;
And who may stand in Your presence
When once You are angry?
[8]You caused judgment to be heard from heaven;
The earth feared and was still,
[9]When God arose to judgment,
To deliver all the oppressed of the earth. *Selah*

[10]Surely the wrath of man shall praise You;
With the remainder of wrath You shall gird Yourself.

[11]Make vows to the LORD your God, and pay *them;*
Let all who are around Him bring presents to Him who ought to be feared.
[12]He shall cut off the spirit of princes;
He is awesome to the kings of the earth.

PSALM 77

The Consoling Memory of God's Redemptive Works

To the Chief Musician. To Jeduthun.
A Psalm of Asaph.

[1]I cried out to God with my voice—
To God with my voice;
And He gave ear to me.
[2]In the day of my trouble I sought the Lord;
My hand was stretched out in the night without ceasing;
My soul refused to be comforted.
[3]I remembered God, and was troubled;
I complained, and my spirit was overwhelmed. *Selah*

[4]You hold my eyelids *open;*
I am so troubled that I cannot speak.
[5]I have considered the days of old,
The years of ancient times.
[6]I call to remembrance my song in the night;
I meditate within my heart,
And my spirit makes diligent search.

[7]Will the Lord cast off forever?

76:title [a]Hebrew *neginoth* **76:2** [a]That is, Jerusalem

QUESTIONS & OBJECTIONS

"Could you be wrong in your claims about Judgment Day and the existence of hell?"

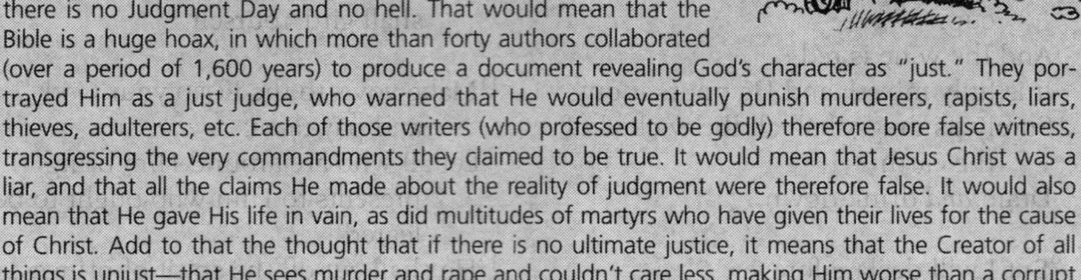

The existence of hell and the surety of the judgment are not the claims of fallible man. The Bible is the source of the claim, and it is utterly infallible.

When someone becomes a Christian, he is admitting that he was in the wrong, and that God is justified in His declarations that we have sinned against Him. However, let's assume for a moment that there is no Judgment Day and no hell. That would mean that the Bible is a huge hoax, in which more than forty authors collaborated (over a period of 1,600 years) to produce a document revealing God's character as "just." They portrayed Him as a just judge, who warned that He would eventually punish murderers, rapists, liars, thieves, adulterers, etc. Each of those writers (who professed to be godly) therefore bore false witness, transgressing the very commandments they claimed to be true. It would mean that Jesus Christ was a liar, and that all the claims He made about the reality of judgment were therefore false. It would also mean that He gave His life in vain, as did multitudes of martyrs who have given their lives for the cause of Christ. Add to that the thought that if there is no ultimate justice, it means that the Creator of all things is unjust—that He sees murder and rape and couldn't care less, making Him worse than a corrupt human judge who refuses to bring criminals to justice.

Here's the bad news if the Bible is right and there is eternal justice: You will find yourself standing before the judgment throne of a holy God, who knows everything you have ever done. Think of it. A holy and perfect Creator has seen your thought-life and every secret sin you have ever committed. You have a multitude of sins, and God must by nature carry out justice. Ask Him to remind you of the sins of your youth. Ask Him to bring to remembrance your secret sexual sins, the lies, the gossip, and other idle words. You may have forgotten your past sins, but God hasn't. Hell will be your just desert (exactly what you deserve), and you will have no one to blame but yourself. This is the claim of the Bible. If you don't believe it, it is still true. It will still happen.

Yet, there is good news—incredibly good news. We deserve judgment, but God offers us mercy through the cross. Jesus paid our fine so that we could leave the courtroom. He destroyed the power of the grave for all who obey Him. Simply obey the gospel, and live. By doing that you will discover that the gospel is indeed the "gospel truth." Jesus said that if you obey Him, He will reveal Himself to you (John 14:26). You will know the truth, and the truth will make you free (John 8:31,32). Get on your knees today, confess and forsake your sins. Tell God you are truly sorry, then trust the Savior as you would trust yourself to a parachute. Then you will find yourself in a terrible dilemma. You will know for certain that hell is a reality. When you get up the courage to warn people you care about, they will smile passively, and say, "Could you be wrong in your claims about Judgment Day and the existence of hell?"

And will He be favorable no more?
8 Has His mercy ceased forever?
Has *His* promise failed forevermore?
9 Has God forgotten to be gracious?
Has He in anger shut up His tender
mercies? *Selah*

10 And I said, "This *is* my anguish;
But I will remember the years of the
right hand of the Most High."
11 I will remember the works of the LORD;
Surely I will remember Your wonders
of old.
12 I will also meditate on all Your work,
And talk of Your deeds.

13 Your way, O God, *is* in the sanctuary;
Who *is* so great a God as *our* God?
14 You *are* the God who does wonders;
You have declared Your strength
among the peoples.
15 You have with *Your* arm redeemed
Your people,
The sons of Jacob and Joseph. *Selah*

16 The waters saw You, O God;
The waters saw You, they were afraid;
The depths also trembled.
17 The clouds poured out water;
The skies sent out a sound;
Your arrows also flashed about.

[18]The voice of Your thunder *was* in the
whirlwind;
The lightnings lit up the world;
The earth trembled and shook.
[19]Your way *was* in the sea,
Your path in the great waters,
And Your footsteps were not known.
[20]You led Your people like a flock
By the hand of Moses and Aaron.

PSALM 78

God's Kindness to Rebellious Israel

A Contemplation[a] of Asaph.

[1]Give ear, O my people, *to* my law;
Incline your ears to the words of my
mouth.
[2]I will open my mouth in a parable;
I will utter dark sayings of old,
[3]Which we have heard and known,
And our fathers have told us.
[4]We will not hide *them* from their
children,
Telling to the generation to come the
praises of the LORD,
And His strength and His wonderful
works that He has done.

[5]For He established a testimony in
Jacob,
And appointed a law in Israel,
Which He commanded our fathers,
That they should make them known
to their children;
[6]That the generation to come might
know *them*,
The children *who* would be born,
That they may arise and declare *them*
to their children,
[7]That they may set their hope in God,
And not forget the works of God,
But keep His commandments;
[8]And may not be like their fathers,
A stubborn and rebellious generation,
A generation *that* did not set its heart
aright,
And whose spirit was not faithful to
God.

[9]The children of Ephraim, *being* armed
and carrying bows,
Turned back in the day of battle.
[10]They did not keep the covenant of
God;
They refused to walk in His law,
[11]And forgot His works
And His wonders that He had shown
them.

[12]Marvelous things He did in the sight
of their fathers,
In the land of Egypt, *in* the field of
Zoan.
[13]He divided the sea and caused them
to pass through;
And He made the waters stand up
like a heap.
[14]In the daytime also He led them with
the cloud,
And all the night with a light of fire.
[15]He split the rocks in the wilderness,
And gave *them* drink in abundance
like the depths.
[16]He also brought streams out of the
rock,
And caused waters to run down like
rivers.

78:title [a]Hebrew *Maschil*

78:2 Messianic prophecy: Jesus fulfilled this in Matt. 13:34,35.

78:5,6 If you want to bring children to the Savior, teach them the Ten Commandments in light of New Testament revelation (lust is adultery, hatred is murder, etc.). Immediately after giving God's moral Law (the Ten Commandments) to Israel, Moses said to teach them diligently. In Deut. 6:6–9, he explains how to do that: speak of the Commandments when you sit with your children at home, as you go for walks together, at their bedtime, and when they get up (nighttime and morning devotions). Bind the Commandments on your hands, in front of your eyes, and at the entry of your house—in other words, do not forget them. Can you name the Ten Commandments? Can your children name them? See Exod. 20:1–17 and Deut. 11:18–21. To help your kids memorize the Ten Commandments, see page 652.

[17]But they sinned even more against Him
By rebelling against the Most High in the wilderness.
[18]And they tested God in their heart
By asking for the food of their fancy.
[19]Yes, they spoke against God:
They said, "Can God prepare a table in the wilderness?
[20]Behold, He struck the rock,
So that the waters gushed out,
And the streams overflowed.
Can He give bread also?
Can He provide meat for His people?"

[21]Therefore the LORD heard *this* and was furious;
So a fire was kindled against Jacob,
And anger also came up against Israel,
[22]Because they did not believe in God,
And did not trust in His salvation.
[23]Yet He had commanded the clouds above,
And opened the doors of heaven,
[24]Had rained down manna on them to eat,
And given them of the bread of heaven.
[25]Men ate angels' food;
He sent them food to the full.

[26]He caused an east wind to blow in the heavens;
And by His power He brought in the south wind.
[27]He also rained meat on them like the dust,
Feathered fowl like the sand of the seas;
[28]And He let *them* fall in the midst of their camp,
All around their dwellings.
[29]So they ate and were well filled,
For He gave them their own desire.
[30]They were not deprived of their craving;
But while their food *was* still in their mouths,
[31]The wrath of God came against them,
And slew the stoutest of them,
And struck down the choice *men* of Israel.

[32]In spite of this they still sinned,
And did not believe in His wondrous works.
[33]Therefore their days He consumed in futility,
And their years in fear.
[34]When He slew them, then they sought Him;
And they returned and sought earnestly for God.
[35]Then they remembered that God *was* their rock,
And the Most High God their Redeemer.

The beginning of anxiety is the end of faith, and the beginning of true faith is the end of anxiety.

GEORGE MUELLER

[36]Nevertheless they flattered Him with their mouth,
And they lied to Him with their tongue;
[37]For their heart was not steadfast with Him,
Nor were they faithful in His covenant.
[38]But He, *being* full of compassion, forgave *their* iniquity,
And did not destroy *them*.
Yes, many a time He turned His anger away,
And did not stir up all His wrath;
[39]For He remembered that they *were but* flesh,
A breath that passes away and does not come again.

[40]How often they provoked Him in the wilderness,
And grieved Him in the desert!
[41]Yes, again and again they tempted God,
And limited the Holy One of Israel.
[42]They did not remember His power:
The day when He redeemed them from the enemy,
[43]When He worked His signs in Egypt,
And His wonders in the field of Zoan;
[44]Turned their rivers into blood,

QUESTIONS & OBJECTIONS

78:39 ***"What do you say to people who believe in reincarnation?"***

Don't get sidetracked into discussing it. I normally ask people what they think they will come back as and what they would like to be in the next life. I may ask what they did to merit coming back in this life as a human being, and who is in charge of dealing out all the new bodies—is it God? But I do it in a light-hearted way. Then I say, "If there is a place called heaven, do you think you are good enough to go there?" Then I take them through the Law. I also mention that the Bible says "it is appointed for men to die once, but after this the judgment" (Heb. 9:27). See also Obad. 1:15 comment.

And their streams, that they could not
drink.
45He sent swarms of flies among them,
which devoured them,
And frogs, which destroyed them.
46He also gave their crops to the
caterpillar,
And their labor to the locust.
47He destroyed their vines with hail,
And their sycamore trees with frost.
48He also gave up their cattle to the hail,
And their flocks to fiery lightning.
49He cast on them the fierceness of His
anger,
Wrath, indignation, and trouble,
By sending angels of destruction
among them.
50He made a path for His anger;
He did not spare their soul from death,
But gave their life over to the plague,
51And destroyed all the firstborn in
Egypt,
The first of *their* strength in the tents
of Ham.
52But He made His own people go forth
like sheep,
And guided them in the wilderness
like a flock;
53And He led them on safely, so that
they did not fear;
But the sea overwhelmed their
enemies.
54And He brought them to His holy
border,
This mountain *which* His right hand
had acquired.
55He also drove out the nations before
them,
Allotted them an inheritance by survey,
And made the tribes of Israel dwell in
their tents.

56Yet they tested and provoked the
Most High God,
And did not keep His testimonies,
57But turned back and acted
unfaithfully like their fathers;
They were turned aside like a
deceitful bow.
58For they provoked Him to anger with
their high places,
And moved Him to jealousy with
their carved images.
59When God heard *this,* He was furious,
And greatly abhorred Israel,
60So that He forsook the tabernacle of
Shiloh,
The tent He had placed among men,
61And delivered His strength into
captivity,
And His glory into the enemy's hand.
62He also gave His people over to the
sword,
And was furious with His inheritance.
63The fire consumed their young men,
And their maidens were not given in
marriage.
64Their priests fell by the sword,
And their widows made no
lamentation.

65Then the Lord awoke as *from* sleep,
Like a mighty man who shouts
because of wine.
66And He beat back His enemies;
He put them to a perpetual reproach.

[67]Moreover He rejected the tent of
Joseph,
And did not choose the tribe of
Ephraim,
[68]But chose the tribe of Judah,
Mount Zion which He loved.
[69]And He built His sanctuary like the
heights,
Like the earth which He has
established forever.

Nothing worse can happen to a church than to be conformed to this world.

CHARLES SPURGEON

[70]He also chose David His servant,
And took him from the sheepfolds;
[71]From following the ewes that had
young He brought him,
To shepherd Jacob His people,
And Israel His inheritance.
[72]So he shepherded them according to
the integrity of his heart,
And guided them by the skillfulness
of his hands.

PSALM 79

A Dirge and a Prayer for Israel, Destroyed by Enemies

A Psalm of Asaph.

[1]O God, the nations have come into
Your inheritance;
Your holy temple they have defiled;
They have laid Jerusalem in heaps.
[2]The dead bodies of Your servants
They have given *as* food for the birds
of the heavens,
The flesh of Your saints to the beasts
of the earth.
[3]Their blood they have shed like water
all around Jerusalem,
And *there was* no one to bury *them*.
[4]We have become a reproach to our
neighbors,
A scorn and derision to those who are
around us.

[5]How long, LORD?
Will You be angry forever?
Will Your jealousy burn like fire?
[6]Pour out Your wrath on the nations
that do not know You,
And on the kingdoms that do not call
on Your name.
[7]For they have devoured Jacob,
And laid waste his dwelling place.

[8]Oh, do not remember former
iniquities against us!
Let Your tender mercies come
speedily to meet us,
For we have been brought very low.
[9]Help us, O God of our salvation,
For the glory of Your name;
And deliver us, and provide
atonement for our sins,
For Your name's sake!
[10]Why should the nations say,
"Where *is* their God?"
Let there be known among the
nations in our sight
The avenging of the blood of Your
servants *which has been* shed.

[11]Let the groaning of the prisoner come
before You;
According to the greatness of Your
power
Preserve those who are appointed to
die;
[12]And return to our neighbors
sevenfold into their bosom
Their reproach with which they have
reproached You, O Lord.

78:69 Bible contradiction? Skeptics argue that some Bible verses say the earth was established forever (Psa.78:69; Eccl. 1:4; 3:14), contradicting those that say the earth will someday perish (Psa. 102:25,26; Matt. 24:35; Heb. 1:10,11; 2 Pet. 3:10).

God has established that the earth will exist forever, though it will be completely remade. At the end of time He is going to make a new heavens and a new earth (see Isa. 65:17; 2 Pet. 3:13), and will make all things new to remove the curse of sin (see Rev. 21:1). See also 2 Kings 2:1 comment

Questions & Objections

80:3

"When I ask someone if he is saved and he sarcastically says, 'Saved from what?' how should I respond?"

He almost has a right to be sarcastic (what Shakespeare called "the lowest form of wit"). As Christians, we should be careful when we use words like "saved," because they make no sense to an unbeliever. We put up signs proclaiming "Jesus saves," and wonder why the world asks which bank He saves at. I would never ask a person if he is saved. In addition, a false convert will say that he is saved, despite the fact that he is trusting in his own righteousness.

I find that the best way to witness is to begin in the natural realm, then ask what the person thinks happens after someone dies—"What's on the other side?" If he thinks there is a heaven, ask if he is good enough to go there, then take him through the Commandments. (See Psa. 51:6 comment.) Once he understands his sin, then the fact that Jesus can "save" him from death and hell will make sense.

13So we, Your people and sheep of Your
pasture,
Will give You thanks forever;
We will show forth Your praise to all
generations.

PSALM 80

Prayer for Israel's Restoration

To the Chief Musician. Set to "The Lilies."[a]
A Testimony[b] of Asaph.
A Psalm.

1Give ear, O Shepherd of Israel,
You who lead Joseph like a flock;
You who dwell *between* the cherubim,
shine forth!
2Before Ephraim, Benjamin, and
Manasseh,
Stir up Your strength,
And come *and* save us!

3Restore us, O God;
Cause Your face to shine,
And we shall be saved!

4O LORD God of hosts,
How long will You be angry
Against the prayer of Your people?
5You have fed them with the bread of
tears,
And given them tears to drink in
great measure.
6You have made us a strife to our
neighbors,
And our enemies laugh among
themselves.

7Restore us, O God of hosts;
Cause Your face to shine,
And we shall be saved!

8You have brought a vine out of Egypt;
You have cast out the nations, and
planted it.
9You prepared *room* for it,
And caused it to take deep root,
And it filled the land.
10The hills were covered with its shadow,
And the mighty cedars with its boughs.
11She sent out her boughs to the Sea,[a]
And her branches to the River.[b]

12Why have You broken down her
hedges,
So that all who pass by the way pluck
her *fruit?*
13The boar out of the woods uproots it,
And the wild beast of the field
devours it.

14Return, we beseech You, O God of
hosts;
Look down from heaven and see,
And visit this vine
15And the vineyard which Your right
hand has planted,
And the branch *that* You made strong
for Yourself.
16*It is* burned with fire, *it is* cut down;
They perish at the rebuke of Your

80:title [a]Hebrew *Shoshannim* [b]Hebrew *Eduth* **80:11** [a]That is, the Mediterranean [b]That is, the Euphrates

countenance.
[17]Let Your hand be upon the man of
Your right hand,
Upon the son of man *whom* You made
strong for Yourself.
[18]Then we will not turn back from You;
Revive us, and we will call upon Your
name.

[19]Restore us, O LORD God of hosts;
Cause Your face to shine,
And we shall be saved!

PSALM 81

An Appeal for Israel's Repentance

To the Chief Musician. On an instrument of Gath.[a]
A Psalm of Asaph.

[1]Sing aloud to God our strength;
Make a joyful shout to the God of
Jacob.
[2]Raise a song and strike the timbrel,
The pleasant harp with the lute.

[3]Blow the trumpet at the time of the
New Moon,
At the full moon, on our solemn feast
day.
[4]For this *is* a statute for Israel,
A law of the God of Jacob.
[5]This He established in Joseph *as* a
testimony,
When He went throughout the land
of Egypt,
Where I heard a language I did not
understand.

[6]"I removed his shoulder from the
burden;
His hands were freed from the baskets.
[7]You called in trouble, and I delivered
you;
I answered you in the secret place of
thunder;
I tested you at the waters of Meribah.
Selah

[8]"Hear, O My people, and I will
admonish you!
O Israel, if you will listen to Me!
[9]There shall be no foreign god among
you;
Nor shall you worship any foreign god.
[10]I *am* the LORD your God,
Who brought you out of the land of
Egypt;
Open your mouth wide, and I will fill
it.

[11]"But My people would not heed My
voice,
And Israel would *have* none of Me.
[12]So I gave them over to their own
stubborn heart,
To walk in their own counsels.

[13]"Oh, that My people would listen to
Me,
That Israel would walk in My ways!
[14]I would soon subdue their enemies,
And turn My hand against their
adversaries.
[15]The haters of the LORD would pretend
submission to Him,
But their fate would endure forever.
[16]He would have fed them also with
the finest of wheat;
And with honey from the rock I
would have satisfied you."

PSALM 82

A Plea for Justice

A Psalm of Asaph.

[1]God stands in the congregation of the
mighty;
He judges among the gods.[a]
[2]How long will you judge unjustly,
And show partiality to the wicked?
Selah

[3]Defend the poor and fatherless;
Do justice to the afflicted and needy.
[4]Deliver the poor and needy;
Free *them* from the hand of the wicked.

[5]They do not know, nor do they
understand;

81:title [a]Hebrew *Al Gittith* **82:1** [a]Hebrew *elohim, mighty ones;* that is, the judges

They walk about in darkness;
All the foundations of the earth are
unstable.

[6]I said, "You *are* gods,[a]
And all of you *are* children of the
Most High.
[7]But you shall die like men,
And fall like one of the princes."

[8]Arise, O God, judge the earth;
For You shall inherit all nations.

. . . . . .

Is "relationship evangelism" biblical? See 1 Thess. 2:8 comment.

. . . . . .

PSALM 83

Prayer to Frustrate Conspiracy Against Israel

A Song. A Psalm of Asaph.

[1]Do not keep silent, O God!
Do not hold Your peace,
And do not be still, O God!
[2]For behold, Your enemies make a
tumult;
And those who hate You have lifted
up their head.
[3]They have taken crafty counsel
against Your people,
And consulted together against Your
sheltered ones.
[4]They have said, "Come, and let us cut
them off from *being* a nation,
That the name of Israel may be
remembered no more."

[5]For they have consulted together
with one consent;
They form a confederacy against You:
[6]The tents of Edom and the Ishmaelites;
Moab and the Hagrites;
[7]Gebal, Ammon, and Amalek;
Philistia with the inhabitants of Tyre;
[8]Assyria also has joined with them;
They have helped the children of Lot.
Selah

[9]Deal with them as *with* Midian,
As *with* Sisera,
As *with* Jabin at the Brook Kishon,
[10]Who perished at En Dor,
Who became *as* refuse on the earth.
[11]Make their nobles like Oreb and like
Zeeb,
Yes, all their princes like Zebah and
Zalmunna,
[12]Who said, "Let us take for ourselves
The pastures of God for a possession."

[13]O my God, make them like the
whirling dust,
Like the chaff before the wind!
[14]As the fire burns the woods,
And as the flame sets the mountains
on fire,
[15]So pursue them with Your tempest,
And frighten them with Your storm.
[16]Fill their faces with shame,
That they may seek Your name, O
LORD.
[17]Let them be confounded and
dismayed forever;
Yes, let them be put to shame and
perish,
[18]That they may know that You, whose
name alone *is* the LORD,
Are the Most High over all the earth.

PSALM 84

The Blessedness of Dwelling in the House of God

To the Chief Musician. On an instrument of Gath.[a] A Psalm of the sons of Korah.

[1]How lovely is Your tabernacle,
O LORD of hosts!

82:6 [a]Hebrew *elohim, mighty ones;* that is, the judges
84:title [a]Hebrew *Al Gittith*

82:7 "Every man must do two things alone: he must do his own believing, and he must do his own dying." *Martin Luther*

[2]My soul longs, yes, even faints
For the courts of the LORD;
My heart and my flesh cry out for the living God.

[3]Even the sparrow has found a home,
And the swallow a nest for herself,
Where she may lay her young—
Even Your altars, O LORD of hosts,
My King and my God.
[4]Blessed *are* those who dwell in Your house;
They will still be praising You. *Selah*

[5]Blessed *is* the man whose strength *is* in You,
Whose heart *is* set on pilgrimage.
[6]*As they* pass through the Valley of Baca,
They make it a spring;
The rain also covers it with pools.
[7]They go from strength to strength;
Each one appears before God in Zion.[a]

> The fruit of the Spirit grows only in the garden of obedience.
>
> **TERRY FULLAM**

[8]O LORD God of hosts, hear my prayer;
Give ear, O God of Jacob! *Selah*
[9]O God, behold our shield,
And look upon the face of Your anointed.

[10]For a day in Your courts *is* better than a thousand.
I would rather be a doorkeeper in the house of my God
Than dwell in the tents of wickedness.
[11]For the LORD God *is* a sun and shield;
The LORD will give grace and glory;
No good *thing* will He withhold
From those who walk uprightly.

[12]O LORD of hosts,
Blessed *is* the man who trusts in You!

PSALM 85

Prayer that the Lord Will Restore Favor to the Land

To the Chief Musician. A Psalm of the sons of Korah.

[1]LORD, You have been favorable to Your land;
You have brought back the captivity of Jacob.
[2]You have forgiven the iniquity of Your people;
You have covered all their sin. *Selah*
[3]You have taken away all Your wrath;
You have turned from the fierceness of Your anger.

[4]Restore us, O God of our salvation,
And cause Your anger toward us to cease.
[5]Will You be angry with us forever?
Will You prolong Your anger to all generations?
[6]Will You not revive us again,
That Your people may rejoice in You?
[7]Show us Your mercy, LORD,
And grant us Your salvation.

[8]I will hear what God the LORD will speak,
For He will speak peace
To His people and to His saints;
But let them not turn back to folly.
[9]Surely His salvation *is* near to those who fear Him,
That glory may dwell in our land.

[10]Mercy and truth have met together;
Righteousness and peace have kissed.
[11]Truth shall spring out of the earth,
And righteousness shall look down from heaven.
[12]Yes, the LORD will give *what is* good;
And our land will yield its increase.

84:7 [a]Septuagint, Syriac, and Vulgate read *The God of gods shall be seen.*

85:10 The cross of Calvary is where righteousness and peace kissed each other.

[13]Righteousness will go before Him,
And shall make His footsteps *our* pathway.

PSALM 86

Prayer for Mercy, with Meditation on the Excellencies of the Lord

A Prayer of David.

[1]Bow down Your ear, O LORD, hear me;
For I *am* poor and needy.
[2]Preserve my life, for I *am* holy;
You are my God;
Save Your servant who trusts in You!
[3]Be merciful to me, O Lord,
For I cry to You all day long.
[4]Rejoice the soul of Your servant,
For to You, O Lord, I lift up my soul.
[5]For You, Lord, *are* good, and ready to forgive,
And abundant in mercy to all those who call upon You.

[6]Give ear, O LORD, to my prayer;
And attend to the voice of my supplications.
[7]In the day of my trouble I will call upon You,
For You will answer me.

[8]Among the gods *there is* none like You, O Lord;
Nor *are there any works* like Your works.
[9]All nations whom You have made
Shall come and worship before You, O Lord,
And shall glorify Your name.
[10]For You *are* great, and do wondrous things;
You alone *are* God.
[11]Teach me Your way, O LORD;
I will walk in Your truth;
Unite my heart to fear Your name.
[12]I will praise You, O Lord my God, with all my heart,
And I will glorify Your name forevermore.
[13]For great *is* Your mercy toward me,
And You have delivered my soul from the depths of Sheol.

[14]O God, the proud have risen against me,
And a mob of violent *men* have sought my life,
And have not set You before them.
[15]But You, O Lord, *are* a God full of compassion, and gracious,
Longsuffering and abundant in mercy and truth.

[16]Oh, turn to me, and have mercy on me!
Give Your strength to Your servant,
And save the son of Your maidservant.
[17]Show me a sign for good,
That those who hate me may see *it* and be ashamed,
Because You, LORD, have helped me and comforted me.

PSALM 87

The Glories of the City of God

A Psalm of the sons of Korah. A Song.

[1]His foundation *is* in the holy mountains.
[2]The LORD loves the gates of Zion
More than all the dwellings of Jacob.
[3]Glorious things are spoken of you,
O city of God! *Selah*

86:5 Unholy huddle. Early in 2008, a couple were snowboarding in New Mexico when they became lost in a snow storm. They had a cell phone to call for help, but decided not to call because they were experienced hikers. They believed they could save themselves. They built a shelter in the snow and spent the night huddled together in the freezing conditions. The next morning they realized that they were not going to be able to make it alone, so they called for help, and then they carved an SOS in the snow. Had they not forsaken their own efforts, they certainly would have perished.

Most of humanity huddles together in this cold world, thinking that they are going to save themselves. They trust in their own religious works. It is only when they realize that their hope of saving themselves is hopeless that they will humble themselves and call upon the name of the Lord. May God help them to understand this, and that time is running out.

[4]"I will make mention of Rahab and
Babylon to those who know Me;
Behold, O Philistia and Tyre, with
Ethiopia:
'This *one* was born there.' "

[5]And of Zion it will be said,
"This *one* and that *one* were born in her;
And the Most High Himself shall
establish her."
[6]The LORD will record,
When He registers the peoples:
"This *one* was born there." *Selah*

[7]Both the singers and the players on
instruments *say*,
"All my springs *are* in you."

PSALM 88

A Prayer for Help in Despondency

A Song. A Psalm of the sons of Korah. To the Chief Musician. Set to "Mahalath Leannoth." A Contemplation[a] of Heman the Ezrahite.

[1]O LORD, God of my salvation,
I have cried out day and night before
You.
[2]Let my prayer come before You;
Incline Your ear to my cry.

[3]For my soul is full of troubles,
And my life draws near to the grave.
[4]I am counted with those who go
down to the pit;
I am like a man *who has* no strength,
[5]Adrift among the dead,
Like the slain who lie in the grave,
Whom You remember no more,
And who are cut off from Your hand.

[6]You have laid me in the lowest pit,
In darkness, in the depths.
[7]Your wrath lies heavy upon me,
And You have afflicted *me* with all
Your waves. *Selah*
[8]You have put away my acquaintances
far from me;
You have made me an abomination to
them;
I am shut up, and I cannot get out;
[9]My eye wastes away because of
affliction.

LORD, I have called daily upon You;
I have stretched out my hands to You.
[10]Will You work wonders for the dead?
Shall the dead arise *and* praise You?
Selah
[11]Shall Your lovingkindness be declared
in the grave?
Or Your faithfulness in the place of
destruction?
[12]Shall Your wonders be known in the
dark?
And Your righteousness in the land of
forgetfulness?

[13]But to You I have cried out, O LORD,
And in the morning my prayer comes
before You.
[14]LORD, why do You cast off my soul?
Why do You hide Your face from me?
[15]I *have been* afflicted and ready to die
from *my* youth;
I suffer Your terrors;
I am distraught.
[16]Your fierce wrath has gone over me;
Your terrors have cut me off.
[17]They came around me all day long
like water;
They engulfed me altogether.
[18]Loved one and friend You have put
far from me,
And my acquaintances into darkness.

PSALM 89

Remembering the Covenant with David, and Sorrow for Lost Blessings

A Contemplation[a] of Ethan the Ezrahite.

[1]I will sing of the mercies of the LORD
forever;
With my mouth will I make known
Your faithfulness to all
generations.
[2]For I have said, "Mercy shall be built
up forever;

88:title [a]Hebrew *Maschil* **89:title** [a]Hebrew *Maschil*

QUESTIONS & OBJECTIONS

89:14

"Why does the Old Testament show a God of wrath and the New Testament a God of mercy?"

The God of the New Testament is the same as the God of the Old Testament. The Bible says that He *never* changes. He is just as merciful in the Old Testament as He is in the New Testament. Read Neh. 9 for a summary of how God mercifully forgave Israel, again and again, after they repeatedly sinned and turned their back on Him. The psalms often speak of God's mercy poured out on sinners.

He is also just as wrath-filled in the New Testament as He is in the Old. He killed a husband and wife in the Book of Acts, simply because they told one lie. Jesus warned that He was to be feared because He has the power to cast the body and soul into hell. The apostle Paul said that he persuaded men to come to the Savior because he knew the "terror of the Lord." Read the dreadful judgments of the New Testament's Book of Revelation. That will put the "fear of God" in you, which incidentally is "the beginning of wisdom."

Perhaps the most fearful display of His wrath is seen in the cross of Jesus Christ. His fury so came upon the Messiah that it seems God enshrouded Jesus in darkness so that creation couldn't gaze upon His unspeakable agony. Whether we like it or not, our God is a consuming fire of holiness (Heb. 12:29). He isn't going to change, so we had better... before the Day of Judgment. If we repent, God, in His mercy, will forgive us and grant us eternal life in heaven with Him.

Your faithfulness You shall establish
in the very heavens."

3"I have made a covenant with My
chosen,
I have sworn to My servant David:
4'Your seed I will establish forever,
And build up your throne to all
generations.' " *Selah*

5And the heavens will praise Your
wonders, O LORD;
Your faithfulness also in the assembly
of the saints.
6For who in the heavens can be
compared to the LORD?
Who among the sons of the mighty
can be likened to the LORD?
7God is greatly to be feared in the
assembly of the saints,
And to be held in reverence by all
those around Him.
8O LORD God of hosts,
Who *is* mighty like You, O LORD?
Your faithfulness also surrounds You.
9You rule the raging of the sea;
When its waves rise, You still them.
10You have broken Rahab in pieces, as
one who is slain;
You have scattered Your enemies with
Your mighty arm.

11The heavens *are* Yours, the earth also
is Yours;
The world and all its fullness, You
have founded them.
12The north and the south, You have
created them;
Tabor and Hermon rejoice in Your
name.
13You have a mighty arm;
Strong is Your hand, *and* high is Your
right hand.
14Righteousness and justice *are* the
foundation of Your throne;
Mercy and truth go before Your face.
15Blessed *are* the people who know the
joyful sound!
They walk, O LORD, in the light of
Your countenance.

89:6 Nothing on this earth or in heaven compares to God. Even the regenerate mind cannot begin to comprehend His infinite greatness.

[16]In Your name they rejoice all day long,
And in Your righteousness they are
exalted.
[17]For You *are* the glory of their strength,
And in Your favor our horn is exalted.
[18]For our shield *belongs* to the LORD,
And our king to the Holy One of Israel.

[19]Then You spoke in a vision to Your
holy one,[a]
And said: "I have given help to *one
who is* mighty;
I have exalted one chosen from the
people.
[20]I have found My servant David;
With My holy oil I have anointed him,
[21]With whom My hand shall be
established;
Also My arm shall strengthen him.
[22]The enemy shall not outwit him,
Nor the son of wickedness afflict him.
[23]I will beat down his foes before his
face,
And plague those who hate him.

[24]"But My faithfulness and My mercy
shall be with him,
And in My name his horn shall be
exalted.
[25]Also I will set his hand over the sea,
And his right hand over the rivers.
[26]He shall cry to Me, 'You *are* my Father,
My God, and the rock of my salvation.'
[27]Also I will make him *My* firstborn,
The highest of the kings of the earth.
[28]My mercy I will keep for him forever,
And My covenant shall stand firm
with him.
[29]His seed also I will make *to endure*
forever,
And his throne as the days of heaven.

[30]"If his sons forsake My law
And do not walk in My judgments,
[31]If they break My statutes
And do not keep My commandments,
[32]Then I will punish their transgression
with the rod,
And their iniquity with stripes.
[33]Nevertheless My lovingkindness I will
not utterly take from him,
Nor allow My faithfulness to fail.
[34]My covenant I will not break,
Nor alter the word that has gone out
of My lips.
[35]Once I have sworn by My holiness;
I will not lie to David:
[36]His seed shall endure forever,
And his throne as the sun before Me;
[37]It shall be established forever like the
moon,
Even *like* the faithful witness in the
sky." *Selah*

[38]But You have cast off and abhorred,
You have been furious with Your
anointed.
[39]You have renounced the covenant of
Your servant;
You have profaned his crown *by
casting it* to the ground.
[40]You have broken down all his hedges;
You have brought his strongholds to
ruin.
[41]All who pass by the way plunder him;
He is a reproach to his neighbors.
[42]You have exalted the right hand of his
adversaries;
You have made all his enemies rejoice.
[43]You have also turned back the edge of
his sword,
And have not sustained him in the
battle.

89:19 [a]Following many Hebrew manuscripts; Masoretic Text, Septuagint, Targum, and Vulgate read *holy ones.*

89:36,37 The moon doesn't have its own light, but simply reflects the light of the sun. Jesus said that the Church is the light for this world, a city set on a hill that cannot be hidden (see Matt. 5:14). Like the moon, the light we reflect is not ours, but the light of the Son. The moon also governs the tides of the earth, and in one sense God has given the Church the ability (under His hand) to influence the tides of revival. There are certain principles—holy living, travailing prayer, and biblical preaching—that God can use to usher a revival of Christianity to this dark and dying world.

QUESTIONS & OBJECTIONS

89:48

"Man is the master of his own destiny!"

If man is in total control of his future, then he should at least be in control of his own body. Instead, he is subject to involuntary yawning, sneezing, breathing, swallowing, sleeping, salivating, dreaming, blinking, and thinking. He can't even control hair and nail growth. He automatically does these things, irrespective of his will. God has set his body in motion and there is little he can do about it. He also has minimal control over his daily bodily functions. His kidneys, bladder, intestines, heart, liver, lungs, etc., work independently of his will.

It is ludicrous to say that man controls his future when he has trouble predicting the stock market, political outcomes, earthquakes, and even the weather, let alone having control over these things.

44 You have made his glory cease,
And cast his throne down to the ground.
45 The days of his youth You have shortened;
You have covered him with shame. *Selah*

46 How long, LORD?
Will You hide Yourself forever?
Will Your wrath burn like fire?
47 Remember how short my time is;
For what futility have You created all the children of men?
48 What man can live and not see death?
Can he deliver his life from the power of the grave? *Selah*

49 Lord, where *are* Your former lovingkindnesses,
Which You swore to David in Your truth?
50 Remember, Lord, the reproach of Your servants—
How I bear in my bosom *the reproach of* all the many peoples,
51 With which Your enemies have reproached, O LORD,
With which they have reproached the footsteps of Your anointed.

52 Blessed *be* the LORD forevermore!
Amen and Amen.

Book Four: Psalms 90—106

PSALM 90

The Eternity of God, and Man's Frailty

A Prayer of Moses the man of God.

1 Lord, You have been our dwelling place[a] in all generations.
2 Before the mountains were brought forth,
Or ever You had formed the earth and the world,
Even from everlasting to everlasting,
You *are* God.

3 You turn man to destruction,
And say, "Return, O children of men."
4 For a thousand years in Your sight
Are like yesterday when it is past,
And *like* a watch in the night.
5 You carry them away *like* a flood;
They are like a sleep.
In the morning they are like grass *which* grows up:
6 In the morning it flourishes and grows up;
In the evening it is cut down and withers.

7 For we have been consumed by Your anger,
And by Your wrath we are terrified.

90:1 [a]Septuagint, Targum, and Vulgate read *refuge.*

89:48 See James 4:14 comment.

QUESTIONS & OBJECTIONS

90:2 "Who made God?"

To one who examines the evidence, there can be no doubt that God exists. *Every* building has a builder. Everything made has a maker. The fact of the existence of the Creator is axiomatic (self-evident). That's why the Bible says, "The fool has said in his heart, 'There is no God'" (Psa. 14:1). The professing atheist denies the common sense given to him by God, and defends his belief by thinking that the question "Who made God?" cannot be answered. This, he thinks, gives him license to deny the existence of God.

The question of who made God can be answered by simply looking at space and asking, "Does space have an end?" Obviously, it doesn't. If there is a brick wall with "The End" written on it, the question arises, "What is behind the brick wall?" Strain the mind though it may, we have to believe (have faith) that space has no beginning and no end. The same applies to God. He has no beginning and no end. He is eternal.

The Bible also informs us that time is a dimension that God created, into which man was subjected (2 Tim. 1:9, Titus 1:2). It even tells us that one day time will no longer exist. That will be called "eternity." God Himself dwells outside of the dimension He created. He dwells in eternity and is not subject to time. God spoke history before it came into being. He can move through time as a man flips through a history book. Because we live in the dimension of time, logic and reason demand that everything *must* have a beginning and an end. We can understand the concept of God's eternal nature the same way we understand the concept of space having no beginning and end—by faith. We simply *have* to believe they are so, even though such thoughts put a strain on our distinctly insufficient cerebrum. See also Isa. 34:4 comment.

8You have set our iniquities before You,
Our secret *sins* in the light of Your
countenance.
9For all our days have passed away in
Your wrath;
We finish our years like a sigh.
10The days of our lives *are* seventy years;
And if by reason of strength *they are*
eighty years,
Yet their boast *is* only labor and sorrow;
For it is soon cut off, and we fly away.
11Who knows the power of Your anger?
For as the fear of You, *so is* Your wrath.
12So teach *us* to number our days,
That we may gain a heart of wisdom.

13Return, O LORD!
How long?
And have compassion on Your servants.
14Oh, satisfy us early with Your mercy,
That we may rejoice and be glad all
our days!
15Make us glad according to the days *in
which* You have afflicted us,
The years *in which* we have seen evil.
16Let Your work appear to Your servants,

The average person dies at 70 years old.

IF YOU ARE:	YOU HAVE ABOUT:
20 years old	2,500 weekends left
30 years old	2,000 weekends left
40 years old	1,500 weekends left
50 years old	1,000 weekends left
60 years old	500 weekends left

According to the U.S Census Bureau, approx. 150,000 people die worldwide every 24 hours.

90:4 Time is God's creation. He Himself is not subject to the dimension of time. See 2 Pet. 3:8 comment.

90:7,8 The ungodly must be made to understand that every hidden sin as well as sins of the heart are seen by God. He will bring every work into judgment, including every secret thing, whether it is good or evil.

"When we merely say that we are bad, the 'wrath' of God seems a barbarous doctrine; as soon as we perceive our bad-ness, it appears inevitable, a mere corollary from God's goodness." *C. S. Lewis*

90:10 See Gen. 5:27 comment.

And Your glory to their children.
[17]And let the beauty of the LORD our God be upon us,
And establish the work of our hands for us;
Yes, establish the work of our hands.

PSALM 91

Safety of Abiding in the Presence of God

[1]He who dwells in the secret place of the Most High
Shall abide under the shadow of the Almighty.
[2]I will say of the LORD, "*He is* my refuge and my fortress;
My God, in Him I will trust."

[3]Surely He shall deliver you from the snare of the fowler[a]
And from the perilous pestilence.
[4]He shall cover you with His feathers,
And under His wings you shall take refuge;
His truth *shall be your* shield and buckler.
[5]You shall not be afraid of the terror by night,
Nor of the arrow *that* flies by day,
[6]*Nor* of the pestilence *that* walks in darkness,
Nor of the destruction *that* lays waste at noonday.

[7]A thousand may fall at your side,
And ten thousand at your right hand;
But it shall not come near you.
[8]Only with your eyes shall you look,
And see the reward of the wicked.

[9]Because you have made the LORD, *who is* my refuge,
Even the Most High, your dwelling place,
[10]No evil shall befall you,
Nor shall any plague come near your dwelling;
[11]For He shall give His angels charge over you,
To keep you in all your ways.
[12]In *their* hands they shall bear you up,
Lest you dash your foot against a stone.
[13]You shall tread upon the lion and the cobra,
The young lion and the serpent you shall trample underfoot.

[14]"Because he has set his love upon Me, therefore I will deliver him;
I will set him on high, because he has known My name.
[15]He shall call upon Me, and I will answer him;
I *will be* with him in trouble;
I will deliver him and honor him.
[16]With long life I will satisfy him,
And show him My salvation."

PSALM 92

Praise to the Lord for His Love and Faithfulness

A Psalm. A Song for the Sabbath day.

[1]*It is* good to give thanks to the LORD,
And to sing praises to Your name, O Most High;
[2]To declare Your lovingkindness in the morning,
And Your faithfulness every night,
[3]On an instrument of ten strings,
On the lute,
And on the harp,
With harmonious sound.
[4]For You, LORD, have made me glad through Your work;

91:3 [a]That is, one who catches birds in a trap or snare

90:12 "Your days at the most cannot be very long, so use them to the best of your ability for the glory of God and the benefit of your generation." *General William Booth*

91:1 This psalm is good medicine for those of us who sometimes feel sick with fear at the thought of evangelism. How can we not draw courage from such incredible promises?

I will triumph in the works of Your
hands.

5O LORD, how great are Your works!
Your thoughts are very deep.
6A senseless man does not know,
Nor does a fool understand this.
7When the wicked spring up like grass,
And when all the workers of iniquity
flourish,
It is that they may be destroyed forever.

8But You, LORD, *are* on high
forevermore.
9For behold, Your enemies, O LORD,
For behold, Your enemies shall perish;
All the workers of iniquity shall be
scattered.

10But my horn You have exalted like a
wild ox;
I have been anointed with fresh oil.
11My eye also has seen *my desire* on my
enemies;
My ears hear *my desire* on the wicked
Who rise up against me.

12The righteous shall flourish like a
palm tree,
He shall grow like a cedar in Lebanon.
13Those who are planted in the house
of the LORD
Shall flourish in the courts of our God.
14They shall still bear fruit in old age;
They shall be fresh and flourishing,
15To declare that the LORD is upright;
He is my rock, and *there is* no
unrighteousness in Him.

PSALM 93

The Eternal Reign of the Lord

1The LORD reigns, He is clothed with
majesty;
The LORD is clothed,
He has girded Himself with strength.
Surely the world is established, so
that it cannot be moved.
2Your throne *is* established from of old;
You *are* from everlasting.

3The floods have lifted up, O LORD,
The floods have lifted up their voice;
The floods lift up their waves.
4The LORD on high *is* mightier
Than the noise of many waters,
Than the mighty waves of the sea.

5Your testimonies are very sure;
Holiness adorns Your house,
O LORD, forever.

PSALM 94

God the Refuge of the Righteous

1O LORD God, to whom vengeance
belongs—
O God, to whom vengeance belongs,
shine forth!
2Rise up, O Judge of the earth;
Render punishment to the proud.
3LORD, how long will the wicked,
How long will the wicked triumph?

92:5,6 The unregenerate person can view God's creation and not begin to comprehend how great God is. His understanding is darkened. He is alienated from the life of God through the ignorance that is in him (Eph. 4:18). This ignorance is a willful blindness brought about by a hardened heart. See John 3:20 comment.

92:13 "Most people think churches are like cafeterias; they pick and choose what they like! They feel the freedom to stay as long as there are no problems. But this does not agree at all with what the Bible teaches. You are not the one who chooses where you go to church. God does! The Bible does not say, 'God has set the members, each one of them, in the body *just as they please*.' Rather it says, 'But now God has set the members, each one of them, in the body *just as He pleased*' (1 Cor. 12:18, emphasis added).

"Remember that, if you're in the place where God wants you, the devil will try to offend you to get you out. He wants to uproot men and women from the place where God plants them. If he can get you out, he has been successful. If you will not budge, even in the midst of great conflict, you will spoil his plans." *John Bevere*

94:1 "God is not disillusioned with us. He never had any illusions to begin with." *Luis Palau*

[4]They utter speech, *and* speak insolent
things;
All the workers of iniquity boast in
themselves.
[5]They break in pieces Your people, O
LORD,
And afflict Your heritage.
[6]They slay the widow and the stranger,
And murder the fatherless.
[7]Yet they say, "The LORD does not see,
Nor does the God of Jacob
understand."

[8]Understand, you senseless among the
people;
And *you* fools, when will you be wise?
[9]He who planted the ear, shall He not
hear?
He who formed the eye, shall He not
see?
[10]He who instructs the nations, shall
He not correct,
He who teaches man knowledge?
[11]The LORD knows the thoughts of man,
That they *are* futile.

[12]Blessed *is* the man whom You
instruct, O LORD,
And teach out of Your law,
[13]That You may give him rest from the
days of adversity,
Until the pit is dug for the wicked.
[14]For the LORD will not cast off His
people,
Nor will He forsake His inheritance.
[15]But judgment will return to
righteousness,
And all the upright in heart will
follow it.

[16]Who will rise up for me against the
evildoers?
Who will stand up for me against the
workers of iniquity?
[17]Unless the LORD *had been* my help,
My soul would soon have settled in
silence.
[18]If I say, "My foot slips,"
Your mercy, O LORD, will hold me up.
[19]In the multitude of my anxieties
within me,
Your comforts delight my soul.

[20]Shall the throne of iniquity, which
devises evil by law,
Have fellowship with You?
[21]They gather together against the life
of the righteous,
And condemn innocent blood.
[22]But the LORD has been my defense,
And my God the rock of my refuge.
[23]He has brought on them their own
iniquity,
And shall cut them off in their own
wickedness;
The LORD our God shall cut them off.

PSALM 95

A Call to Worship and Obedience

[1]Oh come, let us sing to the LORD!
Let us shout joyfully to the Rock of
our salvation.
[2]Let us come before His presence with
thanksgiving;
Let us shout joyfully to Him with
psalms.
[3]For the LORD *is* the great God,
And the great King above all gods.
[4]In His hand *are* the deep places of the
earth;
The heights of the hills *are* His also.

94:7–10 This is the great error of the ungodly. They don't consider the fact that if God can create an ear, He can therefore hear everything they say. If He can create an eye, He therefore can see everything they do.

94:12 Blessed is the man who is instructed out of God's Law. When God uses His Law to bring "the knowledge of sin," it acts as a "tutor" to bring a sinner to the Savior (see Rom. 3:20; Gal. 3:24) .

95:4,5 Scientific facts in the Bible. Only in recent years has man discovered that there are mountains on the ocean floor. This was revealed in the Bible thousands of years ago. While deep in the ocean, Jonah cried, "I went down to the moorings of the mountains..." (Jon. 2:6). The reason the Bible and true science harmonize is that they have the same author. See also Psa. 33:8 comment.

[5]The sea *is* His, for He made it;
And His hands formed the dry *land.*

[6]Oh come, let us worship and bow
down;
Let us kneel before the LORD our Maker.
[7]For He *is* our God,
And we *are* the people of His pasture,
And the sheep of His hand.

Today, if you will hear His voice:
[8]"Do not harden your hearts, as in the
rebellion,[a]
As *in* the day of trial[b] in the wilderness,
[9]When your fathers tested Me;
They tried Me, though they saw My
work.
[10]For forty years I was grieved with *that*
generation,
And said, 'It *is* a people who go astray
in their hearts,
And they do not know My ways.'
[11]So I swore in My wrath,
'They shall not enter My rest.' "

PSALM 96

A Song of Praise to God Coming in Judgment

[1]Oh, sing to the LORD a new song!
Sing to the LORD, all the earth.
[2]Sing to the LORD, bless His name;
Proclaim the good news of His
salvation from day to day.
[3]Declare His glory among the nations,
His wonders among all peoples.

[4]For the LORD *is* great and greatly to be
praised;
He *is* to be feared above all gods.
[5]For all the gods of the peoples *are* idols,
But the LORD made the heavens.
[6]Honor and majesty *are* before Him;
Strength and beauty *are* in His
sanctuary.

[7]Give to the LORD, O families of the
peoples,
Give to the LORD glory and strength.
[8]Give to the LORD the glory *due* His
name;
Bring an offering, and come into His
courts.
[9]Oh, worship the LORD in the beauty
of holiness!
Tremble before Him, all the earth.

Witnessing is the whole work of the whole church for the whole age.

A. T. PIERSON

[10]Say among the nations, "The LORD
reigns;
The world also is firmly established,
It shall not be moved;
He shall judge the peoples righteously."

[11]Let the heavens rejoice, and let the
earth be glad;
Let the sea roar, and all its fullness;
[12]Let the field be joyful, and all that *is*
in it.
Then all the trees of the woods will
rejoice before the LORD.
[13]For He is coming, for He is coming to
judge the earth.
He shall judge the world with
righteousness,
And the peoples with His truth.

95:8 [a]Or *Meribah* [b]Or *Massah*

95:6 "I can safely say, on the authority of all that is revealed in the Word of God, that any man or woman on this earth who is bored and turned off by worship is not ready for heaven." *A. W. Tozer*

96:5 "[The Big Bang] represents the instantaneous suspension of physical laws, the sudden, abrupt flash of lawlessness that allowed something to come out of nothing. It represents a true miracle—transcending physical principles." *Paul Davies*, theoretical physicist, *The Edge of Infinity*

96:11–13 When a murderer is brought to justice, good people rejoice. Justice is sweet to the upright in heart. We are informed that the whole of creation rejoices because God is going to judge the world with righteousness and truth. This is what Paul preached in Acts 17:30,31, and it is what we must preach if we want the world to be saved.

QUESTIONS & OBJECTIONS

97:6

"Do I really need to 'prove' God to anyone or just preach the gospel?"

We do not have to prove to the atheist that God exists. He intuitively knows that God exists but willfully suppresses the truth (see Rom. 1:18). Every person has a God-given conscience, which is the "work of the law written in their hearts" (Rom. 2:15). Just as every sane person knows that it is wrong to lie, steal, kill, and commit adultery, he knows that if there is a moral Law, then there must be a moral Lawgiver.

In addition to the testimony of his impartial conscience, the atheist also has the testimony of creation. It declares the glory of God, His eternal power, and divine nature, so that the person who denies the voice of conscience and the voice of creation is without excuse (Psa. 19:1; Rom. 1:19–21). If he dies in his sins, he will face the wrath of a holy Creator, whether he believes in Him or not.

This is why I don't spend too much effort trying to convince anyone that there is a God. To do so is to waste time and energy. What sinners need is not to be convinced that God exists, but that their sin exists and that they are in terrible danger. The only biblical way to do this is to go through the moral Law and explain that God considers lust to be adultery and hatred to be murder, etc. It is the revelation that God is holy and just, and sees the thought-life, that convinces us that we are in danger of eternal damnation. That is what sinners need to hear to send them to the cross for mercy. So never be discouraged from preaching the gospel, and don't get sidetracked by rabbit-trail issues that don't really matter.

PSALM 97

A Song of Praise to the Sovereign Lord

1The LORD reigns;
Let the earth rejoice;
Let the multitude of isles be glad!

2Clouds and darkness surround Him;
Righteousness and justice *are* the foundation of His throne.
3A fire goes before Him,
And burns up His enemies round about.
4His lightnings light the world;
The earth sees and trembles.
5The mountains melt like wax at the presence of the LORD,
At the presence of the Lord of the whole earth.
6The heavens declare His righteousness,
And all the peoples see His glory.

7Let all be put to shame who serve carved images,
Who boast of idols.
Worship Him, all *you* gods.
8Zion hears and is glad,
And the daughters of Judah rejoice
Because of Your judgments, O LORD.
9For You, LORD, *are* most high above all the earth;
You are exalted far above all gods.

10You who love the LORD, hate evil!
He preserves the souls of His saints;
He delivers them out of the hand of the wicked.
11Light is sown for the righteous,
And gladness for the upright in heart.
12Rejoice in the LORD, you righteous,
And give thanks at the remembrance of His holy name.[a]

PSALM 98

A Song of Praise to the Lord for His Salvation and Judgment

A Psalm.

1Oh, sing to the LORD a new song!
For He has done marvelous things;
His right hand and His holy arm have

97:12 [a]Or *His holiness*

97:2 Righteousness and justice are the very essence of God's character.

97:3–5 This is perhaps a reference to the giving of the Law on Mount Sinai (Exod. 19).

97:10 Do we truly hate evil, or do we secretly embrace lust and take pleasure in violent entertainment?

QUESTIONS & OBJECTIONS

98:9 "Why does God want to torture people in hell?"

God will not "torture" anyone. He will simply give them justice. A criminal who viciously raped three teenage girls may believe that his being thrown into a cold prison cell is torture. The judge knows better. He calls it "justice."

God will "damn" rebellious sinners from all that is good in a prison called "hell." He gave them life and lavished His goodness upon them, and they despised Him, violated His Law, and then refused His mercy. He is extremely kind and "rich" in mercy, and offers complete forgiveness to all who repent and obey the gospel. Those who despise that mercy will get what the Bible calls "equity." Equity, according to the dictionary, is "the quality of being fair or impartial; fairness; impartiality: the equity of Solomon." In law, it is "the application of the dictates of conscience or the principles of natural justice to the settlement of controversies." In other words, impartially doing what is right, fair, and just.

The Bible tells us that God takes no pleasure in the death of the wicked (Ezek. 33:11). His Word even says that "mercy triumphs over judgment" (James 2:13), meaning that God would rather see someone sorrowful and repentant and have their sins forgiven, than receive the full wrath of His justice. But if sinners remain hard and impenitent, His Word warns, "But in accordance with your hardness and your impenitent heart you are treasuring up for yourself wrath in the day of wrath and revelation of the righteous judgment of God, who '*will render to each one according to his deeds*'" (Rom. 2:5,6).

"Sin is man's saying to God throughout life, 'Go away and leave me alone.' Hell is God's finally saying to man, 'You may have your wish.' It is God's leaving man to himself, as man has chosen." *C. S. Lewis*

gained Him the victory.
2The LORD has made known His salvation;
His righteousness He has revealed in the sight of the nations.
3He has remembered His mercy and His faithfulness to the house of Israel;
All the ends of the earth have seen the salvation of our God.

4Shout joyfully to the LORD, all the earth;
Break forth in song, rejoice, and sing praises.
5Sing to the LORD with the harp,
With the harp and the sound of a psalm,
6With trumpets and the sound of a horn;
Shout joyfully before the LORD, the King.

7Let the sea roar, and all its fullness,
The world and those who dwell in it;
8Let the rivers clap *their* hands;
Let the hills be joyful together before the LORD,
9For He is coming to judge the earth.
With righteousness He shall judge the world,
And the peoples with equity.

PSALM 99

Praise to the Lord for His Holiness

1The LORD reigns;
Let the peoples tremble!
He dwells *between* the cherubim;
Let the earth be moved!
2The LORD *is* great in Zion,
And He *is* high above all the peoples.
3Let them praise Your great and awesome name—
He *is* holy.

4The King's strength also loves justice;
You have established equity;
You have executed justice and righteousness in Jacob.

98:7–9 The whole of creation rejoices at the thought of God coming to judge the earth. Justice is a joy to the upright. See Psa. 96:11–13 comment.

[5]Exalt the LORD our God,
And worship at His footstool—
He *is* holy.

[6]Moses and Aaron were among His priests,
And Samuel was among those who called upon His name;
They called upon the LORD, and He answered them.
[7]He spoke to them in the cloudy pillar;
They kept His testimonies and the ordinance He gave them.

If your gospel isn't touching others, it hasn't touched you!

CURRY R. BLAKE

[8]You answered them, O LORD our God;
You were to them God-Who-Forgives,
Though You took vengeance on their deeds.
[9]Exalt the LORD our God,
And worship at His holy hill;
For the LORD our God *is* holy.

PSALM 100

A Song of Praise for the Faithfulness to His People

A Psalm of Thanksgiving.

[1]Make a joyful shout to the LORD, all you lands!
[2]Serve the LORD with gladness;
Come before His presence with singing.
[3]Know that the LORD, He *is* God;
It is He *who* has made us, and not we ourselves;[a]
We are His people and the sheep of His pasture.

[4]Enter into His gates with thanksgiving,
And into His courts with praise.
Be thankful to Him, *and* bless His name.
[5]For the LORD *is* good;
His mercy *is* everlasting,
And His truth *endures* to all generations.

PSALM 101

Promised Faithfulness to the Lord

A Psalm of David.

[1]I will sing of mercy and justice;
To You, O LORD, I will sing praises.

[2]I will behave wisely in a perfect way.
Oh, when will You come to me?
I will walk within my house with a perfect heart.

[3]I will set nothing wicked before my eyes;
I hate the work of those who fall away;
It shall not cling to me.
[4]A perverse heart shall depart from me;
I will not know wickedness.

[5]Whoever secretly slanders his neighbor,
Him I will destroy;
The one who has a haughty look and a proud heart,
Him I will not endure.

[6]My eyes *shall be* on the faithful of the land,
That they may dwell with me;
He who walks in a perfect way,
He shall serve me.
[7]He who works deceit shall not dwell within my house;
He who tells lies shall not continue in my presence.
[8]Early I will destroy all the wicked of the land,
That I may cut off all the evildoers from the city of the LORD.

100:3 [a]Following Kethib, Septuagint, and Vulgate; Qere, many Hebrew manuscripts, and Targum read *we are His.*

101:1 Mercy and judgment met at the cross of Calvary. See Gal. 6:14.

QUESTIONS & OBJECTIONS

102:3,4 *"Why did God create marijuana?"*

Marijuana enthusiasts often point to Gen. 1:11 ("Let the earth bring forth grass") and other verses (Gen. 1:29; 3:18) to justify the smoking of what they refer to as "grass." They say that since God created the plant and declared it "good," it should therefore be enjoyed. It is true that He created it, and that everything He made has some purpose in creation. For example, hemp (from which marijuana is made) is very useful in making strong rope. God also created sand (which is good), and if someone wants to eat sand by the spoonful, they may do so. However, they shouldn't complain if they get a stomachache.

While God had a practical use for marijuana, man decided for some reason to burn it and kill his brain cells by inhaling its harmful fumes. Likewise, man decided to use the beautiful poppy to destroy his life with incredibly addictive heroin. Breathing in the burning fumes of anything is extremely unhealthy, and those who do so aren't thinking very deeply. This is one reason why marijuana is called "dope." Those who smoke "grass" will waste their days, wither their brain, and forget what they are doing.

In the jungles of Asia and South America, missionaries place tobacco leaves in their boots to stop leeches from getting into their shoes and crawling up their legs. Even leeches have the good sense to avoid tobacco. Smokers would be wiser to wrap their lips around the exhaust pipe of their car and breathe in the fumes. Both cigarette smoke and exhaust fumes are full of carcinogens, but cigarette smokers pay for their habit to the tobacco companies, and sadly they pay for their stupidity with their lives.

PSALM 102

The Lord's Eternal Love

A Prayer of the afflicted, when he is overwhelmed and pours out his complaint before the LORD.

1 Hear my prayer, O LORD,
And let my cry come to You.
2 Do not hide Your face from me in the day of my trouble;
Incline Your ear to me;
In the day that I call, answer me speedily.

3 For my days are consumed like smoke,
And my bones are burned like a hearth.
4 My heart is stricken and withered like grass,
So that I forget to eat my bread.
5 Because of the sound of my groaning
My bones cling to my skin.
6 I am like a pelican of the wilderness;
I am like an owl of the desert.
7 I lie awake,
And am like a sparrow alone on the housetop.

8 My enemies reproach me all day long;
Those who deride me swear an oath against me.
9 For I have eaten ashes like bread,
And mingled my drink with weeping,
10 Because of Your indignation and Your wrath;
For You have lifted me up and cast me away.
11 My days *are* like a shadow that lengthens,
And I wither away like grass.

12 But You, O LORD, shall endure forever,
And the remembrance of Your name to all generations.
13 You will arise *and* have mercy on Zion;
For the time to favor her,
Yes, the set time, has come.
14 For Your servants take pleasure in her stones,
And show favor to her dust.
15 So the nations shall fear the name of the LORD,
And all the kings of the earth Your glory.
16 For the LORD shall build up Zion;
He shall appear in His glory.
17 He shall regard the prayer of the destitute,
And shall not despise their prayer.

18 This will be written for the generation to come,
That a people yet to be created may

QUESTIONS & OBJECTIONS

102:25

"Radiometric dating proves the earth is millions of years old."

By Andrew Snelling, Answers in Genesis

Does radiometric dating show that rocks are millions of years old? No! This dating method requires assumptions about the content of the original rocks and the decay rate in the past. Since the Bible is clear about the earth's age of thousands of years, the popular assumptions are wrong.

God's Word unmistakably teaches a young earth and universe ("the heavens"). God has ensured the accurate recording and preservation of His eyewitness account of the earth's history, which Jesus Christ endorsed repeatedly during His earthly ministry.

God took great care to include the necessary chronological details of the universe's creation in six literal days, as well as the unbroken genealogies of mankind from Adam to Jesus. So we have absolutely no doubt that the earth is only around six thousand years old.

Contrary to Scripture, many geologists claim that radiometric "clocks" show rocks to be millions of years old. However, to read any clock accurately we must know where the clock was set at the beginning. It's like making sure that an hourglass clock was set with all the sand in the top bowl at the beginning. However, no geologists were present when the earth and its many rock layers were formed, so they cannot know where the radiometric clocks were set at the beginning.

Also, we have to be sure that the clock has ticked at the same rate from the beginning until now. No geologists have been observing the radiometric clocks for millions of years to check that the rate of radioactive decay has always been the same as the rate today. To the contrary, we now have impeccable evidence that radioactive decay rates were greatly sped up at some point during the past, for example, during the global catastrophic Genesis Flood.

God is beyond time, which He created. He has told us when He created everything and thus how old the universe is. So we finite humans should fearlessly embrace His testimony of a young earth, recorded in His inerrant Word. See also Job 20:4 comment.

"Shells from *living* snails were carbon dated as being 27,000 years old." *Science* magazine, vol. 224, 1984 (emphasis added)

praise the LORD.
19For He looked down from the height
of His sanctuary;
From heaven the LORD viewed the
earth,
20To hear the groaning of the prisoner,
To release those appointed to death,
21To declare the name of the LORD in
Zion,
And His praise in Jerusalem,
22When the peoples are gathered
together,
And the kingdoms, to serve the LORD.

23He weakened my strength in the way;
He shortened my days.
24I said, "O my God,
Do not take me away in the midst of
my days;
Your years *are* throughout all
generations.
25Of old You laid the foundation of the
earth,
And the heavens *are* the work of Your
hands.
26They will perish, but You will endure;
Yes, they will all grow old like a
garment;
Like a cloak You will change them,
And they will be changed.

102:26 Scientific facts in the Bible. Three different places in the Bible (Isa. 51:6; Psa. 102:25,26; Heb. 1:11) indicate that the earth is wearing out. This is what the Second Law of Thermodynamics (the Law of Increasing Entropy) states: that in all physical processes, every ordered system over time tends to become more disordered. Everything is running down and wearing out as energy is becoming less and less available for use. That means the universe will eventually "wear out" to the extent that (theoretically speaking) there will be a "heat death" and therefore no more energy available for use. This wasn't discovered by man until fairly recently, but the Bible states it in clear, succinct terms.

[27]But You *are* the same,
And Your years will have no end.
[28]The children of Your servants will continue,
And their descendants will be established before You."

PSALM 103

Praise for the Lord's Mercies

A Psalm of David.

[1]Bless the LORD, O my soul;
And all that is within me, *bless* His holy name!
[2]Bless the LORD, O my soul,
And forget not all His benefits:
[3]Who forgives all your iniquities,
Who heals all your diseases,
[4]Who redeems your life from destruction,
Who crowns you with lovingkindness and tender mercies,
[5]Who satisfies your mouth with good *things,*
So that your youth is renewed like the eagle's.

[6]The LORD executes righteousness
And justice for all who are oppressed.
[7]He made known His ways to Moses,
His acts to the children of Israel.
[8]The LORD *is* merciful and gracious,
Slow to anger, and abounding in mercy.
[9]He will not always strive *with us,*
Nor will He keep *His anger* forever.
[10]He has not dealt with us according to our sins,
Nor punished us according to our iniquities.

[11]For as the heavens are high above the earth,
So great is His mercy toward those who fear Him;
[12]As far as the east is from the west,
So far has He removed our transgressions from us.
[13]As a father pities *his* children,
So the LORD pities those who fear Him.
[14]For He knows our frame;
He remembers that we *are* dust.

[15]*As for* man, his days *are* like grass;
As a flower of the field, so he flourishes.
[16]For the wind passes over it, and it is gone,
And its place remembers it no more.[a]
[17]But the mercy of the LORD *is* from everlasting to everlasting
On those who fear Him,
And His righteousness to children's children,
[18]To such as keep His covenant,
And to those who remember His commandments to do them.

[19]The LORD has established His throne in heaven,
And His kingdom rules over all.

[20]Bless the LORD, you His angels,
Who excel in strength, who do His word,
Heeding the voice of His word.
[21]Bless the LORD, all *you* His hosts,
You ministers of His, who do His pleasure.
[22]Bless the LORD, all His works,
In all places of His dominion.

Bless the LORD, O my soul!

PSALM 104

Praise to the Sovereign Lord for His Creation and Providence

[1]Bless the LORD, O my soul!

103:16 [a]Compare Job 7:10

102:27 See Heb. 13:8 comment.

103:10 How true it is that God hasn't dealt with us according to our iniquities (vv. 10–18). He hasn't treated us as He treated Ananias and Sapphira (Acts 5:1–10). He has held back His just wrath and instead lavished us with mercy.

QUESTIONS & OBJECTIONS

103:17 ***"God couldn't forgive my sin."***

Those who think they are too sinful for God to accept them don't understand how merciful God is. The Bible says that He is "rich in mercy" (Eph. 2:4). The Scriptures also tell us that "the mercy of the LORD is from everlasting to everlasting on those who fear Him" (Psa. 103:17). God was merciful to King David and forgave him when he committed adultery and murder. He forgave Moses when he committed murder. He also forgave Saul of Tarsus for murdering Christians (Acts 22:4). God promises to save *all* who call on the name of Jesus (Rom. 10:13). Those who think this promise isn't worth the paper it's written on are calling God a liar (see 1 John 5:10). Jesus shed His precious blood to pay for their sins. Wasn't it good enough for them? It was good enough for God. God *commands* them to repent (Acts 17:30). To offer any excuse is to remain in rebellion to His command—no matter how "noble" it may seem to say that they are too sinful.

O LORD my God, You are very great:
You are clothed with honor and
majesty,
2Who cover *Yourself* with light as *with*
a garment,
Who stretch out the heavens like a
curtain.

3He lays the beams of His upper
chambers in the waters,
Who makes the clouds His chariot,
Who walks on the wings of the wind,
4Who makes His angels spirits,
His ministers a flame of fire.

5*You who* laid the foundations of the
earth,
So *that* it should not be moved forever,
6You covered it with the deep as *with* a
garment;
The waters stood above the mountains.
7At Your rebuke they fled;
At the voice of Your thunder they
hastened away.
8They went up over the mountains;
They went down into the valleys,
To the place which You founded for
them.
9You have set a boundary that they
may not pass over,
That they may not return to cover the
earth.

10He sends the springs into the valleys;
They flow among the hills.
11They give drink to every beast of the
field;
The wild donkeys quench their thirst.
12By them the birds of the heavens have
their home;
They sing among the branches.
13He waters the hills from His upper
chambers;
The earth is satisfied with the fruit of
Your works.

14He causes the grass to grow for the
cattle,
And vegetation for the service of man,
That he may bring forth food from
the earth,
15And wine *that* makes glad the heart of
man,
Oil to make *his* face shine,
And bread *which* strengthens man's
heart.
16The trees of the LORD are full *of sap*,
The cedars of Lebanon which He
planted,
17Where the birds make their nests;

104:2 Scientific facts in the Bible. It is interesting to note that scientists are beginning to understand that the universe is expanding or stretching out. At least seven times in Scripture we are told that God *stretches* out the heavens like a curtain. See also Heb. 11:3 comment.

The stork has her home in the fir trees.
18The high hills *are* for the wild goats;
The cliffs are a refuge for the rock
badgers.[a]

19He appointed the moon for seasons;
The sun knows its going down.
20You make darkness, and it is night,
In which all the beasts of the forest
creep about.
21The young lions roar after their prey,
And seek their food from God.
22*When* the sun rises, they gather
together
And lie down in their dens.
23Man goes out to his work
And to his labor until the evening.

24O LORD, how manifold are Your works!
In wisdom You have made them all.
The earth is full of Your
possessions—
25This great and wide sea,
In which *are* innumerable teeming
things,
Living things both small and great.
26There the ships sail about;
There is that Leviathan
Which You have made to play there.

27These all wait for You,
That You may give *them* their food in
due season.
28*What* You give them they gather in;
You open Your hand, they are filled
with good.
29You hide Your face, they are troubled;
You take away their breath, they die
and return to their dust.
30You send forth Your Spirit, they are
created;
And You renew the face of the earth.

31May the glory of the LORD endure
forever;
May the LORD rejoice in His works.
32He looks on the earth, and it trembles;
He touches the hills, and they smoke.

33I will sing to the LORD as long as I live;
I will sing praise to my God while I
have my being.
34May my meditation be sweet to Him;
I will be glad in the LORD.
35May sinners be consumed from the
earth,
And the wicked be no more.

Bless the LORD, O my soul!
Praise the LORD!

104:18 [a]Or *rock hyrax* (compare Leviticus 11:5)

104:19 Scientific facts in the Bible. God created the "lights" in the heavens "for signs and seasons, and for days and years" (Gen. 1:14). Through the marvels of astronomy we now understand that a year is the time required for the earth to travel once around the sun. The seasons are caused by the changing position of the earth in relation to the sun—"astronomers can tell exactly from the earth's motion around the sun when one season ends and the next one begins" (*Worldbook Multimedia Encyclopedia*). We also now understand that a "month [is] the time of one revolution of the moon around the earth with respect to the sun" (*Encyclopedia Britannica*). How could Moses (the accepted author of Genesis) have known 3,500 years ago that the "lights" of the sun and moon were the actual determining factors of the year's length, unless his words were inspired by God? See also Psa. 136:7–9 comment.

104:24 The peppered moth: evolution comes unglued. "Almost all textbooks on evolution include the peppered moth as *the* classic example of evolution by natural selection. There are two types of peppered moths, a light-colored speckled variety and a dark variety. Most peppered moths in England were the light variety, which were camouflaged as they rested on tree trunks. The black variety stood out against the light bark and were easily seen and eaten by birds. But as the industrial revolution created pollution that covered tree trunks with soot, the dark variety was camouflaged better, so birds ate more of the light moths.

"The peppered moth story has been trumpeted since the 1950s as proof positive that evolution by natural selection is true. In 1978, one famous geneticist called the peppered moth 'the clearest case in which a conspicuous evolutionary process has actually been observed.' However, this 'clearest case' of purported Darwinian evolution by natural selection is not true! The nocturnal peppered moth does not rest on the trunks of trees during the day. In fact, despite over 40 years of intense field study, only two *(continued)*

PSALM 105

The Eternal Faithfulness of the Lord

[1]Oh, give thanks to the LORD!
Call upon His name;
Make known His deeds among the
peoples!
[2]Sing to Him, sing psalms to Him;
Talk of all His wondrous works!
[3]Glory in His holy name;
Let the hearts of those rejoice who
seek the LORD!
[4]Seek the LORD and His strength;
Seek His face evermore!
[5]Remember His marvelous works
which He has done,
His wonders, and the judgments of
His mouth,
[6]O seed of Abraham His servant,
You children of Jacob, His chosen ones!

[7]He *is* the LORD our God;
His judgments *are* in all the earth.
[8]He remembers His covenant forever,
The word *which* He commanded, for a
thousand generations,
[9]*The covenant* which He made with
Abraham,
And His oath to Isaac,
[10]And confirmed it to Jacob for a statute,
To Israel *as* an everlasting covenant,
[11]Saying, "To you I will give the land of
Canaan
As the allotment of your inheritance,"
[12]When they were few in number,
Indeed very few, and strangers in it.

[13]When they went from one nation to
another,
From *one* kingdom to another people,
[14]He permitted no one to do them
wrong;
Yes, He rebuked kings for their sakes,
[15]*Saying,* "Do not touch My anointed
ones,
And do My prophets no harm."

[16]Moreover He called for a famine in
the land;
He destroyed all the provision of bread.
[17]He sent a man before them—
Joseph—*who* was sold as a slave.
[18]They hurt his feet with fetters,
He was laid in irons.
[19]Until the time that his word came to
pass,
The word of the LORD tested him.
[20]The king sent and released him,
The ruler of the people let him go free.
[21]He made him lord of his house,
And ruler of all his possessions,

(104:24 continued) peppered moths have ever been seen naturally resting on tree trunks!

"So where did all the evolution textbook pictures of peppered moths on different colored tree trunks come from? They were all staged. The moths were glued, pinned, or placed onto tree trunks and their pictures taken. The scientists who used these pictures in their books to prove evolution *all* conveniently forgot to tell their readers this fact. If the *best* example of evolution is not true, how about all their *other* supposed examples? It makes you wonder, doesn't it?" *Mark Varney*

Evolutionary humor. It's humorous that evolutionists cite the peppered moth as their best example, enabling them to "watch evolution in action." Watch closely: Before the moth's environment changed, some of the moths were mostly white, some were mostly black. After their environment changed, some were mostly white, some were mostly black. No new color or variety came into being, yet we have supposedly just witnessed evolution.

Evolutionist *John Reader (Missing Links)* explains this biased interpretation: "Ever since Darwin's work..., preconceptions have led evidence by the nose." Harvard professor and evolutionist *Steven Jay Gould* admits this scientific bias, "Facts do not 'speak for themselves'; they are read in light of theory."

Even *Charles Darwin* concedes, "Alas, how frequent, how almost universal it is in an author to persuade himself of the truth of his own dogmas." Keep this in mind when scientists proclaim the theory of evolution as "fact." See also Job 35:16 comment.

105:17–19 If God is going to use you to reach the lost, be ready to be "tested." Your own family may turn against you. You may find yourself "laid in irons"—in a hardship in which there seems to be no escape. Don't get discouraged, and don't become passive in your evangelism. See 1 Pet. 1:7.

22 To bind his princes at his pleasure,
And teach his elders wisdom.

23 Israel also came into Egypt,
And Jacob dwelt in the land of Ham.
24 He increased His people greatly,
And made them stronger than their enemies.
25 He turned their heart to hate His people,
To deal craftily with His servants.

26 He sent Moses His servant,
And Aaron whom He had chosen.
27 They performed His signs among them,
And wonders in the land of Ham.

Comfort and prosperity have never enriched the world as much as adversity has.

BILLY GRAHAM

28 He sent darkness, and made *it* dark;
And they did not rebel against His word.
29 He turned their waters into blood,
And killed their fish.
30 Their land abounded with frogs,
Even in the chambers of their kings.
31 He spoke, and there came swarms of flies,
And lice in all their territory.
32 He gave them hail for rain,
And flaming fire in their land.
33 He struck their vines also, and their fig trees,
And splintered the trees of their territory.
34 He spoke, and locusts came,
Young locusts without number,
35 And ate up all the vegetation in their land,
And devoured the fruit of their ground.
36 He also destroyed all the firstborn in their land,
The first of all their strength.

37 He also brought them out with silver and gold,
And *there was* none feeble among His tribes.
38 Egypt was glad when they departed,
For the fear of them had fallen upon them.
39 He spread a cloud for a covering,
And fire to give light in the night.
40 *The people* asked, and He brought quail,
And satisfied them with the bread of heaven.
41 He opened the rock, and water gushed out;
It ran in the dry places *like* a river.

42 For He remembered His holy promise,
And Abraham His servant.
43 He brought out His people with joy,
His chosen ones with gladness.
44 He gave them the lands of the Gentiles,
And they inherited the labor of the nations,
45 That they might observe His statutes
And keep His laws.

Praise the LORD!

PSALM 106

Joy in Forgiveness of Israel's Sins

1 Praise the LORD!

Oh, give thanks to the LORD, for *He is* good!
For His mercy *endures* forever.

2 Who can utter the mighty acts of the LORD?
Who can declare all His praise?
3 Blessed *are* those who keep justice,
And he who does[a] righteousness at all times!

4 Remember me, O LORD, with the favor *You have toward* Your people.
Oh, visit me with Your salvation,
5 That I may see the benefit of Your chosen ones,

106:3 [a]Septuagint, Syriac, Targum, and Vulgate read *those who do.*

That I may rejoice in the gladness of
Your nation,
That I may glory with Your inheritance.

[6]We have sinned with our fathers,
We have committed iniquity,
We have done wickedly.
[7]Our fathers in Egypt did not
understand Your wonders;
They did not remember the multitude
of Your mercies,
But rebelled by the sea—the Red Sea.

[8]Nevertheless He saved them for His
name's sake,
That He might make His mighty
power known.
[9]He rebuked the Red Sea also, and it
dried up;
So He led them through the depths,
As through the wilderness.
[10]He saved them from the hand of him
who hated *them,*
And redeemed them from the hand of
the enemy.
[11]The waters covered their enemies;
There was not one of them left.
[12]Then they believed His words;
They sang His praise.

[13]They soon forgot His works;
They did not wait for His counsel,
[14]But lusted exceedingly in the
wilderness,
And tested God in the desert.
[15]And He gave them their request,
But sent leanness into their soul.

[16]When they envied Moses in the camp,
And Aaron the saint of the LORD,
[17]The earth opened up and swallowed
Dathan,
And covered the faction of Abiram.
[18]A fire was kindled in their company;
The flame burned up the wicked.

[19]They made a calf in Horeb,
And worshiped the molded image.
[20]Thus they changed their glory
Into the image of an ox that eats grass.
[21]They forgot God their Savior,
Who had done great things in Egypt,
[22]Wondrous works in the land of Ham,
Awesome things by the Red Sea.
[23]Therefore He said that He would
destroy them,
Had not Moses His chosen one stood
before Him in the breach,
To turn away His wrath, lest He
destroy *them.*

[24]Then they despised the pleasant land;
They did not believe His word,
[25]But complained in their tents,
And did not heed the voice of the LORD.
[26]Therefore He raised His hand *in an
oath* against them,
To overthrow them in the wilderness,
[27]To overthrow their descendants
among the nations,
And to scatter them in the lands.

[28]They joined themselves also to Baal of
Peor,
And ate sacrifices made to the dead.
[29]Thus they provoked *Him* to anger
with their deeds,
And the plague broke out among them.
[30]Then Phinehas stood up and
intervened,
And the plague was stopped.
[31]And that was accounted to him for
righteousness
To all generations forevermore.

[32]They angered *Him* also at the waters
of strife,[a]
So that it went ill with Moses on
account of them;
[33]Because they rebelled against His
Spirit,
So that he spoke rashly with his lips.

[34]They did not destroy the peoples,
Concerning whom the LORD had
commanded them,
[35]But they mingled with the Gentiles
And learned their works;

106:32 [a]Or *Meribah*

[36]They served their idols,
Which became a snare to them.
[37]They even sacrificed their sons
And their daughters to demons,
[38]And shed innocent blood,
The blood of their sons and daughters,
Whom they sacrificed to the idols of
Canaan;
And the land was polluted with blood.
[39]Thus they were defiled by their own
works,
And played the harlot by their own
deeds.

[40]Therefore the wrath of the LORD was
kindled against His people,
So that He abhorred His own
inheritance.
[41]And He gave them into the hand of
the Gentiles,
And those who hated them ruled over
them.
[42]Their enemies also oppressed them,
And they were brought into
subjection under their hand.
[43]Many times He delivered them;
But they rebelled in their counsel,
And were brought low for their
iniquity.

[44]Nevertheless He regarded their
affliction,
When He heard their cry;
[45]And for their sake He remembered
His covenant,
And relented according to the
multitude of His mercies.
[46]He also made them to be pitied
By all those who carried them away
captive.

[47]Save us, O LORD our God,
And gather us from among the
Gentiles,
To give thanks to Your holy name,
To triumph in Your praise.

[48]Blessed *be* the LORD God of Israel
From everlasting to everlasting!
And let all the people say, "Amen!"

Praise the LORD!

Book Five: Psalms 107—150

PSALM 107

Thanksgiving to the Lord for His Great Works of Deliverance

[1]Oh, give thanks to the LORD, for *He is*
good!
For His mercy *endures* forever.
[2]Let the redeemed of the LORD say *so,*
Whom He has redeemed from the
hand of the enemy,
[3]And gathered out of the lands,
From the east and from the west,
From the north and from the south.

[4]They wandered in the wilderness in a
desolate way;
They found no city to dwell in.
[5]Hungry and thirsty,

106:35–39 Abortion—a result of idolatry. How can people believe in God and yet believe in the killing of children through abortion? Simply because they "serve idols." Idolatry is perhaps the greatest of all sins because it opens the door to unrestrained evil—"My god gives me the right to choose!" etc. It gives sinners license not only to tolerate sin, but to sanction it, fanned by demonic influence. Those who create a god in their own image feel at liberty to play "the harlot by their own deeds."

The following is typical of how easy it is to create your own god:

> Over the years, Ed and Joanne Liverani have found many reasons to summon God. But now, at middle age, they've boiled it down to one essential: "Not to get clobbered by life."
>
> So sometime in the past ten years the Liveranis began to build their own church, salvaging bits of their old religion that they liked and chucking the rest. The first to go were an angry, vengeful God and hell—"That's just something they say to scare you," Ed said. They kept Jesus, "because Jesus is big on love." *The Washington Post* (January 9, 2000)

107:2 How can the redeemed not "say so"? We have been redeemed from the cold hand of death. See v. 14.

Their soul fainted in them.
6Then they cried out to the LORD in
their trouble,
And He delivered them out of their
distresses.
7And He led them forth by the right
way,
That they might go to a city for a
dwelling place.
8Oh, that *men* would give thanks to
the LORD *for* His goodness,
And *for* His wonderful works to the
children of men!
9For He satisfies the longing soul,
And fills the hungry soul with
goodness.

10Those who sat in darkness and in the
shadow of death,
Bound in affliction and irons—
11Because they rebelled against the
words of God,
And despised the counsel of the Most
High,
12Therefore He brought down their
heart with labor;
They fell down, and *there was* none to
help.
13Then they cried out to the LORD in
their trouble,
And He saved them out of their
distresses.
14He brought them out of darkness and
the shadow of death,
And broke their chains in pieces.
15Oh, that *men* would give thanks to
the LORD *for* His goodness,
And *for* His wonderful works to the
children of men!
16For He has broken the gates of bronze,
And cut the bars of iron in two.

17Fools, because of their transgression,
And because of their iniquities, were
afflicted.
18Their soul abhorred all manner of
food,
And they drew near to the gates of
death.
19Then they cried out to the LORD in
their trouble,
And He saved them out of their
distresses.
20He sent His word and healed them,
And delivered *them* from their
destructions.
21Oh, that *men* would give thanks to
the LORD *for* His goodness,
And *for* His wonderful works to the
children of men!
22Let them sacrifice the sacrifices of
thanksgiving,
And declare His works with rejoicing.

23Those who go down to the sea in
ships,
Who do business on great waters,
24They see the works of the LORD,
And His wonders in the deep.
25For He commands and raises the
stormy wind,
Which lifts up the waves of the sea.
26They mount up to the heavens,
They go down again to the depths;
Their soul melts because of trouble.
27They reel to and fro, and stagger like
a drunken man,
And are at their wits' end.
28Then they cry out to the LORD in their
trouble,

107:17 Self-inflicted misery. So much of the world's misery is self-inflicted: AIDS, alcoholism, obesity, guilt, drug addiction, nicotine addiction and its related diseases, etc. Consider the repercussions of adultery, revealed in this unsigned letter: "Eleven years ago, I walked out on a 12-year marriage. My wife was a good person, but for a long time she was under a lot of stress. Instead of helping her, I began an affair with her best friend. It was a disaster. This is what I gave up: 1) seeing my daughter grow up; 2) the respect of many long-time friends; 3) the enjoyment of living as a family; 4) a wife who was loyal, was appreciative and tried to make me happy. This is what I got: 1) two stepchildren who treated me like dirt; 2) a wife who didn't know how to make anything for dinner but reservations; 3) a wife whose only interest in me was how much money she could get; 4) a wife who made disparaging remarks about my family and ruined all my existing friendships; 5) finally, the best thing I got was a bitter, expensive divorce."

"Faith indeed tells what the senses do not tell, but not the contrary of what they see. It is above them and not contrary to them."

Blaise Pascal

And He brings them out of their
distresses.
29He calms the storm,
So that its waves are still.
30Then they are glad because they are
quiet;
So He guides them to their desired
haven.
31Oh, that *men* would give thanks to
the LORD *for* His goodness,
And *for* His wonderful works to the
children of men!
32Let them exalt Him also in the
assembly of the people,
And praise Him in the company of
the elders.

33He turns rivers into a wilderness,
And the watersprings into dry ground;
34A fruitful land into barrenness,
For the wickedness of those who
dwell in it.
35He turns a wilderness into pools of
water,
And dry land into watersprings.
36There He makes the hungry dwell,
That they may establish a city for a
dwelling place,
37And sow fields and plant vineyards,
That they may yield a fruitful harvest.
38He also blesses them, and they
multiply greatly;
And He does not let their cattle
decrease.

39When they are diminished and
brought low
Through oppression, affliction and
sorrow,
40He pours contempt on princes,
And causes them to wander in the
wilderness *where there is* no way;
41Yet He sets the poor on high, far from
affliction,
And makes *their* families like a flock.
42The righteous see *it* and rejoice,
And all iniquity stops its mouth.

43Whoever *is* wise will observe these
things,
And they will understand the
lovingkindness of the LORD.

PSALM 108

Assurance of God's Victory over Enemies

A Song. A Psalm of David.

1O God, my heart is steadfast;
I will sing and give praise, even with
my glory.
2Awake, lute and harp!
I will awaken the dawn.
3I will praise You, O LORD, among the
peoples,
And I will sing praises to You among
the nations.
4For Your mercy *is* great above the
heavens,
And Your truth *reaches* to the clouds.

5Be exalted, O God, above the heavens,
And Your glory above all the earth;
6That Your beloved may be delivered,
Save *with* Your right hand, and hear me.

7God has spoken in His holiness;

"I will rejoice;
I will divide Shechem
And measure out the Valley of Succoth.
8Gilead *is* Mine; Manasseh *is* Mine;
Ephraim also *is* the helmet for My head;
Judah *is* My lawgiver.
9Moab *is* My washpot;
Over Edom I will cast My shoe;
Over Philistia I will triumph."

10Who will bring me *into* the strong city?
Who will lead me to Edom?
11*Is it* not *You,* O God, *who* cast us off?
And *You,* O God, *who* did not go out
with our armies?
12Give us help from trouble,
For the help of man is useless.
13Through God we will do valiantly,
For *it is* He *who* shall tread down our
enemies.[a]

PSALM 109

Plea for Judgment of False Accusers

To the Chief Musician. A Psalm of David.

1Do not keep silent,
O God of my praise!
2For the mouth of the wicked and the
mouth of the deceitful
Have opened against me;
They have spoken against me with a
lying tongue.
3They have also surrounded me with
words of hatred,
And fought against me without a cause.
4In return for my love they are my
accusers,
But I *give myself to* prayer.
5Thus they have rewarded me evil for
good,
And hatred for my love.

6Set a wicked man over him,
And let an accuser[a] stand at his right
hand.
7When he is judged, let him be found
guilty,
And let his prayer become sin.
8Let his days be few,
And let another take his office.
9Let his children be fatherless,
And his wife a widow.
10Let his children continually be
vagabonds, and beg;
Let them seek *their bread*[a] also from
their desolate places.
11Let the creditor seize all that he has,
And let strangers plunder his labor.
12Let there be none to extend mercy to
him,
Nor let there be any to favor his
fatherless children.
13Let his posterity be cut off,
And in the generation following let
their name be blotted out.

14Let the iniquity of his fathers be
remembered before the LORD,
And let not the sin of his mother be
blotted out.
15Let them be continually before the
LORD,
That He may cut off the memory of
them from the earth;
16Because he did not remember to
show mercy,
But persecuted the poor and needy
man,
That he might even slay the broken in
heart.
17As he loved cursing, so let it come to
him;
As he did not delight in blessing, so
let it be far from him.
18As he clothed himself with cursing as
with his garment,
So let it enter his body like water,

108:13 [a]Compare verses 6–13 with 60:5–12 **109:6** [a]Hebrew *satan* **109:10** [a]Following Masoretic Text and Targum; Septuagint and Vulgate read *be cast out*.

109:1–4 When the world turns against you because of your faith and you find yourself in the valley of discouragement, climb up onto the high place of prayer.

109:8 Luke applied this verse to Judas Iscariot. See Acts 1:20.

And like oil into his bones.
19Let it be to him like the garment
which covers him,
And for a belt with which he girds
himself continually.
20*Let* this *be* the LORD's reward to my
accusers,
And to those who speak evil against
my person.

21But You, O GOD the Lord,
Deal with me for Your name's sake;
Because Your mercy *is* good, deliver me.
22For I *am* poor and needy,
And my heart is wounded within me.
23I am gone like a shadow when it
lengthens;
I am shaken off like a locust.
24My knees are weak through fasting,
And my flesh is feeble from lack of
fatness.
25I also have become a reproach to them;
When they look at me, they shake
their heads.

26Help me, O LORD my God!
Oh, save me according to Your mercy,
27That they may know that this *is* Your
hand—
That You, LORD, have done it!
28Let them curse, but You bless;
When they arise, let them be ashamed,
But let Your servant rejoice.
29Let my accusers be clothed with shame,
And let them cover themselves with
their own disgrace as with a
mantle.

30I will greatly praise the LORD with my
mouth;
Yes, I will praise Him among the
multitude.
31For He shall stand at the right hand
of the poor,
To save *him* from those who condemn
him.

PSALM 110

Announcement of the Messiah's Reign

A Psalm of David.

1The LORD said to my Lord,
"Sit at My right hand,
Till I make Your enemies Your
footstool."
2The LORD shall send the rod of Your
strength out of Zion.
Rule in the midst of Your enemies!

3Your people *shall be* volunteers
In the day of Your power;
In the beauties of holiness, from the
womb of the morning,
You have the dew of Your youth.
4The LORD has sworn
And will not relent,
"You *are* a priest forever
According to the order of Melchizedek."

5The Lord *is* at Your right hand;
He shall execute kings in the day of
His wrath.
6He shall judge among the nations,
He shall fill *the places* with dead
bodies,
He shall execute the heads of many
countries.
7He shall drink of the brook by the
wayside;
Therefore He shall lift up the head.

PSALM 111

Praise to God for His Faithfulness and Justice

1Praise the LORD!

I will praise the LORD with *my* whole
heart,
In the assembly of the upright and *in*
the congregation.

2The works of the LORD *are* great,

110:1–7 These verses speak of the coming Messiah. Hebrews 5:5,6 tells us that Jesus is our High Priest "according to the order of Melchizedek" (v. 4), and John 5:22 says that God has committed all judgment to Jesus (v. 6). See also Heb. 4:14; 7:22–26; Acts 10:42.

Studied by all who have pleasure in
them.
3His work *is* honorable and glorious,
And His righteousness endures forever.
4He has made His wonderful works to
be remembered;
The LORD *is* gracious and full of
compassion.
5He has given food to those who fear
Him;
He will ever be mindful of His
covenant.
6He has declared to His people the
power of His works,
In giving them the heritage of the
nations.

7The works of His hands *are* verity
and justice;
All His precepts *are* sure.
8They stand fast forever and ever,
And are done in truth and
uprightness.
9He has sent redemption to His people;
He has commanded His covenant
forever:
Holy and awesome *is* His name.

10The fear of the LORD *is* the beginning
of wisdom;
A good understanding have all those
who do *His commandments.*
His praise endures forever.

PSALM 112

The Blessed State of the Righteous

1Praise the LORD!

Blessed *is* the man *who* fears the LORD,
Who delights greatly in His
commandments.

2His descendants will be mighty on
earth;
The generation of the upright will be
blessed.
3Wealth and riches *will be* in his house,
And his righteousness endures forever.
4Unto the upright there arises light in
the darkness;
He is gracious, and full of
compassion, and righteous.
5A good man deals graciously and lends;
He will guide his affairs with discretion.
6Surely he will never be shaken;
The righteous will be in everlasting
remembrance.
7He will not be afraid of evil tidings;
His heart is steadfast, trusting in the
LORD.
8His heart *is* established;
He will not be afraid,
Until he sees *his desire* upon his
enemies.

9He has dispersed abroad,
He has given to the poor;
His righteousness endures forever;
His horn will be exalted with honor.
10The wicked will see *it* and be grieved;
He will gnash his teeth and melt
away;
The desire of the wicked shall perish.

PSALM 113

The Majesty and Condescension of God

1Praise the LORD!

Praise, O servants of the LORD,
Praise the name of the LORD!
2Blessed be the name of the LORD
From this time forth and forevermore!
3From the rising of the sun to its going
down
The LORD's name *is* to be praised.

4The LORD *is* high above all nations,

112:1 The apostle Paul is one who delighted in the Law of God. See Rom. 7:22.

113:3 As the Declaration of Independence was being signed, *Samuel Adams* stated, "We have this day restored the Sovereign to Whom all men ought to be obedient. He reigns in heaven and from the rising to the setting of the sun, let His kingdom come."

QUESTIONS & OBJECTIONS

115:4–9

"The First Commandment says, 'You shall have no other gods before Me.' That proves He isn't the only God!"

That's true. Man has always made false gods. But there is only one true God, the Creator. An old adage says, "God created man in His own image, and man has been returning the favor ever since." Hindus have millions of gods. Sometimes gods are made of wood or stone; other times man makes up a god in his mind. Whatever the case, making a god to suit yourself is called "idolatry," and is a transgression of both the First and Second of the Ten Commandments.

His glory above the heavens.
5Who *is* like the LORD our God,
Who dwells on high,
6Who humbles Himself to behold
The things that are in the heavens and in the earth?

7He raises the poor out of the dust,
And lifts the needy out of the ash heap,
8That He may seat *him* with princes—
With the princes of His people.
9He grants the barren woman a home,
Like a joyful mother of children.

Praise the LORD!

PSALM 114

The Power of God in His Deliverance of Israel

1When Israel went out of Egypt,
The house of Jacob from a people of strange language,
2Judah became His sanctuary,
And Israel His dominion.

3The sea saw *it* and fled;
Jordan turned back.
4The mountains skipped like rams,
The little hills like lambs.
5What ails you, O sea, that you fled?
O Jordan, *that* you turned back?
6O mountains, *that* you skipped like rams?
O little hills, like lambs?

7Tremble, O earth, at the presence of the Lord,
At the presence of the God of Jacob,
8Who turned the rock *into* a pool of water,
The flint into a fountain of waters.

PSALM 115

The Futility of Idols and the Trustworthiness of God

1Not unto us, O LORD, not unto us,
But to Your name give glory,
Because of Your mercy,
Because of Your truth.
2Why should the Gentiles say,
"So where *is* their God?"

3But our God *is* in heaven;
He does whatever He pleases.
4Their idols *are* silver and gold,
The work of men's hands.
5They have mouths, but they do not speak;
Eyes they have, but they do not see;
6They have ears, but they do not hear;
Noses they have, but they do not smell;
7They have hands, but they do not handle;
Feet they have, but they do not walk;
Nor do they mutter through their throat.
8Those who make them are like them;
So is everyone who trusts in them.

9O Israel, trust in the LORD;
He *is* their help and their shield.
10O house of Aaron, trust in the LORD;
He *is* their help and their shield.

[11]You who fear the LORD, trust in the
LORD;
He *is* their help and their shield.

[12]The LORD has been mindful of *us;*
He will bless us;
He will bless the house of Israel;
He will bless the house of Aaron.
[13]He will bless those who fear the LORD,
Both small and great.

[14]May the LORD give you increase more
and more,
You and your children.
[15]*May* you *be* blessed by the LORD,
Who made heaven and earth.

[16]The heaven, *even* the heavens, *are* the
LORD's;
But the earth He has given to the
children of men.
[17]The dead do not praise the LORD,
Nor any who go down into silence.
[18]But we will bless the LORD
From this time forth and forevermore.

Praise the LORD!

PSALM 116

Thanksgiving for Deliverance from Death

[1]I love the LORD, because He has heard
My voice *and* my supplications.
[2]Because He has inclined His ear to me,
Therefore I will call *upon Him* as long
as I live.

[3]The pains of death surrounded me,
And the pangs of Sheol laid hold of me;
I found trouble and sorrow.
[4]Then I called upon the name of the
LORD:
"O LORD, I implore You, deliver my
soul!"

[5]Gracious *is* the LORD, and righteous;
Yes, our God *is* merciful.
[6]The LORD preserves the simple;
I was brought low, and He saved me.
[7]Return to your rest, O my soul,
For the LORD has dealt bountifully
with you.

[8]For You have delivered my soul from
death,
My eyes from tears,
And my feet from falling.
[9]I will walk before the LORD
In the land of the living.
[10]I believed, therefore I spoke,
"I am greatly afflicted."
[11]I said in my haste,
"All men *are* liars."

[12]What shall I render to the LORD
For all His benefits toward me?
[13]I will take up the cup of salvation,
And call upon the name of the LORD.
[14]I will pay my vows to the LORD
Now in the presence of all His people.

[15]Precious in the sight of the LORD
Is the death of His saints.

[16]O LORD, truly I *am* Your servant;
I *am* Your servant, the son of Your
maidservant;
You have loosed my bonds.
[17]I will offer to You the sacrifice of

115:15 "There are no detailed Darwinian accounts for the evolution of any fundamental biochemical or cellular system, only a variety of wishful speculations. It is remarkable that Darwinism is accepted as a satisfactory explanation for such a vast subject—evolution—with so little rigorous examination of how well its basic theses work in illuminating specific instances of biological adaptation or diversity." *James Shapiro*, molecular biologist ("In the Details . . . What?" *National Review*)

116:11 ". . . 20,000 middle and high-schoolers were surveyed by the Josephson Institute of Ethics—a non-profit organization in Marina del Rey, Calif., devoted to character education. Ninety-two percent of the teenagers admitted having lied to their parents in the previous year, and 73 percent characterized themselves as 'serial liars,' meaning they told lies weekly. Despite these admissions, 91 percent of all respondents said they were 'satisfied with my own ethics and character.'" *Reader's Digest*, November 1999

116:13 *The Holy Grail*

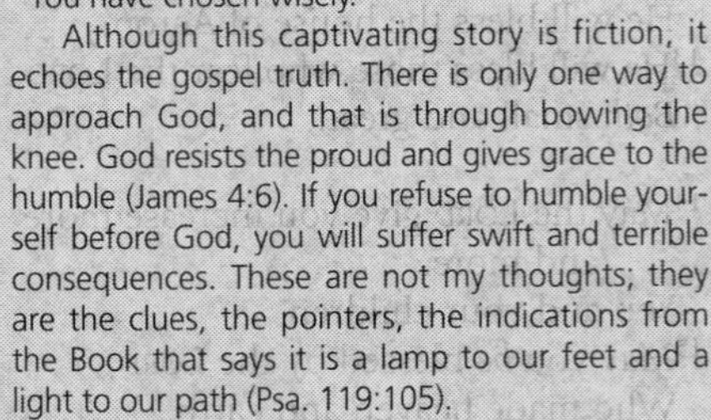

In the blockbuster movie *Indiana Jones and the Last Crusade*, Indiana was in search of the Holy Grail. This is supposedly the cup from which Jesus drank at the Last Supper. Whoever sipped from it would receive everlasting life. Through a series of circumstances, Indiana was forced to make his way past three "challenges."

He has clues written in a book that he holds in his hand. As he makes his way toward the Grail, his first clue is "The penitent man will pass." He repeats the words over and over. Suddenly the meaning dawns on him. He whispers, "The penitent man is *humble before God... kneel!*" He instantly drops to his knees, and as he does so, two spinning blades slice the air where his head had just been. He has made it past the first challenge.

The second is a group of steppingstones with letters of the alphabet on them. The clue is "Proceed in the footsteps of the Word of God." Again, he says the clue repeatedly. Then he whispers, "The name of God is Jehovah," and takes his first step, almost falling to his death as the steppingstone gives way. He then realizes that the name of God in Latin begins with the letter "I." He steps it out and successfully completes the second challenge.

The third challenge is to pass over a huge, bottomless chasm—with no bridge. The clue given is "The path of God. Only a leap from a lion's head will prove his worth." Indiana is understandably terrified at the thought of stepping off the edge over a deep crevasse when there is nothing upon which to step. But he has no choice. He must stand by the stone carving of the lion's head and take a leap of faith. He closes his eyes and steps out onto nothing.

Suddenly his foot touches something solid. The camera angle moves to one side, revealing that the path upon which he had stepped was optically invisible. He walks across the path and then scoops up some sand to toss back onto it, so that those following might see the way more clearly. He has passed the third challenge.

He approaches a table upon which more than a dozen ancient cups are sitting. Most are made of gold or silver. Which one is the Holy Grail? A knight holding a sword tells him that he must choose. He says, "Choose wisely. The true Grail will give you life. The false grail will take it from you." Those who drink from the wrong cup will find that the curse of the Genesis Fall will take place in seconds, rather than the lifetime it normally takes to age and then die.

Indiana ignores the golden cups, picks up a plain one and says, "The cup of a carpenter..." He sips from the cup, and lives. The knight smiles and says, "You have chosen wisely."

Although this captivating story is fiction, it echoes the gospel truth. There is only one way to approach God, and that is through bowing the knee. God resists the proud and gives grace to the humble (James 4:6). If you refuse to humble yourself before God, you will suffer swift and terrible consequences. These are not my thoughts; they are the clues, the pointers, the indications from the Book that says it is a lamp to our feet and a light to our path (Psa. 119:105).

The second clue was the name of God. The Book tells us that God has given Jesus a name that is above every other name. It warns, "There is no other name under heaven given among men, whereby we must be saved" (Acts 4:12). He is the way, the truth, and the life (John 14:6). It couldn't be clearer. The Bible spells it out for us—so be careful where you step.

Now you stand before the great chasm of eternity. You know that you have to humble yourself. You know the only name that can save you. Now you must take a step of faith to prepare for eternity, for without faith it is impossible to please God (Heb. 11:6). Are you fearful to take that step? You have no choice. Death could seize upon you before you finish reading this sentence... and then you will find yourself in eternity, standing guilty before a Holy God, without a Savior.

The Bible tells us that God has "hidden these things from the wise and prudent" (Matt. 11:25). What is hidden from your eyes at the moment will be revealed to you after you have humbled yourself and taken that step. I took it more than thirty years ago and it proved trustworthy. It is a narrow way, but one in which the Lord will uphold you with His hand. The Scriptures make the way apparent for you, so that you can see the path more clearly.

When that step is taken, you may drink from the Cup of Salvation. It isn't made with gold or silver. Nor is it the cold cup of a dead, rich, ritualistic religion. It is a lowly Carpenter's cup—the way of humility and faith, given by the One who said, "Blessed are those who... thirst for righteousness" (Matt. 5:6).

Being a Christian means identifying with something the world despises: righteousness. But the way of righteousness is the way to everlasting life (Prov. 12:28). There is no other way.

(Adapted from *What Hollywood Believes*.)

thanksgiving,
And will call upon the name of the
LORD.

[18]I will pay my vows to the LORD
Now in the presence of all His people,
[19]In the courts of the LORD's house,
In the midst of you, O Jerusalem.

Praise the LORD!

PSALM 117

Let All Peoples Praise the Lord

[1]Praise the LORD, all you Gentiles!
Laud Him, all you peoples!
[2]For His merciful kindness is great
toward us,
And the truth of the LORD *endures*
forever.

Praise the LORD!

PSALM 118

Praise to God for His Everlasting Mercy

[1]Oh, give thanks to the LORD, for *He is*
good!
For His mercy *endures* forever.

[2]Let Israel now say,
"His mercy *endures* forever."
[3]Let the house of Aaron now say,
"His mercy *endures* forever."
[4]Let those who fear the LORD now say,
"His mercy *endures* forever."

[5]I called on the LORD in distress;
The LORD answered me *and set me* in
a broad place.
[6]The LORD *is* on my side;
I will not fear.
What can man do to me?
[7]The LORD is for me among those who
help me;
Therefore I shall see *my desire* on
those who hate me.
[8]*It is* better to trust in the LORD
Than to put confidence in man.
[9]*It is* better to trust in the LORD
Than to put confidence in princes.

[10]All nations surrounded me,
But in the name of the LORD I will
destroy them.
[11]They surrounded me,
Yes, they surrounded me;
But in the name of the LORD I will
destroy them.
[12]They surrounded me like bees;
They were quenched like a fire of
thorns;
For in the name of the LORD I will
destroy them.
[13]You pushed me violently, that I might
fall,
But the LORD helped me.
[14]The LORD *is* my strength and song,
And He has become my salvation.[a]

[15]The voice of rejoicing and salvation
Is in the tents of the righteous;
The right hand of the LORD does
valiantly.
[16]The right hand of the LORD is exalted;
The right hand of the LORD does
valiantly.
[17]I shall not die, but live,
And declare the works of the LORD.
[18]The LORD has chastened me severely,
But He has not given me over to death.

[19]Open to me the gates of righteousness;
I will go through them,
And I will praise the LORD.
[20]This is the gate of the LORD,
Through which the righteous shall
enter.

118:14 [a]Compare Exodus 15:2

118:6 Remember that courage isn't the absence of fear, but the conquering of it. If we really care for the lost, each of us must learn to push aside fear and replace it with faith in God. You do your part, and God will do His.

21I will praise You,
For You have answered me,
And have become my salvation.

22The stone *which* the builders rejected
Has become the chief cornerstone.
23This was the LORD's doing;
It *is* marvelous in our eyes.
24This *is* the day the LORD has made;
We will rejoice and be glad in it.

25Save now, I pray, O LORD;
O LORD, I pray, send now prosperity.
26Blessed *is* he who comes in the name
of the LORD!
We have blessed you from the house
of the LORD.
27God *is* the LORD,
And He has given us light;
Bind the sacrifice with cords to the
horns of the altar.
28You *are* my God, and I will praise You;
You are my God, I will exalt You.

29Oh, give thanks to the LORD, for *He is*
good!
For His mercy *endures* forever.

PSALM 119
Meditations on the Excellencies of the Word of God

א ALEPH
1Blessed *are* the undefiled in the way,
Who walk in the law of the LORD!
2Blessed *are* those who keep His
testimonies,
Who seek Him with the whole heart!
3They also do no iniquity;
They walk in His ways.
4You have commanded *us*
To keep Your precepts diligently.
5Oh, that my ways were directed
To keep Your statutes!
6Then I would not be ashamed,
When I look into all Your
commandments.
7I will praise You with uprightness of
heart,
When I learn Your righteous
judgments.
8I will keep Your statutes;
Oh, do not forsake me utterly!

ב BETH
9How can a young man cleanse his way?
By taking heed according to Your word.
10With my whole heart I have sought
You;
Oh, let me not wander from Your
commandments!
11Your word I have hidden in my heart,
That I might not sin against You.
12Blessed *are* You, O LORD!
Teach me Your statutes.
13With my lips I have declared
All the judgments of Your mouth.
14I have rejoiced in the way of Your
testimonies,
As *much as* in all riches.
15I will meditate on Your precepts,
And contemplate Your ways.
16I will delight myself in Your statutes;
I will not forget Your word.

ג GIMEL
17Deal bountifully with Your servant,
That I may live and keep Your word.

118:22 This is a direct reference to the Messiah. See 1 Pet. 2:7,8.

118:27 We must "bind" our bodies as living sacrifices on the altar of service for God (see Rom. 12:1).

119:2 This wonderful psalm gives us insight into the rewards of meditating on God's Word. It reveals the great key to living a life of victory as a Christian. That key is to seek and serve Him with a "whole heart."

119:10 "Every man is as close to God as he wants to be; he is as holy and as full of the Spirit as he wills to be . . . Yet we must distinguish wanting from wishing. By 'want' I mean wholehearted desire. Certainly there are many who wish they were holy or victorious or joyful but are not willing to meet God's conditions to obtain." *A. W. Tozer*

119:14 "I believe the Bible is the best gift God has given to man. All the good Savior gave to the world was communicated through this Book." *Abraham Lincoln*

[18]Open my eyes, that I may see
Wondrous things from Your law.
[19]I *am* a stranger in the earth;
Do not hide Your commandments
from me.
[20]My soul breaks with longing
For Your judgments at all times.
[21]You rebuke the proud—the cursed,
Who stray from Your commandments.
[22]Remove from me reproach and
contempt,
For I have kept Your testimonies.
[23]Princes also sit *and* speak against me,
But Your servant meditates on Your
statutes.
[24]Your testimonies also *are* my delight
And my counselors.

ד DALETH

[25]My soul clings to the dust;
Revive me according to Your word.
[26]I have declared my ways, and You
answered me;
Teach me Your statutes.
[27]Make me understand the way of Your
precepts;
So shall I meditate on Your wonderful
works.
[28]My soul melts from heaviness;
Strengthen me according to Your word.
[29]Remove from me the way of lying,
And grant me Your law graciously.
[30]I have chosen the way of truth;
Your judgments I have laid *before me.*
[31]I cling to Your testimonies;
O LORD, do not put me to shame!
[32]I will run the course of Your
commandments,
For You shall enlarge my heart.

ה HE

[33]Teach me, O LORD, the way of Your
statutes,
And I shall keep it *to* the end.
[34]Give me understanding, and I shall
keep Your law;
Indeed, I shall observe it with *my*
whole heart.
[35]Make me walk in the path of Your
commandments,
For I delight in it.
[36]Incline my heart to Your testimonies,
And not to covetousness.
[37]Turn away my eyes from looking at
worthless things,
And revive me in Your way.[a]
[38]Establish Your word to Your servant,
Who *is devoted* to fearing You.
[39]Turn away my reproach which I dread,
For Your judgments *are* good.
[40]Behold, I long for Your precepts;
Revive me in Your righteousness.

> Where one man reads the Bible, a hundred read you and me.
>
> **DWIGHT L. MOODY**

ו WAW

[41]Let Your mercies come also to me, O
LORD—
Your salvation according to Your word.
[42]So shall I have an answer for him
who reproaches me,
For I trust in Your word.
[43]And take not the word of truth
utterly out of my mouth,
For I have hoped in Your ordinances.
[44]So shall I keep Your law continually,
Forever and ever.
[45]And I will walk at liberty,
For I seek Your precepts.
[46]I will speak of Your testimonies also
before kings,
And will not be ashamed.
[47]And I will delight myself in Your
commandments,
Which I love.

119:37 [a]Following Masoretic Text, Septuagint, and Vulgate; Targum reads *Your words.*

119:16 "God's Word is our primary weapon in evangelism. It is not designed to destroy life, but to give it. It is not to be used to harm but like a surgeon's scalpel, to save. Just as a builder knows his tools and an artist knows his brushes and pens, we need to know the Bible." *Greg Laurie*

[48]My hands also I will lift up to Your
commandments,
Which I love,
And I will meditate on Your statutes.

ז ZAYIN

[49]Remember the word to Your servant,
Upon which You have caused me to
hope.
[50]This *is* my comfort in my affliction,
For Your word has given me life.
[51]The proud have me in great derision,
Yet I do not turn aside from Your law.
[52]I remembered Your judgments of old,
O LORD,
And have comforted myself.
[53]Indignation has taken hold of me
Because of the wicked, who forsake
Your law.
[54]Your statutes have been my songs
In the house of my pilgrimage.
[55]I remember Your name in the night,
O LORD,
And I keep Your law.
[56]This has become mine,
Because I kept Your precepts.

ח HETH

[57]*You are* my portion, O LORD;
I have said that I would keep Your
words.
[58]I entreated Your favor with *my* whole
heart;
Be merciful to me according to Your
word.
[59]I thought about my ways,
And turned my feet to Your
testimonies.
[60]I made haste, and did not delay
To keep Your commandments.
[61]The cords of the wicked have bound
me,
But I have not forgotten Your law.
[62]At midnight I will rise to give thanks
to You,
Because of Your righteous judgments.
[63]I *am* a companion of all who fear You,
And of those who keep Your precepts.
[64]The earth, O LORD, is full of Your
mercy;
Teach me Your statutes.

ט TETH

[65]You have dealt well with Your servant,
O LORD, according to Your word.
[66]Teach me good judgment and
knowledge,
For I believe Your commandments.
[67]Before I was afflicted I went astray,
But now I keep Your word.
[68]You *are* good, and do good;
Teach me Your statutes.
[69]The proud have forged a lie against me,
But I will keep Your precepts with *my*
whole heart.
[70]Their heart is as fat as grease,
But I delight in Your law.
[71]*It is* good for me that I have been
afflicted,
That I may learn Your statutes.
[72]The law of Your mouth *is* better to me
Than thousands of *coins of* gold and
silver.

י YOD

[73]Your hands have made me and
fashioned me;
Give me understanding, that I may
learn Your commandments.
[74]Those who fear You will be glad
when they see me,
Because I have hoped in Your word.
[75]I know, O LORD, that Your judgments
are right,
And *that* in faithfulness You have
afflicted me.
[76]Let, I pray, Your merciful kindness be
for my comfort,
According to Your word to Your
servant.
[77]Let Your tender mercies come to me,
that I may live;
For Your law *is* my delight.
[78]Let the proud be ashamed,

119:72 "A thorough knowledge of the Bible is worth more than a college education." *Theodore Roosevelt*

For they treated me wrongfully with
falsehood;
But I will meditate on Your precepts.
79Let those who fear You turn to me,
Those who know Your testimonies.
80Let my heart be blameless regarding
Your statutes,
That I may not be ashamed.

כ KAPH

81My soul faints for Your salvation,
But I hope in Your word.
82My eyes fail *from searching* Your word,
Saying, "When will You comfort me?"
83For I have become like a wineskin in
smoke,
Yet I do not forget Your statutes.
84How many *are* the days of Your
servant?
When will You execute judgment on
those who persecute me?
85The proud have dug pits for me,
Which *is* not according to Your law.
86All Your commandments *are* faithful;
They persecute me wrongfully;
Help me!
87They almost made an end of me on
earth,
But I did not forsake Your precepts.
88Revive me according to Your
lovingkindness,
So that I may keep the testimony of
Your mouth.

ל LAMED

89Forever, O LORD,
Your word is settled in heaven.
90Your faithfulness *endures* to all
generations;
You established the earth, and it
abides.
91They continue this day according to
Your ordinances,
For all *are* Your servants.
92Unless Your law *had been* my delight,
I would then have perished in my

"Hold fast to the Bible as the sheet anchor of your liberties; write its precepts in your hearts, and practice them in your lives."

Ulysses S. Grant

affliction.
93I will never forget Your precepts,
For by them You have given me life.
94I *am* Yours, save me;
For I have sought Your precepts.
95The wicked wait for me to destroy me,
But I will consider Your testimonies.
96I have seen the consummation of all
perfection,
But Your commandment *is*
exceedingly broad.

מ MEM

97Oh, how I love Your law!
It *is* my meditation all the day.
98You, through Your commandments,
make me wiser than my enemies;
For they *are* ever with me.
99I have more understanding than all
my teachers,
For Your testimonies *are* my
meditation.
100I understand more than the ancients,

119:97 "If there is anything in my thoughts or style to commend, the credit is due to my parents for instilling in me an early love of the Scriptures." *Daniel Webster*

Because I keep Your precepts.
101I have restrained my feet from every
evil way,
That I may keep Your word.
102I have not departed from Your
judgments,
For You Yourself have taught me.
103How sweet are Your words to my taste,
Sweeter than honey to my mouth!
104Through Your precepts I get
understanding;
Therefore I hate every false way.

נ NUN

105Your word *is* a lamp to my feet
And a light to my path.
106I have sworn and confirmed
That I will keep Your righteous
judgments.
107I am afflicted very much;
Revive me, O LORD, according to Your
word.
108Accept, I pray, the freewill offerings
of my mouth, O LORD,
And teach me Your judgments.
109My life *is* continually in my hand,
Yet I do not forget Your law.
110The wicked have laid a snare for me,
Yet I have not strayed from Your
precepts.
111Your testimonies I have taken as a
heritage forever,
For they *are* the rejoicing of my heart.
112I have inclined my heart to perform
Your statutes
Forever, to the very end.

ס SAMEK

113I hate the double-minded,
But I love Your law.
114You *are* my hiding place and my shield;
I hope in Your word.
115Depart from me, you evildoers,
For I will keep the commandments of
my God!
116Uphold me according to Your word,
that I may live;
And do not let me be ashamed of my
hope.
117Hold me up, and I shall be safe,
And I shall observe Your statutes
continually.
118You reject all those who stray from
Your statutes,
For their deceit *is* falsehood.
119You put away all the wicked of the
earth *like* dross;
Therefore I love Your testimonies.
120My flesh trembles for fear of You,
And I am afraid of Your judgments.

ע AYIN

121I have done justice and
righteousness;
Do not leave me to my oppressors.
122Be surety for Your servant for good;
Do not let the proud oppress me.
123My eyes fail *from seeking* Your
salvation
And Your righteous word.
124Deal with Your servant according to
Your mercy,
And teach me Your statutes.
125I *am* Your servant;
Give me understanding,
That I may know Your testimonies.
126*It is* time for *You* to act, O LORD,
For they have regarded Your law as
void.
127Therefore I love Your commandments
More than gold, yes, than fine gold!
128Therefore all *Your* precepts *concerning*
all *things*
I consider *to be* right;
I hate every false way.

פ PE

129Your testimonies are wonderful;
Therefore my soul keeps them.
130The entrance of Your words gives light;

119:104 "But for this Book [the Bible], we could not know right from wrong…Take all you can of this Book upon reason, and the balance on faith, and you will live and die a happier man." *Abraham Lincoln*

119:128 This verse covers all of God's judgments over sinners—harsh though they may seem to our darkened minds.

119:105 *The Bible Stands Alone*

Compiled by Jordan and Justin Drake

In 1889 a schoolteacher told a ten-year-old boy, "You will never amount to very much." That boy was Albert Einstein. In 1954 a music manager told a young singer, "You ought to go back to driving a truck." That singer was Elvis Presley. In 1962 a record company told a group of singers, "We don't like your sound. Groups with guitars are definitely on their way out." They said that to the Beatles. Man is prone to make mistakes. Those who reject the Bible should take the time to look at the evidence before they come to a verdict.

1. It is unique in its continuity. If just 10 people today were picked who were from the same place, born around the same time, spoke the same language, and made about the same amount of money, and were asked to write on just one controversial subject, they would have trouble agreeing with each other. But the Bible stands alone. It was written over a period of 1,600 years by more than 40 writers from all walks of life. Some were fishermen; some were politicians. Others were generals or kings, shepherds or historians. They were from three different continents, and wrote in three different languages. They wrote on hundreds of controversial subjects yet they wrote with agreement and harmony. They wrote in dungeons, in temples, on beaches, and on hillsides, during peacetime and during war. Yet their words sound like they came from the same source. So even though 10 people today couldn't write on one controversial subject and agree, God picked 40 different people to write the Bible—and it stands the test of time.

2. It is unique in its circulation. The invention of the printing press in 1450 made it possible to print books in large quantities. The first book printed was the Bible. Since then, the Bible has been read by more people and printed more times than any other book in history. By 1930, over one billion Bibles had been distributed by Bible societies around the world. By 1977, Bible societies alone were printing over 200 million Bibles each year, and this doesn't include the rest of the Bible publishing companies. No one who is interested in knowing the truth can ignore such an important book.

3. It is unique in its translation. The Bible has been translated into over 2,400 languages. No other book even comes close.

4. It is unique in its survival. In ancient times, books were copied by hand onto manuscripts which were made from parchment and would decay over time. Ancient books are available today only because someone made copies of the originals to preserve them. For example, the original writings of Julius Caesar are no longer around. We know what he wrote only by the copies we have. Only 10 copies still exist, and they were made 1,000 years after he died. Only 600 copies of Homer's *The Iliad* exist, made 1,300 years after the originals were written. No other book has as many copies of the ancient manuscripts as the Bible. In fact, there are over 24,000 copies of New Testament manuscripts, some written within 35 years of the writer's death.

5. It is unique in withstanding attack. No other book has been so attacked throughout history as the Bible. In A.D. 300 the Roman emperor Diocletian ordered every Bible burned because he thought that by destroying the Scriptures he could destroy Christianity. Anyone caught with a Bible would be executed. But just 25 years later, the Roman emperor Constantine ordered that 50 perfect copies of the Bible be made at government expense. The French philosopher Voltaire, a skeptic who destroyed the faith of many people, boasted that within 100 years of his death, the Bible would disappear from the face of the earth. Voltaire died in 1728, but the Bible lives on.

The Bible has also survived criticism. No book has been more attacked for its accuracy. And yet archeologists are proving every year that the Bible's detailed descriptions of historic events are correct. See also Matt. 4:4 and 1 Pet. 1:25 comments.

It gives understanding to the simple.
131 I opened my mouth and panted,
For I longed for Your commandments.
132 Look upon me and be merciful to me,
As Your custom is toward those who
love Your name.
133 Direct my steps by Your word,
And let no iniquity have dominion
over me.
134 Redeem me from the oppression of
man,
That I may keep Your precepts.

[135]Make Your face shine upon Your
servant,
And teach me Your statutes.
[136]Rivers of water run down from my
eyes,
Because *men* do not keep Your law.

צ TSADDE
[137]Righteous *are* You, O LORD,
And upright *are* Your judgments.
[138]Your testimonies, *which* You have
commanded,
Are righteous and very faithful.
[139]My zeal has consumed me,
Because my enemies have forgotten
Your words.
[140]Your word *is* very pure;
Therefore Your servant loves it.
[141]I *am* small and despised,
Yet I do not forget Your precepts.
[142]Your righteousness *is* an everlasting
righteousness,
And Your law *is* truth.
[143]Trouble and anguish have overtaken
me,
Yet Your commandments *are* my
delights.
[144]The righteousness of Your
testimonies *is* everlasting;
Give me understanding, and I shall
live.

ק QOPH
[145]I cry out with *my* whole heart;
Hear me, O LORD!
I will keep Your statutes.
[146]I cry out to You;
Save me, and I will keep Your
testimonies.
[147]I rise before the dawning of the
morning,
And cry for help;
I hope in Your word.
[148]My eyes are awake through the *night*
watches,
That I may meditate on Your word.
[149]Hear my voice according to Your
lovingkindness;
O LORD, revive me according to Your
justice.
[150]They draw near who follow after
wickedness;
They are far from Your law.
[151]You *are* near, O LORD,
And all Your commandments *are* truth.
[152]Concerning Your testimonies,
I have known of old that You have
founded them forever.

ר RESH
[153]Consider my affliction and deliver me,
For I do not forget Your law.
[154]Plead my cause and redeem me;
Revive me according to Your word.
[155]Salvation *is* far from the wicked,
For they do not seek Your statutes.
[156]Great *are* Your tender mercies, O
LORD;
Revive me according to Your
judgments.
[157]Many *are* my persecutors and my
enemies,
Yet I do not turn from Your
testimonies.
[158]I see the treacherous, and am disgusted,
Because they do not keep Your word.
[159]Consider how I love Your precepts;
Revive me, O LORD, according to Your
lovingkindness.
[160]The entirety of Your word *is* truth,

119:133 Sin may beset the Christian, but those whose steps are in God's Word prevent sin from having dominion over them. See Rom. 6:12–18. See also Gal. 5:16 comment.

119:136 "And you, too, who are moral enough in your conversation, and regular in your attendance on the outward forms of religion, you who never weep over sinners, you who never pray for them, you who never speak to them, you who leave all that to your minister, and think you have nothing to do with it, the voice of your brother's blood crieth from the ground to heaven." *Charles Spurgeon*

119:139 "A zealous man feels that, like a lamp, he is made to burn; and if consumed in burning, he has but done the work for which God appointed him. Such a one will always find a sphere for his zeal. If he cannot preach and work and give money, he will cry and sigh and pray." *J. C. Ryle*

QUESTIONS & OBJECTIONS

119:160

"The Bible has changed down through the ages."

No, it hasn't. God has preserved His Word. In the spring of 1947, the Dead Sea Scrolls were discovered. These manuscripts were copies of large portions of the Old Testament, a thousand years older than any other existing copies. Study of the scrolls has revealed that the Bible hasn't changed in content down through the ages as many skeptics had surmised. (See 1 Pet. 1:25 comment.)

Anyone can now obtain access to computer programs that give the original Hebrew and Greek words, and can see that the only "changes" have been made for clarity. For example, the old English translation of 2 Cor. 12:8 is "For this thing I besought the Lord thrice...," while a contemporary translation is "Concerning this thing I pleaded with the Lord three times..."

And every one of Your righteous
judgments *endures* forever.

ש SHIN

161 Princes persecute me without a cause,
But my heart stands in awe of Your
word.
162 I rejoice at Your word
As one who finds great treasure.
163 I hate and abhor lying,
But I love Your law.
164 Seven times a day I praise You,
Because of Your righteous judgments.
165 Great peace have those who love
Your law,
And nothing causes them to stumble.
166 LORD, I hope for Your salvation,
And I do Your commandments.
167 My soul keeps Your testimonies,
And I love them exceedingly.
168 I keep Your precepts and Your
testimonies,
For all my ways *are* before You.

ת TAU

169 Let my cry come before You, O LORD;
Give me understanding according to
Your word.
170 Let my supplication come before You;
Deliver me according to Your word.
171 My lips shall utter praise,
For You teach me Your statutes.
172 My tongue shall speak of Your word,
For all Your commandments *are*
righteousness.
173 Let Your hand become my help,
For I have chosen Your precepts.
174 I long for Your salvation, O LORD,
And Your law *is* my delight.
175 Let my soul live, and it shall praise You;
And let Your judgments help me.
176 I have gone astray like a lost sheep;
Seek Your servant,
For I do not forget Your
commandments.

. . . . . .

Read a challenging letter from an atheist. See Rom. 9:2,3 comment.

. . . . . .

PSALM 120

Plea for Relief from Bitter Foes

A Song of Ascents.

1 In my distress I cried to the LORD,
And He heard me.
2 Deliver my soul, O LORD, from lying
lips
And from a deceitful tongue.

3 What shall be given to you,
Or what shall be done to you,
You false tongue?
4 Sharp arrows of the warrior,
With coals of the broom tree!

5 Woe is me, that I dwell in Meshech,
That I dwell among the tents of Kedar!
6 My soul has dwelt too long
With one who hates peace.
7 I *am for* peace;
But when I speak, they *are* for war.

SPRINGBOARDS FOR PREACHING AND WITNESSING

The Bible and All It Contains

119:162 A young man once received a letter from a lawyer stating that his grandmother had left him an inheritance. To his astonishment, it was $100,000 plus "my Bible and all it contains."

The youth was delighted to receive the money. However, he knew what the Bible contained, and because he wasn't into religion he didn't bother to open it. Instead, he put it on a high shelf.

He gambled the $100,000, and over the next fifty years he lived as a pauper, scraping for every meal. Finally he became so destitute, he had to move in with his relatives.

When he cleaned out his room, he reached up to get the dusty old Bible from the shelf. As he took it down, his trembling hands dropped it onto the floor, flinging it open to reveal a $100 bill between every page.

The man had lived as a pauper, simply because of his prejudice. He thought he knew what the Bible "contained."

PSALM 121

God the Help of Those Who Seek Him

A Song of Ascents.

1I will lift up my eyes to the hills—
From whence comes my help?
2My help *comes* from the LORD,
Who made heaven and earth.

3He will not allow your foot to be moved;
He who keeps you will not slumber.
4Behold, He who keeps Israel
Shall neither slumber nor sleep.

5The LORD *is* your keeper;
The LORD is your shade at your right hand.
6The sun shall not strike you by day,
Nor the moon by night.

7The LORD shall preserve you from all evil;
He shall preserve your soul.
8The LORD shall preserve your going out and your coming in
From this time forth, and even forevermore.

PSALM 122

The Joy of Going to the House of the Lord

A Song of Ascents. Of David.

1I was glad when they said to me,
"Let us go into the house of the LORD."
2Our feet have been standing
Within your gates, O Jerusalem!

3Jerusalem is built
As a city that is compact together,
4Where the tribes go up,
The tribes of the LORD,
To the Testimony of Israel,
To give thanks to the name of the LORD.
5For thrones are set there for judgment,
The thrones of the house of David.

6Pray for the peace of Jerusalem:
"May they prosper who love you.
7Peace be within your walls,
Prosperity within your palaces."
8For the sake of my brethren and companions,
I will now say, "Peace *be* within you."
9Because of the house of the LORD our God
I will seek your good.

PSALM 123

Prayer for Relief from Contempt

A Song of Ascents.

1Unto You I lift up my eyes,
O You who dwell in the heavens.
2Behold, as the eyes of servants *look* to the hand of their masters,
As the eyes of a maid to the hand of her mistress,
So our eyes *look* to the LORD our God,
Until He has mercy on us.

QUESTIONS & OBJECTIONS

"Atheists do not claim that nothing created everything."

Many atheists refuse to admit they believe the entire universe came into being from nothing, because it is a scientific impossibility and they recognize how silly it sounds. If everything didn't come from nothing, their alternative is to say that creation (nature) created itself. However, a thing cannot make itself. To do so would mean that it had to pre-exist before it existed, and therefore it didn't create itself because it was already in existence. (For where the universe came from, see Isa. 34:4 and Isa. 45:18 comments.) Here are some who have admitted to believing that nothing created everything:

1. "It is now becoming clear that everything can—and probably did—come from nothing." —Robert A. J. Matthews, physicist, Ashton University, England
2. "Space and time both started at the Big Bang and therefore there was nothing before it." —Cornell University's "Ask an Astronomer"
3. "Some physicists believe our universe was created by colliding with another, but Kaku [a theoretical physicist at City University of New York] says it also may have sprung from nothing..." —Scienceline.org
4. "Even if we don't have a precise idea of exactly what took place at the beginning, we can at least see that the origin of the universe from nothing need not be unlawful or unnatural or unscientific." —Paul Davies, physicist, Arizona State University
5. "Assuming the universe came from nothing, it is empty to begin with...Only by the constant action of an agent outside the universe, such as God, could a state of nothingness be maintained. The fact that we have something is just what we would expect if there is no God." —Victor J. Stenger, Prof. Physics, University of Hawaii; author of *God: The Failed Hypothesis*
6. "Few people are aware of the fact that many modern physicists claim that things—perhaps even the entire universe—can indeed arise from nothing via natural processes." —Mark I. Vuletic, *Creation Ex Nihilo—Without God*
7. "To understand these facts we have to turn to science. Where did they all come from, and how did they get so darned outrageous? Well, it all started with nothing." —"Fifty Outrageous Animal Facts," Animal Planet
8. "To the average person it might seem obvious that nothing can happen in nothing. But to a quantum physicist, nothing is, in fact, something." —*Discover Magazine,* "Physics & Math/Cosmology"
9. "It is rather fantastic to realize that the laws of physics can describe how everything was created in a random quantum fluctuation out of nothing, and how over the course of 15 billion years, matter could organize in such complex ways that we have human beings sitting here, talking, doing things intentionally." —Alan Harvey Guth, theoretical physicist and cosmologist, *Discover Magazine*
10. "The fact that life evolved out of nearly nothing, some 10 billion years after the universe evolved out of literally nothing is a fact so staggering that I would be mad to attempt words to do it justice." —Richard Dawkins, *The Ancestor's Tale*

3 Have mercy on us, O LORD, have
mercy on us!
For we are exceedingly filled with
contempt.
4 Our soul is exceedingly filled
With the scorn of those who are at ease,
With the contempt of the proud.

PSALM 124

The Lord the Defense of His People

A Song of Ascents. Of David.

1 "If it had not been the LORD who was
on our side,"
Let Israel now say—
2 "If it had not been the LORD who was
on our side,
When men rose up against us,
3 Then they would have swallowed us
alive,
When their wrath was kindled against
us;
4 Then the waters would have
overwhelmed us,
The stream would have gone over our
soul;
5 Then the swollen waters
Would have gone over our soul."

[6]Blessed *be* the LORD,
Who has not given us *as* prey to their teeth.
[7]Our soul has escaped as a bird from the snare of the fowlers;[a]
The snare is broken, and we have escaped.
[8]Our help *is* in the name of the LORD,
Who made heaven and earth.

PSALM 125

The Lord the Strength of His People

A Song of Ascents.

[1]Those who trust in the LORD
Are like Mount Zion,
Which cannot be moved, *but* abides forever.
[2]As the mountains surround Jerusalem,
So the LORD surrounds His people
From this time forth and forever.

[3]For the scepter of wickedness shall not rest
On the land allotted to the righteous,
Lest the righteous reach out their hands to iniquity.

[4]Do good, O LORD, to *those who are* good,
And to *those who are* upright in their hearts.

[5]As for such as turn aside to their crooked ways,
The LORD shall lead them away
With the workers of iniquity.

Peace *be* upon Israel!

PSALM 126

A Joyful Return to Zion

A Song of Ascents.

[1]When the LORD brought back the captivity of Zion,
We were like those who dream.
[2]Then our mouth was filled with laughter,
And our tongue with singing.
Then they said among the nations,
"The LORD has done great things for them."
[3]The LORD has done great things for us,
And we are glad.

[4]Bring back our captivity, O LORD,
As the streams in the South.

[5]Those who sow in tears
Shall reap in joy.
[6]He who continually goes forth weeping,
Bearing seed for sowing,
Shall doubtless come again with rejoicing,
Bringing his sheaves *with him.*

PSALM 127

Laboring and Prospering with the Lord

A Song of Ascents. Of Solomon.

[1]Unless the LORD builds the house,
They labor in vain who build it;
Unless the LORD guards the city,
The watchman stays awake in vain.
[2]*It is* vain for you to rise up early,
To sit up late,

124:7 [a]That is, persons who catch birds in a trap or snare

125:1 If we are "moved" by adversity, it is because we lack trust in the Lord. The amount of joy we retain in tribulation reveals the depth of our trust in God. The apostle Paul said, "I am exceedingly joyful in all our tribulation" (2 Cor. 7:4).

126:6 Sowing in tears. "But from whence shall I fetch my argument? With what shall I win them? Oh, that I could tell! I would write to them in tears, I would weep out every argument, I would empty my veins for ink, I would petition them on my knees. Oh how thankful I would be if they would be prevailed with to repent and turn!" *Joseph Alleine*

"Jesus Christ wept over Jerusalem, and you will have to weep over sinners if they are to be saved through you." *Charles Spurgeon*

127:3 *What God's Word Says About Abortion*

By Lynn Copeland

God speaks very clearly in the Bible on the value of unborn children.

God's Word says that He personally made each one of us, and has a plan for each life: "Before I formed you in the womb I knew you, before you were born I set you apart" (Jer. 1:5). "Even before I was born, God had chosen me to be His" (Gal. 1:15). "For You created my inmost being; You knit me together in my mother's womb... Your eyes saw my unformed body. All the days ordained for me were written in Your book before one of them came to be" (Psa. 139:13,16). "Your hands shaped me and made me... Did You not clothe me with skin and flesh and knit me together with bones and sinews? You gave me life" (Job 10:8–12). "This is what the Lord says—He who made you, who formed you in the womb" (Isa. 44:2). "Did not He who made me in the womb make them? Did not the same One form us both within our mothers?" (Job 31:15).

Because man is made in God's own image (Gen. 1:27), each life is of great value to God: "Children are a gift from God" (Psa. 127:3). He even calls our children His own: "You took *your* sons and daughters whom you bore to Me and sacrificed them... You slaughtered *My* children" (Ezek. 16:20,21).

The Bible says of our Creator, "In His hand is the life of every living thing and the breath of every human being" (Job 12:10). God, the giver of life, commands us not to take the life of an innocent person: "Do not shed innocent blood" (Jer. 7:6); "Cursed is the man who accepts a bribe to kill an innocent person" (Deut. 27:25). "You shall not murder" (Exod. 20:13).

Taking the life of the unborn is clearly murder —"He didn't *kill* me in the womb, with my mother as my grave" (Jer. 20:17)—and God vowed to punish those who "ripped open the women with child" (Amos 1:13). The unborn child was granted equal protection in the law; if he lost his life, the one who caused his death must lose his own life: "If men who are fighting hit a pregnant woman and she gives birth prematurely but there is no serious injury, the offender must be fined... But if there is serious injury, you are to take life for life" (Exod. 21:22,23).

Life is a gift created by God, and is not to be taken away by abortion. God is "pro-choice," but He tells us clearly the only acceptable choice to make:

"I have set before you life and death, blessings and curses. Now choose life, so that you and your children may live" (Deut. 30:19).

To eat the bread of sorrows;
For so He gives His beloved sleep.

3 Behold, children *are* a heritage from
the LORD,
The fruit of the womb *is* a reward.
4 Like arrows in the hand of a warrior,
So *are* the children of one's youth.
5 Happy *is* the man who has his quiver
full of them;
They shall not be ashamed,
But shall speak with their enemies in
the gate.

PSALM 128

Blessings of Those Who Fear the Lord

A Song of Ascents.

1 Blessed *is* every one who fears the LORD,
Who walks in His ways.

2 When you eat the labor of your hands,
You *shall be* happy, and *it shall be* well
with you.
3 Your wife *shall be* like a fruitful vine
In the very heart of your house,
Your children like olive plants
All around your table.
4 Behold, thus shall the man be blessed
Who fears the LORD.

5 The LORD bless you out of Zion,
And may you see the good of Jerusalem
All the days of your life.
6 Yes, may you see your children's
children.

Peace *be* upon Israel!

PSALM 129

Song of Victory over Zion's Enemies

A Song of Ascents.

1 "Many a time they have afflicted me

from my youth,"
Let Israel now say—
2"Many a time they have afflicted me
from my youth;
Yet they have not prevailed against me.
3The plowers plowed on my back;
They made their furrows long."
4The LORD *is* righteous;
He has cut in pieces the cords of the
wicked.

5Let all those who hate Zion
Be put to shame and turned back.
6Let them be as the grass *on* the
housetops,
Which withers before it grows up,
7With which the reaper does not fill
his hand,
Nor he who binds sheaves, his arms.
8Neither let those who pass by them
say,
"The blessing of the LORD *be* upon you;
We bless you in the name of the LORD!"

PSALM 130

Waiting for the Redemption of the Lord

A Song of Ascents.

1Out of the depths I have cried to You,
O LORD;
2Lord, hear my voice!
Let Your ears be attentive
To the voice of my supplications.

3If You, LORD, should mark iniquities,
O Lord, who could stand?
4But *there is* forgiveness with You,
That You may be feared.

5I wait for the LORD, my soul waits,
And in His word I do hope.
6My soul *waits* for the Lord
More than those who watch for the
morning—
Yes, more than those who watch for
the morning.

7O Israel, hope in the LORD;
For with the LORD *there is* mercy,
And with Him *is* abundant
redemption.
8And He shall redeem Israel
From all his iniquities.

PSALM 131

Simple Trust in the Lord

A Song of Ascents. Of David.

1LORD, my heart is not haughty,
Nor my eyes lofty.
Neither do I concern myself with
great matters,
Nor with things too profound for me.

2Surely I have calmed and quieted my
soul,
Like a weaned child with his mother;
Like a weaned child *is* my soul within
me.

3O Israel, hope in the LORD
From this time forth and forever.

PSALM 132

The Eternal Dwelling of God in Zion

A Song of Ascents.

1LORD, remember David
And all his afflictions;
2How he swore to the LORD,
And vowed to the Mighty One of Jacob:
3"Surely I will not go into the chamber
of my house,
Or go up to the comfort of my bed;
4I will not give sleep to my eyes

130:1–4 Here is true contrition—a humble cry to God for mercy. Those who obtain the mercy of the cross and see the cost of redemption live their lives in the fear of the Lord, knowing that they were not redeemed with silver and gold, but with the precious blood of Christ. See 1 Pet. 1:17–19.

131:1 Beware of "intellectual Christianity." It is easy to become puffed up with a theology that forgets "the simplicity that is in Christ" (2 Cor. 11:3). The quality of our Christian theology will be evidenced by the depth of our concern for the lost.

Or slumber to my eyelids,
5Until I find a place for the LORD,
A dwelling place for the Mighty One of Jacob."

6Behold, we heard of it in Ephrathah;
We found it in the fields of the woods.[a]
7Let us go into His tabernacle;
Let us worship at His footstool.
8Arise, O LORD, to Your resting place,
You and the ark of Your strength.
9Let Your priests be clothed with righteousness,
And let Your saints shout for joy.

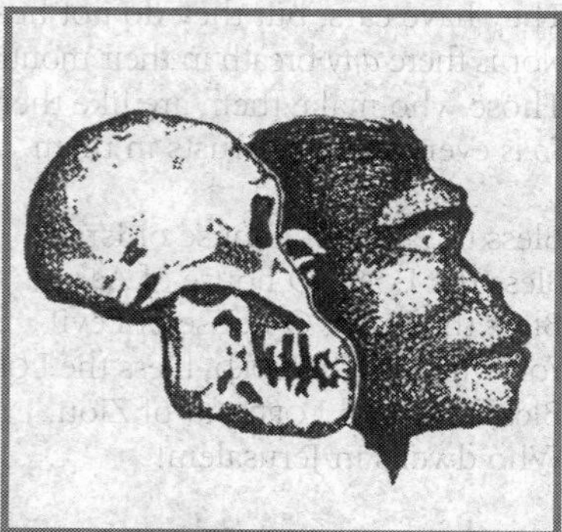

To see how the theory of evolution clashes with the facts, see Acts 14:15 comment.

10For Your servant David's sake,
Do not turn away the face of Your Anointed.

11The LORD has sworn *in* truth to David;
He will not turn from it:
"I will set upon your throne the fruit of your body.
12If your sons will keep My covenant
And My testimony which I shall teach them,
Their sons also shall sit upon your throne forevermore."

13For the LORD has chosen Zion;
He has desired *it* for His dwelling place:
14"This *is* My resting place forever;
Here I will dwell, for I have desired it.
15I will abundantly bless her provision;
I will satisfy her poor with bread.
16I will also clothe her priests with salvation,
And her saints shall shout aloud for joy.
17There I will make the horn of David grow;
I will prepare a lamp for My Anointed.
18His enemies I will clothe with shame,
But upon Himself His crown shall flourish."

PSALM 133

Blessed Unity of the People of God

A Song of Ascents. Of David.

1Behold, how good and how pleasant *it is*
For brethren to dwell together in unity!

2*It is* like the precious oil upon the head,
Running down on the beard,
The beard of Aaron,

Running down on the edge of his garments.
3*It is* like the dew of Hermon,
Descending upon the mountains of Zion;
For there the LORD commanded the blessing—
Life forevermore.

PSALM 134

Praising the Lord in His House at Night

A Song of Ascents.

1Behold, bless the LORD,
All *you* servants of the LORD,
Who by night stand in the house of the LORD!
2Lift up your hands *in* the sanctuary,
And bless the LORD.
3The LORD who made heaven and earth
Bless you from Zion!

132:6 [a]Hebrew *Jaar*

PSALM 135

Praise to God in Creation and Redemption

1Praise the LORD!

Praise the name of the LORD;
Praise *Him,* O you servants of the
LORD!
2You who stand in the house of the
LORD,
In the courts of the house of our God,
3Praise the LORD, for the LORD *is* good;
Sing praises to His name, for *it is*
pleasant.
4For the LORD has chosen Jacob for
Himself,
Israel for His special treasure.

5For I know that the LORD *is* great,
And our Lord *is* above all gods.
6Whatever the LORD pleases He does,
In heaven and in earth,
In the seas and in all deep places.
7He causes the vapors to ascend from
the ends of the earth;
He makes lightning for the rain;
He brings the wind out of His
treasuries.

8He destroyed the firstborn of Egypt,
Both of man and beast.
9He sent signs and wonders into the
midst of you, O Egypt,
Upon Pharaoh and all his servants.
10He defeated many nations
And slew mighty kings—
11Sihon king of the Amorites,
Og king of Bashan,
And all the kingdoms of Canaan—
12And gave their land *as* a heritage,
A heritage to Israel His people.

13Your name, O LORD, *endures* forever,
Your fame, O LORD, throughout all
generations.
14For the LORD will judge His people,
And He will have compassion on His
servants.

15The idols of the nations *are* silver and
gold,
The work of men's hands.
16They have mouths, but they do not
speak;
Eyes they have, but they do not see;
17They have ears, but they do not hear;
Nor is there *any* breath in their mouths.
18Those who make them are like them;
So is everyone who trusts in them.

19Bless the LORD, O house of Israel!
Bless the LORD, O house of Aaron!
20Bless the LORD, O house of Levi!
You who fear the LORD, bless the LORD!
21Blessed be the LORD out of Zion,
Who dwells in Jerusalem!

Praise the LORD!

PSALM 136

Thanksgiving to God for His Enduring Mercy

1Oh, give thanks to the LORD, for *He is*
good!
For His mercy *endures* forever.
2Oh, give thanks to the God of gods!
For His mercy *endures* forever.
3Oh, give thanks to the Lord of lords!

135:7 Scientific facts in the Bible. The Scriptures inform us, "All the rivers run into the sea, yet the sea is not full; to the place from which the rivers come, there they return again" (Eccles. 1:7). This statement alone may not seem profound. But, when considered with other biblical passages, it becomes all the more remarkable. For example, the Mississippi River dumps approximately 6 million gallons of water per second into the Gulf of Mexico. Where does all that water go? And that's just one of thousands of rivers.

The answer lies in the hydrologic cycle, so well brought out in the Bible. Ecclesiastes 11:3 states that "if the clouds are full of rain, they empty themselves upon the earth." Amos 9:6 tells us, "He . . . calls for the waters of the sea, and pours them out on the face of the earth." The idea of a complete water cycle was not fully understood until the seventeenth century. However, more than 2,000 years prior to the discoveries of Pierre Perrault, Edme Mariotte, Edmund Halley, and others, the Scriptures clearly spoke of a water cycle.

QUESTIONS & OBJECTIONS

"If the earth is not millions of years old, how can we see stars millions of light-years away?"

Since God made the sun, moon, and stars "to give light on the earth" (Gen. 1:14–18), those lights would be immediately visible on earth. They fulfilled their purpose on the day God spoke them into being, because He "saw that it was good." No doubt God also made Adam as a fully-grown man—perhaps with the appearance of being 30 years old, even though he was only minutes old. Likewise, herbs and trees were already mature and fruit-bearing, to provide a ready supply of food. That would be the case with all of His creation.

"We should also remember that God is not limited to natural methods as we are. Ironically, the leading secular alternative to the Bible (the big bang) has a light-travel time problem of its own. Known as the 'horizon problem,' the big bang is unable to get light from one side of the universe to the other within its own billions-of-years timeframe. Yet such transport is necessary within the big bang model in order to cause the uniform heat that we find today in the universe's cosmic microwave background. To alleviate this problem, big bang supporters must arbitrarily add another hypothesis like 'inflation' (which has problems of its own)." *Dr. Jason Lisle, Answers in Genesis*

For His mercy *endures* forever:

4 To Him who alone does great wonders,
For His mercy *endures* forever;
5 To Him who by wisdom made the heavens,
For His mercy *endures* forever;
6 To Him who laid out the earth above the waters,
For His mercy *endures* forever;
7 To Him who made great lights,
For His mercy *endures* forever—
8 The sun to rule by day,
For His mercy *endures* forever;
9 The moon and stars to rule by night,
For His mercy *endures* forever.

10 To Him who struck Egypt in their firstborn,
For His mercy *endures* forever;
11 And brought out Israel from among them,
For His mercy *endures* forever;
12 With a strong hand, and with an outstretched arm,
For His mercy *endures* forever;
13 To Him who divided the Red Sea in two,
For His mercy *endures* forever;
14 And made Israel pass through the midst of it,
For His mercy *endures* forever;
15 But overthrew Pharaoh and his army in the Red Sea,
For His mercy *endures* forever;
16 To Him who led His people through the wilderness,
For His mercy *endures* forever;
17 To Him who struck down great kings,
For His mercy *endures* forever;

136:4–6 Worshiping a faithful Creator. We should pray, "Open my eyes that I might continually see the genius of Your mind displayed in creation." If we could walk in such a spirit of illumination, we would walk around awestruck! We would continually worship God. We would be filled with such faith, we would see no problem too great for our God. As the revelation of His greatness astounds us, we would say, "Ah, Lord GOD! Behold, You have made the heavens and the earth by Your great power and outstretched arm. There is nothing too hard for You" (Jer. 32:17).

Such knowledge of His power and ability would cause us to have faith that produces joy, even at the edge of the Red Sea, even in the lion's *mouth*. We can look at the world with all its problems, sins, and pains, and know that with one small breath of Almighty God's Spirit, our nation can be saved. If the mere tip of the finger of God is for us, nothing can be against us.

18And slew famous kings,
For His mercy *endures* forever—
19Sihon king of the Amorites,
For His mercy *endures* forever;
20And Og king of Bashan,
For His mercy *endures* forever—
21And gave their land as a heritage,
For His mercy *endures* forever;
22A heritage to Israel His servant,
For His mercy *endures* forever.

23Who remembered us in our lowly state,
For His mercy *endures* forever;
24And rescued us from our enemies,
For His mercy *endures* forever;
25Who gives food to all flesh,
For His mercy *endures* forever.

26Oh, give thanks to the God of heaven!
For His mercy *endures* forever.

PSALM 137

Longing for Zion in a Foreign Land

1By the rivers of Babylon,
There we sat down, yea, we wept
When we remembered Zion.
2We hung our harps
Upon the willows in the midst of it.
3For there those who carried us away captive asked of us a song,
And those who plundered us *requested* mirth,
Saying, "Sing us *one* of the songs of Zion!"

4How shall we sing the LORD's song
In a foreign land?
5If I forget you, O Jerusalem,
Let my right hand forget *its skill!*
6If I do not remember you,
Let my tongue cling to the roof of my mouth—
If I do not exalt Jerusalem
Above my chief joy.

7Remember, O LORD, against the sons of Edom
The day of Jerusalem,
Who said, "Raze *it*, raze *it*,
To its very foundation!"

8O daughter of Babylon, who are to be destroyed,
Happy the one who repays you as you have served us!
9Happy the one who takes and dashes
Your little ones against the rock!

PSALM 138

The Lord's Goodness to the Faithful

A Psalm of David.

1I will praise You with my whole heart;
Before the gods I will sing praises to You.
2I will worship toward Your holy temple,
And praise Your name
For Your lovingkindness and Your truth;
For You have magnified Your word above all Your name.

There is no doctrine which I would more willingly remove from Christianity than the doctrine of hell, if it lay in my power. But it has the full support of Scripture and, especially, of our Lord's own words; it has always been held by the Christian Church, and it has the support of reason.

C. S. LEWIS

3In the day when I cried out, You answered me,
And made me bold *with* strength in my soul.

4All the kings of the earth shall praise You, O LORD,
When they hear the words of Your mouth.
5Yes, they shall sing of the ways of the LORD,
For great *is* the glory of the LORD.
6Though the LORD *is* on high,
Yet He regards the lowly;
But the proud He knows from afar.

QUESTIONS & OBJECTIONS

139:7,8 ***"If hell is just 'separation from God,' it's no big deal. According to Christians we're in that state now."***

This perceptive atheist has identified a problem with this popular but unbiblical phrase. Modern preachers often tell a sinner that if he dies without Christ's forgiveness he will be "separated from God" forever. It's what I call a "fear of man cliché"—it's a substitute for the uncomfortable topic of hell. There are a number of other unbiblical phrases the modern church has invented that fall in the same category, such as a "Christless eternity" and a "lost eternity." But since the godless don't want God in this life, how is the threat of being without Him in the next life going to awaken them? Modern preachers have fed the sinner the lie that there is an alternative to hell, when there is not. It is not easy to say, but if a sinner dies in his sins, he doesn't go to a "Christless eternity," but to a place of conscious torment called "hell." Death is a mere down payment for his sins; hell is his full wages.

So don't be guilty of failing to preach "the whole counsel of God" (see Acts 20:26,27) and warning the lost of what awaits them on Judgment Day. They will not be able to get away from the God they so despise. Our God fills the heavens and the earth, and there is nowhere we can go that is outside His presence. He presides even over hell (see Psa. 139:7,8; Jer. 23:24; Rev. 14:10). See also Rev. 1:18 and Rev. 20:14 comments.

7 Though I walk in the midst of
trouble, You will revive me;
You will stretch out Your hand
Against the wrath of my enemies,
And Your right hand will save me.
8 The LORD will perfect *that which*
concerns me;
Your mercy, O LORD, *endures* forever;
Do not forsake the works of Your
hands.

PSALM 139

God's Perfect Knowledge of Man

For the Chief Musician. A Psalm of David.

1 O LORD, You have searched me and
known *me.*
2 You know my sitting down and my
rising up;
You understand my thought afar off.
3 You comprehend my path and my
lying down,
And are acquainted with all my ways.
4 For *there is* not a word on my tongue,
But behold, O LORD, You know it
altogether.
5 You have hedged me behind and
before,
And laid Your hand upon me.
6 *Such* knowledge *is* too wonderful for
me;
It is high, I cannot *attain* it.

7 Where can I go from Your Spirit?
Or where can I flee from Your presence?
8 If I ascend into heaven, You *are* there;
If I make my bed in hell, behold, You
are there.
9 *If* I take the wings of the morning,
And dwell in the uttermost parts of
the sea,
10 Even there Your hand shall lead me,
And Your right hand shall hold me.
11 If I say, "Surely the darkness shall fall[a]

139:11 [a]Vulgate and Symmachus read *cover.*

139:2 God's presence. The ungodly are unaware of the immediate presence of a holy Creator. They think that God somehow becomes present when we bow our head in prayer or walk reverently into a lofty cathedral. In truth, our Creator is ever-present. He knows when we sit down and when we stand up (vv. 2–12). He searches our heart and sees our innermost thoughts. He knows every detail of our lives, including every whispered word.

The knowledge that a holy God sees every thought and deed is disconcerting to the guilty, but wonderfully comforting to the forgiven and saved soul (see v. 17). It is with this understanding that we should regularly cry with the psalmist, "Search me, O God, and know my heart; try me, and know my anxieties; and see if there is any wicked way in me, and lead me in the way everlasting" (vv. 23,24).

139:14 *Fearfully and Wonderfully Made*

Do you realize that you sneeze at 120 miles per hour? Did you also know that every time you sneeze, you have been programmed to close your eyes? Where does your hair grow from? How can the thin layer of skin on your head send out a special hair, different from that which grows on the arm, or on the eyelids or eyebrows? Imagine if you had eyebrows or eyelashes that grew to the length of the hair on your head.

Have you ever studied the ordinary garden snail and wondered how its shell is able to grow in proportion to its body? A baby snail has a baby shell. As it doubles in size, it doesn't discard it; the hard shell also doubles in size. Does the snail have a mind brilliant enough to make its own shell?

How does a grubby little caterpillar lose all its legs while inside a cocoon, grow two fresh ones, then form itself into a beautiful butterfly? Consider your fingernails: where did they grow from, and what makes their substance? Notice how your hands hold a book, with the fingers cradling it and the thumbs holding the pages. Both thumbs bend forward, or you couldn't hold the book. Hands have been designed to grip and feel.

How is it that your lungs keep breathing irrespective of your will? You have been doing it without a second thought while looking at your thumbs. In fact, becoming conscious of it can hinder the process. Lungs seem to work best without any conscious thought from the mind. How does your subconscious mind continually feed you with thoughts, even while you sleep? It talks to you and keeps you company, and it never stops. Try to stop it yourself. Close your eyes and think of nothing for five minutes. You can't. Your mind has been set in motion, and it has little to do with your will.

Think of the complexities of the human mind. It is feeding your understanding with knowledge right now by translating ink shapes on these pages, speaking them to your mind, and automatically filing them into your memory bank.

At this moment, your liver, kidneys, heart, pancreas, salivary glands, etc., are all working to keep your body going. You don't even have the power to switch them off and on. As you sleep tonight, your heart will pump seventy-five gallons of blood through your body each hour.

Your lungs are designed to filter oxygen from the air you breathe. These organs contain 300 billion tiny blood vessels called capillaries. Your entire blood supply washes through your lungs once every minute. In your lifetime, the marrow in your bones will create approximately half a ton of red corpuscles.

The focusing muscles in your eyes move an estimated 100,000 times each day. The retina, covering less than a square inch, contains 137 million light-sensitive cells. Even a wide-eyed *Charles Darwin* said, "To suppose that the eye could have been formed by natural selection, seems I freely confess, absurd in the highest degree."

Your brain contains 10 billion neurons, microscopic nerve cells. Your stomach, which produces four pints of gastric juice each day, has 35 million glands lining it. The next time you enjoy a delicious meal, be thankful to God for the 8,000 taste buds that He put into your mouth. Imagine how boring eating would be without them. In addition to taste, the tongue was made to shape speech.

Your ears were designed to capture sound. Its grooves, bumps, and ridges are made to catch passing sound waves and channel them into the eardrum. What if your ears faced backwards or your nose was upside down (what a nightmare in a rainstorm), or your mouth had two tongues? If humanity just happened (with no purposeful design), why don't we see such creatures? In fact, we see the very opposite. From the teeth of a dog to the legs of a grasshopper, one can see practical design in everything that has been made.

Creation reflects the genius of the Creator's hand. Explain how a sparrow knows it is a sparrow and stays with its kind, or how a baby knows to look into the eyes of its mother when no one has taught it to do so. How was a wasp made so that its wings flap at 100 times every second, or the housefly at 190 per second, or the mosquito at an amazing 500 times every second?

The most godless must have a sense of awe and wonder when standing beneath the mighty power of Niagara Falls, gazing into the Grand Canyon, or staring into the infinity of space. How much more should we be humbled by the Maker of these things.

on me,"
Even the night shall be light about me;
12 Indeed, the darkness shall not hide
from You,
But the night shines as the day;
The darkness and the light *are* both
alike *to You.*

13 For You formed my inward parts;
You covered me in my mother's womb.
14 I will praise You, for I am fearfully
and wonderfully made;[a]

139:14 [a]Following Masoretic Text and Targum; Septuagint, Syriac, and Vulgate read *You are fearfully wonderful.*

Marvelous are Your works,
And *that* my soul knows very well.
15My frame was not hidden from You,
When I was made in secret,
And skillfully wrought in the lowest parts of the earth.
16Your eyes saw my substance, being yet unformed.
And in Your book they all were written,
The days fashioned for me,
When *as yet there were* none of them.

17How precious also are Your thoughts to me, O God!
How great is the sum of them!
18*If* I should count them, they would be more in number than the sand;
When I awake, I am still with You.

19Oh, that You would slay the wicked, O God!
Depart from me, therefore, you bloodthirsty men.
20For they speak against You wickedly;
Your enemies take *Your name* in vain.[a]
21Do I not hate them, O LORD, who hate You?
And do I not loathe those who rise up against You?
22I hate them with perfect hatred;
I count them my enemies.

23Search me, O God, and know my heart;
Try me, and know my anxieties;
24And see if *there is any* wicked way in me,
And lead me in the way everlasting.

PSALM 140

Prayer for Deliverance from Evil Men

To the Chief Musician. A Psalm of David.

1Deliver me, O LORD, from evil men;
Preserve me from violent men,
2Who plan evil things in *their* hearts;
They continually gather together *for* war.
3They sharpen their tongues like a serpent;
The poison of asps *is* under their lips. *Selah*

4Keep me, O LORD, from the hands of the wicked;
Preserve me from violent men,
Who have purposed to make my steps stumble.
5The proud have hidden a snare for me, and cords;
They have spread a net by the wayside;
They have set traps for me. *Selah*

6I said to the LORD: "You *are* my God;
Hear the voice of my supplications, O LORD.
7O GOD the Lord, the strength of my salvation,
You have covered my head in the day of battle.
8Do not grant, O LORD, the desires of the wicked;
Do not further his *wicked* scheme,
Lest they be exalted. *Selah*

9"*As for* the head of those who surround me,
Let the evil of their lips cover them;
10Let burning coals fall upon them;
Let them be cast into the fire,
Into deep pits, that they rise not up again.
11Let not a slanderer be established in the earth;
Let evil hunt the violent man to overthrow *him*."

12I know that the LORD will maintain
The cause of the afflicted,
And justice for the poor.

139:20 [a]Septuagint and Vulgate read *They take your cities in vain.*

140:2,3 "The heart is like a viper, hissing and spitting poison at God." *Jonathan Edwards*

"No one has the right to hear the gospel twice, while there remains someone who has not heard it once."

Oswald J. Smith

[13]Surely the righteous shall give thanks
to Your name;
The upright shall dwell in Your
presence.

PSALM 141

Prayer for Safekeeping from Wickedness

A Psalm of David.

[1]LORD, I cry out to You;
Make haste to me!
Give ear to my voice when I cry out
to You.
[2]Let my prayer be set before You *as*
incense,
The lifting up of my hands *as* the
evening sacrifice.

[3]Set a guard, O LORD, over my mouth;
Keep watch over the door of my lips.
[4]Do not incline my heart to any evil
thing,
To practice wicked works
With men who work iniquity;
And do not let me eat of their
delicacies.

[5]Let the righteous strike me;
It shall be a kindness.
And let him rebuke me;
It shall be as excellent oil;
Let my head not refuse it.

For still my prayer *is* against the
deeds of the wicked.
[6]Their judges are overthrown by the
sides of the cliff,
And they hear my words, for they are
sweet.
[7]Our bones are scattered at the mouth
of the grave,
As when one plows and breaks up the
earth.

[8]But my eyes *are* upon You, O GOD the
Lord;
In You I take refuge;
Do not leave my soul destitute.
[9]Keep me from the snares they have
laid for me,
And from the traps of the workers of
iniquity.
[10]Let the wicked fall into their own nets,
While I escape safely.

PSALM 142

A Plea for Relief from Persecutors

A Contemplation[a] of David.
A Prayer when he was in the cave.

[1]I cry out to the LORD with my voice;
With my voice to the LORD I make my
supplication.
[2]I pour out my complaint before Him;
I declare before Him my trouble.

[3]When my spirit was overwhelmed
within me,

142:title [a]Hebrew *Maschil*

141:5 This is a test of our humility. Are we prepared to submit ourselves to godly counsel? "In the eyes of a sinful world, 'humility' is bad self-esteem." *Bruce Garner*

Then You knew my path.
In the way in which I walk
They have secretly set a snare for me.
4Look on *my* right hand and see,
For *there is* no one who acknowledges
me;
Refuge has failed me;
No one cares for my soul.

5I cried out to You, O LORD:
I said, "You *are* my refuge,
My portion in the land of the living.
6Attend to my cry,
For I am brought very low;
Deliver me from my persecutors,
For they are stronger than I.
7Bring my soul out of prison,
That I may praise Your name;
The righteous shall surround me,
For You shall deal bountifully with
me."

PSALM 143

An Earnest Appeal for Guidance and Deliverance

A Psalm of David.

1Hear my prayer, O LORD,
Give ear to my supplications!
In Your faithfulness answer me,
And in Your righteousness.
2Do not enter into judgment with Your
servant,
For in Your sight no one living is
righteous.

3For the enemy has persecuted my
soul;
He has crushed my life to the ground;
He has made me dwell in darkness,
Like those who have long been dead.
4Therefore my spirit is overwhelmed
within me;
My heart within me is distressed.

5I remember the days of old;
I meditate on all Your works;
I muse on the work of Your hands.
6I spread out my hands to You;
My soul *longs* for You like a thirsty
land. *Selah*

7Answer me speedily, O LORD;
My spirit fails!
Do not hide Your face from me,
Lest I be like those who go down into
the pit.
8Cause me to hear Your
lovingkindness in the morning,
For in You do I trust;
Cause me to know the way in which I
should walk,
For I lift up my soul to You.

9Deliver me, O LORD, from my enemies;

THE FUNCTION OF THE LAW

143:2 "It is amazing for a soul to discover that God gave a law to be observed but that its observance is not even taken into account as a means of salvation. Then why was the law given? What good are moral standards? They were not given because God had the illusion that we could conform our lives to them. God knows that we are a degenerate race and that there is nothing good in our carnal nature.

"The law serves another purpose: to show us our sins. Man is confronted with a moral law that is just and good. His mind, while acknowledging that here is the truth, confesses at the same time that he does not live according to this law. And no matter how hard he tries, he realizes he does not reach the ideal. This is how he discovers he is a lost sinner.

"This is the great purpose of the law. It teaches us what sin is and it shows us how wrong we are, just as a mirror reveals to us how filthy we are and what needs cleansing. But just as a mirror does not and cannot wash us but only reveals our condition, so the law cannot correct us but only shows us what great sinners we are.

"The purpose of the law is to make you know your sin so that you will begin to pray with the psalmist, 'Do not enter into judgment with Your servant, for in Your sight no one living is righteous' (Psalm 143:2)." *Richard Wurmbrand*

143:2 How fearful it would be to stand in judgment and be judged by the standard of God's Law. See Gal. 2:16 for what God did so that we could live.

In You I take shelter.[a]
10Teach me to do Your will,
For You *are* my God;
Your Spirit *is* good.
Lead me in the land of uprightness.

11Revive me, O LORD, for Your name's sake!
For Your righteousness' sake bring my soul out of trouble.
12In Your mercy cut off my enemies,
And destroy all those who afflict my soul;
For I *am* Your servant.

PSALM 144

A Song to the Lord Who Preserves and Prospers His People

A Psalm of David.

1Blessed *be* the LORD my Rock,
Who trains my hands for war,
And my fingers for battle—
2My lovingkindness and my fortress,
My high tower and my deliverer,
My shield and *the One* in whom I take refuge,
Who subdues my people[a] under me.

I believe the holier a man becomes, the more he mourns over the unholiness which remains in him.

CHARLES SPURGEON

3LORD, what *is* man, that You take knowledge of him?
Or the son of man, that You are mindful of him?
4Man is like a breath;
His days *are* like a passing shadow.

5Bow down Your heavens, O LORD, and come down;
Touch the mountains, and they shall smoke.
6Flash forth lightning and scatter them;
Shoot out Your arrows and destroy them.
7Stretch out Your hand from above;
Rescue me and deliver me out of great waters,
From the hand of foreigners,
8Whose mouth speaks lying words,
And whose right hand *is* a right hand of falsehood.

9I will sing a new song to You, O God;
On a harp of ten strings I will sing praises to You,
10*The One* who gives salvation to kings,
Who delivers David His servant
From the deadly sword.

11Rescue me and deliver me from the hand of foreigners,
Whose mouth speaks lying words,
And whose right hand *is* a right hand of falsehood—
12That our sons *may be* as plants grown up in their youth;
That our daughters *may be* as pillars,
Sculptured in palace style;
13*That* our barns *may be* full,
Supplying all kinds of produce;
That our sheep may bring forth thousands
And ten thousands in our fields;
14*That* our oxen *may be* well laden;
That there be no breaking in or going out;
That there be no outcry in our streets.
15Happy *are* the people who are in such a state;
Happy *are* the people whose God *is* the LORD!

PSALM 145

A Song of God's Majesty and Love

A Praise of David.

1I will extol You, my God, O King;
And I will bless Your name forever and ever.
2Every day I will bless You,
And I will praise Your name forever and ever.

143:9 [a]Septuagint and Vulgate read *To You I flee.* 144:2 [a]Following Masoretic Text, Septuagint, and Vulgate; Syriac and Targum read *the peoples* (compare 18:47).

QUESTIONS & OBJECTIONS

144:8 "Hitler was a Christian!"

Despite the fact that Adolf Hitler had a Roman Catholic background, he became adamantly anti-Christian and believed in evolution. As other dictators have done, he took over the churches and used their organizational structure to influence the citizens—though the teachings allowed were anything but biblical. *William Shirer*, who chronicled the Nazi regime, stated that "the Nazi regime intended eventually to destroy Christianity in Germany" and substitute paganism.

Hitler's vision for Germany was defined in a thirty-point program for the "National Reich Church," which "categorically claims the exclusive right and the exclusive power to control all churches within the borders of the Reich." Some of the points of the program include the following: The National Church is "determined to exterminate irrevocably the Christian faith"; churches have no pastors or chaplains but only National Reich orators may speak in them; publishing and dissemination of the Bible must immediate cease in Germany. The National Church declared that "the Fuehrer's *Mein Kampf* is the greatest of all documents" and "embodies the purest and truest ethics for the present and future life of our nation." Therefore, churches must remove all Bibles and crucifixes, only *Mein Kampf* may be on the altar, and all crosses must be replaced by "the only unconquerable symbol, the swastika" (*W. L. Shirer*, *The Rise and Fall of the Third Reich*, p. 240).

The following quotes by Hitler reveal his true personal views (taken from *Hitler's Table Talk*):

> National Socialism and religion cannot exist together.... The heaviest blow that ever struck humanity was the coming of Christianity. Bolshevism is Christianity's illegitimate child. Both are inventions of the Jew. The deliberate lie in the matter of religion was introduced into the world by Christianity... Let it not be said that Christianity brought man the life of the soul, for that evolution was in the natural order of things. (pp. 6–7)

> The reason why the ancient world was so pure, light and serene was that it knew nothing of the two great scourges: the pox and Christianity. (p. 75)

> Christianity is an invention of sick brains: one could imagine nothing more senseless, nor any more indecent way of turning the idea of the Godhead into a mockery... Let's be the only people who are immunized against the disease. (pp. 118–119)

> There is something very unhealthy about Christianity. (p. 339)

> I realize that man, in his imperfection, can commit innumerable errors—but to devote myself deliberately to errors, that is something I cannot do. I shall never come personally to terms with the Christian lie. Our epoch in the next 200 years will certainly see the end of the disease of Christianity... My regret will have been that I couldn't... behold [its demise]. (p. 278)

3 Great *is* the LORD, and greatly to be
praised;
And His greatness *is* unsearchable.

4 One generation shall praise Your
works to another,
And shall declare Your mighty acts.
5 I[a] will meditate on the glorious
splendor of Your majesty,
And on Your wondrous works.[b]
6 *Men* shall speak of the might of Your
awesome acts,
And I will declare Your greatness.

7 They shall utter the memory of Your
great goodness,
And shall sing of Your righteousness.

8 The LORD *is* gracious and full of
compassion,
Slow to anger and great in mercy.
9 The LORD *is* good to all,
And His tender mercies *are* over all
His works.

145:5 [a]Following Masoretic Text and Targum; Dead Sea Scrolls, Septuagint, Syriac, and Vulgate read *They*. [b]Literally *on the words of Your wondrous works*

145:8 This is why we have the cross of Calvary. Nothing in man's character drew out God's love for us. It came simply because the Lord is gracious and full of compassion.

[10]All Your works shall praise You, O
LORD,
And Your saints shall bless You.
[11]They shall speak of the glory of Your
kingdom,
And talk of Your power,
[12]To make known to the sons of men
His mighty acts,
And the glorious majesty of His
kingdom.
[13]Your kingdom *is* an everlasting
kingdom,
And Your dominion *endures*
throughout all generations.[a]

[14]The LORD upholds all who fall,
And raises up all *who are* bowed down.
[15]The eyes of all look expectantly to You,
And You give them their food in due
season.
[16]You open Your hand
And satisfy the desire of every living
thing.

[17]The LORD *is* righteous in all His ways,
Gracious in all His works.
[18]The LORD *is* near to all who call upon
Him,
To all who call upon Him in truth.
[19]He will fulfill the desire of those who
fear Him;
He also will hear their cry and save
them.
[20]The LORD preserves all who love Him,
But all the wicked He will destroy.
[21]My mouth shall speak the praise of
the LORD,
And all flesh shall bless His holy name
Forever and ever.

PSALM 146

The Happiness of Those Whose Help Is the Lord

[1]Praise the LORD!

Praise the LORD, O my soul!
[2]While I live I will praise the LORD;
I will sing praises to my God while I
have my being.

[3]Do not put your trust in princes,
Nor in a son of man, in whom *there is*
no help.
[4]His spirit departs, he returns to his
earth;
In that very day his plans perish.

[5]Happy *is he* who *has* the God of Jacob
for his help,
Whose hope *is* in the LORD his God,
[6]Who made heaven and earth,
The sea, and all that *is* in them;
Who keeps truth forever,
[7]Who executes justice for the oppressed,
Who gives food to the hungry.
The LORD gives freedom to the
prisoners.

145:13 [a]Following Masoretic Text and Targum; Dead Sea Scrolls, Septuagint, Syriac, and Vulgate add *The LORD is faithful in all His words, And holy in all His works.*

145:17,18 Notice the word "all" in these verses.

146:6 Evolution's circular reasoning. "Those who argue that the biblical timescale is wrong often commit the fallacy of begging the question—they merely assume the very thing they are trying to prove. Any argument that the earth is billions of years old must presuppose that rates and conditions are basically constant (e.g., no global Flood), and that the world was not supernaturally created in a fully-functioning state. However, the Bible denies these critical presuppositions. So, when an old-earth advocate uses these assumptions to conclude that the Bible is wrong (at least about the age of the earth), he has already tacitly assumed this. His conclusion that the Bible is wrong is based solely upon his assumption that the Bible is wrong. He is reasoning in a vicious circle." *Ken Ham and Jason Lisle*

"Contrary to what most scientists write, the fossil record does not support the Darwinian theory of evolution because it is this theory (there are several) which we use to interpret the fossil record. By doing so we are guilty of circular reasoning if we then say the fossil record supports this theory." *Ronald R. West*, Ph.D.

146:7–9 Here is the ministry of the Savior. Jesus fed the hungry, loosed the prisoners of sin and suffering, opened the eyes of the blind, and raised up those who were bowed down. See also Luke 4:18 comment.

QUESTIONS & OBJECTIONS

147:9

"The Bible calls the hare a cud-chewing animal, which any veterinarian could tell you is false."

This statement is made in Lev. 11:6, where the Hebrew literally means "raises up what has been swallowed." The rabbit does re-eat partially digested fecal pellets that come from a special pouch called the *caecum*. Bacteria in these pellets enrich the diet and provide nutrients to aid digestion. According to the *Encyclopedia Britannica*:

> "Some lagomorphs [rabbits and hares] are capable of re-ingesting moist and nutritionally rich fecal pellets, a practice considered comparable to cud-chewing in ruminants... The upper tooth rows are more widely separated than the lower rows, and chewing is done with a transverse movement."

8The LORD opens *the eyes of* the blind;
The LORD raises those who are bowed down;
The LORD loves the righteous.
9The LORD watches over the strangers;
He relieves the fatherless and widow;
But the way of the wicked He turns upside down.

10The LORD shall reign forever—
Your God, O Zion, to all generations.

Praise the LORD!

PSALM 147

Praise to God for His Word and Providence

1Praise the LORD!
For *it is* good to sing praises to our God;
For *it is* pleasant, *and* praise is beautiful.

2The LORD builds up Jerusalem;
He gathers together the outcasts of Israel.
3He heals the brokenhearted
And binds up their wounds.
4He counts the number of the stars;
He calls them all by name.
5Great *is* our Lord, and mighty in power;
His understanding *is* infinite.
6The LORD lifts up the humble;
He casts the wicked down to the ground.

7Sing to the LORD with thanksgiving;
Sing praises on the harp to our God,
8Who covers the heavens with clouds,
Who prepares rain for the earth,
Who makes grass to grow on the mountains.
9He gives to the beast its food,
And to the young ravens that cry.

10He does not delight in the strength of the horse;
He takes no pleasure in the legs of a man.
11The LORD takes pleasure in those who fear Him,
In those who hope in His mercy.

12Praise the LORD, O Jerusalem!
Praise your God, O Zion!
13For He has strengthened the bars of your gates;
He has blessed your children within you.
14He makes peace *in* your borders,
And fills you with the finest wheat.

15He sends out His command *to the* earth;
His word runs very swiftly.
16He gives snow like wool;

147:4 In Jer. 33:22, the Bible states that "the host of heaven cannot be numbered, nor the sand of the sea measured." When this was written, 2,500 years ago, no one knew how vast the stars were, since only about 1,100 were visible. Now we know that there are *billions* of stars, and that they *cannot* be numbered.

He scatters the frost like ashes;
17He casts out His hail like morsels;
Who can stand before His cold?
18He sends out His word and melts them;
He causes His wind to blow, *and* the
waters flow.

19He declares His word to Jacob,
His statutes and His judgments to
Israel.
20He has not dealt thus with any nation;
And *as for His* judgments, they have
not known them.

Praise the LORD!

PSALM 148

Praise to the Lord from Creation

1Praise the LORD!

Praise the LORD from the heavens;
Praise Him in the heights!
2Praise Him, all His angels;
Praise Him, all His hosts!
3Praise Him, sun and moon;
Praise Him, all you stars of light!
4Praise Him, you heavens of heavens,
And you waters above the heavens!

5Let them praise the name of the LORD,
For He commanded and they were
created.
6He also established them forever and
ever;
He made a decree which shall not
pass away.

7Praise the LORD from the earth,
You great sea creatures and all the
depths;
8Fire and hail, snow and clouds;
Stormy wind, fulfilling His word;
9Mountains and all hills;
Fruitful trees and all cedars;
10Beasts and all cattle;
Creeping things and flying fowl;
11Kings of the earth and all peoples;
Princes and all judges of the earth;
12Both young men and maidens;
Old men and children.

The church is like manure. Pile it up, and it stinks up the neighborhood. Spread it out, and it enriches the world.

LUIS PALAU

13Let them praise the name of the LORD,
For His name alone is exalted;
His glory *is* above the earth and heaven.

148:7 A whale of a time. A Berkeley website for teachers claims that "there are numerous examples of transitional forms in the fossil record, providing an abundance of evidence for change over time." The only example they cite as proof is *Pakicetus*, described as an early ancestor to modern whales. How can scientists tell this? According to the website, "Although pakicetids were land mammals, it is clear that they are related to whales and dolphins based on a number of specializations of the ear, relating to hearing."

In an accompanying illustration, paleontologist Phil Gingerich shows a swimming creature with its forelimbs on the way to becoming flippers, claiming that it is "perfectly intermediate, a missing link between earlier land mammals and later, full-fledged whales."

Although the body he drew does look like a very convincing transitional form, his conclusion was based on only a few fragments of a skull. Not a single bone of the body had been found! Once a more complete skeleton was discovered, it proved that *Pakicetus* looked nothing like the creature he imagined.

Besides, many of God's creatures have similar hearing (how many different ways can you make an ear that hears sound?). The eyes of many of God's creatures are very similar. Pigs have skin that is incredibly close to human skin—closer than primates. We both have noses, ears, eyes, liver, kidneys, lungs, teeth, and a brain. Did man evolve from the pig, rather than the primate? It would seem so if we are going to be consistent with the evolutionist's logic. The pig and man have many features in common.

The creatures that Gingerich was looking at were simply different animals with similar hearing ability, created by the same Creator, and his conclusion was nothing but wild and unscientific speculation. Sadly, this happens all too frequently in the evolutionary world. See also Job 17:14 and Jer. 27:5 comments. (Adapted from *How to Know God Exists*.)

"Sin and the child of God are incompatible. They may occasionally meet; they cannot live together in harmony."

John Stott

14And He has exalted the horn of His
people,
The praise of all His saints—
Of the children of Israel,
A people near to Him.

Praise the LORD!

PSALM 149

Praise to God for His Salvation and Judgment

1Praise the LORD!

Sing to the LORD a new song,
And His praise in the assembly of saints.

2Let Israel rejoice in their Maker;
Let the children of Zion be joyful in
their King.
3Let them praise His name with the
dance;
Let them sing praises to Him with the
timbrel and harp.
4For the LORD takes pleasure in His
people;
He will beautify the humble with
salvation.

5Let the saints be joyful in glory;
Let them sing aloud on their beds.
6*Let* the high praises of God *be* in their
mouth,
And a two-edged sword in their hand,
7To execute vengeance on the nations,
And punishments on the peoples;
8To bind their kings with chains,
And their nobles with fetters of iron;
9To execute on them the written
judgment—
This honor have all His saints.

Praise the LORD!

PSALM 150

Let All Things Praise the Lord

1Praise the LORD!

Praise God in His sanctuary;
Praise Him in His mighty firmament!

2Praise Him for His mighty acts;
Praise Him according to His excellent
greatness!

3Praise Him with the sound of the
trumpet;
Praise Him with the lute and harp!
4Praise Him with the timbrel and
dance;
Praise Him with stringed instruments
and flutes!
5Praise Him with loud cymbals;
Praise Him with clashing cymbals!

6Let everything that has breath praise
the LORD.

Praise the LORD!

Feeding Sheep or Amusing Goats

By Archibald G. Brown

An evil resides in the professed camp of the Lord so gross in its impudence that the most shortsighted can hardly fail to notice it. During the past few years it has developed at an abnormal rate evil for evil. It has worked like leaven until the whole lump ferments. The devil has seldom done a cleverer thing than hinting to the Church that part of their mission is to provide entertainment for the people, with a view to winning them. From speaking out as the Puritans did, the Church has gradually toned down her testimony, then winked at and excused the frivolities of the day. Then she tolerated them in her borders. Now she has adopted them under the plea of reaching the masses.

My first contention is that providing amusement for the people is nowhere spoken of in the Scriptures as a function of the Church. If it is a Christian work why did not Christ speak of it? "Go ye into all the world and preach the gospel to every creature." That is clear enough. So it would have been if He has added, "and provide amusement for those who do not relish the gospel." No such words, however, are to be found. It did not seem to occur to Him. Then again, "He gave some apostles, some prophets, some pastors and teachers, for the work of the ministry." Where do entertainers come in? The Holy Spirit is silent concerning them. Were the prophets persecuted because they amused the people or because they refused? The concert has no martyr roll.

Again, providing amusement is in direct antagonism to the teaching and life of Christ and all His apostles. What was the attitude of the Church to the world? "Ye are the salt," not sugar candy—something the world will spit out, not swallow. Short and sharp was the utterance, "Let the dead bury their dead." He was in awful earnestness!

Had Christ introduced more of the bright and pleasant elements into His mission, He would have been more popular when they went back, because of the searching nature of His teaching. I do not hear Him say, "Run after these people, Peter, and tell them we will have a different style of service tomorrow, something short and attractive with little preaching. We will have a pleasant evening for the people. Tell them they will be sure to enjoy it. Be quick, Peter, we must get the people somehow!" Jesus pitied sinners, sighed and wept over them, but never sought to amuse them. In vain will the Epistles be searched to find any trace of the gospel amusement. Their message is, "Come out, keep out, keep clean out!" Anything approaching fooling is conspicuous by its absence. They had boundless confidence in the gospel and employed no other weapon. After Peter and John were locked up for preaching, the Church had a prayer meeting, but they did not pray, "Lord grant Thy servants that by a wise and discriminating use of innocent recreation we may show these people how happy we are." If they ceased not for preaching Christ, they had not time for arranging entertainments. Scattered by persecution, they went everywhere preaching the gospel. They "turned the world upside down." That is the difference! Lord, clear the Church of all the rot and rubbish the devil has imposed on her and bring us back to apostolic methods.

Lastly, the mission of amusement fails to affect the end desired. It works havoc among young converts. Let the careless and scoffers, who thank God because the Church met them halfway, speak and testify. Let the heavy-laden who found peace through the concert not keep silent! Let the drunkard to whom the dramatic entertainment has been God's link in the chain of their conversion, stand up! There are none to answer. The mission of amusement produces no converts. The need of the hour for today's ministry is believing scholarship joined with earnest spirituality, the one springing from the other as fruit from the root. The need is biblical doctrine, so understood and felt, that it sets men on fire.

Originally attributed to Charles Spurgeon, this seems rather to be an edited version of a sermon by one of his students, Archibald G Brown, "The Devil's Mission of Amusement" (1889), and is included in *Sermons of Archibald G. Brown* (Banner of Truth, 2010).

Proverbs

The Beginning of Knowledge

1 The proverbs of Solomon the son of David, king of Israel:

[2]To know wisdom and instruction,
To perceive the words of understanding,
[3]To receive the instruction of wisdom,
Justice, judgment, and equity;
[4]To give prudence to the simple,
To the young man knowledge and discretion—
[5]A wise *man* will hear and increase learning,
And a man of understanding will attain wise counsel,
[6]To understand a proverb and an enigma,
The words of the wise and their riddles.

[7]The fear of the LORD *is* the beginning of knowledge,
But fools despise wisdom and instruction.

Shun Evil Counsel

[8]My son, hear the instruction of your father,
And do not forsake the law of your mother;
[9]For they *will be* a graceful ornament on your head,
And chains about your neck.
[10]My son, if sinners entice you,
Do not consent.
[11]If they say, "Come with us,
Let us lie in wait to *shed* blood;
Let us lurk secretly for the innocent without cause;
[12]Let us swallow them alive like Sheol,[a]
And whole, like those who go down to the Pit;
[13]We shall find all *kinds* of precious possessions,
We shall fill our houses with spoil;
[14]Cast in your lot among us,
Let us all have one purse"—
[15]My son, do not walk in the way with them,
Keep your foot from their path;
[16]For their feet run to evil,
And they make haste to shed blood.
[17]Surely, in vain the net is spread
In the sight of any bird;
[18]But they lie in wait for their *own* blood,
They lurk secretly for their *own* lives.
[19]So *are* the ways of everyone who is greedy for gain;
It takes away the life of its owners.

The Call of Wisdom

[20]Wisdom calls aloud outside;
She raises her voice in the open squares.

1:12 [a]Or *the grave*

1:2 It is wise to read a proverb for each day of the month. They were written that we might have wisdom, instruction, and understanding.

"It has always been difficult to understand those evangelical Christians who... say they serve the Lord, but they divide their days so as to leave plenty of time to play and loaf and enjoy the pleasures of the world as well. They are at ease while the world burns."

A. W. Tozer

21 She cries out in the chief concourses,[a]
At the openings of the gates in the city
She speaks her words:
22 "How long, you simple ones, will you
love simplicity?
For scorners delight in their scorning,
And fools hate knowledge.
23 Turn at my rebuke;
Surely I will pour out my spirit on you;
I will make my words known to you.
24 Because I have called and you refused,
I have stretched out my hand and no
one regarded,
25 Because you disdained all my counsel,
And would have none of my rebuke,
26 I also will laugh at your calamity;
I will mock when your terror comes,
27 When your terror comes like a storm,
And your destruction comes like a
whirlwind,
When distress and anguish come
upon you.

28 "Then they will call on me, but I will
not answer;
They will seek me diligently, but they
will not find me.
29 Because they hated knowledge
And did not choose the fear of the
LORD,
30 They would have none of my counsel
And despised my every rebuke.
31 Therefore they shall eat the fruit of
their own way,
And be filled to the full with their
own fancies.
32 For the turning away of the simple
will slay them,
And the complacency of fools will
destroy them;
33 But whoever listens to me will dwell
safely,
And will be secure, without fear of
evil."

The Value of Wisdom

2 My son, if you receive my words,
And treasure my commands within
you,
2 So that you incline your ear to wisdom,
And apply your heart to understanding;
3 Yes, if you cry out for discernment,
And lift up your voice for
understanding,

1:21 [a]Septuagint, Syriac, and Targum read *top of the walls;* Vulgate reads *the head of multitudes.*

1:22,23 One just has to observe the gospel being preached in the open air to know the truth of these words. When presented with the knowledge of how to be saved from death and hell, the world delights in scorn. Yet despite their contempt, our Creator offers salvation to a God-hating humanity. He will make His words known to all who turn to His reproof.

2:1–5 The fear of the Lord. This is how to obtain the fear of the Lord, the most necessary virtue: 1) receive the Word of God; 2) hide His commandments within you; 3) incline your ear to wisdom; 4) apply your heart to understanding; 5) cry out for knowledge and discernment; 6) seek it as you would for silver or hidden treasures.

[4]If you seek her as silver,
And search for her as *for* hidden
treasures;
[5]Then you will understand the fear of
the LORD,
And find the knowledge of God.
[6]For the LORD gives wisdom;
From His mouth *come* knowledge and
understanding;
[7]He stores up sound wisdom for the
upright;
He is a shield to those who walk
uprightly;
[8]He guards the paths of justice,
And preserves the way of His saints.
[9]Then you will understand
righteousness and justice,
Equity *and* every good path.

[10]When wisdom enters your heart,
And knowledge is pleasant to your
soul,
[11]Discretion will preserve you;
Understanding will keep you,
[12]To deliver you from the way of evil,
From the man who speaks perverse
things,
[13]From those who leave the paths of
uprightness
To walk in the ways of darkness;
[14]Who rejoice in doing evil,
And delight in the perversity of the
wicked;
[15]Whose ways *are* crooked,
And *who are* devious in their paths;
[16]To deliver you from the immoral
woman,
From the seductress *who* flatters with
her words,
[17]Who forsakes the companion of her
youth,
And forgets the covenant of her God.
[18]For her house leads down to death,
And her paths to the dead;
[19]None who go to her return,
Nor do they regain the paths of life—
[20]So you may walk in the way of
goodness,
And keep *to* the paths of righteousness.
[21]For the upright will dwell in the land,
And the blameless will remain in it;
[22]But the wicked will be cut off from
the earth,
And the unfaithful will be uprooted
from it.

Guidance for the Young

3 My son, do not forget my law,
But let your heart keep my
commands;
[2]For length of days and long life
And peace they will add to you.

[3]Let not mercy and truth forsake you;
Bind them around your neck,
Write them on the tablet of your heart,
[4]*And* so find favor and high esteem
In the sight of God and man.

[5]Trust in the LORD with all your heart,
And lean not on your own
understanding;
[6]In all your ways acknowledge Him,
And He shall direct[a] your paths.

3:6 [a]Or *make smooth* or *straight*

2:12 Wisdom, knowledge, discretion, and understanding will keep you from perversity and sexual sin. They give light to the blind regarding the end result of sin: see v. 18.

3:1–3 The Law leads to mercy and truth. See John 1:17 and Gal. 3:24.

3:3 "You are debtors, for what were ye if compassion had not come to your rescue? Divine compassion, all undeserved and free, has redeemed you from your vain conversation. Surely those who receive mercy should show mercy; those who owe all they have to the pity of God, should not be pitiless to their brethren. The Savior never for a moment tolerates the self-righteous isolation which would make you despise the prodigal, and cavil at his restoration, much less the Cainite spirit which cries, 'Am I my brother's keeper?' No doctrine is rightly received by you if it freezes the genial current of your Christian compassion. You may know the truth of the doctrine, but you do not know the doctrine in truth if it makes you gaze on the wrath to come without emotions of pity for immortal souls." *Charles Spurgeon*

7Do not be wise in your own eyes;
Fear the LORD and depart from evil.
8It will be health to your flesh,[a]
And strength[b] to your bones.

9Honor the LORD with your possessions,
And with the firstfruits of all your increase;
10So your barns will be filled with plenty,
And your vats will overflow with new wine.

11My son, do not despise the chastening of the LORD,
Nor detest His correction;
12For whom the LORD loves He corrects,
Just as a father the son *in whom* he delights.

13Happy *is* the man *who* finds wisdom,
And the man *who* gains understanding;
14For her proceeds *are* better than the profits of silver,
And her gain than fine gold.
15She *is* more precious than rubies,
And all the things you may desire cannot compare with her.
16Length of days *is* in her right hand,
In her left hand riches and honor.
17Her ways *are* ways of pleasantness,
And all her paths *are* peace.
18She *is* a tree of life to those who take hold of her,
And happy *are all* who retain her.

19The LORD by wisdom founded the earth;
By understanding He established the heavens;
20By His knowledge the depths were broken up,
And clouds drop down the dew.

21My son, let them not depart from your eyes—
Keep sound wisdom and discretion;
22So they will be life to your soul
And grace to your neck.
23Then you will walk safely in your way,
And your foot will not stumble.
24When you lie down, you will not be afraid;
Yes, you will lie down and your sleep will be sweet.
25Do not be afraid of sudden terror,
Nor of trouble from the wicked when it comes;
26For the LORD will be your confidence,
And will keep your foot from being caught.

27Do not withhold good from those to whom it is due,
When it is in the power of your hand to do *so*.
28Do not say to your neighbor,
"Go, and come back,
And tomorrow I will give *it*,"
When *you have* it with you.
29Do not devise evil against your neighbor,
For he dwells by you for safety's sake.
30Do not strive with a man without cause,
If he has done you no harm.

31Do not envy the oppressor,

3:8 [a]Literally *navel*, figurative of the body [b]Literally *drink* or *refreshment*

3:5 The world says the opposite: doubt the Word of God and have faith in yourself.

3:6 "It was the Lord who put it into my mind . . . I could feel His hand upon me . . . There is no question the inspiration was from the Holy Spirit because He comforted me with rays of marvelous illumination from the Holy Scriptures . . . No one should fear to undertake any task in the name of our Savior if it is just and if the intention is purely for His holy service. The gospel must still be preached to so many lands in such a short time. This is what convinces me." *Christopher Columbus* (from his diary, in reference to his discovery of "the New World")

3:27,28 We must never lose sight of love for our neighbor. A good deed can be a stronger evangelistic witness than a thousand words. See Prov. 27:10 comment.

3:19 *Good Questions for Evolutionists*

By Ken Ham, Answers in Genesis

Atheistic evolutionists often try to attack creation, the Bible, or the character of God to keep people from asking questions of *their* religion. In other words, they attack Christianity in hopes of not having to defend their own worldview—mainly because they do *not* have good answers to defend their faith.

A good offense may be one of the best defenses you can give. For example, if someone criticizes you for believing that all humanity came from Adam and Eve, a good response could be, "You find it difficult to believe that all the people in the world came from two people, and yet you believe that all the people in the world came from a rock? At least we can demonstrate that people come from people . . ." Questions can be powerful, so here are a few that may help in a conversation.

Questions to clarify:

- What do you mean by evolution?
- What do you mean by science?
- How do you know that is true?
- Has that been observed?

Keep in mind that there are multiple definitions of *evolution* and *science* and you don't want to get caught in a bait and switch. For example, evolution can mean simply change over time or molecules-to-man evolution; and science can mean repeatable, observable knowledge or the philosophy of naturalism (which arbitrarily excludes any supernatural cause).

Issue questions:

- Where did matter and energy come from?
- If everything came about by random processes, then why do laws of nature follow precisely designed formulas like $F=ma$ or $E=mc^2$?
- Where did life come from?
- Where is the evidence for the millions of information-gaining mutations?
- Where are the millions of transitional fossils leading up to the Cambrian period?
- What proof do you have that a global Flood could not have occurred?
- Has anyone repeated changing a single-celled organism, like an ameba, into something like a cow?
- What experiments have been conducted over "millions of years" that verify that it takes millions of years to form rock, sedimentary layers, diamonds, coal, stalactites, and other formations?

Worldview questions:

- If life is ultimately meaningless, then why are you arguing?
- If the material universe is all that there is, what makes you think that logic, truth, and information exist, since they are all non-material?
- If people are simply rearranged chemicals obeying laws of nature, how can anyone criticize what anyone else does?
- Why does the material universe follow immaterial laws?
- Which view of evolution do you believe?
  - Lamarckian—Using traits leads to enhancement of those traits and new kinds.
  - Traditional Darwinism—Natural selection acting over millions of years leads to new kinds.
  - Neo-Darwinism—Natural selection and genetic mutations acting over millions of years leads to new kinds.
  - Punctuated Equilibrium—Natural selection and genetic mutations acting in rapid bursts over millions of years leads to new kinds.

Of course, these are just a small sampling of questions that are good to ask. Keep in mind that such questions are to get evolutionists *to realize* their own professed worldview is false. The individuals are not the enemy—it is the false philosophies that have taken them captive that are the enemy. The unbelievers are made in the image of God and are candidates for salvation in Jesus Christ. So these questions must be asked with gentleness and respect (1 Pet. 3:15). In other words, we should show the same grace to other people that God showed toward us.

And choose none of his ways;
32For the perverse *person is* an
abomination to the LORD,
But His secret counsel *is* with the
upright.
33The curse of the LORD *is* on the house
of the wicked,
But He blesses the home of the just.
34Surely He scorns the scornful,
But gives grace to the humble.
35The wise shall inherit glory,
But shame shall be the legacy of fools.

Security in Wisdom

4 Hear, my children, the instruction of a father,
And give attention to know understanding;
[2]For I give you good doctrine:
Do not forsake my law.
[3]When I was my father's son,
Tender and the only one in the sight of my mother,
[4]He also taught me, and said to me:
"Let your heart retain my words;
Keep my commands, and live.
[5]Get wisdom! Get understanding!
Do not forget, nor turn away from the words of my mouth.
[6]Do not forsake her, and she will preserve you;
Love her, and she will keep you.
[7]Wisdom *is* the principal thing;
Therefore get wisdom.
And in all your getting, get understanding.
[8]Exalt her, and she will promote you;
She will bring you honor, when you embrace her.
[9]She will place on your head an ornament of grace;
A crown of glory she will deliver to you."

[10]Hear, my son, and receive my sayings,
And the years of your life will be many.
[11]I have taught you in the way of wisdom;
I have led you in right paths.
[12]When you walk, your steps will not be hindered,
And when you run, you will not stumble.
[13]Take firm hold of instruction, do not let go;
Keep her, for she *is* your life.

[14]Do not enter the path of the wicked,
And do not walk in the way of evil.
[15]Avoid it, do not travel on it;
Turn away from it and pass on.
[16]For they do not sleep unless they have done evil;
And their sleep is taken away unless they make *someone* fall.
[17]For they eat the bread of wickedness,
And drink the wine of violence.

3:34 An atheist once argued that if God was real He would stop him from leaving a building. Then he turned around and boldly walked out to make his point. God did not stop him from leaving. Did his actions prove anything? Yes, they proved that God does not take dictation from atheists. It doesn't work with presidents either. If I say, "If the President of the United States exists, let him show up outside my house tonight!" I am going to be standing alone in the dark. Such talk is the epitome of arrogance. It was the arrogant Italian dictator Mussolini who stood on a pinnacle as a youth, and said that if God was real He should prove it by striking him dead. His prayer was eventually answered.

4:1–5 Training our children. We are responsible to God to train our children in the way they should go (Prov. 22:6), and must constantly be on guard against humanism, atheism, relativism, evolution, and any other teaching that opposes the Christian worldview. (See also Deut. 11:19 and Eph. 6:4 comments.)

"I think that the most important factor moving us toward a secular society has been the educational factor. Our schools may not teach Johnny how to read properly, but the fact that Johnny is in school until he is sixteen tends toward the elimination of religious superstition. The average American child now acquires a high school education, and this militates against Adam and Eve and all other myths of alleged history." *P. Blanchard*, "Three Cheers for Our Secular State," *The Humanist*

"Education is thus a most powerful ally of humanism. What can a theistic Sunday school's meeting for an hour once a week and teaching only a fraction of the children, do to stem the tide of the five-day program of humanistic teaching?" *Humanism: A New Religion*, 1930

"Fundamental parents have no right to indoctrinate their children in their beliefs. We are preparing their children for the year 2000 and life in a global one-world society, and those children will not fit in." *Senator Paul Hoagland*, 1984

"Give me your four year olds, and in a generation I will build a socialist state." *Vladimir Lenin*

4:7 How do we get this "principal thing" that preserves and promotes? Primarily through prayer and Proverbs. Seek God and feed on this wealth of wisdom daily.

18But the path of the just *is* like the
shining sun,[a]
That shines ever brighter unto the
perfect day.
19The way of the wicked *is* like darkness;
They do not know what makes them
stumble.

20My son, give attention to my words;
Incline your ear to my sayings.
21Do not let them depart from your eyes;
Keep them in the midst of your heart;
22For they *are* life to those who find
them,
And health to all their flesh.
23Keep your heart with all diligence,
For out of it *spring* the issues of life.
24Put away from you a deceitful mouth,
And put perverse lips far from you.
25Let your eyes look straight ahead,
And your eyelids look right before you.
26Ponder the path of your feet,
And let all your ways be established.
27Do not turn to the right or the left;
Remove your foot from evil.

The Peril of Adultery

5 My son, pay attention to my
wisdom;
Lend your ear to my understanding,
2That you may preserve discretion,
And your lips may keep knowledge.
3For the lips of an immoral woman
drip honey,
And her mouth *is* smoother than oil;
4But in the end she is bitter as
wormwood,
Sharp as a two-edged sword.
5Her feet go down to death,
Her steps lay hold of hell.[a]
6Lest you ponder *her* path of life—
Her ways are unstable;
You do not know *them*.

7Therefore hear me now, *my* children,
And do not depart from the words of
my mouth.
8Remove your way far from her,
And do not go near the door of her
house,
9Lest you give your honor to others,
And your years to the cruel *one;*
10Lest aliens be filled with your wealth,
And your labors *go* to the house of a
foreigner;
11And you mourn at last,
When your flesh and your body are
consumed,
12And say:
"How I have hated instruction,
And my heart despised correction!
13I have not obeyed the voice of my
teachers,
Nor inclined my ear to those who
instructed me!
14I was on the verge of total ruin,
In the midst of the assembly and
congregation."

15Drink water from your own cistern,
And running water from your own
well.
16Should your fountains be dispersed
abroad,
Streams of water in the streets?
17Let them be only your own,

4:18 [a]Literally *light* 5:5 [a]Or *Sheol*

4:25 Live for souls. "Now concerning the salvation of our fellow-men; we shall never compass it unless our eyes look right on and our eyelids straight before us. Before we win souls we must live for souls. We need men and women who live to convert others to Christ. The minister had better quit his pulpit if it be not his one burning desire to bring hearts to Jesus' feet. If a divine impulse be not upon him driving him to seek the souls of men, let him go elsewhere with his windy periods. Professors have little right to be in Christ's church unless they are passionately in earnest to increase his kingdom by the salvation of their fellow-men. O my brothers and sisters on whom is the blood-mark of redemption, I charge you concerning this matter to 'let your eyes look right on and let your eyelids look straight before you'! Seek souls as dogs hunt their game; eye, nostril, ear all open, and every muscle strained. Converts are not gained by dreamers. We cannot imitate Jesus as a Savior of men by being dull and heartless. In any point in which we follow our Lord let us do it with all our soul." *Charles Spurgeon*

And not for strangers with you.
18Let your fountain be blessed,
And rejoice with the wife of your youth.
19*As a* loving deer and a graceful doe,
Let her breasts satisfy you at all times;
And always be enraptured with her love.
20For why should you, my son, be enraptured by an immoral woman,
And be embraced in the arms of a seductress?

There is no point on which men make greater mistakes than on the relation which exists between the Law and the gospel.

CHARLES SPURGEON

21For the ways of man *are* before the eyes of the LORD,
And He ponders all his paths.
22His own iniquities entrap the wicked *man,*
And he is caught in the cords of his sin.
23He shall die for lack of instruction,
And in the greatness of his folly he shall go astray.

Dangerous Promises

6 My son, if you become surety for your friend,
If you have shaken hands in pledge for a stranger,
2You are snared by the words of your mouth;
You are taken by the words of your mouth.
3So do this, my son, and deliver yourself;
For you have come into the hand of your friend:
Go and humble yourself;
Plead with your friend.
4Give no sleep to your eyes,
Nor slumber to your eyelids.
5Deliver yourself like a gazelle from the hand *of the hunter,*
And like a bird from the hand of the fowler.[a]

The Folly of Indolence

6Go to the ant, you sluggard!
Consider her ways and be wise,
7Which, having no captain,
Overseer or ruler,
8Provides her supplies in the summer,
And gathers her food in the harvest.
9How long will you slumber, O sluggard?
When will you rise from your sleep?
10A little sleep, a little slumber,
A little folding of the hands to sleep—
11So shall your poverty come on you like a prowler,
And your need like an armed man.

The Wicked Man

12A worthless person, a wicked man,
Walks with a perverse mouth;
13He winks with his eyes,
He shuffles his feet,
He points with his fingers;
14Perversity *is* in his heart,
He devises evil continually,
He sows discord.
15Therefore his calamity shall come suddenly;
Suddenly he shall be broken without remedy.

6:5 [a]That is, one who catches birds in a trap or snare

5:19 Biblical sexuality. It comes as a shock to the world that God's Word speaks so openly about sex. It is a gift of God given for both procreation and pleasure, within the bounds of marriage. Those who refuse to keep sexual intimacy within the bounds of the marriage bed will suffer the consequences of their actions (vv. 20–23). It is interesting to note that a man and a woman can have sexual relations thousands of times within their marriage with no fear of AIDS or any other sexually transmitted diseases. See v. 11.

6:6–8 The ant is similar to the Christian who knows the will of God—to seek and save that which is lost. He understands that God isn't willing that any should perish, so he sets about the task of reaching the lost with the gospel. The ant doesn't need anyone telling him what to do; he just does it. See 1 Cor. 15:58.

[16]These six *things* the LORD hates,
Yes, seven *are* an abomination to Him:
[17]A proud look,
A lying tongue,
Hands that shed innocent blood,
[18]A heart that devises wicked plans,
Feet that are swift in running to evil,
[19]A false witness *who* speaks lies,
And one who sows discord among brethren.

Beware of Adultery

[20]My son, keep your father's command,
And do not forsake the law of your mother.
[21]Bind them continually upon your heart;
Tie them around your neck.
[22]When you roam, they[a] will lead you;
When you sleep, they will keep you;
And *when* you awake, they will speak with you.
[23]For the commandment *is* a lamp,
And the law a light;
Reproofs of instruction *are* the way of life,
[24]To keep you from the evil woman,
From the flattering tongue of a seductress.
[25]Do not lust after her beauty in your heart,
Nor let her allure you with her eyelids.
[26]For by means of a harlot
A man is reduced to a crust of bread;
And an adulteress[a] will prey upon his precious life.
[27]Can a man take fire to his bosom,
And his clothes not be burned?
[28]Can one walk on hot coals,
And his feet not be seared?
[29]So *is* he who goes in to his neighbor's wife;
Whoever touches her shall not be innocent.

[30]*People* do not despise a thief
If he steals to satisfy himself when he is starving.
[31]Yet *when* he is found, he must restore sevenfold;
He may have to give up all the substance of his house.
[32]Whoever commits adultery with a woman lacks understanding;
He *who* does so destroys his own soul.
[33]Wounds and dishonor he will get,
And his reproach will not be wiped away.
[34]For jealousy *is* a husband's fury;
Therefore he will not spare in the day of vengeance.
[35]He will accept no recompense,
Nor will he be appeased though you give many gifts.

7 My son, keep my words,
And treasure my commands within you.

6:22 [a]Literally *it* 6:26 [a]Literally *a man's wife,* that is, of another

THE FUNCTION OF THE LAW

6:23 "The absence of God's holy Law from modern preaching is perhaps as responsible as any other factor for the evangelistic impotence of our churches and missions. Only by the light of the Law can the vermin of sin in the heart be exposed. Satan has effectively used a very clever device to silence the Law, which is needed as an instrument to bring perishing men to Christ.

"It is imperative that preachers of today learn how to declare the spiritual Law of God; for, until we learn how to wound consciences, we shall have no wounds to bind with gospel bandages." *Walter Chantry, Today's Gospel: Authentic or Synthetic?*

"The Law is the God-given light to illuminate the dark soul of man." *Mark A. Spence*

"Unless we see our shortcomings in the light of the Law and holiness of God, we do not see them as sin at all." *J. I. Packer*

6:23–30 Never fall into the trap of thinking that God's Law has no relevance for the Christian. Not only is it a tutor to bring him to Christ (Gal. 3:24), but it leaves him with knowledge that will guide him for the rest of his life. We shouldn't disregard instruction of the tutor after we graduate. The Ten Commandments will keep the Christian from fornication (v. 24), lust (v. 25), adultery (v. 29), and theft (v. 30).

QUESTIONS & OBJECTIONS

6:25

"What if someone doesn't think lust is a violation of the Ten Commandments?"

If a man commits rape and doesn't consider it a violation of the law, it doesn't change the fact that it is. Here is proof that lust is a violation of the Ten Commandments: "You have heard that it was said to those of old, 'You shall not commit adultery' [Seventh Commandment]. But I say to you that whoever looks at a woman to lust for her has already committed adultery with her in his heart" (Matt. 5:27,28). So there you have it from the highest authority on earth—the Word of the Living God. If you have the word of a king or a president, you have it on great authority. But this comes from the authority of the Word of God Himself. So, make sure that you quote the verse and don't just refer to it. Jesus quoted the Scriptures word for word when He was tempted by the devil. God's Word doesn't return void. It is quick and powerful and cuts through to the marrow of a sinner's bones, so quote it when you share the gospel.

Another way to strengthen the lust argument is to reason about it. Tell the sinner that lust is "pornography of the mind." Ask if he considers child pornography to be okay. The odds are he will say it is morally wrong. That is his moral standard. God's standard is higher than his, and He says that lusting after anyone other than your spouse is morally wrong.

Also, never forget that you have on your side the sinner's conscience, which bears witness with the Law (see Rom. 2:15), and of course you have the help of God Himself, who promises that the Holy Spirit will convict of sin. So plant the seed and trust that God will faithfully cause it to grow. See also 2 Sam. 13:1,2 comment.

[2]Keep my commands and live,
And my law as the apple of your eye.
[3]Bind them on your fingers;
Write them on the tablet of your heart.
[4]Say to wisdom, "You *are* my sister,"
And call understanding *your* nearest kin,
[5]That they may keep you from the immoral woman,
From the seductress *who* flatters with her words.

The Crafty Harlot

[6]For at the window of my house
I looked through my lattice,
[7]And saw among the simple,
I perceived among the youths,
A young man devoid of understanding,
[8]Passing along the street near her corner;
And he took the path to her house
[9]In the twilight, in the evening,
In the black and dark night.

[10]And there a woman met him,
With the attire of a harlot, and a crafty heart.
[11]She *was* loud and rebellious,
Her feet would not stay at home.
[12]At times *she was* outside, at times in the open square,
Lurking at every corner.
[13]So she caught him and kissed him;
With an impudent face she said to him:
[14]"*I have* peace offerings with me;
Today I have paid my vows.
[15]So I came out to meet you,
Diligently to seek your face,
And I have found you.
[16]I have spread my bed with tapestry,
Colored coverings of Egyptian linen.
[17]I have perfumed my bed
With myrrh, aloes, and cinnamon.
[18]Come, let us take our fill of love until morning;
Let us delight ourselves with love.
[19]For my husband *is* not at home;
He has gone on a long journey;
[20]He has taken a bag of money with him,
And will come home on the appointed day."

[21]With her enticing speech she caused him to yield,
With her flattering lips she seduced him.
[22]Immediately he went after her, as an ox goes to the slaughter,

Or as a fool to the correction of the
stocks,[a]
23Till an arrow struck his liver.
As a bird hastens to the snare,
He did not know it *would cost* his life.

24Now therefore, listen to me, *my*
children;
Pay attention to the words of my
mouth:
25Do not let your heart turn aside to
her ways,
Do not stray into her paths;
26For she has cast down many wounded,
And all who were slain by her were
strong *men.*
27Her house *is* the way to hell,[a]
Descending to the chambers of death.

The Excellence of Wisdom

8 Does not wisdom cry out,
And understanding lift up her voice?
2She takes her stand on the top of the
high hill,
Beside the way, where the paths meet.
3She cries out by the gates, at the
entry of the city,
At the entrance of the doors:
4"To you, O men, I call,
And my voice *is* to the sons of men.
5O you simple ones, understand
prudence,
And you fools, be of an
understanding heart.
6Listen, for I will speak of excellent
things,
And from the opening of my lips *will
come* right things;
7For my mouth will speak truth;
Wickedness *is* an abomination to my
lips.
8All the words of my mouth *are* with
righteousness;
Nothing crooked or perverse *is* in them.
9They *are* all plain to him who
understands,
And right to those who find knowledge.
10Receive my instruction, and not silver,
And knowledge rather than choice
gold;
11For wisdom *is* better than rubies,
And all the things one may desire
cannot be compared with her.

12"I, wisdom, dwell with prudence,
And find out knowledge *and*
discretion.
13The fear of the LORD *is* to hate evil;
Pride and arrogance and the evil way
And the perverse mouth I hate.
14Counsel *is* mine, and sound wisdom;
I *am* understanding, I have strength.
15By me kings reign,
And rulers decree justice.
16By me princes rule, and nobles,
All the judges of the earth.[a]

If you will not have death unto sin, you shall have sin unto death. There is no alternative. If you do not die to sin, you shall die for sin. If you do not slay sin, sin will slay you.

CHARLES SPURGEON

17I love those who love me,
And those who seek me diligently
will find me.
18Riches and honor *are* with me,
Enduring riches and righteousness.
19My fruit *is* better than gold, yes, than
fine gold,
And my revenue than choice silver.
20I traverse the way of righteousness,
In the midst of the paths of justice,
21That I may cause those who love me
to inherit wealth,
That I may fill their treasuries.

22"The LORD possessed me at the
beginning of His way,
Before His works of old.
23I have been established from
everlasting,
From the beginning, before there was

7:22 [a]Septuagint, Syriac, and Targum read *as a dog to bonds;* Vulgate reads *as a lamb...to bonds.* 7:27 [a]Or *Sheol* 8:16 [a]Masoretic Text, Syriac, Targum, and Vulgate read *righteousness;* Septuagint, Bomberg, and some manuscripts and editions read *earth.*

ever an earth.
[24]When *there were* no depths I was
brought forth,
When *there were* no fountains
abounding with water.
[25]Before the mountains were settled,
Before the hills, I was brought forth;
[26]While as yet He had not made the
earth or the fields,
Or the primal dust of the world.
[27]When He prepared the heavens, I *was*
there,
When He drew a circle on the face of
the deep,
[28]When He established the clouds above,
When He strengthened the fountains
of the deep,
[29]When He assigned to the sea its limit,
So that the waters would not
transgress His command,
When He marked out the
foundations of the earth,
[30]Then I was beside Him *as* a master
craftsman;[a]
And I was daily *His* delight,
Rejoicing always before Him,
[31]Rejoicing in His inhabited world,
And my delight *was* with the sons of
men.

[32]"Now therefore, listen to me, *my*
children,
For blessed *are those who* keep my ways.
[33]Hear instruction and be wise,
And do not disdain *it*.
[34]Blessed is the man who listens to me,
Watching daily at my gates,
Waiting at the posts of my doors.
[35]For whoever finds me finds life,
And obtains favor from the LORD;
[36]But he who sins against me wrongs
his own soul;
All those who hate me love death."

The Way of Wisdom

9 Wisdom has built her house,
She has hewn out her seven pillars;
[2]She has slaughtered her meat,
She has mixed her wine,
She has also furnished her table.

8:30 [a]A Jewish tradition reads *one brought up.*

8:22 Jehovah's Witnesses. When Jehovah's Witnesses maintain that Jesus was "made" of the seed of David (that Jesus was *a* god "created" by Jehovah to die for our sins), they may point to Prov. 8:22–35 for justification. However, the Bible is speaking here of "wisdom" (v. 12).

They also may refer to John 14:28 in which Jesus said, "'I am going to the Father,' for My Father is greater than I," but they fail to consider why Jesus said the Father was greater: "But we see Jesus, *who was made a little lower than the angels, for the suffering of death*... that He, by the grace of God, might taste death for everyone" (Heb. 2:9, emphasis added).

In Rom. 1:3, the word used to refer to the incarnation ("born") is *ginomai*, which means "assembled." A body was prepared for God to manifest Himself in the flesh: "And without controversy great is the mystery of godliness: God was manifested in the flesh, justified in the Spirit, seen by angels, preached among the Gentiles, believed on in the world, received up in glory" (1 Tim. 3:16).

8:23 Eternal truth. French philosopher *Simone Weil* once said, "To be always relevant, you have to say things which are eternal." In other words, if you want to reach people in the present society, then rely on God's eternal truths. Many water down the gospel to make it "culturally relevant" for the current society, but the biblical gospel message applies to all people of all times in all places.

"The apostles and prophets of the early church took their transcendent message from Jerusalem to Rome, from biblically literate to biblically illiterate, from slaves to slave owners, from bond to free, from Jew to Greek; they crossed hard national, social, cultural lines and the message never, ever, ever changed." *John MacArthur*

8:35 "Many people think that the mark of an authentic Christian is doctrinal purity; if a person's beliefs are biblical and doctrinally orthodox, then he is a Christian. People who equate orthodoxy with authenticity find it hard to even consider the possibility that, despite the correctness of all their doctrinal positions, they may have missed the deepest reality of the authentic Christian life. But we must never forget that true Christianity is more than teaching—it is a way of life. In fact, it is life itself. 'He who has the Son has life,' remember? When we talk about life, we are talking about something that is far more than mere morality, far more than doctrinal accuracy." *Ray C. Stedman*

[3]She has sent out her maidens,
She cries out from the highest places
of the city,
[4]"Whoever *is* simple, let him turn in
here!"
As for him who lacks understanding,
she says to him,
[5]"Come, eat of my bread
And drink of the wine I have mixed.
[6]Forsake foolishness and live,
And go in the way of understanding.

[7]"He who corrects a scoffer gets shame
for himself,
And he who rebukes a wicked *man*
only harms himself.
[8]Do not correct a scoffer, lest he hate
you;
Rebuke a wise *man,* and he will love
you.
[9]Give *instruction* to a wise *man,* and he
will be still wiser;
Teach a just *man,* and he will increase
in learning.

[10]"The fear of the LORD *is* the beginning
of wisdom,
And the knowledge of the Holy One
is understanding.
[11]For by me your days will be multiplied,
And years of life will be added to you.
[12]If you are wise, you are wise for
yourself,
And *if* you scoff, you will bear *it* alone."

The Way of Folly

[13]A foolish woman is clamorous;
She is simple, and knows nothing.
[14]For she sits at the door of her house,
On a seat *by* the highest places of the
city,
[15]To call to those who pass by,
Who go straight on their way:
[16]"Whoever *is* simple, let him turn in
here";
And *as for* him who lacks
understanding, she says to him,
[17]"Stolen water is sweet,
And bread *eaten* in secret is pleasant."
[18]But he does not know that the dead
are there,
That her guests *are* in the depths of
hell.[a]

Wise Sayings of Solomon

10 The proverbs of Solomon:

A wise son makes a glad father,
But a foolish son *is* the grief of his
mother.

[2]Treasures of wickedness profit nothing,
But righteousness delivers from death.
[3]The LORD will not allow the righteous
soul to famish,
But He casts away the desire of the
wicked.

[4]He who has a slack hand becomes
poor,
But the hand of the diligent makes rich.
[5]He who gathers in summer *is* a wise

9:18 [a]Or *Sheol*

9:17 Our sinful hearts are so perverse that sin promises excitement. Despite the claim of modern evangelism that we can't find happiness until we come to Jesus, sin is indeed enticing and pleasurable, and can make a man or woman happy. See Jer. 12:1 and Heb. 11:25.

9:18 Warning of hell. "If we that have the care of souls, knew what hell was, had seen the state of the damned, or by any other means, become sensible how dreadful their case was; and at the same time knew that the bigger part of men went thither; and saw our hearers in eminent danger, and that they were not sensible of their danger, and so after being often warned neglected to escape, it would be morally impossible for us to avoid abundantly and most earnestly setting before them the dreadfulness of that misery they were in danger of, and their great exposedness to it, and warning them to fly from it, and even to cry aloud to them." *Jonathan Edwards*

10:2 All the money in the world will not turn the head of the Judge of the Universe. Money may buy a pardon from a civil court, but only righteousness will deliver the guilty from the wrath of Eternal Justice. See Prov. 11:4.

Questions & Objections

10:21

"Since we are not saved by works, why can't I maintain a relationship with God without witnessing?"

This is an honest question. Here is the problem. We know that we are saved because the fruit of God's Spirit will begin manifesting through us. God is love; therefore, we should be filled with love if we have been truly saved (see Rom. 5:5). Think of this scenario. You are in Africa. A child is lying on the ground in front of you starving to death. You have food in your hand. You know God wants you to share the food with the dying child. So the question is, "Why can't I have a good relationship with God, without sharing the food?" You have to answer that yourself.

son;
He who sleeps in harvest *is* a son who
causes shame.

6Blessings *are* on the head of the
righteous,
But violence covers the mouth of the
wicked.
7The memory of the righteous *is* blessed,
But the name of the wicked will rot.

8The wise in heart will receive
commands,
But a prating fool will fall.

9He who walks with integrity walks
securely,
But he who perverts his ways will
become known.

10He who winks with the eye causes
trouble,
But a prating fool will fall.

11The mouth of the righteous *is* a well
of life,
But violence covers the mouth of the
wicked.

12Hatred stirs up strife,
But love covers all sins.

13Wisdom is found on the lips of him
who has understanding,
But a rod *is* for the back of him who
is devoid of understanding.

14Wise *people* store up knowledge,
But the mouth of the foolish *is* near
destruction.

15The rich man's wealth *is* his strong
city;
The destruction of the poor *is* their
poverty.

16The labor of the righteous *leads* to life,
The wages of the wicked to sin.

17He who keeps instruction *is in* the
way of life,
But he who refuses correction goes
astray.

18Whoever hides hatred *has* lying lips,
And whoever spreads slander *is* a fool.

19In the multitude of words sin is not
lacking,
But he who restrains his lips *is* wise.
20The tongue of the righteous *is* choice
silver;
The heart of the wicked *is worth* little.
21The lips of the righteous feed many,
But fools die for lack of wisdom.[a]

22The blessing of the LORD makes *one*
rich,
And He adds no sorrow with it.

23To do evil *is* like sport to a fool,

10:21 [a]Literally *heart*

10:7 Perhaps this is why not too many people name their children Adolf, Judas, or Jezebel.

But a man of understanding has
wisdom.
24The fear of the wicked will come
upon him,
And the desire of the righteous will
be granted.
25When the whirlwind passes by, the
wicked *is* no *more*,
But the righteous *has* an everlasting
foundation.

26As vinegar to the teeth and smoke to
the eyes,
So *is* the lazy *man* to those who send
him.

27The fear of the LORD prolongs days,
But the years of the wicked will be
shortened.
28The hope of the righteous *will be*
gladness,
But the expectation of the wicked will
perish.
29The way of the LORD *is* strength for
the upright,
But destruction *will come* to the
workers of iniquity.

30The righteous will never be removed,
But the wicked will not inhabit the
earth.
31The mouth of the righteous brings
forth wisdom,
But the perverse tongue will be cut out.
32The lips of the righteous know what
is acceptable,
But the mouth of the wicked *what is*
perverse.

11 Dishonest scales *are* an abomination to the LORD,
But a just weight *is* His delight.

2When pride comes, then comes
shame;
But with the humble *is* wisdom.

3The integrity of the upright will guide
them,
But the perversity of the unfaithful
will destroy them.
4Riches do not profit in the day of
wrath,
But righteousness delivers from death.
5The righteousness of the blameless
will direct[a] his way aright,
But the wicked will fall by his own
wickedness.
6The righteousness of the upright will
deliver them,
But the unfaithful will be caught by
their lust.

7When a wicked man dies, *his*

11:5 [a]Or *make smooth* or *straight*

10:32 Knowing what's acceptable. There is no record of David seeking God for His will before he confronted Goliath. How could this be? The Scriptures say, "In all your ways acknowledge Him, and He shall direct your paths" (Prov. 3:6). Shouldn't David have acknowledged the Lord in some way? No doubt, he did pray as he faced his enemy, but there is no proof that David asked God whether he should attack the giant Philistine. The reason for this is clear. The Bible tells us, "The lips of the righteous know what is acceptable." There are certain things that we know are not acceptable. If you saw an elderly woman fall to the ground, would you ask God whether or not you should help her up? Some things should be obvious to the godly. David took one look at the situation and saw that such a thing was completely unacceptable—that this "uncircumcised Philistine" was defying the armies of the Living God.

David could draw that conclusion because he had a relationship with God. His senses were "exercised to discern both good and evil" (Heb. 5:14). He knew the Lord, and those who "know their God shall be strong, and carry out great exploits" (Dan. 11:32).

11:1 We must never forget that God loves honesty in our dealings with others. See v. 3.

11:4 Riches in this life may buy a clever defense lawyer or turn a corrupt judge's head, but on the Day of Wrath the righteousness of Jesus Christ will be the only thing that will deliver the sinner from eternal death. See Rev. 6:15 comment.

11:5–7 Notice the surety of these verses. They *will* come to pass.

expectation will perish,
And the hope of the unjust perishes.
8The righteous is delivered from trouble,
And it comes to the wicked instead.
9The hypocrite with *his* mouth
destroys his neighbor,
But through knowledge the righteous
will be delivered.
10When it goes well with the righteous,
the city rejoices;
And when the wicked perish, *there is*
jubilation.
11By the blessing of the upright the city
is exalted,
But it is overthrown by the mouth of
the wicked.

12He who is devoid of wisdom despises
his neighbor,
But a man of understanding holds his
peace.

13A talebearer reveals secrets,
But he who is of a faithful spirit
conceals a matter.

14Where *there is* no counsel, the people
fall;
But in the multitude of counselors
there is safety.

15He who is surety for a stranger will
suffer,
But one who hates being surety is
secure.

16A gracious woman retains honor,
But ruthless *men* retain riches.
17The merciful man does good for his
own soul,
But *he who is* cruel troubles his own
flesh.
18The wicked *man* does deceptive work,
But he who sows righteousness *will
have* a sure reward.
19As righteousness *leads* to life,
So he who pursues evil *pursues it* to
his own death.
20Those who are of a perverse heart *are*
an abomination to the LORD,
But *the* blameless in their ways *are*
His delight.
21*Though they join* forces,[a] the wicked
will not go unpunished;
But the posterity of the righteous will
be delivered.

22*As* a ring of gold in a swine's snout,
So is a lovely woman who lacks
discretion.

23The desire of the righteous *is* only
good,
But the expectation of the wicked *is*
wrath.

24There is *one* who scatters, yet
increases more;
And there is *one* who withholds more

11:21 [a]Literally *hand to hand*

11:9 If we wouldn't say it in prayer, we shouldn't say it at all.

11:13 The damage of gossip. A woman once spread some juicy gossip about a local pastor. What he had supposedly done became common knowledge around town. Then she found that what she had heard wasn't true. She gallantly went to the pastor and asked for his forgiveness. The pastor forgave her, but then told her to take a pillow full of tiny feathers to a corner of the town, and in high winds, shake the feathers out. Then he told her to try to pick up every feather. He explained that the damage had already been done. She had destroyed his good reputation, and trying to repair the damage was like trying to pick up feathers in high winds.

The Bible says that there is life and death in the power of the tongue (Prov. 18:21; see also James 3:8). Pray with the psalmist, "Set a guard, O LORD, over my mouth; keep watch over the door of my lips" (Psa. 141:3). Remember the old saying, "He who gossips *to* you will gossip *about* you."

11:21 Though the entire world joins forces in a unity of spirit and says that there is no hell, it is still a reality. There *will* be a Judgment Day and justice will be done.

11:24 The wallet is the final frontier. There is nothing wrong with riches. However, those who have wealth must not trust in money (v. 28) and must be willing to share their prosperity with others. See 1 Tim. 6:17–19.

than is right,
But it *leads* to poverty.
25The generous soul will be made rich,
And he who waters will also be
watered himself.
26The people will curse him who
withholds grain,
But blessing *will be* on the head of
him who sells *it*.

27He who earnestly seeks good finds
favor,
But trouble will come to him who
seeks *evil*.

28He who trusts in his riches will fall,
But the righteous will flourish like
foliage.

> What health is to the heart, holiness is to the soul.
>
> **JOHN FLAVEL**

29He who troubles his own house will
inherit the wind,
And the fool *will be* servant to the
wise of heart.

30The fruit of the righteous *is a* tree of
life,
And he who wins souls *is* wise.

31If the righteous will be recompensed
on the earth,
How much more the ungodly and the
sinner.

12

1Whoever loves instruction loves
knowledge,
But he who hates correction *is* stupid.

2A good *man* obtains favor from the
LORD,
But a man of wicked intentions He
will condemn.

3A man is not established by
wickedness,
But the root of the righteous cannot
be moved.

4An excellent[a] wife *is* the crown of her
husband,
But she who causes shame *is* like
rottenness in his bones.

5The thoughts of the righteous *are* right,
But the counsels of the wicked *are*
deceitful.
6The words of the wicked *are*, "Lie in
wait for blood,"
But the mouth of the upright will
deliver them.

7The wicked are overthrown and *are*
no more,
But the house of the righteous will
stand.

8A man will be commended according
to his wisdom,

12:4 [a]Literally *A wife of valor*

11:30 "Even if I were utterly selfish and had no care for anything but my own happiness, I would choose, if God allowed, to be a soul winner, for never did I know perfect, overflowing, unutterable happiness of the purest and most ennobling order till I first heard of one who had sought and found a Savior through my means." *Charles Spurgeon*

Lifestyle evangelism. Here's how to cultivate true lifestyle evangelism: 1) Pray that God uses you to reach the lost. 2) Ask for wisdom to use the time you have effectively for evangelism. Treat every day as though it were your last opportunity to share Christ. One day you will be right. 3) Study how to answer every man who asks you a reason for the hope that is in you (1 Pet. 3:15; see Prov. 16:23). 4) Don't wait for sinners to approach you; go to them (Mark 16:15). Find a "fishing hole" and go there regularly. 5) Use any anxiety as a catalyst to drive you to prayer and trust in God. Don't let the fear of man paralyze you (Phil. 1:28). You will realize the spiritual nature of fear after you conquer it. Confront it with the Word of God: "I can do all things through Christ who strengthens me" (Phil. 4:13). 6) Encourage others, by example and exhortation, in the task of evangelism.

QUESTIONS & OBJECTIONS

12:22

"What if someone says he has broken only the Commandment about lying?"

Committing even one sin, one time, is enough to send someone to hell (see James 2:10). But we know that every person has a multitude of sins. For starters, the person has failed to love God with all of his heart, soul, mind, and strength. He has dishonored his parents' good name by being a liar. Besides that, you can't trust anything he says because he is a self-admitted liar. However, I usually say, "There's bad news. All liars will have their part in the lake of fire" (Rev. 21:8). While telling "white lies" may not seem serious to us, it shows a heart that is willing to deceive, and proves that "the heart is deceitful above all things, and desperately wicked" (Jer. 17:9). I explain that lying is very serious to God. The Bible says that "lying lips are an abomination to the LORD."

But he who is of a perverse heart will
be despised.

9 Better *is the one* who is slighted but
has a servant,
Than he who honors himself but
lacks bread.

10 A righteous *man* regards the life of his
animal,
But the tender mercies of the wicked
are cruel.

11 He who tills his land will be satisfied
with bread,
But he who follows frivolity *is* devoid
of understanding.[a]

12 The wicked covet the catch of evil *men,*
But the root of the righteous yields
fruit.
13 The wicked is ensnared by the
transgression of *his* lips,
But the righteous will come through
trouble.
14 A man will be satisfied with good by
the fruit of *his* mouth,
And the recompense of a man's hands
will be rendered to him.

15 The way of a fool *is* right in his own
eyes,
But he who heeds counsel *is* wise.
16 A fool's wrath is known at once,
But a prudent *man* covers shame.

17 He *who* speaks truth declares
righteousness,
But a false witness, deceit.
18 There is one who speaks like the
piercings of a sword,
But the tongue of the wise *promotes*
health.
19 The truthful lip shall be established
forever,
But a lying tongue *is* but for a moment.
20 Deceit is in the heart of those who
devise evil,
But counselors of peace have joy.
21 No grave trouble will overtake the
righteous,
But the wicked shall be filled with evil.
22 Lying lips *are* an abomination to the
LORD,
But those who deal truthfully *are* His
delight.

23 A prudent man conceals knowledge,
But the heart of fools proclaims
foolishness.

24 The hand of the diligent will rule,

12:11 [a]Literally *heart*

12:15 This verse sums up the philosophy of a world that professes to be wise yet ignores the counsel of God's Word.

12:17 We are to follow the example of Jesus, who "proclaimed the good news of righteousness in the great assembly" (see Psa. 40:6–10).

But the lazy *man* will be put to forced
labor.

25Anxiety in the heart of man causes
depression,
But a good word makes it glad.

26The righteous should choose his
friends carefully,
For the way of the wicked leads them
astray.

27The lazy *man* does not roast what he
took in hunting,
But diligence *is* man's precious
possession.

28In the way of righteousness *is* life,
And in *its* pathway *there is* no death.

13 A wise son *heeds* his father's instruction,
But a scoffer does not listen to rebuke.

2A man shall eat well by the fruit of *his*
mouth,
But the soul of the unfaithful feeds on
violence.
3He who guards his mouth preserves
his life,
But he who opens wide his lips shall
have destruction.

4The soul of a lazy *man* desires, and
has nothing;
But the soul of the diligent shall be
made rich.

5A righteous *man* hates lying,
But a wicked *man* is loathsome and
comes to shame.
6Righteousness guards *him whose* way
is blameless,
But wickedness overthrows the sinner.

7There is one who makes himself rich,
yet *has* nothing;
And one who makes himself poor, yet
has great riches.

8The ransom of a man's life *is* his riches,
But the poor does not hear rebuke.

9The light of the righteous rejoices,
But the lamp of the wicked will be
put out.

10By pride comes nothing but strife,
But with the well-advised *is* wisdom.

11Wealth *gained by* dishonesty will be
diminished,
But he who gathers by labor will
increase.

12Hope deferred makes the heart sick,
But *when* the desire comes, *it is* a tree
of life.

13He who despises the word will be
destroyed,
But he who fears the commandment
will be rewarded.
14The law of the wise *is* a fountain of
life,
To turn *one* away from the snares of
death.

15Good understanding gains favor,
But the way of the unfaithful *is* hard.
16Every prudent *man* acts with
knowledge,
But a fool lays open *his* folly.

17A wicked messenger falls into trouble,
But a faithful ambassador *brings* health.

18Poverty and shame *will come* to him
who disdains correction,

12:25 Are you worried and depressed about the future? Then read and believe the "good word" of God's Word. Nothing banishes fear like faith. Trusting in God's promises is like switching on a bright light in a dark room of gloom.

13:13 The Word will judge and condemn the guilty on the Last Day. Those who fear when they realize that they have sinned against God by transgressing His Law will be rewarded in the gospel. See Gal. 3:24.

But he who regards a rebuke will be
honored.

19A desire accomplished is sweet to the
soul,
But *it is* an abomination to fools to
depart from evil.

20He who walks with wise *men* will be
wise,
But the companion of fools will be
destroyed.

21Evil pursues sinners,
But to the righteous, good shall be
repaid.

22A good *man* leaves an inheritance to
his children's children,
But the wealth of the sinner is stored
up for the righteous.

23Much food *is in* the fallow *ground* of
the poor,
And for lack of justice there is waste.[a]

24He who spares his rod hates his son,
But he who loves him disciplines him
promptly.

25The righteous eats to the satisfying of
his soul,
But the stomach of the wicked shall
be in want.

14 The wise woman builds her house,
But the foolish pulls it down with
her hands.

2He who walks in his uprightness fears
the LORD,
But *he who is* perverse in his ways
despises Him.

3In the mouth of a fool *is* a rod of pride,
But the lips of the wise will preserve
them.

4Where no oxen *are,* the trough *is* clean;
But much increase *comes* by the
strength of an ox.

5A faithful witness does not lie,
But a false witness will utter lies.

6A scoffer seeks wisdom and does not
find it,
But knowledge *is* easy to him who
understands.

7Go from the presence of a foolish man,
When you do not perceive *in him* the
lips of knowledge.

8The wisdom of the prudent *is* to
understand his way,
But the folly of fools *is* deceit.

9Fools mock at sin,
But among the upright *there is* favor.

10The heart knows its own bitterness,
And a stranger does not share its joy.

11The house of the wicked will be
overthrown,
But the tent of the upright will flourish.

12There is a way *that seems* right to a man,
But its end *is* the way of death.

13Even in laughter the heart may sorrow,
And the end of mirth *may be* grief.

14The backslider in heart will be filled
with his own ways,
But a good man *will be satisfied* from
above.[a]

13:23 [a]Literally *what is swept away*

13:19 Sinners love darkness; it is their security. See Prov. 14:9; John 3:19,20.

14:5 See v. 25.

14:14 False converts have no concern for God's will to reach the lost. Those who manage to find themselves in a pulpit will build their own kingdom rather than God's. See also Acts 20:30.

Springboards for Preaching and Witnessing

The Key

14:12 Back in the Old West, a number of men were upstairs in a boarding house amusing themselves with a game of cards when there was a cry from the street below: "Fire! Fire!" The men looked at one another in disbelief. One of the windows grew orange with the flames. "Wait!" said the dealer. "Let's just finish this hand; we've got plenty of time—I have a key to the back door." The men nodded in approval, then quickly picked up the dealt cards.

Precious minutes passed. One of the men became nervous as the flames licked through the now broken window. With darting eyes and a sweat-filled brow, he asked for the key. "Coward!" muttered the dealer as he tossed across the key. Each of them then rushed to the door and waited with bated breath as the key was placed into the lock. "It won't turn!" was the cry. "Let me have it!" said the dealer. As he tried in vain to turn the key, he whispered in horror, *"It's the wrong key!"*

15The simple believes every word,
But the prudent considers well his steps.
16A wise *man* fears and departs from evil,
But a fool rages and is self-confident.
17A quick-tempered *man* acts foolishly,
And a man of wicked intentions is hated.
18The simple inherit folly,
But the prudent are crowned with knowledge.
19The evil will bow before the good,
And the wicked at the gates of the righteous.

20The poor *man* is hated even by his own neighbor,
But the rich *has* many friends.
21He who despises his neighbor sins;
But he who has mercy on the poor, happy *is* he.
22Do they not go astray who devise evil?
But mercy and truth *belong* to those who devise good.

23In all labor there is profit,
But idle chatter[a] *leads* only to poverty.

24The crown of the wise is their riches,
But the foolishness of fools *is* folly.

25A true witness delivers souls,
But a deceitful *witness* speaks lies.

26In the fear of the LORD *there is* strong confidence,
And His children will have a place of refuge.
27The fear of the LORD *is* a fountain of life,
To turn *one* away from the snares of death.

28In a multitude of people is a king's honor,
But in the lack of people *is* the downfall of a prince.

29*He who is* slow to wrath has great understanding,
But *he who is* impulsive[a] exalts folly.

30A sound heart *is* life to the body,
But envy *is* rottenness to the bones.

31He who oppresses the poor reproaches his Maker,
But he who honors Him has mercy on the needy.

14:14 [a]Literally *from above himself* 14:23 [a]Literally *talk of the lips* 14:29 [a]Literally *short of spirit*

14:25 A "witness" is not called upon to give an eloquent speech, but to merely testify to what he has seen and heard.

14:27 Here is a fountain from which most men refuse to drink. Their prejudicial minds think that its waters are bitter, when in truth they are incredibly sweet. The fear of the Lord helps men shake off that beast called "sin"—which is sucking from them their very life's blood.

32The wicked is banished in his
wickedness,
But the righteous has a refuge in his
death.

33Wisdom rests in the heart of him who
has understanding,
But *what is* in the heart of fools is
made known.
34Righteousness exalts a nation,
But sin *is* a reproach to *any* people.

35The king's favor *is* toward a wise
servant,
But his wrath *is against* him who
causes shame.

15 A soft answer turns away wrath,
But a harsh word stirs up anger.
2The tongue of the wise uses
knowledge rightly,
But the mouth of fools pours forth
foolishness.

3The eyes of the LORD *are* in every place,
Keeping watch on the evil and the
good.

4A wholesome tongue *is* a tree of life,
But perverseness in it breaks the spirit.

5A fool despises his father's instruction,
But he who receives correction is
prudent.

6*In* the house of the righteous *there is*
much treasure,
But in the revenue of the wicked is
trouble.

7The lips of the wise disperse
knowledge,
But the heart of the fool *does* not *do* so.

8The sacrifice of the wicked *is* an
abomination to the LORD,
But the prayer of the upright *is* His
delight.
9The way of the wicked *is* an
abomination to the LORD,
But He loves him who follows
righteousness.

10Harsh discipline *is* for him who
forsakes the way,
And he who hates correction will die.

11Hell[a] and Destruction[b] *are* before the
LORD;
So how much more the hearts of the
sons of men.

15:11 [a]Or *Sheol* [b]Hebrew *Abaddon*

14:34 "The moral principles and precepts contained in the Scriptures ought to form the basis of all our civil constitutions and laws. All the miseries and evils which men suffer from—vice, crime, ambition, injustice, oppression, slavery, and war—proceed from their despising or neglecting the precepts contained in the Bible." *Noah Webster*

15:1 Speak softly. This verse needs to be written on the hearts of all who preach the gospel, whether they share their faith with sinners one-on-one or preach open-air. If sinners become angry when you witness to them, speak softly. If you think you are about to be hit, ask the person his name to help diffuse the situation. Don't be afraid to gently change the subject, and don't wait to be a martyr. Jesus said to flee from a city that persecutes you (Matt. 10:23). Paul left one city in a basket (2 Cor. 11:33). For other verses on the spirit in which we should share our faith, see Prov. 16:32.

15:7 God's Law is what gives knowledge (see Rom. 3:20,21). Those who are wise will tell sinners of its righteous requirements.

15:8 When sinners think they are righteous because they give money, attend church, or live what they consider to be a virtuous life, it is an "abomination to the Lord." Even their thoughts are an abomination to Him (v. 26). This is because they stand guilty before Him. Their good works are provoked by a guilty conscience. Like a despicable criminal trying to pervert justice by offering the judge a bribe, they think their good deeds will outweigh their sins (see Heb. 9:14).

"Good works, as they are called, in sinners are nothing but splendid sins." *Augustine*

15:11 For whether God is present even in hell, see Psa. 139:7,8 comment.

[12]A scoffer does not love one who
corrects him,
Nor will he go to the wise.

[13]A merry heart makes a cheerful
countenance,
But by sorrow of the heart the spirit is
broken.

[14]The heart of him who has
understanding seeks knowledge,
But the mouth of fools feeds on
foolishness.

[15]All the days of the afflicted *are* evil,
But he who is of a merry heart *has* a
continual feast.

[16]Better *is* a little with the fear of the
LORD,
Than great treasure with trouble.
[17]Better *is* a dinner of herbs[a] where love
is,
Than a fatted calf with hatred.

[18]A wrathful man stirs up strife,
But *he who is* slow to anger allays
contention.

[19]The way of the lazy *man is* like a
hedge of thorns,
But the way of the upright *is* a highway.

[20]A wise son makes a father glad,
But a foolish man despises his mother.

[21]Folly *is* joy *to him who is* destitute of
discernment,
But a man of understanding walks
uprightly.

[22]Without counsel, plans go awry,
But in the multitude of counselors
they are established.

"I do not believe that any man can preach the gospel who does not preach the Law."

Charles Spurgeon

[23]A man has joy by the answer of his
mouth,
And a word *spoken* in due season,
how good *it is!*

[24]The way of life *winds* upward for the
wise,
That he may turn away from hell[a]
below.

[25]The LORD will destroy the house of
the proud,
But He will establish the boundary of
the widow.

[26]The thoughts of the wicked *are* an
abomination to the LORD,
But *the words* of the pure *are* pleasant.

[27]He who is greedy for gain troubles his

15:17 [a]Or *vegetables* 15:24 [a]Or *Sheol*

15:15 Laughter is the enemy of legalism. Liberty and joy go hand in hand.

15:21 Use your time to further the gospel (see Eph. 5:15,16). So much of today's entertainment is folly. If shallow entertainment gives us joy, it reveals our shallow understanding of the precious nature of time.

15:23 What a joy it is to direct a lost sinner to the Savior. The gospel is always in season. See 2 Tim. 4:2.

own house,
But he who hates bribes will live.

28The heart of the righteous studies how to answer,
But the mouth of the wicked pours forth evil.

29The LORD *is* far from the wicked,
But He hears the prayer of the righteous.

30The light of the eyes rejoices the heart,
And a good report makes the bones healthy.[a]

31The ear that hears the rebukes of life
Will abide among the wise.
32He who disdains instruction despises his own soul,
But he who heeds rebuke gets understanding.
33The fear of the LORD *is* the instruction of wisdom,
And before honor *is* humility.

16 The preparations of the heart *belong* to man,
But the answer of the tongue *is* from the LORD.

2All the ways of a man *are* pure in his own eyes,
But the LORD weighs the spirits.

3Commit your works to the LORD,
And your thoughts will be established.

4The LORD has made all for Himself,
Yes, even the wicked for the day of doom.

5Everyone proud in heart *is* an abomination to the LORD;
Though they join forces,[a] none will go unpunished.

6In mercy and truth
Atonement is provided for iniquity;
And by the fear of the LORD *one* departs from evil.

7When a man's ways please the LORD,
He makes even his enemies to be at peace with him.

8Better *is* a little with righteousness,
Than vast revenues without justice.

9A man's heart plans his way,
But the LORD directs his steps.

10Divination *is* on the lips of the king;
His mouth must not transgress in judgment.
11Honest weights and scales *are* the LORD's;

15:30 [a]Literally *fat* 16:5 [a]Literally *hand to hand*

15:29 "No man is greater than his prayer life. The pastor who is not praying is playing; the people who are not praying are straying. . . We have many organizers, but few agonizers; many players and payers, few pray-ers; many singers, few clingers; lots of pastors, few wrestlers; many fears, few tears; much fashion, little passion; many interferers, few intercessors; many writers, but few fighters. Failing here, we fail everywhere." *Leonard Ravenhill*

16:2 This is never so evident as when you ask a guilty sinner if he thinks he is a good person (see Prov. 21:2; Luke 16:15). When the Law is used properly, it strips a man of self-righteousness. See Luke 18:18–23.

16:5 God resists those who are proud. Grace is only for the humble. (See James 4:6.) Biblical evangelism is always "Law to the proud; grace to the humble." With the Law, we break the hard heart. With the gospel, we heal the broken heart.

16:6 Men will not let go of their beloved sins unless the fear of the Lord grips their sin-loving hearts. Sinners are like a child whose eyes sparkle with delight as he holds a stick of lighted dynamite. He will not let go of it unless he is convinced that he is in terrible danger. The Law of God coupled with future punishment is the convincing agent that God has chosen to awaken the sinner. He must be told that God (who has the power to cast his soul into hell) will judge the world (on Judgment Day) in righteousness (by the perfect and righteous standard of His Law). See Psa. 19:8.

QUESTIONS & OBJECTIONS

16:11

"I have broken the Ten Commandments, but I do good things for people."

Many people do similar things. They may steal from their employer or cheat on their taxes, then give to a charity or spend Thanksgiving helping at a soup kitchen. They think they are balancing the scales: they have done bad, and now they are doing good. However, the Bible reveals that the *motive* of guilty sinners is one of guilt (see Heb. 9:14). They are attempting to bribe the Judge of the Universe. The Judge in this case will not be corrupted. He must punish all sinners. Good works cannot earn mercy; it comes purely by the grace of God. He will dismiss our iniquity only on the grounds of our faith in Jesus—the One who paid our fine in His life's blood.

All the weights in the bag *are* His work.
12*It is* an abomination for kings to
commit wickedness,
For a throne is established by
righteousness.
13Righteous lips *are* the delight of kings,
And they love him who speaks *what is*
right.
14As messengers of death *is* the king's
wrath,
But a wise man will appease it.
15In the light of the king's face *is* life,
And his favor *is* like a cloud of the
latter rain.

16How much better to get wisdom than
gold!
And to get understanding is to be
chosen rather than silver.

17The highway of the upright *is* to
depart from evil;
He who keeps his way preserves his
soul.

18Pride *goes* before destruction,
And a haughty spirit before a fall.
19Better *to be* of a humble spirit with
the lowly,
Than to divide the spoil with the proud.
20He who heeds the word wisely will
find good,
And whoever trusts in the LORD,
happy *is* he.

21The wise in heart will be called
prudent,
And sweetness of the lips increases
learning.

22Understanding *is* a wellspring of life
to him who has it.
But the correction of fools *is* folly.

23The heart of the wise teaches his
mouth,
And adds learning to his lips.

24Pleasant words *are like* a honeycomb,
Sweetness to the soul and health to
the bones.

25There is a way *that seems* right to a
man,
But its end *is* the way of death.

26The person who labors, labors for
himself,

16:20 Faith vs. trust. Unbelievers have a misunderstanding about the word "faith" (an intellectual belief) and the word "trust" (a reliance on a person). Faith in Jesus has nothing to do with an intellectual belief, because it is not in His historical existence. It is rather a trust that we have in Him for our eternal salvation. Faith in the fact that Jesus lived historically will do nothing for you. However, trust in Him as Lord and Savior will give you everlasting life.

16:25 See Prov. 12:15. The way of self-righteousness seems right to men. See also Prov. 15:8 comment.

For his *hungry* mouth drives him *on.*

27An ungodly man digs up evil,
And *it is* on his lips like a burning fire.
28A perverse man sows strife,
And a whisperer separates the best of friends.
29A violent man entices his neighbor,
And leads him in a way *that is* not good.
30He winks his eye to devise perverse things;
He purses his lips *and* brings about evil.

31The silver-haired head *is* a crown of glory,
If it is found in the way of righteousness.

32*He who is* slow to anger *is* better than the mighty,
And he who rules his spirit than he who takes a city.

33The lot is cast into the lap,
But its every decision *is* from the LORD.

17 Better *is* a dry morsel with quietness,
Than a house full of feasting[a] *with* strife.

2A wise servant will rule over a son who causes shame,
And will share an inheritance among the brothers.

3The refining pot *is* for silver and the furnace for gold,
But the LORD tests the hearts.

4An evildoer gives heed to false lips;
A liar listens eagerly to a spiteful tongue.

5He who mocks the poor reproaches his Maker;
He who is glad at calamity will not go unpunished.

6Children's children *are* the crown of old men,
And the glory of children *is* their father.

Any man who declares children to be born perfect was never a father. Your child without evil? You without eyes, you mean!

CHARLES SPURGEON

7Excellent speech is not becoming to a fool,
Much less lying lips to a prince.

8A present *is* a precious stone in the eyes of its possessor;
Wherever he turns, he prospers.

9He who covers a transgression seeks love,
But he who repeats a matter separates friends.

10Rebuke is more effective for a wise *man*
Than a hundred blows on a fool.

11An evil *man* seeks only rebellion;
Therefore a cruel messenger will be sent against him.

12Let a man meet a bear robbed of her cubs,
Rather than a fool in his folly.

17:1 [a]Or *sacrificial meals*

16:32 This is the spirit in which we should share our faith. See Luke 6:28.
"He who masters his passions is a king even while in chains. He who is ruled by his passions is a slave even while sitting on a throne." *Richard Wurmbrand*

17:11 A rebellious heart is an open door to the demonic realm. This was the case with King Saul.

[13]Whoever rewards evil for good,
Evil will not depart from his house.

[14]The beginning of strife *is like* releasing water;
Therefore stop contention before a quarrel starts.

[15]He who justifies the wicked, and he who condemns the just,
Both of them alike *are* an abomination to the LORD.

[16]Why *is there* in the hand of a fool the purchase price of wisdom,
Since *he has* no heart *for it?*

[17]A friend loves at all times,
And a brother is born for adversity.

[18]A man devoid of understanding shakes hands in a pledge,
And becomes surety for his friend.

[19]He who loves transgression loves strife,
And he who exalts his gate seeks destruction.

[20]He who has a deceitful heart finds no good,
And he who has a perverse tongue falls into evil.

[21]He who begets a scoffer *does so* to his sorrow,
And the father of a fool has no joy.

[22]A merry heart does good, *like* medicine,[a]
But a broken spirit dries the bones.

[23]A wicked *man* accepts a bribe behind the back[a]
To pervert the ways of justice.

[24]Wisdom *is* in the sight of him who has understanding,
But the eyes of a fool *are* on the ends of the earth.

[25]A foolish son *is* a grief to his father,
And bitterness to her who bore him.

[26]Also, to punish the righteous *is* not good,
Nor to strike princes for *their* uprightness.

[27]He who has knowledge spares his words,
And a man of understanding is of a calm spirit.
[28]Even a fool is counted wise when he holds his peace;
When he shuts his lips, *he is considered* perceptive.

18

A man who isolates himself seeks his own desire;
He rages against all wise judgment.

[2]A fool has no delight in understanding,
But in expressing his own heart.

[3]When the wicked comes, contempt comes also;
And with dishonor *comes* reproach.

[4]The words of a man's mouth *are* deep

17:22 [a]Or *makes medicine even better* **17:23** [a]Literally *from the bosom*

17:14 See Matt. 12:36 comment.

17:22 Let the joy of the Lord be your strength. See Prov. 15:15 comment.

17:24 True riches are laid before us in the Word of God. Those who ignore these "exceedingly great and precious promises" (2 Pet. 1:4) will never be content.

18:1 Never isolate yourself from other Christians. Those who are not in regular fellowship with other believers make themselves an easier target for the enemy. Satan is as a roaring lion, seeking to devour us (1 Pet. 5:8). The first thing a lion does in stalking its prey is to isolate individual members from the herd. See Heb. 10:25.

waters;
The wellspring of wisdom is a flowing
brook.

5*It is* not good to show partiality to the
wicked,
Or to overthrow the righteous in
judgment.

6A fool's lips enter into contention,
And his mouth calls for blows.
7A fool's mouth *is* his destruction,
And his lips *are* the snare of his soul.
8The words of a talebearer *are* like
tasty trifles,[a]
And they go down into the inmost
body.

9He who is slothful in his work
Is a brother to him who is a great
destroyer.

10The name of the LORD *is* a strong
tower;
The righteous run to it and are safe.
11The rich man's wealth *is* his strong
city,
And like a high wall in his own esteem.

12Before destruction the heart of a man
is haughty,
And before honor *is* humility.

13He who answers a matter before he
hears *it,*
It *is* folly and shame to him.

14The spirit of a man will sustain him
in sickness,
But who can bear a broken spirit?

15The heart of the prudent acquires
knowledge,
And the ear of the wise seeks
knowledge.

16A man's gift makes room for him,
And brings him before great men.

17The first *one* to plead his cause *seems*
right,
Until his neighbor comes and
examines him.

18Casting lots causes contentions to
cease,
And keeps the mighty apart.

19A brother offended *is harder to win*
than a strong city,
And contentions *are* like the bars of a
castle.

20A man's stomach shall be satisfied
from the fruit of his mouth;
From the produce of his lips he shall
be filled.

21Death and life *are* in the power of the
tongue,
And those who love it will eat its fruit.

22*He who* finds a wife finds a good *thing,*
And obtains favor from the LORD.

23The poor *man* uses entreaties,
But the rich answers roughly.

24A man *who has* friends must himself
be friendly,[a]
But there is a friend *who* sticks closer
than a brother.

18:8 [a]A Jewish tradition reads *wounds.* 18:24 [a]Following Greek manuscripts, Syriac, Targum, and Vulgate; Masoretic Text reads *may come to ruin.*

18:13 Be patient when sinners ramble. It is a discredit to our Christian witness to interrupt someone who is trying to tell us something, even though we have heard the empty argument many times before. Love will listen.

18:16 If you are wanting God to use you, He will open the doors in His time.

18:19 Make it a rule of life not to argue over petty doctrinal or prophetic interpretations. Strive to keep the unity of the Spirit. See Phil. 1:27.

19 Better *is* the poor who walks in his integrity
Than *one who is* perverse in his lips, and is a fool.

2Also it is not good *for* a soul *to be* without knowledge,
And he sins who hastens with *his* feet.

3The foolishness of a man twists his way,
And his heart frets against the LORD.

4Wealth makes many friends,
But the poor is separated from his friend.

5A false witness will not go unpunished,
And *he who* speaks lies will not escape.

6Many entreat the favor of the nobility,
And every man *is* a friend to one who gives gifts.
7All the brothers of the poor hate him;
How much more do his friends go far from him!
He may pursue *them with* words, *yet* they abandon *him.*

8He who gets wisdom loves his own soul;
He who keeps understanding will find good.

9A false witness will not go unpunished,
And *he who* speaks lies shall perish.

10Luxury is not fitting for a fool,
Much less for a servant to rule over princes.

11The discretion of a man makes him slow to anger,
And his glory *is* to overlook a transgression.

12The king's wrath *is* like the roaring of a lion,
But his favor *is* like dew on the grass.

13A foolish son *is* the ruin of his father,
And the contentions of a wife *are* a continual dripping.

14Houses and riches *are* an inheritance from fathers,
But a prudent wife *is* from the LORD.

15Laziness casts *one* into a deep sleep,
And an idle person will suffer hunger.

16He who keeps the commandment keeps his soul,
But he who is careless[a] of his ways will die.

17He who has pity on the poor lends to the LORD,
And He will pay back what he has given.

18Chasten your son while there is hope,
And do not set your heart on his destruction.[a]

19*A man of* great wrath will suffer punishment;
For if you rescue *him,* you will have to do it again.

20Listen to counsel and receive instruction,
That you may be wise in your latter days.

21There are many plans in a man's heart,
Nevertheless the LORD's counsel—that will stand.

19:16 [a]Literally *despises*, figurative of recklessness or carelessness 19:18 [a]Literally *to put him to death;* a Jewish tradition reads *on his crying.*

19:3 See Rom. 8:7.

19:5 Those who transgress the Ninth Commandment have a fearful fate. See Rev. 21:8.

19:17 "We make a living by what we get, but we make a life by what we give." *Winston Churchill*

[22]What is desired in a man is kindness,
And a poor man is better than a liar.

[23]The fear of the LORD *leads* to life,
And *he who has it* will abide in satisfaction;
He will not be visited with evil.

[24]A lazy *man* buries his hand in the bowl,[a]
And will not so much as bring it to his mouth again.

[25]Strike a scoffer, and the simple will become wary;
Rebuke one who has understanding, *and* he will discern knowledge.

[26]He who mistreats *his* father *and* chases away *his* mother
Is a son who causes shame and brings reproach.

[27]Cease listening to instruction, my son,
And you will stray from the words of knowledge.

[28]A disreputable witness scorns justice,
And the mouth of the wicked devours iniquity.

[29]Judgments are prepared for scoffers,
And beatings for the backs of fools.

20

Wine *is* a mocker,
Strong drink *is* a brawler,
And whoever is led astray by it is not wise.

[2]The wrath[a] of a king *is* like the roaring of a lion;
Whoever provokes him to anger sins *against* his own life.

[3]*It is* honorable for a man to stop striving,
Since any fool can start a quarrel.

[4]The lazy *man* will not plow because of winter;
He will beg during harvest and *have* nothing.

[5]Counsel in the heart of man *is like* deep water,
But a man of understanding will draw it out.

[6]Most men will proclaim each his own goodness,
But who can find a faithful man?

[7]The righteous *man* walks in his integrity;
His children *are* blessed after him.

[8]A king who sits on the throne of judgment
Scatters all evil with his eyes.

19:24 [a]Septuagint and Syriac read *bosom;* Targum and Vulgate read *armpit.* 20:2 [a]Literally *fear* or *terror* which is produced by the king's wrath

20:1 Alcohol is a poison. When someone is in-*toxic*-ated, he is "poisoned." The body protests with confused thinking, slurred speech, and impaired vision, memory, and judgment. The victim vomits. The next day his head throbs with pain, yet he still drinks the poison. Although hundreds of thousands of innocent people have been maimed on the roads by drunk drivers, the world cannot bring itself to say, "Don't drink." It can only say, "Don't drink and drive." This is because alcohol is an enemy man has succeeded in loving. It destroys his liver, heart, and kidneys. It gives him high blood pressure and causes blood vessels to burst in his skin. It leads him to beat his wife and abuse his kids. It will eventually destroy his ability to enjoy the intimacies of the marriage bed. Yet he still drinks.

He thinks alcohol is a "stimulant." In truth, it is a suppressant that reduces his inhibitions. It dulls the naggings of his conscience so that he can commit sexual and other sins that he couldn't indulge in while sober. A man who gives himself to the demon of alcohol becomes a slave to its addictive properties. It mocks him. It steals his dignity. It takes control of his will. Whoever is deceived by it (and there are millions) is not wise. See Prov. 23:29–35.

20:3 It takes no skill to argue with sinners. We are called to reason—to plead with love and gentleness.

QUESTIONS & OBJECTIONS

"You don't have to be a Christian to be a good person."

A Christian is not a "good person." How can anyone be called a good person when we have no clear definition of the word "good"? Is a rapist a good person because he no longer rapes? Or does a thief become a good person when he gives to charity? Some would say "Yes," and others would say "No."

The only way to define who is good and who isn't is to define the word "good." The dictionary lists 58 definitions, but the principle meaning is to be "morally excellent." In God's view, to be "good" means to be morally perfect, in thought, word, and deed. The Bible tells us that only God is good (see Mark 10:17). Even the word is derived from the word "God." So, once we have a clear definition, it is obvious that a Christian is not a good person. Neither is a non-Christian.

It is true that you don't have to be a Christian to live a good life. Anyone can do the things that Christians do. They can open hospitals, establish schools, feed the poor, build houses, etc. But that won't get anyone to heaven, nor will it save anyone from hell. This is because salvation has nothing to do with our "good" works. How could it? What could you and I ever do to "earn" everlasting life?

But add the fact that we are criminals, having violated the Law of a holy God a multitude of times, and it becomes clear that the only way any of us could ever be saved from hell and enter heaven is by the mercy of the Judge. And that is what the Bible teaches. A Christian is saved by the grace and mercy of God, without works: "For by grace you have been saved through faith, and that not of yourselves; it is the gift of God, not of works, lest anyone should boast" (Eph. 2:8,9).

So, stop pretending to be good, and realize that doing good will do you no good on Judgment Day. Instead, repent and trust the Savior, and then live a good life—not to impress anyone or bribe God, but out of gratitude to Him for His mercy.

9 Who can say, "I have made my heart clean,
I am pure from my sin"?

10 Diverse weights *and* diverse measures,
They *are* both alike, an abomination to the LORD.

11 Even a child is known by his deeds,
Whether what he does *is* pure and right.

12 The hearing ear and the seeing eye,
The LORD has made them both.

13 Do not love sleep, lest you come to poverty;
Open your eyes, *and* you will be satisfied with bread.

14 "*It is* good for nothing,"[a] cries the buyer;
But when he has gone his way, then he boasts.

15 There is gold and a multitude of rubies,
But the lips of knowledge *are* a precious jewel.

20:14 [a]Literally *evil, evil*

20:6 If you ask a man if he thinks he is a good person, he usually will say that he is. That's why we need to use the Law (which the Bible says is "good") to give him understanding about what "good" is (Rom. 7:12). See Prov. 21:2. For details, see Mark 10:17 and John 4:7 comments.

"We miss the mark telling people who are morally good, and very excellent many of them, that Jesus Christ came into the world to make bad men good. He did not. That's a fringe benefit. The first argument God has with a man is not that he's bad, it's that he is dead in trespasses and in sin. And Christianity is the only Gospel in the world, the only message in the world, where a man's God comes and lives inside of him."
Leonard Ravenhill

20:9 No man can do this. Only God can cleanse man's heart of sin and make him pure. See 1 John 1:9.

20:11 Those who deny the reality of the sinful nature haven't had children. See Prov. 29:15 comment.

20:12 Evolution: The Seeing Eye

Man has never developed a camera lens anywhere near the inconceivable intricacy of the human eye. The human eye is an amazing interrelated system of about forty individual subsystems, including the retina, pupil, iris, cornea, lens, and optic nerve. It has more to it than just the 137 million light-sensitive special cells that send messages to the unbelievably complex brain. About 130 million of these cells look like tiny rods, and they handle the black-and-white vision. The other seven million are cone shaped and allow us to see in color. The retina cells receive light impressions, which are then translated into electric pulses and sent directly to the brain through the optic nerve.

A special section of the brain called the visual cortex interprets the pulses as color, contrast, depth, etc., which then allows us to see "pictures" of our world. Incredibly, the eye, optic nerve, and visual cortex are totally separate and distinct subsystems. Yet together they capture, deliver, and interpret up to 1.5 million pulse messages per millisecond! Think about that for a moment. It would take dozens of computers programmed perfectly and operating together flawlessly to even get close to performing this task.

The eye is an example of what is referred to as "irreducible complexity." It would be absolutely impossible for random processes, operating through gradual mechanisms of genetic mutation and natural selection, to be able to create forty separate subsystems when they provide no advantage to the whole until the very last state of development. Ask yourself how the lens, the retina, the optic nerve, and all the other parts in vertebrates that play a role in seeing not only appeared from nothing, but evolved into interrelated and working parts. Evolutionist Robert Jastrow acknowledges that highly trained scientists could not have improved upon "blind chance":

> The eye appears to have been designed; no designer of telescopes could have done better. How could this marvelous instrument have evolved by chance, through a succession of random events? Many people in Darwin's day agreed with theologian William Pauley, who commented, "There cannot be a design without a designer."

You've probably been led to believe that the first simple creatures had rudimentary eyes, and that as creatures slowly evolved their eyes evolved along with them. However, that's not what scientists have found. Not only is there no evidence of this occurring, but some of the most complex eyes have been discovered in the "simplest" creatures.

Riccardo Levi-Setti, professor emeritus of Physics at the University of Chicago, writes of the trilobite's eye:

> This optical doublet is a device so typically associated with human invention that its discovery in trilobites comes as something of a shock. The realization that trilobites developed and used such devices half a billion years ago makes the shock even greater. And a final discovery—that the refracting interface between the two lens elements in a trilobite's eye was designed in accordance with optical constructions worked out by Descartes and Huygens in the mid-seventeenth century—borders on sheer science fiction . . . The design of the trilobite's eye lens could well qualify for a patent disclosure.

How could the amazing, seeing eye have come about purely by blind chance? Based on the evidence, wouldn't a reasonable person conclude that the eye is astonishingly complex and could not have evolved gradually, and that each creature's eyes are uniquely designed?

Even Charles Darwin, the father of evolutionary theory, admitted the incredible complexity of the eye in *The Origin of Species:*

> To suppose that the eye, with all its inimitable contrivances for adjusting the focus to different distances, for admitting different amounts of light, and for the correction of spherical and chromatic aberration, could have formed by natural selection, seems, I freely confess, absurd in the highest degree.

Even more incredible, though, is that Darwin went on to say that he believed the eye could nonetheless have been formed by natural selection. He was right on one point. If a Designer is left out of the equation, such a thought is absurd in the highest degree.

(Adapted from *How to Know God Exists.*)

16 Take the garment of one who is
surety *for* a stranger,
And hold it as a pledge *when it* is for a
seductress.

17 Bread gained by deceit *is* sweet to a
man,
But afterward his mouth will be filled
with gravel.

18Plans are established by counsel;
By wise counsel wage war.

19He who goes about *as* a talebearer reveals secrets;
Therefore do not associate with one who flatters with his lips.

20Whoever curses his father or his mother,
His lamp will be put out in deep darkness.

21An inheritance gained hastily at the beginning
Will not be blessed at the end.

22Do not say, "I will recompense evil";
Wait for the LORD, and He will save you.

23Diverse weights *are* an abomination to the LORD,
And dishonest scales *are* not good.

24A man's steps *are* of the LORD;
How then can a man understand his own way?

25*It is* a snare for a man to devote rashly *something as* holy,
And afterward to reconsider *his* vows.

26A wise king sifts out the wicked,
And brings the threshing wheel over them.

27The spirit of a man *is* the lamp of the LORD,
Searching all the inner depths of his heart.[a]

28Mercy and truth preserve the king,
And by lovingkindness he upholds his throne.

29The glory of young men *is* their strength,
And the splendor of old men *is* their gray head.

30Blows that hurt cleanse away evil,
As *do* stripes the inner depths of the heart.[a]

21 The king's heart *is* in the hand of the LORD,
Like the rivers of water; He turns it wherever He wishes.

2Every way of a man *is* right in his own eyes,
But the LORD weighs the hearts.

3To do righteousness and justice
Is more acceptable to the LORD than sacrifice.

4A haughty look, a proud heart,
And the plowing[a] of the wicked *are* sin.

20:27, 30 [a]Literally *the rooms of the belly* 21:4 [a]Or *lamp*

21:1 This is our great confidence when preaching to sinners. God has control of the hearts of men and women.

21:2 Right in his own eyes. Consider the way dogs cross the road. A dog will wander onto a freeway oblivious to the danger. His tail wags as he steps between cars without a second thought. Cars swerve. Tires squeal. The noise is deafening as vehicles smash into each other. The sleepy dog stops wagging his tail for a moment and looks at the pile of smoldering, broken autos on the freeway. His expression betrays his thoughts. His bone-burying brain doesn't realize for one moment that he is responsible for the disaster.

When man wanders onto the freeway of sin, his tail wags with delight. He thinks that this is what he was made for. His thoughts of any repercussions for his actions are shallow. His mind wanders into lust, then predictably he wanders onto the path of adultery. Suddenly a disaster sits before him. His marriage is shattered, his name is slurred, his children are twisted and scarred. But like the dumb dog, he doesn't realize for one moment that he is solely responsible for his sin.

This is why the perfect Law of God needs to be arrayed before his darkened eyes—to show him that his way is not right in the eyes of a perfect God.

[5]The plans of the diligent *lead* surely
to plenty,
But *those of* everyone *who is* hasty,
surely to poverty.

[6]Getting treasures by a lying tongue
Is the fleeting fantasy of those who
seek death.[a]

[7]The violence of the wicked will
destroy them,[a]
Because they refuse to do justice.

[8]The way of a guilty man *is* perverse;[a]
But *as for* the pure, his work *is* right.

[9]Better to dwell in a corner of a
housetop,
Than in a house shared with a
contentious woman.

· · · · ·

Will sinners go to hell for not believing in Jesus? See John 16:9 comment.

· · · · ·

[10]The soul of the wicked desires evil;
His neighbor finds no favor in his eyes.

[11]When the scoffer is punished, the
simple is made wise;
But when the wise is instructed, he
receives knowledge.

[12]The righteous *God* wisely considers
the house of the wicked,
Overthrowing the wicked for *their*
wickedness.

[13]Whoever shuts his ears to the cry of
the poor
Will also cry himself and not be heard.

[14]A gift in secret pacifies anger,
And a bribe behind the back,[a] strong
wrath.

[15]*It is* a joy for the just to do justice,
But destruction *will come* to the
workers of iniquity.

[16]A man who wanders from the way of
understanding
Will rest in the assembly of the dead.

[17]He who loves pleasure *will be* a poor
man;
He who loves wine and oil will not be
rich.

[18]The wicked *shall be* a ransom for the
righteous,
And the unfaithful for the upright.

[19]Better to dwell in the wilderness,
Than with a contentious and angry
woman.

[20]*There is* desirable treasure,
And oil in the dwelling of the wise,
But a foolish man squanders it.

[21]He who follows righteousness and
mercy
Finds life, righteousness, and honor.

[22]A wise *man* scales the city of the
mighty,
And brings down the trusted
stronghold.

[23]Whoever guards his mouth and
tongue
Keeps his soul from troubles.

21:6 [a]Septuagint reads *Pursue vanity on the snares of death;* Vulgate reads *Is vain and foolish, and shall stumble on the snares of death;* Targum reads *They shall be destroyed, and they shall fall who seek death.* 21:7 [a]Literally *drag them away* 21:8 [a]Or *The way of a man is perverse and strange* 21:14 [a]Literally *in the bosom*

21:6 It has been rightly said that taking the easy path is what makes men and rivers crooked.

21:10 Sinful men have no trouble seeing other people's sins.

21:23 Be slow to speak your personal opinions, and save yourself a great deal of trouble.

[24]A proud *and* haughty *man*—"Scoffer"
is his name;
He acts with arrogant pride.

[25]The desire of the lazy *man* kills him,
For his hands refuse to labor.
[26]He covets greedily all day long,
But the righteous gives and does not
spare.

[27]The sacrifice of the wicked *is* an
abomination;
How much more *when* he brings it
with wicked intent!

[28]A false witness shall perish,
But the man who hears *him* will speak
endlessly.

[29]A wicked man hardens his face,
But *as for* the upright, he establishes[a]
his way.

[30]*There is* no wisdom or understanding
Or counsel against the LORD.

[31]The horse *is* prepared for the day of
battle,
But deliverance *is* of the LORD.

22

A *good* name is to be chosen
rather than great riches,
Loving favor rather than silver and
gold.

[2]The rich and the poor have this in
common,
The LORD *is* the maker of them all.

[3]A prudent *man* foresees evil and
hides himself,
But the simple pass on and are
punished.

[4]By humility *and* the fear of the LORD
Are riches and honor and life.

[5]Thorns *and* snares *are* in the way of
the perverse;
He who guards his soul will be far
from them.

[6]Train up a child in the way he should
go,
And when he is old he will not depart
from it.

[7]The rich rules over the poor,
And the borrower *is* servant to the
lender.

[8]He who sows iniquity will reap sorrow,
And the rod of his anger will fail.

[9]He who has a generous eye will be
blessed,
For he gives of his bread to the poor.

21:29 [a]Qere and Septuagint read *understands*.

21:24 The proud, arrogant, and angry scorner gravitates to open-air preaching. These will be prevalent in the last days (2 Pet. 3:3). The Scriptures reveal that the reason for their contention is that they are given to lust.

21:27 Mankind can never atone for his own sins and buy immortality by giving to charitable causes. Eternal life is a gift of God. See Rom. 6:23; Eph. 2:8,9.

22:1 We must guard our name, character, and reputation for the sake of the gospel. If men think evil of us, let it be only for the cause of righteousness.

22:4 Those who refuse to humble themselves will eventually lose their possessions, their dignity, and their very life. However, those who walk in humility of heart and obey God store up an eternal treasure in heaven. They will preserve their life and be honored by God Himself. See John 12:25.

"Humility is daily clothing of the Christian." *Bruce Garner*

22:6 Training our children. "Let the children . . . be carefully instructed in the principles and obligations of the Christian religion. This is the most essential part of education. The great enemy of the salvation of man, in my opinion, never invented a more effectual means of extirpating [removing] Christianity from the world than by persuading mankind that it was improper to read the Bible at schools." *Benjamin Rush* (See also Prov. 4:1–5 and Eph. 6:4 comments.)

22:6 *Teaching Children the Ten Commandments*

By Kirk Cameron

I love being a father. I'm taking the crash-course in parenting. I have five children under five years old. Yep—my kids are five, four, three, two, and one. Two boys and three girls . . . can you imagine what it'll be like when they're all teenagers at the same time, experimenting with life's options and dating at the same time? If it's true that small children have small problems and big kids have big problems, then in ten years I'm going to fake my own death and move to Tahiti!

Growing up in this world of ungodly values and immoral lifestyles, our kids are already facing difficult challenges, and it's our responsibility as parents to give them a solid foundation on which they can build their lives, dreams, and convictions. I find great comfort in this wonderful proverb. "Train up a child in the way he should go, and when he is old, he will not depart from it."

Now as much as I'd love for this verse of Scripture to be a guaranteed promise of perfect Christian children as long as we raise them in a godly home, I know it doesn't always work that way. Many godly parents in the Bible and today, too, have had sons and daughters who did not walk with the Lord.

But I do know that the principle of preparing the soil for the seed of the gospel can and should start when a child is young. And I believe that the promise of this verse is that if a child learns to turn from sin and trust in Jesus when he is young, then, as he grows older, he will not depart from his Savior because God has already set him apart for His own glory.

Since we know that only the Holy Spirit can actually transform our children from the cute little "me-centered" people that they are into God-loving, God-fearing followers of Christ, the question is: What should I be doing as a parent? How can I train my child "in the way he should go" so that he or she will continue on God's path and become a life-long follower of Jesus Christ?

While there are many great books on the subject (*Shepherding a Child's Heart* by Ted Tripp is our favorite and we refer to it regularly), here is a simple suggestion that has been working very well with our children.

> These are the commandments which the Lord your God commanded you . . . And you shall teach them diligently to your children, and shall talk of them when you sit in your house, and when you walk by the way, and when you lie down, and when you rise up. (Deut. 6:1–7)

This verse means, in simple terms, teach your children the Ten Commandments so that they know them backwards and forwards. This isn't to improve their memory or to help them win an Awana contest; it is to awaken their conscience and prepare the soil of their hearts for the life-giving seed of the gospel.

A personal understanding of the moral Law of God is foundational for anyone (including our children) to become a Christian. God commanded Abraham that he teach it to his children for a reason. Here's why. Galatians 3:24 reads, "Therefore the law was our tutor to bring us to Christ." So God's moral Law (summed up in the Ten Commandments) is a tutor to bring us (and our children) to Jesus Christ. Here's how it works:

1. We know that in order for a child (as well as an adult) to be saved, he or she must turn from their sin and trust in Jesus to save them. If our children are going to personally turn from their sin, they must know what his or her sin is.

2. The Ten Commandments show your child what sin is. Romans 3:20 says, "By the law is the knowledge of sin." First John 3:4 says, "Sin is transgression of the law." Paul says in Rom. 7:7, "I would not have known what sin was except through the law." So Paul is saying that he would not have known what sin was unless the Law (the Ten Commandments) showed him. The Ten Commandments are what made Paul understand that he had sinned against God, helped him see that he was spiritually "dead," and in need of God's forgiveness and new life. (See Rom. 7:7–12.)

The Ten Commandments are like a mirror. They reveal that our hearts are dirty and in need of cleansing. What would you and I do if we didn't have a mirror to look into each morning? Without a mirror, we'd never know whether our face was clean or dirty. In the same way, it is only when we look into the mirror of the Ten Commandments that we can see that our heart is dirty and in desperate need of cleansing. Once children (and others) understand that they are guilty of sin, they are able (with the help of the Holy Spirit) to turn to Jesus to wash that sin away.

3. Simply go through the Ten Commandments with your children, explain what each one means and ask them if they've kept it or broken it (maybe not the Seventh Commandment if your child is too young). Just ask them, "Have you ever told a lie? Have you ever taken something that you knew didn't belong to you? Have you always honored and obeyed your dad and mom? Have you always loved God more than the things He's given you (like toys, family, and friends)?" Your children will see very quickly that they *(continued)*

(22:6 continued)
have broken these Commandments. You may notice that they even feel guilty. That's good, because they are guilty—and closer to the kingdom of God than ever before!

Now that they understand exactly how they've sinned against God and angered Him in the process, they can see their dilemma and need for God's forgiveness. Now, the good news about Jesus taking their punishment for them on the cross will make sense.

> God demonstrated His own love for us in that while we were still sinners, Christ died for us. (Rom. 5:8)

> "For God so loved the world, that He gave His one and only Son, that whoever believes in him will not perish, but have everlasting life." (John 3:16)

Once our children have a keen understanding of their sin, they can now begin to appreciate the great, matchless, and incomprehensible love of God. We know God loves us not because of a warm, fuzzy feeling He gives us; we know God loves us because of what He did for us on the cross. He laid down His own life for us so that we could be forgiven and born again! We broke the Law and Jesus paid our fine—it's as simple as that.

4. Since there can be no salvation without God-given repentance, if our children don't eventually see their need for God's forgiveness, they can't repent, and without repentance, they cannot be saved. Each child has a conscience and knows basic right from wrong. Repentance is simply a determination to turn away from what is wrong.

If you're worried about frightening your child by talking about the seriousness of his or her sin, I've found that my own children are remarkably capable of handling this... because their conscience tells them that it's true and they know that their Mom and Dad and God love them very much and are willing to forgive them. We must first convince them of the disease of sin before they will appreciate the cure of Jesus. Remind them that if they will surrender their hearts to Jesus, God will also give them a "new heart" and help them to begin to love and obey Him like never before.

Recently, my four-year-old daughter Isabella started crying very hard and explained that Jack (her five-year-old brother) had pushed her off the top of her baby brother's crib and hurt her head. Jack, with a look of complete shock and confusion, said, "I didn't do anything. She just fell all by herself. I think I might have scared her or something." As we comforted Isabella, I asked my son very directly, "Did you push your sister and make her fall?" Jack stood firm and denied any culpability. My wife also asked Jack if he was lying or telling the truth. Jack again said he did not push his sister. I told him that I was going to ask him one more question. I told him that if he was honest and told me the truth, he would not be in trouble. But if he did not tell me the truth, he would be in Big trouble. He replied, "What if I've already not told you the truth?" I told him that he must tell me the truth now, regardless of what he's already told me.

Jack looked down at the floor, wrinkled up his face, and began squirming in his chair like a worm on a hook. He knew I was serious, and he was now engaged in a wrestling match with his conscience. Jack finally confessed, "Yes, I pushed her." I told him to tell his mother what he had told me. I took three minutes to discuss the seriousness of lying. It was one of the Commandments that Jack knew so well. We talked about the fact that when he lies to his dad and mom, he is also lying to Jesus. We talked about the fact that in order to lie, Jack had to run away from Jesus to do it.

I tried, as best as I could, to stir up his God-given conscience and help him see the seriousness of his deceit in the eyes of God. I told Jack that a deceitful heart is rotten in God's eyes and that's why he needs the new heart that Jesus can give him. I showed him how to kneel in prayer when you're really sorry and told him I was going to leave him to be alone with Jesus so that he could talk to him and ask for His forgiveness. I left Jack's room and closed the door (except for a crack through which I could hear him praying).

Jack got on his knees, and I could hear him say, "Dear God, I'm sorry I lied to my mommy and daddy and You. I pushed my sister off the crib. Will you please forgive me? Will you please take the trash out of my heart and give me a new heart? And please keep it clean and pure all the time so I don't do sinful things. I ask this in Jesus name. Amen." (See also Josh. 4:21,22 comment.)

10 Cast out the scoffer, and contention
will leave;
Yes, strife and reproach will cease.

11 He who loves purity of heart
And has grace on his lips,
The king *will be* his friend.

12 The eyes of the LORD preserve
knowledge,
But He overthrows the words of the
faithless.

13 The lazy *man* says, "*There is* a lion
outside!

I shall be slain in the streets!"

14The mouth of an immoral woman *is* a
deep pit;
He who is abhorred by the LORD will
fall there.

15Foolishness *is* bound up in the heart
of a child;
The rod of correction will drive it far
from him.

16He who oppresses the poor to
increase his *riches,*
And he who gives to the rich, *will*
surely *come* to poverty.

. . . . . .

For how to witness to Muslims,
see Acts 17:23 comment.

. . . . . .

Sayings of the Wise

17Incline your ear and hear the words
of the wise,
And apply your heart to my
knowledge;
18For *it is* a pleasant thing if you keep
them within you;
Let them all be fixed upon your lips,
19So that your trust may be in the LORD;
I have instructed you today, even you.
20Have I not written to you excellent
things
Of counsels and knowledge,
21That I may make you know the
certainty of the words of truth,
That you may answer words of truth
To those who send to you?

22Do not rob the poor because he *is* poor,
Nor oppress the afflicted at the gate;
23For the LORD will plead their cause,
And plunder the soul of those who
plunder them.

24Make no friendship with an angry man,
And with a furious man do not go,
25Lest you learn his ways
And set a snare for your soul.

26Do not be one of those who shakes
hands in a pledge,
One of those who is surety for debts;
27If you have nothing *with which* to pay,
Why should he take away your bed
from under you?

28Do not remove the ancient landmark
Which your fathers have set.

29Do you see a man *who* excels in his
work?
He will stand before kings;
He will not stand before unknown
men.

23 When you sit down to eat with a
ruler,
Consider carefully what *is* before you;
2And put a knife to your throat
If you *are* a man given to appetite.
3Do not desire his delicacies,
For they *are* deceptive food.

4Do not overwork to be rich;
Because of your own understanding,
cease!
5Will you set your eyes on that which
is not?
For *riches* certainly make themselves
wings;
They fly away like an eagle *toward*
heaven.

6Do not eat the bread of a miser,[a]
Nor desire his delicacies;
7For as he thinks in his heart, so *is* he.
"Eat and drink!" he says to you,

23:6 [a]Literally *one who has an evil eye*

23:2 If you are given to appetite, you are killing yourself. Eat moderately and sensibly so that you can stay healthy and reach out to the unsaved.

QUESTIONS & OBJECTIONS

23:7 ***"Being punished for 'thought-crimes' is absurd."***

The idea that merely thinking could be a crime does seem absurd. But *thought* and *attitude* crimes are a reality in our society. In a hate crime, one is punished not just for committing a specific crime against someone, but for his supposed thoughts toward that person. If a man beat up a heterosexual, for example, he would deserve one sentence. But if he beats up a homosexual, and if it could be proved that he once expressed a negative attitude toward homosexuals, he would get a substantially increased sentence—for the very same crime. Also, students who wish for the death of a teacher or fellow student—and merely mention it on Facebook or in texting, for instance—are taken seriously. They could face punishment because it shows the intent of the heart, even if they are not actively planning it.

If you are caught thinking about assassinating the President of the United States, you will find yourself in serious violation of the law. Again, you don't have to commit the act. You simply have to be thinking about it, and express that thought verbally or in writing. Some may argue that conspiracy to murder the president is different because it is a serious crime. And that's the point. They don't consider pornography of the mind to be a serious crime. God does. Man's moral standards are extremely low, while God's are incredibly high. He is so holy, He requires perfection in thought, word, and deed. If we burn with unlawful sexual thoughts toward another human being, God sees that as adultery (see Matt. 5:27,28). And if we have a seething hatred in our heart for another person, God sees that as murder (see Matt. 5:22; 1 John 3:15).

He judges the thoughts and intents of our heart, and He will see to it that the guilty get their just deserts. Adulterers and murderers will end up damned in a terrible place called hell.

But his heart is not with you.
8The morsel you have eaten, you will
vomit up,
And waste your pleasant words.

9Do not speak in the hearing of a fool,
For he will despise the wisdom of
your words.

10Do not remove the ancient landmark,
Nor enter the fields of the fatherless;
11For their Redeemer *is* mighty;
He will plead their cause against you.

12Apply your heart to instruction,
And your ears to words of knowledge.

13Do not withhold correction from a
child,
For *if* you beat him with a rod, he will
not die.
14You shall beat him with a rod,
And deliver his soul from hell.[a]

15My son, if your heart is wise,
My heart will rejoice—indeed, I myself;
16Yes, my inmost being will rejoice
When your lips speak right things.

17Do not let your heart envy sinners,
But *be zealous* for the fear of the LORD
all the day;
18For surely there is a hereafter,
And your hope will not be cut off.

19Hear, my son, and be wise;
And guide your heart in the way.
20Do not mix with winebibbers,
Or with gluttonous eaters of meat;
21For the drunkard and the glutton will
come to poverty,
And drowsiness will clothe *a man*
with rags.

22Listen to your father who begot you,

23:14 [a]Or *Sheol*

23:12 There is no greater way to do this than to read and meditate on God's Word every day. Say to yourself, "No Bible, no breakfast. No read, no feed." Put your Bible before your belly. See Psa. 1, and mediate on the promises for those who do this.

23:17 See Psa. 73.

Springboards for Preaching and Witnessing

God's Obligation

23:29,30 A young lady from Corona, California, was devastated by the tragic death of her boyfriend. The couple had just celebrated the birth of their first child. He had been to a nightclub, and was returning with friends at 2:00 a.m., when police believe he was speeding and lost control. He wrapped his car around a tree, killing himself and his three passengers.

His mother said that her son "loved to drink." His distraught girlfriend lamented, "I don't know why God would do this to me."

My heart went out to her for her loss, but why was she blaming God for the death of her boyfriend? He was the one who was speeding, probably drunk, at 2:00 a.m. He killed himself. The incident had nothing to do with God, other than that He allowed it, in His sovereign will.

It seems obvious that many nowadays think God is nothing but a divine butler. He is there for our convenience—to come running when we snap our sinful fingers.

God gave us life. He lavished His goodness upon us, and to think that we can treat Him as some sort of lowly servant reveals a great ignorance of who He is. Such error can only end in disillusionment of life and bitterness of soul.

God owes us nothing but justice. He has no obligation at all to bless us with health, wealth, or long life. A civil judge is under no obligation to show mercy to a guilty criminal. If there was an obligation, then it wouldn't be true mercy. Mercy is unmerited. He is, however, obligated to make sure that justice is done.

So it is with God. He is obligated by His very nature to manifest His divine and just wrath against all sin, and that will happen on what the Bible calls "the great and terrible day of the Lord" (the Day of Judgment). But He is also "rich in mercy," and has offered us mercy in the cross . . . and we must receive it while we are on this side of eternity.

And do not despise your mother
when she is old.

23 Buy the truth, and do not sell *it*,
Also wisdom and instruction and
understanding.

24 The father of the righteous will
greatly rejoice,
And he who begets a wise *child* will
delight in him.
25 Let your father and your mother be
glad,
And let her who bore you rejoice.

26 My son, give me your heart,
And let your eyes observe my ways.
27 For a harlot *is* a deep pit,
And a seductress *is* a narrow well.
28 She also lies in wait as *for* a victim,
And increases the unfaithful among
men.

29 Who has woe?
Who has sorrow?
Who has contentions?
Who has complaints?
Who has wounds without cause?
Who has redness of eyes?
30 Those who linger long at the wine,
Those who go in search of mixed wine.
31 Do not look on the wine when it is red,
When it sparkles in the cup,
When it swirls around smoothly;
32 At the last it bites like a serpent,
And stings like a viper.
33 Your eyes will see strange things,
And your heart will utter perverse
things.
34 Yes, you will be like one who lies

23:23 It is tragic that so many Christian ministries demand money from their audience, often with the promise that God will bless them if they give. God knows the motives of the preacher, but the unsaved don't, and are therefore easily deceived by the practice. We should be careful never to give the impression that our motivation is the love of money.

23:24,25 This is the fruit of obedience to the Fifth Commandment.

down in the midst of the sea,
Or like one who lies at the top of the mast, *saying*:
35"They have struck me, *but* I was not hurt;
They have beaten me, but I did not feel *it*.
When shall I awake, that I may seek another *drink*?"

24 Do not be envious of evil men,
Nor desire to be with them;
2For their heart devises violence,
And their lips talk of troublemaking.

3Through wisdom a house is built,
And by understanding it is established;
4By knowledge the rooms are filled
With all precious and pleasant riches.

5A wise man *is* strong,
Yes, a man of knowledge increases strength;
6For by wise counsel you will wage your own war,
And in a multitude of counselors *there is* safety.

Nothing can damn a man but his own righteousness; nothing can save him but the righteousness of Christ.

CHARLES SPURGEON

7Wisdom *is* too lofty for a fool;
He does not open his mouth in the gate.

8He who plots to do evil
Will be called a schemer.
9The devising of foolishness *is* sin,
And the scoffer *is* an abomination to men.

10*If* you faint in the day of adversity,
Your strength *is* small.

11Deliver *those who* are drawn toward death,
And hold back *those* stumbling to the slaughter.
12If you say, "Surely we did not know this,"
Does not He who weighs the hearts consider *it?*
He who keeps your soul, does He *not* know *it?*
And will He *not* render to *each* man according to his deeds?

13My son, eat honey because *it is* good,
And the honeycomb *which is* sweet to your taste;
14So *shall* the knowledge of wisdom *be* to your soul;
If you have found *it,* there is a prospect,
And your hope will not be cut off.

15Do not lie in wait, O wicked *man,* against the dwelling of the righteous;
Do not plunder his resting place;
16For a righteous *man* may fall seven times
And rise again,
But the wicked shall fall by calamity.

17Do not rejoice when your enemy falls,
And do not let your heart be glad when he stumbles;
18Lest the LORD see *it*, and it displease Him,

24:3,4 Jesus Christ and His teachings are the only sure foundation. See Col. 1:9; Matt. 7:24.

24:9 Never be discouraged when a man mocks you as you are preaching the gospel. Your love, gentleness, and reasonableness will be seen to contrast his foolishness.

24:11,12 Surely these verses were written for those slothful servants who shun the task of evangelism. See Matt. 25:14–30.

24:18 "…among all the terrible words spoken concerning the penalty of sin, the most terrible are those which were uttered by our Lord Jesus Christ, the most loving and tender of all teachers. Measure not a man's true tenderness of heart by his avoidance of the subject of 'the wrath to come.'" *Charles Spurgeon*

"More souls have been won for Christ by preachers who did what little they could, than by renowned evangelists."

Richard Wurmbrand

And He turn away His wrath from him.

[19]Do not fret because of evildoers,
Nor be envious of the wicked;
[20]For there will be no prospect for the evil *man;*
The lamp of the wicked will be put out.

[21]My son, fear the LORD and the king;
Do not associate with those given to change;
[22]For their calamity will rise suddenly,
And who knows the ruin those two can bring?

Further Sayings of the Wise

[23]These *things* also *belong* to the wise:

It is not good to show partiality in judgment.
[24]He who says to the wicked, "You *are* righteous,"
Him the people will curse;
Nations will abhor him.
[25]But those who rebuke *the wicked* will have delight,
And a good blessing will come upon them.

[26]He who gives a right answer kisses the lips.

[27]Prepare your outside work,
Make it fit for yourself in the field;
And afterward build your house.

[28]Do not be a witness against your neighbor without cause,
For would you deceive[a] with your lips?
[29]Do not say, "I will do to him just as he has done to me;
I will render to the man according to his work."

[30]I went by the field of the lazy *man,*
And by the vineyard of the man devoid of understanding;
[31]And there it was, all overgrown with thorns;
Its surface was covered with nettles;
Its stone wall was broken down.
[32]When I saw *it,* I considered *it* well;
I looked on *it and* received instruction:
[33]A little sleep, a little slumber,
A little folding of the hands to rest;
[34]So shall your poverty come *like* a prowler,
And your need like an armed man.

Further Wise Sayings of Solomon

25 These also *are* proverbs of Solomon which the men of Hezekiah king of Judah copied:

[2]*It is* the glory of God to conceal a matter,

24:28 [a]Septuagint and Vulgate read *Do not deceive.*

24:25 We are to "preach the word! Be ready in season and out of season," and to "convince, rebuke, exhort, with all longsuffering and teaching" (2 Tim. 4:2). Do this, and you will have the promise of the blessing of God.

But the glory of kings *is* to search out
a matter.

[3]*As* the heavens for height and the
earth for depth,
So the heart of kings *is* unsearchable.

[4]Take away the dross from silver,
And it will go to the silversmith *for*
jewelry.
[5]Take away the wicked from before
the king,
And his throne will be established in
righteousness.

[6]Do not exalt yourself in the presence
of the king,
And do not stand in the place of the
great;
[7]For *it is* better that he say to you,
"Come up here,"
Than that you should be put lower in
the presence of the prince,
Whom your eyes have seen.

[8]Do not go hastily to court;
For what will you do in the end,
When your neighbor has put you to
shame?
[9]Debate your case with your neighbor,
And do not disclose the secret to
another;
[10]Lest he who hears *it* expose your
shame,
And your reputation be ruined.

[11]A word fitly spoken *is like* apples of
gold
In settings of silver.
[12]*Like* an earring of gold and an
ornament of fine gold
Is a wise rebuker to an obedient ear.

[13]Like the cold of snow in time of harvest
Is a faithful messenger to those who
send him,
For he refreshes the soul of his masters.

[14]Whoever falsely boasts of giving
Is like clouds and wind without rain.

[15]By long forbearance a ruler is
persuaded,
And a gentle tongue breaks a bone.

[16]Have you found honey?
Eat only as much as you need,
Lest you be filled with it and vomit.

[17]Seldom set foot in your neighbor's
house,
Lest he become weary of you and
hate you.

[18]A man who bears false witness
against his neighbor
Is like a club, a sword, and a sharp
arrow.

[19]Confidence in an unfaithful *man* in
time of trouble
Is like a bad tooth and a foot out of
joint.

[20]*Like* one who takes away a garment in
cold weather,
And like vinegar on soda,
Is one who sings songs to a heavy heart.

[21]If your enemy is hungry, give him
bread to eat;
And if he is thirsty, give him water to
drink;
[22]For *so* you will heap coals of fire on
his head,
And the LORD will reward you.

[23]The north wind brings forth rain,
And a backbiting tongue an angry
countenance.

25:19 A broken tooth or a foot out of joint cause the most pain when they are put under pressure. How do we react when we are put under pressure to share our faith?

25:21,22 See Lev. 16:12,13 comment.

[24]*It is* better to dwell in a corner of a
housetop,
Than in a house shared with a
contentious woman.

[25]*As* cold water to a weary soul,
So *is* good news from a far country.

[26]A righteous *man* who falters before
the wicked
Is like a murky spring and a polluted
well.

[27]*It is* not good to eat much honey;
So to seek one's own glory *is not* glory.

[28]Whoever *has* no rule over his own
spirit
Is like a city broken down, without
walls.

26

As snow in summer and rain in
harvest,
So honor is not fitting for a fool.

[2]Like a flitting sparrow, like a flying
swallow,
So a curse without cause shall not
alight.

[3]A whip for the horse,
A bridle for the donkey,
And a rod for the fool's back.
[4]Do not answer a fool according to his
folly,
Lest you also be like him.
[5]Answer a fool according to his folly,
Lest he be wise in his own eyes.
[6]He who sends a message by the hand
of a fool
Cuts off *his own* feet *and* drinks
violence.
[7]*Like* the legs of the lame that hang limp
Is a proverb in the mouth of fools.
[8]Like one who binds a stone in a sling
Is he who gives honor to a fool.
[9]*Like* a thorn *that* goes into the hand of
a drunkard
Is a proverb in the mouth of fools.
[10]The great *God* who formed everything
Gives the fool *his* hire and the
transgressor *his* wages.[a]
[11]As a dog returns to his own vomit,
So a fool repeats his folly.
[12]Do you see a man wise in his own eyes?
There is more hope for a fool than for
him.

[13]The lazy *man* says, "*There is* a lion in
the road!
A fierce lion *is* in the streets!"

26:10 [a]The Hebrew is difficult; ancient and modern translators differ greatly.

25:28 We allow the enemy entrance when we give the flesh free reign, having no self-control over our spirit.

26:4 *Abraham Lincoln* once said, "If I were to try to read, much less answer, all the attacks made on me, this shop might as well be closed for any other business. I do the very best I know how, the very best I can, and I mean to keep doing so until the end. If the end brings me out all right, what is said to me won't amount to anything. If the end brings me out wrong, ten angels swearing I was right will make no difference."

26:9 "Is there a poor drunkard here tonight who wants to come? Christ can save a drunkard just as easily as I can turn my hand. He can turn that cup of liquor from you as easily as you turn to it now." *D. L. Moody*

26:10 The word "great" cannot describe how great God is. Worship takes over where words fail. Our God formed *all* things. They didn't evolve after a big bang.

26:12 New Age blasphemy. The inevitable result of man's darkened understanding is that he will think he is God. His pride takes over his brain.

"We no longer feel ourselves to be guests in someone else's home and therefore obliged to make our behavior conform with a set of preexisting cosmic rules. It is our creation now. We make the rules. We establish the parameters of reality. We create the world, and because we do, we no longer feel beholden to outside forces. We no longer have to justify our behavior, for we are now the architects of the universe. We are responsible to nothing outside ourselves, for we are the kingdom, the power, and the glory forever and ever." *Jeremy Rifkin, Algeny*

[14]*As* a door turns on its hinges,
So *does* the lazy *man* on his bed.
[15]The lazy *man* buries his hand in the bowl;[a]
It wearies him to bring it back to his mouth.
[16]The lazy *man is* wiser in his own eyes
Than seven men who can answer sensibly.

[17]He who passes by *and* meddles in a quarrel not his own
Is like one who takes a dog by the ears.

[18]Like a madman who throws firebrands, arrows, and death,
[19]*Is* the man *who* deceives his neighbor,
And says, "I was only joking!"

Is sin so luscious that you will burn in hell forever for it?

CHARLES SPURGEON

[20]Where *there is* no wood, the fire goes out;
And where *there is* no talebearer, strife ceases.
[21]*As* charcoal *is* to burning coals, and wood to fire,
So *is* a contentious man to kindle strife.
[22]The words of a talebearer *are* like tasty trifles,
And they go down into the inmost body.

[23]Fervent lips with a wicked heart
Are like earthenware covered with silver dross.

[24]He who hates, disguises *it* with his lips,
And lays up deceit within himself;
[25]When he speaks kindly, do not believe him,
For *there are* seven abominations in his heart;
[26]*Though his* hatred is covered by deceit,
His wickedness will be revealed before the assembly.

[27]Whoever digs a pit will fall into it,
And he who rolls a stone will have it roll back on him.

[28]A lying tongue hates *those who are* crushed by it,
And a flattering mouth works ruin.

27 Do not boast about tomorrow,
For you do not know what a day may bring forth.

[2]Let another man praise you, and not your own mouth;
A stranger, and not your own lips.

[3]A stone *is* heavy and sand *is* weighty,
But a fool's wrath *is* heavier than both of them.

[4]Wrath *is* cruel and anger a torrent,
But who *is* able to stand before jealousy?

[5]Open rebuke *is* better
Than love carefully concealed.

[6]Faithful *are* the wounds of a friend,
But the kisses of an enemy *are* deceitful.

[7]A satisfied soul loathes the honeycomb,
But to a hungry soul every bitter thing is sweet.

26:15 [a]Compare 19:24

26:17 This is wonderful guidance for the sincere Christian on what not to do. He who meddles will get hurt.

27:1 The only thing we can be sure of is the breath going into our lungs at this moment. We can't be sure of the next breath. That comes only by the permission of God. See James 4:13–15 and Luke 12:20 comment.

27:5 We openly rebuke those in the world for their sin because we love them and are concerned for their eternal welfare.

QUESTIONS & OBJECTIONS

27:10

"How do I reach my neighbors with the gospel?"

Neighbors are like family. We don't want to offend them unnecessarily, because we have to live with them. We need to be rich in good works toward all men, but especially our neighbors. The Bible reveals that this is a legitimate part of evangelism. Jesus said, "Let your light so shine before men, that they may see your good works and glorify your Father in heaven" (Matt. 5:16). It is God's will that "by doing good you may put to silence the ignorance of foolish men" (1 Pet. 2:15). Sinners may disagree with what you believe, but seeing your good works makes them think, "I don't believe what he believes, but *he* sure does. He certainly is sincere in his faith."

A friendly wave, a gift for no reason, fresh-baked goods, etc., can pave the way for evangelism. Offer to mow your neighbors' lawn or help do some painting. Volunteer to pick up their mail and newspapers while they're on vacation. Compliment them on their landscaping and ask for gardening tips. Invite them over for a barbecue or dessert. Pray for an opportunity to share the gospel, and be prepared for it when it comes.

8Like a bird that wanders from its nest
Is a man who wanders from his place.

9Ointment and perfume delight the heart,
And the sweetness of a man's friend *gives delight* by hearty counsel.

10Do not forsake your own friend or your father's friend,
Nor go to your brother's house in the day of your calamity;
Better *is* a neighbor nearby than a brother far away.

11My son, be wise, and make my heart glad,
That I may answer him who reproaches me.

12A prudent *man* foresees evil *and* hides himself;
The simple pass on *and* are punished.

13Take the garment of him who is surety for a stranger,
And hold it in pledge *when* he is surety for a seductress.

14He who blesses his friend with a loud voice, rising early in the morning,
It will be counted a curse to him.

15A continual dripping on a very rainy day
And a contentious woman are alike;
16Whoever restrains her restrains the wind,
And grasps oil with his right hand.

17*As* iron sharpens iron,
So a man sharpens the countenance of his friend.

18Whoever keeps the fig tree will eat its fruit;
So he who waits on his master will be honored.

19As in water face *reflects* face,
So a man's heart *reveals* the man.

20Hell[a] and Destruction[b] are never full;
So the eyes of man are never satisfied.

27:20 [a]Or *Sheol* [b]Hebrew *Abaddon*

27:18 "A tree can weather almost any storm if its root is sound, but when the fig tree which our Lord cursed 'dried up from the roots' it immediately 'withered away.' A church that is soundly rooted cannot be destroyed, but nothing can save a church whose root is dried up. No stimulation, no advertising campaigns, no gifts of money and no beautiful edifice can bring back life to the rootless tree." *A. W. Tozer*

[21]The refining pot *is* for silver and the
furnace for gold,
And a man *is valued* by what others
say of him.

[22]Though you grind a fool in a mortar
with a pestle along with crushed
grain,
Yet his foolishness will not depart
from him.

[23]Be diligent to know the state of your
flocks,
And attend to your herds;
[24]For riches *are* not forever,
Nor does a crown *endure* to all
generations.
[25]*When* the hay is removed, and the
tender grass shows itself,
And the herbs of the mountains are
gathered in,
[26]The lambs *will provide* your clothing,
And the goats the price of a field;
[27]*You shall have* enough goats' milk for
your food,
For the food of your household,
And the nourishment of your
maidservants.

28 The wicked flee when no one
pursues,
But the righteous are bold as a lion.

[2]Because of the transgression of a land,
many *are* its princes;
But by a man of understanding *and*
knowledge
Right will be prolonged.

[3]A poor man who oppresses the poor
Is like a driving rain which leaves no
food.

[4]Those who forsake the law praise the
wicked,
But such as keep the law contend
with them.

[5]Evil men do not understand justice,
But those who seek the LORD
understand all.

[6]Better *is* the poor who walks in his
integrity
Than one perverse *in his* ways, though
he *be* rich.

[7]Whoever keeps the law *is* a discerning
son,
But a companion of gluttons shames
his father.

[8]One who increases his possessions by
usury and extortion
Gathers it for him who will pity the
poor.

[9]One who turns away his ear from

27:20 Men can never satisfy lust; it is an unquenchable inferno. The more it is given fuel, the more it continues to burn. Desire will make him crave sexual pleasure, money, fame, and power. He will continue to "want" until the Lord becomes his shepherd. See Psa. 23:1.

28:4 When the Church forsakes the proclamation of God's Law, iniquity floods the land. *Daniel Webster* stated, "If truth is not diffused, error will be. If God and His Word are not known and received, the devil and his works will gain the ascendancy. If the evangelical volume does not reach every hamlet, the pages of a corrupt and licentious literature will.

"If the power of the gospel is not felt throughout the length and breadth of this land, anarchy and misrule, degradation and misery, corruption and darkness will reign without mitigation or end."

28:5 "God's justice stands forever against the sinner in utter severity. The vague and tenuous hope that God is too kind to punish the ungodly has become a deadly opiate for the consciences of millions. It hushes their fears and allows them to practice all pleasant forms of iniquity while death draws every day nearer and the command to repent goes unregarded. As responsible moral beings, we dare not so trifle with our eternal future." *A. W. Tozer, The Knowledge of the Holy*

28:9 If a professing Christian thinks that he can willfully serve sin by transgressing the moral Law and still have peace with God, he is deceived. See also John 9:31 comment.

hearing the law,
Even his prayer *is* an abomination.

[10]Whoever causes the upright to go
astray in an evil way,
He himself will fall into his own pit;
But the blameless will inherit good.

[11]The rich man *is* wise in his own eyes,
But the poor who has understanding
searches him out.

[12]When the righteous rejoice, *there is*
great glory;
But when the wicked arise, men hide
themselves.

[13]He who covers his sins will not prosper,
But whoever confesses and forsakes
them will have mercy.

[14]Happy *is* the man who is always
reverent,
But he who hardens his heart will fall
into calamity.

[15]*Like* a roaring lion and a charging bear
Is a wicked ruler over poor people.

[16]A ruler who lacks understanding *is* a
great oppressor,
But he who hates covetousness will
prolong *his* days.

[17]A man burdened with bloodshed will
flee into a pit;
Let no one help him.

[18]Whoever walks blamelessly will be
saved,
But *he who is* perverse *in his* ways will
suddenly fall.

[19]He who tills his land will have plenty
of bread,
But he who follows frivolity will have
poverty enough!

[20]A faithful man will abound with
blessings,
But he who hastens to be rich will not
go unpunished.

[21]To show partiality is not good,
Because for a piece of bread a man
will transgress.

[22]A man with an evil eye hastens after
riches,
And does not consider that poverty
will come upon him.

[23]He who rebukes a man will find more
favor afterward
Than he who flatters with the tongue.

[24]Whoever robs his father or his mother,

28:13 Sin cannot be covered so that it is hidden from the eyes of a holy Creator. Biblical conversion comes not only from confessing sin to God, but also from forsaking sin. Those who do that and trust the Savior partake in the mercy of God.

Confessing our sins. "Whereas, it is the duty of nations as well as of men to own their dependence upon the overruling power of God, to confess their sins and transgressions in humble sorrow yet with assured hope that genuine repentance will lead to mercy and pardon, and to recognize the sublime truth, announced in the Holy Scriptures and proven by all history: that those nations only are blessed whose God is the Lord . . .

"We have been the recipients of the choicest bounties of Heaven. We have been preserved these many years in peace and prosperity. We have grown in numbers, wealth and power as no other nation has ever grown. But we have forgotten God. We have forgotten the gracious Hand which preserved us in peace, and multiplied and enriched and strengthened us; and we have vainly imagined, in the deceitfulness of our hearts, that all these blessings were produced by some superior wisdom and virtue of our own.

"Intoxicated with unbroken success, we have become too self-sufficient to feel the necessity of redeeming and preserving grace, too proud to pray to the God that made us!

"It behooves us then to humble ourselves before the offended Power, to confess our national sins and to pray for clemency and forgiveness." *Abraham Lincoln*, 1863, in declaring a day of national fasting, prayer, and humiliation

And says, "*It is* no transgression,"
The same *is* companion to a destroyer.

25 He who is of a proud heart stirs up strife,
But he who trusts in the LORD will be prospered.

26 He who trusts in his own heart is a fool,
But whoever walks wisely will be delivered.

27 He who gives to the poor will not lack,
But he who hides his eyes will have many curses.

28 When the wicked arise, men hide themselves;
But when they perish, the righteous increase.

29 He who is often rebuked, *and* hardens *his* neck,
Will suddenly be destroyed, and that without remedy.

2 When the righteous are in authority, the people rejoice;
But when a wicked *man* rules, the people groan.

3 Whoever loves wisdom makes his father rejoice,
But a companion of harlots wastes *his* wealth.

4 The king establishes the land by justice,
But he who receives bribes overthrows it.

5 A man who flatters his neighbor
Spreads a net for his feet.

6 By transgression an evil man is snared,
But the righteous sings and rejoices.

7 The righteous considers the cause of the poor,
But the wicked does not understand *such* knowledge.

8 Scoffers set a city aflame,
But wise *men* turn away wrath.

9 *If* a wise man contends with a foolish man,
Whether *the fool* rages or laughs, *there is* no peace.

10 The bloodthirsty hate the blameless,
But the upright seek his well-being.[a]

29:10 [a]Literally *soul*

28:26 Never give in to the temptation to trust your feelings over God's promises. See Prov. 3:5,6.

29:1 It is a fearful thought that God would lose patience with those who harden their hearts against Him. Jesus spoke of a man to whom God said, "This night your soul will be required of you" (Luke 12:20). It is prudent to warn sinners that God may lose patience with them and let death seize them, as He did with Ananias and Sapphira (Acts 5:1–10).

29:2 Righteous authority. When believers fulfill their responsibility to elect righteous leaders, the entire country benefits.

"In selecting men for office, let principle be your guide. Regard not the particular sect or denomination of the candidate—look to his character... It is alleged by men of loose principles, or defective views of the subject, that religion and morality are not necessary or important qualifications for political stations. But the Scriptures teach a different doctrine. They direct that rulers should be men who rule in the fear of God, able men, such as fear God, men of truth, hating covetousness...

"When a citizen gives his vote to a man of known immorality, he abuses his civic responsibility; he sacrifices not only his own interest, but that of his neighbor; he betrays the interest of his country." *Noah Webster*

29:9 It has been well said that a wise man will learn more from a fool's question than a fool will learn from a wise man's answer.

"The Church is the one institution that exists for those outside it."

William Tyndale

[11]A fool vents all his feelings,[a]
But a wise *man* holds them back.

[12]If a ruler pays attention to lies,
All his servants *become* wicked.

[13]The poor *man* and the oppressor have
this in common:
The LORD gives light to the eyes of
both.

[14]The king who judges the poor with
truth,
His throne will be established forever.

[15]The rod and rebuke give wisdom,
But a child left *to himself* brings shame
to his mother.

[16]When the wicked are multiplied,
transgression increases;
But the righteous will see their fall.

[17]Correct your son, and he will give
you rest;
Yes, he will give delight to your soul.

[18]Where *there is* no revelation,[a] the
people cast off restraint;
But happy *is* he who keeps the law.

[19]A servant will not be corrected by
mere words;
For though he understands, he will
not respond.

[20]Do you see a man hasty in his words?
There is more hope for a fool than for
him.

[21]He who pampers his servant from
childhood
Will have him as a son in the end.

[22]An angry man stirs up strife,
And a furious man abounds in
transgression.

[23]A man's pride will bring him low,
But the humble in spirit will retain
honor.

[24]Whoever is a partner with a thief
hates his own life;
He swears to tell the truth,[a] but
reveals nothing.

[25]The fear of man brings a snare,
But whoever trusts in the LORD shall
be safe.

[26]Many seek the ruler's favor,
But justice for man *comes* from the
LORD.

[27]An unjust man *is* an abomination to
the righteous,

29:11 [a]Literally *spirit* 29:18 [a]Or *prophetic vision* 29:24 [a]Literally *hears the adjuration*

29:15 A child doesn't learn to do evil; he naturally knows how to be selfish and lie. However, he must be taught to share and be truthful. See Prov. 20:11.

29:25 See Psa. 56:11 comment.

29:25 *How to Start a Witnessing Conversation*

Fear is undoubtedly the greatest hurdle to overcome before we can share our faith. At times we are afraid to even mention the things of God because we fear rejection, or not being able to answer a difficult question, or sounding like a religious nut, etc. But there is a way to bring up the subject of God without mentioning the "uncomfortable" issues of sin, Judgment Day, hell, etc.

Let's start from the beginning. You see a stranger sitting on a park bench. You feel the stirrings of your conscience telling you that if you cared about this man's eternal destiny, you should witness to him. A cold fear grips you at the thought of approaching a complete stranger. So, try this approach. Break the ice by saying a warm, "Good morning!" Then watch for his reaction. More than likely he will be a little surprised by the kindness of your voice, and reply, "Good morning." The ice is melted. Now you can test the waters.

You have a gospel tract in your pocket, so hand it to him along with a friendly, "Did you get one of these?" He takes it because you have stirred his curiosity, and you quickly follow it with, "It's a gospel tract. What do you think happens after someone dies?"

Again, watch for his reaction. More than likely there won't be the slightest offense, because you have simply asked for his opinion. He will probably respond with, "I don't know," so you reply, "Do you think there's a heaven?" or "Do you think about it much?" Now listen closely to his response, which will let you know if you can dive into the waters of personal evangelism. More than likely he will say, "All the time," or "Sometimes."

Again, his response will gauge whether or not he is open to the things of God. Most people are, and that's when you take the plunge. Ask him, "If there is a heaven, do you think you will go there? Are you a good person?" and from there you take him through the Commandments.

This may sound a little complicated, but after doing it a few times, it will become second nature. For details, see comments at 2 Sam. 12:1–14, Psa. 51:7, and John 4:7.

And *he who is* upright in the way *is* an
abomination to the wicked.

The Wisdom of Agur

30 The words of Agur the son of
Jakeh, *his* utterance. This man
declared to Ithiel—to Ithiel and Ucal:

[2]Surely I *am* more stupid than *any* man,
And do not have the understanding
of a man.
[3]I neither learned wisdom
Nor have knowledge of the Holy One.

[4]Who has ascended into heaven, or
descended?
Who has gathered the wind in His fists?
Who has bound the waters in a
garment?
Who has established all the ends of
the earth?
What *is* His name, and what *is* His
Son's name,
If you know?

[5]Every word of God *is* pure;
He *is* a shield to those who put their
trust in Him.
[6]Do not add to His words,
Lest He rebuke you, and you be
found a liar.

[7]Two *things* I request of You
(Deprive me not before I die):
[8]Remove falsehood and lies far from me;
Give me neither poverty nor riches—
Feed me with the food allotted to me;
[9]Lest I be full and deny *You*,

29:27 This is why the world hates the Christian. See John 15:18,19.

30:1,2 This is the foundational key to learning. See 1 Cor. 1:21; 3:18.

30:4 His name is "I AM" and His Son's name is Jesus Christ. See Psa. 2:12.

30:6 *All* Scripture is given by inspiration of God (2 Tim. 3:16), and is His complete revelation to mankind. Many religions accept the words of Scripture, but consider them to be only part of the truth. Those who have added anything to God's Holy Word are in great error.

QUESTIONS & OBJECTIONS

30:5

"The fact that there are so many versions proves that the Bible has mistakes. Which one is right?"

Skeptics often ask which Bible is right, and point to the fact that there are many versions. The implication is that each one is different, and therefore they have no credibility. How could they if they differ?

They are right about the number of versions—there are thousands. There are Chinese versions for Chinese speakers, Russian versions for Russian people, Arabic versions, Korean versions, and so on. There are translations in modern English and in very old English. There are paraphrases, revised versions, large print, pocket size, Greek and Hebrew versions, and even an Amplified version. In fact, the Bible is the most translated book in the world, with at least some portion of it available in over 2,400 languages, spoken by 98 percent of the world's population. All of these have been written so that people of any nation or culture can have access to and understand the Word of God. However, each translation is based on the original biblical texts. Due to the Dead Sea Scrolls, we can know that these texts are reliable. See Psa. 119:105 and 119:160 comments.

And say, "Who *is* the LORD?"
Or lest I be poor and steal,
And profane the name of my God.

[10]Do not malign a servant to his master,
Lest he curse you, and you be found guilty.

[11]*There is* a generation *that* curses its father,
And does not bless its mother.
[12]*There is* a generation *that is* pure in its own eyes,
Yet is not washed from its filthiness.
[13]*There is* a generation—oh, how lofty are their eyes!
And their eyelids are lifted up.
[14]*There is* a generation whose teeth *are like* swords,
And whose fangs *are like* knives,
To devour the poor from off the earth,
And the needy from *among* men.

[15]The leech has two daughters—
Give *and* Give!
There are three *things that* are never satisfied,
Four never say, "Enough!":
[16]The grave,[a]
The barren womb,
The earth *that* is not satisfied with water—
And the fire never says, "Enough!"

[17]The eye *that* mocks *his* father,
And scorns obedience to *his* mother,
The ravens of the valley will pick it out,
And the young eagles will eat it.

[18]There are three *things which* are too wonderful for me,
Yes, four *which* I do not understand:
[19]The way of an eagle in the air,
The way of a serpent on a rock,
The way of a ship in the midst of the sea,
And the way of a man with a virgin.

30:16 [a]Or *Sheol*

30:11,12 What better description do we have of this lawless generation? By transgressing the Fifth Commandment, it reaps the fearful consequences of disobedience and fails to receive the promise given in Eph. 6:1–3. Because they have been left without the light of the moral Law, they consider themselves pure and have therefore become a law to themselves.

30:15,16 Perhaps one more can be added to this list of those who never say "It is enough": the money-hungry television preacher. See 2 Pet. 2:1–3.

[20]This *is* the way of an adulterous
woman:
She eats and wipes her mouth,
And says, "I have done no wickedness."

[21]For three *things* the earth is perturbed,
Yes, for four it cannot bear up:
[22]For a servant when he reigns,
A fool when he is filled with food,
[23]A hateful *woman* when she is married,
And a maidservant who succeeds her
mistress.

[24]There are four *things which* are little
on the earth,
But they *are* exceedingly wise:
[25]The ants *are* a people not strong,
Yet they prepare their food in the
summer;
[26]The rock badgers[a] are a feeble folk,
Yet they make their homes in the crags;
[27]The locusts have no king,
Yet they all advance in ranks;
[28]The spider[a] skillfully grasps with its
hands,
And it is in kings' palaces.

[29]There are three *things which* are
majestic in pace,
Yes, four *which* are stately in walk:
[30]A lion, *which is* mighty among beasts
And does not turn away from any;
[31]A greyhound,[a]
A male goat also,
And a king *whose* troops *are* with him.[b]

[32]If you have been foolish in exalting
yourself,
Or if you have devised evil, *put your*
hand on *your* mouth.
[33]For *as* the churning of milk produces
butter,
And wringing the nose produces blood,
So the forcing of wrath produces strife.

The Words of King Lemuel's Mother

31 The words of King Lemuel, the
utterance which his mother taught
him:

[2]What, my son?
And what, son of my womb?
And what, son of my vows?
[3]Do not give your strength to women,
Nor your ways to that which destroys
kings.

[4]*It is* not for kings, O Lemuel,
It is not for kings to drink wine,
Nor for princes intoxicating drink;
[5]Lest they drink and forget the law,
And pervert the justice of all the
afflicted.
[6]Give strong drink to him who is
perishing,
And wine to those who are bitter of
heart.
[7]Let him drink and forget his poverty,
And remember his misery no more.

[8]Open your mouth for the speechless,
In the cause of all *who are* appointed
to die.[a]
[9]Open your mouth, judge righteously,
And plead the cause of the poor and
needy.

The Virtuous Wife

[10]Who[a] can find a virtuous[b] wife?

30:26 [a]Or *hyraxes* 30:28 [a]Or *lizard* 30:31 [a]Exact identity unknown [b]A Jewish tradition reads *a king against whom there is no uprising.* 31:8 [a]Literally *sons of passing away* 31:10 [a]Verses 10 through 31 are an alphabetic acrostic in Hebrew (compare Psalm 119). [b]Literally *a wife of valor,* in the sense of all forms of excellence

30:20 Seared conscience. Some people seem to have no conscience. In truth, they have a *seared* conscience (see 1 Tim. 4:2)—one that has become so hardened that it has lost its ability to function. A correct use of the Law will resurrect it. When you speak directly to the conscience of a hardened sinner by saying, "You *know* that it's wrong to steal, to lie, to commit adultery, etc.," the conscience affirms the truth of the Commandment. See Rom. 2:15. See 1 Tim. 4:2 comment.

30:25–28 Here are four virtues needed to be an effective witness: initiative (1 Cor. 15:58); wisdom (Matt. 7:24); unity (Phil. 1:27); and persistence (Acts 4:18–20).

QUESTIONS & OBJECTIONS

31:10

"Christianity oppresses women by making them submit to their husbands!"

The Bible does say, "Wives, submit to your own husbands, as to the Lord," but it also instructs, "Husbands, love your wives, just as Christ also loved the church and gave Himself for her" (Eph. 5:22,25). A man who understands that Jesus Christ sacrificed His life's blood for the Church will likewise love his wife sacrificially and passionately. He will honor her, respect her, protect, love, and cherish her as much as he does his own body, as he is instructed to do (Eph. 5:28). He will never say or do anything to harm or demean her. It is in this atmosphere of love and security that a godly wife willingly submits herself to the protective arms of her husband. She does this not because he is better than she is, but simply because this is God's order for His creation.

A godless world rejects the God-given formula for making marriage work. It thinks it knows best, and suffers the heartbreaking consequences of destroyed marriages and ruined lives. The Christian ideal of marriage is not one of an authoritarian and chauvinistic male holding his cringing wife in submission like an obedient dog. It's the very opposite. While most of the great religions treat women as inferior to men, the Bible gives them a place of dignity, honor, and unspeakable worth, expressed so evidently in Prov. 31. See also Exod. 20:17 comment.

For her worth *is* far above rubies.
11The heart of her husband safely trusts her;
So he will have no lack of gain.
12She does him good and not evil
All the days of her life.
13She seeks wool and flax,
And willingly works with her hands.
14She is like the merchant ships,
She brings her food from afar.
15She also rises while it is yet night,
And provides food for her household,
And a portion for her maidservants.
16She considers a field and buys it;
From her profits she plants a vineyard.
17She girds herself with strength,
And strengthens her arms.
18She perceives that her merchandise *is* good,
And her lamp does not go out by night.
19She stretches out her hands to the distaff,
And her hand holds the spindle.
20She extends her hand to the poor,
Yes, she reaches out her hands to the needy.
21She is not afraid of snow for her household,
For all her household *is* clothed with scarlet.
22She makes tapestry for herself;
Her clothing *is* fine linen and purple.
23Her husband is known in the gates,
When he sits among the elders of the land.
24She makes linen garments and sells *them,*
And supplies sashes for the merchants.
25Strength and honor *are* her clothing;
She shall rejoice in time to come.
26She opens her mouth with wisdom,
And on her tongue *is* the law of kindness.
27She watches over the ways of her household,
And does not eat the bread of idleness.
28Her children rise up and call her blessed;
Her husband *also,* and he praises her:
29"Many daughters have done well,
But you excel them all."
30Charm *is* deceitful and beauty *is* passing,
But a woman *who* fears the LORD, she shall be praised.
31Give her of the fruit of her hands,
And let her own works praise her in the gates.

Ecclesiastes

The Vanity of Life

1 The words of the Preacher, the son of David, king in Jerusalem.

2"Vanity[a] of vanities," says the Preacher;
"Vanity of vanities, all *is* vanity."

3What profit has a man from all his labor
In which he toils under the sun?
4*One* generation passes away, and *another* generation comes;
But the earth abides forever.
5The sun also rises, and the sun goes down,
And hastens to the place where it arose.
6The wind goes toward the south,
And turns around to the north;
The wind whirls about continually,
And comes again on its circuit.
7All the rivers run into the sea,
Yet the sea *is* not full;
To the place from which the rivers come,
There they return again.
8All things *are* full of labor;
Man cannot express *it*.
The eye is not satisfied with seeing,
Nor the ear filled with hearing.
9That which has been *is* what will be,
That which *is* done is what will be done,
And *there is* nothing new under the sun.
10Is there anything of which it may be said,
"See, this *is* new"?
It has already been in ancient times before us.
11*There is* no remembrance of former *things*,
Nor will there be any remembrance of *things* that are to come
By *those* who will come after.

The Grief of Wisdom

12I, the Preacher, was king over Israel
in Jerusalem. 13And I set my heart to seek
and search out by wisdom concerning all
that is done under heaven; this burdensome task God has given to the sons of
man, by which they may be exercised. 14I
have seen all the works that are done under the sun; and indeed, all *is* vanity and
grasping for the wind.

1:2 [a]Or *Absurdity, Frustration, Futility, Nonsense*; and so throughout this book

1:2 The reality of death makes this life futile—until we come to know God through the new birth (see John 3:3–8). Sadly, many of the godless have a shallow life philosophy until they are at death's door. See Rom. 8:20–22 for more about this futility.

1:6 See Heb. 11:3 comment for details on this and other scientific facts in the Bible.

"Modern science has confirmed that the air around the planet turns in huge circles, clockwise in one hemisphere and counterclockwise in the other." *Richard Gunther*

[15]*What is* crooked cannot be made
straight,
And what is lacking cannot be
numbered.

[16]I communed with my heart, saying,
"Look, I have attained greatness, and have
gained more wisdom than all who were
before me in Jerusalem. My heart has understood great wisdom and knowledge."
[17]And I set my heart to know wisdom and
to know madness and folly. I perceived
that this also is grasping for the wind.

[18]For in much wisdom *is* much grief,
And he who increases knowledge
increases sorrow.

The Vanity of Pleasure

2 I said in my heart, "Come now, I will
test you with mirth; therefore enjoy
pleasure"; but surely, this also *was* vanity.
[2]I said of laughter—"Madness!"; and of
mirth, "What does it accomplish?" [3]I
searched in my heart *how* to gratify my
flesh with wine, while guiding my heart
with wisdom, and how to lay hold on
folly, till I might see what *was* good for
the sons of men to do under heaven all
the days of their lives.

[4]I made my works great, I built myself
houses, and planted myself vineyards. [5]I
made myself gardens and orchards, and I
planted all *kinds* of fruit trees in them. [6]I
made myself water pools from which to
water the growing trees of the grove. [7]I
acquired male and female servants, and
had servants born in my house. Yes, I had
greater possessions of herds and flocks
than all who were in Jerusalem before me.
[8]I also gathered for myself silver and gold
and the special treasures of kings and of
the provinces. I acquired male and female
singers, the delights of the sons of men,
and musical instruments[a] of all kinds.

[9]So I became great and excelled more
than all who were before me in Jerusalem.
Also my wisdom remained with me.

[10]Whatever my eyes desired I did not
keep from them.
I did not withhold my heart from any
pleasure,
For my heart rejoiced in all my labor;
And this was my reward from all my
labor.
[11]Then I looked on all the works that
my hands had done
And on the labor in which I had toiled;
And indeed all *was* vanity and
grasping for the wind.
There was no profit under the sun.

The End of the Wise and the Fool

[12]Then I turned myself to consider
wisdom and madness and folly;

2:8 [a]Exact meaning unknown

2:4–6 Misguided man is more interested in living in harmony with nature than he is in living in harmony with his Creator. He thinks that Mother Nature has given him life, and he will, therefore, tie himself to a tree rather than let a logging company cut it down. The Christian, however, knows that it is God who gave him life in this world and in the next. May we tie ourselves to the old wooden cross rather than let the world hide it away.

It was in the cross that God demonstrated His lovingkindness, His judgment, and His righteousness. It is there that we find peace with God. This is why Paul gloried in the cross (see Gal. 6:14).

2:11 All is vanity. Seeing the futility of the transient nature of life is often the first sign of spiritual awakening. So never hesitate to speak with the ungodly about the reality of death. Remind them of its appointment. Make them face the fact that it could seize on them at any moment, and make sure you use the Law to bring the knowledge of sin and prepare the heart for grace.

"What has been, and is now, one of the strongest feelings in the human heart? Is it not to find some better place, some lovelier spot, than we have now? It is for this that men are seeking everywhere; and yet, they can have it, if they will; but instead of looking down, they must look up to find it. As men grow in knowledge, they vie with each other more and more to make their homes attractive, but the brightest home on earth is but an empty barn, compared with the mansions that are in the skies." *D. L. Moody*

For what *can* the man *do* who succeeds
the king?—
Only what he has already done.
13Then I saw that wisdom excels folly
As light excels darkness.
14The wise man's eyes *are* in his head,
But the fool walks in darkness.
Yet I myself perceived
That the same event happens to them
all.

15So I said in my heart,
"As it happens to the fool,
It also happens to me,
And why was I then more wise?"
Then I said in my heart,
"This also *is* vanity."
16For *there is* no more remembrance of
the wise than of the fool forever,
Since all that now *is* will be forgotten
in the days to come.
And how does a wise *man* die?
As the fool!

17Therefore I hated life because the work
that was done under the sun *was* distressing to me, for all *is* vanity and grasping
for the wind.

> Today comes but once and comes never to return. We hope it will come again tomorrow; but it does not. It is gone forever, with its inexhaustible possibilities, privileges and responsibilities.
>
> **RECORD OF CHRISTIAN WORK**

18Then I hated all my labor in which I
had toiled under the sun, because I must
leave it to the man who will come after
me. 19And who knows whether he will be
wise or a fool? Yet he will rule over all my
labor in which I toiled and in which I
have shown myself wise under the sun.
This also *is* vanity. 20Therefore I turned
my heart and despaired of all the labor in
which I had toiled under the sun. 21For
there is a man whose labor *is* with wisdom,
knowledge, and skill; yet he must leave
his heritage to a man who has not labored
for it. This also *is* vanity and a great evil.
22For what has man for all his labor, and
for the striving of his heart with which he
has toiled under the sun? 23For all his days
are sorrowful, and his work burdensome;
even in the night his heart takes no rest.
This also is vanity.
24Nothing *is* better for a man *than* that
he should eat and drink, and *that* his soul
should enjoy good in his labor. This also,
I saw, was from the hand of God. 25For
who can eat, or who can have enjoyment,
more than I?[a] 26For *God* gives wisdom
and knowledge and joy to a man who *is*
good in His sight; but to the sinner He
gives the work of gathering and collecting, that he may give to *him who is* good
before God. This also *is* vanity and grasping for the wind.

Everything Has Its Time

3 To everything *there is* a season,
A time for every purpose under
heaven:

2A time to be born,
And a time to die;
A time to plant,
And a time to pluck *what is* planted;
3A time to kill,
And a time to heal;
A time to break down,
And a time to build up;
4A time to weep,
And a time to laugh;
A time to mourn,
And a time to dance;
5A time to cast away stones,
And a time to gather stones;
A time to embrace,
And a time to refrain from embracing;
6A time to gain,
And a time to lose;
A time to keep,
And a time to throw away;
7A time to tear,
And a time to sew;

2:25 [a]Following Masoretic Text, Targum, and Vulgate; some Hebrew manuscripts, Septuagint, and Syriac read *without Him.*

3:6 *Vestigial Organs: Leftovers Again?*

Most likely you have heard that "vestigial organs" are proof that mankind has evolved from more primitive forms. Because these organs supposedly have no purpose, evolutionists assume they have outlived their usefulness and are "leftovers" from our less advanced ancestors.

But even if an organ were no longer needed, wouldn't it only prove *devolution*? This fits well with the Law of Entropy—that all things deteriorate over time. What evolution requires, however, is not the loss but the *addition* of information, where an organism *increases* in complexity. So "vestigial organs" still wouldn't help the evolutionist's case.

Besides, it is not even scientifically possible to prove that something has no use, because its use can always be discovered as more information becomes available. And that is exactly what has happened. It was claimed at the Scopes trial that there are "no less than 180 vestigial structures in the human body, sufficient to make of a man a veritable walking museum of antiquities." Today the list has shrunk to virtually zero. Scientists have discovered that each of these body parts does indeed have a purpose: for example, the appendix is part of the human immune system, and the "tailbone" supports muscles that are necessary for daily bodily functions.

In their zeal to provide "evidence" of evolution, scientists have proclaimed organs as useless simply because they were ignorant of their functions at the time. The functions were there all along, but evolutionists just didn't know it.

The same could be said of God's existence. Atheists may be ignorant of His presence, but that doesn't mean He doesn't exist. If they seek Him, they will find that He was there all along.

(Adapted from *How to Know God Exists.*)

A time to keep silence,
And a time to speak;
8 A time to love,
And a time to hate;
A time of war,
And a time of peace.

The God-Given Task

9 What profit has the worker from that
in which he labors? 10 I have seen the God-
given task with which the sons of men
are to be occupied. 11 He has made everything beautiful in its time. Also He has
put eternity in their hearts, except that no
one can find out the work that God does
from beginning to end.

12 I know that nothing *is* better for them
than to rejoice, and to do good in their
lives, 13 and also that every man should eat
and drink and enjoy the good of all his
labor—it *is* the gift of God.

14 I know that whatever God does,
It shall be forever.
Nothing can be added to it,
And nothing taken from it.
God does *it*, that men should fear
before Him.
15 That which is has already been,
And what is to be has already been;
And God requires an account of what
is past.

Injustice Seems to Prevail

16 Moreover I saw under the sun:

In the place of judgment,
Wickedness *was* there;
And *in* the place of righteousness,
Iniquity *was* there.

17 I said in my heart,

3:11 God has placed eternity in the hearts of humanity. The Adamic race is unique among creation. We crave immortality, but that craving for many is silent until faced with a terminal disease. That's why we must remind sinners that they are part of the ultimate statistic—ten out of ten die—and plead with them to listen to the claims of the gospel of salvation.

"The longest time man has to live, has no more proportion to eternity than a drop of dew has to the ocean." *D. L. Moody*

3:17 God has set a day in which He will judge the world in righteousness (see Acts 17:31). Never forget to include future punishment in your gospel proclamation.

QUESTIONS & OBJECTIONS

3:15 "I have committed sin, but that was in the past."

Everything we have done is "in the past." Even reading this sentence is something you've done in the past. We somehow think that because something sinful was done some time ago, God is no longer angry about the sin. But that defense doesn't work even in our criminal courts: "Judge, I raped and murdered that woman in the past. I haven't raped or murdered anyone since then; therefore you should let me go." Such thoughts are ludicrous. Some years ago the United States extradited a Nazi war criminal after 35 years had passed. In most cases, time doesn't forgive serious crime, and this is especially true with God, because He is not subject to the dimension of time. He sees the sins of our youth as if they were committed yesterday.

"We have a strange illusion that mere time cancels sin. I have heard others, and I have heard myself, recounting cruelties and falsehoods committed in boyhood as if they were no concern of the present speaker's, and even with laughter. But mere time does nothing either to the fact or to the guilt of a sin. The guilt is washed out not by time but by repentance and the blood of Christ." *C. S. Lewis*

"God shall judge the righteous and the
wicked,
For *there is* a time there for every
purpose and for every work."

[18]I said in my heart, "Concerning the
condition of the sons of men, God tests
them, that they may see that they themselves are *like* animals." [19]For what happens to the sons of men also happens to
animals; one thing befalls them: as one
dies, so dies the other. Surely, they all have
one breath; man has no advantage over
animals, for all *is* vanity. [20]All go to one
place: all are from the dust, and all return
to dust. [21]Who knows the spirit of the
sons of men, which goes upward, and the
spirit of the animal, which goes down to
the earth?[a] [22]So I perceived that nothing *is*
better than that a man should rejoice in
his own works, for that *is* his heritage.
For who can bring him to see what will
happen after him?

4 Then I returned and considered all
the oppression that is done under
the sun:

And look! The tears of the oppressed,
But they have no comforter—
On the side of their oppressors *there is*
power,
But they have no comforter.
[2]Therefore I praised the dead who
were already dead,
More than the living who are still alive.
[3]Yet, better than both *is he* who has
never existed,
Who has not seen the evil work that
is done under the sun.

The Vanity of Selfish Toil

[4]Again, I saw that for all toil and every
skillful work a man is envied by his neighbor. This also *is* vanity and grasping for
the wind.

[5]The fool folds his hands
And consumes his own flesh.
[6]Better a handful *with* quietness
Than both hands full, *together with*
toil and grasping for the wind.

[7]Then I returned, and I saw vanity under the sun:

[8]There is one alone, without companion:
He has neither son nor brother.
Yet *there is* no end to all his labors,
Nor is his eye satisfied with riches.
But he never asks,
"For whom do I toil and deprive
myself of good?"
This also *is* vanity and a grave
misfortune.

3:21 [a]Septuagint, Syriac, Targum, and Vulgate read *Who knows whether the spirit... goes upward, and whether... goes downward to the earth?*

The Value of a Friend

9Two *are* better than one,
Because they have a good reward for their labor.
10For if they fall, one will lift up his companion.
But woe to him *who is* alone when he falls,
For *he has* no one to help him up.
11Again, if two lie down together, they will keep warm;
But how can one be warm *alone?*
12Though one may be overpowered by another, two can withstand him.
And a threefold cord is not quickly broken.

Popularity Passes Away

13Better a poor and wise youth
Than an old and foolish king who will be admonished no more.
14For he comes out of prison to be king,
Although he was born poor in his kingdom.
15I saw all the living who walk under the sun;
They were with the second youth who stands in his place.
16*There was* no end of all the people over whom he was made king;
Yet those who come afterward will not rejoice in him.
Surely this also *is* vanity and grasping for the wind.

Fear God, Keep Your Vows

5 Walk prudently when you go to the house of God; and draw near to hear rather than to give the sacrifice of fools, for they do not know that they do evil.

2Do not be rash with your mouth,
And let not your heart utter anything hastily before God.
For God *is* in heaven, and you on earth;
Therefore let your words be few.
3For a dream comes through much activity,
And a fool's voice *is known* by *his* many words.

4When you make a vow to God, do not delay to pay it;
For *He has* no pleasure in fools.
Pay what you have vowed—
5Better not to vow than to vow and not pay.

6Do not let your mouth cause your flesh
to sin, nor say before the messenger *of*
God that it *was* an error. Why should God
be angry at your excuse[a] and destroy the
work of your hands? 7For in the multitude of dreams and many words *there is*
also vanity. But fear God.

The Vanity of Gain and Honor

8If you see the oppression of the poor,
and the violent perversion of justice and
righteousness in a province, do not marvel at the matter; for high official watches
over high official, and higher officials are
over them.
9Moreover the profit of the land is for
all; *even* the king is served from the field.

10He who loves silver will not be satisfied with silver;

5:6 [a]Literally *voice*

4:9–12 Witnessing partner. It's easy to find excuses not to witness by yourself, so find a partner or two and encourage one another in your evangelistic endeavors. Form ties with godly men and women who are liked-minded about the necessity to reach the lost and make plans to go out "fishing" on a regular basis. You may want to begin a weekly PIE night: Pizza, Intercession, and Evangelism. Meet with several others on a Friday night for a big slice of pizza, pray together for 15–20 minutes, then hit the streets or a mall to seek the lost.

5:1 Without the Law it is almost impossible to convince the ungodly that their heart is desperately wicked. Until it brings its light, they measure themselves by themselves, and the tragic result is that they proclaim their own goodness. See Prov. 20:6; Mark 10:17–19.

"The beginning of anxiety is the end of faith, and the beginning of true faith is the end of anxiety."

George Mueller

Nor he who loves abundance, with
increase.
This also *is* vanity.

[11]When goods increase,
They increase who eat them;
So what profit have the owners
Except to see *them* with their eyes?

[12]The sleep of a laboring man *is* sweet,
Whether he eats little or much;
But the abundance of the rich will not
permit him to sleep.

[13]There is a severe evil *which* I have
seen under the sun:
Riches kept for their owner to his hurt.
[14]But those riches perish through
misfortune;
When he begets a son, *there is*
nothing in his hand.
[15]As he came from his mother's womb,
naked shall he return,
To go as he came;
And he shall take nothing from his
labor
Which he may carry away in his hand.
[16]And this also *is* a severe evil—
Just exactly as he came, so shall he go.
And what profit has he who has
labored for the wind?
[17]All his days he also eats in darkness,
And *he has* much sorrow and sickness
and anger.

[18]Here is what I have seen: *It is* good
and fitting *for one* to eat and drink, and to
enjoy the good of all his labor in which
he toils under the sun all the days of his
life which God gives him; for it *is* his heritage. [19]As for every man to whom God
has given riches and wealth, and given
him power to eat of it, to receive his heritage and rejoice in his labor—this *is* the
gift of God. [20]For he will not dwell un-
duly on the days of his life, because God
keeps *him* busy with the joy of his heart.

6 There is an evil which I have seen
under the sun, and it *is* common
among men: [2]A man to whom God has
given riches and wealth and honor, so
that he lacks nothing for himself of all he
desires; yet God does not give him power
to eat of it, but a foreigner consumes it.
This *is* vanity, and it *is* an evil affliction.

[3]If a man begets a hundred *children*
and lives many years, so that the days of
his years are many, but his soul is not satisfied with goodness, or indeed he has no
burial, I say *that* a stillborn child *is* better
than he— [4]for it comes in vanity and departs in darkness, and its name is covered
with darkness. [5]Though it has not seen
the sun or known *anything,* this has more
rest than that man, [6]even if he lives a thousand years twice—but has not seen goodness. Do not all go to one place?

[7]All the labor of man *is* for his mouth,
And yet the soul is not satisfied.
[8]For what more has the wise *man* than
the fool?
What does the poor man have,
Who knows *how* to walk before the
living?
[9]Better *is* the sight of the eyes than the
wandering of desire.

This also *is* vanity and grasping for
the wind.

10Whatever one is, he has been named
already,
For it is known that he *is* man;
And he cannot contend with Him
who is mightier than he.
11Since there are many things that
increase vanity,
How *is* man the better?

12For who knows what *is* good for man
in life, all the days of his vain life which
he passes like a shadow? Who can tell a
man what will happen after him under the
sun?

The Value of Practical Wisdom

7 A good name is better than precious
ointment,
And the day of death than the day of
one's birth;
2Better to go to the house of mourning
Than to go to the house of feasting,
For that *is* the end of all men;
And the living will take *it* to heart.
3Sorrow *is* better than laughter,
For by a sad countenance the heart is
made better.
4The heart of the wise *is* in the house
of mourning,
But the heart of fools *is* in the house
of mirth.

5*It is* better to hear the rebuke of the
wise
Than for a man to hear the song of
fools.
6For like the crackling of thorns under
a pot,
So *is* the laughter of the fool.
This also is vanity.
7Surely oppression destroys a wise
man's reason,
And a bribe debases the heart.

8The end of a thing *is* better than its
beginning;
The patient in spirit *is* better than the
proud in spirit.
9Do not hasten in your spirit to be
angry,
For anger rests in the bosom of fools.
10Do not say,
"Why were the former days better than
these?"
For you do not inquire wisely
concerning this.

11Wisdom *is* good with an inheritance,
And profitable to those who see the
sun.
12For wisdom *is* a defense *as* money *is* a
defense,
But the excellence of knowledge *is*
that wisdom gives life to those
who have it.

How you believe God perceives people
will determine how you respond to them.

JACQUELYN K. HEASLEY

13Consider the work of God;
For who can make straight what He
has made crooked?
14In the day of prosperity be joyful,
But in the day of adversity consider:
Surely God has appointed the one as
well as the other,
So that man can find out nothing *that*
will come after him.

15I have seen everything in my days of
vanity:

There is a just *man* who perishes in

6:12 Thank God for His Word. It is a lamp to our feet and a light to our path. It tells us what is good for us and what the future holds.

7:9 It is wise to go away and pray if you ever find anger in your heart. Faithful friends have been separated for life by a cutting tongue that has been let loose by an angry heart.

his righteousness,
And there is a wicked *man* who
prolongs *life* in his wickedness.

16Do not be overly righteous,
Nor be overly wise:
Why should you destroy yourself?
17Do not be overly wicked,
Nor be foolish:
Why should you die before your time?
18*It is* good that you grasp this,
And also not remove your hand from
the other;
For he who fears God will escape
them all.

19Wisdom strengthens the wise
More than ten rulers of the city.

20For *there is* not a just man on earth
who does good
And does not sin.

21Also do not take to heart everything
people say,
Lest you hear your servant cursing you.
22For many times, also, your own heart
has known
That even you have cursed others.

23All this I have proved by wisdom.
I said, "I will be wise";
But it *was* far from me.
24As for that which is far off and
exceedingly deep,
Who can find it out?
25I applied my heart to know,
To search and seek out wisdom and
the reason *of things,*
To know the wickedness of folly,
Even of foolishness *and* madness.
26And I find more bitter than death
The woman whose heart *is* snares and
nets,
Whose hands *are* fetters.
He who pleases God shall escape
from her,
But the sinner shall be trapped by her.

27"Here is what I have found," says the
Preacher,
"*Adding* one thing to the other to find
out the reason,
28Which my soul still seeks but I
cannot find:
One man among a thousand I have
found,
But a woman among all these I have
not found.
29Truly, this only I have found:
That God made man upright,
But they have sought out many
schemes."

8 Who *is* like a wise *man?*
And who knows the interpretation of
a thing?
A man's wisdom makes his face shine,
And the sternness of his face is
changed.

Obey Authorities for God's Sake

2I *say,* "Keep the king's commandment
for the sake of your oath to God. 3Do not
be hasty to go from his presence. Do not
take your stand for an evil thing, for he
does whatever pleases him."

4Where the word of a king *is, there is*
power;
And who may say to him, "What are
you doing?"
5He who keeps his command will
experience nothing harmful;

7:20 When confronted with their sin, the lost often say that it makes them "human"—and they are right. No human is without sin. See Psa. 143:2; Rom. 3:10–18; and 1 John 1:8–10 for further details on man's standing before God.

8:4 If someone asks how you know that there is an afterlife, tell them that you have the greatest authority on earth. If you have the word of a king, that is something to stand on. But we have the *Word of God*, and that can be relied upon with absolute certainty.

SPRINGBOARDS FOR PREACHING AND WITNESSING

The Future

8:7 If you knew even five minutes into the future, I am certain things would radically change for you. I am not talking about playing blackjack in Vegas; rather, I am thinking about what car or plane you would climb into, or what pill you would consume. I am sure if Heath Ledger had known the future, he would have been more careful about what he swallowed. I am sure if President John F. Kennedy had known just a few minutes into the future, he would have thought twice about climbing into a limo in Dallas. The fact is, we don't know even a moment into the future—but we can know Him who knows the future.

The Bible tells us that God created time and that He can flip through it as you and I flip through the pages of a history book. Those who find that hard to believe simply need to study Matt. 24 or Luke 21, and see how the words of Jesus parallel history before it came into being. The Word of God perfectly predicts the days in which we live. Jesus even predicted that His words would never pass away (see Matt. 24:35), and 2,000 years later we still have them.

What is going to happen in the future? God knows; and it is an unspeakable consolation to know that with all the chaos and uncertainty in this world, there is Someone who is in control. Absolute control.

And a wise man's heart discerns both
time and judgment,
[6]Because for every matter there is a
time and judgment,
Though the misery of man increases
greatly.
[7]For he does not know what will
happen;
So who can tell him when it will occur?
[8]No one has power over the spirit to
retain the spirit,
And no one has power in the day of
death.
There is no release from that war,
And wickedness will not deliver those
who are given to it.

[9]All this I have seen, and applied my
heart to every work that is done under the
sun: *There is* a time in which one man
rules over another to his own hurt.

Death Comes to All

[10]Then I saw the wicked buried, who
had come and gone from the place of holiness, and they were forgotten[a] in the
city where they had so done. This also *is*
vanity. [11]Because the sentence against an
evil work is not executed speedily, therefore the heart of the sons of men is fully
set in them to do evil. [12]Though a sinner
does evil a hundred *times,* and his *days*
are prolonged, yet I surely know that it
will be well with those who fear God,
who fear before Him. [13]But it will not be
well with the wicked; nor will he prolong
his days, *which are* as a shadow, because
he does not fear before God.

[14]There is a vanity which occurs on
earth, that there are just *men* to whom it
happens according to the work of the
wicked; again, there are wicked *men* to
whom it happens according to the work
of the righteous. I said that this also *is*
vanity.

[15]So I commended enjoyment, because
a man has nothing better under the sun
than to eat, drink, and be merry; for this
will remain with him in his labor *all* the
days of his life which God gives him under the sun.

[16]When I applied my heart to know
wisdom and to see the business that is
done on earth, even though one sees no
sleep day or night, [17]then I saw all the

8:10 [a]**Some Hebrew manuscripts, Septuagint, and Vulgate read** ***praised.***

8:11 Instead of appreciating the patience and kindness of God in withholding His wrath, the ungodly embolden themselves in their sin (see Psa. 50:21). Yet, every time they sin, they are storing up God's wrath that will be revealed on the Day of Judgment (see Rom. 2:4,5).

work of God, that a man cannot find out the work that is done under the sun. For though a man labors to discover *it,* yet he will not find *it;* moreover, though a wise *man* attempts to know *it,* he will not be able to find *it.*

9 For I considered all this in my heart, so that I could declare it all: that the righteous and the wise and their works *are* in the hand of God. People know neither love nor hatred *by* anything *they see* before them.
2All things *come* alike to all:

One event *happens* to the righteous
and the wicked;
To the good,[a] the clean, and the
unclean;
To him who sacrifices and him who
does not sacrifice.
As is the good, so *is* the sinner;
He who takes an oath as *he* who fears
an oath.

3This *is* an evil in all that is done under the sun: that one thing *happens* to all. Truly the hearts of the sons of men are full of evil; madness *is* in their hearts while they live, and after that *they go* to the dead.
4But for him who is joined to all the living there is hope, for a living dog is better than a dead lion.

5For the living know that they will die;
But the dead know nothing,
And they have no more reward,
For the memory of them is forgotten.
6Also their love, their hatred, and their
envy have now perished;
Nevermore will they have a share
In anything done under the sun.

7Go, eat your bread with joy,
And drink your wine with a merry
heart;
For God has already accepted your
works.
8Let your garments always be white,
And let your head lack no oil.

9Live joyfully with the wife whom you love all the days of your vain life which He has given you under the sun, all your days of vanity; for that *is* your portion in life, and in the labor which you perform under the sun.

> Tell the students to give up their small ambitions and come eastward to preach the gospel of Christ.
>
> **FRANCIS XAVIER**

10Whatever your hand finds to do, do *it* with your might; for *there is* no work or device or knowledge or wisdom in the grave where you are going.
11I returned and saw under the sun that—

The race *is* not to the swift,
Nor the battle to the strong,
Nor bread to the wise,
Nor riches to men of understanding,
Nor favor to men of skill;
But time and chance happen to them
all.
12For man also does not know his time:
Like fish taken in a cruel net,
Like birds caught in a snare,
So the sons of men *are* snared in an
evil time,
When it falls suddenly upon them.

9:2 [a]Septuagint, Syriac, and Vulgate read *good and bad.*

9:8 Keep your robe of righteousness spotless. See Rev. 3:5,18; 7:9; 16:15 for further details.

"It is of primary importance that the preacher should be clothed with the garment of salvation; that he should be filled with a sense of the immense worth of the truth, the guilt, depravity and danger man is in; the unsearchable love of Christ in the bloody purchase, and his ability and willingness to save redeemed penitents. Without this robe, he will preach a distant Jesus, by an unfelt gospel, and with an unhallowed tongue." *John Leland*

9:11 Evolution: Racing Turtles

The story is told of a symbolic foot race that took place between Russia and the U.S. during the Cold War. The very best athlete from each country competed to see who was superior. The American runner won. The next day, the Soviet newspaper headline read: "Russia comes in second in big race; U.S. comes in next to last."

As this humorous story shows, your perspective makes all the difference. The way you present the evidence has a great impact on the way it is perceived—but it doesn't affect reality. So with that in mind, let's take a close look at an article in the *Encyclopedia Britannica* describing the turtle's evolution:

> The evolution of the turtle is one of the most remarkable in the history of vertebrates. Unfortunately, the origin of this highly successful order is obscured by the *lack of fossils*, although turtles leave *more and better fossil remains* than do other vertebrates. By the middle of the Triassic Period (about 200,000,000 years ago) turtles were numerous and in possession of basic turtle characteristics . . . *Intermediates* between turtles and cotylosaurs, the primitive reptiles from which turtles probably sprang, *are entirely lacking*.

At first glance, this could certainly give the perception that turtles are a marvelous example of evolution. But read it again. Rather than the exciting, clear-cut proof of evolution that it claims to be, here is what it's really saying:

- Due to the lack of fossils, there is no clue to the turtle's origin.
- When it first appeared, the turtle looked just like a turtle and its structure hasn't changed since.
- Despite leaving more fossils, and better fossils, than other vertebrates, there are no intermediate forms.

So the turtle arrived on the scene fully formed, there are no fossils linking it to any other creature, and it remains as a turtle. Sounds like evidence that would delight any creationist. Yet supposedly we've just seen "one of the *most remarkable*" examples of evolution! Your perspective makes all the difference. Do you see a creature that gradually evolved from less complex life forms, linked to its ancestors by numerous transitional forms? Or do you see a creature that was created in its own distinct kind, and is consistently reproducing after its own kind?

Also, with "more and better fossil remains" for the turtle than other vertebrates, but transitional forms still "entirely lacking," what does this say about the intermediates between all other vertebrates? I think the encyclopedia is right about one thing: It is "one of the most remarkable" examples of evolution available—since no such evidence exists, the "nothing" they've found so far is the best there is.

(Adapted from *How to Know God Exists*.)

Wisdom Superior to Folly

13This wisdom I have also seen under
the sun, and it *seemed* great to me: 14*There*
was a little city with few men in it; and a
great king came against it, besieged it, and
built great snares[a] around it. 15Now there
was found in it a poor wise man, and he
by his wisdom delivered the city. Yet no
one remembered that same poor man.
16Then I said:

"Wisdom *is* better than strength.
Nevertheless the poor man's wisdom
is despised,
And his words are not heard.
17Words of the wise, *spoken* quietly,
should be heard
Rather than the shout of a ruler of
fools.
18Wisdom *is* better than weapons of war;
But one sinner destroys much good."

10 Dead flies putrefy[a] the perfumer's
ointment,
And cause it to give off a foul odor;
So does a little folly to one respected
for wisdom *and* honor.
2A wise man's heart *is* at his right hand,
But a fool's heart at his left.
3Even when a fool walks along the way,
He lacks wisdom,
And he shows everyone *that* he *is* a fool.
4If the spirit of the ruler rises against
you,
Do not leave your post;

9:14 [a]Septuagint, Syriac, and Vulgate read *bulwarks*. 10:1 [a]Targum and Vulgate omit *putrefy*.

For conciliation pacifies great offenses.

5 There is an evil I have seen under the
sun,
As an error proceeding from the ruler:
6 Folly is set in great dignity,
While the rich sit in a lowly place.
7 I have seen servants on horses,
While princes walk on the ground
like servants.

· · · · · ·

Did Jesus abolish the Law or not?
See Heb. 7:18,19 comment.

· · · · · ·

8 He who digs a pit will fall into it,
And whoever breaks through a wall
will be bitten by a serpent.
9 He who quarries stones may be hurt
by them,
And he who splits wood may be
endangered by it.
10 If the ax is dull,
And one does not sharpen the edge,
Then he must use more strength;
But wisdom brings success.

11 A serpent may bite when *it is* not
charmed;
The babbler is no different.
12 The words of a wise man's mouth *are*
gracious,
But the lips of a fool shall swallow
him up;
13 The words of his mouth begin with
foolishness,
And the end of his talk *is* raving
madness.
14 A fool also multiplies words.
No man knows what is to be;
Who can tell him what will be after
him?
15 The labor of fools wearies them,
For they do not even know how to go
to the city!

16 Woe to you, O land, when your king
is a child,
And your princes feast in the morning!
17 Blessed *are* you, O land, when your
king *is* the son of nobles,
And your princes feast at the proper
time—
For strength and not for drunkenness!
18 Because of laziness the building decays,
And through idleness of hands the
house leaks.
19 A feast is made for laughter,
And wine makes merry;
But money answers everything.

20 Do not curse the king, even in your
thought;
Do not curse the rich, even in your
bedroom;
For a bird of the air may carry your
voice,
And a bird in flight may tell the matter.

The Value of Diligence

11 Cast your bread upon the waters,
For you will find it after many
days.
2 Give a serving to seven, and also to

10:10 A man was once cutting a tree stump with an obviously blunt axe. He was only bruising the bark as sweat poured from his beaded brow. Someone suggested that he stop for a moment and sharpen the axe, to which he replied, "I'm too busy chopping the tree to stop for anything." If he would only stop for a moment and sharpen the axe, he would slice through the tree with far greater ease.

Stop at the beginning of each day, and "sharpen the axe" through prayer. Seek first the kingdom of God and you will slice through that day with far greater ease.

"We pray for His kingdom to come; we don't bring it in. Oh, the conceit of prayerless activity! P. T. Forsyth said our worst sin is prayerlessness because of what it says about who we really think is in charge of the church and the universe." *Ben Patterson*

11:1 Be continually benevolent. Look at what Jesus said on the subject in Matt. 5:42 and Acts 20:35. The way to an unbeliever's heart is often through his mouth. The gift of a hamburger may speak much louder of your love than a powerful sermon in a deaf ear.

"If you see one hurrying on to destruction, use the utmost of your endeavor to stop him in his course."

George Whitefield

eight,
For you do not know what evil will
be on the earth.

[3]If the clouds are full of rain,
They empty *themselves* upon the earth;
And if a tree falls to the south or the
north,
In the place where the tree falls, there
it shall lie.
[4]He who observes the wind will not
sow,
And he who regards the clouds will
not reap.

[5]As you do not know what *is* the way
of the wind,[a]
Or how the bones *grow* in the womb
of her who is with child,
So you do not know the works of
God who makes everything.
[6]In the morning sow your seed,
And in the evening do not withhold
your hand;
For you do not know which will
prosper,
Either this or that,
Or whether both alike *will be* good.

[7]Truly the light is sweet,
And *it is* pleasant for the eyes to
behold the sun;
[8]But if a man lives many years
And rejoices in them all,
Yet let him remember the days of
darkness,
For they will be many.
All that is coming *is* vanity.

Seek God in Early Life

[9]Rejoice, O young man, in your youth,
And let your heart cheer you in the
days of your youth;
Walk in the ways of your heart,
And in the sight of your eyes;
But know that for all these
God will bring you into judgment.
[10]Therefore remove sorrow from your
heart,
And put away evil from your flesh,
For childhood and youth *are* vanity.

12 Remember now your Creator in
the days
of your youth,

11:5 [a]Or *spirit*

11:3 For the Bible's description of the hydrologic cycle, see Psa. 135:7 comment.

11:6 We need to be busy working, sowing seed wherever we can. We will have eternity to worship God; we have a limited time to reach the lost. Be ready to preach the word in season and out of season (see 2 Tim. 4:2).

"Ultimately evangelism is a matter of the heart between the believer and a sovereign God. It is truly a spiritual matter. And if we are not personally and corporately evangelistic, the first response must be confession and repentance toward the God whose grace is sufficient to give us yet another opportunity." *Thom Rainer*

12:1 This is the greatest advice you can give to young people. Warn them that as they grow old, their hearts will become hard and self-righteous. Strongly exhort them to live their lives soaked in the truth of vv. 13,14.

Before the difficult days come,
And the years draw near when you say,
"I have no pleasure in them":
2While the sun and the light,
The moon and the stars,
Are not darkened,
And the clouds do not return after the rain;
3In the day when the keepers of the house tremble,
And the strong men bow down;
When the grinders cease because they are few,
And those that look through the windows grow dim;
4When the doors are shut in the streets,
And the sound of grinding is low;
When one rises up at the sound of a bird,
And all the daughters of music are brought low.
5Also they are afraid of height,
And of terrors in the way;
When the almond tree blossoms,
The grasshopper is a burden,
And desire fails.
For man goes to his eternal home,
And the mourners go about the streets.
6*Remember your Creator* before the silver cord is loosed,[a]
Or the golden bowl is broken,

God uses broken things. It takes broken soil to produce a crop, broken clouds to give rain, broken grain to give bread, broken bread to give strength. It is the broken alabaster box that gives forth perfume . . . it is Peter, weeping bitterly, who returns to greater power than ever.

VANCE HAVNER

Or the pitcher shattered at the fountain,
Or the wheel broken at the well.
7Then the dust will return to the earth as it was,
And the spirit will return to God who gave it.

8"Vanity of vanities," says the Preacher,
"All *is* vanity."

12:6 [a]Following Qere and Targum; Kethib reads *removed;* Septuagint and Vulgate read *broken.*

12:3 A plea to the unsaved. "Come, friend, I will talk to you personally again—young man, we shall soon grow old, or, perhaps, we shall die before that time, and we shall lie upon our bed—the last bed upon which we shall ever sleep—we shall wake from our last slumber to hear the doleful tidings that there is no hope; the physician will feel our pulse, and solemnly assure our relatives that it is all over!

"And we shall lie in that still room, where all is hushed except the ticking of the clock, and the weeping of our wife and children; and we must die. O! how solemn will it be that hour when we must struggle with that enemy, Death! The death-rattle is in our throat—we can scarce articulate—we try to speak; the death-glaze is on the eye: Death has put his fingers on those windows of the body, and shut out the light for ever; the hands well-nigh refuse to lift themselves, and there we are, close on the borders of the grave! Ah! that moment, when the spirit sees its destiny; that moment, of all moments the most solemn, when the soul looks through the bars of its cage, upon the world to come!

"No, I can not tell you how the spirit feels, if it be an ungodly spirit, when it sees a fiery throne of judgment, and hears the thunders of Almighty wrath, while there is but a moment between it and hell. I cannot picture to you what must be the fright which men will feel, when they realize what they often heard of!" *Charles Spurgeon*

12:7 "I am a creature of a day, passing through life as an arrow through the air. I am a spirit come from God, and returning to God; just hovering over the great gulf; till a few moments hence, I am no more seen! I drop into an unchangeable eternity!" *John Wesley*

"And when I have gone to the last city and preached my last sermon, and when I have offered my last prayer for the last sinner, when this old body of mine is worn and ready to crumble back to dust, and when my loved ones have gathered around my bed and the death gurgle is heard in my throat, when the old world is receding and heaven is opening a way, I stand in the presence of Him whom I have preached and loved and have not seen, I want the first one-thousand years to sit at His feet and say, 'Thank You, Jesus, for saving me that dark and stormy day from a drunkard's and a gambler's hell.'" *E. Howard Cadle*

The Whole Duty of Man

[9]And moreover, because the Preacher
was wise, he still taught the people knowledge; yes, he pondered and sought out *and*
set in order many proverbs. [10]The Preacher
sought to find acceptable words; and *what*
was written *was* upright—words of truth.
[11]The words of the wise are like goads,
and the words of scholars[a] are like well-
driven nails, given by one Shepherd. [12]And
further, my son, be admonished by these.
Of making many books *there is* no end,
and much study *is* wearisome to the flesh.

[13]Let us hear the conclusion of the
whole matter:

Fear God and keep His
    commandments,
For this is man's all.
[14]For God will bring every work into
    judgment,
Including every secret thing,
Whether good or evil.

12:11 [a]Literally *masters of the assemblies*

12:13,14 There is nothing as important in life as this great truth. It will bring us to the cross of Jesus and drive us to seek to present every man perfect in Christ Jesus before that great and terrible Day of the Lord.

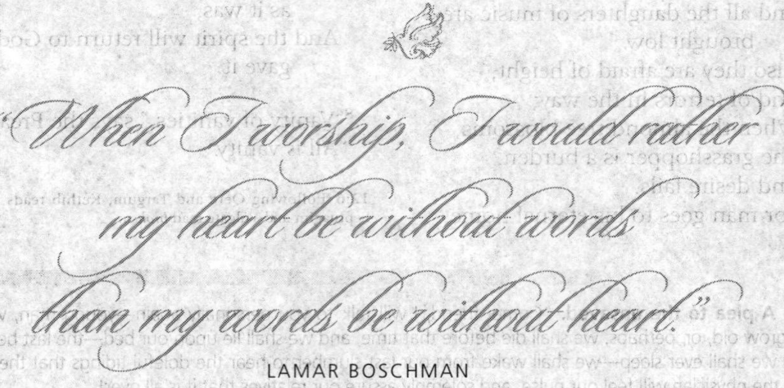

"When I worship, I would rather
my heart be without words
than my words be without heart."
LAMAR BOSCHMAN

The Call to Repentance

The call to repentance is important and must not be neglected. It is entirely accurate to say that it is the *first word of the gospel:*

- Repent was the *first word* of John the Baptist's gospel (Matt. 3:1,2).
- Repent was the *first word* of Jesus' gospel (Matt. 4:17; Mark 1:14,15).
- Repent was the *first word* in the preaching ministry of the twelve disciples (Mark 6:12).
- Repent was the *first word* in the preaching instructions Jesus gave to His disciples after His resurrection (Luke 24:46,47).
- Repent was the *first word* of exhortation in the first Christian sermon (Acts 2:38).
- Repent was the *first word* in the mouth of the apostle Paul through his ministry (Acts 26:19,20).

David Guzik

(For whether repentance is necessary for salvation, see John 3:16 comment.)

Song of Solomon

Song of Solomon

1 The song of songs, which *is* Solomon's.

The Banquet

THE SHULAMITE[a]

[2]Let him kiss me with the kisses of his mouth—
For your[b] love *is* better than wine.
[3]Because of the fragrance of your good ointments,
Your name *is* ointment poured forth;
Therefore the virgins love you.
[4]Draw me away!

THE DAUGHTERS OF JERUSALEM

We will run after you.[a]

THE SHULAMITE

The king has brought me into his chambers.

THE DAUGHTERS OF JERUSALEM

We will be glad and rejoice in you.[b]

We will remember your[c] love more than wine.

THE SHULAMITE

Rightly do they love you.[d]

[5]I *am* dark, but lovely,
O daughters of Jerusalem,
Like the tents of Kedar,
Like the curtains of Solomon.
[6]Do not look upon me, because I *am* dark,
Because the sun has tanned me.
My mother's sons were angry with me;
They made me the keeper of the vineyards,
But my own vineyard I have not kept.

(TO HER BELOVED)

[7]Tell me, O you whom I love,
Where you feed *your flock,*
Where you make *it* rest at noon.
For why should I be as one who veils herself[a]
By the flocks of your companions?

THE BELOVED

[8]If you do not know, O fairest among women,
Follow in the footsteps of the flock,
And feed your little goats
Beside the shepherds' tents.

1:2 [a]A young woman from the town of Shulam or Shunem (compare 6:13). The speaker and audience are identified according to the number, gender, and person of the Hebrew words. Occasionally the identity is not certain. [b]Masculine singular, that is, the Beloved 1:4 [a]Masculine singular, that is, the Beloved [b]Feminine singular, that is, the Shulamite [c]Masculine singular, that is, the Beloved [d]Masculine singular, that is, the Beloved 1:7 [a]Septuagint, Syriac, and Vulgate read *wanders.*

1:3 To the Christian, the name of Jesus is like a wonderful, fragrant ointment that releases the aroma of the love of God. Jesus is the focal point of our salvation: "If anyone does not love the Lord Jesus Christ, let him be accursed" (1 Cor. 16:22).

9I have compared you, my love,
To my filly among Pharaoh's chariots.
10Your cheeks are lovely with ornaments,
Your neck with chains *of gold.*

THE DAUGHTERS OF JERUSALEM
11We will make you[a] ornaments of gold
With studs of silver.

THE SHULAMITE
12While the king *is* at his table,
My spikenard sends forth its fragrance.
13A bundle of myrrh *is* my beloved to me,
That lies all night between my breasts.
14My beloved *is* to me a cluster of henna *blooms*
In the vineyards of En Gedi.

THE BELOVED
15Behold, you *are* fair, my love!
Behold, you *are* fair!
You *have* dove's eyes.

THE SHULAMITE
16Behold, you *are* handsome, my beloved!
Yes, pleasant!
Also our bed *is* green.
17The beams of our houses *are* cedar,
And our rafters of fir.

2 I *am* the rose of Sharon,
And the lily of the valleys.

THE BELOVED
2Like a lily among thorns,
So is my love among the daughters.

THE SHULAMITE
3Like an apple tree among the trees of the woods,
So *is* my beloved among the sons.
I sat down in his shade with great delight,
And his fruit *was* sweet to my taste.

THE SHULAMITE TO THE DAUGHTERS OF JERUSALEM
4He brought me to the banqueting house,
And his banner over me *was* love.
5Sustain me with cakes of raisins,
Refresh me with apples,
For I *am* lovesick.

6His left hand *is* under my head,
And his right hand embraces me.
7I charge you, O daughters of Jerusalem,
By the gazelles or by the does of the field,
Do not stir up nor awaken love
Until it pleases.

The Beloved's Request

THE SHULAMITE
8The voice of my beloved!
Behold, he comes
Leaping upon the mountains,
Skipping upon the hills.
9My beloved is like a gazelle or a young stag.
Behold, he stands behind our wall;

"I have always said, and always will say, that the studious perusal of the Sacred Volume will make better citizens, better fathers, and better husbands."

Thomas Jefferson

1:11 [a]Feminine singular, that is, the Shulamite

He is looking through the windows,
Gazing through the lattice.

[10]My beloved spoke, and said to me:
"Rise up, my love, my fair one,
And come away.
[11]For lo, the winter is past,
The rain is over *and* gone.
[12]The flowers appear on the earth;
The time of singing has come,
And the voice of the turtledove
Is heard in our land.
[13]The fig tree puts forth her green figs,
And the vines *with* the tender grapes
Give a good smell.
Rise up, my love, my fair one,
And come away!

> God sends no one away empty except those who are full of themselves.
>
> **DWIGHT L. MOODY**

[14]"O my dove, in the clefts of the rock,
In the secret *places* of the cliff,
Let me see your face,
Let me hear your voice;
For your voice *is* sweet,
And your face *is* lovely."

HER BROTHERS

[15]Catch us the foxes,
The little foxes that spoil the vines,
For our vines *have* tender grapes.

THE SHULAMITE

[16]My beloved *is* mine, and I *am* his.
He feeds *his flock* among the lilies.

(TO HER BELOVED)

[17]Until the day breaks
And the shadows flee away,
Turn, my beloved,
And be like a gazelle
Or a young stag
Upon the mountains of Bether.[a]

A Troubled Night

THE SHULAMITE

3 By night on my bed I sought the one
I love;
I sought him, but I did not find him.
[2]"I will rise now," *I said,*
"And go about the city;
In the streets and in the squares
I will seek the one I love."
I sought him, but I did not find him.
[3]The watchmen who go about the city
found me;
I said,
"Have you seen the one I love?"

[4]Scarcely had I passed by them,
When I found the one I love.
I held him and would not let him go,
Until I had brought him to the house
of my mother,
And into the chamber of her who

2:17 [a]Literally *Separation*

2:16 Do you love the Lord? Then do His will and reach out to those for whom He shed His precious blood. Too many of us raise our hands in worship *to* God, but refuse to reach out our hands in evangelism *for* God.

3:4 When we are first saved, we long for those we love most to come to the Savior, as Andrew did (see John 1:40–42).

"...we seek to glorify Christ and labor to win others to him. Here is a grand field for all our energies. O Christian people, what are we left in this world for except to bring others to Jesus? Are we not left in this wilderness that we may find out more of the good Shepherd's stray sheep, and work for him and with him to bring them in? I fear we forget this. Are not some of you indifferent as to whether your fellow-men are lost or saved? Have not some of you, in your families, come to this pass—that you see your brother an infidel, your sister frivolous, your parents godless, and yet it does not fret you? I think that if I had a godless relative it would break my night's rest, not now and then, but always. A brother, a father, a child unsaved! What mean ye by taking your ease? If the spirit of Christ be in us, the tears that fell from the eyes of Jesus will find their like upon our cheeks. We shall weep day and night because men are not gathered unto eternal life. Nor will this be a loss to us for blessed are the mourners in Zion. Blessed are they that mourn because others abide in sin and reject the Lord!" *Charles Spurgeon*

conceived me.

[5]I charge you, O daughters of Jerusalem,
By the gazelles or by the does of the field,
Do not stir up nor awaken love
Until it pleases.

The Coming of Solomon

THE SHULAMITE

[6]Who *is* this coming out of the wilderness
Like pillars of smoke,
Perfumed with myrrh and frankincense,
With all the merchant's fragrant powders?
[7]Behold, it *is* Solomon's couch,
With sixty valiant men around it,
Of the valiant of Israel.
[8]They all hold swords,
Being expert in war.
Every man *has* his sword on his thigh
Because of fear in the night.

Merely having an open mind is nothing; the object of opening a mind, as of opening the mouth, is to shut it again on something solid.

G. K. CHESTERTON

[9]Of the wood of Lebanon
Solomon the King
Made himself a palanquin:[a]
[10]He made its pillars *of* silver,
Its support *of* gold,
Its seat *of* purple,
Its interior paved *with* love
By the daughters of Jerusalem.
[11]Go forth, O daughters of Zion,
And see King Solomon with the crown
With which his mother crowned him
On the day of his wedding,
The day of the gladness of his heart.

The Bridegroom Praises the Bride

THE BELOVED

4 Behold, you *are* fair, my love!
Behold, you *are* fair!
You *have* dove's eyes behind your veil.
Your hair *is* like a flock of goats,
Going down from Mount Gilead.
[2]Your teeth *are* like a flock of shorn *sheep*
Which have come up from the washing,
Every one of which bears twins,
And none *is* barren among them.
[3]Your lips *are* like a strand of scarlet,
And your mouth is lovely.
Your temples behind your veil
Are like a piece of pomegranate.
[4]Your neck *is* like the tower of David,
Built for an armory,
On which hang a thousand bucklers,
All shields of mighty men.
[5]Your two breasts *are* like two fawns,
Twins of a gazelle,
Which feed among the lilies.

[6]Until the day breaks
And the shadows flee away,
I will go my way to the mountain of myrrh
And to the hill of frankincense.

[7]You *are* all fair, my love,
And *there is* no spot in you.
[8]Come with me from Lebanon, *my* spouse,
With me from Lebanon.
Look from the top of Amana,
From the top of Senir and Hermon,

3:9 [a]A portable enclosed chair

3:6 "A pastor was asked, 'Is it lawful for a Christian to smoke?' He answered, 'It is altogether wrong for a Christian to smoke: he must be on fire.'

"Lord, it is my desire to be, not simply a burning log in the fireplace, however warm and pleasant, but a flaming torch in Your hand." *Richard Wurmbrand*

4:7 There is no flaw in the Savior. He is the altogether Perfect One. See Eph. 5:27 for the perfection of the Body of Christ.

From the lions' dens,
From the mountains of the leopards.

9 You have ravished my heart,
My sister, *my* spouse;
You have ravished my heart
With one *look* of your eyes,
With one link of your necklace.
10 How fair is your love,
My sister, *my* spouse!
How much better than wine is your love,
And the scent of your perfumes
Than all spices!
11 Your lips, O *my* spouse,
Drip as the honeycomb;
Honey and milk *are* under your tongue;
And the fragrance of your garments
Is like the fragrance of Lebanon.

12 A garden enclosed
Is my sister, *my* spouse,
A spring shut up,
A fountain sealed.
13 Your plants *are* an orchard of pomegranates
With pleasant fruits,
Fragrant henna with spikenard,
14 Spikenard and saffron,
Calamus and cinnamon,
With all trees of frankincense,
Myrrh and aloes,
With all the chief spices—
15 A fountain of gardens,
A well of living waters,
And streams from Lebanon.

THE SHULAMITE

16 Awake, O north *wind*,
And come, O south!
Blow upon my garden,
That its spices may flow out.
Let my beloved come to his garden
And eat its pleasant fruits.

THE BELOVED

5 I have come to my garden, my sister, *my* spouse;
I have gathered my myrrh with my spice;
I have eaten my honeycomb with my honey;
I have drunk my wine with my milk.

(TO HIS FRIENDS)

Eat, O friends!
Drink, yes, drink deeply,
O beloved ones!

The Shulamite's Troubled Evening

THE SHULAMITE

2 I sleep, but my heart is awake;
It is the voice of my beloved!
He knocks, *saying*,
"Open for me, my sister, my love,
My dove, my perfect one;
For my head is covered with dew,
My locks with the drops of the night."

3 I have taken off my robe;
How can I put it on *again*?
I have washed my feet;
How can I defile them?
4 My beloved put his hand
By the latch *of the door*,
And my heart yearned for him.
5 I arose to open for my beloved,
And my hands dripped *with* myrrh,
My fingers with liquid myrrh,
On the handles of the lock.

6 I opened for my beloved,
But my beloved had turned away *and* was gone.
My heart leaped up when he spoke.
I sought him, but I could not find him;
I called him, but he gave me no answer.
7 The watchmen who went about the city found me.
They struck me, they wounded me;

5:2 "Just as the shepherd went everywhere searching for his sheep, just as the woman in the parable went everywhere searching for her coins, so there is a divine search with many variations of the voice that entreats us, calling us back." *A. W. Tozer*

The keepers of the walls
Took my veil away from me.
8I charge you, O daughters of Jerusalem,
If you find my beloved,
That you tell him I *am* lovesick!

THE DAUGHTERS OF JERUSALEM

9What *is* your beloved
More than *another* beloved,
O fairest among women?
What *is* your beloved
More than *another* beloved,
That you so charge us?

The defense of the gospel is most effective when combined with the demeanor of Christ.

ART LINDSLEY

THE SHULAMITE

10My beloved *is* white and ruddy,
Chief among ten thousand.
11His head *is like* the finest gold;
His locks *are* wavy,
And black as a raven.
12His eyes *are* like doves
By the rivers of waters,
Washed with milk,
And fitly set.
13His cheeks *are* like a bed of spices,
Banks of scented herbs.
His lips *are* lilies,
Dripping liquid myrrh.

14His hands *are* rods of gold
Set with beryl.
His body *is* carved ivory
Inlaid *with* sapphires.
15His legs *are* pillars of marble
Set on bases of fine gold.
His countenance *is* like Lebanon,
Excellent as the cedars.
16His mouth *is* most sweet,
Yes, he *is* altogether lovely.
This *is* my beloved,
And this *is* my friend,
O daughters of Jerusalem!

THE DAUGHTERS OF JERUSALEM

6 Where has your beloved gone,
O fairest among women?
Where has your beloved turned aside,
That we may seek him with you?

THE SHULAMITE

2My beloved has gone to his garden,
To the beds of spices,
To feed *his flock* in the gardens,
And to gather lilies.
3I *am* my beloved's,
And my beloved *is* mine.
He feeds *his flock* among the lilies.

Praise of the Shulamite's Beauty

THE BELOVED

4O my love, you *are as* beautiful as
Tirzah,
Lovely as Jerusalem,
Awesome as *an army* with banners!
5Turn your eyes away from me,
For they have overcome me.
Your hair *is* like a flock of goats
Going down from Gilead.
6Your teeth *are* like a flock of sheep
Which have come up from the
washing;
Every one bears twins,
And none *is* barren among them.
7Like a piece of pomegranate
Are your temples behind your veil.

8There are sixty queens
And eighty concubines,

5:6 Do you ever feel forsaken by God? Then don't live by what you "feel." Live by faith in the immutable promises of God. If you have been born again and your lifestyle reveals evidence of regeneration, then know for certain that He will *never* leave you nor forsake you. Believe that with all of your heart. He who promised is faithful (see Heb. 10:23).

6:1 Does this world seek Jesus because of your loving yet uncompromising testimony? Do they see your good works (see Matt. 5:16)? Do they hear the warning of the gospel from your lips?

And virgins without number.
[9]My dove, my perfect one,
Is the only one,
The only one of her mother,
The favorite of the one who bore her.
The daughters saw her
And called her blessed,
The queens and the concubines,
And they praised her.

[10]Who is she who looks forth as the morning,
Fair as the moon,
Clear as the sun,
Awesome as *an army* with banners?

THE SHULAMITE

[11]I went down to the garden of nuts
To see the verdure of the valley,
To see whether the vine had budded
And the pomegranates had bloomed.
[12]Before I was even aware,
My soul had made me
As the chariots of my noble people.[a]

THE BELOVED AND HIS FRIENDS

[13]Return, return, O Shulamite;
Return, return, that we may look upon you!

THE SHULAMITE

What would you see in the Shulamite—
As it were, the dance of the two camps?[a]

Expressions of Praise

THE BELOVED

7 How beautiful are your feet in sandals,
O prince's daughter!
The curves of your thighs *are* like jewels,
The work of the hands of a skillful workman.
[2]Your navel *is* a rounded goblet;
It lacks no blended beverage.
Your waist *is* a heap of wheat
Set about with lilies.
[3]Your two breasts *are* like two fawns,
Twins of a gazelle.
[4]Your neck *is* like an ivory tower,
Your eyes *like* the pools in Heshbon
By the gate of Bath Rabbim.
Your nose *is* like the tower of Lebanon
Which looks toward Damascus.
[5]Your head *crowns* you like *Mount* Carmel,
And the hair of your head *is* like purple;
A king *is* held captive by *your* tresses.

[6]How fair and how pleasant you are,
O love, with your delights!
[7]This stature of yours is like a palm tree,
And your breasts *like* its clusters.
[8]I said, "I will go up to the palm tree,
I will take hold of its branches."
Let now your breasts be like clusters of the vine,
The fragrance of your breath like apples,
[9]And the roof of your mouth like the best wine.

THE SHULAMITE

The wine goes *down* smoothly for my beloved,
Moving gently the lips of sleepers.[a]
[10]I *am* my beloved's,
And his desire *is* toward me.

[11]Come, my beloved,

6:12 [a]Hebrew *Ammi Nadib* 6:13 [a]Hebrew *Mahanaim* 7:9 [a]Septuagint, Syriac, and Vulgate read *lips and teeth*.

7:1 No matter how ugly your feet may look to you, God says that they are beautiful if you preach the gospel of peace (see Isa. 52:7; Rom. 10:15). Never be discouraged. You may have the frown of a sinful world, but you have the smile of God every time you faithfully reach out to the lost.

7:10 The Christian is a chaste virgin, waiting to be presented to Jesus Christ. See 2 Cor. 11:2.

Let us go forth to the field;
Let us lodge in the villages.
12 Let us get up early to the vineyards;
Let us see if the vine has budded,
Whether the grape blossoms are open,
And the pomegranates are in bloom.
There I will give you my love.
13 The mandrakes give off a fragrance,
And at our gates *are* pleasant *fruits,*
All manner, new and old,
Which I have laid up for you, my
beloved.

8 Oh, that you were like my brother,
Who nursed at my mother's breasts!
If I should find you outside,
I would kiss you;
I would not be despised.
2 I would lead you *and* bring you
Into the house of my mother,
She *who* used to instruct me.
I would cause you to drink of spiced
wine,
Of the juice of my pomegranate.

(To the Daughters of Jerusalem)
3 His left hand *is* under my head,
And his right hand embraces me.
4 I charge you, O daughters of
Jerusalem,
Do not stir up nor awaken love
Until it pleases.

Love Renewed in Lebanon

A Relative
5 Who *is* this coming up from the
wilderness,
Leaning upon her beloved?

I awakened you under the apple tree.
There your mother brought you forth;
There she *who* bore you brought *you*
forth.

"A little science estranges men from God, but much science leads them back to Him."

Louis Pasteur

The Shulamite to Her Beloved
6 Set me as a seal upon your heart,
As a seal upon your arm;
For love *is as* strong as death,
Jealousy *as* cruel as the grave;[a]
Its flames *are* flames of fire,
A most vehement[b] flame.

7 Many waters cannot quench love,
Nor can the floods drown it.
If a man would give for love
All the wealth of his house,
It would be utterly despised.

8:6 [a]Or *Sheol* [b]Literally *A flame of* Yah (a poetic form of *YHWH, the* Lord)

7:11 "Christ met unbelievers where they were. He realized what many Christians today still don't seem to understand. Cultivators have to get out in the field. According to one count, the gospels record 132 contacts that Jesus had with people. Six were in the Temple; four in the synagogues, and 122 were out with the people in the mainstream of life." *J. K. Johnston*

8:7 The cross was God's expressed love for you. Don't look to material blessings as a token of His love. One day you may find yourself in a dungeon, with few friends and no material wealth. (This was the apostle Paul's experience—he suffered the loss of *all* things for the sake of the gospel; Phil. 3:8.) So, fortify yourself. Do what Paul did: look only to the cross, and God's love will never be quenched. See Gal. 2:20 for details.

THE SHULAMITE'S BROTHERS

[8]We have a little sister,
And she has no breasts.
What shall we do for our sister
In the day when she is spoken for?
[9]If she *is* a wall,
We will build upon her
A battlement of silver;
And if she *is* a door,
We will enclose her
With boards of cedar.

THE SHULAMITE

[10]I *am* a wall,
And my breasts like towers;
Then I became in his eyes
As one who found peace.
[11]Solomon had a vineyard at Baal
Hamon;
He leased the vineyard to keepers;
Everyone was to bring for its fruit
A thousand silver coins.

(TO SOLOMON)

[12]My own vineyard *is* before me.
You, O Solomon, *may have* a thousand,
And those who tend its fruit two
hundred.

THE BELOVED

[13]You who dwell in the gardens,
The companions listen for your
voice—
Let me hear it!

THE SHULAMITE

[14]Make haste, my beloved,
And be like a gazelle
Or a young stag
On the mountains of spices.

Islam

OFFICIAL NAME: Islam

KEY FIGURE IN HISTORY: Muhammad (A.D. 570–632)

DATE OF ITS ESTABLISHMENT: A.D. 622

ADHERENTS: Worldwide: Estimated 800 million to 1 billion; 58 percent live in South and Southeast Asia; 28 percent in Africa; 9 percent in Near and Middle East; 5 percent other. U.S.: Estimated 6.5 to 8 million.

WHAT IS ISLAM?

Islam is the world's youngest major world religion. It claims to be the restoration of original monotheism and truth and thus supersedes both Judaism and Christianity. It stresses submission to *Allah*, the Arabic name for God, and conformity to the "five pillars" or disciplines of that religion as essential for salvation. From its inception, Islam was an aggressively missionary-oriented religion. Within one century of its formation, and often using military force, Islam had spread across the Middle East, most of North Africa, and as far east as India. While God is, in the understanding of most Muslims, unknowable personally, His will is believed to be perfectly revealed in the holy book, the *Qur'an*. The Qur'an is to be followed completely and its teaching forms a complete guide for life and society.

WHO WAS MUHAMMAD?

Muhammad is believed by Muslims to be the last and greatest prophet of God—"the seal of the prophets." It was through him that the Qur'an was dictated, thus according him the supreme place among the seers of God. A native of Mecca, Muhammad was forced to flee that city in A.D. 622 after preaching vigorously against the paganism of the city. Having secured his leadership in Medina, and with several military victories to his credit, Muhammad returned in triumph to Mecca in A.D. 630. There, he established Islam as the religion of all Arabia.

WHAT IS THE QUR'AN?

The Qur'an is the sacred book of Islam and the perfect word of God for the Muslim. It is claimed that the Qur'an was dictated in Arabic by the angel Gabriel to Muhammad and were God's precise words. As such, it had preexisted from eternity in heaven with God as the "Mother of the Book" and was in that form uncreated and co-eternal with God. Islam teaches that it contains the total and

(continued)

Islam (continued)

perfect revelation and will of God. The Qur'an is about four-fifths the length of the New Testament and is divided into 114 *surahs* or chapters. While Islam respects the Torah, the psalms of David, and the four Gospels, the Qur'an stands alone in its authority and absoluteness. It is believed to be most perfectly understood in Arabic and it is a religious obligation to seek to read and quote it in the original language.

WHAT ARE THE "FIVE PILLARS"?

They are the framework for the Muslims' life and discipline. Successful and satisfactory adherence to the pillars satisfies the will of Allah. They form the basis for the Muslim's hope for salvation along with faith and belief in Allah's existence, the authority of Muhammad as a prophet, and the finality and perfection of the Qur'an. The five pillars are:

The confession of Faith or *Shahada*: It is the declaration that there is no god but Allah and Muhammad is his prophet. Sincerity in the voicing of the confession is necessary for it to be valid. It must be held until death, and repudiation of the *Shahada* nullifies hope for salvation.

Prayer of *Salat*: Five times a day, preceded by ceremonial washing, the Muslim is required to pray facing Mecca. Specific formulas recited from the Qur'an (in Arabic), along with prostrations, are included. Prayer is, in this sense, an expression of submission to the will of Allah. While most of Islam has no hierarchical priesthood, prayers are led in mosques by respected lay leaders. The five times of prayer are before sunrise, noon, midafternoon, sunset, and prior to sleep.

Almsgiving or *Zakat*: The Qur'an teaches the giving of two-and-a-half percent of one's capital wealth to the poor and/or for the propagation of Islam. By doing so, the Muslim's remaining wealth is purified.

The Fast or *Sawm*: During the course of the lunar month of Ramadan, a fast is to be observed by every Muslim from sunrise to sunset. Nothing is to pass over the lips during this time, and they should refrain from sexual relations. After sunset, feasting and other celebrations often occur. The daylight hours are set aside for self-purification. The month is used to remember the giving of the Qur'an to Muhammad.

Pilgrimage or *Hajj*: All Muslims who are economically and physically able are required to journey to Mecca at least once in their lifetime. The required simple pilgrim's dress stresses the notion of equality before God. Another element of the Hajj is the mandatory walk of each pilgrim seven times around the *Kaabah*—the shrine of the black rock, the holiest site of Islam. Muhammad taught that the Kaabah was the original place of worship for Adam and later for Abraham. The Kaabah is thus venerated as the site of true religion, the absolute monotheism of Islam.

THE DOCTRINES OF ISLAM

God: He is numerically and absolutely one. Allah is beyond the understanding of man so that only his will may be revealed and known. He is confessed as the "merciful and compassionate one."

Sin: The most serious sin that can be ascribed to people is that of *shirk* or considering god as more than one. Original sin is viewed as a "lapse" by Adam. Humankind is considered weak and forgetful but not as fallen.

Angels: Islam affirms the reality of angels as messengers and agents of god. Evil spirits or *Jinn* also exist. Satan is a fallen angel. Angels perform important functions for Allah both now and at the end of time.

Final Judgment: The world will be judged at the end of time by Allah. The good deeds and obedience of all people to the five pillars and the Qur'an will serve as the basis of judgment.

Salvation: It is determined by faith, as defined by Islam, as well as by compiling good deeds primarily in conformity to the five pillars.

Marriage: Muslims uphold marriage as honorable and condemn adultery. While many Muslim marriages are monogamous, Islamic states allow as many as four wives. Men consider a woman as less than an equal, and while a man has the right to divorce his wife, the wife has no similar power (see Surah 2:228, 4:34).

Nonetheless, the female has a right to own and dispose of property. Modesty in dress is encouraged for both men and women.

War: The term *jihad* or "struggle" is often considered as both external and internal, both a physical and spiritual struggle. The enemies of Islam or "idolaters," states the Qur'an, may be slain "wherever you find them" (Surah 9:5). (See Surah 47:4.) Paradise is promised for those who die fighting in the cause of Islam (see Surah 3:195, 2:224). Moderate Muslims emphasize the spiritual dimension of Jihad and not its political element.

ANSWERING MUSLIM OBJECTIONS TO CHRISTIANITY

Christians and Jews are acknowledged as "people of the book," although their failure to conform to the confession of Islam labels them as unbelievers. Following are several questions that Muslims have about Christianity.

Is the Trinity a belief in three gods?

Christians are monotheistic and believe that God is one. But both in His work in accomplishing salvation through the person of Jesus Christ and through

(continued)

Islam (continued)

biblical study it has become clear that His oneness in fact comprises three persons—Father, Son (Jesus Christ), and the third person of the Godhead, the Holy Spirit. Mary is not part of the Godhead. The notion of God, who is three-in-one, is part of both the mystery and greatness of God. God is in essence one while in persons three. This truth helps us understand God as truly personal and having the capacity to relate to other persons. As well, Christians confirm the holiness, sovereignty, and greatness of God.

How can Jesus be the Son of God?

Scripture affirms that Jesus was conceived supernaturally by the Holy Spirit and was born of the Virgin Mary. It does not in any way claim that Jesus was directly God the Father's biological and physical son. It rejects the notion of the Arabic word for son, *walad*, meaning physical son, for the word *ibin*, which is the title of relationship. Jesus is the Son in a symbolic manner designating that He was God the Word who became man in order to save humankind from its sin. The virgin birth was supernatural as God the Holy Spirit conceived in Mary, without physical relations, Jesus the Messiah. In this manner even the Qur'an affirms the miraculous birth of Christ (see Surah 19:16–21). Jesus was in this sense "God's unique Son." During His earthly ministry He carried out the will of the Father. Notably the Qur'an affirms Jesus' supernatural birth, life of miracles, His compassion, and ascension to heaven (see Surah 19:16–21,29–31, 3:37–47, 5:110).

How could Jesus have died on the cross especially if He's God's son?

The testimony of history and the *Injil,* or the four Gospels, is that Jesus died on the cross. If it is understood that God is love, and that humankind is lost in sin, then is it not likely that God would have provided a sacrifice for sin? Jesus is God's sacrifice for all the sins of the world and is a bridge from a holy God to fallen and sinful humans.

This truth is revealed in the Injil, John 3:16. Even the Qur'an states in Surah 3:55 that "Allah said: O Isa [Jesus], I am going to terminate [to put to death] the period of your stay (on earth) and cause you to ascend unto Me." What other way could this concept have any meaning apart from Jesus' death for sin and His subsequent resurrection?

Muslims believe that God took Jesus from the cross and substituted Judas in His place, or at least someone who looked like Jesus. He was then taken to heaven where He is alive and from where one day He will return.

ANSWERING MUSLIMS' QUESTIONS TO CHRISTIANS ABOUT ISLAM

What do you think about the prophet Muhammad?

Muhammad was apparently a well-meaning man who sought to oppose paganism and evil in his day. While he succeeded in uniting the Arabian Peninsula and upheld several important virtues, we do not believe he received a fresh revelation from God. Jesus Christ fulfilled not only the final prophetic role from God, but He is the Savior of the world and God the Son. While Islam believes that some Bible passages refer to Muhammad (see Deut. 18:18–19; John 14:16; 15:26; 16:7), that is clearly not the meaning of the texts. Other passages may help in understanding and interpreting the previous texts (see Matt. 21:11; Luke 24:19; John 6:14; 7:40; Acts 1:8–16; 7:37).

What is your opinion of the Qur'an?

It is a greatly valued book for the Muslim. It is not received or believed to be a divine book by the Christian. The statements of the Qur'an are accepted only where they agree with the Bible.

What is your opinion about the five pillars?

Salvation is from God and comes only through the saving work of Jesus Christ. When we put our faith in Him, we may be saved (see John 3:16–21, 31–36).

WITNESSING TO MUSLIMS

- Be courteous and loving.
- Reflect interest in their beliefs. Allow them time to articulate their views.
- Be acquainted with their basic beliefs.
- Be willing to examine passages of the Qur'an concerning their beliefs.
- Stick to the cardinal doctrines of the Christian faith but also take time to respond to all sincere questions.
- Point out the centrality of the person and work of Jesus Christ for salvation.
- Stress that because of Jesus, His cross, and resurrection, one may have the full assurance of salvation, both now and for eternity (see 1 John 5:13).
- Share the plan of salvation with the Muslim. Point out that salvation is a gift and not to be earned.
- Pray for the fullness of the Holy Spirit. Trust Him to provide wisdom and grace.
- Be willing to become a friend and a personal evangelist to Muslims.

Four Simple Laws

1

God is holy and just:

"For God will bring every work into judgment, including every secret thing, whether good or evil" *(Eccles. 12:14)*.

2

The wages of sin is death:

"Sin is the transgression of the Law" *(1 John 3:4, KJV)*.

(See the Ten Commandments on page 1508.)

3

God is rich in mercy:

"But God, who is rich in mercy, because of His great love with which He loved us..." *(Eph. 2:4)*.

4

Eternal life is in Jesus Christ:

"For God so loved the world that He gave His only begotten Son, that whoever believes in Him should not perish but have everlasting life" *(John 3:16)*.

"[God] now commands all men everywhere to repent, because He has appointed a day on which He will judge the world in righteousness" *(Acts 17:30,31)*.

A Model Prayer of Repentance

"God, please forgive me for sinning against You. I understand that, according to Your Law, I deserve to go to hell. However, You are not willing that I perish. Thank You that Jesus suffered and died for me and rose again on the third day. I now repent (turn from my sins), and yield myself to Him to be my Lord and Savior. I will read Your Word daily and obey what I read. In Jesus' name I pray. Amen."

Isaiah

1 The vision of Isaiah the son of Amoz, which he saw concerning Judah and Jerusalem in the days of Uzziah, Jotham, Ahaz, *and* Hezekiah, kings of Judah.

The Wickedness of Judah

2Hear, O heavens, and give ear, O earth!
For the LORD has spoken:
"I have nourished and brought up children,
And they have rebelled against Me;
3The ox knows its owner
And the donkey its master's crib;
But Israel does not know,
My people do not consider."

4Alas, sinful nation,
A people laden with iniquity,
A brood of evildoers,
Children who are corrupters!
They have forsaken the LORD,
They have provoked to anger
The Holy One of Israel,
They have turned away backward.

5Why should you be stricken again?
You will revolt more and more.
The whole head is sick,
And the whole heart faints.
6From the sole of the foot even to the head,
There is no soundness in it,
But wounds and bruises and putrefying sores;
They have not been closed or bound up,
Or soothed with ointment.

7Your country *is* desolate,
Your cities *are* burned with fire;
Strangers devour your land in your presence;
And *it is* desolate, as overthrown by strangers.
8So the daughter of Zion is left as a booth in a vineyard,
As a hut in a garden of cucumbers,
As a besieged city.
9Unless the LORD of hosts
Had left to us a very small remnant,
We would have become like Sodom,
We would have been made like Gomorrah.

10Hear the word of the LORD,
You rulers of Sodom;
Give ear to the law of our God,
You people of Gomorrah:
11"To what purpose *is* the multitude of your sacrifices to Me?"
Says the LORD.
"I have had enough of burnt offerings of rams
And the fat of fed cattle.
I do not delight in the blood of bulls,
Or of lambs or goats.

12"When you come to appear before Me,
Who has required this from your hand,
To trample My courts?
13Bring no more futile sacrifices;

Incense is an abomination to Me.
The New Moons, the Sabbaths, and the calling of assemblies—
I cannot endure iniquity and the sacred meeting.
14Your New Moons and your appointed feasts
My soul hates;
They are a trouble to Me,
I am weary of bearing *them.*
15When you spread out your hands,
I will hide My eyes from you;
Even though you make many prayers,
I will not hear.
Your hands are full of blood.

16"Wash yourselves, make yourselves clean;
Put away the evil of your doings from before My eyes.
Cease to do evil,
17Learn to do good;
Seek justice,
Rebuke the oppressor;[a]
Defend the fatherless,
Plead for the widow.

18"Come now, and let us reason together,"
Says the LORD,
"Though your sins are like scarlet,
They shall be as white as snow;
Though they are red like crimson,
They shall be as wool.
19If you are willing and obedient,
You shall eat the good of the land;
20But if you refuse and rebel,
You shall be devoured by the sword";
For the mouth of the LORD has spoken.

The Degenerate City

21How the faithful city has become a harlot!
It was full of justice;
Righteousness lodged in it,
But now murderers.
22Your silver has become dross,
Your wine mixed with water.
23Your princes *are* rebellious,
And companions of thieves;
Everyone loves bribes,
And follows after rewards.
They do not defend the fatherless,
Nor does the cause of the widow come before them.

24Therefore the Lord says,
The LORD of hosts, the Mighty One of Israel,
"Ah, I will rid Myself of My adversaries,
And take vengeance on My enemies.
25I will turn My hand against you,
And thoroughly purge away your dross,
And take away all your alloy.
26I will restore your judges as at the first,
And your counselors as at the beginning.
Afterward you shall be called the city of righteousness, the faithful city."

27Zion shall be redeemed with justice,

1:17 [a]Some ancient versions read *the oppressed.*

1:18 White as snow. How incredible that the God of the universe would condescend to speak with human beings. But even more incredible is that the Judge of the universe would reason with guilty criminals (see also 43:6). Our sins stand out to a holy God like a crimson, blood-soaked rag, but through the mercy of the cross we can become pure as the driven snow (see Psa. 51:7).

Charles Stanley explains how this truth was brought to life in his photography: "I occasionally use colored filters over my lenses when I photograph in black and white. For instance, a light yellow filter darkens the sky, while brightening the clouds. A red filter enhances the white still more. That particular day, I experimented with viewing a red dot on white paper through a red filter. To my amazement, the dot, when seen through the red filter, appeared white. At that moment I realized the overwhelming truth of God's forgiveness. Our sin, depicted as deep red by Isaiah, becomes white as snow and wool when seen through the red cross of Golgotha. This is the great transformation of forgiveness . . . God in Christ has cleansed you of every stain of sin."

And her penitents with righteousness.
28The destruction of transgressors and
of sinners *shall be* together,
And those who forsake the LORD shall
be consumed.
29For they[a] shall be ashamed of the
terebinth trees
Which you have desired;
And you shall be embarrassed
because of the gardens
Which you have chosen.
30For you shall be as a terebinth whose
leaf fades,
And as a garden that has no water.

> If their houses were on fire, thou wouldst run and help them; and wilt thou not help them when their souls are almost at the fire of hell?
>
> RICHARD BAXTER

31The strong shall be as tinder,
And the work of it as a spark;
Both will burn together,
And no one shall quench *them*.

The Future House of God

2 The word that Isaiah the son of Amoz
saw concerning Judah and Jerusalem.

2Now it shall come to pass in the latter
days
That the mountain of the LORD's
house
Shall be established on the top of the
mountains,
And shall be exalted above the hills;
And all nations shall flow to it.
3Many people shall come and say,
"Come, and let us go up to the
mountain of the LORD,
To the house of the God of Jacob;
He will teach us His ways,
And we shall walk in His paths."
For out of Zion shall go forth the law,
And the word of the LORD from
Jerusalem.
4He shall judge between the nations,
And rebuke many people;
They shall beat their swords into
plowshares,
And their spears into pruning hooks;
Nation shall not lift up sword against
nation,
Neither shall they learn war anymore.

The Day of the Lord

5O house of Jacob, come and let us
walk
In the light of the LORD.

6For You have forsaken Your people,
the house of Jacob,
Because they are filled with eastern
ways;
They *are* soothsayers like the
Philistines,
And they are pleased with the
children of foreigners.
7Their land is also full of silver and
gold,
And there is no end to their treasures;
Their land is also full of horses,
And there is no end to their chariots.
8Their land is also full of idols;
They worship the work of their own
hands,
That which their own fingers have
made.
9People bow down,
And each man humbles himself;
Therefore do not forgive them.

10Enter into the rock, and hide in the
dust,
From the terror of the LORD
And the glory of His majesty.
11The lofty looks of man shall be
humbled,
The haughtiness of men shall be
bowed down,
And the LORD alone shall be exalted
in that day.

12For the day of the LORD of hosts

1:29 [a]Following Masoretic Text, Septuagint, and Vulgate; some Hebrew manuscripts and Targum read *you*.

Shall come upon everything proud
and lofty,
Upon everything lifted up—
And it shall be brought low—
13Upon all the cedars of Lebanon *that*
are high and lifted up,
And upon all the oaks of Bashan;
14Upon all the high mountains,
And upon all the hills *that are* lifted up;
15Upon every high tower,
And upon every fortified wall;
16Upon all the ships of Tarshish,
And upon all the beautiful sloops.
17The loftiness of man shall be bowed
down,
And the haughtiness of men shall be
brought low;
The LORD alone will be exalted in that
day,
18But the idols He shall utterly abolish.

19They shall go into the holes of the
rocks,
And into the caves of the earth,
From the terror of the LORD
And the glory of His majesty,
When He arises to shake the earth
mightily.

20In that day a man will cast away his
idols of silver
And his idols of gold,
Which they made, *each* for himself to
worship,
To the moles and bats,
21To go into the clefts of the rocks,
And into the crags of the rugged rocks,
From the terror of the LORD
And the glory of His majesty,
When He arises to shake the earth
mightily.

22Sever yourselves from such a man,
Whose breath *is* in his nostrils;
For of what account is he?

Judgment on Judah and Jerusalem

3 For behold, the Lord, the LORD of
hosts,
Takes away from Jerusalem and from Judah
The stock and the store,
The whole supply of bread and the
whole supply of water;
2The mighty man and the man of war,
The judge and the prophet,
And the diviner and the elder;
3The captain of fifty and the honorable
man,
The counselor and the skillful artisan,
And the expert enchanter.

4"I will give children *to be* their princes,
And babes shall rule over them.
5The people will be oppressed,
Every one by another and every one
by his neighbor;
The child will be insolent toward the
elder,
And the base toward the honorable."

6When a man takes hold of his brother
In the house of his father, *saying,*
"You have clothing;
You be our ruler,
And *let* these ruins *be* under your
power,"[a]
7In that day he will protest, saying,
"I cannot cure *your* ills,
For in my house *is* neither food nor
clothing;
Do not make me a ruler of the people."

8For Jerusalem stumbled,
And Judah is fallen,

3:6 [a]Literally *hand*

2:17 Notice the references to idolatry in vv. 8 and 18. An idolatrous understanding of God is always at the core of the pride of man. But when the holiness of the Law of God is paraded before a sinful heart, it stirs the conscience and humbles a man. It brings him to his rightful place—on his face before Almighty God.

3:8 Jerusalem came under the judgment of God because they sinned against Him. All sin is primarily against God. David, in his penitent prayer, said, "Against You, You only, have I sinned" (Psa. 51:4). See also Gen. 39:9; 2 Sam. 12:13; Psa. 119:11.

Because their tongue and their doings
Are against the LORD,
To provoke the eyes of His glory.
9The look on their countenance
witnesses against them,
And they declare their sin as Sodom;
They do not hide *it*.
Woe to their soul!
For they have brought evil upon
themselves.

10"Say to the righteous that *it shall be*
well *with them,*
For they shall eat the fruit of their
doings.
11Woe to the wicked! *It shall be* ill *with*
him,
For the reward of his hands shall be
given him.
12*As for* My people, children *are* their
oppressors,
And women rule over them.
O My people! Those who lead you
cause *you* to err,
And destroy the way of your paths."

Oppression and Luxury Condemned

13The LORD stands up to plead,
And stands to judge the people.
14The LORD will enter into judgment
With the elders of His people
And His princes:
"For you have eaten up the vineyard;
The plunder of the poor *is* in your
houses.
15What do you mean by crushing My
people
And grinding the faces of the poor?"
Says the Lord GOD of hosts.

16Moreover the LORD says:

"Because the daughters of Zion are
haughty,
And walk with outstretched necks
And wanton eyes,
Walking and mincing *as* they go,
Making a jingling with their feet,
17Therefore the Lord will strike with a
scab
The crown of the head of the
daughters of Zion,
And the LORD will uncover their
secret parts."

18In that day the Lord will take away
the finery:
The jingling anklets, the scarves, and
the crescents;
19The pendants, the bracelets, and the
veils;
20The headdresses, the leg ornaments,
and the headbands;
The perfume boxes, the charms,
21and the rings;
The nose jewels,
22the festal apparel, and the mantles;
The outer garments, the purses,
23and the mirrors;
The fine linen, the turbans, and the
robes.

24And so it shall be:

Instead of a sweet smell there will be
a stench;
Instead of a sash, a rope;
Instead of well-set hair, baldness;
Instead of a rich robe, a girding of
sackcloth;
And branding instead of beauty.
25Your men shall fall by the sword,
And your mighty in the war.
26Her gates shall lament and mourn,
And she *being* desolate shall sit on the
ground.

4 And in that day seven women shall
take hold of one man, saying,
"We will eat our own food and wear
our own apparel;

3:9 Homosexuals are proud of their lifestyle, parading it to the world, despite God's judgment against homosexuality and despite the health consequences and shortened lifespan it often entails.

SPRINGBOARDS FOR PREACHING AND WITNESSING

The Smell

3:24

No one smells like a smoker. It's true, and what's more, they don't realize how bad they smell. The reason they smell so poorly is that they have deadened the sensitivity of their nose. They literally can't smell the smells that a non-smoker can.

The conscience is like a nose. It sniffs out the stench of sin. Someone who has deadened the sensitivity of his conscience literally can't detect how morally bad he is. That's why we need God's Law. It stirs the conscience so that it can detect sin. When the conscience does its bloodhound duty, it shows us that we don't smell like a rose, but that even our very best deeds stink to high heaven.

If you have never repented of your sins and you are not trusting in Jesus Christ alone, you should realize that your lifestyle is an offense to a holy God. If you ignore your God-given conscience so that you can sin unhindered, all you are doing is storing up His wrath (see Rom. 2:3–11). See Isa. 64:6 and Rom. 3:10–20 to sniff out more details.

Only let us be called by your name,
To take away our reproach."

The Renewal of Zion

2In that day the Branch of the LORD
shall be beautiful and glorious;
And the fruit of the earth *shall be*
excellent and appealing
For those of Israel who have escaped.

3And it shall come to pass that *he who*
is left in Zion and remains in Jerusalem
will be called holy—everyone who is
recorded among the living in Jerusalem.
4When the Lord has washed away the
filth of the daughters of Zion, and purged
the blood of Jerusalem from her midst,
by the spirit of judgment and by the
spirit of burning, 5then the LORD will create above every dwelling place of Mount
Zion, and above her assemblies, a cloud
and smoke by day and the shining of a
flaming fire by night. For over all the glory
there *will be* a covering. 6And there will
be a tabernacle for shade in the daytime
from the heat, for a place of refuge, and
for a shelter from storm and rain.

God's Disappointing Vineyard

5 Now let me sing to my Well-beloved
A song of my Beloved regarding His
vineyard:

My Well-beloved has a vineyard
On a very fruitful hill.
2He dug it up and cleared out its
stones,
And planted it with the choicest vine.
He built a tower in its midst,
And also made a winepress in it;
So He expected *it* to bring forth *good*
grapes,
But it brought forth wild grapes.

3"And now, O inhabitants of Jerusalem
and men of Judah,
Judge, please, between Me and My
vineyard.
4What more could have been done to
My vineyard
That I have not done in it?
Why then, when I expected *it* to
bring forth *good* grapes,
Did it bring forth wild grapes?
5And now, please let Me tell you what
I will do to My vineyard:
I will take away its hedge, and it shall
be burned;
And break down its wall, and it shall
be trampled down.
6I will lay it waste;
It shall not be pruned or dug,
But there shall come up briers and
thorns.
I will also command the clouds
That they rain no rain on it."

7For the vineyard of the LORD of hosts
is the house of Israel,
And the men of Judah are His
pleasant plant.
He looked for justice, but behold,

oppression;
For righteousness, but behold, a cry
for help.

Impending Judgment on Excesses

8Woe to those who join house to house;
They add field to field,
Till *there is* no place
Where they may dwell alone in the
midst of the land!
9In my hearing the LORD of hosts *said,*
"Truly, many houses shall be desolate,
Great and beautiful ones, without
inhabitant.
10For ten acres of vineyard shall yield
one bath,
And a homer of seed shall yield one
ephah."

11Woe to those who rise early in the
morning,
That they may follow intoxicating
drink;
Who continue until night, *till* wine
inflames them!
12The harp and the strings,
The tambourine and flute,
And wine are in their feasts;
But they do not regard the work of
the LORD,
Nor consider the operation of His
hands.

13Therefore my people have gone into
captivity,
Because *they have* no knowledge;
Their honorable men *are* famished,
And their multitude dried up with
thirst.
14Therefore Sheol has enlarged itself
And opened its mouth beyond
measure;
Their glory and their multitude and
their pomp,
And he who is jubilant, shall descend
into it.
15People shall be brought down,
Each man shall be humbled,
And the eyes of the lofty shall be
humbled.
16But the LORD of hosts shall be exalted
in judgment,
And God who is holy shall be
hallowed in righteousness.
17Then the lambs shall feed in their
pasture,
And in the waste places of the fat
ones strangers shall eat.

18Woe to those who draw iniquity with
cords of vanity,
And sin as if with a cart rope;
19That say, "Let Him make speed *and*
hasten His work,
That we may see *it;*
And let the counsel of the Holy One
of Israel draw near and come,
That we may know *it.*"

20Woe to those who call evil good, and
good evil;
Who put darkness for light, and light
for darkness;
Who put bitter for sweet, and sweet
for bitter!

21Woe to *those who are* wise in their
own eyes,
And prudent in their own sight!

22Woe to men mighty at drinking wine,
Woe to men valiant for mixing
intoxicating drink,
23Who justify the wicked for a bribe,
And take away justice from the
righteous man!

24Therefore, as the fire devours the
stubble,
And the flame consumes the chaff,

5:11 What a tragedy it is to see alcohol destroy men and women. Yet its true devastation will be seen on the Day of Judgment. Drunkards will not inherit the kingdom of God (see 1 Cor. 6:9,10). For more on the wisdom of abstaining from alcohol, see Prov. 20:1; 23:29–35; Hos. 4:11.

So their root will be as rottenness,
And their blossom will ascend like
dust;
Because they have rejected the law of
the LORD of hosts,
And despised the word of the Holy
One of Israel.
25Therefore the anger of the LORD is
aroused against His people;
He has stretched out His hand against
them
And stricken them,
And the hills trembled.
Their carcasses *were* as refuse in the
midst of the streets.

For all this His anger is not turned
away,
But His hand *is* stretched out still.

26He will lift up a banner to the nations
from afar,
And will whistle to them from the
end of the earth;
Surely they shall come with speed,
swiftly.
27No one will be weary or stumble
among them,
No one will slumber or sleep;
Nor will the belt on their loins be
loosed,
Nor the strap of their sandals be
broken;
28Whose arrows *are* sharp,
And all their bows bent;
Their horses' hooves will seem like
flint,
And their wheels like a whirlwind.
29Their roaring *will be* like a lion,
They will roar like young lions;
Yes, they will roar
And lay hold of the prey;
They will carry *it* away safely,
And no one will deliver.
30In that day they will roar against them
Like the roaring of the sea.
And if *one* looks to the land,
Behold, darkness *and* sorrow;
And the light is darkened by the
clouds.

Isaiah Called to Be a Prophet

6 In the year that King Uzziah died, I
saw the Lord sitting on a throne, high
and lifted up, and the train of His *robe*
filled the temple. 2Above it stood seraphim; each one had six wings: with two
he covered his face, with two he covered
his feet, and with two he flew. 3And one
cried to another and said:

"Holy, holy, holy *is* the LORD of hosts;
The whole earth *is* full of His glory!"

4And the posts of the door were shaken
by the voice of him who cried out, and the
house was filled with smoke.
5So I said:

"Woe *is* me, for I am undone!
Because I *am* a man of unclean lips,
And I dwell in the midst of a people
of unclean lips;
For my eyes have seen the King,
The LORD of hosts."

6Then one of the seraphim flew to me,
having in his hand a live coal *which* he

5:24 Despised and rejected. Here is a biblical philosophy by which we should live: "Jesus was despised and rejected by men" (see Isa. 53:3). That's the bottom line. If we live for Him, we too will be despised and rejected by men. Anything on top of that is a bonus. When He fed multitudes and healed the sick, they loved Him. But when He spoke of sin, righteousness, and judgment, they hated Him. Jesus said that the world hated Him because He testified that its works were evil. He also said that if the world hated Him, it would hate us. When you and I do what Jesus did, we shouldn't be surprised to get what Jesus got.

6:5–8 Those who see the holiness of God recognize the sinfulness of their own wicked heart and cry out for cleansing. The true convert has his iniquity forgiven at the foot of the cross, and immediately says, "Here I am, Lord! Send me." He willingly commits himself to obeying the Great Commission (see Mark 16:15). For the similarities to Jeremiah's call, see Jer. 1:7–10.

had taken with the tongs from the altar.
[7]And he touched my mouth *with it,* and said:

"Behold, this has touched your lips;
Your iniquity is taken away,
And your sin purged."

[8]Also I heard the voice of the Lord, saying:

"Whom shall I send,
And who will go for Us?"

Then I said, "Here *am* I! Send me."
[9]And He said, "Go, and tell this people:

'Keep on hearing, but do not understand;
Keep on seeing, but do not perceive.'

[10]"Make the heart of this people dull,
And their ears heavy,
And shut their eyes;
Lest they see with their eyes,
And hear with their ears,
And understand with their heart,
And return and be healed."

[11]Then I said, "Lord, how long?"
And He answered:

"Until the cities are laid waste and without inhabitant,
The houses are without a man,
The land is utterly desolate,
[12]The LORD has removed men far away,
And the forsaken places *are* many in the midst of the land.
[13]But yet a tenth *will be* in it,
And will return and be for consuming,
As a terebinth tree or as an oak,
Whose stump *remains* when it is cut down.
So the holy seed *shall be* its stump."

Isaiah Sent to King Ahaz

7 Now it came to pass in the days of
Ahaz the son of Jotham, the son of
Uzziah, king of Judah, *that* Rezin king of
Syria and Pekah the son of Remaliah,
king of Israel, went up to Jerusalem to
make war against it, but could not prevail
against it. [2]And it was told to the house
of David, saying, "Syria's forces are deployed in Ephraim." So his heart and the
heart of his people were moved as the
trees of the woods are moved with the
wind.
[3]Then the LORD said to Isaiah, "Go out
now to meet Ahaz, you and Shear-Jashub[a]
your son, at the end of the aqueduct from
the upper pool, on the highway to the
Fuller's Field, [4]and say to him: 'Take heed,
and be quiet; do not fear or be fainthearted for these two stubs of smoking
firebrands, for the fierce anger of Rezin and
Syria, and the son of Remaliah. [5]Because
Syria, Ephraim, and the son of Remaliah
have plotted evil against you, saying,
[6]"Let us go up against Judah and trouble
it, and let us make a gap in its wall for
ourselves, and set a king over them, the
son of Tabel"— [7]thus says the Lord GOD:

"It shall not stand,
Nor shall it come to pass.
[8]For the head of Syria *is* Damascus,
And the head of Damascus *is* Rezin.
Within sixty-five years Ephraim will be broken,
So that it will not *be* a people.
[9]The head of Ephraim *is* Samaria,
And the head of Samaria *is* Remaliah's son.

7:3 [a]Literally *A Remnant Shall Return*

7:9 Faith is the basis of salvation. If people refuse to believe, they will never come to a point of trusting in the mercy of God. The intellect precedes the heart. If I want to reach the tenth story of a building, my intellect believes that the elevator will get me there, but it will not do so until I trust myself to it by physically stepping into it and pressing the button.

"We know the truth, not only by the reason, but also by the heart." *Blaise Pascal*

If you will not believe,
Surely you shall not be established." ' "

The Immanuel Prophecy

10Moreover the LORD spoke again to
Ahaz, saying, 11"Ask a sign for yourself
from the LORD your God; ask it either in
the depth or in the height above."
12But Ahaz said, "I will not ask, nor
will I test the LORD!"
13Then he said, "Hear now, O house of
David! *Is it* a small thing for you to weary
men, but will you weary my God also?
14Therefore the Lord Himself will give
you a sign: Behold, the virgin shall conceive and bear a Son, and shall call His
name Immanuel.[a] 15Curds and honey He
shall eat, that He may know to refuse the
evil and choose the good. 16For before
the Child shall know to refuse the evil
and choose the good, the land that you
dread will be forsaken by both her kings.
17The LORD will bring the king of Assyria
upon you and your people and your father's house—days that have not come
since the day that Ephraim departed from
Judah."

18And it shall come to pass in that day
That the LORD will whistle for the fly
That *is* in the farthest part of the
rivers of Egypt,
And for the bee that *is* in the land of
Assyria.
19They will come, and all of them will
rest
In the desolate valleys and in the
clefts of the rocks,
And on all thorns and in all pastures.

20In the same day the Lord will shave
with a hired razor,
With those from beyond the River,[a]
with the king of Assyria,
The head and the hair of the legs,
And will also remove the beard.

21It shall be in that day
That a man will keep alive a young
cow and two sheep;
22So it shall be, from the abundance of
milk they give,
That he will eat curds;
For curds and honey everyone will
eat who is left in the land.

23It shall happen in that day,
That wherever there could be a
thousand vines
Worth a thousand *shekels* of silver,
It will be for briers and thorns.
24With arrows and bows men will
come there,
Because all the land will become
briers and thorns.

25And to any hill which could be dug
with the hoe,
You will not go there for fear of briers
and thorns;
But it will become a range for oxen
And a place for sheep to roam.

Assyria Will Invade the Land

8 Moreover the LORD said to me, "Take
a large scroll, and write on it with a
man's pen concerning Maher-Shalal-Hash-
Baz.[a] 2And I will take for Myself faithful
witnesses to record, Uriah the priest and
Zechariah the son of Jeberechiah."
3Then I went to the prophetess, and
she conceived and bore a son. Then the
LORD said to me, "Call his name Maher-
Shalal-Hash-Baz; 4for before the child
shall have knowledge to cry 'My father'
and 'My mother,' the riches of Damascus
and the spoil of Samaria will be taken

7:14 [a]Literally *God-With-Us* 7:20 [a]That is, the Euphrates
8:1 [a]Literally *Speed the Spoil, Hasten the Booty*

7:14 This can only mean a virgin. If it was merely referring to a "young maiden," as some maintain, it would not have been a miraculous "sign" from God. Every day, thousands of young maidens conceive; only once has it happened to a virgin. This messianic prophecy was fulfilled in Luke 1:31–35; Matt. 1:18–23.

away before the king of Assyria."

5The LORD also spoke to me again, saying:

6"Inasmuch as these people refused
The waters of Shiloah that flow softly,
And rejoice in Rezin and in Remaliah's son;
7Now therefore, behold, the Lord brings up over them
The waters of the River,[a] strong and mighty—
The king of Assyria and all his glory;
He will go up over all his channels
And go over all his banks.
8He will pass through Judah,
He will overflow and pass over,
He will reach up to the neck;
And the stretching out of his wings
Will fill the breadth of Your land, O Immanuel.[a]

9"Be shattered, O you peoples, and be broken in pieces!
Give ear, all you from far countries.
Gird yourselves, but be broken in pieces;
Gird yourselves, but be broken in pieces.
10Take counsel together, but it will come to nothing;
Speak the word, but it will not stand,
For God *is* with us."[a]

Fear God, Heed His Word

11For the LORD spoke thus to me with
a strong hand, and instructed me that I
should not walk in the way of this people, saying:

12"Do not say, 'A conspiracy,'
Concerning all that this people call a conspiracy,
Nor be afraid of their threats, nor be troubled.
13The LORD of hosts, Him you shall hallow;
Let Him *be* your fear,
And *let* Him *be* your dread.
14He will be as a sanctuary,
But a stone of stumbling and a rock of offense
To both the houses of Israel,
As a trap and a snare to the inhabitants of Jerusalem.
15And many among them shall stumble;
They shall fall and be broken,
Be snared and taken."

16Bind up the testimony,
Seal the law among my disciples.
17And I will wait on the LORD,
Who hides His face from the house of Jacob;
And I will hope in Him.
18Here am I and the children whom the LORD has given me!
We are for signs and wonders in Israel
From the LORD of hosts,
Who dwells in Mount Zion.

19And when they say to you, "Seek
those who are mediums and wizards, who
whisper and mutter," should not a people
seek their God? *Should they seek* the dead
on behalf of the living? 20To the law and
to the testimony! If they do not speak according to this word, *it is* because *there is*
no light in them.

21They will pass through it hard-
pressed and hungry; and it shall happen,
when they are hungry, that they will be
enraged and curse their king and their
God, and look upward. 22Then they will

8:7 [a]That is, the Euphrates 8:8 [a]Literally *God-With-Us*
8:10 [a]Hebrew *Immanuel*

8:14 To those who fear God, Jesus Christ is the Rock of Salvation, the chief cornerstone upon which everything else is built. But to the proud, He is a rock of offense, a stumbling stone. Truly, blessed are all those who are not offended in Him. See also 28:16 comment.

8:19 For the danger of seeking counsel from mediums, see 1 Chron. 10:13,14 comment.

look to the earth, and see trouble and darkness, gloom of anguish; and *they will be* driven into darkness.

The Government of the Promised Son

9 Nevertheless the gloom *will* not *be*
upon her who *is* distressed,
As when at first He lightly esteemed
The land of Zebulun and the land of
Naphtali,
And afterward more heavily
oppressed *her*,
By the way of the sea, beyond the
Jordan,
In Galilee of the Gentiles.
2The people who walked in darkness
Have seen a great light;
Those who dwelt in the land of the
shadow of death,
Upon them a light has shined.

3You have multiplied the nation
And increased its joy;[a]
They rejoice before You
According to the joy of harvest,
As *men* rejoice when they divide the
spoil.
4For You have broken the yoke of his
burden
And the staff of his shoulder,
The rod of his oppressor,
As in the day of Midian.
5For every warrior's sandal from the
noisy battle,
And garments rolled in blood,
Will be used for burning *and* fuel of
fire.

6For unto us a Child is born,
Unto us a Son is given;
And the government will be upon His
shoulder.
And His name will be called
Wonderful, Counselor, Mighty God,
Everlasting Father, Prince of Peace.
7Of the increase of *His* government
and peace
There will be no end,
Upon the throne of David and over
His kingdom,
To order it and establish it with
judgment and justice
From that time forward, even forever.
The zeal of the Lord of hosts will
perform this.

The Punishment of Samaria

8The Lord sent a word against Jacob,
And it has fallen on Israel.
9All the people will know—
Ephraim and the inhabitant of
Samaria—
Who say in pride and arrogance of
heart:
10"The bricks have fallen down,
But we will rebuild with hewn stones;
The sycamores are cut down,
But we will replace *them* with cedars."
11Therefore the LORD shall set up
The adversaries of Rezin against him,
And spur his enemies on,
12The Syrians before and the Philistines
behind;
And they shall devour Israel with an
open mouth.

For all this His anger is not turned
away,
But His hand *is* stretched out still.

13For the people do not turn to Him
who strikes them,
Nor do they seek the LORD of hosts.
14Therefore the LORD will cut off head
and tail from Israel,

9:3 [a]Following Qere and Targum; Kethib and Vulgate read *not increased joy;* Septuagint reads *Most of the people You brought down in Your joy.*

9:6 What an incredible truth that the little Babe in Bethlehem's manger was God manifest in the flesh (see John 1:14; 1 Tim. 3:16). No man ever spoke like this Man. His words were truly full of wonder. Jesus of Nazareth was Almighty God, the everlasting Father, the Prince of Peace. God prepared Himself a body and filled that body as a hand fills a glove. Jesus was the express image of the invisible God, manifest to destroy death for us.

Palm branch and bulrush in one day.
15The elder and honorable, he *is* the head;
The prophet who teaches lies, he *is* the tail.
16For the leaders of this people cause *them* to err,
And *those who are* led by them are destroyed.
17Therefore the Lord will have no joy in their young men,
Nor have mercy on their fatherless and widows;
For everyone *is* a hypocrite and an evildoer,
And every mouth speaks folly.

> Men do not differ much about what things they will call evils; they differ enormously about what evils they will call excusable.
>
> **G. K. CHESTERTON**

For all this His anger is not turned away,
But His hand *is* stretched out still.

18For wickedness burns as the fire;
It shall devour the briers and thorns,
And kindle in the thickets of the forest;
They shall mount up *like* rising smoke.
19Through the wrath of the LORD of hosts
The land is burned up,
And the people shall be as fuel for the fire;
No man shall spare his brother.
20And he shall snatch on the right hand
And be hungry;
He shall devour on the left hand
And not be satisfied;
Every man shall eat the flesh of his own arm.
21Manasseh *shall devour* Ephraim, and Ephraim Manasseh;
Together they *shall be* against Judah.

For all this His anger is not turned away,
But His hand *is* stretched out still.

10 "Woe to those who decree unrighteous decrees,
Who write misfortune,
Which they have prescribed
2To rob the needy of justice,
And to take what is right from the poor of My people,
That widows may be their prey,
And *that* they may rob the fatherless.
3What will you do in the day of punishment,
And in the desolation *which* will come from afar?
To whom will you flee for help?
And where will you leave your glory?
4Without Me they shall bow down among the prisoners,
And they shall fall among the slain."

For all this His anger is not turned away,
But His hand *is* stretched out still.

Arrogant Assyria Also Judged

5"Woe to Assyria, the rod of My anger
And the staff in whose hand is My indignation.
6I will send him against an ungodly nation,
And against the people of My wrath
I will give him charge,
To seize the spoil, to take the prey,
And to tread them down like the mire of the streets.
7Yet he does not mean so,
Nor does his heart think so;
But *it is* in his heart to destroy,
And cut off not a few nations.

10:5,6 God will often use sinful nations to chasten His people. Then He will punish those nations for their own sin (see v. 12).

8For he says,
'*Are* not my princes altogether kings?
9*Is* not Calno like Carchemish?
Is not Hamath like Arpad?
Is not Samaria like Damascus?
10As my hand has found the kingdoms
of the idols,
Whose carved images excelled those
of Jerusalem and Samaria,
11As I have done to Samaria and her
idols,
Shall I not do also to Jerusalem and
her idols?' "

12Therefore it shall come to pass, when
the Lord has performed all His work on
Mount Zion and on Jerusalem, *that He will*
say, "I will punish the fruit of the arrogant
heart of the king of Assyria, and the glory
of his haughty looks."

13For he says:

"By the strength of my hand I have
done *it,*
And by my wisdom, for I am
prudent;
Also I have removed the boundaries
of the people,
And have robbed their treasuries;
So I have put down the inhabitants
like a valiant *man.*
14My hand has found like a nest the
riches of the people,
And as one gathers eggs *that are* left,
I have gathered all the earth;
And there was no one who moved *his*
wing,
Nor opened *his* mouth with even a
peep."

15Shall the ax boast itself against him
who chops with it?
Or shall the saw exalt itself against
him who saws with it?
As if a rod could wield *itself* against
those who lift it up,
Or as if a staff could lift up, *as if it*
were not wood!
16Therefore the Lord, the Lord[a] of hosts,
Will send leanness among his fat ones;
And under his glory
He will kindle a burning
Like the burning of a fire.
17So the Light of Israel will be for a fire,
And his Holy One for a flame;
It will burn and devour
His thorns and his briers in one day.
18And it will consume the glory of his
forest and of his fruitful field,
Both soul and body;
And they will be as when a sick man
wastes away.
19Then the rest of the trees of his forest
Will be so few in number
That a child may write them.

The Returning Remnant of Israel

20And it shall come to pass in that day
That the remnant of Israel,
And such as have escaped of the
house of Jacob,
Will never again depend on him who
defeated them,
But will depend on the LORD, the
Holy One of Israel, in truth.
21The remnant will return, the remnant
of Jacob,
To the Mighty God.
22For though your people, O Israel, be
as the sand of the sea,
A remnant of them will return;
The destruction decreed shall
overflow with righteousness.
23For the Lord GOD of hosts
Will make a determined end
In the midst of all the land.

24Therefore thus says the Lord GOD of
hosts: "O My people, who dwell in Zion,
do not be afraid of the Assyrian. He shall
strike you with a rod and lift up his staff
against you, in the manner of Egypt. 25For
yet a very little while and the indignation
will cease, as will My anger in their destruction." 26And the LORD of hosts will

10:16 [a]Following Bomberg; Masoretic Text and Dead Sea Scrolls read *YHWH* (*the LORD*).

stir up a scourge for him like the slaughter of Midian at the rock of Oreb; *as* His rod was on the sea, so will He lift it up in the manner of Egypt.

[27]It shall come to pass in that day
That his burden will be taken away
from your shoulder,
And his yoke from your neck,
And the yoke will be destroyed
because of the anointing oil.

[28]He has come to Aiath,
He has passed Migron;
At Michmash he has attended to his
equipment.
[29]They have gone along the ridge,
They have taken up lodging at Geba.
Ramah is afraid,
Gibeah of Saul has fled.
[30]Lift up your voice,
O daughter of Gallim!
Cause it to be heard as far as Laish—
O poor Anathoth![a]
[31]Madmenah has fled,
The inhabitants of Gebim seek refuge.
[32]As yet he will remain at Nob that day;
He will shake his fist at the mount of
the daughter of Zion,
The hill of Jerusalem.

[33]Behold, the Lord,
The LORD of hosts,
Will lop off the bough with terror;
Those of high stature *will be* hewn
down,
And the haughty will be humbled.
[34]He will cut down the thickets of the
forest with iron,
And Lebanon will fall by the Mighty
One.

The Reign of Jesse's Offspring

11 There shall come forth a Rod
from the stem of Jesse,
And a Branch shall grow out of his
roots.
[2]The Spirit of the LORD shall rest upon
Him,
The Spirit of wisdom and
understanding,
The Spirit of counsel and might,
The Spirit of knowledge and of the
fear of the LORD.

[3]His delight *is* in the fear of the LORD,
And He shall not judge by the sight of
His eyes,
Nor decide by the hearing of His ears;
[4]But with righteousness He shall judge
the poor,
And decide with equity for the meek
of the earth;
He shall strike the earth with the rod
of His mouth,
And with the breath of His lips He
shall slay the wicked.
[5]Righteousness shall be the belt of His
loins,
And faithfulness the belt of His waist.

[6]"The wolf also shall dwell with the
lamb,
The leopard shall lie down with the
young goat,
The calf and the young lion and the
fatling together;
And a little child shall lead them.
[7]The cow and the bear shall graze;
Their young ones shall lie down

10:30 [a]Following Masoretic Text, Targum, and Vulgate; Septuagint and Syriac read *Listen to her, O Anathoth.*

11:2 This was so evident in Jesus Christ. This messianic prophecy was fulfilled in John 1:32. Jesus had the spirit of wisdom that dazzled all who heard Him, even His enemies. Each of us need to continually seek wisdom, understanding, knowledge, and especially the fear of the Lord—the beginning of wisdom.

11:6–9 These verses speak of the new heavens and the new earth, where animals will again be vegetarian as they were originally created to be. (Note that the world often misquotes v. 6, saying that the lion shall lie down with the lamb.) There was no killing, death, or bloodshed before the curse, and there will be no more once the curse is removed (see Rev. 22:3). For details, see Gen. 1:30; Isa. 65:25; and Rev. 21:24 comment.

together;
And the lion shall eat straw like the ox.
8The nursing child shall play by the
cobra's hole,
And the weaned child shall put his
hand in the viper's den.
9They shall not hurt nor destroy in all
My holy mountain,
For the earth shall be full of the
knowledge of the LORD
As the waters cover the sea.

10"And in that day there shall be a Root
of Jesse,
Who shall stand as a banner to the
people;
For the Gentiles shall seek Him,
And His resting place shall be
glorious."

11It shall come to pass in that day
That the Lord shall set His hand again
the second time
To recover the remnant of His people
who are left,
From Assyria and Egypt,
From Pathros and Cush,
From Elam and Shinar,
From Hamath and the islands of the
sea.

12He will set up a banner for the nations,
And will assemble the outcasts of
Israel,
And gather together the dispersed of
Judah
From the four corners of the earth.
13Also the envy of Ephraim shall
depart,
And the adversaries of Judah shall be
cut off;
Ephraim shall not envy Judah,
And Judah shall not harass Ephraim.
14But they shall fly down upon the
shoulder of the Philistines toward
the west;
Together they shall plunder the
people of the East;
They shall lay their hand on Edom
and Moab;
And the people of Ammon shall obey
them.
15The LORD will utterly destroy[a] the
tongue of the Sea of Egypt;
With His mighty wind He will shake
His fist over the River,[b]
And strike it in the seven streams,
And make *men* cross over dryshod.
16There will be a highway for the
remnant of His people
Who will be left from Assyria,
As it was for Israel
In the day that he came up from the
land of Egypt.

A Hymn of Praise

12 And in that day you will say:

"O LORD, I will praise You;
Though You were angry with me,
Your anger is turned away, and You
comfort me.
2Behold, God *is* my salvation,
I will trust and not be afraid;
'For YAH, the LORD, *is* my strength and
song;
He also has become my salvation.' "[a]

3Therefore with joy you will draw
water
From the wells of salvation.

4And in that day you will say:

"Praise the LORD, call upon His name;
Declare His deeds among the peoples,
Make mention that His name is

11:15 [a]Following Masoretic Text and Vulgate; Septuagint, Syriac, and Targum read *dry up*. [b]That is, the Euphrates
12:2 [a]Exodus 15:2

12:2,3: Notice how the two verses are linked. Faith always produces joy. Trust in God produces courage. If we know that God has granted us forgiveness of sins and the gift of everlasting life, we will rejoice, and the joy of the Lord will be our strength. If God is for us, nothing can be against us (see Rom. 8:31–39).

exalted.
5Sing to the LORD,
For He has done excellent things;
This *is* known in all the earth.
6Cry out and shout, O inhabitant of Zion,
For great *is* the Holy One of Israel in your midst!"

Proclamation Against Babylon

13 The burden against Babylon which Isaiah the son of Amoz saw.

2"Lift up a banner on the high mountain,
Raise your voice to them;
Wave your hand, that they may enter the gates of the nobles.
3I have commanded My sanctified ones;
I have also called My mighty ones for My anger—
Those who rejoice in My exaltation."

4The noise of a multitude in the mountains,
Like that of many people!
A tumultuous noise of the kingdoms of nations gathered together!
The LORD of hosts musters
The army for battle.
5They come from a far country,
From the end of heaven—
The LORD and His weapons of indignation,
To destroy the whole land.

6Wail, for the day of the LORD *is* at hand!
It will come as destruction from the Almighty.
7Therefore all hands will be limp,
Every man's heart will melt,
8And they will be afraid.
Pangs and sorrows will take hold of *them;*
They will be in pain as a woman in childbirth;
They will be amazed at one another;
Their faces *will be like* flames.

9Behold, the day of the LORD comes,
Cruel, with both wrath and fierce anger,
To lay the land desolate;
And He will destroy its sinners from it.
10For the stars of heaven and their constellations
Will not give their light;
The sun will be darkened in its going forth,
And the moon will not cause its light to shine.

11"I will punish the world for *its* evil,
And the wicked for their iniquity;
I will halt the arrogance of the proud,
And will lay low the haughtiness of the terrible.
12I will make a mortal more rare than fine gold,
A man more than the golden wedge of Ophir.
13Therefore I will shake the heavens,
And the earth will move out of her place,
In the wrath of the LORD of hosts
And in the day of His fierce anger.
14It shall be as the hunted gazelle,

13:11–13 Wrath of the Lord. How terrifying it will be when God Himself causes this earth to tremble with His wrath. Israel was terrified when God gave His Law in peace; how horrifying will it be for the ungodly when He comes in wrath! That is why we must reach out to them now. Paul said of his own motives, "Knowing, therefore, the terror of the Lord, we persuade men" (2 Cor. 5:11). Do we know the terror of the Lord—His just wrath against sin and the horrors of hell? If not, we will lack passion for the lost. Make sure you have a biblical understanding of the character of God. Smash any idols that may inhabit your mind. A god of only love and mercy, who is not also a God of wrath and judgment, is nothing more than a worthless idol.

"Good Mr. Whitefield used to cry, 'Oh, the wrath to come! The wrath to come!' And, verily, I know not what he could have said about it except to utter the exclamation—and there to leave it—for that wrath to come must surpass all human language or imagination!" *Charles Spurgeon*

And as a sheep that no man takes up;
Every man will turn to his own
people,
And everyone will flee to his own land.
15Everyone who is found will be thrust
through,
And everyone who is captured will
fall by the sword.
16Their children also will be dashed to
pieces before their eyes;
Their houses will be plundered
And their wives ravished.

17"Behold, I will stir up the Medes
against them,
Who will not regard silver;
And *as for* gold, they will not delight
in it.
18Also *their* bows will dash the young
men to pieces,
And they will have no pity on the
fruit of the womb;
Their eye will not spare children.
19And Babylon, the glory of kingdoms,
The beauty of the Chaldeans' pride,
Will be as when God overthrew
Sodom and Gomorrah.
20It will never be inhabited,
Nor will it be settled from generation
to generation;
Nor will the Arabian pitch tents there,
Nor will the shepherds make their
sheepfolds there.
21But wild beasts of the desert will lie
there,
And their houses will be full of owls;
Ostriches will dwell there,
And wild goats will caper there.
22The hyenas will howl in their citadels,
And jackals in their pleasant palaces.
Her time *is* near to come,
And her days will not be prolonged."

Using the Law in Evangelism

13:19 Speaking about the destruction of Sodom and Gomorrah, *Jonathan Edwards* said, "Another way that this awful destruction tended to promote this great affair of redemption, was, that hereby God remarkably exhibited the terrors of His Law, to make men sensible of their need of redeeming mercy. The work of redemption never was carried on without this. The Law, from the beginning, is made use of as a schoolmaster to bring men to Christ."

Mercy on Jacob

14 For the LORD will have mercy on
Jacob, and will still choose Israel,
and settle them in their own land. The
strangers will be joined with them, and
they will cling to the house of Jacob. 2Then
people will take them and bring them to
their place, and the house of Israel will
possess them for servants and maids in
the land of the LORD; they will take them
captive whose captives they were, and
rule over their oppressors.

Fall of the King of Babylon

3It shall come to pass in the day the
LORD gives you rest from your sorrow,
and from your fear and the hard bondage
in which you were made to serve, 4that
you will take up this proverb against the
king of Babylon, and say:

"How the oppressor has ceased,
The golden[a] city ceased!
5The LORD has broken the staff of the
wicked,
The scepter of the rulers;
6He who struck the people in wrath
with a continual stroke,
He who ruled the nations in anger,
Is persecuted *and* no one hinders.
7The whole earth is at rest *and* quiet;
They break forth into singing.
8Indeed the cypress trees rejoice over
you,
And the cedars of Lebanon,
Saying, 'Since you were cut down,
No woodsman has come up against us.'

9"Hell from beneath is excited about you,
To meet *you* at your coming;
It stirs up the dead for you,
All the chief ones of the earth;

14:4 [a]Or *insolent*

It has raised up from their thrones
All the kings of the nations.
10They all shall speak and say to you:
'Have you also become as weak as we?
Have you become like us?
11Your pomp is brought down to Sheol,
And the sound of your stringed instruments;
The maggot is spread under you,
And worms cover you.'

The Fall of Lucifer

12"How you are fallen from heaven,
O Lucifer,[a] son of the morning!
How you are cut down to the ground,
You who weakened the nations!
13For you have said in your heart:
'I will ascend into heaven,
I will exalt my throne above the stars of God;
I will also sit on the mount of the congregation
On the farthest sides of the north;
14I will ascend above the heights of the clouds,
I will be like the Most High.'
15Yet you shall be brought down to Sheol,
To the lowest depths of the Pit.

16"Those who see you will gaze at you,
And consider you, *saying:*
'*Is* this the man who made the earth tremble,
Who shook kingdoms,
17Who made the world as a wilderness
And destroyed its cities,
Who did not open the house of his prisoners?'

18"All the kings of the nations,
All of them, sleep in glory,
Everyone in his own house;
19But you are cast out of your grave
Like an abominable branch,
Like the garment of those who are slain,
Thrust through with a sword,
Who go down to the stones of the pit,
Like a corpse trodden underfoot.
20You will not be joined with them in burial,
Because you have destroyed your land
And slain your people.
The brood of evildoers shall never be named.
21Prepare slaughter for his children
Because of the iniquity of their fathers,
Lest they rise up and possess the land,
And fill the face of the world with cities."

Babylon Destroyed

22"For I will rise up against them," says the LORD of hosts,
"And cut off from Babylon the name and remnant,
And offspring and posterity," says the LORD.
23"I will also make it a possession for the porcupine,
And marshes of muddy water;
I will sweep it with the broom of destruction," says the LORD of hosts.

14:12 [a]Literally *Day Star*

14:9 "People seem to forget that there is no door out of hell. If they enter there, they must remain there age after age. Millions on millions of years will roll on, but there is no door, no escape out of hell." *D. L. Moody*

14:12 For a description of Satan's fall, see Ezek. 28:12–17 comment.

14:13–15 This is the same spirit that inhabits the carnal mind of man. He exalts himself above the heavens. He spits out blasphemies against the Creator who gave him life. He stands in judgment over Almighty God and questions His dealings with humanity. To them the Scripture says, "Who are you to reply against God?" (Rom. 9:20). When arrogant sinners question God's actions, it is evident that they don't see themselves as worthy of death and hell themselves. That is why they need the Law. It shows them that they are heinous criminals, and that God is a perfect and righteous Judge. God doesn't owe them an explanation for anything that He does. All He owes them is His just wrath.

Assyria Destroyed

[24]The LORD of hosts has sworn, saying,
"Surely, as I have thought, so it shall come to pass,
And as I have purposed, *so* it shall stand:
[25]That I will break the Assyrian in My land,
And on My mountains tread him underfoot.
Then his yoke shall be removed from them,
And his burden removed from their shoulders.
[26]This *is* the purpose that is purposed against the whole earth,
And this *is* the hand that is stretched out over all the nations.
[27]For the LORD of hosts has purposed,
And who will annul *it*?
His hand *is* stretched out,
And who will turn it back?"

Philistia Destroyed

[28]This is the burden which came in the year that King Ahaz died.

[29]"Do not rejoice, all you of Philistia,
Because the rod that struck you is broken;
For out of the serpent's roots will come forth a viper,
And its offspring *will be* a fiery flying serpent.
[30]The firstborn of the poor will feed,
And the needy will lie down in safety;
I will kill your roots with famine,
And it will slay your remnant.
[31]Wail, O gate! Cry, O city!
All you of Philistia *are* dissolved;
For smoke will come from the north,
And no one *will be* alone in his appointed times."

[32]What will they answer the messengers of the nation?
That the LORD has founded Zion,
And the poor of His people shall take refuge in it.

Proclamation Against Moab

15 The burden against Moab.

Because in the night Ar of Moab is laid waste
And destroyed,
Because in the night Kir of Moab is laid waste
And destroyed,
[2]He has gone up to the temple[a] and Dibon,
To the high places to weep.
Moab will wail over Nebo and over Medeba;
On all their heads *will be* baldness,
And every beard cut off.
[3]In their streets they will clothe themselves with sackcloth;
On the tops of their houses
And in their streets
Everyone will wail, weeping bitterly.
[4]Heshbon and Elealeh will cry out,
Their voice shall be heard as far as Jahaz;
Therefore the armed soldiers[a] of Moab will cry out;
His life will be burdensome to him.

[5]"My heart will cry out for Moab;
His fugitives *shall flee* to Zoar,
Like a three-year-old heifer.[a]
For by the Ascent of Luhith
They will go up with weeping;
For in the way of Horonaim
They will raise up a cry of destruction,
[6]For the waters of Nimrim will be desolate,
For the green grass has withered away;

15:2 [a]Hebrew *bayith,* literally *house* 15:4 [a]Following Masoretic Text, Targum, and Vulgate; Septuagint and Syriac read *loins.* 15:5 [a]Or *The Third Eglath,* an unknown city (compare Jeremiah 48:34)

15:5 O that sinners would weep now in contrition at the foot of the cross, rather than in terror at the Throne of Judgment.

The grass fails, there is nothing green.
7Therefore the abundance they have gained,
And what they have laid up,
They will carry away to the Brook of the Willows.
8For the cry has gone all around the borders of Moab,
Its wailing to Eglaim
And its wailing to Beer Elim.
9For the waters of Dimon[a] will be full of blood;
Because I will bring more upon Dimon,[b]
Lions upon him who escapes from Moab,
And on the remnant of the land."

Moab Destroyed

16 Send the lamb to the ruler of the land,
From Sela to the wilderness,
To the mount of the daughter of Zion.
2For it shall be as a wandering bird thrown out of the nest;
So shall be the daughters of Moab at the fords of the Arnon.

3"Take counsel, execute judgment;
Make your shadow like the night in the middle of the day;
Hide the outcasts,
Do not betray him who escapes.
4Let My outcasts dwell with you, O Moab;
Be a shelter to them from the face of the spoiler.
For the extortioner is at an end,
Devastation ceases,
The oppressors are consumed out of the land.
5In mercy the throne will be established;
And One will sit on it in truth, in the tabernacle of David,
Judging and seeking justice and hastening righteousness."

6We have heard of the pride of Moab—

"There is a Ruler above, and His Providence guides all things. He is our Friend and has plenty of work for all His people to do. It is such a blessing and a privilege to be led into His work instead of into the service of the hard task-masters—the devil and sin."

David Livingstone

He is very proud—
Of his haughtiness and his pride and his wrath;
But his lies *shall* not *be* so.
7Therefore Moab shall wail for Moab;
Everyone shall wail.
For the foundations of Kir Hareseth you shall mourn;
Surely *they are* stricken.

8For the fields of Heshbon languish,
And the vine of Sibmah;
The lords of the nations have broken down its choice plants,
Which have reached to Jazer
And wandered through the wilderness.
Her branches are stretched out,
They are gone over the sea.
9Therefore I will bewail the vine of

15:9 [a]Following Masoretic Text and Targum; Dead Sea Scrolls and Vulgate read *Dibon;* Septuagint reads *Rimon.* [b]Following Masoretic Text and Targum; Dead Sea Scrolls and Vulgate read *Dibon;* Septuagint reads *Rimon.*

Sibmah,
With the weeping of Jazer;
I will drench you with my tears,
O Heshbon and Elealeh;
For battle cries have fallen
Over your summer fruits and your
harvest.

10Gladness is taken away,
And joy from the plentiful field;
In the vineyards there will be no
singing,
Nor will there be shouting;
No treaders will tread out wine in the
presses;
I have made their shouting cease.
11Therefore my heart shall resound like
a harp for Moab,
And my inner being for Kir Heres.

12And it shall come to pass,
When it is seen that Moab is weary
on the high place,
That he will come to his sanctuary to
pray;
But he will not prevail.

13This *is* the word which the LORD has
spoken concerning Moab since that time.
14But now the LORD has spoken, saying,
"Within three years, as the years of a
hired man, the glory of Moab will be despised with all that great multitude, and
the remnant *will be* very small *and* feeble."

Proclamation Against Syria and Israel

17 The burden against Damascus.

"Behold, Damascus will cease from
being a city,
And it will be a ruinous heap.
2The cities of Aroer *are* forsaken;[a]
They will be for flocks
Which lie down, and no one will
make *them* afraid.
3The fortress also will cease from
Ephraim,
The kingdom from Damascus,
And the remnant of Syria;
They will be as the glory of the
children of Israel,"
Says the LORD of hosts.
4"In that day it shall come to pass
That the glory of Jacob will wane,
And the fatness of his flesh grow lean.
5It shall be as when the harvester
gathers the grain,
And reaps the heads with his arm;
It shall be as he who gathers heads of
grain
In the Valley of Rephaim.
6Yet gleaning grapes will be left in it,
Like the shaking of an olive tree,
Two *or* three olives at the top of the
uppermost bough,
Four *or* five in its most fruitful
branches,"
Says the LORD God of Israel.

7In that day a man will look to his
Maker,
And his eyes will have respect for the
Holy One of Israel.
8He will not look to the altars,
The work of his hands;
He will not respect what his fingers
have made,
Nor the wooden images[a] nor the
incense altars.

9In that day his strong cities will be as
a forsaken bough[a]
And an uppermost branch,[b]
Which they left because of the
children of Israel;

17:2 [a]Following Masoretic Text and Vulgate; Septuagint reads *It shall be forsaken forever;* Targum reads *Its cities shall be forsaken and desolate.* 17:8 [a]Hebrew *Asherim,* Canaanite deities 17:9 [a]Septuagint reads *Hivites;* Targum reads *laid waste;* Vulgate reads *as the plows.* [b]Septuagint reads *Amorites;* Targum reads *in ruins;* Vulgate reads *corn.*

17:7,8 We tend to relegate idolatry to the ancients and to primitives, and yet it is the pervasive sin today. Mankind creates gods in his own image because idols have no moral dictates. They satisfy his need for a creator. But when men truly look to their Maker and see Him in His holiness, it always produces the fear of the Lord, and that is the spark of genuine repentance.

SPRINGBOARDS FOR PREACHING AND WITNESSING

17:12

Roaring Waters

A man in a rowboat once found himself caught in fast-moving water, heading for a massive waterfall with jagged rocks 150 feet below. A passerby saw him rowing against the current, but his efforts were futile. Minute by minute he was drawn closer and closer to the roaring falls. The passerby ran to his car, grabbed a rope from the trunk, and threw it to the boat. When it fell across the bow, he screamed, "Grab the rope. I will pull you to the shore!" He couldn't believe his eyes—the man took no notice. He just kept rowing frantically against the current, until he was sucked over the falls to his death.

The Bible tells us that you cannot "do" anything to save yourself. But God Himself did something wonderful to save you from death and hell. He became a person in Jesus Christ, and suffered and died in your place. He paid the fine in His life's blood for the crimes that you committed: "God demonstrates His own love toward us, in that while we were still sinners, Christ died for us" (Rom. 5:8). Then He rose from the dead and defeated death.

There are millions of people on this earth who have never seen the serious nature of sin. They are in the dark about the Judge's ruling. They have no idea that they will end up in hell for crimes that they consider trivial. They know they will have to face God after death, but they think their good works will buy their way out of any trouble in which they may find themselves. And as long as they trivialize their sin, they will deceive themselves into thinking that they can work their way into heaven. But it is as futile as the man who tried to row against the river until he went over the falls.

God Himself has thrown us a rope in Jesus Christ. He is the only One who can save us from death and hell. But we must let go of our own efforts to save ourselves and take hold of the rope. The moment we cease our own religious "rowing" and trust in Jesus, that is when we find peace with God.

And there will be desolation.

10Because you have forgotten the God
of your salvation,
And have not been mindful of the
Rock of your stronghold,
Therefore you will plant pleasant plants
And set out foreign seedlings;
11In the day you will make your plant
to grow,
And in the morning you will make
your seed to flourish;
But the harvest *will be* a heap of ruins
In the day of grief and desperate
sorrow.

12Woe to the multitude of many people
Who make a noise like the roar of the
seas,
And to the rushing of nations
That make a rushing like the rushing
of mighty waters!
13The nations will rush like the rushing
of many waters;
But *God* will rebuke them and they
will flee far away,
And be chased like the chaff of the
mountains before the wind,
Like a rolling thing before the
whirlwind.
14Then behold, at eventide, trouble!
And before the morning, he *is* no more.
This *is* the portion of those who
plunder us,
And the lot of those who rob us.

Proclamation Against Ethiopia

18 Woe to the land shadowed with
buzzing wings,
Which *is* beyond the rivers of Ethiopia,
2Which sends ambassadors by sea,
Even in vessels of reed on the waters,
saying,
"Go, swift messengers, to a nation tall
and smooth *of skin,*
To a people terrible from their
beginning onward,
A nation powerful and treading down,
Whose land the rivers divide."

3All inhabitants of the world and
dwellers on the earth:
When he lifts up a banner on the
mountains, you see *it;*

And when he blows a trumpet, you
hear *it*.
[4]For so the LORD said to me,
"I will take My rest,
And I will look from My dwelling
place
Like clear heat in sunshine,
Like a cloud of dew in the heat of
harvest."
[5]For before the harvest, when the bud
is perfect
And the sour grape is ripening in the
flower,
He will both cut off the sprigs with
pruning hooks
And take away *and* cut down the
branches.
[6]They will be left together for the
mountain birds of prey
And for the beasts of the earth;
The birds of prey will summer on
them,
And all the beasts of the earth will
winter on them.

[7]In that time a present will be brought
to the LORD of hosts
From[a] a people tall and smooth *of skin*,
And from a people terrible from their
beginning onward,
A nation powerful and treading down,
Whose land the rivers divide—
To the place of the name of the LORD
of hosts,
To Mount Zion.

Proclamation Against Egypt

19 The burden against Egypt.

Behold, the LORD rides on a swift
cloud,
And will come into Egypt;
The idols of Egypt will totter at His
presence,
And the heart of Egypt will melt in its
midst.

[2]"I will set Egyptians against Egyptians;
Everyone will fight against his
brother,
And everyone against his neighbor,
City against city, kingdom against
kingdom.
[3]The spirit of Egypt will fail in its
midst;
I will destroy their counsel,
And they will consult the idols and
the charmers,
The mediums and the sorcerers.
[4]And the Egyptians I will give
Into the hand of a cruel master,
And a fierce king will rule over them,"
Says the Lord, the LORD of hosts.

[5]The waters will fail from the sea,
And the river will be wasted and
dried up.
[6]The rivers will turn foul;
The brooks of defense will be
emptied and dried up;
The reeds and rushes will wither.
[7]The papyrus reeds by the River,[a] by
the mouth of the River,
And everything sown by the River,
Will wither, be driven away, and be
no more.
[8]The fishermen also will mourn;
All those will lament who cast hooks
into the River,
And they will languish who spread
nets on the waters.
[9]Moreover those who work in fine flax
And those who weave fine fabric will
be ashamed;
[10]And its foundations will be broken.

18:7 [a]Following Dead Sea Scrolls, Septuagint, and Vulgate; Masoretic Text omits *From;* Targum reads *To.* 19:7 [a]That is, the Nile

18:3 The trumpet has been blown. We are in a battle for the lost. There is no higher calling than to (with God's help) seek to save this dying world. Today, pray for divine encounters and be ready to share the gospel when the opportunity comes. Have your feet shod with the *preparation* of the gospel of peace (see Eph. 6:13–17).

All who make wages *will be* troubled
of soul.

11 Surely the princes of Zoan *are* fools;
Pharaoh's wise counselors give foolish
counsel.
How do you say to Pharaoh, "I *am* the
son of the wise,
The son of ancient kings?"
12 Where *are* they?
Where are your wise men?
Let them tell you now,
And let them know what the LORD of
hosts has purposed against Egypt.
13 The princes of Zoan have become
fools;
The princes of Noph[a] are deceived;
They have also deluded Egypt,
Those who are the mainstay of its
tribes.
14 The LORD has mingled a perverse
spirit in her midst;
And they have caused Egypt to err in
all her work,
As a drunken man staggers in his
vomit.
15 Neither will there be *any* work for
Egypt,
Which the head or tail,
Palm branch or bulrush, may do.[a]

16 In that day Egypt will be like women, and will be afraid and fear because
of the waving of the hand of the LORD of
hosts, which He waves over it. 17 And the
land of Judah will be a terror to Egypt;
everyone who makes mention of it will
be afraid in himself, because of the counsel of the LORD of hosts which He has determined against it.

Egypt, Assyria, and Israel Blessed

18 In that day five cities in the land of
Egypt will speak the language of Canaan
and swear by the LORD of hosts; one will
be called the City of Destruction.[a]
19 In that day there will be an altar to
the LORD in the midst of the land of
Egypt, and a pillar to the LORD at its border. 20 And it will be for a sign and for a
witness to the LORD of hosts in the land of
Egypt; for they will cry to the LORD because of the oppressors, and He will send
them a Savior and a Mighty One, and He
will deliver them. 21 Then the LORD will
be known to Egypt, and the Egyptians
will know the LORD in that day, and will
make sacrifice and offering; yes, they will
make a vow to the LORD and perform *it.*
22 And the LORD will strike Egypt, He will
strike and heal *it;* they will return to the
LORD, and He will be entreated by them
and heal them.

23 In that day there will be a highway
from Egypt to Assyria, and the Assyrian
will come into Egypt and the Egyptian
into Assyria, and the Egyptians will serve
with the Assyrians.

24 In that day Israel will be one of three
with Egypt and Assyria—a blessing in the
midst of the land, 25 whom the LORD of
hosts shall bless, saying, "Blessed *is* Egypt
My people, and Assyria the work of My
hands, and Israel My inheritance."

The Sign Against Egypt and Ethiopia

20 In the year that Tartan[a] came to
Ashdod, when Sargon the king of
Assyria sent him, and he fought against
Ashdod and took it, 2 at the same time the
LORD spoke by Isaiah the son of Amoz,
saying, "Go, and remove the sackcloth
from your body, and take your sandals off

19:13 [a]That is, ancient Memphis 19:15 [a]Compare Isaiah 9:14–16 19:18 [a]Some Hebrew manuscripts, Arabic, Dead Sea Scrolls, Targum, and Vulgate read *Sun;* Septuagint reads *Asedek* (literally *Righteousness*). 20:1 [a]Or *the Commander in Chief*

19:11–13 When people profess atheism, never be intimidated by the thought that they are somehow intellectual. They are not. The Bible says that such a person is a fool (see Psa. 14:1; Rom. 1:22). So, make sure that you move from addressing the intellect (the place of argument; see Rom. 8:7) to addressing the conscience (the place of the knowledge of right and wrong; see Rom. 2:15). This is what Jesus and Paul did, as well as others (see Mark 10:17–22; Rom. 2:19–24).

your feet." And he did so, walking naked
and barefoot.
[3]Then the LORD said, "Just as My servant Isaiah has walked naked and barefoot three years *for* a sign and a wonder
against Egypt and Ethiopia, [4]so shall the
king of Assyria lead away the Egyptians
as prisoners and the Ethiopians as captives, young and old, naked and barefoot,
with their buttocks uncovered, to the
shame of Egypt. [5]Then they shall be
afraid and ashamed of Ethiopia their expectation and Egypt their glory. [6]And the
inhabitant of this territory will say in that
day, 'Surely such *is* our expectation, wherever we flee for help to be delivered from
the king of Assyria; and how shall we
escape?' "

The Fall of Babylon Proclaimed

21 The burden against the Wilderness of the Sea.

As whirlwinds in the South pass
through,
So it comes from the desert, from a
terrible land.
[2]A distressing vision is declared to me;
The treacherous dealer deals
treacherously,
And the plunderer plunders.
Go up, O Elam!
Besiege, O Media!
All its sighing I have made to cease.

[3]Therefore my loins are filled with pain;
Pangs have taken hold of me, like the
pangs of a woman in labor.
I was distressed when *I* heard *it;*
I was dismayed when *I* saw *it.*
[4]My heart wavered, fearfulness
frightened me;
The night for which I longed He
turned into fear for me.
[5]Prepare the table,
Set a watchman in the tower,
Eat and drink.
Arise, you princes,
Anoint the shield!

[6]For thus has the Lord said to me:
"Go, set a watchman,
Let him declare what he sees."
[7]And he saw a chariot *with* a pair of
horsemen,
A chariot of donkeys, *and* a chariot of
camels,
And he listened earnestly with great
care.
[8]Then he cried, "A lion,[a] my Lord!
I stand continually on the watchtower
in the daytime;
I have sat at my post every night.
[9]And look, here comes a chariot of
men *with* a pair of horsemen!"
Then he answered and said,
"Babylon is fallen, is fallen!
And all the carved images of her gods
He has broken to the ground."

[10]Oh, my threshing and the grain of my
floor!
That which I have heard from the
LORD of hosts,
The God of Israel,
I have declared to you.

Proclamation Against Edom

[11]The burden against Dumah.

He calls to me out of Seir,

21:8 [a]Dead Sea Scrolls read *Then the observer cried.*

20:2 Isaiah was stripped to his loincloth. This is the spirit in which every Christian should walk—one of self-denial, humility, and contrition.

21:3,4 We too should be horrified at the fate of the ungodly. Force yourself to consider the horrors of hell, and then let love swallow your fears and motivate you to warn every man, that we may present every man perfect in Christ Jesus (see Col. 1:28). Make sure you open up the Law as Jesus did. Without the Commandments you will have trouble convincing the lost that God is angry at them and that they need a Savior. It is the Law that shows sin in its true light and "brings about wrath" (see Rom. 4:15). Study Rom. 7 for how the Law brought about wrath in Paul's life.

"Watchman, what of the night?
Watchman, what of the night?"
12The watchman said,
"The morning comes, and also the night.
If you will inquire, inquire;
Return! Come back!"

Proclamation Against Arabia

13The burden against Arabia.

In the forest in Arabia you will lodge,
O you traveling companies of Dedanites.
14O inhabitants of the land of Tema,
Bring water to him who is thirsty;
With their bread they met him who fled.
15For they fled from the swords, from the drawn sword,
From the bent bow, and from the distress of war.

16For thus the LORD has said to me:
"Within a year, according to the year of a
hired man, all the glory of Kedar will fail;
17and the remainder of the number of
archers, the mighty men of the people of
Kedar, will be diminished; for the LORD
God of Israel has spoken *it*."

. . . . . .

For "one of the most remarkable" examples of evolution, see Eccles. 9:11 comment.

. . . . . .

Proclamation Against Jerusalem

22 The burden against the Valley of Vision.

What ails you now, that you have all gone up to the housetops,
2You who are full of noise,
A tumultuous city, a joyous city?
Your slain *men are* not slain with the sword,
Nor dead in battle.
3All your rulers have fled together;
They are captured by the archers.
All who are found in you are bound together;
They have fled from afar.
4Therefore I said, "Look away from me,
I will weep bitterly;
Do not labor to comfort me
Because of the plundering of the daughter of my people."

5For *it is* a day of trouble and treading down and perplexity
By the Lord GOD of hosts
In the Valley of Vision—
Breaking down the walls
And of crying to the mountain.
6Elam bore the quiver
With chariots of men *and* horsemen,
And Kir uncovered the shield.
7It shall come to pass *that* your choicest valleys
Shall be full of chariots,
And the horsemen shall set themselves in array at the gate.

8He removed the protection of Judah.
You looked in that day to the armor of the House of the Forest;
9You also saw the damage to the city of David,
That it was great;
And you gathered together the waters of the lower pool.
10You numbered the houses of Jerusalem,
And the houses you broke down
To fortify the wall.
11You also made a reservoir between the two walls
For the water of the old pool.
But you did not look to its Maker,
Nor did you have respect for Him who fashioned it long ago.

12And in that day the Lord GOD of hosts
Called for weeping and for mourning,
For baldness and for girding with sackcloth.
13But instead, joy and gladness,
Slaying oxen and killing sheep,
Eating meat and drinking wine:

"Let us eat and drink, for tomorrow
we die!"

14Then it was revealed in my hearing
by the LORD
of hosts,
"Surely for this iniquity there will be
no atonement
for you,
Even to your death," says the Lord
GOD of hosts.

The Judgment on Shebna

15Thus says the Lord GOD of hosts:

"Go, proceed to this steward,
To Shebna, who *is* over the house,
and say:
16'What have you here, and whom have
you here,
That you have hewn a sepulcher here,
As he who hews himself a sepulcher
on high,
Who carves a tomb for himself in a
rock?
17Indeed, the LORD will throw you
away violently,
O mighty man,
And will surely seize you.
18He will surely turn violently and toss
you like a ball
Into a large country;
There you shall die, and there your
glorious chariots
Shall be the shame of your master's
house.
19So I will drive you out of your office,
And from your position he will pull
you down.[a]

20'Then it shall be in that day,
That I will call My servant Eliakim the
son of Hilkiah;
21I will clothe him with your robe
And strengthen him with your belt;
I will commit your responsibility into
his hand.
He shall be a father to the inhabitants
of Jerusalem
And to the house of Judah.
22The key of the house of David
I will lay on his shoulder;
So he shall open, and no one shall
shut;
And he shall shut, and no one shall
open.
23I will fasten him *as* a peg in a secure
place,
And he will become a glorious throne
to his father's house.

24'They will hang on him all the glory
of his father's house, the offspring and the
posterity, all vessels of small quantity, from
the cups to all the pitchers. 25In that day,'

22:19 [a]Septuagint omits *he will pull you down;* Syriac, Targum, and Vulgate read *I will pull you down.*

22:13 Annihilation. They would not have been so flippant regarding their coming deaths if they knew what awaited them. Many believe in the soul's annihilation, that they simply cease to exist when they die. We must warn the lost that they will instead face a holy God on Judgment Day and give an account of their lives.

"I do not wonder that ingenious persons have invented theories which aim at mitigating the terrors of the world to come to the impenitent. It is natural they should do so, for the facts are so alarming as they are truthfully given us in God's Word, that if we desire to preach comfortable doctrine and such as will quiet the consciences of idle professors, we must dilute the awful truth. The revelation of God concerning the doom of the wicked is so overwhelming as to make it penal, nay, I was about to say damnable, to be indifferent and careless in the work of evangelizing the world. I do not wonder that this error in doctrine springs up just now when abounding callousness of heart needs an excuse for itself. What better pillow for idle heads than the doctrine that the finally impenitent become extinct? The logical reasoning of the sinner is, 'Let us eat and drink, for to-morrow we die,' and the professing Christian is not slow to feel an ease of heart from pressing responsibilities when he accepts so consolatory an opinion. Forbear this sleeping draught, I pray you, for in very deed the sharp stimulant of the truth itself is abundantly needful; even when thus bestirred to duty we are sluggish enough, and need not that these sweet but sleep-producing theories should operate upon us." *Charles Spurgeon*

says the LORD of hosts, 'the peg that is fastened in the secure place will be removed and be cut down and fall, and the burden that *was* on it will be cut off; for the LORD has spoken.' "

Proclamation Against Tyre

23 The burden against Tyre.

Wail, you ships of Tarshish!
For it is laid waste,
So that there is no house, no harbor;
From the land of Cyprus[a] it is revealed to them.

2 Be still, you inhabitants of the coastland,
You merchants of Sidon,
Whom those who cross the sea have filled.[a]
3 And on great waters the grain of Shihor,
The harvest of the River,[a] *is* her revenue;
And she is a marketplace for the nations.

4 Be ashamed, O Sidon;
For the sea has spoken,
The strength of the sea, saying,
"I do not labor, nor bring forth children;
Neither do I rear young men,
Nor bring up virgins."
5 When the report *reaches* Egypt,
They also will be in agony at the report of Tyre.

6 Cross over to Tarshish;
Wail, you inhabitants of the coastland!
7 *Is* this your joyous *city,*
Whose antiquity *is* from ancient days,
Whose feet carried her far off to dwell?
8 Who has taken this counsel against
Tyre, the crowning *city,*
Whose merchants *are* princes,
Whose traders *are* the honorable of the earth?
9 The LORD of hosts has purposed it,
To bring to dishonor the pride of all glory,
To bring into contempt all the honorable of the earth.

10 Overflow through your land like the River,[a]
O daughter of Tarshish;
There is no more strength.
11 He stretched out His hand over the sea,
He shook the kingdoms;
The LORD has given a commandment against Canaan
To destroy its strongholds.
12 And He said, "You will rejoice no more,
O you oppressed virgin daughter of Sidon.
Arise, cross over to Cyprus;
There also you will have no rest."

13 Behold, the land of the Chaldeans,
This people *which* was not;
Assyria founded it for wild beasts of the desert.
They set up its towers,
They raised up its palaces,
And brought it to ruin.

14 Wail, you ships of Tarshish!
For your strength is laid waste.

15 Now it shall come to pass in that day
that Tyre will be forgotten seventy years,
according to the days of one king. At the

23:1 [a]Hebrew *Kittim,* western lands, especially Cyprus 23:2 [a]Following Masoretic Text and Vulgate; Septuagint and Targum read *Passing over the water;* Dead Sea Scrolls read *Your messengers passing over the sea.* 23:3 [a]That is, the Nile 23:10 [a]That is, the Nile

23:15 God knows the future, because He exists outside of the dimension of time that He created. Such a thought is difficult for the finite human mind to comprehend. Still, it does us good to meditate on God's awesome power. It produces awe, wonder, fear, and humility, and fosters the spirit of worship.

end of seventy years it will happen to
Tyre as *in* the song of the harlot:

[16]"Take a harp, go about the city,
You forgotten harlot;
Make sweet melody, sing many songs,
That you may be remembered."

[17]And it shall be, at the end of seventy
years, that the LORD will deal with Tyre.
She will return to her hire, and commit
fornication with all the kingdoms of the
world on the face of the earth. [18]Her gain
and her pay will be set apart for the LORD;
it will not be treasured nor laid up, for
her gain will be for those who dwell before the LORD, to eat sufficiently, and for
fine clothing.

Impending Judgment on the Earth

24 Behold, the LORD makes the earth
empty and makes it waste,
Distorts its surface
And scatters abroad its inhabitants.
[2]And it shall be:
As with the people, so with the priest;
As with the servant, so with his master;
As with the maid, so with her
mistress;
As with the buyer, so with the seller;
As with the lender, so with the
borrower;
As with the creditor, so with the
debtor.
[3]The land shall be entirely emptied
and utterly plundered,
For the LORD has spoken this word.

[4]The earth mourns *and* fades away,
The world languishes *and* fades away;
The haughty people of the earth
languish.
[5]The earth is also defiled under its
inhabitants,
Because they have transgressed the
laws,
Changed the ordinance,
Broken the everlasting covenant.
[6]Therefore the curse has devoured the
earth,
And those who dwell in it are desolate.
Therefore the inhabitants of the earth
are burned,
And few men *are* left.

[7]The new wine fails, the vine
languishes,
All the merry-hearted sigh.
[8]The mirth of the tambourine ceases,
The noise of the jubilant ends,
The joy of the harp ceases.
[9]They shall not drink wine with a song;
Strong drink is bitter to those who
drink it.
[10]The city of confusion is broken down;
Every house is shut up, so that none
may go in.
[11]*There is* a cry for wine in the streets,
All joy is darkened,
The mirth of the land is gone.
[12]In the city desolation is left,
And the gate is stricken with
destruction.
[13]When it shall be thus in the midst of
the land among the people,
It shall be like the shaking of an olive
tree,
Like the gleaning of grapes when the
vintage is done.

[14]They shall lift up their voice, they
shall sing;
For the majesty of the LORD
They shall cry aloud from the sea.
[15]Therefore glorify the LORD in the
dawning light,

24:5,6 "In one-on-one witnessing encounters, a common question asked is, 'Why is there pain and suffering?' If you have your Bible with you at the time, open to this passage and have the person you're talking with read it aloud. When he finishes reading, explain that the Bible tells us that because human beings have broken God's holy Laws, the entire earth is suffering under a curse. You can then redirect the conversation by asking him how many of God's Laws he thinks he has personally broken." *Anna Jackson*

The name of the LORD God of Israel in
the coastlands of the sea.
16From the ends of the earth we have
heard songs:
"Glory to the righteous!"
But I said, "I am ruined, ruined!
Woe to me!
The treacherous dealers have dealt
treacherously,
Indeed, the treacherous dealers have
dealt very treacherously."

17Fear and the pit and the snare
Are upon you, O inhabitant of the
earth.
18And it shall be
That he who flees from the noise of
the fear
Shall fall into the pit,
And he who comes up from the midst
of the pit
Shall be caught in the snare;
For the windows from on high are
open,
And the foundations of the earth are
shaken.

19The earth is violently broken,
The earth is split open,
The earth is shaken exceedingly.
20The earth shall reel to and fro like a
drunkard,
And shall totter like a hut;
Its transgression shall be heavy upon it,
And it will fall, and not rise again.

21It shall come to pass in that day
That the LORD will punish on high the
host of exalted ones,
And on the earth the kings of the earth.
22They will be gathered together,
As prisoners are gathered in the pit,
And will be shut up in the prison;
After many days they will be
punished.
23Then the moon will be disgraced
And the sun ashamed;
For the LORD of hosts will reign
On Mount Zion and in Jerusalem
And before His elders, gloriously.

Praise to God

25 O LORD, You *are* my God.
I will exalt You,
I will praise Your name,
For You have done wonderful *things;*
Your counsels of old *are* faithfulness
and truth.
2For You have made a city a ruin,
A fortified city a ruin,
A palace of foreigners to be a city no
more;
It will never be rebuilt.
3Therefore the strong people will
glorify You;
The city of the terrible nations will
fear You.
4For You have been a strength to the
poor,
A strength to the needy in his
distress,
A refuge from the storm,
A shade from the heat;
For the blast of the terrible ones *is* as
a storm *against* the wall.
5You will reduce the noise of aliens,
As heat in a dry place;
As heat in the shadow of a cloud,
The song of the terrible ones will be
diminished.

6And in this mountain
The LORD of hosts will make for all
people
A feast of choice pieces,
A feast of wines on the lees,
Of fat things full of marrow,
Of well-refined wines on the lees.
7And He will destroy on this mountain

24:21 There is no such thing as a "perfect crime." The Day of Judgment will see that every transgression of the moral Law will receive just retribution. God will bring every work to judgment, including every secret thing whether it is good or evil. What a fearful thing for guilty sinners and for evil spirits. No wonder demons tremble at His name.

The surface of the covering cast over
all people,
And the veil that is spread over all
nations.
[8]He will swallow up death forever,
And the Lord GOD will wipe away
tears from all faces;
The rebuke of His people
He will take away from all the earth;
For the LORD has spoken.

[9]And it will be said in that day:
"Behold, this *is* our God;
We have waited for Him, and He will
save us.
This *is* the LORD;
We have waited for Him;
We will be glad and rejoice in His
salvation."

[10]For on this mountain the hand of the
LORD will rest,
And Moab shall be trampled down
under Him,
As straw is trampled down for the
refuse heap.
[11]And He will spread out His hands in
their midst
As a swimmer reaches out to swim,
And He will bring down their pride
Together with the trickery of their
hands.
[12]The fortress of the high fort of your
walls
He will bring down, lay low,
And bring to the ground, down to the
dust.

A Song of Salvation

26 In that day this song will be sung
in the land of Judah:
"We have a strong city;
God will appoint salvation *for* walls
and bulwarks.
[2]Open the gates,
That the righteous nation which
keeps the truth may enter in.
[3]You will keep *him* in perfect peace,
Whose mind *is* stayed *on You,*
Because he trusts in You.
[4]Trust in the LORD forever,
For in YAH, the LORD, *is* everlasting
strength.[a]
[5]For He brings down those who dwell
on high,
The lofty city;
He lays it low,
He lays it low to the ground,
He brings it down to the dust.
[6]The foot shall tread it down—
The feet of the poor
And the steps of the needy."

[7]The way of the just *is* uprightness;
O Most Upright,
You weigh the path of the just.
[8]Yes, in the way of Your judgments,
O LORD, we have waited for You;
The desire of *our* soul *is* for Your name
And for the remembrance of You.
[9]With my soul I have desired You in
the night,
Yes, by my spirit within me I will seek
You early;
For when Your judgments *are* in the
earth,
The inhabitants of the world will
learn righteousness.

[10]Let grace be shown to the wicked,
Yet he will not learn righteousness;
In the land of uprightness he will deal

26:4 [a]Or *Rock of Ages*

25:8 We are in a battle that we cannot lose: through the cross, death has been swallowed up in victory! The day will come when death, disease, pain, fear, loneliness, etc., will be gone forever. Never be discouraged for a moment. Soak your soul in 1 Cor. 15:54–58; Rev. 21:4.

26:3 Perfect peace is yours right now, if you keep your mind stayed on the Lord. Reject anything that doubts God's promise to never leave you, or to work all things out for good (see Rom. 8:28). Never waver at the promises of God through unbelief. Instead be strong in the Lord, being fully persuaded that what God has promised He is also willing and able to perform (see Rom. 4:20,21).

QUESTIONS & OBJECTIONS

26:21

"If God can 'legally commute our death sentence,' is He under some law?"

God is more than "under some law." He cannot be separated from the moral Law. The Bible says that God is "perfect, holy, just and good." It also says that His Law is "perfect, holy, just, and good." In other words, the moral Law (the Ten Commandments) is a reflection of the very character and nature of God. Scripture calls Him "the habitation of justice" (Jer. 50:7). There wasn't a time in eternity when He wondered, "What is right and what is wrong?" and then came up with the Ten Commandments. The moral Law is eternal. That's why Jesus said that heaven and earth would pass away before one "jot or tittle" (the smallest part) of the Law would fail (see Matt. 5:18). It is written in stone. It will not go away and it will not change. It is immutable, and it calls for the blood of every guilty criminal. For a comparison of God's character and the Law, see page 280.

unjustly,
And will not behold the majesty of the LORD.
11 LORD, *when* Your hand is lifted up, they will not see.
But they will see and be ashamed
For *their* envy of people;
Yes, the fire of Your enemies shall devour them.

12 LORD, You will establish peace for us,
For You have also done all our works in us.
13 O LORD our God, masters besides You
Have had dominion over us;
But by You only we make mention of Your name.
14 *They are* dead, they will not live;
They are deceased, they will not rise.
Therefore You have punished and destroyed them,
And made all their memory to perish.
15 You have increased the nation, O LORD,
You have increased the nation;
You are glorified;
You have expanded all the borders of the land.

16 LORD, in trouble they have visited You,
They poured out a prayer *when* Your chastening *was* upon them.
17 As a woman with child
Is in pain and cries out in her pangs,
When she draws near the time of her delivery,
So have we been in Your sight, O LORD.
18 We have been with child, we have been in pain;
We have, as it were, brought forth wind;
We have not accomplished any deliverance in the earth,
Nor have the inhabitants of the world fallen.

19 Your dead shall live;
Together with my dead body[a] they shall arise.
Awake and sing, you who dwell in dust;
For your dew *is like* the dew of herbs,
And the earth shall cast out the dead.

Take Refuge from the Coming Judgment

20 Come, my people, enter your chambers,
And shut your doors behind you;
Hide yourself, as it were, for a little moment,
Until the indignation is past.
21 For behold, the LORD comes out of His place
To punish the inhabitants of the earth for their iniquity;
The earth will also disclose her blood,

26:19 [a]Following Masoretic Text and Vulgate; Syriac and Targum read *their dead bodies;* Septuagint reads *those in the tombs.*

QUESTIONS & OBJECTIONS

27:1 "Were dinosaurs on Noah's ark?"

By Ken Ham, Answers in Genesis

The history of God's creation (told in Gen. 1—2) tells us that all the land-dwelling creatures were made on Day 6 of Creation Week—the same day God made Adam and Eve. Therefore, it is clear that dinosaurs (being land animals) were made with man.

Also, two of every kind (seven of some) of land animal boarded the Ark. Nothing indicates that any of the land animal kinds were already extinct before the Flood. Besides, the description of "behemoth" in chapter 40 of the Book of Job (Job lived after the Flood) only fits with something like a sauropod dinosaur. The ancestor of "behemoth" must have been on board the Ark.

We also find many dinosaurs that were trapped and fossilized in Flood sediment. Widespread legends of encounters with dragons give another indication that at least some dinosaurs survived the Flood. The only way this could happen is if they were on the Ark.

Juveniles of even the largest land animals do not present a size problem, and, being young, they have their full breeding life ahead of them. Yet most dinosaurs were not very large at all—some were the size of a chicken (although absolutely no relation to birds, as many evolutionists are now saying). Most scientists agree that the average size of a dinosaur is actually the size of a sheep.

For example, God most likely brought Noah two young adult sauropods (e.g., apatosaurs), rather than two full-grown sauropods. The same goes for elephants, giraffes, and other animals that grow to be very large. However, there was adequate room for most fully grown adult animals anyway.

As far as the number of different types of dinosaurs, it should be recognized that, although there are hundreds of names for different varieties (species) of dinosaurs that have been discovered, there are probably only about 50 actual different kinds.

And will no more cover her slain.

27 In that day the LORD with His severe sword, great and strong,
Will punish Leviathan the fleeing serpent,
Leviathan that twisted serpent;
And He will slay the reptile that *is* in
the sea.

The Restoration of Israel

2 In that day sing to her,
"A vineyard of red wine![a]
3 I, the LORD, keep it,
I water it every moment;
Lest any hurt it,
I keep it night and day.
4 Fury *is* not in Me.
Who would set briers *and* thorns
Against Me in battle?
I would go through them,
I would burn them together.
5 Or let him take hold of My strength,
That he may make peace with Me;
And he shall make peace with Me."

6 Those who come He shall cause to

27:2 [a]Following Masoretic Text (Kittel's *Biblia Hebraica*), Bomberg, and Vulgate; Masoretic Text (*Biblia Hebraica Stuttgartensia*), some Hebrew manuscripts, and Septuagint read *delight;* Targum reads *choice vineyard.*

27:5,6 Peace with God. We preach the gospel of peace. If you are given to a lifestyle of reaching out to the lost, you are blessed by God. Jesus said, "Blessed are the peacemakers" (Matt. 5:9). Determine to do all you can to bring men and woman into a right relationship with God. Never say that you can't do it; instead say that you can do all things through Christ who strengthens you (see Phil. 4:13). Every skill you have learned in life came because you applied yourself to it. You learned to crawl, to walk, to feed yourself, to ride a bike, to drive a car, etc. Do the same with evangelism. Study it to show yourself approved, a workman who need not be ashamed. Then practice what you preach. Practice witnessing when you are alone—in the car, in the shower—or witness to your dog. Do it until it becomes second nature to you, and then keep practicing it with the lost, until the knowledge of the glory of the Lord covers this earth as the waters cover the sea.

take root in Jacob;
Israel shall blossom and bud,
And fill the face of the world with fruit.

[7]Has He struck Israel as He struck those who struck him?
Or has He been slain according to the slaughter of those who were slain by Him?
[8]In measure, by sending it away,
You contended with it.
He removes *it* by His rough wind
In the day of the east wind.
[9]Therefore by this the iniquity of Jacob will be covered;
And this *is* all the fruit of taking away his sin:
When he makes all the stones of the altar
Like chalkstones that are beaten to dust,
Wooden images[a] and incense altars shall not stand.

[10]Yet the fortified city *will be* desolate,
The habitation forsaken and left like a wilderness;
There the calf will feed, and there it will lie down
And consume its branches.
[11]When its boughs are withered, they will be broken off;
The women come *and* set them on fire.
For it *is* a people of no understanding;
Therefore He who made them will not have mercy on them,
And He who formed them will show them no favor.

[12]And it shall come to pass in that day
That the LORD will thresh,
From the channel of the River[a] to the Brook of Egypt;
And you will be gathered one by one,
O you children of Israel.

[13]So it shall be in that day:
The great trumpet will be blown;
They will come, who are about to perish in the land of Assyria,
And they who are outcasts in the land of Egypt,
And shall worship the LORD in the holy mount at Jerusalem.

Woe to Ephraim and Jerusalem

28 Woe to the crown of pride, to the drunkards of Ephraim,
Whose glorious beauty *is* a fading flower
Which *is* at the head of the verdant valleys,
To those who are overcome with wine!
[2]Behold, the Lord has a mighty and strong one,
Like a tempest of hail and a destroying storm,
Like a flood of mighty waters overflowing,
Who will bring *them* down to the earth with *His* hand.
[3]The crown of pride, the drunkards of Ephraim,
Will be trampled underfoot;
[4]And the glorious beauty is a fading flower
Which *is* at the head of the verdant valley,
Like the first fruit before the summer,
Which an observer sees;
He eats it up while it is still in his hand.

[5]In that day the LORD of hosts will be
For a crown of glory and a diadem of beauty
To the remnant of His people,
[6]For a spirit of justice to him who sits in judgment,
And for strength to those who turn back the battle at the gate.

[7]But they also have erred through wine,
And through intoxicating drink are out of the way;
The priest and the prophet have erred through intoxicating drink,

27:9 [a]Hebrew *Asherim,* Canaanite deities **27:12** [a]That is, the Euphrates

QUESTIONS & OBJECTIONS

28:15 *"There are no moral absolutes."*

The argument is essentially, "What's good for you may not be good for me, and what's bad for you may not be bad for me." A true moral relativist cannot even be pinned down as to the morality of Nazi Germany. If asked whether Hitler's actions were wrong, he may say, "I would never do something like that myself, but I can't say that it was wrong." To label something as absolutely right or absolutely wrong has strong divine connotations.

So ask a relativist if pedophilia is wrong, and he may say that if it is against the law, it is simply wrong for that society. His framing of civil law is governed by whether people get "hurt," rather than by "right" or "wrong." His argument will be that pedophilia hurts children. But if someone takes pictures of naked children and posts them on the Internet without their knowledge (so that it's not hurting them), then by his criteria it must be morally okay. So press him on the point: Is pedophilia morally wrong? If he says it is not, ask for his name and address, because you need to inform his neighbors and the local police that he is okay with pedophilia. If he admits that it is morally wrong even though society may say it is right, then what Hitler did was also wrong; therefore, there are moral absolutes. At the root of relativism is the desire to get rid of moral accountability. But no matter what the world believes, we are all accountable for keeping an absolute moral standard of a very real God or face a very real hell, and we must warn people of that fact.

Be careful, though, that you don't get mired in pseudo intellectualism. It can be a time-waster, and you and I are to redeem the time. You will simply win an argument, when what you should be doing is showing him that he needs God's forgiveness.

The relativist's conscience is seared, so with the help of God you must awaken it. Say to him, "Let's just assume that there is a heaven. Do you think you would be good enough to go there?" He will almost certainly say that he is (see Prov. 20:6), so take him through the Commandments. You are simply moving from the intellect (the place of argument) to the conscience (the place of the knowledge of right and wrong), so that it will do its God-given duty.

"A great many of those who 'debunk' traditional . . . values have in the background values of their own which they believe to be immune from the debunking process." *C. S. Lewis*

They are swallowed up by wine,
They are out of the way through
intoxicating drink;
They err in vision, they stumble *in*
judgment.
8For all tables are full of vomit *and*
filth;
No place *is clean.*

9"Whom will he teach knowledge?
And whom will he make to
understand the message?
Those *just* weaned from milk?
Those *just* drawn from the breasts?
10For precept *must be* upon precept,
precept upon precept,
Line upon line, line upon line,
Here a little, there a little."

11For with stammering lips and another
tongue
He will speak to this people,
12To whom He said, "This *is* the rest
with which
You may cause the weary to rest,"
And, "This *is* the refreshing";
Yet they would not hear.
13But the word of the LORD was to them,
"Precept upon precept, precept upon
precept,
Line upon line, line upon line,
Here a little, there a little,"
That they might go and fall backward,
and be broken
And snared and caught.

14Therefore hear the word of the LORD,
you scornful men,
Who rule this people who *are* in
Jerusalem,
15Because you have said, "We have
made a covenant with death,

And with Sheol we are in agreement.
When the overflowing scourge passes through,
It will not come to us,
For we have made lies our refuge,
And under falsehood we have hidden ourselves."

A Cornerstone in Zion

[16]Therefore thus says the Lord GOD:

"Behold, I lay in Zion a stone for a foundation,
A tried stone, a precious cornerstone, a sure foundation;
Whoever believes will not act hastily.
[17]Also I will make justice the measuring line,
And righteousness the plummet;
The hail will sweep away the refuge of lies,
And the waters will overflow the hiding place.
[18]Your covenant with death will be annulled,
And your agreement with Sheol will not stand;
When the overflowing scourge passes through,
Then you will be trampled down by it.
[19]As often as it goes out it will take you;
For morning by morning it will pass over,
And by day and by night;
It will be a terror just to understand the report."
[20]For the bed is too short to stretch out *on,*
And the covering so narrow that one cannot wrap himself *in it.*
[21]For the LORD will rise up as *at* Mount Perazim,
He will be angry as in the Valley of Gibeon—
That He may do His work, His awesome work,
And bring to pass His act, His unusual act.
[22]Now therefore, do not be mockers,
Lest your bonds be made strong;
For I have heard from the Lord GOD of hosts,
A destruction determined even upon the whole earth.

Listen to the Teaching of God

[23]Give ear and hear my voice,
Listen and hear my speech.
[24]Does the plowman keep plowing all day to sow?
Does he keep turning his soil and breaking the clods?
[25]When he has leveled its surface,
Does he not sow the black cummin
And scatter the cummin,
Plant the wheat in rows,
The barley in the appointed place,
And the spelt in its place?
[26]For He instructs him in right judgment,
His God teaches him.

[27]For the black cummin is not threshed with a threshing sledge,
Nor is a cartwheel rolled over the cummin;
But the black cummin is beaten out with a stick,
And the cummin with a rod.
[28]Bread *flour* must be ground;
Therefore he does not thresh it forever,
Break *it with* his cartwheel,
Or crush it *with* his horsemen.
[29]This also comes from the LORD of hosts,
Who is wonderful in counsel *and* excellent in guidance.

Woe to Jerusalem

29 "Woe to Ariel,[a] to Ariel, the city *where* David dwelt!

29:1 [a]That is, Jerusalem

28:16 This refers to Jesus, the precious cornerstone of our salvation. See Rom. 9:33 and 1 Pet. 2:4–8.

Add year to year;
Let feasts come around.
[2]Yet I will distress Ariel;
There shall be heaviness and sorrow,
And it shall be to Me as Ariel.
[3]I will encamp against you all around,
I will lay siege against you with a mound,
And I will raise siegeworks against you.
[4]You shall be brought down,
You shall speak out of the ground;
Your speech shall be low, out of the dust;
Your voice shall be like a medium's, out of the ground;
And your speech shall whisper out of the dust.

[5]"Moreover the multitude of your foes
Shall be like fine dust,
And the multitude of the terrible ones
Like chaff that passes away;
Yes, it shall be in an instant, suddenly.
[6]You will be punished by the LORD of hosts
With thunder and earthquake and great noise,
With storm and tempest
And the flame of devouring fire.
[7]The multitude of all the nations who fight against Ariel,
Even all who fight against her and her fortress,
And distress her,
Shall be as a dream of a night vision.
[8]It shall even be as when a hungry man dreams,
And look—he eats;
But he awakes, and his soul is still empty;
Or as when a thirsty man dreams,
And look—he drinks;
But he awakes, and indeed *he is* faint,
And his soul still craves:
So the multitude of all the nations shall be,
Who fight against Mount Zion."

The Blindness of Disobedience

[9]Pause and wonder!
Blind yourselves and be blind!
They are drunk, but not with wine;
They stagger, but not with intoxicating drink.
[10]For the LORD has poured out on you
The spirit of deep sleep,
And has closed your eyes, namely, the prophets;
And He has covered your heads, *namely,* the seers.

[11]The whole vision has become to you
like the words of a book that is sealed,
which *men* deliver to one who is literate,
saying, "Read this, please."
And he says, "I cannot, for it *is* sealed."
[12]Then the book is delivered to one
who is illiterate, saying, "Read this, please."
And he says, "I am not literate."
[13]Therefore the Lord said:

"Inasmuch as these people draw near with their mouths
And honor Me with their lips,
But have removed their hearts far from Me,
And their fear toward Me is taught by the commandment of men,
[14]Therefore, behold, I will again do a marvelous work

29:13 How perfectly this sums up our generation. We have millions who sit within the contemporary Church and sing songs and read words that don't match their sinful lives. Once again, the problem finds its roots in a lack of the fear of God. An insipid and imaginary loving god, devoid of any sense of justice, is preached from pulpits and reproduces itself in the hearts of its hearers. Sinai needs to be thundered from the mouths of preachers whose hearts tremble for fear of the Lord. See Ezek. 33:31 comment.

"It is of no use for any of you to try to be soul-winners if you are not bearing fruit in your own lives. How can you serve the Lord with your lips if you do not serve Him with your lives? How can you preach His gospel with your tongues, when with hands, feet, and heart you are preaching the devil's gospel, and setting up an antichrist by your practical unholiness?" *Charles Spurgeon*

SPRINGBOARDS FOR PREACHING AND WITNESSING

29:16

The A-Frame Roof

A TV news reporter once said, "Tonight we will look at the buying and selling of the world's most valuable commodity—information." He was right; information is the world's most valuable commodity. If you have information about where oil deposits are, or the location of gold or diamonds in the earth, you can be a billionaire overnight. Information can even save your life. If you are in a building that is on fire, and you know the location of the fire escapes, you can find your way out. Without that information, you may die. Your actions will be governed by information—what you know and what you don't know.

This principle is demonstrated by the story of a man who wanted to paint his steep, A-frame roof. As his ladder was too short to reach the top, he threw a strong rope over the roof, went around to the front, and carefully secured the rope to the back of his car. Then he went to the back of the house, climbed up on the roof, tied the rope firmly around his waist and began painting. His wife, not knowing what he had done, came out of the house, car keys in hand, got into the car and drove off. He was pulled over the top of the roof and was seriously injured.

Perhaps you see nothing wrong with believing the theory of evolution or some other theory about our origins. But remember, your information will govern your actions. If you believe a drink contains poison, you won't drink it. If you believe it is okay, you will drink it. If you believe evolution is true, and therefore that the Bible is false, then you won't repent. Why should you? Like the man who secured himself to the car, you will find you are only as secure as that to which you have secured yourself. If your faith is placed in evolution and not in God's promises, you will find that what you have tied yourself to will be your eternal downfall. You will perish because you refused information that would have saved your life.

Among this people,
A marvelous work and a wonder;
For the wisdom of their wise *men*
shall perish,
And the understanding of their
prudent *men* shall be hidden."

15Woe to those who seek deep to hide
their counsel far from the LORD,
And their works are in the dark;
They say, "Who sees us?" and, "Who
knows us?"
16Surely you have things turned around!
Shall the potter be esteemed as the
clay;
For shall the thing made say of him
who made it,
"He did not make me"?
Or shall the thing formed say of him
who formed it,
"He has no understanding"?

Future Recovery of Wisdom

17*Is* it not yet a very little while
Till Lebanon shall be turned into a
fruitful field,
And the fruitful field be esteemed as a
forest?
18In that day the deaf shall hear the
words of the book,
And the eyes of the blind shall see out
of obscurity and out of darkness.
19The humble also shall increase *their*
joy in the LORD,
And the poor among men shall rejoice
In the Holy One of Israel.
20For the terrible one is brought to
nothing,
The scornful one is consumed,
And all who watch for iniquity are cut
off—
21Who make a man an offender by a
word,
And lay a snare for him who reproves
in the gate,
And turn aside the just by empty
words.

22Therefore thus says the LORD, who
redeemed Abraham, concerning the house
of Jacob:

"Jacob shall not now be ashamed,
Nor shall his face now grow pale;

[23]But when he sees his children,
The work of My hands, in his midst,
They will hallow My name,
And hallow the Holy One of Jacob,
And fear the God of Israel.
[24]These also who erred in spirit will
come to understanding,
And those who complained will learn
doctrine."

Futile Confidence in Egypt

30 "Woe to the rebellious children,"
says the LORD,
"Who take counsel, but not of Me,
And who devise plans, but not of My
Spirit,
That they may add sin to sin;
[2]Who walk to go down to Egypt,
And have not asked My advice,
To strengthen themselves in the
strength of Pharaoh,
And to trust in the shadow of Egypt!
[3]Therefore the strength of Pharaoh
Shall be your shame,
And trust in the shadow of Egypt
Shall be *your* humiliation.
[4]For his princes were at Zoan,
And his ambassadors came to Hanes.
[5]They were all ashamed of a people
who could not benefit them,
Or be help or benefit,
But a shame and also a reproach."

[6]The burden against the beasts of the
South.

Through a land of trouble and anguish,
From which *came* the lioness and lion,
The viper and fiery flying serpent,
They will carry their riches on the
backs of young donkeys,
And their treasures on the humps of
camels,
To a people *who* shall not profit;
[7]For the Egyptians shall help in vain
and to no purpose.
Therefore I have called her
Rahab-Hem-Shebeth.[a]

A Rebellious People

[8]Now go, write it before them on a
tablet,
And note it on a scroll,
That it may be for time to come,
Forever and ever:
[9]That this *is* a rebellious people,
Lying children,
Children *who* will not hear the law of
the LORD;
[10]Who say to the seers, "Do not see,"
And to the prophets, "Do not
prophesy to us right things;
Speak to us smooth things, prophesy
deceits.
[11]Get out of the way,
Turn aside from the path,
Cause the Holy One of Israel
To cease from before us."

[12]Therefore thus says the Holy One of
Israel:

"Because you despise this word,
And trust in oppression and
perversity,
And rely on them,
[13]Therefore this iniquity shall be to you
Like a breach ready to fall,
A bulge in a high wall,
Whose breaking comes suddenly, in
an instant.
[14]And He shall break it like the
breaking of the potter's vessel,
Which is broken in pieces;

30:7 [a]Literally *Rahab Sits Idle*

30:9 Those who will not hear the Law will remain in their sins and reap the eternal and terrible consequences of such foolishness. The Scriptures warn that he who is rebuked, and yet refuses to hear, will be destroyed without remedy (see Prov. 29:1).

30:10 It's not what modern preachers say that bothers me. It's what they don't say. They don't talk about sin, or that God requires perfect righteousness, or the reality of hell's existence. And so they rarely preach Christ was crucified to save us from wrath, when that should be the very heart and soul of the message.

He shall not spare.
So there shall not be found among its fragments
A shard to take fire from the hearth,
Or to take water from the cistern."

15 For thus says the Lord GOD, the Holy One of Israel:

"In returning and rest you shall be saved;
In quietness and confidence shall be your strength."
But you would not,
16 And you said, "No, for we will flee on horses"—
Therefore you shall flee!
And, "We will ride on swift *horses*"—
Therefore those who pursue you shall be swift!

17 One thousand *shall flee* at the threat of one,
At the threat of five you shall flee,
Till you are left as a pole on top of a mountain
And as a banner on a hill.

God Will Be Gracious

18 Therefore the LORD will wait, that He may be gracious to you;
And therefore He will be exalted, that He may have mercy on you.
For the LORD *is* a God of justice;
Blessed *are* all those who wait for Him.

19 For the people shall dwell in Zion at Jerusalem;
You shall weep no more.
He will be very gracious to you at the sound of your cry;
When He hears it, He will answer you.
20 And *though* the Lord gives you
The bread of adversity and the water of affliction,
Yet your teachers will not be moved into a corner anymore,
But your eyes shall see your teachers.
21 Your ears shall hear a word behind you, saying,
"This *is* the way, walk in it,"
Whenever you turn to the right hand
Or whenever you turn to the left.
22 You will also defile the covering of your images of silver,
And the ornament of your molded images of gold.
You will throw them away as an unclean thing;
You will say to them, "Get away!"

23 Then He will give the rain for your seed
With which you sow the ground,
And bread of the increase of the earth;
It will be fat and plentiful.
In that day your cattle will feed
In large pastures.
24 Likewise the oxen and the young donkeys that work the ground
Will eat cured fodder,
Which has been winnowed with the shovel and fan.
25 There will be on every high mountain
And on every high hill
Rivers *and* streams of waters,
In the day of the great slaughter,
When the towers fall.
26 Moreover the light of the moon will be as the light of the sun,
And the light of the sun will be sevenfold,
As the light of seven days,
In the day that the LORD binds up the bruise of His people
And heals the stroke of their wound.

Judgment on Assyria

27 Behold, the name of the LORD comes from afar,
Burning *with* His anger,
And *His* burden *is* heavy;

30:20,21 Painful though it may be, we must never let adversity drive us away from God. Lion's dens and Red Seas should send us to our knees and to His Word to hear His voice guiding us.

His lips are full of indignation,
And His tongue like a devouring fire.
28His breath is like an overflowing stream,
Which reaches up to the neck,
To sift the nations with the sieve of futility;
And *there shall be* a bridle in the jaws of the people,
Causing *them* to err.

29You shall have a song
As in the night *when* a holy festival is kept,
And gladness of heart as when one goes with a flute,
To come into the mountain of the LORD,
To the Mighty One of Israel.
30The LORD will cause His glorious voice to be heard,
And show the descent of His arm,
With the indignation of *His* anger
And the flame of a devouring fire,
With scattering, tempest, and hailstones.
31For through the voice of the LORD
Assyria will be beaten down,
As He strikes with the rod.
32And *in* every place where the staff of punishment passes,
Which the LORD lays on him,
It will be with tambourines and harps;
And in battles of brandishing He will fight with it.
33For Tophet *was* established of old,
Yes, for the king it is prepared.
He has made *it* deep and large;
Its pyre *is* fire with much wood;
The breath of the LORD, like a stream of brimstone,
Kindles it.

The Folly of Not Trusting God

31 Woe to those who go down to Egypt for help,
And rely on horses,
Who trust in chariots because *they are* many,
And in horsemen because they are very strong,
But who do not look to the Holy One of Israel,
Nor seek the LORD!
2Yet He also *is* wise and will bring disaster,
And will not call back His words,
But will arise against the house of evildoers,
And against the help of those who work iniquity.
3Now the Egyptians *are* men, and not God;
And their horses are flesh, and not spirit.
When the LORD stretches out His hand,
Both he who helps will fall,
And he who is helped will fall down;
They all will perish together.

God Will Deliver Jerusalem

4For thus the LORD has spoken to me:

"As a lion roars,
And a young lion over his prey
(When a multitude of shepherds is summoned against him,
He will not be afraid of their voice
Nor be disturbed by their noise),
So the LORD of hosts will come down
To fight for Mount Zion and for its hill.
5Like birds flying about,
So will the LORD of hosts defend Jerusalem.
Defending, He will also deliver *it;*
Passing over, He will preserve *it.*"

6Return *to Him* against whom the children of Israel have deeply revolted. 7For
in that day every man shall throw away
his idols of silver and his idols of gold—

31:1 It is easy to be influenced by the godless counsel of this world, and to trust in uncertain riches. See Psa. 1:1,2 to find out where you should get advice.

sin, which your own hands have made for yourselves.

8"Then Assyria shall fall by a sword not of man,
And a sword not of mankind shall devour him.
But he shall flee from the sword,
And his young men shall become forced labor.
9He shall cross over to his stronghold for fear,
And his princes shall be afraid of the banner,"
Says the LORD,
Whose fire *is* in Zion
And whose furnace *is* in Jerusalem.

A Reign of Righteousness

32 Behold, a king will reign in righteousness,
And princes will rule with justice.
2A man will be as a hiding place from the wind,
And a cover from the tempest,
As rivers of water in a dry place,
As the shadow of a great rock in a weary land.
3The eyes of those who see will not be dim,
And the ears of those who hear will listen.
4Also the heart of the rash will understand knowledge,
And the tongue of the stammerers will be ready to speak plainly.

5The foolish person will no longer be called generous,
Nor the miser said *to be* bountiful;
6For the foolish person will speak foolishness,
And his heart will work iniquity:
To practice ungodliness,
To utter error against the LORD,
To keep the hungry unsatisfied,
And he will cause the drink of the thirsty to fail.
7Also the schemes of the schemer *are* evil;
He devises wicked plans
To destroy the poor with lying words,
Even when the needy speaks justice.
8But a generous man devises generous things,
And by generosity he shall stand.

Consequences of Complacency

9Rise up, you women who are at ease,
Hear my voice;
You complacent daughters,
Give ear to my speech.
10In a year and *some* days
You will be troubled, you complacent women;
For the vintage will fail,
The gathering will not come.
11Tremble, you *women* who are at ease;
Be troubled, you complacent ones;
Strip yourselves, make yourselves bare,
And gird *sackcloth* on *your* waists.

12People shall mourn upon their breasts
For the pleasant fields, for the fruitful vine.
13On the land of my people will come up thorns *and* briers,
Yes, on all the happy homes *in* the joyous city;
14Because the palaces will be forsaken,
The bustling city will be deserted.
The forts and towers will become lairs forever,
A joy of wild donkeys, a pasture of flocks—
15Until the Spirit is poured upon us from on high,
And the wilderness becomes a fruitful field,
And the fruitful field is counted as a forest.

The Peace of God's Reign

16Then justice will dwell in the wilderness,
And righteousness remain in the fruitful field.
17The work of righteousness will be

peace,
And the effect of righteousness,
quietness and assurance forever.
18My people will dwell in a peaceful
habitation,
In secure dwellings, and in quiet
resting places,
19Though hail comes down on the forest,
And the city is brought low in
humiliation.

20Blessed *are* you who sow beside all
waters,
Who send out freely the feet of the ox
and the donkey.

A Prayer in Deep Distress

33 Woe to you who plunder, though
you *have* not *been* plundered;
And you who deal treacherously, though
they have not dealt treacherously with you!
When you cease plundering,
You will be plundered;
When you make an end of dealing
treacherously,
They will deal treacherously with you.

2O LORD, be gracious to us;
We have waited for You.
Be their[a] arm every morning,
Our salvation also in the time of
trouble.
3At the noise of the tumult the people
shall flee;
When You lift Yourself up, the nations
shall be scattered;
4And Your plunder shall be gathered
Like the gathering of the caterpillar;
As the running to and fro of locusts,
He shall run upon them.

5The LORD is exalted, for He dwells on
high;
He has filled Zion with justice and
righteousness.
6Wisdom and knowledge will be the
stability of your times,
And the strength of salvation;
The fear of the LORD *is* His treasure.

7Surely their valiant ones shall cry
outside,
The ambassadors of peace shall weep
bitterly.
8The highways lie waste,
The traveling man ceases.
He has broken the covenant,
He has despised the cities,[a]
He regards no man.
9The earth mourns *and* languishes,
Lebanon is shamed *and* shriveled;
Sharon is like a wilderness,
And Bashan and Carmel shake off
their fruits.

Impending Judgment on Zion

10"Now I will rise," says the LORD;
"Now I will be exalted,
Now I will lift Myself up.
11You shall conceive chaff,
You shall bring forth stubble;
Your breath, *as* fire, shall devour you.
12And the people shall be *like* the
burnings of lime;
Like thorns cut up they shall be
burned in the fire.
13Hear, you *who are* afar off, what I
have done;
And you *who are* near, acknowledge
My might."

33:2 [a]Septuagint omits *their*; Syriac, Targum, and Vulgate read *our*. 33:8 [a]Following Masoretic Text and Vulgate; Dead Sea Scrolls read *witnesses;* Septuagint omits *cities;* Targum reads *They have been removed from their cities.*

32:17 The truth of this may not find full realization in this sinful world, but it certainly will in the next. We await a new heavens and a new earth in which righteousness dwells. That sounds boring to a sin-loving world that finds excitement in iniquity. However, who in his right mind wouldn't like a world with no hatred, murder, rape, wars, theft, and lying? Sin leaves humanity without a "right" mind. See 2 Kings 2:1 comment for details on heaven.

"I don't believe in an afterlife, so I don't have to spend my whole life fearing hell, or fearing heaven even more. For whatever the tortures of hell, I think the boredom of heaven would be even worse." *Isaac Asimov*

[14]The sinners in Zion are afraid;
Fearfulness has seized the hypocrites:
"Who among us shall dwell with the devouring fire?
Who among us shall dwell with everlasting burnings?"

God save us from living in comfort while sinners are sinking into hell!

CHARLES SPURGEON

[15]He who walks righteously and speaks uprightly,
He who despises the gain of oppressions,
Who gestures with his hands, refusing bribes,
Who stops his ears from hearing of bloodshed,
And shuts his eyes from seeing evil:
[16]He will dwell on high;
His place of defense *will be* the fortress of rocks;
Bread will be given him,
His water *will be* sure.

The Land of the Majestic King

[17]Your eyes will see the King in His beauty;
They will see the land that is very far off.
[18]Your heart will meditate on terror:
"Where *is* the scribe?
Where *is* he who weighs?
Where *is* he who counts the towers?"
[19]You will not see a fierce people,
A people of obscure speech, beyond perception,
Of a stammering tongue *that you* cannot understand.

[20]Look upon Zion, the city of our appointed feasts;
Your eyes will see Jerusalem, a quiet home,
A tabernacle *that* will not be taken down;
Not one of its stakes will ever be

33:14 Everlasting burnings. The lost twist the motives of Christians who care enough to warn them of hell, accusing them of "hate speech," and yet the warning is a sign of true love and compassion. It is those professed Christians who don't warn the world of the reality of hell whom they should disdain. Jesus rebuked the hypocritical Pharisees because He cared for them. If He did not care, He would have remained silent. Who knows how many of His hypocritical hearers turned from their sin at His rebuke and were among the 3,000 on the Day of Pentecost?

Consider these powerful words from *Edward Payson*, an 18th-century preacher, on our responsibility to warn the lost:

> We all deserve perdition, a thousand times, for our stupid insensibility to the situation of those who are perishing around us. We profess to believe the word of God; but can you all prove that you believe it? Do you all act, as if you believed it? What, believe that many of your acquaintances, your children, are in danger of the fate which has now been described!
>
> Dare you go to God, and say, Lord, I believe thy word, I believe that all thy threatenings will be fulfilled, and then turn away, and coolly pursue your worldly business, without uttering one agonizing cry for those who are exposed to these threatenings? Dare you go and claim relationship to Christ, and profess to have his Spirit, without which you are none of his, and then make no effort, or only a few faint efforts, to save those for whom he shed not tears only, but blood?...
>
> Go, I may say to such, go, inconsistent, cruel, hard-hearted professors; go, slumber over the ruin of immortal souls; wrap yourself up in your selfish temporal interests, and say, I have no time to spare for rescuing others from everlasting burnings. Go, wear out your life in acquiring property for your children, and leave their souls to perish in the fire that never shall be quenched. Go, adorn their bodies, and banish from them, if possible, the seeds of disease; but leave in their bosoms that immortal worm, which will gnaw them for ever. And when God asks, where is thy child? thy brother? thy friend? reply, with impious Cain, I know not, I care not: am I his keeper?

33:15 How many people, once respected and successful, are now in prison or have seen their lives crumble because they haven't walked in righteousness? They have instead given in to fraud and bribery. Those who live in holiness and in righteousness (in Christ) save themselves from certain pains in this life and in the next.

removed,
Nor will any of its cords be broken.
21But there the majestic LORD *will be* for us
A place of broad rivers *and* streams,
In which no galley with oars will sail,
Nor majestic ships pass by
22(For the LORD *is* our Judge,
The LORD *is* our Lawgiver,
The LORD *is* our King;
He will save us);
23Your tackle is loosed,
They could not strengthen their mast,
They could not spread the sail.

Then the prey of great plunder is divided;
The lame take the prey.
24And the inhabitant will not say, "I am sick";
The people who dwell in it *will be* forgiven *their* iniquity.

Judgment on the Nations

34 Come near, you nations, to hear;
And heed, you people!
Let the earth hear, and all that is in it,
The world and all things that come forth from it.
2For the indignation of the LORD is against all nations,
And *His* fury against all their armies;
He has utterly destroyed them,
He has given them over to the slaughter.
3Also their slain shall be thrown out;
Their stench shall rise from their corpses,
And the mountains shall be melted with their blood.
4All the host of heaven shall be dissolved,
And the heavens shall be rolled up like a scroll;
All their host shall fall down
As the leaf falls from the vine,
And as *fruit* falling from a fig tree.

5"For My sword shall be bathed in heaven;
Indeed it shall come down on Edom,
And on the people of My curse, for judgment.
6The sword of the LORD is filled with blood,
It is made overflowing with fatness,
With the blood of lambs and goats,
With the fat of the kidneys of rams.
For the LORD has a sacrifice in Bozrah,
And a great slaughter in the land of Edom.
7The wild oxen shall come down with them,
And the young bulls with the mighty bulls;
Their land shall be soaked with blood,
And their dust saturated with fatness."

8For *it is* the day of the LORD's vengeance,
The year of recompense for the cause of Zion.
9Its streams shall be turned into pitch,
And its dust into brimstone;
Its land shall become burning pitch.
10It shall not be quenched night or day;
Its smoke shall ascend forever.
From generation to generation it shall lie waste;
No one shall pass through it forever and ever.
11But the pelican and the porcupine shall possess it,
Also the owl and the raven shall dwell in it.
And He shall stretch out over it
The line of confusion and the stones of emptiness.

33:22 America's founding fathers based the government's structure, providing separation of powers, on the truth of this verse. See James 4:12 comment.

34:2 We often forget that God sees all humanity, and as nations sin they store up wrath that will be revealed on the terrible Day of Wrath. See Rom. 2:1–11 for an example of what is coming to the ungodly.

QUESTIONS & OBJECTIONS

34:4 "If God could be eternal, so could the universe."

To deal with the dilemma of God and His eternal nature, atheists will often claim that the universe can also be without beginning—abandoning their own accepted science. According to scientist *Stephen Hawking*, "All the evidence seems to indicate that the universe has not existed forever... Rather, the universe, and time itself, had a beginning in the Big Bang." He explains, "In fact, the theory that the universe has existed forever is in serious difficulty with the Second Law of Thermodynamics. The Second Law states that disorder always increases with time. Like the argument about human progress, it indicates that there must have been a beginning. Otherwise, the universe would be in a state of complete disorder by now, and everything would be at the same temperature" (Public Lecture, "The Beginning of Time").

In other words, everything material degenerates. Food rots, metal rusts, and rocks crumble into dust. If the universe had been around forever (trillions and trillions plus years), everything material would have turned to dust. Therefore, it must have had a beginning.

God, on the other hand, is not material. The Bible states that He is "Spirit" (see John 4:24). He is the essence of life itself, the Creator of life, and is invisible (as is "life"), immortal (not touched by death), infinite and eternal (no beginning or end). He exists outside the dimension of time, which He created. For more details, see Isa. 45:18 and Psa. 90:2 comments.

12 They shall call its nobles to the
kingdom,
But none *shall be* there, and all its
princes shall be nothing.

13 And thorns shall come up in its
palaces,
Nettles and brambles in its fortresses;
It shall be a habitation of jackals,
A courtyard for ostriches.
14 The wild beasts of the desert shall
also meet with the jackals,
And the wild goat shall bleat to its
companion;
Also the night creature shall rest there,
And find for herself a place of rest.
15 There the arrow snake shall make her
nest and lay *eggs*
And hatch, and gather *them* under her
shadow;
There also shall the hawks be gathered,
Every one with her mate.

16 "Search from the book of the LORD,
and read:
Not one of these shall fail;
Not one shall lack her mate.
For My mouth has commanded it,
and His Spirit has gathered them.
17 He has cast the lot for them,
And His hand has divided it among
them with a measuring line.
They shall possess it forever;
From generation to generation they
shall dwell in it."

The Future Glory of Zion

35 The wilderness and the wasteland
shall be glad for them,
And the desert shall rejoice and blossom
as the rose;
2 It shall blossom abundantly and
rejoice,
Even with joy and singing.
The glory of Lebanon shall be given

34:9,10 "'Not called!' did you say? 'Not heard the call,' I think you should say. Put your ear down to the Bible, and hear him bid you go and pull sinners out of the fire of sin. Put your ear down to the burdened, agonized heart of humanity, and listen to its pitiful wail for help. Go stand by the gates of hell, and hear the damned entreat you to go to their father's house and bid their brothers and sisters, and servants and masters not to come there. And then look Christ in the face, whose mercy you have professed to obey, and tell him whether you will join heart and soul and body and circumstances in the march to publish his mercy to the world." *William Booth*

to it,
The excellence of Carmel and Sharon.
They shall see the glory of the LORD,
The excellency of our God.

[3]Strengthen the weak hands,
And make firm the feeble knees.
[4]Say to those *who are* fearful-hearted,
"Be strong, do not fear!
Behold, your God will come *with* vengeance,
With the recompense of God;
He will come and save you."

[5]Then the eyes of the blind shall be opened,
And the ears of the deaf shall be unstopped.
[6]Then the lame shall leap like a deer,
And the tongue of the dumb sing.
For waters shall burst forth in the wilderness,
And streams in the desert.
[7]The parched ground shall become a pool,
And the thirsty land springs of water;
In the habitation of jackals, where each lay,
There shall be grass with reeds and rushes.

[8]A highway shall be there, and a road,
And it shall be called the Highway of Holiness.
The unclean shall not pass over it,
But it *shall be* for others.
Whoever walks the road, although a fool,
Shall not go astray.
[9]No lion shall be there,
Nor shall *any* ravenous beast go up on it;
It shall not be found there.
But the redeemed shall walk *there*,
[10]And the ransomed of the LORD shall return,
And come to Zion with singing,
With everlasting joy on their heads.
They shall obtain joy and gladness,
And sorrow and sighing shall flee away.

Sennacherib Boasts Against the Lord

36 Now it came to pass in the four-
teenth year of King Hezekiah *that*
Sennacherib king of Assyria came up
against all the fortified cities of Judah and
took them. [2]Then the king of Assyria sent
the Rabshakeh[a] with a great army from
Lachish to King Hezekiah at Jerusalem.
And he stood by the aqueduct from the
upper pool, on the highway to the
Fuller's Field. [3]And Eliakim the son of
Hilkiah, who was over the household,
Shebna the scribe, and Joah the son of
Asaph, the recorder, came out to him.
[4]Then *the* Rabshakeh said to them, "Say
now to Hezekiah, 'Thus says the great
king, the king of Assyria: "What confidence is this in which you trust? [5]I say
you speak of having plans and power for
war; but *they are* mere words. Now in
whom do you trust, that you rebel against
me? [6]Look! You are trusting in the staff of
this broken reed, Egypt, on which if a

36:2 [a]A title, probably *Chief of Staff* or *Governor*

35:4 The most paralyzing of fears is the fear of man. It stops millions of Christians from reaching out to the lost. This is a terrible thing because it is hindering them from being true and faithful witnesses. Do you want God to say to you, "Well done, good and faithful servant"? Then cast off fear and lift up the shield of faith that God has given to you (see Eph. 6:13–16). If God is for you, nothing can be against you. See yourself as a doctor with a cure to cancer, and say with the disciples, "We cannot but speak the things which we have seen and heard" (Acts 4:20).

"A foolish physician he is, and a most unfaithful friend, that will let a sick man die for fear of troubling him; and cruel wretches are we to our friends, that will rather suffer them to go quietly to hell, then we will anger them, or hazard our reputation with them." *Richard Baxter*

35:10 Jesus gave Himself as a ransom for us (see 1 Tim. 2:6). If He could endure the cross for the joy that was before Him (see Heb. 12:2), we can endure the reproach of this world for that which is in store for us.

man leans, it will go into his hand and pierce it. So *is* Pharaoh king of Egypt to all who trust in him.
[7]"But if you say to me, 'We trust in the LORD our God,' *is it* not He whose high places and whose altars Hezekiah has taken away, and said to Judah and Jerusalem, 'You shall worship before this altar'?" ' [8]Now therefore, I urge you, give a pledge to my master the king of Assyria, and I will give you two thousand horses —if you are able on your part to put riders on them! [9]How then will you repel one captain of the least of my master's servants, and put your trust in Egypt for chariots and horsemen? [10]Have I now come up without the LORD against this land to destroy it? The LORD said to me, 'Go up against this land, and destroy it.' "

> The end of life is not to be happy. The end of life is not to achieve pleasure and avoid pain. The end of life is to do the will of God, come what may.
>
> **DR. MARTIN LUTHER KING, JR.**

[11]Then Eliakim, Shebna, and Joah said to *the* Rabshakeh, "Please speak to your servants in Aramaic, for we understand *it;* and do not speak to us in Hebrew[a] in the hearing of the people who *are* on the wall."
[12]But *the* Rabshakeh said, "Has my master sent me to your master and to you to speak these words, and not to the men who sit on the wall, who will eat and drink their own waste with you?"
[13]Then *the* Rabshakeh stood and called out with a loud voice in Hebrew, and said, "Hear the words of the great king, the king of Assyria! [14]Thus says the king: 'Do not let Hezekiah deceive you, for he will not be able to deliver you; [15]nor let Hezekiah make you trust in the LORD, saying, "The LORD will surely deliver us; this city will not be given into the hand of the king of Assyria." ' [16]Do not listen to Hezekiah; for thus says the king of Assyria: 'Make *peace* with me *by a* present and come out to me; and every one of you eat from his own vine and every one from his own fig tree, and every one of you drink the waters of his own cistern; [17]until I come and take you away to a land like your own land, a land of grain and new wine, a land of bread and vineyards. [18]*Beware* lest Hezekiah persuade you, saying, "The LORD will deliver us." Has any one of the gods of the nations delivered its land from the hand of the king of Assyria? [19]Where *are* the gods of Hamath and Arpad? Where *are* the gods of Sepharvaim? Indeed, have they delivered Samaria from my hand? [20]Who among all the gods of these lands have delivered their countries from my hand, that the LORD should deliver Jerusalem from my hand?' "
[21]But they held their peace and answered him not a word; for the king's commandment was, "Do not answer him."
[22]Then Eliakim the son of Hilkiah, who *was* over the household, Shebna the scribe, and Joah the son of Asaph, the recorder, came to Hezekiah with *their* clothes torn, and told him the words of *the* Rabshakeh.

Isaiah Assures Deliverance

37 And so it was, when King Hezekiah heard *it,* that he tore his clothes, covered himself with sackcloth, and went into the house of the LORD. [2]Then he sent Eliakim, who *was* over the household, Shebna the scribe, and the elders of the priests, covered with sack-

36:11 [a]Literally *Judean*

36:18 Beware of the subtlety of the enemy. He will whisper that God has forsaken you the first time things go seriously wrong for you. God is not a man that He should lie. Trust Him no matter what trials come your way. Believe the promises of God, and doubt the lies of the devil with all of your heart, soul, mind, and strength.

cloth, to Isaiah the prophet, the son of Amoz. [3]And they said to him, "Thus says Hezekiah: 'This day *is* a day of trouble and rebuke and blasphemy; for the children have come to birth, but *there is* no strength to bring them forth. [4]It may be that the LORD your God will hear the words of *the* Rabshakeh, whom his master the king of Assyria has sent to reproach the living God, and will rebuke the words which the LORD your God has heard. Therefore lift up *your* prayer for the remnant that is left.' "

[5]So the servants of King Hezekiah came to Isaiah. [6]And Isaiah said to them, "Thus you shall say to your master, 'Thus says the LORD: "Do not be afraid of the words which you have heard, with which the servants of the king of Assyria have blasphemed Me. [7]Surely I will send a spirit upon him, and he shall hear a rumor and return to his own land; and I will cause him to fall by the sword in his own land." ' "

Sennacherib's Threat and Hezekiah's Prayer

[8]Then *the* Rabshakeh returned, and found the king of Assyria warring against Libnah, for he heard that he had departed from Lachish. [9]And the king heard concerning Tirhakah king of Ethiopia, "He has come out to make war with you." So when he heard *it,* he sent messengers to Hezekiah, saying, [10]"Thus you shall speak to Hezekiah king of Judah, saying: 'Do not let your God in whom you trust deceive you, saying, "Jerusalem shall not be given into the hand of the king of Assyria." [11]Look! You have heard what the kings of Assyria have done to all lands by utterly destroying them; and shall you be delivered? [12]Have the gods of the nations delivered those whom my fathers have destroyed, Gozan and Haran and Rezeph, and the people of Eden who *were* in Telassar? [13]Where *is* the king of Hamath, the king of Arpad, and the king of the city of Sepharvaim, Hena, and Ivah?' "

[14]And Hezekiah received the letter from the hand of the messengers, and read it; and Hezekiah went up to the house of the LORD, and spread it before the LORD. [15]Then Hezekiah prayed to the LORD, saying: [16]"O LORD of hosts, God of Israel, *the One* who dwells *between* the cherubim, You *are* God, You alone, of all the kingdoms of the earth. You have made heaven and earth. [17]Incline Your ear, O LORD, and hear; open Your eyes, O LORD, and see; and hear all the words of Sennacherib, which he has sent to reproach the living God. [18]Truly, LORD, the kings of Assyria have laid waste all the nations and their lands, [19]and have cast their gods into the fire; for they *were* not gods, but the work of men's hands—wood and stone. Therefore they destroyed them. [20]Now therefore, O LORD our God, save us from his hand, that all the kingdoms of the earth may know that You *are* the LORD, You alone."

The Word of the Lord Concerning Sennacherib

[21]Then Isaiah the son of Amoz sent to Hezekiah, saying, "Thus says the LORD God of Israel, 'Because you have prayed to Me against Sennacherib king of Assyria, [22]this *is* the word which the LORD has spoken concerning him:

"The virgin, the daughter of Zion,
Has despised you, laughed you to scorn;
The daughter of Jerusalem

37:7 The heart of the king is in the hand of the Lord. He turns it any way He wishes to accomplish His ends.

37:16 This is similar to the prayer the disciples prayed when they suffered persecution (see Acts 4:24–31). Begin your prayer by looking to the greatness of God, not the greatness of your problem, and ask that God will be glorified (see v. 20). For encouragement, see page 1198.

Has shaken *her* head behind your back!

23"Whom have you reproached and blasphemed?
Against whom have you raised *your* voice,
And lifted up your eyes on high?
Against the Holy One of Israel.
24By your servants you have reproached the Lord,
And said, 'By the multitude of my chariots
I have come up to the height of the mountains,
To the limits of Lebanon;
I will cut down its tall cedars
And its choice cypress trees;
I will enter its farthest height,
To its fruitful forest.
25I have dug and drunk water,
And with the soles of my feet I have dried up
All the brooks of defense.'

26"Did you not hear long ago
How I made it,
From ancient times that I formed it?
Now I have brought it to pass,
That you should be
For crushing fortified cities *into* heaps of ruins.
27Therefore their inhabitants *had* little power;
They were dismayed and confounded;
They were *as* the grass of the field
And the green herb,
As the grass on the housetops
And grain blighted before it is grown.

28"But I know your dwelling place,
Your going out and your coming in,
And your rage against Me.
29Because your rage against Me and your tumult
Have come up to My ears,
Therefore I will put My hook in your nose
And My bridle in your lips,
And I will turn you back
By the way which you came." '

30"This *shall be* a sign to you:

You shall eat this year such as grows of itself,
And the second year what springs from the same;
Also in the third year sow and reap,
Plant vineyards and eat the fruit of them.
31And the remnant who have escaped of the house of Judah
Shall again take root downward,
And bear fruit upward.
32For out of Jerusalem shall go a remnant,
And those who escape from Mount Zion.
The zeal of the LORD of hosts will do this.

33"Therefore thus says the LORD concerning the king of Assyria:

'He shall not come into this city,
Nor shoot an arrow there,
Nor come before it with shield,
Nor build a siege mound against it.
34By the way that he came,
By the same shall he return;
And he shall not come into this city,'
Says the LORD.
35'For I will defend this city, to save it
For My own sake and for My servant David's sake.' "

Sennacherib's Defeat and Death

36Then the angel[a] of the LORD went
out, and killed in the camp of the Assyr-

37:36 [a]Or *Angel*

37:36 This should put the fear of God into the hearts of this godless world. God at any time could send death to all of humanity, and do that which is right and just. Thank God for His mercy.

QUESTIONS & OBJECTIONS

Q 38:10

"What happens when you die?"

By Dr. David R. Reagan

Some of the greatest confusion about life after death relates to the intermediate state between death and eternity. Some people advocate a concept called "soul sleep." They argue that both the saved and unsaved are unconscious after death until the return of Jesus.

But the Bible makes it crystal clear that our spirit does not lose its consciousness at death. The only thing that "falls asleep" is our body—in a symbolic sense. Paul says in 2 Cor. 5:8 that he would prefer to be "absent from the body and at home with the Lord." In Phil. 1:21 he observes, "For me to live is Christ and to die is gain." He then adds in v. 23 that his desire is "to depart and be with Christ." Paul certainly did not expect to be in a coma after he died!

If then our spirits retain their consciousness after death, where do they go? The Bible teaches that prior to the resurrection of Jesus, the spirits of the dead went to a place called Hades ("Sheol" in the Old Testament). The spirits existed there consciously in one of two compartments, either Paradise or Torments. This concept is pictured graphically in Jesus' story of the rich man and Lazarus (Luke 16:19–31).

The Bible indicates that after the death of Jesus on the cross, He descended into Hades and declared to all the spirits there His triumph over Satan (1 Pet. 3:18,19; 4:6). The Bible also indicates that after His resurrection, when He ascended into Heaven, Jesus took Paradise with Him, transferring the spirits of dead saints from Hades to Heaven (Eph. 4:8,9; 2 Cor. 12:1–4). The spirits of dead saints are thereafter pictured as being in Heaven before the throne of God (see Rev. 6:9; 7:9).

The spirits of the righteous dead could not go directly to Heaven before the cross because their sins were not forgiven. Instead, their sins were merely covered by their faith. The forgiveness of their sins had to await the shedding of the blood of Christ (Lev. 17:11; Rom. 5:8,9; Heb. 9:22).

ians one hundred and eighty-five thousand; and when *people* arose early in the
morning, there were the corpses—all
dead. 37So Sennacherib king of Assyria
departed and went away, returned *home,*
and remained at Nineveh. 38Now it came
to pass, as he was worshiping in the
house of Nisroch his god, that his sons
Adrammelech and Sharezer struck him
down with the sword; and they escaped
into the land of Ararat. Then Esarhaddon
his son reigned in his place.

Hezekiah's Life Extended

38 In those days Hezekiah was sick
and near death. And Isaiah the
prophet, the son of Amoz, went to him
and said to him, "Thus says the LORD: 'Set
your house in order, for you shall die and
not live.' "

2Then Hezekiah turned his face toward
the wall, and prayed to the LORD, 3and
said, "Remember now, O LORD, I pray, how
I have walked before You in truth and
with a loyal heart, and have done *what is*
good in Your sight." And Hezekiah wept
bitterly.

4And the word of the LORD came to
Isaiah, saying, 5"Go and tell Hezekiah,
'Thus says the LORD, the God of David
your father: "I have heard your prayer, I
have seen your tears; surely I will add to
your days fifteen years. 6I will deliver you
and this city from the hand of the king of
Assyria, and I will defend this city." ' 7And
this *is* the sign to you from the LORD, that
the LORD will do this thing which He has
spoken: 8Behold, I will bring the shadow
on the sundial, which has gone down
with the sun on the sundial of Ahaz, ten
degrees backward." So the sun returned
ten degrees on the dial by which it had
gone down.

9This is the writing of Hezekiah king
of Judah, when he had been sick and had
recovered from his sickness:

10I said,
"In the prime of my life
I shall go to the gates of Sheol;

I am deprived of the remainder of my
years."
[11]I said,
"I shall not see YAH,
The LORD[a] in the land of the living;
I shall observe man no more among
the inhabitants of the world.[b]
[12]My life span is gone,
Taken from me like a shepherd's tent;
I have cut off my life like a weaver.
He cuts me off from the loom;
From day until night You make an
end of me.
[13]I have considered until morning—
Like a lion,
So He breaks all my bones;
From day until night You make an
end of me.
[14]Like a crane *or* a swallow, so I
chattered;
I mourned like a dove;
My eyes fail *from looking* upward.
O LORD,[a] I am oppressed;
Undertake for me!

[15]"What shall I say?
He has both spoken to me,[a]
And He Himself has done *it*.
I shall walk carefully all my years
In the bitterness of my soul.
[16]O Lord, by these *things men* live;
And in all these *things is* the life of my
spirit;
So You will restore me and make me
live.
[17]Indeed *it was* for *my own* peace
That I had great bitterness;
But You have lovingly *delivered* my
soul from the pit of corruption,
For You have cast all my sins behind
Your back.
[18]For Sheol cannot thank You,
Death cannot praise You;
Those who go down to the pit cannot
hope for Your truth.
[19]The living, the living man, he shall
praise You,
As I *do* this day;
The father shall make known Your
truth to the children.

[20]"The LORD *was ready* to save me;
Therefore we will sing my songs with
stringed instruments
All the days of our life, in the house
of the LORD."

[21]Now Isaiah had said, "Let them take
a lump of figs, and apply *it* as a poultice
on the boil, and he shall recover."
[22]And Hezekiah had said, "What *is* the
sign that I shall go up to the house of the
LORD?"

The Babylonian Envoys

39 At that time Merodach-Baladan[a]
the son of Baladan, king of Babylon, sent letters and a present to Hezekiah, for he heard that he had been sick
and had recovered. [2]And Hezekiah was
pleased with them, and showed them the
house of his treasures—the silver and
gold, the spices and precious ointment,
and all his armory—all that was found
among his treasures. There was nothing
in his house or in all his dominion that
Hezekiah did not show them.

38:11 [a]Hebrew *YAH, YAH* [b]Following some Hebrew manuscripts; Masoretic Text and Vulgate read *rest;* Septuagint omits *among the inhabitants of the world;* Targum reads *land.* 38:14 [a]Following Bomberg; Masoretic Text and Dead Sea Scrolls read *Lord.* 38:15 [a]Following Masoretic Text and Vulgate; Dead Sea Scrolls and Targum read *And shall I say to Him;* Septuagint omits first half of this verse. 39:1 [a]Spelled *Berodach-Baladan* in 2 Kings 20:12

38:17–19 Gratitude is a burning fire that is sparked from the cross of Calvary. Use that combustion to motivate you to reach the lost while there is still time—starting with your family. To learn how to bring your children to Christ, see Deut. 11:19 comment.

"Let us be in earnest about the salvation of our children and friends. Warn that young lady. Yes, Mother, speak to that daughter. Father, speak to that child. Wife, speak to your unconverted husband. Husband, speak to your unconverted wife. Do not let anyone say, 'Nobody cares for my soul.' I never saw parents burdened for their children but that the children soon became anxious to be saved." *D. L. Moody*

[3]Then Isaiah the prophet went to King
Hezekiah, and said to him, "What did
these men say, and from where did they
come to you?"

So Hezekiah said, "They came to me
from a far country, from Babylon."

[4]And he said, "What have they seen in
your house?"

So Hezekiah answered, "They have seen
all that *is* in my house; there is nothing
among my treasures that I have not shown
them."

[5]Then Isaiah said to Hezekiah, "Hear
the word of the LORD of hosts: [6]'Behold,
the days are coming when all that *is* in
your house, and what your fathers have
accumulated until this day, shall be carried to Babylon; nothing shall be left,'
says the LORD. [7]'And they shall take away
some of your sons who will descend from
you, whom you will beget; and they shall
be eunuchs in the palace of the king of
Babylon.' "

[8]So Hezekiah said to Isaiah, "The word
of the LORD which you have spoken *is*
good!" For he said, "At least there will be
peace and truth in my days."

God's People Are Comforted

40 "Comfort, yes, comfort My people!"
Says your God.
[2]"Speak comfort to Jerusalem, and cry out to her,
That her warfare is ended,
That her iniquity is pardoned;
For she has received from the LORD's hand
Double for all her sins."

[3]The voice of one crying in the wilderness:
"Prepare the way of the LORD;
Make straight in the desert[a]
A highway for our God.
[4]Every valley shall be exalted
And every mountain and hill brought low;
The crooked places shall be made straight
And the rough places smooth;
[5]The glory of the LORD shall be revealed,
And all flesh shall see *it* together;
For the mouth of the LORD has spoken."

[6]The voice said, "Cry out!"
And he[a] said, "What shall I cry?"

"All flesh *is* grass,
And all its loveliness *is* like the flower of the field.
[7]The grass withers, the flower fades,
Because the breath of the LORD blows upon it;
Surely the people *are* grass.
[8]The grass withers, the flower fades,
But the word of our God stands forever."

40:3 [a]Following Masoretic Text, Targum, and Vulgate; Septuagint omits *in the desert*. 40:6 [a]Following Masoretic Text and Targum; Dead Sea Scrolls, Septuagint, and Vulgate read *I*.

39:5–8 We must have a humble and even joyful acceptance of what God has in store for us in this life. Whether it seems good or bad, He will work it to our eternal benefit. See Rom. 8:28 for the "safety net" promise.

40:3 We too are called to be a voice in the wilderness, crying out to this world to make a place in their lives for the Lord. This prophecy of John the Baptist was fulfilled in Mark 1:2,3. See Mark 1:4 for the essence of John the Baptist's (and our) message.

40:6–8 The Christian message to this world is that all its pleasures are but for a season. This life is a vapor; it is vanity. There is only One who is eternal, the Word of God, and He will grant eternal life to all who trust in Him. (For the uniqueness of the Bible, see Psa. 119:105 comment.)

"For had they but their thoughts well exercised about the shortness of this life, and the danger that will befall such as do miss of the Lord Jesus Christ, it would make them more wary and sober, and spend more time in the service of God, and be more delighted and diligent in inquiring after the Lord Jesus, who is the deliverer 'from the wrath to come.'" *John Bunyan*

[9]O Zion,
You who bring good tidings,
Get up into the high mountain;
O Jerusalem,
You who bring good tidings,
Lift up your voice with strength,
Lift *it* up, be not afraid;
Say to the cities of Judah, "Behold
your God!"

[10]Behold, the Lord GOD shall come
with a strong *hand,*
And His arm shall rule for Him;
Behold, His reward *is* with Him,
And His work before Him.
[11]He will feed His flock like a shepherd;
He will gather the lambs with His arm,
And carry *them* in His bosom,
And gently lead those who are with
young.

[12]Who has measured the waters[a] in the
hollow of His hand,
Measured heaven with a span
And calculated the dust of the earth
in a measure?
Weighed the mountains in scales
And the hills in a balance?
[13]Who has directed the Spirit of the
LORD,
Or *as* His counselor has taught Him?
[14]With whom did He take counsel, and
who instructed Him,
And taught Him in the path of justice?
Who taught Him knowledge,
And showed Him the way of
understanding?

[15]Behold, the nations *are* as a drop in a
bucket,
And are counted as the small dust on
the scales;
Look, He lifts up the isles as a very
little thing.
[16]And Lebanon *is* not sufficient to burn,
Nor its beasts sufficient for a burnt
offering.
[17]All nations before Him *are* as nothing,
And they are counted by Him less
than nothing and worthless.

[18]To whom then will you liken God?
Or what likeness will you compare to
Him?
[19]The workman molds an image,
The goldsmith overspreads it with
gold,
And the silversmith casts silver chains.
[20]Whoever *is* too impoverished for *such*
a contribution
Chooses a tree *that* will not rot;
He seeks for himself a skillful workman
To prepare a carved image *that* will
not totter.

[21]Have you not known?
Have you not heard?
Has it not been told you from the
beginning?
Have you not understood from the
foundations of the earth?
[22]*It is* He who sits above the circle of
the earth,
And its inhabitants *are* like
grasshoppers,

40:12 [a]Following Masoretic Text, Septuagint, and Vulgate; Dead Sea Scrolls read *waters of the sea;* Targum reads *waters of the world.*

40:9 Lift up your voice like a trumpet and preach the everlasting gospel. Never be afraid to speak for your God. Do not in any way be afraid of your adversaries (see Phil. 1:27,28).

40:12 "Why are we afraid to declare that people in our churches must come to know God Himself? Why do we not tell them that they must get beyond the point of making God a lifeboat for their rescue or a ladder to get them out of a burning building? How can we help our people get over the idea that God exists just to help run their businesses or fly their airplanes?

"God is not a railway porter who carries your suitcase and serves you. God is God. He made heaven and earth. He holds the world in His hand. He measures the dust of the earth in the balance. He spreads the sky out like a mantle. He is the great God Almighty. He is not your servant." *A. W. Tozer*

40:19–21 The preceding verses add to the absolute folly of idolatry.

QUESTIONS & OBJECTIONS

40:28

"Can a Christian believe in evolution?"

A Christian can believe in fairies, if he wishes. While I wouldn't question the salvation of one who did, I may question his spiritual maturity. This is because Christianity doesn't come from what you believe (although that is part of the equation); it comes from Who you know.

Let me explain. The Bible teaches that Jesus Christ was preexistent before He was manifest in human form. He claimed to be the source of life, saying things like "I am the life" (see John 1:4; 11:25; 14:6). When someone repents and believes the gospel (that Jesus Christ died for his sin and rose on the third day), he places his trust in the Savior and comes to "know" God. Then God "seals" the believer with the Holy Spirit. Jesus Christ "who is our life" dwells within the believer (see John 14:16–18). The Scriptures speak of "Christ in you" (see Col. 1:27). Jesus said that He would actually dwell within the Christian through the Holy Spirit (see John 14:16–21; Rom. 8:9–11; Gal. 2:20).

The bottom line is that if you have Jesus Christ, you have life, irrespective of your denomination. God knows those who love Him. If you don't have Jesus Christ (through the new birth of John 3:3), you don't have life. You are still dead in your sins and justly under the condemnation of God (see John 3:17,18). Here are the pivotal verses: "He who has the Son has life; he who does not have the Son of God does not have life. These things I have written to you who believe in the name of the Son of God, that you may know that you have eternal life" (1 John 5:12,13).

If you have the Son of God, then the Holy Spirit will lead you into all truth (see John 16:13). Your theology in time will become "sound," and you will align your beliefs with the truths revealed in Holy Scripture, because it is God's revelation to mankind. If the Bible says there was a literal flood (Jesus did also), the Christian cannot believe otherwise. If the Bible says that the creation took place in six literal, 24-hour days, regardless of what fallible scientists say, the Christian quickly sides with the Bible.

In the case of evolution, Scripture is very clear that God made man in His image, morally cognizant, and not as a primate. He made humans and all the animal kingdom as male and female, and He gave each the ability to reproduce "after their own kind," not to evolve over time into other "kinds" of animals. We see the truth of all of the above both in the fossil record and in the creation that surrounds us. To believe in a theory that says otherwise is to call God a liar. To understand the fallacy of the theory of evolution, see Isa. 45:18 comment.

Who stretches out the heavens like a
  curtain,
And spreads them out like a tent to
  dwell in.
23He brings the princes to nothing;
He makes the judges of the earth
  useless.

24Scarcely shall they be planted,
Scarcely shall they be sown,
Scarcely shall their stock take root in
  the earth,
When He will also blow on them,
And they will wither,
And the whirlwind will take them
  away like stubble.

25"To whom then will you liken Me,
Or *to whom* shall I be equal?" says the
  Holy One.
26Lift up your eyes on high,
And see who has created these *things*,
Who brings out their host by number;
He calls them all by name,
By the greatness of His might
And the strength of *His* power;
Not one is missing.

27Why do you say, O Jacob,
And speak, O Israel:
"My way is hidden from the LORD,
And my just claim is passed over by
  my God"?
28Have you not known?
Have you not heard?
The everlasting God, the LORD,

40:22 The Bible does not teach that the earth is flat, but is a sphere. See Heb. 11:3 comment.

The Creator of the ends of the earth,
Neither faints nor is weary.
His understanding is unsearchable.
29He gives power to the weak,
And to *those who have* no might He
increases strength.
30Even the youths shall faint and be
weary,
And the young men shall utterly fall,
31But those who wait on the LORD
Shall renew *their* strength;
They shall mount up with wings like
eagles,
They shall run and not be weary,
They shall walk and not faint.

Israel Assured of God's Help

41 "Keep silence before Me, O coastlands,
And let the people renew *their* strength!
Let them come near, then let them
speak;
Let us come near together for
judgment.

2"Who raised up one from the east?
Who in righteousness called him to
His feet?
Who gave the nations before him,
And made *him* rule over kings?
Who gave *them* as the dust *to* his
sword,
As driven stubble to his bow?
3Who pursued them, *and* passed
safely
By the way *that* he had not gone with
his feet?
4Who has performed and done *it,*
Calling the generations from the
beginning?
'I, the LORD, am the first;
And with the last I *am* He.'"

5The coastlands saw *it* and feared,
The ends of the earth were afraid;
They drew near and came.
6Everyone helped his neighbor,
And said to his brother,
"Be of good courage!"
7So the craftsman encouraged the
goldsmith;
He who smooths *with* the hammer
inspired him who strikes the anvil,
Saying, "It *is* ready for the soldering";
Then he fastened it with pegs,
That it might not totter.

8"But you, Israel, *are* My servant,
Jacob whom I have chosen,
The descendants of Abraham My
friend.
9*You* whom I have taken from the ends
of the earth,
And called from its farthest regions,
And said to you,
'You *are* My servant,
I have chosen you and have not cast
you away:
10Fear not, for I *am* with you;
Be not dismayed, for I *am* your God.
I will strengthen you,
Yes, I will help you,
I will uphold you with My righteous
right hand.'

11"Behold, all those who were incensed
against you
Shall be ashamed and disgraced;
They shall be as nothing,
And those who strive with you shall
perish.
12You shall seek them and not find
them—
Those who contended with you.
Those who war against you

40:29–31 Here is a promise for the Christian who becomes weary in his labor, but not weary of it. See 2 Cor. 12:9,10 for God's promise to you.

41:8 "A rule I have had for years is: to treat the Lord Jesus Christ as a personal friend. His is not a creed, a mere doctrine, but it is He Himself we have." *Dwight L. Moody*

41:10 When we are fearful to preach or to witness, we must stand firmly upon this wonderful promise. We must not fear. God is with us; He will strengthen, help, and uphold us. See Acts 18:9,10 for how God encouraged Paul.

Shall be as nothing,
As a nonexistent thing.
13For I, the LORD your God, will hold your right hand,
Saying to you, 'Fear not, I will help you.'

14"Fear not, you worm Jacob,
You men of Israel!
I will help you," says the LORD
And your Redeemer, the Holy One of Israel.
15"Behold, I will make you into a new threshing sledge with sharp teeth;
You shall thresh the mountains and beat *them* small,
And make the hills like chaff.
16You shall winnow them, the wind shall carry them away,
And the whirlwind shall scatter them;
You shall rejoice in the LORD,
And glory in the Holy One of Israel.

17"The poor and needy seek water, but *there is* none,
Their tongues fail for thirst.
I, the LORD, will hear them;
I, the God of Israel, will not forsake them.
18I will open rivers in desolate heights,
And fountains in the midst of the valleys;
I will make the wilderness a pool of water,
And the dry land springs of water.
19I will plant in the wilderness the cedar and the acacia tree,
The myrtle and the oil tree;
I will set in the desert the cypress tree *and* the pine
And the box tree together,
20That they may see and know,
And consider and understand together,
That the hand of the LORD has done this,
And the Holy One of Israel has created it.

The Futility of Idols

21"Present your case," says the LORD.
"Bring forth your strong *reasons,*" says the King of Jacob.
22"Let them bring forth and show us what will happen;
Let them show the former things, what they *were,*
That we may consider them,
And know the latter end of them;
Or declare to us things to come.
23Show the things that are to come hereafter,
That we may know that you *are* gods;
Yes, do good or do evil,
That we may be dismayed and see *it* together.
24Indeed you *are* nothing,
And your work *is* nothing;
He who chooses you *is* an abomination.

25"I have raised up one from the north,
And he shall come;
From the rising of the sun he shall call on My name;
And he shall come against princes as *though* mortar,
As the potter treads clay.
26Who has declared from the beginning, that we may know?
And former times, that we may say, '*He is* righteous'?
Surely *there is* no one who shows,
Surely *there is* no one who declares,
Surely *there is* no one who hears your words.

41:20–23 Christianity is not a blind faith, as the lost assume. God has given us more than sufficient evidence so we can "see and know, and consider and understand" that our mighty God exists. He repeatedly states that prophecies prove that He alone is God—only a true God knows what happened at the beginning and can tell what is to come (see v. 6; 45:21; 46:9,10; 48:3–5). When challenged to prove that the Bible is the inspired Word of God, don't hesitate to point to its thousands of fulfilled prophecies as proof. That is why they were given. See also 46:9,10 comment.

[27]The first time *I said* to Zion,
'Look, there they are!'
And I will give to Jerusalem one who brings good tidings.
[28]For I looked, and *there was* no man;
I looked among them, but *there was* no counselor,
Who, when I asked of them, could answer a word.
[29]Indeed they *are* all worthless;[a]
Their works *are* nothing;
Their molded images *are* wind and confusion.

The Servant of the Lord

42 "Behold! My Servant whom I uphold,
My Elect One *in whom* My soul delights!
I have put My Spirit upon Him;
He will bring forth justice to the Gentiles.
[2]He will not cry out, nor raise *His voice,*
Nor cause His voice to be heard in the street.
[3]A bruised reed He will not break,
And smoking flax He will not quench;
He will bring forth justice for truth.
[4]He will not fail nor be discouraged,
Till He has established justice in the earth;
And the coastlands shall wait for His law."

[5]Thus says God the LORD,
Who created the heavens and stretched them out,
Who spread forth the earth and that which comes from it,
Who gives breath to the people on it,
And spirit to those who walk on it:
[6]"I, the LORD, have called You in righteousness,
And will hold Your hand;
I will keep You and give You as a covenant to the people,
As a light to the Gentiles,
[7]To open blind eyes,
To bring out prisoners from the prison,
Those who sit in darkness from the prison house.
[8]I *am* the LORD, that *is* My name;
And My glory I will not give to another,
Nor My praise to carved images.
[9]Behold, the former things have come to pass,
And new things I declare;
Before they spring forth I tell you of them."

Praise to the Lord

[10]Sing to the LORD a new song,
And His praise from the ends of the earth,
You who go down to the sea, and all that is in it,
You coastlands and you inhabitants of them!
[11]Let the wilderness and its cities lift up *their voice,*
The villages *that* Kedar inhabits.
Let the inhabitants of Sela sing,
Let them shout from the top of the mountains.
[12]Let them give glory to the LORD,
And declare His praise in the coastlands.
[13]The LORD shall go forth like a mighty man;
He shall stir up *His* zeal like a man of war.
He shall cry out, yes, shout aloud;
He shall prevail against His enemies.

Promise of the Lord's Help

[14]"I have held My peace a long time,
I have been still and restrained Myself.
Now I will cry like a woman in labor,
I will pant and gasp at once.
[15]I will lay waste the mountains and hills,

41:29 [a]Following Masoretic Text and Vulgate; Dead Sea Scrolls, Syriac, and Targum read *nothing;* Septuagint omits the first line.

42:1–4 This messianic prophecy was fulfilled in Matt. 12:17–21.

42:5 *The DNA Code*

Consider for a moment whether you could ever believe this publication happened by accident. Here's the argument: There was nothing. Then paper appeared, and ink fell from nowhere onto the sheets and shaped itself into perfectly formed letters. Initially, the letters said something like this: "fgsn&k cn1clxc dumh cckvkduh vstupidm ncnx." As you can see, random letters rarely produce words that make sense. But in time, mindless chance formed them into the order of meaningful words separated by spaces. The sentences then grouped themselves to relate to each other, giving them coherence. Punctuation marks, paragraphs, margins, etc., also came into being in the correct placements. Page numbers fell in sequence at the right places, and headers, footers, and footnotes appeared from nowhere on the pages, matching the portions of text to which they related. The paper trimmed itself and bound itself into a book. The ink for the cover fell from different directions, being careful not to incorrectly mingle with the other colors, forming itself into the graphics and title. There are multiple copies of this publication, so it then developed the ability to replicate itself thousands of times over.

With this thought in mind, notice that in the following description, DNA is likened to a book:

> If you think of your genome (all of your chromosomes) as the book that makes you, then the genes are the words that make up the story...The letters that make up the words are called DNA bases, and there are only four of them: adenine (A), guanine (G), cytosine (C), and thymine (T). It's hard to believe that an alphabet with only four letters can make something as wonderful and complex as a person!

To liken DNA to a book is a gross understatement. The amount of information in the 3 billion base pairs in the DNA in every human cell is equivalent to that in 1,000 books of encyclopedia size. It would take a person typing 60 words per minute, eight hours a day, around 50 years to type the human genome. And if all the DNA in your body's 100 trillion cells was put end to end, it would reach to the sun (90 million miles away) and back over 600 times.

Aside from the immense volume of information that your DNA contains, consider whether all the intricate, interrelated parts of this "book" could have come together by sheer chance.

Physical chemist Charles Thaxton writes:

> The DNA code is quite simple in its basic structure (although enormously complex in its functioning). By now most people are familiar with the double helix structure of the DNA molecule. It is like a long ladder, twisted into a spiral. Sugar and phosphate molecules form the sides of the ladder. Four bases make up its "rungs." These are adenine, thymine, guanine, and cytosine. These bases act as the "letters" of a genetic alphabet. They combine in various sequences to form words, sentences, and paragraphs. These base sequences are all the instructions needed to guide the functioning of the cell.
>
> The DNA code is a genetic "language" that communicates information to the cell ...The DNA molecule is exquisitely complex, and extremely precise: the "letters" must be in a very exact sequence. If they are out of order, it is like a typing error in a message. The instructions that it gives the cell are garbled. This is what a mutation is.
>
> The discovery of the DNA code gives the argument from design a new twist. Since life is at its core a chemical code, the origin of life is the origin of a code. A code is a very special kind of order. It represents "specified complexity."

Could DNA's amazing structure have come together by accident? Or does it point to an intelligent Designer? Even the director of the U.S. National Human Genome Research Institute concluded there is a God based on his study of DNA. Francis Collins, the scientist who led the team that cracked the human genome, believes there is a rational basis for a Creator and that scientific discoveries bring man "closer to God":

> When you have for the first time in front of you this 3.1-billion-letter instruction book that conveys all kinds of information and all kinds of mystery about humankind, you can't survey that going through page after page without a sense of awe. I can't help but look at those pages and have a vague sense that this is giving me a glimpse of God's mind.

See also Job 17:14 comment. (Adapted from *How to Know God Exists.*)

And dry up all their vegetation;
I will make the rivers coastlands,
And I will dry up the pools.

16 I will bring the blind by a way they
did not know;
I will lead them in paths they have

not known.
I will make darkness light before them,
And crooked places straight.
These things I will do for them,
And not forsake them.
17 They shall be turned back,
They shall be greatly ashamed,
Who trust in carved images,
Who say to the molded images,
'You *are* our gods.'

18 "Hear, you deaf;
And look, you blind, that you may see.
19 Who *is* blind but My servant,
Or deaf as My messenger *whom* I send?
Who *is* blind as *he who is* perfect,
And blind as the LORD's servant?
20 Seeing many things, but you do not
observe;
Opening the ears, but he does not
hear."

Israel's Obstinate Disobedience

21 The LORD is well pleased for His
righteousness' sake;
He will exalt the law and make *it*
honorable.
22 But this *is* a people robbed and
plundered;
All of them are snared in holes,
And they are hidden in prison houses;
They are for prey, and no one delivers;
For plunder, and no one says,
"Restore!"

23 Who among you will give ear to this?
Who will listen and hear for the time
to come?
24 Who gave Jacob for plunder, and
Israel to the robbers?
Was it not the LORD,
He against whom we have sinned?
For they would not walk in His ways,
Nor were they obedient to His law.
25 Therefore He has poured on him the
fury of His anger
And the strength of battle;
It has set him on fire all around,
Yet he did not know;
And it burned him,
Yet he did not take *it* to heart.

The Function of the Law

42:24 The lost do not consider that they are disobedient and have sinned against a holy God innumerable times. By judging themselves against man's standards, they come up reasonably clean. Adolf Hitler's life, for instance, makes most of us look almost pure.

However, when we use the Law of God as our measure, we see that we are not as clean as we like to think. We need to apply the spiritual nature of God's Law to the conscience of sinners so they can see that their own righteousnesses are as filthy rags in the sight of a holy God (see 64:6).

"God never clothes men until He has first stripped them, nor does He quicken them by the gospel till first they are slain by the Law. When you meet with persons in whom there is no trace of conviction of sin, you may be quite sure that they have not been wrought upon by the Holy Spirit; for 'when He is come, He will reprove the world of sin, and of righteousness, and of judgment.'" *Charles Spurgeon*

The Redeemer of Israel

43 But now, thus says the LORD, who
created you, O Jacob,
And He who formed you, O Israel:
"Fear not, for I have redeemed you;
I have called *you* by your name;
You *are* Mine.

42:21 Jesus magnified the Law and made it honorable in His Sermon on the Mount (Matt. 5—7). For details, see comments at Matt. 5:1; 5:48; Mark 7:5–13.

43:1,2 How incredibly kind of God to redeem us with the precious blood of Christ and to call us *His*. However, believers are not promised a problem-free life. Trials and tribulations, floods and flames can happen to all of us in this life, but as Christians we have God with us in the midst of them.

"Reckon then that to acquire soul-winning power, you will have to go through mental torment and soul distress. You must go into the fire if you are going to pull others out of it, and you will have to dive into the floods if you are going to draw others out of the water. You cannot work a fire escape without feeling the scorch of the conflagration, nor man a lifeboat without being covered with the waves." *Charles Spurgeon*

[2]When you pass through the waters, I
will be with you;
And through the rivers, they shall not
overflow you.
When you walk through the fire, you
shall not be burned,
Nor shall the flame scorch you.
[3]For I *am* the LORD your God,
The Holy One of Israel, your Savior;
I gave Egypt for your ransom,
Ethiopia and Seba in your place.
[4]Since you were precious in My sight,
You have been honored,
And I have loved you;
Therefore I will give men for you,
And people for your life.
[5]Fear not, for I *am* with you;
I will bring your descendants from
the east,
And gather you from the west;
[6]I will say to the north, 'Give them up!'
And to the south, 'Do not keep them
back!'
Bring My sons from afar,
And My daughters from the ends of
the earth—
[7]Everyone who is called by My name,
Whom I have created for My glory;
I have formed him, yes, I have made
him."

[8]Bring out the blind people who have
eyes,
And the deaf who have ears.
[9]Let all the nations be gathered
together,
And let the people be assembled.
Who among them can declare this,
And show us former things?
Let them bring out their witnesses,
that they may be justified;
Or let them hear and say, "*It is* truth."
[10]"You *are* My witnesses," says the LORD,
"And My servant whom I have chosen,
That you may know and believe Me,
And understand that I *am* He.
Before Me there was no God formed,
Nor shall there be after Me.
[11]I, *even* I, *am* the LORD,
And besides Me *there is* no savior.
[12]I have declared and saved,
I have proclaimed,
And *there was* no foreign *god* among
you;
Therefore you *are* My witnesses,"
Says the LORD, "that I *am* God.
[13]Indeed before the day *was*, I *am* He;
And *there is* no one who can deliver
out of My hand;
I work, and who will reverse it?"

[14]Thus says the LORD, your Redeemer,
The Holy One of Israel:
"For your sake I will send to Babylon,
And bring them all down as
fugitives—
The Chaldeans, who rejoice in their
ships.
[15]I *am* the LORD, your Holy One,
The Creator of Israel, your King."

[16]Thus says the LORD, who makes a
way in the sea
And a path through the mighty waters,
[17]Who brings forth the chariot and
horse,
The army and the power
(They shall lie down together, they
shall not rise;
They are extinguished, they are
quenched like a wick):
[18]"Do not remember the former things,

43:10,11 We are called to be witnesses of Jesus Christ. This is the heart of our ministry. We testify to what we have seen and heard, of what we know to be true about the one true God. This is what Paul did when he testified to the Athenians on Mars Hill (see Acts 17:22–31).

43:13 No one can pluck us from the Father's hand (see John 10:29). This is not the "once saved, always saved" concept that gives assurance to any who merely walk an aisle, raise a hand, or recite a prayer to "ask Jesus into their heart." It is an assurance that if you are a good-soil hearer, truly repentant and trusting in Christ alone (soundly saved), then God will keep you from stumbling and present you faultless before the presence of His glory with exceeding joy (see Jude 24).

Nor consider the things of old.
[19]Behold, I will do a new thing,
Now it shall spring forth;
Shall you not know it?
I will even make a road in the
wilderness
And rivers in the desert.
[20]The beast of the field will honor Me,
The jackals and the ostriches,
Because I give waters in the
wilderness
And rivers in the desert,
To give drink to My people, My
chosen.
[21]This people I have formed for Myself;
They shall declare My praise.

Pleading with Unfaithful Israel

[22]"But you have not called upon Me,
O Jacob;
And you have been weary of Me, O
Israel.
[23]You have not brought Me the sheep
for your burnt offerings,
Nor have you honored Me with your
sacrifices.
I have not caused you to serve with
grain offerings,
Nor wearied you with incense.
[24]You have bought Me no sweet cane
with money,
Nor have you satisfied Me with the fat
of your sacrifices;
But you have burdened Me with your
sins,
You have wearied Me with your
iniquities.

[25]"I, *even* I, *am* He who blots out your
transgressions for My own sake;
And I will not remember your sins.
[26]Put Me in remembrance;
Let us contend together;
State your *case*, that you may be
acquitted.
[27]Your first father sinned,
And your mediators have transgressed
against Me.
[28]Therefore I will profane the princes of
the sanctuary;
I will give Jacob to the curse,
And Israel to reproaches.

God's Blessing on Israel

44 "Yet hear me now, O Jacob My
servant,
And Israel whom I have chosen.
[2]Thus says the LORD who made you
And formed you from the womb, *who*
will help you:
'Fear not, O Jacob My servant;
And you, Jeshurun, whom I have
chosen.
[3]For I will pour water on him who is
thirsty,
And floods on the dry ground;
I will pour My Spirit on your
descendants,
And My blessing on your offspring;
[4]They will spring up among the grass
Like willows by the watercourses.'
[5]One will say, 'I *am* the LORD's';
Another will call *himself* by the name
of Jacob;
Another will write *with* his hand, 'The
LORD's,'
And name *himself* by the name of
Israel.

There Is No Other God

[6]"Thus says the LORD, the King of Israel,
And his Redeemer, the LORD of hosts:
"I *am* the First and I *am* the Last;
Besides Me *there is* no God.
[7]And who can proclaim as I do?
Then let him declare it and set it in

43:25 This takes place at the new birth. God blots out, cancels, removes, and annihilates our sins (see also 44:22; Psa. 103:12; Mic. 7:19). For God's attitude toward those in Christ, see Rom. 8:1.

44:2 God formed us in the womb. His incredibly creative and wonderful hand knits every sinew, fashions the eyes, and forms the brain, the blood, skin, and bone (see Psa. 139:13). Such thoughts are too much for us to entertain without being overwhelmed by them. See also Psa. 139:14 comment.

POINTS FOR OPEN-AIR PREACHING

44:13

Chalk It Up

On the sidewalk in front of you, draw a chalk line or place some colorful masking tape in a semi-circle 12–15 feet from your "soapbox." (Be sure to remove it before you leave.) When people stop to listen, ask them, "Could you do me a big favor? To save my voice, could you step up to this line? It will also mean that I don't have to 'yell' at you to be heard (which sounds rude and unloving). Thank you." This will not only help your voice, but it will help to draw others to hear the gospel. A closer, more orderly crowd is more attractive to potential listeners than one that is straggly.

order for Me,
Since I appointed the ancient people.
And the things that are coming and
shall come,
Let them show these to them.
8Do not fear, nor be afraid;
Have I not told you from that time,
and declared *it?*
You *are* My witnesses.
Is there a God besides Me?
Indeed *there is* no other Rock;
I know not *one.*' "

Idolatry Is Foolishness

9Those who make an image, all of
them *are* useless,
And their precious things shall not
profit;
They *are* their own witnesses;
They neither see nor know, that they
may be ashamed.
10Who would form a god or mold an
image
That profits him nothing?
11Surely all his companions would be
ashamed;
And the workmen, they *are* mere men.
Let them all be gathered together,
Let them stand up;
Yet they shall fear,
They shall be ashamed together.

12The blacksmith with the tongs works
one in the coals,
Fashions it with hammers,
And works it with the strength of his
arms.
Even so, he is hungry, and his
strength fails;
He drinks no water and is faint.

13The craftsman stretches out *his* rule,
He marks one out with chalk;
He fashions it with a plane,
He marks it out with the compass,
And makes it like the figure of a man,
According to the beauty of a man,
that it may remain in the house.
14He cuts down cedars for himself,
And takes the cypress and the oak;
He secures *it* for himself among the
trees of the forest.
He plants a pine, and the rain
nourishes *it.*

15Then it shall be for a man to burn,
For he will take some of it and warm
himself;
Yes, he kindles *it* and bakes bread;
Indeed he makes a god and worships
it;
He makes it a carved image, and falls
down to it.
16He burns half of it in the fire;
With this half he eats meat;
He roasts a roast, and is satisfied.
He even warms *himself* and says,
"Ah! I am warm,
I have seen the fire."
17And the rest of it he makes into a god,
His carved image.
He falls down before it and worships
it,
Prays to it and says,
"Deliver me, for you *are* my god!"

18They do not know nor understand;
For He has shut their eyes, so that
they cannot see,
And their hearts, so that they cannot
understand.

[19]And no one considers in his heart,
Nor *is there* knowledge nor
understanding to say,
"I have burned half of it in the fire,
Yes, I have also baked bread on its
coals;
I have roasted meat and eaten *it;*
And shall I make the rest of it an
abomination?
Shall I fall down before a block of
wood?"
[20]He feeds on ashes;
A deceived heart has turned him aside;
And he cannot deliver his soul,
Nor say, "*Is there* not a lie in my right
hand?"

Israel Is Not Forgotten

[21]"Remember these, O Jacob,
And Israel, for you *are* My servant;
I have formed you, you *are* My
servant;
O Israel, you will not be forgotten by
Me!
[22]I have blotted out, like a thick cloud,
your transgressions,
And like a cloud, your sins.
Return to Me, for I have redeemed
you."

[23]Sing, O heavens, for the LORD has
done *it!*
Shout, you lower parts of the earth;
Break forth into singing, you
mountains,
O forest, and every tree in it!
For the LORD has redeemed Jacob,
And glorified Himself in Israel.

Judah Will Be Restored

[24]Thus says the LORD, your Redeemer,
And He who formed you from the
womb:
"I *am* the LORD, who makes all *things,*
Who stretches out the heavens all
alone,
Who spreads abroad the earth by
Myself;
[25]Who frustrates the signs of the
babblers,
And drives diviners mad;
Who turns wise men backward,
And makes their knowledge
foolishness;
[26]Who confirms the word of His
servant,
And performs the counsel of His
messengers;
Who says to Jerusalem, 'You shall be
inhabited,'
To the cities of Judah, 'You shall be
built,'
And I will raise up her waste places;
[27]Who says to the deep, 'Be dry!
And I will dry up your rivers';
[28]Who says of Cyrus, '*He is* My
shepherd,
And he shall perform all My pleasure,
Saying to Jerusalem, "You shall be
built,"
And to the temple, "Your foundation
shall be laid." '

44:24 The origin of life. It is a scientific fact that water freezes at 32°F. It is not a scientific fact that biological life was "spontaneously generated" a few billion years ago. That is evolutionary speculation. Physicist and cosmologist *Robert Jastrow*, an agnostic, addressed this very point:

> Perhaps the appearance of life on the earth is a miracle. Scientists are reluctant to accept that view, but their choices are limited; either life was created on the earth by the will of a being outside the grasp of scientific understanding, or it evolved on our planet spontaneously, through chemical reactions occurring in nonliving matter lying on the surface of the planet.
>
> The first theory places the question of the origin of life beyond the reach of scientific inquiry. It is a statement of faith in the power of a Supreme Being not subject to the laws of science. The second theory is also an act of faith. The act of faith consists in assuming that the scientific view of the origin of life is correct, without having concrete evidence to support that belief. (*Until the Sun Dies*, p. 52)

44:25 God has confounded the proud in their own foolishness. See 1 Cor. 1:18–31 to learn how God did this through the gospel.

Cyrus, God's Instrument

45 "Thus says the LORD to His anointed,
To Cyrus, whose right hand I have held—
To subdue nations before him
And loose the armor of kings,
To open before him the double doors,
So that the gates will not be shut:
2'I will go before you
And make the crooked places[a] straight;
I will break in pieces the gates of bronze
And cut the bars of iron.
3I will give you the treasures of darkness
And hidden riches of secret places,
That you may know that I, the LORD,
Who call *you* by your name,
Am the God of Israel.
4For Jacob My servant's sake,
And Israel My elect,
I have even called you by your name;
I have named you, though you have not known Me.
5I *am* the LORD, and *there is* no other;
There is no God besides Me.
I will gird you, though you have not known Me,
6That they may know from the rising of the sun to its setting
That *there is* none besides Me.
I *am* the LORD, and *there is* no other;
7I form the light and create darkness,
I make peace and create calamity;
I, the LORD, do all these *things*.'

8"Rain down, you heavens, from above,
And let the skies pour down righteousness;
Let the earth open, let them bring forth salvation,
And let righteousness spring up together.
I, the LORD, have created it.

9"Woe to him who strives with his Maker!
Let the potsherd *strive* with the potsherds of the earth!
Shall the clay say to him who forms it, 'What are you making?'
Or shall your handiwork *say*, 'He has no hands'?
10Woe to him who says to *his* father, 'What are you begetting?'
Or to the woman, 'What have you brought forth?' "

11Thus says the LORD,
The Holy One of Israel, and his Maker:
"Ask Me of things to come concerning My sons;
And concerning the work of My hands, you command Me.
12I have made the earth,
And created man on it.
I—My hands—stretched out the heavens,
And all their host I have commanded.
13I have raised him up in righteousness,

45:2 [a]Dead Sea Scrolls and Septuagint read *mountains;* Targum reads *I will trample down the walls;* Vulgate reads *I will humble the great ones of the earth.*

45:5 Answering Jehovah's Witnesses. In their version of the Scriptures, the Jehovah's Witnesses mistranslate John 1:1 to remove references to Jesus' deity. Instead of saying "the Word was God," their New World Translation says: "In [the] beginning the Word was, and the word was with God, and the word was a god." However, this verse leaves no doubt that there is no one else of a divine nature other than the one true God. For other verses that stress that there is no other God, see 43:10; 45:18,21,22; 46:9. For more on the Jehovah's Witnesses, see page 1698.

"The average evangelical Christian who claims to be born again and have eternal life is not doing as much to propagate his or her faith as the busy adherents of the cults handing out their papers on the street corners and visiting from house to house." *A.W. Tozer*

45:7 Unthinking skeptics often point to this verse and accuse God of being evil. But Scripture tells us that God brings calamity (KJV, "evil") on mankind as just punishment for their sins. He does this for the purpose of leading people to repent and turn to Him. But those who fail to do so will be held accountable for their evil deeds and will ultimately face eternal punishment in hell. See also Amos 3:6; Lam. 3:38,39.

45:12 *The Evolutionary Process*

The theory of evolution claims that all the amazing complexity we see throughout creation comes about through undirected processes by means of random mutations and natural selection. Supposedly, if a mutation ("copying error") occurs in the genes, and happens to give the creature some benefit, then this benefit is passed on to offspring through the process of natural selection. If this is truly possible, we shouldn't have any problem seeing plenty of evidence of this taking place.

Microevolution vs. Macroevolution. First, it is important to realize that species do change over time by adaptation. Look at the variety within dogs—from the tiny Chihuahua to the huge Great Dane. These small-scale variations within a kind are sometimes called *micro*evolution. But note that nothing new actually comes into being ("evolves") in microevolution. Though these dogs have incredible differences, they are still dogs. Within the horse family are the donkey, zebra, draft horse, and the dwarf pony. Though different, all are horses. There are tremendous variations among humans. Think of all the different features from Asian to African to Aboriginal to Caucasian. But we are all within the same species, *Homo sapiens*.

Darwin's theory of evolution, however, is based on the concept of *macro*evolution. This is the inference that the small changes seen in adaptation (these variations within species) can accumulate and lead to large changes over long periods of time. In macroevolution, one kind of creature (such as a reptile) becomes another kind of creature (such as a bird), requiring the creation of entirely new features and body types. This would be a bit like observing a car going from 0 to 60 mph in 60 seconds, and inferring that it can then go 0 to 6,000 mph in 100 minutes—and become an airplane in the process.

That's an illogical assumption, and it puts a tremendous responsibility on mutations to accidentally create complex new body parts, and on natural selection to recognize the benefit these new parts will eventually convey and make sure the creatures with those new parts survive. As Stephen J. Gould explains, "The essence of Darwinism lies in a single phrase: natural selection is the creative force of evolutionary change. No one denies that selection will play a negative role in eliminating the unfit. Darwinian theories require that it create the fit as well."

Let's look at how mutations and natural selection supposedly work to create the amazing complexity of life in our world.

Mutations. The first problem we find is that the variations we see in adaptation within a kind are always within limits set by the genetic code. Fifty years of genetic research on the fruit fly have convinced evolutionists that change is limited and confined to a defined population. Despite being bombarded with mutation agents for half a century, the mutant fruit flies continue to exist as fruit flies, leading geneticists to acknowledge that they will not evolve into something else. This confirms Gregor Mendel's findings in the 1800s that there are natural limits to genetic change.

Genetics professor Francisco Ayala is quoted as saying: "I am now convinced from what the paleontologists say that small changes do not accumulate." Small changes aren't the only thing that doesn't add up. But more importantly, the *amount* of change isn't really the issue.

Mutations can only modify or eliminate existing structures; they cannot create new ones. Within a particular type of creature, hair can vary from curly to straight, legs can vary from heavy to thin, beaks from long to short, wings from dark to light, etc. But the creatures still have hair, legs, beaks, and wings—nothing new has been added.

In our DNA "book," a mutation is a mistake—a "typing error." (See Isa. 42:5 comment.) In the genetic blueprint, the letters that define these features can occasionally be rearranged or lost through mutations, but none of this will account for the additions needed by macroevolution. Keep in mind that, in the molecules-to-man theory, everything evolved from simple cells into complex life forms. So if a fish were to grow legs and lungs, or a reptile were to grow wings, that creature's genetic information would have to increase to create the new body parts. This would be equivalent to a telegram giving rise to encyclopedias of meaningful, useful genetic sentences.

Think how much more information there is in the human genome than in the bacterial genome. If macroevolution were true, where did all that vastly complex, new information come from? *Scientists have yet to find even a single mutation that increases genetic information*. As physicist Lee Spetner puts it, "Information cannot be built up by mutations that lose it. A business can't make money by losing it a little at a time."

See also Psa. 36:6 comment.

"To improve a living organism by random mutation is like saying you could improve a Swiss watch by dropping it and bending one of its wheels or axis. Improving life by random mutations has the probability of zero." *Albert Szent-Gyorgi*, Nobel Laureate (Medicine)

(Adapted from *How to Know God Exists*.)

And I will direct all his ways;
He shall build My city
And let My exiles go free,
Not for price nor reward,"
Says the LORD of hosts.

The Lord, the Only Savior

14Thus says the LORD:

"The labor of Egypt and merchandise
of Cush
And of the Sabeans, men of stature,
Shall come over to you, and they shall
be yours;
They shall walk behind you,
They shall come over in chains;
And they shall bow down to you.
They will make supplication to you,
saying, 'Surely God *is* in you,
And *there is* no other;
There is no other God.' "

15Truly You *are* God, who hide Yourself,
O God of Israel, the Savior!
16They shall be ashamed
And also disgraced, all of them;
They shall go in confusion together,
Who are makers of idols.
17*But* Israel shall be saved by the LORD
With an everlasting salvation;
You shall not be ashamed or disgraced
Forever and ever.

18For thus says the LORD,
Who created the heavens,
Who is God,
Who formed the earth and made it,
Who has established it,
Who did not create it in vain,
Who formed it to be inhabited:
"I *am* the LORD, and *there is* no other.
19I have not spoken in secret,
In a dark place of the earth;
I did not say to the seed of Jacob,
'Seek Me in vain';
I, the LORD, speak righteousness,
I declare things that are right.

20"Assemble yourselves and come;
Draw near together,
You *who have* escaped from the nations.
They have no knowledge,
Who carry the wood of their carved
image,
And pray to a god *that* cannot save.
21Tell and bring forth *your case;*
Yes, let them take counsel together.
Who has declared this from ancient
time?
Who has told it from that time?
Have not I, the LORD?
And *there is* no other God besides Me,
A just God and a Savior;
There is none besides Me.

22"Look to Me, and be saved,
All you ends of the earth!
For I *am* God, and *there is* no other.
23I have sworn by Myself;
The word has gone out of My mouth
in righteousness,
And shall not return,
That to Me every knee shall bow,
Every tongue shall take an oath.
24He shall say,
'Surely in the LORD I have
righteousness and strength.
To Him *men* shall come,
And all shall be ashamed
Who are incensed against Him.
25In the LORD all the descendants of
Israel
Shall be justified, and shall glory.' "

Dead Idols and the Living God

46 Bel bows down, Nebo stoops;
Their idols were on the beasts
and on the cattle.

45:22 This is a universal call to humanity to come to the knowledge of salvation. All who look to Jesus will be saved. See also 49:6; 56:6–8; Num. 21:6–9 comment.

45:23 One day, every knee shall bow and every tongue shall confess that Jesus Christ is Lord, to the glory of God the Father. See Rom. 14:11; Phil. 2:10,11.

45:18 *The Origin of the Universe*

Many people refuse to believe in a Creator because they can't fathom how an entity could be eternal. Yet scientists used to teach that the universe itself was eternal—it just always existed—and people were content to believe that. So if anyone believes it is possible for something (such as the universe) to be eternal, to be logically consistent, they would also have to admit it's possible there could be an infinite, omnipotent Being who is eternal.

These days, scientists have concluded that the universe had a beginning. But how did it come into being? According to the Law of Cause and Effect, every effect must have a cause. In other words, everything that happens has a catalyst; everything that came into being has something that caused it. Things don't just happen by themselves.

Most secular scientists say that the universe began in an event known as the Big Bang. The Big Bang theory claims that "nothing" suddenly became time, space, matter, and energy, forming a vast, complex, orderly universe composed of over 100 billion galaxies and containing an estimated trillion, trillion, trillion, trillion tons of matter. Now these scientists have an even greater dilemma: Where did the initial matter come from? How could something come from out of nowhere, by itself? Second, what caused it to go "bang"? What was the catalyst that sent the particles flying?

Famed cosmologist Andrei Linde, professor of Physics at Stanford University, is honest about the evolutionists' dilemma:

> The first, and main, problem is the very existence of the big bang. One may wonder, what came before? If space-time did not exist then, how could everything appear from nothing? What arose first? The universe or the laws determining its evolution? Explaining this initial singularity—where and when it all began—still remains the most intractable problem of modern cosmology.

If a book coming into existence by itself is obvious nonsense (see Isa. 42:5 comment), why is the Big Bang theory any more "scientific"?

Scientists say they may have resolved the cosmic question of where we came from. "In the end, everything comes from space dust," according to Ciska Markwick-Kemper of the University of Manchester in England. This isn't just ordinary space dust, but "dust that was belched from dying stars" about 8 billion light-years from here. Dr. Michael Barlow states that "dust particles in space are the building blocks of comets, planets, and life, yet our knowledge of where this dust was made is still incomplete."

The dilemma is, no matter how far away or how long ago scientists estimate the very first dust particle came from, the logical question remains: Then where did that dust come from?

It's unavoidable—at some point, you're forced to conclude that there must be an uncaused cause (a First Cause) that brought everything else into being. This conclusion agrees with logic, reason, and scientific laws. In all of history, there has never been an instance of anything spontaneously appearing out of nowhere. Something being created from nothing is contrary to all known science. Even Darwin admitted that logically the universe could not have created itself:

> The impossibility of conceiving that this grand and wondrous universe, with our conscious selves, arose through chance, seems to me the chief argument for the existence of God...I am aware that if we admit a first cause, the mind still craves to know whence it came, and how it arose.

Even more difficult to explain is how our incredibly fine-tuned universe could be so amazingly complex and orderly. Evolutionist Stephen Hawking, considered the best-known scientist since Albert Einstein, acknowledges:

> The universe and the laws of physics seem to have been specifically designed for us. If any one of about 40 physical qualities had more than slightly different values, life as we know it could not exist: Either atoms would not be stable, or they wouldn't combine into molecules, or the stars wouldn't form the heavier elements, or the universe would collapse before life could develop, and so on.

In short, the evolutionary view cannot offer a logical, scientific explanation for either the origin or the complexity of the universe. There are only two choices: Either no one created everything out of nothing, or Someone—an intelligent, omnipotent, eternal First Cause—created everything out of nothing. Which makes more sense?

See also Psa. 19:1–4 comment on the Big Bang, and Job 33:4 comment on the origin of life.

"A common sense interpretation of the facts suggests that a superintellect has monkeyed with physics, as well as with chemistry and biology, and that there are no blind forces worth speaking about in nature. The numbers one calculates from the facts seem to me so overwhelming as to put this conclusion almost beyond question." *Sir Frederick Hoyle*

(Adapted from *How to Know God Exists.*)

Your carriages *were* heavily loaded,
A burden to the weary *beast*.
2They stoop, they bow down together;
They could not deliver the burden,
But have themselves gone into captivity.

3"Listen to Me, O house of Jacob,
And all the remnant of the house of Israel,
Who have been upheld *by Me* from birth,
Who have been carried from the womb:
4Even to *your* old age, I *am* He,
And *even* to gray hairs I will carry *you!*
I have made, and I will bear;
Even I will carry, and will deliver *you*.

5"To whom will you liken Me, and make *Me* equal
And compare Me, that we should be alike?
6They lavish gold out of the bag,
And weigh silver on the scales;
They hire a goldsmith, and he makes it a god;
They prostrate themselves, yes, they worship.
7They bear it on the shoulder, they carry it
And set it in its place, and it stands;
From its place it shall not move.
Though *one* cries out to it, yet it cannot answer
Nor save him out of his trouble.

8"Remember this, and show yourselves men;
Recall to mind, O you transgressors.
9Remember the former things of old,
For I *am* God, and *there is* no other;
I am God, and *there is* none like Me,
10Declaring the end from the beginning,
And from ancient times *things* that are not *yet* done,
Saying, 'My counsel shall stand,
And I will do all My pleasure,'
11Calling a bird of prey from the east,
The man who executes My counsel, from a far country.
Indeed I have spoken *it;*
I will also bring it to pass.
I have purposed *it;*
I will also do it.

12"Listen to Me, you stubborn-hearted,
Who *are* far from righteousness:
13I bring My righteousness near, it shall not be far off;
My salvation shall not linger.
And I will place salvation in Zion,
For Israel My glory.

The Humiliation of Babylon

47 "Come down and sit in the dust,
O virgin daughter of Babylon;
Sit on the ground without a throne,
O daughter of the Chaldeans!
For you shall no more be called
Tender and delicate.
2Take the millstones and grind meal.
Remove your veil,
Take off the skirt,
Uncover the thigh,
Pass through the rivers.
3Your nakedness shall be uncovered,
Yes, your shame will be seen;
I will take vengeance,
And I will not arbitrate with a man."

4*As for* our Redeemer, the LORD of hosts *is* His name,
The Holy One of Israel.

5"Sit in silence, and go into darkness,
O daughter of the Chaldeans;

46:9,10 There is no one like God. He knows the beginning from the end. We don't know what each day will bring, and even with modern technology we can hardly get tomorrow's weather forecast right, let alone predict events of the future. Only an omniscient God can reveal the future, and only the Bible contains thousands of fulfilled prophecies, proving its divine inspiration. See Matt. 4:4 comment.

For you shall no longer be called
The Lady of Kingdoms.
6I was angry with My people;
I have profaned My inheritance,
And given them into your hand.
You showed them no mercy;
On the elderly you laid your yoke
very heavily.
7And you said, 'I shall be a lady forever,'
So that you did not take these *things*
to heart,
Nor remember the latter end of them.

8"Therefore hear this now, *you who are*
given to pleasures,
Who dwell securely,
Who say in your heart, 'I *am,* and
there is no one else besides me;
I shall not sit *as* a widow,
Nor shall I know the loss of children';
9But these two *things* shall come to you
In a moment, in one day:
The loss of children, and widowhood.
They shall come upon you in their
fullness
Because of the multitude of your
sorceries,
For the great abundance of your
enchantments.

10"For you have trusted in your
wickedness;
You have said, 'No one sees me';
Your wisdom and your knowledge
have warped you;
And you have said in your heart,
"I *am,* and *there is* no one else besides
me.'
11Therefore evil shall come upon you;
You shall not know from where it
arises.
And trouble shall fall upon you;
You will not be able to put it off.
And desolation shall come upon you
suddenly,
Which you shall not know.

> A tiny group of believers who have the gospel keep mumbling it over and over to themselves. Meanwhile, millions who have never heard it once fall into the flames of eternal hell without ever hearing the salvation story.
>
> **K. P. YOHANNON**

12"Stand now with your enchantments
And the multitude of your sorceries,
In which you have labored from your
youth—
Perhaps you will be able to profit,
Perhaps you will prevail.
13You are wearied in the multitude of
your counsels;
Let now the astrologers, the stargazers,
And the monthly prognosticators
Stand up and save you
From what shall come upon you.
14Behold, they shall be as stubble,
The fire shall burn them;
They shall not deliver themselves
From the power of the flame;

47:10 The ungodly find comfort in their unbelief. Yet, there is a God who sees all, and He is perfect and holy and will bring every work into judgment, including every secret thing (see Eccles. 12:14).

47:14 The power of the flame. The devil loves procrastinators, feeding them lies to fatten their complacency. He would have men and women believe that hell is tolerable, and it seems that some within the Church listen to him. But those who believe that hell exists should reveal it in their preaching. Consider *Charles Spurgeon's* deep concern: "Oh, that you would trust in the Lord Jesus! Repose in him, and in his finished work, and all is well. Did I hear you say, 'I will pray about it'? Better trust at once. Pray as much as you like after you have trusted, but what is the good of unbelieving prayers? 'I will talk with a godly man after the service.' I charge you first trust in Jesus. Go home alone, trusting in Jesus. 'I should like to go into the enquiry-room.' I dare say you would, but we are not willing to pander to popular superstition. We fear that in those rooms men are warmed into a fictitious confidence. Very few of the supposed converts of enquiry-rooms turn out well. Go to your God at once, even where you now are. Cast yourself on Christ, now, at once; ere you stir an inch! In God's name I charge you, believe on the Lord Jesus Christ, for *'he that believeth and is baptized shall be saved; but he that believeth not shall be damned.'"*

It shall not *be* a coal to be warmed by,
Nor a fire to sit before!
15Thus shall they be to you
With whom you have labored,
Your merchants from your youth;
They shall wander each one to his quarter.
No one shall save you.

Israel Refined for God's Glory

48 "Hear this, O house of Jacob,
Who are called by the name of Israel,
And have come forth from the wellsprings of Judah;
Who swear by the name of the LORD,
And make mention of the God of Israel,
But not in truth or in righteousness;
2For they call themselves after the holy city,
And lean on the God of Israel;
The LORD of hosts *is* His name:

3"I have declared the former things from the beginning;
They went forth from My mouth, and I caused them to hear it.
Suddenly I did *them,* and they came to pass.
4Because I knew that you *were* obstinate,
And your neck *was* an iron sinew,
And your brow bronze,
5Even from the beginning I have declared *it* to you;
Before it came to pass I proclaimed *it* to you,
Lest you should say, 'My idol has done them,
And my carved image and my molded image
Have commanded them.'
6"You have heard;
See all this.
And will you not declare *it?*
I have made you hear new things from this time,
Even hidden things, and you did not know them.
7They are created now and not from the beginning;
And before this day you have not heard them,
Lest you should say, 'Of course I knew them.'
8Surely you did not hear,
Surely you did not know;
Surely from long ago your ear was not opened.
For I knew that you would deal very treacherously,
And were called a transgressor from the womb.

9"For My name's sake I will defer My anger,
And *for* My praise I will restrain it from you,
So that I do not cut you off.
10Behold, I have refined you, but not as silver;
I have tested you in the furnace of affliction.
11For My own sake, for My own sake, I will do *it;*
For how should *My name* be profaned?
And I will not give My glory to another.

God's Ancient Plan to Redeem Israel

12"Listen to Me, O Jacob,
And Israel, My called:
I *am* He, I *am* the First,
I *am* also the Last.
13Indeed My hand has laid the

48:1 This is so like the god spoken of by popular preachers. They name the name of the Lord, but they do not know Him in truth or walk in righteousness.

"The American gospel has evolved into a gospel of addition without subtraction. It is the belief that we can add Christ to our lives, but not subtract sin. It is a change in belief without a change in behavior... Obedience is the proof." *Patrick Morley*

foundation of the earth,
And My right hand has stretched out the heavens;
When I call to them,
They stand up together.

14"All of you, assemble yourselves, and hear!
Who among them has declared these *things?*
The LORD loves him;
He shall do His pleasure on Babylon,
And His arm *shall be against* the Chaldeans.
15I, *even* I, have spoken;
Yes, I have called him,
I have brought him, and his way will prosper.

16"Come near to Me, hear this:
I have not spoken in secret from the beginning;
From the time that it was, I *was* there.
And now the Lord GOD and His Spirit
Have[a] sent Me."

17Thus says the LORD, your Redeemer,
The Holy One of Israel:
"I *am* the LORD your God,
Who teaches you to profit,
Who leads you by the way you should go.
18Oh, that you had heeded My commandments!
Then your peace would have been like a river,
And your righteousness like the waves of the sea.
19Your descendants also would have been like the sand,
And the offspring of your body like the grains of sand;
His name would not have been cut off
Nor destroyed from before Me."

20Go forth from Babylon!
Flee from the Chaldeans!
With a voice of singing,
Declare, proclaim this,
Utter it to the end of the earth;
Say, "The LORD has redeemed
His servant Jacob!"
21And they did not thirst
When He led them through the deserts;
He caused the waters to flow from the rock for them;
He also split the rock, and the waters gushed out.

22"*There is* no peace," says the LORD, "for the wicked."

The Servant, the Light to the Gentiles

49 "Listen, O coastlands, to Me,
And take heed, you peoples from afar!
The LORD has called Me from the womb;
From the matrix of My mother He has made mention of My name.
2And He has made My mouth like a sharp sword;
In the shadow of His hand He has hidden Me,
And made Me a polished shaft;
In His quiver He has hidden Me."

3"And He said to me,
'You *are* My servant, O Israel,
In whom I will be glorified.'
4Then I said, 'I have labored in vain,
I have spent my strength for nothing and in vain;
Yet surely my just reward *is* with the LORD,
And my work with my God.' "

5"And now the LORD says,
Who formed Me from the womb *to be*

48:16 [a]The Hebrew verb is singular.

48:18 Here is the root of the problem. The nation that heeds the Commandments will be humbled and find itself at the foot of a blood-stained cross.

SPRINGBOARDS FOR PREACHING AND WITNESSING

Crazy Criminals

49:9 There was a criminal who was condemned to die in the electric chair. The courts had appointed a lawyer on behalf of the criminal, and he had worked hard to get him a reprieve. Finally, it came through, signed by the governor himself. The excited lawyer delivered it by hand to the criminal, but he refused to look at it, and instead arrogantly insisted that the governor appear to him personally, and that if he didn't, he wouldn't believe that he existed.

You have been justly condemned to death and hell by the Law of God. Yet, the same Judge who is holy and righteous is also rich in mercy, and will gladly give you a reprieve. He will dismiss your case because your fine was paid in full by the Savior. Instead of proudly snapping your fingers and insisting upon seeing God, or arguing about the age of the earth or Darwinian evolution, humble yourself and repent and trust the Savior. God will open the prison doors and set you free from sin and death.

His Servant,
To bring Jacob back to Him,
So that Israel is gathered to Him[a]
(For I shall be glorious in the eyes of the LORD,
And My God shall be My strength),

6 Indeed He says,
"It is too small a thing that You should be My Servant
To raise up the tribes of Jacob,
And to restore the preserved ones of Israel;
I will also give You as a light to the Gentiles,
That You should be My salvation to the ends of the earth.' "

7 Thus says the LORD,
The Redeemer of Israel, their Holy One,
To Him whom man despises,
To Him whom the nation abhors,
To the Servant of rulers:
"Kings shall see and arise,
Princes also shall worship,
Because of the LORD who is faithful,
The Holy One of Israel;
And He has chosen You."

8 Thus says the LORD:

"In an acceptable time I have heard You,
And in the day of salvation I have helped You;
I will preserve You and give You
As a covenant to the people,
To restore the earth,
To cause them to inherit the desolate heritages;
9 That You may say to the prisoners, 'Go forth,'
To those who *are* in darkness, 'Show yourselves.'

"They shall feed along the roads,
And their pastures *shall be* on all desolate heights.
10 They shall neither hunger nor thirst,
Neither heat nor sun shall strike them;
For He who has mercy on them will lead them,
Even by the springs of water He will guide them.
11 I will make each of My mountains a road,
And My highways shall be elevated.
12 Surely these shall come from afar;
Look! Those from the north and the west,
And these from the land of Sinim."

13 Sing, O heavens!

49:5 [a]Qere, Dead Sea Scrolls, and Septuagint read *is gathered to Him;* Kethib reads *is not gathered.*

49:8 "His grace in the past and His wrath in the future require repentance in the present. As Paul said elsewhere, 'Now is "the acceptable time," behold, now is "the day of salvation"' (2 Cor. 6:2)." *John MacArthur*

Be joyful, O earth!
And break out in singing, O mountains!
For the LORD has comforted His people,
And will have mercy on His afflicted.

God Will Remember Zion

14But Zion said, "The LORD has forsaken me,
And my Lord has forgotten me."

15"Can a woman forget her nursing child,
And not have compassion on the son of her womb?
Surely they may forget,
Yet I will not forget you.
16See, I have inscribed you on the palms *of My hands;*
Your walls *are* continually before Me.
17Your sons[a] shall make haste;
Your destroyers and those who laid you waste
Shall go away from you.
18Lift up your eyes, look around and see;
All these gather together *and* come to you.
As I live," says the LORD,
"You shall surely clothe yourselves with them all as an ornament,
And bind them *on you* as a bride *does.*

19"For your waste and desolate places,
And the land of your destruction,
Will even now be too small for the inhabitants;
And those who swallowed you up will be far away.
20The children you will have,
After you have lost the others,
Will say again in your ears,
'The place *is* too small for me;
Give me a place where I may dwell.'
21Then you will say in your heart,
'Who has begotten these for me,
Since I have lost my children and am desolate,
A captive, and wandering to and fro?
And who has brought these up?
There I was, left alone;
But these, where *were* they?' "

22Thus says the Lord GOD:

"Behold, I will lift My hand in an oath to the nations,
And set up My standard for the peoples;
They shall bring your sons in *their* arms,
And your daughters shall be carried on *their* shoulders;
23Kings shall be your foster fathers,
And their queens your nursing mothers;
They shall bow down to you with *their* faces to the earth,
And lick up the dust of your feet.
Then you will know that I *am* the LORD,
For they shall not be ashamed who wait for Me."

To love means loving the unlovable. To forgive means pardoning the unpardonable. Faith means believing the unbelievable. Hope means hoping when everything seems hopeless.

G. K. CHESTERTON

24Shall the prey be taken from the mighty,
Or the captives of the righteous[a] be delivered?

25But thus says the LORD:

"Even the captives of the mighty shall be taken away,
And the prey of the terrible be delivered;
For I will contend with him who contends with you,

49:17 [a]Dead Sea Scrolls, Septuagint, Targum, and Vulgate read *builders.* 49:24 [a]Following Masoretic Text and Targum; Dead Sea Scrolls, Syriac, and Vulgate read *the mighty;* Septuagint reads *unjustly.*

And I will save your children.
[26]I will feed those who oppress you
with their own flesh,
And they shall be drunk with their
own blood as with sweet wine.
All flesh shall know
That I, the LORD, *am* your Savior,
And your Redeemer, the Mighty One
of Jacob."

The Servant, Israel's Hope

50 Thus says the LORD:
"Where *is* the certificate of your
mother's divorce,
Whom I have put away?
Or which of My creditors *is it* to
whom I have sold you?
For your iniquities you have sold
yourselves,
And for your transgressions your
mother has been put away.
[2]Why, when I came, *was there* no man?
Why, when I called, *was there* none to
answer?
Is My hand shortened at all that it
cannot redeem?
Or have I no power to deliver?
Indeed with My rebuke I dry up the
sea,
I make the rivers a wilderness;
Their fish stink because *there is* no
water,
And die of thirst.
[3]I clothe the heavens with blackness,
And I make sackcloth their covering."

[4]"The Lord GOD has given Me
The tongue of the learned,
That I should know how to speak
A word in season to *him who is* weary.
He awakens Me morning by morning,
He awakens My ear
To hear as the learned.
[5]The Lord GOD has opened My ear;
And I was not rebellious,
Nor did I turn away.
[6]I gave My back to those who struck
Me,
And My cheeks to those who plucked
out the beard;
I did not hide My face from shame
and spitting.

[7]"For the Lord GOD will help Me;
Therefore I will not be disgraced;
Therefore I have set My face like a
flint,
And I know that I will not be ashamed.
[8]*He is* near who justifies Me;
Who will contend with Me?
Let us stand together.
Who *is* My adversary?
Let him come near Me.
[9]Surely the Lord GOD will help Me;
Who *is* he *who* will condemn Me?
Indeed they will all grow old like a
garment;
The moth will eat them up.

[10]"Who among you fears the LORD?
Who obeys the voice of His Servant?
Who walks in darkness
And has no light?
Let him trust in the name of the LORD
And rely upon his God.
[11]Look, all you who kindle a fire,
Who encircle *yourselves* with sparks:
Walk in the light of your fire and in
the sparks you have kindled—

50:4 You will not know the truth of these words if you do not speak them. Speak with the unsaved. Encourage them to get right with God. Preach Christ crucified, and at times you will sit back and say, "I didn't know I knew that!" God tells us, "Open you mouth wide and I will fill it." That is the order in which God often works. He will give you wisdom as you step out in faith. Stay in the boat and you will never walk on water.

50:6 This messianic prophecy was fulfilled in Matt. 26:67; 27:30.

50:10,11 This sinful world loves the darkness and hates the light. Instead of embracing the light of the glorious gospel, they create their own "light" through false religions or godless explanations of human origins. They believe a lie, and that will lead to their eternal destruction.

This you shall have from My hand:
You shall lie down in torment.

The Lord Comforts Zion

51 "Listen to Me, you who follow after righteousness, You who seek the LORD:
Look to the rock *from which* you were hewn,
And to the hole of the pit *from which* you were dug.
2Look to Abraham your father,
And to Sarah *who* bore you;
For I called him alone,
And blessed him and increased him."

3For the LORD will comfort Zion,
He will comfort all her waste places;
He will make her wilderness like Eden,
And her desert like the garden of the LORD;
Joy and gladness will be found in it,
Thanksgiving and the voice of melody.

4"Listen to Me, My people;
And give ear to Me, O My nation:
For law will proceed from Me,
And I will make My justice rest
As a light of the peoples.
5My righteousness *is* near,
My salvation has gone forth,
And My arms will judge the peoples;
The coastlands will wait upon Me,
And on My arm they will trust.
6Lift up your eyes to the heavens,
And look on the earth beneath.
For the heavens will vanish away like smoke,
The earth will grow old like a garment,
And those who dwell in it will die in like manner;
But My salvation will be forever,
And My righteousness will not be abolished.

7"Listen to Me, you who know righteousness,
You people in whose heart *is* My law:
Do not fear the reproach of men,
Nor be afraid of their insults.
8For the moth will eat them up like a garment,
And the worm will eat them like wool;
But My righteousness will be forever,
And My salvation from generation to generation."

9Awake, awake, put on strength,
O arm of the LORD!
Awake as in the ancient days,
In the generations of old.
Are You not *the arm* that cut Rahab apart,
And wounded the serpent?

10*Are* You not *the One* who dried up the sea,
The waters of the great deep;
That made the depths of the sea a road
For the redeemed to cross over?
11So the ransomed of the LORD shall return,
And come to Zion with singing,
With everlasting joy on their heads.
They shall obtain joy and gladness;
Sorrow and sighing shall flee away.

12"I, *even* I, *am* He who comforts you.
Who *are* you that you should be afraid
Of a man *who* will die,
And of the son of a man *who* will be made like grass?

51:6 Space exploration has given us a window into the heavens to see the infinitude of space. We can view Earth from space like no other generation before us, and know that this big ball of dirt spinning through space will one day be dissolved and reshaped by the mighty hand of Almighty God. See Matt. 24:35; Heb. 1:10–12; 2 Pet. 3:10.

51:7 This is you, dear Christian. You have been given the Holy Spirit. You have the mind of Christ and have God's Law written on your heart (see Heb. 10:16). Step out in faith and speak the words of eternal life with great boldness. Though men may reproach and revile you, you have God's promise that He will be with you and will honor the words you speak for Him. See John 12:26 for a wonderful promise of God.

[13]And you forget the LORD your Maker,
Who stretched out the heavens
And laid the foundations of the earth;
You have feared continually every day
Because of the fury of the oppressor,
When *he has* prepared to destroy.
And where *is* the fury of the oppressor?
[14]The captive exile hastens, that he may
be loosed,
That he should not die in the pit,
And that his bread should not fail.
[15]But I *am* the LORD your God,
Who divided the sea whose waves
roared—
The LORD of hosts *is* His name.
[16]And I have put My words in your
mouth;
I have covered you with the shadow
of My hand,
That I may plant the heavens,
Lay the foundations of the earth,
And say to Zion, 'You *are* My people.' "

God's Fury Removed

[17]Awake, awake!
Stand up, O Jerusalem,
You who have drunk at the hand of
the LORD
The cup of His fury;
You have drunk the dregs of the cup
of trembling,
And drained *it* out.
[18]*There is* no one to guide her
Among all the sons she has brought
forth;
Nor *is there any* who takes her by the
hand
Among all the sons she has brought up.
[19]These two *things* have come to you;
Who will be sorry for you?—
Desolation and destruction, famine
and sword—
By whom will I comfort you?
[20]Your sons have fainted,
They lie at the head of all the streets,
Like an antelope in a net;
They are full of the fury of the LORD,
The rebuke of your God.

[21]Therefore please hear this, you

"Some talk of it as an unreasonable thing to think to fright persons to heaven; but I think it is a reasonable thing to endeavor to fright persons away from hell, that stand upon the brink of it, and are just ready to fall into it, and are senseless of their danger: 'tis a reasonable thing to fright a person out of a house on fire."

Jonathan Edwards

afflicted,
And drunk but not with wine.
[22]Thus says your Lord,
The LORD and your God,
Who pleads the cause of His people:
"See, I have taken out of your hand
The cup of trembling,
The dregs of the cup of My fury;
You shall no longer drink it.
[23]But I will put it into the hand of those
who afflict you,
Who have said to you,[a]
'Lie down, that we may walk over you.'
And you have laid your body like the
ground,
And as the street, for those who walk
over."

God Redeems Jerusalem

52 Awake, awake!
Put on your strength, O Zion;
Put on your beautiful garments,

51:23 [a]Literally *your soul*

O Jerusalem, the holy city!
For the uncircumcised and the unclean
Shall no longer come to you.
2Shake yourself from the dust, arise;
Sit down, O Jerusalem!
Loose yourself from the bonds of
your neck,
O captive daughter of Zion!

3For thus says the LORD:

"You have sold yourselves for nothing,
And you shall be redeemed without
money."

4For thus says the Lord GOD:

"My people went down at first
Into Egypt to dwell there;
Then the Assyrian oppressed them
without cause.
5Now therefore, what have I here,"
says the LORD,
"That My people are taken away for
nothing?
Those who rule over them
Make them wail,"[a] says the LORD,
"And My name *is* blasphemed
continually every day.
6Therefore My people shall know My
name;
Therefore *they shall know* in that day
That I *am* He who speaks:
'Behold, *it is* I.' "

7How beautiful upon the mountains
Are the feet of him who brings good
news,
Who proclaims peace,
Who brings glad tidings of good *things*,
Who proclaims salvation,
Who says to Zion,
"Your God reigns!"
8Your watchmen shall lift up *their*
voices,
With their voices they shall sing
together;
For they shall see eye to eye
When the LORD brings back Zion.
9Break forth into joy, sing together,
You waste places of Jerusalem!
For the LORD has comforted His
people,
He has redeemed Jerusalem.
10The LORD has made bare His holy arm
In the eyes of all the nations;
And all the ends of the earth shall see
The salvation of our God.

11Depart! Depart! Go out from there,
Touch no unclean *thing*;
Go out from the midst of her,
Be clean,
You who bear the vessels of the LORD.
12For you shall not go out with haste,
Nor go by flight;
For the LORD will go before you,
And the God of Israel *will be* your rear
guard.

The Sin-Bearing Servant

13Behold, My Servant shall deal
prudently;
He shall be exalted and extolled and
be very high.
14Just as many were astonished at you,
So His visage was marred more than
any man,
And His form more than the sons of
men;
15So shall He sprinkle[a] many nations.

52:5 [a]Dead Sea Scrolls read *Mock;* Septuagint reads *Marvel and wail;* Targum reads *Boast themselves;* Vulgate reads *Treat them unjustly*. 52:15 [a]Or *startle*

52:7 Do you proclaim the gospel of peace? Then even the lowliest part of you is beautiful in God's eyes. See Nah. 1:15; Rom. 10:15. Remember this when you are despised by this world. Your praise is of God, not of men.

"Had I cared for the comments of people, I should never have been a missionary." *C. T. Studd*

52:14 Depictions of a "suffering Savior" on the cross can never do justice to the agony He endured for us.

"Think lightly of hell, and you will think lightly of the cross. Think little of the sufferings of lost souls, and you will soon think little of the Savior who delivers them." *Charles Spurgeon*

Kings shall shut their mouths at Him;
For what had not been told them they
shall see,
And what they had not heard they
shall consider.

53 Who has believed our report?
And to whom has the arm of the
LORD been revealed?
2For He shall grow up before Him as a
tender plant,
And as a root out of dry ground.
He has no form or comeliness;
And when we see Him,
There is no beauty that we should
desire Him.
3He is despised and rejected by men,
A Man of sorrows and acquainted
with grief.
And we hid, as it were, *our* faces from
Him;
He was despised, and we did not
esteem Him.

4Surely He has borne our griefs
And carried our sorrows;
Yet we esteemed Him stricken,
Smitten by God, and afflicted.
5But He *was* wounded for our
transgressions,
He was bruised for our iniquities;
The chastisement for our peace *was*
upon Him,
And by His stripes we are healed.
6All we like sheep have gone astray;
We have turned, every one, to his
own way;
And the LORD has laid on Him the
iniquity of us all.

7He was oppressed and He was
afflicted,
Yet He opened not His mouth;
He was led as a lamb to the slaughter,
And as a sheep before its shearers is
silent,
So He opened not His mouth.
8He was taken from prison and from
judgment,
And who will declare His generation?
For He was cut off from the land of
the living;
For the transgressions of My people
He was stricken.
9And they[a] made His grave with the
wicked—
But with the rich at His death,
Because He had done no violence,
Nor *was any* deceit in His mouth.

53:9 [a]Literally *he* or *He*

THE FUNCTION OF THE LAW

53:2 As with Psa. 22, one might wonder how any Jewish person who professes to believe God's Word could read Isa. 53 and not see this entire chapter as a prophecy of a "suffering Messiah," fulfilled perfectly in Jesus of Nazareth.

The obstacle to a Jewish person's belief in Jesus as the Messiah could be that he has not had his mouth "stopped" by the Law (see Rom. 3:19). As long as anyone believes he can provide for his own atonement, he won't understand his need for the Savior and therefore won't search the Scriptures.

The evangelist must confront both Gentile and Jew with the spiritual nature of God's Law to show them their guilt (see Jer. 9:25). Open up the Commandments as Jesus did. (See Mark 10:17 and John 4:7 comments.)

Don't take for granted that Jewish people know God's Law as they should. Many Jews today are steeped in tradition, but nullify the Law as did the Jews in the day of Christ. For more on how to witness to Jewish people, see page 1782.

53:1 One would think that a terminally ill world would gladly embrace the cure of the gospel, but few, so few, believe our report (see John 12:38–41).

53:3 The ungodly still despise and reject the name of Jesus Christ. It is used worldwide as a cuss word to express disgust. Adolf Hitler's name wasn't despised enough to be used in such a way.

Though Jesus was anointed with an oil of gladness more than His companions (see Psa. 45:7), He was also a Man of sorrows acquainted with the grief of this world. That is the spirit in which a Christian should walk.

53:4 *Jesus in the Old Testament*

By Todd Friel

What is the one miracle that undeniably proves divinity? The ability to accurately predict the future. As you read Isa. 53, keep in mind that this prophecy about Jesus Christ, the Lamb of God, was written over 600 years before He came to this earth. This accurate prediction of the brutal suffering and death of the Messiah proves that the Bible was written by God:

- Messiah would be so brutally beaten that one could barely tell He was human (Isa. 52:14).
- The Savior would be despised and rejected by men (Isa. 53:3,4).
- Messiah would be beaten and wounded by men to pay the price for our sins (vv. 5,6).
- The Savior would not open His mouth when He was accused (v. 7).
- Messiah would be imprisoned (v. 8).
- The Savior would be killed with criminals but buried in a rich man's grave (v. 9).
- The Messiah would have no deceit in His mouth (v. 9).

Isaiah concludes this amazing description of a murdered Messiah with this stunning sentence, "Yet it pleased the LORD to bruise Him; He has put Him to grief" (v. 10). It was God who crushed His only Son on our behalf (v. 12). When God looked at the cross, He saw you. Now, when God looks at you, He sees Jesus.

This prophecy alone should convince anyone that the Bible is supernatural.

(Adapted from *Don't Stub Your Toe.*)

10Yet it pleased the LORD to bruise Him;
He has put *Him* to grief.
When You make His soul an offering
for sin,
He shall see *His* seed, He shall
prolong *His* days,
And the pleasure of the LORD shall
prosper in His hand.
11He shall see the labor of His soul,[a]
and be satisfied.
By His knowledge My righteous
Servant shall justify many,
For He shall bear their iniquities.
12Therefore I will divide Him a portion
with the great,
And He shall divide the spoil with the
strong,
Because He poured out His soul unto
death,
And He was numbered with the
transgressors,
And He bore the sin of many,
And made intercession for the
transgressors.

A Perpetual Covenant of Peace

54 "Sing, O barren,
You *who* have not borne!
Break forth into singing, and cry aloud,
You *who* have not labored with child!
For more *are* the children of the
desolate
Than the children of the married

53:11 [a]Following Masoretic Text, Targum, and Vulgate; Dead Sea Scrolls and Septuagint read *From the labor of His soul He shall see light.*

53:6 How applicable that God likens humanity to sheep, and how wonderful that God would strike the Shepherd to save us from slaughter. See John 10:11; 1 Pet. 2:24,25.

"Either sin is with you, lying on your shoulders, or it is lying on Christ, the Lamb of God. Now if it is lying on your back, you are lost; but if it is resting on Christ, you are free, and you will be saved. Now choose what you want." *Martin Luther*

53:7 Pilate marveled at the silence of God's Lamb (see Matt. 27:12–14).

53:9 This messianic prophecy was fulfilled in Matt. 27:57–60. See also 1 Pet. 2:22.

53:10 This messianic prophecy was fulfilled in 2 Cor. 5:21. It pleased the LORD to bruise His beloved Son. How great is the love of God for wicked sinners such as us. The greater we see our sin, the greater will we see God's mercy and love so evidently displayed on the cross (see Rom. 7:7–13).

53:11 This messianic prophecy was fulfilled in Rom. 5:15–18. See also 1 John 2:1; Isa. 42:1.

53:12 See Psa. 2:8; Rom. 3:25; Matt. 27:38; Mark 15:27,28.

woman," says the LORD.
2"Enlarge the place of your tent,
And let them stretch out the curtains of your dwellings;
Do not spare;
Lengthen your cords,
And strengthen your stakes.
3For you shall expand to the right and to the left,
And your descendants will inherit the nations,
And make the desolate cities inhabited.

4"Do not fear, for you will not be ashamed;
Neither be disgraced, for you will not be put to shame;
For you will forget the shame of your youth,
And will not remember the reproach of your widowhood anymore.
5For your Maker *is* your husband,
The LORD of hosts *is* His name;
And your Redeemer *is* the Holy One of Israel;
He is called the God of the whole earth.
6For the LORD has called you
Like a woman forsaken and grieved in spirit,
Like a youthful wife when you were refused,"
Says your God.
7"For a mere moment I have forsaken you,
But with great mercies I will gather you.
8With a little wrath I hid My face from you for a moment;
But with everlasting kindness I will have mercy on you,"
Says the LORD, your Redeemer.

9"For this *is* like the waters of Noah to Me;
For as I have sworn
That the waters of Noah would no longer cover the earth,
So have I sworn
That I would not be angry with you, nor rebuke you.
10For the mountains shall depart
And the hills be removed,
But My kindness shall not depart from you,
Nor shall My covenant of peace be removed,"
Says the LORD, who has mercy on you.

11"O you afflicted one,
Tossed with tempest, *and* not comforted,
Behold, I will lay your stones with colorful gems,
And lay your foundations with sapphires.
12I will make your pinnacles of rubies,
Your gates of crystal,
And all your walls of precious stones.
13All your children *shall be* taught by the LORD,
And great *shall be* the peace of your children.
14In righteousness you shall be established;
You shall be far from oppression, for you shall not fear;
And from terror, for it shall not come near you.
15Indeed they shall surely assemble, *but* not because of Me.
Whoever assembles against you shall fall for your sake.

16"Behold, I have created the blacksmith
Who blows the coals in the fire,
Who brings forth an instrument for his work;
And I have created the spoiler to destroy.
17No weapon formed against you shall prosper,
And every tongue *which* rises against you in judgment

54:17 Our confidence before God is only because we stand in the Savior's righteousness. This verse should be read in conjunction with Rom. 8:31–39.

54:9

Was Noah's Flood Global?

By Ken Ham and Tim Lovett, Answers in Genesis

Scientists once understood the fossils (which are buried in water-carried sediments of mud and sand) to be mostly the result of the great Flood. Those who now accept the evolutionary millions of years of gradual accumulation of fossils have, in their way of thinking, explained away the evidence for the global Flood. Hence, many compromising Christians insist on a local flood. Secularists deny the possibility of worldwide Flood at all. If they would think from a biblical perspective, however, they would see the abundant evidence for the Flood. As someone once quipped, "I wouldn't have seen it if I hadn't believed it."

Those who accept the evolutionary time frame with its fossil accumulation also rob the Fall of Adam of its serious consequences. They put the fossils—which testify of disease, suffering, and death—before Adam and Eve sinned and brought death and suffering into the world. In doing this, they also undermine the meaning of the death and resurrection of Christ. Such a scenario also robs all meaning from God's description of His finished creation as "very good."

If the Flood were local, why did Noah have to build an Ark? He could have walked to the other side of the mountains and escaped! Most important, if the Flood were local, people who did not happen to be living in the vicinity would not have been affected by it. They would have escaped God's judgment on sin.

In addition, Jesus believed that the Flood killed every person not on the Ark (Matt. 24:37–39). And what did Christ mean when He likened the coming world judgment to the judgment of "all" men (v. 39) in the days of Noah?

In 2 Pet. 3:5–7, the coming judgment by fire is likened to the former judgment by water in Noah's Flood. A partial judgment in Noah's day, therefore, would mean a partial judgment to come.

If the Flood were only local, how could the waters rise to 15 cubits above the mountains (Gen. 7:20)? Water seeks its own level. It could not rise to cover the local mountains while leaving the rest of the world untouched.

The uppermost parts of Mt. Everest are composed of fossil-bearing, water-deposited layers, so even Mt. Everest was once covered with water—and it's more than 5 miles high. How, then, could the Flood have covered "all the high hills under the whole heaven" (Gen. 7:19)? Before the Flood, the mountains were not as high. The mountains today were formed only toward the end of, and after, the Flood by collision of the tectonic plates and the associated up-thrusting. (Some believe it was during this time that the mountains rose and valleys sank down to the place God establish for them, as mentioned in Psa. 104:6–8.) If we even out the ocean basins and flatten out the mountains, there is enough water to cover the entire earth for a depth of about 1.7 miles!

In addition, if the Flood were merely local, God would have repeatedly broken His promise never to send such a Flood again. (He even put a rainbow in the sky as a covenant between God and man and the animals that He would never repeat such an event; Gen. 9:13–15.) There have been huge "local" floods in recent times (in Bangladesh, for example)—but never another global Flood that killed all life on the land.

You shall condemn.
This *is* the heritage of the servants of
the LORD,
And their righteousness *is* from Me,"
Says the LORD.

An Invitation to Abundant Life

55 "Ho! Everyone who thirsts,
Come to the waters;
And you who have no money,
Come, buy and eat.

SPRINGBOARDS FOR PREACHING AND WITNESSING

Son Stroke

55:1 Two men were crawling through a desert, dying of thirst. One man managed to get to his feet, and stumbled over a small rise. To his utter surprise he found an oasis of cool, fresh water. He fell into the water, drank to his heart's content, and ran back to tell his dying friend the good news.

He said, "There's an oasis of water over that rise. Come with me, drink, and you will live!" The dying man looked up, and said through parched lips, "You liar! I don't believe the water is there . . . and you are a naïve fool to believe it. Don't try to push your so-called water down my throat.

"I have proof that you are deceived—that hill you stumbled over is millions of years old. Besides, it's my life, and I choose to stay here and die, you narrow-minded fool!"

Jesus said, "If anyone thirsts, let him come to Me and drink. He who believes in Me, as the Scripture has said, out of his heart will flow rivers of living water" (John 7:37,38).

Yes, come, buy wine and milk
Without money and without price.
2Why do you spend money for *what is* not bread,
And your wages for *what* does not satisfy?
Listen carefully to Me, and eat *what is* good,
And let your soul delight itself in abundance.
3Incline your ear, and come to Me.
Hear, and your soul shall live;
And I will make an everlasting covenant with you—
The sure mercies of David.
4Indeed I have given him *as* a witness to the people,
A leader and commander for the people.
5Surely you shall call a nation you do not know,
And nations *who* do not know you shall run to you,
Because of the LORD your God,
And the Holy One of Israel;
For He has glorified you."

. . . . . .

For the biblical way to present God's love, see Matt. 10:22 comment.

. . . . . .

6Seek the LORD while He may be found,
Call upon Him while He is near.
7Let the wicked forsake his way,
And the unrighteous man his thoughts;
Let him return to the LORD,
And He will have mercy on him;
And to our God,
For He will abundantly pardon.

55:3 Here is God's universal offer to humanity: "Incline your ear, and come to Me. Hear, and your soul shall live." Those who "thirst" for righteousness and come to Jesus will be filled (see John 7:37).

55:6 This verse suggests that the patience of God is exhaustible. For those who refuse to accept the gospel, the time may come when the Lord will refuse to "be found" (see Prov. 1:24–31). Unbelievers should be made aware that they may not get the deathbed conversion they may be planning on. See also Luke 12:20 comment.

"A good man was one day passing a saloon as a young man was coming out, and thinking to make sport of him he called out, 'Deacon, how far is it to hell?' The deacon gave no answer, but after riding a few rods he turned to look after the scoffer, and found that his horse had thrown him to the ground and broken his neck. I tell you, my friends, I would sooner give that right hand than to trifle with eternal things." *D. L. Moody*

55:7 This is repentance. The sinner is not only to forsake his thoughts, but also his way (actions). It is more than an intellectual acknowledgment that he has sinned. He must *turn* from those sins—he must confess and forsake them (see Prov. 28:13). In doing so, he will be abundantly pardoned. Repentance is not a "work," as some would say. It is God-given to sinners, as is faith. See Acts 5:31; 11:18. For the necessity of true repentance, see John 3:16 comment.

8"For My thoughts *are* not your
thoughts,
Nor *are* your ways My ways," says the
LORD.
9"For *as* the heavens are higher than
the earth,
So are My ways higher than your ways,
And My thoughts than your thoughts.

10"For as the rain comes down, and the
snow from heaven,
And do not return there,
But water the earth,
And make it bring forth and bud,
That it may give seed to the sower
And bread to the eater,
11So shall My word be that goes forth
from My mouth;
It shall not return to Me void,
But it shall accomplish what I please,
And it shall prosper *in the thing* for
which I sent it.

12"For you shall go out with joy,
And be led out with peace;
The mountains and the hills
Shall break forth into singing before
you,
And all the trees of the field shall clap
their hands.
13Instead of the thorn shall come up
the cypress tree,
And instead of the brier shall come
up the myrtle tree;
And it shall be to the LORD for a name,
For an everlasting sign *that* shall not
be cut off."

Salvation for the Gentiles

56 Thus says the LORD:

"Keep justice, and do righteousness,
For My salvation *is* about to come,
And My righteousness to be revealed.
2Blessed *is* the man *who* does this,
And the son of man *who* lays hold on
it;
Who keeps from defiling the Sabbath,
And keeps his hand from doing any
evil."

Before we can begin to see the cross as something done for us, we have to see it as something done by us.

JOHN STOTT

3Do not let the son of the foreigner
Who has joined himself to the LORD
Speak, saying,
"The LORD has utterly separated me
from His people";
Nor let the eunuch say,
"Here I am, a dry tree."
4For thus says the LORD:
"To the eunuchs who keep My
Sabbaths,
And choose what pleases Me,
And hold fast My covenant,
5Even to them I will give in My house
And within My walls a place and a
name
Better than that of sons and daughters;
I will give them[a] an everlasting name
That shall not be cut off.

6"Also the sons of the foreigner
Who join themselves to the LORD, to
serve Him,
And to love the name of the LORD, to
be His servants—
Everyone who keeps from defiling the
Sabbath,
And holds fast My covenant—
7Even them I will bring to My holy

56:5 [a]Literally *him*

55:11 This verse is the reason for our confidence when we preach an uncompromising gospel message, even if we see no visible results (see also 1 Cor. 15:58).

"It is not our business to make the message acceptable, but to make it available. We are not to see that they like it, but that they get it." *Vance Havner*

mountain,
And make them joyful in My house of prayer.
Their burnt offerings and their sacrifices
Will be accepted on My altar;
For My house shall be called a house of prayer for all nations."
8The Lord GOD, who gathers the outcasts of Israel, says,
"Yet I will gather to him
Others besides those who are gathered to him."

Israel's Irresponsible Leaders

9All you beasts of the field, come to devour,
All you beasts in the forest.
10His watchmen *are* blind,
They are all ignorant;
They *are* all dumb dogs,
They cannot bark;
Sleeping, lying down, loving to slumber.
11Yes, *they are* greedy dogs
Which never have enough.
And they *are* shepherds
Who cannot understand;
They all look to their own way,
Every one for his own gain,
From his *own* territory.
12"Come," *one says,* "I will bring wine,
And we will fill ourselves with intoxicating drink;
Tomorrow will be as today,
And much more abundant."

Israel's Futile Idolatry

57 The righteous perishes,
And no man takes *it* to heart;
Merciful men *are* taken away,
While no one considers
That the righteous is taken away from evil.
2He shall enter into peace;
They shall rest in their beds,
Each one walking *in* his uprightness.

3"But come here,
You sons of the sorceress,
You offspring of the adulterer and the harlot!
4Whom do you ridicule?
Against whom do you make a wide mouth
And stick out the tongue?
Are you not children of transgression,
Offspring of falsehood,
5Inflaming yourselves with gods under every green tree,
Slaying the children in the valleys,
Under the clefts of the rocks?
6Among the smooth *stones* of the stream
Is your portion;
They, they, *are* your lot!
Even to them you have poured a drink offering,
You have offered a grain offering.
Should I receive comfort in these?

7"On a lofty and high mountain
You have set your bed;

56:7 This is what Jesus quoted as He cleared the temple, overturning the tables of the money-changers (see Mark 11:15–17). May God do the same thing with money-hungry televangelists.

56:12 The godless see pleasure as their primary goal—something called hedonism. They will have no desire to seek after the righteousness that delivers from death until the Law puts salt on their tongue. The moral Law reveals sin and its terrible consequence. It makes a sin-seeking sinner look for a way to be made right with his Creator. It prepares the heart for the gospel.

57:1,2 Grief at the loss of a loved one can be overwhelming. But we have the strong consolation that God is in control and that He allowed the loss for a reason. Besides, those in Christ who have gone ahead are in a much better place (see. Psa. 72:14; 116:15). Be careful of the emotion of grief. If you lose a loved one, allow yourself to weep; it's a natural grieving process that will help the healing. But don't allow uncontrolled grief to eat away at you. If you find yourself having negative thoughts and memories that cause pain, take control of your thoughts and say, "I will not go there!" Then look to the future and what God would have you do with your life.

Even there you went up
To offer sacrifice.
8Also behind the doors and their posts
You have set up your remembrance;
For you have uncovered yourself *to those other* than Me,
And have gone up to them;
You have enlarged your bed
And made *a covenant* with them;
You have loved their bed,
Where you saw *their* nudity.[a]
9You went to the king with ointment,
And increased your perfumes;
You sent your messengers far off,
And *even* descended to Sheol.
10You are wearied in the length of your way;
Yet you did not say, 'There is no hope.'
You have found the life of your hand;
Therefore you were not grieved.

> Christianity today is man-centered, not God-centered... The image of God currently popular is that of a distracted Father, struggling in heartbroken desperation to get people to accept a Savior of whom they feel no need and in whom they have very little interest.
>
> **A. W. TOZER**

11"And of whom have you been afraid, or feared,
That you have lied
And not remembered Me,
Nor taken *it* to your heart?
Is it not because I have held My peace from of old
That you do not fear Me?
12I will declare your righteousness
And your works,
For they will not profit you.
13When you cry out,
Let your collection *of idols* deliver you.
But the wind will carry them all away,
A breath will take *them*.
But he who puts his trust in Me shall possess the land,
And shall inherit My holy mountain."

Healing for the Backslider

14And one shall say,
"Heap it up! Heap it up!
Prepare the way,
Take the stumbling block out of the way of My people."

15For thus says the High and Lofty One
Who inhabits eternity, whose name *is* Holy:
"I dwell in the high and holy *place*,
With him *who* has a contrite and humble spirit,
To revive the spirit of the humble,
And to revive the heart of the contrite ones.
16For I will not contend forever,
Nor will I always be angry;
For the spirit would fail before Me,
And the souls *which* I have made.
17For the iniquity of his covetousness
I was angry and struck him;
I hid and was angry,
And he went on backsliding in the way of his heart.
18I have seen his ways, and will heal him;
I will also lead him,
And restore comforts to him
And to his mourners.

19"I create the fruit of the lips:
Peace, peace to *him who is* far off and to *him who is* near,"

57:8 [a]Literally *hand*, a euphemism

57:11 One great error of the ungodly is to think that they are getting away with sin. They assume that because God doesn't send lightning when they violate His Commandments, He doesn't care or doesn't see what they do. But with each sin they are storing up His wrath that will be revealed on the Day of Judgment. See Psa. 50:21; Eccles. 8:11.

57:15 Almighty God, who inhabits eternity, condescends to dwell with the lowly of heart (see Psa. 34:18; 51:17; Matt. 5:3). A humble and contrite heart is the essence of repentance.

Says the LORD,
"And I will heal him."
20But the wicked *are* like the troubled
sea,
When it cannot rest,
Whose waters cast up mire and dirt.

21"*There is* no peace,"
Says my God, "for the wicked."

Fasting that Pleases God

58 "Cry aloud, spare not;
Lift up your voice like a trumpet;
Tell My people their transgression,
And the house of Jacob their sins.
2Yet they seek Me daily,
And delight to know My ways,
As a nation that did righteousness,
And did not forsake the ordinance of
their God.
They ask of Me the ordinances of
justice;
They take delight in approaching God.
3'Why have we fasted,' *they say,* 'and
You have not seen?
Why have we afflicted our souls, and
You take no notice?'

"In fact, in the day of your fast you
find pleasure,
And exploit all your laborers.
4Indeed you fast for strife and debate,
And to strike with the fist of
wickedness.
You will not fast as *you do* this day,
To make your voice heard on high.
5Is it a fast that I have chosen,
A day for a man to afflict his soul?
Is it to bow down his head like a
bulrush,
And to spread out sackcloth and ashes?
Would you call this a fast,
And an acceptable day to the LORD?

6"*Is* this not the fast that I have chosen:
To loose the bonds of wickedness,
To undo the heavy burdens,
To let the oppressed go free,
And that you break every yoke?
7*Is it* not to share your bread with the
hungry,
And that you bring to your house the
poor who are cast out;
When you see the naked, that you
cover him,
And not hide yourself from your own
flesh?
8Then your light shall break forth like
the morning,
Your healing shall spring forth
speedily,
And your righteousness shall go
before you;
The glory of the LORD shall be your
rear guard.
9Then you shall call, and the LORD will

58:1 The next time someone tells you that religion is a personal thing and that you should keep it to yourself, think of this verse, because "religion" is empty hypocrisy (as the following verses describe) and *should* be kept to oneself. But God has opened the door of everlasting life through the gospel, and that message should be shouted from the housetops. Lift up your voice like a trumpet, and use God's Law as Jesus did, to show this people their transgressions.

However, when you obey this verse, the ungodly will reprove you. They may tell you to instead speak about God's love, accuse you of being self-righteous, tell you to "judge not lest you be judged," and even insist that Jesus didn't talk about sin. See comments at Matt. 23:13–16; Luke 6:37; and John 8:11.

"Religion is hanging around the cross. Christianity is hanging *on* the cross." *Stephen Hill*

58:7 "Is there a connection between our rediscovered social passion and our growing evangelistic indifference? Evangelism—calling sinful people to repent and follow Jesus—is always a tougher sell than giving a cup of cold water in Jesus' name... Maybe our preference for social activism reveals a more basic problem: that we don't really believe our neighbor's deepest need is to be forgiven by and reconciled to God. We seem to think that if only he or she is fed, or lives in a society brimming with Christian principles, or sees our battles against the world's many injustices, then we will have discharged our responsibility to Christ.

"I'm not sure Jesus would agree. 'For what does it profit a man,' the Lord asks, 'if he gains the whole world and loses or forfeits himself?' May our concern to make a difference in this world not blind us to our neighbors' eternal destiny in the next." *Stan Guthrie*

answer;
You shall cry, and He will say, 'Here I
am.'

"If you take away the yoke from your
midst,
The pointing of the finger, and
speaking wickedness,
10 *If* you extend your soul to the hungry
And satisfy the afflicted soul,
Then your light shall dawn in the
darkness,
And your darkness shall *be* as the
noonday.
11 The LORD will guide you continually,
And satisfy your soul in drought,
And strengthen your bones;
You shall be like a watered garden,
And like a spring of water, whose
waters do not fail.
12 Those from among you
Shall build the old waste places;
You shall raise up the foundations of
many generations;
And you shall be called the Repairer
of the Breach,
The Restorer of Streets to Dwell In.

13 "If you turn away your foot from the
Sabbath,
From doing your pleasure on My holy
day,
And call the Sabbath a delight,
The holy *day* of the LORD honorable,
And shall honor Him, not doing your
own ways,
Nor finding your own pleasure,
Nor speaking *your own* words,
14 Then you shall delight yourself in the
LORD;
And I will cause you to ride on the
high hills of the earth,
And feed you with the heritage of
Jacob your father.
The mouth of the LORD has spoken."

Separated from God

59 Behold, the LORD's hand is not
shortened,
That it cannot save;
Nor His ear heavy,
That it cannot hear.
2 But your iniquities have separated
you from your God;
And your sins have hidden *His* face
from you,
So that He will not hear.
3 For your hands are defiled with blood,
And your fingers with iniquity;
Your lips have spoken lies,
Your tongue has muttered perversity.

4 No one calls for justice,
Nor does *any* plead for truth.
They trust in empty words and speak
lies;
They conceive evil and bring forth
iniquity.
5 They hatch vipers' eggs and weave
the spider's web;
He who eats of their eggs dies,
And *from* that which is crushed a
viper breaks out.

6 Their webs will not become garments,
Nor will they cover themselves with
their works;
Their works *are* works of iniquity,
And the act of violence *is* in their
hands.
7 Their feet run to evil,
And they make haste to shed

58:13,14 We have six days in which to labor, but God has given us one day a week to set aside for rest and to focus on Him. By not striving to provide for ourselves, this shows our trust in Him as the one who has given us our life, our every breath, our loved ones, and eternity in heaven with Him. With grateful hearts we should set aside one day to acknowledge and honor our Creator and Provider.

59:1,2 Many of the ungodly are disillusioned when God doesn't answer their prayers. They need to know that He often doesn't hear them because of their proud and sinful hearts. The psalmist warns that if we regard iniquity in our heart, the Lord will not hear (see Psa. 66:18). We must continually confess and forsake sin, and keep intimate communion with God. See also Isa. 1:15; Mic. 3:4; John 9:31.

Springboards for Preaching and Witnessing

The Persistent Spider

59:5 Many years ago we had in our home a stubborn spider that kept building a web against our house. No matter how many times we swept it away, the spider and its web would reappear the next morning. One day I enlisted the help of one of my sons, as well as a small stick and a can of insect spray. I had my son gently tap the stick on the web while I tried to sound like a fly in distress. The hungry spider came out of its hiding place, and that's when I killed it with the insect spray.

There is a stubborn web of sin that continually plagues mankind. It is the web of violence, corruption, rape, greed, wars, theft, etc. We try to sweep it away through political means. Yet these crimes continue, and the root cause of the problem remains in hiding. We must use the stick of God's Law to gently tap on the human heart. Suddenly, the cause of sin appears. And that is when sin can be put to death with the power of the gospel. So hold still while I "tap" you with God's Law to see if we can find the spider. Do you consider yourself to be a good person—have you kept the Ten Commandments? (For further details on how to go through the Law, see John 4:7 comment.)

innocent blood;
Their thoughts *are* thoughts of iniquity;
Wasting and destruction *are* in their
paths.
8The way of peace they have not
known,
And *there is* no justice in their ways;
They have made themselves crooked
paths;
Whoever takes that way shall not
know peace.

Sin Confessed

9Therefore justice is far from us,
Nor does righteousness overtake us;
We look for light, but there is
darkness!
For brightness, *but* we walk in
blackness!
10We grope for the wall like the blind,
And we grope as if *we had* no eyes;
We stumble at noonday as at twilight;
We are as dead *men* in desolate places.
11We all growl like bears,
And moan sadly like doves;
We look for justice, but *there is* none;
For salvation, *but* it is far from us.
12For our transgressions are multiplied
before You,
And our sins testify against us;
For our transgressions *are* with us,
And *as for* our iniquities, we know
them:
13In transgressing and lying against the
LORD,
And departing from our God,
Speaking oppression and revolt,
Conceiving and uttering from the
heart words of falsehood.
14Justice is turned back,
And righteousness stands afar off;
For truth is fallen in the street,
And equity cannot enter.
15So truth fails,
And he *who* departs from evil makes
himself a prey.

The Redeemer of Zion

Then the LORD saw *it,* and it
displeased Him
That *there was* no justice.
16He saw that *there was* no man,
And wondered that *there was* no
intercessor;
Therefore His own arm brought
salvation for Him;
And His own righteousness, it
sustained Him.
17For He put on righteousness as a
breastplate,

59:12 For the difference among sins, transgressions, and iniquities, see Psa. 32:1,2 comment.

59:15 The moment we depart from sin through genuine repentance, we step into a battle with the world, the flesh, and the devil. See 2 Cor. 4:4 comment.

And a helmet of salvation on His head;
He put on the garments of vengeance for clothing,
And was clad with zeal as a cloak.
18According to *their* deeds, accordingly He will repay,
Fury to His adversaries,
Recompense to His enemies;
The coastlands He will fully repay.
19So shall they fear
The name of the LORD from the west,
And His glory from the rising of the sun;
When the enemy comes in like a flood,
The Spirit of the LORD will lift up a standard against him.

20"The Redeemer will come to Zion,
And to those who turn from transgression in Jacob,"
Says the LORD.

21"As for Me," says the LORD, "this *is*
My covenant with them: My Spirit who *is*
upon you, and My words which I have
put in your mouth, shall not depart from
your mouth, nor from the mouth of your
descendants, nor from the mouth of your
descendants' descendants," says the LORD,
"from this time and forevermore."

The Gentiles Bless Zion

60 Arise, shine;
For your light has come!
And the glory of the LORD is risen upon you.
2For behold, the darkness shall cover the earth,
And deep darkness the people;
But the LORD will arise over you,
And His glory will be seen upon you.
3The Gentiles shall come to your light,
And kings to the brightness of your rising.

4"Lift up your eyes all around, and see:
They all gather together, they come to you;
Your sons shall come from afar,
And your daughters shall be nursed at *your* side.
5Then you shall see and become radiant,
And your heart shall swell with joy;
Because the abundance of the sea shall be turned to you,
The wealth of the Gentiles shall come to you.
6The multitude of camels shall cover your *land,*
The dromedaries of Midian and Ephah;
All those from Sheba shall come;
They shall bring gold and incense,
And they shall proclaim the praises of the LORD.
7All the flocks of Kedar shall be gathered together to you,
The rams of Nebaioth shall minister to you;
They shall ascend with acceptance on My altar,
And I will glorify the house of My glory.

8"Who *are* these *who* fly like a cloud,
And like doves to their roosts?
9Surely the coastlands shall wait for Me;
And the ships of Tarshish *will come* first,
To bring your sons from afar,

60:2 Is the light of the gospel vanishing? "Alas, alas, God's 'way of salvation' is almost entirely unknown today, the nature of Christ's salvation is almost universally misunderstood, and the terms of His salvation misrepresented on every hand. The 'Gospel' which is now being proclaimed is, in nine cases out of every ten, but a perversion of the Truth, and tens of thousands, assured they are bound for heaven, are now hastening to hell as fast as time can take them...

"Unless God is pleased to grant a real revival, it will not be long ere 'the darkness shall cover the earth, and gross darkness the people' (Isa. 60:2), for the light of the true Gospel is rapidly disappearing... Those preachers who tell sinners that they may be saved without forsaking their idols, without repenting, without surrendering to the Lordship of Christ, are as erroneous and dangerous as others who insist that salvation is by works, and that heaven must be earned by our own efforts!" *A. W. Pink*

Their silver and their gold with them,
To the name of the LORD your God,
And to the Holy One of Israel,
Because He has glorified you.

10"The sons of foreigners shall build up your walls,
And their kings shall minister to you;
For in My wrath I struck you,
But in My favor I have had mercy on you.
11Therefore your gates shall be open continually;
They shall not be shut day or night,
That *men* may bring to you the wealth of the Gentiles,
And their kings in procession.
12For the nation and kingdom which will not serve you shall perish,
And *those* nations shall be utterly ruined.

13"The glory of Lebanon shall come to you,
The cypress, the pine, and the box tree together,
To beautify the place of My sanctuary;
And I will make the place of My feet glorious.
14Also the sons of those who afflicted you
Shall come bowing to you,
And all those who despised you shall fall prostrate at the soles of your feet;
And they shall call you The City of the LORD,
Zion of the Holy One of Israel.

15"Whereas you have been forsaken and hated,
So that no one went through *you*,
I will make you an eternal excellence,
A joy of many generations.
16You shall drink the milk of the Gentiles,
And milk the breast of kings;
You shall know that I, the LORD, *am* your Savior
And your Redeemer, the Mighty One of Jacob.

I believe I never was more acceptable to my Master than when I was standing to teach those hearers in the open fields... I now preach to ten times more people than I would if I had been confined to the churches.

GEORGE WHITEFIELD

17"Instead of bronze I will bring gold,
Instead of iron I will bring silver,
Instead of wood, bronze,
And instead of stones, iron.
I will also make your officers peace,
And your magistrates righteousness.
18Violence shall no longer be heard in your land,
Neither wasting nor destruction within your borders;
But you shall call your walls Salvation,
And your gates Praise.

God the Glory of His People

19"The sun shall no longer be your light by day,
Nor for brightness shall the moon give light to you;
But the LORD will be to you an everlasting light,
And your God your glory.
20Your sun shall no longer go down,
Nor shall your moon withdraw itself;
For the LORD will be your everlasting light,
And the days of your mourning shall be ended.
21Also your people *shall* all *be* righteous;
They shall inherit the land forever,
The branch of My planting,
The work of My hands,

60:19 The Scriptures often tell us that God is light. This is more than metaphoric. See Rev. 21:23.

That I may be glorified.
[22]A little one shall become a thousand,
And a small one a strong nation.
I, the LORD, will hasten it in its time."

The Good News of Salvation

61 "The Spirit of the Lord GOD *is* upon Me,
Because the LORD has anointed Me
To preach good tidings to the poor;
He has sent Me to heal the brokenhearted,
To proclaim liberty to the captives,
And the opening of the prison to *those who are* bound;
[2]To proclaim the acceptable year of the LORD,
And the day of vengeance of our God;
To comfort all who mourn,
[3]To console those who mourn in Zion,
To give them beauty for ashes,
The oil of joy for mourning,
The garment of praise for the spirit of heaviness;
That they may be called trees of righteousness,
The planting of the LORD, that He may be glorified."

[4]And they shall rebuild the old ruins,
They shall raise up the former desolations,
And they shall repair the ruined cities,
The desolations of many generations.
[5]Strangers shall stand and feed your flocks,

THE FUNCTION OF THE LAW

61:1 Those who think they are rich and in need of nothing should be presented with the Law, to humble them and prepare their heart for grace. The gospel is to be preached to those who are poor in spirit. In the same way, someone who thinks he is healthy will not see his need of a cure. The Law convinces a sinner that he is sick, while the gospel is the cure. For a detailed description of who the gospel is for, see Luke 4:18 comment. For further details on biblical evangelism, see 2 Sam. 12:1–14 and John 4:7 comments.

And the sons of the foreigner
Shall be your plowmen and your vinedressers.
[6]But you shall be named the priests of the LORD,
They shall call you the servants of our God.
You shall eat the riches of the Gentiles,
And in their glory you shall boast.
[7]Instead of your shame *you shall have* double *honor,*
And *instead of* confusion they shall rejoice in their portion.
Therefore in their land they shall possess double;
Everlasting joy shall be theirs.

[8]"For I, the LORD, love justice;
I hate robbery for burnt offering;
I will direct their work in truth,
And will make with them an everlasting covenant.
[9]Their descendants shall be known

61:3 Here is the order of genuine conversion. A sinner should "mourn" for his sinful state. He should have the spirit of heaviness (be laboring and heavy laden over his sinful heart; see Matt. 11:28). It is these converts who become trees of righteousness because they are the planting of the Lord; they are born of God (see John 1:13). See also Jer. 17:7,8.

"The religion of Christ is the religion of *joy*. Christ came to take away our sins, to roll off our curse, to unbind our chains, to open our prisonhouse, to cancel our debt; in a word, to give us the oil of joy for mourning, the garment of praise for the spirit of heaviness. Is not this joy? Where can we find a joy so real, so deep, so pure, so lasting? There is every element of joy—deep, ecstatic, satisfying, sanctifying joy—in the gospel of Christ. The believer in Jesus is essentially a happy man. The child of God is, from necessity, a joyful man. His sins are forgiven, his soul is justified, his person is adopted, his trials are blessings, his conflicts are victories, his death is immortality, his future is a heaven of inconceivable, unthought-of, untold, and endless blessedness. With such a God, such a Saviour, and such a hope, is he not, ought he not, to be a joyful man?" *Octavius Winslow*

among the Gentiles,
And their offspring among the people.
All who see them shall acknowledge
them,
That they *are* the posterity *whom* the
LORD has blessed."

10 I will greatly rejoice in the LORD,
My soul shall be joyful in my God;
For He has clothed me with the
garments of salvation,
He has covered me with the robe of
righteousness,
As a bridegroom decks *himself* with
ornaments,
And as a bride adorns *herself* with her
jewels.
11 For as the earth brings forth its bud,
As the garden causes the things that
are sown in it to spring forth,
So the Lord GOD will cause
righteousness and praise to
spring forth before all the
nations.

Assurance of Zion's Salvation

62 For Zion's sake I will not hold My
peace,
And for Jerusalem's sake I will not rest,
Until her righteousness goes forth as
brightness,
And her salvation as a lamp *that* burns.
2 The Gentiles shall see your
righteousness,
And all kings your glory.
You shall be called by a new name,
Which the mouth of the LORD will
name.
3 You shall also be a crown of glory
In the hand of the LORD,
And a royal diadem
In the hand of your God.
4 You shall no longer be termed
Forsaken,
Nor shall your land any more be
termed Desolate;
But you shall be called Hephzibah,[a]
and your land Beulah;[b]
For the LORD delights in you,
And your land shall be married.
5 For *as* a young man marries a virgin,
So shall your sons marry you;
And *as* the bridegroom rejoices over
the bride,
So shall your God rejoice over you.

6 I have set watchmen on your walls, O
Jerusalem;
They shall never hold their peace day
or night.
You who make mention of the LORD,
do not keep silent,
7 And give Him no rest till He
establishes
And till He makes Jerusalem a praise
in the earth.

8 The LORD has sworn by His right hand
And by the arm of His strength:
"Surely I will no longer give your grain
As food for your enemies;
And the sons of the foreigner shall
not drink your new wine,
For which you have labored.
9 But those who have gathered it shall
eat it,
And praise the LORD;
Those who have brought it together
shall drink it in My holy courts."

10 Go through,
Go through the gates!
Prepare the way for the people;
Build up,
Build up the highway!
Take out the stones,
Lift up a banner for the peoples!

62:4 [a]Literally *My Delight Is in Her* [b]Literally *Married*

62:10 We obey this verse when we preach the whole counsel of God. The Christian's ministry is to go into all the world and preach the gospel to every creature. Remove any hindrance that will stop dying sinners from seeing the cross.

[11]Indeed the LORD has proclaimed
To the end of the world:
"Say to the daughter of Zion,
'Surely your salvation is coming;
Behold, His reward *is* with Him,
And His work before Him.' "
[12]And they shall call them The Holy
People,
The Redeemed of the LORD;
And you shall be called Sought Out,
A City Not Forsaken.

The Lord in Judgment and Salvation

63 Who *is* this who comes from Edom,
With dyed garments from Bozrah,
This *One who is* glorious in His apparel,
Traveling in the greatness of His
strength?—

"I who speak in righteousness, mighty
to save."

[2]Why *is* Your apparel red,
And Your garments like one who
treads in the winepress?

[3]"I have trodden the winepress alone,
And from the peoples no one *was*
with Me.
For I have trodden them in My anger,
And trampled them in My fury;
Their blood is sprinkled upon My
garments,
And I have stained all My robes.
[4]For the day of vengeance *is* in My
heart,
And the year of My redeemed has
come.
[5]I looked, but *there was* no one to help,
And I wondered
That *there was* no one to uphold;
Therefore My own arm brought
salvation for Me;
And My own fury, it sustained Me.
[6]I have trodden down the peoples in
My anger,
Made them drunk in My fury,
And brought down their strength to
the earth."

God's Mercy Remembered

[7]I will mention the lovingkindnesses
of the LORD
And the praises of the LORD,
According to all that the LORD has
bestowed on us,
And the great goodness toward the
house of Israel,
Which He has bestowed on them
according to His mercies,
According to the multitude of His
lovingkindnesses.
[8]For He said, "Surely they *are* My
people,
Children *who* will not lie."
So He became their Savior.
[9]In all their affliction He was afflicted,
And the Angel of His Presence saved
them;
In His love and in His pity He
redeemed them;
And He bore them and carried them
All the days of old.
[10]But they rebelled and grieved His
Holy Spirit;
So He turned Himself against them as
an enemy,
And He fought against them.

[11]Then he remembered the days of old,
Moses *and* his people, *saying:*
"Where *is* He who brought them up
out of the sea
With the shepherd of His flock?
Where *is* He who put His Holy Spirit
within them,
[12]Who led *them* by the right hand of
Moses,
With His glorious arm,
Dividing the water before them
To make for Himself an everlasting
name,
[13]Who led them through the deep,

63:9 The Angel of the Lord is often a direct reference to God Himself. See Gen. 16:11–13; Exod. 3:1–6.

As a horse in the wilderness,
That they might not stumble?"

14As a beast goes down into the valley,
And the Spirit of the LORD causes him
to rest,
So You lead Your people,
To make Yourself a glorious name.

A Prayer of Penitence

15Look down from heaven,
And see from Your habitation, holy
and glorious.
Where *are* Your zeal and Your strength,
The yearning of Your heart and Your
mercies toward me?
Are they restrained?
16Doubtless You *are* our Father,
Though Abraham was ignorant of us,
And Israel does not acknowledge us.
You, O LORD, *are* our Father;
Our Redeemer from Everlasting *is*
Your name.
17O LORD, why have You made us stray
from Your ways,
And hardened our heart from Your
fear?
Return for Your servants' sake,
The tribes of Your inheritance.
18Your holy people have possessed *it*
but a little while;
Our adversaries have trodden down
Your sanctuary.
19We have become *like* those of old,
over whom You never ruled,
Those who were never called by Your
name.

64 Oh, that You would rend the
heavens!
That You would come down!
That the mountains might shake at
Your presence—
2As fire burns brushwood,
As fire causes water to boil—
To make Your name known to Your
adversaries,
That the nations may tremble at Your
presence!
3When You did awesome things *for
which* we did not look,
You came down,
The mountains shook at Your
presence.
4For since the beginning of the world
Men have not heard nor perceived by
the ear,
Nor has the eye seen any God besides
You,
Who acts for the one who waits for
Him.
5You meet him who rejoices and does
righteousness,
Who remembers You in Your ways.
You are indeed angry, for we have
sinned—
In these ways we continue;
And we need to be saved.

6But we are all like an unclean *thing*,
And all our righteousnesses *are* like
filthy rags;
We all fade as a leaf,
And our iniquities, like the wind,
Have taken us away.
7And *there is* no one who calls on Your
name,
Who stirs himself up to take hold of
You;
For You have hidden Your face from us,
And have consumed us because of
our iniquities.

64:1,2 The prophet's cry was for the world to give God His due honor. This is our prayer also.

64:6 Sinners think that their good deeds commend them to God. Point out that God sees their *good deeds* as filthy rags (literally, as used menstrual cloths)—so imagine how God views their *sins*. To convince a sinner that his self-righteousness is an offense to a holy God, apply the moral Law to the conscience. For the biblical use of the Law, see Mark 10:17–19; Rom. 2:21–24; 3:19,20; 7:7,13; Gal. 3:24; 1 Tim. 1:8–10. See also Luke 16:15.

"The most damnable and pernicious heresy that has ever plagued the mind of man is that somehow he can make himself good enough to deserve to live forever with an all-holy God." *Martin Luther*

[8]But now, O LORD,
You *are* our Father;
We *are* the clay, and You our potter;
And all we *are* the work of Your hand.
[9]Do not be furious, O LORD,
Nor remember iniquity forever;
Indeed, please look—we all *are* Your
people!
[10]Your holy cities are a wilderness,
Zion is a wilderness,
Jerusalem a desolation.
[11]Our holy and beautiful temple,
Where our fathers praised You,
Is burned up with fire;
And all our pleasant things are laid
waste.
[12]Will You restrain Yourself because of
these *things,* O LORD?
Will You hold Your peace, and afflict
us very severely?

The Righteousness of God's Judgment

65 "I was sought by *those who* did not
ask *for Me;*
I was found by *those who* did not
seek Me.
I said, 'Here I am, here I am,'
To a nation *that* was not called by My
name.
[2]I have stretched out My hands all day
long to a rebellious people,
Who walk in a way *that is* not good,
According to their own thoughts;
[3]A people who provoke Me to anger
continually to My face;
Who sacrifice in gardens,
And burn incense on altars of brick;
[4]Who sit among the graves,
And spend the night in the tombs;
Who eat swine's flesh,
And the broth of abominable things is
in their vessels;
[5]Who say, 'Keep to yourself,
Do not come near me,
For I am holier than you!'
These *are* smoke in My nostrils,
A fire that burns all the day.

[6]"Behold, *it is* written before Me:
I will not keep silence, but will
repay—
Even repay into their bosom—
[7]Your iniquities and the iniquities of
your fathers together,"
Says the LORD,
"Who have burned incense on the
mountains
And blasphemed Me on the hills;
Therefore I will measure their former
work into their bosom."

[8]Thus says the LORD:

"As the new wine is found in the
cluster,
And *one* says, 'Do not destroy it,
For a blessing *is* in it,'
So will I do for My servants' sake,
That I may not destroy them all.
[9]I will bring forth descendants from
Jacob,
And from Judah an heir of My
mountains;
My elect shall inherit it,
And My servants shall dwell there.
[10]Sharon shall be a fold of flocks,
And the Valley of Achor a place for
herds to lie down,
For My people who have sought Me.

[11]"But you *are* those who forsake the
LORD,
Who forget My holy mountain,
Who prepare a table for Gad,[a]
And who furnish a drink offering for
Meni.[b]
[12]Therefore I will number you for the
sword,
And you shall all bow down to the
slaughter;
Because, when I called, you did not
answer;
When I spoke, you did not hear,
But did evil before My eyes,
And chose *that* in which I do not
delight."

65:11 [a]Literally *Troop* or *Fortune,* a pagan deity [b]Literally *Number* or *Destiny,* a pagan deity

QUESTIONS & OBJECTIONS

"How can people be happy in heaven, knowing that their unsaved loved ones are suffering in hell?"

Those who ask such questions fall into the category of those who asked Jesus a similar question. The Pharisees said that a certain woman had seven consecutive husbands, so whose wife will she be in heaven (Mark 12:23)? Jesus answered by saying that they neither knew the Scriptures nor the power of God. The unregenerate mind has no concept of God's mind or His infinite power. If God can speak the sun into existence; if He can see every thought of every human heart at the same time; if He can create the human eye with its 137 million light-sensitive cells, then He can handle the minor details of our eternal salvation.

John writes that in heaven "we shall be like Him, for we shall see Him as He is" (1 John 3:2), so perhaps we will be fully satisfied that God is perfectly just and merciful, and that He gave every individual the opportunity to accept or reject Him. However He works it out, God promises that there will not be sorrow or crying in heaven. Our focus in heaven won't be on our loss, but on our gain.

13Therefore thus says the Lord GOD:

"Behold, My servants shall eat,
But you shall be hungry;
Behold, My servants shall drink,
But you shall be thirsty;
Behold, My servants shall rejoice,
But you shall be ashamed;
14Behold, My servants shall sing for joy
of heart,
But you shall cry for sorrow of heart,
And wail for grief of spirit.
15You shall leave your name as a curse
to My chosen;
For the Lord GOD will slay you,
And call His servants by another name;
16So that he who blesses himself in the
earth
Shall bless himself in the God of truth;
And he who swears in the earth
Shall swear by the God of truth;
Because the former troubles are
forgotten,
And because they are hidden from My
eyes.

The Glorious New Creation

17"For behold, I create new heavens and
a new earth;
And the former shall not be
remembered or come to mind.
18But be glad and rejoice forever in
what I create;
For behold, I create Jerusalem *as* a
rejoicing,
And her people a joy.
19I will rejoice in Jerusalem,
And joy in My people;
The voice of weeping shall no longer
be heard in her,
Nor the voice of crying.

20"No more shall an infant from there
live but a few days,
Nor an old man who has not fulfilled
his days;
For the child shall die one hundred
years old,
But the sinner *being* one hundred
years old shall be accursed.
21They shall build houses and inhabit
them;
They shall plant vineyards and eat
their fruit.
22They shall not build and another
inhabit;
They shall not plant and another eat;
For as the days of a tree, *so shall be*
the days of My people,
And My elect shall long enjoy the

65:17 See 2 Pet. 3:13; Rev. 21:1.

work of their hands.
23They shall not labor in vain,
Nor bring forth children for trouble;
For they *shall be* the descendants of the blessed of the LORD,
And their offspring with them.

24"It shall come to pass
That before they call, I will answer;
And while they are still speaking, I will hear.
25The wolf and the lamb shall feed together,
The lion shall eat straw like the ox,
And dust *shall be* the serpent's food.
They shall not hurt nor destroy in all My holy mountain,"
Says the LORD.

True Worship and False

66 Thus says the LORD:
"Heaven is My throne,
And earth *is* My footstool.
Where *is* the house that you will build Me?
And where *is* the place of My rest?
2For all those *things* My hand has made,
And all those *things* exist,"
Says the LORD.
"But on this *one* will I look:
On *him who is* poor and of a contrite spirit,
And who trembles at My word.

3"He who kills a bull *is as if* he slays a man;
He who sacrifices a lamb, *as if* he breaks a dog's neck;
He who offers a grain offering, *as if he offers* swine's blood;
He who burns incense, *as if* he blesses an idol.
Just as they have chosen their own ways,
And their soul delights in their abominations,
4So will I choose their delusions,
And bring their fears on them;
Because, when I called, no one answered,
When I spoke they did not hear;
But they did evil before My eyes,
And chose *that* in which I do not delight."

The Lord Vindicates Zion

5Hear the word of the LORD,
You who tremble at His word:
"Your brethren who hated you,
Who cast you out for My name's sake, said,
'Let the LORD be glorified,
That we may see your joy.'
But they shall be ashamed."

6The sound of noise from the city!
A voice from the temple!
The voice of the LORD,
Who fully repays His enemies!

7"Before she was in labor, she gave birth;
Before her pain came,
She delivered a male child.
8Who has heard such a thing?
Who has seen such things?
Shall the earth be made to give birth in one day?
Or shall a nation be born at once?
For as soon as Zion was in labor,
She gave birth to her children.
9Shall I bring to the time of birth, and not cause delivery?" says the LORD.
"Shall I who cause delivery shut up *the womb*?" says your God.

65:25 This is often misquoted as "The lion will lie down with the lamb."

66:2 If you want God to hear your prayers, keep your heart free from conceit, forsake every idolatrous thought about Him, and tremble at His Word. See yourself as a desperately wicked and condemned criminal who has the rope of execution around his neck, suddenly holding in his hands a pardon from the governor.

66:8 See Jer. 30:3 comment for how the nation of Israel was "born in a day."

Questions & Objections

66:3

"How do you witness to those in cults and other religions?"

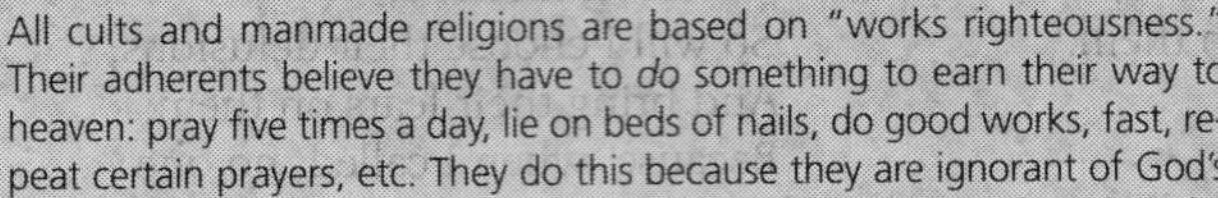

All cults and manmade religions are based on "works righteousness." Their adherents believe they have to *do* something to earn their way to heaven: pray five times a day, lie on beds of nails, do good works, fast, repeat certain prayers, etc. They do this because they are ignorant of God's standard of righteousness. This is why they need the Law of God to show them that the leap they are

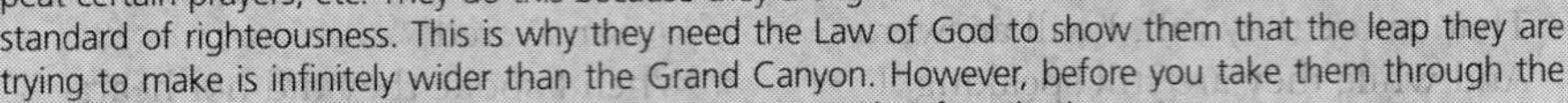

trying to make is infinitely wider than the Grand Canyon. However, before you take them through the Law, help them to see that they are indeed trusting in "works" for salvation.

Let's say there are a couple of cult members at my door. I warmly ask for their names, and then say, "I have a knife in my back. I am dying and have only three minutes to live. What do I need to do to enter heaven/paradise/the kingdom of God?" They look concerned. One says, "A lot." I ask, "What do you mean 'a lot'? I have only *two* minutes to live. Help me." They will normally say they cannot help someone who has just a couple of minutes to live, because their salvation is based on gaining knowledge and doing "good works." The fact that they must *do* things to be saved reveals that they are trusting in their "self-righteousness."

When I then ask if they think they are "good" people, they almost always say they are, and that is the root cause of their deception. While they know they are sinners, they believe their sin is not so bad that they cannot earn their own way out of it and "merit" heaven. So they must be taken through the Law and made to understand that they are *criminals* in the sight of a holy Judge, and are guilty of countless crimes. They must understand that God is perfect and holy, that He considers lust to be adultery and hatred to be murder, and He will see to it that absolute justice is done. That means adulterers, murderers, liars, and thieves will be damned forever. Once they recognize that, they will understand that their "good" works are not good at all, but are in reality a detestable attempt to bribe the Judge of the universe. Hopefully they will trust in His mercy alone to save them.

That is how the thief on the cross was saved—through mercy alone. He didn't go anywhere or *do* anything to save himself. He couldn't, because he was nailed to the cross. He had no other avenue but to humbly turn to Jesus and say, "Lord, remember me when You come into Your kingdom" (Luke 23:42). In doing so, he acknowledged Jesus as Lord, and believed that He would rise from the dead (Rom. 10:9).

That is all that any who are involved in "works righteousness" religions need to do to be saved. They are condemned by the Law. They cannot go anywhere or do anything. All they can do is turn to Jesus and trust in Him alone for their salvation. We are saved by grace through faith, and that not of ourselves; "it is the gift of God, not of works, lest anyone should boast" (Eph. 2:8,9). So plant that seed in the hearts of those who think they can be saved by their own works, then pray that God causes it to grow and produce fruit. (For details on other religions, see pages 478, 1263, 1684, and 1782.)

10"Rejoice with Jerusalem,
And be glad with her, all you who love her;
Rejoice for joy with her, all you who mourn for her;
11That you may feed and be satisfied
With the consolation of her bosom,
That you may drink deeply and be delighted
With the abundance of her glory."

12For thus says the LORD:

"Behold, I will extend peace to her like a river,
And the glory of the Gentiles like a flowing stream.
Then you shall feed;
On *her* sides shall you be carried,
And be dandled on *her* knees.
13As one whom his mother comforts,
So I will comfort you;
And you shall be comforted in Jerusalem."

The Reign and Indignation of God

14When you see *this*, your heart shall rejoice,
And your bones shall flourish like grass;

SPRINGBOARDS FOR PREACHING AND WITNESSING

A Small Prediction

66:8

I am not very good at predicting the future. I thought that there would be a bloodbath when Communist China took back Hong Kong some years ago. I was wrong. Most of us have been wrong with political predictions, baby sex predictions, etc., so I have learned to keep my mouth shut when it comes to the subject. Almost shut—because I have one small prediction to make about you, if you are a skeptic when it comes to Christianity. I will give you a short list of some of the prophecies of the Bible, then make my little prophecy. These were written 2,000 years ago and are called "signs" of the end of the age. Here is what the New Testament says would take place just before the second coming of Jesus Christ:

There would be an increase in wars and hostility between nations, earthquakes, famines, deadly diseases, and vegetarianism. There would also be an empty and dead religious system, money-hungry preachers who would have many followers and slur the name of Christianity, a forsaking of the Ten Commandments ("lawlessness"; Matt. 24:12), and mockery of a worldwide flood (2 Pet. 3:3–6).

Now here is my prediction. If you are a skeptic, you will be saying, "But these signs have always been around!" To be honest, that isn't *my* prediction. The Bible says you would say it (2 Pet. 3:4), and it even says why you are rebelling against the Word of God: because you are full of lust. (How is that for hitting the nail on the head?) Jesus said to watch for one particular "sign": the Jewish repossession of Jerusalem. Israel became a nation in 1948 and the Jews obtained Jerusalem in 1967. They found a homeland for the first time in 2,000 years. What are you waiting for? You had better make peace with God.

The hand of the LORD shall be known
to His servants,
And *His* indignation to His enemies.
15For behold, the LORD will come with
fire
And with His chariots, like a
whirlwind,
To render His anger with fury,
And His rebuke with flames of fire.
16For by fire and by His sword
The LORD will judge all flesh;
And the slain of the LORD shall be many.

17"Those who sanctify themselves and
purify themselves,
To go to the gardens
After an *idol* in the midst,
Eating swine's flesh and the
abomination and the mouse,
Shall be consumed together," says the
LORD.

18"For I *know* their works and their
thoughts. It shall be that I will gather all
nations and tongues; and they shall come
and see My glory. 19I will set a sign among
them; and those among them who escape
I will send to the nations: *to* Tarshish and
Pul[a] and Lud, who draw the bow, and
Tubal and Javan, *to* the coastlands afar off
who have not heard My fame nor seen
My glory. And they shall declare My glory
among the Gentiles. 20Then they shall
bring all your brethren for an offering to
the LORD out of all nations, on horses and
in chariots and in litters, on mules and on
camels, to My holy mountain Jerusalem,"
says the LORD, "as the children of Israel
bring an offering in a clean vessel into the
house of the LORD. 21And I will also take
some of them for priests *and* Levites," says
the LORD.

66:19 [a]Following Masoretic Text and Targum; Septuagint reads *Put* (compare Jeremiah 46:9).

66:15,16 This is the motivation to plead with every man to seek the mercy of a holy God, warning them of the punishment promised in v. 24. See also 2 Thess. 1:7–9.

66:18 "[He] knows the thoughts of all men. The God of hosts—whose sovereign power all creatures obey, and acts for or against us as he wills. Let us humble ourselves before this God, and give all diligence to make him our God. For happy are the people whose God he is, and who have all this power engaged for them." *John Wesley*

22"For as the new heavens and the new
earth
Which I will make shall remain
before Me," says the LORD,
"So shall your descendants and your
name remain.
23And it shall come to pass
That from one New Moon to another,
And from one Sabbath to another,
All flesh shall come to worship before
Me," says the LORD.
24"And they shall go forth and look
Upon the corpses of the men
Who have transgressed against Me.
For their worm does not die,
And their fire is not quenched.
They shall be an abhorrence to all
flesh."

66:24 See Mark 9:44–48.

Evangelistic Survey

The following questions may be helpful for conducting surveys or interviewing people on video. You can begin by approaching someone and asking, "Do you have a few moments to do an interview/answer a survey? It's about what you think happens after someone dies—where do they go?" (That approach lets them know what they are getting into, so there can be no accusations of false pretenses.)

- Where do people go to when they die—do you think there is an afterlife?
- Do you believe God exists? Why or why not?
- Should God punish murderers? If so, how should He punish them?
- It's 1939. You have Adolf Hitler in the sites of a high-power rifle. Do you take him out? Why or why not?
- What do you think a person has to do to go to heaven?
- Do you consider yourself to be a "good" person?
- How many of the Ten Commandments can you name?
- Do you think you have kept the Ten Commandments?
- How many lies have you told in your life?
- Where would you go if you died tonight?
- If there was a way to avoid death, would you be interested?

The question about Hitler is my favorite question to ask, because it reveals the person's basis for morality. Some say, "Absolutely. In a heartbeat." Then I ask if they would take his mother out, if it were 40 years earlier and she was pregnant with Adolf. Would they take Jeffery Dahmer out, before he committed his murders? What about drunk drivers who were going to kill on the road? What about abortion doctors? It shows them that they are trying to play God, and after they have been through the Commandments, they realize that if they are going to be trigger happy to prevent people from doing evil, they have to turn the gun back on themselves.

Jeremiah

1 The words of Jeremiah the son of Hilkiah, of the priests who *were* in
Anathoth in the land of Benjamin, [2]to
whom the word of the LORD came in the
days of Josiah the son of Amon, king of
Judah, in the thirteenth year of his reign.
[3]It came also in the days of Jehoiakim
the son of Josiah, king of Judah, until the end of the eleventh year of Zedekiah the son of Josiah, king of Judah, until the carrying away of Jerusalem captive in the fifth month.

The Prophet Is Called

[4]Then the word of the LORD came to me, saying:

[5]"Before I formed you in the womb I
knew you;
Before you were born I sanctified you;
I ordained you a prophet to the
nations."

[6]Then said I:

"Ah, Lord GOD!
Behold, I cannot speak, for I *am* a
youth."

[7]But the LORD said to me:

"Do not say, 'I *am* a youth,'
For you shall go to all to whom I send
you,
And whatever I command you, you
shall speak.
[8]Do not be afraid of their faces,
For I *am* with you to deliver you,"
says the LORD.

[9]Then the LORD put forth His hand and touched my mouth, and the LORD said to me:

"Behold, I have put My words in your

1:5 This one verse destroys every argument for the murderous act of abortion. God Himself forms us in the womb (see Psa. 139:13; Isa. 44:24). No one is an accident. See also Psa. 127:3 comment.

We, too, have been formed (created by God), known (known by God), sanctified (by the blood of the Savior) and ordained to speak to the nations (given the Great Commission; see Mark 16:15).

1:6,7 "I am tired of hearing the words, 'I can't.' Jeremiah said, 'I am a child,' but the Lord didn't pat him on the back and say, 'Jeremiah, that is very good; I like that in you. Your humility is beautiful.' Oh no! God didn't want any such mock humility. He reproved and rebuked it. I do not like the humility that is too humble to do as it is bid. When my children are too humble to do as they are bid, I pretty soon find a way to make them. I say, 'Go and do it!' The Lord wants us to 'Go and do it.'" *Catherine Booth*

1:9,10 Notice the order. Jeremiah is to root out, pull down, destroy, throw down, then build and plant. Before we can build the kingdom of God by planting the seed of God's Word, we must prepare the ground. It is the function of the moral Law in the hand of the Holy Spirit to break up the soil in the sinner's hard heart—to root out sin, pull down strongholds, and destroy the sinner's self-righteousness so that he understands his need to throw himself on the mercy of God.

mouth.
[10]See, I have this day set you over the
nations and over the kingdoms,
To root out and to pull down,
To destroy and to throw down,
To build and to plant."

[11]Moreover the word of the LORD came
to me, saying, "Jeremiah, what do you
see?"

And I said, "I see a branch of an almond
tree."

[12]Then the LORD said to me, "You have
seen well, for I am ready to perform My
word."

[13]And the word of the LORD came to
me the second time, saying, "What do you
see?"

And I said, "I see a boiling pot, and it
is facing away from the north."

[14]Then the LORD said to me:

"Out of the north calamity shall break
forth
On all the inhabitants of the land.
[15]For behold, I am calling
All the families of the kingdoms of
the north," says the LORD;
"They shall come and each one set his
throne
At the entrance of the gates of
Jerusalem,
Against all its walls all around,
And against all the cities of Judah.
[16]I will utter My judgments
Against them concerning all their
wickedness,
Because they have forsaken Me,
Burned incense to other gods,
And worshiped the works of their
own hands.

[17]"Therefore prepare yourself and arise,
And speak to them all that I
command you.
Do not be dismayed before their
faces,
Lest I dismay you before them.
[18]For behold, I have made you this day
A fortified city and an iron pillar,
And bronze walls against the whole
land—
Against the kings of Judah,
Against its princes,
Against its priests,
And against the people of the land.
[19]They will fight against you,
But they shall not prevail against you.
For I *am* with you," says the LORD, "to
deliver you."

God's Case Against Israel

2 Moreover the word of the LORD came
to me, saying, [2]"Go and cry in the
hearing of Jerusalem, saying, 'Thus says
the LORD:

"I remember you,
The kindness of your youth,
The love of your betrothal,
When you went after Me in the
wilderness,
In a land not sown.
[3]Israel *was* holiness to the LORD,
The firstfruits of His increase.
All that devour him will offend;

1:17 God gives a similar commission to the Christian. We are to prepare ourselves, then arise and speak to this lost and dying world. Sharing the gospel is not an option; it is a command of God. For details on the Great Commission, see page 1386.

1:18,19 May God make us a fortified city, stubborn for the truth. Though the world will be against us, we need nothing else if God is with us (see Rom. 8:31).

2:2 God forbid that we should ever preach without a "cry." We are warning men and women that they will be damned for eternity. Passion should be our fuel.

"Perhaps if there were more of that intense distress for souls that leads to tears, we should more frequently see the results we desire. Sometimes it may be that while we are complaining of the hardness of the hearts of those we are seeking to benefit, the hardness of our own hearts and our feeble apprehension of the solemn reality of eternal things may be the true cause of our want of success." *Hudson Taylor*

Disaster will come upon them," says
the LORD.' "

4Hear the word of the LORD, O house
of Jacob and all the families of the house
of Israel. 5Thus says the LORD:

"What injustice have your fathers
found in Me,
That they have gone far from Me,
Have followed idols,
And have become idolaters?
6Neither did they say, 'Where *is* the
LORD,
Who brought us up out of the land of
Egypt,
Who led us through the wilderness,
Through a land of deserts and pits,
Through a land of drought and the
shadow of death,
Through a land that no one crossed
And where no one dwelt?'
7I brought you into a bountiful
country,
To eat its fruit and its goodness.
But when you entered, you defiled
My land
And made My heritage an
abomination.
8The priests did not say, 'Where *is* the
LORD?'
And those who handle the law did
not know Me;
The rulers also transgressed against Me;
The prophets prophesied by Baal,
And walked after *things that* do not
profit.

9"Therefore I will yet bring charges
against you," says the LORD,
"And against your children's children I
will bring charges.
10For pass beyond the coasts of
Cyprus[a] and see,
Send to Kedar[b] and consider diligently,
And see if there has been such *a thing*.
11Has a nation changed *its* gods,
Which *are* not gods?
But My people have changed their
Glory
For *what* does not profit.
12Be astonished, O heavens, at this,
And be horribly afraid;
Be very desolate," says the LORD.
13"For My people have committed two
evils:
They have forsaken Me, the fountain
of living waters,
And hewn themselves cisterns—
broken cisterns that can hold no
water.

14"*Is* Israel a servant?
Is he a homeborn *slave?*
Why is he plundered?
15The young lions roared at him, *and*
growled;
They made his land waste;
His cities are burned, without
inhabitant.
16Also the people of Noph[a] and
Tahpanhes
Have broken the crown of your head.
17Have you not brought this on
yourself,

2:10 [a]Hebrew *Kittim,* western lands, especially Cyprus [b]In the northern Arabian desert, representative of the eastern cultures **2:16** [a]That is, Memphis in ancient Egypt

2:5 Men may point a sinful finger of accusation at a holy God; but what injustice can be found in God? His ways are perfect (see Mic. 6:3).

2:13 God is the fountain of living waters (see Psa. 36:9; John 4:13,14; 7:37,38), yet a sin-loving world doesn't desire Him (see Rom. 3:11). Instead, it drinks in iniquity like water. How then can we reach the lost with the waters of the gospel, when they have no thirst for it? We can do what Jesus did, and use the Law to bring the knowledge of sin (see Mark 10:17 comment). A man has no desire for the forgiveness of Jesus Christ until he understands that his sin will take him to hell. The Law convinces him of that (see Rom. 7:13) and helps him to see that he needs to be made right with God before the Day of Judgment. It causes him to hunger and thirst for righteousness, because without righteousness he will perish on the Day of Wrath (see Prov. 11:4).

In that you have forsaken the LORD
your God
When He led you in the way?
18And now why take the road to Egypt,
To drink the waters of Sihor?
Or why take the road to Assyria,
To drink the waters of the River?[a]
19Your own wickedness will correct you,
And your backslidings will rebuke you.
Know therefore and see that *it is* an
evil and bitter *thing*
That you have forsaken the LORD your
God,
And the fear of Me *is* not in you,"
Says the Lord GOD of hosts.

20"For of old I have broken your yoke
and burst your bonds;
And you said, 'I will not transgress,'
When on every high hill and under
every green tree
You lay down, playing the harlot.
21Yet I had planted you a noble vine, a
seed of highest quality.
How then have you turned before Me
Into the degenerate plant of an alien
vine?
22For though you wash yourself with
lye, and use much soap,
Yet your iniquity is marked before
Me," says the Lord GOD.

23"How can you say, 'I am not polluted,
I have not gone after the Baals'?
See your way in the valley;
Know what you have done:
You are a swift dromedary breaking
loose in her ways,
24A wild donkey used to the
wilderness,
That sniffs at the wind in her desire;
In her time of mating, who can turn
her away?
All those who seek her will not weary
themselves;
In her month they will find her.
25Withhold your foot from being
unshod, and your throat from
thirst.
But you said, 'There is no hope.
No! For I have loved aliens, and after
them I will go.'

26"As the thief is ashamed when he is
found out,
So is the house of Israel ashamed;
They and their kings and their
princes, and their priests and
their prophets,
27Saying to a tree, 'You *are* my father,'
And to a stone, 'You gave birth to me.'
For they have turned *their* back to
Me, and not *their* face.
But in the time of their trouble
They will say, 'Arise and save us.'
28But where *are* your gods that you
have made for yourselves?
Let them arise,
If they can save you in the time of
your trouble;

2:18 [a]That is, the Euphrates

2:19 "We are closer to revival or judgment than we have ever been. Any nation that forgets God as a corporate people comes under the judgment of God . . . If we look at the history of God's dealings with His people it ought to cause us to tremble. But it is the loss of fear of God that characterizes God's people in America today. When you do not fear God you do not fear sin. There is a direct relationship between a high view of God and a high view of sin." *Henry Blackaby*

2:22 Pontius Pilate thought that his guilt could be washed away without propitiation. The world has the same mentality. Millions believe that mere "washing of the hands" through sorrow or religious acts is all that is required for sin to be remitted. However, without the shedding of blood there is no remission (see Heb. 9:22; 1 John 1:7). See also Psa. 51:1–10.

2:27 Many people don't believe they were made in the image of God, but were merely the product of mindless chance. For the fallacy of evolution, see Isa. 45:18 comment.

"God exists whether or not men may choose to believe in Him. The reason why many people do not believe in God is not so much that it is intellectually impossible to believe in God, but because belief in God forces that thoughtful person to face the fact that he is accountable to such a God." *Robert A. Laidlaw*

For *according to* the number of your
cities
Are your gods, O Judah.

29"Why will you plead with Me?
You all have transgressed against Me,"
says the LORD.
30"In vain I have chastened your children;
They received no correction.
Your sword has devoured your
prophets
Like a destroying lion.

31"O generation, see the word of the
LORD!
Have I been a wilderness to Israel,
Or a land of darkness?
Why do My people say, 'We are lords;
We will come no more to You'?
32Can a virgin forget her ornaments,
Or a bride her attire?
Yet My people have forgotten Me days
without number.

33"Why do you beautify your way to
seek love?
Therefore you have also taught
The wicked women your ways.
34Also on your skirts is found
The blood of the lives of the poor
innocents.
I have not found it by secret search,
But plainly on all these things.
35Yet you say, 'Because I am innocent,
Surely His anger shall turn from me.'
Behold, I will plead My case against
you,
Because you say, 'I have not sinned.'
36Why do you gad about so much to
change your way?
Also you shall be ashamed of Egypt as
you were ashamed of Assyria.
37Indeed you will go forth from him
With your hands on your head;
For the LORD has rejected your
trusted allies,
And you will not prosper by them.

Israel Is Shameless

3 "They say, 'If a man divorces his wife,
And she goes from him
And becomes another man's,
May he return to her again?'
Would not that land be greatly
polluted?
But you have played the harlot with
many lovers;
Yet return to Me," says the LORD.

2"Lift up your eyes to the desolate
heights and see:
Where have you not lain *with men?*
By the road you have sat for them
Like an Arabian in the wilderness;
And you have polluted the land
With your harlotries and your
wickedness.
3Therefore the showers have been
withheld,
And there has been no latter rain.
You have had a harlot's forehead;
You refuse to be ashamed.
4Will you not from this time cry to Me,
'My Father, You *are* the guide of my
youth?
5Will He remain angry forever?
Will He keep it to the end?'
Behold, you have spoken and done
evil things,
As you were able."

A Call to Repentance

6The LORD said also to me in the days
of Josiah the king: "Have you seen what
backsliding Israel has done? She has gone

2:29 The ungodly don't understand that their sin is *against God* (see Psa. 51:4). They believe certain sinful actions are morally acceptable "as long as they don't hurt anyone." But all sin offends God. The true convert understands that he has transgressed against a holy God (see also Jer. 3:13).

3:3 God still withholds showers to chasten nations. The weather is not independent of the will of God. Every drop of rain falls by His permissive will. He lets the rain fall on the just and the unjust (see Matt. 5:45).

up on every high mountain and under
every green tree, and there played the
harlot. 7And I said, after she had done all
these *things,* 'Return to Me.' But she did
not return. And her treacherous sister Judah saw it. 8Then I saw that for all the
causes for which backsliding Israel had
committed adultery, I had put her away
and given her a certificate of divorce; yet
her treacherous sister Judah did not fear,
but went and played the harlot also. 9So
it came to pass, through her casual harlotry, that she defiled the land and committed adultery with stones and trees.
10And yet for all this her treacherous sister Judah has not turned to Me with her
whole heart, but in pretense," says the
LORD.

> Eternity to the godly is a day that has no sunset. Eternity to the wicked is a night that has no sunrise.
>
> **ANONYMOUS**

11Then the LORD said to me, "Backsliding Israel has shown herself more righteous than treacherous Judah. 12Go and
proclaim these words toward the north,
and say:

'Return, backsliding Israel,' says the
LORD;
'I will not cause My anger to fall on you.
For I *am* merciful,' says the LORD;
'I will not remain angry forever.
13Only acknowledge your iniquity,
That you have transgressed against
the LORD your God,
And have scattered your charms
To alien deities under every green
tree,
And you have not obeyed My voice,'
says the LORD.

14"Return, O backsliding children,"
says the LORD; "for I am married to you. I
will take you, one from a city and two
from a family, and I will bring you to
Zion. 15And I will give you shepherds according to My heart, who will feed you
with knowledge and understanding.

16"Then it shall come to pass, when
you are multiplied and increased in the
land in those days," says the LORD, "that
they will say no more, 'The ark of the
covenant of the LORD.' It shall not come
to mind, nor shall they remember it, nor
shall they visit *it,* nor shall it be made
anymore.

17"At that time Jerusalem shall be called
The Throne of the LORD, and all the nations shall be gathered to it, to the name
of the LORD, to Jerusalem. No more shall
they follow the dictates of their evil hearts.

18"In those days the house of Judah
shall walk with the house of Israel, and
they shall come together out of the land
of the north to the land that I have given
as an inheritance to your fathers.

19"But I said:

3:8 Can Christians "backslide"? Some try to justify the concept of "backsliding" by pointing to the use of the word in the Old Testament. However, the word is used in reference to the nation of Israel, not to born-again individuals indwelt by the Holy Spirit. We cannot justify a believer falling away from following Jesus in light of Luke 9:62, where Jesus said that no one who even looks back is fit for the kingdom. The true convert says with Peter, "Lord, to whom shall we go? You have the words of eternal life" (John 6:68). It is the false convert who is like a dog that returns to its vomit and a pig that goes back to the mire. A genuine convert would rather die than despise the Spirit of grace and trample the blood of Christ underfoot.

3:12,13 In a civil court, those who confess their guilt and throw themselves on the mercy of the judge are often given leniency, while those who refuse to admit wrongdoing have the book thrown at them. Our Judge is "rich" in mercy (see Eph. 2:4; Psa. 86:5; 103:8) and therefore willing to extend His mercy to all who acknowledge their sin against Him and turn to Him in genuine repentance. See also 1 John 1:9.

3:15 How we need men in the pulpits who are more than motivational speakers who tickle the ears of their hearers. We need sons of thunder, who are not afraid to put the fear of God in their people, and who speak of knowledge, understanding, and judgment. See Acts 20:28–31.

'How can I put you among the
children
And give you a pleasant land,
A beautiful heritage of the hosts of
nations?'

"And I said:

'You shall call Me, "My Father,"
And not turn away from Me.'
20Surely, *as* a wife treacherously departs
from her husband,
So have you dealt treacherously with
Me,
O house of Israel," says the LORD.

21A voice was heard on the desolate
heights,
Weeping *and* supplications of the
children of Israel.
For they have perverted their way;
They have forgotten the LORD their
God.
22"Return, you backsliding children,
And I will heal your backslidings."

"Indeed we do come to You,
For You are the LORD our God.
23Truly, in vain *is salvation hoped for*
from the hills,
And from the multitude of mountains;
Truly, in the LORD our God
Is the salvation of Israel.
24For shame has devoured
The labor of our fathers from our
youth—
Their flocks and their herds,
Their sons and their daughters.
25We lie down in our shame,
And our reproach covers us.
For we have sinned against the LORD
our God,
We and our fathers,
From our youth even to this day,
And have not obeyed the voice of the
LORD our God."

4 "If you will return, O Israel," says the
LORD,
"Return to Me;
And if you will put away your
abominations out of My sight,
Then you shall not be moved.
2And you shall swear, 'The LORD lives,'
In truth, in judgment, and in
righteousness;
The nations shall bless themselves in
Him,
And in Him they shall glory."

3For thus says the LORD to the men of
Judah and Jerusalem:

"Break up your fallow ground,
And do not sow among thorns.
4Circumcise yourselves to the LORD,
And take away the foreskins of your
hearts,

3:23 The world needs to hear that salvation is only in the Lord. They look in vain for salvation from any other source. He alone is our salvation; it is not a matter of what we do or what we know, but who we know: "He who has the Son has life" (1 John 5:12).

"Every person in your personal world is on one of two lists: saved or lost. First John 5:12 says, 'He that has the Son of God has life. He that does not have the Son of God, does not have life.' There are two destinations for everybody we know. Think of the people you know and love as you hold their eternity in your hands. That's why you are where you are . . . Do whatever it takes and whatever it costs to take the people you know to heaven with you!" *Ron Hutchcraft*

4:2 The world often gravitates to the concept of a god who is "all loving." Such a loving god would never judge people and damn their souls to hell. However, it is more biblical to say that God is love, but He is also the essence of truth, judgment, and righteousness. Therefore, God is bound by His own character to do what is true, just, and right.

"If we exalt one of God's qualities over another, we can get a distorted view of God's character. In fact, overemphasizing any one of God's attributes to the exclusion of others can lead to heresy. For example, teaching only about God's mercy and neglecting His role as a judge will prevent people from understanding God's hatred of sin and the future punishment for wrongdoing." *Bill Bright*

You men of Judah and inhabitants of
Jerusalem,
Lest My fury come forth like fire,
And burn so that no one can quench
it,
Because of the evil of your doings."

An Imminent Invasion

5Declare in Judah and proclaim in Jerusalem, and say:

"Blow the trumpet in the land;
Cry, 'Gather together,'
And say, 'Assemble yourselves,
And let us go into the fortified cities.'
6Set up the standard toward Zion.
Take refuge! Do not delay!
For I will bring disaster from the
north,
And great destruction."

7The lion has come up from his thicket,
And the destroyer of nations is on his
way.
He has gone forth from his place
To make your land desolate.
Your cities will be laid waste,
Without inhabitant.
8For this, clothe yourself with
sackcloth,
Lament and wail.
For the fierce anger of the LORD
Has not turned back from us.

9"And it shall come to pass in that day,"
says the LORD,
"*That* the heart of the king shall perish,
And the heart of the princes;
The priests shall be astonished,
And the prophets shall wonder."

10Then I said, "Ah, Lord GOD!
Surely You have greatly deceived this
people and Jerusalem,
Saying, 'You shall have peace,'
Whereas the sword reaches to the
heart."

11At that time it will be said
To this people and to Jerusalem,
"A dry wind of the desolate heights
blows in the wilderness
Toward the daughter of My people—
Not to fan or to cleanse—
12A wind too strong for these will come
for Me;
Now I will also speak judgment
against them."

13"Behold, he shall come up like clouds,
And his chariots like a whirlwind.
His horses are swifter than eagles.

4:3 Before we sow the seed of the gospel into the hearts of men and women, we need to break up the fallow ground using the Law of God. *Charles Spurgeon*, in speaking of preparing the soil of the heart with the plow of the Law, stated, "One other reason why this soil was so uncongenial was that it was totally unprepared for the seed. There had been no plowing before the seed was sown, and no harrowing afterwards. He that sows without a plow may reap without a sickle. He who preaches the gospel without preaching the Law of God may hold all the results of it in his hand and there will be little for him to hold."

4:4 God's fury against sin is held back by His longsuffering. Our God is a consuming fire (see Heb. 12:29), and it is only His mercy that restrains the lightning of His wrath. See Zech. 2:5 comment. See also Deut. 10:16 comment regarding circumcision of the heart.

"It is because God's wrath is real that His mercy is relevant. Unless you have a real wrath, a real anger, the biblical concepts of long-suffering, of mercy, and of grace are robbed of their meaning." *Alistair Begg*

4:10 Jeremiah is mistaken in his accusation. All of God's judgments are true and righteous altogether (see Psa. 19:9). However, it is a mystery why God allows false prophets to gain positions of authority, where they can deceive so many with their flowery speeches and misrepresentation of God's character.

"Now, was it God that deceived them? No, He had often given them warning of judgments in general and of this in particular; but their own prophets deceive them and cry peace to those to whom the God of heaven does not speak peace. It is a pitiable thing, and that which every good man greatly laments, to see people flattered into their own ruin and promising themselves peace when war is at the door; and this we should complain of to God, who alone can prevent such a fatal delusion." *Matthew Henry*

Woe to us, for we are plundered!"

14O Jerusalem, wash your heart from wickedness,
That you may be saved.
How long shall your evil thoughts lodge within you?
15For a voice declares from Dan
And proclaims affliction from Mount Ephraim:
16"Make mention to the nations,
Yes, proclaim against Jerusalem,
That watchers come from a far country
And raise their voice against the cities of Judah.
17Like keepers of a field they are against her all around,
Because she has been rebellious against Me," says the LORD.
18"Your ways and your doings
Have procured these *things* for you.
This *is* your wickedness,
Because it is bitter,
Because it reaches to your heart."

Sorrow for the Doomed Nation

19O my soul, my soul!
I am pained in my very heart!
My heart makes a noise in me;
I cannot hold my peace,
Because you have heard, O my soul,
The sound of the trumpet,
The alarm of war.
20Destruction upon destruction is cried,
For the whole land is plundered.
Suddenly my tents are plundered,
And my curtains in a moment.
21How long will I see the standard,
And hear the sound of the trumpet?

22"For My people *are* foolish,
They have not known Me.
They *are* silly children,
And they have no understanding.
They *are* wise to do evil,
But to do good they have no knowledge."

23I beheld the earth, and indeed *it was* without form, and void;
And the heavens, they *had* no light.
24I beheld the mountains, and indeed they trembled,
And all the hills moved back and forth.
25I beheld, and indeed *there was* no man,
And all the birds of the heavens had fled.
26I beheld, and indeed the fruitful land *was* a wilderness,
And all its cities were broken down
At the presence of the LORD,
By His fierce anger.

27For thus says the LORD:

"The whole land shall be desolate;
Yet I will not make a full end.
28For this shall the earth mourn,
And the heavens above be black,
Because I have spoken.
I have purposed and will not relent,
Nor will I turn back from it.
29The whole city shall flee from the noise of the horsemen and bowmen.
They shall go into thickets and climb up on the rocks.
Every city *shall be* forsaken,
And not a man shall dwell in it.

30"And *when* you *are* plundered,
What will you do?
Though you clothe yourself with

4:19 This is the heart-cry of the Christian. Those who catch a glimpse of sinful man and the holiness of God groan in prayer and plead in their preaching. They cannot hold their peace because they know that God's wrath abides on sinners, that they are enemies of God, who, without the Savior, will know the judgment of eternal fire.

4:22 Here is a summation of godless humanity, which believes itself wise, but is foolish. The unsaved lack the understanding and the knowledge that is provided by the Law of God (see Jer. 9:23; Hos. 4:6). See also Gen. 3:5 comment.

crimson,
Though you adorn *yourself* with
ornaments of gold,
Though you enlarge your eyes with
paint,
In vain you will make yourself fair;
Your lovers will despise you;
They will seek your life.

31"For I have heard a voice as of a
woman in labor,
The anguish as of her who brings
forth her first child,
The voice of the daughter of Zion
bewailing herself;
She spreads her hands, *saying,*
'Woe is me now, for my soul is weary
Because of murderers!'

. . . . . .

For President Abraham Lincoln's call to national repentance, see Prov. 28:13 comment.

. . . . . .

The Justice of God's Judgment

5 "Run to and fro through the streets of
Jerusalem;
See now and know;
And seek in her open places
If you can find a man,
If there is *anyone* who executes
judgment,
Who seeks the truth,
And I will pardon her.
2Though they say, '*As* the LORD lives,'
Surely they swear falsely."

3O LORD, *are* not Your eyes on the
truth?
You have stricken them,
But they have not grieved;
You have consumed them,
But they have refused to receive
correction.
They have made their faces harder
than rock;
They have refused to return.

4Therefore I said, "Surely these *are*
poor.
They are foolish;
For they do not know the way of the
LORD,
The judgment of their God.
5I will go to the great men and speak
to them,
For they have known the way of the
LORD,
The judgment of their God."

But these have altogether broken the
yoke
And burst the bonds.
6Therefore a lion from the forest shall
slay them,
A wolf of the deserts shall destroy
them;
A leopard will watch over their cities.
Everyone who goes out from there
shall be torn in pieces,
Because their transgressions are many;
Their backslidings have increased.

7"How shall I pardon you for this?
Your children have forsaken Me
And sworn by *those that are* not gods.
When I had fed them to the full,
Then they committed adultery
And assembled themselves by troops
in the harlots' houses.
8They were *like* well-fed lusty stallions;
Every one neighed after his neighbor's
wife.
9Shall I not punish *them* for these
things?" says the LORD.
"And shall I not avenge Myself on such

5:1–5 God testifies that there was not one person in Jerusalem who seeks truth and justice, and Jeremiah agrees with the testimony of the Lord. Even though God chastened them, they refused correction. When tragedy strikes sinful men, rather than being broken in humility before God, many become bitter, angry, and harden their hearts further against God.

a nation as this?

[10]"Go up on her walls and destroy,
But do not make a complete end.
Take away her branches,
For they *are* not the LORD's.
[11]For the house of Israel and the house of Judah
Have dealt very treacherously with Me," says the LORD.

[12]They have lied about the LORD,
And said, "*It is* not He.
Neither will evil come upon us,
Nor shall we see sword or famine.
[13]And the prophets become wind,
For the word *is* not in them.
Thus shall it be done to them."

[14]Therefore thus says the LORD God of hosts:

"Because you speak this word,
Behold, I will make My words in your mouth fire,
And this people wood,
And it shall devour them.
[15]Behold, I will bring a nation against you from afar,
O house of Israel," says the LORD.
"It *is* a mighty nation,
It *is* an ancient nation,
A nation whose language you do not know,
Nor can you understand what they say.
[16]Their quiver *is* like an open tomb;
They *are* all mighty men.
[17]And they shall eat up your harvest and your bread,
Which your sons and daughters should eat.
They shall eat up your flocks and your herds;
They shall eat up your vines and your fig trees;
They shall destroy your fortified cities,
In which you trust, with the sword.

[18]"Nevertheless in those days," says the
LORD, "I will not make a complete end of
you. [19]And it will be when you say, 'Why
does the LORD our God do all these *things*
to us?' then you shall answer them, 'Just
as you have forsaken Me and served foreign gods in your land, so you shall serve
aliens in a land *that is* not yours.'

[20]"Declare this in the house of Jacob
And proclaim it in Judah, saying,
[21]'Hear this now, O foolish people,
Without understanding,
Who have eyes and see not,
And who have ears and hear not:
[22]Do you not fear Me?' says the LORD.
'Will you not tremble at My presence,
Who have placed the sand as the bound of the sea,
By a perpetual decree, that it cannot pass beyond it?
And though its waves toss to and fro,
Yet they cannot prevail;
Though they roar, yet they cannot pass over it.
[23]But this people has a defiant and rebellious heart;

5:21 God Himself calls many people "foolish," including atheists, those who don't call on Him, and those who don't believe His immutable promises (see Psa. 14:1; Luke 24:25).

"I used to think that mountains of evidence from science and history, logically presented, was all that was necessary for men to see and understand the truth about God. Then I read my Bible. The Spirit alone gives life to spiritually dead people. While all the evidence does support the Scripture (and none contradicts it), it is the Spirit of God that overwhelms the soul with the truth of the Bible's words and opens the door to the world of the Spirit. And when that happens, blind men see things that sighted men cannot. With the eyes of faith, we can see heaven and its glories, hell and its horrors, and behold our wonderful Savior, exalted and seated on the throne, ruling, reigning, and worthy to receive all blessing, honor, and glory forever. I thank God for my friends who remind me to look with my 'spiritual eyes' as much as with my natural ones."
Kirk Cameron

"Dim or indistinct views of sin are the origin of most of the errors, heresies, and false doctrines of the present day. If a man does not realize the dangerous nature of his soul's disease, you cannot wonder if he is content with false or imperfect remedies."

J. C. Ryle

They have revolted and departed.
24 They do not say in their heart,
"Let us now fear the LORD our God,
Who gives rain, both the former and the latter, in its season.
He reserves for us the appointed weeks of the harvest."
25 Your iniquities have turned these *things* away,
And your sins have withheld good from you.

26 'For among My people are found wicked *men;*
They lie in wait as one who sets snares;
They set a trap;
They catch men.
27 As a cage is full of birds,
So their houses *are* full of deceit.
Therefore they have become great and grown rich.
28 They have grown fat, they are sleek;
Yes, they surpass the deeds of the wicked;
They do not plead the cause,
The cause of the fatherless;
Yet they prosper,
And the right of the needy they do not defend.
29 Shall I not punish *them* for these *things?*' says the LORD.
'Shall I not avenge Myself on such a nation as this?'

30 "An astonishing and horrible thing
Has been committed in the land:
31 The prophets prophesy falsely,
And the priests rule by their *own* power;
And My people love *to have it* so.
But what will you do in the end?

Impending Destruction from the North

6 "O you children of Benjamin,
Gather yourselves to flee from the midst of Jerusalem!
Blow the trumpet in Tekoa,
And set up a signal-fire in Beth Haccerem;
For disaster appears out of the north,
And great destruction.
2 I have likened the daughter of Zion
To a lovely and delicate woman.
3 The shepherds with their flocks shall come to her.
They shall pitch *their* tents against her all around.
Each one shall pasture in his own place."

4 "Prepare war against her;
Arise, and let us go up at noon.
Woe to us, for the day goes away,
For the shadows of the evening are lengthening.
5 Arise, and let us go by night,
And let us destroy her palaces."

6 For thus has the LORD of hosts said:

"Cut down trees,
And build a mound against Jerusalem.
This *is* the city to be punished.

She *is* full of oppression in her midst.
[7]As a fountain wells up with water,
So she wells up with her wickedness.
Violence and plundering are heard in her.
Before Me continually *are* grief and wounds.
[8]Be instructed, O Jerusalem,
Lest My soul depart from you;
Lest I make you desolate,
A land not inhabited."

[9]Thus says the LORD of hosts:

"They shall thoroughly glean as a vine the remnant of Israel;
As a grape-gatherer, put your hand back into the branches."

[10]To whom shall I speak and give warning,
That they may hear?
Indeed their ear *is* uncircumcised,
And they cannot give heed.
Behold, the word of the LORD is a reproach to them;
They have no delight in it.
[11]Therefore I am full of the fury of the LORD.
I am weary of holding *it* in.
"I will pour it out on the children outside,
And on the assembly of young men together;
For even the husband shall be taken with the wife,
The aged with *him who is* full of days.
[12]And their houses shall be turned over to others,
Fields and wives together;
For I will stretch out My hand
Against the inhabitants of the land,"
says the LORD.
[13]"Because from the least of them even to the greatest of them,
Everyone *is* given to covetousness;
And from the prophet even to the priest,
Everyone deals falsely.
[14]They have also healed the hurt of My people slightly,
Saying, 'Peace, peace!'
When *there is* no peace.
[15]Were they ashamed when they had committed abomination?
No! They were not at all ashamed;
Nor did they know how to blush.
Therefore they shall fall among those who fall;
At the time I punish them,
They shall be cast down," says the LORD.

[16]Thus says the LORD:

"Stand in the ways and see,
And ask for the old paths, where the good way *is*,
And walk in it;
Then you will find rest for your souls.
But they said, 'We will not walk *in it.*'
[17]Also, I set watchmen over you, *saying*,

6:10 God's Word. Do we delight in the Word of the Lord? Do we rejoice in God's Word as one who finds great treasure? (See Psa. 119:162.) The key is to consume the Word of God, to meditate upon the Word, to digest it and let it become part of us. The Bible is a supernatural book, and can give us supernatural energy to do the will of God (see Neh. 8:1–12). Too many fail to read the Bible every day. They find time to feed their stomach each day, but refuse to make time to read God's Word. Don't let your belly take precedence over reading the Bible. Forget your food rather than forget the Word of God. (See Exod. 34:28.)

6:13,14 When preachers in pulpits have no respect for God's Law, they preach a gospel devoid of reference to and omit the reality of future punishment. Idolatry always follows when the Law is rejected. People imagine a god too kind to punish wrongdoing, so they lose the fear of God and therefore neglect to depart from sin. They don't consider repentance to be a prerequisite to salvation and they are told they have peace with God because they simply "believe." Consequently, the contemporary Church is filled with false converts (tares among the wheat, foolish virgins among the wise, bad fish among the good, and sheep among the goats), as well as false apostles, false teachers, and false prophets.

For the necessity of repentance, see John 3:16 comment.

'Listen to the sound of the trumpet!'
But they said, 'We will not listen.'
18Therefore hear, you nations,
And know, O congregation, what *is* among them.
19Hear, O earth!
Behold, I will certainly bring calamity on this people—
The fruit of their thoughts,
Because they have not heeded My words
Nor My law, but rejected it.
20For what purpose to Me
Comes frankincense from Sheba,
And sweet cane from a far country?
Your burnt offerings *are* not acceptable,
Nor your sacrifices sweet to Me."

> The gospel isn't a treasure to be hoarded; it's a gift to be shared.
>
> **GREG LAURIE**

21Therefore thus says the LORD:

"Behold, I will lay stumbling blocks before this people,
And the fathers and the sons together shall fall on them.
The neighbor and his friend shall perish."

22Thus says the LORD:

"Behold, a people comes from the north country,
And a great nation will be raised from the farthest parts of the earth.
23They will lay hold on bow and spear;
They *are* cruel and have no mercy;
Their voice roars like the sea;
And they ride on horses,
As men of war set in array against you, O daughter of Zion."

24We have heard the report of it;
Our hands grow feeble.
Anguish has taken hold of us,
Pain as of a woman in labor.
25Do not go out into the field,
Nor walk by the way.
Because of the sword of the enemy,
Fear *is* on every side.
26O daughter of my people,
Dress in sackcloth
And roll about in ashes!
Make mourning *as for* an only son, most bitter lamentation;
For the plunderer will suddenly come upon us.

27"I have set you *as* an assayer *and* a fortress among My people,
That you may know and test their way.
28They *are* all stubborn rebels, walking as slanderers.
They are bronze and iron,
They *are* all corrupters;
29The bellows blow fiercely,
The lead is consumed by the fire;
The smelter refines in vain,
For the wicked are not drawn off.
30*People* will call them rejected silver,
Because the LORD has rejected them."

Trusting in Lying Words

7 The word that came to Jeremiah from
the LORD, saying, 2"Stand in the gate
of the LORD's house, and proclaim there
this word, and say, 'Hear the word of the
LORD, all *you of* Judah who enter in at
these gates to worship the LORD!' " 3Thus
says the LORD of hosts, the God of Israel:
"Amend your ways and your doings, and
I will cause you to dwell in this place.
4Do not trust in these lying words, saying, 'The temple of the LORD, the temple
of the LORD, the temple of the LORD *are*
these.'

5"For if you thoroughly amend your
ways and your doings, if you thoroughly
execute judgment between a man and his
neighbor, 6*if* you do not oppress the
stranger, the fatherless, and the widow,
and do not shed innocent blood in this
place, or walk after other gods to your
hurt, 7then I will cause you to dwell in
this place, in the land that I gave to your
fathers forever and ever.

7:2 Why Preach Open-air?

By Stuart Scott

When Jeremiah received God's word, he was commanded to stand in the gate of the temple and proclaim the Word of the Lord. Like Jeremiah, we have been given the task of proclaiming God's Word to every person: "Go into all the world and preach the gospel to every creature" (Mark 16:15).

Open-air preaching is the standard method God has always employed throughout Scripture to reach the common people. As *Charles Spurgeon* has said, "Open-air preaching is as old as preaching itself." From Noah, a preacher of righteousness, to the King of kings, Jesus Christ Himself, open-air preaching is God's normal method of getting the word out.

The word for *proclaim* in Hebrew is the word *qara'*, and it means to call, cry, or utter a loud sound, to proclaim aloud or summon. The Greek word used in the New Testament for the word *preach*, as in Mark 16:15, is the word *kerusso*, which means "to officiate as a herald, to publish, proclaim openly." It is always with the sense of formality, gravity, and an authority that must be listened to and obeyed.

From these descriptions, it is obvious that the preaching spoken of in Scripture is not one-to-one witnessing, but the open proclamation of the gospel. Jesus said, "Whatever I tell you in the dark, speak in the light; and what you hear in the ear, preach on the housetops" (Matt. 10:27), and Prov. 1:20,21 says, "Wisdom calls aloud outside; she raises her voice in the open squares. She cries out in the chief concourses, at the openings of the gates in the city she speaks her words."

Here are a few additional verses to consider about preaching the gospel: Jon. 3:2; Matt. 4:17; 10:7; 11:1; Mark 1:4,38; 3:14; Luke 4:18,19; 9:60; Acts 5:42; 10:42; 16:10; 17:3; Rom. 10:15; 15:20; 1 Cor. 1:17; 9:16; Eph. 3:8; Col. 1:28; 2 Tim. 4:2; Rev. 14:6.

I have never known greater joy in nearness to Christ than when standing in the public square, proclaiming the things of God with a loud voice in the open air.

"How would the common people have become indoctrinated with the Gospel had it not been for those far-wandering evangelists... and those daring innovators who found a pulpit on every heap of stones, and an audience chamber in every open space near the abodes of men?" *Charles Spurgeon*

"There is no higher calling than to follow in the footsteps of the Savior and preach in the open air." *Ray Comfort*

8"Behold, you trust in lying words that
cannot profit. 9Will you steal, murder,
commit adultery, swear falsely, burn incense to Baal, and walk after other gods
whom you do not know, 10and *then* come
and stand before Me in this house which
is called by My name, and say, 'We are delivered to do all these abominations'?
11Has this house, which is called by My
name, become a den of thieves in your
eyes? Behold, I, even I, have seen *it*," says
the LORD.

12"But go now to My place which *was*
in Shiloh, where I set My name at the
first, and see what I did to it because of
the wickedness of My people Israel. 13And
now, because you have done all these
works," says the LORD, "and I spoke to you,
rising up early and speaking, but you did
not hear, and I called you, but you did
not answer, 14therefore I will do to the
house which is called by My name, in
which you trust, and to this place which
I gave to you and your fathers, as I have
done to Shiloh. 15And I will cast you out
of My sight, as I have cast out all your
brethren—the whole posterity of Ephraim.

16"Therefore do not pray for this people, nor lift up a cry or prayer for them,
nor make intercession to Me; for I will
not hear you. 17Do you not see what they
do in the cities of Judah and in the streets
of Jerusalem? 18The children gather wood,
the fathers kindle the fire, and the women knead dough, to make cakes for the
queen of heaven; and *they* pour out drink

USING THE LAW IN EVANGELISM

7:9 To show Israel their sin, the LORD pointed to the Ten Commandments to explain their transgressions. They stole (Eighth), murdered (Sixth), committed adultery (Seventh), swore falsely (Ninth), and walked after other gods (First and Second).

offerings to other gods, that they may
provoke Me to anger. 19Do they provoke
Me to anger?" says the LORD. "*Do they* not
provoke themselves, to the shame of their
own faces?"

20Therefore thus says the Lord GOD:
"Behold, My anger and My fury will be
poured out on this place—on man and
on beast, on the trees of the field and on
the fruit of the ground. And it will burn
and not be quenched."

21Thus says the LORD of hosts, the God
of Israel: "Add your burnt offerings to
your sacrifices and eat meat. 22For I did
not speak to your fathers, or command
them in the day that I brought them out
of the land of Egypt, concerning burnt
offerings or sacrifices. 23But this is what I
commanded them, saying, 'Obey My
voice, and I will be your God, and you
shall be My people. And walk in all the
ways that I have commanded you, that it
may be well with you.' 24Yet they did not
obey or incline their ear, but followed the
counsels *and* the dictates of their evil
hearts, and went backward and not forward. 25Since the day that your fathers
came out of the land of Egypt until this
day, I have even sent to you all My servants the prophets, daily rising up early
and sending *them*. 26Yet they did not obey
Me or incline their ear, but stiffened their
neck. They did worse than their fathers.

27"Therefore you shall speak all these
words to them, but they will not obey
you. You shall also call to them, but they
will not answer you.

Judgment on Obscene Religion

28"So you shall say to them, 'This *is* a
nation that does not obey the voice of the
LORD their God nor receive correction.
Truth has perished and has been cut off
from their mouth. 29Cut off your hair and
cast *it* away, and take up a lamentation on
the desolate heights; for the LORD has rejected and forsaken the generation of His
wrath.' 30For the children of Judah have
done evil in My sight," says the LORD.
"They have set their abominations in the
house which is called by My name, to
pollute it. 31And they have built the high

7:18 Worship of Mary. The Roman Catholic church believes that Mary was "conceived immaculate" (born without original sin) and that she was "kept free from every personal sin her whole life long. She is the one who is 'full of grace' (Luke 1:28), 'the all holy.'" In addition, they believe she remained a virgin after giving birth to Jesus, despite the fact that Scripture says she had other children after she bore Jesus (see Matt. 13:55; Mark 6:3; Gal. 1:19). Because Mary was supposedly free from sin and its wages (death), they believe that she was taken up to heaven without experiencing death, in what they call her "Assumption" (Catechism, par. 966).

The Roman Catholic church refers to Mary as "the Mother of God" and the "Queen of Heaven." Even more alarming, the Catholic Catechism teaches that Mary offers salvation:

> ...Taken up to heaven she did not lay aside this saving office but by her manifold intercession continues to bring us the gifts of eternal salvation...Therefore the Blessed Virgin is invoked in the Church under the titles of Advocate, Helper, Benefactress, and Mediatrix. (*Catechism*, par. 969)
>
> Mary had only one Son, Jesus, but in him her spiritual motherhood extends to all whom he came to save. Obediently standing at the side of the new Adam, Jesus Christ, the Virgin is the new Eve, the true mother of all the living, who with a mother's love cooperates in their birth and their formation in the order of grace. Virgin and Mother, Mary is the figure of the Church, its most perfect realization. (*Catechism*, par. 100)

However, the Bible makes clear that there is only one Mediator between God and men—Jesus (1 Tim. 2:5); there is salvation in no other name than Jesus (Acts 4:12); and no one comes to the Father except through Jesus (John 14:6). For more on Catholicism, see page 1810.

7:20 When Adam fell, so did the entire creation (see Gen. 3:17,18). All of creation groans in pain (see Rom. 8:20–22). Everywhere we see signs of the curse: persistent weeds in the soil, diseases in the animal and plant kingdoms, earthquakes, floods, tornadoes, and hurricanes, along with human disease, suffering, and death. All of these things confirm the reality of the Genesis Fall, and both redeemed humanity and creation will be restored in the new heavens and new earth. See Rev. 22:3 comment.

places of Tophet, which *is* in the Valley of
the Son of Hinnom, to burn their sons
and their daughters in the fire, which I
did not command, nor did it come into
My heart.

> Truth is so obscure in these times, and falsehood so established, that, unless we love the truth, we cannot know it.
>
> **BLAISE PASCAL**

32“Therefore behold, the days are coming,” says the LORD, “when it will no more
be called Tophet, or the Valley of the Son
of Hinnom, but the Valley of Slaughter;
for they will bury in Tophet until there is
no room. 33The corpses of this people
will be food for the birds of the heaven
and for the beasts of the earth. And no
one will frighten *them away.* 34Then I will
cause to cease from the cities of Judah
and from the streets of Jerusalem the voice
of mirth and the voice of gladness, the
voice of the bridegroom and the voice of
the bride. For the land shall be desolate.
8 “At that time,” says the LORD, “they
shall bring out the bones of the kings
of Judah, and the bones of its princes,
and the bones of the priests, and the
bones of the prophets, and the bones of
the inhabitants of Jerusalem, out of their
graves. 2They shall spread them before
the sun and the moon and all the host of
heaven, which they have loved and which
they have served and after which they
have walked, which they have sought
and which they have worshiped. They
shall not be gathered nor buried; they
shall be like refuse on the face of the
earth. 3Then death shall be chosen rather
than life by all the residue of those who
remain of this evil family, who remain in
all the places where I have driven them,”
says the LORD of hosts.

The Peril of False Teaching

4“Moreover you shall say to them, ‘Thus
says the LORD:

“Will they fall and not rise?
Will one turn away and not return?
5Why has this people slidden back,
Jerusalem, in a perpetual backsliding?
They hold fast to deceit,
They refuse to return.
6I listened and heard,
But they do not speak aright.
No man repented of his wickedness,
Saying, ‘What have I done?’
Everyone turned to his own course,
As the horse rushes into the battle.

7“Even the stork in the heavens
Knows her appointed times;
And the turtledove, the swift, and the
swallow
Observe the time of their coming.
But My people do not know the
judgment of the LORD.

8“How can you say, ‘We *are* wise,
And the law of the LORD *is* with us’?
Look, the false pen of the scribe
certainly works falsehood.
9The wise men are ashamed,
They are dismayed and taken.
Behold, they have rejected the word
of the LORD;
So what wisdom do they have?
10Therefore I will give their wives to
others,
And their fields to those who will
inherit *them;*
Because from the least even to the
greatest
Everyone is given to covetousness;
From the prophet even to the priest
Everyone deals falsely.
11For they have healed the hurt of the
daughter of My people slightly,
Saying, ‘Peace, peace!’

8:6,7 There will always be self-righteousness in the human heart when there is ignorance of the moral Law and God’s just judgment on sin.

When *there is* no peace.
12Were they ashamed when they had
committed abomination?
No! They were not at all ashamed,
Nor did they know how to blush.
Therefore they shall fall among those
who fall;
In the time of their punishment
They shall be cast down," says the
LORD.

13"I will surely consume them," says the
LORD.
"No grapes *shall be* on the vine,
Nor figs on the fig tree,
And the leaf shall fade;
And *the things* I have given them shall
pass away from them." ' "

14"Why do we sit still?
Assemble yourselves,
And let us enter the fortified cities,
And let us be silent there.
For the LORD our God has put us to
silence
And given us water of gall to drink,
Because we have sinned against the
LORD.

15"*We* looked for peace, but no good
came;
And for a time of health, and there
was trouble!
16The snorting of His horses was heard
from Dan.
The whole land trembled at the
sound of the neighing of His
strong ones;
For they have come and devoured the
land and all that is in it,
The city and those who dwell in it."

17"For behold, I will send serpents
among you,
Vipers which cannot be charmed,
And they shall bite you," says the LORD.

The Prophet Mourns for the People

18I would comfort myself in sorrow;
My heart *is* faint in me.
19Listen! The voice,
The cry of the daughter of my people
From a far country:
"*Is* not the LORD in Zion?
Is not her King in her?"

"Why have they provoked Me to anger
With their carved images—
With foreign idols?"

20"The harvest is past,
The summer is ended,
And we are not saved!"

21For the hurt of the daughter of my
people I am hurt.
I am mourning;
Astonishment has taken hold of me.
22*Is there* no balm in Gilead,
Is there no physician there?
Why then is there no recovery
For the health of the daughter of my
people?

9 Oh, that my head were waters,
And my eyes a fountain of tears,
That I might weep day and night
For the slain of the daughter of my
people!
2Oh, that I had in the wilderness
A lodging place for travelers;
That I might leave my people,
And go from them!

8:12 This gives a picture of true contrition. Those who recognize how abominable their sin is in God's eyes will be broken and will humbly say, "What have I done?" (v. 6). While modern evangelism often goes to great lengths to avoid even hinting at "shame," note that shame is a correct response to sinning against a holy God. See also James 4:9,10.

9:1,2 We weep for the pain of sinners and want to run away from them because of their wickedness. However, we are not called to become monastic monks, but to be in the midst of a crooked and perverse generation, among whom we shine as lights in the world, holding forth the Word of life (see Phil. 2:15). See also 13:17 comment.

For they *are* all adulterers,
An assembly of treacherous men.

3"And *like* their bow they have bent
their tongues *for* lies.
They are not valiant for the truth on
the earth.
For they proceed from evil to evil,
And they do not know Me," says the
LORD.
4"Everyone take heed to his neighbor,
And do not trust any brother;
For every brother will utterly
supplant,
And every neighbor will walk with
slanderers.
5Everyone will deceive his neighbor,
And will not speak the truth;
They have taught their tongue to
speak lies;
They weary themselves to commit
iniquity.
6Your dwelling place *is* in the midst of
deceit;
Through deceit they refuse to know
Me," says the LORD.

7Therefore thus says the LORD of hosts:

"Behold, I will refine them and try them;
For how shall I deal with the
daughter of My people?
8Their tongue *is* an arrow shot out;
It speaks deceit;
One speaks peaceably to his neighbor
with his mouth,
But in his heart he lies in wait.
9Shall I not punish them for these
things?" says the LORD.
"Shall I not avenge Myself on such a
nation as this?"

10I will take up a weeping and wailing
for the mountains,
And for the dwelling places of the
wilderness a lamentation,
Because they are burned up,
So that no one can pass through;
Nor can *men* hear the voice of the
cattle.
Both the birds of the heavens and the
beasts have fled;
They are gone.

11"I will make Jerusalem a heap of ruins,
a den of jackals.
I will make the cities of Judah
desolate, without an inhabitant."

12Who *is* the wise man who may understand this? And *who is he* to whom the
mouth of the LORD has spoken, that he
may declare it? Why does the land perish
and burn up like a wilderness, so that no
one can pass through?
13And the LORD said, "Because they
have forsaken My law which I set before
them, and have not obeyed My voice, nor
walked according to it, 14but they have
walked according to the dictates of their
own hearts and after the Baals, which
their fathers taught them," 15therefore
thus says the LORD of hosts, the God of
Israel: "Behold, I will feed them, this people, with wormwood, and give them water of gall to drink. 16I will scatter them
also among the Gentiles, whom neither
they nor their fathers have known. And I
will send a sword after them until I have
consumed them."

The People Mourn in Judgment

17Thus says the LORD of hosts:

9:6 "If any person is an honest unbeliever and sincerely wants to know God, he will come to a saving faith. Folk with whom I have dealt who say that they cannot believe are not being honest. The fact of the matter is that no man's eyes are blindfolded unless he himself chooses to be blindfolded. If a person really wants to know God and will give up his sin and turn to Christ, God will make Himself real to him. In our day the problem is that a great many folk do not really mean business with God." *J. Vernon McGee*

9:12–14 They forsook God's Law and became idolatrous. America is no different. Many in our nation have turned their backs on the Law and created a god to suit themselves—a god that is nothing more than a celestial Santa Claus. See also Deut. 28:15 comment.

"Consider and call for the mourning
women,
That they may come;
And send for skillful *wailing* women,
That they may come.
18Let them make haste
And take up a wailing for us,
That our eyes may run with tears,
And our eyelids gush with water.
19For a voice of wailing is heard from
Zion:
'How we are plundered!
We are greatly ashamed,
Because we have forsaken the land,
Because we have been cast out of our
dwellings.' "

20Yet hear the word of the LORD, O
women,
And let your ear receive the word of
His mouth;
Teach your daughters wailing,
And everyone her neighbor a
lamentation.
21For death has come through our
windows,
Has entered our palaces,
To kill off the children—*no longer to
be* outside!
And the young men—*no longer* on the
streets!
22Speak, "Thus says the LORD:

'Even the carcasses of men shall fall as
refuse on the open field,
Like cuttings after the harvester,
And no one shall gather *them.*' "

23Thus says the LORD:

"Let not the wise *man* glory in his
wisdom,
Let not the mighty *man* glory in his
might,
Nor let the rich *man* glory in his riches;
24But let him who glories glory in this,
That he understands and knows Me,
That I *am* the LORD, exercising
lovingkindness, judgment, and
righteousness in the earth.
For in these I delight," says the LORD.

25"Behold, the days are coming," says
the LORD, "that I will punish all *who are*
circumcised with the uncircumcised—
26Egypt, Judah, Edom, the people of
Ammon, Moab, and all *who are* in the farthest corners, who dwell in the wilderness. For all *these* nations *are* uncircumcised, and all the house of Israel *are*
uncircumcised in the heart."

Idols and the True God

10 Hear the word which the LORD
speaks to you, O house of Israel.
2Thus says the LORD:

"Do not learn the way of the Gentiles;
Do not be dismayed at the signs of
heaven,
For the Gentiles are dismayed at them.
3For the customs of the peoples *are*
futile;
For *one* cuts a tree from the forest,
The work of the hands of the
workman, with the ax.
4They decorate it with silver and gold;
They fasten it with nails and hammers
So that it will not topple.
5They *are* upright, like a palm tree,
And they cannot speak;
They must be carried,
Because they cannot go *by themselves.*
Do not be afraid of them,
For they cannot do evil,
Nor can they do any good."

6Inasmuch as *there is* none like You, O
LORD

9:23,24 Though a man may have the wisdom of Solomon, the strength of Samson, and the riches of Abraham, he has nothing to glory in compared to the lowliest Christian who knows the Lord (see John 17:3). It is in this knowledge that we find eternal life.

(You *are* great, and Your name *is* great
in might),
[7]Who would not fear You, O King of
the nations?
For this is Your rightful due.
For among all the wise *men* of the
nations,
And in all their kingdoms,
There is none like You.
[8]But they are altogether dull-hearted
and foolish;
A wooden idol *is* a worthless doctrine.
[9]Silver is beaten into plates;
It is brought from Tarshish,
And gold from Uphaz,
The work of the craftsman
And of the hands of the metalsmith;
Blue and purple *are* their clothing;
They *are* all the work of skillful *men*.
[10]But the LORD *is* the true God;
He *is* the living God and the
everlasting King.
At His wrath the earth will tremble,
And the nations will not be able to
endure His indignation.

[11]Thus you shall say to them: "The gods
that have not made the heavens and the
earth shall perish from the earth and from
under these heavens."

[12]He has made the earth by His power,
He has established the world by His
wisdom,
And has stretched out the heavens at
His discretion.
[13]When He utters His voice,
There is a multitude of waters in the
heavens:
"And He causes the vapors to ascend
from the ends of the earth.
He makes lightning for the rain,
He brings the wind out of His
treasuries."[a]

[14]Everyone is dull-hearted, without
knowledge;
Every metalsmith is put to shame by
an image;
For his molded image *is* falsehood,
And *there is* no breath in them.
[15]They *are* futile, a work of errors;
In the time of their punishment they
shall perish.
[16]The Portion of Jacob *is* not like them,
For He *is* the Maker of all *things*,
And Israel *is* the tribe of His
inheritance;
The LORD of hosts *is* His name.

The Coming Captivity of Judah

[17]Gather up your wares from the land,
O inhabitant of the fortress!
[18]For thus says the LORD:
"Behold, I will throw out at this time
The inhabitants of the land,
And will distress them,
That they may find *it so*."

[19]Woe is me for my hurt!
My wound is severe.
But I say, "Truly this *is* an infirmity,
And I must bear it."
[20]My tent is plundered,
And all my cords are broken;
My children have gone from me,
And they *are* no more.
There is no one to pitch my tent
anymore,
Or set up my curtains.

[21]For the shepherds have become dull-
hearted,
And have not sought the LORD;
Therefore they shall not prosper,
And all their flocks shall be scattered.
[22]Behold, the noise of the report has
come,
And a great commotion out of the
north country,
To make the cities of Judah desolate, a
den of jackals.

[23]O LORD, I know the way of man *is*
not in himself;
It is not in man who walks to direct

10:13 [a]Psalm 135:7

his own steps.
[24]O LORD, correct me, but with justice;
Not in Your anger, lest You bring me
to nothing.
[25]Pour out Your fury on the Gentiles,
who do not know You,
And on the families who do not call
on Your name;
For they have eaten up Jacob,
Devoured him and consumed him,
And made his dwelling place desolate.

The Broken Covenant

11 The word that came to Jeremiah
from the LORD, saying, [2]"Hear the
words of this covenant, and speak to the
men of Judah and to the inhabitants of
Jerusalem; [3]and say to them, 'Thus says
the LORD God of Israel: "Cursed *is* the
man who does not obey the words of this
covenant [4]which I commanded your fathers in the day I brought them out of the
land of Egypt, from the iron furnace, saying, 'Obey My voice, and do according to
all that I command you; so shall you be
My people, and I will be your God,' [5]that
I may establish the oath which I have
sworn to your fathers, to give them 'a land
flowing with milk and honey,'[a] as *it is* this
day." ' "

And I answered and said, "So be it,
LORD."

[6]Then the LORD said to me, "Proclaim
all these words in the cities of Judah and
in the streets of Jerusalem, saying: 'Hear
the words of this covenant and do them.
[7]For I earnestly exhorted your fathers in
the day I brought them up out of the land
of Egypt, until this day, rising early and
exhorting, saying, "Obey My voice." [8]Yet
they did not obey or incline their ear, but
everyone followed the dictates of his evil
heart; therefore I will bring upon them all
the words of this covenant, which I commanded *them* to do, but *which* they have
not done.' "

> I am well assured that I did far more good to my Lincolnshire parishioners by preaching three days on my father's tomb than I did by preaching three years in his pulpit.
>
> **JOHN WESLEY**

[9]And the LORD said to me, "A conspiracy has been found among the men
of Judah and among the inhabitants of
Jerusalem. [10]They have turned back to
the iniquities of their forefathers who refused to hear My words, and they have
gone after other gods to serve them; the
house of Israel and the house of Judah
have broken My covenant which I made
with their fathers."

[11]Therefore thus says the LORD: "Behold, I will surely bring calamity on them

11:5 [a]Exodus 3:8

10:23 Man, in his delusion of grandeur, thinks that he is the master of his own destiny, when it is God who holds man's breath in His hand and owns all his ways (see Dan. 5:23).

11:6 Adrenaline rush. Experts tell us that most deaths from skydiving happen because of "human error," insinuating that careful skydivers will be okay. In reality, most premature deaths are from human error: car accidents, drug overdoses, pedestrian deaths, falls down stairs, medical "mistakes," etc. There's a reason that the "Dummies" series of books sell so well. We are "crash dummies" who are prone to error.

Experts think that when a 21-year-old woman jumped on her first free-fall from 10,000 feet, she made a mistake. She began to spin out of control and ended up hitting the ground face-first at 50 mph. She was "eggshelled," and ended up with 15 metal plates in her face. So, think twice before you risk your most precious possession for a quick thrill.

Instead, if you are bored with life and want an adrenaline rush, try open-air preaching. It's more dangerous than skydiving (see Acts 7:57–60), arguably more scary, and infinitely more productive. And if your life is taken from you while you are preaching, at least your death will not be from human error. Rather, it will be by divine permission.

11:11 This is similar to the justice of God being extended in Prov. 1:26–28.

which they will not be able to escape; and though they cry out to Me, I will not listen to them. [12]Then the cities of Judah and the inhabitants of Jerusalem will go and cry out to the gods to whom they offer incense, but they will not save them at all in the time of their trouble. [13]For *according to* the number of your cities were your gods, O Judah; and *according to* the number of the streets of Jerusalem you have set up altars to *that* shameful thing, altars to burn incense to Baal.

[14]"So do not pray for this people, or lift up a cry or prayer for them; for I will not hear *them* in the time that they cry out to Me because of their trouble.

[15]"What has My beloved to do in My house,
Having done lewd deeds with many?
And the holy flesh has passed from you.
When you do evil, then you rejoice.
[16]The LORD called your name,
Green Olive Tree, Lovely *and* of Good Fruit.
With the noise of a great tumult
He has kindled fire on it,
And its branches are broken.

[17]"For the LORD of hosts, who planted you, has pronounced doom against you for the evil of the house of Israel and of the house of Judah, which they have done against themselves to provoke Me to anger in offering incense to Baal."

Jeremiah's Life Threatened

[18]Now the LORD gave me knowledge *of it*, and I know *it;* for You showed me their doings. [19]But I *was* like a docile lamb brought to the slaughter; and I did not know that they had devised schemes against me, *saying,* "Let us destroy the tree with its fruit, and let us cut him off from the land of the living, that his name may be remembered no more."

[20]But, O LORD of hosts,
You who judge righteously,
Testing the mind and the heart,
Let me see Your vengeance on them,
For to You I have revealed my cause.

[21]"Therefore thus says the LORD concerning the men of Anathoth who seek your life, saying, 'Do not prophesy in the name of the LORD, lest you die by our hand'— [22]therefore thus says the LORD of hosts: 'Behold, I will punish them. The young men shall die by the sword, their sons and their daughters shall die by famine; [23]and there shall be no remnant of them, for I will bring catastrophe on the men of Anathoth, *even* the year of their punishment.' "

Jeremiah's Question

12 Righteous *are* You, O LORD, when I plead with You;
Yet let me talk with You about *Your* judgments.
Why does the way of the wicked prosper?
Why are those happy who deal so treacherously?
[2]You have planted them, yes, they have taken root;

11:19 "Now, I know that someday I am going to come to what some people will say is the end of this life. They will probably put me in a box and roll me right down here in front of the church, and some people will gather around, and a few people will cry. But I have told them not to do that because I don't want them to cry. I want them to begin the service with the Doxology and end with the Hallelujah chorus, because I am not going to be there, and I am not going to be dead. I will be more alive than I have ever been in my life, and I will be looking down upon you poor people who are still in the land of dying and have not yet joined me in the land of the living. And I will be alive forevermore, in greater health and vitality and joy than ever, ever, I or anyone has known before." *D. James Kennedy*

12:1 Contrary to the message of modern evangelism, plenty of people are quite prosperous and happy without Jesus. They can *enjoy* the pleasures of sin for a season (see Heb. 11:25). But what they can't have without Jesus is the righteousness that delivers from death (see Prov. 11:4). See 2 Cor. 2:17 comment.

They grow, yes, they bear fruit.
You *are* near in their mouth
But far from their mind.

3 But You, O LORD, know me;
You have seen me,
And You have tested my heart toward You.
Pull them out like sheep for the slaughter,
And prepare them for the day of slaughter.
4 How long will the land mourn,
And the herbs of every field wither?
The beasts and birds are consumed,
For the wickedness of those who dwell there,
Because they said, "He will not see our final end."

The Lord Answers Jeremiah

5 "If you have run with the footmen, and they have wearied you,
Then how can you contend with horses?
And *if* in the land of peace,
In which you trusted, *they wearied you,*
Then how will you do in the floodplain[a] of the Jordan?
6 For even your brothers, the house of your father,
Even they have dealt treacherously with you;
Yes, they have called a multitude after you.
Do not believe them,
Even though they speak smooth words to you.

7 "I have forsaken My house, I have left My heritage;
I have given the dearly beloved of My soul into the hand of her enemies.
8 My heritage is to Me like a lion in the forest;
It cries out against Me;
Therefore I have hated it.
9 My heritage *is* to Me *like* a speckled vulture;
The vultures all around *are* against her.
Come, assemble all the beasts of the field,
Bring them to devour!

10 "Many rulers[a] have destroyed My vineyard,
They have trodden My portion underfoot;
They have made My pleasant portion a desolate wilderness.
11 They have made it desolate;
Desolate, it mourns to Me;
The whole land is made desolate,
Because no one takes *it* to heart.
12 The plunderers have come
On all the desolate heights in the wilderness,
For the sword of the LORD shall devour
From *one* end of the land to the *other* end of the land;
No flesh shall have peace.
13 They have sown wheat but reaped thorns;
They have put themselves to pain *but* do not profit.
But be ashamed of your harvest
Because of the fierce anger of the LORD."

14 Thus says the LORD: "Against all My
evil neighbors who touch the inheritance
which I have caused My people Israel to
inherit—behold, I will pluck them out of
their land and pluck out the house of Judah from among them. 15 Then it shall be,

12:5 [a]Or *thicket* 12:10 [a]Literally *shepherds* or *pastors*

12:2 This is why we must address the conscience of the sin-loving sinner. Many believe in God but they don't fear Him enough to obey Him. They draw near to Him with their lips, but their hearts are far from Him (see Isa. 29:13), treating Him as some sort of divine butler whom they call when they have a need. However, the First Commandment requires that we put God first in our affections, and love Him with all of our heart, soul, mind, and strength, rather than treat Him as a celestial Santa Claus.

after I have plucked them out, that I will return and have compassion on them and bring them back, everyone to his heritage and everyone to his land. [16]And it shall be, if they will learn carefully the ways of My people, to swear by My name, 'As the LORD lives,' as they taught My people to swear by Baal, then they shall be established in the midst of My people. [17]But if they do not obey, I will utterly pluck up and destroy that nation," says the LORD.

Symbol of the Linen Sash

13 Thus the LORD said to me: "Go and get yourself a linen sash, and put it around your waist, but do not put it in water." [2]So I got a sash according to the word of the LORD, and put *it* around my waist.

[3]And the word of the LORD came to me the second time, saying, [4]"Take the sash that you acquired, which *is* around your waist, and arise, go to the Euphrates,[a] and hide it there in a hole in the rock." [5]So I went and hid it by the Euphrates, as the LORD commanded me.

[6]Now it came to pass after many days that the LORD said to me, "Arise, go to the Euphrates, and take from there the sash which I commanded you to hide there." [7]Then I went to the Euphrates and dug, and I took the sash from the place where I had hidden it; and there was the sash, ruined. It was profitable for nothing.

[8]Then the word of the LORD came to me, saying, [9]"Thus says the LORD: 'In this manner I will ruin the pride of Judah and the great pride of Jerusalem. [10]This evil people, who refuse to hear My words, who follow the dictates of their hearts, and walk after other gods to serve them and worship them, shall be just like this sash which is profitable for nothing. [11]For as the sash clings to the waist of a man, so I have caused the whole house of Israel and the whole house of Judah to cling to Me,' says the LORD, 'that they may become My people, for renown, for praise, and for glory; but they would not hear.'

Symbol of the Wine Bottles

[12]"Therefore you shall speak to them this word: 'Thus says the LORD God of Israel: "Every bottle shall be filled with wine." '

"And they will say to you, 'Do we not certainly know that every bottle will be filled with wine?'

[13]"Then you shall say to them, 'Thus says the LORD: "Behold, I will fill all the inhabitants of this land—even the kings who sit on David's throne, the priests, the prophets, and all the inhabitants of Jerusalem—with drunkenness! [14]And I will dash them one against another, even the fathers and the sons together," says the LORD. "I will not pity nor spare nor have mercy, but will destroy them." ' "

Pride Precedes Captivity

[15]Hear and give ear:
Do not be proud,
For the LORD has spoken.
[16]Give glory to the LORD your God
Before He causes darkness,
And before your feet stumble
On the dark mountains,
And while you are looking for light,
He turns it into the shadow of death
And makes *it* dense darkness.
[17]But if you will not hear it,
My soul will weep in secret for *your* pride;
My eyes will weep bitterly
And run down with tears,
Because the LORD's flock has been taken captive.

13:4 [a]Hebrew *Perath*

13:11 This is the very reason for our existence: we are His people, created for the purpose of His renown, praise, and glory.

13:17 Jeremiah is called "the weeping prophet." We need to be more like him.

[18]Say to the king and to the queen mother,
"Humble yourselves;
Sit down,
For your rule shall collapse, the crown of your glory."
[19]The cities of the South shall be shut up,
And no one shall open *them;*
Judah shall be carried away captive, all of it;
It shall be wholly carried away captive.

The greatest form of praise is the sound of consecrated feet seeking out the lost and helpless.

BILLY GRAHAM

[20]Lift up your eyes and see
Those who come from the north.
Where *is* the flock *that* was given to you,
Your beautiful sheep?
[21]What will you say when He punishes you?
For you have taught them
To be chieftains, to be head over you.
Will not pangs seize you,
Like a woman in labor?
[22]And if you say in your heart,
"Why have these things come upon me?"
For the greatness of your iniquity
Your skirts have been uncovered,
Your heels made bare.
[23]Can the Ethiopian change his skin or the leopard its spots?
Then may you also do good who are accustomed to do evil.

[24]"Therefore I will scatter them like stubble
That passes away by the wind of the wilderness.
[25]This is your lot,
The portion of your measures from Me," says the LORD,
"Because you have forgotten Me
And trusted in falsehood.
[26]Therefore I will uncover your skirts over your face,
That your shame may appear.
[27]I have seen your adulteries
And your *lustful* neighings,
The lewdness of your harlotry,
Your abominations on the hills in the fields.
Woe to you, O Jerusalem!
Will you still not be made clean?"

Sword, Famine, and Pestilence

14 The word of the LORD that came to Jeremiah concerning the droughts.

[2]"Judah mourns,
And her gates languish;
They mourn for the land,
And the cry of Jerusalem has gone up.
[3]Their nobles have sent their lads for water;
They went to the cisterns *and* found no water.
They returned with their vessels empty;
They were ashamed and confounded
And covered their heads.
[4]Because the ground is parched,
For there was no rain in the land,
The plowmen were ashamed;
They covered their heads.
[5]Yes, the deer also gave birth in the field,
But left because there was no grass.
[6]And the wild donkeys stood in the desolate heights;
They sniffed at the wind like jackals;
Their eyes failed because *there was* no grass."

13:23 Just as the answer to the first question is "no," the second is likewise impossible. There is none who does good, no, not one (see Psa. 53:3). Jesus said that there is none good but God. See Mark 10:17–19 for how He showed God's standard of goodness.

[7]O LORD, though our iniquities testify
against us,
Do it for Your name's sake;
For our backslidings are many,
We have sinned against You.
[8]O the Hope of Israel, his Savior in
time of trouble,
Why should You be like a stranger in
the land,
And like a traveler *who* turns aside to
tarry for a night?
[9]Why should You be like a man
astonished,
Like a mighty one *who* cannot save?
Yet You, O LORD, *are* in our midst,
And we are called by Your name;
Do not leave us!

[10]Thus says the LORD to this people:

"Thus they have loved to wander;
They have not restrained their feet.
Therefore the LORD does not accept
them;
He will remember their iniquity now,
And punish their sins."

[11]Then the LORD said to me, "Do not
pray for this people, for *their* good. [12]When
they fast, I will not hear their cry; and
when they offer burnt offering and grain
offering, I will not accept them. But I will
consume them by the sword, by the famine, and by the pestilence."
[13]Then I said, "Ah, Lord GOD! Behold,
the prophets say to them, 'You shall not
see the sword, nor shall you have famine,
but I will give you assured peace in this
place.' "
[14]And the LORD said to me, "The
prophets prophesy lies in My name. I
have not sent them, commanded them,
nor spoken to them; they prophesy to
you a false vision, divination, a worthless
thing, and the deceit of their heart.
[15]Therefore thus says the LORD concerning the prophets who prophesy in My
name, whom I did not send, and who say,
'Sword and famine shall not be in this
land'—'By sword and famine those
prophets shall be consumed! [16]And the
people to whom they prophesy shall be
cast out in the streets of Jerusalem because of the famine and the sword; they
will have no one to bury them—them
nor their wives, their sons nor their
daughters—for I will pour their wickedness on them.'
[17]"Therefore you shall say this word to
them:

'Let my eyes flow with tears night and
day,
And let them not cease;
For the virgin daughter of my people
Has been broken with a mighty
stroke, with a very severe blow.
[18]If I go out to the field,
Then behold, those slain with the
sword!
And if I enter the city,
Then behold, those sick from famine!
Yes, both prophet and priest go about
in a land they do not know.' "

The People Plead for Mercy

[19]Have You utterly rejected Judah?
Has Your soul loathed Zion?
Why have You stricken us so that
there is no healing for us?
We looked for peace, but *there was* no
good;
And for the time of healing, and there
was trouble.
[20]We acknowledge, O LORD, our
wickedness
And the iniquity of our fathers,
For we have sinned against You.
[21]Do not abhor *us,* for Your name's sake;
Do not disgrace the throne of Your
glory.
Remember, do not break Your

14:13,14 There are plenty of popular, contemporary false prophets who are wolves in sheep's clothing. They look and sound harmless enough, but they have doctrines of poison, devoid of the judgment of God.

covenant with us.
[22]Are there any among the idols of the
nations that can cause rain?
Or can the heavens give showers?
Are You not He, O LORD our God?
Therefore we will wait for You,
Since You have made all these.

The Lord Will Not Relent

15 Then the LORD said to me, "*Even* if
Moses and Samuel stood before
Me, My mind *would* not *be* favorable toward this people. Cast *them* out of My
sight, and let them go forth. [2]And it shall
be, if they say to you, 'Where should we
go?' then you shall tell them, 'Thus says
the LORD:

"Such as *are* for death, to death;
And such as *are* for the sword, to the
sword;
And such as *are* for the famine, to the
famine;
And such as *are* for the captivity, to
the captivity." '

[3]"And I will appoint over them four
forms *of destruction*," says the LORD: "the
sword to slay, the dogs to drag, the birds
of the heavens and the beasts of the earth
to devour and destroy. [4]I will hand them
over to trouble, to all kingdoms of the
earth, because of Manasseh the son of
Hezekiah, king of Judah, for what he did
in Jerusalem.

[5]"For who will have pity on you, O
Jerusalem?
Or who will bemoan you?
Or who will turn aside to ask how
you are doing?
[6]You have forsaken Me," says the LORD,
"You have gone backward.
Therefore I will stretch out My hand
against you and destroy you;
I am weary of relenting!
[7]And I will winnow them with a
winnowing fan in the gates of the
land;
I will bereave *them* of children;
I will destroy My people,
Since they do not return from their
ways.
[8]Their widows will be increased to Me
more than the sand of the seas;
I will bring against them,
Against the mother of the young men,
A plunderer at noonday;
I will cause anguish and terror to fall
on them suddenly.

[9]"She languishes who has borne seven;
She has breathed her last;
Her sun has gone down
While *it was* yet day;
She has been ashamed and
confounded.
And the remnant of them I will
deliver to the sword
Before their enemies," says the LORD.

Jeremiah's Dejection

[10]Woe is me, my mother,
That you have borne me,
A man of strife and a man of
contention to the whole earth!
I have neither lent for interest,
Nor have men lent to me for interest.
Every one of them curses me.

[11]The LORD said:

"Surely it will be well with your
remnant;
Surely I will cause the enemy to
intercede with you
In the time of adversity and in the
time of affliction.
[12]Can anyone break iron,
The northern iron and the bronze?
[13]Your wealth and your treasures
I will give as plunder without price,

15:1 How wicked they must have been to have exhausted the patience of Almighty God. What a fearful thought.

Because of all your sins,
Throughout your territories.
14And I will make *you* cross over with[a]
your enemies
Into a land *which* you do not know;
For a fire is kindled in My anger,
Which shall burn upon you."
15O LORD, You know;
Remember me and visit me,
And take vengeance for me on my
persecutors.
In Your enduring patience, do not
take me away.
Know that for Your sake I have
suffered rebuke.
16Your words were found, and I ate
them,
And Your word was to me the joy and
rejoicing of my heart;
For I am called by Your name,
O LORD God of hosts.
17I did not sit in the assembly of the
mockers,
Nor did I rejoice;
I sat alone because of Your hand,
For You have filled me with
indignation.
18Why is my pain perpetual
And my wound incurable,
Which refuses to be healed?
Will You surely be to me like an
unreliable stream,
As waters *that* fail?

The Lord Reassures Jeremiah

19Therefore thus says the LORD:

"If you return,
Then I will bring you back;
You shall stand before Me;
If you take out the precious from the
vile,
You shall be as My mouth.
Let them return to you,
But you must not return to them.
20And I will make you to this people a
fortified bronze wall;
And they will fight against you,
But they shall not prevail against you;
For I *am* with you to save you
And deliver you," says the LORD.
21"I will deliver you from the hand of
the wicked,
And I will redeem you from the grip
of the terrible."

Jeremiah's Life-Style and Message

16 The word of the LORD also came to
me, saying, 2"You shall not take a
wife, nor shall you have sons or daughters in this place." 3For thus says the
LORD concerning the sons and daughters
who are born in this place, and concerning their mothers who bore them and
their fathers who begot them in this land:
4"They shall die gruesome deaths; they
shall not be lamented nor shall they be
buried, *but* they shall be like refuse on
the face of the earth. They shall be consumed by the sword and by famine, and
their corpses shall be meat for the birds
of heaven and for the beasts of the earth."
5For thus says the LORD: "Do not enter
the house of mourning, nor go to lament
or bemoan them; for I have taken away
My peace from this people," says the
LORD, "lovingkindness and mercies. 6Both
the great and the small shall die in this
land. They shall not be buried; neither
shall men lament for them, cut themselves,
nor make themselves bald for them. 7Nor
shall *men* break *bread* in mourning for
them, to comfort them for the dead; nor
shall *men* give them the cup of consolation to drink for their father or their
mother. 8Also you shall not go into the
house of feasting to sit with them, to eat

15:14 [a]Following Masoretic Text and Vulgate; Septuagint, Syriac, and Targum read *cause you to serve* (compare 17:4).

15:16 The psalmist said that he rejoiced over God's Word as though he found great treasure (see Psa. 119:162). Take a moment to study history to see what it cost for us to have the precious treasure of the Word of God. Its foundation is soaked in the blood of martyrs.

and drink."
9For thus says the LORD of hosts, the
God of Israel: "Behold, I will cause to
cease from this place, before your eyes
and in your days, the voice of mirth and
the voice of gladness, the voice of the
bridegroom and the voice of the bride.
10"And it shall be, when you show this
people all these words, and they say to
you, 'Why has the LORD pronounced all
this great disaster against us? Or what *is*
our iniquity? Or what *is* our sin that we
have committed against the LORD our
God?' 11then you shall say to them, 'Because your fathers have forsaken Me,'
says the LORD; 'they have walked after
other gods and have served them and
worshiped them, and have forsaken Me
and not kept My law. 12And you have
done worse than your fathers, for behold,
each one follows the dictates of his own
evil heart, so that no one listens to Me.
13Therefore I will cast you out of this land
into a land that you do not know, neither
you nor your fathers; and there you shall
serve other gods day and night, where I
will not show you favor.'

God Will Restore Israel

14"Therefore behold, the days are
coming," says the LORD, "that it shall no
more be said, 'The LORD lives who
brought up the children of Israel from the
land of Egypt,' 15but, 'The LORD lives who
brought up the children of Israel from the
land of the north and from all the lands
where He had driven them.' For I will
bring them back into their land which I
gave to their fathers.
16"Behold, I will send for many fishermen," says the LORD, "and they shall fish
them; and afterward I will send for many
hunters, and they shall hunt them from
every mountain and every hill, and out
of the holes of the rocks. 17For My eyes
are on all their ways; they are not hidden
from My face, nor is their iniquity hidden
from My eyes. 18And first I will repay
double for their iniquity and their sin,
because they have defiled My land; they
have filled My inheritance with the carcasses of their detestable and abominable
idols."

19O LORD, my strength and my fortress,
My refuge in the day of affliction,
The Gentiles shall come to You
From the ends of the earth and say,
"Surely our fathers have inherited lies,
Worthlessness and unprofitable *things*."
20Will a man make gods for himself,
Which *are* not gods?

21"Therefore behold, I will this once
cause them to know,

THE FUNCTION OF THE LAW

16:10,11 The same pattern can be seen in contemporary America. When our righteous God and His holy Law are forsaken, humanity has no sense of sin and immediately creates gods with no moral dictates.

"It is exceeding necessary for us to know this use of the Law. For he that is not an open and a public murderer, an adulterer, or a thief, holds himself to be an upright and godly man; as did the Pharisee, so blinded and possessed spiritually of the devil, that he could neither see nor feel his sins, nor his miserable case, but exalted himself touching his good works and deserts. Such hypocrites and haughty saints can God by no better means humble and soften, than by and through the Law; for that is the right club or hammer, the thunderclap from heaven, the axe of God's wrath, that strikes through, beats down, and batters such stock-blind, hardened hypocrites.

For this cause, it is no small matter that we should rightly understand what the Law is, whereto it serves, and what is its proper work and office. We do not reject the Law and the works thereof, but on the contrary, confirm them, and teach that we ought to do good works, and that the Law is very good and profitable, if we merely give it its right, and keep it to its own proper work and office." *Martin Luther*

16:17 All things are naked and open to the eyes of Him to whom we must give account (see Heb. 4:13). See Rom. 2:3–11 for the fate of those who refuse to repent of their sins.

I will cause them to know
My hand and My might;
And they shall know that My name *is*
the LORD.

Judah's Sin and Punishment

17 "The sin of Judah *is* written with a
pen of iron;
With the point of a diamond *it is*
engraved
On the tablet of their heart,
And on the horns of your altars,
2While their children remember
Their altars and their wooden images[a]
By the green trees on the high hills.
3O My mountain in the field,
I will give as plunder your wealth, all
your treasures,
And your high places of sin within all
your borders.
4And you, even yourself,
Shall let go of your heritage which I
gave you;
And I will cause you to serve your
enemies
In the land which you do not know;
For you have kindled a fire in My
anger *which* shall burn forever."

5Thus says the LORD:

"Cursed *is* the man who trusts in man
And makes flesh his strength,
Whose heart departs from the LORD.
6For he shall be like a shrub in the
desert,
And shall not see when good comes,
But shall inhabit the parched places
in the wilderness,
In a salt land *which is* not inhabited.

7"Blessed *is* the man who trusts in the
LORD,
And whose hope is the LORD.
8For he shall be like a tree planted by
the waters,
Which spreads out its roots by the
river,
And will not fear[a] when heat comes;
But its leaf will be green,
And will not be anxious in the year of
drought,
Nor will cease from yielding fruit.

9"The heart *is* deceitful above all *things*,
And desperately wicked;
Who can know it?
10I, the LORD, search the heart,
I test the mind,
Even to give every man according to
his ways,
According to the fruit of his doings.

11"*As* a partridge that broods but does
not hatch,
So is he who gets riches, but not by
right;
It will leave him in the midst of his
days,
And at his end he will be a fool."

12A glorious high throne from the
beginning
Is the place of our sanctuary.
13O LORD, the hope of Israel,

17:2 [a]Hebrew *Asherim*, Canaanite deities 17:8 [a]*Qere* and *Targum* read *see.*

17:7,8 Those who trust in Jesus Christ are blessed beyond words. Trust in Him with all your heart, and never lean on your own understanding. Stand on this promise and the similar promise of Psa. 1.

17:9,10 This is diametrically opposed to the testimony of the world, which believes that man is basically good. Ask any non-Christian, or someone you think may be a false convert, if he thinks he is a good person. He will almost always proclaim his own goodness (see Prov. 20:6). When someone dies, the world will say that he was a good man, despite his wicked life. Their error is in measuring themselves by the standards of man, rather than by the perfect standard of God—who sees not only actions but attitudes and thoughts. God's Law judges lust as adultery (Matt. 5:27,28) and hatred as murder (1 John 3:15). God Himself says that our hearts are not good (only He is good; see Mark 10:18) but in reality are "desperately wicked." For a diagnosis of the sinner's heart ailment, see Matt. 13:15–17; Mark 7:21–23.

All who forsake You shall be ashamed.

"Those who depart from Me
Shall be written in the earth,
Because they have forsaken the LORD,
The fountain of living waters."

Jeremiah Prays for Deliverance

14Heal me, O LORD, and I shall be
healed;
Save me, and I shall be saved,
For You *are* my praise.
15Indeed they say to me,
"Where *is* the word of the LORD?
Let it come now!"
16As for me, I have not hurried away
from *being* a shepherd *who*
follows You,
Nor have I desired the woeful day;
You know what came out of my lips;
It was right there before You.
17Do not be a terror to me;
You *are* my hope in the day of doom.
18Let them be ashamed who persecute
me,
But do not let me be put to shame;
Let them be dismayed,
But do not let me be dismayed.
Bring on them the day of doom,
And destroy them with double
destruction!

Hallow the Sabbath Day

19Thus the LORD said to me: "Go and
stand in the gate of the children of the
people, by which the kings of Judah
come in and by which they go out, and in
all the gates of Jerusalem; 20and say to
them, 'Hear the word of the LORD, you
kings of Judah, and all Judah, and all the
inhabitants of Jerusalem, who enter by
these gates. 21Thus says the LORD: "Take
heed to yourselves, and bear no burden
on the Sabbath day, nor bring *it* in by the
gates of Jerusalem; 22nor carry a burden
out of your houses on the Sabbath day,
nor do any work, but hallow the Sabbath
day, as I commanded your fathers. 23But
they did not obey nor incline their ear,
but made their neck stiff, that they might
not hear nor receive instruction.

24"And it shall be, if you heed Me carefully," says the LORD, "to bring no burden
through the gates of this city on the Sabbath day, but hallow the Sabbath day, to
do no work in it, 25then shall enter the
gates of this city kings and princes sitting
on the throne of David, riding in chariots
and on horses, they and their princes, accompanied by the men of Judah and the
inhabitants of Jerusalem; and this city
shall remain forever. 26And they shall come
from the cities of Judah and from the
places around Jerusalem, from the land of
Benjamin and from the lowland, from the
mountains and from the South, bringing
burnt offerings and sacrifices, grain offerings and incense, bringing sacrifices of
praise to the house of the LORD.

27"But if you will not heed Me to hallow the Sabbath day, such as not carrying
a burden when entering the gates of Jerusalem on the Sabbath day, then I will kindle a fire in its gates, and it shall devour
the palaces of Jerusalem, and it shall not
be quenched." ' "

The Potter and the Clay

18 The word which came to Jeremiah
from the LORD, saying: 2"Arise and
go down to the potter's house, and there
I will cause you to hear My words." 3Then
I went down to the potter's house, and
there he was, making something at the
wheel. 4And the vessel that he made of
clay was marred in the hand of the potter;
so he made it again into another vessel, as
it seemed good to the potter to make.

5Then the word of the LORD came to
me, saying: 6"O house of Israel, can I not
do with you as this potter?" says the
LORD. "Look, as the clay *is* in the potter's
hand, so *are* you in My hand, O house of
Israel! 7The instant I speak concerning a

17:23 See Zech. 7:11,12 comment.

Questions & Objections

18:8 ***"The Bible says 'God repented.' Doesn't that show He is capable of sin?"***

Man is sinful, and when the Scriptures speak of man "repenting," it is in reference to him changing his mind and turning from sin. It means to "confess and forsake" his sins (see Prov. 28:13). However, Num. 23:19 tells us that "God is not a man, that He should lie, nor a son of man, that He should repent." God is without sin, so any reference to God's "repentance" is merely His relenting by not bringing about a promised punishment if sinners turn from their sins. The King James translation has at least twenty-six references to God "repenting," and each time it is in the context of punishing or rewarding a person or group of people. For example, Jon. 3:10 says, "Then God saw their works, that they turned from their evil way; and God relented [KJV, "repented"] from the disaster that He had said He would bring upon them, and He did not do it." Because He did not punish them as He warned, it may appear to them that He "changed" His mind, but His promised punishment was contingent on their repentance.

nation and concerning a kingdom, to
pluck up, to pull down, and to destroy *it,*
8if that nation against whom I have spoken turns from its evil, I will relent of the
disaster that I thought to bring upon it.
9And the instant I speak concerning a nation and concerning a kingdom, to build
and to plant *it,* 10if it does evil in My sight
so that it does not obey My voice, then I
will relent concerning the good with which
I said I would benefit it.

11"Now therefore, speak to the men of
Judah and to the inhabitants of Jerusalem,
saying, 'Thus says the LORD: "Behold, I
am fashioning a disaster and devising a
plan against you. Return now every one
from his evil way, and make your ways
and your doings good." ' "

God's Warning Rejected

12And they said, "That is hopeless! So
we will walk according to our own plans,
and we will every one obey the dictates of
his evil heart."

13Therefore thus says the LORD:

"Ask now among the Gentiles,
Who has heard such things?
The virgin of Israel has done a very
horrible thing.
14Will *a man* leave the snow water of
Lebanon,
Which comes from the rock of the field?
Will the cold flowing waters be
forsaken for strange waters?

15"Because My people have forgotten Me,
They have burned incense to
worthless idols.
And they have caused themselves to
stumble in their ways,
From the ancient paths,
To walk in pathways and not on a
highway,
16To make their land desolate *and* a
perpetual hissing;
Everyone who passes by it will be
astonished
And shake his head.
17I will scatter them as with an east
wind before the enemy;
I will show them[a] the back and not
the face
In the day of their calamity."

Jeremiah Persecuted

18Then they said, "Come and let us devise plans against Jeremiah; for the law
shall not perish from the priest, nor
counsel from the wise, nor the word from
the prophet. Come and let us attack him
with the tongue, and let us not give heed
to any of his words."

19Give heed to me, O LORD,

18:17 [a]Following Septuagint, Syriac, Targum, and Vulgate; Masoretic Text reads *look them in.*

POINTS FOR OPEN-AIR PREACHING

19:2

Location, Location, Location

A good place for open-air preaching is anywhere people gather—beaches, parks, or waiting in line—where they're not in a hurry. Select a place that has plenty of foot traffic, away from the noise of the street, a fountain, or machinery. It is ideal to have somewhere that will acoustically hold your voice, and where you can be slightly elevated. You shouldn't have problems speaking in public places in the United States; it is your First Amendment right to speak on American soil.

I typically keep going back to the same area as long as people will listen to the gospel. This is because it is good for regulars to hear the gospel more than once. You will find that you can befriend these people, and some may even seek you out with questions. Another reason I stick with the same place is because of the old adage, "If it's not broke, why fix it?" This is also true when you find an effective fishing hole for handing out tracts and witnessing.

And listen to the voice of those who
contend with me!
20Shall evil be repaid for good?
For they have dug a pit for my life.
Remember that I stood before You
To speak good for them,
To turn away Your wrath from them.
21Therefore deliver up their children to
the famine,
And pour out their *blood*
By the force of the sword;
Let their wives *become* widows
And bereaved of their children.
Let their men be put to death,
Their young men *be* slain
By the sword in battle.
22Let a cry be heard from their houses,
When You bring a troop suddenly
upon them;
For they have dug a pit to take me,
And hidden snares for my feet.
23Yet, LORD, You know all their counsel
Which is against me, to slay *me.*
Provide no atonement for their
iniquity,
Nor blot out their sin from Your sight;
But let them be overthrown before
You.
Deal *thus* with them
In the time of Your anger.

The Sign of the Broken Flask

19 Thus says the LORD: "Go and get a
potter's earthen flask, and *take*
some of the elders of the people and
some of the elders of the priests. 2And go
out to the Valley of the Son of Hinnom,
which *is* by the entry of the Potsherd Gate;
and proclaim there the words that I will
tell you, 3and say, 'Hear the word of the
LORD, O kings of Judah and inhabitants
of Jerusalem. Thus says the LORD of hosts,
the God of Israel: "Behold, I will bring
such a catastrophe on this place, that whoever hears of it, his ears will tingle.
4"Because they have forsaken Me and
made this an alien place, because they
have burned incense in it to other gods
whom neither they, their fathers, nor the
kings of Judah have known, and have
filled this place with the blood of the innocents 5(they have also built the high
places of Baal, to burn their sons with fire
for burnt offerings to Baal, which I did
not command or speak, nor did it come
into My mind), 6therefore behold, the
days are coming," says the LORD, "that
this place shall no more be called Tophet
or the Valley of the Son of Hinnom, but
the Valley of Slaughter. 7And I will make
void the counsel of Judah and Jerusalem

18:20 When you are persecuted for the gospel's sake, pour your heart out to the Lord. Cast all your care upon Him. This is what the disciples did in the Book of Acts. Keep in mind the admonitions in Matt. 5:44 and Rom. 12:14.

19:7 When the enemy comes against you, commit yourself to Him who judges righteously, then stand back and watch Him take vengeance where necessary—in His time and in His way. Don't take vengeance into your own hands, and don't hold any grudges. Let them all go.

in this place, and I will cause them to fall
by the sword before their enemies and by
the hands of those who seek their lives;
their corpses I will give as meat for the
birds of the heaven and for the beasts of
the earth. 8I will make this city desolate
and a hissing; everyone who passes by it
will be astonished and hiss because of all
its plagues. 9And I will cause them to eat
the flesh of their sons and the flesh of
their daughters, and everyone shall eat
the flesh of his friend in the siege and in
the desperation with which their enemies
and those who seek their lives shall drive
them to despair." '

10"Then you shall break the flask in
the sight of the men who go with you,
11and say to them, 'Thus says the LORD of
hosts: "Even so I will break this people
and this city, as *one* breaks a potter's vessel, which cannot be made whole again;
and they shall bury *them* in Tophet till
there is no place to bury. 12Thus I will do
to this place," says the LORD, "and to its
inhabitants, and make this city like
Tophet. 13And the houses of Jerusalem
and the houses of the kings of Judah shall
be defiled like the place of Tophet, because of all the houses on whose roofs
they have burned incense to all the host
of heaven, and poured out drink offerings to other gods." ' "

14Then Jeremiah came from Tophet,
where the LORD had sent him to prophesy; and he stood in the court of the
Lord's house and said to all the people,
15"Thus says the LORD of hosts, the God
of Israel: 'Behold, I will bring on this city
and on all her towns all the doom that I
have pronounced against it, because they
have stiffened their necks that they might
not hear My words.' "

The Word of God to Pashhur

20 Now Pashhur the son of Immer,
the priest who *was* also chief governor in the house of the LORD, heard that
Jeremiah prophesied these things. 2Then
Pashhur struck Jeremiah the prophet, and
put him in the stocks that *were* in the
high gate of Benjamin, which *was* by the
house of the LORD.

3And it happened on the next day that
Pashhur brought Jeremiah out of the
stocks. Then Jeremiah said to him, "The
LORD has not called your name Pashhur,
but Magor-Missabib.[a] 4For thus says the
LORD: 'Behold, I will make you a terror to
yourself and to all your friends; and they
shall fall by the sword of their enemies,
and your eyes shall see *it*. I will give all
Judah into the hand of the king of Babylon, and he shall carry them captive to
Babylon and slay them with the sword.
5Moreover I will deliver all the wealth of
this city, all its produce, and all its precious things; all the treasures of the kings
of Judah I will give into the hand of their
enemies, who will plunder them, seize
them, and carry them to Babylon. 6And
you, Pashhur, and all who dwell in your
house, shall go into captivity. You shall go
to Babylon, and there you shall die, and
be buried there, you and all your friends,
to whom you have prophesied lies.' "

Jeremiah's Unpopular Ministry

7O LORD, You induced me, and I was
persuaded;
You are stronger than I, and have
prevailed.
I am in derision daily;
Everyone mocks me.
8For when I spoke, I cried out;
I shouted, "Violence and plunder!"
Because the word of the LORD was
made to me
A reproach and a derision daily.
9Then I said, "I will not make mention
of Him,

20:3 [a]Literally *Fear on Every Side*

20:9 Persecution almost persuaded Jeremiah not to speak in God's name, but God's Word burned so within Jeremiah that he could not keep it to himself (see Psa. 39:3). How much more should we be forthright in presenting the good news of eternal life through our Savior Jesus! See also John 17:14 comment.

Nor speak anymore in His name."
But *His word* was in my heart like a
burning fire
Shut up in my bones;
I was weary of holding *it* back,
And I could not.
10For I heard many mocking:
"Fear on every side!"
"Report," *they say,* "and we will report
it!"
All my acquaintances watched for my
stumbling, *saying,*
"Perhaps he can be induced;
Then we will prevail against him,
And we will take our revenge on him."
11But the LORD *is* with me as a mighty,
awesome One.
Therefore my persecutors will
stumble, and will not prevail.
They will be greatly ashamed, for they
will not prosper.
Their everlasting confusion will never
be forgotten.
12But, O LORD of hosts,
You who test the righteous,
And see the mind and heart,
Let me see Your vengeance on them;
For I have pleaded my cause before
You.

13Sing to the LORD! Praise the LORD!
For He has delivered the life of the
poor
From the hand of evildoers.

14Cursed *be* the day in which I was born!
Let the day not be blessed in which
my mother bore me!
15Let the man *be* cursed
Who brought news to my father,
saying,
"A male child has been born to you!"
Making him very glad.
16And let that man be like the cities
Which the LORD overthrew, and did
not relent;
Let him hear the cry in the morning
And the shouting at noon,
17Because he did not kill me from the
womb,
That my mother might have been my
grave,
And her womb always enlarged *with
me.*
18Why did I come forth from the womb
to see labor and sorrow,
That my days should be consumed
with shame?

Jerusalem's Doom Is Sealed

21 The word which came to Jeremiah from the LORD when King
Zedekiah sent to him Pashhur the son of
Melchiah, and Zephaniah the son of Maaseiah, the priest, saying, 2"Please inquire
of the LORD for us, for Nebuchadnezzar[a]
king of Babylon makes war against us.
Perhaps the LORD will deal with us according to all His wonderful works, that
the king may go away from us."
3Then Jeremiah said to them, "Thus
you shall say to Zedekiah, 4'Thus says the
LORD God of Israel: "Behold, I will turn
back the weapons of war that *are* in your
hands, with which you fight against the
king of Babylon and the Chaldeans[a] who
besiege you outside the walls; and I will
assemble them in the midst of this city. 5I
Myself will fight against you with an outstretched hand and with a strong arm,
even in anger and fury and great wrath. 6I
will strike the inhabitants of this city,
both man and beast; they shall die of a
great pestilence. 7And afterward," says
the LORD, "I will deliver Zedekiah king of
Judah, his servants and the people, and

21:2 [a]Hebrew *Nebuchadrezzar,* and so elsewhere 21:4 [a]Or *Babylonians*

21:4,5 These are some of the most frightening verses in the Bible. This is the Creator, whose terrifying power is displayed in earthquakes, tornadoes, and lightning, saying that He will fight against the king. If God is against us, who can be for us?

such as are left in this city from the pestilence and the sword and the famine, into
the hand of Nebuchadnezzar king of
Babylon, into the hand of their enemies,
and into the hand of those who seek their
life; and he shall strike them with the
edge of the sword. He shall not spare them,
or have pity or mercy." '

8"Now you shall say to this people,
'Thus says the LORD: "Behold, I set before
you the way of life and the way of death.
9He who remains in this city shall die by
the sword, by famine, and by pestilence;
but he who goes out and defects to the
Chaldeans who besiege you, he shall live,
and his life shall be as a prize to him.
10For I have set My face against this city
for adversity and not for good," says the
LORD. "It shall be given into the hand of
the king of Babylon, and he shall burn it
with fire." '

Message to the House of David

11"And concerning the house of the
king of Judah, *say,* 'Hear the word of the
LORD, 12O house of David! Thus says the
LORD:

"Execute judgment in the morning;
And deliver *him who is* plundered
Out of the hand of the oppressor,
Lest My fury go forth like fire
And burn so that no one can quench
it,
Because of the evil of your doings.

> Lord, grant that the fire of my heart may melt the lead in my feet.
>
> UNKNOWN

13"Behold, I *am* against you, O
inhabitant of the valley,
And rock of the plain," says the LORD,
"Who say, 'Who shall come down
against us?
Or who shall enter our dwellings?'
14But I will punish you according to the
fruit of your doings," says the
LORD;
"I will kindle a fire in its forest,
And it shall devour all things around
it." ' "

22 Thus says the LORD: "Go down to
the house of the king of Judah,
and there speak this word, 2and say, 'Hear
the word of the LORD, O king of Judah,
you who sit on the throne of David, you
and your servants and your people who
enter these gates! 3Thus says the LORD:
"Execute judgment and righteousness, and
deliver the plundered out of the hand of
the oppressor. Do no wrong and do no
violence to the stranger, the fatherless, or
the widow, nor shed innocent blood in
this place. 4For if you indeed do this thing,
then shall enter the gates of this house,
riding on horses and in chariots, accompanied by servants and people, kings
who sit on the throne of David. 5But if
you will not hear these words, I swear by
Myself," says the LORD, "that this house
shall become a desolation." ' "

6For thus says the LORD to the house
of the king of Judah:

"You *are* Gilead to Me,
The head of Lebanon;
Yet I surely will make you a
wilderness,
Cities *which* are not inhabited.
7I will prepare destroyers against you,
Everyone with his weapons;
They shall cut down your choice
cedars
And cast *them* into the fire.

8And many nations will pass by this
city; and everyone will say to his neighbor, 'Why has the LORD done so to this
great city?' 9Then they will answer, 'Because they have forsaken the covenant of

21:8 See Deut. 30:15–19.

the LORD their God, and worshiped other gods and served them.' "

[10]Weep not for the dead, nor bemoan
him;
Weep bitterly for him who goes away,
For he shall return no more,
Nor see his native country.

Message to the Sons of Josiah

[11]For thus says the LORD concerning
Shallum[a] the son of Josiah, king of Judah,
who reigned instead of Josiah his father,
who went from this place: "He shall not
return here anymore, [12]but he shall die in
the place where they have led him captive, and shall see this land no more.

[13]"Woe to him who builds his house by
unrighteousness
And his chambers by injustice,
Who uses his neighbor's service
without wages
And gives him nothing for his work,
[14]Who says, 'I will build myself a wide
house with spacious chambers,
And cut out windows for it,
Paneling *it* with cedar
And painting *it* with vermilion.'

[15]"Shall you reign because you enclose
yourself in cedar?
Did not your father eat and drink,
And do justice and righteousness?
Then *it was* well with him.
[16]He judged the cause of the poor and
needy;
Then *it was* well.
Was not this knowing Me?" says the
LORD.
[17]"Yet your eyes and your heart *are* for
nothing but your covetousness,
For shedding innocent blood,
And practicing oppression and
violence."

[18]Therefore thus says the LORD concerning Jehoiakim the son of Josiah, king of Judah:

"They shall not lament for him,
Saying, 'Alas, my brother!' or 'Alas,
my sister!'
They shall not lament for him,
Saying, 'Alas, master!' or 'Alas, his
glory!'
[19]He shall be buried with the burial of
a donkey,
Dragged and cast out beyond the
gates of Jerusalem.

[20]"Go up to Lebanon, and cry out,
And lift up your voice in Bashan;
Cry from Abarim,
For all your lovers are destroyed.
[21]I spoke to you in your prosperity,
But you said, 'I will not hear.'
This *has been* your manner from your
youth,
That you did not obey My voice.
[22]The wind shall eat up all your rulers,
And your lovers shall go into
captivity;
Surely then you will be ashamed and
humiliated
For all your wickedness.
[23]O inhabitant of Lebanon,
Making your nest in the cedars,
How gracious will you be when pangs
come upon you,
Like the pain of a woman in labor?

Message to Coniah

[24]"As I live," says the LORD, "though
Coniah[a] the son of Jehoiakim, king of Judah, were the signet on My right hand,
yet I would pluck you off; [25]and I will give
you into the hand of those who seek your

22:11 [a]Also called *Jehoahaz* 22:24 [a]Also called *Jeconiah* and *Jehoiachin*

22:13,14 The entire world is built on unrighteousness, and is committed to making a fast buck by ripping off the innocent. Jesus spoke of a rich man who said that he would build bigger barns to store his goods for himself, but he wasn't rich toward God. God called him a fool, and said, "This night your soul will be required of you" (Luke 12:20).

life, and into the hand *of those* whose face you fear—the hand of Nebuchadnezzar king of Babylon and the hand of the Chaldeans. 26So I will cast you out, and your mother who bore you, into another country where you were not born; and there you shall die. 27But to the land to which they desire to return, there they shall not return.

28"Is this man Coniah a despised,
broken idol—
A vessel in which *is* no pleasure?
Why are they cast out, he and his
descendants,
And cast into a land which they do
not know?
29O earth, earth, earth,
Hear the word of the LORD!
30Thus says the LORD:
'Write this man down as childless,
A man *who* shall not prosper in his
days;
For none of his descendants shall
prosper,
Sitting on the throne of David,
And ruling anymore in Judah.' "

The Branch of Righteousness

23 "Woe to the shepherds who destroy and scatter the sheep of My pasture!" says the LORD. 2Therefore thus says the LORD God of Israel against the shepherds who feed My people: "You have scattered My flock, driven them away, and not attended to them. Behold, I will attend to you for the evil of your doings," says the LORD. 3"But I will gather the remnant of My flock out of all countries where I have driven them, and bring them back to their folds; and they shall be fruitful and increase. 4I will set up shepherds over them who will feed them; and they shall fear no more, nor be dismayed, nor shall they be lacking," says the LORD.

5"Behold, *the* days are coming," says
the LORD,
"That I will raise to David a Branch of
righteousness;
A King shall reign and prosper,
And execute judgment and
righteousness in the earth.
6In His days Judah will be saved,
And Israel will dwell safely;
Now this *is* His name by which He
will be called:

THE LORD OUR RIGHTEOUSNESS.[a]

7"Therefore, behold, *the* days are coming," says the LORD, "that they shall no longer say, 'As the LORD lives who brought up the children of Israel from the land of Egypt,' 8but, 'As the LORD lives who brought up and led the descendants of the house of Israel from the north country and from all the countries where I had driven them.' And they shall dwell in their own land."

False Prophets and Empty Oracles

9My heart within me is broken
Because of the prophets;
All my bones shake.
I am like a drunken man,
And like a man whom wine has
overcome,
Because of the LORD,
And because of His holy words.
10For the land is full of adulterers;
For because of a curse the land
mourns.
The pleasant places of the wilderness
are dried up.
Their course of life is evil,
And their might *is* not right.

11"For both prophet and priest are
profane;
Yes, in My house I have found their
wickedness," says the LORD.
12"Therefore their way shall be to them

23:6 [a]Hebrew *YHWH Tsidkenu*

23:5,6 This messianic prophecy was fulfilled in Matt. 1:1 and 1 Cor. 1:30. See also Zech. 6:12 comment.

Like slippery *ways;*
In the darkness they shall be driven on
And fall in them;
For I will bring disaster on them,
The year of their punishment," says
the LORD.

13"And I have seen folly in the prophets
of Samaria:
They prophesied by Baal
And caused My people Israel to err.
14Also I have seen a horrible thing in
the prophets of Jerusalem:
They commit adultery and walk in
lies;
They also strengthen the hands of
evildoers,
So that no one turns back from his
wickedness.
All of them are like Sodom to Me,
And her inhabitants like Gomorrah.

15"Therefore thus says the LORD of
hosts concerning the prophets:

'Behold, I will feed them with
wormwood,
And make them drink the water of
gall;
For from the prophets of Jerusalem
Profaneness has gone out into all the
land.' "

16Thus says the LORD of hosts:

"Do not listen to the words of the
prophets who prophesy to you.
They make you worthless;
They speak a vision of their own
heart,
Not from the mouth of the LORD.
17They continually say to those who
despise Me,
'The LORD has said, "You shall have
peace" ';
And *to* everyone who walks according
to the dictates of his own heart,
they say,
'No evil shall come upon you.' "

18For who has stood in the counsel of
the LORD,
And has perceived and heard His
word?
Who has marked His word and heard
it?
19Behold, a whirlwind of the LORD has
gone forth in fury—
A violent whirlwind!
It will fall violently on the head of the
wicked.
20The anger of the LORD will not turn
back
Until He has executed and performed
the thoughts of His heart.
In the latter days you will understand
it perfectly.

21"I have not sent these prophets, yet
they ran.
I have not spoken to them, yet they
prophesied.
22But if they had stood in My counsel,
And had caused My people to hear
My words,
Then they would have turned them
from their evil way
And from the evil of their doings.

23"*Am* I a God near at hand," says the
LORD,
"And not a God afar off?
24Can anyone hide himself in secret
places,
So I shall not see him?" says the LORD;

23:17 This is the message of modern evangelism. A blasphemous world is told that God loves them and that they can have peace with Him by "asking Jesus into their heart." That is not the gospel. God's wrath abides on sinners and the only way they can make peace with a holy God is to repent and trust Jesus Christ as Lord and Savior. See v. 22. They must surrender to His will. See also 2 Cor. 2:17 comment.

23:24 This small verse shares the grandest of truths. God sees all. He knows all. As human beings, we can hardly contain two thoughts at the same time. God is also omnipresent (see Psa. 139:7–10). He is nothing like we imagine Him to be.

QUESTIONS & OBJECTIONS

23:32 *"Statistics show that religious people are just as bad as the rest."*

The modern church has proclaimed a false gospel that has produced millions of false converts (those we commonly call "backsliders"). These people are normally bitter at Christianity. They feel cheated, and so they should. They heard a false gospel and had a false conversion, and the Bible warns that those who experience such will end up in a worse state than before their "conversion" (see 2 Pet. 2:20).

However, even more tragic than the false converts who fall away from the faith is the category of false converts who stay within the Church. They profess the Christian faith, but as statistics confirm, their hypocritical lifestyles don't match what they profess. The Bible calls them "goats" among the "sheep." In the Middle East it's difficult to discern goats from sheep as they flock together. However, a good shepherd can tell the difference. The day will come when the Good Shepherd will separate the sheep from the goats. The sheep (true converts) will go into everlasting life, and the goats (false converts) will go into everlasting damnation (se Matt. 25:32–46).

Here is the difference between the true gospel and the false gospel. The false message says that you should come to Christ "because something is missing in your life—you have a God-shaped hole in your heart. God has a wonderful plan for your life." But there is no biblical precedent for a message of life-improvement upon conversion. None. In fact, the Bible promises us trials, tribulations, temptations, and persecution.

The reason any of us should come to Christ is because we are deceitfully wicked sinners, and we desperately need a Savior. Without the mercy of God in Christ, we will come under God's just wrath, and end up in hell. We should come to Christ for no other reason. (See 2 Cor. 2:17 comment.)

The false message is very popular for obvious reasons, and that is why many who preach the false gospel have such large followings. However, some people are beginning to notice the discrepancy and asking why. It is my earnest prayer that they reform the message they are preaching.

"Do I not fill heaven and earth?" says
the LORD.

25"I have heard what the prophets
have said who prophesy lies in My name,
saying, 'I have dreamed, I have dreamed!'
26How long will *this* be in the heart of the
prophets who prophesy lies? Indeed *they*
are prophets of the deceit of their own
heart, 27who try to make My people forget My name by their dreams which everyone tells his neighbor, as their fathers forgot My name for Baal.

28"The prophet who has a dream, let
him tell a dream;
And he who has My word, let him
speak My word faithfully.
What *is* the chaff to the wheat?" says
the LORD.

29"*Is* not My word like a fire?" says the
LORD,
"And like a hammer *that* breaks the
rock in pieces?

30"Therefore behold, I *am* against the
prophets," says the LORD, "who steal My
words every one from his neighbor. 31Be-
hold, I *am* against the prophets," says the
LORD, "who use their tongues and say, 'He
says.' 32Behold, I *am* against those who
prophesy false dreams," says the LORD,
"and tell them, and cause My people to
err by their lies and by their recklessness.
Yet I did not send them or command
them; therefore they shall not profit this
people at all," says the LORD.
33"So when these people or the
prophet or the priest ask you, saying,

23:28 All that is asked of us is that we be true and faithful witnesses.

23:29 Use the Word of God as much as you can in your preaching and witnessing. It is a powerful two-edged sword that cuts to the bone of sinners (see Heb. 4:12). Use the Law to break the hard heart, then share the glorious gospel to heal the broken heart.

'What is the oracle of the LORD?' you shall
then say to them, 'What oracle?'[a] I will
even forsake you," says the LORD. 34"And
as for the prophet and the priest and the
people who say, 'The oracle of the LORD!'
I will even punish that man and his
house. 35Thus every one of you shall say
to his neighbor, and every one to his
brother, 'What has the LORD answered?'
and, 'What has the LORD spoken?' 36And
the oracle of the LORD you shall mention
no more. For every man's word will be
his oracle, for you have perverted the
words of the living God, the LORD of
hosts, our God. 37Thus you shall say to the
prophet, 'What has the LORD answered
you?' and, 'What has the LORD spoken?'
38But since you say, 'The oracle of the
LORD!' therefore thus says the LORD: 'Because you say this word, "The oracle of
the LORD!" and I have sent to you, saying,
"Do not say, 'The oracle of the LORD!' "
39therefore behold, I, even I, will utterly
forget you and forsake you, and the city
that I gave you and your fathers, and *will
cast you* out of My presence. 40And I will
bring an everlasting reproach upon you,
and a perpetual shame, which shall not
be forgotten.' "

The Sign of Two Baskets of Figs

24 The LORD showed me, and there
were two baskets of figs set before
the temple of the LORD, after Nebuchadnezzar king of Babylon had carried away
captive Jeconiah the son of Jehoiakim,
king of Judah, and the princes of Judah
with the craftsmen and smiths, from Jerusalem, and had brought them to Babylon.
2One basket *had* very good figs, like the
figs *that are* first ripe; and the other basket *had* very bad figs which could not be
eaten, they were so bad. 3Then the LORD
said to me, "What do you see, Jeremiah?"
And I said, "Figs, the good figs, very
good; and the bad, very bad, which cannot be eaten, they are so bad."
4Again the word of the LORD came to
me, saying, 5"Thus says the LORD, the
God of Israel: 'Like these good figs, so
will I acknowledge those who are carried
away captive from Judah, whom I have
sent out of this place for *their own* good,
into the land of the Chaldeans. 6For I will
set My eyes on them for good, and I will
bring them back to this land; I will build
them and not pull *them* down, and I will
plant them and not pluck *them* up. 7Then
I will give them a heart to know Me, that
I *am* the LORD; and they shall be My people, and I will be their God, for they shall
return to Me with their whole heart.

. . . . . .

*For the Holy Spirit's role in salvation,
see John 16:8–11 comment.*

. . . . . .

8'And as the bad figs which cannot be
eaten, they are so bad'—surely thus says
the LORD—'so will I give up Zedekiah the
king of Judah, his princes, the residue of
Jerusalem who remain in this land, and
those who dwell in the land of Egypt. 9I
will deliver them to trouble into all the
kingdoms of the earth, for *their* harm, *to
be* a reproach and a byword, a taunt and
a curse, in all places where I shall drive
them. 10And I will send the sword, the
famine, and the pestilence among them,
till they are consumed from the land that
I gave to them and their fathers.' "

Seventy Years of Desolation

25 The word that came to Jeremiah
concerning all the people of Judah, in the fourth year of Jehoiakim the

23:33 [a]Septuagint, Targum, and Vulgate read '*You are the burden.*'

24:7 This is what happens at conversion. We, who didn't know God, now know Him. He opens our blind eyes to His majesty. Nothing is the same as it was before. Nothing. See 2 Cor. 5:17 for what happens to a person who surrenders to Jesus Christ.

son of Josiah, king of Judah (which *was*
the first year of Nebuchadnezzar king of
Babylon), 2which Jeremiah the prophet
spoke to all the people of Judah and to all
the inhabitants of Jerusalem, saying:
3"From the thirteenth year of Josiah the
son of Amon, king of Judah, even to this
day, this *is* the twenty-third year in which
the word of the LORD has come to me;
and I have spoken to you, rising early
and speaking, but you have not listened.
4And the LORD has sent to you all His servants the prophets, rising early and sending *them,* but you have not listened nor
inclined your ear to hear. 5They said, 'Repent now everyone of his evil way and
his evil doings, and dwell in the land that
the LORD has given to you and your fathers forever and ever. 6Do not go after
other gods to serve them and worship
them, and do not provoke Me to anger
with the works of your hands; and I will
not harm you.' 7Yet you have not listened
to Me," says the LORD, "that you might
provoke Me to anger with the works of
your hands to your own hurt.

8"Therefore thus says the LORD of
hosts: 'Because you have not heard My
words, 9behold, I will send and take all
the families of the north,' says the LORD,
'and Nebuchadnezzar the king of Babylon, My servant, and will bring them
against this land, against its inhabitants,
and against these nations all around, and
will utterly destroy them, and make them
an astonishment, a hissing, and perpetual
desolations. 10Moreover I will take from
them the voice of mirth and the voice of
gladness, the voice of the bridegroom and
the voice of the bride, the sound of the
millstones and the light of the lamp. 11And
this whole land shall be a desolation *and*
an astonishment, and these nations shall
serve the king of Babylon seventy years.

12'Then it will come to pass, when seventy years are completed, *that* I will punish the king of Babylon and that nation,
the land of the Chaldeans, for their iniquity,' says the LORD; 'and I will make it a
perpetual desolation. 13So I will bring on
that land all My words which I have pronounced against it, all that is written in
this book, which Jeremiah has prophesied
concerning all the nations. 14(For many
nations and great kings shall be served by
them also; and I will repay them according to their deeds and according to the
works of their own hands.)' "

Judgment on the Nations

15For thus says the LORD God of Israel
to me: "Take this wine cup of fury from
My hand, and cause all the nations, to
whom I send you, to drink it. 16And they
will drink and stagger and go mad because of the sword that I will send among
them."

17Then I took the cup from the LORD's
hand, and made all the nations drink, to
whom the LORD had sent me: 18Jerusalem
and the cities of Judah, its kings and its
princes, to make them a desolation, an
astonishment, a hissing, and a curse, as *it
is* this day; 19Pharaoh king of Egypt, his
servants, his princes, and all his people;
20all the mixed multitude, all the kings of
the land of Uz, all the kings of the land
of the Philistines (namely, Ashkelon,
Gaza, Ekron, and the remnant of Ashdod); 21Edom, Moab, and the people of
Ammon; 22all the kings of Tyre, all the
kings of Sidon, and the kings of the

25:3 When it comes to the task of evangelism, leave the results up to God. We plant, someone else waters, but it is God who makes the seed grow (see 1 Cor. 3:6). Think of Noah, Jeremiah, and many others who faithfully labored for many years. How many of us would be faithful enough to preach to the lost for *twenty-three years* if they weren't listening? Rather than aiming for "decisions for Jesus," the key is to see the planting of the gospel seed ("sowing in tears") as your success. Keep that attitude and you will always retain your joy when you seek the lost: "Those who sow in tears shall reap in joy. He who continually goes forth weeping, bearing seed for sowing, shall doubtless come again with rejoicing, bringing his sheaves with him" (Psa. 126:5,6). See also Ezek. 2:5,7; Gal. 6:9.

coastlands which *are* across the sea;
23 Dedan, Tema, Buz, and all *who are* in
the farthest corners; 24 all the kings of
Arabia and all the kings of the mixed
multitude who dwell in the desert; 25 all
the kings of Zimri, all the kings of Elam,
and all the kings of the Medes; 26 all the
kings of the north, far and near, one with
another; and all the kingdoms of the
world which *are* on the face of the earth.
Also the king of Sheshach[a] shall drink
after them.

27 "Therefore you shall say to them,
'Thus says the LORD of hosts, the God of
Israel: "Drink, be drunk, and vomit! Fall
and rise no more, because of the sword
which I will send among you." ' 28 And it
shall be, if they refuse to take the cup
from your hand to drink, then you shall
say to them, 'Thus says the LORD of hosts:
"You shall certainly drink! 29 For behold, I
begin to bring calamity on the city which
is called by My name, and should you be
utterly unpunished? You shall not be unpunished, for I will call for a sword on all
the inhabitants of the earth," says the
LORD of hosts.'

30 "Therefore prophesy against them all
these words, and say to them:

'The LORD will roar from on high,
And utter His voice from His holy
habitation;
He will roar mightily against His fold.
He will give a shout, as those who
tread *the grapes,*
Against all the inhabitants of the
earth.
31 A noise will come to the ends of the
earth—
For the LORD has a controversy with
the nations;
He will plead His case with all flesh.
He will give those *who are* wicked to
the sword,' says the LORD."

32 Thus says the LORD of hosts:

"Behold, disaster shall go forth
From nation to nation,
And a great whirlwind shall be raised
up
From the farthest parts of the earth.

33 "And at that day the slain of the LORD
shall be from *one* end of the earth even to
the *other* end of the earth. They shall not
be lamented, or gathered, or buried; they
shall become refuse on the ground.

> Jesus told me to go. He never said I would come back. Isn't this the life of a Christian?
>
> **CELSO (A COLOMBIAN EVANGELIST)**

34 "Wail, shepherds, and cry!
Roll about *in the ashes,*
You leaders of the flock!
For the days of your slaughter and
your dispersions are fulfilled;
You shall fall like a precious vessel.
35 And the shepherds will have no way
to flee,
Nor the leaders of the flock to escape.
36 A voice of the cry of the shepherds,
And a wailing of the leaders to the
flock *will be heard.*
For the LORD has plundered their
pasture,
37 And the peaceful dwellings are cut
down
Because of the fierce anger of the LORD.
38 He has left His lair like the lion;
For their land is desolate

25:26 [a]A code word for Babylon (compare 51:41)

25:31 We must never forget that the final Day of Judgment will come to all mankind. It will be the climax of the ages, when God will ensure that justice is done. What a wonderful day for the cause of righteousness, and what a fearful thing for guilty humanity.

25:36 When those who profess to be shepherds of the flock of God fail to be faithful in their gospel proclamation, they fill the Church with false converts (goats among the sheep). See also Isa. 56:11.

Because of the fierceness of the
Oppressor,
And because of His fierce anger."

Jeremiah Saved from Death

26 In the beginning of the reign of
Jehoiakim the son of Josiah, king
of Judah, this word came from the LORD,
saying, 2"Thus says the LORD: 'Stand in
the court of the LORD's house, and speak
to all the cities of Judah, which come to
worship *in* the LORD's house, all the words
that I command you to speak to them.
Do not diminish a word. 3Perhaps everyone will listen and turn from his evil way,
that I may relent concerning the calamity
which I purpose to bring on them because of the evil of their doings.' 4And you
shall say to them, 'Thus says the LORD: "If
you will not listen to Me, to walk in My
law which I have set before you, 5to heed
the words of My servants the prophets
whom I sent to you, both rising up early
and sending *them* (but you have not
heeded), 6then I will make this house like
Shiloh, and will make this city a curse to
all the nations of the earth." ' "

7So the priests and the prophets and
all the people heard Jeremiah speaking
these words in the house of the LORD.
8Now it happened, when Jeremiah had
made an end of speaking all that the LORD
had commanded *him* to speak to all the
people, that the priests and the prophets
and all the people seized him, saying,
"You will surely die! 9Why have you
prophesied in the name of the LORD, saying, 'This house shall be like Shiloh, and
this city shall be desolate, without an inhabitant'?" And all the people were gathered against Jeremiah in the house of the
LORD.

10When the princes of Judah heard
these things, they came up from the
king's house to the house of the LORD and
sat down in the entry of the New Gate of
the LORD's *house*. 11And the priests and
the prophets spoke to the princes and all
the people, saying, "This man deserves to
die! For he has prophesied against this
city, as you have heard with your ears."

12Then Jeremiah spoke to all the
princes and all the people, saying: "The
LORD sent me to prophesy against this
house and against this city with all the
words that you have heard. 13Now therefore, amend your ways and your doings,
and obey the voice of the LORD your God;
then the LORD will relent concerning the
doom that He has pronounced against

The Function of the Law

26:3–6 "No unrepentant sinner will ever get into heaven; unless they forsake their sin they cannot enter there. The Law of God is very plain on this point: 'Except a man repent.' That's the language of Scripture. And when this is so plainly set down, why is it that men fold their arms and say, 'God will take me into heaven anyway.'" *D. L. Moody*

To bring a sinner to a point of genuine repentance takes the knowledge of sin, which comes only by the moral Law. See Rom. 3:19,20; 7:7,13 for the function of God's Law. For the necessity of repentance, see John 3:16 comment.

26:18 [a]Literally *house* [b]Compare Micah 3:12

26:2 In our presentation of the gospel, many of us are guilty of diminishing the significance of biblical words such as "repentance," "hell," "Judgment Day," and "sin." Perhaps we downplay these words because we fear persecution and are trying to make ourselves more acceptable to the unsaved. For how to present the gospel biblically, see 2 Sam. 12:1–14 comment.

"It is a poor sermon that gives no offense; that neither makes the hearer displeased with himself nor with the preacher." *George Whitefield*

26:8 One result of Jeremiah's obedience to his commission (v. 2) was a death threat. We should never be surprised if the world hates us, because we speak the words of God and we belong to Jesus Christ. See also Acts 7:59 and Rev. 12:11 comments, and page 1198.

26:13 What a great and wonderful mystery—that God will deflect His wrath toward the most heinous of sinners, because of the cross. He forgives us for Christ's sake. See Rom. 5:8,9.

you. 14As for me, here I am, in your hand; do with me as seems good and proper to you. 15But know for certain that if you put me to death, you will surely bring innocent blood on yourselves, on this city, and on its inhabitants; for truly the LORD has sent me to you to speak all these words in your hearing."

16So the princes and all the people said to the priests and the prophets, "This man does not deserve to die. For he has spoken to us in the name of the LORD our God."

17Then certain of the elders of the land rose up and spoke to all the assembly of the people, saying: 18"Micah of Moresheth prophesied in the days of Hezekiah king of Judah, and spoke to all the people of Judah, saying, 'Thus says the LORD of hosts:

"Zion shall be plowed *like* a field,
Jerusalem shall become heaps of
ruins,
And the mountain of the temple[a]
Like the bare hills of the forest." '[b]

19Did Hezekiah king of Judah and all Judah ever put him to death? Did he not fear the LORD and seek the LORD's favor? And the LORD relented concerning the doom which He had pronounced against them. But we are doing great evil against ourselves."

20Now there was also a man who prophesied in the name of the LORD, Urijah the son of Shemaiah of Kirjath Jearim, who prophesied against this city and against this land according to all the words of Jeremiah. 21And when Jehoiakim the king, with all his mighty men and all the princes, heard his words, the king sought to put him to death; but when Urijah heard *it,* he was afraid and fled, and went to Egypt. 22Then Jehoiakim the king sent men to Egypt: Elnathan the son of Achbor, and *other* men *who went* with him to Egypt. 23And they brought Urijah from Egypt and brought him to Jehoiakim the king, who killed him with the sword and cast his dead body into the graves of the common people.

24Nevertheless the hand of Ahikam the son of Shaphan was with Jeremiah, so that they should not give him into the hand of the people to put him to death.

Symbol of the Bonds and Yokes

27 In the beginning of the reign of Jehoiakim[a] the son of Josiah, king of Judah, this word came to Jeremiah from the LORD, saying,[b] 2"Thus says the LORD to me: 'Make for yourselves bonds and yokes, and put them on your neck, 3and send them to the king of Edom, the king of Moab, the king of the Ammonites, the king of Tyre, and the king of Sidon, by the hand of the messengers who come to Jerusalem to Zedekiah king of Judah. 4And command them to say to their masters, "Thus says the LORD of hosts, the God of Israel—thus you shall say to your masters: 5'I have made the earth, the man and the beast that *are* on the ground, by My great power and by My outstretched arm, and have given it to whom it seemed proper to Me. 6And now I have given all these lands into the hand of Nebuchadnezzar the king of Babylon, My servant; and the beasts of the field I have also given him to serve him. 7So all nations shall serve him and his son and his son's son, until the time of his land comes; and then many nations and great kings shall make him serve them. 8And it shall be, *that* the nation and kingdom which will not serve Nebuchadnezzar the king of Babylon, and which will not put its neck under the yoke of the king of Babylon, that nation I will punish,' says the LORD, 'with the sword, the famine, and the pestilence, until I have consumed them by his hand. 9Therefore do not listen to your prophets, your diviners, your dreamers, your soothsayers, or your sorcerers, who speak to you, saying, "You shall not serve the king of Babylon." 10For they

27:1 [a]Following Masoretic Text, Targum, and Vulgate; some Hebrew manuscripts, Arabic, and Syriac read *Zedekiah* (compare 27:3, 12; 28:1). [b]Septuagint omits verse 1.

27:5 *Transitional Forms*

If evolution were true, and humans and chimps did have a common ancestor, we would expect to find something that is half-monkey/half-man. These intermediate stages where one species supposedly evolves into another species are called "transitional forms."

Because evolution is said to have happened in the past, we have to look to paleontology, the science of the study of fossils, to find evidence on the history of life. Well-known French paleontologist Pierre-Paul Grassé said, "Naturalists must remember that the process of evolution is revealed only through fossil forms . . . Only paleontology can provide them with the evidence of evolution and reveal its course or mechanisms."

If life gradually evolved from one species to another, then the fossil record should reveal *millions* of transitional forms. Darwin understood that evolutionary theory was dependent on these "missing links." He wrote in *Origin of Species:*

> Why, if species have descended from other species by fine gradations, do we not everywhere see innumerable transitional forms? Why is not all nature in confusion, instead of the species being, as we see them, well defined? . . . As by this theory innumerable transitional forms must have existed, why do we not find them embedded in countless numbers in the crust of the earth?

Darwin acknowledged that the absence of intermediates put his theory in doubt, but he attributed their lack to the scarcity of fossils at that time. However, nearly 150 years later, the situation hasn't changed. After scientists have searched diligently *for a century and a half* for evidence, we now have over 100 million fossils catalogued in the world's museums, with 250,000 different species. Surely this should be enough to give us an accurate picture of our past. Remember, paleontology holds the key to whether this theory is true. So do we see the gradual progression from simple life forms to more complex? Did we find the millions of transitional forms that would be expected if evolution were true?

Excited evolutionists believed that they found one back in 1999. *Archaeoraptor*, supposedly a transitional form between dinosaurs and birds, was quickly exposed as a fraud. (For details, see Acts 14:15 comment.) Storrs L. Olson, Curator of Birds at the National Museum of Natural History at the Smithsonian Institution, stated that the feathered dinosaur that was pictured is "simply imaginary and has no place outside of science fiction," and added, "The idea of feathered dinosaurs . . . is now fast becoming one of the grander scientific hoaxes of our age."

Aside from "feathered dinosaurs," many other proposed "missing links" have been debunked. For example, *Pakicetus*, a supposed transition between land mammals and whales, is one that fails to live up to its claims. (For details, see Psa. 148:7 comment.) As for man's evolutionary history, in a PBS documentary, Richard Leakey, the world's foremost paleoanthropologist, admitted:

> If pressed about man's ancestry, I would have to unequivocally say that all we have is a huge question mark. To date, there has been nothing found to truthfully purport as a transitional species to man, including Lucy . . . If further pressed, I would have to state that there is more evidence to suggest an *abrupt arrival of man rather than a gradual process of evolving*.

Even the classic example of horse evolution is fictionalized. Evolutionist Boyce Rensberger addressed a symposium attended by 150 scientists at the Field Museum of Natural History in Chicago, which considered problems facing the theory of evolution. He describes what the fossil evidence reveals for horses:

> The popularly told example of horse evolution, suggesting a gradual sequence of changes from four-toed, fox-sized creatures, living nearly 50 million years ago, to today's much larger one-toed horse, has long been known to be wrong. Instead of gradual change, fossils of each intermediate species *appear fully distinct, persist unchanged*, and then become extinct. Transitional forms are unknown.

This is the case not just for horses, but throughout the entire animal kingdom. Rather than the millions of transitional forms evolutionists would expect to find, all we have at best are a handful of disputable examples. Harvard paleontologist Stephen Jay Gould writes,

> The extreme rarity of transitional forms in the fossil record persists as the trade secret of paleontology. The evolutionary trees that adorn our textbooks have data only at the tips and nodes of their branches; the rest is inference, however reasonable, not the evidence of fossils . . . All paleontologists know that the fossil record contains precious little in the way of intermediate forms; transitions between major groups are characteristically abrupt.

See also 1 Cor. 15:39 comment.

(Adapted from *How to Know God Exists.*)

prophesy a lie to you, to remove you far from your land; and I will drive you out, and you will perish. 11But the nations that bring their necks under the yoke of the king of Babylon and serve him, I will let them remain in their own land,' says the LORD, 'and they shall till it and dwell in it.' " ' "

12I also spoke to Zedekiah king of Judah according to all these words, saying, "Bring your necks under the yoke of the king of Babylon, and serve him and his people, and live! 13Why will you die, you and your people, by the sword, by the famine, and by the pestilence, as the LORD has spoken against the nation that will not serve the king of Babylon? 14Therefore do not listen to the words of the prophets who speak to you, saying, 'You shall not serve the king of Babylon,' for they prophesy a lie to you; 15for I have not sent them," says the LORD, "yet they prophesy a lie in My name, that I may drive you out, and that you may perish, you and the prophets who prophesy to you."

> The devil doesn't mind how many sermons we preach or prepare if it will keep us from preparing ourselves.
>
> **VANCE HAVNER**

16Also I spoke to the priests and to all this people, saying, "Thus says the LORD: 'Do not listen to the words of your prophets who prophesy to you, saying, "Behold, the vessels of the LORD's house will now shortly be brought back from Babylon"; for they prophesy a lie to you. 17Do not listen to them; serve the king of Babylon, and live! Why should this city be laid waste? 18But if they *are* prophets, and if the word of the LORD is with them, let them now make intercession to the LORD of hosts, that the vessels which are left in the house of the LORD, *in* the house of the king of Judah, and at Jerusalem, do not go to Babylon.'

19"For thus says the LORD of hosts concerning the pillars, concerning the Sea, concerning the carts, and concerning the remainder of the vessels that remain in this city, 20which Nebuchadnezzar king of Babylon did not take, when he carried away captive Jeconiah the son of Jehoiakim, king of Judah, from Jerusalem to Babylon, and all the nobles of Judah and Jerusalem— 21yes, thus says the LORD of hosts, the God of Israel, concerning the vessels that remain in the house of the LORD, and in the house of the king of Judah and of Jerusalem: 22'They shall be carried to Babylon, and there they shall be until the day that I visit them,' says the LORD. 'Then I will bring them up and restore them to this place.' "

Hananiah's Falsehood and Doom

28 And it happened in the same year, at the beginning of the reign of Zedekiah king of Judah, in the fourth year *and* in the fifth month, *that* Hananiah the son of Azur the prophet, who *was* from Gibeon, spoke to me in the house of the LORD in the presence of the priests and of all the people, saying, 2"Thus speaks the LORD of hosts, the God of Israel, saying: 'I have broken the yoke of the king of Babylon. 3Within two full years I will bring back to this place all the vessels of the LORD's house, that Nebuchadnezzar king of Babylon took away from this place and carried to Babylon. 4And I will bring back to this place Jeconiah the son of Jehoiakim, king of Judah, with all the captives of Judah who went to Babylon,' says the LORD, 'for I will break the yoke of the king of Babylon.' "

5Then the prophet Jeremiah spoke to the prophet Hananiah in the presence of the priests and in the presence of all the people who stood in the house of the LORD, 6and the prophet Jeremiah said, "Amen! The LORD do so; the LORD perform your words which you have prophesied, to bring back the vessels of the LORD's house and all who were carried away captive, from Babylon to this place.

7Nevertheless hear now this word that I speak in your hearing and in the hearing of all the people: 8The prophets who have been before me and before you of old prophesied against many countries and great kingdoms—of war and disaster and pestilence. 9As for the prophet who prophesies of peace, when the word of the prophet comes to pass, the prophet will be known *as* one whom the LORD has truly sent."

10Then Hananiah the prophet took the yoke off the prophet Jeremiah's neck and broke it. 11And Hananiah spoke in the presence of all the people, saying, "Thus says the LORD: 'Even so I will break the yoke of Nebuchadnezzar king of Babylon from the neck of all nations within the space of two full years.' " And the prophet Jeremiah went his way.

12Now the word of the LORD came to Jeremiah, after Hananiah the prophet had broken the yoke from the neck of the prophet Jeremiah, saying, 13"Go and tell Hananiah, saying, 'Thus says the LORD: "You have broken the yokes of wood, but you have made in their place yokes of iron." 14For thus says the LORD of hosts, the God of Israel: "I have put a yoke of iron on the neck of all these nations, that they may serve Nebuchadnezzar king of Babylon; and they shall serve him. I have given him the beasts of the field also." ' "

15Then the prophet Jeremiah said to Hananiah the prophet, "Hear now, Hananiah, the LORD has not sent you, but you make this people trust in a lie. 16Therefore thus says the LORD: 'Behold, I will cast you from the face of the earth. This year you shall die, because you have taught rebellion against the LORD.' "

17So Hananiah the prophet died the same year in the seventh month.

Jeremiah's Letter to the Captives

29 Now these *are* the words of the letter that Jeremiah the prophet sent from Jerusalem to the remainder of the elders who were carried away captive—to the priests, the prophets, and all the people whom Nebuchadnezzar had carried away captive from Jerusalem to Babylon. 2(This happened after Jeconiah the king, the queen mother, the eunuchs, the princes of Judah and Jerusalem, the craftsmen, and the smiths had departed from Jerusalem.) 3*The letter was sent* by the hand of Elasah the son of Shaphan, and Gemariah the son of Hilkiah, whom Zedekiah king of Judah sent to Babylon, to Nebuchadnezzar king of Babylon, saying,

4Thus says the LORD of hosts, the
God of Israel, to all who were
carried away captive, whom I have
caused to be carried away from
Jerusalem to Babylon:

5Build houses and dwell *in them;*
plant gardens and eat their fruit.
6Take wives and beget sons and
daughters; and take wives for your
sons and give your daughters to
husbands, so that they may bear
sons and daughters—that you may
be increased there, and not
diminished. 7And seek the peace of
the city where I have caused you to
be carried away captive, and pray to
the LORD for it; for in its peace you
will have peace. 8For thus says the
LORD of hosts, the God of Israel: Do
not let your prophets and your
diviners who are in your midst
deceive you, nor listen to your
dreams which you cause to be
dreamed. 9For they prophesy falsely

28:10–17 Hananiah was a false prophet, whose words sounded spiritual, but who had not been sent by God. He therefore caused the people to trust in a lie. The only truly reliable "Thus says the Lord" is what we have written in Holy Scripture. Too many have discredited God's name and brought reproach to the cause of the gospel by saying "God told me," when it was merely their own mind, the voice of their conscience, or the voice of their spiritually proud heart.

to you in My name; I have not sent
them, says the LORD.

10For thus says the LORD: After
seventy years are completed at
Babylon, I will visit you and perform
My good word toward you, and
cause you to return to this place.
11For I know the thoughts that I
think toward you, says the LORD,
thoughts of peace and not of evil, to
give you a future and a hope.
12Then you will call upon Me and
go and pray to Me, and I will listen
to you. 13And you will seek Me and
find *Me,* when you search for Me
with all your heart. 14I will be
found by you, says the LORD, and I
will bring you back from your
captivity; I will gather you from all
the nations and from all the places
where I have driven you, says the
LORD, and I will bring you to the
place from which I cause you to be
carried away captive.

15Because you have said, "The LORD
has raised up prophets for us in
Babylon"— 16therefore thus says the
LORD concerning the king who sits
on the throne of David, concerning
all the people who dwell in this city,
and concerning your brethren who
have not gone out with you into
captivity— 17thus says the LORD of
hosts: Behold, I will send on them
the sword, the famine, and the
pestilence, and will make them like
rotten figs that cannot be eaten,
they are so bad. 18And I will pursue
them with the sword, with famine,
and with pestilence; and I will
deliver them to trouble among all
the kingdoms of the earth—to be a
curse, an astonishment, a hissing,
and a reproach among all the
nations where I have driven them,
19because they have not heeded My
words, says the LORD, which I sent
to them by My servants the prophets,
rising up early and sending *them;*
neither would you heed, says the
LORD. 20Therefore hear the word of
the LORD, all you of the captivity,
whom I have sent from Jerusalem
to Babylon.

21Thus says the LORD of hosts, the
God of Israel, concerning Ahab the
son of Kolaiah, and Zedekiah the
son of Maaseiah, who prophesy a
lie to you in My name: Behold, I
will deliver them into the hand of
Nebuchadnezzar king of Babylon,
and he shall slay them before your
eyes. 22And because of them a curse
shall be taken up by all the captivity
of Judah who *are* in Babylon, saying,
"The LORD make you like Zedekiah
and Ahab, whom the king of
Babylon roasted in the fire";
23because they have done disgraceful things in Israel, have committed
adultery with their neighbors'
wives, and have spoken lying words
in My name, which I have not
commanded them. Indeed I know,
and *am* a witness, says the LORD.

29:8,9 Search the Scriptures to make sure that everything you hear lines up with the Word of God. If it's not biblical, reject it as you would a drop of deadly poison.

29:13 This conditional invitation differs considerably from the arrogant view often expressed by the unsaved sinner: "I will believe when God shows Himself to me!" (For a response to this argument, see John 1:18 comment.) All who seek God with a *sincere heart* will find Him. See 1 Chron. 28:9 comment.

"I have learned that when anyone becomes in earnest about his soul's salvation and he begins to seek God, it does not take long for an anxious sinner to meet an anxious Savior. 'Ye shall seek me, and find me, when ye shall search for me with all your heart' (Jer. 29:13). Those who seek for Him with all their hearts, find Christ." *D. L. Moody*

SPRINGBOARDS FOR PREACHING AND WITNESSING

Why People Have Affairs

29:23 In 2008, a book was published called *When Good People Have Affairs*, giving seventeen motives for people committing adultery. One motive cited is the "accidental affair." This is when a woman has an innocent drink with her boss, and then goes back to his apartment to discuss business and ends up in bed with him. I am sure her husband will completely understand the next day when she tells him that she accidentally committed adultery.

No doubt the book will become a bestseller because human beings love to be told that they are good people. This deals with the "sin" problem. Good people don't go to hell. The trouble is that the word "good" is relative. Your definition may be different from mine, and Hitler's definition of "good" is no doubt different from ours.

The dilemma regarding how to define "good" is resolved by looking at how God defines it. In His Book, "good" means moral perfection, in thought, word, and deed. In that case, none of us is good. Therefore, the book's title is an oxymoron, because good people don't commit adultery. Sinners do, and sinners who commit adultery will receive terrible justice from a holy God for transgression of His Law.

24You shall also speak to Shemaiah
the Nehelamite, saying, 25Thus
speaks the LORD of hosts, the God
of Israel, saying: You have sent
letters in your name to all the
people who *are* at Jerusalem, to
Zephaniah the son of Maaseiah the
priest, and to all the priests, saying,
26"The LORD has made you priest
instead of Jehoiada the priest, so
that there should be officers *in* the
house of the LORD over every man
who is demented and considers
himself a prophet, that you should
put him in prison and in the stocks.
27Now therefore, why have you not
rebuked Jeremiah of Anathoth who
makes himself a prophet to you?
28For he has sent to us *in* Babylon,
saying, 'This *captivity is* long; build
houses and dwell *in them,* and plant
gardens and eat their fruit.' "

29Now Zephaniah the priest read this
letter in the hearing of Jeremiah the
prophet. 30Then the word of the
LORD came to Jeremiah, saying:
31Send to all those in captivity,
saying, Thus says the LORD concerning Shemaiah the Nehelamite:
Because Shemaiah has prophesied
to you, and I have not sent him,
and he has caused you to trust in a
lie— 32therefore thus says the LORD:
Behold, I will punish Shemaiah the
Nehelamite and his family: he shall
not have anyone to dwell among
this people, nor shall he see the
good that I will do for My people,
says the LORD, because he has
taught rebellion against the LORD.

Restoration of Israel and Judah

30 The word that came to Jeremiah
from the LORD, saying, 2"Thus
speaks the LORD God of Israel, saying:
'Write in a book for yourself all the words
that I have spoken to you. 3For behold,
the days are coming,' says the LORD, 'that
I will bring back from captivity My people Israel and Judah,' says the LORD. 'And
I will cause them to return to the land
that I gave to their fathers, and they shall
possess it.' "

30:3 God warned Israel many times that He would scatter them throughout the nations for their continual sin. That dispersion took place in 70 A.D., leaving the Jewish people without a homeland for approximately 2,000 years (see Hos. 3:4,5). However, God promised to gather them again from among the countries where they were scattered (see Ezek. 20:34). On May 14, 1948, Israel was declared a nation by the United Nations—a nation was born in a day (see Isa. 66:8). See also Ezek. 36:11,24; Isa. 43:5,6; and Ezek. 11:17 comment.

[4]Now these *are* the words that the LORD spoke concerning Israel and Judah.
[5]"For thus says the LORD:

'We have heard a voice of trembling,
Of fear, and not of peace.
[6]Ask now, and see,
Whether a man is ever in labor with child?
So why do I see every man *with* his hands on his loins
Like a woman in labor,
And all faces turned pale?
[7]Alas! For that day *is* great,
So that none *is* like it;
And it *is* the time of Jacob's trouble,
But he shall be saved out of it.

'For it shall come to pass in that day,'
Says the LORD of hosts,
'*That* I will break his yoke from your neck,
And will burst your bonds;
Foreigners shall no more enslave them.
[9]But they shall serve the LORD their God,
And David their king,
Whom I will raise up for them.

[10]'Therefore do not fear, O My servant Jacob,' says the LORD,
'Nor be dismayed, O Israel;
For behold, I will save you from afar,
And your seed from the land of their captivity.
Jacob shall return, have rest and be quiet,
And no one shall make *him* afraid.
[11]For I *am* with you,' says the LORD, 'to save you;
Though I make a full end of all nations where I have scattered you,
Yet I will not make a complete end of you.
But I will correct you in justice,
And will not let you go altogether unpunished.'

[12]"For thus says the LORD:

'Your affliction *is* incurable,
Your wound *is* severe.
[13]*There is* no one to plead your cause,
That you may be bound up;
You have no healing medicines.
[14]All your lovers have forgotten you;
They do not seek you;
For I have wounded you with the wound of an enemy,
With the chastisement of a cruel one,
For the multitude of your iniquities,
Because your sins have increased.
[15]Why do you cry about your affliction?
Your sorrow *is* incurable.
Because of the multitude of your iniquities,
Because your sins have increased,
I have done these things to you.

[16]'Therefore all those who devour you shall be devoured;
And all your adversaries, every one of them, shall go into captivity;
Those who plunder you shall become plunder,
And all who prey upon you I will make a prey.
[17]For I will restore health to you
And heal you of your wounds,' says the LORD,
'Because they called you an outcast

30:15 How frightening it would be if God treated this wicked world according to its sins! He is presently storing up His wrath, because He is rich in mercy and is not willing that any perish (see Rom. 2:5; John 3:36; 2 Pet. 3:9). But the day will come when He will be revealed in flaming fire to take vengeance (see 2 Thess. 1:7,8). Knowing that it is a fearful thing to fall into the hands of the living God, we must persuade men to run to the shelter of the cross (see 2 Cor. 5:11).

"If sinners will be damned, at least let them leap to hell over our bodies. And if they perish, let them perish with our arms about their knees, imploring them to stay. If hell must be filled, at least let it be filled in the teeth of our exertions, and let not one go there unwarned and unprayed for." *Charles Spurgeon*

saying:
"This *is* Zion;
No one seeks her." '

18"Thus says the LORD:

'Behold, I will bring back the captivity of Jacob's tents,
And have mercy on his dwelling places;
The city shall be built upon its own mound,
And the palace shall remain according to its own plan.
19Then out of them shall proceed thanksgiving
And the voice of those who make merry;
I will multiply them, and they shall not diminish;
I will also glorify them, and they shall not be small.
20Their children also shall be as before,
And their congregation shall be established before Me;
And I will punish all who oppress them.
21Their nobles shall be from among them,
And their governor shall come from their midst;
Then I will cause him to draw near,
And he shall approach Me;
For who *is* this who pledged his heart to approach Me?' says the LORD.
22'You shall be My people,
And I will be your God.' "

23Behold, the whirlwind of the LORD
Goes forth with fury,
A continuing whirlwind;
It will fall violently on the head of the wicked.
24The fierce anger of the LORD will not return until He has done it,
And until He has performed the intents of His heart.

In the latter days you will consider it.

The Remnant of Israel Saved

31 "At the same time," says the LORD,
"I will be the God of all the families of Israel, and they shall be My people."
2Thus says the LORD:

"The people who survived the sword
Found grace in the wilderness—
Israel, when I went to give him rest."

3The LORD has appeared of old to me, *saying:*
"Yes, I have loved you with an everlasting love;
Therefore with lovingkindness I have drawn you.
4Again I will build you, and you shall be rebuilt,
O virgin of Israel!
You shall again be adorned with your tambourines,
And shall go forth in the dances of those who rejoice.
5You shall yet plant vines on the mountains of Samaria;
The planters shall plant and eat *them* as ordinary food.
6For there shall be a day
When the watchmen will cry on Mount Ephraim,
'Arise, and let us go up *to* Zion,
To the LORD our God.' "

7For thus says the LORD:

"Sing with gladness for Jacob,

31:3 It was His love that drew us to our Savior. No man can come to the Son unless the Father draws him (see John 6:44). We see a glimpse of the depth of God's love through His blood shed on the cross.

"Dost thou believe, that if he had not loved thee and given himself for thee, the gnawing worm and the unquenchable fire would have been thy portion forever? O then, where is thy gratitude, thy love?" *Edward Payson*

And shout among the chief of the
nations;
Proclaim, give praise, and say,
'O LORD, save Your people,
The remnant of Israel!'
8Behold, I will bring them from the
north country,
And gather them from the ends of the
earth,
Among them the blind and the lame,
The woman with child
And the one who labors with child,
together;
A great throng shall return there.
9They shall come with weeping,
And with supplications I will lead
them.
I will cause them to walk by the rivers
of waters,
In a straight way in which they shall
not stumble;
For I am a Father to Israel,
And Ephraim *is* My firstborn.

10"Hear the word of the LORD, O nations,
And declare *it* in the isles afar off, and
say,
'He who scattered Israel will gather
him,
And keep him as a shepherd *does* his
flock.'
11For the LORD has redeemed Jacob,
And ransomed him from the hand of
one stronger than he.
12Therefore they shall come and sing in
the height of Zion,
Streaming to the goodness of the
LORD—
For wheat and new wine and oil,
For the young of the flock and the
herd;
Their souls shall be like a well-
watered garden,
And they shall sorrow no more at all.
13"Then shall the virgin rejoice in the
dance,
And the young men and the old,
together;
For I will turn their mourning to joy,
Will comfort them,
And make them rejoice rather than
sorrow.
14I will satiate the soul of the priests
with abundance,
And My people shall be satisfied with
My goodness, says the LORD."

Mercy on Ephraim

15Thus says the LORD:

"A voice was heard in Ramah,
Lamentation *and* bitter weeping,
Rachel weeping for her children,
Refusing to be comforted for her
children,
Because they *are* no more."

16Thus says the LORD:

"Refrain your voice from weeping,
And your eyes from tears;
For your work shall be rewarded, says
the LORD,
And they shall come back from the
land of the enemy.
17There is hope in your future, says the
LORD,
That *your* children shall come back to
their own border.

18"I have surely heard Ephraim
bemoaning himself:
'You have chastised me, and I was
chastised,
Like an untrained bull;
Restore me, and I will return,
For You *are* the LORD my God.
19Surely, after my turning, I repented;

31:9 Israel knew God as a "Father" only of the nation. Jesus spoke of Him as Father to the individual. As His children, Christians have a personal relationship with Him and know Him intimately.

31:15 Matthew quotes this verse in reference to Herod's slaughter of male babies in his attempt to kill the infant Jesus (see Matt. 2:18).

And after I was instructed, I struck
myself on the thigh;
I was ashamed, yes, even humiliated,
Because I bore the reproach of my
youth.'
[20]*Is* Ephraim My dear son?
Is he a pleasant child?
For though I spoke against him,
I earnestly remember him still;
Therefore My heart yearns for him;
I will surely have mercy on him, says
the LORD.

[21]"Set up signposts,
Make landmarks;
Set your heart toward the highway,
The way in *which* you went.
Turn back, O virgin of Israel,
Turn back to these your cities.
[22]How long will you gad about,
O you backsliding daughter?
For the LORD has created a new thing
in the earth—
A woman shall encompass a man."

For how to use the Ten Commandments in witnessing, see Psa. 51:6 comment.

Future Prosperity of Judah

[23]Thus says the LORD of hosts, the God
of Israel: "They shall again use this
speech in the land of Judah and in its
cities, when I bring back their captivity:
'The LORD bless you, O home of justice,
and mountain of holiness!' [24]And there
shall dwell in Judah itself, and in all its
cities together, farmers and those going
out with flocks. [25]For I have satiated the
weary soul, and I have replenished every
sorrowful soul."
[26]After this I awoke and looked around,
and my sleep was sweet to me.
[27]"Behold, the days are coming, says
the LORD, that I will sow the house of Israel and the house of Judah with the seed
of man and the seed of beast. [28]And it
shall come to pass, *that* as I have watched

THE FUNCTION OF THE LAW

31:33 This is the New Covenant, mediated by Jesus through His blood (see Luke 22:20; Heb. 10:16). Through the gospel God's perfect Law is written upon our hearts, causing us to walk in His statutes. This is wonderful beyond words. This is why the true convert delights to seek and save that which is lost. Evangelism is an expression of both love for God and love for one's neighbor. That is the essence of the Law of God.

"The highest service to which a man may attain on earth is to preach the law of God." *John Wycliffe*

over them to pluck up, to break down, to
throw down, to destroy, and to afflict, so
I will watch over them to build and to
plant, says the LORD. [29]In those days they
shall say no more:

'The fathers have eaten sour grapes,
And the children's teeth are set on
edge.'

[30]But every one shall die for his own iniquity; every man who eats the sour grapes,
his teeth shall be set on edge.

A New Covenant

[31]"Behold, the days are coming, says
the LORD, when I will make a new covenant with the house of Israel and with the
house of Judah— [32]not according to the
covenant that I made with their fathers in
the day *that* I took them by the hand to
lead them out of the land of Egypt, My
covenant which they broke, though I was
a husband to them,[a] says the LORD. [33]But
this *is* the covenant that I will make with
the house of Israel after those days, says
the LORD: I will put My law in their minds,
and write it on their hearts; and I will be
their God, and they shall be My people.
[34]No more shall every man teach his
neighbor, and every man his brother, saying, 'Know the LORD,' for they all shall
know Me, from the least of them to the

31:32 [a]Following Masoretic Text, Targum, and Vulgate; Septuagint and Syriac read *and I turned away from them.*

31:34 *Jesus in the Old Testament*

By Todd Friel

For 800 years, the children of Israel lived under the Mosaic sacrificial covenant system. Because this system covered their sins but didn't remove them, people still lived with guilt. Despite rivers of blood from countless lamb sacrifices, forgiveness was still longed for.

Suddenly, a prophet named Jeremiah announced a new covenant that would *forgive* their sins and remove their guilt once and for all: "For I will forgive their iniquity, and their sin I will remember no more" (Jer. 31:34). The question was, how would God do this?

On the night Jesus was betrayed, He was in Jerusalem to celebrate the Passover (when the death angel passed over the children of Israel). For 1,500 years the Jews had celebrated Passover by sacrificing an unblemished, male lamb. At the Passover meal, they would drink wine at four times. The third cup was called the Cup of Redemption—essentially a "toast" to the lamb whose blood had been shed that day for the covering of their sins.

However, at this meal, Jesus announced, "This cup is the new covenant in My blood. This do, as often as you drink it, in remembrance of *Me*" (1 Cor. 11:25). Jesus basically proclaimed, "Don't toast those lambs that could merely cover sins. Toast me, the Lamb of God who *takes away* the sins of the world." No longer would animal blood be shed for the covering of sins. Jesus Christ would be sacrificed one time for the complete forgiveness of sins.

With one sentence, Jesus broke centuries of tradition and announced the fulfillment of the New Covenant promised over six hundred years earlier. See Isa. 53:4 comment.

(Adapted from *Don't Stub Your Toe.*)

greatest of them, says the LORD. For I will forgive their iniquity, and their sin I will remember no more."

35Thus says the LORD,
Who gives the sun for a light by day,
The ordinances of the moon and the stars for a light by night,
Who disturbs the sea,
And its waves roar
(The LORD of hosts *is* His name):

36"If those ordinances depart
From before Me, says the LORD,
Then the seed of Israel shall also cease
From being a nation before Me forever."

37Thus says the LORD:

"If heaven above can be measured,
And the foundations of the earth searched out beneath,
I will also cast off all the seed of Israel
For all that they have done, says the LORD.

38"Behold, the days are coming, says
the LORD, that the city shall be built for
the LORD from the Tower of Hananel to the
Corner Gate. 39The surveyor's line shall
again extend straight forward over the
hill Gareb; then it shall turn toward Goath.
40And the whole valley of the dead bodies and of the ashes, and all the fields as
far as the Brook Kidron, to the corner of
the Horse Gate toward the east, *shall be*
holy to the LORD. It shall not be plucked
up or thrown down anymore forever."

Jeremiah Buys a Field

32 The word that came to Jeremiah
from the LORD in the tenth year of
Zedekiah king of Judah, which was the
eighteenth year of Nebuchadnezzar. 2For
then the king of Babylon's army besieged
Jerusalem, and Jeremiah the prophet was
shut up in the court of the prison, which
was in the king of Judah's house. 3For
Zedekiah king of Judah had shut him up,
saying, "Why do you prophesy and say,
'Thus says the LORD: "Behold, I will give
this city into the hand of the king of
Babylon, and he shall take it; 4and Zedekiah king of Judah shall not escape from
the hand of the Chaldeans, but shall
surely be delivered into the hand of the
king of Babylon, and shall speak with

31:35 *Confessions of a Rocket Scientist*

You don't have to be a rocket scientist to recognize a problem with evolution, but it doesn't hurt. Wernher von Braun is, without a doubt, the world's most famous rocket scientist. As head of NASA's Marshall Space Flight Center, he lead the development of the Saturn V booster rocket that helped land the first men on the moon in July 1969. In a letter to the California State Board of Education, which was debating the teaching of evolution, he offered his observations on whether "the case for design" was a viable scientific theory:

> One cannot be exposed to the law and order of the universe without concluding that there must be design and purpose behind it all. In the world round us, we can behold the obvious manifestations of an ordered, structured plan or design . . . The better we understand the intricacies of the universe and all it harbors, the more reason we have found to marvel at the inherent design upon which it is based.
>
> While the admission of a design for the universe ultimately raises the question of a Designer (a subject outside of science), *the scientific method does not allow us to exclude data which lead to the conclusion that the universe, life and man are based on design. To be forced to believe only one conclusion—that everything in the universe happened by chance—would violate the very objectivity of science itself*. Certainly there are those who argue that the universe evolved out of a random process, but what random process could produce the brain of a man or the system or the human eye? . . .
>
> They [evolutionists] challenge science to prove the existence of God. But must we really light a candle to see the sun?
>
> Many men who are intelligent and of good faith say they cannot visualize a Designer. Well, can a physicist visualize an electron? The electron is materially inconceivable and yet it is so perfectly known through its effects that we use it to illuminate our cities, guide our airlines through the night skies and take the most accurate measurements. What strange rationale makes some physicists accept the inconceivable electrons as real while refusing to accept the reality of a Designer on the ground that they cannot conceive Him? . . .
>
> We in NASA were often asked what the real reason was for the amazing string of successes we had with our Apollo flights to the Moon. I think the only honest answer we could give was that we tried to never overlook anything. It is in that same sense of scientific honesty that I endorse the presentation of alternative theories for the origin of the universe, life and man in the science classroom. It would be an error to overlook the possibility that the universe was planned rather than happening by chance.

This brilliant scientist owed the success of his team to the fact that they "never overlook anything." Those who are truly interested in scientific evidence will likewise need to have enough "scientific honesty" to not overlook the possibility that our intricate, ordered universe has an intelligent Designer. See also Isa. 45:18 comment.

(Adapted from *How to Know God Exists.*)

him face to face,[a] and see him eye to eye;
5then he shall lead Zedekiah to Babylon,
and there he shall be until I visit him,"
says the LORD; "though you fight with the
Chaldeans, you shall not succeed" '?"
6And Jeremiah said, "The word of the
LORD came to me, saying, 7'Behold, Hanamel the son of Shallum your uncle will
come to you, saying, "Buy my field which
is in Anathoth, for the right of redemption
is yours to buy *it*." ' 8Then Hanamel
my uncle's son came to me in the court of

32:4 [a]Literally *mouth to mouth*

32:3 The world asks us similar questions: "Why do you speak of the existence of hell?" The answer is, "Because it is the truth. It exists." Jeremiah spoke only the words of God. To follow his example, be sure to use the Law to make hell reasonable. Leave it out and the necessity of hell makes no sense.

"Oh sirs, deal with sin as sin, and speak of heaven and hell as they are, and not as if you were in jest." *John Flavel*

32:4 See 34:3 comment.

the prison according to the word of the LORD, and said to me, 'Please buy my field that *is* in Anathoth, which *is* in the country of Benjamin; for the right of inheritance *is* yours, and the redemption yours; buy *it* for yourself.' Then I knew that this was the word of the LORD. 9So I bought the field from Hanamel, the son of my uncle who *was* in Anathoth, and weighed *out to* him the money—seventeen shekels of silver. 10And I signed the deed and sealed *it,* took witnesses, and weighed the money on the scales. 11So I took the purchase deed, *both* that which was sealed *according* to the law and custom, and that which was open; 12and I gave the purchase deed to Baruch the son of Neriah, son of Mahseiah, in the presence of Hanamel my uncle's *son,* and in the presence of the witnesses who signed the purchase deed, before all the Jews who sat in the court of the prison.

13"Then I charged Baruch before them, saying, 14'Thus says the LORD of hosts, the God of Israel: "Take these deeds, both this purchase deed which is sealed and this deed which is open, and put them in an earthen vessel, that they may last many days." 15For thus says the LORD of hosts, the God of Israel: "Houses and fields and vineyards shall be possessed again in this land." '

Jeremiah Prays for Understanding

16"Now when I had delivered the purchase deed to Baruch the son of Neriah, I prayed to the LORD, saying: 17'Ah, Lord GOD! Behold, You have made the heavens and the earth by Your great power and outstretched arm. There is nothing too hard for You. 18*You* show lovingkindness to thousands, and repay the iniquity of the fathers into the bosom of their children after them—the Great, the Mighty God, whose name *is* the LORD of hosts. 19*You are* great in counsel and mighty in work, for Your eyes *are* open to all the ways of the sons of men, to give everyone according to his ways and according to the fruit of his doings. 20You have set signs and wonders in the land of Egypt, to this day, and in Israel and among *other* men; and You have made Yourself a name, as it is this day. 21You have brought Your people Israel out of the land of Egypt with signs and wonders, with a strong hand and an outstretched arm, and with great terror; 22You have given them this land, of which You swore to their fathers to give them—"a land flowing with milk and honey."[a] 23And they came in and took possession of it, but they have not obeyed Your voice or walked in Your law. They have done nothing of all that You commanded them to do; therefore You have caused all this calamity to come upon them.

24'Look, the siege mounds! They have come to the city to take it; and the city has been given into the hand of the Chaldeans who fight against it, because of the sword and famine and pestilence. What You have spoken has happened; there You see *it!* 25And You have said to me, O Lord GOD, "Buy the field for money, and take witnesses"!—yet the city has been given into the hand of the Chaldeans.' "

God's Assurance of the People's Return

26Then the word of the LORD came to Jeremiah, saying, 27"Behold, I *am* the LORD, the God of all flesh. Is there anything too hard for Me? 28Therefore thus says the LORD: 'Behold, I will give this city into the hand of the Chaldeans, into the hand of

32:22 [a]Exodus 3:8

32:17 "Ah, Lord GOD!" is an expression of overwhelming awe that God could create such a creation as surrounds us. Words cannot express our wonder. When one has such a revelation, it leads to the great truth that nothing is too hard for God (see Luke 1:37). This is a good verse to memorize, so that when you find yourself looking up at a mountain of adversity, you will remember that it is but a small molehill compared to Almighty God. See also Psa. 33:8 comment.

Nebuchadnezzar king of Babylon, and he
shall take it. 29 And the Chaldeans who
fight against this city shall come and set
fire to this city and burn it, with the
houses on whose roofs they have offered
incense to Baal and poured out drink offerings to other gods, to provoke Me to
anger; 30 because the children of Israel
and the children of Judah have done only
evil before Me from their youth. For the
children of Israel have provoked Me only
to anger with the work of their hands,'
says the LORD. 31 'For this city has been to
Me *a provocation of* My anger and My fury
from the day that they built it, even to
this day; so I will remove it from before
My face 32 because of all the evil of the
children of Israel and the children of Judah, which they have done to provoke Me
to anger—they, their kings, their princes,
their priests, their prophets, the men of
Judah, and the inhabitants of Jerusalem.

> I have learned that true Christianity consists, not in a set of options, or of forms and ceremonies, but in holiness of heart and life.
>
> **JOHN WESLEY**

33 And they have turned to Me the back,
and not the face; though I taught them,
rising up early and teaching *them,* yet
they have not listened to receive instruction. 34 But they set their abominations in
the house which is called by My name, to
defile it. 35 And they built the high places
of Baal which *are* in the Valley of the Son
of Hinnom, to cause their sons and their
daughters to pass through *the fire* to Molech, which I did not command them, nor
did it come into My mind that they should
do this abomination, to cause Judah to
sin.'

36 "Now therefore, thus says the LORD,
the God of Israel, concerning this city of
which you say, 'It shall be delivered into
the hand of the king of Babylon by the
sword, by the famine, and by the pestilence: 37 Behold, I will gather them out of
all countries where I have driven them in
My anger, in My fury, and in great wrath;
I will bring them back to this place, and
I will cause them to dwell safely. 38 They
shall be My people, and I will be their
God; 39 then I will give them one heart
and one way, that they may fear Me forever, for the good of them and their children after them. 40 And I will make an
everlasting covenant with them, that I
will not turn away from doing them good;
but I will put My fear in their hearts so
that they will not depart from Me. 41 Yes,
I will rejoice over them to do them good,
and I will assuredly plant them in this
land, with all My heart and with all My
soul.'

42 "For thus says the LORD: 'Just as I
have brought all this great calamity on
this people, so I will bring on them all the
good that I have promised them. 43 And
fields will be bought in this land of which
you say, "*It is* desolate, without man or
beast; it has been given into the hand of
the Chaldeans." 44 Men will buy fields for
money, sign deeds and seal *them,* and
take witnesses, in the land of Benjamin,
in the places around Jerusalem, in the
cities of Judah, in the cities of the mountains, in the cities of the lowland, and in
the cities of the South; for I will cause
their captives to return,' says the LORD."

Excellence of the Restored Nation

33 Moreover the word of the LORD
came to Jeremiah a second time,
while he was still shut up in the court of
the prison, saying, 2 "Thus says the LORD
who made it, the LORD who formed it to

32:38–40 The wonderful gospel went to the Jews first, then to the Gentiles. Notice that the sign of those born of the Spirit of God is that they will fear Him. This is lacking in many "converts" of modern evangelism, because preachers don't use the Law to show that God ought to be feared.

establish it (the LORD *is* His name): 3'Call
to Me, and I will answer you, and show
you great and mighty things, which you
do not know.'
4"For thus says the LORD, the God of
Israel, concerning the houses of this city
and the houses of the kings of Judah,
which have been pulled down *to fortify*[a]
against the siege mounds and the sword:
5'They come to fight with the Chaldeans,
but *only* to fill their places[a] with the dead
bodies of men whom I will slay in My
anger and My fury, all for whose wickedness I have hidden My face from this city.
6Behold, I will bring it health and healing; I will heal them and reveal to them
the abundance of peace and truth. 7And I
will cause the captives of Judah and the
captives of Israel to return, and will rebuild those places as at the first. 8I will
cleanse them from all their iniquity by
which they have sinned against Me, and I
will pardon all their iniquities by which
they have sinned and by which they have
transgressed against Me. 9Then it shall be
to Me a name of joy, a praise, and an
honor before all nations of the earth, who
shall hear all the good that I do to them;
they shall fear and tremble for all the
goodness and all the prosperity that I
provide for it.'
10"Thus says the LORD: 'Again there
shall be heard in this place—of which
you say, "It *is* desolate, without man and
without beast"—in the cities of Judah, in
the streets of Jerusalem that are desolate,
without man and without inhabitant and
without beast, 11the voice of joy and the
voice of gladness, the voice of the bridegroom and the voice of the bride, the
voice of those who will say:

"Praise the LORD of hosts,
For the LORD *is* good,
For His mercy *endures* forever"—

and of those *who will* bring the sacrifice of
praise into the house of the LORD. For I
will cause the captives of the land to return as at the first,' says the LORD.
12"Thus says the LORD of hosts: 'In this
place which is desolate, without man and
without beast, and in all its cities, there
shall again be a dwelling place of shepherds causing *their* flocks to lie down.
13In the cities of the mountains, in the
cities of the lowland, in the cities of the
South, in the land of Benjamin, in the
places around Jerusalem, and in the cities
of Judah, the flocks shall again pass under the hands of him who counts *them*,'
says the LORD.
14'Behold, the days are coming,' says
the LORD, 'that I will perform that good
thing which I have promised to the house
of Israel and to the house of Judah:

15'In those days and at that time
I will cause to grow up to David
A Branch of righteousness;
He shall execute judgment and
righteousness in the earth.
16In those days Judah will be saved,
And Jerusalem will dwell safely.
And this *is the name* by which she will
be called:

THE LORD OUR RIGHTEOUSNESS.'[a]

17"For thus says the LORD: 'David shall
never lack a man to sit on the throne of
the house of Israel; 18nor shall the priests,
the Levites, lack a man to offer burnt offerings before Me, to kindle grain offerings, and to sacrifice continually.' "

33:4 [a]Compare Isaiah 22:10 33:5 [a]Compare 2 Kings 23:14
33:16 [a]Compare 23:5, 6

33:3 This word was given to Jeremiah, but all the promises of God in Christ are "Yes" and "Amen" (see 2 Cor. 1:20). This is an open challenge to call upon the Lord for great and mighty things.

"I do not think that God's people often go astray in the most difficult cases, for they do take them to the Lord in prayer. It is in simple matters that we make our greatest blunders, because we think we know what to do and, therefore, we do not wait upon the Lord for guidance." *Charles Spurgeon*

The Permanence of God's Covenant

[19]And the word of the LORD came to Jeremiah, saying, [20]"Thus says the LORD: 'If you can break My covenant with the day and My covenant with the night, so that there will not be day and night in their season, [21]then My covenant may also be broken with David My servant, so that he shall not have a son to reign on his throne, and with the Levites, the priests, My ministers. [22]As the host of heaven cannot be numbered, nor the sand of the sea measured, so will I multiply the descendants of David My servant and the Levites who minister to Me.' "

[23]Moreover the word of the LORD came to Jeremiah, saying, [24]"Have you not considered what these people have spoken, saying, 'The two families which the LORD has chosen, He has also cast them off'? Thus they have despised My people, as if they should no more be a nation before them.

[25]"Thus says the LORD: 'If My covenant *is* not with day and night, *and if* I have not appointed the ordinances of heaven and earth, [26]then I will cast away the descendants of Jacob and David My servant, *so* that I will not take *any* of his descendants *to be* rulers over the descendants of Abraham, Isaac, and Jacob. For I will cause their captives to return, and will have mercy on them.' "

Zedekiah Warned by God

34 The word which came to Jeremiah from the LORD, when Nebuchadnezzar king of Babylon and all his army, all the kingdoms of the earth under his dominion, and all the people, fought against Jerusalem and all its cities, saying, [2]"Thus says the LORD, the God of Israel: 'Go and speak to Zedekiah king of Judah and tell him, "Thus says the LORD: 'Behold, I will give this city into the hand of the king of Babylon, and he shall burn it with fire. [3]And you shall not escape from his hand, but shall surely be taken and delivered into his hand; your eyes shall see the eyes of the king of Babylon, he shall speak with you face to face,[a] and you shall go to Babylon.' " ' [4]Yet hear the word of the LORD, O Zedekiah king of Judah! Thus says the LORD concerning you: 'You shall not die by the sword. [5]You shall die in peace; as in the ceremonies of your fathers, the former kings who were before you, so they shall burn incense for you and lament for you, *saying,* "Alas, lord!" For I have pronounced the word, says the LORD.' "

[6]Then Jeremiah the prophet spoke all these words to Zedekiah king of Judah in Jerusalem, [7]when the king of Babylon's army fought against Jerusalem and all the cities of Judah that were left, against Lachish and Azekah; for *only* these fortified cities remained of the cities of Judah.

Treacherous Treatment of Slaves

[8]*This is* the word that came to Jeremiah from the LORD, after King Zedekiah had made a covenant with all the people who *were* at Jerusalem to proclaim liberty to them: [9]that every man should set free his male and female slave—a Hebrew man or woman—that no one should keep a Jewish brother in bondage. [10]Now when all the princes and all the people, who had entered into the covenant, heard

34:3 [a]Literally *mouth to mouth*

33:22 See Psa. 147:4 comment.

34:3 Here is a wonderful illustration of how God confounds the wicked in their own craftiness. If the proud are searching for "mistakes" in the Bible, this appears to be a big one. Here God told Zedekiah, through the prophet, that he would see the king of Babylon, yet Ezek. 12:13 says that Zedekiah will not see Babylon. There you have it—a glaring "mistake" in the Word of God. For the answer to this "dilemma," see 39:6,7.

Never doubt the Word of God because of the twisting of Scripture or because one verse is interpreted without another. Every one of skeptics' "mistakes" in the Bible can be explained with a little humble searching of the Scriptures. See Mark 15:26 comment.

"In the vast plain to the north I have sometimes seen, in the morning sun, the smoke of a thousand villages where no missionary has ever been."

Robert Moffat

that everyone should set free his male and
female slaves, that no one should keep
them in bondage anymore, they obeyed
and let *them* go. [11]But afterward they
changed their minds and made the male
and female slaves return, whom they had
set free, and brought them into subjection as male and female slaves.

[12]Therefore the word of the LORD
came to Jeremiah from the LORD, saying,
[13]"Thus says the LORD, the God of Israel:
'I made a covenant with your fathers in
the day that I brought them out of the
land of Egypt, out of the house of bondage, saying, [14]"At the end of seven years
let every man set free his Hebrew brother,
who has been sold to him; and when he
has served you six years, you shall let him
go free from you." But your fathers did not
obey Me nor incline their ear. [15]Then you
recently turned and did what was right in
My sight—every man proclaiming liberty
to his neighbor; and you made a covenant before Me in the house which is
called by My name. [16]Then you turned
around and profaned My name, and every
one of you brought back his male and female slaves, whom you had set at liberty,
at their pleasure, and brought them back
into subjection, to be your male and female slaves.'

[17]"Therefore thus says the LORD: 'You
have not obeyed Me in proclaiming liberty, every one to his brother and every
one to his neighbor. Behold, I proclaim
liberty to you,' says the LORD—'to the
sword, to pestilence, and to famine! And
I will deliver you to trouble among all the
kingdoms of the earth. [18]And I will give
the men who have transgressed My covenant, who have not performed the words
of the covenant which they made before
Me, when they cut the calf in two and
passed between the parts of it— [19]the
princes of Judah, the princes of Jerusalem, the eunuchs, the priests, and all the
people of the land who passed between
the parts of the calf— [20]I will give them
into the hand of their enemies and into
the hand of those who seek their life.
Their dead bodies shall be for meat for
the birds of the heaven and the beasts of
the earth. [21]And I will give Zedekiah king
of Judah and his princes into the hand of
their enemies, into the hand of those who
seek their life, and into the hand of the
king of Babylon's army which has gone
back from you. [22]Behold, I will command,'
says the LORD, 'and cause them to return
to this city. They will fight against it and
take it and burn it with fire; and I will
make the cities of Judah a desolation
without inhabitant.' "

The Obedient Rechabites

35 The word which came to Jeremiah from the LORD in the days of
Jehoiakim the son of Josiah, king of Judah,
saying, [2]"Go to the house of the Rechabites, speak to them, and bring them into
the house of the LORD, into one of the
chambers, and give them wine to drink."

[3]Then I took Jaazaniah the son of Jeremiah, the son of Habazziniah, his brothers and all his sons, and the whole house
of the Rechabites, [4]and I brought them
into the house of the LORD, into the

chamber of the sons of Hanan the son of Igdaliah, a man of God, which *was* by the chamber of the princes, above the chamber of Maaseiah the son of Shallum, the keeper of the door. [5]Then I set before the sons of the house of the Rechabites bowls full of wine, and cups; and I said to them, "Drink wine."

[6]But they said, "We will drink no wine, for Jonadab the son of Rechab, our father, commanded us, saying, 'You shall drink no wine, you nor your sons, forever. [7]You shall not build a house, sow seed, plant a vineyard, nor have *any of these*; but all your days you shall dwell in tents, that you may live many days in the land where you are sojourners.' [8]Thus we have obeyed the voice of Jonadab the son of Rechab, our father, in all that he charged us, to drink no wine all our days, we, our wives, our sons, or our daughters, [9]nor to build ourselves houses to dwell in; nor do we have vineyard, field, or seed. [10]But we have dwelt in tents, and have obeyed and done according to all that Jonadab our father commanded us. [11]But it came to pass, when Nebuchadnezzar king of Babylon came up into the land, that we said, 'Come, let us go to Jerusalem for fear of the army of the Chaldeans and for fear of the army of the Syrians.' So we dwell at Jerusalem."

[12]Then came the word of the LORD to Jeremiah, saying, [13]"Thus says the LORD of hosts, the God of Israel: 'Go and tell the men of Judah and the inhabitants of Jerusalem, "Will you not receive instruction to obey My words?" says the LORD. [14]"The words of Jonadab the son of Rechab, which he commanded his sons, not to drink wine, are performed; for to this day they drink none, and obey their father's commandment. But although I have spoken to you, rising early and speaking, you did not obey Me. [15]I have also sent to you all My servants the prophets, rising up early and sending *them*, saying, 'Turn now everyone from his evil way, amend your doings, and do not go after other gods to serve them; then you will dwell in the land which I have given you and your fathers.' But you have not inclined your ear, nor obeyed Me. [16]Surely the sons of Jonadab the son of Rechab have performed the commandment of their father, which he commanded them, but this people has not obeyed Me." '

[17]"Therefore thus says the LORD God of hosts, the God of Israel: 'Behold, I will bring on Judah and on all the inhabitants of Jerusalem all the doom that I have pronounced against them; because I have spoken to them but they have not heard, and I have called to them but they have not answered.' "

[18]And Jeremiah said to the house of the Rechabites, "Thus says the LORD of hosts, the God of Israel: 'Because you have obeyed the commandment of Jonadab your father, and kept all his precepts and done according to all that he commanded you, [19]therefore thus says the LORD of hosts, the God of Israel: "Jonadab the son of Rechab shall not lack a man to stand before Me forever." ' "

The Scroll Read in the Temple

36 Now it came to pass in the fourth year of Jehoiakim the son of Josiah, king of Judah, *that* this word came to Jeremiah from the LORD, saying: [2]"Take a scroll of a book and write on it all the words that I have spoken to you against Israel, against Judah, and against all the nations, from the day I spoke to you, from the days of Josiah even to this day.

35:13 "To be entirely safe from the devil's snares the man of God must be completely obedient to the Word of the Lord. The driver on the highway is safe, not when he reads the signs but when he obeys them." *A. W. Tozer*

36:1–3 Sinners must hear all the adversity that the Law threatens so that they may turn from their evil ways, and God may forgive their iniquity and their sin through the gospel.

3It may be that the house of Judah will hear all the adversities which I purpose to bring upon them, that everyone may turn from his evil way, that I may forgive their iniquity and their sin."

4Then Jeremiah called Baruch the son of Neriah; and Baruch wrote on a scroll of a book, at the instruction of Jeremiah,[a] all the words of the LORD which He had spoken to him. 5And Jeremiah commanded Baruch, saying, "I *am* confined, I cannot go into the house of the LORD. 6You go, therefore, and read from the scroll which you have written at my instruction,[a] the words of the LORD, in the hearing of the people in the LORD's house on the day of fasting. And you shall also read them in the hearing of all Judah who come from their cities. 7It may be that they will present their supplication before the LORD, and everyone will turn from his evil way. For great *is* the anger and the fury that the LORD has pronounced against this people." 8And Baruch the son of Neriah did according to all that Jeremiah the prophet commanded him, reading from the book the words of the LORD in the LORD's house.

9Now it came to pass in the fifth year of Jehoiakim the son of Josiah, king of Judah, in the ninth month, *that* they proclaimed a fast before the LORD to all the people in Jerusalem, and to all the people who came from the cities of Judah to Jerusalem. 10Then Baruch read from the book the words of Jeremiah in the house of the LORD, in the chamber of Gemariah the son of Shaphan the scribe, in the upper court at the entry of the New Gate of the LORD's house, in the hearing of all the people.

The Scroll Read in the Palace

11When Michaiah the son of Gemariah, the son of Shaphan, heard all the words of the LORD from the book, 12he then went down to the king's house, into the scribe's chamber; and there all the princes were sitting—Elishama the scribe, Delaiah the son of Shemaiah, Elnathan the son of Achbor, Gemariah the son of Shaphan, Zedekiah the son of Hananiah, and all the princes. 13Then Michaiah declared to them all the words that he had heard when Baruch read the book in the hearing of the people. 14Therefore all the princes sent Jehudi the son of Nethaniah, the son of Shelemiah, the son of Cushi, to Baruch, saying, "Take in your hand the scroll from which you have read in the hearing of the people, and come." So Baruch the son of Neriah took the scroll in his hand and came to them. 15And they said to him, "Sit down now, and read it in our hearing." So Baruch read *it* in their hearing.

16Now it happened, when they had heard all the words, that they looked in fear from one to another, and said to Baruch, "We will surely tell the king of all these words." 17And they asked Baruch, saying, "Tell us now, how did you write all these words—at his instruction?"[a]

18So Baruch answered them, "He proclaimed with his mouth all these words to me, and I wrote *them* with ink in the book."

19Then the princes said to Baruch, "Go and hide, you and Jeremiah; and let no one know where you are."

The King Destroys Jeremiah's Scroll

20And they went to the king, into the court; but they stored the scroll in the chamber of Elishama the scribe, and told all the words in the hearing of the king. 21So the king sent Jehudi to bring the scroll, and he took it from Elishama the scribe's chamber. And Jehudi read it in the hearing of the king and in the hearing of all the princes who stood beside the king. 22Now the king was sitting in the winter house in the ninth month, with *a fire* burning on the hearth before him. 23And it happened, when Jehudi had read three or four columns, *that the king* cut it with the scribe's knife and cast *it* into the

36:4 [a]Literally *from Jeremiah's mouth* 36:6 [a]Literally *from my mouth* 36:17 [a]Literally *with his mouth*

fire that *was* on the hearth, until all the scroll was consumed in the fire that *was* on the hearth. 24 Yet they were not afraid, nor did they tear their garments, the king nor any of his servants who heard all these words. 25 Nevertheless Elnathan, Delaiah, and Gemariah implored the king not to burn the scroll; but he would not listen to them. 26 And the king commanded Jerahmeel the king's[a] son, Seraiah the son of Azriel, and Shelemiah the son of Abdeel, to seize Baruch the scribe and Jeremiah the prophet, but the LORD hid them.

Jeremiah Rewrites the Scroll

27 Now after the king had burned the scroll with the words which Baruch had written at the instruction of Jeremiah,[a] the word of the LORD came to Jeremiah, saying: 28 "Take yet another scroll, and write on it all the former words that were in the first scroll which Jehoiakim the king of Judah has burned. 29 And you shall say to Jehoiakim king of Judah, 'Thus says the LORD: "You have burned this scroll, saying, 'Why have you written in it that the king of Babylon will certainly come and destroy this land, and cause man and beast to cease from here?' " 30 Therefore thus says the LORD concerning Jehoiakim king of Judah: "He shall have no one to sit on the throne of David, and his dead body shall be cast out to the heat of the day and the frost of the night. 31 I will punish him, his family, and his servants for their iniquity; and I will bring on them, on the inhabitants of Jerusalem, and on the men of Judah all the doom that I have pronounced against them; but they did not heed." ' "

32 Then Jeremiah took another scroll and gave it to Baruch the scribe, the son of Neriah, who wrote on it at the instruction of Jeremiah[a] all the words of the book which Jehoiakim king of Judah had burned in the fire. And besides, there were added to them many similar words.

Zedekiah's Vain Hope

37 Now King Zedekiah the son of Josiah reigned instead of Coniah the son of Jehoiakim, whom Nebuchadnezzar king of Babylon made king in the land of Judah. 2 But neither he nor his servants nor the people of the land gave heed to the words of the LORD which He spoke by the prophet Jeremiah.

3 And Zedekiah the king sent Jehucal the son of Shelemiah, and Zephaniah the son of Maaseiah, the priest, to the prophet Jeremiah, saying, "Pray now to the LORD our God for us." 4 Now Jeremiah was coming and going among the people, for they had not *yet* put him in prison. 5 Then Pharaoh's army came up from Egypt; and when the Chaldeans who were besieging Jerusalem heard news of them, they departed from Jerusalem.

6 Then the word of the LORD came to the prophet Jeremiah, saying, 7 "Thus says the LORD, the God of Israel, 'Thus you shall say to the king of Judah, who sent you to Me to inquire of Me: "Behold, Pharaoh's army which has come up to help you will return to Egypt, to their own land. 8 And the Chaldeans shall come back and fight against this city, and take it and burn it with fire." ' 9 Thus says the LORD: 'Do not deceive yourselves, saying, "The Chaldeans will surely depart from us," for they will not depart. 10 For though you had defeated the whole army of the Chaldeans who fight against you, and there remained *only* wounded men among them, they would rise up, every man in his tent, and burn the city with fire.' "

Jeremiah Imprisoned

11 And it happened, when the army of

36:26 [a]Hebrew *Hammelech* 36:27 [a]Literally *from Jeremiah's mouth* 36:32 [a]Literally *from Jeremiah's mouth*

36:22–24 This is how proud skeptics treat the Word of God—with utter disdain. They don't tremble at His Word.

POINTS FOR OPEN-AIR PREACHING

37:18

Stay Out of Jail

There are two basic rules for open-air preaching. The first is to make sure there are no stones in the area. The second is to have identification, and if a police officer approaches you, be extra polite and very humble of heart. Make sure you keep your hands out of your pockets and don't make any sudden movements. He wants to see his family that night, so if he thinks you have a weapon he may just shoot you, and we don't want that. We need you on the front-lines.

If a police officer or security guard tries to shut you down, be very polite. Don't talk about First Amendment rights, as that will probably upset him. Instead, ask the officer or security guard if you are breaking the law. If you are, you will gladly leave. If you aren't breaking any law, gently state that you are going to continue speaking. For details on your legal rights, see page 350.

the Chaldeans left *the siege* of Jerusalem
for fear of Pharaoh's army, [12]that Jeremiah
went out of Jerusalem to go into the land
of Benjamin to claim his property there
among the people. [13]And when he was in
the Gate of Benjamin, a captain of the
guard *was* there whose name *was* Irijah
the son of Shelemiah, the son of Hananiah;
and he seized Jeremiah the prophet, saying, "You are defecting to the Chaldeans!"

[14]Then Jeremiah said, "False! I am not
defecting to the Chaldeans." But he did
not listen to him.

So Irijah seized Jeremiah and brought
him to the princes. [15]Therefore the princes
were angry with Jeremiah, and they struck
him and put him in prison in the house
of Jonathan the scribe. For they had made
that the prison.

[16]When Jeremiah entered the dungeon
and the cells, and Jeremiah had remained
there many days, [17]then Zedekiah the king
sent and took him *out*. The king asked
him secretly in his house, and said, "Is
there *any* word from the LORD?"

And Jeremiah said, "There is." Then
he said, "You shall be delivered into the
hand of the king of Babylon!"

[18]Moreover Jeremiah said to King
Zedekiah, "What offense have I committed against you, against your servants, or
against this people, that you have put me
in prison? [19]Where now *are* your prophets who prophesied to you, saying, 'The
king of Babylon will not come against you
or against this land'? [20]Therefore please
hear now, O my lord the king. Please, let
my petition be accepted before you, and
do not make me return to the house of
Jonathan the scribe, lest I die there."

[21]Then Zedekiah the king commanded
that they should commit Jeremiah to the
court of the prison, and that they should
give him daily a piece of bread from the
bakers' street, until all the bread in the
city was gone. Thus Jeremiah remained
in the court of the prison.

Jeremiah in the Dungeon

38 Now Shephatiah the son of Mattan, Gedaliah the son of Pashhur,
Jucal[a] the son of Shelemiah, and Pashhur
the son of Malchiah heard the words that
Jeremiah had spoken to all the people,
saying, [2]"Thus says the LORD: 'He who remains in this city shall die by the sword,
by famine, and by pestilence; but he who
goes over to the Chaldeans shall live; his
life shall be as a prize to him, and he shall
live.'[a] [3]Thus says the LORD: 'This city shall
surely be given into the hand of the king
of Babylon's army, which shall take it.' "

[4]Therefore the princes said to the
king, "Please, let this man be put to death,
for thus he weakens the hands of the men
of war who remain in this city, and the

38:1 [a]Same as *Jehucal* (compare 37:3) **38:2** [a]Compare 21:9

38:2 Here is the truth of the gospel. Whoever desires to save his life will lose it, but whoever loses his life for Jesus' sake will save it (see Luke 9:24).

hands of all the people, by speaking such words to them. For this man does not seek the welfare of this people, but their harm."

5Then Zedekiah the king said, "Look, he *is* in your hand. For the king can *do* nothing against you." 6So they took Jeremiah and cast him into the dungeon of Malchiah the king's[a] son, which *was* in the court of the prison, and they let Jeremiah down with ropes. And in the dungeon *there was* no water, but mire. So Jeremiah sank in the mire.

7Now Ebed-Melech the Ethiopian, one of the eunuchs, who was in the king's house, heard that they had put Jeremiah in the dungeon. When the king was sitting at the Gate of Benjamin, 8Ebed-Melech went out of the king's house and spoke to the king, saying: 9"My lord the king, these men have done evil in all that they have done to Jeremiah the prophet, whom they have cast into the dungeon, and he is likely to die from hunger in the place where he is. For *there is* no more bread in the city." 10Then the king commanded Ebed-Melech the Ethiopian, saying, "Take from here thirty men with you, and lift Jeremiah the prophet out of the dungeon before he dies." 11So Ebed-Melech took the men with him and went into the house of the king under the treasury, and took from there old clothes and old rags, and let them down by ropes into the dungeon to Jeremiah. 12Then Ebed-Melech the Ethiopian said to Jeremiah, "Please put these old clothes and rags under your armpits, under the ropes." And Jeremiah did so. 13So they pulled Jeremiah up with ropes and lifted him out of the dungeon. And Jeremiah remained in the court of the prison.

Zedekiah's Fears and Jeremiah's Advice

14Then Zedekiah the king sent and had Jeremiah the prophet brought to him at the third entrance of the house of the LORD. And the king said to Jeremiah, "I will ask you something. Hide nothing from me."

15Jeremiah said to Zedekiah, "If I declare *it* to you, will you not surely put me to death? And if I give you advice, you will not listen to me."

16So Zedekiah the king swore secretly to Jeremiah, saying, "*As* the LORD lives, who made our very souls, I will not put you to death, nor will I give you into the hand of these men who seek your life."

17Then Jeremiah said to Zedekiah, "Thus says the LORD, the God of hosts, the God of Israel: 'If you surely surrender to the king of Babylon's princes, then your soul shall live; this city shall not be burned with fire, and you and your house shall live. 18But if you do not surrender to the king of Babylon's princes, then this city shall be given into the hand of the Chaldeans; they shall burn it with fire, and you shall not escape from their hand.' "

19And Zedekiah the king said to Jeremiah, "I am afraid of the Jews who have defected to the Chaldeans, lest they deliver me into their hand, and they abuse me."

20But Jeremiah said, "They shall not deliver *you*. Please, obey the voice of the LORD which I speak to you. So it shall be well with you, and your soul shall live. 21But if you refuse to surrender, this *is* the word that the LORD has shown me: 22'Now

38:6 [a]Hebrew *Hammelech*

38:4 They beseeched the king for the death of the prophet. The world is passionate about stopping the mouth of the evangelistic Christian. In their error, they are convinced that Christians want the ruin, not the good, of humanity.

38:19,20 We plead with the dying world, as though God were speaking through us, to be reconciled to God. We seek to pacify the sinner's fears that his "friends" will leave him and that the world will mock him, while stressing that this is the only way to be saved from death—what will it profit a man if he gains the whole world and loses his own soul (see Mark 8:36)? Nothing is more important than his eternal salvation.

behold, all the women who are left in the
king of Judah's house *shall be* surrendered
to the king of Babylon's princes, and
those *women* shall say:

"Your close friends have set upon you
And prevailed against you;
Your feet have sunk in the mire,
And they have turned away again."

23'So they shall surrender all your
wives and children to the Chaldeans. You
shall not escape from their hand, but
shall be taken by the hand of the king of
Babylon. And you shall cause this city to
be burned with fire.' "

24Then Zedekiah said to Jeremiah,
"Let no one know of these words, and
you shall not die. 25But if the princes hear
that I have talked with you, and they
come to you and say to you, 'Declare to
us now what you have said to the king,
and also what the king said to you; do
not hide *it* from us, and we will not put
you to death,' 26then you shall say to
them, 'I presented my request before the
king, that he would not make me return
to Jonathan's house to die there.' "

27Then all the princes came to Jeremiah and asked him. And he told them
according to all these words that the king
had commanded. So they stopped speaking with him, for the conversation had
not been heard. 28Now Jeremiah remained
in the court of the prison until the day
that Jerusalem was taken. And he was
there when Jerusalem was taken.

The Fall of Jerusalem

39 In the ninth year of Zedekiah king
of Judah, in the tenth month,
Nebuchadnezzar king of Babylon and all
his army came against Jerusalem, and besieged it. 2In the eleventh year of Zedekiah, in the fourth month, on the ninth
day of the month, the city was penetrated.

3Then all the princes of the king of
Babylon came in and sat in the Middle
Gate: Nergal-Sharezer, Samgar-Nebo, Sar-
sechim, Rabsaris,[a] Nergal-Sarezer, Rabmag,[b] with the rest of the princes of the
king of Babylon.

4So it was, when Zedekiah the king of
Judah and all the men of war saw them,
that they fled and went out of the city by
night, by way of the king's garden, by the
gate between the two walls. And he went
out by way of the plain.[a] 5But the Chaldean army pursued them and overtook
Zedekiah in the plains of Jericho. And
when they had captured him, they brought
him up to Nebuchadnezzar king of Babylon, to Riblah in the land of Hamath,
where he pronounced judgment on him.
6Then the king of Babylon killed the sons
of Zedekiah before his eyes in Riblah; the
king of Babylon also killed all the nobles
of Judah. 7Moreover he put out Zedekiah's
eyes, and bound him with bronze fetters
to carry him off to Babylon. 8And the
Chaldeans burned the king's house and
the houses of the people with fire, and
broke down the walls of Jerusalem. 9Then
Nebuzaradan the captain of the guard
carried away captive to Babylon the remnant of the people who remained in the
city and those who defected to him, with
the rest of the people who remained.
10But Nebuzaradan the captain of the
guard left in the land of Judah the poor
people, who had nothing, and gave them
vineyards and fields at the same time.

Jeremiah Goes Free

11Now Nebuchadnezzar king of Babylon gave charge concerning Jeremiah to
Nebuzaradan the captain of the guard,
saying, 12"Take him and look after him,
and do him no harm; but do to him just
as he says to you." 13So Nebuzaradan the
captain of the guard sent Nebushasban,
Rabsaris, Nergal-Sharezer, Rabmag, and
all the king of Babylon's chief officers;
14then they sent *someone* to take Jeremiah
from the court of the prison, and committed him to Gedaliah the son of Ahikam,
the son of Shaphan, that he should take

39:3 [a]A title, probably *Chief Officer;* also verse 13 [b]A title, probably *Troop Commander;* also verse 13 **39:4** [a]Or *the Arabah,* that is, the Jordan Valley

him home. So he dwelt among the people.

15 Meanwhile the word of the LORD had come to Jeremiah while he was shut up in the court of the prison, saying, 16 "Go and speak to Ebed-Melech the Ethiopian, saying, 'Thus says the LORD of hosts, the God of Israel: "Behold, I will bring My words upon this city for adversity and not for good, and they shall be *performed* in that day before you. 17 But I will deliver you in that day," says the LORD, "and you shall not be given into the hand of the men of whom you *are* afraid. 18 For I will surely deliver you, and you shall not fall by the sword; but your life shall be as a prize to you, because you have put your trust in Me," says the LORD.' "

Jeremiah with Gedaliah the Governor

40 The word that came to Jeremiah from the LORD after Nebuzaradan the captain of the guard had let him go from Ramah, when he had taken him bound in chains among all who were carried away captive from Jerusalem and Judah, who were carried away captive to Babylon.

2 And the captain of the guard took Jeremiah and said to him: "The LORD your God has pronounced this doom on this place. 3 Now the LORD has brought *it,* and has done just as He said. Because you *people* have sinned against the LORD, and not obeyed His voice, therefore this thing has come upon you. 4 And now look, I free you this day from the chains that *were* on your hand. If it seems good to you to come with me to Babylon, come, and I will look after you. But if it seems wrong for you to come with me to Babylon, remain here. See, all the land *is* before you; wherever it seems good and convenient for you to go, go there."

5 Now while Jeremiah had not yet gone back, *Nebuzaradan said,* "Go back to Gedaliah the son of Ahikam, the son of Shaphan, whom the king of Babylon has made governor over the cities of Judah, and dwell with him among the people. Or go wherever it seems convenient for you to go." So the captain of the guard gave him rations and a gift and let him go. 6 Then Jeremiah went to Gedaliah the son of Ahikam, to Mizpah, and dwelt with him among the people who were left in the land.

7 And when all the captains of the armies who *were* in the fields, they and their men, heard that the king of Babylon had made Gedaliah the son of Ahikam

39:6–8 Warning sinners of judgment. Jeremiah warned King Zedekiah repeatedly that God would judge His people. The prophet pleaded with the king, but still he would not do what Jeremiah said. One cannot but wonder what the king thought about after he was blinded and bound with chains. Perhaps his thoughts were of the last thing he saw—the unspeakable agony of seeing his own beloved sons butchered before his eyes. Or perhaps the words of Jeremiah flashed before his tormented mind, warning him that all of Israel (including his sons) could have been saved if only he had obeyed the voice of the Lord. We can't begin to imagine the remorse he felt.

How this must typify the ungodly who have been bound by the bronze fetters of sin, "taken captive by [the devil] to do his will" (2 Tim. 2:26). We warn that there is judgment coming (both temporal and eternal) to those who live for the devil, but most remain in unbelief. Their master is he who came "to steal, and to kill, and to destroy" (John 10:10). He blinds the minds of those who don't believe (see 2 Cor. 4:4). Like Zedekiah, so many see their own sons and daughters die before their very eyes. AIDS and other sin-related diseases, as well as alcohol, drugs, and suicide, kill many before their time. Multitudes give themselves to the burning fires of sexual lust, and so the devil breaks down the walls of entire nations.

Yet, there is still time to warn them. There is still time to pray that God will open their understanding. God instructed Jeremiah to tell an Ethiopian named Ebedmelech that He would deliver him from judgment. He said, "'For I will surely deliver you, and you shall not fall by the sword; but your life shall be as a prize to you, because you have put your trust in Me,' says the LORD" (Jer. 39:18). This is the message Christians are to deliver. He who keeps his life will lose it, but those who trust in the Lord will be safe on the Day of Judgment. On that Day, the sword of the Word of God will not fall upon him, because it fell on the Savior 2,000 years ago.

governor in the land, and had committed to him men, women, children, and the poorest of the land who had not been carried away captive to Babylon, 8then they came to Gedaliah at Mizpah—Ishmael the son of Nethaniah, Johanan and Jonathan the sons of Kareah, Seraiah the son of Tanhumeth, the sons of Ephai the Netophathite, and Jezaniah[a] the son of a Maachathite, they and their men. 9And Gedaliah the son of Ahikam, the son of Shaphan, took an oath before them and their men, saying, "Do not be afraid to serve the Chaldeans. Dwell in the land and serve the king of Babylon, and it shall be well with you. 10As for me, I will indeed dwell at Mizpah and serve the Chaldeans who come to us. But you, gather wine and summer fruit and oil, put *them* in your vessels, and dwell in your cities that you have taken." 11Likewise, when all the Jews who *were* in Moab, among the Ammonites, in Edom, and who *were* in all the countries, heard that the king of Babylon had left a remnant of Judah, and that he had set over them Gedaliah the son of Ahikam, the son of Shaphan, 12then all the Jews returned out of all places where they had been driven, and came to the land of Judah, to Gedaliah at Mizpah, and gathered wine and summer fruit in abundance.

13Moreover Johanan the son of Kareah and all the captains of the forces that *were* in the fields came to Gedaliah at Mizpah, 14and said to him, "Do you certainly know that Baalis the king of the Ammonites has sent Ishmael the son of Nethaniah to murder you?" But Gedaliah the son of Ahikam did not believe them.

15Then Johanan the son of Kareah spoke secretly to Gedaliah in Mizpah, saying, "Let me go, please, and I will kill Ishmael the son of Nethaniah, and no one will know *it*. Why should he murder you, so that all the Jews who are gathered to you would be scattered, and the remnant in Judah perish?"

16But Gedaliah the son of Ahikam said to Johanan the son of Kareah, "You shall not do this thing, for you speak falsely concerning Ishmael."

Insurrection Against Gedaliah

41 Now it came to pass in the seventh month *that* Ishmael the son of Nethaniah, the son of Elishama, of the royal family and of the officers of the king, came with ten men to Gedaliah the son of Ahikam, at Mizpah. And there they ate bread together in Mizpah. 2Then Ishmael the son of Nethaniah, and the ten men who were with him, arose and struck Gedaliah the son of Ahikam, the son of Shaphan, with the sword, and killed him whom the king of Babylon had made governor over the land. 3Ishmael also struck down all the Jews who were with him, *that is*, with Gedaliah at Mizpah, and the Chaldeans who were found there, the men of war.

4And it happened, on the second day after he had killed Gedaliah, when as yet no one knew *it*, 5that certain men came from Shechem, from Shiloh, and from Samaria, eighty men with their beards shaved and their clothes torn, having cut themselves, with offerings and incense in their hand, to bring *them* to the house of the LORD. 6Now Ishmael the son of Nethaniah went out from Mizpah to meet them, weeping as he went along; and it happened as he met them that he said to them, "Come to Gedaliah the son of Ahikam!" 7So it was, when they came into the midst of the city, that Ishmael the son of Nethaniah killed them *and cast them* into the midst of a pit, he and the men who were with him. 8But ten men were

40:8 [a]Spelled *Jaazaniah* in 2 Kings 25:23

41:8 The Ten Commandments have been put to death by many within the Church. Yet, the Law is the means by which God uncovers the treasures hidden in the field of this world. It is a tutor that brings men to Christ (see Gal. 3:24).

found among them who said to Ishmael, "Do not kill us, for we have treasures of wheat, barley, oil, and honey in the field." So he desisted and did not kill them among their brethren. [9]Now the pit into which Ishmael had cast all the dead bodies of the men whom he had slain, because of Gedaliah, *was* the same one Asa the king had made for fear of Baasha king of Israel. Ishmael the son of Nethaniah filled it with *the* slain. [10]Then Ishmael carried away captive all the rest of the people who *were* in Mizpah, the king's daughters and all the people who remained in Mizpah, whom Nebuzaradan the captain of the guard had committed to Gedaliah the son of Ahikam. And Ishmael the son of Nethaniah carried them away captive and departed to go over to the Ammonites.

[11]But when Johanan the son of Kareah and all the captains of the forces that *were* with him heard of all the evil that Ishmael the son of Nethaniah had done, [12]they took all the men and went to fight with Ishmael the son of Nethaniah; and they found him by the great pool that *is* in Gibeon. [13]So it was, when all the people who *were* with Ishmael saw Johanan the son of Kareah, and all the captains of the forces who *were* with him, that they were glad. [14]Then all the people whom Ishmael had carried away captive from Mizpah turned around and came back, and went to Johanan the son of Kareah. [15]But Ishmael the son of Nethaniah escaped from Johanan with eight men and went to the Ammonites.

[16]Then Johanan the son of Kareah, and all the captains of the forces that were with him, took from Mizpah all the rest of the people whom he had recovered from Ishmael the son of Nethaniah after he had murdered Gedaliah the son of Ahikam—the mighty men of war and the women and the children and the eunuchs, whom he had brought back from Gibeon. [17]And they departed and dwelt in the habitation of Chimham, which is near Bethlehem, as they went on their way to Egypt, [18]because of the Chaldeans; for they were afraid of them, because Ishmael the son of Nethaniah had murdered Gedaliah the son of Ahikam, whom the king of Babylon had made governor in the land.

The Flight to Egypt Forbidden

42 Now all the captains of the forces, Johanan the son of Kareah, Jezaniah the son of Hoshaiah, and all the people, from the least to the greatest, came near [2]and said to Jeremiah the prophet, "Please, let our petition be acceptable to you, and pray for us to the LORD your God, for all this remnant (since we are left *but* a few of many, as you can see), [3]that the LORD your God may show us the way in which we should walk and the thing we should do."

[4]Then Jeremiah the prophet said to them, "I have heard. Indeed, I will pray to the LORD your God according to your words, and it shall be, *that* whatever the LORD answers you, I will declare *it* to you. I will keep nothing back from you."

[5]So they said to Jeremiah, "Let the LORD be a true and faithful witness between us, if we do not do according to everything which the LORD your God sends us by you. [6]Whether *it is* pleasing or displeasing, we will obey the voice of the LORD our God to whom we send you, that it may be well with us when we obey the voice of the LORD our God."

[7]And it happened after ten days that the word of the LORD came to Jeremiah. [8]Then he called Johanan the son of Kareah, all the captains of the forces which *were* with him, and all the people from the

42:5,6 How tragic that, despite the fact that they acknowledged God as a "true and faithful witness," they refused to believe Him (see 43:1–4). Jesus is called the Faithful and True Witness (see Rev. 3:14), but how few believe His words of warning.

least even to the greatest, 9and said to them, "Thus says the LORD, the God of Israel, to whom you sent me to present your petition before Him: 10'If you will still remain in this land, then I will build you and not pull *you* down, and I will plant you and not pluck *you* up. For I relent concerning the disaster that I have brought upon you. 11Do not be afraid of the king of Babylon, of whom you are afraid; do not be afraid of him,' says the LORD, 'for I *am* with you, to save you and deliver you from his hand. 12And I will show you mercy, that he may have mercy on you and cause you to return to your own land.'

13"But if you say, 'We will not dwell in this land,' disobeying the voice of the LORD your God, 14saying, 'No, but we will go to the land of Egypt where we shall see no war, nor hear the sound of the trumpet, nor be hungry for bread, and there we will dwell'— 15Then hear now the word of the LORD, O remnant of Judah! Thus says the LORD of hosts, the God of Israel: 'If you wholly set your faces to enter Egypt, and go to dwell there, 16then it shall be *that* the sword which you feared shall overtake you there in the land of Egypt; the famine of which you were afraid shall follow close after you there *in* Egypt; and there you shall die. 17So shall it be with all the men who set their faces to go to Egypt to dwell there. They shall die by the sword, by famine, and by pestilence. And none of them shall remain or escape from the disaster that I will bring upon them.'

18"For thus says the LORD of hosts, the God of Israel: 'As My anger and My fury have been poured out on the inhabitants of Jerusalem, so will My fury be poured out on you when you enter Egypt. And you shall be an oath, an astonishment, a curse, and a reproach; and you shall see this place no more.'

19"The LORD has said concerning you, O remnant of Judah, 'Do not go to Egypt!' Know certainly that I have admonished you this day. 20For you were hypocrites in your hearts when you sent me to the LORD your God, saying, 'Pray for us to the LORD our God, and according to all that the LORD your God says, so declare to us and we will do *it*.' 21And I have this day declared *it* to you, but you have not obeyed the voice of the LORD your God, or anything which He has sent you by me. 22Now therefore, know certainly that you shall die by the sword, by famine, and by pestilence in the place where you desire to go to dwell."

. . . . . .

For how to witness to Jews, see Rom. 3:1 comment.

. . . . . .

Jeremiah Taken to Egypt

43 Now it happened, when Jeremiah had stopped speaking to all the people all the words of the LORD their God, for which the LORD their God had sent him to them, all these words, 2that Azariah the son of Hoshaiah, Johanan the son of Kareah, and all the proud men spoke, saying to Jeremiah, "You speak falsely! The LORD our God has not sent you to say, 'Do not go to Egypt to dwell there.' 3But Baruch the son of Neriah has set you against us, to deliver us into the hand of the Chaldeans, that they may put us to death or carry us away captive to Babylon." 4So Johanan the son of Kareah, all the captains of the forces, and all the people would not obey the voice of the LORD, to remain in the land of Judah. 5But Johanan the son of Kareah and all the captains of the forces took all the

43:2–4 Some who reject your message will claim that you are not speaking for God and will even twist your motives, calling your good "evil." Pridefully believing that they are okay with God, they will not obey His command to repent. Like Jeremiah, we are to faithfully speak the truth anyway.

remnant of Judah who had returned to
dwell in the land of Judah, from all nations where they had been driven— 6men,
women, children, the king's daughters, and
every person whom Nebuzaradan the captain of the guard had left with Gedaliah
the son of Ahikam, the son of Shaphan,
and Jeremiah the prophet and Baruch the
son of Neriah. 7So they went to the land
of Egypt, for they did not obey the voice
of the LORD. And they went as far as Tahpanhes.

8Then the word of the LORD came to
Jeremiah in Tahpanhes, saying, 9"Take large
stones in your hand, and hide them in
the sight of the men of Judah, in the clay
in the brick courtyard which *is* at the entrance to Pharaoh's house in Tahpanhes;
10and say to them, 'Thus says the LORD of
hosts, the God of Israel: "Behold, I will
send and bring Nebuchadnezzar the king
of Babylon, My servant, and will set his
throne above these stones that I have hidden. And he will spread his royal pavilion
over them. 11When he comes, he shall
strike the land of Egypt *and deliver* to death
those appointed for death, and to captivity
those appointed for captivity, and to the
sword *those appointed* for the sword. 12I[a]
will kindle a fire in the houses of the gods
of Egypt, and he shall burn them and
carry them away captive. And he shall array himself with the land of Egypt, as a
shepherd puts on his garment, and he
shall go out from there in peace. 13He
shall also break the *sacred* pillars of Beth
Shemesh[a] that *are* in the land of Egypt;
and the houses of the gods of the Egyptians he shall burn with fire." ' "

Israelites Will Be Punished in Egypt

44 The word that came to Jeremiah
concerning all the Jews who
dwell in the land of Egypt, who dwell at
Migdol, at Tahpanhes, at Noph,[a] and in
the country of Pathros, saying, 2"Thus
says the LORD of hosts, the God of Israel:
'You have seen all the calamity that I have
brought on Jerusalem and on all the cities
of Judah; and behold, this day they *are* a
desolation, and no one dwells in them,
3because of their wickedness which they
have committed to provoke Me to anger,
in that they went to burn incense *and* to
serve other gods whom they did not know,
they nor you nor your fathers. 4However
I have sent to you all My servants the
prophets, rising early and sending *them*,
saying, "Oh, do not do this abominable
thing that I hate!" 5But they did not listen
or incline their ear to turn from their
wickedness, to burn no incense to other
gods. 6So My fury and My anger were
poured out and kindled in the cities of
Judah and in the streets of Jerusalem; and
they are wasted *and* desolate, as it is this
day.'

7"Now therefore, thus says the LORD,
the God of hosts, the God of Israel: 'Why
do you commit *this* great evil against yourselves, to cut off from you man and woman, child and infant, out of Judah, leaving none to remain, 8in that you provoke
Me to wrath with the works of your
hands, burning incense to other gods in
the land of Egypt where you have gone to
dwell, that you may cut yourselves off
and be a curse and a reproach among all
the nations of the earth? 9Have you forgotten the wickedness of your fathers, the
wickedness of the kings of Judah, the
wickedness of their wives, your own
wickedness, and the wickedness of your
wives, which they committed in the land
of Judah and in the streets of Jerusalem?
10They have not been humbled, to this
day, nor have they feared; they have not
walked in My law or in My statutes that I
set before you and your fathers.'

11"Therefore thus says the LORD of

43:12 [a]Following Masoretic Text and Targum; Septuagint, Syriac, and Vulgate read *He.* 43:13 [a]Literally *House of the Sun,* ancient On; later called Heliopolis 44:1 [a]That is, ancient Memphis

44:10 Here are the traits of the ungodly. See Matt. 5:1–10 for the character of godliness.

hosts, the God of Israel: 'Behold, I will set My face against you for catastrophe and for cutting off all Judah. [12]And I will take the remnant of Judah who have set their faces to go into the land of Egypt to dwell there, and they shall all be consumed *and* fall in the land of Egypt. They shall be consumed by the sword *and* by famine. They shall die, from the least to the greatest, by the sword and by famine; and they shall be an oath, an astonishment, a curse and a reproach! [13]For I will punish those who dwell in the land of Egypt, as I have punished Jerusalem, by the sword, by famine, and by pestilence, [14]so that none of the remnant of Judah who have gone into the land of Egypt to dwell there shall escape or survive, lest they return to the land of Judah, to which they desire to return and dwell. For none shall return except those who escape.' "

[15]Then all the men who knew that their wives had burned incense to other gods, with all the women who stood by, a great multitude, and all the people who dwelt in the land of Egypt, in Pathros, answered Jeremiah, saying: [16]"*As for* the word that you have spoken to us in the name of the LORD, we will not listen to you! [17]But we will certainly do whatever has gone out of our own mouth, to burn incense to the queen of heaven and pour out drink offerings to her, as we have done, we and our fathers, our kings and our princes, in the cities of Judah and in the streets of Jerusalem. For *then* we had plenty of food, were well-off, and saw no trouble. [18]But since we stopped burning incense to the queen of heaven and pouring out drink offerings to her, we have lacked everything and have been consumed by the sword and by famine."

[19]*The women also said,* "And when we burned incense to the queen of heaven and poured out drink offerings to her, did we make cakes for her, to worship her, and pour out drink offerings to her without our husbands' *permission?*"

[20]Then Jeremiah spoke to all the people—the men, the women, and all the people who had given him *that* answer—saying: [21]"The incense that you burned in the cities of Judah and in the streets of Jerusalem, you and your fathers, your kings and your princes, and the people of the land, did not the LORD remember them, and did it *not* come into His mind? [22]So the LORD could no longer bear *it,* because of the evil of your doings *and* because of the abominations which you committed. Therefore your land is a desolation, an astonishment, a curse, and without an inhabitant, as *it is* this day. [23]Because you have burned incense and because you have sinned against the LORD, and have not obeyed the voice of the LORD or walked in His law, in His statutes or in His testimonies, therefore this calamity has happened to you, as *at* this day."

[24]Moreover Jeremiah said to all the people and to all the women, "Hear the word of the LORD, all Judah who *are* in the land of Egypt! [25]Thus says the LORD of hosts, the God of Israel, saying: 'You and your wives have spoken with your mouths and fulfilled with your hands, saying, "We will surely keep our vows that we have made, to burn incense to the queen of heaven and pour out drink offerings to her." You will surely keep your vows and perform your vows!' [26]Therefore hear the word of the LORD, all Judah who dwell in the land of Egypt: 'Behold, I have sworn by My great name,' says the LORD, 'that My name shall no more be named in the mouth of any man of Judah in all the land of Egypt, saying, "The Lord GOD lives." [27]Behold, I will watch over them for adversity and not for good. And all the men of Judah who *are* in the land of Egypt shall be consumed by the sword and by famine, until there is an end to

44:16,17 Rebellion is the essence of sin. The wicked in his proud countenance does not seek God or listen to His voice (see Psa. 10:4).

them. [28]Yet a small number who escape the sword shall return from the land of Egypt to the land of Judah; and all the remnant of Judah, who have gone to the land of Egypt to dwell there, shall know whose words will stand, Mine or theirs. [29]And this *shall be* a sign to you,' says the LORD, 'that I will punish you in this place, that you may know that My words will surely stand against you for adversity.'

[30]"Thus says the LORD: 'Behold, I will give Pharaoh Hophra king of Egypt into the hand of his enemies and into the hand of those who seek his life, as I gave Zedekiah king of Judah into the hand of Nebuchadnezzar king of Babylon, his enemy who sought his life.' "

Assurance to Baruch

45 The word that Jeremiah the prophet spoke to Baruch the son of Neriah, when he had written these words in a book at the instruction of Jeremiah,[a] in the fourth year of Jehoiakim the son of Josiah, king of Judah, saying, [2]"Thus says the LORD, the God of Israel, to you, O Baruch: [3]'You said, "Woe is me now! For the LORD has added grief to my sorrow. I fainted in my sighing, and I find no rest." '

[4]"Thus you shall say to him, 'Thus says the LORD: "Behold, what I have built I will break down, and what I have planted I will pluck up, that is, this whole land. [5]And do you seek great things for yourself? Do not seek *them;* for behold, I will bring adversity on all flesh," says the LORD. "But I will give your life to you as a prize in all places, wherever you go." ' "

Judgment on Egypt

46 The word of the LORD which came to Jeremiah the prophet against the nations. [2]Against Egypt.

Concerning the army of Pharaoh Necho, king of Egypt, which was by the River Euphrates in Carchemish, and which Nebuchadnezzar king of Babylon defeated in the fourth year of Jehoiakim the son of Josiah, king of Judah:

[3]"Order the buckler and shield,
And draw near to battle!
[4]Harness the horses,
And mount up, you horsemen!
Stand forth with *your* helmets,
Polish the spears,
Put on the armor!
[5]Why have I seen them dismayed *and* turned back?
Their mighty ones are beaten down;
They have speedily fled,
And did not look back,
For fear *was* all around," says the LORD.
[6]"Do not let the swift flee away,
Nor the mighty man escape;
They will stumble and fall
Toward the north, by the River Euphrates.

[7]"Who *is* this coming up like a flood,
Whose waters move like the rivers?
[8]Egypt rises up like a flood,
And *its* waters move like the rivers;
And he says, 'I will go up *and* cover the earth,
I will destroy the city and its inhabitants.'
[9]Come up, O horses, and rage, O chariots!
And let the mighty men come forth:
The Ethiopians and the Libyans who handle the shield,
And the Lydians who handle *and* bend the bow.

45:1 [a]Literally *from Jeremiah's mouth*

45:1–5 Baruch played second fiddle to Jeremiah, and God rewarded him for his service. This is the promise that is given to all who serve God through Jesus Christ. Our life is given to us. See Matt. 25:14–30 for the faithfulness that God requires of His own.

46:1 We tend to think that God dealt only with the nation of Israel. But He is intimately familiar with all nations. He is sovereign and can judge whom He will when He wills.

10For this *is* the day of the Lord GOD of hosts,
A day of vengeance,
That He may avenge Himself on His adversaries.
The sword shall devour;
It shall be satiated and made drunk with their blood;
For the Lord GOD of hosts has a sacrifice
In the north country by the River Euphrates.

11"Go up to Gilead and take balm,
O virgin, the daughter of Egypt;
In vain you will use many medicines;
You shall not be cured.
12The nations have heard of your shame,
And your cry has filled the land;
For the mighty man has stumbled against the mighty;
They both have fallen together."

Babylonia Will Strike Egypt

13The word that the LORD spoke to Jeremiah the prophet, how Nebuchadnezzar
king of Babylon would come *and* strike
the land of Egypt.

14"Declare in Egypt, and proclaim in Migdol;
Proclaim in Noph[a] and in Tahpanhes;
Say, 'Stand fast and prepare yourselves,
For the sword devours all around you.'
15Why are your valiant *men* swept away?
They did not stand
Because the LORD drove them away.
16He made many fall;
Yes, one fell upon another.
And they said, 'Arise!
Let us go back to our own people
And to the land of our nativity
From the oppressing sword.'
17They cried there,
'Pharaoh, king of Egypt, *is but* a noise.
He has passed by the appointed time!'

18"*As* I live," says the King,
Whose name *is* the LORD of hosts,
"Surely as Tabor *is* among the mountains
And as Carmel by the sea, *so* he shall come.
19O you daughter dwelling in Egypt,
Prepare yourself to go into captivity!
For Noph[a] shall be waste and desolate, without inhabitant.

20"Egypt *is* a very pretty heifer,
But destruction comes, it comes from the north.
21Also her mercenaries are in her midst like fat bulls,
For they also are turned back,
They have fled away together.
They did not stand,
For the day of their calamity had come upon them,
The time of their punishment.
22Her noise shall go like a serpent,
For they shall march with an army
And come against her with axes,
Like those who chop wood.

23"They shall cut down her forest," says the LORD,
"Though it cannot be searched,
Because they *are* innumerable,
And more numerous than grasshoppers.
24The daughter of Egypt shall be ashamed;
She shall be delivered into the hand
Of the people of the north."

25The LORD of hosts, the God of Israel,
says: "Behold, I will bring punishment on
Amon[a] of No,[b] and Pharaoh and Egypt,
with their gods and their kings—Pharaoh
and those who trust in him. 26And I will
deliver them into the hand of those who
seek their lives, into the hand of Nebuchadnezzar king of Babylon and the hand
of his servants. Afterward it shall be inhabited as in the days of old," says the
LORD.

46:14 [a]That is, ancient Memphis 46:19 [a]That is, ancient Memphis 46:25 [a]A sun god [b]That is, ancient Thebes

God Will Preserve Israel

27"But do not fear, O My servant Jacob,
And do not be dismayed, O Israel!
For behold, I will save you from afar,
And your offspring from the land of their captivity;
Jacob shall return, have rest and be at ease;
No one shall make *him* afraid.
28Do not fear, O Jacob My servant," says the LORD,
"For I *am* with you;
For I will make a complete end of all the nations
To which I have driven you,
But I will not make a complete end of you.
I will rightly correct you,
For I will not leave you wholly unpunished."

Judgment on Philistia

47 The word of the LORD that came to Jeremiah the prophet against the Philistines, before Pharaoh attacked Gaza.
2Thus says the LORD:

"Behold, waters rise out of the north,
And shall be an overflowing flood;
They shall overflow the land and all that is in it,
The city and those who dwell within;
Then the men shall cry,
And all the inhabitants of the land shall wail.
3At the noise of the stamping hooves of his strong horses,
At the rushing of his chariots,
At the rumbling of his wheels,
The fathers will not look back for *their* children,
Lacking courage,
4Because of the day that comes to plunder all the Philistines,
To cut off from Tyre and Sidon every helper who remains;
For the LORD shall plunder the Philistines,
The remnant of the country of Caphtor.
5Baldness has come upon Gaza,
Ashkelon is cut off
With the remnant of their valley.
How long will you cut yourself?

6"O you sword of the LORD,
How long until you are quiet?
Put yourself up into your scabbard,
Rest and be still!
7How can it be quiet,
Seeing the LORD has given it a charge
Against Ashkelon and against the seashore?
There He has appointed it."

Judgment on Moab

48 Against Moab.
Thus says the LORD of hosts, the God of Israel:

"Woe to Nebo!
For it is plundered,
Kirjathaim is shamed *and* taken;
The high stronghold[a] is shamed and dismayed—
2No more praise of Moab.
In Heshbon they have devised evil against her:
'Come, and let us cut her off as a nation.'
You also shall be cut down, O Madmen![a]
The sword shall pursue you;
3A voice of crying *shall be* from Horonaim:
'Plundering and great destruction!'
4"Moab is destroyed;
Her little ones have caused a cry to be heard;[a]

48:1 [a]Hebrew *Misgab* 48:2 [a]A city of Moab 48:4 [a]Following Masoretic Text, Targum, and Vulgate; Septuagint reads *Proclaim it in Zoar.*

47:3 Fathers instinctively protect their children. How great must their fear have been to ignore such God-given intuition.

5For in the Ascent of Luhith they
ascend with continual weeping;
For in the descent of Horonaim the
enemies have heard a cry of
destruction.

6"Flee, save your lives!
And be like the juniper[a] in the
wilderness.
7For because you have trusted in your
works and your treasures,
You also shall be taken.
And Chemosh shall go forth into
captivity,
His priests and his princes together.
8And the plunderer shall come against
every city;
No one shall escape.
The valley also shall perish,
And the plain shall be destroyed,
As the LORD has spoken.

I am a creature of a day, passing through life as an arrow through the air. I am a spirit come from God, and returning to God; just hovering over the great gulf; till a few moments hence, I am no more seen! I drop into an unchangeable eternity!

JOHN WESLEY

9"Give wings to Moab,
That she may flee and get away;
For her cities shall be desolate,
Without any to dwell in them.
10Cursed *is* he who does the work of
the LORD deceitfully,
And cursed *is* he who keeps back his
sword from blood.

11"Moab has been at ease from his[a]
youth;
He has settled on his dregs,
And has not been emptied from
vessel to vessel,
Nor has he gone into captivity.
Therefore his taste remained in him,
And his scent has not changed.

12"Therefore behold, the days are
coming," says the LORD,
"That I shall send him wine-workers
Who will tip him over
And empty his vessels
And break the bottles.
13Moab shall be ashamed of Chemosh,
As the house of Israel was ashamed of
Bethel, their confidence.

14"How can you say, 'We *are* mighty
And strong men for the war'?
15Moab is plundered and gone up *from*
her cities;
Her chosen young men have gone
down to the slaughter," says the
King,
Whose name is the LORD of hosts.

16"The calamity of Moab *is* near at hand,
And his affliction comes quickly.
17Bemoan him, all you who are around
him;
And all you who know his name,
Say, 'How the strong staff is broken,
The beautiful rod!'

18"O daughter inhabiting Dibon,
Come down from *your* glory,
And sit in thirst;
For the plunderer of Moab has come
against you,
He has destroyed your strongholds.
19O inhabitant of Aroer,
Stand by the way and watch;
Ask him who flees
And her who escapes;
Say, 'What has happened?'
20Moab is shamed, for he is broken
down.
Wail and cry!
Tell it in Arnon, that Moab is
plundered.

21"And judgment has come on the plain
country:
On Holon and Jahzah and Mephaath,

48:6 [a]Or *Aroer,* a city of Moab 48:11 [a]The Hebrew uses masculine and feminine pronouns interchangeably in this chapter.

22On Dibon and Nebo and Beth
Diblathaim,
23On Kirjathaim and Beth Gamul and
Beth Meon,
24On Kerioth and Bozrah,
On all the cities of the land of Moab,
Far or near.
25The horn of Moab is cut off,
And his arm is broken," says the LORD.

26"Make him drunk,
Because he exalted *himself* against the
LORD.
Moab shall wallow in his vomit,
And he shall also be in derision.
27For was not Israel a derision to you?
Was he found among thieves?
For whenever you speak of him,
You shake *your head in scorn.*
28You who dwell in Moab,
Leave the cities and dwell in the rock,
And be like the dove *which* makes her
nest
In the sides of the cave's mouth.

29"We have heard the pride of Moab
(He *is* exceedingly proud),
Of his loftiness and arrogance and
pride,
And of the haughtiness of his heart."

30"I know his wrath," says the LORD,
"But it *is* not right;
His lies have made nothing right.
31Therefore I will wail for Moab,
And I will cry out for all Moab;
I[a] will mourn for the men of Kir Heres.
32O vine of Sibmah! I will weep for you
with the weeping of Jazer.
Your plants have gone over the sea,
They reach to the sea of Jazer.
The plunderer has fallen on your
summer fruit and your vintage.
33Joy and gladness are taken
From the plentiful field
And from the land of Moab;
I have caused wine to fail from the
winepresses;
No one will tread with joyous
shouting—
Not joyous shouting!

34"From the cry of Heshbon to Elealeh
and to Jahaz
They have uttered their voice,
From Zoar to Horonaim,
Like a three-year-old heifer;[a]
For the waters of Nimrim also shall
be desolate.

35"Moreover," says the LORD,
"I will cause to cease in Moab
The one who offers *sacrifices* in the
high places
And burns incense to his gods.
36Therefore My heart shall wail like
flutes for Moab,
And like flutes My heart shall wail
For the men of Kir Heres.
Therefore the riches they have
acquired have perished.

37"For every head *shall be* bald, and
every beard clipped;
On all the hands *shall be* cuts, and on
the loins sackcloth—
38A general lamentation
On all the housetops of Moab,
And in its streets;
For I have broken Moab like a vessel
in which *is* no pleasure," says the
LORD.
39"They shall wail:
'How she is broken down!
How Moab has turned her back with
shame!'
So Moab shall be a derision

48:31 [a]Following Dead Sea Scrolls, Septuagint, and Vulgate; Masoretic Text reads *He.* 48:34 [a]Or *The Third Eglath,* an unknown city (compare Isaiah 15:5)

48:27 Christianity is an object of disdain for the proud of heart. They shake their heads in contempt for our naiveté in believing such obvious myths. Yet, they will give an account for every idle word to Him who judges righteously. What a fearful thing.

And a dismay to all those about her."
[40]For thus says the LORD:

"Behold, one shall fly like an eagle,
And spread his wings over Moab.
[41]Kerioth is taken,
And the strongholds are surprised;
The mighty men's hearts in Moab on that day shall be
Like the heart of a woman in birth pangs.
[42]And Moab shall be destroyed as a people,
Because he exalted *himself* against the LORD.
[43]Fear and the pit and the snare *shall be* upon you,
O inhabitant of Moab," says the LORD.
[44]"He who flees from the fear shall fall into the pit,
And he who gets out of the pit shall be caught in the snare.
For upon Moab, upon it I will bring
The year of their punishment," says the LORD.

[45]"Those who fled stood under the shadow of Heshbon
Because of exhaustion.
But a fire shall come out of Heshbon,
A flame from the midst of Sihon,
And shall devour the brow of Moab,
The crown of the head of the sons of tumult.
[46]Woe to you, O Moab!
The people of Chemosh perish;
For your sons have been taken captive,
And your daughters captive.

[47]"Yet I will bring back the captives of Moab
In the latter days," says the LORD.

Thus far is the judgment of Moab.

Judgment on Ammon

49 Against the Ammonites.
Thus says the LORD:

"Has Israel no sons?
Has he no heir?
Why *then* does Milcom[a] inherit Gad,
And his people dwell in its cities?
[2]Therefore behold, the days are coming," says the LORD,
"That I will cause to be heard an alarm of war
In Rabbah of the Ammonites;
It shall be a desolate mound,
And her villages shall be burned with fire.
Then Israel shall take possession of his inheritance," says the LORD.

[3]"Wail, O Heshbon, for Ai is plundered!
Cry, you daughters of Rabbah,
Gird yourselves with sackcloth!
Lament and run to and fro by the walls;
For Milcom shall go into captivity
With his priests and his princes together.
[4]Why do you boast in the valleys,
Your flowing valley, O backsliding daughter?
Who trusted in her treasures, *saying,*
'Who will come against me?'
[5]Behold, I will bring fear upon you,"
Says the Lord GOD of hosts,
"From all those who are around you;
You shall be driven out, everyone headlong,
And no one will gather those who wander off.
[6]But afterward I will bring back
The captives of the people of Ammon," says the LORD.

Judgment on Edom

[7]Against Edom.
Thus says the LORD of hosts:

"*Is* wisdom no more in Teman?
Has counsel perished from the prudent?
Has their wisdom vanished?

49:1 [a]Hebrew *Malcam,* literally *their king,* a god of the Ammonites; also called *Molech* (compare verse 3)

[8]Flee, turn back, dwell in the depths,
O inhabitants of Dedan!
For I will bring the calamity of Esau
upon him,
The time *that* I will punish him.
[9]If grape-gatherers came to you,
Would they not leave *some* gleaning
grapes?
If thieves by night,
Would they not destroy until they
have enough?
[10]But I have made Esau bare;
I have uncovered his secret places,[a]
And he shall not be able to hide
himself.
His descendants are plundered,
His brethren and his neighbors,
And he *is* no more.
[11]Leave your fatherless children,
I will preserve *them* alive;
And let your widows trust in Me."

. . . . . .

Is "hell-fire" preaching effective?
See Acts 24:25 comment.

. . . . . .

[12]For thus says the LORD: "Behold, those
whose judgment *was* not to drink of the
cup have assuredly drunk. And *are* you
the one who will altogether go unpunished? You shall not go unpunished, but
you shall surely drink *of it.* [13]For I have
sworn by Myself," says the LORD, "that
Bozrah shall become a desolation, a reproach, a waste, and a curse. And all its
cities shall be perpetual wastes."

[14]I have heard a message from the
LORD,
And an ambassador has been sent to
the nations:
"Gather together, come against her,
And rise up to battle!

[15]"For indeed, I will make you small
among nations,
Despised among men.
[16]Your fierceness has deceived you,
The pride of your heart,
O you who dwell in the clefts of the
rock,
Who hold the height of the hill!
Though you make your nest as high
as the eagle,
I will bring you down from there,"
says the LORD.[a]

[17]"Edom also shall be an astonishment;
Everyone who goes by it will be
astonished
And will hiss at all its plagues.
[18]As in the overthrow of Sodom and
Gomorrah
And their neighbors," says the LORD,
"No one shall remain there,
Nor shall a son of man dwell in it.

[19]"Behold, he shall come up like a lion
from the floodplain[a] of the
Jordan
Against the dwelling place of the
strong;
But I will suddenly make him run
away from her.
And who *is* a chosen *man that* I may
appoint over her?
For who *is* like Me?
Who will arraign Me?
And who *is* that shepherd
Who will withstand Me?"

[20]Therefore hear the counsel of the
LORD that He has taken against
Edom,
And His purposes that He has
proposed against the inhabitants
of Teman:
Surely the least of the flock shall draw
them out;
Surely He shall make their dwelling
places desolate with them.
[21]The earth shakes at the noise of their
fall;
At the cry its noise is heard at the Red
Sea.
[22]Behold, He shall come up and fly like

49:10 [a]Compare Obadiah 5, 6 **49:16** [a]Compare Obadiah 3, 4
49:19 [a]Or *thicket*

the eagle,
And spread His wings over Bozrah;
The heart of the mighty men of Edom
in that day shall be
Like the heart of a woman in birth
pangs.

Judgment on Damascus

23Against Damascus.

"Hamath and Arpad are shamed,
For they have heard bad news.
They are fainthearted;
There is trouble on the sea;
It cannot be quiet.
24Damascus has grown feeble;
She turns to flee,
And fear has seized *her.*
Anguish and sorrows have taken her
like a woman in labor.
25Why is the city of praise not deserted,
the city of My joy?
26Therefore her young men shall fall in
her streets,
And all the men of war shall be cut
off in that day," says the LORD of
hosts.
27"I will kindle a fire in the wall of
Damascus,
And it shall consume the palaces of
Ben-Hadad."[a]

Judgment on Kedar and Hazor

28Against Kedar and against the kingdoms of Hazor, which Nebuchadnezzar
king of Babylon shall strike.
Thus says the LORD:

"Arise, go up to Kedar,
And devastate the men of the East!
29Their tents and their flocks they shall
take away.
They shall take for themselves their
curtains,
All their vessels and their camels;
And they shall cry out to them,
'Fear is on every side!'

30"Flee, get far away! Dwell in the
depths,
O inhabitants of Hazor!" says the LORD.
"For Nebuchadnezzar king of Babylon
has taken counsel against you,
And has conceived a plan against you.

31"Arise, go up to the wealthy nation
that dwells securely," says the
LORD,
"Which has neither gates nor bars,
Dwelling alone.
32Their camels shall be for booty,
And the multitude of their cattle for
plunder.
I will scatter to all winds those in the
farthest corners,
And I will bring their calamity from
all its sides," says the LORD.
33"Hazor shall be a dwelling for jackals,
a desolation forever;
No one shall reside there,
Nor son of man dwell in it."

Judgment on Elam

34The word of the LORD that came to
Jeremiah the prophet against Elam, in the
beginning of the reign of Zedekiah king
of Judah, saying, 35"Thus says the LORD of
hosts:

'Behold, I will break the bow of Elam,
The foremost of their might.
36Against Elam I will bring the four
winds
From the four quarters of heaven,
And scatter them toward all those
winds;
There shall be no nations where the
outcasts of Elam will not go.
37For I will cause Elam to be dismayed
before their enemies
And before those who seek their life.
I will bring disaster upon them,
My fierce anger,' says the LORD;
'And I will send the sword after them
Until I have consumed them.
38I will set My throne in Elam,
And will destroy from there the king
and the princes,' says the LORD.

49:27 [a]Compare Amos 1:4

39"But it shall come to pass in the
latter days:
I will bring back the captives of
Elam,' says the LORD."

Judgment on Babylon and Babylonia

50 The word that the LORD spoke against Babylon *and* against the land of the Chaldeans by Jeremiah the prophet.

2"Declare among the nations,
Proclaim, and set up a standard;
Proclaim—do not conceal *it*—
Say, 'Babylon is taken, Bel is shamed.
Merodach[a] is broken in pieces;
Her idols are humiliated,
Her images are broken in pieces.'
3For out of the north a nation comes
up against her,
Which shall make her land desolate,
And no one shall dwell therein.
They shall move, they shall depart,
Both man and beast.

4"In those days and in that time," says
the LORD,
"The children of Israel shall come,
They and the children of Judah
together;
With continual weeping they shall
come,
And seek the LORD their God.
5They shall ask the way to Zion,
With their faces toward it, *saying*,
'Come and let us join ourselves to the
LORD
In a perpetual covenant
That will not be forgotten.'

6"My people have been lost sheep.
Their shepherds have led them astray;
They have turned them away *on* the
mountains.
They have gone from mountain to hill;
They have forgotten their resting place.
7All who found them have devoured
them;
And their adversaries said, 'We have
not offended,
Because they have sinned against the
LORD, the habitation of justice,
The LORD, the hope of their fathers.'

8"Move from the midst of Babylon,
Go out of the land of the Chaldeans;
And be like the rams before the
flocks.
9For behold, I will raise and cause to
come up against Babylon
An assembly of great nations from the
north country,
And they shall array themselves
against her;
From there she shall be captured.
Their arrows *shall be* like *those* of an
expert warrior;[a]
None shall return in vain.
10And Chaldea shall become plunder;
All who plunder her shall be
satisfied," says the LORD.

11"Because you were glad, because you
rejoiced,
You destroyers of My heritage,
Because you have grown fat like a
heifer threshing grain,
And you bellow like bulls,
12Your mother shall be deeply ashamed;
She who bore you shall be ashamed.

50:2 [a]A Babylonian god; sometimes spelled *Marduk* 50:9 [a]Following some Hebrew manuscripts, Septuagint, and Syriac; Masoretic Text, Targum, and Vulgate read *a warrior who makes childless.*

49:39 After being destroyed as a nation, they were restored in recent years under the name Khuzistan (a province in Iran). It is in the southwest portion of the country, bordering Iraq and the Persian Gulf. Elamites were among those present to hear the gospel on the Day of Pentecost.

50:4–7 How different things would have been if God's people had been faithful to Him. He set before them the way of life and the way of death (21:8; Deut. 30:15,19). He told them to choose which they would have. He spoke to them of incredible blessings if they would obey His voice, and warned them of terrible curses for rebellion (see Deut. 28).

50:7 The Old Story

It is clear from Scripture that a genuine convert is one who hears and "understands" (see Matt. 13:23). Perhaps this is why Philip the evangelist asked the Ethiopian eunuch if he *understood* what he was reading (Acts 8:30). This understanding seems to refer not only to sin, but also to the gospel. In the Parable of the Sower, the enemy is able to snatch the good seed from the wayside hearer because he lacks understanding. He doesn't *understand* that it is the message of everlasting life, so he gives it no value: "When anyone hears the word of the kingdom, and does not understand it, then the wicked one comes and snatches away what was sown in his heart" (Matt. 13:19).

My great desire is for sinners to *understand* the gospel and be saved. Although God alone saves the sinner, from the sowing to the reaping, I believe that, as a preacher of the gospel, my job is to strive (with the help of God) to bring about "understanding." So rather than using "enticing words of man's wisdom" (1 Cor. 2:4), I keep the message simple in the hope that the sinner will grasp what I am trying to say.

My gospel presentation may begin with a parable about a man stealing another man's lamb (as with Nathan and David), or with a quote by Athenian poets (as with Paul when he preached in Athens). I may use metaphors, similes, statistics, quotes, personal experiences, and of course I present the Law, the gospel, and the necessity of repentance and faith.

Incorporating the Law into the gospel presentation does many things. It primarily brings the knowledge of sin (see Rom. 7:7), showing the sinner that he is a criminal and that God is his Judge. The Law (in the hand of the Holy Spirit) stops his mouth of justification and leaves him guilty before God (see Rom. 3:19,20). It reveals that he deserves nothing but judgment for his crimes. Like a faithful prosecutor, the Law of God points its accusing finger, and so the sinner's stirred conscience bears witness and likewise points its finger at the criminal (see Rom. 2:15). The verdict is "guilty," and the condemnation is just. I do my best to put him in the courtroom on the Day of Judgment, with the hope that he will understand the mercy that God offers him in Christ.

I may equate repentance to a criminal who becomes law-abiding and shows his sincerity by returning stolen goods. I perhaps will explain saving faith by differentiating it from an intellectual belief, and likening it to *trusting* a pilot or a parachute. I speak of the cross by explaining that it's like a civil judge paying a criminal's fine, thus satisfying the law and at the same time extending mercy. All these things are aimed at (with the help of God) bringing *understanding* to the sinner. If he doesn't understand the gospel, he won't value it and seek the Savior.

I then explain, "It was a *legal* transaction. You broke God's Law (the Ten Commandments), and Jesus paid your fine in His life's blood. That means that God can *legally* dismiss your case. You can leave the courtroom on the Day of Judgment because your fine has been paid. *Does that make sense?*"

Again and again, I can see the light go on in the eyes of my hearers. Many suddenly understood the gospel when I explained it that way. While this is certainly not a magic formula, and I can't point to a Bible verse that uses this exact language, I can say that legality is the essence of the cross. It was God's love for justice, and for guilty sinners, that drove Him to Calvary.

Man is unique among God's creation. He is forensic by nature. He intuitively understands the principles of law, retribution, justice, and mercy, because he is made in the image of God. That's why every civilization sets up court systems and why the moral Law resonates with a sinner's conscience. Scripture tells us that all mankind has "the work of the law written in their hearts, their conscience also bearing witness, and between themselves their thoughts accusing or else excusing them" (Rom. 2:15). So when Paul uses the Law to bring the knowledge of sin to his hearers, he knows that it will find reverberation in their hearts:

> You, therefore, who teach another, do you not teach yourself? You who preach that a man should not steal, do you steal? You who say, "Do not commit adultery," do you commit adultery? You who abhor idols, do you rob temples? You who make your boast in the law, do you dishonor God through breaking the law? For "the name of God is blasphemed among the Gentiles because of you," as it is written. (Rom. 2:21–24)

God is the "habitation of justice" (see Jer. 50:7). We are guilty criminals. Our fine has been paid, and upon our repentance and faith in Jesus, we can leave the courtroom. Carefully explaining the gospel message, using legal vernacular to those whose understanding is "darkened," sheds new light on what they perceived to be just an old and irrelevant story.

Behold, the least of the nations *shall*
be a wilderness,
A dry land and a desert.
13 Because of the wrath of the LORD
She shall not be inhabited,
But she shall be wholly desolate.
Everyone who goes by Babylon shall
be horrified
And hiss at all her plagues.

14 "Put yourselves in array against
Babylon all around,
All you who bend the bow;
Shoot at her, spare no arrows,
For she has sinned against the LORD.
15 Shout against her all around;
She has given her hand,
Her foundations have fallen,
Her walls are thrown down;
For it *is* the vengeance of the LORD.
Take vengeance on her.
As she has done, so do to her.
16 Cut off the sower from Babylon,
And him who handles the sickle at
harvest time.
For fear of the oppressing sword
Everyone shall turn to his own
people,
And everyone shall flee to his own
land.

17 "Israel *is* like scattered sheep;
The lions have driven *him* away.
First the king of Assyria devoured him;
Now at last this Nebuchadnezzar king
of Babylon has broken his bones."

18 Therefore thus says the LORD of hosts,
the God of Israel:

"Behold, I will punish the king of
Babylon and his land,
As I have punished the king of Assyria.
19 But I will bring back Israel to his
home,
And he shall feed on Carmel and
Bashan;
His soul shall be satisfied on Mount
Ephraim and Gilead.
20 In those days and in that time," says
the LORD,
"The iniquity of Israel shall be sought,
but *there shall be* none;
And the sins of Judah, but they shall
not be found;
For I will pardon those whom I
preserve.

21 "Go up against the land of Merathaim,
against it,
And against the inhabitants of Pekod.
Waste and utterly destroy them," says
the LORD,
"And do according to all that I have
commanded you.
22 A sound of battle is in the land,
And of great destruction.
23 How the hammer of the whole earth
has been cut apart and broken!
How Babylon has become a
desolation among the nations!
24 I have laid a snare for you;
You have indeed been trapped, O
Babylon,
And you were not aware;
You have been found and also caught,
Because you have contended against
the LORD.
25 The LORD has opened His armory,
And has brought out the weapons of
His indignation;
For this *is* the work of the Lord GOD
of hosts
In the land of the Chaldeans.
26 Come against her from the farthest
border;
Open her storehouses;
Cast her up as heaps of ruins,
And destroy her utterly;
Let nothing of her be left.
27 Slay all her bulls,
Let them go down to the slaughter.
Woe to them!
For their day has come, the time of
their punishment.
28 The voice of those who flee and
escape from the land of Babylon
Declares in Zion the vengeance of the
LORD our God,
The vengeance of His temple.

29"Call together the archers against
Babylon.
All you who bend the bow, encamp
against it all around;
Let none of them escape.[a]
Repay her according to her work;
According to all she has done, do to
her;
For she has been proud against the
LORD,
Against the Holy One of Israel.
30Therefore her young men shall fall in
the streets,
And all her men of war shall be cut
off in that day," says the LORD.
31"Behold, I *am* against you,
O most haughty one!" says the Lord
GOD of hosts;
"For your day has come,
The time *that* I will punish you.[a]
32The most proud shall stumble and
fall,
And no one will raise him up;
I will kindle a fire in his cities,
And it will devour all around him."

33Thus says the LORD of hosts:

"The children of Israel *were* oppressed,
Along with the children of Judah;
All who took them captive have held
them fast;
They have refused to let them go.
34Their Redeemer *is* strong;
The LORD of hosts *is* His name.
He will thoroughly plead their case,
That He may give rest to the land,
And disquiet the inhabitants of
Babylon.

35"A sword *is* against the Chaldeans,"
says the LORD,
"Against the inhabitants of Babylon,
And against her princes and her wise
men.
36A sword *is* against the soothsayers,
and they will be fools.
A sword *is* against her mighty men,
and they will be dismayed.
37A sword *is* against their horses,
Against their chariots,
And against all the mixed peoples
who *are* in her midst;
And they will become like women.
A sword *is* against her treasures, and
they will be robbed.
38A drought[a] *is* against her waters, and
they will be dried up.
For it *is* the land of carved images,
And they are insane with *their* idols.

I value all things only by the price they shall gain in eternity.

JOHN WESLEY

39"Therefore the wild desert beasts shall
dwell *there* with the jackals,
And the ostriches shall dwell in it.
It shall be inhabited no more forever,
Nor shall it be dwelt in from
generation to generation.
40As God overthrew Sodom and
Gomorrah
And their neighbors," says the LORD,
"*So* no one shall reside there,
Nor son of man dwell in it.

41"Behold, a people shall come from the
north,
And a great nation and many kings
Shall be raised up from the ends of
the earth.
42They shall hold the bow and the
lance;
They *are* cruel and shall not show
mercy.
Their voice shall roar like the sea;
They shall ride on horses,
Set in array, like a man for the battle,
Against you, O daughter of Babylon.

43"The king of Babylon has heard the

50:29 [a]Qere, some Hebrew manuscripts, Septuagint, and Targum add *to her*. **50:31** [a]Following Masoretic Text and Targum; Septuagint and Vulgate read *The time of your punishment.* **50:38** [a]Following Masoretic Text, Targum, and Vulgate; Syriac reads *sword;* Septuagint omits *A drought is.*

report about them,
And his hands grow feeble;
Anguish has taken hold of him,
Pangs as of a woman in childbirth.

44"Behold, he shall come up like a lion
from the floodplain[a] of the
Jordan
Against the dwelling place of the
strong;
But I will make them suddenly run
away from her.
And who *is* a chosen *man that* I may
appoint over her?
For who *is* like Me?
Who will arraign Me?
And who *is* that shepherd
Who will withstand Me?"

45Therefore hear the counsel of the
LORD that He has taken against
Babylon,
And His purposes that He has
proposed against the land of the
Chaldeans:
Surely the least of the flock shall draw
them out;
Surely He will make their dwelling
place desolate with them.
46At the noise of the taking of Babylon
The earth trembles,
And the cry is heard among the nations.

The Utter Destruction of Babylon

51 Thus says the LORD:

"Behold, I will raise up against Babylon,
Against those who dwell in Leb Kamai,[a]
A destroying wind.
2And I will send winnowers to
Babylon,
Who shall winnow her and empty her
land.
For in the day of doom
They shall be against her all around.
3Against *her* let the archer bend his
bow,
And lift himself up against *her* in his
armor.
Do not spare her young men;
Utterly destroy all her army.
4Thus the slain shall fall in the land of
the Chaldeans,
And *those* thrust through in her
streets.
5For Israel is not forsaken, nor Judah,
By his God, the LORD of hosts,
Though their land was filled with sin
against the Holy One of Israel."

6Flee from the midst of Babylon,
And every one save his life!
Do not be cut off in her iniquity,
For this *is* the time of the LORD's
vengeance;
He shall recompense her.
7Babylon *was* a golden cup in the
LORD's hand,
That made all the earth drunk.
The nations drank her wine;
Therefore the nations are deranged.
8Babylon has suddenly fallen and been
destroyed.
Wail for her!
Take balm for her pain;
Perhaps she may be healed.

9We would have healed Babylon,
But she is not healed.
Forsake her, and let us go everyone to
his own country;
For her judgment reaches to heaven
and is lifted up to the skies.
10The LORD has revealed our
righteousness.
Come and let us declare in Zion the
work of the LORD our God.

11Make the arrows bright!
Gather the shields!
The LORD has raised up the spirit of
the kings of the Medes.
For His plan *is* against Babylon to
destroy it,
Because it *is* the vengeance of the
LORD,
The vengeance for His temple.

50:44 [a]Or *thicket* **51:1** [a]A code word for Chaldea (Babylonia); may be translated *The Midst of Those Who Rise Up Against Me*

[12]Set up the standard on the walls of
Babylon;
Make the guard strong,
Set up the watchmen,
Prepare the ambushes.
For the LORD has both devised and
done
What He spoke against the
inhabitants of Babylon.
[13]O you who dwell by many waters,
Abundant in treasures,
Your end has come,
The measure of your covetousness.
[14]The LORD of hosts has sworn by
Himself:
"Surely I will fill you with men, as
with locusts,
And they shall lift up a shout against
you."

[15]He has made the earth by His power;
He has established the world by His
wisdom,
And stretched out the heaven by His
understanding.
[16]When He utters *His* voice—
There is a multitude of waters in the
heavens:
"He causes the vapors to ascend from
the ends of the earth;
He makes lightnings for the rain;
He brings the wind out of His
treasuries."[a]

[17]Everyone is dull-hearted, without
knowledge;
Every metalsmith is put to shame by
the carved image;
For his molded image *is* falsehood,
And *there is* no breath in them.
[18]They *are* futile, a work of errors;
In the time of their punishment they
shall perish.
[19]The Portion of Jacob *is* not like them,
For He *is* the Maker of all things;
And *Israel is* the tribe of His
inheritance.
The LORD of hosts is His name.

[20]"You *are* My battle-ax *and* weapons of
war:
For with you I will break the nation
in pieces;
With you I will destroy kingdoms;
[21]With you I will break in pieces the
horse and its rider;
With you I will break in pieces the
chariot and its rider;
[22]With you also I will break in pieces
man and woman;
With you I will break in pieces old
and young;
With you I will break in pieces the
young man and the maiden;
[23]With you also I will break in pieces
the shepherd and his flock;
With you I will break in pieces the
farmer and his yoke of oxen;
And with you I will break in pieces
governors and rulers.

[24]"And I will repay Babylon
And all the inhabitants of Chaldea
For all the evil they have done
In Zion in your sight," says the LORD.

[25]"Behold, I *am* against you, O
destroying mountain,
Who destroys all the earth," says the
LORD.

51:16 [a]Psalm 135:7

51:15–17 God made all things with the utterance of His voice. He spoke creation into existence by His Word. Then this same "Word" became flesh and dwelt among us (see John 1:1–3). How incredible.

Max Planck, the father of Quantum Mechanics and Nobel Prize winner in physics, stated, "As a man who has devoted his whole life to the most clear-headed science, to the study of matter, I can tell you as a result of my research about atoms this much: There is no matter as such. All matter originates and exists only by virtue of a force which brings the particle of an atom to vibration and holds this most minute solar system of the atom together. We must assume behind this force the existence of a conscious and intelligent mind. This mind is the matrix of all matter."

"And I will stretch out My hand
against you,
Roll you down from the rocks,
And make you a burnt mountain.
26They shall not take from you a stone
for a corner
Nor a stone for a foundation,
But you shall be desolate forever,"
says the LORD.

27Set up a banner in the land,
Blow the trumpet among the nations!
Prepare the nations against her,
Call the kingdoms together against her:
Ararat, Minni, and Ashkenaz.
Appoint a general against her;
Cause the horses to come up like the
bristling locusts.
28Prepare against her the nations,
With the kings of the Medes,
Its governors and all its rulers,
All the land of his dominion.
29And the land will tremble and sorrow;
For every purpose of the LORD shall
be performed against Babylon,
To make the land of Babylon a
desolation without inhabitant.
30The mighty men of Babylon have
ceased fighting,
They have remained in their
strongholds;
Their might has failed,
They became *like* women;
They have burned her dwelling places,
The bars of her *gate* are broken.
31One runner will run to meet another,
And one messenger to meet another,
To show the king of Babylon that his
city is taken on *all* sides;
32The passages are blocked,
The reeds they have burned with fire,
And the men of war are terrified.

33For thus says the LORD of hosts, the
God of Israel:

"The daughter of Babylon *is* like a
threshing floor
When it is time to thresh her;
Yet a little while
And the time of her harvest will come."

34"Nebuchadnezzar the king of Babylon
Has devoured me, he has crushed me;
He has made me an empty vessel,
He has swallowed me up like a
monster;
He has filled his stomach with my
delicacies,
He has spit me out.
35Let the violence *done* to me and my
flesh *be* upon Babylon,"
The inhabitant of Zion will say;
"And my blood be upon the
inhabitants of Chaldea!"
Jerusalem will say.

36Therefore thus says the LORD:

"Behold, I will plead your case and
take vengeance for you.
I will dry up her sea and make her
springs dry.
37Babylon shall become a heap,
A dwelling place for jackals,
An astonishment and a hissing,
Without an inhabitant.
38They shall roar together like lions,
They shall growl like lions' whelps.
39In their excitement I will prepare
their feasts;
I will make them drunk,
That they may rejoice,
And sleep a perpetual sleep
And not awake," says the LORD.
40"I will bring them down
Like lambs to the slaughter,
Like rams with male goats.

41"Oh, how Sheshach[a] is taken!
Oh, how the praise of the whole earth
is seized!
How Babylon has become desolate
among the nations!
42The sea has come up over Babylon;
She is covered with the multitude of
its waves.
43Her cities are a desolation,

51:41 [a]A code word for Babylon (compare Jeremiah 25:26)

A dry land and a wilderness,
A land where no one dwells,
Through which no son of man passes.
44 I will punish Bel in Babylon,
And I will bring out of his mouth
what he has swallowed;
And the nations shall not stream to
him anymore.
Yes, the wall of Babylon shall fall.

45 "My people, go out of the midst of her!
And let everyone deliver himself from
the fierce anger of the LORD.
46 And lest your heart faint,
And you fear for the rumor that *will
be* heard in the land
(A rumor will come *one* year,
And after that, in *another* year
A rumor *will come,*
And violence in the land,
Ruler against ruler),
47 Therefore behold, the days are coming
That I will bring judgment on the
carved images of Babylon;
Her whole land shall be ashamed,
And all her slain shall fall in her midst.
48 Then the heavens and the earth and
all that *is* in them
Shall sing joyously over Babylon;
For the plunderers shall come to her
from the north," says the LORD.

49 As Babylon *has caused* the slain of
Israel to fall,
So at Babylon the slain of all the earth
shall fall.
50 You who have escaped the sword,
Get away! Do not stand still!
Remember the LORD afar off,
And let Jerusalem come to your mind.

51 We are ashamed because we have
heard reproach.
Shame has covered our faces,
For strangers have come into the
sanctuaries of the LORD's house.

52 "Therefore behold, the days are
coming," says the LORD,
"That I will bring judgment on her
carved images,
And throughout all her land the
wounded shall groan.
53 Though Babylon were to mount up to
heaven,
And though she were to fortify the
height of her strength,
Yet from Me plunderers would come
to her," says the LORD.

The church needs to get back to the real task to which we are called: evangelizing the lost. Only when multitudes of individuals in our society turn to Christ will society itself experience any significant transformation.

JOHN MACARTHUR

54 The sound of a cry *comes* from
Babylon,
And great destruction from the land
of the Chaldeans,
55 Because the LORD is plundering
Babylon
And silencing her loud voice,
Though her waves roar like great
waters,
And the noise of their voice is uttered,
56 Because the plunderer comes against
her, against Babylon,
And her mighty men are taken.
Every one of their bows is broken;
For the LORD *is* the God of
recompense,
He will surely repay.

57 "And I will make drunk
Her princes and wise men,
Her governors, her deputies, and her
mighty men.
And they shall sleep a perpetual sleep
And not awake," says the King,
Whose name *is* the LORD of hosts.

58 Thus says the LORD of hosts:

"The broad walls of Babylon shall be
utterly broken,

And her high gates shall be burned
with fire;
The people will labor in vain,
And the nations, because of the fire;
And they shall be weary."

Jeremiah's Command to Seraiah

59 The word which Jeremiah the prophet commanded Seraiah the son of Neriah, the son of Mahseiah, when he went with Zedekiah the king of Judah to Babylon in the fourth year of his reign. And Seraiah *was* the quartermaster. 60 So Jeremiah wrote in a book all the evil that would come upon Babylon, all these words that are written against Babylon. 61 And Jeremiah said to Seraiah, "When you arrive in Babylon and see it, and read all these words, 62 then you shall say, 'O LORD, You have spoken against this place to cut it off, so that none shall remain in it, neither man nor beast, but it shall be desolate forever.' 63 Now it shall be, when you have finished reading this book, *that* you shall tie a stone to it and throw it out into the Euphrates. 64 Then you shall say, 'Thus Babylon shall sink and not rise from the catastrophe that I will bring upon her. And they shall be weary.' "

Thus far *are* the words of Jeremiah.

The Fall of Jerusalem Reviewed

52 Zedekiah *was* twenty-one years old when he became king, and he reigned eleven years in Jerusalem. His mother's name *was* Hamutal the daughter of Jeremiah of Libnah. 2 He also did evil in the sight of the LORD, according to all that Jehoiakim had done. 3 For because of the anger of the LORD *this* happened in Jerusalem and Judah, till He finally cast them out from His presence. Then Zedekiah rebelled against the king of Babylon.

4 Now it came to pass in the ninth year of his reign, in the tenth month, on the tenth *day* of the month, *that* Nebuchadnezzar king of Babylon and all his army came against Jerusalem and encamped against it; and *they* built a siege wall against it all around. 5 So the city was besieged until the eleventh year of King Zedekiah. 6 By the fourth month, on the ninth day of the month, the famine had become so severe in the city that there was no food for the people of the land. 7 Then the city *wall* was broken through, and all the men of war fled and went out of the city at night by way of the gate between the two walls, which *was* by the king's garden, even though the Chaldeans *were* near the city all around. And they went by way of the plain.[a]

8 But the army of the Chaldeans pursued the king, and they overtook Zedekiah in the plains of Jericho. All his army was scattered from him. 9 So they took the king and brought him up to the king of Babylon at Riblah in the land of Hamath, and he pronounced judgment on him. 10 Then the king of Babylon killed the sons of Zedekiah before his eyes. And he killed all the princes of Judah in Riblah. 11 He also put out the eyes of Zedekiah; and the king of Babylon bound him in bronze fetters, took him to Babylon, and put him in prison till the day of his death.

The Temple and City Plundered and Burned

12 Now in the fifth month, on the tenth *day* of the month (which *was* the nineteenth year of King Nebuchadnezzar king of Babylon), Nebuzaradan, the captain of the guard, *who* served the king of Babylon, came to Jerusalem. 13 He burned the house of the LORD and the king's house;

52:7 [a]Or *the Arabah,* that is, the Jordan Valley

52:10,11 How unspeakably terrible for the king to have to witness the death of his beloved sons. How terrible it is for the ungodly to see their children die at the hands of the enemy who came to steal, kill, and destroy—through drug or alcohol abuse, AIDS, or suicide due to guilt or hopelessness—because they refused to surrender to the Lord. The sins of the parents are often passed on to the children, who often pick up the same destructive behaviors.

all the houses of Jerusalem, that is, all the houses of the great, he burned with fire. [14]And all the army of the Chaldeans who *were* with the captain of the guard broke down all the walls of Jerusalem all around. [15]Then Nebuzaradan the captain of the guard carried away captive *some* of the poor people, the rest of the people who remained in the city, the defectors who had deserted to the king of Babylon, and the rest of the craftsmen. [16]But Nebuzaradan the captain of the guard left *some* of the poor of the land as vinedressers and farmers.

[17]The bronze pillars that *were* in the house of the LORD, and the carts and the bronze Sea that *were* in the house of the LORD, the Chaldeans broke in pieces, and carried all their bronze to Babylon. [18]They also took away the pots, the shovels, the trimmers, the bowls, the spoons, and all the bronze utensils with which the *priests* ministered. [19]The basins, the firepans, the bowls, the pots, the lampstands, the spoons, and the cups, whatever *was* solid gold and whatever *was* solid silver, the captain of the guard took away. [20]The two pillars, one Sea, the twelve bronze bulls which *were* under *it, and* the carts, which King Solomon had made for the house of the LORD—the bronze of all these articles was beyond measure. [21]Now *concerning* the pillars: the height of one pillar *was* eighteen cubits, a measuring line of twelve cubits could measure its circumference, and its thickness *was* four fingers; *it was* hollow. [22]A capital of bronze *was* on it; and the height of one capital *was* five cubits, with a network and pomegranates all around the capital, all of bronze. The second pillar, with pomegranates was the same. [23]There were ninety-six pomegranates on the sides; all the pomegranates, all around on the network, *were* one hundred.

The People Taken Captive to Babylonia

[24]The captain of the guard took Seraiah the chief priest, Zephaniah the second priest, and the three doorkeepers. [25]He also took out of the city an officer who had charge of the men of war, seven men of the king's close associates who were found in the city, the principal scribe of the army who mustered the people of the land, and sixty men of the people of the land who were found in the midst of the city. [26]And Nebuzaradan the captain of the guard took these and brought them to the king of Babylon at Riblah. [27]Then the king of Babylon struck them and put them to death at Riblah in the land of Hamath. Thus Judah was carried away captive from its own land.

[28]These *are* the people whom Nebuchadnezzar carried away captive: in the seventh year, three thousand and twenty-three Jews; [29]in the eighteenth year of Nebuchadnezzar he carried away captive from Jerusalem eight hundred and thirty-two persons; [30]in the twenty-third year of Nebuchadnezzar, Nebuzaradan the captain of the guard carried away captive of the Jews seven hundred and forty-five persons. All the persons *were* four thousand six hundred.

Jehoiachin Released from Prison

[31]Now it came to pass in the thirty-seventh year of the captivity of Jehoiachin king of Judah, in the twelfth month, on the twenty-fifth *day* of the month, *that* Evil-Merodach[a] king of Babylon, in the *first* year of his reign, lifted up the head of Jehoiachin king of Judah and brought him out of prison. [32]And he spoke kindly to him and gave him a more prominent seat than those of the kings who *were* with him in Babylon. [33]So Jehoiachin changed from his prison garments, and he ate bread regularly before the king all the days of his life. [34]And as for his provisions, there was a regular ration given him by the king of Babylon, a portion for each day until the day of his death, all the days of his life.

52:31 [a]Or *Awil-Marduk*

Lamentations

Jerusalem in Affliction

1 How lonely sits the city
That was full of people!
How like a widow is she,
Who *was* great among the nations!
The princess among the provinces
Has become a slave!

2 She weeps bitterly in the night,
Her tears *are* on her cheeks;
Among all her lovers
She has none to comfort *her.*
All her friends have dealt treacherously with her;
They have become her enemies.

3 Judah has gone into captivity,
Under affliction and hard servitude;
She dwells among the nations,
She finds no rest;
All her persecutors overtake her in dire straits.

4 The roads to Zion mourn
Because no one comes to the set feasts.
All her gates are desolate;
Her priests sigh,
Her virgins are afflicted,
And she *is* in bitterness.

5 Her adversaries have become the master,
Her enemies prosper;
For the LORD has afflicted her
Because of the multitude of her transgressions.
Her children have gone into captivity before the enemy.

6 And from the daughter of Zion
All her splendor has departed.
Her princes have become like deer
That find no pasture,
That flee without strength
Before the pursuer.

7 In the days of her affliction and roaming,
Jerusalem remembers all her pleasant things
That she had in the days of old.
When her people fell into the hand of the enemy,
With no one to help her,
The adversaries saw her
And mocked at her downfall.[a]

1:7 [a]Vulgate reads *her Sabbaths.*

1:5 The Book of Lamentations describes the spirit in which every Christian should walk. The Bible says that Jesus was a Man of sorrows, acquainted with grief (see Isa. 53:3). Those who acquaint themselves with the sufferings of this life, and the sufferings of the next for those who die in their sins, will lament in horror and then preach with passion. The lost, with the same loves and fears as we have, are held captive by the enemy (see 2 Tim. 2:26) and await unawares the most terrible of fates, but for the grace of God. Tragically, they do not consider their eternal destiny (see v. 9).

[8]Jerusalem has sinned gravely,
Therefore she has become vile.[a]
All who honored her despise her
Because they have seen her
nakedness;
Yes, she sighs and turns away.

[9]Her uncleanness *is* in her skirts;
She did not consider her destiny;
Therefore her collapse was awesome;
She had no comforter.
"O LORD, behold my affliction,
For *the* enemy is exalted!"

[10]The adversary has spread his hand
Over all her pleasant things;
For she has seen the nations enter her
sanctuary,
Those whom You commanded
Not to enter Your assembly.

[11]All her people sigh,
They seek bread;
They have given their valuables for
food to restore life.
"See, O LORD, and consider,
For I am scorned."

[12]"*Is it* nothing to you, all you who pass
by?
Behold and see
If there is any sorrow like my sorrow,
Which has been brought on me,
Which the LORD has inflicted
In the day of His fierce anger.

[13]"From above He has sent fire into my
bones,
And it overpowered them;
He has spread a net for my feet
And turned me back;
He has made me desolate
And faint all the day.

[14]"The yoke of my transgressions was
bound;[a]
They were woven together by His
hands,
And thrust upon my neck.
He made my strength fail;
The Lord delivered me into the hands
of *those whom* I am not able to
withstand.

[15]"The Lord has trampled underfoot all
my mighty *men* in my midst;
He has called an assembly against me
To crush my young men;
The Lord trampled *as* in a winepress
The virgin daughter of Judah.

[16]"For these *things* I weep;
My eye, my eye overflows with water;
Because the comforter, who should
restore my life,
Is far from me.
My children are desolate
Because the enemy prevailed."

[17]Zion spreads out her hands,
But no one comforts her;
The LORD has commanded
concerning Jacob
That those around him *become* his
adversaries;
Jerusalem has become an unclean
thing among them.

[18]"The LORD is righteous,
For I rebelled against His
commandment.
Hear now, all peoples,
And behold my sorrow;
My virgins and my young men

1:8 [a]Septuagint and Vulgate read *moved* or *removed*. **1:14** [a]Following Masoretic Text and Targum; Septuagint, Syriac, and Vulgate read *watched over.*

1:12 How could this not be the cry of Christ on the cross, as the world looks on the One whom they pierced (see John 19:37)? Yet this same cross is meaningless to millions who pass it by. They don't understand that it is the key to the door of everlasting life. A ladder leaning against your fourth-story window is meaningless, until you see that your house is on fire and you have no other escape. So the cross makes no sense until the Law shows the sinner his terrible danger.

Have gone into captivity.

[19]“I called for my lovers,
But they deceived me;
My priests and my elders
Breathed their last in the city,
While they sought food
To restore their life.

[20]“See, O LORD, that I *am* in distress;
My soul is troubled;
My heart is overturned within me,
For I have been very rebellious.
Outside the sword bereaves,
At home *it is* like death.

> What should a man or woman feel in the transaction of the new birth? There ought to be that real and genuine cry of pain . . . There should be the terror of seeing ourselves in violent contrast to the holy, holy, holy God.
>
> **A. W. TOZER**

[21]“They have heard that I sigh,
But no one comforts me.
All my enemies have heard of my
trouble;
They are glad that You have done *it.*
Bring on the day You have
announced,
That they may become like me.

[22]“Let all their wickedness come before
You,
And do to them as You have done to
me
For all my transgressions;
For my sighs *are* many,
And my heart *is* faint.”

God’s Anger with Jerusalem

2 How the Lord has covered the
daughter of Zion
With a cloud in His anger!
He cast down from heaven to the
earth
The beauty of Israel,
And did not remember His footstool
In the day of His anger.

[2]The Lord has swallowed up and has
not pitied
All the dwelling places of Jacob.
He has thrown down in His wrath
The strongholds of the daughter of
Judah;
He has brought *them* down to the
ground;
He has profaned the kingdom and its
princes.

[3]He has cut off in fierce anger
Every horn of Israel;
He has drawn back His right hand
From before the enemy.
He has blazed against Jacob like a
flaming fire
Devouring all around.

[4]Standing like an enemy, He has bent
His bow;
With His right hand, like an adversary,
He has slain all *who were* pleasing to
His eye;
On the tent of the daughter of Zion,
He has poured out His fury like fire.

[5]The Lord was like an enemy.
He has swallowed up Israel,
He has swallowed up all her palaces;
He has destroyed her strongholds,
And has increased mourning and
lamentation
In the daughter of Judah.

[6]He has done violence to His
tabernacle,
As if it were a garden;
He has destroyed His place of
assembly;
The LORD has caused
The appointed feasts and Sabbaths to
be forgotten in Zion.
In His burning indignation He has
spurned the king and the priest.

[7]The Lord has spurned His altar,

He has abandoned His sanctuary;
He has given up the walls of her palaces
Into the hand of the enemy.
They have made a noise in the house of the LORD
As on the day of a set feast.

8The LORD has purposed to destroy
The wall of the daughter of Zion.
He has stretched out a line;
He has not withdrawn His hand from destroying;
Therefore He has caused the rampart and wall to lament;
They languished together.

9Her gates have sunk into the ground;
He has destroyed and broken her bars.
Her king and her princes *are* among the nations;
The Law *is* no *more,*
And her prophets find no vision from the LORD.

10The elders of the daughter of Zion
Sit on the ground *and* keep silence;
They throw dust on their heads
And gird themselves with sackcloth.
The virgins of Jerusalem
Bow their heads to the ground.

11My eyes fail with tears,
My heart is troubled;
My bile is poured on the ground
Because of the destruction of the daughter of my people,
Because the children and the infants
Faint in the streets of the city.

12They say to their mothers,
"Where *is* grain and wine?"
As they swoon like the wounded
In the streets of the city,
As their life is poured out
In their mothers' bosom.

13How shall I console you?
To what shall I liken you,
O daughter of Jerusalem?
What shall I compare with you, that I may comfort you,
O virgin daughter of Zion?
For your ruin *is* spread wide as the sea;
Who can heal you?

14Your prophets have seen for you
False and deceptive visions;
They have not uncovered your iniquity,
To bring back your captives,
But have envisioned for you false prophecies and delusions.

15All who pass by clap *their* hands at you;
They hiss and shake their heads
At the daughter of Jerusalem:
"*Is* this the city that is called
'The perfection of beauty,
The joy of the whole earth'?"

16All your enemies have opened their mouth against you;
They hiss and gnash *their* teeth.
They say, "We have swallowed *her* up!
Surely this *is* the day we have waited for;
We have found *it,* we have seen *it!*"

17The LORD has done what He

2:14 Speaking of sin. There are many professing Christians who, for some reason, avoid the subject of sin in speaking to the lost. They refuse to expose the guilt of sinners. They will have to give an account to the One they call "Lord" and profess to serve.

"No matter how many persons we touch with the gospel we have failed unless, along with the message of invitation, we have boldly declared the exceeding sinfulness of man and the transcendent holiness of the Most High God. They who degrade or compromise the truth in order to reach larger numbers, dishonor God and deeply injure the souls of men.

"The temptation to modify the teachings of Christ with the hope that larger numbers may 'accept' Him is cruelly strong in this day of speed, size, noise, and crowds. But if we know what is good for us, we'll resist it with every power at our command." *A. W. Tozer*

purposed;
He has fulfilled His word
Which He commanded in days of old.
He has thrown down and has not
pitied,
And He has caused an enemy to
rejoice over you;
He has exalted the horn of your
adversaries.

18 Their heart cried out to the Lord,
"O wall of the daughter of Zion,
Let tears run down like a river day
and night;
Give yourself no relief;
Give your eyes no rest.

. . . . . .

To read a challenging letter from an atheist, see Rom. 9:2,3 comment.

. . . . . .

19 "Arise, cry out in the night,
At the beginning of the watches;
Pour out your heart like water before
the face of the Lord.
Lift your hands toward Him
For the life of your young children,
Who faint from hunger at the head of
every street."

20 "See, O LORD, and consider!
To whom have You done this?
Should the women eat their offspring,
The children they have cuddled?[a]
Should the priest and prophet be slain
In the sanctuary of the Lord?

21 "Young and old lie
On the ground in the streets;
My virgins and my young men
Have fallen by the sword;
You have slain *them* in the day of Your
anger,
You have slaughtered *and* not pitied.

22 "You have invited as to a feast day
The terrors that surround me.
In the day of the LORD's anger
There was no refugee or survivor.
Those whom I have borne and
brought up
My enemies have destroyed."

The Prophet's Anguish and Hope

3 I *am* the man *who* has seen affliction
by the rod of His wrath.
2 He has led me and made *me* walk
In darkness and not *in* light.
3 Surely He has turned His hand
against me
Time and time again throughout the
day.

4 He has aged my flesh and my skin,
And broken my bones.
5 He has besieged me
And surrounded *me* with bitterness
and woe.
6 He has set me in dark places
Like the dead of long ago.

7 He has hedged me in so that I cannot
get out;
He has made my chain heavy.
8 Even when I cry and shout,
He shuts out my prayer.
9 He has blocked my ways with hewn
stone;
He has made my paths crooked.

10 He *has been* to me a bear lying in wait,
Like a lion in ambush.
11 He has turned aside my ways and
torn me in pieces;
He has made me desolate.
12 He has bent His bow
And set me up as a target for the arrow.

13 He has caused the arrows of His
quiver
To pierce my loins.[a]
14 I have become the ridicule of all my
people—
Their taunting song all the day.
15 He has filled me with bitterness,
He has made me drink wormwood.

2:20 [a]Vulgate reads *a span long.* **3:13** [a]Literally *kidneys*

Springboards for Preaching and Witnessing

Dentists Do Not Exist

3:16 "On a recent trip to the dentist, while the dentist was working on my teeth he said to me, 'I do not believe in God.' Now this dentist knows what I do for a living and how important my faith is to me, yet for numerous reasons (one main one being his hands were in my mouth) I uncharacteristically remained silent, allowing him to explain: 'How can God exist and still allow all the suffering and pain in the world?' I remained quiet until he was finished (and of course put his drill away) and told him that 'I do not believe in dentists.' This confused him greatly so I clarified for him that if there are dentists in the world, how can so many people have broken, infected, and missing teeth? He answered me, 'I cannot help anyone who does not come to me to have their teeth fixed.' That reply is the same for faith. God cannot help people until they come to Him in repentance and faith, . . . and ask Him for help."
Tony Perkins

16He has also broken my teeth with
gravel,
And covered me with ashes.
17You have moved my soul far from
peace;
I have forgotten prosperity.
18And I said, "My strength and my hope
Have perished from the LORD."

19Remember my affliction and roaming,
The wormwood and the gall.
20My soul still remembers
And sinks within me.
21This I recall to my mind,
Therefore I have hope.

22*Through* the LORD's mercies we are not
consumed,
Because His compassions fail not.
23*They are* new every morning;
Great *is* Your faithfulness.
24"The LORD *is* my portion," says my soul,
"Therefore I hope in Him!"

25The LORD *is* good to those who wait
for Him,
To the soul *who* seeks Him.
26*It is* good that *one* should hope and
wait quietly
For the salvation of the LORD.
27*It is* good for a man to bear
The yoke in his youth.

28Let him sit alone and keep silent,
Because *God* has laid *it* on him;
29Let him put his mouth in the dust—
There may yet be hope.
30Let him give *his* cheek to the one who
strikes him,
And be full of reproach.

31For the Lord will not cast off forever.
32Though He causes grief,
Yet He will show compassion
According to the multitude of His
mercies.
33For He does not afflict willingly,
Nor grieve the children of men.

34To crush under one's feet
All the prisoners of the earth,
35To turn aside the justice *due* a man
Before the face of the Most High,
36Or subvert a man in his cause—
The Lord does not approve.

37Who *is* he *who* speaks and it comes to
pass,

3:22–26 In these verses, Jeremiah, in the midst of the desert of despair and God's judgment, remembers the wonderful oasis of God's mercy and compassion. This is the same hope for all who are currently under God's wrath. God is utterly faithful. His mercies are new every morning, and if they call upon the Lord they will not be consumed.

Here, three things are named as being good: God is good to those who wait for Him; it is good to hope and wait for the salvation of the Lord, and it is good for a man to bear the yoke (submit to discipline) in his youth.

When the Lord has not commanded it?
38Is it not from the mouth of the Most High
That woe and well-being proceed?
39Why should a living man complain,
A man for the punishment of his sins?

40Let us search out and examine our ways,
And turn back to the LORD;
41Let us lift our hearts and hands
To God in heaven.
42We have transgressed and rebelled;
You have not pardoned.

43You have covered *Yourself* with anger
And pursued us;
You have slain *and* not pitied.
44You have covered Yourself with a cloud,
That prayer should not pass through.
45You have made us an offscouring and refuse
In the midst of the peoples.

46All our enemies
Have opened their mouths against us.
47Fear and a snare have come upon us,
Desolation and destruction.
48My eyes overflow with rivers of water
For the destruction of the daughter of my people.

49My eyes flow and do not cease,
Without interruption,
50Till the LORD from heaven
Looks down and sees.
51My eyes bring suffering to my soul
Because of all the daughters of my city.

52My enemies without cause
Hunted me down like a bird.
53They silenced[a] my life in the pit
And threw stones at me.
54The waters flowed over my head;
I said, "I am cut off!"

55I called on Your name, O LORD,
From the lowest pit.
56You have heard my voice:
"Do not hide Your ear
From my sighing, from my cry for help."
57You drew near on the day I called on You,
And said, "Do not fear!"

58O Lord, You have pleaded the case for my soul;
You have redeemed my life.
59O LORD, You have seen *how* I am wronged;
Judge my case.
60You have seen all their vengeance,
All their schemes against me.

Oh, to realize that souls, precious, never dying souls, are perishing all around us, going out into the blackness of darkness and despair, eternally lost, and yet to feel no anguish, shed no tears, know no travail! How little we know of the compassion of Jesus!

OSWALD J. SMITH

61You have heard their reproach, O LORD,
All their schemes against me,
62The lips of my enemies
And their whispering against me all the day.
63Look at their sitting down and their rising up;
I *am* their taunting song.

64Repay them, O LORD,
According to the work of their hands.
65Give them a veiled[a] heart;
Your curse *be* upon them!

3:53 [a]Septuagint reads *put to death.* 3:65 [a]A Jewish tradition reads *sorrow of.*

3:48 Do we ever shed tears for the destruction of humanity? Do our eyes overflow with water? Do we even care for the eternal salvation of the lost? Then our evangelistic lifestyle should be evident. (Also see Paul's lament in his letter to the Romans, 9:1–3.)

66In Your anger,
Pursue and destroy them
From the heavens of the LORD.

The Degradation of Zion

4 How the gold has become dim!
How changed the fine gold!
The stones of the sanctuary are
scattered
At the head of every street.

2The precious sons of Zion,
Valuable as fine gold,
How they are regarded as clay pots,
The work of the hands of the potter!

3Even the jackals present their breasts
To nurse their young;
But the daughter of my people *is* cruel,
Like ostriches in the wilderness.

4The tongue of the infant clings
To the roof of its mouth for thirst;
The young children ask for bread,
But no one breaks *it* for them.

5Those who ate delicacies
Are desolate in the streets;
Those who were brought up in scarlet
Embrace ash heaps.

6The punishment of the iniquity of the
daughter of my people
Is greater than the punishment of the
sin of Sodom,
Which was overthrown in a moment,
With no hand to help her!

7Her Nazirites[a] were brighter than snow
And whiter than milk;
They were more ruddy in body than
rubies,
Like sapphire in their appearance.

8*Now* their appearance is blacker than
soot;
They go unrecognized in the streets;
Their skin clings to their bones,
It has become as dry as wood.

9*Those* slain by the sword are better off
Than *those* who die of hunger;
For these pine away,
Stricken *for lack* of the fruits of the
field.

10The hands of the compassionate
women
Have cooked their own children;
They became food for them
In the destruction of the daughter of
my people.

11The LORD has fulfilled His fury,
He has poured out His fierce anger.
He kindled a fire in Zion,
And it has devoured its foundations.

12The kings of the earth,
And all inhabitants of the world,
Would not have believed
That the adversary and the enemy
Could enter the gates of Jerusalem—

13Because of the sins of her prophets
And the iniquities of her priests,
Who shed in her midst
The blood of the just.

14They wandered blind in the streets;
They have defiled themselves with
blood,
So that no one would touch their
garments.

15They cried out to them,
"Go away, unclean!
Go away, go away,
Do not touch us!"
When they fled and wandered,

4:7 [a]Or *nobles*

4:6 Think of how fearful it would have been in Sodom to see fire and brimstone fall from the heavens. Yet this wrath was greater. These incidents should compel us to warn men and women everywhere to flee to the cross.

Those among the nations said,
"They shall no longer dwell *here.*"

16The face[a] of the LORD scattered them;
He no longer regards them.
The people do not respect the priests
Nor show favor to the elders.

17Still our eyes failed us,
Watching vainly for our help;
In our watching we watched
For a nation *that* could not save *us.*

18They tracked our steps
So that we could not walk in our streets.
Our end was near;
Our days were over,
For our end had come.

19Our pursuers were swifter
Than the eagles of the heavens.
They pursued us on the mountains
And lay in wait for us in the wilderness.

20The breath of our nostrils, the anointed of the LORD,
Was caught in their pits,
Of whom we said, "Under his shadow
We shall live among the nations."

21Rejoice and be glad, O daughter of Edom,
You who dwell in the land of Uz!
The cup shall also pass over to you
And you shall become drunk and make yourself naked.

22*The punishment of* your iniquity is accomplished,
O daughter of Zion;
He will no longer send you into captivity.
He will punish your iniquity,
O daughter of Edom;
He will uncover your sins!

A Prayer for Restoration

5 Remember, O LORD, what has come upon us;
Look, and behold our reproach!
2Our inheritance has been turned over to aliens,
And our houses to foreigners.
3We have become orphans and waifs,
Our mothers *are* like widows.

4We pay for the water we drink,
And our wood comes at a price.
5*They* pursue at our heels;[a]
We labor *and* have no rest.
6We have given our hand *to* the Egyptians
And the Assyrians, to be satisfied with bread.

7Our fathers sinned *and are* no more,
But we bear their iniquities.
8Servants rule over us;
There is none to deliver *us* from their hand.
9We get our bread *at the risk* of our lives,
Because of the sword in the wilderness.

10Our skin is hot as an oven,
Because of the fever of famine.
11They ravished the women in Zion,
The maidens in the cities of Judah.
12Princes were hung up by their hands,
And elders were not respected.
13Young men ground at the millstones;
Boys staggered under *loads of* wood.
14The elders have ceased *gathering at* the gate,
And the young men from their music.

15The joy of our heart has ceased;
Our dance has turned into mourning.
16The crown has fallen *from* our head.
Woe to us, for we have sinned!
17Because of this our heart is faint;
Because of these *things* our eyes grow dim;
18Because of Mount Zion which is desolate,
With foxes walking about on it.

4:16 [a]Targum reads *anger.* 5:5 [a]Literally *necks*

[19]You, O LORD, remain forever;
Your throne from generation to generation.
[20]Why do You forget us forever,
And forsake us for so long a time?
[21]Turn us back to You, O LORD, and we will be restored;
Renew our days as of old,
[22]Unless You have utterly rejected us,
And are very angry with us!

5:22 The time came when God lost patience with His people. Never rest on the thought that His patience is inexhaustible. To have such an image of God is to serve an idol and give license to sin.

Join the Fellowship of the Unashamed

By David MacAdam

The author of the following letter is unknown, but is believed to be a young pastor in Zimbabwe who was martyred for his faith in Jesus Christ. It was found in his study:

> I'm part of the fellowship of the unashamed. I have the Holy Spirit's power. The die has been cast. I have stepped over the line. The decision has been made—I'm a disciple of His. I won't look back, let up, slow down, back away, or be still. My past is redeemed, my present makes sense, my future is secure. I'm finished and done with low living, sight walking, smooth knees, colorless dreams, tamed visions, worldly talking, cheap giving, and dwarfed goals.
>
> I no longer need preeminence, prosperity, position, promotions, plaudits, or popularity. I don't have to be right, first, tops, recognized, praised, regarded, or rewarded. I now live by faith, lean in His presence, walk by patience, am uplifted by prayer, and I labor with power.
>
> My face is set, my gait is fast, my goal is heaven, my road is narrow, my way rough, my companions few, my Guide reliable, my mission clear. I cannot be bought, compromised, detoured, lured away, turned back, deluded, or delayed. I will not flinch in the face of sacrifices, hesitate in the presence of the enemy, pander at the pool of popularity, or meander in the maze of mediocrity.
>
> I won't give up, shut up, let up, until I have stayed up, stored up, prayed up, paid up, preached up for the cause of Christ. I am a disciple of Jesus. I must go till He comes, give till I drop, preach till all know, and work till He stops me. And, when He comes for His own, He will have no problem recognizing me . . . my banner will be clear.

After His resurrection, Jesus appeared to His disciples and commissioned them to join the Fellowship of the Unashamed. "But you shall receive power when the Holy Spirit has come upon you; and you shall be witnesses to Me in Jerusalem, and in all Judea and Samaria, and to the end of the earth" (Acts 1:8).

The word "witness" in the original Greek text is *martus*, from which we get the English word "martyr." The Holy Spirit empowers the believer to be a bold witness to the identity and work of Christ. He is not only willing to die for Him, but also to live for Him on a day-to-day basis.

The Christian faith is unique in that its Founder is the indispensable dynamic for its every demand. Jesus said, "Without Me you can do nothing" (John 15:5). The only one who can live the Christian life is Christ. By active faith in His indwelling life we are promised the fruit of Christlike character (the fruit of the Spirit—Gal. 5:22,23); Christlike conduct (the fruit of righteousness—Phil. 1:11); Christlike ministry (the fruit of the gospel—Col. 1:6) and God-honoring worship (the fruit of our lips giving thanks to His name—Heb. 13:15).

Authentic Christian faith makes Christ the origin of our activity and not just the object. For from Him and through Him and to Him are all things!

We overcome not just by the blood of the Lamb and the word of our testimony but by virtue of the fact that we do not love our lives so much as to shrink from death (Rev. 12:11). The great witness of our authenticity is the fact that we have already surrendered our lives to the cross. We do not need to strive to preserve ourselves. Christ lives in us and empowers us to offer ourselves to a world that desperately needs Him.

May our banner be clear!

Ezekiel

Ezekiel's Vision of God

1 Now it came to pass in the thirtieth year, in the fourth *month,* on the fifth *day* of the month, as I *was* among the captives by the River Chebar, *that* the heavens were opened and I saw visions[a] of God. 2On the fifth *day* of the month, which *was* in the fifth year of King Jehoiachin's captivity, 3the word of the LORD came expressly to Ezekiel the priest, the son of Buzi, in the land of the Chaldeans[a] by the River Chebar; and the hand of the LORD was upon him there.

4Then I looked, and behold, a whirlwind was coming out of the north, a great cloud with raging fire engulfing itself; and brightness *was* all around it and radiating out of its midst like the color of amber, out of the midst of the fire. 5Also from within it *came* the likeness of four living creatures. And this *was* their appearance: they had the likeness of a man. 6Each one had four faces, and each one had four wings. 7Their legs *were* straight, and the soles of their feet *were* like the soles of calves' feet. They sparkled like the color of burnished bronze. 8The hands of a man *were* under their wings on their four sides; and each of the four had faces and wings. 9Their wings touched one another. *The creatures* did not turn when they went, but each one went straight forward.

10As for the likeness of their faces, *each* had the face of a man; each of the four had the face of a lion on the right side, each of the four had the face of an ox on the left side, and each of the four had the face of an eagle. 11Thus *were* their faces. Their wings stretched upward; two *wings* of each one touched one another, and two covered their bodies. 12And each one went straight forward; they went wherever the spirit wanted to go, and they did not turn when they went.

13As for the likeness of the living creatures, their appearance *was* like burning coals of fire, like the appearance of torches going back and forth among the living creatures. The fire was bright, and out of the fire went lightning. 14And the living creatures ran back and forth, in appearance like a flash of lightning.

15Now as I looked at the living creatures, behold, a wheel *was* on the earth beside each living creature with its four faces. 16The appearance of the wheels and their workings *was* like the color of beryl, and all four had the same likeness. The appearance of their workings *was,* as it were, a wheel in the middle of a wheel. 17When they moved, they went toward

1:1 [a]Following Masoretic Text, Septuagint, and Vulgate; Syriac and Targum read *a vision.* 1:3 [a]Or *Babylonians,* and so elsewhere in this book

1:13,14 This incredible description of the Supernatural is too much for the human mind to comprehend. One can be excused for not knowing what is literal and what is symbolic. One day we will know which was which.

any one of four directions; they did not turn aside when they went. 18As for their rims, they were so high they were awesome; and their rims *were* full of eyes, all around the four of them. 19When the living creatures went, the wheels went beside them; and when the living creatures were lifted up from the earth, the wheels were lifted up. 20Wherever the spirit wanted to go, they went, *because* there the spirit went; and the wheels were lifted together with them, for the spirit of the living creatures[a] *was* in the wheels. 21When those went, *these* went; when those stood, *these* stood; and when those were lifted up from the earth, the wheels were lifted up together with them, for the spirit of the living creatures[a] *was* in the wheels.

22The likeness of the firmament above the heads of the living creatures[a] *was* like the color of an awesome crystal, stretched out over their heads. 23And under the firmament their wings *spread out* straight, one toward another. Each one had two which covered one side, and each one had two which covered the other side of the body. 24When they went, I heard the noise of their wings, like the noise of many waters, like the voice of the Almighty, a tumult like the noise of an army; and when they stood still, they let down their wings. 25A voice came from above the firmament that *was* over their heads; whenever they stood, they let down their wings.

26And above the firmament over their heads *was* the likeness of a throne, in appearance like a sapphire stone; on the likeness of the throne *was* a likeness with the appearance of a man high above it. 27Also from the appearance of His waist and upward I saw, as it were, the color of amber with the appearance of fire all around within it; and from the appearance of His waist and downward I saw, as it were, the appearance of fire with brightness all around. 28Like the appearance of a rainbow in a cloud on a rainy day, so *was* the appearance of the brightness all around it. This *was* the appearance of the likeness of the glory of the LORD.

Ezekiel Sent to Rebellious Israel

So when I saw *it,* I fell on my face, and I heard a voice of One speaking.

2 And He said to me, "Son of man, stand on your feet, and I will speak to you." 2Then the Spirit entered me when He spoke to me, and set me on my feet; and I heard Him who spoke to me. 3And He said to me: "Son of man, I am sending you to the children of Israel, to a rebellious nation that has rebelled against Me; they and their fathers have transgressed against Me to this very day. 4For *they are* impudent and stubborn children. I am sending you to them, and you shall say to them, 'Thus says the Lord GOD.' 5As for them, whether they hear or whether they refuse—for they *are* a rebellious house—yet they will know that a prophet has been among them.

6"And you, son of man, do not be afraid of them nor be afraid of their words, though briers and thorns *are* with you and you dwell among scorpions; do not be afraid of their words or dismayed by their looks, though they *are* a rebellious house. 7You shall speak My words to them, whether they hear or whether

1:20 [a]Literally *living creature;* Septuagint and Vulgate read *spirit of life;* Targum reads *creatures.* 1:21 [a]Literally *living creature;* Septuagint and Vulgate read *spirit of life;* Targum reads *creatures.* 1:22 [a]Following Septuagint, Targum, and Vulgate; Masoretic Text reads *living creature.*

1:28 "The light of God's glory shines two ways: it sheds light on the knowledge of God so we can see Him more clearly, but it also sheds light on us so that we can see our own sin more clearly. Remember, the closer you approach the light, the brighter it shines on you. This is the marvelous two-edged sword of intimacy. We see Him more clearly and we see ourselves more clearly. It is the perfect safeguard against pride. You can mark His word on this: true intimacy breeds true humility!" *Beth Moore*

2:7 All we can do is faithfully preach the gospel and make the issues of sin, righteousness, and judgment as clear as possible, with the help of God. The rest is between the sinner and God.

they refuse, for they *are* rebellious. 8But you, son of man, hear what I say to you. Do not be rebellious like that rebellious house; open your mouth and eat what I give you."

9Now when I looked, there was a hand stretched out to me; and behold, a scroll of a book *was* in it. 10Then He spread it before me; and *there was* writing on the inside and on the outside, and written on it *were* lamentations and mourning and woe.

3 Moreover He said to me, "Son of man, eat what you find; eat this scroll, and go, speak to the house of Israel." 2So I opened my mouth, and He caused me to eat that scroll.

3And He said to me, "Son of man, feed your belly, and fill your stomach with this scroll that I give you." So I ate, and it was in my mouth like honey in sweetness.

4Then He said to me: "Son of man, go to the house of Israel and speak with My words to them. 5For you *are* not sent to a people of unfamiliar speech and of hard language, *but* to the house of Israel, 6not to many people of unfamiliar speech and of hard language, whose words you cannot understand. Surely, had I sent you to them, they would have listened to you. 7But the house of Israel will not listen to you, because they will not listen to Me; for all the house of Israel *are* impudent and hard-hearted. 8Behold, I have made your face strong against their faces, and your forehead strong against their foreheads. 9Like adamant stone, harder than flint, I have made your forehead; do not be afraid of them, nor be dismayed at their looks, though they *are* a rebellious house."

10Moreover He said to me: "Son of man, receive into your heart all My words that I speak to you, and hear with your ears. 11And go, get to the captives, to the children of your people, and speak to them and tell them, 'Thus says the Lord GOD,' whether they hear, or whether they refuse."

12Then the Spirit lifted me up, and I heard behind me a great thunderous voice: "Blessed *is* the glory of the LORD from His place!" 13*I* also *heard* the noise of the wings of the living creatures that touched one another, and the noise of the wheels beside them, and a great thunderous noise. 14So the Spirit lifted me up and took me away, and I went in bitterness, in the heat of my spirit; but the hand of the LORD was strong upon me. 15Then I came to the captives at Tel Abib, who dwelt by the River Chebar; and I sat where they sat, and remained there astonished among them seven days.

Ezekiel Is a Watchman

16Now it came to pass at the end of seven days that the word of the LORD came to me, saying, 17"Son of man, I have made you a watchman for the house of Israel; therefore hear a word from My mouth, and give them warning from Me: 18When I say to the wicked, 'You shall surely die,' and you give him no warning, nor speak to warn the wicked from his wicked way, to save his life, that same wicked *man* shall die in his iniquity; but his blood I will require at your hand. 19Yet, if you warn

3:1,2 We feed on God's Word by meditating on it (see Psa. 1). We chew on it, then absorb it into our being for sustenance that will energize us to do the will of God.

3:8,9 Once we have taken God's Word to heart (v. 10), may God give us an obstinate forehead for the truth of the gospel. We need to be as stubborn as a mule as we carry the Savior into this world.

3:18,19 Memorize these verses and share them with professing Christians who do not seem to care about the unsaved. If we neglect to warn those who are about to die, their blood is on our hands. Civil law says that if we let another human being die when it is within our ability to save them, we are guilty of something called "depraved indifference." How much more are we guilty if we know that sinners are going to a terrifying hell and we do nothing to turn them to the Savior? See 1 Cor. 9:16 for Paul's reasoning on our responsibility to the lost. See also Ezek. 33:8,9 comment.

the wicked, and he does not turn from his wickedness, nor from his wicked way, he shall die in his iniquity; but you have delivered your soul.

[20]"Again, when a righteous *man* turns from his righteousness and commits iniquity, and I lay a stumbling block before him, he shall die; because you did not give him warning, he shall die in his sin, and his righteousness which he has done shall not be remembered; but his blood I will require at your hand. [21]Nevertheless if you warn the righteous *man* that the righteous should not sin, and he does not sin, he shall surely live because he took warning; also you will have delivered your soul."

[22]Then the hand of the LORD was upon me there, and He said to me, "Arise, go out into the plain, and there I shall talk with you."

[23]So I arose and went out into the plain, and behold, the glory of the LORD stood there, like the glory which I saw by the River Chebar; and I fell on my face. [24]Then the Spirit entered me and set me on my feet, and spoke with me and said to me: "Go, shut yourself inside your house. [25]And you, O son of man, surely they will put ropes on you and bind you with them, so that you cannot go out among them. [26]I will make your tongue cling to the roof of your mouth, so that you shall be mute and not be one to rebuke them, for they *are* a rebellious house. [27]But when I speak with you, I will open your mouth, and you shall say to them, 'Thus says the Lord GOD.' He who hears, let him hear; and he who refuses, let him refuse; for they *are* a rebellious house.

The Siege of Jerusalem Portrayed

4 "You also, son of man, take a clay tablet and lay it before you, and portray on it a city, Jerusalem. [2]Lay siege against it, build a siege wall against it, and heap up a mound against it; set camps against it also, and place battering rams against it all around. [3]Moreover take for yourself an iron plate, and set it *as* an iron wall between you and the city. Set your face against it, and it shall be besieged, and you shall lay siege against it. This *will be* a sign to the house of Israel.

[4]"Lie also on your left side, and lay the iniquity of the house of Israel upon it. *According* to the number of the days that you lie on it, you shall bear their iniquity. [5]For I have laid on you the years of their iniquity, according to the number of the days, three hundred and ninety days; so you shall bear the iniquity of the house of Israel. [6]And when you have completed them, lie again on your right side; then you shall bear the iniquity of the house of Judah forty days. I have laid on you a day for each year.

[7]"Therefore you shall set your face toward the siege of Jerusalem; your arm *shall be* uncovered, and you shall prophesy against it. [8]And surely I will restrain you so that you cannot turn from one side to another till you have ended the days of your siege.

[9]"Also take for yourself wheat, barley, beans, lentils, millet, and spelt; put them into one vessel, and make bread of them for yourself. *During* the number of days that you lie on your side, three hundred and ninety days, you shall eat it. [10]And your food which you eat *shall be* by weight, twenty shekels a day; from time to time you shall eat it. [11]You shall also drink water by measure, one-sixth of a hin; from time to time you shall drink. [12]And you shall eat it *as* barley cakes; and bake it using fuel of human waste in their sight."

[13]Then the LORD said, "So shall the children of Israel eat their defiled bread among the Gentiles, where I will drive them."

[14]So I said, "Ah, Lord GOD! Indeed I

4:1–6 Ezekiel, like Jesus of Nazareth, is called the "son of man." He symbolically bore the iniquity of his people. Jesus literally bore the sin of the world (see John 1:29; 1 Pet. 2:24).

have never defiled myself from my youth till now; I have never eaten what died of itself or was torn by beasts, nor has abominable flesh ever come into my mouth."

15Then He said to me, "See, I am giving you cow dung instead of human waste, and you shall prepare your bread over it."

16Moreover He said to me, "Son of man, surely I will cut off the supply of bread in Jerusalem; they shall eat bread by weight and with anxiety, and shall drink water by measure and with dread, 17that they may lack bread and water, and be dismayed with one another, and waste away because of their iniquity.

A Sword Against Jerusalem

5 "And you, son of man, take a sharp sword, take it as a barber's razor, and pass *it* over your head and your beard; then take scales to weigh and divide the hair. 2You shall burn with fire one-third in the midst of the city, when the days of the siege are finished; then you shall take one-third and strike around *it* with the sword, and one-third you shall scatter in the wind: I will draw out a sword after them. 3You shall also take a small number of them and bind them in the edge of your *garment.* 4Then take some of them again and throw them into the midst of the fire, and burn them in the fire. From there a fire will go out into all the house of Israel.

5"Thus says the Lord GOD: 'This *is* Jerusalem; I have set her in the midst of the nations and the countries all around her. 6She has rebelled against My judgments by doing wickedness more than the nations, and against My statutes more than the countries that *are* all around her; for they have refused My judgments, and they have not walked in My statutes.' 7Therefore thus says the Lord GOD: 'Because you have multiplied *disobedience* more than the nations that *are* all around you, have not walked in My statutes nor kept My judgments, nor even done[a] according to the judgments of the nations that *are* all around you'— 8therefore thus says the Lord GOD: 'Indeed I, even I, *am* against you and will execute judgments in your midst in the sight of the nations. 9And I will do among you what I have never done, and the like of which I will never do again, because of all your abominations. 10Therefore fathers shall eat *their* sons in your midst, and sons shall eat their fathers; and I will execute judgments among you, and all of you who remain I will scatter to all the winds.

11'Therefore, *as* I live,' says the Lord GOD, 'surely, because you have defiled My sanctuary with all your detestable things and with all your abominations, therefore I will also diminish *you;* My eye will not spare, nor will I have any pity. 12One-third of you shall die of the pestilence, and be consumed with famine in your midst; and one-third shall fall by the sword all around you; and I will scatter another third to all the winds, and I will draw out a sword after them.

13'Thus shall My anger be spent, and I will cause My fury to rest upon them, and I will be avenged; and they shall know that I, the LORD, have spoken *it* in My zeal, when I have spent My fury upon them. 14Moreover I will make you a waste and a reproach among the nations that *are* all around you, in the sight of all who pass by.

15'So it[a] shall be a reproach, a taunt, a lesson, and an astonishment to the nations that *are* all around you, when I execute judgments among you in anger and in fury and in furious rebukes. I, the LORD, have spoken. 16When I send against them the terrible arrows of famine which

5:7 [a]Following Masoretic Text, Septuagint, Targum, and Vulgate; many Hebrew manuscripts and Syriac read *but have done* (compare 11:12). 5:15 [a]Septuagint, Syriac, Targum, and Vulgate read *you.*

5:8–13 We can know the seriousness of the crime by the severity of the punishment given. See Lev. 26:33 and Deut. 28:64 for God's promises to scatter His people throughout the earth because of their sin.

Questions & Objections

"How can a perfect God be furious?"

There are some crimes that *outrage* society. It often takes the murder of a child to stir a sense of anger in sinful humanity, but God's wrath is stirred even by hatred, which He considers equivalent to murder. All sins are crimes against God's Law (1 John 3:4) and are extremely offensive to Him.

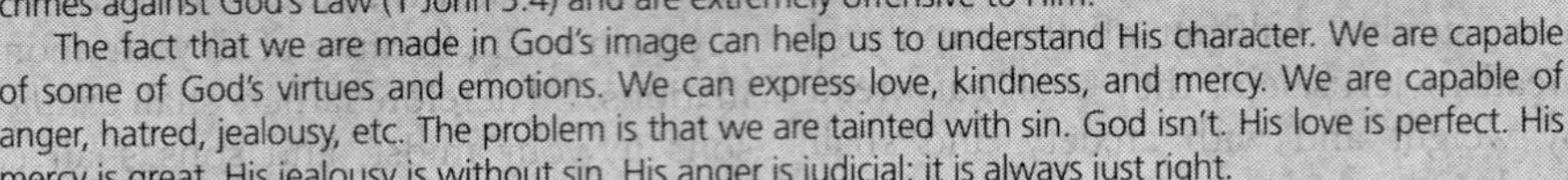

The fact that we are made in God's image can help us to understand His character. We are capable of some of God's virtues and emotions. We can express love, kindness, and mercy. We are capable of anger, hatred, jealousy, etc. The problem is that we are tainted with sin. God isn't. His love is perfect. His mercy is great. His jealousy is without sin. His anger is judicial; it is always just right.

"Let such know that Jehovah, the one and only living and true God, is a jealous God, and a revenger; he is jealous for the comfort of his worshippers, jealous for his land (Joel 2:18), and will not have that injured. He is a revenger, and He is furious.

"He has fury (so the word is), not as man has it, in whom it is an ungoverned passion (so He has said, Fury is not in me, Isa. 27:4), but He has it in such a way as becomes the righteous God, to put an edge upon His justice, and to make it appear more terrible to those who otherwise would stand in no awe of it. He is Lord of anger (so the Hebrew phrase is for that which we read, He is furious); He has anger, but He has it at command and under government. Our anger is often lord over us, as theirs that have no rule over their own spirits, but God is always Lord of His anger and weighs a path to it (Psa. 78:50)."
Matthew Henry

shall be for destruction, which I will send
to destroy you, I will increase the famine
upon you and cut off your supply of bread.
17So I will send against you famine and
wild beasts, and they will bereave you.
Pestilence and blood shall pass through
you, and I will bring the sword against
you. I, the LORD, have spoken.' "

Judgment on Idolatrous Israel

6 Now the word of the LORD came to
me, saying: 2"Son of man, set your face
toward the mountains of Israel, and prophesy against them, 3and say, 'O mountains
of Israel, hear the word of the Lord GOD!
Thus says the Lord GOD to the mountains,
to the hills, to the ravines, and to the valleys: "Indeed I, *even* I, will bring a sword
against you, and I will destroy your high
places. 4Then your altars shall be desolate,
your incense altars shall be broken, and I
will cast down your slain *men* before your
idols. 5And I will lay the corpses of the
children of Israel before their idols, and I
will scatter your bones all around your
altars. 6In all your dwelling places the
cities shall be laid waste, and the high
places shall be desolate, so that your altars
may be laid waste and made desolate,
your idols may be broken and made to
cease, your incense altars may be cut
down, and your works may be abolished.
7The slain shall fall in your midst, and you
shall know that I *am* the LORD.

8"Yet I will leave a remnant, so that
you may have *some* who escape the sword
among the nations, when you are scattered through the countries. 9Then those
of you who escape will remember Me
among the nations where they are carried
captive, because I was crushed by their
adulterous heart which has departed from
Me, and by their eyes which play the harlot after their idols; they will loathe themselves for the evils which they committed
in all their abominations. 10And they shall
know that I *am* the LORD; I have not said
in vain that I would bring this calamity
upon them."

11"Thus says the Lord GOD: "Pound your
fists and stamp your feet, and say, 'Alas,
for all the evil abominations of the house

6:3 "High places" were places of idolatrous worship.

of Israel! For they shall fall by the sword,
by famine, and by pestilence. [12]He who is
far off shall die by the pestilence, he who
is near shall fall by the sword, and he
who remains and is besieged shall die by
the famine. Thus will I spend My fury
upon them. [13]Then you shall know that I
am the LORD, when their slain are among
their idols all around their altars, on
every high hill, on all the mountaintops,
under every green tree, and under every
thick oak, wherever they offered sweet
incense to all their idols. [14]So I will stretch
out My hand against them and make the
land desolate, yes, more desolate than the
wilderness toward Diblah, in all their
dwelling places. Then they shall know
that I *am* the LORD.' " ' "

Judgment on Israel Is Near

7 Moreover the word of the LORD came
to me, saying, [2]"And you, son of man,
thus says the Lord GOD to the land of
Israel:

'An end! The end has come upon the
four corners of the land.
[3]Now the end *has come* upon you,
And I will send My anger against you;
I will judge you according to your
ways,
And I will repay you for all your
abominations.
[4]My eye will not spare you,
Nor will I have pity;
But I will repay your ways,
And your abominations will be in
your midst;
Then you shall know that I *am* the
LORD!'

[5]"Thus says the Lord GOD:

'A disaster, a singular disaster;
Behold, it has come!
[6]An end has come,
The end has come;
It has dawned for you;
Behold, it has come!
[7]Doom has come to you, you who
dwell in the land;
The time has come,
A day of trouble *is* near,
And not of rejoicing in the
mountains.
[8]Now upon you I will soon pour out
My fury,
And spend My anger upon you;
I will judge you according to your
ways,
And I will repay you for all your
abominations.

[9]'My eye will not spare,
Nor will I have pity;
I will repay you according to your
ways,
And your abominations will be in
your midst.
Then you shall know that I *am* the
LORD who strikes.

This generation of Christians is responsible for this generation of souls on the earth!

KEITH GREEN

[10]'Behold, the day!
Behold, it has come!
Doom has gone out;
The rod has blossomed,
Pride has budded.
[11]Violence has risen up into a rod of
wickedness;
None of them *shall remain,*
None of their multitude,
None of them;
Nor *shall there be* wailing for them.
[12]The time has come,
The day draws near.
'Let not the buyer rejoice,
Nor the seller mourn,
For wrath *is* on their whole
multitude.
[13]For the seller shall not return to what
has been sold,
Though he may still be alive;

For the vision concerns the whole
multitude,
And it shall not turn back;
No one will strengthen himself
Who lives in iniquity.

14'They have blown the trumpet and
made everyone ready,
But no one goes to battle;
For My wrath *is* on all their multitude.
15The sword *is* outside,
And the pestilence and famine within.
Whoever *is* in the field
Will die by the sword;
And whoever *is* in the city,
Famine and pestilence will devour
him.

. . . . . .

Will people who have never heard of Jesus go to hell? See Rom. 2:12 comment.

. . . . . .

16'Those who survive will escape and
be on the mountains
Like doves of the valleys,
All of them mourning,
Each for his iniquity.
17Every hand will be feeble,
And every knee will be *as* weak *as*
water.
18They will also be girded with
sackcloth;
Horror will cover them;
Shame *will be* on every face,
Baldness on all their heads.

19'They will throw their silver into the
streets,
And their gold will be like refuse;
Their silver and their gold will not be
able to deliver them
In the day of the wrath of the LORD;
They will not satisfy their souls,
Nor fill their stomachs,
Because it became their stumbling
block of iniquity.

20'As for the beauty of his ornaments,
He set it in majesty;
But they made from it
The images of their abominations—
Their detestable things;
Therefore I have made it
Like refuse to them.
21I will give it as plunder
Into the hands of strangers,
And to the wicked of the earth as spoil;
And they shall defile it.
22I will turn My face from them,
And they will defile My secret place;
For robbers shall enter it and defile it.

23'Make a chain,
For the land is filled with crimes of
blood,
And the city is full of violence.
24Therefore I will bring the worst of the
Gentiles,
And they will possess their houses;
I will cause the pomp of the strong to
cease,
And their holy places shall be defiled.
25Destruction comes;
They will seek peace, but *there shall be*
none.
26Disaster will come upon disaster,
And rumor will be upon rumor.
Then they will seek a vision from a
prophet;
But the law will perish from the priest,
And counsel from the elders.

27'The king will mourn,
The prince will be clothed with
desolation,

7:19 The love of money will always be an overwhelming temptation until a man deals with the stumbling block of his iniquity (see 1 Tim. 6:9,10). Once sin is forgiven and he is given a new heart with new desires, the saved can see through the folly of chasing riches. It has been well said, "Man seeks both wealth and wisdom. Having found one, he seldom seeks the other." The love of money may turn the head of a judge and cause him to pervert justice, but all the gold and silver in the world will not turn the head of the Judge of the universe on the Day of Wrath.

THE FUNCTION OF THE LAW

7:26 "If it were known that God Himself were going to speak once again to man, what eagerness and excitement there would be! For nearly nineteen hundred years He has been silent. No inspired message has been added to the Bible for nearly nineteen hundred years. How eagerly all men would listen if God should speak once more. Yet men forget that the Bible is God's own Word, and that it is as truly His message today as when it was delivered of old. The Law that was given at Sinai has lost none of its solemnity. Time cannot wear out its authority or the fact of its authorship." *D. L. Moody*

And the hands of the common people
will tremble.
I will do to them according to their
way,
And according to what they deserve I
will judge them;
Then they shall know that I *am* the
LORD!' "

Abominations in the Temple

8 And it came to pass in the sixth year, in the sixth *month,* on the fifth *day* of the month, as I sat in my house with the elders of Judah sitting before me, that the hand of the Lord GOD fell upon me there. 2Then I looked, and there was a likeness, like the appearance of fire—from the appearance of His waist and downward, fire; and from His waist and upward, like the appearance of brightness, like the color of amber. 3He stretched out the form of a hand, and took me by a lock of my hair; and the Spirit lifted me up between earth and heaven, and brought me in visions of God to Jerusalem, to the door of the north gate of the inner *court,* where the seat of the image of jealousy *was,* which provokes to jealousy. 4And behold, the glory of the God of Israel *was* there, like the vision that I saw in the plain.

5Then He said to me, "Son of man, lift your eyes now toward the north." So I lifted my eyes toward the north, and there, north of the altar gate, was this image of jealousy in the entrance.

6Furthermore He said to me, "Son of man, do you see what they are doing, the great abominations that the house of Israel commits here, to make Me go far away from My sanctuary? Now turn again, you will see greater abominations." 7So He brought me to the door of the court; and when I looked, there was a hole in the wall. 8Then He said to me, "Son of man, dig into the wall"; and when I dug into the wall, there was a door.

9And He said to me, "Go in, and see the wicked abominations which they are doing there." 10So I went in and saw, and there—every sort of creeping thing, abominable beasts, and all the idols of the house of Israel, portrayed all around on the walls. 11And there stood before them seventy men of the elders of the house of Israel, and in their midst stood Jaazaniah the son of Shaphan. Each man had a censer in his hand, and a thick cloud of incense went up. 12Then He said to me, "Son of man, have you seen what the elders of the house of Israel do in the dark, every man in the room of his idols? For they say, 'The LORD does not see us, the LORD has forsaken the land.' "

13And He said to me, "Turn again, *and* you will see greater abominations that they are doing." 14So He brought me to the door of the north gate of the LORD's house; and to my dismay, women were sitting there weeping for Tammuz.

15Then He said to me, "Have you seen *this,* O son of man? Turn again, you will see greater abominations than these." 16So He brought me into the inner court of the LORD's house; and there, at the door of the temple of the LORD, between

8:12 The error of the unsaved is that they think the Lord does not see their secret sins. There isn't a word that enters our mind or comes off our tongue that God isn't intimately acquainted with. All the ways of men are known to God (see Psa. 139:3; Jer. 16:17; 32:19).

the porch and the altar, *were* about twenty-five men with their backs toward the temple of the LORD and their faces toward the east, and they were worshiping the sun toward the east.

17And He said to me, "Have you seen *this,* O son of man? Is it a trivial thing to the house of Judah to commit the abominations which they commit here? For they have filled the land with violence; then they have returned to provoke Me to anger. Indeed they put the branch to their nose. 18Therefore I also will act in fury. My eye will not spare nor will I have pity; and though they cry in My ears with a loud voice, I will not hear them."

The Wicked Are Slain

9 Then He called out in my hearing with a loud voice, saying, "Let those who have charge over the city draw near, each *with* a deadly weapon in his hand." 2And suddenly six men came from the direction of the upper gate, which faces north, each with his battle-ax in his hand. One man among them *was* clothed with linen and had a writer's inkhorn at his side. They went in and stood beside the bronze altar.

3Now the glory of the God of Israel had gone up from the cherub, where it had been, to the threshold of the temple.[a] And He called to the man clothed with linen, who *had* the writer's inkhorn at his side; 4and the LORD said to him, "Go through the midst of the city, through the midst of Jerusalem, and put a mark on the foreheads of the men who sigh and cry over all the abominations that are done within it."

5To the others He said in my hearing, "Go after him through the city and kill; do not let your eye spare, nor have any pity. 6Utterly slay old *and* young men, maidens and little children and women; but do not come near anyone on whom *is* the mark; and begin at My sanctuary." So they began with the elders who *were* before the temple. 7Then He said to them, "Defile the temple, and fill the courts with the slain. Go out!" And they went out and killed in the city.

8So it was, that while they were killing them, I was left *alone;* and I fell on my face and cried out, and said, "Ah, Lord GOD! Will You destroy all the remnant of Israel in pouring out Your fury on Jerusalem?"

9Then He said to me, "The iniquity of the house of Israel and Judah is exceedingly great, and the land is full of bloodshed, and the city full of perversity; for they say, 'The LORD has forsaken the land, and the LORD does not see!' 10And as for Me also, My eye will neither spare, nor will I have pity, *but* I will recompense their deeds on their own head."

11Just then, the man clothed with linen, who *had* the inkhorn at his side, reported back and said, "I have done as You commanded me."

The Glory Departs from the Temple

10 And I looked, and there in the firmament that was above the head of the cherubim, there appeared something like a sapphire stone, having the appearance of the likeness of a throne. 2Then He spoke to the man clothed with linen, and said, "Go in among the wheels, under the cherub, fill your hands with

9:3 [a]Literally *house*

9:3–6 God has sealed His own with His Holy Spirit (see 2 Cor. 1:22; Eph. 1:13; 4:30), and they grieve over the wickedness of man. He will one day place a seal on the foreheads of His servants, to protect them during the end times (see Rev. 7:2,3; 9:4).

10:2 See Rev. 8:5 for a similar instance of God's judgment.

"The fire being taken from between the wheels, under the cherubim, seems to have signified the wrath of God to be executed upon Jerusalem. It intimated that the fire of Divine wrath, which kindles judgment upon a people, is just and holy; and in the great day, the earth, and all the works that are therein, will be burnt up." *Matthew Henry*

coals of fire from among the cherubim, and scatter *them* over the city." And he went in as I watched.

[3]Now the cherubim were standing on the south side of the temple[a] when the man went in, and the cloud filled the inner court. [4]Then the glory of the LORD went up from the cherub, *and paused* over the threshold of the temple; and the house was filled with the cloud, and the court was full of the brightness of the LORD's glory. [5]And the sound of the wings of the cherubim was heard *even* in the outer court, like the voice of Almighty God when He speaks.

[6]Then it happened, when He commanded the man clothed in linen, saying, "Take fire from among the wheels, from among the cherubim," that he went in and stood beside the wheels. [7]And the cherub stretched out his hand from among the cherubim to the fire that *was* among the cherubim, and took *some of it* and put *it* into the hands of the *man* clothed with linen, who took *it* and went out. [8]The cherubim appeared to have the form of a man's hand under their wings.

[9]And when I looked, there were four wheels by the cherubim, one wheel by one cherub and another wheel by each other cherub; the wheels appeared *to have* the color of a beryl stone. [10]*As for* their appearance, all four looked alike—as it were, a wheel in the middle of a wheel. [11]When they went, they went toward *any of* their four directions; they did not turn aside when they went, but followed in the direction the head was facing. They did not turn aside when they went. [12]And their whole body, with their back, their hands, their wings, and the wheels that the four had, *were* full of eyes all around. [13]As for the wheels, they were called in my hearing, "Wheel."

[14]Each one had four faces: the first face *was* the face of a cherub, the second face the face of a man, the third the face of a lion, and the fourth the face of an eagle. [15]And the cherubim were lifted up. This *was* the living creature I saw by the River Chebar. [16]When the cherubim went, the wheels went beside them; and when the cherubim lifted their wings to mount up from the earth, the same wheels also did not turn from beside them. [17]When *the cherubim*[a] stood still, *the wheels* stood still, and when *one*[b] was lifted up, *the other*[c] lifted itself up, for the spirit of the living creature *was* in them.

[18]Then the glory of the LORD departed from the threshold of the temple and stood over the cherubim. [19]And the cherubim lifted their wings and mounted up from the earth in my sight. When they went out, the wheels *were* beside them; and they stood at the door of the east gate of the LORD's house, and the glory of the God of Israel *was* above them.

> A man can no more diminish God's glory by refusing to worship Him than a lunatic can put out the sun by scribbling the word 'darkness' on the walls of his cell.
>
> **C. S. LEWIS**

[20]This *is* the living creature I saw under the God of Israel by the River Chebar, and I knew they *were* cherubim. [21]Each one had four faces and each one four wings, and the likeness of the hands of a man *was* under their wings. [22]And the likeness of their faces *was* the same *as* the faces which I had seen by the River Chebar, their appearance and their persons. They each went straight forward.

Judgment on Wicked Counselors

11 Then the Spirit lifted me up and brought me to the East Gate of the LORD's house, which faces eastward; and there at the door of the gate were twenty-five men, among whom I saw Jaazaniah the son of Azzur, and Pelatiah the son of Benaiah, princes of the people. [2]And He

10:3 [a]Literally *house,* also in verses 4 and 18 10:17 [a]Literally *they* [b]Literally *they* [c]Literally *they*

said to me: "Son of man, these *are* the men who devise iniquity and give wicked counsel in this city, 3who say, '*The time is* not near to build houses; this *city is* the caldron, and we *are* the meat.' 4Therefore prophesy against them, prophesy, O son of man!"

5Then the Spirit of the LORD fell upon me, and said to me, "Speak! 'Thus says the LORD: "Thus you have said, O house of Israel; for I know the things that come into your mind. 6You have multiplied your slain in this city, and you have filled its streets with the slain." 7Therefore thus says the Lord GOD: "Your slain whom you have laid in its midst, they *are* the meat, and this *city is* the caldron; but I shall bring you out of the midst of it. 8You have feared the sword; and I will bring a sword upon you," says the Lord GOD. 9"And I will bring you out of its midst, and deliver you into the hands of strangers, and execute judgments on you. 10You shall fall by the sword. I will judge you at the border of Israel. Then you shall know that I *am* the LORD. 11This *city* shall not be your caldron, nor shall you be the meat in its midst. I will judge you at the border of Israel. 12And you shall know that I *am* the LORD; for you have not walked in My statutes nor executed My judgments, but have done according to the customs of the Gentiles which *are* all around you." ' "

13Now it happened, while I was prophesying, that Pelatiah the son of Benaiah died. Then I fell on my face and cried with a loud voice, and said, "Ah, Lord GOD! Will You make a complete end of the remnant of Israel?"

God Will Restore Israel

14Again the word of the LORD came to me, saying, 15"Son of man, your brethren, your relatives, your countrymen, and all the house of Israel in its entirety, *are* those about whom the inhabitants of Jerusalem have said, 'Get far away from the LORD; this land has been given to us as a possession.' 16Therefore say, 'Thus says the Lord GOD: "Although I have cast them far off among the Gentiles, and although I have scattered them among the countries, yet I shall be a little sanctuary for them in the countries where they have gone." ' 17Therefore say, 'Thus says the Lord GOD: "I will gather you from the peoples, assemble you from the countries where you have been scattered, and I will give you the land of Israel." ' 18And they will go there, and they will take away all its detestable things and all its abominations from there. 19Then I will give them one heart, and I will put a new spirit within them,[a] and take the stony heart

11:19 [a]Literally *you*

11:5 It is a fearful revelation to the ungodly to realize that God sees their thoughts. This understanding brought me to the foot of the cross when I discovered that God saw my lust-filled heart and therefore considered me an adulterer (see Matt. 5:27,28).

11:17 The Bible's fascinating facts. In Isaiah 66:7,8 (700 B.C.), the prophet Isaiah gives a strange prophecy: "Before she was in labor, she gave birth; before her pain came, she delivered a male child. Who has heard such a thing? Who has seen such things? Shall the earth be made to give birth in one day? Or shall a nation be born at once? For as soon as Zion was in labor, she gave birth to her children." In 1922 the League of Nations gave Great Britain the mandate (political authority) over Palestine. On May 14, 1948, Britain withdrew her mandate, and the nation of Israel was "born in a day." There are more than 25 Bible prophecies concerning Palestine that have been literally fulfilled. Probability estimations conclude that the chances of these being accidentally fulfilled are less than one chance in 33 million.

11:19 New heart and spirit. This is the miracle of the new birth (see John 3:3). Many people, when questioned about their faith, will say that they have been born again. They confuse it with being sprinkled as a baby or having a change of mind about God. So make sure you explain that the new birth comes through understanding the nature of sin and exercising "repentance toward God and faith toward our Lord Jesus Christ" (Acts 20:21) for eternal salvation. It takes place when God gives a new heart with new desires, gives a new spirit, and makes a sinner a new creature in Christ (see 2 Cor. 5:17). Without the new birth (being born again), there is no salvation. See also Ezek. 18:31; 36:26,27; Psa. 51:10,11.

out of their flesh, and give them a heart of flesh, 20that they may walk in My statutes and keep My judgments and do them; and they shall be My people, and I will be their God. 21But *as for those* whose hearts follow the desire for their detestable things and their abominations, I will recompense their deeds on their own heads," says the Lord GOD.

22So the cherubim lifted up their wings, with the wheels beside them, and the glory of the God of Israel *was* high above them. 23And the glory of the LORD went up from the midst of the city and stood on the mountain, which *is* on the east side of the city.

24Then the Spirit took me up and brought me in a vision by the Spirit of God into Chaldea,[a] to those in captivity. And the vision that I had seen went up from me. 25So I spoke to those in captivity of all the things the LORD had shown me.

Judah's Captivity Portrayed

12 Now the word of the LORD came to me, saying: 2"Son of man, you dwell in the midst of a rebellious house, which has eyes to see but does not see, and ears to hear but does not hear; for they *are* a rebellious house.

3"Therefore, son of man, prepare your belongings for captivity, and go into captivity by day in their sight. You shall go from your place into captivity to another place in their sight. It may be that they will consider, though they *are* a rebellious house. 4By day you shall bring out your belongings in their sight, as though going into captivity; and at evening you shall go in their sight, like those who go into captivity. 5Dig through the wall in their sight, and carry *your belongings* out through it. 6In their sight you shall bear *them* on *your* shoulders *and* carry *them* out at twilight; you shall cover your face, so that you cannot see the ground, for I have made you a sign to the house of Israel."

7So I did as I was commanded. I brought out my belongings by day, as though going into captivity, and at evening I dug through the wall with my hand. I brought *them* out at twilight, *and* I bore *them* on *my* shoulder in their sight.

8And in the morning the word of the LORD came to me, saying, 9"Son of man, has not the house of Israel, the rebellious house, said to you, 'What are you doing?' 10Say to them, 'Thus says the Lord GOD: "This burden *concerns* the prince in Jerusalem and all the house of Israel who are among them." ' 11Say, 'I *am* a sign to you. As I have done, so shall it be done to them; they shall be carried away into captivity.' 12And the prince who *is* among them shall bear *his belongings* on *his* shoulder at twilight and go out. They shall dig through the wall to carry *them* out through it. He shall cover his face, so that he cannot see the ground with *his* eyes. 13I will also spread My net over him, and he shall be caught in My snare. I will bring him to Babylon, *to* the land of the Chaldeans; yet he shall not see it, though he shall die there. 14I will scatter to every wind all who *are* around him to help him, and all his troops; and I will draw out the sword after them.

15"Then they shall know that I *am* the LORD, when I scatter them among the nations and disperse them throughout the countries. 16But I will spare a few of their men from the sword, from famine, and from pestilence, that they may declare all their abominations among the Gentiles wherever they go. Then they shall know that I *am* the LORD."

Judgment Not Postponed

17Moreover the word of the LORD came

11:24 [a]Or *Babylon,* and so elsewhere in this book

12:2 The essence of sin is a rebellious heart. It is not that sinners cannot see, but that they will not. This verse sums up contemporary, secular America, where eyes and ears are firmly shut against God's truth.

to me, saying, 18“Son of man, eat your
bread with quaking, and drink your water with trembling and anxiety. 19And say
to the people of the land, ‘Thus says the
Lord GOD to the inhabitants of Jerusalem
and to the land of Israel: “They shall eat
their bread with anxiety, and drink their
water with dread, so that her land may be
emptied of all who are in it, because of
the violence of all those who dwell in it.
20Then the cities that are inhabited shall
be laid waste, and the land shall become
desolate; and you shall know that I *am*
the LORD.” ’ ”

> The gospel is light but only the Spirit can give sight. When seeking to bring the lost to Christ we must pray continually that they may receive the gift of seeing. And we must pit our prayer against that dark spirit who blinds the hearts of men.
>
> **A. W. TOZER**

21And the word of the LORD came to
me, saying, 22“Son of man, what *is* this
proverb *that* you *people* have about the
land of Israel, which says, ‘The days are
prolonged, and every vision fails’? 23Tell
them therefore, ‘Thus says the Lord GOD:
“I will lay this proverb to rest, and they
shall no more use it as a proverb in Israel.” ’ But say to them, ‘ “The days are at
hand, and the fulfillment of every vision.
24For no more shall there be any false vision or flattering divination within the
house of Israel. 25For I *am* the LORD. I
speak, and the word which I speak will
come to pass; it will no more be postponed; for in your days, O rebellious
house, I will say the word and perform
it,” says the Lord GOD.’ ”
26Again the word of the LORD came to
me, saying, 27“Son of man, look, the house
of Israel is saying, ‘The vision that he sees
is for many days *from now,* and he prophesies of times far off.’ 28Therefore say to
them, ‘Thus says the Lord GOD: “None of
My words will be postponed any more,
but the word which I speak will be
done,” says the Lord GOD.’ ”

Woe to Foolish Prophets

13 And the word of the LORD came to
me, saying, 2“Son of man, prophesy against the prophets of Israel who
prophesy, and say to those who prophesy
out of their own heart, ‘Hear the word of
the LORD!’ ”
3Thus says the Lord GOD: “Woe to the
foolish prophets, who follow their own
spirit and have seen nothing! 4O Israel,
your prophets are like foxes in the deserts.
5You have not gone up into the gaps to
build a wall for the house of Israel to
stand in battle on the day of the LORD.
6They have envisioned futility and false
divination, saying, ‘Thus says the LORD!’
But the LORD has not sent them; yet they
hope that the word may be confirmed.
7Have you not seen a futile vision, and
have you not spoken false divination?
You say, ‘The LORD says,’ but I have not
spoken.”
8Therefore thus says the Lord GOD:
“Because you have spoken nonsense and
envisioned lies, therefore I *am* indeed
against you,” says the Lord GOD. 9“My
hand will be against the prophets who
envision futility and who divine lies; they
shall not be in the assembly of My people, nor be written in the record of the
house of Israel, nor shall they enter into
the land of Israel. Then you shall know
that I *am* the Lord GOD.
10“Because, indeed, because they have
seduced My people, saying, ‘Peace!’ when
there is no peace—and one builds a wall,
and they plaster it with untempered *mortar*— 11say to those who plaster *it* with
untempered *mortar,* that it will fall. There
will be flooding rain, and you, O great

12:25 Every promise that God has made He will fulfill, whether it is of blessing or cursing.

hailstones, shall fall; and a stormy wind
shall tear *it* down. [12]Surely, when the wall
has fallen, will it not be said to you,
'Where *is* the mortar with which you
plastered *it?*' "

[13]Therefore thus says the Lord GOD: "I
will cause a stormy wind to break forth in
My fury; and there shall be a flooding
rain in My anger, and great hailstones in
fury to consume *it.* [14]So I will break down
the wall you have plastered with untempered *mortar,* and bring it down to the
ground, so that its foundation will be uncovered; it will fall, and you shall be consumed in the midst of it. Then you shall
know that I *am* the LORD.

[15]"Thus will I accomplish My wrath
on the wall and on those who have plastered it with untempered *mortar;* and I
will say to you, 'The wall *is* no *more,* nor
those who plastered it, [16]*that is,* the prophets of Israel who prophesy concerning
Jerusalem, and who see visions of peace
for her when *there is* no peace,' " says the
Lord GOD.

[17]"Likewise, son of man, set your face
against the daughters of your people,
who prophesy out of their own heart;
prophesy against them, [18]and say, 'Thus
says the Lord GOD: "Woe to the *women*
who sew *magic* charms on their sleeves[a]
and make veils for the heads of people of
every height to hunt souls! Will you hunt
the souls of My people, and keep yourselves alive? [19]And will you profane Me
among My people for handfuls of barley
and for pieces of bread, killing people
who should not die, and keeping people
alive who should not live, by your lying
to My people who listen to lies?"

[20]'Therefore thus says the Lord GOD:
"Behold, I *am* against your *magic* charms
by which you hunt souls there like birds.
I will tear them from your arms, and let
the souls go, the souls you hunt like birds.
[21]I will also tear off your veils and deliver
My people out of your hand, and they
shall no longer be as prey in your hand.
Then you shall know that I *am* the LORD.

[22]"Because with lies you have made
the heart of the righteous sad, whom I
have not made sad; and you have
strengthened the hands of the wicked, so
that he does not turn from his wicked
way to save his life. [23]Therefore you shall
no longer envision futility nor practice
divination; for I will deliver My people
out of your hand, and you shall know
that I *am* the LORD." ' "

Idolatry Will Be Punished

14 Now some of the elders of Israel
came to me and sat before me.
[2]And the word of the LORD came to me,
saying, [3]"Son of man, these men have set
up their idols in their hearts, and put before them that which causes them to
stumble into iniquity. Should I let Myself
be inquired of at all by them?

[4]"Therefore speak to them, and say to
them, 'Thus says the Lord GOD: "Everyone of the house of Israel who sets up his
idols in his heart, and puts before him
what causes him to stumble into iniquity,
and then comes to the prophet, I the
LORD will answer him who comes, according to the multitude of his idols,
[5]that I may seize the house of Israel by
their heart, because they are all estranged
from Me by their idols." '

[6]"Therefore say to the house of Israel,

13:18 [a]Literally *over all the joints of My hands;* Vulgate reads *under every elbow;* Septuagint and Targum read *on all elbows of the hands.*

13:15,16 Although this passage speaks of prophets who have visions of peace for Jerusalem when there was no peace (see v. 10), these verses should make us tremble. The modern message of evangelism is too quick to say that a sinner has peace with God merely because he has recited a "sinner's prayer." If there is no genuine repentance, there is no peace. The sinner is still under the wrath of God.

"If I am content to heal a hurt slightly, saying 'Peace, peace,' where there is no peace; if I forget the poignant word 'Let love be without dissimulation [hypocrisy]' and blunt the edge of truth, speaking not right things but smooth things, then I know nothing of Calvary love." *Amy Carmichael*

'Thus says the Lord GOD: "Repent, turn away from your idols, and turn your faces away from all your abominations. [7]For anyone of the house of Israel, or of the strangers who dwell in Israel, who separates himself from Me and sets up his idols in his heart and puts before him what causes him to stumble into iniquity, then comes to a prophet to inquire of him concerning Me, I the LORD will answer him by Myself. [8]I will set My face against that man and make him a sign and a proverb, and I will cut him off from the midst of My people. Then you shall know that I *am* the LORD.

[9]"And if the prophet is induced to speak anything, I the LORD have induced that prophet, and I will stretch out My hand against him and destroy him from among My people Israel. [10]And they shall bear their iniquity; the punishment of the prophet shall be the same as the punishment of the one who inquired, [11]that the house of Israel may no longer stray from Me, nor be profaned anymore with all their transgressions, but that they may be My people and I may be their God," says the Lord GOD.' "

Judgment on Persistent Unfaithfulness

[12]The word of the LORD came again to me, saying: [13]"Son of man, when a land sins against Me by persistent unfaithfulness, I will stretch out My hand against it; I will cut off its supply of bread, send famine on it, and cut off man and beast from it. [14]Even *if* these three men, Noah, Daniel, and Job, were in it, they would deliver *only* themselves by their righteousness," says the Lord GOD.

[15]"If I cause wild beasts to pass through the land, and they empty it, and make it so desolate that no man may pass through because of the beasts, [16]*even though* these three men *were* in it, *as* I live," says the Lord GOD, "they would deliver neither sons nor daughters; only they would be delivered, and the land would be desolate.

[17]"Or *if* I bring a sword on that land, and say, 'Sword, go through the land,' and I cut off man and beast from it, [18]even *though* these three men *were* in it, *as* I live," says the Lord GOD, "they would deliver neither sons nor daughters, but only they themselves would be delivered.

[19]"Or *if* I send a pestilence into that land and pour out My fury on it in blood, and cut off from it man and beast, [20]even *though* Noah, Daniel, and Job *were* in it, *as* I live," says the Lord GOD, "they would deliver neither son nor daughter; they would deliver *only* themselves by their righteousness."

[21]For thus says the Lord GOD: "How much more it shall be when I send My four severe judgments on Jerusalem—the sword and famine and wild beasts and pestilence—to cut off man and beast from it? [22]Yet behold, there shall be left in it a remnant who will be brought out, *both* sons and daughters; surely they will come out to you, and you will see their ways and their doings. Then you will be comforted concerning the disaster that I have brought upon Jerusalem, all that I have brought upon it. [23]And they will comfort you, when you see their ways and their doings; and you shall know that I have done nothing without cause that I have done in it," says the Lord GOD.

The Outcast Vine

15

Then the word of the LORD came to me, saying: [2]"Son of man, how is the wood of the vine *better* than any other wood, the vine branch which is among the trees of the forest? [3]Is wood taken from it to make any object? Or can *men* make a peg from it to hang any ves-

---

14:14–20 Each of these three men knew the power of God's deliverance. Noah was delivered from the flood, Daniel from the mouth of lions, and Job from terrible tribulation.

14:21 These are the same four judgments that are meted out in Rev. 6:8.

sel on? 4Instead, it is thrown into the fire
for fuel; the fire devours both ends of it,
and its middle is burned. Is it useful for
any work? 5Indeed, when it was whole,
no object could be made from it. How
much less will it be useful for *any* work
when the fire has devoured it, and it is
burned?

6"Therefore thus says the Lord GOD:
'Like the wood of the vine among the
trees of the forest, which I have given to
the fire for fuel, so I will give up the inhabitants of Jerusalem; 7and I will set My
face against them. They will go out from
one fire, but *another* fire shall devour them.
Then you shall know that I *am* the LORD,
when I set My face against them. 8Thus I
will make the land desolate, because they
have persisted in unfaithfulness,' says the
Lord GOD."

God's Love for Jerusalem

16 Again the word of the LORD came
to me, saying, 2"Son of man, cause
Jerusalem to know her abominations,
3and say, 'Thus says the Lord GOD to Jerusalem: "Your birth and your nativity *are*
from the land of Canaan; your father *was*
an Amorite and your mother a Hittite.
4*As for* your nativity, on the day you were
born your navel cord was not cut, nor
were you washed in water to cleanse *you;*
you were not rubbed with salt nor wrapped
in swaddling cloths. 5No eye pitied you,
to do any of these things for you, to have
compassion on you; but you were thrown
out into the open field, when you yourself were loathed on the day you were
born.

6"And when I passed by you and saw
you struggling in your own blood, I said
to you in your blood, 'Live!' Yes, I said to
you in your blood, 'Live!' 7I made you
thrive like a plant in the field; and you
grew, matured, and became very beautiful. *Your* breasts were formed, your hair
grew, but you *were* naked and bare.

8"When I passed by you again and
looked upon you, indeed your time *was*
the time of love; so I spread My wing
over you and covered your nakedness.
Yes, I swore an oath to you and entered
into a covenant with you, and you became Mine," says the Lord GOD.

*Does water baptism save us?
See Acts 10:47 comment.*

9"Then I washed you in water; yes, I
thoroughly washed off your blood, and I
anointed you with oil. 10I clothed you in
embroidered cloth and gave you sandals
of badger skin; I clothed you with fine
linen and covered you with silk. 11I
adorned you with ornaments, put bracelets on your wrists, and a chain on your
neck. 12And I put a jewel in your nose,
earrings in your ears, and a beautiful crown
on your head. 13Thus you were adorned
with gold and silver, and your clothing
was of fine linen, silk, and embroidered
cloth. You ate *pastry of* fine flour, honey,
and oil. You were exceedingly beautiful,
and succeeded to royalty. 14Your fame went
out among the nations because of your
beauty, for it *was* perfect through My
splendor which I had bestowed on you,"
says the Lord GOD.

Jerusalem's Harlotry

15"But you trusted in your own beauty,
played the harlot because of your fame,
and poured out your harlotry on everyone passing by who *would have* it. 16You
took some of your garments and adorned
multicolored high places for yourself, and
played the harlot on them. *Such* things
should not happen, nor be. 17You have
also taken your beautiful jewelry from
My gold and My silver, which I had given

15:6–8 Israel was under the fierce wrath of God because they forsook His Law, gave themselves to idolatry, which took them into sin. It is a predictable and downward path to judgment.

you, and made for yourself male images and played the harlot with them. 18You took your embroidered garments and covered them, and you set My oil and My incense before them. 19Also My food which I gave you—the pastry of fine flour, oil, and honey *which* I fed you—you set it before them as sweet incense; and *so* it was," says the Lord GOD.

20"Moreover you took your sons and your daughters, whom you bore to Me, and these you sacrificed to them to be devoured. *Were* your *acts* of harlotry a small matter, 21that you have slain My children and offered them up to them by causing them to pass through *the fire?* 22And in all your abominations and acts of harlotry you did not remember the days of your youth, when you were naked and bare, struggling in your blood.

> It is the duty of every Christian to be Christ to his neighbor.
>
> **MARTIN LUTHER**

23"Then it was so, after all your wickedness—'Woe, woe to you!' says the Lord GOD— 24*that* you also built for yourself a shrine, and made a high place for yourself in every street. 25You built your high places at the head of every road, and made your beauty to be abhorred. You offered yourself to everyone who passed by, and multiplied your acts of harlotry. 26You also committed harlotry with the Egyptians, your very fleshly neighbors, and increased your acts of harlotry to provoke Me to anger.

27"Behold, therefore, I stretched out My hand against you, diminished your allotment, and gave you up to the will of those who hate you, the daughters of the Philistines, who were ashamed of your lewd behavior. 28You also played the harlot with the Assyrians, because you were insatiable; indeed you played the harlot with them and still were not satisfied. 29Moreover you multiplied your acts of harlotry as far as the land of the trader, Chaldea; and even then you were not satisfied.

30"How degenerate is your heart!" says the Lord GOD, "seeing you do all these *things,* the deeds of a brazen harlot.

Jerusalem's Adultery

31"You erected your shrine at the head of every road, and built your high place in every street. Yet you were not like a harlot, because you scorned payment. 32*You are* an adulterous wife, *who* takes strangers instead of her husband. 33Men make payment to all harlots, but you made your payments to all your lovers, and hired them to come to you from all around for your harlotry. 34You are the opposite of *other* women in your harlotry, because no one solicited you to be a harlot. In that you gave payment but no payment was given you, therefore you are the opposite."

Jerusalem's Lovers Will Abuse Her

35'Now then, O harlot, hear the word of the LORD! 36Thus says the Lord GOD: "Because your filthiness was poured out and your nakedness uncovered in your harlotry with your lovers, and with all your abominable idols, and because of the blood of your children which you gave to them, 37surely, therefore, I will gather all your lovers with whom you took pleasure, all those you loved, *and* all those you hated; I will gather them from all around against you and will uncover your nakedness to them, that they may see all your nakedness. 38And I will judge you as women who break wedlock or shed blood are judged; I will bring blood upon you in fury and jealousy. 39I will also give you into their hand, and they shall throw down your shrines and break down your high places. They shall also

---

16:20,21 God calls our children His own. To see how precious life is from the moment of conception, see Psa. 127:3 comment.

strip you of your clothes, take your beautiful jewelry, and leave you naked and
bare.
40“They shall also bring up an assembly against you, and they shall stone you
with stones and thrust you through with
their swords. 41They shall burn your houses
with fire, and execute judgments on you
in the sight of many women; and I will
make you cease playing the harlot, and
you shall no longer hire lovers. 42So I will
lay to rest My fury toward you, and My
jealousy shall depart from you. I will be
quiet, and be angry no more. 43Because
you did not remember the days of your
youth, but agitated Me[a] with all these
things, surely I will also recompense your
deeds on *your own* head,” says the Lord
GOD. “And you shall not commit lewdness in addition to all your abominations.

More Wicked than Samaria and Sodom

44“Indeed everyone who quotes proverbs will use *this* proverb against you: ‘Like
mother, like daughter!’ 45You *are* your
mother’s daughter, loathing husband and
children; and you *are* the sister of your
sisters, who loathed their husbands and
children; your mother *was* a Hittite and
your father an Amorite.
46“Your elder sister *is* Samaria, who
dwells with her daughters to the north of
you; and your younger sister, who dwells
to the south of you, *is* Sodom and her
daughters. 47You did not walk in their ways
nor act according to their abominations;
but, as *if that were* too little, you became
more corrupt than they in all your ways.
48“*As* I live,” says the Lord GOD, “neither your sister Sodom nor her daughters
have done as you and your daughters
have done. 49Look, this was the iniquity
of your sister Sodom: She and her daughter
had pride, fullness of food, and abundance
of idleness; neither did she strengthen the
hand of the poor and needy. 50And they
were haughty and committed abomination
before Me; therefore I took them away as
I saw *fit.*[a]
51“Samaria did not commit half of
your sins; but you have multiplied your
abominations more than they, and have
justified your sisters by all the abominations which you have done. 52You who
judged your sisters, bear your own shame
also, because the sins which you committed were more abominable than theirs;
they are more righteous than you. Yes, be
disgraced also, and bear your own shame,
because you justified your sisters.
53“When I bring back their captives,
the captives of Sodom and her daughters,
and the captives of Samaria and her
daughters, then *I will also bring back* the
captives of your captivity among them,
54that you may bear your own shame and
be disgraced by all that you did when you
comforted them. 55When your sisters,
Sodom and her daughters, return to their
former state, and Samaria and her daughters return to their former state, then you
and your daughters will return to your
former state. 56For your sister Sodom was
not a byword in your mouth in the days
of your pride, 57before your wickedness
was uncovered. It was like the time of the
reproach of the daughters of Syria[a] and
all *those* around her, and of the daughters
of the Philistines, who despise you everywhere. 58You have paid for your lewdness
and your abominations,” says the LORD.
59For thus says the Lord GOD: “I will deal
with you as you have done, who despised
the oath by breaking the covenant.

An Everlasting Covenant

60“Nevertheless I will remember My
covenant with you in the days of your
youth, and I will establish an everlasting
covenant with you. 61Then you will remember your ways and be ashamed, when
you receive your older and your younger
sisters; for I will give them to you for
daughters, but not because of My cove-

16:43 [a]Following Septuagint, Syriac, Targum, and Vulgate; Masoretic Text reads *were agitated with Me.* 16:50 [a]Vulgate reads *you saw;* Septuagint reads *he saw;* Targum reads *as was revealed to Me.* 16:57 [a]Following Masoretic Text, Septuagint, Targum, and Vulgate; many Hebrew manuscripts and Syriac read *Edom.*

POINTS FOR OPEN-AIR PREACHING

Evolving Conversation

17:2

One fear of those who open-air preach is the inability to gather and hold a crowd. To engage the crowd, one way to draw responses is to address trivia questions to those in the crowd who embrace evolution. Simply say, "This next question is only for those who believe in evolution." Then ask these questions (giving away dollar bills for correct answers): "What was Darwin's first name?" (*Charles*) "What was the name of his first book?" (*The Voyage of the Beagle*) "What is the age of the earth: thousands, millions, or billions of years old?"

While people are calling out answers, look for the most outspoken person. Then ask him, "What's your name? Fred, you obviously believe in the theory of evolution. Why?"

Don't feel that you need to be an expert on the theory of evolution or even have to give your thoughts on the age of the earth. All you have to remember is that you are completely in control of the *direction* of the conversation and can move from the "intellect" to the "conscience" anytime you wish. Simply ask him questions about why he believes what he believes about the theory, then ask if he believes in the existence of God—is there a heaven, etc.? If he says that he doesn't believe in God or an afterlife, say, "*If* heaven does exist, are you good enough to go there? Are you a good person?" This moves away from the intellect to the conscience. Then take him through the Commandments. If he says that he is not a good person, ask, "So have you broken the Ten Commandments?" and take him through each one for his (and for the crowd's) sake. Then preach Judgment Day, the cross, the resurrection, repentance, and faith. See Psa. 51:6 comment.

nant with you. [62]And I will establish My
covenant with you. Then you shall know
that I *am* the LORD, [63]that you may remember and be ashamed, and never open
your mouth anymore because of your
shame, when I provide you an atonement
for all you have done," says the Lord
GOD.' "

The Eagles and the Vine

17 And the word of the LORD came to
me, saying, [2]"Son of man, pose a
riddle, and speak a parable to the house
of Israel, [3]and say, 'Thus says the Lord GOD:

"A great eagle with large wings and
long pinions,
Full of feathers of various colors,
Came to Lebanon
And took from the cedar the highest
branch.
[4]He cropped off its topmost young twig
And carried it to a land of trade;
He set it in a city of merchants.
[5]Then he took some of the seed of the
land
And planted it in a fertile field;
He placed *it* by abundant waters
And set it like a willow tree.
[6]And it grew and became a spreading
vine of low stature;
Its branches turned toward him,
But its roots were under it.
So it became a vine,
Brought forth branches,
And put forth shoots.

[7]"But there was another[a] great eagle
with large wings and many
feathers;
And behold, this vine bent its roots
toward him,
And stretched its branches toward him,
From the garden terrace where it had
been planted,
That he might water it.
[8]It was planted in good soil by many
waters,
To bring forth branches, bear fruit,
And become a majestic vine." '

[9]"Say, 'Thus says the Lord GOD:

"Will it thrive?
Will he not pull up its roots,
Cut off its fruit,
And leave it to wither?

17:7 [a]Following Septuagint, Syriac, and Vulgate; Masoretic Text and Targum read *one*.

All of its spring leaves will wither,
And no great power or many people
Will be needed to pluck it up by its
roots.
[10]Behold, *it is* planted,
Will it thrive?
Will it not utterly wither when the
east wind touches it?
It will wither in the garden terrace
where it grew." ' "

[11]Moreover the word of the LORD came
to me, saying, [12]"Say now to the rebellious house: 'Do you not know what these
things mean?' Tell *them,* 'Indeed the king
of Babylon went to Jerusalem and took its
king and princes, and led them with him
to Babylon. [13]And he took the king's offspring, made a covenant with him, and
put him under oath. He also took away
the mighty of the land, [14]that the kingdom might be brought low and not lift itself up, *but* that by keeping his covenant
it might stand. [15]But he rebelled against
him by sending his ambassadors to Egypt,
that they might give him horses and many
people. Will he prosper? Will he who does
such *things* escape? Can he break a
covenant and still be delivered?

[16]'*As* I live,' says the Lord GOD, 'surely
in the place *where* the king *dwells* who
made him king, whose oath he despised
and whose covenant he broke—with him
in the midst of Babylon he shall die. [17]Nor
will Pharaoh with *his* mighty army and
great company do anything in the war,
when they heap up a siege mound and
build a wall to cut off many persons.
[18]Since he despised the oath by breaking
the covenant, and in fact gave his hand
and still did all these *things,* he shall not
escape.' "
[19]Therefore thus says the Lord GOD:
"*As* I live, surely My oath which he despised, and My covenant which he broke,
I will recompense on his own head. [20]I
will spread My net over him, and he shall
be taken in My snare. I will bring him to
Babylon and try him there for the treason
which he committed against Me. [21]All his
fugitives[a] with all his troops shall fall by
the sword, and those who remain shall be
scattered to every wind; and you shall
know that I, the LORD, have spoken."

Israel Exalted at Last

[22]Thus says the Lord GOD: "I will take
also *one* of the highest branches of the
high cedar and set *it* out. I will crop off
from the topmost of its young twigs a tender one, and will plant *it* on a high and
prominent mountain. [23]On the mountain
height of Israel I will plant it; and it will
bring forth boughs, and bear fruit, and be
a majestic cedar. Under it will dwell birds
of every sort; in the shadow of its branches they will dwell. [24]And all the trees of
the field shall know that I, the LORD, have
brought down the high tree and exalted
the low tree, dried up the green tree and
made the dry tree flourish; I, the LORD,
have spoken and have done *it.*"

A False Proverb Refuted

18 The word of the LORD came to me
again, saying, [2]"What do you mean
when you use this proverb concerning
the land of Israel, saying:

'The fathers have eaten sour grapes,
And the children's teeth are set on
edge'?

[3]"As I live," says the Lord GOD, "you
shall no longer use this proverb in Israel.

[4]"Behold, all souls are Mine;

17:21 [a]Following Masoretic Text and Vulgate; many Hebrew manuscripts and Syriac read *choice men;* Targum reads *mighty men;* Septuagint omits *All his fugitives.*

17:19 Zedekiah heard the gracious offer of God's mercy many times, and yet he refused it. Millions are like the stubborn king. There are times when we want to give up on them, but how can we? Never stop pleading with the lost. As long as there is breath in their lungs, there must be hope in our hearts.

"You are not here in the world for yourself. You have been sent here for others. The world is waiting for you!"

Catherine Booth

The soul of the father
As well as the soul of the son is Mine;
The soul who sins shall die.
5But if a man is just
And does what is lawful and right;
6If he has not eaten on the mountains,
Nor lifted up his eyes to the idols of
the house of Israel,
Nor defiled his neighbor's wife,
Nor approached a woman during her
impurity;
7If he has not oppressed anyone,
But has restored to the debtor his
pledge;
Has robbed no one by violence,
But has given his bread to the hungry
And covered the naked with clothing;
8If he has not exacted usury
Nor taken any increase,
But has withdrawn his hand from
iniquity
And executed true judgment between
man and man;
9*If* he has walked in My statutes
And kept My judgments faithfully—
He *is* just;
He shall surely live!"
Says the Lord GOD.

10"If he begets a son *who is* a robber
Or a shedder of blood,
Who does any of these *things*
11And does none of those *duties,*
But has eaten on the mountains
Or defiled his neighbor's wife;
12If he has oppressed the poor and
needy,
Robbed by violence,
Not restored the pledge,
Lifted his eyes to the idols,
Or committed abomination;
13If he has exacted usury
Or taken increase—
Shall he then live?
He shall not live!
If he has done any of these
abominations,
He shall surely die;
His blood shall be upon him.

14"*If,* however, he begets a son
Who sees all the sins which his father
has done,
And considers but does not do
likewise;
15*Who* has not eaten on the mountains,
Nor lifted his eyes to the idols of the
house of Israel,
Nor defiled his neighbor's wife;
16Has not oppressed anyone,
Nor withheld a pledge,
Nor robbed by violence,
But has given his bread to the hungry
And covered the naked with clothing;

18:4 Skeptics say they don't believe in the "soul." Yet the soul is simply the life that inhabits the body. It is the real you. Genesis 35:18 says of Rachel, "her soul was departing (for she died)..." If someone lost all of his limbs in a terrible accident, though he has only half of his physical body he is still a whole person. He is the same complete soul. See also 1 Kings 17:21,22 comment.

"You don't have a soul. You are a soul. You have a body." *C. S. Lewis*

Springboards for Preaching and Witnessing

Plane Speaking

18:20 Two hundred years ago, "rational" thinking folks would have mocked you if you spoke of the possibility of massive jumbo jets floating through the air filled with human beings. Any sensible person knew that massively heavy objects couldn't possibly float through the air, as though they were lighter than a feather. They "knew" this because of an invisible law: the law of gravity. But we now know that this is possible, because of another law that overcomes gravity. When an object moves at a certain speed, it supersedes the invisible law of gravity and enters into another invisible law—the law of aerodynamics. Gravity remains, but the heavy object breaks free from its influence.

The Bible says that all of humanity is subject to an invisible law: "the law of sin and death." That law says that the soul who sins will die. Those who deny that it exists should simply take a trip to a graveyard (they will one day). Universal death proves that this law is a reality. However, because of the cross of Jesus Christ, we can break free from the law of sin and death. The moment you repent and trust in the risen Savior, you move into the influence of another invisible law. This is a higher law—"the law of life in Christ Jesus"—and it is simple to prove. You need only to step into the plane. Tragically, most don't, because of a closed mind. "For the law of the Spirit of life in Christ Jesus has made me free from the law of sin and death" (Rom. 8:2).

17 *Who* has withdrawn his hand from
the poor[a]
And not received usury or increase,
But has executed My judgments
And walked in My statutes—
He shall not die for the iniquity of his
father;
He shall surely live!

18 "*As for* his father,
Because he cruelly oppressed,
Robbed his brother by violence,
And did what *is* not good among his
people,
Behold, he shall die for his iniquity.

Turn and Live

19 "Yet you say, 'Why should the son
not bear the guilt of the father?' Because
the son has done what is lawful and right,
and has kept all My statutes and observed
them, he shall surely live. 20 The soul who
sins shall die. The son shall not bear the
guilt of the father, nor the father bear the
guilt of the son. The righteousness of the
righteous shall be upon himself, and the
wickedness of the wicked shall be upon
himself.

21 "But if a wicked man turns from all
his sins which he has committed, keeps
all My statutes, and does what is lawful
and right, he shall surely live; he shall not
die. 22 None of the transgressions which
he has committed shall be remembered
against him; because of the righteousness
which he has done, he shall live. 23 Do I
have any pleasure at all that the wicked
should die?" says the Lord GOD, "*and* not
that he should turn from his ways and
live?

24 "But when a righteous man turns
away from his righteousness and commits
iniquity, and does according to all the
abominations that the wicked *man* does,
shall he live? All the righteousness which
he has done shall not be remembered;
because of the unfaithfulness of which he
is guilty and the sin which he has committed,
because of them he shall die.

. . . . . .

Do vestigial organs prove evolution? See Eccles. 3:6 comment.

. . . . . .

25 "Yet you say, 'The way of the Lord is
not fair.' Hear now, O house of Israel, is it
not My way which is fair, and your ways
which are not fair? 26 When a righteous
man turns away from his righteousness,
commits iniquity, and dies in it, it is because
of the iniquity which he has done
that he dies. 27 Again, when a wicked *man*

18:17 [a]Following Masoretic Text, Targum, and Vulgate; Septuagint reads *iniquity* (compare verse 8).

turns away from the wickedness which
he committed, and does what is lawful and
right, he preserves himself alive. 28Be-
cause he considers and turns away from
all the transgressions which he committed, he shall surely live; he shall not die.
29Yet the house of Israel says, 'The way of
the Lord is not fair.' O house of Israel, is
it not My ways which are fair, and your
ways which are not fair?
30"Therefore I will judge you, O house
of Israel, every one according to his ways,"
says the Lord GOD. "Repent, and turn
from all your transgressions, so that iniquity will not be your ruin. 31Cast away
from you all the transgressions which
you have committed, and get yourselves
a new heart and a new spirit. For why
should you die, O house of Israel? 32For I
have no pleasure in the death of one who
dies," says the Lord GOD. "Therefore turn
and live!"

Israel Degraded

19 "Moreover take up a lamentation
for the princes of Israel, 2and say:

'What *is* your mother? A lioness:
She lay down among the lions;
Among the young lions she nourished
her cubs.
3She brought up one of her cubs,
And he became a young lion;
He learned to catch prey,
And he devoured men.
4The nations also heard of him;
He was trapped in their pit,
And they brought him with chains to
the land of Egypt.

5'When she saw that she waited, *that*
her hope was lost,
She took another of her cubs *and*
made him a young lion.
6He roved among the lions,
And became a young lion;
He learned to catch prey;
He devoured men.
7He knew their desolate places,[a]
And laid waste their cities;
The land with its fullness was desolated
By the noise of his roaring.
8Then the nations set against him from
the provinces on every side,
And spread their net over him;
He was trapped in their pit.
9They put him in a cage with chains,
And brought him to the king of
Babylon;

19:7 [a]Septuagint reads *He stood in insolence;* Targum reads *He destroyed its palaces;* Vulgate reads *He learned to make widows.*

18:25,29 God is not "fair." The average person is guilty of committing tens of thousands of crimes against God in his lifetime. He has no justification. With the voice of his conscience, he knows it is wrong to lie, steal, commit adultery in his heart, etc. He knows intuitively that God gave him life (see Rom. 1:18–20), but instead of showing any gratitude, he uses His holy name as a cuss word to express disgust. Hell is therefore his just reward, if God is "fair."

But God is "unfair." He offers the sinner a complete pardon for his sins. Jesus paid his fine 2,000 years ago, and that means God (as Judge) can legally dismiss his case upon his repentance and faith in Jesus. *None* of his transgressions will be remembered. Because of God's great mercy, He does not give us what is "fair" and just: "He has not dealt with us according to our sins, nor punished us according to our iniquities" (Psa. 103:10).

18:30 Do we remove words that might offend, such as "repentance" and "hell," to make the message more acceptable, or to make ourselves acceptable to a God-hating world? God forbid that our concern should be for our own comfort, rather than for the eternal welfare of the world.

"From Athens to Los Angeles, first century to twenty-first century and everywhere in between, repentance may not be popular, but it's still the gospel." *John MacArthur*

18:31 This should be the heart-cry of every Christian. We should be horrified at sinners' disregard for their eternal salvation. See also 36:26,27 comment.

18:32 God has no pleasure in the death of sinners and in damning them if they refuse to repent. Mercy rejoices over judgment. As His ambassadors we should echo His plea that sinners "turn and live!" See 33:11 comment.

They brought him in nets,
That his voice should no longer be
heard on the mountains of Israel.

10'Your mother *was* like a vine in your
bloodline,[a]
Planted by the waters,
Fruitful and full of branches
Because of many waters.
11She had strong branches for scepters
of rulers.
She towered in stature above the
thick branches,
And was seen in her height amid the
dense foliage.
12But she was plucked up in fury,
She was cast down to the ground,
And the east wind dried her fruit.
Her strong branches were broken and
withered;
The fire consumed them.
13And now she *is* planted in the
wilderness,
In a dry and thirsty land.
14Fire has come out from a rod of her
branches
And devoured her fruit,
So that she has no strong branch— a
scepter for ruling.' "

This *is* a lamentation, and has become a lamentation.

The Rebellions of Israel

20 It came to pass in the seventh year, in the fifth *month,* on the tenth *day* of the month, *that* certain of the elders of Israel came to inquire of the LORD, and sat before me.
2Then the word of the LORD came to me, saying,
3"Son of man, speak to the elders of Israel, and say to them, 'Thus says the Lord GOD: "Have you come to inquire of Me? *As* I live," says the Lord GOD, "I will not be inquired of by you." '
4Will you judge them, son of man, will you judge *them?* Then make known to them the abominations of their fathers.
5"Say to them, 'Thus says the Lord GOD: "On the day when I chose Israel and raised My hand in an oath to the descendants of the house of Jacob, and made Myself known to them in the land of Egypt, I raised My hand in an oath to them, saying, 'I *am* the LORD your God.'
6On that day I raised My hand in an oath to them, to bring them out of the land of Egypt into a land that I had searched out for them, 'flowing with milk and honey,'[a] the glory of all lands.
7Then I said to them, 'Each of you, throw away the abominations which are before his eyes, and do not defile yourselves with the idols of Egypt. I *am* the LORD your God.'
8But they rebelled against Me and would not obey Me. They did not all cast away the abominations which were before their eyes, nor did they forsake the idols of Egypt. Then I said, 'I will pour out My fury on them and fulfill My anger against them in the midst of the land of Egypt.'

> You blame me for weeping, but how can I help it when you will not weep for yourselves, though your immortal souls are on the verge of destruction?
>
> **GEORGE WHITEFIELD**

9But I acted for My name's sake, that it should not be profaned before the Gentiles among whom they *were,* in whose sight I had made Myself known to them, to bring them out of the land of Egypt.
10"Therefore I made them go out of the land of Egypt and brought them into the wilderness.
11And I gave them My statutes and showed them My judgments, 'which, *if* a man does, he shall live by them.'[a]

19:10 [a]Literally *blood,* following Masoretic Text, Syriac, and Vulgate; Septuagint reads *like a flower on a pomegranate tree;* Targum reads *in your likeness.* 20:6 [a]Exodus 3:8 20:11 [a]Leviticus 18:5

20:11,12 See Col. 2:16 comments regarding the Sabbath.

12Moreover I also gave them My Sabbaths, to be a sign between them and Me, that they might know that I *am* the LORD who sanctifies them. 13Yet the house of Israel rebelled against Me in the wilderness; they did not walk in My statutes; they despised My judgments, 'which, *if* a man does, he shall live by them';[a] and they greatly defiled My Sabbaths. Then I said I would pour out My fury on them in the wilderness, to consume them. 14But I acted for My name's sake, that it should not be profaned before the Gentiles, in whose sight I had brought them out. 15So I also raised My hand in an oath to them in the wilderness, that I would not bring them into the land which I had given *them,* 'flowing with milk and honey,'[a] the glory of all lands, 16because they despised My judgments and did not walk in My statutes, but profaned My Sabbaths; for their heart went after their idols. 17Nevertheless My eye spared them from destruction. I did not make an end of them in the wilderness.

18"But I said to their children in the wilderness, 'Do not walk in the statutes of your fathers, nor observe their judgments, nor defile yourselves with their idols. 19I *am* the LORD your God: Walk in My statutes, keep My judgments, and do them; 20hallow My Sabbaths, and they will be a sign between Me and you, that you may know that I *am* the LORD your God.'

21"Notwithstanding, the children rebelled against Me; they did not walk in My statutes, and were not careful to observe My judgments, 'which, *if* a man does, he shall live by them';[a] but they profaned My Sabbaths. Then I said I would pour out My fury on them and fulfill My anger against them in the wilderness. 22Nevertheless I withdrew My hand and acted for My name's sake, that it should not be profaned in the sight of the Gentiles, in whose sight I had brought them out. 23Also I raised My hand in an oath to those in the wilderness, that I would scatter them among the Gentiles and disperse them throughout the countries, 24because they had not executed My judgments, but had despised My statutes, profaned My Sabbaths, and their eyes were fixed on their fathers' idols.

25"Therefore I also gave them up to statutes *that were* not good, and judgments by which they could not live; 26and I pronounced them unclean because of their ritual gifts, in that they caused all their firstborn to pass through *the fire,* that I might make them desolate and that they might know that I am the LORD." '

27"Therefore, son of man, speak to the house of Israel, and say to them, 'Thus says the Lord GOD: "In this too your fathers have blasphemed Me, by being unfaithful to Me. 28When I brought them into the land *concerning* which I had raised My hand in an oath to give them, and they saw all the high hills and all the thick trees, there they offered their sacrifices and provoked Me with their offerings. There they also sent up their sweet aroma and poured out their drink offerings. 29Then I said to them, 'What *is* this high place to which you go?' So its name is called Bamah[a] to this day." ' 30Therefore say to the house of Israel, 'Thus says the Lord GOD: "Are you defiling yourselves in the manner of your fathers, and committing harlotry according to their abominations? 31For when you offer your gifts and make your sons pass through the fire, you defile yourselves with all your idols, even to this day. So shall I be inquired of by you, O house of Israel? *As* I live," says the Lord GOD, "I will not be inquired of by you. 32What you have in your mind shall never be, when you say, 'We will be like the Gentiles, like the families in other countries, serving wood and stone.'

God Will Restore Israel

33"*As* I live," says the Lord GOD, "surely with a mighty hand, with an outstretched arm, and with fury poured out, I will rule

20:13 [a]Leviticus 18:5 **20:15** [a]Exodus 3:8 **20:21** [a]Leviticus 18:5 **20:29** [a]Literally *High Place*

over you. 34I will bring you out from the peoples and gather you out of the countries where you are scattered, with a mighty hand, with an outstretched arm, and with fury poured out. 35And I will bring you into the wilderness of the peoples, and there I will plead My case with you face to face. 36Just as I pleaded My case with your fathers in the wilderness of the land of Egypt, so I will plead My case with you," says the Lord GOD.

37"I will make you pass under the rod, and I will bring you into the bond of the covenant; 38I will purge the rebels from among you, and those who transgress against Me; I will bring them out of the country where they dwell, but they shall not enter the land of Israel. Then you will know that I *am* the LORD.

39"As for you, O house of Israel," thus says the Lord GOD: "Go, serve every one of you his idols—and hereafter—if you will not obey Me; but profane My holy name no more with your gifts and your idols. 40For on My holy mountain, on the mountain height of Israel," says the Lord GOD, "there all the house of Israel, all of them in the land, shall serve Me; there I will accept them, and there I will require your offerings and the firstfruits of your sacrifices, together with all your holy things. 41I will accept you as a sweet aroma when I bring you out from the peoples and gather you out of the countries where you have been scattered; and I will be hallowed in you before the Gentiles. 42Then you shall know that I *am* the LORD, when I bring you into the land of Israel, into the country *for* which I raised My hand in an oath to give to your fathers. 43And there you shall remember your ways and all your doings with which you were defiled; and you shall loathe yourselves in your own sight because of all the evils that you have committed. 44Then you shall know that I *am* the LORD, when I have dealt with you for My name's sake, not according to your wicked ways nor according to your corrupt doings, O house of Israel," says the Lord GOD.' "

Fire in the Forest

45Furthermore the word of the LORD came to me, saying, 46"Son of man, set your face toward the south; preach against the south and prophesy against the forest land, the South,[a] 47and say to the forest of the South, 'Hear the word of the LORD! Thus says the Lord GOD: "Behold, I will kindle a fire in you, and it shall devour every green tree and every dry tree in you; the blazing flame shall not be quenched, and all faces from the south to the north shall be scorched by it. 48All flesh shall see that I, the LORD, have kindled it; it shall not be quenched." ' "

49Then I said, "Ah, Lord GOD! They say of me, 'Does he not speak parables?' "

Babylon, the Sword of God

21 And the word of the LORD came to me, saying, 2"Son of man, set your face toward Jerusalem, preach against the holy places, and prophesy against the land of Israel; 3and say to the land of Israel, 'Thus says the LORD: "Behold, I *am* against you, and I will draw My sword out of its sheath and cut off both righteous and wicked from you. 4Because I will cut off both righteous and wicked from you, therefore My sword shall go out of its sheath against all flesh from south *to* north, 5that all flesh may know that I, the LORD, have drawn My sword out of its

20:46 [a]Hebrew *Negev*

20:39 It is a fearful thing when God stops striving with a man to turn from his sin, and instead gives him over to a reprobate mind. See Rom. 1:28.

20:43 This is an example of genuine repentance. After Job had a revelation of God's nature, he said, "I have heard of You by the hearing of the ear, but now my eye sees You. Therefore I abhor myself, and repent in dust and ashes" (Job 42:5,6). See also Joel 2:12,13; Jer. 8:6,12.

sheath; it shall not return anymore." '
[6]Sigh therefore, son of man, with a breaking heart, and sigh with bitterness before
their eyes. [7]And it shall be when they say
to you, 'Why are you sighing?' that you shall answer, 'Because of the news; when it comes, every heart will melt, all hands will be feeble, every spirit will faint, and all knees will be weak *as* water. Behold, it is coming and shall be brought to pass,' says the Lord GOD."

[8]Again the word of the LORD came to
me, saying, [9]"Son of man, prophesy and
say, 'Thus says the LORD!' Say:

'A sword, a sword is sharpened
And also polished!
[10]Sharpened to make a dreadful
slaughter,
Polished to flash like lightning!
Should we then make mirth?
It despises the scepter of My son,
As it does all wood.
[11]And He has given it to be polished,
That it may be handled;
This sword is sharpened, and it is
polished
To be given into the hand of the
slayer.'

[12]"Cry and wail, son of man;
For it will be against My people,
Against all the princes of Israel.
Terrors including the sword will be
against My people;
Therefore strike *your* thigh.

[13]"Because *it is* a testing,
And what if *the sword* despises even
the scepter?
The scepter shall be no *more*,"
says the Lord GOD.

[14]"You therefore, son of man, prophesy,
And strike *your* hands together.
The third time let the sword do
double *damage*.
It *is* the sword *that* slays,
The sword that slays the great *men*,
That enters their private chambers.
[15]I have set the point of the sword
against all their gates,
That the heart may melt and many
may stumble.
Ah! *It is* made bright;
It is grasped for slaughter:

[16]"Swords at the ready!
Thrust right!
Set your blade!
Thrust left—
Wherever your edge is ordered!

[17]"I also will beat My fists together,
And I will cause My fury to rest;
I, the LORD, have spoken."

[18]The word of the LORD came to me
again, saying: [19]"And son of man, appoint
for yourself two ways for the sword of the king of Babylon to go; both of them shall go from the same land. Make a sign; put
it at the head of the road to the city. [20]Appoint a road for the sword to go to Rabbah of the Ammonites, and to Judah, into

---

21:6,7 Do we "sigh" at the thought of Judgment Day? Does terror grip us at the thought of guilty sinners facing the wrath of a holy God? Love is the catalyst for zeal for the lost.

"Missionary zeal does not grow out of intellectual beliefs, nor out of theological arguments, but out of love." *Roland Allen*

"The attitude of the average Christian today is relax and be raptured. But He is coming... and when God gets angry you've no idea what it is. Like a thousand volcanoes exploding. He has appointed a day in which He is going to judge the world, and the poor blind world doesn't know much about it and the poor blind church doesn't think much about it now." *Leonard Ravenhill*

21:9–11 For every murder and rape, God sharpens and draws back the sword of eternal justice. For every lie, for hatred, greed, lust, envy, jealousy, pride, for adultery, fornication, unbridled anger, for every idle word, Almighty God holds the sword that is wielded by the arm of His Law.

fortified Jerusalem. 21For the king of
Babylon stands at the parting of the road,
at the fork of the two roads, to use divination: he shakes the arrows, he consults
the images, he looks at the liver. 22In his
right hand is the divination for Jerusalem: to set up battering rams, to call for
a slaughter, to lift the voice with shouting, to set battering rams against the
gates, to heap up a *siege* mound, and to
build a wall. 23And it will be to them like
a false divination in the eyes of those who
have sworn oaths with them; but he will
bring their iniquity to remembrance, that
they may be taken.

24"Therefore thus says the Lord GOD:
'Because you have made your iniquity to
be remembered, in that your transgressions are uncovered, so that in all your
doings your sins appear—because you
have come to remembrance, you shall be
taken in hand.

25'Now to you, O profane, wicked
prince of Israel, whose day has come,
whose iniquity *shall* end, 26thus says the
Lord GOD:

"Remove the turban, and take off the
crown;
Nothing *shall remain* the same.
Exalt the humble, and humble the
exalted.
27Overthrown, overthrown,
I will make it overthrown!
It shall be no *longer,*
Until He comes whose right it is,
And I will give it *to Him.*" '

A Sword Against the Ammonites

28"And you, son of man, prophesy and
say, 'Thus says the Lord GOD concerning
the Ammonites and concerning their reproach,' and say:

'A sword, a sword is drawn,
Polished for slaughter,
For consuming, for flashing—
29While they see false visions for you,
While they divine a lie to you,
To bring you on the necks of the
wicked, the slain
Whose day has come,
Whose iniquity *shall* end.

30'Return *it* to its sheath.
I will judge you
In the place where you were created,
In the land of your nativity.
31I will pour out My indignation on
you;
I will blow against you with the fire of
My wrath,
And deliver you into the hands of
brutal men *who are* skillful to
destroy.
32You shall be fuel for the fire;
Your blood shall be in the midst of
the land.
You shall not be remembered,
For I the LORD have spoken.' "

Sins of Jerusalem

22 Moreover the word of the LORD
came to me, saying, 2"Now, son of
man, will you judge, will you judge the
bloody city? Yes, show her all her abominations! 3Then say, 'Thus says the Lord
GOD: "The city sheds blood in her own
midst, that her time may come; and she
makes idols within herself to defile herself. 4You have become guilty by the
blood which you have shed, and have defiled yourself with the idols which you
have made. You have caused your days to
draw near, and have come to *the end of*
your years; therefore I have made you a
reproach to the nations, and a mockery
to all countries. 5*Those* near and *those* far
from you will mock you as infamous *and*
full of tumult.

6"Look, the princes of Israel: each one
has used his power to shed blood in you.
7In you they have made light of father
and mother; in your midst they have oppressed the stranger; in you they have
mistreated the fatherless and the widow.
8You have despised My holy things and
profaned My Sabbaths. 9In you are men
who slander to cause bloodshed; in you
are those who eat on the mountains; in

your midst they commit lewdness. 10In you men uncover their fathers' nakedness; in you they violate women who are set apart during their impurity. 11One commits abomination with his neighbor's wife; another lewdly defiles his daughter-in-law; and another in you violates his sister, his father's daughter. 12In you they take bribes to shed blood; you take usury and increase; you have made profit from your neighbors by extortion, and have forgotten Me," says the Lord GOD.

> First we practice sin, then defend it, then boast of it.
>
> **THOMAS MANTON**

13"Behold, therefore, I beat My fists at the dishonest profit which you have made, and at the bloodshed which has been in your midst. 14Can your heart endure, or can your hands remain strong, in the days when I shall deal with you? I, the LORD, have spoken, and will do *it.* 15I will scatter you among the nations, disperse you throughout the countries, and remove your filthiness completely from you. 16You shall defile yourself in the sight of the nations; then you shall know that I *am* the LORD." ' "

Israel in the Furnace

17The word of the LORD came to me, saying, 18"Son of man, the house of Israel has become dross to Me; they *are* all bronze, tin, iron, and lead, in the midst of a furnace; they have become dross from silver. 19Therefore thus says the Lord GOD: 'Because you have all become dross, therefore behold, I will gather you into the midst of Jerusalem. 20*As men* gather silver, bronze, iron, lead, and tin into the midst of a furnace, to blow fire on it, to melt *it;* so I will gather *you* in My anger and in My fury, and I will leave *you there* and melt you. 21Yes, I will gather you and blow on you with the fire of My wrath, and you shall be melted in its midst. 22As silver is melted in the midst of a furnace, so shall you be melted in its midst; then you shall know that I, the LORD, have poured out My fury on you.' "

Israel's Wicked Leaders

23And the word of the LORD came to me, saying, 24"Son of man, say to her: 'You *are* a land that is not cleansed[a] or rained on in the day of indignation.' 25The conspiracy of her prophets[a] in her midst is like a roaring lion tearing the prey; they have devoured people; they have taken treasure and precious things; they have made many widows in her midst. 26Her priests have violated My law and profaned My holy things; they have not distinguished between the holy and unholy, nor have they made known *the difference* between the unclean and the clean; and they have hidden their eyes from My Sabbaths, so that I am profaned among them. 27Her princes in her midst *are* like wolves tearing the prey, to shed blood, to destroy people, and to get dishonest gain. 28Her prophets plastered them with untempered *mortar,* seeing false visions, and divining lies for them, saying, 'Thus says the Lord GOD,' when the LORD had not spoken. 29The people of the land have used oppressions, committed robbery, and mistreated the poor and needy; and they wrongfully oppress the stranger. 30So I sought for a man among them who would make a wall, and stand in the gap before Me on behalf of the land, that I should not destroy it; but I found no one. 31Therefore I have poured out My indignation on

22:24 [a]Following Masoretic Text, Syriac, and Vulgate; Septuagint reads *showered upon*. 22:25 [a]Following Masoretic Text and Vulgate; Septuagint reads *princes*; Targum reads *scribes*.

22:26 When a nation violates God's Law, it no longer makes any distinction between good and evil. Abortion, pornography, homosexuality, adultery, lying, and stealing become accepted parts of its culture.

them; I have consumed them with the fire of My wrath; and I have recompensed their deeds on their own heads," says the Lord GOD.

Two Harlot Sisters

23 The word of the LORD came again to me, saying:

2"Son of man, there were two women,
The daughters of one mother.
3They committed harlotry in Egypt,
They committed harlotry in their youth;
Their breasts were there embraced,
Their virgin bosom was there pressed.
4Their names: Oholah[a] the elder and Oholibah[b] her sister;
They were Mine,
And they bore sons and daughters.
As for their names,
Samaria *is* Oholah, and Jerusalem *is* Oholibah.

The Older Sister, Samaria

5"Oholah played the harlot even though she was Mine;
And she lusted for her lovers, the neighboring Assyrians,
6*Who were* clothed in purple,
Captains and rulers,
All of them desirable young men,
Horsemen riding on horses.
7Thus she committed her harlotry with them,
All of them choice men of Assyria;
And with all for whom she lusted,
With all their idols, she defiled herself.
8She has never given up her harlotry *brought* from Egypt,
For in her youth they had lain with her,
Pressed her virgin bosom,
And poured out their immorality upon her.

9"Therefore I have delivered her
Into the hand of her lovers,
Into the hand of the Assyrians,
For whom she lusted.
10They uncovered her nakedness,
Took away her sons and daughters,
And slew her with the sword;
She became a byword among women,
For they had executed judgment on her.

The Younger Sister, Jerusalem

11"Now although her sister Oholibah
saw *this,* she became more corrupt in her
lust than she, and in her harlotry more
corrupt than her sister's harlotry.

12"She lusted for the neighboring Assyrians,
Captains and rulers,
Clothed most gorgeously,
Horsemen riding on horses,
All of them desirable young men.
13Then I saw that she was defiled;
Both *took* the same way.
14But she increased her harlotry;
She looked at men portrayed on the

23:4 [a]Literally *Her Own Tabernacle* [b]Literally *My Tabernacle Is in Her*

22:30,31 Stand in the gap. We must stand in the gap and plead for this world. Had it not been for the prayers of the godly, the wrath of God may have already judged many nations. Never underestimate the power, influence, and authority God has given you through faith in Jesus. Through His name you have the ear of the Father in heaven. See Psa. 106:23.

"Prayer is far-reaching in its influence and worldwide in its effects. It affects all men, affects them everywhere, and affects them in all things. It touches man's interest in time and eternity. It lays hold upon God and moves Him to interfere in the affairs of earth. It moves the angels to minister to men in this life. It restrains and defeats the devil in his schemes to ruin man. Prayer goes everywhere and lays its hand upon everything." *E. M. Bounds*

23:3 God forbid that any of us would play the harlot by flirting with this sinful world. James 4:4 warns us against being adulterers by having friendship with the world.

wall,
Images of Chaldeans portrayed in
vermilion,
15Girded with belts around their waists,
Flowing turbans on their heads,
All of them looking like captains,
In the manner of the Babylonians of
Chaldea,
The land of their nativity.
16As soon as her eyes saw them,
She lusted for them
And sent messengers to them in
Chaldea.

17"Then the Babylonians came to her,
into the bed of love,
And they defiled her with their
immorality;
So she was defiled by them, and
alienated herself from them.
18She revealed her harlotry and
uncovered her nakedness.
Then I alienated Myself from her,
As I had alienated Myself from her
sister.

19"Yet she multiplied her harlotry
In calling to remembrance the days of
her youth,
When she had played the harlot in
the land of Egypt.
20For she lusted for her paramours,
Whose flesh *is like* the flesh of
donkeys,
And whose issue *is like* the issue of
horses.
21Thus you called to remembrance the
lewdness of your youth,
When the Egyptians pressed your
bosom
Because of your youthful breasts.

Judgment on Jerusalem

22"Therefore, Oholibah, thus says the
Lord GOD:

'Behold, I will stir up your lovers
against you,
From whom you have alienated
yourself,
And I will bring them against you
from every side:
23The Babylonians,
All the Chaldeans,
Pekod, Shoa, Koa,
All the Assyrians with them,
All of them desirable young men,
Governors and rulers,
Captains and men of renown,
All of them riding on horses.
24And they shall come against you
With chariots, wagons, and war-
horses,
With a horde of people.

23:16 The four-Letter word. If you could sum up in one word what is keeping most of this world from coming to Christ, what would that word be? Perhaps you would say "unbelief," or "rebellion" or "sin." True, but I believe "lust" is at the forefront of sin. The Bible says that the corruption we see in the world has its roots in lust (see 1 Pet. 1:14). It is the shining light for Hollywood, soap operas, the Internet, magazine covers, TV programs, car advertising, clothing, popular music, and much of contemporary culture. In 2 Pet. 3:3 we are told that men mock God because they love their lust. So what would make any sane man turn from lust's powerful pleasure? Two things: One is that we can never separate lust from death. If we embrace lust, we embrace death, because lust brings forth sin and sin produces death (see James 1:15). A realization of that eternal truth should cause common sense to kick in. No sane man wants to embrace death and, on top of that, end up in hell.

The second reason a man turns from the pleasures of lust is knowing what it cost the Savior for our forgiveness. If my father sold everything he had to raise money to pay a fine for me to avoid prison, what sort of wretch would I be to go straight back into crime because I enjoyed it? The prodigal son made a sensible choice: he "came to himself" (Luke 15:17). That is the point to which we are trying to bring the lost. We want them to exercise common sense (now there is an oxymoron). We are saying, "Come to your senses and call on the name of the Lord. He will not only change your unclean desires, but He will also save you from death and hell." When the power of the gospel changes a sinful, lust-loving heart, no amount of atheistic arguments or evolutionary silliness comes close to making a Christian even slightly doubt the reality of God.

They shall array against you
Buckler, shield, and helmet all
around.

'I will delegate judgment to them,
And they shall judge you according to
their judgments.
25I will set My jealousy against you,
And they shall deal furiously with
you;
They shall remove your nose and
your ears,
And your remnant shall fall by the
sword;
They shall take your sons and your
daughters,
And your remnant shall be devoured
by fire.
26They shall also strip you of your
clothes
And take away your beautiful jewelry.

27'Thus I will make you cease your
lewdness and your harlotry
Brought from the land of Egypt,
So that you will not lift your eyes to
them,
Nor remember Egypt anymore.'

28"For thus says the Lord GOD: 'Surely
I will deliver you into the hand of those
you hate, into the hand *of those* from
whom you alienated yourself. 29They will
deal hatefully with you, take away all you
have worked for, and leave you naked
and bare. The nakedness of your harlotry
shall be uncovered, both your lewdness
and your harlotry. 30I will do these *things*
to you because you have gone as a harlot
after the Gentiles, because you have become defiled by their idols. 31You have
walked in the way of your sister; therefore I will put her cup in your hand.'
32"Thus says the Lord GOD:

'You shall drink of your sister's cup,
The deep and wide one;
You shall be laughed to scorn
And held in derision;
It contains much.
33You will be filled with drunkenness
and sorrow,
The cup of horror and desolation,
The cup of your sister Samaria.
34You shall drink and drain it,
You shall break its shards,
And tear at your own breasts;
For I have spoken,'
Says the Lord GOD.

35"Therefore thus says the Lord GOD:

'Because you have forgotten Me and
cast Me behind your back,
Therefore you shall bear the *penalty*
Of your lewdness and your harlotry.' "

Both Sisters Judged

36The LORD also said to me: "Son of
man, will you judge Oholah and Oholibah? Then declare to them their abominations. 37For they have committed adultery, and blood *is* on their hands. They
have committed adultery with their idols,
and even sacrificed their sons whom they
bore to Me, passing them through *the fire*,
to devour *them*. 38Moreover they have
done this to Me: They have defiled My
sanctuary on the same day and profaned
My Sabbaths. 39For after they had slain
their children for their idols, on the same
day they came into My sanctuary to profane it; and indeed thus they have done
in the midst of My house.
40"Furthermore you sent for men to
come from afar, to whom a messenger
was sent; and there they came. And you
washed yourself for them, painted your
eyes, and adorned yourself with ornaments. 41You sat on a stately couch, with
a table prepared before it, on which you
had set My incense and My oil. 42The

23:37 It is hard to conceive of the wickedness of any parents taking their own offspring and sacrificing them to an idol.

sound of a carefree multitude *was* with
her, and Sabeans *were* brought from the
wilderness with men of the common sort,
who put bracelets on their wrists and
beautiful crowns on their heads. 43Then I
said concerning *her who had grown* old in
adulteries, 'Will they commit harlotry with
her now, and she *with them?*' 44Yet they
went in to her, as men go in to a woman
who plays the harlot; thus they went in to
Oholah and Oholibah, the lewd women.
45But righteous men will judge them after
the manner of adulteresses, and after the
manner of women who shed blood, because they *are* adulteresses, and blood *is*
on their hands.

46"For thus says the Lord GOD: 'Bring
up an assembly against them, give them
up to trouble and plunder. 47The assembly shall stone them with stones and execute them with their swords; they shall
slay their sons and their daughters, and
burn their houses with fire. 48Thus I will
cause lewdness to cease from the land,
that all women may be taught not to practice your lewdness. 49They shall repay
you for your lewdness, and you shall pay
for your idolatrous sins. Then you shall
know that I *am* the Lord GOD.' "

Symbol of the Cooking Pot

24 Again, in the ninth year, in the
tenth month, on the tenth *day* of
the month, the word of the LORD came to
me, saying, 2"Son of man, write down the
name of the day, this very day—the king
of Babylon started his siege against Jerusalem this very day. 3And utter a parable
to the rebellious house, and say to them,
'Thus says the Lord GOD:

"Put on a pot, set it on,
And also pour water into it.
4Gather pieces *of meat* in it,
Every good piece,
The thigh and the shoulder.
Fill *it* with choice cuts;
5Take the choice of the flock.
Also pile *fuel* bones under it,
Make it boil well,
And let the cuts simmer in it."

6"Therefore thus says the Lord GOD:

"Woe to the bloody city,
To the pot whose scum *is* in it,
And whose scum is not gone from it!
Bring it out piece by piece,
On which no lot has fallen.
7For her blood is in her midst;
She set it on top of a rock;
She did not pour it on the ground,
To cover it with dust.
8That it may raise up fury and take
vengeance,
I have set her blood on top of a rock,
That it may not be covered."

9"Therefore thus says the Lord GOD:

"Woe to the bloody city!
I too will make the pyre great.
10Heap on the wood,
Kindle the fire;
Cook the meat well,
Mix in the spices,
And let the cuts be burned up.

11"Then set the pot empty on the coals,
That it may become hot and its
bronze may burn,
That its filthiness may be melted in it,
That its scum may be consumed.
12She has grown weary with lies,
And her great scum has not gone
from her.
Let her scum *be* in the fire!
13In your filthiness *is* lewdness.
Because I have cleansed you, and you
were not cleansed,
You will not be cleansed of your
filthiness anymore,
Till I have caused My fury to rest
upon you.
14I, the LORD, have spoken *it;*
It shall come to pass, and I will do *it;*
I will not hold back,
Nor will I spare,
Nor will I relent;
According to your ways

And according to your deeds
They[a] will judge you,"
Says the Lord GOD.' "

The Prophet's Wife Dies

[15]Also the word of the LORD came to me, saying, [16]"Son of man, behold, I take away from you the desire of your eyes with one stroke; yet you shall neither mourn nor weep, nor shall your tears run down. [17]Sigh in silence, make no mourning for the dead; bind your turban on your head, and put your sandals on your feet; do not cover *your* lips, and do not eat man's bread *of sorrow*."

[18]So I spoke to the people in the morning, and at evening my wife died; and the next morning I did as I was commanded.

[19]And the people said to me, "Will you not tell us what these *things signify* to us, that you behave so?"

[20]Then I answered them, "The word of the LORD came to me, saying, [21]'Speak to the house of Israel, "Thus says the Lord GOD: 'Behold, I will profane My sanctuary, your arrogant boast, the desire of your eyes, the delight of your soul; and your sons and daughters whom you left behind shall fall by the sword. [22]And you shall do as I have done; you shall not cover *your* lips nor eat man's bread *of sorrow*. [23]Your turbans shall be on your heads and your sandals on your feet; you shall neither mourn nor weep, but you shall pine away in your iniquities and mourn with one another. [24]Thus Ezekiel is a sign to you; according to all that he has done you shall do; and when this comes, you shall know that I *am* the Lord GOD.' "

[25]'And you, son of man—*will it* not *be* in the day when I take from them their stronghold, their joy and their glory, the desire of their eyes, and that on which they set their minds, their sons and their daughters: [26]*that* on that day one who escapes will come to you to let *you* hear *it* with *your* ears? [27]On that day your mouth will be opened to him who has escaped; you shall speak and no longer be mute. Thus you will be a sign to them, and they shall know that I *am* the LORD.' "

Proclamation Against Ammon

25 The word of the LORD came to me, saying, [2]"Son of man, set your face against the Ammonites, and prophesy against them. [3]Say to the Ammonites, 'Hear the word of the Lord GOD! Thus says the Lord GOD: "Because you said, 'Aha!' against My sanctuary when it was profaned, and against the land of Israel when it was desolate, and against the house of Judah when they went into captivity, [4]indeed, therefore, I will deliver you as a possession to the men of the East, and they shall set their encampments among you and make their dwellings among you; they shall eat your fruit, and they shall drink your milk. [5]And I will make Rabbah a stable for camels and Ammon a resting place for flocks. Then you shall know that I *am* the LORD."

[6]'For thus says the Lord GOD: "Because you clapped *your* hands, stamped your feet, and rejoiced in heart with all your disdain for the land of Israel, [7]indeed, therefore, I will stretch out My hand against you, and give you as plunder to the nations; I will cut you off from the peoples, and I will cause you to perish from the countries; I will destroy you, and you shall know that I *am* the LORD."

Proclamation Against Moab

[8]'Thus says the Lord GOD: "Because Moab and Seir say, 'Look! The house of Judah *is* like all the nations,' [9]therefore, behold, I will clear the territory of Moab of cities, of the cities on its frontier, the glory of the country, Beth Jeshimoth, Baal Meon, and Kirjathaim. [10]To the men of the East I will give it as a possession, together with the Ammonites, that the Ammonites may not be remembered among the nations. [11]And I will execute judgments upon Moab, and they shall know that I *am* the LORD."

24:14 [a]Septuagint, Syriac, Targum, and Vulgate read *I*.

Proclamation Against Edom

12'Thus says the Lord GOD: "Because of what Edom did against the house of Judah by taking vengeance, and has greatly offended by avenging itself on them," 13therefore thus says the Lord GOD: "I will also stretch out My hand against Edom, cut off man and beast from it, and make it desolate from Teman; Dedan shall fall by the sword. 14I will lay My vengeance on Edom by the hand of My people Israel, that they may do in Edom according to My anger and according to My fury; and they shall know My vengeance," says the Lord GOD.

Proclamation Against Philistia

15'Thus says the Lord GOD: "Because the Philistines dealt vengefully and took vengeance with a spiteful heart, to destroy because of the old hatred," 16therefore thus says the Lord GOD: "I will stretch out My hand against the Philistines, and I will cut off the Cherethites and destroy the remnant of the seacoast. 17I will execute great vengeance on them with furious rebukes; and they shall know that I *am* the LORD, when I lay My vengeance upon them." ' "

Proclamation Against Tyre

26 And it came to pass in the eleventh year, on the first *day* of the month, *that* the word of the LORD came to me, saying, 2"Son of man, because Tyre has said against Jerusalem, 'Aha! She is broken who *was* the gateway of the peoples; now she is turned over to me; I shall be filled; she is laid waste.'

3"Therefore thus says the Lord GOD: 'Behold, I *am* against you, O Tyre, and will cause many nations to come up against you, as the sea causes its waves to come up. 4And they shall destroy the walls of Tyre and break down her towers; I will also scrape her dust from her, and make her like the top of a rock. 5It shall be *a place for* spreading nets in the midst of the sea, for I have spoken,' says the Lord GOD; 'it shall become plunder for the nations. 6Also her daughter *villages* which *are* in the fields shall be slain by the sword. Then they shall know that I am the LORD.'

7"For thus says the Lord GOD: 'Behold, I will bring against Tyre from the north Nebuchadnezzar[a] king of Babylon, king of kings, with horses, with chariots, and with horsemen, and an army with many people. 8He will slay with the sword your daughter *villages* in the fields; he will heap up a siege mound against you, build a wall against you, and raise a defense against you. 9He will direct his battering rams against your walls, and with his axes he will break down your towers. 10Because of the abundance of his horses, their dust will cover you; your walls will shake at the noise of the horsemen, the wagons, and the chariots, when he enters your gates, as men enter a city that has been breached. 11With the hooves of his horses he will trample all your streets; he will slay your people by the sword, and your strong pillars will fall to the ground. 12They will plunder your riches and pillage your merchandise; they will break down your walls and destroy your pleasant houses; they will lay your stones, your timber, and your soil in the midst of the water. 13I will put an end to the sound of your songs, and the sound of your harps shall be heard no more. 14I will make you like the top of a rock; you shall be *a place for* spreading nets, and you shall never be rebuilt, for I the LORD have spoken,' says the Lord GOD.

15"Thus says the Lord GOD to Tyre: 'Will

26:7 [a]Hebrew *Nebuchadrezzar,* and so elsewhere in this book

26:4 To prevent Nebuchadnezzar from obtaining her treasures, the residents of Tyre moved onto an island half a mile off the coast. The conqueror destroyed the coastal city and left. Over two centuries later, Alexander the Great used the ruins of the city to build a causeway to the island, thus fulfilling this prophecy.

the coastlands not shake at the sound of
your fall, when the wounded cry, when
slaughter is made in the midst of you?
16Then all the princes of the sea will
come down from their thrones, lay aside
their robes, and take off their embroidered garments; they will clothe themselves with trembling; they will sit on the
ground, tremble *every* moment, and be
astonished at you. 17And they will take
up a lamentation for you, and say to you:

"How you have perished,
O one inhabited by seafaring men,
O renowned city,
Who was strong at sea,
She and her inhabitants,
Who caused their terror *to be* on all
her inhabitants!
18Now the coastlands tremble on the
day of your fall;
Yes, the coastlands by the sea are
troubled at your departure." '

19"For thus says the Lord GOD: 'When
I make you a desolate city, like cities that
are not inhabited, when I bring the deep
upon you, and great waters cover you,
20then I will bring you down with those
who descend into the Pit, to the people of
old, and I will make you dwell in the lowest part of the earth, in places desolate
from antiquity, with those who go down
to the Pit, so that you may never be inhabited; and I shall establish glory in the
land of the living. 21I will make you a terror, and you *shall be* no *more;* though you
are sought for, you will never be found
again,' says the Lord GOD."

Lamentation for Tyre

27 The word of the LORD came again
to me, saying, 2"Now, son of man,
take up a lamentation for Tyre, 3and say
to Tyre, 'You who are situated at the entrance of the sea, merchant of the peoples
on many coastlands, thus says the Lord
GOD:

"O Tyre, you have said,
'I *am* perfect in beauty.'
4Your borders *are* in the midst of the
seas.
Your builders have perfected your
beauty.
5They made all *your* planks of fir trees
from Senir;
They took a cedar from Lebanon to
make you a mast.
6*Of* oaks from Bashan they made your
oars;
The company of Ashurites have inlaid
your planks
With ivory from the coasts of Cyprus.[a]
7Fine embroidered linen from Egypt
was what you spread for your
sail;
Blue and purple from the coasts of
Elishah was what covered you.

8"Inhabitants of Sidon and Arvad were
your oarsmen;
Your wise men, O Tyre, were in you;
They became your pilots.
9Elders of Gebal and its wise men
Were in you to caulk your seams;
All the ships of the sea
And their oarsmen were in you
To market your merchandise.

10"Those from Persia, Lydia,[a] and Libya[b]
Were in your army as men of war;
They hung shield and helmet in you;
They gave splendor to you.
11Men of Arvad with your army *were*
on your walls *all* around,
And the men of Gammad were in

27:6 [a]Hebrew *Kittim,* western lands, especially Cyprus 27:10 [a]Hebrew *Lud* [b]Hebrew *Put*

27:1 In times of old, God spoke through the prophets, but we now have His mind revealed through His Word. Be careful of those who say, "God told me . . ." Such people are often not open to any human counsel or correction. If we disagree with them, we would be disagreeing with "God." Such talk is often rooted in pride.

your towers;
They hung their shields on your walls
all around;
They made your beauty perfect.

12"Tarshish *was* your merchant because
of your many luxury goods. They gave
you silver, iron, tin, and lead for your
goods. 13Javan, Tubal, and Meshech *were*
your traders. They bartered human lives
and vessels of bronze for your merchandise. 14Those from the house of Togarmah traded for your wares with horses,
steeds, and mules. 15The men of Dedan
were your traders; many isles *were* the
market of your hand. They brought you
ivory tusks and ebony as payment. 16Syria
was your merchant because of the abundance of goods you made. They gave you
for your wares emeralds, purple, embroidery, fine linen, corals, and rubies. 17Judah
and the land of Israel *were* your traders.
They traded for your merchandise wheat
of Minnith, millet, honey, oil, and balm.
18Damascus *was* your merchant because
of the abundance of goods you made, because of your many luxury items, with
the wine of Helbon and with white wool.
19Dan and Javan paid for your wares, tra-
versing back and forth. Wrought iron,
cassia, and cane were among your merchandise. 20Dedan *was* your merchant in
saddlecloths for riding. 21Arabia and all the
princes of Kedar *were* your regular merchants. They traded with you in lambs,
rams, and goats. 22The merchants of Sheba
and Raamah *were* your merchants. They
traded for your wares the choicest spices,
all kinds of precious stones, and gold.
23Haran, Canneh, Eden, the merchants of
Sheba, Assyria, *and* Chilmad *were* your
merchants. 24These *were* your merchants
in choice items—in purple clothes, in
embroidered garments, in chests of multicolored apparel, in sturdy woven cords,
which were in your marketplace.

25"The ships of Tarshish were carriers of
your merchandise.
You were filled and very glorious in
the midst of the seas.
26Your oarsmen brought you into many
waters,
But the east wind broke you in the
midst of the seas.

27"Your riches, wares, and merchandise,
Your mariners and pilots,
Your caulkers and merchandisers,
All your men of war who *are* in you,
And the entire company which *is* in
your midst,
Will fall into the midst of the seas on
the day of your ruin.
28The common-land will shake at the
sound of the cry of your pilots.

29 "All who handle the oar,
The mariners,
All the pilots of the sea
Will come down from their ships *and*
stand on the shore.
30They will make their voice heard
because of you;
They will cry bitterly and cast dust on
their heads;
They will roll about in ashes;
31They will shave themselves
completely bald because of you,
Gird themselves with sackcloth,
And weep for you
With bitterness of heart *and* bitter
wailing.
32In their wailing for you
They will take up a lamentation,
And lament for you:
'What *city is* like Tyre,
Destroyed in the midst of the sea?

33'When your wares went out by sea,
You satisfied many people;
You enriched the kings of the earth
With your many luxury goods and
your merchandise.
34But you are broken by the seas in the
depths of the waters;
Your merchandise and the entire
company will fall in your midst.
35All the inhabitants of the isles will be
astonished at you;

Their kings will be greatly afraid,
And *their* countenance will be troubled.
[36]The merchants among the peoples will hiss at you;
You will become a horror, and *be* no more forever.' " ' "

Proclamation Against the King of Tyre

28 The word of the LORD came to me
again, saying, [2]"Son of man, say to
the prince of Tyre, 'Thus says the Lord
GOD:

"Because your heart *is* lifted up,
And you say, 'I *am* a god,
I sit *in* the seat of gods,
In the midst of the seas,'
Yet you *are* a man, and not a god,
Though you set your heart as the heart of a god
[3](Behold, you *are* wiser than Daniel!
There is no secret that can be hidden from you!
[4]With your wisdom and your understanding
You have gained riches for yourself,
And gathered gold and silver into your treasuries;
[5]By your great wisdom in trade you have increased your riches,
And your heart is lifted up because of your riches),"

[6]'Therefore thus says the Lord GOD:

"Because you have set your heart as the heart of a god,
[7]Behold, therefore, I will bring strangers against you,
The most terrible of the nations;
And they shall draw their swords against the beauty of your wisdom,
And defile your splendor.
[8]They shall throw you down into the Pit,
And you shall die the death of the slain
In the midst of the seas.

[9]"Will you still say before him who slays you,
'I *am* a god'?
But you *shall be* a man, and not a god,
In the hand of him who slays you.
[10]You shall die the death of the uncircumcised
By the hand of aliens;
For I have spoken," says the Lord GOD.' "

Lamentation for the King of Tyre

[11]Moreover the word of the LORD came
to me, saying, [12]"Son of man, take up a
lamentation for the king of Tyre, and say
to him, 'Thus says the Lord GOD:

"You *were* the seal of perfection,
Full of wisdom and perfect in beauty.
[13]You were in Eden, the garden of God;
Every precious stone *was* your covering:
The sardius, topaz, and diamond,
Beryl, onyx, and jasper,
Sapphire, turquoise, and emerald with gold.
The workmanship of your timbrels and pipes
Was prepared for you on the day you

28:2 This has been man's desire ever since Satan tempted Adam and Eve that they could "be like God" (see Gen. 3:5). Mormonism teaches that you can become a god; the New Age teaches that you are god; and Hinduism teaches that you can become part of the Universal Consciousness. However, there is only one true God, the Creator of all things. See Deut. 4:35; Isa. 40:25; 43:10; 44:6; 45:21,22; 46:9.

28:12–17 Tyre was judged by God because she lifted herself up through pride and had the ultimate delusions of grandeur (v. 2). Though this proclamation is against the king of Tyre, much of this chapter is thought to describe the fall of Satan. Satan was present in the Garden of Eden as well as on the mountain of God (vv. 13,14), but pride likewise led to his downfall. See Isa. 14:12–15 for similar wording about the king of Babylon (also thought to describe Satan). No doubt Satan inspired them both.

were created.

[14]"You *were* the anointed cherub who covers;
I established you;
You were on the holy mountain of God;
You walked back and forth in the midst of fiery stones.
[15]You *were* perfect in your ways from the day you were created,
Till iniquity was found in you.

[16]"By the abundance of your trading
You became filled with violence within,
And you sinned;
Therefore I cast you as a profane thing
Out of the mountain of God;
And I destroyed you, O covering cherub,
From the midst of the fiery stones.

[17]"Your heart was lifted up because of your beauty;
You corrupted your wisdom for the sake of your splendor;
I cast you to the ground,
I laid you before kings,
That they might gaze at you.

[18]"You defiled your sanctuaries
By the multitude of your iniquities,
By the iniquity of your trading;
Therefore I brought fire from your midst;
It devoured you,
And I turned you to ashes upon the earth
In the sight of all who saw you.
[19]All who knew you among the peoples are astonished at you;
You have become a horror,
And *shall be* no more forever." ' "

Proclamation Against Sidon

[20]Then the word of the LORD came to
me, saying, [21]"Son of man, set your face
toward Sidon, and prophesy against her,
[22]and say, 'Thus says the Lord GOD:

"Behold, I *am* against you, O Sidon;
I will be glorified in your midst;
And they shall know that I *am* the LORD,
When I execute judgments in her and am hallowed in her.
[23]For I will send pestilence upon her,
And blood in her streets;
The wounded shall be judged in her midst
By the sword against her on every side;
Then they shall know that I *am* the LORD.

[24]"And there shall no longer be a
pricking brier or a painful thorn for the
house of Israel from among all *who are*
around them, who despise them. Then
they shall know that I *am* the Lord GOD."

Israel's Future Blessing

[25]"Thus says the Lord GOD: "When I
have gathered the house of Israel from
the peoples among whom they are scattered, and am hallowed in them in the
sight of the Gentiles, then they will dwell
in their own land which I gave to My servant Jacob. [26]And they will dwell safely
there, build houses, and plant vineyards;
yes, they will dwell securely, when I execute judgments on all those around them
who despise them. Then they shall know
that I *am* the LORD their God." ' "

Proclamation Against Egypt

29 In the tenth year, in the tenth
month, on the twelfth *day* of the
month, the word of the LORD came to me,
saying, [2]"Son of man, set your face against
Pharaoh king of Egypt, and prophesy
against him, and against all Egypt. [3]Speak,
and say, 'Thus says the Lord GOD:

"Behold, I *am* against you,
O Pharaoh king of Egypt,
O great monster who lies in the midst of his rivers,

Who has said, 'My River[a] *is* my own;
I have made *it* for myself.'
4But I will put hooks in your jaws,
And cause the fish of your rivers to stick to your scales;
I will bring you up out of the midst of your rivers,
And all the fish in your rivers will stick to your scales.
5I will leave you in the wilderness,
You and all the fish of your rivers;
You shall fall on the open field;
You shall not be picked up or gathered.[a]
I have given you as food
To the beasts of the field
And to the birds of the heavens.

6"Then all the inhabitants of Egypt
Shall know that I *am* the LORD,
Because they have been a staff of reed to the house of Israel.
7When they took hold of you with the hand,
You broke and tore all their shoulders;[a]
When they leaned on you,
You broke and made all their backs quiver."

8'Therefore thus says the Lord GOD:
"Surely I will bring a sword upon you
and cut off from you man and beast. 9And
the land of Egypt shall become desolate
and waste; then they will know that I *am*
the LORD, because he said, 'The River *is*
mine, and I have made *it*.' 10Indeed, therefore, I *am* against you and against your
rivers, and I will make the land of Egypt
utterly waste and desolate, from Migdol[a]
to Syene, as far as the border of Ethiopia.
11Neither foot of man shall pass through
it nor foot of beast pass through it, and it
shall be uninhabited forty years. 12I will
make the land of Egypt desolate in the
midst of the countries *that are* desolate;
and among the cities *that are* laid waste,
her cities shall be desolate forty years;
and I will scatter the Egyptians among
the nations and disperse them throughout the countries."

13'Yet, thus says the Lord GOD: "At the
end of forty years I will gather the Egyptians from the peoples among whom they
were scattered. 14I will bring back the
captives of Egypt and cause them to return to the land of Pathros, to the land of
their origin, and there they shall be a
lowly kingdom. 15It shall be the lowliest
of kingdoms; it shall never again exalt itself above the nations, for I will diminish
them so that they will not rule over the
nations anymore. 16No longer shall it be
the confidence of the house of Israel, but
will remind them of *their* iniquity when
they turned to follow them. Then they
shall know that I *am* the Lord GOD." ' "

Babylonia Will Plunder Egypt

17And it came to pass in the twenty-
seventh year, in the first *month*, on the
first *day* of the month, *that* the word of
the LORD came to me, saying, 18"Son of
man, Nebuchadnezzar king of Babylon
caused his army to labor strenuously
against Tyre; every head *was* made bald,
and every shoulder rubbed raw; yet neither he nor his army received wages from
Tyre, for the labor which they expended
on it. 19Therefore thus says the Lord GOD:
'Surely I will give the land of Egypt to
Nebuchadnezzar king of Babylon; he
shall take away her wealth, carry off her
spoil, and remove her pillage; and that
will be the wages for his army. 20I have
given him the land of Egypt *for* his labor,
because they worked for Me,' says the
Lord GOD.

29:3 [a]That is, the Nile 29:5 [a]Following Masoretic Text, Septuagint, and Vulgate; some Hebrew manuscripts and Targum read *buried*. 29:7 [a]Following Masoretic Text and Vulgate; Septuagint and Syriac read *hand*. 29:10 [a]Or *tower*

29:15 Egypt has been called "the greatest power the world had ever seen," but it has never risen to the place of power that it once had.

[21]"In that day I will cause the horn of the house of Israel to spring forth, and I will open your mouth to speak in their midst. Then they shall know that I *am* the LORD.' "

Egypt and Her Allies Will Fall

30 The word of the LORD came to me again, saying, [2]"Son of man, prophesy and say, 'Thus says the Lord GOD:

"Wail, 'Woe to the day!'
[3]For the day *is* near,
Even the day of the LORD *is* near;
It will be a day of clouds, the time of the Gentiles.
[4]The sword shall come upon Egypt,
And great anguish shall be in Ethiopia,
When the slain fall in Egypt,
And they take away her wealth,
And her foundations are broken down.

[5]"Ethiopia, Libya,[a] Lydia,[b] all the mingled people, Chub, and the men of the lands who are allied, shall fall with them by the sword."

[6]'Thus says the LORD:

"Those who uphold Egypt shall fall,
And the pride of her power shall come down.
From Migdol *to* Syene
Those within her shall fall by the sword,"
Says the Lord GOD.

[7]"They shall be desolate in the midst of the desolate countries,
And her cities shall be in the midst of the cities *that are* laid waste.
[8]Then they will know that I *am* the LORD,
When I have set a fire in Egypt
And all her helpers are destroyed.
[9]On that day messengers shall go forth from Me in ships
To make the careless Ethiopians afraid,
And great anguish shall come upon them,
As on the day of Egypt;
For indeed it is coming!"

[10]'Thus says the Lord GOD:

"I will also make a multitude of Egypt to cease
By the hand of Nebuchadnezzar king of Babylon.
[11]He and his people with him, the most terrible of the nations,
Shall be brought to destroy the land;
They shall draw their swords against Egypt,
And fill the land with the slain.
[12]I will make the rivers dry,
And sell the land into the hand of the wicked;
I will make the land waste, and all that is in it,
By the hand of aliens.
I, the LORD, have spoken."

[13]'Thus says the Lord GOD:

"I will also destroy the idols,
And cause the images to cease from Noph;[a]
There shall no longer be princes from the land of Egypt;
I will put fear in the land of Egypt.
[14]I will make Pathros desolate,
Set fire to Zoan,
And execute judgments in No.[a]
[15]I will pour My fury on Sin,[a] the strength of Egypt;
I will cut off the multitude of No,

30:5 [a]Hebrew *Put* [b]Hebrew *Lud* 30:13 [a]That is, ancient Memphis 30:14 [a]That is, ancient Thebes 30:15 [a]That is, ancient Pelusium

30:4 "Deism" is the popular belief that God created the universe but that He is merely a Higher Power that has no interest in the affairs of men or nations. This chapter destroys such a notion.

16 And set a fire in Egypt;
Sin shall have great pain,
No shall be split open,
And Noph *shall be in* distress daily.
17 The young men of Aven[a] and Pi
Beseth shall fall by the sword,
And these *cities* shall go into captivity.
18 At Tehaphnehes[a] the day shall also be
darkened,[b]
When I break the yokes of Egypt
there.
And her arrogant strength shall cease
in her;
As for her, a cloud shall cover her,
And her daughters shall go into
captivity.
19 Thus I will execute judgments on
Egypt,
Then they shall know that I *am* the
LORD."'"

Proclamation Against Pharaoh

20 And it came to pass in the eleventh
year, in the first *month,* on the seventh *day*
of the month, *that* the word of the LORD
came to me, saying, 21 "Son of man, I have
broken the arm of Pharaoh king of Egypt;
and see, it has not been bandaged for
healing, nor a splint put on to bind it, to
make it strong enough to hold a sword.
22 Therefore thus says the Lord GOD:
'Surely I *am* against Pharaoh king of Egypt,
and will break his arms, both the strong
one and the one that was broken; and I
will make the sword fall out of his hand.
23 I will scatter the Egyptians among the
nations, and disperse them throughout
the countries. 24 I will strengthen the arms
of the king of Babylon and put My sword
in his hand; but I will break Pharaoh's
arms, and he will groan before him with
the groanings of a mortally wounded
man. 25 Thus I will strengthen the arms of
the king of Babylon, but the arms of
Pharaoh shall fall down; they shall know
that I *am* the LORD, when I put My sword
into the hand of the king of Babylon and
he stretches it out against the land of Egypt.
26 I will scatter the Egyptians among the
nations and disperse them throughout
the countries. Then they shall know that
I *am* the LORD.'"

Egypt Cut Down Like a Great Tree

31 Now it came to pass in the eleventh year, in the third *month,* on
the first *day* of the month, *that* the word
of the LORD came to me, saying, 2 "Son of
man, say to Pharaoh king of Egypt and to
his multitude:

'Whom are you like in your greatness?
3 Indeed Assyria *was* a cedar in
Lebanon,
With fine branches that shaded the
forest,
And of high stature;
And its top was among the thick
boughs.
4 The waters made it grow;
Underground waters gave it height,
With their rivers running around the
place where it was planted,
And sent out rivulets to all the trees
of the field.

5 'Therefore its height was exalted
above all the trees of the field;
Its boughs were multiplied,
And its branches became long
because of the abundance of
water,
As it sent them out.
6 All the birds of the heavens made
their nests in its boughs;
Under its branches all the beasts of
the field brought forth their
young;
And in its shadow all great nations
made their home.
7 'Thus it was beautiful in greatness
and in the length of its branches,
Because its roots reached to abundant
waters.
8 The cedars in the garden of God
could not hide it;

30:17 [a]That is, ancient On (Heliopolis) 30:18 [a]Spelled *Tahpanhes* in Jeremiah 43:7 and elsewhere [b]Following many Hebrew manuscripts, Bomberg, Septuagint, Syriac, Targum, and Vulgate; Masoretic Text reads *refrained.*

The fir trees were not like its boughs,
And the chestnut[a] trees were not like
its branches;
No tree in the garden of God was like
it in beauty.
9I made it beautiful with a multitude
of branches,
So that all the trees of Eden envied it,
That *were* in the garden of God.'

10"Therefore thus says the Lord GOD:
'Because you have increased in height, and
it set its top among the thick boughs, and
its heart was lifted up in its height, 11there-
fore I will deliver it into the hand of the
mighty one of the nations, and he shall
surely deal with it; I have driven it out for
its wickedness. 12And aliens, the most
terrible of the nations, have cut it down
and left it; its branches have fallen on the
mountains and in all the valleys; its
boughs lie broken by all the rivers of the
land; and all the peoples of the earth have
gone from under its shadow and left it.

13'On its ruin will remain all the birds
of the heavens,
And all the beasts of the field will
come to its branches—

14'So that no trees by the waters may ever
again exalt themselves for their height,
nor set their tops among the thick boughs,
that no tree which drinks water may ever
be high enough to reach up to them.

'For they have all been delivered to
death,
To the depths of the earth,
Among the children of men who go
down to the Pit.'

15"Thus says the Lord GOD: 'In the day
when it went down to hell, I caused
mourning. I covered the deep because of
it. I restrained its rivers, and the great waters were held back. I caused Lebanon to
mourn for it, and all the trees of the field
wilted because of it. 16I made the nations
shake at the sound of its fall, when I cast
it down to hell together with those who
descend into the Pit; and all the trees of
Eden, the choice and best of Lebanon, all
that drink water, were comforted in the
depths of the earth. 17They also went down
to hell with it, with those *slain* by the
sword; and *those who were* its *strong* arm
dwelt in its shadows among the nations.
18'To which of the trees in Eden will
you then be likened in glory and greatness? Yet you shall be brought down with
the trees of Eden to the depths of the
earth; you shall lie in the midst of the uncircumcised, with *those* slain by the
sword. This *is* Pharaoh and all his multitude,' says the Lord GOD."

Lamentation for Pharaoh and Egypt

32 And it came to pass in the twelfth
year, in the twelfth *month*, on the
first *day* of the month, *that* the word of the
LORD came to me, saying, 2"Son of man,
take up a lamentation for Pharaoh king of
Egypt, and say to him:

'You are like a young lion among the
nations,
And you *are* like a monster in the
seas,
Bursting forth in your rivers,
Troubling the waters with your feet,
And fouling their rivers.

3'Thus says the Lord GOD:

31:8 [a]Hebrew *armon*

31:10,11 God Himself caused Assyria to become incredibly great, like a huge and beautiful tree. If we ever find ourselves exalted by the Lord, we must make sure that our branches hang low in humility of heart, or we too will be cut down to size. See Dan. 4:30–33 comment.

32:2 Pharaoh compared himself to a great lion. He exalted himself and was cut down because of pride. God resists the proud (see James 4:6). He humbles those who become great in their own eyes.

31:16 *The Mormon View of Heaven and Hell*

Mormons believe that, after the final judgment, almost everyone will go to some form of heaven. They believe there are three levels of heaven: celestial, terrestrial, and telestial. All of them are superior to this life. Mormons seek to go to the top level, where they return to "Heavenly Father" and become a god of their own planet and produce lots of spirit children.

- **Celestial kingdom:** This is where Heavenly Father and Jesus Christ reside. Only faithful Mormons who live according to the gospel of Jesus Christ, are cleansed from sin by the Atonement, and meet all the requirements will enter this highest kingdom. This celestial kingdom also has three levels with different privileges and powers.
- **Terrestrial kingdom:** Righteous people who are not Mormons—those who refuse to accept the gospel of Jesus Christ but who live honorable lives—will receive a place in the terrestrial kingdom. Most Mormons will also end up here.
- **Telestial kingdom:** The lowest level is for the wicked and ungodly—liars, thieves, adulterers, murderers, etc. Those who continue in their sins and do not repent until after they have died will eventually receive a place in the telestial kingdom. Even the glory of the telestial kingdom "surpasses all understanding" (*Doctrine and Covenants*, 76:81–90).

Mormon apostle John Widtsoe said, "In the Church of Jesus Christ of Latter-day Saints, there is no hell. All will find a measure of salvation; all must pay for any infringement of the law; but the payment will be as the Lord may decide" (Joseph Smith, *Seeker After Truth*, p. 178). However, 10th LDS President Joseph Fielding Smith wrote, "The Church does teach that there is a place called hell. Of course we do not believe that all those who do not receive the gospel will eventually be cast into hell" (*Answers to Gospel Questions*, 2:210).

Mormons call the place of punishment "outer darkness," but they are taught that it is only for the "sons of perdition": the devil and his angels, and a few apostate Mormons. Even Hitler might qualify for the low level of heaven, which Joseph Smith said is so wonderful that if we could get just one little glimpse into the lowest heaven, "we would be tempted to commit suicide to get there."

For how to witness to Mormons, see Mark 11:25 comment.

(Adapted from *World Religions in a Nutshell*.)

"I will therefore spread My net over you
with a company of many people,
And they will draw you up in My net.
4Then I will leave you on the land;
I will cast you out on the open fields,
And cause to settle on you all the
birds of the heavens.
And with you I will fill the beasts of
the whole earth.
5I will lay your flesh on the
mountains,
And fill the valleys with your carcass.

6"I will also water the land with the
flow of your blood,
Even to the mountains;
And the riverbeds will be full of you.
7When *I* put out your light,
I will cover the heavens, and make its
stars dark;
I will cover the sun with a cloud,
And the moon shall not give her light.
8All the bright lights of the heavens I
will make dark over you,
And bring darkness upon your land,"
Says the Lord GOD.

9"I will also trouble the hearts of many
peoples, when I bring your destruction
among the nations, into the countries
which you have not known. 10Yes, I will
make many peoples astonished at you,
and their kings shall be horribly afraid of
you when I brandish My sword before
them; and they shall tremble *every* moment,
every man for his own life, in the
day of your fall.

11"For thus says the Lord GOD: "The
sword of the king of Babylon shall come
upon you. 12By the swords of the mighty
warriors, all of them the most terrible of
the nations, I will cause your multitude
to fall.

"They shall plunder the pomp of
Egypt,

And all its multitude shall be
destroyed.
13Also I will destroy all its animals
From beside its great waters;
The foot of man shall muddy them no
more,
Nor shall the hooves of animals
muddy them.
14Then I will make their waters clear,
And make their rivers run like oil,"
Says the Lord GOD.

15"When I make the land of Egypt
desolate,
And the country is destitute of all that
once filled it,
When I strike all who dwell in it,
Then they shall know that I *am* the
LORD.

16"This is the lamentation
With which they shall lament her;
The daughters of the nations shall
lament her;
They shall lament for her, for Egypt,
And for all her multitude,"
Says the Lord GOD.'"

Egypt and Others Consigned to the Pit

17It came to pass also in the twelfth
year, on the fifteenth *day* of the month,
that the word of the LORD came to me,
saying:

18"Son of man, wail over the multitude
of Egypt,
And cast them down to the depths of
the earth,
Her and the daughters of the famous
nations,
With those who go down to the Pit:
19'Whom do you surpass in beauty?
Go down, be placed with the
uncircumcised.'

20"They shall fall in the midst of *those*
slain by the sword;
She is delivered to the sword,
Drawing her and all her multitudes.
21The strong among the mighty
Shall speak to him out of the midst of
hell
With those who help him:
'They have gone down,
They lie with the uncircumcised, slain
by the sword.'

22"Assyria *is* there, and all her company,
With their graves all around her,
All of them slain, fallen by the sword.
23Her graves are set in the recesses of
the Pit,
And her company is all around her
grave,
All of them slain, fallen by the sword,
Who caused terror in the land of the
living.

24"There *is* Elam and all her multitude,
All around her grave,
All of them slain, fallen by the sword,
Who have gone down uncircumcised
to the lower parts of the earth,
Who caused their terror in the land of
the living;
Now they bear their shame with those
who go down to the Pit.
25They have set her bed in the midst of
the slain,
With all her multitude,
With her graves all around it,
All of them uncircumcised, slain by
the sword;
Though their terror was caused
In the land of the living,

32:21 "Almost every natural man that hears of hell, flatters himself that he shall escape it; he depends upon himself for his own security; he flatters himself in what he has done, in what he is now doing, or what he intends to do. Every one lays out matters in his own mind how he shall avoid damnation, and flatters himself that he contrives well for himself, and that his schemes will not fail. They hear indeed that there are but few saved, and that the greater part of men that have died heretofore are gone to hell; but each one imagines that he lays out matters better for his own escape than others have done." *Jonathan Edwards*

SPRINGBOARDS FOR PREACHING AND WITNESSING

Christians—the Raving Lunatics

33:5 A woman's car broke down late one moonless night in an unfamiliar area. She was afraid, so she wound the vehicle's windows up tight, locked the doors, and turned on the car radio to keep her company. She decided that it would be wise to wait until the morning light before going for help.

A short time later a frantic man appeared at her window and began to yell at her. Frightened, she gestured for him to go away. He left and then returned seconds later with a rock in his hand, smashed the window of her car, and pulled her out, much to the woman's horrified protests.

As they fell to the ground a massive train slammed into her car, causing it to burst into flames.

You may consider Christians to be raving lunatics, but all we are frantically trying to do is warn you that you are in terrible danger. The train of God's moral Law is merciless. Your ignorance of the imminent peril doesn't make it disappear. Please, soften your heart and listen to us before it is too late.

Yet they bear their shame
With those who go down to the Pit;
It was put in the midst of the slain.

26"There *are* Meshech and Tubal and all their multitudes,
With all their graves around it,
All of them uncircumcised, slain by the sword,
Though they caused their terror in the land of the living.
27They do not lie with the mighty
Who are fallen of the uncircumcised,
Who have gone down to hell with their weapons of war;
They have laid their swords under their heads,
But their iniquities will be on their bones,
Because of the terror of the mighty in the land of the living.
28Yes, you shall be broken in the midst of the uncircumcised,
And lie with *those* slain by the sword.

29"There *is* Edom,
Her kings and all her princes,
Who despite their might
Are laid beside *those* slain by the sword;
They shall lie with the uncircumcised,
And with those who go down to the Pit.
30There *are* the princes of the north,
All of them, and all the Sidonians,
Who have gone down with the slain
In shame at the terror which they caused by their might;
They lie uncircumcised with *those* slain by the sword,
And bear their shame with those who go down to the Pit.

31"Pharaoh will see them
And be comforted over all his multitude,
Pharaoh and all his army,
Slain by the sword,"
Says the Lord GOD.

32"For I have caused My terror in the land of the living;
And he shall be placed in the midst of the uncircumcised
With *those* slain by the sword,
Pharaoh and all his multitude,"
Says the Lord GOD.

The Watchman and His Message

33 Again the word of the LORD came
to me, saying, 2"Son of man, speak
to the children of your people, and say to
them: 'When I bring the sword upon a
land, and the people of the land take a
man from their territory and make him
their watchman, 3when he sees the sword
coming upon the land, if he blows the
trumpet and warns the people, 4then
whoever hears the sound of the trumpet
and does not take warning, if the sword
comes and takes him away, his blood
shall be on his *own* head. 5He heard the
sound of the trumpet, but did not take

warning; his blood shall be upon himself.
But he who takes warning will save his
life. 6But if the watchman sees the sword
coming and does not blow the trumpet,
and the people are not warned, and the
sword comes and takes *any* person from
among them, he is taken away in his iniquity; but his blood I will require at the
watchman's hand.'

7"So you, son of man: I have made you
a watchman for the house of Israel; therefore you shall hear a word from My
mouth and warn them for Me. 8When I
say to the wicked, 'O wicked *man,* you
shall surely die!' and you do not speak to
warn the wicked from his way, that
wicked *man* shall die in his iniquity; but
his blood I will require at your hand.
9Nevertheless if you warn the wicked to
turn from his way, and he does not turn
from his way, he shall die in his iniquity;
but you have delivered your soul.

10"Therefore you, O son of man, say to
the house of Israel: 'Thus you say, "If our
transgressions and our sins *lie* upon us,
and we pine away in them, how can we
then live?" ' 11Say to them: '*As* I live,' says
the Lord GOD, 'I have no pleasure in the
death of the wicked, but that the wicked
turn from his way and live. Turn, turn
from your evil ways! For why should you
die, O house of Israel?'

The Fairness of God's Judgment

12"Therefore you, O son of man, say to
the children of your people: 'The righteousness of the righteous man shall not
deliver him in the day of his transgression; as for the wickedness of the wicked,
he shall not fall because of it in the day
that he turns from his wickedness; nor
shall the righteous be able to live because
of *his righteousness* in the day that he sins.'
13When I say to the righteous *that* he
shall surely live, but he trusts in his own
righteousness and commits iniquity, none
of his righteous works shall be remembered; but because of the iniquity that he
has committed, he shall die. 14Again, when
I say to the wicked, 'You shall surely die,'
if he turns from his sin and does what is
lawful and right, 15*if* the wicked restores
the pledge, gives back what he has stolen,
and walks in the statutes of life without
committing iniquity, he shall surely live;
he shall not die. 16None of his sins which
he has committed shall be remembered
against him; he has done what is lawful
and right; he shall surely live.

17"Yet the children of your people say,
'The way of the LORD is not fair.' But it is
their way which is not fair! 18When the

33:8,9 These verses should make every one of us tremble, when we realize how many professed Christians within the Church don't bother to warn a soul of the coming judgment of God. It would seem that Paul had these verses in mind when he spoke of his responsibility to God and man (see Acts 18:6; 20:26,27). To help your hearers consider the seriousness of the situation (whether you are speaking to a crowd or just one person), you may like to say, "If you refuse to repent and you die in your sins, if your eyes and mine meet on the Day of Judgment, I am free from your blood because I haven't held back from telling you the truth." See also 3:18,19 comment.

"Someone asked, Will the heathen who have never heard the gospel be saved? It is more a question with me whether we—who have the gospel and fail to give it to those who have not—can be saved." *Charles Spurgeon*

33:11 God takes no pleasure in the death of the wicked. He is not willing that any perish, but that all come to repentance (see 2 Pet. 3:9). This is why it is biblical to tell sinners that God does not want them to go to hell. It is not His will. He does not send anyone to hell, in the same way a righteous judge does not delight to send anyone to prison. The criminal's crimes send him to prison; the judge merely executes justice. In the case of our salvation, God prefers mercy over judgment, but if we refuse His mercy shown in Jesus' sacrifice for us, we will get exactly what we deserve. See Psa. 98:9 comment.

33:12,13 Without the illumination of the moral Law, man is in darkness as to his true sinful condition in God's eyes (see Rom. 7:7,13). The Law demands *perfect* righteousness (see Psa. 19:7). Even one transgression against its holy precepts will condemn us (see James 2:10), but in reality, the most righteous of human souls has a *multitude* of sins (see Jer. 30:15; James 5:20).

righteous turns from his righteousness and commits iniquity, he shall die because of it. [19]But when the wicked turns from his wickedness and does what is lawful and right, he shall live because of it. [20]Yet you say, 'The way of the LORD is not fair.' O house of Israel, I will judge every one of you according to his own ways."

The Fall of Jerusalem

[21]And it came to pass in the twelfth year of our captivity, in the tenth *month,* on the fifth *day* of the month, *that* one who had escaped from Jerusalem came to me and said, "The city has been captured!" [22]Now the hand of the LORD had been upon me the evening before the man came who had escaped. And He had opened my mouth; so when he came to me in the morning, my mouth was opened, and I was no longer mute.

The Cause of Judah's Ruin

[23]Then the word of the LORD came to me, saying: [24]"Son of man, they who inhabit those ruins in the land of Israel are saying, 'Abraham was only one, and he inherited the land. But we *are* many; the land has been given to us as a possession.'

[25]"Therefore say to them, 'Thus says the Lord GOD: "You eat *meat* with blood, you lift up your eyes toward your idols, and shed blood. Should you then possess the land? [26]You rely on your sword, you commit abominations, and you defile one another's wives. Should you then possess the land?" '

[27]"Say thus to them, 'Thus says the Lord GOD: "*As* I live, surely those who *are* in the ruins shall fall by the sword, and the one who *is* in the open field I will give to the beasts to be devoured, and those who *are* in the strongholds and caves shall die of the pestilence. [28]For I will make the land most desolate, her arrogant strength shall cease, and the mountains of Israel shall be so desolate that no one will pass through. [29]Then they shall know that I *am* the LORD, when I have made the land most desolate because of all their abominations which they have committed." '

Hearing and Not Doing

[30]"As for you, son of man, the children of your people are talking about you beside the walls and in the doors of the houses; and they speak to one another, everyone saying to his brother, 'Please come and hear what the word is that comes from the LORD.' [31]So they come to you as people do, they sit before you *as* My people, and they hear your words, but they do not do them; for with their mouth they show much love, *but* their hearts pursue their *own* gain. [32]Indeed you *are* to them as a very lovely song of one who has a pleasant voice and can play well on an instrument; for they hear your words, but they do not do them. [33]And when this comes to pass—surely it will come—then they will know that a prophet has been among them."

33:31,32 A pleasant voice. God forbid that any preacher should become merely a pleasant voice, entertaining and tickling the ears of his hearers. Yet many of America's popular preachers have stripped the gospel of that which is designed to awaken its hearers, and replaced it with a message of life-enhancement. And I suspect that they have no idea what they have done. They are like a doctor who was well-liked because he never used a needle to inoculate his ever-increasing number of patients against a deadly disease. He did not like the feeling he got when the needle brought them pain, so he discarded it in the name of love. When his patients began to die of an agonizing disease, his professed love was seen for what it was—a terrible betrayal. Millions of unconverted churchgoers sit in pews with a Bible on their lap, asleep in their sins within earshot of the pulpit.

Listen to these sobering words of warning from *J. C. Ryle*: "It is a fearful thing to fall into the hands of the living God, but never so fearful as when men fall from under the gospel. The saddest road to hell is that which runs under the pulpit, past the Bible, and through the midst of warnings and invitations." How much sadder is it when no warning is given. Many a church service has become nothing but entertainment for those who profess to know God, while in works they deny Him (see Titus 1:16; Matt. 15:8). Jesus said, "Why do you call Me 'Lord, Lord,' and not do the things which I say?" (Luke 6:46).

Irresponsible Shepherds

34 And the word of the LORD came to me, saying, 2 "Son of man, prophesy against the shepherds of Israel, prophesy and say to them, 'Thus says the Lord GOD to the shepherds: "Woe to the shepherds of Israel who feed themselves! Should not the shepherds feed the flocks? 3 You eat the fat and clothe yourselves with the wool; you slaughter the fatlings, *but* you do not feed the flock. 4 The weak you have not strengthened, nor have you healed those who were sick, nor bound up the broken, nor brought back what was driven away, nor sought what was lost; but with force and cruelty you have ruled them. 5 So they were scattered because *there was* no shepherd; and they became food for all the beasts of the field when they were scattered. 6 My sheep wandered through all the mountains, and on every high hill; yes, My flock was scattered over the whole face of the earth, and no one was seeking or searching *for them.*"

7 'Therefore, you shepherds, hear the word of the LORD: 8 "*As* I live," says the Lord GOD, "surely because My flock became a prey, and My flock became food for every beast of the field, because *there was* no shepherd, nor did My shepherds search for My flock, but the shepherds fed themselves and did not feed My flock"— 9 therefore, O shepherds, hear the word of the LORD! 10 Thus says the Lord GOD: "Behold, I *am* against the shepherds, and I will require My flock at their hand; I will cause them to cease feeding the sheep, and the shepherds shall feed themselves no more; for I will deliver My flock from their mouths, that they may no longer be food for them."

God, the True Shepherd

11 'For thus says the Lord GOD: "Indeed I Myself will search for My sheep and seek them out. 12 As a shepherd seeks out his flock on the day he is among his scattered sheep, so will I seek out My sheep and deliver them from all the places where they were scattered on a cloudy and dark day. 13 And I will bring them out from the peoples and gather them from the countries, and will bring them to their own land; I will feed them on the mountains of Israel, in the valleys and in all the inhabited places of the country. 14 I will feed them in good pasture, and their fold shall be on the high mountains of Israel. There they shall lie down in a good fold and feed in rich pasture on the mountains of Israel. 15 I will feed My flock, and I will make them lie down," says the Lord GOD. 16 "I will seek what was lost and bring back what was driven away, bind up the broken and strengthen what was sick; but I will destroy the fat and the strong, and feed them in judgment."

17 'And *as for* you, O My flock, thus says the Lord GOD: "Behold, I shall judge between sheep and sheep, between rams and goats. 18 *Is it* too little for you to have eaten up the good pasture, that you must tread down with your feet the residue of your pasture—and to have drunk of the clear waters, that you must foul the residue with your feet? 19 And *as for* My flock, they eat what you have trampled with your feet, and they drink what you have fouled with your feet."

20 'Therefore thus says the Lord GOD to them: "Behold, I Myself will judge between the fat and the lean sheep. 21 Because you have pushed with side and shoulder, butted all the weak ones with your horns, and scattered them abroad, 22 therefore I will save My flock, and they shall no longer be a prey; and I will judge between sheep and sheep. 23 I will estab-

---

34:2–5 It is hard to read this and not think of the many "shepherds" who fleece their flock with a false gospel of prosperity that makes no reference to sin, righteousness, or judgment.

34:13 This was a promise that God reiterated many times (see Deut. 30:3; Isa. 11:11; Jer. 16:15; 23:3; Zeph. 3:20; Zech. 10:10). The fulfillment of this promise started in 1949, when the Jews took hold of the land of Palestine and began to return from throughout the earth. The Jews regained Jerusalem in 1967.

SPRINGBOARDS FOR PREACHING AND WITNESSING

Are You Lost?

34:16 The dictionary gives numerous meanings for the word "lost." One definition is "having gone astray or missed the way; bewildered as to place, direction, etc." There is one thing worse than being lost. It is being lost and not knowing it. Perhaps that describes you. Let's find out by asking three searching questions. The first is, Do you know the origin of the species of which you are a part? If you don't accept the Genesis explanation for our origins, the odds are you haven't any idea where humans came from.

The second question is, What is the purpose of human existence? Why are you here? If you don't accept the biblical explanation for mankind's purpose (that we are created by God, for God), then you will have no idea why you are here. Third question: Where are you going? In other words, what happens after death? More than likely you will be confined to the arena of speculation. You don't know what eternity holds for you. The best you have is a guess—a stab in the dark. So there you have it. You don't know where you came from, you don't know what you are doing here, and you don't know where you are going. You are "lost." As the Bible says, you are like a sheep that has gone astray, and the Scriptures tell us that the Good Shepherd came "to seek and save that which was lost."

lish one shepherd over them, and he shall feed them—My servant David. He shall feed them and be their shepherd. 24And I, the LORD, will be their God, and My servant David a prince among them; I, the LORD, have spoken.

25"I will make a covenant of peace with them, and cause wild beasts to cease from the land; and they will dwell safely in the wilderness and sleep in the woods. 26I will make them and the places all around My hill a blessing; and I will cause showers to come down in their season; there shall be showers of blessing. 27Then the trees of the field shall yield their fruit, and the earth shall yield her increase. They shall be safe in their land; and they shall know that I *am* the LORD, when I have broken the bands of their yoke and delivered them from the hand of those who enslaved them. 28And they shall no longer be a prey for the nations, nor shall beasts of the land devour them; but they shall dwell safely, and no one shall make *them* afraid. 29I will raise up for them a garden of renown, and they shall no longer be consumed with hunger in the land, nor bear the shame of the Gentiles anymore. 30Thus they shall know that I, the LORD their God, *am* with them, and they, the house of Israel, *are* My people," says the Lord GOD.'

31"You are My flock, the flock of My pasture; you *are* men, *and* I *am* your God," says the Lord GOD.

Judgment on Mount Seir

35 Moreover the word of the LORD came to me, saying, 2"Son of man, set your face against Mount Seir and prophesy against it, 3and say to it, 'Thus says the Lord GOD:

"Behold, O Mount Seir, I *am* against you;
I will stretch out My hand against you,
And make you most desolate;
4I shall lay your cities waste,
And you shall be desolate.
Then you shall know that I *am* the LORD.

5"Because you have had an ancient hatred, and have shed *the blood of* the children of Israel by the power of the sword at the time of their calamity, when their iniquity *came to an* end, 6therefore, *as* I live," says the Lord GOD, "I will prepare you for blood, and blood shall pursue

34:23 This refers ultimately to Jesus, the Good Shepherd, who lays down His life for the sheep (see John 10:14–16). See also Zech. 13:7 comment.

you; since you have not hated blood, therefore blood shall pursue you. [7]Thus I will make Mount Seir most desolate, and cut off from it the one who leaves and the one who returns. [8]And I will fill its mountains with the slain; on your hills and in your valleys and in all your ravines those who are slain by the sword shall fall. [9]I will make you perpetually desolate, and your cities shall be uninhabited; then you shall know that I *am* the LORD.

[10]"Because you have said, 'These two nations and these two countries shall be mine, and we will possess them,' although the LORD was there, [11]therefore, *as* I live," says the Lord GOD, "I will do according to your anger and according to the envy which you showed in your hatred against them; and I will make Myself known among them when I judge you. [12]Then you shall know that I *am* the LORD. I have heard all your blasphemies which you have spoken against the mountains of Israel, saying, 'They are desolate; they are given to us to consume.' [13]Thus with your mouth you have boasted against Me and multiplied your words against Me; I have heard *them.*"

[14]'Thus says the Lord GOD: "The whole earth will rejoice when I make you desolate. [15]As you rejoiced because the inheritance of the house of Israel was desolate, so I will do to you; you shall be desolate, O Mount Seir, as well as all of Edom—all of it! Then they shall know that I *am* the LORD." '

Blessing on Israel

36 "And you, son of man, prophesy to the mountains of Israel, and say, 'O mountains of Israel, hear the word of the LORD! [2]Thus says the Lord GOD: "Because the enemy has said of you, 'Aha! The ancient heights have become our possession,' " ' [3]therefore prophesy, and say, 'Thus says the Lord GOD: "Because they made *you* desolate and swallowed you up on every side, so that you became the possession of the rest of the nations, and you are taken up by the lips of talkers and slandered by the people"— [4]therefore, O mountains of Israel, hear the word of the Lord GOD! Thus says the Lord GOD to the mountains, the hills, the rivers, the valleys, the desolate wastes, and the cities that have been forsaken, which became plunder and mockery to the rest of the nations all around— [5]therefore thus says the Lord GOD: "Surely I have spoken in My burning jealousy against the rest of the nations and against all Edom, who gave My land to themselves as a possession, with wholehearted joy *and* spiteful minds, in order to plunder its open country." '

[6]"Therefore prophesy concerning the land of Israel, and say to the mountains, the hills, the rivers, and the valleys, 'Thus says the Lord GOD: "Behold, I have spoken in My jealousy and My fury, because you have borne the shame of the nations." [7]Therefore thus says the Lord GOD: "I have raised My hand in an oath that surely the nations that *are* around you shall bear their own shame. [8]But you, O mountains of Israel, you shall shoot forth your branches and yield your fruit to My people Israel, for they are about to come. [9]For indeed I *am* for you, and I will turn to you, and you shall be tilled and sown. [10]I will multiply men upon you, all the house of Israel, all of it; and the cities shall be inhabited and the ruins rebuilt. [11]I will multiply upon you man and beast; and they shall increase and bear young; I will make you inhabited as in former times, and do better *for you* than at your beginnings. Then you shall know that I *am* the LORD. [12]Yes, I will cause men to walk on you, My people Israel; they shall take possession of you, and you shall be their inheritance; no more

35:12,13 When we listen to modern speech, it is fearful to think that God hears every blasphemy and that His wrath is being stored with every word. See Rom. 2:5 for the promise of retribution.

shall you bereave them *of children*."
13'Thus says the Lord GOD: "Because
they say to you, 'You devour men and bereave your nation *of children*,' 14therefore
you shall devour men no more, nor bereave your nation anymore," says the Lord
GOD. 15"Nor will I let you hear the taunts
of the nations anymore, nor bear the reproach of the peoples anymore, nor shall
you cause your nation to stumble anymore," says the Lord GOD.' "

The Renewal of Israel

16Moreover the word of the LORD came
to me, saying: 17"Son of man, when the
house of Israel dwelt in their own land,
they defiled it by their own ways and
deeds; to Me their way was like the uncleanness of a woman in her customary
impurity. 18Therefore I poured out My
fury on them for the blood they had shed
on the land, and for their idols *with which*
they had defiled it. 19So I scattered them
among the nations, and they were dispersed throughout the countries; I judged
them according to their ways and their
deeds. 20When they came to the nations,
wherever they went, they profaned My
holy name—when they said of them,
'These *are* the people of the LORD, *and* yet
they have gone out of His land.' 21But I
had concern for My holy name, which the
house of Israel had profaned among the
nations wherever they went.
22"Therefore say to the house of Israel,
'Thus says the Lord GOD: "I do not do *this*
for your sake, O house of Israel, but for
My holy name's sake, which you have profaned among the nations wherever you
went. 23And I will sanctify My great
name, which has been profaned among
the nations, which you have profaned in
their midst; and the nations shall know
that I *am* the LORD," says the Lord GOD,
"when I am hallowed in you before their
eyes. 24For I will take you from among
the nations, gather you out of all countries, and bring you into your own land.
25Then I will sprinkle clean water on you,
and you shall be clean; I will cleanse you
from all your filthiness and from all your
idols. 26I will give you a new heart and
put a new spirit within you; I will take
the heart of stone out of your flesh and
give you a heart of flesh. 27I will put My
Spirit within you and cause you to walk
in My statutes, and you will keep My
judgments and do *them*. 28Then you shall
dwell in the land that I gave to your fathers; you shall be My people, and I will
be your God. 29I will deliver you from all
your uncleannesses. I will call for the grain
and multiply it, and bring no famine
upon you. 30And I will multiply the fruit
of your trees and the increase of your
fields, so that you need never again bear
the reproach of famine among the nations. 31Then you will remember your
evil ways and your deeds that *were* not
good; and you will loathe yourselves in
your own sight, for your iniquities and
your abominations. 32Not for your sake
do I do *this*," says the Lord GOD, "let it be
known to you. Be ashamed and confounded for your own ways, O house of
Israel!"
33"Thus says the Lord GOD: "On the
day that I cleanse you from all your iniq-

36:22–25 This passage makes it clear that any salvation from God (whether it be the deliverance of the nation of Israel, or of the sinner through the gospel) doesn't come by anything we have done. He cleanses us of our sin (see 1 John 1:7; Heb. 10:22) and enables us to do His will—all for His glory and for the sake of His holy name. Salvation is by grace and grace alone, through faith alone, without works. Any good works we do merely confirm God's grace. Works are the fruit that confirm that the tree is planted in the grace of the Lord.

36:26,27 This wonderful promise of God finds fulfillment upon conversion. God takes our heart of stone and gives us a heart of flesh so that we desire to do His will. He causes us to love what He loves and hate what He hates. He puts His Holy Spirit within us and we are born again as new creatures in Christ (see John 3:3; 2 Cor. 5:17).

uities, I will also enable *you* to dwell in the cities, and the ruins shall be rebuilt. [34]The desolate land shall be tilled instead of lying desolate in the sight of all who pass by. [35]So they will say, 'This land that was desolate has become like the garden of Eden; and the wasted, desolate, and ruined cities *are now* fortified *and* inhabited.' [36]Then the nations which are left all around you shall know that I, the LORD, have rebuilt the ruined places *and* planted what was desolate. I, the LORD, have spoken *it,* and I will do *it.*"

[37]'Thus says the Lord GOD: "I will also let the house of Israel inquire of Me to do this for them: I will increase their men like a flock. [38]Like a flock *offered as* holy *sacrifices,* like the flock at Jerusalem on its feast days, so shall the ruined cities be filled with flocks of men. Then they shall know that I *am* the LORD." ' "

The Dry Bones Live

37 The hand of the LORD came upon me and brought me out in the Spirit of the LORD, and set me down in the midst of the valley; and it *was* full of bones. [2]Then He caused me to pass by them all around, and behold, *there were* very many in the open valley; and indeed *they were* very dry. [3]And He said to me, "Son of man, can these bones live?"

So I answered, "O Lord GOD, You know."

[4]Again He said to me, "Prophesy to these bones, and say to them, 'O dry bones, hear the word of the LORD! [5]Thus says the Lord GOD to these bones: "Surely I will cause breath to enter into you, and you shall live. [6]I will put sinews on you and bring flesh upon you, cover you with skin and put breath in you; and you shall live. Then you shall know that I *am* the LORD." ' "

[7]So I prophesied as I was commanded; and as I prophesied, there was a noise, and suddenly a rattling; and the bones came together, bone to bone. [8]Indeed, as I looked, the sinews and the flesh came upon them, and the skin covered them over; but *there was* no breath in them.

[9]Also He said to me, "Prophesy to the breath, prophesy, son of man, and say to the breath, 'Thus says the Lord GOD: "Come from the four winds, O breath, and breathe on these slain, that they may live." ' " [10]So I prophesied as He commanded me, and breath came into them, and they lived, and stood upon their feet, an exceedingly great army.

[11]Then He said to me, "Son of man, these bones are the whole house of Israel. They indeed say, 'Our bones are dry, our hope is lost, and we ourselves are cut off!' [12]Therefore prophesy and say to them, 'Thus says the Lord GOD: "Behold, O My people, I will open your graves and cause you to come up from your graves, and bring you into the land of Israel. [13]Then you shall know that I *am* the LORD, when I have opened your graves, O My people, and brought you up from your graves. [14]I will put My Spirit in you, and you shall live, and I will place you in your own land. Then you shall know that I, the LORD, have spoken *it* and performed *it,*" says the LORD.' "

One Kingdom, One King

[15]Again the word of the LORD came to me, saying, [16]"As for you, son of man, take a stick for yourself and write on it: 'For Judah and for the children of Israel, his companions.' Then take another stick and write on it, 'For Joseph, the stick of Ephraim, and *for* all the house of Israel,

37:1–10 While these verses are directed at the "whole house of Israel" (v. 11), it is easy to see their evangelistic application. The world sits in the valley of the shadow of death. Those who do not know the Lord are dead in their trespasses and sins (see Eph. 2:1), and we have been commanded to preach the Word of the Lord to their dry bones. May God breathe His Spirit into them, raising up a great army to reach this lost and dying world.

his companions.' 17Then join them one to another for yourself into one stick, and they will become one in your hand.

18"And when the children of your people speak to you, saying, 'Will you not show us what you *mean* by these?'— 19say to them, 'Thus says the Lord GOD: "Surely I will take the stick of Joseph, which *is* in the hand of Ephraim, and the tribes of Israel, his companions; and I will join them with it, with the stick of Judah, and make them one stick, and they will be one in My hand." ' 20And the sticks on which you write will be in your hand before their eyes.

21"Then say to them, 'Thus says the Lord GOD: "Surely I will take the children of Israel from among the nations, wherever they have gone, and will gather them from every side and bring them into their own land; 22and I will make them one nation in the land, on the mountains of Israel; and one king shall be king over them all; they shall no longer be two nations, nor shall they ever be divided into two kingdoms again. 23They shall not defile themselves anymore with their idols, nor with their detestable things, nor with any of their transgressions; but I will deliver them from all their dwelling places in which they have sinned, and will cleanse them. Then they shall be My people, and I will be their God.

24"David My servant *shall be* king over them, and they shall all have one shepherd; they shall also walk in My judgments and observe My statutes, and do them. 25Then they shall dwell in the land that I have given to Jacob My servant, where your fathers dwelt; and they shall dwell there, they, their children, and their children's children, forever; and My servant David *shall be* their prince forever. 26Moreover I will make a covenant of peace with them, and it shall be an everlasting covenant with them; I will establish them and multiply them, and I will set My sanctuary in their midst forevermore. 27My tabernacle also shall be with them; indeed I will be their God, and they shall be My people. 28The nations also will know that I, the LORD, sanctify Israel, when My sanctuary is in their midst forevermore." ' "

Gog and Allies Attack Israel

38 Now the word of the LORD came to me, saying, 2"Son of man, set your face against Gog, of the land of Magog, the prince of Rosh,[a] Meshech, and Tubal, and prophesy against him, 3and say, 'Thus says the Lord GOD: "Behold, I *am* against you, O Gog, the prince of Rosh, Meshech, and Tubal. 4I will turn you around, put hooks into your jaws, and lead you out, with all your army, horses, and horsemen, all splendidly clothed, a great company *with* bucklers and shields, all of them handling swords. 5Persia, Ethiopia,[a] and Libya[b] are with them, all of them *with* shield and helmet; 6Gomer and all its troops; the house of Togarmah *from* the far north and all its troops— many people *are* with you.

7"Prepare yourself and be ready, you and all your companies that are gathered about you; and be a guard for them. 8After many days you will be visited. In the latter years you will come into the land of those brought back from the sword *and* gathered from many people on the mountains of Israel, which had long been desolate; they were brought out of the nations, and now all of them dwell safely. 9You will ascend, coming like a storm, covering the land like a cloud, you and all your troops and many peoples with you."

10'Thus says the Lord GOD: "On that day it shall come to pass *that* thoughts

38:2 [a]Targum, Vulgate, and Aquila read *chief prince of* (also verse 3). 38:5 [a]Hebrew *Cush* [b]Hebrew *Put*

38:4 No one can thwart the perfect will of God. He puts hooks in the jaws of nations and takes them wherever He wills. See also 2 Kings 19:28.

will arise in your mind, and you will make an evil plan: [11]You will say, 'I will go up against a land of unwalled villages; I will go to a peaceful people, who dwell safely, all of them dwelling without walls, and having neither bars nor gates'— [12]to take plunder and to take booty, to stretch out your hand against the waste places *that are again* inhabited, and against a people gathered from the nations, who have acquired livestock and goods, who dwell in the midst of the land. [13]Sheba, Dedan, the merchants of Tarshish, and all their young lions will say to you, 'Have you come to take plunder? Have you gathered your army to take booty, to carry away silver and gold, to take away livestock and goods, to take great plunder?' " '

[14]"Therefore, son of man, prophesy and say to Gog, 'Thus says the Lord GOD: "On that day when My people Israel dwell safely, will you not know *it?* [15]Then you will come from your place out of the far north, you and many peoples with you, all of them riding on horses, a great company and a mighty army. [16]You will come up against My people Israel like a cloud, to cover the land. It will be in the latter days that I will bring you against My land, so that the nations may know Me, when I am hallowed in you, O Gog, before their eyes." [17]Thus says the Lord GOD: "Are *you* he of whom I have spoken in former days by My servants the prophets of Israel, who prophesied for years in those days that I would bring you against them?

Judgment on Gog

[18]"And it will come to pass at the same time, when Gog comes against the land of Israel," says the Lord GOD, "*that* My fury will show in My face. [19]For in My jealousy *and* in the fire of My wrath I have spoken: 'Surely in that day there shall be a great earthquake in the land of Israel, [20]so that the fish of the sea, the birds of the heavens, the beasts of the field, all creeping things that creep on the earth, and all men who *are* on the face of the earth shall shake at My presence. The mountains shall be thrown down, the steep places shall fall, and every wall shall fall to the ground.' [21]I will call for a sword against Gog throughout all My mountains," says the Lord GOD. "Every man's sword will be against his brother. [22]And I

38:22 Russia and Israel. A number of books of the Bible speak of future events. Ezekiel 38 (written approximately 600 B.C.) prophesies that in these times ("the latter days," v. 16), Russia (referred to as the "Prince of Rosh," see *Smith's Bible Dictionary*, p. 584) will combine with Iran, Libya (in Hebrew called "Put"), and communistic Ethiopia (in Hebrew called "Cush") and attack Israel (vv. 5–8). This will take place after an Israeli peace initiative has been successful (v. 11). The Bible even gives the Russian reasoning for and the direction of the attack (vv. 10–15), as well as the location of the battle (Armageddon—Rev. 16:16). This is generally interpreted as meaning "the mountain of Megiddo," which is located on the north side of the plains of Jezreel. Russia has had a foothold in the Middle East for many years: "The Soviets are entrenched around the rim of the Middle East heartland, in Afghanistan, South Yemen, Ethiopia, and Libya" ("Countdown in the Middle East," *Reader's Digest*, May 1982).

Israel will never have lasting peace until she obeys God. If she will obey His statutes and keep His commandments, He will give her rain in due season, an abundance of food, freedom from fear, victory over the enemy, and peace within the land (Lev. 26:1–13). Sadly, from what we see of the Scriptures, Israel will only seek God as a last resort, when she sees that she cannot prevail against the might and power of the Russian invasion (Joel 2:12–20). Deuteronomy 4:30 gives warning that it would take tribulation to turn Israel to God in the latter days. When Israel finally turns to God in true repentance, He will take pity on His people and remove far from them the "northern army" (Joel 2:20).

Another sign of the latter days will be a clear understanding of the judgments and the will of God. No other generation has seen Russia mustering forces against Israel, the Arab-Israeli conflict in the Middle East and the Jews in Jerusalem. No other generation has had the scientific knowledge to help it understand "strange" Scriptures, nor have they had access to the Bible as we have. We can understand perfectly the times in which we live: "The anger of the LORD will not turn back until He has executed and performed the thoughts of His heart. In the latter days you will understand it perfectly" (Jer. 23:20). Keep one eye on the Middle East—and the other toward the heavens. See also Rev. 9:9 and 16:16 comments.

will bring him to judgment with pestilence and bloodshed; I will rain down on
him, on his troops, and on the many peoples who *are* with him, flooding rain,
great hailstones, fire, and brimstone.
23Thus I will magnify Myself and sanctify
Myself, and I will be known in the eyes of
many nations. Then they shall know that
I *am* the LORD."'

Gog's Armies Destroyed

39 "And you, son of man, prophesy
against Gog, and say, 'Thus says
the Lord GOD: "Behold, I *am* against you,
O Gog, the prince of Rosh,[a] Meshech,
and Tubal; 2and I will turn you around
and lead you on, bringing you up from
the far north, and bring you against the
mountains of Israel. 3Then I will knock
the bow out of your left hand, and cause
the arrows to fall out of your right hand.
4You shall fall upon the mountains of Israel, you and all your troops and the peoples who *are* with you; I will give you to
birds of prey of every sort and *to* the
beasts of the field to be devoured. 5You
shall fall on the open field; for I have spoken," says the Lord GOD. 6"And I will send
fire on Magog and on those who live in
security in the coastlands. Then they
shall know that I *am* the LORD. 7So I will
make My holy name known in the midst
of My people Israel, and I will not *let them*
profane My holy name anymore. Then
the nations shall know that *I am* the
LORD, the Holy One in Israel. 8Surely it is
coming, and it shall be done," says the
Lord GOD. "This *is* the day of which I
have spoken.

9"Then those who dwell in the cities of
Israel will go out and set on fire and burn
the weapons, both the shields and bucklers, the bows and arrows, the javelins
and spears; and they will make fires with
them for seven years. 10They will not take
wood from the field nor cut down *any*
from the forests, because they will make
fires with the weapons; and they will
plunder those who plundered them, and
pillage those who pillaged them," says
the Lord GOD.

The Burial of Gog

11"It will come to pass in that day *that*
I will give Gog a burial place there in Israel, the valley of those who pass by east
of the sea; and it will obstruct travelers,
because there they will bury Gog and all
his multitude. Therefore they will call *it*
the Valley of Hamon Gog.[a] 12For seven
months the house of Israel will be burying them, in order to cleanse the land.
13Indeed all the people of the land will be
burying, and they will gain renown for it
on the day that I am glorified," says the
Lord GOD. 14"They will set apart men regularly employed, with the help of a search
party,[a] to pass through the land and bury
those bodies remaining on the ground, in
order to cleanse it. At the end of seven
months they will make a search. 15The
search party will pass through the land;
and *when anyone* sees a man's bone, he
shall set up a marker by it, till the buriers
have buried it in the Valley of Hamon Gog.
16*The* name of *the* city *will* also *be* Hamo-
nah. Thus they shall cleanse the land."'

A Triumphant Festival

17"And as for you, son of man, thus
says the Lord GOD, 'Speak to every sort of
bird and to every beast of the field:

"Assemble yourselves and come;
Gather together from all sides to My
sacrificial meal
Which I am sacrificing for you,
A great sacrificial meal on the
mountains of Israel,
That you may eat flesh and drink
blood.
18You shall eat the flesh of the mighty,
Drink the blood of the princes of the
earth,
Of rams and lambs,
Of goats and bulls,

39:1 [a]Targum, Vulgate and Aquila read *chief prince of.*
39:11 [a]Literally *The Multitude of Gog* **39:14** [a]Literally *those who pass through*

All of them fatlings of Bashan.
19You shall eat fat till you are full,
And drink blood till you are drunk,
At My sacrificial meal
Which I am sacrificing for you.
20You shall be filled at My table
With horses and riders,
With mighty men
And with all the men of war," says the
Lord GOD.

Israel Restored to the Land

21"I will set My glory among the nations; all the nations shall see My judgment which I have executed, and My hand
which I have laid on them. 22So the house
of Israel shall know that I *am* the LORD
their God from that day forward. 23The
Gentiles shall know that the house of Israel went into captivity for their iniquity;
because they were unfaithful to Me, therefore I hid My face from them. I gave them
into the hand of their enemies, and they
all fell by the sword. 24According to their
uncleanness and according to their transgressions I have dealt with them, and hidden My face from them." '

25"Therefore thus says the Lord GOD:
'Now I will bring back the captives of Jacob,
and have mercy on the whole house of
Israel; and I will be jealous for My holy
name— 26after they have borne their
shame, and all their unfaithfulness in
which they were unfaithful to Me, when
they dwelt safely in their *own* land and no
one made *them* afraid. 27When I have
brought them back from the peoples and
gathered them out of their enemies' lands,
and I am hallowed in them in the sight of
many nations, 28then they shall know
that I *am* the LORD their God, who sent
them into captivity among the nations,
but also brought them back to their land,
and left none of them captive any longer.
29And I will not hide My face from them
anymore; for I shall have poured out My
Spirit on the house of Israel,' says the
Lord GOD."

A New City, a New Temple

40 In the twenty-fifth year of our
captivity, at the beginning of the
year, on the tenth *day* of the month, in
the fourteenth year after the city was captured, on the very same day the hand of
the LORD was upon me; and He took me
there. 2In the visions of God He took me
into the land of Israel and set me on a
very high mountain; on it toward the
south *was* something like the structure of
a city. 3He took me there, and behold,
there was a man whose appearance *was*
like the appearance of bronze. He had a
line of flax and a measuring rod in his
hand, and he stood in the gateway.

4And the man said to me, "Son of
man, look with your eyes and hear with
your ears, and fix your mind on everything I show you; for you *were* brought
here so that I might show *them* to you.
Declare to the house of Israel everything
you see." 5Now there was a wall all around
the outside of the temple.[a] In the man's
hand was a measuring rod six cubits *long,*
each being a cubit and a handbreadth; and
he measured the width of the wall structure, one rod; and the height, one rod.

The Eastern Gateway of the Temple

6Then he went to the gateway which
faced east; and he went up its stairs and
measured the threshold of the gateway,
which was one rod wide, and the other
threshold *was* one rod wide. 7Each gate

40:5 [a]Literally *house,* and so elsewhere in this book

39:23 All of God's terrible judgments against Israel were according to righteousness. He simply did what was right and just by punishing them for their sins (see Deut. 31:17). The Day of Judgment will be the ultimate Day when God manifests His righteous judgments according to the sins of humanity, right down to every idle word men speak (see Matt. 12:36). What a fearful thing it will be to fall into the hands of the Living God. We must warn this sinful world so that we can present every man and woman perfect in Christ Jesus (see Col. 1:28).

"If you want to find out if you have the heart of a servant, you will find out when you are treated like one."

Elisabeth Elliot

chamber *was* one rod long and one rod
wide; between the gate chambers *was a
space of* five cubits; and the threshold of
the gateway by the vestibule of the inside
gate *was* one rod. 8He also measured the
vestibule of the inside gate, one rod. 9Then
he measured the vestibule of the gateway,
eight cubits; and the gateposts, two cubits.
The vestibule of the gate *was* on the inside. 10In the eastern gateway *were* three
gate chambers on one side and three on
the other; the three *were* all the same size;
also the gateposts were of the same size
on this side and that side.

11He measured the width of the entrance to the gateway, ten cubits; *and* the
length of the gate, thirteen cubits. 12*There
was* a space in front of the gate chambers,
one cubit *on this side* and one cubit on that
side; the gate chambers *were* six cubits on
this side and six cubits on that side.
13Then he measured the gateway from
the roof of *one* gate chamber to the roof of
the other; the width *was* twenty-five cubits, as door faces door. 14He measured
the gateposts, sixty cubits high, and the
court all around the gateway *extended* to
the gatepost. 15*From* the front of the entrance gate to the front of the vestibule of
the inner gate *was* fifty cubits. 16*There were*
beveled window *frames* in the gate chambers and in their intervening archways on
the inside of the gateway all around, and
likewise in the vestibules. *There were* windows all around on the inside. And on
each gatepost *were* palm trees.

The Outer Court

17Then he brought me into the outer
court; and *there were* chambers and a pavement made all around the court; thirty
chambers faced the pavement. 18The pavement was by the side of the gateways,
corresponding to the length of the gateways; *this was* the lower pavement. 19Then
he measured the width from the front of
the lower gateway to the front of the inner court exterior, one hundred cubits
toward the east and the north.

The Northern Gateway

20On the outer court was also a gateway facing north, and he measured its
length and its width. 21Its gate chambers,
three on this side and three on that side,
its gateposts and its archways, had the
same measurements as the first gate; its
length *was* fifty cubits and its width
twenty-five cubits. 22Its windows and
those of its archways, and also its palm
trees, *had* the same measurements as the
gateway facing east; it was ascended by
seven steps, and its archway *was* in front
of it. 23A gate of the inner court was opposite the northern gateway, just as the
eastern *gateway;* and he measured from
gateway to gateway, one hundred cubits.

The Southern Gateway

24After that he brought me toward the
south, and there a gateway was facing
south; and he measured its gateposts and
archways according to these same measurements. 25*There were* windows in it and
in its archways all around like those windows; its length *was* fifty cubits and its
width twenty-five cubits. 26Seven steps led
up to it, and its archway *was* in front of

them; and it had palm trees on its gateposts, one on this side and one on that
side. 27*There was* also a gateway on the inner court, facing south; and he measured
from gateway to gateway toward the
south, one hundred cubits.

Gateways of the Inner Court

28Then he brought me to the inner
court through the southern gateway; he
measured the southern gateway according to these same measurements. 29Also
its gate chambers, its gateposts, and its
archways *were* according to these same
measurements; *there were* windows in it
and in its archways all around; *it was* fifty
cubits long and twenty-five cubits wide.
30*There were* archways all around, twenty-
five cubits long and five cubits wide. 31Its
archways faced the outer court, palm trees
were on its gateposts, and going up to it
were eight steps.

32And he brought me into the inner
court facing east; he measured the gateway according to these same measurements. 33Also its gate chambers, its gateposts, and its archways *were* according to
these same measurements; and *there were*
windows in it and in its archways all
around; *it was* fifty cubits long and twenty-
five cubits wide. 34Its archways faced the
outer court, and palm trees *were* on its
gateposts on this side and on that side;
and going up to it *were* eight steps.

35Then he brought me to the north
gateway and measured *it* according to
these same measurements— 36also its gate
chambers, its gateposts, and its archways.
It had windows all around; its length *was*
fifty cubits and its width twenty-five cubits. 37Its gateposts faced the outer court,
palm trees *were* on its gateposts on this
side and on that side, and going up to it
were eight steps.

Where Sacrifices Were Prepared

38*There was* a chamber and its entrance
by the gateposts of the gateway, where
they washed the burnt offering. 39In the
vestibule of the gateway *were* two tables
on this side and two tables on that side,
on which to slay the burnt offering, the
sin offering, and the trespass offering.
40At the outer side of the vestibule, as one
goes up to the entrance of the northern
gateway, *were* two tables; and on the
other side of the vestibule of the gateway
were two tables. 41Four tables *were* on this
side and four tables on that side, by the
side of the gateway, eight tables on which
they slaughtered *the sacrifices.* 42*There were*
also four tables of hewn stone for the
burnt offering, one cubit and a half long,
one cubit and a half wide, and one cubit
high; on these they laid the instruments
with which they slaughtered the burnt
offering and the sacrifice. 43Inside *were*
hooks, a handbreadth wide, fastened all
around; and the flesh of the sacrifices *was*
on the tables.

Chambers for Singers and Priests

44Outside the inner gate *were* the
chambers for the singers in the inner court,
one facing south at the side of the northern gateway, and the other facing north at
the side of the southern[a] gateway. 45Then
he said to me, "This chamber which faces
south *is* for the priests who have charge
of the temple. 46The chamber which faces
north *is* for the priests who have charge
of the altar; these *are* the sons of Zadok,
from the sons of Levi, who come near the
LORD to minister to Him."

**Dimensions of the Inner Court
and Vestibule**

47And he measured the court, one hundred cubits long and one hundred cubits
wide, foursquare. The altar *was* in front
of the temple. 48Then he brought me to
the vestibule of the temple and measured
the doorposts of the vestibule, five cubits
on this side and five cubits on that side;
and the width of the gateway was three
cubits on this side and three cubits on
that side. 49The length of the vestibule

40:44 [a]Following Septuagint; Masoretic Text and Vulgate read *eastern.*

was twenty cubits, and the width eleven cubits; and by the steps which led up to it *there were* pillars by the doorposts, one on this side and another on that side.

Dimensions of the Sanctuary

41 Then he brought me into the sanctuary[a] and measured the doorposts, six cubits wide on one side and six cubits wide on the other side—the width of the tabernacle. 2The width of the entryway *was* ten cubits, and the side walls of the entrance *were* five cubits on this side and five cubits on the other side; and he measured its length, forty cubits, and its width, twenty cubits.

3Also he went inside and measured the doorposts, two cubits; and the entrance, six cubits *high;* and the width of the entrance, seven cubits. 4He measured the length, twenty cubits; and the width, twenty cubits, beyond the sanctuary; and he said to me, "This *is* the Most Holy *Place.*"

The Side Chambers on the Wall

5Next, he measured the wall of the temple, six cubits. The width of each side chamber all around the temple *was* four cubits on every side. 6The side chambers *were* in three stories, one above the other, thirty chambers in each story; they rested on ledges which *were* for the side chambers all around, that they might be supported, but not fastened to the wall of the temple. 7As one went up from story to story, the side chambers became wider all around, because their supporting ledges in the wall of the temple ascended like steps; therefore the width of the structure increased as one went up *from* the lowest *story* to the highest by way of the middle one. 8I also saw an elevation all around the temple; it was the foundation of the side chambers, a full rod, *that is,* six cubits *high.* 9The thickness of the outer wall of the side chambers *was* five cubits, and so also the remaining terrace by the place of the side chambers of the temple. 10And between *it and* the *wall* chambers was a width of twenty cubits all around the temple on every side. 11The doors of the side chambers opened on the terrace, one door toward the north and another toward the south; and the width of the terrace *was* five cubits all around.

The Building at the Western End

12The building that faced the separating courtyard at its western end *was* seventy cubits wide; the wall of the building *was* five cubits thick all around, and its

41:1 [a]Hebrew *heykal,* here the main room of the temple, sometimes called the *holy place* (compare Exodus 26:33)

41:1 Features unique to Ezekiel's temple
By Lambert Dolphin

No wall of partition to exclude Gentiles (compare Eph. 2:14). The Gentiles were previously welcome in the Outer Courts, but excluded from the Inner Courts on pain of death.
No Court of Women (compare Gal. 3:28; Outer Court and Inner Court only)
No Laver (see Ezek. 36:24–27; John 15:3)
No Table of Shewbread (see Mic. 5:4; John 6:35)
No Lampstand or Menorah (see Isa. 49:6; John 8:12)
No Golden Altar of Incense (Zech. 8:20–23; John 14:6)
No Veil (Isa. 25:6–8; Matt. 27:51)
No Ark of the Covenant (Jer. 3:16; John 10:30–33)

Major changes to the Altar: The sacrificial Altar will be approached by a ramp from the east. Previous altars were all approached from the south. Now there will be stairs to the altar, not a ramp as previously. The top of the altar is now described by the Hebrew word "*ariel*" (Isa. 29:1), meaning "hearth of God" or "lion of God" (Rev. 5:5).

If the previous temples, as well as the Tabernacle of Moses, are pictures of man as the dwelling place of God, then Ezekiel's temple may be intended to teach us about the marvelously new resurrection bodies waiting for every believer when he leaves this present life (2 Cor. 5:1–5).

length ninety cubits.

Dimensions and Design of the Temple Area

[13]So he measured the temple, one hundred cubits long; and the separating courtyard with the building and its walls *was* one hundred cubits long; [14]also the width of the eastern face of the temple, including the separating courtyard, *was* one hundred cubits. [15]He measured the length of the building behind it, facing the separating courtyard, with its galleries on the one side and on the other side, one hundred cubits, as well as the inner temple and the porches of the court, [16]their doorposts and the beveled window frames. And the galleries all around their three stories opposite the threshold were paneled with wood from the ground to the windows—the windows were covered— [17]from the space above the door, even to the inner room,[a] as well as outside, and on every wall all around, inside and outside, by measure.

[18]And *it was* made with cherubim and palm trees, a palm tree between cherub and cherub. *Each* cherub had two faces, [19]so that the face of a man *was* toward a palm tree on one side, and the face of a young lion toward a palm tree on the other side; thus *it was* made throughout the temple all around. [20]From the floor to the space above the door, and on the wall of the sanctuary, cherubim and palm trees *were* carved.

[21]The doorposts of the temple *were* square, *as was* the front of the sanctuary; their appearance was similar. [22]The altar *was* of wood, three cubits high, and its length two cubits. Its corners, its length, and its sides *were* of wood; and he said to me, "This *is* the table that *is* before the LORD."

[23]The temple and the sanctuary had two doors. [24]The doors had two panels *apiece,* two folding panels: two *panels* for one door and two panels for the other *door.* [25]Cherubim and palm trees *were* carved on the doors of the temple just as they *were* carved on the walls. A wooden canopy *was* on the front of the vestibule outside. [26]*There were* beveled window *frames* and palm trees on one side and on the other, on the sides of the vestibule—also on the side chambers of the temple and on the canopies.

The Chambers for the Priests

42 Then he brought me out into the outer court, by the way toward the north; and he brought me into the chamber which *was* opposite the separating courtyard, and which *was* opposite the building toward the north. [2]Facing the length, *which was* one hundred cubits (the width was fifty cubits), was the north door. [3]Opposite the inner court of twenty *cubits,* and opposite the pavement of the outer court, *was* gallery against gallery in three *stories.* [4]In front of the chambers, toward the inside, *was* a walk ten cubits wide, at a distance of one cubit; and their doors faced north. [5]Now the upper chambers *were* shorter, because the galleries took away *space* from them more than from the lower and middle stories of the building. [6]For they *were* in three *stories* and did not have pillars like the pillars of the courts; therefore *the upper level* was shortened more than the lower and middle levels from the ground up. [7]And a wall which *was* outside ran parallel to the chambers, at the front of the chambers, toward the outer court; its length *was* fifty cubits. [8]The length of the chambers toward the outer court *was* fifty cubits, whereas that facing the temple *was* one hundred cubits. [9]At the lower chambers *was* the entrance on the east side, as one goes into them from the outer court.

[10]Also *there were* chambers in the thickness of the wall of the court toward the east, opposite the separating courtyard and opposite the building. [11]*There was* a walk in front of them also, and their appearance *was* like the chambers which *were* toward the north; they *were* as long and

41:17 [a]Literally *house,* here *the Most Holy Place*

as wide as the others, and all their exits
and entrances *were* according to plan.
12And corresponding to the doors of the
chambers that *were* facing south, as one
enters them, *there was* a door in front of
the walk, the way directly in front of the
wall toward the east.
13Then he said to me, "The north
chambers *and* the south chambers, which
are opposite the separating courtyard, *are*
the holy chambers where the priests who
approach the LORD shall eat the most holy
offerings. There they shall lay the most
holy offerings—the grain offering, the sin
offering, and the trespass offering—for
the place *is* holy. 14When the priests enter
them, they shall not go out of the holy
chamber into the outer court; but there
they shall leave their garments in which
they minister, for they *are* holy. They shall
put on other garments; then they may approach *that* which *is* for the people."

Outer Dimensions of the Temple

15Now when he had finished measuring the inner temple, he brought me out
through the gateway that faces toward
the east, and measured it all around. 16He
measured the east side with the measuring rod,[a] five hundred rods by the measuring rod all around. 17He measured the
north side, five hundred rods by the measuring rod all around. 18He measured the
south side, five hundred rods by the measuring rod. 19He came around to the west
side *and* measured five hundred rods by
the measuring rod. 20He measured it on
the four sides; it had a wall all around,
five hundred *cubits* long and five hundred
wide, to separate the holy areas from the
common.

The Temple, the Lord's Dwelling Place

43 Afterward he brought me to the
gate, the gate that faces toward the
east. 2And behold, the glory of the God of
Israel came from the way of the east. His
voice *was* like the sound of many waters;
and the earth shone with His glory. 3*It was*
like the appearance of the vision which I
saw—like the vision which I saw when I[a]
came to destroy the city. The visions *were*
like the vision which I saw by the River
Chebar; and I fell on my face. 4And the
glory of the LORD came into the temple
by way of the gate which faces toward the
east. 5The Spirit lifted me up and brought
me into the inner court; and behold, the
glory of the LORD filled the temple.
6Then I heard *Him* speaking to me
from the temple, while a man stood beside me. 7And He said to me, "Son of man,
this is the place of My throne and the
place of the soles of My feet, where I will
dwell in the midst of the children of Israel forever. No more shall the house of
Israel defile My holy name, they nor their
kings, by their harlotry or with the carcasses of their kings on their high places.
8When they set their threshold by My
threshold, and their doorpost by My
doorpost, with a wall between them and
Me, they defiled My holy name by the
abominations which they committed;
therefore I have consumed them in My
anger. 9Now let them put their harlotry
and the carcasses of their kings far away
from Me, and I will dwell in their midst
forever.

42:16 [a]Compare 40:5 43:3 [a]Some Hebrew manuscripts and Vulgate read *He*.

43:2 "After Ezekiel had surveyed the temple of God, he had a vision of the glory of God. When Christ crucified, and the things freely given to us of God, through Him, are shown to us by the Holy Ghost, they make us ashamed for our sins. This frame of mind prepares us for fuller discoveries of the mysteries of redeeming love; and the whole of the Scriptures should be opened and applied, that men may see their sins, and repent of them. We are not now to offer any atoning sacrifices, for by one offering Christ has perfected for ever those that are sanctified, Heb. 10:14; but the sprinkling of his blood is needful in all our approaches to God the Father. Our best services can be accepted only as sprinkled with the blood which cleanses from all sin." *Matthew Henry*

10"Son of man, describe the temple to
the house of Israel, that they may be
ashamed of their iniquities; and let them
measure the pattern. 11And if they are
ashamed of all that they have done, make
known to them the design of the temple
and its arrangement, its exits and its entrances, its entire design and all its ordinances, all its forms and all its laws. Write
it down in their sight, so that they may
keep its whole design and all its ordinances, and perform them. 12This *is* the
law of the temple: The whole area surrounding the mountaintop *is* most holy.
Behold, this *is* the law of the temple.

Dimensions of the Altar

13"These are the measurements of the
altar in cubits (the *cubit is* one cubit and
a handbreadth): the base one cubit high
and one cubit wide, with a rim all around
its edge of one span. This *is* the height of
the altar: 14from the base on the ground to
the lower ledge, two cubits; the width of
the ledge, one cubit; from the smaller ledge
to the larger ledge, four cubits; and the
width of the ledge, *one* cubit. 15The altar
hearth *is* four cubits high, with four horns
extending upward from the hearth. 16The
altar hearth *is* twelve cubits long, twelve
wide, square at its four corners; 17the ledge,
fourteen *cubits* long and fourteen wide on
its four sides, with a rim of half a cubit
around it; its base, one cubit all around;
and its steps face toward the east."

Consecrating the Altar

18And He said to me, "Son of man,
thus says the Lord GOD: 'These *are* the ordinances for the altar on the day when it
is made, for sacrificing burnt offerings on
it, and for sprinkling blood on it. 19You
shall give a young bull for a sin offering
to the priests, the Levites, who are of the
seed of Zadok, who approach Me to minister to Me,' says the Lord GOD. 20'You
shall take some of its blood and put *it* on
the four horns of the altar, on the four
corners of the ledge, and on the rim around
it; thus you shall cleanse it and make
atonement for it. 21Then you shall also take
the bull of the sin offering, and burn it in
the appointed place of the temple, outside the sanctuary. 22On the second day
you shall offer a kid of the goats without
blemish for a sin offering; and they shall
cleanse the altar, as they cleansed *it* with
the bull. 23When you have finished cleansing *it*, you shall offer a young bull without blemish, and a ram from the flock
without blemish. 24When you offer them
before the LORD, the priests shall throw
salt on them, and they will offer them up
as a burnt offering to the LORD. 25Every
day for seven days you shall prepare a
goat *for* a sin offering; they shall also prepare a young bull and a ram from the
flock, both without blemish. 26Seven days
they shall make atonement for the altar
and purify it, and so consecrate *it*. 27When
these days are over it shall be, on the
eighth day and thereafter, that the priests
shall offer your burnt offerings and your
peace offerings on the altar; and I will accept you,' says the Lord GOD."

The East Gate and the Prince

44 Then He brought me back to the
outer gate of the sanctuary which
faces toward the east, but it *was* shut.
2And the LORD said to me, "This gate shall
be shut; it shall not be opened, and no
man shall enter by it, because the LORD
God of Israel has entered by it; therefore
it shall be shut. 3*As for* the prince, *because*
he *is* the prince, he may sit in it to eat
bread before the LORD; he shall enter by
way of the vestibule of the gateway, and
go out the same way."

Those Admitted to the Temple

4Also He brought me by way of the

44:4 The day will come when the glory of the Lord will cover this earth as the waters cover the sea (see Num. 14:21; Hab. 2:14).

north gate to the front of the temple; so I
looked, and behold, the glory of the LORD
filled the house of the LORD; and I fell on
my face. 5And the LORD said to me, "Son
of man, mark well, see with your eyes
and hear with your ears, all that I say to
you concerning all the ordinances of the
house of the LORD and all its laws. Mark
well who may enter the house and all
who go out from the sanctuary.
6"Now say to the rebellious, to the
house of Israel, 'Thus says the Lord GOD:
"O house of Israel, let Us have no more of
all your abominations. 7When you brought
in foreigners, uncircumcised in heart and
uncircumcised in flesh, to be in My sanctuary to defile it—My house—and when
you offered My food, the fat and the
blood, then they broke My covenant because of all your abominations. 8And you
have not kept charge of My holy things,
but you have set *others* to keep charge of
My sanctuary for you." 9Thus says the Lord
GOD: "No foreigner, uncircumcised in
heart or uncircumcised in flesh, shall enter My sanctuary, including any foreigner
who *is* among the children of Israel.

Laws Governing Priests

10"And the Levites who went far from
Me, when Israel went astray, who strayed
away from Me after their idols, they shall
bear their iniquity. 11Yet they shall be
ministers in My sanctuary, *as* gatekeepers
of the house and ministers of the house;
they shall slay the burnt offering and the
sacrifice for the people, and they shall
stand before them to minister to them.
12Because they ministered to them before
their idols and caused the house of Israel
to fall into iniquity, therefore I have
raised My hand in an oath against them,"
says the Lord GOD, "that they shall bear
their iniquity. 13And they shall not come
near Me to minister to Me as priest, nor
come near any of My holy things, nor
into the Most Holy *Place;* but they shall
bear their shame and their abominations
which they have committed. 14Neverthe-
less I will make them keep charge of the
temple, for all its work, and for all that
has to be done in it.
15"But the priests, the Levites, the sons
of Zadok, who kept charge of My sanctuary when the children of Israel went
astray from Me, they shall come near Me
to minister to Me; and they shall stand
before Me to offer to Me the fat and the
blood," says the Lord GOD. 16"They shall
enter My sanctuary, and they shall come
near My table to minister to Me, and they
shall keep My charge. 17And it shall be,
whenever they enter the gates of the inner court, that they shall put on linen
garments; no wool shall come upon them
while they minister within the gates of
the inner court or within the house. 18They
shall have linen turbans on their heads
and linen trousers on their bodies; they
shall not clothe themselves with *anything*
that causes sweat. 19When they go out to
the outer court, to the outer court to the
people, they shall take off their garments
in which they have ministered, leave
them in the holy chambers, and put on
other garments; and in their holy garments they shall not sanctify the people.
20"They shall neither shave their heads,
nor let their hair grow long, but they
shall keep their hair well trimmed. 21No
priest shall drink wine when he enters
the inner court. 22They shall not take as
wife a widow or a divorced woman, but
take virgins of the descendants of the
house of Israel, or widows of priests.
23"And they shall teach My people *the*
difference between the holy and the unholy, and cause them to discern between
the unclean and the clean. 24In controversy they shall stand as judges, *and* judge
it according to My judgments. They shall
keep My laws and My statutes in all My
appointed meetings, and they shall hallow My Sabbaths.
25"They shall not defile *themselves* by
coming near a dead person. Only for father or mother, for son or daughter, for
brother or unmarried sister may they defile themselves. 26After he is cleansed, they
shall count seven days for him. 27And on

QUESTIONS & OBJECTIONS

44:24

"I don't believe we'll be judged by the Ten Commandments."

The Bible makes it clear that there will be a Day of Judgment. The Scriptures warn, "Though they join forces, the wicked will not go unpunished" (Prov. 11:21). However, will the standard of judgment be the Ten Commandments, or something else? Some believe it will be the words of Jesus that will judge mankind, based on John 12:48: "He who rejects Me, and does not receive My words, has that which judges him—the word that I have spoken will judge him in the last day."

What words of Jesus will humanity be judged by? The Scriptures say the Lord would "magnify the law, and make it honourable" (Isa. 42:21, KJV). This was the essence of the Messiah's teaching ministry. The religious leaders had twisted and demeaned the Law so that its original intent was lost. But Jesus magnified it, showing that lust was adultery, that anger without cause violated its holy precepts, etc. He reminded them that not one jot or tittle of the Law would fail.

When Paul preached on Mars Hill, he warned the idolatrous Athenians, who had violated the First and Second Commandments, that God would "judge the world in righteousness" (Acts 17:31). The "righteousness" of which he spoke is the "righteousness which is of the law" (Rom. 10:5; see also 8:4). Scripture tells us that the moral Law is the standard by which God will judge mankind: "For as many as have sinned without law will also perish without law, and as many as have sinned in the law *will be judged by the law*" (Rom. 2:12, emphasis added). James 2:12 also warns that the moral Law will be the standard of judgment: "So speak and so do as those who will be judged by the law of liberty."

Those who may be tempted to say that the "law of liberty" isn't the moral Law but "the law of Christ" should consider the context. The preceding verse tells us what James had in mind: "For He who said, 'Do not commit adultery' [7th Commandment], also said, 'Do not murder' [6th Commandment]. Now if you do not commit adultery, but you do murder, you have become a transgressor of the law" (James 2:11).

the day that he goes to the sanctuary to
minister in the sanctuary, he must offer
his sin offering in the inner court," says
the Lord GOD.
28"It shall be, in regard to their inheritance, *that* I *am* their inheritance. You shall
give them no possession in Israel, for I
am their possession. 29They shall eat the
grain offering, the sin offering, and the
trespass offering; every dedicated thing in
Israel shall be theirs. 30The best of all firstfruits of any kind, and every sacrifice of
any kind from all your sacrifices, shall be
the priest's; also you shall give to the
priest the first of your ground meal, to
cause a blessing to rest on your house.
31The priests shall not eat anything, bird
or beast, that died naturally or was torn
by wild beasts.

The Holy District

45 "Moreover, when you divide the
land by lot into inheritance, you
shall set apart a district for the LORD, a
holy section of the land; its length *shall be*
twenty-five thousand *cubits,* and the width
ten thousand. It *shall be* holy throughout
its territory all around. 2Of this there shall
be a square plot for the sanctuary, five
hundred by five hundred *rods,* with fifty
cubits around it for an open space. 3So this
is the district you shall measure: twenty-
five thousand *cubits* long and ten thousand wide; in it shall be the sanctuary, the
Most Holy *Place.* 4It shall be a holy *section*
of the land, belonging to the priests, the
ministers of the sanctuary, who come
near to minister to the LORD; it shall be a
place for their houses and a holy place for
the sanctuary. 5*An area* twenty-five thousand *cubits* long and ten thousand wide
shall belong to the Levites, the ministers
of the temple; they shall have twenty
chambers as a possession.[a]

45:5 [a]Following Masoretic Text, Targum, and Vulgate; Septuagint reads *a possession, cities of dwelling.*

Properties of the City and the Prince

6“You shall appoint as the property of the city *an area* five thousand *cubits* wide and twenty-five thousand long, adjacent to the district of the holy *section;* it shall belong to the whole house of Israel.

7“The prince shall have *a section* on one side and the other of the holy district and the city’s property; and bordering on the holy district and the city’s property, extending westward on the west side and eastward on the east side, the length *shall be* side by side with one of the *tribal* portions, from the west border to the east border. 8The land shall be his possession in Israel; and My princes shall no more oppress My people, but they shall give *the rest of* the land to the house of Israel, according to their tribes.”

Laws Governing the Prince

9‘Thus says the Lord GOD: “Enough, O princes of Israel! Remove violence and plundering, execute justice and righteousness, and stop dispossessing My people,” says the Lord GOD. 10“You shall have honest scales, an honest ephah, and an honest bath. 11The ephah and the bath shall be of the same measure, so that the bath contains one-tenth of a homer, and the ephah one-tenth of a homer; their measure shall be according to the homer. 12The shekel *shall be* twenty gerahs; twenty shekels, twenty-five shekels, *and* fifteen shekels shall be your mina.

13“This *is* the offering which you shall offer: you shall give one-sixth of an ephah from a homer of wheat, and one-sixth of an ephah from a homer of barley. 14The ordinance concerning oil, the bath of oil, *is* one-tenth of a bath from a kor. *A kor is* a homer or ten baths, for ten baths *are* a homer. 15And one lamb shall be given from a flock of two hundred, from the rich pastures of Israel. These shall be for grain offerings, burnt offerings, and peace offerings, to make atonement for them,” says the Lord GOD. 16“All the people of the land shall give this offering for the prince in Israel. 17Then it shall be the prince’s part *to give* burnt offerings, grain offerings, and drink offerings, at the feasts, the New Moons, the Sabbaths, and at all the appointed seasons of the house of Israel. He shall prepare the sin offering, the grain offering, the burnt offering, and the peace offerings to make atonement for the house of Israel.”

Keeping the Feasts

18‘Thus says the Lord GOD: “In the first *month,* on the first *day* of the month, you shall take a young bull without blemish and cleanse the sanctuary. 19The priest shall take some of the blood of the sin offering and put *it* on the doorposts of the temple, on the four corners of the ledge of the altar, and on the gateposts of the gate of the inner court. 20And so you shall do on the seventh *day* of the month for everyone who has sinned unintentionally or in ignorance. Thus you shall make atonement for the temple.

21“In the first *month,* on the fourteenth day of the month, you shall observe the Passover, a feast of seven days; unleavened bread shall be eaten. 22And on that day the prince shall prepare for himself and for all the people of the land a bull *for* a sin offering. 23On the seven days of the feast he shall prepare a burnt offering to the LORD, seven bulls and seven rams without blemish, daily for seven days, and a kid of the goats daily *for* a sin offering. 24And he shall prepare a grain offering of one ephah for each bull and one

45:10 A slightly rigged scale that no one notices could make much money over time, but we must never forget that God sees that unjust scale and that He loves righteousness and hates robbery.

45:20 We still violate God’s Law, even if we sin in ignorance. Even though someone is ignorant of the law of gravity, they suffer the consequences of violating its laws. God does, however, take ignorance into account (see Acts 17:30). See also Lev. 4:27,28; 5:17.

ephah for each ram, together with a hin
of oil for each ephah.
25“In the seventh *month*, on the fifteenth day of the month, at the feast, he
shall do likewise for seven days, according to the sin offering, the burnt offering,
the grain offering, and the oil.”

The Manner of Worship

46 Thus says the Lord GOD: “The
gateway of the inner court that
faces toward the east shall be shut the six
working days; but on the Sabbath it shall
be opened, and on the day of the New
Moon it shall be opened. 2The prince shall
enter by way of the vestibule of the gateway from the outside, and stand by the
gatepost. The priests shall prepare his
burnt offering and his peace offerings. He
shall worship at the threshold of the gate.
Then he shall go out, but the gate shall
not be shut until evening. 3Likewise the
people of the land shall worship at the
entrance to this gateway before the LORD
on the Sabbaths and the New Moons.
4The burnt offering that the prince offers
to the LORD on the Sabbath day *shall be*
six lambs without blemish, and a ram
without blemish; 5and the grain offering
shall be one ephah for a ram, and the grain
offering for the lambs, as much as he
wants to give, as well as a hin of oil with
every ephah. 6On the day of the New
Moon *it shall be* a young bull without
blemish, six lambs, and a ram; they shall
be without blemish. 7He shall prepare a
grain offering of an ephah for a bull, an
ephah for a ram, as much as he wants to
give for the lambs, and a hin of oil with
every ephah. 8When the prince enters, he
shall go in by way of the vestibule of the
gateway, and go out the same way.
9“But when the people of the land come
before the LORD on the appointed feast
days, whoever enters by way of the north
gate to worship shall go out by way of the
south gate; and whoever enters by way of
the south gate shall go out by way of the
north gate. He shall not return by way of
the gate through which he came, but
shall go out through the opposite gate.
10The prince shall then be in their midst.
When they go in, he shall go in; and when
they go out, he shall go out. 11At the fes-
tivals and the appointed feast days the
grain offering shall be an ephah for a bull,
an ephah for a ram, as much as he wants
to give for the lambs, and a hin of oil with
every ephah.
12“Now when the prince makes a voluntary burnt offering or voluntary peace
offering to the LORD, the gate that faces
toward the east shall then be opened for
him; and he shall prepare his burnt offering and his peace offerings as he did on
the Sabbath day. Then he shall go out,
and after he goes out the gate shall be
shut.

> It is not enough for us to be where God is worshipped, if we do not ourselves worship him, and that not with bodily exercise only, which profits little, but with the heart.
>
> **MATTHEW HENRY**

13“You shall daily make a burnt offering to the LORD *of* a lamb of the first year
without blemish; you shall prepare it every
morning. 14And you shall prepare a grain
offering with it every morning, a sixth of
an ephah, and a third of a hin of oil to
moisten the fine flour. This grain offering
is a perpetual ordinance, to be made regularly to the LORD. 15Thus they shall prepare the lamb, the grain offering, and
the oil, *as* a regular burnt offering every
morning.”

The Prince and Inheritance Laws

16“Thus says the Lord GOD: “If the
prince gives a gift *of some* of his inheritance to any of his sons, it shall belong to
his sons; it is their possession by inheritance. 17But if he gives a gift of some of
his inheritance to one of his servants, it
shall be his until the year of liberty, after
which it shall return to the prince. But

his inheritance shall belong to his sons; it shall become theirs. [18]Moreover the prince shall not take any of the people's inheritance by evicting them from their property; he shall provide an inheritance for his sons from his own property, so that none of My people may be scattered from his property." ' "

How the Offerings Were Prepared

[19]Now he brought me through the entrance, which *was* at the side of the gate, into the holy chambers of the priests which face toward the north; and there a place *was* situated at their extreme western end. [20]And he said to me, "This *is* the place where the priests shall boil the trespass offering and the sin offering, *and* where they shall bake the grain offering, so that they do not bring *them* out into the outer court to sanctify the people."

[21]Then he brought me out into the outer court and caused me to pass by the four corners of the court; and in fact, in every corner of the court *there was another* court. [22]In the four corners of the court *were* enclosed courts, forty *cubits* long and thirty wide; all four corners *were* the same size. [23]*There was* a row *of building stones* all around in them, all around the four of them; and cooking hearths were made under the rows of stones all around. [24]And he said to me, "These *are* the kitchens where the ministers of the temple shall boil the sacrifices of the people."

The Healing Waters and Trees

47 Then he brought me back to the door of the temple; and there was water, flowing from under the threshold of the temple toward the east, for the front of the temple faced east; the water was flowing from under the right side of the temple, south of the altar. [2]He brought me out by way of the north gate, and led me around on the outside to the outer gateway that faces east; and there was water, running out on the right side.

[3]And when the man went out to the east with the line in his hand, he measured one thousand cubits, and he brought me through the waters; the water *came up to my* ankles. [4]Again he measured one thousand and brought me through the waters; the water *came up to my* knees. Again he measured one thousand and brought me through; the water *came up to my* waist. [5]Again he measured one thousand, *and it was* a river that I could not cross; for the water was too deep, water in which one must swim, a river that could not be crossed. [6]He said to me, "Son of man, have you seen *this*?" Then he brought me and returned me to the bank of the river.

[7]When I returned, there, along the bank of the river, *were* very many trees on one side and the other. [8]Then he said to me: "This water flows toward the eastern region, goes down into the valley, and enters the sea. *When it* reaches the sea, *its* waters are healed. [9]And it shall be *that* every living thing that moves, wherever the rivers go, will live. There will be a very great multitude of fish, because these waters go there; for they will be healed, and everything will live wherever the river goes. [10]It shall be *that* fishermen will stand by it from En Gedi to En Eglaim; they will be *places* for spreading their nets. Their fish will be of the same kinds as the fish of the Great Sea, exceedingly many. [11]But its swamps and marshes will not be healed; they will be given over to salt. [12]Along the bank of the river, on this side and that, will grow all *kinds of* trees used for food; their leaves will not wither, and their fruit will not fail. They will bear fruit every month, because their water

47:1,2 How committed are we to reaching the lost? Too often we creep out into the waters of evangelism, but only up to our ankles. We would find a new liberty if we abandoned ourselves to the task of bringing others to the "pure river of water of life" (see Rev. 22:1).

47:12 Much of modern-day medicine comes from the leaves of plants. How kind of God to give antidotes to disease. These leaves, however, will provide the ultimate "healing of the nations" (see Rev. 22:2).

flows from the sanctuary. Their fruit will
be for food, and their leaves for medicine."

Borders of the Land

13Thus says the Lord GOD: "These *are*
the borders by which you shall divide the
land as an inheritance among the twelve
tribes of Israel. Joseph *shall have two* portions. 14You shall inherit it equally with
one another; for I raised My hand in an
oath to give it to your fathers, and this
land shall fall to you as your inheritance.
15"This *shall be* the border of the land
on the north: from the Great Sea, *by* the
road to Hethlon, as one goes to Zedad,
16Hamath, Berothah, Sibraim (which *is*
between the border of Damascus and the
border of Hamath), to Hazar Hatticon
(which *is* on the border of Hauran).
17Thus the boundary shall be from the Sea
to Hazar Enan, the border of Damascus;
and as for the north, northward, it is the
border of Hamath. *This is* the north side.
18"On the east side you shall mark out
the border from between Hauran and
Damascus, and between Gilead and the
land of Israel, along the Jordan, and along
the eastern side of the sea. *This is* the east
side.
19"The south side, toward the South,[a]
shall be from Tamar to the waters of
Meribah by Kadesh, along the brook to
the Great Sea. *This is* the south side, toward
the South.
20"The west side *shall be* the Great Sea,
from the *southern* boundary until one
comes to a point opposite Hamath. This
is the west side.
21"Thus you shall divide this land
among yourselves according to the tribes
of Israel. 22It shall be that you will divide
it by lot as an inheritance for yourselves,
and for the strangers who dwell among
you and who bear children among you.
They shall be to you as native-born among
the children of Israel; they shall have an
inheritance with you among the tribes of
Israel. 23And it shall be *that* in whatever
tribe the stranger dwells, there you shall
give *him* his inheritance," says the Lord
GOD.

Division of the Land

48 "Now these *are* the names of the
tribes: From the northern border
along the road to Hethlon at the entrance
of Hamath, to Hazar Enan, the border of
Damascus northward, in the direction of
Hamath, *there shall be* one *section for* Dan
from its east to its west side; 2by the border of Dan, from the east side to the west,
one *section for* Asher; 3by the border of
Asher, from the east side to the west, one
section for Naphtali; 4by the border of
Naphtali, from the east side to the west,
one *section for* Manasseh; 5by the border
of Manasseh, from the east side to the
west, one *section for* Ephraim; 6by the border of Ephraim, from the east side to the
west, one *section for* Reuben; 7by the border of Reuben, from the east side to the
west, one *section for* Judah; 8by the border
of Judah, from the east side to the west,
shall be the district which you shall set
apart, twenty-five thousand *cubits* in width,
and *in* length the same as one of the *other*
portions, from the east side to the west,
with the sanctuary in the center.
9"The district that you shall set apart
for the LORD *shall be* twenty-five thousand
cubits in length and ten thousand in width.
10To these—to the priests—the holy district shall belong: on the north twenty-
five thousand *cubits in length*, on the west
ten thousand in width, on the east ten
thousand in width, and on the south
twenty-five thousand in length. The
sanctuary of the LORD shall be in the center. 11*It shall be* for the priests of the sons
of Zadok, who are sanctified, who have
kept My charge, who did not go astray
when the children of Israel went astray, as
the Levites went astray. 12And *this* district
of land that is set apart shall be to them a
thing most holy by the border of the
Levites.
13"Opposite the border of the priests,

47:19 [a]Hebrew *Negev*

the Levites *shall have an area* twenty-five
thousand *cubits* in length and ten thousand in width; its entire length *shall be*
twenty-five thousand and its width ten
thousand. 14And they shall not sell or exchange any of it; they may not alienate
this best *part* of the land, for *it is* holy to
the LORD.

15"The five thousand *cubits* in width
that remain, along the edge of the twenty-
five thousand, shall be for general use by
the city, for dwellings and common-land;
and the city shall be in the center. 16These
shall be its measurements: the north side
four thousand five hundred *cubits,* the
south side four thousand five hundred,
the east side four thousand five hundred,
and the west side four thousand five hundred. 17The common-land of the city shall
be: to the north two hundred and fifty
cubits, to the south two hundred and fifty,
to the east two hundred and fifty, and to
the west two hundred and fifty. 18The rest
of the length, alongside the district of the
holy *section, shall be* ten thousand *cubits*
to the east and ten thousand to the west.
It shall be adjacent to the district of the
holy *section,* and its produce shall be food
for the workers of the city. 19The workers
of the city, from all the tribes of Israel,
shall cultivate it. 20The entire district *shall*
be twenty-five thousand *cubits* by twenty-
five thousand *cubits,* foursquare. You
shall set apart the holy district with the
property of the city.

21"The rest *shall belong* to the prince,
on one side and on the other of the holy
district and of the city's property, next to
the twenty-five thousand *cubits* of the
holy district as far as the eastern border,
and westward next to the twenty-five
thousand as far as the western border, adjacent to the *tribal* portions; *it shall belong*
to the prince. It shall be the holy district,
and the sanctuary of the temple *shall be* in
the center. 22Moreover, apart from the
possession of the Levites and the possession of the city *which are* in the midst of
what *belongs* to the prince, *the area* between the border of Judah and the border
of Benjamin shall belong to the prince.

23"As for the rest of the tribes, from the
east side to the west, Benjamin *shall have*
one *section;* 24by the border of Benjamin,
from the east side to the west, Simeon
shall have one *section;* 25by the border of
Simeon, from the east side to the west,
Issachar *shall have* one *section;* 26by the
border of Issachar, from the east side to
the west, Zebulun *shall have* one *section;*
27by the border of Zebulun, from the east
side to the west, Gad *shall have* one *sec-*
tion; 28by the border of Gad, on the south
side, toward the South,[a] the border shall
be from Tamar *to* the waters of Meribah
by Kadesh, along the brook to the Great
Sea. 29This *is* the land which you shall divide by lot as an inheritance among the
tribes of Israel, and these *are* their portions," says the Lord GOD.

The Gates of the City and Its Name

30"These *are* the exits of the city. On
the north side, measuring four thousand
five hundred *cubits* 31(the gates of the city
shall be named after the tribes of Israel),
the three gates northward: one gate for
Reuben, one gate for Judah, and one gate
for Levi; 32on the east side, four thousand
five hundred *cubits,* three gates: one gate
for Joseph, one gate for Benjamin, and
one gate for Dan; 33on the south side,
measuring four thousand five hundred
cubits, three gates: one gate for Simeon,
one gate for Issachar, and one gate for Zebulun; 34on the west side, four thousand
five hundred *cubits* with their three gates:
one gate for Gad, one gate for Asher, and
one gate for Naphtali. 35All the way around
shall be eighteen thousand *cubits;* and the
name of the city from *that* day *shall be:*
THE LORD *IS* THERE."[a]

48:28 [a]Hebrew *Negev* **48:35** [a]Hebrew *YHWH Shammah*

We Are Slaves for Jesus

By The Voice of the Martyrs

On a recent trip to Laos, VOM workers enjoyed fellowship with Christians from several people groups, including the Khmu. Although the Khmu are the original inhabitants of Laos, many Laotians look down on them as culturally backward. Sometimes people call them *kha*, meaning "slave," an insulting reference to a time when the Khmu were taken captive by invaders.

The Khmu, of course, resent being called slaves. But the Greek word for "slave," *doulos*, is also the second most common word used to describe Christians in Greek manuscripts of the New Testament. The word *doulos* occurs more than 100 times in Greek manuscripts, second only to *mathetes*, meaning "disciple."

It is difficult to find the word "slave" in most translations of the Bible. From the first translation of the New Testament—Greek to Latin—the shocking term for "slave" was toned down with a more socially acceptable word meaning "servant." A look at the word "servant" in *Strong's Exhaustive Concordance* reveals the additional, enriching meaning behind the word.

Greek manuscripts of the New Testament use several different Greek words for "servant," including *diakonos*, *sakir*, and *misthios*. These words convey the meaning of a servant who performs a service and who may sometimes be paid. However, a *doulos* is more than a servant. A *doulos* is bought for a price and is bound to serve his master.

As bought and paid for *douloi* (plural of *doulos*), we understand that "freedom in Christ" does not mean we are free to serve Jesus only when we feel like it. Remaining in Christ, being bound to Him as a slave to a master, provides true freedom from the desires and priorities of the world. In 1 Peter 2:16, the apostle writes that although we are "as free," we should live as *douloi*, or fully committed slaves of God.

References to freedom in the New Testament do not imply freedom from Jesus, but rather freedom from sin or religious customs of men. In one sense, even Jesus was not "free" to do what He wanted. In John 8:29, Jesus says that He came to do the will of His Father. We, His *douloi*, are commanded to follow in His steps. Although Jesus calls us His friends (John 15:15), He lovingly and jealously regards us as His committed slaves. Jesus uses the *doulos* metaphor notably and powerfully in Matt. 20:27 and 25:21, Mark 9:35, and John 15:20. The term *doulos* continues to appear throughout the New Testament, including several times in the Book of Revelation as a title of honor for the saints.

As slaves of Jesus, one reason we may be persecuted is that the world sees our commitment to following Him and is angry that it can never own us; we have been bought by the blood of Christ. Our true freedom is being bound in a relationship with our Master, and the world can never take this freedom away from us.

The VOM workers asked the Khmu Christians how they felt about losing homes and being beaten because they are Christians. Surprisingly, many of the Khmu replied that these sufferings encourage them. They said that their own suffering proves that Jesus is God because He told them in the Bible that Christians would be persecuted.

We wonder if these *kha*, loyal slaves of Jesus Christ, know that Jesus Himself took the nature of a slave. Jesus became a *kha* for us all, submitting to the Father with unquestioned obedience in order to secure our salvation (Phil. 2:5–11). Likewise, He requires us to be of an obedient mind and complete the will of His Father, no matter what we may face.

To many in the world we will always look like losers, but Jesus' "strength is made perfect in weakness" (2 Cor. 12:9). Like Jesus, we are more than conquerors. Through the power of the Holy Spirit, we are victorious over the flesh, the world, and ultimately the grave.

Whenever we Christians are insulted in the courts, in the press or in the classroom, we—like the *kha*—are free to rejoice that these attacks from the world prove that Jesus is God. We are free to ignore seemingly terrible consequences in order to share His saving grace and love with more passion. As *douloi* of Jesus who were paid for with the price of His blood, He owns us. We are His. He is our Lord.

(Adapted from *The Voice of the Martyrs* newsletter, Sept. 2010, www.persecution.com.)

Daniel

Daniel and His Friends Obey God

1 In the third year of the reign of Jehoiakim king of Judah, Nebuchadnezzar
king of Babylon came to Jerusalem and
besieged it. 2And the Lord gave Jehoiakim king of Judah into his hand, with
some of the articles of the house of God,
which he carried into the land of Shinar
to the house of his god; and he brought
the articles into the treasure house of his
god.
3Then the king instructed Ashpenaz,
the master of his eunuchs, to bring some
of the children of Israel and some of the
king's descendants and some of the nobles, 4young men in whom *there was* no
blemish, but good-looking, gifted in all
wisdom, possessing knowledge and quick
to understand, who *had* ability to serve in
the king's palace, and whom they might
teach the language and literature of the
Chaldeans. 5And the king appointed for
them a daily provision of the king's delicacies and of the wine which he drank,
and three years of training for them, so
that at the end of *that time* they might
serve before the king. 6Now from among
those of the sons of Judah were Daniel,
Hananiah, Mishael, and Azariah. 7To them
the chief of the eunuchs gave names: he
gave Daniel *the name* Belteshazzar; to
Hananiah, Shadrach; to Mishael, Meshach;
and to Azariah, Abed-Nego.
8But Daniel purposed in his heart that
he would not defile himself with the portion of the king's delicacies, nor with the
wine which he drank; therefore he requested of the chief of the eunuchs that
he might not defile himself. 9Now God
had brought Daniel into the favor and
goodwill of the chief of the eunuchs.
10And the chief of the eunuchs said to
Daniel, "I fear my lord the king, who has
appointed your food and drink. For why
should he see your faces looking worse
than the young men who *are* your age?
Then you would endanger my head before the king."
11So Daniel said to the steward[a] whom
the chief of the eunuchs had set over
Daniel, Hananiah, Mishael, and Azariah,
12"Please test your servants for ten days,
and let them give us vegetables to eat and
water to drink. 13Then let our appearance
be examined before you, and the appearance of the young men who eat the portion of the king's delicacies; and as you
see fit, *so* deal with your servants." 14So
he consented with them in this matter,
and tested them ten days.
15And at the end of ten days their features appeared better and fatter in flesh

1:11 [a]Hebrew *Melzar,* also in verse 16

1:4 In Christ, God has made us without blemish in His sight. In His Word He has given us everything we need—wisdom, knowledge, and understanding. Soak your soul in the Word of God, and pray that God gives you the boldness to speak what you know.

than all the young men who ate the portion of the king's delicacies. [16]Thus the steward took away their portion of delicacies and the wine that they were to drink, and gave them vegetables.

[17]As for these four young men, God gave them knowledge and skill in all literature and wisdom; and Daniel had understanding in all visions and dreams.

[18]Now at the end of the days, when the king had said that they should be brought in, the chief of the eunuchs brought them in before Nebuchadnezzar. [19]Then the king interviewed[a] them, and among them all none was found like Daniel, Hananiah, Mishael, and Azariah; therefore they served before the king. [20]And in all matters of wisdom *and* understanding about which the king examined them, he found them ten times better than all the magicians *and* astrologers who *were* in all his realm. [21]Thus Daniel continued until the first year of King Cyrus.

Nebuchadnezzar's Dream

2 Now in the second year of Nebuchadnezzar's reign, Nebuchadnezzar had dreams; and his spirit was *so* troubled that his sleep left him. [2]Then the king gave the command to call the magicians, the astrologers, the sorcerers, and the Chaldeans to tell the king his dreams. So they came and stood before the king. [3]And the king said to them, "I have had a dream, and my spirit is anxious to know the dream."

[4]Then the Chaldeans spoke to the king in Aramaic,[a] "O king, live forever! Tell your servants the dream, and we will give the interpretation."

[5]The king answered and said to the Chaldeans, "My decision is firm: if you do not make known the dream to me, and its interpretation, you shall be cut in pieces, and your houses shall be made an ash heap. [6]However, if you tell the dream and its interpretation, you shall receive from me gifts, rewards, and great honor. Therefore tell me the dream and its interpretation."

[7]They answered again and said, "Let the king tell his servants the dream, and we will give its interpretation."

[8]The king answered and said, "I know for certain that you would gain time, because you see that my decision is firm: [9]if you do not make known the dream to me, *there is only* one decree for you! For you have agreed to speak lying and corrupt words before me till the time has changed. Therefore tell me the dream, and I shall know that you can give me its interpretation."

[10]The Chaldeans answered the king, and said, "There is not a man on earth who can tell the king's matter; therefore no king, lord, or ruler has *ever* asked such things of any magician, astrologer, or Chaldean. [11]*It is* a difficult thing that the king requests, and there is no other who can tell it to the king except the gods, whose dwelling is not with flesh."

[12]For this reason the king was angry and very furious, and gave the command to destroy all the wise *men* of Babylon. [13]So the decree went out, and they began killing the wise *men;* and they sought Daniel and his companions, to kill *them.*

God Reveals Nebuchadnezzar's Dream

[14]Then with counsel and wisdom Daniel answered Arioch, the captain of

1:19 [a]Literally *talked with them* 2:4 [a]The original language of Daniel 2:4b through 7:28 is Aramaic.

2:11–14 The wisdom of man is foolishness with God. The wisest of the wise of this world are but babbling baboons when it comes to understanding the simplest of the things of God. The natural mind cannot receive them (see 1 Cor. 2:14). The simplest Christian, however, has the mind of Christ (1 Cor. 2:16) and has access to the wisdom of God. The godless wisdom of this world can give no explanation for why we exist, what causes death, and how to avoid it. These mysteries are revealed by the Spirit of God to all who trust in the Savior.

the king's guard, who had gone out to kill
the wise *men* of Babylon; 15he answered
and said to Arioch the king's captain, "Why
is the decree from the king so urgent?"
Then Arioch made the decision known to
Daniel.

16So Daniel went in and asked the king
to give him time, that he might tell the
king the interpretation. 17Then Daniel went
to his house, and made the decision known
to Hananiah, Mishael, and Azariah, his
companions, 18that they might seek mercies from the God of heaven concerning
this secret, so that Daniel and his companions might not perish with the rest of
the wise *men* of Babylon. 19Then the secret
was revealed to Daniel in a night vision.
So Daniel blessed the God of heaven.

20Daniel answered and said:

"Blessed be the name of God forever
and ever,
For wisdom and might are His.
21And He changes the times and the
seasons;
He removes kings and raises up
kings;
He gives wisdom to the wise
And knowledge to those who have
understanding.
22He reveals deep and secret things;
He knows what *is* in the darkness,
And light dwells with Him.

23"I thank You and praise You,
O God of my fathers;
You have given me wisdom and
might,
And have now made known to me
what we asked of You,
For You have made known to us the
king's demand."

Daniel Explains the Dream

24Therefore Daniel went to Arioch,
whom the king had appointed to destroy
the wise *men* of Babylon. He went and
said thus to him: "Do not destroy the wise
men of Babylon; take me before the king,
and I will tell the king the interpretation."

25Then Arioch quickly brought Daniel
before the king, and said thus to him, "I
have found a man of the captives[a] of Judah, who will make known to the king
the interpretation."

26The king answered and said to Daniel,
whose name *was* Belteshazzar, "Are you
able to make known to me the dream
which I have seen, and its interpretation?"

27Daniel answered in the presence of
the king, and said, "The secret which the
king has demanded, the wise *men*, the astrologers, the magicians, and the soothsayers cannot declare to the king. 28But
there is a God in heaven who reveals secrets, and He has made known to King
Nebuchadnezzar what will be in the latter days. Your dream, and the visions of
your head upon your bed, were these:
29As for you, O king, thoughts came *to*
your *mind while* on your bed, *about* what
would come to pass after this; and He
who reveals secrets has made known to
you what will be. 30But as for me, this secret has not been revealed to me because
I have more wisdom than anyone living,
but for *our* sakes who make known the
interpretation to the king, and that you
may know the thoughts of your heart.

31"You, O king, were watching; and
behold, a great image! This great image,
whose splendor *was* excellent, stood before
you; and its form *was* awesome. 32This

2:25 [a]Literally *of the sons of the captivity*

2:23 The Christian has a unique knowledge that is foreign to this world. The next time you witness to a professing atheist ask, "What is the purpose for humanity's existence?" He will more than likely say that we are here to strive for happiness. Say, "That's what you *do* while you are here, but what is the actual *purpose* for existence?" You know that you exist to love God and enjoy Him forever, but the world sees no logical reason to exist. That is a good and humbling realization for an unsaved person to come to: that without God, he is utterly lost with no rhyme or reason for his existence.

image's head *was* of fine gold, its chest and arms of silver, its belly and thighs[a] of bronze, 33its legs of iron, its feet partly of iron and partly of clay.[a] 34You watched while a stone was cut out without hands, which struck the image on its feet of iron and clay, and broke them in pieces. 35Then the iron, the clay, the bronze, the silver, and the gold were crushed together, and became like chaff from the summer threshing floors; the wind carried them away so that no trace of them was found. And the stone that struck the image became a great mountain and filled the whole earth.

36"This is the dream. Now we will tell the interpretation of it before the king. 37You, O king, *are* a king of kings. For the God of heaven has given you a kingdom, power, strength, and glory; 38and wherever the children of men dwell, or the beasts of the field and the birds of the heaven, He has given *them* into your hand, and has made you ruler over them all—you *are* this head of gold. 39But after you shall arise another kingdom inferior to yours; then another, a third kingdom of bronze, which shall rule over all the earth. 40And the fourth kingdom shall be as strong as iron, inasmuch as iron breaks in pieces and shatters everything; and like iron that crushes, *that kingdom* will break in pieces and crush all the others. 41Whereas you saw the feet and toes, partly of potter's clay and partly of iron, the kingdom shall be divided; yet the strength of the iron shall be in it, just as you saw the iron mixed with ceramic clay. 42And *as* the toes of the feet *were* partly of iron and partly of clay, *so* the kingdom shall be partly strong and partly fragile. 43As you saw iron mixed with ceramic clay, they will mingle with the seed of men; but they will not adhere to one another, just as iron does not mix with clay. 44And in the days of these kings the God of heaven will set up a kingdom which shall never be destroyed; and the kingdom shall not be left to other people; it shall break in pieces and consume all these kingdoms, and it shall stand forever. 45Inasmuch as you saw that the stone was cut out of the mountain without hands, and that it broke in pieces the iron, the bronze, the clay, the silver, and the gold—the great God has made known to the king what will come to pass after this. The dream is certain, and its interpretation is sure."

Daniel and His Friends Promoted

46Then King Nebuchadnezzar fell on his face, prostrate before Daniel, and commanded that they should present an offering and incense to him. 47The king answered Daniel, and said, "Truly your God *is* the God of gods, the Lord of kings, and a revealer of secrets, since you could reveal this secret." 48Then the king promoted Daniel and gave him many great gifts; and he made him ruler over the whole province of Babylon, and chief administrator over all the wise *men* of Babylon. 49Also Daniel petitioned the king, and he set Shadrach, Meshach, and Abed-Nego over the affairs of the province of Babylon; but Daniel *sat* in the gate[a] of the king.

The Image of Gold

3 Nebuchadnezzar the king made an image of gold, whose height *was* sixty cubits *and* its width six cubits. He set it up in the plain of Dura, in the province of Babylon. 2And King Nebuchadnezzar sent *word* to gather together the satraps, the administrators, the gover-

2:32 [a]Or *sides* 2:33 [a]Or *baked clay,* and so in verses 34, 35, and 42 2:49 [a]That is, the king's court

2:39,40 "This chapter describes a succession of five empires or national entities. Historians have confirmed that the succession of empires predicted in this chapter followed one another just as predicted here. Hundreds of years before these nations ever formed, Daniel foresaw the rise and fall of Assyria, Medo-Persia, Greece, and Rome." *Richard Gunther*

nors, the counselors, the treasurers, the judges, the magistrates, and all the officials of the provinces, to come to the dedication of the image which King Nebuchadnezzar had set up. 3So the satraps, the administrators, the governors, the counselors, the treasurers, the judges, the magistrates, and all the officials of the provinces gathered together for the dedication of the image that King Nebuchadnezzar had set up; and they stood before the image that Nebuchadnezzar had set up. 4Then a herald cried aloud: "To you it is commanded, O peoples, nations, and languages, 5*that* at the time you hear the sound of the horn, flute, harp, lyre, *and* psaltery, in symphony with all kinds of music, you shall fall down and worship the gold image that King Nebuchadnezzar has set up; 6and whoever does not fall down and worship shall be cast immediately into the midst of a burning fiery furnace."

7So at that time, when all the people heard the sound of the horn, flute, harp, *and* lyre, in symphony with all kinds of music, all the people, nations, and languages fell down *and* worshiped the gold image which King Nebuchadnezzar had set up.

Daniel's Friends Disobey the King

8Therefore at that time certain Chaldeans came forward and accused the Jews. 9They spoke and said to King Nebuchadnezzar, "O king, live forever! 10You, O king, have made a decree that everyone who hears the sound of the horn, flute, harp, lyre, *and* psaltery, in symphony with all kinds of music, shall fall down and worship the gold image; 11and whoever does not fall down and worship shall be cast into the midst of a burning fiery furnace. 12There are certain Jews whom you have set over the affairs of the province of Babylon: Shadrach, Meshach, and Abed-Nego; these men, O king, have not paid due regard to you. They do not serve your gods or worship the gold image which you have set up."

13Then Nebuchadnezzar, in rage and fury, gave the command to bring Shadrach, Meshach, and Abed-Nego. So they brought these men before the king. 14Nebuchadnezzar spoke, saying to them, "*Is it* true, Shadrach, Meshach, and Abed-Nego, *that* you do not serve my gods or worship the gold image which I have set up? 15Now if you are ready at the time you hear the sound of the horn, flute, harp, lyre, *and* psaltery, in symphony with all kinds of music, and you fall down and worship the image which I have made, *good!* But if you do not worship, you shall be cast immediately into the midst of a burning fiery furnace. And who *is* the god who will deliver you from my hands?"

16Shadrach, Meshach, and Abed-Nego answered and said to the king, "O Nebuchadnezzar, we have no need to answer you in this matter. 17If that *is the case,* our God whom we serve is able to deliver us from the burning fiery furnace, and He will deliver *us* from your hand, O king.

3:1 After Daniel interpreted the dream, the king fell at his feet and acknowledged that Daniel's God was "the God of gods" (see 2:46,47). But it's not enough to intellectually acknowledge the existence of God. We need to be born again (see John 3:3–5), with a new heart and new desires that long to please God. Contemporary preachers often hold mass crusades in countries like India and get thousands of "decisions." Yet, because the Law isn't used to bring to the knowledge of sin, these "converts" remain in their idolatry, and simply add Jesus to their list of worshiped gods.

3:12 These godly Jews refused to transgress the First and Second Commandments by bowing before idols.

3:15 King Nebuchadnezzar exalted himself above God. This is normal human behavior. Sinful men stand in judgment over God and question His decrees. They imagine themselves to be cleverer than God, thinking that they can outwit Him by sinning and then repenting at the last minute. Though they can see, they presume that He is blind to their sin. They slur His character by thinking that He will tolerate their hypocrisy. Like the arrogant king of Babylon, they think that God lacks even the power to deliver from their mighty hands.

18 But if not, let it be known to you, O king,
that we do not serve your gods, nor will
we worship the gold image which you
have set up."

Saved in Fiery Trial

19 Then Nebuchadnezzar was full of
fury, and the expression on his face
changed toward Shadrach, Meshach, and
Abed-Nego. He spoke and commanded
that they heat the furnace seven times
more than it was usually heated. 20 And
he commanded certain mighty men of
valor who *were* in his army to bind
Shadrach, Meshach, and Abed-Nego, *and*
cast *them* into the burning fiery furnace.
21 Then these men were bound in their
coats, their trousers, their turbans, and
their *other* garments, and were cast into
the midst of the burning fiery furnace.
22 Therefore, because the king's command
was urgent, and the furnace exceedingly
hot, the flame of the fire killed those men
who took up Shadrach, Meshach, and
Abed-Nego. 23 And these three men, Shadrach, Meshach, and Abed-Nego, fell down
bound into the midst of the burning fiery
furnace.

24 Then King Nebuchadnezzar was astonished; and he rose in haste *and* spoke,
saying to his counselors, "Did we not cast
three men bound into the midst of the
fire?"

They answered and said to the king,
"True, O king."

25 "Look!" he answered, "I see four men
loose, walking in the midst of the fire;
and they are not hurt, and the form of the
fourth is like the Son of God."[a]

Nebuchadnezzar Praises God

26 Then Nebuchadnezzar went near the
mouth of the burning fiery furnace *and*
spoke, saying, "Shadrach, Meshach, and
Abed-Nego, servants of the Most High
God, come out, and come *here*." Then
Shadrach, Meshach, and Abed-Nego came
from the midst of the fire. 27 And the
satraps, administrators, governors, and
the king's counselors gathered together,
and they saw these men on whose bodies
the fire had no power; the hair of their
head was not singed nor were their garments affected, and the smell of fire was
not on them.

28 Nebuchadnezzar spoke, saying,
"Blessed be the God of Shadrach, Meshach, and Abed-Nego, who sent His Angel[a] and delivered His servants who
trusted in Him, and they have frustrated
the king's word, and yielded their bodies,
that they should not serve nor worship
any god except their own God! 29 Therefore I make a decree that any people, nation, or language which speaks anything
amiss against the God of Shadrach, Meshach, and Abed-Nego shall be cut in
pieces, and their houses shall be made an
ash heap; because there is no other God
who can deliver like this."

30 Then the king promoted Shadrach,
Meshach, and Abed-Nego in the province
of Babylon.

Nebuchadnezzar's Second Dream

4 Nebuchadnezzar the king,

To all peoples, nations, and languages

3:25 [a]Or *a son of the gods* 3:28 [a]Or *angel*

3:17,18 The three faithful men refused to compromise—even at the risk of their lives. As we can see from their words, "But if not..." their conviction did not come from a promise that God would deliver them. They were full of faith. They lived by faith, and they were prepared to die in faith. We, too, are called to be faithful in the face of death. Neither do we have a promise of deliverance from the hands of ungodly men. God allowed Stephen to be martyred, as well as eleven of the original apostles and millions of other martyrs down through the ages. See Acts 7:59 comment.

3:19 The smiling face of the world changes when we refuse to compromise the issue of sin.

3:24 It is a great testimony to the world if they see that we are not bound by ties in fiery trials. Our joy can remain even in the midst of a furnace because our names are written in heaven.

that dwell in all the earth:
Peace be multiplied to you.

2I thought it good to declare the signs
and wonders that the Most High
God has worked for me.

3How great *are* His signs,
And how mighty His wonders!
His kingdom *is* an everlasting
kingdom,
And His dominion *is* from generation
to generation.

4I, Nebuchadnezzar, was at rest in my
house, and flourishing in my palace.
5I saw a dream which made me
afraid, and the thoughts on my bed
and the visions of my head troubled
me. 6Therefore I issued a decree to
bring in all the wise *men* of Babylon
before me, that they might make
known to me the interpretation of
the dream. 7Then the magicians, the
astrologers, the Chaldeans, and the
soothsayers came in, and I told them
the dream; but they did not make
known to me its interpretation. 8But
at last Daniel came before me (his
name *is* Belteshazzar, according to
the name of my god; in him *is* the
Spirit of the Holy God), and I told
the dream before him, *saying:*
9"Belteshazzar, chief of the
magicians, because I know that the
Spirit of the Holy God *is* in you, and
no secret troubles you, explain to me
the visions of my dream that I have
seen, and its interpretation.

10"These *were* the visions of my head
while on my bed:

I was looking, and behold,
A tree in the midst of the earth,
And its height was great.
11The tree grew and became strong;
Its height reached to the heavens,
And it could be seen to the ends of all
the earth.
12Its leaves *were* lovely,
Its fruit abundant,
And in it *was* food for all.
The beasts of the field found shade
under it,
The birds of the heavens dwelt in its
branches,
And all flesh was fed from it.

13"I saw in the visions of my head
while on my bed, and there was a
watcher, a holy one, coming down
from heaven. 14He cried aloud and
said thus:

'Chop down the tree and cut off its
branches,
Strip off its leaves and scatter its fruit.
Let the beasts get out from under it,
And the birds from its branches.
15Nevertheless leave the stump and
roots in the earth,
Bound with a band of iron and
bronze,
In the tender grass of the field.
Let it be wet with the dew of heaven,
And *let* him graze with the beasts
On the grass of the earth.
16Let his heart be changed from *that of*
a man,
Let him be given the heart of a beast,
And let seven times[a] pass over him.

17'This decision *is* by the decree of the
watchers,
And the sentence by the word of the
holy ones,
In order that the living may know
That the Most High rules in the
kingdom of men,
Gives it to whomever He will,
And sets over it the lowest of men.'

18"This dream I, King Nebuchadnezzar,
have seen. Now you, Belteshazzar,
declare its interpretation, since all the
wise *men* of my kingdom are not able
to make known to me the interpreta-

4:16 [a]Possibly *seven years*, and so in verses 23, 25, and 32

tion; but you *are* able, for the Spirit
of the Holy God *is* in you."

Daniel Explains the Second Dream

19Then Daniel, whose name *was* Belteshazzar, was astonished for a time,
and his thoughts troubled him. *So* the
king spoke, and said, "Belteshazzar,
do not let the dream or its interpretation trouble you." Belteshazzar
answered and said, "My lord, *may* the
dream concern those who hate you,
and its interpretation concern your
enemies!

20"The tree that you saw, which grew
and became strong, whose height
reached to the heavens and which
could be seen by all the earth, 21whose
leaves *were* lovely and its fruit abundant, in which *was* food for all, under
which the beasts of the field dwelt,
and in whose branches the birds of
the heaven had their home— 22it *is*
you, O king, who have grown and
become strong; for your greatness has
grown and reaches to the heavens,
and your dominion to the end of the
earth.

23"And inasmuch as the king saw a
watcher, a holy one, coming down
from heaven and saying, 'Chop down
the tree and destroy it, but leave its
stump and roots in the earth, *bound*
with a band of iron and bronze in the
tender grass of the field; let it be wet
with the dew of heaven, and let him
graze with the beasts of the field, till
seven times pass over him'; 24this is
the interpretation, O king, and this is
the decree of the Most High, which
has come upon my lord the king:

25They shall drive you from men,
your dwelling shall be with the
beasts of the field, and they shall
make you eat grass like oxen. They
shall wet you with the dew of
heaven, and seven times shall pass
over you, till you know that the
Most High rules in the kingdom of
men, and gives it to whomever He
chooses.

Nearly all men can stand adversity, but if you want to test a man's character, give him power.

ABRAHAM LINCOLN

26"And inasmuch as they gave the
command to leave the stump *and*
roots of the tree, your kingdom
shall be assured to you, after you
come to know that Heaven rules.
27Therefore, O king, let my advice
be acceptable to you; break off your
sins by *being* righteous, and your
iniquities by showing mercy to *the*
poor. Perhaps there may be a
lengthening of your prosperity."

Nebuchadnezzar's Humiliation

28All *this* came upon King Nebuchadnezzar. 29At the end of the twelve
months he was walking about the
royal palace of Babylon. 30The king
spoke, saying, "Is not this great

4:24 Notice that Daniel was not afraid of the king. Because he feared God, he spoke the truth even though it wasn't a pleasant interpretation.

4:30–33 Amazingly, the king succumbed to pride despite having been forewarned of this very thing—and its dire consequences. We are to warn the lost of the consequences of their sin and plead with them to submit to God, but many will tragically reject our pleas.

To strip a man of his pride, show him the requirements of God's holy Law. It reveals that he has the heart of a beast (v. 16) and brings him to a point of understanding that the Most High rules in the kingdom of men and gives it to whomever He chooses (v. 32). Like the prodigal son of Jesus' parable, when the sinner sees his sinfulness in the bright light of God's Law, he sees that his desire is for pig food and he comes to his senses (vv. 34–37). See Luke 15:16–19 and 2 Chron. 6:37,38 comment.

Babylon, that I have built for a royal
dwelling by my mighty power and
for the honor of my majesty?"

31While the word *was still* in the king's
mouth, a voice fell from heaven:
"King Nebuchadnezzar, to you it is
spoken: the kingdom has departed
from you! 32And they shall drive you
from men, and your dwelling *shall be*
with the beasts of the field. They
shall make you eat grass like oxen;
and seven times shall pass over you,
until you know that the Most High
rules in the kingdom of men, and
gives it to whomever He chooses."

33That very hour the word was fulfilled concerning Nebuchadnezzar;
he was driven from men and ate
grass like oxen; his body was wet
with the dew of heaven till his hair
had grown like eagles' *feathers* and
his nails like birds' *claws*.

Nebuchadnezzar Praises God

34And at the end of the time[a] I,
Nebuchadnezzar, lifted my eyes to
heaven, and my understanding
returned to me; and I blessed the
Most High and praised and honored
Him who lives forever:

For His dominion *is* an everlasting
dominion,
And His kingdom *is* from generation
to generation.
35All the inhabitants of the earth *are*
reputed as nothing;
He does according to His will in the
army of heaven
And *among* the inhabitants of the
earth.
No one can restrain His hand
Or say to Him, "What have You done?"

36At the same time my reason
returned to me, and for the glory of
my kingdom, my honor and splendor returned to me. My counselors
and nobles resorted to me, I was
restored to my kingdom, and
excellent majesty was added to me.
37Now I, Nebuchadnezzar, praise
and extol and honor the King of
heaven, all of whose works *are* truth,
and His ways justice. And those who
walk in pride He is able to put down.

Belshazzar's Feast

5 Belshazzar the king made a great feast for a thousand of his lords, and drank wine in the presence of the thousand.
2While he tasted the wine, Belshazzar gave the command to bring the gold and silver vessels which his father Nebuchadnezzar had taken from the temple which *had been* in Jerusalem, that the king and his lords, his wives, and his concubines might drink from them.
3Then they brought the gold vessels that had been taken from the temple of the house of God which *had been* in Jerusalem; and the king and his lords, his wives, and his concubines drank from them.
4They drank wine, and praised the gods of gold and silver, bronze and iron, wood and stone.

5In the same hour the fingers of a man's hand appeared and wrote opposite the lampstand on the plaster of the wall of the king's palace; and the king saw the part of the hand that wrote.
6Then the king's countenance changed, and his thoughts troubled him, so that the joints of his hips were loosened and his knees

4:34 [a]Literally *days*

5:5,6 Our aim when preaching the gospel is to make the issue clear to sinners. We must put the writing on the wall—that God has seen their sin and will judge them for it. When God gave His Law, "so terrifying was the sight that Moses said, 'I am exceedingly afraid and trembling' " (Heb. 12:21). It is the thundering of the Law, echoing in the resurrected conscience, that makes the sinner's knees tremble. Felix "was afraid" when Paul reasoned with him about "righteousness, self-control, and the judgment to come" (Acts 24:25).

knocked against each other. 7The king
cried aloud to bring in the astrologers,
the Chaldeans, and the soothsayers. The
king spoke, saying to the wise *men* of
Babylon, "Whoever reads this writing, and
tells me its interpretation, shall be clothed
with purple and *have* a chain of gold
around his neck; and he shall be the third
ruler in the kingdom." 8Now all the king's
wise *men* came, but they could not read
the writing, or make known to the king
its interpretation. 9Then King Belshazzar
was greatly troubled, his countenance was
changed, and his lords were astonished.

10The queen, because of the words of
the king and his lords, came to the banquet hall. The queen spoke, saying, "O
king, live forever! Do not let your thoughts
trouble you, nor let your countenance
change. 11There is a man in your kingdom
in whom *is* the Spirit of the Holy God.
And in the days of your father, light and
understanding and wisdom, like the wisdom of the gods, were found in him; and
King Nebuchadnezzar your father—your
father the king—made him chief of the
magicians, astrologers, Chaldeans, *and*
soothsayers. 12Inasmuch as an excellent
spirit, knowledge, understanding, interpreting dreams, solving riddles, and explaining enigmas[a] were found in this
Daniel, whom the king named Belteshazzar, now let Daniel be called, and he will
give the interpretation."

The Writing on the Wall Explained

13Then Daniel was brought in before
the king. The king spoke, and said to
Daniel, "*Are* you that Daniel who is one
of the captives[a] from Judah, whom my father the king brought from Judah? 14I
have heard of you, that the Spirit of God
is in you, and *that* light and understanding and excellent wisdom are found in
you. 15Now the wise *men,* the astrologers,
have been brought in before me, that they
should read this writing and make known
to me its interpretation, but they could
not give the interpretation of the thing.
16And I have heard of you, that you can
give interpretations and explain enigmas.
Now if you can read the writing and make
known to me its interpretation, you shall
be clothed with purple and *have* a chain
of gold around your neck, and shall be
the third ruler in the kingdom."

17Then Daniel answered, and said before the king, "Let your gifts be for yourself, and give your rewards to another;
yet I will read the writing to the king, and
make known to him the interpretation.
18O king, the Most High God gave Nebuchadnezzar your father a kingdom and
majesty, glory and honor. 19And because
of the majesty that He gave him, all peoples, nations, and languages trembled and
feared before him. Whomever he wished,
he executed; whomever he wished, he
kept alive; whomever he wished, he set
up; and whomever he wished, he put
down. 20But when his heart was lifted up,
and his spirit was hardened in pride, he
was deposed from his kingly throne, and
they took his glory from him. 21Then he
was driven from the sons of men, his
heart was made like the beasts, and his
dwelling *was* with the wild donkeys.
They fed him with grass like oxen, and
his body was wet with the dew of heaven,
till he knew that the Most High God rules
in the kingdom of men, and appoints
over it whomever He chooses.

22"But you his son, Belshazzar, have not
humbled your heart, although you knew
all this. 23And you have lifted yourself up
against the Lord of heaven. They have
brought the vessels of His house before
you, and you and your lords, your wives
and your concubines, have drunk wine
from them. And you have praised the
gods of silver and gold, bronze and iron,
wood and stone, which do not see or
hear or know; and the God who *holds*
your breath in His hand and owns all
your ways, you have not glorified. 24Then
the fingers[a] of the hand were sent from
Him, and this writing was written.

5:12 [a]Literally *untying knots,* and so in verse 16 5:13 [a]Literally *of the sons of the captivity* 5:24 [a]Literally *palm*

The Function of the Law

5:26,27 "We are called to do what Daniel did, to interpret the spiritual nature of God's Law for a sin-loving world. God has numbered our days and weighed us in the balance of His Law. Salvation is only through repentance and trust in the Savior.

"Some people have their own balances. A great many are making balances to be weighed in. But after all we must be weighed in God's balances, the balances of the sanctuary. It is a favorite thing with infidels to set their own standard, to measure themselves by other people. But that will not do in the Day of Judgment. Now we will use God's Law as a balance weight. When men find fault with the lives of professing Christians, it is a tribute to the Law of God." *D. L. Moody*

25"And this is the inscription that was written:

MENE,[a] MENE, TEKEL,[b] UPHARSIN.[c]

26This *is* the interpretation of *each* word. MENE: God has numbered your kingdom, and finished it; 27TEKEL: You have been weighed in the balances, and found wanting; 28PERES: Your kingdom has been divided, and given to the Medes and Persians."[a] 29Then Belshazzar gave the command, and they clothed Daniel with purple and *put* a chain of gold around his neck, and made a proclamation concerning him that he should be the third ruler in the kingdom.

Belshazzar's Fall

30That very night Belshazzar, king of the Chaldeans, was slain. 31And Darius the Mede received the kingdom, *being* about sixty-two years old.

The Plot Against Daniel

6 It pleased Darius to set over the kingdom one hundred and twenty satraps, to be over the whole kingdom; 2and over these, three governors, of whom Daniel *was* one, that the satraps might give account to them, so that the king would suffer no loss. 3Then this Daniel distinguished himself above the governors and satraps, because an excellent spirit *was* in him; and the king gave thought to setting him over the whole realm. 4So the governors and satraps sought to find *some* charge against Daniel concerning the kingdom; but they could find no charge or fault, because he *was* faithful; nor was there any error or fault found in him. 5Then these men said, "We shall not find any charge against this Daniel unless we find *it* against him concerning the law of his God."

6So these governors and satraps thronged before the king, and said thus to him: "King Darius, live forever! 7All the governors of the kingdom, the administrators and satraps, the counselors and advisors, have consulted together to establish a royal statute and to make a firm decree, that whoever petitions any god or man for thirty days, except you, O king, shall be cast into the den of lions. 8Now, O king, establish the decree and sign the writing, so that it cannot be changed, according to the law of the Medes and Persians, which does not alter." 9Therefore King Darius signed the written decree.

5:25 [a]Literally *a mina* (50 shekels) from the verb "to number" [b]Literally *a shekel* from the verb "to weigh" [c]Literally *and half-shekels* from the verb "to divide" 5:28 [a]Aramaic *Paras,* consonant with *Peres*

5:30 "If someone had told the king an hour before that the time had come when he must step into the balances and be weighed, he would have laughed at the thought. But the vital hour had come... That night the king's blood mingled with the wine of the banquet hall. Judgment came upon him unexpectedly, suddenly: and probably ninety-nine out of every hundred judgments come in this way. Death comes upon us unexpectedly; it comes upon us suddenly." *D. L. Moody*

6:4 May this sinful world find us faultless in appearance, in conduct, and in speech (see Phil. 2:15). The lost look on our outward appearance, and if they don't like how we look, they may not listen to us. You may have the liberty to wear large rings through your nose, but if that's not the culture in which you are living, the rings may become a distraction or a stumbling block to your hearers. If there is any offense from our hearers, may it come only from the message we speak.

Daniel in the Lions' Den

[10]Now when Daniel knew that the writing was signed, he went home. And in his upper room, with his windows open toward Jerusalem, he knelt down on his knees three times that day, and prayed and gave thanks before his God, as was his custom since early days.

[11]Then these men assembled and found Daniel praying and making supplication before his God. [12]And they went before the king, and spoke concerning the king's decree: "Have you not signed a decree that every man who petitions any god or man within thirty days, except you, O king, shall be cast into the den of lions?"

The king answered and said, "The thing *is* true, according to the law of the Medes and Persians, which does not alter."

[13]So they answered and said before the king, "That Daniel, who is one of the captives[a] from Judah, does not show due regard for you, O king, or for the decree that you have signed, but makes his petition three times a day."

[14]And the king, when he heard *these* words, was greatly displeased with himself, and set *his* heart on Daniel to deliver him; and he labored till the going down of the sun to deliver him. [15]Then these men approached the king, and said to the king, "Know, O king, that *it is* the law of the Medes and Persians that no decree or statute which the king establishes may be changed."

[16]So the king gave the command, and they brought Daniel and cast *him* into the den of lions. *But* the king spoke, saying to Daniel, "Your God, whom you serve continually, He will deliver you." [17]Then a stone was brought and laid on the mouth of the den, and the king sealed it with his own signet ring and with the signets of his lords, that the purpose concerning Daniel might not be changed.

Daniel Saved from the Lions

[18]Now the king went to his palace and spent the night fasting; and no musicians[a] were brought before him. Also his sleep went from him. [19]Then the king arose very early in the morning and went in haste to the den of lions. [20]And when he came to the den, he cried out with a lamenting voice to Daniel. The king spoke, saying to Daniel, "Daniel, servant of the living God, has your God, whom you serve continually, been able to deliver you from the lions?"

[21]Then Daniel said to the king, "O king, live forever! [22]My God sent His angel and shut the lions' mouths, so that they have not hurt me, because I was found innocent before Him; and also, O king, I have done no wrong before you."

[23]Now the king was exceedingly glad for him, and commanded that they should take Daniel up out of the den. So Daniel was taken up out of the den, and no injury whatever was found on him, because he believed in his God.

Darius Honors God

[24]And the king gave the command, and they brought those men who had accused Daniel, and they cast *them* into the den of lions—them, their children, and their wives; and the lions overpowered them, and broke all their bones in pieces before they ever came to the bottom of the den.

6:13 [a]Literally *of the sons of the captivity* **6:18** [a]Exact meaning unknown

6:10 Like his three friends (see 3:17,18), Daniel would not compromise his faith in God, even in the face of death.

6:22 For us, God also stopped the mouths of the ten hungry lions of the Ten Commandments. He sent the Messiah to take the curse of the Law on our behalf (see Gal. 3:13) and save us from being devoured by their sharp teeth. We will therefore be found innocent before God of the Day of Judgment.

6:24 When a man fights against the ways of God, he often passes his godless sentiments on to his loved ones and leads his family into a fearful fate.

25Then King Darius wrote:

To all peoples, nations, and languages
that dwell in all the earth:

Peace be multiplied to you.

26I make a decree that in every
dominion of my kingdom *men must*
tremble and fear before the God of
Daniel.

For He *is* the living God,
And steadfast forever;
His kingdom *is the one* which shall
not be destroyed,
And His dominion *shall endure* to the
end.
27He delivers and rescues,
And He works signs and wonders
In heaven and on earth,
Who has delivered Daniel from the
power of the lions.

28So this Daniel prospered in the reign
of Darius and in the reign of Cyrus the
Persian.

Vision of the Four Beasts

7 In the first year of Belshazzar king of
Babylon, Daniel had a dream and visions of his head *while* on his bed. Then
he wrote down the dream, telling the
main facts.[a]
2Daniel spoke, saying, "I saw in my vision by night, and behold, the four winds
of heaven were stirring up the Great Sea.
3And four great beasts came up from the
sea, each different from the other. 4The
first *was* like a lion, and had eagle's wings.
I watched till its wings were plucked off;
and it was lifted up from the earth and
made to stand on two feet like a man, and
a man's heart was given to it.
5"And suddenly another beast, a second, like a bear. It was raised up on one
side, and *had* three ribs in its mouth between its teeth. And they said thus to it:
'Arise, devour much flesh!'
6"After this I looked, and there was another, like a leopard, which had on its back
four wings of a bird. The beast also had
four heads, and dominion was given to it.
7"After this I saw in the night visions,
and behold, a fourth beast, dreadful and
terrible, exceedingly strong. It had huge
iron teeth; it was devouring, breaking in
pieces, and trampling the residue with its
feet. It *was* different from all the beasts
that *were* before it, and it had ten horns.
8I was considering the horns, and there
was another horn, a little one, coming up
among them, before whom three of the
first horns were plucked out by the roots.
And there, in this horn, *were* eyes like the
eyes of a man, and a mouth speaking
pompous words.

Vision of the Ancient of Days

9"I watched till thrones were put in
place,
And the Ancient of Days was seated;
His garment *was* white as snow,
And the hair of His head *was* like
pure wool.
His throne *was* a fiery flame,
Its wheels a burning fire;
10A fiery stream issued
And came forth from before Him.
A thousand thousands ministered to
Him;
Ten thousand times ten thousand
stood before Him.
The court[a] was seated,
And the books were opened.

11"I watched then because of the sound
of the pompous words which the horn
was speaking; I watched till the beast was
slain, and its body destroyed and given to
the burning flame. 12As for the rest of the
beasts, they had their dominion taken
away, yet their lives were prolonged for a
season and a time.

13"I was watching in the night visions,
And behold, *One* like the Son of Man,

7:1 [a]Literally *the head* (or *chief*) *of the words* 7:10 [a]Or *judgment*

7:9,10 *A Dream of Judgment Day*

This passage refers to the great and terrible day of the Lord. (See also 2 Thess. 1:6–10; Rev. 1:13–18; 20:11–15.) This should ever be in the mind of the Christian. This is why we preach Christ—not to improve the lifestyle of the unsaved, and not to "change" their lives. We preach Christ so that sinners may be saved from the wrath that is to come.

May the following letter, written by a pastor, stir your heart to do all that you can to lead sinners to genuine conversion:

Dear Brother Ray,

I have been a pastor for 25 years. I always thought I was doing a reasonably good job. Kind of like the folks who consider themselves "good people." I had tried to preach, what I thought, was the whole counsel of God. I prayed, over the years, with many people to accept Jesus and make Him Lord of their lives.

My wife, Judy, and I moved to Ruidoso, New Mexico, about six years ago to plant a church. Shortly after arriving I was convicted that something was horribly wrong with my ministry. I read the Scriptures and prayed earnestly that God would show me what was wrong. The feeling continued to grow and I became depressed and moody. I asked Judy to pray for me and explained my problem. I didn't know if this was the Holy Spirit convicting or Satan attacking. She prayed that God would reveal the cause of my depression and make Himself clear as He revealed any problem with my ministry for Him.

That night I had the most terrifying, realistic, blood-chilling nightmare any man has ever had. I am a Vietnam veteran and I know a little about nightmares. Nothing in my experience has ever come close, nor do I ever want it to, to the horror of that night!

I dreamed that it was Judgment Day and I was standing right next to the throne of God. I noticed that to my left and my right were pastors as far as I could see. I thought this was odd that the Lord would reserve this front-row space for pastors only.

I looked out across a space of only a few yards and there were millions, maybe billions, of people, yet I could see each one of their eyes staring at me. As I studied this group I noticed that I knew many of them from times at the altar or ones who had sat under my teaching. I was pleased to see that they had made it to heaven, but confused because they didn't look happy. They looked very angry and hateful.

Then I heard the voice of the Lord say, "Away, I never knew you." I was suddenly frightened that what I was seeing were those who thought they were saved. Then I saw all of them pointing a finger at each of us pastors and saying together, in one voice that shook my soul, "We sat in your church and thought we were saved. Why didn't you tell us we were lost?"

Tears were pouring down my face and the faces of all of those pastors. I watched as one by one those people were cast into hell. One and then another, and another, and another..., until they were all gone. I died inside as each one screamed in agony and gnashed their teeth, cursing us as they went into the lake of fire.

Then I was looking into the face of Jesus and He said to me, "Is this the part where I'm supposed to say, 'Well done, my good and faithful servant'?" I woke up with a scream and my heart pounding and I was begging Jesus to forgive me.

I died a million deaths that night. Since that night I have done two things on a daily basis. I do everything I can to preach the Law before grace in the hope that conviction of sin will bring a sinner to true salvation. The other thing that I do is pray for every person I have ever preached to, asking God to repair any damage I have done. I also never believe anyone when they tell me they are saved. It is my duty to challenge them and search out the solidness of their salvation.

I am learning to be more effective and confident as I teach others how to share their faith by using the Law. I have seen several people saved, who thought they were saved, as I have used the "Way of the Master" material to teach them evangelism.

I do want to hear those words, "Well done, my good and faithful servant," and thanks to you and your team I have a better chance of hearing them. Thank you! I just wanted to let you know, some pastors are waking up to the truth. The desire of my heart is to please God. I pray that my days of being a man-pleaser are over along with the nightmares. I also pray that God will use me to bring other pastors into the truth of the Gospel message so that they will not have to face the nightmare that I did.

Steve Kreins

Coming with the clouds of heaven!
He came to the Ancient of Days,
And they brought Him near before
Him.
14Then to Him was given dominion
and glory and a kingdom,

That all peoples, nations, and
languages should serve Him.
His dominion *is* an everlasting
dominion,
Which shall not pass away,
And His kingdom *the one*
Which shall not be destroyed.

Daniel's Visions Interpreted

15“I, Daniel, was grieved in my spirit
within *my* body, and the visions of my
head troubled me. 16I came near to one of
those who stood by, and asked him the
truth of all this. So he told me and made
known to me the interpretation of these
things: 17‘Those great beasts, which are
four, *are* four kings[a] *which* arise out of the
earth. 18But the saints of the Most High
shall receive the kingdom, and possess the
kingdom forever, even forever and ever.’
19“Then I wished to know the truth
about the fourth beast, which was different from all the others, exceedingly dreadful, *with* its teeth of iron and its nails of
bronze, *which* devoured, broke in pieces,
and trampled the residue with its feet;
20and the ten horns that *were* on its head,
and the other *horn* which came up, before which three fell, namely, that horn
which had eyes and a mouth which spoke
pompous words, whose appearance *was*
greater than his fellows.
21“I was watching; and the same horn
was making war against the saints, and
prevailing against them, 22until the Ancient
of Days came, and a judgment was made
in favor of the saints of the Most High, and
the time came for the saints to possess the
kingdom.
23“Thus he said:

‘The fourth beast shall be
A fourth kingdom on earth,
Which shall be different from all *other*
kingdoms,
And shall devour the whole earth,
Trample it and break it in pieces.
24The ten horns *are* ten kings
Who shall arise from this kingdom.
And another shall rise after them;
He shall be different from the first *ones*,
And shall subdue three kings.
25He shall speak *pompous* words against
the Most High,
Shall persecute[a] the saints of the Most
High,
And shall intend to change times and
law.
Then *the saints* shall be given into his
hand
For a time and times and half a time.

26‘But the court shall be seated,
And they shall take away his
dominion,
To consume and destroy *it* forever.
27Then the kingdom and dominion,
And the greatness of the kingdoms
under the whole heaven,
Shall be given to the people, the
saints of the Most High.
His kingdom *is* an everlasting
kingdom,
And all dominions shall serve and
obey Him.’

28“This *is* the end of the account.[a] As
for me, Daniel, my thoughts greatly troubled me, and my countenance changed;
but I kept the matter in my heart.”

Vision of a Ram and a Goat

8 In the third year of the reign of King
Belshazzar a vision appeared *to* me—
to me, Daniel—after the one that appeared
to me the first time. 2I saw in the vision,
and it so happened while I was looking,
that I *was* in Shushan, the citadel, which
is in the province of Elam; and I saw in
the vision that I was by the River Ulai.
3Then I lifted my eyes and saw, and there,
standing beside the river, was a ram which
had two horns, and the two horns *were*
high; but one *was* higher than the other,
and the higher *one* came up last. 4I saw
the ram pushing westward, northward,
and southward, so that no animal could

7:17 [a]Representing their kingdoms (compare verse 23)
7:25 [a]Literally *wear out* 7:28 [a]Literally *the word*

withstand him; nor *was there any* that
could deliver from his hand, but he did
according to his will and became great.
5And as I was considering, suddenly a
male goat came from the west, across the
surface of the whole earth, without touching the ground; and the goat *had* a notable
horn between his eyes. 6Then he came to
the ram that had two horns, which I had
seen standing beside the river, and ran at
him with furious power. 7And I saw him
confronting the ram; he was moved with
rage against him, attacked the ram, and
broke his two horns. There was no power
in the ram to withstand him, but he cast
him down to the ground and trampled
him; and there was no one that could deliver the ram from his hand.

> The first of April is the day we remember what we are the other 364 days of the year.
>
> **MARK TWAIN**

8Therefore the male goat grew very
great; but when he became strong, the
large horn was broken, and in place of it
four notable ones came up toward the
four winds of heaven. 9And out of one of
them came a little horn which grew exceedingly great toward the south, toward
the east, and toward the Glorious *Land.*
10And it grew up to the host of heaven;
and it cast down *some* of the host and
some of the stars to the ground, and trampled them. 11He even exalted *himself* as
high as the Prince of the host; and by him
the daily *sacrifices* were taken away, and
the place of His sanctuary was cast down.
12Because of transgression, an army was
given over *to the horn* to oppose the daily
sacrifices; and he cast truth down to the
ground. He did *all this* and prospered.
13Then I heard a holy one speaking;
and *another* holy one said to that certain
one who was speaking, "How long *will*
the vision *be, concerning* the daily *sacrifices* and the transgression of desolation,
the giving of both the sanctuary and the
host to be trampled underfoot?"
14And he said to me, "For two thousand three hundred days;[a] then the sanctuary shall be cleansed."

Gabriel Interprets the Vision

15Then it happened, when I, Daniel,
had seen the vision and was seeking the
meaning, that suddenly there stood before me one having the appearance of a
man. 16And I heard a man's voice between
the banks of the Ulai, who called, and said,
"Gabriel, make this *man* understand the
vision." 17So he came near where I stood,
and when he came I was afraid and fell
on my face; but he said to me, "Understand, son of man, that the vision *refers* to
the time of the end."
18Now, as he was speaking with me, I
was in a deep sleep with my face to the
ground; but he touched me, and stood
me upright. 19And he said, "Look, I am
making known to you what shall happen
in the latter time of the indignation; for at
the appointed time the end *shall be.* 20The
ram which you saw, having the two horns
—*they are* the kings of Media and Persia.
21And the male goat *is* the kingdom[a] of
Greece. The large horn that *is* between its
eyes *is* the first king. 22As for the broken
horn and the four that stood up in its place,
four kingdoms shall arise out of that nation, but not with its power.

23"And in the latter time of their
kingdom,
When the transgressors have reached
their fullness,
A king shall arise,
Having fierce features,
Who understands sinister schemes.
24His power shall be mighty, but not by
his own power;
He shall destroy fearfully,
And shall prosper and thrive;
He shall destroy the mighty, and *also*
the holy people.

8:14 [a]Literally *evening-mornings* **8:21** [a]Literally *king,* representing his kingdom (compare 7:17, 23)

25“Through his cunning
He shall cause deceit to prosper
under his rule;[a]
And he shall exalt *himself* in his heart.
He shall destroy many in *their*
prosperity.
He shall even rise against the Prince
of princes;
But he shall be broken without *human*
means.[b]

26“And the vision of the evenings and
mornings
Which was told is true;
Therefore seal up the vision,
For *it refers* to many days *in the future*.”

27And I, Daniel, fainted and was sick
for days; afterward I arose and went about
the king’s business. I was astonished by
the vision, but no one understood it.

Daniel’s Prayer for the People

9 In the first year of Darius the son of
Ahasuerus, of the lineage of the Medes,
who was made king over the realm of
the Chaldeans— 2in the first year of his
reign I, Daniel, understood by the books
the number of the years *specified* by the
word of the LORD through Jeremiah the
prophet, that He would accomplish seventy years in the desolations of Jerusalem.
3Then I set my face toward the Lord
God to make request by prayer and supplications, with fasting, sackcloth, and
ashes. 4And I prayed to the LORD my God,
and made confession, and said, “O Lord,
great and awesome God, who keeps His
covenant and mercy with those who love
Him, and with those who keep His commandments, 5we have sinned and committed iniquity, we have done wickedly
and rebelled, even by departing from
Your precepts and Your judgments. 6Nei-
ther have we heeded Your servants the
prophets, who spoke in Your name to our
kings and our princes, to our fathers and
all the people of the land. 7O Lord, righteousness *belongs* to You, but to us shame
of face, as *it is* this day—to the men of

THE FUNCTION OF THE LAW

9:11 “That’s the trouble with the sinners . . . they’ve turned against God, broken His Commandments, trampled His Law under their feet, and their sins hang upon them; until they show signs of repentance their sin will remain. But the moment they see their iniquity and come to God, forgiveness will be given them and their iniquity will be taken out of their way.” *D. L. Moody*

Judah, to the inhabitants of Jerusalem and
all Israel, those near and those far off in all
the countries to which You have driven
them, because of the unfaithfulness which
they have committed against You.
8“O Lord, to us *belongs* shame of face,
to our kings, our princes, and our fathers,
because we have sinned against You. 9To
the Lord our God *belong* mercy and forgiveness, though we have rebelled against
Him. 10We have not obeyed the voice of
the LORD our God, to walk in His laws,
which He set before us by His servants
the prophets. 11Yes, all Israel has transgressed Your law, and has departed so as
not to obey Your voice; therefore the curse
and the oath written in the Law of Moses
the servant of God have been poured out
on us, because we have sinned against
Him. 12And He has confirmed His words,
which He spoke against us and against
our judges who judged us, by bringing
upon us a great disaster; for under the
whole heaven such has never been done
as what has been done to Jerusalem.
13“As *it is* written in the Law of Moses,
all this disaster has come upon us; yet we
have not made our prayer before the
LORD our God, that we might turn from
our iniquities and understand Your truth.
14Therefore the LORD has kept the disaster in mind, and brought it upon us; for
the LORD our God *is* righteous in all the
works which He does, though we have
not obeyed His voice. 15And now, O Lord
our God, who brought Your people out of
the land of Egypt with a mighty hand, and

8:25 [a]Literally *hand* [b]Literally *hand*

made Yourself a name, as *it is* this day—
we have sinned, we have done wickedly!
16"O Lord, according to all Your righteousness, I pray, let Your anger and Your
fury be turned away from Your city Jerusalem, Your holy mountain; because for
our sins, and for the iniquities of our fathers, Jerusalem and Your people *are* a reproach to all *those* around us. 17Now
therefore, our God, hear the prayer of
Your servant, and his supplications, and
for the Lord's sake cause Your face to
shine on Your sanctuary, which is desolate. 18O my God, incline Your ear and
hear; open Your eyes and see our desolations, and the city which is called by Your
name; for we do not present our supplications before You because of our righteous deeds, but because of Your great
mercies. 19O Lord, hear! O Lord, forgive!
O Lord, listen and act! Do not delay for
Your own sake, my God, for Your city
and Your people are called by Your name."

The Seventy-Weeks Prophecy

20Now while I *was* speaking, praying,
and confessing my sin and the sin of my
people Israel, and presenting my supplication before the LORD my God for the
holy mountain of my God, 21yes, while I
was speaking in prayer, the man Gabriel,
whom I had seen in the vision at the beginning, being caused to fly swiftly, reached
me about the time of the evening offering. 22And he informed *me,* and talked
with me, and said, "O Daniel, I have now
come forth to give you skill to understand.
23At the beginning of your supplications
the command went out, and I have come
to tell *you,* for you *are* greatly beloved;
therefore consider the matter, and understand the vision:

24"Seventy weeks[a] are determined
For your people and for your holy city,
To finish the transgression,
To make an end of[b] sins,
To make reconciliation for iniquity,
To bring in everlasting righteousness,
To seal up vision and prophecy,
And to anoint the Most Holy.

25"Know therefore and understand,
That from the going forth of the command
To restore and build Jerusalem
Until Messiah the Prince,
There shall be seven weeks and sixty-two weeks;
The street[a] shall be built again, and the wall,[b]
Even in troublesome times.

26"And after the sixty-two weeks
Messiah shall be cut off, but not for Himself;
And the people of the prince who is to come
Shall destroy the city and the sanctuary.
The end of it *shall be* with a flood,
And till the end of the war desolations are determined.
27Then he shall confirm a covenant with many for one week;
But in the middle of the week
He shall bring an end to sacrifice and offering.
And on the wing of abominations shall be one who makes desolate,
Even until the consummation, which is determined,
Is poured out on the desolate."

Vision of the Glorious Man

10 In the third year of Cyrus king of
Persia a message was revealed to

9:24 [a]Literally *sevens,* and so throughout the chapter [b]Following Qere, Septuagint, Syriac, and Vulgate; Kethib and Theodotion read *To seal up.* 9:25 [a]Or *open square* [b]Or *moat*

9:27 While prophetic interpretations are fascinating, don't let them become a distraction from your commission: to preach the gospel to every creature (see Mark 16:15). We have too many who run from conference to conference, filling their minds with theories to a point where they have neither time nor concern for those who could be snatched any moment into eternal damnation.

QUESTIONS & OBJECTIONS

10:12,13 ***"It's harmful for Christians to think of fellow human beings as enemies."***

I can understand why you are concerned about the metaphor of a war. However, there is nothing metaphoric about the spiritual battle in which we find ourselves.

The Salvation "Army," a Christian organization, was originally structured by "General" William Booth to remind their "soldiers" that they are involved in a very real battle. The war in which we are involved is with the demonic realm. The world may use the phrase "he has his demons," but Christians see demons as being more than figurative. The Bible says that we "wrestle" against demonic forces (see Eph. 6:12). This is why the Bible exhorts Christians to "fight the good fight" of faith, and to endure hardship as a "good soldier of Jesus Christ" (see 1 Tim. 6:12; 2 Tim. 2:3).

This is a spiritual battle for your life. You aren't the enemy, but the Bible says that you have been taken captive by him (see 2 Tim. 2:26) and that Satan has blinded your mind (see 2 Cor. 4:4). That is why we can tell you that God offers you everlasting life and you don't even see what is being offered.

So don't be concerned; we don't see you as the enemy. We are not fighting against you; we are fighting *for* you. We love you and are consumed with concern for your eternal salvation. There is nothing more important than where you will spend eternity.

"While women weep, as they do now, I'll fight; while children go hungry, as they do now, I'll fight; while men go to prison, in and out, in and out, as they do now, I'll fight; while there is a drunkard left, while there is a poor lost girl upon the streets, while there remains one dark soul without the light of God, I'll fight—I'll fight to the very end!" *William Booth*

Daniel, whose name was called Belteshazzar. The message *was* true, but the
appointed time *was* long;[a] and he understood the message, and had understanding of the vision. 2In those days I, Daniel,
was mourning three full weeks. 3I ate no
pleasant food, no meat or wine came into
my mouth, nor did I anoint myself at all,
till three whole weeks were fulfilled.

4Now on the twenty-fourth day of the
first month, as I was by the side of the
great river, that *is,* the Tigris,[a] 5I lifted my
eyes and looked, and behold, a certain
man clothed in linen, whose waist *was*
girded with gold of Uphaz! 6His body *was*
like beryl, his face like the appearance of
lightning, his eyes like torches of fire, his
arms and feet like burnished bronze in
color, and the sound of his words like the
voice of a multitude.

7And I, Daniel, alone saw the vision,
for the men who were with me did not
see the vision; but a great terror fell upon
them, so that they fled to hide themselves. 8Therefore I was left alone when I
saw this great vision, and no strength remained in me; for my vigor was turned to
frailty in me, and I retained no strength.
9Yet I heard the sound of his words; and
while I heard the sound of his words I was
in a deep sleep on my face, with my face
to the ground.

Prophecies Concerning Persia and Greece

10Suddenly, a hand touched me, which
made me tremble on my knees and *on* the
palms of my hands. 11And he said to me,
"O Daniel, man greatly beloved, understand the words that I speak to you, and
stand upright, for I have now been sent
to you." While he was speaking this word
to me, I stood trembling.

12Then he said to me, "Do not fear,
Daniel; for from the first day that you set
your heart to understand, and to humble
yourself before your God, your words were
heard; and I have come because of your

10:1 [a]Or *and of great conflict* 10:4 [a]Hebrew *Hiddekel*

10:7–9 This sounds very similar to the experience of Saul of Tarsus on the road to Damascus. See Acts 22:9 comment.

Questions & Objections

"What if someone says he doesn't believe the Bible is God's Word?"

I would say, "Let's not argue about the inspiration of the Bible for a moment," and then take him through the Commandments. Jesus did not say, "Go into all the world and convince people that the Bible is the Word of God." It is the *gospel* that is the power of God to salvation (see Rom. 1:16). Someone can become a Christian and not even know that the Bible exists.

We often hear that Christianity stands or falls on the validity of Scripture. I respectfully disagree. Christianity is not true because the Bible confirms it; it is true with or without the Scriptures. I absolutely believe that the Bible is the Word of God and that all Scripture is given by inspiration of God. There is no argument there. But my salvation is not dependent upon that fact, because I was not converted by the Bible. I was converted by the power of God, and when I picked up a Bible it simply explained what had happened to me.

In our sincere efforts to convince a sinful world, we tend to use intellectual arguments (I am often guilty of this) when the ultimate proof is the power of God transforming the human heart. But I did not come to Christ through an intellectual argument, and my faith does not stand on human wisdom, so why should I try to bring others through that door?

If the whole scientific world came together and "disproved" the Bible, and archaeologists found what were "proved" to be the bones of Jesus, it would not shake my faith in the slightest. Not at all. This is what Paul speaks about in 1 Cor. 2:4,5 when he says that the Christian's faith does not rest "in the wisdom of men but in the power of God." Remember, early Christians were not converted by the Scriptures. Instead, they were saved by believing a spoken message. The New Testament had not yet been compiled, there was no such thing as the printing press, and most could not read anyway.

If you believe that the foundation for our faith is the written Scriptures rather than in the person of Jesus Christ, consider these questions. When did Christianity begin? Was it on the Day of Pentecost when 3,000 were converted by the power of God, or did it have to wait until the New Testament was compiled in 200 A.D.?

So don't feel that it is your mandate to convince anyone of the inspiration of the Word of God. You will never do it while they love their sins. For every reasonable argument you come up with, the skeptic will come back with a hundred and one atrocities and injustices in the Bible.

Instead, give the arrow of the gospel thrust by using the Law of God to bring the knowledge of sin. Make the sinner thirst after righteousness, without which he will perish. Then, once he is born again and comes to know the Lord, the Scriptures will open up to him. Until that time, the things of God will seem foolishness to him, as the Scriptures say (see 1 Cor. 2:14).

words. 13But the prince of the kingdom
of Persia withstood me twenty-one days;
and behold, Michael, one of the chief
princes, came to help me, for I had been
left alone there with the kings of Persia.
14Now I have come to make you understand what will happen to your people in
the latter days, for the vision *refers* to
many days yet *to come*."

15When he had spoken such words to
me, I turned my face toward the ground
and became speechless. 16And suddenly,
one having the likeness of the sons[a] of
men touched my lips; then I opened my
mouth and spoke, saying to him who
stood before me, "My lord, because of the
vision my sorrows have overwhelmed
me, and I have retained no strength. 17For
how can this servant of my lord talk with
you, my lord? As for me, no strength remains in me now, nor is any breath left in
me."

18Then again, *the one* having the likeness of a man touched me and strengthened me. 19And he said, "O man greatly
beloved, fear not! Peace *be* to you; be
strong, yes, be strong!"

So when he spoke to me I was strengthened, and said, "Let my lord speak, for
you have strengthened me."

20Then he said, "Do you know why I

10:16 [a]Theodotion and Vulgate read *the son;* Septuagint reads *a hand.*

have come to you? And now I must return to fight with the prince of Persia; and when I have gone forth, indeed the prince of Greece will come. 21But I will tell you what is noted in the Scripture of Truth. (No one upholds me against these, except Michael your prince.

11 "Also in the first year of Darius the Mede, I, *even* I, stood up to confirm and strengthen him.) 2And now I will tell you the truth: Behold, three more kings will arise in Persia, and the fourth shall be far richer than *them* all; by his strength, through his riches, he shall stir up all against the realm of Greece. 3Then a mighty king shall arise, who shall rule with great dominion, and do according to his will. 4And when he has arisen, his kingdom shall be broken up and divided toward the four winds of heaven, but not among his posterity nor according to his dominion with which he ruled; for his kingdom shall be uprooted, even for others besides these.

Warring Kings of North and South

5"Also the king of the South shall become strong, as well as *one* of his princes; and he shall gain power over him and have dominion. His dominion *shall be* a great dominion. 6And at the end of *some* years they shall join forces, for the daughter of the king of the South shall go to the king of the North to make an agreement; but she shall not retain the power of her authority,[a] and neither he nor his authority[b] shall stand; but she shall be given up, with those who brought her, and with him who begot her, and with him who strengthened her in *those* times. 7But from a branch of her roots *one* shall arise in his place, who shall come with an army, enter the fortress of the king of the North, and deal with them and prevail. 8And he shall also carry their gods captive to Egypt, with their princes[a] *and* their precious articles of silver and gold; and he shall continue *more* years than the king of the North.

9"Also *the king of the North* shall come to the kingdom of the king of the South, but shall return to his own land. 10However his sons shall stir up strife, and assemble a multitude of great forces; and *one* shall certainly come and overwhelm and pass through; then he shall return to his fortress and stir up strife.

11"And the king of the South shall be moved with rage, and go out and fight with him, with the king of the North, who shall muster a great multitude; but the multitude shall be given into the hand of his *enemy.* 12When he has taken away the multitude, his heart will be lifted up; and he will cast down tens of thousands, but he will not prevail. 13For the king of the North will return and muster a multitude greater than the former, and shall certainly come at the end of some years with a great army and much equipment.

14"Now in those times many shall rise up against the king of the South. Also, violent men[a] of your people shall exalt themselves in fulfillment of the vision, but they shall fall. 15So the king of the North shall come and build a siege mound, and take a fortified city; and the forces[a] of the South shall not withstand *him.* Even his choice troops *shall have* no strength to resist. 16But he who comes against him shall do according to his own will, and no one shall stand against him. He shall stand in the Glorious Land with destruction in his power.[a]

17"He shall also set his face to enter with the strength of his whole kingdom, and upright ones[a] with him; thus shall he do. And he shall give him the daughter of women to destroy it; but she shall not stand *with him,* or be for him. 18After this he shall turn his face to the coastlands, and shall take many. But a ruler shall bring the reproach against them to an end; and with the reproach removed, he shall turn

11:6 [a]Literally *arm* [b]Literally *arm* **11:8** [a]Or *molded images* **11:14** [a]Or *robbers,* literally *sons of breakage* **11:15** [a]Literally *arms* **11:16** [a]Literally *hand* **11:17** [a]Or *bring equitable terms*

back on him. [19]Then he shall turn his
face toward the fortress of his own land;
but he shall stumble and fall, and not be
found.
[20]"There shall arise in his place one
who imposes taxes *on* the glorious kingdom; but within a few days he shall be
destroyed, but not in anger or in battle.
[21]And in his place shall arise a vile person, to whom they will not give the
honor of royalty; but he shall come in
peaceably, and seize the kingdom by intrigue. [22]With the force[a] of a flood they
shall be swept away from before him and
be broken, and also the prince of the
covenant. [23]And after the league *is made*
with him he shall act deceitfully, for he
shall come up and become strong with a
small *number of* people. [24]He shall enter
peaceably, even into the richest places of
the province; and he shall do *what* his fathers have not done, nor his forefathers:
he shall disperse among them the plunder, spoil, and riches; and he shall devise
his plans against the strongholds, but
only for a time.
[25]"He shall stir up his power and his
courage against the king of the South
with a great army. And the king of the
South shall be stirred up to battle with a
very great and mighty army; but he shall
not stand, for they shall devise plans
against him. [26]Yes, those who eat of the
portion of his delicacies shall destroy him;
his army shall be swept away, and many
shall fall down slain. [27]Both these kings'
hearts *shall be* bent on evil, and they shall
speak lies at the same table; but it shall
not prosper, for the end *will* still *be* at the
appointed time. [28]While returning to his
land with great riches, his heart shall be
moved against the holy covenant; so he
shall do *damage* and return to his own
land.

The Northern King's Blasphemies

[29]"At the appointed time he shall return and go toward the south; but it shall
not be like the former or the latter. [30]For
ships from Cyprus[a] shall come against
him; therefore he shall be grieved, and
return in rage against the holy covenant,
and do *damage*.
"So he shall return and show regard
for those who forsake the holy covenant.
[31]And forces[a] shall be mustered by him,
and they shall defile the sanctuary fortress; then they shall take away the daily
sacrifices, and place *there* the abomination
of desolation. [32]Those who do wickedly
against the covenant he shall corrupt with
flattery; but the people who know their
God shall be strong, and carry out *great*
exploits. [33]And those of the people who
understand shall instruct many; yet *for*
many days they shall fall by sword and
flame, by captivity and plundering. [34]Now
when they fall, they shall be aided with a
little help; but many shall join with them
by intrigue. [35]And *some* of those of understanding shall fall, to refine them, purify *them,* and make *them* white, *until* the
time of the end; because *it is* still for the
appointed time.
[36]"Then the king shall do according to
his own will: he shall exalt and magnify
himself above every god, shall speak blasphemies against the God of gods, and shall
prosper till the wrath has been accomplished; for what has been determined
shall be done. [37]He shall regard neither
the God[a] of his fathers nor the desire of
women, nor regard any god; for he shall
exalt himself above *them* all. [38]But in their
place he shall honor a god of fortresses;
and a god which his fathers did not know

11:22 [a]Literally *arms* **11:30** [a]Hebrew *Kittim,* western lands, especially Cyprus **11:31** [a]Literally *arms* **11:37** [a]Or *gods*

11:36 Is this the Antichrist, a king in history, or perhaps both? While there are respected Bible teachers who profess to understand these mysteries of Scripture, take a moment to listen to their passion. Is it for the lost? Do they care about the terrible fate of the unsaved? Do they preach Christ crucified? Do they challenge their Christian hearers to reach out to the unsaved? If not, be careful that you don't become like them.

12:1 Which Jesus?

By Mark Spence

If a stranger approaches you and says he knows your buddy "John," but all the facts are wrong concerning him, you could safely conclude that he is referring to a different John. With that in mind, there are many religions that claim they know and believe in Jesus, but that does not mean they are referring to the same Jesus Christ of the Bible. For example:

- Mormons believe Jesus was the spirit brother of Lucifer. That is not the Jesus of the Bible.
- Jehovah Witnesses believe Jesus was Michael the Archangel. That is not in the Bible!
- Muslims believe Jesus was just a prophet. That is definitely not what the Bible teaches.
- Baha'i teaches Jesus was simply a messenger.

Notice how none of these religions teach what the Bible says, that Jesus was God in human flesh.

You see, the real Jesus sparked more controversy than any other religious leader in history. He made radical claims; He spoke, not from, but with authority; and He forgave people of their sins, which was a hook on which God alone could hang His hat. Jesus healed without medicine, fed thousands from a boy's lunch, and calmed the raging sea.

He claimed to be the Way, the Truth, and the Life, and said that no man would come to the Father, but through Him. He claimed to be the Bread of Life, the Light of the world, the good Shepherd, the true Vine, and the Resurrection and the Life, and He was ultimately crucified because He claimed to be God. He was able to conquer death by rising from the grave as He said He would. How is that possible? Because He is the Christ, the Savior of the world.

So, if someone comes to you talking about Jesus, but he doesn't sound like the Jesus of the Bible, that's probably because he isn't.

he shall honor with gold and silver, with
precious stones and pleasant things. 39Thus
he shall act against the strongest fortresses
with a foreign god, which he shall acknowledge, *and* advance *its* glory; and he
shall cause them to rule over many, and
divide the land for gain.

The Northern King's Conquests

40"At the time of the end the king of
the South shall attack him; and the king
of the North shall come against him like
a whirlwind, with chariots, horsemen, and
with many ships; and he shall enter the
countries, overwhelm *them,* and pass
through. 41He shall also enter the Glorious
Land, and many *countries* shall be overthrown; but these shall escape from his
hand: Edom, Moab, and the prominent
people of Ammon. 42He shall stretch out
his hand against the countries, and the
land of Egypt shall not escape. 43He shall
have power over the treasures of gold and
silver, and over all the precious things of
Egypt; also the Libyans and Ethiopians
shall follow at his heels. 44But news from
the east and the north shall trouble him;
therefore he shall go out with great fury
to destroy and annihilate many. 45And he
shall plant the tents of his palace between
the seas and the glorious holy mountain;
yet he shall come to his end, and no one
will help him.

Prophecy of the End Time

12 "At that time Michael shall stand
up,
The great prince who stands *watch* over
the sons of your people;
And there shall be a time of trouble,
Such as never was since there was a
nation,
Even to that time.
And at that time your people shall be
delivered,
Every one who is found written in the
book.
2And many of those who sleep in the
dust of the earth shall awake,
Some to everlasting life,
Some to shame *and* everlasting
contempt.
3Those who are wise shall shine
Like the brightness of the firmament,
And those who turn many to
righteousness

Like the stars forever and ever.

[4]"But you, Daniel, shut up the words,
and seal the book until the time of the end;
many shall run to and fro, and knowledge shall increase."
[5]Then I, Daniel, looked; and there
stood two others, one on this riverbank
and the other on that riverbank. [6]And *one*
said to the man clothed in linen, who *was*
above the waters of the river, "How long
shall the fulfillment of these wonders *be?*"
[7]Then I heard the man clothed in
linen, who *was* above the waters of the
river, when he held up his right hand and
his left hand to heaven, and swore by Him
who lives forever, that *it shall be* for a
time, times, and half *a time;* and when the
power of the holy people has been completely shattered, all these *things* shall be
finished.
[8]Although I heard, I did not understand. Then I said, "My lord, what *shall be*
the end of these *things?*"
[9]And he said, "Go *your way,* Daniel, for
the words *are* closed up and sealed till
the time of the end. [10]Many shall be purified, made white, and refined, but the
wicked shall do wickedly; and none of
the wicked shall understand, but the wise
shall understand.

"To be a Christian without prayer is no more possible than to be alive without breathing."

Martin Luther

[11]"And from the time *that* the daily
sacrifice is taken away, and the abomination of desolation is set up, *there shall be*
one thousand two hundred and ninety
days. [12]Blessed *is* he who waits, and comes
to the one thousand three hundred and
thirty-five days.
[13]"But you, go *your way* till the end;
for you shall rest, and will arise to your
inheritance at the end of the days."

12:2 An atheist on heaven and hell. Penn Jillette, the taller, louder half of the magic/comedy act "Penn and Teller," is a well-known atheist. He is so committed to atheism that he claims, "I cross the word 'God' off every [dollar] bill I touch."

However, late in 2008, Penn said that after one of his shows, a businessman approached him and gave him a Gideon New Testament. Penn noted, "It was really wonderful. I believe he knew that I was an atheist, but he was not defensive, and he looked me right in the eyes... and then gave me this Bible. I've always said that I don't respect people who don't proselytize. I don't respect that at all. If you believe that there's a heaven and hell, and people could be going to hell, or not getting eternal life, or whatever, and you think that, 'Well, it's not really worth telling them this because it would make it socially awkward'—*How much do you have to hate somebody to believe that everlasting life is possible and not tell them that?* I mean if I believed beyond a shadow of a doubt that a truck was coming at you, and you didn't believe it, and that truck was bearing down on you, there is a certain point where I tackle you—and this is more important than that... He cared enough about me to proselytize and give me a Bible."

"Every person in your personal world is on one of two lists: saved or lost. First John 5:12 says, 'He that has the Son of God has life. He that does not have the Son of God, does not have life.' There are two destinations for everybody we know. Think of the people you know and love as you hold their eternity in your hands. That's why you are where you are... Do whatever it takes and whatever it costs to take the people you know to heaven with you!" *Ron Hutchcraft*

12:3 Be one who is wise: turn many to righteousness. There is no higher calling.

Hosea

1 The word of the LORD that came to
Hosea the son of Beeri, in the days of
Uzziah, Jotham, Ahaz, *and* Hezekiah,
kings of Judah, and in the days of Jeroboam the son of Joash, king of Israel.

The Family of Hosea

2 When the LORD began to speak by
Hosea, the LORD said to Hosea:

"Go, take yourself a wife of harlotry
And children of harlotry,
For the land has committed great
harlotry
By departing from the LORD."

3 So he went and took Gomer the daughter of Diblaim, and she conceived and bore
him a son.
4 Then the LORD said to him:

"Call his name Jezreel,
For in a little *while*
I will avenge the bloodshed of Jezreel
on the house of Jehu,
And bring an end to the kingdom of
the house of Israel.
5 It shall come to pass in that day
That I will break the bow of Israel in
the Valley of Jezreel."

6 And she conceived again and bore a
daughter. Then *God* said to him:

"Call her name Lo-Ruhamah,[a]
For I will no longer have mercy on
the house of Israel,
But I will utterly take them away.[b]
7 Yet I will have mercy on the house of
Judah,
Will save them by the LORD their
God,
And will not save them by bow,
Nor by sword or battle,
By horses or horsemen."

8 Now when she had weaned Lo-
Ruhamah, she conceived and bore a son.
9 Then *God* said:

"Call his name Lo-Ammi,[a]
For you *are* not My people,
And I will not be your *God*.

The Restoration of Israel

10 "Yet the number of the children of
Israel
Shall be as the sand of the sea,

1:6 [a]Literally *No-Mercy* [b]Or *That I may forgive them at all*
1:9 [a]Literally *Not-My-People*

1:8–11 "Some think that these promises will not have accomplishment in full, till the general conversion of the Jews in the latter days. Also this promise is applied to the gospel, and the bringing in both the Jews and Gentiles to it, by St. Paul, Ro 9:25,26, and by St. Peter, 1Pe 2:10. To believe in Christ, is to have him for our Head, and willingly to commit ourselves to his guidance and government. And let us pray for the coming of the glorious day, when there shall be one Lord through all the earth." *Matthew Henry*

Which cannot be measured or
numbered.
And it shall come to pass
In the place where it was said to
them,
'You *are* not My people,'[a]
There it shall be said to them,
'*You are* sons of the living God.'
11 Then the children of Judah and the
children of Israel
Shall be gathered together,
And appoint for themselves one head;
And they shall come up out of the
land,
For great *will be* the day of Jezreel!

2 Say to your brethren, 'My people,'[a]
And to your sisters, 'Mercy[b] *is shown.*'

God's Unfaithful People

2 "Bring charges against your mother, bring charges;
For she *is* not My wife, nor *am* I her
Husband!
Let her put away her harlotries from
her sight,
And her adulteries from between her
breasts;
3 Lest I strip her naked
And expose her, as in the day she was
born,
And make her like a wilderness,
And set her like a dry land,
And slay her with thirst.

4 "I will not have mercy on her children,
For they *are* the children of harlotry.
5 For their mother has played the
harlot;
She who conceived them has behaved
shamefully.
For she said, 'I will go after my lovers,
Who give *me* my bread and my water,
My wool and my linen,
My oil and my drink.'

6 "Therefore, behold,
I will hedge up your way with thorns,
And wall her in,
So that she cannot find her paths.
7 She will chase her lovers,
But not overtake them;
Yes, she will seek them, but not find
them.
Then she will say,
'I will go and return to my first
husband,
For then *it was* better for me than
now.'
8 For she did not know
That I gave her grain, new wine, and
oil,
And multiplied her silver and gold—
Which they prepared for Baal.

9 "Therefore I will return and take away
My grain in its time
And My new wine in its season,
And will take back My wool and My
linen,
Given to cover her nakedness.
10 Now I will uncover her lewdness in
the sight of her lovers,
And no one shall deliver her from My
hand.
11 I will also cause all her mirth to cease,
Her feast days,
Her New Moons,
Her Sabbaths—
All her appointed feasts.

12 "And I will destroy her vines and her
fig trees,
Of which she has said,
'These *are* my wages that my lovers

1:10 [a]Hebrew *lo-ammi* (compare verse 9) **2:1** [a]Hebrew *Ammi* (compare 1:9, 10) [b]Hebrew *Ruhamah* (compare 1:6)

2:8,9 It is good to point out, when witnessing, that God lavishes His goodness on the ungodly. He gives them eyes to see His creation, ears to enjoy good music, and taste buds to enjoy the wonderful array of food that He has created. He has given them life itself, yet they live in rebellion to His will and use His holy name as a cuss word to express disgust. This reveals the sin of ingratitude, and therefore a failure to obey the First Commandment.

have given me.'
So I will make them a forest,
And the beasts of the field shall eat
them.
13 I will punish her
For the days of the Baals to which she
burned incense.
She decked herself with her earrings
and jewelry,
And went after her lovers;
But Me she forgot," says the LORD.

God's Mercy on His People

14 "Therefore, behold, I will allure her,
Will bring her into the wilderness,
And speak comfort to her.
15 I will give her her vineyards from
there,
And the Valley of Achor as a door of
hope;
She shall sing there,
As in the days of her youth,
As in the day when she came up from
the land of Egypt.

> I fear the preachers have been more studious to please than to awaken, or there would have been a deeper work.
>
> **JOHN WESLEY**

16 "And it shall be, in that day,"
Says the LORD,
"*That* you will call Me 'My Husband,'[a]
And no longer call Me 'My Master,'[b]
17 For I will take from her mouth the
names of the Baals,
And they shall be remembered by
their name no more.
18 In that day I will make a covenant for
them
With the beasts of the field,
With the birds of the air,
And *with* the creeping things of the
ground.
Bow and sword of battle I will shatter
from the earth,
To make them lie down safely.

19 "I will betroth you to Me forever;
Yes, I will betroth you to Me
In righteousness and justice,
In lovingkindness and mercy;
20 I will betroth you to Me in faithfulness,
And you shall know the LORD.

21 "It shall come to pass in that day
That I will answer," says the LORD;
"I will answer the heavens,
And they shall answer the earth.
22 The earth shall answer
With grain,
With new wine,
And with oil;
They shall answer Jezreel.[a]
23 Then I will sow her for Myself in the
earth,
And I will have mercy on *her who had*
not obtained mercy;[a]
Then I will say to *those who were* not
My people,[b]
'You *are* My people!'
And they shall say, '*You are* my God!' "

Israel Will Return to God

3 Then the LORD said to me, "Go again,
love a woman *who is* loved by a lover[a]
and is committing adultery, just like the
love of the LORD for the children of Israel,
who look to other gods and love *the*
raisin cakes *of the pagans.*"
2 So I bought her for myself for fifteen
shekels of silver, and one and one-half
homers of barley. 3 And I said to her, "You
shall stay with me many days; you shall
not play the harlot, nor shall you have a
man—so, too, *will* I *be* toward you."
4 For the children of Israel shall abide
many days without king or prince, without sacrifice or *sacred* pillar, without
ephod or teraphim. 5 Afterward the children of Israel shall return and seek the
LORD their God and David their king. They
shall fear the LORD and His goodness in
the latter days.

2:16 [a]Hebrew *Ishi* [b]Hebrew *Baali* 2:22 [a]Literally *God Will Sow* 2:23 [a]Hebrew *lo-ruhamah* [b]Hebrew *lo-ammi* 3:1 [a]Literally *friend* or *husband*

SPRINGBOARDS FOR PREACHING AND WITNESSING

The Challenge

2:20 A sincere atheist challenged me to live the life of an unbeliever for just one month. In return, he would live the life of a Christian. The rule is that each person has to be open-minded to the fact that he may be wrong in his beliefs. The Christian is not to read the Bible, and he's not to go to church. The atheist will in turn read the Bible and go to church.

While I appreciate the kind gesture, it really illustrates that we Christians have a communication problem with some people. It's completely our fault. We haven't made the issue clear. So I'm going to try to make it very understandable. I will repeat and deliberately emphasize it, so that it hits the target. In doing this I risk sounding sarcastic. If that's how it comes across, I apologize.

Here we go: A Christian is someone who knows the Lord. Let me repeat that. Christians know the Lord. Actually know Him. Experientially. They know a Person, not a lifestyle. I'm talking about the God of the universe. They know Him.

I will now personalize this, but I am speaking on behalf of everyone who knows the Lord. I don't "*believe*" that He exists. I *know* Him. Personally. I have a living relationship with the Creator. I talk to Him through prayer, and He guides me through His Word and by His Holy Spirit, who lives in me. I have known the Lord since April 25, 1972, at 1:30 in the morning.

Perhaps I'm not making myself clear, so I will try an analogy. It's like actually knowing someone. Personally. It's like having a friendship with Him—a 24-hour-a-day, 365-days-a-year, intimate relationship. Therefore, it is self-evident that I can't live for a month being open to not knowing Him. All the so-called "mistakes" in the Bible can't change that fact. All the hypocrisy committed by religious people in the past can't change it. All the atheists on God's earth saying that He doesn't exist doesn't change it in the slightest. Darwin's theory can't change it. The storms of this life can't change it. If I get cancer and die a horrible death, it doesn't change the fact that I know the Lord. I not only know Him, but I love Him. I love Him with all of my heart, soul, mind, and strength. He is my life. He's my joy, my Creator, my Savior, my Lord, and my God.

My earnest hope and prayer is that you would soften your sinful hearts, and repent and trust Jesus Christ, so that you too can testify to the unchanging truth that "This is eternal life, that they may know You, the only true God, and Jesus Christ whom You have sent" (John 17:3). See 1 Sam. 2:12 comment.

God's Charge Against Israel

4 Hear the word of the LORD,
You children of Israel,
For the LORD *brings* a charge against
the inhabitants of the land:

"There is no truth or mercy
Or knowledge of God in the land.
2 *By* swearing and lying,
Killing and stealing and committing
adultery,
They break all restraint,
With bloodshed upon bloodshed.
3 Therefore the land will mourn;
And everyone who dwells there will
waste away
With the beasts of the field
And the birds of the air;
Even the fish of the sea will be taken
away.

4 "Now let no man contend, or rebuke
another;
For your people *are* like those who
contend with the priest.
5 Therefore you shall stumble in the
day;
The prophet also shall stumble with
you in the night;
And I will destroy your mother.
6 My people are destroyed for lack of
knowledge.
Because you have rejected knowledge,
I also will reject you from being priest
for Me;
Because you have forgotten the law of
your God,
I also will forget your children.

7 "The more they increased,
The more they sinned against Me;
I will change[a] their glory[b] into shame.

4:7 [a]Following Masoretic Text, Septuagint, and Vulgate; scribal tradition, Syriac, and Targum read *They will change*. [b]Following Masoretic Text, Septuagint, Syriac, Targum, and Vulgate; scribal tradition reads *My glory*.

The Function of the Law

4:1–3 When truth is not preached, mercy isn't understood, and the world therefore lacks the knowledge of God's character. The result is an idolatrous perception of God, which leads to lawlessness (transgression of the moral Law). Notice that Israel's sins were violations of the Ten Commandments (v. 2), such as lying, killing, stealing, and committing adultery. Their lawlessness resulted in judgment upon the land—droughts, etc.

"The Law, the Ten Commandments, is a reflection of the character and nature of God. Through the Law, we understand God, and what He expects of us. Through the Law, we see ourselves in truth. So to neglect the critical importance of the Law is to leave ourselves in ignorance of the nature of God and of ourselves." *Matthew Johnson*

8They eat up the sin of My people;
They set their heart on their iniquity.
9And it shall be: like people, like
priest.
So I will punish them for their ways,
And reward them for their deeds.
10For they shall eat, but not have
enough;
They shall commit harlotry, but not
increase;
Because they have ceased obeying the
LORD.

The Idolatry of Israel

11"Harlotry, wine, and new wine enslave
the heart.
12My people ask counsel from their
wooden *idols,*
And their staff informs them.
For the spirit of harlotry has caused
them to stray,
And they have played the harlot
against their God.
13They offer sacrifices on the
mountaintops,
And burn incense on the hills,
Under oaks, poplars, and terebinths,
Because their shade is good.
Therefore your daughters commit
harlotry,
And your brides commit adultery.

14"I will not punish your daughters
when they commit harlotry,
Nor your brides when they commit
adultery;
For *the men* themselves go apart with
harlots,
And offer sacrifices with a ritual
harlot.[a]
Therefore people *who* do not
understand will be trampled.

15"Though you, Israel, play the harlot,
Let not Judah offend.
Do not come up to Gilgal,
Nor go up to Beth Aven,
Nor swear an oath, *saying,* 'As the
LORD lives'—

16"For Israel is stubborn
Like a stubborn calf;
Now the LORD will let them forage
Like a lamb in open country.

17"Ephraim is joined to idols,
Let him alone.
18Their drink is rebellion,
They commit harlotry continually.
Her rulers dearly[a] love dishonor.
19The wind has wrapped her up in its
wings,
And they shall be ashamed because of
their sacrifices.

4:14 [a]Compare Deuteronomy 23:18 **4:18** [a]Hebrew is difficult; a Jewish tradition reads *Her rulers shamefully love, 'Give!'*

4:6 This is one of the most commonly quoted verses in the Old Testament, but rarely is it quoted in full. This is not referring to general knowledge; people are not destroyed due to ignorance of book learning. Rather, people were destroyed through a lack of knowledge *of God's Law* (v. 6). If a nation forsakes the Law of God, it has no knowledge of sin (see Rom. 7:7).

Those who have no knowledge of sin cannot repent (how can they, if they don't know what sin is?); and if they don't repent, the Bible warns that they will perish (see Luke 13:3).

Impending Judgment on Israel and Judah

5 "Hear this, O priests!
Take heed, O house of Israel!
Give ear, O house of the king!
For yours *is* the judgment,
Because you have been a snare to Mizpah
And a net spread on Tabor.
2 The revolters are deeply involved in slaughter,
Though I rebuke them all.
3 I know Ephraim,
And Israel is not hidden from Me;
For now, O Ephraim, you commit harlotry;
Israel is defiled.

4 "They do not direct their deeds
Toward turning to their God,
For the spirit of harlotry is in their midst,
And they do not know the LORD.
5 The pride of Israel testifies to his face;
Therefore Israel and Ephraim stumble in their iniquity;
Judah also stumbles with them.

6 "With their flocks and herds
They shall go to seek the LORD,
But they will not find *Him;*
He has withdrawn Himself from them.
7 They have dealt treacherously with the LORD,
For they have begotten pagan children.
Now a New Moon shall devour them and their heritage.

8 "Blow the ram's horn in Gibeah,
The trumpet in Ramah!
Cry aloud *at* Beth Aven,
'*Look* behind you, O Benjamin!'
9 Ephraim shall be desolate in the day of rebuke;
Among the tribes of Israel I make known what is sure.

10 "The princes of Judah are like those who remove a landmark;
I will pour out My wrath on them like water.
11 Ephraim is oppressed *and* broken in judgment,
Because he willingly walked by *human* precept.
12 Therefore I *will be* to Ephraim like a moth,
And to the house of Judah like rottenness.

The men who have guided the destiny of the United States have found the strength for their tasks by going to their knees.

LYNDON B. JOHNSON

13 "When Ephraim saw his sickness,
And Judah *saw* his wound,
Then Ephraim went to Assyria
And sent to King Jareb;
Yet he cannot cure you,
Nor heal you of your wound.
14 For I *will be* like a lion to Ephraim,
And like a young lion to the house of Judah.
I, *even* I, will tear *them* and go away;
I will take *them* away, and no one shall rescue.
15 I will return again to My place
Till they acknowledge their offense.
Then they will seek My face;

5:15 We must help the lost see their sin so that they can acknowledge their offense against a holy God. Only then will they seek the Savior.

"Everything God has done proves that He is in earnest about the salvation of men's souls. He has proved it by giving His only Son to die for us. The Son of God was in earnest when He died. What is Calvary but a proof of that? And the Lord wants us to be in earnest when it comes to this great question of the soul's salvation. I never saw men seeking Him with all their hearts but they soon found Him." *D. L. Moody*

In their affliction they will earnestly
seek Me."

A Call to Repentance

6 Come, and let us return to the LORD;
For He has torn, but He will heal us;
He has stricken, but He will bind us up.
2After two days He will revive us;
On the third day He will raise us up,
That we may live in His sight.
3Let us know,
Let us pursue the knowledge of the LORD.
His going forth is established as the morning;
He will come to us like the rain,
Like the latter *and* former rain to the earth.

Impenitence of Israel and Judah

4"O Ephraim, what shall I do to you?
O Judah, what shall I do to you?
For your faithfulness is like a morning cloud,
And like the early dew it goes away.
5Therefore I have hewn *them* by the prophets,
I have slain them by the words of My mouth;
And your judgments *are like* light *that* goes forth.
6For I desire mercy and not sacrifice,
And the knowledge of God more than burnt offerings.
7"But like men[a] they transgressed the covenant;
There they dealt treacherously with Me.
8Gilead *is* a city of evildoers
And defiled with blood.
9As bands of robbers lie in wait for a man,
So the company of priests murder on the way to Shechem;
Surely they commit lewdness.
10I have seen a horrible thing in the house of Israel:
There *is* the harlotry of Ephraim;
Israel is defiled.
11Also, O Judah, a harvest is appointed for you,
When I return the captives of My people.

7 "When I would have healed Israel,
Then the iniquity of Ephraim was uncovered,
And the wickedness of Samaria.
For they have committed fraud;
A thief comes in;
A band of robbers takes spoil outside.
2They do not consider in their hearts
That I remember all their wickedness;
Now their own deeds have surrounded them;
They are before My face.

6:7 [a]Or *like Adam*

6:1,2 Return to the Lord. "God has made all his waves and his billows go over you; the Law has sounded its trumpet in your ear and brought your sin to remembrance; conscience has started up in alarm from its long sleep and cries like a mighty man that wakes up from his slumber and finds the camp besieged. You are troubled and sore broken; your heart is melted like wax in the midst of your bowels, so that while you are sitting in the house of God to-day you are complaining.—'I am the man that has seen affliction;' and perhaps worse than that you are groaning, 'His wrath lies hard upon me, I cannot look up'...

"Oh! may you, nay hearer, you upon whom I fix my eye this morning, you whose case is the case of Israel in Hosea, may you say, 'Come, and let us return unto the Lord, for he has torn, and he will heal us; he has smitten, and he will bind us up.' I desire to come straight up to you who are in this condition and put my hand inside yours, holding you fast while I strive in God's name to reason with you, beseeching God the Holy Spirit to reason better than I can, sweetly moving your soul, till you say, 'I will arise and go unto my Father.'" *Charles Spurgeon*

6:6 Didn't God command offerings and sacrifices? For details on God's view of them, see 1 Sam. 15:22 comment.

7:1,2 The ungodly have no idea that God sees every wicked deed they commit, and that He requires an account of it, down to the words of the mouth and the thoughts of the heart. See Rom. 2:1–12 for details.

[3]They make a king glad with their
wickedness,
And princes with their lies.

[4]"They *are* all adulterers.
Like an oven heated by a baker—
He ceases stirring *the fire* after
kneading the dough,
Until it is leavened.
[5]In the day of our king
Princes have made *him* sick, inflamed
with wine;
He stretched out his hand with
scoffers.
[6]They prepare their heart like an oven,
While they lie in wait;
Their baker[a] sleeps all night;
In the morning it burns like a flaming
fire.
[7]They are all hot, like an oven,
And have devoured their judges;
All their kings have fallen.
None among them calls upon Me.

[8]"Ephraim has mixed himself among
the peoples;
Ephraim is a cake unturned.
[9]Aliens have devoured his strength,
But he does not know *it;*
Yes, gray hairs are here and there on
him,
Yet he does not know *it.*
[10]And the pride of Israel testifies to his
face,
But they do not return to the LORD
their God,
Nor seek Him for all this.

Futile Reliance on the Nations

[11]"Ephraim also is like a silly dove,
without sense—
They call to Egypt,
They go to Assyria.
[12]Wherever they go, I will spread My
net on them;
I will bring them down like birds of
the air;
I will chastise them
According to what their congregation
has heard.

[13]"Woe to them, for they have fled from
Me!
Destruction to them,
Because they have transgressed
against Me!
Though I redeemed them,
Yet they have spoken lies against Me.
[14]They did not cry out to Me with their
heart
When they wailed upon their beds.

"They assemble together for[a] grain and
new wine,
They rebel against Me;[b]
[15]Though I disciplined *and*
strengthened their arms,
Yet they devise evil against Me;
[16]They return, *but* not to the Most High;[a]
They are like a treacherous bow.
Their princes shall fall by the sword
For the cursings of their tongue.
This *shall be* their derision in the land
of Egypt.

The Apostasy of Israel

8 "*Set* the trumpet[a] to your mouth!
He shall come like an eagle against
the house of the LORD,
Because they have transgressed My
covenant
And rebelled against My law.
[2]Israel will cry to Me,
'My God, we know You!'

7:6 [a]Following Masoretic Text and Vulgate; Syriac and Targum read *Their anger;* Septuagint reads *Ephraim.* 7:14 [a]Following Masoretic Text and Targum; Vulgate reads *thought upon;* Septuagint reads *slashed themselves for* (compare 1 Kings 18:28). [b]Following Masoretic Text, Syriac, and Targum; Septuagint omits *They rebel against Me;* Vulgate reads *They departed from Me.* 7:16 [a]Or *upward* 8:1 [a]Hebrew *shophar,* ram's horn

8:1 "This Bible is God's Bible, and when I see it, I seem to hear a voice springing up from it, saying, 'I am the book of God; man, read me. I am God's writing; open my leaf, for I was penned by God; read it, for he is my author, and you will see him visible and manifest everywhere.' 'I have written to him the great things of my law.'" *Charles Spurgeon*

"A man's greatest misery is to be without God—that is, to have no inward connection to the One who is life and existence itself."

Augustine

[3]Israel has rejected the good;
The enemy will pursue him.

[4]"They set up kings, but not by Me;
They made princes, but I did not
acknowledge *them.*
From their silver and gold
They made idols for themselves—
That they might be cut off.
[5]Your calf is rejected, O Samaria!
My anger is aroused against them—
How long until they attain to
innocence?
[6]For from Israel *is* even this:
A workman made it, and it *is* not God;
But the calf of Samaria shall be
broken to pieces.

[7]"They sow the wind,
And reap the whirlwind.
The stalk has no bud;
It shall never produce meal.
If it should produce,
Aliens would swallow it up.
[8]Israel is swallowed up;
Now they are among the Gentiles
Like a vessel in which *is* no pleasure.
[9]For they have gone up to Assyria,
Like a wild donkey alone by itself;
Ephraim has hired lovers.
[10]Yes, though they have hired among
the nations,
Now I will gather them;
And they shall sorrow a little,[a]
Because of the burden[b] of the king of
princes.

[11]"Because Ephraim has made many
altars for sin,
They have become for him altars for
sinning.
[12]I have written for him the great
things of My law,
But they were considered a strange
thing.
[13]*For* the sacrifices of My offerings they
sacrifice flesh and eat *it,*
But the LORD does not accept them.
Now He will remember their iniquity
and punish their sins.
They shall return to Egypt.

[14]"For Israel has forgotten his Maker,
And has built temples;[a]
Judah also has multiplied fortified
cities;
But I will send fire upon his cities,
And it shall devour his palaces."

Judgment of Israel's Sin

9 Do not rejoice, O Israel, with joy
like *other* peoples,
For you have played the harlot against
your God.
You have made love *for* hire on every
threshing floor.
[2]The threshing floor and the winepress
Shall not feed them,
And the new wine shall fail in her.
[3]They shall not dwell in the LORD's
land,
But Ephraim shall return to Egypt,
And shall eat unclean *things* in Assyria.
[4]They shall not offer wine *offerings* to

8:10 [a]Or *begin to diminish* [b]Or *oracle* 8:14 [a]Or *palaces*

the LORD,
Nor shall their sacrifices be pleasing
to Him.
It shall be like bread of mourners to
them;
All who eat it shall be defiled.
For their bread *shall be* for their *own*
life;
It shall not come into the house of the
LORD.

5What will you do in the appointed
day,
And in the day of the feast of the LORD?
6For indeed they are gone because of
destruction.
Egypt shall gather them up;
Memphis shall bury them.
Nettles shall possess their valuables of
silver;
Thorns *shall be* in their tents.

7The days of punishment have come;
The days of recompense have come.
Israel knows!
The prophet *is* a fool,
The spiritual man *is* insane,
Because of the greatness of your
iniquity and great enmity.
8The watchman of Ephraim *is* with my
God;
But the prophet *is* a fowler's[a] snare in
all his ways—
Enmity in the house of his God.
9They are deeply corrupted,
As in the days of Gibeah.
He will remember their iniquity;
He will punish their sins.

10"I found Israel
Like grapes in the wilderness;
I saw your fathers
As the firstfruits on the fig tree in its
first season.
But they went to Baal Peor,
And separated themselves *to that*
shame;
They became an abomination like the
thing they loved.
11*As for* Ephraim, their glory shall fly
away like a bird—
No birth, no pregnancy, and no
conception!
12Though they bring up their children,
Yet I will bereave them to the last man.
Yes, woe to them when I depart from
them!
13Just as I saw Ephraim like Tyre,
planted in a pleasant place,
So Ephraim will bring out his
children to the murderer."

14Give them, O LORD—
What will You give?
Give them a miscarrying womb
And dry breasts!

15"All their wickedness *is* in Gilgal,
For there I hated them.
Because of the evil of their deeds
I will drive them from My house;
I will love them no more.
All their princes *are* rebellious.
16Ephraim is stricken,
Their root is dried up;
They shall bear no fruit.
Yes, were they to bear children,
I would kill the darlings of their
womb."

17My God will cast them away,
Because they did not obey Him;
And they shall be wanderers among
the nations.

Israel's Sin and Captivity

10 Israel empties *his* vine;
He brings forth fruit for himself.

9:8 [a]That is, one who catches birds in a trap or snare

9:7 Unrepentant sin comes back with a terrible vengeance, both on individuals and on nations.

9:15 This image of God is hard to reconcile with the world's belief that "God is a God of love." He is also a God of justice, righteousness, and truth, and any hatred is judicial. Divine hatred is without sin (1 John 1:5). See also Psa. 5:5

According to the multitude of his
fruit
He has increased the altars;
According to the bounty of his land
They have embellished *his* sacred
pillars.
2Their heart is divided;
Now they are held guilty.
He will break down their altars;
He will ruin their sacred pillars.

3For now they say,
"We have no king,
Because we did not fear the LORD.
And as for a king, what would he do
for us?"
4They have spoken words,
Swearing falsely in making a covenant.
Thus judgment springs up like hem-
lock in the furrows of the field.

5The inhabitants of Samaria fear
Because of the calf[a] of Beth Aven.
For its people mourn for it,
And its priests shriek for it—
Because its glory has departed from it.
6*The idol* also shall be carried to
Assyria
As a present for King Jareb.
Ephraim shall receive shame,
And Israel shall be ashamed of his
own counsel.

7*As for* Samaria, her king is cut off
Like a twig on the water.
8Also the high places of Aven, the sin
of Israel,
Shall be destroyed.
The thorn and thistle shall grow on
their altars;
They shall say to the mountains,
"Cover us!"
And to the hills, "Fall on us!"

9"O Israel, you have sinned from the
days of Gibeah;
There they stood.
The battle in Gibeah against the
children of iniquity[a]
Did not overtake them.
10When *it is* My desire, I will chasten
them.
Peoples shall be gathered against
them
When I bind them for their two
transgressions.[a]
11Ephraim *is* a trained heifer
That loves to thresh *grain;*
But I harnessed her fair neck,
I will make Ephraim pull *a plow.*
Judah shall plow;
Jacob shall break his clods."

12Sow for yourselves righteousness;
Reap in mercy;
Break up your fallow ground,
For *it is* time to seek the LORD,
Till He comes and rains righteousness
on you.

13You have plowed wickedness;
You have reaped iniquity.
You have eaten the fruit of lies,
Because you trusted in your own way,
In the multitude of your mighty men.
14Therefore tumult shall arise among
your people,
And all your fortresses shall be
plundered
As Shalman plundered Beth Arbel in
the day of battle—
A mother dashed in pieces upon *her*
children.

10:5 [a]Literally *calves* 10:9 [a]So read many Hebrew manuscripts, Septuagint, and Vulgate; Masoretic Text reads *unruliness.* 10:10 [a]Or *in their two habitations*

10:12 This is a summation of the Christian message to the world. Those who understand the righteousness of God will see their need for His mercy, which is found only in Jesus Christ. However, there can be no mercy until the hard soil of the heart has been broken up by the plow of the Law (see Rom. 7:7,13). It prepares the heart for the seed of the gospel (see Gal. 3:24).

"There must be plowing before there is sowing if there is to be reaping after the sowing!" *Charles Spurgeon*

[15]Thus it shall be done to you, O
Bethel,
Because of your great wickedness.
At dawn the king of Israel
Shall be cut off utterly.

God's Continuing Love for Israel

11 "When Israel *was* a child, I loved
him,
And out of Egypt I called My son.
[2]*As* they called them,[a]
So they went from them;[b]
They sacrificed to the Baals,
And burned incense to carved images.

[3]"I taught Ephraim to walk,
Taking them by their arms;[a]
But they did not know that I healed
them.
[4]I drew them with gentle cords,[a]
With bands of love,
And I was to them as those who take
the yoke from their neck.[b]
I stooped *and* fed them.

[5]"He shall not return to the land of
Egypt;
But the Assyrian shall be his king,
Because they refused to repent.
[6]And the sword shall slash in his cities,
Devour his districts,
And consume *them*,
Because of their own counsels.
[7]My people are bent on backsliding
from Me.
Though they call to the Most High,[a]
None at all exalt *Him*.

[8]"How can I give you up, Ephraim?
How can I hand you over, Israel?
How can I make you like Admah?
How can I set you like Zeboiim?
My heart churns within Me;
My sympathy is stirred.
[9]I will not execute the fierceness of My
anger;
I will not again destroy Ephraim.
For I *am* God, and not man,
The Holy One in your midst;
And I will not come with terror.[a]

The first joint priority of the churches of any city should be that of making it hard for people to go to hell from that city.

DAVID SHIBLEY

[10]"They shall walk after the LORD.
He will roar like a lion.
When He roars,
Then *His* sons shall come trembling
from the west;
[11]They shall come trembling like a bird
from Egypt,
Like a dove from the land of Assyria.
And I will let them dwell in their
houses,"
Says the LORD.

God's Charge Against Ephraim

[12]"Ephraim has encircled Me with lies,
And the house of Israel with deceit;
But Judah still walks with God,
Even with the Holy One[a] *who is*
faithful.

12 "Ephraim feeds on the wind,
And pursues the east wind;
He daily increases lies and desolation.
Also they make a covenant with the
Assyrians,
And oil is carried to Egypt.

[2]"The LORD also *brings* a charge against
Judah,
And will punish Jacob according to
his ways;

11:2 [a]Following Masoretic Text and Vulgate; Septuagint reads *Just as I called them*; Targum interprets as *I sent prophets to a thousand of them*. [b]Following Masoretic Text, Targum, and Vulgate; Septuagint reads *from My face*. 11:3 [a]Some Hebrew manuscripts, Septuagint, Syriac, and Vulgate read *My arms*. 11:4 [a]Literally *cords of a man* [b]Literally *jaws* 11:7 [a]Or *upward* 11:9 [a]Or *I will not enter a city* 11:12 [a]Or *holy ones*

11:1 This messianic prophecy was fulfilled in Matt. 2:12–15.

According to his deeds He will
recompense him.
[3]He took his brother by the heel in the
womb,
And in his strength he struggled with
God.[a]
[4]Yes, he struggled with the Angel and
prevailed;
He wept, and sought favor from Him.
He found Him *in* Bethel,
And there He spoke to us—
[5]That is, the LORD God of hosts.
The LORD *is* His memorable name.
[6]So you, by *the help of* your God, return;
Observe mercy and justice,
And wait on your God continually.

[7]"A cunning Canaanite!
Deceitful scales *are* in his hand;
He loves to oppress.
[8]And Ephraim said,
'Surely I have become rich,
I have found wealth for myself;
In all my labors
They shall find in me no iniquity that
is sin.'

[9]"But I *am* the LORD your God,
Ever since the land of Egypt;
I will again make you dwell in tents,
As in the days of the appointed feast.
[10]I have also spoken by the prophets,
And have multiplied visions;
I have given symbols through the
witness of the prophets."

[11]Though Gilead *has* idols—
Surely they are vanity—
Though they sacrifice bulls in Gilgal,
Indeed their altars *shall be* heaps in
the furrows of the field.
[12]Jacob fled to the country of Syria;
Israel served for a spouse,
And for a wife he tended *sheep*.
[13]By a prophet the LORD brought Israel
out of Egypt,
And by a prophet he was preserved.
[14]Ephraim provoked *Him* to anger most
bitterly;
Therefore his Lord will leave the guilt
of his bloodshed upon him,
And return his reproach upon him.

Relentless Judgment on Israel

13 When Ephraim spoke, trembling,
He exalted *himself* in Israel;
But when he offended through Baal
worship, he died.
[2]Now they sin more and more,
And have made for themselves
molded images,
Idols of their silver, according to their
skill;
All of it *is* the work of craftsmen.
They say of them,
"Let the men who sacrifice[a] kiss the
calves!"
[3]Therefore they shall be like the
morning cloud
And like the early dew that passes
away,
Like chaff blown off from a threshing
floor
And like smoke from a chimney.

12:3 [a]Compare Genesis 32:28 13:2 [a]*Or those who offer human sacrifice*

12:10 The witness of the prophets. "When the Lord would win his people Israel from their iniquities, he did not leave a stone unturned, but gave them precept upon precept, line upon line, here a little and there a little. He taught them sometimes with a rod in his hand, when he smote them with sore famine and pestilence, and invasion; at other times he sought to win them with bounties, for he multiplied their corn and their wine and their oil, and he laid no famine upon them. But all the teachings of his providence were unavailing, and whilst his hand was stretched out, still they continued to rebel against the Most High. He hewed them by the prophets. He sent them first one, and then another: the golden mouthed Isaiah was followed by the plaintive Jeremy; while at his heels in quick succession, there followed many far-seeing, thunder-speaking seers. But though prophet followed prophet in quick succession, each of them uttering the burning words of the Most High, yet they would have none of his rebukes, but they hardened their hearts, and went on still in their iniquities." *Charles Spurgeon*

[4]"Yet I *am* the LORD your God
Ever since the land of Egypt,
And you shall know no God but Me;
For *there is* no savior besides Me.
[5]I knew you in the wilderness,
In the land of great drought.
[6]When they had pasture, they were filled;
They were filled and their heart was exalted;
Therefore they forgot Me.

[7]"So I will be to them like a lion;
Like a leopard by the road I will lurk;
[8]I will meet them like a bear deprived *of her cubs;*
I will tear open their rib cage,
And there I will devour them like a lion.
The wild beast shall tear them.

[9]"O Israel, you are destroyed,[a]
But your help[b] *is* from Me.
[10]I will be your King;[a]
Where *is any other,*
That he may save you in all your cities?
And your judges to whom you said,
'Give me a king and princes'?
[11]I gave you a king in My anger,
And took *him* away in My wrath.

[12]"The iniquity of Ephraim *is* bound up;
His sin *is* stored up.
[13]The sorrows of a woman in childbirth shall come upon him.
He *is* an unwise son,
For he should not stay long where children are born.

[14]"I will ransom them from the power of the grave;[a]
I will redeem them from death.
O Death, I will be your plagues![b]
O Grave,[c] I will be your destruction![d]
Pity is hidden from My eyes."

[15]Though he is fruitful among *his* brethren,
An east wind shall come;
The wind of the LORD shall come up from the wilderness.
Then his spring shall become dry,
And his fountain shall be dried up.
He shall plunder the treasury of every desirable prize.
[16]Samaria is held guilty,[a]
For she has rebelled against her God.
They shall fall by the sword,
Their infants shall be dashed in pieces,
And their women with child ripped open.

Israel Restored at Last

14 O Israel, return to the LORD your God,
For you have stumbled because of your iniquity;
[2]Take words with you,
And return to the LORD.
Say to Him,
"Take away all iniquity;
Receive *us* graciously,
For we will offer the sacrifices[a] of our lips.
[3]Assyria shall not save us,
We will not ride on horses,
Nor will we say anymore to the work of our hands, '*You are* our gods.'
For in You the fatherless finds mercy."

[4]"I will heal their backsliding,

13:9 [a]Literally *it* or *he destroyed you* [b]Literally *in your help* 13:10 [a]Septuagint, Syriac, Targum, and Vulgate read *Where is your king?* 13:14 [a]Or *Sheol* [b]Septuagint reads *where is your punishment?* [c]Or *Sheol* [d]Septuagint reads *where is your sting?* 13:16 [a]Septuagint reads *shall be disfigured* 14:2 [a]Literally *bull calves;* Septuagint reads *fruit.*

13:4 Jesus Christ, the Savior of the world, was God in human form. See 1 Tim. 3:16.

13:14 Words cannot express the wonder of this promise from God. Through Jesus' sacrifice on the cross, He destroyed the power of the grave. The precious blood of Christ has redeemed us from death; that last enemy has been overcome and will eventually be vanquished forever (see 1 Cor. 15:26). This is the greatest news humanity could ever dream of hearing. What an absolute tragedy for any to refuse to obey the gospel and find everlasting life. See 1 Cor. 15:51–55.

I will love them freely,
For My anger has turned away from him.
5 I will be like the dew to Israel;
He shall grow like the lily,
And lengthen his roots like Lebanon.
6 His branches shall spread;
His beauty shall be like an olive tree,
And his fragrance like Lebanon.
7 Those who dwell under his shadow shall return;
They shall be revived *like* grain,
And grow like a vine.
Their scent[a] *shall be* like the wine of Lebanon.

8 "Ephraim *shall say,* 'What have I to do anymore with idols?'
I have heard and observed him.
I *am* like a green cypress tree;
Your fruit is found in Me."
9 Who *is* wise?
Let him understand these things.
Who is prudent?
Let him know them.
For the ways of the LORD *are* right;
The righteous walk in them,
But transgressors stumble in them.

14:7 [a]Literally *remembrance*

14:4 The word "backslider" in Scripture is usually used in a national sense. Most of those individuals we call "backsliders" never slid forward in the first place. They are false converts who are strangers to genuine repentance. See Luke 9:62 and 2 Cor. 2:17 comments.

A simple way to study the Bible is to **COMB** the words:
C: Context; **O:** Other related verses;
M: Meaning of words;
B: Background

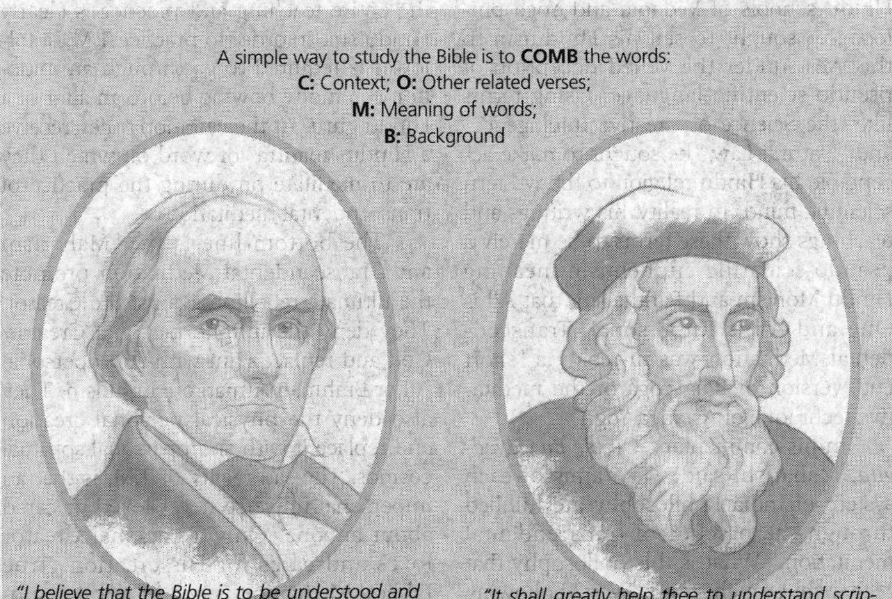

"I believe that the Bible is to be understood and received in the plain and obvious meaning of its passages; for I cannot persuade myself that a book intended for the instruction and conversion of the whole world should cover its true meaning in any such mystery and doubt that none but critics and philosophers can discover it."

Daniel Webster

"It shall greatly help thee to understand scripture if thou mark not only what is spoken or written, but of whom, and to whom, and with what words, at what time, where, to what intent, and with what circumstances, considering what goeth before and what followeth."

John Wycliffe

Transcendental Meditation and Maharishi Mahesh Yogi

By Dr. Ron Carlson

Maharishi Mahesh Yogi, founder of Transcendental Meditation, died February 6, 2008, in his Dutch home in Vlodrop, Netherlands. For nearly five decades he had promoted throughout the world the Hindu practice known as T.M. He built T.M. into a multi-million dollar organization, which includes Maharishi International University in Fairfield, Iowa. The Natural Law Party, active in American politics, also came out of his movement.

Maharishi, who promoted the Indian Hindu schools of Vedanta and Yoga philosophy, sought to sell his Hinduism to the West under the veiled deception of pseudo-scientific language. Using terms like "the Science of Creative Intelligence" and "Natural Law," he sought to make acceptable his Hindu religion to the western scientific mind. In reality, his writings and teachings show these terms to be merely a pseudo-scientific euphemism meaning Hindu Monism and Pantheism, that All is One and All is Impersonal. Transcendental Meditation was in reality a "short cut" version of Raja Yoga or the meditative technique of Astanga Yoga.

In his commentary, *On the Bhagavadgita*, Maharishi said, "The aims of each system of Indian philosophy are fulfilled through the practice of transcendental meditation." What is this philosophy that Maharishi brought to the West? Following the Vedanta school of Hinduism, Maharishi taught the unity of all things: that the entire universe and all existence are of one impersonal essence or nature. Maharishi teaches that the physical, personal world is illusion; only the transcendent and spiritual are real. Man in his true nature is said to be impersonal. The illusion of the physical, personal existence of man merely produces suffering in life. To eliminate suffering, says Maharishi, one must eliminate the physical, personal realm of existence.

In order to transcend this illusory, physical world and achieve a state of enlightenment, or oneness with the impersonal cosmos, Maharishi said a person must use the yoga technique of Transcendental Meditation. Though it was claimed by followers not to be religious, the entire teaching and practice is clearly Hinduism. In order to practice T.M., a follower is required to go through an initiation ceremony bowing before an altar of a Hindu guru. At the ceremony they receive a Hindu "mantra" or word on which they are to meditate on during the practice of transcendental meditation.

The bottom line is that Maharishi and Transcendental Meditation promote the ultimate rebellion against the Creator. They deny the infinite personal Creator/God and replace Him with an impersonal All or Brahman/Atman of Hinduism. They also deny the physical personal creation and replace it with an impersonal spiritual cosmos. The sad reality of T.M. is that an impersonal universe never loved or cared about anyone. Only a personal Creator loves and cares for His creation. True Biblical Meditation is not an inward, subjective descent into yourself as T.M. promotes, but an outward objective ascent to the personal Creator who "so loved the world that He gave his only begotten Son, that whosoever believes in Him shall not perish, but have everlasting life!"

Joel

1 The word of the LORD that came to
Joel the son of Pethuel.

The Land Laid Waste

[2]Hear this, you elders,
And give ear, all you inhabitants of the land!
Has *anything like* this happened in your days,
Or even in the days of your fathers?
[3]Tell your children about it,
Let your children *tell* their children,
And their children another generation.

[4]What the chewing locust[a] left, the swarming locust has eaten;
What the swarming locust left, the crawling locust has eaten;
And what the crawling locust left, the consuming locust has eaten.

[5]Awake, you drunkards, and weep;
And wail, all you drinkers of wine,
Because of the new wine,
For it has been cut off from your mouth.
[6]For a nation has come up against My land,
Strong, and without number;
His teeth *are* the teeth of a lion,
And he has the fangs of a fierce lion.
[7]He has laid waste My vine,
And ruined My fig tree;
He has stripped it bare and thrown *it* away;
Its branches are made white.

[8]Lament like a virgin girded with sackcloth
For the husband of her youth.
[9]The grain offering and the drink offering
Have been cut off from the house of the LORD;
The priests mourn, who minister to the LORD.
[10]The field is wasted,
The land mourns;
For the grain is ruined,
The new wine is dried up,
The oil fails.

[11]Be ashamed, you farmers,
Wail, you vinedressers,
For the wheat and the barley;
Because the harvest of the field has perished.
[12]The vine has dried up,
And the fig tree has withered;

1:4 [a]Exact identity of these locusts is unknown.

1:3 If Christian parents neglect to have daily family devotions and to take time to build a solid Christian foundation during their children's impressionable years, they should not be mystified when the children turn from the things of God during their teenage years (see Psa. 78:4,5). For more on this topic, see Josh. 4:21,22 and Prov. 22:6 comments.

The pomegranate tree,
The palm tree also,
And the apple tree—
All the trees of the field are withered;
Surely joy has withered away from
the sons of men.

Mourning for the Land

13Gird yourselves and lament, you
priests;
Wail, you who minister before the
altar;
Come, lie all night in sackcloth,
You who minister to my God;
For the grain offering and the drink
offering
Are withheld from the house of your
God.
14Consecrate a fast,
Call a sacred assembly;
Gather the elders
And all the inhabitants of the land
Into the house of the LORD your God,
And cry out to the LORD.

15Alas for the day!
For the day of the LORD *is* at hand;
It shall come as destruction from the
Almighty.
16Is not the food cut off before our eyes,
Joy and gladness from the house of
our God?
17The seed shrivels under the clods,
Storehouses are in shambles;
Barns are broken down,
For the grain has withered.
18How the animals groan!
The herds of cattle are restless,
Because they have no pasture;
Even the flocks of sheep suffer
punishment.[a]

19O LORD, to You I cry out;
For fire has devoured the open
pastures,
And a flame has burned all the trees
of the field.
20The beasts of the field also cry out to
You,
For the water brooks are dried up,
And fire has devoured the open
pastures.

The Day of the Lord

2 Blow the trumpet in Zion,
And sound an alarm in My holy
mountain!
Let all the inhabitants of the land
tremble;
For the day of the LORD is coming,
For it is at hand:
2A day of darkness and gloominess,
A day of clouds and thick darkness,
Like the morning *clouds* spread over
the mountains.
A people *come,* great and strong,
The like of whom has never been;
Nor will there ever be any *such* after
them,
Even for many successive generations.

3A fire devours before them,
And behind them a flame burns;
The land *is* like the Garden of Eden
before them,
And behind them a desolate
wilderness;
Surely nothing shall escape them.
4Their appearance is like the
appearance of horses;
And like swift steeds, so they run.
5With a noise like chariots
Over mountaintops they leap,
Like the noise of a flaming fire that

1:18 [a]Septuagint and Vulgate read *are made desolate.*

1:14–20 This sort of heart-cry to God should find itself manifest in passionate preaching to the unsaved (see 2:1).

2:1 Lift up your voice like a trumpet and show this people their transgression. Open up the moral Law to bring the knowledge of sin (see Rom. 3:19,20; 7:7; 7:13), then preach that Christ has redeemed us from the curse of the Law, having become a curse for us, and that God commands all men everywhere to repent, because He has appointed a day on which He will judge the world in righteousness (see Acts 17:30,31).

devours the stubble,
Like a strong people set in battle array.

6Before them the people writhe in pain;
All faces are drained of color.[a]
7They run like mighty men,
They climb the wall like men of war;
Every one marches in formation,
And they do not break ranks.
8They do not push one another;
Every one marches in his own column.[a]
Though they lunge between the weapons,
They are not cut down.[b]
9They run to and fro in the city,
They run on the wall;
They climb into the houses,
They enter at the windows like a thief.

10The earth quakes before them,
The heavens tremble;
The sun and moon grow dark,
And the stars diminish their brightness.
11The LORD gives voice before His army,
For His camp is very great;
For strong *is the One* who executes His word.
For the day of the LORD *is* great and very terrible;
Who can endure it?

A Call to Repentance

12"Now, therefore," says the LORD,
"Turn to Me with all your heart,
With fasting, with weeping, and with mourning."
13So rend your heart, and not your garments;
Return to the LORD your God,
For He *is* gracious and merciful,
Slow to anger, and of great kindness;
And He relents from doing harm.
14Who knows *if* He will turn and relent,
And leave a blessing behind Him—
A grain offering and a drink offering
For the LORD your God?

15Blow the trumpet in Zion,
Consecrate a fast,
Call a sacred assembly;
16Gather the people,
Sanctify the congregation,
Assemble the elders,
Gather the children and nursing babes;
Let the bridegroom go out from his chamber,
And the bride from her dressing room.
17Let the priests, who minister to the LORD,
Weep between the porch and the altar;
Let them say, "Spare Your people, O LORD,
And do not give Your heritage to reproach,
That the nations should rule over them.
Why should they say among the peoples,
'Where *is* their God?' "

The Land Refreshed

18Then the LORD will be zealous for His land,
And pity His people.
19The LORD will answer and say to His people,
"Behold, I will send you grain and new

2:6 [a]Septuagint, Targum, and Vulgate read *gather blackness.*
2:8 [a]Literally *his own highway* [b]That is, they are not halted by losses

2:12,13 True repentance is more than an outward show of sorrow. It comes from a deep knowledge that we have offended God—a "godly sorrow" that produces repentance leading to salvation (see 2 Cor. 7:10). David lacked repentance until he understood that his sin with Bathsheba was *against God* and God alone (see Psa. 51:4). Too much of today's "repentance" is superficial because there is only a superficial knowledge of sin. This is why the moral Law must be used to bring the knowledge of sin (see Rom. 3:19,20; 7:13). It is when we see sin in its true light that we can appropriate the words of James: "Lament and mourn and weep! Let your laughter be turned to mourning and your joy to gloom" (James 4:9).

wine and oil,
And you will be satisfied by them;
I will no longer make you a reproach
among the nations.

20 "But I will remove far from you the
northern *army,*
And will drive him away into a barren
and desolate land,
With his face toward the eastern sea
And his back toward the western sea;
His stench will come up,
And his foul odor will rise,
Because he has done monstrous
things."

21 Fear not, O land;
Be glad and rejoice,
For the LORD has done marvelous
things!
22 Do not be afraid, you beasts of the
field;
For the open pastures are springing
up,
And the tree bears its fruit;
The fig tree and the vine yield their
strength.
23 Be glad then, you children of Zion,
And rejoice in the LORD your God;
For He has given you the former rain
faithfully,[a]
And He will cause the rain to come
down for you—
The former rain,
And the latter rain in the first *month.*
24 The threshing floors shall be full of
wheat,
And the vats shall overflow with new
wine and oil.

25 "So I will restore to you the years that
the swarming locust has eaten,
The crawling locust,
The consuming locust,
And the chewing locust,[a]
My great army which I sent among
you.
26 You shall eat in plenty and be
satisfied,
And praise the name of the LORD your
God,
Who has dealt wondrously with you;
And My people shall never be put to
shame.
27 Then you shall know that I *am* in the
midst of Israel:
I *am* the LORD your God
And there is no other.
My people shall never be put to shame.

God's Spirit Poured Out

28 "And it shall come to pass afterward
That I will pour out My Spirit on all
flesh;
Your sons and your daughters shall
prophesy,
Your old men shall dream dreams,
Your young men shall see visions.
29 And also on *My* menservants and on
My maidservants
I will pour out My Spirit in those days.

30 "And I will show wonders in the
heavens and in the earth:
Blood and fire and pillars of smoke.
31 The sun shall be turned into
darkness,
And the moon into blood,
Before the coming of the great and
awesome day of the LORD.
32 And it shall come to pass
That whoever calls on the name of the
LORD
Shall be saved.
For in Mount Zion and in Jerusalem
there shall be deliverance,

2:23 [a]Or *the teacher of righteousness* **2:25** [a]Compare 1:4

2:29 God's Spirit was poured out on those who repented on the Day of Pentecost. See Acts 2:16–21. "Whenever, in any century, whether in a single heart or in a company of believers, there has been a fresh effusion of the Spirit, there has followed inevitably a fresh endeavor in the work of evangelizing the world." *A. J. Gordon*

As the LORD has said,
Among the remnant whom the LORD
calls.

God Judges the Nations

3 "For behold, in those days and at
that time,
When I bring back the captives of Judah
and Jerusalem,
2I will also gather all nations,
And bring them down to the Valley of
Jehoshaphat;
And I will enter into judgment with
them there
On account of My people, My
heritage Israel,
Whom they have scattered among the
nations;
They have also divided up My land.
3They have cast lots for My people,
Have given a boy *as payment* for a
harlot,
And sold a girl for wine, that they
may drink.

4"Indeed, what have you to do with Me,
O Tyre and Sidon, and all the coasts
of Philistia?
Will you retaliate against Me?
But if you retaliate against Me,
Swiftly and speedily I will return your
retaliation upon your own head;
5Because you have taken My silver and
My gold,
And have carried into your temples
My prized possessions.
6Also the people of Judah and the
people of Jerusalem
You have sold to the Greeks,
That you may remove them far from
their borders.

7"Behold, I will raise them
Out of the place to which you have
sold them,
And will return your retaliation upon
your own head.
8I will sell your sons and your
daughters
Into the hand of the people of Judah,
And they will sell them to the
Sabeans,[a]
To a people far off;
For the LORD has spoken."

9Proclaim this among the nations:
"Prepare for war!
Wake up the mighty men,
Let all the men of war draw near,
Let them come up.
10Beat your plowshares into swords
And your pruning hooks into spears;
Let the weak say, 'I *am* strong.' "
11Assemble and come, all you nations,
And gather together all around.
Cause Your mighty ones to go down
there, O LORD.

12"Let the nations be wakened, and
come up to the Valley of
Jehoshaphat;
For there I will sit to judge all the
surrounding nations.
13Put in the sickle, for the harvest is
ripe.
Come, go down;
For the winepress is full,
The vats overflow—
For their wickedness *is* great."

14Multitudes, multitudes in the valley
of decision!
For the day of the LORD *is* near in the

3:8 [a]Literally *Shebaites* (compare Isaiah 60:6 and Ezekiel 27:22)

2:31,32 Revelation 6 describes this fearful scenario. Even then, whoever calls on the name of the Lord will be saved (v. 32). "Whoever" means anyone. No one can say that God's invitation doesn't include them. The gospel applies universally. But as Paul pointed out, the lost cannot call on Him of whom they have not heard—we must first "preach the gospel of peace" (see Rom. 10:13–15).

3:13,14 May God help us to sow and allow us to reap. See Mark 4:29.

valley of decision.
[15]The sun and moon will grow dark,
And the stars will diminish their
brightness.
[16]The LORD also will roar from Zion,
And utter His voice from Jerusalem;
The heavens and earth will shake;
But the LORD will be a shelter for His
people,
And the strength of the children of
Israel.

> At this moment, I have in my heart a prayer. I ask only to be a good and faithful servant of my Lord and my people.
>
> **HARRY S. TRUMAN**

[17]"So you shall know that I *am* the LORD
your God,
Dwelling in Zion My holy mountain.
Then Jerusalem shall be holy,
And no aliens shall ever pass through
her again."

God Blesses His People

[18]And it will come to pass in that day
That the mountains shall drip with
new wine,
The hills shall flow with milk,
And all the brooks of Judah shall be
flooded with water;
A fountain shall flow from the house
of the LORD
And water the Valley of Acacias.

[19]"Egypt shall be a desolation,
And Edom a desolate wilderness,
Because of violence *against* the people
of Judah,
For they have shed innocent blood in
their land.
[20]But Judah shall abide forever,
And Jerusalem from generation to
generation.
[21]For I will acquit them of the guilt of
bloodshed, whom I had not
acquitted;
For the LORD dwells in Zion."

Islam

With approximately 1.5 billion adherents, Islam is the world's second largest religion. It is also the fastest growing religion today, with one of every five people in the world being a Muslim. Christianity is currently the largest religion, followed by one-third of the world's population. But if current trends continue, Islam will become the most popular world religion sometime in the mid-21st century.

Despite the Middle East being the birthplace of Islam, the majority of Muslims (about 75 percent) are non-Arabs. Although we hear a lot about Muslims in the news, most of us don't know much about their beliefs or how to reach them with the gospel. As with most religions, Islam has some similarities with Christianity, but it's the differences that we want to consider.

BACKGROUND

Approximately 1,500 years ago in Mecca, Saudi Arabia, a man named Muhammad was contemplating inside a cave when he claimed he was visited by an angel named Gabriel. The angel gave him messages, and continued to reveal things to him over a 23-year period. Muhammad used these teachings to form the basis of a religion called Islam. The word "Islam" means "surrender" or "submission." People who believe the teachings of Islam are known as Muslims.

Yet Muslims do not believe that Muhammad and his followers were the first Muslims. Others mentioned in the Bible—such as Abraham (Koran, Sura 3:67)—were Muslims, even though they lived hundreds of years before Muhammad.

In fact, Muslims believe that Islam was the original religion from the time of creation, and that Adam was the first prophet of Allah. Other biblical characters such as Noah, Moses, David, Solomon, John the Baptist, and Jesus were also prophets of Allah. In all, there have been about 124,000 prophets sent for specific times, but Muhammad is considered the last and the greatest, and is known as the "seal of the prophets."

(continued)

Islam (continued)

After Muhammad's death, his followers disagreed on who should be his successor, and they divided into two main groups: the Sunnis and the Shi'ites. About 85 percent of the world's Muslims are Sunnis and 15 percent are Shi'ites. The two branches differ somewhat in their practices and traditions.

SCRIPTURES

Muslims believe their holy book, the Koran (or Quran), was dictated to the Muslim prophet Muhammad by an angel from Allah. Muhammad recited the messages to his followers, who either wrote the words down or memorized them. The Koran was not arranged into the form of a book until after Muhammad's death. Sometime later, a Muslim leader collected all the writings that were part of the official Koran, and he ordered other versions to be burned.

The Koran is divided into 114 chapters, called suras, which cover the topics of ethics, history, law, and theology. It is slightly smaller than the New Testament. Although the Koran is printed in many languages, Muslims believe Arabic is the language of Allah, and that the true meaning of the Koran can be fully learned only in Arabic. Muslims who memorize the Koran usually memorize it in Arabic, even if they don't understand the language. Because they believe it is the word of Allah, Muslims handle copies of the Koran with great care. They wash their hands before reading it, and they keep it in a safe place—never on the floor. In Muslim countries, anyone who intentionally damages a Koran can be arrested.

Islam teaches that Allah was the source of both the Bible and the Koran. Muslims believe that some of the previous prophets were given books that are considered to be divinely inspired: 1) The *Tawrat* (Torah), given to Moses; 2) The *Zabur* (Psalms), given to David; 3) The *Injil* (Gospel), given to Jesus; 4) The Koran, given to Muhammad. Muslims are taught that the first three have been corrupted, so to correct the errors Allah appointed Muhammad to receive the Koran. It supersedes all previous revelation, and Allah has preserved it from corruption. (Perhaps this would be a good question to ask a Muslim: If all books were originally true and given by Allah, who is able to preserve his word, why is he able to keep the Koran free from corruption, but he wasn't able to preserve the first three?)

In addition, Muslims try to live as Muhammad did by following the *hadith*, collections of records of the things Muhammad and his companions did and said. Several *hadith* collectors gathered reports of Muhammad's life, similar to the different Gospel accounts of Jesus' life.

WHO IS GOD?

Like in Christianity and Judaism, Islam teaches monotheism—a belief that there is only one God. Muslims worship Allah, who they believe created the universe in six days and is in complete control of all things. While he is eternal, omnipotent, omnipresent, and omniscient, Muslims believe that Allah himself is not knowable, and they cannot have a personal relationship with him. Rather than fellowship with Allah, Islam is concerned only with allegiance to him and total submission to his will.

The Koran does not say that Allah seeks to redeem those lost in sin, and it states repeatedly that he does not love sinners (Sura 3:32; 4:107).

The Muslim belief that there are no gods other than Allah is recited daily in the *shahada*. Like with Judaism, they believe in God's absolute oneness and reject the Trinity. To ascribe any partners to Allah is to commit the unforgivable sin of *shirk*.

WHO IS JESUS?

Muslims believe that, prior to Muhammad, Allah sent many great prophets who spoke for God to specific people, and whose message was meant for that time. Jesus, then, was simply one of many prophets according to Islam. The Koran does acknowledge Jesus' virgin birth, holy life, and many miracles, but says He was no more than a man. Jesus (whom they call Isa) must never be called "God," "Lord," or the "Son of God." The Koran has many verses stating that Jesus is not the son of Allah, and adds that anyone who says Allah has a son is a liar (Sura 37:152). Many Muslims think calling Jesus "the Son of God" means that Allah had physical relations, which is highly offensive.

The Koran teaches that Jesus did not die, but was taken directly to heaven. Muslims believe that Allah would not allow Jesus, a prophet, to die on the cross. Such a death would mean defeat—if Jesus were killed, that would mean He failed and His enemies won. So they believe someone else, possibly Judas, was made to look like Jesus and died on the cross in place of Jesus. Of course, since they believe Jesus didn't die, then He also did not rise from the dead.

HEAVEN AND HELL

Muslims believe that everyone will attain either the punishment of hell or the reward of heaven (Paradise): "For those who reject Allah, is a terrible Penalty: but for those who believe and work righteous deeds, is Forgiveness, and a magnificent Reward" (Sura 35:7).

Hell is where unbelievers and sinners will spend eternity. One translation of the Koran states: "The unbelievers among the People of the Book [Christians and Jews] and the pagans shall burn for ever in the fire of hell. They are the vilest of all creatures" (Sura 98:1–8).

The "magnificent reward" that Muslims hope to achieve is Paradise—"gardens of bliss" where they will be joined by their spouses (resurrected as virgins) and waited on by immortal youths. There they will enjoy sensual pleasures: choice food and

(continued)

drink, nice clothes and jewelry, lovely companions, and beautiful virgins (Sura 56:12–37).

SIN AND SALVATION

Muslims believe human beings are born sinless and are good by nature. Since they don't have a fallen nature, they don't think they need a Savior. They depend on their own efforts to please Allah.

Muslims believe that Allah will judge everyone on Judgment Day according to their deeds (helping others, testifying to the truth of God, leading a virtuous life). If they have done more good deeds than bad, they hope Allah will forgive their sins and let them into Paradise when they die. But they can't be sure.

The Koran tells them that the good deeds they do will cancel out bad deeds (Sura 11:114), but no one knows how many good deeds are enough. Although they believe they can ask Allah to forgive their sins, Allah may or may not forgive them. The Koran says, "Allah . . . punishes whom he pleases and forgives whom he pleases" (Sura 5:40).

Because the tally of good deeds vs. bad is known only to Allah, Muslims cannot know whether they are saved until Judgment Day. The Koran says: "Then those whose balance (of good deeds) is heavy, they will be successful. But those whose balance is light, will be those who have lost their souls; in hell will they abide" (Sura 23:102–103).

To go to Paradise, the Koran says Muslims should believe in Allah, the prophets of Islam, the Koran, angels, and Judgment Day (Sura 4:136). They must repent and obey Islamic law, but even doing those things will not necessarily assure Muslims of salvation.

In other words, though Allah is frequently called Forgiving and Merciful in the Koran, forgiveness and mercy don't appear to be applied to the sinner's account—sin must still be atoned for by each individual's works.

MUSLIM CUSTOMS

All Muslims have five important duties that they are obligated to fulfill. These duties, called the "Five Pillars," are referred to by their Arabic names:

1. *Shahada*: Confess the faith by reciting, "There is no God but Allah, and Muhammad is his messenger."
2. *Salat*: Pray five times a day at specific times while facing the city of Mecca, the birthplace of Muhammad. Wherever they live, all Muslims must face Mecca during their times of prayer, and perform ceremonial washing beforehand. The five daily prayers are recited in Arabic.
3. *Zakat*: Give money to help the poor. Muslim adults are required to give 2.5 percent of their wealth to charity every year. Some Muslim youth do volunteer work as a form of helping the needy.
4. *Sawm*: Fast from sunrise to sunset during the Muslim holy month of Ramadan, to remember the giving of the Koran to Muhammad. After sunset, Muslims may get together with family and friends to eat a meal called *iftar*. Muslims celebrate the end of Ramadan with a three-day festival called *Eid al-Fitr*. Schools and businesses close in Muslim countries for the holidays.
5. *Hajj*: Take a pilgrimage to Mecca at least once if possible. Mecca is a holy city for Muslims; by law, non-Muslims may not enter it. On the road to Mecca, highway signs direct non-Muslims to exit before reaching the city. Once a year, approximately 2 million Muslims from all over the world come to Mecca for the *Hajj*, a ritual lasting several days. For many Muslims, the *Hajj* is the high point of their lives.

The Five Pillars form the framework for the Muslim's life and practice. Faithfully adhering to these pillars is how Muslims hope to satisfy Allah and achieve salvation.

TIPS FOR WITNESSING

- Often Christians feel that it's their job to try to explain the deity of Jesus to a Muslim. However, keep in mind these verses: "He said to them, 'But who do you say that I am?' Simon Peter answered and said, 'You are the Christ, the Son of the living God.' Jesus answered and said to him, 'Blessed are you, Simon Bar-Jonah, for flesh and blood has not revealed this to you, *but My Father who is in heaven*" (Matt. 16:15–17, emphasis added). Let God reveal to him who Jesus is.
- Also, it's not wise to try to explain the Trinity unless the person brings it up. Keep in mind that in Islam, the greatest of sins, called *shirk*, is to attribute "partners" to God. To say that God is a Trinity of persons is an unforgivable sin to a Muslim.
- Muslims have the highest regard for their Koran —keeping it above their waist, placing it on the highest shelf, and never letting it touch the ground. If you witness to them using a marked-up, highlighted Bible, they will consider it very irreverent and disrespectful.
- Muslims believe Allah punishes people for their own sins. Many believe it would be unfair for Jesus to be punished and to die for the sins of others. C. S. Lewis suggests thinking about sins as if they were debts. It makes sense for those in debt to seek help from someone who owes nothing and can afford to help those who do. Jesus did not sin, so He is able to help those who come to Him for salvation from their sins.

For more ideas on how to reach Muslims, see Acts 17:22 comment.

(Adapted from *World Religions in a Nutshell*.)

Amos

1 The words of Amos, who was among
the sheepbreeders[a] of Tekoa, which
he saw concerning Israel in the days of
Uzziah king of Judah, and in the days of
Jeroboam the son of Joash, king of Israel,
two years before the earthquake.
2And he said:

"The LORD roars from Zion,
And utters His voice from Jerusalem;
The pastures of the shepherds mourn,
And the top of Carmel withers."

Judgment on the Nations

3Thus says the LORD:

"For three transgressions of Damascus,
and for four,
I will not turn away its *punishment*,
Because they have threshed Gilead
with implements of iron.
4But I will send a fire into the house of
Hazael,
Which shall devour the palaces of
Ben-Hadad.
5I will also break the *gate* bar of
Damascus,
And cut off the inhabitant from the
Valley of Aven,
And the one who holds the scepter
from Beth Eden.
The people of Syria shall go captive to
Kir,"
Says the LORD.

6Thus says the LORD:

"For three transgressions of Gaza, and
for four,
I will not turn away its *punishment*,
Because they took captive the whole
captivity
To deliver *them* up to Edom.
7But I will send a fire upon the wall of
Gaza,
Which shall devour its palaces.
8I will cut off the inhabitant from
Ashdod,
And the one who holds the scepter
from Ashkelon;
I will turn My hand against Ekron,
And the remnant of the Philistines
shall perish,"
Says the Lord GOD.

9Thus says the LORD:

"For three transgressions of Tyre, and
for four,
I will not turn away its *punishment*,
Because they delivered up the whole
captivity to Edom,
And did not remember the covenant
of brotherhood.
10But I will send a fire upon the wall of
Tyre,
Which shall devour its palaces."

11Thus says the LORD:

"For three transgressions of Edom, and

1:1 [a]Compare 2 Kings 3:4

for four,
I will not turn away its *punishment,*
Because he pursued his brother with
the sword,
And cast off all pity;
His anger tore perpetually,
And he kept his wrath forever.
12But I will send a fire upon Teman,
Which shall devour the palaces of
Bozrah."

13Thus says the LORD:

"For three transgressions of the people
of Ammon, and for four,
I will not turn away its *punishment,*
Because they ripped open the women
with child in Gilead,
That they might enlarge their territory.
14But I will kindle a fire in the wall of
Rabbah,
And it shall devour its palaces,
Amid shouting in the day of battle,
And a tempest in the day of the
whirlwind.
15Their king shall go into captivity,
He and his princes together,"
Says the LORD.

2 Thus says the LORD:

"For three transgressions of Moab, and
for four,
I will not turn away its *punishment,*
Because he burned the bones of the
king of Edom to lime.
2But I will send a fire upon Moab,
And it shall devour the palaces of
Kerioth;
Moab shall die with tumult,
With shouting *and* trumpet sound.
3And I will cut off the judge from its
midst,
And slay all its princes with him,"
Says the LORD.

THE FUNCTION OF THE LAW

2:4 "Without grace all men are of this kind, but especially the self-righteous. Hence Scripture says and concludes: 'All men are liars' (Ps 116:11); and again (Ps 39:5) 'Every man at his best state is altogether vanity'; and (Ps 14:3) 'There is none that does good, no, not one.' But despair follows when a man becomes aware of the reason why he is keeping the Law and recognizes that to love God's Law is impossible for him, since he finds nothing good in himself but only hatred of the good and lust for the bad.

"Then he recognizes that works cannot do justice to the Law. Therefore he despairs of works and disregards them. He ought to have love, but he does not find any and of and by himself can have none. The result must be a poor, miserable, humbled spirit, a man oppressed and frightened through the Law by his conscience, which demands and requires of him what he has not a penny to pay. Yet the Law alone is of benefit to such presumptuous people, for it was given to work this knowledge and humiliation. This is its [the Law's] proper work . . ."
Martin Luther

Judgment on Judah

4Thus says the LORD:

"For three transgressions of Judah, and
for four,
I will not turn away its *punishment,*
Because they have despised the law of
the LORD,
And have not kept His
commandments.
Their lies lead them astray,
Lies which their fathers followed.
5But I will send a fire upon Judah,
And it shall devour the palaces of
Jerusalem."

Judgment on Israel

6Thus says the LORD:

"For three transgressions of Israel, and
for four,

1:13 This was the murder of mother and child. There is no depth of wickedness of which man is incapable. May those who have murdered their own children through abortion come to Christ before the day of God's wrath. See also Psa. 127:3 comment.

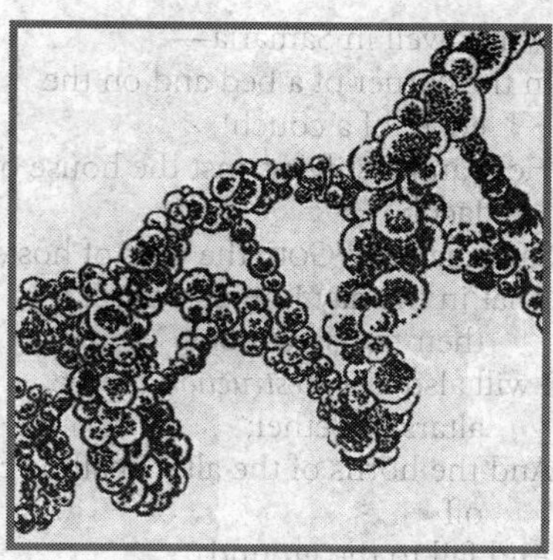

Do DNA similarities really show a common ancestor? See Job 17:14 comment.

I will not turn away its *punishment*,
Because they sell the righteous for silver,
And the poor for a pair of sandals.
7They pant after[a] the dust of the earth
which is on the head of the poor,
And pervert the way of the humble.
A man and his father go in to the *same* girl,
To defile My holy name.
8They lie down by every altar on clothes taken in pledge,
And drink the wine of the condemned *in* the house of their god.

9"Yet *it was* I *who* destroyed the Amorite before them,
Whose height *was* like the height of the cedars,
And he *was as* strong as the oaks;
Yet I destroyed his fruit above
And his roots beneath.
10Also *it was* I *who* brought you up from the land of Egypt,
And led you forty years through the wilderness,
To possess the land of the Amorite.
11I raised up some of your sons as prophets,
And some of your young men as Nazirites.
Is it not so, O you children of Israel?"
Says the LORD.
12"But you gave the Nazirites wine to drink,
And commanded the prophets saying,
'Do not prophesy!'

13"Behold, I am weighed down by you,
As a cart full of sheaves is weighed down.
14Therefore flight shall perish from the swift,
The strong shall not strengthen his power,
Nor shall the mighty deliver himself;
15He shall not stand who handles the bow,
The swift of foot shall not escape,
Nor shall he who rides a horse deliver himself.
16The most courageous men of might
Shall flee naked in that day,"
Says the LORD.

Authority of the Prophet's Message

3 Hear this word that the LORD has spoken against you, O children of Israel, against the whole family which I brought up from the land of Egypt, saying:

2"You only have I known of all the families of the earth;
Therefore I will punish you for all your iniquities."

3Can two walk together, unless they are agreed?
4Will a lion roar in the forest, when he has no prey?
Will a young lion cry out of his den,

2:7 [a]Or *trample on*

2:7 Sinners don't understand that sexual sin has terrible repercussions. When a man becomes involved in sexual sin, he not only sins against his own body (see 1 Cor. 6:18) and the body of the woman, but he sins *against God* (see Psa. 51:4). He violates God's perfect Law with the mere look of lust (see Matt. 5:27,28), so how much more does he sin against God when he carries out his sexual imaginations?

if he has caught nothing?
[5]Will a bird fall into a snare on the earth, where there is no trap for it?
Will a snare spring up from the earth, if it has caught nothing at all?
[6]If a trumpet is blown in a city, will not the people be afraid?
If there is calamity in a city, will not the LORD have done *it*?

[7]Surely the Lord GOD does nothing,
Unless He reveals His secret to His servants the prophets.
[8]A lion has roared!
Who will not fear?
The Lord GOD has spoken!
Who can but prophesy?

Punishment of Israel's Sins

[9]"Proclaim in the palaces at Ashdod,[a]
And in the palaces in the land of Egypt, and say:
'Assemble on the mountains of Samaria;
See great tumults in her midst,
And the oppressed within her.
[10]For they do not know to do right,'
Says the LORD,
'Who store up violence and robbery in their palaces.' "

[11]Therefore thus says the Lord GOD:

" An adversary *shall be* all around the land;
He shall sap your strength from you,
And your palaces shall be plundered."

[12]Thus says the LORD:

"As a shepherd takes from the mouth of a lion
Two legs or a piece of an ear,
So shall the children of Israel be taken out
Who dwell in Samaria—
In the corner of a bed and on the edge[a] of a couch!
[13]Hear and testify against the house of Jacob,"
Says the Lord GOD, the God of hosts,
[14]"That in the day I punish Israel for their transgressions,
I will also visit *destruction* on the altars of Bethel;
And the horns of the altar shall be cut off
And fall to the ground.
[15]I will destroy the winter house along with the summer house;
The houses of ivory shall perish,
And the great houses shall have an end,"
Says the LORD.

4 Hear this word, you cows of Bashan, who *are* on the mountain of Samaria,
Who oppress the poor,
Who crush the needy,
Who say to your husbands,[a] "Bring *wine*, let us drink!"
[2]The Lord GOD has sworn by His holiness:
"Behold, the days shall come upon you
When He will take you away with fishhooks,
And your posterity with fishhooks.
[3]You will go out *through* broken *walls*,
Each one straight ahead of her,
And you will be cast into Harmon,"
Says the LORD.

[4]"Come to Bethel and transgress,
At Gilgal multiply transgression;
Bring your sacrifices every morning,

3:9 [a]Following Masoretic Text; Septuagint reads *Assyria*. 3:12 [a]The Hebrew is uncertain. 4:1 [a]Literally *their lords* or *their masters*

3:3 Humanity is at enmity with God (see John 3:36; Rom. 8:7; Col. 1:21), so that God and man cannot "walk" together. The Lion of the tribe of Judah (see Rev. 5:5), whose ferocious wrath roars against sin, has commanded us to preach the gospel to every creature. Therefore, we cannot but speak the things which we have seen and heard; it is our moral obligation (see Acts 4:20; 5:20,29; 1 Cor. 9:16).

Your tithes every three days.[a]
5Offer a sacrifice of thanksgiving with leaven,
Proclaim *and* announce the freewill offerings;
For this you love,
You children of Israel!"
Says the Lord GOD.

Israel Did Not Accept Correction

6"Also I gave you cleanness of teeth in all your cities,
And lack of bread in all your places;
Yet you have not returned to Me,"
Says the LORD.

7"I also withheld rain from you,
When *there were* still three months to the harvest.
I made it rain on one city,
I withheld rain from another city.
One part was rained upon,
And where it did not rain the part withered.
8So two *or* three cities wandered to another city to drink water,
But they were not satisfied;
Yet you have not returned to Me,"
Says the LORD.

9"I blasted you with blight and mildew.
When your gardens increased,
Your vineyards,
Your fig trees,
And your olive trees,
The locust devoured *them;*
Yet you have not returned to Me,"
Says the LORD.

10"I sent among you a plague after the manner of Egypt;
Your young men I killed with a sword,
Along with your captive horses;
I made the stench of your camps come up into your nostrils;
Yet you have not returned to Me,"
Says the LORD.

11"I overthrew *some* of you,
As God overthrew Sodom and Gomorrah,
And you were like a firebrand plucked from the burning;
Yet you have not returned to Me,"
Says the LORD.

12"Therefore thus will I do to you, O Israel;
Because I will do this to you,
Prepare to meet your God, O Israel!"

13For behold,
He who forms mountains,
And creates the wind,
Who declares to man what his[a] thought *is*,
And makes the morning darkness,
Who treads the high places of the earth—
The LORD God of hosts *is* His name.

A Lament for Israel

5 Hear this word which I take up against you, a lamentation, O house of Israel:

2The virgin of Israel has fallen;
She will rise no more.
She lies forsaken on her land;
There is no one to raise her up.

3For thus says the Lord GOD:

"The city that goes out by a thousand
Shall have a hundred left,

4:4 [a]Or *years* (compare Deuteronomy 14:28) 4:13 [a]Or *His*

4:6–10 At times, the power of hunger, thirst, pestilence and plague may not be enough to soften the hard hearts of wicked men. America was brought very low by the horror of 9/11, but it wasn't long until she crawled her way back into sin. Adversity sometimes makes people look to God, but often they prefer to find solace in sin. So don't make the mistake of waiting for misfortune to come to the ungodly, thinking that it will give you opportunity to witness. It may harden them or distract them from your words.

4:13 *Albert Einstein's Debt*

There are many who, in a vain attempt to show atheism to be "intellectual," have claimed that Albert Einstein was an atheist. However, the father of all scientists made a number of statements that clearly refute such a claim. He said, "In the view of such harmony in the cosmos which I, with my limited human mind, am able to recognize, there are yet people who say there is no God. But what makes me really angry is that they quote me for support of such views."

Einstein stated, "I'm not an atheist. I don't think I can call myself a pantheist. The problem involved is too vast for our limited minds. We are in the position of a little child entering a huge library filled with books in many languages. The child knows someone must have written those books. It does not know how. It does not understand the languages in which they are written. The child dimly suspects a mysterious order in the arrangement of the books but doesn't know what it is. That, it seems to me, is the attitude of even the most intelligent human being toward God. We see the universe marvelously arranged and obeying certain laws but only dimly understand these laws."

He even revealed his insightful mind in admitting, "I see a pattern, but my imagination cannot picture the maker of the pattern. I see a clock, but I cannot envision the clockmaker. The human mind is unable to conceive of the four dimensions, so how can it conceive of a God, before whom a thousand years and a thousand dimensions are as one?" He also said, "I want to know how God created this world. I am not interested in this or that phenomenon, in the spectrum of this or that element. I want to know His thoughts. The rest are details."

Those who take the time to read the Bible can know how God created this world (see Gen. 1), and they can read the thoughts of God throughout Holy Scripture. The problem is that the Bible is not merely a history book as some maintain. It is a moral book, and for that reason sinful man refuses to open its pages. The psalmist informs us that "the entrance of Your Word gives light" (Psa. 119:130), and the Bible further tells us that men love darkness rather than light because their deeds are evil. They refuse to come to the light because it exposes their sinful deeds (see John 3:19,20).

In light of these thoughts, it's interesting that at the age of thirty-four a reasonably young Einstein unashamedly boasted, "I have firmly resolved to bite the dust, when my time comes, with the minimum of medical assistance, and up to then I will sin to my wicked heart's content."

However, time tends to make most thinking men somewhat philosophical. Two months before his death in 1955, he said, "To one bent on age, death will come as a release. I feel this quite strongly now that I have grown old myself and have come to regard death like an old debt, at long last to be discharged. Still, instinctively one does everything possible to postpone the final settlement. Such is the game that Nature plays with us."

It seems that the great genius spoke biblical truth unawares. However, it isn't Nature that seeks a "final settlement"; it is the Law of God. Like a criminal who has transgressed civil law, he (like the rest of humanity) was in debt to eternal justice because he had transgressed God's Law. This great debt he spoke of could not be satisfied with mere silver and gold. It is a debt that demands capital punishment. It calls for the death penalty for guilty transgressors . . . and eternal damnation in hell. Its terrible decree demands, "The soul who sins shall die," but it is a demand that was fully satisfied by the One who cried from Calvary's cross, "It is finished!" The debt was paid in full by the precious blood of Jesus.

(Adapted from *God Doesn't Believe in Atheists*.)

And that which goes out by a hundred
Shall have ten left to the house of
Israel."

A Call to Repentance

[4]For thus says the LORD to the house of Israel:

"Seek Me and live;
[5]But do not seek Bethel,
Nor enter Gilgal,
Nor pass over to Beersheba;
For Gilgal shall surely go into
captivity,
And Bethel shall come to nothing.
[6]Seek the LORD and live,
Lest He break out like fire *in* the
house of Joseph,
And devour *it*,
With no one to quench *it* in Bethel—

[7]You who turn justice to wormwood,
And lay righteousness to rest in the earth!"

[8]He made the Pleiades and Orion;
He turns the shadow of death into morning
And makes the day dark as night;
He calls for the waters of the sea
And pours them out on the face of the earth;
The LORD *is* His name.
[9]He rains ruin upon the strong,
So that fury comes upon the fortress.

To offer a sinner the gift of salvation based upon the work of Christ, while at the same time allowing him to retain the idea that the gift carries with it no moral implications, is to do him untold injury where it hurts him worst.

A. W. TOZER

[10]They hate the one who rebukes in the gate,
And they abhor the one who speaks uprightly.
[11]Therefore, because you tread down the poor
And take grain taxes from him,
Though you have built houses of hewn stone,
Yet you shall not dwell in them;
You have planted pleasant vineyards,
But you shall not drink wine from them.
[12]For I know your manifold transgressions
And your mighty sins:
Afflicting the just *and* taking bribes;
Diverting the poor *from justice* at the gate.
[13]Therefore the prudent keep silent at that time,
For it *is* an evil time.

[14]Seek good and not evil,
That you may live;
So the LORD God of hosts will be with you,
As you have spoken.
[15]Hate evil, love good;
Establish justice in the gate.
It may be that the LORD God of hosts
Will be gracious to the remnant of Joseph.

The Day of the Lord

[16]Therefore the LORD God of hosts, the
Lord, says this:

"*There shall be* wailing in all streets,
And they shall say in all the highways,
'Alas! Alas!'
They shall call the farmer to mourning,
And skillful lamenters to wailing.
[17]In all vineyards *there shall be* wailing,
For I will pass through you,"
Says the LORD.

[18]Woe to you who desire the day of the LORD!
For what good *is* the day of the LORD to you?
It *will be* darkness, and not light.
[19]It *will be* as though a man fled from a lion,
And a bear met him!
Or *as though* he went into the house,
Leaned his hand on the wall,
And a serpent bit him!

5:4–8 This is the message we have from God: "Seek Me and live." He turns the shadow of death into morning through the rising of the Son. How unspeakably wonderful that the glorious light of the resurrection banished the dark shadow of death forever, for all who trust in the Savior!

5:12 God's Law shows the sinner that his "trivial discrepancies" are actually "manifold transgressions" and "mighty sins."

5:14,15 For the relationship between good and evil, see Gen. 3:5 comment.

[20]*Is* not the day of the LORD darkness,
and not light?
Is it not very dark, with no brightness
in it?

[21]"I hate, I despise your feast days,
And I do not savor your sacred
assemblies.
[22]Though you offer Me burnt offerings
and your grain offerings,
I will not accept *them,*
Nor will I regard your fattened peace
offerings.
[23]Take away from Me the noise of your
songs,
For I will not hear the melody of your
stringed instruments.
[24]But let justice run down like water,
And righteousness like a mighty
stream.

[25]"Did you offer Me sacrifices and
offerings
In the wilderness forty years, O house
of Israel?
[26]You also carried Sikkuth[a] your king[b]
And Chiun,[c] your idols,
The star of your gods,
Which you made for yourselves.
[27]Therefore I will send you into
captivity beyond Damascus,"
Says the LORD, whose name *is* the
God of hosts.

Warnings to Zion and Samaria

6 Woe to you *who are* at ease in Zion,
And trust in Mount Samaria,
Notable persons in the chief nation,
To whom the house of Israel comes!
[2]Go over to Calneh and see;
And from there go to Hamath the great;
Then go down to Gath of the
Philistines.
Are you better than these kingdoms?
Or is their territory greater than your
territory?

[3]*Woe to* you who put far off the day of
doom,
Who cause the seat of violence to
come near;
[4]Who lie on beds of ivory,
Stretch out on your couches,
Eat lambs from the flock
And calves from the midst of the stall;
[5]Who sing idly to the sound of
stringed instruments,
And invent for yourselves musical
instruments like David;
[6]Who drink wine from bowls,
And anoint yourselves with the best
ointments,
But are not grieved for the affliction of
Joseph.
[7]Therefore they shall now go captive
as the first of the captives,
And those who recline at banquets
shall be removed.

[8]The Lord GOD has sworn by Himself,
The LORD God of hosts says:
"I abhor the pride of Jacob,
And hate his palaces;
Therefore I will deliver up *the* city
And all that is in it."

[9]Then it shall come to pass, that if ten
men remain in one house, they shall die.
[10]And when a relative *of the dead,* with
one who will burn *the bodies,* picks up the
bodies[a] to take them out of the house, he

5:26 [a]A pagan deity [b]Septuagint and Vulgate read *tabernacle of Moloch.* [c]A pagan deity

6:3 Those who live in the knowledge of the great and terrible day of the Lord keep their heart from sin. They know that only in Christ can they have "boldness in the day of judgment" (1 John 4:17).

6:4–7 There is nothing wrong with being prosperous, eating fine foods, etc., but not at the neglect of any concern for those afflicted with the fatal disease of sin. This was the sin of the rich man whom Jesus speaks of in Luke 16:1–13. This was the sin of the Laodicean church, which thought that it was rich and in need of nothing (see Rev. 3:19). How this describes the contemporary Church, which is self-indulgent and has little concern for the unsaved.

will say to one inside the house, "*Are there* any more with you?"

Then someone will say, "None."

And he will say, "Hold your tongue! For we dare not mention the name of the LORD."

[11]For behold, the LORD gives a command:
He will break the great house into bits,
And the little house into pieces.

[12]Do horses run on rocks?
Does *one* plow *there* with oxen?
Yet you have turned justice into gall,
And the fruit of righteousness into wormwood,
[13]You who rejoice over Lo Debar,[a]
Who say, "Have we not taken Karnaim[b] for ourselves
By our own strength?"

It is no fault of Christianity that a hypocrite falls into sin.

JEROME

[14]"But, behold, I will raise up a nation against you,
O house of Israel,"
Says the LORD God of hosts;
"And they will afflict you from the entrance of Hamath
To the Valley of the Arabah."

Vision of the Locusts

7 Thus the Lord GOD showed me: Behold, He formed locust swarms at the beginning of the late crop; indeed *it was* the late crop after the king's mowings. [2]And so it was, when they had finished eating the grass of the land, that I said:

"O Lord GOD, forgive, I pray!
Oh, that Jacob may stand,
For he *is* small!"
[3]*So* the LORD relented concerning this.
"It shall not be," said the LORD.

Vision of the Fire

[4]Thus the Lord GOD showed me: Behold, the Lord GOD called for conflict by fire, and it consumed the great deep and devoured the territory. [5]Then I said:

"O Lord GOD, cease, I pray!
Oh, that Jacob may stand,
For he *is* small!"
[6]*So* the LORD relented concerning this.
"This also shall not be," said the Lord GOD.

Vision of the Plumb Line

[7]Thus He showed me: Behold, the Lord stood on a wall *made* with a plumb line, with a plumb line in His hand. [8]And the LORD said to me, "Amos, what do you see?"

And I said, "A plumb line."

Then the Lord said:

"Behold, I am setting a plumb line
In the midst of My people Israel;
I will not pass by them anymore.
[9]The high places of Isaac shall be desolate,
And the sanctuaries of Israel shall be laid waste.
I will rise with the sword against the house of Jeroboam."

Amaziah's Complaint

[10]Then Amaziah the priest of Bethel sent to Jeroboam king of Israel, saying, "Amos has conspired against you in the midst of the house of Israel. The land is not able to bear all his words. [11]For thus Amos has said:

'Jeroboam shall die by the sword,
And Israel shall surely be led away captive
From their own land.' "

[12]Then Amaziah said to Amos:

"Go, you seer!
Flee to the land of Judah.
There eat bread,

6:10 [a]Literally *bones* 6:13 [a]Literally *Nothing* [b]Literally *Horns,* symbol of strength

And there prophesy.
13But never again prophesy at Bethel,
For it *is* the king's sanctuary,
And it *is* the royal residence."

14Then Amos answered, and said to Amaziah:

"I *was* no prophet,
Nor *was* I a son of a prophet,
But I *was* a sheepbreeder[a]
And a tender of sycamore fruit.
15Then the LORD took me as I followed the flock,
And the LORD said to me,
'Go, prophesy to My people Israel.'
16Now therefore, hear the word of the LORD:
You say, 'Do not prophesy against Israel,
And do not spout against the house of Isaac.'

17"Therefore thus says the LORD:

'Your wife shall be a harlot in the city;
Your sons and daughters shall fall by the sword;
Your land shall be divided by *survey* line;
You shall die in a defiled land;
And Israel shall surely be led away captive
From his own land.'"

Vision of the Summer Fruit

8 Thus the Lord GOD showed me: Behold, a basket of summer fruit. 2And
He said, "Amos, what do you see?"
So I said, "A basket of summer fruit."
Then the LORD said to me:

"The end has come upon My people Israel;
I will not pass by them anymore.
3And the songs of the temple
Shall be wailing in that day,"
Says the Lord GOD—
"Many dead bodies everywhere,
They shall be thrown out in silence."

4Hear this, you who swallow up[a] the needy,
And make the poor of the land fail,

5Saying:

"When will the New Moon be past,
That we may sell grain?
And the Sabbath,
That we may trade wheat?
Making the ephah small and the shekel large,
Falsifying the scales by deceit,
6That we may buy the poor for silver,
And the needy for a pair of sandals—
Even sell the bad wheat?"

7The LORD has sworn by the pride of Jacob:
"Surely I will never forget any of their works.
8Shall the land not tremble for this,
And everyone mourn who dwells in it?
All of it shall swell like the River,[a]

7:14 [a]Compare 2 Kings 3:4 8:4 [a]Or *trample on* (compare 2:7) 8:8 [a]That is, the Nile; some Hebrew manuscripts, Septuagint, Syriac, Targum, and Vulgate read *River*; Masoretic Text reads *the light*.

8:1,2 National sins. "There are such things as national sins, and there are consequently such things as national punishments. In looking back upon the history of the world, though skeptics might entertain a doubt as to individual transgression and personal punishment, they must confess that there have been such things as national judgments sent from the hand of God. If I could take you to-day to the dreary wilderness of Babylon, I would bid you listen to the hooting of the owl, and shiver amid the lonely ruins. I would remind you that this was the throne of one of the greatest monarchies. You ask, 'And why were these people swept from off the face of the earth? Why has the palace been consumed with fire, and the beautiful city become desolate?' We can give you but one answer, that the sin of this people at last became so intolerable that from the very force of its own rottenness it crumbled to decay." *Charles Spurgeon*

Heave and subside
Like the River of Egypt.

[9]"And it shall come to pass in that day,"
says the Lord GOD,
"That I will make the sun go down at noon,
And I will darken the earth in broad daylight;
[10]I will turn your feasts into mourning,
And all your songs into lamentation;
I will bring sackcloth on every waist,
And baldness on every head;
I will make it like mourning for an only *son*,
And its end like a bitter day.

[11]"Behold, the days are coming," says the Lord GOD,
"That I will send a famine on the land,
Not a famine of bread,
Nor a thirst for water,
But of hearing the words of the LORD.
[12]They shall wander from sea to sea,
And from north to east;
They shall run to and fro, seeking the word of the LORD,
But shall not find *it*.

I want to know one thing: the way to heaven. God himself has condescended to teach me the way. He has written it down in a book. Oh, give me that book! At any price give me the book of God. Let me be a man of one book.

JOHN WESLEY

[13]"In that day the fair virgins
And strong young men
Shall faint from thirst.
[14]Those who swear by the sin[a] of Samaria,
Who say,
'As your god lives, O Dan!'
And, 'As the way of Beersheba lives!'
They shall fall and never rise again."

The Destruction of Israel

9 I saw the Lord standing by the altar, and He said:
"Strike the doorposts, that the thresholds may shake,
And break them on the heads of them all.
I will slay the last of them with the sword.
He who flees from them shall not get away,
And he who escapes from them shall not be delivered.

[2]"Though they dig into hell,[a]
From there My hand shall take them;
Though they climb up to heaven,
From there I will bring them down;
[3]And though they hide themselves on top of Carmel,
From there I will search and take them;
Though they hide from My sight at the bottom of the sea,
From there I will command the serpent, and it shall bite them;
[4]Though they go into captivity before their enemies,
From there I will command the sword,
And it shall slay them.
I will set My eyes on them for harm and not for good."

[5]The Lord GOD of hosts,
He who touches the earth and it melts,
And all who dwell there mourn;
All of it shall swell like the River,[a]
And subside like the River of Egypt.
[6]He who builds His layers in the sky,
And has founded His strata in the earth;

8:14 [a]Or *Ashima*, a Syrian goddess 9:2 [a]Or *Sheol* 9:5 [a]That is, the Nile

9:6 For a description of the hydrologic cycle, see Psa. 135:7 comment.

9:2 *Hell in the Old Testament*

By Todd Friel

When witnessing to Jewish people, it is not uncommon for them to claim that the Scriptures (specifically the Old Testament) do not talk about hell. While we must remember that the Bible is a progressive revelation—that is, more and more details and information are revealed over time—the Old Testament makes it clear that hell exists.

Sheol is the Hebrew word for the place of the dead. It can mean several things based on context: a grave or pit or the abode of the dead below the earth. Sheol is translated "grave" 31 times and is translated as "hell" 31 times in the Old Testament. Following is a sampling of verses that mention hell or describe the afterlife.

- "For a fire is kindled in My anger, and shall burn to the lowest hell; it shall consume the earth with her increase, and set on fire the foundations of the mountains." (Deut. 32:22)
- "The dead tremble, those under the waters and those inhabiting them. Sheol is naked before Him, and Destruction has no covering." (Job 26:5,6)
- "The wicked shall be turned into hell, and all the nations that forget God." (Psa. 9:17)
- "Your hand will find all Your enemies; Your right hand will find those who hate You. You shall make them as a fiery oven in the time of Your anger; the Lord shall swallow them up in His wrath, and the fire shall devour them." (Psa. 21:8,9)
- "If I ascend into heaven, You are there; If I make my bed in hell, behold, You are there." (Psa. 139:8)
- "The way of life winds upward for the wise, that he may turn away from hell below." (Prov. 15:24)
- "Hell and Destruction are never full; so the eyes of man are never satisfied." (Prov. 27:20)
- "The strong shall be as tinder, and the work of it as a spark; both will burn together, and no one shall quench them." (Isa. 1:31)
- "Therefore Sheol has enlarged itself and opened its mouth beyond measure; their glory and their multitude and their pomp, and he who is jubilant, shall descend into it." (Isa. 5:14)
- "Hell from beneath is excited about you, to meet you at your coming; it stirs up the dead for you, all the chief ones of the earth; it has raised up from their thrones all the kings of the nations." (Isa. 14:9)
- "You shall conceive chaff, you shall bring forth stubble; your breath, as fire, shall devour you. And the people shall be like the burnings of lime; like thorns cut up they shall be burned in the fire." (Isa. 33:11,12)
- "And many of those who sleep in the dust of the earth shall awake, some to everlasting life, some to shame and everlasting contempt." (Dan. 12:2)
- "Though they dig into hell, from there My hand shall take them; though they climb up to heaven, from there I will bring them down." (Amos 9:2)

While the Sadducees of the New Testament did not believe in the afterlife, the Pharisees believed in both heaven and hell and the resurrection of the dead (see Isa. 26:19).

It would be wise to memorize at least one of these verses so you can share it in your next witnessing encounter with a Jewish person.

For more scriptural details on hell, see Rev. 1:18 comment.

Who calls for the waters of the sea,
And pours them out on the face of
the earth—
The LORD is His name.

7"*Are* you not like the people of
Ethiopia to Me,
O children of Israel?" says the LORD.
"Did I not bring up Israel from the
land of Egypt,
The Philistines from Caphtor,
And the Syrians from Kir?

8"Behold, the eyes of the Lord GOD *are*
on the sinful kingdom,
And I will destroy it from the face of
the earth;
Yet I will not utterly destroy the
house of Jacob,"
Says the LORD.

9"For surely I will command,
And will sift the house of Israel
among all nations,
As *grain* is sifted in a sieve;
Yet not the smallest grain shall fall to
the ground.
10All the sinners of My people shall die

by the sword,
Who say, 'The calamity shall not
overtake nor confront us.'

Israel Will Be Restored

11"On that day I will raise up
The tabernacle[a] of David, which has
fallen down,
And repair its damages;
I will raise up its ruins,
And rebuild it as in the days of old;
12That they may possess the remnant of
Edom,[a]
And all the Gentiles who are called by
My name,"
Says the LORD who does this thing.

13"Behold, the days are coming," says
the LORD,
"When the plowman shall overtake the
reaper,
And the treader of grapes him who
sows seed;
The mountains shall drip with sweet
wine,
And all the hills shall flow *with it.*
14I will bring back the captives of My
people Israel;
They shall build the waste cities and
inhabit *them;*
They shall plant vineyards and drink
wine from them;
They shall also make gardens and eat
fruit from them.
15I will plant them in their land,
And no longer shall they be pulled up
From the land I have given them,"
Says the LORD your God.

9:11 [a]Literally *booth,* figure of a deposed dynasty **9:12** [a]Septuagint reads *mankind.*

Memorizing Scripture

It's important for all Christians to have the Word of God hidden in their hearts. However, just as with witnessing, we all know we should do it, but we often don't know how. There are a number of ways to memorize the Word of God. The following is one suggestion, and is the method I use.

On a 3×5 index card, write out the memory verse. On the top left, write a topic to categorize the verse, and on the top right, record the verse reference. Place the reference again under the verse.

Read the verse two or three times out loud. Pay attention to the sound of the verse, and listen for any helpful memory aids, such as words in alphabetical order.

As you begin to memorize the verse, say the Topic > Reference > Verse > Reference, one portion at a time. Here's an example:

God's Love
Romans 5:8
"But God demonstrates His own love"
Romans 5:8

(continued)

Memorizing Scripture (continued)

God's Love
Romans 5:8
"But God demonstrates His own love toward us"
Romans 5:8

God's Love
Romans 5:8
"But God demonstrates His own love toward us, in that while we were still sinners,"
Romans 5:8

God's Love
Romans 5:8
"But God demonstrates His own love toward us, in that while we were still sinners, Christ died for us."
Romans 5:8

God's Love Romans 5:8

"But God demonstrates His own love toward us, in that while we were still sinners, Christ died for us."

Romans 5:8

Repeat each phrase until you can correctly quote everything up to that point. Then repeat the whole thing a few more times to get it lodged in your memory. Quote it throughout the day:

God's Love
Romans 5:8
"But God demonstrates His own love toward us, in that while we were still sinners, Christ died for us."
Romans 5:8

Think about it as you lay down at night, and when you wake up in the morning.

You may also find it helpful to record, on the reverse side of the card, what the verse means to you and your meditations on the verse.

THE MOST IMPORTANT STEP: REVIEW

It's very easy to memorize Scripture. It's not quite as easy, however, to remember what you memorized last week . . . or even three days ago—not to mention what you memorized six months ago.

To help you recall them, you may want to carry about twenty verses with you. After you have begun memorizing each new verse, add it to a keyring. Review these verses daily during your quiet time, as well as when you stand in line, eat lunch, wait at a traffic light, etc.—anytime you have a free minute, you can quickly review one or two verses.

If you purchase an index card box and dividers, it will help you greatly (of course, you can make your own storage device if these are not available). Label the dividers as follows:

Sunday | Monday | Tuesday | Wednesday | Thursday | Friday | Saturday

Once you have about twenty cards on your keyring, remove the first one, which should now be well-memorized, and place it behind "Sunday." With the next verse you add to your keyring, remove the oldest, and place it behind "Monday." Do this with each new verse you add, removing the oldest, putting it in the next day of the week.

Now, every Sunday, take out the cards for "Sunday" and review them. On Monday, get the cards for "Monday." Each day of the week, you will now be reviewing the twenty verses that you carry with you, plus a new set of verses previously memorized. This will help the verses to become firmly lodged in your memory.

You may want to find a friend to help you practice reviewing your verses. As you recite each verse, your friend can make sure you say the complete verse and reference correctly.

(Reprinted from *The School of Biblical Evangelism.*)

Obadiah

1 The Coming Judgment on Edom

The vision of Obadiah.

Thus says the Lord GOD concerning
Edom
(We have heard a report from the
LORD,
And a messenger has been sent
among the nations, *saying,*
"Arise, and let us rise up against her
for battle"):

2"Behold, I will make you small among
the nations;
You shall be greatly despised.
3The pride of your heart has deceived
you,
You who dwell in the clefts of the
rock,
Whose habitation is high;
You who say in your heart, 'Who will
bring me down to the ground?'
4Though you ascend *as* high as the
eagle,
And though you set your nest among
the stars,
From there I will bring you down,"
says the LORD.

5"If thieves had come to you,
If robbers by night—
Oh, how you will be cut off!—
Would they not have stolen till they
had enough?
If grape-gatherers had come to you,
Would they not have left *some*
gleanings?

6"Oh, how Esau shall be searched out!
How his hidden treasures shall be
sought after!
7All the men in your confederacy
Shall force you to the border;
The men at peace with you
Shall deceive you *and* prevail against
you.
Those who eat your bread shall lay a
trap[a] for you.
No one is aware of it.

8"Will I not in that day," says the LORD,
"Even destroy the wise *men* from
Edom,
And understanding from the
mountains of Esau?
9Then your mighty men, O Teman,

7 [a]Or *wound,* or *plot*

1:3 Pride deceives the human heart. It stops the search for God (see Psa. 10:4) and blinds the eyes to reality. Pride makes a fool think that he is wise, as a grasshopper might think it's a giant. Pride tells a man that he is good when his heart is desperately wicked, and that he is right when the entire world can see that he is wrong. It is the root of the tree of self-righteousness. Thank God for His Law! It strips a man of the deceit of pride and humbles him by showing him the truth.

shall be dismayed,
To the end that everyone from the
mountains of Esau
May be cut off by slaughter.

Edom Mistreated His Brother

10"For violence against your brother
Jacob,
Shame shall cover you,
And you shall be cut off forever.
11In the day that you stood on the
other side—
In the day that strangers carried
captive his forces,
When foreigners entered his gates
And cast lots for Jerusalem—
Even you *were* as one of them.

12"But you should not have gazed on the
day of your brother
In the day of his captivity;[a]
Nor should you have rejoiced over
the children of Judah
In the day of their destruction;
Nor should you have spoken proudly
In the day of distress.
13You should not have entered the gate
of My people
In the day of their calamity.
Indeed, you should not have gazed
on their affliction
In the day of their calamity,
Nor laid *hands* on their substance
In the day of their calamity.
14You should not have stood at the
crossroads
To cut off those among them who
escaped;
Nor should you have delivered up
those among them who remained
In the day of distress.

15"For the day of the LORD upon all the
nations *is* near;
As you have done, it shall be done to
you;
Your reprisal shall return upon your
own head.
16For as you drank on My holy
mountain,
So shall all the nations drink
continually;
Yes, they shall drink, and swallow,
And they shall be as though they had
never been.

Israel's Final Triumph

17"But on Mount Zion there shall be
deliverance,
And there shall be holiness;
The house of Jacob shall possess their
possessions.
18The house of Jacob shall be a fire,
And the house of Joseph a flame;

12 [a]Literally *on the day he became a foreigner*

1:15 Karma. It is popular in Western culture to embrace something called "karma." Hindus, Buddhists, New Agers, and others believe in this concept of a cycle of cause and effect. It is popular because it sounds reasonable—you bear the consequences for your own actions—and seems to give an explanation for suffering. The problem with the philosophy of karma is that it is tied to the error of reincarnation. Supposedly what you did in your past life affects you now, and what you do in this life will determine your future reincarnation.

The idea of karma requires an impersonal "force" that is able to see all people everywhere, keep track of all their deeds, determine whether each is good or bad, tally the results to see if each individual should be rewarded or punished, and assign their identity in the next life. That would require an entity that is eternal, intelligent, omniscient, omnipotent, moral, fair, and just. This describes our holy, righteous Judge rather than some unknowable, impersonal, universal force.

Although the idea of karma is erroneous, we can use it as a springboard for witnessing. If you encounter people who embrace the concept, simply ask them how they are doing—are they living a good life? How do they think they will do in the next? Most believe they are doing okay. Then say, "Let's suppose that there is a heaven. Do you think you are good enough to get in? Are you a good person?" Take them through the Ten Commandments to show God's perfect standard, and then tell them about grace, repentance, and faith.

But the house of Esau *shall be* stubble;
They shall kindle them and devour
them,
And no survivor shall *remain* of the
house of Esau,"
For the LORD has spoken.

19 The South[a] shall possess the
mountains of Esau,
And the Lowland shall possess
Philistia.
They shall possess the fields of
Ephraim
And the fields of Samaria.
Benjamin *shall possess* Gilead.
20 And the captives of this host of the
children of Israel
Shall possess the land of the Canaanites
As far as Zarephath.
The captives of Jerusalem who are in
Sepharad
Shall possess the cities of the South.[a]
21 Then saviors[a] shall come to Mount
Zion
To judge the mountains of Esau,
And the kingdom shall be the LORD's.

19 [a]Hebrew *Negev* 20 [a]Hebrew *Negev* 21 [a]Or *deliverers*

1:21 "For Yours is the kingdom and the power and the glory forever" (Matt. 6:13).

Hinduism

While you may not have encountered many who follow Hinduism, you have undoubtedly heard of some of its practices. Reincarnation, yoga, meditation, and "being one with God" are all concepts of Hinduism that have influenced our culture. Back in the 1960s, The Beatles helped to popularize Hinduism by promoting Maharishi Mahesh Yogi, a spiritual guru, and through their song "My Sweet Lord." The "Lord" sung about here is not Jesus, but the Hindu deity Krishna.

BACKGROUND

Hinduism is said to be the oldest and most complex of all religious systems. (In reality, nothing is older than Christianity, which began at the moment of creation.) It is not easy to give the history of Hinduism, because it has no defined beginning and no specific founder or theology. Hinduism originated in the Indus Valley in modern Pakistan more than three thousand years ago, and now is the world's third largest religion behind Christianity and Islam. It has about 900 million adherents, with a little over a million in the U.S. and the vast majority living in India.

Hindu society is based on a "caste" system, which ranks people by their occupational class:

- *Brahmins*—priests
- *Kshatriyas*—soldiers, king-warrior class
- *Vaishyas*—merchants, farmers, laborers, craftspeople
- *Harijahns*—the "untouchables"

The higher a person's caste, the more that person is blessed with the benefits and luxuries life has to offer. Although the caste system was outlawed in 1948, it is still important to the Hindu people of India and is still recognized as the proper way to stratify society.

Hinduism actually encompasses a wide variety of religious beliefs, and has been influential in the foundations of other religions, such as Transcendental Meditation, Buddhism, and the New Age Movement. Hindus are tolerant of other religions since they believe that all paths eventually lead to God—because all is God.

KARMA

A guiding principle in Hinduism is what is known as "the law of karma"—a law of cause and effect, in which each individual creates his destiny through his thoughts, words, and deeds. Good actions will lead to good consequences, and bad actions will have the opposite effect.

Often the law of karma isn't accounted for during this life, so it carries over into future lives, trapping individuals in a cycle of reincarnation. Those who have built up a lot of bad karma may be born into a lower caste or even as an animal or insect. It may take many more lifetimes of suffering before they are again reborn as humans. Selfless acts and

(continued)

Hinduism (continued)

thoughts as well as devotion to God help one to be reborn at a higher level. This circle of birth, death, and rebirth is known as *samsara*.

Tragically, this belief in karma has great social implications. Because people are considered responsible for their current lot in life, it is believed that those who are suffering or less fortunate are just getting what they deserve based on their karma. Their present suffering helps them to atone for the evil they committed in their previous life. For this reason, charity is almost unheard of.

SCRIPTURES

There is no single source of authority, but Hinduism's vast collection of sacred text includes the following:

- *Vedas*: These four "books of knowledge" are considered the most authoritative. Compiled over about 1,000 years, with no known author, they are a collection of hymns to the various Hindu gods.
- *Upanishads*: The *Upanishads* discuss the idea that behind all gods is the one ultimate reality, Brahman.
- *Ramayana and Mahabharata*: These two epics in Hindu literature tell of the mythical incarnations of Vishnu. The *Mahabharata* ("great epic of India") is an approximately 100,000-verse poem, the most famous part of which is the *Bhagavad Gita*. The *Bhagavad Gita* is the most popular of all Hindu texts and explains how to reach Nirvana.
- *Puranas*: These contain myths, lore, and legends of the Hindu gods.

WHO IS GOD?

In one sense Hinduism is monotheistic, in that it recognizes one supreme deity known as Brahman, or ultimate reality. Brahman is the universe and all it contains; in other words, God is everything and everything is God, a belief known as pantheism. That "everything" includes us: as part of Brahman, that means we are also God. Hinduism has no concept of a personal, knowable God who is separate from His creation. Brahman alone is all that exists.

In another sense Hinduism is polytheistic, with the worship of multiple deities—though they are all considered manifestations of the one ultimate reality. Brahman is personalized as three separate entities: Brahma (the Creator), Vishnu (the Preserver), and Shiva (the Destroyer). Most Hindus also worship Krishna and Rama, two of Vishnu's ten incarnations, or *avatars*. In addition, forces of nature, animals, and humans can all be deified, giving Hindus a pantheon of 330 million gods and goddesses to worship.

WHO IS JESUS?

Hindus are happy to consider Jesus to be one of the many *avatars*, or incarnations, of the impersonal Brahman. But they do not accept Him as the *only* incarnation of God. In no sense is He the unique Son of God, part of the Triune Godhead of the Bible.

HEAVEN AND HELL

Hinduism does not teach a literal heaven and hell. The closest they come to the concept of hell is the suffering endured through numerous lifetimes on earth. The closest thing to heaven would be to lose their individual identify and be absorbed into the universal oneness.

SIN AND SALVATION

Hinduism has no concept of sin against God; instead, it teaches that man's greatest problem is his ignorance that he is God. In Hindu belief, since Brahman is all that exists, everything else is ultimately an illusion, or *maya*. Our material world, our physical bodies, and our personal existence are all illusions. In essence, then, our ignorance is equivalent to the "Fall" of man: We have forgotten that we are part of Brahman, and have attached ourselves to the desires of the individual self. It is these desires and their consequences that bring suffering, and that subject us to the law of karma.

Though there is no concept of "salvation," the goal of Hindus is to remove the karmic debt and end the cycle of rebirths. By overcoming the ignorance of their divinity and detaching from self, the individual can achieve "liberation" from the wheel of life, called *moksha*. Released from their physical, personal existence, individuals become free from all pain and suffering, and disappear into the impersonal Brahman, like a drop in the ocean.

There are three paths to achieve this liberation:

- *The Way of Works*: Liberation can be obtained through social and religious obligations.
- *The Way of Devotion*: This is the most popular way, and includes acts of worship to any of the numerous gods (*avatars*). Whether in the home or in a temple, worship is primarily done individually rather than as a congregation. Most Hindus worship daily through offerings, rituals, and prayers.
- *The Way of Knowledge*: This way attempts to reach a higher consciousness until one finally realizes his identity with Brahman. This is achieved through study of philosophical writings, yoga, and deep meditation.

HOW TO REACH A HINDU

Once again, here is another religion that is based on good works. As far as the Hindu is concerned, there is no God who warns of Judgment Day, no heaven, and no hell. So the same principle of using the Law to bring the knowledge of sin applies to Hindus.

For more information on Hinduism, see page 603.

(Adapted from *World Religions in a Nutshell*.)

Jonah

Jonah's Disobedience

1 Now the word of the LORD came to
Jonah the son of Amittai, saying,
2"Arise, go to Nineveh, that great city,
and cry out against it; for their wickedness has come up before Me." 3But Jonah
arose to flee to Tarshish from the presence of the LORD. He went down to Joppa,
and found a ship going to Tarshish; so
he paid the fare, and went down into it,
to go with them to Tarshish from the
presence of the LORD.

The Storm at Sea

4But the LORD sent out a great wind on
the sea, and there was a mighty tempest
on the sea, so that the ship was about to
be broken up.
5Then the mariners were afraid; and
every man cried out to his god, and threw
the cargo that *was* in the ship into the sea,
to lighten the load.[a] But Jonah had gone
down into the lowest parts of the ship,
had lain down, and was fast asleep.
6So the captain came to him, and said
to him, "What do you mean, sleeper?
Arise, call on your God; perhaps your
God will consider us, so that we may not
perish."
7And they said to one another, "Come,

1:5 [a]Literally *from upon them*

1:1–3 How each of us can identify with Jonah! We too have been told to "go" and speak to the world about its great wickedness that has come before God.

We may identify with the prophet, but God forbid that we should imitate him. He fled "from the presence of the Lord." A fish would do better to try to flee from the presence of the ocean. Although God may manifest Himself in certain places, it is to follow in the folly of Adam to imagine that we can run from His presence (see Gen. 3:8). God is omnipresent.

For the biblical way to confront sinners, see 2 Sam. 12:1–14 comment.

1:4,5 Mighty tempest. The storms of this life tell a thinking person that all is not well between humanity and God. The tempest of His anger sent the Genesis curse across the sea of humanity and this earthly abode. Earthquakes, hurricanes, floods, tornadoes, famine, drought, disease, and death tell us that we do not have harmony with Heaven.

It is because of death that every sensible man cries out to his god. Every civilization has a measure of faith in some god. We have yet to discover an atheistic civilization. Primitive man is ignorant, but he is not that ignorant. In his darkened mind, he worships the sun or an idol made by his hands. He practices some form of sacrifice to try to appease his god because he can see that he lives on the brink of death.

He tries through his own religious effects to "lighten the ship." But religion cannot save him from death. His own labors are not able to deliver him. It is not by any works of righteousness that we are saved, but only according to His mercy (see Eph. 2:8,9; Titus 3:5).

1:6 Until God's Law comes in the hand of the Captain of our salvation (see Heb. 2:10), we are asleep in our sins. It strikes us and says, "Awake, you who sleep, arise from the dead, and Christ will give you light" (Eph. 5:14). It is God's Law that causes the sinner to revive and makes him aware of his plight. It reveals to him that he will perish unless God intervenes with His great mercy.

let us cast lots, that we may know for
whose cause this trouble *has come* upon
us." So they cast lots, and the lot fell on
Jonah. 8Then they said to him, "Please tell
us! For whose cause *is* this trouble upon
us? What is your occupation? And where
do you come from? What is your country?
And of what people are you?"

> If you want to run from God, the devil will always provide the transportation.
>
> **DR. JERRY VINES**

9So he said to them, "I *am* a Hebrew;
and I fear the LORD, the God of heaven,
who made the sea and the dry *land.*"

Jonah Thrown into the Sea

10Then the men were exceedingly
afraid, and said to him, "Why have you
done this?" For the men knew that he fled
from the presence of the LORD, because
he had told them. 11Then they said to him,
"What shall we do to you that the sea
may be calm for us?"—for the sea was
growing more tempestuous.
12And he said to them, "Pick me up
and throw me into the sea; then the sea
will become calm for you. For I know that
this great tempest *is* because of me."
13Nevertheless the men rowed hard to
return to land, but they could not, for the
sea continued to grow more tempestuous
against them. 14Therefore they cried out
to the LORD and said, "We pray, O LORD,
please do not let us perish for this man's
life, and do not charge us with innocent
blood; for You, O LORD, have done as it
pleased You." 15So they picked up Jonah
and threw him into the sea, and the sea
ceased from its raging. 16Then the men
feared the LORD exceedingly, and offered
a sacrifice to the LORD and took vows.

Jonah's Prayer and Deliverance

17Now the LORD had prepared a great
fish to swallow Jonah. And Jonah was in
the belly of the fish three days and three
nights.

2 Then Jonah prayed to the LORD his
God from the fish's belly. 2And he said:

"I cried out to the LORD because of my
affliction,
And He answered me.

"Out of the belly of Sheol I cried,
And You heard my voice.
3For You cast me into the deep,
Into the heart of the seas,
And the floods surrounded me;
All Your billows and Your waves
passed over me.
4Then I said, 'I have been cast out of
Your sight;

1:11,12 The more we sin, the more we provoke the tempestuous wrath of Almighty God. But wonder of wonders, the Man from Nazareth said, "Pick Me up and throw Me into the sea of God's wrath." "Greater love has no one than this, than to lay down one's life for his friends" (John 15:13). The man Christ Jesus became sin for us, and in Him our sins are cast into the sea of God's forgetfulness. It is in Him that we have peace with God. The storm of God's anger is calm for all who trust in the Savior.

1:13 Even when sinful men are presented with the good news of the gospel—that they can be saved simply by God's grace through faith—many refuse to trust in the mercy of God. Their pride causes them to try to save themselves. Their guilt-ridden conscience drives them to works of righteousness that cannot save them. And the storm of God's wrath worsens.

1:14 When all hope of saving themselves is stripped from them, men will turn to the mercy of God, and trust in the One who died that they might live. They cry, "Not My will, but Yours, be done" (Luke 22:42).

1:17 Those who know God understand His incredible power and have no trouble believing this literally happened. If He so desired, God could have had Jonah swallow the big fish. *Nothing* is impossible for Him. Those whose god is limited worship an idol, and forsake the only One who can offer them mercy (see 2:8).

Jesus not only believed this happened, but He likened His time in the grave to Jonah's experience in the belly of the fish (see Matt. 12:40).

2:7 How to Pray for the Lost

by Derek Gentle

Salvation is an inside job and we are dependent upon God to do an internal heart-changing work in those for whom we are burdened . . . What are some things we can pray for them?

We can pray for God to send *conviction*, that they will sense the urgency of their need. At Pentecost, Peter's sermon was interrupted by his listeners, "Now when they heard this, they were cut to the heart, and said to Peter and the rest of the apostles, 'Men and brethren, what shall we do?'" (Acts 2:37). Conviction is when God calls us to account and shows us our fault.

We can ask God to send *enlightenment*. Paul was commissioned by God to go to the Gentiles, "To open their eyes, in order to turn them from darkness to light, and from the power of Satan to God, that they may receive forgiveness of sins and an inheritance among those who are sanctified by faith in Me" (Acts 26:18).

We can pray that God would *call* and *draw*, attracting them to Christ. While we, in our natural condition, are turned off by God, He has a way of engineering circumstances that cause us to be drawn to Him. "He called you by our gospel, for the obtaining of the glory of our Lord Jesus Christ" (2 Thess. 2:14). Jesus said, "No one can come to Me unless the Father who sent Me draws him; and I will raise him up at the last day" (John 6:44).

We can ask God to *destroy mental strongholds*, to remove the barriers between them and Christ. Being a lost person is hard work. God gives witness to Himself in powerful ways. And the person who doesn't want to turn to Christ has to defend himself against the guilt and feelings of foolishness for rejecting Him. So they build defensive walls to keep those feelings out—and to keep God from "meddling" in their lives. Some of these wall are made of intellectual rationalizations, some of the memories of bad experiences at church or with people who professed to be Christians. Some walls are made with the bricks of procrastination. But all the walls are a hardened bunker to keep God away. Prayer, however, can penetrate these walls: "The weapons with which we fight are not human weapons, but are mighty for God in overthrowing strong fortresses. For we overthrow arrogant 'reckonings,' and every stronghold that towers high in defiance of the knowledge of God, and we carry off every thought as if into slavery—into subjection to Christ" (2 Cor. 10:4,5, *Weymouth*).

Yet I will look again toward Your holy
temple.'
5The waters surrounded me, *even* to
my soul;
The deep closed around me;
Weeds were wrapped around my
head.
6I went down to the moorings of the
mountains;
The earth with its bars *closed* behind
me forever;
Yet You have brought up my life from
the pit,
O LORD, my God.

7"When my soul fainted within me,
I remembered the LORD;
And my prayer went *up* to You,
Into Your holy temple.

8"Those who regard worthless idols
Forsake their own Mercy.
9But I will sacrifice to You
With the voice of thanksgiving;
I will pay what I have vowed.
Salvation is of the LORD."

10So the LORD spoke to the fish, and it
vomited Jonah onto dry *land*.

2:2–6 Perhaps here we have insight into the sufferings of the Savior. The waters of the wrath of God encompassed Him as His soul was made an offering for sin (see Isa. 53:10). A crown of thorns was wrapped around His head as He took upon Himself the Genesis curse. Jesus Himself said that He went into the heart of the earth (Matt. 12:40), into the pit of death.

But death could not hold Him; God spoke to death and brought Jesus' soul up from the grave (v. 10; see also Acts 2:24).

2:9 Salvation is of the Lord. This is the reason we should forsake any manmade methods to attain salvation and trust solely in God for our salvation. God saves men by grace and grace alone.

QUESTIONS & OBJECTIONS

3:3,4 *"Is open-air preaching for every Christian?"*

Yes and no. Yes, if you desperately want to reach the world with the gospel. No, if you are not that desperate. Mark 16:15 is commonly called "the Great Commission," and it tells us to "Go into all the world and preach the gospel to every creature." The word "preach" means to "herald" with a raised voice. Not only did Jesus preach the gospel in the open air, but so did Paul, Stephen, Peter, Wesley, Whitefield, Spurgeon, and many others throughout Church history.

In fact, *Charles Spurgeon*, the Prince of Preachers, said, "No sort of defense is needed for preaching out-of-doors; but it would need very potent arguments to prove that a man had done his duty who has never preached beyond the walls of his meetinghouse." *John Wesley* said, "What marvel the devil does not love field-preaching! Neither do I: I love a commodious room, a soft cushion, a handsome pulpit. But where is my zeal if I do not trample all these underfoot to save one more soul?"

When I witness one-to-one, I am excited that one person is listening to the words of everlasting life. In a good open air, I can witness one-to-two hundred. How much better it is to offer the cure to death and hell to two hundred than one dying sinner. I wish every Christian could say with the apostles, "We cannot but speak the things which we have seen and heard" (Acts 4:20), to a point where they would open-air preach to those unaware that they are on their way to hell.

Jonah Preaches at Nineveh

3 Now the word of the LORD came to
Jonah the second time, saying, 2"Arise,
go to Nineveh, that great city, and preach
to it the message that I tell you." 3So Jonah
arose and went to Nineveh, according to
the word of the LORD. Now Nineveh was
an exceedingly great city, a three-day
journey[a] *in extent.* 4And Jonah began to
enter the city on the first day's walk.
Then he cried out and said, "Yet forty
days, and Nineveh shall be overthrown!"

The People of Nineveh Believe

5So the people of Nineveh believed
God, proclaimed a fast, and put on sackcloth, from the greatest to the least of
them. 6Then word came to the king of
Nineveh; and he arose from his throne
and laid aside his robe, covered *himself*
with sackcloth and sat in ashes. 7And he
caused *it* to be proclaimed and published
throughout Nineveh by the decree of the
king and his nobles, saying,

Let neither man nor beast, herd
nor flock, taste anything; do not
let them eat, or drink water. 8But
let man and beast be covered
with sackcloth, and cry mightily

3:3 [a]Exact meaning unknown

3:1,2 Don't be a chicken. My wife and I have a chicken coop, and I have noticed something interesting about the birds. They are curious creatures. They will boldly run up to see what I have in my hand. However, if I reach out to pick them up, they will cower like … chickens. They squat, spread their wings, and physically tremble (as if I was going to grab them, wring their neck, and eat them or something).

I am like a chicken. There are certain things I can boldly do, but the moment God's hand comes upon me to witness to someone, I tremble. Like Jonah, I want to flee from the presence of the Lord. What stops me from running is a mixture of compassion for the unsaved and a fear of God. How could I not obey Almighty God when He has commanded me to speak to the lost? How could I say, "World, go to hell; I couldn't care less"?

Notice what happened when Jonah ran from the presence of the Lord. God sent a great storm, and Jonah ended up being swallowed by a big fish. So I have a choice. I can disobey God and have Him chasten me with some sort of storm (Heb. 12:5,6 says He chastens those He loves), something I know from experience is not at all pleasant. Or I can obey Him and have the joy of doing what pleases Him. I choose the latter, and I far prefer the joy of the Lord to feeling down in the mouth.

Our responsibility is not only to preach the gospel, but to make sure the message we share is the one God gave us (v. 2). For details on biblical evangelism, see 2 Cor. 2:17 comment.

to God; yes, let every one turn
from his evil way and from the
violence that is in his hands.
9Who can tell *if* God will turn
and relent, and turn away from
His fierce anger, so that we may
not perish?

10Then God saw their works, that they
turned from their evil way; and God relented from the disaster that He had said
He would bring upon them, and He did
not do it.

. . . . . .

Check out "The Rush."
See Luke 16:17 comment.

. . . . . .

Jonah's Anger and God's Kindness

4 But it displeased Jonah exceedingly,
and he became angry. 2So he prayed
to the LORD, and said, "Ah, LORD, was not
this what I said when I was still in my
country? Therefore I fled previously to
Tarshish; for I know that You *are* a gracious and merciful God, slow to anger
and abundant in lovingkindness, One
who relents from doing harm. 3Therefore
now, O LORD, please take my life from me,
for *it is* better for me to die than to live!"
4Then the LORD said, "*Is it* right for
you to be angry?"
5So Jonah went out of the city and sat
on the east side of the city. There he made
himself a shelter and sat under it in the
shade, till he might see what would become of the city. 6And the LORD God prepared a plant[a] and made it come up over
Jonah, that it might be shade for his head
to deliver him from his misery. So Jonah
was very grateful for the plant. 7But as
morning dawned the next day God prepared a worm, and it *so* damaged the
plant that it withered. 8And it happened,
when the sun arose, that God prepared a
vehement east wind; and the sun beat on
Jonah's head, so that he grew faint. Then
he wished death for himself, and said, "*It*
is better for me to die than to live."
9Then God said to Jonah, "*Is it* right
for you to be angry about the plant?"
And he said, "*It is* right for me to be
angry, even to death!"
10But the LORD said, "You have had
pity on the plant for which you have not
labored, nor made it grow, which came
up in a night and perished in a night.
11And should I not pity Nineveh, that great
city, in which are more than one hundred
and twenty thousand persons who cannot discern between their right hand and
their left—and much livestock?"

4:6 [a]Hebrew *kikayon*, exact identity unknown

3:5 True belief produces repentance. The people of Nineveh *believed* God, and the genuineness of their belief in Him produced the evident works of repentance (v. 10). Measure the faith of those you have witnessed to by asking, "Do you believe what you have just heard?" If they say they don't, question what part didn't make sense. If they say they do believe it, ask where they would go if they were to die in their sins. If they say, "Heaven," ask, "Why?" It is usually because they are still clinging to self-righteousness and you need to go back with the axe of the Law and chop out that root. If they say, "Hell," ask what they are going to do about it. They will usually say, "Pray, and change my ways," so repeat what you have told them: "Repent and trust in Jesus." If they agree, ask, "When are you going to do that?" You want them to see the urgency. *Today* is the day of salvation (see 2 Cor. 6:2).

3:7,8 May our King, too, cause the good news of the gospel to be proclaimed and published throughout this world. This should be our constant prayer—that God will raise up and send forth messengers who will call people to turn from their evil ways. Repentance from sin is more important than food or drink. (See also John 4:34; Luke 24:47.)

3:10 For whether God "repented" or changed His mind, see Jer. 18:8 comment.

4:1,2 Bitterness, jealousy, and resentment steal our joy. They do to the soul what rust does to steel. How much better is it to be filled with a love that rejoices when good things happen to other people?

"Humility will show up in my life by how I show an interest in others." *Bruce Garner*

Worldly Guests

Do you remember what it was like to fly before smoking was banned on airplanes? It was horrible. Breathing recycled air was bad enough without having to endure second-hand smoke. Of course, the airlines provided a smoking "section": smokers were confined to the back five rows. Unfortunately, the smoke was not.

Don't ever be deceived into thinking that you can allow the pollution of the world to enter your home and not contaminate your family. You won't be able to confine it. Someone sent me an article by Jeremy Archer in which he spoke of having allowed some worldly guests to enter his home. While their behavior was questionable, they entertained his family, and he justified the friendship by saying that Jesus was accused of being a friend of sinners. Sometimes the conversations revolved around drinking, violence, drugs, the occult, sex, theft, lying, and other vices. But he said that they justified it because it was all discussed in an entertaining manner.

Their guests were having a growing influence on his family. As time passed, the behavior grew worse. Then people began partying, making obscene gestures, and even started having sex right in front of him and his family. As I read the article I remember thinking, *How could he let this happen... in front of his family! How could he be looking at them!* Then I read the final words of the article. He concluded, "Together we turned off the television."

So many professing Christians allow their families to be polluted in the name of entertainment. Some Christians, realizing how their children are being affected, get rid of the TV altogether. Others learn the art of self-control, and then control the remote control. Whatever you do, *be in control*. If you have the liberty to watch television, make sure you watch only that which is governed by Phil. 4:8:

> ...whatever things are true, whatever things are noble, whatever things are just, whatever things are pure, whatever things are lovely, whatever things are of good report, if there is any virtue and if there is anything praiseworthy—meditate on these things.

Even then, you may leave your kids watching a wholesome program, but the inserted advertisements may be filthy. So be extra careful that the world doesn't corrupt them through this means. When the mud flows, shut the door.

The world says that you can't shelter your children from wickedness. While that may be true, you can certainly give it a good try. What sort of parents would let their children roam around outside knowing that vicious dogs were loose in the area? It's your responsibility to protect them. That doesn't mean your children become monks in a monastery. It simply means that, as their parents, you keep them away from those things that you know will harm them. God sees innocence as a virtue, not a vice, so keep your children innocent toward that which is evil (Rom. 16:19). The Bible instructs us to set nothing wicked before our eyes (Psa. 101:3), and to not do anything that would cause anyone—especially a child—to stumble. Are you careful to monitor the types of entertainment that come into your home?

That includes keeping a very close watch on the music you allow your children to have—even professed Christian music. Much of it simply comes from the world's musicians who have seen big bucks in gospel music. They have tossed a few clichés and the name of Jesus into their music, and naïve Christians buy into it and let their children feed on it.

Most kids spend several hours a day being influenced by television and music. One way to keep your children from spending much time indulging in questionable entertainment is to give them responsibilities around the home. This will also prepare them for the real world that they will have to face.

Also be aware of the types of friends your children have. If they are from non-Christian families, make sure your kids are influencing them with the gospel, rather than them influencing your children with the things of the world. Peer pressure can greatly sway kids when it comes to musical tastes, fashions, attitudes toward drugs, sex, etc. This is why you need a good, communicative relationship with them. Ask your children what their friends talk about and what they believe. Pray with them for their friends' salvation.

Remember, it is the Christian parents' responsibility to bring up their children in the training and admonition of the Lord (Eph. 6:4). Be sure you protect your children from all ungodly influences—both inside your home and out.

(Adapted from *How to Bring Your Children to Christ... & Keep Them There*.)

Micah

1 The word of the LORD that came to
Micah of Moresheth in the days of
Jotham, Ahaz, *and* Hezekiah, kings of
Judah, which he saw concerning Samaria
and Jerusalem.

The Coming Judgment on Israel

2 Hear, all you peoples!
Listen, O earth, and all that is in it!
Let the Lord GOD be a witness against you,
The Lord from His holy temple.

3 For behold, the LORD is coming out of His place;
He will come down
And tread on the high places of the earth.
4 The mountains will melt under Him,
And the valleys will split
Like wax before the fire,
Like waters poured down a steep place.
5 All this is for the transgression of Jacob
And for the sins of the house of Israel.
What *is* the transgression of Jacob?
Is it not Samaria?
And what *are* the high places of Judah?
Are they not Jerusalem?

6 "Therefore I will make Samaria a heap of ruins in the field,
Places for planting a vineyard;
I will pour down her stones into the valley,
And I will uncover her foundations.
7 All her carved images shall be beaten to pieces,
And all her pay as a harlot shall be burned with the fire;
All her idols I will lay desolate,
For she gathered *it* from the pay of a harlot,
And they shall return to the pay of a harlot."

Mourning for Israel and Judah

8 Therefore I will wail and howl,
I will go stripped and naked;
I will make a wailing like the jackals
And a mourning like the ostriches,
9 For her wounds *are* incurable.

1:1–4 A witness against you. Notice the word "let" in v. 2. Those who allow God to speak to them will understand that He has witnessed every transgression of His Law. Those who refuse to hear will eventually find to their horror that He has witnessed every secret sin, but by then it will be too late to partake in His mercy. They will see Him when He comes in flaming fire and will drink the wine of His wrath. How we must meditate on verses that warn us of that day, when mountains will melt under Him and great valleys will split like wax before a fire, like waters pouring down a steep place. In light of these thoughts, do we plead with sinners? Are we horrified at their fate? Do our eyes run with water as we pray for them? If they don't, it may be because we have never truly meditated on the terror they will face at the coming of Almighty God.

For it has come to Judah;
It has come to the gate of My people—
To Jerusalem.

10Tell *it* not in Gath,
Weep not at all;
In Beth Aphrah[a]
Roll yourself in the dust.
11Pass by in naked shame, you inhabitant of Shaphir;
The inhabitant of Zaanan[a] does not go out.
Beth Ezel mourns;
Its place to stand is taken away from you.

Most Christian ministries would like to send their recruits to Bible college for five years. I would like to send our recruits to hell for five minutes. That would do more than anything else to prepare them for a lifetime of compassionate ministry.

WILLIAM BOOTH

12For the inhabitant of Maroth pined[a] for good,
But disaster came down from the LORD
To the gate of Jerusalem.
13O inhabitant of Lachish,
Harness the chariot to the swift steeds
(She *was* the beginning of sin to the daughter of Zion),
For the transgressions of Israel were found in you.

14Therefore you shall give presents to Moresheth Gath;[a]
The houses of Achzib[b] *shall be* a lie to the kings of Israel.
15I will yet bring an heir to you, O inhabitant of Mareshah;[a]
The glory of Israel shall come to Adullam.
16Make yourself bald and cut off your hair,
Because of your precious children;
Enlarge your baldness like an eagle,
For they shall go from you into captivity.

Woe to Evildoers

2 Woe to those who devise iniquity,
And work out evil on their beds!
At morning light they practice it,
Because it is in the power of their hand.
2They covet fields and take *them* by violence,
Also houses, and seize *them*.
So they oppress a man and his house,
A man and his inheritance.

3Therefore thus says the LORD:

"Behold, against this family I am devising disaster,
From which you cannot remove your necks;
Nor shall you walk haughtily,
For this *is* an evil time.
4In that day *one* shall take up a proverb against you,
And lament with a bitter lamentation, saying:
'We are utterly destroyed!
He has changed the heritage of my people;
How He has removed *it* from me!
To a turncoat He has divided our fields.' "

5Therefore you will have no one to de-

1:10 [a]Literally *House of Dust* 1:11 [a]Literally *Going Out* 1:12 [a]Literally *was sick* 1:14 [a]Literally *Possession of Gath* [b]Literally *Lie* 1:15 [a]Literally *Inheritance*

2:1–3 How this passage speaks of Hollywood, where evil men dig into the depths of their imaginations and make it a reality through their profession. They have the power in their hand to encourage violence in the land and to destroy the family unit by glamorizing adultery. They don't understand that God will bring upon them the fruit of their sin.

termine boundaries[a] by lot
In the assembly of the LORD.

Lying Prophets

6"Do not prattle," *you say to those* who prophesy.
So they shall not prophesy to you;[a]
They shall not return insult for insult.[b]
7*You who are* named the house of Jacob:
"Is the Spirit of the LORD restricted?
Are these His doings?
Do not My words do good
To him who walks uprightly?
8"Lately My people have risen up as an enemy—
You pull off the robe with the garment
From those who trust *you,* as they pass by,
Like men returned from war.
9The women of My people you cast out
From their pleasant houses;
From their children
You have taken away My glory forever.

10"Arise and depart,
For this *is* not *your* rest;
Because it is defiled, it shall destroy,
Yes, with utter destruction.
11If a man should walk in a false spirit
And speak a lie, *saying,*
'I will prophesy to you of wine and drink,'
Even he would be the prattler of this people.

Israel Restored

12"I will surely assemble all of you, O Jacob,
I will surely gather the remnant of Israel;
I will put them together like sheep of the fold,[a]
Like a flock in the midst of their pasture;
They shall make a loud noise because of *so many* people.
13The one who breaks open will come up before them;
They will break out,
Pass through the gate,
And go out by it;
Their king will pass before them,
With the LORD at their head."

Wicked Rulers and Prophets

3 And I said:

"Hear now, O heads of Jacob,
And you rulers of the house of Israel:
Is it not for you to know justice?
2You who hate good and love evil;
Who strip the skin from My people,[a]
And the flesh from their bones;
3Who also eat the flesh of My people,
Flay their skin from them,
Break their bones,
And chop *them* in pieces
Like *meat* for the pot,
Like flesh in the caldron."

4Then they will cry to the LORD,
But He will not hear them;
He will even hide His face from them at that time,
Because they have been evil in their deeds.

5Thus says the LORD concerning the prophets
Who make my people stray;
Who chant "Peace"
While they chew with their teeth,
But who prepare war against him
Who puts nothing into their mouths:
6"Therefore you shall have night without vision,
And you shall have darkness without divination;
The sun shall go down on the prophets,
And the day shall be dark for them.

2:5 [a]Literally *one casting a surveyor's line* 2:6 [a]Literally *to these* [b]Vulgate reads *He shall not take shame.* 2:12 [a]Hebrew *Bozrah* 3:2 [a]Literally *them*

[7]So the seers shall be ashamed,
And the diviners abashed;
Indeed they shall all cover their lips;
For *there is* no answer from God."

[8]But truly I am full of power by the
Spirit of the LORD,
And of justice and might,
To declare to Jacob his transgression
And to Israel his sin.
[9]Now hear this,
You heads of the house of Jacob
And rulers of the house of Israel,
Who abhor justice
And pervert all equity,
[10]Who build up Zion with bloodshed
And Jerusalem with iniquity:
[11]Her heads judge for a bribe,
Her priests teach for pay,
And her prophets divine for money.
Yet they lean on the LORD, and say,
"Is not the LORD among us?
No harm can come upon us."
[12]Therefore because of you
Zion shall be plowed *like* a field,
Jerusalem shall become heaps of
ruins,
And the mountain of the temple[a]
Like the bare hills of the forest.

The Lord's Reign in Zion

4 Now it shall come to pass in the latter days
That the mountain of the LORD's house
Shall be established on the top of the
mountains,
And shall be exalted above the hills;
And peoples shall flow to it.
[2]Many nations shall come and say,
"Come, and let us go up to the
mountain of the LORD,
To the house of the God of Jacob;
He will teach us His ways,
And we shall walk in His paths."
For out of Zion the law shall go forth,
And the word of the LORD from
Jerusalem.
[3]He shall judge between many
peoples,
And rebuke strong nations afar off;
They shall beat their swords into
plowshares,
And their spears into pruning hooks;
Nation shall not lift up sword against
nation,
Neither shall they learn war
anymore.[a]

[4]But everyone shall sit under his vine
and under his fig tree,
And no one shall make *them* afraid;
For the mouth of the LORD of hosts
has spoken.
[5]For all people walk each in the name
of his god,
But we will walk in the name of the
LORD our God
Forever and ever.

Zion's Future Triumph

[6]"In that day," says the LORD,
"I will assemble the lame,
I will gather the outcast
And those whom I have afflicted;

3:12 [a]Literally *house* 4:3 [a]Compare Isaiah 2:2–4

3:8 Power to witness. Jesus said that when we receive the Holy Spirit, we receive power (see Acts 1:8). Why have we been given this power? To speak against sin and be witnesses to Jesus' saving grace. We are to declare to the world the Law that God gave to Moses, which measures how all have sinned against God. Sin cannot be understood in truth until we realize that we are transgressors (see Rom. 7:7; 1 John 3:4). Any knowledge of sin, without the light of God's Law, will be shallow. It is God's Law that shows sin to be exceedingly sinful (see Rom. 7:13).

4:1–5 What an unspeakable treasure we have in the Scriptures. God has given us a Book that explains our origins, the nature of our Creator, the reason for our existence, why we die, and the antidote to that terrible dilemma—it shows us how to live forever. In addition, God Himself tells us what will happen in the future.

Peace among the nations, which has been but a dream for millennia, will be reality in the coming kingdom, where all men will have peace with God and with each other.

7 I will make the lame a remnant,
And the outcast a strong nation;
So the LORD will reign over them in
Mount Zion
From now on, even forever.
8 And you, O tower of the flock,
The stronghold of the daughter of
Zion,
To you shall it come,
Even the former dominion shall come,
The kingdom of the daughter of
Jerusalem."

9 Now why do you cry aloud?
Is there no king in your midst?
Has your counselor perished?
For pangs have seized you like a
woman in labor.
10 Be in pain, and labor to bring forth,
O daughter of Zion,
Like a woman in birth pangs.
For now you shall go forth from the
city,
You shall dwell in the field,
And to Babylon you shall go.
There you shall be delivered;
There the LORD will redeem you
From the hand of your enemies.

11 Now also many nations have
gathered against you,
Who say, "Let her be defiled,
And let our eye look upon Zion."
12 But they do not know the thoughts of
the LORD,
Nor do they understand His counsel;
For He will gather them like sheaves
to the threshing floor.

13 "Arise and thresh, O daughter of Zion;
For I will make your horn iron,
And I will make your hooves bronze;
You shall beat in pieces many
peoples;
I will consecrate their gain to the LORD,
And their substance to the Lord of the
whole earth."

5 Now gather yourself in troops,
O daughter of troops;
He has laid siege against us;
They will strike the judge of Israel
with a rod on the cheek.

The Coming Messiah

2 "But you, Bethlehem Ephrathah,
Though you are little among the
thousands of Judah,
Yet out of you shall come forth to Me
The One to be Ruler in Israel,
Whose goings forth *are* from of old,
From everlasting."

3 Therefore He shall give them up,
Until the time *that* she who is in labor
has given birth;
Then the remnant of His brethren
Shall return to the children of Israel.
4 And He shall stand and feed *His flock*
In the strength of the LORD,
In the majesty of the name of the
LORD His God;
And they shall abide,
For now He shall be great
To the ends of the earth;
5 And this *One* shall be peace.

Judgment on Israel's Enemies

When the Assyrian comes into our
land,

5:2 Fulfilled prophecy. This prophecy of the Messiah's birthplace was fulfilled in Luke 2:4–7. See also Matt. 2:4–6; John 7:42.

The evidence of biblical prophecy has been a key to unlock the door to many a skeptic. Those who take the time to study messianic and other prophecies, *knowing that the dates of the Old Testament Scriptures can be authenticated*, can only come away with the knowledge that the Bible is a supernatural Book. However, always keep in mind that knowledge of the Bible's inspiration will not in itself bring a sinner to the foot of the cross. There must also be a knowledge of sin, which comes by the moral Law (see Rom. 7:7,13). This is why the apostle Paul "explained and solemnly testified of the kingdom of God, persuading them concerning Jesus from both the Law of Moses and the Prophets" (Acts 28:23).

And when he treads in our palaces,
Then we will raise against him
Seven shepherds and eight princely
men.
6They shall waste with the sword the
land of Assyria,
And the land of Nimrod at its
entrances;
Thus He shall deliver *us* from the
Assyrian,
When he comes into our land
And when he treads within our
borders.

7Then the remnant of Jacob
Shall be in the midst of many peoples,
Like dew from the LORD,
Like showers on the grass,
That tarry for no man
Nor wait for the sons of men.
8And the remnant of Jacob
Shall be among the Gentiles,
In the midst of many peoples,
Like a lion among the beasts of the
forest,
Like a young lion among flocks of
sheep,
Who, if he passes through,
Both treads down and tears in pieces,
And none can deliver.
9Your hand shall be lifted against your
adversaries,
And all your enemies shall be cut off.

10"And it shall be in that day," says the
LORD,
"That I will cut off your horses from
your midst
And destroy your chariots.
11I will cut off the cities of your land
And throw down all your
strongholds.
12I will cut off sorceries from your hand,
And you shall have no soothsayers.
13Your carved images I will also cut off,
And your sacred pillars from your
midst;
You shall no more worship the work
of your hands;
14I will pluck your wooden images[a]
from your midst;
Thus I will destroy your cities.
15And I will execute vengeance in anger
and fury
On the nations that have not heard."[a]

God Pleads with Israel

6 Hear now what the LORD says:

"Arise, plead your case before the
mountains,
And let the hills hear your voice.
2Hear, O you mountains, the LORD's
complaint,
And you strong foundations of the
earth;
For the LORD has a complaint against
His people,
And He will contend with Israel.

3"O My people, what have I done to
you?
And how have I wearied you?
Testify against Me.
4For I brought you up from the land
of Egypt,

5:14 [a]Hebrew *Asherim*, Canaanite deities 5:15 [a]Or *obeyed*

5:13 Many modern cultures worship graven images, which are anything that is venerated—whether it is an image of a rat, a Buddha, Mary, dead "saints," or even an icon of Jesus on the cross. For those who would disagree with such thoughts, read carefully Exod. 20:4,5. The Ten Commandments couldn't make it any clearer that we are not to bow down to any image. God alone is to be worshiped. It is a tragedy that the Roman Catholic church removed the Second Commandant from their catechism and split the Tenth Commandment into two to hide the fact that it is missing. For details, see page 1810.

6:3–5 The Bible says that man hates God without cause (see John 15:25). When bad things happen, many people put God on trial for His perceived "transgressions," but they neglect to acknowledge His great kindness and provision. Any time we feel the urge to complain about our circumstances, we need to remember that we have been redeemed from our bondage to sin.

I redeemed you from the house of
bondage;
And I sent before you Moses, Aaron,
and Miriam.
5O My people, remember now
What Balak king of Moab counseled,
And what Balaam the son of Beor
answered him,
From Acacia Grove[a] to Gilgal,
That you may know the righteousness
of the LORD."

6With what shall I come before the
LORD,
And bow myself before the High God?
Shall I come before Him with burnt
offerings,
With calves a year old?
7Will the LORD be pleased with
thousands of rams,
Ten thousand rivers of oil?
Shall I give my firstborn *for* my
transgression,
The fruit of my body *for* the sin of my
soul?

8He has shown you, O man, what *is*
good;
And what does the LORD require of
you
But to do justly,
To love mercy,
And to walk humbly with your God?

Punishment of Israel's Injustice

9The LORD's voice cries to the city—
Wisdom shall see Your name:

"Hear the rod!
Who has appointed it?
10Are there yet the treasures of
wickedness
In the house of the wicked,
And the short measure *that is* an
abomination?
11Shall I count pure *those* with the
wicked scales,
And with the bag of deceitful weights?
12For her rich men are full of violence,
Her inhabitants have spoken lies,
And their tongue is deceitful in their
mouth.

13"Therefore I will also make *you* sick by
striking you,
By making *you* desolate because of
your sins.
14You shall eat, but not be satisfied;
Hunger[a] *shall be* in your midst.
You may carry *some* away,[b] but shall
not save *them;*
And what you do rescue I will give
over to the sword.

15"You shall sow, but not reap;
You shall tread the olives, but not
anoint yourselves with oil;
And *make* sweet wine, but not drink
wine.
16For the statutes of Omri are kept;
All the works of Ahab's house *are done;*
And you walk in their counsels,
That I may make you a desolation,
And your inhabitants a hissing.
Therefore you shall bear the reproach
of My people."[a]

Sorrow for Israel's Sins

7 Woe is me!
For I am like those who gather summer fruits,
Like those who glean vintage grapes;
There is no cluster to eat
Of the first-ripe fruit *which* my soul

6:5 [a]Hebrew *Shittim* (compare Numbers 25:1; Joshua 2:1; 3:1) 6:14 [a]Or *Emptiness* or *Humiliation* [b]Targum and Vulgate read *You shall take hold.* 6:16 [a]Following Masoretic Text, Targum, and Vulgate; Septuagint reads *of nations.*

6:6,7 God does not want our sacrifices. He wants us to present *ourselves* as living sacrifices (see Rom. 12:1).

6:8 Rather than do what is good and walk in humility with God, sinners walk away from Him in prideful rebellion. The cross of Jesus is the great expression of God doing justly and loving mercy, so that we could walk humbly with Him. See 7:18.

"Does a friend or family member need to be told that God is a God of justice? . . . Lovingly warn someone who has not acted justly that God judges those who do wrong."

Bill Bright

desires.
[2]The faithful *man* has perished from the earth,
And *there is* no one upright among men.
They all lie in wait for blood;
Every man hunts his brother with a net.

[3]That they may successfully do evil with both hands—
The prince asks *for gifts,*
The judge *seeks* a bribe,
And the great *man* utters his evil desire;
So they scheme together.
[4]The best of them *is* like a brier;
The most upright *is sharper* than a thorn hedge;
The day of your watchman and your punishment comes;
Now shall be their perplexity.

[5]Do not trust in a friend;
Do not put your confidence in a companion;
Guard the doors of your mouth
From her who lies in your bosom.
[6]For son dishonors father,
Daughter rises against her mother,
Daughter-in-law against her mother-in-law;
A man's enemies *are* the men of his own household.
[7]Therefore I will look to the LORD;
I will wait for the God of my salvation;
My God will hear me.

Israel's Confession and Comfort

[8]Do not rejoice over me, my enemy;
When I fall, I will arise;
When I sit in darkness,
The LORD *will be* a light to me.
[9]I will bear the indignation of the LORD,
Because I have sinned against Him,
Until He pleads my case
And executes justice for me.

7:6 Jesus quoted this verse in regard to the persecution that comes to those who live godly in Christ Jesus (see Matt. 10:35,36; Luke 12:53). The gospel is a sword that divides us from this evil world. When someone becomes a Christian, he is like an ex-criminal who has become a police officer. He has betrayed the evil cause of this world and sided with the opposition. However, when friends and family turn against us, we have the strong consolation that God is our Father. He will lift us up when we fall and be a light to us in the darkest of hours (see vv. 7,8).

7:9 He executes justice. God's anger against our sins is not only justified, it should be expected if God is good by nature. No judge in a civil court would be considered a "good" judge if he allowed crimes to go unpunished. If he is good, he *must* see that justice is done, and if God is perfectly good, He must see that perfect justice is carried out on the Day of Wrath. The demands of a perfect, unbending Law leave every one of us in terrible trouble. Who of us hasn't lusted and therefore violated the Seventh Commandment (see Matt. 5:27,28)? Who hasn't borne false witness, stolen, etc.? The Law leaves us guilty and "brings about wrath" (see Rom. 4:15), and it is that knowledge that drives us to the cross. See also Luke 15:21 comment.

He will bring me forth to the light;
I will see His righteousness.
10Then *she who is* my enemy will see,
And shame will cover her who said to me,
"Where is the LORD your God?"
My eyes will see her;
Now she will be trampled down
Like mud in the streets.

From beginning to ending, there is not a word or syllable or revelation in the Word of God that has contradicted, or ever will contradict, any true, substantiated scientific fact.

W. A. CRISWELL

11*In* the day when your walls are to be built,
In that day the decree shall go far and wide.[a]
12*In* that day they[a] shall come to you
From Assyria and the fortified cities,[b]
From the fortress[c] to the River,[d]
From sea to sea,
And mountain *to* mountain.
13Yet the land shall be desolate
Because of those who dwell in it,
And for the fruit of their deeds.

God Will Forgive Israel

14Shepherd Your people with Your staff,
The flock of Your heritage,
Who dwell solitarily *in* a woodland,
In the midst of Carmel;
Let them feed *in* Bashan and Gilead,
As in days of old.

15"As in the days when you came out of the land of Egypt,
I will show them[a] wonders."

16The nations shall see and be ashamed of all their might;
They shall put *their* hand over *their* mouth;
Their ears shall be deaf.
17They shall lick the dust like a serpent;
They shall crawl from their holes like snakes of the earth.
They shall be afraid of the LORD our God,
And shall fear because of You.
18Who *is* a God like You,
Pardoning iniquity
And passing over the transgression of the remnant of His heritage?

He does not retain His anger forever,
Because He delights *in* mercy.
19He will again have compassion on us,
And will subdue our iniquities.

You will cast all our[a] sins
Into the depths of the sea.
20You will give truth to Jacob
And mercy to Abraham,
Which You have sworn to our fathers
From days of old.

7:11 [a]Or *the boundary shall be extended* 7:12 [a]Literally *he,* collective of the captives [b]Hebrew *arey mazor,* possibly *cities of Egypt* [c]Hebrew *mazor*, possibly *Egypt* [d]That is, the Euphrates 7:15 [a]Literally *him,* collective for the captives 7:19 [a]Literally *their*

7:18 Bible contradiction? Skeptics argue that some verses say God's anger does not last forever (Psa. 30:5; Jer. 3:12; Mic. 7:18), contradicting others that say God's anger lasts forever (Jer. 17:4; Matt. 25:46).

There are two types of God's anger mentioned in these verses. The first is a reference to His temporal anger against sin. Because He is merciful, He forgives those who turn to Him in true repentance. For example, in Jer. 3:11–13 God is speaking to sinful Israel: "I will not remain angry forever. Only acknowledge your iniquity, that you have transgressed against the LORD your God." However, Matt. 25:46 is a fearful reference to those who are the damned—those who refuse to repent and therefore die in their sins. One is a temporal anger, the other is eternal.

Optical Illusions

Seeing is believing?

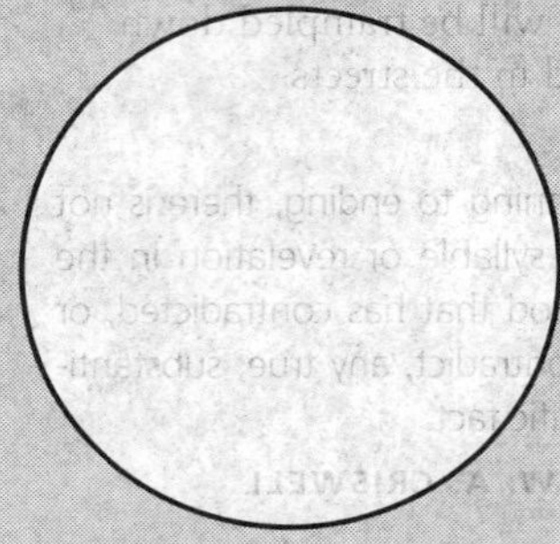

1. Stare intently at the four dots in the center of the left image for 40 seconds. Then stare at the empty circle for 30 seconds.

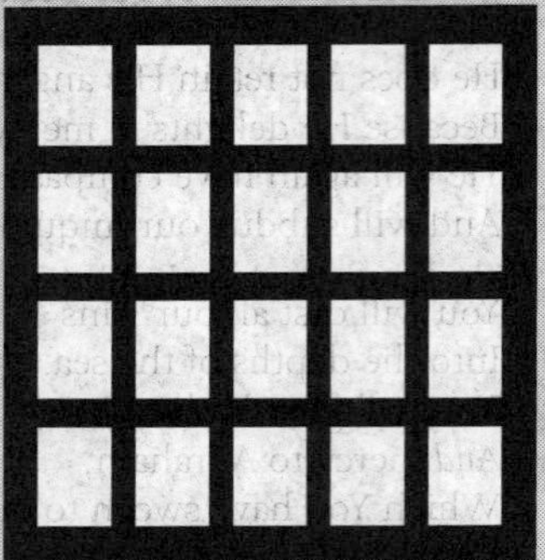

2. Are there dots between the white boxes?

3. How many "prongs" —two or three?

4. The distance of the line to the left of the arrow is the same as the distance to the right.

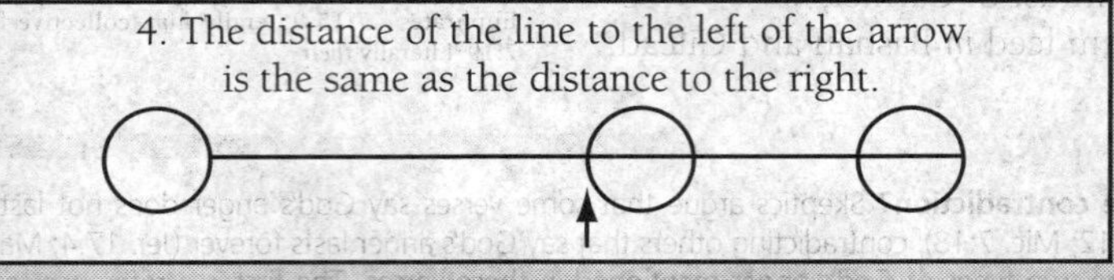

The Atheist Test: Imagine a circle represents all the knowledge in the universe (someone who had all knowledge would know every hair on every head, every thought of every heart, every grain of sand, every event in human history, etc.). Let's surmise that you know an incredible 1 percent of all knowledge. Is it possible that, in the 99 percent of the knowledge you haven't yet come across, there is ample evidence to prove that God does exist?

(See John 20:25 comment.)

Nahum

1 The burden[a] against Nineveh. The
book of the vision of Nahum the Elko-
shite.

God's Wrath on His Enemies

2God *is* jealous, and the LORD avenges;
The LORD avenges and *is* furious.
The LORD will take vengeance on His
adversaries,
And He reserves *wrath* for His
enemies;
3The LORD *is* slow to anger and great
in power,
And will not at all acquit *the wicked.*

The LORD has His way
In the whirlwind and in the storm,
And the clouds *are* the dust of His
feet.
4He rebukes the sea and makes it dry,
And dries up all the rivers.
Bashan and Carmel wither,
And the flower of Lebanon wilts.
5The mountains quake before Him,
The hills melt,
And the earth heaves[a] at His
presence,
Yes, the world and all who dwell in it.

6Who can stand before His
indignation?
And who can endure the fierceness of
His anger?
His fury is poured out like fire,
And the rocks are thrown down by
Him.

1:1 [a]Or *oracle* 1:5 [a]Targum reads *burns.*

1:2–6 The attributes of God. Here is a revelation of God's divine attributes. He is jealous. He takes vengeance. He becomes furious and wrath-filled. Yet, our all-powerful God is also slow to anger. He holds back His terrible wrath because He is rich in mercy (see Eph. 2:4). He is not willing that any perish (see 2 Pet. 3:9), but warns that He will by no means acquit the wicked. He not only gives us His word that justice will be done, but reason also demands it. It is reasonable that murderers, rapists, thieves, etc., be punished. If His creation—massive mountains, tremendous winds, vast seas and rivers—bows at His presence, how much more will sinful man be subject to His power? No one can stand before His indignation. See also Num. 14:18 comment. For how the moral Law reflects God's character, see page 280.

"Learn ye, my friends, to look upon God as being as severe in His justice as if He were not loving, and yet as loving as if He were not severe. His love does not diminish His justice, nor does His justice, in the least degree, make warfare upon His love. The two things are sweetly linked together in the atonement of Christ. But, mark, we can never understand the fullness of the atonement till we have first grasped the Scriptural truth of God's immense justice. There was never an ill word spoken, nor an ill thought conceived, nor an evil deed done, for which God will not have punishment from some one or another. He will either have satisfaction from you, or else from Christ. If you have no atonement to bring through Christ, you must for ever lie paying the debt which you never can pay, in eternal misery; for as surely as God is God, He will sooner lose His Godhead than suffer one sin to go unpunished, or one particle of rebellion unrevenged." *Charles Spurgeon*

[7]The LORD *is* good,
A stronghold in the day of trouble;
And He knows those who trust in Him.
[8]But with an overflowing flood
He will make an utter end of its place,
And darkness will pursue His
enemies.

[9]What do you conspire against the
LORD?
He will make an utter end *of it*.
Affliction will not rise up a second
time.
[10]For while tangled *like* thorns,
And while drunken *like* drunkards,
They shall be devoured like stubble
fully dried.
[11]From you comes forth *one*
Who plots evil against the LORD,
A wicked counselor.

[12]Thus says the LORD:

"Though *they are* safe, and likewise
many,
Yet in this manner they will be cut
down
When he passes through.
Though I have afflicted you,
I will afflict you no more;
[13]For now I will break off his yoke
from you,
And burst your bonds apart."

[14]The LORD has given a command
concerning you:
"Your name shall be perpetuated no
longer.
Out of the house of your gods
I will cut off the carved image and the
molded image.
I will dig your grave,
For you are vile."

[15]Behold, on the mountains
The feet of him who brings good
tidings,
Who proclaims peace!
O Judah, keep your appointed feasts,
Perform your vows.
For the wicked one shall no more
pass through you;
He is utterly cut off.

The Destruction of Nineveh

2 He who scatters[a] has come up be-
fore your face.
Man the fort!
Watch the road!
Strengthen *your* flanks!
Fortify *your* power mightily.

[2]For the LORD will restore the
excellence of Jacob
Like the excellence of Israel,
For the emptiers have emptied them
out
And ruined their vine branches.

[3]The shields of his mighty men *are*
made red,
The valiant men *are* in scarlet.
The chariots *come* with flaming
torches
In the day of his preparation,
And the spears are brandished.[a]
[4]The chariots rage in the streets,
They jostle one another in the broad
roads;

2:1 [a]Vulgate reads *He who destroys.* 2:3 [a]Literally *the cypresses are shaken;* Septuagint and Syriac read *the horses rush about;* Vulgate reads *the drivers are stupefied.*

1:7 It was God's goodness that provided Jesus' sacrifice on the cross, and that is our stronghold in the day of trouble. Through trust in Him, wicked men are not merely acquitted, but are justified and made righteous before God.

1:9 See Psa. 2 for the foolishness of conspiring against the Lord.

1:15 Where are your feet taking you? As God's people, we should be going into all the world, declaring the good news to the lost so they too can have peace with God. God sees as beautiful the lowly feet of those who preach His glorious gospel. See Isa. 52:7 comment and Rom. 10:15.

They seem like torches,
They run like lightning.

[5]He remembers his nobles;
They stumble in their walk;
They make haste to her walls,
And the defense is prepared.
[6]The gates of the rivers are opened,
And the palace is dissolved.
[7]It is decreed:[a]
She shall be led away captive,
She shall be brought up;
And her maidservants shall lead *her*
as with the voice of doves,
Beating their breasts.

[8]Though Nineveh of old *was* like a
pool of water,
Now they flee away.
"Halt! Halt!" *they cry;*
But no one turns back.
[9]Take spoil of silver!
Take spoil of gold!
There is no end of treasure,
Or wealth of every desirable prize.
[10]She is empty, desolate, and waste!
The heart melts, and the knees shake;
Much pain *is* in every side,
And all their faces are drained of color.[a]

[11]Where *is* the dwelling of the lions,
And the feeding place of the young
lions,
Where the lion walked, the lioness
and lion's cub,
And no one made *them* afraid?
[12]The lion tore in pieces enough for his
cubs,
Killed for his lionesses,
Filled his caves with prey,
And his dens with flesh.

[13]"Behold, I *am* against you," says the
LORD of hosts, "I will burn your[a] chariots
in smoke, and the sword shall devour your
young lions; I will cut off your prey from
the earth, and the voice of your messengers shall be heard no more."

The Woe of Nineveh

3 Woe to the bloody city!
It *is* all full of lies *and* robbery.
Its victim never departs.
[2]The noise of a whip
And the noise of rattling wheels,
Of galloping horses,
Of clattering chariots!
[3]Horsemen charge with bright sword
and glittering spear.
There is a multitude of slain,
A great number of bodies,
Countless corpses—
They stumble over the corpses—
[4]Because of the multitude of harlotries
of the seductive harlot,
The mistress of sorceries,
Who sells nations through her
harlotries,
And families through her sorceries.

[5]"Behold, I *am* against you," says the
LORD of hosts;
"I will lift your skirts over your face,
I will show the nations your
nakedness,
And the kingdoms your shame.
[6]I will cast abominable filth upon you,
Make you vile,
And make you a spectacle.
[7]It shall come to pass *that* all who look
upon you
Will flee from you, and say,
'Nineveh is laid waste!
Who will bemoan her?'
Where shall I seek comforters for you?"

[8]Are you better than No Amon[a]
That was situated by the River,[b]

2:7 [a]Hebrew *Huzzab* 2:10 [a]Compare Joel 2:6 2:13 [a]Literally *her* 3:8 [a]That is, ancient Thebes; Targum and Vulgate read *populous Alexandria.* [b]Literally *rivers,* that is, the Nile and the surrounding canals

3:1 Modern America has many bloody cities. During the 1990s, there were over 200,000 murders in the United States. Our crimes will not escape God's just retribution.

That had the waters around her,
Whose rampart *was* the sea,
Whose wall *was* the sea?
9Ethiopia and Egypt *were* her strength,
And *it was* boundless;
Put and Lubim were your[a] helpers.
10Yet she *was* carried away,

She went into captivity;
Her young children also were dashed to pieces
At the head of every street;
They cast lots for her honorable men,
And all her great men were bound in chains.
11You also will be drunk;
You will be hidden;
You also will seek refuge from the enemy.

> Faith isn't the ability to believe long and far into the misty future. It's simply taking God at His word and taking the next step.
>
> **JONI EARECKSON TADA**

12All your strongholds *are* fig trees with ripened figs:
If they are shaken,
They fall into the mouth of the eater.
13Surely, your people in your midst *are* women!
The gates of your land are wide open for your enemies;
Fire shall devour the bars of your *gates.*

14Draw your water for the siege!
Fortify your strongholds!
Go into the clay and tread the mortar!
Make strong the brick kiln!
15There the fire will devour you,
The sword will cut you off;
It will eat you up like a locust.

Make yourself many—like the locust!
Make yourself many—like the *swarming* locusts!
16You have multiplied your merchants more than the stars of heaven.
The locust plunders and flies away.
17Your commanders *are* like *swarming* locusts,
And your generals like great grasshoppers,
Which camp in the hedges on a cold day;
When the sun rises they flee away,
And the place where they *are* is not known.

18Your shepherds slumber, O king of Assyria;
Your nobles rest *in the dust.*
Your people are scattered on the mountains,
And no one gathers them.
19Your injury *has* no healing,
Your wound is severe.
All who hear news of you
Will clap *their* hands over you,
For upon whom has not your wickedness passed continually?

3:9 [a]Septuagint reads *her.*

3:19 A century earlier, God's judgment was withheld when Nineveh repented at Jonah's warning. Now filled with idolatry, corruption, and violence, the wicked city could not escape God's judgment.

Habakkuk

1 The burden[a] which the prophet Habakkuk saw.

The Prophet's Question

[2]O LORD, how long shall I cry,
And You will not hear?
Even cry out to You, "Violence!"
And You will not save.
[3]Why do You show me iniquity,
And cause *me* to see trouble?
For plundering and violence *are* before me;
There is strife, and contention arises.
[4]Therefore the law is powerless,
And justice never goes forth.
For the wicked surround the righteous;
Therefore perverse judgment proceeds.

The Lord's Reply

[5]"Look among the nations and watch—
Be utterly astounded!
For *I will* work a work in your days
Which you would not believe, though it were told *you*.
[6]For indeed I am raising up the Chaldeans,
A bitter and hasty nation
Which marches through the breadth of the earth,
To possess dwelling places *that are* not theirs.
[7]They are terrible and dreadful;
Their judgment and their dignity proceed from themselves.
[8]Their horses also are swifter than leopards,
And more fierce than evening wolves.
Their chargers charge ahead;
Their cavalry comes from afar;
They fly as the eagle *that* hastens to eat.

[9]"They all come for violence;
Their faces are set *like* the east wind.
They gather captives like sand.
[10]They scoff at kings,
And princes are scorned by them.
They deride every stronghold,
For they heap up earthen *mounds* and seize it.
[11]Then *his* mind[a] changes, and he

1:1 [a]Or *oracle* 1:11 [a]Literally *spirit* or *wind*

1:1–5 The Christian carries a "burden." We look around us at the unspeakable atrocities and carnage of humanity and cry out in despair to God. When we speak out about the fruits of sin, we find that the world contends with us. The unsaved suffer horribly with the disease of sin and yet refuse the cure.

One fruit of a sinful world is a system of law that eliminates any reference to God, who is the final authority, the one whose laws are perfect and just. When a nation forsakes God's moral Law, it produces erroneous judgments. But as desperate as things seem, God can "do exceedingly abundantly above all that we ask or think" (see Eph. 3:20). He allows us to see iniquity for what it is so that we might be driven to prayer and see Him fulfill His wondrous purposes.

transgresses;
He commits offense,
Ascribing this power to his god."

The Prophet's Second Question

12Are You not from everlasting,
O LORD my God, my Holy One?
We shall not die.
O LORD, You have appointed them for judgment;
O Rock, You have marked them for correction.
13*You are* of purer eyes than to behold evil,
And cannot look on wickedness.
Why do You look on those who deal treacherously,
And hold Your tongue when the wicked devours
A *person* more righteous than he?
14*Why* do You make men like fish of the sea,
Like creeping things *that have* no ruler over them?

> What is the testimony of your closet? Can it bear witness to your sighs and groans and tears over the wickedness and desolations of the world?
>
> CHARLES FINNEY

15They take up all of them with a hook,
They catch them in their net,
And gather them in their dragnet.
Therefore they rejoice and are glad.
16Therefore they sacrifice to their net,
And burn incense to their dragnet;
Because by them their share *is* sumptuous
And their food plentiful.
17Shall they therefore empty their net,
And continue to slay nations without pity?

2 I will stand my watch
And set myself on the rampart,
And watch to see what He will say to me,
And what I will answer when I am corrected.

The Just Live by Faith

2Then the LORD answered me and said:

"Write the vision
And make *it* plain on tablets,
That he may run who reads it.
3For the vision *is* yet for an appointed time;
But at the end it will speak, and it will not lie.
Though it tarries, wait for it;
Because it will surely come,
It will not tarry.

4"Behold the proud,
His soul is not upright in him;
But the just shall live by his faith.

Woe to the Wicked

5"Indeed, because he transgresses by wine,
He is a proud man,
And he does not stay at home.

2:5 [a]Or *Sheol*

1:13 God's eyes are too pure to look upon evil (see Psa. 5:4). Without the help of the Holy Spirit, it is almost impossible for any of us to even begin to understand the nature of God's holiness (see Isa. 6:1–5). The ungodly think of Him as an old man in the sky or refer to Him as "the man upstairs" without any concept of His absolute purity. When a sinner begins to understand the perfect holiness of God's Law and its absolute requirements, it dawns on him that God is nothing like humanity (see Psa. 50:21).

2:1 A *standing* soldier will not sleep on his watch. When Jesus told His disciples to watch and pray in the Garden of Gethsemane, they did neither. Had they done as He said, they may not have forsaken Him and run like cowards when He was arrested. Yet, it was all in God's incredible plan. We can, however, learn from their experience.

2:4 Faith, and faith alone, makes us right with God (see Eph. 2:8,9).

Because he enlarges his desire as hell,[a]
And he *is* like death, and cannot be
satisfied,
He gathers to himself all nations
And heaps up for himself all peoples.
6"Will not all these take up a proverb against him,
And a taunting riddle against him,
and say,
'Woe to him who increases
What is not his—how long?
And to him who loads himself with
many pledges'?[a]
7Will not your creditors[a] rise up
suddenly?
Will they not awaken who oppress
you?
And you will become their booty.
8Because you have plundered many
nations,
All the remnant of the people shall
plunder you,
Because of men's blood
And the violence of the land *and* the
city,
And of all who dwell in it.

9"Woe to him who covets evil gain for
his house,
That he may set his nest on high,
That he may be delivered from the
power of disaster!
10You give shameful counsel to your
house,
Cutting off many peoples,
And sin *against* your soul.
11For the stone will cry out from the
wall,
And the beam from the timbers will
answer it.

12"Woe to him who builds a town with
bloodshed,
Who establishes a city by iniquity!
13Behold, *is it* not of the LORD of hosts
That the peoples labor to feed the
fire,[a]
And nations weary themselves in vain?
14For the earth will be filled
With the knowledge of the glory of
the LORD,
As the waters cover the sea.

15"Woe to him who gives drink to his
neighbor,
Pressing[a] *him to* your bottle,
Even to make *him* drunk,
That you may look on his nakedness!
16You are filled with shame instead of
glory.
You also—drink!
And be exposed as uncircumcised![a]
The cup of the LORD's right hand *will
be* turned against you,
And utter shame will be on your
glory.
17For the violence *done to* Lebanon will
cover you,
And the plunder of beasts *which* made
them afraid,
Because of men's blood
And the violence of the land *and* the
city,
And of all who dwell in it.

18"What profit is the image, that its
maker should carve it,
The molded image, a teacher of lies,
That the maker of its mold should
trust in it,
To make mute idols?
19Woe to him who says to wood,
'Awake!'
To silent stone, 'Arise! It shall teach!'
Behold, it is overlaid with gold and
silver,
Yet in it there is no breath at all.

20"But the LORD is in His holy temple.
Let all the earth keep silence before
Him."

The Prophet's Prayer

3 A prayer of Habakkuk the prophet,
on Shigionoth.[a]

2:6 [a]Syriac and Vulgate read *thick clay.* 2:7 [a]Literally *those who bite you* 2:13 [a]Literally *for what satisfies fire,* that is, for what is of no lasting value 2:15 [a]Literally *Attaching* or *Joining* 2:16 [a]Dead Sea Scrolls and Septuagint read *And reel!;* Syriac and Vulgate read *And fall fast asleep!* 3:1 [a]Exact meaning unknown

[2]O LORD, I have heard Your speech
and was afraid;
O LORD, revive Your work in the
midst of the years!
In the midst of the years make *it*
known;
In wrath remember mercy.

[3]God came from Teman,
The Holy One from Mount Paran.
Selah

His glory covered the heavens,
And the earth was full of His praise.
[4]*His* brightness was like the light;
He had rays *flashing* from His hand,
And there His power *was* hidden.
[5]Before Him went pestilence,
And fever followed at His feet.

[6]He stood and measured the earth;
He looked and startled the nations.
And the everlasting mountains were
scattered,
The perpetual hills bowed.
His ways *are* everlasting.
[7]I saw the tents of Cushan in affliction;
The curtains of the land of Midian
trembled.

[8]O LORD, were *You* displeased with the
rivers,
Was Your anger against the rivers,
Was Your wrath against the sea,
That You rode on Your horses,
Your chariots of salvation?
[9]Your bow was made quite ready;
Oaths were sworn over *Your* arrows.[a]
Selah

You divided the earth with rivers.
[10]The mountains saw You *and*
trembled;
The overflowing of the water passed by.
The deep uttered its voice,
And lifted its hands on high.
[11]The sun and moon stood still in their
habitation;
At the light of Your arrows they went,
At the shining of Your glittering spear.

"I can see how it might be possible for someone to look around on earth and not believe in God, but I cannot conceive how anyone could look up into the heavens and say there is no God."

Abraham Lincoln

[12]You marched through the land in
indignation;
You trampled the nations in anger.
[13]You went forth for the salvation of
Your people,
For salvation with Your Anointed.
You struck the head from the house
of the wicked,
By laying bare from foundation to
neck. *Selah*
[14]You thrust through with his own arrows
The head of his villages.
They came out like a whirlwind to
scatter me;
Their rejoicing was like feasting on
the poor in secret.
[15]You walked through the sea with
Your horses,
Through the heap of great waters.
[16]When I heard, my body trembled;
My lips quivered at *the* voice;
Rottenness entered my bones;
And I trembled in myself,
That I might rest in the day of
trouble.

3:9 [a]Literally *rods* or *tribes* (compare verse 14)

When he comes up to the people,
He will invade them with his troops.

A Hymn of Faith

17 Though the fig tree may not blossom,
Nor fruit be on the vines;
Though the labor of the olive may fail,
And the fields yield no food;
Though the flock may be cut off from the fold,
And there be no herd in the stalls—
18 Yet I will rejoice in the LORD,
I will joy in the God of my salvation.

19 The LORD God[a] is my strength;
He will make my feet like deer's *feet*,
And He will make me walk on my high hills.

To the Chief Musician. With my stringed instruments.

3:19 [a]Hebrew *YHWH Adonai*

3:17–19 When we rejoice because our names are written in heaven, we can have joy even though the fig tree fails to yield its crop, the car runs out of gas, the bank account runs dry, and the cupboard is bare. Our citizenship is in heaven. That is our true home.

"Heaven is not here, it's There. If we were given all we wanted here, our hearts would settle for this world rather than the next. God is forever luring us up and away from this one, wooing us to Himself and His still invisible Kingdom, where we will certainly find what we so keenly long for." *Elisabeth Elliot*

What Makes a Group Non-Christian?

By Matthew J. Slick

There are many non-Christian religions and cults in America: Mormonism, Jehovah's Witnesses, Christian Science, Unity, The Way International, Unitarianism, etc. They all claim special revelation and privilege. The dictionary defines a cult as "a system of religious worship or ritual; devoted attachment to, or extravagant admiration for, a person, principle, etc.; a group of followers." This is a typical secular definition and by it, any believer in any god is a cultist, even atheists since they have an admiration for a principle and are a group of followers of the philosophy of atheism. Therefore, this is too broad a definition since it doesn't sufficiently address the issue of true and false religious systems.

The definition I use for "non-Christian cult" or "non-Christian religion" encompasses groups that may or may not include the Bible in their set of authoritative scriptures. If a group does include the Bible, it distorts the true biblical doctrines that affect salvation sufficiently so as to void salvation. If it doesn't use the Bible, it is a non-Christian religion and does not participate in the benefit of divine revelation.

The term "cult" can range from any group of worshipers of any god who pay no attention to the Bible, to a small, highly paranoid, apocalyptic people who gather around a charismatic leader who uses the Bible to control them. Groups like the Mormons and Jehovah's Witnesses object to the label "cult" because it often gets an emotional reaction and is a label they want to avoid.

Most Christian bookstores have "cult" sections that include Mormons, Jehovah's Witnesses, etc., so I am not alone in describing what a non-Christian, Bible-based cult is. Nevertheless, a group is non-Christian when it denies the essential doctrines of the Bible:

- The deity of Christ, which involves the Trinity
- The resurrection of Jesus
- Salvation by grace alone

(continued)

What Makes a Group Non-Christian? (continued)

All of the cults add to the finished work of Jesus on the cross. Some cult groups even add to the Bible, e.g., Mormonism has the Book of Mormon, Doctrine and Covenants, and *The Pearl of Great Price*. Christian Science has added *Science and Health with Key to the Scriptures*. The Jehovah's Witnesses, however, have actually changed the text of the Bible to make it fit what they want it to.

Cults add their own efforts, their own works of righteousness to the finished work of salvation accomplished by Jesus on the cross. All cults say that Jesus' sacrifice is sufficient, yet our works must be "mixed with" or "added to" His in order to prove that we are saved and worthy of salvation. They say one thing but believe another. They maintain that they must try their best to please God and prove to Him that they are sincere, have worked hard, and are then worthy to be with Him. In other words, they do their best and God takes care of the rest.

This is absolutely wrong. The Bible says that we are saved by grace, not by works: "For by grace you have been saved through faith . . . not as a result of works, that no one should boast" (Eph. 2:8,9, NASB); we are not saved by anything we do: "For we maintain that a man is justified by faith apart from works of the law" (Rom. 3:28, NASB). Because if there was anything that we could do to merit the forgiveness of our sins, then Jesus died needlessly: "nevertheless knowing that a man is not justified by the works of the law but through faith in Christ Jesus, even we have believed in Christ Jesus, that we may be justified by faith in Christ, and not by the works of the law; since by the works of the law shall no flesh be justified . . . I do not nullify the grace of God; for if righteousness comes through the law, then Christ died needlessly" (Gal. 2:16,21, NASB).

People in cults will often cite James 2:26, which says that *faith without works is dead*, in an attempt to demonstrate that works are part of becoming saved. While it is true that faith without works is dead, it isn't the works that save us. James is saying that if you have real and true faith, it will result in real and true works of Christianity. In other words, you do good works *because* you are saved, not to *get* saved. He isn't saying that our works are what saves us, or that they, in combination with the finished work of Christ, save us. This agrees with Paul who tells us that faith is what saves us: "Therefore, having been justified by faith, we have peace with God through our Lord Jesus Christ" (Rom. 5:1, NASB). This faith is real faith, or true saving faith, not just an empty mental acknowledgment of God's existence, which is what those who *say* they have faith but show no corresponding godliness are guilty of. Incidentally, you should realize that faith is only as good as the object in which you place it. Just having faith in something doesn't mean you're saved. That is why it is important to have the true Jesus, because if you have great faith but it is in the wrong Jesus, then your faith is useless.

In Mormonism, Jesus is the brother of the devil begotten through sexual intercourse with a god who came from another planet. In Jehovah's Witnesses, he is Michael the Archangel who became a man. In the New Age Movement, he is a man in tune with the divine consciousness. Which is true? The only true Jesus is the one of the Bible, the one who is prayed to (1 Cor. 1:1,2; Acts 7:55–60); worshiped (Matt. 2:2,11; 14:33; John 9:35–38; Heb. 1:8); and called God (John 20:28; Col. 2:9). The Jesus of the cults is not prayed to, worshiped, or called God. And since the Jesus of the Bible is the only one who reveals the Father (Luke 10:22) so that you may have eternal life (John 17:3), you must have the true Jesus who alone is the way, the truth, and the life (John 14:6).

Another common denominator among cults is their methods of twisting Scripture. Some of the errors they commit in interpreting Scripture are: 1) taking Scripture out of context; 2) reading into the Scriptures information that is not there; 3) picking and choosing only Scriptures that suit their needs; 4) ignoring other explanations; 5) combining Scriptures that don't have anything to do with each other; 5) quoting a verse without giving its location; 6) incorrect definitions of key words; and 7) mistranslations. These are only a few of the many ways cults misuse Scripture.

If you want to be able to witness well to a person in a cult, you need to understand their doctrines as well as your own. It would be a good idea to study Christian doctrine regarding the Bible, God, Jesus, the Holy Spirit, salvation, creation, man, etc., to become better equipped. Through study you will be able to answer questions that often come up in witnessing encounters. A Christian should know his doctrine well enough to be able to recognize not only what is true, but also what is false in a religious system (1 Pet. 3:15; 2 Tim. 2:15).

Jesus warned us that in the last days false Christs and false prophets would arise and deceive many (Matt. 24:24). The Lord knew that there would be a rise of the spirit of antichrist (1 John 4:1–3) in the last days. Its manifestation is here in the forms of Mormonism, Jehovah's Witnesses, and the New Age Movement, among others.

(Reprinted from *The School of Biblical Evangelism.*)

Zephaniah

1 The word of the LORD which came to
Zephaniah the son of Cushi, the son
of Gedaliah, the son of Amariah, the son
of Hezekiah, in the days of Josiah the
son of Amon, king of Judah.

The Great Day of the Lord

2"I will utterly consume everything
From the face of the land,"
Says the LORD;
3"I will consume man and beast;
I will consume the birds of the
heavens,
The fish of the sea,
And the stumbling blocks[a] along with
the wicked.
I will cut off man from the face of the
land,"
Says the LORD.

4"I will stretch out My hand against
Judah,
And against all the inhabitants of
Jerusalem.
I will cut off every trace of Baal from
this place,
The names of the idolatrous priests[a]
with the *pagan* priests—
5Those who worship the host of
heaven on the housetops;
Those who worship and swear *oaths*
by the LORD,
But who *also* swear by Milcom;[a]
6Those who have turned back from
following the LORD,
And have not sought the LORD, nor
inquired of Him."

7Be silent in the presence of the Lord
GOD;
For the day of the LORD *is* at hand,
For the LORD has prepared a sacrifice;
He has invited[a] His guests.

8"And it shall be,
In the day of the LORD's sacrifice,
That I will punish the princes and the
king's children,
And all such as are clothed with
foreign apparel.
9In the same day I will punish

1:3 [a]Figurative of idols 1:4 [a]Hebrew *chemarim* 1:5 [a]Or *Malcam*, an Ammonite god, also called *Molech* (compare Leviticus 18:21) 1:7 [a]Literally *set apart, consecrated*

1:5 How many people today read their daily horoscope and bow to what it says about their future? It is not just "harmless entertainment" to appeal to the sun, moon, and stars for advice on how to live. See Deut. 4:19; 2 Kings 23:5.

1:7 When an unsaved person rails against God for His judgments or becomes "angry" at God, he reveals the sin of idolatry. He doesn't fear God because he doesn't see Him as He is, and he doesn't see himself as he is. Use the Law of God to put God in the judgment seat and the sinner on the stand as a devious criminal. It will cause him to be silent before his Maker—to lay his hand upon his sinful mouth and not speak foolishness (see Rom. 3:20).

All those who leap over the threshold,[a]
Who fill their masters' houses with
violence and deceit.

10"And there shall be on that day," says
the LORD,
"The sound of a mournful cry from the
Fish Gate,
A wailing from the Second Quarter,
And a loud crashing from the hills.
11Wail, you inhabitants of Maktesh![a]
For all the merchant people are cut
down;
All those who handle money are cut
off.

12"And it shall come to pass at that time
That I will search Jerusalem with
lamps,
And punish the men
Who are settled in complacency,[a]
Who say in their heart,
'The LORD will not do good,
Nor will He do evil.'
13Therefore their goods shall become
booty,
And their houses a desolation;
They shall build houses, but not
inhabit *them;*
They shall plant vineyards, but not
drink their wine."

14The great day of the LORD is near;
It is near and hastens quickly.
The noise of the day of the LORD is
bitter;
There the mighty men shall cry out.
15That day is a day of wrath,
A day of trouble and distress,
A day of devastation and desolation,
A day of darkness and gloominess,
A day of clouds and thick darkness,
16A day of trumpet and alarm
Against the fortified cities
And against the high towers.

17"I will bring distress upon men,
And they shall walk like blind men,
Because they have sinned against the
LORD;
Their blood shall be poured out like
dust,
And their flesh like refuse."

18Neither their silver nor their gold
Shall be able to deliver them
In the day of the LORD's wrath;
But the whole land shall be devoured
By the fire of His jealousy,
For He will make speedy riddance
Of all those who dwell in the land.

. . . . .

For the amazing complexity of the "simple" cell, see Job 33:4 comment.

. . . . .

A Call to Repentance

2 Gather yourselves together, yes,
gather together,
O undesirable[a] nation,
2Before the decree is issued,
Or the day passes like chaff,
Before the LORD's fierce anger comes
upon you,
Before the day of the LORD's anger
comes upon you!
3Seek the LORD, all you meek of the
earth,
Who have upheld His justice.

1:9 [a]Compare 1 Samuel 5:5 1:11 [a]Literally *Mortar,* a market district of Jerusalem 1:12 [a]Literally *on their lees,* that is, settled like the dregs of wine 2:1 [a]Or *shameless*

1:18 The only thing that can deliver us from God's wrath is righteousness (see 2:3). See also Ezek.7:19 and Prov. 10:2 comment.

2:3 This is the universal call to salvation, which is to be preached to the entire world (see Mark 16:15). It is an exhortation to thirst after the righteousness of God in Christ. Riches will not profit in the day of wrath (see 1:18); only the righteousness of Christ will shelter the sinner in the day of the Lord's anger and deliver him from death (see Rom. 5:17).

For the way to help sinners thirst after righteousness, see 2 Sam. 12:1–14 comment.

Seek righteousness, seek humility.
It may be that you will be hidden
In the day of the LORD's anger.

Judgment on Nations

4For Gaza shall be forsaken,
And Ashkelon desolate;
They shall drive out Ashdod at noonday,
And Ekron shall be uprooted.
5Woe to the inhabitants of the seacoast,
The nation of the Cherethites!
The word of the LORD *is* against you,
O Canaan, land of the Philistines:
"I will destroy you;
So there shall be no inhabitant."

6The seacoast shall be pastures,
With shelters[a] for shepherds and folds for flocks.
7The coast shall be for the remnant of the house of Judah;
They shall feed *their* flocks there;
In the houses of Ashkelon they shall lie down at evening.
For the LORD their God will intervene for them,
And return their captives.

8"I have heard the reproach of Moab,
And the insults of the people of Ammon,
With which they have reproached My people,
And made arrogant threats against their borders.
9Therefore, as I live,"
Says the LORD of hosts, the God of Israel,
"Surely Moab shall be like Sodom,
And the people of Ammon like Gomorrah—
Overrun with weeds and saltpits,
And a perpetual desolation.
The residue of My people shall plunder them,
And the remnant of My people shall possess them."

10This they shall have for their pride,
Because they have reproached and made arrogant threats
Against the people of the LORD of hosts.
11The LORD *will be* awesome to them,
For He will reduce to nothing all the gods of the earth;
People shall worship Him,
Each one from his place,
Indeed all the shores of the nations.

Our world cannot afford to be lied to about such a crucial issue as hell. Every believer must see this present hour as a God-sent opportunity to warn the lost of the dangers of hell.

BILL BRIGHT

12"You Ethiopians also,
You shall be slain by My sword."

13And He will stretch out His hand against the north,
Destroy Assyria,
And make Nineveh a desolation,
As dry as the wilderness.
14The herds shall lie down in her midst,
Every beast of the nation.
Both the pelican and the bittern
Shall lodge on the capitals *of* her *pillars;*
Their voice shall sing in the windows;
Desolation *shall be* at the threshold;
For He will lay bare the cedar work.
15This is the rejoicing city
That dwelt securely,
That said in her heart,
"I *am it,* and *there is* none besides me."
How has she become a desolation,
A place for beasts to lie down!
Everyone who passes by her
Shall hiss and shake his fist.

The Wickedness of Jerusalem

3 Woe to her who is rebellious and polluted,
To the oppressing city!

2:6 [a]Literally *excavations,* either underground huts or cisterns

[2]She has not obeyed *His* voice,
She has not received correction;
She has not trusted in the LORD,
She has not drawn near to her God.

[3]Her princes in her midst *are* roaring
lions;
Her judges *are* evening wolves
That leave not a bone till morning.
[4]Her prophets are insolent,
treacherous people;
Her priests have polluted the
sanctuary,
They have done violence to the law.
[5]The LORD *is* righteous in her midst,
He will do no unrighteousness.
Every morning He brings His justice
to light;
He never fails,
But the unjust knows no shame.

[6]"I have cut off nations,
Their fortresses are devastated;
I have made their streets desolate,
With none passing by.
Their cities are destroyed;
There is no one, no inhabitant.
[7]I said, 'Surely you will fear Me,
You will receive instruction'—
So that her dwelling would not be
cut off,
Despite everything for which I
punished her.
But they rose early and corrupted all
their deeds.

A Faithful Remnant

[8]"Therefore wait for Me," says the LORD,
"Until the day I rise up for plunder;[a]
My determination *is* to gather the
nations
To My assembly of kingdoms,

The Function of the Law

3:4 False prophets—whether those during Zephaniah's time, the Pharisees in Jesus' day, or the false prophets of our day—all do "violence to the Law." They show contempt for the Law, refusing to preach it despite the example of Jesus (see Luke 10:25,26; 18:18–20) and the many verses that speak of the Law's God-given function to bring sinners to the Savior (see Rom. 3:19,20; 7:7; Gal. 3:24; 1 Tim. 1:8–10). Also see Amos 2:4; Mark 7:9.

"The Law is very much to be insisted on, and the preaching of the gospel is likely to be in vain without it." *Jonathan Edwards*

3:8 [a]Septuagint and Syriac read *for witness;* Targum reads *for the day of My revelation for judgment;* Vulgate reads *for the day of My resurrection that is to come.*

3:2 The ungodly often think that all that God requires of them is to "believe" in Him. However, God does not require just *belief* (the demons believe and tremble); He demands *obedience*. We are to bow to the Lordship of the One who gave us life. He is *the* Lord and if the world refuses to bow to His absolute sovereignty now in mercy, they will bow later in judgment.

"Salvation comes not by 'accepting the finished work' or 'deciding for Christ.' It comes by believing on the Lord Jesus Christ, the whole, living, victorious Lord who, as God and man, fought our fight and won it, accepted our debt as His own and paid it, took our sins and died under them and rose again to set us free. This is the true Christ, and nothing less will do.

"But something less is among us, nevertheless, and we do well to identify it so that we may repudiate it. That something is a poetic fiction, a product of the romantic imagination and maudlin religious fancy. It is a Jesus, gentle, dreamy, shy, sweet and feminine, almost effeminate, and marvelously adaptable to whatever society He may find Himself in . . . He is used as a means to almost any carnal end, but he is never acknowledged as Lord. These quasi Christians follow a quasi Christ. They want his help but not his interference. They will flatter him but never obey him." *A. W. Tozer*

3:8 What a fearful day it will be when Almighty God reveals His just anger against all evil. As Jesus predicted (see Matt. 24:38), people will be as they were in the days of Noah, eating and drinking, with no thoughts of God's anger against sin or concerns about judgment. Yet, each time the ungodly sin against God's Law, they store up His wrath that will be revealed on Judgment Day. Take the time to study Rom. 2:1–16, and pray that God gives you an empathy that will drive you to reach out to the lost, to plead with them to flee from His wrath. Make sure you have Paul's testimony: "Knowing, therefore, the terror of the Lord, we persuade men" (2 Cor. 5:11).

To pour on them My indignation,
All My fierce anger;
All the earth shall be devoured
With the fire of My jealousy.

9"For then I will restore to the peoples
a pure language,
That they all may call on the name of
the LORD,
To serve Him with one accord.
10From beyond the rivers of Ethiopia
My worshipers,
The daughter of My dispersed ones,
Shall bring My offering.
11In that day you shall not be shamed
for any of your deeds
In which you transgress against Me;
For then I will take away from your
midst
Those who rejoice in your pride,
And you shall no longer be haughty
In My holy mountain.
12I will leave in your midst
A meek and humble people,
And they shall trust in the name of
the LORD.
13The remnant of Israel shall do no
unrighteousness
And speak no lies,
Nor shall a deceitful tongue be found
in their mouth;
For they shall feed *their* flocks and lie
down,
And no one shall make *them* afraid."

Joy in God's Faithfulness

14Sing, O daughter of Zion!
Shout, O Israel!
Be glad and rejoice with all *your* heart,
O daughter of Jerusalem!
15The LORD has taken away your
judgments,
He has cast out your enemy.
The King of Israel, the LORD, *is* in
your midst;
You shall see[a] disaster no more.

16In that day it shall be said to
Jerusalem:
"Do not fear;
Zion, let not your hands be weak.
17The LORD your God in your midst,
The Mighty One, will save;
He will rejoice over you with
gladness,
He will quiet *you* with His love,
He will rejoice over you with
singing."

. . . . . .

Do sacrifices take away sin or not?
See Num. 15:24–28 comment.

. . . . . .

18"I will gather those who sorrow over
the appointed assembly,
Who are among you,
To whom its reproach *is* a burden.
19Behold, at that time
I will deal with all who afflict you;
I will save the lame,
And gather those who were driven out;
I will appoint them for praise and fame
In every land where they were put to
shame.
20At that time I will bring you back,
Even at the time I gather you;
For I will give you fame and praise
Among all the peoples of the earth,
When I return your captives before
your eyes,"
Says the LORD.

3:15 [a]Some Hebrew manuscripts, Septuagint, and Bomberg read *see;* Masoretic Text and Vulgate read *fear.*

3:17 In Christ, we find God's love and favor; we can call Almighty God "Father," even "Daddy" ("Abba") (see Rom. 8:15). Read this verse with Rom. 8:35–39.

Intelligence Tests

(Do not read these questions yourself. If you do, you will fail to see their evangelistic potential. Instead, have someone ask you the questions.)

1. How many of each animal did Moses take into the ark?
2. What is the name of the raised print that deaf people use?
3. Is it possible to end a sentence with the word "the"?
4. Spell the word "shop." What do you do when you come to a green light?
5. It is noon. You look at the clock. The big hand is on three. The little hand is on five. What time is it?
6. Spell the word "silk." What do cows drink?
7. Listen carefully: You are the driver of a train. There are thirty people on board. At the first stop ten people get off. At the next stop five people get on. Now for the question: What is the name of the train driver?

Answers:

1. None. It was Noah.
2. Deaf people don't use raised print.
3. The question is an example of one.
4. Go.
5. Noon.
6. Water.
7. You are the driver of the train.

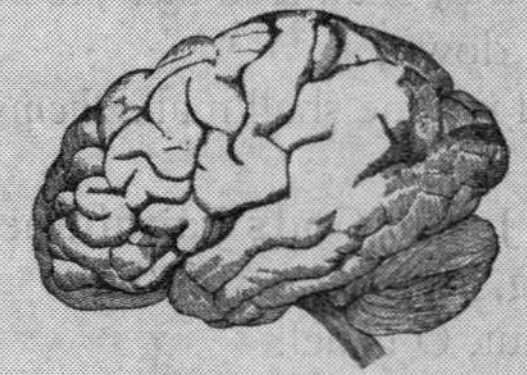

The Bible warns, "He who trusts in his own heart is a fool" (Prov. 28:26). The tests are an excellent way to humble an unsaved person and show him that he can't trust his own judgments. This may be followed with, "If you make a mistake with something as simple as this, could you be wrong in your beliefs about God, Judgment Day, the existence of hell, etc.?"

Haggai

The Command to Build God's House

1 In the second year of King Darius, in
the sixth month, on the first day of
the month, the word of the LORD came
by Haggai the prophet to Zerubbabel the
son of Shealtiel, governor of Judah, and
to Joshua the son of Jehozadak, the high
priest, saying, 2"Thus speaks the LORD of
hosts, saying: 'This people says, "The
time has not come, the time that the
LORD's house should be built." ' "
3Then the word of the LORD came by
Haggai the prophet, saying, 4"*Is it* time for
you yourselves to dwell in your paneled
houses, and this temple[a] *to lie* in ruins?"
5Now therefore, thus says the LORD of
hosts: "Consider your ways!

6"You have sown much, and bring in
little;
You eat, but do not have enough;
You drink, but you are not filled with
drink;
You clothe yourselves, but no one is
warm;
And he who earns wages,
Earns wages *to put* into a bag with
holes."

7Thus says the LORD of hosts: "Consider your ways! 8Go up to the mountains
and bring wood and build the temple,
that I may take pleasure in it and be glorified," says the LORD. 9"*You* looked for
much, but indeed *it came to* little; and
when you brought it home, I blew it away.
Why?" says the LORD of hosts. "Because of
My house that *is in* ruins, while every one
of you runs to his own house. 10Therefore
the heavens above you withhold the dew,
and the earth withholds its fruit. 11For I
called for a drought on the land and the
mountains, on the grain and the new
wine and the oil, on whatever the ground
brings forth, on men and livestock, and
on all the labor of *your* hands."

The People's Obedience

12Then Zerubbabel the son of Shealtiel, and Joshua the son of Jehozadak, the
high priest, with all the remnant of the
people, obeyed the voice of the LORD
their God, and the words of Haggai the
prophet, as the LORD their God had sent
him; and the people feared the presence
of the LORD. 13Then Haggai, the LORD's
messenger, spoke the LORD's message to
the people, saying, "I *am* with you, says
the LORD." 14So the LORD stirred up the
spirit of Zerubbabel the son of Shealtiel,

1:4 [a]Literally *house,* and so in verse 8

1:6–11 This is the terrible result of a nation that prioritizes its own desires above the things of God. We exist to bring Him glory (see v. 8). With the Spirit of God dwelling in us, we are the temple of the living God. (See Eph. 2:21,22; 1 Cor. 3:16; 2 Cor. 6:16.) As we share the gospel and tell people how to be born again, we can help to build the temple of the Lord—a duty we dare not neglect.

POINTS FOR OPEN-AIR PREACHING

2:5

Fear in Perspective

Always keep in mind that you will never be free from fear, especially just before you get up to open-air preach. Overcome it through thoughts of the fate of the ungodly, the sacrifice of the cross, and the fact that God is watching you. I have known men who said that it was less fearful for them to skydive for the first time than to open-air preach. So think of the worst-case scenario if something goes wrong with both. In skydiving, if the parachute fails to open or becomes twisted, you fall to an unspeakably terrifying death. In open-air preaching, you may make a fool of yourself and dent your ego. There is no comparison. So just do it, and God will be with you. For ways to overcome fear, see Prov. 29:25 comment.

governor of Judah, and the spirit of Joshua the son of Jehozadak, the high priest, and the spirit of all the remnant of the people; and they came and worked on the house of the LORD of hosts, their God,
15on the twenty-fourth day of the sixth month, in the second year of King Darius.

The Coming Glory of God's House

2 In the seventh *month,* on the twenty-first of the month, the word of the LORD came by Haggai the prophet, saying:
2"Speak now to Zerubbabel the son of Shealtiel, governor of Judah, and to Joshua the son of Jehozadak, the high priest, and to the remnant of the people, saying:
3'Who is left among you who saw this temple[a] in its former glory? And how do you see it now? In comparison with it, *is this* not in your eyes as nothing?
4Yet now be strong, Zerubbabel,' says the LORD; 'and be strong, Joshua, son of Jehozadak, the high priest; and be strong, all you people of the land,' says the LORD, 'and work; for I *am* with you,' says the LORD of hosts.
5'*According to* the word that I covenanted with you when you came out of Egypt, so My Spirit remains among you; do not fear!'
6"For thus says the LORD of hosts: 'Once more (it *is* a little while) I will shake heaven and earth, the sea and dry land;
7and I will shake all nations, and they shall come to the Desire of All Nations,[a] and I will fill this temple with glory,' says the LORD of hosts.
8'The silver *is* Mine, and the gold *is* Mine,' says the LORD of hosts.
9'The glory of this latter temple shall be greater than the former,' says the LORD of hosts. 'And in this place I will give peace,' says the LORD of hosts."

The People Are Defiled

10On the twenty-fourth *day* of the ninth *month,* in the second year of Darius, the word of the LORD came by Haggai the prophet, saying,
11"Thus says the LORD of hosts: 'Now, ask the priests *concerning the* law, saying,
12"If one carries holy meat in the fold of his garment, and with the edge he touches bread or stew, wine or oil, or any food, will it become holy?" ' "

> I would think it a greater happiness to gain one soul to Christ than mountains of silver and gold to myself.
>
> **MATTHEW HENRY**

Then the priests answered and said, "No."
13And Haggai said, "If *one who is* unclean *because* of a dead body touches any of these, will it be unclean?"

So the priests answered and said, "It shall be unclean."
14Then Haggai answered and said, " 'So is this people, and so is this nation before Me,' says the LORD, 'and so is every work of their hands; and what they offer there is unclean.

2:3 [a]Literally *house,* and so in verses 7 and 9 2:7 [a]Or *the desire of all nations*

Promised Blessing

15'And now, carefully consider from this
day forward: from before stone was laid
upon stone in the temple of the LORD—
16since those *days,* when *one* came to a
heap of twenty ephahs, there were *but* ten;
when *one* came to the wine vat to draw
out fifty baths from the press, there were
but twenty. 17I struck you with blight and
mildew and hail in all the labors of your
hands; yet you did not *turn* to Me,' says
the LORD. 18'Consider now from this day
forward, from the twenty-fourth day of
the ninth month, from the day that the
foundation of the LORD's temple was laid
—consider it: 19Is the seed still in the barn?
As yet the vine, the fig tree, the pomegranate, and the olive tree have not yielded
fruit. But from this day I will bless *you.*' "

Zerubbabel Chosen as a Signet

20And again the word of the LORD came
to Haggai on the twenty-fourth day of the
month, saying, 21"Speak to Zerubbabel,
governor of Judah, saying:

'I will shake heaven and earth.
22I will overthrow the throne of
kingdoms;
I will destroy the strength of the
Gentile kingdoms.
I will overthrow the chariots
And those who ride in them;
The horses and their riders shall
come down,
Every one by the sword of his brother.

23'In that day,' says the LORD of hosts,
'I will take you, Zerubbabel My servant,
the son of Shealtiel,' says the LORD, 'and
will make you like a signet *ring;* for I have
chosen you,' says the LORD of hosts."

"That we may not complain of what is, let us see God's hand in all events; and, that we may not be afraid of what shall be, let us see all events in God's hands."

Swallow Your Pride

The life and death of Jesus Christ is a standing rebuke to every form of pride of which men are capable:

- **Pride of birth and rank:** "Is this not the carpenter's son?" (Matt. 13:55)
- **Pride of wealth:** "The Son of Man has nowhere to lay His head." (Matt. 8:20)
- **Pride of personal appearance:** "There is no beauty that we should desire Him." (Isaiah 53:2)
- **Pride of reputation:** "A friend of tax collectors and sinners!" (Matt. 11:19)
- **Pride of learning:** "How does this Man know letters, having never studied?" (John 7:15)
- **Pride of superiority:** "I am among you as the One who serves." (Luke 22:27)
- **Pride of success:** "He was despised and rejected by men." (Isa. 53:3)
- **Pride of ability:** "I can of Myself do nothing." (John 5:30)
- **Pride of intellect:** "As My Father taught Me, I speak these things." (John 8:28)
- **Pride of self-will**: "I do not seek my own will, but the will of the Father who sent me." (John 5:30)
- **Pride in death:** "He . . . became obedient to the point of death, even the death of the cross." (Phil. 2:8)

Unitarianism

By Matthew J. Slick

Unitarianism is the belief that God exists in one person, not three. It is a denial of the doctrine of the Trinity as well as the full divinity of Jesus. Therefore, it is not Christian. Several groups fall under this umbrella, including Jehovah's Witnesses, Christadelphianism, and The Way International. Another term for this type of belief is "monarchianism." Unitarians have no dogma and hold to a common system of believing as you will about God, salvation, sin, etc. They also hold to the universal redemption of all mankind.

In the context of universalism, the Unitarianism discussed here is the belief that denies the Trinity, the deity of Christ, the personhood of the Holy Spirit, eternal punishment, and the vicarious atonement of Jesus. Unitarian Universalists use many biblical concepts and terms but with non-biblical meanings. Unitarianism is not Christian.

There is a group known as the Unitarian Universalists Association, which was formed in the U.S. in 1961 when the American Unitarian Association and the Universalist Church of America merged. Its membership is around 175,000.

The General Convention of the Unitarian Universalists formulated the five principles of the Universalist Faith in 1899:

- The Universal Fatherhood of God
- The spiritual authority and leadership of His Son Jesus Christ
- The trustworthiness of the Bible as containing a revelation from God
- The certainty of just retribution for sin
- The final harmony of all souls with God

Additional beliefs generally held by Unitarian Universalists are:

- Jesus became the Son of God at His baptism.
- The Holy Spirit is not a person, does not have a will, etc.
- There will be rewards and punishments according to one's actions, but this does not include the traditional doctrine of hell.
- Human reason and experience should be the final authority in determining spiritual truth.

This last point is perhaps the most revealing of Unitarian Universalists. They believe, "In the end religious authority lies not in a book or person or institution, but in ourselves. We are a 'non-creedal' religion: we do not ask anyone to subscribe to a creed." Instead of God and His Word being the final authority on truth and error, right and wrong, Unitarian Universalists subject God and His Word to their understanding, feeling, and reason. This is exemplified in the following quotes from the official Unitarian Universalist website (www.uua.org):

- "I want a religion that respects the differences between people and affirms every person as an individual."
- "I want a church that values children, that welcomes them on their own terms—a church they are eager to attend on Sunday morning."
- "I want a congregation that cherishes freedom and encourages open dialogue on questions of faith, one in which it is okay to change your mind."
- "I want a religious community that affirms spiritual exploration and reason as ways of finding truth."
- "I want a church that acts locally and thinks globally on the great issues of our time—world peace; women's rights; racial justice; homelessness; gay, lesbian, bisexual, and transgender rights; and protection of the environment."

Notice that each of the five statements begins with "I want..." This is not the humble attitude of one indwelt by the Holy Spirit of God. It is not the attitude of one who wants to put God first.

It can plainly be seen that this is a religion based on personal hopes and desires and not on the Bible.

I cannot help thinking of the five "I will's" listed in Isa. 14:13,14:

> For you have said in your heart:
> "*I will* ascend into heaven,
> *I will* exalt my throne above the stars of God;
> *I will* also sit on the mount of the congregation
> on the farthest sides of the north;
> *I will* ascend above the heights of the clouds,
> *I will* be like the Most High."

Many commentators believe that these five "I wills" were uttered by Satan as he sought to be exalted and equal to God. They reflect the arrogance of the evil one as his heart was filled with pride and he put his own will before God's. He placed his desires before God's. But notice what Isaiah says in the next verse: "Yet you shall be brought down to Sheol, to the lowest depths of the Pit" (Isa. 14:15).

Jesus said, "Out of the abundance of the heart the mouth speaks" (Matt. 12:34). We can see that the Unitarian Universalists speak first from their own desires, according to their own wisdom, and not according to the wisdom of God. What does God say about this?

"For the wisdom of this world is foolishness with God" (1 Cor. 3:19).

(Reprinted from *The School of Biblical Evangelism*.)

Zechariah

A Call to Repentance

1 In the eighth month of the second year of Darius, the word of the LORD came to Zechariah the son of Berechiah, the son of Iddo the prophet, saying, 2"The LORD has been very angry with your fathers. 3Therefore say to them, 'Thus says the LORD of hosts: "Return to Me," says the LORD of hosts, "and I will return to you," says the LORD of hosts. 4"Do not be like your fathers, to whom the former prophets preached, saying, 'Thus says the LORD of hosts: "Turn now from your evil ways and your evil deeds." ' But they did not hear nor heed Me," says the LORD.

5"Your fathers, where *are* they?
And the prophets, do they live forever?
6Yet surely My words and My statutes,
Which I commanded My servants the prophets,
Did they not overtake your fathers?

"So they returned and said:

'Just as the LORD of hosts determined to do to us,
According to our ways and according to our deeds,
So He has dealt with us.' " ' "

Vision of the Horses

7On the twenty-fourth day of the eleventh month, which is the month Shebat, in the second year of Darius, the word of the LORD came to Zechariah the son of Berechiah, the son of Iddo the prophet: 8I saw by night, and behold, a man riding on a red horse, and it stood among the myrtle trees in the hollow; and behind him *were* horses: red, sorrel, and white. 9Then I said, "My lord, what *are* these?" So the angel who talked with me said to me, "I will show you what they *are*."

10And the man who stood among the myrtle trees answered and said, "These *are the ones* whom the LORD has sent to walk to and fro throughout the earth."

11So they answered the Angel of the LORD, who stood among the myrtle trees, and said, "We have walked to and fro throughout the earth, and behold, all the earth is resting quietly."

The Lord Will Comfort Zion

12Then the Angel of the LORD answered and said, "O LORD of hosts, how long will You not have mercy on Jerusalem and on the cities of Judah, against

1:3 The title "LORD of Hosts" (used 46 times in this book) means that all created agencies and forces are under the leadership or dominion of God, who not only made them, but maintains them (see Gen. 2:1; Isa. 45:12). Notice that God tells sinners that if they will forsake their evil ways and deeds and turn to Him, He will turn to them. This was the case with the prodigal son. After leaving the pigsty, he found that his father was *waiting* for him to return (see Luke 15:20).

which You were angry these seventy years?"

[13]And the LORD answered the angel who talked to me, *with* good *and* comforting words. [14]So the angel who spoke with me said to me, "Proclaim, saying, 'Thus says the LORD of hosts:

"I am zealous for Jerusalem
And for Zion with great zeal.
[15]I am exceedingly angry with the nations at ease;
For I was a little angry,
And they helped—*but* with evil *intent*."

[16]"Therefore thus says the LORD:

"I am returning to Jerusalem with mercy;
My house shall be built in it," says the LORD of hosts,
"And a *surveyor's* line shall be stretched out over Jerusalem." '

[17]"Again proclaim, saying, 'Thus says the LORD of hosts:

"My cities shall again spread out through prosperity;
The LORD will again comfort Zion,
And will again choose Jerusalem." ' "

Vision of the Horns

[18]Then I raised my eyes and looked, and there *were* four horns. [19]And I said to the angel who talked with me, "What *are* these?"

So he answered me, "These *are* the horns that have scattered Judah, Israel, and Jerusalem."

[20]Then the LORD showed me four craftsmen. [21]And I said, "What are these coming to do?"

So he said, "These *are* the horns that scattered Judah, so that no one could lift up his head; but the craftsmen[a] are coming to terrify them, to cast out the horns of the nations that lifted up *their* horn against the land of Judah to scatter it."

Vision of the Measuring Line

2 Then I raised my eyes and looked, and behold, a man with a measuring line in his hand. [2]So I said, "Where are you going?"

And he said to me, "To measure Jerusalem, to see what *is* its width and what *is* its length."

[3]And there *was* the angel who talked with me, going out; and another angel was coming out to meet him, [4]who said to him, "Run, speak to this young man, saying: 'Jerusalem shall be inhabited *as* towns without walls, because of the multitude of men and livestock in it. [5]For I,' says the LORD, 'will be a wall of fire all around her, and I will be the glory in her midst.' "

Future Joy of Zion and Many Nations

[6]"Up, up! Flee from the land of the north," says the LORD; "for I have spread you abroad like the four winds of heaven," says the LORD. [7]"Up, Zion! Escape, you who dwell with the daughter of Babylon."

[8]For thus says the LORD of hosts: "He sent Me after glory, to the nations which plunder you; for he who touches you touches the apple of His eye. [9]For surely I will shake My hand against them, and they shall become spoil for their servants.

1:21 [a]Literally *these*

1:18–21 God bless the brethren who dedicate their time to studying the mysteries of Bible prophecy. Such time is well-spent if it equips the Christian to reach out to the lost. Spiritual indulgence without the exercise of evangelism, however, leads to spiritual obesity.

2:5 God often manifests Himself as fire, as He did with Moses in the burning bush (see Exod. 3:2). He is called a "consuming fire" (see Deut. 4:24; Heb. 12:29), and He is coming "in flaming fire taking vengeance on those who do not know God, and on those who do not obey the gospel of our Lord Jesus Christ" (2 Thess. 1:8). See also Exod. 33:18–23, and Deut. 4:24 and Jer. 4:4 comments.

Then you will know that the LORD of
hosts has sent Me.
10“Sing and rejoice, O daughter of Zion!
For behold, I am coming and I will dwell
in your midst,” says the LORD. 11“Many
nations shall be joined to the LORD in that
day, and they shall become My people.
And I will dwell in your midst. Then you
will know that the LORD of hosts has sent
Me to you. 12And the LORD will take possession of Judah as His inheritance in the
Holy Land, and will again choose Jerusalem. 13Be silent, all flesh, before the
LORD, for He is aroused from His holy
habitation!”

Vision of the High Priest

3 Then he showed me Joshua the high
priest standing before the Angel of
the LORD, and Satan standing at his right
hand to oppose him. 2And the LORD said
to Satan, “The LORD rebuke you, Satan!
The LORD who has chosen Jerusalem rebuke you! *Is* this not a brand plucked
from the fire?”
3Now Joshua was clothed with filthy
garments, and was standing before the
Angel.
4Then He answered and spoke to
those who stood before Him, saying, “Take
away the filthy garments from him.” And
to him He said, “See, I have removed your
iniquity from you, and I will clothe you
with rich robes.”
5And I said, “Let them put a clean turban on his head.”

> Let us save men by all means under heaven; let us prevent men going down to hell. We are not half as earnest as we ought to be.
>
> **CHARLES SPURGEON**

So they put a clean turban on his head,
and they put the clothes on him. And the
Angel of the LORD stood by.

The Coming Branch

6Then the Angel of the LORD admonished Joshua, saying, 7“Thus says the LORD
of hosts:

‘If you will walk in My ways,
And if you will keep My command,
Then you shall also judge My house,
And likewise have charge of My
courts;
I will give you places to walk
Among these who stand here.

8‘Hear, O Joshua, the high priest,
You and your companions who sit

2:11 See Mal. 1:11 comment.

3:1 The Bible tells us that the enemy with which we wrestle is not flesh and blood, but is demonic. It is easy to be fooled into believing that much of what happens to us is natural in origin. Study your enemy (see Eph. 6:12–20) to learn his strengths and weaknesses. Sin gives him territory while righteousness disarms him, so clothe yourself in the righteousness of Christ. When we give ourselves to any sin, we give ourselves to the enemy. Beware of the subtle hidden sins of the heart, such as conceit, jealousy, bitterness, and envy. Guard your heart with all diligence.

3:2 Every Christian is a “brand plucked from the fire.” We have been saved from the fire that shall never be quenched, and our commission is to pull sinners “out of the fire, hating even the garment defiled by the flesh” (Jude 23).

“Born in 1703, John Wesley was the fifteenth child, and second surviving son of Susanna and Samuel Wesley. His father was the pastor of Epworth . . . [When John was age five] the Wesleys’ home caught on fire in the night. All the children were removed safely from the house, but when they were counted, John was missing. A farmer from nearby spotted little John looking out of an upstairs window amid the leaping flames. Several neighbors climbed on each other’s shoulders, until the man on top was able to put his arms around the boy and pull him out of the flames to safety. Only moments after he was rescued, the entire house exploded in flames. Ever after, for the rest of his life, John Wesley referred to himself ‘as a brand plucked from the burning,’ quoting Zechariah 3:2.” *Leslie F. Church, Knight of the Burning Heart: The Story of John Wesley*

before you,
For they are a wondrous sign;
For behold, I am bringing forth My
Servant the BRANCH.
9For behold, the stone
That I have laid before Joshua:
Upon the stone *are* seven eyes.
Behold, I will engrave its inscription,'
Says the LORD of hosts,
'And I will remove the iniquity of that
land in one day.
10In that day,' says the LORD of hosts,
'Everyone will invite his neighbor
Under his vine and under his fig tree.' "

Vision of the Lampstand and Olive Trees

4 Now the angel who talked with me
came back and wakened me, as a
man who is wakened out of his sleep.
2And he said to me, "What do you see?"
So I said, "I am looking, and there *is* a
lampstand of solid gold with a bowl on
top of it, and on the *stand* seven lamps
with seven pipes to the seven lamps.
3Two olive trees *are* by it, one at the right
of the bowl and the other at its left." 4So
I answered and spoke to the angel who
talked with me, saying, "What *are* these,
my lord?"
5Then the angel who talked with me
answered and said to me, "Do you not
know what these are?"
And I said, "No, my lord."
6So he answered and said to me:
"This *is* the word of the LORD to
Zerubbabel:
'Not by might nor by power, but by
My Spirit,'
Says the LORD of hosts.
7'Who *are* you, O great mountain?
Before Zerubbabel *you shall become* a
plain!
And he shall bring forth the capstone
With shouts of "Grace, grace to it!" ' "
8Moreover the word of the LORD came
to me, saying:
9"The hands of Zerubbabel
Have laid the foundation of this
temple;[a]
His hands shall also finish *it*.
Then you will know
That the LORD of hosts has sent Me to
you.
10For who has despised the day of
small things?
For these seven rejoice to see
The plumb line in the hand of
Zerubbabel.
They are the eyes of the LORD,
Which scan to and fro throughout the
whole earth."
11Then I answered and said to him,
"What *are* these two olive trees—at the
right of the lampstand and at its left?" 12And

4:9 [a]Literally *house*

4:1 Sleeping giant. The church in America is like a sleeping giant that needs to be awakened. Studies show that only two percent of evangelicals share their faith. The problem is the millions of spurious converts who sit within the Church—tares among the wheat, foolish virgins among the wise, goats among the sheep, etc. These people are in the midst of the American church, but they are not part of the true Church. If they were awakened to their true state, instead of a mere 2 percent we would see 100 percent sharing their faith, because they had a passion to do the will of God.

4:6 We tend, in our carnality, to lean toward might and power, but God does all things by His Spirit. He convicts us by His Spirit; we are born of His Spirit; we are baptized with His Spirit, and He guides us by the Spirit. (See John 16:8; 3:7,8; 1 Cor. 12:13; John 16:13.)

4:9 See Ezek. 47:1,2 comment.

4:12 "Many do not recognize the fact as they ought, that Satan has got men fast asleep in sin and that it is his great device to keep them so. He does not care what we do if he can do that. We may sing songs about the sweet by and by, preach sermons and say prayers until doomsday, and he will never concern himself about us, if we don't wake anybody up. But if we awake the sleeping sinner he will gnash on us with his teeth. This is our work—to wake people up." *Catherine Booth*

I further answered and said to him,
"What *are these* two olive branches that
drip into the receptacles[a] of the two gold
pipes from which the golden *oil* drains?"
13Then he answered me and said, "Do
you not know what these *are?*"
And I said, "No, my lord."
14So he said, "These *are* the two anointed ones, who stand beside the Lord
of the whole earth."

Vision of the Flying Scroll

5 Then I turned and raised my eyes,
and saw there a flying scroll.
2And he said to me, "What do you
see?"
So I answered, "I see a flying scroll. Its
length *is* twenty cubits and its width ten
cubits."
3Then he said to me, "This *is* the curse
that goes out over the face of the whole
earth: 'Every thief shall be expelled,' according *to* this side of *the scroll;* and, 'Every
perjurer shall be expelled,' according *to*
that side of it."

4"I will send out *the curse,*" says the
LORD of hosts;
"It shall enter the house of the thief
And the house of the one who swears
falsely by My name.
It shall remain in the midst of his
house
And consume it, with its timber and
stones."

Vision of the Woman in a Basket

5Then the angel who talked with me
came out and said to me, "Lift your eyes
now, and see what this *is* that goes forth."
6So I asked, "What *is* it?" And he said,
"It *is* a basket[a] that is going forth."
He also said, "This *is* their resemblance
throughout the earth: 7Here *is* a lead disc
lifted up, and this *is* a woman sitting inside the basket"; 8then he said, "This *is*
Wickedness!" And he thrust her down
into the basket, and threw the lead cover[a]
over its mouth. 9Then I raised my eyes
and looked, and there *were* two women,
coming with the wind in their wings; for
they had wings like the wings of a stork,
and they lifted up the basket between
earth and heaven.
10So I said to the angel who talked with
me, "Where are they carrying the basket?"
11And he said to me, "To build a house
for it in the land of Shinar;[a] when it is
ready, *the basket* will be set there on its
base."

Vision of the Four Chariots

6 Then I turned and raised my eyes and
looked, and behold, four chariots *were*
coming from between two mountains,
and the mountains *were* mountains of
bronze. 2With the first chariot *were* red
horses, with the second chariot black
horses, 3with the third chariot white horses, and with the fourth chariot dappled
horses—strong *steeds.* 4Then I answered
and said to the angel who talked with me,
"What *are* these, my lord?"
5And the angel answered and said to
me, "These *are* four spirits of heaven,
who go out from *their* station before the
Lord of all the earth. 6The one with the
black horses is going to the north country, the white are going after them, and
the dappled are going toward the south
country." 7Then the strong *steeds* went out,
eager to go, that they might walk to and
fro throughout the earth. And He said,
"Go, walk to and fro throughout the earth."
So they walked to and fro throughout the
earth. 8And He called to me, and spoke to
me, saying, "See, those who go toward

4:12 [a]Literally *into the hands of* 5:6 [a]Hebrew *ephah*, a measuring container, and so elsewhere 5:8 [a]Literally *stone* 5:11 [a]That is, Babylon

5:1–3 This is the curse of the moral Law. Its long arm will pursue every lawbreaker and make sure that justice is served.

6:2,3 Compare Rev. 6:2–8.

the north country have given rest to My Spirit in the north country."

The Command to Crown Joshua

[9]Then the word of the LORD came to me, saying: [10]"Receive *the gift* from the captives—from Heldai, Tobijah, and Jedaiah, who have come from Babylon—and go the same day and enter the house of Josiah the son of Zephaniah. [11]Take the silver and gold, make an elaborate crown, and set *it* on the head of Joshua the son of Jehozadak, the high priest. [12]Then speak to him, saying, 'Thus says the LORD of hosts, saying:

"Behold, the Man whose name *is* the
BRANCH!
From His place He shall branch out,
And He shall build the temple of the
LORD;
[13]Yes, He shall build the temple of the
LORD.
He shall bear the glory,
And shall sit and rule on His throne;
So He shall be a priest on His throne,
And the counsel of peace shall be
between them both." '

[14]"Now the elaborate crown shall be for a memorial in the temple of the LORD for Helem,[a] Tobijah, Jedaiah, and Hen the son of Zephaniah. [15]Even those from afar shall come and build the temple of the LORD. Then you shall know that the LORD of hosts has sent Me to you. And *this* shall come to pass if you diligently obey the voice of the LORD your God."

Obedience Better than Fasting

7 Now in the fourth year of King Darius it came to pass *that* the word of the LORD came to Zechariah, on the fourth *day* of the ninth month, Chislev, [2]when *the people*[a] sent Sherezer,[b] with Regem-Melech and his men, *to* the house of God,[c] to pray before the LORD, [3]*and* to ask the priests who *were* in the house of the LORD of hosts, and the prophets, saying, "Should I weep in the fifth month and fast as I have done for so many years?"

[4]Then the word of the LORD of hosts came to me, saying, [5]"Say to all the people of the land, and to the priests: 'When you fasted and mourned in the fifth and seventh *months* during those seventy years, did you really fast for Me—for Me? [6]When you eat and when you drink, do you not eat and drink *for yourselves?* [7]*Should you* not *have obeyed* the words which the LORD proclaimed through the former prophets when Jerusalem and the cities around it were inhabited and prosperous, and the South[a] and the Lowland were inhabited?' "

Disobedience Resulted in Captivity

[8]Then the word of the LORD came to Zechariah, saying, [9]"Thus says the LORD of hosts:

'Execute true justice,
Show mercy and compassion
Everyone to his brother.
[10]Do not oppress the widow or the
fatherless,
The alien or the poor.
Let none of you plan evil in his heart
Against his brother.'

[11]"But they refused to heed, shrugged their shoulders, and stopped their ears so that they could not hear. [12]Yes, they made their hearts like flint, refusing to hear the law and the words which the LORD of

6:14 [a]Following Masoretic Text, Targum, and Vulgate; Syriac reads *for Heldai* (compare verse 10); Septuagint reads *for the patient ones.* 7:2 [a]Literally *they* (compare verse 5) [b]Or *Sar-Ezer* [c]Hebrew *Bethel* 7:7 [a]Hebrew *Negev*

6:12 This messianic prophecy refers to Jesus as the chief cornerstone who will build the temple of the LORD. See Eph. 2:20–22.

7:7 Prosperity can dull our ears to the voice of God. He may allow adversity in our lives to bring us to our knees. It has a way of making us see our dependency on Him, and to pray. See Prov. 30:8,9.

hosts had sent by His Spirit through the former prophets. Thus great wrath came from the LORD of hosts. 13Therefore it happened, *that* just as He proclaimed and they would not hear, so they called out and I would not listen," says the LORD of hosts. 14"But I scattered them with a whirlwind among all the nations which they had not known. Thus the land became desolate after them, so that no one passed through or returned; for they made the pleasant land desolate."

Jerusalem, Holy City of the Future

8 Again the word of the LORD of hosts came, saying, 2"Thus says the LORD of hosts:

'I am zealous for Zion with great zeal;
With great fervor I am zealous for her.'

3"Thus says the LORD:

'I will return to Zion,
And dwell in the midst of Jerusalem.
Jerusalem shall be called the City of Truth,
The Mountain of the LORD of hosts,
The Holy Mountain.'

4"Thus says the LORD of hosts:

'Old men and old women shall again sit
In the streets of Jerusalem,
Each one with his staff in his hand
Because of great age.
5The streets of the city
Shall be full of boys and girls
Playing in its streets.'

6"Thus says the LORD of hosts:

'If it is marvelous in the eyes of the remnant of this people in these days,
Will it also be marvelous in My eyes?'
Says the LORD of hosts.

7"Thus says the LORD of hosts:

'Behold, I will save My people from the land of the east
And from the land of the west;
8I will bring them *back*,
And they shall dwell in the midst of Jerusalem.
They shall be My people
And I will be their God,
In truth and righteousness.'

9"Thus says the LORD of hosts:

'Let your hands be strong,
You who have been hearing in these days
These words by the mouth of the prophets,
Who *spoke* in the day the foundation was laid
For the house of the LORD of hosts,
That the temple might be built.
10For before these days
There were no wages for man nor any hire for beast;
There was no peace from the enemy for whoever went out or came in;
For I set all men, everyone, against his neighbor.

11But now I *will* not *treat* the remnant of this people as in the former days,' says the LORD of hosts.

12'For the seed *shall be* prosperous,
The vine shall give its fruit,
The ground shall give her increase,
And the heavens shall give their dew—

7:11,12 The unsaved refuse to hear; they pull away, stop their ears, and harden their hearts lest they should "hear the Law." God's Ten Commandments offend them (see Rom. 8:7). See also Neh. 9:29; Isa. 65:12; Prov. 1:24–28.

I will cause the remnant of this people
To possess all these.
13And it shall come to pass
That just as you were a curse among the nations,
O house of Judah and house of Israel,
So I will save you, and you shall be a blessing.
Do not fear,
Let your hands be strong.'

14"For thus says the LORD of hosts:

'Just as I determined to punish you
When your fathers provoked Me to wrath,'
Says the LORD of hosts,
'And I would not relent,
15So again in these days
I am determined to do good
To Jerusalem and to the house of Judah.
Do not fear.
16These *are* the things you shall do:
Speak each man the truth to his neighbor;
Give judgment in your gates for truth, justice, and peace;
17Let none of you think evil in your[a] heart against your neighbor;
And do not love a false oath.
For all these *are things* that I hate,'
Says the LORD."

18Then the word of the LORD of hosts
came to me, saying, 19"Thus says the LORD
of hosts:

'The fast of the fourth *month*,
The fast of the fifth,
The fast of the seventh,
And the fast of the tenth,
Shall be joy and gladness and cheerful feasts
For the house of Judah.
Therefore love truth and peace.'

20"Thus says the LORD of hosts:

'Peoples shall yet come,
Inhabitants of many cities;
21The inhabitants of one *city* shall go to another, saying,
"Let us continue to go and pray before the LORD,
And seek the LORD of hosts.
I myself will go also."
22Yes, many peoples and strong nations
Shall come to seek the LORD of hosts in Jerusalem,
And to pray before the LORD.'

23"Thus says the LORD of hosts: 'In those
days ten men from every language of the
nations shall grasp the sleeve of a Jewish
man, saying, "Let us go with you, for we
have heard *that* God *is* with you." ' "

Israel Defended Against Enemies

9 The burden[a] of the word of the LORD
Against the land of Hadrach,
And Damascus its resting place
(For the eyes of men
And all the tribes of Israel
Are on the LORD);
2Also *against* Hamath, *which* borders on it,
And *against* Tyre and Sidon, though they are very wise.

8:17 [a]Literally *his* 9:1 [a]Or *oracle*

8:12 Compare Isa. 30:23. If we will honor God, He will honor us.

8:21 "We give ourselves to prayer. We preach a gospel that saves to the uttermost, and witness to its power. We do not argue about worldliness; we witness. We do not discuss philosophy; we preach the gospel. We do not speculate about the destiny of sinners; we pluck them as brands from the burning. We ask no man's patronage. We beg no man's money. We fear no man's frown . . . Let no man join us who is afraid, and we want none but those who are saved, sanctified and aflame with the fire of the Holy Ghost."
Samuel Chadwick

[3]For Tyre built herself a tower,
Heaped up silver like the dust,
And gold like the mire of the streets.
[4]Behold, the Lord will cast her out;
He will destroy her power in the sea,
And she will be devoured by fire.

[5]Ashkelon shall see *it* and fear;
Gaza also shall be very sorrowful;
And Ekron, for He dried up her
expectation.
The king shall perish from Gaza,
And Ashkelon shall not be inhabited.

[6]"A mixed race shall settle in Ashdod,
And I will cut off the pride of the
Philistines.
[7]I will take away the blood from his
mouth,
And the abominations from between
his teeth.
But he who remains, even he *shall be*
for our God,
And shall be like a leader in Judah,
And Ekron like a Jebusite.
[8]I will camp around My house
Because of the army,
Because of him who passes by and
him who returns.
No more shall an oppressor pass
through them,
For now I have seen with My eyes.

The Coming King

[9]"Rejoice greatly, O daughter of Zion!
Shout, O daughter of Jerusalem!
Behold, your King is coming to you;
He *is* just and having salvation,
Lowly and riding on a donkey,
A colt, the foal of a donkey.
[10]I will cut off the chariot from Ephraim
And the horse from Jerusalem;
The battle bow shall be cut off.
He shall speak peace to the nations;
His dominion *shall be* 'from sea to sea,
And from the River to the ends of the
earth.'[a]

God Will Save His People

[11]"As for you also,
Because of the blood of your
covenant,
I will set your prisoners free from the
waterless pit.
[12]Return to the stronghold,
You prisoners of hope.
Even today I declare
That I will restore double to you.
[13]For I have bent Judah, My *bow*,
Fitted the bow with Ephraim,
And raised up your sons, O Zion,
Against your sons, O Greece,
And made you like the sword of a
mighty man."

> Contrary to popular belief, you *can* take it with you . . . Living a holy life, leading others to Christ as we share our faith, doing good works in Christ's name, all of these things are materials that may be sent on ahead.
>
> **BILLY GRAHAM**

[14]Then the LORD will be seen over
them,
And His arrow will go forth like
lightning.
The Lord GOD will blow the trumpet,
And go with whirlwinds from the
south.
[15]The LORD of hosts will defend them;
They shall devour and subdue with
slingstones.
They shall drink *and* roar as if with
wine;
They shall be filled *with blood* like
basins,
Like the corners of the altar.
[16]The LORD their God will save them in
that day,
As the flock of His people.

9:10 [a]Psalm 72:8

9:9 This messianic prophecy was fulfilled in Matt. 21:4–11; John 12:12–16.

For they *shall be like* the jewels of a
crown,
Lifted like a banner over His land—
17For how great is its[a] goodness
And how great its[b] beauty!
Grain shall make the young men
thrive,
And new wine the young women.

Restoration of Judah and Israel

10 Ask the LORD for rain
In the time of the latter rain.[a]
The LORD will make flashing clouds;
He will give them showers of rain,
Grass in the field for everyone.

2For the idols[a] speak delusion;
The diviners envision lies,
And tell false dreams;
They comfort in vain.
Therefore *the people* wend their way
like sheep;
They are in trouble because *there is* no
shepherd.

3"My anger is kindled against the
shepherds,
And I will punish the goatherds.
For the LORD of hosts will visit His
flock,
The house of Judah,
And will make them as His royal
horse in the battle.
4From him comes the cornerstone,
From him the tent peg,
From him the battle bow,
From him every ruler[a] together.
5They shall be like mighty men,
Who tread down *their enemies*
In the mire of the streets in the battle.
They shall fight because the LORD is
with them,
And the riders on horses shall be put
to shame.

6"I will strengthen the house of Judah,
And I will save the house of Joseph.
I will bring them back,
Because I have mercy on them.
They shall be as though I had not cast
them aside;
For I *am* the LORD their God,
And I will hear them.
7*Those of* Ephraim shall be like a
mighty man,
And their heart shall rejoice as if with
wine.
Yes, their children shall see *it* and be
glad;
Their heart shall rejoice in the LORD.
8I will whistle for them and gather
them,
For I will redeem them;
And they shall increase as they once
increased.

9"I will sow them among the peoples,
And they shall remember Me in far
countries;
They shall live, together with their
children,
And they shall return.
10I will also bring them back from the
land of Egypt,
And gather them from Assyria.
I will bring them into the land of
Gilead and Lebanon,
Until no *more room* is found for them.
11He shall pass through the sea with
affliction,
And strike the waves of the sea:
All the depths of the River[a] shall dry
up.
Then the pride of Assyria shall be
brought down,
And the scepter of Egypt shall depart.

12"So I will strengthen them in the LORD,
And they shall walk up and down in

9:17 [a]Or *His* [b]Or *His* 10:1 [a]That is, spring rain 10:2 [a]Hebrew *teraphim* 10:4 [a]Or *despot* 10:11 [a]That is, the Nile

10:2 Jesus was moved with compassion when He saw multitudes who were like sheep without a shepherd. See Matt. 9:36.

His name,"
Says the LORD.

Desolation of Israel

11 Open your doors, O Lebanon,
That fire may devour your cedars.
2Wail, O cypress, for the cedar has
fallen,
Because the mighty *trees* are ruined.
Wail, O oaks of Bashan,
For the thick forest has come down.
3*There is* the sound of wailing
shepherds!
For their glory is in ruins.
There is the sound of roaring lions!
For the pride[a] of the Jordan is in
ruins.

Prophecy of the Shepherds

4Thus says the LORD my God, "Feed the flock for slaughter, 5whose owners slaughter them and feel no guilt; those who sell them say, 'Blessed be the LORD, for I am rich'; and their shepherds do not pity them. 6For I will no longer pity the inhabitants of the land," says the LORD. "But indeed I will give everyone into his neighbor's hand and into the hand of his king. They shall attack the land, and I will not deliver *them* from their hand."

7So I fed the flock for slaughter, in particular the poor of the flock.[a] I took for myself two staffs: the one I called Beauty,[b] and the other I called Bonds;[c] and I fed the flock. 8I dismissed the three shepherds in one month. My soul loathed them, and their soul also abhorred me. 9Then I said, "I will not feed you. Let what is dying die, and what is perishing perish. Let those that are left eat each other's flesh." 10And I took my staff, Beauty, and cut it in two, that I might break the covenant which I had made with all the peoples. 11So it was broken on that day. Thus the poor[a] of the flock, who were watching me, knew that it *was* the word of the LORD. 12Then I said to them, "If it is agreeable to you, give *me* my wages; and if not, refrain." So they weighed out for my wages thirty *pieces* of silver.

13And the LORD said to me, "Throw it to the potter"—that princely price they set on me. So I took the thirty *pieces* of silver and threw them into the house of the LORD for the potter. 14Then I cut in two my other staff, Bonds, that I might break the brotherhood between Judah and Israel.

15And the LORD said to me, "Next, take for yourself the implements of a foolish shepherd. 16For indeed I will raise up a shepherd in the land *who* will not care for those who are cut off, nor seek the young, nor heal those that are broken, nor feed those that still stand. But he will eat the flesh of the fat and tear their hooves in pieces.

17"Woe to the worthless shepherd,
Who leaves the flock!
A sword *shall be* against his arm
And against his right eye;
His arm shall completely wither,
And his right eye shall be totally
blinded."

The Coming Deliverance of Judah

12 The burden[a] of the word of the LORD against Israel. Thus says the LORD, who stretches out the heavens, lays the foundation of the earth, and forms the spirit of man within him: 2"Behold, I will make Jerusalem a cup of drunkenness to all the surrounding peoples, when they lay siege against Judah and Jerusalem. 3And it shall happen in that day that I will make Jerusalem a very heavy stone for all peoples; all who would heave it away will surely be cut in pieces, though all nations of the earth are gath-

11:3 [a]Or *floodplain, thicket* 11:7 [a]Following Masoretic Text, Targum, and Vulgate; Septuagint reads *for the Canaanites.* [b]Or *Grace,* and so in verse 10 [c]Or *Unity,* and so in verse 14 11:11 [a]Following Masoretic Text, Targum, and Vulgate; Septuagint reads *the Canaanites.* 12:1 [a]Or *oracle*

11:12,13 This messianic prophecy was fulfilled in Matt. 26:14,15; 27:3–10.

ered against it. 4In that day," says the
LORD, "I will strike every horse with confusion, and its rider with madness; I will
open My eyes on the house of Judah,
and will strike every horse of the peoples
with blindness. 5And the governors of
Judah shall say in their heart, 'The inhabitants of Jerusalem *are* my strength in
the LORD of hosts, their God.' 6In that
day I will make the governors of Judah
like a firepan in the woodpile, and like a
fiery torch in the sheaves; they shall devour all the surrounding peoples on the
right hand and on the left, but Jerusalem
shall be inhabited again in her own
place—Jerusalem.

7"The LORD will save the tents of Judah
first, so that the glory of the house of
David and the glory of the inhabitants of
Jerusalem shall not become greater than
that of Judah. 8In that day the LORD will
defend the inhabitants of Jerusalem; the
one who is feeble among them in that day
shall be like David, and the house of
David *shall be* like God, like the Angel of
the LORD before them. 9It shall be in that
day *that* I will seek to destroy all the nations that come against Jerusalem.

Mourning for the Pierced One

10"And I will pour on the house of
David and on the inhabitants of Jerusalem the Spirit of grace and supplication; then they will look on Me whom
they pierced. Yes, they will mourn for
Him as one mourns for *his* only *son*, and
grieve for Him as one grieves for a firstborn. 11In that day there shall be a great
mourning in Jerusalem, like the mourning at Hadad Rimmon in the plain of
Megiddo.[a] 12And the land shall mourn,
every family by itself: the family of the
house of David by itself, and their wives
by themselves; the family of the house of
Nathan by itself, and their wives by
themselves; 13the family of the house of
Levi by itself, and their wives by themselves; the family of Shimei by itself, and
their wives by themselves; 14all the families that remain, every family by itself,
and their wives by themselves.

· · · · · ·

Was Jesus God in human form?
See Matt. 8:2 comment.

· · · · · ·

Idolatry Cut Off

13 "In that day a fountain shall be
opened for the house of David
and for the inhabitants of Jerusalem, for
sin and for uncleanness.

2"It shall be in that day," says the LORD
of hosts, "*that* I will cut off the names of
the idols from the land, and they shall no
longer be remembered. I will also cause
the prophets and the unclean spirit to depart from the land. 3It shall come to pass
that if anyone still prophesies, then his father and mother who begot him will say
to him, 'You shall not live, because you
have spoken lies in the name of the
LORD.' And his father and mother who

12:11 [a]Hebrew *Megiddon*

12:10 This messianic prophecy of Jesus' crucifixion was fulfilled in John 19:34,37. See also Psa. 22:16.

12:11 The phrase "in that day" appears seven times in this chapter, referring to the coming Day of the Lord. See 14:1; Rev. 1:7.

"We do not grudge to the seed of Israel after the flesh the first application of this very precious promise. There will be a day when those who have so long refused to acknowledge Jesus as the Messiah shall discern the marks of his mission, and shall mourn that they have pierced him. When the tribes of Israel shall lament their sin with holy earnestness, there shall be no mourning to exceed it, they shall weep even as in the mourning of Hadadrimmon in the valley of Megiddo, when the well-beloved Josiah was slain. Discovering that their nation rejected the Son of God, when they crucified Jesus of Nazareth, their deeply religious spirit shall be filled with the utmost bitterness of repentance, and each man and each woman shall cry for pardon to the Lord of mercy." *Charles Spurgeon*

begot him shall thrust him through when he prophesies.

[4]"And it shall be in that day *that* every prophet will be ashamed of his vision when he prophesies; they will not wear a robe of coarse hair to deceive. [5]But he will say, 'I *am* no prophet, I *am* a farmer; for a man taught me to keep cattle from my youth.' [6]And *one* will say to him, 'What are these wounds between your arms?'[a] Then he will answer, '*Those* with which I was wounded in the house of my friends.'

The Shepherd Savior

[7]"Awake, O sword, against My
Shepherd,
Against the Man who is My
Companion,"
Says the LORD of hosts.
"Strike the Shepherd,
And the sheep will be scattered;
Then I will turn My hand against the
little ones.
[8]And it shall come to pass in all the
land,"
Says the LORD,
"*That* two-thirds in it shall be cut off
and die,
But *one*-third shall be left in it:
[9]I will bring the *one*-third through the
fire,
Will refine them as silver is refined,
And test them as gold is tested.
They will call on My name,
And I will answer them.
I will say, 'This *is* My people';
And each one will say, 'The LORD *is*
my God.' "

The Day of the Lord

14 Behold, the day of the LORD is coming,
And your spoil will be divided in your midst.
[2]For I will gather all the nations to
battle against Jerusalem;
The city shall be taken,
The houses rifled,
And the women ravished.
Half of the city shall go into captivity,
But the remnant of the people shall
not be cut off from the city.

[3]Then the LORD will go forth
And fight against those nations,
As He fights in the day of battle.
[4]And in that day His feet will stand on
the Mount of Olives,
Which faces Jerusalem on the east.
And the Mount of Olives shall be split
in two,
From east to west,
Making a very large valley;
Half of the mountain shall move
toward the north
And half of it toward the south.

[5]Then you shall flee *through* My
mountain valley,
For the mountain valley shall reach to
Azal.
Yes, you shall flee
As you fled from the earthquake
In the days of Uzziah king of Judah.

Thus the LORD my God will come,
And all the saints with You.[a]

[6]It shall come to pass in that day
That there will be no light;
The lights will diminish.
[7]It shall be one day
Which is known to the LORD—
Neither day nor night.
But at evening time it shall happen
That it will be light.

[8]And in that day it shall be
That living waters shall flow from

13:6 [a]Or *hands* 14:5 [a]Or *you;* Septuagint, Targum, and Vulgate read *Him.*

13:7 This messianic prophecy, repeated by Jesus in Matt. 26:31,32, was fulfilled in Matt. 26:56; Mark 14:50. See Ezek. 34:23 comment.

Jerusalem,
Half of them toward the eastern sea
And half of them toward the western sea;
In both summer and winter it shall occur.
9And the LORD shall be King over all the earth.
In that day it shall be—
"The LORD *is* one,"[a]
And His name one.

10All the land shall be turned into a plain from Geba to Rimmon south of Jerusalem. *Jerusalem*[a] shall be raised up and inhabited in her place from Benjamin's Gate to the place of the First Gate and the Corner Gate, and *from* the Tower of Hananel to the king's winepresses.

11*The people* shall dwell in it;
And no longer shall there be utter destruction,
But Jerusalem shall be safely inhabited.

12And this shall be the plague with which the LORD will strike all the people who fought against Jerusalem:

Their flesh shall dissolve while they stand on their feet,
Their eyes shall dissolve in their sockets,
And their tongues shall dissolve in their mouths.

13It shall come to pass in that day
That a great panic from the LORD will be among them.
Everyone will seize the hand of his neighbor,
And raise his hand against his neighbor's hand;
14Judah also will fight at Jerusalem.
And the wealth of all the surrounding nations
Shall be gathered together:
Gold, silver, and apparel in great abundance.

15Such also shall be the plague
On the horse *and* the mule,
On the camel and the donkey,
And on all the cattle that will be in those camps.
So *shall* this plague *be*.

The Nations Worship the King

16And it shall come to pass *that* everyone who is left of all the nations which came against Jerusalem shall go up from year to year to worship the King, the LORD of hosts, and to keep the Feast of Tabernacles. 17And it shall be *that* whichever of the families of the earth do not come up to Jerusalem to worship the King, the LORD of hosts, on them there will be no rain. 18If the family of Egypt will not come up and enter in, they *shall have* no *rain;* they shall receive the plague with which the LORD strikes the nations who do not come up to keep the Feast of Tabernacles. 19This shall be the punishment of Egypt and the punishment of all the nations that do not come up to keep the Feast of Tabernacles.

20In that day "HOLINESS TO THE LORD" shall be *engraved* on the bells of the horses. The pots in the LORD's house shall be like the bowls before the altar. 21Yes, every pot in Jerusalem and Judah shall be holiness to the LORD of hosts.[a] Everyone who sacrifices shall come and take them and cook in them. In that day there shall no longer be a Canaanite in the house of the LORD of hosts.

14:9 [a]Compare Deuteronomy 6:4 14:10 [a]Literally *She*
14:21 [a]Or *on every pot...shall be (engraved) "HOLINESS TO THE LORD OF HOSTS"*

14:8 How wonderful will that day be! The knowledge of the glory of the Lord will cover the earth, as the waters cover the sea (see Hab. 2:14). In the meanwhile, we have a limited time to take the living waters of the gospel to this lost and dying world. Don't waste your life chasing things that don't matter. Pray that God gives you such love for the lost that it will swallow your fears.

Malachi

1 The burden[a] of the word of the LORD
to Israel by Malachi.

Israel Beloved of God

2"I have loved you," says the LORD.
"Yet you say, 'In what way have You loved us?'
Was not Esau Jacob's brother?"
Says the LORD.
"Yet Jacob I have loved;
3But Esau I have hated,
And laid waste his mountains and his heritage
For the jackals of the wilderness."

4Even though Edom has said,
"We have been impoverished,
But we will return and build the desolate places,"

Thus says the LORD of hosts:

"They may build, but I will throw down;
They shall be called the Territory of Wickedness,
And the people against whom the LORD will have indignation forever.
5Your eyes shall see,
And you shall say,
'The LORD is magnified beyond the border of Israel.'

Polluted Offerings

6"A son honors *his* father,
And a servant *his* master.
If then I am the Father,
Where *is* My honor?
And if I *am* a Master,
Where *is* My reverence?
Says the LORD of hosts
To you priests who despise My name.
Yet you say, 'In what way have we despised Your name?'

7"You offer defiled food on My altar,
But say,
'In what way have we defiled You?'
By saying,
'The table of the LORD is contemptible.'
8And when you offer the blind as a sacrifice,
Is it not evil?
And when you offer the lame and sick,
Is it not evil?
Offer it then to your governor!
Would he be pleased with you?
Would he accept you favorably?"
Says the LORD of hosts.

9"But now entreat God's favor,
That He may be gracious to us.

1:1 [a]Or *oracle*

1:2,3 The Bible often uses hyperbole, contrasting love with hate, for the sake of emphasis. To say that God is "all loving," as the ungodly so often maintain, is to create an idol to worship. God is love, but He is also just, holy, and righteous. He loves us because He chooses to; He is not a slave to sentiment.

1:8 The sacrifice of ourselves to the service of God is now acceptable because of Calvary (see Rom. 12:1,2).

While this is being *done* by your hands,
Will He accept you favorably?"
Says the LORD of hosts.
10"Who *is there* even among you who would shut the doors,
So that you would not kindle fire *on* My altar in vain?
I have no pleasure in you,"
Says the LORD of hosts,
"Nor will I accept an offering from your hands.
11For from the rising of the sun, even to its going down,
My name *shall be* great among the Gentiles;
In every place incense *shall be* offered to My name,
And a pure offering;
For My name shall be great among the nations,"
Says the LORD of hosts.

12"But you profane it,
In that you say,
'The table of the LORD[a] is defiled;
And its fruit, its food, *is* contemptible.'
13You also say,
'Oh, what a weariness!'
And you sneer at it,"
Says the LORD of hosts.
"And you bring the stolen, the lame, and the sick;
Thus you bring an offering!
Should I accept this from your hand?"
Says the LORD.
14"But cursed *be* the deceiver
Who has in his flock a male,
And takes a vow,
But sacrifices to the Lord what is blemished—
For I *am* a great King,"
Says the LORD of hosts,
"And My name *is to be* feared among the nations.

Corrupt Priests

2 "And now, O priests, this commandment is for you.
2If you will not hear,
And if you will not take *it* to heart,
To give glory to My name,"
Says the LORD of hosts,
"I will send a curse upon you,
And I will curse your blessings.
Yes, I have cursed them already,
Because you do not take *it* to heart.

3"Behold, I will rebuke your descendants
And spread refuse on your faces,
The refuse of your solemn feasts;
And *one* will take you away with it.
4Then you shall know that I have sent this commandment to you,
That My covenant with Levi may continue,"
Says the LORD of hosts.
5"My covenant was with him, *one* of life and peace,
And I gave them to him *that he might* fear *Me;*
So he feared Me
And was reverent before My name.
6The law of truth[a] was in his mouth,
And injustice was not found on his lips.
He walked with Me in peace and equity,
And turned many away from iniquity.

7"For the lips of a priest should keep knowledge,
And *people* should seek the law from his mouth;
For he is the messenger of the LORD of hosts.
8But you have departed from the way;

1:12 [a]Following Bomberg; Masoretic Text reads *Lord.* **2:6** [a]Or *true instruction*

1:11 It was never God's intention to confine salvation to the Jews, as the early Church surmised (see Acts 10:45; 11:18). The call to salvation is universal. See John 3:16; Rom. 3:29; 10:11–13.

"We must be global Christians with a global vision because our God is a global God." *John Stott*

Questions & Objections

2:10 *"We're all children of God."*

The world often says that *all* humans are children of God—no matter what race, color, or creed—therefore it doesn't matter which religion (if any) we follow. That sounds virtuous, but it is not what the Bible teaches. While mankind was made in God's image—with a moral compass that sets us apart from the animal kingdom—the Bible makes it clear that we are not all His "children." Rather, in our unredeemed state we are called "children of wrath" (see Eph. 2:3). This is because we have a nature that is hostile to God (see Rom. 8:7). Jesus told the religious leaders of His time that the devil was their father: "You are of your father the devil, and the desires of your father you want to do" (John 8:44). We become children of God only when we are born of His Spirit (see John 3:3), and it is only then that we can call God "Father" (see Rom. 8:15). When that happens, the Holy Spirit will bear witness with us that we are children of God (see Rom. 8:16).

You have caused many to stumble at
the law.
You have corrupted the covenant of
Levi,"
Says the LORD of hosts.
9"Therefore I also have made you
contemptible and base
Before all the people,
Because you have not kept My ways
But have shown partiality in the law."

The Function of the Law

2:5-8 The covenant of the Law was given that we might fear God. Those who preach the gospel with no reference to God's Law will reap "converts" who have no reverence for God. Verse 5 underscores the Third Commandment, which demands reverence for God's holy name.

The end of these "converts" can be seen in Matt. 7:21–23. They continue to practice "lawlessness" despite doing religious works in His name. The genuine convert, however, will have the Law of truth in his mouth. He will magnify God's Law and make it honorable (see Isa. 42:21). He has named the name of Christ and departed from iniquity (see 2 Tim. 2:19). Iniquity is not found in his lips, and he turns many away from iniquity because his preaching makes continual reference to the Law that sinners have violated.

Jesus rebuked the lawyers, those who should have been preaching God's Law to bring the knowledge of sin to Israel. He said, "You have taken away the key of knowledge" (Luke 11:52). It is the key of the Law that leads to the door of the Savior. It is a "tutor to bring us to Christ" (see Gal. 3:24).

If you want sinners to be saved, don't be afraid to confront them with the Ten Commandments. For details and instructions on how to do this, see Luke 11:52 and John 4:7 comments.

Treachery of Infidelity

10Have we not all one Father?
Has not one God created us?
Why do we deal treacherously with
one another
By profaning the covenant of the
fathers?
11Judah has dealt treacherously,
And an abomination has been committed in Israel and in Jerusalem,
For Judah has profaned
The LORD's holy *institution* which He
loves:
He has married the daughter of a
foreign god.
12May the LORD cut off from the tents of
Jacob
The man who does this, being awake
and aware,[a]
Yet who brings an offering to the
LORD of hosts!

13And this is the second thing you do:
You cover the altar of the LORD with
tears,
With weeping and crying;
So He does not regard the offering
anymore,
Nor receive *it* with goodwill from
your hands.
14Yet you say, "For what reason?"

2:12 [a]Talmud and Vulgate read *teacher and student.*

Because the LORD has been witness
Between you and the wife of your youth,
With whom you have dealt treacherously;
Yet she is your companion
And your wife by covenant.
15But did He not make *them* one,
Having a remnant of the Spirit?
And why one?
He seeks godly offspring.
Therefore take heed to your spirit,
And let none deal treacherously with the wife of his youth.

16"For the LORD God of Israel says
That He hates divorce,
For it covers one's garment with violence,"
Says the LORD of hosts.
"Therefore take heed to your spirit,
That you do not deal treacherously."

17You have wearied the LORD with your words;
Yet you say,
"In what way have we wearied *Him?*"
In that you say,
"Everyone who does evil
Is good in the sight of the LORD,
And He delights in them,"
Or, "Where *is* the God of justice?"

The Coming Messenger

3 "Behold, I send My messenger,
And he will prepare the way before Me.
And the Lord, whom you seek,
Will suddenly come to His temple,
Even the Messenger of the covenant,
In whom you delight.
Behold, He is coming,"
Says the LORD of hosts.

2"But who can endure the day of His coming?
And who can stand when He appears?
For He *is* like a refiner's fire
And like launderers' soap.
3He will sit as a refiner and a purifier of silver;
He will purify the sons of Levi,
And purge them as gold and silver,
That they may offer to the LORD
An offering in righteousness.

4"Then the offering of Judah and Jerusalem
Will be pleasant to the LORD,
As in the days of old,

2:15 How to raise godly offspring. If you want "godly offspring," it is essential that you make the time to establish a family altar. Build it out of the unmovable rocks of resolution. You will need to be resolute about this because it will be a battle. Your flesh will fight it, and you can be sure there will be a continual spiritual battle within your mind. "Circumstances" will constantly crop up. Your kids will occasionally groan when you announce that it is time for devotions. Loved ones may subtly, subconsciously discourage you. However, your time of family devotions should be a priority for your whole family. Don't be legalistic about it, but as much as possible, put all other things aside before you postpone or cancel family devotions.

It will be an altar of sacrifice, as you sacrifice your time, your energy, and sometimes your dignity. For years, our kids heard, "Six o'clock—reading time." My wife and I dropped whatever we were doing, and the children learned to do the same, and we gathered as a family. Making it a priority for your family's growth will speak volumes about its importance in their lives.

Again, you will find that there are many *excuses* for not having devotions. You may be pressed for time, feel tired, or think you are unable to teach the Bible. However, there is one very powerful reason why you should have daily devotions: the eternal salvation of your children. (Adapted from *How to Bring Your Children to Christ... & Keep Them There.*)

For suggestions on having a family devotional time, see Josh. 4:21,22 comment.

2:17 This is what we see in this generation. Evildoers think they are good people, while advocating the killing of children in the womb, homosexual marriages, and other things that are offensive to God. All the while they think their behavior is fine in God's eyes. That is why the Law must be thundered from the pulpits and echoed in the streets.

3:1 This prophecy of John the Baptist was fulfilled in Matt. 11:10; Luke 1:13–17; 1:76. See also Isa. 40:3.

As in former years.
[5]And I will come near you for judgment;
I will be a swift witness
Against sorcerers,
Against adulterers,
Against perjurers,
Against those who exploit wage
earners and widows and
orphans,
And against those who turn away an
alien—
Because they do not fear Me,"
Says the LORD of hosts.

[6]"For I *am* the LORD, I do not change;
Therefore you are not consumed, O
sons of Jacob.
[7]Yet from the days of your fathers
You have gone away from My
ordinances
And have not kept *them*.
Return to Me, and I will return to you,"
Says the LORD of hosts.
"But you said,
'In what way shall we return?'

Do Not Rob God

[8]"Will a man rob God?
Yet you have robbed Me!
But you say,
'In what way have we robbed You?'
In tithes and offerings.
[9]You are cursed with a curse,
For you have robbed Me,
Even this whole nation.
[10]Bring all the tithes into the storehouse,
That there may be food in My house,
And try Me now in this,"
Says the LORD of hosts,
"If I will not open for you the windows
of heaven
And pour out for you *such* blessing
That *there will* not *be room* enough *to
receive it*.

[11]"And I will rebuke the devourer for
your sakes,
So that he will not destroy the fruit of
your ground,
Nor shall the vine fail to bear fruit for
you in the field,"
Says the LORD of hosts;
[12]And all nations will call you blessed,
For you will be a delightful land,"
Says the LORD of hosts.

The People Complain Harshly

[13]"Your words have been harsh against
Me,"
Says the LORD,
"Yet you say,
'What have we spoken against You?'
[14]You have said,
'It is useless to serve God;
What profit *is it* that we have kept His
ordinance,
And that we have walked as
mourners
Before the LORD of hosts?

THE FUNCTION OF THE LAW

3:5 The reason for sorcery, adultery, false witness, and other transgressions of God's Law is a lack of the fear of God. Never hesitate to preach the fear of God. It causes sinners to depart from sin (see Prov. 16:6). Preach the thunderings and lightnings of Mount Sinai and future punishment!

The preaching of the Law without retribution will not be effective in winning souls for Christ. It has been well said that God's Law without consequence is nothing but good advice. The world will agree with "You shall not kill." That makes sense. They will smile at "You shall not commit adultery." They know it destroys families. They will give assent to "You shall not bear false witness." They know that it harms friendships. The Ten Commandments certainly are good advice. However, when you preach the Law with the message that God "will judge the world in righteousness" (as Paul preached in Athens; see Acts 17:22–31), your listeners may be provoked to say, "We will hear you again on this matter" (Acts 17:32). And sinners will be soundly saved.

3:6 Those ignorant of Holy Scripture say, "The God of the Old Testament is a God of wrath, while the God of the New Testament is loving and kind." He never changes. He is just as wrath-filled in the New Testament, and just as kind in the Old. For details, see Psa. 89:14 comment.

[15]So now we call the proud blessed,
For those who do wickedness are raised up;
They even tempt God and go free.' "

A Book of Remembrance

[16]Then those who feared the LORD spoke to one another,
And the LORD listened and heard *them;*
So a book of remembrance was written before Him
For those who fear the LORD
And who meditate on His name.

[17]"They shall be Mine," says the LORD of hosts,
"On the day that I make them My jewels.[a]
And I will spare them
As a man spares his own son who serves him."
[18]Then you shall again discern
Between the righteous and the wicked,
Between one who serves God
And one who does not serve Him.

The Great Day of God

4 "For behold, the day is coming,
Burning like an oven,
And all the proud, yes, all who do wickedly will be stubble.
And the day which is coming shall burn them up,"
Says the LORD of hosts,
"That will leave them neither root nor branch.
[2]But to you who fear My name
The Sun of Righteousness shall arise
With healing in His wings;
And you shall go out
And grow fat like stall-fed calves.
[3]You shall trample the wicked,
For they shall be ashes under the soles of your feet
On the day that I do *this,*"
Says the LORD of hosts.

[4]"Remember the Law of Moses, My servant,
Which I commanded him in Horeb for all Israel,
With the statutes and judgments.
[5]Behold, I will send you Elijah the prophet
Before the coming of the great and dreadful day of the LORD.
[6]And he will turn
The hearts of the fathers to the children,
And the hearts of the children to their fathers,
Lest I come and strike the earth with a curse."

3:17 [a]Literally *special treasure*

THE FUNCTION OF THE LAW

4:4,5 We are not to forget the Law once we have trusted the Savior. Like John the Baptist, its function is to prepare the way of the Lord (see Gal. 3:24). Does the student, after he graduates, forget the knowledge given by his tutor? That knowledge may now be used to instruct lost sinners on why they, too, need the Savior.

May we go "in the spirit and power of Elijah" as we speak of the "coming of the great and dreadful day of the Lord." Be sure to precede the message of grace with the just and holy Law. In doing so, you will make grace amazing.

3:16 Those who love and fear God cannot *but* speak of His wondrous love and kindness, especially in light of the cross. (See also Psa. 66:16.) Notice here and in 4:2 the importance of the fear of the Lord—a doctrine that is despised by the world as well as by many who profess to be part of the Church.

3:18 Are we serving God by seeking the lost? Or do we lift our hands in worship to God, but refuse to reach out our hands in evangelism for God? Worship without service is empty hypocrisy. It is to draw near to Him with our lips, but have our hearts far from Him (see Isa. 29:13). It is to worship Him in vain (see Mark 7:7). If the average church made as much noise about God on Mondays as it makes to God on Sundays, we would see revival.

4:5,6 This prophecy of John the Baptist was fulfilled in Matt. 11:14; 17:10–13; Luke 1:17.

The New Testament

Matthew

The Genealogy of Jesus Christ

1 The book of the genealogy of Jesus Christ, the Son of David, the Son of Abraham:

[2]Abraham begot Isaac, Isaac begot Jacob, and Jacob begot Judah and his brothers. [3]Judah begot Perez and Zerah by Tamar, Perez begot Hezron, and Hezron begot Ram. [4]Ram begot Amminadab, Amminadab begot Nahshon, and Nahshon begot Salmon. [5]Salmon begot Boaz by Rahab, Boaz begot Obed by Ruth, Obed begot Jesse, [6]and Jesse begot David the king.

David the king begot Solomon by her *who had been the wife*[a] of Uriah. [7]Solomon begot Rehoboam, Rehoboam begot Abijah, and Abijah begot Asa.[a] [8]Asa begot Jehoshaphat, Jehoshaphat begot Joram, and Joram begot Uzziah. [9]Uzziah begot Jotham, Jotham begot Ahaz, and Ahaz begot Hezekiah. [10]Hezekiah begot Manasseh, Manasseh begot Amon,[a] and Amon begot Josiah. [11]Josiah begot Jeconiah and his brothers about the time they were carried away to Babylon.

[12]And after they were brought to Babylon, Jeconiah begot Shealtiel, and Shealtiel begot Zerubbabel. [13]Zerubbabel begot Abiud, Abiud begot Eliakim, and Eliakim begot Azor. [14]Azor begot Zadok, Zadok begot Achim, and Achim begot Eliud. [15]Eliud begot Eleazar, Eleazar begot Matthan, and Matthan begot Jacob. [16]And Jacob begot Joseph the husband of Mary, of whom was born Jesus who is called Christ.

[17]So all the generations from Abraham to David *are* fourteen generations, from David until the captivity in Babylon *are* fourteen generations, and from the captivity in Babylon until the Christ *are* fourteen generations.

Christ Born of Mary

[18]Now the birth of Jesus Christ was as follows: After His mother Mary was be-

1:6 [a]Words in italic type have been added for clarity. They are not found in the original Greek. 1:7 [a]NU-Text reads *Asaph.* 1:10 [a]NU-Text reads *Amos.*

1:1 Genealogy errors? Some point to the different genealogies of Jesus as "errors" in the Bible. However, Matthew gives the paternal genealogy of the Messiah (through His legal father), and Luke (3:23) gives His maternal genealogy (through His mother). Some skeptics also claim that Jesus cannot be the Son of God if Joseph was His father, "as the two genealogies attest," and that the prophecy that the Messiah would descend from the line of David was thus unfulfilled.

However, Luke 3:23 says "as was supposed," meaning Jesus was *thought to be* the son of Joseph. He wasn't. He was the Son of God (God manifest in human form). Matthew 1:16 says, "Joseph the husband of Mary, of whom was born Jesus who is called Christ." In neither case is Joseph called the father of Jesus.

In both of these lists, the genealogy goes through the lineage of David (Luke 3:31 and Matt. 1:6). Mary is a descendant of David through Nathan, giving Jesus the physical right to David's throne. Joseph, as the adoptive father, gives Jesus the legal right to David's throne. See also Luke 3:23 comment.

trothed to Joseph, before they came together, she was found with child of the Holy Spirit. 19Then Joseph her husband, being a just *man,* and not wanting to make her a public example, was minded to put her away secretly. 20But while he thought about these things, behold, an angel of the Lord appeared to him in a dream, saying, "Joseph, son of David, do not be afraid to take to you Mary your wife, for that which is conceived in her is of the Holy Spirit. 21And she will bring forth a Son, and you shall call His name JESUS, for He will save His people from their sins."

22So all this was done that it might be fulfilled which was spoken by the Lord through the prophet, saying: 23*"Behold, the virgin shall be with child, and bear a Son, and they shall call His name Immanuel,"*[a] which is translated, "God with us."

24Then Joseph, being aroused from sleep, did as the angel of the Lord commanded him and took to him his wife, 25and did not know her till she had brought forth her firstborn Son.[a] And he called His name JESUS.

Wise Men from the East

2 Now after Jesus was born in Bethlehem of Judea in the days of Herod the king, behold, wise men from the East came to Jerusalem, 2saying, "Where is He who has been born King of the Jews? For we have seen His star in the East and have come to worship Him."

3When Herod the king heard *this,* he was troubled, and all Jerusalem with him. 4And when he had gathered all the chief priests and scribes of the people together, he inquired of them where the Christ was to be born.

5So they said to him, "In Bethlehem of Judea, for thus it is written by the prophet:

6*'But you, Bethlehem, in the land of*
Judah,
Are not the least among the rulers of
Judah;
For out of you shall come a Ruler
Who will shepherd My people
Israel.'"[a]

7Then Herod, when he had secretly called the wise men, determined from them what time the star appeared. 8And he sent them to Bethlehem and said, "Go and search carefully for the young Child, and when you have found *Him,* bring back word to me, that I may come and worship Him also."

9When they heard the king, they departed; and behold, the star which they had seen in the East went before them, till it came and stood over where the young Child was. 10When they saw the star, they rejoiced with exceedingly great joy. 11And when they had come into the house, they saw the young Child with Mary His mother, and fell down and worshiped Him. And when they had opened their treasures, they presented gifts to

1:23 [a]Isaiah 7:14. Words in oblique type in the New Testament are quoted from the Old Testament. **1:25** [a]NU-Text reads *a Son.* **2:6** [a]Micah 5:2

1:20–23 Some say this was not a "virgin" but merely a "young maiden." Isaiah 7:14 says that God Himself will give a "sign." A young maiden becoming pregnant is not a sign from God, but an everyday occurrence. A *virgin* conceiving is a supernatural sign. See Luke 1:31–35.

2:1 Wise men still seek Him. How is it that these wise men, who were not Jews, were aware of the birth of the "King of the Jews"? That they not only understood who He was, but desired to worship Him (v. 2) shows that God is able to reveal Himself to people in all lands and call them to Himself. These wise men "rejoiced with exceedingly great joy" as God used a star to guide them to the Christ Child, then they "fell down and worshiped Him" (vv. 9–11). They made great personal and financial sacrifices to see this Child: they traveled a great distance, spent months away from their homes, and gave extravagant gifts to this newborn King.

Those who are wise today will listen for His voice, follow His guidance, and be willing to sacrifice everything for so great a privilege as meeting the King. See Phil. 3:8.

Him: gold, frankincense, and myrrh.

[12]Then, being divinely warned in a dream that they should not return to Herod, they departed for their own country another way.

The Flight into Egypt

[13]Now when they had departed, behold, an angel of the Lord appeared to Joseph in a dream, saying, "Arise, take the young Child and His mother, flee to Egypt, and stay there until I bring you word; for Herod will seek the young Child to destroy Him."

[14]When he arose, he took the young Child and His mother by night and departed for Egypt, [15]and was there until the death of Herod, that it might be fulfilled which was spoken by the Lord through the prophet, saying, *"Out of Egypt I called My Son."*[a]

Massacre of the Innocents

[16]Then Herod, when he saw that he was deceived by the wise men, was exceedingly angry; and he sent forth and put to death all the male children who were in Bethlehem and in all its districts, from two years old and under, according to the time which he had determined from the wise men. [17]Then was fulfilled what was spoken by Jeremiah the prophet, saying:

[18]*"A voice was heard in Ramah,*
Lamentation, weeping, and great
mourning,
Rachel weeping for her children,
Refusing to be comforted,
Because they are no more."[a]

The Home in Nazareth

[19]Now when Herod was dead, behold, an angel of the Lord appeared in a dream to Joseph in Egypt, [20]saying, "Arise, take the young Child and His mother, and go to the land of Israel, for those who sought the young Child's life are dead." [21]Then he arose, took the young Child and His mother, and came into the land of Israel.

[22]But when he heard that Archelaus was reigning over Judea instead of his father Herod, he was afraid to go there. And being warned by God in a dream, he turned aside into the region of Galilee. [23]And he came and dwelt in a city called Nazareth, that it might be fulfilled which was spoken by the prophets, "He shall be called a Nazarene."

John the Baptist Prepares the Way

3 In those days John the Baptist came preaching in the wilderness of Judea, [2]and saying, "Repent, for the kingdom of heaven is at hand!" [3]For this is he who was spoken of by the prophet Isaiah, saying:

"The voice of one crying in the
wilderness:
'Prepare the way of the Lord;
Make His paths straight.' "[a]

[4]Now John himself was clothed in camel's hair, with a leather belt around his waist; and his food was locusts and wild honey. [5]Then Jerusalem, all Judea, and all the region around the Jordan went out to him [6]and were baptized by him in the Jordan, confessing their sins.

[7]But when he saw many of the Pharisees and Sadducees coming to his baptism, he said to them, "Brood of vipers! Who warned you to flee from the wrath to come? [8]Therefore bear fruits worthy of repentance, [9]and do not think to say to yourselves, 'We have Abraham as *our* father.' For I say to you that God is able to raise up children to Abraham from these stones. [10]And even now the ax is laid to the root of the trees. Therefore every tree which does not bear good fruit is cut down and thrown into the fire. [11]I indeed baptize you with water unto repentance, but He who is coming after me is mightier than I, whose sandals I am not worthy to carry. He will baptize you with the

2:15 [a]Hosea 11:1 2:18 [a]Jeremiah 31:15 3:3 [a]Isaiah 40:3

Holy Spirit and fire.[a] 12His winnowing
fan *is* in His hand, and He will thoroughly clean out His threshing floor, and
gather His wheat into the barn; but He
will burn up the chaff with unquenchable fire."

John Baptizes Jesus

13Then Jesus came from Galilee to
John at the Jordan to be baptized by him.
14And John *tried to* prevent Him, saying,
"I need to be baptized by You, and are
You coming to me?"

15But Jesus answered and said to him,
"Permit *it to be so* now, for thus it is fitting
for us to fulfill all righteousness." Then
he allowed Him.

16When He had been baptized, Jesus
came up immediately from the water;
and behold, the heavens were opened to
Him, and He[a] saw the Spirit of God descending like a dove and alighting upon
Him. 17And suddenly a voice *came* from
heaven, saying, "This is My beloved Son,
in whom I am well pleased."

Satan Tempts Jesus

4 Then Jesus was led up by the Spirit
into the wilderness to be tempted by
the devil. 2And when He had fasted forty
days and forty nights, afterward He was
hungry. 3Now when the tempter came to
Him, he said, "If You are the Son of God,
command that these stones become
bread."

4But He answered and said, "It is written, *'Man shall not live by bread alone,*
but by every word that proceeds from the
mouth of God.' "[a]

5Then the devil took Him up into the
holy city, set Him on the pinnacle of the
temple, 6and said to Him, "If You are the
Son of God, throw Yourself down. For it
is written:

> *'He shall give His angels charge over*
> *you,'*

and,

3:11 [a]M-Text omits *and fire.* 3:16 [a]Or *he* 4:4 [a]Deuteronomy 8:3

3:1 Open-air preaching. John the Baptist was an open-air preacher. Jesus was an open-air preacher. He preached the greatest sermon of all time, the "Sermon on the Mount," in the open-air. Peter preached in the open-air at Pentecost and Paul chose to stand on Mars Hill and preach open-air to the Athenians.

If we are serious about reaching this world, let us follow in the footsteps of Jesus and the apostles and preach where sinners gather. In thirty minutes, a good open-air preacher can reach more sinners than the average church does in twelve months.

Thank God that the disciples didn't stay in the upper room. They didn't carpet the building, pad the pews, then put a notice outside the front door saying, "Tonight: Gospel outreach service, 7 P.M.—all welcome." They went into the open air.

The gospel is for the world, not the Church. One-third of the word "gospel" is "go." Two-thirds of "God" is "go"; but like King Og, we seem to have it backwards. We take sinners to meetings rather than meetings to sinners. The Church prefers to fish on dry land rather than get its feet wet. *Charles Finney* put his finger on the reason why: "It is the great business of every Christian to save souls. People complain that they do not know how to take hold of this matter. Why, the reason is plain enough; they have never studied it. They have never taken the proper pains to qualify themselves for the work. If you do not make it a matter of study, how you may successfully act in building up the kingdom of Christ, you are acting a very wicked and absurd part as a Christian."

He who loves his neighbor as himself will be concerned for his eternal welfare. He who couldn't care less that every day multitudes of living people are being swallowed by the jaws of hell has a heart of stone indeed.

3:2 Repentance—its necessity for salvation. The first word John the Baptist preached to Israel was "repent." However, it must be remembered that Israel had the Law and therefore had the "knowledge of sin" (Rom. 7:7). Unregenerate humanity needs the moral Law to show them what sin is (1 John 3:4). Without the knowledge that the "tutor" brings (see Gal. 3:24), they remain in ignorance about sin's true nature and therefore their need for biblical repentance. See Luke 13:3.

4:6 "The devil can cite Scripture for his purpose." *William Shakespeare*

4:4 *Archaeology and History Attest to the Reliability of the Bible*

By Richard M. Fales, Ph.D.

No other ancient book is questioned or maligned like the Bible. Critics looking for the flyspeck in the masterpiece allege that there was a long span between the time the events in the New Testament occurred and when they were recorded. They claim a gap exists archaeologically between the earliest copies made and the autographs of the New Testament. In reality, the alleged spaces and so-called gaps exist only in the minds of the critics.

Manuscript Evidence. Aristotle's *Ode to Poetics* was written between 384 and 322 B.C. The earliest copy of this work is dated A.D. 1100, and there are only forty-nine extant manuscripts. The gap between the original writing and the earliest copy is 1,400 years. There are only seven extant manuscripts of Plato's Tetralogies, written 427–347 B.C. The earliest copy is A.D. 900—a gap of over 1,200 years. What about the New Testament? Jesus was crucified in A.D. 30. The New Testament was written between A.D. 48 and 95. The oldest manuscripts date to the last quarter of the first century, and the second oldest A.D. 125. This gives us a narrow gap of thirty-five to forty years from the originals written by the apostles.

From the early centuries, we have some 5,300 Greek manuscripts of the New Testament. Altogether, including Syriac, Latin, Coptic, and Aramaic, we have a whopping 24,633 texts of the ancient New Testament to confirm the wording of the Scriptures. So the bottom line is, there was no great period between the events of the New Testament and the New Testament writings. Nor is there a great time lapse between the original writings and the oldest copies. With the great body of manuscript evidence, it can be proved, beyond a doubt, that the New Testament says exactly the same things today as it originally did nearly 2,000 years ago.

Corroborating Writings. Another point of contention arises when Bible critics have knowingly or unknowingly misled people by implying that Old and New Testament books were either excluded from or added into the canon of Scripture at the great ecumenical councils of A.D. 336, 382, 397, and 419. In fact, one result of these gatherings was to confirm the Church's belief that the books already in the Bible were divinely inspired. Therefore, the Church, at these meetings, neither added to nor took away from the books of the Bible. At that time, the thirty-nine Old Testament books had already been accepted, and the New Testament, as it was written, simply grew up with the ancient Church. Each document, being accepted as it was penned in the first century, was then passed on to Christians of the next century. So, this foolishness about the Roman Emperor Constantine dropping books from the Bible is simply uneducated rumor.

Fulfilled Prophecies. Prophecies from the Old and New Testaments that have been fulfilled also add credibility to the Bible. The Scriptures predicted the rise and fall of great empires like Greece and Rome (Dan. 2:39,40), and foretold the destruction of cities like Tyre and Sidon (Isa. 23). Tyre's demise is recorded by ancient historians, who tell how Alexander the Great lay siege to the city for seven months. King Nebuchadnezzar of Babylon had failed in a 13-year attempt to capture the seacoast city and completely destroy its inhabitants. During the siege of 573 B.C., much of the population of Tyre moved to its new island home approximately half a mile from the land city. Here it remained surrounded by walls as high as 150 feet until judgment fell in 332 B.C. with the arrival of Alexander the Great. In the seven-month siege, he fulfilled the remainder of the prophecies (Zech. 9:4; Ezek. 26:12) concerning the city at sea by completely destroying Tyre, killing 8,000 of its inhabitants and selling 30,000 of its population into slavery. To reach the island, he scraped up the dust and rubble of the old land city of Tyre, just like the Bible predicted, and cast them into the sea, building a 200-foot-wide causeway out to the island.

Alexander's death and the murder of his two sons was also foretold in the Scripture.

Another startling prophecy was Jesus' detailed prediction of Jerusalem's destruction, and the further spreading of the Jewish diaspora throughout the world, which is recorded in Luke 21. In A.D. 70, not only was Jerusalem destroyed by Titus, the future emperor of Rome, but another prediction of Jesus Christ in Matt. 24:1,2 came to pass—the complete destruction of the temple of God.

Messianic Prophecies. In the Book of Daniel, the Bible prophesied the coming of the one and only Jewish Messiah prior to the temple's demise. The Old Testament prophets declared He would be born in Bethlehem (Mic. 5:2) to a virgin (Isa. 7:14), be betrayed for thirty pieces of silver (Zech. 11:12,13), die by crucifixion (Psa. 22), and be buried in a rich man's tomb (Isa. 53:9). There was only one person who fits all of the messianic prophecies of the Old Testament who lived before A.D. 70: Jesus of Nazareth, the Son of Mary.

Yes, the Bible is an amazing book. (See also 1 Pet. 1:25 comment.)

'In their hands they shall bear you up,
Lest you dash your foot against a
stone.' "[a]

7Jesus said to him, "It is written again,
'You shall not tempt the Lord your God.'"[a]
8Again, the devil took Him up on an
exceedingly high mountain, and showed
Him all the kingdoms of the world and
their glory. 9And he said to Him, "All
these things I will give You if You will fall
down and worship me."
10Then Jesus said to him, "Away with
you,[a] Satan! For it is written, *'You shall*
worship the LORD your God, and Him
only you shall serve.'"[b]
11Then the devil left Him, and behold,
angels came and ministered to Him.

Jesus Begins His Galilean Ministry

12Now when Jesus heard that John
had been put in prison, He departed to
Galilee. 13And leaving Nazareth, He came
and dwelt in Capernaum, which is by the
sea, in the regions of Zebulun and Naphtali, 14that it might be fulfilled which was
spoken by Isaiah the prophet, saying:

15*"The land of Zebulun and the land of*
Naphtali,
By the way of the sea, beyond the
Jordan,
Galilee of the Gentiles:
16*The people who sat in darkness have*
seen a great light,
And upon those who sat in the region
and shadow of death
Light has dawned."[a]

17From that time Jesus began to
preach and to say, "Repent, for the kingdom of heaven is at hand."

Four Fishermen Called as Disciples

18And Jesus, walking by the Sea of Galilee, saw two brothers, Simon called Peter,
and Andrew his brother, casting a net into
the sea; for they were fishermen. 19Then
He said to them, "Follow Me, and I will
make you fishers of men." 20They immediately left *their* nets and followed Him.
21Going on from there, He saw two
other brothers, James *the son* of Zebedee,
and John his brother, in the boat with
Zebedee their father, mending their nets.
He called them, 22and immediately they
left the boat and their father, and followed Him.

Jesus Heals a Great Multitude

23And Jesus went about all Galilee,
teaching in their synagogues, preaching
the gospel of the kingdom, and healing
all kinds of sickness and all kinds of disease among the people. 24Then His fame
went throughout all Syria; and they
brought to Him all sick people who were
afflicted with various diseases and torments, and those who were demon-possessed, epileptics, and paralytics; and He
healed them. 25Great multitudes followed Him—from Galilee, and *from* Decapolis, Jerusalem, Judea, and beyond
the Jordan.

4:6 [a]Psalm 91:11, 12 4:7 [a]Deuteronomy 6:16 4:10 [a]M-Text reads *Get behind Me.* [b]Deuteronomy 6:13 4:16 [a]Isaiah 9:1, 2

4:9 The devil tempted Jesus to become a Satan worshiper.

4:16 This life is the valley of the shadow of death. Sinners sit in darkness—waiting to die. The light of the Savior banishes the shadow of death.

4:17 Like John the Baptist, Jesus' first word in preaching to Israel was "repent." Israel already had the "knowledge of sin" (which only the Law can bring), but now they needed to repent—to turn from their sins as revealed by the Law.

4:19 "The expression 'fishing for men' is an important one for us to understand. Another way to translate it would be 'catching men alive' (women, too, of course). We find this unique phrase only two times in the Bible, first in Matt. 4:19 and then in 2 Tim. 2:26, where it describes those who have been ensnared by Satan. Thus, Scripture provides a striking contrast: either we will catch men and women alive or the devil will." *Greg Laurie*

5:1 *The Sermon on the Mount*

This sermon not only reveals God's divine nature, it puts into our hands the most powerful of evangelistic weapons. It is the greatest evangelistic sermon ever preached by the greatest evangelist who ever lived. The straightedge of God's Law reveals how crooked we are:

v. 3: The unregenerate heart isn't poor in spirit. It is proud, self-righteous, and boastful (every man is pure in his own eyes—Prov. 16:2).

v. 4: The unsaved don't mourn over their sin; they love the darkness and hate the light (John 3:19).

v. 5: The ungodly are not meek and lowly of heart. Their sinful condition is described in Rom. 3:13–18.

v. 6: Sinners don't hunger and thirst after righteousness. Instead, they drink iniquity like water (Job 15:16).

v. 7: The world is shallow in its ability to show true mercy. It is by nature cruel and vindictive (Gen. 6:5).

v. 8: The heart of the unregenerate is not pure; it is desperately wicked (Jer. 17:9).

Those who are born again manifest the fruit of the Spirit, live godly in Christ Jesus (vv. 3–9), and therefore suffer persecution (vv. 10–12). However, their purpose on earth is to be salt and light: to be a moral influence, and bring light to those who sit in the shadow of death (vv. 13–16).

Look now at how the Messiah expounds the Law and makes it "honorable" (Isa. 42:21). He establishes that He didn't come to destroy the Law (v. 17); not even the smallest part of it will pass away (v. 18). It will be the divine standard of judgment (James 2:12; Rom. 2:12; Acts 17:31). Those who teach it "shall be called great in the kingdom of heaven" (v. 19). The Law should be taught to sinners because it was made for them (1 Tim. 1:8–10), and is a "tutor" that brings the "knowledge of sin" (Rom. 3:19,20; 7:7). Its function is to destroy self-righteousness and bring sinners to the cross (Gal. 3:24).

The righteousness of the scribes and Pharisees was merely outward, but God requires truth in the inward parts (Psa. 51:6). Jesus shows this by unveiling the Law's *spiritual* nature (Rom. 7:14). The Sixth Commandment forbids murder. However, Jesus shows that it also condemns anger "without a cause," and even evil-speaking (vv. 21–26): "for every idle word men may speak, they will give account of it in the day of judgment" (Matt. 12:36). The Seventh Commandment forbids adultery, but Jesus revealed that this also includes lust, and it even condemns divorce, except in the case of sexual sin of the spouse (vv. 27–32).

Jesus opens up the Ninth Commandment (vv. 33–37), and then shows that love is the spirit of the Law—"The purpose of the commandment is love from a pure heart" (1 Tim. 1:5). This is summarized in what is commonly called the Golden Rule: "Therefore, whatever you want men to do to you, do also to them, *for this is the Law and the Prophets*" (Matt. 7:12, emphasis added). "Owe no one anything except to love one another, for he who loves another has fulfilled the law. For the commandments, 'You shall not commit adultery,' 'You shall not murder,' 'You shall not steal,' 'You shall not bear false witness,' 'You shall not covet,' and if there is any other commandment, are all summed up in this saying, namely, 'You shall love your neighbor as yourself.' Love does no harm to a neighbor; therefore love is the fulfillment of the law" (Rom. 13:8–10).

When a sinner is born again he is able to do this (vv. 38–47). He now possesses "the divine nature" (2 Pet. 1:4). In Christ he is made perfect and thus satisfies the demands of a "perfect" Law (Psa. 19:7; James 1:25). Without the righteousness of Christ, he cannot be perfect as his Father in heaven is perfect (v. 48). The Law annihilated his self-righteousness, leaving him undone and condemned. His only hope was in the cross of Jesus Christ. After his conversion, knowledge of the Law that brought him there keeps him at the foot of the cross.

John Wesley said, "Therefore I cannot spare the Law one moment, no more than I can spare Christ, seeing I now want it as much to keep me to Christ, as I ever wanted it to bring me to Him. Otherwise this 'evil heart of unbelief' would immediately 'depart from the living God.' Indeed each is continually sending me to the other—the Law to Christ, and Christ to the Law."

The Beatitudes

5 And seeing the multitudes, He went up on a mountain, and when He was seated His disciples came to Him. 2 Then He opened His mouth and taught them, saying:

3 "Blessed *are* the poor in spirit,
For theirs is the kingdom of heaven.
4 Blessed *are* those who mourn,
For they shall be comforted.

[5]Blessed *are* the meek,
For they shall inherit the earth.
[6]Blessed *are* those who hunger and thirst for righteousness,
For they shall be filled.
[7]Blessed *are* the merciful,
For they shall obtain mercy.
[8]Blessed *are* the pure in heart,
For they shall see God.
[9]Blessed *are* the peacemakers,
For they shall be called sons of God.
[10]Blessed *are* those who are persecuted for righteousness' sake,
For theirs is the kingdom of heaven.

[11]"Blessed are you when they revile and
persecute you, and say all kinds of evil
against you falsely for My sake. [12]Rejoice
and be exceedingly glad, for great is your
reward in heaven, for so they persecuted
the prophets who were before you.

Believers Are Salt and Light

[13]"You are the salt of the earth; but if
the salt loses its flavor, how shall it be
seasoned? It is then good for nothing but
to be thrown out and trampled underfoot
by men.
[14]"You are the light of the world. A
city that is set on a hill cannot be hidden.
[15]Nor do they light a lamp and put it under a basket, but on a lampstand, and it
gives light to all *who are* in the house.
[16]Let your light so shine before men, that
they may see your good works and glorify your Father in heaven.

Christ Fulfills the Law

[17]"Do not think that I came to destroy
the Law or the Prophets. I did not come
to destroy but to fulfill. [18]For assuredly, I
say to you, till heaven and earth pass
away, one jot or one tittle will by no
means pass from the law till all is fulfilled. [19]Whoever therefore breaks one of
the least of these commandments, and
teaches men so, shall be called least in
the kingdom of heaven; but whoever
does and teaches *them*, he shall be called
great in the kingdom of heaven. [20]For I
say to you, that unless your righteousness
exceeds *the righteousness* of the scribes

5:2 Sin, righteousness, and judgment. "The Sermon on the Mount is the greatest example we have of how to 'reprove the world of sin, of righteousness, and of judgment.' In Matthew chapter 5, Christ reproves the multitudes of sin by showing the essence of the Law. In chapter 6, He teaches on true righteousness, the essence of which is to cause men to glorify our Father which is in heaven, not to draw attention to ourselves. Then, in chapter 7, He teaches concerning judgment. He warns the multitudes that if they judge others as guilty for doing the same things they themselves are practicing, instead of pulling the log out of their own eye first, they are obviously hypocrites. If we will follow this method of preaching the gospel, then we can expect the Holy Spirit to help us. For Jesus Himself promised that this divine Helper would reprove the world of sin, of righteousness, and of judgment. He does this by causing our words to make saving impressions on the minds of men." *Joel Crumpton*

5:6 We should come to the Savior thirsting for *righteousness*, not *happiness* as modern evangelism maintains: "Riches do not profit in the day of wrath, but *righteousness* delivers from death" (Prov. 11:4, emphasis added).

5:7 Jesus didn't come to destroy the Law and the Prophets, but to fulfill them (Matt. 5:17). It was our transgressions that necessitated the Savior. If we hadn't sinned, there would have been no need for a sacrifice. We broke the Law, and Jesus paid the fine. God loved the world with such passion that He sent His only Son to the cross of Calvary, so that we might trust in Him alone. In so doing, we would not perish under the wrath of His Law, but have everlasting life (John 3:16).

5:13 "The pulpit, not the media, is to be the most powerful voice in our land." *Bill Gothard*

5:14 Set on a hill. Some people say that religion is a personal thing and it should be kept to oneself. However, Jesus tells us that the gospel of salvation is the good news of everlasting life and is for this dying world. We should be set on a hill. We should be preaching on the housetops, lifting up our voice like a trumpet to show this people their transgression. The Bible tells us that God's Law is light (Prov. 6:23). When the light of the Law and the glorious gospel of Christ shine together, they expose and banish the shadows of sin and death.

POINTS FOR OPEN-AIR PREACHING

5:10–12

Never Fear Hecklers

The best thing that can happen to an open-air meeting is to have a good heckler. Jesus gave us some of the greatest gems of Scripture because someone either made a statement or asked a question in an open-air setting. A good heckler can increase a crowd of 20 people to 200 in a matter of minutes. The air becomes electric. Suddenly, you have 200 people listening intently to how you will answer a heckler. All you have to do is remember the attributes of 2 Tim. 2:23–26: be patient, gentle, humble, etc. Don't worry if you can't answer a question. Just say, "I can't answer that, but I'll try to get the answer for you if you really want to know." With Bible "difficulties," I regularly fall back on the powerful statement of *Mark Twain:* "Most people are bothered by those passages of Scripture they don't understand, but for me I have always noticed that the passages that bother me are those I do understand."

A "good" heckler is one who will provoke your thoughts. He will stand up, speak up, then shut up so that you can preach. Occasionally, you will get hecklers who have the first two qualifications, but they just won't be quiet. If they will not let you get a word in, move your location. Most of the crowd will follow. Better to have 10 listeners who can hear than 200 who can't. If the heckler follows, move again . . . then the crowd will usually turn on him.

One ploy that often works with a heckler who is out solely to hinder the gospel is to wait until he is quiet and say to the crowd (making sure the heckler is listening also), "I want to show you how people are like sheep. When I move, watch this man follow me because he can't get a crowd by himself." His pride usually keeps him from following.

If you have a "mumbling heckler" who won't speak up, ignore him and talk over the top of him. This will usually get him angry enough to speak up and draw hearers. There is a fine line between him getting angry enough to draw a crowd, and hitting you; you will find it in time.

If you are fortunate enough to get a heckler, don't panic. Show him genuine respect, not only because he can double your crowd, but because the Bible says to honor all men, so you don't want to offend him unnecessarily. Ask the heckler his name, so that if you want to ask him a question and he is talking to someone, you don't have to say, "Hey, you!"

Often, people will walk through the crowd so they can get close to you and will whisper something like, "I think you are a #@*!$!" Answer loud enough for the crowd to hear, "God bless you." Do it with a smile so that it looks as though the person has just whispered a word of encouragement to you. This will stop him from doing it again. The Bible says to bless those who curse you, and to do good to those who hate you.

Remember that you are not fighting against flesh and blood. Hecklers will stoop very low and be cutting and cruel in their remarks. If you have some physical disability, they will play on it. Try to smile back at them. Look past the words. If you are reviled for the name of Jesus, "rejoice and be exceedingly glad." Read Matt. 5:10–12 until it is written on the corridors of your mind.

The most angry hecklers are usually what we call "backsliders." These are actually false converts who never slid forward in the first place. They "asked Jesus into their heart" but never truly repented. Ask him, "Did you know the Lord?" (see Heb. 8:11). If he answers "Yes," then he is admitting that he is willfully denying Him, and if he answers "No," then he was never a Christian in the first place—"This is eternal life, that they may know You, the only true God, and Jesus Christ whom You have sent" (John 17:3). See also 1 Cor. 2:4 comment.

and Pharisees, you will by no means enter the kingdom of heaven.

Murder Begins in the Heart

21"You have heard that it was said to
those of old, *'You shall not murder,*[a] and
whoever murders will be in danger of the
judgment.' 22But I say to you that whoever is angry with his brother without a
cause[a] shall be in danger of the judgment. And whoever says to his brother,
'Raca!' shall be in danger of the council.
But whoever says, 'You fool!' shall be in
danger of hell fire. 23Therefore if you
bring your gift to the altar, and there remember that your brother has something
against you, 24leave your gift there before

5:21 [a]Exodus 20:13; Deuteronomy 5:17 5:22 [a]NU-Text omits *without a cause.*

The Function of the Law

5:22 "Herein is the Law of God above all other laws, that it is a spiritual law. Other laws may forbid compassing and imagining, which are treason in the heart, but cannot take cognizance thereof, unless there be some overt act; but the Law of God takes notice of the iniquity regarded in the heart, though it go no further." *Matthew Henry*

"The precepts of philosophy, and of the Hebrew code, laid hold of actions only. [Jesus] pushed His scrutinies into the heart of man, erected His tribunal in the region of his thoughts, and purified the waters at the fountain head." *Thomas Jefferson*

the altar, and go your way. First be reconciled to your brother, and then come and offer your gift. 25 Agree with your adversary quickly, while you are on the way with him, lest your adversary deliver you to the judge, the judge hand you over to the officer, and you be thrown into prison. 26 Assuredly, I say to you, you will by no means get out of there till you have paid the last penny.

Adultery in the Heart

27 "You have heard that it was said to those of old,[a] *'You shall not commit adultery.'*[b] 28 But I say to you that whoever looks at a woman to lust for her has already committed adultery with her in his heart. 29 If your right eye causes you to sin, pluck it out and cast *it* from you; for it is more profitable for you that one of your members perish, than for your whole body to be cast into hell. 30 And if your right hand causes you to sin, cut it off and cast *it* from you; for it is more profitable for you that one of your members perish, than for your whole body to be cast into hell.

Marriage Is Sacred and Binding

31 "Furthermore it has been said, 'Whoever divorces his wife, let him give her a certificate of divorce.' 32 But I say to you that whoever divorces his wife for any reason except sexual immorality[a] causes her to commit adultery; and whoever marries a woman who is divorced commits adultery.

Jesus Forbids Oaths

33 "Again you have heard that it was said to those of old, 'You shall not swear falsely, but shall perform your oaths to the Lord.' 34 But I say to you, do not swear at all: neither by heaven, for it is God's throne; 35 nor by the earth, for it is His footstool; nor by Jerusalem, for it is

5:27 [a]NU-Text and M-Text omit *to those of old.* [b]Exodus 20:14; Deuteronomy 5:18 5:32 [a]Or *fornication*

5:16 "If doing a good act in public will excite others to do more good, then 'Let your light shine to all.' Miss no opportunity to do good." *John Wesley*

5:20 Self-righteousness. These words would have astounded Jesus' hearers. If anyone was righteous, it was the scribes and Pharisees. Their hope of gaining everlasting life from the Law was therefore shattered. That is what we must do: shatter the self-righteous beliefs of those poor souls who try to earn salvation by their works. Jesus shows us how in the following verses by explaining that God requires truth even in the inward parts.

5:21,22 Leading sinners to Jesus: *God sees the thought-life.* He weighs our motives and judges the intent of the heart: "Whoever hates his brother is a murderer" (1 John 3:15). See Matt. 5:27,28 comment.

5:22 Hell: For verses warning of its reality, see Matt. 5:29,30.

5:27,28 Leading sinners to Jesus: *God knows what is in the heart.* If we have lust in our hearts, God considers us to be adulterers (v. 28). "God will bring every work into judgment, including every secret thing, whether good or evil" (Eccles. 12:14). "But in accordance with your hardness and your impenitent heart you are treasuring up for yourself wrath in the day of wrath and revelation of the righteous judgment of God, who 'will render to each one according to his deeds'" (Rom. 2:5,6). See Mark 7:20–23 comment

5:28 Men often try to justify lust by saying that there is nothing wrong with looking at a pretty girl. True, the Bible doesn't condemn looking; it condemns "lust." The conscience knows the difference.

5:29,30 Hell: For verses warning of its reality, see Matt. 10:28.

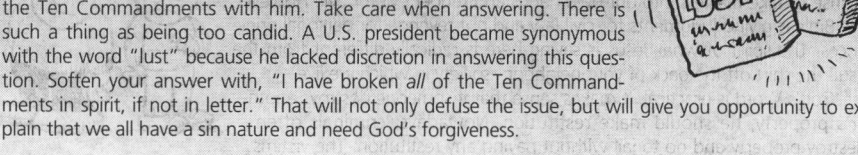

QUESTIONS & OBJECTIONS

5:28 ***"What should I say if someone asks, 'Have you ever lusted?'"***

An individual may challenge you on this issue while you're going through the Ten Commandments with him. Take care when answering. There is such a thing as being too candid. A U.S. president became synonymous with the word "lust" because he lacked discretion in answering this question. Soften your answer with, "I have broken *all* of the Ten Commandments in spirit, if not in letter." That will not only defuse the issue, but will give you opportunity to explain that we all have a sin nature and need God's forgiveness.

the city of the great King. 36Nor shall you
swear by your head, because you cannot
make one hair white or black. 37But let
your 'Yes' be 'Yes,' and your 'No,' 'No.'
For whatever is more than these is from
the evil one.

Go the Second Mile

38"You have heard that it was said, *'An
eye for an eye and a tooth for a tooth.'*[a]
39But I tell you not to resist an evil person. But whoever slaps you on your right
cheek, turn the other to him also. 40If
anyone wants to sue you and take away
your tunic, let him have *your* cloak also.
41And whoever compels you to go one
mile, go with him two. 42Give to him who
asks you, and from him who wants to
borrow from you do not turn away.

Love Your Enemies

43"You have heard that it was said,
'You shall love your neighbor[a] and hate
your enemy.' 44But I say to you, love your
enemies, bless those who curse you, do
good to those who hate you, and pray for
those who spitefully use you and persecute you,[a] 45that you may be sons of your
Father in heaven; for He makes His sun
rise on the evil and on the good, and

5:38 [a]Exodus 21:24; Leviticus 24:20; Deuteronomy 19:21 5:43 [a]Compare Leviticus 19:18 5:44 [a]NU-Text omits three clauses from this verse, leaving, *"But I say to you, love your enemies and pray for those who persecute you."*

5:44 Prayer. There are several reasons why as Christians we should pray for those who persecute us: 1) we are commanded to; 2) prayer is an antidote against bitterness; and 3) it can lead to the salvation of the persecutor.

Capital punishment. Some maintain that this verse shows Jesus did not believe in capital punishment. However, just because we have love for an enemy doesn't give us the right to allow him to escape punishment for murder. The Bible says, "Let every soul be subject to the governing authorities. For there is no authority except from God, and the authorities that exist are appointed by God. Therefore whoever resists the authority resists the ordinance of God, and those who resist will bring judgment on themselves... *But if you do evil, be afraid; for he does not bear the sword in vain; for he is God's minister, an avenger to execute wrath on him who practices evil"* (Rom. 13:1–4, emphasis added).

The Bible says that if I deliberately take a life, I should lose my own (see Num. 35:30,31). Genesis 9:6 says, "Whoever sheds man's blood, by man his blood shall be shed; for in the image of God He made man." This shows the value that God places on human life. The seriousness of a crime is revealed in the punishment dealt to the criminal. It is interesting to note that when Oklahoma City bomber Timothy McVeigh requested the death penalty, 250 relatives of the victims he killed asked to watch his execution. Their desire to actually see justice done shows the value they place on the loved ones they lost. Despite claims to the contrary, capital punishment does deter crime. The person executed will not do it again.

Still, there are respected Christian leaders whose conscience will not allow them to advocate capital punishment. This is understandable in light of the fact that innocent people may fall through the cracks of a godless justice system. However, despite civil law's imperfections, we are told to be subject to the governing authorities. It was God who instigated the death penalty in the beginning. The Judge of the Universe pronounced the death sentence upon all humanity when He said, "The soul who sins shall die" (Ezek. 18:20).

QUESTIONS & OBJECTIONS

"In saying 'an eye for an eye,' the Bible encourages taking the law into our own hands."

This verse is so often misquoted by the world. Many believe it is giving a license to take matters into our own hands and render evil for evil. However, the Bible is giving judgments for civil law and not revenge for personal grievances. The spirit of what Jesus is saying here is radically different from the "sue the shirt off the back of your neighbor" society in which we live.

God's Word is practical. It makes sense that if someone destroys another's property, he should make restitution. Nowadays, criminals often destroy property and go to jail without paying any restitution. The victims remain uncompensated for their losses. So if someone steals your ox, he is to restore the ox. If someone steals and wrecks your car, he is to buy you another one . . . a car for a car, an eye for an eye, a tooth for a tooth.

sends rain on the just and on the unjust.
46For if you love those who love you,
what reward have you? Do not even the
tax collectors do the same? 47And if you
greet your brethren[a] only, what do you
do more *than others*? Do not even the tax
collectors[b] do so? 48Therefore you shall
be perfect, just as your Father in heaven
is perfect.

Do Good to Please God

6 "Take heed that you do not do your
charitable deeds before men, to be
seen by them. Otherwise you have no reward from your Father in heaven. 2Therefore,
when you do a charitable deed, do
not sound a trumpet before you as the
hypocrites do in the synagogues and in
the streets, that they may have glory
from men. Assuredly, I say to you, they
have their reward. 3But when you do a
charitable deed, do not let your left hand
know what your right hand is doing,
4that your charitable deed may be in se-

5:47 [a]M-Text reads *friends.* [b]NU-Text reads *Gentiles.*

5:48 Be perfect. Some believe Jesus didn't really mean "perfect" here, because that would require that we be "without defect, flawless." Instead, they think He was telling us to be "mature." If that were true, then He would be saying, "Therefore you shall be mature, just as your Father in heaven is mature." However, calling God "mature" implies that He was once immature. Such a thought is contrary to Scripture. God never changes (Mal. 3:6); He has always been perfect and doesn't need to mature.

Throughout the Sermon on the Mount, Jesus expounded the perfect Law of a perfect Creator. God's work is perfect (Deut. 32:4), His way is perfect (Psa. 18:30), and His Law is perfect (Psa. 19:7; James 1:25). Jesus then climaxes His exposition with the demand of the Law—perfection in thought, word, and deed.

In magnifying the Law and making it honorable, He put righteousness beyond the reach of sinful humanity. He destroyed the vain hope that we can get right with a perfect Creator by our own imperfect efforts, i.e., by the works of the Law. (See Mark 7:5–13 comment.)

Instead, we must seek righteousness by another means—through faith alone in the Savior (Rom. 3:21,22). In doing so, Jesus was showing us the right use of the Law—as a "tutor to bring us to Christ" (Gal. 3:24). This is what Jesus did with the rich young ruler. The young man asked, "Good Teacher, what good thing shall I do that I may have eternal life?" (Matt. 19:16). Jesus corrected his misuse of the word "good," gave him five of the Ten Commandments, and then said, "If you want to be perfect . . ." (v. 21). The young man's hope of "doing" something to be saved was dashed and he went away sorrowful. However, this is not a negative incident; it is positive when a sinner's vain hope is dashed. If he cannot find salvation "by the works of the law," he may just seek it "by the hearing of faith" (Gal. 3:2). This is why we should use the Law when reasoning with the lost and press home its requirement of absolute perfection. (See James 2:10,11.) On hearing the demands of a perfect Law, it is not uncommon to hear a guilty sinner say, "Wow! Nobody's perfect." That's the point of the Law.

Our mission is to preach Christ and to warn sinners, "that we may present every man perfect in Christ Jesus" (Col. 1:28). See also Eph. 4:13 comment.

"It is true that [many] are praying for world-wide revival. But it would be more timely, and more scriptural, for prayer to be made to the Lord of the harvest, that He would raise up and thrust forth laborers who would fearlessly and faithfully preach those truths which are calculated to bring about a revival."

A. W. Pink

cret; and your Father who sees in secret
will Himself reward you openly.[a]

The Model Prayer

5"And when you pray, you shall not
be like the hypocrites. For they love to
pray standing in the synagogues and on
the corners of the streets, that they may
be seen by men. Assuredly, I say to you,
they have their reward. 6But you, when
you pray, go into your room, and when
you have shut your door, pray to your
Father who *is* in the secret *place;* and
your Father who sees in secret will reward you openly.[a] 7And when you pray,
do not use vain repetitions as the heathen
do. For they think that they will be heard
for their many words.

8"Therefore do not be like them. For
your Father knows the things you have
need of before you ask Him. 9In this
manner, therefore, pray:

Our Father in heaven,
Hallowed be Your name.
10Your kingdom come.
Your will be done
On earth as *it is* in heaven.
11Give us this day our daily bread.
12And forgive us our debts,
As we forgive our debtors.
13And do not lead us into temptation,
But deliver us from the evil one.
For Yours is the kingdom and the
power and the glory forever.
Amen.[a]

14"For if you forgive men their trespasses, your heavenly Father will also forgive you. 15But if you do not forgive men
their trespasses, neither will your Father
forgive your trespasses.

Fasting to Be Seen Only by God

16"Moreover, when you fast, do not be
like the hypocrites, with a sad countenance. For they disfigure their faces that
they may appear to men to be fasting. Assuredly, I say to you, they have their reward. 17But you, when you fast, anoint
your head and wash your face, 18so that
you do not appear to men to be fasting,
but to your Father who *is* in the secret
place; and your Father who sees in secret
will reward you openly.[a]

Lay Up Treasures in Heaven

19"Do not lay up for yourselves treasures on earth, where moth and rust destroy and where thieves break in and steal;
20but lay up for yourselves treasures in
heaven, where neither moth nor rust destroys and where thieves do not break in
and steal. 21For where your treasure is,
there your heart will be also.

6:4 [a]NU-Text omits *openly*. 6:6 [a]NU-Text omits *openly*. 6:13 [a]NU-Text omits *For Yours* through *Amen*. 6:18 [a]NU-Text and M-Text omit *openly*.

6:12 Scripture is clear: if we refuse to forgive others, we will not be forgiven. See v. 15; Matt. 18:21–35.

Principles of Growth for the New and Growing Christian

6:9 Prayer—"Wait for a Minute"

God always answers prayer. Sometimes He says yes; sometimes He says no; and sometimes He says, "Wait for a minute." And since to the Lord a day is the same as a thousand years (2 Pet. 3:8), that could mean a ten-year wait for us. So ask in faith, but rest in peace-filled patience.

Surveys show that more than 90% of Americans pray daily. No doubt they pray for health, wealth, happiness, etc. They also pray when grandma gets sick, and when grandma doesn't get better (or dies), many end up disillusioned or bitter. This is because they don't understand what the Bible says about prayer. It teaches, among other things, that our sin will keep God from even hearing our prayer (Psa. 66:18), and that if we pray with doubt, we will not get an answer (James 1:6,7).

Here's how to be heard:

- Pray with faith (Heb. 11:6).
- Pray with clean hands and a pure heart (Psa. 24:3,4).
- Pray genuine heartfelt prayers, rather than vain repetitions (Matt. 6:7).
- Make sure you are praying to the God revealed in the Scriptures (Exod. 20:3–6).

1. How do you "pray with faith"? Someone once told me, "Ray, you're a man of great faith in God," thinking they were paying me a compliment. They weren't. What if I said to you, "I'm a man of great faith in my doctor"? It's a compliment to the doctor. If I have great faith in him, it means that I see him as being a man of integrity, a man of great ability—that he is trustworthy. I give "glory" to the man through my faith in him. The Bible says that Abraham "did not waver at the promise of God through unbelief, but was strengthened in faith, giving glory to God, and being fully convinced that what He had promised He was also able to perform" (Rom. 4:20,21). Abraham was a man of great faith in God. Remember, that is not a compliment to Abraham. He merely caught a glimpse of God's incredible ability, His impeccable integrity, and His wonderful faithfulness to keep every promise He makes. Abraham's faith gave "glory" to a faithful God.

As far as God is concerned, if you belong to Jesus, you are a VIP. You can boldly come before the throne of grace (Heb. 4:16). You have access to the King *because you are the son or daughter of the King*. When you were a child, did you have to grovel to get your needs met by your mom or dad? I hope not.

So, when you pray, don't say, "Oh God, I *hope* you will supply my needs." Instead say something like, "Father, thank You that You keep *every* promise You make. Your Word says that You will supply *all* my needs according to Your riches in glory by Christ Jesus (Phil. 4:19). Therefore, I thank You that You will do this thing for my family. I ask this in the wonderful name of Jesus. Amen."

2. How do you get "clean hands and a pure heart"? Simply by confessing your sins to God through Jesus Christ, whose blood cleanses from all sin (1 John 1:7–9). God will not only forgive your every sin, He promises to *forget* them (Heb. 8:12). He will even justify you based on the sacrifice of the Savior. This means He will count it as though you have never sinned in the first place. He will make you pure in His sight—sinless. He will even "purge" your conscience, so that you will no longer have a sense of guilt that you sinned. That's what it means to be "justified by faith." That's why you need to soak yourself in holy Scripture; read the letters to the churches and see the wonderful things God has done for us through the cross of Calvary. If you don't bother to read the "will," you won't have any idea what has been given to you.

3. How do you pray "genuine heartfelt prayers"? Simply by keeping yourself in the love of God. If the love of God is in you, you will never pray hypocritical or selfish prayers. Just talk to your heavenly Father as candidly and intimately as a young child, nestled on Daddy's lap, would talk to his earthly father. How would you feel if every day your child pulled out a pre-written statement to dryly recite to you, rather than pouring out the events and emotions of that day? God wants to hear from your heart. When your prayer life is pleasing to God, He will reward you openly (Matt. 6:6).

4. How do you know you're praying to "the God revealed in Scripture"? Study the Word. Don't accept the image of God portrayed by the world, even though it appeals to the natural mind. A kind, gentle Santa Claus figure, dispensing good things with no sense of justice or truth, appeals to guilty sinners. Look to the thunderings and lightnings of Mount Sinai. Gaze at Jesus on the cross of Calvary—hanging in unspeakable agony because of the justice of a holy God. Such thoughts tend to banish idolatry.

For the next principle of growth, see 2 Cor. 4:4 comment.

The Lamp of the Body

22 “The lamp of the body is the eye. If
therefore your eye is good, your whole
body will be full of light. 23 But if your eye
is bad, your whole body will be full of
darkness. If therefore the light that is in
you is darkness, how great *is* that darkness!

You Cannot Serve God and Riches

24 “No one can serve two masters; for
either he will hate the one and love the
other, or else he will be loyal to the one
and despise the other. You cannot serve
God and mammon.

Do Not Worry

25 “Therefore I say to you, do not
worry about your life, what you will eat
or what you will drink; nor about your
body, what you will put on. Is not life
more than food and the body more than
clothing? 26 Look at the birds of the air,
for they neither sow nor reap nor gather
into barns; yet your heavenly Father
feeds them. Are you not of more value
than they? 27 Which of you by worrying
can add one cubit to his stature?

28 “So why do you worry about clothing? Consider the lilies of the field, how
they grow: they neither toil nor spin;
29 and yet I say to you that even Solomon
in all his glory was not arrayed like one of
these. 30 Now if God so clothes the grass
of the field, which today is, and tomorrow is thrown into the oven, *will He* not
much more *clothe* you, O you of little
faith?

31 “Therefore do not worry, saying,
‘What shall we eat?’ or ‘What shall we
drink?’ or ‘What shall we wear?’ 32 For after all these things the Gentiles seek. For
your heavenly Father knows that you
need all these things. 33 But seek first the
kingdom of God and His righteousness,
and all these things shall be added to
you. 34 Therefore do not worry about tomorrow, for tomorrow will worry about
its own things. Sufficient for the day *is* its
own trouble.

Do Not Judge

7 “Judge not, that you be not judged.
2 For with what judgment you judge,
you will be judged; and with the measure you use, it will be measured back to

6:26 Man is the pinnacle of God’s earthly creation. He is not a mere part of the evolutionary process having to yield to the rights of animals. Jesus said that mankind is “of more value” than birds and sheep (Matt. 12:12). He is to subdue the earth and have dominion over it (Gen. 1:28) by bringing its vast resources into submission. All were created for him by the infinite genius and loving hand of Almighty God. See also Psa. 8:6 comment.

6:31–33 Seek first His kingdom. Think about how the Lord must feel when He sees us spending so much more energy satisfying and gratifying self while neglecting our commitments to Him. We spend so little time obeying His commandment to warn sinners to flee from the wrath to come. When we consider what He’s done for us, our excuses fall short. It is as we seek *first* His kingdom that “all these things shall be added to you” (v. 33).

“The unmortified Christian and the heathen are of the same religion, and the deity they truly worship is the god of this world. What shall we eat? What shall we drink? What shall we wear? And how shall we pass away our time? Which way may we gather and perpetuate our names and families in the earth? It is a mournful reflection, but a truth which will not be denied, that these worldly lusts fill up a great part of the study, care and conversation of Christendom.

“The false notion that they may be children of God while in a state of disobedience to his holy commandments, and disciples of Jesus though they revolt from his cross, and members of his true church, which is without spot or wrinkle, notwithstanding their lives are full of spots and wrinkles, is of all other deceptions upon themselves the most pernicious to their eternal condition for they are at peace in sin and under a security in their transgression.” *William Penn*

7:1 See also Luke 6:37 comment for how to respond to this statement.

“People tell me, ‘Judge not lest ye be judged.’ I always tell them, ‘Twist not Scripture lest ye be like Satan.’” *Paul Washer*

THE FUNCTION OF THE LAW

7:6 "Just as the world was not ready for the New Testament before it received the Old, just as the Jews were not prepared for the ministry of Christ until John the Baptist had gone before Him with his claimant call to repentance, so the unsaved are in no condition today for the gospel till the Law be applied to their hearts, for 'by the Law is the knowledge of sin.' It is a waste of time to sow seed on ground which has never been ploughed or spaded! To present the vicarious sacrifice of Christ to those whose dominant passion is to take fill of sin, is to give that which is holy to the dogs." *A. W. Pink*

you. [3]And why do you look at the speck in your brother's eye, but do not consider the plank in your own eye? [4]Or how can you say to your brother, 'Let me remove the speck from your eye'; and look, a plank *is* in your own eye? [5]Hypocrite! First remove the plank from your own eye, and then you will see clearly to remove the speck from your brother's eye.

[6]"Do not give what is holy to the dogs; nor cast your pearls before swine, lest they trample them under their feet, and turn and tear you in pieces.

Keep Asking, Seeking, Knocking

[7]"Ask, and it will be given to you; seek, and you will find; knock, and it will be opened to you. [8]For everyone who asks receives, and he who seeks finds, and to him who knocks it will be opened. [9]Or what man is there among you who, if his son asks for bread, will give him a stone? [10]Or if he asks for a fish, will he give him a serpent? [11]If you then, being evil, know how to give good gifts to your children, how much more will your Father who is in heaven give good things to those who ask Him! [12]Therefore, whatever you want men to do to you, do also to them, for this is the Law and the Prophets.

The Narrow Way

[13]"Enter by the narrow gate; for wide *is* the gate and broad *is* the way that leads to destruction, and there are many who go in by it. [14]Because[a] narrow *is* the gate and difficult *is* the way which leads to life, and there are few who find it.

You Will Know Them by Their Fruits

[15]"Beware of false prophets, who come to you in sheep's clothing, but inwardly they are ravenous wolves. [16]You will know them by their fruits. Do men gather grapes from thornbushes or figs from thistles? [17]Even so, every good tree bears good fruit, but a bad tree bears bad fruit. [18]A good tree cannot bear bad fruit, nor *can* a bad tree bear good fruit. [19]Every tree that does not bear good fruit is cut down and thrown into the fire. [20]Therefore by their fruits you will know them.

I Never Knew You

[21]"Not everyone who says to Me, 'Lord, Lord,' shall enter the kingdom of heaven, but he who does the will of My Father in heaven. [22]Many will say to Me in that day, 'Lord, Lord, have we not prophesied in Your name, cast out demons in Your name, and done many wonders in Your name?' [23]And then I will declare to them, 'I never knew you; depart from Me, you who practice lawlessness!'

Build on the Rock

[24]"Therefore whoever hears these sayings of Mine, and does them, I will liken him to a wise man who built his house on the rock: [25]and the rain descended, the

7:14 [a]NU-Text and M-Text read *How . . . !*

7:22,23 These are perhaps the most frightening verses in the Bible. Vast multitudes of professing Christians fit into the category spoken of here. They call Jesus "Lord," but they practice lawlessness. They profess faith in Jesus, but have no regard for the divine Law. They tell "fibs" or "white" lies, take things that belong to others, have a roaming eye for the opposite sex, etc. They are liars, thieves, and adulterers at heart, who will be cast from the gates of heaven into the jaws of hell. See 1 John 2:19 comment.

floods came, and the winds blew and beat on that house; and it did not fall, for it was founded on the rock.

26“But everyone who hears these sayings of Mine, and does not do them, will be like a foolish man who built his house on the sand: 27and the rain descended, the floods came, and the winds blew and beat on that house; and it fell. And great was its fall.”

28And so it was, when Jesus had ended these sayings, that the people were astonished at His teaching, 29for He taught them as one having authority, and not as the scribes.

Jesus Cleanses a Leper

8 When He had come down from the mountain, great multitudes followed Him. 2And behold, a leper came and worshiped Him, saying, “Lord, if You are willing, You can make me clean.”

3Then Jesus put out *His* hand and touched him, saying, “I am willing; be cleansed.” Immediately his leprosy was cleansed.

4And Jesus said to him, “See that you tell no one; but go your way, show yourself to the priest, and offer the gift that Moses commanded, as a testimony to them.”

Jesus Heals a Centurion’s Servant

5Now when Jesus had entered Capernaum, a centurion came to Him, pleading with Him, 6saying, “Lord, my servant is lying at home paralyzed, dreadfully tormented.”

7And Jesus said to him, “I will come and heal him.”

8The centurion answered and said, “Lord, I am not worthy that You should come under my roof. But only speak a word, and my servant will be healed. 9For I also am a man under authority, having soldiers under me. And I say to this *one,* ‘Go,’ and he goes; and to another, ‘Come,’ and he comes; and to my servant, ‘Do this,’ and he does *it.*”

10When Jesus heard *it,* He marveled, and said to those who followed, “Assuredly, I say to you, I have not found such great faith, not even in Israel! 11And I say to you that many will come from

---

7:26 False converts. The foolish man was the one who heard the sayings of Jesus, but did not obey them. It’s not the world that hears the sayings of Jesus and doesn’t obey them. Most know only the “Golden Rule” and “Judge not,” and even then their understanding is darkened. However, the Church is filled with false converts who sit among God’s people and hear His words, but don’t obey them. They build their house on sand rather than on the firm foundation of Jesus Christ and His words. *A. W. Tozer* said, “It is my opinion that tens of thousands of people, if not millions, have been brought into some kind of religious experience by accepting Christ, and they have not been saved.” See Matt. 13:24–30 comment.

8:2 Was Jesus God in human form? See John 8:58.

Jehovah’s Witnesses: Jesus was God manifest in the flesh. The Bible tells us, “As Peter was coming in, Cornelius met him and fell down at his feet and worshiped him. But Peter lifted him up, saying, ‘Stand up; I myself am also a man’ ” (Acts 10:25,26). Peter refused worship in light of the Law that said, “You shall worship the LORD your God, and Him only you shall serve” (Matt. 4:10). In Rev. 19:10, when the apostle John saw an angel, he said, “I fell at his feet to worship him. But he said to me, ‘See that you do not do that! . . . Worship God!’ ” Even the angel of the Lord refused to be worshiped.

However, here are many more verses showing that Jesus allowed Himself to be worshiped, simply because He was God “manifest in the flesh”: “While He spoke these things to them, behold, a ruler came and worshiped Him, saying, ‘My daughter has just died, but come and lay Your hand on her and she will live’” (Matt. 9:18); “Then those who were in the boat came and worshiped Him, saying, ‘Truly You are the Son of God’” (Matt. 14:33); “Then she came and worshiped Him, saying, ‘Lord, help me!’” (Matt.15:25); “And as they went to tell His disciples, behold, Jesus met them, saying, ‘Rejoice!’ So they came and held Him by the feet and worshiped Him” (Matt. 28:9); “When they saw Him, they worshiped Him; but some doubted” (Matt. 28:17). He received their worship because He was “the image of the invisible God” (Col. 1:15)—“*God was manifested in the flesh*, justified in the Spirit, seen by angels, preached among the Gentiles, believed on in the world, received up in glory” (1 Tim. 3:16, emphasis added). See also the chart “The Deity of Jesus” at John 10:36.

QUESTIONS & OBJECTIONS

8:14 "How should I witness to someone who belongs to a denomination, but I suspect isn't trusting the Savior?"

The most effective way to speak about the issues of eternity to a religious person is not to get sidetracked from the essentials of salvation. Upon hearing a person's background, we may feel an obligation to speak to issues such as infant baptism, transubstantiation, etc. However, it is wise rather to build on the points of agreement between the Bible and the person's denomination, such as the virgin birth, the cross, and so on.

One point of agreement will almost certainly be the Ten Commandments. They are the key to bringing any religious person to a saving knowledge of the gospel. After someone is converted to Jesus Christ, the Bible will come alive and he will be led into all truth by the indwelling Holy Spirit. God's Word will then give him light, and he will forsake religious tradition as he is led by God.

While there are strong biblical arguments that may convince unregenerate people that their church's traditions contradict Holy Scripture, there is a difficulty. Some religious people hold the teachings of their church to be on a par with, or of greater authority than, Holy Scripture. It is therefore often futile to try to convince them intellectually that their trust should be in the person of Jesus Christ, rather than in their own righteousness or in their church traditions. For this reason we should aim at the conscience, instead of the intellect. Take them through the Law of God (the Commandments) to show that they are condemned despite their works, and strongly emphasize that we are saved by grace, and grace alone, rather than by trusting in our own righteousness or religious traditions.

If they are open to the gospel, and are interested in what God's Word says in reference to their church's teachings, they will listen to Scripture. For example, in Matt. 8:14 we see that Peter (whom the Roman Catholic church maintains was the first pope) was married, as were many of the other apostles (see 1 Cor. 9:5).

east and west, and sit down with Abraham, Isaac, and Jacob in the kingdom of
heaven. 12But the sons of the kingdom
will be cast out into outer darkness.
There will be weeping and gnashing of
teeth." 13Then Jesus said to the centurion, "Go your way; and as you have believed, *so* let it be done for you." And his
servant was healed that same hour.

Peter's Mother-in-Law Healed

14Now when Jesus had come into Peter's house, He saw his wife's mother lying sick with a fever. 15So He touched her
hand, and the fever left her. And she arose
and served them.[a]

Many Healed in the Evening

16When evening had come, they
brought to Him many who were demon-
possessed. And He cast out the spirits with
a word, and healed all who were sick,
17that it might be fulfilled which was
spoken by Isaiah the prophet, saying:

"He Himself took our infirmities
And bore our sicknesses."[a]

The Cost of Discipleship

18And when Jesus saw great multitudes about Him, He gave a command to
depart to the other side. 19Then a certain
scribe came and said to Him, "Teacher, I
will follow You wherever You go."
20And Jesus said to him, "Foxes have
holes and birds of the air *have* nests, but
the Son of Man has nowhere to lay *His*
head."
21Then another of His disciples said to
Him, "Lord, let me first go and bury my
father."
22But Jesus said to him, "Follow Me,
and let the dead bury their own dead."

Wind and Wave Obey Jesus

23Now when He got into a boat, His
disciples followed Him. 24And suddenly

8:15 [a]NU-Text and M-Text read *Him.* 8:17 [a]Isaiah 53:4

a great tempest arose on the sea, so that the boat was covered with the waves. But He was asleep. 25 Then His disciples came to *Him* and awoke Him, saying, "Lord, save us! We are perishing!"

26 But He said to them, "Why are you fearful, O you of little faith?" Then He arose and rebuked the winds and the sea, and there was a great calm. 27 So the men marveled, saying, "Who can this be, that even the winds and the sea obey Him?"

Two Demon-Possessed Men Healed

28 When He had come to the other side, to the country of the Gergesenes,[a] there met Him two demon-possessed *men,* coming out of the tombs, exceedingly fierce, so that no one could pass that way. 29 And suddenly they cried out, saying, "What have we to do with You, Jesus, You Son of God? Have You come here to torment us before the time?"

30 Now a good way off from them there was a herd of many swine feeding. 31 So the demons begged Him, saying, "If You cast us out, permit us to go away[a] into the herd of swine."

32 And He said to them, "Go." So when they had come out, they went into the herd of swine. And suddenly the whole herd of swine ran violently down the steep place into the sea, and perished in the water.

33 Then those who kept *them* fled; and they went away into the city and told everything, including what *had happened* to the demon-possessed *men.* 34 And behold, the whole city came out to meet Jesus. And when they saw Him, they begged *Him* to depart from their region.

Jesus Forgives and Heals a Paralytic

9 So He got into a boat, crossed over, and came to His own city. 2 Then behold, they brought to Him a paralytic lying on a bed. When Jesus saw their faith, He said to the paralytic, "Son, be of good cheer; your sins are forgiven you."

3 And at once some of the scribes said within themselves, "This Man blasphemes!"

THE FUNCTION OF THE LAW

9:12 "Sinners that think they need no physician will not endure the healer's hand. The Law is therefore necessary to give knowledge of sin, so that proud man, who thought he was whole, may be humbled by the discovery of his own great wickedness, and sigh and pant after the grace that is set forth in Christ." *Martin Luther*

4 But Jesus, knowing their thoughts, said, "Why do you think evil in your hearts? 5 For which is easier, to say, *'Your* sins are forgiven you,' or to say, 'Arise and walk'? 6 But that you may know that the Son of Man has power on earth to forgive sins"—then He said to the paralytic, "Arise, take up your bed, and go to your house." 7 And he arose and departed to his house.

> Before we can pray 'Thy Kingdom come,' we must be willing to pray 'my kingdom go.'
>
> **ALAN REDPATH**

8 Now when the multitudes saw *it,* they marveled[a] and glorified God, who had given such power to men.

Matthew the Tax Collector

9 As Jesus passed on from there, He saw a man named Matthew sitting at the tax office. And He said to him, "Follow Me." So he arose and followed Him.

10 Now it happened, as Jesus sat at the table in the house, *that* behold, many tax collectors and sinners came and sat down with Him and His disciples. 11 And when the Pharisees saw *it,* they said to His disciples, "Why does your Teacher eat with tax collectors and sinners?"

12 When Jesus heard *that,* He said to them, "Those who are well have no need of a physician, but those who are sick.

8:28 [a]NU-Text reads *Gadarenes.* 8:31 [a]NU-Text reads *send us.* 9:8 [a]NU-Text reads *were afraid.*

13But go and learn what *this* means: *'I desire mercy and not sacrifice.'*[a] For I did not come to call the righteous, but sinners, to repentance."[b]

Jesus Is Questioned About Fasting

14Then the disciples of John came to Him, saying, "Why do we and the Pharisees fast often,[a] but Your disciples do not fast?"

15And Jesus said to them, "Can the friends of the bridegroom mourn as long as the bridegroom is with them? But the days will come when the bridegroom will be taken away from them, and then they will fast. 16No one puts a piece of unshrunk cloth on an old garment; for the patch pulls away from the garment, and the tear is made worse. 17Nor do they put new wine into old wineskins, or else the wineskins break, the wine is spilled, and the wineskins are ruined. But they put new wine into new wineskins, and both are preserved."

A Girl Restored to Life and a Woman Healed

18While He spoke these things to them, behold, a ruler came and worshiped Him, saying, "My daughter has just died, but come and lay Your hand on her and she will live." 19So Jesus arose and followed him, and so *did* His disciples.

20And suddenly, a woman who had a flow of blood for twelve years came from behind and touched the hem of His garment. 21For she said to herself, "If only I may touch His garment, I shall be made well." 22But Jesus turned around, and when He saw her He said, "Be of good cheer, daughter; your faith has made you well." And the woman was made well from that hour.

23When Jesus came into the ruler's house, and saw the flute players and the noisy crowd wailing, 24He said to them, "Make room, for the girl is not dead, but sleeping." And they ridiculed Him. 25But when the crowd was put outside, He went in and took her by the hand, and the girl arose. 26And the report of this went out into all that land.

Two Blind Men Healed

27When Jesus departed from there, two blind men followed Him, crying out and saying, "Son of David, have mercy on us!"

28And when He had come into the house, the blind men came to Him. And Jesus said to them, "Do you believe that I am able to do this?"

They said to Him, "Yes, Lord."

29Then He touched their eyes, saying, "According to your faith let it be to you." 30And their eyes were opened. And Jesus sternly warned them, saying, "See *that* no one knows *it*." 31But when they had departed, they spread the news about Him in all that country.

9:13 [a]Hosea 6:6 [b]NU-Text omits *to repentance*. 9:14 [a]NU-Text brackets *often* as disputed.

9:20 Evolution and blood. "Platelets" play an important role in preventing the loss of blood by beginning a chain reaction that results in blood clotting. As blood begins to flow from a cut or scratch, platelets respond to help the blood clot and to stop the bleeding after a short time.

Platelets promote the clotting process by clumping together and forming a plug at the site of a wound and then releasing proteins called "clotting factors." These proteins start a series of chemical reactions that are extremely complicated. Every step of the clotting must go smoothly if a clot is to form. If one of the clotting factors is missing or defective, the clotting process does not work. A serious genetic disorder known as "hemophilia" results from a defect in one of the clotting factor genes. Because they lack one of the clotting factors, hemophilia sufferers may bleed uncontrollably from even small cuts or scrapes.

To form a blood clot there must be twelve specific individual chemical reactions in our blood. If evolution is true, and if this 12-step process didn't happen in the first generation (i.e., if any one of these specific reactions failed to operate in their exact reaction and order), no creatures would have survived. They all would have bled to death! See also Job 4:4 comment.

A Mute Man Speaks

32As they went out, behold, they
brought to Him a man, mute and demon-
possessed. 33And when the demon was
cast out, the mute spoke. And the multitudes marveled, saying, "It was never
seen like this in Israel!"

34But the Pharisees said, "He casts out
demons by the ruler of the demons."

The Compassion of Jesus

35Then Jesus went about all the cities
and villages, teaching in their synagogues, preaching the gospel of the kingdom, and healing every sickness and
every disease among the people.[a] 36But
when He saw the multitudes, He was
moved with compassion for them, because they were weary[a] and scattered,
like sheep having no shepherd. 37Then
He said to His disciples, "The harvest
truly is plentiful, but the laborers *are* few.
38Therefore pray the Lord of the harvest
to send out laborers into His harvest."

The Twelve Apostles

10 And when He had called His
twelve disciples to *Him*, He gave
them power *over* unclean spirits, to cast
them out, and to heal all kinds of sickness and all kinds of disease. 2Now the
names of the twelve apostles are these:
first, Simon, who is called Peter, and Andrew his brother; James the *son* of
Zebedee, and John his brother; 3Philip
and Bartholomew; Thomas and Matthew
the tax collector; James the *son* of Alphaeus, and Lebbaeus, whose surname was[a]
Thaddaeus; 4Simon the Cananite,[a] and
Judas Iscariot, who also betrayed Him.

Sending Out the Twelve

5These twelve Jesus sent out and commanded them, saying: "Do not go into
the way of the Gentiles, and do not enter
a city of the Samaritans. 6But go rather to
the lost sheep of the house of Israel. 7And
as you go, preach, saying, 'The kingdom of
heaven is at hand.' 8Heal the sick, cleanse
the lepers, raise the dead,[a] cast out demons. Freely you have received, freely
give. 9Provide neither gold nor silver nor
copper in your money belts, 10nor bag for
your journey, nor two tunics, nor sandals,
nor staffs; for a worker is worthy of his
food.

> The most important thing you could ever do is to tell others about the sacrifice Jesus made for them. The greatest possible difference you could make with the rest of your life is to help others be in heaven with you.
>
> **RON HUTCHCRAFT**

11"Now whatever city or town you enter, inquire who in it is worthy, and stay
there till you go out. 12And when you go
into a household, greet it. 13If the household is worthy, let your peace come upon
it. But if it is not worthy, let your peace
return to you. 14And whoever will not receive you nor hear your words, when you
depart from that house or city, shake off

9:35 [a]NU-Text omits *among the people.* 9:36 [a]NU-Text and M-Text read *harassed.* 10:3 [a]NU-Text omits *Lebbaeus, whose surname was.* 10:4 [a]NU-Text reads *Cananaean.* 10:8 [a]NU-Text reads *raise the dead, cleanse the lepers;* M-Text omits *raise the dead.*

9:38 If we are not laborers, we won't obey this command, because our conscience will condemn us. The devil therefore gets two victories: not only does the professing Christian not labor in the harvest fields, but neither does he pray for laborers.

10:5 Bible contradiction? Skeptics argue that, because Jesus told His disciples not to go to certain groups of people, this proves He didn't love Gentiles or Samaritans—which contradicts the command to "love your neighbor" (Matt. 22:39).

However, the plan of God was to preach the gospel to the Jews first before taking it to the Gentiles. This wasn't because of a lack of love and concern for them, but because the Jews already had the Law which prepared them for the message of grace.

10:22 God's Love: The Biblical Presentation

The essence of the modern gospel message is "God loves you and has a wonderful plan for your life." However, our idea of "wonderful" is a little different from the world's. Take a sinner through the pages of the Book of Acts and show him the terrifying scene of stones breaking the bones of Stephen. Then smile and whisper, "*Wonderful...*" Listen together to the sound of a cat-o'-nine-tails as it rips the flesh off the back of the apostle Paul. Follow together the word "suffering" through the Epistles, and see if you can get the world to whisper, "Wonderful!" After such a ride down Honesty Road, they may think the pleasures of sin are a little more attractive than the call to "suffer affliction with the people of God."

Who in the world is going to listen if we are so blatantly honest about the Christian life? Perhaps not as many as are attracted by the talk of a wonderful plan. However, the answer to our dilemma is to make the issue one of *righteousness*, rather than *happiness*. This is what Jesus did. He used the Ten Commandments to show sinners the righteous standard of God (Luke 10:25–27; 18:18–20). Once the world sees the perfect standard by which they will be judged, they will begin to fear God, and through the fear of the Lord, men depart from sin (Prov. 16:6). They will begin to hunger and thirst after the righteousness that is in Jesus Christ alone.

If you study the New Testament you will see that God's love is almost always given in direct correlation to the cross: herein is love, for God so loved, God commended His love, etc. (See John 3:16; Rom. 5:5,6,8; Gal. 2:20; Eph.2:4,5; 5:2,25; 1 John 3:16; 4:10; and Rev. 1:5, among others.) The cross is the focal point of God's love for the world. How can we point to the cross without making reference to sin?

How can we refer to sin without the Law (Rom. 7:7)? The biblical way to express God's love to a sinner is to show him how great his sin is (using the Law—see Rom. 7:13; Gal. 3:24), and then give him the incredible grace of God in Christ. This was the key to reaching so many on the Day of Pentecost. They were "devout" Jews who knew the Law and its holy demands, and therefore readily accepted the mercy of God in Christ to escape its fearful wrath.

When you use the Law to show the world their true state, get ready for sinners to thank you. For the first time in their lives, they will see the Christian message as an expression of love and concern for their eternal welfare, rather than of merely proselytizing for a better lifestyle while on this earth.

John MacArthur said, "We need to adjust our presentation of the gospel. We cannot dismiss the fact that God hates sin and punishes sinners with eternal torment. How can we begin a gospel presentation by telling people on their way to hell that God has a wonderful plan for their lives?"

the dust from your feet. 15 Assuredly, I say
to you, it will be more tolerable for the
land of Sodom and Gomorrah in the day
of judgment than for that city!

Persecutions Are Coming

16 "Behold, I send you out as sheep in
the midst of wolves. Therefore be wise as
serpents and harmless as doves. 17 But beware of men, for they will deliver you up
to councils and scourge you in their synagogues. 18 You will be brought before
governors and kings for My sake, as a testimony to them and to the Gentiles. 19 But
when they deliver you up, do not worry
about how or what you should speak.
For it will be given to you in that hour
what you should speak; 20 for it is not you
who speak, but the Spirit of your Father
who speaks in you.

21 "Now brother will deliver up
brother to death, and a father *his* child;

10:16 This passage contradicts the promise of modern evangelism, that "God loves you and has a wonderful plan for your life." That message promises a life of roses without thorns. In reality, Jesus told His disciples that He was sending them among sharp thorns. Their own families would betray them and have them put to death for their faith (v. 21). This is the life Jesus promised believers: we would be hated for His name's sake and would be persecuted. See also John 15:18–21 comment.

and children will rise up against parents and cause them to be put to death. [22]And you will be hated by all for My name's sake. But he who endures to the end will be saved. [23]When they persecute you in this city, flee to another. For assuredly, I say to you, you will not have gone through the cities of Israel before the Son of Man comes.

[24]"A disciple is not above *his* teacher, nor a servant above his master. [25]It is enough for a disciple that he be like his teacher, and a servant like his master. If they have called the master of the house Beelzebub,[a] how much more *will they call* those of his household! [26]Therefore do not fear them. For there is nothing covered that will not be revealed, and hidden that will not be known.

Jesus Teaches the Fear of God

[27]"Whatever I tell you in the dark, speak in the light; and what you hear in the ear, preach on the housetops. [28]And do not fear those who kill the body but cannot kill the soul. But rather fear Him who is able to destroy both soul and body in hell. [29]Are not two sparrows sold for a copper coin? And not one of them falls to the ground apart from your Father's will. [30]But the very hairs of your head are all numbered. [31]Do not fear therefore; you are of more value than many sparrows.

Confess Christ Before Men

[32]"Therefore whoever confesses Me before men, him I will also confess before My Father who is in heaven. [33]But whoever denies Me before men, him I will also deny before My Father who is in heaven.

Christ Brings Division

[34]"Do not think that I came to bring peace on earth. I did not come to bring peace but a sword. [35]For I have come to *'set a man against his father, a daughter against her mother, and a daughter-in-law against her mother-in-law'*; [36]and *'a man's enemies will be those of his own household.'*[a] [37]He who loves father or mother more than Me is not worthy of Me. And he who loves son or daughter more than Me is not worthy of Me. [38]And he who does not take his cross and follow after Me is not worthy of Me. [39]He who finds his life will lose it, and he who loses his life for My sake will find it.

10:25 [a]**NU-Text and M-Text read** ***Beelzebul.*** **10:36** [a]**Micah 7:6**

10:23 Don't wait around to be martyred. Leave when trouble brews. Paul once left a potentially explosive situation by being lowered down a wall in a basket. Sometimes backing off can be humbling, but wise.

Bible error? Did Jesus say that He would return during the lifetime of His disciples? "Another alternative is to take the promise literally and immediately and to interpret the phrase 'before the Son of Man comes' as a reference to the fact that Jesus rejoined the disciples after their mission. This view may be supported by several facts. First, the phrase 'before the Son of Man comes' is never used by Matthew to describe the Second Coming. Second, it fits with a literal understanding of the first part of the verse. The disciples went literally and immediately into 'the cities of Israel' to preach, and Jesus literally and immediately rejoined them after their itinerant ministry." *Norman Geisler* and *Thomas Howe, When Critics Ask*

10:27,28 Faithful, not fearful, witnesses. We are to be faithful witnesses for Jesus. When it comes to preaching the gospel, we are to fear only God.

If you are fearful when it comes to witnessing, here's something you can do that doesn't take much courage. When you go to a gas station, leave a small tract in the credit card slot at the pump. The next person will have to take it out to put his credit card in, and will appreciate having something to read while he's filling his gas tank. Each time you go to the grocery store, discreetly go down the beer aisle, placing tracts in the top slot in beer cases. Tuck tracts into pockets in the clothing department, inside magazines, and in the racks in the checkout line, where they'll be easily seen and enjoy a captive audience.

10:28 Hell: For verses warning of its reality, see Matt. 18:9.

10:37 "People who need people to walk with God, don't walk with God. They walk with people." *Emeal Zwayne*

A Cup of Cold Water

40"He who receives you receives Me, and he who receives Me receives Him who sent Me. 41He who receives a prophet in the name of a prophet shall receive a prophet's reward. And he who receives a righteous man in the name of a righteous man shall receive a righteous man's reward. 42And whoever gives one of these little ones only a cup of cold *water* in the name of a disciple, assuredly, I say to you, he shall by no means lose his reward."

John the Baptist Sends Messengers to Jesus

11 Now it came to pass, when Jesus finished commanding His twelve disciples, that He departed from there to teach and to preach in their cities.

2And when John had heard in prison about the works of Christ, he sent two of[a] his disciples 3and said to Him, "Are You the Coming One, or do we look for another?"

4Jesus answered and said to them, "Go and tell John the things which you hear and see: 5*The* blind see and *the* lame walk; *the* lepers are cleansed and *the* deaf hear; *the* dead are raised up and *the* poor have the gospel preached to them. 6And blessed is he who is not offended because of Me."

7As they departed, Jesus began to say to the multitudes concerning John: "What did you go out into the wilderness to see? A reed shaken by the wind? 8But what did you go out to see? A man clothed in soft garments? Indeed, those who wear soft *clothing* are in kings' houses. 9But what did you go out to see?

"We must all mutually share in the knowledge that our existence only attains its true value when we have experienced in ourselves the truth of the declaration: 'He who loses his life shall find it.'"

Albert Schweitzer

A prophet? Yes, I say to you, and more than a prophet. 10For this is *he* of whom it is written:

'Behold, I send My messenger before
Your face,
Who will prepare Your way before
You.'[a]

11"Assuredly, I say to you, among those born of women there has not risen one greater than John the Baptist; but he who is least in the kingdom of heaven is greater than he. 12And from the days of

11:2 [a]NU-Text reads *by* for *two of.* 11:10 [a]Malachi 3:1

11:11 "If God has called you to be a missionary, your Father would be grieved for you to shrivel down into a king." *Charles Spurgeon*

11:12,13 The Law and the prophets were doing their job in Israel. The prophets established the inspiration of Holy Scripture, while the Law brought the knowledge of sin. When John began to preach that Israel should repent, they flocked to him for the baptism of repentance because the Law convinced them of sin. Just as a drowning man may become "violent" to be saved (and at times have to be knocked out by a lifeguard), so the Law makes a man *desperate* to be saved. It makes him take hold of the kingdom of God "by force."

QUESTIONS & OBJECTIONS

11:24 ***"God is unfair in that Hitler and a sweet old lady (who never trusted in Jesus) will both go to hell."***

Sinners often accuse God of being unjust, because they assume that everyone will receive the same punishment in hell. God's judgment, however, will be according to righteousness (Acts 17:31). This verse shows that there will be *degrees* of punishment. See also Mark 6:11.

John the Baptist until now the kingdom
of heaven suffers violence, and the violent take it by force. 13For all the prophets and the law prophesied until John.
14And if you are willing to receive *it,* he is
Elijah who is to come. 15He who has ears
to hear, let him hear!
16"But to what shall I liken this generation? It is like children sitting in the
marketplaces and calling to their companions, 17and saying:

'We played the flute for you,
And you did not dance;
We mourned to you,
And you did not lament.'

18For John came neither eating nor drinking, and they say, 'He has a demon.' 19The
Son of Man came eating and drinking,
and they say, 'Look, a glutton and a
winebibber, a friend of tax collectors and
sinners!' But wisdom is justified by her
children."[a]

Woe to the Impenitent Cities

20Then He began to rebuke the cities
in which most of His mighty works had
been done, because they did not repent:
21"Woe to you, Chorazin! Woe to you,
Bethsaida! For if the mighty works which
were done in you had been done in Tyre
and Sidon, they would have repented
long ago in sackcloth and ashes. 22But I
say to you, it will be more tolerable for
Tyre and Sidon in the day of judgment
than for you. 23And you, Capernaum, who
are exalted to heaven, will be[a] brought
down to Hades; for if the mighty works
which were done in you had been done
in Sodom, it would have remained until
this day. 24But I say to you that it shall be
more tolerable for the land of Sodom in
the day of judgment than for you."

Jesus Gives True Rest

25At that time Jesus answered and
said, "I thank You, Father, Lord of
heaven and earth, that You have hidden
these things from *the* wise and prudent
and have revealed them to babes. 26Even
so, Father, for so it seemed good in Your
sight. 27All things have been delivered to
Me by My Father, and no one knows the
Son except the Father. Nor does anyone
know the Father except the Son, and *the
one* to whom the Son wills to reveal *Him.*
28Come to Me, all *you* who labor and are
heavy laden, and I will give you rest.
29Take My yoke upon you and learn from
Me, for I am gentle and lowly in heart, and
you will find rest for your souls. 30For
My yoke *is* easy and My burden is light."

Jesus Is Lord of the Sabbath

12 At that time Jesus went through
the grainfields on the Sabbath. And

11:19 [a]NU-Text reads *works.* 11:23 [a]NU-Text reads *will you be exalted to heaven? No, you will be.*

11:14 This verse is often used to try to justify belief in reincarnation. However, Elijah wasn't reincarnated as John the Baptist. John merely came in the "spirit and power of Elijah" (Luke 1:17). It is appointed unto man *once* to die (see Heb. 9:27).

His disciples were hungry, and began to pluck heads of grain and to eat. [2]And when the Pharisees saw *it,* they said to Him, "Look, Your disciples are doing what is not lawful to do on the Sabbath!"

[3]But He said to them, "Have you not read what David did when he was hungry, he and those who were with him: [4]how he entered the house of God and ate the showbread which was not lawful for him to eat, nor for those who were with him, but only for the priests? [5]Or have you not read in the law that on the Sabbath the priests in the temple profane the Sabbath, and are blameless? [6]Yet I say to you that in this place there is *One* greater than the temple. [7]But if you had known what *this* means, *'I desire mercy and not sacrifice,'*[a] you would not have condemned the guiltless. [8]For the Son of Man is Lord even[a] of the Sabbath."

Healing on the Sabbath

[9]Now when He had departed from there, He went into their synagogue. [10]And behold, there was a man who had a withered hand. And they asked Him, saying, "Is it lawful to heal on the Sabbath?"—that they might accuse Him.

> The best means of resisting the devil is to destroy whatever of the world remains in us, in order to raise for God, upon its ruins, a building all of love. Then shall we begin, in this fleeting life, to love God as we shall love him in eternity.
>
> **JOHN WESLEY**

[11]Then He said to them, "What man is there among you who has one sheep, and if it falls into a pit on the Sabbath, will not lay hold of it and lift *it* out? [12]Of how much more value then is a man than a sheep? Therefore it is lawful to do good on the Sabbath." [13]Then He said to the man, "Stretch out your hand." And he stretched *it* out, and it was restored as whole as the other. [14]Then the Pharisees went out and plotted against Him, how they might destroy Him.

Behold, My Servant

[15]But when Jesus knew *it,* He withdrew from there. And great multitudes[a] followed Him, and He healed them all. [16]Yet He warned them not to make Him known, [17]that it might be fulfilled which was spoken by Isaiah the prophet, saying:

[18]*"Behold! My Servant whom I have chosen,*
My Beloved in whom My soul is well pleased!
I will put My Spirit upon Him,
And He will declare justice to the Gentiles.
[19]*He will not quarrel nor cry out,*
Nor will anyone hear His voice in the streets.
[20]*A bruised reed He will not break,*
And smoking flax He will not quench,
Till He sends forth justice to victory;
[21]*And in His name Gentiles will trust."*[a]

A House Divided Cannot Stand

[22]Then one was brought to Him who was demon-possessed, blind and mute; and He healed him, so that the blind and[a] mute man both spoke and saw. [23]And all the multitudes were amazed and said, "Could this be the Son of David?"

[24]Now when the Pharisees heard *it* they said, "This *fellow* does not cast out demons except by Beelzebub,[a] the ruler of the demons."

[25]But Jesus knew their thoughts, and said to them: "Every kingdom divided against itself is brought to desolation, and every city or house divided against itself will not stand. [26]If Satan casts out Satan, he is divided against himself. How then will his kingdom stand? [27]And if I cast out demons by Beelzebub, by whom do your sons cast *them* out? Therefore they shall be your judges. [28]But if I cast out

12:7 [a]Hosea 6:6 12:8 [a]NU-Text and M-Text omit *even.* 12:15 [a]NU-Text brackets *multitudes* as disputed. 12:21 [a]Isaiah 42:1–4 12:22 [a]NU-Text omits *blind and.* 12:24 [a]NU-Text and M-Text read *Beelzebul.*

QUESTIONS & OBJECTIONS

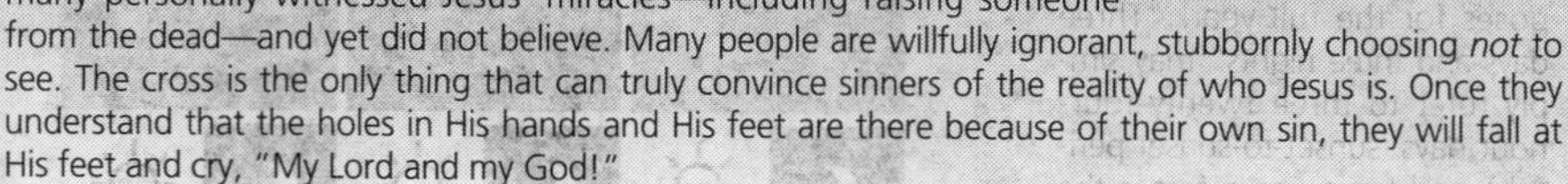

12:39 ***"If God gives me some 'sign,' then I will believe."***

The unsaved often want a "sign" from God. This is in spite of the testimony of creation, their conscience, the Bible, and the Christian. Think of how many personally witnessed Jesus' miracles—including raising someone from the dead—and yet did not believe. Many people are willfully ignorant, stubbornly choosing *not* to see. The cross is the only thing that can truly convince sinners of the reality of who Jesus is. Once they understand that the holes in His hands and His feet are there because of their own sin, they will fall at His feet and cry, "My Lord and my God!"

demons by the Spirit of God, surely the
kingdom of God has come upon you.
29Or how can one enter a strong man's
house and plunder his goods, unless he
first binds the strong man? And then he
will plunder his house. 30He who is not
with Me is against Me, and he who does
not gather with Me scatters abroad.

The Unpardonable Sin

31"Therefore I say to you, every sin
and blasphemy will be forgiven men, but
the blasphemy *against* the Spirit will not
be forgiven men. 32Anyone who speaks a
word against the Son of Man, it will be
forgiven him; but whoever speaks against
the Holy Spirit, it will not be forgiven
him, either in this age or in the *age* to
come.

A Tree Known by Its Fruit

33"Either make the tree good and its
fruit good, or else make the tree bad and
its fruit bad; for a tree is known by *its* fruit.
34Brood of vipers! How can you, being
evil, speak good things? For out of the
abundance of the heart the mouth speaks.
35A good man out of the good treasure of
his heart[a] brings forth good things, and
an evil man out of the evil treasure brings
forth evil things. 36But I say to you that
for every idle word men may speak, they
will give account of it in the day of judgment.
37For by your words you will be
justified, and by your words you will be
condemned."

The Scribes and Pharisees Ask for a Sign

38Then some of the scribes and Pharisees
answered, saying, "Teacher, we want
to see a sign from You."
39But He answered and said to them,
"An evil and adulterous generation seeks

12:35 [a]NU-Text and M-Text omit *of his heart.*

12:36 Idle words divide the body. In 1 Kings 3:16–27, the Bible tells of two harlots claiming to be the mother of one child. Solomon revealed his God-given wisdom by suggesting that the child be cut in two, thus exposing the true mother. The false mother preferred to divide the body rather than back down from her claim.

It is interesting to note that both women dwelt in the same house, just as both the wheat and the tares sit alongside each other in the House of God (Matt. 13:24–30,38). Each of the women called Solomon "lord," and both the wheat and tares call Jesus "Lord" (Matt. 7:21). It is not always easy to discern the wheat from the tares because it takes the wisdom of Solomon to do so. Here is wisdom: *the false convert will show his spirit by, without hesitation, dividing the Body of Christ in two, rather than gracefully making a withdrawal*. He will cut a body of believers in half with vicious gossip. He sows discord among the brethren. He is a slave to his tongue, which is a "world of iniquity...set on fire by hell" (James 3:6).

However, the true convert sets a watch at the door of his mouth, and will immediately back away from words that could divide a local church. He knows that "the beginning of strife is like releasing water" (Prov. 17:14). He does not become involved in idle talk. He is a peacemaker, a child of God. The fear of God is his guide. He knows that there is not a word on his tongue that God does not know, and that on Judgment Day he will give an account for every idle word he speaks.

12:40 How long was Jesus in the tomb?

To first-century Jews, any part of a day could be counted as if it were a full day, just as a child born December 31 at 11:59 p.m. is deductible for income-tax purposes for the full year. "Three days and three nights" may simply refer to three twenty-four-hour days (sunset-to-sunset periods), and Jesus was in fact in the tomb during part of three different days.

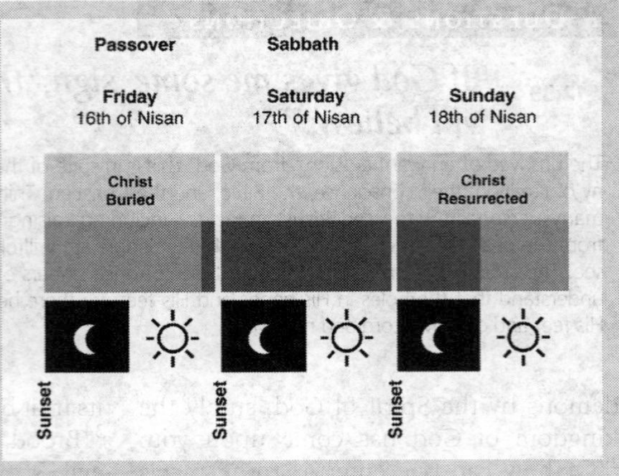

after a sign, and no sign will be given to
it except the sign of the prophet Jonah.
40For as Jonah was three days and three
nights in the belly of the great fish, so will
the Son of Man be three days and three
nights in the heart of the earth. 41The
men of Nineveh will rise up in the judgment with this generation and condemn it, because they repented at the preaching of Jonah; and indeed a greater than Jonah
is here. 42The queen of the South will rise
up in the judgment with this generation and condemn it, for she came from the ends of the earth to hear the wisdom of Solomon; and indeed a greater than Solomon *is* here.

> The gospel is not something we come to church to hear; it is something we go from church to tell.
>
> **VANCE HAVNER**

An Unclean Spirit Returns

43"When an unclean spirit goes out of
a man, he goes through dry places, seeking rest, and finds none. 44Then he says,
'I will return to my house from which I
came.' And when he comes, he finds *it*
empty, swept, and put in order. 45Then
he goes and takes with him seven other spirits more wicked than himself, and they enter and dwell there; and the last *state* of that man is worse than the first. So shall it also be with this wicked generation."

Jesus' Mother and Brothers Send for Him

46While He was still talking to the
multitudes, behold, His mother and brothers stood outside, seeking to speak
with Him. 47Then one said to Him, "Look,
Your mother and Your brothers are standing outside, seeking to speak with You."
48But He answered and said to the one
who told Him, "Who is My mother and
who are My brothers?" 49And He stretched
out His hand toward His disciples and said, "Here are My mother and My brothers!
50For whoever does the will of My
Father in heaven is My brother and sister and mother."

The Parable of the Sower

13 On the same day Jesus went out of
the house and sat by the sea. 2And
great multitudes were gathered together to Him, so that He got into a boat and sat; and the whole multitude stood on the shore.

3Then He spoke many things to them
in parables, saying: "Behold, a sower
went out to sow. 4And as he sowed, some
seed fell by the wayside; and the birds
came and devoured them. 5Some fell on
stony places, where they did not have much earth; and they immediately sprang

up because they had no depth of earth.
6But when the sun was up they were
scorched, and because they had no root
they withered away. 7And some fell
among thorns, and the thorns sprang up
and choked them. 8But others fell on
good ground and yielded a crop: some a
hundredfold, some sixty, some thirty.
9He who has ears to hear, let him hear!"

The Purpose of Parables

10And the disciples came and said to
Him, "Why do You speak to them in
parables?"

11He answered and said to them, "Because it has been given to you to know
the mysteries of the kingdom of heaven,
but to them it has not been given. 12For
whoever has, to him more will be given,
and he will have abundance; but whoever does not have, even what he has will
be taken away from him. 13Therefore I
speak to them in parables, because seeing
they do not see, and hearing they do not
hear, nor do they understand. 14And in
them the prophecy of Isaiah is fulfilled,
which says:

'Hearing you will hear and shall not
understand,
And seeing you will see and not
perceive;
15*For the hearts of this people have*
grown dull.
Their ears are hard of hearing,
And their eyes they have closed,
Lest they should see with their eyes
and hear with their ears,
Lest they should understand with
their hearts and turn,
So that I should[a] *heal them.'*[b]

16But blessed *are* your eyes for they see,
and your ears for they hear; 17for assuredly, I say to you that many prophets
and righteous *men* desired to see what
you see, and did not see *it,* and to hear
what you hear, and did not hear *it.*

The Parable of the Sower Explained

18"Therefore hear the parable of the
sower: 19When anyone hears the word of
the kingdom, and does not understand *it,*
then the wicked *one* comes and snatches
away what was sown in his heart. This is
he who received seed by the wayside.
20But he who received the seed on stony
places, this is he who hears the word and
immediately receives it with joy; 21yet he
has no root in himself, but endures only
for a while. For when tribulation or persecution arises because of the word, immediately he stumbles. 22Now he who
received seed among the thorns is he
who hears the word, and the cares of this
world and the deceitfulness of riches
choke the word, and he becomes unfruitful. 23But he who received seed on the
good ground is he who hears the word
and understands *it,* who indeed bears
fruit and produces: some a hundredfold,
some sixty, some thirty."

The Parable of the Wheat and the Tares

24Another parable He put forth to
them, saying: "The kingdom of heaven is

13:15 [a]NU-Text and M-Text read *would.* [b]Isaiah 6:9, 10

13:16 These are not the words of merely a "great teacher." These are the words of God in human form. He was speaking of Himself—blessed are those who see Him and hear His words. He was either the greatest egotist who ever lived, or He was the source of life in the flesh.

13:19 The key difference between the "wayside" hearer in this verse and the "good soil" hearer in v. 23 is understanding. This is why we must use the Law as a "tutor" to bring the knowledge of sin (Gal. 3:24; Rom. 3:20). Unless there is understanding as to his true plight, the sinner will not flee to the Savior.

"I had rather be fully understood by ten than admired by ten thousand." *Jonathan Edwards*

13:24–30 The wheat and the tares are the true and the false converts sitting alongside each other until the time of harvest. (See vv. 37–43.) For more on true and false converts, see Matt. 25:12 comment.

"There are probably more unsaved church people than we can begin to imagine." *Gary Labro*

like a man who sowed good seed in his field; 25 but while men slept, his enemy came and sowed tares among the wheat and went his way. 26 But when the grain had sprouted and produced a crop, then the tares also appeared. 27 So the servants of the owner came and said to him, 'Sir, did you not sow good seed in your field? How then does it have tares?' 28 He said to them, 'An enemy has done this.' The servants said to him, 'Do you want us then to go and gather them up?' 29 But he said, 'No, lest while you gather up the tares you also uproot the wheat with them. 30 Let both grow together until the harvest, and at the time of harvest I will say to the reapers, "First gather together the tares and bind them in bundles to burn them, but gather the wheat into my barn." ' "

The Parable of the Mustard Seed

31 Another parable He put forth to them, saying: "The kingdom of heaven is like a mustard seed, which a man took and sowed in his field, 32 which indeed is the least of all the seeds; but when it is grown it is greater than the herbs and becomes a tree, so that the birds of the air come and nest in its branches."

The Parable of the Leaven

33 Another parable He spoke to them: "The kingdom of heaven is like leaven, which a woman took and hid in three measures[a] of meal till it was all leavened."

Prophecy and the Parables

34 All these things Jesus spoke to the multitude in parables; and without a parable He did not speak to them, 35 that it might be fulfilled which was spoken by the prophet, saying:

"I will open My mouth in parables;
I will utter things kept secret from the
foundation of the world."[a]

The Parable of the Tares Explained

36 Then Jesus sent the multitude away and went into the house. And His disciples came to Him, saying, "Explain to us the parable of the tares of the field."

37 He answered and said to them: "He who sows the good seed is the Son of Man. 38 The field is the world, the good seeds are the sons of the kingdom, but the tares are the sons of the wicked *one*. 39 The enemy who sowed them is the devil, the harvest is the end of the age, and the reapers are the angels. 40 Therefore as the tares are gathered and burned in the fire, so it will be at the end of this age. 41 The Son of Man will send out His angels, and they will gather out of His kingdom all things that offend, and those who practice lawlessness, 42 and will cast them into the furnace of fire. There will be wailing and gnashing of teeth. 43 Then the righteous will shine forth as the sun in the kingdom of their Father. He who has ears to hear, let him hear!

The Parable of the Hidden Treasure

44 "Again, the kingdom of heaven is like treasure hidden in a field, which a man found and hid; and for joy over it he goes and sells all that he has and buys that field.

The Parable of the Pearl of Great Price

45 "Again, the kingdom of heaven is like a merchant seeking beautiful pearls, 46 who, when he had found one pearl of great price, went and sold all that he had and bought it.

The Parable of the Dragnet

47 "Again, the kingdom of heaven is like

13:33 [a]Greek *sata,* approximately two pecks in all 13:35 [a]Psalm 78:2

13:34,35 Messianic prophecy fulfilled: "I will open my mouth in a parable: I will utter dark sayings of old" (Psa 78:2). See Matt 26:15 comment.

a dragnet that was cast into the sea and gathered some of every kind, [48]which, when it was full, they drew to shore; and they sat down and gathered the good into vessels, but threw the bad away. [49]So it will be at the end of the age. The angels will come forth, separate the wicked from among the just, [50]and cast them into the furnace of fire. There will be wailing and gnashing of teeth."

[51]Jesus said to them,[a] "Have you understood all these things?"

They said to Him, "Yes, Lord."[b]

[52]Then He said to them, "Therefore every scribe instructed concerning[a] the kingdom of heaven is like a householder who brings out of his treasure *things* new and old."

Jesus Rejected at Nazareth

[53]Now it came to pass, when Jesus had finished these parables, that He departed from there. [54]When He had come to His own country, He taught them in their synagogue, so that they were astonished and said, "Where did this *Man* get this wisdom and *these* mighty works? [55]Is this not the carpenter's son? Is not His mother called Mary? And His brothers James, Joses,[a] Simon, and Judas? [56]And His sisters, are they not all with us? Where then did this *Man* get all these things?" [57]So they were offended at Him.

But Jesus said to them, "A prophet is not without honor except in his own country and in his own house." [58]Now He did not do many mighty works there because of their unbelief.

John the Baptist Beheaded

14 At that time Herod the tetrarch heard the report about Jesus [2]and said to his servants, "This is John the Baptist; he is risen from the dead, and therefore these powers are at work in him." [3]For Herod had laid hold of John and bound him, and put *him* in prison for the sake of Herodias, his brother Philip's wife. [4]Because John had said to him, "It is not lawful for you to have her." [5]And although he wanted to put him to death, he feared the multitude, because they counted him as a prophet.

[6]But when Herod's birthday was celebrated, the daughter of Herodias danced before them and pleased Herod. [7]Therefore he promised with an oath to give her whatever she might ask.

> Mass crusades, to which I have committed my life, will never finish the job; but one to one will.
>
> **BILLY GRAHAM**

[8]So she, having been prompted by her mother, said, "Give me John the Baptist's head here on a platter."

[9]And the king was sorry; nevertheless, because of the oaths and because of those who sat with him, he commanded *it* to be given to *her*. [10]So he sent and had John beheaded in prison. [11]And his head was brought on a platter and given to the girl, and she brought *it* to her mother. [12]Then his disciples came and took away the body and buried it, and went and told Jesus.

Feeding the Five Thousand

[13]When Jesus heard *it*, He departed from there by boat to a deserted place by

13:51 [a]NU-Text omits *Jesus said to them.* [b]NU-Text omits *Lord.* 13:52 [a]Or *for* 13:55 [a]NU-Text reads *Joseph.*

13:47–50 Notice the good fish and the bad fish were in the net together. The world is not caught in the dragnet of the kingdom of heaven; they remain in the world. The "fish" that are caught are those who respond to the gospel—the evangelistic "catch." They remain together until the Day of Judgment.

14:10 "The man whose little sermon is 'repent' sets himself against his age, and will for the time being be battered mercilessly by the age whose moral tone he challenges. There is but one end for such a man—'off with his head!' You had better not try to preach repentance until you have pledged your head to heaven." *Joseph Parker*

Himself. But when the multitudes heard it, they followed Him on foot from the cities. 14And when Jesus went out He saw a great multitude; and He was moved with compassion for them, and healed their sick. 15When it was evening, His disciples came to Him, saying, "This is a deserted place, and the hour is already late. Send the multitudes away, that they may go into the villages and buy themselves food."

16But Jesus said to them, "They do not need to go away. You give them something to eat."

17And they said to Him, "We have here only five loaves and two fish."

18He said, "Bring them here to Me." 19Then He commanded the multitudes to sit down on the grass. And He took the five loaves and the two fish, and looking up to heaven, He blessed and broke and gave the loaves to the disciples; and the disciples gave to the multitudes. 20So they all ate and were filled, and they took up twelve baskets full of the fragments that remained. 21Now those who had eaten were about five thousand men, besides women and children.

Jesus Walks on the Sea

22Immediately Jesus made His disciples get into the boat and go before Him to the other side, while He sent the multitudes away. 23And when He had sent the multitudes away, He went up on the mountain by Himself to pray. Now when evening came, He was alone there. 24But the boat was now in the middle of the sea,[a] tossed by the waves, for the wind was contrary.

25Now in the fourth watch of the night Jesus went to them, walking on the sea. 26And when the disciples saw Him walking on the sea, they were troubled, saying, "It is a ghost!" And they cried out for fear.

27But immediately Jesus spoke to them, saying, "Be of good cheer! It is I; do not be afraid."

28And Peter answered Him and said, "Lord, if it is You, command me to come to You on the water."

29So He said, "Come." And when Peter had come down out of the boat, he walked on the water to go to Jesus. 30But when he saw that the wind *was* boisterous,[a] he was afraid; and beginning to sink he cried out, saying, "Lord, save me!"

31And immediately Jesus stretched out *His* hand and caught him, and said to him, "O you of little faith, why did you doubt?" 32And when they got into the boat, the wind ceased.

33Then those who were in the boat came and[a] worshiped Him, saying, "Truly You are the Son of God."

14:24 [a]NU-Text reads *many furlongs away from the land.*
14:30 [a]NU-Text brackets *that* and *boisterous* as disputed.
14:33 [a]NU-Text omits *came and.*

14:15–21 Sharing the Bread of Life. Compare this incident with 2 Kings 4:42–44, in which one hundred men were fed twenty loaves of barley bread. Elisha instructed, "Give it to the people, that they may eat; for thus says the LORD: 'They shall eat and have some left over.'" In both incidents, the people were given bread to eat and had some left over. We have eaten from the Bread of Life, and now we must take that Bread to a starving world.

"The disciples watched miraculous healings for hours and then approached the Master and told Him three things: 1) the hour was late; 2) they were in a 'deserted place'; and 3) the multitude needed to eat. Jesus told His disciples that they should be the source of the multitude being fed. The boy's lunch (John 6:9) was the best they could bring, and Jesus did a miracle when they brought the best they had. Then He had them pick up what remained. There were twelve baskets, for twelve disciples. I believe Jesus was saying: 'Now that I showed you how, go feed your own multitude.'" *Mike Smalley*

14:28 Peter had the concept, and Jesus put His blessing on Peter's idea. Peter knew Jesus intimately; he knew the mind of the Master. He knew that his desire wasn't an impertinent presumption, but just a longing to follow the Lord into the realm of the supernatural. Jesus said, "If anyone serves Me, let him follow Me; and where I am, there My servant will be also. If anyone serves Me, him My Father will honor" (John 12:26).

Many Touch Him and Are Made Well

34When they had crossed over, they came to the land of[a] Gennesaret. 35And when the men of that place recognized Him, they sent out into all that surrounding region, brought to Him all who were sick, 36and begged Him that they might only touch the hem of His garment. And as many as touched *it* were made perfectly well.

Defilement Comes from Within

15 Then the scribes and Pharisees who were from Jerusalem came to Jesus, saying, 2"Why do Your disciples transgress the tradition of the elders? For they do not wash their hands when they eat bread."

3He answered and said to them, "Why do you also transgress the commandment of God because of your tradition? 4For God commanded, saying, *'Honor your father and your mother';*[a] and, *'He who curses father or mother, let him be put to death.'*[b] 5But you say, 'Whoever says to his father or mother, "Whatever profit you might have received from me *is a gift to God*"— 6then he need not honor his father or mother.'[a] Thus you have made the commandment[b] of God of no effect by your tradition. 7Hypocrites! Well did Isaiah prophesy about you, saying:

8'These people draw near to Me with
their mouth,
And[a] *honor Me with their lips,*
But their heart is far from Me.
9And in vain they worship Me,
Teaching as doctrines the
commandments of men.' "[a]

10When He had called the multitude to *Himself*, He said to them, "Hear and understand: 11Not what goes into the mouth defiles a man; but what comes out of the mouth, this defiles a man."

12Then His disciples came and said to Him, "Do You know that the Pharisees were offended when they heard this saying?"

13But He answered and said, "Every plant which My heavenly Father has not planted will be uprooted. 14Let them alone. They are blind leaders of the blind. And if the blind leads the blind, both will fall into a ditch."

For whether the lost will "be separated from God" for eternity, see Psa. 139:7,8 comment.

15Then Peter answered and said to Him, "Explain this parable to us."

16So Jesus said, "Are you also still without understanding? 17Do you not yet understand that whatever enters the mouth goes into the stomach and is eliminated? 18But those things which proceed out of the mouth come from the heart, and they defile a man. 19For out of the

14:34 [a]NU-Text reads *came to land at.* 15:4 [a]Exodus 20:12; Deuteronomy 5:16 [b]Exodus 21:17 15:6 [a]NU-Text omits *or mother.* [b]NU-Text reads *word.* 15:8 [a]NU-Text omits *draw near to Me with their mouth, And.* 15:9 [a]Isaiah 29:13

15:19 The spiritual nature of the Law. Notice how the sins named are transgressions of the moral Law, the Ten Commandments. If civil law can prove that you are planning to assassinate the president, you can be prosecuted and severely punished. That law, however, is limited in its search for evidence—it can't see what a man thinks. Not so with the all-seeing eye of our Creator. His Law searches the heart. He sees "evil thoughts," and requires truth in the inward parts (Psa. 51:6). To *think* hatred is to commit murder (1 John 3:15) and transgress the Sixth Commandment. To *think* lustfully is to commit adultery (Matt. 5:27,28) and transgress the Seventh. Fornication breaks the same Commandment (Gal. 5:19). Then Jesus names theft (Eighth Commandment), false witness (Ninth), and blasphemies (Third). A person cannot lust without breaking the Tenth, and by their nature, these sins transgress the remaining four Commandments. All sin traces in some way back to the moral Law, for sin is transgression of the Law (1 John 3:4). This is why the Law must be used to bring the knowledge of sin to religious people who are trusting in their own righteous deeds for their salvation.

heart proceed evil thoughts, murders, adulteries, fornications, thefts, false witness, blasphemies. [20]These are *the things* which defile a man, but to eat with unwashed hands does not defile a man."

A Gentile Shows Her Faith

[21]Then Jesus went out from there and departed to the region of Tyre and Sidon. [22]And behold, a woman of Canaan came from that region and cried out to Him, saying, "Have mercy on me, O Lord, Son of David! My daughter is severely demon-possessed."

[23]But He answered her not a word. And His disciples came and urged Him, saying, "Send her away, for she cries out after us."

> Save some, O Christians! By all means, save some. From yonder flames and outer darkness, and the weeping, wailing, and gnashing of teeth, seek to save some! Let this, as in the case of the apostle, be your great, ruling object in life, that by all means you might save some.
>
> CHARLES SPURGEON

[24]But He answered and said, "I was not sent except to the lost sheep of the house of Israel."

[25]Then she came and worshiped Him, saying, "Lord, help me!"

[26]But He answered and said, "It is not good to take the children's bread and throw *it* to the little dogs."

[27]And she said, "Yes, Lord, yet even the little dogs eat the crumbs which fall from their masters' table."

[28]Then Jesus answered and said to her, "O woman, great *is* your faith! Let it be to you as you desire." And her daughter was healed from that very hour.

Jesus Heals Great Multitudes

[29]Jesus departed from there, skirted the Sea of Galilee, and went up on the mountain and sat down there. [30]Then great multitudes came to Him, having with them *the* lame, blind, mute, maimed, and many others; and they laid them down at Jesus' feet, and He healed them. [31]So the multitude marveled when they saw *the* mute speaking, *the* maimed made whole, *the* lame walking, and *the* blind seeing; and they glorified the God of Israel.

Feeding the Four Thousand

[32]Now Jesus called His disciples to *Himself* and said, "I have compassion on the multitude, because they have now continued with Me three days and have nothing to eat. And I do not want to send them away hungry, lest they faint on the way."

[33]Then His disciples said to Him, "Where could we get enough bread in the wilderness to fill such a great multitude?"

[34]Jesus said to them, "How many loaves do you have?"

And they said, "Seven, and a few little fish."

[35]So He commanded the multitude to sit down on the ground. [36]And He took the seven loaves and the fish and gave thanks, broke *them* and gave *them* to His disciples; and the disciples *gave* to the multitude. [37]So they all ate and were filled, and they took up seven large baskets full of the fragments that were left. [38]Now those who ate were four thousand men, besides women and children. [39]And He sent away the multitude, got into the boat, and came to the region of Magdala.[a]

The Pharisees and Sadducees Seek a Sign

16 Then the Pharisees and Sadducees came, and testing Him asked that He would show them a sign from heaven. [2]He answered and said to them, "When it is evening you say, '*It will be* fair weather, for the sky is red'; [3]and in the morning, '*It will be* foul weather today, for the sky is red and threatening.' Hypocrites![a] You

15:39 [a]NU-Text reads *Magadan*. **16:3** [a]NU-Text omits *Hypocrites*.

SPRINGBOARDS FOR PREACHING AND WITNESSING

All About Him

16:13 Most non-Christians have no idea that the entire Bible is about one Person, Jesus of Nazareth. It speaks of Him from the Book of Genesis to the Book of Revelation. It tells us that He created all things, including the eyes you are using to see these words, the lungs that are breathing in the oxygen He created, to feed the brain that He made so you can process them (see John 1:1–3).

Of course, His name hasn't always been Jesus of Nazareth. The Bible tells us that He is God the Son, eternally preexistent before the incarnation, and is "the image of the invisible God" (Col. 1:15). He created a body for Himself and became a Man to suffer and die for the sin of the world.

Consider how the New Testament exalts Jesus of Nazareth. It calls Him "Lord" nearly 250 times. He is the One to whom all humanity will one day bow the knee. He is also called the "Christ" well over 500 times. This is because "Christ" ("Messiah," or anointed One) is a title rather than a name.

He is called "Son of Man" over 80 times, because He truly was a Man who had the ability to feel pain, experience thirst, and know the torment of fear. He is called "Son of God" more than 40 times, because He was truly God in human form, manifesting His authority over His creation by walking on water, stilling storms, healing disease, and conquering death.

There has never been anyone like Jesus of Nazareth. Take the time to open the New Testament and read about Him—who He was, and what He did for you. You have nothing to lose and everything to gain. If in this life you refuse to humble yourself and bow the knee to Him as Savior so that your sins can be forgiven, you will bow the knee to Him as Lord on Judgment Day so that justice will be done. That will be a fearful thing . . . with terrible eternal consequences.

know how to discern the face of the sky,
but you cannot *discern* the signs of the
times. [4]A wicked and adulterous generation seeks after a sign, and no sign shall
be given to it except the sign of the
prophet[a] Jonah." And He left them and
departed.

The Leaven of the Pharisees and Sadducees

[5]Now when His disciples had come to
the other side, they had forgotten to take
bread. [6]Then Jesus said to them, "Take
heed and beware of the leaven of the
Pharisees and the Sadducees."

[7]And they reasoned among themselves,
saying, "*It is* because we have taken no
bread."

[8]But Jesus, being aware of *it,* said to
them, "O you of little faith, why do you
reason among yourselves because you
have brought no bread?[a] [9]Do you not yet
understand, or remember the five loaves
of the five thousand and how many baskets you took up? [10]Nor the seven loaves
of the four thousand and how many large
baskets you took up? [11]How is it you do
not understand that I did not speak to
you concerning bread?—*but* to beware of
the leaven of the Pharisees and Sadducees." [12]Then they understood that He
did not tell *them* to beware of the leaven
of bread, but of the doctrine of the Pharisees and Sadducees.

Peter Confesses Jesus as the Christ

[13]When Jesus came into the region of
Caesarea Philippi, He asked His disciples,
saying, "Who do men say that I, the Son
of Man, am?"

[14]So they said, "Some *say* John the
Baptist, some Elijah, and others Jeremiah
or one of the prophets."

[15]He said to them, "But who do you
say that I am?"

[16]Simon Peter answered and said, "You
are the Christ, the Son of the living God."

[17]Jesus answered and said to him,
"Blessed are you, Simon Bar-Jonah, for
flesh and blood has not revealed *this* to
you, but My Father who is in heaven.
[18]And I also say to you that you are Peter,
and on this rock I will build My church,
and the gates of Hades shall not prevail
against it. [19]And I will give you the keys

16:4 [a]NU-Text omits *the prophet.* **16:8** [a]NU-Text reads *you have no bread.*

SPRINGBOARDS FOR PREACHING AND WITNESSING

16:26

Money or Water?

If you were offered a handful of $1,000 bills or a glass of cool water, which would you choose? The $1,000 bills, of course—*anyone in his right mind would.* However, if you were crawling through a desert, dying of thirst, and you were offered a glass of water or a handful of $1,000 bills, which would you take? The water, of course—*anyone in his right mind would.* That's called "circumstantial priorities." Your priorities change according to your circumstances.

If there was a way to find *everlasting* life, would you want to know about it? The answer is "yes," of course—*anyone in his right mind would.* What the Bible contains may surprise you. The Scriptures speak of riches beyond our wildest dreams—the "riches" of everlasting life—and they are offered in the form of cool, clear water: "Let him who thirsts come. Whoever desires, let him take the water of life freely" (Rev. 22:17). At the moment, you may not be interested in the offer, but on Judgment Day your circumstances will radically change. Then it will be too late.

of the kingdom of heaven, and whatever
you bind on earth will be bound in
heaven, and whatever you loose on earth
will be loosed[a] in heaven."
20Then He commanded His disciples
that they should tell no one that He was
Jesus the Christ.

Jesus Predicts His Death and Resurrection

21From that time Jesus began to show
to His disciples that He must go to Jerusalem, and suffer many things from the
elders and chief priests and scribes, and
be killed, and be raised the third day.
22Then Peter took Him aside and began to rebuke Him, saying, "Far be it from
You, Lord; this shall not happen to You!"
23But He turned and said to Peter,
"Get behind Me, Satan! You are an offense to Me, for you are not mindful of
the things of God, but the things of men."

Take Up the Cross and Follow Him

24Then Jesus said to His disciples, "If
anyone desires to come after Me, let him
deny himself, and take up his cross, and
follow Me. 25For whoever desires to save
his life will lose it, but whoever loses his
life for My sake will find it. 26For what
profit is it to a man if he gains the whole
world, and loses his own soul? Or what
will a man give in exchange for his soul?
27For the Son of Man will come in the
glory of His Father with His angels, and
then He will reward each according to his
works.

Jesus Transfigured on the Mount

28Assuredly, I say to you, there are
some standing here who shall not taste
death till they see the Son of Man coming
in His kingdom."

16:19 [a]Or *will have been bound . . . will have been loosed*

16:17 Don't see it as your job to convince a Muslim, Mormon, or other unbeliever that Jesus is God. That's the Father's job. Our part is to share the simple message of the gospel.

16:18 Jesus is not saying that Peter is the "rock" upon which He will build His Church. That would contradict Scripture. First Corinthians 3:11 makes it clear that Jesus is the only foundation, and the "rock" is the revelation that He is the Christ, the Son of the Living God. See Rom. 9:33.

"Give me one hundred preachers who fear nothing but sin and desire nothing but God, and I care not a straw whether they be clergymen or laymen, such alone will shake the gates of hell and set up the kingdom of God upon earth." *John Wesley*

16:23 If you are going to do something in the area of evangelism, be sure you set your face like a "flint" to do so (Isa. 50:7). A flint is a very hard stone that produces sparks when struck. That's what Peter found when he tried to deter Jesus from doing God's will. The enemy will try to discourage you, and often where you least expect it.

16:27 **Second coming of Jesus:** See Matt. 24:27.

"God loves with a great love the man whose heart is bursting with a passion for the impossible."

William Booth

17 Now after six days Jesus took Peter, James, and John his brother,
led them up on a high mountain by
themselves; 2and He was transfigured before them. His face shone like the sun,
and His clothes became as white as the
light. 3And behold, Moses and Elijah appeared to them, talking with Him. 4Then
Peter answered and said to Jesus, "Lord,
it is good for us to be here; if You wish,
let us[a] make here three tabernacles: one
for You, one for Moses, and one for Elijah."
5While he was still speaking, behold, a
bright cloud overshadowed them; and
suddenly a voice came out of the cloud,
saying, "This is My beloved Son, in whom
I am well pleased. Hear Him!" 6And
when the disciples heard *it,* they fell on
their faces and were greatly afraid. 7But
Jesus came and touched them and said,
"Arise, and do not be afraid." 8When they
had lifted up their eyes, they saw no one
but Jesus only.
9Now as they came down from the
mountain, Jesus commanded them, saying, "Tell the vision to no one until the
Son of Man is risen from the dead."
10And His disciples asked Him, saying,
"Why then do the scribes say that Elijah
must come first?"
11Jesus answered and said to them,
"Indeed, Elijah is coming first[a] and will
restore all things. 12But I say to you that
Elijah has come already, and they did not
know him but did to him whatever they
wished. Likewise the Son of Man is also
about to suffer at their hands." 13Then
the disciples understood that He spoke to
them of John the Baptist.

A Boy Is Healed

14And when they had come to the
multitude, a man came to Him, kneeling
down to Him and saying, 15"Lord, have
mercy on my son, for he is an epileptic[a]
and suffers severely; for he often falls into
the fire and often into the water. 16So I
brought him to Your disciples, but they
could not cure him."
17Then Jesus answered and said, "O
faithless and perverse generation, how
long shall I be with you? How long shall
I bear with you? Bring him here to Me."
18And Jesus rebuked the demon, and it
came out of him; and the child was cured
from that very hour.
19Then the disciples came to Jesus privately and said, "Why could we not cast
it out?"
20So Jesus said to them, "Because of
your unbelief;[a] for assuredly, I say to
you, if you have faith as a mustard seed,
you will say to this mountain, 'Move from

17:4 [a]NU-Text reads *I will.* 17:11 [a]NU-Text omits *first.* 17:15 [a]Literally *moonstruck* 17:20 [a]NU-Text reads *little faith.*

17:1–8 The new birth is a Mount of Transfiguration experience. It is divine revelation as to who Jesus is: He is the One to whom the Law (Moses) and the prophets (Elijah) testify. Those who hear the voice of the Father hear the voice of the Son. They fall on their faces before Jesus and see no one but Him.

17:10 See Matt. 11:13 comment.

QUESTIONS & OBJECTIONS

18:9 ***"My God would never create hell."***

Those who say this are right: their "god" would never create hell, because he *couldn't*. He doesn't exist. He is a figment of their imagination, a god they have created to suit themselves. It's called "idolatry," and it's the oldest sin in the Book. Idolaters will not inherit the kingdom of God. The one true God, however, could and did create hell for those who reject His mercy. They will reap His just wrath. (For the reasonableness of hell, see Psa. 55:15 comment.)

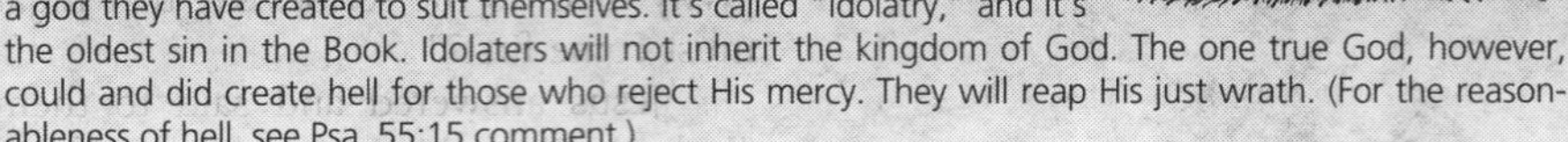

here to there,' and it will move; and nothing will be impossible for you. 21However,
ever, this kind does not go out except by
prayer and fasting."[a]

Jesus Again Predicts His Death and Resurrection

22Now while they were staying[a] in
Galilee, Jesus said to them, "The Son of
Man is about to be betrayed into the
hands of men, 23and they will kill Him,
and the third day He will be raised up."
And they were exceedingly sorrowful.

Peter and His Master Pay Their Taxes

24When they had come to Caper-
naum,[a] those who received the *temple* tax
came to Peter and said, "Does your Teacher not pay the *temple* tax?"
25He said, "Yes."
And when he had come into the house,
Jesus anticipated him, saying, "What do
you think, Simon? From whom do the
kings of the earth take customs or taxes,
from their sons or from strangers?"
26Peter said to Him, "From strangers."
Jesus said to him, "Then the sons are
free. 27Nevertheless, lest we offend them,
go to the sea, cast in a hook, and take the
fish that comes up first. And when you
have opened its mouth, you will find a
piece of money;[a] take that and give it to
them for Me and you."

Who Is the Greatest?

18 At that time the disciples came to
Jesus, saying, "Who then is greatest in the kingdom of heaven?"
2Then Jesus called a little child to
Him, set him in the midst of them, 3and
said, "Assuredly, I say to you, unless you
are converted and become as little children, you will by no means enter the
kingdom of heaven. 4Therefore whoever
humbles himself as this little child is the
greatest in the kingdom of heaven.
5Whoever receives one little child like
this in My name receives Me.

Jesus Warns of Offenses

6"Whoever causes one of these little
ones who believe in Me to sin, it would
be better for him if a millstone were hung
around his neck, and he were drowned
in the depth of the sea. 7Woe to the
world because of offenses! For offenses
must come, but woe to that man by
whom the offense comes!
8"If your hand or foot causes you to
sin, cut it off and cast *it* from you. It is
better for you to enter into life lame or
maimed, rather than having two hands or
two feet, to be cast into the everlasting
fire. 9And if your eye causes you to sin,

17:21 [a]NU-Text omits this verse. **17:22** [a]NU-Text reads *gathering together*. **17:24** [a]NU-Text reads *Capharnaum* (here and elsewhere). **17:27** [a]Greek *stater,* the exact amount to pay the temple tax (didrachma) for two

17:20 "The prayer power has never been tried to its full capacity. If we want to see mighty works of Divine power and grace wrought in the place of weakness, failure and disappointment, let us answer God's standing challenge, 'Call to me, and I will answer you, and show you great and mighty things, which you do not know' [Jer. 33:3]." *Hudson Taylor*

pluck it out and cast *it* from you. It is better for you to enter into life with one eye,
rather than having two eyes, to be cast
into hell fire.

The Parable of the Lost Sheep

10“Take heed that you do not despise
one of these little ones, for I say to you
that in heaven their angels always see the
face of My Father who is in heaven. 11For
the Son of Man has come to save that
which was lost.[a]

> Can we go too fast in saving souls? If anyone still wants a reply, let him ask the lost souls in hell.
>
> **WILLIAM BOOTH**

12“What do you think? If a man has a
hundred sheep, and one of them goes
astray, does he not leave the ninety-nine
and go to the mountains to seek the one
that is straying? 13And if he should find
it, assuredly, I say to you, he rejoices more
over that *sheep* than over the ninety-nine
that did not go astray. 14Even so it is not
the will of your Father who is in heaven
that one of these little ones should perish.

Dealing with a Sinning Brother

15“Moreover if your brother sins against
you, go and tell him his fault between
you and him alone. If he hears you, you
have gained your brother. 16But if he will
not hear, take with you one or two more,
that *‘by the mouth of two or three witnesses every word may be established.’*[a]
17And if he refuses to hear them, tell *it* to
the church. But if he refuses even to hear
the church, let him be to you like a heathen and a tax collector.

18“Assuredly, I say to you, whatever you
bind on earth will be bound in heaven,
and whatever you loose on earth will be
loosed in heaven.

19“Again I say[a] to you that if two of
you agree on earth concerning anything
that they ask, it will be done for them by
My Father in heaven. 20For where two or
three are gathered together in My name, I
am there in the midst of them.”

The Parable of the Unforgiving Servant

21Then Peter came to Him and said,
“Lord, how often shall my brother sin
against me, and I forgive him? Up to seven
times?”

22Jesus said to him, “I do not say to
you, up to seven times, but up to seventy
times seven. 23Therefore the kingdom of
heaven is like a certain king who wanted
to settle accounts with his servants.
24And when he had begun to settle accounts, one was brought to him who
owed him ten thousand talents. 25But as
he was not able to pay, his master commanded that he be sold, with his wife
and children and all that he had, and that
payment be made. 26The servant therefore fell down before him, saying, ‘Master, have patience with me, and I will pay
you all.’ 27Then the master of that servant
was moved with compassion, released
him, and forgave him the debt.

28“But that servant went out and
found one of his fellow servants who
owed him a hundred denarii; and he laid
hands on him and took *him* by the throat,
saying, ‘Pay me what you owe!’ 29So his
fellow servant fell down at his feet[a] and
begged him, saying, ‘Have patience with

18:11 [a]NU-Text omits this verse. **18:16** [a]Deuteronomy 19:15 **18:19** [a]NU-Text and M-Text read *Again, assuredly, I say.* **18:29** [a]NU-Text omits *at his feet.* [b]NU-Text and M-Text omit *all.*

18:9 Hell: For verses warning of its reality, see Matt. 23:33.

18:11 “We would not see nor realize it (what a distressing and horrible fall in which we lie), if it were not for the Law, and we would have to remain forever lost, if we were not again helped out of it through Christ. Therefore the Law and the gospel are given to the end that we may learn to know both how guilty we are and to what we should again return.” *Martin Luther*

me, and I will pay you all.'[b] 30And he would not, but went and threw him into prison till he should pay the debt. 31So when his fellow servants saw what had been done, they were very grieved, and came and told their master all that had been done. 32Then his master, after he had called him, said to him, 'You wicked servant! I forgave you all that debt because you begged me. 33Should you not also have had compassion on your fellow servant, just as I had pity on you?' 34And his master was angry, and delivered him to the torturers until he should pay all that was due to him.

35"So My heavenly Father also will do to you if each of you, from his heart, does not forgive his brother his trespasses."[a]

Marriage and Divorce

19 Now it came to pass, when Jesus had finished these sayings, *that* He departed from Galilee and came to the region of Judea beyond the Jordan. 2And great multitudes followed Him, and He healed them there.

3The Pharisees also came to Him, testing Him, and saying to Him, "Is it lawful for a man to divorce his wife for *just* any reason?"

4And He answered and said to them, "Have you not read that He who made[a] *them* at the beginning *'made them male and female,'*[b] 5and said, *'For this reason a man shall leave his father and mother and be joined to his wife, and the two shall become one flesh'?*[a] 6So then, they are no longer two but one flesh. Therefore what God has joined together, let not man separate."

7They said to Him, "Why then did Moses command to give a certificate of divorce, and to put her away?"

8He said to them, "Moses, because of the hardness of your hearts, permitted you to divorce your wives, but from the beginning it was not so. 9And I say to you, whoever divorces his wife, except for sexual immorality,[a] and marries another, commits adultery; and whoever marries her who is divorced commits adultery."

10His disciples said to Him, "If such is the case of the man with *his* wife, it is better not to marry."

Jesus Teaches on Celibacy

11But He said to them, "All cannot accept this saying, but only *those* to whom it has been given: 12For there are eunuchs who were born thus from *their* mother's womb, and there are eunuchs who were made eunuchs by men, and there are eunuchs who have made themselves eunuchs for the kingdom of heaven's sake. He who is able to accept *it,* let him accept *it.*"

18:35 [a]NU-Text omits *his trespasses.* **19:4** [a]NU-Text reads *created.* [b]Genesis 1:27; 5:2 **19:5** [a]Genesis 2:24 **19:9** [a]Or *fornication*

19:3–6 Jesus confirmed that the creation of Adam and Eve was a real historical event when He quoted Gen. 1:27 and 2:24 in His teaching. Genesis is quoted more than sixty times in seventeen books of the New Testament. See also Mark 10:6–9 and 2 Cor. 11:3 comments.

19:4 Evolution—the origin of sexes. Almost all forms of complex life have both male and female: horses, dogs, humans, moths, monkeys, fish, elephants, birds, etc. The male needs the female to reproduce, and the female needs the male to reproduce. *One cannot carry on life without the other.* Which then came first according to the evolutionary theory? If a male came into being before a female, how did the male of each species reproduce *without* females? How is it possible that a male and a female spontaneously came into being independently, yet they have complex, complementary reproductive systems? If each sex was able to reproduce without the other, why (and how) would they have developed a reproductive system that requires both sexes in order for the species to survive? Answer: God made them male and female. See also 1 Kings 4:33 comment.

"I myself am convinced that the theory of evolution, especially the extent to which it has been applied, will be one of the great jokes in the history books of the future. Posterity will marvel that so flimsy and dubious an hypothesis could be accepted with the incredible credulity that it has." *Malcolm Muggeridge*, British journalist and philosopher

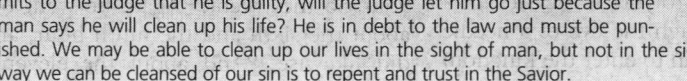

QUESTIONS & OBJECTIONS

19:16 ***"I need to get my life cleaned up first."***

Those who think that they can clean up their lives don't see their true plight. They are standing guilty before a wrath-filled God. They have been condemned by His Law (John 3:18; Rom. 3:19). If a man commits rape and murder and admits to the judge that he is guilty, will the judge let him go just because the man says he will clean up his life? He is in debt to the law and must be punished. We may be able to clean up our lives in the sight of man, but not in the sight of God. The only way we can be cleansed of our sin is to repent and trust in the Savior.

Jesus Blesses Little Children

[13]Then little children were brought to
Him that He might put *His* hands on
them and pray, but the disciples rebuked
them. [14]But Jesus said, "Let the little children come to Me, and do not forbid them;
for of such is the kingdom of heaven."
[15]And He laid *His* hands on them and departed from there.

Jesus Counsels the Rich Young Ruler

[16]Now behold, one came and said to
Him, "Good[a] Teacher, what good thing
shall I do that I may have eternal life?"
[17]So He said to him, "Why do you call
Me good?[a] No one *is* good but One, *that
is,* God.[b] But if you want to enter into life,
keep the commandments."
[18]He said to Him, "Which ones?"
Jesus said, " *'You shall not murder,' 'You
shall not commit adultery,' 'You shall not
steal,' 'You shall not bear false witness,'*
[19]*'Honor your father and your mother,'*[a]
and, *'You shall love your neighbor as yourself.'* "[b]
[20]The young man said to Him, "All
these things I have kept from my youth.[a]
What do I still lack?"
[21]Jesus said to him, "If you want to be
perfect, go, sell what you have and give
to the poor, and you will have treasure in
heaven; and come, follow Me."
[22]But when the young man heard that

19:16 [a]NU-Text omits *Good.* 19:17 [a]NU-Text reads *Why do you ask Me about what is good?* [b]NU-Text reads *There is One who is good.* 19:19 [a]Exodus 20:12–16; Deuteronomy 5:16–20 [b]Leviticus 19:18 19:20 [a]NU-Text omits *from my youth.*

USING THE LAW IN EVANGELISM

19:17–22 Here is the Master Evangelist showing us how to deal with a proud, self-righteous person—a typical sinner. This is noticeably different from the approach of modern evangelism. When the man asked how he could obtain eternal life, Jesus did not ask, "Would you like to have the assurance that if you died tonight you would go straight to heaven? You can have that confidence right now simply by acknowledging that you have sinned against God, and by trusting in the finished work of Calvary's cross. Would you like me to lead you in prayer right now so that you can have that assurance?" Instead, Jesus pointed him to the Law so that he could recognize his sin. Biblical evangelism always follows the principle of Law to the proud, and grace to the humble. *John Newton* said, "My grand point in preaching is to break the hard heart and to heal the broken one."

This young man is a prime example of an unregenerate person. He had no understanding of the word "good." Jesus reproved him, then gently gave him five horizontal Commandments—those dealing with his fellow man. When the man revealed his self-righteousness, Jesus showed him that in his vertical relationship with God he had transgressed the First of the Ten Commandments. God wasn't foremost in his life. The rich young man loved his money, and the Scriptures make it clear that we cannot serve God and mammon (money). The Law brought him "the knowledge of sin" (see Rom. 3:20).

In light of the way most Christians share the gospel, Jesus failed because He didn't get a "decision." However, heaven doesn't rejoice over "decisions." It reserves its rejoicing for repentance, and there can be no repentance without a God-given knowledge of sin—and that, according to Scripture, can come only by the Law (Rom. 7:7). See also Mark 10:17 and John 4:7 comments.

saying, he went away sorrowful, for he had great possessions.

With God All Things Are Possible

23Then Jesus said to His disciples, "Assuredly, I say to you that it is hard for a rich man to enter the kingdom of heaven. 24And again I say to you, it is easier for a camel to go through the eye of a needle than for a rich man to enter the kingdom of God."

25When His disciples heard *it,* they were greatly astonished, saying, "Who then can be saved?"

26But Jesus looked at *them* and said to them, "With men this is impossible, but with God all things are possible."

27Then Peter answered and said to Him, "See, we have left all and followed You. Therefore what shall we have?"

28So Jesus said to them, "Assuredly I say to you, that in the regeneration, when the Son of Man sits on the throne of His glory, you who have followed Me will also sit on twelve thrones, judging the twelve tribes of Israel. 29And everyone who has left houses or brothers or sisters or father or mother or wife[a] or children or lands, for My name's sake, shall receive a hundredfold, and inherit eternal life. 30But many *who are* first will be last, and the last first.

The Parable of the Workers in the Vineyard

20 "For the kingdom of heaven is like a landowner who went out early in the morning to hire laborers for his vineyard. 2Now when he had agreed with the laborers for a denarius a day, he sent them into his vineyard. 3And he went out about the third hour and saw others standing idle in the marketplace, 4and said to them, 'You also go into the vineyard, and whatever is right I will give you.' So they went. 5Again he went out about the sixth and the ninth hour, and did likewise. 6And about the eleventh hour he went out and found others standing idle,[a] and said to them, 'Why have you been standing here idle all day?' 7They said to him, 'Because no one hired us.' He said to them, 'You also go into the vineyard, and whatever is right you will receive.'[a]

8"So when evening had come, the owner of the vineyard said to his steward, 'Call the laborers and give them *their* wages, beginning with the last to the first.' 9And when those came who *were hired* about the eleventh hour, they each received a denarius. 10But when the first came, they supposed that they would receive more; and they likewise received each a denarius. 11And when they had received *it,* they complained against the landowner, 12saying, 'These last *men* have worked *only* one hour, and you made them equal to us who have borne the burden and the heat of the day.' 13But he answered one of them and said, 'Friend, I am doing you no wrong. Did you not agree with me for a denarius? 14Take

19:29 [a]NU-Text omits *or wife.* 20:6 [a]NU-Text omits *idle.* 20:7 [a]NU-Text omits the last clause of this verse.

19:24 The eye of a needle. A common interpretation is that Jerusalem had a main gate, beside which was a smaller gate called "the eye of a needle." When the main gate was closed, a camel had to forsake its load, then get on its knees and crawl through the smaller gate to enter the city. This is what a rich man must do to enter the celestial city. He must forsake his riches and humble himself to enter. Interesting though it may sound, it is unlikely that this is correct, because of the response of both the disciples and Jesus. If that's what Jesus was saying, the disciples would have more than likely responded with something like, "That makes sense." Instead, they were "greatly astonished" (v. 25). What Jesus had said *astonished* them. He didn't then respond to their astonishment by saying that it was "difficult" for a camel to get through the eye of the needle. Rather, He used the word "impossible." It would seem therefore that the analogy was to a literal camel and a literal needle.

"The gate of heaven, though it is so wide that the greatest sinner may enter, is nevertheless so low that pride can never pass through it." *Charles Spurgeon*

what is yours and go your way. I wish to
give to this last man *the same* as to you.
15Is it not lawful for me to do what I wish
with my own things? Or is your eye evil
because I am good?' 16So the last will be
first, and the first last. For many are
called, but few chosen."[a]

Jesus a Third Time Predicts His Death and Resurrection

17Now Jesus, going up to Jerusalem,
took the twelve disciples aside on the road
and said to them, 18"Behold, we are going
up to Jerusalem, and the Son of Man will
be betrayed to the chief priests and to the
scribes; and they will condemn Him to
death, 19and deliver Him to the Gentiles
to mock and to scourge and to crucify.
And the third day He will rise again."

Greatness Is Serving

20Then the mother of Zebedee's sons
came to Him with her sons, kneeling
down and asking something from Him.
21And He said to her, "What do you
wish?"

She said to Him, "Grant that these two
sons of mine may sit, one on Your right
hand and the other on the left, in Your
kingdom."

22But Jesus answered and said, "You
do not know what you ask. Are you able
to drink the cup that I am about to drink,
and be baptized with the baptism that I
am baptized with?"[a]

They said to Him, "We are able."

23So He said to them, "You will indeed
drink My cup, and be baptized with the
baptism that I am baptized with;[a] but to
sit on My right hand and on My left is not
Mine to give, but *it is for those* for whom
it is prepared by My Father."

24And when the ten heard *it*, they
were greatly displeased with the two
brothers. 25But Jesus called them to *Himself* and said, "You know that the rulers of
the Gentiles lord it over them, and those
who are great exercise authority over
them. 26Yet it shall not be so among you;
but whoever desires to become great
among you, let him be your servant.
27And whoever desires to be first among
you, let him be your slave— 28just as the
Son of Man did not come to be served,
but to serve, and to give His life a ransom
for many."

Two Blind Men Receive Their Sight

29Now as they went out of Jericho, a
great multitude followed Him. 30And behold, two blind men sitting by the road,
when they heard that Jesus was passing
by, cried out, saying, "Have mercy on us,
O Lord, Son of David!"

31Then the multitude warned them
that they should be quiet; but they cried
out all the more, saying, "Have mercy on
us, O Lord, Son of David!"

32So Jesus stood still and called them,
and said, "What do you want Me to do for
you?"

33They said to Him, "Lord, that our eyes
may be opened." 34So Jesus had compassion and touched their eyes. And immediately their eyes received sight, and
they followed Him.

The Triumphal Entry

21 Now when they drew near Jerusalem, and came to Bethphage,[a]
at the Mount of Olives, then Jesus sent

20:16 [a]NU-Text omits the last sentence of this verse. 20:22 [a]NU-Text omits *and be baptized with the baptism that I am baptized with.* 20:23 [a]NU-Text omits *and be baptized with the baptism that I am baptized with.* 21:1 [a]M-Text reads *Bethsphage.*

20:28 "If the sinless Christ, who is literally God in human flesh and Lord of all, would so humble Himself for us, we dare not denigrate humility or aspire to self-esteem instead of lowliness... Do you want to be blessed? Develop a servant's heart. If Jesus can step down from His glorious equality with God to become a man, and then further humble Himself to be a servant and wash the feet of twelve undeserving sinners—then humble Himself to die so horribly on our behalf—surely we ought to be willing to suffer any indignity to serve Him." *John MacArthur*

QUESTIONS & OBJECTIONS

21:2,3 *"Jesus wasn't sinless—He stole a donkey."*

Skeptics try to find sin in Jesus Christ, but they cannot. He was morally perfect. This objection is about the best anyone can do, along with the claim that He disobeyed His parents, or He lost His temper when He cleared the temple. (See Mark 11:15 and Luke 2:46 comments.)

In Matt. 21:1–6, Jesus instructed His disciples to go and get the colt and its mother, and told them what to say if someone asked what they were doing. Jesus said the owner would give permission: "immediately he will send them" (v. 3). It happened as Jesus told them it would, and the donkeys were released as He said they would be. Mark 11:6 says even more clearly that the disciples were permitted to take the donkeys by those who stood there: "So they let them go." It isn't stealing if the owner gives permission.

Matthew notes that this was a fulfillment of a prophecy given over five centuries earlier (Zech. 9:9), that the Messiah would enter Jerusalem riding on a donkey's colt. It is not too difficult to imagine that our omniscient God knew where to find a suitable colt and a willing owner.

two disciples, 2saying to them, "Go into
the village opposite you, and immediately you will find a donkey tied, and a
colt with her. Loose *them* and bring *them*
to Me. 3And if anyone says anything to
you, you shall say, 'The Lord has need of
them,' and immediately he will send
them."

4All[a] this was done that it might be fulfilled which was spoken by the prophet,
saying:

5*"Tell the daughter of Zion,*
'Behold, your King is coming to you,
Lowly, and sitting on a donkey,
A colt, the foal of a donkey.'"[a]

6So the disciples went and did as Jesus
commanded them. 7They brought the
donkey and the colt, laid their clothes on
them, and set *Him*[a] on them. 8And a very
great multitude spread their clothes on
the road; others cut down branches from
the trees and spread *them* on the road.
9Then the multitudes who went before
and those who followed cried out, saying:

"Hosanna to the Son of David!
'Blessed is He who comes in the name
of the LORD!'[a]
Hosanna in the highest!"

10And when He had come into Jerusalem, all the city was moved, saying,
"Who is this?"

11So the multitudes said, "This is Jesus,
the prophet from Nazareth of Galilee."

Jesus Cleanses the Temple

12Then Jesus went into the temple of
God[a] and drove out all those who bought
and sold in the temple, and overturned
the tables of the money changers and the
seats of those who sold doves. 13And He
said to them, "It is written, *'My house shall*
be called a house of prayer,'[a] but you
have made it a *'den of thieves.'"*[b]

14Then *the* blind and *the* lame came to
Him in the temple, and He healed them.
15But when the chief priests and scribes

21:4 [a]NU-Text omits *All.* 21:5 [a]Zechariah 9:9 21:7 [a]NU-Text reads *and He sat.* 21:9 [a]Psalm 118:26 21:12 [a]NU-Text omits *of God.* 21:13 [a]Isaiah 56:7 [b]Jeremiah 7:11

21:12,13 See Mark 11:15 comment.

"Genuine outrage is not just a permissible reaction to the hard-pressed Christian; God himself feels it, and so should the Christian in the presence of pain, cruelty, violence, and injustice. God, who is the Father of Jesus Christ, is neither impersonal nor beyond good and evil. By the absolute immutability of His character, He is implacably opposed to evil and outraged by it." *Os Guinness*

"Tolerance is a virtue for those who have no convictions." *G. K. Chesterton*

saw the wonderful things that He did, and
the children crying out in the temple and
saying, "Hosanna to the Son of David!"
they were indignant 16and said to Him,
"Do You hear what these are saying?"

And Jesus said to them, "Yes. Have
you never read,

'Out of the mouth of babes and nursing
infants
You have perfected praise'? "[a]

17Then He left them and went out of
the city to Bethany, and He lodged there.

> Believe what you do believe, or else you will never persuade anybody else to believe it.
>
> **CHARLES SPURGEON**

The Fig Tree Withered

18Now in the morning, as He returned
to the city, He was hungry. 19And seeing
a fig tree by the road, He came to it and
found nothing on it but leaves, and said
to it, "Let no fruit grow on you ever
again." Immediately the fig tree withered
away.

The Lesson of the Withered Fig Tree

20And when the disciples saw *it,* they
marveled, saying, "How did the fig tree
wither away so soon?"

21So Jesus answered and said to them,
"Assuredly, I say to you, if you have faith
and do not doubt, you will not only do
what was done to the fig tree, but also if
you say to this mountain, 'Be removed
and be cast into the sea,' it will be done.
22And whatever things you ask in prayer,
believing, you will receive."

Jesus' Authority Questioned

23Now when He came into the temple,
the chief priests and the elders of the
people confronted Him as He was teaching, and said, "By what authority are You
doing these things? And who gave You
this authority?"

24But Jesus answered and said to
them, "I also will ask you one thing,
which if you tell Me, I likewise will tell
you by what authority I do these things:
25The baptism of John—where was it
from? From heaven or from men?"

And they reasoned among themselves,
saying, "If we say, 'From heaven,' He will
say to us, 'Why then did you not believe
him?' 26But if we say, 'From men,' we fear
the multitude, for all count John as a
prophet." 27So they answered Jesus and
said, "We do not know."

And He said to them, "Neither will I
tell you by what authority I do these
things.

The Parable of the Two Sons

28"But what do you think? A man had
two sons, and he came to the first and
said, 'Son, go, work today in my vineyard.' 29He answered and said, 'I will

21:16 [a]Psalm 8:2

21:22 *Robert Speer* said, "The evangelization of the world depends first of all upon a revival of prayer. Deeper than the need for workers; deeper far, than the need for money; deep down at the bottom of our spiritual lives is the need for the forgotten secret of prevailing, worldwide prayer. Missions have progressed slowly abroad because piety and prayer have been slow at home."

Robert Speer is right; prayer is evidence of our utter dependence on God. Without Him we can do nothing. However, never forget that Jesus said there was a lack of laborers in His time, and there is a lack of laborers in our time (see Matt. 9:37). It is easier to pray for this world than to preach the gospel to them. So make sure that you don't substitute the sacrifice of prayer for the obedience of evangelism; to do so is to play the hypocrite.

"We Christians too often substitute prayer for playing the game. Prayer is good; but when used as a substitute for obedience, it is nothing but a blatant hypocrisy, a despicable Pharisaism . . . To your knees, man! And to your Bible! Decide at once! Don't hedge! Time flies! Cease your insults to God. Quit consulting flesh and blood. Stop your lame, lying, and cowardly excuses. Enlist!" *C. T. Studd*

not,' but afterward he regretted it and
went. 30 Then he came to the second and
said likewise. And he answered and said,
'I *go,* sir,' but he did not go. 31 Which of
the two did the will of *his* father?"

They said to Him, "The first."

Jesus said to them, "Assuredly, I say to
you that tax collectors and harlots enter
the kingdom of God before you. 32 For
John came to you in the way of righteousness, and you did not believe him;
but tax collectors and harlots believed
him; and when you saw *it,* you did not afterward relent and believe him.

The Parable of the Wicked Vinedressers

33 "Hear another parable: There was a
certain landowner who planted a vineyard and set a hedge around it, dug a
winepress in it and built a tower. And he
leased it to vinedressers and went into a
far country. 34 Now when vintage-time
drew near, he sent his servants to the
vinedressers, that they might receive its
fruit. 35 And the vinedressers took his servants, beat one, killed one, and stoned
another. 36 Again he sent other servants,
more than the first, and they did likewise
to them. 37 Then last of all he sent his son
to them, saying, 'They will respect my
son.' 38 But when the vinedressers saw the
son, they said among themselves, 'This is
the heir. Come, let us kill him and seize
his inheritance.' 39 So they took him and
cast *him* out of the vineyard and killed
him.

40 "Therefore, when the owner of the
vineyard comes, what will he do to those
vinedressers?"

41 They said to Him, "He will destroy
those wicked men miserably, and lease *his*
vineyard to other vinedressers who will
render to him the fruits in their seasons."

42 Jesus said to them, "Have you never
read in the Scriptures:

'The stone which the builders rejected
Has become the chief cornerstone.
This was the LORD's doing,
And it is marvelous in our eyes'?[a]

43 "Therefore I say to you, the kingdom of God will be taken from you and
given to a nation bearing the fruits of it.
44 And whoever falls on this stone will be
broken; but on whomever it falls, it will
grind him to powder."

45 Now when the chief priests and
Pharisees heard His parables, they perceived that He was speaking of them.
46 But when they sought to lay hands on
Him, they feared the multitudes, because
they took Him for a prophet.

The Parable of the Wedding Feast

22 And Jesus answered and spoke to
them again by parables and said:
2 "The kingdom of heaven is like a certain
king who arranged a marriage for his son,
3 and sent out his servants to call those
who were invited to the wedding; and
they were not willing to come. 4 Again, he
sent out other servants, saying, 'Tell those
who are invited, "See, I have prepared my
dinner; my oxen and fatted cattle *are*
killed, and all things *are* ready. Come to
the wedding."' 5 But they made light of it
and went their ways, one to his own
farm, another to his business. 6 And the
rest seized his servants, treated *them*
spitefully, and killed *them.* 7 But when the
king heard *about it,* he was furious. And
he sent out his armies, destroyed those
murderers, and burned up their city.
8 Then he said to his servants, 'The wedding is ready, but those who were invited
were not worthy. 9 Therefore go into the

21:42 [a]Psalm 118:22, 23

21:44 Those who fall upon the stone of Jesus Christ are broken. He will not despise a broken and contrite heart. However, when Jesus comes in flaming fire, taking vengeance on those who do not know God (2 Thess. 1:8), His judgment will "grind them to powder." When you grind something to powder, you do a thorough job. He will judge right down to the thoughts and intents of the heart.

highways, and as many as you find, invite
to the wedding.' 10So those servants went
out into the highways and gathered together all whom they found, both bad
and good. And the wedding *hall* was
filled with guests.
11"But when the king came in to see
the guests, he saw a man there who did
not have on a wedding garment. 12So he
said to him, 'Friend, how did you come
in here without a wedding garment?' And
he was speechless. 13Then the king said
to the servants, 'Bind him hand and foot,
take him away, and[a] cast *him* into outer
darkness; there will be weeping and
gnashing of teeth.'
14"For many are called, but few *are*
chosen."

The Pharisees: Is It Lawful to Pay Taxes to Caesar?

15Then the Pharisees went and plotted
how they might entangle Him in *His* talk.
16And they sent to Him their disciples
with the Herodians, saying, "Teacher, we
know that You are true, and teach the
way of God in truth; nor do You care
about anyone, for You do not regard the
person of men. 17Tell us, therefore, what
do You think? Is it lawful to pay taxes to
Caesar, or not?"
18But Jesus perceived their wickedness, and said, "Why do you test Me, *you*
hypocrites? 19Show Me the tax money."
So they brought Him a denarius.
20And He said to them, "Whose image
and inscription *is* this?"
21They said to Him, "Caesar's."
And He said to them, "Render therefore to Caesar the things that are Caesar's,
and to God the things that are God's."
22When they had heard *these words,* they
marveled, and left Him and went their
way.

The Sadducees: What About the Resurrection?

23The same day the Sadducees, who
say there is no resurrection, came to Him
and asked Him, 24saying: "Teacher, Moses
said that if a man dies, having no children, his brother shall marry his wife and
raise up offspring for his brother. 25Now
there were with us seven brothers. The
first died after he had married, and having no offspring, left his wife to his
brother. 26Likewise the second also, and
the third, even to the seventh. 27Last of
all the woman died also. 28Therefore, in
the resurrection, whose wife of the seven
will she be? For they all had her."
29Jesus answered and said to them,
"You are mistaken, not knowing the Scriptures nor the power of God. 30For in the
resurrection they neither marry nor are
given in marriage, but are like angels of
God[a] in heaven. 31But concerning the
resurrection of the dead, have you not read
what was spoken to you by God, saying,

22:13 [a]NU-Text omits *take him away, and.* 22:30 [a]NU-Text omits *of God.*

22:29 Mistakes in the Bible. In his ignorance man searches for what he considers "mistakes" in the Bible to justify his godless beliefs. He is like a man with a magnifying glass who diligently searches for a tiny dirt speck on the Mona Lisa, so he can justify discarding the whole painting as junk. In the following article from *The Almost Christian* (written in 1661), *Matthew Mead* addresses the problem:

> There is a proud heart in every natural man. There was much pride in Adam's sin—and there is much of it in all Adam's sons. Pride is a radical sin, and from hence arises this over-inflated opinion of a man's spiritual state and condition: "The Pharisee stood up and prayed about himself: God, I thank you that I am not like other men—robbers, evildoers, adulterers" (Luke 18:11). This is the unsaved man's motto.
>
> A proud man has an eye to see his beauty—but not his deformity. He sees his abilities—but not his spots. He sees his seeming righteousness—but not his real wretchedness. It must be a work of grace—which must show a man the lack of grace. The haughty eye looks upward—but the humble eye looks downward, and therefore this is the believer's motto, "I am the least of saints—and the greatest of sinners!"

32*'I am the God of Abraham, the God of
Isaac, and the God of Jacob'?*[a] God is not
the God of the dead, but of the living."
33And when the multitudes heard *this,*
they were astonished at His teaching.

The Scribes: Which Is the First Commandment of All?

34But when the Pharisees heard that He
had silenced the Sadducees, they gathered together. 35Then one of them, a lawyer, asked *Him a question,* testing Him,
and saying, 36"Teacher, which *is* the great
commandment in the law?"
37Jesus said to him, "*'You shall love
the LORD your God with all your heart,
with all your soul, and with all your
mind.'*[a] 38This is *the* first and great commandment. 39And *the* second *is* like it:
*'You shall love your neighbor as your-
self.'*[a] 40On these two commandments
hang all the Law and the Prophets."

Jesus: How Can David Call His Descendant Lord?

41While the Pharisees were gathered together, Jesus asked them, 42saying, "What
do you think about the Christ? Whose
Son is He?"
They said to Him, "*The Son* of David."
43He said to them, "How then does
David in the Spirit call Him *'Lord,'* saying:

44*'The LORD said to my Lord,*
"Sit at My right hand,
Till I make Your enemies Your
footstool"'?[a]

45If David then calls Him *'Lord,'* how is He
his Son?" 46And no one was able to answer Him a word, nor from that day on
did anyone dare question Him anymore.

Woe to the Scribes and Pharisees

23 Then Jesus spoke to the multitudes and to His disciples, 2say-
ing: "The scribes and the Pharisees sit in
Moses' seat. 3Therefore whatever they tell
you to observe,[a] *that* observe and do, but
do not do according to their works; for
they say, and do not do. 4For they bind
heavy burdens, hard to bear, and lay *them*
on men's shoulders; but they *themselves*
will not move them with one of their fingers. 5But all their works they do to be
seen by men. They make their phylacter-
ies broad and enlarge the borders of their
garments. 6They love the best places at
feasts, the best seats in the synagogues,
7greetings in the marketplaces, and to be
called by men, 'Rabbi, Rabbi.' 8But you,
do not be called 'Rabbi'; for One is your
Teacher, the Christ,[a] and you are all
brethren. 9Do not call anyone on earth
your father; for One is your Father, He
who is in heaven. 10And do not be called
teachers; for One is your Teacher, the
Christ. 11But he who is greatest among
you shall be your servant. 12And whoever
exalts himself will be humbled, and he
who humbles himself will be exalted.
13"But woe to you, scribes and Pharisees, hypocrites! For you shut up the
kingdom of heaven against men; for you
neither go in *yourselves,* nor do you allow
those who are entering to go in. 14Woe to
you, scribes and Pharisees, hypocrites!

22:32 [a]Exodus 3:6, 15 22:37 [a]Deuteronomy 6:5 22:39 [a]Leviticus 19:18 22:44 [a]Psalm 110:1 23:3 [a]NU-Text omits *to observe.* 23:8 [a]NU-Text omits *the Christ.*

22:36–40 At war with the Law. "There is a war between you and God's Law. The Ten Commandments are against you. The first comes forward and says, 'Let him be cursed. For he denies Me. He has another god beside Me. His god is his belly and he yields his homage to his lust.' All the Ten Commandments, like ten great cannons, are pointed at you today. For you have broken all of God's statutes and lived in daily neglect of all His commands.

"Soul, thou wilt find it a hard thing to go at war with the Law. When the Law came in peace, Sinai was altogether on a smoke and even Moses said, 'I exceeding fear and quake!' What will you do when the Law of God comes in terror; when the trumpet of the archangel shall tear you from your grave; when the eyes of God shall burn their way into your guilty soul; when the great books shall be opened and all your sin and shame shall be punished . . . Can you stand against an angry Law in that Day?" *Charles Spurgeon*

QUESTIONS & OBJECTIONS

23:13–16 ***"You shouldn't talk about sin because Jesus didn't condemn anybody. He was always loving and kind."***

Jesus did indeed condemn some people for their sin. In Matt. 23 He called the religious leaders "hypocrites" seven times. He told them that they were "fools and blind," sons of hell, full of hypocrisy and sin. He climaxed His sermon by saying, "Serpents, brood of vipers! How can you escape the condemnation of hell?" (v. 33). He then warned that He would say to the wicked, "Depart from Me, you cursed, into the everlasting fire prepared for the devil and his angels" (Matt. 25:41).

For you devour widows' houses, and for
a pretense make long prayers. Therefore
you will receive greater condemnation.[a]
15"Woe to you, scribes and Pharisees,
hypocrites! For you travel land and sea to win one proselyte, and when he is won, you make him twice as much a son of hell as yourselves.

. . . . . .

For the Bible's uniqueness, see Psa. 119:105 comment.

. . . . . .

16"Woe to you, blind guides, who say,
'Whoever swears by the temple, it is nothing; but whoever swears by the gold of
the temple, he is obliged *to perform it.*'
17Fools and blind! For which is greater,
the gold or the temple that sanctifies[a] the
gold? 18And, 'Whoever swears by the altar, it is nothing; but whoever swears by the gift that is on it, he is obliged *to perform it.*' 19Fools and blind! For which is
greater, the gift or the altar that sanctifies
the gift? 20Therefore he who swears by
the altar, swears by it and by all things on
it. 21He who swears by the temple, swears
by it and by Him who dwells[a] in it. 22And
he who swears by heaven, swears by the throne of God and by Him who sits on it.
23"Woe to you, scribes and Pharisees,
hypocrites! For you pay tithe of mint and anise and cummin, and have neglected the weightier *matters* of the law: justice and mercy and faith. These you ought to have done, without leaving the others
undone. 24Blind guides, who strain out a
gnat and swallow a camel!
25"Woe to you, scribes and Pharisees,
hypocrites! For you cleanse the outside of the cup and dish, but inside they are full
of extortion and self-indulgence.[a] 26Blind
Pharisee, first cleanse the inside of the cup and dish, that the outside of them may be clean also.
27"Woe to you, scribes and Pharisees,
hypocrites! For you are like whitewashed tombs which indeed appear beautiful outwardly, but inside are full of dead *men's*
bones and all uncleanness. 28Even so you
also outwardly appear righteous to men, but inside you are full of hypocrisy and lawlessness.
29"Woe to you, scribes and Pharisees,
hypocrites! Because you build the tombs of the prophets and adorn the monuments of the righteous, 30and say, 'If we
had lived in the days of our fathers, we would not have been partakers with them in the blood of the prophets.'
31"Therefore you are witnesses against
yourselves that you are sons of those who murdered the prophets. 32Fill up, then,
the measure of your fathers' *guilt.* 33Ser-

23:14 [a]NU-Text omits this verse. 23:17 [a]NU-Text reads *sanctified.* 23:21 [a]M-Text reads *dwelt.* 23:25 [a]M-Text reads *unrighteousness.*

23:9 Jesus commanded His followers not to call any man "father." The Pharisees loved to be seen and praised by men. They cherished their titles—Rabbi (Matt. 23:8) and Father (Acts 7:2; 22:1). Jesus condemned these titles because of their hypocrisy. Paul used them rightly in reference to those whom he had begotten through the gospel (1 Cor. 4:15).

pents, brood of vipers! How can you escape the condemnation of hell? 34There-
fore, indeed, I send you prophets, wise
men, and scribes: *some* of them you will
kill and crucify, and *some* of them you
will scourge in your synagogues and persecute from city to city, 35that on you may
come all the righteous blood shed on the
earth, from the blood of righteous Abel to
the blood of Zechariah, son of Berechiah,
whom you murdered between the temple
and the altar. 36Assuredly, I say to you,
all these things will come upon this generation.

> Preaching the gospel is to us a matter of life and death; we throw our whole soul into it. We live and are happy if you believe in Jesus and are saved. But we are almost ready to die if you refuse the gospel of Christ.
>
> CHARLES SPURGEON

Jesus Laments over Jerusalem

37"O Jerusalem, Jerusalem, the one
who kills the prophets and stones those
who are sent to her! How often I wanted
to gather your children together, as a hen
gathers her chicks under *her* wings, but
you were not willing! 38See! Your house
is left to you desolate; 39for I say to you,
you shall see Me no more till you say,
*'Blessed is He who comes in the name of
the LORD!'* "[a]

Jesus Predicts the Destruction of the Temple

24 Then Jesus went out and departed
from the temple, and His disciples
came up to show Him the buildings of
the temple. 2And Jesus said to them, "Do
you not see all these things? Assuredly, I
say to you, not *one* stone shall be left here
upon another, that shall not be thrown
down."

The Signs of the Times and the End of the Age

3Now as He sat on the Mount of Olives,
the disciples came to Him privately, saying, "Tell us, when will these things be?
And what *will be* the sign of Your coming,
and of the end of the age?"
4And Jesus answered and said to
them: "Take heed that no one deceives
you. 5For many will come in My name,
saying, 'I am the Christ,' and will deceive
many. 6And you will hear of wars and rumors of wars. See that you are not troubled; for all[a] *these things* must come to
pass, but the end is not yet. 7For nation
will rise against nation, and kingdom
against kingdom. And there will be
famines, pestilences,[a] and earthquakes in
various places. 8All these *are* the beginning of sorrows.
9"Then they will deliver you up to
tribulation and kill you, and you will be
hated by all nations for My name's sake.
10And then many will be offended, will
betray one another, and will hate one another. 11Then many false prophets will
rise up and deceive many. 12And because
lawlessness will abound, the love of many
will grow cold. 13But he who endures to
the end shall be saved. 14And this gospel

23:39 [a]Psalm 118:26 24:6 [a]NU-Text omits *all.* 24:7 [a]NU-Text omits *pestilences.*

23:33 Hell: For verses warning of its reality, see Matt. 25:41.

24:2 Jewish historian Josephus wrote of the temple's destruction by Romans in A.D. 70: "They carried away every stone of the sacred temple, partially in a frenzied search for every last piece of the gold ornamentation melted in the awful heat of the fire. They then plowed the ground level, and since it had already been sown with its defenders' blood, they sowed it with salt" (*Wars of the Jews*). See also Mark 13:2.

24:3 For more signs of the end times, see Mark 13:4.

24:7 The Bible informs us that in the last days there will be earthquakes in different places. This was stated 2,000 years ago, and there is little historical data regarding the size, frequency, and location of earthquakes. One thing is certain: earthquakes in different places are a sign of these times.

of the kingdom will be preached in all the world as a witness to all the nations, and then the end will come.

The Great Tribulation

15"Therefore when you see the *'abomination of desolation,'*[a] spoken of by Daniel the prophet, standing in the holy place" (whoever reads, let him understand),
16"then let those who are in Judea flee to the mountains. 17Let him who is on the housetop not go down to take anything out of his house. 18And let him who is in the field not go back to get his clothes.
19But woe to those who are pregnant and to those who are nursing babies in those days! 20And pray that your flight may not be in winter or on the Sabbath. 21For then there will be great tribulation, such as has not been since the beginning of the world until this time, no, nor ever shall be. 22And unless those days were shortened, no flesh would be saved; but for the elect's sake those days will be shortened.

23"Then if anyone says to you, 'Look, here *is* the Christ!' or 'There!' do not believe *it.* 24For false christs and false prophets will rise and show great signs and wonders to deceive, if possible, even the elect. 25See, I have told you beforehand.

26"Therefore if they say to you, 'Look, He is in the desert!' do not go out; *or* 'Look, *He is* in the inner rooms!' do not believe *it.* 27For as the lightning comes from the east and flashes to the west, so also will the coming of the Son of Man be. 28For wherever the carcass is, there the eagles will be gathered together.

The Coming of the Son of Man

29"Immediately after the tribulation of those days the sun will be darkened, and the moon will not give its light; the stars will fall from heaven, and the powers of the heavens will be shaken. 30Then the sign of the Son of Man will appear in heaven, and then all the tribes of the earth will mourn, and they will see the Son of Man coming on the clouds of heaven with power and great glory.
31And He will send His angels with a great sound of a trumpet, and they will gather together His elect from the four winds, from one end of heaven to the other.

The Parable of the Fig Tree

32"Now learn this parable from the fig tree: When its branch has already become tender and puts forth leaves, you know that summer *is* near. 33So you also, when you see all these things, know that it[a] is near—at the doors! 34Assuredly, I say to you, this generation will by no means pass away till all these things take place. 35Heaven and earth will pass away, but My words will by no means pass away.

No One Knows the Day or Hour

36"But of that day and hour no one knows, not even the angels of heaven,[a] but My Father only. 37But as the days of Noah *were,* so also will the coming of the Son of Man be. 38For as in the days before the flood, they were eating and drinking, marrying and giving in marriage, until the day that Noah entered the ark, 39and did not know until the flood came and took them all away, so also will the coming of the Son of Man be. 40Then two *men* will be in the field: one will be

24:15 [a]Daniel 11:31; 12:11 24:33 [a]Or *He* 24:36 [a]NU-Text adds *nor the Son.*

24:14 "No one is beyond the reach of God to present the gospel to them." *Garry T. Ansdell*

24:27 Second coming of Jesus: See Matt. 24:39.

24:35 God is able to ensure that His written Word, the Bible, will endure. See Psa. 119:105 comment.

24:37–39 Jesus referred to Noah as an actual historical person, and the Flood as a bona fide historical event.

24:39 Second coming of Jesus: See Matt. 25:31.

24:38,39 *Ten Points to Consider About the Flood*

By Ken Ham, Answers in Genesis

1. Flood Legends: Hundreds of legends of a massive flood are found in cultures all over the world. This is a great confirmation of the biblical account and exactly what we would expect as nations traveled around the world passing down the account of the Flood. Various aspects of the Flood would be lost and other parts embellished, and that is precisely what we find.

2. Layers: The amount of sediment that was deposited by the waters of the Flood is incredible (estimates are around 700 million cubic kilometers or 168 million cubic miles). Wow! Only a global Flood can explain such extensive layers of rock that everyone agrees was deposited by water.

3. Fossils: Ninety-five percent of the fossils in the layers are marine organisms. That is what we would expect from a global Flood that overtakes the land. Of the remaining 5 percent, 95 percent are plants/trees/algae. The remaining fossils (including vertebrates) are rare.

4. The Door: After Noah's family entered the Ark, the Lord shut the only door (Gen. 7:16). Jesus is the only door by which we can enter to escape the eternal condemnation of hell (John 10:7–9).

5. Kinds not Species: Genesis 7:14 uses the word "kind" (*min*), which could be equated with the modern *species, genus, family*, or even *order* in special cases (most often it is closer to a family level). Often people mistakenly think *kind* means the modern concept of "species." But "species" is simply that—a term used in the modern classification system. So equating the two is not wise. When it comes to kinds, there is a dog kind (including wolves, coyotes, dingoes, domestic dogs, etc.), cat kind (including lions, tigers, bobcats, domestic cats, etc.), elephant kind (including Asian elephants, African elephants, mammoths, mastodons, etc.), and so on. This reduces the number of animals that Noah needed on the Ark—two of each kind (two dogs, two cats, etc.), not two of each species. See Acts 10:12 comment.

6. Global in Extent: Throughout Genesis 6—8, the Bible repeatedly uses universal language to describe the Flood: "*all* the high hills under the *whole* heaven" (7:19), "mountains were covered" (7:20), etc. Such language indicates that God was accentuating the massive extent of a global Flood. In the same way that the Flood was a universal judgment, so will be the coming judgment of fire (2 Pet. 3:5–7). See Isa. 54:9 and 2 Pet. 2:5 comments.

7. Ararat: The Bible indicates that the Ark landed "on the mountains of Ararat" (see Gen. 8:4; it doesn't mention any specific mountain), a region extending from eastern Turkey to western Iran. Many people search for the remains of the Ark on Mt. Ararat, but Noah and his family could have landed anywhere in that region.

8. Eating Meat: Man was originally vegetarian (Gen. 1:29), but God first permitted man to eat meat after the Flood (Gen. 9:3). See Gen. 1:30 comment.

9. Animal Death: The vast majority of the rock layers that contain fossils are a testament to the Flood of Noah's day (of course, there have been local catastrophes, like volcanoes, that have produced layers since the Flood). But these fossil layers could *not* be evidence of millions of years since we find evidence of death in these layers. Death was the result of sin entering creation in Gen. 3 after Adam and Eve ate of the fruit. In fact, the first recorded death of an animal came *after* Adam and Eve sinned (Gen. 3:21). It was a direct result of man's sin, so there is a relationship between human sin and animal death. See Gen. 8:20 and Rev. 21:4 comments.

10. Carnivores: Although animals were originally vegetarian (Gen. 1:30), after man's sin brought a curse on all creation, they began eating meat. While the Bible doesn't tell us exactly when animals started eating each other, it's obvious this happened before the Flood. The fossil record—most of which was formed by the Flood of Noah's day—contains the fossils of animal bones in the stomachs of other animals. Thus, some animals were eating each other before the Flood. This makes sense because the Bible says that all flesh had corrupted itself (Gen. 6:12).

taken and the other left. [41]Two *women*
will be grinding at the mill: one will be
taken and the other left. [42]Watch therefore, for you do not know what hour[a]
your Lord is coming. [43]But know this,
that if the master of the house had known
what hour the thief would come, he
would have watched and not allowed his

24:42 [a]NU-Text reads *day*.

house to be broken into. 44Therefore you
also be ready, for the Son of Man is coming at an hour you do not expect.

The Faithful Servant and the Evil Servant

45"Who then is a faithful and wise servant, whom his master made ruler over
his household, to give them food in due
season? 46Blessed *is* that servant whom
his master, when he comes, will find so
doing. 47Assuredly, I say to you that he
will make him ruler over all his goods.
48But if that evil servant says in his heart,
'My master is delaying his coming,'[a]
49and begins to beat *his* fellow servants,
and to eat and drink with the drunkards,
50the master of that servant will come on
a day when he is not looking for *him* and
at an hour that he is not aware of, 51and
will cut him in two and appoint *him* his
portion with the hypocrites. There shall
be weeping and gnashing of teeth.

The Parable of the Wise and Foolish Virgins

25 "Then the kingdom of heaven shall
be likened to ten virgins who
took their lamps and went out to meet
the bridegroom. 2Now five of them were
wise, and five *were* foolish. 3Those who
were foolish took their lamps and took no
oil with them, 4but the wise took oil in
their vessels with their lamps. 5But while
the bridegroom was delayed, they all
slumbered and slept.

6"And at midnight a cry was *heard:*
'Behold, the bridegroom is coming;[a] go
out to meet him!' 7Then all those virgins
arose and trimmed their lamps. 8And the
foolish said to the wise, 'Give us *some* of
your oil, for our lamps are going out.'
9But the wise answered, saying, '*No,* lest
there should not be enough for us and
you; but go rather to those who sell, and
buy for yourselves.' 10And while they
went to buy, the bridegroom came, and
those who were ready went in with him
to the wedding; and the door was shut.

11"Afterward the other virgins came
also, saying, 'Lord, Lord, open to us!' 12But
he answered and said, 'Assuredly, I say to
you, I do not know you.'

13"Watch therefore, for you know neither the day nor the hour[a] in which the
Son of Man is coming.

The Parable of the Talents

14"For *the kingdom of heaven is* like a
man traveling to a far country, *who* called
his own servants and delivered his goods
to them. 15And to one he gave five talents, to another two, and to another one,
to each according to his own ability; and
immediately he went on a journey. 16Then
he who had received the five talents went
and traded with them, and made another
five talents. 17And likewise he who *had
received* two gained two more also. 18But
he who had received one went and dug
in the ground, and hid his lord's money.
19After a long time the lord of those servants came and settled accounts with
them.

20"So he who had received five talents

24:48 [a]NU-Text omits *his coming.* 25:6 [a]NU-Text omits *is coming.* 25:13 [a]NU-Text omits the rest of this verse.

25:12 False converts. The foolish virgins called Him "Lord," but Jesus said, "I do not know you." They were false converts. Jesus warned, "Not everyone who says to Me, 'Lord, Lord,' shall enter the kingdom of heaven, but he who does the will of My Father in heaven. Many will say to Me in that day, 'Lord, Lord, have we not prophesied in Your name, cast out demons in Your name, and done many wonders in Your name?' And then I will declare to them, 'I never knew you; depart from Me, you who practice lawlessness!'" (Matt. 7:21–23). This is why we must forsake traditional quick-fix evangelism and do all things according to the pattern given to us in Scripture. For the key to biblical evangelism, see Luke 11:52 comment.

"The vast majority of people who are members of churches in America today are not Christians. I say that without the slightest fear of contradiction. I base it on empirical evidence of twenty-four years of examining thousands of people." *D. James Kennedy*

came and brought five other talents, saying, 'Lord, you delivered to me five talents; look, I have gained five more talents besides them.' 21His lord said to him, 'Well *done,* good and faithful servant; you were faithful over a few things, I will make you ruler over many things. Enter into the joy of your lord.' 22He also who had received two talents came and said, 'Lord, you delivered to me two talents; look, I have gained two more talents besides them.' 23His lord said to him, 'Well *done,* good and faithful servant; you have been faithful over a few things, I will make you ruler over many things. Enter into the joy of your lord.'

24"Then he who had received the one talent came and said, 'Lord, I knew you to be a hard man, reaping where you have not sown, and gathering where you have not scattered seed. 25And I was afraid, and went and hid your talent in the ground. Look, *there* you have *what is* yours.'

26"But his lord answered and said to him, 'You wicked and lazy servant, you knew that I reap where I have not sown, and gather where I have not scattered seed. 27So you ought to have deposited my money with the bankers, and at my coming I would have received back my own with interest. 28So take the talent from him, and give *it* to him who has ten talents.

29'For to everyone who has, more will be given, and he will have abundance; but from him who does not have, even what he has will be taken away. 30And cast the unprofitable servant into the outer darkness. There will be weeping and gnashing of teeth.'

The Son of Man Will Judge the Nations

31"When the Son of Man comes in His glory, and all the holy[a] angels with Him, then He will sit on the throne of His glory. 32All the nations will be gathered before Him, and He will separate them one from another, as a shepherd divides *his* sheep from the goats. 33And He will set the sheep on His right hand, but the goats on the left. 34Then the King will say to those on His right hand, 'Come, you blessed of My Father, inherit the kingdom prepared for you from the foundation of the world: 35for I was hungry and you gave Me food; I was thirsty and you gave Me drink; I was a stranger and you took Me in; 36I *was* naked and you clothed Me; I was sick and you visited Me; I was in prison and you came to Me.'

37"Then the righteous will answer Him, saying, 'Lord, when did we see You hungry and feed *You,* or thirsty and give *You* drink? 38When did we see You a stranger and take *You* in, or naked and clothe *You?* 39Or when did we see You sick, or in prison, and come to You?' 40And the King will answer and say to them, 'Assuredly, I say to you, inasmuch as you did *it* to one of the least of these My brethren, you did *it* to Me.'

41"Then He will also say to those on the left hand, 'Depart from Me, you cursed, into the everlasting fire prepared for the devil and his angels: 42for I was hungry and you gave Me no food; I was thirsty and you gave Me no drink; 43I was a

25:31 [a]NU-Text omits *holy.*

25:31 Second coming of Jesus: See Matt. 26:64.

25:32 Judgment Day: For verses that warn of its reality, see John 5:28,29.

25:41 Hell: For verses warning of its reality, see Mark 9:43–48.

"Now observe, brethren, if I, or you, or any of us, or all of us, shall have spent our lives merely in amusing men, or educating men, or moralizing men, when we shall come to give our account at the last great day we shall be in a very sorry condition, and we shall have but a very sorry record to render; for of what avail will it be to a man to be educated when he comes to be damned? Of what service will it be to him to have been amused when the trumpet sounds, and heaven and earth are shaking, and the pit opens wide her jaws of fire and swallows up the soul unsaved? Of what avail even to have moralized a man if still he is on the left hand of the judge, and if still, "Depart, ye cursed," shall be his portion?'" *Charles Spurgeon*

stranger and you did not take Me in, naked and you did not clothe Me, sick and in prison and you did not visit Me.’
44“Then they also will answer Him,[a] saying, ‘Lord, when did we see You hungry or thirsty or a stranger or naked or sick or in prison, and did not minister to You?’ 45Then He will answer them, saying, ‘Assuredly, I say to you, inasmuch as you did not do *it* to one of the least of these, you did not do *it* to Me.’ 46And these will go away into everlasting punishment, but the righteous into eternal life.”

> I desire to have both heaven and hell in my eye.
>
> **JOHN WESLEY**

The Plot to Kill Jesus

26 Now it came to pass, when Jesus had finished all these sayings, *that* He said to His disciples, 2“You know that after two days is the Passover, and the Son of Man will be delivered up to be crucified.”

3Then the chief priests, the scribes,[a] and the elders of the people assembled at the palace of the high priest, who was called Caiaphas, 4and plotted to take Jesus by trickery and kill *Him.* 5But they said, “Not during the feast, lest there be an uproar among the people.”

The Anointing at Bethany

6And when Jesus was in Bethany at the house of Simon the leper, 7a woman came to Him having an alabaster flask of very costly fragrant oil, and she poured *it* on His head as He sat *at the table.* 8But when His disciples saw *it,* they were indignant, saying, “Why this waste? 9For this fragrant oil might have been sold for much and given to *the* poor.”

10But when Jesus was aware of *it,* He said to them, “Why do you trouble the woman? For she has done a good work for Me. 11For you have the poor with you always, but Me you do not have always. 12For in pouring this fragrant oil on My body, she did *it* for My burial. 13Assuredly, I say to you, wherever this gospel is preached in the whole world, what this woman has done will also be told as a memorial to her.”

Judas Agrees to Betray Jesus

14Then one of the twelve, called Judas Iscariot, went to the chief priests 15and said, “What are you willing to give me if I deliver Him to you?” And they counted out to him thirty pieces of silver. 16So from that time he sought opportunity to betray Him.

Jesus Celebrates Passover with His Disciples

17Now on the first *day of the Feast* of the Unleavened Bread the disciples came to Jesus, saying to Him, “Where do You want us to prepare for You to eat the Passover?”

18And He said, “Go into the city to a certain man, and say to him, ‘The Teacher says, “My time is at hand; I will keep the Passover at your house with My disciples.” ’ ”

19So the disciples did as Jesus had directed them; and they prepared the Passover.

25:44 [a]NU-Text and M-Text omit *Him.* **26:3** [a]NU-Text omits *the scribes.*

25:46 For believers, life here on earth is as bad it gets; for those who refuse Jesus as their Savior, life here on earth is as good as it gets.

“Has this world been so kind to you that you should leave with regret? There are better things ahead than any we leave behind.” *C. S. Lewis*

26:15 Messianic prophecy fulfilled: “Then I said to them, ‘If it is agreeable to you, give me my wages; and if not, refrain.’ So they weighed out for my wages thirty pieces of silver” (Zech. 11:12). See Matt. 26:60 comment.

20When evening had come, He sat down with the twelve. 21Now as they were eating, He said, "Assuredly, I say to you, one of you will betray Me."

22And they were exceedingly sorrowful, and each of them began to say to Him, "Lord, is it I?"

23He answered and said, "He who dipped *his* hand with Me in the dish will betray Me. 24The Son of Man indeed goes just as it is written of Him, but woe to that man by whom the Son of Man is betrayed! It would have been good for that man if he had not been born."

25Then Judas, who was betraying Him, answered and said, "Rabbi, is it I?"

He said to him, "You have said it."

Jesus Institutes the Lord's Supper

26And as they were eating, Jesus took bread, blessed[a] and broke *it,* and gave *it* to the disciples and said, "Take, eat; this is My body."

27Then He took the cup, and gave thanks, and gave *it* to them, saying, "Drink from it, all of you. 28For this is My blood of the new[a] covenant, which is shed for many for the remission of sins. 29But I say to you, I will not drink of this fruit of the vine from now on until that day when I drink it new with you in My Father's kingdom."

30And when they had sung a hymn, they went out to the Mount of Olives.

Jesus Predicts Peter's Denial

31Then Jesus said to them, "All of you will be made to stumble because of Me this night, for it is written:

'I will strike the Shepherd,
And the sheep of the flock will be
scattered.'[a]

32But after I have been raised, I will go before you to Galilee."

33Peter answered and said to Him, "Even if all are made to stumble because of You, I will never be made to stumble."

34Jesus said to him, "Assuredly, I say to you that this night, before the rooster crows, you will deny Me three times."

35Peter said to Him, "Even if I have to die with You, I will not deny You!"

And so said all the disciples.

The Prayer in the Garden

36Then Jesus came with them to a place called Gethsemane, and said to the disciples, "Sit here while I go and pray over there." 37And He took with Him Peter and the two sons of Zebedee, and He began to be sorrowful and deeply distressed. 38Then He said to them, "My soul is exceedingly sorrowful, even to death. Stay here and watch with Me."

39He went a little farther and fell on His face, and prayed, saying, "O My Father, if it is possible, let this cup pass from Me; nevertheless, not as I will, but as You *will.*"

40Then He came to the disciples and found them sleeping, and said to Peter, "What! Could you not watch with Me one hour? 41Watch and pray, lest you enter into temptation. The spirit indeed *is* willing, but the flesh *is* weak."

42Again, a second time, He went away and prayed, saying, "O My Father, if this cup cannot pass away from Me unless[a] I drink it, Your will be done." 43And He came and found them asleep again, for their eyes were heavy.

26:26 [a]M-Text reads *gave thanks for.* **26:28** [a]NU-Text omits *new.* **26:31** [a]Zechariah 13:7 **26:42** [a]NU-Text reads *if this may not pass away unless.*

26:26 This could only have been a *symbolic* statement. The bread was obviously not His *physical* body, as He was standing in front of them.

26:27,28 This could not have been Jesus' literal blood, because He was present with them. His words were *spiritual.* After Jesus told His disciples that they must eat of His flesh and drink of His blood, He said that the words that He spoke were spirit and life (John 6:63). When we are born of the Spirit (John 3:3–7), we "taste and see that the Lord is good" (Psa. 34:8).

44So He left them, went away again,
and prayed the third time, saying the
same words. 45Then He came to His disciples and said to them, "Are *you* still
sleeping and resting? Behold, the hour is
at hand, and the Son of Man is being betrayed into the hands of sinners. 46Rise, let
us be going. See, My betrayer is at hand."

Betrayal and Arrest in Gethsemane

47And while He was still speaking, behold, Judas, one of the twelve, with a great
multitude with swords and clubs, came
from the chief priests and elders of the
people.

48Now His betrayer had given them a
sign, saying, "Whomever I kiss, He is the
One; seize Him." 49Immediately he went
up to Jesus and said, "Greetings, Rabbi!"
and kissed Him.

50But Jesus said to him, "Friend, why
have you come?"

Then they came and laid hands on Jesus and took Him. 51And suddenly, one
of those *who were* with Jesus stretched
out *his* hand and drew his sword, struck
the servant of the high priest, and cut off
his ear.

52But Jesus said to him, "Put your
sword in its place, for all who take the
sword will perish[a] by the sword. 53Or do
you think that I cannot now pray to My
Father, and He will provide Me with
more than twelve legions of angels? 54How
then could the Scriptures be fulfilled,
that it must happen thus?"

55In that hour Jesus said to the multitudes, "Have you come out, as against a
robber, with swords and clubs to take
Me? I sat daily with you, teaching in the
temple, and you did not seize Me. 56But
all this was done that the Scriptures of
the prophets might be fulfilled."

Then all the disciples forsook Him
and fled.

Jesus Faces the Sanhedrin

57And those who had laid hold of Jesus led *Him* away to Caiaphas the high
priest, where the scribes and the elders
were assembled. 58But Peter followed Him
at a distance to the high priest's courtyard. And he went in and sat with the
servants to see the end.

59Now the chief priests, the elders,[a]
and all the council sought false testimony
against Jesus to put Him to death, 60but

26:52 [a]M-Text reads *die.* 26:59 [a]NU-Text omits *the elders.*

26:41 Watch and pray. "Real praying is a costly exercise but it pays far more than it costs. It is not easy work but it is most profitable of all work. We can accomplish more by time and strength put into prayer than we can by putting the same amount of time and strength into anything else." *R. A. Torrey*

"Do you ever get that wistful feeling that there are other things more effective, even more desirable, than prayer? This explains why far too many of us are busy in attempting great things for God, rather than expecting great things from God in a humble attitude of prayer." *Robert Foster*

26:54 Archaeology confirms the Bible. The Scriptures make more than forty references to the great Hittite Empire. However, until one hundred years ago there was no archaeological evidence to substantiate the biblical claim that the Hittites existed. Skeptics claimed that the Bible was in error, until their mouths were suddenly stopped. In 1906, Hugo Winckler uncovered a huge library of 10,000 clay tablets, which completely documented the lost Hittite Empire. We now know that at its height, the Hittite civilization rivaled Egypt and Assyria in its glory and power. See Luke 1:27 comment.

"It may be stated categorically that no archaeological discovery has ever controverted a biblical reference. Scores of archaeological findings have been made which confirm in clear outline or exact detail historical statements in the Bible. And, by the same token, proper evaluation of biblical descriptions has often led to amazing discoveries." *Dr. Nelson Glueck*

"Archaeology has confirmed countless passages which have been rejected by critics as unhistorical or contradictory to known facts... Yet archaeological discoveries have shown that these critical charges... are wrong and that the Bible is trustworthy in the very statements which have been set aside as untrustworthy ...We do not know of any cases where the Bible has been proved wrong." *Dr. Joseph P. Free*

found none. Even though many false witnesses came forward, they found none.[a]
But at last two false witnesses[b] came forward [61]and said, "This *fellow* said, 'I am
able to destroy the temple of God and to
build it in three days.' "
[62]And the high priest arose and said to
Him, "Do You answer nothing? What *is it*
these men testify against You?" [63]But Jesus kept silent. And the high priest answered and said to Him, "I put You under
oath by the living God: Tell us if You are
the Christ, the Son of God!"
[64]Jesus said to him, "*It is as* you said.
Nevertheless, I say to you, hereafter you
will see the Son of Man sitting at the right
hand of the Power, and coming on the
clouds of heaven."
[65]Then the high priest tore his clothes,
saying, "He has spoken blasphemy! What
further need do we have of witnesses?
Look, now you have heard His blasphemy! [66]What do you think?"
They answered and said, "He is deserving of death."
[67]Then they spat in His face and beat
Him; and others struck *Him* with the
palms of their hands, [68]saying, "Prophesy
to us, Christ! Who is the one who struck
You?"

Peter Denies Jesus, and Weeps Bitterly

[69]Now Peter sat outside in the courtyard. And a servant girl came to him, saying, "You also were with Jesus of Galilee."
[70]But he denied it before *them* all, saying, "I do not know what you are saying."
[71]And when he had gone out to the
gateway, another *girl* saw him and said to
those *who were* there, "This *fellow* also was
with Jesus of Nazareth."
[72]But again he denied with an oath, "I
do not know the Man!"
[73]And a little later those who stood by
came up and said to Peter, "Surely you
also are *one* of them, for your speech betrays you."
[74]Then he began to curse and swear,
saying, "I do not know the Man!"
Immediately a rooster crowed. [75]And
Peter remembered the word of Jesus who
had said to him, "Before the rooster crows,
you will deny Me three times." So he went
out and wept bitterly.

Jesus Handed Over to Pontius Pilate

27 When morning came, all the chief
priests and elders of the people
plotted against Jesus to put Him to death.
[2]And when they had bound Him, they
led Him away and delivered Him to Pontius[a] Pilate the governor.

Judas Hangs Himself

[3]Then Judas, His betrayer, seeing that
He had been condemned, was remorseful
and brought back the thirty pieces of silver to the chief priests and elders, [4]say-
ing, "I have sinned by betraying innocent
blood."
And they said, "What *is that* to us? You
see *to it!*"
[5]Then he threw down the pieces of silver in the temple and departed, and went
and hanged himself.
[6]But the chief priests took the silver

26:60 [a]NU-Text puts a comma after *but found none,* does not capitalize *Even,* and omits *they found none.* [b]NU-Text omits *false witnesses.* 27:2 [a]NU-Text omits *Pontius.*

26:60 Messianic prophecy fulfilled: "Do not deliver me to the will of my adversaries; for false witnesses have risen against me, and such as breathe out violence" (Psa. 27:12). See Matt. 26:62,63 comment.

26:62,63 Messianic prophecy fulfilled: "He was oppressed and He was afflicted, yet He opened not His mouth; He was led as a lamb to the slaughter, and as a sheep before its shearers is silent, so He opened not his mouth" (Isa. 53:7). See Matt. 27:39–44 comment.

26:64 Second coming of Jesus: See Mark 8:38.

27:5 "I have had few difficulties, many friends, great success; I have gone from wife to wife, and from house to house, visited great countries of the world, but I am fed up with inventing devices to fill up 24 hours of the day." *Ralph Barton* (cartoonist), in his suicide note

pieces and said, "It is not lawful to put them into the treasury, because they are the price of blood." 7And they consulted together and bought with them the potter's field, to bury strangers in. 8Therefore that field has been called the Field of Blood to this day.

9Then was fulfilled what was spoken by Jeremiah the prophet, saying, *"And they took the thirty pieces of silver, the value of Him who was priced,* whom they of the children of Israel priced, 10*and gave them for the potter's field, as the LORD directed me."*[a]

Jesus Faces Pilate

11Now Jesus stood before the governor. And the governor asked Him, saying, "Are You the King of the Jews?"

Jesus said to him, *"It is as you say."* 12And while He was being accused by the chief priests and elders, He answered nothing.

13Then Pilate said to Him, "Do You not hear how many things they testify against You?" 14But He answered him not one word, so that the governor marveled greatly.

Taking the Place of Barabbas

15Now at the feast the governor was accustomed to releasing to the multitude one prisoner whom they wished. 16And at that time they had a notorious prisoner called Barabbas.[a] 17Therefore, when they had gathered together, Pilate said to them, "Whom do you want me to release to you? Barabbas, or Jesus who is called Christ?" 18For he knew that they had handed Him over because of envy.

19While he was sitting on the judgment seat, his wife sent to him, saying, "Have nothing to do with that just Man, for I have suffered many things today in a dream because of Him."

20But the chief priests and elders persuaded the multitudes that they should ask for Barabbas and destroy Jesus. 21The governor answered and said to them, "Which of the two do you want me to release to you?"

They said, "Barabbas!"

22Pilate said to them, "What then shall I do with Jesus who is called Christ?"

They all said to him, "Let Him be crucified!"

23Then the governor said, "Why, what evil has He done?"

We have grasped the mystery of the atom and rejected the Sermon on the Mount... The world has achieved brilliance without conscience. Ours is a world of nuclear giants and ethical infants.

GENERAL OMAR BRADLEY

But they cried out all the more, saying, "Let Him be crucified!"

24When Pilate saw that he could not prevail at all, but rather *that* a tumult was rising, he took water and washed *his* hands before the multitude, saying, "I am innocent of the blood of this just Person.[a] You see *to it.*"

25And all the people answered and said, "His blood *be* on us and on our children."

26Then he released Barabbas to them; and when he had scourged Jesus, he delivered *Him* to be crucified.

The Soldiers Mock Jesus

27Then the soldiers of the governor took Jesus into the Praetorium and gathered the whole garrison around Him.

27:10 [a]Jeremiah 32:6–9 **27:16** [a]NU-Text reads *Jesus Barabbas.* **27:24** [a]NU-Text omits *just.*

27:9,10 Notice that Scripture doesn't say "that which was *written in* Jeremiah." This was "spoken" by Jeremiah the prophet, but it was not recorded in the Book of Jeremiah. A similar prophecy was given in Zech. 11:12,13.

[28]And they stripped Him and put a scarlet robe on Him. [29]When they had twisted a crown of thorns, they put *it* on His head, and a reed in His right hand. And they bowed the knee before Him and mocked Him, saying, "Hail, King of the Jews!" [30]Then they spat on Him, and took the reed and struck Him on the head. [31]And when they had mocked Him, they took the robe off Him, put His *own* clothes on Him, and led Him away to be crucified.

The King on a Cross

[32]Now as they came out, they found a man of Cyrene, Simon by name. Him they compelled to bear His cross. [33]And when they had come to a place called Golgotha, that is to say, Place of a Skull, [34]they gave Him sour[a] wine mingled with gall to drink. But when He had tasted *it,* He would not drink.

[35]Then they crucified Him, and divided His garments, casting lots,[a] that it might be fulfilled which was spoken by the prophet:

"They divided My garments among
them,
And for My clothing they cast lots."[b]

[36]Sitting down, they kept watch over Him there. [37]And they put up over His head the accusation written against Him:

THIS IS JESUS
THE KING OF THE JEWS.

[38]Then two robbers were crucified with Him, one on the right and another on the left.

[39]And those who passed by blasphemed Him, wagging their heads [40]and saying, "You who destroy the temple and build *it* in three days, save Yourself! If You are the Son of God, come down from the cross."

[41]Likewise the chief priests also, mocking with the scribes and elders,[a] said, [42]"He saved others; Himself He cannot save. If He is the King of Israel,[a] let Him now come down from the cross, and we will believe Him.[b] [43]He trusted in God; let Him deliver Him now if He will have Him; for He said, 'I am the Son of God.' "

[44]Even the robbers who were crucified with Him reviled Him with the same thing.

Jesus Dies on the Cross

[45]Now from the sixth hour until the ninth hour there was darkness over all the land. [46]And about the ninth hour Jesus cried out with a loud voice, saying, "Eli, Eli, lama sabachthani?" that is, *"My God, My God, why have You forsaken Me?"*[a]

[47]Some of those who stood there, when they heard *that,* said, "This Man is calling for Elijah!" [48]Immediately one of them ran and took a sponge, filled *it* with sour wine and put *it* on a reed, and offered it to Him to drink.

[49]The rest said, "Let Him alone; let us see if Elijah will come to save Him."

27:34 [a]NU-Text omits *sour.* 27:35 [a]NU-Text and M-Text omit the rest of this verse. [b]Psalm 22:18 27:41 [a]M-Text reads *with the scribes, the Pharisees, and the elders.* 27:42 [a]NU-Text reads *He is the King of Israel!* [b]NU-Text and M-Text read *we will believe in Him.* 27:46 [a]Psalm 22:1

27:26–29 Paintings of a "suffering Savior" on the cross can never do justice to the agonies He suffered for us. Isaiah 52:14 tells us "His visage was marred more than any man, and His form more than the sons of men."

27:39–44 Messianic prophecy fulfilled: "But I am a worm, and no man; a reproach of men, and despised by the people. All those who see Me ridicule Me; they shoot out the lip, they shake the head, saying, 'He trusted in the LORD, let Him rescue Him; let Him deliver Him, since He delights in Him!'" (Psa. 22:6–8). See Mark 14:10 comment.

27:46 "The pain was absolutely unbearable. In fact, it was literally beyond words to describe; they had to invent a new word: *excruciating*. Literally, excruciating means 'out of the cross.'" *Alexander Metherell, M.D., Ph.D.*

50And Jesus cried out again with a
loud voice, and yielded up His spirit.
51Then, behold, the veil of the temple
was torn in two from top to bottom; and
the earth quaked, and the rocks were
split, 52and the graves were opened; and
many bodies of the saints who had fallen
asleep were raised; 53and coming out of
the graves after His resurrection, they
went into the holy city and appeared to
many.

> She is a traitor to the Master who sent her if she is so beguiled by the beauties of taste and art as to forget that to 'preach Christ...and Him crucified' is the only object for which she exists among the sons of men. The business of the Church is salvation of souls.
>
> **CHARLES SPURGEON**

54So when the centurion and those
with him, who were guarding Jesus, saw
the earthquake and the things that had
happened, they feared greatly, saying,
"Truly this was the Son of God!"
55And many women who followed Jesus from Galilee, ministering to Him, were
there looking on from afar, 56among
whom were Mary Magdalene, Mary the
mother of James and Joses,[a] and the
mother of Zebedee's sons.

Jesus Buried in Joseph's Tomb

57Now when evening had come, there
came a rich man from Arimathea, named
Joseph, who himself had also become a
disciple of Jesus. 58This man went to Pilate and asked for the body of Jesus. Then
Pilate commanded the body to be given
to him. 59When Joseph had taken the
body, he wrapped it in a clean linen cloth,
60and laid it in his new tomb which he
had hewn out of the rock; and he rolled
a large stone against the door of the
tomb, and departed. 61And Mary Magdalene was there, and the other Mary, sitting opposite the tomb.

Pilate Sets a Guard

62On the next day, which followed the
Day of Preparation, the chief priests and
Pharisees gathered together to Pilate,
63saying, "Sir, we remember, while He
was still alive, how that deceiver said, 'After three days I will rise.' 64Therefore
command that the tomb be made secure
until the third day, lest His disciples come
by night[a] and steal Him *away,* and say to
the people, 'He has risen from the dead.'
So the last deception will be worse than
the first."
65Pilate said to them, "You have a
guard; go your way, make *it* as secure as
you know how." 66So they went and made
the tomb secure, sealing the stone and
setting the guard.

He Is Risen

28 Now after the Sabbath, as the first
day of the week began to dawn,
Mary Magdalene and the other Mary
came to see the tomb. 2And behold, there
was a great earthquake; for an angel of
the Lord descended from heaven, and
came and rolled back the stone from the
door,[a] and sat on it. 3His countenance
was like lightning, and his clothing as
white as snow. 4And the guards shook for
fear of him, and became like dead *men.*
5But the angel answered and said to
the women, "Do not be afraid, for I know
that you seek Jesus who was crucified.
6He is not here; for He is risen, as He said.
Come, see the place where the Lord lay.
7And go quickly and tell His disciples
that He is risen from the dead, and indeed He is going before you into Galilee;
there you will see Him. Behold, I have told
you."
8So they went out quickly from the
tomb with fear and great joy, and ran to
bring His disciples word.

The Women Worship the Risen Lord

9And as they went to tell His disci-

27:56 [a]NU-Text reads *Joseph.* 27:64 [a]NU-Text omits *by night.* 28:2 [a]NU-Text omits *from the door.*

QUESTIONS & OBJECTIONS

28:9

"There are contradictions in the resurrection accounts. Did Christ appear first to the women or to His disciples?"

Both Matthew and Mark list women as the first to see the resurrected Christ. Mark says, "He appeared first to Mary Magdalene" (16:9). But Paul lists Peter (Cephas) as the first one to see Christ after His resurrection (1 Cor. 15:5).

Jesus appeared first to Mary Magdalene, then to the other women, and then to Peter. Paul was not giving a complete list, but only the important one for his purpose. Since only men's testimony was considered legal or official in the first century, it is understandable that the apostle would not list the women as witnesses in his defense of the resurrection here.

The order of the appearances of Christ is as follows:

CHRIST'S RESURRECTION APPEARANCES

APPEARED TO:	REFERENCES:
1. Mary	John 20:10–18
2. Mary and women	Matt. 28:1–10
3. Peter	1 Cor. 15:5
4. Two disciples	Luke 24:13–35
5. Ten apostles	Luke 24:36–49; John 20:19–23
6. Eleven apostles	John 20:24–31
7. Seven apostles	John 21
8. All apostles	Matt. 28:16–20; Mark 16:14–18
9. 500 brethren	1 Cor. 15:6
10. James	1 Cor. 15:7
11. All apostles	Acts 1:4–8
12. Paul	Acts 9:1–9; 1 Cor. 15:8

ples,[a] behold, Jesus met them, saying, "Rejoice!" So they came and held Him by the feet and worshiped Him. [10]Then Jesus said to them, "Do not be afraid. Go *and* tell My brethren to go to Galilee, and there they will see Me."

The Soldiers Are Bribed

[11]Now while they were going, behold, some of the guard came into the city and reported to the chief priests all the things that had happened. [12]When they had assembled with the elders and consulted together, they gave a large sum of money to the soldiers, [13]saying, "Tell them, 'His disciples came at night and stole Him *away* while we slept.' [14]And if this comes to the governor's ears, we will appease him and make you secure." [15]So they took the money and did as they were instructed; and this saying is commonly reported among the Jews until this day.

The Great Commission

[16]Then the eleven disciples went away into Galilee, to the mountain which Jesus

28:9 [a]NU-Text omits the first clause of this verse.

28:9 If Jesus was not God, He would have been transgressing the Law of God by receiving their worship.

POINTS FOR OPEN-AIR PREACHING

28:19,20

Make the Bullet Hit the Target

It is obvious from Scripture that God requires us not only to preach to sinners, but also to teach them. The servant of the Lord must be "able to teach, patient, in humility correcting" those who oppose them (2 Tim. 2:24,25). For a long while I thought I was to leap among sinners, scatter the seed, then leave. But our responsibility goes further. We are to bring the sinner to a point of understanding his need before God. Psalm 25:8 says, "Good and upright is the LORD; therefore He teaches sinners in the way." Psalm 51:13 adds, "Then I will teach transgressors Your ways, and sinners shall be converted to You." The Great Commission is to "make disciples of all the nations...teaching them to observe all things" (Matt. 28:19,20). The disciples obeyed the command "daily in the temple, and in every house, they did not cease teaching and preaching Jesus as the Christ" (Acts 5:42).

The "good-soil" hearer is he who "hears...and *understands*" (Matt. 13:23). Philip the evangelist saw fit to ask his potential convert, the Ethiopian, "Do you understand what you are reading?" Some preachers are like a loud gun that misses the target. It may sound effective, but if the bullet misses the target, the exercise is in vain. He may be the largest-lunged, chandelier-swinging, pulpit-pounding preacher this side of the Book of Acts, but if the sinner leaves the meeting failing to understand his desperate need of God's forgiveness, then the preacher has failed. He has missed the target, which is the understanding of the sinner. This is why the Law of God must be used in preaching. It is a "tutor" to bring "the knowledge of sin" (Gal. 3:24; Rom. 3:20). It teaches and instructs. A sinner will come to "know His will, and approve the things that are excellent," if he is "instructed out of the Law" (Rom. 2:18). See Acts 20:21 comment.

had appointed for them. [17]When they
saw Him, they worshiped Him; but some
doubted.
[18]And Jesus came and spoke to them,
saying, "All authority has been given to
Me in heaven and on earth. [19]Go therefore[a] and make disciples of all the nations, baptizing them in the name of the
Father and of the Son and of the Holy
Spirit, [20]teaching them to observe all
things that I have commanded you; and
lo, I am with you always, *even* to the end
of the age." Amen.[a]

28:19 [a]M-Text omits *therefore*. 28:20 [a]NU-Text omits *Amen*.

28:19 "We cannot pick and choose which commands of our Lord we will follow. Jesus Christ's last command to the Christian community was, 'You are to go into all the world and preach the Good News to everyone, everywhere' (Mark 16:15, TLB). This command, which the Church calls the Great Commission, was not intended merely for the eleven remaining disciples, or just for the apostles or for those in present times who may have the gift of evangelism. This command is the duty of every man and woman who confesses Christ as Lord." *Bill Bright*

"Men are mirrors, or 'carriers' of Christ to other men. Usually it is those who know Him who bring Him to others. That's why the Church, the whole body of Christians showing Him to one another, is so important. It is easy to think that the Church has a lot of different objects—education, building, missions, holding services...The Church exists for nothing else but to draw men into Christ, to make them little Christs. If they are not doing that, all the cathedrals, clergy, missions, sermons, even the Bible itself, are simply a waste of time. God became Man for no other purpose. It is even doubtful, you know, whether the whole universe was created for any other purpose." *C. S. Lewis*

"Go therefore and make disciples of all the nations..."

MATT. 28:19

The Great Commission

"Jesus came and spoke to them, saying, 'All authority has been given to Me in heaven and on earth. Go therefore and make disciples of all the nations, baptizing them in the name of the Father and of the Son and of the Holy Spirit, teaching them to observe all things that I have commanded you; and lo, I am with you always, even to the end of the age.'" *(Matt. 28:18–20)*

"Then He said to them, 'Follow Me, and I will make you fishers of men.'" *(Matt. 4:19)*

"Then He said to them, 'Thus it is written, and thus it was necessary for the Christ to suffer and to rise from the dead the third day, and that repentance and remission of sins should be preached in His name to all nations, beginning at Jerusalem.'" *(Luke 24:46,47)*

"And He said to them, '...But you shall receive power when the Holy Spirit has come upon you; and you shall be witnesses to Me in Jerusalem, and in all Judea and Samaria, and to the end of the earth.'" *(Acts 1:8)*

And He said to them, 'Go into all the world and preach the gospel to every creature.'" *(Mark 16:15)*

"So Jesus said to them again, '...As the Father has sent Me, I also send you.'" *(John 20:21)*

"Then He said to His disciples, 'The harvest truly is plentiful, but the laborers are few. Therefore pray the Lord of the harvest to send out laborers into His harvest.'" *(Matt. 9:37,38)*

"But why do you call Me 'Lord, Lord,' and not do the things which I say?" *(Luke 6:46)*

(See John 4:7 comment on how to effectively share your faith.)

Mark

John the Baptist Prepares the Way

1 The beginning of the gospel of Jesus
Christ, the Son of God. 2As it is written in the Prophets:[a]

"Behold, I send My messenger before
Your face,
Who will prepare Your way before
You."[b]
3 *"The voice of one crying in the*
wilderness:
'Prepare the way of the LORD;
Make His paths straight.' "[a]

4John came baptizing in the wilderness and preaching a baptism of repentance for the remission of sins. 5Then all
the land of Judea, and those from Jerusalem, went out to him and were all baptized by him in the Jordan River, confessing their sins.

6Now John was clothed with camel's
hair and with a leather belt around his
waist, and he ate locusts and wild honey.
7And he preached, saying, "There comes
One after me who is mightier than I,
whose sandal strap I am not worthy to
stoop down and loose. 8I indeed baptized
you with water, but He will baptize you
with the Holy Spirit."

John Baptizes Jesus

9It came to pass in those days *that* Jesus came from Nazareth of Galilee, and
was baptized by John in the Jordan.
10And immediately, coming up from[a] the
water, He saw the heavens parting and
the Spirit descending upon Him like a
dove. 11Then a voice came from heaven,
"You are My beloved Son, in whom I am
well pleased."

Satan Tempts Jesus

12Immediately the Spirit drove Him
into the wilderness. 13And He was there
in the wilderness forty days, tempted by
Satan, and was with the wild beasts; and
the angels ministered to Him.

Jesus Begins His Galilean Ministry

14Now after John was put in prison,
Jesus came to Galilee, preaching the gos-
pel of the kingdom[a] of God, 15and saying,
"The time is fulfilled, and the kingdom of
God is at hand. Repent, and believe in
the gospel."

Four Fishermen Called as Disciples

16And as He walked by the Sea of Gali-

THE FUNCTION OF THE LAW

1:3 Commenting on the Law's capacity to bring the knowledge of sin, Bible commentator *Matthew Henry* said, "Of this excellent use is the Law: it converts the soul, opens the eyes, prepares the way of the Lord in the desert, rends the rocks, levels the mountains, makes a people prepared for the Lord."

1:2 [a]NU-Text reads *Isaiah the prophet.* [b]Malachi 3:1 1:3 [a]Isaiah 40:3 1:10 [a]NU-Text reads *out of.* 1:14 [a]NU-Text omits *of the kingdom.*

QUESTIONS & OBJECTIONS

1:4,5

"Is water baptism essential to salvation?"

While we should preach that all men are commanded to repent and be baptized (Acts 2:38), adding any other requirement to salvation by grace becomes "works" in disguise. Even though numerous Scriptures speak of the importance of water baptism, adding *anything* to the work of the cross demeans the sacrifice of the Savior. It implies that His finished work wasn't enough. But the Bible makes clear that we are saved by grace, and grace alone (Eph. 2:8,9). Baptism is simply a step of obedience to the Lord following our repentance and confession of sin. Our obedience—water baptism, prayer, good works, fellowship, witnessing, etc.—issues from our faith in Christ. Salvation is not based on what we do, but on Who we have: "He who has the Son has life" (1 John 5:12). See also Acts 2:38 comment.

lee, He saw Simon and Andrew his
brother casting a net into the sea; for they
were fishermen. 17Then Jesus said to them,
"Follow Me, and I will make you become
fishers of men." 18They immediately left
their nets and followed Him.
19When He had gone a little farther
from there, He saw James the *son* of
Zebedee, and John his brother, who also
were in the boat mending their nets. 20And
immediately He called them, and they
left their father Zebedee in the boat with
the hired servants, and went after Him.

Jesus Casts Out an Unclean Spirit

21Then they went into Capernaum,
and immediately on the Sabbath He entered the synagogue and taught. 22And
they were astonished at His teaching, for
He taught them as one having authority,
and not as the scribes.
23Now there was a man in their synagogue with an unclean spirit. And he
cried out, 24saying, "Let *us* alone! What
have we to do with You, Jesus of Nazareth? Did You come to destroy us? I know
who You are—the Holy One of God!"
25But Jesus rebuked him, saying, "Be
quiet, and come out of him!" 26And when
the unclean spirit had convulsed him and
cried out with a loud voice, he came out
of him. 27Then they were all amazed, so
that they questioned among themselves,
saying, "What is this? What new doctrine
is this? For with authority[a] He commands
even the unclean spirits, and they obey
Him." 28And immediately His fame
spread throughout all the region around
Galilee.

Peter's Mother-in-Law Healed

29Now as soon as they had come out
of the synagogue, they entered the house
of Simon and Andrew, with James and
John. 30But Simon's wife's mother lay sick
with a fever, and they told Him about her
at once. 31So He came and took her by
the hand and lifted her up, and immediately the fever left her. And she served
them.

Many Healed After Sabbath Sunset

32At evening, when the sun had set,
they brought to Him all who were sick
and those who were demon-possessed.

1:27 [a]NU-Text reads *What is this? A new doctrine with authority.*

1:15 Jesus preached repentance because His hearers knew the Law. Since He was sent to "the lost sheep of the house of Israel" (Matt. 15:24), His ministry was originally confined to Jews. The Scriptures often use the phrase "to the Jew first." Romans 3:1,2 tells us that Jews had the advantage of having the Law of God. They knew what sin was, and therefore understood their need for repentance. Those without a knowledge of sin (which only the Law can bring—see Rom. 7:7) need to hear the message of the Law before they are able (with God's help) to repent.

1:17 *The Parable of the Fishless Fishermen Fellowship*

They were surrounded by streams and lakes full of hungry fish. They met regularly to discuss the call to fish, the abundance of fish, and the thrill of catching fish. They got excited about fishing!

Someone suggested that they needed a philosophy of fishing, so they carefully defined and redefined fishing, and the purpose of fishing. They developed fishing strategies and tactics. Then they realized that they had been going at it backwards. They had approached fishing from the point of view of the fisherman, and not from the point of view of the fish. How do fish view the world? How does the fisherman appear to the fish? What do fish eat, and when? These are all good things to know. So they began research studies and attended conferences on fishing. Some traveled to faraway places to study different kinds of fish with different habits. Some got doctorates in fishology. But no one had yet gone fishing.

So a committee was formed to send out fishermen. As prospective fishing places outnumbered fishermen, the committee needed to determine priorities. A priority list of fishing places was posted on bulletin boards in all of the fellowship halls. But still, no one was fishing. A survey was launched to find out why. Most did not answer the survey, but from those who did, it was discovered that some felt called to study fish, a few to furnish fishing equipment, and several to go around encouraging the fishermen. What with meetings, conferences, and seminars, they just simply didn't have time to fish.

Now, Jake was a newcomer to the Fisherman's Fellowship. After one stirring meeting of the fellowship, he went fishing and caught a large fish. At the next meeting, he told his story and was honored for his catch. He was told that he had a special "gift of fishing." He was then scheduled to speak at all the fellowship chapters and tell how he did it.

With all the speaking invitations and his election to the board of directors of the Fisherman's Fellowship, Jake no longer had time to go fishing. But soon he began to feel restless and empty. He longed to feel the tug on the line once again. So he canceled the speaking, he resigned from the board, and he said to a friend, "Let's go fishing." They did, just the two of them, and they caught fish.

The members of the Fisherman's Fellowship were many, the fish were plentiful, but the fishers were few! *Anonymous*

33And the whole city was gathered together at the door. 34Then He healed many
who were sick with various diseases, and
cast out many demons; and He did not
allow the demons to speak, because they
knew Him.

Preaching in Galilee

35Now in the morning, having risen a
long while before daylight, He went out
and departed to a solitary place; and
there He prayed. 36And Simon and those
who were with Him searched for Him.
37When they found Him, they said to
Him, "Everyone is looking for You."
38But He said to them, "Let us go into
the next towns, that I may preach there
also, because for this purpose I have come
forth."
39And He was preaching in their synagogues throughout all Galilee, and casting out demons.

Jesus Cleanses a Leper

40Now a leper came to Him, imploring
Him, kneeling down to Him and saying to
Him, "If You are willing, You can make
me clean."
41Then Jesus, moved with compassion, stretched out *His* hand and touched
him, and said to him, "I am willing; be
cleansed." 42As soon as He had spoken,

1:35 Prayer—the secret weapon: See Mark 6:46. There are some days in which we think we are too busy to take time for prayer. But the busier our schedules become, the more we need to ask God to order our day and invite Him to work through us to accomplish His will. "I have so much to do [today] that I should spend the first three hours in prayer." *Martin Luther*

"I have been driven many times upon my knees by the overwhelming conviction that I had nowhere else to go. My own wisdom, and that of all about me, seemed insufficient for that day." *Abraham Lincoln*

immediately the leprosy left him, and he
was cleansed. 43And He strictly warned
him and sent him away at once, 44and
said to him, "See that you say nothing to
anyone; but go your way, show yourself
to the priest, and offer for your cleansing
those things which Moses commanded,
as a testimony to them."

45However, he went out and began to
proclaim *it* freely, and to spread the matter, so that Jesus could no longer openly
enter the city, but was outside in deserted
places; and they came to Him from every
direction.

Jesus Forgives and Heals a Paralytic

2 And again He entered Capernaum
after *some* days, and it was heard that
He was in the house. 2Immediately[a] many
gathered together, so that there was no
longer room to receive *them,* not even
near the door. And He preached the
word to them. 3Then they came to Him,
bringing a paralytic who was carried by
four *men*. 4And when they could not
come near Him because of the crowd,
they uncovered the roof where He was.
So when they had broken through, they
let down the bed on which the paralytic
was lying.

5When Jesus saw their faith, He said
to the paralytic, "Son, your sins are forgiven you."

6And some of the scribes were sitting
there and reasoning in their hearts,
7"Why does this *Man* speak blasphemies
like this? Who can forgive sins but God
alone?"

8But immediately, when Jesus perceived in His spirit that they reasoned
thus within themselves, He said to them,
"Why do you reason about these things
in your hearts? 9Which is easier, to say to
the paralytic, '*Your* sins are forgiven you,'
or to say, 'Arise, take up your bed and
walk'? 10But that you may know that the
Son of Man has power on earth to forgive
sins"—He said to the paralytic, 11"I say to
you, arise, take up your bed, and go to
your house." 12Immediately he arose, took
up the bed, and went out in the presence
of them all, so that all were amazed and
glorified God, saying, "We never saw
anything like this!"

Matthew the Tax Collector

13Then He went out again by the sea;
and all the multitude came to Him, and
He taught them. 14As He passed by, He
saw Levi the *son* of Alphaeus sitting at the
tax office. And He said to him, "Follow
Me." So he arose and followed Him.

15Now it happened, as He was dining
in *Levi's* house, that many tax collectors
and sinners also sat together with Jesus
and His disciples; for there were many,
and they followed Him. 16And when the
scribes and[a] Pharisees saw Him eating
with the tax collectors and sinners, they
said to His disciples, "How *is it* that He
eats and drinks with tax collectors and
sinners?"

17When Jesus heard *it,* He said to
them, "Those who are well have no need
of a physician, but those who are sick. I
did not come to call *the* righteous, but
sinners, to repentance."[a]

2:2 [a]NU-Text omits *Immediately.* 2:16 [a]NU-Text reads *of the.* 2:17 [a]NU-Text omits *to repentance.*

2:2 "In my preaching of the Word, I took special notice of this one thing, namely, that the Lord did lead me to begin where His Word begins with sinners; that is, to condemn all flesh, and to open and allege that the curse of God, by the Law, doth belong to and lay hold on all men as they come into the world, because of sin." *John Bunyan*

2:17 "Christ's call is to save the lost, not the stiff-necked; He came not to call scoffers but sinners to repentance; not to build and furnish comfortable chapels, churches, and cathedrals at home in which to rock Christian professors to sleep by means of clever essays, stereotyped prayers, and artistic musical performances, but to capture men from the devil's clutches and the very jaws of hell. This can be accomplished only by a red-hot, unconventional, unfettered devotion, in the power of the Holy Spirit, to the Lord Jesus Christ." *C. T. Studd*

Jesus Is Questioned About Fasting

18The disciples of John and of the
Pharisees were fasting. Then they came
and said to Him, "Why do the disciples of
John and of the Pharisees fast, but Your
disciples do not fast?"
19And Jesus said to them, "Can the
friends of the bridegroom fast while the
bridegroom is with them? As long as they
have the bridegroom with them they cannot fast. 20But the days will come when
the bridegroom will be taken away from
them, and then they will fast in those
days. 21No one sews a piece of unshrunk
cloth on an old garment; or else the new
piece pulls away from the old, and the
tear is made worse. 22And no one puts
new wine into old wineskins; or else the
new wine bursts the wineskins, the wine
is spilled, and the wineskins are ruined.
But new wine must be put into new
wineskins."

Jesus Is Lord of the Sabbath

23Now it happened that He went
through the grainfields on the Sabbath;
and as they went His disciples began to
pluck the heads of grain. 24And the Pharisees said to Him, "Look, why do they do
what is not lawful on the Sabbath?"
25But He said to them, "Have you
never read what David did when he was
in need and hungry, he and those with
him: 26how he went into the house of
God *in the days* of Abiathar the high
priest, and ate the showbread, which is
not lawful to eat except for the priests,
and also gave some to those who were
with him?"
27And He said to them, "The Sabbath
was made for man, and not man for the
Sabbath. 28Therefore the Son of Man is
also Lord of the Sabbath."

Healing on the Sabbath

3 And He entered the synagogue again,
and a man was there who had a withered hand. 2So they watched Him closely, whether He would heal him on the
Sabbath, so that they might accuse Him.

"In every true searcher of Nature there is a kind of religious reverence, for he finds it impossible to imagine that he is the first to have thought out the exceedingly delicate threads that connect his perceptions."

Albert Einstein

3And He said to the man who had the
withered hand, "Step forward." 4Then
He said to them, "Is it lawful on the Sabbath to do good or to do evil, to save life
or to kill?" But they kept silent. 5And
when He had looked around at them
with anger, being grieved by the hardness of their hearts, He said to the man,
"Stretch out your hand." And he stretched
it out, and his hand was restored as
whole as the other.[a] 6Then the Pharisees
went out and immediately plotted with
the Herodians against Him, how they
might destroy Him.

A Great Multitude Follows Jesus

7But Jesus withdrew with His disciples
to the sea. And a great multitude from
Galilee followed Him, and from Judea
8and Jerusalem and Idumea and beyond
the Jordan; and those from Tyre and Sidon, a great multitude, when they heard
how many things He was doing, came to
Him. 9So He told His disciples that a

3:5 [a]NU-Text omits *as whole as the other.*

small boat should be kept ready for Him because of the multitude, lest they should crush Him. 10For He healed many, so that as many as had afflictions pressed about Him to touch Him. 11And the unclean spirits, whenever they saw Him, fell down before Him and cried out, saying, "You are the Son of God." 12But He sternly warned them that they should not make Him known.

The Twelve Apostles

13And He went up on the mountain and called to *Him* those He Himself wanted. And they came to Him. 14Then He appointed twelve,[a] that they might be with Him and that He might send them out to preach, 15and to have power to heal sicknesses and[a] to cast out demons: 16Simon,[a] to whom He gave the name Peter; 17James the *son* of Zebedee and John the brother of James, to whom He gave the name Boanerges, that is, "Sons of Thunder"; 18Andrew, Philip, Bartholomew, Matthew, Thomas, James the *son* of Alphaeus, Thaddaeus, Simon the Cananite; 19and Judas Iscariot, who also betrayed Him. And they went into a house.

A House Divided Cannot Stand

20Then the multitude came together again, so that they could not so much as eat bread. 21But when His own people heard *about this*, they went out to lay hold of Him, for they said, "He is out of His mind."

22And the scribes who came down from Jerusalem said, "He has Beelzebub," and, "By the ruler of the demons He casts out demons."

23So He called them to *Himself* and said to them in parables: "How can Satan cast out Satan? 24If a kingdom is divided against itself, that kingdom cannot stand. 25And if a house is divided against itself, that house cannot stand. 26And if Satan has risen up against himself, and is divided, he cannot stand, but has an end. 27No one can enter a strong man's house and plunder his goods, unless he first binds the strong man. And then he will plunder his house.

The Unpardonable Sin

28"Assuredly, I say to you, all sins will be forgiven the sons of men, and whatever blasphemies they may utter; 29but he who blasphemes against the Holy Spirit never has forgiveness, but is subject to eternal condemnation"— 30because they said, "He has an unclean spirit."

Jesus' Mother and Brothers Send for Him

31Then His brothers and His mother came, and standing outside they sent to Him, calling Him. 32And a multitude was sitting around Him; and they said to Him, "Look, Your mother and Your brothers[a]

3:14 [a]NU-Text adds *whom He also named apostles.* 3:15 [a]NU-Text omits *to heal sicknesses and.* 3:16 [a]NU-Text reads *and He appointed the twelve: Simon*.... 3:32 [a]NU-Text and M-Text add *and Your sisters.*

3:29 The unpardonable sin. It is often maintained that the "unpardonable sin" is when someone "rejects Jesus Christ as Lord and Savior." However, v. 30 defines exactly what the sin is. The scribes said that Jesus did His miracles by an "unclean spirit," attributing the work of the Holy Spirit to Satan's power. (In Matt. 12:28, Jesus clearly identifies who is doing the work by saying that He "cast out demons by the Spirit of God.") If sinners do not acknowledge the Holy Spirit's work in their lives as being from God, they cannot be saved and enter the kingdom of God.

It is only by the Holy Spirit that men are convicted of their sin and need for righteousness (John 16:8), and it is only by the Holy Spirit that anyone can discern spiritual truths and understand the salvation God offers in Christ (1 Cor. 2:12–14). Therefore, those who are "stiff-necked" and who "always resist the Holy Spirit" (Acts 7:51) will die in their sins. Because they refuse to acknowledge their sin, they refuse to repent and trust the Savior. For this reason, anyone who rejects the Holy Spirit's convicting influence and does not repent will not be forgiven, "either in this age or in the age to come" (Matt. 12:32).

3:31–35 Jesus here affords Mary with no more honor than any believer. See also Luke 8:20,21; 11:27,28.

are outside seeking You."
33But He answered them, saying, "Who
is My mother, or My brothers?" 34And He
looked around in a circle at those who sat
about Him, and said, "Here are My mother
and My brothers! 35For whoever does the
will of God is My brother and My sister
and mother."

The Parable of the Sower

4 And again He began to teach by the
sea. And a great multitude was gathered to Him, so that He got into a boat
and sat *in it* on the sea; and the whole
multitude was on the land facing the sea.
2Then He taught them many things by
parables, and said to them in His teaching:
3"Listen! Behold, a sower went out to
sow. 4And it happened, as he sowed, *that*
some *seed* fell by the wayside; and the
birds of the air[a] came and devoured it.
5Some fell on stony ground, where it did
not have much earth; and immediately it
sprang up because it had no depth of
earth. 6But when the sun was up it was
scorched, and because it had no root it
withered away. 7And some *seed* fell among
thorns; and the thorns grew up and choked
it, and it yielded no crop. 8But other *seed*
fell on good ground and yielded a crop
that sprang up, increased and produced:
some thirtyfold, some sixty, and some a
hundred."
9And He said to them,[a] "He who has
ears to hear, let him hear!"

The Purpose of Parables

10But when He was alone, those around
Him with the twelve asked Him about
the parable. 11And He said to them, "To
you it has been given to know the mystery of the kingdom of God; but to those
who are outside, all things come in parables, 12so that

'Seeing they may see and not perceive,
And hearing they may hear and not
understand;
Lest they should turn,
And their sins be forgiven them.'"[a]

> That is the reason we have so many 'mushroom' converts, because their stony ground is not plowed up; they have not got a conviction of the Law; they are stony-ground hearers.
>
> **GEORGE WHITEFIELD**

The Parable of the Sower Explained

13And He said to them, "Do you not
understand this parable? How then will
you understand all the parables? 14The
sower sows the word. 15And these are the
ones by the wayside where the word is
sown. When they hear, Satan comes immediately and takes away the word that
was sown in their hearts. 16These like-

4:4 [a]NU-Text and M-Text omit *of the air.* 4:9 [a]NU-Text and M-Text omit *to them.* 4:12 [a]Isaiah 6:9, 10

4:13 The key to the parables. The parable of the sower is the key to unlock the mysteries of all the other parables. If we understand this parable (that when the gospel is preached there are true and false conversions), then all the parables Jesus told will make sense: the foolish virgins (false) and the wise virgins (genuine), the good and bad fish, the wheat and tares, etc. See also John 1:13 and 3:16 comments.

4:14 Sowing the seed of the gospel. A student at Jacksonville University in Florida was given a tract. The student crumpled the pamphlet up and tossed it into a trash bin in his dorm. Later, his dorm mate picked it out of the trash, read it, and was soundly saved. He is now a pastor of a church in Florida.

"A Christian I met in a home group said his job was raking litter off the Avon River. It was dull, boring work and he often wondered what life was all about. One day he raked a soggy piece of paper off the water and decided it was interesting enough to keep, so he carefully placed it in his bag and took it home. That evening he dried the paper in front of a heater and carefully unfolded it, then he read it . . . it was a gospel tract. He became a Christian that evening." *Richard Gunther*

"Nothing surpasses a tract for sowing the seed of the Good News." *Billy Graham*

See the next page for ideas on where to distribute tracts. See also 1 Cor. 9:22 and Rev. 22:2 comments.

Where to Leave Tracts

- In library books
- In shopping carts
- In clothes pockets in stores
- In letters to loved ones
- With a generous tip
- On seats in restaurant lobbies
- With fast-food employees, cashiers, flight attendants, cab drivers, and gas station workers
- In restrooms
- At rest areas
- On ATM machines and bank counters
- In envelopes with bill payments
- In elevators
- On hotel dressers for the maid
- On ice machines
- On newspaper racks
- In waiting rooms of doctors' offices and hospitals
- On seats at airports, subways, and bus stations
- In plane seat pockets
- Inside magazines
- In cabs
- In laundromats

wise are the ones sown on stony ground
who, when they hear the word, immediately receive it with gladness; 17and they
have no root in themselves, and so endure only for a time. Afterward, when
tribulation or persecution arises for the
word's sake, immediately they stumble.
18Now these are the ones sown among
thorns; *they are* the ones who hear the
word, 19and the cares of this world, the
deceitfulness of riches, and the desires for
other things entering in choke the word,
and it becomes unfruitful. 20But these are
the ones sown on good ground, those
who hear the word, accept *it,* and bear
fruit: some thirtyfold, some sixty, and
some a hundred."

Light Under a Basket

21Also He said to them, "Is a lamp
brought to be put under a basket or under a bed? Is it not to be set on a lampstand? 22For there is nothing hidden
which will not be revealed, nor has anything been kept secret but that it should
come to light. 23If anyone has ears to
hear, let him hear."
24Then He said to them, "Take heed
what you hear. With the same measure
you use, it will be measured to you; and
to you who hear, more will be given.
25For whoever has, to him more will be
given; but whoever does not have, even
what he has will be taken away from him."

The Parable of the Growing Seed

26And He said, "The kingdom of God
is as if a man should scatter seed on the
ground, 27and should sleep by night and
rise by day, and the seed should sprout
and grow, he himself does not know how.
28For the earth yields crops by itself: first
the blade, then the head, after that the
full grain in the head. 29But when the
grain ripens, immediately he puts in the
sickle, because the harvest has come."

The Parable of the Mustard Seed

30Then He said, "To what shall we
liken the kingdom of God? Or with what
parable shall we picture it? 31*It is* like a
mustard seed which, when it is sown on
the ground, is smaller than all the seeds
on earth; 32but when it is sown, it grows
up and becomes greater than all herbs,
and shoots out large branches, so that the
birds of the air may nest under its shade."

Jesus' Use of Parables

33And with many such parables He
spoke the word to them as they were able
to hear *it.* 34But without a parable He did
not speak to them. And when they were
alone, He explained all things to His disciples.

4:31 Skeptics claim that this verse is an error, that the mustard seed is not the smallest seed on earth. But keep in mind that Jesus is not leading a botany class; He is explaining the kingdom of God using an analogy that would be understood by His audience. He is saying that of the seeds sown by the Jews in Israel, it is the smallest. His point is to show the great expanse of the kingdom of God from the smallest of beginnings.

Wind and Wave Obey Jesus

35 On the same day, when evening had come, He said to them, "Let us cross over to the other side." 36 Now when they had left the multitude, they took Him along in the boat as He was. And other little boats were also with Him. 37 And a great windstorm arose, and the waves beat into the boat, so that it was already filling. 38 But He was in the stern, asleep on a pillow. And they awoke Him and said to Him, "Teacher, do You not care that we are perishing?"

39 Then He arose and rebuked the wind, and said to the sea, "Peace, be still!" And the wind ceased and there was a great calm. 40 But He said to them, "Why are you so fearful? How *is it* that you have no faith?"[a] 41 And they feared exceedingly, and said to one another, "Who can this be, that even the wind and the sea obey Him!"

A Demon-Possessed Man Healed

5 Then they came to the other side of the sea, to the country of the Gadarenes.[a] 2 And when He had come out of the boat, immediately there met Him out of the tombs a man with an unclean spirit, 3 who had *his* dwelling among the tombs; and no one could bind him,[a] not even with chains, 4 because he had often been bound with shackles and chains. And the chains had been pulled apart by him, and the shackles broken in pieces; neither could anyone tame him. 5 And always, night and day, he was in the mountains and in the tombs, crying out and cutting himself with stones.

6 When he saw Jesus from afar, he ran and worshiped Him. 7 And he cried out with a loud voice and said, "What have I to do with You, Jesus, Son of the Most High God? I implore You by God that You do not torment me."

8 For He said to him, "Come out of the man, unclean spirit!" 9 Then He asked him, "What *is* your name?"

And he answered, saying, "My name *is* Legion; for we are many." 10 Also he begged Him earnestly that He would not send them out of the country.

11 Now a large herd of swine was feeding there near the mountains. 12 So all the demons begged Him, saying, "Send us to the swine, that we may enter them." 13 And at once Jesus[a] gave them permission. Then the unclean spirits went out and entered the swine (there were about two thousand); and the herd ran violently down the steep place into the sea, and drowned in the sea.

14 So those who fed the swine fled, and they told *it* in the city and in the country. And they went out to see what it was that had happened. 15 Then they came to Jesus, and saw the one *who had been* demon-possessed and had the legion, sitting and clothed and in his right mind. And they were afraid. 16 And those who saw it told them how it happened to him *who had been* demon-possessed, and about the swine. 17 Then they began to plead with Him to depart from their region.

18 And when He got into the boat, he who had been demon-possessed begged Him that he might be with Him. 19 However, Jesus did not permit him, but said to him, "Go home to your friends, and tell them what great things the Lord has done for you, and how He has had compassion on you." 20 And he departed and began to proclaim in Decapolis all that Jesus had done for him; and all marveled.

A Girl Restored to Life and a Woman Healed

21 Now when Jesus had crossed over

4:40 [a]NU-Text reads *Have you still no faith?* 5:1 [a]NU-Text reads *Gerasenes.* 5:3 [a]NU-Text adds *anymore.* 5:13 [a]NU-Text reads *And He gave.*

4:38 "Christians alone are in a position to rescue the perishing. We dare not settle down to try to live as if things were 'normal.' Nothing is normal while sin and lust and death roam the world, pouncing upon one and another till the whole population has been destroyed." *A. W. Tozer*

again by boat to the other side, a great
multitude gathered to Him; and He was
by the sea. 22And behold, one of the rulers
of the synagogue came, Jairus by name.
And when he saw Him, he fell at His feet
23and begged Him earnestly, saying, "My
little daughter lies at the point of death.
Come and lay Your hands on her, that she
may be healed, and she will live." 24So *Je-*
sus went with him, and a great multitude
followed Him and thronged Him.

25Now a certain woman had a flow of
blood for twelve years, 26and had suffered many things from many physicians.
She had spent all that she had and was no
better, but rather grew worse. 27When
she heard about Jesus, she came behind
Him in the crowd and touched His garment. 28For she said, "If only I may touch
His clothes, I shall be made well."

29Immediately the fountain of her
blood was dried up, and she felt in *her*
body that she was healed of the affliction.
30And Jesus, immediately knowing in
Himself that power had gone out of Him,
turned around in the crowd and said,
"Who touched My clothes?"

31But His disciples said to Him, "You
see the multitude thronging You, and
You say, 'Who touched Me?' "

32And He looked around to see her
who had done this thing. 33But the woman, fearing and trembling, knowing what
had happened to her, came and fell down
before Him and told Him the whole
truth. 34And He said to her, "Daughter,
your faith has made you well. Go in
peace, and be healed of your affliction."

35While He was still speaking, *some*
came from the ruler of the synagogue's
house who said, "Your daughter is dead.
Why trouble the Teacher any further?"

36As soon as Jesus heard the word that
was spoken, He said to the ruler of the
synagogue, "Do not be afraid; only believe." 37And He permitted no one to follow Him except Peter, James, and John
the brother of James. 38Then He came to
the house of the ruler of the synagogue,
and saw a tumult and those who wept
and wailed loudly. 39When He came in,
He said to them, "Why make this commotion and weep? The child is not dead,
but sleeping."

40And they ridiculed Him. But when
He had put them all outside, He took the
father and the mother of the child, and
those *who were* with Him, and entered
where the child was lying. 41Then He
took the child by the hand, and said to
her, "Talitha, cumi," which is translated,
"Little girl, I say to you, arise." 42Immedi-
ately the girl arose and walked, for she
was twelve years *of age.* And they were
overcome with great amazement. 43But
He commanded them strictly that no one
should know it, and said that *something*
should be given her to eat.

Jesus Rejected at Nazareth

6 Then He went out from there and
came to His own country, and His
disciples followed Him. 2And when the
Sabbath had come, He began to teach in
the synagogue. And many hearing *Him*
were astonished, saying, "Where *did* this
Man *get* these things? And what wisdom
is this which is given to Him, that such
mighty works are performed by His
hands! 3Is this not the carpenter, the Son

6:2 Enriching every sphere. "Socrates taught for 40 years, Plato for 50, Aristotle for 40, and Jesus for only 3. Yet the influence of Christ's 3-year ministry infinitely transcends the impact left by the combined 130 years of teaching from these men who were among the greatest philosophers of all antiquity. Jesus painted no pictures; yet, some of the finest paintings of Raphael, Michelangelo, and Leonardo da Vinci received their inspiration from Him.

"Jesus wrote no poetry; but Dante, Milton, and scores of the world's greatest poets were inspired by Him. Jesus composed no music; still Haydn, Handel, Beethoven, Bach, and Mendelssohn reached their highest perfection of melody in the hymns, symphonies, and oratories they composed in His praise. Every sphere of human greatness has been enriched by this humble Carpenter of Nazareth." *Henry G. Bosch*

of Mary, and brother of James, Joses,
Judas, and Simon? And are not His sisters here with us?" So they were offended
at Him.
4 But Jesus said to them, "A prophet is
not without honor except in his own
country, among his own relatives, and in
his own house." 5 Now He could do no
mighty work there, except that He laid
His hands on a few sick people and
healed *them.* 6 And He marveled because
of their unbelief. Then He went about the
villages in a circuit, teaching.

Sending Out the Twelve

7 And He called the twelve to *Himself,*
and began to send them out two *by* two,
and gave them power over unclean spirits. 8 He commanded them to take nothing for the journey except a staff—no
bag, no bread, no copper in *their* money
belts— 9 but to wear sandals, and not to
put on two tunics.
10 Also He said to them, "In whatever
place you enter a house, stay there till
you depart from that place. 11 And whoever[a] will not receive you nor hear you,
when you depart from there, shake off
the dust under your feet as a testimony
against them.[b] Assuredly, I say to you, it
will be more tolerable for Sodom and Gomorrah in the day of judgment than for
that city!"
12 So they went out and preached that
people should repent. 13 And they cast out
many demons, and anointed with oil many
who were sick, and healed *them.*

John the Baptist Beheaded

14 Now King Herod heard *of Him,* for
His name had become well known. And
he said, "John the Baptist is risen from
the dead, and therefore these powers are
at work in him."
15 Others said, "It is Elijah."
And others said, "It is the Prophet, or[a]
like one of the prophets."
16 But when Herod heard, he said,
"This is John, whom I beheaded; he has
been raised from the dead!" 17 For Herod
himself had sent and laid hold of John,
and bound him in prison for the sake of
Herodias, his brother Philip's wife; for he
had married her. 18 Because John had said
to Herod, "It is not lawful for you to have
your brother's wife."

> You and I must continue to drive at men's hearts till they are broken. Then we must keep on preaching Christ crucified until their hearts are bound up.
>
> **CHARLES SPURGEON**

19 Therefore Herodias held it against
him and wanted to kill him, but she
could not; 20 for Herod feared John,
knowing that he *was* a just and holy man,
and he protected him. And when he
heard him, he did many things, and
heard him gladly.
21 Then an opportune day came when
Herod on his birthday gave a feast for his
nobles, the high officers, and the chief
men of Galilee. 22 And when Herodias'
daughter herself came in and danced,
and pleased Herod and those who sat
with him, the king said to the girl, "Ask

6:11 [a]NU-Text reads *whatever place.* [b]NU-Text omits the rest of this verse. **6:15** [a]NU-Text and M-Text omit *or.*

6:3 Jesus' siblings. Jesus had four brothers and at least two sisters. Therefore Mary was no longer a virgin *after* she gave birth to Jesus. The Greek word used here is *adelphos*—brother (not half-brother). It is also unlikely that these were the cousins of Jesus or Jewish brethren. These children were spoken of as being with Mary, without a shadow of a hint that they were not her children. The word "mother" is mentioned at the same time (Mark 3:31; Luke 8:19; John 2:12; Acts 1:14). Likewise, Matt. 1:25 does not say that Mary remained a virgin for life, but that she had no physical union with her husband *until* Jesus was born.

"By a Carpenter mankind was made, and only by that Carpenter can mankind be remade." *Deriderius Erasmas*

me whatever you want, and I will give *it*
to you." 23 He also swore to her, "Whatever
you ask me, I will give you, up to half my
kingdom."

24 So she went out and said to her
mother, "What shall I ask?"

And she said, "The head of John the
Baptist!"

25 Immediately she came in with haste
to the king and asked, saying, "I want
you to give me at once the head of John
the Baptist on a platter."

26 And the king was exceedingly sorry;
yet, because of the oaths and because of
those who sat with him, he did not want
to refuse her. 27 Immediately the king sent
an executioner and commanded his head
to be brought. And he went and beheaded
him in prison, 28 brought his head on a
platter, and gave it to the girl; and the girl
gave it to her mother. 29 When his disciples heard *of it,* they came and took away
his corpse and laid it in a tomb.

Feeding the Five Thousand

30 Then the apostles gathered to Jesus
and told Him all things, both what they
had done and what they had taught.
31 And He said to them, "Come aside by
yourselves to a deserted place and rest a
while." For there were many coming and
going, and they did not even have time to
eat. 32 So they departed to a deserted place
in the boat by themselves.

33 But the multitudes[a] saw them departing, and many knew Him and ran
there on foot from all the cities. They arrived before them and came together to
Him. 34 And Jesus, when He came out,
saw a great multitude and was moved
with compassion for them, because they
were like sheep not having a shepherd.
So He began to teach them many things.
35 When the day was now far spent, His
disciples came to Him and said, "This is a
deserted place, and already the hour *is*
late. 36 Send them away, that they may go
into the surrounding country and villages
and buy themselves bread;[a] for they have
nothing to eat."

37 But He answered and said to them,
"You give them something to eat."

And they said to Him, "Shall we go
and buy two hundred denarii worth of
bread and give them *something* to eat?"

38 But He said to them, "How many
loaves do you have? Go and see."

And when they found out they said,
"Five, and two fish."

39 Then He commanded them to make
them all sit down in groups on the green
grass. 40 So they sat down in ranks, in
hundreds and in fifties. 41 And when He
had taken the five loaves and the two
fish, He looked up to heaven, blessed and
broke the loaves, and gave *them* to His
disciples to set before them; and the two
fish He divided among *them* all. 42 So they
all ate and were filled. 43 And they took
up twelve baskets full of fragments and of
the fish. 44 Now those who had eaten the
loaves were about[a] five thousand men.

Jesus Walks on the Sea

45 Immediately He made His disciples
get into the boat and go before Him to
the other side, to Bethsaida, while He
sent the multitude away. 46 And when He
had sent them away, He departed to the
mountain to pray. 47 Now when evening
came, the boat was in the middle of the

6:33 [a]NU-Text and M-Text read *they.* 6:36 [a]NU-Text reads *something to eat* and omits the rest of this verse. 6:44 [a]NU-Text and M-Text omit *about.*

6:23 The power of lust. Lust blinds a man to reason (v. 22), leading him to yield up to "half [his] kingdom." He will abandon his wife, his children, his home, and his reputation, and run off with another woman. Herod feared John the Baptist because he knew that John was a just and holy man. He even protected him and heard him gladly, yet because Herod had a sinful eye he further violated the Law of God and had John murdered. Herod feared man more than he feared God (v. 26).

In truth, lust doesn't want half of your kingdom, it wants your head on a plate. See James 1:15.

6:46 Prayer—the secret weapon: See Luke 5:16.

sea; and He *was* alone on the land. 48Then He saw them straining at rowing, for the wind was against them. Now about the fourth watch of the night He came to them, walking on the sea, and would have passed them by. 49And when they saw Him walking on the sea, they supposed it was a ghost, and cried out; 50for they all saw Him and were troubled. But immediately He talked with them and said to them, "Be of good cheer! It is I; do not be afraid." 51Then He went up into the boat to them, and the wind ceased. And they were greatly amazed in themselves beyond measure, and marveled. 52For they had not understood about the loaves, because their heart was hardened.

Many Touch Him and Are Made Well

53When they had crossed over, they came to the land of Gennesaret and anchored there. 54And when they came out of the boat, immediately the people recognized Him, 55ran through that whole surrounding region, and began to carry about on beds those who were sick to wherever they heard He was. 56Wherever He entered, into villages, cities, or the country, they laid the sick in the marketplaces, and begged Him that they might just touch the hem of His garment. And as many as touched Him were made well.

Defilement Comes from Within

7 Then the Pharisees and some of the scribes came together to Him, having come from Jerusalem. 2Now when[a] they saw some of His disciples eat bread with defiled, that is, with unwashed hands, they found fault. 3For the Pharisees and all the Jews do not eat unless they wash *their* hands in a special way, holding the tradition of the elders. 4*When they come* from the marketplace, they do not eat unless they wash. And there are many other things which they have received and hold, *like* the washing of cups, pitchers, copper vessels, and couches.

5Then the Pharisees and scribes asked Him, "Why do Your disciples not walk according to the tradition of the elders, but eat bread with unwashed hands?"

6He answered and said to them, "Well did Isaiah prophesy of you hypocrites, as it is written:

'This people honors Me with their lips,
But their heart is far from Me.
7*And in vain they worship Me,*
Teaching as doctrines the
commandments of men.'[a]

8For laying aside the commandment of God, you hold the tradition of men[a]—the washing of pitchers and cups, and many other such things you do."

9He said to them, "*All too* well you reject the commandment of God, that you may keep your tradition. 10For Moses said, *'Honor your father and your mother'*;[a] and, *'He who curses father or mother, let him be put to death.'*[b] 11But you say, 'If a man says to his father or mother, "Whatever profit you might have received from me *is* Corban"—' (that is, a gift *to God*), 12then you no longer let him do anything for his father or his mother, 13making the word of God of no effect through your tradition which you have handed down. And many such things you do."

14When He had called all the multitude to *Himself,* He said to them, "Hear Me, everyone, and understand: 15There is

7:2 [a]NU-Text omits *when* and *they found fault.* 7:7 [a]Isaiah 29:13 7:8 [a]NU-Text omits the rest of this verse. 7:10 [a]Exodus 20:12; Deuteronomy 5:16 [b]Exodus 21:17

7:5–13 The Bible says that the Messiah would magnify the Law and make it honorable (Isa. 42:21). Jesus did this many times, particularly in the Sermon on the Mount. The Pharisees had dishonored the Law by merely giving God lip service. They made the Commandment void through their tradition, teaching for doctrines the commandments of men. The Savior brought honor back to the Law by teaching that the Law was spiritual by nature, and that outward observance was not enough. God required truth in the inward parts (the thought-life, intent, and motives).

The Function of the Law

7:21 "Now, if you have your hearts broken up by the Law, you will find the heart is more deceitful than the devil. I can say this myself, I am very much afraid of mine, it is so bad. The heart is like a dark cellar, full of lizards, cockroaches, beetles, and all kinds of reptiles and insects, which in the dark we see not, but the Law takes down the shutters and lets in the light, and so we see the evil. Thus sin becoming apparent by the Law, it is written the Law makes the offense to abound." *Charles Spurgeon*

nothing that enters a man from outside
which can defile him; but the things which
come out of him, those are the things that
defile a man. 16If anyone has ears to hear,
let him hear!"[a]

17When He had entered a house away
from the crowd, His disciples asked Him
concerning the parable. 18So He said to
them, "Are you thus without understanding also? Do you not perceive that whatever enters a man from outside cannot
defile him, 19because it does not enter his
heart but his stomach, and is eliminated,
thus purifying all foods?"[a] 20And He said,
"What comes out of a man, that defiles a
man. 21For from within, out of the heart
of men, proceed evil thoughts, adulteries,
fornications, murders, 22thefts, covetousness, wickedness, deceit, lewdness, an evil
eye, blasphemy, pride, foolishness. 23All
these evil things come from within and
defile a man."

A Gentile Shows Her Faith

24From there He arose and went to the
region of Tyre and Sidon.[a] And He entered
a house and wanted no one to know *it,*
but He could not be hidden. 25For a
woman whose young daughter had an
unclean spirit heard about Him, and she
came and fell at His feet. 26The woman
was a Greek, a Syro-Phoenician by birth,
and she kept asking Him to cast the demon out of her daughter. 27But Jesus said
to her, "Let the children be filled first, for
it is not good to take the children's bread
and throw *it* to the little dogs."

28And she answered and said to Him,
"Yes, Lord, yet even the little dogs under
the table eat from the children's crumbs."

29Then He said to her, "For this saying
go your way; the demon has gone out of
your daughter."

30And when she had come to her
house, she found the demon gone out,
and her daughter lying on the bed.

Jesus Heals a Deaf-Mute

31Again, departing from the region of
Tyre and Sidon, He came through the
midst of the region of Decapolis to the
Sea of Galilee. 32Then they brought to
Him one who was deaf and had an impediment in his speech, and they begged
Him to put His hand on him. 33And He
took him aside from the multitude, and
put His fingers in his ears, and He spat
and touched his tongue. 34Then, looking
up to heaven, He sighed, and said to him,
"Ephphatha," that is, "Be opened."

35Immediately his ears were opened,
and the impediment of his tongue was
loosed, and he spoke plainly. 36Then He
commanded them that they should tell
no one; but the more He commanded

7:16 [a]NU-Text omits this verse. 7:19 [a]NU-Text ends quotation with *eliminated,* setting off the final clause as Mark's comment that Jesus has declared all foods clean. 7:24 [a]NU-Text omits *and Sidon.*

7:20–23 Leading sinners to Jesus: *Man's heart is sinful.* Jeremiah 17:9 affirms the condition of man's heart: "The heart is deceitful above all things, and desperately wicked; who can know it?" Verse 10 then warns us that God not only knows the secret things of the heart but will reward us accordingly: "I, the LORD, search the heart, I test the mind, even to give every man according to his ways, according to the fruit of his doings." See Mark 12:29–31 comment.

7:21,22 Notice that what defiles a man is directly referenced to the moral Law (the Ten Commandments): adulteries (Seventh), fornications (Seventh), murders (Sixth), thefts (Eighth), covetousness (Tenth), blasphemy (Third). Sin is transgression of the Law (1 John 3:4).

them, the more widely they proclaimed
it. 37And they were astonished beyond
measure, saying, "He has done all things
well. He makes both the deaf to hear and
the mute to speak."

Feeding the Four Thousand

8 In those days, the multitude being
very great and having nothing to eat,
Jesus called His disciples *to Him* and said
to them, 2"I have compassion on the multitude, because they have now continued
with Me three days and have nothing to
eat. 3And if I send them away hungry to
their own houses, they will faint on the
way; for some of them have come from
afar."

4Then His disciples answered Him,
"How can one satisfy these people with
bread here in the wilderness?"

5He asked them, "How many loaves
do you have?"

> As the fisherman longs to take the fish in his net, as the hunter pants to bear home his spoil, as the mother pines to clasp her lost child to her bosom, so do we faint for the salvation of souls.
>
> **CHARLES SPURGEON**

And they said, "Seven."

6So He commanded the multitude to
sit down on the ground. And He took the
seven loaves and gave thanks, broke *them*
and gave *them* to His disciples to set before
them; and they set *them* before the multitude. 7They also had a few small fish; and
having blessed them, He said to set them
also before *them.* 8So they ate and were
filled, and they took up seven large baskets of leftover fragments. 9Now those
who had eaten were about four thousand. And He sent them away, 10immedi-
ately got into the boat with His disciples,
and came to the region of Dalmanutha.

The Pharisees Seek a Sign

11Then the Pharisees came out and began to dispute with Him, seeking from
Him a sign from heaven, testing Him.
12But He sighed deeply in His spirit, and
said, "Why does this generation seek a
sign? Assuredly, I say to you, no sign shall
be given to this generation."

Beware of the Leaven of the Pharisees and Herod

13And He left them, and getting into
the boat again, departed to the other side.
14Now the disciples[a] had forgotten to
take bread, and they did not have more
than one loaf with them in the boat.
15Then He charged them, saying, "Take
heed, beware of the leaven of the Pharisees and the leaven of Herod."

16And they reasoned among themselves, saying, "*It is* because we have no
bread."

17But Jesus, being aware of *it,* said to
them, "Why do you reason because you
have no bread? Do you not yet perceive
nor understand? Is your heart still[a] hardened? 18Having eyes, do you not see? And
having ears, do you not hear? And do you
not remember? 19When I broke the five
loaves for the five thousand, how many
baskets full of fragments did you take
up?"

They said to Him, "Twelve."

20"Also, when I broke the seven for
the four thousand, how many large baskets full of fragments did you take up?"

And they said, "Seven."

21So He said to them, "How *is it* you
do not understand?"

A Blind Man Healed at Bethsaida

22Then He came to Bethsaida; and they
brought a blind man to Him, and begged
Him to touch him. 23So He took the blind
man by the hand and led him out of the
town. And when He had spit on his eyes
and put His hands on him, He asked him
if he saw anything.

24And he looked up and said, "I see
men like trees, walking."

8:14 [a]NU-Text and M-Text read *they.* 8:17 [a]NU-Text omits *still.*

[25]Then He put *His* hands on his eyes again and made him look up. And he was restored and saw everyone clearly. [26]Then He sent him away to his house, saying, "Neither go into the town, nor tell anyone in the town."[a]

Peter Confesses Jesus as the Christ

[27]Now Jesus and His disciples went out to the towns of Caesarea Philippi; and on the road He asked His disciples, saying to them, "Who do men say that I am?"

[28]So they answered, "John the Baptist; but some *say,* Elijah; and others, one of the prophets."

[29]He said to them, "But who do you say that I am?"

Peter answered and said to Him, "You are the Christ."

[30]Then He strictly warned them that they should tell no one about Him.

For the biblical way to confront sinners, see Psa. 41:4 comment.

Jesus Predicts His Death and Resurrection

[31]And He began to teach them that the Son of Man must suffer many things, and be rejected by the elders and chief priests and scribes, and be killed, and after three days rise again. [32]He spoke this word openly. Then Peter took Him aside and began to rebuke Him. [33]But when He had turned around and looked at His disciples, He rebuked Peter, saying, "Get behind Me, Satan! For you are not mindful of the things of God, but the things of men."

Take Up the Cross and Follow Him

[34]When He had called the people to *Himself,* with His disciples also, He said to them, "Whoever desires to come after Me, let him deny himself, and take up his cross, and follow Me. [35]For whoever desires to save his life will lose it, but whoever loses his life for My sake and the gospel's will save it. [36]For what will it profit a man if he gains the whole world, and loses his own soul? [37]Or what will a man give in exchange for his soul? [38]For whoever is ashamed of Me and My words in this adulterous and sinful generation, of him the Son of Man also will be ashamed when He comes in the glory of His Father with the holy angels."

Jesus Transfigured on the Mount

9 And He said to them, "Assuredly, I say to you that there are some standing here who will not taste death till they see the kingdom of God present with power."

[2]Now after six days Jesus took Peter, James, and John, and led them up on a high mountain apart by themselves; and He was transfigured before them. [3]His clothes became shining, exceedingly white, like snow, such as no launderer on earth can whiten them. [4]And Elijah appeared to them with Moses, and they were talking with Jesus. [5]Then Peter an-

8:26 [a]NU-Text reads *"Do not even go into the town."*

8:33 If you are going to do anything for the kingdom of God, be ready for unexpected discouragement. This may come through a Christian brother or sister—the place least expected. Satan spoke directly through Peter in an attempt to stop Jesus from doing the will of the Father. It was David's elder brother who tried to discourage him from slaying Goliath (see 1 Sam. 17:28).

8:38 Here is an effective way to unashamedly share your faith and show that you care about strangers: When you are eating in a restaurant, tell the waiter, "We're going to be asking the blessing for our food in a minute, and wanted to know if there's anything you'd like us to pray for?"

"I reckon him a Christian indeed who is not ashamed of the gospel or a shame to it." *Matthew Henry*

8:38 Second coming of Jesus: See Luke 12:40.

9:4 See Luke 9:30 comment.

swered and said to Jesus, "Rabbi, it is
good for us to be here; and let us make
three tabernacles: one for You, one for
Moses, and one for Elijah"— 6because he
did not know what to say, for they were
greatly afraid.
7And a cloud came and overshadowed
them; and a voice came out of the cloud,
saying, "This is My beloved Son. Hear
Him!" 8Suddenly, when they had looked
around, they saw no one anymore, but
only Jesus with themselves.
9Now as they came down from the
mountain, He commanded them that
they should tell no one the things they
had seen, till the Son of Man had risen
from the dead. 10So they kept this word
to themselves, questioning what the rising from the dead meant.
11And they asked Him, saying, "Why
do the scribes say that Elijah must come
first?"
12Then He answered and told them,
"Indeed, Elijah is coming first and restores all things. And how is it written
concerning the Son of Man, that He must
suffer many things and be treated with
contempt? 13But I say to you that Elijah
has also come, and they did to him whatever they wished, as it is written of him."

A Boy Is Healed

14And when He came to the disciples,
He saw a great multitude around them,
and scribes disputing with them. 15Im-
mediately, when they saw Him, all the
people were greatly amazed, and running
to *Him,* greeted Him. 16And He asked the
scribes, "What are you discussing with
them?"
17Then one of the crowd answered and
said, "Teacher, I brought You my son,
who has a mute spirit. 18And wherever it
seizes him, it throws him down; he foams
at the mouth, gnashes his teeth, and becomes rigid. So I spoke to Your disciples,
that they should cast it out, but they
could not."
19He answered him and said, "O faithless generation, how long shall I be with

"Most people are bothered by those passages of Scriptures they don't understand, but for me I have always noticed that the passages that bother me are those I do understand."

Mark Twain

you? How long shall I bear with you?
Bring him to Me." 20Then they brought
him to Him. And when he saw Him, immediately the spirit convulsed him, and
he fell on the ground and wallowed,
foaming at the mouth.
21So He asked his father, "How long
has this been happening to him?"
And he said, "From childhood. 22And
often he has thrown him both into the
fire and into the water to destroy him.
But if You can do anything, have compassion on us and help us."
23Jesus said to him, "If you can believe,[a] all things *are* possible to him who
believes."
24Immediately the father of the child
cried out and said with tears, "Lord, I believe; help my unbelief!"
25When Jesus saw that the people came
running together, He rebuked the unclean spirit, saying to it, "Deaf and dumb
spirit, I command you, come out of him
and enter him no more!" 26Then *the spirit*

9:23 [a]NU-Text reads *"If You can!' All things. . . ."*

QUESTIONS & OBJECTIONS

9:47 ***"Hell isn't a place. This life is hell."***

Skeptics who say this are trying to dismiss the reality of hell. They might like to think that life as we know it couldn't get any worse, but the sufferings in this life will be heaven compared to the suffering in the next life—for those who die in their sins. This life is the closest thing to hell that Christians will ever know, and the closest thing to heaven that sinners will ever know.

For a biblical description of hell, see Rev. 1:18 comment.

cried out, convulsed him greatly, and came out of him. And he became as one dead, so that many said, "He is dead." 27But Jesus took him by the hand and lifted him up, and he arose.

28And when He had come into the house, His disciples asked Him privately, "Why could we not cast it out?"

29So He said to them, "This kind can come out by nothing but prayer and fasting."[a]

Jesus Again Predicts His Death and Resurrection

30Then they departed from there and passed through Galilee, and He did not want anyone to know *it.* 31For He taught His disciples and said to them, "The Son of Man is being betrayed into the hands of men, and they will kill Him. And after He is killed, He will rise the third day." 32But they did not understand this saying, and were afraid to ask Him.

Who Is the Greatest?

33Then He came to Capernaum. And when He was in the house He asked them, "What was it you disputed among yourselves on the road?" 34But they kept silent, for on the road they had disputed among themselves who *would be the* greatest. 35And He sat down, called the twelve, and said to them, "If anyone desires to be first, he shall be last of all and servant of all." 36Then He took a little child and set him in the midst of them. And when He had taken him in His arms, He said to them, 37"Whoever receives one of these little children in My name receives Me; and whoever receives Me, receives not Me but Him who sent Me."

Jesus Forbids Sectarianism

38Now John answered Him, saying, "Teacher, we saw someone who does not follow us casting out demons in Your name, and we forbade him because he does not follow us."

39But Jesus said, "Do not forbid him, for no one who works a miracle in My name can soon afterward speak evil of Me. 40For he who is not against us is on our[a] side. 41For whoever gives you a cup of water to drink in My name, because you belong to Christ, assuredly, I say to you, he will by no means lose his reward.

Jesus Warns of Offenses

42"But whoever causes one of these little ones who believe in Me to stumble, it would be better for him if a millstone were hung around his neck, and he were thrown into the sea. 43If your hand

9:29 [a]NU-Text omits *and fasting.* 9:40 [a]M-Text reads *against you is on your side.*

9:34,35 "Not everybody could be famous, but everybody can be great because greatness is determined by service." *Martin Luther King, Jr.*

9:43–48 Hell: For verses warning of its reality, see Luke 16:23.

"It has been estimated that of the 40 parables Jesus told, more than half dealt with God's eternal judgment and hell... He doesn't want any man or woman uniquely made in His image to spend eternity in hell." *Greg Laurie*

causes you to sin, cut it off. It is better for
you to enter into life maimed, rather than
having two hands, to go to hell, into the
fire that shall never be quenched—
44where

'Their worm does not die
And the fire is not quenched.'[a]

45And if your foot causes you to sin, cut
it off. It is better for you to enter life lame,
rather than having two feet, to be cast
into hell, into the fire that shall never be
quenched— 46where

'Their worm does not die
And the fire is not quenched.'[a]

47And if your eye causes you to sin, pluck
it out. It is better for you to enter the
kingdom of God with one eye, rather
than having two eyes, to be cast into hell
fire— 48where

'Their worm does not die
And the fire is not quenched.'[a]

Tasteless Salt Is Worthless

49"For everyone will be seasoned with
fire,[a] and every sacrifice will be seasoned
with salt. 50Salt *is* good, but if the salt
loses its flavor, how will you season it?
Have salt in yourselves, and have peace
with one another."

Marriage and Divorce

10 Then He arose from there and
came to the region of Judea by the
other side of the Jordan. And multitudes
gathered to Him again, and as He was accustomed, He taught them again.
2The Pharisees came and asked Him,
"Is it lawful for a man to divorce *his* wife?"
testing Him.
3And He answered and said to them,
"What did Moses command you?"
4They said, "Moses permitted *a man* to
write a certificate of divorce, and to dismiss *her*."
5And Jesus answered and said to
them, "Because of the hardness of your
heart he wrote you this precept. 6But
from the beginning of the creation, God
'made them male and female.'[a] 7*'For this
reason a man shall leave his father and
mother and be joined to his wife,* 8*and the
two shall become one flesh'*;[a] so then they
are no longer two, but one flesh. 9There-
fore what God has joined together, let not
man separate."
10In the house His disciples also asked
Him again about the same *matter*. 11So He
said to them, "Whoever divorces his wife
and marries another commits adultery
against her. 12And if a woman divorces
her husband and marries another, she
commits adultery."

Jesus Blesses Little Children

13Then they brought little children to
Him, that He might touch them; but the
disciples rebuked those who brought *them*.
14But when Jesus saw *it*, He was greatly
displeased and said to them, "Let the lit-

9:44 [a]NU-Text omits this verse. 9:46 [a]NU-Text omits the last clause of verse 45 and all of verse 46. 9:48 [a]Isaiah 66:24 9:49 [a]NU-Text omits the rest of this verse. 10:6 [a]Genesis 1:27; 5:2 10:8 [a]Genesis 2:24

9:50 Salty Christians. "Salvation is a radical thing. It is a call to all that Christ has demanded us to do. Real Christianity will make a salty difference, in our family, in our waking up, in our work, in our relationships, in the way we spend our money, and in the way we spend our leisure time. Real Christianity is not casual. It is dynamic. It goes beyond mere intellectual assent to correct doctrine.

"Real Christians who want to know real Christianity, who are not content with games and masks and only images of the truth, must rise from our comfortable pews and leave our 'one-stop Christian service centers' and go out into the world and make a salty difference!" *Guy Rice Doud*

10:6–9 By quoting from both chapters 1 and 2 of Genesis, Jesus shows that these chapters are not contradictory, as some claim. Chapter 2 merely gives the details of chapter 1. A sports commentator is not in error when (after a game) he gives in-depth analysis and fails to repeat every detail in chronological order. He is merely reviewing the completed game by mentioning the highlights. See also Gen. 2:4 comment.

Questions & Objections

10:18 "I'm as good as any Christian!"

That is true. A Christian, by himself, isn't good. Jesus said that only God is good. The Bible tells us that, without Christ, man is corrupt and filthy; "there is none who does good, no, not one" (Psa. 14:3). In God's sight, even our "good deeds" are as filthy rags (Isa. 64:6). The only "goodness," or righteousness, that the believer has comes from Christ when we repent and trust in Him (2 Cor. 5:21; Phil. 3:9). See also Rom. 3:9 comment.

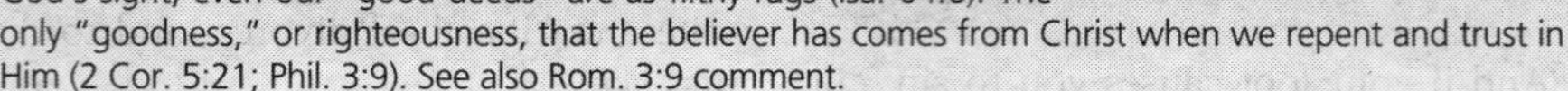

tle children come to Me, and do not forbid them; for of such is the kingdom of
God. 15Assuredly, I say to you, whoever
does not receive the kingdom of God as a
little child will by no means enter it."
16And He took them up in His arms, laid
His hands on them, and blessed them.

Using the Law in Evangelism

10:17 Here is a potential convert. He *runs* to Jesus (he is earnest), he kneels down (he is humble), he asks how he can inherit eternal life (what more could we want in a convert?). But notice what Jesus *didn't* do. He didn't speak of the love of God or a wonderful plan, or lead him in a "sinner's prayer."

Instead, He reproved the man's understanding of "good." This is because most unsaved people have an erroneous understanding of what "good" is. To see this, ask sinners if they think they are good people, and you will find that 99 percent say they are. Proverbs 20:6 tells us, "Most men will proclaim each his own goodness." Imitate Jesus. Reveal the righteousness of God by showing sinners His standard of "goodness"—the moral Law (see v. 19). It was the Law that exposed the man's hidden sin: he was a transgressor of the First Commandment. His money was his god, and one cannot serve God and money (see Matt. 6:24).

Notice it was "love" that motivated Jesus to speak this way to this young man (v. 21). Love sinners enough to do your best to make sure they don't have a false conversion. They must have the knowledge of sin before they come to the Savior (see Rom. 3:19,20; 7:7,13). See also Matt. 19:17–22 and Rom. 2:21 comments.

Jesus Counsels the Rich Young Ruler

17Now as He was going out on the
road, one came running, knelt before Him,
and asked Him, "Good Teacher, what
shall I do that I may inherit eternal life?"
18So Jesus said to him, "Why do you
call Me good? No one *is* good but One,
that is, God. 19You know the commandments: *'Do not commit adultery,' 'Do not
murder,' 'Do not steal,' 'Do not bear false
witness,'* 'Do not defraud,' *'Honor your
father and your mother.'* "[a]
20And he answered and said to Him,
"Teacher, all these things I have kept
from my youth."
21Then Jesus, looking at him, loved
him, and said to him, "One thing you
lack: Go your way, sell whatever you
have and give to the poor, and you will
have treasure in heaven; and come, take
up the cross, and follow Me."
22But he was sad at this word, and

10:19 [a]Exodus 20:12–16; Deuteronomy 5:16–20

10:21 "Poor youth! He had a good mind to be a Christian, and to inherit eternal life, but thought it too dear, if it could be purchased at no less an expense than of his estate! And thus many, both young and old, now-a-days, come running to worship our blessed Lord in public, and kneel before him in private, and inquire at his gospel, what they must do to inherit eternal life: but when they find they must renounce the self-enjoyment of riches, and forsake all in affection to follow him, they cry, 'The Lord pardon us in this thing! We pray thee, have us excused'... He will not!" *George Whitefield*

"Christianity has always insisted that the cross we bear precedes the crown we wear." *Martin Luther King, Jr.*

"No pain, no palm; no thorns, no throne; no gall, no glory; no cross, no crown..." *William Penn*

went away sorrowful, for he had great possessions.

With God All Things Are Possible

23 Then Jesus looked around and said to His disciples, "How hard it is for those who have riches to enter the kingdom of God!" 24 And the disciples were astonished at His words. But Jesus answered again and said to them, "Children, how hard it is for those who trust in riches[a] to enter the kingdom of God! 25 It is easier for a camel to go through the eye of a needle than for a rich man to enter the kingdom of God."

26 And they were greatly astonished, saying among themselves, "Who then can be saved?"

> The diver plunges deep to find pearls, and we must accept any labor or hazard to win a soul.
>
> **CHARLES SPURGEON**

27 But Jesus looked at them and said, "With men *it is* impossible, but not with God; for with God all things are possible."

28 Then Peter began to say to Him, "See, we have left all and followed You."

29 So Jesus answered and said, "Assuredly, I say to you, there is no one who has left house or brothers or sisters or father or mother or wife[a] or children or lands, for My sake and the gospel's, 30 who shall not receive a hundredfold now in this time—houses and brothers and sisters and mothers and children and lands, with persecutions—and in the age to come, eternal life. 31 But many *who are* first will be last, and the last first."

Jesus a Third Time Predicts His Death and Resurrection

32 Now they were on the road, going up to Jerusalem, and Jesus was going before them; and they were amazed. And as they followed they were afraid. Then He took the twelve aside again and began to tell them the things that would happen to Him: 33 "Behold, we are going up to Jerusalem, and the Son of Man will be betrayed to the chief priests and to the scribes; and they will condemn Him to death and deliver Him to the Gentiles; 34 and they will mock Him, and scourge Him, and spit on Him, and kill Him. And the third day He will rise again."

Greatness Is Serving

35 Then James and John, the sons of Zebedee, came to Him, saying, "Teacher, we want You to do for us whatever we ask."

36 And He said to them, "What do you want Me to do for you?"

37 They said to Him, "Grant us that we may sit, one on Your right hand and the other on Your left, in Your glory."

38 But Jesus said to them, "You do not know what you ask. Are you able to drink the cup that I drink, and be baptized with the baptism that I am baptized with?"

39 They said to Him, "We are able."

So Jesus said to them, "You will indeed drink the cup that I drink, and with the baptism I am baptized with you will be baptized; 40 but to sit on My right hand and on My left is not Mine to give, but *it is for those* for whom it is prepared."

41 And when the ten heard *it,* they began to be greatly displeased with James and John. 42 But Jesus called them to *Himself* and said to them, "You know that those who are considered rulers over the Gentiles lord it over them, and their great ones exercise authority over them. 43 Yet

10:24 [a]NU-Text omits *for those who trust in riches.* 10:29 [a]NU-Text omits *or wife.*

10:44 "A Christian man is the most free lord of all, subject to no one. A Christian man is the dutiful servant of all, subject to everyone." *Martin Luther*

it shall not be so among you; but whoever desires to become great among you shall be your servant. 44And whoever of you desires to be first shall be slave of all. 45For even the Son of Man did not come to be served, but to serve, and to give His life a ransom for many."

Jesus Heals Blind Bartimaeus

46Now they came to Jericho. As He went out of Jericho with His disciples and a great multitude, blind Bartimaeus, the son of Timaeus, sat by the road begging. 47And when he heard that it was Jesus of Nazareth, he began to cry out and say, "Jesus, Son of David, have mercy on me!"

48Then many warned him to be quiet; but he cried out all the more, "Son of David, have mercy on me!"

49So Jesus stood still and commanded him to be called.

Then they called the blind man, saying to him, "Be of good cheer. Rise, He is calling you."

50And throwing aside his garment, he rose and came to Jesus.

51So Jesus answered and said to him, "What do you want Me to do for you?"

The blind man said to Him, "Rabboni, that I may receive my sight."

52Then Jesus said to him, "Go your way; your faith has made you well." And immediately he received his sight and followed Jesus on the road.

The Triumphal Entry

11 Now when they drew near Jerusalem, to Bethphage[a] and Bethany, at the Mount of Olives, He sent two of His disciples; 2and He said to them, "Go into the village opposite you; and as soon as you have entered it you will find a colt tied, on which no one has sat. Loose it and bring *it.* 3And if anyone says to you, 'Why are you doing this?' say, 'The Lord has need of it,' and immediately he will send it here."

4So they went their way, and found the[a] colt tied by the door outside on the street, and they loosed it. 5But some of those who stood there said to them, "What are you doing, loosing the colt?"

6And they spoke to them just as Jesus had commanded. So they let them go. 7Then they brought the colt to Jesus and threw their clothes on it, and He sat on it. 8And many spread their clothes on the road, and others cut down leafy branches from the trees and spread *them* on the road. 9Then those who went before and those who followed cried out, saying:

"Hosanna!
'Blessed is He who comes in the name of the LORD!'[a]
10Blessed *is* the kingdom of our father David
That comes in the name of the Lord![a]
Hosanna in the highest!"

11And Jesus went into Jerusalem and into the temple. So when He had looked around at all things, as the hour was already late, He went out to Bethany with the twelve.

The Fig Tree Withered

12Now the next day, when they had

11:1 [a]M-Text reads *Bethsphage.* 11:4 [a]NU-Text and M-Text read *a.* 11:9 [a]Psalm 118:26 11:10 [a]NU-Text omits *in the name of the Lord.*

11:2,3 1) The colt had never been used. As a Christian, you have been set apart (sanctified), made a new creature—born again, specifically for the Master's use.

2) The colt was loosed. We have been set free from sin and death to serve the Living God. Our purpose in life is to carry Jesus of Nazareth to the cross of Calvary, so that a dying world will look to Him and find everlasting life.

3) The Lord "needed" the lowly colt. Almighty God has condescended to choose the foolishness of human preaching to save those who believe. The laborers are few, so you are therefore needed to preach Jesus Christ and Him crucified.

QUESTIONS & OBJECTIONS

11:15 ***"Jesus wasn't sinless—He became angry when He cleared the temple."***

This incident is recorded in all four Gospels. John 2:14–16 give us a fuller picture: "He found in the temple those who sold oxen and sheep and doves, and the money changers doing business. When He had made a whip of cords, He drove them all out of the temple, with the sheep and the oxen, and poured out the changers' money and overturned the tables."

There is no loss of temper here. What He did was deliberate and premeditated. He took the time to make a whip of small cords, then He cleared the temple of the day's equivalent of money-grabbing televangelists. The temple of God should be a house of prayer, but Jesus called it a "den of thieves" (v. 17), because the moneychangers were not interested in God but in taking financial advantage of those who came to worship. Anger at hypocrisy is not a sin; it is a virtue.

come out from Bethany, He was hungry.
13And seeing from afar a fig tree having
leaves, He went to see if perhaps He
would find something on it. When He
came to it, He found nothing but leaves,
for it was not the season for figs. 14In response Jesus said to it, "Let no one eat
fruit from you ever again."

And His disciples heard *it*.

Jesus Cleanses the Temple

15So they came to Jerusalem. Then Jesus went into the temple and began to
drive out those who bought and sold in
the temple, and overturned the tables of
the money changers and the seats of
those who sold doves. 16And He would
not allow anyone to carry wares through
the temple. 17Then He taught, saying to
them, "Is it not written, *'My house shall
be called a house of prayer for all nations'?*[a] But you have made it a *'den of
thieves.'* "[b]

18And the scribes and chief priests
heard it and sought how they might destroy Him; for they feared Him, because
all the people were astonished at His
teaching. 19When evening had come, He
went out of the city.

The Lesson of the Withered Fig Tree

20Now in the morning, as they passed
by, they saw the fig tree dried up from
the roots. 21And Peter, remembering, said
to Him, "Rabbi, look! The fig tree which
You cursed has withered away."

22So Jesus answered and said to them,
"Have faith in God. 23For assuredly, I say
to you, whoever says to this mountain,
'Be removed and be cast into the sea,' and
does not doubt in his heart, but believes
that those things he says will be done, he
will have whatever he says. 24Therefore I
say to you, whatever things you ask when
you pray, believe that you receive *them*,
and you will have *them*.

Forgiveness and Prayer

25"And whenever you stand praying, if
you have anything against anyone, forgive him, that your Father in heaven may
also forgive you your trespasses. 26But if

11:17 [a]Isaiah 56:7 [b]Jeremiah 7:11

11:22 Faith in God. It is amazing how many people find it difficult to have faith in a perfect God, but they trust their lives without question to fallible men. The eighth leading cause of death in the U.S. is "medical mistakes."

11:23 Prayer—the secret weapon: This is an open invitation for Christians to beseech God for genuine revival. We should never be satisfied until every living human being is safe in Christ: "Show me a thoroughly satisfied man and I will show you a failure." *Thomas Edison*

11:25 *How to Witness to Mormons*

Even though Mormons use language that sounds Christian, it is a manmade religion and it is heresy. A religion cannot teach that Jesus is the brother of Lucifer, that you and I can become gods, and that we are saved by grace "after all we can do," and still be labeled part of Christianity. It is our responsibility to reach out to Mormons with the truth and love. So how do we do that?

There are at least two approaches to use in witnessing to Mormons. We can either debate the doctrines of Mormonism (baptism for the dead, "burning" in the bosom, Joseph Smith as a prophet of God, the validity of the Book of Mormon, the Trinity, "God was once a man," "protective" underwear, etc.), or we can present the gospel biblically. One creates an atmosphere of contention and often leaves the Christian feeling frustrated, while the other creates an atmosphere of concern for the eternal welfare of the Mormon. Our goal should be to win a soul to Christ rather than merely win a doctrinal argument.

One point of frustration for the Christian is that Mormons often agree when they hear words such as "salvation," or Jesus as "Savior." The problem is that their understanding of the words differs from the biblical revelation of the words. "Salvation" for a Mormon can mean the salvation of all humanity—when the "Savior" will eventually raise everyone from the dead.

Rather than speak of "going to heaven," the Christian should ask what the Mormon has to do to be at peace with "Heavenly Father." This is language they can understand, and will reveal the basis for their salvation. Are they trusting in self-righteousness, or solely in the righteousness of Christ?

Mark J. Cares writes: "Although Mormons commonly appear self-assured and self-righteous, many are undergoing great stress. This is because Mormonism holds up perfection as an attainable goal. The one Bible passage the Mormon church constantly holds up before its membership is Matt. 5:48: 'Be ye therefore perfect, even as your Father which is in heaven is perfect.' They then expound on it with numerous exhortations to strive for perfection. Spencer W. Kimball, for example, wrote: 'Being perfect means to triumph over sin. This is a mandate from the Lord. He is just and wise and kind. He would never require anything from his children which was not for their benefit and which was not attainable. Perfection therefore is an achievable goal' (*Life and Teachings of Jesus and His Apostles,* Church of Jesus Christ of Latter-day Saints).

"This emphasis on perfection permeates every aspect of a Mormon's life. Its most common form is the unending demand on them to be 'worthy.' Every privilege in Mormonism is conditioned on a person's worthiness. Kimball wrote: 'All blessings are conditional. I know of none that are not' (*Remember Me*, Church of Jesus Christ of Latter-day Saints).

"Christians need to recognize that this constant striving for perfection—and the resultant stress it produces—offers an excellent opening to talk to Mormons about Jesus and the imputed perfection we receive through Him.

"**Reinforce their predicament.** Average hard-working Mormons view this striving for perfection as a heavy but manageable burden. They can cultivate illusions of perfection because the Mormon church has greatly watered down the concept of sin. Consequently, the Christian witness needs to show Mormons both the severity of their predicament and the impossibility of their becoming perfect. In other words, they need to have a face-to-face confrontation with the stern message of God's Law, because 'through the Law we become conscious of sin' (Rom. 3:21).

"The best way to accomplish this is to tell them, lovingly but firmly, that they are going to 'outer darkness.' (Outer darkness is the closest concept in Mormonism to an eternal hell.) Most Mormons have never been told this, nor have they ever considered that possibility for themselves, since Mormonism teaches that nearly everyone will enter one of Mormonism's three kingdoms of heaven. [See Ezek. 31:16 comment.] Therefore, until you introduce the thought of eternal suffering, they will not feel any real urgency to take your witness to heart. On the contrary, most, if they are willing to talk at all, will view any religious conversation as nothing more than an interesting intellectual discussion.

"Christians often hesitate to be this blunt. They feel that if anything will turn Mormons off, telling them that they are going to outer darkness surely will. I shared that fear when I began using this approach. To my amazement, however, rejection wasn't the reaction I received. Most have been shocked, but they were also eager to know why I would say such a thing. The key is to speak this truth with love, in such a way that our concern for their souls is readily apparent.

"Alerting Mormons to the very real danger of their going to outer darkness opens the door to telling them the basis for that judgment—which is, they are not meeting God's requirement for living with Him (they are not presently perfect). The

(continued)

(11:25 continued)
key to explaining this is the present imperative, be perfect, in Matt. 5:48."

Share with them the hope that is found only in the true Jesus: "For by one offering He has *perfected forever* those who are being sanctified" (Heb. 10:14, emphasis added).

See also Psa. 51:6 comment for how to go through the Law, and 1 Cor. 15:58 comment on how not to be discouraged in witnessing.

you do not forgive, neither will your Father in heaven forgive your trespasses."[a]

Jesus' Authority Questioned

[27]Then they came again to Jerusalem. And as He was walking in the temple, the chief priests, the scribes, and the elders came to Him. [28]And they said to Him, "By what authority are You doing these things? And who gave You this authority to do these things?"

[29]But Jesus answered and said to them, "I also will ask you one question; then answer Me, and I will tell you by what authority I do these things: [30]The baptism of John—was it from heaven or from men? Answer Me."

[31]And they reasoned among themselves, saying, "If we say, 'From heaven,' He will say, 'Why then did you not believe him?' [32]But if we say, 'From men' "—they feared the people, for all counted John to have been a prophet indeed. [33]So they answered and said to Jesus, "We do not know."

And Jesus answered and said to them, "Neither will I tell you by what authority I do these things."

The Parable of the Wicked Vinedressers

12 Then He began to speak to them in parables: "A man planted a vineyard and set a hedge around *it,* dug *a place for* the wine vat and built a tower. And he leased it to vinedressers and went into a far country. [2]Now at vintage-time he sent a servant to the vinedressers, that he might receive some of the fruit of the vineyard from the vinedressers. [3]And they took *him* and beat him and sent *him* away empty-handed. [4]Again he sent them another servant, and at him they threw stones,[a] wounded *him* in the head, and sent *him* away shamefully treated. [5]And again he sent another, and him they killed; and many others, beating some and killing some. [6]Therefore still having one son, his beloved, he also sent him to them last, saying, 'They will respect my son.' [7]But those vinedressers said among themselves, 'This is the heir. Come, let us kill him, and the inheritance will be ours.' [8]So they took him and killed *him* and cast *him* out of the vineyard.

[9]"Therefore what will the owner of the vineyard do? He will come and destroy the vinedressers, and give the vineyard to others. [10]Have you not even read this Scripture:

'The stone which the builders rejected
Has become the chief cornerstone.
[11] *This was the LORD's doing,*
And it is marvelous in our eyes'? "[a]

[12]And they sought to lay hands on Him, but feared the multitude, for they knew He had spoken the parable against them. So they left Him and went away.

The Pharisees: Is It Lawful to Pay Taxes to Caesar?

[13]Then they sent to Him some of the Pharisees and the Herodians, to catch Him in *His* words. [14]When they had come, they said to Him, "Teacher, we know that You are true, and care about no one; for You do not regard the person of men, but teach the way of God in truth. Is it lawful to pay taxes to Caesar, or not? [15]Shall we pay, or shall we not pay?"

But He, knowing their hypocrisy, said

11:26 [a]NU-Text omits this verse. 12:4 [a]NU-Text omits *and at him they threw stones.* 12:11 [a]Psalm 118:22, 23

to them, "Why do you test Me? Bring Me a denarius that I may see *it*." [16]So they brought *it*.

And He said to them, "Whose image and inscription *is* this?" They said to Him, "Caesar's."

[17]And Jesus answered and said to them, "Render to Caesar the things that are Caesar's, and to God the things that are God's."

And they marveled at Him.

The Sadducees: What About the Resurrection?

[18]Then *some* Sadducees, who say there is no resurrection, came to Him; and they asked Him, saying: [19]"Teacher, Moses wrote to us that if a man's brother dies, and leaves *his* wife behind, and leaves no children, his brother should take his wife and raise up offspring for his brother. [20]Now there were seven brothers. The first took a wife; and dying, he left no offspring. [21]And the second took her, and he died; nor did he leave any offspring. And the third likewise. [22]So the seven had her and left no offspring. Last of all the woman died also. [23]Therefore, in the resurrection, when they rise, whose wife will she be? For all seven had her as wife."

[24]Jesus answered and said to them, "Are you not therefore mistaken, because you do not know the Scriptures nor the power of God? [25]For when they rise from the dead, they neither marry nor are given in marriage, but are like angels in heaven. [26]But concerning the dead, that they rise, have you not read in the book of Moses, in the *burning* bush *passage*, how God spoke to him, saying, *'I am the God of Abraham, the God of Isaac, and the God of Jacob'?*[a] [27]He is not the God of the dead, but the God of the living. You are therefore greatly mistaken."

The Scribes: Which Is the First Commandment of All?

[28]Then one of the scribes came, and having heard them reasoning together, perceiving[a] that He had answered them well, asked Him, "Which is the first commandment of all?"

[29]Jesus answered him, "The first of all the commandments *is*: *'Hear, O Israel, the LORD our God, the LORD is one.* [30]*And you shall love the LORD your God with all your heart, with all your soul, with all your mind, and with all your strength.'*[a] This *is* the first commandment.[b] [31]And the second, like *it*, *is* this: *'You shall love your neighbor as yourself.'*[a] There is no other commandment greater than these."

[32]So the scribe said to Him, "Well *said*, Teacher. You have spoken the truth, for there is one God, and there is no other but He. [33]And to love Him with all the heart, with all the understanding, with all the soul,[a] and with all the strength, and to love one's neighbor as oneself, is more than all the whole burnt offerings and sacrifices."

[34]Now when Jesus saw that he answered wisely, He said to him, "You are not far from the kingdom of God."

But after that no one dared question Him.

Jesus: How Can David Call His Descendant Lord?

[35]Then Jesus answered and said, while He taught in the temple, "How *is it* that the scribes say that the Christ is the Son of David? [36]For David himself said by the Holy Spirit:

12:26 [a]Exodus 3:6, 15 12:28 [a]NU-Text reads *seeing*. 12:30 [a]Deuteronomy 6:4, 5 [b]NU-Text omits this sentence. 12:31 [a]Leviticus 19:18 12:33 [a]NU-Text omits *with all the soul*.

12:29–31 Leading sinners to Jesus: *No one has ever kept the Commandments.* "The LORD looks down from heaven upon the children of men, to see if there are any who understand, who seek God. They have all turned aside, they have together become corrupt; there is none who does good, no, not one" (Psa. 14:2,3). To go through the Ten Commandments, see Psa. 51:6 comment.

12:34 It is understanding of the Law that brings a sinner closer to the kingdom of God.

PRINCIPLES OF GROWTH FOR THE NEW AND GROWING CHRISTIAN

12:41–44 *Tithing—The Final Frontier*

It has been said that the wallet is the "final frontier." It is often the final area to be conquered—the last thing that we surrender to God. Jesus spoke much about money. He said that we cannot serve God and mammon (Matt. 6:24). "Mammon" was the common Aramaic word for riches, which is related to a Hebrew word signifying "that which is to be trusted." In other words, we cannot trust both God and money. Either money is our source of joy, our great love, our sense of security, the supplier of our needs—or God is.

When you open your purse or wallet, give generously and regularly to your local church. A guide to how much you should give can be found in the "tithe" of the Old Testament: 10 percent of your income. Whatever amount you give, make sure you give *something* to the work of God (see Mal. 3:8–11). Give because you *want* to, not because you *have* to. God loves a cheerful giver (2 Cor. 9:6,7), so learn to hold your money with a loose hand.

'The LORD said to my Lord,
"Sit at My right hand,
Till I make Your enemies Your
footstool."'[a]

37Therefore David himself calls Him *'Lord'*;
how is He *then* his Son?"

And the common people heard Him gladly.

Beware of the Scribes

38Then He said to them in His teaching, "Beware of the scribes, who desire to go around in long robes, *love* greetings in
the marketplaces, 39the best seats in the
synagogues, and the best places at feasts,
40who devour widows' houses, and for a
pretense make long prayers. These will receive greater condemnation."

The Widow's Two Mites

41Now Jesus sat opposite the treasury
and saw how the people put money into
the treasury. And many *who were* rich put
in much. 42Then one poor widow came
and threw in two mites,[a] which make a
quadrans. 43So He called His disciples to
Himself and said to them, "Assuredly, I say to you that this poor widow has put in more than all those who have given to
the treasury; 44for they all put in out of
their abundance, but she out of her poverty put in all that she had, her whole livelihood."

Jesus Predicts the Destruction of the Temple

13 Then as He went out of the temple, one of His disciples said to Him, "Teacher, see what manner of stones and what buildings *are here!*"

2And Jesus answered and said to him,
"Do you see these great buildings? Not

12:36 [a]Psalm 110:1 12:42 [a]Greek *lepta*, very small copper coins worth a fraction of a penny

13:2 Fulfilled prophecy. This prophecy was fulfilled in A.D. 70 when Titus destroyed Jerusalem. "Now the outward face of the temple in its front wanted nothing that was likely to surprise either men's minds or their eyes; for it was covered all over with plates of gold of great weight, and, at the first rising of the sun, reflected back a very fiery splendor, and made those who forced themselves to look upon it to turn their eyes away, just as they would have done at the sun's own rays. But this temple appeared to strangers, when they were coming to it at a distance, like a mountain covered with snow; for as to those parts of it that were not gilt, they were exceeding white. On its top it had spikes with sharp points, to prevent any pollution of it by birds sitting upon it. Of its stones, some of them were forty-five cubits in length, five in height, and six in breadth." (*The History of the Destruction of Jerusalem*, *The Works of Flavius Josephus*)

"[The wall] was so thoroughly laid even with the ground by those that dug it up to the foundation, that there was left nothing to make those that came thither believe it had ever been inhabited." *Josephus*, *The Wars of the Jews* (See also Matt. 24:2.)

one stone shall be left upon another, that shall not be thrown down."

The Signs of the Times and the End of the Age

3Now as He sat on the Mount of Olives opposite the temple, Peter, James, John, and Andrew asked Him privately, 4"Tell us, when will these things be? And what *will be* the sign when all these things will be fulfilled?"

> The bottom of the soul may be in repose, even while we are in many outward troubles; just as the bottom of the sea is calm, while the surface is strongly agitated.
>
> **JOHN WESLEY**

5And Jesus, answering them, began to say: "Take heed that no one deceives you. 6For many will come in My name, saying, 'I am *He,*' and will deceive many. 7But when you hear of wars and rumors of wars, do not be troubled; for *such things* must happen, but the end *is* not yet. 8For nation will rise against nation, and kingdom against kingdom. And there will be earthquakes in various places, and there will be famines and troubles.[a] These *are* the beginnings of sorrows.

9"But watch out for yourselves, for they will deliver you up to councils, and you will be beaten in the synagogues. You will be brought[a] before rulers and kings for My sake, for a testimony to them. 10And the gospel must first be preached to all the nations. 11But when they arrest *you* and deliver you up, do not worry beforehand, or premeditate[a] what you will speak. But whatever is given you in that hour, speak that; for it is not you who speak, but the Holy Spirit. 12Now brother will betray brother to death, and a father *his* child; and children will rise up against parents and cause them to be put to death. 13And you will be hated by all for My name's sake. But he who endures to the end shall be saved.

The Great Tribulation

14"So when you see the *'abomination of desolation,'*[a] spoken of by Daniel the prophet,[b] standing where it ought not" (let the reader understand), "then let those who are in Judea flee to the mountains. 15Let him who is on the housetop not go down into the house, nor enter to take anything out of his house. 16And let him who is in the field not go back to get his clothes. 17But woe to those who are pregnant and to those who are nursing babies in those days! 18And pray that your flight may not be in winter. 19For *in* those days there will be tribulation, such

13:8 [a]NU-Text omits *and troubles.* **13:9** [a]NU-Text and M-Text read *will stand.* **13:11** [a]NU-Text omits *or premeditate.* **13:14** [a]Daniel 11:31; 12:11 [b]NU-Text omits *spoken of by Daniel the prophet.*

13:4 For more signs of the end times, see Luke 21:7.

13:5 "Evolution is a fairy tale for grown-ups. This theory has helped nothing in the progress of science. It is useless." *Professor Louis Bounoure*, Director of Research, National Center of Scientific Research

"Scientists who go about teaching that evolution is a fact of life are great con-men, and the story they are telling may be the greatest hoax ever. In explaining evolution, we do not have one iota of fact." *Dr. T. N. Tahmisian*, Atomic Energy Commission

"One must conclude that, contrary to the established and current wisdom, a scenario describing the genesis of life on earth by chance and natural causes which can be accepted on the basis of *fact* and not *faith* has not yet been written." *Hubert Yockey*, Information Theorist

"In fact, evolution became in a sense a scientific religion; almost all scientists have accepted it and many are prepared to 'bend' their observations to fit in with it." *H. S. Lipson*, professor of physics, University of Manchester, UK

13:10 "The world can be witnessed to in a single generation. We can welcome Him back with our present of the finished task set by Him so long ago when He said, 'This gospel of the kingdom must be preached for a witness to all nations; then shall the end come.'" *Winkie Pratney*

QUESTIONS & OBJECTIONS

13:24–27 ***"The second coming of Jesus was a failed prediction. The generation He was speaking to did pass away, but these things haven't happened."***

This passage begins by saying, "But in those days..." Jesus will return. The days referred to are those described in the preceding verses. The chapter promises that the gospel must first be preached in all the world, tremendous persecution of Christians will occur, false prophets and false christs will arise, and there will be a great tribulation that is unparalleled in history.

The questioner's error is in thinking that "this generation" in v. 30 refers to the generation Jesus was speaking to. He is overlooking the immediately preceding verses for the point: "Now learn this parable from the fig tree: When its branch has already become tender, and puts forth leaves, you know that summer is near. So you also, *when you see these things happening*, know that it is near—at the doors!" (vv. 28,29, emphasis added).

Just as one who sees the leaves sprouting on a fig tree knows that summer is near, Jesus said that the generation *who sees all these signs* will also see His return "with great power and glory." (In the same way, one who sees his wife in labor will also live to see his newborn child—the events happen in pretty quick succession.)

as has not been since the beginning of the
creation which God created until this
time, nor ever shall be. 20And unless the
Lord had shortened those days, no flesh
would be saved; but for the elect's sake,
whom He chose, He shortened the days.
21"Then if anyone says to you, 'Look,
here *is* the Christ!' or, 'Look, *He is* there!'
do not believe it. 22For false christs and
false prophets will rise and show signs
and wonders to deceive, if possible, even
the elect. 23But take heed; see, I have told
you all things beforehand.

The Coming of the Son of Man

24"But in those days, after that tribulation, the sun will be darkened, and the
moon will not give its light; 25the stars of
heaven will fall, and the powers in the
heavens will be shaken. 26Then they will
see the Son of Man coming in the clouds
with great power and glory. 27And then
He will send His angels, and gather together His elect from the four winds,
from the farthest part of earth to the farthest part of heaven.

The Parable of the Fig Tree

28"Now learn this parable from the fig
tree: When its branch has already become
tender, and puts forth leaves, you know
that summer is near. 29So you also, when
you see these things happening, know
that it[a] is near—at the doors! 30Assured-
ly, I say to you, this generation will by no
means pass away till all these things take
place. 31Heaven and earth will pass away,
but My words will by no means pass
away.

No One Knows the Day or Hour

32"But of that day and hour no one
knows, not even the angels in heaven,
nor the Son, but only the Father. 33Take
heed, watch and pray; for you do not
know when the time is. 34*It is* like a man
going to a far country, who left his house
and gave authority to his servants, and to
each his work, and commanded the doorkeeper to watch. 35Watch therefore, for
you do not know when the master of the
house is coming—in the evening, at midnight, at the crowing of the rooster, or in
the morning— 36lest, coming suddenly,
he find you sleeping. 37And what I say to
you, I say to all: Watch!"

The Plot to Kill Jesus

14 After two days it was the Passover
and *the Feast* of Unleavened Bread.
And the chief priests and the scribes sought
how they might take Him by trickery and

13:29 [a]Or *He*

put *Him* to death. 2But they said, "Not during the feast, lest there be an uproar of the people."

The Anointing at Bethany

3And being in Bethany at the house of Simon the leper, as He sat at the table, a woman came having an alabaster flask of very costly oil of spikenard. Then she broke the flask and poured *it* on His head. 4But there were some who were indignant among themselves, and said, "Why was this fragrant oil wasted? 5For it might have been sold for more than three hundred denarii and given to the poor." And they criticized her sharply.

6But Jesus said, "Let her alone. Why do you trouble her? She has done a good work for Me. 7For you have the poor with you always, and whenever you wish you may do them good; but Me you do not have always. 8She has done what she could. She has come beforehand to anoint My body for burial. 9Assuredly, I say to you, wherever this gospel is preached in the whole world, what this woman has done will also be told as a memorial to her."

Judas Agrees to Betray Jesus

10Then Judas Iscariot, one of the twelve, went to the chief priests to betray Him to them. 11And when they heard *it,* they were glad, and promised to give him money. So he sought how he might conveniently betray Him.

Jesus Celebrates the Passover with His Disciples

12Now on the first day of Unleavened Bread, when they killed the Passover *lamb,* His disciples said to Him, "Where do You want us to go and prepare, that You may eat the Passover?"

13And He sent out two of His disciples and said to them, "Go into the city, and a man will meet you carrying a pitcher of water; follow him. 14Wherever he goes in, say to the master of the house, 'The Teacher says, "Where is the guest room in which I may eat the Passover with My disciples?" ' 15Then he will show you a large upper room, furnished *and* prepared; there make ready for us."

16So His disciples went out, and came into the city, and found it just as He had said to them; and they prepared the Passover.

17In the evening He came with the twelve. 18Now as they sat and ate, Jesus said, "Assuredly, I say to you, one of you who eats with Me will betray Me."

19And they began to be sorrowful, and to say to Him one by one, "*Is* it I?" And another *said,* "*Is* it I?"[a]

20He answered and said to them, "*It is* one of the twelve, who dips with Me in the dish. 21The Son of Man indeed goes just as it is written of Him, but woe to that man by whom the Son of Man is betrayed! It would have been good for that man if he had never been born."

Jesus Institutes the Lord's Supper

22And as they were eating, Jesus took bread, blessed and broke *it,* and gave *it* to them and said, "Take, eat;[a] this is My body."

23Then He took the cup, and when He had given thanks He gave *it* to them, and they all drank from it. 24And He said to them, "This is My blood of the new[a] covenant, which is shed for many. 25Assuredly, I say to you, I will no longer drink of the fruit of the vine until that day when I drink it new in the kingdom of God."

14:19 [a]**NU-Text omits this sentence.** **14:22** [a]**NU-Text omits** *eat.* **14:24** [a]**NU-Text omits** *new.*

14:10 Messianic prophecy fulfilled: "Even my own familiar friend in whom I trusted, who ate my bread, has lifted up his heel against me" (Psa. 41:9). See Mark 14:65 comment.

14:24 The wine was not His literal blood, which was still in His body. He was referring to it as being *symbolic* of His blood.

[26]And when they had sung a hymn, they went out to the Mount of Olives.

Jesus Predicts Peter's Denial

[27]Then Jesus said to them, "All of you will be made to stumble because of Me this night,[a] for it is written:

'I will strike the Shepherd,
And the sheep will be scattered.'[b]

[28]"But after I have been raised, I will go before you to Galilee."

[29]Peter said to Him, "Even if all are made to stumble, yet I *will* not *be*."

[30]Jesus said to him, "Assuredly, I say to you that today, *even* this night, before the rooster crows twice, you will deny Me three times."

[31]But he spoke more vehemently, "If I have to die with You, I will not deny You!"

And they all said likewise.

The Prayer in the Garden

[32]Then they came to a place which
was named Gethsemane; and He said to
His disciples, "Sit here while I pray." [33]And
He took Peter, James, and John with Him,
and He began to be troubled and deeply
distressed. [34]Then He said to them, "My
soul is exceedingly sorrowful, *even* to
death. Stay here and watch."

[35]He went a little farther, and fell on
the ground, and prayed that if it were
possible, the hour might pass from Him.
[36]And He said, "Abba, Father, all things
are possible for You. Take this cup away
from Me; nevertheless, not what I will,
but what You *will*."

[37]Then He came and found them sleeping, and said to Peter, "Simon, are you
sleeping? Could you not watch one hour?
[38]Watch and pray, lest you enter into
temptation. The spirit indeed *is* willing,
but the flesh *is* weak."

[39]Again He went away and prayed,
and spoke the same words. [40]And when
He returned, He found them asleep again,
for their eyes were heavy; and they did
not know what to answer Him.

[41]Then He came the third time and
said to them, "Are you still sleeping and
resting? It is enough! The hour has come;
behold, the Son of Man is being betrayed
into the hands of sinners. [42]Rise, let us be
going. See, My betrayer is at hand."

Betrayal and Arrest in Gethsemane

[43]And immediately, while He was still
speaking, Judas, one of the twelve, with a
great multitude with swords and clubs,
came from the chief priests and the scribes
and the elders. [44]Now His betrayer had
given them a signal, saying, "Whomever I
kiss, He is the One; seize Him and lead
Him away safely."

[45]As soon as he had come, immediately he went up to Him and said to Him,
"Rabbi, Rabbi!" and kissed Him.

> Before we can begin to see the cross as something done for us, we have to see it as something done by us.
>
> **JOHN STOTT**

[46]Then they laid their hands on Him
and took Him. [47]And one of those who
stood by drew his sword and struck the
servant of the high priest, and cut off his
ear.

[48]Then Jesus answered and said to
them, "Have you come out, as against a
robber, with swords and clubs to take
Me? [49]I was daily with you in the temple
teaching, and you did not seize Me. But
the Scriptures must be fulfilled."

14:27 [a]NU-Text omits *because of Me this night.* [b]Zechariah 13:7

14:38 "The reason why many fail in battle is because they wait until the hour of battle. The reason why others succeed is because they have gained their victory on their knees long before the battle came . . . Anticipate your battles; fight them on your knees before temptation comes, and you will always have victory." *R. A. Torrey*

QUESTIONS & OBJECTIONS

14:62 ***"The chief priests didn't see Jesus coming with the clouds or sitting in power, so He's a false prophet."***

You forget that the hour is coming when all who are in their graves will hear His voice (see John 5:28). There is going to be a resurrection of the just and the unjust (see Acts 24:15). *Every* eye will see Him. The chief priests will bow the knee before Him. So will Hitler and every murderer, rapist, thief, and liar. All will bow down to Jesus Christ and confess Him as Lord of the universe (see Rom. 14:11; Phil. 2:10,11). He is the Creator of all things (see Col. 1:16), and every human being will see Him in His glory, including you. When they saw the resurrected Christ, shining with a brightness greater than the sun, Paul trembled in terror and John fell at His feet as if dead (see Acts 26:13–15; Rev. 1:16,17).

So it would be wise to stop rejecting Him as a false prophet. Instead confess and forsake your sins, and put your trust in Him while He extends His mercy to sinful men and women. He has waited for 2,000 years because He is not willing that any perish, but that all come to repentance (see 2 Pet. 3:9). Everything Jesus said would happen has happened throughout history (see Matt. 24; Luke 21), so you can bet your very soul that those men Jesus said would see His coming as sure as hell will see it.

50Then they all forsook Him and fled.

A Young Man Flees Naked

51Now a certain young man followed
Him, having a linen cloth thrown around
his naked *body*. And the young men laid
hold of him, 52and he left the linen cloth
and fled from them naked.

Jesus Faces the Sanhedrin

53And they led Jesus away to the high
priest; and with him were assembled all
the chief priests, the elders, and the
scribes. 54But Peter followed Him at a
distance, right into the courtyard of the
high priest. And he sat with the servants
and warmed himself at the fire.
55Now the chief priests and all the
council sought testimony against Jesus to
put Him to death, but found none. 56For
many bore false witness against Him, but
their testimonies did not agree.
57Then some rose up and bore false
witness against Him, saying, 58"We heard
Him say, 'I will destroy this temple made
with hands, and within three days I will
build another made without hands.' "
59But not even then did their testimony
agree.
60And the high priest stood up in the
midst and asked Jesus, saying, "Do You
answer nothing? What *is it* these men testify against You?" 61But He kept silent
and answered nothing.
Again the high priest asked Him, saying to Him, "Are You the Christ, the Son
of the Blessed?"
62Jesus said, "I am. And you will see
the Son of Man sitting at the right hand
of the Power, and coming with the clouds
of heaven."
63Then the high priest tore his clothes
and said, "What further need do we have
of witnesses? 64You have heard the blasphemy! What do you think?"
And they all condemned Him to be
deserving of death.
65Then some began to spit on Him,
and to blindfold Him, and to beat Him,
and to say to Him, "Prophesy!" And the
officers struck Him with the palms of
their hands.[a]

Peter Denies Jesus, and Weeps

66Now as Peter was below in the
courtyard, one of the servant girls of the
high priest came. 67And when she saw
Peter warming himself, she looked at him
and said, "You also were with Jesus of
Nazareth."
68But he denied it, saying, "I neither
know nor understand what you are saying." And he went out on the porch, and
a rooster crowed.

14:65 [a]NU-Text reads *received Him with slaps.*

[69]And the servant girl saw him again, and began to say to those who stood by, "This is *one* of them." [70]But he denied it again.

And a little later those who stood by said to Peter again, "Surely you are *one* of them; for you are a Galilean, and your speech shows *it*."[a]

[71]Then he began to curse and swear, "I do not know this Man of whom you speak!"

[72]A second time *the* rooster crowed. Then Peter called to mind the word that Jesus had said to him, "Before the rooster crows twice, you will deny Me three times." And when he thought about it, he wept.

Jesus Faces Pilate

15 Immediately, in the morning, the chief priests held a consultation with the elders and scribes and the whole council; and they bound Jesus, led *Him* away, and delivered *Him* to Pilate. [2]Then Pilate asked Him, "Are You the King of the Jews?"

He answered and said to him, "*It is as* you say."

[3]And the chief priests accused Him of many things, but He answered nothing. [4]Then Pilate asked Him again, saying, "Do You answer nothing? See how many things they testify against You!"[a] [5]But Jesus still answered nothing, so that Pilate marveled.

Taking the Place of Barabbas

[6]Now at the feast he was accustomed to releasing one prisoner to them, whomever they requested. [7]And there was one named Barabbas, *who was* chained with his fellow rebels; they had committed murder in the rebellion. [8]Then the multitude, crying aloud,[a] began to ask *him to do* just as he had always done for them. [9]But Pilate answered them, saying, "Do you want me to release to you the King of the Jews?" [10]For he knew that the chief priests had handed Him over because of envy.

[11]But the chief priests stirred up the crowd, so that he should rather release Barabbas to them. [12]Pilate answered and said to them again, "What then do you want me to do *with Him* whom you call the King of the Jews?"

[13]So they cried out again, "Crucify Him!"

[14]Then Pilate said to them, "Why, what evil has He done?"

But they cried out all the more, "Crucify Him!"

[15]So Pilate, wanting to gratify the crowd, released Barabbas to them; and he delivered Jesus, after he had scourged *Him*, to be crucified.

The Soldiers Mock Jesus

[16]Then the soldiers led Him away into the hall called Praetorium, and they called together the whole garrison. [17]And they clothed Him with purple; and they twisted a crown of thorns, put it on His *head*, [18]and began to salute Him, "Hail, King of the Jews!" [19]Then they struck Him on the head with a reed and spat on Him; and bowing the knee, they worshiped Him. [20]And when they had mocked Him, they took the purple off Him, put His own clothes on Him, and led Him out to crucify Him.

The King on a Cross

[21]Then they compelled a certain man,

14:70 [a]NU-Text omits *and your speech shows it.* 15:4 [a]NU-Text reads *of which they accuse You.* 15:8 [a]NU-Text reads *going up.*

14:65 Messianic prophecy fulfilled: "I gave My back to those who struck Me, and My cheeks to those who plucked out the beard; I did not hide My face from shame and spitting" (Isa. 50:6). See Mark 15:24 comment.

15:12 "Public opinion is held in reverence. It settles everything. Some think it is the voice of God." *Mark Twain*

Simon a Cyrenian, the father of Alexander and Rufus, as he was coming out of
the country and passing by, to bear His
cross. 22And they brought Him to the
place Golgotha, which is translated, Place
of a Skull. 23Then they gave Him wine
mingled with myrrh to drink, but He did
not take *it.* 24And when they crucified
Him, they divided His garments, casting
lots for them to determine what every
man should take.

25Now it was the third hour, and they
crucified Him. 26And the inscription of
His accusation was written above:

THE KING OF THE JEWS.

27With Him they also crucified two
robbers, one on His right and the other
on His left. 28So the Scripture was fulfilled[a] which says, *"And He was numbered with the transgressors."*[b]

29And those who passed by blasphemed
Him, wagging their heads and saying,
"Aha! *You* who destroy the temple and
build *it* in three days, 30save Yourself,
and come down from the cross!"

31Likewise the chief priests also,
mocking among themselves with the
scribes, said, "He saved others; Himself
He cannot save. 32Let the Christ, the King
of Israel, descend now from the cross,
that we may see and believe."[a]

Even those who were crucified with
Him reviled Him.

Jesus Dies on the Cross

33Now when the sixth hour had come,
there was darkness over the whole land
until the ninth hour. 34And at the ninth
hour Jesus cried out with a loud voice,
saying, "Eloi, Eloi, lama sabachthani?"
which is translated, *"My God, My God,
why have You forsaken Me?"*[a]

35Some of those who stood by, when
they heard *that,* said, "Look, He is calling
for Elijah!" 36Then someone ran and
filled a sponge full of sour wine, put *it* on
a reed, and offered *it* to Him to drink,
saying, "Let Him alone; let us see if Elijah
will come to take Him down."

37And Jesus cried out with a loud
voice, and breathed His last.

> Young men and old men, and sisters of all ages, if you love the Lord, get a passion for souls. Do you not see them? They are going down to hell by the thousands.
>
> **CHARLES SPURGEON**

38Then the veil of the temple was torn
in two from top to bottom. 39So when the
centurion, who stood opposite Him, saw
that He cried out like this and breathed
His last,[a] he said, "Truly this Man was the
Son of God!"

40There were also women looking on
from afar, among whom were Mary Magdalene, Mary the mother of James the
Less and of Joses, and Salome, 41who also
followed Him and ministered to Him
when He was in Galilee, and many other
women who came up with Him to
Jerusalem.

15:28 [a]Isaiah 53:12 [b]NU-Text omits this verse. 15:32 [a]M-Text reads *believe Him.* 15:34 [a]Psalm 22:1 15:39 [a]NU-Text reads *that He thus breathed His last.*

15:24 Messianic prophecy fulfilled: "They divide My garments among them, and for My clothing they cast lots" (Psa. 22:18). See Luke 1:32,33 comment.

15:25 Bible contradiction? Mark tells us that Jesus was crucified at the third hour. But skeptics claim there is a contradiction because John says it was at least three hours later, since at "about the *sixth* hour" Jesus was still with Pilate before the Jewish crowd (John 19:14). Matthew (27:45) and Luke (23:44) also have Jesus already on the cross at the sixth hour, so they, too, appear to contradict John's account.

So what time of day was Jesus crucified? This has a very simple explanation. Matthew, Mark, and Luke used the Jewish system of keeping the time, where the day was reckoned as starting at 6 a.m. (sunrise). John, on the other hand, used the Roman system, which (like our time) counts the day as starting at midnight. In both cases, Jesus was crucified at 9 a.m.

15:26 *Contradictions in the Bible—Why Are They There?*

The Bible has many *seeming* contradictions within its pages. For example, the four Gospels give four differing accounts as to what was written on the sign that hung on the cross. Matthew said, "This is Jesus the King of the Jews" (27:37). However, Mark contradicts that with "The King of the Jews" (15:26). Luke says something different: "This is the King of the Jews" (23:38), and John maintains that the sign said "Jesus of Nazareth, the King of the Jews" (19:19). Those who are *looking* for contradictions may therefore say, "See—the Bible is *full* of mistakes!" and choose to reject it entirely as being untrustworthy. However, those who trust God have no problem harmonizing the Gospels. There is no contradiction if the sign simply said, "This is Jesus of Nazareth, the King of the Jews."

The godly base their confidence on two truths: 1) "all Scripture is given by inspiration of God" (2 Tim. 3:16); and 2) an elementary rule of Scripture is that God has deliberately included *seeming* contradictions in His Word to "snare" the proud. He has "hidden" things from the "wise and prudent" and "revealed them to babes" (Luke 10:21), purposely choosing foolish things to confound the wise (1 Cor. 1:27). If an ungodly man refuses to humble himself and obey the gospel, and instead desires to build a case against the Bible, God gives him enough material to build his own gallows.

This incredible principle is clearly illustrated in the account of the capture of Zedekiah, king of Judah. Jeremiah the prophet told Zedekiah that God would judge him. He was informed that he would be "delivered into his hand; your eyes shall see the eyes of the king of Babylon, he shall speak with you face to face, and you shall go to Babylon" (Jer. 34:3). This is confirmed in Jer. 39:5–7 where we are told that he was captured and brought to King Nebuchadnezzar, then they "bound him with bronze fetters to carry him off to Babylon." However, in Ezek. 12:13, God warned, "I will bring him to Babylon . . . *yet he shall not see it*, though he shall die there" (emphasis added).

Here is material to build a case against the Bible! It is an *obvious* mistake. Three Bible verses say that the king would go to Babylon, and yet the Bible in another place says that he would not see Babylon. How can someone be taken somewhere and not see it? It makes no sense at all—unless Zedekiah was *blinded*. And that is precisely what happened. Zedekiah saw Nebuchadnezzar face to face, saw his sons killed before his eyes, then "the king of Babylon . . . put out Zedekiah's eyes" before taking him to Babylon (Jer. 39:6,7).

This is the underlying principle behind the many "contradictions" of Holy Scripture (such as how many horses David had, who was the first to arrive at the tomb after the resurrection of Jesus, etc.).

God has turned the tables on proud, arrogant, self-righteous man. When man proudly stands outside of the kingdom of God, and seeks to justify his sinfulness through evidence he thinks discredits the Bible, he doesn't realize that God has simply lowered the door of life, so that only those willing to exercise childlike faith and bow in humility may enter.

It is interesting to note that the seeming contradictions in the four Gospels attest to the fact that there was no corroboration between the writers.

Jesus Buried in Joseph's Tomb

42 Now when evening had come, because it was the Preparation Day, that is,
the day before the Sabbath, 43 Joseph of
Arimathea, a prominent council member,
who was himself waiting for the kingdom
of God, coming and taking courage, went
in to Pilate and asked for the body of Jesus.
44 Pilate marveled that He was already
dead; and summoning the centurion, he
asked him if He had been dead for some
time. 45 So when he found out from the
centurion, he granted the body to Joseph.
46 Then he bought fine linen, took Him
down, and wrapped Him in the linen.
And he laid Him in a tomb which had
been hewn out of the rock, and rolled a
stone against the door of the tomb. 47 And
Mary Magdalene and Mary *the mother* of
Joses observed where He was laid.

He Is Risen

16 Now when the Sabbath was past,
Mary Magdalene, Mary *the mother*
of James, and Salome bought spices, that
they might come and anoint Him. 2 Very
early in the morning, on the first *day* of
the week, they came to the tomb when
the sun had risen. 3 And they said among
themselves, "Who will roll away the

15:39 ## *The Witness (An interesting insight into what may have been)*

By Danny Hotea

As was my custom, I rose early that day to pay homage to the gods by prayers and burnt offerings. To which I vowed my obedience on that fateful morning, I cannot now remember. There were so many.

Leaving the place of worship, I endeavored to sit quietly and read the creeds of Rome as written by the emperor himself. It was my duty not only as a centurion, but as a Roman citizen, to understand the purpose of almighty Caesar and Rome. However, just as I began pouring over the open scroll, a nameless messenger came panting with word from Pontius Pilate, governor of Judea, ordering my garrison to his palace immediately.

I arrived with three hundred men as if by flight. The sun had hardly risen, and the air held an unseen weight, as if to distinguish this day from all others. The men, all clad in leather and metal with swords swaying from their belts and spears stabbing at the sky in protest of their unusually early arousal, wobbled restlessly in rigid formation, awaiting my command. The sound of spiked sandals scraping the stone palace floor echoed down the long, stone hallway adding tension to mystery. They undoubtedly supposed that I knew the reason for it all. But I didn't—until another messenger came with another scroll describing our purpose exactly.

Jerusalem was a place known for its concentrated reserve of mindless zealots. And I had experience in stamping out the feeble efforts of disorderly vagrants and disorganized militias meant to unshackle the Jews from Rome's iron grip. One in particular came to mind as I read the final sentence of that day's orders. It was the most recent and pathetic uprising. A small army of poorly armed religious rebels managed to assassinate an insignificant gatekeeper in the governor's palace. The idea that a handful of superstitious peasants could overthrow Rome was ridiculous and, if it weren't so sad, it would be laughable. Their leader had been a thin, sweaty man with hardly any beard, balding head and shifting eyes. A Jew. A brainless dreamer suffering from resentment. His name was Barabbas. He was hardly a match for Rome. I caught him in the streets attempting to hide beneath a vendor's blankets after his pitiful militia had been butchered and left for the dogs. I was his judge and jury. And since only Romans have the right to a trial, I stuffed him in a smaller-than-usual cell after the garrison had their day's exercise of beating him with rods and slapping him with gloved fists.

That day had another experience for me altogether. As we pushed our way into the Praetorium hauling the scourged offender to the platform, where another Man stood, the mob sang out in a chorus of hatred, "Crucify Him!" The governor addressed the riotous masses with careful words, offering them a choice between the bloodied and uncondemned Man now occupying the platform with him, or the pathetic zealot, Barabbas, who had failed an attempt to destroy Rome. Immediately they sent out blood-curdling screams consenting to the murder of the One and the release of the other. It was apparent, by their screams, that this Man had not offended Rome. He had offended the Jews.

A messenger interrupted the procedure, which was doubtlessly an urgent matter, after which I was signaled to bring Him into the governor's inner court.

The conversation that took place proved this Man's character. He spoke only when questioned and claimed that the governor's authority was given to him by the Offender's Father, which made little sense to me at the time. When He said He was a King, I wondered whether Barabbas, the sweaty zealot, had similar thoughts. But, all in all, this Man had authority incomparable to any I had seen before. This fact was startling considering I had seen the Caesar and all his delegates more often than Pontius himself.

What seemed like moments later, my garrison had elbowed their way through the riotous crowds to the place of execution, hauling two offenders of Rome and One offender of the Jews.

His head had been crowned with thorns, no doubt a torturous invention of the guiltless soldiers in my garrison. His beard replaced with bleeding flesh. His back opened wide by a Roman scourge to an infectious environment full of illness bred in the hearts of vehement enemies. Yet, it seemed that these were the slightest of His pains judging by the weight of grief He bore on His countenance. His visage carried an eternal load of unfamiliar burdens.

As was my custom, I drove the first nail into the left wrist of each offender inaugurating their torturous departure from this world and instructing my garrison how to proceed with the crucifixion. The two vagrants wrestled pathetically against the soldier's grip that held their filthy arms against the knotted wood, spitting out blasphemies against the gods of Rome and sprinkling our faces with bloody specs of mucus. But they could do little more than wiggle their palms and claw at my wrists with their broken nails until the iron spike

(continued)

(15:39 continued)

impaled the wrist and its owner's arm was pinned against the wood, twitching like a wounded animal. I often delighted in the sound of their earsplitting screams and hellish moans that filled the air and the sight of their epileptic convulsions of agony as their crosses were set upright. It became somewhat of a drama to which I looked forward with secret pleasure, even more than the gladiators and the chariot races where countless men had lost their lives to entertain Rome. I could hardly keep from smiling, at times.

But this Man, although He was innocent, displayed no reluctance in placing His arm against the wood. His eyes fastened on the soldier holding His arm and on me, His sadistic executioner. I expected the typical reaction as the iron penetrated His skin. But this Man was not typical in any sense of the word. Instead of spraying my face with spittle, He groaned and looked away, scrapping His thorny crown against the lumber behind His head. Unlike the other two, this Man did not moan in melodies of agony as the cross sat upright, disjointing its resident.

Tears ran down His scabbed face as He viewed the masses streaming past the foot of His cross. Their venomous words struck the air like frothy waves pounding some seaside cliff. And, unlike the other two, whose hoarse-voiced cursing baptized each passerby with vulgar threats and swollen words of every sort, He spoke kindly to a few standing at the foot of His cross. Had He not been a Jew, I would have been compelled to defend His dying reputation for sheer sympathy's sake.

At the instant before He died, the sky blackened as if it had been split open like a carcass and all its guilt bled out onto the clouds. The earth convulsed, shaking and tossing my men and me like mere toys. At that instant I knew this Man was no mere Man.

He wielded an exclusive power. The image of Rome, as if it were a colossal statue carved of iron, lay in heaps beneath His cross as a mound of chaff vulnerable to the slightest breath of wind. The sight of His emaciated corpse stabbed at my conscience. Had I done wrong? If not, then why such agony of heart? I was bleeding now and my zeal for Rome poured from the bowels of my heart like the streamlets coursing from His side and brow. He had slain me; not I Him. His naked body, reduced to shards of stinking flesh hanging lifelessly on the cross, seemed more alive than I did standing with my hand-polished helmet and Roman embroidery hanging like empirical curtains from my shoulders. I was ashamed of myself.

I turned away to prevent my tears from being noticed. Regret welled up in my soul and poured out onto my cheeks with burning tears. I tried desperately to compose myself to no avail. Once more, I turned to look at Him, and my knees betrayed me to the ground beneath. My forehead kissed the ground in an unguarded slump. I gritted my teeth and formed the words, "Truly, this was the Son of God!"

I have never been the same since.

stone from the door of the tomb for us?"
4But when they looked up, they saw that
the stone had been rolled away—for it
was very large. 5And entering the tomb,
they saw a young man clothed in a long
white robe sitting on the right side; and
they were alarmed.

6But he said to them, "Do not be
alarmed. You seek Jesus of Nazareth, who
was crucified. He is risen! He is not here.
See the place where they laid Him. 7But
go, tell His disciples—and Peter—that
He is going before you into Galilee; there
you will see Him, as He said to you."

8So they went out quickly[a] and fled
from the tomb, for they trembled and
were amazed. And they said nothing to
anyone, for they were afraid.

Mary Magdalene Sees the Risen Lord

9Now when *He* rose early on the first
day of the week, He appeared first to
Mary Magdalene, out of whom He had
cast seven demons. 10She went and told
those who had been with Him, as they
mourned and wept. 11And when they
heard that He was alive and had been
seen by her, they did not believe.

Jesus Appears to Two Disciples

12After that, He appeared in another
form to two of them as they walked and
went into the country. 13And they went
and told *it* to the rest, *but* they did not believe them either.

The Great Commission

14Later He appeared to the eleven as
they sat at the table; and He rebuked
their unbelief and hardness of heart, be-

16:8 [a]NU-Text and M-Text omit *quickly*.

Questions & Objections

16:6

"How many angels were at the tomb—one or two?"

The question has arisen simply because Matthew (28:2–7) and Mark mention one angel, whereas Luke (24:4–7) and John (20:12,13) refer to two. There is no conflict if there were two angels but Matthew and Mark simply quote the one who was a spokesperson.

cause they did not believe those who had
seen Him after He had risen. 15And He
said to them, "Go into all the world and
preach the gospel to every creature. 16He
who believes and is baptized will be
saved; but he who does not believe will
be condemned. 17And these signs will
follow those who believe: In My name
they will cast out demons; they will speak
with new tongues; 18they[a] will take up
serpents; and if they drink anything
deadly, it will by no means hurt them;
they will lay hands on the sick, and they
will recover."

Christ Ascends to God's Right Hand

19So then, after the Lord had spoken
to them, He was received up into heaven,
and sat down at the right hand of God.
20And they went out and preached everywhere, the Lord working with *them* and
confirming the word through the accompanying signs. Amen.[a]

16:18 [a]NU-Text reads *and in their hands they will.* **16:20** [a]Verses 9–20 are bracketed in NU-Text as not original. They are lacking in Codex Sinaiticus and Codex Vaticanus, although nearly all other manuscripts of Mark contain them.

16:15 Here is some fascinating information. The original Greek meaning of "Go into all the world and preach the gospel to every creature" opens up some interesting thoughts. The word for "go" is very captivating. It is *poreuomai*, meaning "go." The word "all" also carries with it gripping connotations. It is *hapas*, and actually means "all." And if that doesn't rivet you, look closely at the word "every." It is *pas*, and literally means "every." So when Jesus commanded us, "Go into all the world and preach the gospel to every creature," to be true and faithful to the original text, what He was actually saying was, "Go into all the world and preach the gospel to every creature." We are so fortunate to have access to knowledge like this.

If the command to "preach the gospel to every creature" were given only to the eleven disciples, preaching of the gospel would have stopped when they died. *Every* Christian is a "disciple." The word in Greek is *mathetes* and simply means "a learner." It is used in reference to the eleven, as well as to believers such as Joseph of Arimathea (Matt. 27:57), Ananias (Acts 9:10), and others (Acts 9:36; 16:1; 21:16). In Luke 14:26,27 Jesus used the term in reference to *any* who would believe in Him.

"Here is our commissioning and sending. There are no exceptions—every Christian is commanded to go!"
Trevor Yaxley

16:17,18 In reference to true converts, Jesus said, "By their *fruits* you will know them" (Matt. 7:20), not by their gifts. Many false converts have had "power" gifts. See Matt. 7:21–23.

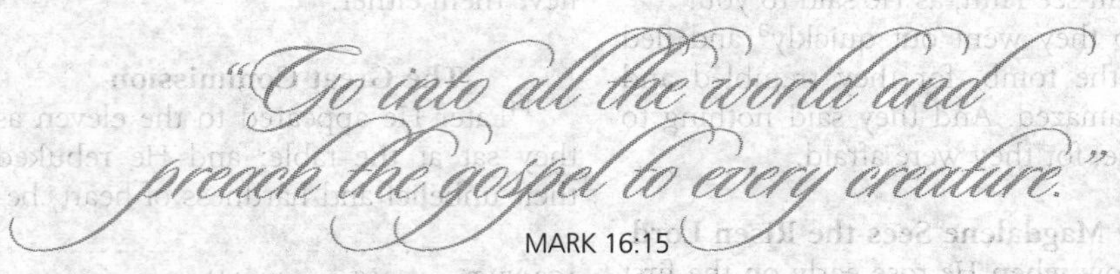
"Go into all the world and
preach the gospel to every creature."
MARK 16:15

Luke

Dedication to Theophilus

1 Inasmuch as many have taken in hand
to set in order a narrative of those
things which have been fulfilled[a] among
us, 2just as those who from the beginning were eyewitnesses and ministers of
the word delivered them to us, 3it seemed
good to me also, having had perfect understanding of all things from the very
first, to write to you an orderly account,
most excellent Theophilus, 4that you may
know the certainty of those things in
which you were instructed.

John's Birth Announced to Zacharias

5There was in the days of Herod, the
king of Judea, a certain priest named
Zacharias, of the division of Abijah. His
wife *was* of the daughters of Aaron, and
her name *was* Elizabeth. 6And they were
both righteous before God, walking in all
the commandments and ordinances of the
Lord blameless. 7But they had no child,
because Elizabeth was barren, and they
were both well advanced in years.

8So it was, that while he was serving
as priest before God in the order of his
division, 9according to the custom of the
priesthood, his lot fell to burn incense
when he went into the temple of the Lord.
10And the whole multitude of the people
was praying outside at the hour of incense.
11Then an angel of the Lord appeared to
him, standing on the right side of the altar of incense. 12And when Zacharias saw
him, he was troubled, and fear fell upon
him.

13But the angel said to him, "Do not
be afraid, Zacharias, for your prayer is
heard; and your wife Elizabeth will bear
you a son, and you shall call his name
John. 14And you will have joy and gladness, and many will rejoice at his birth.
15For he will be great in the sight of the
Lord, and shall drink neither wine nor
strong drink. He will also be filled with
the Holy Spirit, even from his mother's
womb. 16And he will turn many of the
children of Israel to the Lord their God.
17He will also go before Him in the spirit
and power of Elijah, *'to turn the hearts of
the fathers to the children,'*[a] and the disobedient to the wisdom of the just, to
make ready a people prepared for the
Lord."

18And Zacharias said to the angel, "How
shall I know this? For I am an old man,
and my wife is well advanced in years."

19And the angel answered and said to
him, "I am Gabriel, who stands in the

1:1 [a]Or *are most surely believed* 1:17 [a]Malachi 4:5, 6

1:3 Historical accuracy. "Given the large portion of the New Testament written by him, it's extremely significant that Luke has been established to be a scrupulously accurate historian, even in the smallest details. One prominent archaeologist carefully examined Luke's references to thirty-two countries, fifty-four cities, and nine islands, finding not a single mistake." *John McRay*

presence of God, and was sent to speak to you and bring you these glad tidings. 20But behold, you will be mute and not able to speak until the day these things take place, because you did not believe my words which will be fulfilled in their own time."

21And the people waited for Zacharias, and marveled that he lingered so long in the temple. 22But when he came out, he could not speak to them; and they perceived that he had seen a vision in the temple, for he beckoned to them and remained speechless.

> I trust that you will find no rest for your feet till you have been the means of leading many to that blessed Savior who is your confidence and hope.
>
> **CHARLES SPURGEON**

23So it was, as soon as the days of his service were completed, that he departed to his own house. 24Now after those days his wife Elizabeth conceived; and she hid herself five months, saying, 25"Thus the Lord has dealt with me, in the days when He looked on *me,* to take away my reproach among people."

Christ's Birth Announced to Mary

26Now in the sixth month the angel Gabriel was sent by God to a city of Galilee named Nazareth, 27to a virgin betrothed to a man whose name was Joseph, of the house of David. The virgin's name *was* Mary. 28And having come in, the angel said to her, "Rejoice, highly favored *one,* the Lord *is* with you; blessed *are* you among women!"[a]

29But when she saw *him,*[a] she was troubled at his saying, and considered what manner of greeting this was. 30Then the angel said to her, "Do not be afraid, Mary, for you have found favor with God. 31And behold, you will conceive in your womb and bring forth a Son, and shall call His name JESUS. 32He will be great, and will be called the Son of the Highest; and the Lord God will give Him the throne of His father David. 33And He will reign over the house of Jacob forever, and of His kingdom there will be no end."

34Then Mary said to the angel, "How can this be, since I do not know a man?"

35And the angel answered and said to her, "*The* Holy Spirit will come upon you, and the power of the Highest will overshadow you; therefore, also, that Holy One who is to be born will be called the Son of God. 36Now indeed, Elizabeth your relative has also conceived a son in her old age; and this is now the sixth month for her who was called barren. 37For with God nothing will be impossible."

38Then Mary said, "Behold the maidservant of the Lord! Let it be to me according to your word." And the angel departed from her.

Mary Visits Elizabeth

39Now Mary arose in those days and went into the hill country with haste, to a city of Judah, 40and entered the house of Zacharias and greeted Elizabeth. 41And it happened, when Elizabeth heard the greet-

1:28 [a]NU-Text omits *blessed are you among women.* 1:29 [a]NU-Text omits *when she saw him.*

1:27 Archaeology confirms the Bible. Following the 1993 discovery in Israel of a stone containing the inscriptions "House of David" and "King of Israel," *Time* magazine stated, "This writing—dated to the 9th century B.C., only a century after David's reign—described a victory by a neighboring king over the Israelites... The skeptics' claim that David never existed is now hard to defend." *Time*, December 18, 1995

1:31–35 See Matt. 1:20–23 comment.

1:32,33 Messianic prophecy fulfilled: "Of the increase of His government and peace there will be no end, upon the throne of David and over His kingdom, to order it and establish it with judgment and justice from that time forward, even forever. The zeal of the Lord of hosts will perform this" (Isa. 9:7). See Luke 3:23 comment.

ing of Mary, that the babe leaped in her
womb; and Elizabeth was filled with the
Holy Spirit. 42Then she spoke out with a
loud voice and said, "Blessed *are* you
among women, and blessed *is* the fruit of
your womb! 43But why *is* this *granted* to
me, that the mother of my Lord should
come to me? 44For indeed, as soon as the
voice of your greeting sounded in my
ears, the babe leaped in my womb for
joy. 45Blessed *is* she who believed, for
there will be a fulfillment of those things
which were told her from the Lord."

The Song of Mary

46And Mary said:

"My soul magnifies the Lord,
47And my spirit has rejoiced in God my
Savior.
48For He has regarded the lowly state
of His maidservant;
For behold, henceforth all
generations will call me blessed.
49For He who is mighty has done great
things for me,
And holy *is* His name.
50And His mercy *is* on those who fear
Him
From generation to generation.
51He has shown strength with His arm;
He has scattered *the* proud in the
imagination of their hearts.
52He has put down the mighty from
their thrones,
And exalted *the* lowly.
53He has filled *the* hungry with good
things,
And *the* rich He has sent away empty.
54He has helped His servant Israel,
In remembrance of *His* mercy,
55As He spoke to our fathers,
To Abraham and to his seed forever."

56And Mary remained with her about
three months, and returned to her house.

Birth of John the Baptist

57Now Elizabeth's full time came for
her to be delivered, and she brought forth
a son. 58When her neighbors and relatives
heard how the Lord had shown great
mercy to her, they rejoiced with her.

Circumcision of John the Baptist

59So it was, on the eighth day, that they
came to circumcise the child; and they
would have called him by the name of his
father, Zacharias. 60His mother answered
and said, "No; he shall be called John."
61But they said to her, "There is no
one among your relatives who is called by
this name." 62So they made signs to his
father—what he would have him called.
63And he asked for a writing tablet, and
wrote, saying, "His name is John." So they
all marveled. 64Immediately his mouth
was opened and his tongue *loosed,* and he
spoke, praising God. 65Then fear came
on all who dwelt around them; and all
these sayings were discussed throughout
all the hill country of Judea. 66And all
those who heard *them* kept *them* in their
hearts, saying, "What kind of child will
this be?" And the hand of the Lord was
with him.

Zacharias' Prophecy

67Now his father Zacharias was filled
with the Holy Spirit, and prophesied,
saying:

68"Blessed *is* the Lord God of Israel,
For He has visited and redeemed His
people,
69And has raised up a horn of salvation
for us
In the house of His servant David,
70As He spoke by the mouth of His
holy prophets,
Who *have been* since the world began,
71That we should be saved from our
enemies
And from the hand of all who hate us,
72To perform the mercy *promised* to
our fathers
And to remember His holy covenant,
73The oath which He swore to our
father Abraham:
74To grant us that we,

Being delivered from the hand of our
enemies,
Might serve Him without fear,
75In holiness and righteousness before
Him all the days of our life.

76"And you, child, will be called the
prophet of the Highest;
For you will go before the face of the
Lord to prepare His ways,
77To give knowledge of salvation to His
people
By the remission of their sins,
78Through the tender mercy of our
God,
With which the Dayspring from on
high has visited[a] us;
79To give light to those who sit in
darkness and the shadow of
death,
To guide our feet into the way of
peace."

80So the child grew and became
strong in spirit, and was in the deserts till
the day of his manifestation to Israel.

Christ Born of Mary

2 And it came to pass in those days
that a decree went out from Caesar
Augustus that all the world should be
registered. 2This census first took place
while Quirinius was governing Syria. 3So
all went to be registered, everyone to his
own city.
4Joseph also went up from Galilee, out
of the city of Nazareth, into Judea, to the
city of David, which is called Bethlehem,
because he was of the house and lineage
of David, 5to be registered with Mary, his
betrothed wife,[a] who was with child. 6So
it was, that while they were there, the
days were completed for her to be delivered. 7And she brought forth her firstborn Son, and wrapped Him in swaddling cloths, and laid Him in a manger,
because there was no room for them in
the inn.

Glory in the Highest

8Now there were in the same country
shepherds living out in the fields, keeping watch over their flock by night. 9And
behold,[a] an angel of the Lord stood before them, and the glory of the Lord shone
around them, and they were greatly
afraid. 10Then the angel said to them,
"Do not be afraid, for behold, I bring you
good tidings of great joy which will be to
all people. 11For there is born to you this
day in the city of David a Savior, who is
Christ the Lord. 12And this *will be* the
sign to you: You will find a Babe wrapped
in swaddling cloths, lying in a manger."
13And suddenly there was with the
angel a multitude of the heavenly host
praising God and saying:

14"Glory to God in the highest,
And on earth peace, goodwill toward
men!"[a]

15So it was, when the angels had gone
away from them into heaven, that the
shepherds said to one another, "Let us
now go to Bethlehem and see this thing
that has come to pass, which the Lord
has made known to us." 16And they came
with haste and found Mary and Joseph,
and the Babe lying in a manger. 17Now
when they had seen *Him,* they made

1:78 [a]NU-Text reads *shall visit.* 2:5 [a]NU-Text omits *wife.* 2:9 [a]NU-Text omits *behold.* 2:14 [a]NU-Text reads *toward men of goodwill.*

1:74 Fear of man. When God commissioned Moses to go speak to Pharaoh, Moses revealed that he had a problem. His seeming humility ("Who am I . . . ?") was actually the fear of man (Exod. 3:11; 4:1). Although he argued with God that he wasn't eloquent, God promised to be with him and teach him what to say (Exod. 4:10–14). Likewise, we have no excuse for entertaining the fear of man when it comes to seeking the lost, because we are not called to use eloquent speech. We have the indwelling Christ, and through Him and His strength we can "do all things" (Phil. 4:13).

1:79 See Psa. 23:4 comment.

widely[a] known the saying which was told
them concerning this Child. 18And all those
who heard *it* marveled at those things
which were told them by the shepherds.
19But Mary kept all these things and pondered *them* in her heart. 20Then the shepherds returned, glorifying and praising
God for all the things that they had heard
and seen, as it was told them.

Circumcision of Jesus

21And when eight days were completed for the circumcision of the Child,[a]
His name was called JESUS, the name
given by the angel before He was conceived in the womb.

Jesus Presented in the Temple

22Now when the days of her purification according to the law of Moses were
completed, they brought Him to Jerusalem to present *Him* to the Lord 23(as it
is written in the law of the Lord, *"Every
male who opens the womb shall be called
holy to the Lord"*),[a] 24and to offer a sacrifice according to what is said in the law
of the Lord, *"A pair of turtledoves or two
young pigeons."*[a]

Simeon Sees God's Salvation

25And behold, there was a man in
Jerusalem whose name *was* Simeon, and
this man *was* just and devout, waiting for
the Consolation of Israel, and the Holy
Spirit was upon him. 26And it had been
revealed to him by the Holy Spirit that he
would not see death before he had seen
the Lord's Christ. 27So he came by the
Spirit into the temple. And when the parents brought in the Child Jesus, to do for
Him according to the custom of the law,
28he took Him up in his arms and blessed
God and said:

29"Lord, now You are letting Your
servant depart in peace,
According to Your word;
30For my eyes have seen Your salvation
31Which You have prepared before the
face of all peoples,
32A light to *bring* revelation to the
Gentiles,
And the glory of Your people Israel."

33And Joseph and His mother[a] marveled at those things which were spoken
of Him. 34Then Simeon blessed them, and
said to Mary His mother, "Behold, this
Child is destined for the fall and rising of
many in Israel, and for a sign which will
be spoken against 35(yes, a sword will
pierce through your own soul also), that
the thoughts of many hearts may be revealed."

Anna Bears Witness to the Redeemer

36Now there was one, Anna, a prophetess, the daughter of Phanuel, of the
tribe of Asher. She was of a great age, and
had lived with a husband seven years
from her virginity; 37and this woman *was*
a widow of about eighty-four years,[a] who
did not depart from the temple, but served
God with fastings and prayers night and
day. 38And coming in that instant she
gave thanks to the Lord,[a] and spoke of
Him to all those who looked for redemption in Jerusalem.

The Family Returns to Nazareth

39So when they had performed all
things according to the law of the Lord,

2:17 [a]NU-Text omits *widely*. 2:21 [a]NU-Text reads *for His circumcision*. 2:23 [a]Exodus 13:2, 12, 15 2:24 [a]Leviticus 12:8 2:33 [a]NU-Text reads *And His father and mother*. 2:37 [a]NU-Text reads *a widow until she was eighty-four*. 2:38 [a]NU-Text reads *to God*.

2:38 "In the Incarnation, God masterminds the announcement of the good news of the birth of Christ. He sends prophets well in advance to foretell the coming of the Messiah. He commissions an angel to announce the birth to a virgin. He sets a new star in the heavens to summon wise men from the East. He sends a company of singing angels to pronounce Christ's birth to the shepherds in the fields. He quickens Anna the prophetess to declare the arrival of the Messiah on his day of circumcision. Though Christ was born in a lowly manger, there was nothing quiet about his birth." *John Witte, Jr.*

QUESTIONS & OBJECTIONS

2:46 ***"Jesus wasn't sinless—He dishonored His parents."***

This biblical incident is a favorite of skeptics, as they try to find fault with Jesus. The accusation is that Jesus dishonored His parents by staying behind in Jerusalem, when they were traveling back to Nazareth. Therefore, He was in violation of the Fifth Commandment. Of course, the charge is completely unfounded. In Luke 2:42–49 we are told that His mother and Joseph left Jerusalem "supposing Him to have been in the company." He wasn't, and an entire day went by before they realized it. It took three days for them to return to Jerusalem and find Him. He was in the temple teaching the elders, as He said, about His "Father's business." Any responsible parents would never leave a city "supposing" that their twelve-year-old was with them. That was poor parenting, not disobedience.

they returned to Galilee, to their *own* city,
Nazareth. 40And the Child grew and became strong in spirit,[a] filled with wisdom;
and the grace of God was upon Him.

The Boy Jesus Amazes the Scholars

41His parents went to Jerusalem every
year at the Feast of the Passover. 42And
when He was twelve years old, they went
up to Jerusalem according to the custom of
the feast. 43When they had finished the
days, as they returned, the Boy Jesus lingered behind in Jerusalem. And Joseph
and His mother[a] did not know *it;* 44but
supposing Him to have been in the company, they went a day's journey, and
sought Him among *their* relatives and acquaintances. 45So when they did not find
Him, they returned to Jerusalem, seeking
Him. 46Now so it was *that* after three
days they found Him in the temple, sitting in the midst of the teachers, both listening to them and asking them questions.
47And all who heard Him were astonished
at His understanding and answers. 48So
when they saw Him, they were amazed;
and His mother said to Him, "Son, why
have You done this to us? Look, Your father and I have sought You anxiously."
49And He said to them, "Why did you
seek Me? Did you not know that I must
be about My Father's business?" 50But
they did not understand the statement
which He spoke to them.

Jesus Advances in Wisdom and Favor

51Then He went down with them and
came to Nazareth, and was subject to them,
but His mother kept all these things in
her heart. 52And Jesus increased in wisdom and stature, and in favor with God
and men.

John the Baptist Prepares the Way

3 Now in the fifteenth year of the reign
of Tiberius Caesar, Pontius Pilate being governor of Judea, Herod being tet-

2:40 [a]NU-Text omits *in spirit.* 2:43 [a]NU-Text reads *And His parents.*

2:44 Assuming God is with us. Multitudes sit in churches "supposing" that Jesus is with them, but they don't know Him (see Matt. 7:21–23). They are false converts who will be sorted out on Judgment Day. They have never obeyed the command to repent and trust that Savior. That's disobedience.

The world is filled with people who, like Mary and Joseph, suppose that God is with them. To them He is nothing but a divine butler, who is expected to come running when they want something to be done. Such is the trail that often leads to atheism.

The soil of history is stained in the blood that tyrants have shed, because they supposed that their holy war had divine favor. When Abraham Lincoln heard someone say he hoped the Lord was on the Union's side, the president responded, "I am not at all concerned about that, for I know that the Lord is always on the side of the right. But it is my constant anxiety and prayer that I and this nation should be on the Lord's side."

Mary and Joseph had the supposition that Jesus was with them. But they were wrong. Let's not make the same mistake.

rarch of Galilee, his brother Philip tetrarch
of Iturea and the region of Trachonitis,
and Lysanias tetrarch of Abilene, [2]while
Annas and Caiaphas were high priests,[a]
the word of God came to John the son of
Zacharias in the wilderness. [3]And he went
into all the region around the Jordan,
preaching a baptism of repentance for the
remission of sins, [4]as it is written in the
book of the words of Isaiah the prophet,
saying:

"The voice of one crying in the
wilderness:
'Prepare the way of the Lord;
Make His paths straight.
[5]*Every valley shall be filled*
And every mountain and hill brought
low;
The crooked places shall be made
straight
And the rough ways smooth;
[6]*And all flesh shall see the salvation of*
God.' "[a]

John Preaches to the People

[7]Then he said to the multitudes that
came out to be baptized by him, "Brood
of vipers! Who warned you to flee from
the wrath to come? [8]Therefore bear fruits
worthy of repentance, and do not begin
to say to yourselves, 'We have Abraham
as *our* father.' For I say to you that God is
able to raise up children to Abraham
from these stones. [9]And even now the ax
is laid to the root of the trees. Therefore
every tree which does not bear good fruit
is cut down and thrown into the fire."
[10]So the people asked him, saying,

THE FUNCTION OF THE LAW

3:4 "Ever more the Law must prepare the way for the gospel. To overlook this in instructing souls is almost certain to result in false hope, the introduction of a false standard of Christian experience, and to fill the Church with false converts... Time will make this plain." *Charles Finney*

"What shall we do then?"
[11]He answered and said to them, "He
who has two tunics, let him give to him
who has none; and he who has food, let
him do likewise."
[12]Then tax collectors also came to be
baptized, and said to him, "Teacher, what
shall we do?"
[13]And he said to them, "Collect no
more than what is appointed for you."
[14]Likewise the soldiers asked him,
saying, "And what shall we do?"
So he said to them, "Do not intimidate
anyone or accuse falsely, and be content
with your wages."
[15]Now as the people were in expectation, and all reasoned in their hearts
about John, whether he was the Christ *or*
not, [16]John answered, saying to all, "I indeed baptize you with water; but One
mightier than I is coming, whose sandal
strap I am not worthy to loose. He will
baptize you with the Holy Spirit and fire.
[17]His winnowing fan *is* in His hand, and
He will thoroughly clean out His threshing floor, and gather the wheat into His
barn; but the chaff He will burn with unquenchable fire."

3:2 [a]NU-Text and M-Text read *in the high priesthood of Annas and Caiaphas.* 3:6 [a]Isaiah 40:3–5

3:1,2 Archaeology confirms the Bible. A hidden burial chamber, dating to the first century, was discovered in 1990 two miles from the Temple Mount. One bore the bones of a man in his 60s, with the inscription "Yehosef bar Qayafa"—meaning "Joseph, son of Caiaphas." Experts believe this was Caiaphas, the high priest of Jerusalem, who was involved in the arrest of Jesus, interrogated Him, and handed Him over to Pontius Pilate for execution.

A few decades earlier, excavations at Caesarea Maritama, the ancient seat of Roman government in Judea, uncovered a stone slab whose complete inscription may have read: "Pontius Pilate, the prefect of Judea, has dedicated to the people of Caesarea a temple in honor of Tiberius."

The discovery is truly significant, establishing that the man depicted in the Gospels as Judea's Roman governor had the authority ascribed to him by the Gospel writers. *Jeffery L. Sheler*, "Is the Bible True?" *Reader's Digest*, June 2000

18 And with many other exhortations
he preached to the people. 19 But Herod
the tetrarch, being rebuked by him concerning Herodias, his brother Philip's
wife,[a] and for all the evils which Herod
had done, 20 also added this, above all,
that he shut John up in prison.

John Baptizes Jesus

21 When all the people were baptized,
it came to pass that Jesus also was baptized; and while He prayed, the heaven
was opened. 22 And the Holy Spirit descended in bodily form like a dove upon
Him, and a voice came from heaven which
said, "You are My beloved Son; in You I
am well pleased."

The Genealogy of Jesus Christ

23 Now Jesus Himself began *His ministry at* about thirty years of age, being (as
was supposed) *the* son of Joseph, *the son*
of Heli, 24 *the son* of Matthat,[a] *the son* of
Levi, *the son* of Melchi, *the son* of Janna,
the son of Joseph, 25 *the son* of Mattathiah,
the son of Amos, *the son* of Nahum, *the son*
of Esli, *the son* of Naggai, 26 *the son* of
Maath, *the son* of Mattathiah, *the son* of
Semei, *the son* of Joseph, *the son* of Judah,
27 *the son* of Joannas, *the son* of Rhesa, *the
son* of Zerubbabel, *the son* of Shealtiel, *the
son* of Neri, 28 *the son* of Melchi, *the son* of
Addi, *the son* of Cosam, *the son* of Elmo-
dam, *the son* of Er, 29 *the son* of Jose, *the
son* of Eliezer, *the son* of Jorim, *the son* of
Matthat, *the son* of Levi, 30 *the son* of Simeon,
the son of Judah, *the son* of Joseph, *the son*
of Jonan, *the son* of Eliakim, 31 *the son* of
Melea, *the son* of Menan, *the son* of Mat-
tathah, *the son* of Nathan, *the son* of
David, 32 *the son* of Jesse, *the son* of Obed,
the son of Boaz, *the son* of Salmon, *the son*
of Nahshon, 33 *the son* of Amminadab, *the
son* of Ram, *the son* of Hezron, *the son* of
Perez, *the son* of Judah, 34 *the son* of Jacob,
the son of Isaac, *the son* of Abraham, *the
son* of Terah, *the son* of Nahor, 35 *the son* of
Serug, *the son* of Reu, *the son* of Peleg, *the
son* of Eber, *the son* of Shelah, 36 *the son* of
Cainan, *the son* of Arphaxad, *the son* of
Shem, *the son* of Noah, *the son* of Lamech,
37 *the son* of Methuselah, *the son* of Enoch,
the son of Jared, *the son* of Mahalalel, *the
son* of Cainan, 38 *the son* of Enosh, *the son*
of Seth, *the son* of Adam, *the son* of God.

Satan Tempts Jesus

4 Then Jesus, being filled with the
Holy Spirit, returned from the Jordan
and was led by the Spirit into[a] the wilderness, 2 being tempted for forty days
by the devil. And in those days He ate
nothing, and afterward, when they had

3:19 [a]NU-Text reads *his brother's wife.* 3:24 [a]This and several other names in the genealogy are spelled somewhat differently in the NU-Text. Since the New King James Version uses the Old Testament spelling for persons mentioned in the New Testament, these variations, which come from the Greek, have not been footnoted. 4:1 [a]NU-Text reads *in.*

3:17 "When I pastored a country church, a farmer didn't like the sermons I preached on hell. He said, 'Preach about the meek and lowly Jesus.' I said, 'That's where I got my information about hell.'" *Vance Havner*

3:21 "More than twenty times the Gospels call attention to Jesus' practice of prayer. It is given special mention during events of momentous decision in His life—His baptism (Luke 3:21); the selection of the twelve apostles (Luke 6:12); on the Mount of Transfiguration (Luke 9:29); the Last Supper (Matt. 26:27); in Gethsemane (Luke 22:39–46); and on the cross (Luke 23:46)." *Robert E. Coleman*

3:23 Bible contradiction? Skeptics argue that there is a contradiction regarding who Joseph's father was. Matthew 1:16 says, "Jacob begot Joseph the husband of Mary," while this verse says Joseph was the son of Heli. Joseph's father was Jacob, as Matthew states. Luke follows Mary's genealogy, though he doesn't name any women in his list. He therefore lists the name of Joseph (her husband), who was Heli's son-in-law (in legal terms, his son by marriage). See also Matt. 1:1 comment.

Messianic prophecy fulfilled: "The scepter shall not depart from Judah, nor a lawgiver from between his feet, until Shiloh comes; and to Him shall be the obedience of the people" (Gen. 49:10). See Luke 23:32–34 comment.

ended, He was hungry.
3And the devil said to Him, "If You are
the Son of God, command this stone to
become bread."
4But Jesus answered him, saying,[a] "It
is written, *'Man shall not live by bread
alone, but by every word of God.'* "[b]
5Then the devil, taking Him up on a
high mountain, showed Him[a] all the kingdoms of the world in a moment of time.
6And the devil said to Him, "All this authority I will give You, and their glory; for
this has been delivered to me, and I give
it to whomever I wish. 7Therefore, if You
will worship before me, all will be Yours."
8And Jesus answered and said to him,
"Get behind Me, Satan![a] For[b] it is written,
*'You shall worship the Lord your God,
and Him only you shall serve.'* "[c]
9Then he brought Him to Jerusalem,
set Him on the pinnacle of the temple,
and said to Him, "If You are the Son of
God, throw Yourself down from here.
10For it is written:

*'He shall give His angels charge over
you,
To keep you,'*

11and,

*'In their hands they shall bear you up,
Lest you dash your foot against a
stone.'* "[a]

12And Jesus answered and said to him,
"It has been said, *'You shall not tempt the
Lord your God.'* "[a]
13Now when the devil had ended
every temptation, he departed from Him
until an opportune time.

Jesus Begins His Galilean Ministry

14Then Jesus returned in the power of
the Spirit to Galilee, and news of Him
went out through all the surrounding region. 15And He taught in their synagogues, being glorified by all.

Jesus Rejected at Nazareth

16So He came to Nazareth, where He
had been brought up. And as His custom
was, He went into the synagogue on the
Sabbath day, and stood up to read. 17And
He was handed the book of the prophet
Isaiah. And when He had opened the
book, He found the place where it was
written:

18*"The Spirit of the LORD is upon Me,
Because He has anointed Me
To preach the gospel to the poor;
He has sent Me to heal the
brokenhearted,*[a]
*To proclaim liberty to the captives
And recovery of sight to the blind,
To set at liberty those who are
oppressed;*
19*To proclaim the acceptable year of
the LORD."*[a]

20Then He closed the book, and gave *it*
back to the attendant and sat down. And

4:4 [a]Deuteronomy 8:3 [b]NU-Text omits *but by every word of God.* 4:5 [a]NU-Text reads *And taking Him up, he showed Him.* 4:8 [a]NU-Text omits *Get behind Me, Satan.* [b]NU-Text and M-Text omit *For.* [c]Deuteronomy 6:13 4:11 [a]Psalm 91:11, 12 4:12 [a]Deuteronomy 6:16 4:18 [a]NU-Text omits *to heal the brokenhearted.* 4:19 [a]Isaiah 61:1, 2

4:4 "If you wish to know God, you must know His Word. If you wish to perceive His power, you must see how He works by His Word. If you wish to know His purpose before it comes to pass, you can only discover it by His Word." *Charles Spurgeon*

4:8 "To worship is to quicken the conscience by the holiness of God, to feed the mind with the truth of God, to purge the imagination by the beauty of God, to open the heart to the love of God, to devote the will to the purpose of God." *William Temple*

4:10,11 When Jesus was being tempted, the devil quoted Scripture but twisted its meaning. Jesus responded by countering with the true application of God's Word (vv. 4–13). We must know the truth in order to counter error, or we will be misled by those who take Scripture out of context and misinterpret it. That's why we should not "live by bread alone, but by every word of God" (v. 4).

the eyes of all who were in the synagogue
were fixed on Him. 21And He began to
say to them, "Today this Scripture is fulfilled in your hearing." 22So all bore witness to Him, and marveled at the gracious
words which proceeded out of His mouth.
And they said, "Is this not Joseph's son?"

23He said to them, "You will surely say
this proverb to Me, 'Physician, heal yourself! Whatever we have heard done in Capernaum,[a] do also here in Your country.' "
24Then He said, "Assuredly, I say to you,
no prophet is accepted in his own country. 25But I tell you truly, many widows
were in Israel in the days of Elijah, when
the heaven was shut up three years and
six months, and there was a great famine
throughout all the land; 26but to none of
them was Elijah sent except to Zarephath,[a] *in the region* of Sidon, to a woman
who was a widow. 27And many lepers
were in Israel in the time of Elisha the
prophet, and none of them was cleansed
except Naaman the Syrian."

28So all those in the synagogue, when
they heard these things, were filled with
wrath, 29and rose up and thrust Him out
of the city; and they led Him to the brow
of the hill on which their city was built,
that they might throw Him down over
the cliff. 30Then passing through the
midst of them, He went His way.

Jesus Casts Out an Unclean Spirit

31Then He went down to Capernaum,
a city of Galilee, and was teaching them
on the Sabbaths. 32And they were astonished at His teaching, for His word was
with authority. 33Now in the synagogue
there was a man who had a spirit of an
unclean demon. And he cried out with a
loud voice, 34saying, "Let *us* alone! What
have we to do with You, Jesus of
Nazareth? Did You come to destroy us? I
know who You are—the Holy One of
God!"

35But Jesus rebuked him, saying, "Be
quiet, and come out of him!" And when
the demon had thrown him in *their* midst,
it came out of him and did not hurt him.
36Then they were all amazed and spoke
among themselves, saying, "What a word
this *is!* For with authority and power He
commands the unclean spirits, and they
come out." 37And the report about Him
went out into every place in the surrounding region.

Peter's Mother-in-Law Healed

38Now He arose from the synagogue
and entered Simon's house. But Simon's
wife's mother was sick with a high fever,

4:23 [a]Here and elsewhere the NU-Text spelling is *Capharnaum.* 4:26 [a]Greek *Sarepta*

4:18 Who is the gospel for? Jesus gives us a summation of who the gospel is for: the poor, the brokenhearted, the captives, the blind, the oppressed. Jesus is not referring to those who lack financial resources when He speaks of the *poor.* The word means "meek, humble, lowly" and refers to the "poor in spirit" (Matt. 5:3)—the blessed ones to whom the kingdom of God belongs. The poor are those who know that they are destitute of righteousness.

The *brokenhearted* refers not to unhappy people who have been jilted by a sweetheart, but to those who, like Peter and Isaiah, are contrite and sorrowing for their sin. *Matthew Henry* wrote of Jesus, "For He was sent to heal the brokenhearted, to give peace to those that were troubled and humbled for sins, and to bring them to rest who were weary and heavy-laden, under the burden of guilt and corruption."

The *captives* are those "taken captive by [the devil] to do his will" (2 Tim. 2:26).

The *blind* are those whom "the god of this age has blinded…[to] the light of the gospel of the glory of Christ" (2 Cor. 4:4).

The *oppressed* are those who are "oppressed by the devil" (Acts 10:38).

In other words, Jesus came to preach the Good News of God's forgiveness to those who recognize their spiritual poverty and are broken by the realization that they have sinned against a just and holy God.

The gospel of grace is for the humble, not the proud. "God resists the proud, but gives grace to the humble" (James 4:6). The Scriptures tell us, "Everyone proud in heart is an abomination to the LORD" (Prov. 16:5). God looks on the man who is poor and of a contrite spirit, and who trembles at His Word (Isa. 66:2). Only the sick need a physician, and only those who are convinced of the disease of sin will appreciate and appropriate the cure of the gospel.

and they made request of Him concerning her. 39So He stood over her and rebuked the fever, and it left her. And immediately she arose and served them.

Many Healed After Sabbath Sunset

40When the sun was setting, all those
who had any that were sick with various
diseases brought them to Him; and He
laid His hands on every one of them and
healed them. 41And demons also came
out of many, crying out and saying, "You
are the Christ,[a] the Son of God!"

And He, rebuking *them,* did not allow
them to speak, for they knew that He was
the Christ.

Jesus Preaches in Galilee

42Now when it was day, He departed
and went into a deserted place. And the
crowd sought Him and came to Him, and
tried to keep Him from leaving them;
43but He said to them, "I must preach the
kingdom of God to the other cities also,
because for this purpose I have been sent."
44And He was preaching in the synagogues of Galilee.[a]

Four Fishermen Called as Disciples

5 So it was, as the multitude pressed
about Him to hear the word of God,
that He stood by the Lake of Gennesaret,
2and saw two boats standing by the lake;
but the fishermen had gone from them
and were washing *their* nets. 3Then He
got into one of the boats, which was
Simon's, and asked him to put out a little from the land. And He sat down and
taught the multitudes from the boat.
4When He had stopped speaking, He
said to Simon, "Launch out into the deep
and let down your nets for a catch."

5But Simon answered and said to
Him, "Master, we have toiled all night
and caught nothing; nevertheless at Your
word I will let down the net." 6And when
they had done this, they caught a great
number of fish, and their net was breaking. 7So they signaled to *their* partners in
the other boat to come and help them.
And they came and filled both the boats,
so that they began to sink. 8When Simon
Peter saw *it,* he fell down at Jesus' knees,
saying, "Depart from me, for I am a sinful
man, O Lord!"

9For he and all who were with him
were astonished at the catch of fish which
they had taken; 10and so also *were* James
and John, the sons of Zebedee, who were
partners with Simon. And Jesus said to
Simon, "Do not be afraid. From now on
you will catch men." 11So when they had
brought their boats to land, they forsook
all and followed Him.

4:41 [a]NU-Text omits *the Christ.* 4:44 [a]NU-Text reads *Judea.*

4:40 Scientific facts in the Bible. For ages, scientists believed in a geocentric view of the universe. The differences between night and day were believed to be caused by the sun revolving around the earth. Today, we know that the earth's rotation on its axis is responsible for the sun's rising and setting. But around 3,500 years ago, it was written, "Have you commanded the morning since your days began, and caused the dawn to know its place…? It [the earth] takes on form like clay under a seal" (Job 38:12,14). The Hebrew word for "takes on form" means "to turn," and alludes to the rolling cylindrical seal used to stamp an impression on clay—an accurate analogy of the earth's rotation. See also Heb. 11:3 comment.

"The study of the Book of Job and its comparison with the latest scientific discoveries has brought me to the matured conviction that the Bible is an inspired book and was written by the One who made the stars." *Charles Burckhalter*, Chabot Observatory

5:10 "We cannot be fishers of men if we remain among the men in the same element with them. Fish will not be fishers. The sinner will not convert the sinner. The ungodly man will not convert the ungodly man. What is more to the point, the worldly Christian will not convert the world. If you are of the world, no doubt the world will love its own, but you cannot save the world. If you are dark and belong to the kingdom of darkness, you cannot remove the darkness. If you march with the armies of the wicked one, you cannot defeat them. I believe that one reason why the Church of God at this present moment has so little influence over the world is because the world has so much influence over the church." *Charles Spurgeon*

Jesus Cleanses a Leper

12And it happened when He was in a
certain city, that behold, a man who was
full of leprosy saw Jesus; and he fell on
his face and implored Him, saying, "Lord,
if You are willing, You can make me clean."
13Then He put out *His* hand and
touched him, saying, "I am willing; be
cleansed." Immediately the leprosy left
him. 14And He charged him to tell no one,
"But go and show yourself to the priest,
and make an offering for your cleansing,
as a testimony to them, just as Moses
commanded."
15However, the report went around
concerning Him all the more; and great
multitudes came together to hear, and to
be healed by Him of their infirmities.
16So He Himself *often* withdrew into the
wilderness and prayed.

Jesus Forgives and Heals a Paralytic

17Now it happened on a certain day,
as He was teaching, that there were Pharisees and teachers of the law sitting by,
who had come out of every town of Galilee, Judea, and Jerusalem. And the power
of the Lord was *present* to heal them.[a]
18Then behold, men brought on a bed a
man who was paralyzed, whom they
sought to bring in and lay before Him.
19And when they could not find how
they might bring him in, because of the
crowd, they went up on the housetop
and let him down with *his* bed through
the tiling into the midst before Jesus.
20When He saw their faith, He said to
him, "Man, your sins are forgiven you."
21And the scribes and the Pharisees
began to reason, saying, "Who is this who
speaks blasphemies? Who can forgive sins
but God alone?"
22But when Jesus perceived their
thoughts, He answered and said to them,
"Why are you reasoning in your hearts?
23Which is easier, to say, 'Your sins are
forgiven you,' or to say, 'Rise up and
walk'? 24But that you may know that the
Son of Man has power on earth to forgive
sins"—He said to the man who was paralyzed, "I say to you, arise, take up your
bed, and go to your house."
25Immediately he rose up before
them, took up what he had been lying
on, and departed to his own house, glorifying God. 26And they were all amazed,
and they glorified God and were filled
with fear, saying, "We have seen strange
things today!"

Matthew the Tax Collector

27After these things He went out and
saw a tax collector named Levi, sitting at
the tax office. And He said to him, "Follow Me." 28So he left all, rose up, and followed Him.
29Then Levi gave Him a great feast in
his own house. And there were a great
number of tax collectors and others who
sat down with them. 30And their scribes
and the Pharisees[a] complained against
His disciples, saying, "Why do You eat
and drink with tax collectors and sinners?"
31Jesus answered and said to them,
"Those who are well have no need of a
physician, but those who are sick. 32I
have not come to call *the* righteous, but
sinners, to repentance."

Jesus Is Questioned About Fasting

33Then they said to Him, "Why do[a]
the disciples of John fast often and make

5:17 [a]NU-Text reads *present with Him to heal.* 5:30 [a]NU-Text reads *But the Pharisees and their scribes.* 5:33 [a]NU-Text omits *Why do,* making the verse a statement.

5:16 Prayer—the secret weapon: Prayer was the ignition to every revival fire in history. Prayer was the key to the doorway of ministry for every preacher used by God in the past. For the soldier of Christ, true prayer should be a way of life, not just a call for help in the heat of battle. See Luke 6:12.

5:32 Repentance—its necessity for salvation. See Luke 13:3.

"There are only two kinds of men: the righteous, who believe themselves sinners; the rest, sinners, who believe themselves righteous." *Blaise Pascal*

prayers, and likewise those of the Pharisees, but Yours eat and drink?"
34And He said to them, "Can you
make the friends of the bridegroom fast
while the bridegroom is with them? 35But
the days will come when the bridegroom
will be taken away from them; then they
will fast in those days."
36Then He spoke a parable to them:
"No one puts a piece from a new garment
on an old one;[a] otherwise the new makes
a tear, and also the piece that was *taken*
out of the new does not match the old.
37And no one puts new wine into old
wineskins; or else the new wine will burst
the wineskins and be spilled, and the
wineskins will be ruined. 38But new wine
must be put into new wineskins, and
both are preserved.[a] 39And no one, having drunk old *wine,* immediately[a] desires
new; for he says, 'The old is better.' "[b]

Jesus Is Lord of the Sabbath

6 Now it happened on the second Sabbath after the first[a] that He went
through the grainfields. And His disciples
plucked the heads of grain and ate *them,*
rubbing *them* in *their* hands. 2And some
of the Pharisees said to them, "Why are
you doing what is not lawful to do on
the Sabbath?"
3But Jesus answering them said, "Have
you not even read this, what David did
when he was hungry, he and those who
were with him: 4how he went into the
house of God, took and ate the showbread, and also gave some to those with
him, which is not lawful for any but the
priests to eat?" 5And He said to them, "The
Son of Man is also Lord of the Sabbath."

Healing on the Sabbath

6Now it happened on another Sabbath, also, that He entered the synagogue
and taught. And a man was there whose
right hand was withered. 7So the scribes
and Pharisees watched Him closely,
whether He would heal on the Sabbath,
that they might find an accusation against
Him. 8But He knew their thoughts, and
said to the man who had the withered
hand, "Arise and stand here." And he arose
and stood. 9Then Jesus said to them, "I
will ask you one thing: Is it lawful on the
Sabbath to do good or to do evil, to save
life or to destroy?"[a] 10And when He had
looked around at them all, He said to the
man,[a] "Stretch out your hand." And he
did so, and his hand was restored as whole
as the other.[b] 11But they were filled with
rage, and discussed with one another what
they might do to Jesus.

The Twelve Apostles

12Now it came to pass in those days
that He went out to the mountain to pray,
and continued all night in prayer to God.
13And when it was day, He called His disciples to *Himself;* and from them He chose
twelve whom He also named apostles:
14Simon, whom He also named Peter,
and Andrew his brother; James and John;
Philip and Bartholomew; 15Matthew and
Thomas; James the *son* of Alphaeus, and
Simon called the Zealot; 16Judas *the son*
of James, and Judas Iscariot who also became a traitor.

Jesus Heals a Great Multitude

17And He came down with them and
stood on a level place with a crowd of His
disciples and a great multitude of people
from all Judea and Jerusalem, and from
the seacoast of Tyre and Sidon, who came
to hear Him and be healed of their dis-

5:36 [a]NU-Text reads *No one tears a piece from a new garment and puts it on an old one.* 5:38 [a]NU-Text omits *and both are preserved.* 5:39 [a]NU-Text omits *immediately.* [b]NU-Text reads *good.* 6:1 [a]NU-Text reads *on a Sabbath.* 6:9 [a]M-Text reads *to kill.* 6:10 [a]NU-Text and M-Text read *to him.* [b]NU-Text omits *as whole as the other.*

6:12 Prayer—the secret weapon: See Luke 22:41. "The one concern of the devil is to keep Christians from praying. He fears nothing from prayerless studies, prayerless works, and prayerless religion. He laughs at our toil, mocks at our wisdom, but trembles when we pray." *Samuel Chadwick*

QUESTIONS & OBJECTIONS

6:27

"Religion has caused more wars than anything else in history."

Not quite. When it comes to committing atrocities, religion comes in second. Atheistic communism comes in at number one. It has caused the death of more than one hundred million people.

But it is true that millions have been oppressed and murdered because man has used religion for political gain. Nazi Germany had "God with us" engraved in German on the belts of Nazi soldiers. America said, "Praise the Lord and pass the ammunition." The law may even allow you to start the Christian Nazi Party, if you so desire. You can become a "reverend" for a few dollars through the tabloid classifieds and then further your political agenda with the world's blessing, no matter how much it smears the name of Christ.

Jesus tells us in John 16:2,3 that there will be some who, in their error, commit atrocities and murder in the name of God: "The time is coming that whoever kills you will think that he offers God service." However, He informs us that these are not true believers: "And these things they will do to you because they have not known the Father nor Me" (John 16:3). The Bible also tells us that "no murderer has eternal life abiding in him" (1 John 3:15). Jesus told His followers to love their enemies. So if a man puts a knife into someone's back in the name of Christianity, something obviously isn't right. If we human beings can detect it, how much more will God? He will deal with it on Judgment Day.

eases, [18]as well as those who were tormented with unclean spirits. And they were healed. [19]And the whole multitude sought to touch Him, for power went out from Him and healed *them* all.

The Beatitudes

[20]Then He lifted up His eyes toward His disciples, and said:

"Blessed *are you* poor,
For yours is the kingdom of God.
[21]Blessed *are you* who hunger now,
For you shall be filled.
Blessed *are you* who weep now,
For you shall laugh.
[22]Blessed are you when men hate you,
And when they exclude you,
And revile *you*, and cast out your
name as evil,
For the Son of Man's sake.
[23]Rejoice in that day and leap for joy!
For indeed your reward *is* great in heaven,
For in like manner their fathers did to the prophets.

Jesus Pronounces Woes

[24]"But woe to you who are rich,
For you have received your consolation.
[25]Woe to you who are full,
For you shall hunger.
Woe to you who laugh now,
For you shall mourn and weep.
[26]Woe to you[a] when all[b] men speak

6:26 [a]NU-Text and M-Text omit *to you.* [b]M-Text omits *all.*

6:26 A soft gospel. Those who speak about "the love of Jesus," but refuse to preach the gospel of love revealed in the bloodied cross, *will* have the smile of the world. Their listeners have itching ears and they are more than pleased to scratch them with a soft gospel. They are of the world; they speak of the world, and the world gladly hears them. Jesus gave warning to those who fall into this subtle trap: "Woe to you when all men speak well of you."

The cross is the only God-given means of salvation from death, and we will bear reproach as long as we cling to its frame. It is only for a season—some day we will exchange it for a crown. In the meantime, let our faith in Jesus be spoken of throughout the whole world whether it be with a smile or a frown. The praise of men is a volatile minefield of pleasant flowers. In a moment it can swing from a fragrant "Hosanna!" to an explosive "Crucify Him!" Ask any baseball hero who has had a bad season. God's approval, however, is eternal.

QUESTIONS & OBJECTIONS

6:37

"Judge not lest you be judged. You therefore have no right to judge me when it comes to my sins!"

The world often takes this verse out of context and uses it to accuse Christians of being "judgmental" when they speak of sin. In the context of this verse Jesus is telling His disciples not to judge one another, something the Bible condemns (Rom. 14:10; James 4:11). In Luke 6:41,42 He speaks of seeing a speck in a *brother's* eye. He also tells us that when we judge, we should use "righteous judgment" (John 7:24). If someone steals, lies, commits adultery, etc., the Christian can make a (righteous) moral judgment and say that the actions were morally wrong, and that these sins will have eternal consequences.

It is important to make it clear that whenever we speak about sin we are making a moral judgment, but it is based on God's standards, not ours. The moral Law is the righteous standard by which all of us will be judged. So, helping people see how they will do when they stand before God on Judgment Day is not being judgmental; it is being compassionate. *Chuck Colson* said, "True tolerance is not a total lack of judgment. It's knowing what should be tolerated—and refusing to tolerate that which shouldn't."

well of you,
For so did their fathers to the false
prophets.

Love Your Enemies

27"But I say to you who hear: Love
your enemies, do good to those who hate
you, 28bless those who curse you, and
pray for those who spitefully use you.
29To him who strikes you on the *one*
cheek, offer the other also. And from him
who takes away your cloak, do not withhold *your* tunic either. 30Give to everyone
who asks of you. And from him who
takes away your goods do not ask *them*
back. 31And just as you want men to do
to you, you also do to them likewise.
32"But if you love those who love you,
what credit is that to you? For even sinners love those who love them. 33And if
you do good to those who do good to
you, what credit is that to you? For even
sinners do the same. 34And if you lend *to*
those from whom you hope to receive
back, what credit is that to you? For even
sinners lend to sinners to receive as much
back. 35But love your enemies, do good,
and lend, hoping for nothing in return;
and your reward will be great, and you
will be sons of the Most High. For He is
kind to the unthankful and evil. 36There-
fore be merciful, just as your Father also
is merciful.

Do Not Judge

37"Judge not, and you shall not be
judged. Condemn not, and you shall not
be condemned. Forgive, and you will be
forgiven. 38Give, and it will be given to
you: good measure, pressed down, shaken
together, and running over will be put
into your bosom. For with the same measure that you use, it will be measured
back to you."
39And He spoke a parable to them:
"Can the blind lead the blind? Will they
not both fall into the ditch? 40A disciple
is not above his teacher, but everyone
who is perfectly trained will be like his
teacher. 41And why do you look at the
speck in your brother's eye, but do not
perceive the plank in your own eye? 42Or
how can you say to your brother,
'Brother, let me remove the speck that *is*

6:27 The Church is commanded to love her enemies, just as Israel was instructed to do in Exod. 23:4,5.

6:28 This is the spirit in which we should share our faith. See Col. 4:5,6.

6:38 "You gain by giving that which you can't buy with money." *Edwin Cole*

in your eye,' when you yourself do not see the plank that is in your own eye? Hypocrite! First remove the plank from your own eye, and then you will see clearly to remove the speck that is in your brother's eye.

A Tree Is Known by Its Fruit

[43]"For a good tree does not bear bad fruit, nor does a bad tree bear good fruit.
[44]For every tree is known by its own fruit. For *men* do not gather figs from thorns, nor do they gather grapes from a bramble bush. [45]A good man out of the good treasure of his heart brings forth good; and an evil man out of the evil treasure of his heart[a] brings forth evil. For out of the abundance of the heart his mouth speaks.

Build on the Rock

[46]"But why do you call Me 'Lord, Lord,' and not do the things which I say?
[47]Whoever comes to Me, and hears My sayings and does them, I will show you whom he is like: [48]He is like a man building a house, who dug deep and laid the foundation on the rock. And when the flood arose, the stream beat vehemently against that house, and could not shake it, for it was founded on the rock.[a] [49]But he who heard and did nothing is like a man who built a house on the earth without a foundation, against which the stream beat vehemently; and immediately it fell.[a] And the ruin of that house was great."

Jesus Heals a Centurion's Servant

7 Now when He concluded all His sayings in the hearing of the people, He entered Capernaum. [2]And a certain centurion's servant, who was dear to him, was sick and ready to die. [3]So when he heard about Jesus, he sent elders of the Jews to Him, pleading with Him to come and heal his servant. [4]And when they came to Jesus, they begged Him earnestly, saying that the one for whom He should do this was deserving, [5]"for he loves our nation, and has built us a synagogue."

[6]Then Jesus went with them. And when He was already not far from the house, the centurion sent friends to Him, saying to Him, "Lord, do not trouble Yourself, for I am not worthy that You should enter under my roof. [7]Therefore I did not even think myself worthy to come to You. But say the word, and my servant will be healed. [8]For I also am a man placed under authority, having soldiers under me. And I say to one, 'Go,' and he goes; and to another, 'Come,' and he comes; and to my servant, 'Do this,' and he does *it*."

[9]When Jesus heard these things, He marveled at him, and turned around and said to the crowd that followed Him, "I say to you, I have not found such great faith, not even in Israel!" [10]And those who were sent, returning to the house, found the servant well who had been sick.[a]

Jesus Raises the Son of the Widow of Nain

[11]Now it happened, the day after, *that* He went into a city called Nain; and many of His disciples went with Him, and a large crowd. [12]And when He came near the gate of the city, behold, a dead man was being carried out, the only son of his mother; and she was a widow. And a large crowd from the city was with her.
[13]When the Lord saw her, He had compassion on her and said to her, "Do not weep." [14]Then He came and touched the open coffin, and those who carried *him* stood still. And He said, "Young man, I

6:45 [a]NU-Text omits *treasure of his heart.* 6:48 [a]NU-Text reads *for it was well built.* 6:49 [a]NU-Text reads *collapsed.* 7:10 [a]NU-Text omits *who had been sick.*

6:46 "You cannot say, 'No, Lord,' and mean both words; one annuls the other. If you say no to Him, then He is not your Lord." *D. James Kennedy*

say to you, arise." 15So he who was dead
sat up and began to speak. And He presented him to his mother.
16Then fear came upon all, and they
glorified God, saying, "A great prophet
has risen up among us"; and, "God has
visited His people." 17And this report
about Him went throughout all Judea
and all the surrounding region.

John the Baptist Sends Messengers to Jesus

18Then the disciples of John reported
to him concerning all these things. 19And
John, calling two of his disciples to *him,*
sent *them* to Jesus,[a] saying, "Are You the
Coming One, or do we look for another?"
20When the men had come to Him,
they said, "John the Baptist has sent us to
You, saying, 'Are You the Coming One,
or do we look for another?' " 21And that
very hour He cured many of infirmities,
afflictions, and evil spirits; and to many
blind He gave sight.

> You can be forgiven all your sin in half the tick of a clock, and pass from death to life more swiftly than I can utter the words.
>
> **CHARLES SPURGEON**

22Jesus answered and said to them,
"Go and tell John the things you have
seen and heard: that *the* blind see, *the*
lame walk, *the* lepers are cleansed, *the*
deaf hear, *the* dead are raised, *the* poor
have the gospel preached to them. 23And
blessed is *he* who is not offended because
of Me."
24When the messengers of John had
departed, He began to speak to the multitudes concerning John: "What did you
go out into the wilderness to see? A reed
shaken by the wind? 25But what did you
go out to see? A man clothed in soft garments? Indeed those who are gorgeously
appareled and live in luxury are in kings'
courts. 26But what did you go out to see?
A prophet? Yes, I say to you, and more
than a prophet. 27This is *he* of whom it is
written:

'Behold, I send My messenger before
Your face,
Who will prepare Your way before
You.[a]

28For I say to you, among those born of
women there is not a greater prophet than
John the Baptist;[a] but he who is least in
the kingdom of God is greater than he."
29And when all the people heard *Him,*
even the tax collectors justified God, having been baptized with the baptism of
John. 30But the Pharisees and lawyers rejected the will of God for themselves, not
having been baptized by him.
31And the Lord said,[a] "To what then
shall I liken the men of this generation,
and what are they like? 32They are like
children sitting in the marketplace and
calling to one another, saying:

'We played the flute for you,
And you did not dance;
We mourned to you,
And you did not weep.'

33For John the Baptist came neither eating bread nor drinking wine, and you say,
'He has a demon.' 34The Son of Man has
come eating and drinking, and you say,
'Look, a glutton and a winebibber, a friend
of tax collectors and sinners!' 35But wisdom is justified by all her children."

A Sinful Woman Forgiven

36Then one of the Pharisees asked
Him to eat with him. And He went to the
Pharisee's house, and sat down to eat.
37And behold, a woman in the city who
was a sinner, when she knew that *Jesus*
sat at the table in the Pharisee's house,
brought an alabaster flask of fragrant oil,
38and stood at His feet behind *Him* weeping; and she began to wash His feet with

7:19 [a]NU-Text reads *the Lord.* 7:27 [a]Malachi 3:1 7:28 [a]NU-Text reads *there is none greater than John.* 7:31 [a]NU-Text and M-Text omit *And the Lord said.*

"[The Bible] is a Book worth more than all the other books which were ever printed."

Patrick Henry

her tears, and wiped *them* with the hair of
her head; and she kissed His feet and anointed *them* with the fragrant oil. [39]Now
when the Pharisee who had invited Him
saw *this,* he spoke to himself, saying,
"This Man, if He were a prophet, would
know who and what manner of woman
this is who is touching Him, for she is a
sinner."
[40]And Jesus answered and said to him,
"Simon, I have something to say to you."
So he said, "Teacher, say it."

. . . . . .

For evidence of the Bible's reliability, see Matt. 4:4 comment.

. . . . . .

[41]"There was a certain creditor who
had two debtors. One owed five hundred
denarii, and the other fifty. [42]And when
they had nothing with which to repay, he
freely forgave them both. Tell Me, therefore, which of them will love him more?"
[43]Simon answered and said, "I suppose the *one* whom he forgave more."
And He said to him, "You have rightly
judged." [44]Then He turned to the woman
and said to Simon, "Do you see this woman? I entered your house; you gave Me
no water for My feet, but she has washed
My feet with her tears and wiped *them*
with the hair of her head. [45]You gave Me
no kiss, but this woman has not ceased to
kiss My feet since the time I came in.
[46]You did not anoint My head with oil,
but this woman has anointed My feet
with fragrant oil. [47]Therefore I say to
you, her sins, *which are* many, are forgiven, for she loved much. But to whom
little is forgiven, *the same* loves little."
[48]Then He said to her, "Your sins are
forgiven."
[49]And those who sat at the table with
Him began to say to themselves, "Who is
this who even forgives sins?"
[50]Then He said to the woman, "Your
faith has saved you. Go in peace."

Many Women Minister to Jesus

8 Now it came to pass, afterward, that
He went through every city and village, preaching and bringing the glad
tidings of the kingdom of God. And the
twelve *were* with Him, [2]and certain women who had been healed of evil spirits
and infirmities—Mary called Magdalene,
out of whom had come seven demons,
[3]and Joanna the wife of Chuza, Herod's
steward, and Susanna, and many others
who provided for Him[a] from their substance.

The Parable of the Sower

[4]And when a great multitude had gathered, and they had come to Him from
every city, He spoke by a parable: [5]"A
sower went out to sow his seed. And as
he sowed, some fell by the wayside; and
it was trampled down, and the birds of
the air devoured it. [6]Some fell on rock;
and as soon as it sprang up, it withered
away because it lacked moisture. [7]And
some fell among thorns, and the thorns
sprang up with it and choked it. [8]But
others fell on good ground, sprang up,

8:3 [a]NU-Text and M-Text read *them*. 8:10 [a]Isaiah 6:9

and yielded a crop a hundredfold." When He had said these things He cried, "He who has ears to hear, let him hear!"

The Purpose of Parables

9 Then His disciples asked Him, saying, "What does this parable mean?"

10 And He said, "To you it has been given to know the mysteries of the kingdom of God, but to the rest *it is given* in parables, that

'Seeing they may not see,
And hearing they may not
understand.'[a]

The Parable of the Sower Explained

11 "Now the parable is this: The seed is the word of God. 12 Those by the wayside are the ones who hear; then the devil comes and takes away the word out of their hearts, lest they should believe and be saved. 13 But the ones on the rock *are those* who, when they hear, receive the word with joy; and these have no root, who believe for a while and in time of temptation fall away. 14 Now the ones *that* fell among thorns are those who, when they have heard, go out and are choked with cares, riches, and pleasures of life, and bring no fruit to maturity. 15 But the ones *that* fell on the good ground are those who, having heard the word with a noble and good heart, keep *it* and bear fruit with patience.

The Parable of the Revealed Light

16 "No one, when he has lit a lamp, covers it with a vessel or puts *it* under a bed, but sets *it* on a lampstand, that those who enter may see the light. 17 For nothing is secret that will not be revealed, nor *anything* hidden that will not be known and come to light. 18 Therefore take heed how you hear. For whoever has, to him *more* will be given; and whoever does not have, even what he seems to have will be taken from him."

Jesus' Mother and Brothers Come to Him

19 Then His mother and brothers came to Him, and could not approach Him because of the crowd. 20 And it was told Him *by some,* who said, "Your mother and Your brothers are standing outside, desiring to see You."

21 But He answered and said to them, "My mother and My brothers are these who hear the word of God and do it."

Wind and Wave Obey Jesus

22 Now it happened, on a certain day, that He got into a boat with His disciples. And He said to them, "Let us cross over to the other side of the lake." And they launched out. 23 But as they sailed He fell asleep. And a windstorm came down on the lake, and they were filling *with water,* and were in jeopardy. 24 And they came to Him and awoke Him, saying, "Master, Master, we are perishing!"

Then He arose and rebuked the wind and the raging of the water. And they ceased, and there was a calm. 25 But He said to them, "Where is your faith?"

And they were afraid, and marveled, saying to one another, "Who can this be? For He commands even the winds and water, and they obey Him!"

A Demon-Possessed Man Healed

26 Then they sailed to the country of the Gadarenes,[a] which is opposite Galilee. 27 And when He stepped out on the land, there met Him a certain man from the city who had demons for a long time. And he wore no clothes,[a] nor did he live

8:26 [a]NU-Text reads *Gerasenes.* **8:27** [a]NU-Text reads *who had demons and for a long time wore no clothes.*

8:20,21 This was an opportunity for Jesus to exalt His mother above the rest of humanity. Blessed though she was in bearing Him, He gave her no more honor than any of the common people who heard the Word of God and obeyed it. See Luke 11:27,28 comment.

QUESTIONS & OBJECTIONS

8:39 *"How do you witness to family members?"*

Here is some advice that may save you a great deal of grief. As a new Christian, I did almost irreparable damage by acting like a wild bull in a crystal showroom. I bullied my mom, my dad, and many of my friends into making a "decision for Christ." I was sincere, zealous, loving, kind, and stupid. I didn't understand that salvation doesn't come through making a "decision," but through repentance, and that repentance comes through godly sorrow over sin (2 Cor. 7:10). The Bible teaches that no one can come to the Son unless the Father "draws" him (John 6:44). If you are able to get a "decision" but the person has no conviction of sin, you will almost certainly end up with a stillborn on your hands.

In my "zeal without knowledge" I actually inoculated the very ones I was so desperately trying to reach. There is nothing more important to you than the salvation of your loved ones, and you don't want to blow it. If you do, you may find that you don't have a second chance. Fervently pray for them, thanking God for their salvation. Let them see your faith. Let them *feel* your kindness, your genuine love, and your gentleness. Buy gifts for no reason. Do chores when you are not asked to. Go the extra mile. Put yourself in their position. You know that you have found everlasting life—death has lost its sting! Your joy is unspeakable. But as far as they are concerned, you have been brainwashed and become part of a weird sect. So your loving actions will speak more loudly than ten thousand eloquent sermons.

Therefore, when you share the gospel with your loved ones, make sure you have knowledge that will guide your zeal. Using the Law will help you to gently address the conscience and bring the knowledge of sin inoffensively. Although it would be nice to have a loved one say, "Tell me about your faith in Jesus Christ," that may not happen. You may have to gently and lovingly *make* an opportunity to speak to them. You may have only one shot, so pray for wisdom and sensitivity to God's timing. Keep your cool, or you may end up with a lifetime of regret—believe me. Continue to persevere in prayer for them, that God would open their eyes to the truth. In the meantime, witness to other Christians' unsaved loved ones, and trust that God will have some faithful Christian witness to yours. I have seen this happen in my own experience. God is faithful to the faithful.

in a house but in the tombs. 28When he
saw Jesus, he cried out, fell down before
Him, and with a loud voice said, "What
have I to do with You, Jesus, Son of the
Most High God? I beg You, do not torment me!" 29For He had commanded the
unclean spirit to come out of the man.
For it had often seized him, and he was
kept under guard, bound with chains
and shackles; and he broke the bonds
and was driven by the demon into the
wilderness.

30Jesus asked him, saying, "What is
your name?"

And he said, "Legion," because many
demons had entered him. 31And they
begged Him that He would not command
them to go out into the abyss.

32Now a herd of many swine was
feeding there on the mountain. So they
begged Him that He would permit them
to enter them. And He permitted them.
33Then the demons went out of the man
and entered the swine, and the herd ran
violently down the steep place into the
lake and drowned.

34When those who fed *them* saw what
had happened, they fled and told *it* in the
city and in the country. 35Then they went
out to see what had happened, and came
to Jesus, and found the man from whom
the demons had departed, sitting at the
feet of Jesus, clothed and in his right mind.
And they were afraid. 36They also who
had seen *it* told them by what means he
who had been demon-possessed was
healed. 37Then the whole multitude of
the surrounding region of the Gadarenes[a]
asked Him to depart from them, for they
were seized with great fear. And He got
into the boat and returned.

38Now the man from whom the
demons had departed begged Him that
he might be with Him. But Jesus sent him

8:37 [a]NU-Text reads *Gerasenes.*

away, saying, [39]"Return to your own
house, and tell what great things God has
done for you." And he went his way and
proclaimed throughout the whole city
what great things Jesus had done for him.

A Girl Restored to Life and a Woman Healed

[40]So it was, when Jesus returned, that
the multitude welcomed Him, for they
were all waiting for Him. [41]And behold,
there came a man named Jairus, and he
was a ruler of the synagogue. And he fell
down at Jesus' feet and begged Him to
come to his house, [42]for he had an only
daughter about twelve years of age, and
she was dying.

> If you are saved, the work is only half done until you are employed to bring others to Christ.
>
> **CHARLES SPURGEON**

But as He went, the multitudes thronged
Him. [43]Now a woman, having a flow of
blood for twelve years, who had spent all
her livelihood on physicians and could
not be healed by any, [44]came from behind and touched the border of His garment. And immediately her flow of blood
stopped.

[45]And Jesus said, "Who touched Me?"

When all denied it, Peter and those
with him[a] said, "Master, the multitudes
throng and press You, and You say, 'Who
touched Me?' "[b]

[46]But Jesus said, "Somebody touched
Me, for I perceived power going out from
Me." [47]Now when the woman saw that
she was not hidden, she came trembling;
and falling down before Him, she declared to Him in the presence of all the
people the reason she had touched Him
and how she was healed immediately.

[48]And He said to her, "Daughter, be of
good cheer;[a] your faith has made you
well. Go in peace."

[49]While He was still speaking, someone came from the ruler of the synagogue's
house, saying to him, "Your daughter is
dead. Do not trouble the Teacher."[a]

[50]But when Jesus heard *it,* He answered him, saying, "Do not be afraid;
only believe, and she will be made well."
[51]When He came into the house, He permitted no one to go in[a] except Peter, James,
and John,[b] and the father and mother of
the girl. [52]Now all wept and mourned for
her; but He said, "Do not weep; she is not
dead, but sleeping." [53]And they ridiculed
Him, knowing that she was dead.

[54]But He put them all outside,[a] took
her by the hand and called, saying, "Little girl, arise." [55]Then her spirit returned,
and she arose immediately. And He commanded that she be given *something* to
eat. [56]And her parents were astonished,
but He charged them to tell no one what
had happened.

Sending Out the Twelve

9 Then He called His twelve disciples
together and gave them power and
authority over all demons, and to cure
diseases. [2]He sent them to preach the
kingdom of God and to heal the sick.
[3]And He said to them, "Take nothing for
the journey, neither staffs nor bag nor
bread nor money; and do not have two
tunics apiece.

[4]"Whatever house you enter, stay
there, and from there depart. [5]And whoever will not receive you, when you go
out of that city, shake off the very dust
from your feet as a testimony against
them."

[6]So they departed and went through
the towns, preaching the gospel and healing everywhere.

Herod Seeks to See Jesus

[7]Now Herod the tetrarch heard of all
that was done by Him; and he was perplexed, because it was said by some that

8:45 [a]NU-Text omits *and those with him.* [b]NU-Text omits *and You say, 'Who touched Me?'* 8:48 [a]NU-Text omits *be of good cheer.* 8:49 [a]NU-Text adds *anymore.* 8:51 [a]NU-Text adds *with Him.* [b]NU-Text and M-Text read *Peter, John, and James.* 8:54 [a]NU-Text omits *put them all outside.*

John had risen from the dead, [8]and by some that Elijah had appeared, and by others that one of the old prophets had risen again. [9]Herod said, "John I have beheaded, but who is this of whom I hear such things?" So he sought to see Him.

Feeding the Five Thousand

[10]And the apostles, when they had returned, told Him all that they had done. Then He took them and went aside privately into a deserted place belonging to the city called Bethsaida. [11]But when the multitudes knew *it,* they followed Him; and He received them and spoke to them about the kingdom of God, and healed those who had need of healing. [12]When the day began to wear away, the twelve came and said to Him, "Send the multitude away, that they may go into the surrounding towns and country, and lodge and get provisions; for we are in a deserted place here."

[13]But He said to them, "You give them something to eat."

And they said, "We have no more than five loaves and two fish, unless we go and buy food for all these people." [14]For there were about five thousand men.

Then He said to His disciples, "Make them sit down in groups of fifty." [15]And they did so, and made them all sit down. [16]Then He took the five loaves and the two fish, and looking up to heaven, He blessed and broke *them,* and gave *them* to the disciples to set before the multitude. [17]So they all ate and were filled, and twelve baskets of the leftover fragments were taken up by them.

Peter Confesses Jesus as the Christ

[18]And it happened, as He was alone praying, *that* His disciples joined Him, and He asked them, saying, "Who do the crowds say that I am?"

[19]So they answered and said, "John the Baptist, but some *say* Elijah; and others *say* that one of the old prophets has risen again."

[20]He said to them, "But who do you say that I am?"

Peter answered and said, "The Christ of God."

Jesus Predicts His Death and Resurrection

[21]And He strictly warned and commanded them to tell this to no one, [22]saying, "The Son of Man must suffer many things, and be rejected by the elders and chief priests and scribes, and be killed, and be raised the third day."

Take Up the Cross and Follow Him

[23]Then He said to *them* all, "If anyone desires to come after Me, let him deny himself, and take up his cross daily,[a] and follow Me. [24]For whoever desires to save his life will lose it, but whoever loses his life for My sake will save it. [25]For what profit is it to a man if he gains the whole world, and is himself destroyed or lost? [26]For whoever is ashamed of Me and My words, of him the Son of Man will be ashamed when He comes in His *own* glory, and *in His* Father's, and of the holy angels.

Jesus Transfigured on the Mount

[27]But I tell you truly, there are some standing here who shall not taste death till they see the kingdom of God."

[28]Now it came to pass, about eight days after these sayings, that He took Peter, John, and James and went up on the mountain to pray. [29]As He prayed, the appearance of His face was altered, and His robe *became* white *and* glistening. [30]And behold, two men talked with Him, who

9:23 [a]M-Text omits *daily.*

9:25 "[A] watchful eye must be kept on ourselves lest, while we are building great monuments of renown and bliss here, we neglect to have our names enrolled in the Annals of Heaven." *James Madison*

were Moses and Elijah, 31who appeared in glory and spoke of His decease which He was about to accomplish at Jerusalem. 32But Peter and those with him were heavy with sleep; and when they were fully awake, they saw His glory and the two men who stood with Him. 33Then it happened, as they were parting from Him, *that* Peter said to Jesus, "Master, it is good for us to be here; and let us make three tabernacles: one for You, one for Moses, and one for Elijah"—not knowing what he said.

34While he was saying this, a cloud came and overshadowed them; and they were fearful as they entered the cloud. 35And a voice came out of the cloud, saying, "This is My beloved Son.[a] Hear Him!" 36When the voice had ceased, Jesus was found alone. But they kept quiet, and told no one in those days any of the things they had seen.

A Boy Is Healed

37Now it happened on the next day, when they had come down from the mountain, that a great multitude met Him. 38Suddenly a man from the multitude cried out, saying, "Teacher, I implore You, look on my son, for he is my only child. 39And behold, a spirit seizes him, and he suddenly cries out; it convulses him so that he foams *at the mouth;* and it departs from him with great difficulty, bruising him. 40So I implored Your disciples to cast it out, but they could not."

41Then Jesus answered and said, "O faithless and perverse generation, how long shall I be with you and bear with you? Bring your son here." 42And as he was still coming, the demon threw him down and convulsed *him.* Then Jesus rebuked the unclean spirit, healed the child, and gave him back to his father.

Jesus Again Predicts His Death

43And they were all amazed at the majesty of God.

But while everyone marveled at all the things which Jesus did, He said to His disciples, 44"Let these words sink down into your ears, for the Son of Man is about to be betrayed into the hands of men." 45But they did not understand this saying, and it was hidden from them so that they did not perceive it; and they were afraid to ask Him about this saying.

9:35 [a]NU-Text reads *This is My Son, the Chosen One.*

9:30 The Mount of Transfiguration. When Jesus was transfigured on the Holy Mountain, Moses and Elijah appeared in a vision and communed with Him. Moses represented the Law and Elijah represented the prophets.

Scripture gives us insight into what they spoke about: they communed about the cross (vv. 30,31). When Peter suggested paying homage to Moses, Elijah, and Jesus, it seems God wasn't impressed with the proposal. He spoke from heaven, telling the disciples to listen to Jesus. Then Moses and Elijah disappeared, and Jesus was left alone with the disciples.

When a person hears from the Father and understands who Jesus is, Moses and Elijah disappear. We see only Jesus. He is the Alpha and Omega, the Beginning and the End, the Author and Finisher of our faith. He is the only One to whom we bow the knee. Too many who profess to have heard the Father's voice spend too much time at the feet of Moses, bowing their knee to the Law. They are legalists who have no zeal for the lost. Their only concern is "do not touch, do not taste, do not handle" (Col. 2:21).

Many also spend too much time bowing down to Elijah. Prophecy is their joy. Prophecy shouldn't have us gazing into the future; it should have us gazing at the Savior and His will for the lost.

Charles Spurgeon said, "Here is another who spent all his time in interpreting the prophecies, so that everything he reads of in the newspapers he could see in Daniel or Revelation. Some say he is wise, but I would rather spend my time in winning souls. I would sooner bring one sinner to Jesus than unravel all the mysteries of the divine Word, for salvation is the one thing we are to live for."

The death and resurrection of the Savior didn't occur so that we could dabble in the future, but to open the door of salvation to hell-bound sinners. Those who hear the Father's voice hear the Son. They walk in His steps. They come down from the mountain to continue His work on earth: to seek and save what is lost.

Who Is the Greatest?

46 Then a dispute arose among them as
to which of them would be greatest.
47 And Jesus, perceiving the thought of
their heart, took a little child and set him
by Him, 48 and said to them, "Whoever
receives this little child in My name receives Me; and whoever receives Me receives Him who sent Me. For he who is
least among you all will be great."

Jesus Forbids Sectarianism

49 Now John answered and said, "Master, we saw someone casting out demons
in Your name, and we forbade him because he does not follow with us."
50 But Jesus said to him, "Do not forbid
him, for he who is not against us[a] is on
our[b] side."

A Samaritan Village Rejects the Savior

51 Now it came to pass, when the time
had come for Him to be received up, that
He steadfastly set His face to go to Jerusalem, 52 and sent messengers before His
face. And as they went, they entered a village of the Samaritans, to prepare for
Him. 53 But they did not receive Him, because His face was *set* for the journey to
Jerusalem. 54 And when His disciples
James and John saw *this,* they said, "Lord,
do You want us to command fire to come
down from heaven and consume them,
just as Elijah did?"[a]
55 But He turned and rebuked them,[a]
and said, "You do not know what manner
of spirit you are of. 56 For the Son of Man
did not come to destroy men's lives but
to save *them.*"[a] And they went to another
village.

The Cost of Discipleship

57 Now it happened as they journeyed
on the road, *that* someone said to Him,
"Lord, I will follow You wherever You
go."
58 And Jesus said to him, "Foxes have
holes and birds of the air *have* nests, but
the Son of Man has nowhere to lay *His*
head."
59 Then He said to another, "Follow
Me."
But he said, "Lord, let me first go and
bury my father."
60 Jesus said to him, "Let the dead bury
their own dead, but you go and preach
the kingdom of God."
61 And another also said, "Lord, I will
follow You, but let me first go *and* bid
them farewell who are at my house."
62 But Jesus said to him, "No one, having put his hand to the plow, and looking
back, is fit for the kingdom of God."

The Seventy Sent Out

10 After these things the Lord appointed seventy others also,[a] and
sent them two by two before His face into
every city and place where He Himself
was about to go. 2 Then He said to them,
"The harvest truly *is* great, but the laborers *are* few; therefore pray the Lord of the
harvest to send out laborers into His har-

9:50 [a]NU-Text reads *you.* [b]NU-Text reads *your.* 9:54 [a]NU-Text omits *just as Elijah did.* 9:55 [a]NU-Text omits the rest of this verse. 9:56 [a]NU-Text omits the first sentence of this verse. 10:1 [a]NU-Text reads *seventy-two others.*

9:62 "Backsliders"—who are they? It is fairly common to hear someone give a testimony by saying something like, "I gave my heart to Jesus when I was a child. Then I fell away from the Lord and became involved in drugs, robbery, rape, murder, pornography, gambling, adultery, extortion, and other things I would rather not mention. All this time I still knew the Lord. Then I came back to Him when I was thirty years old."

These words usually come from those who don't understand that the Bible speaks many times of true and false conversion. Almost all of those we place in the category of "backsliders" are not backsliders. They never slid forward in the first place. They are false converts—"stony-ground" or "thorny-ground" hearers (Mark 4:16–19), who fall away in a time of temptation, tribulation, or persecution. The true convert puts his hand to the plow and doesn't look back, because he is fit for the kingdom. "Backsliders" don't just *look* back, they actually *go* back, showing that something is radically wrong. See 2 Cor. 2:17 comment.

Principles of Growth for the New and Growing Christian

10:2

Evangelism—Our Most Sobering Task

Late in December 1996, a large family gathered for a joyous Christmas. There were so many gathered that night, five of the children slept in the converted garage, kept warm during the night by an electric heater placed near the door.

During the early hours of the morning, the heater suddenly burst into flames, blocking the doorway. In seconds the room became a blazing inferno. The frantic 911 call revealed the unspeakable terror as one of the children could be heard screaming, *"I'm on fire!"* The distraught father rushed into the flames to try to save his beloved children, receiving burns to 50 percent of his body. Tragically, all five children burned to death. They died because steel bars on the windows thwarted their escape. There was only one door, and it was blocked by the flames.

Imagine you're back in time, just minutes before the heater burst into flames. You peer through the darkness at the peaceful sight of five sleeping youngsters, knowing that at any moment the room will erupt into an inferno and burn the flesh of horrified children. *Can you in good conscience walk away?* No! You *must* awaken them and warn them to run from that death trap!

The world sleeps peacefully in the darkness of ignorance. There is only one Door by which they may escape death. The steel bars of sin prevent their salvation, and at the same time call for the flames of Eternal Justice. What a fearful thing Judgment Day will be! The fires of the wrath of Almighty God will burn for eternity. The Church has been entrusted with the task of awakening them before it's too late. We cannot turn our backs and walk away in complacency. *Think of how the father ran into the flames.* His love knew no bounds. Our devotion to the sober task God has given us will be in direct proportion to our love for the lost. There are only a few who run headlong into the flames to warn them to flee (Luke 10:2). *Please* be one of them. We really have no choice. The apostle Paul said, "Woe is me if I do not preach the gospel!" (1 Cor. 9:16).

The "Prince of Preachers," *Charles Spurgeon*, said, "We need to be ashamed at the bare suspicion of unconcern." A Christian *cannot* be apathetic about the salvation of the world. The love of God in him will motivate him to seek and save that which is lost.

You probably have a limited amount of time after your conversion to impact your unsaved friends and family with the gospel. After their initial shock, they will put you in a neat little ribbon-tied box, and keep you at arm's length. So it's important that you take advantage of the short time you have while you still have their ears. For advice on how to do this, see Luke 8:39 comment.

It is also important to realize that we should share our faith with others *whenever* we can. The Bible says that there are only two times we should do this: "in season and out of season" (2 Tim. 4:2). The apostle Paul *pleaded* for prayer for his own personal witness. He said, "[Pray] for me, that utterance may be given to me, that I may open my mouth boldly to make known the mystery of the gospel, for which I am an ambassador in chains; that in it I may speak boldly, as I ought to speak" (Eph. 6:19,20).

Remember that you have the sobering responsibility of speaking to other people's loved ones. Perhaps another Christian has prayed earnestly that God would use a faithful witness to speak to his beloved mom or dad, and *you* are the answer to that prayer. You are the true and faithful witness God wants to use.

Keep the fate of the ungodly before your eyes. Too many of us settle down on a padded pew and become introverted. Our world becomes a monastery without walls. Our friends are confined solely to those *within* the Church, when Jesus was the "friend of sinners." So take the time to deliberately befriend the lost for the sake of their salvation. Remember that each and every person who dies in his sins has an appointment with the Judge of the Universe. Hell opens wide its terrible jaws. There is no more sobering task than to be entrusted with the gospel of salvation, working with God for the eternal well-being of dying humanity.

For the next principle of growth, see Heb. 6:18 comment.

vest. 3Go your way; behold, I send you
out as lambs among wolves. 4Carry neither money bag, knapsack, nor sandals;
and greet no one along the road. 5But
whatever house you enter, first say, 'Peace
to this house.' 6And if a son of peace is
there, your peace will rest on it; if not, it
will return to you. 7And remain in the
same house, eating and drinking such
things as they give, for the laborer is worthy of his wages. Do not go from house to
house. 8Whatever city you enter, and they

QUESTIONS & OBJECTIONS

10:3

"Is it wise to send new converts out into the battlefield before they're grounded in the Word and apologetics?"

It is the best thing you can do for them. The woman at the well didn't go to a seminary before she testified of the Savior, and she brought a whole village to Him (see John 4:28–42). After finding Christ, Andrew immediately told Simon Peter (see John 1:40,41). The first thing Philip did was find Nathanael and immediately tell him about the Savior (see John 1:43–46). If new converts came to Christ under the sound of the Law, they know enough to go and do likewise with the lost. They will make mistakes. They may get bruised. But that is how we learned to walk in this life, and the same is true spiritually.

receive you, eat such things as are set before you. 9 And heal the sick there, and
say to them, 'The kingdom of God has
come near to you.' 10 But whatever city you
enter, and they do not receive you, go out
into its streets and say, 11 'The very dust
of your city which clings to us[a] we wipe
off against you. Nevertheless know this,
that the kingdom of God has come near
you.' 12 But[a] I say to you that it will be
more tolerable in that Day for Sodom
than for that city.

Woe to the Impenitent Cities

13 "Woe to you, Chorazin! Woe to you,
Bethsaida! For if the mighty works which
were done in you had been done in Tyre
and Sidon, they would have repented
long ago, sitting in sackcloth and ashes.
14 But it will be more tolerable for Tyre
and Sidon at the judgment than for you.
15 And you, Capernaum, who are exalted
to heaven, will be brought down to
Hades.[a] 16 He who hears you hears Me, he
who rejects you rejects Me, and he who
rejects Me rejects Him who sent Me."

The Seventy Return with Joy

17 Then the seventy[a] returned with joy,
saying, "Lord, even the demons are subject to us in Your name."

18 And He said to them, "I saw Satan
fall like lightning from heaven. 19 Behold,
I give you the authority to trample on
serpents and scorpions, and over all the
power of the enemy, and nothing shall by
any means hurt you. 20 Nevertheless do
not rejoice in this, that the spirits are subject to you, but rather[a] rejoice because
your names are written in heaven."

Jesus Rejoices in the Spirit

21 In that hour Jesus rejoiced in the
Spirit and said, "I thank You, Father, Lord
of heaven and earth, that You have hidden these things from *the* wise and prudent and revealed them to babes. Even
so, Father, for so it seemed good in Your
sight. 22 All[a] things have been delivered to
Me by My Father, and no one knows who
the Son is except the Father, and who the
Father is except the Son, and *the one* to
whom the Son wills to reveal *Him*."

23 Then He turned to *His* disciples and
said privately, "Blessed *are* the eyes which
see the things you see; 24 for I tell you that
many prophets and kings have desired to

10:11 [a]NU-Text reads *our feet.* 10:12 [a]NU-Text and M-Text omit *But.* 10:15 [a]NU-Text reads *will you be exalted to heaven? You will be thrust down to Hades!* 10:17 [a]NU-Text reads *seventy-two.* 10:20 [a]NU-Text and M-Text omit *rather.* 10:22 [a]M-Text reads *And turning to the disciples He said, "All…*

10:14 The world often mocks the thought of hell, by saying that God is unjust in sending all sinners there regardless of whether their sins are menial or heinous. God's punishment, however, will be according to righteousness. Here we see that the more sinful cities of Chorazin and Bethsaida will receive a more harsh judgment than Tyre and Sidon. For a description of hell, see Rev. 1:18 comment.

10:20 "The joy of heaven will arm us against the assaults of our spiritual enemies and put our mouths out of taste for those pleasures with which the tempter baits his hooks." *Matthew Henry*

see what you see, and have not seen *it,*
and to hear what you hear, and have not
heard *it.*”

The Parable of the Good Samaritan

25And behold, a certain lawyer stood
up and tested Him, saying, “Teacher, what
shall I do to inherit eternal life?”

26He said to him, “What is written in
the law? What is your reading *of it?*”

27So he answered and said, *“‘You shall
love the Lord your God with all your
heart, with all your soul, with all your
strength, and with all your mind,*[a] and
‘your neighbor as yourself.’”[b]

28And He said to him, “You have answered rightly; do this and you will live.”

29But he, wanting to justify himself,
said to Jesus, “And who is my neighbor?”

30Then Jesus answered and said: “A
certain *man* went down from Jerusalem
to Jericho, and fell among thieves, who
stripped him of his clothing, wounded
him, and departed, leaving *him* half dead.
31Now by chance a certain priest came
down that road. And when he saw him,
he passed by on the other side. 32Like-
wise a Levite, when he arrived at the
place, came and looked, and passed by
on the other side. 33But a certain Samaritan, as he journeyed, came where he was.
And when he saw him, he had compassion. 34So he went to *him* and bandaged
his wounds, pouring on oil and wine; and
he set him on his own animal, brought
him to an inn, and took care of him.
35On the next day, when he departed,[a]
he took out two denarii, gave *them* to the
innkeeper, and said to him, ‘Take care of
him; and whatever more you spend, when
I come again, I will repay you.’ 36So which
of these three do you think was neighbor
to him who fell among the thieves?”

37And he said, “He who showed mercy
on him.”

Then Jesus said to him, “Go and do
likewise.”

Mary and Martha Worship and Serve

38Now it happened as they went that
He entered a certain village; and a certain
woman named Martha welcomed Him
into her house. 39And she had a sister
called Mary, who also sat at Jesus’[a] feet
and heard His word. 40But Martha was
distracted with much serving, and she
approached Him and said, “Lord, do You
not care that my sister has left me to serve
alone? Therefore tell her to help me.”

41And Jesus[a] answered and said to
her, “Martha, Martha, you are worried and
troubled about many things. 42But one
thing is needed, and Mary has chosen
that good part, which will not be taken
away from her.”

10:27 [a]Deuteronomy 6:5 [b]Leviticus 19:18 **10:35** [a]NU-Text omits *when he departed.* **10:39** [a]NU-Text reads *the Lord's.* **10:41** [a]NU-Text reads *the Lord.*

10:26 This man was proud and self-righteous. He “stood up” and tested Jesus. He needed the Law to humble him and bring him the knowledge of sin. When the Law accused him, he tried to justify his guilt: “But he, wanting to justify himself, said to Jesus, ‘And who is my neighbor?’” (v. 29). Jesus then explained the spiritual nature of the Commandments to show the man how far he had fallen short of the glory of God that is revealed in the Law (vv. 30–37).

10:27 Love God with the whole heart. Three children were watching a new television set their father had just purchased for them. When their dad arrived home, they didn't even get up and greet him at the door. Instead, they were watching TV. The father walked over to it, turned it off and said, “Kids, I purchased that television set because I love you and want you to be happy. But if it comes between you and your love for me, I am going to sell it, because you are loving the gift more than the giver.”

If we love anything more than God (our mother, father, brother, sister, spouse, children, job, sports, or even our own life), we are loving the gift more than the Giver. To love anything more than we love God is to transgress the First Commandment. See also Luke 14:26 comment.

10:34 “When you see that men have been wounded by the Law, then it is time to pour in the gospel oil.” *Samuel Bolton*

The Model Prayer

11 Now it came to pass, as He was
praying in a certain place, when
He ceased, *that* one of His disciples said
to Him, "Lord, teach us to pray, as John
also taught his disciples."
2So He said to them, "When you pray,
say:

Our Father in heaven,[a]
Hallowed be Your name.
Your kingdom come.[b]
Your will be done
On earth as *it is* in heaven.
3Give us day by day our daily bread.
4And forgive us our sins,
For we also forgive everyone who is
indebted to us.
And do not lead us into temptation,
But deliver us from the evil one."[a]

A Friend Comes at Midnight

5And He said to them, "Which of you
shall have a friend, and go to him at midnight and say to him, 'Friend, lend me three
loaves; 6for a friend of mine has come to
me on his journey, and I have nothing to
set before him'; 7and he will answer from
within and say, 'Do not trouble me; the
door is now shut, and my children are with
me in bed; I cannot rise and give to you'?
8I say to you, though he will not rise and
give to him because he is his friend, yet
because of his persistence he will rise and
give him as many as he needs.

Keep Asking, Seeking, Knocking

9"So I say to you, ask, and it will be
given to you; seek, and you will find;
knock, and it will be opened to you. 10For
everyone who asks receives, and he who
seeks finds, and to him who knocks it
will be opened. 11If a son asks for bread[a]
from any father among you, will he give
him a stone? Or if *he asks* for a fish, will
he give him a serpent instead of a fish?
12Or if he asks for an egg, will he offer
him a scorpion? 13If you then, being evil,
know how to give good gifts to your children, how much more will *your* heavenly
Father give the Holy Spirit to those who
ask Him!"

A House Divided Cannot Stand

14And He was casting out a demon,
and it was mute. So it was, when the demon had gone out, that the mute spoke;
and the multitudes marveled. 15But some
of them said, "He casts out demons by
Beelzebub,[a] the ruler of the demons."
16Others, testing *Him,* sought from Him
a sign from heaven. 17But He, knowing
their thoughts, said to them: "Every kingdom divided against itself is brought to
desolation, and a house *divided* against a
house falls. 18If Satan also is divided against
himself, how will his kingdom stand? Because you say I cast out demons by Beelzebub. 19And if I cast out demons by
Beelzebub, by whom do your sons cast
them out? Therefore they will be your
judges. 20But if I cast out demons with
the finger of God, surely the kingdom of
God has come upon you. 21When a strong
man, fully armed, guards his own palace,
his goods are in peace. 22But when a
stronger than he comes upon him and
overcomes him, he takes from him all his
armor in which he trusted, and divides
his spoils. 23He who is not with Me is
against Me, and he who does not gather
with Me scatters.

An Unclean Spirit Returns

24"When an unclean spirit goes out of
a man, he goes through dry places, seek-

11:2 [a]NU-Text omits *Our* and *in heaven.* [b]NU-Text omits the rest of this verse. 11:4 [a]NU-Text omits *But deliver us from the evil one.* 11:11 [a]NU-Text omits the words from *bread* through *for* in the next sentence. 11:15 [a]NU-Text and M-Text read *Beelzebul.*

11:2 Prayer. "Prayer is the open admission that without Christ we can do nothing. And prayer is the turning away from ourselves to God in the confidence that He will provide the help we need. Prayer humbles *us* as needy and exalts *God* as all-sufficient." *John Piper*

"Prayer doesn't get man's will done in heaven; it gets God's will done on earth." *Ronald Dunn*

SPRINGBOARDS FOR PREACHING AND WITNESSING

Sting Operation

11:39 Some years ago, Southern California police carried out an interesting "sting" operation. They had a list of thousands of wanted criminals who had somehow evaded jail. Instead of risking their lives by going and attempting to arrest each one, they sent all the criminals a letter telling them they had won a large amount of money in a drawing.

The police put signs and banners on a building, and placed balloons and even a clown on the outside to create a festive atmosphere to welcome the "winners." As each criminal entered the building, he heard music and celebration. He was then ushered into a room where he smiled as his hand was shaken. The facial expression changed from one of joy to unbelief as each was told, "Congratulations—you have just won time in prison!" Dozens of criminals made their way through the main doors, were arrested and ushered out the back door. It was interesting that many of these lawbreakers declared, "I *thought* it was a sting operation!" but their greed wouldn't let them stay away.

ing rest; and finding none, he says, 'I will
return to my house from which I came.'
[25]And when he comes, he finds *it* swept
and put in order. [26]Then he goes and
takes with *him* seven other spirits more
wicked than himself, and they enter and
dwell there; and the last *state* of that man
is worse than the first."

Keeping the Word

[27]And it happened, as He spoke these
things, that a certain woman from the
crowd raised her voice and said to Him,
"Blessed *is* the womb that bore You, and
the breasts which nursed You!"

[28]But He said, "More than that, blessed
are those who hear the word of God and
keep it!"

Seeking a Sign

[29]And while the crowds were thickly
gathered together, He began to say, "This
is an evil generation. It seeks a sign, and
no sign will be given to it except the sign
of Jonah the prophet.[a] [30]For as Jonah became a sign to the Ninevites, so also the
Son of Man will be to this generation.
[31]The queen of the South will rise up in
the judgment with the men of this generation and condemn them, for she came
from the ends of the earth to hear the
wisdom of Solomon; and indeed a greater
than Solomon *is* here. [32]The men of Nineveh will rise up in the judgment with
this generation and condemn it, for they
repented at the preaching of Jonah; and
indeed a greater than Jonah *is* here.

The Lamp of the Body

[33]"No one, when he has lit a lamp,
puts *it* in a secret place or under a basket,
but on a lampstand, that those who come
in may see the light. [34]The lamp of the
body is the eye. Therefore, when your eye
is good, your whole body also is full of
light. But when *your eye* is bad, your body
also *is* full of darkness. [35]Therefore take
heed that the light which is in you is not
darkness. [36]If then your whole body *is*
full of light, having no part dark, *the* whole
body will be full of light, as when the
bright shining of a lamp gives you light."

Woe to the Pharisees and Lawyers

[37]And as He spoke, a certain Pharisee
asked Him to dine with him. So He went
in and sat down to eat. [38]When the Pharisee saw *it,* he marveled that He had not
first washed before dinner.

[39]Then the Lord said to him, "Now you
Pharisees make the outside of the cup
and dish clean, but your inward part is

11:29 [a]NU-Text omits *the prophet.*

11:27,28 Rather than exalting Mary above the rest of the common people, Jesus said that the greater blessing belongs to those who hear the Word of God and obey it.

11:52 *The Key to Reaching the Lost*

Have you ever thought, "There must be a key to reaching the lost"? There is—and it's rusty through lack of use. The Bible does actually call it "the key," and its purpose is to bring us to Christ, to unlock the Door of the Savior (John 10:9).

Much of the Church still doesn't even know it exists. Not only is it biblical, but it can be shown through history that the Church used it to unlock the doors of revival. The problem is that it was lost around the turn of the twentieth century. Keys have a way of getting lost.

Jesus used it (Mark 10:17–22). So did Paul (Rom. 2:21–24), Timothy (1 Tim. 1:8–11), and James (James 2:10). Stephen used it when he preached (Acts 7:53). Peter found that it had been used to open the door to release 3,000 imprisoned souls on the Day of Pentecost. Jesus said that the lawyers had "taken away" the key, and even refused to use it to let people enter into the kingdom of God.

Satan has tried to prejudice the modern Church against the key. He has maligned it, misused it, twisted it, and, of course, hidden it—he hates it because of what it does. To discover what this key is, let's look at what God's Word says on the subject. All I ask is that you set aside your traditions and prejudices.

In Acts 28:23 the Bible tells us that Paul sought to persuade his hearers "concerning Jesus from both the Law of Moses and the Prophets." Here we have two effective means of persuading the unsaved "concerning Jesus."

First, fulfilled prophecy *proves* the inspiration of Scripture. The predictions of the prophets present a powerful case for the inspiration of the Bible. Any skeptic who reads the prophetic words of Isaiah, Ezekiel, Joel, etc., or the words of Jesus in Matthew 24 cannot but be challenged that this is no ordinary book.

The other means by which Paul persuaded sinners concerning Jesus was from "the Law of Moses." The Bible tells us that the Law is good if it is used lawfully (1 Tim. 1:8). It was given by God as a "tutor to bring us to Christ" (Gal. 3:24). Paul wrote that he "would not have known sin except through the law" (Rom. 7:7). The Law of God (the Ten Commandments) is evidently the "key of knowledge" Jesus spoke of in Luke 11:52. He was speaking to "lawyers"—those who should have been teaching God's Law so that sinners would receive the "knowledge of sin," and thus recognize their need of the Savior.

Prophecy speaks to the *intellect* of the sinner, while the Law speaks to his *conscience*. One produces *faith* in the Word of God; the other brings *knowledge* of sin in the heart of the sinner. The Law is the God-given "key" to unlock the Door of salvation. See also Matt. 19:17–22 comment.

"I do not believe that any man can preach the gospel who does not preach the Law. The Law is the needle, and you cannot draw the silken thread of the gospel through a man's heart unless you first send the needle of the Law to make way for it." *Charles Spurgeon*

full of greed and wickedness. 40Foolish
ones! Did not He who made the outside
make the inside also? 41But rather give
alms of such things as you have; then indeed all things are clean to you.

42"But woe to you Pharisees! For you tithe the mint and rue and all manner of herbs, and pass by justice and the love of God. These you ought to have done, without leaving the others undone.
43Woe to
you Pharisees! For you love the best seats in the synagogues and greetings in the
marketplaces. 44Woe to you, scribes and
Pharisees, hypocrites![a] For you are like graves which are not seen, and the men who walk over *them* are not aware *of them*."

45Then one of the lawyers answered and said to Him, "Teacher, by saying these things You reproach us also."

46And He said, "Woe to you also, lawyers! For you load men with burdens hard to bear, and you yourselves do not touch the burdens with one of your fingers.
47Woe to you! For you build the tombs of the prophets, and your fathers killed them.
48In fact, you bear witness that you approve the deeds of your fathers; for they indeed killed them, and you build their tombs.
49Therefore the wisdom of God also said, 'I will send them prophets and apostles, and *some* of
them they will kill and persecute,' 50that
the blood of all the prophets which was shed from the foundation of the world may be required of this generation,
51from the blood of Abel to the blood of

11:44 [a]NU-Text omits *scribes and Pharisees, hypocrites*.

Zechariah who perished between the altar and the temple. Yes, I say to you, it
shall be required of this generation.
52“Woe to you lawyers! For you have
taken away the key of knowledge. You
did not enter in yourselves, and those who
were entering in you hindered.”
53And as He said these things to
them,[a] the scribes and the Pharisees began to assail *Him* vehemently, and to cross-
examine Him about many things, 54lying
in wait for Him, and seeking to catch Him
in something He might say, that they
might accuse Him.[a]

Beware of Hypocrisy

12 In the meantime, when an innumerable multitude of people had
gathered together, so that they trampled
one another, He began to say to His disciples first *of all,* “Beware of the leaven of
the Pharisees, which is hypocrisy. 2For
there is nothing covered that will not be
revealed, nor hidden that will not be
known. 3Therefore whatever you have
spoken in the dark will be heard in the
light, and what you have spoken in the
ear in inner rooms will be proclaimed on
the housetops.

Jesus Teaches the Fear of God

4“And I say to you, My friends, do not
be afraid of those who kill the body, and
after that have no more that they can do.
5But I will show you whom you should
fear: Fear Him who, after He has killed,
has power to cast into hell; yes, I say to
you, fear Him!
6“Are not five sparrows sold for two
copper coins?[a] And not one of them is
forgotten before God. 7But the very hairs
of your head are all numbered. Do not
fear therefore; you are of more value than
many sparrows.

Confess Christ Before Men

8“Also I say to you, whoever confesses
Me before men, him the Son of Man also
will confess before the angels of God.
9But he who denies Me before men will
be denied before the angels of God.
10“And anyone who speaks a word
against the Son of Man, it will be forgiven
him; but to him who blasphemes against
the Holy Spirit, it will not be forgiven.

> If Jesus had preached the same message that ministers preach today, He would never have been crucified.
>
> LEONARD RAVENHILL

11“Now when they bring you to the
synagogues and magistrates and authorities, do not worry about how or what you
should answer, or what you should say.
12For the Holy Spirit will teach you in
that very hour what you ought to say.”

The Parable of the Rich Fool

13Then one from the crowd said to
Him, “Teacher, tell my brother to divide
the inheritance with me.”

11:53 [a]NU-Text reads *And when He left there.* 11:54 [a]NU-Text omits *and seeking* and *that they might accuse Him.* 12:6 [a]Greek *assarion,* a coin of very small value

12:5 “People will never set their faces decidedly towards heaven, and live like pilgrims, until they really feel that they are in danger of hell...Let us expound and beat out the Ten Commandments, and show the length, and breadth, and depth, and height of their requirements. This is the way of our Lord in the Sermon on the Mount [Matt. 5:30]. We cannot do better than follow His plan. We may depend on it: men will never come to Jesus, and stay with Jesus, and live for Jesus, unless they really know why they are to come, and what is their need. Those whom the Spirit draws to Jesus are those whom the Spirit has convinced of sin. Without thorough conviction of sin, men may seem to come to Jesus and follow Him for a season, but they will soon fall away and return to the world.” *J. C. Ryle*

12:8 “Our Lord needs no secret agents! Those who are not willing to confess Christ publicly are not willing to confess Christ. Perhaps acceptance of Christ begins as a very personal and private experience, but it can never stay that way.” *Guy Rice Doud*

QUESTIONS & OBJECTIONS

12:20

"I'll wait until I am old, then I'll get right with God."

You may not get the chance. God may just lose patience with you and end your life. Perhaps you don't think He would do such a thing. Then read Gen. 38:7 to see how God killed a man who was wicked. Jesus told of a man who boasted that he had so many goods that he would have to build bigger barns. God called the man a fool and took his life that night.

Those who say they will repent in their own time lack the fear of God. Their understanding of His nature is erroneous. If they caught a glimpse of His holiness, His righteousness, and His consuming justice, they wouldn't trifle with His mercy. Such arrogance needs to be confronted with the thunders of Mount Sinai. He is not wise who thinks he can outwit his Creator, enjoy a lifetime of sin, and repent at the last minute. Deathbed repentance is very rare. God killed a husband and wife because they told a lie (Acts 5:1–10). He lost patience with them. Most people think that God's patience is eternal. It evidently is not. The Bible says that it is through the fear of the Lord that men depart from sin (Prov. 16:6). If they don't fear God, they will be complacent about their eternal salvation (Matt. 10:28).

14But He said to him, "Man, who made
Me a judge or an arbitrator over you?"
15And He said to them, "Take heed and
beware of covetousness,[a] for one's life
does not consist in the abundance of the
things he possesses."
16Then He spoke a parable to them,
saying: "The ground of a certain rich man
yielded plentifully. 17And he thought within himself, saying, 'What shall I do, since
I have no room to store my crops?' 18So
he said, 'I will do this: I will pull down
my barns and build greater, and there I
will store all my crops and my goods.
19And I will say to my soul, "Soul, you
have many goods laid up for many years;
take your ease; eat, drink, *and* be merry."'
20But God said to him, 'Fool! This night
your soul will be required of you; then
whose will those things be which you
have provided?'
21"So *is* he who lays up treasure for
himself, and is not rich toward God."

Do Not Worry

22Then He said to His disciples, "Therefore I say to you, do not worry about
your life, what you will eat; nor about the
body, what you will put on. 23Life is
more than food, and the body *is more*
than clothing. 24Consider the ravens, for
they neither sow nor reap, which have
neither storehouse nor barn; and God
feeds them. Of how much more value are
you than the birds? 25And which of you
by worrying can add one cubit to his
stature? 26If you then are not able to do
the least, why are you anxious for the rest?
27Consider the lilies, how they grow:
they neither toil nor spin; and yet I say to
you, even Solomon in all his glory was
not arrayed like one of these. 28If then
God so clothes the grass, which today is
in the field and tomorrow is thrown into
the oven, how much more *will He clothe*
you, O *you* of little faith?
29"And do not seek what you should
eat or what you should drink, nor have
an anxious mind. 30For all these things
the nations of the world seek after, and
your Father knows that you need these
things. 31But seek the kingdom of God,
and all these things[a] shall be added to
you.
32"Do not fear, little flock, for it is your
Father's good pleasure to give you the
kingdom. 33Sell what you have and give
alms; provide yourselves money bags
which do not grow old, a treasure in the
heavens that does not fail, where no thief
approaches nor moth destroys. 34For
where your treasure is, there your heart
will be also.

12:15 [a]NU-Text reads *all covetousness.* **12:31** [a]NU-Text reads *His kingdom, and these things.*

The Faithful Servant and the Evil Servant

35“Let your waist be girded and *your* lamps burning; 36and you yourselves be like men who wait for their master, when he will return from the wedding, that when he comes and knocks they may open to him immediately. 37Blessed *are* those servants whom the master, when he comes, will find watching. Assuredly, I say to you that he will gird himself and have them sit down *to eat,* and will come and serve them. 38And if he should come in the second watch, or come in the third watch, and find *them* so, blessed are those servants. 39But know this, that if the master of the house had known what hour the thief would come, he would have watched and[a] not allowed his house to be broken into. 40Therefore you also be ready, for the Son of Man is coming at an hour you do not expect.”

41Then Peter said to Him, “Lord, do You speak this parable *only* to us, or to all *people?*”

42And the Lord said, “Who then is that faithful and wise steward, whom *his* master will make ruler over his household, to give *them their* portion of food in due season? 43Blessed *is* that servant whom his master will find so doing when he comes. 44Truly, I say to you that he will make him ruler over all that he has. 45But if that servant says in his heart, ‘My master is delaying his coming,’ and begins to beat the male and female servants, and to eat and drink and be drunk, 46the master of that servant will come on a day when he is not looking for *him,* and at an hour when he is not aware, and will cut him in two and appoint *him* his portion with the unbelievers. 47And that servant who knew his master’s will, and did not prepare *himself* or do according to his will, shall be beaten with many *stripes.* 48But he who did not know, yet committed things deserving of stripes, shall be beaten with few. For everyone to whom much is given, from him much will be required; and to whom much has been committed, of him they will ask the more.

Christ Brings Division

49“I came to send fire on the earth, and how I wish it were already kindled! 50But I have a baptism to be baptized with, and how distressed I am till it is accomplished! 51Do *you* suppose that I came to give peace on earth? I tell you, not at all, but rather division. 52For from now on five in one house will be divided: three against two, and two against three. 53Father will be divided against son and son against father, mother against daughter and daughter against mother, mother-in-law against her daughter-in-law and daughter-in-law against her mother-in-law.”

Discern the Time

54Then He also said to the multitudes, “Whenever you *see* a cloud rising out of the west, immediately you say, ‘A shower is coming’; and so it is. 55And when you see the south wind blow, you say, ‘There will be hot weather’; and there is. 56Hypocrites! You can discern the face of the sky and of the earth, but how *is it* you do not discern this time?

Make Peace with Your Adversary

57“Yes, and why, even of yourselves,

12:39 [a]**NU-Text reads** ***he would not have allowed.***

12:33 “You know, when a man is going up in a balloon, he takes in sand as a ballast, and when he wants to mount a little higher, he throws out a little of the ballast, and then he will mount a little higher; he throws out a little more ballast, and he mounts still higher; and the higher he gets the more he throws out—and so the nearer we get to God the more we have to throw out of the things of this world. Let go of them; do not let us first set our hearts and affections on them, but do what the Master tells us—lay up for ourselves treasures in heaven.” *D. L. Moody*

12:40 Second coming of Jesus: See Luke 21:27.

do you not judge what is right? 58 When you go with your adversary to the magistrate, make every effort along the way to settle with him, lest he drag you to the judge, the judge deliver you to the officer, and the officer throw you into prison. 59 I tell you, you shall not depart from there till you have paid the very last mite."

Repent or Perish

13 There were present at that season some who told Him about the Galileans whose blood Pilate had mingled with their sacrifices. 2 And Jesus answered and said to them, "Do you suppose that these Galileans were worse sinners than all *other* Galileans, because they suffered such things? 3 I tell you, no; but unless you repent you will all likewise perish.

> The last words of Jesus to the church (in Revelation) were 'Repent!'
>
> **LEONARD RAVENHILL**

4 Or those eighteen on whom the tower in Siloam fell and killed them, do you think that they were worse sinners than all *other* men who dwelt in Jerusalem? 5 I tell you, no; but unless you repent you will all likewise perish."

The Parable of the Barren Fig Tree

6 He also spoke this parable: "A certain *man* had a fig tree planted in his vineyard, and he came seeking fruit on it and found none. 7 Then he said to the keeper of his vineyard, 'Look, for three years I have come seeking fruit on this fig tree and find none. Cut it down; why does it use up the ground?' 8 But he answered and said to him, 'Sir, let it alone this year also, until I dig around it and fertilize *it.* 9 And if it bears fruit, *well.* But if not, after that[a] you can cut it down.' "

A Spirit of Infirmity

10 Now He was teaching in one of the synagogues on the Sabbath. 11 And behold, there was a woman who had a spirit of infirmity eighteen years, and was bent over and could in no way raise *herself* up. 12 But when Jesus saw her, He called *her* to *Him* and said to her, "Woman, you are loosed from your infirmity." 13 And He laid *His* hands on her, and immediately she was made straight, and glorified God.

14 But the ruler of the synagogue answered with indignation, because Jesus had healed on the Sabbath; and he said to the crowd, "There are six days on which men ought to work; therefore come and be healed on them, and not on the Sabbath day."

15 The Lord then answered him and said, "Hypocrite![a] Does not each one of you on the Sabbath loose his ox or donkey from the stall, and lead *it* away to water it? 16 So ought not this woman, being a daughter of Abraham, whom Satan has bound—think of it—for eighteen years, be loosed from this bond on the Sabbath?" 17 And when He said these things, all His adversaries were put to shame; and all the multitude rejoiced for all the

13:9 [a]NU-Text reads *And if it bears fruit after that, well. But if not, you can cut it down.* 13:15 [a]NU-Text and M-Text read *Hypocrites.*

13:3 Repentance—its necessity for salvation. See Luke 24:47.

13:5 Hosea 4:6 tells us why sinners will perish. "My people are destroyed for lack of knowledge. Because you have rejected knowledge, I also will reject you...; because you have forgotten the law of your God, I also will forget your children." The reason God's people were destroyed was a lack of knowledge *of God's Law*. A sinner who is ignorant of the moral Law has no understanding of the nature of sin (Rom. 7:7–9). If he doesn't understand what sin is, he will not repent; and if he fails to repent, he will perish. He perishes through lack of knowledge of the Law.

"The gospel has not been clearly preached if the hearer doesn't know that not to make a decision is a decision." *Dan Arnold*

glorious things that were done by Him.

The Parable of the Mustard Seed

18 Then He said, "What is the kingdom of God like? And to what shall I compare it? 19 It is like a mustard seed, which a man took and put in his garden; and it grew and became a large[a] tree, and the birds of the air nested in its branches."

The Parable of the Leaven

20 And again He said, "To what shall I liken the kingdom of God? 21 It is like leaven, which a woman took and hid in three measures[a] of meal till it was all leavened."

The Narrow Way

22 And He went through the cities and villages, teaching, and journeying toward Jerusalem. 23 Then one said to Him, "Lord, are there few who are saved?"

And He said to them, 24 "Strive to enter through the narrow gate, for many, I say to you, will seek to enter and will not be able. 25 When once the Master of the house has risen up and shut the door, and you begin to stand outside and knock at the door, saying, 'Lord, Lord, open for us,' and He will answer and say to you, 'I do not know you, where you are from,' 26 then you will begin to say, 'We ate and drank in Your presence, and You taught in our streets.' 27 But He will say, 'I tell you I do not know you, where you are from. Depart from Me, all you workers of iniquity.' 28 There will be weeping and gnashing of teeth, when you see Abraham and Isaac and Jacob and all the prophets in the kingdom of God, and yourselves thrust out. 29 They will come from the east and the west, from the north and the south, and sit down in the kingdom of God. 30 And indeed there are last who will be first, and there are first who will be last."

31 On that very day[a] some Pharisees came, saying to Him, "Get out and depart from here, for Herod wants to kill You."

32 And He said to them, "Go, tell that fox, 'Behold, I cast out demons and perform cures today and tomorrow, and the third *day* I shall be perfected.' 33 Nevertheless I must journey today, tomorrow, and the *day* following; for it cannot be that a prophet should perish outside of Jerusalem.

Jesus Laments over Jerusalem

34 "O Jerusalem, Jerusalem, the one who kills the prophets and stones those who are sent to her! How often I wanted to gather your children together, as a hen *gathers* her brood under *her* wings, but you were not willing! 35 See! Your house is left to you desolate; and assuredly,[a] I say to you, you shall not see Me until *the time* comes when you say, *'Blessed is He who comes in the name of the Lord!'* "[b]

A Man with Dropsy Healed on the Sabbath

14 Now it happened, as He went into the house of one of the rulers of the Pharisees to eat bread on the Sabbath,

13:19 [a]NU-Text omits *large.* 13:21 [a]Greek *sata,* approximately two pecks in all 13:31 [a]NU-Text reads *In that very hour.* 13:35 [a]NU-Text and M-Text omit *assuredly.* [b]Psalm 118:26

13:20,21 This is a picture of the false convert in the midst of God's people: "This shall have its accomplishment in the destruction of the corrupt and hypocritical part of the Church." *Matthew Henry*

13:34 "The more we become what we shall be, the more will compassion rule our hearts. The Lord Jesus Christ, who is the pattern and mirror of perfect manhood, what said He concerning the sins and the woes of Jerusalem? He knew Jerusalem must perish; did He bury his pity beneath the fact of the divine decree, and steel His heart by the thought of the sovereignty or the justice that would be resplendent in the city's destruction? No, not He, but with eyes gushing like founts, he cried, 'O Jerusalem, Jerusalem, how often would I have gathered your children together as a hen gathers her chickens under her wings! and you would not.' If you would be like Jesus, you must be tender and very pitiful . . . I beseech you, let your hearts be moved with pity, do not endure to see the spiritual death of mankind. Be in agony as often as you contemplate the ruin of any soul of the seed of Adam." *Charles Spurgeon*

that they watched Him closely. 2And behold, there was a certain man before Him
who had dropsy. 3And Jesus, answering,
spoke to the lawyers and Pharisees, saying, "Is it lawful to heal on the Sabbath?"[a]
4But they kept silent. And He took *him*
and healed him, and let him go. 5Then
He answered them, saying, "Which of you,
having a donkey[a] or an ox that has fallen
into a pit, will not immediately pull him
out on the Sabbath day?" 6And they could
not answer Him regarding these things.

Take the Lowly Place

7So He told a parable to those who
were invited, when He noted how they
chose the best places, saying to them:
8"When you are invited by anyone to a
wedding feast, do not sit down in the
best place, lest one more honorable than
you be invited by him; 9and he who invited you and him come and say to you,
'Give place to this man,' and then you begin with shame to take the lowest place.
10But when you are invited, go and sit
down in the lowest place, so that when
he who invited you comes he may say to
you, 'Friend, go up higher.' Then you will
have glory in the presence of those who
sit at the table with you. 11For whoever
exalts himself will be humbled, and he
who humbles himself will be exalted."
12Then He also said to him who invited Him, "When you give a dinner or a
supper, do not ask your friends, your
brothers, your relatives, nor rich neighbors, lest they also invite you back, and
you be repaid. 13But when you give a
feast, invite *the* poor, *the* maimed, *the*
lame, *the* blind. 14And you will be
blessed, because they cannot repay you;
for you shall be repaid at the resurrection
of the just."

The Parable of the Great Supper

15Now when one of those who sat at
the table with Him heard these things, he
said to Him, "Blessed *is* he who shall eat
bread[a] in the kingdom of God!"
16Then He said to him, "A certain man
gave a great supper and invited many,
17and sent his servant at supper time to
say to those who were invited, 'Come, for
all things are now ready.' 18But they all
with one *accord* began to make excuses.
The first said to him, 'I have bought a
piece of ground, and I must go and see it.
I ask you to have me excused.' 19And another said, 'I have bought five yoke of
oxen, and I am going to test them. I ask
you to have me excused.' 20Still another
said, 'I have married a wife, and therefore
I cannot come.' 21So that servant came
and reported these things to his master.
Then the master of the house, being angry, said to his servant, 'Go out quickly
into the streets and lanes of the city, and
bring in here *the* poor and *the* maimed
and *the* lame and *the* blind.' 22And the
servant said, 'Master, it is done as you
commanded, and still there is room.'
23Then the master said to the servant, 'Go
out into the highways and hedges, and
compel *them* to come in, that my house
may be filled. 24For I say to you that none

"The salvation of a single soul is more important than the production or preservation of all the epics and tragedies in the world."

C. S. Lewis

14:3 [a]NU-Text adds *or not.* 14:5 [a]NU-Text and M-Text read *son.* 14:15 [a]M-Text reads *dinner.*

QUESTIONS & OBJECTIONS

14:26 ***"Jesus taught hatred by saying that a Christian should 'hate' his father and mother."***

Jesus used what is called "hyperbole"—a statement of extremes, contrasting love with hate for emphasis' sake. The Bible often does this (Prov. 13:24; 29:24). Jesus tells us that the first and greatest Commandment is to love God with all of our heart, soul, and mind (Matt. 22:37,38). As much as we treasure our spouse and family, and even our own life, there should be no one whom we love and value more than God, no one who takes precedence in our life. To place love for another (including ourself) above God is idolatry.

of those men who were invited shall taste
my supper.' "

Leaving All to Follow Christ

25Now great multitudes went with
Him. And He turned and said to them,
26"If anyone comes to Me and does not
hate his father and mother, wife and children, brothers and sisters, yes, and his
own life also, he cannot be My disciple.
27And whoever does not bear his cross
and come after Me cannot be My disciple.
28For which of you, intending to build a
tower, does not sit down first and count
the cost, whether he has *enough* to finish
it— 29lest, after he has laid the foundation, and is not able to finish, all who see
it begin to mock him, 30saying, 'This man
began to build and was not able to finish'? 31Or what king, going to make war
against another king, does not sit down
first and consider whether he is able with
ten thousand to meet him who comes
against him with twenty thousand? 32Or
else, while the other is still a great way
off, he sends a delegation and asks conditions of peace. 33So likewise, whoever
of you does not forsake all that he has
cannot be My disciple.

Tasteless Salt Is Worthless

34"Salt *is* good; but if the salt has lost
its flavor, how shall it be seasoned? 35It is
neither fit for the land nor for the
dunghill, *but* men throw it out. He who
has ears to hear, let him hear!"

The Parable of the Lost Sheep

15 Then all the tax collectors and the
sinners drew near to Him to hear
Him. 2And the Pharisees and scribes complained, saying, "This Man receives sinners and eats with them." 3So He spoke
this parable to them, saying:
4"What man of you, having a hundred
sheep, if he loses one of them, does not
leave the ninety-nine in the wilderness,
and go after the one which is lost until he
finds it? 5And when he has found *it,* he
lays *it* on his shoulders, rejoicing. 6And
when he comes home, he calls together
his friends and neighbors, saying to them,

14:23 It is essential that all Christians understand that they are missionaries, and that the world that lies outside of their church's doors is the mission field. "It is one thing for a minister to be an advocate and supporter of missions: it is another and very different thing for him to understand that missions are the chief end of the church, and therefore the chief end for which his congregation exists. It is only when this truth masters him in its spiritual power that he will be able to give the subject of missions its true place in his ministry." *E. R. Hendrix*

"Preach abroad . . . It is the cooping yourselves up in rooms that has dampened the work of God, which never was and never will be carried out to any purpose without going into the highways and hedges and compelling men and women to come in." *Jonathan Edwards*

14:28 "The convert that must pay a heavy price for his faith in Christ is the one that will persevere to the end. He begins with the wind in his face, and should the storm grow in strength he will not turn back for he has been conditioned to endure it." *A. W. Tozer*

15:4 How Much Do Lost People Matter?

By Steven D. Mathewson

When the religious leaders of Jesus' day criticized him for hanging out with sinners, Jesus told three stories about lost items: a lost sheep (Luke 15:1–7), a lost coin (Luke 15:8–10), and a lost son (Luke 15:11–32).

The shepherd left 99 sheep in open country to search for one lost sheep. He didn't say, "Oh well, 99 percent isn't bad. You're going to lose one once in a while."

The peasant woman swept the reed-covered dirt floor until she spied the lost coin. She didn't say, "Oh well, it's only a day's wage."

The father checks the road for the sign of his lost son's return. He didn't say, "Forget him. If he's going to be such an idiot, then I'll pour my life into my older son."

In each case, the value of what's lost dictated an intensive search. Jesus is saying that the value of lost people demands an intensive response. Our failures to reach our communities stem more from faulty perspective than from faulty technique. Intensive searches happen only when we place a premium on the lost item. Technique usually takes care of itself when we share Jesus' perspective.

When we bump into people during the day, how do we view them? We notice that Todd is unfriendly. The truth is, he is lost. We think of Rob as a kind grandfather and a reliable neighbor. The truth is, he is lost. We view Sharon as a gorgeous blond with great potential as an interior decorator. The truth is, she's lost.

If people are really lost, and if these lost people are valuable, then an intensive search-and-rescue mission is in order. When we value lost people as Jesus did, outreach will happen, and more people will sing, "I once was lost, but now am found, 'twas blind, but now I see."

'Rejoice with me, for I have found my
sheep which was lost!' 7I say to you that
likewise there will be more joy in heaven
over one sinner who repents than over
ninety-nine just persons who need no repentance.

The Parable of the Lost Coin

8"Or what woman, having ten silver
coins,[a] if she loses one coin, does not
light a lamp, sweep the house, and search
carefully until she finds *it*? 9And when
she has found *it*, she calls *her* friends and
neighbors together, saying, 'Rejoice with
me, for I have found the piece which I
lost!' 10Likewise, I say to you, there is joy
in the presence of the angels of God over
one sinner who repents."

The Parable of the Lost Son

11Then He said: "A certain man had
two sons. 12And the younger of them said
to *his* father, 'Father, give me the portion
of goods that falls *to me*.' So he divided to
them *his* livelihood. 13And not many days
after, the younger son gathered all together, journeyed to a far country, and
there wasted his possessions with prodigal living. 14But when he had spent all,
there arose a severe famine in that land,
and he began to be in want. 15Then he
went and joined himself to a citizen of
that country, and he sent him into his
fields to feed swine. 16And he would gladly
have filled his stomach with the pods that
the swine ate, and no one gave him *anything*.

17"But when he came to himself, he
said, 'How many of my father's hired servants have bread enough and to spare,
and I perish with hunger! 18I will arise

15:8 [a]Greek *drachma*, a valuable coin often worn in a ten-piece garland by married women

15:10 Heaven does not rejoice over those who make "decisions." It reserves its rejoicing for sinners who repent.

"Have you taught for a long time in your Sunday school class and have you had only one girl saved? Do not be satisfied with that one, but, at the same time, do not forget to thank the Lord for that one. If you are not grateful to God for letting you win one soul for Him, you are not likely to be allowed to win another." *Charles Spurgeon*

and go to my father, and will say to him, "Father, I have sinned against heaven and before you, 19 and I am no longer worthy to be called your son. Make me like one of your hired servants." '

20 "And he arose and came to his father. But when he was still a great way off, his father saw him and had compassion, and ran and fell on his neck and kissed him. 21 And the son said to him, 'Father, I have sinned against heaven and in your sight, and am no longer worthy to be called your son.'

22 "But the father said to his servants, 'Bring[a] out the best robe and put *it* on him, and put a ring on his hand and sandals on *his* feet. 23 And bring the fatted calf here and kill *it*, and let us eat and be merry; 24 for this my son was dead and is alive again; he was lost and is found.' And they began to be merry.

25 "Now his older son was in the field. And as he came and drew near to the house, he heard music and dancing. 26 So he called one of the servants and asked what these things meant. 27 And he said to him, 'Your brother has come, and because he has received him safe and sound, your father has killed the fatted calf.'

28 "But he was angry and would not go in. Therefore his father came out and pleaded with him. 29 So he answered and said to *his* father, 'Lo, these many years I have been serving you; I never transgressed your commandment at any time; and yet you never gave me a young goat, that I might make merry with my friends. 30 But as soon as this son of yours came, who has devoured your livelihood with harlots, you killed the fatted calf for him.'

31 "And he said to him, 'Son, you are always with me, and all that I have is yours. 32 It was right that we should make merry and be glad, for your brother was dead and is alive again, and was lost and is found.' "

The Parable of the Unjust Steward

16 He also said to His disciples: "There was a certain rich man who had a steward, and an accusation was brought to him that this man was wasting his goods. 2 So he called him and said to him, 'What is this I hear about you? Give an account of your stewardship, for you can no longer be steward.'

3 "Then the steward said within himself, 'What shall I do? For my master is taking the stewardship away from me. I cannot dig; I am ashamed to beg. 4 I have resolved what to do, that when I am put out of the stewardship, they may receive me into their houses.'

5 "So he called every one of his master's debtors to *him*, and said to the first, 'How

15:22 [a]NU-Text reads *Quickly bring.*

15:17 "Do you esteem the pleasures of sin so sweet, so solid, so lasting—that it is your interest to run the risk of intolerable, eternal misery, rather than part with them? Can you form such an estimate as this while in your senses?

"No! He is a mad-man with whom fleshly pleasures for a little time, the sordid pleasures of sin—outweigh an eternity of perfect happiness. He is certainly not in his right mind—who would rather be tormented in hell forever—than lead a holy life, and labor to escape the wrath to come!" *Samuel Davies*

15:21 All sin is against God. Often sinners will try to justify their vices because there is no "victim" involved (such as in adult pornography). However, *all* sin is an offense against God. When Joseph was sexually propositioned by Potiphar's wife, he spoke of it as being a sin against God (Gen. 39:9). When David sinned with Bathsheba, he acknowledged that he had sinned against the LORD (2 Sam. 12:13). The prodigal son recognized that he had sinned against heaven (Luke 15:21). God is always the offended Party when someone commits sin. However, the real victim of sin will be the sinner. His sin will damn him, because he is a victim of his own foolishness.

15:32 "The evangelist who preaches for eternity is never great on numbers. He is not apt to count hundreds of converts where there is no restitution, no confession, and no glad cry which proclaims, 'The lost is found, the dead is made alive again!' " *E. M. Bounds*

much do you owe my master?' [6]And he said, 'A hundred measures[a] of oil.' So he said to him, 'Take your bill, and sit down quickly and write fifty.' [7]Then he said to another, 'And how much do you owe?' So he said, 'A hundred measures[a] of wheat.' And he said to him, 'Take your bill, and write eighty.' [8]So the master commended the unjust steward because he had dealt shrewdly. For the sons of this world are more shrewd in their generation than the sons of light.

> The conscience of a man, when he is really quickened and awakened by the Holy Spirit, speaks the truth. It rings the great alarm bell. And if he turns over in his bed, that great alarm bell rings out again and again, 'The wrath to come! The wrath to come! The wrath to come.'
>
> **CHARLES SPURGEON**

[9]"And I say to you, make friends for yourselves by unrighteous mammon, that when you fail,[a] they may receive you into an everlasting home. [10]He who *is* faithful in *what is* least is faithful also in much; and he who is unjust in *what is* least is unjust also in much. [11]Therefore if you have not been faithful in the unrighteous mammon, who will commit to your trust the true *riches?* [12]And if you have not been faithful in what is another man's, who will give you what is your own?

[13]"No servant can serve two masters; for either he will hate the one and love the other, or else he will be loyal to the one and despise the other. You cannot serve God and mammon."

The Law, the Prophets, and the Kingdom

[14]Now the Pharisees, who were lovers of money, also heard all these things, and they derided Him. [15]And He said to them, "You are those who justify yourselves before men, but God knows your hearts. For what is highly esteemed among men is an abomination in the sight of God.

[16]"The law and the prophets *were* until John. Since that time the kingdom of God has been preached, and everyone is pressing into it. [17]And it is easier for heaven and earth to pass away than for one tittle of the law to fail.

[18]"Whoever divorces his wife and marries another commits adultery; and whoever marries her who is divorced from *her* husband commits adultery.

The Rich Man and Lazarus

[19]"There was a certain rich man who was clothed in purple and fine linen and fared sumptuously every day. [20]But there was a certain beggar named Lazarus, full of sores, who was laid at his gate, [21]desiring to be fed with the crumbs which fell[a] from the rich man's table. Moreover the dogs came and licked his sores. [22]So it was that the beggar died, and was carried by the angels to Abraham's bosom. The rich man also died and was buried. [23]And being in torments in Hades, he

16:6 [a]Greek *batos,* eight or nine gallons each (Old Testament *bath*) 16:7 [a]Greek *koros,* ten or twelve bushels each (Old Testament *kor*) 16:9 [a]NU-Text reads *it fails.* 16:21 [a]NU-Text reads *with what fell.*

16:10 If I am not a straight-shooter with a pistol, He won't let me near the cannon.

16:13 If you were given $1,000 every time you witnessed to someone, would you be more zealous in your evangelism? If so, you are serving money rather than God.

16:15 A little girl was once looking at a sheep as it ate green grass. She thought to herself how nice and white the sheep looked against the green grass. Then it began to snow. The little girl then thought how dirty the sheep looked against the white snow. It was the same sheep, but with a different background. When we compare ourselves to the background of man's standards, we come up reasonably clean. However, when we compare ourselves to the snow-white righteousness of the Law of God, we see that we are all as an unclean thing, and our righteous deeds are as filthy rags (Isa. 64:6).

Springboards for Preaching and Witnessing

16:17

The Rush

You've always wanted to skydive, but the thought scared you too much to try it. That is, until you met someone who had made over 100 jumps. He talked you into it by explaining how safe it was. His enthusiasm was contagious. He spoke of the freedom of falling through the air... the adrenaline rush... the unspeakable exhilaration.

Now you are standing on the edge of a plane, looking down on the earth far, far below. Everything has been checked. Double-checked. This is safer than driving on the freeway—a thought that helps you deal with the fear. Modern parachutes are state-of-the-art. Besides, there is a backup chute. Still, your heart is beating rapidly with apprehension.

Suddenly, you *jump!* You have trained so much for this moment, you instinctively spread your hands and legs. The speed is unbelievable. The power of the air forcing itself against your body is incredible. It's like a dream. You are defying the law of gravity, racing through the air at more than 120 mph!

The earth is coming closer. All normal sense of time lost. Speed, thrust of air, unspeakable joy. You glance at the altimeter on your wrist. Only another ten seconds and you will pull the rip cord and feel the jolt of the parachute opening. All that you had been told was true. The adrenaline rush is like nothing you have experienced. If only it could last a little longer. Reluctantly, you pull the cord. It opens, *but there is no jolt!*

You tilt your head back to see a horrifying sight: the parachute has twisted and is trailing like a flapping streamer. Your heart races with fear, pounding in your chest. Your eyes bulge in terror. Your chest heaves as you gasp for air. You try to keep a clear mind and remember your training ...pull the second cord. *Nothing happens!* You pull again. Again! Harder. *Harder!* Nothing. Your throat lets out a scream, a groan of panic. Your heart is pounding so hard you think your chest will burst. Sweat breaks through your skin. A thousand thoughts speed through your mind. Your family! Your fate!...Safer than driving on the freeway! You whisper, "What a fool I was...to think that I could defy the law of gravity." Now a merciless law waits for the moment of impact. The ground accelerates toward you. No words can describe the terror gripping your mind. A voice is speaking to you. It is the voice of good sense. It is the voice you ignored so often: "You have played the fool. You have given up your life, your most precious possession, for a cheap thrill. You have exchanged your loved ones for a rush of adrenaline. What a fool...*what a fool!*"

One word stands alone to describe how you feel about what you've done. One word screams within the corridors of your terrified mind as the earth races toward you, as death readies to embrace you. One word, a word that you have never understood fully until this moment. That terrible word is *remorse!*

The world, the flesh, and the devil whisper to you about how pleasurable sin is. That God isn't angry at sin. God is love. It is safe to jump into the arms of iniquity and abandon yourself to a free fall through its vast domain.

You go where angels fear to tread. But it is worth it. The rush is everything sin promised. You drink in iniquity like water. You love the darkness. Conscience speaks again and again, but you ignore its warning. You are defying the moral Law and loving every minute.

Now you stand before the Judge on Judgment Day. You pull your first line by telling God what a good person you are. Nothing happens. The moral Law rushes at you. In panic, you pull the second line and tell God that you believed in Him. *Again, nothing happens.* It is no use. Your mouth is stopped. The moral Law accelerates toward you even faster, promising to so impact you that it will "grind [you] to powder" (Luke 20:18). Death and hell wait to embrace you. Unspeakable terror fills your heart. Conscience speaks so clearly now: "What a fool you have been. You rejected the mercy of God in Jesus Christ. You have given up your loved ones in exchange for the joys of a sinful lifestyle. You relinquished your most precious possession, *your very life*, for the cheap thrill of sin. What a fool! What a fool!" One word will stay with you for eternity. One word alone will echo forever within your tormented mind. Remorse! You whisper the word, "Remorse...*remorse.*"

Suddenly you are staring at the ceiling of your bedroom, still mouthing the word through dry lips. *Remorse!* The sheets are soaked with sweat. *It was just a dream.* You look out the window and see the sun breaking through the green trees. It was just a dream! It's morning now. A peaceful new day. Today's the day you go skydiving. It will be your first time.

QUESTIONS & OBJECTIONS

"Since God is loving, why would He send people to a place of torment?"

By Mark Spence

Why should we think God has less sense of justice than mankind? God is loving, but that's not all He is. He is also a good judge. Should a loving *human* judge allow criminals to go free? Of course not. If we, with our finite justice system, think it is necessary to punish criminals in civil court, how much more should an infinite God judge our crimes, our sins against Him?

The Bible tells us God alone is holy. He is the standard of all that is right and good. His nature is pure. Think of it like this: If I were to light a match and place the flame next to a dried out leaf, what would happen? The fire would consume the leaf. Why? Because they're different, their natures are opposed one to the other.

In the same way, God and man have opposing natures. On the Day of Judgment, sinful man will not be able to stand in the presence of a holy God because of their opposing natures. It isn't that God is unloving, but that He is holy. He is described as a "consuming fire" who dwells in "unapproachable light" (Heb. 12:29; 1 Tim. 6:16). In our sinful state, we don't stand a chance. Our only hope is to somehow take on the same nature as God. We must be born again. When we turn from our sins and place our faith in the resurrected Christ, God imputes His righteousness to us.

It is imperative that we are given this new nature, since each of us is headed toward our own personal Judgment Day. The Bible says, "He is coming to judge the earth. He shall judge the world with righteousness" (Psa. 96:13). So the next time someone tells you a loving God would never send anyone to hell, simply explain the difference between God's and man's opposing natures. The problem isn't with God; the problem is our sin.

lifted up his eyes and saw Abraham afar
off, and Lazarus in his bosom.
24"Then he cried and said, 'Father
Abraham, have mercy on me, and send
Lazarus that he may dip the tip of his finger in water and cool my tongue; for I am
tormented in this flame.' 25But Abraham
said, 'Son, remember that in your lifetime
you received your good things, and likewise Lazarus evil things; but now he is
comforted and you are tormented. 26And
besides all this, between us and you there
is a great gulf fixed, so that those who
want to pass from here to you cannot,
nor can those from there pass to us.'
27"Then he said, 'I beg you therefore,
father, that you would send him to my father's house, 28for I have five brothers,
that he may testify to them, lest they also
come to this place of torment.' 29Abra-
ham said to him, 'They have Moses and
the prophets; let them hear them.' 30And
he said, 'No, father Abraham; but if one
goes to them from the dead, they will repent.' 31But he said to him, 'If they do not
hear Moses and the prophets, neither will
they be persuaded though one rise from
the dead.' "

Jesus Warns of Offenses

17 Then He said to the disciples, "It
is impossible that no offenses
should come, but woe *to him* through
whom they do come! 2It would be better
for him if a millstone were hung around
his neck, and he were thrown into the
sea, than that he should offend one of
these little ones. 3Take heed to yourselves. If your brother sins against you,[a]
rebuke him; and if he repents, forgive

17:3 [a]NU-Text omits *against you.*

16:23 Hell: For verses warning of its reality, see Rev. 20:15.

16:24 "Love your fellowmen, and cry about them if you cannot bring them to Christ. If you cannot save them, you can weep over them. If you cannot give them a drop of water in hell, you can give them your heart's tears while they are still in this body." *Charles Spurgeon*

him. 4And if he sins against you seven times in a day, and seven times in a day returns to you,[a] saying, 'I repent,' you shall forgive him."

Faith and Duty

5And the apostles said to the Lord, "Increase our faith."

6So the Lord said, "If you have faith as a mustard seed, you can say to this mulberry tree, 'Be pulled up by the roots and be planted in the sea,' and it would obey you. 7And which of you, having a servant plowing or tending sheep, will say to him when he has come in from the field, 'Come at once and sit down to eat'? 8But will he not rather say to him, 'Prepare something for my supper, and gird yourself and serve me till I have eaten and drunk, and afterward you will eat and drink'? 9Does he thank that servant because he did the things that were commanded him? I think not.[a] 10So likewise you, when you have done all those things which you are commanded, say, 'We are unprofitable servants. We have done what was our duty to do.' "

Ten Lepers Cleansed

11Now it happened as He went to Jerusalem that He passed through the midst of Samaria and Galilee. 12Then as He entered a certain village, there met Him ten men who were lepers, who stood afar off. 13And they lifted up *their* voices and said, "Jesus, Master, have mercy on us!"

14So when He saw *them,* He said to them, "Go, show yourselves to the priests." And so it was that as they went, they were cleansed.

15And one of them, when he saw that he was healed, returned, and with a loud voice glorified God, 16and fell down on *his* face at His feet, giving Him thanks. And he was a Samaritan.

17So Jesus answered and said, "Were there not ten cleansed? But where *are* the nine? 18Were there not any found who returned to give glory to God except this foreigner?" 19And He said to him, "Arise, go your way. Your faith has made you well."

The Coming of the Kingdom

20Now when He was asked by the Pharisees when the kingdom of God would come, He answered them and said, "The kingdom of God does not come with observation; 21nor will they say, 'See here!' or 'See there!'[a] For indeed, the kingdom of God is within you."

22Then He said to the disciples, "The days will come when you will desire to see one of the days of the Son of Man, and you will not see *it.* 23And they will say to you, 'Look here!' or 'Look there!'[a] Do not go after *them* or follow *them.* 24For as the lightning that flashes out of one *part* under heaven shines to the other *part* under heaven, so also the Son of Man will be in His day. 25But first He must suffer many things and be rejected by this generation. 26And as it was in the days of Noah, so it will be also in the days of the Son of Man: 27They ate, they drank, they married wives, they were given in marriage, until the day that Noah entered the ark, and the flood came and destroyed them all. 28Likewise as it was also in the days of Lot: They ate, they drank, they bought, they sold, they planted, they built; 29but on the day that Lot went out of Sodom it rained fire and brimstone from heaven and destroyed *them* all. 30Even so will it be in the day when the Son of Man is revealed.

31"In that day, he who is on the house-

17:4 [a]M-Text omits *to you.* 17:9 [a]NU-Text ends verse with *commanded;* M-Text omits *him.* 17:21 [a]NU-Text reverses *here* and *there.* 17:23 [a]NU-Text reverses *here* and *there.*

17:4 "Forgiveness is not just an occasional act: it is a permanent attitude." *Martin Luther King, Jr.*

17:26,27 Jesus referred to Noah as an actual historical person, and the Flood as a bona fide historical event. See Matt. 24:38,39 comment for details on the Flood.

top, and his goods *are* in the house, let
him not come down to take them away.
And likewise the one who is in the field,
let him not turn back. 32Remember Lot's
wife. 33Whoever seeks to save his life will
lose it, and whoever loses his life will preserve it. 34I tell you, in that night there
will be two *men* in one bed: the one will
be taken and the other will be left. 35Two
women will be grinding together: the one
will be taken and the other left. 36Two
men will be in the field: the one will be
taken and the other left."[a]

37And they answered and said to Him,
"Where, Lord?"

So He said to them, "Wherever the
body is, there the eagles will be gathered
together."

The Parable of the Persistent Widow

18 Then He spoke a parable to them,
that men always ought to pray
and not lose heart, 2saying: "There was in
a certain city a judge who did not fear
God nor regard man. 3Now there was a
widow in that city; and she came to him,
saying, 'Get justice for me from my adversary.' 4And he would not for a while;
but afterward he said within himself,
'Though I do not fear God nor regard man,
5yet because this widow troubles me I
will avenge her, lest by her continual
coming she weary me.' "

6Then the Lord said, "Hear what the
unjust judge said. 7And shall God not
avenge His own elect who cry out day
and night to Him, though He bears long
with them? 8I tell you that He will avenge
them speedily. Nevertheless, when the
Son of Man comes, will He really find
faith on the earth?"

The Parable of the Pharisee and the Tax Collector

9Also He spoke this parable to some
who trusted in themselves that they were
righteous, and despised others: 10"Two
men went up to the temple to pray, one a
Pharisee and the other a tax collector.
11The Pharisee stood and prayed thus with
himself, 'God, I thank You that I am not
like other men—extortioners, unjust,
adulterers, or even as this tax collector.
12I fast twice a week; I give tithes of all
that I possess.' 13And the tax collector,
standing afar off, would not so much as
raise *his* eyes to heaven, but beat his
breast, saying, 'God, be merciful to me a
sinner!' 14I tell you, this man went down
to his house justified *rather* than the other;
for everyone who exalts himself will be
humbled, and he who humbles himself
will be exalted."

Jesus Blesses Little Children

15Then they also brought infants to
Him that He might touch them; but when
the disciples saw *it,* they rebuked them.
16But Jesus called them to *Him* and said,
"Let the little children come to Me, and do
not forbid them; for of such is the kingdom
of God. 17Assuredly, I say to you, whoever
does not receive the kingdom of God as a
little child will by no means enter it."

Jesus Counsels the Rich Young Ruler

18Now a certain ruler asked Him, saying, "Good Teacher, what shall I do to inherit eternal life?"

19So Jesus said to him, "Why do you

17:36 [a]NU-Text and M-Text omit verse 36.

17:32 Some dismiss the Book of Genesis as just an allegory, but Jesus believed the Genesis account of Lot's wife.

17:33 "He is no fool who gives what he cannot keep to gain that which he cannot lose." *Jim Elliot*

18:1 Prayerlessness. "Prayerlessness is an insult to God. Every prayerless day is a statement by a helpless individual, 'I do not need God today.' Failing to pray reflects idolatry—a trust in substitutes for God. We rely on our money instead of God's provision. We rest on our own flawed thinking rather than on God's perfect wisdom. We take charge of our lives rather than trusting God. Prayerlessness short-circuits the working of God. Neglecting prayer, therefore, is not a weakness; it is a sinful choice." *Ben Jennings*

Questions & Objections

18:19

"As a Christian, I think non-Christians can be good, normal people."

It deeply concerns me when I hear a professing Christian telling an unbeliever that he is a good person. Jesus said there is no one good but God (Mark 10:18). Anyone who says human beings are good is calling Jesus a liar. My concern isn't just that the unbeliever is being confirmed in his deception, but it makes me doubt the genuine nature of the Christian's salvation, because he seems to have no biblical understanding of sin himself. This deception comes when the Law is not used to bring the knowledge of sin (see Rom. 3:19,20) and to show sin to be "exceedingly sinful" (see Rom. 7:13).

Not surprisingly, Christians who think sinners are "good" believe that preaching the gospel simply means to tell them "Jesus loves you," something for which there is no precedent in Scripture. Wherever the love of Christ is preached, it is almost always in direct correlation to the cross (see Matt. 10:22 comment). And the cross makes no sense without mentioning sin, and sin makes no sense without preaching the Law, for "sin is the transgression of the law" (1 John 3:4, KJV).

I thought I was a good person until I understood that in *God's* eyes, "good" means to be morally perfect. The only just rule by which we can measure our morality is the Ten Commandments. It was through the moral Law that I learned God considers lust to be adultery and hatred to be murder. When I measured myself by *that* standard, I realized I was not good. At all.

It is also not surprising in this case that unbelievers would have kind words for the Christian. This is because they are not offended by his message. However, to fail to warn sinners of the terrible consequences of sin (damnation in hell), and to instead tell them that they are good people, is the ultimate betrayal. Jesus warned, "Woe to you when all men speak well of you, for so did their fathers to the false prophets" (Luke 6:26).

call Me good? No one *is* good but One,
that is, God. 20You know the commandments: *'Do not commit adultery,' 'Do not
murder,' 'Do not steal,' 'Do not bear false
witness,' 'Honor your father and your
mother.' '*[a]

> A world of nice people, content in their own niceness, looking no further, turned away from God, would be just as desperately in need of salvation as a miserable world—and might even be more difficult to save.
>
> **C. S. LEWIS**

21And he said, "All these things I have
kept from my youth."
22So when Jesus heard these things,
He said to him, "You still lack one thing.
Sell all that you have and distribute to the
poor, and you will have treasure in heaven;
and come, follow Me."
23But when he heard this, he became
very sorrowful, for he was very rich.

With God All Things Are Possible

24And when Jesus saw that he became
very sorrowful, He said, "How hard it is
for those who have riches to enter the
kingdom of God! 25For it is easier for a
camel to go through the eye of a needle
than for a rich man to enter the kingdom
of God."
26And those who heard it said, "Who
then can be saved?"
27But He said, "The things which are impossible with men are possible with God."

18:20 [a]Exodus 20:12–16; Deuteronomy 5:16–20

18:20 Jesus gave him five "horizontal" Commandments having to do with his fellow man. When he said that he had kept them, Jesus then used the First of the Ten Commandments to show this man that his god was his money, and you cannot serve God and money.

18:24,25 There is hope for the rich: see Luke 19:2.

QUESTIONS & OBJECTIONS

"What if someone says they've never lied, stolen, lusted, blasphemed—if they deny having any sin at all?"

Ask the person if he has kept the First of the Ten Commandments. Has he always loved God above all else—with all of his heart, soul, mind, and strength (Mark 12:30)? If he says that he has, gently say, "The Bible says that 'there is none who seeks after God' (Rom. 3:11). *Nobody* (except Jesus Christ) has kept the First of the Ten Commandments. One of you is lying—either you or God—and the Bible says that it is *impossible* for God to lie" (Heb. 6:18; Titus 1:2).

28Then Peter said, "See, we have left
all[a] and followed You."
29So He said to them, "Assuredly, I say
to you, there is no one who has left house
or parents or brothers or wife or children,
for the sake of the kingdom of God, 30who
shall not receive many times more in this
present time, and in the age to come eternal life."

Jesus a Third Time Predicts His Death and Resurrection

31Then He took the twelve aside and
said to them, "Behold, we are going up to
Jerusalem, and all things that are written
by the prophets concerning the Son of
Man will be accomplished. 32For He will
be delivered to the Gentiles and will be
mocked and insulted and spit upon.
33They will scourge *Him* and kill Him.
And the third day He will rise again."
34But they understood none of these
things; this saying was hidden from them,
and they did not know the things which
were spoken.

A Blind Man Receives His Sight

35Then it happened, as He was coming near Jericho, that a certain blind man
sat by the road begging. 36And hearing a
multitude passing by, he asked what it
meant. 37So they told him that Jesus of
Nazareth was passing by. 38And he cried
out, saying, "Jesus, Son of David, have
mercy on me!"
39Then those who went before warned
him that he should be quiet; but he cried
out all the more, "Son of David, have
mercy on me!"
40So Jesus stood still and commanded
him to be brought to Him. And when he
had come near, He asked him, 41saying,
"What do you want Me to do for you?"
He said, "Lord, that I may receive my
sight."

> I would freely give my eyes if you might but see Christ, and I would willingly give my hands if you might but lay hold on Him.
>
> **CHARLES SPURGEON**

42Then Jesus said to him, "Receive
your sight; your faith has made you well."
43And immediately he received his sight,
and followed Him, glorifying God. And
all the people, when they saw *it*, gave
praise to God.

Jesus Comes to Zacchaeus' House

19 Then *Jesus* entered and passed
through Jericho. 2Now behold,
there was a man named Zacchaeus who
was a chief tax collector, and he was rich.
3And he sought to see who Jesus was, but
could not because of the crowd, for he was
of short stature. 4So he ran ahead and
climbed up into a sycamore tree to see
Him, for He was going to pass that *way*.
5And when Jesus came to the place, He
looked up and saw him,[a] and said to him,

18:28 [a]NU-Text reads *our own.* **19:5** [a]NU-Text omits *and saw him.*

"Zacchaeus, make haste and come down, for today I must stay at your house." 6So he made haste and came down, and received Him joyfully. 7But when they saw *it,* they all complained, saying, "He has gone to be a guest with a man who is a sinner."

8Then Zacchaeus stood and said to the Lord, "Look, Lord, I give half of my goods to the poor; and if I have taken anything from anyone by false accusation, I restore fourfold."

9And Jesus said to him, "Today salvation has come to this house, because he also is a son of Abraham; 10for the Son of Man has come to seek and to save that which was lost."

The Parable of the Minas

11Now as they heard these things, He spoke another parable, because He was near Jerusalem and because they thought the kingdom of God would appear immediately. 12Therefore He said: "A certain nobleman went into a far country to receive for himself a kingdom and to return. 13So he called ten of his servants, delivered to them ten minas,[a] and said to them, 'Do business till I come.' 14But his citizens hated him, and sent a delegation after him, saying, 'We will not have this *man* to reign over us.'

15"And so it was that when he returned, having received the kingdom, he then commanded these servants, to whom he had given the money, to be called to him, that he might know how much every man had gained by trading. 16Then came the first, saying, 'Master, your mina has earned ten minas.' 17And he said to him, 'Well *done,* good servant; because you were faithful in a very little, have authority over ten cities.' 18And the second came, saying, 'Master, your mina has earned five minas.' 19Likewise he said to him, 'You also be over five cities.'

20"Then another came, saying, 'Master, here is your mina, which I have kept put away in a handkerchief. 21For I feared you, because you are an austere man. You collect what you did not deposit, and reap what you did not sow.' 22And he said to him, 'Out of your own mouth I will judge you, *you* wicked servant. You knew that I was an austere man, collecting what I did not deposit and reaping what I did not sow. 23Why then did you

19:13 [a]The *mina* (Greek *mna,* Hebrew *minah*) was worth about three months' salary.

19:10 Our purpose on earth. "If God's primary purpose for the saved were loving fellowship, He would take believers immediately to heaven, where spiritual fellowship is perfect, unhindered by sin, disharmony, or loneliness. If His primary purpose for the saved were the learning of His Word, He would also take believers immediately to heaven, where His Word is perfectly known and understood. And if God's primary purpose for the saved were to give Him praise, He would, again, take believers immediately to heaven, where praise is perfect and unending. There is only one reason the Lord allows His Church to remain on earth: *to seek and to save the lost*, just as Christ's only reason for coming to earth was to seek and to save the lost. 'As the Father has sent Me,' He declared, 'I also send you' (John 20:21). Therefore, believers who are not committed to winning the lost for Jesus Christ should reexamine their relationship to the Lord and certainly their divine reason for existence. Fellowship, teaching, and praise are not the mission of the Church but are rather the preparation of the Church to fulfill its mission of winning the lost. And just as in athletics, training should never be confused with or substituted for actually competing in the game, which is the reason for all the training." *John MacArthur*

"Christ said, 'I came into this world for one reason—to reach and save lost souls!' Yet, this was not only Jesus' mission. He made it our mission as well: 'And he said unto them, Go ye into all the world, and preach the gospel to every creature'" (Mark 16:15). *David Wilkerson*

19:17 "Dietrich Bonhoeffer wrote that 'only he who believes is obedient, and only he who is obedient believes.' Neither proposition can stand alone. Christians often think we are doing the Lord's work when we are not. Jesus himself warned us about this. We cannot serve two masters. The one we choose will determine whether at our death we hear, 'Well done, good and faithful servant,' or 'I never knew you.'" *Daniel L. Weiss*

not put my money in the bank, that at my coming I might have collected it with interest?'

[24]"And he said to those who stood by, 'Take the mina from him, and give *it* to him who has ten minas.' [25](But they said to him, 'Master, he has ten minas.') [26]'For I say to you, that to everyone who has will be given; and from him who does not have, even what he has will be taken away from him. [27]But bring here those enemies of mine, who did not want me to reign over them, and slay *them* before me.' "

The Triumphal Entry

[28]When He had said this, He went on ahead, going up to Jerusalem. [29]And it came to pass, when He drew near to Bethphage[a] and Bethany, at the mountain called Olivet, *that* He sent two of His disciples, [30]saying, "Go into the village opposite *you*, where as you enter you will find a colt tied, on which no one has ever sat. Loose it and bring *it here.* [31]And if anyone asks you, 'Why are you loosing *it?*' thus you shall say to him, 'Because the Lord has need of it.' "

> Let eloquence be flung to the dogs rather than souls be lost. What we want is to win souls. They are not won by flowery speeches.
>
> **CHARLES SPURGEON**

[32]So those who were sent went their way and found *it* just as He had said to them. [33]But as they were loosing the colt, the owners of it said to them, "Why are you loosing the colt?"

[34]And they said, "The Lord has need of him." [35]Then they brought him to Jesus. And they threw their own clothes on the colt, and they set Jesus on him. [36]And as He went, *many* spread their clothes on the road.

[37]Then, as He was now drawing near the descent of the Mount of Olives, the whole multitude of the disciples began to rejoice and praise God with a loud voice for all the mighty works they had seen, [38]saying:

" 'Blessed is the King who comes in the name of the LORD!'[a]
Peace in heaven and glory in the highest!"

[39]And some of the Pharisees called to Him from the crowd, "Teacher, rebuke Your disciples."

[40]But He answered and said to them, "I tell you that if these should keep silent, the stones would immediately cry out."

Jesus Weeps over Jerusalem

[41]Now as He drew near, He saw the city and wept over it, [42]saying, "If you had known, even you, especially in this your day, the things *that make* for your peace! But now they are hidden from your eyes. [43]For days will come upon you when your enemies will build an embankment around you, surround you and close you in on every side, [44]and level you, and your children within you, to the ground; and they will not leave in you one stone upon another, because you did not know the time of your visitation."

Jesus Cleanses the Temple

[45]Then He went into the temple and began to drive out those who bought and sold in it,[a] [46]saying to them, "It is written, *'My house is*[a] *a house of prayer,'*[b] but you have made it a *'den of thieves.'* "[c]

19:29 [a]M-Text reads *Bethsphage.* 19:38 [a]Psalm 118:26 19:45 [a]NU-Text reads *those who were selling.* 19:46 [a]NU-Text reads *shall be.* [b]Isaiah 56:7 [c]Jeremiah 7:11

19:31 How incredible to think that the Lord had need of a little donkey. But He did. He chose to be carried into Jerusalem on a lowly donkey. God has also chosen lowly creatures like us to carry the Savior to this sinful world. How incredible. See also Matt. 21:2,3 comment.

QUESTIONS & OBJECTIONS

Q 20:3,4

"If Christianity is true, why are so many atrocities committed in the name of Christ?"

Jesus often asked questions of His questioners, to help them think it through logically and see whether their question was even valid. So follow His example. People who pose this question seem to be saying that whenever atrocities are committed by adherents of a certain belief system, then that belief system cannot be true. Let's see how that applies to the belief of atheism. Atheistic governments have slaughtered millions of their people; for example, Mao Zedong was responsible for the deaths of approximately 75 million in China, while Stalin used famine and murder to kill another 10 to 60 million in the Soviet Union. So could we use that same reasoning to conclude that atheism cannot be true? How would your questioner answer that?

When it comes to religion, it is popular these days to defend the Islamic religion regardless of the actions of its most committed followers. Despite the countless atrocities that have been committed, and continue to be committed, in the name of Allah and based on commands in the Koran, many people make a distinction between the "radical" Muslims who commit these acts and the "peaceful" religion of Islam itself. Ask your questioner if he is ready to condemn Islam and all Muslims based on the actions of a minority. Most likely, he isn't—he is interested in condemning only Christianity.

[47]And He was teaching daily in the temple. But the chief priests, the scribes, and the leaders of the people sought to destroy Him, [48]and were unable to do anything; for all the people were very attentive to hear Him.

Jesus' Authority Questioned

20 Now it happened on one of those days, as He taught the people in the temple and preached the gospel, *that* the chief priests and the scribes, together with the elders, confronted *Him* [2]and spoke to Him, saying, "Tell us, by what authority are You doing these things? Or who is he who gave You this authority?"

[3]But He answered and said to them, "I also will ask you one thing, and answer Me: [4]The baptism of John—was it from heaven or from men?"

[5]And they reasoned among themselves, saying, "If we say, 'From heaven,' He will say, 'Why then[a] did you not believe him?' [6]But if we say, 'From men,' all the people will stone us, for they are persuaded that John was a prophet." [7]So they answered that they did not know where *it was* from.

[8]And Jesus said to them, "Neither will I tell you by what authority I do these things."

The Parable of the Wicked Vinedressers

[9]Then He began to tell the people this parable: "A certain man planted a vineyard, leased it to vinedressers, and went into a far country for a long time. [10]Now at vintage-time he sent a servant to the vinedressers, that they might give him some of the fruit of the vineyard. But the vinedressers beat him and sent *him* away empty-handed. [11]Again he sent another servant; and they beat him also, treated *him* shamefully, and sent *him* away empty-handed. [12]And again he sent a third; and they wounded him also and cast *him* out.

[13]"Then the owner of the vineyard said, 'What shall I do? I will send my beloved son. Probably they will respect *him* when they see him.' [14]But when the vinedressers saw him, they reasoned among themselves, saying, 'This is the heir. Come, let us kill him, that the inheritance may be ours.' [15]So they cast him out of the vineyard and killed *him*. Therefore what will the owner of the vineyard do to them? [16]He will come and destroy those vinedressers and give the vineyard to others."

And when they heard *it* they said, "Certainly not!"

20:5 [a]NU-Text and M-Text omit *then*.

[17]Then He looked at them and said, "What then is this that is written:

*'The stone which the builders rejected
Has become the chief cornerstone'?*[a]

[18]Whoever falls on that stone will be broken; but on whomever it falls, it will grind him to powder."

[19]And the chief priests and the scribes that very hour sought to lay hands on Him, but they feared the people[a]—for they knew He had spoken this parable against them.

The Pharisees: Is It Lawful to Pay Taxes to Caesar?

[20]So they watched *Him,* and sent spies who pretended to be righteous, that they might seize on His words, in order to deliver Him to the power and the authority of the governor.

[21]Then they asked Him, saying, "Teacher, we know that You say and teach rightly, and You do not show personal favoritism, but teach the way of God in truth: [22]Is it lawful for us to pay taxes to Caesar or not?"

[23]But He perceived their craftiness, and said to them, "Why do you test Me?[a] [24]Show Me a denarius. Whose image and inscription does it have?"

They answered and said, "Caesar's."

[25]And He said to them, "Render therefore to Caesar the things that are Caesar's, and to God the things that are God's."

[26]But they could not catch Him in His words in the presence of the people. And they marveled at His answer and kept silent.

The Sadducees: What About the Resurrection?

[27]Then some of the Sadducees, who deny that there is a resurrection, came to *Him* and asked Him, [28]saying: "Teacher, Moses wrote to us *that* if a man's brother dies, having a wife, and he dies without children, his brother should take his wife and raise up offspring for his brother.

"To men who think praying their main business . . . does God commit the keys of his kingdom, and by them does he work his spiritual wonders in this world."

E. M. Bounds

[29]Now there were seven brothers. And the first took a wife, and died without children. [30]And the second[a] took her as wife, and he died childless. [31]Then the third took her, and in like manner the seven also; and they left no children,[a] and died. [32]Last of all the woman died also. [33]Therefore, in the resurrection, whose wife does she become? For all seven had her as wife."

[34]Jesus answered and said to them, "The sons of this age marry and are given in marriage. [35]But those who are counted worthy to attain that age, and the resurrection from the dead, neither marry nor are given in marriage; [36]nor can they die anymore, for they are equal to the angels and are sons of God, being sons of the resurrection. [37]But even Moses showed in the *burning* bush *passage* that the dead are raised, when he called the Lord *'the God of Abraham, the God of Isaac, and the God of Jacob.'*[a] [38]For He is not the

20:17 [a]Psalm 118:22 20:19 [a]M-Text reads *but they were afraid.* 20:23 [a]NU-Text omits *Why do you test Me?* 20:30 [a]NU-Text ends verse 30 here. 20:31 [a]NU-Text and M-Text read *the seven also left no children.* 20:37 [a]Exodus 3:6, 15

God of the dead but of the living, for all live to Him."

39 Then some of the scribes answered and said, "Teacher, You have spoken well." 40 But after that they dared not question Him anymore.

Jesus: How Can David Call His Descendant Lord?

41 And He said to them, "How can they say that the Christ is the Son of David? 42 Now David himself said in the Book of Psalms:

'The Lord said to my Lord,
"Sit at My right hand,
43 *Till I make Your enemies Your*
footstool."' [a]

44 Therefore David calls Him *'Lord';* how is He then his Son?"

> He that pleads for Christ should himself be moved with the prospect of Judgment Day.
>
> CHARLES SPURGEON

Beware of the Scribes

45 Then, in the hearing of all the people, He said to His disciples, 46 "Beware of the scribes, who desire to go around in long robes, love greetings in the marketplaces, the best seats in the synagogues, and the best places at feasts, 47 who devour widows' houses, and for a pretense make long prayers. These will receive greater condemnation."

The Widow's Two Mites

21 And He looked up and saw the rich putting their gifts into the treasury, 2 and He saw also a certain poor widow putting in two mites. 3 So He said, "Truly I say to you that this poor widow has put in more than all; 4 for all these out of their abundance have put in offerings for God,[a] but she out of her poverty put in all the livelihood that she had."

Jesus Predicts the Destruction of the Temple

5 Then, as some spoke of the temple, how it was adorned with beautiful stones and donations, He said, 6 "These things which you see—the days will come in which not *one* stone shall be left upon another that shall not be thrown down."

The Signs of the Times and the End of the Age

7 So they asked Him, saying, "Teacher, but when will these things be? And what sign *will there be* when these things are about to take place?"

8 And He said: "Take heed that you not be deceived. For many will come in My name, saying, 'I am *He,*' and, 'The time has drawn near.' Therefore[a] do not go after them. 9 But when you hear of wars and commotions, do not be terrified; for these things must come to pass first, but the end *will* not *come* immediately."

10 Then He said to them, "Nation will rise against nation, and kingdom against kingdom. 11 And there will be great earthquakes in various places, and famines and pestilences; and there will be fearful sights and great signs from heaven. 12 But before all these things, they will lay their hands on you and persecute *you,* delivering *you* up to the synagogues and prisons. You will be brought before kings and rulers for My name's sake. 13 But it will turn out for you as an occasion for testimony. 14 Therefore settle *it* in your hearts not to meditate beforehand on what you will answer; 15 for I will give you a mouth and wisdom which all your

20:43 [a]Psalm 110:1 21:4 [a]NU-Text omits *for God.* 21:8 [a]NU-Text omits *Therefore.*

20:47 See Matt. 11:24 comment.

21:7 For more signs of the end times, see 1 Tim. 4:1.

QUESTIONS & OBJECTIONS

21:24 ***"If the Jews are God's 'chosen people,' why have they been so oppressed?"***

Israel's blessings were dependent upon her obedience. If the nation sinned, it would be chastened. This is God's warning to the Jews, followed by His promised restoration: "Then the LORD will scatter you among all peoples, from one end of the earth to the other, and there you shall serve other gods, which neither you nor your fathers have known—wood and stone. And among those nations you shall find no rest, nor shall the sole of your foot have a resting place; but there the LORD will give you a trembling heart, failing eyes, and anguish of soul" (Deut. 28:64,65).

"In the latter years you will come into the land of those brought back from the sword and gathered from many people on the mountains of Israel, which had long been desolate; they were brought out of the nations, and now all of them dwell safely" (Ezek. 38:8).

adversaries will not be able to contradict
or resist. 16You will be betrayed even by
parents and brothers, relatives and friends;
and they will put *some* of you to death.
17And you will be hated by all for My
name's sake. 18But not a hair of your head
shall be lost. 19By your patience possess
your souls.

> My main ambition in life is to be on the devil's most wanted list.
>
> **LEONARD RAVENHILL**

The Destruction of Jerusalem

20"But when you see Jerusalem surrounded by armies, then know that its
desolation is near. 21Then let those who
are in Judea flee to the mountains, let
those who are in the midst of her depart,
and let not those who are in the country
enter her. 22For these are the days of
vengeance, that all things which are written may be fulfilled. 23But woe to those
who are pregnant and to those who are
nursing babies in those days! For there
will be great distress in the land and
wrath upon this people. 24And they will
fall by the edge of the sword, and be led
away captive into all nations. And Jerusalem will be trampled by Gentiles until
the times of the Gentiles are fulfilled.

The Coming of the Son of Man

25"And there will be signs in the sun,
in the moon, and in the stars; and on the
earth distress of nations, with perplexity,
the sea and the waves roaring; 26men's
hearts failing them from fear and the expectation of those things which are coming on the earth, for the powers of the
heavens will be shaken. 27Then they will
see the Son of Man coming in a cloud
with power and great glory. 28Now when
these things begin to happen, look up
and lift up your heads, because your redemption draws near."

The Parable of the Fig Tree

29Then He spoke to them a parable:
"Look at the fig tree, and all the trees.
30When they are already budding, you
see and know for yourselves that summer
is now near. 31So you also, when you see
these things happening, know that the
kingdom of God is near. 32Assuredly, I
say to you, this generation will by no
means pass away till all things take place.
33Heaven and earth will pass away, but
My words will by no means pass away.

21:26 It has been said that there are three types of people in this world: those who are fearful, those who don't know enough to be fearful, and those who know their Bibles.

21:27 **Second coming of Jesus:** See Acts 1:11.

The Importance of Watching

34"But take heed to yourselves, lest your hearts be weighed down with carousing, drunkenness, and cares of this life, and that Day come on you unexpectedly. 35For it will come as a snare on all those who dwell on the face of the whole earth. 36Watch therefore, and pray always that you may be counted worthy[a] to escape all these things that will come to pass, and to stand before the Son of Man."

37And in the daytime He was teaching in the temple, but at night He went out and stayed on the mountain called Olivet. 38Then early in the morning all the people came to Him in the temple to hear Him.

The Plot to Kill Jesus

22 Now the Feast of Unleavened Bread drew near, which is called Passover. 2And the chief priests and the scribes sought how they might kill Him, for they feared the people.

3Then Satan entered Judas, surnamed Iscariot, who was numbered among the twelve. 4So he went his way and conferred with the chief priests and captains, how he might betray Him to them. 5And they were glad, and agreed to give him money. 6So he promised and sought opportunity to betray Him to them in the absence of the multitude.

Jesus and His Disciples Prepare the Passover

7Then came the Day of Unleavened Bread, when the Passover must be killed. 8And He sent Peter and John, saying, "Go and prepare the Passover for us, that we may eat."

9So they said to Him, "Where do You want us to prepare?"

10And He said to them, "Behold, when you have entered the city, a man will meet you carrying a pitcher of water; follow him into the house which he enters. 11Then you shall say to the master of the house, 'The Teacher says to you, "Where

"He who kneels the most, stands best."

D. L. Moody

is the guest room where I may eat the Passover with My disciples?" ' 12Then he will show you a large, furnished upper room; there make ready."

13So they went and found it just as He had said to them, and they prepared the Passover.

Jesus Institutes the Lord's Supper

14When the hour had come, He sat down, and the twelve[a] apostles with Him. 15Then He said to them, "With *fervent* desire I have desired to eat this Passover with you before I suffer; 16for I say to you, I will no longer eat of it until it is fulfilled in the kingdom of God."

17Then He took the cup, and gave thanks, and said, "Take this and divide *it* among yourselves; 18for I say to you,[a] I will not drink of the fruit of the vine until the kingdom of God comes."

19And He took bread, gave thanks and broke *it,* and gave *it* to them, saying, "This is My body which is given for you; do this in remembrance of Me."

20Likewise He also *took* the cup after

21:36 [a]NU-Text reads *may have strength.* 22:14 [a]NU-Text omits *twelve.* 22:18 [a]NU-Text adds *from now on.*

supper, saying, "This cup *is* the new covenant in My blood, which is shed for you. 21But behold, the hand of My betrayer *is* with Me on the table. 22And truly the Son of Man goes as it has been determined, but woe to that man by whom He is betrayed!"

23Then they began to question among themselves, which of them it was who would do this thing.

The Disciples Argue About Greatness

24Now there was also a dispute among them, as to which of them should be considered the greatest. 25And He said to them, "The kings of the Gentiles exercise lordship over them, and those who exercise authority over them are called 'benefactors.' 26But not so *among* you; on the contrary, he who is greatest among you, let him be as the younger, and he who governs as he who serves. 27For who *is* greater, he who sits at the table, or he who serves? *Is* it not he who sits at the table? Yet I am among you as the One who serves.

28"But you are those who have continued with Me in My trials. 29And I bestow upon you a kingdom, just as My Father bestowed *one* upon Me, 30that you may eat and drink at My table in My kingdom, and sit on thrones judging the twelve tribes of Israel."

Jesus Predicts Peter's Denial

31And the Lord said,[a] "Simon, Simon! Indeed, Satan has asked for you, that he may sift *you* as wheat. 32But I have prayed for you, that your faith should not fail; and when you have returned to *Me,* strengthen your brethren."

33But he said to Him, "Lord, I am ready to go with You, both to prison and to death."

34Then He said, "I tell you, Peter, the rooster shall not crow this day before you will deny three times that you know Me."

Supplies for the Road

35And He said to them, "When I sent you without money bag, knapsack, and sandals, did you lack anything?"

So they said, "Nothing."

36Then He said to them, "But now, he who has a money bag, let him take *it,* and likewise a knapsack; and he who has no sword, let him sell his garment and buy one. 37For I say to you that this which is written must still be accomplished in Me: *'And He was numbered with the transgressors.'*[a] For the things concerning Me have an end."

38So they said, "Lord, look, here *are* two swords."

And He said to them, "It is enough."

The Prayer in the Garden

39Coming out, He went to the Mount of Olives, as He was accustomed, and His disciples also followed Him. 40When He came to the place, He said to them, "Pray that you may not enter into temptation."

41And He was withdrawn from them about a stone's throw, and He knelt down

22:31 [a]NU-Text omits *And the Lord said.* 22:37 [a]Isaiah 53:12

22:31,32 The purpose of sifting. "In Luke 22:31, the word *sift* is translated from the Greek *siniazo,* meaning 'to sift, shake in a sieve; by inward agitation to try one's faith to the verge of overthrow.'

"Jesus did not pray that Simon Peter would escape this intense shaking. He prayed that his faith would not fail in the process... Satan had requested permission to shake Simon Peter so severely that he would lose his faith, but God had a different purpose for the shaking. He allowed the enemy to shake everything in Simon Peter that *needed* to be shaken.

"There are five purposes for shaking an object: 1) to bring it closer to its foundation; 2) to remove what is dead; 3) to harvest what is ripe; 4) to awaken it; and 5) to unify or mix together so it can no longer be separated. As a result of this tremendous shaking, all of Simon Peter's self-confidence would be gone, and all that would remain was God's sure foundation. He would be awakened to his true condition, the dead would be removed and the ripe fruit harvested, bringing him closer to his true foundation. He would no longer function independently but would be interdependent on the Lord." *John Bevere, The Bait of Satan*

and prayed, 42saying, "Father, if it is Your
will, take this cup away from Me; nevertheless not My will, but Yours, be done."
43Then an angel appeared to Him from
heaven, strengthening Him. 44And being
in agony, He prayed more earnestly.
Then His sweat became like great drops
of blood falling down to the ground.[a]
45When He rose up from prayer, and
had come to His disciples, He found them
sleeping from sorrow. 46Then He said to
them, "Why do you sleep? Rise and pray,
lest you enter into temptation."

Betrayal and Arrest in Gethsemane

47And while He was still speaking, behold, a multitude; and he who was called
Judas, one of the twelve, went before
them and drew near to Jesus to kiss Him.
48But Jesus said to him, "Judas, are you
betraying the Son of Man with a kiss?"
49When those around Him saw what
was going to happen, they said to Him,
"Lord, shall we strike with the sword?"
50And one of them struck the servant of
the high priest and cut off his right ear.
51But Jesus answered and said, "Permit even this." And He touched his ear
and healed him.
52Then Jesus said to the chief priests,
captains of the temple, and the elders who
had come to Him, "Have you come out, as
against a robber, with swords and clubs?
53When I was with you daily in the temple, you did not try to seize Me. But this
is your hour, and the power of darkness."

Peter Denies Jesus, and Weeps Bitterly

54Having arrested Him, they led *Him*
and brought Him into the high priest's
house. But Peter followed at a distance.
55Now when they had kindled a fire in
the midst of the courtyard and sat down
together, Peter sat among them. 56And a
certain servant girl, seeing him as he sat
by the fire, looked intently at him and
said, "This man was also with Him."
57But he denied Him,[a] saying, "Woman, I do not know Him."
58And after a little while another saw
him and said, "You also are of them."
But Peter said, "Man, I am not!"
59Then after about an hour had passed,
another confidently affirmed, saying,
"Surely this *fellow* also was with Him, for
he is a Galilean."
60But Peter said, "Man, I do not know
what you are saying!"
Immediately, while he was still speaking, the rooster[a] crowed. 61And the Lord
turned and looked at Peter. Then Peter
remembered the word of the Lord, how
He had said to him, "Before the rooster
crows,[a] you will deny Me three times."

22:44 [a]NU-Text brackets verses 43 and 44 as not in the original text. 22:57 [a]NU-Text reads *denied it*. 22:60 [a]NU-Text and M-Text read *a rooster*. 22:61 [a]NU-Text adds *today*.

22:41 Prayer—the secret weapon: See Acts 1:14.

22:44 This is not just hyperbole like "sweating bullets," but is an actual medical condition known as *hematidrosis*.

22:47 Modern evangelism. The Bible tells us that Judas led a "multitude" to Jesus. His motive, however, wasn't to bring them to the Savior for salvation. Modern evangelism is also bringing "multitudes" to Jesus. Their motive may be different from Judas's, but the end result is the same. Just as the multitudes that Judas directed to Christ fell back from the Son of God, statistics show that up to 90 percent of those coming to Christ under the methods of modern evangelism fall away from the faith. Their latter end becomes worse than the first. They openly crucify the Son of God afresh.

In their zeal without knowledge, those who prefer the ease of modern evangelism to biblical evangelism betray the cause of the gospel with a kiss. What may look like love for the sinner's welfare is in truth eternally detrimental to him.

Like Peter (v. 50), our zeal without knowledge is actually cutting off the ears of sinners. Those we erroneously call "backsliders" won't listen to our reasonings. As far as they are concerned, they have tried Christianity once, and it didn't work. What a victory for the prince of darkness, and what an unspeakable tragedy for the Church! See Luke 11:52 and 2 Cor. 2:17 comments.

62So Peter went out and wept bitterly.

Jesus Mocked and Beaten

63Now the men who held Jesus mocked Him and beat Him. 64And having blindfolded Him, they struck Him on the face and asked Him,[a] saying, "Prophesy! Who is the one who struck You?" 65And many other things they blasphemously spoke against Him.

Jesus Faces the Sanhedrin

66As soon as it was day, the elders of the people, both chief priests and scribes, came together and led Him into their council, saying, 67"If You are the Christ, tell us."

> Men occasionally stumble over the truth, but most of them pick themselves up and hurry off as if nothing had happened.
>
> **WINSTON CHURCHILL**

But He said to them, "If I tell you, you will by no means believe. 68And if I also ask *you,* you will by no means answer Me or let *Me* go.[a] 69Hereafter the Son of Man will sit on the right hand of the power of God."

70Then they all said, "Are You then the Son of God?"

So He said to them, "You *rightly* say that I am."

71And they said, "What further testimony do we need? For we have heard it ourselves from His own mouth."

Jesus Handed Over to Pontius Pilate

23 Then the whole multitude of them arose and led Him to Pilate. 2And they began to accuse Him, saying, "We found this *fellow* perverting the[a] nation, and forbidding to pay taxes to Caesar, saying that He Himself is Christ, a King."

3Then Pilate asked Him, saying, "Are You the King of the Jews?"

He answered him and said, "*It is as* you say."

4So Pilate said to the chief priests and the crowd, "I find no fault in this Man."

5But they were the more fierce, saying, "He stirs up the people, teaching throughout all Judea, beginning from Galilee to this place."

Jesus Faces Herod

6When Pilate heard of Galilee,[a] he asked if the Man were a Galilean. 7And as soon as he knew that He belonged to Herod's jurisdiction, he sent Him to Herod, who was also in Jerusalem at that time. 8Now when Herod saw Jesus, he was exceedingly glad; for he had desired for a long *time* to see Him, because he had heard many things about Him, and he hoped to see some miracle done by Him. 9Then he questioned Him with many words, but He answered him nothing. 10And the chief priests and scribes stood and vehemently accused Him. 11Then Herod, with his men of war, treated Him with contempt and mocked *Him,* arrayed Him in a gorgeous robe, and sent Him back to Pilate. 12That very day Pilate and Herod became friends with each other, for previously they had been at enmity with each other.

Taking the Place of Barabbas

13Then Pilate, when he had called together the chief priests, the rulers, and the people, 14said to them, "You have brought this Man to me, as one who misleads the people. And indeed, having examined *Him* in your presence, I have found no fault in this Man concerning those things of which you accuse Him; 15no, neither did Herod, for I sent you back to him;[a] and indeed nothing deserving of death has been done by Him. 16I will therefore chastise Him and release *Him*" 17(for it was necessary for him to release one to them at the feast).[a]

22:64 [a]NU-Text reads *And having blindfolded Him, they asked Him.* 22:68 [a]NU-Text omits *also* and *Me or let Me go.* 23:2 [a]NU-Text reads *our.* 23:6 [a]NU-Text omits *of Galilee.* 23:15 [a]NU-Text reads *for he sent Him back to us.* 23:17 [a]NU-Text omits verse 17.

18And they all cried out at once, saying, "Away with this *Man,* and release to us Barabbas"— 19who had been thrown into prison for a certain rebellion made in the city, and for murder.

20Pilate, therefore, wishing to release Jesus, again called out to them. 21But they shouted, saying, "Crucify *Him,* crucify Him!"

22Then he said to them the third time, "Why, what evil has He done? I have found no reason for death in Him. I will therefore chastise Him and let *Him* go."

23But they were insistent, demanding with loud voices that He be crucified. And the voices of these men and of the chief priests prevailed.[a] 24So Pilate gave sentence that it should be as they requested. 25And he released to them[a] the one they requested, who for rebellion and murder had been thrown into prison; but he delivered Jesus to their will.

The King on a Cross

26Now as they led Him away, they laid hold of a certain man, Simon a Cyrenian, who was coming from the country, and on him they laid the cross that he might bear *it* after Jesus.

27And a great multitude of the people followed Him, and women who also mourned and lamented Him. 28But Jesus, turning to them, said, "Daughters of Jerusalem, do not weep for Me, but weep for yourselves and for your children. 29For indeed the days are coming in which they will say, 'Blessed *are* the barren, wombs that never bore, and breasts which never nursed!' 30Then they will begin *'to say to the mountains, "Fall on us!" and to the hills, "Cover us!"'*[a] 31For if they do these things in the green wood, what will be done in the dry?"

32There were also two others, criminals, led with Him to be put to death.

33And when they had come to the place called Calvary, there they crucified Him, and the criminals, one on the right hand and the other on the left. 34Then Jesus said, "Father, forgive them, for they do not know what they do."[a]

And they divided His garments and cast lots. 35And the people stood looking on. But even the rulers with them sneered, saying, "He saved others; let Him save Himself if He is the Christ, the chosen of God."

36The soldiers also mocked Him, coming and offering Him sour wine, 37and saying, "If You are the King of the Jews, save Yourself."

38And an inscription also was written over Him in letters of Greek, Latin, and Hebrew:[a]

THIS IS THE KING OF THE JEWS.

39Then one of the criminals who were hanged blasphemed Him, saying, "If You are the Christ,[a] save Yourself and us."

40But the other, answering, rebuked him, saying, "Do you not even fear God, seeing you are under the same condemnation? 41And we indeed justly, for we receive the due reward of our deeds; but this Man has done nothing wrong." 42Then he said to Jesus, "Lord,[a] remember me when You come into Your kingdom."

43And Jesus said to him, "Assuredly, I say to you, today you will be with Me in Paradise."

Jesus Dies on the Cross

44Now it was[a] about the sixth hour,

23:23 [a]NU-Text omits *and of the chief priests.* 23:25 [a]NU-Text and M-Text omit *to them.* 23:30 [a]Hosea 10:8 23:34 [a]NU-Text brackets the first sentence as a later addition. 23:38 [a]NU-Text omits *written* and *in letters of Greek, Latin, and Hebrew.* 23:39 [a]NU-Text reads *Are You not the Christ?* 23:42 [a]NU-Text reads *And he said, "Jesus, remember me.* 23:44 [a]NU-Text adds *already.*

23:32–34 Messianic prophecy fulfilled: "He poured out His soul unto death, and He was numbered with the transgressors, and He bore the sin of many, and made intercession for the transgressors" (Isa. 53:12). See Luke 24:39 comment.

23:53 *The Hands of the Carpenter*

It was Joseph of Arimathaea who had the honor of taking the body of Jesus down from the cross. Think what it would be like to have to pull the cold and lifeless hands of the Son of God from the thick, barbed Roman nails. These were carpenter's hands, which once held nails and wood, now being held by nails and wood. These were the hands that broke bread and fed multitudes, now being broken to feed multitudes. They once applied clay to a blind man's eyes, touched lepers, healed the sick, washed the disciple's feet, and took children in His arms. These were the hands that, more than once, loosed the cold hand of death, now held firmly by its icy grip.

These were the fingers that wrote in the sand when the adulterous woman was cast at His feet, and for the love of God, fashioned a whip that purged His Father's house. These were the same fingers that took bread and dipped it in a dish, and gave it to Judas as a gesture of deep love and friendship. Here was the Bread of Life itself, being dipped in the cup of suffering, as the ultimate gesture of God's love for the evil world that Judas represented.

Joseph's shame, that he had been afraid to own the Savior, sickened him as he tore the blood-sodden feet from the six-inch cold steel spikes that fastened them to the cross. These were the "beautiful feet" of Him that preached the gospel of peace, that Mary washed with her hair, that walked upon the Sea of Galilee, now crimson with a sea of blood.

As Joseph reached out his arms to get Him down from the cross, perhaps he stared for an instant at the inanimate face of the Son of God. His heart wrenched as he looked upon Him whom they had pierced. This face, which once radiated with the glory of God on the Mount of Transfiguration, which so many had looked upon with such veneration, was now blood-stained from the needle-sharp crown of thorns, deathly pale and twisted from unspeakable suffering as the sin of the world was laid upon Him.

His eyes, which once sparkled with the life of God, now stared at nothingness, as He was brought into the dust of death. His lips, which spoke such gracious words and calmed the fears of so many, were swollen and bruised from the beating given to Him by the hardened fists of cruel soldiers.

As it is written, "His visage was marred more than any man" (Isa. 52:14).

Nicodemus may have reached up to help Joseph with the body. As the cold blood of the Lamb of God covered his hand he was reminded of the blood of the Passover lamb he had seen shed so many times. The death of each spotless animal had been so quick and merciful, but this death had been unspeakably cruel, vicious, inhumane, and brutal. It seemed that all the hatred that sin-loving humanity had for the Light formed itself into a dark and evil spear, and was thrust with cruel delight into the perfect Lamb of God.

Perhaps as he carefully pried the crown from His head, looked at the gaping hole in His side, the deep mass of abrasions upon His back, and the mutilated wounds in His hands and feet, a sense of outrage engrossed him, that this could happen to such a Man as this. But the words of the prophet Isaiah rang within his heart:

> He was wounded for our transgressions, He was bruised for our iniquities; the chastisement for our peace was upon Him, and by His stripes we are healed... the LORD has laid on Him the iniquity of us all... He was led as a lamb to the slaughter... For the transgressions of My people He was stricken... Yet it pleased the LORD to bruise Him... By His knowledge My righteous Servant shall justify many, for He shall bear their iniquities. (Isa. 53:5–11)

Jesus of Nazareth was stripped of His robe, that we might be robed in pure righteousness. He suffered a deathly thirst, that our thirst for life might be quenched. He agonized under the curse of the Law, that we might relish the blessing of the gospel. He took upon Himself the hatred of the world, so that we could experience the love of God. Hell was let loose upon Him so that heaven could be let loose upon us. Jesus of Nazareth tasted the bitterness of death, so that we might taste the sweetness of life everlasting. The Son of God willingly passed over His life, that death might freely pass over the sons and daughters of Adam.

May Calvary's cross be as real to us as it was to those who stood on its bloody soil on that terrible day. May we also gaze upon the face of the crucified Son of God, and may shame grip our hearts if ever the fear of man comes near our souls. May we identify with the apostle Paul, who could have gloried in his dramatic and miraculous experience on the road to Damascus. Instead, he whispered in awe of God's great love:

> God forbid that I should boast except in the cross of our Lord Jesus Christ, by whom the world has been crucified to me, and I to the world. (Gal. 6:14)

and there was darkness over all the earth until the ninth hour. [45]Then the sun was darkened,[a] and the veil of the temple was torn in two. [46]And when Jesus had cried out with a loud voice, He said, "Father, *'into Your hands I commit My spirit.'* "[a] Having said this, He breathed His last.

[47]So when the centurion saw what had happened, he glorified God, saying, "Certainly this was a righteous Man!"

[48]And the whole crowd who came together to that sight, seeing what had been done, beat their breasts and returned. [49]But all His acquaintances, and the women who followed Him from Galilee, stood at a distance, watching these things.

Jesus Buried in Joseph's Tomb

[50]Now behold, *there was* a man named Joseph, a council member, a good and just man. [51]He had not consented to their decision and deed. *He was* from Arimathea, a city of the Jews, who himself was also waiting[a] for the kingdom of God. [52]This man went to Pilate and asked for the body of Jesus. [53]Then he took it down, wrapped it in linen, and laid it in a tomb *that was* hewn out of the rock, where no one had ever lain before. [54]That day was the Preparation, and the Sabbath drew near.

[55]And the women who had come with Him from Galilee followed after, and they observed the tomb and how His body was laid. [56]Then they returned and prepared spices and fragrant oils. And they rested on the Sabbath according to the commandment.

He Is Risen

24 Now on the first *day* of the week, very early in the morning, they, and certain *other women* with them,[a] came to the tomb bringing the spices which they had prepared. [2]But they found the stone rolled away from the tomb. [3]Then they went in and did not find the body of the Lord Jesus. [4]And it happened, as they were greatly[a] perplexed about this, that behold, two men stood by them in shining garments. [5]Then, as they were afraid and bowed *their* faces to the earth, they said to them, "Why do you seek the living among the dead? [6]He is not here, but is risen! Remember how He spoke to you when He was still in Galilee, [7]saying, 'The Son of Man must be delivered into the hands of sinful men, and be crucified, and the third day rise again.' "

[8]And they remembered His words. [9]Then they returned from the tomb and told all these things to the eleven and to all the rest. [10]It was Mary Magdalene, Joanna, Mary *the mother* of James, and the other *women* with them, who told these things to the apostles. [11]And their words seemed to them like idle tales, and they did not believe them. [12]But Peter arose and ran to the tomb; and stooping down, he saw the linen cloths lying[a] by themselves; and he departed, marveling to himself at what had happened.

The Road to Emmaus

[13]Now behold, two of them were traveling that same day to a village called Emmaus, which was seven miles[a] from Jerusalem. [14]And they talked together of all these things which had happened. [15]So it was, while they conversed and reasoned, that Jesus Himself drew near and went with them. [16]But their eyes were restrained, so that they did not know Him.

[17]And He said to them, "What kind of

23:45 [a]NU-Text reads *obscured.* 23:46 [a]Psalm 31:5 23:51 [a]NU-Text reads *who was waiting.* 24:1 [a]NU-Text omits *and certain other women with them.* 24:4 [a]NU-Text omits *greatly.* 24:12 [a]NU-Text omits *lying.* 24:13 [a]Literally *sixty stadia*

24:1 Who arrived at the tomb first? Some say there seems to be a contradiction as to who arrived first at the tomb. However, there is no contradiction when the Gospels are read in harmony. When the women arrived at the edge of the garden, they looked and saw that the stone had been rolled back from the tomb. Mary concluded that the body had been stolen, and ran back to Peter and John in Jerusalem. The other women continued to the tomb, and went on inside where they encountered the angels.

conversation *is* this that you have with one another as you walk and are sad?"[a]

18Then the one whose name was Cleopas answered and said to Him, "Are You the only stranger in Jerusalem, and have You not known the things which happened there in these days?"

19And He said to them, "What things?"

So they said to Him, "The things concerning Jesus of Nazareth, who was a Prophet mighty in deed and word before God and all the people, 20and how the chief priests and our rulers delivered Him to be condemned to death, and crucified Him. 21But we were hoping that it was He who was going to redeem Israel. Indeed, besides all this, today is the third day since these things happened. 22Yes, and certain women of our company, who arrived at the tomb early, astonished us. 23When they did not find His body, they came saying that they had also seen a vision of angels who said He was alive. 24And certain of those *who were* with us went to the tomb and found *it* just as the women had said; but Him they did not see."

25Then He said to them, "O foolish ones, and slow of heart to believe in all that the prophets have spoken! 26Ought not the Christ to have suffered these things and to enter into His glory?" 27And beginning at Moses and all the Prophets, He expounded to them in all the Scriptures the things concerning Himself.

The Disciples' Eyes Opened

28Then they drew near to the village where they were going, and He indicated that He would have gone farther. 29But they constrained Him, saying, "Abide with us, for it is toward evening, and the day is far spent." And He went in to stay with them.

30Now it came to pass, as He sat at the table with them, that He took bread, blessed and broke *it,* and gave it to them. 31Then their eyes were opened and they knew Him; and He vanished from their sight.

> God does not expect us to submit our faith to Him without reason, but the very limits of our reason make faith a necessity.
>
> **AUGUSTINE**

32And they said to one another, "Did not our heart burn within us while He talked with us on the road, and while He opened the Scriptures to us?" 33So they rose up that very hour and returned to Jerusalem, and found the eleven and those *who were* with them gathered together, 34saying, "The Lord is risen indeed, and has appeared to Simon!" 35And they told about the things *that had happened* on the road, and how He was known to them in the breaking of bread.

Jesus Appears to His Disciples

36Now as they said these things, Jesus Himself stood in the midst of them, and said to them, "Peace to you." 37But they

24:17 [a]NU-Text reads *as you walk? And they stood still, looking sad.*

24:25 "About this time there lived Jesus, a wise man, if indeed one ought to call him a man. For he was one who wrought surprising feats and was a teacher of such people as accepted the truth gladly. He won over many Jews and many Greeks. He was the Christ. When Pilate, upon hearing him accused by men of the highest standing among us, had condemned him to be crucified, those who had in the first place come to love him did not give up their affection for him. On the third day he appeared to them restored to life, for the prophets of God had prophesied these and countless other marvelous things about him. And the tribe of Christians, so called after him, has still to this day not disappeared." *Josephus, Testimonium Flavianum*

24:39 Messianic prophecy fulfilled: "For dogs have surrounded Me; the congregation of the wicked has enclosed Me. They pierced My hands and My feet" (Psa. 22:16). See John 1:11 comment.

QUESTIONS & OBJECTIONS

24:44,45 ***"What if someone claims to have read the Bible and says it's just a book of fairy tales?"***

Call his bluff. Gently ask, "What is the thread of continuity that runs through the Bible—the consistent theme from the Old Testament through the New Testament?" More than likely he won't know. So explain, "The Old Testament was God's promise that He would destroy death. The New Testament tells how He did it." Then appeal directly to the conscience by asking if he has kept the Ten Commandments (see Psa. 51:6 and John 4:7 comments).

For more about the Bible's reliability, see Matt. 4:4 and 2 Tim. 3:16 comments.

were terrified and frightened, and supposed they had seen a spirit. 38And He
said to them, "Why are you troubled?
And why do doubts arise in your hearts?
39Behold My hands and My feet, that it is
I Myself. Handle Me and see, for a spirit
does not have flesh and bones as you see
I have."
40When He had said this, He showed
them His hands and His feet.[a] 41But
while they still did not believe for joy, and
marveled, He said to them, "Have you
any food here?" 42So they gave Him a
piece of a broiled fish and some honeycomb.[a] 43And He took *it* and ate in their
presence.

The Scriptures Opened

44Then He said to them, "These *are*
the words which I spoke to you while I
was still with you, that all things must be
fulfilled which were written in the Law of
Moses and *the* Prophets and *the* Psalms
concerning Me." 45And He opened their
understanding, that they might comprehend the Scriptures.
46Then He said to them, "Thus it is
written, and thus it was necessary for the
Christ to suffer and to rise[a] from the dead
the third day, 47and that repentance and
remission of sins should be preached in
His name to all nations, beginning at Jerusalem. 48And you are witnesses of these
things. 49Behold, I send the Promise of My
Father upon you; but tarry in the city of
Jerusalem[a] until you are endued with
power from on high."

The Ascension

50And He led them out as far as
Bethany, and He lifted up His hands and
blessed them. 51Now it came to pass,
while He blessed them, that He was parted
from them and carried up into heaven.
52And they worshiped Him, and returned to Jerusalem with great joy, 53and
were continually in the temple praising
and[a] blessing God. Amen.[b]

24:40 [a]Some printed New Testaments omit this verse. It is found in nearly all Greek manuscripts. 24:42 [a]NU-Text omits *and some honeycomb.* 24:46 [a]NU-Text reads *written, that the Christ should suffer and rise.* 24:49 [a]NU-Text omits *of Jerusalem.* 24:53 [a]NU-Text omits *praising and.* [b]NU-Text omits *Amen.*

24:43 Jesus' resurrected body was physical. He was visible, could be touched, and could eat food. He was not a spirit, but had flesh and bones. Our resurrected bodies will also be physical; see Rom. 8:23.

24:47 Repentance—its necessity for salvation. See Acts 2:38.

"There are many who speak only of the forgiveness of sin, but who say little or nothing about repentance. If there is nevertheless no forgiveness of sins without repentance, so also forgiveness of sins cannot be understood without repentance. Therefore, if forgiveness of sins is preached without repentance, it follows that the people imagine they have already received the forgiveness of sins, and thereby they become cocksure and fearless, which is then greater error and sin than all the error that preceded our time."
Melanchthon

Resurrection Proofs

How Do We Know Jesus Rose from the Dead?

The resurrection of Jesus Christ is the cornerstone of the Christian faith. As the apostle Paul said, "If Christ has not been raised, your faith is worthless; you are still in your sins" (1 Corinthians 15:17). But Christianity is not a "blind faith." God has given us "many infallible proofs" of Jesus' resurrection (Acts 1:3) and invites us to examine the evidence.

HIS RESURRECTION WAS FORETOLD

Jesus Himself said that He would be killed and on the third day rise again. The risen Jesus spoke to two disciples on the road to Emmaus, telling them, "These are My words that I spoke to you while I was still with you—that everything written about Me in the Law of Moses, the Prophets, and the Psalms must be fulfilled" (Luke 24:47). The suffering death of the Savior was foretold in numerous Old Testament prophecies, down to minute details, all of which were precisely fulfilled.

JESUS DIED

Some skeptics have proposed the "swoon theory"—that Jesus didn't really die on the cross but instead passed out and later revived in the tomb. But He was brutally beaten, flogged with a cat-o'-nine-tails tearing His flesh, hung on a cross with thick spikes driven through His hands and feet, then—to ensure that He was dead—He was pierced in the side with a spear. The Roman soldiers were professional executioners who knew how to do a thorough job. No one in this condition could have survived, then awakened to roll away a two-ton stone and slipped by the Roman guards posted at the sealed tomb. That Jesus died and was buried is reported even by secular sources of the time.

THE TOMB WAS EMPTY

Even Jesus' enemies did not dispute that the tomb was empty. Instead, they claimed that the body was stolen while the guards slept—even though the guards faced execution if they fell asleep on the job. It would have been impossible for the cowardly disciples, who fled upon Jesus' arrest, to overpower a squadron of professional soldiers. And why would they? They each faced persecution and death for their eyewitness testimony, fully convinced that Jesus Christ rose from the grave. What would they gain by dying for a known lie?

The Jewish leaders certainly wouldn't have stolen the body. Their goal was to stop the spread of Christianity, so having people believe in Jesus' resurrection was the furthest thing from their minds. If the body could have been found anywhere, they surely would have searched until they produced it and put this new religion to rest.

HE WAS SEEN ALIVE AFTER THE RESURRECTION

These were not "hallucinations" or brief sightings—Jesus ate, drank, and spoke at length with His disciples. Jesus appeared at least 11 times over a 40-day period, and to *over 500* eyewitnesses! In writing of this amazing eyewitness testimony, the apostle Paul noted that "most of [them] remain to the present." With witnesses still alive for cross-examination, skeptics could have easily verified the truth of the claim.

Dr. Simon Greenleaf, a founder of Harvard Law School, was one of the greatest legal minds in this country. He concluded that the resurrection of Christ was one of the best supported events in history, according to the laws of legal evidence used in court. In fact, Greenleaf was so convinced by the overwhelming evidence, he committed his life to Christ!

LIVES ARE RADICALLY TRANSFORMED

Overnight, the fearful disciples became bold, fearless witnesses, proclaiming the resurrection of Jesus Christ. After seeing the ultimate proof of Jesus' deity, thousands of Jews abandoned centuries-old religious rituals to follow the Messiah. Truly, the Son of God has power over life and death, and He is alive to transform lives today. All who repent and trust in Him will "know Him and the power of His resurrection"—they too will encounter the risen Lord and be given eternal life.

(Reprinted from *The Way of the Master New Testament.*)

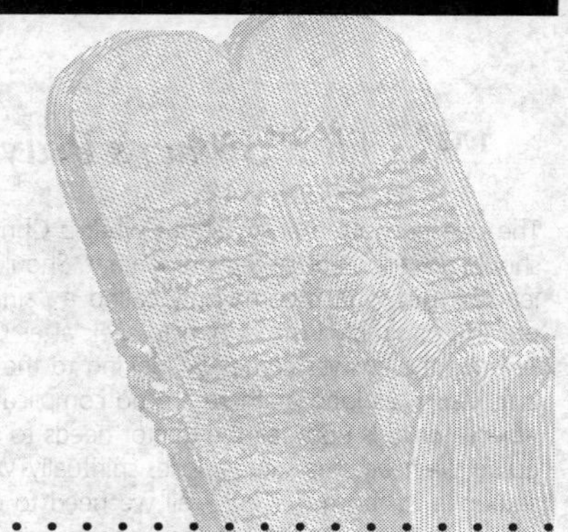

John

The Eternal Word

1 In the beginning was the Word, and the Word was with God, and the Word was God. 2He was in the beginning with God. 3All things were made through Him, and without Him nothing was made that was made. 4In Him was life, and the life was the light of men. 5And the light shines in the darkness, and the darkness did not comprehend[a] it.

John's Witness: The True Light

6There was a man sent from God, whose name *was* John. 7This man came for a witness, to bear witness of the Light, that all through him might believe. 8He was not that Light, but *was sent* to bear witness of that Light. 9That was the true Light which gives light to every man coming into the world.[a]

10He was in the world, and the world was made through Him, and the world did not know Him. 11He came to His own,[a] and His own[b] did not receive Him. 12But as many as received Him, to them He gave the right to become children of God, to those who believe in His name: 13who were born, not of blood, nor of the will of the flesh, nor of the will of man, but of God.

The Word Becomes Flesh

14And the Word became flesh and dwelt among us, and we beheld His glory, the glory as of the only begotten of the Father, full of grace and truth.

15John bore witness of Him and cried out, saying, "This was He of whom I said,

1:5 [a]Or *overcome* 1:9 [a]Or *That was the true Light which, coming into the world, gives light to every man.* 1:11 [a]That is, His own things or domain [b]That is, His own people

1:3,4 Rejection of the Bible's account of creation as given in the Book of Genesis could rightly be called "Genecide," because it eradicated man's purpose of existence and left a whole generation with no certainty as to its beginning. Consequently, theories and tales of our origin have crept like primeval slime from the minds of those who don't know God. This intellectual genocide has given the godless a temporary license to labor to the extremes of their imagination, giving birth to painful conjecture of human beginnings. They speak in speculation, the uncertain language of those who drift aimlessly across the endless sea of secular philosophy. See Job 35:16 comment for the tentative nature of science.

The Scriptures, on the other hand, deal only with truth and certainty. They talk of fact, reality, and purpose for man's existence. The darkness of the raging sea of futility retreats where the lighthouse of Genesis begins.

1:9 On the Day of Judgment no one can plead ignorance. God has given light to every man. See 2 Cor. 4:6.

1:11 Messianic prophecy fulfilled: "He is despised and rejected by men, a Man of sorrows and acquainted with grief. And we hid, as it were, our faces from Him; He was despised, and we did not esteem Him" (Isa. 53:3). See John 1:32 comment.

1:13 New birth—its necessity for salvation: See John 3:7.

1:13 The "Sinner's Prayer"—To Pray or Not To Pray?

The question often arises about what a Christian should do if someone seems repentant. Should we lead him in what's commonly called a "sinner's prayer" or simply instruct him to seek after God? Perhaps the answer comes by looking to the natural realm. As long as there are no complications when a child is born, all the doctor needs to do is *guide the head*. The same applies spiritually. When someone is "born of God," all we need to do is guide the head—make sure he *understands* what he is doing.

Philip the evangelist did this with the Ethiopian eunuch, asking him, "Do you understand what you are reading?" (Acts 8:30). In the parable of the sower, the true convert ("good soil" hearer) is he who hears "and understands" (Matt. 13:23). This understanding comes by the Law in the hand of the Spirit (Rom. 7:7). If a sinner is ready for the Savior, it is because he has been drawn by the Holy Spirit (John 6:44). This is why we must be careful to allow the Holy Spirit to do His work and not rush in where angels fear to tread. Praying a "sinner's prayer" with someone who isn't genuinely repentant may leave you with a stillborn on your hands. So rather than *lead* him in a prayer of repentance, encourage him to pray himself.

When Nathan confronted David about his sin, he didn't lead the king in a prayer of repentance. If a man committed adultery, and his wife is willing to take him back, should you have to write out an apology for him to read to her? No. Sorrow for his betrayal of her trust should spill from his lips. She doesn't want eloquent words, but simply sorrow of heart. The same applies to a prayer of repentance. The words aren't as important as the presence of "godly sorrow." The sinner should be told to repent—to confess and forsake his sins. He could do this as a whispered prayer, then you could pray for him. If he's not sure what to say, perhaps David's prayer of repentance (Psa. 51) could be used as a model, but his own words are more desirable.

'He who comes after me is preferred before me, for He was before me.' "
16And[a] of His fullness we have all received, and grace for grace. 17For the law
was given through Moses, *but* grace and
truth came through Jesus Christ. 18No
one has seen God at any time. The only
begotten Son,[a] who is in the bosom of the
Father, He has declared *Him*.

A Voice in the Wilderness

19Now this is the testimony of John,
when the Jews sent priests and Levites
from Jerusalem to ask him, "Who are you?"
20He confessed, and did not deny, but
confessed, "I am not the Christ."
21And they asked him, "What then? Are
you Elijah?"
He said, "I am not."
"Are you the Prophet?"
And he answered, "No."
22Then they said to him, "Who are you,
that we may give an answer to those who
sent us? What do you say about yourself?"
23He said: "I *am*

'The voice of one crying in the
wilderness:
"Make straight the way of the Lord," '[a]

1:16 [a]NU-Text reads *For.* 1:18 [a]NU-Text reads *only begotten God.* 1:23 [a]Isaiah 40:3

1:13 How to get false converts. Our aim should be to ensure that sinners are born of the Spirit—of the will of God and not of the will of man. Too many of our "decisions" are not a work of the Spirit, but a work of our sincere but manipulative practices. It is simple to secure a decision for Jesus by using this popular method: "Do you know whether you are going to heaven when you die? God wants you to have that assurance. All you need to do is: 1) realize that you are a sinner ('All have sinned and fall short of the glory of God'), and 2) believe that Jesus died on the cross for you. Would you like me to pray with you right now so that you can give your heart to Jesus? Then you will have the assurance that you are going to heaven when you die." For the *biblical* way to present the gospel, see John 4:7 comment. For more on false converts, see Matt. 25:12 comment.

1:17 "A wrong understanding of the harmony between Law and grace would produce 'error on the left and the right hand.'" *John Newton*

QUESTIONS & OBJECTIONS

"I will believe if God will appear to me."

A proud and ignorant sinner who says this has no understanding of the nature of his Creator. When God "appeared" to certain men in the Old Testament, He manifested himself in other forms, such as a burning bush or "the Angel of the Lord." However, no man has seen the essence of God at any time (see John 1:18). (In Exod. 33:11, the expression "the LORD spoke to Moses face to face" is an example of anthropomorphism.)

When Moses asked to see God's glory, God told him, "I will make all My goodness pass before you . . . [but] you cannot see My face; for no man shall see Me, and live" (Exod. 33:18–23). If all of God's "goodness" were shown to a sinner, he would instantly die. God's "goodness" would just spill wrath upon evil man. We can understand that if an earthly judge is a good man, he would be outraged by a vicious murder and must do his best to ensure the wicked criminal is brought to justice. It is the judge's goodness that makes him passionate for justice to be done.

It is the goodness of God that will make sure every murderer and rapist is brought to justice on Judgment Day. However, God is so good, so pure and holy, that He is utterly provoked to just retribution by any evil (anger, greed, envy, pride, lust, lying, jealousy, hatred, etc.). However, the Lord told Moses, "So it shall be, while My glory passes by, that I will put you in the cleft of the rock, and will cover you with My hand while I pass by." When Moses simply gazed at where God had been, his own face so shone with the glory of God that Israel could not even look at him (see Exod. 34:29–35). The only way a sinner can see a holy God and live is to be hidden in the Rock of Jesus Christ (see 1 Cor. 10:4).

as the prophet Isaiah said."
[24]Now those who were sent were from
the Pharisees. [25]And they asked him, saying, "Why then do you baptize if you are
not the Christ, nor Elijah, nor the
Prophet?"
[26]John answered them, saying, "I baptize with water, but there stands One
among you whom you do not know. [27]It
is He who, coming after me, is preferred
before me, whose sandal strap I am not
worthy to loose."
[28]These things were done in Betha-
bara[a] beyond the Jordan, where John was
baptizing.

The Lamb of God

[29]The next day John saw Jesus coming
toward him, and said, "Behold! The Lamb
of God who takes away the sin of the
world! [30]This is He of whom I said, 'After
me comes a Man who is preferred before
me, for He was before me.' [31]I did not
know Him; but that He should be revealed to Israel, therefore I came baptizing with water."
[32]And John bore witness, saying, "I
saw the Spirit descending from heaven
like a dove, and He remained upon Him.
[33]I did not know Him, but He who sent
me to baptize with water said to me,
'Upon whom you see the Spirit descending, and remaining on Him, this is He
who baptizes with the Holy Spirit.' [34]And
I have seen and testified that this is the
Son of God."

The First Disciples

[35]Again, the next day, John stood with
two of his disciples. [36]And looking at Jesus
as He walked, he said, "Behold the Lamb
of God!"
[37]The two disciples heard him speak,
and they followed Jesus. [38]Then Jesus

1:28 [a]NU-Text and M-Text read *Bethany.*

1:32 Messianic prophecy fulfilled: "The Spirit of the LORD shall rest upon Him, the Spirit of wisdom and understanding, the Spirit of counsel and might, the Spirit of knowledge and of the fear of the LORD" (Isa. 11:2). See John 6:14 comment.

turned, and seeing them following, said to them, "What do you seek?"

They said to Him, "Rabbi" (which is to say, when translated, Teacher), "where are You staying?"

39He said to them, "Come and see." They came and saw where He was staying, and remained with Him that day (now it was about the tenth hour).

40One of the two who heard John *speak,* and followed Him, was Andrew, Simon Peter's brother. 41He first found his own brother Simon, and said to him, "We have found the Messiah" (which is translated, the Christ). 42And he brought him to Jesus.

Now when Jesus looked at him, He said, "You are Simon the son of Jonah.[a] You shall be called Cephas" (which is translated, A Stone).

Philip and Nathanael

43The following day Jesus wanted to go to Galilee, and He found Philip and said to him, "Follow Me." 44Now Philip was from Bethsaida, the city of Andrew and Peter. 45Philip found Nathanael and said to him, "We have found Him of whom Moses in the law, and also the prophets, wrote—Jesus of Nazareth, the son of Joseph."

46And Nathanael said to him, "Can anything good come out of Nazareth?"

Philip said to him, "Come and see."

47Jesus saw Nathanael coming toward Him, and said of him, "Behold, an Israelite indeed, in whom is no deceit!"

48Nathanael said to Him, "How do You know me?"

Jesus answered and said to him, "Before Philip called you, when you were under the fig tree, I saw you."

49Nathanael answered and said to Him, "Rabbi, You are the Son of God! You are the King of Israel!"

50Jesus answered and said to him, "Because I said to you, 'I saw you under the fig tree,' do you believe? You will see greater things than these." 51And He said to him, "Most assuredly, I say to you, hereafter[a] you shall see heaven open, and the angels of God ascending and descending upon the Son of Man."

Water Turned to Wine

2 On the third day there was a wedding in Cana of Galilee, and the mother of Jesus was there. 2Now both Jesus and His disciples were invited to the wedding. 3And when they ran out of wine, the

1:42 [a]NU-Text reads *John.* 1:51 [a]NU-Text omits *hereafter.*

1:41 After we have found the Messiah, we are to tell others about Him. The only "failure" when it comes to reaching out to the lost is not to be doing it.

"Many churches report no new members on confession of faith. Why these meager results with this tremendous expenditure of energy and money? Why are so few people coming into the Kingdom? I will tell you—there is not a definite effort put forth to persuade a definite person to receive a definite Savior at a definite time, and that definite time is now." *Billy Sunday*

"Our forefathers must be asking, 'How is it that we did so much with so little, and you do so little with so much?'" *R. Albert Mohler Jr.*

1:46 Come and see. Jesus called Philip to follow Him, then Philip immediately found Nathanael and told him about the Savior. Nathanael's question is a typical reaction of the contemporary world to those who follow the Savior. To the cynical, Christians are intellectual wimps, prudes, rejects—unlearned cripples who need some sort of crutch to get them through life. So it is understandable for them to ask, "Can any good thing come out of Christianity?" Down through the ages, its good name has been tainted with the stained brush of hypocrisy, dead religion, and more recently, fanatical sects and televangelism.

Philip merely answered Nathanael's cynicism with the same thing Jesus said to Andrew: "Come and see." Skeptic, come and see. Atheist, come and see. Intellectual, come and see. Just come with a humble and teachable heart, and you who are sightless *will* see and know that this Man from Nazareth is the Son of God.

1:47 Nathanael was "an Israelite indeed, in whom is no deceit." He was a Jew in *deed*, not just in *word*. As an honest Jew he didn't twist the Law, as did the Pharisees. He read it in truth. The Law and the prophets had pointed him to Jesus and he was therefore ready to come to the Savior.

2:6–11 *The Significance of the First Miracle*

1. The turning of water into blood was the first public miracle that Moses did in Egypt (Exod. 7:20), and the water into wine was the first public miracle that Jesus did in the world (John 2:11).

2. The signs that God gave to Egypt in the Old Testament were plagues, destruction, and death, and the signs that Jesus did in the world in the New Testament were healings, blessings, and life.

3. The turning of water to blood initiated Moses (a type of the Savior—Deut. 18:15) leading his people out of the bondage of Egypt into an earthly liberty; the turning of water into wine initiated Jesus taking His people out of the bondage of the corruption of the world into the glorious liberty of the children of God (Rom. 8:21).

4. The turning of water to blood culminated in the firstborn in Egypt being delivered to death, while turning the water into wine culminated in the Firstborn being delivered from death (Col. 1:18).

5. The Law was a ministry of death, the gospel a ministry of life. One was written on cold tablets of stone, the other on the warm fleshly tablets of the heart. One was a ministration of sin unto condemnation and bondage, the other a ministration of righteousness unto life and liberty (2 Cor. 3:7–9).

6. When Moses changed the water into blood, all the fish in the river died. When Jesus initiated the new covenant, the catch of the fish are made alive in the net of the kingdom of God (Matt. 4:19).

7. The river of blood was symbolic of death for Egypt, but the water into wine is symbolic of life for the world. The letter of the Law kills, but the Spirit makes alive (2 Cor. 3:6).

8. When Moses turned the waters of Egypt into blood, the river reeked and made the Egyptians search for another source of water supply (Exod. 7:21,24). When the Law of Moses does its work in the sinner, it makes life odious for him. The weight of sin on his back becomes unbearable as he begins to labor and be heavy laden under its weight. Like the Egyptians, he begins to search for another spring of water; he begins to "thirst for righteousness," because he knows that without a right standing with God, he will perish.

9. Moses turned water into blood, and Jesus' blood turned into water (1 John 5:6). They both poured from His side (John 19:34), perhaps signifying that both Law and grace found harmony in the Savior's death—"Mercy and truth have met together; righteousness and peace have kissed" (Psa. 85:10).

10. The water of the old covenant ran out. It could do nothing but leave the sinner with a thirst for righteousness. But as with the wine at Cana, God saved the best until last. The new wine given on the Day of Pentecost (Acts 2:13; Eph. 5:18) was the Bridegroom giving us the new and "better" covenant (Heb. 8:5,6).

mother of Jesus said to Him, "They have
no wine."
4Jesus said to her, "Woman, what does
your concern have to do with Me? My
hour has not yet come."
5His mother said to the servants,
"Whatever He says to you, do *it*."
6Now there were set there six waterpots of stone, according to the manner of
purification of the Jews, containing twenty
or thirty gallons apiece. 7Jesus said to
them, "Fill the waterpots with water." And
they filled them up to the brim. 8And He
said to them, "Draw *some* out now, and
take *it* to the master of the feast." And
they took *it*. 9When the master of the
feast had tasted the water that was made
wine, and did not know where it came
from (but the servants who had drawn
the water knew), the master of the feast
called the bridegroom. 10And he said to
him, "Every man at the beginning sets
out the good wine, and when the *guests*
have well drunk, then the inferior. You
have kept the good wine until now!"
11This beginning of signs Jesus did in
Cana of Galilee, and manifested His
glory; and His disciples believed in Him.
12After this He went down to Capernaum, He, His mother, His brothers, and
His disciples; and they did not stay there
many days.

Jesus Cleanses the Temple

13Now the Passover of the Jews was at
hand, and Jesus went up to Jerusalem.
14And He found in the temple those who
sold oxen and sheep and doves, and the
money changers doing business. 15When
He had made a whip of cords, He drove

them all out of the temple, with the sheep
and the oxen, and poured out the changers' money and overturned the tables.
16And He said to those who sold doves,
"Take these things away! Do not make
My Father's house a house of merchandise!" 17Then His disciples remembered
that it was written, *"Zeal for Your house
has eaten*[a] *Me up."*[b]

18So the Jews answered and said to
Him, "What sign do You show to us,
since You do these things?"

19Jesus answered and said to them,
"Destroy this temple, and in three days I
will raise it up."

20Then the Jews said, "It has taken
forty-six years to build this temple, and
will You raise it up in three days?"

21But He was speaking of the temple
of His body. 22Therefore, when He had
risen from the dead, His disciples remembered that He had said this to
them;[a] and they believed the Scripture
and the word which Jesus had said.

The Discerner of Hearts

23Now when He was in Jerusalem at
the Passover, during the feast, many believed in His name when they saw the
signs which He did. 24But Jesus did not
commit Himself to them, because He
knew all *men,* 25and had no need that
anyone should testify of man, for He
knew what was in man.

The New Birth

3 There was a man of the Pharisees
named Nicodemus, a ruler of the Jews.
2This man came to Jesus by night and
said to Him, "Rabbi, we know that You
are a teacher come from God; for no one
can do these signs that You do unless
God is with him."

3Jesus answered and said to him, "Most
assuredly, I say to you, unless one is born
again, he cannot see the kingdom of God."

4Nicodemus said to Him, "How can a
man be born when he is old? Can he enter a second time into his mother's womb
and be born?"

5Jesus answered, "Most assuredly, I say
to you, unless one is born of water and
the Spirit, he cannot enter the kingdom

2:17 [a]NU-Text and M-Text read *will eat.* [b]Psalm 69:9
2:22 [a]NU-Text and M-Text omit *to them.*

2:13–17 Cleansing the temple. When Jesus went to the temple, He found it to be filled with those buying and selling merchandise. According to the Jewish historian Josephus, at each Passover, over 250,000 animals were sacrificed. The priests sold licenses to the dealers and therefore would have had a great source of income from the Passover. When the Bible called them "changers of money," it was an appropriate term.

There is, however, another theft going on in another temple. Mankind was made as a dwelling place for his Creator. God made him a little lower than the angels, crowned him with glory and honor, and set him over the works of His hands (Heb. 2:7), yet sin has given the dwelling place to the devil. The thief, who came to steal, kill, and destroy, is making merchandise out of mankind. Instead of the heart of man being a temple of the Living God (2 Cor. 6:16)—a house of prayer—iniquity has made it a den of thieves.

When someone repents and calls upon the name of Jesus Christ, He turns the tables on the devil. The ten stinging cords of the Ten Commandments in the hand of the Savior cleanse the temple of sin. *Charles Spurgeon* had a resolute grasp of the Law. In preaching to sinners, he said, "I would that this whip would fall upon your backs, that you might be flogged out of your self-righteousness and made to fly to Jesus Christ and find shelter there."

2:24,25 "We may deceive all the people sometimes; we may deceive some of the people all the time, but not all the people all the time, and not God at any time." *Abraham Lincoln*

"Character is what you are in the dark." *D. L. Moody*

3:2 Grace to the humble. Nicodemus was a humble Jew (he acknowledged the deity of the Son of God), and he knew the Law (he was a "teacher of Israel," v. 10); therefore, Jesus gave him the good news of the gospel. He was convinced of the disease of sin and consequently ready to hear of the cure.

3:3 "These verses aren't necessarily about what Nicodemus asked Jesus; they are about what Jesus knew. The last verse of the previous chapter said that He knew what was in man. Jesus knew what was in the heart of Nicodemus: he was a Law-breaker, and he needed to be born again." *Garry T. Ansdell, D.D.*

Questions & Objections

3:3 *"I have been born again many times."*

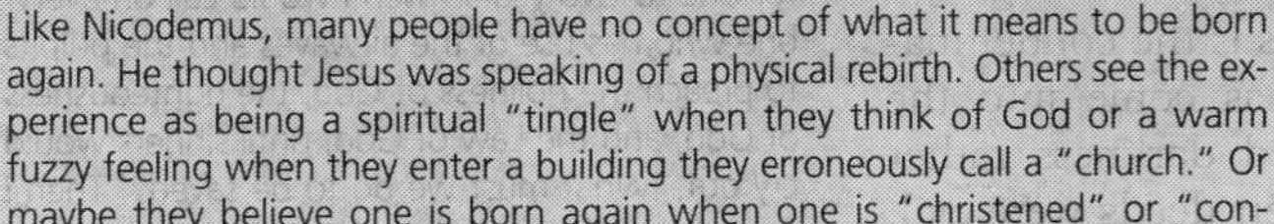

Like Nicodemus, many people have no concept of what it means to be born again. He thought Jesus was speaking of a physical rebirth. Others see the experience as being a spiritual "tingle" when they think of God or a warm fuzzy feeling when they enter a building they erroneously call a "church." Or maybe they believe one is born again when one is "christened" or "confirmed." However, the new birth spoken of by Jesus is absolutely essential for sinners to enter heaven. If they are not born again, they will not enter the kingdom of God. Therefore it is necessary to establish the fact that one becomes a Christian by being born again, pointing out that Jesus Himself said that the experience was crucial. The difference between *believing* in Jesus and being born again is like believing in a parachute, and putting one on. The difference will be seen when you jump. (See Rom. 13:14.)

How is one born again? Simply through repentance toward God and faith in the Lord Jesus Christ (Acts 20:21). Confess and forsake your sins, and trust in Jesus alone for your eternal salvation. When you do, you will receive spiritual life through the Holy Spirit who comes to live within you. See also Eph. 4:18 and 1 Pet. 1:23 comments.

of God. 6 That which is born of the flesh
is flesh, and that which is born of the
Spirit is spirit. 7 Do not marvel that I said
to you, 'You must be born again.' 8 The
wind blows where it wishes, and you
hear the sound of it, but cannot tell
where it comes from and where it goes.
So is everyone who is born of the Spirit."
9 Nicodemus answered and said to
Him, "How can these things be?"
10 Jesus answered and said to him, "Are
you the teacher of Israel, and do not know
these things? 11 Most assuredly, I say to
you, We speak what We know and testify
what We have seen, and you do not receive
Our witness. 12 If I have told you
earthly things and you do not believe,
how will you believe if I tell you heavenly
things? 13 No one has ascended to heaven
but He who came down from heaven,
that is, the Son of Man who is in heaven.[a]
14 And as Moses lifted up the serpent in
the wilderness, even so must the Son of
Man be lifted up, 15 that whoever believes
in Him should not perish but[a] have eternal
life. 16 For God so loved the world that
He gave His only begotten Son, that whoever
believes in Him should not perish
but have everlasting life. 17 For God did
not send His Son into the world to condemn
the world, but that the world

3:13 [a]NU-Text omits *who is in heaven.* 3:15 [a]NU-Text omits *not perish but.*

3:7 New birth—its necessity for salvation. This is a fulfillment of Ezek. 36:26: "I will give you a new heart and put a new spirit within you; I will take the heart of stone out of your flesh and give you a heart of flesh." Man cannot enter heaven in his spiritually dead state; he must be born again to have spiritual life. Jesus said that He is life (John 14:6; 11:25,26), and that we must come to Him to have life (John 5:39,40; 1 John 5:11,12). Those who trust in Christ are "born again, not of corruptible seed but incorruptible, through the word of God which lives and abides forever" (1 Pet. 1:23). See also 2 Cor. 5:17.

"Ever since Adam sinned, the earth has been the land of the walking dead—spiritually dead. What is the disease that killed man? 'The wages of sin is death.' So from God's point of view, salvation involves the raising of spiritually dead men to life. But before God could give life to the dead, He had to totally eradicate the fatal disease that killed men—sin. So the cross was God's method of dealing with the disease called sin, and the resurrection of Christ was and is God's method of giving life to the dead!" *Bob George, Classic Christianity*

3:14,15 When the Israelites doubted God, He sent serpents among them with a deadly venom—but He also sent a cure. For details, see Num. 21:6–9 comment.

3:16 Salvation is possible for every person. See John 4:14.

through Him might be saved.
[18]"He who believes in Him is not condemned; but he who does not believe is condemned already, because he has not believed in the name of the only begotten Son of God. [19]And this is the condemnation, that the light has come into the world, and men loved darkness rather than light, because their deeds were evil. [20]For everyone practicing evil hates the light and does not come to the light, lest his deeds should be exposed. [21]But he who does the truth comes to the light, that his deeds may be clearly seen, that they have been done in God."

USING THE LAW IN EVANGELISM

3:16 "If I had my way, I would declare a moratorium on public preaching of 'the plan of salvation' in America for one to two years. Then I would call on everyone who has use of the airwaves and the pulpits to preach the holiness of God, the righteousness of God, and the Law of God, until sinners would cry out, 'What must we do to be saved?' Then I would take them off in a corner and whisper the gospel to them. Don't use John 3:16. Such drastic action is needed because we have gospel-hardened a generation of sinners by telling them how to be saved before they have any understanding why they need to be saved." *Paris Reidhead*

John the Baptist Exalts Christ

[22]After these things Jesus and His disciples came into the land of Judea, and there He remained with them and baptized. [23]Now John also was baptizing in Aenon near Salim, because there was much water there. And they came and were baptized. [24]For John had not yet been thrown into prison.

[25]Then there arose a dispute between *some* of John's disciples and the Jews about purification. [26]And they came to John and said to him, "Rabbi, He who was with you beyond the Jordan, to whom you have testified—behold, He is baptizing, and all are coming to Him!"

[27]John answered and said, "A man can receive nothing unless it has been given to him from heaven. [28]You yourselves bear me witness, that I said, 'I am not the Christ,' but, 'I have been sent before Him.' [29]He who has the bride is the bridegroom; but the friend of the bridegroom, who stands and hears him, rejoices greatly because of the bridegroom's voice. Therefore this joy of mine is fulfilled. [30]He must increase, but I *must* decrease. [31]He who comes from above is above all; he who is of the earth is earthly and speaks of the earth. He who comes from heaven is above all. [32]And what He has seen and heard, that He testifies; and no one receives His testimony. [33]He who has received His testimony has certified that God is true. [34]For He whom God has sent speaks the words of God, for God does

3:16,17 Leading sinners to Jesus: *God Himself provided our way of escape.* "God demonstrates His own love toward us, in that while we were still sinners, Christ died for us" (Rom. 5:8). "For He made Him who knew no sin to be sin for us, that we might become the righteousness of God in Him" (2 Cor. 5:21). "He was wounded for our transgressions, He was bruised for our iniquities; the chastisement for our peace was upon Him, and by His stripes we are healed. All we like sheep have gone astray; we have turned, every one, to his own way; and the LORD has laid on Him the iniquity of us all" (Isa. 53:5,6). See Rom. 10:9 comment.

3:19 Jesus said that we loved the darkness of sin rather than the light of righteousness, because the human heart finds pleasure in sin. If you don't believe it, visit the "adult" section of your local video store. Look at the covers to see the type of entertainment the hearts of men and women crave—unspeakable violence, inconceivable horror, and unending sexual perversion.

3:20 The same sunlight that melts wax also hardens clay. As God's light shines on man, the sinner's heart determines his response. One whose heart is tender will respond to God; one whose heart is bent on evil will harden his heart further against God and will remain in darkness. Sinners should note: After Pharaoh repeatedly hardened his heart against God (Exod. 8:15,32), God then hardened Pharaoh's heart (Exod. 10:27). Those who continually reject God will be given up to "uncleanness, vile passions, and a debased mind" (Rom. 1:24,26,28).

3:16 Is Repentance Necessary for Salvation?

It is true that numerous Bible verses speak of the promise of salvation with no mention of repentance. These verses merely say to "believe" on Jesus Christ and you shall be saved (Acts 16:31; Rom. 10:9). However, the Bible makes it clear that God is holy and man is sinful, and that sin makes a separation between the two (Isa. 59:1,2). Without repentance from sin, wicked men cannot have fellowship with a holy God. We are *dead* in our trespasses and sins (Eph. 2:1) and until we forsake them through repentance, we cannot be made alive in Christ. The Scriptures speak of "repentance to life" (Acts 11:18). We turn *from* sin *to* the Savior. This is why Paul preached "repentance toward God and faith toward our Lord Jesus Christ" (Acts 20:21).

The first public word Jesus preached was "repent" (Matt. 4:17). John the Baptist began his ministry the same way (Matt. 3:2). Jesus told His hearers that without repentance, they would perish (Luke 13:3). If belief is all that is necessary for salvation, then the logical conclusion is that one need never repent. However, the Bible tells us that a false convert "believes" and yet is not saved (Luke 8:13); he remains a "worker of iniquity." Look at the warning of Scripture: "If we say that we have fellowship with Him, and walk in darkness, we lie and do not practice the truth" (1 John 1:6). The Scriptures also say, "He who covers his sins will not prosper, but whoever confesses and forsakes them [repentance] will have mercy" (Prov. 28:13). Jesus said that there was joy in heaven over one sinner who "repents" (Luke 15:10). If there is no repentance, there is no joy because there is no salvation.

As Peter preached on the Day of Pentecost, he commanded his hearers to repent "for the remission of sins" (Acts 2:38). Without repentance, there is no remission of sins; we are still under God's wrath. Peter further said, "Repent...and be converted, that your sins may be blotted out" (Acts 3:19). We cannot be "converted" unless we repent. God Himself "commands *all* men *everywhere* [leaving no exceptions] to repent" (Acts 17:30, emphasis added). Peter said a similar thing at Pentecost: "Repent, and let *every one* of you be baptized" (Acts 2:38).

If repentance was not necessary for salvation, why then did Jesus command that *repentance* be preached to all nations (Luke 24:47)? With so many Scriptures speaking of the necessity of repentance for salvation, one can only wonder why anyone would not preach repentance, as we have been commanded to.

not give the Spirit by measure. [35]The Father loves the Son, and has given all
things into His hand. [36]He who believes
in the Son has everlasting life; and he who
does not believe the Son shall not see life,
but the wrath of God abides on him."

A Samaritan Woman Meets Her Messiah

4 Therefore, when the Lord knew that
the Pharisees had heard that Jesus
made and baptized more disciples than
John [2](though Jesus Himself did not baptize, but His disciples), [3]He left Judea and
departed again to Galilee. [4]But He needed to go through Samaria.
[5]So He came to a city of Samaria
which is called Sychar, near the plot of
ground that Jacob gave to his son Joseph.
[6]Now Jacob's well was there. Jesus therefore, being wearied from *His* journey, sat
thus by the well. It was about the sixth

3:36 He who believes. The Greek word used here for the first occurrence of "believes" is *pisteuo*—which means "to trust." However, in the second occurrence in this verse ("he who does not believe"), the word used for "believes" is *apeitheo*—which means "disobedient." The disobedient will not see the salvation of God, no matter what prayer they have prayed, because they refuse to surrender their will to the Lordship of Jesus Christ. He is coming "in flaming fire taking vengeance on those who do not know God, and on those who *do not obey the gospel* of our Lord Jesus Christ" (2 Thess. 1:8, emphasis added).

Under God's wrath. Those without Christ are dead in their sins, separated from the life of God, and will not have spiritual life unless they trust in Jesus Christ. Their sin makes them objects of God's wrath.

Somehow we think that time forgives sin. This is not so. The more we sin, the more we store up God's wrath. See Rom. 2:5.

hour.
[7]A woman of Samaria came to draw
water. Jesus said to her, "Give Me a
drink." [8]For His disciples had gone away
into the city to buy food.
[9]Then the woman of Samaria said to
Him, "How is it that You, being a Jew, ask
a drink from me, a Samaritan woman?"
For Jews have no dealings with Samaritans.
[10]Jesus answered and said to her, "If
you knew the gift of God, and who it is
who says to you, 'Give Me a drink,' you
would have asked Him, and He would
have given you living water."
[11]The woman said to Him, "Sir, You
have nothing to draw with, and the well is
deep. Where then do You get that living
water? [12]Are You greater than our father
Jacob, who gave us the well, and drank
from it himself, as well as his sons and his
livestock?"
[13]Jesus answered and said to her,
"Whoever drinks of this water will thirst
again, [14]but whoever drinks of the water
that I shall give him will never thirst. But
the water that I shall give him will become in him a fountain of water springing up into everlasting life."
[15]The woman said to Him, "Sir, give
me this water, that I may not thirst, nor

4:7 Personal Witnessing—How Jesus Did It

How to address the sinner's conscience and speak with someone who doesn't believe in hell

Verses 7–26 give us the Master's example of how to share our faith. Notice that Jesus spoke to the woman at the well when she was alone. We will often find that people are more open and honest when they are alone. So, if possible, pick a person who is sitting by himself. From these verses, we can see four clear principles to follow.

First: Jesus began in the natural realm (v. 7). He spoke of something she could relate to—water. Most of us can strike up a conversation with a stranger in the natural realm. It may be a friendly "How are you doing?" or a warm "Good morning!" If the person responds with a sense of warmth, we may then ask, "Do you live around here?" and from there develop a conversation.

Second: Jesus swung the conversation to the spiritual realm (v. 10). He simply mentioned the things of God. This will take courage. We may say something like, "Did you go to church on Sunday?" or "Did you see that Christian TV program last week?" If the person responds positively, the question "Do you have a Christian background?" will probe his background. He may answer, "I went to church when I was a child, but I drifted away from it."

Another simple way to swing to the spiritual is to offer the person a gospel tract and ask, "Did you get one of these?" When he takes it, simply say, "It's a gospel tract. Do you come from a Christian background?"

Third: Jesus brought conviction using the Law of God (vv. 16–18). Jesus gently spoke to her conscience by alluding to the fact that she had transgressed the Seventh of the Ten Commandments. He used the Law to bring "the knowledge of sin" (see Rom. 3:19,20). We can do the same by asking, "Do you think that you have kept the Ten Commandments?" Most people think they have, so quickly follow with, "Have you ever told a lie?" This might seem confrontational, but if it is asked in a spirit of love and gentleness, there won't be any offense. Remember that the "work of the Law [is] written in their hearts" and that the conscience will bear "witness" (Rom. 2:15). Jesus confronted the rich young ruler in Luke 18:18–21 with five of the Ten Commandments and there was no offense. Have confidence that the conscience will do its work and affirm the truth of each Commandment. Don't be afraid to gently ask, "Have you ever stolen something, even if it's small?" Learn how to open up the spirituality of the Law and show how God considers lust to be the same as adultery (Matt. 5:27,28) and hatred the same as murder (1 John 3:15). Make sure you get an admission of guilt.

Ask the person, "If God judges you by the Ten Commandments on Judgment Day, do you think you will be innocent or guilty?" If he says he will be innocent, ask, "Why is that?" If he admits his guilt, ask, "Do you think you will go to heaven or hell?"

From there the conversation may go one of three ways:

1. *He may confidently say, "I don't believe in hell."* Gently respond, "That doesn't matter. You still have to face God on Judgment Day *whether you believe in it or not.* If I step onto the freeway when a massive truck is heading for me and I say, 'I don't believe in trucks,' my lack of belief isn't

(continued)

(4:7 continued)

going to change reality."

Then tenderly tell him he has *already* admitted to you that he has lied, stolen, and committed adultery in his heart, and that God gave him a conscience so that he would know right from wrong. His conscience and the conviction of the Holy Spirit will do the rest.

That's why it is essential to draw out an admission of guilt *before* you mention Judgment Day or the existence of hell.

2. *He may say that he's guilty, but that he will go to heaven.* This is usually because he thinks that God is "good," and that He will therefore overlook sin in his case. Point out that if a judge in a criminal case has a guilty murderer standing before him, the judge, if he is a good man, can't just let him go. He must ensure that the guilty man is punished. If God is good, He must (by nature) punish murderers, rapists, thieves, liars, adulterers, fornicators, and those who have lived in rebellion to the inner light that God has given to every man.

3. *He may admit that he is guilty and therefore going to hell.* Ask him if that concerns him. Speak to him about how much he values his eyes and how much more therefore he should value the salvation of his soul. (For the biblical description of hell, see Rev. 1:18 comment.) If possible, take the person through the linked verses in this Bible, beginning at the Matt. 5:21,22 comment.

Fourth: Jesus revealed Himself as the Messiah (v. 26). Once the Law has humbled the person, he is ready for grace. Remember, the Bible says that God resists the proud and gives grace to the humble (James 4:6). The gospel is for the humble (see Luke 4:18 comment). Only the sick need a physician, and only those who will admit that they have the disease of sin will truly embrace the cure of the gospel.

Learn how to present the work of the cross —that God sent His Son to suffer and die in our place. Tell the sinner of the love of God in Christ; that Jesus rose from the dead and defeated death. Take him back to civil law and say, "It's as simple as this: We broke God's Law, and Jesus paid our fine. If you will repent and trust in the Savior, God will forgive your sins and dismiss your case." Ask him if he understands what you have told him. If he is willing to confess and forsake his sins, and trust the Savior with his eternal salvation, have him pray and ask God to forgive him. Then pray for him. Get him a Bible. Instruct him to read it daily and obey what he reads, and encourage him to get into a Bible-believing, Christ-preaching church.

come here to draw."
16Jesus said to her, "Go, call your husband, and come here."
17The woman answered and said, "I
have no husband."
Jesus said to her, "You have well said,
'I have no husband,' 18for you have had
five husbands, and the one whom you
now have is not your husband; in that
you spoke truly."
19The woman said to Him, "Sir, I perceive that You are a prophet. 20Our fathers
worshiped on this mountain, and you *Jews*
say that in Jerusalem is the place where
one ought to worship."
21Jesus said to her, "Woman, believe
Me, the hour is coming when you will
neither on this mountain, nor in Jerusalem, worship the Father. 22You worship
what you do not know; we know what
we worship, for salvation is of the Jews.
23But the hour is coming, and now is,
when the true worshipers will worship
the Father in spirit and truth; for the Father is seeking such to worship Him.
24God *is* Spirit, and those who worship
Him must worship in spirit and truth."
25The woman said to Him, "I know that
Messiah is coming" (who is called Christ).
"When He comes, He will tell us all things."
26Jesus said to her, "I who speak to you
am *He*."

The Whitened Harvest

27And at this *point* His disciples came,
and they marveled that He talked with a
woman; yet no one said, "What do You
seek?" or, "Why are You talking with her?"
28The woman then left her waterpot,
went her way into the city, and said to the
men, 29"Come, see a Man who told me all
things that I ever did. Could this be the
Christ?" 30Then they went out of the city
and came to Him.

4:14 Salvation is possible for every person. See John 6:51.

"I believe that lack of efficient personal work is one of the failures of the Church today. The people of the Church are like squirrels in a cage. Lots of activity, but accomplishing nothing. It doesn't require a Christian life to sell oyster soup or run a bazaar or a rummage sale..."

Billy Sunday

31In the meantime His disciples urged
Him, saying, "Rabbi, eat."
32But He said to them, "I have food to
eat of which you do not know."
33Therefore the disciples said to one
another, "Has anyone brought Him *any-*
thing to eat?"
34Jesus said to them, "My food is to do
the will of Him who sent Me, and to finish His work. 35Do you not say, 'There are
still four months and *then* comes the harvest'? Behold, I say to you, lift up your
eyes and look at the fields, for they are already white for harvest! 36And he who
reaps receives wages, and gathers fruit for
eternal life, that both he who sows and he
who reaps may rejoice together. 37For in
this the saying is true: 'One sows and another reaps.' 38I sent you to reap that for
which you have not labored; others have
labored, and you have entered into their
labors."

The Savior of the World

39And many of the Samaritans of that
city believed in Him because of the word
of the woman who testified, "He told me
all that I *ever* did." 40So when the Samaritans had come to Him, they urged Him
to stay with them; and He stayed there
two days. 41And many more believed because of His own word.
42Then they said to the woman, "Now
we believe, not because of what you said,
for we ourselves have heard *Him* and we
know that this is indeed the Christ,[a] the
Savior of the world."

Welcome at Galilee

43Now after the two days He departed
from there and went to Galilee. 44For Jesus Himself testified that a prophet has
no honor in his own country. 45So when
He came to Galilee, the Galileans received Him, having seen all the things He
did in Jerusalem at the feast; for they also
had gone to the feast.

4:42 [a]NU-Text omits *the Christ*.

4:34 The "food" that nourished the Savior was to carry out the work of evangelism—to seek and to save that which was lost.

4:36 "I would think it a greater happiness to gain one soul to Christ than mountains of silver and gold to myself." *Matthew Henry*

4:37,38 The measure of success. Don't be tempted to measure evangelistic "success" by the number of "decisions" obtained. We tend to rejoice over decisions, when heaven reserves its rejoicing for repentance—"There is joy in the presence of the angels of God over one sinner who repents" (Luke 15:10). It is easy to get "decisions for Jesus" using the modern method of well-chosen words and psychological manipulation. Rather, see success as having the opportunity to sow the seed of God's Word into the hearts of your hearers. If you faithfully sow, someone else will reap. If you have the privilege of reaping, then someone has faithfully sown before you. One sows, another reaps, but it is God who gives the increase (see 1 Cor. 3:6,7).

QUESTIONS & OBJECTIONS

"Should a woman testify in the open air?"

Some believe that women should never testify in the open air, because they would be in direct violation of Scripture: "Let a woman learn in silence with all submission. And I do not permit a woman to teach or to have authority over a man, but to be in silence" (1 Tim. 2:11,12). However, this is clearly a reference to church conduct, not to reaching out to the lost. Paul is merely reaffirming church structure he had already put in place within the local church: "Let your women keep silent *in the churches*, for they are not permitted to speak; but they are to be submissive, as the law also says. And if they want to learn something, let them ask their own husbands at home; for it is shameful for women to speak *in church*" (1 Cor. 14:34,35, emphasis added).

If Paul was speaking of the task of evangelism when he said women should be "in silence," then all Christian women should ignore the command to go into all the world and preach the gospel to every creature. Instead, they should remain silent. Again, if this is a general admonition regarding a Christian woman's conduct, she should testify neither one-to-one nor one-to-a-hundred.

However, there is no reason to believe that the Great Commission was restricted to men. God saw fit to give women the power to be witnesses on the Day of Pentecost (see Acts 1:14; 2:1–4). God had promised this power for witnessing to women as well as men: "And on My menservants and on My *maidservants* I will pour out My Spirit in those days..." (Acts 2:18, emphasis added).

The Bible doesn't say "How beautiful are the feet of those (*men*) who preach the gospel of peace" (Rom. 10:15) or "Go (*men*) into all the world and preach the gospel to every creature" (Mark 16:15). In both cases the Greek word used for "preach" is *kerusso,* meaning "to herald (as a public crier)." Whether a man or a woman, you are commanded to preach the gospel—to raise your voice as a town crier.

After the woman at the well met the Savior, she publicly witnessed to men (see John 4:28). Did she do this on a one-to-one basis, and become silent if more than one man gathered in the open air to listen to her testify? Thank God that she wasn't silent: "And many of the Samaritans of that city believed in Him because of the word of the woman who testified, 'He told me all that I ever did'" (John 4:39).

When giving the do's and don'ts of preaching in the open air, *R. A. Torrey* said, "None but consecrated men and women will ever succeed in open-air meetings." The Salvation Army was famous for open-air preaching: "The Salvation Army gave women equal responsibility with men for preaching and welfare work and on one occasion William Booth remarked, 'My best men are women!'"

Scripture names a number of women who were Paul's "fellow workers" in the gospel (see Rom. 16:3,9,12). This is a reference to the task of evangelism (*sunergos*) as "those who helped [Paul] in spreading the gospel" (*Bauer-Arndt-Gingrich Greek Lexicon*). Paul used this term not only for men (Rom. 16:21; Phil. 2:25; 4:3), but also for women, as in the case of Priscilla (see Rom. 16:3), Euodia, and Syntyche (see Phil. 4:2,3). Other women Paul commends for their "labor in the Lord" include Mary, Tryphena, Tryphosa, and Persis (see Rom. 16:6,12).

Charles Spurgeon included women when he spoke of Jesus making His hearers "fishers of men." He said, "You men and women that sit before me, you are by the shore of a great sea of human life swarming with the souls of men. You live in the midst of millions; but if you will follow Jesus, and be faithful to him, and true to him, and do what he bids you, he will make you fishers of men."

I thank God that He chose women rather than men to be first to herald the good news of the resurrected Savior. These faithful women took the good news to a group of hardhearted, faithless men, who were cringing in fear behind locked doors. That makes me wonder if the men who want women to be silent preach in the open air themselves. Could it be that they are embarrassed by the fact that women are doing what they don't have the courage to do themselves?

We have a subtle enemy who wants to silence those few laborers we have at present. May God raise up more women who will follow the example of the woman at the well, and may many believe because of their faithful testimony.

A Nobleman's Son Healed

46So Jesus came again to Cana of
Galilee where He had made the water
wine. And there was a certain nobleman
whose son was sick at Capernaum.
47When he heard that Jesus had come out
of Judea into Galilee, he went to Him and
implored Him to come down and heal
his son, for he was at the point of death.
48Then Jesus said to him, "Unless you

people see signs and wonders, you will by no means believe."

49The nobleman said to Him, "Sir, come down before my child dies!"

50Jesus said to him, "Go your way; your son lives." So the man believed the word that Jesus spoke to him, and he went his way. 51And as he was now going down, his servants met him and told *him*, saying, "Your son lives!"

52Then he inquired of them the hour when he got better. And they said to him, "Yesterday at the seventh hour the fever left him." 53So the father knew that *it was* at the same hour in which Jesus said to him, "Your son lives." And he himself believed, and his whole household.

54This again *is* the second sign Jesus did when He had come out of Judea into Galilee.

A Man Healed at the Pool of Bethesda

5 After this there was a feast of the Jews, and Jesus went up to Jerusalem. 2Now there is in Jerusalem by the Sheep *Gate* a pool, which is called in Hebrew, Bethesda,[a] having five porches. 3In these lay a great multitude of sick people, blind, lame, paralyzed, waiting for the moving of the water. 4For an angel went down at a certain time into the pool and stirred up the water; then whoever stepped in first, after the stirring of the water, was made well of whatever disease he had.[a] 5Now a certain man was there who had an infirmity thirty-eight years. 6When Jesus saw him lying there, and knew that he already had been *in that condition* a long time, He said to him, "Do you want to be made well?"

7The sick man answered Him, "Sir, I have no man to put me into the pool when the water is stirred up; but while I am coming, another steps down before me."

8Jesus said to him, "Rise, take up your bed and walk." 9And immediately the man was made well, took up his bed, and walked.

And that day was the Sabbath. 10The Jews therefore said to him who was cured, "It is the Sabbath; it is not lawful for you to carry your bed."

> Sin and hell are married unless repentance proclaims the divorce.
>
> **CHARLES SPURGEON**

11He answered them, "He who made me well said to me, 'Take up your bed and walk.' "

12Then they asked him, "Who is the Man who said to you, 'Take up your bed and walk'?" 13But the one who was healed did not know who it was, for Jesus had withdrawn, a multitude being in *that* place. 14Afterward Jesus found him in the temple, and said to him, "See, you have been made well. Sin no more, lest a worse thing come upon you."

15The man departed and told the Jews that it was Jesus who had made him well.

Honor the Father and the Son

16For this reason the Jews persecuted Jesus, and sought to kill Him,[a] because He had done these things on the Sabbath. 17But Jesus answered them, "My Father

5:2 [a]NU-Text reads *Bethzatha.* 5:4 [a]NU-Text omits *waiting for the moving of the water* at the end of verse 3, and all of verse 4. 5:16 [a]NU-Text omits *and sought to kill Him*

5:14 We once lay as feeble, fragile, and frail folk, helpless and hopeless, pathetically paralyzed by the devil—"taken captive by him to do his will" (2 Tim. 2:26)—until Jesus spoke a word to us. We were on a deathbed of sin with no one able to help us, but we heard the voice of the Word of God saying, "Arise from the dead, and Christ will give you light" (Eph. 5:14).

Now a thankful heart for the unspeakable gift makes us want to be always in the presence of God. Unlike the healed man, however, we need not go to the temple to thank the Father, for He now abides in the heart of the believer. The work of Calvary has made the believer the temple of the Living God (see 2 Cor. 6:16).

has been working until now, and I have
been working."
18Therefore the Jews sought all the
more to kill Him, because He not only
broke the Sabbath, but also said that God
was His Father, making Himself equal
with God. 19Then Jesus answered and
said to them, "Most assuredly, I say to
you, the Son can do nothing of Himself,
but what He sees the Father do; for whatever He does, the Son also does in like
manner. 20For the Father loves the Son,
and shows Him all things that He Himself does; and He will show Him greater
works than these, that you may marvel.
21For as the Father raises the dead and
gives life to *them*, even so the Son gives life
to whom He will. 22For the Father judges
no one, but has committed all judgment
to the Son, 23that all should honor the
Son just as they honor the Father. He who
does not honor the Son does not honor
the Father who sent Him.

Life and Judgment Are Through the Son

24"Most assuredly, I say to you, he who
hears My word and believes in Him who
sent Me has everlasting life, and shall not
come into judgment, but has passed from
death into life. 25Most assuredly, I say to
you, the hour is coming, and now is,
when the dead will hear the voice of the
Son of God; and those who hear will live.
26For as the Father has life in Himself, so
He has granted the Son to have life in
Himself, 27and has given Him authority
to execute judgment also, because He is
the Son of Man. 28Do not marvel at this;
for the hour is coming in which all who
are in the graves will hear His voice 29and
come forth—those who have done good,
to the resurrection of life, and those who
have done evil, to the resurrection of condemnation. 30I can of Myself do nothing.
As I hear, I judge; and My judgment is
righteous, because I do not seek My own
will but the will of the Father who sent
Me.

The Fourfold Witness

31"If I bear witness of Myself, My witness is not true. 32There is another who
bears witness of Me, and I know that the
witness which He witnesses of Me is true.
33You have sent to John, and he has
borne witness to the truth. 34Yet I do not
receive testimony from man, but I say
these things that you may be saved. 35He
was the burning and shining lamp, and
you were willing for a time to rejoice in his
light. 36But I have a greater witness than
John's; for the works which the Father
has given Me to finish—the very works

5:17 Jesus' claims. Jesus was either God in human form, or a crackpot. There is no middle ground. In vv. 17–29 He said:

- Whatever He saw the Father do, He did.
- God showed Jesus everything He did and He had even greater things to show Him, which would cause the people to be astonished.
- Just as God raised the dead and gave life to them, so Jesus gives life to whomever He will.
- God Himself had appointed Jesus of Nazareth as the Judge of all mankind.
- Humanity should honor Jesus as much as they honor the Father.
- Those who didn't honor Jesus didn't honor God.
- All who heard His words and trusted in the Father escape the wrath of the Law.
- All who trusted Him passed from death to life.
- The hour would come when *everyone* in their graves would hear the voice of Jesus and be raised from the dead.
- As God is the source of all life, so He has given Jesus life in Himself.

5:28 Jesus' unique words: Jesus is saying that His voice will raise *billions* who have died. Psalm 29:3–9 describes the powerful voice of God. See John 6:38 comment.

5:29 Judgment Day: For verses that warn of its reality, see Acts 17:31.

that I do—bear witness of Me, that the
Father has sent Me. 37And the Father Himself, who sent Me, has testified of Me. You
have neither heard His voice at any time,
nor seen His form. 38But you do not have
His word abiding in you, because whom
He sent, Him you do not believe. 39You
search the Scriptures, for in them you
think you have eternal life; and these are
they which testify of Me. 40But you are
not willing to come to Me that you may
have life.
41"I do not receive honor from men.
42But I know you, that you do not have
the love of God in you. 43I have come in
My Father's name, and you do not receive
Me; if another comes in his own name,
him you will receive. 44How can you believe, who receive honor from one another, and do not seek the honor that
comes from the only God? 45Do not think
that I shall accuse you to the Father;
there is *one* who accuses you—Moses, in
whom you trust. 46For if you believed
Moses, you would believe Me; for he
wrote about Me. 47But if you do not believe his writings, how will you believe
My words?"

Feeding the Five Thousand

6 After these things Jesus went over the
Sea of Galilee, which is *the Sea* of Tiberias. 2Then a great multitude followed
Him, because they saw His signs which
He performed on those who were diseased. 3And Jesus went up on the mountain, and there He sat with His disciples.
4Now the Passover, a feast of the Jews,
was near. 5Then Jesus lifted up *His* eyes,
and seeing a great multitude coming to-

Halloween is an incredible opportunity for sharing the gospel. See 1 Tim. 4:1 comment.

ward Him, He said to Philip, "Where shall
we buy bread, that these may eat?" 6But
this He said to test him, for He Himself
knew what He would do.
7Philip answered Him, "Two hundred
denarii worth of bread is not sufficient for
them, that every one of them may have a
little."
8One of His disciples, Andrew, Simon
Peter's brother, said to Him, 9"There is a
lad here who has five barley loaves and
two small fish, but what are they among
so many?"
10Then Jesus said, "Make the people
sit down." Now there was much grass in
the place. So the men sat down, in number about five thousand. 11And Jesus
took the loaves, and when He had given
thanks He distributed *them* to the disciples, and the disciples[a] to those sitting
down; and likewise of the fish, as much

6:11 [a]NU-Text omits *to the disciples, and the disciples.*

5:39,40 Many people think they are Christians because as a child they "asked Jesus into their heart." They were sincere and read the Bible, but eventually stopped believing. It is important to understand that salvation doesn't come from just reading the Bible, but by obedience to its words (see Heb. 5:9). Most children who are encouraged to "ask Jesus into their heart" have false conversions. This is because few children have the maturity to understand the nature of their personal sin, so they don't exercise biblical repentance—which is essential for salvation. They may have a relationship with the church, but not with Christ. They therefore tend to fall away from the faith (church) when they hit their teenage years. The opposite sex suddenly becomes more attractive than Jonah and the great fish. For how to bring children to genuine salvation, see Deut. 11:19 and Prov. 22:6 comments. To see why sinners need to come to Jesus to have life, see John 3:7 and Gen. 2:17 comments.

as they wanted. [12]So when they were
filled, He said to His disciples, "Gather up
the fragments that remain, so that nothing is lost." [13]Therefore they gathered
them up, and filled twelve baskets with
the fragments of the five barley loaves
which were left over by those who had
eaten. [14]Then those men, when they had
seen the sign that Jesus did, said, "This is
truly the Prophet who is to come into the
world."

Jesus Walks on the Sea

[15]Therefore when Jesus perceived that
they were about to come and take Him
by force to make Him king, He departed
again to the mountain by Himself alone.
[16]Now when evening came, His disciples went down to the sea, [17]got into the
boat, and went over the sea toward Capernaum. And it was already dark, and
Jesus had not come to them. [18]Then the
sea arose because a great wind was blowing. [19]So when they had rowed about
three or four miles,[a] they saw Jesus walking on the sea and drawing near the boat;
and they were afraid. [20]But He said to
them, "It is I; do not be afraid." [21]Then
they willingly received Him into the boat,
and immediately the boat was at the land
where they were going.

The Bread from Heaven

[22]On the following day, when the people who were standing on the other side
of the sea saw that there was no other
boat there, except that one which His disciples had entered,[a] and that Jesus had
not entered the boat with His disciples,
but His disciples had gone away alone—
[23]however, other boats came from Tiberias, near the place where they ate bread
after the Lord had given thanks— [24]when
the people therefore saw that Jesus was
not there, nor His disciples, they also got
into boats and came to Capernaum, seeking Jesus. [25]And when they found Him
on the other side of the sea, they said to
Him, "Rabbi, when did You come here?"
[26]Jesus answered them and said,
"Most assuredly, I say to you, you seek
Me, not because you saw the signs, but
because you ate of the loaves and were
filled. [27]Do not labor for the food which
perishes, but for the food which endures
to everlasting life, which the Son of Man
will give you, because God the Father has
set His seal on Him."
[28]Then they said to Him, "What shall
we do, that we may work the works of
God?"
[29]Jesus answered and said to them,
"This is the work of God, that you believe
in Him whom He sent."
[30]Therefore they said to Him, "What
sign will You perform then, that we may
see it and believe You? What work will
You do? [31]Our fathers ate the manna in
the desert; as it is written, *'He gave them
bread from heaven to eat.'* "[a]
[32]Then Jesus said to them, "Most assuredly, I say to you, Moses did not give
you the bread from heaven, but My Father
gives you the true bread from heaven.

6:19 [a]Literally *twenty-five or thirty stadia* 6:22 [a]NU-Text omits *that* and *which His disciples had entered.* 6:31 [a]Exodus 16:4; Nehemiah 9:15; Psalm 78:24

6:14 Messianic prophecy fulfilled: "The LORD your God will raise up for you a Prophet like me from your midst, from your brethren. Him you shall hear" (Deut. 18:15). See John 19:29 comment.

6:27 "Evangelism is about experiencing God. If you choose to be obedient, He will take you on a journey so exciting that your life will never be the same." *Bill Fay, Share Jesus Without Fear*

"Evangelism is the cure to the disease of church boredom." *Todd P. McCollum*

"I can tell you that there is no greater joy than leading someone to faith in Jesus Christ. Even if they reject your message, it still feels great to obey Christ. Yet regardless of how we feel, we need to remember this is what He has commanded." *D. James Kennedy*

6:28,29 Most religions teach that certain works are required in order to be saved. Here God tells us the only "work" He considers: "believe in Him whom He sent."

33 For the bread of God is He who comes
down from heaven and gives life to the
world."

34 Then they said to Him, "Lord, give
us this bread always."

> When your will is God's will, you will have your will.
> **CHARLES SPURGEON**

35 And Jesus said to them, "I am the
bread of life. He who comes to Me shall
never hunger, and he who believes in Me
shall never thirst. 36 But I said to you that
you have seen Me and yet do not believe.
37 All that the Father gives Me will come
to Me, and the one who comes to Me I
will by no means cast out. 38 For I have
come down from heaven, not to do My
own will, but the will of Him who sent
Me. 39 This is the will of the Father who
sent Me, that of all He has given Me I
should lose nothing, but should raise it
up at the last day. 40 And this is the will of
Him who sent Me, that everyone who
sees the Son and believes in Him may
have everlasting life; and I will raise him
up at the last day."

Rejected by His Own

41 The Jews then complained about
Him, because He said, "I am the bread
which came down from heaven." 42 And
they said, "Is not this Jesus, the son of
Joseph, whose father and mother we
know? How is it then that He says, 'I have
come down from heaven'?"

43 Jesus therefore answered and said to
them, "Do not murmur among yourselves. 44 No one can come to Me unless
the Father who sent Me draws him; and I
will raise him up at the last day. 45 It is
written in the prophets, *'And they shall
all be taught by God.'*[a] Therefore everyone who has heard and learned[b] from the
Father comes to Me. 46 Not that anyone
has seen the Father, except He who is
from God; He has seen the Father. 47 Most
assuredly, I say to you, he who believes in
Me[a] has everlasting life. 48 I am the bread
of life. 49 Your fathers ate the manna in the
wilderness, and are dead. 50 This is the
bread which comes down from heaven,
that one may eat of it and not die. 51 I am
the living bread which came down from
heaven. If anyone eats of this bread, he
will live forever; and the bread that I shall
give is My flesh, which I shall give for the
life of the world."

52 The Jews therefore quarreled among
themselves, saying, "How can this Man
give us *His* flesh to eat?"

53 Then Jesus said to them, "Most assuredly, I say to you, unless you eat the

6:45 [a]Isaiah 54:13 [b]M-Text reads *hears and has learned.*
6:47 [a]NU-Text omits *in Me.*

6:38 Jesus' unique words: Jesus said that He had "come down from heaven," that He was pre-existent. He says elsewhere: "I am from above...I am not of this world" (8:23), and "I proceeded forth and came from God" (8:42). For more on His pre-existence, see John 17:5. See also John 6:47 comment.

6:45 Taught by God. "Read and read again, and do not despair of help to understand the will and mind of God though you think they are fast locked up from you. Neither trouble your heads though you have not commentaries and exposition. Pray and read, read and pray; for a little from God is better than a great deal from men. Also, what is from men is uncertain, and is often lost and tumbled over by men; but what is from God is fixed as a nail in a sure place. There is nothing that so abides with us as what we receive from God; and the reason why the Christians in this day are at such a loss as to some things is that they are contented with what comes from men's mouths, without searching and kneeling before God to know of Him the truth of things. Things we receive at God's hands come to us as truths from the minting house, though old in themselves, yet new to us. Old truths are always new to us if they come with the smell of heaven upon them." *John Bunyan*

6:47 Jesus' unique words: He was saying that He had the authority to grant *everlasting life* to all who trust in Him. See John 6:53,54 comment.

6:51 Salvation is possible for every person. See John 7:37.

flesh of the Son of Man and drink His blood, you have no life in you. 54Whoever eats My flesh and drinks My blood has eternal life, and I will raise him up at the last day. 55For My flesh is food indeed,[a] and My blood is drink indeed. 56He who eats My flesh and drinks My blood abides in Me, and I in him. 57As the living Father sent Me, and I live because of the Father, so he who feeds on Me will live because of Me. 58This is the bread which came down from heaven—not as your fathers ate the manna, and are dead. He who eats this bread will live forever."

59These things He said in the synagogue as He taught in Capernaum.

Many Disciples Turn Away

60Therefore many of His disciples, when they heard *this*, said, "This is a hard saying; who can understand it?"

61When Jesus knew in Himself that His disciples complained about this, He said to them, "Does this offend you? 62*What* then if you should see the Son of Man ascend where He was before? 63It is the Spirit who gives life; the flesh profits nothing. The words that I speak to you are spirit, and *they* are life. 64But there are some of you who do not believe." For Jesus knew from the beginning who they were who did not believe, and who would betray Him. 65And He said, "Therefore I have said to you that no one can come to Me unless it has been granted to him by My Father."

66From that *time* many of His disciples went back and walked with Him no more. 67Then Jesus said to the twelve, "Do you also want to go away?"

68But Simon Peter answered Him, "Lord, to whom shall we go? You have the words of eternal life. 69Also we have come to believe and know that You are the Christ, the Son of the living God."[a]

70Jesus answered them, "Did I not choose you, the twelve, and one of you is a devil?" 71He spoke of Judas Iscariot, *the son* of Simon, for it was he who would betray Him, being one of the twelve.

Jesus' Brothers Disbelieve

7 After these things Jesus walked in Galilee; for He did not want to walk in Judea, because the Jews[a] sought to kill Him. 2Now the Jews' Feast of Tabernacles was at hand. 3His brothers therefore said to Him, "Depart from here and go into Judea, that Your disciples also may see the works that You are doing. 4For no one does anything in secret while he himself seeks to be known openly. If You do these things, show Yourself to the world." 5For even His brothers did not believe in Him.

6Then Jesus said to them, "My time has not yet come, but your time is always ready. 7The world cannot hate you; but it hates Me because I testify of it that its

6:55 [a]NU-Text reads *true food* and *true drink*. 6:69 [a]NU-Text reads *You are the Holy One of God*. 7:1 [a]That is, the ruling authorities

6:53,54 Jesus' unique words: These are the words of a madman . . . or God in human form. He was not advocating cannibalism, but was speaking in a spiritual sense. Just as we need to eat and drink in order to live, so we must "eat" the Bread of Life (John 6:48,51) and "drink" His "blood, which is shed for you" (Luke 22:20) in order to have spiritual life. Unless we trust in Christ, relying on Him daily for our life-sustaining nourishment, we have no life in us and remain dead in our sins. (See Eph. 4:18 comment.) See also John 8:51 comment.

6:65 "The impulse to pursue God originates with God." *A. W. Tozer*

6:68 The uniqueness of Jesus. "This Jesus of Nazareth, without money and arms, conquered more millions than Alexander, Caesar, Mohammed, and Napoleon; without science and learning, He shed more light on things human and divine than all philosophers and scholars combined; without the eloquence of schools, He spoke such words of life as were never spoken before or since, and produced effects which lie beyond the reach of orator or poet; without writing a single line, He set more pens in motion, and furnished themes for more sermons, orations, discussions, learned volumes, works of art, and songs of praise than the whole army of great men of ancient and modern times." *Philip Schaff, The Person of Christ*

works are evil. 8You go up to this feast. I am not yet[a] going up to this feast, for My time has not yet fully come." 9When He had said these things to them, He remained in Galilee.

The Heavenly Scholar

10But when His brothers had gone up, then He also went up to the feast, not openly, but as it were in secret. 11Then the Jews sought Him at the feast, and said, "Where is He?" 12And there was much complaining among the people concerning Him. Some said, "He is good"; others said, "No, on the contrary, He deceives the people." 13However, no one spoke openly of Him for fear of the Jews.

14Now about the middle of the feast Jesus went up into the temple and taught. 15And the Jews marveled, saying, "How does this Man know letters, having never studied?"

16Jesus[a] answered them and said, "My doctrine is not Mine, but His who sent Me. 17If anyone wills to do His will, he shall know concerning the doctrine, whether it is from God or *whether* I speak on My own *authority.* 18He who speaks from himself seeks his own glory; but He who seeks the glory of the One who sent Him is true, and no unrighteousness is in Him. 19Did not Moses give you the law, yet none of you keeps the law? Why do you seek to kill Me?"

20The people answered and said, "You have a demon. Who is seeking to kill You?"

21Jesus answered and said to them, "I did one work, and you all marvel. 22Moses therefore gave you circumcision (not that it is from Moses, but from the fathers), and you circumcise a man on the Sabbath. 23If a man receives circumcision on the Sabbath, so that the law of Moses should not be broken, are you angry with Me because I made a man completely well on the Sabbath? 24Do not judge according to appearance, but judge with righteous judgment."

Could This Be the Christ?

25Now some of them from Jerusalem said, "Is this not He whom they seek to kill? 26But look! He speaks boldly, and they say nothing to Him. Do the rulers know indeed that this is truly[a] the Christ? 27However, we know where this Man is from; but when the Christ comes, no one knows where He is from."

28Then Jesus cried out, as He taught in the temple, saying, "You both know Me, and you know where I am from; and I have not come of Myself, but He who sent Me is true, whom you do not know. 29But[a] I know Him, for I am from Him, and He sent Me."

30Therefore they sought to take Him; but no one laid a hand on Him, because His hour had not yet come. 31And many of the people believed in Him, and said, "When the Christ comes, will He do more signs than these which this *Man* has done?"

Jesus and the Religious Leaders

32The Pharisees heard the crowd murmuring these things concerning Him, and the Pharisees and the chief priests sent officers to take Him. 33Then Jesus said to

7:8 [a]NU-Text omits *yet.* 7:16 [a]NU-Text and M-Text read *So Jesus.* 7:26 [a]NU-Text omits *truly.* 7:29 [a]NU-Text and M-Text omit *But.*

7:17 In reference to creation, respected Bible teacher *Derek Prince* said, "I am simple-minded enough to believe that it happened the way the Bible described it. I have been a professor at Britain's largest university [Cambridge] for nine years. I hold various degrees and academic distinctions, and I feel in many ways I am quite sophisticated intellectually, but I don't feel in any way intellectually inferior when I say that I believe the Bible record of creation. Prior to believing the Bible I have studied many other attempts to explain man's origin and found them all unsatisfying and in many cases self-contradictory. I turned to study the Bible as a professional philosopher—not as a believer—and I commented to myself, 'At least it can't be any sillier than some of the other things I've heard,' and to my astonishment, I discovered it had the answer."

"I know men and I tell you that Jesus Christ is no mere man..." (See what Napoleon had to say about Jesus in John 7:46.)

Napoleon Bonaparte

them,[a] "I shall be with you a little while
longer, and *then* I go to Him who sent
Me. 34You will seek Me and not find *Me,*
and where I am you cannot come."
35Then the Jews said among themselves, "Where does He intend to go that
we shall not find Him? Does He intend to
go to the Dispersion among the Greeks and
teach the Greeks? 36What is this thing
that He said, 'You will seek Me and not find
Me, and where I am you cannot come'?"

The Promise of the Holy Spirit

37On the last day, that great *day* of the
feast, Jesus stood and cried out, saying,
"If anyone thirsts, let him come to Me and
drink. 38He who believes in Me, as the
Scripture has said, out of his heart will
flow rivers of living water." 39But this He
spoke concerning the Spirit, whom those
believing[a] in Him would receive; for the
Holy[b] Spirit was not yet *given,* because
Jesus was not yet glorified.

Who Is He?

40Therefore many[a] from the crowd,
when they heard this saying, said, "Truly
this is the Prophet." 41Others said, "This
is the Christ."

But some said, "Will the Christ come
out of Galilee? 42Has not the Scripture said
that the Christ comes from the seed of
David and from the town of Bethlehem,
where David was?" 43So there was a division among the people because of Him.
44Now some of them wanted to take Him,
but no one laid hands on Him.

Rejected by the Authorities

45Then the officers came to the chief
priests and Pharisees, who said to them,
"Why have you not brought Him?"
46The officers answered, "No man ever
spoke like this Man!"
47Then the Pharisees answered them,
"Are you also deceived? 48Have any of the
rulers or the Pharisees believed in Him?
49But this crowd that does not know the
law is accursed."
50Nicodemus (he who came to Jesus by
night,[a] being one of them) said to them,
51"Does our law judge a man before it
hears him and knows what he is doing?"
52They answered and said to him, "Are
you also from Galilee? Search and look,
for no prophet has arisen[a] out of Galilee."

7:33 [a]NU-Text and M-Text omit *to them.* 7:39 [a]NU-Text reads *who believed.* [b]NU-Text omits Holy. 7:40 [a]NU-Text reads *some.* 7:50 [a]NU-Text reads *before.* 7:52 [a]NU-Text reads *is to rise.*

7:37 Salvation is possible for every person. See Acts 2:21.

7:46 The uniqueness of Jesus. "I know men and I tell you that Jesus Christ is no mere man. Between Him and every other person in the world there is no possible term of comparison. Alexander, Caesar, Charlemagne, and I have founded empires. But on what did we rest the creations of our genius? Upon force. Jesus Christ founded His empire upon love; and at this hour millions of men would die for Him." *Napoleon Bonaparte*

7:52 This showed their ignorance of Scripture (see Isa. 9:1,2), and of the fact that Jesus was born in Bethlehem.

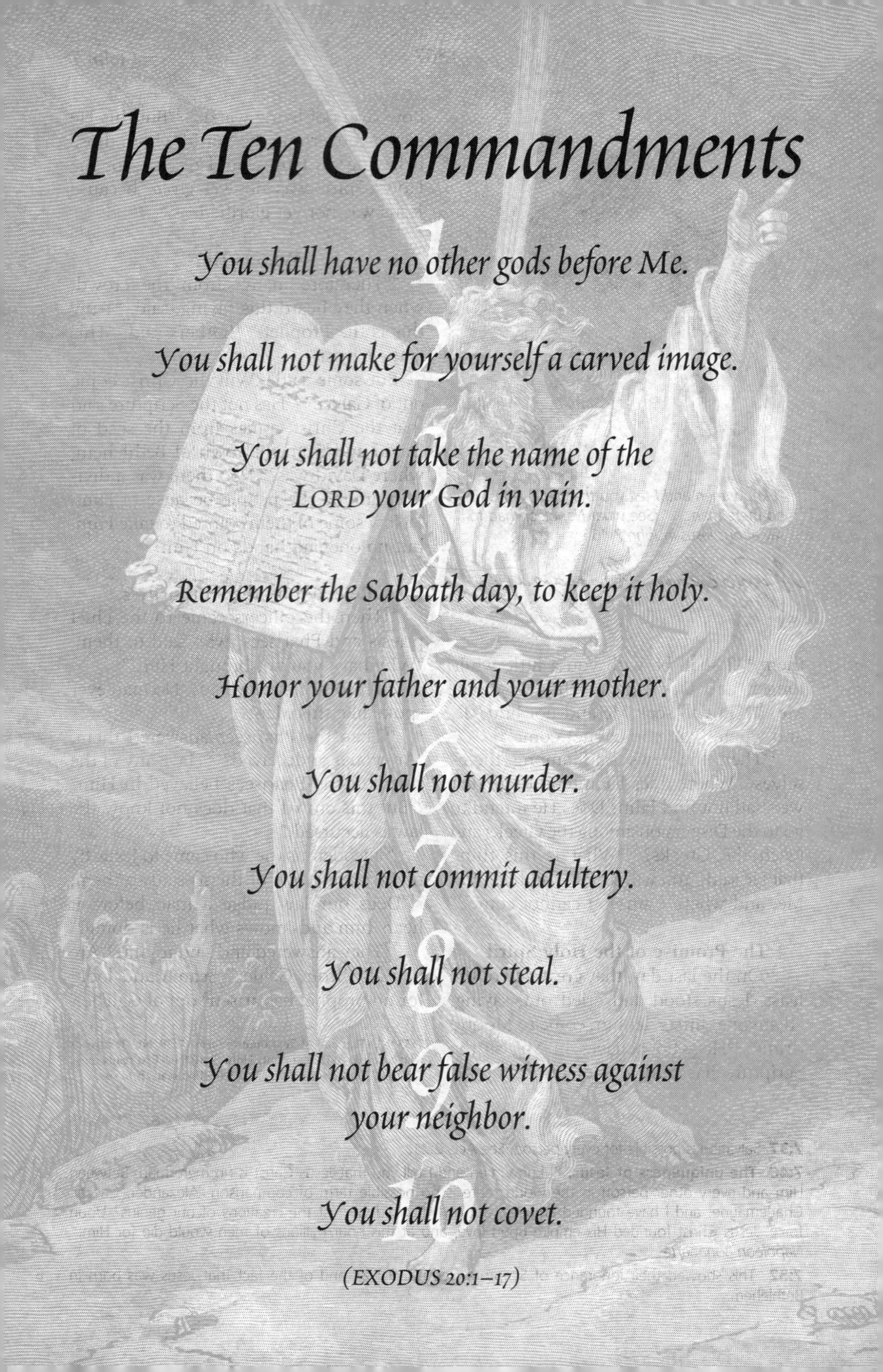

The Ten Commandments

1

You shall have no other gods before Me.

2

You shall not make for yourself a carved image.

3

You shall not take the name of the
LORD your God in vain.

4

Remember the Sabbath day, to keep it holy.

5

Honor your father and your mother.

6

You shall not murder.

7

You shall not commit adultery.

8

You shall not steal.

9

You shall not bear false witness against
your neighbor.

10

You shall not covet.

(EXODUS 20:1–17)

QUESTIONS & OBJECTIONS

8:9

"You are trying to make me feel guilty by quoting the Ten Commandments."

Ask the person which one of the Ten Commandments makes him feel guilty. Simply state, "The Bible says, 'You shall not steal.' If you feel guilty when you hear that, why do you think that is? Could it be because you *are* guilty?" God gave us our conscience so we would know when we break His Law; the guilt we feel when we do something wrong tells us that we need to repent. (See also Rom. 2:15 comment.)

An Adulteress Faces the Light of the World

[53]And everyone went to his *own* house.[a]

8 But Jesus went to the Mount of Olives.

[2]Now early[a] in the morning He came
again into the temple, and all the people
came to Him; and He sat down and
taught them. [3]Then the scribes and Pharisees brought to Him a woman caught in
adultery. And when they had set her in
the midst, [4]they said to Him, "Teacher,
this woman was caught[a] in adultery, in
the very act. [5]Now Moses, in the law, commanded[a] us that such should be stoned.[b]
But what do You say?"[c] [6]This they said,
testing Him, that they might have *something* of which to accuse Him. But Jesus
stooped down and wrote on the ground
with *His* finger, as though He did not
hear.[a]
[7]So when they continued asking Him,
He raised Himself up[a] and said to them,
"He who is without sin among you, let
him throw a stone at her first." [8]And
again He stooped down and wrote on the
ground. [9]Then those who heard *it*, being
convicted by *their* conscience,[a] went out
one by one, beginning with the oldest
even to the last. And Jesus was left alone,
and the woman standing in the midst.
[10]When Jesus had raised Himself up and
saw no one but the woman, He said to

USING THE LAW IN EVANGELISM

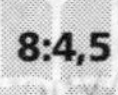

8:4,5

The wrath of the Law brought this woman to the feet of the Savior. That's the function of the Law: to condemn. Some may say that we shouldn't condemn anyone, when all the Law does is reveal to the sinner that he is "condemned already" (John 3:18). The Law shows him his danger and therefore his desperate need for the Savior. See Gal. 3:19 comment.

7:53 [a]The words *And everyone* through *sin no more* (8:11) are bracketed by NU-Text as not original. They are present in over 900 manuscripts. 8:2 [a]M-Text reads *very early.* 8:4 [a]M-Text reads *we found this woman.* 8:5 [a]M-Text reads *in our law Moses commanded.* [b]NU-Text and M-Text read *to stone such.* [c]M-Text adds *about her.* 8:6 [a]NU-Text and M-Text omit *as though He did not hear.* 8:7 [a]M-Text reads *He looked up.* 8:9 [a]NU-Text and M-Text omit *being convicted by their conscience.*

8:6 It is likely that Jesus wrote the Ten Commandments on the ground. They had been talking about the Law, and each of the men were convicted by their conscience (v. 9), which is the effect of the Law (Rom. 2:15). The Law was written in stone (uncompromising), this was written in sand (removable)—besides, what else does God write with His finger? See Exod. 31:18.

8:10–12 What a fearful thing it is when we face God's Law. The very stones call for our blood. The Law cries out for justice; it has no mercy. It demands, "The soul who sins shall die" (Ezek. 18:4). But the Judge who rules can, at His own discretion, administer the *spirit* of the Law, and its spirit says that mercy rejoices over judgment—God is rich in mercy to all who call upon Him. The letter kills, but the Spirit brings life. God is not willing that the wrath of the Law fall upon guilty sinners, because He would rather acquit the criminal from the courtroom... and He can do so because of Calvary.

A. N. Martin said, "The moment God's Law ceases to be the most powerful factor in influencing the moral sensitivity of any individual or nation, there will be indifference to Divine wrath, and when indifference comes in it always brings in its train indifference to salvation."

QUESTIONS & OBJECTIONS

8:11 ***"Jesus didn't condemn the woman caught in the act of adultery, but condemned those who judged her. Therefore you shouldn't judge others."***

The Christian is not "judging others" but simply telling the world of *God's* judgment—that God (not the Christian) has judged all the world as being guilty before Him (Rom. 3:19,23). Jesus was able to offer that woman forgiveness for her sin, because He was on His way to die on the cross for her. She acknowledged Him as "Lord," but He still told her, "Go and sin no more." If she didn't repent, she would perish (see Luke 13:3).

her,[a] "Woman, where are those accusers
of yours?[b] Has no one condemned you?"
11She said, "No one, Lord."
And Jesus said to her, "Neither do I
condemn you; go and[a] sin no more."
12Then Jesus spoke to them again, saying, "I am the light of the world. He who
follows Me shall not walk in darkness,
but have the light of life."

> Faith never knows where it is being led, but it loves and knows the One who is leading.
>
> **OSWALD CHAMBERS**

Jesus Defends His Self-Witness

13The Pharisees therefore said to Him,
"You bear witness of Yourself; Your witness is not true."
14Jesus answered and said to them,
"Even if I bear witness of Myself, My witness is true, for I know where I came
from and where I am going; but you do
not know where I come from and where
I am going. 15You judge according to the
flesh; I judge no one. 16And yet if I do
judge, My judgment is true; for I am not
alone, but I *am* with the Father who sent
Me. 17It is also written in your law that
the testimony of two men is true. 18I am
One who bears witness of Myself, and the
Father who sent Me bears witness of Me."
19Then they said to Him, "Where is
Your Father?"
Jesus answered, "You know neither
Me nor My Father. If you had known Me,
you would have known My Father also."
20These words Jesus spoke in the treasury, as He taught in the temple; and no
one laid hands on Him, for His hour had
not yet come.

Jesus Predicts His Departure

21Then Jesus said to them again, "I am
going away, and you will seek Me, and
will die in your sin. Where I go you cannot come."
22So the Jews said, "Will He kill Himself, because He says, 'Where I go you
cannot come'?"
23And He said to them, "You are from
beneath; I am from above. You are of this
world; I am not of this world. 24Therefore
I said to you that you will die in your
sins; for if you do not believe that I am
He, you will die in your sins."
25Then they said to Him, "Who are
You?"
And Jesus said to them, "Just what I
have been saying to you from the beginning. 26I have many things to say and to
judge concerning you, but He who sent
Me is true; and I speak to the world those
things which I heard from Him."
27They did not understand that He
spoke to them of the Father.
28Then Jesus said to them, "When you
lift up the Son of Man, then you will
know that I am *He,* and *that* I do nothing
of Myself; but as My Father taught Me, I
speak these things. 29And He who sent
Me is with Me. The Father has not left Me

8:10 [a]NU-Text omits *and saw no one but the woman;* M-Text reads *He saw her and said.* [b]NU-Text and M-Text omit *of yours.* **8:11** [a]NU-Text and M-Text add *from now on.*

alone, for I always do those things that please Him." 30As He spoke these words, many believed in Him.

The Truth Shall Make You Free

31Then Jesus said to those Jews who believed Him, "If you abide in My word, you are My disciples indeed. 32And you shall know the truth, and the truth shall make you free."

33They answered Him, "We are Abraham's descendants, and have never been in bondage to anyone. How *can* You say, 'You will be made free'?"

34Jesus answered them, "Most assuredly, I say to you, whoever commits sin is a slave of sin. 35And a slave does not abide in the house forever, *but* a son abides forever. 36Therefore if the Son makes you free, you shall be free indeed.

Abraham's Seed and Satan's

37"I know that you are Abraham's descendants, but you seek to kill Me, because My word has no place in you. 38I speak what I have seen with My Father, and you do what you have seen with[a] your father."

39They answered and said to Him, "Abraham is our father."

Jesus said to them, "If you were Abraham's children, you would do the works of Abraham. 40But now you seek to kill Me, a Man who has told you the truth which I heard from God. Abraham did not do this. 41You do the deeds of your father."

Then they said to Him, "We were not born of fornication; we have one Father—God."

42Jesus said to them, "If God were your Father, you would love Me, for I proceeded forth and came from God; nor have I come of Myself, but He sent Me. 43Why do you not understand My speech? Because you are not able to listen to My word. 44You are of *your* father the devil, and the desires of your father you want to do. He was a murderer from the beginning, and does not stand in the truth, because there is no truth in him. When he speaks a lie, he speaks from his own *resources,* for he is a liar and the father of it. 45But because I tell the truth, you do not believe Me. 46Which of you convicts Me of sin? And if I tell the truth, why do you not believe Me? 47He who is of God hears God's words; therefore you do not hear, because you are not of God."

Before Abraham Was, I AM

48Then the Jews answered and said to Him, "Do we not say rightly that You are a Samaritan and have a demon?"

49Jesus answered, "I do not have a demon; but I honor My Father, and you dishonor Me. 50And I do not seek My *own* glory; there is One who seeks and judges. 51Most assuredly, I say to you, if anyone keeps My word he shall never see death."

52Then the Jews said to Him, "Now we know that You have a demon! Abraham is dead, and the prophets; and You say, 'If anyone keeps My word he shall never taste death.' 53Are You greater than our father Abraham, who is dead? And the prophets are dead. Who do You make Yourself out to be?"

54Jesus answered, "If I honor Myself, My honor is nothing. It is My Father who

8:38 [a]NU-Text reads *heard from.*

8:44 Names of the enemy. The devil is called the god of this age, the ruler of this world, and the ruler of darkness (2 Cor. 4:4; John 12:31; Eph. 6:12). He seeks to hinder the work of God and suppress God's Word (Matt. 13:38,39; 1 Thess. 2:18). He is a liar, the father of lies, and a murderer (John 8:44). The devil is your adversary and a devourer (1 Pet. 5:8). He is the promoter of pride (Gen. 3:5; 1 Tim. 3:6), the stimulator of lust (Eph. 2:2,3), and the tempter (Luke 4:1–13).

8:51 Jesus' unique words: *Anyone* who obeys Him would not die. This is not advocating works as a means of salvation, but obedience as a *sign* of our salvation. We keep His word because we love Him (John 14:23). See 1 John 2:17 and John 8:58 comment.

honors Me, of whom you say that He is
your[a] God. 55Yet you have not known
Him, but I know Him. And if I say, 'I do
not know Him,' I shall be a liar like you;
but I do know Him and keep His word.
56Your father Abraham rejoiced to see My
day, and he saw *it* and was glad."

57Then the Jews said to Him, "You are
not yet fifty years old, and have You seen
Abraham?"

58Jesus said to them, "Most assuredly, I
say to you, before Abraham was, I AM."

59Then they took up stones to throw at
Him; but Jesus hid Himself and went out
of the temple,[a] going through the midst
of them, and so passed by.

A Man Born Blind Receives Sight

9 Now as *Jesus* passed by, He saw a
man who was blind from birth. 2And
His disciples asked Him, saying, "Rabbi,
who sinned, this man or his parents, that
he was born blind?"

3Jesus answered, "Neither this man
nor his parents sinned, but that the
works of God should be revealed in him.
4I[a] must work the works of Him who sent
Me while it is day; *the* night is coming
when no one can work. 5As long as I am
in the world, I am the light of the world."

6When He had said these things, He
spat on the ground and made clay with
the saliva; and He anointed the eyes of
the blind man with the clay. 7And He said
to him, "Go, wash in the pool of Siloam"
(which is translated, Sent). So he went
and washed, and came back seeing.

8Therefore the neighbors and those
who previously had seen that he was
blind[a] said, "Is not this he who sat and
begged?"

9Some said, "This is he." Others *said*,
"He is like him."[a]

8:54 [a]NU-Text and M-Text read *our.* 8:59 [a]NU-Text omits the rest of this verse. 9:4 [a]NU-Text reads *We.* 9:8 [a]NU-Text reads *a beggar.* 9:9 [a]NU-Text reads *"No, but he is like him."*

THE FUNCTION OF THE LAW

9:7 When we apply the tablets of the Law to the eyes of sinners, it causes them to have reason to go to the cleansing pool of the gospel. This man would not have had a reason to go to the pool until he perceived that he was unclean. That's the function of the Law—to convince a man he is unclean (Rom. 7:13).

"No man will ever put on the robe of Christ's righteousness till he is stripped of his fig leaves, nor will he wash in the fount of mercy till he perceives his filthiness. Therefore, my brethren, we must not cease to declare the Law, its demands, its threatenings, and the sinner's multiplied breaches of it." *Charles Spurgeon*

8:58 Jesus' unique words: Jesus was affirming that He was God manifest in the flesh. He is the Great "I AM," the Eternal One who revealed Himself to Moses in the burning bush (Exod. 3:14). See also John 11:25 comment.

Was Jesus God in human form? If you are given a small slice of cheese from a large block (the taste being constant throughout the whole block), and you spit out the cheese saying you hate the taste, then you reject the whole block. Jesus was God manifest in human form. If the Jews rejected Him, they rejected the Father also—he who is of God hears God's words (John 8:47). John later stated in his epistle, "Whoever denies the Son does not have the Father either; he who acknowledges the Son has the Father also" (1 John 2:23). See John 10:30.

9:4 *John Wesley* was asked what he would do with his life if he knew that he would die at midnight the next day. His answer was something like this: "I would just carry on with what I am doing. I will arise at 5:00 a.m. for prayer, then take a house meeting at 6.00 a.m. At 12 noon, I will be preaching at an open-air meeting. At 3:00 p.m. I have another meeting in another town. At 6:00 p.m. I have a house meeting; at 10:00 p.m. I have a prayer meeting and at 12:00 midnight, I would go to be with my Lord."

If we knew we were to die at 12 o'clock tomorrow night, would we have to step up our evangelistic efforts, or could we in all good conscience carry on just as we are?

"The evangelistic harvest is always urgent. The destiny of men and of nations is always being decided. Every generation is strategic. We are not responsible for the past generation, and we cannot bear the full responsibility for the next one; but we do have our generation. God will hold us responsible as to how well we fulfill our responsibilities to this age and take advantage of our opportunities." *Billy Graham*

He said, "I am *he.*"

10Therefore they said to him, "How were your eyes opened?"

11He answered and said, "A Man called Jesus made clay and anointed my eyes and said to me, 'Go to the pool of[a] Siloam and wash.' So I went and washed, and I received sight."

12Then they said to him, "Where is He?"

He said, "I do not know."

The Pharisees Excommunicate the Healed Man

13They brought him who formerly was blind to the Pharisees. 14Now it was a Sabbath when Jesus made the clay and opened his eyes. 15Then the Pharisees also asked him again how he had received his sight. He said to them, "He put clay on my eyes, and I washed, and I see."

16Therefore some of the Pharisees said, "This Man is not from God, because He does not keep the Sabbath."

Others said, "How can a man who is a sinner do such signs?" And there was a division among them.

17They said to the blind man again, "What do you say about Him because He opened your eyes?"

He said, "He is a prophet."

18But the Jews did not believe concerning him, that he had been blind and received his sight, until they called the parents of him who had received his sight. 19And they asked them, saying, "Is this your son, who you say was born blind? How then does he now see?"

20His parents answered them and said, "We know that this is our son, and that he was born blind; 21but by what means he now sees we do not know, or who opened his eyes we do not know. He is of age; ask him. He will speak for himself." 22His parents said these *things* because they feared the Jews, for the Jews had agreed already that if anyone confessed *that* He *was* Christ, he would be put out of the synagogue. 23Therefore his parents said, "He is of age; ask him."

24So they again called the man who was blind, and said to him, "Give God the glory! We know that this Man is a sinner."

25He answered and said, "Whether He is a sinner *or not* I do not know. One thing I know: that though I was blind, now I see."

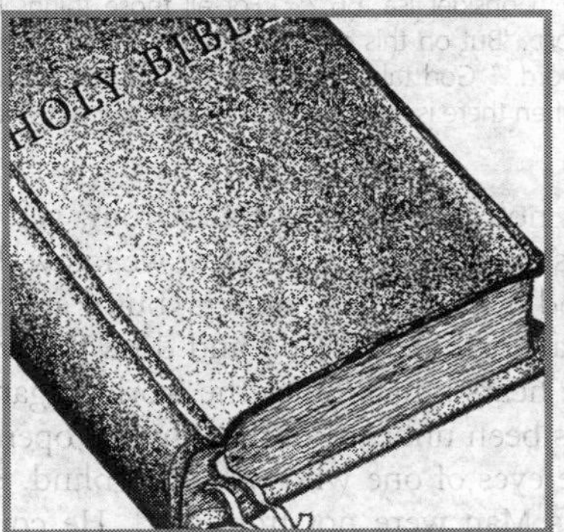

The Bible is unique and proves itself to be supernatural in origin. See Psa. 119:105 comment.

26Then they said to him again, "What did He do to you? How did He open your eyes?"

27He answered them, "I told you already, and you did not listen. Why do you want to hear *it* again? Do you also want to become His disciples?"

28Then they reviled him and said, "You are His disciple, but we are Moses' disciples. 29We know that God spoke to Moses; *as for* this *fellow,* we do not know where He is from."

30The man answered and said to them, "Why, this is a marvelous thing, that you

9:11 [a]NU-Text omits *the pool of.*

9:25 This is the testimony of the newly saved. There are many questions for which they have no answers. But one thing they do know: "though I was blind, now I see." It has been well said that the man with an experience is not at the mercy of a man with an argument.

QUESTIONS & OBJECTIONS

9:31

"If God doesn't hear some prayers, how can He be omniscient?"

God is omniscient and "hears" all things, but if we remain in rebellion to Him, clinging to sin, He will take no notice of our prayers. Here are two such verses (there are others): "If I regard iniquity in my heart, the Lord will not hear" (Psa. 66:18). "But your iniquities have separated you from your God; and your sins have hidden His face from you, so that He will not hear" (Isa. 59:2).

The Scriptures tell us that He "resists" the proud and gives grace to the humble (see James 4:6). That is why a proud person can think there is no God: he believes that his prayers didn't make it above the ceiling, and he is right. He needs to approach God in humility of heart. That way He will be attentive to his prayer.

Consider Isa. 66:2: "'For all those things My hand has made, and all those things exist,' says the LORD. 'But on this one I will look: on him who is poor and of a contrite spirit, and who trembles at My word.'" God takes notice of the humble prayer. He forgives sin and reveals Himself (in salvation), only when there is repentance and faith in Jesus. See also Prov. 28:9.

do not know where He is from; yet He
has opened my eyes! [31]Now we know that
God does not hear sinners; but if anyone
is a worshiper of God and does His will,
He hears him. [32]Since the world began it
has been unheard of that anyone opened
the eyes of one who was born blind. [33]If
this Man were not from God, He could
do nothing."

[34]They answered and said to him, "You
were completely born in sins, and are
you teaching us?" And they cast him out.

True Vision and True Blindness

[35]Jesus heard that they had cast him
out; and when He had found him, He
said to him, "Do you believe in the Son of
God?"[a]

[36]He answered and said, "Who is He,
Lord, that I may believe in Him?"

[37]And Jesus said to him, "You have
both seen Him and it is He who is talking
with you."

[38]Then he said, "Lord, I believe!" And
he worshiped Him.

[39]And Jesus said, "For judgment I have
come into this world, that those who do
not see may see, and that those who see
may be made blind."

[40]Then *some* of the Pharisees who were
with Him heard these words, and said to
Him, "Are we blind also?"

[41]Jesus said to them, "If you were blind,
you would have no sin; but now you say,
'We see.' Therefore your sin remains.

Jesus the True Shepherd

10 "Most assuredly, I say to you, he
who does not enter the sheepfold
by the door, but climbs up some other
way, the same is a thief and a robber. [2]But
he who enters by the door is the shepherd
of the sheep. [3]To him the doorkeeper
opens, and the sheep hear his voice; and
he calls his own sheep by name and leads
them out. [4]And when he brings out his
own sheep, he goes before them; and the
sheep follow him, for they know his
voice. [5]Yet they will by no means follow a
stranger, but will flee from him, for they
do not know the voice of strangers."
[6]Jesus used this illustration, but they did
not understand the things which He
spoke to them.

9:35 [a]NU-Text reads *Son of Man.*

10:2 True believers are likened to sheep, which: know the voice of their shepherd; are easily led (they submit without resistance); flock together (in unity); need a shepherd (or they stray); were a type of Israel (Matt. 10:6); imitate one another; are productive (wool, leather, meat, and milk); were a sign of God's blessing (see Deut. 7:13); will be divided from the "goats" at the Judgment; were offered in sacrifice.

Jesus the Good Shepherd

7Then Jesus said to them again, "Most
assuredly, I say to you, I am the door of
the sheep. 8All who *ever* came before Me[a]
are thieves and robbers, but the sheep
did not hear them. 9I am the door. If anyone enters by Me, he will be saved, and
will go in and out and find pasture. 10The
thief does not come except to steal, and
to kill, and to destroy. I have come that
they may have life, and that they may
have *it* more abundantly.

11"I am the good shepherd. The good
shepherd gives His life for the sheep.
12But a hireling, *he who is* not the shepherd, one who does not own the sheep,
sees the wolf coming and leaves the
sheep and flees; and the wolf catches the
sheep and scatters them. 13The hireling
flees because he is a hireling and does not
care about the sheep. 14I am the good
shepherd; and I know My *sheep,* and am
known by My own. 15As the Father knows
Me, even so I know the Father; and I lay
down My life for the sheep. 16And other
sheep I have which are not of this fold;
them also I must bring, and they will hear
My voice; and there will be one flock *and*
one shepherd.

17"Therefore My Father loves Me, because I lay down My life that I may take
it again. 18No one takes it from Me, but I
lay it down of Myself. I have power to lay
it down, and I have power to take it again.
This command I have received from My
Father."

19Therefore there was a division again
among the Jews because of these sayings.
20And many of them said, "He has a demon
and is mad. Why do you listen to Him?"

21Others said, "These are not the words
of one who has a demon. Can a demon
open the eyes of the blind?"

The Shepherd Knows His Sheep

22Now it was the Feast of Dedication
in Jerusalem, and it was winter. 23And Jesus walked in the temple, in Solomon's
porch. 24Then the Jews surrounded Him
and said to Him, "How long do You keep
us in doubt? If You are the Christ, tell us
plainly."

25Jesus answered them, "I told you,
and you do not believe. The works that I

10:8 [a]M-Text omits *before Me.*

10:9 A Hebrew servant who was given his freedom had the option to stay with a master he loved. If he chose to give up his freedom, his master took him to the doorpost and pierced his ear with an awl, "and he shall serve him forever" (Exod. 21:5,6). In the same way, the sinner, upon conversion, is given freedom from sin and becomes a servant of Jesus Christ (1 Cor. 7:22) to serve Him forever. He presents his body as a living sacrifice. His ear is forever open to the Door of the Savior (John 10:9).

10:10 The abundant life. Jesus did not come to bring us a "better" life. In this verse, the word "abundant" does not mean better, richer, and happier. It simply means life in its "fullness." If you study Paul's life, you will find that it was full. It was full of trials, tribulations, temptations, and persecutions. He was hated, beaten, mocked, whipped, stoned, imprisoned, and finally martyred. He told Timothy that "all who desire to live godly in Christ Jesus will suffer persecution" (2 Tim. 3:12).

Telling sinners that God's purpose is to give mankind happiness and fulfillment and allow them to get the best out of life is a perversion of the gospel message. Nowhere in Scripture do we see that message being preached, yet it is the essence of the modern proclamation. It leaves the sinner ignorant of the fact that he is a criminal and that God is his Judge, and is the recipe for a false conversion. If we keep the analogy in the courtroom (criminal and judge), it keeps us from straying into the error of the modern gospel. See 2 Cor. 2:17 comment for details on why we should not entice sinners with the promise of a wonderful new life.

10:11 Hundreds of years earlier, David had written that the Lord was his shepherd, and now that Shepherd had become flesh. Here is a continuance of the most famous of psalms, Psalm 23. This was the "Great Shepherd" Himself (Heb. 13:20), the One who takes away the "want" of the covetous human heart. He was the path of righteousness, who brought light to the valley of the shadow of death. Here was the Bread of Life, placed by God on a table in the presence of our enemies. Heaven's cup "ran over," and brought the Father's goodness and mercy to us, so that we might dwell in the House of the Lord forever.

10:16 The Mormons misrepresent this verse. It is an obvious reference to the Gentiles. See John 11:52; Rom. 15:9–12; Eph. 2:11–18.

do in My Father's name, they bear witness of Me. [26]But you do not believe, because you are not of My sheep, as I said
to you.[a] [27]My sheep hear My voice, and I
know them, and they follow Me. [28]And I
give them eternal life, and they shall
never perish; neither shall anyone snatch
them out of My hand. [29]My Father, who
has given *them* to Me, is greater than all;
and no one is able to snatch *them* out of
My Father's hand. [30]I and My Father are
one."

> Preach Christ or nothing: don't dispute or discuss except with your eye on the cross.
>
> **CHARLES SPURGEON**

Renewed Efforts to Stone Jesus

[31]Then the Jews took up stones again to
stone Him. [32]Jesus answered them, "Many
good works I have shown you from My
Father. For which of those works do you
stone Me?"

[33]The Jews answered Him, saying, "For
a good work we do not stone You, but for
blasphemy, and because You, being a
Man, make Yourself God."

[34]Jesus answered them, "Is it not written in your law, *'I said, "You are gods"'*?[a]
[35]If He called them gods, to whom the
word of God came (and the Scripture
cannot be broken), [36]do you say of Him
whom the Father sanctified and sent into
the world, 'You are blaspheming,' because I said, 'I am the Son of God'? [37]If I
do not do the works of My Father, do not
believe Me; [38]but if I do, though you do
not believe Me, believe the works, that
you may know and believe[a] that the Father *is* in Me, and I in Him." [39]Therefore
they sought again to seize Him, but He
escaped out of their hand.

The Believers Beyond Jordan

[40]And He went away again beyond the
Jordan to the place where John was baptizing at first, and there He stayed.
[41]Then many came to Him and said,
"John performed no sign, but all the
things that John spoke about this Man
were true." [42]And many believed in Him
there.

The Death of Lazarus

11 Now a certain *man* was sick,
Lazarus of Bethany, the town of
Mary and her sister Martha. [2]It was *that*
Mary who anointed the Lord with fragrant oil and wiped His feet with her hair,
whose brother Lazarus was sick. [3]There-
fore the sisters sent to Him, saying,
"Lord, behold, he whom You love is
sick."

[4]When Jesus heard *that,* He said, "This
sickness is not unto death, but for the
glory of God, that the Son of God may be
glorified through it."

[5]Now Jesus loved Martha and her sister and Lazarus. [6]So, when He heard that
he was sick, He stayed two more days in
the place where He was. [7]Then after this
He said to *the* disciples, "Let us go to
Judea again."

[8]*The* disciples said to Him, "Rabbi,
lately the Jews sought to stone You, and

10:26 [a]NU-Text omits *as I said to you.* 10:34 [a]Psalm 82:6
10:38 [a]NU-Text reads *understand.*

10:27 See 2 Tim. 2:19 comment.

10:30 Was Jesus God in human form? See John 10:38.

10:38 Was Jesus God in human form? See John 14:10.

11:6 God's ways are distinctively and consistently different from ours. God did not rescue Daniel out of the lion's den as we would have. He didn't turn off the fiery furnace into which Shadrach, Meshach, and Abed-Nego were cast, as we would. He didn't kill Pharaoh and save the Israelites from the Red Sea; instead He worked His wondrous purposes *in* the lion's den, *in* the furnace, and *in* the Red Sea. Lion's teeth, fire, and water are no big deal to the God who created them. Death, at the presence of the Light of the world, is but a shadow that quickly dissipates in the brilliance of the noon-day sun.

10:36 *The Deity of Jesus*

From *Christ Before the Manger* by *Ron Rhodes*

A strong argument for the deity of Christ is the fact that many of the names, titles, and attributes ascribed to Yahweh are also ascribed to Jesus Christ.

DESCRIPTION	FATHER	JESUS
Yahweh ("I AM")	Exodus 3:14 Deuteronomy 32:39 Isaiah 43:10	John 8:24 John 8:58 John 18:4–6
God	Genesis 1:1 Deuteronomy 6:4 Psalm 45:6,7	Isaiah 7:14 Isaiah 9:6 John 1:1,14 John 20:28 Titus 2:13 Hebrews 1:8 2 Peter 1:1 Matthew 1:23 1 John 5:20
Alpha and Omega (First and Last)	Isaiah 41:4 Isaiah 48:12 Revelation 1:8	Revelation 1:17,18 Revelation 2:8 Revelation 22:12–16
Lord	Isaiah 45:23	Matthew 12:8 Acts 7:59,60 Acts 10:36 Romans 10:12 1 Corinthians 2:8 1 Corinthians 12:3 Philippians 2:10,11
Savior	Isaiah 43:3 Isaiah 43:11 Isaiah 49:26 Isaiah 63:8 Luke 1:47 1 Timothy 4:10	Matthew 1:21 Luke 2:11 John 1:29 John 4:42 2 Timothy 1:10 Titus 2:13 Hebrews 5:9
King	Psalm 95:3 Isaiah 43:15 1 Timothy 6:14–16	Revelation 17:14 Revelation 19:16
Judge	Genesis 18:25 Deuteronomy 32:36 Psalm 50:4,6 Psalm 58:11 Psalm 75:7 Psalm 96:13	John 5:22 2 Corinthians 5:10 2 Timothy 4:1
Light	2 Samuel 22:29 Psalm 27:1	John 1:4,9 John 3:19 John 8:12 John 9:5
Rock	Deuteronomy 32:3,4 2 Samuel 22:32 Psalm 89:26	Romans 9:33 1 Corinthians 10:3,4 1 Peter 2:4–8

(continued)

(10:36 continued)

DESCRIPTION	FATHER	JESUS
Redeemer	Psalm 130:7,8 Isaiah 43:1 Isaiah 48:17 Isaiah 49:26 Isaiah 54:5	Acts 20:28 Ephesians 1:7 Hebrews 9:12
Our Righteousness	Isaiah 45:24	Jeremiah 23:6 Romans 3:21,22
Husband	Isaiah 54:5 Hosea 2:16	Matthew 25:1 Mark 2:18,19 2 Corinthians 11:2 Ephesians 5:25–32 Revelation 21:2,9
Shepherd	Genesis 49:24 Psalm 23:1 Psalm 80:1	John 10:11,16 Hebrews 13:20 1 Peter 2:25 1 Peter 5:4
Creator	Genesis 1:1 Job 33:4 Psalm 95:5,6 Psalm 102:24,25 Isaiah 40:28 Isaiah 43:1 Acts 4:24	John 1:2,3,10 Colossians 1:15–18 Hebrews 1:1–3,10
Giver of Life	Genesis 2:7 Deuteronomy 32:39 1 Samuel 2:6 Psalm 36:9	John 5:21 John 10:28 John 11:25
Forgiver of Sin	Exodus 34:6,7 Nehemiah 9:17 Daniel 9:9 Jonah 4:2	Matthew 9:2 Mark 2:1–12 Acts 26:18 Colossians 2:13 Colossians 3:13
Lord our Healer	Exodus 15:26	Acts 9:34
Omnipresent	Psalm 139:7–12 Proverbs 15:3	Matthew 18:20 Matthew 28:20 Ephesians 3:17 Ephesians 4:10
Omniscient	1 Kings 8:39 Jeremiah 17:10,16	Matthew 9:4 Matthew 11:27 Luke 5:4–6 John 2:25 John 16:30 John 21:17 Acts 1:24
Omnipotent	Isaiah 40:10–31 Isaiah 45:5–13 Revelation 19:6	Matthew 28:18 Mark 1:29–34 John 10:18 Jude 24
Eternal	Psalm 102:26,27 Habakkuk 3:6	Isaiah 9:6 Micah 5:2 John 8:58

(continued)

(10:36 continued)

DESCRIPTION	FATHER	JESUS
Preexistent	Genesis 1:1	John 1:15,30 John 3:13,31,32 John 6:62 John 16:28 John 17:5
Immutable	Malachi 3:6 James 1:17	Hebrews 13:8
Receiver of worship	Matthew 4:10 John 4:24 Revelation 5:14 Revelation 7:11 Revelation 11:16 Revelation 19:4,10	Matthew 2:8,11 Matthew 14:33 Matthew 28:9 John 9:38 Philippians 2:10,11 Hebrews 1:6
Hope	Jeremiah 17:7	1 Timothy 1:1
Speaker with divine authority	"Thus saith the Lord . . ." —used hundreds of times	Matthew 23:34–37 John 3:5 John 7:46 "Truly, truly, I say . . ."
Who raised Jesus from the dead?	Acts 2:24,32 Romans 8:11 1 Corinthians 6:14	John 2:19–22 John 10:17,18 Matthew 27:40
Who gets the glory?	Isaiah 42:8 Isaiah 48:11	Hebrews 13:21 John 17:5

are You going there again?"
[9]Jesus answered, "Are there not twelve
hours in the day? If anyone walks in the
day, he does not stumble, because he sees
the light of this world. [10]But if one walks
in the night, he stumbles, because the
light is not in him." [11]These things He
said, and after that He said to them, "Our
friend Lazarus sleeps, but I go that I may
wake him up."
[12]Then His disciples said, "Lord, if he
sleeps he will get well." [13]However, Jesus
spoke of his death, but they thought that
He was speaking about taking rest in
sleep.
[14]Then Jesus said to them plainly,
"Lazarus is dead. [15]And I am glad for
your sakes that I was not there, that you
may believe. Nevertheless let us go to
him."
[16]Then Thomas, who is called the
Twin, said to his fellow disciples, "Let us
also go, that we may die with Him."

I Am the Resurrection and the Life

[17]So when Jesus came, He found that
he had already been in the tomb four
days. [18]Now Bethany was near Jerusalem,
about two miles[a] away. [19]And many of
the Jews had joined the women around
Martha and Mary, to comfort them concerning their brother.
[20]Now Martha, as soon as she heard
that Jesus was coming, went and met
Him, but Mary was sitting in the house.
[21]Now Martha said to Jesus, "Lord, if You
had been here, my brother would not
have died. [22]But even now I know that
whatever You ask of God, God will give
You."
[23]Jesus said to her, "Your brother will
rise again."
[24]Martha said to Him, "I know that he
will rise again in the resurrection at the
last day."

11:18 [a]Literally *fifteen stadia*

11:14 How to Preach at a Funeral for Someone You Suspect Died Unsaved

By Mike Smalley

1. Start in the natural realm and swing to the spiritual.

2. Say something positive about the person who has died—either personally, or their marriage, kids, work ethic, their generation, etc. This should build rapport with the audience. Use a humorous story that relates to the above.

3. Don't feel pressured to mention where the deceased may have gone after death (God is the only One who truly knows).

4. Never insinuate that he went to heaven.

5. Use this as a springboard: "Good friends often remind us of things that we don't want to deal with, but that are very important. Bob, today, reminds us that we *all* must die."

6. Use anecdotes that convey eternal truths.

7. Go quickly but thoroughly through each of the Ten Commandments.

8. Warn briefly about sin, death, judgment, and eternity.

9. Give a clear gospel presentation.

10. Appeal to the audience to repent today.

"When anyone dies, I ask myself, 'Was I faithful?' Did I speak all the truth? And did I speak it from my very soul every time I preached?" *Charles Spurgeon*

[25]Jesus said to her, "I am the resurrection and the life. He who believes in Me,
though he may die, he shall live. [26]And
whoever lives and believes in Me shall
never die. Do you believe this?"

[27]She said to Him, "Yes, Lord, I believe
that You are the Christ, the Son of God,
who is to come into the world."

Jesus and Death, the Last Enemy

[28]And when she had said these things,
she went her way and secretly called
Mary her sister, saying, "The Teacher has
come and is calling for you." [29]As soon as
she heard *that,* she arose quickly and
came to Him. [30]Now Jesus had not yet
come into the town, but was[a] in the place
where Martha met Him. [31]Then the Jews
who were with her in the house, and
comforting her, when they saw that Mary
rose up quickly and went out, followed
her, saying, "She is going to the tomb to
weep there."[a]

[32]Then, when Mary came where Jesus
was, and saw Him, she fell down at His
feet, saying to Him, "Lord, if You had been
here, my brother would not have died."

[33]Therefore, when Jesus saw her weeping, and the Jews who came with her
weeping, He groaned in the spirit and was
troubled. [34]And He said, "Where have
you laid him?"

They said to Him, "Lord, come and
see."

[35]Jesus wept. [36]Then the Jews said,
"See how He loved him!"

11:30 [a]NU-Text adds *still.* **11:31** [a]NU-Text reads *supposing that she was going to the tomb to weep there.*

11:25 The uniqueness of Jesus. "A man who was merely a man and said the sort of things Jesus said wouldn't be a great moral teacher. He'd either be a lunatic—on a level with the man who says he's a poached egg—or else he'd be the Devil of Hell. You must make your choice. Either this man was, and is, the Son of God: or else a madman or something worse. You can shut Him up for a fool, you can spit at Him and kill Him as a demon; or you can fall at His feet and call Him Lord and God. But don't let us come with any patronizing nonsense about His being a great human teacher. He hasn't left that open to us. He didn't intend to." *C. S. Lewis, The Case for Christianity*

Jesus' unique words: See John 14:6 comment.

11:35 In one sense, this verse is a mystery because Jesus knew what He was about to do. He was about to give Mary and Martha the greatest gift, outside of salvation, that they could ever hope for. Yet, He wept.

The prophets tell us that the Messiah would be a "Man of sorrows and acquainted with grief" (Isa. 53:3). He was moved with compassion for the multitudes, wept over Jerusalem, and knew what it was to "weep with those who weep" (Rom. 12:15). Even though heaven is before us, it pains the Head of the Body when the foot hurts. Jesus is a High Priest who could "sympathize with our weaknesses" (Heb. 4:15).

37And some of them said, "Could not this Man, who opened the eyes of the blind, also have kept this man from dying?"

Lazarus Raised from the Dead

38Then Jesus, again groaning in Himself, came to the tomb. It was a cave, and a stone lay against it. 39Jesus said, "Take away the stone."

Martha, the sister of him who was dead, said to Him, "Lord, by this time there is a stench, for he has been *dead* four days."

40Jesus said to her, "Did I not say to you that if you would believe you would see the glory of God?" 41Then they took away the stone *from the place* where the dead man was lying.[a] And Jesus lifted up *His* eyes and said, "Father, I thank You that You have heard Me. 42And I know that You always hear Me, but because of the people who are standing by I said *this,* that they may believe that You sent Me." 43Now when He had said these things, He cried with a loud voice, "Lazarus, come forth!" 44And he who had died came out bound hand and foot with graveclothes, and his face was wrapped with a cloth. Jesus said to them, "Loose him, and let him go."

The Plot to Kill Jesus

45Then many of the Jews who had come to Mary, and had seen the things Jesus did, believed in Him. 46But some of them went away to the Pharisees and told them the things Jesus did. 47Then the chief priests and the Pharisees gathered a council and said, "What shall we do? For this Man works many signs. 48If we let Him alone like this, everyone will believe in Him, and the Romans will come and take away both our place and nation."

49And one of them, Caiaphas, being high priest that year, said to them, "You know nothing at all, 50nor do you consider that it is expedient for us[a] that one man should die for the people, and not that the whole nation should perish." 51Now this he did not say on his own *authority;* but being high priest that year he prophesied that Jesus would die for the nation, 52and not for that nation only, but also that He would gather together in one the children of God who were scattered abroad.

53Then, from that day on, they plotted to put Him to death. 54Therefore Jesus no longer walked openly among the Jews, but went from there into the country near the wilderness, to a city called Ephraim, and there remained with His disciples.

55And the Passover of the Jews was near, and many went from the country up to Jerusalem before the Passover, to purify themselves. 56Then they sought Jesus, and spoke among themselves as they stood in the temple, "What do you think—that He will not come to the feast?" 57Now both the chief priests and

11:41 [a]NU-Text omits *from the place where the dead man was lying.* 11:50 [a]NU-Text reads *you.*

11:43,44 The words of Jesus cut through the icy grip of death like a white-hot blade through soft powdered snow. The same Word that brought life in the beginning breathed life into the decomposing corpse of Lazarus. Suddenly, from the blackened shadow of the tomb appeared a figure wrapped in cloth. As he stood at the entrance of the tomb, his face and body were covered with grave clothes. God took him by the hand and led him to the light.

What a picture of what is before us! The hour is coming when all who are in their graves will hear His voice. The victory Lazarus had over death was bad news for the devil and the undertaker, but it was only a temporary triumph, for the undertaker would eventually get his deathly fee. Lazarus would ultimately depart from this earth, but the time is coming when death shall be no more. On that day, we will exchange these vile, perishing bodies for incorruptible bodies that will never feel pain, disease, or death: "So when this corruptible has put on incorruption, and this mortal has put on immortality, then shall be brought to pass the saying that is written: 'Death is swallowed up in victory' " (1 Cor. 15:54).

For those who trust in Jesus, this body is but a chrysalis, which may become wrinkled and crusty with age, but it is just a shell that will be discarded as the new butterfly emerges.

the Pharisees had given a command, that if anyone knew where He was, he should report *it,* that they might seize Him.

The Anointing at Bethany

12 Then, six days before the Passover, Jesus came to Bethany, where Lazarus was who had been dead,[a] whom He had raised from the dead. [2]There they made Him a supper; and Martha served, but Lazarus was one of those who sat at the table with Him. [3]Then Mary took a pound of very costly oil of spikenard, anointed the feet of Jesus, and wiped His feet with her hair. And the house was filled with the fragrance of the oil.

> Men have been helped to live by remembering that they must die.
> **CHARLES SPURGEON**

[4]But one of His disciples, Judas Iscariot, Simon's *son,* who would betray Him, said, [5]"Why was this fragrant oil not sold for three hundred denarii[a] and given to the poor?" [6]This he said, not that he cared for the poor, but because he was a thief, and had the money box; and he used to take what was put in it.

[7]But Jesus said, "Let her alone; she has kept[a] this for the day of My burial. [8]For the poor you have with you always, but Me you do not have always."

The Plot to Kill Lazarus

[9]Now a great many of the Jews knew that He was there; and they came, not for Jesus' sake only, but that they might also see Lazarus, whom He had raised from the dead. [10]But the chief priests plotted to put Lazarus to death also, [11]because on account of him many of the Jews went away and believed in Jesus.

The Triumphal Entry

[12]The next day a great multitude that had come to the feast, when they heard that Jesus was coming to Jerusalem, [13]took branches of palm trees and went out to meet Him, and cried out:

"Hosanna!
'Blessed is He who comes in the name of the LORD!'[a]
The King of Israel!"

[14]Then Jesus, when He had found a young donkey, sat on it; as it is written:

[15]*"Fear not, daughter of Zion;*
Behold, your King is coming,
Sitting on a donkey's colt."[a]

[16]His disciples did not understand these things at first; but when Jesus was glorified, then they remembered that these things were written about Him and *that* they had done these things to Him.

[17]Therefore the people, who were with Him when He called Lazarus out of his tomb and raised him from the dead, bore witness. [18]For this reason the people also met Him, because they heard that He had done this sign. [19]The Pharisees therefore said among themselves, "You see that you are accomplishing nothing. Look, the world has gone after Him!"

12:1 [a]NU-Text omits *who had been dead.* 12:5 [a]About one year's wages for a worker 12:7 [a]NU-Text reads *that she may keep.* 12:13 [a]Psalm 118:26 12:15 [a]Zechariah 9:9

12:9 The raising of Lazarus happened for the inestimable profit of humanity. It was the long-awaited fulfillment of what was spoken of by the prophets of old. It was a beam of wondrous and glistening light in the darkest and most hopeless of all caves.

12:14 Instead of riding triumphantly through the streets of Jerusalem on a kingly white stallion, Jesus chose to ride on a young donkey, a lowly beast of burden. Imagine how humbling it would be for the president of the United States to ride through New York on the back of a donkey. But this is what the King of kings did. This time He came in lowliness, humbling Himself and becoming obedient to the death of the cross. The next time He will come in flaming fire, on a white horse with ten thousands of His saints.

The Fruitful Grain of Wheat

20 Now there were certain Greeks among those who came up to worship at the feast. 21 Then they came to Philip, who was from Bethsaida of Galilee, and asked him, saying, "Sir, we wish to see Jesus."

22 Philip came and told Andrew, and in turn Andrew and Philip told Jesus.

23 But Jesus answered them, saying, "The hour has come that the Son of Man should be glorified. 24 Most assuredly, I say to you, unless a grain of wheat falls into the ground and dies, it remains alone; but if it dies, it produces much grain. 25 He who loves his life will lose it, and he who hates his life in this world will keep it for eternal life. 26 If anyone serves Me, let him follow Me; and where I am, there My servant will be also. If anyone serves Me, him *My* Father will honor.

Jesus Predicts His Death on the Cross

27 "Now My soul is troubled, and what shall I say? 'Father, save Me from this hour'? But for this purpose I came to this hour. 28 Father, glorify Your name."

Then a voice came from heaven, *saying,* "I have both glorified *it* and will glorify *it* again."

29 Therefore the people who stood by and heard *it* said that it had thundered. Others said, "An angel has spoken to Him."

30 Jesus answered and said, "This voice did not come because of Me, but for your sake. 31 Now is the judgment of this world; now the ruler of this world will be cast out. 32 And I, if I am lifted up from the earth, will draw all *peoples* to Myself." 33 This He said, signifying by what death He would die.

34 The people answered Him, "We have heard from the law that the Christ remains forever; and how *can* You say, 'The Son of Man must be lifted up'? Who is this Son of Man?"

35 Then Jesus said to them, "A little while longer the light is with you. Walk while you have the light, lest darkness overtake you; he who walks in darkness does not know where he is going. 36 While you have the light, believe in the light, that you may become sons of light." These things Jesus spoke, and departed, and was hidden from them.

Who Has Believed Our Report?

37 But although He had done so many signs before them, they did not believe in Him, 38 that the word of Isaiah the prophet might be fulfilled, which he spoke:

"Lord, who has believed our report?
And to whom has the arm of the LORD
been revealed?"[a]

39 Therefore they could not believe, because Isaiah said again:

40 *"He has blinded their eyes and*
hardened their hearts,
Lest they should see with their eyes,
Lest they should understand with
their hearts and turn,
So that I should heal them."[a]

41 These things Isaiah said when[a] he saw His glory and spoke of Him.

Walk in the Light

42 Nevertheless even among the rulers many believed in Him, but because of the

12:38 [a]Isaiah 53:1 12:40 [a]Isaiah 6:10 12:41 [a]NU-Text reads *because.*

12:25 "The greatest proof of Christianity for others is not how far a man can logically analyze his reasons for believing, but how far in practice he will stake his life on his belief." *T. S. Eliot*

12:32 "We must praise Your goodness that You have left nothing undone to draw us to Yourself. But one thing we ask of You, our God, not to cease to work in our improvement. Let us tend towards You, no matter by what means, and be fruitful in good works, for the sake of Jesus Christ our Lord." *Ludwig van Beethoven*

12:38 One would think that a terminally ill world would gladly embrace the cure of the gospel, but few, so few believe our report.

Pharisees they did not confess *Him,* lest they should be put out of the synagogue; [43]for they loved the praise of men more than the praise of God.

[44]Then Jesus cried out and said, "He who believes in Me, believes not in Me but in Him who sent Me. [45]And he who sees Me sees Him who sent Me. [46]I have come *as* a light into the world, that whoever believes in Me should not abide in darkness. [47]And if anyone hears My words and does not believe,[a] I do not judge him; for I did not come to judge the world but to save the world. [48]He who rejects Me, and does not receive My words, has that which judges him—the word that I have spoken will judge him in the last day. [49]For I have not spoken on My own *authority;* but the Father who sent Me gave Me a command, what I should say and what I should speak. [50]And I know that His command is everlasting life. Therefore, whatever I speak, just as the Father has told Me, so I speak."

Jesus Washes the Disciples' Feet

13 Now before the Feast of the Passover, when Jesus knew that His hour had come that He should depart from this world to the Father, having loved His own who were in the world, He loved them to the end.

[2]And supper being ended,[a] the devil having already put it into the heart of Judas Iscariot, Simon's *son,* to betray Him, [3]Jesus, knowing that the Father had given all things into His hands, and that He had come from God and was going to God, [4]rose from supper and laid aside His garments, took a towel and girded Himself. [5]After that, He poured water into a basin and began to wash the disciples' feet, and to wipe *them* with the towel with which He was girded. [6]Then He came to Simon Peter. And *Peter* said to Him, "Lord, are You washing my feet?"

[7]Jesus answered and said to him, "What I am doing you do not understand now, but you will know after this."

[8]Peter said to Him, "You shall never wash my feet!"

Jesus answered him, "If I do not wash you, you have no part with Me."

[9]Simon Peter said to Him, "Lord, not my feet only, but also *my* hands and *my* head!"

[10]Jesus said to him, "He who is bathed needs only to wash *his* feet, but is completely clean; and you are clean, but not all of you." [11]For He knew who would betray Him; therefore He said, "You are not all clean."

[12]So when He had washed their feet, taken His garments, and sat down again, He said to them, "Do you know what I have done to you? [13]You call Me Teacher

12:47 [a]**NU-Text reads *keep them.*** **13:2** [a]**NU-Text reads *And during supper.***

12:42 What is behind fear? Are you fearful to share your faith? Most of us are. To conquer it, see fear as a barometer of your pride. The more fear you have, the greater is the pride in your heart. Consider what we fear most. It is not that our faith will be shaken, or that someone will outwit us in an argument. Rather, it is a fear of looking foolish, of being called "religious" or "brainwashed," or of being rejected for our beliefs. A proud person is concerned about (fearful of) those things. Because he has a high view of himself, a proud person fears being ridiculed or rejected. However, a truly humble person is not concerned about himself and how others view him because his view of himself is low. It is the sin of pride that keeps us from coming to the cross, and it is the sin of pride that stops us preaching the old rugged cross. We do not want to carry its shame and reproach.

13:2 While "the devil made me do it" will not be a valid defense on Judgment Day, if more people would believe that the devil is at work in their lives, our prisons would be less populated and human suffering would be greatly reduced.

So often we hear of people feeling "compelled" to kill, and thinking the impulses were their own. If potential homosexuals understood the influence of unclean spirits, they would be less likely to follow every grimy impulse that comes into their minds. Those who believe that our battle is not against flesh and blood, but demonic personalities, will then be less prone to be tools of darkness.

and Lord, and you say well, for *so* I am. 14If I then, *your* Lord and Teacher, have washed your feet, you also ought to wash one another's feet. 15For I have given you an example, that you should do as I have done to you. 16Most assuredly, I say to you, a servant is not greater than his master; nor is he who is sent greater than he who sent him. 17If you know these things, blessed are you if you do them.

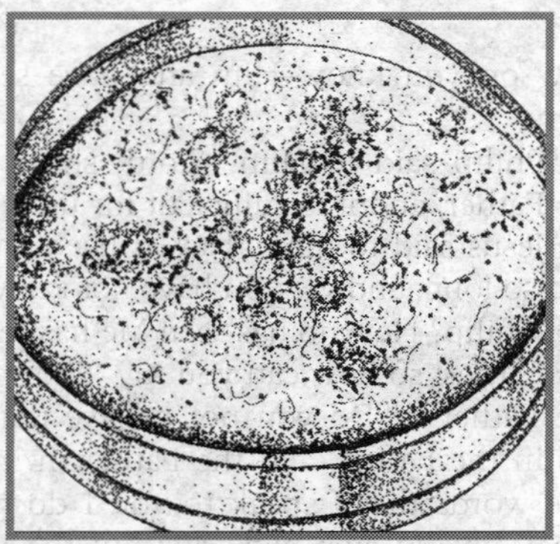

The Bible gave instructions on how to avoid diseases, thousands of years before man discovered their cause. See Heb. 11:3 comment.

Jesus Identifies His Betrayer

18"I do not speak concerning all of you. I know whom I have chosen; but that the Scripture may be fulfilled, *'He who eats bread with Me*[a] *has lifted up his heel against Me.'*[b] 19Now I tell you before it comes, that when it does come to pass, you may believe that I am *He*. 20Most assuredly, I say to you, he who receives whomever I send receives Me; and he who receives Me receives Him who sent Me."

21When Jesus had said these things, He was troubled in spirit, and testified and said, "Most assuredly, I say to you, one of you will betray Me." 22Then the disciples looked at one another, perplexed about whom He spoke.

23Now there was leaning on Jesus' bosom one of His disciples, whom Jesus loved. 24Simon Peter therefore motioned to him to ask who it was of whom He spoke.

25Then, leaning back[a] on Jesus' breast, he said to Him, "Lord, who is it?"

26Jesus answered, "It is he to whom I shall give a piece of bread when I have dipped *it*." And having dipped the bread, He gave *it* to Judas Iscariot, *the son* of Simon. 27Now after the piece of bread, Satan entered him. Then Jesus said to him, "What you do, do quickly." 28But no one at the table knew for what reason He said this to him. 29For some thought, because Judas had the money box, that Jesus had said to him, "Buy *those things* we need for the feast," or that he should give something to the poor.

30Having received the piece of bread, he then went out immediately. And it was night.

The New Commandment

31So, when he had gone out, Jesus said, "Now the Son of Man is glorified, and God is glorified in Him. 32If God is glorified in Him, God will also glorify Him in Himself, and glorify Him immediately. 33Little children, I shall be with you a little while longer. You will seek Me; and as I said to the Jews, 'Where I am going, you cannot come,' so now I say to you. 34A new commandment I give to you, that you love one another; as I have loved you, that you also love one another. 35By this all will know that you are My disciples, if you have love for one another."

Jesus Predicts Peter's Denial

36Simon Peter said to Him, "Lord, where are You going?"

Jesus answered him, "Where I am going you cannot follow Me now, but you shall follow Me afterward."

37Peter said to Him, "Lord, why can I not follow You now? I will lay down my life for Your sake."

13:18 [a]NU-Text reads *My bread.* [b]Psalm 41:9 13:25 [a]NU-Text and M-Text add *thus.*

QUESTIONS & OBJECTIONS

14:6

"It's intolerant to say that Jesus is the only way to God!"

Jesus is the One who said that He is the only way to the Father. For Christians to say that there are other ways to find peace with God is to bear false testimony. In one sweeping statement, Jesus discards all other religions as a means of finding forgiveness of sins. This agrees with other Scriptures: "Nor is there salvation in any other, for there is no other name under heaven given among men by which we must be saved" (Acts 4:12), and "For there is one God and one Mediator between God and men, the Man Christ Jesus" (1 Tim. 2:5). See also "Why Christianity?" on page xxv.

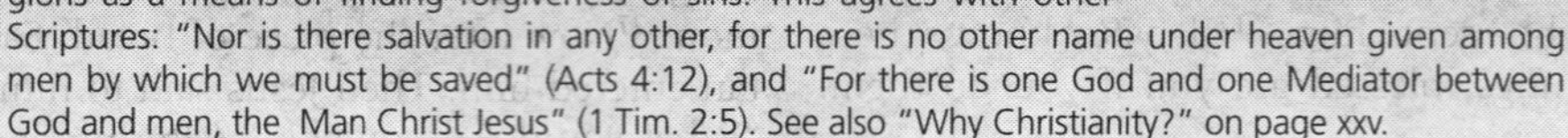

38Jesus answered him, "Will you lay
down your life for My sake? Most assuredly, I say to you, the rooster shall not
crow till you have denied Me three times.

The Way, the Truth, and the Life

14 "Let not your heart be troubled;
you believe in God, believe also in
Me. 2In My Father's house are many mansions;[a] if *it were* not *so,* I would have told
you. I go to prepare a place for you.[b]
3And if I go and prepare a place for you,
I will come again and receive you to Myself; that where I am, *there* you may be
also. 4And where I go you know, and the
way you know." 5Thomas said to Him,
"Lord, we do not know where You are going, and how can we know the way?" 6Je-
sus said to him, "I am the way, the truth,
and the life. No one comes to the Father
except through Me.

The Father Revealed

7"If you had known Me, you would
have known My Father also; and from
now on you know Him and have seen
Him."

8Philip said to Him, "Lord, show us
the Father, and it is sufficient for us."

9Jesus said to him, "Have I been with
you so long, and yet you have not known
Me, Philip? He who has seen Me has seen
the Father; so how can you say, 'Show us
the Father'? 10Do you not believe that I
am in the Father, and the Father in Me?
The words that I speak to you I do not
speak on My own *authority;* but the Father who dwells in Me does the works.
11Believe Me that I *am* in the Father and
the Father in Me, or else believe Me for
the sake of the works themselves.

The Answered Prayer

12"Most assuredly, I say to you, he who
believes in Me, the works that I do he will
do also; and greater *works* than these he

14:2 [a]Literally *dwellings* [b]NU-Text adds a word which would cause the text to read either *if it were not so, would I have told you that I go to prepare a place for you?* or *if it were not so I would have told you; for I go to prepare a place for you.*

14:2 Faith in God clears the muddy waters of fear. The Christian who has confidence in Jesus Christ knows that his eternal footsteps have been ordered by the Lord, and that there is a mansion prepared for him that his wildest imaginations could not conceive. If these things weren't so, Jesus would have told us. *He is not a liar.* His word is sure and steadfast, a mooring for the soul, and those who come into the harbor of a calm faith in God have perfect peace in the troubled storms of this world.

14:3 "We talk about heaven being so far away. It is within speaking distance to those who belong there. Heaven is a prepared place for a prepared people." *Dwight L. Moody*

14:6 Jesus' unique words: *Paige Patterson* stated, "It comes down to a question of truth. Every false religious expression is a religion of darkness. That doesn't mean there are no good things in that faith. But if Jesus is to be taken seriously when He says, 'No one comes to the Father but through Me,' every other proposal is one of darkness." See John 14:21 comment.

14:10 Was Jesus God in human form? See John 17:22.

QUESTIONS & OBJECTIONS

14:21

"I made a commitment, but nothing happened."

Some people do not get past "square one" because they trust in their feelings rather than God. His promises are true, despite our feelings. If I make a promise to my wife, that promise is true whether she is feeling happy or sad. If she doubts my word, then she brings a slur to my integrity.

Anyone who genuinely repents and trusts in Christ will be saved. The Bible makes this promise: "He who has My commandments and keeps them, it is he who loves Me. And he who loves Me will be loved by My Father, and I will love him and manifest Myself to him" (John 14:21). There is the promise, and there is the condition. Any person who loves and obeys Jesus will begin a supernatural relationship with Him and the Father. He said, "And this is eternal life, that they may know You, the only true God, and Jesus Christ whom You have sent" (John 17:3). That does not mean you will hear voices or see visions. God will instead make you a new person from within. He will send His Spirit to live within you. You will have a new heart with new desires. You will suddenly become conscious of God and His creation. The Bible will open up to you and become a living Word, and you will have an inner witness that you are saved, that your name is written in heaven, and that death has lost its sting (1 John 5:10–12).

will do, because I go to My Father. 13And
whatever you ask in My name, that I will
do, that the Father may be glorified in the
Son. 14If you ask[a] anything in My name,
I will do *it*.

Jesus Promises Another Helper

15"If you love Me, keep[a] My commandments. 16And I will pray the Father,
and He will give you another Helper, that
He may abide with you forever— 17the
Spirit of truth, whom the world cannot
receive, because it neither sees Him nor
knows Him; but you know Him, for He
dwells with you and will be in you. 18I will
not leave you orphans; I will come to you.

Indwelling of the Father and the Son

19"A little while longer and the world
will see Me no more, but you will see Me.
Because I live, you will live also. 20At that
day you will know that I *am* in My Father,
and you in Me, and I in you. 21He who
has My commandments and keeps them,
it is he who loves Me. And he who loves
Me will be loved by My Father, and I will
love him and manifest Myself to him."
22Judas (not Iscariot) said to Him,
"Lord, how is it that You will manifest
Yourself to us, and not to the world?"
23Jesus answered and said to him, "If
anyone loves Me, he will keep My word;
and My Father will love him, and We will
come to him and make Our home with
him. 24He who does not love Me does not
keep My words; and the word which you
hear is not Mine but the Father's who sent
Me.

The Gift of His Peace

25"These things I have spoken to you
while being present with you. 26But the

14:14 [a]NU-Text adds *Me*. 14:15 [a]NU-Text reads *you will keep*.

14:14 In 1 Kings 3:5, the LORD appeared to Solomon in a dream by night, and said, "Ask! What shall I give you?" God asks us the same question. Be like Solomon and ask for wisdom. God promises to give it liberally (James 1:5). He who gets wisdom loves his own soul (Prov. 19:8). If you have wisdom, you will think right, do right, and speak right. Remember: He who wins souls is wise (Prov. 11:30).

14:15 We show our love for God by our obedience. If we do not obey, we do not truly love Him (see vv. 23,24). There are many who call Him "Lord, Lord," but do not do what He says. Matthew 7:21–23 tells us their fearful fate.

14:21 Jesus' unique words: Jesus promises that He and the Father will reveal themselves to all who love and obey Him. This is the ultimate challenge to any skeptic. See John 17:5 comment.

SPRINGBOARDS FOR PREACHING AND WITNESSING

Revolting Natives

15:13 An African chief got wind of a mutiny being planned in his tribe. In an effort to quash the revolt, he called the tribe together and said that *anyone* caught in rebellion would be given one hundred lashes, *without mercy*.

A short time later, to the chief's dismay he found that his own brother was behind the revolt. He was trying to overthrow him so he could be head of the tribe. Everyone thought the chief would break his word. But being a just man, he had his brother tied to a tree. Then he had himself tied next to him, *and he took those one hundred lashes across his own bare flesh, in his brother's place*. In doing so, he not only kept his word (justice was done), but he also demonstrated his great love and forgiveness toward his brother.

Helper, the Holy Spirit, whom the Father
will send in My name, He will teach you
all things, and bring to your remembrance all things that I said to you.
27 Peace I leave with you, My peace I give
to you; not as the world gives do I give to
you. Let not your heart be troubled, neither let it be afraid. 28 You have heard Me
say to you, 'I am going away and coming
back to you.' If you loved Me, you would
rejoice because I said,[a] 'I am going to the
Father,' for My Father is greater than I.
29 "And now I have told you before it
comes, that when it does come to pass,
you may believe. 30 I will no longer talk
much with you, for the ruler of this
world is coming, and he has nothing in
Me. 31 But that the world may know that I
love the Father, and as the Father gave
Me commandment, so I do. Arise, let us
go from here.

The True Vine

15 "I am the true vine, and My Father
is the vinedresser. 2 Every branch
in Me that does not bear fruit He takes
away;[a] and every *branch* that bears fruit
He prunes, that it may bear more fruit.
3 You are already clean because of the
word which I have spoken to you. 4 Abide
in Me, and I in you. As the branch cannot
bear fruit of itself, unless it abides in the
vine, neither can you, unless you abide
in Me.
5 "I am the vine, you *are* the branches.
He who abides in Me, and I in him, bears
much fruit; for without Me you can do
nothing. 6 If anyone does not abide in Me,
he is cast out as a branch and is withered;
and they gather them and throw *them*
into the fire, and they are burned. 7 If you
abide in Me, and My words abide in you,
you will[a] ask what you desire, and it shall
be done for you. 8 By this My Father is
glorified, that you bear much fruit; so
you will be My disciples.

Love and Joy Perfected

9 "As the Father loved Me, I also have
loved you; abide in My love. 10 If you
keep My commandments, you will abide
in My love, just as I have kept My Father's
commandments and abide in His love.
11 "These things I have spoken to you,
that My joy may remain in you, and *that*

14:28 [a]NU-Text omits *I said*. **15:2** [a]Or *lifts up* **15:7** [a]NU-Text omits *you will*.

14:28 Bible contradiction? Skeptics argue that this verse contradicts John 10:30: "I and My Father are one." Is Jesus equal to or lesser than God?

Jesus was God manifest in human form (see John 1:1–14). He was one with God in His preexistence (before He came to this earth), but in His earthly form He was "made a little lower than the angels, for the suffering of death crowned with glory and honor, that He, by the grace of God, might taste death for everyone" (Heb. 2:9). In His incarnation He was made lower than the Father in that He set aside the glory He had in heaven and in His human weakness He became tired, hungry, and thirsty, and was limited to time and space.

your joy may be full. 12This is My commandment, that you love one another as I have loved you. 13Greater love has no one than this, than to lay down one's life for his friends. 14You are My friends if you do whatever I command you. 15No longer do I call you servants, for a servant does not know what his master is doing; but I have called you friends, for all things that I heard from My Father I have made known to you. 16You did not choose Me, but I chose you and appointed you that you should go and bear fruit, and *that* your fruit should remain, that whatever you ask the Father in My name He may give you. 17These things I command you, that you love one another.

> There must be true and deep conviction of sin. This the preacher must labor to produce, for where this is not felt, the new birth has not taken place.
>
> **CHARLES SPURGEON**

The World's Hatred

18"If the world hates you, you know that it hated Me before *it hated* you. 19If you were of the world, the world would love its own. Yet because you are not of the world, but I chose you out of the world, therefore the world hates you. 20Remember the word that I said to you, 'A servant is not greater than his master.' If they persecuted Me, they will also persecute you. If they kept My word, they will keep yours also. 21But all these things they will do to you for My name's sake, because they do not know Him who sent Me. 22If I had not come and spoken to them, they would have no sin, but now they have no excuse for their sin. 23He who hates Me hates My Father also. 24If I had not done among them the works which no one else did, they would have no sin; but now they have seen and also hated both Me and My Father. 25But *this happened* that the word might be fulfilled which is written in their law, *'They hated Me without a cause.'*[a]

The Coming Rejection

26"But when the Helper comes, whom I shall send to you from the Father, the Spirit of truth who proceeds from the Father, He will testify of Me. 27And you also will bear witness, because you have been with Me from the beginning.

16 "These things I have spoken to you, that you should not be made to stumble. 2They will put you out of the synagogues; yes, the time is coming that whoever kills you will think that he offers God service. 3And these things they will do to you[a] because they have not known the Father nor Me. 4But these things I have told you, that when the[a] time comes, you may remember that I told you of them.

"And these things I did not say to you at the beginning, because I was with you.

The Work of the Holy Spirit

5"But now I go away to Him who sent Me, and none of you asks Me, 'Where are You going?' 6But because I have said these things to you, sorrow has filled your heart. 7Nevertheless I tell you the truth. It is to your advantage that I go away; for if I do not go away, the Helper will not come to you; but if I depart, I will send Him to you. 8And when He has come, He will convict the world of sin, and of righteousness, and of judgment: 9of sin, because they do not believe in Me; 10of righteousness, because I go to My Father and you see Me no more; 11of judgment,

15:25 [a]Psalm 69:4 16:3 [a]NU-Text and M-Text omit *to you.* 16:4 [a]NU-Text reads *their.*

15:18–21 Some preachers promise a life of peace and happiness, but the Bible promises something else: *"all* who desire to live godly in Christ Jesus *will* suffer persecution" (2 Tim. 3:12). See Matt. 10:16 and Phil. 1:29 comments.

because the ruler of this world is judged.
12"I still have many things to say to
you, but you cannot bear *them* now.
13However, when He, the Spirit of truth,
has come, He will guide you into all
truth; for He will not speak on His own
authority, but whatever He hears He will
speak; and He will tell you things to come.
14He will glorify Me, for He will take of
what is Mine and declare *it* to you. 15All
things that the Father has are Mine.
Therefore I said that He will take of Mine
and declare *it* to you.[a]

Sorrow Will Turn to Joy

16"A little while, and you will not see
Me; and again a little while, and you will
see Me, because I go to the Father."
17Then *some* of His disciples said
among themselves, "What is this that He
says to us, 'A little while, and you will not
see Me; and again a little while, and you
will see Me'; and, 'because I go to the
Father'?" 18They said therefore, "What is
this that He says, 'A little while'? We do
not know what He is saying."
19Now Jesus knew that they desired to
ask Him, and He said to them, "Are you
inquiring among yourselves about what I
said, 'A little while, and you will not see
Me; and again a little while, and you will
see Me'? 20Most assuredly, I say to you
that you will weep and lament, but the
world will rejoice; and you will be sorrowful, but your sorrow will be turned
into joy. 21A woman, when she is in labor,
has sorrow because her hour has come;
but as soon as she has given birth to the
child, she no longer remembers the anguish, for joy that a human being has
been born into the world. 22Therefore

16:15 [a]NU-Text and M-Text read *He takes of Mine and will declare it to you.*

16:8–11 The Holy Spirit's role in salvation. The question may arise about the Holy Spirit's role in the salvation of sinners. The answer is clear from Scripture. We are drawn by, convicted by, born of, and kept by the Holy Spirit. Why then do we need to use the Law when witnessing? Why don't we just leave the salvation of sinners up to the Holy Spirit? Simply because, just as God has condescended to choose the foolishness of preaching to save those who believe, so He has chosen the moral Law to bring the knowledge of sin.

Jesus Himself tells us how the Holy Spirit works in the salvation of the lost. He said that when the Holy Spirit comes "He will convict the world of sin [which is *transgression* of the Law—1 John 3:4], and of righteousness [which is *of* the Law—Rom. 8:4], and of judgment [which is *by* the Law—Rom. 2:12]." So when we use the Law to bring the knowledge of sin to the lost, we simply become instruments the Holy Spirit uses to lead sinners to the Savior. See also Acts 10:38 comment.

"When 100 years ago earnest scholars decreed that the Law had no relationship to the preaching of the gospel, they deprived the Holy Spirit in the area where their influence prevailed of the only instrument with which He had ever armed Himself to prepare sinners for grace." *Paris Reidhead*

"The Holy Spirit convicts us…He shows us the Ten Commandments; the Law is the schoolmaster that leads us to Christ. We look in the mirror of the Ten Commandments, and we see ourselves in that mirror." *Billy Graham*

16:9 Why will sinners go to hell? Much damage has been done to the cause of the gospel by telling the world that they will go to hell "because they don't believe in Jesus." This makes no sense to the ungodly. It seems unreasonable that God would eternally damn them for not believing something. However, the verse can be explained this way: If a man jumps out of a plane without a parachute, he will perish because he transgressed the law of gravity. Had he put on a parachute, he would have been saved. In one sense, he perished because he didn't put on the parachute. But the primary reason he died was because he broke the law of gravity.

If a sinner refuses to trust in Jesus Christ before he passes through the door of death, he will perish. This isn't because he refused to trust the Savior, but because he transgressed the Law of God. Had he "put on the Lord Jesus Christ" (Rom. 13:14), he would have been saved; but because he refused to repent, he will suffer the full consequences of his sin. Sin is not "failing to believe in Jesus." Sin is "transgression of the Law" (1 John 3:4, KJV).

16:22 Jesus said, "Blessed are those who mourn, for they shall be comforted" (Matt. 5:4). As Christians, we can rejoice even while we truly sorrow—because our rejoicing is in the hope of heaven.

QUESTIONS & OBJECTIONS

17:3 *"I don't believe God is knowable."*

It is amazing how it's human nature to assume that because we believe or don't believe something, that makes it true. Some may not believe in the law of gravity, and may feel they have "evidence" to back up their belief. However, gravity exists whether they believe in it or not. The truth is, God is knowable. Jesus testified, "And this is eternal life, that they may know You, the only true God, and Jesus Christ whom You have sent" (John 17:3). We not only have the testimony of the Scriptures to tell us this, but we have the testimony of multitudes of Christians who know the Lord personally. It is more truthful to say, "I don't *want* to know God." Sinful man runs from Him as did Adam in the garden of Eden. See also Hos. 2:20 comment.

you now have sorrow; but I will see you again and your heart will rejoice, and your joy no one will take from you.

23"And in that day you will ask Me nothing. Most assuredly, I say to you, whatever you ask the Father in My name He will give you. 24Until now you have asked nothing in My name. Ask, and you will receive, that your joy may be full.

Jesus Christ Has Overcome the World

25"These things I have spoken to you in figurative language; but the time is coming when I will no longer speak to you in figurative language, but I will tell you plainly about the Father. 26In that day you will ask in My name, and I do not say to you that I shall pray the Father for you; 27for the Father Himself loves you, because you have loved Me, and have believed that I came forth from God. 28I came forth from the Father and have come into the world. Again, I leave the world and go to the Father."

29His disciples said to Him, "See, now You are speaking plainly, and using no figure of speech! 30Now we are sure that You know all things, and have no need that anyone should question You. By this we believe that You came forth from God."

31Jesus answered them, "Do you now believe? 32Indeed the hour is coming, yes, has now come, that you will be scattered, each to his own, and will leave Me alone. And yet I am not alone, because the Father is with Me. 33These things I have spoken to you, that in Me you may have peace. In the world you will[a] have tribulation; but be of good cheer, I have overcome the world."

Jesus Prays for Himself

17 Jesus spoke these words, lifted up His eyes to heaven, and said: "Father, the hour has come. Glorify Your Son, that Your Son also may glorify You, 2as You have given Him authority over all flesh, that He should[a] give eternal life to as many as You have given Him. 3And this is eternal life, that they may know You, the only true God, and Jesus Christ whom You have sent. 4I have glorified You on the earth. I have finished the work which You have given Me to do. 5And now, O Father, glorify Me together with Yourself, with the glory which I had with You before the world was.

16:33 [a]NU-Text and M-Text omit *will*. 17:2 [a]M-Text reads *shall*.

17:5 Jesus' unique words: Jesus declared that He was with the Father before the world came into existence, and that the Father loved Him before the foundation of the world (v. 24). Hebrews 7:3 tells us that He had no beginning. He not only existed before Abraham (John 8:58), He existed before the creation of the world (John 1:1–3).

Jesus Prays for His Disciples

6“I have manifested Your name to the
men whom You have given Me out of the
world. They were Yours, You gave them
to Me, and they have kept Your word.
7Now they have known that all things
which You have given Me are from You.
8For I have given to them the words
which You have given Me; and they have
received *them,* and have known surely
that I came forth from You; and they have
believed that You sent Me.

9“I pray for them. I do not pray for the
world but for those whom You have
given Me, for they are Yours. 10And all
Mine are Yours, and Yours are Mine, and
I am glorified in them. 11Now I am no
longer in the world, but these are in the
world, and I come to You. Holy Father,
keep through Your name those whom
You have given Me,[a] that they may be one
as We *are.* 12While I was with them in the
world,[a] I kept them in Your name. Those
whom You gave Me I have kept;[b] and
none of them is lost except the son of
perdition, that the Scripture might be fulfilled. 13But now I come to You, and these
things I speak in the world, that they may
have My joy fulfilled in themselves. 14I
have given them Your word; and the
world has hated them because they are
not of the world, just as I am not of the
world. 15I do not pray that You should
take them out of the world, but that You
should keep them from the evil one.
16They are not of the world, just as I am
not of the world. 17Sanctify them by Your
truth. Your word is truth. 18As You sent
Me into the world, I also have sent them
into the world. 19And for their sakes I
sanctify Myself, that they also may be
sanctified by the truth.

Jesus Prays for All Believers

20“I do not pray for these alone, but
also for those who will[a] believe in Me
through their word; 21that they all may be
one, as You, Father, *are* in Me, and I in

17:11 [a]NU-Text and M-Text read *keep them through Your name which You have given Me.* 17:12 [a]NU-Text omits *in the world.* [b]NU-Text reads *in Your name which You gave Me. And I guarded them;* (or *it;*). 17:20 [a]NU-Text and M-Text omit *will.*

17:14 Do you feel discouraged by negative reactions to the gospel? You shouldn’t. According to the Gospels, the religious leaders tried to kill Jesus ten times. Let’s look to Scripture and see what happened when Paul preached the biblical gospel:

- The crowd began “contradicting and blaspheming.” (Acts 13:45)
- Paul and Barnabas were persecuted and thrown out of the region. (Acts 13:50)
- The crowd plotted to stone them, forcing them to flee. (Acts 14:5)
- Paul was stoned and left for dead. (Acts 14:19)
- Both Paul and Silas were beaten with “many stripes” and thrown in prison. (Acts 16:23)
- Paul’s hearers “opposed him and blasphemed.” (Acts 18:6)
- His hearers were “full of wrath” and seized Paul’s companions. (Acts 19:26–29)
- The Holy Spirit warned Paul that bonds and afflictions awaited him wherever he preached the gospel. (Acts 20:23)
- His listeners called for his death. (Acts 22:21,22)
- As soon as he began to speak, he was smacked in the mouth. (Acts 23:1,2)
- After Paul spoke there was “great dissension” in the crowd and he was nearly “pulled to pieces.” (Acts 23:10)
- More than forty Jews conspired to murder him. (Acts 23:12,13)
- He is called a “plague,” a “creator of dissension,” and a “ringleader” of a “sect.” (Acts 24:5)

17:18 “Evangelism is not a professional job for a few trained men, but is instead the unrelenting responsibility of every person who belongs to the company of Jesus.” *Elton Trueblood*

17:21 “Has it ever occurred to you that one hundred pianos all tuned to the same fork are automatically tuned to each other? They are of one accord by being tuned, not to each other, but to another standard to which each one must individually bow. So one hundred worshipers [meeting] together, each one looking away to Christ, are in heart nearer to each other than they could possibly be, were they to become ‘unity’ conscious and turn their eyes away from God to strive for closer fellowship.” *A. W. Tozer*

You; that they also may be one in Us, that
the world may believe that You sent Me.
22And the glory which You gave Me I
have given them, that they may be one
just as We are one: 23I in them, and You
in Me; that they may be made perfect in
one, and that the world may know that
You have sent Me, and have loved them
as You have loved Me.

24"Father, I desire that they also whom
You gave Me may be with Me where I am,
that they may behold My glory which You
have given Me; for You loved Me before
the foundation of the world. 25O righteous
Father! The world has not known You, but
I have known You; and these have known
that You sent Me. 26And I have declared to
them Your name, and will declare *it,* that
the love with which You loved Me may be
in them, and I in them."

Betrayal and Arrest in Gethsemane

18 When Jesus had spoken these
words, He went out with His disciples over the Brook Kidron, where there
was a garden, which He and His disciples
entered. 2And Judas, who betrayed Him,
also knew the place; for Jesus often met
there with His disciples. 3Then Judas, having received a detachment *of troops,* and
officers from the chief priests and Pharisees, came there with lanterns, torches,
and weapons. 4Jesus therefore, knowing
all things that would come upon Him,
went forward and said to them, "Whom
are you seeking?"

5They answered Him, "Jesus of Nazareth."

Jesus said to them, "I am *He.*" And Judas, who betrayed Him, also stood with
them. 6Now when He said to them, "I am
He," they drew back and fell to the
ground.

7Then He asked them again, "Whom
are you seeking?"

And they said, "Jesus of Nazareth."

8Jesus answered, "I have told you that

"Let men of science and learning expound their knowledge and prize and probe with their researches every detail of the records which have been preserved to us from those dim ages. All they will do is fortify the grand simplicity and essential accuracy of the recorded truths which have lighted so far the pilgrimage of men."

Winston Churchill

I am *He.* Therefore, if you seek Me, let
these go their way," 9that the saying might
be fulfilled which He spoke, "Of those
whom You gave Me I have lost none."

10Then Simon Peter, having a sword,
drew it and struck the high priest's servant, and cut off his right ear. The servant's
name was Malchus.

11So Jesus said to Peter, "Put your
sword into the sheath. Shall I not drink
the cup which My Father has given Me?"

Before the High Priest

12Then the detachment *of troops* and
the captain and the officers of the Jews
arrested Jesus and bound Him. 13And
they led Him away to Annas first, for he
was the father-in-law of Caiaphas who
was high priest that year. 14Now it was

17:22 Was Jesus God in human form? See Col. 1:15,16.

Caiaphas who advised the Jews that it was expedient that one man should die for the people.

Peter Denies Jesus

15 And Simon Peter followed Jesus, and so *did* another[a] disciple. Now that disciple was known to the high priest, and went with Jesus into the courtyard of the high priest. 16 But Peter stood at the door outside. Then the other disciple, who was known to the high priest, went out and spoke to her who kept the door, and brought Peter in. 17 Then the servant girl who kept the door said to Peter, "You are not also *one* of this Man's disciples, are you?"

He said, "I am not."

18 Now the servants and officers who had made a fire of coals stood there, for it was cold, and they warmed themselves. And Peter stood with them and warmed himself.

Jesus Questioned by the High Priest

19 The high priest then asked Jesus about His disciples and His doctrine.

20 Jesus answered him, "I spoke openly to the world. I always taught in synagogues and in the temple, where the Jews always meet,[a] and in secret I have said nothing. 21 Why do you ask Me? Ask those who have heard Me what I said to them. Indeed they know what I said."

22 And when He had said these things, one of the officers who stood by struck Jesus with the palm of his hand, saying, "Do You answer the high priest like that?"

23 Jesus answered him, "If I have spoken evil, bear witness of the evil; but if well, why do you strike Me?"

24 Then Annas sent Him bound to Caiaphas the high priest.

Peter Denies Twice More

25 Now Simon Peter stood and warmed himself. Therefore they said to him, "You are not also *one* of His disciples, are you?"

He denied *it* and said, "I am not!"

26 One of the servants of the high priest, a relative *of him* whose ear Peter cut off, said, "Did I not see you in the garden with Him?" 27 Peter then denied again; and immediately a rooster crowed.

In Pilate's Court

28 Then they led Jesus from Caiaphas to the Praetorium, and it was early morning. But they themselves did not go into the Praetorium, lest they should be defiled, but that they might eat the Passover. 29 Pilate then went out to them and said, "What accusation do you bring against this Man?"

30 They answered and said to him, "If He were not an evildoer, we would not have delivered Him up to you."

31 Then Pilate said to them, "You take Him and judge Him according to your law."

Therefore the Jews said to him, "It is not lawful for us to put anyone to death," 32 that the saying of Jesus might be fulfilled which He spoke, signifying by what death He would die.

33 Then Pilate entered the Praetorium again, called Jesus, and said to Him, "Are You the King of the Jews?"

34 Jesus answered him, "Are you speaking for yourself about this, or did others tell you this concerning Me?"

35 Pilate answered, "Am I a Jew? Your own nation and the chief priests have delivered You to me. What have You done?"

36 Jesus answered, "My kingdom is not of this world. If My kingdom were of this world, My servants would fight, so that I should not be delivered to the Jews; but now My kingdom is not from here."

18:15 [a]M-Text reads *the other.* 18:20 [a]NU-Text reads *where all the Jews meet.*

18:17 Who of us who know the Lord cannot identify with Peter? We have felt the paralyzing power of the fear of man grip our hearts and fasten our lips. Peter stood by the fire and warmed his cold body, but what he really needed was a fiery coal from the altar of God to touch his frozen lips (see Isa. 6:5–8).

SPRINGBOARDS FOR PREACHING AND WITNESSING

What Is Truth?

18:38 What do we truly know in this life—of what can we be sure? To find out, I have some strange questions for you. Here is the first. When is "now"? Tell me if you can. Seriously, pinpoint "now." You can never pinpoint when it is, because by the time you do, it is gone. "Now" is elusive. In an instant it becomes "then." Here is another question. Where is "here"? Point to it. If you say it is where you are, six billion others on earth would disagree with you. "Here" is where they are, and to them, where you are pointing is "there." Another one: Which way is "up"? If you point toward the sky, millions of folks Down-under would disagree with you. If they point to the sky to show the direction of up, they will be pointing in the opposite direction. Remember, we live on a big, round ball. The same applies with the direction of down. Here is another one. What color is the sky on a cloudless day? If you said "blue," you are wrong. It is colorless. If you don't believe it, view it from space. There is no "sky" at all. How about a "sunrise"? Have you ever seen one? No one has. The sun never actually "rises" or "sets." Remember, it is the earth turning that creates that impression.

So, of what can you be sure in this life? Some say death and taxes. That is not true either—plenty of people avoid taxes. So if we cannot be sure of anything but death, what on earth is reality (truth)? If you leave God out of the equation, you have no answer. What is truth? Is there any such thing? Do you know? Again, if you ignore Almighty God (the "I AM" who transcends time and space), you will end up as lost as the misguided Pilate of Scripture as he stood bewildered in front of Jesus Christ. The Roman governor asked the rhetorical question, "What is truth?" Pilate gazed on Him who was Truth itself (see John 14:6), and you are just as close to Him (see Rom. 10:8,9; Acts 17:27,28). Are you going to wash your hands of Jesus Christ, like Pilate did? Or will you obey Him, and know the truth of the words, "And you shall know the truth, and the truth shall make you free" (John 8:32)?

37Pilate therefore said to Him, "Are You a king then?"

Jesus answered, "You say *rightly* that I am a king. For this cause I was born, and for this cause I have come into the world, that I should bear witness to the truth. Everyone who is of the truth hears My voice."

38Pilate said to Him, "What is truth?" And when he had said this, he went out again to the Jews, and said to them, "I find no fault in Him at all.

Taking the Place of Barabbas

39"But you have a custom that I should release someone to you at the Passover. Do you therefore want me to release to you the King of the Jews?"

40Then they all cried again, saying, "Not this Man, but Barabbas!" Now Barabbas was a robber.

The Soldiers Mock Jesus

19 So then Pilate took Jesus and scourged *Him*. 2And the soldiers twisted a crown of thorns and put *it* on His head, and they put on Him a purple robe. 3Then they said,[a] "Hail, King of the Jews!" And they struck Him with their hands.

4Pilate then went out again, and said to them, "Behold, I am bringing Him out to you, that you may know that I find no fault in Him."

Pilate's Decision

5Then Jesus came out, wearing the crown of thorns and the purple robe. And *Pilate* said to them, "Behold the Man!"

6Therefore, when the chief priests and officers saw Him, they cried out, saying,

19:3 [a]NU-Text reads *And they came up to Him and said.*

19:1,2 It was plain that the direction this Pilate was taking was not a good one, and he knew it. He could see that it was going to land him on ground he preferred not to touch. He tried vainly to alter his course by having Jesus scourged, in the hope that it would appease the Jews. After the whipping, the twisted soldiers twisted a crown of thorns and put it on His head. This was perhaps symbolic of the Messiah taking upon Himself the curse placed upon creation when Adam sinned (Gen. 3:18).

"Crucify *Him*, crucify *Him!*"

Pilate said to them, "You take Him and crucify *Him*, for I find no fault in Him."

[7]The Jews answered him, "We have a law, and according to our[a] law He ought to die, because He made Himself the Son of God."

[8]Therefore, when Pilate heard that saying, he was the more afraid, [9]and went again into the Praetorium, and said to Jesus, "Where are You from?" But Jesus gave him no answer.

[10]Then Pilate said to Him, "Are You not speaking to me? Do You not know that I have power to crucify You, and power to release You?"

[11]Jesus answered, "You could have no power at all against Me unless it had been given you from above. Therefore the one who delivered Me to you has the greater sin."

[12]From then on Pilate sought to release Him, but the Jews cried out, saying, "If you let this Man go, you are not Caesar's friend. Whoever makes himself a king speaks against Caesar."

[13]When Pilate therefore heard that saying, he brought Jesus out and sat down in the judgment seat in a place that is called *The* Pavement, but in Hebrew, Gabbatha.
[14]Now it was the Preparation Day of the Passover, and about the sixth hour. And he said to the Jews, "Behold your King!"

[15]But they cried out, "Away with *Him*, away with *Him!* Crucify Him!"

Pilate said to them, "Shall I crucify your King?"

The chief priests answered, "We have no king but Caesar!"

[16]Then he delivered Him to them to be crucified. Then they took Jesus and led *Him* away.[a]

The King on a Cross

[17]And He, bearing His cross, went out to a place called *the Place* of a Skull, which is called in Hebrew, Golgotha,
[18]where they crucified Him, and two others with Him, one on either side, and Jesus in the center. [19]Now Pilate wrote a title and put *it* on the cross. And the writing was:

JESUS OF NAZARETH,
THE KING OF THE JEWS.

[20]Then many of the Jews read this title, for the place where Jesus was crucified was near the city; and it was written in Hebrew, Greek, *and* Latin.

[21]Therefore the chief priests of the Jews said to Pilate, "Do not write, 'The King of the Jews,' but, 'He said, "I am the King of the Jews." ' "

[22]Pilate answered, "What I have written, I have written."

> We must school and train ourselves to deal personally with the unconverted. We must not excuse ourselves, but force ourselves to the irksome task until it becomes easy.
>
> **CHARLES SPURGEON**

[23]Then the soldiers, when they had crucified Jesus, took His garments and made four parts, to each soldier a part, and also the tunic. Now the tunic was without seam, woven from the top in one piece. [24]They said therefore among themselves, "Let us not tear it, but cast lots for it, whose it shall be," that the Scripture might be fulfilled which says:

"They divided My garments among them,
And for My clothing they cast lots."[a]

Therefore the soldiers did these things.

Behold Your Mother

[25]Now there stood by the cross of Jesus His mother, and His mother's sister, Mary the *wife* of Clopas, and Mary Magdalene. [26]When Jesus therefore saw His mother, and the disciple whom He loved standing by, He said to His mother, "Woman, behold your son!" [27]Then He said

19:7 [a]NU-Text reads *the law.* 19:16 [a]NU-Text omits *and led Him away.* 19:24 [a]Psalm 22:18

QUESTIONS & OBJECTIONS

19:33,34 **"Is it possible that Jesus simply fainted on the cross, and revived while He was in the tomb?"**

Jesus had been whipped and beaten, and was bleeding from His head, back, hands, and feet for at least six hours. While he was on the cross, a soldier pierced His side with a spear and blood and water gushed out. Professional soldiers would certainly have completed their assigned task and ensured His death. See details on the resurrection, see pages 1486 and 1716.

"It is impossible that a being who had stolen half-dead out of the sepulcher, who crept about weak and ill, wanting medical treatment, who required bandaging, strengthening, and indulgence, and who still at last yielded to his sufferings, could have given to the disciples the impression that he was a conqueror over death and the grave, the Prince of Life: an impression which lay at the bottom of their future ministry. Such a resuscitation could only have weakened the impression which he had made upon them in life and in death, at the most could only have given it an elegiac voice, but could by no possibility have changed their sorrow into enthusiasm, have elevated their reverence into worship." *David Friedrich Strauss, New Life of Jesus* (quoted in *Who Moved the Stone?* by *Frank Morison*)

"Clearly the weight of historical and medical evidence indicates that Jesus was dead before the wound to His side was inflicted and supports the traditional view that the spear, thrust between His right rib, probably perforated not only the right lung but also the pericardium and heart and thereby ensured His death. Accordingly, interpretations based on the assumption that Jesus did not die on the cross appear to be at odds with modern medical knowledge." *Journal of the American Medical Society*, March 21, 1986

to the disciple, "Behold your mother!" And from that hour that disciple took her to his own *home*.

It Is Finished

28After this, Jesus, knowing[a] that all things were now accomplished, that the Scripture might be fulfilled, said, "I thirst!" 29Now a vessel full of sour wine was sitting there; and they filled a sponge with sour wine, put *it* on hyssop, and put *it* to His mouth. 30So when Jesus had received the sour wine, He said, "It is finished!" And bowing His head, He gave up His spirit.

Jesus' Side Is Pierced

31Therefore, because it was the Preparation *Day*, that the bodies should not remain on the cross on the Sabbath (for that Sabbath was a high day), the Jews asked Pilate that their legs might be broken, and *that* they might be taken away. 32Then the soldiers came and broke the legs of the first and of the other who was crucified with Him. 33But when they came to Jesus and saw that He was already dead, they did not break His legs. 34But one of the soldiers pierced His side with a spear, and immediately blood and water came out. 35And he who has seen has testified, and his testimony is true; and he knows that he is telling the truth, so that you may believe. 36For these things

19:28 [a]M-Text reads *seeing*.

19:29 Messianic prophecy fulfilled: "They also gave me gall for my food, and for my thirst they gave me vinegar to drink" (Psa. 69:21). See John 19:33,36 comment.

19:31,32 Archaeology confirms the Bible. "During the past four decades, spectacular discoveries have produced data corroborating the historical backdrop of the Gospels. In 1968, for example, the skeletal remains of a crucified man were found in a burial cave in northern Jerusalem. . . There was evidence that his wrists may have been pierced with nails. The knees had been doubled up and turned sideways and an iron nail (still lodged in the heel bone of one foot) driven through both heels. The shinbones appeared to have been broken, perhaps corroborating the Gospel of John." *Jeffery L. Sheler*, "Is the Bible True?" *Reader's Digest*, June 2000

were done that the Scripture should be fulfilled, *"Not one of His bones shall be broken."*[a] [37]And again another Scripture says, *"They shall look on Him whom they pierced."*[a]

Jesus Buried in Joseph's Tomb

[38]After this, Joseph of Arimathea, being a disciple of Jesus, but secretly, for fear of the Jews, asked Pilate that he might take away the body of Jesus; and Pilate gave *him* permission. So he came and took the body of Jesus. [39]And Nicodemus, who at first came to Jesus by night, also came, bringing a mixture of myrrh and aloes, about a hundred pounds. [40]Then they took the body of Jesus, and bound it in strips of linen with the spices, as the custom of the Jews is to bury. [41]Now in the place where He was crucified there was a garden, and in the garden a new tomb in which no one had yet been laid. [42]So there they laid Jesus, because of the Jews' Preparation *Day,* for the tomb was nearby.

The Empty Tomb

20 Now the first *day* of the week Mary Magdalene went to the tomb early, while it was still dark, and saw *that* the stone had been taken away from the tomb. [2]Then she ran and came to Simon Peter, and to the other disciple, whom Jesus loved, and said to them, "They have taken away the Lord out of the tomb, and we do not know where they have laid Him."

[3]Peter therefore went out, and the other disciple, and were going to the tomb. [4]So they both ran together, and the other disciple outran Peter and came to the tomb first. [5]And he, stooping down and looking in, saw the linen cloths lying *there;* yet he did not go in. [6]Then Simon Peter came, following him, and went into the tomb; and he saw the linen cloths lying *there,* [7]and the handkerchief that had been around His head, not lying with the linen cloths, but folded together in a place by itself. [8]Then the other disciple, who came to the tomb first, went in also; and he saw and believed. [9]For as yet they did not know the Scripture, that He must rise again from the dead. [10]Then the disciples went away again to their own homes.

Mary Magdalene Sees the Risen Lord

[11]But Mary stood outside by the tomb weeping, and as she wept she stooped down *and looked* into the tomb. [12]And she saw two angels in white sitting, one at the head and the other at the feet, where the body of Jesus had lain. [13]Then they said to her, "Woman, why are you weeping?"

She said to them, "Because they have taken away my Lord, and I do not know where they have laid Him."

[14]Now when she had said this, she turned around and saw Jesus standing *there,* and did not know that it was Jesus. [15]Jesus said to her, "Woman, why are you weeping? Whom are you seeking?"

She, supposing Him to be the gardener, said to Him, "Sir, if You have carried Him away, tell me where You have laid Him, and I will take Him away."

[16]Jesus said to her, "Mary!"

She turned and said to Him,[a] "Rabboni!" (which is to say, Teacher).

[17]Jesus said to her, "Do not cling to Me, for I have not yet ascended to My Father; but go to My brethren and say to them, 'I am ascending to My Father and your Father, and *to* My God and your God.' "

[18]Mary Magdalene came and told the

19:36 [a]Exodus 12:46; Numbers 9:12; Psalm 34:20 **19:37** [a]Zechariah 12:10 **20:16** [a]NU-Text adds *in Hebrew.*

19:33,36 Messianic prophecy fulfilled: As Exod. 12:46 instructs, none of the Passover lamb's bones were to be broken. When Jesus, our Passover Lamb, was sacrificed for our sins, none of His bones were broken. See Acts 2:31 comment.

QUESTIONS & OBJECTIONS

"Seeing is believing. If I can't see it, I don't believe it exists."

We believe in many things that we can't see. (See Optical Illusions on page 1280.) Ask a skeptic if he has ever seen the wind. Has he seen history? Has he ever seen his brain? We see the *effects* of the wind, but the wind is invisible. We have records of history, but it is by "faith" that we believe certain historical events happened. Television waves are invisible, but an antenna and a receiver can detect their presence. The unregenerate man likewise has a "receiver." However, the receiver (his spirit) is dead because of sin (Eph. 2:1). He needs to be plugged into the life of God; then he will come alive and be aware of the invisible spiritual realm.

disciples that she had seen the Lord,[a] and
that He had spoken these things to her.

The Apostles Commissioned

[19]Then, the same day at evening, being the first *day* of the week, when the
doors were shut where the disciples were
assembled,[a] for fear of the Jews, Jesus
came and stood in the midst, and said to
them, "Peace *be* with you." [20]When He
had said this, He showed them *His* hands
and His side. Then the disciples were
glad when they saw the Lord.

[21]So Jesus said to them again, "Peace
to you! As the Father has sent Me, I also
send you." [22]And when He had said this,
He breathed on *them,* and said to them,
"Receive the Holy Spirit. [23]If you forgive
the sins of any, they are forgiven them; if
you retain the *sins* of any, they are retained."

Seeing and Believing

[24]Now Thomas, called the Twin, one
of the twelve, was not with them when
Jesus came. [25]The other disciples therefore said to him, "We have seen the Lord."

So he said to them, "Unless I see in
His hands the print of the nails, and put
my finger into the print of the nails, and
put my hand into His side, I will not believe."

[26]And after eight days His disciples
were again inside, and Thomas with
them. Jesus came, the doors being shut,
and stood in the midst, and said, "Peace
to you!" [27]Then He said to Thomas,
"Reach your finger here, and look at My
hands; and reach your hand *here,* and put
it into My side. Do not be unbelieving,

20:18 [a]NU-Text reads *disciples, "I have seen the Lord,"*...
20:19 [a]NU-Text omits *assembled.*

20:18 The first evangelist was a woman. She took the good news of the resurrection to the men, who were hiding behind locked doors

20:22 Why did Jesus breathe on His disciples and say, "Receive the Holy Spirit," when He had already told them that the Holy Spirit could come only after His ascension (John 16:7)? Perhaps it was at that moment that the Body of Christ on earth was conceived within the womb. Perhaps it was then that He *planted* the seed of the life of the Church, but after the gestation period, on the Day of Pentecost, the Body of Christ was then *birthed* on earth.

The first seed of Adam's race began with the breath of God (Gen. 2:7), but the "last Adam" began with the breath of God in Christ. The first man had been formed from the dust of the ground, and when the Lord God breathed into his nostrils the breath of life, he became a "living being," but Christ was made a "life-giving spirit" (1 Cor. 15:45).

Jesus picked up fallen dust from the ground of Israel, shaped them for three years, and now He breathed life into them, as He did in Genesis with the dust He had formed into Adam's body. It was but a gentle breath at conception, which became a rushing mighty wind on the Day of Pentecost (Acts 2:2), and caused the living Body of Christ to stand on its feet on earth.

20:23 If someone has turned from sin and is trusting in Jesus Christ alone for his eternal salvation, every believer has power to inform him that his sin is forgiven, based on his professed faith in the Savior.

but believing."
28And Thomas answered and said to
Him, "My Lord and my God!"
29Jesus said to him, "Thomas,[a] because you have seen Me, you have believed. Blessed *are* those who have not
seen and *yet* have believed."

That You May Believe

30And truly Jesus did many other signs
in the presence of His disciples, which
are not written in this book; 31but these
are written that you may believe that Jesus is the Christ, the Son of God, and that
believing you may have life in His name.

Breakfast by the Sea

21 After these things Jesus showed
Himself again to the disciples at
the Sea of Tiberias, and in this way He
showed *Himself:* 2Simon Peter, Thomas
called the Twin, Nathanael of Cana in
Galilee, the *sons* of Zebedee, and two others of His disciples were together. 3Simon
Peter said to them, "I am going fishing."
They said to him, "We are going with
you also." They went out and immediately[a] got into the boat, and that night
they caught nothing. 4But when the
morning had now come, Jesus stood on
the shore; yet the disciples did not know
that it was Jesus. 5Then Jesus said to
them, "Children, have you any food?"
They answered Him, "No."
6And He said to them, "Cast the net on
the right side of the boat, and you will
find *some.*" So they cast, and now they
were not able to draw it in because of the
multitude of fish.
7Therefore that disciple whom Jesus
loved said to Peter, "It is the Lord!" Now
when Simon Peter heard that it was the
Lord, he put on *his* outer garment (for he
had removed it), and plunged into the
sea. 8But the other disciples came in the
little boat (for they were not far from
land, but about two hundred cubits),
dragging the net with fish. 9Then, as soon
as they had come to land, they saw a fire
of coals there, and fish laid on it, and
bread. 10Jesus said to them, "Bring some
of the fish which you have just caught."

A dead calm is our enemy, a storm may prove our helper. Controversy may arouse thought, and through thought may come the Divine change.

CHARLES SPURGEON

11Simon Peter went up and dragged
the net to land, full of large fish, one hundred and fifty-three; and although there
were so many, the net was not broken.
12Jesus said to them, "Come *and* eat breakfast." Yet none of the disciples dared ask
Him, "Who are You?"—knowing that it
was the Lord. 13Jesus then came and took

20:29 [a]NU-Text and M-Text omit *Thomas.* **21:3** [a]NU-Text omits *immediately.*

20:26 Scientific facts in the Bible. Babies are circumcised on the eighth day because this is the day that the coagulating factor in the blood, called *prothrombin*, is the highest. Medical science has discovered that this is when the human body's immune system is at its peak.

Just as the eighth day was the God-given timing for circumcision (Gen. 17:12), there is a God-given timing for every person who is "circumcised with the circumcision made without hands" (Col. 2:11). Jesus appeared to Thomas on the eighth day. What Thomas saw cut away the flesh of his unbelieving heart. He became a Jew inwardly as his circumcision became "that of the heart, in the Spirit, not in the letter" (Rom. 2:29). Thomas bowed his heart to Jesus of Nazareth as his Lord and his God. He needed a miracle, and God graciously gave it to him.

Each of us is dealt with individually by God; some get incredible spiritual manifestations at conversion. Others quietly trust the promises of God, and God reveals Himself to them through faith rather than feelings of great joy. What matters is not *how* each of us came to Christ, but that we became new creatures in Christ, because that is the *real* miracle that proves the reality of salvation. This is what Paul meant when he wrote, "For in Christ Jesus neither circumcision nor uncircumcision avails anything, but a new creation" (Gal. 6:15).

"God, if you are there, strike me dead!"
(See Prov. 3:34 comment.)

Benito Mussolini

the bread and gave it to them, and likewise the fish.
[14]This *is* now the third time Jesus
showed Himself to His disciples after He
was raised from the dead.

Jesus Restores Peter

[15]So when they had eaten breakfast,
Jesus said to Simon Peter, "Simon, *son* of
Jonah,[a] do you love Me more than
these?"
He said to Him, "Yes, Lord; You know
that I love You."
He said to him, "Feed My lambs."
[16]He said to him again a second time,
"Simon, *son* of Jonah,[a] do you love Me?"
He said to Him, "Yes, Lord; You know
that I love You."
He said to him, "Tend My sheep."
[17]He said to him the third time, "Simon,
son of Jonah,[a] do you love Me?" Peter was
grieved because He said to him the third
time, "Do you love Me?"
And he said to Him, "Lord, You know
all things; You know that I love You."
Jesus said to him, "Feed My sheep.
[18]Most assuredly, I say to you, when you
were younger, you girded yourself and
walked where you wished; but when you
are old, you will stretch out your hands,
and another will gird you and carry *you*
where you do not wish." [19]This He spoke,
signifying by what death he would glorify
God. And when He had spoken this, He
said to him, "Follow Me."

The Beloved Disciple and His Book

[20]Then Peter, turning around, saw the
disciple whom Jesus loved following,
who also had leaned on His breast at the
supper, and said, "Lord, who is the one
who betrays You?" [21]Peter, seeing him, said
to Jesus, "But Lord, what *about* this man?"
[22]Jesus said to him, "If I will that he remain till I come, what *is that* to you? You
follow Me."
[23]Then this saying went out among
the brethren that this disciple would not
die. Yet Jesus did not say to him that he
would not die, but, "If I will that he remain till I come, what *is that* to you?"
[24]This is the disciple who testifies of
these things, and wrote these things; and
we know that his testimony is true.
[25]And there are also many other things
that Jesus did, which if they were written
one by one, I suppose that even the
world itself could not contain the books
that would be written. Amen.

21:15 [a]NU-Text reads *John*. **21:16** [a]NU-Text reads *John*.
21:17 [a]NU-Text reads *John*.

"As the Father has sent Me,
I also send you."

JOHN 20:21

Helpful Verses to Use When Witnessing

Exod. 20:1–17 (the Ten Commandments)

Psa. 51 (as an example of a prayer of repentance)

Isa. 53:5,6: But He was wounded for our transgressions, He was bruised for our iniquities; the chastisement for our peace was upon Him, and by His stripes we are healed. All we like sheep have gone astray; we have turned, every one, to his own way; and the LORD has laid on Him the iniquity of us all.

Isa. 64:6: …all our righteousnesses are like filthy rags…

Ezek. 18:4: "… the soul who sins shall die."

Matt. 5:27,28: "…whoever looks at a woman to lust for her has already committed adultery with her in his heart."

Matt. 7:21: "Not everyone who says to Me, 'Lord, Lord,' shall enter the kingdom of heaven, but he who does the will of My Father in heaven."

Matt. 12:36: "But I say to you that for every idle word men may speak, they will give account of it in the day of judgment."

Luke 13:3: "…unless you repent you will all likewise perish."

Luke 16:15: "You are those who justify yourselves before men, but God knows your hearts. For what is highly esteemed among men is an abomination in the sight of God."

John 3:3: "…unless one is born again, he cannot see the kingdom of God."

John 3:16: "For God so loved the world that He gave His only begotten Son, that whoever believes in Him should not perish but have everlasting life."

John 3:18: "He who believes in Him is not condemned; but he who does not believe is condemned already, because he has not believed in the name of the only begotten Son of God."

John 3:36: "He who believes in the Son has everlasting life; and he who does not believe the Son shall not see life, but the wrath of God abides on him."

John 14:6: Jesus said to him, "I am the way, the truth, and the life. No one comes to the Father except through Me."

John 14:21: "He who has My commandments and keeps them, it is he who loves Me. And he who loves Me will be loved by My Father, and I will love him and manifest Myself to him."

Acts 4:12: "Nor is there salvation in any other, for there is no other name under heaven given among men by which we must be saved."

Acts 17:30,31: "Truly, these times of ignorance God overlooked, but now commands all men everywhere to repent, because He has appointed a day on which He will judge the world in righteousness… "

Rom. 2:5,6: But in accordance with your hardness and your impenitent heart you are treasuring up for yourself wrath in the day of wrath and revelation of the righteous judgment of God, who "will render to each one according to his deeds."

Rom. 3:12: "There is none who does good, no, not one."

Rom. 5:8: But God demonstrates His own love toward us, in that while we were still sinners, Christ died for us.

1 Cor. 6:9,10: Neither fornicators, nor idolaters, nor adulterers, nor homosexuals, … nor thieves…will inherit the kingdom of God.

Col. 1:21: And you, who once were alienated and enemies in your mind by wicked works…

Eph. 2:8,9: For by grace you have been saved through faith, and that not of yourselves; it is the gift of God, not of works, lest anyone should boast.

Heb. 9:27: And as it is appointed for men to die once, but after this the judgment…

James 2:10: For whoever shall keep the whole law, and yet stumble in one point, he is guilty of all.

James 2:19: Even the demons believe—and tremble!

1 John 1:9,10: If we confess our sins, He is faithful and just to forgive us our sins and to cleanse us from all unrighteousness. If we say that we have not sinned, we make Him a liar, and His word is not in us.

1 John 3:15: Whoever hates his brother is a murderer…

Rev. 21:8: "…all liars shall have their part in the lake which burns with fire…"

Acts

Prologue

1 The former account I made, O Theophilus, of all that Jesus began both to do and teach, [2]until the day in which He was taken up, after He through the Holy Spirit had given commandments to the apostles whom He had chosen, [3]to whom He also presented Himself alive after His suffering by many infallible proofs, being seen by them during forty days and speaking of the things pertaining to the kingdom of God.

The Holy Spirit Promised

[4]And being assembled together with *them,* He commanded them not to depart from Jerusalem, but to wait for the Promise of the Father, "which," *He said,* "you have heard from Me; [5]for John truly baptized with water, but you shall be baptized with the Holy Spirit not many days from now." [6]Therefore, when they had come together, they asked Him, saying, "Lord, will You at this time restore the kingdom to Israel?" [7]And He said to them, "It is not for you to know times or seasons which the Father has put in His own authority. [8]But you shall receive power when the Holy Spirit has come upon you; and you shall be witnesses to Me[a] in Jerusalem, and in all Judea and Samaria, and to the end of the earth."

Jesus Ascends to Heaven

[9]Now when He had spoken these things, while they watched, He was taken up, and a cloud received Him out of their sight. [10]And while they looked steadfastly toward heaven as He went up, behold, two men stood by them in white apparel, [11]who also said, "Men of Galilee, why do you stand gazing up into heaven? This *same* Jesus, who was taken up from you into heaven, will so come in like manner

1:8 [a]NU-Text reads *My witnesses.*

1:5 Water baptism doesn't save us. In Acts 2:38, Peter's hearers repented and believed the gospel *before* they were baptized. In Acts 10:47, those who believed the gospel received the Holy Spirit (they passed from death to life) *before* they were baptized.

1:8 Have you received the Holy Spirit (been born again)? If so, then you have been given power to witness and been sent into all the world to share the gospel. See page 1386 and Prov. 29:25 comment.

"If a person is filled with the Holy Spirit, his witness will not be optional or mandatory—it will be inevitable." *Richard Halverson*

1:10,11 The inference is, "Don't stand here gazing up into the heavens. God has granted everlasting life to sinful humanity. Go and wait for the power to take the gospel to the world." We haven't been saved to gaze up to heaven, but to take the light to those who sit in the dark shadow of death. How can any person, who professes to have the love of God in him sit passively while sinners die daily and go to hell? Paul said, "Woe is me if I do not preach the gospel!" (1 Cor. 9:16).

1:11 Second coming of Jesus: See 1 Cor. 4:5.

QUESTIONS & OBJECTIONS

1:3 "Your religion is all about faith."

Much of what we do in life has its foundation in trust. We trust our dentist when he drills, our taxi driver when he drives, our pilots when they fly us. We trust our history books, our teachers, and some still even trust politicians. Marriage is a trust relationship. So are business partnerships and friendships. We trust elevators, planes, cars, brakes, chairs, doctors, surgeons, brokers, and television anchors. We place our faith in these items and people based on evidence that they are trustworthy. This is why it's hard to understand why skeptics mock the thought of trust in God.

The questioner's statement implies that Christians are living by a naïve, "blind" faith based on something for which we have no evidence, when the opposite is the case. Our faith is rational and reasonable, and is based on credible, verifiable, historical evidence. The God who created us has given us all the evidence we need to come to know Him, and He invites us, "Come now, and let us reason together" (Isa. 1:18).

The fact that some do not recognize the evidence doesn't mean it is not there. God has given light to every man (see John 1:9)—through this wonderful creation, through the undeniable voice of the conscience, and through plain old common sense. We have the Bible's thousands of fulfilled prophecies, "many infallible proofs" of the resurrection (see Acts 1:3), and He even promises to reveal Himself to those who obey Him (see John 14:21).

It is also important to explain the difference between believing something (the Bible), and trusting Someone (Jesus Christ). Skeptics think that a Christian is someone who simply "believes" in God's existence. When the Bible speaks of "faith" in God, it is not a reference to an intellectual acknowledgment that He exists (we all intuitively know that). It is speaking of an implicit *trust* in His person and His promises. There's nothing difficult about having trust or "faith" when the One you are trusting is utterly trustworthy. For evidence of God, see also Rom. 1:20 comment.

as you saw Him go into heaven."

The Upper Room Prayer Meeting

12 Then they returned to Jerusalem
from the mount called Olivet, which is
near Jerusalem, a Sabbath day's journey.
13 And when they had entered, they went
up into the upper room where they were
staying: Peter, James, John, and Andrew;
Philip and Thomas; Bartholomew and
Matthew; James *the son* of Alphaeus and
Simon the Zealot; and Judas *the son* of
James. 14 These all continued with one accord in prayer and supplication,[a] with the women and Mary the mother of Jesus, and with His brothers.

Matthias Chosen

15 And in those days Peter stood up in
the midst of the disciples[a] (altogether the
number of names was about a hundred
and twenty), and said, 16 "Men *and*
brethren, this Scripture had to be fulfilled, which the Holy Spirit spoke before by the mouth of David concerning Judas, who became a guide to those who arrested Jesus; 17 for he was numbered with
us and obtained a part in this ministry."

18 (Now this man purchased a field
with the wages of iniquity; and falling

1:14 [a]NU-Text omits *and supplication.* 1:15 [a]NU-Text reads *brethren.*

1:14 Prayer—the secret weapon: See Acts 4:24.

1:18 Bible contradiction? Skeptics argue that this verse contradicts Matt. 27:5, which says that Judas "went and hanged himself." So how did Judas die?

Note that this verse doesn't state how he died; it just mentions what happened to his body. So there is no contradiction. The body begins to decompose shortly after death, and one exposed to air will decompose even more quickly. It seems that Judas's dead body was left hanging, and fell because of decomposition. This seems very clear in that we are told that his "entrails gushed out."

headlong, he burst open in the middle and all his entrails gushed out. [19]And it became known to all those dwelling in Jerusalem; so that field is called in their own language, Akel Dama, that is, Field of Blood.)

[20]"For it is written in the Book of Psalms:

'Let his dwelling place be desolate,
And let no one live in it';[a]

and,

'Let[b] another take his office.'[c]

[21]"Therefore, of these men who have accompanied us all the time that the Lord Jesus went in and out among us, [22]beginning from the baptism of John to that day when He was taken up from us, one of these must become a witness with us of His resurrection."

[23]And they proposed two: Joseph called Barsabas, who was surnamed Justus, and Matthias. [24]And they prayed and said, "You, O Lord, who know the hearts of all, show which of these two You have chosen [25]to take part in this ministry and apostleship from which Judas by transgression fell, that he might go to his own place." [26]And they cast their lots, and the lot fell on Matthias. And he was numbered with the eleven apostles.

Coming of the Holy Spirit

2 When the Day of Pentecost had fully come, they were all with one accord[a] in one place. [2]And suddenly there came a sound from heaven, as of a rushing mighty wind, and it filled the whole house where they were sitting. [3]Then there appeared to them divided tongues, as of fire, and *one* sat upon each of them. [4]And they were all filled with the Holy Spirit and began to speak with other tongues, as the Spirit gave them utterance.

The Crowd's Response

[5]And there were dwelling in Jerusalem Jews, devout men, from every nation under heaven. [6]And when this sound occurred, the multitude came together, and were confused, because everyone heard them speak in his own language. [7]Then they were all amazed and marveled, saying to one another, "Look, are not all these who speak Galileans? [8]And how *is it that* we hear, each in our own language in which we were born? [9]Parthians and Medes and Elamites, those dwelling in Mesopotamia, Judea and Cappadocia, Pontus and Asia, [10]Phrygia and Pamphylia, Egypt and the parts of Libya adjoining Cyrene, visitors from Rome, both Jews and proselytes, [11]Cretans and Arabs—we hear them speaking in our own tongues the wonderful works of God." [12]So they were all amazed and perplexed, saying to one another, "Whatever could this mean?"

[13]Others mocking said, "They are full of new wine."

Peter's Sermon

[14]But Peter, standing up with the eleven, raised his voice and said to them, "Men of Judea and all who dwell in Jerusalem, let this be known to you, and heed my words. [15]For these are not drunk, as you suppose, since it is *only* the third hour of the day. [16]But this is what was spoken by the prophet Joel:

[17]*'And it shall come to pass in the last days, says God,*

1:20 [a]Psalm 69:25 [b]Psalm 109:8 [c]Greek *episkopen,* position of overseer **2:1** [a]NU-Text reads *together.*

1:21–26 As Israel crossed over the Jordan on dry ground, God instructed them to place twelve stones as immovable witnesses—a memorial to tell the Israelite children what God had done for them (Josh. 4:1–7). Likewise, the Church was established with twelve witnesses so that we would know and tell what God has done for us through Christ.

POINTS FOR OPEN-AIR PREACHING

2:14

How to Draw a Crowd

One of the most difficult things to do is draw a crowd to hear the gospel. Today's society has been programmed to want immediate action, and open-air preaching isn't too attractive to guilty sinners. Therefore we have to be as wise as serpents and as gentle as doves. A serpent gets its heart's desire subtly. Our desire is for sinners to gather under the sound of the gospel.

Ask people passing by what they think is the greatest killer of drivers in the U.S. This stirs their curiosity. Some begin calling out "Alcohol!" or "Falling asleep at the wheel!" Tell them it's not and repeat the question a few more times, saying that you will give a dollar to the person who gets the answer. Tell them that they will never guess what it is that kills more drivers than anything else in America. A few more shouts emit from the crowd. People are now waiting around for the answer. What is it that kills more drivers than anything else in the United States? What is it that could be the death of you and me? You won't believe this, but it is "trees." Millions of them line our highways, waiting for a driver to kill. When one is struck, the tree stays still, sending the driver into eternity.

Then tell the crowd that you have another question for them. Ask what they think is the most common food on which people choke to death in U.S. restaurants. Over the next couple of minutes, go through the same scenario. People call out "Steak!" "Chicken bones!" Believe it or not, the answer is "hard-boiled egg yoke."

By now you have a crowd that is enjoying what is going on. Ask them what they think is the most dangerous job in America. Someone calls out "cop." It's not. Someone else may name another dangerous profession like "firefighter." Say, "Good one . . . but wrong." Give a suggestion by saying, "Why doesn't someone say 'electrician'?" Someone takes the suggestion and says, "Electrician!" Say, "Sorry, it's not electrician." The most dangerous job in the United States . . . is to be the president. Out of forty or so, four have been murdered while on the job.

Then tell the crowd you have another question: "Does anyone in the crowd consider himself to be a good person?" By now you will have noted who in the crowd has the self-confidence to speak out. Point to one or two and ask, "Sir, do you consider yourself to be a good person?" The Bible tells us that "most men will proclaim each his own goodness" (Prov. 20:6), and he does. He smiles and says, "Yes, I do consider myself to be a good person." Ask him if he has ever told a lie. Has he stolen, lusted, blasphemed, etc.? That's when all heaven breaks loose. There is conviction of sin. Sinners hear the gospel, and angels rejoice.

MORE QUESTIONS FOR CROWD DRAWING

- Who wrote, "Ask not what your country can do for you. Ask what you can do for your country"? *(President Kennedy's speechwriter)*
- What is the only fish that can blink with both eyes? *(A shark)*
- Who was John Lennon's first girlfriend? *(Thelma Pickles)*
- How long does it take the average person to fall asleep: 2 minutes, 7 minutes, or 4 hours? *(7 minutes)*
- How long is a goldfish's memory span: 3 seconds, 3 minutes, or 3 hours? *(3 seconds)*
- How many muscles does a cat have in each ear: 2, 32, or 426? *(32)*

That I will pour out of My Spirit on all flesh;
Your sons and your daughters shall prophesy,
Your young men shall see visions,
Your old men shall dream dreams.
18 *And on My menservants and on My maidservants*
I will pour out My Spirit in those days;
And they shall prophesy.
19 *I will show wonders in heaven above*
And signs in the earth beneath:
Blood and fire and vapor of smoke.
20 *The sun shall be turned into darkness,*
And the moon into blood,
Before the coming of the great and awesome day of the LORD.
21 *And it shall come to pass*
That whoever calls on the name of the LORD
Shall be saved.'[a]

2:21 [a]Joel 2:28–32

[22]"Men of Israel, hear these words: Jesus of Nazareth, a Man attested by God to
you by miracles, wonders, and signs
which God did through Him in your
midst, as you yourselves also know—
[23]Him, being delivered by the determined purpose and foreknowledge of
God, you have taken[a] by lawless hands,
have crucified, and put to death; [24]whom
God raised up, having loosed the pains of
death, because it was not possible that He
should be held by it. [25]For David says
concerning Him:

'I foresaw the LORD always before my face,
For He is at my right hand, that I may not be shaken.
[26]Therefore my heart rejoiced, and my tongue was glad;
Moreover my flesh also will rest in hope.
[27]For You will not leave my soul in Hades,
Nor will You allow Your Holy One to see corruption.
[28]You have made known to me the ways of life;
You will make me full of joy in Your presence.'[a]

[29]"Men *and* brethren, let *me* speak
freely to you of the patriarch David, that
he is both dead and buried, and his tomb
is with us to this day. [30]Therefore, being a
prophet, and knowing that God had
sworn with an oath to him that of the
fruit of his body, according to the flesh,
He would raise up the Christ to sit on his
throne,[a] [31]he, foreseeing this, spoke concerning the resurrection of the Christ,
that His soul was not left in Hades, nor
did His flesh see corruption. [32]This Jesus
God has raised up, of which we are all
witnesses. [33]Therefore being exalted to
the right hand of God, and having received from the Father the promise of the
Holy Spirit, He poured out this which
you now see and hear.
[34]"For David did not ascend into the
heavens, but he says himself:

'The Lord said to my Lord,
"Sit at My right hand,
[35]Till I make Your enemies Your footstool."'[a]

[36]"Therefore let all the house of Israel
know assuredly that God has made this
Jesus, whom you crucified, both Lord
and Christ."
[37]Now when they heard *this*, they were
cut to the heart, and said to Peter and the
rest of the apostles, "Men *and* brethren,
what shall we do?"
[38]Then Peter said to them, "Repent,
and let every one of you be baptized in

USING THE LAW IN EVANGELISM

2:37 Peter's audience was composed of "devout men" (v. 5) who were gathered at Pentecost to celebrate the giving of God's Law on Mount Sinai. Even though these were godly Jews, Peter told them that they were "lawless"—they had violated God's Law by murdering Jesus (v. 23). He drove home that fact by saying, "Therefore let all the house of Israel know assuredly that God has made this Jesus, *whom you crucified*, both Lord and Christ" (v. 36, emphasis added). It was then that they saw that their sin was personal. They were "cut to the heart" and cried out for help. Only after the Law convicted them of their guilt did Peter tell his hearers the good news of the fine being paid for them in Christ (v. 38).

2:23 [a]NU-Text omits *have taken*. 2:28 [a]Psalm 16:8–11
2:30 [a]NU-Text omits *according to the flesh, He would raise up the Christ* and completes the verse with *He would seat one on his throne.* 2:35 [a]Psalm 110:1

2:21 Salvation is possible for every person. See Rom. 10:13.

2:31 Messianic prophecy fulfilled: "For You will not leave my soul in Sheol, nor will You allow Your Holy One to see corruption" (Psa. 16:10). See 1 Pet. 2:24 comment.

2:38 Repentance—its necessity for salvation. See Acts 3:19.

PRINCIPLES OF GROWTH FOR THE NEW AND GROWING CHRISTIAN

2:38 *Water Baptism—Sprinkle or Immerse?*

The Bible says, "Repent, and let every one of you be baptized in the name of Jesus Christ for the remission of sins" (Acts 2:38). There is no question about whether you *should* be baptized. The questions are how, when, and by whom?

It would seem clear from Scripture that those who were baptized were fully immersed in water. Here's one reason why: "Now John also was baptizing in Aenon near Salim, because there was much water there" (John 3:23). If John were merely sprinkling believers, he would have needed only a cupful of water. Baptism by immersion also pictures our death to sin, burial, and resurrection to new life in Christ. (See Rom. 6:4; Col. 2:12.)

The Philippian jailer and his family were baptized at midnight, the same hour they believed (Acts 16:30–33). The Ethiopian eunuch was baptized as soon as he believed (Acts 8:35–37), as was Paul (Acts 9:17,18). Baptism is a step of obedience, and God blesses our obedience. So what are you waiting for?

Who should baptize you? It is clear from Scripture that other believers had the privilege, but check with your pastor; he may want the honor himself.

For the next principle of growth, see Mark 12:41–44 comment.

the name of Jesus Christ for the remission
of sins; and you shall receive the gift of
the Holy Spirit. 39For the promise is to
you and to your children, and to all who
are afar off, as many as the Lord our God
will call."

A Vital Church Grows

40And with many other words he testified and exhorted them, saying, "Be
saved from this perverse generation."
41Then those who gladly[a] received his
word were baptized; and that day about
three thousand souls were added *to them.*
42And they continued steadfastly in the
apostles' doctrine and fellowship, in the
breaking of bread, and in prayers. 43Then
fear came upon every soul, and many
wonders and signs were done through
the apostles. 44Now all who believed
were together, and had all things in common, 45and sold their possessions and
goods, and divided them among all, as
anyone had need.
46So continuing daily with one accord
in the temple, and breaking bread from
house to house, they ate their food with
gladness and simplicity of heart, 47praising God and having favor with all the
people. And the Lord added to the church[a] daily those who were being saved.

A Lame Man Healed

3 Now Peter and John went up together
to the temple at the hour of prayer,

2:41 [a]NU-Text omits *gladly.* 2:47 [a]NU-Text omits *to the church.*

2:41 "Isn't it staggering when you think that one sermon on the day of Pentecost produced 3,000 people? And we had some cities yesterday where 3,000 sermons were preached and nobody was saved. And it doesn't even faze us." *Leonard Ravenhill*

2:44–46 The need for church. "None of us is self-sufficient in our spiritual lives. We need God, and we need each other. A lot of people go to church because they think God takes roll. For them, the important thing is to make sure their name gets checked off every Sunday on the heavenly roster. But that's not the way it works. Church is not some kind of moral obligation, some habit or tradition that is 'the right thing to do.' Church is a place where we worship God, share our faith with the community of believers, build each other up, and get empowered to go out into the world and *live out our faith!*

"Similarly, some people think of their spiritual life as if they were one person in a telephone booth, talking to God on a private line. They don't want to be bothered by the demands of 'organized religion' and don't think they need anyone else. 'Oh yeah, I'm spiritual,' they say, 'I just don't like church.' To those folks I say: You cannot grow spiritually in isolation." *Rich DeVos*

POINTS FOR OPEN-AIR PREACHING

3:4

Crowd Etiquette

If you have other Christians with you, have them form an audience and look as though they are listening to your preaching. This will encourage others to stop and listen. Tell the Christians to never stand with their back to the preacher. I have seen open-air meetings when a fellow laborer is preaching, and what are the Christians doing? They are talking among themselves. Why then should anyone stop and listen if those in front of the speaker aren't even attentive? It is so easy to chat with friends when you've heard the gospel a million times before. I have found myself doing it, but it is so disheartening for the preacher to speak to the backs of a crowd.

Also, instruct Christians not to argue with hecklers. That will ruin an open-air meeting. I have seen an old lady hit a heckler with her umbrella and turn the crowd from listening to the gospel to watching the fight she has just started. Who can blame them? Remember, the enemy will do everything he can to distract your listeners. Don't let him. See 2 Tim. 2:24–26 comment.

the ninth *hour.* 2And a certain man lame
from his mother's womb was carried,
whom they laid daily at the gate of the
temple which is called Beautiful, to ask
alms from those who entered the temple;
3who, seeing Peter and John about to go
into the temple, asked for alms. 4And
fixing his eyes on him, with John, Peter
said, "Look at us." 5So he gave them his
attention, expecting to receive something
from them. 6Then Peter said, "Silver and
gold I do not have, but what I do have I
give you: In the name of Jesus Christ of
Nazareth, rise up and walk." 7And he
took him by the right hand and lifted
him up, and immediately his feet and
ankle bones received strength. 8So he,
leaping up, stood and walked and entered the temple with them—walking,
leaping, and praising God. 9And all the
people saw him walking and praising
God. 10Then they knew that it was he
who sat begging alms at the Beautiful
Gate of the temple; and they were filled
with wonder and amazement at what
had happened to him.

Preaching in Solomon's Portico

11Now as the lame man who was
healed held on to Peter and John, all the
people ran together to them in the porch
which is called Solomon's, greatly amazed.
12So when Peter saw *it,* he responded to
the people: "Men of Israel, why do you
marvel at this? Or why look so intently at
us, as though by our own power or godliness we had made this man walk? 13The
God of Abraham, Isaac, and Jacob, the
God of our fathers, glorified His Servant
Jesus, whom you delivered up and denied in the presence of Pilate, when he
was determined to let *Him* go. 14But you
denied the Holy One and the Just, and
asked for a murderer to be granted to
you, 15and killed the Prince of life, whom
God raised from the dead, of which we
are witnesses. 16And His name, through
faith in His name, has made this man
strong, whom you see and know. Yes, the
faith which *comes* through Him has given
him this perfect soundness in the presence of you all.

> It's not my job to convict or convert people; it's my job to *converse* with people. The Holy Spirit will do the work of convicting and converting.
>
> **CARL KERBY**

17"Yet now, brethren, I know that you
did *it* in ignorance, as *did* also your
rulers. 18But those things which God
foretold by the mouth of all His prophets,
that the Christ would suffer, He has thus
fulfilled. 19Repent therefore and be con-

3:19 Repentance—its necessity for salvation. See Acts 17:30.

verted, that your sins may be blotted out,
so that times of refreshing may come
from the presence of the Lord, 20and that
He may send Jesus Christ, who was
preached to you before,[a] 21whom heaven
must receive until the times of restoration
of all things, which God has spoken by
the mouth of all His holy prophets since
the world began. 22For Moses truly said
to the fathers, *'The LORD your God will
raise up for you a Prophet like me from
your brethren. Him you shall hear in all
things, whatever He says to you.* 23*And it
shall be that every soul who will not hear
that Prophet shall be utterly destroyed
from among the people.'*[a] 24Yes, and all
the prophets, from Samuel and those
who follow, as many as have spoken,
have also foretold[a] these days. 25You are
sons of the prophets, and of the covenant
which God made with our fathers, saying
to Abraham, *'And in your seed all the
families of the earth shall be blessed.'*[a]
26To you first, God, having raised up His
Servant Jesus, sent Him to bless you, in
turning away every one *of you* from your
iniquities."

Peter and John Arrested

4 Now as they spoke to the people, the
priests, the captain of the temple,
and the Sadducees came upon them,
2being greatly disturbed that they taught
the people and preached in Jesus the resurrection from the dead. 3And they laid
hands on them, and put *them* in custody
until the next day, for it was already
evening. 4However, many of those who
heard the word believed; and the number of the men came to be about five
thousand.

Addressing the Sanhedrin

5And it came to pass, on the next day,
that their rulers, elders, and scribes, 6as
well as Annas the high priest, Caiaphas,
John, and Alexander, and as many as
were of the family of the high priest, were
gathered together at Jerusalem. 7And
when they had set them in the midst,
they asked, "By what power or by what
name have you done this?"
8Then Peter, filled with the Holy Spirit,
said to them, "Rulers of the people and
elders of Israel: 9If we this day are judged
for a good deed *done* to a helpless man,
by what means he has been made well,
10let it be known to you all, and to all the
people of Israel, that by the name of Jesus
Christ of Nazareth, whom you crucified,
whom God raised from the dead, by Him
this man stands here before you whole.

> Moses could mediate on the law, Mohammed could brandish a sword, Buddha could give personal counsel, Confucius could offer wise sayings. But none of these men was qualified to offer an atonement for the sins of the world.
>
> **R. C. SPROUL**

11This is the *'stone which was rejected by
you builders, which has become the chief
cornerstone.'*[a] 12Nor is there salvation in
any other, for there is no other name under heaven given among men by which
we must be saved."

The Name of Jesus Forbidden

13Now when they saw the boldness of
Peter and John, and perceived that they
were uneducated and untrained men,
they marveled. And they realized that
they had been with Jesus. 14And seeing
the man who had been healed standing
with them, they could say nothing
against it. 15But when they had commanded them to go aside out of the
council, they conferred among themselves, 16saying, "What shall we do to
these men? For, indeed, that a notable
miracle has been done through them *is*
evident to all who dwell in Jerusalem,
and we cannot deny *it.* 17But so that it

3:20 [a]NU-Text and M-Text read *Christ Jesus, who was ordained for you before.* 3:23 [a]Deuteronomy 18:15, 18, 19 3:24 [a]NU-Text and M-Text read *proclaimed.* 3:25 [a]Genesis 22:18; 26:4; 28:14 4:11 [a]Psalm 118:22

4:12 *Is Suffering the Entrance to Heaven?*

A well-known televangelist once said on a worldwide TV talk show, "I believe that every person who died in the Holocaust went to heaven." He was very sincere, and if he was seeking the commendation of the world, he surely got it with that statement. Who wouldn't consider what he said to be utterly compassionate? However, let's look at the implications of his heartfelt beliefs. His statement seemed to limit salvation to the *Jews* who died in the Holocaust, because he added that "their blood laid a foundation for the nation of Israel." If the slaughtered Jews made it to heaven, did the many *Gypsies* who died in the Holocaust also obtain eternal salvation? If his statement includes Gentiles, is the salvation he spoke of limited to those who died at the hands of Nazis? Did the many *Frenchmen* who met their death at the hands of cruel Nazis go to heaven also?

Perhaps he was saying that the death of Jesus on the cross covered *all* of humanity, and that all will eventually be saved—something called "universalism." This means that salvation will also come to Hitler and the Nazis who killed the Jews. However, I doubt if he was saying that. Such a statement would have brought the scorn of his Jewish host, and of the world whose compassion has definite limits.

If pressed, he probably didn't mean that only the Jews in the camps went to heaven, because that smacks of *racism*. He was likely saying that those who died were saved because they died in such *tragic circumstances*. Then Jesus was lying when He said, "I am the way, the truth, and the life. No one comes to the Father except through Me" (John 14:6). There is another way to heaven: death in a Nazi concentration camp. Does that mean that the many Jews who died under *communism* went to heaven? Or is salvation limited to *German* concentration camps?

If their salvation came because of the grim circumstances surrounding their death, does a Jew therefore enter heaven after suffering for hours before dying in a car wreck... if he was killed by a drunk driver who happened to be German? Bear in mind that his suffering may have been much greater than someone who died within minutes in a Nazi gas chamber.

Many unsaved think we *can* merit entrance into heaven by our suffering. Their error was confirmed by this sincere, compassionate man of God. They may now disregard the truth, "Nor is there salvation in any other, for there is no other name under heaven given among men by which we must be saved" (Acts 4:12). They can now save themselves by the means of their own death ...if they suffer enough.

Imagine the damage done by saying that there is another means of salvation outside of Jesus Christ, on a program watched by untold millions around the world. Who on earth needs to repent and trust in Jesus, if millions entered the kingdom without being born again? No one.

spreads no further among the people, let
us severely threaten them, that from now
on they speak to no man in this name."
[18]So they called them and commanded them not to speak at all nor
teach in the name of Jesus. [19]But Peter
and John answered and said to them,
"Whether it is right in the sight of God to
listen to you more than to God, you
judge. [20]For we cannot but speak the
things which we have seen and heard."
[21]So when they had further threatened
them, they let them go, finding no way of
punishing them, because of the people,
since they all glorified God for what had
been done. [22]For the man was over forty
years old on whom this miracle of healing had been performed.

Prayer for Boldness

[23]And being let go, they went to their
own *companions* and reported all that the
chief priests and elders had said to them.
[24]So when they heard that, they raised

4:24 Fossil evidence points to creation. "The creation account in Genesis and the theory of evolution could not be reconciled. One must be right and the other wrong. The story of the fossils agrees with the account of Genesis. In the oldest rocks we did not find a series of fossils covering the gradual changes from the most primitive creatures to developed forms but rather, in the oldest rocks, developed species suddenly appeared. Between every species there was a complete absence of intermediate fossils." *D. B. Gower* (biochemist), "Scientist Rejects Evolution," *Kentish Times* (See also Jer. 27:5 comment.)

their voice to God with one accord and said: "Lord, You *are* God, who made heaven and earth and the sea, and all that is in them, 25who by the mouth of Your servant David[a] have said:

'Why did the nations rage,
And the people plot vain things?
26*The kings of the earth took their*
stand,
And the rulers were gathered together
Against the LORD *and against His*
Christ.'[a]

27"For truly against Your holy Servant Jesus, whom You anointed, both Herod and Pontius Pilate, with the Gentiles and the people of Israel, were gathered together 28to do whatever Your hand and Your purpose determined before to be done. 29Now, Lord, look on their threats, and grant to Your servants that with all boldness they may speak Your word, 30by stretching out Your hand to heal, and that signs and wonders may be done through the name of Your holy Servant Jesus."

31And when they had prayed, the place where they were assembled together was shaken; and they were all filled with the Holy Spirit, and they spoke the word of God with boldness.

Sharing in All Things

32Now the multitude of those who believed were of one heart and one soul; neither did anyone say that any of the things he possessed was his own, but they had all things in common. 33And with great power the apostles gave witness to the resurrection of the Lord Jesus. And great grace was upon them all. 34Nor was there anyone among them who lacked; for all who were possessors of lands or houses sold them, and brought the proceeds of the things that were sold, 35and laid *them* at the apostles' feet; and they distributed to each as anyone had need.

36And Joses,[a] who was also named Barnabas by the apostles (which is translated Son of Encouragement), a Levite of the country of Cyprus, 37having land, sold *it,* and brought the money and laid *it* at the apostles' feet.

Lying to the Holy Spirit

5 But a certain man named Ananias, with Sapphira his wife, sold a possession. 2And he kept back *part* of the proceeds, his wife also being aware *of it,* and brought a certain part and laid *it* at the apostles' feet. 3But Peter said, "Ananias, why has Satan filled your heart to lie to the Holy Spirit and keep back *part* of the price of the land for yourself? 4While it remained, was it not your own? And after it was sold, was it not in your own control? Why have you conceived this thing in your heart? You have not lied to men but to God."

5Then Ananias, hearing these words, fell down and breathed his last. So great fear came upon all those who heard these things. 6And the young men arose and wrapped him up, carried *him* out, and buried *him.*

7Now it was about three hours later when his wife came in, not knowing what had happened. 8And Peter answered her, "Tell me whether you sold the land for so much?"

She said, "Yes, for so much."

9Then Peter said to her, "How is it that you have agreed together to test the Spirit of the Lord? Look, the feet of those who

4:25 [a]NU-Text reads *who through the Holy Spirit, by the mouth of our father, Your servant David.* 4:26 [a]Psalm 2:1, 2 4:36 [a]NU-Text reads *Joseph.*

4:24 Prayer—the secret weapon: See Acts 12:12.

4:29 When we are afraid to witness to sinners, we can stand firmly upon the wonderful promise of God given in Isa. 41:10: We need not fear or be dismayed because He is with us. He will strengthen, help, and uphold us with His righteous right hand.

have buried your husband *are* at the
door, and they will carry you out."
10Then immediately she fell down at his
feet and breathed her last. And the young
men came in and found her dead, and
carrying *her* out, buried *her* by her husband. 11So great fear came upon all the
church and upon all who heard these
things.

Continuing Power in the Church

12And through the hands of the apostles many signs and wonders were done
among the people. And they were all
with one accord in Solomon's Porch. 13Yet
none of the rest dared join them, but the
people esteemed them highly. 14And believers were increasingly added to the
Lord, multitudes of both men and
women, 15so that they brought the sick
out into the streets and laid *them* on beds
and couches, that at least the shadow of
Peter passing by might fall on some of
them. 16Also a multitude gathered from
the surrounding cities to Jerusalem,
bringing sick people and those who were
tormented by unclean spirits, and they
were all healed.

Imprisoned Apostles Freed

17Then the high priest rose up, and all
those who *were* with him (which is the
sect of the Sadducees), and they were
filled with indignation, 18and laid their
hands on the apostles and put them in
the common prison. 19But at night an angel of the Lord opened the prison doors
and brought them out, and said, 20"Go,
stand in the temple and speak to the people all the words of this life."

21And when they heard *that,* they entered the temple early in the morning and
taught. But the high priest and those with
him came and called the council together, with all the elders of the children
of Israel, and sent to the prison to have
them brought.

Apostles on Trial Again

22But when the officers came and did
not find them in the prison, they returned and reported, 23saying, "Indeed
we found the prison shut securely, and
the guards standing outside[a] before the
doors; but when we opened them, we
found no one inside!" 24Now when the
high priest,[a] the captain of the temple,
and the chief priests heard these things,
they wondered what the outcome would
be. 25So one came and told them, saying,[a]
"Look, the men whom you put in prison
are standing in the temple and teaching
the people!"

26Then the captain went with the officers and brought them without violence,
for they feared the people, lest they
should be stoned. 27And when they had
brought them, they set *them* before the
council. And the high priest asked them,
28saying, "Did we not strictly command
you not to teach in this name? And look,

"We have been assured, Sir, in the Sacred Writings, that 'except the Lord build the house, they labor in vain that build it.' I firmly believe this; and I also believe that without his concurring aid we shall succeed in this political building no better than the builders of Babel."

Benjamin Franklin

5:23 [a]NU-Text and M-Text omit *outside.* 5:24 [a]NU-Text omits *the high priest.* 5:25 [a]NU-Text and M-Text omit *saying.*

you have filled Jerusalem with your doctrine, and intend to bring this Man's blood on us!"

29But Peter and the *other* apostles answered and said: "We ought to obey God rather than men. 30The God of our fathers raised up Jesus whom you murdered by hanging on a tree. 31Him God has exalted to His right hand *to be* Prince and Savior, to give repentance to Israel and forgiveness of sins. 32And we are His witnesses to these things, and *so* also *is* the Holy Spirit whom God has given to those who obey Him."

For the Bible's inspiration, see 2 Tim. 3:16 comment.

Gamaliel's Advice

33When they heard *this,* they were furious and plotted to kill them. 34Then one in the council stood up, a Pharisee named Gamaliel, a teacher of the law held in respect by all the people, and commanded them to put the apostles outside for a little while. 35And he said to them: "Men of Israel, take heed to yourselves what you intend to do regarding these men. 36For some time ago Theudas rose up, claiming to be somebody. A number of men, about four hundred, joined him. He was slain, and all who obeyed him were scattered and came to nothing. 37After this man, Judas of Galilee rose up in the days of the census, and drew away many people after him. He also perished, and all who obeyed him were dispersed. 38And now I say to you, keep away from these men and let them alone; for if this plan or this work is of men, it will come to nothing; 39but if it is of God, you cannot overthrow it—lest you even be found to fight against God."

40And they agreed with him, and when they had called for the apostles and beaten *them,* they commanded that they should not speak in the name of Jesus, and let them go. 41So they departed from the presence of the council, rejoicing that they were counted worthy to suffer shame for His[a] name. 42And daily in the temple, and in every house, they did not cease teaching and preaching Jesus *as* the Christ.

Seven Chosen to Serve

6 Now in those days, when *the number of* the disciples was multiplying, there arose a complaint against the Hebrews by the Hellenists,[a] because their widows were neglected in the daily distribution. 2Then the twelve summoned the multitude of the disciples and said, "It is not desirable that we should leave the word of God and serve tables. 3Therefore, brethren, seek out from among you seven men of *good* reputation, full of the Holy Spirit and wisdom, whom we may appoint over this business; 4but we will give ourselves continually to prayer and to the ministry of the word."

5And the saying pleased the whole multitude. And they chose Stephen, a man full of faith and the Holy Spirit, and Philip, Prochorus, Nicanor, Timon, Parmenas, and Nicolas, a proselyte from Antioch, 6whom they set before the apostles; and when they had prayed, they laid hands on them.

7Then the word of God spread, and the number of the disciples multiplied greatly in Jerusalem, and a great many of the priests were obedient to the faith.

Stephen Accused of Blasphemy

8And Stephen, full of faith[a] and power, did great wonders and signs among the people. 9Then there arose some from what is called the Synagogue of the Freedmen (Cyrenians, Alexandrians, and those from Cilicia and Asia), disputing with Stephen. 10And they were not able to resist the wisdom and the Spirit by which he spoke. 11Then they secretly in-

5:41 [a]NU-Text reads *the name;* M-Text reads *the name of Jesus.*
6:1 [a]That is, Greek-speaking Jews **6:8** [a]NU-Text reads *grace.*

duced men to say, "We have heard him speak blasphemous words against Moses and God." 12And they stirred up the people, the elders, and the scribes; and they came upon *him,* seized him, and brought *him* to the council. 13They also set up false witnesses who said, "This man does not cease to speak blasphemous[a] words against this holy place and the law; 14for we have heard him say that this Jesus of Nazareth will destroy this place and change the customs which Moses delivered to us." 15And all who sat in the council, looking steadfastly at him, saw his face as the face of an angel.

Stephen's Address: The Call of Abraham

7 Then the high priest said, "Are these things so?"

2And he said, "Brethren and fathers, listen: The God of glory appeared to our father Abraham when he was in Mesopotamia, before he dwelt in Haran, 3and said to him, *'Get out of your country and from your relatives, and come to a land that I will show you.'*[a] 4Then he came out of the land of the Chaldeans and dwelt in Haran. And from there, when his father was dead, He moved him to this land in which you now dwell. 5And *God* gave him no inheritance in it, not even *enough* to set his foot on. But even when *Abraham* had no child, He promised to give it to him for a possession, and to his descendants after him. 6But God spoke in this way: that his descendants would dwell in a foreign land, and that they would bring them into bondage and oppress *them* four hundred years. 7*'And the nation to whom they will be in bondage I will judge,'*[a] said God, *'and after that they shall come out and serve Me in this place.'*[b] 8Then He gave him the covenant of circumcision; and so *Abraham* begot Isaac and circumcised him on the eighth day; and Isaac *begot* Jacob, and Jacob *begot* the twelve patriarchs.

The Patriarchs in Egypt

9"And the patriarchs, becoming envious, sold Joseph into Egypt. But God was with him 10and delivered him out of all his troubles, and gave him favor and wisdom in the presence of Pharaoh, king of Egypt; and he made him governor over Egypt and all his house. 11Now a famine and great trouble came over all the land of Egypt and Canaan, and our fathers found no sustenance. 12But when Jacob heard that there was grain in Egypt, he sent out our fathers first. 13And the second *time* Joseph was made known to his brothers, and Joseph's family became known to the Pharaoh. 14Then Joseph sent and called his father Jacob and all his relatives to *him,* seventy-five[a] people. 15So Jacob went down to Egypt; and he died, he and our fathers. 16And they were carried back to Shechem and laid in the tomb that Abraham bought for a sum of money from the sons of Hamor, *the father* of Shechem.

God Delivers Israel by Moses

17"But when the time of the promise drew near which God had sworn to Abraham, the people grew and multiplied in Egypt 18till another king arose who did not know Joseph. 19This man dealt treacherously with our people, and oppressed

6:13 [a]NU-Text omits *blasphemous.* 7:3 [a]Genesis 12:1 7:7 [a]Genesis 15:14 [b]Exodus 3:12 7:14 [a]Or *seventy* (compare Exodus 1:5)

7:5 The Bible's fascinating facts. In Genesis, the Book of Beginnings, God said that Ishmael (the progenitor of the Arab race, see *Time,* April 4, 1988) would be a "wild man…and every man's hand [shall be] against him. And he shall dwell in the presence of all his brethren" (Gen. 16:12). Almost four thousand years later, who could deny that this prophecy is being fulfilled in the Arab race? The Arabs and the Jews are "brethren" having Abraham as their ancestor. The whole Middle East conflict is caused by their dwelling together.

our forefathers, making them expose their babies, so that they might not live. [20]At this time Moses was born, and was well pleasing to God; and he was brought up in his father's house for three months. [21]But when he was set out, Pharaoh's daughter took him away and brought him up as her own son. [22]And Moses was learned in all the wisdom of the Egyptians, and was mighty in words and deeds.

[23]"Now when he was forty years old, it came into his heart to visit his brethren, the children of Israel. [24]And seeing one of *them* suffer wrong, he defended and avenged him who was oppressed, and struck down the Egyptian. [25]For he supposed that his brethren would have understood that God would deliver them by his hand, but they did not understand. [26]And the next day he appeared to two of them as they were fighting, and *tried to* reconcile them, saying, 'Men, you are brethren; why do you wrong one another?' [27]But he who did his neighbor wrong pushed him away, saying, *'Who made you a ruler and a judge over us?* [28]*Do you want to kill me as you did the Egyptian yesterday?'*[a] [29]Then, at this saying, Moses fled and became a dweller in the land of Midian, where he had two sons.

[30]"And when forty years had passed, an Angel of the Lord[a] appeared to him in a flame of fire in a bush, in the wilderness of Mount Sinai. [31]When Moses saw *it,* he marveled at the sight; and as he drew near to observe, the voice of the Lord came to him, [32]*saying, 'I am the God of your fathers—the God of Abraham, the God of Isaac, and the God of Jacob.'*[a] And Moses trembled and dared not look. [33]*'Then the Lord said to him, "Take your sandals off your feet, for the place where you stand is holy ground.* [34]*I have surely seen the oppression of My people who are in Egypt; I have heard their groaning and have come down to deliver them. And now come, I will send you to Egypt."'*[a]

[35]"This Moses whom they rejected, saying, *'Who made you a ruler and a judge?'*[a] is the one God sent *to be* a ruler and a deliverer by the hand of the Angel who appeared to him in the bush. [36]He brought them out, after he had shown wonders and signs in the land of Egypt, and in the Red Sea, and in the wilderness forty years.

Israel Rebels Against God

[37]"This is that Moses who said to the children of Israel,[a] *'The Lord your God will raise up for you a Prophet like me from your brethren. Him you shall hear.'*[b]

[38]"This is he who was in the congregation in the wilderness with the Angel

7:28 [a]Exodus 2:14 7:30 [a]NU-Text omits *of the Lord.* 7:32 [a]Exodus 3:6, 15 7:34 [a]Exodus 3:5, 7, 8, 10 7:35 [a]Exodus 2:14 7:37 [a]Deuteronomy 18:15 [b]NU-Text and M-Text omit *Him you shall hear.*

7:22 Don't be concerned that you aren't "gifted" as a speaker when it comes to reaching the lost. Moses "was learned in all the wisdom of the Egyptians, and was mighty in words and in deeds," yet God didn't use him to deliver Israel until 40 years later. It took all that time of tending sheep to produce in him a meekness of character. We are told, "The humble He guides in justice, and the humble He teaches His way" (Psa. 25:9). The "wisdom" that Moses gained in Egypt was not wisdom from above. When he saw injustice, he took the law into his own hands and committed murder. God doesn't need the wisdom of this world. He merely desires a pure, humble, peace-loving, compassionate soul to use as a mouthpiece for the gospel. He wants us to be a lighthouse of His love. The moment we receive the Spirit of Christ, we receive the gift of those virtues. We don't need to tend sheep for 40 years when we have the character of the Good Shepherd manifesting through us.

7:26 "We do wrong, we think wrong, and our efforts to deal with wrong are themselves corrupted by wrong." *Chuck Colson*

7:33 Moses was told to remove his sandals because by God's presence even the ground on which he stood was made holy. Through faith in Christ, the believer himself is made holy. Now his feet are shod with the gospel of peace (Eph. 6:15), to take the word of salvation to those who stand on unholy ground.

who spoke to him on Mount Sinai, and *with* our fathers, the one who received the living oracles to give to us, [39]whom our fathers would not obey, but rejected. And in their hearts they turned back to Egypt, [40]saying to Aaron, *'Make us gods to go before us; as for this Moses who brought us out of the land of Egypt, we do not know what has become of him.'*[a] [41]And they made a calf in those days, offered sacrifices to the idol, and rejoiced in the works of their own hands. [42]Then God turned and gave them up to worship the host of heaven, as it is written in the book of the Prophets:

'Did you offer Me slaughtered animals
and sacrifices during forty years
in the wilderness,
O house of Israel?
[43]*You also took up the tabernacle of*
Moloch,
And the star of your god Remphan,
Images which you made to worship;
And I will carry you away beyond
Babylon.'[a]

God's True Tabernacle

[44]"Our fathers had the tabernacle of witness in the wilderness, as He appointed, instructing Moses to make it according to the pattern that he had seen, [45]which our fathers, having received it in turn, also brought with Joshua into the land possessed by the Gentiles, whom God drove out before the face of our fathers until the days of David, [46]who found favor before God and asked to find a dwelling for the God of Jacob. [47]But Solomon built Him a house.

[48]"However, the Most High does not dwell in temples made with hands, as the prophet says:

[49]*'Heaven is My throne,*
And earth is My footstool.
What house will you build for Me?
says the L*ORD*,
Or what is the place of My rest?
[50]*Has My hand not made all these*
things?'[a]

Israel Resists the Holy Spirit

[51]"*You* stiff-necked and uncircumcised in heart and ears! You always resist the Holy Spirit; as your fathers *did*, so *do* you. [52]Which of the prophets did your fathers not persecute? And they killed those who foretold the coming of the Just One, of whom you now have become the betrayers and murderers, [53]who have received the law by the direction of angels and have not kept *it*."

Stephen the Martyr

[54]When they heard these things they were cut to the heart, and they gnashed at him with *their* teeth. [55]But he, being full of the Holy Spirit, gazed into heaven and saw the glory of God, and Jesus standing at the right hand of God, [56]and said, "Look! I see the heavens opened and the Son of Man standing at the right hand of God!"

[57]Then they cried out with a loud voice, stopped their ears, and ran at him with one accord; [58]and they cast *him* out of the city and stoned *him*. And the witnesses laid down their clothes at the feet

7:40 [a]Exodus 32:1, 23 7:43 [a]Amos 5:25–27 7:50 [a]Isaiah 66:1, 2

7:55 As I was open-air preaching one day, a man looked to the heavens not to see the glory of God, but to shout obscenities at Jesus Christ that would make your hair curl in tight knots. He concluded his conversation by telling the Lord to strike him dead. He then turned to me and screamed, "Nothing happened!" I said, "Yes, it did. You have just stored up wrath for yourself, which will be revealed on the Day of Wrath."

Why would a man lack *any* fear of God? I believe it's because we insist on telling a sinful world that God loves them and has a wonderful plan for their lives. This is the gospel according to the contemporary Church. We give the world a choice: Do they choose God's wonderful plan, or is their own life's plan more wonderful? For the answer to this dilemma and the biblical way to witness, see Matt. 10:22 comment.

History reveals the fate of the apostles:

PHILIP: Crucified, Phrygia, A.D. 54
MATTHEW: Beheaded, Ethiopia, A.D. 60
JOHN: Abandoned, Isle of Patmos, A.D. 63
BARNABAS: Burned to death, Cyprus, A.D. 64
MARK: Dragged to death, Alexandria, A.D. 64
JAMES (THE LESS): Clubbed to death, Jerusalem, A.D. 66
PAUL: Beheaded, Rome, A.D. 66
PETER: Crucified, Rome, A.D. 69
ANDREW: Crucified, Achaia, A.D. 70
THOMAS: Speared to death, Calamina, A.D. 70
LUKE: Hanged, Athens, A.D. 93

7:59 Death for Christians. Actually, no one can "kill" a Christian. It's been well-said that death isn't the termination of existence, but the entrance into an eternal and unchanging state. The Christian has been "sealed" with the life of God Himself. All a murderer does is promote those who trust in Christ from this pain-filled futile existence into eternal reality. Then, in the coming kingdom, we will enjoy forever an earth where "the wolf and the lamb shall feed together, the lion shall eat straw like the ox" (Isa. 65:25).

"You can kill us, but you cannot do us any real harm." *Justin Martyr* (martyred A.D. 165)

of a young man named Saul. 59And they
stoned Stephen as he was calling on *God*
and saying, "Lord Jesus, receive my
spirit." 60Then he knelt down and cried
out with a loud voice, "Lord, do not
charge them with this sin." And when he
had said this, he fell asleep.

Saul Persecutes the Church

8 Now Saul was consenting to his
death.

At that time a great persecution
arose against the church which was at
Jerusalem; and they were all scattered
throughout the regions of Judea and
Samaria, except the apostles. 2And devout men carried Stephen *to his burial,*
and made great lamentation over him.

3As for Saul, he made havoc of the
church, entering every house, and dragging off men and women, committing
them to prison.

Christ Is Preached in Samaria

4Therefore those who were scattered
went everywhere preaching the word.
5Then Philip went down to the[a] city of
Samaria and preached Christ to them.
6And the multitudes with one accord
heeded the things spoken by Philip, hearing and seeing the miracles which he did.
7For unclean spirits, crying with a loud
voice, came out of many who were possessed; and many who were paralyzed
and lame were healed. 8And there was
great joy in that city.

The Sorcerer's Profession of Faith

9But there was a certain man called Simon, who previously practiced sorcery in
the city and astonished the people of
Samaria, claiming that he was someone
great, 10to whom they all gave heed, from
the least to the greatest, saying, "This
man is the great power of God." 11And
they heeded him because he had astonished them with his sorceries for a long
time. 12But when they believed Philip as

8:5 [a]Or *a*

he preached the things concerning the kingdom of God and the name of Jesus Christ, both men and women were baptized. [13]Then Simon himself also believed; and when he was baptized he continued with Philip, and was amazed, seeing the miracles and signs which were done.

The Sorcerer's Sin

[14]Now when the apostles who were at Jerusalem heard that Samaria had received the word of God, they sent Peter and John to them, [15]who, when they had come down, prayed for them that they might receive the Holy Spirit. [16]For as yet He had fallen upon none of them. They had only been baptized in the name of the Lord Jesus. [17]Then they laid hands on them, and they received the Holy Spirit.

[18]And when Simon saw that through the laying on of the apostles' hands the Holy Spirit was given, he offered them money, [19]saying, "Give me this power also, that anyone on whom I lay hands may receive the Holy Spirit."

[20]But Peter said to him, "Your money perish with you, because you thought that the gift of God could be purchased with money! [21]You have neither part nor portion in this matter, for your heart is not right in the sight of God. [22]Repent therefore of this your wickedness, and pray God if perhaps the thought of your heart may be forgiven you. [23]For I see that you are poisoned by bitterness and bound by iniquity."

[24]Then Simon answered and said, "Pray to the Lord for me, that none of the things which you have spoken may come upon me."

[25]So when they had testified and preached the word of the Lord, they returned to Jerusalem, preaching the gospel in many villages of the Samaritans.

Christ Is Preached to an Ethiopian

[26]Now an angel of the Lord spoke to Philip, saying, "Arise and go toward the south along the road which goes down from Jerusalem to Gaza." This is desert. [27]So he arose and went. And behold, a man of Ethiopia, a eunuch of great authority under Candace the queen of the Ethiopians, who had charge of all her treasury, and had come to Jerusalem to worship, [28]was returning. And sitting in his chariot, he was reading Isaiah the prophet. [29]Then the Spirit said to Philip, "Go near and overtake this chariot."

[30]So Philip ran to him, and heard him reading the prophet Isaiah, and said, "Do you understand what you are reading?"

[31]And he said, "How can I, unless someone guides me?" And he asked Philip to come up and sit with him. [32]The place in the Scripture which he read was this:

"He was led as a sheep to the slaughter;
And as a lamb before its shearer is silent,
So He opened not His mouth.
[33]*In His humiliation His justice was taken away,*
And who will declare His generation?
For His life is taken from the earth."[a]

8:33 [a]Isaiah 53:7, 8

8:19 Using God's power. "Waste of power is a tragedy. God does not waste the great power of his Spirit on those who want it simply for their own sake, to be more holy, or good, or gifted. His great task is to carry on the work for which Jesus sacrificed his throne and his life—the redemption of fallen humanity." *Alan Redpath*

8:26,27 "God has placed you where He has placed no one else. No one else in the world has the same relationships you have. No one will stand in the same grocery store line at exactly the same moment you do. No one else will come across a hungering diplomat in the desert at exactly the same time you do. God has not put you in those places merely to model the truth. Listen for the voice of the Spirit to whisper in your ear. Watch for the stranger on the road. And be aware of your opportunities to go where He would send you." *Chuck Swindoll*

34 So the eunuch answered Philip and said, "I ask you, of whom does the prophet say this, of himself or of some other man?" 35 Then Philip opened his mouth, and beginning at this Scripture, preached Jesus to him. 36 Now as they went down the road, they came to some water. And the eunuch said, "See, *here is* water. What hinders me from being baptized?"

37 Then Philip said, "If you believe with all your heart, you may."

And he answered and said, "I believe that Jesus Christ is the Son of God."[a]

38 So he commanded the chariot to stand still. And both Philip and the eunuch went down into the water, and he baptized him. 39 Now when they came up out of the water, the Spirit of the Lord caught Philip away, so that the eunuch saw him no more; and he went on his way rejoicing. 40 But Philip was found at Azotus. And passing through, he preached in all the cities till he came to Caesarea.

The Damascus Road: Saul Converted

9 Then Saul, still breathing threats and murder against the disciples of the Lord, went to the high priest 2 and asked letters from him to the synagogues of Damascus, so that if he found any who were of the Way, whether men or women, he might bring them bound to Jerusalem.

3 As he journeyed he came near Damascus, and suddenly a light shone around him from heaven. 4 Then he fell to the ground, and heard a voice saying to him, "Saul, Saul, why are you persecuting Me?"

> No man who preaches the gospel without zeal is sent from God to preach at all.
>
> **CHARLES SPURGEON**

5 And he said, "Who are You, Lord?"

Then the Lord said, "I am Jesus, whom you are persecuting.[a] It *is* hard for you to kick against the goads."

6 So he, trembling and astonished, said, "Lord, what do You want me to do?"

Then the Lord *said* to him, "Arise and go into the city, and you will be told what you must do."

8:37 [a]NU-Text and M-Text omit this verse. It is found in Western texts, including the Latin tradition. 9:5 [a]NU-Text and M-Text omit the last sentence of verse 5 and begin verse 6 with *But arise and go.*

8:35 Wisdom in witnessing. The Bible says, "He who wins souls is wise" (Prov. 11:30). If we are wise, we will discern the condition of a person's heart, remembering the biblical principle of "Law to the proud, grace to the humble." If he is a sincere Nicodemus, tell him the good news; if he is like the arrogant lawyer (Luke 10:25–29) who has no understanding of sin, righteousness, and judgment, use the Law to stir his conscience and convict him. If he has a knowledge of sin, give him the gospel. (See Matt. 19:17–22 comment.)

When the fruit is ripe, it should practically fall off the tree, as with the Ethiopian eunuch. God led Philip to a soul that was ripe for salvation! If you have to twist and pull an apple off a branch, you will probably find it to be sour. Be careful you don't try to harvest before fruit is ready.

8:39 God does the "follow-up." The exciting thing about true conversion is that there will be little need for what is commonly called "follow-up." A true convert will not need to be followed. He will put his hand to the plow and not look back (Luke 9:62). Of course, he will have to be fed, discipled, and nurtured. These things are biblical and most necessary. This can be done simply by encouraging him to read the Bible daily, answering questions he may have, and teaching him principles of fellowship, prayer, evangelism, etc.

Sometimes there is confusion between "follow-up" (we need to follow the new convert because he will fall away if we don't) and discipleship (instructing him to continue in the word of Christ, John 8:31). Look what happened after the Ethiopian eunuch was saved—he was left without follow-up. The Spirit of God transported Philip away and left the new convert in the wilderness. This is because his salvation wasn't dependent on Philip, but upon his relationship with the indwelling Lord. Those whom God saves, He keeps. If He is the author of their faith, He will be the finisher. If He has begun a good work in them, He will complete it. He is able to keep them from falling and present them faultless before the presence of His glory with exceeding joy.

7And the men who journeyed with
him stood speechless, hearing a voice but
seeing no one. 8Then Saul arose from the
ground, and when his eyes were opened
he saw no one. But they led him by the
hand and brought *him* into Damascus.
9And he was three days without sight,
and neither ate nor drank.

Ananias Baptizes Saul

10Now there was a certain disciple at
Damascus named Ananias; and to him
the Lord said in a vision, "Ananias."

And he said, "Here I am, Lord."

11So the Lord *said* to him, "Arise and
go to the street called Straight, and inquire at the house of Judas for *one* called
Saul of Tarsus, for behold, he is praying.
12And in a vision he has seen a man
named Ananias coming in and putting *his*
hand on him, so that he might receive his
sight."

13Then Ananias answered, "Lord, I
have heard from many about this man,
how much harm he has done to Your
saints in Jerusalem. 14And here he has authority from the chief priests to bind all
who call on Your name."

15But the Lord said to him, "Go, for he
is a chosen vessel of Mine to bear My
name before Gentiles, kings, and the children of Israel. 16For I will show him how
many things he must suffer for My name's
sake."

17And Ananias went his way and entered the house; and laying his hands on
him he said, "Brother Saul, the Lord Jesus,[a] who appeared to you on the road as
you came, has sent me that you may receive your sight and be filled with the
Holy Spirit." 18Immediately there fell
from his eyes *something* like scales, and he
received his sight at once; and he arose
and was baptized.

19So when he had received food, he
was strengthened. Then Saul spent some
days with the disciples at Damascus.

Saul Preaches Christ

20Immediately he preached the Christ[a]
in the synagogues, that He is the Son of
God.

Buddhists seek salvation by works. For how to witness to them, *see page 478.*

21Then all who heard were amazed,
and said, "Is this not he who destroyed
those who called on this name in
Jerusalem, and has come here for that
purpose, so that he might bring them
bound to the chief priests?"

22But Saul increased all the more in
strength, and confounded the Jews who
dwelt in Damascus, proving that this *Jesus* is the Christ.

Saul Escapes Death

23Now after many days were past, the
Jews plotted to kill him. 24But their plot
became known to Saul. And they watched

9:17 [a]M-Text omits *Jesus*. 9:20 [a]NU-Text reads *Jesus*.

9:21 "In the New Testament church it says they were all amazed—and now in our churches everybody wants to be amused." *Leonard Ravenhill*

9:22 Do not be discouraged if, as a new Christian, you feel inadequate to share your faith. The very fact that you were once enjoying the pleasures of sin and are now walking that path of righteousness is a testimony that Jesus is the Christ. Many no doubt heard of the conversion of Saul of Tarsus without hearing him preach. A changed life is a testimony in itself.

QUESTIONS & OBJECTIONS

"What should I say to someone who has lost a loved one through cancer?"

Be very careful not to give the impression that God was punishing the person for his sins. Instead, speak about the fact that all around us we can see the evidence of a "fallen creation." Explain how in the beginning there was no disease, pain, suffering, or death. But when sin entered the world, it brought suffering with it. Then gently turn the conversation away from the person who died to the person who is still living. Ask if he has been thinking about God, and if he has kept the Ten Commandments. Then take the opportunity to go through the spiritual nature of God's Law. Someone who has lost a loved one often begins to ask soul-searching questions about God, death, and eternity. Many people are so hardhearted that it takes a tragedy to make them receptive to God.

the gates day and night, to kill him.
25Then the disciples took him by night
and let *him* down through the wall in a
large basket.

Saul at Jerusalem

26And when Saul had come to
Jerusalem, he tried to join the disciples;
but they were all afraid of him, and did
not believe that he was a disciple. 27But
Barnabas took him and brought *him* to
the apostles. And he declared to them
how he had seen the Lord on the road,
and that He had spoken to him, and how
he had preached boldly at Damascus in
the name of Jesus. 28So he was with them
at Jerusalem, coming in and going out.
29And he spoke boldly in the name of the
Lord Jesus and disputed against the Hellenists, but they attempted to kill him.
30When the brethren found out, they
brought him down to Caesarea and sent
him out to Tarsus.

The Church Prospers

31Then the churches[a] throughout all
Judea, Galilee, and Samaria had peace
and were edified. And walking in the fear
of the Lord and in the comfort of the
Holy Spirit, they were multiplied.

Aeneas Healed

32Now it came to pass, as Peter went
through all *parts of the country,* that he
also came down to the saints who dwelt
in Lydda. 33There he found a certain man
named Aeneas, who had been bedridden
eight years and was paralyzed. 34And Peter said to him, "Aeneas, Jesus the Christ
heals you. Arise and make your bed."
Then he arose immediately. 35So all who
dwelt at Lydda and Sharon saw him and
turned to the Lord.

Dorcas Restored to Life

36At Joppa there was a certain disciple
named Tabitha, which is translated Dorcas. This woman was full of good works
and charitable deeds which she did. 37But
it happened in those days that she became sick and died. When they had
washed her, they laid *her* in an upper
room. 38And since Lydda was near Joppa,
and the disciples had heard that Peter
was there, they sent two men to him, imploring *him* not to delay in coming to
them. 39Then Peter arose and went with
them. When he had come, they brought
him to the upper room. And all the wid-

9:31 [a]NU-Text reads *church . . . was edified.*

9:31 Fear of the Lord. "The fear of the Lord involves a sober awareness of what He loves, of what He despises, and of the consequences of disobedience and rebellion against Him. It leads to a sincere desire to please Him, heartfelt gratefulness for His mercy, and unending delight in His loving presence. So when we choose to 'fear the Lord' we will heed Romans 12:9, 'Abhor what is evil. Cling to what is good.'" *Berit Kjos*

ows stood by him weeping, showing the
tunics and garments which Dorcas had
made while she was with them. 40But Peter put them all out, and knelt down and
prayed. And turning to the body he said,
"Tabitha, arise." And she opened her
eyes, and when she saw Peter she sat up.
41Then he gave her *his* hand and lifted
her up; and when he had called the saints
and widows, he presented her alive.
42And it became known throughout all
Joppa, and many believed on the Lord.
43So it was that he stayed many days in
Joppa with Simon, a tanner.

Cornelius Sends a Delegation

10 There was a certain man in Caesarea called Cornelius, a centurion of what was called the Italian Regiment, 2a devout *man* and one who feared
God with all his household, who gave
alms generously to the people, and
prayed to God always. 3About the ninth
hour of the day he saw clearly in a vision
an angel of God coming in and saying to
him, "Cornelius!"

4And when he observed him, he was
afraid, and said, "What is it, lord?"

So he said to him, "Your prayers and
your alms have come up for a memorial
before God. 5Now send men to Joppa,
and send for Simon whose surname is
Peter. 6He is lodging with Simon, a tanner, whose house is by the sea.[a] He will
tell you what you must do." 7And when
the angel who spoke to him had departed, Cornelius called two of his
household servants and a devout soldier
from among those who waited on him
continually. 8So when he had explained
all *these* things to them, he sent them to
Joppa.

Peter's Vision

9The next day, as they went on their
journey and drew near the city, Peter
went up on the housetop to pray, about
the sixth hour. 10Then he became very
hungry and wanted to eat; but while they
made ready, he fell into a trance 11and
saw heaven opened and an object like a
great sheet bound at the four corners, descending to him and let down to the
earth. 12In it were all kinds of four-footed
animals of the earth, wild beasts, creeping things, and birds of the air. 13And a
voice came to him, "Rise, Peter; kill and
eat."

14But Peter said, "Not so, Lord! For I
have never eaten anything common or
unclean."

The Law searches to the dividing asunder of joints and marrow, and it is a discerner of the thoughts and intents of the heart. Its excessive light strikes us like Saul of Tarsus, to the earth, and makes us cry for mercy.

CHARLES SPURGEON

15And a voice *spoke* to him again the
second time, "What God has cleansed
you must not call common." 16This was
done three times. And the object was
taken up into heaven again.

Summoned to Caesarea

17Now while Peter wondered within
himself what this vision which he had
seen meant, behold, the men who had
been sent from Cornelius had made inquiry for Simon's house, and stood before
the gate. 18And they called and asked
whether Simon, whose surname was Peter, was lodging there.

19While Peter thought about the vision, the Spirit said to him, "Behold,
three men are seeking you. 20Arise therefore, go down and go with them, doubting nothing; for I have sent them."

21Then Peter went down to the men
who had been sent to him from Cornelius,[a] and said, "Yes, I am he whom
you seek. For what reason have you
come?"

22And they said, "Cornelius *the* centu-

10:6 [a]NU-Text and M-Text omit the last sentence of this verse. **10:21** [a]NU-Text and M-Text omit *who had been sent to him from Cornelius*.

10:12 Variety Within Created Kinds

By Dr. Georgia Purdom, Answers in Genesis

Did all species evolve from one common ancestor? Genesis 1 repeats ten times that God created the different types of plants and animals each "according to its [or their] kind." The word *kind* is used again in Gen. 6:19,20 and 7:13–16 when God instructed Noah to take two of every kind of land animal onto the Ark; and in Gen. 8:17 God commanded these animals to reproduce after the Flood. Today's species show the potential variation that God designed within the original kinds, but this variety remains limited—cats are still cats, and dogs are dogs.

What does the word *kind* mean?

Since two of each *kind* of land animal (and seven of some) were brought aboard the Ark for the purpose of preserving their offspring upon the earth (Gen. 7:3), it seems clear that a "kind" represents the basic reproductive boundary of an organism. That is, the offspring of an organism is always the same *kind* as its parents, even though it may display considerable variation.

Dogs, for example, exhibit tremendous variety. Yet diverse breeds of dogs can produce offspring with each other—indicating that all dogs are of the same *kind.* Dogs will not interbreed with cats, however, since they are a different kind. Modern breeding research therefore confirms the biblical concept of animal and plant kinds.

Creation researchers have found that "kind" is often at the level of "family" in our modern classification scheme. For example, zebras, horses, and donkeys all belong to the family Equidae and can mate with each other to form hybrid animals such as mules (from a horse and donkey) and zonkeys (from a zebra and donkey). However, there is no reason to assume a one-to-one correspondence between our manmade system and the biblical terminology. So "kind" may be at a higher taxonomic level in some cases, lower in others.

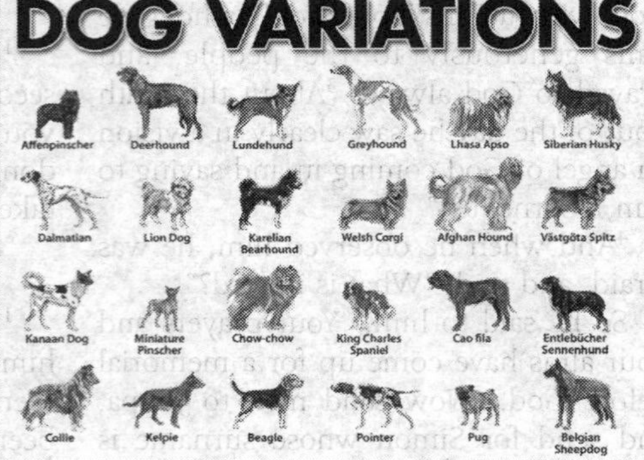

God placed the potential for tremendous variety within the original created kinds. This original variation, altered by genetic mutations and other mechanisms after the Fall (such as natural selection), led to the great diversity of living things we see today. See Isa. 45:12 comment.

rion, a just man, one who fears God and
has a good reputation among all the nation of the Jews, was divinely instructed
by a holy angel to summon you to his
house, and to hear words from you."
23Then he invited them in and lodged
them.

On the next day Peter went away with
them, and some brethren from Joppa accompanied him.

Peter Meets Cornelius

24And the following day they entered
Caesarea. Now Cornelius was waiting for
them, and had called together his relatives and close friends. 25As Peter was
coming in, Cornelius met him and fell
down at his feet and worshiped *him.*
26But Peter lifted him up, saying, "Stand
up; I myself am also a man." 27And as he
talked with him, he went in and found
many who had come together. 28Then he
said to them, "You know how unlawful it
is for a Jewish man to keep company with
or go to one of another nation. But God
has shown me that I should not call any
man common or unclean. 29Therefore I
came without objection as soon as I was
sent for. I ask, then, for what reason have
you sent for me?"

30So Cornelius said, "Four days ago I
was fasting until this hour; and at the

ninth hour[a] I prayed in my house, and behold, a man stood before me in bright clothing, 31and said, 'Cornelius, your prayer has been heard, and your alms are remembered in the sight of God. 32Send therefore to Joppa and call Simon here, whose surname is Peter. He is lodging in the house of Simon, a tanner, by the sea.[a] When he comes, he will speak to you.' 33So I sent to you immediately, and you have done well to come. Now therefore, we are all present before God, to hear all the things commanded you by God."

Preaching to Cornelius' Household

34Then Peter opened *his* mouth and said: "In truth I perceive that God shows no partiality. 35But in every nation whoever fears Him and works righteousness is accepted by Him. 36The word which *God* sent to the children of Israel, preaching peace through Jesus Christ—He is Lord of all— 37that word you know, which was proclaimed throughout all Judea, and began from Galilee after the baptism which John preached: 38how God anointed Jesus of Nazareth with the Holy Spirit and with power, who went about doing good and healing all who were oppressed by the devil, for God was with Him. 39And we are witnesses of all things which He did both in the land of the Jews and in Jerusalem, whom they[a] killed by hanging on a tree. 40Him God raised up on the third day, and showed Him openly, 41not to all the people, but to witnesses chosen before by God, *even* to us who ate and drank with Him after He arose from the dead. 42And He commanded us to preach to the people, and to testify that it is He who was ordained by God *to be* Judge of the living and the dead. 43To Him all the prophets witness that, through His name, whoever believes in Him will receive remission of sins."

The Holy Spirit Falls on the Gentiles

44While Peter was still speaking these words, the Holy Spirit fell upon all those who heard the word. 45And those of the circumcision who believed were astonished, as many as came with Peter, because the gift of the Holy Spirit had been poured out on the Gentiles also. 46For they heard them speak with tongues and magnify God.

Then Peter answered, 47"Can anyone forbid water, that these should not be baptized who have received the Holy Spirit just as we *have?*" 48And he commanded them to be baptized in the name of the Lord. Then they asked him to stay a few days.

10:30 [a]NU-Text reads *Four days ago to this hour, at the ninth hour.* **10:32** [a]NU-Text omits the last sentence of this verse. **10:39** [a]NU-Text and M-Text add *also*.

10:38 The Trinity at work in redemption. "In every major phase of the redemption, each Person of the Godhead is directly involved. Their involvement in each successive phase may be set out as follows:

1. *Incarnation*. The Father incarnated the Son in the womb of Mary by the Holy Spirit (see Luke 1:35).
2. *Baptism in the Jordan River*. The Spirit descended on the Son, and the Father spoke His approval from heaven (see Matt. 3:14–17).
3. *Public ministry*. The Father anointed the Son with the Spirit (see Acts 10:38).
4. *The crucifixion*. Jesus offered Himself to the Father through the Spirit (see Heb. 9:14).
5. *The resurrection*. The Father resurrected the Son by the Spirit (see Acts 2:32; Rom. 1:4).
6. *Pentecost*. From the Father the Son received the Spirit, whom He then poured out on His disciples (see Acts 2:33).

Each Person of the Godhead—and I mean this reverently—was jealous to be included in the process of redeeming humanity." *Derek Prince*, *Atonement*

10:47 Baptism. If we are saved by being water baptized (as certain Scriptures *seem* to imply), then we are saved by works and not grace. The Holy Spirit fell on the Gentiles *before* they were baptized. This means they were saved (by God's grace) *before* they went near water. Paul said that Christ sent him not to baptize, but to preach (1 Cor. 1:17). That's because it is the gospel that saves us, not our works in response to it. As this verse shows, baptism is an act of obedience *after* salvation.

Peter Defends God's Grace

11 Now the apostles and brethren
who were in Judea heard that the
Gentiles had also received the word of
God. 2And when Peter came up to
Jerusalem, those of the circumcision contended with him, 3saying, "You went in to
uncircumcised men and ate with them!"
4But Peter explained *it* to them in order from the beginning, saying: 5"I was in
the city of Joppa praying; and in a trance
I saw a vision, an object descending like
a great sheet, let down from heaven by
four corners; and it came to me. 6When I
observed it intently and considered, I saw
four-footed animals of the earth, wild
beasts, creeping things, and birds of the
air. 7And I heard a voice saying to me,
'Rise, Peter; kill and eat.' 8But I said, 'Not
so, Lord! For nothing common or unclean has at any time entered my mouth.'

> If people are to be saved by a message, it must contain at least some measure of knowledge. There must be light as well as fire.
>
> **CHARLES SPURGEON**

9But the voice answered me again from
heaven, 'What God has cleansed you
must not call common.' 10Now this was
done three times, and all were drawn up
again into heaven. 11At that very moment, three men stood before the house
where I was, having been sent to me from
Caesarea. 12Then the Spirit told me to go
with them, doubting nothing. Moreover
these six brethren accompanied me, and
we entered the man's house. 13And he
told us how he had seen an angel standing in his house, who said to him, 'Send
men to Joppa, and call for Simon whose
surname is Peter, 14who will tell you
words by which you and all your household will be saved.' 15And as I began to
speak, the Holy Spirit fell upon them, as
upon us at the beginning. 16Then I remembered the word of the Lord, how He
said, 'John indeed baptized with water,
but you shall be baptized with the Holy
Spirit.' 17If therefore God gave them the
same gift as *He gave* us when we believed
on the Lord Jesus Christ, who was I that
I could withstand God?"
18When they heard these things they
became silent; and they glorified God,
saying, "Then God has also granted to the
Gentiles repentance to life."

Barnabas and Saul at Antioch

19Now those who were scattered after
the persecution that arose over Stephen
traveled as far as Phoenicia, Cyprus, and
Antioch, preaching the word to no one
but the Jews only. 20But some of them
were men from Cyprus and Cyrene, who,
when they had come to Antioch, spoke to
the Hellenists, preaching the Lord Jesus.
21And the hand of the Lord was with
them, and a great number believed and
turned to the Lord.
22Then news of these things came to
the ears of the church in Jerusalem, and
they sent out Barnabas to go as far as Antioch. 23When he came and had seen the
grace of God, he was glad, and encouraged them all that with purpose of heart
they should continue with the Lord.
24For he was a good man, full of the Holy
Spirit and of faith. And a great many people were added to the Lord.
25Then Barnabas departed for Tarsus
to seek Saul. 26And when he had found
him, he brought him to Antioch. So it
was that for a whole year they assembled
with the church and taught a great many
people. And the disciples were first called
Christians in Antioch.

Relief to Judea

27And in these days prophets came
from Jerusalem to Antioch. 28Then one of
them, named Agabus, stood up and
showed by the Spirit that there was going
to be a great famine throughout all the
world, which also happened in the days
of Claudius Caesar. 29Then the disciples,
each according to his ability, determined
to send relief to the brethren dwelling in

Judea. 30This they also did, and sent it to the elders by the hands of Barnabas and Saul.

Herod's Violence to the Church

12 Now about that time Herod the king stretched out *his* hand to harass some from the church. 2Then he killed James the brother of John with the sword. 3And because he saw that it pleased the Jews, he proceeded further to seize Peter also. Now it was *during* the Days of Unleavened Bread. 4So when he had arrested him, he put *him* in prison, and delivered *him* to four squads of soldiers to keep him, intending to bring him before the people after Passover.

Peter Freed from Prison

5Peter was therefore kept in prison, but constant[a] prayer was offered to God for him by the church. 6And when Herod was about to bring him out, that night Peter was sleeping, bound with two chains between two soldiers; and the guards before the door were keeping the prison. 7Now behold, an angel of the Lord stood by *him,* and a light shone in the prison; and he struck Peter on the side and raised him up, saying, "Arise quickly!" And his chains fell off *his* hands. 8Then the angel said to him, "Gird yourself and tie on your sandals"; and so he did. And he said to him, "Put on your garment and follow me." 9So he went out and followed him, and did not know that what was done by the angel was real, but thought he was seeing a vision. 10When they were past the first and the second guard posts, they came to the iron gate that leads to the city, which opened to them of its own accord; and they went out and went down one street, and immediately the angel departed from him.

11And when Peter had come to himself, he said, "Now I know for certain that the Lord has sent His angel, and has delivered me from the hand of Herod and *from* all the expectation of the Jewish people."

12So, when he had considered *this,* he came to the house of Mary, the mother of John whose surname was Mark, where many were gathered together praying. 13And as Peter knocked at the door of the

THE FUNCTION OF THE LAW

12:7 "The very first end of the Law [is], namely, convicting men of sin; awakening those who are still asleep on the brink of hell... The ordinary method of God is to convict sinners by the Law, and that only. The gospel is not the means which God hath ordained, or which our Lord Himself used, for this end." *John Wesley*

"Few, very few, are ever awakened or convinced by the encouragements and promises of the gospel, but almost all by the denunciations of the law." *Timothy Dwight*

12:5 [a]NU-Text reads *constantly* (or *earnestly*).

12:6 The chains of sin and death. Peter lay soundly asleep in Herod's prison. This is faith in action. Faith snoozes, even in a storm. Stephen had been stoned, James had just been killed with a sword,... and Peter sleeps. He was bound with chains between two soldiers. More guards stood before the door of the prison. Suddenly an angel of the Lord appeared and stood by him, "and a light shone in the prison." There is a strong inference that the light didn't awaken Peter from his sleep, because the Scriptures then tell us that the angel struck him on the side. As he arose, his chains fell off, he girded himself, tied on his shoes, put on his garment, and followed the angel. After that, the iron gate leading to the city opened of its own accord, and Peter was free.

The sinner is in the prison of his sins. He has been taken captive by the devil. He is bound by the chains of sin, under the sentence of death. He is asleep in his sins. He lives in a dream world. But it isn't the gospel light that will awaken him. How can "Good News" alarm a sinner? Rather, the Law must strike him. He needs to be struck with the lightning of Sinai and awakened by its thunderings. That will rouse him to his plight of being on the threshold of death. Then he will arise and the gospel will remove the chains of sin and death. It will be "the power of God unto salvation." Then he will gird himself with truth, tie on his gospel shoes, put on his garment of righteousness, follow the Lord, and the iron gate of the Celestial City will open of its own accord.

gate, a girl named Rhoda came to answer.
14When she recognized Peter's voice, because of *her* gladness she did not open
the gate, but ran in and announced that
Peter stood before the gate. 15But they
said to her, "You are beside yourself!" Yet
she kept insisting that it was so. So they
said, "It is his angel."
16Now Peter continued knocking; and
when they opened *the door* and saw him,
they were astonished. 17But motioning to
them with his hand to keep silent, he declared to them how the Lord had brought
him out of the prison. And he said, "Go,
tell these things to James and to the
brethren." And he departed and went to
another place.

Each individual is unique from the moment of conception. For how we are fearfully and wonderfully made, see Psa. 139:14 comment.

18Then, as soon as it was day, there
was no small stir among the soldiers
about what had become of Peter. 19But
when Herod had searched for him and
not found him, he examined the guards
and commanded that *they* should be put
to death.
And he went down from Judea to Caesarea, and stayed *there.*

Herod's Violent Death

20Now Herod had been very angry
with the people of Tyre and Sidon; but
they came to him with one accord, and
having made Blastus the king's personal
aide their friend, they asked for peace,
because their country was supplied with
food by the king's *country.*
21So on a set day Herod, arrayed in
royal apparel, sat on his throne and gave
an oration to them. 22And the people
kept shouting, "The voice of a god and
not of a man!" 23Then immediately an angel of the Lord struck him, because he
did not give glory to God. And he was
eaten by worms and died.
24But the word of God grew and multiplied.

Barnabas and Saul Appointed

25And Barnabas and Saul returned
from[a] Jerusalem when they had fulfilled
their ministry, and they also took with
them John whose surname was Mark.

13 Now in the church that was at Antioch there were certain prophets
and teachers: Barnabas, Simeon who was
called Niger, Lucius of Cyrene, Manaen
who had been brought up with Herod
the tetrarch, and Saul. 2As they ministered to the Lord and fasted, the Holy
Spirit said, "Now separate to Me Barnabas and Saul for the work to which I
have called them." 3Then, having fasted
and prayed, and laid hands on them, they
sent *them* away.

Preaching in Cyprus

4So, being sent out by the Holy Spirit,
they went down to Seleucia, and from
there they sailed to Cyprus. 5And when
they arrived in Salamis, they preached
the word of God in the synagogues of the
Jews. They also had John as *their* assistant.
6Now when they had gone through

12:25 [a]NU-Text and M-Text read *to.*

12:12 Prayer—the secret weapon: See Acts 21:5.

the island[a] to Paphos, they found a certain sorcerer, a false prophet, a Jew whose name *was* Bar-Jesus, 7who was with the proconsul, Sergius Paulus, an intelligent man. This man called for Barnabas and Saul and sought to hear the word of God. 8But Elymas the sorcerer (for so his name is translated) withstood them, seeking to turn the proconsul away from the faith. 9Then Saul, who also *is called* Paul, filled with the Holy Spirit, looked intently at him 10and said, "O full of all deceit and all fraud, *you* son of the devil, *you* enemy of all righteousness, will you not cease perverting the straight ways of the Lord? 11And now, indeed, the hand of the Lord *is* upon you, and you shall be blind, not seeing the sun for a time."

> Some have used the terrors of the Lord to terrify, but Paul used them to persuade.
>
> **CHARLES SPURGEON**

And immediately a dark mist fell on him, and he went around seeking someone to lead him by the hand. 12Then the proconsul believed, when he saw what had been done, being astonished at the teaching of the Lord.

At Antioch in Pisidia

13Now when Paul and his party set sail from Paphos, they came to Perga in Pamphylia; and John, departing from them, returned to Jerusalem. 14But when they departed from Perga, they came to Antioch in Pisidia, and went into the synagogue on the Sabbath day and sat down. 15And after the reading of the Law and the Prophets, the rulers of the synagogue sent to them, saying, "Men *and* brethren, if you have any word of exhortation for the people, say on."

16Then Paul stood up, and motioning with *his* hand said, "Men of Israel, and you who fear God, listen: 17The God of this people Israel[a] chose our fathers, and exalted the people when they dwelt as strangers in the land of Egypt, and with an uplifted arm He brought them out of it. 18Now for a time of about forty years He put up with their ways in the wilderness. 19And when He had destroyed seven nations in the land of Canaan, He distributed their land to them by allotment.

20"After that He gave *them* judges for about four hundred and fifty years, until Samuel the prophet. 21And afterward they asked for a king; so God gave them Saul the son of Kish, a man of the tribe of Benjamin, for forty years. 22And when He had removed him, He raised up for them David as king, to whom also He gave testimony and said, '*I have found David*[a] the *son* of Jesse, *a man after My own heart, who will do all My will.*'[b] 23From this man's seed, according to *the* promise, God raised up for Israel a Savior—Jesus—[a] 24after John had first preached, before His coming, the baptism of repentance to all the people of Israel. 25And as John was finishing his course, he said, 'Who do you think I am? I am not *He.* But behold, there comes One after me, the sandals of whose feet I am not worthy to loose.'

26"Men *and* brethren, sons of the family of Abraham, and those among you who fear God, to you the word of this salvation has been sent. 27For those who dwell in Jerusalem, and their rulers, because they did not know Him, nor even the voices of the Prophets which are read every Sabbath, have fulfilled *them* in con-

13:6 [a]NU-Text reads *the whole island.* 13:17 [a]M-Text omits *Israel.* 13:22 [a]Psalm 89:20 [b]1 Samuel 13:14 13:23 [a]M-Text reads *for Israel salvation.*

13:22 The psalms reveal that David was sometimes vindictive and even hateful in prayer. However, he proved to be "a man after [God's] own heart" in his dealings with King Saul. He was full of mercy and grace in the face of murderous hostility. This may be because he had the good sense to pour out his heart to God, dealing with his anger in the privacy of prayer.

demning *Him.* 28And though they found no cause for death *in Him,* they asked Pilate that He should be put to death. 29Now when they had fulfilled all that was written concerning Him, they took *Him* down from the tree and laid *Him* in a tomb. 30But God raised Him from the dead. 31He was seen for many days by those who came up with Him from Galilee to Jerusalem, who are His witnesses to the people. 32And we declare to you glad tidings—that promise which was made to the fathers. 33God has fulfilled this for us their children, in that He has raised up Jesus. As it is also written in the second Psalm:

'You are My Son,
Today I have begotten You.'[a]

34And that He raised Him from the dead, no more to return to corruption, He has spoken thus:

'I will give you the sure mercies of
David.'[a]

35Therefore He also says in another *Psalm:*

'You will not allow Your Holy One to
see corruption.'[a]

36"For David, after he had served his own generation by the will of God, fell asleep, was buried with his fathers, and saw corruption; 37but He whom God raised up saw no corruption. 38Therefore let it be known to you, brethren, that through this Man is preached to you the forgiveness of sins; 39and by Him everyone who believes is justified from all things from which you could not be justified by the law of Moses. 40Beware therefore, lest what has been spoken in the prophets come upon you:

41*'Behold, you despisers,*
Marvel and perish!
For I work a work in your days,
A work which you will by no means
believe,
Though one were to declare it to you.'"[a]

Blessing and Conflict at Antioch

42So when the Jews went out of the synagogue,[a] the Gentiles begged that these words might be preached to them the next Sabbath. 43Now when the congregation had broken up, many of the Jews and devout proselytes followed Paul and Barnabas, who, speaking to them, persuaded them to continue in the grace of God.

44On the next Sabbath almost the whole city came together to hear the word of God. 45But when the Jews saw the multitudes, they were filled with envy; and contradicting and blaspheming, they opposed the things spoken by Paul. 46Then Paul and Barnabas grew bold and said, "It was necessary that the word of God should be spoken to you first; but since you reject it, and judge yourselves unworthy of everlasting life, behold, we turn to the Gentiles. 47For so

13:33 [a]Psalm 2:7 13:34 [a]Isaiah 55:3 13:35 [a]Psalm 16:10 13:41 [a]Habakkuk 1:5 13:42 [a]Or *And when they went out of the synagogue of the Jews;* NU-Text reads *And when they went out, they begged.*

13:38 Notice to whom Paul was speaking. This was to Jews who knew the Law (v. 15). He therefore preached the gospel of grace—Christ crucified and risen from the dead.

13:39 Justification. "[Justification] is the judicial act of God, by which He pardons all the sins of those who believe in Christ, and accounts, accepts, and treats them as righteous in the eye of the Law, i.e., as conformed to all its demands. In addition to the pardon of sin, justification declares that all the claims of the Law are satisfied in respect of the justified. It is the act of a judge and not of a sovereign. The Law is not relaxed or set aside, but is declared to be fulfilled in the strictest sense; and so the person justified is declared to be entitled to all the advantages and rewards arising from perfect obedience to the Law." *Easton Bible Dictionary*

QUESTIONS & OBJECTIONS

13:47

"If I submit to God, I'll just become a puppet!"

"A brilliant young man questioned Dr. Henrietta Mears about surrendering his life to God. He was convinced that becoming a Christian would mean the destruction of his personality, that he'd be altered in some strange way, and that he'd lose control of his own mind. He feared becoming a mere puppet in God's hands.

"So Miss Mears asked him to watch as she turned on a lamp. One moment it was dark, then she turned on the switch. She explained, 'The lamp surrendered itself to the electric current and light has filled the room. The lamp didn't destroy its personality when it surrendered to the current. On the contrary—the very thing happened for which the lamp was created: it gave light.'"
Vonette Bright

the Lord has commanded us:

'I have set you as a light to the Gentiles,
That you should be for salvation to the ends of the earth.' "[a]

48 Now when the Gentiles heard this, they were glad and glorified the word of the Lord. And as many as had been appointed to eternal life believed.

49 And the word of the Lord was being spread throughout all the region. 50 But the Jews stirred up the devout and prominent women and the chief men of the city, raised up persecution against Paul and Barnabas, and expelled them from their region. 51 But they shook off the dust from their feet against them, and came to Iconium. 52 And the disciples were filled with joy and with the Holy Spirit.

At Iconium

14 Now it happened in Iconium that they went together to the synagogue of the Jews, and so spoke that a great multitude both of the Jews and of the Greeks believed. 2 But the unbelieving Jews stirred up the Gentiles and poisoned their minds against the brethren. 3 Therefore they stayed there a long time, speaking boldly in the Lord, who was bearing witness to the word of His grace, granting signs and wonders to be done by their hands. 4 But the multitude of the city was divided: part sided with the Jews, and part with the apostles. 5 And when a violent attempt was made by both the Gentiles and Jews, with their rulers, to abuse and stone them, 6 they became aware of it and fled to Lystra and Derbe, cities of Lycaonia, and to the surrounding region. 7 And they were preaching the gospel there.

Idolatry at Lystra

8 And in Lystra a certain man without strength in his feet was sitting, a cripple from his mother's womb, who had never walked. 9 *This* man heard Paul speaking. Paul, observing him intently and seeing that he had faith to be healed, 10 said with a loud voice, "Stand up straight on your feet!" And he leaped and walked. 11 Now when the people saw what Paul had done, they raised their voices, saying in the Lycaonian *language,* "The gods have come down to us in the likeness of men!" 12 And Barnabas they called Zeus, and Paul, Hermes, because he was the chief speaker. 13 Then the priest of Zeus, whose temple was in front of their city, brought oxen and garlands to the gates, intending to sacrifice with the multitudes.

14 But when the apostles Barnabas and Paul heard this, they tore their clothes and ran in among the multitude, crying out 15 and saying, "Men, why are you do-

13:47 [a]Isaiah 49:6

14:15 "Missing Links" Still Missing

In 1999, a Chinese farmer completely fooled the worldwide scientific community into thinking it had found the "missing link" between carnivorous dinosaurs and modern birds. Called *Archaeoraptor*, it was simply the head and body of a primitive bird that he had glued to the tail and hind limbs of a dromaeosaur dinosaur.

"Did dinos soar? Imaginations certainly took flight over *Archaeoraptor Liaoningensis*, a birdlike fossil with a meat-eater's tail that was spirited out of northeastern China, 'discovered' at a Tucson, Arizona, gem and mineral show last year, and displayed at the National Geographic Society in Washington, D.C. Some 110,000 visitors saw the exhibit, which closed January 17; millions more read about the find in November's *National Geographic*. Now, paleontologists are eating crow. Instead of 'a true missing link' connecting dinosaurs to birds, the specimen appears to be a composite, its unusual appendage likely tacked on by a Chinese farmer, not evolution.

"*Archaeoraptor* is hardly the first 'missing link' to snap under scrutiny. In 1912, fossil remains of an ancient hominid were found in England's Piltdown quarries and quickly dubbed man's apelike ancestor. It took decades to reveal the hoax." *U.S. News & World Report*, February 14, 2000

The Piltdown Man fraud is explained in *Our Times: The Illustrated History of the 20th Century*: "Charles Dawson, a British lawyer and amateur geologist, announced in 1912 his discovery of pieces of a human skull and an apelike jaw in a gravel pit near the town of Piltdown, England . . . Dawson's announcement stopped the scorn cold. Experts instantly declared Piltdown Man (estimated to be 300,000 to one million years old) the evolutionary find of the century. Darwin's missing link had been identified.

"Or so it seemed for the next 40 or so years. Then, in the early fifties . . . scientists began to suspect misattribution. In 1953, that suspicion gave way to a full-blown scandal: Piltdown Man was a hoax. Radiocarbon tests proved that its skull belonged to a 600-year old woman, and its jaw to a 500-year old orangutan from the East Indies."

Piltdown Man is not the only supposed human ancestor that has been debunked. Many alleged "missing links" are based on only a single fossil fragment and the wishful thinking of evolutionists. The famed Nebraska Man was derived from a single tooth, which was later found to be from an extinct pig. Java Man, found in the early 20th century, was nothing more than a piece of skull, a fragment of a thigh bone, and three molar teeth. The rest came from the deeply fertile imaginations of plaster of Paris workers. Java Man is now regarded as fully human. Heidelberg Man came from a jawbone, a large chin section, and a few teeth. Most scientists reject the jawbone because it's similar to that of modern man. Still, many evolutionists believe that he's 250,000 years old. No doubt they pinpointed his birthday with carbon dating. However, *Time* magazine (June 11, 1990) published a science article subtitled, "Geologists show that carbon dating can be way off." (See Job 20:4 and Psa. 102:25 comments.) And don't look to Neanderthal Man for any evidence of evolution. He died of exposure. His skull was exposed as being fully human, not ape. Not only was his stooped posture found to be caused by disease, but he spoke and was artistic and religious.

"There are gaps in the fossil graveyard, places where there should be intermediate forms, but where there is nothing whatsoever instead. No paleontologist . . . denies that this is so. It is simply a fact. Darwin's theory and the fossil record are in conflict." *David Berlinsky*

"The evolutionists seem to know everything about the missing link except the fact that it is missing." *G. K. Chesterton*

ing these things? We also are men with
the same nature as you, and preach to
you that you should turn from these useless things to the living God, who made
the heaven, the earth, the sea, and all
things that are in them, [16]who in bygone
generations allowed all nations to walk in
their own ways. [17]Nevertheless He did
not leave Himself without witness, in that
He did good, gave us rain from heaven
and fruitful seasons, filling our hearts
with food and gladness." [18]And with
these sayings they could scarcely restrain
the multitudes from sacrificing to them.

Stoning, Escape to Derbe

[19]Then Jews from Antioch and Iconium came there; and having persuaded
the multitudes, they stoned Paul *and*
dragged *him* out of the city, supposing
him to be dead. [20]However, when the disciples gathered around him, he rose up

14:17 *Who Has the Most Evidence: Creationists or Evolutionists?*

By Ken Ham, Answers in Genesis

In this ongoing war between creation and evolution, Christians are always looking for the strongest evidence for creation, wanting to have "our" facts/evidences to counter "theirs."

However, it is not a matter of "their evidence vs. ours." *All* evidence is actually interpreted, and *all* scientists actually have the same observations—the *same* data—available to them. Creationists and evolutionists, Christians and non-Christians, all have the *same* evidence—the same facts. Think about it: we all have the same earth, the same fossil layers, the same animals and plants, the same stars—the facts are all the same.

The difference is in the way we all *interpret* the facts. And why do we interpret facts differently? It is because we start with different *presuppositions* or starting points. These then become the basis for other conclusions. All reasoning is based on presuppositions. This becomes especially relevant when dealing with past events.

So it's not a battle over sorting out *different* evidences. It's really a battle over the *same* evidence. The difference is, whose interpretation are you going to trust? Will you start with an all-knowing God, who has always been there, created everything, and cannot lie . . . or would you dare start with fallible ideas about the past from sinful men who were not there?

and went into the city. And the next day
he departed with Barnabas to Derbe.

Strengthening the Converts

[21]And when they had preached the
gospel to that city and made many disciples, they returned to Lystra, Iconium,
and Antioch, [22]strengthening the souls of
the disciples, exhorting *them* to continue
in the faith, and *saying,* "We must
through many tribulations enter the
kingdom of God." [23]So when they had
appointed elders in every church, and
prayed with fasting, they commended
them to the Lord in whom they had believed. [24]And after they had passed
through Pisidia, they came to Pamphylia.
[25]Now when they had preached the word
in Perga, they went down to Attalia.
[26]From there they sailed to Antioch,
where they had been commended to the
grace of God for the work which they had
completed.
[27]Now when they had come and gathered the church together, they reported
all that God had done with them, and
that He had opened the door of faith to
the Gentiles. [28]So they stayed there a long
time with the disciples.

Conflict over Circumcision

15 And certain *men* came down from
Judea and taught the brethren,
"Unless you are circumcised according to
the custom of Moses, you cannot be
saved." [2]Therefore, when Paul and Barnabas had no small dissension and dispute
with them, they determined that Paul
and Barnabas and certain others of them
should go up to Jerusalem, to the apostles and elders, about this question.
[3]So, being sent on their way by the
church, they passed through Phoenicia
and Samaria, describing the conversion

14:19 Open-air preaching. "The [street] preachers needed to have faces set like flints, and so indeed they had. John Furz says, 'As soon as I began to preach, a man came forward and presented a gun at my face; swearing that he would blow my brains out if I spoke another word. However, I continued speaking and he continued swearing, sometimes putting the muzzle of the gun to my mouth, sometimes against my ear. While we were singing the last hymn, he got behind me, fired the gun, and burned off part of my hair.'

"After this, my brethren, we ought never to speak of petty interruptions or annoyances. The proximity of a blunderbuss in the hands of a son of Belial is not very conducive to collected thought and clear utterance." *Charles Spurgeon*

of the Gentiles; and they caused great joy
to all the brethren. 4And when they had
come to Jerusalem, they were received by
the church and the apostles and the elders; and they reported all things that
God had done with them. 5But some of
the sect of the Pharisees who believed
rose up, saying, "It is necessary to circumcise them, and to command *them* to
keep the law of Moses."

The Jerusalem Council

6Now the apostles and elders came together to consider this matter. 7And
when there had been much dispute, Peter rose up *and* said to them: "Men *and*
brethren, you know that a good while
ago God chose among us, that by my
mouth the Gentiles should hear the word
of the gospel and believe. 8So God, who
knows the heart, acknowledged them by
giving them the Holy Spirit, just as *He did*
to us, 9and made no distinction between
us and them, purifying their hearts by
faith. 10Now therefore, why do you test
God by putting a yoke on the neck of the
disciples which neither our fathers nor
we were able to bear? 11But we believe
that through the grace of the Lord Jesus
Christ[a] we shall be saved in the same
manner as they."

12Then all the multitude kept silent
and listened to Barnabas and Paul declaring how many miracles and wonders God
had worked through them among the
Gentiles. 13And after they had become
silent, James answered, saying, "Men *and*
brethren, listen to me: 14Simon has declared how God at the first visited the
Gentiles to take out of them a people for
His name. 15And with this the words of
the prophets agree, just as it is written:

16*'After this I will return*
And will rebuild the tabernacle of
David, which has fallen down;
I will rebuild its ruins,
And I will set it up;
17*So that the rest of mankind may seek*
the LORD,
Even all the Gentiles who are called by
My name,
Says the LORD who does all these
things.'[a]

18"Known to God from eternity are all
His works.[a] 19Therefore I judge that we
should not trouble those from among the
Gentiles who are turning to God, 20but
that we write to them to abstain from
things polluted by idols, *from* sexual immorality,[a] *from* things strangled, and *from*
blood. 21For Moses has had throughout
many generations those who preach him
in every city, being read in the synagogues every Sabbath."

The Jerusalem Decree

22Then it pleased the apostles and elders, with the whole church, to send
chosen men of their own company to Antioch with Paul and Barnabas, *namely,* Judas who was also named Barsabas,[a] and
Silas, leading men among the brethren.
23They wrote this, *letter* by them:

The apostles, the elders, and the
brethren,

To the brethren who are of the
Gentiles in Antioch, Syria, and
Cilicia:

Greetings.

15:11 [a]NU-Text and M-Text omit *Christ.* 15:17 [a]Amos 9:11, 12 15:18 [a]NU-Text (combining with verse 17) reads *Says the Lord, who makes these things known from eternity (of old).* 15:20 [a]Or *fornication* 15:22 [a]NU-Text and M-Text read *Barsabbas.*

15:18 God does not think as we do. He is omniscient—He knows all things. That means He never has an idea. If a concept suddenly came to Him, then He would be ignorant of the thought before it formed in His mind. However, God does not have thoughts "come to His mind." Because He is omniscient, His mind has all thoughts resident.

"As by this theory innumerable transitional forms must have existed, why do we not find them embedded in countless numbers in the crust of the earth? The number of intermediate links between all living and extinct species must have been inconceivably great!"

Charles Darwin

[24]Since we have heard that some who
went out from us have troubled you
with words, unsettling your souls,
saying, "*You must* be circumcised
and keep the law"[a]—to whom we
gave no *such* commandment—[25]it
seemed good to us, being assembled
with one accord, to send chosen
men to you with our beloved Barnabas and Paul, [26]men who have risked
their lives for the name of our Lord
Jesus Christ. [27]We have therefore
sent Judas and Silas, who will also
report the same things by word of
mouth. [28]For it seemed good to the
Holy Spirit, and to us, to lay upon
you no greater burden than these
necessary things: [29]that you abstain
from things offered to idols, from
blood, from things strangled, and
from sexual immorality.[a] If you keep
yourselves from these, you will do
well.

Farewell.

Continuing Ministry in Syria

[30]So when they were sent off, they
came to Antioch; and when they had
gathered the multitude together, they delivered the letter. [31]When they had read
it, they rejoiced over its encouragement.
[32]Now Judas and Silas, themselves being
prophets also, exhorted and strengthened
the brethren with many words. [33]And after they had stayed *there* for a time, they
were sent back with greetings from the
brethren to the apostles.[a]

[34]However, it seemed good to Silas to
remain there.[a] [35]Paul and Barnabas also remained in Antioch, teaching and preaching the word of the Lord, with many others also.

Division over John Mark

[36]Then after some days Paul said to
Barnabas, "Let us now go back and visit
our brethren in every city where we have
preached the word of the Lord, *and see*
how they are doing." [37]Now Barnabas
was determined to take with them John
called Mark. [38]But Paul insisted that they
should not take with them the one who
had departed from them in Pamphylia,
and had not gone with them to the work.
[39]Then the contention became so sharp
that they parted from one another. And
so Barnabas took Mark and sailed to
Cyprus; [40]but Paul chose Silas and departed, being commended by the brethren to the grace of God. [41]And he went
through Syria and Cilicia, strengthening
the churches.

Timothy Joins Paul and Silas

16 Then he came to Derbe and
Lystra. And behold, a certain disciple was there, named Timothy, *the* son
of a certain Jewish woman who believed,
but his father *was* Greek. [2]He was well
spoken of by the brethren who were at

15:24 [a]NU-Text omits *saying, "You must be circumcised and keep the law."* 15:29 [a]Or *fornication* 15:33 [a]NU-Text reads *to those who had sent them.* 15:34 [a]NU-Text and M-Text omit this verse.

Lystra and Iconium. [3]Paul wanted to have
him go on with him. And he took *him*
and circumcised him because of the Jews
who were in that region, for they all
knew that his father was Greek. [4]And as
they went through the cities, they delivered to them the decrees to keep, which
were determined by the apostles and elders at Jerusalem. [5]So the churches were
strengthened in the faith, and increased
in number daily.

The Macedonian Call

[6]Now when they had gone through
Phrygia and the region of Galatia, they
were forbidden by the Holy Spirit to
preach the word in Asia. [7]After they had
come to Mysia, they tried to go into
Bithynia, but the Spirit[a] did not permit
them. [8]So passing by Mysia, they came
down to Troas. [9]And a vision appeared to
Paul in the night. A man of Macedonia
stood and pleaded with him, saying,
"Come over to Macedonia and help us."
[10]Now after he had seen the vision, immediately we sought to go to Macedonia,
concluding that the Lord had called us to
preach the gospel to them.

Lydia Baptized at Philippi

[11]Therefore, sailing from Troas, we ran
a straight course to Samothrace, and the
next *day* came to Neapolis, [12]and from
there to Philippi, which is the foremost
city of that part of Macedonia, a colony.
And we were staying in that city for some
days. [13]And on the Sabbath day we went
out of the city to the riverside, where
prayer was customarily made; and we sat
down and spoke to the women who met
there. [14]Now a certain woman named Lydia heard *us.* She was a seller of purple
from the city of Thyatira, who worshiped
God. The Lord opened her heart to heed
the things spoken by Paul. [15]And when
she and her household were baptized,
she begged *us,* saying, "If you have
judged me to be faithful to the Lord,
come to my house and stay." So she persuaded us.

Paul and Silas Imprisoned

[16]Now it happened, as we went to
prayer, that a certain slave girl possessed
with a spirit of divination met us, who

16:7 [a]NU-Text adds *of Jesus.*

16:6 "I think a good rule of thumb to follow would be to presume the Lord wants you to share the gospel with everyone unless He leads you not to." *Danny Lehmann*

16:16 Those who think they are contacting their dead loved ones through the occult are actually contacting "familiar spirits" (demons), a forbidden practice (Lev. 19:31; 20:6; Deut. 18:10–12). See 1 Chron. 10:13,14 comment.

16:16–18 The woman (or the demon) was speaking the truth. These men *were* servants of the Most High God, and they *were* showing the way of salvation. Why then was Paul grieved? Satan is very subtle. Rather than openly oppose the truth, he will often attempt to conceal it by maintaining that the occult and God are compatible. If you are open-air preaching, don't be surprised to have someone who is obviously demonically controlled loudly agree with you, so that it looks to the crowd that you are both preaching the same message. This *is* very frustrating.

For two years I was heckled almost daily by a woman named Petra. She dressed in black, carried a wooden staff, and said she was a prophet to the nation. As in the days of Noah, only eight would be saved. She maintained that she was one of them, and that she determined who the other seven would be. She also claimed that my spirit visited her spirit in the night (it did not!). The problem was that she would "Amen" much of what I preached, adding her thoughts at the points I made. She would do this at the top of her very loud voice. It must have appeared to newcomers to the crowd that we were a team, preaching the same thing. This was why I was delighted when (every now and then) she would get angry with something I said and let out a string of cuss words, revealing to the crowd that we were *not* on the same side.

The question arises as to whether Paul did the right thing by casting out the demon. I'm not sure he did. If the woman was not repentant, she may have received seven more demons (Matt. 12:43–45). After his action, great persecution came against the disciples, but God in His goodness worked it out for their good, as well as for the good of the Philippian jailer and his family (see vv. 24–34).

brought her masters much profit by for-
tune-telling. 17This girl followed Paul and
us, and cried out, saying, "These men are
the servants of the Most High God, who
proclaim to us the way of salvation."
18And this she did for many days.

But Paul, greatly annoyed, turned and
said to the spirit, "I command you in the
name of Jesus Christ to come out of her."
And he came out that very hour. 19But
when her masters saw that their hope of
profit was gone, they seized Paul and
Silas and dragged *them* into the marketplace to the authorities.

20And they brought them to the magistrates, and said, "These men, being
Jews, exceedingly trouble our city; 21and
they teach customs which are not lawful
for us, being Romans, to receive or observe." 22Then the multitude rose up together against them; and the magistrates
tore off their clothes and commanded
them to be beaten with rods. 23And when
they had laid many stripes on them, they
threw *them* into prison, commanding the
jailer to keep them securely. 24Having received such a charge, he put them into
the inner prison and fastened their feet in
the stocks.

The Philippian Jailer Saved

25But at midnight Paul and Silas were
praying and singing hymns to God, and
the prisoners were listening to them.
26Suddenly there was a great earthquake,
so that the foundations of the prison were
shaken; and immediately all the doors
were opened and everyone's chains were
loosed. 27And the keeper of the prison,
awaking from sleep and seeing the prison
doors open, supposing the prisoners had
fled, drew his sword and was about to
kill himself. 28But Paul called with a loud
voice, saying, "Do yourself no harm, for
we are all here."

29Then he called for a light, ran in,
and fell down trembling before Paul and
Silas. 30And he brought them out and
said, "Sirs, what must I do to be saved?"

31So they said, "Believe on the Lord Jesus Christ, and you will be saved, you
and your household." 32Then they spoke
the word of the Lord to him and to all
who were in his house. 33And he took
them the same hour of the night and
washed *their* stripes. And immediately he
and all his *family* were baptized. 34Now
when he had brought them into his
house, he set food before them; and he
rejoiced, having believed in God with all
his household.

Paul Refuses to Depart Secretly

35And when it was day, the magistrates
sent the officers, saying, "Let those men
go."

36So the keeper of the prison reported
these words to Paul, saying, "The magistrates have sent to let you go. Now therefore depart, and go in peace."

16:25 *Ira Sankey*, before he became D. L. Moody's famous song leader (and a powerful preacher himself), was assigned to night duty in the American Civil War. While he was on duty, he lifted his eyes toward heaven and began to sing, praising the Lord while he was alone. At least, he thought he was alone.

Years later, after the war had ended, Sankey was on a ship traveling across the Atlantic Ocean. Since he was now a famous singer, a crowd of people approached him and asked him to sing. He lifted his eyes toward heaven and sang a beautiful hymn.

After his song, a man from the crowd asked him if, on a certain night during the Civil War, he had performed night duty for a certain infantry unit. "Yes, I did," was his reply.

The man continued, "I was on the opposite side of the war, and I was hiding in a bush near your camp. With my rifle aimed at your head, I was about to shoot you when you looked toward heaven and began to sing. I thought, 'Well, I like music, and this guy has a nice voice. I'll sit here, let him sing the song, . . . and then shoot him. He's not going anywhere.' But then I realized what you were singing. It was the same hymn my mother used to sing at my bedside when I was a child. And it's the same hymn you sang tonight! I tried, but that night during the Civil War, I was powerless to shoot you."

Ira Sankey pointed that man to Christ. He and thousands of others were saved under Sankey's ministry. All this stemmed from the fact that Sankey praised the Lord at all times.

QUESTIONS & OBJECTIONS

17:2

"Christians can't use 'circular reasoning' by trying to prove the Bible by quoting from the Bible!"

The "circular reasoning" argument is absurd. That's like saying you can't prove that the President lives in the White House by *looking into* the White House. It is looking into the White House that will provide the necessary proof. The fulfilled prophecies, the amazing consistency, and the many scientific statements of the Bible prove it to be the Word of God. They provide evidence that it is supernatural in origin.

See also Psa. 119:105 comment.

37But Paul said to them, "They have
beaten us openly, uncondemned Romans, *and* have thrown *us* into prison.
And now do they put us out secretly? No
indeed! Let them come themselves and
get us out."
38And the officers told these words to
the magistrates, and they were afraid
when they heard that they were Romans.
39Then they came and pleaded with them
and brought *them* out, and asked *them* to
depart from the city. 40So they went out
of the prison and entered *the house of*
Lydia; and when they had seen the brethren, they encouraged them and departed.

Preaching Christ at Thessalonica

17 Now when they had passed
through Amphipolis and Apollo-
nia, they came to Thessalonica, where
there was a synagogue of the Jews. 2Then
Paul, as his custom was, went in to them,
and for three Sabbaths reasoned with
them from the Scriptures, 3explaining
and demonstrating that the Christ had to
suffer and rise again from the dead, and
saying, "This Jesus whom I preach to you
is the Christ." 4And some of them were
persuaded; and a great multitude of the
devout Greeks, and not a few of the leading women, joined Paul and Silas.

Assault on Jason's House

5But the Jews who were not persuaded, becoming envious,[a] took some of
the evil men from the marketplace, and
gathering a mob, set all the city in an uproar and attacked the house of Jason, and
sought to bring them out to the people.
6But when they did not find them, they
dragged Jason and some brethren to the
rulers of the city, crying out, "These who
have turned the world upside down have
come here too. 7Jason has harbored
them, and these are all acting contrary to
the decrees of Caesar, saying there is another king—Jesus." 8And they troubled
the crowd and the rulers of the city when
they heard these things. 9So when they
had taken security from Jason and the
rest, they let them go.

· · · · · ·

For what great leaders have said about the Bible, see page 1750.

· · · · · ·

Ministering at Berea

10Then the brethren immediately sent
Paul and Silas away by night to Berea.
When they arrived, they went into the
synagogue of the Jews. 11These were
more fair-minded than those in Thessalonica, in that they received the word
with all readiness, and searched the
Scriptures daily *to find out* whether these
things were so. 12Therefore many of them
believed, and also not a few of the
Greeks, prominent women as well as men.

17:5 [a]NU-Text omits *who were not persuaded;* M-Text omits *becoming envious.*

Questions & Objections

17:16

"When Paul spoke in Athens, why did he begin his preaching with creation as opposed to the Law?"

In Acts 17:16 we are told that Paul was grieved because the whole city of Athens was given over to idolatry. So, in vv. 22–28, he tells his hearers that they had other gods before the God of creation. He is in essence opening up the First and Second Commandments: "I am the Lord your God . . . You shall have no other gods before Me. You shall not make for yourself a carved image" (Exod. 20:2–4). Then, in vv. 29–31, he rebukes them for their idolatry and preaches repentance and future punishment by the Law (God's standard of "righteousness"). So I wouldn't say that he began with creation as opposed to the Law. It was what he used to point them to the Law.

Think of how Jesus approached the woman at the well (in John 4). He began to speak to her about water, but then He spoke to her about her violation of the Seventh Commandment. When Nathan was commissioned by God to reprove David for his sins, Nathan began in the natural realm, and then pointed out David's transgression: "Why have you despised the commandment of the LORD?" (2 Sam. 12:9).

Although Paul mentioned creation, he didn't stay there for long, because speaking about creation doesn't convict a man of his sins. There is no guilty conscience accusing hearers as long as we speak apologetically. The goal is to use the Law to bring the knowledge of sin (see Rom. 3:20).

Be careful not to get caught up in a sword fight about evolution or atheism. These subjects should merely be seen as a means to an end. The end is the preaching of the reality of Judgment Day and the terror of hell—the cross, repentance, and faith—and the biblical way to get there is through the Law.

13But when the Jews from Thessalonica
learned that the word of God was
preached by Paul at Berea, they came there
also and stirred up the crowds. 14Then immediately the brethren sent Paul away, to
go to the sea; but both Silas and Timothy
remained there. 15So those who conducted
Paul brought him to Athens; and receiving
a command for Silas and Timothy to come
to him with all speed, they departed.

The Philosophers at Athens

16Now while Paul waited for them at
Athens, his spirit was provoked within
him when he saw that the city was given
over to idols. 17Therefore he reasoned in
the synagogue with the Jews and with the
Gentile worshipers, and in the marketplace daily with those who happened to
be there. 18Then[a] certain Epicurean and
Stoic philosophers encountered him.
And some said, "What does this babbler
want to say?"

Others said, "He seems to be a pro-
claimer of foreign gods," because he
preached to them Jesus and the resurrection.

19And they took him and brought him
to the Areopagus, saying, "May we know
what this new doctrine *is* of which you
speak? 20For you are bringing some strange
things to our ears. Therefore we want to
know what these things mean." 21For all
the Athenians and the foreigners who
were there spent their time in nothing
else but either to tell or to hear some new
thing.

Addressing the Areopagus

22Then Paul stood in the midst of the
Areopagus and said, "Men of Athens, I
perceive that in all things you are very religious; 23for as I was passing through
and considering the objects of your worship, I even found an altar with this inscription:

TO THE UNKNOWN GOD.

Therefore, the One whom you worship
without knowing, Him I proclaim to you:
24God, who made the world and everything in it, since He is Lord of heaven and
earth, does not dwell in temples made
with hands. 25Nor is He worshiped with
men's hands, as though He needed anything, since He gives to all life, breath,

17:18 [a]NU-Text and M-Text add *also*.

POINTS FOR OPEN-AIR PREACHING

17:22

Give Yourself a Lift

If you are going to preach in the open-air, elevate yourself. For eighteen months, I preached without any elevation and hardly attracted any listeners. As soon as I did it "soapbox" style, people stopped to listen. Their attitude was "What has this guy got to say?" They had an excuse to stop.

Also, elevation will give you protection. I was once almost eaten by an angry 6'6" gentleman who kept fuming, "God is love!" We were eye to eye...while I was elevated. On another occasion, a very heavy gentleman who had a mean countenance placed it about 6" from mine and whispered, "Jesus said to love your enemies." I nodded in agreement. Then he asked in a deep voice, "Who is your enemy?" I shrugged. His voice deepened and spilled forth in a chilling tone, *"Lucifer!"* I was standing beside my stepladder at the time so he pushed me backwards with his stomach. He kept doing so until I was moved back about 20 feet. I prayed, "Wisdom, Lord," then said, "You are either going to hit me or hug me." He hugged me and walked off. That wouldn't have happened if I had been elevated.

Elevation will also give you added authority. Often hecklers will walk right up to you and ask questions quietly. This is an attempt to stifle the preaching, and it will work if you are not higher than your heckler. If they come too close to me, I talk over their heads and tell them to go back to the heckler's gallery. They actually obey me because they get the impression I am bigger than they are.

When Ezra preached the Law, he was elevated (Neh. 8:4,5). John Wesley used elevation to preach. Jesus preached the greatest sermon ever on a mount (Matt. 5–7), and Paul went up Mars' Hill to preach (Acts 17:22). So if you can't find a hilltop to preach from, use a soapbox or a stepladder. See Acts 3:4 comment.

and all things. 26And He has made from one blood[a] every nation of men to dwell on all the face of the earth, and has determined their preappointed times and the boundaries of their dwellings, 27so that they should seek the Lord, in the hope that they might grope for Him and find Him, though He is not far from each one of us; 28for in Him we live and move and have our being, as also some of your own poets have said, 'For we are also His offspring.' 29Therefore, since we are the offspring of God, we ought not to think that the Divine Nature is like gold or silver or stone, something shaped by art and man's devising. 30Truly, these times of ignorance God overlooked, but now commands all men everywhere to repent, 31because He has appointed a day on which He will judge the world in righteousness by the Man whom He has ordained. He has given assurance of this to

17:26 [a]NU-Text omits *blood.*

17:24 Evolution should not be taught. *Dr. Colin Patterson*, senior paleontologist, British Museum of Natural History, gave a keynote address at the American Museum of Natural History, New York City, in 1981. In it, he explained his sudden "anti-evolutionary" view: "One morning I woke up and...it struck me that I had been working on this stuff for twenty years and there was not one thing I knew about it. That's quite a shock to learn that one can be misled so long...I've tried putting a simple question to various people: 'Can you tell me anything you know about evolution, any one thing, any one thing that is true?' I tried that question on the geology staff at the Field Museum of Natural History and the only answer I got was silence. I tried it on the members of the Evolutionary Morphology Seminar in the University of Chicago, a very prestigious body of evolutionists, and all I got there was silence for a long time and eventually one person said, 'I do know one thing—it ought not to be taught in high school.'"

17:26 Mormons believe that God cursed Cain with black skin and a flat nose. However, the "mark" was set upon Cain *before* the Flood. In that Flood all flesh perished except for Noah, his wife, his three sons, and their wives. If the curse upon Cain was dark skin, the only way the race could have survived was for Noah to be a direct descendent of Cain. However, Noah's genealogy did not come from Cain, but from Seth (Gen. 5:3,6–32).

17:23 *How to Witness to Muslims*

In Acts 17:22–31 the apostle Paul built on areas of "common ground" as he prepared his listeners for the good news of the gospel. Even though he was addressing Gentiles whose beliefs were erroneous, he did not rebuke them for having a doctrine of devils (see 1 Cor. 10:20). Neither did he present the great truth that Jesus of Nazareth was Almighty God manifest in human form. This may have initially offended his hearers and closed the door to what he wanted to convey. Instead, he built on what they already knew.

There are three main areas of common ground upon which Christians may stand with Muslims. First, that there is one God—the Creator of all things. Second, that Jesus of Nazareth was a prophet of God, as the Bible makes clear (see Acts 3:20–22).

The Qur'an (Koran) says, "Behold! The angel said 'O Mary! Allah giveth you Glad Tidings of a word from Him. His name will be (Christ Jesus) the son of Mary, held in honor in this world and the hereafter and of (the company of) those nearest to Allah'" (Surah 3:45). In Surah 19:19, the angel said to Mary, "I am only a messenger of thy Lord to announce to you a gift of a holy son." Surah 3:55 says, "Allah said: 'O Jesus! I will take you and raise you to Myself.'"

Based on these and other references to Jesus in the Qur'an, a Muslim will not object when you establish that Jesus was a prophet from God.

This brings us to the third area of common ground. Muslims also respect Moses as a prophet of God. Therefore, there should be little contention when Christians speak of God (as Creator), Jesus the prophet, and the Law of the prophet Moses.

Most Muslims do have some knowledge of their sinfulness, but few see sin in its true light. It is therefore essential to take them through the spiritual nature of the Ten Commandments. But before you do, be sure to share the following anecdote. Imagine a man has been convicted of raping, beating, and robbing a helpless woman. He pleads guilty, but says to the judge, "Judge, I am genuinely sorry, and I won't do it again." Will a good judge let him go simply because he is sorry for his crime and promises not to do it again? Of course not. A criminal *should* be sorry (he has done wrong), and of course he should not commit the crime again. It is important to make sure the Muslim agrees with this point, because more than likely when you go through the Commandments and he acknowledges that he has broken them, he will say that *he simply tells God he is sorry, and he repents (he won't commit the crime again).* However, a good judge would never let a heinous criminal go free because of sorrow and a promise not to commit the crime again, and it is even more so with a holy God. A holy God must see that justice is done. The Muslim must be made to understand this, before you go through the Commandments.

Although the First Commandment is, "You shall have no other gods before Me," it may be unwise to start out by telling a Muslim that Allah is a false god. Such talk may close the door before you are able to speak to his conscience. Rather, present the Law in a similar order in which Jesus gave it in Luke 18:20. He addressed the man's sins of the flesh, mentioning commandments that have to do with his fellow man. Therefore, ask your hearer if he has ever told a lie. If he admits that he has, ask him what that makes him. Don't call him a liar. Instead, gently press him to tell you what someone is called who has lied. Try to get him to say that he is a "liar."

Then ask him if he has ever stolen something, even if it is small. If he has, ask what that makes him (a thief). Then quote from the prophet Jesus: "Whoever looks at a woman to lust for her has already committed adultery with her in his heart" (Matt. 5:28). Ask if he has ever looked at a woman with lust. If he is reasonable, he will admit that he has sinned in that area. Then gently tell him that, *by his own admission*, he is a "lying, thieving, adulterer at heart." Say, "If God judges you by the Law of Moses on Judgment Day, will you be innocent or guilty?"

At this point, he may be tempted to say that he will be innocent, because he confesses his sins to God and hopes God is merciful. However, the Qur'an says: "Every soul that has sinned, if it possessed all that is on earth, would fain give it in ransom" (Surah 10:54). In other words, if he possessed the whole world and offered it to God as a sacrifice for his sins, it would not be enough to provide atonement for his sins.

This is when you remind him of the story about the earthly judge. Repentance does not mean acquittal from the courtroom. There must be punishment for crime. So now you can bring in the truth of the atonement, continuing with the courtroom analogy.

Say to him, "Remember that if a criminal is guilty he should not be forgiven just because he is sorry or vows never to do it again. The judge will, however, let him go *if someone pays the fine for him.*"

Now tell him that Moses gave instructions to

(continued)

(17:23 continued)
Israel to shed the blood of a spotless lamb to provide a temporary atonement for their sin; and that Jesus was the Lamb that God provided to make atonement for the sins of the world. Through faith in Jesus, he can have atonement with God. All his sins can be washed away, once and for all. God can grant him the gift of everlasting life through faith in Jesus Christ on the basis of His death and resurrection.

The uniqueness of Jesus of Nazareth was that He claimed He had power on earth to forgive sins (Matt. 9:2–6). No other prophet of any of the great religions made this claim. Only Jesus can provide peace with God. That is why He said, "I am the way, the truth, and the life. No one comes to the Father except through Me" (John 14:6). God commands sinners to repent and trust in Jesus as Lord and Savior, or they will perish.

To try to justify himself, your listener may say something like, "The Bible has changed. It has been altered. There are many different versions, but the Koran has never changed." Explain that there are many different versions, printed in different languages and in modern English, to help people understand the Bible, but the content of the Scriptures remains the same. The Dead Sea Scrolls prove that God has preserved the Scriptures. Tell him that the 100 percent accurate prophecies of Scripture (Matt. 24; Luke 21; 2 Tim. 3; etc.) prove that this is the Book of the Creator.

Your task is to present the truth of the gospel. It is God who makes it come alive (1 Cor. 3:6,7). It is God who brings conviction of sin (John 16:7,8). It is God who reveals who Jesus is (Matt. 16:16,17). All God requires is your faithful presentation of the truth (Matt. 25:21). For more on Muslim beliefs, see pages 919 and 1244.

all by raising Him from the dead."
32And when they heard of the resurrection of the dead, some mocked, while others said, "We will hear you again on this *matter*." 33So Paul departed from among them. 34However, some men joined him and believed, among them Dionysius the Areopagite, a woman named Damaris, and others with them.

USING THE LAW IN EVANGELISM

17:29 Paul was preaching the essence of the First and Second Commandments to show his hearers that they were idolaters. See Acts 28:23 comment.

Ministering at Corinth

18 After these things Paul departed from Athens and went to Corinth.
2And he found a certain Jew named Aquila, born in Pontus, who had recently come from Italy with his wife Priscilla (because Claudius had commanded all the Jews to depart from Rome); and he came to them.
3So, because he was of the same trade, he stayed with them and worked; for by occupation they were tentmakers.
4And he reasoned in the synagogue every Sabbath, and persuaded both Jews and Greeks.
5When Silas and Timothy had come from Macedonia, Paul was compelled by

17:30 Repentance—its necessity for salvation. See Acts 20:21. Instead of desperate sinners knocking on the door of heaven, we incorrectly paint a picture of Jesus pleading at the heart of the sinner. This type of "invitation" gives the impression that the sinner will be doing God a favor if he responds. The gospel is not an invitation because invitations can be politely turned down without fear of reprisal. Scripture says that "God . . . *commands* all men everywhere to repent" (Acts 17:30, emphasis added).

"If my six-year-old daughter was out on the road playing in front of my house and I saw a huge truck barreling around the corner, what would I do in that moment? Out of my love for my daughter I would not gently invite her to step away from the street. I would *command* her to change her direction, and get off the road! Why? Because of my love for her. I know that the truck would not be able to stop in time and it would run her over and kill her. The same is true of the Father's love for us. Out of His love, he commands us to repent, because at any moment the truck of sin and death could run us over for playing on the road of rebellion!" *Rob Price*

17:31 Judgment Day: For verses that warn of its reality, see Rom. 2:16. We preach Christ and Him crucified for the sins of the world, seeking to warn every man of the great and coming Day of the Lord, in which God will judge the world in righteousness. The standard of judgment will be a perfect Law (Psa. 19:7), and those who fail to meet its perfect requirements will come under its terrible wrath. See Acts 18:9 comment.

QUESTIONS & OBJECTIONS

17:26 "Where do all the races come from?"

Some have wondered, if we are all descendants of Adam and Eve, why are there so many races? The Bible informed us 2,000 years ago that God has made all nations from "one blood." We are all of the same race—the "human race," descendants of Adam and Eve, something science is slowly coming to realize. Reuters news service reported the following article by *Maggie Fox:*

> Science may have caught up with the Bible, which says that Adam and Eve are the ancestors of all humans alive today.
>
> Peter Underhill of Stanford University in California remarked on findings published in the November 2000 issue of the journal *Nature Genetics*...Geneticists have long agreed there is no genetic basis to race—only to ethnic and geographic groups. "People look at a very conspicuous trait like skin color and they say, 'Well, this person's so different'...but that's only skin deep," Underhill said. "When you look at the level of the Y chromosome you find that, gee, there is very little difference between them. And skin color differences are strictly a consequence of climate."

"When the families scattered from Babel, they each took different combinations of genes with them. In such small populations, trivial differences (such as skin color) can arise quickly in only a few generations. Even evolutionists admit this is true. But different shades of skin and slightly different genetic traits are trivial and do not constitute different 'races.'" *Carl Kerby, Reasons for Hope*

See also 1 Cor. 11:9 comment.

the Spirit, and testified to the Jews *that*
Jesus *is* the Christ. 6But when they opposed him and blasphemed, he shook *his*
garments and said to them, "Your blood
be upon your *own* heads; I *am* clean.
From now on I will go to the Gentiles."
7And he departed from there and entered
the house of a certain *man* named Justus,[a]
one who worshiped God, whose house
was next door to the synagogue. 8Then
Crispus, the ruler of the synagogue, believed on the Lord with all his household.
And many of the Corinthians, hearing,
believed and were baptized.
9Now the Lord spoke to Paul in the
night by a vision, "Do not be afraid, but
speak, and do not keep silent; 10for I am
with you, and no one will attack you to
hurt you; for I have many people in this
city." 11And he continued *there* a year and
six months, teaching the word of God
among them.

18:7 [a]NU-Text reads *Titius Justus.*

18:4 Paul did not go to the synagogue to keep the Sabbath holy. He went there to *reason* with the Jews about Christ. His manner was to become like a Jew to the Jews. His heart's desire was to reach his own nation with the gospel. See 1 Cor. 9:20–22.

18:9 "God [has] appointed a day in which He will judge the world, and we sigh and cry until it shall end the reign of wickedness, and give rest to the oppressed. Brethren, we must preach the coming of the Lord, and preach it somewhat more than we have done, *because it is the driving power of the gospel*. Too many have kept back these truths, and thus the bone has been taken out of the arm of the gospel. Its point has been broken; its edge has been blunted. The doctrine of judgment to come is the power by which men are to be aroused. There is another life; the Lord will come a second time; judgment will arrive; the wrath of God will be revealed. *Where this is not preached, I am bold to say the gospel is not preached.*

"It is absolutely necessary to the preaching of the gospel of Christ that men be warned as to what will happen if they continue in their sins. Ho, ho sir surgeon, you are too delicate to tell the man that he is ill! You hope to heal the sick without their knowing it. You therefore flatter them; and what happens? They laugh at you; they dance upon their own graves. At last they die! Your delicacy is cruelty; your flatteries are poisons; *you are a murderer*. Shall we keep men in a fool's paradise? Shall we lull them into soft slumbers from which they will awake in hell? Are we to become helpers of their damnation by our smooth speeches? In the name of God we will not." *Charles Spurgeon*

[12]When Gallio was proconsul of Achaia,
the Jews with one accord rose up against
Paul and brought him to the judgment
seat, [13]saying, "This *fellow* persuades men
to worship God contrary to the law."
[14]And when Paul was about to open
his mouth, Gallio said to the Jews, "If it
were a matter of wrongdoing or wicked
crimes, O Jews, there would be reason
why I should bear with you. [15]But if it is
a question of words and names and your
own law, look *to it* yourselves; for I do not
want to be a judge of such *matters*."
[16]And he drove them from the judgment
seat. [17]Then all the Greeks[a] took Sosthenes, the ruler of the synagogue, and
beat *him* before the judgment seat. But
Gallio took no notice of these things.

Paul Returns to Antioch

[18]So Paul still remained a good while.
Then he took leave of the brethren and
sailed for Syria, and Priscilla and Aquila
were with him. He had *his* hair cut off at
Cenchrea, for he had taken a vow. [19]And
he came to Ephesus, and left them there;
but he himself entered the synagogue and
reasoned with the Jews. [20]When they
asked *him* to stay a longer time with them,
he did not consent, [21]but took leave of
them, saying, "I must by all means keep
this coming feast in Jerusalem;[a] but I will
return again to you, God willing." And he
sailed from Ephesus.
[22]And when he had landed at Caesarea, and gone up and greeted the
church, he went down to Antioch. [23]After
he had spent some time *there*, he departed and went over the region of Galatia and Phrygia in order, strengthening all
the disciples.

> The great benefit of open-air preaching is that we get so many new comers to hear the gospel who otherwise would never hear it.
>
> **CHARLES SPURGEON**

Ministry of Apollos

[24]Now a certain Jew named Apollos,
born at Alexandria, an eloquent man *and*
mighty in the Scriptures, came to Ephesus. [25]This man had been instructed in
the way of the Lord; and being fervent in
spirit, he spoke and taught accurately the
things of the Lord, though he knew only
the baptism of John. [26]So he began to
speak boldly in the synagogue. When
Aquila and Priscilla heard him, they took
him aside and explained to him the way
of God more accurately. [27]And when he
desired to cross to Achaia, the brethren
wrote, exhorting the disciples to receive
him; and when he arrived, he greatly
helped those who had believed through

18:17 [a]NU-Text reads *they all*. **18:21** [a]NU-Text omits *I must through Jerusalem*.

18:10 Never be discouraged by thinking that you are the only one God can use to reach the lost. Elijah, fearing that all the other prophets had been killed, said, "I alone am left; and they seek to take my life" (1 Kings 19:10). Yet God had reserved 7,000 faithful followers who hadn't bowed their knee to worship Baal (v. 18). Because God has His laborers, we need never panic when it comes to our loved ones being reached with the gospel. If we faithfully reach out and touch the lives of other people's loved ones, God (in His perfect timing) can use others to touch the lives of the ones we love so dearly. Claim your family in prayer, then thank God for His faithfulness in answering those prayers.

18:19 "The proper goal in apologetics is not to force someone to admit that we have proved our position, but simply to remove objections so that a nonbeliever cannot hide behind intellectual objections." *John S. Hammett*

18:26 "It is better to be divided by truth than united in error; it is better to speak truth that hurts and then heals than to speak a lie; it is better to be hated for telling the truth than to be loved for telling a lie; it is better to stand alone with truth than to be wrong with the multitude . . . The religion of today is 'get-along-ism.' It is time for men and women of God to stand, [even] if they have to stand alone." *Adrian Rogers*

grace; 28for he vigorously refuted the Jews publicly, showing from the Scriptures that Jesus is the Christ.

Paul at Ephesus

19 And it happened, while Apollos was at Corinth, that Paul, having passed through the upper regions, came to Ephesus. And finding some disciples 2he said to them, "Did you receive the Holy Spirit when you believed?"

So they said to him, "We have not so much as heard whether there is a Holy Spirit."

3And he said to them, "Into what then were you baptized?"

So they said, "Into John's baptism."

4Then Paul said, "John indeed baptized with a baptism of repentance, saying to the people that they should believe on Him who would come after him, that is, on Christ Jesus."

5When they heard *this,* they were baptized in the name of the Lord Jesus. 6And when Paul had laid hands on them, the Holy Spirit came upon them, and they spoke with tongues and prophesied. 7Now the men were about twelve in all.

8And he went into the synagogue and spoke boldly for three months, reasoning and persuading concerning the things of the kingdom of God. 9But when some were hardened and did not believe, but spoke evil of the Way before the multitude, he departed from them and withdrew the disciples, reasoning daily in the school of Tyrannus. 10And this continued for two years, so that all who dwelt in Asia heard the word of the Lord Jesus, both Jews and Greeks.

Miracles Glorify Christ

11Now God worked unusual miracles by the hands of Paul, 12so that even handkerchiefs or aprons were brought from his body to the sick, and the diseases left them and the evil spirits went out of them. 13Then some of the itinerant Jewish exorcists took it upon themselves to call the name of the Lord Jesus over those who had evil spirits, saying, "We[a] exorcise you by the Jesus whom Paul preaches." 14Also there were seven sons of Sceva, a Jewish chief priest, who did so.

15And the evil spirit answered and said, "Jesus I know, and Paul I know; but who are you?"

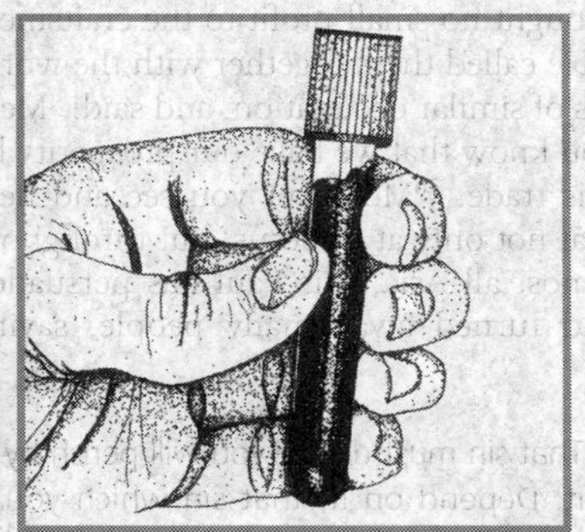

The platelets in blood reveal the folly of evolution. See Matt. 9:20 comment.

16Then the man in whom the evil spirit was leaped on them, overpowered[a] them, and prevailed against them,[b] so that they fled out of that house naked and wounded. 17This became known both to all Jews and Greeks dwelling in Ephesus; and fear fell on them all, and the name of the Lord Jesus was magnified. 18And many who had believed came confessing and telling their deeds. 19Also, many of those who had practiced magic brought their books together and burned *them* in the sight of all. And they counted up the value of them, and *it* totaled fifty thousand *pieces* of silver. 20So the word of the Lord grew mightily and prevailed.

The Riot at Ephesus

21When these things were accomplished, Paul purposed in the Spirit, when he had passed through Macedonia and Achaia, to go to Jerusalem, saying, "After I have been there, I must also see

19:13 [a]NU-Text reads *I.* **19:16** [a]M-Text reads *and they overpowered.* [b]NU-Text reads *both of them.*

Rome." [22]So he sent into Macedonia two of those who ministered to him, Timothy and Erastus, but he himself stayed in Asia for a time.

[23]And about that time there arose a great commotion about the Way. [24]For a certain man named Demetrius, a silversmith, who made silver shrines of Diana,[a] brought no small profit to the craftsmen. [25]He called them together with the workers of similar occupation, and said: "Men, you know that we have our prosperity by this trade. [26]Moreover you see and hear that not only at Ephesus, but throughout almost all Asia, this Paul has persuaded and turned away many people, saying that they are not gods which are made with hands. [27]So not only is this trade of ours in danger of falling into disrepute, but also the temple of the great goddess Diana may be despised and her magnificence destroyed,[a] whom all Asia and the world worship."

> That sin must die, or you will perish by it. Depend on it, that sin which you would save from the slaughter will slaughter you.
>
> **CHARLES SPURGEON**

[28]Now when they heard *this,* they were full of wrath and cried out, saying, "Great *is* Diana of the Ephesians!" [29]So the whole city was filled with confusion, and rushed into the theater with one accord, having seized Gaius and Aristarchus, Macedonians, Paul's travel companions. [30]And when Paul wanted to go in to the people, the disciples would not allow him. [31]Then some of the officials of Asia, who were his friends, sent to him pleading that he would not venture into the theater. [32]Some therefore cried one thing and some another, for the assembly was confused, and most of them did not know why they had come together. [33]And they drew Alexander out of the multitude, the Jews putting him forward. And Alexander motioned with his hand, and wanted to make his defense to the people. [34]But when they found out that he was a Jew, all with one voice cried out for about two hours, "Great *is* Diana of the Ephesians!"

[35]And when the city clerk had quieted the crowd, he said: "Men of Ephesus, what man is there who does not know that the city of the Ephesians is temple guardian of the great goddess Diana, and of the *image* which fell down from Zeus? [36]Therefore, since these things cannot be denied, you ought to be quiet and do nothing rashly. [37]For you have brought these men here who are neither robbers of temples nor blasphemers of your[a] goddess. [38]Therefore, if Demetrius and his fellow craftsmen have a case against anyone, the courts are open and there are proconsuls. Let them bring charges against one another. [39]But if you have any other inquiry to make, it shall be determined in the lawful assembly. [40]For we are in danger of being called in question for today's uproar, there being no reason which we may give to account for this disorderly gathering." [41]And when he had said these things, he dismissed the assembly.

For the key to reaching the lost, see Luke 11:52 comment.

Journeys in Greece

20 After the uproar had ceased, Paul called the disciples to *himself,* embraced *them,* and departed to go to Macedonia. [2]Now when he had gone over that region and encouraged them with many words, he came to Greece [3]and stayed three months. And when the Jews plotted against him as he was about to sail to Syria, he decided to return through

19:24 [a]Greek *Artemis* 19:27 [a]NU-Text reads *she be deposed from her magnificence.* 19:37 [a]NU-Text reads *our.*

Macedonia. [4]And Sopater of Berea accompanied him to Asia—also Aristarchus
and Secundus of the Thessalonians, and
Gaius of Derbe, and Timothy, and Tychicus and Trophimus of Asia. [5]These men,
going ahead, waited for us at Troas. [6]But
we sailed away from Philippi after the
Days of Unleavened Bread, and in five
days joined them at Troas, where we
stayed seven days.

Ministering at Troas

[7]Now on the first *day* of the week,
when the disciples came together to
break bread, Paul, ready to depart the
next day, spoke to them and continued
his message until midnight. [8]There were
many lamps in the upper room where
they[a] were gathered together. [9]And in a
window sat a certain young man named
Eutychus, who was sinking into a deep
sleep. He was overcome by sleep; and as
Paul continued speaking, he fell down
from the third story and was taken up
dead. [10]But Paul went down, fell on him,
and embracing *him* said, "Do not trouble
yourselves, for his life is in him." [11]Now
when he had come up, had broken bread
and eaten, and talked a long while, even
till daybreak, he departed. [12]And they
brought the young man in alive, and they
were not a little comforted.

From Troas to Miletus

[13]Then we went ahead to the ship and
sailed to Assos, there intending to take
Paul on board; for so he had given orders,
intending himself to go on foot. [14]And
when he met us at Assos, we took him on
board and came to Mitylene. [15]We sailed
from there, and the next *day* came opposite Chios. The following *day* we arrived
at Samos and stayed at Trogyllium. The
next *day* we came to Miletus. [16]For Paul
had decided to sail past Ephesus, so that
he would not have to spend time in Asia;
for he was hurrying to be at Jerusalem, if
possible, on the Day of Pentecost.

The Ephesian Elders Exhorted

[17]From Miletus he sent to Ephesus
and called for the elders of the church.
[18]And when they had come to him, he
said to them: "You know, from the first
day that I came to Asia, in what manner I
always lived among you, [19]serving the
Lord with all humility, with many tears
and trials which happened to me by the
plotting of the Jews; [20]how I kept back
nothing that was helpful, but proclaimed
it to you, and taught you publicly and
from house to house, [21]testifying to Jews,
and also to Greeks, repentance toward
God and faith toward our Lord Jesus
Christ. [22]And see, now I go bound in the
spirit to Jerusalem, not knowing the
things that will happen to me there, [23]ex-
cept that the Holy Spirit testifies in every
city, saying that chains and tribulations
await me. [24]But none of these things
move me; nor do I count my life dear to
myself,[a] so that I may finish my race with
joy, and the ministry which I received
from the Lord Jesus, to testify to the
gospel of the grace of God.
[25]"And indeed, now I know that you
all, among whom I have gone preaching
the kingdom of God, will see my face no
more. [26]Therefore I testify to you this day
that I *am* innocent of the blood of all *men*.
[27]For I have not shunned to declare to

20:8 [a]NU-Text and M-Text read *we.* **20:24** [a]NU-Text reads *But I do not count my life of any value or dear to myself.*

20:9 Eutychus had some good excuses for dozing off: Paul's sermon was long; the many lights no doubt made the room hot; he was a young man staying up until midnight; he was "overcome" by sleep.

It is the midnight hour. We sit on the window of eternity. We can fall into eternity in a heartbeat. If the stale air of this world's influence makes us sink into a sleep of apathy, we must seek refreshing from the presence of the Lord. When our Christian life seems to be a dry and lifeless sermon without end, and the joy of feeding on God's Word is no longer in our hearts, we must get on our knees and return to our first love.

20:21 Repentance—its necessity for salvation. See 2 Pet. 3:9.

POINTS FOR OPEN-AIR PREACHING

20:21

Aim for Repentance Rather Than a Decision

As you witness, divorce yourself from the thought that you are merely seeking "decisions for Christ." What we should be seeking is repentance within the heart. This is the purpose of the Law, to bring the knowledge of sin. How can a man repent if he doesn't know what sin is? If there is no repentance, there is no salvation. Jesus said, "Unless you repent you will all likewise perish" (Luke 13:3). God is not willing that any should perish, but that all should come to repentance (2 Pet. 3:9).

Many don't understand that the salvation of a soul is not a resolution to change a way of life, but "repentance toward God and faith toward our Lord Jesus Christ." The modern concept of success in evangelism is to relate how many people were "saved" (that is, how many prayed the "sinner's prayer"). This produces a "no decisions, no success" mentality. This shouldn't be, because Christians who seek decisions in evangelism become discouraged after a time of witnessing if "no one came to the Lord." The Bible tells us that as we sow the good seed of the gospel, one sows and another reaps. If you faithfully sow the seed, someone will reap. If you reap, it is because someone has sown in the past, but it is God who causes the seed to grow. If His hand is not on the person you are leading in a prayer of committal, if there is no God-given repentance, then you will end up with a stillbirth on your hands, and that is nothing to rejoice about. We should measure our success by how faithfully we sowed the seed. In that way, we will avoid becoming discouraged. For whether to lead someone in a prayer, see John 1:13 comment.

"If you have not repented, you will not see the inside of the kingdom of God." *Billy Graham*

you the whole counsel of God. 28There-
fore take heed to yourselves and to all the
flock, among which the Holy Spirit has
made you overseers, to shepherd the
church of God[a] which He purchased with
His own blood. 29For I know this, that after my departure savage wolves will come
in among you, not sparing the flock.
30Also from among yourselves men will
rise up, speaking perverse things, to draw
away the disciples after themselves.
31Therefore watch, and remember that
for three years I did not cease to warn
everyone night and day with tears.
32"So now, brethren, I commend you
to God and to the word of His grace,
which is able to build you up and give
you an inheritance among all those who
are sanctified. 33I have coveted no one's
silver or gold or apparel. 34Yes,[a] you
yourselves know that these hands have
provided for my necessities, and for those
who were with me. 35I have shown you in

20:28 [a]M-Text reads *of the Lord and God.* **20:34** [a]NU-Text and M-Text omit *Yes.*

20:24 A missionary society wrote to *David Livingstone* and suggested that if he could ensure them of safe roads, they would send him some help. He responded with the following note: "If you have men who will only come if they have a good road, I don't want them. I want men who will come if there is no road at all."

20:26 "My anxious desire is that every time I preach, I may clear myself of the blood of all men; that if I step from this platform to my coffin, I may have told out all I knew of the way of salvation." *Charles Spurgeon*

20:27 How to witness. Here is a suggested structure of a gospel message:

Begin in the natural realm if you are not in a normal church setting. Perhaps you could springboard off some well-publicized tragedy, then ask if your hearers ever wonder how they are going to die. Say that we will all die because we have broken an eternal law—the Law of God, often referred to as the Ten Commandments. Then open up each Commandment, emphasizing its spiritual nature (lust is seen by God as adultery, hatred is murder—that God sees man's thoughts, and nothing is hidden from His eyes).

Stress the fact of Judgment Day—that God is holy and will bring every work into judgment, including every secret thing whether it is good or evil. Don't be afraid to use the word "hell." Tell them that it is God's place of punishment for sin. Emphasize that He doesn't want them to go there, that He has made provision for their forgiveness. Then preach Christ and Him crucified, risen from the dead. Thoroughly lace the message with God's Word—verbally quote relevant Scriptures. Then preach the necessity of repentance (that it is *commanded*), and the importance of faith *in* and obedience *to* God's Word. See Acts 20:21 comment.

every way, by laboring like this, that you must support the weak. And remember the words of the Lord Jesus, that He said, 'It is more blessed to give than to receive.' "

[36]And when he had said these things, he knelt down and prayed with them all. [37]Then they all wept freely, and fell on Paul's neck and kissed him, [38]sorrowing most of all for the words which he spoke, that they would see his face no more. And they accompanied him to the ship.

Warnings on the Journey to Jerusalem

21 Now it came to pass, that when we had departed from them and set sail, running a straight course we came to Cos, the following *day* to Rhodes, and from there to Patara. [2]And finding a ship sailing over to Phoenicia, we went aboard and set sail. [3]When we had sighted Cyprus, we passed it on the left, sailed to Syria, and landed at Tyre; for there the ship was to unload her cargo. [4]And finding disciples,[a] we stayed there seven days. They told Paul through the Spirit not to go up to Jerusalem. [5]When we had come to the end of those days, we departed and went on our way; and they all accompanied us, with wives and children, till *we were* out of the city. And we knelt down on the shore and prayed. [6]When we had taken our leave of one another, we boarded the ship, and they returned home.

[7]And when we had finished *our* voyage from Tyre, we came to Ptolemais, greeted the brethren, and stayed with them one day. [8]On the next *day* we who were Paul's companions[a] departed and came to Caesarea, and entered the house of Philip the evangelist, who was *one* of the seven, and stayed with him. [9]Now this man had four virgin daughters who prophesied. [10]And as we stayed many days, a certain prophet named Agabus came down from Judea. [11]When he had come to us, he took Paul's belt, bound his *own* hands and feet, and said, "Thus says the Holy Spirit, 'So shall the Jews at Jerusalem bind the man who owns this belt, and deliver *him* into the hands of the Gentiles.' "

[12]Now when we heard these things, both we and those from that place pleaded with him not to go up to Jerusalem. [13]Then Paul answered, "What do you mean by weeping and breaking my heart? For I am ready not only to be bound, but also to die at Jerusalem for the name of the Lord Jesus."

[14]So when he would not be persuaded, we ceased, saying, "The will of the Lord be done."

Paul Urged to Make Peace

[15]And after those days we packed and went up to Jerusalem. [16]Also some of the disciples from Caesarea went with us and brought with them a certain Mnason of Cyprus, an early disciple, with whom we were to lodge.

[17]And when we had come to Jerusalem, the brethren received us gladly. [18]On the following *day* Paul went in with us to James, and all the elders were present. [19]When he had greeted them, he told in detail those things which God had done among the Gentiles through his ministry. [20]And when they heard *it,* they glorified the Lord. And they said to him, "You see, brother, how many myriads of Jews there are who have believed, and they are all zealous for the law; [21]but they have been informed about you that you teach all the Jews who are among the Gentiles to forsake Moses, saying that they ought not to circumcise *their* children nor to walk according to the customs. [22]What then? The assembly must certainly meet, for they will[a] hear that you have come. [23]Therefore do what we

21:4 [a]NU-Text reads *the disciples.* **21:8** [a]NU-Text omits *who were Paul's companions.* **21:22** [a]NU-Text reads *What then is to be done? They will certainly.*

21:5 Prayer—the secret weapon: See Mark 11:23.

POINTS FOR OPEN-AIR PREACHING

Raw Nerves

21:30

When you're preaching open-air, don't let angry reactions from the crowd concern you. A dentist knows where to work on a patient when he touches a raw nerve. When you touch a raw nerve in the heart of the sinner, it means that you are in business. Anger is a thousand times better than apathy. Anger is a sign of conviction. If I have an argument with my wife and suddenly realize that I am in the wrong, I can come to her in a repentant attitude and apologize, or I can save face by lashing out in anger.

Read Acts 19 and see how Paul was a dentist with an eye for decay. He probed raw nerves wherever he went. At one point, he had to be carried shoulder height by soldiers because of the "violence of the mob" (Acts 21:35). Now there's a successful preacher! He didn't seek the praise of men. *John Wesley* told his evangelist trainees that when they preached, people should either get angry or get converted. No doubt, he wasn't speaking about the "Jesus loves you" gospel, but about sin, Law, righteousness, judgment, and hell. See Matt. 28:19,20 comment.

tell you: We have four men who have
taken a vow. 24Take them and be purified
with them, and pay their expenses so that
they may shave *their* heads, and that all
may know that those things of which
they were informed concerning you are
nothing, but *that* you yourself also walk
orderly and keep the law. 25But concerning the Gentiles who believe, we have
written *and* decided that they should observe no such thing, except[a] that they
should keep themselves from *things* offered to idols, from blood, from things
strangled, and from sexual immorality."

Arrested in the Temple

26Then Paul took the men, and the
next day, having been purified with them,
entered the temple to announce the expi-
ration of the days of purification, at
which time an offering should be made
for each one of them.

27Now when the seven days were almost ended, the Jews from Asia, seeing
him in the temple, stirred up the whole
crowd and laid hands on him, 28crying
out, "Men of Israel, help! This is the man
who teaches all *men* everywhere against
the people, the law, and this place; and
furthermore he also brought Greeks into
the temple and has defiled this holy
place." 29(For they had previously[a] seen
Trophimus the Ephesian with him in the
city, whom they supposed that Paul had
brought into the temple.)

30And all the city was disturbed; and
the people ran together, seized Paul, and
dragged him out of the temple; and immediately the doors were shut. 31Now as
they were seeking to kill him, news came
to the commander of the garrison that all
Jerusalem was in an uproar. 32He immediately took soldiers and centurions, and
ran down to them. And when they saw
the commander and the soldiers, they
stopped beating Paul. 33Then the commander came near and took him, and
commanded *him* to be bound with two
chains; and he asked who he was and
what he had done. 34And some among
the multitude cried one thing and some
another.

So when he could not ascertain the
truth because of the tumult, he commanded him to be taken into the barracks. 35When he reached the stairs, he
had to be carried by the soldiers because
of the violence of the mob. 36For the multitude of the people followed after, crying
out, "Away with him!"

Addressing the Jerusalem Mob

37Then as Paul was about to be led
into the barracks, he said to the commander, "May I speak to you?"

He replied, "Can you speak Greek?
38Are you not the Egyptian who some

21:25 [a]NU-Text omits *that they should observe no such thing, except.* **21:29** [a]M-Text omits *previously.*

time ago stirred up a rebellion and led the four thousand assassins out into the wilderness?"

39But Paul said, "I am a Jew from Tarsus, in Cilicia, a citizen of no mean city; and I implore you, permit me to speak to the people."

40So when he had given him permission, Paul stood on the stairs and motioned with his hand to the people. And when there was a great silence, he spoke to *them* in the Hebrew language, saying,

22 "Brethren and fathers, hear my defense before you now." 2And when they heard that he spoke to them in the Hebrew language, they kept all the more silent.

Then he said: 3"I am indeed a Jew, born in Tarsus of Cilicia, but brought up in this city at the feet of Gamaliel, taught according to the strictness of our fathers' law, and was zealous toward God as you all are today. 4I persecuted this Way to the death, binding and delivering into prisons both men and women, 5as also the high priest bears me witness, and all the council of the elders, from whom I also received letters to the brethren, and went to Damascus to bring in chains even those who were there to Jerusalem to be punished.

6"Now it happened, as I journeyed and came near Damascus at about noon, suddenly a great light from heaven shone around me. 7And I fell to the ground and heard a voice saying to me, 'Saul, Saul, why are you persecuting Me?' 8So I answered, 'Who are You, Lord?' And He said to me, 'I am Jesus of Nazareth, whom you are persecuting.'

9"And those who were with me indeed saw the light and were afraid,[a] but they did not hear the voice of Him who spoke to me. 10So I said, 'What shall I do, Lord?' And the Lord said to me, 'Arise and go into Damascus, and there you will be told all things which are appointed for you to do.' 11And since I could not see for the glory of that light, being led by the hand of those who were with me, I came into Damascus.

12"Then a certain Ananias, a devout man according to the law, having a good testimony with all the Jews who dwelt *there,* 13came to me; and he stood and said to me, 'Brother Saul, receive your sight.' And at that same hour I looked up at him. 14Then he said, 'The God of our fathers has chosen you that you should know His will, and see the Just One, and hear the voice of His mouth. 15For you will be His witness to all men of what you have seen and heard. 16And now why are you waiting? Arise and be baptized, and wash away your sins, calling on the name of the Lord.'

> The greatest enemy to human souls is the self-righteous spirit which makes men look to themselves for salvation.
>
> **CHARLES SPURGEON**

17"Now it happened, when I returned to Jerusalem and was praying in the temple, that I was in a trance 18and saw Him saying to me, 'Make haste and get out of Jerusalem quickly, for they will not receive your testimony concerning Me.' 19So I said, 'Lord, they know that in every synagogue I imprisoned and beat those who believe on You. 20And when the blood of Your martyr Stephen was shed, I also was standing by consenting to his death,[a] and guarding the clothes of those who were

22:9 [a]NU-Text omits *and were afraid.* 22:20 [a]NU-Text omits *to his death.*

22:9 Contradiction in the Bible? Some may think that this is a mistake in the Scriptures, because in Acts 9:7 Paul said that those who were with him *heard* the voice. However, John 12:29 gives us insight into what God's voice sounds like. People *heard* His voice but thought that it thundered (see also 2 Sam. 22:14; Job 37:4,5; 40:9). They obviously heard it but the words were not coherent to them.

"Labor to keep alive in your breast that spark of celestial fire called conscience."

George Washington

killing him.' [21]Then He said to me, 'Depart, for I will send you far from here to
the Gentiles.' "

Paul's Roman Citizenship

[22]And they listened to him until this
word, and *then* they raised their voices
and said, "Away with such a *fellow* from
the earth, for he is not fit to live!" [23]Then,
as they cried out and tore off *their* clothes
and threw dust into the air, [24]the commander ordered him to be brought into
the barracks, and said that he should be
examined under scourging, so that he
might know why they shouted so against
him. [25]And as they bound him with
thongs, Paul said to the centurion who
stood by, "Is it lawful for you to scourge a
man who is a Roman, and uncondemned?"
[26]When the centurion heard *that,* he
went and told the commander, saying,
"Take care what you do, for this man is a
Roman."

[27]Then the commander came and said
to him, "Tell me, are you a Roman?"

He said, "Yes."

[28]The commander answered, "With a
large sum I obtained this citizenship."

And Paul said, "But I was born *a citizen.*"

[29]Then immediately those who were
about to examine him withdrew from
him; and the commander was also afraid
after he found out that he was a Roman,
and because he had bound him.

The Sanhedrin Divided

[30]The next day, because he wanted to
know for certain why he was accused by
the Jews, he released him from *his* bonds,
and commanded the chief priests and all
their council to appear, and brought Paul
down and set him before them.

23 Then Paul, looking earnestly at
the council, said, "Men *and*
brethren, I have lived in all good conscience before God until this day." [2]And
the high priest Ananias commanded
those who stood by him to strike him on
the mouth. [3]Then Paul said to him, "God
will strike you, *you* whitewashed wall!
For you sit to judge me according to the
law, and do you command me to be
struck contrary to the law?"

[4]And those who stood by said, "Do
you revile God's high priest?"

[5]Then Paul said, "I did not know,
brethren, that he was the high priest; for
it is written, *'You shall not speak evil of a
ruler of your people.'* "[a]

[6]But when Paul perceived that one
part were Sadducees and the other Pharisees, he cried out in the council, "Men
and brethren, I am a Pharisee, the son of
a Pharisee; concerning the hope and resurrection of the dead I am being judged!"

[7]And when he had said this, a dissension arose between the Pharisees and the
Sadducees; and the assembly was divided. [8]For Sadducees say that there is no
resurrection—and no angel or spirit; but
the Pharisees confess both. [9]Then there
arose a loud outcry. And the scribes of the
Pharisees' party arose and protested, saying, "We find no evil in this man; but if a

23:5 [a]Exodus 22:28

spirit or an angel has spoken to him, let us not fight against God."[a]

[10]Now when there arose a great dissension, the commander, fearing lest Paul might be pulled to pieces by them, commanded the soldiers to go down and take him by force from among them, and bring him into the barracks.

The Plot Against Paul

[11]But the following night the Lord stood by him and said, "Be of good cheer, Paul; for as you have testified for Me in Jerusalem, so you must also bear witness at Rome."

> I have known what it is to use up all my ammunition, and then I have, as it were, rammed myself into the great gospel gun and fired myself at the hearers—all my experience of God's goodness, all my consciousness of sin, and all my sense of the power of the gospel.
>
> **CHARLES SPURGEON**

[12]And when it was day, some of the Jews banded together and bound themselves under an oath, saying that they would neither eat nor drink till they had killed Paul. [13]Now there were more than forty who had formed this conspiracy. [14]They came to the chief priests and elders, and said, "We have bound ourselves under a great oath that we will eat nothing until we have killed Paul. [15]Now you, therefore, together with the council, suggest to the commander that he be brought down to you tomorrow,[a] as though you were going to make further inquiries concerning him; but we are ready to kill him before he comes near."

[16]So when Paul's sister's son heard of their ambush, he went and entered the barracks and told Paul. [17]Then Paul called one of the centurions to *him* and said, "Take this young man to the commander, for he has something to tell him." [18]So he took him and brought *him* to the commander and said, "Paul the prisoner called me to *him* and asked *me* to bring this young man to you. He has something to say to you."

[19]Then the commander took him by the hand, went aside, and asked privately, "What is it that you have to tell me?"

[20]And he said, "The Jews have agreed to ask that you bring Paul down to the council tomorrow, as though they were going to inquire more fully about him. [21]But do not yield to them, for more than forty of them lie in wait for him, men who have bound themselves by an oath that they will neither eat nor drink till they have killed him; and now they are ready, waiting for the promise from you."

[22]So the commander let the young man depart, and commanded *him,* "Tell no one that you have revealed these things to me."

Sent to Felix

[23]And he called for two centurions, saying, "Prepare two hundred soldiers, seventy horsemen, and two hundred spearmen to go to Caesarea at the third hour of the night; [24]and provide mounts to set Paul on, and bring *him* safely to Felix the governor." [25]He wrote a letter in the following manner:

[26]Claudius Lysias,

To the most excellent governor Felix:

Greetings.

[27]This man was seized by the Jews and was about to be killed by them. Coming with the troops I rescued him, having learned that he was a Roman. [28]And when I wanted to know the reason they accused him, I brought him before their council. [29]I found

23:9 [a]**NU-Text omits last clause and reads** ***what if a spirit or an angel has spoken to him?*** **23:15** [a]**NU-Text omits** ***tomorrow.***

out that he was accused
concerning questions of their law,
but had nothing charged against
him deserving of death or chains.
30And when it was told me that
the Jews lay in wait for the man,[a]
I sent him immediately to you,
and also commanded his
accusers to state before you the
charges against him.

Farewell.

31Then the soldiers, as they were commanded, took Paul and brought *him* by
night to Antipatris. 32The next day they
left the horsemen to go on with him, and
returned to the barracks. 33When they
came to Caesarea and had delivered the
letter to the governor, they also presented
Paul to him. 34And when the governor
had read *it*, he asked what province he
was from. And when he understood that
he was from Cilicia, 35he said, "I will hear
you when your accusers also have come."
And he commanded him to be kept in
Herod's Praetorium.

Accused of Sedition

24 Now after five days Ananias the
high priest came down with the
elders and a certain orator *named* Tertul-
lus. These gave evidence to the governor
against Paul.

2And when he was called upon, Ter-
tullus began his accusation, saying: "Seeing that through you we enjoy great
peace, and prosperity is being brought to
this nation by your foresight, 3we accept
it always and in all places, most noble Felix, with all thankfulness. 4Nevertheless,
not to be tedious to you any further, I beg
you to hear, by your courtesy, a few
words from us. 5For we have found this
man a plague, a creator of dissension
among all the Jews throughout the world,
and a ringleader of the sect of the
Nazarenes. 6He even tried to profane the
temple, and we seized him,[a] and wanted
to judge him according to our law. 7But
the commander Lysias came by and with
great violence took *him* out of our hands,
8commanding his accusers to come to
you. By examining him yourself you may
ascertain all these things of which we accuse him." 9And the Jews also assented,[a]
maintaining that these things were so.

The Defense Before Felix

10Then Paul, after the governor had
nodded to him to speak, answered: "Inasmuch as I know that you have been for
many years a judge of this nation, I do
the more cheerfully answer for myself,
11because you may ascertain that it is no
more than twelve days since I went up to
Jerusalem to worship. 12And they neither
found me in the temple disputing with
anyone nor inciting the crowd, either in
the synagogues or in the city. 13Nor can
they prove the things of which they now
accuse me. 14But this I confess to you,
that according to the Way which they call
a sect, so I worship the God of my fathers, believing all things which are written in the Law and in the Prophets. 15I
have hope in God, which they themselves
also accept, that there will be a resurrection of *the* dead,[a] both of *the* just and *the*
unjust. 16This *being* so, I myself always
strive to have a conscience without offense toward God and men.

17"Now after many years I came to
bring alms and offerings to my nation,
18in the midst of which some Jews from
Asia found me purified in the temple,
neither with a mob nor with tumult.

23:30 [a]NU-Text reads *there would be a plot against the man.* 24:6 [a]NU-Text ends the sentence here and omits the rest of verse 6, all of verse 7, and the first clause of verse 8. 24:9 [a]NU-Text and M-Text read *joined the attack.* 24:15 [a]NU-Text omits *of the dead.*

24:5 The apostle Paul was called a "plague," a "creator of dissension," and a "ringleader" of a "sect." The prophet Elijah was called a "troubler of Israel" (1 Kings 18:17). Those who stand for righteousness will be considered troublemakers in the world's eyes.

Questions & Objections

24:15

"Are Catholics, Methodists, Lutherans, Episcopals, etc., all false Christians?"

The Bible doesn't mention "Catholics, Methodists, Lutherans, Episcopals," etc. Instead, the Scriptures simply have two categories for humanity: the "just" and the "unjust." The "just" are those whom God has justified (made right with Himself through their repentance and faith in Jesus). The "unjust" are those who are still in their sins. The Bible warns that God will see that every wicked person gets exactly what he deserves: "So it will be at the end of the age. The angels will come forth, separate the wicked from among the just, and cast them into the furnace of fire. There will be wailing and gnashing of teeth" (Matt. 13:49,50). That's good news for those who care about justice.

So the question is, how is a person "justified"? The Bible says that we are freely justified by God's mercy. We are guilty criminals, but God acquits us from the courtroom because Jesus paid our fine. Everlasting life is a free gift of God (see Rom. 6:23). No one has to be "religious" to try to earn salvation from death. So who are the true Christians? Here is the Bible's answer: "Nevertheless the solid foundation of God stands, having this seal: 'The Lord knows those who are His,' and, 'Let everyone who names the name of Christ depart from iniquity'" (2 Tim. 2:19). So make sure you are the Lord's, and that if you name the name of Christ, you depart from iniquity (violation of God's Law).

19They ought to have been here before
you to object if they had anything against
me. 20Or else let those who are *here* themselves say if they found any wrongdoing[a]
in me while I stood before the council,
21unless *it is* for this one statement which
I cried out, standing among them, 'Concerning the resurrection of the dead I am
being judged by you this day.' "

Felix Procrastinates

22But when Felix heard these things,
having more accurate knowledge of *the*
Way, he adjourned the proceedings and
said, "When Lysias the commander
comes down, I will make a decision on
your case." 23So he commanded the centurion to keep Paul and to let *him* have
liberty, and told him not to forbid any of
his friends to provide for or visit him.

24And after some days, when Felix came
with his wife Drusilla, who was Jewish,
he sent for Paul and heard him concerning the faith in Christ. 25Now as he reasoned about righteousness, self-control,
and the judgment to come, Felix was
afraid and answered, "Go away for now;
when I have a convenient time I will call
for you." 26Meanwhile he also hoped that
money would be given him by Paul, that
he might release him.[a] Therefore he sent
for him more often and conversed with
him.

27But after two years Porcius Festus
succeeded Felix; and Felix, wanting to do
the Jews a favor, left Paul bound.

Paul Appeals to Caesar

25 Now when Festus had come to
the province, after three days he
went up from Caesarea to Jerusalem.
2Then the high priest[a] and the chief men
of the Jews informed him against Paul;
and they petitioned him, 3asking a favor
against him, that he would summon him
to Jerusalem—while *they* lay in ambush
along the road to kill him. 4But Festus answered that Paul should be kept at Caesarea, and that he himself was going *there*

24:20 [a]NU-Text and M-Text read *say what wrongdoing they found.* 24:26 [a]NU-Text omits *that he might release him.* 25:2 [a]NU-Text reads *chief priests.*

24:25 "What we think about God influences our friendship with Him... The Bible is our only safe source of knowledge about God—and it requires thinking. God's persistent invitation in every age remains: '"Come now, let us *reason* together," says the Lord' (Isa. 1:18)." *Joni Eareckson Tada*

Questions & Objections

24:25 "Is 'hell-fire' preaching effective?"

Preaching the reality of hell, without using the Law to bring the knowledge of sin, can do a great deal of damage to the cause of the gospel. A sinner cannot conceive of the thought that God would send anyone to hell, as long as he is deceived into thinking that God's standard of righteousness is the same as his. Paul "reasoned" with Felix regarding righteousness, self-control, and the coming judgment (Acts 24:25). This is the righteousness that is of the Law and judgment by the Law. Felix was afraid because he suddenly understood that his intemperance made him a guilty sinner in the sight of a holy God. The reality of hell suddenly became *reasonable* to him when the Law was used to bring the knowledge of sin.

Imagine if the police burst into your home, arrested you, and shouted, "You are going away for a long time!" Such conduct would probably leave you bewildered and angry. What they have done seems unreasonable.

However, imagine if the law burst into your home and instead told you specifically why you were in trouble: "We have discovered 10,000 marijuana plants growing in your back yard. You are going away for a long time!" At least then you would understand *why* you were in trouble. Knowledge of the law you have transgressed furnished you with that understanding. It makes judgment *reasonable*. Hell-fire preaching without use of the Law to show the sinner why God is angry with him will more than likely leave him bewildered and angry about what he considers *unreasonable* punishment.

shortly. 5"Therefore," he said, "let those
who have authority among you go down
with *me* and accuse this man, to see if
there is any fault in him."

6And when he had remained among
them more than ten days, he went down
to Caesarea. And the next day, sitting on
the judgment seat, he commanded Paul
to be brought. 7When he had come, the
Jews who had come down from Jerusalem
stood about and laid many serious
complaints against Paul, which they
could not prove, 8while he answered for
himself, "Neither against the law of the
Jews, nor against the temple, nor against
Caesar have I offended in anything at all."

9But Festus, wanting to do the Jews a
favor, answered Paul and said, "Are you
willing to go up to Jerusalem and there
be judged before me concerning these
things?"

10So Paul said, "I stand at Caesar's judgment
seat, where I ought to be judged. To
the Jews I have done no wrong, as you
very well know. 11For if I am an offender,
or have committed anything deserving of
death, I do not object to dying; but if
there is nothing in these things of which
these men accuse me, no one can deliver
me to them. I appeal to Caesar."

12Then Festus, when he had conferred
with the council, answered, "You have appealed
to Caesar? To Caesar you shall go!"

Paul Before Agrippa

13And after some days King Agrippa
and Bernice came to Caesarea to greet
Festus. 14When they had been there
many days, Festus laid Paul's case before
the king, saying: "There is a certain man
left a prisoner by Felix, 15about whom
the chief priests and the elders of the
Jews informed *me*, when I was in Jerusalem,
asking for a judgment against him.
16To them I answered, 'It is not the custom
of the Romans to deliver any man to
destruction[a] before the accused meets the
accusers face to face, and has opportunity
to answer for himself concerning the
charge against him.' 17Therefore when
they had come together, without any delay,
the next day I sat on the judgment
seat and commanded the man to be
brought in. 18When the accusers stood
up, they brought no accusation against
him of such things as I supposed, 19but

25:16 [a]NU-Text omits *to destruction*, although it is implied.

had some questions against him about
their own religion and about a certain Jesus, who had died, whom Paul affirmed
to be alive. [20]And because I was uncertain
of such questions, I asked whether he
was willing to go to Jerusalem and there
be judged concerning these matters.
[21]But when Paul appealed to be reserved
for the decision of Augustus, I commanded him to be kept till I could send
him to Caesar."

[22]Then Agrippa said to Festus, "I also
would like to hear the man myself."

"Tomorrow," he said, "you shall hear
him."

[23]So the next day, when Agrippa and
Bernice had come with great pomp, and
had entered the auditorium with the commanders and the prominent men of the
city, at Festus' command Paul was brought
in. [24]And Festus said: "King Agrippa and
all the men who are here present with us,
you see this man about whom the whole
assembly of the Jews petitioned me, both
at Jerusalem and here, crying out that he
was not fit to live any longer. [25]But when
I found that he had committed nothing
deserving of death, and that he himself
had appealed to Augustus, I decided to
send him. [26]I have nothing certain to
write to my lord concerning him. Therefore I have brought him out before you,
and especially before you, King Agrippa,
so that after the examination has taken
place I may have something to write. [27]For
it seems to me unreasonable to send a
prisoner and not to specify the charges
against him."

Paul's Early Life

26 Then Agrippa said to Paul, "You
are permitted to speak for yourself."

So Paul stretched out his hand and answered for himself: [2]"I think myself happy,
King Agrippa, because today I shall answer for myself before you concerning all
the things of which I am accused by the
Jews, [3]especially because you are expert
in all customs and questions which have
to do with the Jews. Therefore I beg you
to hear me patiently.

[4]"My manner of life from my youth,
which was spent from the beginning
among my own nation at Jerusalem, all
the Jews know. [5]They knew me from the
first, if they were willing to testify, that
according to the strictest sect of our religion I lived a Pharisee. [6]And now I stand
and am judged for the hope of the
promise made by God to our fathers. [7]To
this *promise* our twelve tribes, earnestly
serving *God* night and day, hope to attain.
For this hope's sake, King Agrippa, I am
accused by the Jews. [8]Why should it be
thought incredible by you that God raises
the dead?

> I care not how beautifully you sing; how eloquently you teach; how liberally you give; how circumspectly you walk—if you are not endeavoring to bring souls to Jesus Christ, you're not right with God. You . . . are guilty of high treason against heaven's King.
>
> **ADRIAN ROGERS**

[9]"Indeed, I myself thought I must do
many things contrary to the name of Jesus
of Nazareth. [10]This I also did in Jerusalem, and many of the saints I shut up in
prison, having received authority from
the chief priests; and when they were put
to death, I cast my vote against *them.*
[11]And I punished them often in every
synagogue and compelled *them* to blaspheme; and being exceedingly enraged
against them, I persecuted *them* even to
foreign cities.

Paul Recounts His Conversion

[12]"While thus occupied, as I journeyed to Damascus with authority and
commission from the chief priests, [13]at
midday, O king, along the road I saw a
light from heaven, brighter than the sun,
shining around me and those who journeyed with me. [14]And when we all had
fallen to the ground, I heard a voice speak-

QUESTIONS & OBJECTIONS

26:28 **"What should I say to someone who acknowledges his sins, but says, 'I just hope God is forgiving'?"**

These people could be referred to as "awakened, but not alarmed." Explain that God *is* forgiving—but only to those who repent of their sins. Ask him, "If you died right now, where would you go?" If he says, "Hell," ask if that concerns him. If it does concern him, ask, "What are you going to do?" Then tell him that God *commands* him to repent and trust the Savior. If it doesn't concern him, speak of the value of his life, the threat of *eternal* damnation, and the biblical description of hell. Caution him that he doesn't have the promise of tomorrow, and plead with him to come to his senses.

"Almost persuaded to be a Christian is like the man who was almost pardoned, but he was hanged; like the man who was almost rescued, but he was burned in the house. A man that is almost saved is damned." *Charles Spurgeon*

ing to me and saying in the Hebrew language, 'Saul, Saul, why are you persecuting Me? *It is* hard for you to kick against
the goads.' [15]So I said, 'Who are You,
Lord?' And He said, 'I am Jesus, whom
you are persecuting. [16]But rise and stand
on your feet; for I have appeared to you
for this purpose, to make you a minister
and a witness both of the things which
you have seen and of the things which I
will yet reveal to you. [17]I will deliver you
from the *Jewish* people, as well as *from* the
Gentiles, to whom I now[a] send you, [18]to
open their eyes, *in order* to turn *them*
from darkness to light, and *from* the
power of Satan to God, that they may receive forgiveness of sins and an inheritance among those who are sanctified by
faith in Me.'

Paul's Post-Conversion Life

[19]"Therefore, King Agrippa, I was not
disobedient to the heavenly vision, [20]but
declared first to those in Damascus and
in Jerusalem, and throughout all the region of Judea, and *then* to the Gentiles,
that they should repent, turn to God, and
do works befitting repentance. [21]For
these reasons the Jews seized me in the
temple and tried to kill *me*. [22]Therefore,
having obtained help from God, to this
day I stand, witnessing both to small and
great, saying no other things than those
which the prophets and Moses said
would come— [23]that the Christ would
suffer, that He would be the first to rise
from the dead, and would proclaim light
to the *Jewish* people and to the Gentiles."

Agrippa Parries Paul's Challenge

[24]Now as he thus made his defense,
Festus said with a loud voice, "Paul, you

26:17 [a]NU-Text and M-Text omit *now.*

26:20 The problem with modern evangelism. Many Christians obtain "decisions" by using the following method: "Do you know that you are going to heaven when you die?" Most will say, "I *hope* so." The Christian then says, "You can *know* so. The Bible says 'All have sinned.' Jesus died on the cross for our sins, and if you give your heart to Him today, you can know for sure that you are going to heaven. Would you like to have that assurance that you will go to heaven when you die?" He will almost always say, "Yes." The person is then led in what is commonly called a "sinner's prayer."

There are a few difficulties with this popular approach: 1) There is no mention of Judgment Day, the very *reason* men are commanded to repent; 2) There is no mention of hell; and 3) The Law isn't used to bring the knowledge of sin. The apostle Paul said that the Law was the *only* means by which he came to know what sin was (Rom. 7:7). The modern approach may get a decision or gain a church member, but if there is no biblical repentance, there will be a false conversion. See John 4:7 comment.

are beside yourself! Much learning is driving you mad!"

[25]But he said, "I am not mad, most noble Festus, but speak the words of truth and reason. [26]For the king, before whom I also speak freely, knows these things; for I am convinced that none of these things escapes his attention, since this thing was not done in a corner. [27]King Agrippa, do you believe the prophets? I know that you do believe."

[28]Then Agrippa said to Paul, "You almost persuade me to become a Christian."

[29]And Paul said, "I would to God that not only you, but also all who hear me today, might become both almost and altogether such as I am, except for these chains."

[30]When he had said these things, the king stood up, as well as the governor and Bernice and those who sat with them; [31]and when they had gone aside, they talked among themselves, saying, "This man is doing nothing deserving of death or chains."

[32]Then Agrippa said to Festus, "This man might have been set free if he had not appealed to Caesar."

The Voyage to Rome Begins

27 And when it was decided that we should sail to Italy, they delivered Paul and some other prisoners to *one* named Julius, a centurion of the Augustan Regiment. [2]So, entering a ship of Adramyttium, we put to sea, meaning to sail along the coasts of Asia. Aristarchus, a Macedonian of Thessalonica, was with us. [3]And the next *day* we landed at Sidon. And Julius treated Paul kindly and gave *him* liberty to go to his friends and receive care. [4]When we had put to sea from there, we sailed under *the shelter of* Cyprus, because the winds were contrary. [5]And when we had sailed over the sea which is off Cilicia and Pamphylia, we came to Myra, *a city* of Lycia. [6]There the centurion found an Alexandrian ship sailing to Italy, and he put us on board. [7]When we had sailed slowly many days, and arrived with difficulty off Cnidus, the wind not permitting us to proceed, we sailed under *the shelter of* Crete off Salmone. [8]Passing it with difficulty, we came to a place called Fair Havens, near the city *of* Lasea.

Paul's Warning Ignored

[9]Now when much time had been spent, and sailing was now dangerous because the Fast was already over, Paul advised them, [10]saying, "Men, I perceive that this voyage will end with disaster and much loss, not only of the cargo and ship, but also our lives." [11]Nevertheless the centurion was more persuaded by the helmsman and the owner of the ship than by the things spoken by Paul. [12]And because the harbor was not suitable to winter in, the majority advised to set sail from there also, if by any means they could reach Phoenix, a harbor of Crete opening toward the southwest and northwest, *and* winter *there*.

In the Tempest

[13]When the south wind blew softly, supposing that they had obtained *their* desire, putting out to sea, they sailed close by Crete. [14]But not long after, a tempestuous head wind arose, called Euroclydon.[a] [15]So when the ship was caught, and could not head into the wind, we let *her* drive. [16]And running under *the shelter of* an island called Clauda,[a] we secured the skiff with difficulty. [17]When they had taken it on board, they used cables to undergird the ship; and fearing lest they should run aground on the Syrtis[a] *Sands*, they struck sail and so were driven. [18]And because we were exceedingly tempest-tossed, the next *day* they lightened the ship. [19]On the third *day* we threw the ship's tackle overboard with our own hands. [20]Now when neither sun nor stars appeared for many days, and no

27:14 [a]NU-Text reads *Euraquilon.* **27:16** [a]NU-Text reads *Cauda.* **27:17** [a]M-Text reads *Syrtes.*

small tempest beat on *us*, all hope that we
would be saved was finally given up.
21But after long abstinence from food,
then Paul stood in the midst of them and
said, "Men, you should have listened to
me, and not have sailed from Crete and
incurred this disaster and loss. 22And
now I urge you to take heart, for there
will be no loss of life among you, but
only of the ship. 23For there stood by me
this night an angel of the God to whom I
belong and whom I serve, 24saying, 'Do
not be afraid, Paul; you must be brought
before Caesar; and indeed God has
granted you all those who sail with you.'
25Therefore take heart, men, for I believe
God that it will be just as it was told me.
26However, we must run aground on a
certain island."

What comes into our minds when we think about God is the most important thing about us.

A. W. TOZER

27Now when the fourteenth night had
come, as we were driven up and down in
the Adriatic *Sea*, about midnight the
sailors sensed that they were drawing
near some land. 28And they took soundings and found *it* to be twenty fathoms;
and when they had gone a little farther,
they took soundings again and found *it* to
be fifteen fathoms. 29Then, fearing lest we
should run aground on the rocks, they
dropped four anchors from the stern, and
prayed for day to come. 30And as the
sailors were seeking to escape from the
ship, when they had let down the skiff
into the sea, under pretense of putting
out anchors from the prow, 31Paul said to
the centurion and the soldiers, "Unless
these men stay in the ship, you cannot be
saved." 32Then the soldiers cut away the
ropes of the skiff and let it fall off.
33And as day was about to dawn, Paul
implored *them* all to take food, saying,
"Today is the fourteenth day you have
waited and continued without food, and
eaten nothing. 34Therefore I urge you to
take nourishment, for this is for your survival, since not a hair will fall from the
head of any of you." 35And when he had
said these things, he took bread and gave
thanks to God in the presence of them
all; and when he had broken *it* he began
to eat. 36Then they were all encouraged,
and also took food themselves. 37And in
all we were two hundred and seventy-six
persons on the ship. 38So when they had
eaten enough, they lightened the ship
and threw out the wheat into the sea.

Shipwrecked on Malta

39When it was day, they did not recognize the land; but they observed a bay
with a beach, onto which they planned to
run the ship if possible. 40And they let go
the anchors and left *them* in the sea,
meanwhile loosing the rudder ropes; and
they hoisted the mainsail to the wind and
made for shore. 41But striking a place where
two seas met, they ran the ship aground;
and the prow stuck fast and remained
immovable, but the stern was being broken up by the violence of the waves.
42And the soldiers' plan was to kill the
prisoners, lest any of them should swim
away and escape. 43But the centurion,
wanting to save Paul, kept them from
their purpose, and commanded that
those who could swim should jump *overboard* first and get to land, 44and the rest,
some on boards and some on *parts* of the
ship. And so it was that they all escaped
safely to land.

Paul's Ministry on Malta

28 Now when they had escaped,
they then found out that the island was called Malta. 2And the natives
showed us unusual kindness; for they
kindled a fire and made us all welcome,
because of the rain that was falling and
because of the cold. 3But when Paul had
gathered a bundle of sticks and laid *them*
on the fire, a viper came out because of
the heat, and fastened on his hand. 4So

when the natives saw the creature hanging from his hand, they said to one another, "No doubt this man is a murderer,
whom, though he has escaped the sea,
yet justice does not allow to live." 5But he
shook off the creature into the fire and
suffered no harm. 6However, they were
expecting that he would swell up or suddenly fall down dead. But after they had
looked for a long time and saw no harm
come to him, they changed their minds
and said that he was a god.

7In that region there was an estate of
the leading citizen of the island, whose
name was Publius, who received us and
entertained us courteously for three days.
8And it happened that the father of Publius lay sick of a fever and dysentery. Paul
went in to him and prayed, and he laid
his hands on him and healed him. 9So
when this was done, the rest of those on
the island who had diseases also came and
were healed. 10They also honored us in
many ways; and when we departed, they
provided such things as were necessary.

Arrival at Rome

11After three months we sailed in an
Alexandrian ship whose figurehead was
the Twin Brothers, which had wintered at
the island. 12And landing at Syracuse, we
stayed three days. 13From there we circled round and reached Rhegium. And
after one day the south wind blew; and
the next day we came to Puteoli, 14where
we found brethren, and were invited to
stay with them seven days. And so we
went toward Rome. 15And from there,
when the brethren heard about us, they
came to meet us as far as Appii Forum
and Three Inns. When Paul saw them, he
thanked God and took courage.

16Now when we came to Rome, the
centurion delivered the prisoners to the
captain of the guard; but Paul was permitted to dwell by himself with the soldier who guarded him.

Paul's Ministry at Rome

17And it came to pass after three days
that Paul called the leaders of the Jews
together. So when they had come together, he said to them: "Men *and*
brethren, though I have done nothing
against our people or the customs of our
fathers, yet I was delivered as a prisoner
from Jerusalem into the hands of the Romans, 18who, when they had examined
me, wanted to let *me* go, because there
was no cause for putting me to death.
19But when the Jews[a] spoke against *it*, I
was compelled to appeal to Caesar, not
that I had anything of which to accuse
my nation. 20For this reason therefore I
have called for you, to see *you* and speak
with *you*, because for the hope of Israel I
am bound with this chain."

21Then they said to him, "We neither
received letters from Judea concerning
you, nor have any of the brethren who
came reported or spoken any evil of you.
22But we desire to hear from you what
you think; for concerning this sect, we
know that it is spoken against everywhere."

23So when they had appointed him a
day, many came to him at *his* lodging, to
whom he explained and solemnly testified of the kingdom of God, persuading
them concerning Jesus from both the
Law of Moses and the Prophets, from
morning till evening. 24And some were
persuaded by the things which were spoken, and some disbelieved. 25So when they
did not agree among themselves, they departed after Paul had said one word: "The
Holy Spirit spoke rightly through Isaiah
the prophet to our[a] fathers, 26saying,

28:19 [a]That is, the ruling authorities **28:25** [a]NU-Text reads *your.*

28:23 The goal of evangelism is to persuade people concerning Jesus. He is the way, the truth, and the life. There is salvation in no other name.

USING THE LAW IN EVANGELISM

28:23 Notice that Paul used *both* prophecy and the Law of Moses in his evangelism. Prophecy appeals to a man's intellect and creates faith in the Word of God. As he realizes that the Bible is no ordinary book—that it contains numerous indisputable prophecies that prove its supernatural origin—he begins to give Scripture credibility. However, the Law of Moses appeals to a man's conscience and brings conviction of sin. A "decision" for Jesus purely in the realm of the intellect—with no biblical knowledge of sin, which comes only by the Law (Rom. 7:7)—will almost certainly produce a false convert. See Rom. 2:21 comment.

"The Law's part in transformation is to make a person aware of his sin and of his need for divine forgiveness and redemption and to set the standard of acceptable morality.

"Until a person acknowledges his basic sinfulness and inability to perfectly fulfill the demands of God's Law, he will not come repentantly to seek salvation. Until he despairs of himself and his own sinfulness, he will not come in humble faith to be filled with Christ's righteousness. A person who says he wants salvation but refuses to recognize and repent of his sin deceives himself.

"Grace means nothing to a person who does not know he is sinful and that such sinfulness means he is separated from God and damned. It is therefore pointless to preach grace until the impossible demands of the Law and the reality of guilt before God are preached." *John MacArthur*

'Go to this people and say:
"Hearing you will hear, and shall not
understand;
And seeing you will see, and not
perceive;
27 *For the hearts of this people have*
grown dull.
Their ears are hard of hearing,
And their eyes they have closed,
Lest they should see with their eyes
and hear with their ears,
Lest they should understand with
their hearts and turn,
So that I should heal them." '[a]

28 "Therefore let it be known to you
that the salvation of God has been sent to
the Gentiles, and they will hear it!" 29 And
when he had said these words, the Jews
departed and had a great dispute among
themselves.[a]

30 Then Paul dwelt two whole years in
his own rented house, and received all who
came to him, 31 preaching the kingdom of
God and teaching the things which concern the Lord Jesus Christ with all confidence, no one forbidding him.

28:27 [a]Isaiah 6:9, 10 28:29 [a]NU-Text omits this verse.

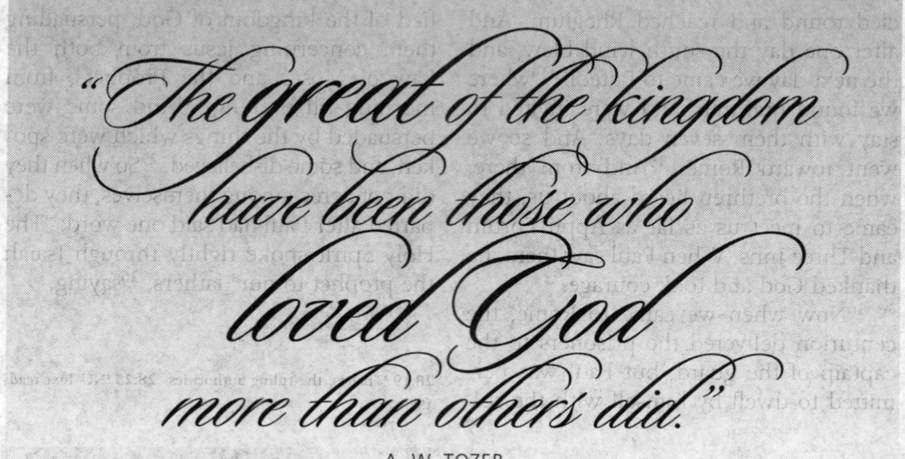

"The great of the kingdom have been those who loved God more than others did."
A. W. TOZER

Romans

Greeting

1 Paul, a bondservant of Jesus Christ, called *to be* an apostle, separated to the gospel of God [2]which He promised before through His prophets in the Holy Scriptures, [3]concerning His Son Jesus Christ our Lord, who was born of the seed of David according to the flesh, [4]*and* declared *to be* the Son of God with power according to the Spirit of holiness, by the resurrection from the dead. [5]Through Him we have received grace and apostleship for obedience to the faith among all nations for His name, [6]among whom you also are the called of Jesus Christ;

[7]To all who are in Rome, beloved of God, called *to be* saints:

Grace to you and peace from God our Father and the Lord Jesus Christ.

Desire to Visit Rome

[8]First, I thank my God through Jesus Christ for you all, that your faith is spoken of throughout the whole world. [9]For God is my witness, whom I serve with my spirit in the gospel of His Son, that without ceasing I make mention of you always in my prayers, [10]making request if, by some means, now at last I may find a way in the will of God to come to you. [11]For I long to see you, that I may impart to you some spiritual gift, so that you may be established— [12]that is, that I may be encouraged together with you by the mutual faith both of you and me.

[13]Now I do not want you to be unaware, brethren, that I often planned to come to you (but was hindered until now), that I might have some fruit among you also, just as among the other Gentiles. [14]I am a debtor both to Greeks and to barbarians, both to wise and to unwise. [15]So, as much as is in me, *I am* ready to preach the gospel to you who are in Rome also.

The Just Live by Faith

[16]For I am not ashamed of the gospel of Christ,[a] for it is the power of God to salvation for everyone who believes, for the Jew first and also for the Greek. [17]For in it the righteousness of God is revealed from faith to faith; as it is written, *"The just shall live by faith."*[a]

God's Wrath on Unrighteousness

[18]For the wrath of God is revealed from heaven against all ungodliness and unrighteousness of men, who suppress the truth in unrighteousness, [19]because what may be known of God is manifest in

1:16 [a]NU-Text omits *of Christ.* 1:17 [a]Habakkuk 2:4

1:14 "So long as there is a human being who does not know Jesus Christ, I am his debtor to serve him until he does." *Oswald Chambers*

Questions & Objections

"There is no reason to believe that a supernatural, intelligent Creator exists."

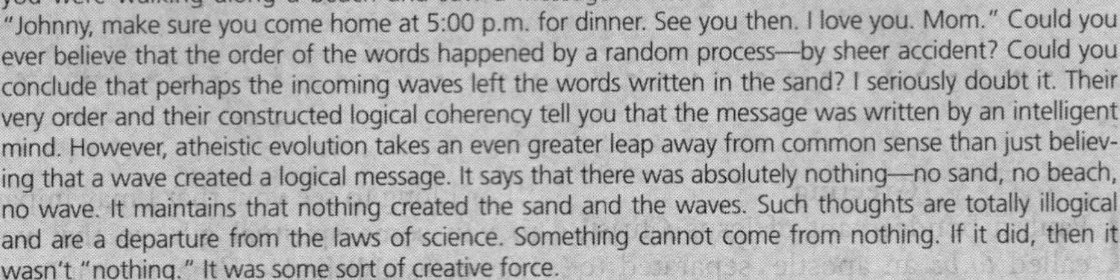

There are trillions of reasons to believe in a supernatural, intelligent Creator. From DNA, to the basic atom, to the amazingly designed tiny fleas, to massive elephants, to the sun and its circuit, to the millions of stars and the entire universe, there is incredible complexity and order throughout creation. Let's say you were walking along a beach and saw a message written in the sand: "Johnny, make sure you come home at 5:00 p.m. for dinner. See you then. I love you. Mom." Could you ever believe that the order of the words happened by a random process—by sheer accident? Could you conclude that perhaps the incoming waves left the words written in the sand? I seriously doubt it. Their very order and their constructed logical coherency tell you that the message was written by an intelligent mind. However, atheistic evolution takes an even greater leap away from common sense than just believing that a wave created a logical message. It says that there was absolutely nothing—no sand, no beach, no wave. It maintains that nothing created the sand and the waves. Such thoughts are totally illogical and are a departure from the laws of science. Something cannot come from nothing. If it did, then it wasn't "nothing." It was some sort of creative force.

What proof is there that this God exists? Even though through my natural senses I cannot see, hear, touch, taste, or smell Him, there is one other sense that I must not overlook. It is called "common" sense. When I look at a building, how can I know that there was a builder? I cannot see him, hear him, touch, taste, or smell him. Common sense tells me that the building is absolute 100 percent scientific proof that there was a builder. There cannot be a building without a builder. Buildings don't build themselves. I don't need faith to believe in a builder; all I need is eyes that can see and a brain that works.

This same concept is true for paintings and painters. When I look at a painting, how can I know there was a painter? Common sense tells me that the painting is absolute 100 percent scientific proof that there was a painter. Paintings don't happen by themselves. I couldn't want better proof that there was a painter than to have the painting in front of me. I don't need faith to believe in a painter; all I need is eyes that can see and a brain that works.

Exactly the same reasoning applies with the existence of God. How can we know God exists? We cannot see Him, hear Him, touch, taste, or smell Him. Common sense tells us that creation is absolute 100 percent scientific proof that there was a Creator. We cannot have a creation without a Creator. We don't need faith to believe in a Creator. All we need is eyes that can see and a brain that works. This is exactly what the Bible says: "For since the creation of the world His invisible attributes are clearly seen, being understood by the things that are made, even His eternal power and Godhead, so that they are without excuse" (Rom. 1:20).

So, just as I don't need faith to believe in a builder because I have the building in front of me, so I don't need faith to believe in a Creator, because I have creation in front of me. However, if I want the builder to do something for me, then I need to have faith in him. The same is true with God: "But without faith it is impossible to please Him, for he who comes to God must believe that He is, and that He is a rewarder of those who diligently seek Him" (Heb. 11:6).

Albert Einstein may not have trusted in Jesus Christ as his Lord and Savior, but he believed in the existence of God. He said, "In the view of such harmony in the cosmos which I, with my limited human mind, am able to recognize, there are yet people who say there is no God. But what makes me really angry is that they quote me for support of such views." A little child and the genius of Albert Einstein have one thing in common: common sense.

"This most beautiful system of the sun, planets, and comets could only proceed from the counsel and dominion of an intelligent and powerful Being." *Sir Isaac Newton*

"The more I study nature, the more I stand amazed at the work of the Creator." *Louis Pasteur*

them, for God has shown *it* to them.
20For since the creation of the world His
invisible *attributes* are clearly seen, being
understood by the things that are made,
even His eternal power and Godhead, so
that they are without excuse, 21because,

although they knew God, they did not
glorify *Him* as God, nor were thankful,
but became futile in their thoughts, and
their foolish hearts were darkened. 22Pro-
fessing to be wise, they became fools,
23and changed the glory of the incorrupt-

ible God into an image made like corruptible man—and birds and four-footed animals and creeping things.

[24]Therefore God also gave them up to uncleanness, in the lusts of their hearts, to dishonor their bodies among themselves, [25]who exchanged the truth of God for the lie, and worshiped and served the creature rather than the Creator, who is blessed forever. Amen.

> My main business is the saving of souls. This one thing I do.
>
> **CHARLES SPURGEON**

[26]For this reason God gave them up to vile passions. For even their women exchanged the natural use for what is against nature. [27]Likewise also the men, leaving the natural use of the woman, burned in their lust for one another, men with men committing what is shameful, and receiving in themselves the penalty of their error which was due.

[28]And even as they did not like to retain God in *their* knowledge, God gave them over to a debased mind, to do those things which are not fitting; [29]being filled with all unrighteousness, sexual immorality,[a] wickedness, covetousness, maliciousness; full of envy, murder, strife, deceit, evil-mindedness; *they are* whisperers, [30]backbiters, haters of God, violent, proud, boasters, inventors of evil things, disobedient to parents, [31]undiscerning, untrustworthy, unloving, unforgiving,[a] unmerciful; [32]who, knowing the righteous judgment of God, that those who practice such things are deserving of death, not only do the same but also approve of those who practice them.

God's Righteous Judgment

2 Therefore you are inexcusable, O man, whoever you are who judge, for in whatever you judge another you condemn yourself; for you who judge practice the same things. [2]But we know that the judgment of God is according to truth against those who practice such things. [3]And do you think this, O man, you who judge those practicing such things, and doing the same, that you will escape the judgment of God? [4]Or do you despise the riches of His goodness, forbearance, and longsuffering, not knowing that the goodness of God leads you to repentance? [5]But in accordance with your hardness and your impenitent heart you are treasuring up for yourself wrath in the day of wrath and revelation of the righteous judgment of God, [6]who ***"will render to each one according to his deeds"***:[a] [7]eternal life to those who by patient continuance in doing good seek for glory, honor, and immortality; [8]but to those who are self-seeking and do not obey the truth, but obey unrighteousness—indignation and wrath, [9]tribulation and anguish, on every soul of man who does evil, of the Jew first and also of the Greek; [10]but glory,

1:29 [a]NU-Text omits *sexual immorality.* 1:31 [a]NU-Text omits *unforgiving.* 2:6 [a]Psalm 62:12; Proverbs 24:12

1:27 Homosexuality. Despite claims to the contrary, no scientific evidence has been found that homosexuals are "born that way." In fact, God's Word is clear that sexual activity is to be only within the bounds of marriage, between one man and one woman. Homosexuality goes against God's created order and expressed will. If a homosexual claims to be born that way, gently explain that all people are born with a sin nature, but that our nature makes us children of wrath. See also 1 Tim. 1:9,10 and Jude 7 comments.

2:4 This verse is sandwiched between statements of God's judgment and wrath. If Paul was saying that we should speak only of God's goodness to sinners, he wasn't practicing what he preached.

"I never knew but one person in the whole course of my ministry who acknowledged that the first motions of religion in his own heart arose from a sense of the goodness of God, 'What shall I render to the Lord, who has dealt so bountifully with me?' But I think all besides who have come within my notice have rather been first awakened to fly from the wrath to come by the passion of fear." *Isaac Watts*

QUESTIONS & OBJECTIONS

2:12

"What about people who have never heard of Jesus Christ—are they all going to hell?"

The inference is that those who have never heard the gospel are basically good people who do not deserve to go to hell. So, tell the questioner that they will be fine—if they are good people. However, in God's eyes "good" is moral perfection in thought, word, and deed. So if they have broken even one Law—lied, stolen, murdered (hated), or committed adultery (lusted)—they will get what they deserve. (See Rom. 1—3.) God will do what is right and just, and will punish wrongdoing no matter where it is found. That is why we send missionaries to these people—so they can be saved from their sins through faith in Jesus.

Second, the person is really questioning God's character. If some people were never given a chance to hear and be saved, then God must be unable to reach them and uncaring in letting them go to hell. But Scripture tells us that God wants all men to be saved and to come to the knowledge of the truth (1 Tim. 2:4), and that He has given light to every man (John 1:9). We have the light of creation, telling us there is a Creator, and the light of conscience, telling us there is a moral Law (and therefore a Lawgiver). All who respond to the light they are given will be given more. Everyone who seeks God in truth will find Him—they will be given the light of the gospel.

Because God is omnipotent and omnipresent, no one is beyond His reach: "And He has made from one blood every nation of men to dwell on all the face of the earth, and has determined their preappointed times and the boundaries of their dwellings, *so that they should seek the Lord*, in the hope that they might grope for Him and find Him, though He is not far from each one of us" (Acts 17:26,27, emphasis added).

We see examples in Scripture of people in faraway lands seeking the true God, such as the three wise men in Persia (Matt. 2) and the Roman centurion Cornelius (Acts 10). Cornelius was *sincere* but wasn't worshiping God in truth, so God gave him a vision and sent him someone who "will tell you what you must do." This is why God sent Philip to speak with the Ethiopian eunuch (Acts 8:26–29).

We have countless examples today where people, like Cornelius, are given visions and dreams about Jesus. There are thousands of Muslims coming to Christ every year after Jesus has supernaturally revealed Himself to them. Others who realize the religion in which they were raised is just not true may have a dream telling them to go to the marketplace at noon, where a missionary passes by to hand them a Bible. Even in countries hostile to the gospel, God knows those whose hearts are seeking Him, and He will find a way to get the gospel to them.

So once you have assured the person that God is not willing that *any* should perish—no matter where they live—then say, "Now, let's get back to you . . ." See also John 16:9 comment.

"When men earnestly seek the Lord and are in earnest about their salvation, they will soon find Christ. You do not need to go up to the heights to bring Him down, or down to the depths to bring Him up, or go off to some distant city to find Him. This day He is near to every one of us." *D. L. Moody*

honor, and peace to everyone who works
what is good, to the Jew first and also to
the Greek. [11]For there is no partiality with
God.
[12]For as many as have sinned without
law will also perish without law, and as
many as have sinned in the law will be
judged by the law [13](for not the hearers
of the law *are* just in the sight of God, but
the doers of the law will be justified; [14]for
when Gentiles, who do not have the law,
by nature do the things in the law, these,
although not having the law, are a law to
themselves, [15]who show the work of the
law written in their hearts, their conscience also bearing witness, and between themselves *their* thoughts accusing
or else excusing *them*) [16]in the day when
God will judge the secrets of men by Jesus Christ, according to my gospel.

The Jews Guilty as the Gentiles

[17]Indeed[a] you are called a Jew, and rest
on the law, and make your boast in God,
[18]and know *His* will, and approve the
things that are excellent, being instructed

2:17 [a]NU-Text reads *But if.*

Using the Law in Evangelism

2:21 Paul has just been speaking about the human conscience bearing witness with God's Law (v. 15). Now he applies the Law to the conscience to bring "the knowledge of sin." He *personalizes* the Eighth Commandment: "You who preach that a man should not steal, do *you* steal?" (v. 21, emphasis added). The conscience agrees with the Commandment that it is morally wrong to steal. This is why I find it so beneficial to ask someone who professes to be a "good" person how many lies he thinks he has told in his life. When he says, "Hundreds," I ask, "What do you call someone who tells lies?" When he answers, "A liar," he is being shown the *personal* nature of his sins. Then Paul uses the Seventh Commandment, personalizing it by asking, "Do *you* commit adultery?" (v. 22, emphasis added). When you take someone through the moral Law, on this Commandment don't forget to explain that Jesus said if we even look with lust, we commit adultery in our hearts (see Matt. 5:27,28). See also Mark 10:17 and James 2:8 comments.

Dr. J Gresham Machen said, "A new and more powerful proclamation of [the] Law is perhaps the most pressing need of the hour; men would have little difficulty with the gospel if they had only learned the lesson of the Law."

out of the law, [19]and are confident that
you yourself are a guide to the blind, a
light to those who are in darkness, [20]an
instructor of the foolish, a teacher of
babes, having the form of knowledge and
truth in the law. [21]You, therefore, who
teach another, do you not teach yourself?
You who preach that a man should not
steal, do you steal? [22]You who say, "Do
not commit adultery," do you commit
adultery? You who abhor idols, do you
rob temples? [23]You who make your boast
in the law, do you dishonor God through
breaking the law? [24]For *"the name of God
is blasphemed among the Gentiles because of you,"*[a] as it is written.

Circumcision of No Avail

[25]For circumcision is indeed profitable
if you keep the law; but if you are a
breaker of the law, your circumcision has
become uncircumcision. [26]Therefore, if
an uncircumcised man keeps the righteous requirements of the law, will not his
uncircumcision be counted as circumcision? [27]And will not the physically uncircumcised, if he fulfills the law, judge you
who, *even* with *your* written *code* and circumcision, *are* a transgressor of the law?
[28]For he is not a Jew who *is one* outwardly, nor *is* circumcision that which *is*
outward in the flesh; [29]but *he is* a Jew
who *is one* inwardly; and circumcision *is*
that of the heart, in the Spirit, not in the
letter; whose praise *is* not from men but
from God.

God's Judgment Defended

3 What advantage then has the Jew, or
what *is* the profit of circumcision?
[2]Much in every way! Chiefly because to
them were committed the oracles of
God. [3]For what if some did not believe?
Will their unbelief make the faithfulness
of God without effect? [4]Certainly not!
Indeed, let God be true but every man a
liar. As it is written:

2:24 [a]Isaiah 52:5; Ezekiel 36:22

2:15 The sinner's conscience. Human understanding is "darkened" (Eph. 4:18), but the conscience is the area where God has given light to every man. The word "con-science" means "with knowledge." The conscience is the headline warning of sin; the Scriptures give the fine print. None of us can say that we don't know it is wrong to lie, steal, murder, or commit adultery; that knowledge is written in large print on our heart. However, in the Scriptures we see the true nature of sin: that God requires truth even in the inward parts (see Psa. 51:6). The fine print reveals that lust is adultery of the heart, hatred is murder of the heart, fibs are bearing false witness, etc.

"Conscience is the internal perception of God's moral Law." *Oswald Chambers*

2:15,16 Leading sinners to Jesus: *There are two witnesses to our crimes.* In addition to our conscience, God Himself accuses us. See 1 Cor. 6:9,10 comment.

2:16 Judgment Day: For verses that warn of its reality, see Rom. 14:10.

QUESTIONS & OBJECTIONS

3:1 "How should I witness to a Jew?"

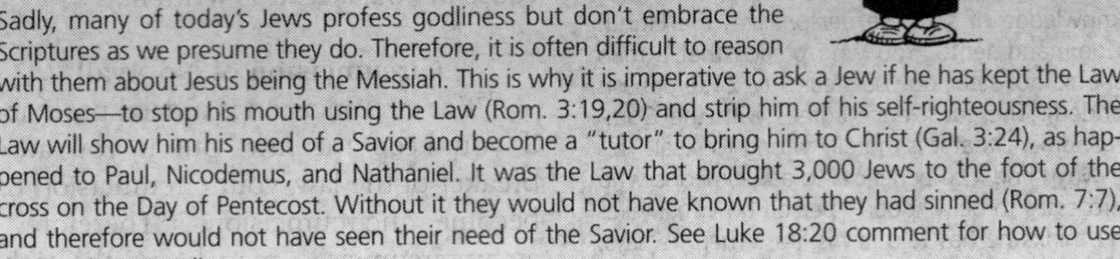

Sadly, many of today's Jews profess godliness but don't embrace the Scriptures as we presume they do. Therefore, it is often difficult to reason with them about Jesus being the Messiah. This is why it is imperative to ask a Jew if he has kept the Law of Moses—to stop his mouth using the Law (Rom. 3:19,20) and strip him of his self-righteousness. The Law will show him his need of a Savior and become a "tutor" to bring him to Christ (Gal. 3:24), as happened to Paul, Nicodemus, and Nathaniel. It was the Law that brought 3,000 Jews to the foot of the cross on the Day of Pentecost. Without it they would not have known that they had sinned (Rom. 7:7), and therefore would not have seen their need of the Savior. See Luke 18:20 comment for how to use the Law in evangelism.

"That You may be justified in Your
words,
And may overcome when You are
judged."[a]

5But if our unrighteousness demonstrates the righteousness of God, what
shall we say? *Is* God unjust who inflicts
wrath? (I speak as a man.) 6Certainly not!
For then how will God judge the world?
7For if the truth of God has increased
through my lie to His glory, why am I also
still judged as a sinner? 8And *why* not *say,*
"Let us do evil that good may come"?—as
we are slanderously reported and as some
affirm that we say. Their condemnation is
just.

All Have Sinned

9What then? Are we better *than they?*
Not at all. For we have previously charged
both Jews and Greeks that they are all
under sin.
10As it is written:

"There is none righteous, no, not one;
11*There is none who understands;*
There is none who seeks after God.
12*They have all turned aside;*
They have together become
unprofitable;
There is none who does good, no, not
one."[a]
13*"Their throat is an open tomb;*
With their tongues they have
practiced deceit";[a]
"The poison of asps is under their
lips";[b]
14*"Whose mouth is full of cursing and*
bitterness."[a]
15*"Their feet are swift to shed blood;*
16*Destruction and misery are in their*
ways;
17*And the way of peace they have not*
known."[a]
18*"There is no fear of God before their*
eyes."[a]

19Now we know that whatever the law
says, it says to those who are under the
law, that every mouth may be stopped,
and all the world may become guilty before God. 20Therefore by the deeds of the
law no flesh will be justified in His sight,
for by the law is the knowledge of sin.

3:4 [a]Psalm 51:4 3:12 [a]Psalms 14:1–3; 53:1–3; Ecclesiastes 7:20 3:13 [a]Psalm 5:9 [b]Psalm 140:3 3:14 [a]Psalm 10:7 3:17 [a]Isaiah 59:7, 8 3:18 [a]Psalm 36:1

3:19 "Every unredeemed human being, Jew or Gentile, is under the Law of God and accountable to God. The final verdict, then, is that unredeemed mankind has no defense whatever and is guilty of all charges. The defense must rest, as it were, before it has opportunity to say anything, because the omniscient and all-wise God has infallibly demonstrated the impossibility of any grounds of acquittal. Absolute silence is the only possible response." *John MacArthur*

QUESTIONS & OBJECTIONS

3:9

"Do you think that Christians are better than non-Christians?"

The Christian is no better than a non-Christian, but he is infinitely *better off*. It is like two men on a plane, one of whom is wearing a parachute while the other is not. Neither is better than the other, but the man with the parachute is certainly better off than the man who is not wearing a parachute. The difference will be seen when they jump from the plane at 20,000 feet. Jesus warned that if we "jump" into death without Him, we would perish.

Even harsher than the law of gravity is the Law of an infinitely holy and just Creator. Scripture states that sinners are God's enemy (Rom.5:10) and that "it is a fearful thing to fall into the hands of the living God" (Heb. 10:31).

God's Righteousness Through Faith

[21]But now the righteousness of God
apart from the law is revealed, being witnessed by the Law and the Prophets,
[22]even the righteousness of God, through
faith in Jesus Christ, to all and on all[a]
who believe. For there is no difference;
[23]for all have sinned and fall short of the
glory of God, [24]being justified freely by
His grace through the redemption that is
in Christ Jesus, [25]whom God set forth *as*
a propitiation by His blood, through
faith, to demonstrate His righteousness,
because in His forbearance God had
passed over the sins that were previously
committed, [26]to demonstrate at the present time His righteousness, that He
might be just and the justifier of the one
who has faith in Jesus.

Boasting Excluded

[27]Where *is* boasting then? It is excluded. By what law? Of works? No, but
by the law of faith. [28]Therefore we conclude that a man is justified by faith apart
from the deeds of the law. [29]Or *is He* the
God of the Jews only? *Is He* not also the
God of the Gentiles? Yes, of the Gentiles
also, [30]since *there is* one God who will
justify the circumcised by faith and the
uncircumcised through faith. [31]Do we
then make void the law through faith?
Certainly not! On the contrary, we establish the law.

THE FUNCTION OF THE LAW

3:19 The purpose of the Law is to stop the sinner's mouth of justification. The Law tells him what sin is (see 1 John 3:4) and stops him proclaiming his own goodness. Its intent is to drive him to the cross. *John Wesley* said, "The first use of [the Law], without question, is to convince the world of sin. By this is the sinner discovered to himself. All his fig-leaves are torn away, and he sees that he is 'wretched and poor and miserable, blind and naked.' The Law flashes conviction on every side. He feels himself a mere sinner. He has nothing to pay. His 'mouth is stopped' and he stands 'guilty before God.'"

"Ask Paul why [the Law] was given. Here is his answer, 'That every mouth may be stopped, and all the world may become guilty before God' (Rom. 3:19). The Law stops every man's mouth. I can always tell a man who is near the kingdom of God; his mouth is stopped. This, then, is why God gives us the Law—to show us ourselves in our true colors." *D. L. Moody*

Abraham Justified by Faith

4 What then shall we say that Abraham
our father has found according to the
flesh?[a] [2]For if Abraham was justified by
works, he has *something* to boast about,
but not before God. [3]For what does the
Scripture say? *"Abraham believed God,*
and it was accounted to him for right-
eousness."[a] [4]Now to him who works, the
wages are not counted as grace but as
debt.

3:22 [a]NU-Text omits *and on all.* 4:1 [a]Or *Abraham our (fore)father according to the flesh has found?* 4:3 [a]Genesis 15:6

THE FUNCTION OF THE LAW

3:20 Sin is like smog—it is not visible while you are in its midst. The Law takes the sinner above the smog of his own perspective and shows him heaven's viewpoint. It gives the sinner knowledge of his sin. *John Bunyan* stated, "The man who does not know the nature of the Law cannot know the nature of sin."

"The trouble with people who are not seeking for a Savior, and for salvation, is that they do not understand the nature of sin. It is the peculiar function of the Law to bring such an understanding to a man's mind and conscience. That is why great evangelical preachers 300 years ago in the time of the Puritans, and 200 years ago in the time of Whitefield and others, always engaged in what they called a preliminary 'Law work.'" *Martyn Lloyd-Jones*

"The first duty of the gospel preacher is to declare God's Law and show the nature of sin." *Martin Luther*

David Celebrates the Same Truth

5But to him who does not work but believes on Him who justifies the ungodly, his faith is accounted for righteousness, 6just as David also describes the blessedness of the man to whom God imputes righteousness apart from works:

7*"Blessed are those whose lawless*
deeds are forgiven,
And whose sins are covered;
8*Blessed is the man to whom the LORD*
shall not impute sin."[a]

Abraham Justified Before Circumcision

9*Does* this blessedness then *come* upon the circumcised *only,* or upon the uncircumcised also? For we say that faith was accounted to Abraham for righteousness.
10How then was it accounted? While he was circumcised, or uncircumcised? Not while circumcised, but while uncircumcised. 11And he received the sign of circumcision, a seal of the righteousness of the faith which *he had while still* uncircumcised, that he might be the father of all those who believe, though they are uncircumcised, that righteousness might be imputed to them also, 12and the father of circumcision to those who not only *are* of the circumcision, but who also walk in the steps of the faith which our father Abraham *had while still* uncircumcised.

The Promise Granted Through Faith

13For the promise that he would be the heir of the world *was* not to Abraham or to his seed through the law, but through the righteousness of faith. 14For if those who are of the law *are* heirs, faith is made void and the promise made of no effect, 15because the law brings about wrath; for where there is no law *there is* no transgression.

16Therefore *it is* of faith that *it might be* according to grace, so that the promise might be sure to all the seed, not only to those who are of the law, but also to those who are of the faith of Abraham, who is the father of us all 17(as it is written, *"I have made you a father of many nations"*[a]) in the presence of Him whom he believed—God, who gives life to the dead and calls those things which do not exist as though they did; 18who, contrary to hope, in hope believed, so that he became the father of many nations, according to what was spoken, *"So shall your descendants be."*[a] 19And not being weak in faith, he did not consider his own body, already dead (since he was about a hundred years old), and the deadness of Sarah's womb. 20He did not waver at the promise of God through unbelief, but

4:8 [a]Psalm 32:1, 2 4:17 [a]Genesis 17:5 4:18 [a]Genesis 15:5

4:20 There is a wise saying: If it sounds too good to be true, it probably is. That is solid advice when you are dealing with sinful mankind. But the promises of God—of forgiveness of sin, of peace with God through trusting in the Savior, of a new heaven and a new earth—come from a faithful Creator, and there is no greater insult to God than not to believe His promises.

was strengthened in faith, giving glory to God, 21and being fully convinced that what He had promised He was also able to perform. 22And therefore *"it was accounted to him for righteousness."*[a]

23Now it was not written for his sake alone that it was imputed to him, 24but also for us. It shall be imputed to us who believe in Him who raised up Jesus our Lord from the dead, 25who was delivered up because of our offenses, and was raised because of our justification.

Faith Triumphs in Trouble

5 Therefore, having been justified by faith, we have[a] peace with God through our Lord Jesus Christ, 2through whom also we have access by faith into this grace in which we stand, and rejoice in hope of the glory of God. 3And not only *that,* but we also glory in tribulations, knowing that tribulation produces perseverance; 4and perseverance, character; and character, hope. 5Now hope does not disappoint, because the love of God has been poured out in our hearts by the Holy Spirit who was given to us.

Christ in Our Place

6For when we were still without strength, in due time Christ died for the ungodly. 7For scarcely for a righteous man will one die; yet perhaps for a good man someone would even dare to die. 8But God demonstrates His own love toward us, in that while we were still sinners, Christ died for us. 9Much more then, having now been justified by His blood, we shall be saved from wrath through Him. 10For if when we were enemies we were reconciled to God through the death of His Son, much more, having been reconciled, we shall be saved by His life. 11And not only *that,* but we also rejoice in God through our Lord Jesus Christ, through whom we have now received the reconciliation.

Death in Adam, Life in Christ

12Therefore, just as through one man sin entered the world, and death through sin, and thus death spread to all men, because all sinned— 13(For until the law sin was in the world, but sin is not imputed when there is no law. 14Nevertheless death reigned from Adam to Moses, even over those who had not sinned according to the likeness of the transgression of Adam, who is a type of Him who was to come. 15But the free gift *is* not like the offense. For if by the one man's offense many died, much more the grace of God and the gift by the grace of the one Man, Jesus Christ, abounded to many. 16And the gift *is* not like *that which came* through the one who sinned. For the judgment *which came* from one *offense resulted* in condemnation, but the free gift *which came* from many offenses *resulted* in justification. 17For if by the one man's offense death reigned through the one, much more those who receive abundance of grace and of the gift of righteousness will reign

4:22 [a]Genesis 15:6 **5:1** [a]Another ancient reading is, *let us have peace.*

5:8 "God proved His love on the cross. When Christ hung, and bled, and died, it was God saying to the world, 'I love you.'" *Billy Graham*

5:14 Many years ago, a man jumped off a high bridge in an effort to end his life. Fortunately, he lived through the ordeal but broke his back as a result of the fall, and ended up in a wheelchair. His attempt to take his life caused a great deal of distress, to those in control of the bridge, to paramedics, to traffic, and especially to his family. Authorities wanted to press charges against him but they couldn't; since this was the city's first suicide attempt, they had no law forbidding such an act. He escaped the consequences of the law of man, but suffered the painful consequences of breaking another law, the law of gravity.

In the same way, even before there was a written moral Law, every person in Adam has sinned and therefore suffered the consequences of breaking the Law: "The soul who sins shall die" (Ezek. 18:4). Death reigned as king, with a dominion from Adam to Moses. Although others didn't eat from the Tree of Knowledge of Good and Evil as did Adam, they still sinned against God.

QUESTIONS & OBJECTIONS

5:12

"Why is there suffering? That proves there is no loving God."

Study the soil for a moment. It naturally produces weeds. No one plants them; no one waters them. They even stubbornly push through cracks of a dry sidewalk. Millions of useless weeds sprout like there's no tomorrow, strangling our crops and ruining our lawns. Pull them out by the roots, and there will be more tomorrow. They are nothing but a curse!

Consider how much of the earth is uninhabitable. There are millions of square miles of barren deserts in Africa and other parts of the world. Most of Australia is nothing but miles and miles of useless desolate land. Not only that, but the earth is constantly shaken with massive earthquakes. Its shores are lashed with hurricanes; tornadoes rip through creation with incredible fury; devastating floods soak the land; and terrible droughts parch the soil.

Sharks, tigers, lions, snakes, spiders, and disease-carrying mosquitoes attack humanity and suck its life's blood. The earth's inhabitants are afflicted with disease, pain, suffering, and death. Think of how many people are plagued with cancer, Alzheimer's, multiple sclerosis, heart disease, emphysema, Parkinson's, and a number of other debilitating illnesses. Consider all the children with leukemia, or people born with crippling diseases or without the mental capability to even feed themselves. All these things should convince thinking minds that something is radically wrong.

Did God blow it when He created humanity? What sort of tyrant must our Creator be if this was His master plan?

Sadly, many use the issue of suffering as an excuse to reject any thought of God, when its existence is the *very reason* we should believe Him. Suffering stands as terrible testimony to the truth of the explanation given by the Word of God. But how can we know that the Bible is true? Simply by studying the prophecies of Matt. 24, Luke 21, and 2 Tim. 3. A few minutes of openhearted inspection will convince any honest skeptic that this is no ordinary book. It is the supernatural testament of our Creator about why there is suffering . . . and what we can do about it.

The Bible tells us that God cursed the earth because of Adam's transgression. Weeds are a curse. So is disease. Sin and suffering cannot be separated. The Scriptures inform us that we live in a *fallen* creation. In the beginning, God created man perfect, and he lived in a perfect world without suffering. *It was heaven on earth.* When sin came into the world, death and misery came with it.

Those who understand the message of Holy Scripture eagerly await a new heaven and a new earth "in which righteousness dwells." In that coming Kingdom there will be no more pain, suffering, disease, or death. We are told that no eye has ever seen, nor has any ear heard, nor has any man's mind ever imagined the wonderful things that God has in store for those who love Him (1 Cor. 2:9). Think for a moment what it would be like if food grew with the fervor of weeds. Consider how wonderful it would be if the deserts became incredibly fertile, if creation stopped devouring humanity. Imagine if the weather worked *for* us instead of against us, if disease completely disappeared, if pain was a thing of the past, if death was no more.

The dilemma is that we are like a child whose insatiable appetite for chocolate has caused his face to break out with ugly sores. He looks in the mirror and sees a sight that makes him depressed. But instead of giving up his beloved chocolate, he consoles himself by stuffing more into his mouth. Yet, the source of his pleasure is actually the cause of his suffering.

The whole face of the earth is nothing but ugly sores of suffering. Everywhere we look we see unspeakable pain. But instead of believing God's explanation and asking Him to forgive us and change our appetite, we run deeper into sin's sweet embrace. There we find solace in its temporal pleasures, thus intensifying our pain, both in this life and in the life to come.

---

in life through the One, Jesus Christ.)
18Therefore, as through one man's offense *judgment came* to all men, resulting in condemnation, even so through one Man's righteous act *the free gift came* to all men, resulting in justification of life.
19For as by one man's disobedience many were made sinners, so also by one Man's obedience many will be made righteous.
20Moreover the law entered that the offense might abound. But where sin abounded, grace abounded much more,
21so that as sin reigned in death, even so grace might reign through righteousness to eternal life through Jesus Christ our Lord.

Dead to Sin, Alive to God

6 What shall we say then? Shall we continue in sin that grace may abound? [2]Certainly not! How shall we who died to sin live any longer in it? [3]Or do you not know that as many of us as were baptized into Christ Jesus were baptized into His death? [4]Therefore we were buried with Him through baptism into death, that just as Christ was raised from the dead by the glory of the Father, even so we also should walk in newness of life.

> I would sooner bring one sinner to Jesus Christ than unpick all the mysteries of the divine Word, for salvation is the thing we are to live for.
>
> **CHARLES SPURGEON**

[5]For if we have been united together in the likeness of His death, certainly we also shall be *in the likeness* of *His* resurrection, [6]knowing this, that our old man was crucified with *Him,* that the body of sin might be done away with, that we should no longer be slaves of sin. [7]For he who has died has been freed from sin. [8]Now if we died with Christ, we believe that we shall also live with Him, [9]knowing that Christ, having been raised from the dead, dies no more. Death no longer has dominion over Him. [10]For *the death* that He died, He died to sin once for all; but *the life* that He lives, He lives to God. [11]Likewise you also, reckon yourselves to be dead indeed to sin, but alive to God in Christ Jesus our Lord.

[12]Therefore do not let sin reign in your mortal body, that you should obey it in its lusts. [13]And do not present your members *as* instruments of unrighteousness to sin, but present yourselves to God as being alive from the dead, and your members *as* instruments of righteousness to God. [14]For sin shall not have dominion over you, for you are not under law but under grace.

From Slaves of Sin to Slaves of God

[15]What then? Shall we sin because we are not under law but under grace? Certainly not! [16]Do you not know that to whom you present yourselves slaves to obey, you are that one's slaves whom you obey, whether of sin *leading* to death, or of obedience *leading* to righteousness? [17]But God be thanked that *though* you were slaves of sin, yet you obeyed from the heart that form of doctrine to which you were delivered. [18]And having been set free from sin, you became slaves of righteousness. [19]I speak in human *terms* because of the weakness of your flesh. For just as you presented your members *as* slaves of uncleanness, and of lawlessness *leading* to *more* lawlessness, so now present your members *as* slaves *of* righteousness for holiness.

[20]For when you were slaves of sin, you were free in regard to righteousness. [21]What fruit did you have then in the things of which you are now ashamed? For the end of those things *is* death. [22]But now having been set free from sin, and having become slaves of God, you have your fruit to holiness, and the end, everlasting life. [23]For the wages of sin *is* death, but the gift of God *is* eternal life in Christ Jesus our Lord.

5:20 "God's grace cannot be faithfully preached to unbelievers until His Law is preached and man's corrupt nature is exposed. It is impossible for a person to fully realize his need for God's grace until he sees how terribly he has failed the standards of God's Law. It is impossible for him to realize his need for mercy until he realizes the magnitude of his guilt." *John MacArthur*

6:6 See 1 Pet. 4:1 comment.

6:14 In Christ we are sheltered under the umbrella of grace from the rain of the wrath of the Law. Paul is not saying that the Law has been done away with. Jesus Himself said that He hadn't come to do away with the Law. We "establish" the Law in Christ (Rom. 3:31). We corroborate it. It still remains as the standard of God's righteousness, and it will be the means by which He will judge the world (see Ezek. 44:24 comment).

Springboards for Preaching and Witnessing

Be Wise

6:23

One key to good health is to check the genetic makeup of your ancestors. Did your great-grandmother have problems with diabetes or osteoporosis? Then adjust your sugar and calcium accordingly. Did your grandfather die of heart disease? Then lay off too much fat and get plenty of exercise. Find out the potential problems, then work toward their avoidance.

That's what I did when I was 22 years old. I looked at my ancestors and saw that they had all died. All of them. So I began to see if there was any way for the potential problem of death to be avoided. First, I found the cause of death (something the scientific community cannot figure out). It is a terminal genetic disease called "sin." Then, to my utter amazement (by the grace of God), I discovered the cure: repentance toward God and implicit trust in Jesus Christ. After all these years, my amazement is still there.

A wise man once said that when he became a Christian, he gave up what he could not keep (his temporal life) to gain what he could not lose (the eternal life of God). Be wise; give up your life. Surrender it to God, and put your trust in the only Savior, Jesus Christ. If you are genuine in your commitment to Him, you will never look back, and you will never regret it. Not for a millisecond . . . and you will live in eternal amazement.

Freed from the Law

7 Or do you not know, brethren (for I
speak to those who know the law),
that the law has dominion over a man as
long as he lives? 2For the woman who
has a husband is bound by the law to *her*
husband as long as he lives. But if the
husband dies, she is released from the
law of *her* husband. 3So then if, while *her*
husband lives, she marries another man,
she will be called an adulteress; but if
her husband dies, she is free from that
law, so that she is no adulteress, though
she has married another man. 4There-
fore, my brethren, you also have become
dead to the law through the body of
Christ, that you may be married to another—to Him who was raised from the
dead, that we should bear fruit to God.
5For when we were in the flesh, the sinful passions which were aroused by the
law were at work in our members to bear
fruit to death. 6But now we have been
delivered from the law, having died to
what we were held by, so that we should
serve in the newness of the Spirit and
not *in* the oldness of the letter.

Sin's Advantage in the Law

7What shall we say then? *Is* the law
sin? Certainly not! On the contrary, I would
not have known sin except through the
law. For I would not have known covetousness unless the law had said, *"You
shall not covet."*[a] 8But sin, taking opportunity by the commandment, produced
in me all *manner of* evil desire. For apart
from the law sin *was* dead. 9I was alive

7:7 [a]Exodus 20:17; Deuteronomy 5:21

7:7 "Even with the light of nature, and the light of conscience, and the light of tradition, there are some things we should never have believed to be sins had we not been taught so by the Law." *Charles Spurgeon*

"The only way we can know whether we are sinning is by knowing His moral Law." *Jonathan Edwards*

7:9 "It is right for a preacher of the gospel first, by a revelation of the Law and of sin, to rebuke everything and make sin of everything that is not the living fruit of the Spirit and faith in Christ, so that men may be led to know themselves and their own wretchedness, and become humble and ask for help. No one knows that lime has heat until he pours water upon it. Then the heat has occasion to show itself. The water did not create the heat in the lime, but it has made itself manifest. It is similar to the will of man and the Law.

"'I was alive without the law once: but when the commandment came, sin revived' (Rom. 7:9). So it is with the work-righteous and the proud unbelievers. Because they do not know the Law of God, which is directed against them, it is impossible for them to know their sin. Therefore also they are not amenable to instruction. If they would know the Law, they would also know their sin; and sin to which they are now dead would become alive in them." *Martin Luther*

THE FUNCTION OF THE LAW

7:11 "To slay the sinner is then the first use of the Law, to destroy the life and strength wherein he trusts and convince him that he is dead while he lives; not only under the sentence of death, but actually dead to God, void of all spiritual life, dead in trespasses and sins." *John Wesley*

once without the law, but when the commandment came, sin revived and I died.
[10]And the commandment, which *was* to
bring life, I found to *bring* death. [11]For sin,
taking occasion by the commandment,
deceived me, and by it killed *me*. [12]Therefore the law *is* holy, and the commandment holy and just and good.

Law Cannot Save from Sin

[13]Has then what is good become death
to me? Certainly not! But sin, that it might appear sin, was producing death in me through what is good, so that sin through the commandment might become exceedingly sinful. [14]For we know
that the law is spiritual, but I am carnal,
sold under sin. [15]For what I am doing, I
do not understand. For what I will to do, that I do not practice; but what I hate,
that I do. [16]If, then, I do what I will not
to do, I agree with the law that *it is* good.
[17]But now, *it is* no longer I who do it, but
sin that dwells in me. [18]For I know that
in me (that is, in my flesh) nothing good dwells; for to will is present with me, but *how* to perform what is good I do not
find. [19]For the good that I will *to do,* I do
not do; but the evil I will not *to do,* that I
practice. [20]Now if I do what I will not *to
do,* it is no longer I who do it, but sin that dwells in me.
[21]I find then a law, that evil is present
with me, the one who wills to do good.
[22]For I delight in the law of God according
to the inward man. [23]But I see another law
in my members, warring against the law of my mind, and bringing me into captivity to the law of sin which is in my members. [24]O wretched man that I am! Who
will deliver me from this body of death?
[25]I thank God—through Jesus Christ our
Lord!

So then, with the mind I myself serve the law of God, but with the flesh the law of sin.

Free from Indwelling Sin

8 *There* is therefore now no condemnation to those who are in Christ Jesus,[a] who do not walk according to the flesh,

8:1 [a]NU-Text omits the rest of this verse.

7:18,19 There is disagreement about whether Paul is speaking of his pre-conversion experience or the battle the Christian has with sin. It would seem that both interpretations may be applied. God bless the Christian who is able to obtain "sinless perfection." He is a better man than most Christians. Rather, the majority of believers can identify with *George Whitefield*: "After we are renewed, yet we are renewed but in part, indwelling sin continues in us, there is a mixture of corruption in every one of our duties; so that after we are converted, were Jesus Christ only to accept us according to our works, our works would damn us, for we cannot put up a prayer but it is far from that perfection which the moral Law requireth. I do not know what you may think, but I can say that I cannot pray but I sin—cannot preach to you or others but I sin—I can do nothing without sin; and, as one expresseth it, my repentance wants to be repented of, and my tears to be washed in the precious blood of my dear Redeemer."

7:22 In speaking of the Christian's attitude to the Law, *John Wesley* said, "Yea, love and value it for the sake of Him from whom it came, and of Him to whom it leads. Let it be thy glory and joy, next to the cross of Christ. Declare its praise, and make it honorable before all men."

"Never, never let us despise [the Law]. It is the symptom of an ignorant ministry, and unhealthy state of religion, when the Law is reckoned unimportant. The true Christian delights in God's Law." *J. C. Ryle*

7:24,25 *Mahatma Gandhi* acknowledged the inability of his religion to atone for sin. Despite his moral lifestyle and good works, he admitted, "It is a constant torture to me that I am still so far from Him whom I know to be my very life and being. I know it is my own wretchedness and wickedness that keeps me from Him." All works-based religions lead to futility and death. It is only in Jesus Christ that sinners can find forgiveness for their sins and deliverance from death and hell. For more on Hinduism, see pages 603 and 1263.

but according to the Spirit. [2]For the law of the Spirit of life in Christ Jesus has made me free from the law of sin and death. [3]For what the law could not do in that it was weak through the flesh, God *did* by sending His own Son in the likeness of sinful flesh, on account of sin: He condemned sin in the flesh, [4]that the righteous requirement of the law might be fulfilled in us who do not walk according to the flesh but according to the Spirit. [5]For those who live according to the flesh set their minds on the things of the flesh, but those *who live* according to the Spirit, the things of the Spirit. [6]For to be carnally minded *is* death, but to be spiritually minded *is* life and peace. [7]Because the carnal mind *is* enmity against God; for it is not subject to the law of God, nor indeed can be. [8]So then, those who are in the flesh cannot please God.

[9]But you are not in the flesh but in the Spirit, if indeed the Spirit of God dwells in you. Now if anyone does not have the Spirit of Christ, he is not His. [10]And if Christ *is* in you, the body *is* dead because of sin, but the Spirit *is* life because of righteousness. [11]But if the Spirit of Him who raised Jesus from the dead dwells in you, He who raised Christ from the dead will also give life to your mortal bodies through His Spirit who dwells in you.

Sonship Through the Spirit

[12]Therefore, brethren, we are debtors—not to the flesh, to live according to the flesh. [13]For if you live according to the flesh you will die; but if by the Spirit you put to death the deeds of the body, you will live. [14]For as many as are led by the Spirit of God, these are sons of God. [15]For you did not receive the spirit of bondage again to fear, but you received the Spirit of adoption by whom we cry out, "Abba, Father." [16]The Spirit Himself bears witness with our spirit that we are children of God, [17]and if children, then heirs—heirs of God and joint heirs with Christ, if indeed we suffer with *Him*, that we may also be glorified together.

. . . . . .

How did the apostles die?
See Acts 7:59.

. . . . . .

From Suffering to Glory

[18]For I consider that the sufferings of this present time are not worthy *to be compared* with the glory which shall be revealed in us. [19]For the earnest expectation of the creation eagerly waits for the revealing of the sons of God. [20]For the creation was subjected to futility, not willingly, but because of Him who subjected *it* in hope; [21]because the creation itself also will be delivered from the bondage of corruption into the glorious liberty of the children of God. [22]For we know that the whole creation groans and labors with birth pangs together until now. [23]Not only *that*, but we also who have the firstfruits of the Spirit, even we ourselves groan within ourselves, eagerly waiting for the adoption, the redemption of our body. [24]For we were saved in this hope, but hope that is seen is not hope; for why does one still hope for what he sees? [25]But if we hope for what we do not see,

8:2 A higher Law. One hundred fifty years ago it would have been thought insane that a jumbo jet, filled with people, could fly. The law of gravity made it impossible for even a feather to remain in the air. Yet, we know that when a certain object moves at a particular speed, it moves out of the law of gravity into a higher law—the law of aerodynamics—even though the law of gravity still remains. The world thinks the Christian is insane to live for Jesus Christ. But we know that, even though there is the law of sin and death, we live in a higher law—the law of the Spirit of life in Christ Jesus.

8:6 "Let no man think of fighting hell's legions if he is still fighting an internal warfare. Carnage without will sicken him if he has carnality within. It is the man who has surrendered to the Lord who will never surrender to his enemies." *Leonard Ravenhill*

QUESTIONS & OBJECTIONS

8:22 "Mother Nature sure blew it…"

Hurricanes, tornadoes, floods, droughts, and earthquakes kill tens of thousands of people each year. Multitudes endure crippling diseases, endless suffering, and unspeakable pain (see Rom. 5:12 comment). Many non-Christians credit a heartless Mother Nature for giving us all this grief. They fail to consider that "Mother Nature" has a Senior Partner—Father God.

However, if God is responsible for all this heartache, that presents an interesting dilemma. If God is an "all-loving" Father figure, as we are told, we seem to have three choices: 1) God blew it when He made everything (He's creative but incompetent); 2) God is a tyrant, who gets His kicks from seeing kids die of leukemia; 3) something between God and man is radically wrong. These are our choices…and those who take time to consider the evidence will lean toward number three. Something between man and God *is* radically wrong, and the Bible tells us what it is. It was Adam's sin that brought a curse upon all creation, and mankind has been in continual rebellion against God since then.

There is a war going on. We are told that mankind is an enemy of God in his mind through wicked works (Col. 1:21). That's not too hard to see. Man is continually committing violent acts such as murder and rape, lying, stealing, etc., as the daily news confirms. He uses God's name as a curse word, while Mother Nature gets the glory for His creation—unless there's a horrible disaster; then man calls that "an act of God."

An applicable acronym for WAR is We Are Right. Any country going to war does so because it has the conviction that it is in the right. However, a quick look at God's Law shows us who is right and who is wrong. We, not God, are the guilty party. If we want His blessing back on our nation and in our lives, we must make peace with Him, and that is possible only through faith in Jesus Christ.

we eagerly wait for *it* with perseverance.
26 Likewise the Spirit also helps in our
weaknesses. For we do not know what
we should pray for as we ought, but the
Spirit Himself makes intercession for us[a]
with groanings which cannot be uttered.
27 Now He who searches the hearts knows
what the mind of the Spirit *is*, because He
makes intercession for the saints according to *the will of* God.
28 And we know that all things work
together for good to those who love God,
to those who are the called according to
His purpose. 29 For whom He foreknew,
He also predestined *to be* conformed to
the image of His Son, that He might be
the firstborn among many brethren.
30 Moreover whom He predestined, these
He also called; whom He called, these He
also justified; and whom He justified,
these He also glorified.

God's Everlasting Love

31 What then shall we say to these
things? If God *is* for us, who *can be* against
us? 32 He who did not spare His own Son,
but delivered Him up for us all, how shall
He not with Him also freely give us all
things? 33 Who shall bring a charge against
God's elect? *It is* God who justifies. 34 Who
is he who condemns? *It is* Christ who died,
and furthermore is also risen, who is even
at the right hand of God, who also makes
intercession for us. 35 Who shall separate
us from the love of Christ? *Shall* tribulation, or distress, or persecution, or famine,
or nakedness, or peril, or sword? 36 As it
is written:

"For Your sake we are killed all day long;
We are accounted as sheep for the slaughter."[a]

37 Yet in all these things we are more
than conquerors through Him who loved
us. 38 For I am persuaded that neither
death nor life, nor angels nor principalities nor powers, nor things present nor
things to come, 39 nor height nor depth,

8:26 [a]NU-Text omits *for us*. 8:36 [a]Psalm 44:22

nor any other created thing, shall be able
to separate us from the love of God which
is in Christ Jesus our Lord.

Israel's Rejection of Christ

9 I tell the truth in Christ, I am not
lying, my conscience also bearing me
witness in the Holy Spirit, 2that I have
great sorrow and continual grief in my
heart. 3For I could wish that I myself
were accursed from Christ for my brethren, my countrymen[a] according to the
flesh, 4who are Israelites, to whom *per-*
tain the adoption, the glory, the covenants, the giving of the law, the service *of*
God, and the promises; 5of whom *are* the
fathers and from whom, according to the
flesh, Christ *came,* who is over all, *the*
eternally blessed God. Amen.

Israel's Rejection and God's Purpose

6But it is not that the word of God has
taken no effect. For they *are* not all Israel
who *are* of Israel, 7nor *are they* all children because they are the seed of Abraham; but, *"In Isaac your seed shall be*
called."[a] 8That is, those who *are* the children of the flesh, these *are* not the children
of God; but the children of the promise
are counted as the seed. 9For this *is* the
word of promise: *"At this time I will come*
and Sarah shall have a son."[a]
10And not only *this,* but when Rebecca
also had conceived by one man, *even* by
our father Isaac 11(for *the children* not yet
being born, nor having done any good or
evil, that the purpose of God according to
election might stand, not of works but of
Him who calls), 12it was said to her, *"The*
older shall serve the younger."[a] 13As it is
written, *"Jacob I have loved, but Esau I*
have hated."[a]

Israel's Rejection and God's Justice

14What shall we say then? *Is there* un-

9:3 [a]Or *relatives* 9:7 [a]Genesis 21:12 9:9 [a]Genesis 18:10, 14
9:12 [a]Genesis 25:23 9:13 [a]Malachi 1:2, 3

8:39 The cost of our redemption was the blood of God's Son. The Father's love for us was and is so great, He didn't hesitate for a moment, but delivered Him up freely for us as a Lamb for the slaughter. With that as the case, then what good thing will He withhold from those who walk uprightly in Christ? What demon can make one peep, or mutter an accusation against us, when we have such evidence of God's love set before our eyes? What trial could ever separate us from the devotion of God in Christ?

Shall the shepherd, who put his life in great jeopardy by climbing down a precipice to rescue a lost sheep, carry it back carelessly? Will he now let it starve after he risked his very life to rescue it? Will he now stand by idly and let wolves devour the sheep? The Chief Shepherd descended into death itself to deliver us. He has already proven His great love by willingly giving His life for the sheep, so no tribulation, distress, persecution, famine, or even sharp sword will cut us off from such love.

9:1 "When a man calls himself an atheist, he is not attacking God; he is attacking his own conscience." *Michael Pearl*

9:2,3 A letter from an atheist. "You are really convinced that you've got all the answers. You've really got yourself tricked into believing that you're 100% right. Well, let me tell you just one thing. Do you consider yourself to be compassionate of other humans? If you're right about God, as you say you are, and you believe that, then how can you sleep at night? When you speak with me, you are speaking with someone who you believe is walking directly into eternal damnation, into an endless onslaught of horrendous pain which your 'loving' god created, yet you stand by and do nothing.

"If you believed one bit that thousands every day were falling into an eternal and unchangeable fate, you should be running the streets mad with rage at their blindness. That's equivalent to standing on a street corner and watching every person that passes you walk blindly directly into the path of a bus and die, yet you stand idly by and do nothing. You're just twiddling your thumbs, happy in the knowledge that one day that 'Walk' signal will shine your way across the road.

"Think about it. Imagine the horrors hell must have in store if the Bible is true. You're just going to allow that to happen and not care about saving anyone but yourself? If you're right, then you're an uncaring, unemotional and purely selfish (expletive) that has no right to talk about subjects such as love and caring."

If we have great heaviness and sorrow in *our* heart for the lost, we'll warn them of the reality of hell (see 2 Thess. 1:7–9 comment) and how to avoid it. See John 4:7 comment for witnessing tips.

righteousness with God? Certainly not!
[15]For He says to Moses, *"I will have mercy
on whomever I will have mercy, and I will
have compassion on whomever I will have
compassion."*[a] [16]So then *it is* not of him
who wills, nor of him who runs, but of
God who shows mercy. [17]For the Scripture says to the Pharaoh, *"For this very
purpose I have raised you up, that I may
show My power in you, and that My
name may be declared in all the earth."*[a]
[18]Therefore He has mercy on whom He
wills, and whom He wills He hardens.
[19]You will say to me then, "Why does
He still find fault? For who has resisted
His will?" [20]But indeed, O man, who are
you to reply against God? Will the thing
formed say to him who formed *it*, "Why
have you made me like this?" [21]Does not
the potter have power over the clay, from
the same lump to make one vessel for
honor and another for dishonor?
[22]*What* if God, wanting to show *His*
wrath and to make His power known,
endured with much longsuffering the
vessels of wrath prepared for destruction,
[23]and that He might make known the
riches of His glory on the vessels of mercy,
which He had prepared beforehand for
glory, [24]even us whom He called, not of
the Jews only, but also of the Gentiles?
[25]As He says also in Hosea:

"I will call them My people, who were
not My people,
And her beloved, who was not
beloved."[a]
[26]*"And it shall come to pass in the place*
where it was said to them,
'You are not My people,'
There they shall be called sons of the
living God."[a]

[27]Isaiah also cries out concerning Israel:[a]

"Though the number of the children of
Israel be as the sand of the sea,
The remnant will be saved.
[28]*For He will finish the work and cut it*
short in righteousness,
Because the LORD will make a short
work upon the earth."[a]

[29]And as Isaiah said before:

"Unless the LORD of Sabaoth[a] *had left*
us a seed,
We would have become like Sodom,
And we would have been made like
Gomorrah."[b]

Present Condition of Israel

[30]What shall we say then? That Gentiles, who did not pursue righteousness,
have attained to righteousness, even the
righteousness of faith; [31]but Israel, pursuing the law of righteousness, has not attained to the law of righteousness.[a] [32]Why?
Because *they did* not *seek it* by faith, but as
it were, by the works of the law.[a] For they
stumbled at that stumbling stone. [33]As it
is written:

"Behold, I lay in Zion a stumbling stone
and rock of offense,
And whoever believes on Him will not
be put to shame."[a]

Israel Needs the Gospel

10 Brethren, my heart's desire and
prayer to God for Israel[a] is that
they may be saved. [2]For I bear them witness that they have a zeal for God, but
not according to knowledge. [3]For they
being ignorant of God's righteousness,

9:15 [a]Exodus 33:19 9:17 [a]Exodus 9:16 9:25 [a]Hosea 2:23 9:26 [a]Hosea 1:10 9:27 [a]Isaiah 10:22, 23 9:28 [a]NU-Text reads *For the LORD will finish the work and cut it short upon the earth.* 9:29 [a]Literally, in Hebrew, *Hosts* [b]Isaiah 1:9 9:31 [a]NU-Text omits *of righteousness.* 9:32 [a]NU-Text reads *by works.* 9:33 [a]Isaiah 8:14; 28:16 10:1 [a]NU-Text reads *them.*

9:32 For those who are trusting in good works, see Eph. 2:8,9 and Titus 3:5.

10:1 The heart of a person who is close to God must be consumed with prayer for the salvation of the world. That theme will permeate his prayers.

QUESTIONS & OBJECTIONS

10:1 "Will all Jews go to hell if they don't accept Jesus as the Messiah?"

Some people argue that Jews do not need to be saved because they are already "God's chosen people." But the fact that they were chosen as a nation to glorify God does not mean that individual Jewish people are saved.

Jews, like all of humanity, are commanded to repent and trust the Savior (Acts 2:38), and warned that if they don't repent, they will perish (Luke 13:3). Jesus, who was Jewish (see John 4:9), is the promised Jewish Messiah (see John 4:25,26). The disciples were Jewish. Christianity was birthed in the land of the Jews. The first three thousand converts to Christianity were Jews (see Acts 2:41), as well as the next two thousand (see Acts 4:4). The apostle Paul was Jewish (see Acts 23:6), commissioned to testify to Jews about their need for "repentance toward God and faith toward our Lord Jesus Christ" (see Acts 20:21). The God of Israel (the Jews) made sure the gospel was offered to the Jews first, before the Gentiles (see Rom. 1:16).

God offers eternal life to all humanity, whether Jew or Gentile, "red and yellow, black and white, *all* are precious in His sight." *Whoever* believes in Jesus should not perish but have eternal life (see John 3:15). If anyone ends up in hell it will not be because of their ethnicity or their color, but because of their sin. Rapists, murderers, thieves, liars, blasphemers, adulterers, etc., will get exactly what they deserve, and if Jews die in their sins, their Jewish heritage will not save them from the justice of a holy God. Only the blood of Jesus of Nazareth, the God-given Jewish Messiah, can do that. See Jer. 4:4 comment and Rom. 2:28,29. For details on Judaism, see page 1782.

and seeking to establish their own righteousness, have not submitted to the righteousness of God. [4]For Christ *is* the end of
the law for righteousness to everyone who
believes.

[5]For Moses writes about the righteousness which is of the law, *"The man
who does those things shall live by them."*[a]
[6]But the righteousness of faith speaks in
this way, *"Do not say in your heart, 'Who
will ascend into heaven?' "*[a] (that is, to
bring Christ down *from above*) [7]or, *" 'Who
will descend into the abyss?' "*[a] (that is, to
bring Christ up from the dead). [8]But
what does it say? *"The word is near you,
in your mouth and in your heart"*[a] (that is,
the word of faith which we preach): [9]that
if you confess with your mouth the Lord
Jesus and believe in your heart that God
has raised Him from the dead, you will
be saved. [10]For with the heart one believes unto righteousness, and with the
mouth confession is made unto salvation.
[11]For the Scripture says, *"Whoever believes on Him will not be put to shame."*[a]
[12]For there is no distinction between Jew
and Greek, for the same Lord over all is
rich to all who call upon Him. [13]For
*"whoever calls on the name of the LORD
shall be saved."*[a]

Israel Rejects the Gospel

[14]How then shall they call on Him in
whom they have not believed? And how
shall they believe in Him of whom they
have not heard? And how shall they hear
without a preacher? [15]And how shall they
preach unless they are sent? As it is written:

10:5 [a]Leviticus 18:5 10:6 [a]Deuteronomy 30:12 10:7 [a]Deuteronomy 30:13 10:8 [a]Deuteronomy 30:14 10:11 [a]Isaiah 28:16 10:13 [a]Joel 2:32

10:9 Leading sinners to Jesus: *We must confess and forsake our sins to receive God's mercy.* Here is a model prayer of repentance, from Psa. 51: "Have mercy upon me, O God, according to Your lovingkindness; according to the multitude of Your tender mercies, blot out my transgressions. Wash me thoroughly from my iniquity, and cleanse me from my sin. For I acknowledge my transgressions, and my sin is always before me. Against You, You only, have I sinned, and done this evil in Your sight. I believe that Jesus suffered and died in my place. I believe that He rose from the dead. I put my trust in Him this day as my Lord and my Savior. I will read Your Word daily and obey what I read. In Jesus' name I pray. Amen." See Rom. 10:12 comment.

QUESTIONS & OBJECTIONS

10:3 *"Why are there so many different religions?"*

It has been well said that "religion" is man's way of trying to deal with his guilt. Different religions have different ways of attempting to rid their adherents of sin and its consequences. They fast, pray, deny themselves legitimate pleasures, or chasten themselves, often to a point of inflicting pain. They do this because they have a concept of what they think God (or "the gods") is like, so they seek to establish their own righteousness, being "ignorant of God's righteousness."

The Good News of the Christian faith is that no one need suffer the pains of religious works. Christ's blood can cleanse our conscience from the "dead works" of religion (Heb. 9:14). Jesus took our punishment upon Himself, and He is the only One who can save us from sin and death. See Acts 4:12 and John 14:6. See also "Why Christianity?" on page xxv.

"How beautiful are the feet of those
who preach the gospel of peace,[a]
Who bring glad tidings of good
things!"[b]

16 But they have not all obeyed the gospel. For Isaiah says, *"LORD, who has be-*
lieved our report?"[a] 17 So then faith *comes*
by hearing, and hearing by the word of
God.

18 But I say, have they not heard? Yes
indeed:

"Their sound has gone out to all the
earth,
And their words to the ends of the
world."[a]

19 But I say, did Israel not know? First
Moses says:

"I will provoke you to jealousy by those
who are not a nation,
I will move you to anger by a foolish
nation."[a]

20 But Isaiah is very bold and says:

"I was found by those who did not seek
Me;
I was made manifest to those who did
not ask for Me."[a]

21 But to Israel he says:

"All day long I have stretched out My
hands
To a disobedient and contrary
people."[a]

10:15 [a]NU-Text omits *preach the gospel of peace, Who.* [b]Isaiah 52:7; Nahum 1:15 10:16 [a]Isaiah 53:1 10:18 [a]Psalm 19:4 10:19 [a]Deuteronomy 32:21 10:20 [a]Isaiah 65:1 10:21 [a]Isaiah 65:2

10:12 Leading sinners to Jesus: *Here are God's promises to all who call upon Him:* "If we confess our sins, He is faithful and just to forgive us our sins and to cleanse us from all unrighteousness" (1 John 1:9). "He who believes in the Son of God has the witness in himself; he who does not believe God has made Him a liar, because he has not believed the testimony that God has given of His Son. And this is the testimony: that God has given us eternal life, and this life is in His Son. He who has the Son has life; he who does not have the Son of God does not have life. These things I have written to you who believe in the name of the Son of God, that you may know that you have eternal life, and that you may continue to believe in the name of the Son of God" (1 John 5:10–13). For principles of growth for new Christians, see Matt. 6:9 comment.

10:13 Salvation is possible for every person. See also 1 Tim. 2:4.

10:15 If we take the gospel to a world that desperately needs to hear it, God considers even the lowest part of us to be beautiful.

Israel's Rejection Not Total

11 I say then, has God cast away His people? Certainly not! For I also am an Israelite, of the seed of Abraham, of the tribe of Benjamin. 2 God has not cast away His people whom He foreknew. Or do you not know what the Scripture says of Elijah, how he pleads with God against Israel, saying, 3 *"LORD, they have killed Your prophets and torn down Your altars, and I alone am left, and they seek my life"*?[a] 4 But what does the divine response say to him? *"I have reserved for Myself seven thousand men who have not bowed the knee to Baal."*[a] 5 Even so then, at this present time there is a remnant according to the election of grace. 6 And if by grace, then *it is* no longer of works; otherwise grace is no longer grace.[a] But if *it is* of works, it is no longer grace; otherwise work is no longer work.

7 What then? Israel has not obtained what it seeks; but the elect have obtained it, and the rest were blinded. 8 Just as it is written:

"God has given them a spirit of stupor,
Eyes that they should not see
And ears that they should not hear,
To this very day."[a]

9 And David says:

"Let their table become a snare and a trap,
A stumbling block and a recompense to them.
10 *Let their eyes be darkened, so that they do not see,*
And bow down their back always."[a]

Israel's Rejection Not Final

11 I say then, have they stumbled that they should fall? Certainly not! But through their fall, to provoke them to jealousy, salvation *has come* to the Gentiles. 12 Now if their fall *is* riches for the world, and their failure riches for the Gentiles, how much more their fullness!

13 For I speak to you Gentiles; inasmuch as I am an apostle to the Gentiles, I magnify my ministry, 14 if by any means I may provoke to jealousy *those who are* my flesh and save some of them. 15 For if their being cast away *is* the reconciling of the world, what *will* their acceptance *be* but life from the dead?

16 For if the firstfruit *is* holy, the lump *is* also *holy;* and if the root *is* holy, so *are* the branches. 17 And if some of the branches were broken off, and you, being a wild olive tree, were grafted in among them, and with them became a partaker of the root and fatness of the olive tree, 18 do not boast against the branches. But if you do boast, *remember that* you do not support the root, but the root *supports* you.

> God, send me anywhere, only go with me. Lay any burden on me, only sustain me. And sever any tie in my heart except the tie that binds my heart to Yours.
>
> **DAVID LIVINGSTONE**

19 You will say then, "Branches were broken off that I might be grafted in." 20 Well *said.* Because of unbelief they were broken off, and you stand by faith. Do not be haughty, but fear. 21 For if God did not spare the natural branches, He may not spare you either. 22 Therefore consider the goodness and severity of God: on those who fell, severity; but toward you, goodness,[a] if you continue in *His* goodness. Otherwise you also will be cut off. 23 And they also, if they do not continue in unbelief, will be grafted in, for God is able to graft them in again. 24 For if you were cut out of the olive tree which is wild by nature, and were grafted contrary to nature into a cultivated olive tree, how much more will these, who *are* natural *branches,* be grafted into their own olive tree?

11:3 [a]1 Kings 19:10,14 11:4 [a]1 Kings 19:18 11:6 [a]NU-Text omits the rest of this verse. 11:8 [a]Deuteronomy 29:4; Isaiah 29:10 11:10 [a]Psalm 69:22, 23 11:22 [a]NU-Text adds *of God.*

[25]For I do not desire, brethren, that
you should be ignorant of this mystery,
lest you should be wise in your own
opinion, that blindness in part has happened to Israel until the fullness of the
Gentiles has come in. [26]And so all Israel
will be saved,[a] as it is written:

"The Deliverer will come out of Zion,
And He will turn away ungodliness
from Jacob;
[27]*For this is My covenant with them,*
When I take away their sins."[a]

[28]Concerning the gospel *they are* enemies for your sake, but concerning the
election *they are* beloved for the sake of
the fathers. [29]For the gifts and the calling
of God *are* irrevocable. [30]For as you were
once disobedient to God, yet have now
obtained mercy through their disobedience, [31]even so these also have now been
disobedient, that through the mercy
shown you they also may obtain mercy.
[32]For God has committed them all to disobedience, that He might have mercy on
all.

[33]Oh, the depth of the riches both of
the wisdom and knowledge of God! How
unsearchable *are* His judgments and His
ways past finding out!

[34]*"For who has known the mind of the*
LORD?
Or who has become His counselor?"[a]
[35]*"Or who has first given to Him*
And it shall be repaid to him?"[a]

[36]For of Him and through Him and to
Him *are* all things, to whom *be* glory forever. Amen.

Living Sacrifices to God

12 I beseech you therefore, brethren,
by the mercies of God, that you

"I was honored today with having a few stones, dirt, rotten eggs, and pieces of dead cats thrown at me."

George Whitefield

present your bodies a living sacrifice, holy,
acceptable to God, *which is* your reasonable service. [2]And do not be conformed
to this world, but be transformed by the
renewing of your mind, that you may
prove what *is* that good and acceptable and
perfect will of God.

Serve God with Spiritual Gifts

[3]For I say, through the grace given to
me, to everyone who is among you, not
to think *of himself* more highly than he
ought to think, but to think soberly, as
God has dealt to each one a measure of
faith. [4]For as we have many members in
one body, but all the members do not
have the same function, [5]so we, *being*
many, are one body in Christ, and individually members of one another. [6]Hav-
ing then gifts differing according to the
grace that is given to us, *let us use them:* if
prophecy, *let us prophesy* in proportion to
our faith; [7]or ministry, *let us use it* in *our*
ministering; he who teaches, in teaching;

11:26 [a]Or *delivered* 11:27 [a]Isaiah 59:20, 21 11:34 [a]Isaiah 40:13; Jeremiah 23:18 11:35 [a]Job 41:11

12:1 "If by excessive labor we die before reaching the average age of man, worn out in the Master's service, then glory be to God. We shall have so much less of earth and so much more of heaven. It is our duty and our privilege to exhaust our lives for Jesus. We are not to be living specimens of men in fine preservation, but living sacrifices, whose lot is to be consumed." *Charles Spurgeon*

8he who exhorts, in exhortation; he who gives, with liberality; he who leads, with diligence; he who shows mercy, with cheerfulness.

Behave Like a Christian

9*Let* love *be* without hypocrisy. Abhor what is evil. Cling to what is good. 10*Be* kindly affectionate to one another with brotherly love, in honor giving preference to one another; 11not lagging in diligence, fervent in spirit, serving the Lord; 12rejoicing in hope, patient in tribulation, continuing steadfastly in prayer; 13distributing to the needs of the saints, given to hospitality.

14Bless those who persecute you; bless and do not curse. 15Rejoice with those who rejoice, and weep with those who weep. 16Be of the same mind toward one another. Do not set your mind on high things, but associate with the humble. Do not be wise in your own opinion.

17Repay no one evil for evil. Have regard for good things in the sight of all men. 18If it is possible, as much as depends on you, live peaceably with all men. 19Beloved, do not avenge yourselves, but *rather* give place to wrath; for it is written, *"Vengeance is Mine, I will repay,"*[a] says the Lord. 20Therefore

"If your enemy is hungry, feed him;
If he is thirsty, give him a drink;
For in so doing you will heap coals of
fire on his head."[a]

21Do not be overcome by evil, but overcome evil with good.

Submit to Government

13 Let every soul be subject to the governing authorities. For there is no authority except from God, and the authorities that exist are appointed by God. 2Therefore whoever resists the authority resists the ordinance of God, and those who resist will bring judgment on themselves. 3For rulers are not a terror to good works, but to evil. Do you want to be unafraid of the authority? Do what is good, and you will have praise from the same. 4For he is God's minister to you for good. But if you do evil, be afraid; for he does not bear the sword in vain; for he is God's minister, an avenger to *execute* wrath on him who practices evil. 5Therefore *you* must be subject, not only because of wrath but also for conscience' sake. 6For because of this you also pay taxes, for they are God's ministers attending continually to this very thing. 7Render therefore to all their due: taxes to whom taxes *are due,* customs to whom customs, fear to whom fear, honor to whom honor.

Are there contradictions in the Bible? See Mark 15:26 comment.

Love Your Neighbor

8Owe no one anything except to love one another, for he who loves another has fulfilled the law. 9For the commandments, *"You shall not commit adultery," "You shall not murder," "You shall not steal," "You shall not bear false witness,"*[a] *"You shall not covet,"*[b] and if *there is* any other commandment, are *all* summed up in this saying, namely, *"You shall love your neighbor as yourself."*[c] 10Love does no harm to a neighbor; therefore love *is* the fulfillment of the law.

Put on Christ

11And *do* this, knowing the time, that now *it is* high time to awake out of sleep; for now our salvation *is* nearer than when we *first* believed. 12The night is far spent, the day is at hand. Therefore let us cast off the works of darkness, and let us put on the armor of light. 13Let us walk properly, as in the day, not in revelry and

12:19 [a]Deuteronomy 32:35 12:20 [a]Proverbs 25:21, 22
13:9 [a]NU-Text omits *"You shall not bear false witness."* [b]Exodus 20:13–15, 17; Deuteronomy 5:17–19, 21 [c]Leviticus 19:18

(Can Hinduism provide deliverance from sin? See Rom. 7:24,25 comment.)

Mahatma Gandhi

drunkenness, not in lewdness and lust, not in strife and envy. [14]But put on the Lord Jesus Christ, and make no provision for the flesh, to *fulfill its* lusts.

The Law of Liberty

14 Receive one who is weak in the faith, *but* not to disputes over doubtful things. [2]For one believes he may eat all things, but he who is weak eats *only* vegetables. [3]Let not him who eats despise him who does not eat, and let not him who does not eat judge him who eats; for God has received him. [4]Who are you to judge another's servant? To his own master he stands or falls. Indeed, he will be made to stand, for God is able to make him stand.

[5]One person esteems *one* day above another; another esteems every day *alike.* Let each be fully convinced in his own mind. [6]He who observes the day, observes *it* to the Lord;[a] and he who does not observe the day, to the Lord he does not observe *it.* He who eats, eats to the Lord, for he gives God thanks; and he who does not eat, to the Lord he does not eat, and gives God thanks. [7]For none of us lives to himself, and no one dies to himself. [8]For if we live, we live to the Lord; and if we die, we die to the Lord. Therefore, whether we live or die, we are the Lord's. [9]For to this end Christ died and rose[a] and lived again, that He might be Lord of both the dead and the living. [10]But why do you judge your brother? Or why do you show contempt for your brother? For we shall all stand before the judgment seat of Christ.[a] [11]For it is written:

"As I live, says the LORD,
Every knee shall bow to Me,
And every tongue shall confess to
God."[a]

[12]So then each of us shall give account of himself to God. [13]Therefore let us not judge one another anymore, but rather resolve this, not to put a stumbling block or a cause to fall in *our* brother's way.

The Law of Love

[14]I know and am convinced by the Lord Jesus that *there is* nothing unclean of itself; but to him who considers anything to be unclean, to him *it is* unclean. [15]Yet if your brother is grieved because of *your* food, you are no longer walking in love. Do not destroy with your food the one for whom Christ died. [16]Therefore do not let your good be spoken of as evil; [17]for

14:6 [a]NU-Text omits the rest of this sentence. 14:9 [a]NU-Text omits *and rose.* 14:10 [a]NU-Text reads *of God.* 14:11 [a]Isaiah 45:23

13:14 Salvation comes through trusting Jesus Christ in the same way you trust a parachute. You don't just "believe" in it, you *put it on*. See Gal. 3:27.

14:2 Vegetarianism. See 1 Tim. 4:3,4 comment.

14:10 Judgment Day: For verses that warn of its reality, see 2 Cor. 5:10.

QUESTIONS & OBJECTIONS

14:12 *"How do I witness to someone I know?"*

For most of us, it is far easier to witness to a stranger than to someone we know and respect. An effective way to soften the message without compromise is to speak in the "first person" or in testimonial form. Say something like, "I didn't realize that the Bible warns that for every idle word I have spoken, I will have to give an account on Judgment Day. I thought that as long as I believed in God and tried to live a good life, I would go to heaven when I died. I was so wrong. Jesus said that if I as much as looked with lust, I had committed adultery in my heart, and that there was nothing I could do to wash away my sins. I knew that if God judged me by the Ten Commandments on Judgment Day, I would end up guilty, and go to hell. It was when I acknowledged my sins that I began to understand why Jesus died. It was to take the punishment for my sins, and the sins of the world."

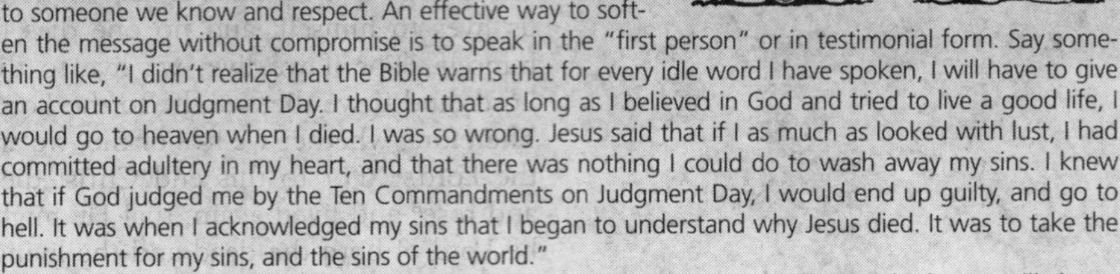

Then, depending on the person's openness, you may ask, "How do you think you will do on Judgment Day, if God judges you by the Ten Commandments?"

the kingdom of God is not eating and
drinking, but righteousness and peace
and joy in the Holy Spirit. 18For he who
serves Christ in these things[a] *is* acceptable to God and approved by men.

19Therefore let us pursue the things
which make for peace and the things by
which one may edify another. 20Do not
destroy the work of God for the sake of
food. All things indeed *are* pure, but *it is*
evil for the man who eats with offense.
21*It is* good neither to eat meat nor drink
wine nor *do anything* by which your
brother stumbles or is offended or is made
weak.[a] 22Do you have faith?[a] Have *it* to
yourself before God. Happy *is* he who does
not condemn himself in what he approves.
23But he who doubts is condemned if he
eats, because *he does* not *eat* from faith;
for whatever *is* not from faith is sin.[a]

Bearing Others' Burdens

15 We then who are strong ought to
bear with the scruples of the
weak, and not to please ourselves. 2Let
each of us please *his* neighbor for *his*
good, leading to edification. 3For even
Christ did not please Himself; but as it is
written, *"The reproaches of those who reproached You fell on Me."*[a] 4For whatever
things were written before were written
for our learning, that we through the patience and comfort of the Scriptures
might have hope. 5Now may the God of
patience and comfort grant you to be
like-minded toward one another, according to Christ Jesus, 6that you may with
one mind *and* one mouth glorify the God
and Father of our Lord Jesus Christ.

Glorify God Together

7Therefore receive one another, just as
Christ also received us,[a] to the glory of
God. 8Now I say that Jesus Christ has become a servant to the circumcision for
the truth of God, to confirm the promises
made to the fathers, 9and that the Gentiles
might glorify God for *His* mercy, as it is
written:

14:18 [a]NU-Text reads *this.* 14:21 [a]NU-Text omits *or is offended or is made weak.* 14:22 [a]NU-Text reads *The faith which you have—have.* 14:23 [a]M-Text puts Romans 16:25–27 here. 15:3 [a]Psalm 69:9 15:7 [a]NU-Text and M-Text read *you.*

14:20 "Would you judge of the lawfulness or unlawfulness of pleasure, of the innocence or malignity of actions? Take this rule: whatever weakens your reason, impairs the tenderness of your conscience, obscures your sense of God, or takes off the relish of spiritual things; in short, whatever increases the strength and authority of your body over your mind—that thing is sin to you, however innocent it may be in itself."
Susanna Wesley

"For this reason I will confess to You
among the Gentiles,
And sing to Your name."[a]

10And again he says:

"Rejoice, O Gentiles, with His
people!"[a]

11And again:

"Praise the LORD, all you Gentiles!
Laud Him, all you peoples!"[a]

12And again, Isaiah says:

"There shall be a root of Jesse;
And He who shall rise to reign over
the Gentiles,
In Him the Gentiles shall hope."[a]

13Now may the God of hope fill you with all joy and peace in believing, that you may abound in hope by the power of the Holy Spirit.

From Jerusalem to Illyricum

14Now I myself am confident concerning you, my brethren, that you also are full of goodness, filled with all knowledge, able also to admonish one another.[a] 15Nevertheless, brethren, I have written more boldly to you on *some* points, as reminding you, because of the grace given to me by God, 16that I might be a minister of Jesus Christ to the Gentiles, ministering the gospel of God, that the offering of the Gentiles might be acceptable, sanctified by the Holy Spirit. 17Therefore I have reason to glory in Christ Jesus in the things *which pertain* to God. 18For I will not dare to speak of any of those things which Christ has not accomplished through me, in word and deed, to make the Gentiles obedient— 19in mighty signs and wonders, by the power of the Spirit of God, so that from Jerusalem and round about to Illyricum I have fully preached the gospel of Christ. 20And so I have made it my aim to preach the gospel, not where Christ was named, lest I should build on another man's foundation, 21but as it is written:

"To whom He was not announced, they
shall see;
And those who have not heard shall
understand."[a]

Plan to Visit Rome

22For this reason I also have been much hindered from coming to you. 23But now no longer having a place in these parts, and having a great desire these many years to come to you, 24whenever I journey to Spain, I shall come to you.[a] For I hope to see you on my journey, and to be helped on my way there by you, if first I may enjoy your *company* for a while.

15:9 [a]2 Samuel 22:50; Psalm 18:49 15:10 [a]Deuteronomy 32:43 15:11 [a]Psalm 117:1 15:12 [a]Isaiah 11:10 15:14 [a]M-Text reads *others*. 15:21 [a]Isaiah 52:15 15:24 [a]NU-Text omits *I shall come to you* (and joins *Spain* with the next sentence).

15:13 "Understand that you must not look upon the possession of joy and peace as being the absolutely necessary consequence of your being saved. A man may be in the lifeboat, but that lifeboat may be so tossed about that he may still feel himself exceedingly ill, and think himself to be still in peril. It is not his sense of safety that makes him safe; he is safe because he is in the lifeboat, whether he is sensible of this or not. Understand then that joy and peace are not infallible or indispensable evidences of safety, and that they certainly are not unchanging evidences. The brightest Christians lose their joy, and some of those that stand well in the things of God, and concerning whom you would entertain no doubt, entertain a great many suspicions, however, about themselves. Joy and peace are the element of a Christian, but he is sometimes out of his element: joy and peace are his usual states, but there are times when, with fightings within and wars without, his joy departs, and his peace is broken. The leaves on the tree prove that the tree is alive, but the absence of leaves will not prove that the tree is dead." *Charles Spurgeon*

15:16 "Consider as sin any minute of life spent on something other than saving souls for eternity from this world doomed to destruction." *Richard Wurmbrand*

[25]But now I am going to Jerusalem to minister to the saints. [26]For it pleased those from Macedonia and Achaia to make a certain contribution for the poor among the saints who are in Jerusalem. [27]It pleased them indeed, and they are their debtors. For if the Gentiles have been partakers of their spiritual things, their duty is also to minister to them in material things. [28]Therefore, when I have performed this and have sealed to them this fruit, I shall go by way of you to Spain. [29]But I know that when I come to you, I shall come in the fullness of the blessing of the gospel[a] of Christ.

[30]Now I beg you, brethren, through the Lord Jesus Christ, and through the love of the Spirit, that you strive together with me in prayers to God for me, [31]that I may be delivered from those in Judea who do not believe, and that my service for Jerusalem may be acceptable to the saints, [32]that I may come to you with joy by the will of God, and may be refreshed together with you. [33]Now the God of peace *be* with you all. Amen.

Sister Phoebe Commended

16 I commend to you Phoebe our sister, who is a servant of the church in Cenchrea, [2]that you may receive her in the Lord in a manner worthy of the saints, and assist her in whatever business she has need of you; for indeed she has been a helper of many and of myself also.

Greeting Roman Saints

[3]Greet Priscilla and Aquila, my fellow workers in Christ Jesus, [4]who risked their own necks for my life, to whom not only I give thanks, but also all the churches of the Gentiles. [5]Likewise *greet* the church that is in their house.

Greet my beloved Epaenetus, who is the firstfruits of Achaia[a] to Christ. [6]Greet Mary, who labored much for us. [7]Greet Andronicus and Junia, my countrymen and my fellow prisoners, who are of note among the apostles, who also were in Christ before me.

[8]Greet Amplias, my beloved in the Lord. [9]Greet Urbanus, our fellow worker in Christ, and Stachys, my beloved. [10]Greet Apelles, approved in Christ. Greet those who are of the *household* of Aristobulus. [11]Greet Herodion, my countryman.[a] Greet those who are of the *household* of Narcissus who are in the Lord.

> No pursuit of mortal men is to be compared with that of soul-winning.
>
> **CHARLES SPURGEON**

[12]Greet Tryphena and Tryphosa, who have labored in the Lord. Greet the beloved Persis, who labored much in the Lord. [13]Greet Rufus, chosen in the Lord, and his mother and mine. [14]Greet Asyncritus, Phlegon, Hermas, Patrobas, Hermes, and the brethren who are with them. [15]Greet Philologus and Julia, Nereus and his sister, and Olympas, and all the saints who are with them.

[16]Greet one another with a holy kiss. The[a] churches of Christ greet you.

Avoid Divisive Persons

[17]Now I urge you, brethren, note those who cause divisions and offenses, contrary to the doctrine which you learned, and avoid them. [18]For those who are such do not serve our Lord Jesus[a] Christ, but their own belly, and by

15:29 [a]NU-Text omits *of the gospel.* 16:5 [a]NU-Text reads *Asia.* 16:11 [a]Or *relative* 16:16 [a]NU-Text reads *All the churches.* 16:18 [a]NU-Text and M-Text omit *Jesus.*

16:5 Believers in many countries today must meet secretly in homes to worship. These "house churches" follow the New Testament model for fellowship, prayer, and study of the Scriptures better than do many modern churches that have the finest facilities. The true *Church* is actually the body of believers, and can worship the Lord with or without a building.

smooth words and flattering speech deceive the hearts of the simple. [19]For your
obedience has become known to all.
Therefore I am glad on your behalf; but I
want you to be wise in what is good, and
simple concerning evil. [20]And the God of
peace will crush Satan under your feet
shortly.

The grace of our Lord Jesus Christ *be* with you. Amen.

Greetings from Paul's Friends

[21]Timothy, my fellow worker, and Lucius, Jason, and Sosipater, my countrymen, greet you.

[22]I, Tertius, who wrote *this* epistle,
greet you in the Lord.

[23]Gaius, my host and *the host* of the
whole church, greets you. Erastus, the
treasurer of the city, greets you, and
Quartus, a brother. [24]The grace of our Lord
Jesus Christ *be* with you all. Amen.[a]

Benediction

[25]Now to Him who is able to establish
you according to my gospel and the
preaching of Jesus Christ, according to
the revelation of the mystery kept secret
since the world began [26]but now made
manifest, and by the prophetic Scriptures
made known to all nations, according to
the commandment of the everlasting
God, for obedience to the faith— [27]to
God, alone wise, *be* glory through Jesus
Christ forever. Amen.[a]

16:24 [a]NU-Text omits this verse. **16:27** [a]M-Text puts Romans 16:25–27 after Romans 14:23.

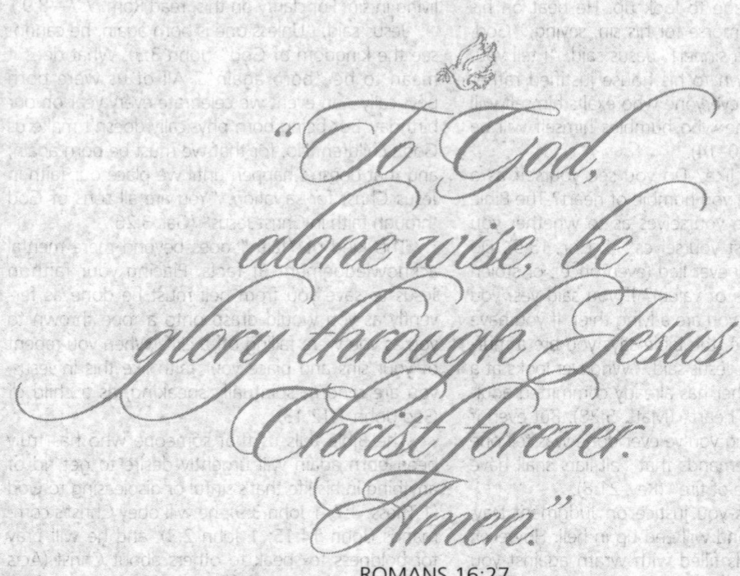
"To God,
alone wise, be
glory through Jesus
Christ forever.
Amen."
ROMANS 16:27

Examine Yourself

By Anna Jackson

Jesus said, "Many will say to Me in that day, 'Lord, Lord, have we not prophesied in Your name, cast out demons in Your name, and done many wonders in Your name?' And then I will declare to them, 'I never knew you; *depart from Me, you who practice lawlessness!*'" (Matt. 7:22,23).

Did you know that about 62% of Americans claim to have a "relationship with Jesus Christ"? These people go peacefully into death, believing they are safely on their way to heaven; but Jesus says "many" of them will be shocked and horrified on Judgment Day. How can you be sure you are not one of them?

Jesus told a story about two men who prayed; one was a religious man and the other wasn't. The religious man saw himself as a good person. He stood and prayed aloud about himself, "God, I thank you that I am not like other men—extortioners, unjust, adulterers..." But the other man knew he wasn't a good person at all. He was humbled in his heart before God. He stood at a distance, without even the courage to look up. He beat on his chest in extreme remorse for his sin, saying, "God, be merciful to me a sinner!" Jesus said, "I tell you, this man went down to his house justified rather than the other; for everyone who exalts himself will be humbled, and he who humbles himself will be exalted" (Luke 18:10–14).

Which are you like? Do you see yourself as a good person, or are you humble of heart? The Bible urges us, "Examine yourselves as to whether you are in the faith. Test yourselves" (2 Cor. 13:5). Do that now: Have you ever lied (even once), or stolen anything (regardless of value)? If you said yes, you have admitted that you are a lying thief. If you have ever hated someone, the Bible says you are a murderer (1 John 3:15). Jesus said, "Whoever looks at a woman to lust for her has already committed adultery with her in his heart" (Matt. 5:28). But even if the only wrong thing you've ever done was tell one lie, God's justice demands that "all liars shall have their part in the lake of fire" (Rev. 21:8).

So if God gives you justice on Judgment Day, you will be guilty, and will end up in hell. However, even though God is filled with wrath against you for your sin, He is also merciful, and has made a way for you to be forgiven. God sent His sinless Son, Jesus, to willingly suffer and die on the cross, then He rose from the dead and defeated death. But it may surprise you to learn that just believing these facts won't get you to heaven. In fact, the Bible tells us that even the demons "believe" (James 2:19). So what do you need to do?

Jesus said, "Unless you repent you will all likewise perish" (Luke 13:5). Have you repented? Before you say "yes" too quickly, many people think "repent" means to feel sorry for doing bad things and to ask God for forgiveness. But that's not true. Of course you should feel sorry—cut to the heart with guilt for your sins—but there's a difference between feeling sorry and repenting. The Bible tells us that "your sorrow led to repentance" (2 Cor. 7:9). Sorrow is a feeling, but repentance is an action—"repentance from dead works" (Heb. 6:1). The Bible tells us to "repent, turn to God, and do works befitting repentance" (Acts 26:20).

How can you tell if you have really repented? The Bible says you will "produce fruit in keeping with repentance" (Matt. 3:8). So examine yourself critically. What actions have you repented of? What "fruit" of repentance have you produced? According to the Bible's definition, have you really repented? The bottom line is that Jesus says unless you repent you will perish. (Does this mean real Christians never sin? Of course not; see 1 John 1:8. But there is a clear distinction between stumbling into sin and living in sin. For clarity on this, read Rom. 7:7—8:9.)

Jesus said, "Unless one is born again, he cannot see the kingdom of God" (John 3:3). What does it mean to be "born again"? All of us were born physically—an event we celebrate every year on our birthday. But being born physically doesn't make us God's children. No, for that we must be born again; and that doesn't happen until we place our faith in Jesus Christ for salvation. "You are all sons of God through faith in Christ Jesus" (Gal. 3:26).

This kind of "faith" goes beyond mere mental acknowledgement of facts. Placing your faith in Jesus to save you from hell must be done as fervently as you would grasp onto a rope thrown to you as you were falling off a cliff. When you repent of your sins and place your faith like this in Jesus, you are reborn, spiritually speaking, as a child of God (John 1:12,13).

The Bible tells us that someone who has truly been born again will urgently desire to get rid of anything in his life that's sinful or displeasing to God (1 Thess. 4:7, 1 John 3:9), he will obey Christ's commands (John 14:15; 1 John 2:3), and he will pray for boldness to speak to others about Christ (Acts 4:29). The Bible says, "If we would judge ourselves, we would not be judged" (1 Cor. 11:31). So judge yourself now, before you have to face God on Judgment Day.

Don't be like the religious man in Jesus' story. Humble yourself before God today. Truly repent. Place your faith in Jesus Christ, and be genuinely born again. Take time now to "make your call and election sure" (2 Pet. 1:10). Don't wait another minute; this breath may be the last one God grants you.

1 Corinthians

Greeting

1 Paul, called *to be* an apostle of Jesus
Christ through the will of God, and
Sosthenes *our* brother,

[2]To the church of God which is at Corinth, to those who are sanctified in Christ Jesus, called *to be* saints, with all who in every place call on the name of Jesus Christ our Lord, both theirs and ours:

[3]Grace to you and peace from God our Father and the Lord Jesus Christ.

Spiritual Gifts at Corinth

[4]I thank my God always concerning
you for the grace of God which was given
to you by Christ Jesus, [5]that you were enriched in everything by Him in all utterance and all knowledge, [6]even as the testimony of Christ was confirmed in you,
[7]so that you come short in no gift, eagerly
waiting for the revelation of our Lord Jesus Christ, [8]who will also confirm you to
the end, *that you may be* blameless in the
day of our Lord Jesus Christ. [9]God is
faithful, by whom you were called into
the fellowship of His Son, Jesus Christ
our Lord.

Sectarianism Is Sin

[10]Now I plead with you, brethren, by
the name of our Lord Jesus Christ, that
you all speak the same thing, and *that*
there be no divisions among you, but *that*
you be perfectly joined together in the
same mind and in the same judgment.
[11]For it has been declared to me concerning you, my brethren, by those of
Chloe's *household,* that there are contentions among you. [12]Now I say this, that
each of you says, "I am of Paul," or "I am
of Apollos," or "I am of Cephas," or "I am
of Christ." [13]Is Christ divided? Was Paul
crucified for you? Or were you baptized
in the name of Paul?

[14]I thank God that I baptized none of
you except Crispus and Gaius, [15]lest anyone should say that I had baptized in my
own name. [16]Yes, I also baptized the household of Stephanas. Besides, I do not know
whether I baptized any other. [17]For Christ
did not send me to baptize, but to preach
the gospel, not with wisdom of words,
lest the cross of Christ should be made of
no effect.

Christ the Power and Wisdom of God

[18]For the message of the cross is foolishness to those who are perishing, but to
us who are being saved it is the power of
God. [19]For it is written:

"I will destroy the wisdom of the wise,

1:18 "To convince the world of the truth of Christianity, it must first be convinced of sin. It is only sin that renders Christ intelligible." *Andrew Murray*

Springboards for Preaching and Witnessing

The Sinking Ship

1:18 Imagine for a moment that you are standing on the seashore gazing at a large ocean liner. The sun is shining. There is no wind and the sea is calm. To your amazement, about thirty people suddenly dive off the end of the ship and cling to a lifeboat.

You shake your head in disbelief at their foolishness. Then without warning, the great ocean liner strikes an iceberg and suddenly sinks, taking all on board with it.

Those who *looked* like fools in abandoning the ship were actually wise, and those who seemed wise by staying on board were, in truth, fools.

The world scoffs at those who abandon the ship of this world and cling to the lifeboat of the Savior. But Christians know that this great pleasure-cruiser will eventually come into contact with the immovable iceberg of the Law of God, sink into hell... and take all those on board with it.

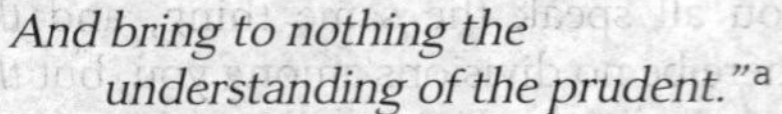

And bring to nothing the
understanding of the prudent."[a]

[20]Where *is* the wise? Where *is* the
scribe? Where *is* the disputer of this age?
Has not God made foolish the wisdom of
this world? [21]For since, in the wisdom of
God, the world through wisdom did not
know God, it pleased God through the
foolishness of the message preached to
save those who believe. [22]For Jews request a sign, and Greeks seek after wisdom; [23]but we preach Christ crucified, to
the Jews a stumbling block and to the
Greeks[a] foolishness, [24]but to those who
are called, both Jews and Greeks, Christ
the power of God and the wisdom of
God. [25]Because the foolishness of God is
wiser than men, and the weakness of God
is stronger than men.

Glory Only in the Lord

[26]For you see your calling, brethren,
that not many wise according to the flesh,
not many mighty, not many noble, *are
called.* [27]But God has chosen the foolish
things of the world to put to shame the
wise, and God has chosen the weak things
of the world to put to shame the things
which are mighty; [28]and the base things

1:19 [a]Isaiah 29:14 1:23 [a]NU-Text reads *Gentiles.*

1:23 There were some in John Wesley's day who refused to preach the Law to bring the knowledge of sin. They justified their method by saying that they preached "Christ and Him crucified." So Wesley points to Paul's method of preaching Christ crucified:

"...when Felix sent for Paul, on purpose that he might 'hear him concerning the faith in Christ;' instead of preaching Christ in *your* sense (which would probably have caused the Governor, either to mock or to contradict and blaspheme,) 'he reasoned of righteousness, temperance, and judgment to come,' till Felix (hardened as he was) 'trembled,' (Acts 24:24,25). Go thou and tread in his steps. Preach Christ to the careless sinner, by reasoning 'of righteousness, temperance, and judgment to come!'" *John Wesley*

1:25 "Everything that can be invented has been invented." *Charles H. Duell*, Commissioner, U.S. Office of Patents, 1899

1:27,28 Many years ago, I ran a children's club. At the end of the club I told about one hundred kids to line up for some candy. There was an immediate rush, and the line sorted itself into what I saw as being a line of greed. The bigger, selfish kids were at the front, and the small and timid ones were at the back. I then did something that gave me great satisfaction. I told them to turn about face. Everyone did. Then I said to stay where they were, and I took great delight in going to the other end of the line and giving the candy to the smaller, timid kids first.

In a world where the rich get richer and the poor get stomped on, we are informed that God has gone to the other end of the line with the message of everlasting life. How has He done that? Simply by choosing that which is weak, base, and despised. You can see this by asking a skeptic, "Do you believe that the following biblical accounts actually happened?"

(continued)

QUESTIONS & OBJECTIONS

1:26 ***"Even the Bible says Christians are not very smart."***

Those who think this verse means Christians are not wise are skipping over the words "according to the flesh." There are different types of wisdom. There is the wisdom of this world ("according to the flesh"), and there is the wisdom of God. The message of this passage is that God has chosen a seemingly foolish message, requiring humility and childlike faith, to confound those proud folks who think they are wise.

If you look around the Christian faith, you won't find many of those proud people who are puffed up in their own "fleshly" wisdom. The same thing is true with 1 Cor. 3:18: it speaks of anyone who "seems to be wise in this age," and goes on to explain that "the wisdom of this world is foolishness with God" (v. 19). Again, this is referring to those who are wise in their own eyes—they only think they are wise. So the atheist isn't wiser than the dumbest of Christians. Rather, according to the Bible, the atheist is a fool (see Psa. 14:1).

of the world and the things which are despised God has chosen, and the things
which are not, to bring to nothing the
things that are, 29that no flesh should glory
in His presence. 30But of Him you are in
Christ Jesus, who became for us wisdom
from God—and righteousness and sanctification and redemption— 31that, as it
is written, *"He who glories, let him glory
in the LORD."*[a]

Christ Crucified

2 And I, brethren, when I came to you,
did not come with excellence of speech
or of wisdom declaring to you the testimony[a] of God. 2For I determined not to
know anything among you except Jesus
Christ and Him crucified. 3I was with you
in weakness, in fear, and in much trembling. 4And my speech and my preaching *were* not with persuasive words of
human[a] wisdom, but in demonstration of
the Spirit and of power, 5that your faith
should not be in the wisdom of men but
in the power of God.

Spiritual Wisdom

6However, we speak wisdom among
those who are mature, yet not the wis-

1:31 [a]Jeremiah 9:24 2:1 [a]NU-Text reads *mystery.* 2:4 [a]NU-Text omits *human.*

(1:27,28 continued) Adam and Eve, Noah's ark, Jonah and the whale, Joshua and the walls of Jericho, Samson and his long hair, Daniel and the lion's den, Moses and the Red Sea

Of course he doesn't. To say that he believed such fantastic stories would mean that he would have to surrender his intellectual dignity. Who in his right mind would ever do that? The answer is simply *those who understand that God has chosen foolish, base, weak, and despised things of the world to confound those who think they are wise.*

"He is not seeking a powerful people to represent Him. Rather, He looks for all those who are weak, foolish, despised, and written off: and He inhabits them with His own strength." *Graham Cooke*

1:30 How amazing that God accounts His righteousness to us, so that we are not just prodigal sons who are forgiven but who underneath it all still smell like a pigsty. We are washed clean, clothed with a pure robe of righteousness, and given a ring of inheritance (see Luke 15:22).

2:1–4 Qualifications for evangelism:

1. A witness need not have "excellence of speech or of wisdom." He should simply declare what he has seen and heard.
2. He must not get sidetracked with unnecessary details, but focus on the essentials of Christ's death on the cross.
3. He must have "weakness" (not trusting in his own strength or ability).
4. He must have "fear" (in Greek, *phobos,* "that which is caused by being scared").
5. He must have "much trembling" (awareness of his insufficiency).

Do you meet these qualifications?

POINTS FOR OPEN-AIR PREACHING

2:4

Watch for "Red Herrings" or "Rabbit Trails"

The Bible warns us to avoid foolish questions because they start arguments (2 Tim. 2:23). Most of us have fallen into the trap of jumping at every objection to the gospel. However, these questions can often be arguments in disguise to sidetrack you from the "weightier matters of the Law" (Matt. 23:23). While apologetics (arguments for God's existence, creation vs. evolution, etc.) are legitimate in evangelism, they should merely be "bait," with the Law of God being the "hook" that brings the conviction of sin. Those who witness solely in the realm of apologetical argument may just get an intellectual decision rather than a repentant conversion. The sinner may come to a point of acknowledging that the Bible is the Word of God, and Jesus is Lord—but even the devil knows that.

Always pull the sinner back to his responsibility before God on Judgment Day, as Jesus did in Luke 13:1–5. Whenever you are in an open-air situation, be wary of those who are intent on distracting workers from witnessing. They argue about prophecy, how much water one should baptize with, or in whose name they should be baptized. It is grievous to see five or six Christians standing around arguing with some sectarian nitpicker, while sinners are sinking into hell. See Acts 21:30 comment.

dom of this age, nor of the rulers of this
age, who are coming to nothing. [7]But we
speak the wisdom of God in a mystery,
the hidden *wisdom* which God ordained
before the ages for our glory, [8]which none
of the rulers of this age knew; for had
they known, they would not have crucified the Lord of glory.

[9]But as it is written:

"Eye has not seen, nor ear heard,
Nor have entered into the heart of man
The things which God has prepared for those who love Him."[a]

[10]But God has revealed *them* to us
through His Spirit. For the Spirit searches
all things, yes, the deep things of God.
[11]For what man knows the things of a
man except the spirit of the man which is
in him? Even so no one knows the things
of God except the Spirit of God. [12]Now
we have received, not the spirit of the
world, but the Spirit who is from God,
that we might know the things that have
been freely given to us by God.

[13]These things we also speak, not in
words which man's wisdom teaches but
which the Holy[a] Spirit teaches, comparing spiritual things with spiritual. [14]But
the natural man does not receive the
things of the Spirit of God, for they are
foolishness to him; nor can he know
them, because they are spiritually discerned. [15]But he who is spiritual judges
all things, yet he himself is *rightly* judged
by no one. [16]For *"who has known the
mind of the LORD that he may instruct
Him?"*[a] But we have the mind of Christ.

2:9 [a]Isaiah 64:4 2:13 [a]NU-Text omits *Holy.* 2:16 [a]Isaiah 40:13

2:5 If someone has been converted to the Christian faith by the wisdom of men, all it would take is the wisdom of *un*converted men to talk him out of his faith. However, if he is transformed by the power of God, he is not solely motivated to Christianity by his intellect. The Holy Spirit has convicted him of sin, righteousness, and judgment. The motivation is the Law of God working upon his conscience. That has given him the knowledge that he has offended a holy God. His repentance is therefore directed at God, who responds in mercy. Those who are converted by God cannot be talked out of their faith because they were not talked into it.

2:11 "Groanings which cannot be uttered are often prayers which cannot be refused." *Charles Spurgeon*

2:16 The mind of God. Evolutionist *Stephen Hawking* wrote, "It would be very difficult to explain why the universe should have begun in just this way, except as the act of a God who intended to create beings like us" *(A Brief History of Time).* He also stated: "Then we shall... be able to take part in the discussion of the question of why it is that we and the universe exist. If we find the answer to that, it would be the ultimate triumph of human reason—for then we would know the mind of God." *(continued)*

QUESTIONS & OBJECTIONS

"I've tried to read the Bible, but I can't understand it."

The Scriptures tell us that the "natural man" cannot understand the things of the Spirit of God. Most Americans would find it difficult to understand the Chinese language. However, a child who is *born* into a Chinese family can understand every word. That's why you must be born again with God's Spirit living within you (John 3:3). The moment you become part of God's family, the Bible will begin to make sense.

Sectarianism Is Carnal

3 And I, brethren, could not speak to
you as to spiritual *people* but as to
carnal, as to babes in Christ. [2]I fed you
with milk and not with solid food; for
until now you were not able *to receive it,*
and even now you are still not able; [3]for
you are still carnal. For where *there are*
envy, strife, and divisions among you,
are you not carnal and behaving like
mere men? [4]For when one says, "I am of
Paul," and another, "I *am* of Apollos," are
you not carnal?

Watering, Working, Warning

[5]Who then is Paul, and who *is* Apollos, but ministers through whom you believed, as the Lord gave to each one? [6]I
planted, Apollos watered, but God gave
the increase. [7]So then neither he who
plants is anything, nor he who waters,
but God who gives the increase. [8]Now he
who plants and he who waters are one,
and each one will receive his own reward
according to his own labor.

[9]For we are God's fellow workers; you
are God's field, *you are* God's building.
[10]According to the grace of God which
was given to me, as a wise master builder
I have laid the foundation, and another
builds on it. But let each one take heed
how he builds on it. [11]For no other foun-

(2:16 continued) We can get a glimpse of the incredible mind of God simply by looking at His creation. Take one (very) small part—the mind of man: The brain is a soft lump of tissue weighing about 3 pounds. It is one of the most watery organs of the body, its outer tissue being 85 percent water. There is very little relationship between brain size and intelligence. Some very bright people have smaller brains than those who are less intelligent. The brain feels no pain because it has no pain receptors. It floats in fluid inside the skull, and the fluid (derived from blood) acts as a shock absorber. The brain stops growing in size at about age 15.

Its surface is covered with folds. If it were laid out flat, the brain surface would cover two average student desks. The brain has about 16 times as many nerve cells as there are people on Earth. With its 100 billion neurons, it can record 86 million bits of information each day of our lives. Supporting, protecting, and nourishing these 10 billion neurons are 1 trillion glial cells, which make up half the mass of the brain.

The brain continues sending out electrical wave signals as long as 37 hours after death. Since nerve cells can't reproduce, you have fewer of them as you get older. People at age 70 or 80 may have only 75 percent of the nerve cells they were born with. Nerve impulses travel more quickly than cars do, with some up to 250 miles per hour. If all the nerves were laid end to end, they would stretch almost 45 miles. If all the nerve cell connections—axons and dendrites—from a human brain could be placed end to end, they would encircle the Earth many times. The dendrites alone could stretch an estimated 100,000 miles.

Let's now look to the heavens: "They defined the exact shape of the closest major galaxy, a beautiful spiral named Andromeda, containing more than 300 billion stars. The nearest of these is (an incredible) thirteen quintillion (13,000,000,000,000,000,000) miles, or 2.2 million light-years, beyond the Milky Way, a distance calculated by comparing the star's apparent brightness with a star of similar brightness and known distance from Earth. And beyond Andromeda lay billions of other galaxies." *Solar System* (Time-Life Books)

The incredible complexity of the human brain and the vastness of the heavens speak of the awesome power of the Creator's mind, and together they "declare the glory of God" (Psa. 19:1).

3:6,7 See John 4:37,38 comment.

QUESTIONS & OBJECTIONS

3:17 *"Does someone go to hell for committing suicide?"*

Those who are adamant that a person who takes his life is committing a mortal sin, and will go to hell, are basing their belief on church doctrine rather than on the Bible. Scripture is silent on the subject. There are no verses that say "He who takes his own life shall be damned." According to Scripture, only *one* sin does not have forgiveness, and that is blasphemy of the Holy Spirit (see Mark 3:29 comment). That means there *is* forgiveness for every other sin.

Some quote 1 Cor. 3:17, which says that God will destroy someone who "defiles" the temple of the Holy Spirit. Yet, there is disagreement about what it means to *defile* the temple. Does this include suicide? Does it include illicit drug abuse (slow suicide), prescription drug abuse, cigarettes (deliberately breathing in poisons that will eventually kill), tattoos, over-eating (digging a grave with your spoon), or alcohol abuse?

God forbid that we add to the pain of someone who has lost a loved one through the tragedy of suicide, by making a judgment about their eternal destiny. God is the ultimate Judge, and we should therefore leave the issue in His hands. It would be wise to follow the biblical example and not come to any verdict in the case of suicide.

dation can anyone lay than that which is
laid, which is Jesus Christ. 12Now if anyone builds on this foundation *with* gold,
silver, precious stones, wood, hay, straw,
13each one's work will become clear; for
the Day will declare it, because it will be
revealed by fire; and the fire will test each
one's work, of what sort it is. 14If anyone's work which he has built on *it* endures, he will receive a reward. 15If anyone's work is burned, he will suffer loss;
but he himself will be saved, yet so as
through fire.
16Do you not know that you are the
temple of God and *that* the Spirit of God
dwells in you? 17If anyone defiles the
temple of God, God will destroy him. For
the temple of God is holy, which *temple*
you are.

Avoid Worldly Wisdom

18Let no one deceive himself. If anyone among you seems to be wise in this
age, let him become a fool that he may
become wise. 19For the wisdom of this
world is foolishness with God. For it is
written, *"He catches the wise in their own*
craftiness";[a] 20and again, *"The LORD*
knows the thoughts of the wise, that they
are futile."[a] 21Therefore let no one boast

3:19 [a]Job 5:13 3:20 [a]Psalm 94:11

3:13,14 "If we work on marble, it will perish; if on brass, time will efface it; if we rear up temples, they will crumble into dust; but if we work on immortal minds and imbue them with principles, with the just fear of God and the love of our fellow men, we engrave on those tablets something that will brighten to all eternity." *Daniel Webster*

3:19 The world's ignorant maxims: 1. *"All good things must come to an end."* This isn't true for the Christian; see Eph. 2:4–7. **2.** *"Which came first, the chicken or the egg?"* The chicken; see Gen. 1:20. **3.** *"There's no such thing as a free lunch."* See Matt. 14:19. **4.** *"You can't take it with you."* The Christian's works "follow" him; see Rev. 14:13. **5.** *"There are only two things in life that are sure—death and taxes."* Plenty of people avoid taxes; none avoid death. See Heb. 9:27. **6.** *"Crime doesn't pay."* It does… up until Judgment Day; see Rom. 2:6. **7.** *"As miserable as sin."* Sin gives pleasure; see Heb. 11:25. **8.** *"That's impossible!"* With God, *nothing* is impossible; see Mark 10:27. **9.** *"No one knows!"* God does; see 1 John 3:20. **10.** *"It's the perfect crime."* Judgment Day will prove that there is no such thing as a crime that escapes justice; see Heb. 4:13. **11.** *"Seeing is believing."* Any magician knows that isn't true. The eyes are easily fooled; see Prov. 28:26. **12.** *"God helps those who help themselves."* God helps those who *cannot* help themselves; see Rom. 5:6.

The Bible tells us that it is the Law of the Lord that make wise the simple (see Psa. 19:7).

in men. For all things are yours:
22whether Paul or Apollos or Cephas, or
the world or life or death, or things present or things to come—all are yours.
23And you *are* Christ's, and Christ *is* God's.

Stewards of the Mysteries of God

4 Let a man so consider us, as servants
of Christ and stewards of the mysteries of God. 2Moreover it is required in
stewards that one be found faithful. 3But
with me it is a very small thing that I
should be judged by you or by a human
court.[a] In fact, I do not even judge myself. 4For I know of nothing against myself, yet I am not justified by this; but He
who judges me is the Lord. 5Therefore
judge nothing before the time, until the
Lord comes, who will both bring to light
the hidden things of darkness and reveal
the counsels of the hearts. Then each
one's praise will come from God.

Fools for Christ's Sake

6Now these things, brethren, I have
figuratively transferred to myself and
Apollos for your sakes, that you may learn
in us not to think beyond what is written,
that none of you may be puffed up on behalf of one against the other. 7For who
makes you differ *from another?* And what
do you have that you did not receive?
Now if you did indeed receive *it,* why do
you boast as if you had not received *it?*
8You are already full! You are already
rich! You have reigned as kings without
us—and indeed I could wish you did
reign, that we also might reign with you!
9For I think that God has displayed us,
the apostles, last, as men condemned to
death; for we have been made a spectacle
to the world, both to angels and to men.
10We *are* fools for Christ's sake, but you
are wise in Christ! We *are* weak, but you
are strong! You *are* distinguished, but we
are dishonored! 11To the present hour we
both hunger and thirst, and we are poorly
clothed, and beaten, and homeless.
12And we labor, working with our own
hands. Being reviled, we bless; being persecuted, we endure; 13being defamed, we
entreat. We have been made as the filth
of the world, the offscouring of all things
until now.

Paul's Paternal Care

14I do not write these things to shame
you, but as my beloved children I warn
you. 15For though you might have ten
thousand instructors in Christ, yet *you do*
not *have* many fathers; for in Christ Jesus
I have begotten you through the gospel.
16Therefore I urge you, imitate me. 17For
this reason I have sent Timothy to you,
who is my beloved and faithful son in the
Lord, who will remind you of my ways in
Christ, as I teach everywhere in every
church.
18Now some are puffed up, as though
I were not coming to you. 19But I will

4:3 [a]Literally *day*

4:5 Second coming of Jesus: See Phil. 4:5.

4:15 See Matt. 23:9 comment.

4:16 Pastors often ask me how they can be more effective in reaching their city. This is what I tell them. Ask your congregation how many are concerned for their city. There will be a forest of hands. Ask how many are praying daily for the city. Many hands will appear. Then ask how many are sharing their faith on a regular basis. Give a gauge by asking how many have verbally spoken about the way of salvation to twelve people in the preceding twelve months. About 5 percent will raise their hands.

I once attended an interdenominational prayer meeting, where I could tell who attended a particular church simply by the way they prayed. I could recognize phrases of their pastors in their prayers. It confirmed that congregations imitate their pastor. This is why I would advise a pastor to join a secular health club, or a golf club, or someplace where he will rub shoulders with the ungodly. I encourage him to regularly tell his congregation of his witnessing experiences and to share his fears—to show not only that he witnesses to the unsaved, but that he has the same fears they have. In this way he can "shepherd the flock of God" (1 Pet. 5:2), and it won't be long before they imitate him.

come to you shortly, if the Lord wills, and I will know, not the word of those who are puffed up, but the power. [20]For the kingdom of God *is* not in word but in power. [21]What do you want? Shall I come to you with a rod, or in love and a spirit of gentleness?

Immorality Defiles the Church

5 It is actually reported *that there is* sexual immorality among you, and such sexual immorality as is not even named[a] among the Gentiles—that a man has his father's wife! [2]And you are puffed up, and have not rather mourned, that he who has done this deed might be taken away from among you. [3]For I indeed, as absent in body but present in spirit, have already judged (as though I were present) him who has so done this deed. [4]In the name of our Lord Jesus Christ, when you are gathered together, along with my spirit, with the power of our Lord Jesus Christ, [5]deliver such a one to Satan for the destruction of the flesh, that his spirit may be saved in the day of the Lord Jesus.[a]

[6]Your glorying *is* not good. Do you not know that a little leaven leavens the whole lump? [7]Therefore purge out the old leaven, that you may be a new lump, since you truly are unleavened. For indeed Christ, our Passover, was sacrificed for us.[a] [8]Therefore let us keep the feast, not with old leaven, nor with the leaven of malice and wickedness, but with the unleavened *bread* of sincerity and truth.

Immorality Must Be Judged

[9]I wrote to you in my epistle not to keep company with sexually immoral people. [10]Yet *I* certainly *did* not *mean* with the sexually immoral people of this world, or with the covetous, or extortioners, or idolaters, since then you would need to go out of the world. [11]But now I have written to you not to keep company with anyone named a brother, who is sexually immoral, or covetous, or an idolater, or a reviler, or a drunkard, or an extortioner—not even to eat with such a person.

> In many ministries, there is not enough of probing the heart and arousing the conscience by the revelation of man's alienation from God, and by the declaration of the selfishness and the wickedness of such a state.
>
> **CHARLES SPURGEON**

[12]For what *have* I *to do* with judging those also who are outside? Do you not judge those who are inside? [13]But those who are outside God judges. Therefore *"put away from yourselves the evil person."*[a]

Do Not Sue the Brethren

6 Dare any of you, having a matter against another, go to law before the unrighteous, and not before the saints? [2]Do you not know that the saints will judge the world? And if the world will be judged by you, are you unworthy to judge the smallest matters? [3]Do you not know that we shall judge angels? How much more, things that pertain to this life? [4]If then you have judgments concerning things pertaining to this life, do you appoint those who are least esteemed by the church to judge? [5]I say this to your shame. Is it so, that there is

5:1 [a]NU-Text omits *named.* 5:5 [a]NU-Text omits *Jesus.* 5:7 [a]NU-Text omits *for us.* 5:13 [a]Deuteronomy 17:7; 19:19; 22:21, 24; 24:7

5:8 "The issue is not our emotions or our preferences. The issue is truth. *Sincerity in religious matters is never enough*. We do not doubt the sincerity of those who follow Islam or Hinduism. We admire them for their dedication to what they believe. But sincerity only matters when it is applied to the proper object. You can be sincerely wrong and you will still be wrong. You can sincerely drink rat poison and you will be sincerely dead. *Believing the wrong thing doesn't make it right*. All truth is narrow. Years ago we all learned that 2 + 2 = 4. It doesn't equal 5 or 3, no matter how sincere you are." *Ray Pritchard*

not a wise man among you, not even
one, who will be able to judge between
his brethren? 6But brother goes to law
against brother, and that before unbelievers!

7Now therefore, it is already an utter
failure for you that you go to law against
one another. Why do you not rather accept wrong? Why do you not rather *let
yourselves* be cheated? 8No, you yourselves do wrong and cheat, and *you do*
these things *to your* brethren! 9Do you
not know that the unrighteous will not
inherit the kingdom of God? Do not be
deceived. Neither fornicators, nor idolaters, nor adulterers, nor homosexuals,[a]
nor sodomites, 10nor thieves, nor covetous, nor drunkards, nor revilers, nor
extortioners will inherit the kingdom of
God. 11And such were some of you. But
you were washed, but you were sanctified,
but you were justified in the name of the
Lord Jesus and by the Spirit of our God.

Glorify God in Body and Spirit

12All things are lawful for me, but all
things are not helpful. All things are lawful for me, but I will not be brought under the power of any. 13Foods for the
stomach and the stomach for foods, but
God will destroy both it and them. Now
the body *is* not for sexual immorality but
for the Lord, and the Lord for the body.
14And God both raised up the Lord and
will also raise us up by His power.

15Do you not know that your bodies
are members of Christ? Shall I then take
the members of Christ and make *them*
members of a harlot? Certainly not! 16Or
do you not know that he who is joined to
a harlot is one body *with her*? For *"the
two,"* He says, *"shall become one flesh."*[a]
17But he who is joined to the Lord is one
spirit *with Him*.

18Flee sexual immorality. Every sin
that a man does is outside the body, but
he who commits sexual immorality sins
against his own body. 19Or do you not
know that your body is the temple of the
Holy Spirit *who is* in you, whom you have
from God, and you are not your own?
20For you were bought at a price; therefore glorify God in your body[a] and in
your spirit, which are God's.

6:9 [a]That is, catamites 6:16 [a]Genesis 2:24 6:20 [a]NU-Text ends the verse at *body*.

6:9,10 Leading sinners to Jesus: *Sinners will not enter the kingdom of God.* "Who can say, 'I have made my heart clean, I am pure from my sin'?" (Prov. 20:9). "For there is not a just man on earth who does good and does not sin" (Eccles. 7:20). "If we say that we have no sin, we deceive ourselves, and the truth is not in us" (1 John 1:8). "For all have sinned and fall short of the glory of God" (Rom. 3:23). See Rev. 21:8 comment.

6:9–11 Homosexuals are deceived if they think they find in Scripture that their lifestyle is okay with God, and that they cannot change. This list of sins (which encompass most, if not all, of the Ten Commandments) makes it clear who will not be included in the kingdom of God. However, Paul says to those who are now believers, "And such *were* some of you" (v. 11). No matter what their sins, God can wash sinners clean and make them righteous in His sight. See Jude 7 comment.

The "gay Christian." People often ask how to respond to those who are homosexuals and yet consider themselves to be Christians. While a fornicator, a homosexual, an adulterer, a thief, and a liar can become a Christian, it is important to understand that they cannot remain in their sins. If someone does, he is simply a pretender (a hypocrite). To be a Christian, you must turn from your sinful lifestyle, commonly called "repentance."

So, how do you tell someone that, without causing undue offense? I would witness to him using God's Law (the Ten Commandments). I wouldn't mention the homosexual issue until he is humbled, and sin is seen in its true light. There is a very good reason for this. No proud person can see the nature of his own sins. He is blinded by pride. If you have done marriage counseling, you will know this to be true. If there is no humility, there won't be an open ear to reason. So the Law should be used to humble the human heart, show sin in its true light, and hopefully show the person his error, and his great danger.

6:19 "Coming under the loving Lordship of Jesus Christ means an end to our 'rights' as well as to our wrongs. It means the end of life on our own terms." *Larry Tomczak*

Principles of Marriage

7 Now concerning the things of which you wrote to me:

It is good for a man not to touch a woman. [2]Nevertheless, because of sexual immorality, let each man have his own wife, and let each woman have her own husband. [3]Let the husband render to his wife the affection due her, and likewise also the wife to her husband. [4]The wife does not have authority over her own body, but the husband *does.* And likewise the husband does not have authority over his own body, but the wife *does.* [5]Do not deprive one another except with consent for a time, that you may give yourselves to fasting and prayer; and come together again so that Satan does not tempt you because of your lack of self-control. [6]But I say this as a concession, not as a commandment. [7]For I wish that all men were even as I myself. But each one has his own gift from God, one in this manner and another in that.

[8]But I say to the unmarried and to the widows: It is good for them if they remain even as I am; [9]but if they cannot exercise self-control, let them marry. For it is better to marry than to burn *with passion.*

Keep Your Marriage Vows

[10]Now to the married I command, *yet* not I but the Lord: A wife is not to depart from *her* husband. [11]But even if she does depart, let her remain unmarried or be reconciled to *her* husband. And a husband is not to divorce *his* wife.

[12]But to the rest I, not the Lord, say: If any brother has a wife who does not believe, and she is willing to live with him, let him not divorce her. [13]And a woman who has a husband who does not believe, if he is willing to live with her, let her not divorce him. [14]For the unbelieving husband is sanctified by the wife, and the unbelieving wife is sanctified by the husband; otherwise your children would be unclean, but now they are holy. [15]But if the unbeliever departs, let him depart; a brother or a sister is not under bondage in such *cases.* But God has called us to peace. [16]For how do you know, O wife, whether you will save *your* husband? Or how do you know, O husband, whether you will save *your* wife?

Live as You Are Called

[17]But as God has distributed to each one, as the Lord has called each one, so let him walk. And so I ordain in all the churches. [18]Was anyone called while circumcised? Let him not become uncircumcised. Was anyone called while uncircumcised? Let him not be circumcised. [19]Circumcision is nothing and uncircumcision is nothing, but keeping the commandments of God *is what matters.* [20]Let each one remain in the same calling in which he was called. [21]Were you called *while* a slave? Do not be concerned about

---

7:2–5 Biblical sexuality. The gift of sex came from God; it didn't come about through an evolutionary process. It was given by God for procreation and pleasure. Scripture says that the only time a husband and wife should refrain from the joys of sex is when they are praying and fasting. The Bible also says that a man should be ravished (enraptured) always with her love (Prov. 5:18–20). The only stipulation is that it is his wife he is to be enraptured with—not the woman down the street.

Those who forsake marriage thinking that they can enjoy sex outside the bonds of the institution risk getting AIDS and numerous other sexually transmitted diseases—several of which are incurable. It is interesting to note that a man and a woman can engage in sex ten thousand times within marriage and never even once risk contracting any sexually transmitted disease.

One who commits fornication (from the Greek *Porneia,* "illicit sexual intercourse") takes what could lawfully be his as a gift from God, and corrupts it. He is like a child who one night steals a crisp, new twenty-dollar bill from his father's wallet, not realizing that his father intended to give it to him as a gift in the morning.

The fornicator not only sins against God and incurs the wrath of eternal justice, but he sins against his conscience, and his own body (1 Cor. 6:18). Fornicators will not inherit the kingdom of God (1 Cor. 6:9).

it; but if you can be made free, rather use *it.* 22For he who is called in the Lord *while* a slave is the Lord's freedman. Likewise he who is called *while* free is Christ's slave. 23You were bought at a price; do not become slaves of men. 24Brethren, let each one remain with God in that *state* in which he was called.

To the Unmarried and Widows

25Now concerning virgins: I have no commandment from the Lord; yet I give judgment as one whom the Lord in His mercy has made trustworthy. 26I suppose therefore that this is good because of the present distress—that *it is* good for a man to remain as he is: 27Are you bound to a wife? Do not seek to be loosed. Are you loosed from a wife? Do not seek a wife. 28But even if you do marry, you have not sinned; and if a virgin marries, she has not sinned. Nevertheless such will have trouble in the flesh, but I would spare you.

29But this I say, brethren, the time *is* short, so that from now on even those who have wives should be as though they had none, 30those who weep as though they did not weep, those who rejoice as though they did not rejoice, those who buy as though they did not possess, 31and those who use this world as not misusing *it.* For the form of this world is passing away.

32But I want you to be without care. He who is unmarried cares for the things of the Lord—how he may please the Lord. 33But he who is married cares about the things of the world—how he may please *his* wife. 34There is[a] a difference between a wife and a virgin. The unmarried woman cares about the things of the Lord, that she may be holy both in body and in spirit. But she who is married cares about the things of the world—how she may please *her* husband. 35And this I say for your own profit, not that I may put a leash on you, but for what is proper, and that you may serve the Lord without distraction.

36But if any man thinks he is behaving improperly toward his virgin, if she is past the flower of youth, and thus it must be, let him do what he wishes. He does not sin; let them marry. 37Nevertheless he who stands steadfast in his heart, having no necessity, but has power over his own will, and has so determined in his heart that he will keep his virgin,[a] does well. 38So then he who gives *her*[a] in marriage does well, but he who does not give *her* in marriage does better.

39A wife is bound by law as long as her husband lives; but if her husband dies, she is at liberty to be married to whom she wishes, only in the Lord. 40But she is happier if she remains as she is, according to my judgment—and I think I also have the Spirit of God.

Be Sensitive to Conscience

8 Now concerning things offered to idols: We know that we all have knowledge. Knowledge puffs up, but love edifies. 2And if anyone thinks that he knows anything, he knows nothing yet as he ought to know. 3But if anyone

7:34 [a]M-Text adds *also.* 7:37 [a]Or *virgin daughter* 7:38 [a]NU-Text reads *his own virgin.*

7:22 "Make no reserve, exercise no choice but obey his command. When you know what he commands, do not hesitate, question, or try to avoid it, but 'do it': do it at once, do it heartily, do it cheerfully, do it to the full. It is but a little thing that, as our Lord has bought us with the price of his own blood, we should be his servants. The apostles frequently call themselves the bond-slaves of Christ. Where our Authorized Version softly puts it 'servant' it really is 'bond-slave.' The early saints delighted to count themselves Christ's absolute property, bought by him, owned by him, and wholly at his disposal. Paul even went so far as to rejoice that he had the marks of his Master's brand on him, and he cries, 'Let no man trouble me: for I bear in my body the marks of the Lord Jesus' [Gal. 6:17]. There was the end of all debate: he was the Lord's, and the marks of the scourges, the rods, and the stones were the broad-arrow of the King which marked Paul's body as the property of Jesus the Lord." *Charles Spurgeon*

QUESTIONS & OBJECTIONS

8:10 "Conscience is given to us by society."

It is interesting that every culture has a sense of morality, and that no matter how "primitive" they are, they acknowledge some sort of Creator. I am not aware of any past culture that has been found to be atheistic. Every culture acknowledges God because the knowledge of His existence is manifest through the conscience, as well as through creation (see Rom. 1:19–21).

The word "conscience" comes from two words and means "with knowledge" (*con* means "with" and *science* means "knowledge"). Here is the dictionary definition: "knowledge within oneself, a moral sense; lit. with-knowledge."

Consider the experience of a minister who went to Papua New Guinea and met with a tribe that had no prior contact with Christianity. He asked if they believed that certain behaviors were wrong. They admitted that things like stealing, cannibalism (which some of them were practicing), and adultery were wrong. When he asked how they knew it was wrong, they said they knew it in their being…in their heart. That's the conscience. With no contact with the Bible or with Christians, instinctively they knew the difference between right and wrong.

However, let's say that this objection is right—that it is society and not God that entirely shapes the human conscience. Let's imagine that a man has been rescued by authorities after 20 years of being raised by wolves. He is found to be intelligent and completely sane, but has had no moral instruction from any human being in those 20 years.

He is cleaned up, given a nice suit, and taken to New York where he is overawed by what he sees. He is still given no moral instruction. When he is left alone, the first thing he does is find a pretty young woman. He rapes and murders her, then he steals her money and is captured while spending it.

In court, his attorney's defense is that he didn't know right from wrong—society had given him no moral instruction. Is the judge going to let him go? Of course not, because although the human conscience may be *influenced* by society, it is not given to us by society. We each have the moral Law written on our heart (Rom. 2:15), and it speaks of issues of right and wrong. The conscience is given to us by God, so that every sane human being intuitively knows that some things are "right" and some things are "wrong" regardless of what was taught to us. That is why we will all be without excuse on the Day of Judgment.

loves God, this one is known by Him.
[4]Therefore concerning the eating of
things offered to idols, we know that an
idol *is* nothing in the world, and that
there is no other God but one. [5]For even
if there are so-called gods, whether in
heaven or on earth (as there are many
gods and many lords), [6]yet for us *there is*
one God, the Father, of whom *are* all
things, and we for Him; and one Lord Jesus Christ, through whom *are* all things,
and through whom we *live*.
[7]However, *there is* not in everyone that
knowledge; for some, with consciousness
of the idol, until now eat *it* as a thing offered to an idol; and their conscience, being weak, is defiled. [8]But food does not
commend us to God; for neither if we eat
are we the better, nor if we do not eat are
we the worse.
[9]But beware lest somehow this liberty
of yours become a stumbling block to
those who are weak. [10]For if anyone sees
you who have knowledge eating in an
idol's temple, will not the conscience of
him who is weak be emboldened to eat
those things offered to idols? [11]And because of your knowledge shall the weak
brother perish, for whom Christ died?
[12]But when you thus sin against the
brethren, and wound their weak conscience, you sin against Christ. [13]Therefore,

8:4 See Psa. 115:4–9 comment.

8:9 Although we have incredible liberty as Christians, we are servants of all. If something we are at liberty to do offends an unsaved person, we must stop doing it, for the sake of the gospel. It has been said that if Paul saw a Jew, he would hide his ham sandwich behind his back. We need to walk in that same spirit.

if food makes my brother stumble, I will
never again eat meat, lest I make my
brother stumble.

A Pattern of Self-Denial

9 Am I not an apostle? Am I not free?
Have I not seen Jesus Christ our Lord?
Are you not my work in the Lord? 2If I
am not an apostle to others, yet doubtless I am to you. For you are the seal of
my apostleship in the Lord.
3My defense to those who examine me
is this: 4Do we have no right to eat and
drink? 5Do we have no right to take along
a believing wife, as *do* also the other apostles, the brothers of the Lord, and Cephas?
6Or *is it* only Barnabas and I *who* have no
right to refrain from working? 7Who ever
goes to war at his own expense? Who
plants a vineyard and does not eat of its
fruit? Or who tends a flock and does not
drink of the milk of the flock?
8Do I say these things as a *mere* man?
Or does not the law say the same also? 9For
it is written in the law of Moses, *"You
shall not muzzle an ox while it treads out
the grain."*[a] Is it oxen God is concerned
about? 10Or does He say *it* altogether for
our sakes? For our sakes, no doubt, *this* is
written, that he who plows should plow
in hope, and he who threshes in hope
should be partaker of his hope. 11If we
have sown spiritual things for you, *is it* a
great thing if we reap your material
things? 12If others are partakers of *this*
right over you, *are* we not even more?
Nevertheless we have not used this
right, but endure all things lest we hinder
the gospel of Christ. 13Do you not know
that those who minister the holy things
eat *of the things* of the temple, and those
who serve at the altar partake of *the offerings of* the altar? 14Even so the Lord has
commanded that those who preach the
gospel should live from the gospel.
15But I have used none of these things,
nor have I written these things that it
should be done so to me; for it *would be*
better for me to die than that anyone
should make my boasting void. 16For if I
preach the gospel, I have nothing to boast
of, for necessity is laid upon me; yes, woe
is me if I do not preach the gospel! 17For
if I do this willingly, I have a reward; but
if against my will, I have been entrusted
with a stewardship. 18What is my reward
then? That when I preach the gospel, I
may present the gospel of Christ[a] without
charge, that I may not abuse my authority in the gospel.

Serving All Men

19For though I am free from all *men,*
I have made myself a servant to all, that I
might win the more; 20and to the Jews I became as a Jew, that I might win Jews; to
those *who are* under the law, as under the
law,[a] that I might win those *who are* under the law; 21to those *who are* without
law, as without law (not being without
law toward God,[a] but under law toward
Christ[b]), that I might win those *who are*
without law; 22to the weak I became as[a]
weak, that I might win the weak. I have
become all things to all *men,* that I might
by all means save some. 23Now this I do
for the gospel's sake, that I may be partaker of it with *you.*

Striving for a Crown

24Do you not know that those who
run in a race all run, but one receives the

9:9 [a]Deuteronomy 25:4 9:18 [a]NU-Text omits *of Christ.*
9:20 [a]NU-Text adds *though not being myself under the law*
9:21 [a]NU-Text reads *God's law.* [b]NU-Text reads *Christ's law.*
9:22 [a]NU-Text omits *as.*

9:16 Second Kings 7:9 tells of lepers who had seen a great victory and initially kept the good news to themselves. But their consciences spoke to them of their moral obligation to tell others: "Then they said to one another, 'We are not doing right. This day is a day of good news, and we remain silent.'" How much more should we feel an obligation to take the Good News of everlasting life to a dying world? We must speak about what we have seen and heard. Like Paul, we are a "debtor" to those who haven't heard the gospel (Rom. 1:14). Woe to us if we do not preach the gospel!

9:22 *How to Use Gospel Tracts*

If Paul meant "by all means," he no doubt would have used gospel tracts as a means to reach the lost. Never underestimate the power of a good gospel tract. After *George Whitefield* read one called "The Life of God in the Soul of a Man," he said, "God showed me I must be born again or be damned." He went on to pray, "Lord, if I am not a Christian, or if I am not a real one, for Jesus Christ's sake show me what Christianity is, that I may not be damned at last!" Then his journal tells us "from that moment... did I know that I must become a new creature." A Christian book relates the true story of a diver who saw a piece of paper clutched in the shell of an oyster. The man grabbed it, found that it was a gospel tract and said, "I can't hold out any longer. His mercy is so great that He has caused His Word to follow me even to the bottom of the ocean." God used a tract to save the man.

Why should a Christian use tracts? Simply because *God* uses them. He used a tract to save the great missionary Hudson Taylor, as well as innumerable others. That fact alone should be enough incentive for a Christian to always use tracts to reach the lost, but there are even more reasons why we should use them. Here are a few:

- Tracts can provide an opening for us to share our faith. We can watch people's reaction as we give them tracts, and see if they are open to listening to spiritual things.
- They can do the witnessing for us. If we are too timid to speak to people about the things of God, we can at least give them tracts, or leave tracts lying around so that others will pick them up.
- They speak to the individuals when they are ready. They don't read it until they want to.
- They can find their way into people's homes when we can't.
- They don't get into arguments; they just state their case.

Dr. Oswald J. Smith said, "The only way to carry out the Great Commission will be by the means of the printed page." *Charles Spurgeon* stated, "When preaching and private talk are not available, you need to have a tract ready... Get good striking tracts, or none at all. But a touching gospel tract may be the seed of eternal life. Therefore, do not go out without your tracts."

If you want people to accept your literature, try to greet them before offering them a tract. If you can get them to respond to a warm "Good morning," or "How are you doing?" that will almost always break the ice and they will take it. After the greeting, don't ask, "Would you like this?" They will probably respond, "What is it?" Instead, say, "Did you get one of these?" That will stir their curiosity and make them feel as though they are missing out on something. So they are.

Perhaps you almost pass out at the thought of passing out a tract. Don't worry; you are not alone. We all battle fear. The answer to fear is found in the prayer closet. Ask God to give you a compassion that will swallow your fears. Meditate on the fate of the ungodly. Give hell some deep thought. Confront what it is that makes you fearful.

Do you like roller coasters? Some Christians want to try bungee-jumping or skydiving. Isn't it strange? We are prepared to risk our lives for the love of fear—and yet we are willing to let a sinner go to hell for fear of giving out a tract. Ask yourself how many piles of bloodied stones you can find where Christians have been stoned to death for preaching the gospel. How much singed soil can you find where they have been burned at the stake? Part of our fear is a fear of rejection. We are fearful of looking foolish. That's a subtle form of pride. The other part of our battle with fear comes directly from the enemy. He knows that fear paralyzes. We must resist the devil and his lies. If God is with us, nothing can be against us.

If you have never given out tracts, why not begin today? Leave them in a shopping cart, or put them in your bills when you pay them. Then each night as you shut your eyes to sleep, you will have something special to pray about—that God will use the tracts you put somewhere. You will also have a deep sense of satisfaction that you played a small part in carrying out the Great Commission to reach this dying world with the gospel of everlasting life. Don't waste your life. Do something for the kingdom of God while you are able to. Always remember: treat every day as though it were your last—one day you will be right. See also Mark 4:14 and Rev. 22:2 comments.

prize? Run in such a way that you may
obtain *it.*
25 And everyone who competes
for the prize is temperate in all things.
Now they *do it* to obtain a perishable
crown, but we *for* an imperishable *crown.*
26 Therefore I run thus: not with uncertainty. Thus I fight: not as *one who* beats
the air.
27 But I discipline my body and

bring *it* into subjection, lest, when I have preached to others, I myself should become disqualified.

Old Testament Examples

10 Moreover, brethren, I do not want you to be unaware that all our fathers were under the cloud, all passed through the sea, [2]all were baptized into Moses in the cloud and in the sea, [3]all ate the same spiritual food, [4]and all drank the same spiritual drink. For they drank of that spiritual Rock that followed them, and that Rock was Christ. [5]But with most of them God was not well pleased, for *their bodies* were scattered in the wilderness.

[6]Now these things became our examples, to the intent that we should not lust after evil things as they also lusted. [7]And do not become idolaters as *were* some of them. As it is written, *"The people sat down to eat and drink, and rose up to play."*[a] [8]Nor let us commit sexual immorality, as some of them did, and in one day twenty-three thousand fell; [9]nor let us tempt Christ, as some of them also tempted, and were destroyed by serpents; [10]nor complain, as some of them also complained, and were destroyed by the destroyer. [11]Now all[a] these things happened to them as examples, and they were written for our admonition, upon whom the ends of the ages have come.

[12]Therefore let him who thinks he stands take heed lest he fall. [13]No temptation has overtaken you except such as is common to man; but God *is* faithful, who will not allow you to be tempted beyond what you are able, but with the temptation will also make the way of escape, that you may be able to bear *it*.

Flee from Idolatry

[14]Therefore, my beloved, flee from idolatry. [15]I speak as to wise men; judge for yourselves what I say. [16]The cup of blessing which we bless, is it not the communion of the blood of Christ? The bread which we break, is it not the communion of the body of Christ? [17]For we, *though* many, are one bread *and* one body; for we all partake of that one bread.

[18]Observe Israel after the flesh: Are not those who eat of the sacrifices partakers of the altar? [19]What am I saying then? That an idol is anything, or what is offered to idols is anything? [20]Rather, that the things which the Gentiles sacrifice they sacrifice to demons and not to God, and I do not want you to have fellowship with demons. [21]You cannot drink the cup of the Lord and the cup of demons; you cannot partake of the Lord's table and of the table of demons. [22]Or do we provoke the Lord to jealousy? Are we stronger than He?

10:7 [a]Exodus 32:6 **10:11** [a]NU-Text omits *all*.

10:1 This chapter shows how subtle idolatry can be. If we create an idol of God in our minds, that idol will not speak to us when we fall into the sin of lust. However, if we keep before us the true revelation of God's omniscient holiness, when Potiphar's wife calls we will flee from sexual sin. Despite our protests that lust easily overcomes our weak wills, v. 13 leaves each of us without excuse. See how that verse is linked to v. 14.

10:4 Just as Moses struck the rock to bring forth life-sustaining water for the Israelites in the desert (Exod.17:6), it was Moses' Law that came down upon the Rock (Christ) at the cross.

10:9 See Num. 21:6–9 and John 3:14,15 comments.

10:14 Idolatry. Those who deny the fact that God is angry at sin insinuate that sinful man (with his measure of desire to see justice) is more just than God. This is an incredible affront to the integrity of God. The following *Time* magazine letter to the editor epitomizes idolatry (the oldest sin in the Book):

> Excellent topic! I truly enjoyed reading "Does Heaven Exist?" I am a devout Christian, and I don't give much thought to heaven. My spirituality isn't based on an anthropomorphic, kick-butt God who will throw four generations of children into eternal damnation because some distant forefather ticked him off [see Prov. 28:5]. Heaven is the flip side of the absolutely barbaric notion of hell that evolved under that kick-butt mindset... To me, God is a symbol for something unfathomable, an utter mystery that fills my heart with joy and my spirit with song.

QUESTIONS & OBJECTIONS

"Why is Christianity better than other religions?"

In all major religions, the followers strive to rid themselves of sin through various practices. They may pray in a prescribed way, do various good works, deny themselves legitimate sexual pleasure, follow dietary restrictions, lie on beds of nails, etc. The uniqueness of Jesus is shown in His statement, "The Son of Man has power on earth to forgive sins" (Matt. 9:6). No other religious leader has ever made this claim. Jesus Christ alone can wash away every sin anyone has ever committed, because of what He did on the cross. By paying the penalty for our sin, He can release us from the torture of guilt. We cannot do anything in the way of religious works to wash away our sins. Forgiveness is a free gift of God (Eph. 2:8,9). To see what "religion" does (or rather doesn't do), read Mahatma Gandhi's words in Rom. 7:24,25 comment. See also "Why Christianity?" on page xxv.

All to the Glory of God

23All things are lawful for me,[a] but not
all things are helpful; all things are lawful
for me,[b] but not all things edify. 24Let no
one seek his own, but each one the other's
well-being.
25Eat whatever is sold in the meat market, asking no questions for conscience'
sake; 26for *"the earth is the* LORD'S, *and all
its fullness."*[a]
27If any of those who do not believe
invites you *to dinner,* and you desire to
go, eat whatever is set before you, asking
no question for conscience' sake. 28But if
anyone says to you, "This was offered to
idols," do not eat it for the sake of the one
who told you, and for conscience' sake;[a]
for *"the earth is the* LORD'S, *and all its fullness."*[b] 29"Conscience," I say, not your
own, but that of the other. For why is my
liberty judged by another *man's* conscience? 30But if I partake with thanks,
why am I evil spoken of for *the food* over
which I give thanks?
31Therefore, whether you eat or drink,
or whatever you do, do all to the glory of
God. 32Give no offense, either to the Jews
or to the Greeks or to the church of God,
33just as I also please all *men* in all *things,*
not seeking my own profit, but the *profit*
of many, that they may be saved.

11 Imitate me, just as I also *imitate*
Christ.

Head Coverings

2Now I praise you, brethren, that you
remember me in all things and keep the
traditions just as I delivered *them* to you.
3But I want you to know that the head of
every man is Christ, the head of woman
is man, and the head of Christ *is* God.
4Every man praying or prophesying, having *his* head covered, dishonors his head.
5But every woman who prays or prophesies with *her* head uncovered dishonors
her head, for that is one and the same as
if her head were shaved. 6For if a woman
is not covered, let her also be shorn. But
if it is shameful for a woman to be shorn
or shaved, let her be covered. 7For a man
indeed ought not to cover *his* head, since
he is the image and glory of God; but
woman is the glory of man. 8For man is

10:23 [a]NU-Text omits *for me.* [b]NU-Text omits *for me.* **10:26** [a]Psalm 24:1 **10:28** [a]NU-Text omits the rest of this verse. [b]Psalm 24:1

10:20 To many, Eastern religions have a sense of romantic mysticism. It must therefore be a surprise to find that India has 220 million cows that are worshiped as the supreme givers of life (God). The cow's hooves are bathed in religious ceremonies. Their urine is considered holy and is used to anoint believers. The animal's dung is also applied to the skin of the faithful in religious rituals. They believe that all the gods inhabit some part of the cow's body. A Christian revival in India would not only provide eternal salvation for the country, but would also release enough meat to feed their hungry population.

not from woman, but woman from man.
9Nor was man created for the woman, but
woman for the man. 10For this reason the
woman ought to have *a symbol of* authority
on *her* head, because of the angels. 11Nev-
ertheless, neither *is* man independent of
woman, nor woman independent of man,
in the Lord. 12For as woman *came* from
man, even so man also *comes* through
woman; but all things are from God.

> If any man's life at home is unworthy, he should go several miles away before he stands up to preach. When he stands up, he should say nothing.
>
> **CHARLES SPURGEON**

13Judge among yourselves. Is it proper
for a woman to pray to God with her
head uncovered? 14Does not even nature
itself teach you that if a man has long hair,
it is a dishonor to him? 15But if a woman
has long hair, it is a glory to her; for *her*
hair is given to her[a] for a covering. 16But
if anyone seems to be contentious, we have
no such custom, nor *do* the churches of
God.

Conduct at the Lord's Supper

17Now in giving these instructions I
do not praise *you,* since you come together not for the better but for the worse.
18For first of all, when you come together
as a church, I hear that there are divisions
among you, and in part I believe it. 19For
there must also be factions among you,
that those who are approved may be recognized among you. 20Therefore when
you come together in one place, it is not
to eat the Lord's Supper. 21For in eating,
each one takes his own supper ahead of
others; and one is hungry and another is
drunk. 22What! Do you not have houses
to eat and drink in? Or do you despise
the church of God and shame those who
have nothing? What shall I say to you?
Shall I praise you in this? I do not praise
you.

Institution of the Lord's Supper

23For I received from the Lord that
which I also delivered to you: that the Lord
Jesus on the *same* night in which He was
betrayed took bread; 24and when He had
given thanks, He broke *it* and said, "Take,
eat;[a] this is My body which is broken[b] for
you; do this in remembrance of Me." 25In
the same manner *He* also *took* the cup after supper, saying, "This cup is the new
covenant in My blood. This do, as often
as you drink *it,* in remembrance of Me."
26For as often as you eat this bread
and drink this cup, you proclaim the Lord's
death till He comes.

Examine Yourself

27Therefore whoever eats this bread or
drinks *this* cup of the Lord in an unwor-

11:15 [a]M-Text omits *to her.* **11:24** [a]NU-Text omits *Take, eat.* [b]NU-Text omits *broken.*

11:8 It has been well said that woman was made from Adam's rib—close to his heart, under his protective arm (Gen. 2:21,22).

11:9 Earth's population refutes evolution. "The evolutionary scientists who believe that man existed for over a million years have an almost insurmountable problem. Using the assumption of forty-three years for an average human generation, the population growth over a million years would produce 23,256 consecutive generations. We calculate the expected population by starting with one couple one million years ago and use the same assumptions of a forty-three-year generation and 2.5 children per family . . . The evolutionary theory of a million years of growth would produce trillions × trillions × trillions × trillions of people that should be alive today on our planet. To put this in perspective, this number is vastly greater than the total number of atoms in our vast universe. If mankind had lived on earth for a million years, we would all be standing on enormously high mountains of bones from the trillions of skeletons of those who had died in past generations. However, despite the tremendous archaeological and scientific investigation in the last two centuries, the scientists have not found a fraction of the trillions of skeletons predicted by the theory of evolutionary scientists." *Grant R. Jeffery, The Signature of God*

QUESTIONS & OBJECTIONS

12:14 *"Since individuals in the body of Christ have different functions, why should all of us witness?"*

The main passage likening the Church to the human body is 1 Cor. 12:14–31, describing how each part fulfills its own function in a healthy body. But notice in v. 28 that this passage pertains to in-reach (within the local church), not outreach (evangelism). There is no mention of evangelists here because it is in the context of the Church coming together; when all those functions are working well, we have a healthy Church. Then, when the Church is healthy, it will (as one body) do what it has been commanded to do by the Head: to reach out to the lost.

We are like survivors in a lifeboat of the *Titanic*. All around us are drowning people. We need every hand onboard to help reach those who are dying and pull them into the boat. We think and move as one mind and one body. Nothing else matters. Love is our motivation. Every hand is needed—because there is a terrible lack of rescuers. Why? Because some think their role is to sit in the lifeboat, and, knowing that people are perishing, busy themselves polishing the brass.

If that's the case, one has to question if they are really part of the body, because the Head has commanded us to reach out to those who are perishing (see Mark 16:15). A hand that doesn't do what the Head commands it to isn't healthy.

As we reach out to people, we must also be sure to do it the way the Bible instructs us to. Otherwise, we are just pulling corpses into the boat—and we see the fruit of this within the contemporary Church. See also Eph. 4:11 comment.

"I look upon this world as a wrecked vessel. God has given me a lifeboat and said to me: Moody, save all you can." *Dwight L. Moody*

thy manner will be guilty of the body and
blood[a] of the Lord. [28]But let a man examine himself, and so let him eat of the
bread and drink of the cup. [29]For he who
eats and drinks in an unworthy manner[a]
eats and drinks judgment to himself, not
discerning the Lord's[b] body. [30]For this
reason many *are* weak and sick among
you, and many sleep. [31]For if we would
judge ourselves, we would not be judged.
[32]But when we are judged, we are chastened by the Lord, that we may not be
condemned with the world.
[33]Therefore, my brethren, when you
come together to eat, wait for one another. [34]But if anyone is hungry, let him
eat at home, lest you come together for
judgment. And the rest I will set in order
when I come.

Spiritual Gifts: Unity in Diversity

12 Now concerning spiritual *gifts*,
brethren, I do not want you to be
ignorant: [2]You know that[a] you were Gentiles, carried away to these dumb idols,
however you were led. [3]Therefore I make
known to you that no one speaking by
the Spirit of God calls Jesus accursed, and
no one can say that Jesus is Lord except
by the Holy Spirit.
[4]There are diversities of gifts, but the
same Spirit. [5]There are differences of
ministries, but the same Lord. [6]And there
are diversities of activities, but it is the
same God who works all in all. [7]But the
manifestation of the Spirit is given to
each one for the profit *of all:* [8]for to one is
given the word of wisdom through the
Spirit, to another the word of knowledge
through the same Spirit, [9]to another faith
by the same Spirit, to another gifts of
healings by the same[a] Spirit, [10]to another
the working of miracles, to another prophecy, to another discerning of spirits, to
another *different* kinds of tongues, to another the interpretation of tongues. [11]But
one and the same Spirit works all these
things, distributing to each one individually as He wills.

Unity and Diversity in One Body

[12]For as the body is one and has many

11:27 [a]NU-Text and M-Text read *the blood.* 11:29 [a]NU-Text omits *in an unworthy manner.* [b]NU-Text omits *Lord's.* 12:2 [a]NU-Text and M-Text add *when.* 12:9 [a]NU-Text reads *one.*

members, but all the members of that one body, being many, are one body, so also *is* Christ. [13]For by one Spirit we were all baptized into one body—whether Jews or Greeks, whether slaves or free—and have all been made to drink into[a] one Spirit. [14]For in fact the body is not one member but many.

[15]If the foot should say, "Because I am not a hand, I am not of the body," is it therefore not of the body? [16]And if the ear should say, "Because I am not an eye, I am not of the body," is it therefore not of the body? [17]If the whole body *were* an eye, where *would be* the hearing? If the whole *were* hearing, where *would be* the smelling? [18]But now God has set the members, each one of them, in the body just as He pleased. [19]And if they were all one member, where *would* the body *be?*

Love will find a way. Indifference will find an excuse.

ANONYMOUS

[20]But now indeed *there are* many members, yet one body. [21]And the eye cannot say to the hand, "I have no need of you"; nor again the head to the feet, "I have no need of you." [22]No, much rather, those members of the body which seem to be weaker are necessary. [23]And those *members* of the body which we think to be less honorable, on these we bestow greater honor; and our unpresentable *parts* have greater modesty, [24]but our presentable *parts* have no need. But God composed the body, having given greater honor to that *part* which lacks it, [25]that there should be no schism in the body, but *that* the members should have the same care for one another. [26]And if one member suffers, all the members suffer with *it;* or if one member is honored, all the members rejoice with *it.*

[27]Now you are the body of Christ, and members individually. [28]And God has appointed these in the church: first apostles, second prophets, third teachers, after that miracles, then gifts of healings, helps, administrations, varieties of tongues. [29]*Are* all apostles? *Are* all prophets? *Are* all teachers? *Are* all workers of miracles? [30]Do all have gifts of healings? Do all speak with tongues? Do all interpret? [31]But earnestly desire the best[a] gifts. And yet I show you a more excellent way.

The Greatest Gift

13 Though I speak with the tongues of men and of angels, but have not love, I have become sounding brass or a clanging cymbal. [2]And though I have *the gift of* prophecy, and understand all mysteries and all knowledge, and though I have all faith, so that I could remove mountains, but have not love, I am nothing. [3]And though I bestow all my goods to feed *the poor,* and though I give my body to be burned,[a] but have not love, it profits me nothing.

[4]Love suffers long *and* is kind; love does not envy; love does not parade itself, is not puffed up; [5]does not behave rudely, does not seek its own, is not provoked, thinks no evil; [6]does not rejoice in iniquity, but rejoices in the truth; [7]bears all things, believes all things, hopes all things, endures all things.

[8]Love never fails. But whether *there are* prophecies, they will fail; whether *there are* tongues, they will cease; whether *there is* knowledge, it will vanish away. [9]For we know in part and we prophesy in part. [10]But when that which is perfect has come, then that which is in part will be done away.

[11]When I was a child, I spoke as a child, I understood as a child, I thought as a child; but when I became a man, I

12:13 [a]NU-Text omits *into.* **12:31** [a]NU-Text reads *greater.* **13:3** [a]NU-Text reads *so I may boast.*

12:25 "Satan always hates Christian fellowship; it is his policy to keep Christians apart. Anything which can divide saints from one another he delights in." *Charles Spurgeon*

13:2 **Speaking the Truth in Love to Jehovah's Witnesses**

By Clint DeBoer

I was raised as a Jehovah's Witness and remained one until age 11. Coming out of this cult, I entered my teenage years as a bitter atheist where I remained until I graduated from college. Through God's amazing grace I was saved in 1994 after reading the Bible and realizing that it was indeed the true Word of God.

Repeatedly God has blessed me with the passion and privilege to witness to the Jehovah's Witnesses. You've almost certainly had them come knocking on your door on a Saturday afternoon and you may have even engaged a Jehovah's Witness in a theological discussion. In talking to other Christians I find that when presented with a face-to-face encounter with a Jehovah's Witness there are usually two responses:

1) A "frontal assault" via debate or heated discussion; or

2) A polite "no thanks, I'm already a Christian" followed by an all too abrupt closing of the door.

For the mature Christian, what's usually missing is the realization that this is a true witnessing opportunity—one that has arrived right at your doorstep.

In my earliest attempts at grabbing the proverbial bull by the horns, I tried engaging them in direct debates, often quoting from several texts I had studied regarding the cultic practices of the Jehovah's Witnesses. After several failed "conversion" attempts, often ending with thoroughly frustrated Jehovah's Witnesses unwilling to ever return to my residence, I arrived at a startling realization: Jehovah's Witnesses are real people, with real needs and real feelings. They can feel frustration, anger, fear, and confusion. I then realized that the reason my frontal assaults on the Jehovah's Witnesses never seemed to work was because I had not put myself in their place and taken their feelings into account.

A wise man once said, "When you want to get someone's attention, you don't shine a flashlight in their eyes." In presenting my arguments and facts without giving them time to prepare, I had forgotten they were human beings searching for the truth. I had not been speaking this truth in love.

Months later, when I was again presented with an opportunity to speak with Jehovah's Witnesses at my door, I engaged them in conversation, and agreed to do a weekly Bible study with them in order to further discuss what exactly they believed. They agreed, with the understanding that along the way I would ask questions whenever we arrived at a topic or subject with which I disagreed or failed to understand. The amazing difference was that instead of blindsiding them with questions and points of contention, I was giving them an opportunity to prepare themselves for a topic of discussion.

But more importantly, I began to care about them personally and yearn for their salvation.

In this way, I am able to meet with Witnesses on a weekly basis and take them off the streets, focusing on critical topics such as the requirement that one be born again to enter the kingdom of God, the unbiblical theology of a two-class system of believers, and the true identity of Jesus Christ.

put away childish things. [12]For now we
see in a mirror, dimly, but then face to
face. Now I know in part, but then I shall
know just as I also am known.
[13]And now abide faith, hope, love, these
three; but the greatest of these *is* love.

Prophecy and Tongues

14 Pursue love, and desire spiritual *gifts,* but especially that you may
prophesy. [2]For he who speaks in a
tongue does not speak to men but to
God, for no one understands *him;* however, in the spirit he speaks mysteries.
[3]But he who prophesies speaks edification and exhortation and comfort to men.
[4]He who speaks in a tongue edifies himself, but he who prophesies edifies the
church. [5]I wish you all spoke with tongues,
but even more that you prophesied; for[a]
he who prophesies *is* greater than he who speaks with tongues, unless indeed he interprets, that the church may receive edification.

Tongues Must Be Interpreted

[6]But now, brethren, if I come to you
speaking with tongues, what shall I profit you unless I speak to you either by revelation, by knowledge, by prophesying, or

14:5 [a]NU-Text reads *and.*

"We do not know one-millionth of one percent about anything." (See 1 Cor. 8:2.)

Thomas Edison

by teaching? [7]Even things without life, whether flute or harp, when they make a sound, unless they make a distinction in the sounds, how will it be known what is piped or played? [8]For if the trumpet makes an uncertain sound, who will prepare for battle? [9]So likewise you, unless you utter by the tongue words easy to understand, how will it be known what is spoken? For you will be speaking into the air. [10]There are, it may be, so many kinds of languages in the world, and none of them *is* without significance. [11]Therefore, if I do not know the meaning of the language, I shall be a foreigner to him who speaks, and he who speaks *will be* a foreigner to me. [12]Even so you, since you are zealous for spiritual *gifts, let it be* for the edification of the church *that* you seek to excel.

[13]Therefore let him who speaks in a tongue pray that he may interpret. [14]For if I pray in a tongue, my spirit prays, but my understanding is unfruitful. [15]What is *the conclusion* then? I will pray with the spirit, and I will also pray with the understanding. I will sing with the spirit, and I will also sing with the understanding. [16]Otherwise, if you bless with the spirit, how will he who occupies the place of the uninformed say "Amen" at your giving of thanks, since he does not understand what you say? [17]For you indeed give thanks well, but the other is not edified.

[18]I thank my God I speak with tongues more than you all; [19]yet in the church I would rather speak five words with my understanding, that I may teach others also, than ten thousand words in a tongue.

Tongues a Sign to Unbelievers

[20]Brethren, do not be children in understanding; however, in malice be babes, but in understanding be mature.

[21]In the law it is written:

"With men of other tongues and other lips
I will speak to this people;
And yet, for all that, they will not hear Me,"[a]

says the Lord.

[22]Therefore tongues are for a sign, not to those who believe but to unbelievers; but prophesying is not for unbelievers but for those who believe. [23]Therefore if the whole church comes together in one place, and all speak with tongues, and there come in *those who are* uninformed or unbelievers, will they not say that you are out of your mind? [24]But if all prophesy, and an unbeliever or an uninformed person comes in, he is convinced by all, he is convicted by all. [25]And thus[a] the secrets of his heart are revealed; and so, falling down on *his* face, he will worship God and report that God is truly among you.

Order in Church Meetings

[26]How is it then, brethren? Whenever you come together, each of you has a psalm, has a teaching, has a tongue, has a revelation, has an interpretation. Let all

14:21 [a]Isaiah 28:11, 12 **14:25** [a]NU-Text omits *And thus.*

things be done for edification. [27]If anyone speaks in a tongue, *let there be* two or at the most three, *each* in turn, and let one interpret. [28]But if there is no interpreter, let him keep silent in church, and let him speak to himself and to God. [29]Let two or three prophets speak, and let the others judge. [30]But if *anything* is revealed to another who sits by, let the first keep silent. [31]For you can all prophesy one by one, that all may learn and all may be encouraged. [32]And the spirits of the prophets are subject to the prophets. [33]For God is not *the author* of confusion but of peace, as in all the churches of the saints.

> It was not the volume of sin that sent Christ to the cross; it was the fact of sin.
>
> **RAVI ZACHARIAS**

[34]Let your[a] women keep silent in the churches, for they are not permitted to speak; but *they are* to be submissive, as the law also says. [35]And if they want to learn something, let them ask their own husbands at home; for it is shameful for women to speak in church.

[36]Or did the word of God come *originally* from you? Or *was it* you only that it reached? [37]If anyone thinks himself to be a prophet or spiritual, let him acknowledge that the things which I write to you are the commandments of the Lord. [38]But if anyone is ignorant, let him be ignorant.[a]

[39]Therefore, brethren, desire earnestly to prophesy, and do not forbid to speak with tongues. [40]Let all things be done decently and in order.

The Risen Christ, Faith's Reality

15 Moreover, brethren, I declare to you the gospel which I preached to you, which also you received and in which you stand, [2]by which also you are saved, if you hold fast that word which I preached to you—unless you believed in vain.

[3]For I delivered to you first of all that which I also received: that Christ died for our sins according to the Scriptures, [4]and that He was buried, and that He rose again the third day according to the Scriptures, [5]and that He was seen by Cephas, then by the twelve. [6]After that He was seen by over five hundred brethren at once, of whom the greater part remain to the present, but some have fallen asleep. [7]After that He was seen by James, then by all the apostles. [8]Then last of all He was seen by me also, as by one born out of due time.

[9]For I am the least of the apostles, who am not worthy to be called an apostle, because I persecuted the church of God. [10]But by the grace of God I am what I am, and His grace toward me was not in

14:34 [a]NU-Text omits *your.* 14:38 [a]NU-Text reads *if anyone does not recognize this, he is not recognized.*

15:6 "The fact that Abraham Lincoln was born, became president, or was assassinated cannot be proven using scientific methods. To be 'scientific' it must be *repeatable* (as in the testing of gravity). The proofs that Lincoln did exist and was a historical figure are: 1) the written evidence; 2) eyewitness testimony; and 3) physical evidence that remains to this day—the Ford Theatre, birth records, and newspaper articles regarding his election. All these facts are acceptable in a court of law as proof to a judge and jury.

"The resurrection of Jesus Christ from the dead is 'evidential': 1) the empty tomb still exists; 2) His birth record is documented all the way back to Adam and Eve; 3) the four Gospels record His death; 4) the location, and even the names of the political leaders who sentenced Him are historically recorded; 5) there were more than five hundred eyewitnesses who saw Jesus after the resurrection, recorded by the New Testament writers; 6) the very existence of the Christian faith, based on His death and resurrection; 7) the cultural and political evidence of the time, including the Roman calendar separating all of time into 'Before Christ' (B.C.) and 'in the year of our Lord' (A.D.)." *Garry T. Ansdell*

15:10 "There is nothing but God's grace. We walk upon it; we breathe it; we live and die by it; it makes the nails and axles of the universe." *Robert Louis Stevenson*

QUESTIONS & OBJECTIONS

15:22 ***"If God is perfect, why did He make an imperfect creation?"***

The Bible tells us that the Genesis creation was "very good." There was no sin and therefore no suffering or death. Why then did God give Adam and Eve the ability to sin, knowing full well that they would sin and bring death and pain to the human race? Some believe that if Adam had been created without the ability to choose, then he would have been a "robot." A father *cannot* make his children love him. They choose to love him because they have a free will. Others point out that humanity would never have seen the depth of the love of God, as displayed in the cross, unless Adam had sinned, and that fact could be one reason why God allowed sin to enter the world.

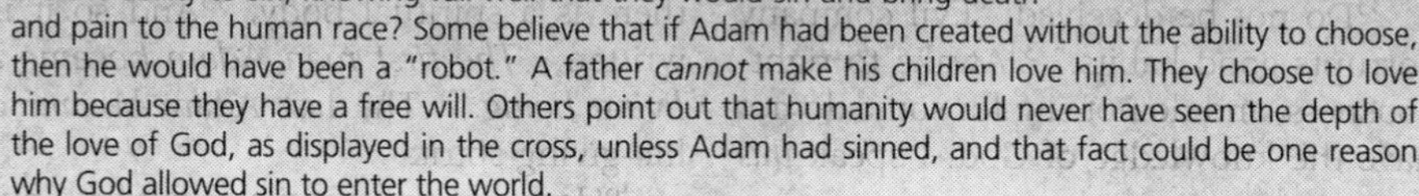

vain; but I labored more abundantly than they all, yet not I, but the grace of God *which was* with me. 11Therefore, whether *it was* I or they, so we preach and so you believed.

The Risen Christ, Our Hope

12Now if Christ is preached that He has been raised from the dead, how do some among you say that there is no resurrection of the dead? 13But if there is no resurrection of the dead, then Christ is not risen. 14And if Christ is not risen, then our preaching is empty and your faith *is* also empty. 15Yes, and we are found false witnesses of God, because we have testified of God that He raised up Christ, whom He did not raise up—if in fact the dead do not rise. 16For if *the* dead do not rise, then Christ is not risen. 17And if Christ is not risen, your faith *is* futile; you are still in your sins! 18Then also those who have fallen asleep in Christ have perished. 19If in this life only we have hope in Christ, we are of all men the most pitiable.

The Last Enemy Destroyed

20But now Christ is risen from the dead, *and* has become the firstfruits of those who have fallen asleep. 21For since by man *came* death, by Man also *came* the resurrection of the dead. 22For as in Adam all die, even so in Christ all shall be made alive. 23But each one in his own order: Christ the firstfruits, afterward those *who are* Christ's at His coming. 24Then *comes* the end, when He delivers the kingdom to God the Father, when He puts an end to all rule and all authority and power. 25For He must reign till He has put all enemies under His feet. 26The last enemy *that* will be destroyed *is* death. 27For *"He has put all things under His feet."*[a] But when He says "all things are put under Him," *it is* evident that He who put all things under Him is excepted. 28Now when all things are made subject to Him, then the Son Himself will also be subject to Him who put all things under Him, that God may be all in all.

Effects of Denying the Resurrection

29Otherwise, what will they do who are baptized for the dead, if the dead do not rise at all? Why then are they baptized for the dead? 30And why do we

15:27 [a]Psalm 8:6

15:14 If Jesus Christ didn't rise from the tomb, then the Bible is a fraud and any hope of resurrection is therefore in vain. However, God has given us irrefutable evidence in His Word to strengthen our faith in His promises—historical, scientific, medical, archaeological, and prophetic evidence.

15:17 "How can anyone lose who chooses to become a Christian? If, when he dies, there turns out to be no God and his faith was in vain, he has lost nothing—in fact, he has been happier in life than his nonbelieving friends. If, however, there is a God and a heaven and hell, then he has gained heaven and his skeptical friends will have lost everything in hell!" *Blaise Pascal*

stand in jeopardy every hour? 31I affirm,
by the boasting in you which I have in
Christ Jesus our Lord, I die daily. 32If, in
the manner of men, I have fought with
beasts at Ephesus, what advantage *is it* to
me? If *the* dead do not rise, *"Let us eat*
and drink, for tomorrow we die!"[a]

33Do not be deceived: "Evil company
corrupts good habits." 34Awake to righteousness, and do not sin; for some do not
have the knowledge of God. I speak *this*
to your shame.

A Glorious Body

35But someone will say, "How are the
dead raised up? And with what body do
they come?" 36Foolish one, what you sow
is not made alive unless it dies. 37And
what you sow, you do not sow that body
that shall be, but mere grain—perhaps
wheat or some other *grain.* 38But God
gives it a body as He pleases, and to each
seed its own body.

39All flesh *is* not the same flesh, but
there is one *kind of* flesh[a] of men, another
flesh of animals, another of fish, *and* another of birds.

40*There are* also celestial bodies and
terrestrial bodies; but the glory of the celestial *is* one, and the *glory* of the terrestrial *is* another. 41*There is* one glory of the
sun, another glory of the moon, and another glory of the stars; for *one* star differs
from *another* star in glory.

42So also *is* the resurrection of the
dead. *The body* is sown in corruption, it is
raised in incorruption. 43It is sown in dishonor, it is raised in glory. It is sown in
weakness, it is raised in power. 44It is
sown a natural body, it is raised a spiritual body. There is a natural body, and
there is a spiritual body. 45And so it is
written, *"The first man Adam became a*
living being."[a] The last Adam *became* a
life-giving spirit.

46However, the spiritual is not first, but
the natural, and afterward the spiritual.
47The first man *was* of the earth, *made* of
dust; the second Man *is* the Lord[a] from
heaven. 48As *was* the *man* of dust, so also
are those *who are made* of dust; and as *is*
the heavenly *Man,* so also *are* those *who*
are heavenly. 49And as we have borne the
image of the *man* of dust, we shall also
bear[a] the image of the heavenly *Man.*

Our Final Victory

50Now this I say, brethren, that flesh
and blood cannot inherit the kingdom of
God; nor does corruption inherit incorruption. 51Behold, I tell you a mystery:
We shall not all sleep, but we shall all be
changed— 52in a moment, in the twinkling of an eye, at the last trumpet. For
the trumpet will sound, and the dead will

15:32 [a]Isaiah 22:13 15:39 [a]NU-Text and M-Text omit *of flesh.* 15:45 [a]Genesis 2:7 15:47 [a]NU-Text omits *the Lord.* 15:49 [a]M-Text reads *let us also bear.*

15:29 Mormon practices. Mormons are well-known for their interest in genealogy because they believe it is their responsibility to be baptized on behalf of the dead. They believe those who have died without accepting Mormonism can still make it to heaven if their names are taken to the Temple and someone is baptized on their behalf. Because they no longer have a body, the ordinance is done for them by proxy, giving the dead the opportunity to accept Mormonism in the spirit world. Mormons base this practice on 1 Cor. 15:29, but Paul disassociates himself from the pagan practice by using the word "they," not "we."

Some Mormons are even married on behalf of the dead, by going through the marriage ceremony in their place. This supposedly enables a dead person to make it out of "Spirit Prison" and into a higher level of heaven. For more on Mormon beliefs, see page 1684.

15:31 "We are not merely imperfect creatures who must be improved: we are, as Newman said, rebels who must lay down our arms...To surrender a self-will inflamed and swollen with years of usurpation is a kind of death...Hence the necessity to die daily: however often we think we have broken the rebellious self, we shall still find it alive." *C. S. Lewis, The Problem of Pain*

15:34 False converts. Paul acknowledges that there were false converts in their midst; to their shame, some among them did not know God, were dead to righteousness, and were continuing to sin. We also should feel a sense of shame at the state of the lukewarm contemporary Church, where only 2 percent have any real concern for the salvation of the world.

15:39 The Cambrian Explosion

Rather than transitional forms between species, as evolutionists claim, what the fossil record reveals is that each species appears fully distinct and remains unchanged. Despite what you've been taught in school, the fossil evidence does not show that all life evolved from a single common ancestor through minor changes.

Instead, during the period that paleontologists call the Cambrian Explosion, virtually all the major animal forms appeared suddenly without any trace of less complex ancestors. No new body plans have come into existence since then. The Cambrian Explosion is also known as "The Biological Big Bang," because the majority of complex life forms show up virtually overnight. If the entire period of life on earth was a 24-hour day, the Cambrian period would be less than two minutes. Like the Big Bang that supposedly began our universe, out of nowhere, nothing suddenly became everything. (See Psa. 121:2 comment.)

T. S. Kemp, curator of the zoological collections at the Oxford University Museum of Natural History, is one of the world's foremost experts on Cambrian fossils. In discussing the sudden appearance of new species, Kemp writes, "With few exceptions, radically new kinds of organisms appear for the first time in the fossil record already fully evolved, with most of their characteristic features present... It is not at all what might have been expected."

Nature clearly does not reveal the gradually changing picture that evolution requires. Instead, life forms are strictly separated into very distinct categories. Paleontologist Robert Carroll, an evolutionist authority, admits this fact in his book *Patterns and Processes of Vertebrate Evolution:* "Although an almost incomprehensible number of species inhabit Earth today, they do not form a continuous spectrum of barely distinguishable intermediates. Instead, nearly all species can be recognized as belonging to a relatively limited number of clearly distinct major groups, with very few illustrating intermediate structures or ways of life."

So according to the evidence produced by paleontology—the scientists' guide to whether or not evolution is true (see Jer. 27:5 comment)—life did *not* evolve gradually over a long period from simple to complex forms. Instead, the fossils show exactly what we would expect to find if biblical creation is true: all the major animal groups appeared fully formed, all at one time, genetically separated into kinds, and with limited change.

Regarding the Cambrian fauna, prominent British evolutionist Richard Dawkins made the following observation: "And we find many of them already in an advanced state of evolution, the very first time they appear. It is as though they were just planted there, without any evolutionary history. Needless to say, this appearance of sudden planting has delighted creationists..."

Naturally, Dawkins surmises why there may be a lack of any intermediates and attributes the "very important gaps" to "imperfections in the fossil record." He then adds, "If you are a creationist you may think that this is special pleading"—and he's correct. He goes on to say: "Both schools of [evolutionary] thought agree that the only alternative explanation of the sudden appearance of so many complex animal types in the Cambrian era is divine creation, and both would reject this alternative."

Dawkins was right. Creationists *are* delighted that the scientific evidence so consistently reveals the truth about the origins of this incredible creation. But we would be delighted beyond words if evolutionists would overcome their bias against the truth and acknowledge our incredible Creator. (Adapted from *How to Know God Exists*).

"The abrupt manner in which whole groups of species suddenly appear in certain formations, has been urged by several paleontologists... as a fatal objection to the belief in the transmutation of species. If numerous species, belonging to the same genera or families, have really started into life at once, the fact would be fatal to the theory of evolution through natural selection." *Charles Darwin, Origin of Species*

be raised incorruptible, and we shall be
changed. 53 For this corruptible must put
on incorruption, and this mortal *must* put
on immortality. 54 So when this corruptible has put on incorruption, and this
mortal has put on immortality, then shall
be brought to pass the saying that is written: *"Death is swallowed up in victory."*[a]

55 *"O Death, where is your sting?*[a]
O Hades, where is your victory?"[b]

56 The sting of death *is* sin, and the strength
of sin *is* the law. 57 But thanks *be* to God,

15:54 [a]Isaiah 25:8 15:55 [a]Hosea 13:14 [b]NU-Text reads *O Death, where is your victory? O Death, where is your sting?*

QUESTIONS & OBJECTIONS

"Adam was a mythical figure who never really lived."

Adam is a key figure in Scripture. He is described as the "first Adam," the one who brought sin into the world. He made it necessary for Jesus, the "last Adam," to atone for all humans, and then rise from the grave with the promise of complete redemption for fallen man and fallen creation. If Adam was just a myth, we would not be able to fully understand the work of Jesus.

If Adam and Eve were not real, then we ought to doubt whether their children were real too, and their children…and then we ought to doubt the first 11 chapters of Genesis, and so on. All the genealogies accept Adam as being a literal person, so their children Cain and Abel (Gen. 4:9,10; Luke 11:50,51) must be real too. Jesus was descended from Adam, and it is impossible to be descended from a myth.

who gives us the victory through our
Lord Jesus Christ.
58Therefore, my beloved brethren, be
steadfast, immovable, always abounding
in the work of the Lord, knowing that
your labor is not in vain in the Lord.

. . . . . .

For how to speak with someone who doesn't believe in the afterlife, see Psa. 49:15 comment.

. . . . . .

Collection for the Saints

16 Now concerning the collection for
the saints, as I have given orders
to the churches of Galatia, so you must
do also: 2On the first *day* of the week let
each one of you lay something aside,
storing up as he may prosper, that there
be no collections when I come. 3And when
I come, whomever you approve by *your*
letters I will send to bear your gift to Jerusalem.
4But if it is fitting that I go also,
they will go with me.

Personal Plans

5Now I will come to you when I pass
through Macedonia (for I am passing
through Macedonia). 6And it may be that
I will remain, or even spend the winter
with you, that you may send me on my
journey, wherever I go. 7For I do not wish
to see you now on the way; but I hope to
stay a while with you, if the Lord permits.
8But I will tarry in Ephesus until Pentecost.
9For a great and effective door has
opened to me, and *there are* many adversaries.
10And if Timothy comes, see that he
may be with you without fear; for he does
the work of the Lord, as I also *do.* 11Therefore
let no one despise him. But send him
on his journey in peace, that he may come
to me; for I am waiting for him with the

15:58 Discouragement in witnessing. It is easy to become discouraged after trying to reason with sinners. But to do so is to demean the influence of the Holy Spirit in our witness. If the salvation of a single soul depended solely upon us, we *should* be depressed if we see little visible and immediate fruit for our labors. However, the Bible tells us that "salvation is of the Lord." We *do* play a part as a co-laborer with Christ—He may instruct us to roll the stone away, but it is the Lord alone who calls the sinner from the tomb of his deathly state. He gives us opportunity, but He opens the heart of the sinner, and it is Him alone that makes the sinner come to life.

Our confidence should then be in *Him*. Jesus said, "With God nothing will be impossible" (Luke 1:37). We therefore can *always* abound in the Lord, knowing that our labors (even with cults) are not in vain. His Word cannot return void. Our part is simply to be true and faithful in our witness, then to stand back and watch the miracle work of our God. Who knows, perhaps the words we placed in the heart of the person may bear fruit years after they were spoken, and we will have the joy of unwrapping the grave clothes when God, in His time, calls them.

15:55 *Last Words of Famous People*

Fearful Last Words:

Cardinal Borgia: "I have provided in the course of my life for everything except death, and now, alas, I am to die unprepared."

Elizabeth the First: "All my possessions for one moment of time."

Kurt Cobain (suicide note): "Frances and Courtney, I'll be at your altar. Please keep going Courtney, for Frances. For her life will be so much happier without me. I love you. *I love you.*"

Ludwig van Beethoven: "Too bad, too bad! It's too late!"

Thomas Hobbs: "I am about to take my last voyage, a great leap in the dark."

Anne Boleyn: "O God, have pity on my soul. O God, have pity on my soul."

Prince Henry of Wales: "Tie a rope round my body, pull me out of bed, and lay me in ashes, that I may die with repentant prayers to an offended God. O! I in vain wish for that time I lost with you and others in vain recreations."

Socrates: "All the wisdom of this world is but a tiny raft upon which we must set sail when we leave this earth. If only there was a firmer foundation upon which to sail, perhaps some divine word."

Sigmund Freud: "The meager satisfaction that man can extract from reality leaves him starving."

Tony Hancock (British comedian): "Nobody will ever know I existed. Nothing to leave behind me. Nothing to pass on. Nobody to mourn me. That's the bitterest blow of all."

Phillip III, King of France: "What an account I shall have to give to God! How I should like to live otherwise than I have lived."

Luther Burbank: "I don't feel good."

Voltaire (skeptic): "I am abandoned by God and man! I will give you half of what I am worth if you will give me six months' life. Then I shall go to hell; and you will go with me. O Christ! O Jesus Christ!" (The talented French writer once said of Jesus, "Curse the wretch!" He stated, "Every sensible man, every honorable man, must hold the Christian sect in horror...Christianity is the most ridiculous, the most absurd and bloody religion that has ever infected the world.")

Philosophical Last Words:

Karl Marx: "Go on, get out! Last words are for fools who haven't said enough!"

Aldous Huxley (humanist): "It is a bit embarrassing to have been concerned with the human problem all one's life and find at the end that one has no more to offer by way of advice than 'Try and be a little kinder.'"

Napoleon: "I marvel that where the ambitious dreams of myself and of Alexander and of Caesar should have vanished into thin air, a Judean peasant—Jesus—should be able to stretch his hands across the centuries, and control the destinies of men and nations."

Leonardo da Vinci: "I have offended God and mankind because my work did not reach the quality it should have."

Leo Tolstoy: "Even in the valley of the shadow of death, two and two do not make six."

Benjamin Franklin: "A dying man can do nothing easy."

Grotius: "I have lived my life in a laborious doing of nothing."

Unexpected Demise:

H. G. Wells: "Go away: I'm all right."

General John Sedgwick (during the heat of battle in 1864): "They couldn't hit an elephant at this dist——!"

Bing Crosby: "That was a great game of golf."

Mahatma Ghandi: "I am late by ten minutes. I hate being late. I like to be at the prayer punctually at the stroke of five."

Diana (Spencer), Princess of Wales: "My God. What's happened?" (per police files)

Douglas Fairbanks, Sr.: "Never felt better."

Franklin D. Roosevelt: "I have a terrific headache."

Sal Mineo: (stabbed through the heart): "Oh God! No! Help! Someone help!"

Jesse James: "It's awfully hot today."

Lee Harvey Oswald: "I will be glad to discuss this proposition with my attorney, and that after I talk with one, we could either discuss it with him or discuss it with my attorney, if the attorney thinks it is a wise thing to do, but at the present time I have nothing more to say to you."

Unusual Last Words:

Vincent Van Gogh: "I shall never get rid of this depression."

James Dean: "My fun days are over."

W. C. Fields: "I'm looking for a loophole."

(continued)

(15:55 continued)

Oscar Wilde: "My wallpaper and I are fighting a duel to the death. One or the other of us has to go…"

Louis XVII: "I have something to tell you…"

Assurance of Salvation:

General William Booth (to his son): "And the homeless children, Bramwell, look after the homeless. Promise me…"

Charles Dickens: "I commit my soul to the mercy of God, through our Lord and Savior Jesus Christ, and I exhort my dear children humbly to try and guide themselves by the teaching of the New Testament."

Jonathan Edwards: "Trust in God and you shall have nothing to fear."

Alexander Hamilton: "I have a tender reliance on the mercy of the Almighty, through the merits of the Lord Jesus Christ. I am a sinner. I look to Him for mercy."

Patrick Henry: "Doctor, I wish you to observe how real and beneficial the religion of Christ is to a man about to die…" In his will he wrote: "This is all the inheritance I give to my dear family. The religion of Christ which will give them one which will make them rich indeed."

Martin Luther: "Into Thy hands I commend my spirit! Thou hast redeemed me, O God of truth."

John Milton (British poet): "Death is the great key that opens the palace of Eternity."

Lew Wallace (wrote *Ben Hur*): "Thy will be done."

D. L. Moody: "I see earth receding; heaven is opening. God is calling me."

John Owen: "I am going to Him whom my soul loveth, or rather who has loved me with an everlasting love, which is the sole ground of all my consolation."

William Shakespeare: "I commend my soul into the hands of God my Creator, hoping and assuredly believing, through the only merits of Jesus Christ my Savior, to be made partaker of life everlasting; and my body to the earth, whereof it was made."

Sir Walter Raleigh (at his execution): "So the heart be right, it is no matter which way the head lieth."

Daniel Webster (just before his death): "The great mystery is Jesus Christ—the gospel. What would the condition of any of us be if we had not the hope of immortality?…Thank God, the gospel of Jesus Christ brought life and immortality to light." His last words were: "I still live."

David Livingstone: "Build me a hut to die in. I am going home."

Andrew Jackson: "My dear children, do not grieve for me…I am my God's. I belong to Him. I go but a short time before you, and…I hope and trust to meet you all in heaven."

Isaac Watts (hymn-writer): "It is a great mercy that I have no manner of fear or dread of death. I could, if God please, lay my head back and die without terror this afternoon."

brethren.
12Now concerning *our* brother Apollos,
I strongly urged him to come to you with
the brethren, but he was quite unwilling
to come at this time; however, he will
come when he has a convenient time.

Final Exhortations

13Watch, stand fast in the faith, be
brave, be strong. 14Let all *that* you *do* be
done with love.
15I urge you, brethren—you know the
household of Stephanas, that it is the
firstfruits of Achaia, and *that* they have
devoted themselves to the ministry of the
saints— 16that you also submit to such,
and to everyone who works and labors
with *us*.
17I am glad about the coming of
Stephanas, Fortunatus, and Achaicus, for
what was lacking on your part they supplied. 18For they refreshed my spirit and
yours. Therefore acknowledge such men.

Greetings and a Solemn Farewell

19The churches of Asia greet you. Aquila
and Priscilla greet you heartily in the
Lord, with the church that is in their
house. 20All the brethren greet you.
Greet one another with a holy kiss.
21The salutation with my own hand—
Paul's.
22If anyone does not love the Lord Jesus Christ, let him be accursed.[a] O Lord,
come![b]
23The grace of our Lord Jesus Christ *be*
with you. 24My love *be* with you all in
Christ Jesus. Amen.

16:22 [a]Greek *anathema* [b]Aramaic *Maranatha*

2 Corinthians

Greeting

1 Paul, an apostle of Jesus Christ by the will of God, and Timothy *our* brother,

To the church of God which is at Corinth, with all the saints who are in all Achaia:

[2]Grace to you and peace from God our Father and the Lord Jesus Christ.

Comfort in Suffering

[3]Blessed *be* the God and Father of our Lord Jesus Christ, the Father of mercies and God of all comfort, [4]who comforts us in all our tribulation, that we may be able to comfort those who are in any trouble, with the comfort with which we ourselves are comforted by God. [5]For as the sufferings of Christ abound in us, so our consolation also abounds through Christ. [6]Now if we are afflicted, *it is* for your consolation and salvation, which is effective for enduring the same sufferings which we also suffer. Or if we are comforted, *it is* for your consolation and salvation. [7]And our hope for you *is* steadfast, because we know that as you are partakers of the sufferings, so also *you will partake* of the consolation.

Delivered from Suffering

[8]For we do not want you to be ignorant, brethren, of our trouble which came to us in Asia: that we were burdened beyond measure, above strength, so that we despaired even of life. [9]Yes, we had the sentence of death in ourselves, that we should not trust in ourselves but in God who raises the dead, [10]who delivered us from so great a death, and does[a] deliver us; in whom we trust that He will still deliver *us,* [11]you also helping together in prayer for us, that thanks may be given by many persons on our[a] behalf for the gift *granted* to us through many.

Paul's Sincerity

[12]For our boasting is this: the testimony of our conscience that we conducted ourselves in the world in simplicity and godly sincerity, not with fleshly wisdom but by the grace of God, and more abundantly toward you. [13]For we are not writing any other things to you than what you read or understand. Now I trust you will understand, even to the end [14](as also you have understood us in part), that we are your boast as you also *are* ours, in the day of the Lord Jesus.

Sparing the Church

[15]And in this confidence I intended to come to you before, that you might have

1:10 [a]NU-Text reads *shall.* **1:11** [a]M-Text reads *your behalf.*

1:4,5 This chapter is in direct conflict with the message of modern evangelism, which promises a life of happiness, joy, peace, and fulfillment. The Christian life is filled with trials that keep us on our knees.

a second benefit— [16]to pass by way of you to Macedonia, to come again from Macedonia to you, and be helped by you on my way to Judea. [17]Therefore, when I was planning this, did I do it lightly? Or the things I plan, do I plan according to the flesh, that with me there should be Yes, Yes, and No, No? [18]But *as* God *is* faithful, our word to you was not Yes and No. [19]For the Son of God, Jesus Christ, who was preached among you by us—by me, Silvanus, and Timothy—was not Yes and No, but in Him was Yes. [20]For all the promises of God in Him *are* Yes, and in Him Amen, to the glory of God through us. [21]Now He who establishes us with you in Christ and has anointed us *is* God, [22]who also has sealed us and given us the Spirit in our hearts as a guarantee.

[23]Moreover I call God as witness against my soul, that to spare you I came no more to Corinth. [24]Not that we have dominion over your faith, but are fellow workers for your joy; for by faith you stand.

2 But I determined this within myself, that I would not come again to you in sorrow. [2]For if I make you sorrowful, then who is he who makes me glad but the one who is made sorrowful by me?

Forgive the Offender

[3]And I wrote this very thing to you, lest, when I came, I should have sorrow over those from whom I ought to have joy, having confidence in you all that my joy is *the joy* of you all. [4]For out of much affliction and anguish of heart I wrote to you, with many tears, not that you should be grieved, but that you might know the love which I have so abundantly for you.

[5]But if anyone has caused grief, he has not grieved me, but all of you to some extent—not to be too severe. [6]This punishment which *was inflicted* by the majority *is* sufficient for such a man, [7]so that, on the contrary, you *ought* rather to forgive and comfort *him,* lest perhaps such a one be swallowed up with too much sorrow. [8]Therefore I urge you to reaffirm *your* love to him. [9]For to this end I also wrote, that I might put you to the test, whether you are obedient in all things. [10]Now whom you forgive anything, I also *forgive.* For if indeed I have forgiven anything, I have forgiven that one[a] for your sakes in the presence of Christ, [11]lest Satan should take advantage of us; for we are not ignorant of his devices.

Triumph in Christ

[12]Furthermore, when I came to Troas to *preach* Christ's gospel, and a door was opened to me by the Lord, [13]I had no rest in my spirit, because I did not find Titus my brother; but taking my leave of them, I departed for Macedonia.

[14]Now thanks *be* to God who always leads us in triumph in Christ, and through us diffuses the fragrance of His knowledge in every place. [15]For we are to God the fragrance of Christ among those who are being saved and among those who are perishing. [16]To the one *we are* the aroma of death *leading* to death, and to the other the aroma of life *leading* to life. And who *is* sufficient for these things? [17]For we are not, as so many,[a] peddling the word of God; but as of sincerity, but as from God, we speak in the sight of God in Christ.

Christ's Epistle

3 Do we begin again to commend ourselves? Or do we need, as some *others,* epistles of commendation to you or *letters* of commendation from you? [2]You are our epistle written in our hearts,

2:10 [a]NU-Text reads *For indeed, what I have forgiven, if I have forgiven anything, I did it.* 2:17 [a]M-Text reads *the rest.*

2:17 Opticians now offer glasses with titanium frames. Titanium twists and bends but retains its integrity. It always goes back to its original shape. That's what a Christian should be like. We bend; we are flexible on certain issues. However, we always retain our integrity. We refuse to compromise the truth of God's Word. See also 2 Cor. 4:2.

2:17 *The Gospel: Why not preach that Jesus gives happiness, peace, and joy?*

Two men are seated on a plane. The first is given a parachute and told to put it on as it would improve his flight. He's a little skeptical at first, since he can't see how wearing a parachute on a plane could possibly improve his flight.

He decides to experiment and see if the claims are true. As he puts it on, he notices the weight of it upon his shoulders and he finds he has difficulty in sitting upright. However, he consoles himself with the fact he was told that the parachute would improve his flight. So he decides to give it a little time.

As he waits he notices that some of the other passengers are laughing at him for wearing a parachute on a plane. He begins to feel somewhat humiliated. As they continue to point and laugh at him, he can stand it no longer. He slinks in his seat, unstraps the parachute and throws it to the floor. Disillusionment and bitterness fill his heart, because as far as he was concerned he was told an outright lie.

The second man is given a parachute, *but listen to what he is told*. He's told to put it on because at any moment he'll be jumping 25,000 feet out of the plane. He gratefully puts the parachute on. He doesn't notice the weight of it upon his shoulders, nor that he can't sit upright. His mind is consumed with the thought of what would happen to him if he jumped without the parachute.

Let's now analyze the motive and the result of each passenger's experience. The first man's motive for putting the parachute on was solely to improve his flight. The result of his experience was that he was humiliated by the passengers, disillusioned, and somewhat embittered against those who gave him the parachute. As far as he's concerned, it will be a long time before anyone gets one of those things on his back again.

The second man put the parachute on solely to escape the jump to come. And because of his knowledge of what would happen to him if he jumped without it, he has a deep-rooted joy and peace in his heart knowing that he's saved from sure death. This knowledge gives him the ability to withstand the mockery of the other passengers. His attitude toward those who gave him the parachute is one of heartfelt gratitude.

Now listen to what the modern gospel says: "Put on the Lord Jesus Christ. He'll give you love, joy, peace, fulfillment, and lasting happiness." In other words, Jesus will improve your flight. The sinner responds, and in an experimental fashion puts on the Savior to see if the claims are true. And what does he get? The promised temptation, tribulation, and persecution—the other "passengers" mock him. So what does he do? He takes off the Lord Jesus Christ; he's offended for the Word's sake; he's disillusioned and somewhat embittered . . . and quite rightly so.

He was promised love, joy, peace, and fulfillment, and all he got were trials and humiliation. His bitterness is directed toward those who gave him the so-called "good news." His latter end becomes worse than the first, and he's another inoculated and bitter "backslider."

Instead of preaching that Jesus improves the flight, we should be warning sinners that they have to jump out of a plane. That it's appointed for man to die once and then face judgment (Heb. 9:27). When a sinner understands the horrific consequences of breaking the Law of God, he will flee to the Savior, solely to escape the wrath that's to come. If we are true and faithful witnesses, that's what we'll be preaching—that there is wrath to come—that God "commands all men everywhere to repent, *because* He has appointed a day on which He will judge the world in righteousness" (Acts 17:30,31, emphasis added).

The issue isn't one of happiness, but one of righteousness. It doesn't matter how happy a sinner is, or how much he is enjoying the pleasures of sin for a season, without the righteousness of Christ, he will perish on the day of wrath. Proverbs 11:4 says, "Riches do not profit in the day of wrath, but righteousness delivers from death." Peace and joy are legitimate *fruits* of salvation, but it's not legitimate to use these fruits as a drawing card *for* salvation. If we continue to do so, the sinner will respond with an impure motive, lacking repentance.

Can you remember why the *second* passenger had joy and peace in his heart? It was because he knew that the parachute was going to save him from sure death. In the same way, as believers we have joy and peace in believing because we know that the righteousness of Christ is going to deliver us from the wrath that is to come.

With that thought in mind, let's take a close look at an incident aboard the plane. We have a brand-new flight attendant. It's her first day. She's carrying a tray of boiling hot coffee. She wants to leave an impression on the passengers and she certainly does! As she's walking down the aisle

(continued)

(2:17 continued)
she trips over someone's foot and slops the hot coffee all over the lap of our second passenger. What's his reaction as that boiling liquid hits his tender flesh? Does he say, "Man, that hurt!"? Yes, he does. But then does he rip the parachute from his shoulders, throw it to the floor, and say, "The stupid parachute!"? No, why should he? He didn't put the parachute on for a better flight. He put it on to save him from the jump to come. If anything, the hot coffee incident causes him to cling tighter to the parachute and even look forward to the jump.

If we have put on the Lord Jesus Christ for the right motive—to flee from the wrath that's to come—when tribulation strikes, when the flight gets bumpy, we won't get angry at God, and we won't lose our joy and peace. Why should we? We didn't come to Christ for a better lifestyle, but to flee from the wrath to come.

If anything, tribulation drives the true believer *closer* to the Savior. Sadly, we have multitudes of professing Christians who lose their joy and peace when the flight gets bumpy. Why? They are the product of a man-centered gospel. They came lacking repentance, without which they cannot be saved.

See also John 3:16 comment.

known and read by all men; [3]clearly you
are an epistle of Christ, ministered by us,
written not with ink but by the Spirit of
the living God, not on tablets of stone but
on tablets of flesh, *that is,* of the heart.

The Spirit, Not the Letter

[4]And we have such trust through
Christ toward God. [5]Not that we are sufficient of ourselves to think of anything
as *being* from ourselves, but our sufficiency *is* from God, [6]who also made us
sufficient as ministers of the new covenant, not of the letter but of the Spirit;[a]
for the letter kills, but the Spirit gives life.

Glory of the New Covenant

[7]But if the ministry of death, written
and engraved on stones, was glorious, so
that the children of Israel could not look
steadily at the face of Moses because of
the glory of his countenance, which *glory*
was passing away, [8]how will the ministry
of the Spirit not be more glorious? [9]For if
the ministry of condemnation *had* glory,
the ministry of righteousness exceeds
much more in glory. [10]For even what was
made glorious had no glory in this respect, because of the glory that excels.
[11]For if what is passing away *was* glorious, what remains *is* much more glorious.
[12]Therefore, since we have such hope,
we use great boldness of speech— [13]un-
like Moses, *who* put a veil over his face so
that the children of Israel could not look
steadily at the end of what was passing
away. [14]But their minds were blinded.
For until this day the same veil remains
unlifted in the reading of the Old Testament, because the *veil* is taken away in
Christ. [15]But even to this day, when
Moses is read, a veil lies on their heart.
[16]Nevertheless when one turns to the
Lord, the veil is taken away. [17]Now the
Lord is the Spirit; and where the Spirit of
the Lord *is,* there *is* liberty. [18]But we all,

3:6 [a]Or *spirit*

THE FUNCTION OF THE LAW

3:5,6 "God be thanked when the Law so works as to take off the sinner from all confidence in himself! To make the leper confess that he is incurable is going a great way toward compelling him to go to that divine Savior, who alone is able to heal him. This is the whole end of the Law toward men whom God will save." *Charles Spurgeon*

3:12 "The big problem is that many Christians speak with forked tongues. They speak a strange lingo called the 'language of Zion' and can only be understood by using a special unscrambler, which most [people] do not possess. So we have to learn to speak plainly and not in code." *Dan Wooding*

3:14–16 "Be cold, sober, wise, circumspect. Keep yourself low by the ground avoiding high questions. Expound the Law truly and open the veil of Moses to condemn all flesh and prove all men sinners, and set at broach the mercy of our Lord Jesus, and let wounded consciences drink of Him." *William Tyndale*

with unveiled face, beholding as in a mirror the glory of the Lord, are being transformed into the same image from glory to
glory, just as by the Spirit of the Lord.

The Light of Christ's Gospel

4 Therefore, since we have this ministry, as we have received mercy, we do
not lose heart. 2But we have renounced
the hidden things of shame, not walking
in craftiness nor handling the word of
God deceitfully, but by manifestation of
the truth commending ourselves to every
man's conscience in the sight of God.
3But even if our gospel is veiled, it is
veiled to those who are perishing, 4whose
minds the god of this age has blinded,
who do not believe, lest the light of the
gospel of the glory of Christ, who is the
image of God, should shine on them.

> If we suffer persecution and affliction in a right manner, we attain a larger measure of conformity to Christ... than we could have done merely by imitating his mercy in abundance of good works.
>
> **JOHN WESLEY**

5For we do not preach ourselves, but
Christ Jesus the Lord, and ourselves your
bondservants for Jesus' sake. 6For it is
the God who commanded light to shine
out of darkness, who has shone in our
hearts to *give* the light of the knowledge
of the glory of God in the face of Jesus
Christ.

Cast Down but Unconquered

7But we have this treasure in earthen
vessels, that the excellence of the power
may be of God and not of us. 8*We are*
hard-pressed on every side, yet not
crushed; *we are* perplexed, but not in despair; 9persecuted, but not forsaken; struck
down, but not destroyed— 10always carrying about in the body the dying of the
Lord Jesus, that the life of Jesus also may
be manifested in our body. 11For we who
live are always delivered to death for Jesus' sake, that the life of Jesus also may be
manifested in our mortal flesh. 12So then
death is working in us, but life in you.
13And since we have the same spirit of
faith, according to what is written, *"I believed and therefore I spoke,"*[a] we also
believe and therefore speak, 14knowing
that He who raised up the Lord Jesus will
also raise us up with Jesus, and will present *us* with you. 15For all things *are* for
your sakes, that grace, having spread
through the many, may cause thanksgiving to abound to the glory of God.

Seeing the Invisible

16Therefore we do not lose heart. Even
though our outward man is perishing, yet
the inward *man* is being renewed day by
day. 17For our light affliction, which is
but for a moment, is working for us a far
more exceeding *and* eternal weight of
glory, 18while we do not look at the things
which are seen, but at the things which
are not seen. For the things which are

4:13 [a]Psalm 116:10

3:18 We often delight in sifting gnats, making issues out of things that aren't important. If someone becomes a Christian, some in the Church seem intent on shaping him to be conformed to their own image, rather than the image of Christ. They feel that he should dress, look, believe, speak, eat, and breathe just as they do.

When someone comes to the Lord, he may not look as we think he should. His hair may be long, his clothes may be radical, he may have an earring in his ear, but if these things are wrong, God will speak in his ear. In the meantime, He may be ministering to him about the need to return stolen goods, or about seeking forgiveness from those he has wronged in the past. Those are the things that matter to God.

4:2 "I believe in preaching without compromise against sin." *Franklin Graham*

"Some evangelists are prepared to be anything to anybody as long as they get somebody at the altar for something." *Leonard Ravenhill*

PRINCIPLES OF GROWTH FOR THE NEW AND GROWING CHRISTIAN

Warfare—Praise the Lord and Pass the Ammunition

Before you became a Christian, you floated downstream with the other dead fish. But now, God has put His life within you, and you will find yourself swimming against a threefold current: the world, the devil, and the flesh. Let's look at these three resistant enemies.

Our first enemy is the world, which refers to the sinful, rebellious, world system. The world loves the darkness and hates the light (John 3:20), and is governed by the "prince of the power of the air" (Eph. 2:2). The Bible says the Christian has escaped the corruption that is in the world through lust. "Lust" is unlawful desire, and is the life's blood of the world—whether it be lust for sexual sin, for power, for money, for material things. Lust is a monster that will never be gratified, so don't feed it. It will grow bigger and bigger until it weighs heavy upon your back, and will be the death of you (James 1:15).

There is nothing wrong with sex, power, money, or material things, but when desire for these becomes predominant, it becomes idolatry (Col. 3:5). We are told, "Do not love the world or the things in the world. If anyone loves the world, the love of the Father is not in him"; whoever is "a friend of the world makes himself an enemy of God" (1 John 2:15; James 4:4).

The second enemy is the devil, who is the "god of this age" (2 Cor. 4:4). He was your spiritual father before you joined the family of God (John 8:44; Eph. 2:2). Jesus called the devil a thief who came to steal, kill, and destroy (John 10:10).

The way to overcome him and his demons is to make sure you are outfitted with the spiritual armor of God (Eph. 6:10–20). Become intimately familiar with it. Sleep in it. Never take it off. Bind the sword to your hand so you never lose its grip. The reason for this brings us to the third enemy.

The third enemy is what the Bible calls the "flesh." This is your sinful nature. The domain for the battle is your mind.

If you have a mind to, you *will* be attracted to the world and all its sin. The mind is the control panel for the eyes and the ears, the center of your appetites. All sin begins in the "heart" (Prov. 4:23; Matt. 15:19). We think of sin before we commit it. James 1:15 warns that lust brings forth sin, and sin when it's conceived brings forth death. Every day of life, we have a choice. To sin or not to sin—that is the question. The answer is the fear of God. If you don't fear God, you will sin to your sinful heart's delight.

Did you know that God kills people? He killed a man for what he did sexually (Gen. 38:9,10), killed another man for being greedy (Luke 12:15–21), and killed a husband and wife for telling one lie (Acts 5:1–10). Knowledge of God's goodness—His righteous judgments against evil—should put the fear of God in us and help us to not indulge in sin.

If we know that the eyes of the Lord are in every place, keeping watch on the evil and the good, and that He will bring every work to judgment, we will live accordingly. Such weighty thoughts are valuable, for "by the fear of the LORD one departs from evil" (Prov. 16:6).

For the next principle of growth, see Heb. 10:25 comment.

seen *are* temporary, but the things which
are not seen *are* eternal.

Assurance of the Resurrection

5 For we know that if our earthly house,
this tent, is destroyed, we have a building from God, a house not made with
hands, eternal in the heavens. 2For in this
we groan, earnestly desiring to be clothed
with our habitation which is from heav-
en, 3if indeed, having been clothed, we
shall not be found naked. 4For we who
are in *this* tent groan, being burdened,
not because we want to be unclothed,
but further clothed, that mortality may
be swallowed up by life. 5Now He who
has prepared us for this very thing *is*
God, who also has given us the Spirit as
a guarantee.
6So *we are* always confident, knowing

4:6 Just as in the beginning the earth was without form and void, and in darkness (Gen. 1:2), the understanding of unregenerate man is darkened (Eph. 4:18). It is without form and void until God says, "Let there be light."

QUESTIONS & OBJECTIONS

5:14,15 *"Because Jesus died on the cross, we are all forgiven of every sin."*

The belief that all humanity will be saved is called universalism. But the forgiveness that is in Jesus Christ is conditional upon "repentance toward God and faith toward our Lord Jesus Christ" (Acts 20:21). It is a gift that God offers to everyone, but individuals must receive it by repenting and trusting in Christ, or they will remain dead in their sins. No one has biblical grounds to continue in sin, assuming that they are safe just because Jesus died on the cross. See 1 John 3:4–6.

that while we are at home in the body we
are absent from the Lord. [7]For we walk
by faith, not by sight. [8]We are confident,
yes, well pleased rather to be absent from
the body and to be present with the Lord.

The Judgment Seat of Christ

[9]Therefore we make it our aim, whether
present or absent, to be well pleasing to
Him. [10]For we must all appear before the
judgment seat of Christ, that each one
may receive the things *done* in the body,
according to what he has done, whether
good or bad. [11]Knowing, therefore, the
terror of the Lord, we persuade men; but
we are well known to God, and I also
trust are well known in your consciences.

Be Reconciled to God

[12]For we do not commend ourselves
again to you, but give you opportunity to
boast on our behalf, that you may have
an answer for those who boast in appearance and not in heart. [13]For if we are beside ourselves, *it is* for God; or if we are
of sound mind, *it is* for you. [14]For the
love of Christ compels us, because we
judge thus: that if One died for all, then
all died; [15]and He died for all, that those
who live should live no longer for themselves, but for Him who died for them
and rose again.

[16]Therefore, from now on, we regard
no one according to the flesh. Even though
we have known Christ according to the
flesh, yet now we know *Him thus* no
longer. [17]Therefore, if anyone *is* in Christ,
he is a new creation; old things have
passed away; behold, all things have become new. [18]Now all things *are* of God,
who has reconciled us to Himself through
Jesus Christ, and has given us the ministry of reconciliation, [19]that is, that God
was in Christ reconciling the world to
Himself, not imputing their trespasses to
them, and has committed to us the word
of reconciliation.

[20]Now then, we are ambassadors for
Christ, as though God were pleading
through us: we implore *you* on Christ's
behalf, be reconciled to God. [21]For He
made Him who knew no sin *to be* sin for
us, that we might become the righteousness of God in Him.

5:10 Judgment Day: For verses that warn of its reality, see 2 Thess. 1:7–9.

5:11 "We fear men so much because we fear God so little. One fear causes another. When man's terror scares you, turn your thoughts to the wrath of God." *William Gurnall*

5:17 New birth—its necessity for salvation. See Titus 3:5. "It is easier to denature plutonium than to denature the evil spirit of man." *Albert Einstein*

5:21 "Christians are continually trying to *change* their lives; but God calls us to experience the *exchanged* life. Christianity is not a self-improvement program. It isn't a reformation project. It is resurrection! It is new life! And it is expressed in terms of a total exchange of identity. Jesus Christ identified Himself with us in our death in order that we might be identified with Him in His resurrection. We give Christ all that we were—spiritually dead, guilty sinners—and Christ gives us all that He is—resurrected life, forgiveness, righteousness, acceptance." *Bob George, Classic Christianity* (See Gal. 2:20.)

SPRINGBOARDS FOR PREACHING AND WITNESSING

The Olympic High Diver

6:2

An Olympic gold-medalist high-diving champion was once plagued with insomnia. As he tossed and turned upon his bed, he began thinking deeply about the success he had attained in his field. He meditated on the gold medals he had won. To his dismay he realized that his success had not achieved what he had hoped. The excitement of winning, the photographers, the medals, and the fame had given him some sense of pleasure, but the fact of death awaiting him left him with a complete sense of futility.

He rose from the bed and made his way to his diving pool. Because of a full moon, he didn't even bother to turn the lights on. As he climbed the high diving board, he watched his shadow cast by the moonlight on the far wall. The routine had become so commonplace to him that he could confidently walk that board in the semi-darkness.

At the end of the diving board, he prepared for the dive. He placed his feet together, then pulled his arms up to a horizontal position. As he did so, his eyes caught a glimpse of his shadow on the far wall. All he could see was a perfect cross. His mind immediately raced back to his Sunday school days: "God demonstrates His own love toward us, in that while we were still sinners, Christ died for us" (Rom. 5:8). All of a sudden he felt unclean as he considered the Commandments he had broken. The sinless Son of God had come to pay the penalty for his sins. With tears in his eyes, the great athlete turned around, slowly made his way down to the bottom of the diving board, fell to his knees, and yielded his life to Jesus Christ. He was able to go back to bed and sleep peacefully.

In the morning he arose with a new sense of forgiveness of his sins. He made his way back to the pool, but to his utter astonishment, *it was completely empty*. The previous evening, the caretaker had emptied it and was just beginning the process of refilling.

Marks of the Ministry

6 We then, *as* workers together *with Him*
also plead with *you* not to receive the
grace of God in vain. [2]For He says:

"In an acceptable time I have heard you,
And in the day of salvation I have helped you."[a]

Behold, now *is* the accepted time; behold, now *is* the day of salvation.
[3]We give no offense in anything, that
our ministry may not be blamed. [4]But in
all *things* we commend ourselves as ministers of God: in much patience, in tribulations, in needs, in distresses, [5]in stripes,
in imprisonments, in tumults, in labors,
in sleeplessness, in fastings; [6]by purity,
by knowledge, by longsuffering, by kindness, by the Holy Spirit, by sincere love,
[7]by the word of truth, by the power of
God, by the armor of righteousness on
the right hand and on the left, [8]by honor
and dishonor, by evil report and good report; as deceivers, and *yet* true; [9]as unknown, and *yet* well known; as dying,
and behold we live; as chastened, and *yet*
not killed; [10]as sorrowful, yet always rejoicing; as poor, yet making many rich; as
having nothing, and *yet* possessing all
things.

Be Holy

[11]O Corinthians! We have spoken
openly to you, our heart is wide open.
[12]You are not restricted by us, but you are
restricted by your *own* affections. [13]Now
in return for the same (I speak as to children), you also be open.
[14]Do not be unequally yoked together
with unbelievers. For what fellowship

6:2 [a]Isaiah 49:8

6:1 "It's very sobering to find how many people whom I would presume to be saved feel little or no urgency regarding their spiritual condition, the condition of the church, or that of our nation…Whereas I once thought the battlefield was 'out there' among those rejecting Christ, I see things differently now… The front-line of the battle is in the hearts of God's people." *Rob Cummins*

has righteousness with lawlessness? And
what communion has light with darkness? 15And what accord has Christ with
Belial? Or what part has a believer with
an unbeliever? 16And what agreement has
the temple of God with idols? For you[a]
are the temple of the living God. As God
has said:

"I will dwell in them
And walk among them.
I will be their God,
And they shall be My people."[b]

17Therefore

"Come out from among them
And be separate, says the Lord.
Do not touch what is unclean,
And I will receive you."[a]
18*"I will be a Father to you,*
And you shall be My sons and
daughters,
Says the LORD *Almighty."*[a]

7 Therefore, having these promises,
beloved, let us cleanse ourselves from
all filthiness of the flesh and spirit, perfecting holiness in the fear of God.

The Corinthians' Repentance

2Open *your hearts* to us. We have
wronged no one, we have corrupted no
one, we have cheated no one. 3I do not
say *this* to condemn; for I have said before that you are in our hearts, to die together and to live together. 4Great *is* my
boldness of speech toward you, great *is*
my boasting on your behalf. I am filled
with comfort. I am exceedingly joyful in
all our tribulation.

5For indeed, when we came to Macedonia, our bodies had no rest, but we
were troubled on every side. Outside
were conflicts, inside *were* fears. 6Never-
theless God, who comforts the downcast,
comforted us by the coming of Titus,
7and not only by his coming, but also by
the consolation with which he was comforted in you, when he told us of your
earnest desire, your mourning, your zeal
for me, so that I rejoiced even more.

8For even if I made you sorry with my
letter, I do not regret it; though I did regret it. For I perceive that the same epistle made you sorry, though only for a
while. 9Now I rejoice, not that you were
made sorry, but that your sorrow led to
repentance. For you were made sorry in a
godly manner, that you might suffer loss
from us in nothing. 10For godly sorrow
produces repentance *leading* to salvation,
not to be regretted; but the sorrow of the
world produces death. 11For observe this
very thing, that you sorrowed in a godly

6:16 [a]NU-Text reads *we.* [b]Leviticus 26:12; Jeremiah 32:38; Ezekiel 37:27 6:17 [a]Isaiah 52:11; Ezekiel 20:34, 41 6:18 [a]2 Samuel 7:14

7:4 "Receive every inward and outward trouble, every disappointment, pain, uneasiness, temptation, darkness and desolation with both hands, as to a true opportunity and blessed occasion of dying to self and entering into a fuller fellowship with thy self-denying, suffering Savior." *John Wesley*

7:10 Godly sorrow. A pastor was once approached by his six-year-old son who said he wanted to "ask Jesus into his heart." The father, suspecting that the child lacked the knowledge of sin, told him that he could do so when he was older, then sent him off to bed.

A short time later, the boy got out of bed and asked his father if he could give his life to the Savior. The father still wasn't persuaded of the son's understanding, so, not wanting the child's salvation to be spurious, he sent him back to his room.

A third time the son returned. This time the father questioned him about whether he had broken any of the Ten Commandments. The young boy didn't think he had. When asked if he was a liar, the child said he wasn't. The father thought for a moment, then asked him how many lies he had to tell to be a liar. When it was established that one lie made a person a liar, the child thought for a moment, realized he had lied, and broke down in uncontrollable tears. When the father then asked if he wanted to "ask Jesus into his heart," the child *cringed* and shook his head. He was fearful because now he knew that he had sinned against God. At this point, he could do more than experimentally "ask Jesus into his heart." He could find a place of godly sorrow, repentance toward God, and faith toward our Lord Jesus Christ (Acts 20:21).

"If your sorrow is because of certain consequences which have come on your family because of your sin, this is remorse, not true repentance. If, on the other hand, you are grieved because you also sinned against God and His holy laws, then you are on the right road." (See 2 Cor. 7:10.)

Billy Graham

manner: What diligence it produced in you, *what* clearing *of yourselves, what* indignation, *what* fear, *what* vehement desire, *what* zeal, *what* vindication! In all *things* you proved yourselves to be clear in this matter. [12]Therefore, although I wrote to you, *I did* not *do it* for the sake of him who had done the wrong, nor for the sake of him who suffered wrong, but that our care for you in the sight of God might appear to you.

The Joy of Titus

[13]Therefore we have been comforted in your comfort. And we rejoiced exceedingly more for the joy of Titus, because his spirit has been refreshed by you all. [14]For if in anything I have boasted to him about you, I am not ashamed. But as we spoke all things to you in truth, even so our boasting to Titus was found true. [15]And his affections are greater for you as he remembers the obedience of you all, how with fear and trembling you received him. [16]Therefore I rejoice that I have confidence in you in everything.

Excel in Giving

8 Moreover, brethren, we make known to you the grace of God bestowed on the churches of Macedonia: [2]that in a great trial of affliction the abundance of their joy and their deep poverty abounded in the riches of their liberality. [3]For I bear witness that according to *their* ability, yes, and beyond *their* ability, *they were* freely willing, [4]imploring us with much urgency that we would receive[a] the gift and the fellowship of the ministering to the saints. [5]And not *only* as we had hoped, but they first gave themselves to the Lord, and *then* to us by the will of God. [6]So we urged Titus, that as he had begun, so he would also complete this grace in you as well. [7]But as you abound in everything—in faith, in speech, in knowledge, in all diligence, and in your love for us—*see* that you abound in this grace also.

Christ Our Pattern

[8]I speak not by commandment, but I am testing the sincerity of your love by the diligence of others. [9]For you know the grace of our Lord Jesus Christ, that though He was rich, yet for your sakes He became poor, that you through His poverty might become rich.

[10]And in this I give advice: It is to your advantage not only to be doing what you began and were desiring to do a year ago; [11]but now you also must complete the doing *of it;* that as *there was* a readiness to desire *it,* so *there* also *may be* a completion out of what *you* have. [12]For if there is first a willing mind, *it is* accepted according to what one has, *and* not according to what he does not have.

[13]For *I do* not *mean* that others should

8:4 [a]NU-Text and M-Text omit *that we would receive,* thus changing text to *urgency for the favor and fellowship* . . . .

be eased and you burdened; 14but by an
equality, *that* now at this time your abundance *may supply* their lack, that their
abundance also may *supply* your lack—
that there may be equality. 15As it is written, *"He who gathered much had nothing
left over, and he who gathered little had no
lack."*[a]

> You must have, more or less, a distinct sense of the dreadful wrath of God and of the terrors of the judgment to come, or you will lack energy in your work and so lack one of the essentials of success.
>
> CHARLES SPURGEON

Collection for the Judean Saints

16But thanks *be* to God who puts[a] the
same earnest care for you into the heart
of Titus. 17For he not only accepted the
exhortation, but being more diligent, he
went to you of his own accord. 18And we
have sent with him the brother whose
praise *is* in the gospel throughout all the
churches, 19and not only *that,* but who
was also chosen by the churches to travel
with us with this gift, which is administered by us to the glory of the Lord Himself
and *to show* your ready mind, 20avoiding
this: that anyone should blame us in this
lavish gift which is administered by us—
21providing honorable things, not only in
the sight of the Lord, but also in the sight
of men.

22And we have sent with them our
brother whom we have often proved diligent in many things, but now much more
diligent, because of the great confidence
which *we have* in you. 23If *anyone inquires*
about Titus, *he is* my partner and fellow
worker concerning you. Or if our brethren *are inquired about, they are* messengers of the churches, the glory of Christ.
24Therefore show to them, and[a] before
the churches, the proof of your love and
of our boasting on your behalf.

Administering the Gift

9 Now concerning the ministering to
the saints, it is superfluous for me to
write to you; 2for I know your willingness, about which I boast of you to the
Macedonians, that Achaia was ready a
year ago; and your zeal has stirred up the
majority. 3Yet I have sent the brethren, lest
our boasting of you should be in vain in
this respect, that, as I said, you may be
ready; 4lest if *some* Macedonians come
with me and find you unprepared, we
(not to mention you!) should be ashamed
of this confident boasting.[a] 5Therefore I
thought it necessary to exhort the brethren to go to you ahead of time, and prepare your generous gift beforehand, which
you had previously promised, that it may
be ready as *a matter of* generosity and
not as a grudging obligation.

The Cheerful Giver

6But this *I say:* He who sows sparingly
will also reap sparingly, and he who sows
bountifully will also reap bountifully. 7*So
let* each one *give* as he purposes in his
heart, not grudgingly or of necessity; for
God loves a cheerful giver. 8And God *is*
able to make all grace abound toward you,
that you, always having all sufficiency in
all *things,* may have an abundance for
every good work. 9As it is written:

"He has dispersed abroad,
He has given to the poor;

8:15 [a]Exodus 16:18 8:16 [a]NU-Text reads *has put.* 8:24 [a]NU-Text and M-Text omit *and.* 9:4 [a]NU-Text reads *this confidence.*

9:2 "If you never have sleepless hours, if you never have weeping eyes, if your hearts never swell as if they would burst, you need not anticipate that you will be called zealous. You do not know the beginning of true zeal, for the foundation of Christian zeal lies in the heart. The heart must be heavy with grief and yet must beat high with holy ardor. The heart must be vehement in desire, panting continually for God's glory, or else we shall never attain to anything like the zeal which God would have us know." *Charles Spurgeon*

His righteousness endures forever."[a]

10 Now may[a] He who supplies seed to the sower, and bread for food, supply and multiply the seed you have *sown* and increase the fruits of your righteousness, 11 while *you are* enriched in everything for all liberality, which causes thanksgiving through us to God. 12 For the administration of this service not only supplies the needs of the saints, but also is abounding through many thanksgivings to God, 13 while, through the proof of this ministry, they glorify God for the obedience of your confession to the gospel of Christ, and for *your* liberal sharing with them and all *men,* 14 and by their prayer for you, who long for you because of the exceeding grace of God in you. 15 Thanks *be* to God for His indescribable gift!

The Spiritual War

10 Now I, Paul, myself am pleading with you by the meekness and gentleness of Christ—who in presence *am* lowly among you, but being absent am bold toward you. 2 But I beg *you* that when I am present I may not be bold with that confidence by which I intend to be bold against some, who think of us as if we walked according to the flesh. 3 For though we walk in the flesh, we do not war according to the flesh. 4 For the weapons of our warfare *are* not carnal but mighty in God for pulling down strongholds, 5 casting down arguments and every high thing that exalts itself against the knowledge of God, bringing every thought into captivity to the obedience of Christ, 6 and being ready to punish all disobedience when your obedience is fulfilled.

Reality of Paul's Authority

7 Do you look at things according to the outward appearance? If anyone is convinced in himself that he is Christ's, let him again consider this in himself, that just as he *is* Christ's, even so we *are* Christ's.[a] 8 For even if I should boast somewhat more about our authority, which the Lord gave us[a] for edification and not for your destruction, I shall not be ashamed— 9 lest I seem to terrify you by letters. 10 "For *his* letters," they say, "*are* weighty and powerful, but *his* bodily presence *is* weak, and *his* speech contemptible." 11 Let such a person consider this, that what we are in word by letters when we are absent, such *we will* also *be* in deed when we are present.

Limits of Paul's Authority

12 For we dare not class ourselves or compare ourselves with those who commend themselves. But they, measuring themselves by themselves, and comparing themselves among themselves, are not wise. 13 We, however, will not boast beyond measure, but within the limits of the sphere which God appointed us—a sphere which especially includes you. 14 For we are not overextending ourselves (as though *our authority* did not extend to you), for it was to you that we came with the gospel of Christ; 15 not boasting of things beyond measure, *that is,* in other men's labors, but having hope, *that* as your faith is increased, we shall be greatly enlarged by you in our sphere, 16 to preach the gospel in the *regions* beyond you, *and* not to boast in another man's sphere of accomplishment.

17 But *"he who glories, let him glory in the LORD."*[a] 18 For not he who commends himself is approved, but whom the Lord commends.

Concern for Their Faithfulness

11 Oh, that you would bear with me in a little folly—and indeed you do bear with me. 2 For I am jealous for you with godly jealousy. For I have betrothed you to one husband, that I may present *you as* a chaste virgin to Christ. 3 But I fear, lest somehow, as the serpent deceived Eve by his craftiness, so your

9:9 [a]Psalm 112:9 9:10 [a]NU-Text reads *Now He who supplies…will supply….* 10:7 [a]NU-Text reads *even as we are.* 10:8 [a]NU-Text omits *us.* 10:17 [a]Jeremiah 9:24

minds may be corrupted from the simplicity[a] that is in Christ. 4For if he who comes preaches another Jesus whom we have not preached, or *if* you receive a different spirit which you have not received, or a different gospel which you have not accepted—you may well put up with it!

Paul and False Apostles

5For I consider that I am not at all inferior to the most eminent apostles. 6Even though *I am* untrained in speech, yet *I am* not in knowledge. But we have been thoroughly manifested[a] among you in all things.

7Did I commit sin in humbling myself that you might be exalted, because I preached the gospel of God to you free of charge? 8I robbed other churches, taking wages *from them* to minister to you. 9And when I was present with you, and in need, I was a burden to no one, for what I lacked the brethren who came from Macedonia supplied. And in everything I kept myself from being burdensome to you, and so I will keep *myself*. 10As the truth of Christ is in me, no one shall stop me from this boasting in the regions of Achaia. 11Why? Because I do not love you? God knows!

12But what I do, I will also continue to do, that I may cut off the opportunity from those who desire an opportunity to be regarded just as we are in the things of which they boast. 13For such *are* false apostles, deceitful workers, transforming themselves into apostles of Christ. 14And no wonder! For Satan himself transforms himself into an angel of light. 15Therefore *it is* no great thing if his ministers also transform themselves into ministers of righteousness, whose end will be according to their works.

Reluctant Boasting

16I say again, let no one think me a fool. If otherwise, at least receive me as a fool, that I also may boast a little. 17What I speak, I speak not according to the Lord, but as it were, foolishly, in this confidence of boasting. 18Seeing that many boast according to the flesh, I also will

11:3 [a]NU-Text adds *and purity*. **11:6** [a]NU-Text omits *been*.

11:3 When the serpent deceived Eve, he cast doubt on God's Word, causing her to mistrust God Himself (Gen. 3:1–5). God said, "You shall surely die," but Eve chose to believe that God was deceitful. To partake of the fruit was an act of rebellion against the God who had not only given Adam and Eve life but had lavished His goodness upon them.

We must remember that Satan is the father of lies (John 8:44), and he usually uses enough of the truth to make the lie believable. Here Paul cautions believers to reject any message that differs from the true gospel as revealed in the Word of God. See Eph. 4:18 and Luke 4:10,11 comments.

Also, notice that Paul believed the Genesis account of the Fall. See 2 Pet. 3:6 comment.

11:14 Mormonism's "angel of light." The Scriptures warn against preaching "another Jesus" (2 Cor. 11:4) and that Satan himself can appear to us as an "angel of light." Joseph Smith, the founder of Mormonism, said it was an "angel" clothed in light that gave him "another testament"—which turns out to be another "gospel" entirely.

Rather than the good news that Jesus paid for our sin, this new "gospel" that the "angel" gave to Smith involves a lifelong labor to *earn* salvation—a salvation by works and not by faith alone. The Book of Mormon says, "For we know that it is by grace that we are saved, *after all we can do*" (2 Nephi 25:23, emphasis added). *Spencer W. Kimball*, a Mormon prophet and church president, said:

> One of the most fallacious doctrines originated by Satan and propounded by man is that man is saved alone by the grace of God; that belief in Jesus Christ alone is all that is needed for salvation. (*Miracle of Forgiveness*, p. 206)

Yet the Bible makes it very clear that salvation has nothing to do with our works: "For by grace you have been saved through faith, and that not of yourselves; it is the gift of God, not of works, lest anyone should boast" (Eph. 2:8,9). Titus 3:5 says, "Not by works of righteousness which we have done, but according to His mercy He saved us." For details on how Mormons attempt to earn salvation, see page 1684.

(Adapted from *World Religions in a Nutshell*.)

boast. 19For you put up with fools gladly,
since you *yourselves* are wise! 20For you
put up with it if one brings you into
bondage, if one devours *you*, if one takes
from you, if one exalts himself, if one
strikes you on the face. 21To *our* shame I
say that we were too weak for that! But in
whatever anyone is bold—I speak foolishly—I am bold also.

Suffering for Christ

22Are they Hebrews? So *am* I. Are they
Israelites? So *am* I. Are they the seed of
Abraham? So *am* I. 23Are they ministers
of Christ?—I speak as a fool—I *am* more:
in labors more abundant, in stripes above
measure, in prisons more frequently, in
deaths often. 24From the Jews five times I
received forty *stripes* minus one. 25Three
times I was beaten with rods; once I was
stoned; three times I was shipwrecked; a
night and a day I have been in the deep;
26*in* journeys often, *in* perils of waters, *in*
perils of robbers, *in* perils of *my own*
countrymen, *in* perils of the Gentiles, *in*
perils in the city, *in* perils in the wilderness, *in* perils in the sea, *in* perils among
false brethren; 27in weariness and toil, in
sleeplessness often, in hunger and thirst,
in fastings often, in cold and nakedness— 28besides the other things, what
comes upon me daily: my deep concern
for all the churches. 29Who is weak, and
I am not weak? Who is made to stumble,
and I do not burn *with indignation*?

30If I must boast, I will boast in the
things which concern my infirmity.
31The God and Father of our Lord Jesus
Christ, who is blessed forever, knows
that I am not lying. 32In Damascus the
governor, under Aretas the king, was
guarding the city of the Damascenes with
a garrison, desiring to arrest me; 33but I
was let down in a basket through a window in the wall, and escaped from his
hands.

The Vision of Paradise

12 It is doubtless[a] not profitable for
me to boast. I will come to visions

"Three times I was beaten with rods;
once I was stoned; three times I was
shipwrecked; a night and a day I have
been in the deep" (v. 25).

For other trials and tribulations Paul suffered for preaching the gospel, see John 17:14 comment.

and revelations of the Lord: 2I know a
man in Christ who fourteen years ago—
whether in the body I do not know, or
whether out of the body I do not know,
God knows—such a one was caught up
to the third heaven. 3And I know such a
man—whether in the body or out of the
body I do not know, God knows— 4how
he was caught up into Paradise and heard
inexpressible words, which it is not lawful for a man to utter. 5Of such a one I
will boast; yet of myself I will not boast,
except in my infirmities. 6For though I
might desire to boast, I will not be a fool;
for I will speak the truth. But I refrain,
lest anyone should think of me above
what he sees me *to be* or hears from me.

The Thorn in the Flesh

7And lest I should be exalted above
measure by the abundance of the revelations, a thorn in the flesh was given to
me, a messenger of Satan to buffet me,
lest I be exalted above measure. 8Con-
cerning this thing I pleaded with the Lord
three times that it might depart from me.
9And He said to me, "My grace is sufficient for you, for My strength is made
perfect in weakness." Therefore most
gladly I will rather boast in my infirmi-

12:1 [a]NU-Text reads *necessary, though not profitable, to boast.*

ties, that the power of Christ may rest
upon me. [10]Therefore I take pleasure in
infirmities, in reproaches, in needs, in persecutions, in distresses, for Christ's sake.
For when I am weak, then I am strong.

Signs of an Apostle

[11]I have become a fool in boasting;[a]
you have compelled me. For I ought to
have been commended by you; for in
nothing was I behind the most eminent
apostles, though I am nothing. [12]Truly the
signs of an apostle were accomplished
among you with all perseverance, in signs
and wonders and mighty deeds. [13]For
what is it in which you were inferior to
other churches, except that I myself was
not burdensome to you? Forgive me this
wrong!

Love for the Church

[14]Now *for* the third time I am ready to
come to you. And I will not be burdensome to you; for I do not seek yours, but
you. For the children ought not to lay up
for the parents, but the parents for the
children. [15]And I will very gladly spend
and be spent for your souls; though the
more abundantly I love you, the less I am
loved.

[16]But be that *as it may,* I did not burden you. Nevertheless, being crafty, I
caught you by cunning! [17]Did I take advantage of you by any of those whom I
sent to you? [18]I urged Titus, and sent our
brother with *him.* Did Titus take advantage of you? Did we not walk in the same
spirit? Did *we* not *walk* in the same steps?

[19]Again, do you think[a] that we excuse
ourselves to you? We speak before God
in Christ. But *we do* all things, beloved,
for your edification. [20]For I fear lest,
when I come, I shall not find you such as
I wish, and *that* I shall be found by you
such as you do not wish; lest *there be* contentions, jealousies, outbursts of wrath,
selfish ambitions, backbitings, whisperings, conceits, tumults; [21]lest, when I come
again, my God will humble me among
you, and I shall mourn for many who have
sinned before and have not repented of
the uncleanness, fornication, and lewdness which they have practiced.

> It is good to renew ourselves, from time to time, by closely examining the state of our souls, as if we had never done it before; for nothing tends more to the full assurance of faith, than to keep ourselves by this means in humility, and the exercise of all good works.
>
> **JOHN WESLEY**

Coming with Authority

13 This *will be* the third *time* I am
coming to you. *"By the mouth of*
two or three witnesses every word shall
be established."[a] [2]I have told you before,
and foretell as if I were present the second time, and now being absent I write[a]
to those who have sinned before, and to
all the rest, that if I come again I will not
spare— [3]since you seek a proof of Christ
speaking in me, who is not weak toward
you, but mighty in you. [4]For though He
was crucified in weakness, yet He lives by
the power of God. For we also are weak

12:11 [a]NU-Text omits *in boasting.* 12:19 [a]NU-Text reads *You have been thinking for a long time....* 13:1 [a]Deuteronomy 19:15 13:2 [a]NU-Text omits *I write.*

12:9 "God whispers to us in our pleasures, speaks to us in our conscience, but shouts in our pains: It is His megaphone to rouse a deaf world." *C. S. Lewis, The Problem of Pain*

12:11 "The humble man feels no jealousy or envy. He can praise God when others are preferred and blessed before him. He can bear to hear others praised and himself forgotten, because in God's presence he has learned to say with Paul, 'I am nothing.'" *Andrew Murray*

"God creates out of nothing. Therefore until man is nothing, God can make nothing out of him." *Martin Luther*

12:15 "You have nothing to do but to save souls. Therefore spend and be spent in this work." *John Wesley*

in Him, but we shall live with Him by the
power of God toward you.
5Examine yourselves *as to* whether you
are in the faith. Test yourselves. Do you
not know yourselves, that Jesus Christ is
in you?—unless indeed you are disqualified. 6But I trust that you will know that
we are not disqualified.

Paul Prefers Gentleness

7Now I[a] pray to God that you do no
evil, not that we should appear approved,
but that you should do what is honorable, though we may seem disqualified.
8For we can do nothing against the truth,
but for the truth. 9For we are glad when
we are weak and you are strong. And this
also we pray, that you may be made complete. 10Therefore I write these things being absent, lest being present I should
use sharpness, according to the authority
which the Lord has given me for edification and not for destruction.

Greetings and Benediction

11Finally, brethren, farewell. Become
complete. Be of good comfort, be of one
mind, live in peace; and the God of love
and peace will be with you.
12Greet one another with a holy kiss.
13All the saints greet you.
14The grace of the Lord Jesus Christ,
and the love of God, and the communion
of the Holy Spirit *be* with you all. Amen.

13:7 [a]NU-Text reads *we.*

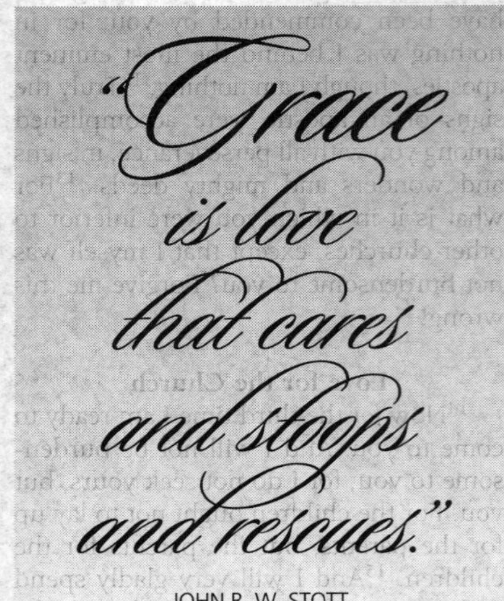

"Grace
is love
that cares
and stoops
and rescues."
JOHN R. W. STOTT

13:3 The Christian life. "The Christian life is more than difficult; it is humanly impossible to live. Only Jesus Christ can live it through you as He dwells within you. The Christian life is not a person trying to imitate Christ; rather, it is Christ imparting His life to and living His life through the person. The Christian life is not what you do for Him; it is what He does for and through you. He wants to think with your mind, express Himself through your emotions, and speak through your voice, though you may be unconscious of it." *Bill Bright*

13:5 Examine yourself. Contrary to Scripture, the modern gospel assures people that if they sincerely pray a "sinner's prayer," they should never doubt their salvation. Some go so far as to say that any doubts are from the devil. With eternity at stake, however, Paul admonishes believers to test themselves to make sure their faith is sound and secure.

Think of what you would do if you were wearing a parachute and waiting to jump out of a plane. You would have faith in the parachute, but you would also regularly check to make sure that the straps are firm. Once you have put on the Lord Jesus Christ through conversion (repentance and faith), you should regularly examine yourself to see how firm your relationship is with the Lord. Are you reading the Word daily? Do you have regular prayer? Are you fighting sin, or giving in to it? Are you living in holiness? Are you confessing sin? How is your relationship with other Christians? Is there any hidden bitterness against anyone? Are you sharing your faith? What is your greatest passion? Is it the Lord, or are material things more important? Do you love the world and the things in the world? On a scale of one to ten, how would you rate your walk with God? It should be a ten. If it is not, strive to make it a ten. See also page 1630.

Galatians

Greeting

1 Paul, an apostle (not from men nor through man, but through Jesus Christ and God the Father who raised Him from the dead), [2]and all the brethren who are with me,

To the churches of Galatia:

[3]Grace to you and peace from God the Father and our Lord Jesus Christ, [4]who gave Himself for our sins, that He might deliver us from this present evil age, according to the will of our God and Father, [5]to whom *be* glory forever and ever. Amen.

Only One Gospel

[6]I marvel that you are turning away so soon from Him who called you in the grace of Christ, to a different gospel, [7]which is not another; but there are some who trouble you and want to pervert the gospel of Christ. [8]But even if we, or an angel from heaven, preach any other gospel to you than what we have preached to you, let him be accursed. [9]As we have said before, so now I say again, if anyone preaches any other gospel to you than what you have received, let him be accursed.

[10]For do I now persuade men, or God? Or do I seek to please men? For if I still pleased men, I would not be a bondservant of Christ.

Call to Apostleship

[11]But I make known to you, brethren, that the gospel which was preached by me is not according to man. [12]For I neither received it from man, nor was I taught *it*, but *it came* through the revelation of Jesus Christ.

1:3 Many who don't know the Savior claim to have made their "peace with God." But there is no peace with God without accepting the grace of God, which is given only to those who repent.

1:4 Jesus willingly "gave" Himself for the sins of the world. No one took His life from Him.

1:6 These are strong words from the same apostle who wrote the "love chapter" of 1 Cor. 13. His words reveal his passion for the truth and his knowledge of the consequences of preaching "a different gospel." This should make the gospel preacher strive to make sure his hearers understand that salvation is by grace alone. Any message saying that we must add anything to the work of the cross to be saved is another gospel.

"Satan, the god of all dissension, stirreth up daily new sects, and last of all, which of all other I should never have foreseen or once suspected, he has raised up a sect such as teach... that men should not be terrified by the Law, but gently exhorted by the preaching of the grace of Christ." *Martin Luther*

1:8 "Avoid a sugared gospel as you would shun sugar of lead. Seek that gospel which rips up and tears and cuts and wounds and hacks and even kills, for that is the gospel that makes alive again. And when you have found it, give good heed to it. Let it enter into your inmost being. As the rains soaks into the ground, so pray the Lord to let His gospel soak into your soul." *Charles Spurgeon*

[13]For you have heard of my former conduct in Judaism, how I persecuted the church of God beyond measure and *tried to* destroy it. [14]And I advanced in Judaism beyond many of my contemporaries in my own nation, being more exceedingly zealous for the traditions of my fathers.

[15]But when it pleased God, who separated me from my mother's womb and called *me* through His grace, [16]to reveal His Son in me, that I might preach Him among the Gentiles, I did not immediately confer with flesh and blood, [17]nor did I go up to Jerusalem to those *who were* apostles before me; but I went to Arabia, and returned again to Damascus.

Contacts at Jerusalem

[18]Then after three years I went up to Jerusalem to see Peter,[a] and remained with him fifteen days. [19]But I saw none of the other apostles except James, the Lord's brother. [20](Now *concerning* the things which I write to you, indeed, before God, I do not lie.)

[21]Afterward I went into the regions of Syria and Cilicia. [22]And I was unknown by face to the churches of Judea which *were* in Christ. [23]But they were hearing only, "He who formerly persecuted us now preaches the faith which he once *tried to* destroy." [24]And they glorified God in me.

Defending the Gospel

2 Then after fourteen years I went up again to Jerusalem with Barnabas, and also took Titus with *me.* [2]And I went up by revelation, and communicated to them that gospel which I preach among the Gentiles, but privately to those who were of reputation, lest by any means I might run, or had run, in vain. [3]Yet not even Titus who *was* with me, being a Greek, was compelled to be circumcised. [4]And *this occurred* because of false brethren secretly brought in (who came in by stealth to spy out our liberty which we have in Christ Jesus, that they might bring us into bondage), [5]to whom we did not yield submission even for an hour, that the truth of the gospel might continue with you.

. . . . . .

Does God "hate the sin but love the sinner"? See 1 Tim. 1:9,10 comment.

. . . . . .

[6]But from those who seemed to be something—whatever they were, it makes no difference to me; God shows personal favoritism to no man—for those who seemed *to be something* added nothing to me. [7]But on the contrary, when they saw that the gospel for the uncircumcised had been committed to me, as *the gospel* for the circumcised *was* to Peter [8](for He who worked effectively in Peter for the apostleship to the circumcised also worked effectively in me toward the Gentiles), [9]and when James, Cephas, and John, who seemed to be pillars, perceived the grace that had been given to me, they gave me and Barnabas the right hand of fellowship, that we *should go* to the Gentiles and they to the circumcised. [10]*They desired* only that we should remember the poor, the very thing which I also was eager to do.

No Return to the Law

[11]Now when Peter[a] had come to Anti-

1:18 [a]NU-Text reads *Cephas.* 2:11 [a]NU-Text reads *Cephas.*

1:16 God also wants to reveal His Son in us. We can do this by following in Paul's steps and preaching Jesus Christ and Him crucified.

2:4 The Bible speaks of false brethren, false apostles, false prophets, false teachers, and false conversion (Mark 4:3–20).

2:10 Good works have a legitimate place in evangelism. When the Salvation Army first began, their message was "soap, soup, and salvation." See Titus 3:8.

THE FUNCTION OF THE LAW

2:19 The Law's function is to bring death to the sinner in the same way civil law brings capital punishment to a guilty murderer. However, our offense was paid for by the Savior, leaving us free to receive the pardon of the gospel. The Law has no demand on the Christian. See 2 Kings 24:4 comment.

och, I withstood him to his face, because he was to be blamed; [12]for before certain men came from James, he would eat with the Gentiles; but when they came, he withdrew and separated himself, fearing those who were of the circumcision. [13]And the rest of the Jews also played the hypocrite with him, so that even Barnabas was carried away with their hypocrisy.

[14]But when I saw that they were not straightforward about the truth of the gospel, I said to Peter before *them* all, "If you, being a Jew, live in the manner of Gentiles and not as the Jews, why do you[a] compel Gentiles to live as Jews?[b] [15]We *who are* Jews by nature, and not sinners of the Gentiles, [16]knowing that a man is not justified by the works of the law but by faith in Jesus Christ, even we have believed in Christ Jesus, that we might be justified by faith in Christ and not by the works of the law; for by the works of the law no flesh shall be justified.

[17]"But if, while we seek to be justified by Christ, we ourselves also are found sinners, *is* Christ therefore a minister of sin? Certainly not! [18]For if I build again those things which I destroyed, I make myself a transgressor. [19]For I through the law died to the law that I might live to God. [20]I have been crucified with Christ; it is no longer I who live, but Christ lives in me; and the *life* which I now live in the flesh I live by faith in the Son of God, who loved me and gave Himself for me. [21]I do not set aside the grace of God; for if righteousness *comes* through the law, then Christ died in vain."

Justification by Faith

3 O foolish Galatians! Who has bewitched you that you should not obey the truth,[a] before whose eyes Jesus Christ was clearly portrayed among you[b] as crucified? [2]This only I want to learn from you: Did you receive the Spirit by the works of the law, or by the hearing of faith? [3]Are you so foolish? Having begun in the Spirit, are you now being made perfect by the flesh? [4]Have you suffered so many things in vain—if indeed *it was* in vain?

[5]Therefore He who supplies the Spirit to you and works miracles among you, *does He do it* by the works of the law, or by the hearing of faith?— [6]just as Abraham *"believed God, and it was accounted to him for righteousness."*[a] [7]Therefore know that *only* those who are of faith are sons of Abraham. [8]And the Scripture, foreseeing that God would justify the Gentiles by faith, preached the gospel to Abraham beforehand, *saying, "In you all the nations shall be blessed."*[a] [9]So then

2:14 [a]NU-Text reads *how can you.* [b]Some interpreters stop the quotation here. 3:1 [a]NU-Text omits *that you should not obey the truth.* [b]NU-Text omits *among you.* 3:6 [a]Genesis 15:6 3:8 [a]Genesis 12:3; 18:18; 22:18; 26:4; 28:14

2:16 For those trusting in good works, see Gal. 3:11. "Neither the Jewish Law of ten commands nor its law of ceremonies was ever intended to save anybody. By a set of pictures it set forth the way of salvation, but it was not itself the way. It was a map, not a country; a model of the road, not the road itself." *Charles Spurgeon*

2:20 Dying to self. "The path toward humility is death to self. When self is dead, humility has been perfected. Jesus humbled Himself unto death, and by His example the way is opened for us to follow. A dead man or woman does not react to an offense. The truth is, if we become offended by the words of others, then death to self has not been finished. When we humble ourselves despite injustice and there is perfect peace of heart, then death to self is complete. Death is the seed, while humility is the ripened fruit." *Alice Smith, Beyond the Veil: God's Call to Intimate Intercession* (See also Gal. 5:24.)

those who *are* of faith are blessed with
believing Abraham.

The Law Brings a Curse

10For as many as are of the works of
the law are under the curse; for it is written, *"Cursed is everyone who does not
continue in all things which are written in
the book of the law, to do them."*[a] 11But
that no one is justified by the law in the
sight of God *is* evident, for *"the just shall
live by faith."*[a] 12Yet the law is not of faith,
but *"the man who does them shall live by
them."*[a]

13Christ has redeemed us from the
curse of the law, having become a curse
for us (for it is written, *"Cursed is everyone who hangs on a tree"*[a]), 14that the
blessing of Abraham might come upon
the Gentiles in Christ Jesus, that we
might receive the promise of the Spirit
through faith.

The Changeless Promise

15Brethren, I speak in the manner of
men: Though *it is* only a man's covenant,
yet *if it is* confirmed, no one annuls or
adds to it. 16Now to Abraham and his
Seed were the promises made. He does
not say, "And to seeds," as of many, but
as of one, *"And to your Seed,"*[a] who is
Christ. 17And this I say, *that* the law, which
was four hundred and thirty years later,
cannot annul the covenant that was confirmed before by God in Christ,[a] that it
should make the promise of no effect.
18For if the inheritance *is* of the law, *it is*
no longer of promise; but God gave *it* to
Abraham by promise.

Purpose of the Law

19What purpose then *does* the law *serve?*
It was added because of transgressions,
till the Seed should come to whom the
promise was made; *and it was* appointed
through angels by the hand of a mediator. 20Now a mediator does not *mediate*
for one *only*, but God is one.

21*Is* the law then against the promises
of God? Certainly not! For if there had
been a law given which could have given
life, truly righteousness would have been
by the law. 22But the Scripture has confined all under sin, that the promise by
faith in Jesus Christ might be given to
those who believe. 23But before faith came,
we were kept under guard by the law,
kept for the faith which would afterward
be revealed. 24Therefore the law was our
tutor *to bring us* to Christ, that we might
be justified by faith. 25But after faith has
come, we are no longer under a tutor.

Sons and Heirs

26For you are all sons of God through
faith in Christ Jesus. 27For as many of you
as were baptized into Christ have put on
Christ. 28There is neither Jew nor Greek,
there is neither slave nor free, there is
neither male nor female; for you are all
one in Christ Jesus. 29And if you *are*
Christ's, then you are Abraham's seed,
and heirs according to the promise.

4 Now I say *that* the heir, as long as he
is a child, does not differ at all from a
slave, though he is master of all, 2but is
under guardians and stewards until the
time appointed by the father. 3Even so
we, when we were children, were in bondage under the elements of the world.
4But when the fullness of the time had
come, God sent forth His Son, born[a] of a
woman, born under the law, 5to redeem

3:10 [a]Deuteronomy 27:26 3:11 [a]Habakkuk 2:4 3:12 [a]Leviticus 18:5 3:13 [a]Deuteronomy 21:23 3:16 [a]Genesis 12:7; 13:15; 24:7 3:17 [a]NU-Text omits *in Christ.* 4:4 [a]Or *made*

3:10 Those who try to keep the Law are usually ignorant of its holy demands. It requires perfection in thought, word, and deed. The proclamation of the spiritual nature of the Law (that God requires truth in the inward parts) strips a sinner of self-righteousness. See James 2:10 comment.

3:11 No one will earn his way into heaven by keeping the Ten Commandments. They were not given for that purpose. The Law is like a mirror. All it can do is reflect what we are in truth—unclean and desperately in need of cleansing. For those trusting in good works, see Eph. 2:8,9.

3:19 *What is the Purpose of the Law?*

By Charles Spurgeon

Beloved, the Law is a great deluge which would have drowned the world with worse than the water of Noah's flood; it is a great fire which would have burned the earth with a destruction worse than that which fell on Sodom; it is a stern angel with a sword, athirst for blood, and winged to slay; it is a great destroyer sweeping down the nations; it is the great messenger of God's vengeance sent into the world. Apart from the gospel of Jesus Christ, the Law is nothing but the condemning voice of God thundering against mankind. 'Wherefore then serveth the Law?' seems a very natural question. Can the Law be of any benefit to man? Can the Judge who puts on a black cap and condemns us all, this Lord Chief Justice Law, can he help in salvation? Yes, he can; and you shall see how he does it, if God shall help us while we preach.

Now, if you are unrepentant, you have never obeyed your Maker. Every step you have taken has added to your crimes. When God has fanned your heaving lungs, you have breathed out your poisonous breath in rebellion against Him. How should God feel toward you? You have walked over the principles of righteousness with your unsanctified feet. You have lifted up your hands, filled with poisoned weapons, against the throne of the Almighty. You have spurned every principle of right, of love and of happiness. You are the enemy of God, the foe of man and a child of the devil in league with hell. Ought not God hate you with all His heart?

Yet, in the midst of your rebellion He has borne with you. All this you have done, and He has kept silent. Dare you think that He will never reprove?

Lo, I see, the Law given upon Mount Sinai. The very hill doth quake with fear. Lightnings and thunders are the attendants of those dreadful syllables which make the hearts of Israel to melt. Sinai seemeth altogether on the smoke. The Lord came from Paran, and the Holy One from Mount Sinai; "He came with ten thousands of his saints." Out of His mouth went a fiery Law for them. It was a dread Law even when it was given, and since then from that Mount of Sinai an awful lava of vengeance has run down, to deluge, to destroy, to burn, and to consume the whole human race, if it had not been that Jesus Christ had stemmed its awful torrent and bidden its waves of fire be still. If you could see the world without Christ in it, simply under the Law, you would see a world in ruins, a world with God's black seal put upon it, stamped and sealed for condemnation; you would see men, who, if they knew their condition, would have their hands on their loins and be groaning all their days—you would see men and women condemned, lost, and ruined; and in the uttermost regions you would see the pit that is digged for the wicked, into which the whole earth must have been cast if the Law had its way, apart from the gospel of Jesus Christ our Redeemer.

My hearer, does not the Law of God convince you of sin? Under the hand of God's Spirit does it not make you feel that you have been guilty, that you deserve to be lost, that you have incurred the fierce anger of God? Look here: have you not broken these Ten Commandments; even in the letter, have you not broken them? Who is there among you who has always honored his mother and father? Who is there among you who has always spoken the truth? Have we not sometimes borne false witness against our neighbors? Is there one person here who has not made to himself another god, and loved himself, or his business, or his friends, more than he has Jehovah, the God of the whole earth? Which of you has not coveted his neighbor's house, or his manservant, or his ox, or his donkey? We are all guilty with regard to every letter of the Law; we have all of us transgressed the Commandments.

And if we really understood these Commandments, and felt that they condemned us, they would have this useful influence on us of showing us our danger, and so leading us to fly to Christ. But, my hearers, does not this Law condemn you, because even if you should say you have not broken the letter of it, yet you have violated the spirit of it. What, though you have never killed, yet we are told, he that is angry with his brother is a murderer.

This Law does not only mean what it says in words, but it has deep things hidden in its bowels. It says, "Thou shall not commit adultery," but it means as Jesus has it, "He that looketh on a woman to lust after her has committed adultery with her already in his heart." It says, "Thou shall not take the name of the Lord thy God in vain." It meaneth that we should reverence God in every place, and have His fear before our eyes, and should always pay respect to His ordinances and evermore walk in His fear and love. My brethren, surely there is not one here so foolhardy in self-righteousness as to say, "I am innocent." The spirit of the Law condemns us. And this is its useful property; it humbles us, makes us know we are guilty, and so we are led to receive the Savior.

The Function of the Law

3:24 "Lower the Law and you dim the light by which man perceives his guilt; this is a very serious loss to the sinner rather than a gain; for it lessens the likelihood of his conviction and conversion. I say you have deprived the gospel of its ablest auxiliary [its most powerful weapon] when you have set aside the Law. You have taken away from it the schoolmaster that is to bring men to Christ... *They will never accept grace till they tremble before a just and holy Law.* Therefore the Law serves a most necessary purpose, and it must not be removed from its place." *Charles Spurgeon*

"We cannot come to Christ to be justified until we have first been to Moses to be condemned. But once we have gone to Moses and acknowledged our sin, guilt and condemnation, we must not stay there." *John R. W. Stott*

those who were under the law, that we
might receive the adoption as sons.
6And because you are sons, God has
sent forth the Spirit of His Son into your
hearts, crying out, "Abba, Father!" 7There-
fore you are no longer a slave but a son,
and if a son, then an heir of[a] God through
Christ.

Fears for the Church

8But then, indeed, when you did not
know God, you served those which by
nature are not gods. 9But now after you
have known God, or rather are known by
God, how *is it that* you turn again to the
weak and beggarly elements, to which
you desire again to be in bondage? 10You
observe days and months and seasons and
years. 11I am afraid for you, lest I have labored for you in vain.
12Brethren, I urge you to become like
me, for I *became* like you. You have not
injured me at all. 13You know that because of physical infirmity I preached the
gospel to you at the first. 14And my trial
which was in my flesh you did not despise or reject, but you received me as an
angel of God, *even* as Christ Jesus.
15What[a] then was the blessing you *enjoyed?* For I bear you witness that, if possible, you would have plucked out your
own eyes and given them to me. 16Have I
therefore become your enemy because I
tell you the truth?
17They zealously court you, *but* for no
good; yes, they want to exclude you, that
you may be zealous for them. 18But it is
good to be zealous in a good thing always, and not only when I am present
with you. 19My little children, for whom
I labor in birth again until Christ is
formed in you, 20I would like to be present with you now and to change my
tone; for I have doubts about you.

Two Covenants

21Tell me, you who desire to be under
the law, do you not hear the law? 22For it
is written that Abraham had two sons:
the one by a bondwoman, the other by a
freewoman. 23But he *who was* of the bondwoman was born according to the flesh,
and he of the freewoman through promise, 24which things are symbolic. For these
are the[a] two covenants: the one from
Mount Sinai which gives birth to bondage, which is Hagar— 25for this Hagar is

4:7 [a]NU-Text reads *through God* and omits *through Christ.*
4:15 [a]NU-Text reads *Where.* 4:24 [a]NU-Text and M-Text omit *the.*

3:21 "Although the Law disclosed and increases sin, it is still not against the promises of God but is, in fact, for them. For in its true and proper work and purpose it humbles a man and prepares him—if he uses the Law correctly—to yearn and seek for grace." *Martin Luther*

4:5 There is no difference between Jew and Gentile. Both must be put "under the Law" first, before the gospel can redeem them. Why would any sinner see any need to be redeemed, if he didn't first see himself as a lawbreaker? Until each Commandment is applied to the conscience, sinners will not see sin as being "exceedingly sinful" (Rom. 7:13). The Law must also be preached in conjunction with future punishment. It has been well observed that "Law without consequence is nothing but good advice." The world must be made to understand that God is going to judge the world "in righteousness" (Acts 17:31).

QUESTIONS & OBJECTIONS

4:6

"How can you know that you are saved?"

A three-year-old boy was once staring at a heater, fascinated by its bright orange glow. His father saw him and warned, "Don't touch that heater, son. It may look pretty, but it's hot." The little boy believed him, and moved away from the heater.

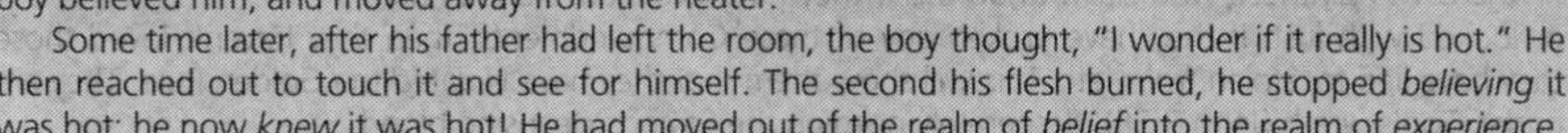

Some time later, after his father had left the room, the boy thought, "I wonder if it really is hot." He then reached out to touch it and see for himself. The second his flesh burned, he stopped *believing* it was hot; he now *knew* it was hot! He had moved out of the realm of *belief* into the realm of *experience.*

Christians believed in God's existence before their conversion. However, when they obeyed the Word of God, turned from their sins, and embraced Jesus Christ, they stopped merely believing. The moment they reached out and touched the heater bar of God's mercy, they moved out of *belief* into the realm of *experience*. This experience is so radical, Jesus referred to it as being "born again."

The Bible says that those who don't know God are spiritually dead (Eph. 2:1; 4:18). We are born with physical life, but not spiritual life. Picture unbelievers as corpses walking around who, by repenting and placing their faith in Christ, receive His very life. There is a radical difference between a corpse and a living, breathing human, just as there is when sinners pass from spiritual death to life. The apostle Paul said if you are "in Christ," you are a brand new creature (2 Cor. 5:17).

Those who now have God's Spirit living in them will love what He loves and desire to do His will; they will have a hunger for His Word, a love for other believers, and a burden for the lost. The Holy Spirit also confirms in their spirit that they are now children of God (Rom. 8:16). Those who believe on the name of the Son of God can *know* that they have eternal life (1 John 5:12,13).

Paul wrote to the church at Corinth, "My speech and my preaching were not with persuasive words of human wisdom, but in demonstration of the Spirit and of power, that your faith should not be in the wisdom of men but in the power of God" (1 Cor. 2:4,5). What Paul was saying was, "I deliberately did not talk you into your faith, but I let God's power transform you." He didn't reach them through an intellectual assent, but through the realm of personal experience.

Suppose two people—a heater manufacturer and a skin specialist—walked into the room just after that child had burned his hand on the heater. Both assured the boy that he couldn't possibly have been burned. But all the experts, theories, and arguments in the world will not dissuade that boy, because of his experience.

Those who have been transformed by God's power need never fear scientific or other arguments, because the man with an experience is not at the mercy of a man with an argument. "For our gospel did not come to you in word only, but also in power, and in the Holy Spirit and in much assurance . . ." (1 Thess. 1:5).

Mount Sinai in Arabia, and corresponds
to Jerusalem which now is, and is in bondage with her children— 26but the Jerusalem above is free, which is the mother
of us all. 27For it is written:

"Rejoice, O barren,
You who do not bear!
Break forth and shout,
You who are not in labor!
For the desolate has many more children
Than she who has a husband."[a]

28Now we, brethren, as Isaac *was*, are
children of promise. 29But, as he who was
born according to the flesh then persecuted him *who was born* according to the
Spirit, even so *it is* now. 30Nevertheless
what does the Scripture say? *"Cast out
the bondwoman and her son, for the son
of the bondwoman shall not be heir with
the son of the freewoman."*[a] 31So then,
brethren, we are not children of the bondwoman but of the free.

Christian Liberty

5 Stand fast therefore in the liberty by
which Christ has made us free,[a] and

4:27 [a]Isaiah 54:1 4:30 [a]Genesis 21:10 5:1 [a]NU-Text reads *For freedom Christ has made us free; stand fast therefore.*

QUESTIONS & OBJECTIONS

"I believe I will go to heaven because I live by the Golden Rule."

Much of the world knows the Golden Rule simply as "do unto others as you would have them do unto you" (see Luke 6:31). According to this verse, if we can live by this rule and love our neighbor as much as we love ourselves, we fulfill the Law. Ask those who claim to do this if they have ever lied, stolen, hated, or looked with lust. If they have broken any of these Commandments, then they haven't loved those they have lied to, stolen from, etc. This will show them that they have *violated* the Golden Rule. They are under God's wrath (John 3:36), desperately needing the Savior's cleansing blood.

do not be entangled again with a yoke of
bondage. 2Indeed I, Paul, say to you that
if you become circumcised, Christ will
profit you nothing. 3And I testify again
to every man who becomes circumcised
that he is a debtor to keep the whole
law. 4You have become estranged from
Christ, you who *attempt to* be justified by
law; you have fallen from grace. 5For we
through the Spirit eagerly wait for the
hope of righteousness by faith. 6For in
Christ Jesus neither circumcision nor
uncircumcision avails anything, but faith
working through love.

Love Fulfills the Law

7You ran well. Who hindered you
from obeying the truth? 8This persuasion
does not *come* from Him who calls you.
9A little leaven leavens the whole lump.
10I have confidence in you, in the Lord,
that you will have no other mind; but he
who troubles you shall bear his judgment,
whoever he is.

11And I, brethren, if I still preach circumcision, why do I still suffer persecution? Then the offense of the cross has
ceased. 12I could wish that those who trouble you would even cut themselves off!

13For you, brethren, have been called
to liberty; only do not *use* liberty as an
opportunity for the flesh, but through
love serve one another. 14For all the law
is fulfilled in one word, *even* in this: *"You*
shall love your neighbor as yourself."[a]
15But if you bite and devour one another,
beware lest you be consumed by one another!

Walking in the Spirit

16I say then: Walk in the Spirit, and
you shall not fulfill the lust of the flesh.
17For the flesh lusts against the Spirit,
and the Spirit against the flesh; and these
are contrary to one another, so that you
do not do the things that you wish. 18But
if you are led by the Spirit, you are not
under the law.

> The preacher's work is to throw sinners down in utter helplessness, so that they may be compelled to look up to Him who alone can help them.
>
> **CHARLES SPURGEON**

19Now the works of the flesh are evident, which are: adultery,[a] fornication, uncleanness, lewdness, 20idolatry, sorcery,
hatred, contentions, jealousies, outbursts
of wrath, selfish ambitions, dissensions,
heresies, 21envy, murders,[a] drunkenness,
revelries, and the like; of which I tell you
beforehand, just as I also told *you* in time
past, that those who practice such things

5:14 [a]Leviticus 19:18 5:19 [a]NU-Text omits *adultery*. 5:21 [a]NU-Text omits *murders*.

5:11 The cross will cause offense to the proud and self-righteous—those whose understanding is darkened. To those who understand their need of grace (the humble), it is a tree of life.

5:16 *Ten Ways to Break the Stronghold of Pornography*

1 Would you ever take pornography to church and view it during worship? You may as well, because God is just as present in your bedroom as He is in the church building.

2 Face the fact that you may not be saved. Examine yourself to ensure that Christ is living in you (2 Cor. 13:5). See Rom. 6:11–22; 8:1–14; Eph. 5:3–8.

3 Realize that when you give yourself to pornography, you are committing adultery (Matt. 5:27,28).

4 Grasp the serious nature of your sin. Jesus said that it would be better for you to be blind and go to heaven, than for your eye to cause you to sin and end up in hell (Matt. 5:29).

5 Those who profess to be Christians yet give themselves to pornographic material evidently lack the fear of God (Prov.16:6). Cultivate the fear of God by reading Prov. 2:1–5.

6 Read Psa. 51 and make it your own prayer.

7 Memorize James 1:14,15 and 1 Cor. 10:13. Follow Jesus' example (Matt. 4:3–11) and quote the Word of God when you are tempted (see Eph. 6:12–20).

8 Make no provision for your flesh (Rom. 13:14; 1 Pet. 2:11). Get rid of every access to pornographic material—the Internet, printed literature, TV, videos, and movies. Stop feeding the fire.

9 Guard your heart with all diligence (Prov. 4:23). Don't let the demonic realm have access to your thought-life. If you give yourself to it, you will become its slave (Rom. 6:16). Read the Bible daily, without fail. As you submit to God, the devil will flee (James 4:7,8).

10 The next time temptation comes, do fifty push-ups, then fifty sit-ups. If you are still burning, repeat the process (see 1 Cor. 9:27).

will not inherit the kingdom of God.
[22]But the fruit of the Spirit is love, joy,
peace, longsuffering, kindness, goodness,
faithfulness, [23]gentleness, self-control.
Against such there is no law. [24]And those
who are Christ's have crucified the flesh
with its passions and desires. [25]If we live
in the Spirit, let us also walk in the Spirit.
[26]Let us not become conceited, provoking
one another, envying one another.

Bear and Share the Burdens

6 Brethren, if a man is overtaken in any
trespass, you who *are* spiritual restore such a one in a spirit of gentleness,
considering yourself lest you also be
tempted. [2]Bear one another's burdens,
and so fulfill the law of Christ. [3]For if
anyone thinks himself to be something,
when he is nothing, he deceives himself.
[4]But let each one examine his own work,
and then he will have rejoicing in himself alone, and not in another. [5]For each
one shall bear his own load.

Be Generous and Do Good

[6]Let him who is taught the word share
in all good things with him who teaches.
[7]Do not be deceived, God is not
mocked; for whatever a man sows, that
he will also reap. [8]For he who sows to his
flesh will of the flesh reap corruption, but
he who sows to the Spirit will of the
Spirit reap everlasting life. [9]And let us not

5:19 Men will often deceive themselves by believing that the Ten Commandments condemn only adultery, leaving them free to have sex outside the bonds of marriage. However, the Law condemns all unlawful sex. First Tim. 1:8–10 tells us that the Law was also made for fornicators).

6:7 "Many people think they can break the Ten Commandments right and left and get by with it. That reminds me of the whimsical story of the man who jumped off the Empire State Building in New York City. As he went sailing by the fiftieth floor, a man looked out the window and said to him, 'Well, how is it?' The falling man replied, 'So far, so good.' That is not where the law of gravity enforces itself. Fifty more floors down and the man will find out, 'So far, not so good.' The interesting thing is that a law must be enforced to be a law and therefore God says in Ezek. 18:4, 'The soul that sins, it shall die.' The Law must be enforced and the breaker of the Law must pay the penalty." *J. Vernon McGee*

grow weary while doing good, for in due
season we shall reap if we do not lose
heart. 10Therefore, as we have opportunity,
let us do good to all, especially to those
who are of the household of faith.

Glory Only in the Cross

11See with what large letters I have
written to you with my own hand! 12As
many as desire to make a good showing
in the flesh, these *would* compel you to be
circumcised, only that they may not suffer persecution for the cross of Christ.
13For not even those who are circumcised
keep the law, but they desire to have you
circumcised that they may boast in your
flesh. 14But God forbid that I should boast
except in the cross of our Lord Jesus Christ,
by whom[a] the world has been crucified to
me, and I to the world. 15For in Christ Jesus neither circumcision nor uncircumcision avails anything, but a new creation.

Blessing and a Plea

16And as many as walk according to
this rule, peace and mercy *be* upon them,
and upon the Israel of God.
17From now on let no one trouble me,
for I bear in my body the marks of the
Lord Jesus.
18Brethren, the grace of our Lord Jesus
Christ *be* with your spirit. Amen.

6:14 [a]Or *by which* (the cross)

6:14 "All heaven is interested in the cross of Christ, all hell terribly afraid of it, while men are the only beings who more or less ignore its meaning." *Oswald Chambers*

Mormonism

OFFICIAL NAME: Church of Jesus Christ of Latter-day Saints (LDS, Mormons)

FOUNDER: Joseph Smith Jr., on April 6, 1830

CURRENT LEADER: Gordon B. Hinckley (b. 1910)

HEADQUARTERS: Salt Lake City, Utah

MEMBERSHIP (1998): Worldwide: 10.3 million in 28,670 wards and branches in 162 countries; United States: 5.1 million in all 50 states and D.C.; Canada: 152,000.

MISSIONARIES (1998): 58,700

The Church of Jesus Christ of Latter-day Saints was founded by Joseph F. Smith Jr. (1805–1844). Smith claimed to have had a visitation from God in 1820 in which God directed him to establish the true church. Consequently he organized the Mormon Church on April 6, 1830, with six original members. Beginning with a few hundred followers the church moved to Ohio, Missouri, and Illinois before Smith's death at the hands of a mob at the Carthage, Ill., jail. Smith had been arrested for encouraging the destruction of the *Expositor*, a Nauvoo, Ill., newspaper. After Smith's death, Brigham Young was affirmed as president of the church by a majority of the church's leaders and led several thousand followers to Utah where they established Salt Lake City in 1847. Joseph Smith's widow, Emma, resided in Independence, Mo. Those who affirmed her son, Joseph Smith, as the true successor of his father and as prophet of the church helped found the Reorganized Church of Jesus Christ of Latter Day Saints, now headquartered in Independence, Mo., in 1852.

MAJOR BELIEFS OF MORMONS

ONE TRUE CHURCH: The Mormon church claims to be the only true church. In God's supposed revelation to Joseph Smith, Jesus Christ told him to join no other church for "they were all wrong . . . their creeds were an abomination . . . those professors [members] were all corrupt" (*The Pearl of Great Price*, Joseph Smith History—1:19). Mormons teach that after the New Testament all churches became heretical and no true saints existed until the "Church of the Latter-day Saints" was organized, hence their name. Non-Mormons are thus called "Gentiles." The new revelations given to Smith, the institution of the prophet and apostles in the church, the restoration of the divine priesthoods, and the temple ceremonies make the church authentic. True and full salvation or exaltation is found only in the LDS Church.

(continued)

Mormonism (continued)

Biblical Response: The true church of Jesus Christ has had an ongoing presence and witness in the world since Pentecost. Jesus Christ promised that His church, *true* baptized and regenerate believers, would not fail (Matt. 16:17,18). The marks of a true church include faithfulness to the teaching of the first apostles (Acts 2:42)—not the creation of new doctrines.

AUTHORITY OF THE PROPHET: The *president* or *prophet* of the Church is thought to be the sole spokesman and revelator of God. Joseph Smith was the initial prophet, but each successive president holds that position. Through him God's will can be made known to the church. All revelations are made scripture and no Mormon can attain godhood without accepting Joseph Smith as a true prophet. The Mormon scriptures state that Latter-day Saints "shalt give heed unto all his [the prophet's] words and commandments... For his word ye shall receive as if from mine [God's] own mouth" (*Doctrine and Covenants* 21:4–5).

Biblical Response: Old and New Testament prophets were God's spokesmen. Their words were always consistent with the Bible and pointed to God's Son, Jesus Christ. A test of genuineness for prophets was that any prediction they proclaimed would come true (Deut. 18:20–22). For example, Joseph Smith predicted that the temple of the church would be built in Independence, Mo., within his lifetime (*Doctrine and Covenants* 84:2–5). No temple has yet been built there. New Testament prophets spoke, along with teachers, pastors, and evangelists, in evangelizing with and edifying the church (Eph. 4:11–13).

MORMON SCRIPTURE: Mormons accept four books as scripture and the word of God. The King James Version of the Bible is one of them, but only "as far as it is translated correctly"—seemingly allowing for possible questions about its authority. Joseph Smith made over 600 corrections to its text. Other "standard works" are the *Book of Mormon*, *Doctrine and Covenants*, and *The Pearl of Great Price*. The Bible is missing "plain and precious parts" according to the *Book of Mormon* (1 Nephi 13:26) which the other three volumes complete. The *Book of Mormon* has the "fullness of the gospel" and tells the story of a supposed migration of Israelites in 600 B.C. to the American continent. These Israelites subsequently lapsed into apostasy although their story was preserved on golden plates written in Reformed Egyptian. Joseph Smith, it is said, translated the plates by the "gift and power of God" (*Doctrine and Covenants* 135:3). Reformed Egyptian does not exist as a language. The golden plates were returned to the angel Moroni after they were transcribed and Moroni returned them to heaven. The *Book of Mormon* does not contain explicit Mormon doctrine. *Doctrine and Covenants* contains the revelations of the Mormon prophets—138 in number along with two "declarations." Here most of Mormon doctrine can be found including the priesthood, baptism for the dead, godhood, and polygamy. *The Pearl of Great Price* contains Smith's religious history, the Articles of Faith, the Book of Abraham, and the Book of Moses.

Biblical Response: The Bible explicitly warns against adding to or detracting from its teaching (Rev. 22:18; Deut. 4:2). The New Testament contains the inspired and totally accurate witness of contemporary disciples and followers of Jesus. It alone claims to be fully inspired of God and usable for the establishment of doctrine (2 Tim. 3:15–17; 2 Pet. 1:19–21).

ESTABLISHMENT OF TEMPLES: The first Mormon temple was constructed in Kirtland, Ohio, in 1836. Subsequently, a temple was constructed in Nauvoo, Ill., in 1846. Presently there are at least 53 operating temples throughout the world including the one finished in Salt Lake City in 1893. The purpose and function of temples is for the practice of eternal ordinances including primarily baptism for the dead, endowments, and celestial marriages. Baptism in the Mormon church, for both the living and the dead, is essential for the fullness of salvation. The dead often are baptized by proxy which affords them after death the opportunity to become Mormons. Celestial marriage for "time and eternity" is also a temple ordinance. It is necessary for godhood and seals the marriage forever. Temples form an essential part of Mormon salvation. Only Mormons in possession of a "temple recommend" by their bishop may enter a temple.

Biblical Response: The Temple of the Old Testament was a place of symbolic sacrifice forefiguring the sacrifice of Christ. Worship in the Jewish temple in Jerusalem was a practice of early Jewish believers (Acts 2:46). Otherwise there is no mention of any such practice in the New Testament. Never was the Jewish temple used for baptism for the dead, marriage, or other secret ceremonies. It was the place in the Old Testament where the glory of God occasionally dwelt. Today the individual believer is God's dwelling place, not a physical building (1 Cor. 3:16).

GOD IS AN EXALTED MAN: Elohim, the god of this universe, was previously a man in a prior existence. As a result of having kept the requirements of Mormonism, he was exalted to godhood and inherited his own universe. God is confined to a "body of flesh and bones" (*Doctrine and Covenants* 130:22) and yet is thought to be omniscient and omnipotent. He obviously cannot be omnipresent. There are an infinite number of gods with their own worlds—these too were previously men. The Holy Ghost, Jesus Christ, and "Heavenly Father" comprise three separate and distinct gods. Heavenly Father sires spiritual children in heaven destined for human life on earth. All humans, as well as Jesus Christ and Lucifer, are god's heavenly children. (See *Doctrine and Covenants* 130:22; God, Jesus, and the Spirit thus had beginnings.)

(continued)

Mormonism (continued)

Biblical Response: God is Spirit and is not confined to a physical body (John 4:24). Jesus Christ was incarnated through a miraculous and non-physical conception through the Virgin Mary. He was fully God from the beginning (John 1:1). Together with the person of the Holy Spirit they form the triune (three-in-one) eternal God.

JESUS IS GOD'S "SON": Jesus was Heavenly Father's firstborn spirit child in heaven. He was begotten by God through Mary as in a "literal, full and complete sense" in the same "sense in which he is the son of Mary" (Bruce McConkie, *A New Witness for the Articles of Faith* [Salt Lake City: Deseret Book Co., 1993], 67). These two elements of Jesus being literally God's son form his uniqueness in Mormon theology. In the Garden of Gethsemane as well as on the cross Jesus atoned for Adam's sin and guaranteed all humankind resurrection and immortality. Jesus visited the Israelites or Indians of North America after his resurrection and established the true church among them. We are the spiritual, but literal, younger brothers and sisters of Christ. Some Mormon documents claim that Jesus was married at Cana in Galilee (John 2) and had children himself.

Biblical Response: Jesus is viewed as God, the Word or Son, eternally existent with the Father and worthy of identity as God (John 1:1–14). He was born of the Virgin Mary who had conceived him supernaturally by the Holy Spirit. He lived a perfect life, died on the cross for the sins of the world, and was raised from the dead. He will come again and reign as Lord of lords.

HUMANS ARE GODS IN EMBRYO: Every human being has the potential of becoming a god by keeping the requirements of Mormonism. A well-known statement within Mormonism is, "As man is god once was, as god is man may become." From a prior spirit existence in heaven, humans may be born on earth in order to exercise freedom to choose good or evil and to have a body for the resurrection. Basically humans are good, but they will be punished for their sin. But by keeping Mormon teaching and obeying the church and the Prophet, after the resurrection worthy Mormon males may pass the celestial guards, bring their wives with them, and achieve a status similar to Elohim—the god of this world. The consequences of their sin are erased by their allegiance to the tenets of Mormonism. In resurrection faithful Mormons receive exaltation to godhood and will exercise dominion over their world.

Biblical Response: Human beings are God's special creation. There is no evidence from Scripture of preexistence, rather God acknowledges that it was in the womb of our mothers that He formed us (Isaiah 44:2). A sinful nature is part of humanity's experience. Liberation from the power and presence of sin is experienced as a result of faith in Christ. At that point God's image is begun to be remade in every Christian. Although the believer is being transformed to Christlikeness, the Bible does not teach literal godhood as the inheritance of the saints (Rom. 8:29; Rev. 1:5–6).

MORMON PLAN OF SALVATION: The Mormon plan of salvation is built on the idea that all people have eternal life, but only the most faithful Mormons have godhood or enter the celestial Kingdom. In order to obtain this ultimate step, Mormons must exercise faith in the God of Mormonism, its Christ, and the Church of Jesus Christ of Latter-day Saints; exercise repentance; and be baptized in the LDS Church. Additionally Mormons must keep the "Word of Wisdom" by abstaining from alcohol, tobacco, and caffeine; tithe to the church; attend weekly sacrament meetings; support the Mormon prophet; do temple works; and be active in their support of the church.

Biblical Response: Salvation, according to the Bible, is due to God's grace and love. He provided Jesus as the sacrifice for the sins of the world. It is through faith in the crucified and risen Jesus that we may be saved. Works are excluded (John 1:12; 3:16; Rom. 10:9–13; Eph. 2:8–9).

EVANGELIZING MORMONS

- Know clearly the Christian faith and the gospel.
- Be aware of the unique Mormon doctrines as presented here.
- Remember, Mormons use Christian vocabulary (gospel, atonement, god) but radically redefine their meanings. Define clearly what you mean when you use biblical words.
- Present a clear testimony of your faith in Christ alone for your salvation.
- Show your Mormon friend that the Bible teaches salvation alone through the cross of Christ (John 3:16; Rom. 10:4,10–13; Eph. 2:8–9). Emphasize that salvation is a gift to be received, not a merit to be earned.
- Warn the Mormon about trusting in feelings (i.e., the burning in the bosom) for a validation of Mormonism's truth claim. Without historical, objective verification, feelings are useless.
- When Mormons use a Bible verse, read carefully the verses before and afterward to make clear the exact meaning and purpose of the passage. Don't let them take Bible verses out of context. Read carefully the full reference in the Bible before deciding what any one verse means.
- Keep the central doctrines of the faith as the focus of your discussion.
- Do the basics: pray, trust the Holy Spirit, and be loving, patient, and steadfast.

Phil Roberts, Director of Interfaith Evangelism.

Ephesians

Greeting

1 Paul, an apostle of Jesus Christ by the will of God,

To the saints who are in Ephesus, and faithful in Christ Jesus:

2 Grace to you and peace from God our Father and the Lord Jesus Christ.

Redemption in Christ

3 Blessed *be* the God and Father of our Lord Jesus Christ, who has blessed us with every spiritual blessing in the heavenly *places* in Christ, 4 just as He chose us in Him before the foundation of the world, that we should be holy and without blame before Him in love, 5 having predestined us to adoption as sons by Jesus Christ to Himself, according to the good pleasure of His will, 6 to the praise of the glory of His grace, by which He made us accepted in the Beloved.

7 In Him we have redemption through His blood, the forgiveness of sins, according to the riches of His grace 8 which He made to abound toward us in all wisdom and prudence, 9 having made known to us the mystery of His will, according to His good pleasure which He purposed in Himself, 10 that in the dispensation of the fullness of the times He might gather together in one all things in Christ, both[a] which are in heaven and which are on earth—in Him. 11 In Him also we have obtained an inheritance, being predestined according to the purpose of Him who works all things according to the counsel of His will, 12 that we who first trusted in Christ should be to the praise of His glory.

13 In Him you also *trusted,* after you heard the word of truth, the gospel of your

1:10 [a]NU-Text and M-Text omit *both*.

1:1 Sainthood. There are those who believe that someone must be dead for many years, and have performed miracles, before he can be "exalted" to sainthood. Not so. Paul is writing to *living* people and, as he often begins his letters, he refers to them as "saints." The word "saint" comes from the same Hebrew root as "sanctified" and "holy," which mean "set apart." The moment we are born again, God sets us apart from the world (sanctifies us) for His use. In addressing the Corinthian church, Paul writes: "to those who are *sanctified* in Christ Jesus, called to be *saints,* with *all* who in every place call on the name of Jesus Christ our Lord" (1 Cor. 1:2, emphasis added). A saint is not someone who has lived a "holy" life, but a forgiven sinner who has called on the name of Jesus and been made righteous by the grace of God.

1:9 The will of God is no longer a mystery ("having *made* known . . ."). The next verse makes His will clear: He wants to gather the redeemed together. We can work within His will by seeking to save that which is lost. He is not willing that *any* perish, but that *all* come to repentance. He has commanded us to "Go." We don't need to wait for another moment. To wait upon God for His will, when it is so plainly given, is to sit in disobedience. If you are paralyzed by fear, leave a gospel tract in a shopping cart. Crawl before you walk. Do *something* to bring the message of eternal salvation to a dying world.

QUESTIONS & OBJECTIONS

"I know I'm a sinner, but I confess my sins to God daily. I tell Him that I'm sorry and I won't sin again."

If you find yourself in court with a $50,000 fine, will a judge let you go simply because you say you're sorry and you won't commit the crime again? Of course not. You should be sorry for breaking the law and, of course, you shouldn't commit the crime again. But only when your $50,000 fine is paid will you be free from the demands of the law.

God will not forgive a sinner on the basis that he is sorry. Of course we should be sorry for sin—we have a conscience to tell us that adultery, rape, lust, murder, hatred, lying, stealing, etc., are wrong. And of course we shouldn't sin again. However, God will release us from the demands for eternal justice only on the basis that someone else paid our fine. Two thousand years ago, Jesus Christ died on the cross to pay for the sins of the world. His words on the cross were, "It is finished!" (John 19:30). In other words, the debt has been paid in full. All who repent and trust in Him receive forgiveness of sins. Their case is dismissed on the basis of His suffering death.

salvation; in whom also, having believed,
you were sealed with the Holy Spirit of
promise, 14who[a] is the guarantee of our
inheritance until the redemption of the
purchased possession, to the praise of His
glory.

Prayer for Spiritual Wisdom

15Therefore I also, after I heard of your
faith in the Lord Jesus and your love for
all the saints, 16do not cease to give thanks
for you, making mention of you in my
prayers: 17that the God of our Lord Jesus
Christ, the Father of glory, may give to
you the spirit of wisdom and revelation
in the knowledge of Him, 18the eyes of
your understanding[a] being enlightened;
that you may know what is the hope of
His calling, what are the riches of the
glory of His inheritance in the saints,
19and what *is* the exceeding greatness of
His power toward us who believe, according to the working of His mighty
power 20which He worked in Christ when
He raised Him from the dead and seated
Him at His right hand in the heavenly
places, 21far above all principality and
power and might and dominion, and every
name that is named, not only in this age
but also in that which is to come.
22And He put all *things* under His feet,
and gave Him *to be* head over all *things* to
the church, 23which is His body, the fullness of Him who fills all in all.

By Grace Through Faith

2 And you *He made alive,* who were
dead in trespasses and sins, 2in which
you once walked according to the course

1:14 [a]NU-Text reads *which.* 1:18 [a]NU-Text and M-Text read *hearts.*

1:13 Many think that to "believe" in Jesus is merely an intellectual assent. However, when the Bible speaks of believing in Jesus Christ, it means to *trust* in Him in the same way you trust yourself to an elevator. It is more than a mere acknowledgment of its ability to transport.

1:19 Our God's power is so great that He could easily turn 800 billion enemy tanks into fine powder with the flutter of an eyelash. Never, never lose sight of the victory! Don't let the lies of enemy propaganda penetrate your mind. Remember the command, "Fear not, for I am with you; be not dismayed, for I am your God. I will strengthen you, yes, . . . I will uphold you with My righteous right hand" (Isa. 41:10).

To be discouraged is to dishonor God. If He is with us, we must never lose courage. A blind, anemic, weak-kneed flea on crutches would have a greater chance of defeating a herd of a thousand wild stampeding elephants than the enemy has of defeating God!

1:21 *The Names of Jesus*

Jesus is given many names and titles, and the day will come when all of humanity will kneel before Him and acknowledge Him as "Lord." Here are some of His other titles, in the hope that the lost will soften their heart toward Him and trust in His mercy:

Adam, the Last (1 Cor. 15:45)
Advocate (1 John 2:1)
Almighty (Rev. 1:8)
Alpha & Omega (Rev. 1:8; 21:6)
Amen (Rev. 3:14)
Anchor (Heb. 6:19)
Ancient of Days (Dan. 7:9–11 with Rev. 1:13–16)
Anointed, His (Psa. 2:2). See also Messiah.
Apostle (Heb. 3:1)
Arm of the Lord (Isa. 53:1)
Author (Heb. 12:2)
Balm of Gilead (Jer. 8:22)
Beginning (Col. 1:18)
Beginning & the End (Rev. 1:8; 21:6; 22:13)
Begotten (One and Only; John 3:16)
Beloved (Eph. 1:6)
Bishop of your souls (1 Pet. 2:25)
Branch (Isa. 11:1; Jer. 23:5; Zech. 3:8; 6:12; Rev. 11:1)
Bread (John 6:32,33; 6:35)
Bridegroom (Matt. 9:15; John 3:29; Rev. 21:9)
Bright & Morning Star, see Star.
Brightness of His (God's) glory (Heb. 1:3)
Captain of their salvation (Heb. 2:10)
Carpenter['s son] (Matt. 13:55; Mark 6:3)
Chief [among ten thousand] (Song 5:10)
Child [the young] (Isa. 9:6; Matt 2:8–21)
Chosen of God (Luke 23:35)
Christ (Matt. 1:17; Mark 8:29; John 1:41; Rom. 1:16; 1 Cor. 1:23)
Comforter (Isa. 61:2; John 14:16)
Commander (Isa. 55:4)
Companion of God (Zech. 13:7)
Consolation of Israel (Luke 2:25)
Cornerstone (Eph. 2:20; Isa. 28:16)
Counselor (Isa. 9:6; Isa. 40:13)
Creator of all things (Col. 1:16)
Dayspring from on high (Luke 1:78)
Day Star (2 Pet. 1:19). See also Bright & Morning Star.
Deliverer (Rom. 11:26)
Desire of all nations (Hag. 2:7)
Door [of the sheepfold] (John 10:7, 9)
End, see Beginning & the End.
End of the Law (Rom 10:4)
Express image of His (God's) person (Heb. 1:3)
Faithful Witness (Rev. 1:5; 3:14; 19:11)
Faithful & True (Rev. 19:11)
First & the Last (Rev. 1:17)
Firstborn from the dead (Rev. 1:5)
Firstborn over all creation (Col. 1:15)
Firstfruits (1 Cor. 15:20,23)
Foundation (Isa. 28:16; 1 Cor. 3:11)
Fountain (Jer. 2:13; Zech. 13:1)
Forerunner (Heb. 6:20)
Friend of sinners (Matt. 11:19; Luke 7:34)
Fullness of the Godhead (Col. 2:9)
Gift of God (John 4:10; 2 Cor. 9:15)
Glory of God (Isa. 60:1)
God (John 1:1; Matt. 1:23; Rom. 9:5; 1 Tim. 3:16; Heb. 1:8)
Good Teacher (Matt. 19:16)
Great High Priest (Heb. 4:14)
Guide (Psa. 48:14)
Head (even Christ) (Eph. 4:15)
Heir of all things (Heb. 1:2)
Helper (Heb. 13:6)
Hiding Place (Isa. 32:2)
High Priest (Heb. 3:1; 7:1)
Holy Child (Acts 4:30)
Holy One [& the Just] (Acts 2:27; 3:14)
Hope of Israel (Jer. 17:13)
Horn of salvation (Psa. 18:2; Luke 1:69)
I AM (John 8:24,58)
Image of [the invisible] God (2 Cor. 4:4; Col. 1:15)
Immanuel (Isa. 7:14; Matt. 1:23)
Intercessor (Heb. 7:25)
Jehovah (Isa. 26:4; 40:3)
Jesus (Matt. 1:21)
Judge (Mic. 5:1; Acts 10:42)
Just One (Acts 7:52)
King (Zech. 14:16)
King of kings (1 Tim. 6:15; Rev. 17:14)
Lamb [of God] (John 1:29, 36; 1 Pet 1:19; Rev. 5:6,12; 7:17)
Last, see First. (Rev. 22:13)
Last Adam (1 Cor. 15:45)
Lawgiver (Isa. 33:22)
Life (John 11:25; 1 John 1:2)
Life-giving Spirit (1 Cor. 15:45)
Light (John 12:35)
Lion of the tribe of Judah (Rev. 5:5)
Lord (1 Cor. 12:3; 2 Pet. 1:11). See also Master.
Lord of lords (1 Tim. 6:15; Rev. 17:14)
Man (John 19:5; Acts 17:31; 1 Tim. 2:5). See also Son of Man.
Master (Matt. 8:19)
Mediator (1 Tim. 2:5)
Merciful High Priest (Heb. 2:17)
Mercy Seat (Rom. 3:24,25)
Messiah (Dan. 9:25; John 1:41; 4:25)
Mighty God (Isa. 9:6; 63:1)
Minister of the Sanctuary (Heb. 8:2)

(continued)

(1:21 continued)

Nazarene (Mark 1:24)
Offering (Eph. 5:2; Heb. 10:10)
Offspring of David (Rev. 22:16). See also Root.
Omega. See Alpha & Omega.
One and Only Son, see Son. (John 3:16)
Passover (1 Cor. 5:7)
Peace, our (Eph. 2:14)
Physician (Matt. 9:12; Luke 4:23)
Potentate (1 Tim. 6:15)
Prince of Life (Acts 3:15; 5:31)
Prince of Peace (Isa. 9:6)
Prophet (Acts 3:22,23)
Propitiation (1 John 2:2; 4:10)
Priest (Heb. 4:14)
Rabbi (John 3:2; Matt. 26:25; John 20:16)
Ransom (1 Tim. 2:6)
Redeemer, Redemption (Isa. 59:20; 60:16; 1 Cor. 1:30)
Refuge (Isa. 25:4)
Resurrection (John 11:25)
Righteousness (Jer. 23:6; 33:16; 1 Cor. 1:30)
Rock (1 Cor. 10:4)
Rod (Isa. 11:1)
Root (Rev. 22:16)
Rose of Sharon (Song 2:1)
Ruler (Matt. 2:6)
Sacrifice (Eph. 5:2)
Sanctification (1 Cor. 1:30)
Savior [of the world] (Luke 1:47; 2:11; 1 John 4:14)
Second Man (1 Cor. 15:47)
Seed of Abraham (Gal. 3:16,19)
Servant (Isa. 42:1; 49:5–7; Matt. 12:18)
Shepherd (John 10:11,14; 1 Peter 5:4)
Shiloh (Gen. 49:10)
Son (Isa. 9:6; 1 John 4:14)
Son of Man (Matt. 9:6; 12:40)
Sower (Matt. 13:37)
Star (Num. 24:17)
Stone (Psa. 118:22)
Stumbling Stone (Rom. 9:33; 1 Pet. 2:8)
Sun of Righteousness (Mal. 4:2)
Teacher (Matt. 26:18; John 3:2; 11:28). See also Master.
Testator (Heb. 9:15–17)
True Bread, see Bread.
Truth (John 14:6)
Vine (John 15:1,5)
Way (John 14:6)
Wonderful (Isa. 9:6)
Word (John 1:1)

of this world, according to the prince of
the power of the air, the spirit who now
works in the sons of disobedience, [3]among
whom also we all once conducted ourselves in the lusts of our flesh, fulfilling
the desires of the flesh and of the mind,
and were by nature children of wrath,
just as the others.

[4]But God, who is rich in mercy, because of His great love with which He
loved us, [5]even when we were dead in
trespasses, made us alive together with
Christ (by grace you have been saved),
[6]and raised *us* up together, and made *us*
sit together in the heavenly *places* in
Christ Jesus, [7]that in the ages to come He
might show the exceeding riches of His
grace in *His* kindness toward us in Christ
Jesus. [8]For by grace you have been saved
through faith, and that not of yourselves;
it is the gift of God, [9]not of works, lest
anyone should boast. [10]For we are His
workmanship, created in Christ Jesus for
good works, which God prepared beforehand that we should walk in them.

Brought Near by His Blood

[11]Therefore remember that you, once
Gentiles in the flesh—who are called Uncircumcision by what is called the Circumcision made in the flesh by hands—
[12]that at that time you were without
Christ, being aliens from the common-
wealth of Israel and strangers from the
covenants of promise, having no hope and
without God in the world. [13]But now in

2:3 Unsaved people often try to justify themselves when confronted with their sinfulness, by saying, "It's only *natural* that we sin." They're right—sin does come naturally to us. We naturally lie, steal, lust, etc. The lifestyles of the ungodly can be clearly seen in soap operas, movies, talk shows, and tabloids. However, because it's natural doesn't make it right. By nature we are children of wrath. See Titus 3:3 comment.

2:8,9 These verses make it clear that no one will be saved through their own goodness. Nothing we can do could ever merit everlasting life. It can come only as a gift, by the grace of God. Note that we are not saved *by* our faith—it is not faith itself that saves us. Faith is the medium God uses to extend His grace to us. For those trusting in good works, see Titus 3:5.

SPRINGBOARDS FOR PREACHING AND WITNESSING

The Love of God

2:4,5 Imagine a place on the earth that never saw the sun. Day in, day out, it is covered with thick clouds. From the time a person was born until the time he died he never saw even a glimpse of the sun. Suppose you visited this place and tried to convince the inhabitants of the reality, the beauty, and the power of the sun. "Where I come from," you say, "a huge yellow ball rises up over the sea each day and floats across the sky, no strings attached, giving warmth and light to those upon the earth. The reason you don't experience it is because you are cut off from it by the clouds." Although the thought may seem fantastic to those people, the fact that they don't believe in it does not change the reality that it exists.

Christ Jesus you who once were far off have been brought near by the blood of Christ.

Christ Our Peace

[14]For He Himself is our peace, who has made both one, and has broken down the middle wall of separation, [15]having abolished in His flesh the enmity, *that is,* the law of commandments *contained* in ordinances, so as to create in Himself one new man *from* the two, *thus* making peace, [16]and that He might reconcile them both to God in one body through the cross, thereby putting to death the enmity. [17]And He came and preached peace to you who were afar off and to those who were near. [18]For through Him we both have access by one Spirit to the Father.

Christ Our Cornerstone

[19]Now, therefore, you are no longer strangers and foreigners, but fellow citizens with the saints and members of the household of God, [20]having been built on the foundation of the apostles and prophets, Jesus Christ Himself being the chief corner*stone,* [21]in whom the whole building, being fitted together, grows into a holy temple in the Lord, [22]in whom you also are being built together for a dwelling place of God in the Spirit.

The Mystery Revealed

3 For this reason I, Paul, the prisoner of Christ Jesus for you Gentiles— [2]if indeed you have heard of the dispensation of the grace of God which was given to me for you, [3]how that by revelation He made known to me the mystery (as I have briefly written already, [4]by which, when you read, you may understand my knowledge in the mystery of Christ), [5]which in other ages was not made known to the sons of men, as it has now been revealed by the Spirit to His holy apostles and prophets: [6]that the Gentiles should be fellow heirs, of the same body, and partakers of His promise in Christ through the gospel, [7]of which I became a minister according to the gift of the grace of God given to me by the effective working of His power.

Purpose of the Mystery

[8]To me, who am less than the least of all the saints, this grace was given, that I should preach among the Gentiles the unsearchable riches of Christ, [9]and to make all see what *is* the fellowship[a] of the mystery, which from the beginning of the ages has been hidden in God who created all things through Jesus Christ;[b] [10]to the

3:9 [a]NU-Text and M-Text read *stewardship (dispensation).* [b]NU-Text omits *through Jesus Christ.*

2:13 There is nothing more valuable in the universe than the precious blood of our Savior. We were separated from God and without hope, but the blood of Jesus brought us to God.

3:7 It is God's power, working in us through His Holy Spirit, that equips us to share the gospel. (See Acts 1:8.) God provides the ability; all He wants from us is our *avail*ability.

intent that now the manifold wisdom of God might be made known by the church to the principalities and powers in the heavenly *places,* [11]according to the eternal purpose which He accomplished in Christ Jesus our Lord, [12]in whom we have boldness and access with confidence through faith in Him. [13]Therefore I ask that you do not lose heart at my tribulations for you, which is your glory.

Appreciation of the Mystery

[14]For this reason I bow my knees to the Father of our Lord Jesus Christ,[a] [15]from whom the whole family in heaven and earth is named, [16]that He would grant you, according to the riches of His glory, to be strengthened with might through His Spirit in the inner man, [17]that Christ may dwell in your hearts through faith; that you, being rooted and grounded in love, [18]may be able to comprehend with all the saints what *is* the width and length and depth and height— [19]to know the love of Christ which passes knowledge; that you may be filled with all the fullness of God.

[20]Now to Him who is able to do exceedingly abundantly above all that we ask or think, according to the power that works in us, [21]to Him *be* glory in the church by Christ Jesus to all generations, forever and ever. Amen.

Walk in Unity

4 I, therefore, the prisoner of the Lord, beseech you to walk worthy of the calling with which you were called, [2]with all lowliness and gentleness, with longsuffering, bearing with one another in love, [3]endeavoring to keep the unity of the Spirit in the bond of peace. [4]*There is* one body and one Spirit, just as you were called in one hope of your calling; [5]one Lord, one faith, one baptism; [6]one God and Father of all, who *is* above all, and through all, and in you[a] all.

Spiritual Gifts

[7]But to each one of us grace was given according to the measure of Christ's gift.

3:14 [a]NU-Text omits *of our Lord Jesus Christ.* **4:6** [a]NU-Text omits *you;* M-Text reads *us.*

3:9 Life's origins—the ever-changing mind of science. According to an NBC News report in August 1999, there was a "remarkable" discovery in Australia. They said the *Journal of Science* reported that they had found what they considered to be proof that life appeared on earth 2.7 billion years ago—a billion years earlier than previously thought. They now admit that they were wrong in their first estimate (a mere 1,000,000,000 years off), but with this discovery they are now sure that they have the truth...until their next discovery.

CBS News reported in October 1999 that discoveries were made of the bones of an unknown animal in Asia that may be as much as 40 million years old. This changed scientific minds as to *where* man first originated. Scientists once believed that primates evolved in Africa, but now they think they may be wrong, and that man's ancestors may have originated in Asia. So they believe... until the next discovery.

USA Today (March 21, 2001) reported, "Paleontologists have discovered a new skeleton in the closet of human ancestry that is likely to force science to revise, if not scrap, current theories of human origins." *Reuters* reported that the discovery left "scientists of human evolution... *confused,*" saying, "Lucy may not even be a direct human ancestor after all." See also Job 35:16 comment.

What is science? "We are invited, brethren, most earnestly to go away from the old-fashioned belief of our forefathers because of the supposed discoveries of science. What is science? The method by which man tries to hide his ignorance. It should not be so, but so it is. You are not to be dogmatical in theology, my brethren, it is wicked; but for scientific men it is the correct thing. You are never to assert anything very strongly; but scientists may boldly assert what they cannot prove, and may demand a faith far more credulous than any we possess. Forsooth, you and I are to take our Bibles and shape and mould our belief according to the ever-shifting teachings of so-called scientific men. What folly is this! Why, the march of science, falsely so called, through the world may be traced by exploded fallacies and abandoned theories. Former explorers once adored are now ridiculed; the continual wreckings of false hypotheses is a matter of universal notoriety. You may tell where the supposed learned have encamped by the debris left behind of suppositions and theories as plentiful as broken bottles." *Charles Spurgeon*

QUESTIONS & OBJECTIONS

4:13

"How do you respond when someone says, 'Well, no one is perfect'?"

Agree with him. The person is seeking to justify his sinful heart by spreading the blame around all of humanity, and at the same time inferring that the standard God requires is too high. Say, "That's right; you are not perfect. You are a self-admitted liar, thief, etc., and you have to stand before a perfect God whose Law you have violated and give an account of your actions. What are you going to say? You can't justify yourself. And you are right about no one being perfect. We have all sinned, and we are all heading for hell."

The person's words reveal a subtle form of self-righteousness, and you have to chop that out with the sharp axe of the Law. So cut deep and get it all out. You want to bring him to a point of acknowledging, "I have sinned against God." His sin is personal. Study Paul's use of the Law in Rom. 2:21–23. He stirred the conscience and made it personal. Nathan did the same thing with David when he said, "You are the man!" Study the opening verses of Psa. 51 to see how personal David knew his transgression was—knowledge that came from the prophet's rebuke. His actions weren't "imperfect"; he calls what he did "evil." See Matt. 5:48 comment.

8Therefore He says:

"When He ascended on high,
He led captivity captive,
And gave gifts to men."[a]

9(Now this, *"He ascended"*—what does it
mean but that He also first[a] descended
into the lower parts of the earth? 10He
who descended is also the One who ascended far above all the heavens, that He
might fill all things.)

11And He Himself gave some *to be*
apostles, some prophets, some evangelists, and some pastors and teachers, 12for
the equipping of the saints for the work
of ministry, for the edifying of the body
of Christ, 13till we all come to the unity of
the faith and of the knowledge of the Son
of God, to a perfect man, to the measure
of the stature of the fullness of Christ;
14that we should no longer be children,
tossed to and fro and carried about with
every wind of doctrine, by the trickery of
men, in the cunning craftiness of deceitful plotting, 15but, speaking the truth in
love, may grow up in all things into Him
who is the head—Christ— 16from whom
the whole body, joined and knit together
by what every joint supplies, according
to the effective working by which every
part does its share, causes growth of the
body for the edifying of itself in love.

The New Man

17This I say, therefore, and testify in
the Lord, that you should no longer walk

4:8 [a]Psalm 68:18 4:9 [a]NU-Text omits *first*.

4:11 The "gift" of evangelism. Often Christians pass off their responsibility to reach out to the lost by saying that it is not their "gifting." However, there is no such thing as the "gift of evangelism." That's like saying, "He has the gift of feeding starving children." It is not a gift. Rather, he has love enough to take food to the hungry. Another word for *evangelism* is "love." The Scriptures here are speaking of the God-given ability of the evangelist to equip the *saints* for the work of ministry—that's all believers.

"It occurred to me that in our work with secular organizations, the leader shapes the heart and passion of the corporate entity. In our work with non-profit organizations, we have found the same principle to be operative. When it comes to the focus of the organization, the people who serve there tend to take on many of the core personality traits of the leader toward fulfilling the mandate of the organization. If this is true, and most churches seem to lack the fervor and focus for evangelism, is it reasonable to conclude that it may be because of the lack of zeal most pastors have for identifying, befriending, loving and evangelizing non-Christian people?" *George Barna, Evangelism That Works*

QUESTIONS & OBJECTIONS

4:19 *"I don't feel guilty."*

Some people don't feel guilty when they sin because they have "seared" their conscience. Repeated sin sears the conscience until its muffled voice is no longer heard. This is a tragedy because the conscience is the voice of warning. Those who delight in sin, because they have dulled their conscience, are like a man who removes the batteries from his smoke detector because he doesn't want to be bothered by its alarm.

To awaken a deadened conscience, simply take the person through the Law. Address the conscience directly by saying, "You know it's wrong to lie, steal, commit adultery, etc." As you do so, the conscience will confirm the truth of the Commandments. Always preach the Law along with future punishment, then pray the Holy Spirit will convict the person of sin, righteousness, and judgment to come.

as the rest of[a] the Gentiles walk, in the futility of their mind, 18having their understanding darkened, being alienated from
the life of God, because of the ignorance
that is in them, because of the blindness
of their heart; 19who, being past feeling,
have given themselves over to lewdness,
to work all uncleanness with greediness.
20But you have not so learned Christ,
21if indeed you have heard Him and have
been taught by Him, as the truth is in Jesus: 22that you put off, concerning your
former conduct, the old man which
grows corrupt according to the deceitful
lusts, 23and be renewed in the spirit of
your mind, 24and that you put on the
new man which was created according to
God, in true righteousness and holiness.

4:17 [a]NU-Text omits *the rest of.*

4:15 The love of Jesus. "The powerful preaching of Jesus is piercing precisely because everything He says is not only true, but comes from a heart of love. Jesus, first of all, loves His Father in heaven and would never compromise the message that sinners must be delivered or be damned. That is the reason Jesus came to earth—to save sinners. It's true. Jesus loved you and me too much to not speak plainly of our greatest problem (sin and the wrath of God) and the glorious solution (the good news of the gospel).

"I recently heard a missionary, Paul Washer, tell how a doctor ruined his mother's day by telling her she had cancer. The news ruined her whole weekend and made her cry. But, obviously, the doctor was doing the most compassionate thing he could by telling her the truth and offering her an opportunity to do something about her problem before it was too late. If the doctor had avoided the dreadful subject of cancer, he would have acted immorally, unethically, and should have had his license taken away. Likewise, Washer states, there are many pastors today who need to have their licenses taken away due to their lack of courage to speak of that which is most vital to the sinner—his need to recognize his own sin, turn from that sin (along with its eternal penalty) and turn to the Savior, resulting in pardon, peace, and paradise. I agree with Washer and pray that God gives me courage to speak the truth in love like Jesus did." *Kirk Cameron*

4:18 Darkened understanding. When New Age followers say, "I am God," rather than revealing their delusions of grandeur, they are revealing their darkened understanding of their concept of God. The god of this world has blinded their minds. If, in their ignorance, sinners continually harden their hearts against the truth of God, they will eventually be unable to feel the Holy Spirit's conviction, and will be given over to a life of sin (Rom. 1:21–24). To reach them we must use God's Law to provide understanding (Rom. 3:20). It breaks the hard heart, and reveals to the sinner that he is cut off from the life of God (Rom. 7:9).

Alienated from the life of God. Atheists attest to the fact that their spirit (their God-conscious part) is dead. (See Gen. 2:17 comment.) They know God exists intellectually—because of their conscience and creation—but they are not aware of His omnipresence because they are dead spiritually. They are like a fish in the ocean that is not aware of the ocean.

"We are born dead in trespasses and sins, alienated, cut off, detached from the life of God. The day that man believed the devil's lie (which is sin), he forfeited the life that distinguished him from the animal kingdom—the life of God. When sin came in, the life went out." *Ian Thomas*

Do Not Grieve the Spirit

25Therefore, putting away lying, *"Let
each one of you speak truth with his
neighbor,"*[a] for we are members of one
another. 26*"Be angry, and do not sin"*:[a] do
not let the sun go down on your wrath,
27nor give place to the devil. 28Let him
who stole steal no longer, but rather let
him labor, working with *his* hands what
is good, that he may have something to
give him who has need. 29Let no corrupt
word proceed out of your mouth, but
what is good for necessary edification,
that it may impart grace to the hearers.

> Your one business in life is to lead men to believe in Jesus Christ by the power of the Holy Spirit. Every other thing should be made subservient to this one objective.
>
> **CHARLES SPURGEON**

30And do not grieve the Holy Spirit of
God, by whom you were sealed for the
day of redemption. 31Let all bitterness,
wrath, anger, clamor, and evil speaking
be put away from you, with all malice.
32And be kind to one another, tenderhearted, forgiving one another, even as
God in Christ forgave you.

Walk in Love

5 Therefore be imitators of God as dear
children. 2And walk in love, as Christ
also has loved us and given Himself for
us, an offering and a sacrifice to God for
a sweet-smelling aroma.

3But fornication and all uncleanness
or covetousness, let it not even be named
among you, as is fitting for saints; 4nei-
ther filthiness, nor foolish talking, nor
coarse jesting, which are not fitting, but
rather giving of thanks. 5For this you
know,[a] that no fornicator, unclean person, nor covetous man, who is an idolater, has any inheritance in the kingdom
of Christ and God. 6Let no one deceive
you with empty words, for because of
these things the wrath of God comes
upon the sons of disobedience. 7There-
fore do not be partakers with them.

Walk in Light

8For you were once darkness, but now
you are light in the Lord. Walk as children of light 9(for the fruit of the Spirit[a] *is*
in all goodness, righteousness, and
truth), 10finding out what is acceptable to
the Lord. 11And have no fellowship with
the unfruitful works of darkness, but
rather expose *them*. 12For it is shameful
even to speak of those things which are
done by them in secret. 13But all things
that are exposed are made manifest by
the light, for whatever makes manifest is
light. 14Therefore He says:

"Awake, you who sleep,
Arise from the dead,
And Christ will give you light."

Walk in Wisdom

15See then that you walk circumspectly, not as fools but as wise, 16re-
deeming the time, because the days are
evil.

17Therefore do not be unwise, but understand what the will of the Lord *is*.
18And do not be drunk with wine, in

4:25 [a]Zechariah 8:16 4:26 [a]Psalm 4:4 5:5 [a]NU-Text reads *For know this.* 5:9 [a]NU-Text reads *light.*

4:29 If you wouldn't say it in prayer, don't say it at all.

5:5 A covetous person transgresses the Tenth, First, and Second Commandments. When he loves material things more than he loves God, he is setting his affections on the gift, rather than on the Giver. What father wouldn't be grieved if his beloved child loved his toys more than the father who gave him the toys? A child should love his father first and foremost. He should love the *giver* more than the *gift*.

5:17 Those who don't understand the will of the Lord are unwise. See Eph. 1:9 comment.

PRINCIPLES OF GROWTH FOR THE NEW AND GROWING CHRISTIAN

5:20 *Thanksgiving—Do the Right Thing*

For the Christian, every day should be Thanksgiving Day. We should be thankful even in the midst of problems. The apostle Paul said, "I am exceedingly joyful in all our tribulation" (2 Cor. 7:4). He knew that God was working all things together for his good, even his trials (Rom. 8:28).

Problems *will* come your way. God will see to it personally that you grow as a Christian. He will allow storms in your life, in order to send your roots deep into the soil of His Word. We also pray more in the midst of problems. It's been well said that you will see more from your knees than on your tiptoes.

A man once watched a butterfly struggling to get out of its cocoon. In an effort to help it, he took a razor blade and carefully slit the edge of the cocoon. The butterfly escaped from its problem . . . but immediately died. It is God's way to have the butterfly struggle. It is the struggle that causes its tiny heart to beat fast, sending the life's blood into its wings.

Trials have their purpose. They make us struggle in the cocoon in which we often find ourselves. It is there that the life's blood of faith in God helps us spread our wings.

Faith and thanksgiving are close friends. If you have faith in God, you will be thankful because you know His loving hand is upon you, even though you are in a lion's den. That will give you a deep sense of joy, which is the barometer of the depth of faith you have in God. Let me give you an example. Imagine if I said I'd give one million dollars to everyone who ripped out the last page of this publication and mailed it to me. Of course, you don't believe I would do that. But imagine if you did, and that you knew 1,000 people who had sent in the page, and every one received their million dollars—no strings attached. More than that, you actually called me, and I assured you personally that I would keep my word. If you believed me, *wouldn't* you have joy? If you didn't believe me—no joy. The amount of joy you have would be a barometer of how much you believed my promise.

We have so much for which to be thankful. God has given us "exceedingly great and precious promises" (2 Pet. 1:4) that are more to be desired than gold. Do yourself a big favor: believe those promises, thank God continually for them, and let your joy be full.

For the next principle of growth, see Acts 2:38 comment.

which is dissipation; but be filled with
the Spirit, [19]speaking to one another in
psalms and hymns and spiritual songs,
singing and making melody in your heart
to the Lord, [20]giving thanks always for all
things to God the Father in the name of
our Lord Jesus Christ, [21]submitting to
one another in the fear of God.[a]

Marriage—Christ and the Church

[22]Wives, submit to your own husbands, as to the Lord. [23]For the husband
is head of the wife, as also Christ is head
of the church; and He is the Savior of the
body. [24]Therefore, just as the church is
subject to Christ, so *let* the wives *be* to
their own husbands in everything.

[25]Husbands, love your wives, just as
Christ also loved the church and gave
Himself for her, [26]that He might sanctify
and cleanse her with the washing of water by the word, [27]that He might present
her to Himself a glorious church, not
having spot or wrinkle or any such thing,
but that she should be holy and without
blemish. [28]So husbands ought to love
their own wives as their own bodies; he
who loves his wife loves himself. [29]For no
one ever hated his own flesh, but nourishes and cherishes it, just as the Lord
does the church. [30]For we are members of
His body,[a] of His flesh and of His bones.
[31]*"For this reason a man shall leave his father and mother and be joined to his wife,
and the two shall become one flesh."*[a]
[32]This is a great mystery, but I speak concerning Christ and the church. [33]Never-

5:21 [a]NU-Text reads *Christ*. 5:30 [a]NU-Text omits the rest of this verse. 5:31 [a]Genesis 2:24

5:22–25 See Prov. 31:10 comment.

theless let each one of you in particular
so love his own wife as himself, and let
the wife *see* that she respects *her* husband.

Children and Parents

6 Children, obey your parents in the
Lord, for this is right. 2*"Honor your
father and mother,"* which is the first
commandment with promise: 3*"that it
may be well with you and you may live
long on the earth."*[a]

> The only real argument against the Bible is an unholy life. When a man argues against the Word of God, follow him home, and see if you cannot discover the reason of his enmity to the Word of the Lord. It lies in some sort of sin.
>
> **CHARLES SPURGEON**

4And you, fathers, do not provoke
your children to wrath, but bring them
up in the training and admonition of the
Lord.

Bondservants and Masters

5Bondservants, be obedient to those
who are your masters according to the
flesh, with fear and trembling, in sincerity of heart, as to Christ; 6not with eyeservice, as men-pleasers, but as bondservants of Christ, doing the will of God
from the heart, 7with goodwill doing service, as to the Lord, and not to men,
8knowing that whatever good anyone
does, he will receive the same from the
Lord, whether *he is* a slave or free.
9And you, masters, do the same things
to them, giving up threatening, knowing
that your own Master also[a] is in heaven,
and there is no partiality with Him.

The Whole Armor of God

10Finally, my brethren, be strong in
the Lord and in the power of His might.
11Put on the whole armor of God, that
you may be able to stand against the
wiles of the devil. 12For we do not wrestle against flesh and blood, but against
principalities, against powers, against the
rulers of the darkness of this age,[a] against
spiritual *hosts* of wickedness in the heavenly *places.* 13Therefore take up the
whole armor of God, that you may be
able to withstand in the evil day, and
having done all, to stand.
14Stand therefore, having girded your
waist with truth, having put on the
breastplate of righteousness, 15and having shod your feet with the preparation of
the gospel of peace; 16above all, taking
the shield of faith with which you will be

6:3 [a]Deuteronomy 5:16 6:9 [a]NU-Text reads *He who is both their Master and yours.* 6:12 [a]NU-Text reads *rulers of this darkness.*

6:1,2 Teaching children God's Law. Paul uses the Commandment to bring the knowledge of sin. The biblical way to bring a child to the Savior is to teach him God's Law. Immediately after Moses had read the Ten Commandments to Israel, he said that they should teach them to their children as they sit and as they walk, when they lie down and rise up. The Commandments should be placed where they can be constant reminders (see Deut. 6:4–9). Why should our children be taught the Ten Commandments? Simply because they will show the child what sin is. As the child matures and discovers sin in his heart, and he begins to understand that God requires truth in the inward parts, the threat of the Law will drive him to the foot of a blood-stained cross. What child can look at Eph. 6:1,2 and say that he is guiltless and therefore free of its warning? To help children memorize the Ten Commandments, see page 652; see also Prov. 22:6 comment.

6:4 "I am much afraid that schools will prove to be the great gates of hell unless they diligently labor in explaining the Holy Scriptures, engraving them in the hearts of youth. I advise no one to place his child where the Scriptures do not reign paramount. Every institution in which men are not increasingly occupied with the Word of God must become corrupt." *Martin Luther* (See also Prov. 4:1–5 comment.)

6:10 "Do not pray for easy lives. Pray to be stronger men. Do not pray for tasks commensurate with your strength. Pray for strength commensurate with your tasks." *Phillips Brooks*

able to quench all the fiery darts of the
wicked one. 17And take the helmet of salvation, and the sword of the Spirit, which
is the word of God; 18praying always with
all prayer and supplication in the Spirit,
being watchful to this end with all perseverance and supplication for all the
saints— 19and for me, that utterance may
be given to me, that I may open my
mouth boldly to make known the mystery of the gospel, 20for which I am an
ambassador in chains; that in it I may speak
boldly, as I ought to speak.

A Gracious Greeting

21But that you also may know my affairs *and* how I am doing, Tychicus, a
beloved brother and faithful minister in
the Lord, will make all things known to
you; 22whom I have sent to you for this
very purpose, that you may know our affairs, and *that* he may comfort your hearts.
23Peace to the brethren, and love with
faith, from God the Father and the Lord
Jesus Christ. 24Grace *be* with all those who
love our Lord Jesus Christ in sincerity.
Amen.

6:15 Don't go barefoot. In v. 11 we are told to put on the *whole* armor of God. Many Christians are truthful. They have their heart free of sin, they are sure of their salvation, they rightly use the Word of God. But they are shoeless—they are not prepared to share the gospel. Those who do not advance the cause of the gospel are stationary soldiers; any evangelistic movement is too painful for them. If they are not seeking to save the lost, they are not taking ground for the kingdom of God. Paul climaxed his admonition to the Ephesians by highlighting what the battle is for. He pleads with them to pray for him to have boldness to reach out to the unsaved, citing his moral responsibility (v. 20).

6:17 "We must thrust the sword of the Spirit into the hearts of men." *Charles Spurgeon*

6:18 "Let's move from theology to kneeology! Power for victory in spiritual warfare is found in prayer." *Robert R. Lawrence*

6:19 Beware of the subtlety of passive prayer. We have been commanded to preach the gospel. Make sure you don't pacify a guilty conscience by simply praying for the salvation of the lost, but not preaching to them. It is the *gospel* that is the power of God to salvation (Rom. 1:16). How shall they hear without a preacher? See Rom. 10:14.

Jehovah's Witnesses

The Jehovah's Witnesses are best known for their door-to-door evangelism. With over 6 million active Witnesses making house calls each year, there's a very good chance they've knocked on your door at least once. In fact, no religious group in the world spends as many hours proselytizing as the Jehovah's Witnesses. With followers in 235 countries—1 million in the U.S—they spent over 1.2 *billion* hours in 2005 "proclaiming the good news" of Jehovah and His Kingdom. What is the so-called "good news" that they are proclaiming that attracts 300,000 new members each year?

BACKGROUND

The Jehovah's Witnesses religious movement was started about 130 years ago by a young man named Charles Russell. As a teenager, he left his church because he rejected its biblical teachings on eternal punishment in hell. So Russell reasoned that when man dies, he simply stops existing. He also denied that Jesus was God in human flesh, rejecting the Trinity and many other essential Christian doctrines.

When he was 18 years old, Russell started a Bible study where he began to spread his beliefs. Then he published his own magazine, now known as *The Watchtower*. Some people were fascinated by his "end-of-the-world" predictions, and in 1884 he started the Watchtower Bible and Tract Society, which is headquartered in Brooklyn, New York.

Originally, those who followed Russell were called "Russelites." The name "Jehovah's Witnesses" didn't catch on until almost fifty years later, and is based on Isa. 43:10: "Ye are my witnesses, saith Jehovah, and my servant whom I have chosen" (American Standard Version).

The Watchtower Society boldly claims to be the *only* channel of divine truth today, and that no one can be saved apart from their organization.

(continued)

Jehovah's Witnesses (continued)

SCRIPTURES

Since many of their doctrines are easily refuted by the Scriptures, in 1961 the Watchtower Society published their own Bible. Called the *New World Translation* (NWT), it blatantly alters many verses that revealed the errors of the Watchtower teaching.

In addition, *The Watchtower* magazine is one of their main sources of doctrine. The Watchtower Society teaches that only *they* can interpret the Bible, and no individual can learn the truth apart from them. Jehovah's Witnesses are therefore encouraged to study their Bible only in conjunction with the other Watchtower publications, so the Watchtower Society can tell them what it really means.

> The Bible is an organizational book and belongs to the Christian congregation as an organization, not to individuals, regardless of how sincerely they may believe that they can interpret the Bible. For this reason, the Bible cannot be properly understood without Jehovah's visible organization in mind. (*Watchtower*, Oct. 1, 1967)

WHO IS GOD?

Jehovah's Witnesses reject the biblical concept of a triune God. Saying that it's "difficult to love and worship a complicated, freakish-looking, three-headed God," they reason that God cannot be a Trinity. After all, God made man in His image, and "no one has ever seen a three-headed human creature" (*Let God Be True*).

Based on Isa. 43:10, they believe the only true God is known as "Jehovah," the Almighty. Although He is eternal and omnipotent, He is not omnipresent.

In addition, Jehovah's Witnesses deny the deity of the Holy Spirit. They believe the Holy Spirit is not a person but is only "the active force of God."

WHO IS JESUS?

The Watchtower Society teaches that Jesus is not God incarnate but is just a created being. He is called God's "only begotten Son" because He is the first and only being created directly by Jehovah. As the "first-born of all creation," Jesus was then used by God to create all other things.

Before Jesus came to earth He was Michael the archangel, and is the "second greatest personage of the universe." Through the virgin birth, He was later re-created on earth as a perfect man. Jesus became the Messiah at His baptism, and at that time He was anointed to become the King of the coming Kingdom.

Jehovah's Witnesses also deny the bodily resurrection of Christ. They believe that after Jesus was buried, God disposed of His physical body. Jesus was raised as a *spirit* creature and temporarily "materialized" different physical bodies to make Himself visible to His disciples. Now back in heaven as a spirit, He is once again known as Michael the archangel.

HEAVEN AND HELL

The Watchtower Society denies the existence of hell as a place of everlasting punishment for the wicked. They argue, "The doctrine of a burning hell where the wicked are tortured eternally after death cannot be true mainly for four reasons: (1) It is wholly unscriptural; (2) it is unreasonable; (3) it is contrary to God's love; and (4) it is repugnant to justice" (*Let God Be True*).

The Jehovah's Witnesses (like the Seventh-Day Adventists) believe in "soul sleep"—that humans don't have immortal souls, so when the body dies there is no longer any conscience existence. (For the biblical view, see Isa. 38:10 comment.) They teach that hell, or Sheol, is simply the common grave of mankind. From there, those who are righteous will be resurrected; those who are ultimately condemned by God will be annihilated and cease to exist.

The Watchtower theology of heaven is based on their interpretation of the Book of Revelation. They teach that when the saints go marching in, you're not going to be in that number because the only ones who will enter the Pearly Gates are the 144,000 "anointed ones." According to the Watchtower, all of these tickets to heaven have already been "sold out." Only these 144,000 are born again, are members of the spiritual body of Christ, and can expect to reign with Christ in heaven.

So for the vast majority of remaining Jehovah's Witnesses, known as the "other sheep" or the "great crowd," Christ's sacrifice provides only a chance at eternal life on earth. They will never go to heaven or see Jesus/Michael. Their only hope is to live in the Paradise established on earth after Armageddon. These "other sheep" expect to be given a physical *eternal life* on earth, in contrast to *immortality* as spirits in heaven for the 144,000.

Note that, like the Mormon church, Jehovah's Witnesses redefine biblical words, making it difficult to witness to them. You can try to convince them that "unless one is born again, he cannot see the kingdom of God" (John 3:3), and they will agree with you. They believe only the 144,000 who are born again will go to "the kingdom of God," while they are content to end up in Paradise on earth—therefore, they don't need to be born again.

SIN AND SALVATION

Jehovah's Witnesses believe that in the Fall, all mankind inherited "imperfection" from Adam and Eve and hence are sinners who are subject to death. But they believe sin was only *partially* atoned for by Christ. As a perfect man, Christ's death paid the ransom that removed the effects of *Adam's* sin, but individuals still have to work to earn forgiveness for *their* present and future sins. In other words, original sin that brought death was canceled by Christ's

(continued)

Jehovah's Witnesses (continued)

atonement—yet men can still die by their own rebellion and sin.

For Jehovah's Witnesses, salvation requires a complicated combination of belief and good works: "[Belief] involves taking in accurate knowledge of God's purposes and his way of salvation. Then faith has to be exercised in Jesus Christ as the Chief Agent of salvation... This places the Christian in a saved condition, but he must now persevere in doing God's will and continue to adhere to all of God's requirements for the rest of his life. Only then will he be saved to eternal life" (*Watchtower*, Dec. 15, 1989).

Jehovah is said to be a God of "grace" only because without Jesus' death for our sins, no one would have the *opportunity* to merit salvation. In addition to faith in Jesus' sacrifice, requirements for salvation include baptism by immersion, repentance, active association with the Watchtower Society, righteous conduct, and absolute loyalty to Jehovah. Even then, there is no assurance of salvation, only hope for a resurrection. Those who fail to live up to these requirements, or who are disfellowshiped by the Watchtower Society, have no hope of salvation.

Jehovah's Witnesses are told that serving as loyal spokesmen for the Society is "a sacred duty, a requirement on which our life depends." Witnesses are compelled to knock on door after door to try to spread their beliefs—and earn their salvation. Witnesses are expected to spend five hours a week going door-to-door, to sell twelve subscriptions to *The Watchtower* magazine each month, and to conduct a monthly "Bible study" in the homes of their converts. They then have to submit detailed reports of their activity, and their performance will affect their status in the local congregation or "Kingdom Hall"—adding more pressure for them to work harder. With a lifetime of works to try to earn their salvation, it is hard to see how their gospel is "good news" at all.

JEHOVAH'S WITNESS CUSTOMS

No crosses: Because Jehovah's Witnesses teach that Jesus was executed on a "torture stake," they reject the traditional symbol of Christianity, the cross, as being of pagan origin. They believe displaying a cross (whether on a necklace or church) is idol worship—so you won't see any on their buildings.

Forbidden activities: The Watchtower Society also forbids many activities that are not explicitly forbidden in the Bible: such as smoking, blood transfusions, boxing, or participating in a raffle, as well as things related to the current earthly kingdom, like saluting the flag, reciting the Pledge of Allegiance, standing for or singing the national anthem, voting, and performing military or civic service. The Society also forbids celebrating personal birthdays, Christmas, Easter, Mother's Day and Father's Day, as well as most other holidays, believing that they have pagan roots.

No association: So that Jehovah's Witnesses are not corrupted by contact with others, they are not allowed to associate with non-Witnesses—even those in their own family. The only exception is if a non-Witness family member is living in the same household.

HOW TO REACH A JEHOVAH'S WITNESS

As you're talking with Jehovah's Witnesses, keep in mind that they believe they worship the true God of the Bible, while Christians are lost souls who have been misled by the devil into worshiping a pagan three-headed deity. So don't be surprised if they are not very receptive to your message.

Also keep in mind that members are taught to obediently follow all the teachings of their leaders, and any who question their teaching are severely reprimanded or even disfellowshiped. Because a member who leaves the organization must be shunned by all other Witnesses—including his family—he is not going to give up his beliefs easily.

So what is the best way to reach a Jehovah's Witness? Should you try to convince him that Jesus is God, or of the existence of hell? Well, if you have the confidence to, try it. Many ex-Witnesses say they were forced to reexamine their beliefs because someone planted just one seed of doubt in their minds about the truthfulness of the Watchtower teachings. The Word of God is living and powerful, and *will* have an impact.

If you can quickly demonstrate from Scripture that Jesus is God, Jehovah's Witnesses will have to reconsider their understanding of God. They will now have two Persons who are God—Father and Son. For example, have them read Isa. 7:14 and 9:6. Point out that the Messiah would be "Immanuel" ("God with us") and would be called "Mighty God"—the same name used for Jehovah in Isa. 10:21.

But be careful you don't try to win the fight simply by arguing doctrine—and then failing to share the gospel biblically. If you don't address the conscience, you will end up trapped in the intellect with nowhere to go. So next time the Jehovah's Witnesses come calling, take the opportunity to speak with them. Don't worry about straightening out all the areas of disagreement, but gently point them to the moral Law, the Ten Commandments. Show them that as lawbreakers they will be guilty before a holy God, and that no amount of works will ever save them.

And remember—those who are caught in this cult are spending one billion hours spreading their false teaching. Be sure you're a faithful witness for the Lord Jesus Christ and spend your time wisely in spreading what is truly "good news"!

(Adapted from *World Religions in a Nutshell*.)

Philippians

Greeting

1 Paul and Timothy, bondservants of Jesus Christ,

To all the saints in Christ Jesus who are in Philippi, with the bishops[a] and deacons:

2Grace to you and peace from God our Father and the Lord Jesus Christ.

Thankfulness and Prayer

3I thank my God upon every remembrance of you, 4always in every prayer of mine making request for you all with joy, 5for your fellowship in the gospel from the first day until now, 6being confident of this very thing, that He who has begun a good work in you will complete *it* until the day of Jesus Christ; 7just as it is right for me to think this of you all, because I have you in my heart, inasmuch as both in my chains and in the defense and confirmation of the gospel, you all are partakers with me of grace. 8For God is my witness, how greatly I long for you all with the affection of Jesus Christ.

9And this I pray, that your love may abound still more and more in knowledge and all discernment, 10that you may approve the things that are excellent, that you may be sincere and without offense till the day of Christ, 11being filled with the fruits of righteousness which *are* by Jesus Christ, to the glory and praise of God.

Christ Is Preached

12But I want you to know, brethren, that the things *which happened* to me have actually turned out for the furtherance of the gospel, 13so that it has become evident to the whole palace guard, and to all the rest, that my chains are in Christ; 14and most of the brethren in the Lord, having become confident by my chains, are much more bold to speak the word without fear.

15Some indeed preach Christ even from envy and strife, and some also from goodwill: 16The former[a] preach Christ

1:1 [a]Literally *overseers* 1:16 [a]NU-Text reverses the contents of verses 16 and 17.

1:6 Do you ever think about how many faces there are upon the earth? As you line up in a store, do you sometimes feel like a tiny grain of sand in the massive desert? Then lift your head and look to the heavens—God Almighty is your Maker. Like a giant heavenly zoom lens, He focused in on you from eternity. He foreknew every sinew of your fearfully and wonderfully made body. He is the lover of your soul. He breathed life into your human frame, and is at work in you to will and to do for His good pleasure (Phil. 2:13).

His good pleasure is to conform you to the image of His Son. Never let discouragement fall upon your mind, for God will complete the good work He has begun in you. He picked you out of the ranks of the masses, called you by His grace, justified you through faith, and glorified you in Christ.

1:14 The Church should never dread persecution, as it can work *for* rather than *against* the furtherance of the gospel. The winds of persecution only spread the flames of the gospel.

QUESTIONS & OBJECTIONS

"How can we be sure our motive for witnessing is right so we won't be ineffective?"

Ask God to search out your motives. However, even if your heart is not in the right place (I'm not talking about sin, but that you are going because of a sense of guilt or obligation), you should still go. If you were rescued from a burning building by a fireman who left the firehouse because he felt guilty not coming to the fire, as far as you are concerned, his motive for rescuing you is irrelevant. All that matters is that he did. So don't get hung up on why you reach out to the lost, just do it, while there is still time. Paul rejoiced even though Christ was preached from the mouth of a hypocrite. This is because the quality is in the seed, not in the sower. This gives great consolation to those of us who feel we lack ability.

However, some who are worried about motive may lack motivation themselves. Love for God and for the lost is all we need. Jesus told us to go, and He gave us the Holy Spirit to help us. So if you are waiting for the "prompting" of the Holy Spirit to witness, just ask yourself if the people you are waiting to witness to fit the category Jesus mentioned in Mark 16:15: "Go into all the world and preach the gospel to every [person]." The word "every" puts them in the "need to hear the gospel" category. If you were sitting in one of the *Titanic*'s lifeboats, with plenty of room on board, would you look to the captain for his approval before you reached out to each drowning person, when he has already commanded you to reach everyone you can? Of course not. A good rule of thumb is: if they are breathing, they need to hear the gospel. Regardless of motive, the important thing is that Christ is preached.

from selfish ambition, not sincerely, supposing to add affliction to my chains;
[17]but the latter out of love, knowing that
I am appointed for the defense of the gospel. [18]What then? Only *that* in every way,
whether in pretense or in truth, Christ is
preached; and in this I rejoice, yes, and
will rejoice.

To Live Is Christ

[19]For I know that this will turn out for
my deliverance through your prayer and
the supply of the Spirit of Jesus Christ,
[20]according to my earnest expectation and
hope that in nothing I shall be ashamed,
but with all boldness, as always, so now
also Christ will be magnified in my body,
whether by life or by death. [21]For to me,
to live *is* Christ, and to die *is* gain. [22]But
if *I* live on in the flesh, this *will mean* fruit
from *my* labor; yet what I shall choose I
cannot tell. [23]For[a] I am hard-pressed between the two, having a desire to depart
and be with Christ, *which is* far better.
[24]Nevertheless to remain in the flesh *is*
more needful for you. [25]And being confident of this, I know that I shall remain
and continue with you all for your progress and joy of faith, [26]that your rejoicing
for me may be more abundant in Jesus
Christ by my coming to you again.

Striving and Suffering for Christ

[27]Only let your conduct be worthy of
the gospel of Christ, so that whether I
come and see you or am absent, I may
hear of your affairs, that you stand fast in
one spirit, with one mind striving together for the faith of the gospel, [28]and
not in any way terrified by your adversaries, which is to them a proof of perdition, but to you of salvation,[a] and that from
God. [29]For to you it has been granted on
behalf of Christ, not only to believe in
Him, but also to suffer for His sake,
[30]having the same conflict which you saw
in me and now hear *is* in me.

Unity Through Humility

2 Therefore if *there is* any consolation
in Christ, if any comfort of love, if
any fellowship of the Spirit, if any affec-

1:23 [a]NU-Text and M-Text read *But*. 1:28 [a]NU-Text reads *of your salvation*.

1:20 Paul lived for the furtherance of the gospel. God's will was his will.

tion and mercy, [2]fulfill my joy by being like-minded, having the same love, *being* of one accord, of one mind. [3]*Let* nothing *be done* through selfish ambition or conceit, but in lowliness of mind let each esteem others better than himself. [4]Let each of you look out not only for his own interests, but also for the interests of others.

The Humbled and Exalted Christ

[5]Let this mind be in you which was also in Christ Jesus, [6]who, being in the form of God, did not consider it robbery to be equal with God, [7]but made Himself of no reputation, taking the form of a bondservant, *and* coming in the likeness of men. [8]And being found in appearance as a man, He humbled Himself and became obedient to *the point of* death, even the death of the cross. [9]Therefore God also has highly exalted Him and given Him the name which is above every name, [10]that at the name of Jesus every knee should bow, of those in heaven, and of those on earth, and of those under the earth, [11]and *that* every tongue should confess that Jesus Christ *is* Lord, to the glory of God the Father.

Light Bearers

[12]Therefore, my beloved, as you have always obeyed, not as in my presence only, but now much more in my absence, work out your own salvation with fear and trembling; [13]for it is God who works in you both to will and to do for *His* good pleasure.

Preach Christ or nothing: don't dispute or discuss except with your eye on the cross.

CHARLES SPURGEON

[14]Do all things without complaining and disputing, [15]that you may become blameless and harmless, children of God without fault in the midst of a crooked and perverse generation, among whom

1:29 "Suffering and sacrifice are essential to the Christian life just as they were essential to Christ's life. 'When Christ calls a man,' [Dietrich] Bonhoeffer wrote, 'He bids him come and die' *(The Cost of Discipleship)*. This doesn't always—or even usually—necessitate our physical deaths, but Christ calls us first and foremost to die to sin and to ourselves. Leave your home, sell everything you own, turn the other cheek, do not store up earthly treasures, love your enemies, take up your cross and follow me. None of Christ's commands call believers to a life of comfort. All require patience, suffering, and sacrifice." *Daniel L. Weiss*

2:3 Beware of the subtle sin of conceit. When pride (a feeling of superiority) manifests through us, it is often evident and we can humble ourselves. But conceit (an exaggerated estimate of abilities) hides. It conceals itself deep within the wicked human heart, and it needs the psalmist's earnest plea: "Search me, O God, and know my heart; ... and see if there is any wicked way in me" (Psa. 139:23,24).

2:8 The death of the cross. "Oh sinner, why provoke your Maker? Your judgment does not linger and your damnation does not slumber. When the Law was broken and mankind was exposed to its fearful penalty, God offered justice to the universe and mercy for sinners, which He displayed in the atonement. To make this universal offer of pardon without justice would violate His Law. A due regard for public interest forbade the Lawgiver to forgive and set aside the penalty without finding a way to secure obedience to the Law. Therefore, His compassion for mankind and His regard for the Law were so great that He was willing to suffer in the person of His Son, who became a substitute for the penalty of the Law. This was the most stupendous exhibition of self-denial that was ever made: the Father giving His only begotten and beloved Son; the Son veiling the glories of His uncreated Godhead and becoming obedient to death, even the death of the cross, that we may never die." *Charles Finney*

2:13 "I used to ask God to help me. Then I asked if I might help Him. I ended up by asking Him to do His work through me." *Hudson Taylor*

2:15 Too often the Church becomes exclusive. We fellowship only with Christians—a monastery without walls. We become salt among salt, light among light. In reality, the Church should be "in the midst... among whom... in the world." Verse 16 tells us what we should be doing "in the midst."

"I would not give much for your religion unless it can be seen. Lamps do not talk, but they do shine." *Charles Spurgeon*

SPRINGBOARDS FOR PREACHING AND WITNESSING

The Name Above All Names

2:9 The most hated name in the world is not Osama bin Laden, Hitler, or Judas Iscariot. None of those names are internationally used as a cuss word. By far the winner of the Most Despised Name award is Jesus Christ. He is an all-time Hollywood favorite. His name is used as a cuss word in books and magazines, on radio and TV, all over the Internet, and in everyday speech. Jesus predicted that the world would hate Him because He testified that its works are evil (see John 7:7). The world hates Jesus for the same reason devious criminals hate the police.

Using His name as a cuss word is not the only way to deal with this problem of Jesus of Nazareth. You can try to wash your hands of Him by doing what the Mormons did—make up their own "Jesus," who is the brother of Lucifer. Or you can do what Islam did—create a Jesus who is not the Son of God and did not die on the cross.

Or you could try to change the historical revelation of Jesus. Some claim that Jesus never performed miracles, that He was just a man who married and had kids, or that He died and was buried. Others have suggested that Jesus was fathered by a Roman soldier who raped Mary.

The Book of Acts tells us that the religious leaders of the day forbade preaching "in His name." They hated the name of Jesus. Two thousand years later, not much has changed. A National Day of Prayer chairman refused to pray in the name of Jesus so as not to offend any Jewish participants. They seem to presume that Jews hate Him—one of their own. I am Jewish, and I don't hate His name. I love it.

I cannot help but wonder how those who are offended by Jesus' name would react if I concluded a prayer with, "In the name of the perfect Son of God, who was born of a virgin, suffered and died for the sin of the world, rose again on the third day for our justification, and is coming in flaming fire to bring vengeance on those who don't know God and refuse to obey the gospel of salvation. Hallelujah! Praise His glorious name. Oh how I love Him. Amen."

you shine as lights in the world, 16holding fast the word of life, so that I may rejoice in the day of Christ that I have not run in vain or labored in vain.

17Yes, and if I am being poured out *as a drink offering* on the sacrifice and service of your faith, I am glad and rejoice with you all. 18For the same reason you also be glad and rejoice with me.

Timothy Commended

19But I trust in the Lord Jesus to send Timothy to you shortly, that I also may be encouraged when I know your state. 20For I have no one like-minded, who will sincerely care for your state. 21For all seek their own, not the things which are of Christ Jesus. 22But you know his proven character, that as a son with *his* father he served with me in the gospel. 23Therefore I hope to send him at once, as soon as I see how it goes with me. 24But I trust in the Lord that I myself shall also come shortly.

Epaphroditus Praised

25Yet I considered it necessary to send to you Epaphroditus, my brother, fellow worker, and fellow soldier, but your messenger and the one who ministered to my need; 26since he was longing for you all, and was distressed because you had heard that he was sick. 27For indeed he was sick almost unto death; but God had mercy on him, and not only on him but on me also, lest I should have sorrow upon sorrow. 28Therefore I sent him the more eagerly, that when you see him again you may rejoice, and I may be less sorrowful. 29Receive him therefore in the Lord with all gladness, and hold such men in esteem; 30because for the work of Christ he came close to death, not regarding his life, to supply what was lacking in your service toward me.

All for Christ

3 Finally, my brethren, rejoice in the Lord. For me to write the same things to you *is* not tedious, but for you *it is* safe.

2Beware of dogs, beware of evil workers, beware of the mutilation! 3For we are the circumcision, who worship God in the

3:9 *Using the Law with Catholics*

By Bruce Garner

Countless missionaries and pastors in Catholic-majority countries around the world have confirmed an awful reality: professions of faith and "sinner's prayers" were plentiful among Catholics. Disciples were scarce. The little fruit that remains even after the most sincere and seemingly successful evangelistic efforts shows us a vital truth: When we present them with the gospel, Catholics need to be confronted with the Law.

It took me years to realize it, but a Lawless gospel does not show a sincere Catholic his guilt before a holy and just God. If we ask him only to "believe" in Christ, we will find no objection. He *does* "believe in Christ," or he would not be a Catholic. If we ask our Catholic friend to "receive Christ," he may readily accept. As one man told me, "I receive Him every time I go to Mass."

A Lawless gospel will become, in the mind of a person brought up in Catholicism, merely another good work—an evangelical sacrament. The Church has taught the Catholic faithful that they must do many good works to be accepted by God: attend Mass, go to confession, do penance, etc. When a witnessing Christian merely assures Catholics of God's love and asks them to "believe in Jesus," "receive Christ," or "pray this prayer," it becomes simply another good work for them to do. Little surprise, then, that they readily do what we ask. They have been doing good deeds all their lives, so there is certainly no harm in doing another.

But when that same Christian shows up the next day to make a "follow up" visit with what he imagines is a new convert to Christ, he often discovers that the reality is quite different. After all, our Catholic friend had no intention of "switching religions."

Since sincere Catholics are trying to "be good enough" to get to heaven, we do them grave harm when we fail to present the Law. The Law will show them that they are already under judgment. The Law will show them the awesome holiness of God, their just Judge. The Law will show them their utter inability to ever do enough to satisfy His righteous demands. Only then will they despair of their own good works and turn for mercy to the Savior.

Spirit,[a] rejoice in Christ Jesus, and have
no confidence in the flesh, 4though I also
might have confidence in the flesh. If anyone else thinks he may have confidence
in the flesh, I more so: 5circumcised the
eighth day, of the stock of Israel, *of* the
tribe of Benjamin, a Hebrew of the Hebrews; concerning the law, a Pharisee;
6concerning zeal, persecuting the church;
concerning the righteousness which is in
the law, blameless.

7But what things were gain to me, these
I have counted loss for Christ. 8Yet indeed
I also count all things loss for the excellence of the knowledge of Christ Jesus my
Lord, for whom I have suffered the loss of
all things, and count them as rubbish,
that I may gain Christ 9and be found in
Him, not having my own righteousness,
which *is* from the law, but that which is
through faith in Christ, the righteousness
which is from God by faith; 10that I may
know Him and the power of His resurrection, and the fellowship of His sufferings, being conformed to His death, 11if,

3:3 [a]NU-Text and M-Text read *who worship in the Spirit of God.*

3:8 The greatest discovery. Dr. James Simpson, born in 1811, was responsible for the discovery of chloroform's anesthetic qualities, leading to its medical use worldwide. He also laid a solid foundation for gynecology and predicted the discovery of the X-ray. Dr. Simpson was president of the Royal Medical Society and Royal Physician to the Queen, the highest medical position of his day. He once stated, "Christianity works because it is supremely true and therefore supremely livable. There is nothing incompatible between religion and science."

When asked what his greatest discovery was, Dr. Simpson replied: "It was not chloroform. It was to know I am a sinner and that I could be saved by the grace of God. A man has missed the whole meaning of life if he has not entered into an active, living relationship with God through Christ." The greatest discovery in history has not been the law of gravity, calculus, telescopes, or the telegraph. The greatest discovery an individual could ever make is finding Jesus Christ and making Him both Lord and Savior.

by any means, I may attain to the resurrection from the dead.

Pressing Toward the Goal

[12]Not that I have already attained, or am already perfected; but I press on, that I may lay hold of that for which Christ Jesus has also laid hold of me. [13]Brethren, I do not count myself to have apprehended; but one thing *I do,* forgetting those things which are behind and reaching forward to those things which are ahead, [14]I press toward the goal for the prize of the upward call of God in Christ Jesus.

[15]Therefore let us, as many as are mature, have this mind; and if in anything you think otherwise, God will reveal even this to you. [16]Nevertheless, to *the degree* that we have already attained, let us walk by the same rule,[a] let us be of the same mind.

Our Citizenship in Heaven

[17]Brethren, join in following my example, and note those who so walk, as you have us for a pattern. [18]For many walk, of whom I have told you often, and now tell you even weeping, *that they are* the enemies of the cross of Christ: [19]whose end *is* destruction, whose god *is their* belly, and *whose* glory *is* in their shame—who set their mind on earthly things. [20]For our citizenship is in heaven, from which we also eagerly wait for the Savior, the Lord Jesus Christ, [21]who will transform our lowly body that it may be conformed to His glorious body, according to the working by which He is able even to subdue all things to Himself.

"Man is never so tall as when he kneels before God—never so great as when he humbles himself before God. And the man who kneels to God can stand up to anything."

Louis H. Evans

4 Therefore, my beloved and longed-for brethren, my joy and crown, so stand fast in the Lord, beloved.

Be United, Joyful, and in Prayer

[2]I implore Euodia and I implore Syntyche to be of the same mind in the Lord. [3]And[a] I urge you also, true companion, help these women who labored with me in the gospel, with Clement also, and the rest of my fellow workers, whose names *are* in the Book of Life.

[4]Rejoice in the Lord always. Again I will say, rejoice!

3:16 [a]NU-Text omits *rule* and the rest of the verse. 4:3 [a]NU-Text and M-Text read *Yes.*

3:13 "Oh God, let this horrible war quickly come to an end that we may all return home and engage in the only work that is worthwhile—and that is the salvation of men." *General "Stonewall" Jackson*

3:21 New bodies for Christians. The unsaved have no idea of our hope. They presume that when we die we will spend eternity in heaven as a spirit or an angel. In truth, God's kingdom is coming to earth, and God's will *will* be done on earth as it is in heaven. We will be neither spirits nor angels, but we will have new bodies similar to the resurrected body of the Savior, never again to be plagued by disease, decay, death, or even dandruff. See Luke 24:36–43.

4:3 True companions are those who "labor" in the gospel. These are the ones of whom Jesus said there was a great lack (Luke 10:2). The fruit of genuine converts (those whose names are in the Book of Life) is a concern for the lost. Love cannot sit in passivity while sinners sink into hell.

[5]Let your gentleness be known to all
men. The Lord *is* at hand.
[6]Be anxious for nothing, but in everything by prayer and supplication, with
thanksgiving, let your requests be made
known to God; [7]and the peace of God,
which surpasses all understanding, will
guard your hearts and minds through
Christ Jesus.

Meditate on These Things

[8]Finally, brethren, whatever things are
true, whatever things *are* noble, whatever
things *are* just, whatever things *are* pure,
whatever things *are* lovely, whatever
things *are* of good report, if *there is* any
virtue and if *there is* anything praiseworthy—meditate on these things. [9]The
things which you learned and received
and heard and saw in me, these do, and
the God of peace will be with you.

Philippian Generosity

[10]But I rejoiced in the Lord greatly
that now at last your care for me has
flourished again; though you surely did
care, but you lacked opportunity. [11]Not
that I speak in regard to need, for I have
learned in whatever state I am, to be content: [12]I know how to be abased, and I
know how to abound. Everywhere and in
all things I have learned both to be full
and to be hungry, both to abound and to
suffer need. [13]I can do all things through
Christ[a] who strengthens me.
[14]Nevertheless you have done well that
you shared in my distress. [15]Now you
Philippians know also that in the beginning of the gospel, when I departed from
Macedonia, no church shared with me
concerning giving and receiving but you
only. [16]For even in Thessalonica you sent
aid once and again for my necessities.
[17]Not that I seek the gift, but I seek the
fruit that abounds to your account. [18]In-
deed I have all and abound. I am full,
having received from Epaphroditus the
things *sent* from you, a sweet-smelling
aroma, an acceptable sacrifice, well pleasing to God. [19]And my God shall supply all
your need according to His riches in glory
by Christ Jesus. [20]Now to our God and
Father *be* glory forever and ever. Amen.

Greeting and Blessing

[21]Greet every saint in Christ Jesus.
The brethren who are with me greet you.
[22]All the saints greet you, but especially
those who are of Caesar's household.
[23]The grace of our Lord Jesus Christ
be with you all.[a] Amen.

4:13 [a]NU-Text reads *Him who.* **4:23** [a]NU-Text reads *your spirit.*

4:5 Second coming of Jesus: See 1 Thess. 5:2.

4:6 "Realistically, the way you regard prayer is the way you regard God, for prayer is communicating with Him. No other way exists in which to relate with Him! Put simply, low levels of prayer signal a demotion of God in our attitude. High levels of prayer indicate an expectation for a fullness of His presence and power." *Ben Jennings*

4:7 "Christians ought not to be smothered in fear. There is a spiritual readiness, where we return to having the peace of God stand guard over our hearts and minds. What an incredible witness it is to a lost and fearful society when the Christian acts like a child of God, living under the loving sovereignty of the heavenly Father. Christians need to walk in peace, so no matter what happens they will be able to bear witness to a watching world." *Henry Blackaby*

4:13 Although God assured the prophet Jeremiah that He formed him, knew him, sanctified and ordained him, he still was paralyzed by the fear of man (Jer. 1:5,6). When the fear of man seeks to paralyze us, we must stop saying "I cannot speak," and instead say, "I can do all things through Christ who strengthens me." This verse obliterates every excuse we try to offer for not preaching the gospel to every creature. It counters the fear of man, the fear of rejection, the fear of public speaking, and the fear of offering a stranger a gospel tract.

Hudson Taylor said, "All God's giants have been weak men, who did great things for God because they believed that God would be with them."

Defending Salvation Through Christ Alone

By Jason Carlson

Don't all religions lead to God? Isn't one faith as good as another? Isn't it arrogant to say that only one religion leads to salvation? These are some common questions that people in our pluralistic world are wrestling with today. In a world full of religious options, many people of goodwill, including evangelical Christians, have trouble with the idea that there would only be one way to enter into a saving relationship with God. However, this is exactly what God's Word tells us: salvation is only found in a relationship with Jesus Christ (Acts 4:12; John 14:6).

The problem that many Christians often face when communicating this biblical truth is that many non-Christians will simply reply, "But I don't believe the Bible." So, how can we as Christians convey this critical biblical truth to people who don't necessarily accept the Scriptures as God's word? This is where a simple little philosophical argument can be extremely helpful; it's called the "Law of Non-Contradiction."

In the philosophical discipline of Logic, there are numerous rules that govern the process of forming a coherent and rational argument. One of these rules is the Law of Non-Contradiction. The Law of Non-Contradiction formally stated is that "A cannot be non-A." In plain language, this simply means that something that is true cannot be anything but that thing which is true. For example, if it is true that Jason Carlson alone wrote this article, nobody but Jason Carlson could have written this article. Either Jason Carlson alone wrote it or he did not. To say that Jason Carlson and Jane Doe both individually wrote this article would be a violation of the Law of Non-Contradiction.

When it comes to the questions of religious pluralism and promoting the Christian claim of exclusivity (salvation is found in Jesus Christ alone), the Law of Non-Contradiction can serve as a valuable resource in a Christian's apologetic tool-box. Here's how it works:

All religions in the world make absolute truth claims regarding the way to salvation...

- Christians proclaim that salvation comes by grace through faith in Jesus Christ.
- Hindus claim that salvation (liberation) is achieved when a person transcends this world of illusion by building up enough positive karma (good works) to escape the cycle of reincarnation.
- Muslims state that the possibility of salvation* results from submitting one's life to Allah and faithfully carrying-out the Five Pillars of Islam.
- Buddhists say that salvation (Nirvana) is the result of detaching one's self from the desires of the physical, material world.

Each of the world's religions claims to promote the true path to salvation, but each of these religions provides a distinct and contrary path from all of the others. Thus, one of these paths to salvation is true, or none of them are true, but they cannot all be true at the same time; this would be a violation of the Law of Non-Contradiction.

For the Christian who uses this apologetic argument in response to the questions of religious pluralism and to promote the Christian claim of exclusivity, it is important to understand that this argument does not prove that Jesus is the one true path to salvation. What this argument demonstrates is that from a philosophical standpoint, it is irrational to claim that all religions are equally valid paths to salvation. The idea of religious pluralism ("all roads lead to God") is philosophically invalid according to the Law of Non-Contradiction.

In order to show that Jesus Christ is the one true way to salvation, Christians must be ready (1 Pet. 3:15) with other apologetic tools: arguments for the historicity of Jesus Christ, the reliability of the gospels, and the resurrection of Jesus Christ, etc.

*In Islam there is no certainty of salvation. Allah, the god of Islam, is capricious by nature and therefore even the most devout Muslim has no certainty of salvation. The only certainty of salvation in Islam is to die as a martyr in Jihad or holy war.

Colossians

Greeting

1 Paul, an apostle of Jesus Christ by the
will of God, and Timothy our brother,

2 To the saints and faithful brethren in
Christ *who are* in Colosse:

Grace to you and peace from God our
Father and the Lord Jesus Christ.[a]

Their Faith in Christ

3 We give thanks to the God and Father
of our Lord Jesus Christ, praying always for
you, 4 since we heard of your faith in Christ
Jesus and of your love for all the saints;
5 because of the hope which is laid up for
you in heaven, of which you heard before
in the word of the truth of the gospel,
6 which has come to you, as *it has* also in
all the world, and is bringing forth fruit,[a]
as *it is* also among you since the day you
heard and knew the grace of God in truth;
7 as you also learned from Epaphras, our
dear fellow servant, who is a faithful minister of Christ on your behalf, 8 who also
declared to us your love in the Spirit.

Preeminence of Christ

9 For this reason we also, since the day
we heard it, do not cease to pray for you,
and to ask that you may be filled with the
knowledge of His will in all wisdom and
spiritual understanding; 10 that you may
walk worthy of the Lord, fully pleasing
Him, being fruitful in every good work
and increasing in the knowledge of God;
11 strengthened with all might, according
to His glorious power, for all patience and
longsuffering with joy; 12 giving thanks to
the Father who has qualified us to be partakers of the inheritance of the saints in
the light. 13 He has delivered us from the
power of darkness and conveyed *us* into
the kingdom of the Son of His love, 14 in
whom we have redemption through His
blood,[a] the forgiveness of sins.

15 He is the image of the invisible God,
the firstborn over all creation. 16 For by
Him all things were created that are in
heaven and that are on earth, visible and
invisible, whether thrones or dominions
or principalities or powers. All things were
created through Him and for Him. 17 And
He is before all things, and in Him all
things consist. 18 And He is the head of the
body, the church, who is the beginning,
the firstborn from the dead, that in all
things He may have the preeminence.

1:2 [a]NU-Text omits *and the Lord Jesus Christ.* 1:6 [a]NU-Text and M-Text add *and growing.* 1:14 [a]NU-Text and M-Text omit *through His blood.*

1:3,4 Some people applaud when sinners step forward to make a decision for Christ. It is more biblical to hold the applause until the genuineness of their repentance is evidenced by "fruit." See v. 6.

1:15,16 Was Jesus God in human form? The One who created all things and brought life into being is the Word of God, who became flesh in the person of Jesus of Nazareth (John 1:3,4,14). See Col. 2:9.

QUESTIONS & OBJECTIONS

1:20 *"I've made my peace with the 'Man upstairs.'"*

When people refer to God as "the Man upstairs," they reveal that they have no concept of (nor living relationship with) Him. They will use such words because they feel uncomfortable saying His name. Often they will have a measure of reverence for God, but not enough to obey Him. Ask if the person thinks he will go to heaven when he dies. He'll almost certainly say he will, and a little probing will reveal that he's trusting in his own goodness to save him. However, the only way sinners can have peace with the God they have offended is through the shed blood of the Savior.

Therefore, it's important to take the person through the Ten Commandments and strip him of his self-righteousness and his false sense of assurance of salvation. As you do so, you may feel bad that you are making him uncomfortable, but if you care about his eternal salvation, you must ask yourself, "Which is worse: a few moments of conviction under the sound of God's Law, or eternity in the lake of fire?" Unless there is a knowledge of sin (which comes by the Law—Rom. 7:7), there will be no repentance.

Reconciled in Christ

19For it pleased *the Father that* in Him
all the fullness should dwell, 20and by Him
to reconcile all things to Himself, by Him,
whether things on earth or things in heav-
en, having made peace through the blood
of His cross.
21And you, who once were alienated
and enemies in your mind by wicked
works, yet now He has reconciled 22in the
body of His flesh through death, to present
you holy, and blameless, and above reproach in His sight— 23if indeed you continue in the faith, grounded and steadfast,
and are not moved away from the hope of
the gospel which you heard, which was
preached to every creature under heaven,
of which I, Paul, became a minister.

Sacrificial Service for Christ

24I now rejoice in my sufferings for
you, and fill up in my flesh what is lacking
in the afflictions of Christ, for the sake of
His body, which is the church, 25of which
I became a minister according to the
stewardship from God which was given
to me for you, to fulfill the word of God,
26the mystery which has been hidden from
ages and from generations, but now has
been revealed to His saints. 27To them God
willed to make known what are the riches
of the glory of this mystery among the
Gentiles: which[a] is Christ in you, the hope
of glory. 28Him we preach, warning every
man and teaching every man in all wisdom, that we may present every man perfect in Christ Jesus. 29To this *end* I also labor, striving according to His working
which works in me mightily.

Not Philosophy but Christ

2 For I want you to know what a great
conflict I have for you and those in
Laodicea, and *for* as many as have not
seen my face in the flesh, 2that their hearts
may be encouraged, being knit together
in love, and *attaining* to all riches of the
full assurance of understanding, to the
knowledge of the mystery of God, both of
the Father and[a] of Christ, 3in whom are
hidden all the treasures of wisdom and
knowledge.
4Now this I say lest anyone should de-

1:27 [a]M-Text reads *who.* 2:2 [a]NU-Text omits *both of the Father and.*

1:21 This runs contrary to the secular concept of man's relationship to his Creator. We are alienated from God, separated from Him by our iniquities (Isa. 59:2). We are His enemies, and our works are wicked.

1:27 Salvation doesn't come from *what* we know, but from *Who* we know. Jesus said, "This is eternal life, that they may know You, the only true God, and Jesus Christ whom You have sent" (John 17:3).

ceive you with persuasive words. 5For
though I am absent in the flesh, yet I am
with you in spirit, rejoicing to see your
good order and the steadfastness of your
faith in Christ.

6As you therefore have received Christ
Jesus the Lord, so walk in Him, 7rooted
and built up in Him and established in the
faith, as you have been taught, abounding in it[a] with thanksgiving.

8Beware lest anyone cheat you through
philosophy and empty deceit, according
to the tradition of men, according to the
basic principles of the world, and not according to Christ. 9For in Him dwells all
the fullness of the Godhead bodily; 10and
you are complete in Him, who is the
head of all principality and power.

Not Legalism but Christ

11In Him you were also circumcised
with the circumcision made without
hands, by putting off the body of the sins[a]
of the flesh, by the circumcision of Christ,
12buried with Him in baptism, in which
you also were raised with *Him* through
faith in the working of God, who raised
Him from the dead. 13And you, being dead
in your trespasses and the uncircumcision of your flesh, He has made alive together with Him, having forgiven you all
trespasses, 14having wiped out the handwriting of requirements that was against
us, which was contrary to us. And He has
taken it out of the way, having nailed it to
the cross. 15Having disarmed principalities and powers, He made a public spectacle of them, triumphing over them in it.

16So let no one judge you in food or in
drink, or regarding a festival or a new

2:7 [a]NU-Text omits *in it*. 2:11 [a]NU-Text omits *of the sins*.

1:28 Our primary task. A lighthouse keeper gained a reputation as being a very kind man. He would give free fuel to ships that miscalculated the amount of fuel needed to reach their destination port. One night during a storm, lightning struck his lighthouse and put out his light. He immediately turned on his generator but it soon ran out of fuel—and he had given all his reserves to passing ships. During the dark night, a ship struck the rocks and many lives were lost.

At his trial, the judge knew of the lighthouse keeper's reputation as a kind man and wept as he gave sentence. He accused the lighthouse keeper of neglecting his primary responsibility: to keep the light shining.

The Church can so often get caught up in legitimate acts of kindness—standing for political righteousness, feeding the hungry, etc.—but our primary task is to warn sinners of danger. We are to keep the light of the gospel shining so sinners can avoid the jagged-edged rocks of wrath and escape being eternally damned.

My friend, I stand in judgment now,
and feel that you're to blame somehow.
On earth I walked with you by day,
and never did you show the way.

You knew the Savior in truth and glory,
But never did you tell the story.
My knowledge then was very dim.
You could have led me safe to Him.
Though we lived together, here on earth,
you never told me of the second birth.
And now I stand before eternal hell,
because of heaven's glory you did not tell!
(Anonymous)

"The only way to turn back darkness is to let the radiant light of the gospel shine." *Greg Laurie*

"Each person we meet on a daily basis who does not know Christ is hell-bound. That may make some folks bristle—but it's a fact. When we refuse to warn people that their actions and lifestyles have eternal consequences, we're not doing them any favors. If everybody feels good about his or her sin, why would anyone repent?" *Franklin Graham*

2:9 Was Jesus God in human form? Some may ask how Jesus could be both God and man. It has been well said that when God, the Creator and Sustainer of the universe, became a man, He didn't cease to be God. He created a body, and then filled that body as a hand fills a glove (Heb. 10:5). See 1 Tim. 3:16.

2:16 *Freedom from Sabbath-keeping*

Some today insist that Christians must keep the Sabbath day, that those who worship on the first day of the week (Sunday) are in great error. They reason that "Sun-day" comes from the pagan worship of the Sun god, that Jesus and Paul kept the Sabbath day as an example for us to follow, and that the Roman Catholic church is responsible for the change in the day of worship. Those who continue to worship on Sunday will receive the mark of the beast.

Let's briefly look at these arguments. First, nowhere does the Fourth Commandment say that Christians are to *worship* on the Sabbath. It commands that we *rest* on that day: "Remember the Sabbath day, to keep it holy. Six days shall you labor and do all your work, but the seventh day is the Sabbath of the LORD your God. In it you shall do no work...For in six days the LORD made the heavens and the earth, the sea, and all that is in them, and rested the seventh day. Therefore the LORD blessed the Sabbath day and hallowed it" (Exod. 20:8–11).

Sabbath-keepers worship on Saturday. However, the word "Satur-day" comes from the Latin for "Saturn's day," a pagan day of worship of the planet Saturn (astrology).

If a Christian's salvation depends upon his keeping a certain day, surely God would have told us. At one point, the apostles gathered specifically to discuss the relationship of believers to the Law of Moses. Acts chapter 15 was God's opportunity to make His will clear to His children. All He had to do to save millions from damnation was say, "Remember to keep the Sabbath holy," and millions of Christ-centered, God-loving, Bible-believing Christians would have gladly kept it. Instead, the only commands the apostles gave were to "abstain from things offered to idols, from blood, from things strangled, and from sexual immorality" (Acts 15:29).

There isn't even one command in the New Testament for Christians to keep the Sabbath holy. In fact, we are told not to let others judge us regarding Sabbaths (Col. 2:16), and that man was not made for the Sabbath, but the Sabbath for man (Mark 2:27). The Sabbath was given as a sign to Israel (Exod. 31:13–17); nowhere is it given as a sign to the Church. Thousands of years after the Commandment was given, we can still see the sign that separates Israel from the world—they continue to set aside the Sabbath.

The apostles came together on the first day of the week to break bread (Acts 20:7). The collection was taken on the first day of the week (1 Cor. 16:2). When do Sabbath-keepers gather together to break bread or take up the collection? It is not on the same day as the early Church. They tell us that the Roman Catholic church changed their day of worship from Saturday to Sunday, but what has that got to do with the disciples keeping the first day of the week? That was the Roman Catholic church in the early centuries, not the Church of the Book of Acts.

Romans 14:5–10 tells us that one man esteems one day of the week above another; another esteems every day alike. Then Scripture tells us that everyone should be fully persuaded in his own mind. We are not to judge each other regarding the day on which we worship.

Jesus did keep the Sabbath. He had to keep the whole Law to be the perfect sacrifice. The Bible makes it clear that the Law has been satisfied in Christ. The reason Paul went to the synagogue each Sabbath wasn't to keep the Law; that would have been contrary to everything he taught about being saved by grace alone (Eph. 2:8,9). It was so he could preach the gospel to the Jews, as evident in the Book of Acts. Paul had an incredible evangelistic zeal for Israel to be saved (Rom. 10:1). To the Jew he became as a Jew, that he might win the Jews (1 Cor. 9:19,20). That meant he went to where they gathered on the day they gathered —not to keep the law, but to preach the gospel to them. He also went to anywhere people were gathered at any time (marketplace, riverbank, etc.) to preach the gospel.

D. L. Moody said, "The Law can only chase a man to Calvary, no further." Christ redeemed us from the curse of the Law so we are no longer in bondage to it. If we try to keep one part of the Law (even out of love for God), we are obligated to keep the whole Law (Gal. 3:10)—all 613 precepts.

If those who insist on keeping the Sabbath were as zealous about the salvation of the lost as they are about other Christians keeping the Sabbath, we would see revival.

moon or sabbaths, [17]which are a shadow of things to come, but the substance is of Christ. [18]Let no one cheat you of your reward, taking delight in *false* humility and worship of angels, intruding into those things which he has not[a] seen, vainly puffed up by his fleshly mind, [19]and not holding fast to the Head, from whom all

2:18 [a]NU-Text omits *not*.

the body, nourished and knit together by
joints and ligaments, grows with the increase *that is* from God.
[20]Therefore,[a] if you died with Christ
from the basic principles of the world,
why, as *though* living in the world, do you
subject yourselves to regulations— [21]"Do
not touch, do not taste, do not handle,"
[22]which all concern things which perish
with the using—according to the commandments and doctrines of men? [23]These
things indeed have an appearance of wisdom in self-imposed religion, *false* humility, and neglect of the body, *but are* of no
value against the indulgence of the flesh.

Not Carnality but Christ

3 If then you were raised with Christ,
seek those things which are above,
where Christ is, sitting at the right hand
of God. [2]Set your mind on things above,
not on things on the earth. [3]For you died,
and your life is hidden with Christ in God.
[4]When Christ *who is* our life appears, then
you also will appear with Him in glory.
[5]Therefore put to death your members
which are on the earth: fornication, uncleanness, passion, evil desire, and covetousness, which is idolatry. [6]Because of
these things the wrath of God is coming
upon the sons of disobedience, [7]in which
you yourselves once walked when you
lived in them.
[8]But now you yourselves are to put off
all these: anger, wrath, malice, blasphemy,
filthy language out of your mouth. [9]Do
not lie to one another, since you have put
off the old man with his deeds, [10]and
have put on the new *man* who is renewed
in knowledge according to the image of
Him who created him, [11]where there is
neither Greek nor Jew, circumcised nor
uncircumcised, barbarian, Scythian, slave
nor free, but Christ *is* all and in all.

Character of the New Man

[12]Therefore, as *the* elect of God, holy

The Function of the Law

2:21 Some may wonder whether using the Law in evangelism produces legalism. When the Law is used to show a sinner that sin is "exceedingly sinful"—that nothing can commend him to God—he clings to the cross knowing that he is saved by grace and grace alone. This knowledge gives the Christian the understanding that even after a lifetime of good works, fasting, praying, seeking the lost, etc., his "works" don't commend him to God; he is still saved by grace and grace alone.

However, when the Law *isn't* used before the cross, and a sinner simply makes a "decision for Christ," he comes with a lack of understanding about the true nature of sin. After his commitment, he thinks that his good works, his fasting, praying, evangelism, etc., commend him to God. He is the one who thinks that what he eats, what he wears, and what he does become relevant to his salvation. He is the one who is liable to say "do not touch, do not taste, do not handle"—the one who becomes "legalistic." Using the Law in evangelism before the cross liberates a new convert from legalism.

Robbie Flockhart, when he preached in the streets of Edinburgh, used to say, "You must preach the Law, for the gospel is a silken thread and you cannot get it into the hearts of men unless you have made a way for it with a sharp needle—the sharp needle of the Law will pull the silken thread of the gospel after it."

2:20 [a]NU-Text and M-Text omit *Therefore.*

2:16 "I am no preacher of the old legal Sabbath. I am a preacher of the gospel. The Sabbath of the Jew is to him a task; the Lord's Day of the Christian, the first day of the week, is to him a joy, a day of rest, of peace, and of thanksgiving. And if you Christian men can earnestly drive away all distractions, so that you can really rest today, it will be good for your bodies, good for your souls, good mentally, good spiritually, good temporally, and good eternally." *Charles Spurgeon*

3:3 "There was a day when I died, utterly died, died to George Mueller, his opinions, preferences, tastes, and will—died to the world, its approval or censure—died to the approval or blame even of my brethren and friends—and since then I have only to show myself approved to God." *George Mueller*

3:6 The Bible calls us children of disobedience. Children know naturally how to be selfish and lie. Rebellion is rooted deep in the human heart until we are born again and become children of God (John 1:12).

and beloved, put on tender mercies, kindness, humility, meekness, longsuffering;
13bearing with one another, and forgiving
one another, if anyone has a complaint
against another; even as Christ forgave
you, so you also *must do.* 14But above all
these things put on love, which is the bond
of perfection. 15And let the peace of God
rule in your hearts, to which also you
were called in one body; and be thankful.
16Let the word of Christ dwell in you
richly in all wisdom, teaching and ad-
monishing one another in psalms and
hymns and spiritual songs, singing with
grace in your hearts to the Lord. 17And
whatever you do in word or deed, *do* all
in the name of the Lord Jesus, giving
thanks to God the Father through Him.

The Christian Home

18Wives, submit to your own husbands,
as is fitting in the Lord.

19Husbands, love your wives and do
not be bitter toward them.

20Children, obey your parents in all
things, for this is well pleasing to the Lord.

21Fathers, do not provoke your children, lest they become discouraged.

22Bondservants, obey in all things your
masters according to the flesh, not with
eyeservice, as men-pleasers, but in sincerity of heart, fearing God. 23And whatever
you do, do it heartily, as to the Lord and
not to men, 24knowing that from the Lord
you will receive the reward of the inheritance; for[a] you serve the Lord Christ. 25But
he who does wrong will be repaid for what
he has done, and there is no partiality.

4 Masters, give your bondservants what
is just and fair, knowing that you also
have a Master in heaven.

Christian Graces

2Continue earnestly in prayer, being
vigilant in it with thanksgiving; 3mean-
while praying also for us, that God would
open to us a door for the word, to speak
the mystery of Christ, for which I am also
in chains, 4that I may make it manifest, as
I ought to speak.

> I am told that Christians do not love each other. I am very sorry if that be true, but I rather doubt it, for I suspect that those who do not love each other are not Christians.
>
> **CHARLES SPURGEON**

5Walk in wisdom toward those *who
are* outside, redeeming the time. 6*Let* your
speech always *be* with grace, seasoned with
salt, that you may know how you ought
to answer each one.

Final Greetings

7Tychicus, a beloved brother, faithful
minister, and fellow servant in the Lord,
will tell you all the news about me. 8I am
sending him to you for this very purpose,
that he[a] may know your circumstances

3:24 [a]NU-Text omits *for.* 4:8 [a]NU-Text reads *you may know our circumstances and he may.*

3:10 Feminists bristle at the Bible's statement that God made man in *His* image. This verse doesn't mean that God is a man, or that He looks like man (John 4:24). It means that when God made man and woman, He endowed them with a mind, emotions, and will. Humans are rational, moral beings with an inherent God-consciousness. However, in revealing Himself to mankind, God describes Himself in the male gender using terms such as Father, Son, Bridegroom, etc. Those who consider God to be female and call Him "Mother" are engaging in idolatry. To change who God has revealed Himself to be is to create a god in their own image.

4:3,4 Paul asks the Colossian church to pray that God would open doors of opportunity for him to evangelize. Reaching out to the unsaved was the apostle's number one priority (see Rom. 9:1–3). He often uses the phrase "as I ought to speak." He didn't see evangelism as a ministry only for people with a "gift" to reach the unsaved; he saw it as a moral responsibility, as each of us should. The only "gift" we need for evangelizing is the Holy Spirit, and every born-again believer has received Him.

and comfort your hearts, 9with Onesimus,
a faithful and beloved brother, who is *one*
of you. They will make known to you all
things which *are happening* here.

. . . .

For scientific facts in the Bible,
see Heb. 11:3 comment.

. . . .

10Aristarchus my fellow prisoner greets
you, with Mark the cousin of Barnabas
(about whom you received instructions:
if he comes to you, welcome him), 11and
Jesus who is called Justus. These *are my*
only fellow workers for the kingdom of
God who are of the circumcision; they
have proved to be a comfort to me.
12Epaphras, who is *one* of you, a bondservant of Christ, greets you, always laboring fervently for you in prayers, that you
may stand perfect and complete[a] in all the
will of God. 13For I bear him witness that
he has a great zeal[a] for you, and those who
are in Laodicea, and those in Hierapolis.
14Luke the beloved physician and Demas
greet you. 15Greet the brethren who are
in Laodicea, and Nymphas and the church
that *is* in his[a] house.

Closing Exhortations and Blessing

16Now when this epistle is read among
you, see that it is read also in the church
of the Laodiceans, and that you likewise
read the *epistle* from Laodicea. 17And say
to Archippus, "Take heed to the ministry
which you have received in the Lord, that
you may fulfill it."
18This salutation by my own hand—
Paul. Remember my chains. Grace *be* with
you. Amen.

4:12 [a]NU-Text reads *fully assured.* 4:13 [a]NU-Text reads *concern.* 4:15 [a]NU-Text reads *Nympha…her house.*

4:4 Witnessing to telemarketers. If you are ever bugged by telemarketers, take the opportunity to share your faith. Simply say, "May I ask *you* a question?" Telemarketers will usually say yes. Ask, "Have you kept the Ten Commandments?" Then ask, "Have you ever told a lie?" Most admit to at least telling "fibs" or "white lies." When they admit it, ask what that makes them. If they refuse to call themselves a liar, say, "If *I* told a lie, what would I be called?" When they say, "Liar," ask, "Have you ever stolen something, even if it's small?" Be gentle and loving in your tone. Then say, "Jesus said that if you look with lust, you commit adultery in your heart. Have you ever looked with lust?"

Don't be afraid to inquire how they will do on Judgment Day—will they be innocent or guilty…heaven or hell? The worst thing that can happen is that they hang up in your ear. If that happens, you can rejoice that they were convicted enough to do so. You not only had the privilege of planting the seed of God's Word in the heart of a stranger, but you proved yourself to be faithful to the Lord, you conquered the fear of man, and now you can rejoice that you were rejected for the sake of righteousness. If they hang up, spend a moment in prayer for them. If they are open to hearing more, take them through the cross, repentance, and faith. Ask if they have a Bible at home, encourage them to read it daily, and then thank them for listening to you.

4:5,6 This is the spirit in which we should share our faith. See 1 Thess. 5:14.

4:12 Transforming prayer. "Prayer can move mountains. It can change human hearts, families, neighborhoods, cities, and nations. It's the ultimate source of power because it is, in reality, the power of Almighty God.

"Prayer can do what political action cannot, what education cannot, what military might cannot, and what planning committees cannot. All these are impotent by comparison.

"By prayer the kingdom of God is built, and by prayer the kingdom of Satan is destroyed. Where there is no prayer, there are no great works, and there is no building of the kingdom. Where there is much prayer and fervent prayer, there are great gains for the kingdom: God's rule is established, His power is directed, His will is done, society is transformed, lost persons are saved, and saints are enabled to 'stand against the devil's schemes' (Eph. 6:11). If that isn't enough to compel us to 'devote [ourselves] to prayer' and 'always [wrestle] in prayer' (Col. 4:2,12), I don't know what is!" *Alvin J. Vander Griend*, "Your Prayers Matter," *Discipleship Journal*

The Resurrection:

Does Circumstantial Evidence Confirm It?

Timothy McVeigh, the man behind the Oklahoma City bombing,...received a lethal injection for killing 168 innocent people, even though no one saw him commit this heinous crime. All the evidence against McVeigh was circumstantial.

Indirect testimony: That's what circumstantial evidence is. It's an accumulation of facts from which one can draw intelligent conclusions.

As a newspaper reporter covering the courts, former journalist Lee Strobel saw how circumstantial evidence is used to expose what really happened during a crime. So, in the midst of a spiritual quest, Strobel began to wonder: Could circumstantial evidence verify that the resurrection of Christ really happened?

Well, he took his question to philosopher J. P. Moreland. In a challenging voice, Strobel asked Moreland: "Can you give me five pieces of solid circumstantial evidence that convince you Jesus rose from the dead?"

Certainly, Moreland responded. **First**, there's the evidence of the skeptics. Some of those who were most hostile to Jesus prior to his death became his most ardent supporters afterwards.

Second, the ancient Jews had a number of immensely important religious rituals. These included the offering of animal sacrifices, obeying the Mosaic law, and keeping the Sabbath. But within five weeks of Jesus' death, more than 10,000 Jews had suddenly altered or abandoned these rituals. Moreland asked: Why would they relinquish rites that had long given them their national identity? The implication is that something enormously significant had occurred.

Third, we see the emergence of new rituals: the sacraments of Communion and Baptism. The early Jews baptized in the name of the Father, the Son, and the Holy Spirit, "which," Moreland said, "meant they had elevated Jesus to the full status of God."

Fourth, we see the rapid rise of a new church, beginning shortly after the death of Jesus. Within twenty years this new church (begun by the companions of a dead carpenter) had reached Caesar's palace in Rome, and eventually spread throughout the Roman empire.

And **fifth**, Moreland said, there's the most convincing circumstantial evidence of all: the fact that every one of Jesus' disciples was willing to suffer and die for his beliefs. These men spent the rest of their lives witnessing about Christ. They frequently went without food; they were mocked, beaten, and thrown into prison. In the end, all but one died a painful martyr's death.

Would they have done this for a lie? Of course not. They did it because they were convinced beyond a doubt that they had seen the risen Christ.

Even if we doubted 2,000-year-old evidence, we have all the circumstantial evidence we could possibly want—right in front of us. It is, Moreland said, "the ongoing encounter with the resurrected Christ that happens all over the world, in every culture, to people from all kinds of backgrounds and personalities. They all will testify that more than any single thing in their lives, Jesus Christ has changed them."

Circumstantial evidence earned Timothy McVeigh a death sentence. But sacred circumstantial evidence about the resurrection of Jesus Christ can lead all of us, including McVeigh, to a much better verdict: everlasting life in the presence of God.

From "BreakPoint with Charles Colson," April 19, 2001, reprinted with permission of Prison Fellowship, PO Box 17500, Washington, DC 20041-7500, www.pfm.org.

1 Thessalonians

Greeting

1 Paul, Silvanus, and Timothy,

To the church of the Thessalonians in God the Father and the Lord Jesus Christ:

Grace to you and peace from God our Father and the Lord Jesus Christ.[a]

Their Good Example

[2]We give thanks to God always for you all, making mention of you in our prayers, [3]remembering without ceasing your work of faith, labor of love, and patience of hope in our Lord Jesus Christ in the sight of our God and Father, [4]knowing, beloved brethren, your election by God. [5]For our gospel did not come to you in word only, but also in power, and in the Holy Spirit and in much assurance, as you know what kind of men we were among you for your sake.

[6]And you became followers of us and of the Lord, having received the word in much affliction, with joy of the Holy Spirit, [7]so that you became examples to all in Macedonia and Achaia who believe. [8]For from you the word of the Lord has sounded forth, not only in Macedonia and Achaia, but also in every place. Your faith toward God has gone out, so that we do not need to say anything. [9]For they themselves declare concerning us what manner of entry we had to you, and how you turned to God from idols to serve the living and true God, [10]and to wait for His Son from heaven, whom He raised from the dead, *even* Jesus who delivers us from the wrath to come.

Paul's Conduct

2 For you yourselves know, brethren, that our coming to you was not in vain. [2]But even[a] after we had suffered before and were spitefully treated at Philippi, as you know, we were bold in our God to speak to you the gospel of God in much conflict. [3]For our exhortation *did* not *come* from error or uncleanness, nor *was it* in deceit.

[4]But as we have been approved by

1:1 [a]NU-Text omits *from God our Father and the Lord Jesus Christ.* 2:2 [a]NU-Text and M-Text omit *even.*

1:5 God backs up His Word with power. When the unsaved ask for proof, we have it. If any person obeys the command to repent and trust Jesus Christ, he will experience the power of the gospel. God will transform him on the inside by giving him a new heart with new desires. Instead of drinking in iniquity like water, he will begin to thirst after righteousness. He will be born again. God will make him a new creature, all of which will give him "much assurance."

1:9 This reveals the essence of Paul's message to the Thessalonians. He preached against their sin of idolatry (transgression of the First and Second Commandments). This is also the essence of his message to the Athenians (see Acts 17:29).

God to be entrusted with the gospel, even
so we speak, not as pleasing men, but God
who tests our hearts. 5For neither at any
time did we use flattering words, as you
know, nor a cloak for covetousness—God
is witness. 6Nor did we seek glory from
men, either from you or from others,
when we might have made demands as
apostles of Christ. 7But we were gentle
among you, just as a nursing *mother* cherishes her own children. 8So, affectionately
longing for you, we were well pleased to
impart to you not only the gospel of God,
but also our own lives, because you had
become dear to us. 9For you remember,
brethren, our labor and toil; for laboring
night and day, that we might not be a
burden to any of you, we preached to you
the gospel of God.

10You *are* witnesses, and God *also*, how
devoutly and justly and blamelessly we behaved ourselves among you who believe;
11as you know how we exhorted, and
comforted, and charged[a] every one of you,
as a father *does* his own children, 12that
you would walk worthy of God who calls
you into His own kingdom and glory.

Their Conversion

13For this reason we also thank God
without ceasing, because when you received the word of God which you heard
from us, you welcomed *it* not *as* the word
of men, but as it is in truth, the word of
God, which also effectively works in you
who believe. 14For you, brethren, became
imitators of the churches of God which
are in Judea in Christ Jesus. For you also
suffered the same things from your own
countrymen, just as they *did* from the
Judeans, 15who killed both the Lord Jesus
and their own prophets, and have persecuted us; and they do not please God and
are contrary to all men, 16forbidding us
to speak to the Gentiles that they may be
saved, so as always to fill up *the measure
of* their sins; but wrath has come upon
them to the uttermost.

2:11 [a]NU-Text and M-Text read *implored.*

2:4 It is a great betrayal of trust to fashion our message to please men. We must never fail to call hell "hell" and sin "sin," rather than use timid clichés such as a "Christless eternity" and "indiscretions."

"Never mind *who* frowns, if God smiles." *Catherine Booth*

2:6 "The canvas never quarrels with the painter. He is free to paint on it what he likes, be it a beggar or a king. The Christian accepts any condition in life as coming from God. If he is successful, he does not boast of it. Can a brush boast that a beautiful picture has been drawn with it? Only the master painter deserves glory. Such is our relationship with Christ. A Christian seeks glory from no one." *Richard Wurmbrand*

2:8 Relationship evangelism. Don't let the common philosophy of "relationship evangelism" steal your zeal. This is the idea that you must befriend people and build a relationship before witnessing to them. If you believe that, consider two questions. First, who are the hardest people to witness to? Isn't it your unsaved relatives? Why then would we want to wait until we build relationships with people before witnessing to them? If we witness to strangers and offend them, we lose nothing. But if we have developed a good relationship with a person and offend him, we risk losing that relationship. Building relationships actually makes it harder to witness. The truth is, we often will use any excuse not to confront people with the offense of the cross, and building a rapport with them is less threatening than sharing the truth of the gospel.

The second question is, what happens to people if they die while you are taking the time to build relationships with them? There is no nice way to put it—they will go to hell for eternity if they die in their sins. They will end up in the lake of fire, so how can you even consider taking that risk?

So make it easier on yourself. Witness to strangers. Make it a way of life to witness to people you don't know, and if you must build a relationship with them, feel at liberty to build for 3 or 4 minutes until the relationship grows, then share the truth, as you should.

"You need to be the living proof of your message by the way you live, but that's not enough. Someone could watch you for the next fifty years. They are not going to say, 'Joey is such a nice guy. I'll bet Jesus died on the cross for my sins.' They won't figure that out. You have to tell them!" *Ron Hutchcraft*

2:9,10 We must strive to be devout, just, and blameless in the sight of a sinful world. God forbid that any souls should stumble because they see what they perceive to be hypocrisy in our lives.

QUESTIONS & OBJECTIONS

2:13

"There is no absolute truth. You can't be sure of anything!"

Those who say that there are no absolutes are often very adamant about their belief. If they say that they are *absolutely* sure, then they are wrong because their own statement is an absolute. If they are not 100 percent sure, then there is a chance that they are wrong and they are risking their eternal salvation by trusting in a wrong belief. God tells us that there is an objective, absolute truth that is not subject to man's interpretations or whims, on which we can base our eternity. That truth is the Word of God (John 17:7). See also Judg. 21:25 comment.

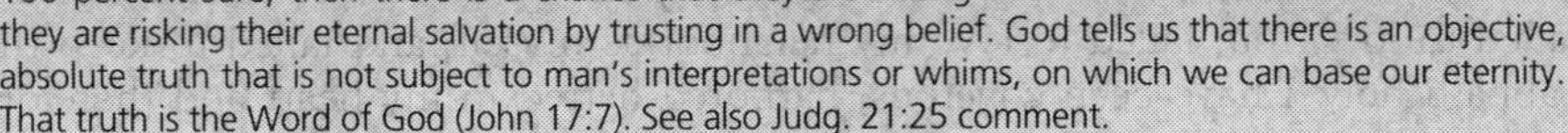

"No one can know truth except the one who obeys truth. You think you know truth. People memorize the Scriptures by the yard, but that is not a guarantee of knowing the truth. Truth is not a text. Truth is in the text, but it takes the text plus the Holy Spirit to bring truth to a human soul . . ." *A. W. Tozer*

Longing to See Them

17 But we, brethren, having been taken
away from you for a short time in presence, not in heart, endeavored more eagerly to see your face with great desire.
18 Therefore we wanted to come to you—
even I, Paul, time and again—but Satan
hindered us. 19 For what *is* our hope, or
joy, or crown of rejoicing? *Is it* not even
you in the presence of our Lord Jesus
Christ at His coming? 20 For you are our
glory and joy.

Concern for Their Faith

3 Therefore, when we could no longer
endure it, we thought it good to be
left in Athens alone, 2 and sent Timothy,
our brother and minister of God, and our
fellow laborer in the gospel of Christ, to
establish you and encourage you concerning your faith, 3 that no one should
be shaken by these afflictions; for you
yourselves know that we are appointed
to this. 4 For, in fact, we told you before
when we were with you that we would
suffer tribulation, just as it happened, and
you know. 5 For this reason, when I could
no longer endure it, I sent to know your
faith, lest by some means the tempter had
tempted you, and our labor might be in
vain.

Encouraged by Timothy

6 But now that Timothy has come to us
from you, and brought us good news of
your faith and love, and that you always
have good remembrance of us, greatly
desiring to see us, as we also *to see* you—
7 therefore, brethren, in all our affliction
and distress we were comforted concerning you by your faith. 8 For now we live,
if you stand fast in the Lord.

2:16 Some lack the fear of God and believe that it is their right to suppress the truth of God's Word. However, those who hinder the progress of the gospel will come under the severe wrath of the Almighty. It would be better that a millstone be placed around their neck and they be cast into the depths of the sea, rather than hinder a single person from coming to peace with their Creator.

We can take strong consolation in the fact that God will have His way. Whoever calls on the name of the Lord *will* be saved and the wicked *will* be punished. He has delusions of grandeur indeed who thinks he can stop the will of God from coming to pass. Though they join forces, the wicked will not go unpunished (Prov. 11:21). God will judge the world in righteousness. It would be infinitely easier to build a bacon-burger restaurant on the Temple Mount in Jerusalem than to stop God from saving those who call upon Him and from having His Day of Justice.

2:19 "Aspire to be something more than the mass of church members. Lift up your cry to God and beseech him to fire you with a nobler ambition than that which possesses the common Christian—that you may be found faithful unto God at the last, and may win many crowns for your Lord and Master, Christ." *Charles Spurgeon*

Two Prayers

"DEAR GOD, I have sinned against You by breaking Your Commandments. Despite the conscience You gave me, I have looked with lust and therefore committed adultery in my heart. I have lied, stolen, failed to love You, failed to love my neighbor as myself, and failed to keep the Sabbath holy. I have been covetous, harbored hatred in my heart and therefore been guilty of murder in Your sight. I have used Your holy name in vain, have made a god to suit myself, and because of the nature of my sin, I have dishonored my parents. If I stood before You in Your burning holiness on Judgment Day, if every secret sin I have committed and every idle word I have spoken came out as evidence of my crimes against You, I would be utterly guilty, and justly deserve hell. I am unspeakably thankful that Jesus took my place by suffering and dying on the cross. He was bruised for my iniquities. He paid my fine so that I could leave the courtroom. He revealed how much You love me. I believe that He then rose from the dead (according to the Scriptures). I now confess and forsake my sin and yield myself to Him to be my Lord and Savior. I will no longer live for myself. I present my body, soul, and spirit to You as a living sacrifice, to serve You in the furtherance of Your Kingdom. I will read Your Word daily and obey what I read. It is solely because of Calvary's cross that I will live forever. I am eternally Yours. In Jesus' name I pray. Amen."

"Choose this day whom you will serve..."

"SATAN, the Bible tells me that you are the god of this world. You are the father of lies. You deceive the nations and blind the minds of those who do not believe. God warns that I cannot enter His Kingdom because I have lied, stolen, looked with lust and therefore committed adultery in my heart. I have harbored hatred, which the Bible says is the same as murder. I have blasphemed, refused to put God first, violated the Sabbath, coveted other people's goods, dishonored my parents, and have been guilty of the sin of idolatry—I even made a god to suit myself. I did all this despite the presence of my conscience. I know that it was God who gave me life. I have seen the splendor of a sunrise. I have heard the sounds of nature. I have enjoyed pleasures of an incredible array of food, all of which came from His generous hand. I realize that if I die in my sins I will never know pleasure again. I know that Jesus Christ shed His life's blood for my sins and rose again to destroy the power of death, but today I refuse to confess and forsake my sins. On the Day of Judgment, if I am cast into the lake of fire I will have no one to blame but myself. It is not God's will that I perish. He demonstrated His love toward me through the death of His Son, who came to give me life. It was you who came to steal, kill, and destroy. You are my spiritual father. I choose to continue to serve you and do your will. This is because I love the darkness and hate the light. If I do not come to my senses, I will be eternally yours. Amen."

9For what thanks can we render to
God for you, for all the joy with which
we rejoice for your sake before our God,
10night and day praying exceedingly that
we may see your face and perfect what is
lacking in your faith?

Prayer for the Church

11Now may our God and Father Himself, and our Lord Jesus Christ, direct our
way to you. 12And may the Lord make
you increase and abound in love to one
another and to all, just as we *do* to you,
13so that He may establish your hearts
blameless in holiness before our God and
Father at the coming of our Lord Jesus
Christ with all His saints.

Plea for Purity

4 Finally then, brethren, we urge and
exhort in the Lord Jesus that you
should abound more and more, just as you
received from us how you ought to walk
and to please God; 2for you know what
commandments we gave you through
the Lord Jesus.
3For this is the will of God, your sanctification: that you should abstain from
sexual immorality; 4that each of you
should know how to possess his own vessel in sanctification and honor, 5not in
passion of lust, like the Gentiles who do
not know God; 6that no one should take
advantage of and defraud his brother in
this matter, because the Lord *is* the avenger
of all such, as we also forewarned you
and testified. 7For God did not call us to
uncleanness, but in holiness. 8Therefore
he who rejects *this* does not reject man,
but God, who has also given[a] us His Holy
Spirit.

A Brotherly and Orderly Life

9But concerning brotherly love you
have no need that I should write to you,
for you yourselves are taught by God to
love one another; 10and indeed you do so
toward all the brethren who are in all
Macedonia. But we urge you, brethren,
that you increase more and more; 11that
you also aspire to lead a quiet life, to mind
your own business, and to work with
your own hands, as we commanded you,
12that you may walk properly toward
those who are outside, and *that* you may
lack nothing.

The Comfort of Christ's Coming

13But I do not want you to be ignorant,
brethren, concerning those who have
fallen asleep, lest you sorrow as others
who have no hope. 14For if we believe that
Jesus died and rose again, even so God
will bring with Him those who sleep in
Jesus.[a]

> In proportion as a church is holy, in that proportion will its testimony for Christ be powerful.
>
> **CHARLES SPURGEON**

15For this we say to you by the word
of the Lord, that we who are alive *and* remain until the coming of the Lord will by
no means precede those who are asleep.
16For the Lord Himself will descend from
heaven with a shout, with the voice of an
archangel, and with the trumpet of God.
And the dead in Christ will rise first.
17Then we who are alive *and* remain shall
be caught up together with them in the
clouds to meet the Lord in the air. And
thus we shall always be with the Lord.
18Therefore comfort one another with
these words.

The Day of the Lord

5 But concerning the times and the seasons, brethren, you have no need that
I should write to you. 2For you yourselves

4:8 [a]NU-Text reads *who also gives.* 4:14 [a]Or *those who through Jesus sleep*

5:2 Second coming of Jesus: See Heb. 9:28.

know perfectly that the day of the Lord so comes as a thief in the night. 3For when they say, "Peace and safety!" then sudden destruction comes upon them, as labor pains upon a pregnant woman. And they shall not escape. 4But you, brethren, are not in darkness, so that this Day should overtake you as a thief. 5You are all sons of light and sons of the day. We are not of the night nor of darkness. 6Therefore let us not sleep, as others *do*, but let us watch and be sober. 7For those who sleep, sleep at night, and those who get drunk are drunk at night. 8But let us who are of the day be sober, putting on the breastplate of faith and love, and *as* a helmet the hope of salvation. 9For God did not appoint us to wrath, but to obtain salvation through our Lord Jesus Christ, 10who died for us, that whether we wake or sleep, we should live together with Him.

11Therefore comfort each other and edify one another, just as you also are doing.

Various Exhortations

12And we urge you, brethren, to recognize those who labor among you, and are over you in the Lord and admonish you, 13and to esteem them very highly in love for their work's sake. Be at peace among yourselves.

14Now we exhort you, brethren, warn those who are unruly, comfort the fainthearted, uphold the weak, be patient with all. 15See that no one renders evil for evil to anyone, but always pursue what is good both for yourselves and for all.

16Rejoice always, 17pray without ceasing, 18in everything give thanks; for this is the will of God in Christ Jesus for you.

19Do not quench the Spirit. 20Do not despise prophecies. 21Test all things; hold fast what is good. 22Abstain from every form of evil.

· · · · · ·

For how to witness to homosexuals, see 1 Tim. 1:9,10 comment.

· · · · · ·

Blessing and Admonition

23Now may the God of peace Himself sanctify you completely; and may your whole spirit, soul, and body be preserved blameless at the coming of our Lord Jesus Christ. 24He who calls you *is* faithful, who also will do *it*.

25Brethren, pray for us.

26Greet all the brethren with a holy kiss.

27I charge you by the Lord that this epistle be read to all the holy[a] brethren.

28The grace of our Lord Jesus Christ *be* with you. Amen.

5:27 [a]NU-Text omits *holy*.

5:14 This is the spirit in which we should share our faith. See 2 Tim. 2:24.

5:17 *General "Stonewall" Jackson*, one of the country's greatest generals, gives a good example of how to "pray without ceasing":

> When we take our meals, there is the grace. When I take a draught of water, I always pause... to lift up my heart to God in thanks and prayer for the water of life. Whenever I [send] a letter... I send a petition along with it, for God's blessing upon its mission and upon the person to whom it is sent.
>
> When I [open] a letter... I stop to pray to God that He may prepare me for its contents... When I go to my class-room and await the arrangement of the cadets in their places, that is my time to intercede with God for them.

5:17 "Prayers are not limited to place and time. If you are not in the right place to pray, you're not in the right place." *Chuck Missler*

"Prayer is the shield to the soul, a delight to God, and a scourge to Satan." *John Bunyan*

2 Thessalonians

Greeting

1 Paul, Silvanus, and Timothy,

To the church of the Thessalonians in
God our Father and the Lord Jesus Christ:

[2]Grace to you and peace from God our
Father and the Lord Jesus Christ.

God's Final Judgment and Glory

[3]We are bound to thank God always
for you, brethren, as it is fitting, because
your faith grows exceedingly, and the love
of every one of you all abounds toward
each other, [4]so that we ourselves boast of
you among the churches of God for your
patience and faith in all your persecutions
and tribulations that you endure, [5]*which
is* manifest evidence of the righteous judgment
of God, that you may be counted
worthy of the kingdom of God, for which
you also suffer; [6]since *it is* a righteous
thing with God to repay with tribulation
those who trouble you, [7]and to *give* you
who are troubled rest with us when the
Lord Jesus is revealed from heaven with
His mighty angels, [8]in flaming fire taking
vengeance on those who do not know
God, and on those who do not obey the
gospel of our Lord Jesus Christ. [9]These
shall be punished with everlasting destruction
from the presence of the Lord
and from the glory of His power, [10]when
He comes, in that Day, to be glorified in
His saints and to be admired among all
those who believe,[a] because our testimony
among you was believed.

[11]Therefore we also pray always for you

1:10 [a]NU-Text and M-Text read *have believed.*

1:6 The world doesn't understand why the Christian turns the other cheek. This isn't because he is weak. Rather than take the law into his own hands, he simply commits himself to "Him who judges righteously" (1 Pet. 2:23). If God sees fit to repay, He will. The Scriptures tell us, "'Vengeance is Mine, I will repay,' says the Lord" (Rom. 12:19).

1:7–9 Judgment Day: Such a thought should stir in us a passion for evangelism. It is a fearful thing to fall into the hands of the living God. For verses that warn of its reality, see 2 Tim. 4:1. See also Psa. 139:7,8 comment.

"The wrath of God does not end with death. This is a truth which the preacher cannot mention without trembling, nor without wondering that he does not tremble more. The eternity of punishment is a thought which crushes the heart. You have buried the man, but you have not buried his sins. His sins live and are immortal. They have gone before him to judgment, or they will follow after him to bear their witness as to the evil of his heart and the rebellion of his life. The Lord God is slow to anger, but when he is once aroused to it, as he will be against those who finally reject his Son, he will put forth all his omnipotence to crush his enemies." *Charles Spurgeon*

1:10 Our beliefs govern our actions. Those who don't believe that they are in danger of God's wrath will not flee from it.

that our God would count you worthy of
this calling, and fulfill all the good pleasure
of *His* goodness and the work of faith
with power, 12that the name of our Lord
Jesus Christ may be glorified in you, and
you in Him, according to the grace of our
God and the Lord Jesus Christ.

The Great Apostasy

2 Now, brethren, concerning the coming of our Lord Jesus Christ and our
gathering together to Him, we ask you,
2not to be soon shaken in mind or troubled, either by spirit or by word or by
letter, as if from us, as though the day of
Christ[a] had come. 3Let no one deceive you
by any means; for *that Day will not come*
unless the falling away comes first, and
the man of sin[a] is revealed, the son of
perdition, 4who opposes and exalts himself above all that is called God or that is
worshiped, so that he sits as God[a] in the
temple of God, showing himself that he
is God.

> I further believe, although certain persons deny it, that the influence of fear is to be exercised over the minds of men, and that it ought to operate upon the mind of the preacher himself: 'Noah . . . moved with fear, prepared an ark to the saving of his house' (Heb. 11:7).
>
> **CHARLES SPURGEON**

5Do you not remember that when I
was still with you I told you these things?
6And now you know what is restraining,
that he may be revealed in his own time.
7For the mystery of lawlessness is already
at work; only He[a] who now restrains *will
do so* until He[b] is taken out of the way.
8And then the lawless one will be revealed,
whom the Lord will consume with the
breath of His mouth and destroy with the

"I never thought much of the courage of a lion-tamer. Inside the cage he is at least safe from people."

George Bernard Shaw

brightness of His coming. 9The coming of
the *lawless one* is according to the working
of Satan, with all power, signs, and lying
wonders, 10and with all unrighteous deception among those who perish, because they did not receive the love of the
truth, that they might be saved. 11And for
this reason God will send them strong
delusion, that they should believe the lie,
12that they all may be condemned who
did not believe the truth but had pleasure
in unrighteousness.

Stand Fast

13But we are bound to give thanks to
God always for you, brethren beloved by
the Lord, because God from the beginning chose you for salvation through
sanctification by the Spirit and belief in
the truth, 14to which He called you by our

2:2 [a]NU-Text reads *the Lord.* 2:3 [a]NU-Text reads *lawlessness.* 2:4 [a]NU-Text omits *as God.* 2:7 [a]Or *he* [b]Or *he*

2:11,12 If sinners refuse to truly embrace the gospel, God in His righteousness will give them over to "strong delusion" and a "debased mind" (Rom. 1:28). Those who refuse to come to the light will be given over to darkness. See John 3:20 comment.

gospel, for the obtaining of the glory of
our Lord Jesus Christ. [15]Therefore, brethren, stand fast and hold the traditions
which you were taught, whether by word
or our epistle.

[16]Now may our Lord Jesus Christ
Himself, and our God and Father, who
has loved us and given *us* everlasting
consolation and good hope by grace,
[17]comfort your hearts and establish you in
every good word and work.

Pray for Us

3 Finally, brethren, pray for us, that
the word of the Lord may run *swiftly*
and be glorified, just as *it is* with you,
[2]and that we may be delivered from unreasonable and wicked men; for not all
have faith.

[3]But the Lord is faithful, who will establish you and guard *you* from the evil
one. [4]And we have confidence in the
Lord concerning you, both that you do
and will do the things we command you.

[5]Now may the Lord direct your hearts
into the love of God and into the patience
of Christ.

Warning Against Idleness

[6]But we command you, brethren, in
the name of our Lord Jesus Christ, that
you withdraw from every brother who
walks disorderly and not according to the
tradition which he[a] received from us. [7]For
you yourselves know how you ought to
follow us, for we were not disorderly
among you; [8]nor did we eat anyone's bread
free of charge, but worked with labor and
toil night and day, that we might not be
a burden to any of you, [9]not because we
do not have authority, but to make ourselves an example of how you should follow us.

[10]For even when we were with you,
we commanded you this: If anyone will
not work, neither shall he eat. [11]For we
hear that there are some who walk among
you in a disorderly manner, not working
at all, but are busybodies. [12]Now those
who are such we command and exhort
through our Lord Jesus Christ that they
work in quietness and eat their own bread.

Archaeological discoveries confirm the Bible's account of historical events. See Matt. 26:54 comment.

[13]But *as for* you, brethren, do not grow
weary *in* doing good. [14]And if anyone does
not obey our word in this epistle, note
that person and do not keep company with
him, that he may be ashamed. [15]Yet do not
count *him* as an enemy, but admonish
him as a brother.

Benediction

[16]Now may the Lord of peace Himself
give you peace always in every way. The
Lord *be* with you all.

[17]The salutation of Paul with my own
hand, which is a sign in every epistle; so
I write.

[18]The grace of our Lord Jesus Christ *be*
with you all. Amen.

3:6 [a]NU-Text and M-Text read *they*.

3:1 Paul again requests prayer for the evangelistic enterprise. "The word of the Lord" refers to the salvation message. "Unreasonable and wicked men" (v. 2) continually seek to stop the gospel from being able to "run swiftly."

Ten Reasons Why Christians Should Share the Gospel

1. We have been commanded to do so.
We have been commanded to preach the gospel to all creation. Jesus said, "Go into all the world and preach the gospel to every creature" (Mark 16:15). We need no other reason.

2. Hell exists.
Jesus said, "But I will show you whom you should fear: Fear Him who, after He has killed, has power to cast into hell; yes, I say to you, fear Him!" (Luke 12:5). If hell didn't exist, we would have a legitimate excuse for passivity. But we have God's Word (and reason) to tell us what awaits guilty sinners. How coldhearted would we be to not warn of its reality!

3. We strive to love our neighbor as much as we love ourselves.
A firefighter rescuing people from a burning building may be fearful and prefer to be home with his family, but he ignores his fears and denies himself. Like him, our thoughts are not on ourselves but on the fate of the perishing. "And on some have compassion, making a distinction; but others save with fear, pulling them out of the fire, hating even the garment defiled by the flesh" (Jude 22,23).

4. Obedience is evidence of salvation.
The Bible says that Jesus is the author of eternal salvation to those who *obey* Him (see Heb. 5:9). We are not saved by our obedience; we are obedient *because* we are saved. Jesus said, "But why do you call Me 'Lord, Lord,' and not do the things which I say?" (Luke 6:46).

5. To remain in silence is a sin.
As soon as the Holy Spirit was given, the apostles began to preach the gospel. God had granted everlasting life to dying humanity! They could not stay in the Upper Room because God's love provoked them to reach out to the lost. "To him who knows to do good and does not do it, to him it is sin" (James 4:17).

6. Evangelism deepens our walk with God.
Nothing teaches a fisherman like fishing. Interacting with the lost results in greater confidence and faith in God. ". . . hearing of your love and faith which you have toward the Lord Jesus and toward all the saints, that the sharing of your faith may become effective by the acknowledgment of every good thing which is in you in Christ Jesus" (Philem. 4–6).

7. It causes us to search the Scriptures.
Wanting to know how to answer every man will send us to God's Word. "Be diligent to present yourself approved to God, a worker who does not need to be ashamed, rightly dividing the word of truth" (2 Tim. 2:15).

8. It deepens our gratitude for the cross.
As we continually preach the cross, it will deepen our understanding of what God did for us in Christ. We will find ourselves practicing what we preach, so we will be frequently thinking about the cross. "I determined not to know anything among you except Jesus Christ and Him crucified" (1 Cor. 2:2).

9. It deepens our prayer life.
We reveal our love for the lost by pondering their fate, and as a result we cannot help but cry out to God for them. "My heart's desire and prayer to God for Israel is that they may be saved (Rom. 10:1).

Our fears and sense of inadequacy will also drive us to our knees—the safest place for a Christian. "Therefore I take pleasure in infirmities, in reproaches, in needs, in persecutions, in distresses, for Christ's sake. For when I am weak, then I am strong" (2 Cor. 12:10).

10. We have been commanded to imitate Paul.
Paul showed his love for God and for sinners by his obedience to the Great Commission. ". . . I also please all men in all things, not seeking my own profit, but the profit of many, that they may be saved. Imitate me, just as I also imitate Christ" (1 Cor. 10:33—11:1).

1 Timothy

Greeting

1 Paul, an apostle of Jesus Christ, by
the commandment of God our Savior
and the Lord Jesus Christ, our hope,

2 To Timothy, a true son in the faith:

Grace, mercy, *and* peace from God our
Father and Jesus Christ our Lord.

No Other Doctrine

3 As I urged you when I went into
Macedonia—remain in Ephesus that you
may charge some that they teach no other
doctrine, 4 nor give heed to fables and endless genealogies, which cause disputes
rather than godly edification which is in
faith. 5 Now the purpose of the commandment is love from a pure heart, *from* a
good conscience, and *from* sincere faith,
6 from which some, having strayed, have
turned aside to idle talk, 7 desiring to be
teachers of the law, understanding neither what they say nor the things which
they affirm.

8 But we know that the law *is* good if
one uses it lawfully, 9 knowing this: that
the law is not made for a righteous person, but for *the* lawless and insubordinate, for *the* ungodly and for sinners, for
the unholy and profane, for murderers of
fathers and murderers of mothers, for
manslayers, 10 for fornicators, for sodomites, for kidnappers, for liars, for perjurers, and if there is any other thing that is
contrary to sound doctrine, 11 according
to the glorious gospel of the blessed God
which was committed to my trust.

Glory to God for His Grace

12 And I thank Christ Jesus our Lord
who has enabled me, because He counted
me faithful, putting *me* into the ministry,
13 although I was formerly a blasphemer,

1:5 In the context of this passage (vv. 5–11), Paul is speaking of the Law of God when he refers to the "commandment." Its purpose is to bring a sinner to genuine conversion, with the evidence of the fruit of love from a pure heart, a good conscience, and true faith. The purpose of a mirror is to send us to the water that we might be made clean. The purpose of the Law is to reveal sin and send us to be washed clean by the blood of Jesus Christ.

1:8 The way to use the Law "lawfully" is to use it in evangelism as a "tutor" to bring sinners to Christ (Gal. 3:24). See vv. 9,10.

"I have found by long experience that the severest threatenings of the Law of God have a prominent place in leading men to Christ. They must see themselves lost before they will cry for mercy. They will not escape from danger until they see it." *A. B. Earle*

1:12 Here are three wonderful truths for evangelism:

1. God has enabled you to be His witness (Acts 1:8).
2. God considers you faithful, entrusting you with the stewardship of the gospel (1 Cor. 9:16,17).
3. God has placed you into the ministry (Mark 16:15).

THE FUNCTION OF THE LAW

1:8 "As that which is straight discovers that which is crooked, so there is no way of coming to that knowledge of sin which is necessary to repentance, but by comparing our hearts and lives with the Law.

"Paul had a very quick and piercing judgment and yet never attained the right knowledge of indwelling sin till the Spirit by the Law made it known to him. Though brought up at the feet of Gamaliel, a doctor of the Law, though himself a strict observer of it, yet without the Law. He had the letter of the Law, but he had not the spiritual meaning of it—the shell, but not the kernel. He had the Law in his hand and in his head, but he had it not in his heart. But when the commandment came (not to his eyes only, but to his heart), sin revived, as the dust in a room rises when the sunshine is let into it. Paul then saw that in sin which he had never seen before—sin in its consequences, sin with death at the heels of it, sin and the curse entailed upon it. 'The Spirit, by the commandment, convinced me that I was in a state of sin, and in a state of death because of sin.' Of this excellent use is the Law; it is a lamp and a light; it opens the eyes, prepares the way of the Lord." *Matthew Henry*

a persecutor, and an insolent man; but I
obtained mercy because I did *it* ignorantly in unbelief. 14And the grace of our
Lord was exceedingly abundant, with
faith and love which are in Christ Jesus.
15This *is* a faithful saying and worthy of
all acceptance, that Christ Jesus came
into the world to save sinners, of whom I
am chief. 16However, for this reason I obtained mercy, that in me first Jesus Christ
might show all longsuffering, as a pattern
to those who are going to believe on Him
for everlasting life. 17Now to the King eternal, immortal, invisible, to God who alone
is wise,[a] *be* honor and glory forever and
ever. Amen.

Fight the Good Fight

18This charge I commit to you, son
Timothy, according to the prophecies
previously made concerning you, that by
them you may wage the good warfare,
19having faith and a good conscience,
which some having rejected, concerning
the faith have suffered shipwreck, 20of
whom are Hymenaeus and Alexander,
whom I delivered to Satan that they may
learn not to blaspheme.

Pray for All Men

2 Therefore I exhort first of all that supplications, prayers, intercessions, *and*
giving of thanks be made for all men,
2for kings and all who are in authority,
that we may lead a quiet and peaceable
life in all godliness and reverence. 3For
this *is* good and acceptable in the sight
of God our Savior, 4who desires all men
to be saved and to come to the knowledge of the truth. 5For *there is* one God
and one Mediator between God and
men, *the* Man Christ Jesus, 6who gave
Himself a ransom for all, to be testified in
due time, 7for which I was appointed a
preacher and an apostle—I am speaking
the truth in Christ[a] *and* not lying—a
teacher of the Gentiles in faith and truth.

Men and Women in the Church

8I desire therefore that the men pray
everywhere, lifting up holy hands, without wrath and doubting; 9in like manner
also, that the women adorn themselves in
modest apparel, with propriety and moderation, not with braided hair or gold or

1:17 [a]NU-Text reads *to the only God.* 2:7 [a]NU-Text omits *in Christ.*

1:18 For instructions for the soldier of Christ, see 1 Tim. 6:12; 2 Tim. 2:3,4; Eph. 6:11–17.

2:1 Intercessory prayer. "God gave us intercessory prayer so we could partner with Him in transforming society, saving the lost, and establishing His kingdom. To be sure, God is perfectly capable of doing these things without us. He is all-wise, full of love, and almighty. In His wisdom He always knows what is best. In His love He always chooses what is best. And in His power He is able to do what is best. He doesn't need us. Nevertheless, in His sovereign good pleasure, He has chosen to involve us, through our prayers, in accomplishing His will. Our intercessory prayers are important to God; they should also be important to us." *Alvin J. Vander Griend*, "Your Prayers Matter," *Discipleship Journal*

2:4 Salvation is possible for every person. See 2 Pet. 3:9.

QUESTIONS & OBJECTIONS

"How should I witness to a homosexual?"

1:9,10

Rather than offend homosexuals by directly confronting the issue of their sinful lifestyle, modern evangelism often tries to soften the approach by saying that "God hates the sin, but loves the sinner." This isn't a new concept. *Charles Finney* stated, "God is not angry merely against the sin abstracted from the sinner, but against the sinner himself. Some persons have labored hard to set up this ridiculous and absurd abstraction, and would fain make it appear that God is angry at sin, yet not at the sinner. He hates the theft, but loves the thief. He abhors adultery, but is pleased with the adulterer. Now this is supreme nonsense. The sin has no moral character apart from the sinner. The act is nothing apart from the actor. The very thing that God hates and disapproves is not the mere event—the thing done in distinction from the doer; but it is the *doer himself*. It grieves and displeases Him that a rational moral agent, under His government, should array himself against his own God and Father, against all that is right and just in the universe. This is the thing that offends God. The sinner himself is the direct and the only object of his anger.

"So the Bible shows. God is angry with the wicked [Psa. 7:11], not with the abstract sin. If the wicked turn not, God will whet His sword—He has bent His bow and made it ready—not to shoot at the *sin*, but the *sinner*—the wicked man who has done the abominable thing. This is the only doctrine of either the Bible or of common sense on this subject" *(The Guilt of Sin)*.

The biblical way to witness to a homosexual is not to argue with him about his lifestyle but to use the Law to bring the knowledge of sin. This will show him that he is guilty of breaking God's holy Law, and he is damned *despite* his sexual preference. The Law was made for homosexuals, as well as other lawbreakers. See Psa. 5:5, 2 Pet. 2:6–8, and Jude 7 comments.

pearls or costly clothing, 10but, which is
proper for women professing godliness,
with good works. 11Let a woman learn in
silence with all submission. 12And I do not
permit a woman to teach or to have authority over a man, but to be in silence.
13For Adam was formed first, then Eve.
14And Adam was not deceived, but the woman being deceived, fell into transgression.
15Nevertheless she will be saved in child-

2:5 "We know God only through Jesus Christ. Without this Mediator, is taken away all communication with God; through Jesus Christ we know God. All those who have pretended to know God, and prove Him without Jesus Christ, have only impotent proofs.

"But, to prove Jesus Christ we have the prophecies which are good and valid proofs. And those prophecies, being fulfilled, and truly proved by the event, indicate the certainty of these truths, and therefore the truth of the divinity of Jesus Christ. In Him, and by Him, then, we know God. Otherwise, and without Scripture, without original sin, without a necessary Mediator, we can not absolutely prove God, nor teach a good doctrine and sound morals." *Blaise Pascal*

2:8 "The neglect of prayer is a grand hindrance to holiness." *John Wesley*

2:13 Common ancestry. "Researchers suggest that virtually all modern men—99% of them, says one scientist—are closely related genetically and share genes with one male ancestor, dubbed 'Y-chromosome Adam.' We are finding that humans have very, very shallow genetic roots which go back very recently to one ancestor... That indicates that there was an origin in a specific location on the globe, and then it spread out from there." *U.S. News & World Report*, December 4, 1995

"In new genetic studies of modern human origins, scientists think they have found strong evidence that there was an ancestral 'Adam' about 188,000 years ago to go with the previously discovered 'Eve.' The scientists used certain male-specific segments of the Y chromosome, the chromosome passed from father to son, to trace the common ancestor of every man now on earth to that period.

"Earlier analysis of the DNA of the mitochondria... indicated that all humans have as a common ancestor one woman who lived in Africa some 200,000 years ago—and inevitably has been stuck with the name Eve. All human mitochondrial DNA now extant, it seemed, derived from a single ancestral mitochondrial molecule from that place and time." *The New York Times*

See also Acts 17:26 comment.

QUESTIONS & OBJECTIONS

2:14 ***"God made me like this. Sin is His fault!"***

If this excuse will not work in a civil court, it certainly will not work on Judgment Day. Even with an expert defense lawyer, it would take a pretty inept judge to fall for the old "God made me do it" defense. We are responsible moral agents. The "buck" stopped at Adam. He tried to blame both God and Eve for his sin; Eve blamed the serpent. It is human nature to try, but it doesn't work with God.

bearing if they continue in faith, love,
and holiness, with self-control.

Qualifications of Overseers

3 This *is* a faithful saying: If a man desires the position of a bishop,[a] he desires a good work. 2A bishop then must
be blameless, the husband of one wife,
temperate, sober-minded, of good behavior, hospitable, able to teach; 3not
given to wine, not violent, not greedy for
money,[a] but gentle, not quarrelsome, not
covetous; 4one who rules his own house
well, having *his* children in submission
with all reverence 5(for if a man does not
know how to rule his own house, how
will he take care of the church of God?);
6not a novice, lest being puffed up with
pride he fall into the *same* condemnation
as the devil. 7Moreover he must have a
good testimony among those who are
outside, lest he fall into reproach and the
snare of the devil.

Qualifications of Deacons

8Likewise deacons *must be* reverent, not
double-tongued, not given to much wine,
not greedy for money, 9holding the mystery of the faith with a pure conscience.
10But let these also first be tested; then let
them serve as deacons, being *found* blameless. 11Likewise, *their* wives *must be* reverent, not slanderers, temperate, faithful in
all things. 12Let deacons be the husbands
of one wife, ruling *their* children and their
own houses well. 13For those who have
served well as deacons obtain for themselves a good standing and great boldness
in the faith which is in Christ Jesus.

The Great Mystery

14These things I write to you, though I
hope to come to you shortly; 15but if I am
delayed, *I write* so that you may know
how you ought to conduct yourself in the
house of God, which is the church of the
living God, the pillar and ground of the
truth. 16And without controversy great is
the mystery of godliness:

God[a] was manifested in the flesh,
Justified in the Spirit,
Seen by angels,
Preached among the Gentiles,
Believed on in the world,
Received up in glory.

The Great Apostasy

4 Now the Spirit expressly says that in
latter times some will depart from the

3:1 [a]Literally *overseer* 3:3 [a]NU-Text omits *not greedy for money.* 3:16 [a]NU-Text reads *Who.*

2:14 Why God created the serpent and allowed him to tempt Eve is a mystery. (See 1 Cor. 15:22 comment for one possibility.) However, those who would be quick to accuse God of wrongdoing would be wise to lay a hand on their mouth. We don't have to question His integrity because we know that all of His judgments are true and righteous altogether (Psa. 19:9). See also 2 Cor. 11:3 comment.

3:9 "Without God there is no virtue because there is no prompting of the conscience . . . without God there is a coarsening of the society; without God democracy will not and cannot long endure . . . If we ever forget that we are One Nation Under God, then we will be a nation gone under." *Ronald Reagan*

3:16 **Was Jesus God in human form?** See Heb. 1:1–3.

3:16 Seen by Angels

By Bruce Garner

When you examine the life of Christ, one evidence that this is no mere man is the fact that His life and work were witnessed and supported by angels. Jesus lived His life, I am confident, as an *incomprehensible spectacle* to angels.

The Bible tells us that angels are ministering spirits. Just like humans, they are creations of God, but are of a higher order than you and I. They were created for God's service. The Greek word literally means "messengers." They are simply creatures that God has created to serve Him and to serve believers. And they are seen throughout the life of Jesus Christ.

They praised God at Jesus' birth. Angels filled the heavens in a moment, praised God, and sang the first Christmas song, celebrating that the Word had become flesh (see Luke 2:13,14).

They served Jesus after His temptation by Satan. They met Him in the desert and ministered to Him after His days of fasting and temptation by Satan (see Matt. 4:11).

An angel strengthened Jesus as He prayed in Gethsemane. As Jesus agonized, to the point where His sweat became as drops of blood due to the severe physical and spiritual stress He was under, when His prayers were concluded, an angel came to Him and strengthened Him (see Luke 22:43).

Thousands of angels were available to rescue Him from His crucifixion. A mob with weapons and sticks has come to arrest Jesus. The boldest and most impetuous of His disciples strides forward and lops off a man's ear. Jesus stopped this well-intentioned but practically meaningless defense, healed the man, and said this:

> "Put your sword in its place, for all who take the sword will perish by the sword. Or do you think that I cannot now pray to My Father, and He will provide Me with more than twelve legions of angels? How then could the Scriptures be fulfilled, that it must happen thus?" (Matt. 26:52–54)

A Roman legion was 6,000 men. Jesus is saying to Peter, "Put your sword away. It's not necessary. Don't you know that I have more than 72,000 angels who would be here at a moment's notice to rescue Me?" And here's the part that moved my heart, because it speaks so deeply of the courage, strength, and absolute self-sacrifice that marks Jesus Christ as not only a man among men but the God-man. At the very moment that vile, wicked men laid hands on Him, more than 72,000 angels stood ready to come at a moment in His defense. In the Old Testament, you will find that on one occasion, the Angel of the Lord killed 185,000 men of a foreign army in one night. And that was one angel! It's as if Jesus says, "This moment is so great that twelve legions and more—72,000 angels—stand ready to come rescue Me, but put that sword away, Peter, because this is exactly what the Scriptures said must happen." Though the Bible simply does not tell us much about angels, I can imagine these created beings, perfect in holiness, amazing in power, are without a doubt the most feared fighting force that has ever intersected human history. They were ready . . . waiting . . . just a word from the Father to put an end to it . . . to stop our salvation, to set our redemption aside. It would take just one word from the Father, but both Father and Son refused. And the Son went on to endure the crucifixion that those men had come to deliver Him to, and wicked hands laid Him on a cross and made a public spectacle of Him, beating Him and cursing Him, and tearing out His beard, and blaspheming Him, and He did it all—for you . . . and for me. That's love.

And that makes such an astonishing difference in your day-to-day life. If you know God loves you like that, it pushes all your questions about Him and against Him out of the way, because you know for a fact that He refused rescue so that you could be saved and forgiven. That an amazing rescuing force stayed its hand because the Father and the Son did not will it to come. And the angels could have come at any moment, and you and I would have remained lost . . . forever.

All of that in this single phrase. When Jesus was on earth, after becoming manifested in the flesh, after living a righteous life, after being justified by the Spirit, He was seen by angels.

faith, giving heed to deceiving spirits and
doctrines of demons, 2speaking lies in
hypocrisy, having their own conscience
seared with a hot iron, 3forbidding to marry, *and commanding* to abstain from foods
which God created to be received with
thanksgiving by those who believe and
know the truth. 4For every creature of
God *is* good, and nothing is to be refused if it is received with thanksgiving;
5for it is sanctified by the word of God
and prayer.

QUESTIONS & OBJECTIONS

4:2 "Can you appeal to the conscience if it is seared?"

Definitely. A "seared" conscience is not a "dead" conscience. In Scripture, the conscience is referred to as "weak" (1 Cor. 8:7–12), "good" (1 Tim. 1:5), "pure" (1 Tim. 3:9), "defiled" (Titus 1:15), and "evil" (Heb. 10:22), but it is never called "dead." In John 8:9 one might think that the accusing, self-righteous Pharisees would have had dead consciences, but when Jesus spoke of their sin, "Then those who heard it, being convicted by their conscience, went out one by one, beginning with the oldest even to the last." Not one of them escaped the accusatory voice of the conscience. It was Rom. 2:15 in action: "who show the work of the law written in their hearts, their conscience also bearing witness, and between themselves their thoughts accusing or else excusing them."

Some may wonder about casting our "pearls before swine" by witnessing to those whose consciences seem seared. When do we stop offering the gospel to the hardened unsaved? Scripture uses the analogy of a pig to describe someone who makes a profession of faith, but goes back to the world (see 2 Pet. 2:22). The pig, considered an unclean animal, wallows in filth to cool its flesh. If someone's "conversion" is spurious, it is only a matter of time until he has to go back to the filth of the world to cool his flesh. We often call these people "backsliders," but they are in reality "false converts," and most of us would agree that they are the hardest to reach with the true gospel. This is because they usually say they were born again, read the Bible, went to church, witnessed, sang praise songs, etc., but then they "saw the error of being a Christian." However, we each need to decide for ourselves whether to stop witnessing to such people. If we do stop, that doesn't mean we give up on them. God forbid. We may stop sharing the gospel because they are contentious, but we should never stop praying for their salvation, until the day death seizes them. Then, and only then, is the battle over.

A Good Servant of Jesus Christ

6If you instruct the brethren in these
things, you will be a good minister of Jesus Christ, nourished in the words of
faith and of the good doctrine which you
have carefully followed. 7But reject profane and old wives' fables, and exercise
yourself toward godliness. 8For bodily
exercise profits a little, but godliness is
profitable for all things, having promise
of the life that now is and of that which is
to come. 9This *is* a faithful saying and worthy of all acceptance. 10For to this *end* we
both labor and suffer reproach,[a] because

4:10 [a]NU-Text reads *we labor and strive.*

4:1 For more signs of the end times, see 2 Tim. 3:1.

Halloween. The celebration can be traced back to the Druid festival of the dead. The Roman Pantheon, built by Emperor Hadrian in A.D. 100 as a temple to the goddess Cybele and other Roman gods, became the principle place of worship. In 609, Emperor Phocas seized Rome and gave the Pantheon to Pope Boniface IV. Boniface consecrated it to the Virgin Mary and kept using the temple to pray for the dead, only now it was "Christianized," as men added the unscriptural teaching of purgatory. In 834, Gregory IV extended the feast for all the church and it became known as All Saint's Day, still remembering the dead.

Samhain, a Druid god of the dead, was honored at Hallowe'en ("All Hallows Eve") in Britain, Germany, France, and the Celtic countries. Samhain called together all wicked souls who died within the past year and who were destined to inhabit animals. The Druids believed that souls of the dead came back to their homes to be entertained by those still living. Suitable food and shelter were provided for these spirits or else they would cast spells, steal infants, destroy crops, kill farm animals, and create terror as they haunted the living. This is the action that "Trick-or-Treat" copies today. The Samhain celebration used nuts, apples, skeletons, witches, and black cats. Divination and auguries were practiced as well as magic to seek answers for the future. Even today witchcraft practitioners declare October 31 as the most favorable time to practice their arts.

Many Christians use Halloween as an opportunity to reach the lost by giving candy and gospel tracts to trick-or-treaters. *What other day do scores of people come to your door for gospel tracts?*

4:2 "If we can break the least of the known commands of God, without any self-condemnation, it is plain that the god of this world hath hardened our hearts. If we do not soon recover from this, we shall be 'past feeling,' and our consciences (as St. Paul speaks) will be 'seared as with a hot iron.'" *John Wesley*

we trust in the living God, who is *the* Savior of all men, especially of those who believe. 11These things command and teach.

Take Heed to Your Ministry

12Let no one despise your youth, but
be an example to the believers in word,
in conduct, in love, in spirit,[a] in faith, in
purity. 13Till I come, give attention to reading, to exhortation, to doctrine. 14Do not
neglect the gift that is in you, which was
given to you by prophecy with the laying
on of the hands of the eldership. 15Medi-
tate on these things; give yourself entirely
to them, that your progress may be evident to all. 16Take heed to yourself and to
the doctrine. Continue in them, for in
doing this you will save both yourself and
those who hear you.

Treatment of Church Members

5 Do not rebuke an older man, but exhort *him* as a father, younger men as
brothers, 2older women as mothers,
younger women as sisters, with all purity.

Honor True Widows

3Honor widows who are really widows. 4But if any widow has children or
grandchildren, let them first learn to show
piety at home and to repay their parents;
for this is good and[a] acceptable before
God. 5Now she who is really a widow,
and left alone, trusts in God and continues in supplications and prayers night

THE FUNCTION OF THE LAW

"When once God the Holy Spirit applies the Law to the conscience, secret sins are dragged to light, little sins are magnified to their true size, and things apparently harmless become exceedingly sinful. Before that dread searcher of the hearts and trier of the reins makes His entrance into the soul, it appears righteous, just, lovely, and holy; but when He reveals the hidden evils, the scene is changed. Offenses which were once styled peccadilloes, trifles, freaks of youth, follies, indulgences, little slips, etc., then appear in their true color, as breaches of the Law of God, deserving condign punishment." *Charles Spurgeon*

"The proper effect of the Law is to lead us out of our tents and tabernacles, that is to say, from the quietness and security wherein we dwell, and from trusting in ourselves, and to bring us before the presence of God, to reveal his wrath to us, and to set us before our sins." *Martin Luther*

"The man that has an awakened conscience is the least likely to be deceived of any man in the world: 'tis the drowsy, insensible, stupid conscience that is most easily blinded. The more sensible conscience is in a diseased soul, the less easily is it quieted without a real healing. The more sensible conscience is made of the dreadfulness of sin, and of the greatness of a man's own guilt of it, the less likely is he to rest in his own righteousness, or to be pacified with nothing but shadows. A man that has been thoroughly terrified with a sense of his danger and misery is not easily flattered and made to believe himself safe, without any good grounds." *Jonathan Edwards*

4:12 [a]NU-Text omits *in spirit.* 5:4 [a]NU-Text and M-Text omit *good and.*

4:3,4 Vegetarianism. One of the signs of the end of this age is that people would try to impose a lifestyle on others where certain foods are not to be eaten. This could be a reference to vegetarianism, which has gained popularity these days. But the Scriptures tell us that *every* creature of God is good for food, and *nothing* is to be refused.

Vegetarianism is not always the blessing it is made out to be. In India in 1942, three million people died of starvation. Alongside the bodies of men, women, and children lay the carcasses of hundreds of thousands of "sacred" cows—potential beef-steaks. They were God-given protein that would have saved the lives of multitudes. See Psa. 66:15 and Rev. 22:3 comments.

4:7 One way to prevent physical injuries and pain is to keep yourself fit. Exercise. After warning Timothy to refuse false doctrine, Paul told him to exercise himself to godliness. Paul kept fit through exercise and striving. He said, "I myself always strive to have a conscience without offense toward God and men" (Acts 24:16). Do the same. Listen to the voice of conscience. It is your friend, not your enemy.

5:5 "I have no confidence at all in polished speech or brilliant literary effort to bring about a revival, but I have all the confidence in the world in the poor saint who would weep her eyes out because people are living in sin." *Charles Spurgeon*

and day. 6But she who lives in pleasure is dead while she lives. 7And these things command, that they may be blameless. 8But if anyone does not provide for his own, and especially for those of his household, he has denied the faith and is worse than an unbeliever.

9Do not let a widow under sixty years old be taken into the number, *and not unless* she has been the wife of one man, 10well reported for good works: if she has brought up children, if she has lodged strangers, if she has washed the saints' feet, if she has relieved the afflicted, if she has diligently followed every good work.

> Try after sermons to talk to strangers. The preacher may have missed the mark, but you need not miss it. Or the preacher may have struck the mark, and you can help to make the impression deeper by a kind word.
>
> **CHARLES SPURGEON**

11But refuse *the* younger widows; for when they have begun to grow wanton against Christ, they desire to marry, 12having condemnation because they have cast off their first faith. 13And besides they learn *to be* idle, wandering about from house to house, and not only idle but also gossips and busybodies, saying things which they ought not. 14Therefore I desire that *the* younger *widows* marry, bear children, manage the house, give no opportunity to the adversary to speak reproachfully. 15For some have already turned aside after Satan. 16If any believing man or[a] woman has widows, let them relieve them, and do not let the church be burdened, that it may relieve those who are really widows.

Honor the Elders

17Let the elders who rule well be counted worthy of double honor, especially those who labor in the word and doctrine. 18For the Scripture says, *"You shall not muzzle an ox while it treads out the grain,"*[a] and, "The laborer *is* worthy of his wages."[b] 19Do not receive an accusation against an elder except from two or three witnesses. 20Those who are sinning rebuke in the presence of all, that the rest also may fear.

21I charge *you* before God and the Lord Jesus Christ and the elect angels that you observe these things without prejudice, doing nothing with partiality. 22Do not lay hands on anyone hastily, nor share in other people's sins; keep yourself pure.

23No longer drink only water, but use a little wine for your stomach's sake and your frequent infirmities.

24Some men's sins are clearly evident, preceding *them* to judgment, but those of some *men* follow later. 25Likewise, the good works *of some* are clearly evident, and those that are otherwise cannot be hidden.

Honor Masters

6 Let as many bondservants as are under the yoke count their own masters worthy of all honor, so that the name of God and *His* doctrine may not be blasphemed. 2And those who have believing masters, let them not despise *them* because they are brethren, but rather serve *them* because those who are benefited are believers and beloved. Teach and exhort these things.

Error and Greed

3If anyone teaches otherwise and does not consent to wholesome words, *even* the words of our Lord Jesus Christ, and to the doctrine which accords with godliness, 4he is proud, knowing nothing, but is obsessed with disputes and arguments over words, from which come envy, strife, reviling, evil suspicions, 5useless wranglings[a] of men of corrupt minds and destitute of the truth, who suppose that godliness is a *means of* gain. From such withdraw yourself.[b]

5:16 [a]NU-Text omits *man or.* 5:18 [a]Deuteronomy 25:4 [b]Luke 10:7 6:5 [a]NU-Text and M-Text read *constant friction.* [b]NU-Text omits this sentence.

QUESTIONS & OBJECTIONS

"What if someone doesn't believe 'taking God's name in vain' is a sin?"

The lost may argue that they don't consider casually saying "God" to be blasphemy. In fact, the phrase "omigod" is so embedded in the vocabulary of youth today that it is shortened to "OMG" for ease in text messaging. It is just a meaningless word to them. In other words, they don't esteem the name of God. The Hebrew word used for "vain" means nothingness, emptiness, vanity. According to *John F. Walvoord*, to misuse God's name means literally, "to lift it up to or attach it to emptiness." The Third Commandment forbids using God's name flippantly or in profanity. So using the Lord's name lightly or without thinking is the very essence of taking it "in vain."

Another argument you may encounter is that the Seventh Commandment refers only to adultery, not fornication (sex before marriage). But 1 Tim. 1:8–10 makes clear that the Law also pertains to fornicators and homosexuals. God's design is for sex to occur only between a husband and wife, and *any* sexual relations outside the bounds of marriage are forbidden. In an effort to counter homosexual marriage, many have used the argument that it is wrong simply because a child is better raised with a mother and a father than with two parents of the same gender. However, homosexuality is morally wrong because it violates *God's* Law.

Finally, there are some who claim the Ninth Commandment, "You shall not bear false witness," refers solely to giving false witness in a court of law, and therefore doesn't include everyday lying. Another untruth. First Tim. 1:8–10 also says that the Law was made for "liars." So, as much as the world would like to do away with the Law, or at least water it down, it is immutable. It is not going away, and it will be the unbending standard of judgment on the day when God judges the hearts of men and women (see Rom. 2:12).

6 Now godliness with contentment is
great gain. 7 For we brought nothing into
this world, *and it is* certain[a] we can carry
nothing out. 8 And having food and clothing, with these we shall be content. 9 But
those who desire to be rich fall into temptation and a snare, and *into* many foolish
and harmful lusts which drown men in
destruction and perdition. 10 For the love
of money is a root of all *kinds of* evil, for
which some have strayed from the faith
in their greediness, and pierced themselves through with many sorrows.

· · · · · ·

For how to address the sinner's conscience, see John 4:7 comment.

· · · · · ·

The Good Confession

11 But you, O man of God, flee these
things and pursue righteousness, godliness, faith, love, patience, gentleness.
12 Fight the good fight of faith, lay hold on
eternal life, to which you were also called
and have confessed the good confession
in the presence of many witnesses. 13 I
urge you in the sight of God who gives
life to all things, and *before* Christ Jesus
who witnessed the good confession before
Pontius Pilate, 14 that you keep *this* commandment without spot, blameless until
our Lord Jesus Christ's appearing, 15 which
He will manifest in His own time, *He who
is* the blessed and only Potentate, the
King of kings and Lord of lords, 16 who
alone has immortality, dwelling in unapproachable light, whom no man has seen
or can see, to whom *be* honor and everlasting power. Amen.

Instructions to the Rich

17 Command those who are rich in this

6:7 [a]NU-Text omits *and it is certain.*

6:8 "You say, 'If I had a little more, I should be very satisfied.' You make a mistake. If you are not content with what you have, you would not be satisfied if it were doubled." *Charles Spurgeon*

QUESTIONS & OBJECTIONS

6:20 *"Didn't the Church persecute Galileo?"*

Skeptics often try to demean Scripture by saying that the Christian Church persecuted Galileo when he maintained that the Earth circled the sun. As a professor of astronomy at the University of Pisa, Galileo was required to teach the accepted theory of his time that the sun and all the planets revolved around the Earth. Later at the University of Padua he was exposed to a new theory, proposed by Nicolaus Copernicus, that the Earth and all the other planets revolved around the sun. Galileo's observations with his new telescope convinced him of the truth of Copernicus's sun-centered or heliocentric theory. His scientific beliefs didn't contradict the Scriptures, but they contradicted the teaching of the Roman Catholic church. In 1633 during the Inquisition he was convicted of heresy and ordered to recant (publicly withdraw) his support of Copernicus. The Roman Catholic church sentenced him to life imprisonment, but because of his advanced age allowed him to serve his term under house arrest at his villa outside of Florence, Italy. The Christian Church therefore should not be blamed for his imprisonment. It was the Roman Catholic church that persecuted Galileo.

"Under the sentence of imprisonment Galileo remained till his death in 1642. It is, however, untrue to speak of him as in any proper sense a 'prisoner.' As his Protestant biographer, von Gebler, tells us, 'One glance at the truest historical source for the famous trial would convince anyone that Galileo spent altogether twenty-two days in the buildings of the Holy Office [during the Inquisition], and even then not in a prison cell with barred windows, but in the handsome and commodious apartment of an official of the Inquisition.'" *(Catholic Encyclopedia)*

present age not to be haughty, nor to
trust in uncertain riches but in the living
God, who gives us richly all things to enjoy. [18]*Let them* do good, that they be rich
in good works, ready to give, willing to
share, [19]storing up for themselves a good
foundation for the time to come, that
they may lay hold on eternal life.

Guard the Faith

[20]O Timothy! Guard what was committed to your trust, avoiding the profane
and idle babblings and contradictions of
what is falsely called knowledge— [21]by
professing it some have strayed concerning the faith.

Grace *be* with you. Amen.

"How many observe Christ's birthday! How few, his precepts! O 'tis easier to keep holidays than commandments."

BENJAMIN FRANKLIN

6:15 "It may surprise you that Aldous Huxley, often a critic of orthodox and evangelical Christianity, has been quoted as saying: 'My kingdom go is the necessary correlary to Thy kingdom come.'...

"Certainly His kingdom can never be realized in my life until my own selfish kingdom is deposed. It is when I resign, when I am no longer king of my domain that Jesus Christ will become King of my life." *A. W. Tozer*

6:15,16 "We can only know one thing about God—that He is what we are not. Our wretchedness alone is an image of this. The more we contemplate it, the more we contemplate Him." *Simone Weil*

"God is a circle whose center is everywhere and circumference nowhere." *Voltaire*

6:18 "Do all the good you can, by all the means you can, in all the places you can, at all the times you can, to all the people you can, as long as you ever can." *John Wesley*

2 Timothy

Greeting

1 Paul, an apostle of Jesus Christ[a] by the will of God, according to the promise of life which is in Christ Jesus,

2 To Timothy, a beloved son:

Grace, mercy, *and* peace from God the Father and Christ Jesus our Lord.

Timothy's Faith and Heritage

3 I thank God, whom I serve with a
pure conscience, as *my* forefathers *did,* as
without ceasing I remember you in my
prayers night and day, 4 greatly desiring
to see you, being mindful of your tears,
that I may be filled with joy, 5 when I call
to remembrance the genuine faith that is
in you, which dwelt first in your grandmother
Lois and your mother Eunice,
and I am persuaded is in you also.
6 Therefore I remind you to stir up the gift
of God which is in you through the laying
on of my hands. 7 For God has not
given us a spirit of fear, but of power and
of love and of a sound mind.

Not Ashamed of the Gospel

8 Therefore do not be ashamed of the
testimony of our Lord, nor of me His
prisoner, but share with me in the sufferings
for the gospel according to the
power of God, 9 who has saved us and
called *us* with a holy calling, not according
to our works, but according to His
own purpose and grace which was given
to us in Christ Jesus before time began,
10 but has now been revealed by the appearing
of our Savior Jesus Christ, *who*
has abolished death and brought life and
immortality to light through the gospel,
11 to which I was appointed a preacher,
an apostle, and a teacher of the Gentiles.[a]
12 For this reason I also suffer these things;
nevertheless I am not ashamed, for I
know whom I have believed and am persuaded
that He is able to keep what I
have committed to Him until that Day.

Be Loyal to the Faith

13 Hold fast the pattern of sound words
which you have heard from me, in faith
and love which are in Christ Jesus. 14 That
good thing which was committed to you,
keep by the Holy Spirit who dwells in us.
15 This you know, that all those in Asia
have turned away from me, among whom

1:1 [a]NU-Text and M-Text read *Christ Jesus.* 1:11 [a]NU-Text omits *of the Gentiles.*

1:8,9 "We want the power of God to be manifested, but sometimes we fail to seek purity on our part." *Anonymous*

1:10 "Surely God would not have created such a being as man, with an ability to grasp the infinite, to exist only for a day. No, no, man was made for immortality." *Abraham Lincoln*

are Phygellus and Hermogenes. [16]The
Lord grant mercy to the household of
Onesiphorus, for he often refreshed me,
and was not ashamed of my chain; [17]but
when he arrived in Rome, he sought me
out very zealously and found *me.* [18]The
Lord grant to him that he may find mercy
from the Lord in that Day—and you
know very well how many ways he ministered *to me*[a] at Ephesus.

Be Strong in Grace

2 You therefore, my son, be strong in
the grace that is in Christ Jesus. [2]And
the things that you have heard from me
among many witnesses, commit these to
faithful men who will be able to teach
others also. [3]You therefore must endure[a]
hardship as a good soldier of Jesus Christ.
[4]No one engaged in warfare entangles
himself with the affairs of *this* life, that
he may please him who enlisted him as a
soldier. [5]And also if anyone competes in
athletics, he is not crowned unless he
competes according to the rules. [6]The
hardworking farmer must be first to partake of the crops. [7]Consider what I say,
and may[a] the Lord give you understanding in all things.

[8]Remember that Jesus Christ, of the
seed of David, was raised from the dead
according to my gospel, [9]for which I suffer
trouble as an evildoer, *even* to the point
of chains; but the word of God is not
chained. [10]Therefore I endure all things
for the sake of the elect, that they also
may obtain the salvation which is in
Christ Jesus with eternal glory.

[11]*This is* a faithful saying:

For if we died with *Him,*
We shall also live with *Him.*

"The New Testament is the very best book that ever was or ever will be known in the world."

Charles Dickens

[12]If we endure,
We shall also reign with *Him.*
If we deny *Him,*
He also will deny us.
[13]If we are faithless,
He remains faithful;
He cannot deny Himself.

Approved and Disapproved Workers

[14]Remind *them* of these things, charging *them* before the Lord not to strive
about words to no profit, to the ruin of
the hearers. [15]Be diligent to present yourself approved to God, a worker who does
not need to be ashamed, rightly dividing
the word of truth. [16]But shun profane *and*
idle babblings, for they will increase to

1:18 [a]*To me* is from the Vulgate and a few Greek manuscripts. 2:3 [a]NU-Text reads *You must share.* 2:7 [a]NU-Text reads *the Lord will give you.*

2:3 "A barracks is meant to be a place where real soldiers were to be fed and equipped for war, not a place to settle down in or as a comfortable snuggery in which to enjoy ourselves. I hope that if ever they, our soldiers, do settle down God will burn their barracks over their heads!" *Catherine Booth*

2:15 "The next time someone says, 'That's just *your* interpretation,' have the person read the verse and ask him how he might interpret it differently. Ask him to give reasons why he would choose one interpretation over another. Ask him if his interpretation matches what the author intended to say. The question is not, 'Whose interpretation is this?' but 'Is this interpretation correct?'" *Todd Friel*

QUESTIONS & OBJECTIONS

2:19 *"The Church is full of hypocrites."*

Hypocrites may show up at a church building every Sunday, but there are no hypocrites in the Church (Christ's body). *Hypocrite* comes from the Greek word for "actor," or pretender. Hypocrisy is "the practice of professing beliefs, feelings, or virtues that one does not hold." The Church is made up of true believers; hypocrites are "pretenders" who sit among God's people. God knows those who love Him, and the Bible warns that He will sort out the true converts from the false on the Day of Judgment. All hypocrites will end up in hell (Matt. 24:51).

more ungodliness. 17And their message
will spread like cancer. Hymenaeus and
Philetus are of this sort, 18who have strayed
concerning the truth, saying that the resurrection is already past; and they overthrow the faith of some. 19Nevertheless
the solid foundation of God stands, having this seal: "The Lord knows those who
are His," and, "Let everyone who names
the name of Christ[a] depart from iniquity."
20But in a great house there are not
only vessels of gold and silver, but also of
wood and clay, some for honor and some
for dishonor. 21Therefore if anyone
cleanses himself from the latter, he will be
a vessel for honor, sanctified and useful
for the Master, prepared for every good
work. 22Flee also youthful lusts; but pursue righteousness, faith, love, peace with
those who call on the Lord out of a pure
heart. 23But avoid foolish and ignorant disputes, knowing that they generate strife.
24And a servant of the Lord must not
quarrel but be gentle to all, able to teach,
patient, 25in humility correcting those who
are in opposition, if God perhaps will
grant them repentance, so that they may
know the truth, 26and *that* they may come
to their senses *and escape* the snare of the
devil, having been taken captive by him
to *do* his will.

Perilous Times and Perilous Men

3 But know this, that in the last days
perilous times will come: 2For men
will be lovers of themselves, lovers of
money, boasters, proud, blasphemers, disobedient to parents, unthankful, unholy,

2:19 [a]NU-Text and M-Text read *the Lord.*

2:19 True and false converts. False converts lack genuine contrition for sin. They make a profession of faith but are deficient in biblical repentance: "They profess to know God, but in works they deny Him, being abominable, disobedient, and disqualified for every good work" (Titus 1:16). A true convert, however, has a knowledge of sin and has godly sorrow, truly repents, and produces the "things that accompany salvation" (Heb. 6:9). This is evident by the fruit of the Spirit, the fruit of righteousness, etc. However, only God truly knows the genuine from the false.

"Our churches are full of the nicest, kindest people who have never known the despair of guilt or the breathless wonder of forgiveness." *P. T. Forsyth*

2:21 "When you are willing, God will call you. When you are prepared, God will empower you. When you are empowered, God will test you. When you are tested, God will strengthen you. When you are strengthened, God will use you, and when you are used, God will reward you." *Ross Rhodes*

"Clay is molded into a vessel, but the ultimate use of the vessel depends on the part where nothing exists. Doors and windows are cut out of the wall of a house, but the ultimate use of the house depends on the parts where nothing exists. I wish to become such a useful nothing." *Richard Wurmbrand*

2:24 This is the spirit in which we should share our faith. It has been well said, "Never argue with a fool. Someone watching might not be able to tell the difference." As we witness, we must be kind and gentle to those who oppose us. It is not our job to convince them with brilliant arguments, but simply to share the truth, so that God may bring them to repentance. See 2 Tim. 4:2.

POINTS FOR OPEN-AIR PREACHING

2:24–26

"Watch It, Blind Man!"

There is one passage in Scripture to which I point for all those who want to witness or preach in the open-air. It is 2 Tim. 2:24–26. Memorize it. Scripture tells us that sinners are blind. They *cannot* see. What would you think if I were to stomp up to a blind man who had just stumbled, and say, "Watch where you're going, blind man!"? Such an attitude is completely unreasonable. The man *cannot* see.

The same applies to the lost—spiritual sight is beyond their ability. Consider the words used in Scripture: "Unless one is born again, he *cannot see* the kingdom of God...Whose minds the god of this age has blinded...But the natural man does not receive the things of the Spirit of God, for they are foolishness to him; nor *can* he know them...having their understanding *darkened*...because of the *blindness* of their heart...*never able* to come to the knowledge of the truth" (emphasis added).

With these thoughts in mind, read 2 Tim. 2:24–26 again and look at the adjectives used by Paul to describe the attitude we are to have with sinners: "must not quarrel...be gentle...patient...in humility." Just as it is unreasonable to be impatient with a blind man, so it is with the sinner. See also Matt. 5:10–12 comment.

3unloving, unforgiving, slanderers, without self-control, brutal, despisers of good,
4traitors, headstrong, haughty, lovers of
pleasure rather than lovers of God, 5hav-
ing a form of godliness but denying its
power. And from such people turn away!
6For of this sort are those who creep into
households and make captives of gullible
women loaded down with sins, led away
by various lusts, 7always learning and
never able to come to the knowledge of
the truth. 8Now as Jannes and Jambres
resisted Moses, so do these also resist the
truth: men of corrupt minds, disapproved
concerning the faith; 9but they will progress no further, for their folly will be
manifest to all, as theirs also was.

The Man of God and the Word of God

10But you have carefully followed my
doctrine, manner of life, purpose, faith,
longsuffering, love, perseverance, 11per-
secutions, afflictions, which happened to
me at Antioch, at Iconium, at Lystra—
what persecutions I endured. And out of
them all the Lord delivered me. 12Yes, and
all who desire to live godly in Christ Jesus
will suffer persecution. 13But evil men and
impostors will grow worse and worse,
deceiving and being deceived. 14But you
must continue in the things which you
have learned and been assured of, knowing from whom you have learned *them*,
15and that from childhood you have

3:1 Fulfillment of Bible prophecy. Few in the Church would deny that Bible prophecy is being fulfilled before our very eyes. These are certainly "perilous" times. Men's hearts are failing them for fear of what is coming on the earth. There are suicide bombings, terrorist acts, nation rising against nation and kingdom against kingdom. The neighbors of Israel are boldly escalating their hatred of the Jews. Lawlessness and the love of sin abound on every side. Economies are collapsing, and as political leaders try to keep a brave face, I can see fear deep in their eyes. They fail to even acknowledge the God who gave them life, and I think of the psalmist's prayer, "Arise, O LORD, do not let man prevail; let the nations be judged in Your sight. Put them in fear, O LORD, that the nations may know themselves to be but men" (Psa. 9:19,20).

In the midst of speaking about the dark and frightening signs of the end of the age, Jesus shone a beacon of wonderful light: "And this gospel of the kingdom will be preached in all the world as a witness to all the nations, and then the end will come" (Matt. 24:14). You and I can be a part of fulfillment of Bible prophecy. God has entrusted us (as the Church) to be lighthouse keepers, especially at the end of this age. We are to steer perishing sinners into the God-given safe haven. So make sure you show your brilliance by embracing the work that God has called us to do. If ever you were needed, it is now.

For more signs of the end times, see 2 Pet. 3:3.

3:5 "The chief danger of the 20th century will be religion without the Holy Spirit, Christianity without Christ, forgiveness without repentance, salvation without regeneration, politics without God, and heaven without hell." *General William Booth*

known the Holy Scriptures, which are able to make you wise for salvation through faith which is in Christ Jesus.
[16]All Scripture *is* given by inspiration of God, and *is* profitable for doctrine, for reproof, for correction, for instruction in righteousness, [17]that the man of God may be complete, thoroughly equipped for every good work.

Preach the Word

4 I charge *you* therefore before God and the Lord Jesus Christ, who will judge the living and the dead at[a] His appearing and His kingdom: [2]Preach the word! Be ready in season *and* out of season. Convince, rebuke, exhort, with all longsuffering and teaching. [3]For the time will come when they will not endure sound doctrine, but according to their own desires, *because* they have itching ears, they will heap up for themselves teachers; [4]and they will turn *their* ears away from the truth, and be turned aside to fables. [5]But you be watchful in all things, endure afflictions, do the work of an evangelist, fulfill your ministry.

Paul's Valedictory

[6]For I am already being poured out as a drink offering, and the time of my departure is at hand. [7]I have fought the good fight, I have finished the race, I have kept the faith. [8]Finally, there is laid up for me the crown of righteousness, which the Lord, the righteous Judge, will give to me on that Day, and not to me only but also to all who have loved His appearing.

The Abandoned Apostle

[9]Be diligent to come to me quickly; [10]for Demas has forsaken me, having loved this present world, and has departed for Thessalonica—Crescens for Galatia, Titus for Dalmatia. [11]Only Luke is with me. Get Mark and bring him with you, for he is useful to me for ministry. [12]And Tychicus I have sent to Ephesus. [13]Bring the cloak

4:1 [a]NU-Text omits *therefore* and reads *and by* for *at.*

3:16 The Bible's Inspiration. "The authors, speaking under the inspiration of the Holy Spirit, . . . wrote on hundreds of controversial subjects with absolute harmony from the beginning to the end. There is one unfolding story from Genesis to Revelation: the redemption of mankind through the Messiah—the Old Testament through the coming Messiah, the New Testament from the Messiah that has come. In Genesis, you have paradise lost, in Revelation you have paradise gained. You can't understand Revelation without understanding Genesis. It's all interwoven on hundreds of controversial subjects.

"Now here's the picture: 1,600 years, 60 generations, 40-plus authors, different walks of life, different places, different times, different moods, different continents, three languages, writing on hundreds of controversial subjects and yet when they are brought together, there is absolute harmony from beginning to end . . . There is no other book in history to even compare to the uniqueness of this continuity." *Josh McDowell*

"We account the Scriptures of God to be the most sublime philosophy. I find more sure marks of authenticity in the Bible than in any profane history whatsoever." *Sir Isaac Newton*

"The Bible is endorsed by the ages. Our civilization is built upon its words. In no other Book is there such a collection of inspired wisdom, reality, and hope." *Dwight D. Eisenhower*

3:17 What better "good work" can there be than to use the Law of God to bring sinners to repentance? For the biblical way to witness, see John 4:7 comment.

4:1 Judgment Day: For verses that warn of its reality, see Heb. 9:27.

4:2 This is the spirit in which we should share our faith. See Titus 3:2,3.

Open season. When it comes to seeking and saving the lost, it's always "hunting" season. We should be ready to preach the gospel to everyone we meet, at all times.

"We want in the church of Christ a band of well-trained sharpshooters, who will pick the people out individually and be always on the watch for all who come into the place, not annoying them, but making sure that they do not go away without having had a personal warning, invitation, and exhortation to come to Christ." *Charles Spurgeon*

4:3 "Scratching people where they itch and addressing their 'felt needs' is a stratagem of the poor steward of the oracles of God. This was the recipe for success for the false prophets of the Old Testament." *R. C. Sproul*

4:9 Evolution: Too Fast to See

To skirt around the fact that the evidence refutes Darwin's theory of gradualism (see 1 Cor. 15:39 comment), some scientists have proposed their own theory: *punctuated equilibrium.* This theory, championed by Stephen Gould and others, proposes that evolution happened in rapid spurts (by some mysterious genetic mechanism) followed by long periods of stability. They suggest that species had to evolve quickly based on sudden changes in their environment, such as a flood or drought.

There are a couple of problems with this theory as well. First, according to the website "Understanding Evolution," which explains evolution to teachers, "Factors in the environment...are not generally thought to influence the direction of mutation." They state that experiments showed mutations "did not occur because the organism was placed in a situation where the mutation would be useful." Again, mutations are completely random and *not* based on the environment (see Psa. 36:6 comment). So if there is no evidence to show that mutations could cause creatures to evolve gradually over millions of years, why would we think they could somehow manage to evolve very rapidly?

Second, there is nothing in the fossil record that would lead us to believe this was the case. Very conveniently for proponents of this theory, evolution supposedly occurred so quickly that there wasn't time to leave any fossils as evidence. The theory of punctuated equilibrium was proposed only as a way to explain the *lack* of fossil evidence. I'm afraid the only thing actually evolving is their theory.

In his book *Darwinism: The Refutation of a Myth*, Swedish embryologist Soren Lovtrup writes, "I suppose that nobody will deny that it is a great misfortune if an entire branch of science becomes addicted to a false theory. But this is what has happened in biology...I believe that one day the Darwinian myth will be ranked the greatest deceit in the history of science." See Isa. 45:12 and 1 Kings 4:33 comments.

(Adapted from *How to Know God Exists.*)

that I left with Carpus at Troas when you
come—and the books, especially the
parchments.
14Alexander the coppersmith did me
much harm. May the Lord repay him according to his works. 15You also must beware of him, for he has greatly resisted
our words.

. . . . . .

For how to use gospel tracts, see 1 Cor. 9:22 comment.

. . . . . .

16At my first defense no one stood with
me, but all forsook me. May it not be
charged against them.

The Lord Is Faithful

17But the Lord stood with me and
strengthened me, so that the message
might be preached fully through me, and
that all the Gentiles might hear. Also I
was delivered out of the mouth of the
lion. 18And the Lord will deliver me from
every evil work and preserve *me* for His
heavenly kingdom. To Him *be* glory forever and ever. Amen!

Come Before Winter

19Greet Prisca and Aquila, and the
household of Onesiphorus. 20Erastus stayed
in Corinth, but Trophimus I have left in
Miletus sick.
21Do your utmost to come before winter.
Eubulus greets you, as well as Pudens,
Linus, Claudia, and all the brethren.

Farewell

22The Lord Jesus Christ[a] be with your
spirit. Grace be with you. Amen.

4:22 [a]NU-Text omits *Jesus Christ.*

4:17 "To win men to acceptance of Jesus Christ as Saviour and Lord is the only reason Christians are left in this world." *R. A. Torrey*

Open-air Preaching

By Charles Spurgeon

I am somewhat pleased when I occasionally hear of a brother's being locked up by the police, for it does him good, and it does the people good also. It is a fine sight to see the minister of the Gospel marched off by the servant of the law! It excites sympathy for him, and the next step is sympathy for his message. Many who felt no interest in him before are eager to hear him when he is ordered to leave off, and still more so when he is taken to the station. The vilest of mankind respect a man who gets into trouble in order to do them good, and if they see unfair opposition excited they grow quite zealous in the man's defense.

As to style in preaching out-of-doors, it should certainly be very different from much of that which prevails within, and perhaps if a speaker were to acquire a style fully adapted to a street audience, he would be wise to bring it indoors with him. A great deal of sermonizing may be defined as saying nothing at extreme length; but out-of-doors verbosity is not admired; you must say something and have done with it and go on to say something more, or your hearers will let you know.

"Now then," cries a street critic, "let us have it, old fellow." Or else the observation is made, "Now then, pitch it out! You'd better go home and learn your lesson." "Cut it short, old boy," is a very common admonition, and I wish the presenters of this advice gratis could let it be heard inside Ebenezer and Zoar and some other places sacred to long-winded orations. Where these outspoken criticisms are not employed, the hearers rebuke prosiness by quietly walking away. Very unpleasant this, to find your congregation dispersing, but a very plain intimation that your ideas are also much dispersed.

In the street, a man must keep himself alive, and use many illustrations and anecdotes, and sprinkle a quaint remark here and there. To dwell long on a point will never do. Reasoning must be brief, clear, and soon done with. The discourse must not be labored or involved, neither must the second head depend upon the first, for the audience is a changing one, and each point must be complete in itself. The chain of thought must be taken to pieces and each link melted down and turned into bullets: you will need not so much Saladin's saber to cut through a muslin handkerchief as Coeur de Lion's battle-axe to break a bar of iron. Come to the point at once, and come there with all your might.

Short sentences of words and short passages of thought are needed for out-of-doors. Long paragraphs and long arguments had better be reserved for other occasions. In quiet country crowds there is much force in an eloquent silence, now and then interjected; it gives people time to breathe, and also to reflect. Do not, however, attempt this in a London street; you must go ahead, or someone else may run off with your congregation. In a regular field sermon pauses are very effective, and are useful in several ways, both to speaker and listeners, but to a passing company who are not inclined for anything like worship, quick, short, sharp address is most adapted.

In the streets a man must from beginning to end be intense, and for that very reason he must be condensed and concentrated in his thought and utterance. It would never do to begin by saying, "My text, dear friends, is a passage from the inspired Word, containing doctrines of the utmost importance, and bringing before us in the clearest manner the most valuable practical instruction. I invite your careful attention and the exercise of your most candid judgment while we consider it under various aspects and place it in different lights, in order that we may be able to perceive its position in the analogy of the faith. In its exegesis we shall find an arena for the cultured intellect, and the refined sensibilities. As the purling brook meanders among the meads and fertilizes the pastures, so a stream of sacred truth flows through the remarkable words which now lie before us. It will be well for us to divert the crystal current to the reservoir of our meditation, that we may quaff the cup of wisdom with the lips of satisfaction."

There, gentlemen, is not that rather above the average of word-spinning, and is not the art very generally in vogue in these days? If you go out to the obelisk in Blackfriars Road, and talk in that fashion, you will be saluted with "Go on, old buffer," or "Ain't he fine? My eye!" A very vulgar youth will cry, "What a mouth for a tater!" and another will shout in a tone of mock solemnity, "Amen!" If you give them chaff they will cheerfully return it into your own bosom. Good measure, pressed down and running over will they mete out to you. Shams and shows will have no mercy from a street gathering.

(From Spurgeon's "Open-Air Preaching: A Sketch of Its History and Remarks Thereon.")

I Have a Problem

"FATHER, I HAVE a problem. It's weighing heavy on me. It's all I can think about, night and day. Before I bring it to you in prayer, I suppose I should pray for those who are less fortunate than me—those in this world who have hardly enough food for this day, and for those who don't have a roof over their heads at night. I also pray for families who have lost loved ones in sudden death, for parents whose children have leukemia, for the many people who are dying of brain tumors, for the hundreds of thousands who are laid waste with other terrible cancers, for people whose bodies have been suddenly shattered in car wrecks, for those who are lying in hospitals with agonizing burns over their bodies, whose faces have been burned beyond recognition. I pray for people with emphysema, whose eyes fill with terror as they struggle for every breath merely to live, for those who are tormented beyond words by irrational fears, for the elderly who are wracked with the pains of aging, whose only 'escape' is death.

"I pray for people who are watching their loved ones fade before their eyes through the grief of Alzheimer's disease, for the many thousands who are suffering the agony of AIDS, for those who are in such despair that they are contemplating suicide, for people who are tormented by the demons of alcoholism and drug addiction. I pray for children who have been abandoned by their parents, for those who are sexually abused, for wives held in quiet despair, beaten and abused by cruel drunken husbands, for people whose minds have been destroyed by mental disorders, for those who have lost everything in floods, tornadoes, hurricanes, and earthquakes. I pray for the blind, who never see the faces of the ones they love or the beauty of a sunrise, for those whose bodies are deformed by painful arthritis, for the many whose lives will be taken from them today by murderers, for those wasting away on their deathbeds in hospitals.

"Most of all, I cry out for the millions who don't know the forgiveness that is in Jesus Christ...for those who in a moment of time will be swept into hell by the cold hand of death, and find to their utter horror the unspeakable vengeance of eternal fire. They will be eternally damned to everlasting punishment. O God, I pray for them.

"Strange. I can't seem to remember what my problem was. In Jesus' name I pray. Amen."

Titus

Greeting

1 Paul, a bondservant of God and an apostle of Jesus Christ, according to the faith of God's elect and the acknowledgment of the truth which accords with godliness, [2]in hope of eternal life which God, who cannot lie, promised before time began, [3]but has in due time manifested His word through preaching, which was committed to me according to the commandment of God our Savior;

[4]To Titus, a true son in *our* common faith:

Grace, mercy, *and* peace from God the Father and the Lord Jesus Christ[a] our Savior.

Qualified Elders

[5]For this reason I left you in Crete, that you should set in order the things that are lacking, and appoint elders in every city as I commanded you—[6]if a man is blameless, the husband of one wife, having faithful children not accused of dissipation or insubordination. [7]For a bishop[a] must be blameless, as a steward of God, not self-willed, not quick-tempered, not given to wine, not violent, not greedy for money, [8]but hospitable, a lover of what is good, sober-minded, just, holy, self-controlled, [9]holding fast the faithful word as he has been taught, that he may be able, by sound doctrine, both to exhort and convict those who contradict.

The Elders' Task

[10]For there are many insubordinate, both idle talkers and deceivers, especially those of the circumcision, [11]whose mouths must be stopped, who subvert whole households, teaching things which they ought not, for the sake of dishonest gain. [12]One of them, a prophet of their own, said, "Cretans *are* always liars, evil beasts, lazy gluttons." [13]This testimony is true. Therefore rebuke them sharply, that they may be sound in the faith, [14]not giving heed to Jewish fables and commandments of men who turn from the truth. [15]To the pure all things are pure, but to those who are defiled and unbelieving nothing is pure; but even their mind and conscience

1:4 [a]NU-Text reads *and Christ Jesus.* 1:7 [a]Literally *overseer*

1:1 Those in the world cry out for truth. They have no idea of their origin, why they exist, or what death holds in store for them. Sin has left them lost and in darkness. The truth will set them free (John 8:31,32), but there can be no understanding of the truth without repentance and faith. It comes *after* godliness.

1:9 The steward of God is not to see himself as being above the lowly task of evangelism.

1:11 The way to "stop the mouth" is to use the Law of God. See Rom. 3:19 comment.

1:15 Those who defile the conscience remove the battery from their own smoke detector.

QUESTIONS & OBJECTIONS

"Which is right, Calvinism or Arminianism?"

How do God's sovereign grace and man's responsibility to turn to Him fit together? For example, Ezek. 33:11 says, "'As I live,' says the Lord God, 'I have no pleasure in the death of the wicked, but that the wicked turn from his way and live. Turn, turn from your evil ways! For why should you die . . . ?" God Himself tells the sinner to "turn" from his evil ways or he will die.

It is clear from Scripture that He grants us repentance (Acts 5:31; 11:18), and He also gives us faith as a gift (Rom. 12:3). But He then commands *all* men everywhere to repent and to have faith (believe). See Mark 1:15; Acts 17:30. We read that God "is not willing that *any* should perish but that *all* should come to repentance" (2 Pet. 3:9, emphasis added).

Also, James 4:8 addresses sinners directly telling them to draw near to God, cleanse their hands, and purify their hearts. Jesus rebuked His disciples and called them "foolish" because they didn't believe (Mark 16:14; Luke 24:25).

Charles Spurgeon proclaimed divine sovereignty yet he also preached man's responsibility, although he admitted that he didn't understand how they fit together. Consider his exhortations to the sinner: "*Believe* in Jesus, and though you are now in slippery places your feet shall soon be set upon a rock of safety"; "Sinner, *fly* to Christ"; "O sinner, *humble yourself* under the mighty hand of God . . ." And it is the sinner's responsibility to trust in the Savior: "Trust Christ with your soul and He will save it. I know you will not do this unless the Holy Spirit constrains you, *but this does not remove your responsibility*."

The Armenian and Calvinist views are diametrically opposed to each other, yet believers on both sides point to a thousand verses to back their theology. If you choose one view or the other, don't let your choice cut you off from others who may believe differently. The two opposing truths can walk together. All that is missing is some information for them to harmonize. The day will come when we will understand everything (1 Cor. 13:12), and it is then we will be so glad that we didn't cause division by arguing about which one is right.

Sadly, church history has shown us that Christ-centered men of God have clashed over these issues (e.g., Wesley and Whitefield). More recently, I have seen brethren make a theological stand and much to their dismay, they were marked by their home church as "troublemakers." Fine missionaries have been pulled from the field, pastors fired from the ministry, and churches have split, simply because of different views of God's sovereignty.

So, if you do get it worked out, be careful that you strive to keep unity among the brethren, and then focus on your God-given commission. Firefighters exist to fight fires, not to fight each other. They must have unity of purpose. Every moment that you and I spend arguing about theological interpretations is time we have lost forever, that could have been spent in prayer for the unsaved or in seeking to save that which is lost.

are defiled. [16]They profess to know God,
but in works they deny Him, being
abominable, disobedient, and disqualified
for every good work.

Qualities of a Sound Church

2 But as for you, speak the things which
are proper for sound doctrine: [2]that
the older men be sober, reverent, temperate,
sound in faith, in love, in patience;
[3]the older women likewise, that they be
reverent in behavior, not slanderers, not
given to much wine, teachers of good
things— [4]that they admonish the young
women to love their husbands, to love
their children, [5]to be discreet, chaste,
homemakers, good, obedient to their own
husbands, that the word of God may not
be blasphemed.

[6]Likewise, exhort the young men to be

1:16 There are many who profess to know God, but they lack the things that accompany salvation—the fruit of righteousness, holiness, repentance, good works, and the fruit of the Spirit. We must repent, turn to God, and do works befitting repentance (Acts 26:20).

2:6–8 We must be sober-minded, rich in good works, sound in doctrine, living in the fear of God and without corruption—all for the sake of our testimony.

sober-minded, 7in all things showing
yourself *to be* a pattern of good works; in
doctrine *showing* integrity, reverence, incorruptibility,[a] 8sound speech that cannot be condemned, that one who is an
opponent may be ashamed, having nothing evil to say of you.[a]

> He is no Christian who does not seek to serve his God. The very motto of the Christian should be 'I serve.'
>
> **CHARLES SPURGEON**

9*Exhort* bondservants to be obedient
to their own masters, to be well pleasing
in all *things,* not answering back, 10not
pilfering, but showing all good fidelity,
that they may adorn the doctrine of God
our Savior in all things.

Trained by Saving Grace

11For the grace of God that brings salvation has appeared to all men, 12teaching
us that, denying ungodliness and worldly
lusts, we should live soberly, righteously,
and godly in the present age, 13looking
for the blessed hope and glorious appearing of our great God and Savior Jesus
Christ, 14who gave Himself for us, that
He might redeem us from every lawless
deed and purify for Himself *His* own special people, zealous for good works.

15Speak these things, exhort, and rebuke with all authority. Let no one despise you.

Graces of the Heirs of Grace

3 Remind them to be subject to rulers
and authorities, to obey, to be ready
for every good work, 2to speak evil of no
one, to be peaceable, gentle, showing all
humility to all men. 3For we ourselves
were also once foolish, disobedient, deceived, serving various lusts and pleasures, living in malice and envy, hateful
and hating one another. 4But when the
kindness and the love of God our Savior

2:7 [a]NU-Text omits *incorruptibility.* 2:8 [a]NU-Text and M-Text read *us.*

2:12 "The fact is that the New Testament message embraces a great deal more than an offer of free pardon. It is a message of pardon, and for that may God be praised; but it is also a message of repentance. It is a message of atonement, but it is also a message of temperance and righteousness and godliness in this present world. It tells us that we must accept a Savior, but it tells us also that we must deny ungodliness and worldly lusts. The gospel message includes the idea of amendment, of separation from the world, of cross-carrying and loyalty to the kingdom of God even unto death…

"To offer a sinner the gift of salvation based upon the work of Christ, while at the same time allowing him to retain the idea that the gift carries with it no moral implications, is to do him untold injury where it hurts him worst." *A. W. Tozer*

3:2 This is the spirit in which we should share our faith. See James 3:17.

3:3 The deceitfulness of sin. Two women from Southern California were about to cross the Mexican border to return to the U.S. when they saw what looked like a very small, sick animal in the ditch beside their car. As they examined it in the darkness of the night, they saw that it was a tiny Chihuahua. There they decided to take it home with them and nurse it back to health. However, because they were afraid that they were breaking the law, they put it in the trunk of their car, and drove across the border. Once they were in the U.S., they retrieved the animal and nursed it until they arrived home.

One of the women was so concerned for the ailing dog that she actually took it to bed with her, and reached out several times during the night to touch the tiny animal and reassure it that she was still present. The dog was so sick the next morning, she decided to take it to the veterinarian. That's when she found out that the animal wasn't a tiny sick dog. It was a Mexican water rat, dying of rabies.

The world, in the blackness of its ignorance, thinks that sin is a puppy to be played with. It is the light of God's Law that enlightens the sinner to the fact that he is in bed with a deadly rat.

We were once "deceived, serving various lusts and pleasures," but now, if we are truly converted, our eyes have been opened. We see sin for the sugar-coated venom that it is. This is why we should never have a holier-than-thou attitude toward the unsaved (see also 1 Cor. 6:9–11).

toward man appeared, [5]not by works of
righteousness which we have done, but
according to His mercy He saved us,
through the washing of regeneration and
renewing of the Holy Spirit, [6]whom He
poured out on us abundantly through
Jesus Christ our Savior, [7]that having been
justified by His grace we should become
heirs according to the hope of eternal life.
[8]This is a faithful saying, and these
things I want you to affirm constantly, that
those who have believed in God should be
careful to maintain good works. These
things are good and profitable to men.

Avoid Dissension

[9]But avoid foolish disputes, genealogies, contentions, and strivings about the
law; for they are unprofitable and useless.
[10]Reject a divisive man after the first and
second admonition, [11]knowing that such
a person is warped and sinning, being
self-condemned.

Final Messages

[12]When I send Artemas to you, or
Tychicus, be diligent to come to me at
Nicopolis, for I have decided to spend the

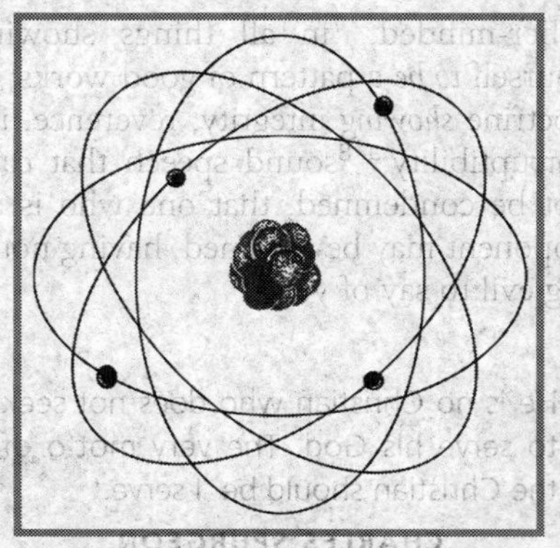

The Bible tells us that God created everything with things that are not seen. *See Heb. 11:3 comment.*

winter there. [13]Send Zenas the lawyer and
Apollos on their journey with haste, that
they may lack nothing. [14]And let our *people* also learn to maintain good works, to
meet urgent needs, that they may not be
unfruitful.

Farewell

[15]All who *are* with me greet you. Greet
those who love us in the faith.

Grace *be* with you all. Amen.

3:5 New birth—its necessity for salvation. See 1 Pet. 1:3.

For those trusting in good works, see Gal. 2:16 comment.

3:10 It is wise to avoid those brethren who only want to argue about doctrine. Rather, put your energy into reaching the lost.

Worship of the loving God is man's whole reason for existence.
That is why we are born and that is why we are born again from above.
That is why we were created and that is why we have been recreated.
That is why there was a genesis at the beginning, and
that is why there is a re-genesis, called regeneration.

A. W. TOZER

Philemon

Greeting

Paul, a prisoner of Christ Jesus, and Timothy *our* brother,

To Philemon our beloved *friend* and fellow laborer, 2to the beloved[a] Apphia, Archippus our fellow soldier, and to the church in your house:

3Grace to you and peace from God our Father and the Lord Jesus Christ.

Philemon's Love and Faith

4I thank my God, making mention of you always in my prayers, 5hearing of your love and faith which you have toward the Lord Jesus and toward all the saints, 6that the sharing of your faith may become effective by the acknowledgment of every good thing which is in you[a] in Christ Jesus. 7For we have[a] great joy[b] and consolation in your love, because the hearts of the saints have been refreshed by you, brother.

The Plea for Onesimus

8Therefore, though I might be very bold in Christ to command you what is fitting, 9*yet* for love's sake I rather appeal *to you*—being such a one as Paul, the aged, and now also a prisoner of Jesus Christ— 10I appeal to you for my son Onesimus, whom I have begotten *while* in my chains, 11who once was unprofitable to you, but now is profitable to you and to me.

12I am sending him back.[a] You therefore receive him, that is, my own heart, 13whom I wished to keep with me, that on your behalf he might minister to me in my chains for the gospel. 14But without your consent I wanted to do nothing, that your good deed might not be by compulsion, as it were, but voluntary.

15For perhaps he departed for a while for this *purpose*, that you might receive him forever, 16no longer as a slave but more than a slave—a beloved brother, especially to me but how much more to you, both in the flesh and in the Lord.

Philemon's Obedience Encouraged

17If then you count me as a partner,

2 [a]NU-Text reads *to our sister Apphia.* 6 [a]NU-Text and M-Text read *us.* 7 [a]NU-Text reads *had.* [b]M-Text reads *thanksgiving.* 12 [a]NU-Text reads *back to you in person, that is, my own heart.*

4–6 For the sharing of our faith to be "effective" (active, operative, and powerful), we must not confine our love to the Lord Jesus and the saints. Philemon's love went beyond the walls of the church building. He communicated his faith. This is what made Paul prayerfully thankful.

11 Now that the runaway slave was a Christian, upon return to Philemon he would be "profitable." The world gains unspeakable profit from the presence of Christians. People who once were filled with corruption, upon conversion live as law-abiding, useful members of society. Onesimus ("useful") would be a faithful servant for God's kingdom. He would work not only for his earthly master, but also for his heavenly Master, to whom he had submitted himself as a willing slave.

receive him as *you would* me. 18But if he
has wronged you or owes anything, put
that on my account. 19I, Paul, am writing
with my own hand. I will repay—not to
mention to you that you owe me even
your own self besides. 20Yes, brother, let
me have joy from you in the Lord; refresh
my heart in the Lord.
21Having confidence in your obedience, I write to you, knowing that you
will do even more than I say. 22But,
meanwhile, also prepare a guest room for
me, for I trust that through your prayers
I shall be granted to you.

Farewell

23Epaphras, my fellow prisoner in
Christ Jesus, greets you, 24*as do* Mark,
Aristarchus, Demas, Luke, my fellow laborers.
25The grace of our Lord Jesus Christ *be*
with your spirit. Amen.

"The Bible is the best book in the world. It contains more than all the libraries I have seen."

John Adams

Great Leaders Speak About the Bible

"Here is a Book worth more than all the other books which were ever printed." *Patrick Henry*

"That book, Sir, is the Rock upon which our republic rests." *Andrew Jackson*

"The more profoundly we study this wonderful Book, and the more closely we observe its divine precepts, the better citizens we will become and the higher will be our destiny as a nation." *William McKinley*

"The best religion the world has ever known is the religion of the Bible. It builds up all that is good." *Rutherford B. Hayes*

"There are a good many problems before the American people today, and before me as President, but I expect to find the solution of those problems just in the proportion that I am faithful in the study of the Word of God." *Woodrow Wilson*

"The whole inspiration of our civilization springs from the teachings of Christ and the lessons of the prophets. To read the Bible for these fundamentals is a necessity of American life." *Herbert Hoover*

"I say to you, Search the Scriptures! The Bible is the book of all others, to be read at all ages, and in all conditions of human life; not to be read once or twice or thrice through, and then laid aside, but to be read in small portions of one or two chapters every day, and never to be intermitted, unless by some overruling necessity." *John Quincy Adams*

"We cannot read the history of our rise and development as a nation, without reckoning the place the Bible has occupied in shaping the advances of the Republic." *Franklin D. Roosevelt*

"In all my perplexities and distresses, the Bible has never failed to give me light and strength." *Robert E. Lee*

"Within the covers of the Bible are all the answers for all the problems men face. The Bible can touch hearts, order minds and refresh souls." *Ronald Reagan*

"I have read the Bible through many times, and now make it a practice to read it through once every year. It is a book of all others for lawyers, as well as divines; and I pity the man who cannot find in it a rich supply of thought and of rules for conduct. It fits a man for life—it prepares him for death." *Daniel Webster*

Hebrews

God's Supreme Revelation

1 God, who at various times and in various ways spoke in time past to the fathers by the prophets, 2has in these last days spoken to us by *His* Son, whom He has appointed heir of all things, through whom also He made the worlds; 3who being the brightness of *His* glory and the express image of His person, and upholding all things by the word of His power, when He had by Himself[a] purged our[b] sins, sat down at the right hand of the Majesty on high, 4having become so much better than the angels, as He has by inheritance obtained a more excellent name than they.

The Son Exalted Above Angels

5For to which of the angels did He ever say:

"You are My Son,
Today I have begotten You"?[a]

And again:

"I will be to Him a Father,
And He shall be to Me a Son"?[b]

6But when He again brings the firstborn into the world, He says:

"Let all the angels of God worship Him."[a]

7And of the angels He says:

"Who makes His angels spirits
And His ministers a flame of fire."[a]

8But to the Son *He says:*

"Your throne, O God, is forever and ever;
A scepter of righteousness is the scepter of Your kingdom.
9 *You have loved righteousness and hated lawlessness;*
Therefore God, Your God, has anointed You

1:3 [a]NU-Text omits *by Himself.* [b]NU-Text omits *our.* 1:5 [a]Psalm 2:7 [b]2 Samuel 7:14 1:6 [a]Deuteronomy 32:43 (Septuagint, Dead Sea Scrolls); Psalm 97:7 1:7 [a]Psalm 104:4 1:9 [a]Psalm 45:6, 7

1:1 The Bible's inspiration. The Bible doesn't attempt to defend its inspiration. But here is an interesting thing: Genesis opens with the words "God said" nine times in the first chapter. The statement "Thus says the Lord" appears 23 times in the last Old Testament book, Malachi. So you have "God says" from Genesis to Malachi. "The Lord spoke" appears 560 times in the first five books of the Bible and at least 3,800 times in the whole of the Old Testament! Isaiah claims at least 40 times that his message came directly from the Lord; Ezekiel, 60 times; and Jeremiah, 100 times. See also Deut. 18:20–22 and Matt. 4:4 comments.

"Defend the Bible? I would as soon defend a lion!" *Charles Spurgeon*

1:2,3 "There is a Being who made all things, who holds all things in His power, and is therefore to be feared." *Sir Isaac Newton*

1:5 *Jehovah's Witnesses: Witnessing Tips*

By David A. Reed, Ex-Jehovah's Witness elder

Encounters between Christians and Jehovah's Witnesses typically revolve around a discussion of deity. The reason for this is twofold. First, this is the area where Watchtower theology deviates most dramatically from orthodox Christianity. In contrast to the Trinitarian concept of one God in three Persons—Father, Son, and Holy Spirit—the JWs have been taught to believe that God the Father alone is "Jehovah," the only true God; that Jesus Christ is Michael the archangel, the first angelic being created by God; and that the Holy Spirit is neither God nor a person, but rather God's impersonal "active force." Second, the subject of deity is a frequent confrontational focus because *both* Jehovah's Witnesses and Christians (at least those who like to witness to JWs) feel confident and well-prepared to defend their stand and attack the opposing viewpoint.

Due to the profound theological differences, such discussions often take the form of spiritual trench warfare—a long series of arguments and counterarguments, getting nowhere and ending in mutual frustration. But this need not be the case, especially if the Christian will "become all things to all men" by taking a moment to put himself in the Witness's shoes, so to speak (see 1 Cor. 9:22). In the JW's mind he himself is a worshiper of the true God of the Bible, while you are a lost soul who has been misled by the devil into worshiping a pagan three-headed deity. He is, no doubt, quite sincere in these beliefs and feels both threatened and offended by the doctrine of the Trinity. To give any serious consideration to your arguments in support of the Trinity is simply unthinkable to the JW; he would be sinning against Jehovah God to entertain such a thought.

So, in order to make any headway with the Witness, it is necessary to bridge the gap—to find common ground that will enable him to rethink his theology. Rather than plunging into a defense of "the doctrine of the Trinity," which can be mind-boggling even to a Christian, take things one step at a time.

A good first step would be to consider the question, "Is Jesus Christ really an angel?" It will be frightening to the Jehovah's Witness to open this cherished belief of his to critical re-examination, but not nearly as frightening as to start off discussing evidence that God is triune.

Since the Watchtower Society speaks of "Jesus Christ, whom we understand from the Scriptures to be Michael the archangel" (*The Watchtower,* Feb. 15, 1979, p. 31), put the JW on the spot and ask him to show you "the Scriptures" that say Jesus is Michael. There are none. The Watchtower Society *New World Translation* (NWT) mentions Michael five times as: 1) "one of the foremost princes" (Dan. 10:13); 2) "the prince of [Daniel's] people" (Dan. 10:21); 3) "the great prince who is standing in behalf of the sons of [Daniel's] people" (Dan. 12:1); 4) "the archangel" who "had a difference with the devil and was disputing about Moses' body" but "did not dare to bring a judgment against him in abusive terms" (Jude 9); and 5) a participant in heavenly conflict when "Michael and his angels battled with the dragon" (Rev. 12:7).

Ask the Jehovah's Witness which one of these verses says that Michael is Jesus Christ. Help him to see that it is necessary to read Scripture *plus* a complicated Watchtower argument to reach that conclusion. Rather than being merely "*one of* the foremost princes," Jesus Christ is "Lord of lords and King of kings" (Rev. 17:14, NWT) and is "far above every government and authority and power and lordship and every name named, not only in this system of things, but also in that to come" (Eph. 1:21, NWT). And, unlike "Michael who did not dare condemn the Devil with insulting words, but said, 'The Lord rebuke you!'" (Jude 9, *Today's English Version*), Jesus Christ displayed His authority over the devil when He freely commanded him, "Go away, Satan!" (Matt. 4:10, NWT).

In arguing that Jesus is Michael the archangel, the Watchtower Society also points to another verse that does not use the name Michael but says that "the Lord himself will descend from heaven with a commanding call, with an archangel's voice and with God's trumpet..." (1 Thess. 4:16, NWT). However, the expression "with an archangel's voice" simply means that the archangel, like God's trumpet, will herald the coming of the Lord, not that the Lord is an archangel.

Point out to the JW that none of the verses he has attempted to use as proof-texts even comes close to stating that Jesus Christ is Michael the archangel. In fact, Scripture clearly teaches the opposite: namely, that the Son of God is *superior* to the angels. The entire first chapter of Hebrews is devoted to this theme. Have the Witness read Hebrews chapter one aloud with you, and, as you do so, interrupt to point out the sharp contrast between angels and the Son of God. "For to what angel did God ever say, 'Thou are my Son...?' And again, when he brings the first-born into the world, he says, 'Let all God's angels worship him'" (vv. 5,6, *Revised Standard Version*).

Remind the JW that angels consistently refuse

(continued)

(1:5 continued)
worship ("Be careful! Do not do that! ...Worship God," Rev. 22:8,9, NWT), but the Father's command concerning the Son is, "Let all God's angels worship him" (Heb. 1:6). That is how the Watchtower's own *New World Translation* read for some 20 years until, in 1970, the Society changed it to read "do obeisance to him" instead of "worship him"—part of their consistent campaign to eliminate from their Bible all references to the deity of Christ. (See John 10:36 comment.)

True, you have not yet proved the "doctrine of the Trinity" in this discussion. But you have laid a good foundation by giving the Jehovah's Witness convincing evidence that Jesus Christ is not an angel (he is now faced with the question of who Jesus really is), and you have shown that the Watchtower Society has misled him, even resorting to altering Scripture to do so. Now you are in a much better position to go on to present the gospel. For more information on Jehovahs' Witnesses, see page 1698.

With the oil of gladness more than
Your companions."[a]

[10]And:

"You, LORD, in the beginning laid the
foundation of the earth,
And the heavens are the work of Your
hands.
[11]*They will perish, but You remain;*
And they will all grow old like a
garment;
[12]*Like a cloak You will fold them up,*
And they will be changed.
But You are the same,
And Your years will not fail."[a]

[13]But to which of the angels has He ever said:

"Sit at My right hand,
Till I make Your enemies Your
footstool"?[a]

[14]Are they not all ministering spirits sent forth to minister for those who will inherit salvation?

Do Not Neglect Salvation

2 Therefore we must give the more
earnest heed to the things we have
heard, lest we drift away. [2]For if the word
spoken through angels proved steadfast,
and every transgression and disobedience
received a just reward, [3]how shall we escape if we neglect so great a salvation,
which at the first began to be spoken by
the Lord, and was confirmed to us by
those who heard *Him*, [4]God also bearing
witness both with signs and wonders,
with various miracles, and gifts of the
Holy Spirit, according to His own will?

The Son Made Lower than Angels

[5]For He has not put the world to come,
of which we speak, in subjection to an-

1:12 [a]Psalm 102:25–27 1:13 [a]Psalm 110:1

1:10 The divine foot. Professor *Richard Lewontin*, an evolutionary biologist and geneticist, reveals the reason evolutionists are so against Intelligent Design—regardless of whether or not the facts support it:

> We take the side of science *in spite* of the patent absurdity of some of its constructs, *in spite* of its failure to fulfill many of its extravagant promises of health and life, *in spite* of the tolerance of the scientific community for unsubstantiated just-so stories, because we have a prior commitment, a commitment to materialism. It is not that the methods and institutions of science somehow compel us to accept a material explanation of the phenomenal world, but, on the contrary, that we are forced by our *a priori* adherence to material causes to create an apparatus of investigation and a set of concepts that produce material explanations, no matter how counter-intuitive, no matter how mystifying to the uninitiated. Moreover, that materialism is an absolute, for we cannot allow a Divine Foot in the door. ("Billions and billions of demons," *The New York Review*, emphasis in original)

The reason evolutionists stubbornly hold to their absurd beliefs, even though they are unsubstantiated, is that they "cannot allow a Divine Foot in the door." We have news for Mr. Lewontin. It is too late. God is in the house. For details on the fallacy of evolution, see Isa. 45:18 comment.

1:11 See Psa. 102:26 comment.

SPRINGBOARDS FOR PREACHING AND WITNESSING

The Titanic

2:10 The story of the *Titanic* has incredibly close parallels to the biblical plan of salvation. Just as the great pleasure ship struck an iceberg and sank, this great world—with all its inhabitants—is slowly sinking into the cold grip of death. As with the *Titanic*, where only those passengers who believed that they were in impending danger looked to the lifeboats, so only those who believe that they are in mortal danger will look to the Lifeboat of the Savior, Jesus Christ. The great "iceberg" that will take the world to an icy grave is the moral Law, the Ten Commandments.

Here is the evidence that we are sinking: Jesus said that if we look with lust, we commit adultery in our heart. No one who has had sex outside of marriage, or any liar, or any thief will enter heaven. The Bible says that if we hate someone, we are guilty of murder. We fail to put God first. We make a god in our image. We break all the Commandments. If we stay with the "ship," we will perish on the Day of Judgment, when all of our sins come out as evidence of our guilt. God, however, is rich in mercy and doesn't want anyone to go to hell. He made a way for us to be saved. Jesus Christ, the One whom the Bible calls the "Captain of our salvation," gave His life so that we could have a place in the lifeboat. He took our punishment upon Himself, suffering on the cross for us. We broke God's Law, but He paid our fine. Then He rose from the dead, defeating death. The moment we repent and trust in Him alone for our eternal salvation, God will forgive us and grant us the gift of eternal life.

Don't hesitate. You may wait until it's too late! It was reported that some of the lifeboats that left the *Titanic* early were only half full. Many more on board could have been saved, but they refused to believe that the great "unsinkable" ship was sinking. They perished because their faith was misguided. Don't be like them. Believe the gospel. Repent and trust Jesus Christ today . . . and God will never let you down.

gels. [6]But one testified in a certain place,
saying:

"What is man that You are mindful of
him,
Or the son of man that You take care
of him?
[7] *You have made him a little lower than*
the angels;
You have crowned him with glory and
honor,[a]
And set him over the works of Your
hands.
[8] *You have put all things in subjection*
under his feet."[a]

For in that He put all in subjection under
him, He left nothing *that is* not put
under him. But now we do not yet see
all things put under him. [9]But we see
Jesus, who was made a little lower than
the angels, for the suffering of death
crowned with glory and honor, that He,
by the grace of God, might taste death for
everyone.

Bringing Many Sons to Glory

[10]For it was fitting for Him, for whom
are all things and by whom *are* all things,
in bringing many sons to glory, to make the
captain of their salvation perfect through
sufferings. [11]For both He who sanctifies
and those who are being sanctified *are* all
of one, for which reason He is not ashamed
to call them brethren, [12]saying:

"I will declare Your name to My
brethren;
In the midst of the assembly I will sing
praise to You."[a]

2:7 [a]NU-Text and M-Text omit the rest of verse 7. 2:8 [a]Psalm 8:4–6 2:12 [a]Psalm 22:22

2:6 "Young man, the secret of my success is that at an early age I discovered I was not God." *Oliver Wendell Holmes, Jr.*

13And again:

"I will put My trust in Him."[a]

And again:

"Here am I and the children whom
God has given Me."[b]

14Inasmuch then as the children have
partaken of flesh and blood, He Himself
likewise shared in the same, that through
death He might destroy him who had the
power of death, that is, the devil, 15and
release those who through fear of death
were all their lifetime subject to bondage.
16For indeed He does not give aid to angels, but He does give aid to the seed of
Abraham. 17Therefore, in all things He
had to be made like *His* brethren, that He
might be a merciful and faithful High Priest
in things *pertaining* to God, to make propitiation for the sins of the people. 18For
in that He Himself has suffered, being
tempted, He is able to aid those who are
tempted.

The Son Was Faithful

3 Therefore, holy brethren, partakers
of the heavenly calling, consider the
Apostle and High Priest of our confession, Christ Jesus, 2who was faithful to
Him who appointed Him, as Moses also
was faithful in all His house. 3For this
One has been counted worthy of more
glory than Moses, inasmuch as He who
built the house has more honor than the
house. 4For every house is built by someone, but He who built all things *is* God.
5And Moses indeed *was* faithful in all His
house as a servant, for a testimony of
those things which would be spoken
afterward, 6but Christ as a Son over His
own house, whose house we are if we
hold fast the confidence and the rejoicing of the hope firm to the end.[a]

Be Faithful

7Therefore, as the Holy Spirit says:

THE FUNCTION OF THE LAW

3:12 "While [every true believer] cries out, 'O what love have I unto thy Law! All the day long is my study in it;' he sees daily, in that divine mirror, more and more of his own sinfulness. He sees more and more clearly that he is fullness a sinner in all things—that neither his heart nor his ways are right before God, and that every moment sends him to Christ.

"Therefore I cannot spare the Law one moment, no more than I can spare Christ, seeing I now want it as much to keep me to Christ, as I ever wanted it to bring me to Him. Otherwise this 'evil heart of unbelief' would immediately 'depart from the living God.' Indeed each is continually sending me to the other—the Law to Christ, and Christ to the Law." *John Wesley*

"Today, if you will hear His voice,
8*Do not harden your hearts as in the*
rebellion,
In the day of trial in the wilderness,
9*Where your fathers tested Me, tried*
Me,
And saw My works forty years.
10*Therefore I was angry with that*
generation,
And said, 'They always go astray in
their heart,
And they have not known My ways.'
11*So I swore in My wrath,*
'They shall not enter My rest.' "[a]

12Beware, brethren, lest there be in any
of you an evil heart of unbelief in departing from the living God; 13but exhort one
another daily, while it is called *"Today,"*
lest any of you be hardened through the
deceitfulness of sin. 14For we have become partakers of Christ if we hold the
beginning of our confidence steadfast to
the end, 15while it is said:

"Today, if you will hear His voice,
Do not harden your hearts as in the
rebellion."[a]

2:13 [a]2 Samuel 22:3; Isaiah 8:17 [b]Isaiah 8:18 3:6 [a]NU-Text omits *firm to the end.* 3:11 [a]Psalm 95:7–11 3:15 [a]Psalm 95:7, 8

Failure of the Wilderness Wanderers

16For who, having heard, rebelled? Indeed, *was it* not all who came out of Egypt, *led* by Moses? 17Now with whom was He angry forty years? *Was it* not with those who sinned, whose corpses fell in the wilderness? 18And to whom did He swear that they would not enter His rest, but to those who did not obey? 19So we see that they could not enter in because of unbelief.

The Promise of Rest

4 Therefore, since a promise remains of entering His rest, let us fear lest any of you seem to have come short of it. 2For indeed the gospel was preached to us as well as to them; but the word which they heard did not profit them,[a] not being mixed with faith in those who heard *it.* 3For we who have believed do enter that rest, as He has said:

"So I swore in My wrath,
'They shall not enter My rest,' "[a]

although the works were finished from the foundation of the world. 4For He has spoken in a certain place of the seventh *day* in this way: *"And God rested on the seventh day from all His works";*[a] 5and again in this *place: "They shall not enter My rest."*[a]

6Since therefore it remains that some *must* enter it, and those to whom it was first preached did not enter because of disobedience, 7again He designates a certain day, saying in David, *"Today,"* after such a long time, as it has been said:

"Today, if you will hear His voice,
Do not harden your hearts."[a]

8For if Joshua had given them rest, then He would not afterward have spoken of another day. 9There remains therefore a rest for the people of God. 10For he who has entered His rest has himself also ceased from his works as God *did* from His.

The Word Discovers Our Condition

11Let us therefore be diligent to enter

4:2 [a]NU-Text and M-Text read *profit them,* since they were not united by faith with those who heeded it. 4:3 [a]Psalm 95:11 4:4 [a]Genesis 2:2 4:5 [a]Psalm 95:11 4:7 [a]Psalm 95:7, 8

4:4 Creation in six days. Most theologians throughout church history agree that in using the phrase "the evening and the morning were the first day," the creation account in Genesis is speaking of a literal 24-hour day, rather than a general time or a period of years. (See Gen. 1:5 comment.)

"To understand the meaning of 'day' in Gen. 1, we need to determine how the Hebrew word for 'day,' *yom*, is used in the context of Scripture . . . A number, and the phrase 'evening and morning,' are used for each of the six days of creation (Gen. 1:5,8,13,19,23,31). Outside Gen. 1, *yom* is used with a number 359 times, and each time it means an ordinary day—why would Genesis 1 be the exception?

"Outside Gen. 1, *yom* is used with the word 'evening' or 'morning' 23 times. 'Evening' and 'morning' appear in association, but without *yom*, 38 times. All 61 times the text refers to an ordinary day—why would Genesis 1 be the exception?

"In Genesis 1:5, *yom* occurs in context with the word 'night.' Outside of Gen. 1, 'night' is used with *yom* 53 times—and each time it means an ordinary day. Why would Gen. 1 be the exception? Even the usage of the word 'light' with *yom* in this passage determines the meaning as ordinary day.

"There are words in biblical Hebrew (such as *olam* or *qedem*) that are very suitable for communicating long periods of time, or indefinite time, but *none* of these words are used in Gen. 1. Alternatively, the days or years could have been compared with grains of sand if long periods were meant. If we are prepared to let the words of the language speak to us in accord with the context and normal definitions, without being influenced by outside ideas, then the word for 'day' found in Gen. 1—which is qualified by a number, the phrase 'evening and morning' and for Day 1 the words 'light and darkness'—*obviously* means an ordinary day (about 24 hours)." *Ken Ham, et al., The New Answers Book*

4:7 Isaiah 55:6 exhorts the lost to "seek the LORD while He may be found, call upon Him while He is near." God's offer of grace will end, so sinners are commanded to seek the Lord "while He may be found." They must then "call" upon Him. An intellectual belief in His existence is not saving faith. Romans 10:13 says "whoever *calls* on the name of the LORD shall be saved" (emphasis added).

THE FUNCTION OF THE LAW

4:12 "It is the ordinary method of the Spirit of God to convict sinners by the Law. It is this which, being set home on the conscience, generally breaketh the rocks in pieces. It is more especially this part of the Word of God which is quick and powerful, full of life and energy and sharper than any two-edged sword." *John Wesley*

"The Law cuts into the core of the evil, it reveals the seat of the malady, and informs us that the leprosy lies deep within." *Charles Spurgeon*

that rest, lest anyone fall according to the same example of disobedience. 12For the word of God *is* living and powerful, and sharper than any two-edged sword, piercing even to the division of soul and spirit, and of joints and marrow, and is a discerner of the thoughts and intents of the heart. 13And there is no creature hidden from His sight, but all things *are* naked and open to the eyes of Him to whom we *must give* account.

Our Compassionate High Priest

14Seeing then that we have a great High Priest who has passed through the heavens, Jesus the Son of God, let us hold fast *our* confession. 15For we do not have a High Priest who cannot sympathize with our weaknesses, but was in all *points* tempted as *we are, yet* without sin. 16Let us therefore come boldly to the throne of grace, that we may obtain mercy and find grace to help in time of need.

Qualifications for High Priesthood

5 For every high priest taken from among men is appointed for men in things *pertaining* to God, that he may offer both gifts and sacrifices for sins. 2He can have compassion on those who are ignorant and going astray, since he himself is also subject to weakness. 3Because of this he is required as for the people, so also for himself, to offer *sacrifices* for sins. 4And no man takes this honor to himself, but he who is called by God, just as Aaron *was*.

A Priest Forever

5So also Christ did not glorify Himself to become High Priest, but *it was* He who said to Him:

"You are My Son,
Today I have begotten You."[a]

6As *He* also says in another *place:*

"You are a priest forever

5:5 [a]Psalm 2:7

4:12 Soldier of Christ, throw away your sheath, it is not part of your armor. Strap the two-edged sword firmly in your hand. The way to keep the sword on hand is to have it in your mouth. In Jer. 1:7–9, God told the prophet not to be afraid to speak. God then put His words in Jeremiah's mouth, and in chapter 5 we are given a report of his transformation: "Thus says the LORD God of hosts: 'Because you speak this word, behold, I will make My words in your mouth fire, and this people wood, and it shall devour them'" (v. 14).

4:15 Some believe that because Scripture says Jesus was "in all points tempted as we are" that He must have struggled with temptations to lie, steal, sin sexually, etc. But Scripture explains that all the attractions of this world fit into three categories: the lust of the flesh, the lust of the eyes, and the pride of life (1 John 2:16). Jesus was tempted by the devil in these three areas and, as the "last Adam," He successfully passed the tests. These are the same tests that the first Adam underwent and failed (Gen. 3:6). Adam and Eve saw that the tree was good for food ("lust of the flesh"; compare Luke 4:3,4), was pleasant to the eyes ("lust of the eyes"; compare Luke 4:5–8), and was desirable to make one wise ("pride of life"; compare Luke 4:9–12). We will "pass the test" and not succumb to these temptations by following Jesus' example. He quoted the truths of the Word of God, using the sword of the Spirit to refute the lies of the enemy.

4:16 If you have a zeal for the lost, you will be a target for the enemy of your soul. He wants you to be beset by sin. His devious obsession is for iniquity to defile your conscience, and therefore take away your confidence before God. God forbid that we should allow that to happen. May each of us be so saturated in prayer and in the grace of God that we can boldly come before His throne with our head held high in faith and effectively stand in the gap for a dark and sinful world.

According to the order of
Melchizedek";[a]
[7]who, in the days of His flesh, when He had offered up prayers and supplications, with vehement cries and tears to Him who was able to save Him from death, and was heard because of His godly fear, [8]though He was a Son, *yet* He learned obedience by the things which He suffered. [9]And having been perfected, He became the author of eternal salvation to all who obey Him, [10]called by God as High Priest *"according to the order of Melchizedek,"* [11]of whom we have much to say, and hard to explain, since you have become dull of hearing.

Spiritual Immaturity

[12]For though by this time you ought to be teachers, you need *someone* to teach you again the first principles of the oracles of God; and you have come to need milk and not solid food. [13]For everyone who partakes *only* of milk *is* unskilled in the word of righteousness, for he is a babe. [14]But solid food belongs to those who are of full age, *that is,* those who by reason of use have their senses exercised to discern both good and evil.

The Peril of Not Progressing

6 Therefore, leaving the discussion of the elementary *principles* of Christ, let us go on to perfection, not laying again the foundation of repentance from dead works and of faith toward God, [2]of the doctrine of baptisms, of laying on of hands, of resurrection of the dead, and of eternal judgment. [3]And this we will[a] do if God permits.

[4]For *it is* impossible for those who were once enlightened, and have tasted the heavenly gift, and have become partakers of the Holy Spirit, [5]and have tasted the good word of God and the powers of the age to come, [6]if they fall away,[a] to renew them again to repentance, since they crucify again for themselves the Son of God, and put *Him* to an open shame.

[7]For the earth which drinks in the rain that often comes upon it, and bears herbs useful for those by whom it is cultivated, receives blessing from God; [8]but if it bears thorns and briers, *it is* rejected and near to being cursed, whose end *is* to be burned.

No sinner looks to the Savior with a dry eye or a hard heart. Aim, therefore, at heart-breaking, at bringing home condemnation to the conscience and weaning the mind from sin. Be not content till the whole mind is deeply and vitally changed in reference to sin.

CHARLES SPURGEON

A Better Estimate

[9]But, beloved, we are confident of better things concerning you, yes, things that accompany salvation, though we speak in this manner. [10]For God *is* not unjust to forget your work and labor of[a] love which you have shown toward His name, *in that* you have ministered to the saints, and do minister. [11]And we desire that each one of you show the same diligence to the full assurance of hope until the end, [12]that you do not become sluggish, but imitate those who through faith and patience inherit the promises.

God's Infallible Purpose in Christ

[13]For when God made a promise to Abraham, because He could swear by no one greater, He swore by Himself, [14]saying, *"Surely blessing I will bless you, and multiplying I will multiply you."*[a] [15]And so, after he had patiently endured, he ob-

5:6 [a]Psalm 110:4 6:3 [a]M-Text reads *let us do.* 6:6 [a]Or *and have fallen away* 6:10 [a]NU-Text omits *labor of.* 6:14 [a]Genesis 22:17

5:9 "I don't believe in any religion apart from doing the will of God." *Catherine Booth*

PRINCIPLES OF GROWTH FOR THE NEW AND GROWING CHRISTIAN

6:18 ***Faith—Elevators Can Let You Down***

I have heard people say, "I just find it hard to have faith in God," not realizing the implications of their words. These are the same people who often accept the daily weather forecast, believe the newspapers, and trust their lives to a pilot they have never seen whenever they board a plane. We exercise faith every day. We rely on our car's brakes. We trust history books, medical journals, and elevators. Yet elevators can let us down. History books can be wrong. Planes can crash. How much more then should we trust the sure and true promises of Almighty God. He will never let us down . . . if we trust Him.

Cynics often argue, "You can't trust the Bible—it's full of mistakes." It is. The first mistake was when man rejected God, and the Scriptures show men and women making the same tragic mistake again and again. It's also full of what *seem to be* contradictions. For example, the Scriptures tell us "with God nothing will be impossible" (Luke 1:37); there is nothing Almighty God can't do. Yet we are also told that it is "impossible for God to lie" (Heb. 6:18). So there is something God cannot do! Isn't that an obvious "mistake" in the Bible? No, it isn't.

Lying, deception, bearing false witness, etc., is so repulsive to God, so disgusting to Him, so against His holy character, that the Scriptures draw on the strength of the word "impossible" to substantiate the claim. He cannot, could not, and would not lie.

That means that in a world where we are continually let down, we can totally rely on, trust in, and count on His promises. They are sure, certain, indisputable, true, trustworthy, reliable, faithful, unfailing, dependable, steadfast, and an anchor for the soul. In other words, you can truly believe them, and because of that, you can throw yourself blindfolded and without reserve, into His mighty hands. He will *never, ever* let you down. Do you believe that?

For the next principle of growth, see 1 Pet. 2:2 comment.

tained the promise. 16For men indeed
swear by the greater, and an oath for confirmation *is* for them an end of all dispute. 17Thus God, determining to show
more abundantly to the heirs of promise
the immutability of His counsel, confirmed
it by an oath, 18that by two immutable
things, in which it *is* impossible for God
to lie, we might[a] have strong consolation,
who have fled for refuge to lay hold of the
hope set before *us.*
19This *hope* we have as an anchor of
the soul, both sure and steadfast, and
which enters the *Presence* behind the veil,
20where the forerunner has entered for
us, *even* Jesus, having become High Priest
forever according to the order of Melchizedek.

The King of Righteousness

7 For this Melchizedek, king of Salem,
priest of the Most High God, who
met Abraham returning from the slaughter of the kings and blessed him, 2to
whom also Abraham gave a tenth part of
all, first being translated "king of righteousness," and then also king of Salem,
meaning "king of peace," 3without father,
without mother, without genealogy, having neither beginning of days nor end of
life, but made like the Son of God, remains a priest continually.
4Now consider how great this man *was,*
to whom even the patriarch Abraham
gave a tenth of the spoils. 5And indeed
those who are of the sons of Levi, who receive the priesthood, have a commandment to receive tithes from the people according to the law, that is, from their
brethren, though they have come from the
loins of Abraham; 6but he whose genealogy is not derived from them received
tithes from Abraham and blessed him
who had the promises. 7Now beyond all
contradiction the lesser is blessed by the
better. 8Here mortal men receive tithes,
but there he *receives them,* of whom it is
witnessed that he lives. 9Even Levi, who
receives tithes, paid tithes through Abraham, so to speak, 10for he was still in the

6:18 [a]M-Text omits *might.*

loins of his father when Melchizedek met him.

Need for a New Priesthood

[11]Therefore, if perfection were through the Levitical priesthood (for under it the people received the law), what further need *was there* that another priest should rise according to the order of Melchizedek, and not be called according to the order of Aaron? [12]For the priesthood being changed, of necessity there is also a change of the law. [13]For He of whom these things are spoken belongs to another tribe, from which no man has officiated at the altar.

[14]For *it is* evident that our Lord arose from Judah, of which tribe Moses spoke nothing concerning priesthood.[a] [15]And it is yet far more evident if, in the likeness of Melchizedek, there arises another priest [16]who has come, not according to the law of a fleshly commandment, but according to the power of an endless life. [17]For He testifies:[a]

"You are a priest forever
According to the order of
Melchizedek."[b]

[18]For on the one hand there is an annulling of the former commandment because of its weakness and unprofitableness, [19]for the law made nothing perfect; on the other hand, *there is the* bringing in of a better hope, through which we draw near to God.

Greatness of the New Priest

[20]And inasmuch as *He was* not *made priest* without an oath [21](for they have become priests without an oath, but He with an oath by Him who said to Him:

"The LORD has sworn
And will not relent,
'You are a priest forever[a]
According to the order of
Melchizedek' "),[b]

[22]by so much more Jesus has become a surety of a better covenant.

[23]Also there were many priests, because they were prevented by death from continuing. [24]But He, because He continues forever, has an unchangeable priesthood. [25]Therefore He is also able to save to the uttermost those who come to God through Him, since He always lives to make intercession for them.

[26]For such a High Priest was fitting for us, *who is* holy, harmless, undefiled, separate from sinners, and has become higher than the heavens; [27]who does not need daily, as those high priests, to offer up sacrifices, first for His own sins and then for the people's, for this He did once for

7:14 [a]NU-Text reads *priests.* **7:17** [a]NU-Text reads *it is testified.* [b]Psalm 110:4 **7:21** [a]NU-Text ends the quotation here. [b]Psalm 110:4

7:18,19 Bible contradiction? Skeptics claim that this passage and Eph. 2:13–15 abolish the Law, in contradiction to Matt. 5:17: "Do not think that I came to destroy the Law or the Prophets. I did not come to destroy but to fulfill."

The skeptic has no understanding of the reason Christ suffered and died. He came to fulfill the Law so that those who trust in Him could be justified (declared not guilty and made clean in the sight of God).

Think of two brothers who each have large court fines. They have no money and are about to be sentenced to prison. Their kindly father loves them and pays their fines. He satisfies the demands of the law by fulfilling the court's requirements. Both men are then free to go. However, one of them refuses to accept the payment. He is therefore still under the law's penalty and is sentenced to a long prison term. He was thrown in prison even though the father satisfied the law's demand through his payment.

Jesus didn't come to do away with the moral Law. It is eternal and will be the standard of judgment on Judgment Day (see Ezek. 44:24 comment). He came to satisfy its demands for those who trust Him—making provision for our forgiveness by paying our fine in His life's blood.

Christians (both Jew and Gentile) are no longer under the wrath of the Law, because they trust in Jesus Christ. However, those who are outside of Christ (refusing His blood payment) are still under its wrath (see John 3:36).

SPRINGBOARDS FOR PREACHING AND WITNESSING

8:6

Solid Ice

There once was a man who was traveling on foot through a snowstorm in a strange country. He had to get to a certain town by nightfall and was somewhat perturbed when he came to an ice-covered river. *How thick was the ice?* Could he trust it to hold him? He began crawling on the ice on his stomach, inch-by-inch, tapping with his fingers. Sweat poured from his forehead. He was filled with the fear that at any moment he could plunge to an icy death.

An hour later, he had progressed only about 40 feet. He suddenly stopped crawling. He could hear singing! He turned his head to see a horse and cart, laden with people. The driver was singing at the top of his voice as he drove his cart across the ice. The driver knew that lake was solid ice and his faith was such that he had total confidence, with not an ounce of fear. Such are the solid promises of God.

all when He offered up Himself. 28For the
law appoints as high priests men who have weakness, but the word of the oath, which came after the law, *appoints* the Son who has been perfected forever.

The New Priestly Service

8 Now *this is* the main point of the things we are saying: We have such a High Priest, who is seated at the right hand of the throne of the Majesty in the heavens, 2a Minister of the sanctuary and of the true tabernacle which the Lord erected, and not man.

3For every high priest is appointed to offer both gifts and sacrifices. Therefore *it is* necessary that this One also have something to offer. 4For if He were on earth, He would not be a priest, since there are priests who offer the gifts according to the law; 5who serve the copy and shadow of the heavenly things, as Moses was divinely instructed when he was about to make the tabernacle. For He said, *"See that you make all things according to the pattern shown you on the mountain."*[a]
6But now He has obtained a more excellent ministry, inasmuch as He is also Mediator of a better covenant, which was established on better promises.

A New Covenant

7For if that first *covenant* had been faultless, then no place would have been sought for a second. 8Because finding fault with them, He says: *"Behold, the days are coming, says the LORD, when I will make a new covenant with the house of Israel and with the house of Judah— 9not according to the covenant that I made with their fathers in the day when I took them by the hand to lead them out of the land of Egypt; because they did not continue in My covenant, and I disregarded them, says the LORD. 10For this is the covenant that I will make with the house of Israel after those days, says the LORD: I will put My laws in their mind and write them on*

8:5 [a]Exodus 25:40

8:5 Following the God-given pattern. When God spoke to Moses about the tabernacle, He told him to do all things according to the pattern. He didn't say, "Do the best you can"—it had to be 100 percent accurate, according to the instructions God had given him. How much more then should we follow the pattern God has given us for bringing men and women into the knowledge of eternal salvation? Our failure to use the Law lawfully, as a "tutor" to bring sinners to Christ (Gal. 3:24), has resulted in the ruin of millions of souls—something which will not be fully realized until Judgment Day.

The pattern of evangelistic endeavor is made plain in the Book of Romans. To obtain God's blessing, we must never deviate from the biblical paradigm set so clearly before us in the inspired words of the apostle Paul. *Winston Churchill* noted that the nose of the bulldog is slanted backward so he can continue to breathe without letting go. Get your teeth into the importance of using the Law of God to bring the knowledge of sin, and don't let it go for any reason. Let it be said of you, "The law of his God is in his heart; none of his steps shall slide" (Psa. 37:31). See 2 Cor. 2:17 comment.

their hearts; and I will be their God, and
they shall be My people. [11]*None of them*
shall teach his neighbor, and none his
brother, saying, 'Know the LORD,' for all
shall know Me, from the least of them to
the greatest of them. [12]*For I will be mer-*
ciful to their unrighteousness, and their
sins and their lawless deeds[a] *I will re-*
member no more."[b]
[13]In that He says, *"A new covenant,"*
He has made the first obsolete. Now what
is becoming obsolete and growing old is
ready to vanish away.

The Earthly Sanctuary

9 Then indeed, even the first *covenant*
had ordinances of divine service and
the earthly sanctuary. [2]For a tabernacle
was prepared: the first *part,* in which *was*
the lampstand, the table, and the showbread, which is called the sanctuary;
[3]and behind the second veil, the part of
the tabernacle which is called the Holiest
of All, [4]which had the golden censer and
the ark of the covenant overlaid on all
sides with gold, in which *were* the gold-
en pot that had the manna, Aaron's rod
that budded, and the tablets of the
covenant; [5]and above it were the cherubim of glory overshadowing the mercy
seat. Of these things we cannot now
speak in detail.

Limitations of the Earthly Service

[6]Now when these things had been
thus prepared, the priests always went
into the first part of the tabernacle, performing *the services.* [7]But into the second
part the high priest *went* alone once a
year, not without blood, which he offered
for himself and *for* the people's sins *com-*
mitted in ignorance; [8]the Holy Spirit indicating this, that the way into the Holiest
of All was not yet made manifest while
the first tabernacle was still standing. [9]It

"O Lord, Almighty and everlasting God, by Thy holy Word Thou hast created the heaven, and the earth, and the sea; blessed and glorified be Thy name, and praised be Thy majesty, which hath deigned to use us, Thy humble servants, that Thy holy name may be proclaimed in this second part of the earth."

Christopher Columbus

was symbolic for the present time in
which both gifts and sacrifices are offered
which cannot make him who performed
the service perfect in regard to the conscience— [10]*concerned* only with foods
and drinks, various washings, and fleshly
ordinances imposed until the time of reformation.

The Heavenly Sanctuary

[11]But Christ came *as* High Priest of the
good things to come,[a] with the greater
and more perfect tabernacle not made
with hands, that is, not of this creation.
[12]Not with the blood of goats and calves,
but with His own blood He entered the

8:12 [a]NU-Text omits *and their lawless deeds.* [b]Jeremiah 31:31–34 9:11 [a]NU-Text reads *that have come.*

8:10 God puts His Law into our minds, giving us a new mind—the "mind of Christ" (1 Cor. 2:16), and renewing us in the "spirit" of our minds. He gives us a "new and living way" (Heb. 10:20). Now God's ways are our ways and God's thoughts become our thoughts. We are led by the Spirit, walking "in His ways" (Psa. 119:3). This is the miracle of the new birth. We are completely new creatures in Christ (2 Cor. 5:17).

9:2 *Jesus Pictured in the Old Testament Tabernacle*

By Todd Friel

Hebrews 8—10 tell us that the Old Testament Tabernacle, the traveling tent in which the Jews worshiped while wandering through the desert, was a picture (a "type" or shadow) of Jesus Christ Himself. As you read this list, ask yourself, "Could human authors have possibly agreed to such an intricate story spanning 1,500 years?"

The Door: The children of Israel could enter through the door (which always faced east) into the outer courtyard.

The Laver: The bronze laver was where the priests washed their hands and feet daily. They could not enter the Holy Place without washing.

Holy Place: Only the priests could enter the Holy Place. They would do so daily. This was also called the tent of meeting.

Candlestick (Golden Lampstand): This seven-branched candlestick was made of pure gold. It burned olive oil night and day, serving as the only light in the tabernacle. In darkness the other articles would have been impossible to see.

Table of Showbread: The table was to the right as one entered the Holy Place. On it were twelve loaves of bread representing God's covenant people, Israel. The table was a place of communion and fellowship.

Golden Altar (Altar of Incense): This altar was used to burn incense continuously. Its fragrance wafted across the mercy seat and above the other furniture. The incense on the altar represented prayer and speaks to us of intercession. Coals to heat this altar came from the altar of sacrifice, after the blood of the sacrifice dripped on them. This was God's supremely holy altar.

Holy of Holies: The Holy of Holies (or Most Holy) was separated from the Holy Place by a veil. This part of the tabernacle was entered only by the High Priest on one day of the year, the Day of Atonement.

Veil: Made of blue, purple, and scarlet yarn and fine linen. No priest could enter except through the veil. It was the only way to approach the Ark of the Covenant. If the priest passed through it without being sacrificially clean, God would strike him dead, as He cannot have sin in His presence.

Ark of the Covenant: The Ark occupied the Holy of Holies. On top of the ark was a lid called the mercy seat. Hovering above the mercy seat were two cherubim with outstretched wings. The ark contained the stone tablets of the covenant, a golden pot of manna, and Aaron's rod that budded.

Priests: The priests were mediators between God and man. The priestly and Levitical offices were fixed by birth. The High Priest was the head priest.

Sacrifice: Yearly, an unblemished lamb was slaughtered for the covering of sins of the individual. They would place their hands on the lamb, symbolically transferring their sins to the lamb that would be slaughtered for the covering, but not forgiveness, of sins.

Day of Atonement: Every year, on the Day of Atonement, the blood of a goat was sprinkled on the mercy seat to cover the sins of the people. It was there above the mercy seat that God hovered in the pillar of cloud. In His *mercy* and in connection with the blood of the offering, the Lord covered Israel's sins. Remember, sins were only covered, as an animal sacrifice was not sufficient to forgive sins. It was merely a shadow of the only Lamb of God, Jesus Christ, whose death could take away the sins of the world.

Jesus: The Fulfillment to the Temple—1,500 Years Later

Christ is the Door: "Jesus said, 'I am the door. If anyone enters by Me, he will be saved'" (John 10:9).

Christ is the Laver: "Peter said to Him, 'You shall never wash my feet!' Jesus answered him, 'If I do not wash you, you have no part with Me'" (John 13:8).

Christ is the Lampstand: "Then Jesus spoke to them again, saying, 'I am the light of the world. He who follows Me shall not walk in darkness, but have the light of life'" (John 8:12).

Christ is the Showbread: "Jesus said to them, 'I am the bread of life. He who comes to Me shall never hunger, and he who believes in Me shall never thirst'" (John 6:35).

Christ is the Altar of Incense: "Therefore He is also able to save to the uttermost those who come to God through Him, since He always lives to make intercession for them" (Heb. 7:25).

Christ is the Veil: "Therefore, brethren, having boldness to enter the Holiest by the blood of Jesus, by a new and living way which He consecrated for us, through the veil, that is, His flesh" (Heb. 10:19,20).

Christ is the Mercy Seat: "Christ Jesus, whom God set forth as a propitiation by His blood, through faith" (Rom. 3:24,25).

Christ is the High Priest: "For such a High Priest fitting for us, who is holy, harmless, undefiled,

(continued)

(9:2 continued)

separate from sinners, and has become higher than the heavens" (Heb. 7:26). "Christ came as High Priest of the good things to come, with the greater and more perfect tabernacle not made with hands, that is, not of this creation" (Heb. 9:11).

Christ is the Sacrifice: "Not with the blood of goats and calves, but with His own blood He entered the Most Holy Place once for all, having obtained eternal redemption" (Heb. 9:12). "By that will we have been sanctified through the offering of the body of Jesus Christ once for all" (Heb. 10:10).

Most Holy Place once for all, having obtained eternal redemption. 13For if the
blood of bulls and goats and the ashes of
a heifer, sprinkling the unclean, sanctifies
for the purifying of the flesh, 14how much
more shall the blood of Christ, who
through the eternal Spirit offered Himself
without spot to God, cleanse your conscience from dead works to serve the living God? 15And for this reason He is the
Mediator of the new covenant, by means
of death, for the redemption of the transgressions under the first covenant, that
those who are called may receive the
promise of the eternal inheritance.

The Mediator's Death Necessary

16For where there *is* a testament, there
must also of necessity be the death of the
testator. 17For a testament *is* in force after

THE FUNCTION OF THE LAW

9:14 "You understand that the work of the Law is the revealing of sin. Furthermore, when I speak of sin, I include all kinds of sin—external, internal, hypocrisy, unbelief, love of self, and contempt for or ignorance of God—which are certainly the very roots of all human works. In the justification of sinners the first work of God is to reveal our sin; to confound our conscience, make us tremble, terrify us, briefly, to condemn us.

"The beginning of repentance consists of that work of the Law by which the Spirit of God terrifies and confounds consciences…Just as the Christian life must certainly begin with the knowledge of sin, so Christian doctrine must begin with the function of the Law." *Melanchthon*

men are dead, since it has no power at all
while the testator lives. 18Therefore not
even the first *covenant* was dedicated without blood. 19For when Moses had spoken
every precept to all the people according
to the law, he took the blood of calves
and goats, with water, scarlet wool, and
hyssop, and sprinkled both the book itself and all the people, 20saying, *"This is
the blood of the covenant which God has
commanded you."*[a] 21Then likewise he
sprinkled with blood both the tabernacle
and all the vessels of the ministry. 22And
according to the law almost all things are
purified with blood, and without shedding of blood there is no remission.

Greatness of Christ's Sacrifice

23Therefore *it was* necessary that the
copies of the things in the heavens should
be purified with these, but the heavenly
things themselves with better sacrifices
than these. 24For Christ has not entered
the holy places made with hands, *which
are* copies of the true, but into heaven itself, now to appear in the presence of
God for us; 25not that He should offer
Himself often, as the high priest enters
the Most Holy Place every year with blood
of another— 26He then would have had
to suffer often since the foundation of the
world; but now, once at the end of the
ages, He has appeared to put away sin by
the sacrifice of Himself. 27And as it is ap-

9:20 [a]Exodus 24:8

9:22 Leading sinners to Jesus: *Forgiveness of sin requires the shedding of blood.* God was the first person to kill an animal, as recorded in Gen. 3:21. As Adam and Eve sinned and lost their righteousness, God shed the blood of an innocent animal to provide a covering for them. The fig leaves of self-righteousness will not cover a sinner on the Day of Judgment. God alone can provide the covering through the shed blood of the Savior (1 John 1:7–10). See John 3:16,17 comment.

pointed for men to die once, but after this the judgment, [28]so Christ was offered once to bear the sins of many. To those who eagerly wait for Him He will appear a second time, apart from sin, for salvation.

Animal Sacrifices Insufficient

10 For the law, having a shadow of the good things to come, *and* not the very image of the things, can never with these same sacrifices, which they offer continually year by year, make those who approach perfect. [2]For then would they not have ceased to be offered? For the worshipers, once purified, would have had no more consciousness of sins. [3]But in those *sacrifices there is* a reminder of sins every year. [4]For *it is* not possible that the blood of bulls and goats could take away sins.

Christ's Death Fulfills God's Will

[5]Therefore, when He came into the world, He said:

"Sacrifice and offering You did not desire,
But a body You have prepared for Me.
[6]*In burnt offerings and sacrifices for sin*
You had no pleasure.
[7]*Then I said, 'Behold, I have come—*
In the volume of the book it is written of Me—
To do Your will, O God.' "[a]

[8]Previously saying, *"Sacrifice and offering, burnt offerings, and offerings for sin You did not desire, nor had pleasure in them"* (which are offered according to the law), [9]then He said, *"Behold, I have come to do Your will, O God."*[a] He takes away the first that He may establish the second. [10]By that will we have been sanctified through the offering of the body of Jesus Christ once *for all.*

Christ's Death Perfects the Sanctified

[11]And every priest stands ministering daily and offering repeatedly the same sacrifices, which can never take away sins. [12]But this Man, after He had offered one sacrifice for sins forever, sat down at the right hand of God, [13]from that time waiting till His enemies are made His footstool. [14]For by one offering He has perfected forever those who are being sanctified.

[15]But the Holy Spirit also witnesses to us; for after He had said before,

[16]*"This is the covenant that I will make with them after those days, says the LORD: I will put My laws into their hearts, and in their minds I will write them,"*[a]
[17]*then He adds, "Their sins and their lawless deeds I will remember no more."*[a]
[18]Now where there is remission of these,

10:7 [a]Psalm 40:6–8 10:9 [a]NU-Text and M-Text omit *O God.*
10:16 [a]Jeremiah 31:33 10:17 [a]Jeremiah 31:34

9:27 Judgment Day: For verses that warn of its reality, see 2 Pet. 2:4,5,9.

Reincarnation. This verse shows that there is no such thing as reincarnation. It is merely wishful thinking for guilty sinners. Many of the world's largest religions teach their adherents that if they don't "get it right" in this lifetime, they will have multiple opportunities in future lives. That people don't need to trust in Jesus before they die is one of Satan's greatest lies.

9:28 Second coming of Jesus: See Heb. 10:37.

10:16 This is the promise of the gospel of salvation. The experience of "conversion" is when God puts His Law in the heart of those who repent and trust in the Savior. He causes them to walk in His statutes (Ezek. 36:26,27), and gives believers the desire to obey the moral Law. This is different from "the work of the Law" (Rom. 2:15) that God has placed in every unregenerate heart. It is the work of the Law that resonates with the conscience and confirms the truth of the Law. But through the miracle of the new birth, the Christian no longer desires to lie, steal, covet, commit adultery, etc.; he has a new heart with new desires that "delight" to do God's will (see Psa. 40:8). He is a new creature in Christ (2 Cor. 5:17). See Psa. 40:7–9 comment.

PRINCIPLES OF GROWTH FOR THE NEW AND GROWING CHRISTIAN

10:25 *Fellowship—Flutter by Butterfly*

Pray about where you should fellowship. Make sure your church home calls sin what it is: sin. Do they believe the promises of God? Are they loving? Does the pastor treat his wife with respect? Is he a man of the Word? Does he have a humble heart and a gentle spirit? Listen closely to his teaching. It should glorify God, magnify Jesus, and edify the believer.

One evidence that you have been truly saved is that you will have a love for other Christians (1 John 3:14). You will want to fellowship with them. The old saying that birds of a feather flock together is true of Christians. You gather together for the breaking of bread (communion), for teaching from the Word, and for fellowship. You share the same inspirations, illuminations, inclinations, temptations, aspirations, motivations, and perspirations. You are working together for the same thing: the furtherance of the kingdom of God on earth. This is why you attend church—not because you have to, but because you want to.

Don't become a "spiritual butterfly." If you are flitting from church to church, how will your pastor know what type of food you are digesting? The Bible says that your shepherd is accountable to God for you (Heb. 13:17), so make yourself known to your pastor. Pray for him regularly. Pray also for his wife, his family, and the church leaders. Being a pastor is no easy task. Most people don't realize how long it takes to prepare a fresh sermon each week. They don't appreciate the time spent in prayer and in study of the Word. If the pastor repeats a joke or a story, remember, he's human. So give him a great deal of grace, and double honor. Never murmur about him. If you don't like something he has said, pray about it, then leave the issue with God. If that doesn't satisfy you, leave the church, rather than divide it through murmuring and complaining. God hates those who cause division among the brethren (Prov. 6:16–19). See Psa. 92:13 comment.

For the next principle of growth, see Eph. 5:20 comment.

there is no longer an offering for sin.

Hold Fast Your Confession

[19]Therefore, brethren, having boldness to enter the Holiest by the blood of
Jesus, [20]by a new and living way which
He consecrated for us, through the veil,
that is, His flesh, [21]and *having* a High
Priest over the house of God, [22]let us
draw near with a true heart in full assurance of faith, having our hearts sprinkled from an evil conscience and our bodies
washed with pure water. [23]Let us hold
fast the confession of *our* hope without wavering, for He who promised *is* faithful. [24]And let us consider one another in
order to stir up love and good works,
[25]not forsaking the assembling of ourselves together, as *is* the manner of some, but exhorting *one another,* and so much the more as you see the Day approaching.

The Just Live by Faith

[26]For if we sin willfully after we have received the knowledge of the truth, there no longer remains a sacrifice for
sins, [27]but a certain fearful expectation of judgment, and fiery indignation which
will devour the adversaries. [28]Anyone who has rejected Moses' law dies without mercy on the testimony of two or three
witnesses. [29]Of how much worse punishment, do you suppose, will he be thought worthy who has trampled the Son of God underfoot, counted the blood of the covenant by which he was sanctified a common thing, and insulted the Spirit of
grace? [30]For we know Him who said,

10:22 The sinner's conscience. "O soul! Thou are at war with thy conscience. Thou have tried to quiet it, but it will prick you. Oh, there be some of you to whom conscience is a ghost haunting you by day and night. You know the good, though you choose the evil; you prick your fingers with the thorn of conscience when you try to pluck the rose of sin." *Charles Spurgeon*

10:23 "Never be afraid to trust an unknown future to a known God." *Corrie ten Boom*

QUESTIONS & OBJECTIONS

10:31

"You are using scare tactics by talking about hell and Judgment Day."

In the late 1980s, TV commercials in the U.S. asked, "What goes through the mind of a driver who is not wearing a seat belt in a head-on collision?" Then they showed a crash dummy having its head crushed by a steering wheel in a collision, and said, "The steering wheel!" Those were scare tactics, but no one complained because they were legitimate scare tactics. We should fear what happens in a head-on collision if we are foolish enough to not put on a seat belt.

Fear itself is not a bad thing. Fear stops us from stepping off a 500-foot cliff. It keeps us away from fire. It holds us back from sticking a fork into a live power outlet. These types of fear are self-preserving, but the ultimate self-preserving fear is the fear of the Lord. That fear is called "the beginning of wisdom," and because of it, the Bible says men "depart from sin."

To warn of hell is fearful, but it is absolutely legitimate, because the Bible says that it is a fearful thing for a sinner to fall into the hands of the living God.

"Vengeance is Mine, I will repay,"[a] says
the Lord.[b] And again, *"The LORD will
judge His people."*[c] 31It is a fearful thing
to fall into the hands of the living God.
32But recall the former days in which,
after you were illuminated, you endured
a great struggle with sufferings: 33partly
while you were made a spectacle both by
reproaches and tribulations, and partly
while you became companions of those
who were so treated; 34for you had compassion on me[a] in my chains, and joyfully
accepted the plundering of your goods,
knowing that you have a better and an
enduring possession for yourselves in
heaven.[b] 35Therefore do not cast away
your confidence, which has great reward.
36For you have need of endurance, so
that after you have done the will of God,
you may receive the promise:

37*"For yet a little while,*
And He[a] who is coming will come
and will not tarry.
38*Now the[a] just shall live by faith;*
But if anyone draws back,
My soul has no pleasure in him."[b]

39But we are not of those who draw back
to perdition, but of those who believe to
the saving of the soul.

By Faith We Understand

11 Now faith is the substance of things
hoped for, the evidence of things
not seen. 2For by it the elders obtained a
good testimony.
3By faith we understand that the
worlds were framed by the word of God,
so that the things which are seen were
not made of things which are visible.

Faith at the Dawn of History

4By faith Abel offered to God a more
excellent sacrifice than Cain, through
which he obtained witness that he was
righteous, God testifying of his gifts; and
through it he being dead still speaks.
5By faith Enoch was taken away so
that he did not see death, *"and was not
found, because God had taken him"*;[a] for
before he was taken he had this testimony, that he pleased God. 6But without
faith *it is* impossible to please *Him,* for he
who comes to God must believe that He
is, and *that* He is a rewarder of those who
diligently seek Him.
7By faith Noah, being divinely warned

10:30 [a]Deuteronomy 32:35 [b]NU-Text omits *says the Lord.* [c]Deuteronomy 32:36 10:34 [a]NU-Text reads *the prisoners* instead of *me in my chains.* [b]NU-Text omits *in heaven.* 10:37 [a]Or *that which* 10:38 [a]NU-Text reads *My just one.* [b]Habakkuk 2:3, 4 11:5 [a]Genesis 5:24

10:37 Second coming of Jesus: See James 5:8.

11:3 Scientific Facts in the Bible

1. Only in recent years has science discovered that everything we see is composed of invisible atoms. Here, Scripture tells us that the "things which are seen were not made of things which are visible" (Heb. 11:3).

2. Medical science has only recently discovered that blood-clotting in a newborn reaches its peak on the eighth day, then drops. The Bible consistently says that male infants must be circumcised on the eighth day (Lev. 12:3).

3. At a time when some believed that the earth sat on a large animal or a giant (1500 B.C.), the Bible spoke of the earth's free float in space: "He hangs the earth on nothing" (Job 26:7).

4. The prophet Isaiah also tells us that the earth is round: "It is He who sits above the circle of the earth" (Isa. 40:22). This is not a reference to a flat disk, as some skeptics maintain, but to a sphere. Secular man discovered this 2,400 years later. Though it was once commonly believed that the earth was flat, it was the Scriptures that inspired Christopher Columbus to sail around the world (see Prov. 3:6 comment).

5. God told Job in 1500 B.C.: "Can you send out lightnings, that they may go, and say to you, 'Here we are!'?" (Job 38:35). The Bible here is making what appears to be a scientifically ludicrous statement—that light can be *sent*, and then manifest itself in speech. But did you know that radio waves travel at the speed of light? This is why you can have *instantaneous* wireless communication with someone on the other side of the earth. Science didn't discover this until 1864 when "British scientist James Clerk Maxwell suggested that electricity and light waves were two forms of the same thing" (*Modern Century Illustrated Encyclopedia*).

6. Job 38:19 asks, "Where is the way to the dwelling of light?" Man has only recently discovered that light (electromagnetic radiation) has a "way," traveling at 186,000 miles per second.

7. Science has discovered that stars emit radio waves, which are received on earth as a high pitch. God mentioned this in Job 38:7: "When the morning stars sang together . . ."

8. "Most cosmologists (scientists who study the structures and evolution of the universe) agree that the Genesis account of creation, in imagining an initial void, may be uncannily close to the truth" (*Time*, Dec. 1976).

9. Solomon described a "cycle" of air currents two thousand years before scientists "discovered" them. "The wind goes toward the south, and turns around to the north; the wind whirls about continually, and comes again on its circuit" (Eccles. 1:6).

10. Science expresses the universe in five terms: time, space, matter, power, and motion. Genesis 1:1,2 revealed such truths to the Hebrews in 1450 B.C.: "In the beginning [*time*] God created [*power*] the heaven [*space*] and the earth [*matter*] . . . And the Spirit of God moved [*motion*] upon the face of the waters" (KJV). The first thing God tells man is that He controls all aspects of the universe.

11. The great biological truth concerning the importance of blood in our body's mechanism has been fully comprehended only in recent years. Up until 120 years ago, sick people were "bled," and many died because of the practice. If you lose your blood, you lose your life. Yet Lev. 17:11, written 3,500 years ago, declared that blood is the source of life: "For the life of the flesh is in the blood."

12. *Encyclopedia Britannica* documents that in 1845, a young doctor in Vienna named Dr. Ignaz Semmelweis was horrified at the terrible death rate of women who gave birth in hospitals. As many as 30 percent died after giving birth. Semmelweis noted that doctors would examine the bodies of patients who died, then, without washing their hands, go straight to the next ward and examine expectant mothers. This was their normal practice, because the presence of microscopic diseases was unknown. Semmelweis insisted that doctors wash their hands before examinations, and the death rate immediately dropped to 2 percent.

Look at the specific instructions God gave His people for when they encounter disease: "And when he who has a discharge is cleansed of his discharge, then he shall count for himself seven days for his cleansing, wash his clothes, and bathe his body in running water; then he shall be clean" (Lev. 15:13). Until recent years, doctors washed their hands in a bowl of water, leaving invisible germs on their hands. However, the Bible says specifically to wash hands under "running water."

13. Luke 17:34–36 says the Second Coming of Jesus Christ will occur while some are asleep at night and others are working at daytime activities in the field. This is a clear indication of a revolving earth, with day and night at the same time.

14. "During the devastating Black Death of the fourteenth century, patients who were sick or dead were kept in the same rooms as the rest of the family. People often wondered why the disease was affecting so many people at one time. They attributed these epidemics to 'bad air' or 'evil

(continued)

(11:3 continued)
spirits.' However, careful attention to the medical commands of God as revealed in Leviticus would have saved untold millions of lives. Arturo Castiglione wrote about the overwhelming importance of this biblical medical law: 'The laws against leprosy in Leviticus 13 may be regarded as the first model of sanitary legislation' (*A History of Medicine*)." *Grant R. Jeffery, The Signature of God*

With all these truths revealed in Scripture, how could a thinking person deny that the Bible is supernatural in origin? There is no other book in any of the world's religions (Vedas, Bhagavad-Gita, Koran, Book of Mormon, etc.) that contains scientific truth. In fact, they contain statements that are clearly unscientific. *Hank Hanegraaff* said, "Faith in Christ is not some blind leap into a dark chasm, but a faith based on established evidence."

of things not yet seen, moved with godly fear, prepared an ark for the saving of his household, by which he condemned the world and became heir of the righteousness which is according to faith.

Faithful Abraham

8By faith Abraham obeyed when he was called to go out to the place which he would receive as an inheritance. And he went out, not knowing where he was going. 9By faith he dwelt in the land of promise as *in* a foreign country, dwelling in tents with Isaac and Jacob, the heirs with him of the same promise; 10for he waited for the city which has foundations, whose builder and maker *is* God.

11By faith Sarah herself also received strength to conceive seed, and she bore a child[a] when she was past the age, because she judged Him faithful who had promised. 12Therefore from one man, and him as good as dead, were born *as many* as the stars of the sky in multitude—innumerable as the sand which is by the seashore.

The Heavenly Hope

13These all died in faith, not having received the promises, but having seen them afar off were assured of them,[a] embraced *them* and confessed that they were strangers and pilgrims on the earth. 14For those who say such things declare plainly that they seek a homeland. 15And truly if they had called to mind that *country* from which they had come out, they would have had opportunity to return. 16But now they desire a better, that is, a heavenly *country*. Therefore God is not ashamed to be called their God, for He has prepared a city for them.

The Faith of the Patriarchs

17By faith Abraham, when he was tested, offered up Isaac, and he who had received the promises offered up his only begotten *son*, 18of whom it was said, *"In Isaac your seed shall be called,"*[a] 19concluding that God *was* able to raise *him* up, even from the dead, from which he also received him in a figurative sense.

20By faith Isaac blessed Jacob and Esau concerning things to come.

21By faith Jacob, when he was dying, blessed each of the sons of Joseph, and worshiped, *leaning* on the top of his staff.

22By faith Joseph, when he was dying, made mention of the departure of the children of Israel, and gave instructions concerning his bones.

The Faith of Moses

23By faith Moses, when he was born, was hidden three months by his parents, because they saw *he was* a beautiful child; and they were not afraid of the king's

11:11 [a]NU-Text omits *she bore a child.* 11:13 [a]NU-Text and M-Text omit *were assured of them.* 11:18 [a]Genesis 21:12

11:7 The writer of the Book of Hebrews believed the Genesis account of Noah's Flood.

11:11 Scientific facts in the Bible. Genesis 3:15 reveals that a female possesses a "seed" for childbearing. This was not the common knowledge until a few centuries ago. It was widely believed that only the male possessed the "seed of life" and that the woman was nothing more than a "glorified incubator."

QUESTIONS & OBJECTIONS

11:25 "I'm doing fine. I don't need God."

Many people feel this way because of the modern gospel message. It says that Jesus will help their marriage, remove their drug problem, fill the emptiness in their heart, give them peace and joy, etc. In doing so, it restricts the gospel's field of influence. If the message of the cross is only for people who have bad marriages, are lonely, and have problems, then those who are happy won't see their need for the Savior.

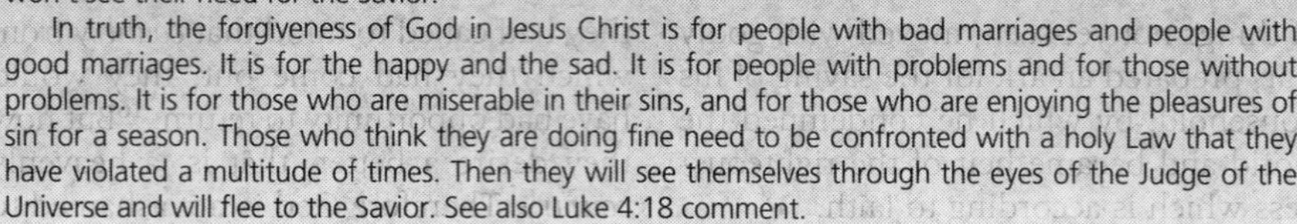

In truth, the forgiveness of God in Jesus Christ is for people with bad marriages and people with good marriages. It is for the happy and the sad. It is for people with problems and for those without problems. It is for those who are miserable in their sins, and for those who are enjoying the pleasures of sin for a season. Those who think they are doing fine need to be confronted with a holy Law that they have violated a multitude of times. Then they will see themselves through the eyes of the Judge of the Universe and will flee to the Savior. See also Luke 4:18 comment.

command.
[24]By faith Moses, when he became of
age, refused to be called the son of Pharaoh's daughter, [25]choosing rather to suffer affliction with the people of God than
to enjoy the passing pleasures of sin, [26]es-
teeming the reproach of Christ greater riches than the treasures in[a] Egypt; for he looked to the reward.
[27]By faith he forsook Egypt, not fearing the wrath of the king; for he endured
as seeing Him who is invisible. [28]By faith
he kept the Passover and the sprinkling of blood, lest he who destroyed the firstborn should touch them.
[29]By faith they passed through the Red Sea as by dry *land, whereas* the Egyptians, attempting to do so, were drowned.

By Faith They Overcame

[30]By faith the walls of Jericho fell down
after they were encircled for seven days.
[31]By faith the harlot Rahab did not perish with those who did not believe, when she had received the spies with peace.
[32]And what more shall I say? For the time would fail me to tell of Gideon and Barak and Samson and Jephthah, also *of* David and Samuel and the prophets:
[33]who through faith subdued kingdoms, worked righteousness, obtained promises,
stopped the mouths of lions, [34]quenched
the violence of fire, escaped the edge of the sword, out of weakness were made strong, became valiant in battle, turned
to flight the armies of the aliens. [35]Women
received their dead raised to life again.
Others were tortured, not accepting deliverance, that they might obtain a better resurrection. [36]Still others had trial of
mockings and scourgings, yes, and of
chains and imprisonment. [37]They were
stoned, they were sawn in two, were tempted,[a] were slain with the sword. They wandered about in sheepskins and goatskins, being destitute, afflicted, tormented— [38]of whom the world was not worthy.

11:26 [a]NU-Text and M-Text read *of.* 11:37 [a]NU-Text omits *were tempted.*

11:25 As we witness, we should remember that there *is* pleasure in sin for a season. Contrary to the claims of modern evangelism, the world *can* find happiness without Jesus. The prophet Jeremiah complained to the Lord, "Why does the way of the wicked prosper? Why are those happy who deal so treacherously?" (Jer. 12:1). However, this sinful world cannot find *righteousness* without Jesus, and it is righteousness that they will need on the Day of Wrath (Prov. 11:4). See Rev. 6:15 comment.

"Oh, what folly it is: for a cup of pleasure—drink a sea of wrath! Sin will be bitter in the end. The *pleasure* of sin is soon gone—but the sting remains!" *Thomas Watson*

SPRINGBOARDS FOR PREACHING AND WITNESSING

The New Convert

11:29 A new convert was reading his Bible when he called out, "Wow! Praise the Lord!" A liberal minister heard him, and asked him what the noise was about. The young Christian replied with great enthusiasm, "This is incredible. It says here that God performed a miracle of deliverance by opening up the Red Sea for the Israelites to march through!"

The minister replied, "Owing to tidal patterns around that time of year, the Red Sea was a swamp that was only three inches deep."

Somewhat subdued, the young man continued reading, but soon exclaimed, "Wow! Praise the Lord!" "What's the matter now?" asked the minister. To which the Christian replied, *"God has just drowned the whole Egyptian army in three inches of water!"*

Over 3,000 times, the Bible speaks of its inspiration by God. His Word is true, and you can believe every word of it.

They wandered in deserts and mountains,
in dens and caves of the earth.
39And all these, having obtained a good
testimony through faith, did not receive
the promise, 40God having provided something better for us, that they should not
be made perfect apart from us.

The Race of Faith

12 Therefore we also, since we are
surrounded by so great a cloud of
witnesses, let us lay aside every weight,
and the sin which so easily ensnares *us*,
and let us run with endurance the race
that is set before us, 2looking unto Jesus,
the author and finisher of *our* faith, who
for the joy that was set before Him endured the cross, despising the shame,
and has sat down at the right hand of the
throne of God.

The Discipline of God

3For consider Him who endured such
hostility from sinners against Himself, lest
you become weary and discouraged in
your souls. 4You have not yet resisted to
bloodshed, striving against sin. 5And you
have forgotten the exhortation which
speaks to you as to sons:

"My son, do not despise the chastening
of the LORD,
Nor be discouraged when you are
rebuked by Him;
6*For whom the LORD loves He*
chastens,
And scourges every son whom He
receives."[a]

12:6 [a]Proverbs 3:11, 12

12:3 Evangelistic discouragement. "One night when [Dwight L.] Moody was going home, it suddenly occurred to him that he had not spoken to a single person that day about accepting Christ. *A day lost*, he thought to himself. But as he walked up the street he saw a man by a lamppost. He promptly walked up to the man and asked, 'Are you a Christian?' . . .

"Nor did Moody find soul-winning easy. In fact, even Christians often criticized him for having 'zeal without knowledge.' Others called him 'Crazy Moody.' Once when he spoke to a perfect stranger about Christ, the man said, 'That is none of your business . . . If you were not a sort of a preacher I would knock you into the gutter for your impertinence.'

"The next day, a businessman friend sent for Moody. The businessman told Moody that the stranger he had spoken to was a friend of his. 'Moody, you've got zeal without knowledge: you insulted a friend of mine on the street last night. You went up to him, a perfect stranger, and asked him if he were a Christian.'

"Moody went out of his friend's office almost brokenhearted. For some time he worried about this. Then late one night a man pounded on the door of his home. It was the stranger he had supposedly insulted. The stranger said, 'Mr. Moody, I have not had a good night's sleep since that night you spoke to me under the lamppost, and I have come around at this unearthly hour of the night for you to tell me what I have to do to be saved.'" *Harry Albus*

7If[a] you endure chastening, God deals with you as with sons; for what son is there whom a father does not chasten? 8But if you are without chastening, of which all have become partakers, then you are illegitimate and not sons. 9Furthermore, we have had human fathers who corrected *us,* and we paid *them* respect. Shall we not much more readily be in subjection to the Father of spirits and live? 10For they indeed for a few days chastened *us* as seemed *best* to them, but He for *our* profit, that *we* may be partakers of His holiness. 11Now no chastening seems to be joyful for the present, but painful; nevertheless, afterward it yields the peaceable fruit of righteousness to those who have been trained by it.

Renew Your Spiritual Vitality

12Therefore strengthen the hands which hang down, and the feeble knees, 13and make straight paths for your feet, so that what is lame may not be dislocated, but rather be healed.

14Pursue peace with all *people,* and holiness, without which no one will see the Lord: 15looking carefully lest anyone fall short of the grace of God; lest any root of bitterness springing up cause trouble, and by this many become defiled; 16lest there *be* any fornicator or profane person like Esau, who for one morsel of food sold his birthright. 17For you know that afterward, when he wanted to inherit the blessing, he was rejected, for he found no place for repentance, though he sought it diligently with tears.

The Glorious Company

18For you have not come to the mountain that[a] may be touched and that burned with fire, and to blackness and darkness[b] and tempest, 19and the sound of a trumpet and the voice of words, so that those who heard *it* begged that the word should not be spoken to them anymore. 20(For they could not endure what was commanded: *"And if so much as a beast touches the mountain, it shall be stoned*[a] *or shot with an arrow."*[b] 21And so terrifying was the sight *that* Moses said, *"I am exceedingly afraid* and trembling."[a])

22But you have come to Mount Zion and to the city of the living God, the heavenly Jerusalem, to an innumerable company of angels, 23to the general assembly and church of the firstborn *who are* registered in heaven, to God the Judge of all, to the spirits of just men made perfect, 24to Jesus the Mediator of the new covenant, and to the blood of sprinkling that speaks better things than *that of* Abel.

For how to convince a sinner of the reasonableness of judgment, *see Psa. 55:15 comment.*

Hear the Heavenly Voice

25See that you do not refuse Him who speaks. For if they did not escape who refused Him who spoke on earth, much more *shall we not escape* if we turn away

12:7 [a]NU-Text and M-Text read *It is for discipline that you endure; God....* 12:18 [a]NU-Text reads *to that which.* [b]NU-Text reads *gloom.* 12:20 [a]NU-Text and M-Text omit the rest of this verse. [b]Exodus 19:12, 13 12:21 [a]Deuteronomy 9:19

12:14 "Let us awake to a sense of the perilous state of many professing Christians. 'Without holiness no man shall see the Lord'; without sanctification there is no salvation (Heb. 12:14). Then what an enormous amount of so-called religion there is which is perfectly useless!" *J. C. Ryle*

QUESTIONS & OBJECTIONS

"If God exists, why doesn't He speak for Himself, audibly?"

He did speak audibly to Israel when He gave them the Ten Commandments, and the Bible says that Israel was so fearful at what they saw and heard, they pleaded that He no longer speak to them (see Exod. 20:18,19; Heb. 12:19). When He spoke on the Mount of Transfiguration, He terrified the disciples (see Matt. 17:5,6). When He once spoke audibly to Jesus, the people thought that they heard thunder (see John 12:28,29). So why didn't God just whisper on these occasions? Perhaps He did.

However, God (in His infinite wisdom) has chosen what the Bible calls "the foolishness of the message preached" to bring the gospel to humanity (see 1 Cor. 1:21). He has condescended to use lowly man to deliver the message of everlasting life to dying humanity.

When it comes to God speaking to us, it is important to make sure that we don't exaggerate our importance. We are but very tiny specks on a tiny speck of a planet, moving through the massive infinitude of space. If you want a special audience with the President, he likely will not come running to speak especially to you when, how, and where you want. Only a person with delusions of grandeur indeed would expect such treatment.

How much more so with the Creator of the universe? You are not going to get a special audience with God. So humble yourself, repent of your sins, and trust the Savior, then seek God through prayer and reading of His Word. Prayer is you speaking to God, and the Bible is God speaking to you. Make sure you listen carefully to what He says. Your eternity depends on it.

from Him who *speaks* from heaven,
26 whose voice then shook the earth; but
now He has promised, saying, *"Yet once
more I shake*[a] *not only the earth, but also
heaven."*[b] 27 Now this, *"Yet once more,"*
indicates the removal of those things that are being shaken, as of things that are made, that the things which cannot be shaken may remain.
28 Therefore, since we are receiving a kingdom which cannot be shaken, let us have grace, by which we may[a] serve God acceptably with reverence and godly fear.
29 For our God *is* a consuming fire.

Concluding Moral Directions

13 Let brotherly love continue. 2 Do
not forget to entertain strangers, for by so *doing* some have unwittingly entertained angels.
3 Remember the prison-
ers as if chained with them—those who are mistreated—since you yourselves are in the body also.
4 Marriage *is* honorable among all, and the bed undefiled; but fornicators and adulterers God will judge.
5 *Let your* conduct *be* without covetousness; *be* content with such things as you have. For He Himself has said, *"I will
never leave you nor forsake you."*[a] 6 So we
may boldly say:

"The LORD is my helper;
I will not fear.
What can man do to me?"[a]

Concluding Religious Directions

7 Remember those who rule over you, who have spoken the word of God to you, whose faith follow, considering the
outcome of *their* conduct. 8 Jesus Christ *is*
the same yesterday, today, and forever.
9 Do not be carried about[a] with various

12:26 [a]NU-Text reads *will shake.* [b]Haggai 2:6 12:28 [a]M-Text omits *may.* 13:5 [a]Deuteronomy 31:6, 8; Joshua 1:5 13:6 [a]Psalm 118:6 13:9 [a]NU-Text and M-Text read *away.*

12:29 "Our God is a consuming fire. He consumes pride, lust, materialism, and other sin." *Leonard Ravenhill*

13:8 Jesus has never changed. He has no variableness or shadow of turning (James 1:17). Hebrews 1:12 says of Him, "You are the same, and Your years will not fail."

and strange doctrines. For *it is* good that
the heart be established by grace, not
with foods which have not profited those
who have been occupied with them.
10 We have an altar from which those
who serve the tabernacle have no right to
eat. 11 For the bodies of those animals,
whose blood is brought into the sanctuary by the high priest for sin, are burned
outside the camp. 12 Therefore Jesus also,
that He might sanctify the people with
His own blood, suffered outside the gate.
13 Therefore let us go forth to Him, outside the camp, bearing His reproach.
14 For here we have no continuing city,
but we seek the one to come. 15 Therefore
by Him let us continually offer the sacrifice of praise to God, that is, the fruit of
our lips, giving thanks to His name. 16 But
do not forget to do good and to share, for
with such sacrifices God is well pleased.

To be a soul winner is the happiest thing in this world. And with every soul you bring to Jesus Christ, you seem to get a new heaven here upon earth.
CHARLES SPURGEON

17 Obey those who rule over you, and
be submissive, for they watch out for
your souls, as those who must give account. Let them do so with joy and not
with grief, for that would be unprofitable
for you.

Prayer Requested

18 Pray for us; for we are confident that
we have a good conscience, in all things
desiring to live honorably. 19 But I especially urge *you* to do this, that I may be
restored to you the sooner.

"When thou prayest, rather let thy heart be without words than thy words be without heart."

John Bunyan

Benediction, Final Exhortation, Farewell

20 Now may the God of peace who
brought up our Lord Jesus from the dead,
that great Shepherd of the sheep, through
the blood of the everlasting covenant,
21 make you complete in every good work
to do His will, working in you[a] what is well
pleasing in His sight, through Jesus Christ,
to whom *be* glory forever and ever. Amen.
22 And I appeal to you, brethren, bear
with the word of exhortation, for I have
written to you in few words. 23 Know that
our brother Timothy has been set free,
with whom I shall see you if he comes
shortly.
24 Greet all those who rule over you, and
all the saints. Those from Italy greet you.
25 Grace *be* with you all. Amen.

13:21 [a]NU-Text and M-Text read *us.*

13:15 "And forasmuch as ingratitude is one of the most odious of vices, let me not be unmindful gratefully to acknowledge the favours I receive from Heaven . . . For all Thy innumerable benefits; for life and reason, and the use of speech, for health and joy and every pleasant hour, my Good God, I thank Thee." *Benjamin Franklin*

James

Greeting to the Twelve Tribes

1 James, a bondservant of God and of the Lord Jesus Christ,

To the twelve tribes which are scattered abroad:

Greetings.

Profiting from Trials

[2]My brethren, count it all joy when you fall into various trials, [3]knowing that the testing of your faith produces patience. [4]But let patience have *its* perfect work, that you may be perfect and complete, lacking nothing. [5]If any of you lacks wisdom, let him ask of God, who gives to all liberally and without reproach, and it will be given to him. [6]But let him ask in faith, with no doubting, for he who doubts is like a wave of the sea driven and tossed by the wind. [7]For let not that man suppose that he will receive anything from the Lord; [8]*he is* a double-minded man, unstable in all his ways.

The Perspective of Rich and Poor

[9]Let the lowly brother glory in his exaltation, [10]but the rich in his humiliation, because as a flower of the field he will pass away. [11]For no sooner has the sun risen with a burning heat than it withers the grass; its flower falls, and its beautiful appearance perishes. So the rich man also will fade away in his pursuits.

Loving God Under Trials

[12]Blessed *is* the man who endures temptation; for when he has been approved, he will receive the crown of life which the Lord has promised to those who love Him. [13]Let no one say when he is tempted, "I am tempted by God"; for God cannot be tempted by evil, nor does He Himself tempt anyone. [14]But each one is tempted when he is drawn away by his own desires and enticed. [15]Then, when desire has conceived, it gives birth to sin; and sin, when it is full-grown, brings forth death.

1:3 Satan tempts us in order to bring out the worst in us; God tests us to bring out the best. (See v. 12.)

1:5 One mark of wisdom is the saving of souls (Prov. 11:30). With an open-ended promise such as this, we should plead with God for wisdom (see Prov. 2:1–7). Proverbs 19:8 tells us that he who gets wisdom loves his own soul.

1:15 The ungodly hold firmly onto the lighted stick of dynamite called "sin." They relish its flickering flame. Lust may delight the human heart, but its terrible consequences are sin, death, and hell.

"Human nature rises against restraint: 'I had not known lust except the Law had said, 'Thou shall not covet.' The depravity of man is excited to rebellion by the promulgation of laws. So evil are we, that we conceive at once the desire to commit an act, simply because it is forbidden." *Charles Spurgeon*

THE FUNCTION OF THE LAW

1:25 "God, being a perfect God, had to give a perfect Law, and the Law was given not to save men, but to measure them. I want you to understand this clearly, because I believe hundreds and thousands stumble at this point. They try to save themselves by trying to keep the Law; but it was never meant for men to save themselves by."
D. L. Moody

16Do not be deceived, my beloved
brethren. 17Every good gift and every perfect gift is from above, and comes down
from the Father of lights, with whom there
is no variation or shadow of turning. 18Of
His own will He brought us forth by the
word of truth, that we might be a kind of
firstfruits of His creatures.

Qualities Needed in Trials

19So then,[a] my beloved brethren, let
every man be swift to hear, slow to speak,
slow to wrath; 20for the wrath of man does
not produce the righteousness of God.

Doers—Not Hearers Only

21Therefore lay aside all filthiness and
overflow of wickedness, and receive with
meekness the implanted word, which is
able to save your souls.
22But be doers of the word, and not
hearers only, deceiving yourselves. 23For
if anyone is a hearer of the word and not
a doer, he is like a man observing his natural face in a mirror; 24for he observes
himself, goes away, and immediately forgets what kind of man he was. 25But he
who looks into the perfect law of liberty
and continues *in it,* and is not a forgetful
hearer but a doer of the work, this one
will be blessed in what he does.
26If anyone among you[a] thinks he is
religious, and does not bridle his tongue
but deceives his own heart, this one's
religion *is* useless. 27Pure and undefiled
religion before God and the Father is this:
to visit orphans and widows in their trouble, *and* to keep oneself unspotted from
the world.

Beware of Personal Favoritism

2 My brethren, do not hold the faith of
our Lord Jesus Christ, *the Lord* of
glory, with partiality. 2For if there should
come into your assembly a man with
gold rings, in fine apparel, and there
should also come in a poor man in filthy
clothes, 3and you pay attention to the
one wearing the fine clothes and say to
him, "You sit here in a good place," and
say to the poor man, "You stand there,"
or, "Sit here at my footstool," 4have you
not shown partiality among yourselves,
and become judges with evil thoughts?
5Listen, my beloved brethren: Has God
not chosen the poor of this world *to be* rich
in faith and heirs of the kingdom which
He promised to those who love Him?
6But you have dishonored the poor man.
Do not the rich oppress you and drag you
into the courts? 7Do they not blaspheme
that noble name by which you are called?

1:19 [a]NU-Text reads *Know this* or *This you know.* 1:26 [a]NU-Text omits *among you.*

1:22 This is particularly applicable to the many commands to evangelize this world.

1:23–25 The only way you and I can see ourselves in truth is to look into a mirror. Yet a mirror can only do its job and reflect truth if there is bright light. In Scripture, the Law of God is called both a mirror (James 1:23–25; 2:11,12) and light (Prov. 6:23). Many of today's "converts" aren't shown the mirror of the Law. We think that a long look at what they are in truth will be too painful for them, so "All have sinned" is all we tell them. Without the conviction of their own sin, they are stillborn with no life in them.

2:7 Witnessing to blasphemers. If you hear God's name taken in vain, don't tell the person it's offensive; instead, use it as an opening for the gospel. Greet him, talk about something in the natural realm, then give him a gospel tract. Gently say, "I noticed that you used God's name in vain. Do you know what you're actually doing when you do that?" Most people will say no. Then say, "Instead of using a filth word to express disgust, you're putting God's name in place of that word. That's called 'blasphemy,' and the Bible says, 'The Lord will not hold him guiltless who takes His name in vain.'"

USING THE LAW IN EVANGELISM

2:8 In vv. 8–12 James uses the Law (in conjunction with future punishment) to bring the knowledge of sin. See John 8:4,5 comment.

"It is of great importance that the sinner should be made to feel his guilt, and not to the impression that he is unfortunate. Do not be afraid, but show him the breadth of the divine Law, and the exceeding strictness of its precepts. Make him see how it condemns his thoughts and life. By a convicted sinner, I mean one who feels himself condemned by the Law of God, as a guilty sinner.

"I remark that this [the Law] is the rule, and the only just rule by which the guilt of sin can be measured . . . Every man need only consult his own conscience faithfully and he will see that it is equally affirmed by the mind's own intuition to be right." *Charles Finney*

[8]If you really fulfill *the* royal law according to the Scripture, *"You shall love your neighbor as yourself,"*[a] you do well;
[9]but if you show partiality, you commit sin, and are convicted by the law as transgressors.
[10]For whoever shall keep the whole law, and yet stumble in one *point*, he is guilty of all.
[11]For He who said, *"Do not commit adultery,"*[a] also said, *"Do not murder."*[b] Now if you do not commit adultery, but you do murder, you have become a transgressor of the law.
[12]So speak and so do as those who will be judged by the law of liberty.
[13]For judgment is without mercy to the one who has shown no mercy. Mercy triumphs over judgment.

Faith Without Works Is Dead

[14]What *does it* profit, my brethren, if someone says he has faith but does not have works? Can faith save him?
[15]If a brother or sister is naked and destitute of daily food,
[16]and one of you says to them, "Depart in peace, be warmed and filled," but you do not give them the things which are needed for the body, what *does it* profit?
[17]Thus also faith by itself, if it does not have works, is dead.

[18]But someone will say, "You have faith, and I have works." Show me your faith without your[a] works, and I will show you my faith by my[b] works.
[19]You believe that there is one God. You do well. Even the demons believe—and tremble!
[20]But do you want to know, O foolish man, that faith without works is dead?[a]
[21]Was not Abraham our father justified

2:8 [a]Leviticus 19:18 2:11 [a]Exodus 20:14; Deuteronomy 5:18 [b]Exodus 20:13; Deuteronomy 5:17 2:18 [a]NU-Text omits *your.* [b]NU-Text omits *my.* 2:20 [a]NU-Text reads *useless.*

2:10 Galatians 3:10 warns that the sinner must continue to do "*all* things" that are written in the Law. The strict demands of the Law cannot be kept by sinful man and should send the sinner to the Savior. See Matt. 5:48 comment.

"God's Law is unified; it all hangs together and is inseparable. It is like hitting a window with a hammer. You may hit it only once, and that rather lightly, but the whole window is shattered." *John MacArthur*

2:16 "Science may have found a cure for most evils; but it has found no remedy for the worst of them all: the apathy of human beings." *Helen Keller*

2:17 Faith without works. A Christian farmer in western Kansas felt sure that God spoke to him to give his $40,000 hail insurance to missions. So, in faith he gave the money, trusting that God would protect his crop. Sure enough, the hail came and severely damaged all his neighbor's crops, but not his.

In contrast, there is a well-known story about a brilliant tightrope artist named Blondin, who pushed a wheelbarrow across Niagara Falls. After he had walked to the other side, the crowd roared with applause at his amazing feat.

He asked a small boy in the crowd if he believed that Blondin could walk back. The boy said, "Yes, sir!" He then asked if the boy thought he could do it with him in the wheelbarrow. The boy said he believed he could do it, to which the famous tightrope walker said, *"Good! Jump in then and I will take you!"* The boy would not get in.

Here are two different types of faith. The farmer had faith that he had heard from God; he was so sure that he was prepared to step out. But the boy's faith was (understandably) lacking; he was not prepared to step out, and get in. Many sincere folks have a measure of faith in Jesus, but they have never *trusted* in Him. In that sense, their faith, because it does not have works with it, is dead.

by works when he offered Isaac his son on the altar? 22Do you see that faith was working together with his works, and by works faith was made perfect? 23And the Scripture was fulfilled which says, *"Abraham believed God, and it was accounted to him for righteousness."*[a] And he was called the friend of God. 24You see then that a man is justified by works, and not by faith only.

25Likewise, was not Rahab the harlot also justified by works when she received the messengers and sent *them* out another way?

26For as the body without the spirit is dead, so faith without works is dead also.

The Untamable Tongue

3 My brethren, let not many of you become teachers, knowing that we shall receive a stricter judgment. 2For we all stumble in many things. If anyone does not stumble in word, he *is* a perfect man, able also to bridle the whole body. 3Indeed,[a] we put bits in horses' mouths that they may obey us, and we turn their whole body. 4Look also at ships: although they are so large and are driven by fierce winds, they are turned by a very small rudder wherever the pilot desires. 5Even so the tongue is a little member and boasts great things.

See how great a forest a little fire kindles! 6And the tongue *is* a fire, a world of iniquity. The tongue is so set among our members that it defiles the whole body, and sets on fire the course of nature; and it is set on fire by hell. 7For every kind of beast and bird, of reptile and creature of the sea, is tamed and has been tamed by mankind. 8But no man can tame the tongue. *It is* an unruly evil, full of deadly poison. 9With it we bless our God and Father, and with it we curse men, who have been made in the similitude of God.

What can be wiser than in the highest sense to bless our fellow men—to snatch a soul from the gulf that yawns, to lift it up to the heaven that glorifies, to deliver an immortal from the thralldom of Satan, and to bring him into the liberty of Christ?

CHARLES SPURGEON

10Out of the same mouth proceed blessing and cursing. My brethren, these things ought not to be so. 11Does a spring send forth fresh *water* and bitter from the same opening? 12Can a fig tree, my brethren, bear olives, or a grapevine bear figs? Thus no spring yields both salt water and fresh.[a]

Heavenly Versus Demonic Wisdom

13Who *is* wise and understanding among you? Let him show by good conduct *that* his works *are done* in the meekness of wisdom. 14But if you have bitter envy and self-seeking in your hearts, do not boast and lie against the truth. 15This wisdom does not descend from above, but *is* earthly, sensual, demonic. 16For where envy and self-seeking *exist,* confusion and every evil thing *are* there. 17But the wis-

2:23 [a]Genesis 15:6 3:3 [a]NU-Text reads *Now if.* 3:12 [a]NU-Text reads *Neither can a salty spring produce fresh water.*

2:19 "No man is better for knowing that God in the beginning created the heaven and the earth. The devil knows that, and so did Ahab and Judas Iscariot. No man is better for knowing that God so loved the world of men that He gave His only begotten Son to die for their redemption. In hell there are millions who know that. Theological truth is useless until it is obeyed. The purpose behind all doctrine is to secure moral action." *A. W. Tozer*

2:20 "What is it [evolution] based upon? Upon nothing whatever but faith, upon belief in the reality of the unseen—belief in the fossils that cannot be produced, belief in the embryological experiments that refuse to come off. It is faith unjustified by works." *Arthur N. Field*

3:6 The tongue weighs practically nothing, but so few people are able to hold it. Here we are told that the tongue is set on fire by hell. At Pentecost, God gave man a new tongue—set on fire by heaven. The mouths of the unsaved reveal their wicked hearts (see Rom. 3:13,14).

dom that is from above is first pure, then
peaceable, gentle, willing to yield, full of
mercy and good fruits, without partiality
and without hypocrisy. 18Now the fruit of
righteousness is sown in peace by those
who make peace.

Pride Promotes Strife

4 Where do wars and fights *come* from
among you? Do *they* not *come* from
your *desires for* pleasure that war in your
members? 2You lust and do not have.
You murder and covet and cannot obtain.
You fight and war. Yet[a] you do not have
because you do not ask. 3You ask and do
not receive, because you ask amiss, that
you may spend *it* on your pleasures.
4Adulterers and[a] adulteresses! Do you not
know that friendship with the world is
enmity with God? Whoever therefore
wants to be a friend of the world makes
himself an enemy of God. 5Or do you
think that the Scripture says in vain, "The
Spirit who dwells in us yearns jealously"?
6But He gives more grace. Therefore
He says:

"God resists the proud,
But gives grace to the humble."[a]

Humility Cures Worldliness

7Therefore submit to God. Resist the
devil and he will flee from you. 8Draw near
to God and He will draw near to you.
Cleanse *your* hands, *you* sinners; and purify
your hearts, *you* double-minded. 9Lament
and mourn and weep! Let your laughter be
turned to mourning and *your* joy to gloom.

USING THE LAW IN EVANGELISM

4:2–4 James here uses the Law once again to bring the knowledge of sin—speaking of lust, adultery, murder, and covetousness.

"First, then, before you can speak peace to your hearts, you must be made to see, made to feel, made to weep over, made to bewail, your actual transgressions against the Law of God." *George Whitefield*

10Humble yourselves in the sight of the
Lord, and He will lift you up.

· · · · · ·

Are the lost God's friend or enemy? See 2 Chron. 20:7 comment.

· · · · · ·

Do Not Judge a Brother

11Do not speak evil of one another,
brethren. He who speaks evil of a brother
and judges his brother, speaks evil of the
law and judges the law. But if you judge
the law, you are not a doer of the law but
a judge. 12There is one Lawgiver,[a] who is
able to save and to destroy. Who[b] are you
to judge another?[c]

Do Not Boast About Tomorrow

13Come now, you who say, "Today or
tomorrow we will[a] go to such and such a
city, spend a year there, buy and sell, and

4:2 [a]NU-Text and M-Text omit *Yet.* 4:4 [a]NU-Text omits *Adulterers and.* 4:6 [a]Proverbs 3:34 4:12 [a]NU-Text adds *and Judge.* [b]NU-Text and M-Text read *But who.* [c]NU-Text reads *a neighbor.* 4:13 [a]M-Text reads *let us.*

3:17 This is the spirit in which we should share our faith. See Prov. 15:1.

Beware of "religious" types. They tend to gravitate toward the evangelistic enterprise. They will contend with you about doctrine and steal your time from the work of evangelism. You will recognize them by their lack of gentleness, mercy, and willingness to yield to reason.

4:6 Biblical evangelism is always "Law to the proud and grace to the humble." With the Law we break the hard heart; with the gospel we heal the broken one. See Matt. 19:17–22 comment.

4:7 "The best means of resisting the devil is to destroy whatever of the world remains in us, in order to raise for God, upon its ruins, a building all of love. Then shall we begin, in this fleeting life, to love God as we shall love him in eternity." *John Wesley*

4:9,10 These are the inner workings of a genuinely repentant heart—lamenting, mourning, weeping (contrition), heaviness, and humility. These are the ones the Lord lifts up. See Psa. 147:6.

Springboards for Preaching and Witnessing

The Will to Live

4:14

Millions of people spend dozens of hours each week watching dead people on TV. From Elvis to Lucy to Jimmy Stewart, the faces of folks who no longer exist entertain us. Time not only snatched their looks, it snatched their lives. Today, good-looking Hollywood stars are making movies so that tomorrow's generation can also pass the time by watching dead people on TV.

Time makes today tomorrow's memory. Each weekend seems to pass us by like blurred telephone poles flashing past the window of the speeding train of life.

If I bought a new car and saw in the owner's manual that it had a certain type of engine, I shouldn't be surprised to lift the hood and find the engine to be exactly as the manual stated. The maker's handbook gives me insight into the unseen workings of the vehicle. This is also true with human beings. The Maker's manual tells us how each of us thinks and why we react the way we do. It lifts the hood and reveals the inner workings of *Homo sapiens.*

In doing so, the Bible discloses an often-overlooked tool that we can use to reach the lost. That tool is the "fear of death." For the Christian who may find such an approach to be negative, it may be looked at in a *positive* light. The tool may also be called "the will to live." Every human being in his right mind has a fear of death (Heb. 2:15). *He doesn't want to die.* He sits wide-eyed, staring out the window of the speeding train watching life pass him by.

Here is how to use that tool when speaking to an unsaved person: "Let's assume that the average person dies at 70 years old. Then if you are 20 years old, you have approximately 2,500 weekends left to live. If you have turned 30, you have 2,000 weekends left until the day you die. If you are 40 years old, you have only 1,500 weekends left. If you are 50, then you have just 1,000 weekends, and if you are 60, you have a mere 500 weekends left until the day death comes to you."

Even as a Christian that thought concerns me. I somehow can relate to "weekends," while "years" puts death into the distance. It shakes me enough to ask myself, *What I am doing with my life?* It sickens me that I am doing so little to reach the lost. It also deeply concerns me that I have dry eyes when I pray. My train will take me into the presence of God. For those trusting in Jesus Christ, death has been defeated. But the train of the unregenerate will take them to horrific disaster. Their end will be eternal hell. In light of such terrible thoughts, all my activities outside of warning the world of their destination seem trivial.

It has been wisely stated that every one of us is unique…*just like everyone else.* In truth, each unique individual is uniquely predictable. Every sinner has a fear of death. No one can deny that he naturally has a will to live. Therefore, it makes sense to confront him with reality by reminding him that he has an "appointment" to keep. Bluntly tell him how many weekends he has left. Then appeal to his reason by saying, "If there was one chance in a million that Jesus Christ 'has abolished death and brought life and immortality to light through the gospel' (2 Tim. 1:10), you owe it to your good sense to look into it."

make a profit"; 14whereas you do not know
what *will happen* tomorrow. For what *is*
your life? It is even a vapor that appears
for a little time and then vanishes away.
15Instead you *ought* to say, "If the Lord
wills, we shall live and do this or that."
16But now you boast in your arrogance.
All such boasting is evil.
17Therefore, to him who knows to do
good and does not do *it,* to him it is sin.

Rich Oppressors Will Be Judged

5 Come now, *you* rich, weep and howl
for your miseries that are coming up-

4:12 The idea for the American government's divided powers came directly from Scripture. Isaiah 33:22 says, "For the LORD is our Judge [the judicial branch], the LORD is our Lawgiver [the legislative branch], the LORD is our King [the executive branch]." Our Founding Fathers knew that separated powers were needed because of man's inherent sinfulness and desire for control—and what better model could there be for a government than the Lord who governs the universe!

"The teachings of the Bible are so interwoven and entwined with our whole civic and social life that it would be literally—I do not mean figuratively, I mean literally—impossible for us to figure to ourselves what life would be if these teachings were removed." *Theodore Roosevelt*

4:17 "To sin by silence when they should protest makes cowards out of men." *Abraham Lincoln*

on *you!* 2Your riches are corrupted, and your garments are moth-eaten. 3Your gold and silver are corroded, and their corrosion will be a witness against you and will eat your flesh like fire. You have heaped up treasure in the last days. 4Indeed the wages of the laborers who mowed your fields, which you kept back by fraud, cry out; and the cries of the reapers have reached the ears of the Lord of Sabaoth.[a] 5You have lived on the earth in pleasure and luxury; you have fattened your hearts as[a] in a day of slaughter. 6You have condemned, you have murdered the just; he does not resist you.

The Dead Sea Scrolls confirm that the Bible hasn't changed through the years. See 1 Pet. 1:25 comment.

Be Patient and Persevering

7Therefore be patient, brethren, until the coming of the Lord. See *how* the farmer waits for the precious fruit of the earth, waiting patiently for it until it receives the early and latter rain. 8You also be patient. Establish your hearts, for the coming of the Lord is at hand.

9Do not grumble against one another, brethren, lest you be condemned.[a] Behold, the Judge is standing at the door! 10My brethren, take the prophets, who spoke in the name of the Lord, as an example of suffering and patience. 11Indeed we count them blessed who endure. You have heard of the perseverance of Job and seen the end *intended by* the Lord—that the Lord is very compassionate and merciful.

12But above all, my brethren, do not swear, either by heaven or by earth or with any other oath. But let your "Yes" be "Yes," and *your* "No," "No," lest you fall into judgment.[a]

Meeting Specific Needs

13Is anyone among you suffering? Let him pray. Is anyone cheerful? Let him sing psalms. 14Is anyone among you sick? Let him call for the elders of the church, and let them pray over him, anointing him with oil in the name of the Lord. 15And the prayer of faith will save the sick, and the Lord will raise him up. And if he has committed sins, he will be forgiven. 16Confess *your* trespasses[a] to one another, and pray for one another, that you may be healed. The effective, fervent prayer of a righteous man avails much. 17Elijah was a man with a nature like ours, and he prayed earnestly that it would not rain; and it did not rain on the land for three years and six months. 18And he prayed again, and the heaven gave rain, and the earth produced its fruit.

Bring Back the Erring One

19Brethren, if anyone among you wanders from the truth, and someone turns him back, 20let him know that he who turns a sinner from the error of his way will save a soul[a] from death and cover a multitude of sins.

5:4 [a]Literally, in Hebrew, *Hosts* 5:5 [a]NU-Text omits *as.* 5:9 [a]NU-Text and M-Text read *judged.* 5:12 [a]M-Text reads *hypocrisy.* 5:16 [a]NU-Text reads *Therefore confess your sins.* 5:20 [a]NU-Text reads *his soul.*

5:8 Second coming of Jesus: See Jude 14.

5:16 "Prayer is the honest thoughts of the heart and mind converted into a form of communication, either verbal or mental, directed toward God." *Emeal Zwayne*

5:20 There is no higher calling than to turn a sinner from the error of his ways. A surgeon may extend someone's life, but death eventually takes the person. Our work has *eternal* consequences.

Judaism

There are approximately 14 million Jewish people in the world today, with close to 6 million living in the U.S. and about 5 million in Israel. Although Christians believe in the God of Abraham, Isaac, and Jacob and are followers of the Jewish Messiah, we don't have as much in common with our Jewish friends as you may think.

Judaism is ranked as the sixth largest organized religion in the world, but it may surprise you to find that many Jewish people don't believe in God. More than half of all Jews in Israel today call themselves "secular," and according to polls, only 30 percent of all Jews are "absolutely certain" that God exists, 34 percent are "somewhat certain," 24 percent aren't sure, and 12 percent believe there is no God.

So it's possible to be secular, agnostic, or *an atheist* and still be Jewish. Some Jews even believe in reincarnation. If your mother is Jewish, that makes you Jewish, no matter what you believe. So being Jewish is not the same thing as following the religion of Judaism. Being Jewish is like having a *citizenship*; but following Judaism is living a certain lifestyle. To Jewish people, what they believe about God and the afterlife isn't as important as how they live.

BACKGROUND

There are three main branches, or movements, in contemporary Judaism:

Orthodox: Orthodox is the most strict form, and until 200 years ago, it was the only kind of Judaism. Orthodox or "traditional" Jews emphasize tradition and pride themselves on faithfully keeping the Laws of Moses. They make up 10 percent of the Jewish population in America.

Reform: On the other end of the scale is the liberal or "modern" movement, called Reform. The Reform movement began in the 18th century to bring Judaism's "old and outmoded ways of thinking" up to date. Reform Jews say they keep the good values of Judaism, but don't have to keep strict religious laws. These are most of the Jews you will meet today.

Conservative: In between the Orthodox and Reform are the Conservatives. Conservative Judaism arose in the 19th century, as a middle ground between the other two branches. They are traditional but believe the rabbis can change Jewish laws to suit the times. About 30 percent of American Jews are Conservative.

Because Judaism emphasizes behavior instead of theology, there is a wide variety of beliefs even within each of the branches. With such diversity, it's difficult to generalize about their beliefs.

WHO IS GOD?

Orthodox Jews believe there is only one God. He is a Spirit who is all-knowing, all-powerful, ever-present, and eternal. Jews often recite something called the Shema: "Hear, O Israel: The Lord our God, the Lord is one!" (Deut. 6:4).

Reform Jews, however, can interpret the "God concept" however they like, and that's still within the boundaries of their Judaism. They can be atheists, naturalists, religious humanists, but they all agree on one concept: "The truth is that we do not know the truth." So if you want to know what Reform Jews believe about God today, it really depends on which Jewish person you ask.

SCRIPTURES

Orthodox Jews (the strict believers) believe the *Torah* was written by God through the hand of Moses. The Torah is the Hebrew name for the first five books of the Bible: Genesis, Exodus, Leviticus, Numbers, and Deuteronomy. They also believe the rest of the Old Testament, which is called the *Tanakh*, but don't give it as much authority as the Torah. There is also the *Talmud*—the teachings of the Jewish rabbis—which they believe has great authority.

But Reform Jews (the more liberal ones) don't necessarily believe that the Scriptures were written by God. Most believe they were merely written by men. They feel it's a good book for preserving history and culture, and helps to live a good life, but the bottom line is, it wasn't written by God, so it's not binding.

HEAVEN AND HELL

Orthodox Jews do believe there is life after death in the *Olam Ha-Ba*—the World to Come. They believe that the righteous of all nations will live forever with God in a perfect place of peace and prosperity, and that the unrighteous will suffer—but they don't all agree on where those people will go. Some believe nothing happens when you die. Others believe you go to She'ol, or Gehenna, a place of purification (kind of like a Jewish purgatory). Then you either go directly to Paradise, or you are destroyed and cease to exist, or you continue to live in a state of unending remorse. Again, today's Judaism leaves it open to personal opinion.

In the Reform and Conservative branches, most have no concept of personal life after death. What is most important is the here and now—being a good person, and making the world a better place.

SIN AND SALVATION

None of the branches of Judaism believe in original sin. They teach that man is created in the image of God and is born morally pure. They either think of humanity as neutral—with the potential for both good and bad—or as basically good. Although men

(continued)

Judaism (continued)

do sin, they believe that God's justice is tempered with mercy.

Many Jewish people never ask the question, "What do I have to do to get into heaven?"since Judaism teaches that all good people from all nations will go to heaven. And because most Jews don't believe in hell, they don't think of needing to be "saved" from anything. Remember, they believe they already have a favored standing with God as His "chosen people."

Many Jews do believe that studying the Torah, praying, and doing good deeds will earn them a *better* place in heaven, but they get a "Free Pass" as descendants of Abraham, Isaac, and Jacob. Scripture has something to say about that kind of thinking: "And do not think to say to yourselves, 'We have Abraham as our father.' For I say to you that God is able to raise up children to Abraham from these stones" (Matt. 3:9).

THE MESSIAH

So, what do Jewish people think about the Messiah today? Again, it depends on who you ask. Most Jewish people aren't waiting with anticipation for a coming Messiah. The Orthodox Jews are still holding to that hope, but they fail to see the Messiah as divine, or as having to suffer as the Scriptures prophesied that He would. They believe that the Messiah is simply going to be a great political leader who brings peace to Israel and extends his rule over all the earth. One thing most Jewish people do agree on today is that Jesus is not that Messiah.

The other branches place their hope not in a person but in a "messianic age"—a Utopian age that mankind is progressing toward.

JEWISH CUSTOMS

It is traditional for most Jews to celebrate certain life events, such as circumcision of male newborns, and a *bar mitzvah* (for boys) or *bat mitzvah* (for girls)—which is a coming-of-age ceremony at age 13. Many also observe the Sabbath as a weekly day of rest.

Most Jewish people observe at least some of the Jewish holidays, though it's often to connect with their heritage more than for religious reasons. The most solemn are the High Holy Days: Rosh Hashanah and Yom Kippur. Yom Kippur, the Day of Atonement, is when Jews fast and pray for the forgiveness of their sins.

The most popular of all the holidays is Passover, which remembers the Israelites' deliverance from slavery in Egypt. During the week of Passover they eat *matzo*, which is unleavened bread, and hold a *Seder*, or Passover meal.

HOW TO REACH A JEWISH PERSON

First, here are some tips on what *not* to do as you talk with a Jewish person:

- Don't be intimidated by thinking that all Jewish people are well acquainted with the Scriptures. Although they do give the Old Testament respect, there's a very good chance you know the Bible better than they do.
- Unless it's in a phrase like "Orthodox Jews," using the word "Jews" can sound anti-Semitic. It's best to refer to "Jewish people" instead.
- Since they view Jewishness as a way of life, avoid using the term "convert," which implies leaving behind their Jewishness. Instead, talk about becoming a "follower of Jesus."
- While it's fine to mention "Y'shua" as the Hebrew name of Jesus, people will not realize you are referring to the historical person Jesus of Nazareth unless you also use the name "Jesus."
- The term "Savior" is not understood by Jewish people, so instead speak of a Redeemer and use the word "Messiah." Because of the Passover *Seder*, the concept of "redemption" is more familiar, so use that term rather than "salvation." You can explain that as God freed the Israelites from slavery in Egypt, so He wants to free us from the slavery to sin in our lives.

So, how do we reach a Jewish person? There are many different ways you could try. Paul said he reasoned with the Jews both out of the Law of Moses and out of the Prophets, so you could show them how Jesus fulfills the Jewish prophecies of the coming Messiah. (For a few of the many fulfilled prophecies, see the "Messianic Prophecies" chart on the following page.) But sadly, many Jews don't care about this evidence because they don't have much regard for the Scriptures. And, if you have someone who esteems the Old Testament, he may argue that you're just "reading Jesus into the Scriptures."

Another approach is to try to answer all of the person's objections to Christianity. For example, how we as Christians can believe in the Trinity and yet believe in only one God, not three, or that Jesus will set up His earthly kingdom at His *second* coming, not His first. All this information is good, but be forewarned: if you are speaking to someone who has a proud heart, this may stir up a zesty argument.

That's why when we talk with a Jewish person about God, we must start with the Law of Moses. It's really very simple, so don't complicate it. Find out if the person is proud or humble by asking the question, "Would you consider yourself to be a good person?" If he says "yes," then take him through the Ten Commandments, just like Jesus did with the rich young ruler (see Mark 10:17). Let those ten great cannons humble him and show him that he'll be guilty on Judgment Day and will need God's forgiveness, which can be found only in the Messiah, Jesus Christ.

If his heart is humble, then unashamedly reveal the love of God displayed on the cross—that God Himself provided a Lamb for our atonement. Then trust in His great faithfulness to bring the person to everlasting life that is in Jesus alone.

(continued)

Messianic Prophecies

PROPHECY	FULFILLMENT
Messiah will be from the lineage of Abraham (Gen. 18:18); Isaac (Gen. 21:12); Jacob (Gen. 28:13,14); Judah (Gen. 49:10); Jesse (Isa. 11:1,2,10); and David (Jer. 23:5,6).	"Jesus . . . the son of David, the son of Jesse, . . . the son of Judah, the son of Jacob, the son of Isaac, the son of Abraham." (Luke 3:31–34)
Messiah will be born of a virgin. (Isa. 7:14)	"An angel of the Lord appeared to him in a dream, saying, 'Joseph, son of David, do not be afraid to take to you Mary your wife, for that which is conceived in her is of the Holy Spirit. And she will bring forth a Son, and you shall call His name JESUS, for He will save His people from their sins.'" (Matt. 1:20,21)
Messiah will be born in Bethlehem. (Mic. 5:2)	"Now after Jesus was born in Bethlehem of Judea in the days of Herod the king, behold, wise men from the East came to Jerusalem, saying, 'Where is He who has been born King of the Jews?'" (Matt. 2:1,2)
Messiah will be declared the Son of God. (Psa. 2:7)	"Suddenly a voice came from heaven, saying, 'This is My beloved Son, in whom I am well pleased.'" (Matt. 3:17)
Messiah will perform miraculous healings. (Isa. 35:5,6)	"Jesus answered and said to them, 'Go and tell John the things you have seen and heard: that the blind see, the lame walk, the lepers are cleansed, the deaf hear, the dead are raised, the poor have the gospel preached to them.'" (Luke 7:21,22)
Messiah will be betrayed for thirty pieces of silver. (Zech. 11:12)	"Then one of the twelve, called Judas Iscariot, went to the chief priests and said, 'What are you willing to give me if I deliver Him to you?' And they counted out to him thirty pieces of silver." (Matt. 26:14,15)
Messiah will be crucified. (Psa. 22:16)	"And He, bearing His cross, went out to a place called . . . Golgotha, where they crucified Him, and two others with Him, one on either side, and Jesus in the center." (John 19:17,18)
Messiah will not have any bones broken. (Psa. 34:20)	"Then the soldiers came and broke the legs of the first and of the other who was crucified with Him. But when they came to Jesus and saw that He was already dead, they did not break His legs." (John 19:32,33)
Messiah will be resurrected. (Psa. 16:10)	"[David], foreseeing this, spoke concerning the resurrection of the Christ, that His soul was not left in Hades, nor did His flesh see corruption. This Jesus God has raised up, of which we are all witnesses." (Acts 2:31,32)
Messiah will ascend to heaven. (Psa. 16:10)	"So then, after the Lord had spoken to them, He was received up into heaven, and sat down at the right hand of God." (Mark 16:19)

(Adapted from *World Religions in a Nutshell.*)

1 Peter

Greeting to the Elect Pilgrims

1 Peter, an apostle of Jesus Christ,

To the pilgrims of the Dispersion in Pontus, Galatia, Cappadocia, Asia, and Bithynia, [2]elect according to the foreknowledge of God the Father, in sanctification of the Spirit, for obedience and sprinkling of the blood of Jesus Christ:

Grace to you and peace be multiplied.

A Heavenly Inheritance

[3]Blessed *be* the God and Father of our Lord Jesus Christ, who according to His abundant mercy has begotten us again to a living hope through the resurrection of Jesus Christ from the dead, [4]to an inheritance incorruptible and undefiled and that does not fade away, reserved in heaven for you, [5]who are kept by the power of God through faith for salvation ready to be revealed in the last time.

[6]In this you greatly rejoice, though now for a little while, if need be, you have been grieved by various trials, [7]that the genuineness of your faith, *being* much more precious than gold that perishes, though it is tested by fire, may be found to praise, honor, and glory at the revelation of Jesus Christ, [8]whom having not seen[a] you love. Though now you do not see *Him,* yet believing, you rejoice with joy inexpressible and full of glory, [9]receiving the end of your faith—the salvation of *your* souls.

[10]Of this salvation the prophets have inquired and searched carefully, who prophesied of the grace *that would come* to you, [11]searching what, or what manner of time, the Spirit of Christ who was in them was indicating when He testified beforehand the sufferings of Christ and the glories that would follow. [12]To them it was revealed that, not to themselves, but to us[a] they were ministering the things which now have been reported to you through those who have preached the gospel to you by the Holy Spirit sent from heaven—things which angels desire to look into.

Living Before God Our Father

[13]Therefore gird up the loins of your mind, be sober, and rest *your* hope fully upon the grace that is to be brought to you at the revelation of Jesus Christ; [14]as obedient children, not conforming yourselves to the former lusts, *as* in your ignorance; [15]but as He who called you *is* holy, you also be holy in all *your* conduct, [16]because it is written, *"Be holy, for I am holy."*[a]

[17]And if you call on the Father, who without partiality judges according to each

1:8 [a]M-Text reads *known.* 1:12 [a]NU-Text and M-Text read *you.* 1:16 [a]Leviticus 11:44, 45; 19:2; 20:7

1:3 New birth—its necessity for salvation. See 1 Pet. 1:23.

SPRINGBOARDS FOR PREACHING AND WITNESSING

The Beloved Son

1:4

A true story is told of a millionaire who had a portrait of his beloved son painted before the son went to war. He was tragically killed in battle, and shortly afterward, the heartbroken millionaire died. His will stated that all his riches were to be auctioned, specifying that the painting must sell first.

Many showed up at the auction, where a mass of the rich man's wealth was displayed. When the painting was held up for sale, there were no bids made. It was an unknown painting by an unknown painter of the rich man's uncelebrated son, so sadly, there was little interest.

After a few moments, a butler who worked for the man remembered how much the millionaire loved his son, decided to bid for it, and purchased the portrait for a very low price.

Suddenly, to everyone's surprise the auctioneer brought down his gavel and declared the auction closed. The rich man's will had secretly specified that the person who cared enough to purchase the painting of his beloved son was also to be given all the riches of his estate.

This is precisely what God has done through the gospel. He who accepts the beloved Son of God also receives all the riches of His estate—the gift of eternal life and "pleasures forevermore" (Psa. 16:11). They become "joint heirs" with the Son (Rom. 8:16,17).

one's work, conduct yourselves throughout the time of your stay *here* in fear;
18knowing that you were not redeemed
with corruptible things, *like* silver or gold,
from your aimless conduct *received* by
tradition from your fathers, 19but with the
precious blood of Christ, as of a lamb
without blemish and without spot. 20He
indeed was foreordained before the foundation of the world, but was manifest in
these last times for you 21who through
Him believe in God, who raised Him from
the dead and gave Him glory, so that
your faith and hope are in God.

The Enduring Word

22Since you have purified your souls
in obeying the truth through the Spirit[a]
in sincere love of the brethren, love one
another fervently with a pure heart, 23hav-
ing been born again, not of corruptible
seed but incorruptible, through the word
of God which lives and abides forever,[a]
24because

"All flesh is as grass,
And all the glory of man[a] *as the flower*

1:22 [a]NU-Text omits *through the Spirit.* 1:23 [a]NU-Text omits *forever.* 1:24 [a]NU-Text reads *all its glory.*

1:8 The source of joy. "Joy is not the same as pleasure or happiness. A wicked and evil man may have pleasure, while any ordinary mortal is capable of being happy. Pleasure generally comes from things, and always through the senses; happiness comes from humans through fellowship. Joy comes from loving God and neighbor. Pleasure is quick and violent, like a flash of lightning. Joy is steady and abiding, like a fixed star. Pleasure depends on external circumstances, such as money, food, travel, etc. Joy is independent of them, for it comes from a good conscience and love of God." *Fulton J. Sheen*

1:15 "To ask that God's love should be content with us as we are is to ask that God should cease to be God: because He is what He is, His love must, in the nature of things, be impeded and repelled by certain stains in our present character, and because He already loves us He must labor to make us lovable." *C. S. Lewis*

1:23 New birth—its necessity for salvation. If you speak to someone who professes to know God and you are not certain of their salvation, simply ask if they have been "born again" (see John 3:1–7). If you find that they are not sure (this is one sign that they haven't—1 John 5:10) or they say that they haven't, here is how you can bring focus to its importance. Tell them that the difference between *believing* in God and being *born again* is like the difference between *believing* in a parachute and *putting it on*. There is a big difference when you jump from the plane. Then say, "Do you know what convinced me that I had to be born again? It was the Ten Commandments." Then take them through the spiritual nature of the Law, which brings the knowledge of sin (Rom. 7:7). See 1 John 5:1.

1:25 *The Dead Sea Scrolls— "The greatest manuscript discovery of all times."*

By William F. Albright

The discovery of the Dead Sea Scrolls (DSS) at Qumran [in 1947] had significant effects in corroborating evidence for the Scriptures. The ancient texts, found hidden in pots in cliff-top caves by a monastic religious community, confirm the reliability of the Old Testament text. These texts, which were copied and studied by the Essenes, include one complete Old Testament book (Isaiah) and thousands of fragments, representing every Old Testament book except Esther.

The manuscripts date from the third century B.C. to the first century A.D. and give the earliest window found so far into the texts of the Old Testament books and their predictive prophecies. The Qumran texts have become an important witness for the divine origin of the Bible, providing further evidence against the criticism of such crucial books as Daniel and Isaiah.

Dating the Manuscripts. Carbon-14 dating is a reliable form of scientific dating when applied to uncontaminated material several thousand years old. Results indicated an age of 1917 years with a 200-year (10 percent) variant.

Paleography (ancient writing forms) and orthography (spelling) indicated that some manuscripts were inscribed before 100 B.C. Albright set the date of the complete Isaiah scroll to around 100 B.C.—"there can happily not be the slightest doubt in the world about the genuineness of the manuscript."

Archaeological Dating. Collaborative evidence for an early date came from archaeology. Pottery accompanying the manuscripts was late Hellenistic (c. 150–63 B.C.) and Early Roman (c. 63 B.C. to A.D. 100). Coins found in the monastery ruins proved by their inscriptions to have been minted between 135 B.C. and A.D. 135. The weave and pattern of the cloth supported an early date. There is no reasonable doubt that the Qumran manuscripts came from the century before Christ and the first century A.D.

Significance of the Dating. Previous to the DSS, the earliest known manuscript of the Old Testament was the Masoretic Text (A.D. 900) and two others (dating about A.D. 1000) from which, for example, the King James version of the Old Testament derived its translation. Perhaps most would have considered the Masoretic text as a very late text and therefore questioned the reliability of the Old Testament wholesale. The Dead Sea Scrolls eclipse these texts by 1,000 years and provide little reason to question their reliability, and further, present only confidence for the text. The beauty of the Dead Sea Scrolls lies in the close match they have with the Masoretic text—demonstrable evidence of reliability and preservation of the authentic text through the centuries. So the discovery of the DSS provides evidence for the following:

1) Confirmation of the Hebrew Text
2) Support for the Masoretic Text
3) Support for the Greek translation of the Hebrew Text (the Septuagint). Since the New Testament often quotes from the Greek Old Testament, the DSS furnish the reader with further confidence for the Masoretic texts in this area where it can be tested.

(Adapted from *Norman Geisler*, "Dead Sea Scrolls," *Baker Encyclopedia of Christian Apologetics*)

of the grass.
The grass withers,
And its flower falls away,
25 *But the word of the LORD endures*
forever."[a]

Now this is the word which by the gospel was preached to you.

2 Therefore, laying aside all malice, all deceit, hypocrisy, envy, and all evil speaking, 2 as newborn babes, desire the
pure milk of the word, that you may grow
thereby,[a] 3 if indeed you have tasted that
the Lord *is* gracious.

The Chosen Stone and His Chosen People

4 Coming to Him *as to* a living stone,
rejected indeed by men, but chosen by God
and precious, 5 you also, as living stones,
are being built up a spiritual house, a

1:25 [a]Isaiah 40:6–8 2:2 [a]NU-Text adds *up to salvation.*

2:2 "Had the doctrines of Jesus been preached always as pure as they came from His lips, the whole civilized world would now have been Christians." *Thomas Jefferson*

PRINCIPLES OF GROWTH FOR THE NEW AND GROWING CHRISTIAN

2:2

Feeding on the Word—Daily Nutrition

A healthy baby has a healthy appetite. If you have truly been "born" of the Spirit of God, you *will* have a healthy appetite. The Bible says, "As newborn babes, desire the pure milk of the word, that you may grow thereby" (1 Pet. 2:2). Feed yourself daily without fail. Job said, "I have treasured the words of His mouth more than my necessary food" (Job 23:12). The more you eat, the quicker you will grow, and the less bruising you will have. Speed up the process and save yourself some pain—vow to read God's Word every day, *without fail*. Say to yourself, "No Bible, no breakfast. No read, no feed." Be like Job, and put your Bible *before* your belly. If you do that, God promises that you will be like a fruitful, strong, and healthy tree (Psa. 1). Each day, find somewhere quiet and thoroughly soak your soul in the Word of God.

There may be times when you read through its pages with great enthusiasm, and other times when it seems dry and even boring. But food profits your body whether you enjoy it or not. As a child, you no doubt ate desserts with great enthusiasm. Perhaps vegetables weren't so exciting. If you were a normal child, you probably had to be *encouraged* to eat them at first. Then, as you matured in life you were taught to discipline yourself to eat vegetables, because they benefit you physically even though they may not bring pleasure to your taste buds.

For the next principle of growth, see Matt. 6:9 comment.

holy priesthood, to offer up spiritual sacrifices acceptable to God through Jesus
Christ. [6]Therefore it is also contained in
the Scripture,

"Behold, I lay in Zion
A chief cornerstone, elect, precious,
And he who believes on Him will by
no means be put to shame."[a]

[7]Therefore, to you who believe, *He* is
precious; but to those who are disobedient,[a]

"The stone which the builders rejected
Has become the chief cornerstone,"[b]

[8]and

"A stone of stumbling
And a rock of offense."[a]

They stumble, being disobedient to the word, to which they also were appointed.
[9]But you *are* a chosen generation, a royal priesthood, a holy nation, His own special people, that you may proclaim the praises of Him who called you out of darkness into His marvelous light; [10]who once
were not a people but *are* now the people of God, who had not obtained mercy but now have obtained mercy.

Living Before the World

[11]Beloved, I beg *you* as sojourners and pilgrims, abstain from fleshly lusts which war against the soul, [12]having your conduct honorable among the Gentiles, that when they speak against you as evildoers, they may, by *your* good works which they observe, glorify God in the day of visitation.

Submission to Government

[13]Therefore submit yourselves to every ordinance of man for the Lord's sake, whether to the king as supreme, [14]or to
governors, as to those who are sent by him for the punishment of evildoers and *for the* praise of those who do good. [15]For
this is the will of God, that by doing good you may put to silence the ignorance of

2:6 [a]Isaiah 28:16 2:7 [a]NU-Text reads *to those who disbelieve.* [b]Psalm 118:22 2:8 [a]Isaiah 8:14

2:5 "If Jesus Christ be God and died for me, no sacrifice I make can be too great for Him." *C. T. Studd*

2:7 Perhaps the number one fruit of salvation will be that Jesus will become precious to the believer. See 1 Cor. 16:22.

QUESTIONS & OBJECTIONS

"How should I witness to my coworkers?"

When we interact with people on a daily basis, we have many opportunities for sharing our faith. First, be sure you are respectful to your employer and set a good example in your work ethic by working "heartily, as to the Lord" (Col. 3:23). When others around you grumble and complain, if you have a calm, forgiving, steadfast spirit, it will make an impression. As you respond in a Christlike way to angry coworkers and stressful circumstances, people will see a difference in your life.

If your boss forbids it, don't witness on work time. Instead, keep a pile of Million Dollar Bills or some other tract on your desk but don't give them out. If someone asks for one, let them take it. Displaying a favorite Scripture or a devotional calendar, or quietly reading your Bible during lunchtime, may prompt others to inquire about your faith.

To not infringe on your employer's time, invite unsaved coworkers out to lunch (not the opposite sex) and witness to them there. Just ask for their thoughts on what happens after death. That will let you know if they are open to the gospel. If you detect contention, apologize and instead use closet prayer. Make a list of workers and uphold them before God, asking for divine openings.

In the meantime, let your love shine. Always be friendly and courteous, and show genuine interest in your coworkers' lives. Share their joys and sorrows by congratulating them in their good times and offering to pray for them in their bad times. Be sure you do pray for them, then follow up by asking them about the situation you prayed for. They will be moved by your concern. If coworkers are discussing what they did during the previous weekend, you can share your excitement about attending church services or a special church event. Ask about their plans for celebrating Christmas or Easter; be nonjudgmental of their answer, and be ready to explain why you celebrate as you do.

Bringing home-baked goods or leaving a small gift with a note on a coworker's desk can sometimes have a greater impact than a thousand eloquent sermons. We can show our faith by our works. Others may not like a tree of righteousness, but they cannot help but like its fruit.

foolish men— 16as free, yet not using liberty as a cloak for vice, but as bondservants of God. 17Honor all *people*. Love the
brotherhood. Fear God. Honor the king.

Submission to Masters

18Servants, *be* submissive to *your* masters with all fear, not only to the good and
gentle, but also to the harsh. 19For this *is*
commendable, if because of conscience
toward God one endures grief, suffering
wrongfully. 20For what credit *is it* if, when
you are beaten for your faults, you take it
patiently? But when you do good and
suffer, if you take it patiently, this *is* commendable before God. 21For to this you
were called, because Christ also suffered
for us,[a] leaving us[b] an example, that you
should follow His steps:

22*"Who committed no sin,*
Nor was deceit found in His mouth";[a]

23who, when He was reviled, did not revile
in return; when He suffered, He did not
threaten, but committed *Himself* to Him
who judges righteously; 24who Himself
bore our sins in His own body on the
tree, that we, having died to sins, might

2:21 [a]NU-Text reads *you*. [b]NU-Text and M-Text read *you*.
2:22 [a]Isaiah 53:9

2:15 Good works have a legitimate place in evangelism. Since the way to a man's heart is often through his taste buds, buying him a hamburger may reach him more effectively than an argument.

"Kindness has converted more sinners than zeal, eloquence, or learning." *Frederick W. Faber*

2:24 Messianic prophecy fulfilled: "But He was wounded for our transgressions, He was bruised for our iniquities; the chastisement for our peace was upon Him, and by His stripes we are healed" (Isa. 53:5). See Matt.13:34,35 comment.

live for righteousness—by whose stripes
you were healed. 25For you were like sheep
going astray, but have now returned to
the Shepherd and Overseer[a] of your souls.

Submission to Husbands

3 Wives, likewise, *be* submissive to your
own husbands, that even if some do
not obey the word, they, without a word,
may be won by the conduct of their wives,
2when they observe your chaste conduct
accompanied by fear. 3Do not let your
adornment be *merely* outward—arranging
the hair, wearing gold, or putting on *fine*
apparel— 4rather *let it be* the hidden person of the heart, with the incorruptible
beauty of a gentle and quiet spirit, which
is very precious in the sight of God. 5For
in this manner, in former times, the holy
women who trusted in God also adorned
themselves, being submissive to their own
husbands, 6as Sarah obeyed Abraham,
calling him lord, whose daughters you
are if you do good and are not afraid
with any terror.

A Word to Husbands

7Husbands, likewise, dwell with *them*
with understanding, giving honor to the
wife, as to the weaker vessel, and as *being*
heirs together of the grace of life, that your
prayers may not be hindered.

Called to Blessing

8Finally, all *of you be* of one mind, having compassion for one another; love as
brothers, *be* tenderhearted, *be* courteous;[a]
9not returning evil for evil or reviling for
reviling, but on the contrary blessing,
knowing that you were called to this, that
you may inherit a blessing. 10For

"He who would love life
And see good days,
Let him refrain his tongue from evil,
And his lips from speaking deceit.
11*Let him turn away from evil and do*
good;
Let him seek peace and pursue it.
12*For the eyes of the LORD are on the*
righteous,
And His ears are open to their prayers;
But the face of the LORD is against
those who do evil."[a]

Suffering for Right and Wrong

13And who *is* he who will harm you if
you become followers of what is good?
14But even if you should suffer for righteousness' sake, *you are* blessed. *"And do*
not be afraid of their threats, nor be trou-
bled."[a] 15But sanctify the Lord God[a] in
your hearts, and always *be* ready to *give* a
defense to everyone who asks you a reason for the hope that is in you, with meekness and fear; 16having a good conscience,
that when they defame you as evildoers,
those who revile your good conduct in
Christ may be ashamed. 17For *it is* better,

2:25 [a]Greek *Episkopos* 3:8 [a]NU-Text reads *humble.* 3:12 [a]Psalm 34:12–16 3:14 [a]Isaiah 8:12 3:15 [a]NU-Text reads *Christ as Lord.*

3:1,2 Do not "preach at" loved ones, or express frustration or anger because they don't believe. Try to win them with your works rather than just your words. Buy them gifts, do them favors, show them love and kindness. Make sure that you are free from the slightest hint of hypocrisy.

3:8,9 Witnessing tips. "When you approach a careless individual, be sure to treat him kindly. Let him see that you are talking with him, not because you seek a quarrel with him, but because you love his soul and desire his best good in time and eternity. If you are harsh and overbearing, you will probably drive him farther away from the way of life.

"Be serious! Avoid all lightness of manner or language. Levity will produce anything but a right impression. You ought to feel that you are engaged in a very serious work, which is going to affect the character of your friend or neighbor and probably determine his destiny for eternity. Who could trifle and use levity in such circumstances if his heart were sincere?

"Be respectful. Some think it is necessary to be abrupt, rude, and coarse in their discussions with the careless and impenitent. No mistake can be greater. The apostle Peter has given us a better rule on the subject, where he says: 'Be pitiful, be courteous: not rendering evil for evil, or railing for railing: but contrariwise blessing.'" *Charles Finney*

QUESTIONS & OBJECTIONS

"If God is a God of love, why hasn't He dealt with evil?"

By Ron Meade

In Dr. Robert Morey's book *The New Atheism and the Erosion of Freedom*, he talks with an atheist about this issue. The atheist assumes that everything is relative, and there are no absolutes (he is absolutely sure of that). Morey replies that the first thing an atheist must do is prove the existence of evil. By what process can an atheist identify evil? He must have a universal absolute to do so. Without an absolute reference point for "good" (which only God can provide), no one can identify what is good or evil. Thus without the existence of God, there is no "evil" or "good" in an absolute sense. Everything is relative. The problem of evil does not negate the existence of God. It actually requires it.

Many assume that because evil still exists today, God has not dealt with it. How can atheists assume that God has not already solved the problem of evil in such a way that neither His goodness nor omnipotence is limited? On what grounds do they limit what God can and cannot do to solve the problem? God has already solved the problem of evil. And He did it in a way in which He did not contradict His nature or the nature of man.

We assume God will solve the problem of evil in one single act. But why can't He deal with evil in a progressive way? Can't He deal with it throughout time as we know it, and then bring it to the climax on the Day of Judgment?

God sent His Son to die on the cross in order to solve the problem of evil. Christ atoned for evil and secured the eventual removal of all evil from the earth. One day evil will be quarantined in one spot called "hell." Then there will be a perfect world devoid of all evil. If God declared that all evil would, at this moment, cease to exist, you and I and all of humanity would go up in a puff of smoke. Divine judgment demands that sin be punished.

if it is the will of God, to suffer for doing good than for doing evil.

Christ's Suffering and Ours

[18]For Christ also suffered once for sins, the just for the unjust, that He might bring us[a] to God, being put to death in the flesh but made alive by the Spirit,
[19]by whom also He went and preached to
the spirits in prison, [20]who formerly were
disobedient, when once the Divine longsuffering waited[a] in the days of Noah, while *the* ark was being prepared, in which a few, that is, eight souls, were saved
through water. [21]There is also an antitype
which now saves us—baptism (not the removal of the filth of the flesh, but the answer of a good conscience toward God), through the resurrection of Jesus Christ,
[22]who has gone into heaven and is at the right hand of God, angels and authorities and powers having been made subject to Him.

4 Therefore, since Christ suffered for us[a] in the flesh, arm yourselves also with the same mind, for he who has suf-

3:18 [a]NU-Text and M-Text read *you.* 3:20 [a]NU-Text and M-Text read *when the longsuffering of God waited patiently.* 4:1 [a]NU-Text omits *for us.*

3:15 Always be ready to "contend earnestly for the faith" (Jude 3). Learn how to prove God's existence. Study the theory of evolution and the evidence for creation. Become proficient in presenting the spiritual nature of God's Law. Say, "I can do all things through Christ who strengthens me," and thereby walk above the snare of the fear of man.

Note that this verse is not a prescription for what is commonly called "lifestyle evangelism." We are not being told to wait until we are asked about our faith—we may be waiting for a long time. As soldiers of Christ we are not only to *defend* the faith, but we are to *advance* the cause of the gospel. The word "go" in the Great Commission means just that—go.

3:20 Peter believed the Genesis account of Noah's Flood—that it was a worldwide deluge in which only eight people were saved.

QUESTIONS & OBJECTIONS

4:1 "Do you sin, as a Christian?"

If a Christian sins, it is *against* his will. One who is regenerate *falls* rather than *dives* into sin; he resists rather than embraces it. Any dead fish can float downstream. It takes a live one to swim against the flow. Christians still experience temptations and can sometimes fall into sin, but they are no longer slaves to sin (Rom. 6:6). They have God's Holy Spirit within them to help them say no to temptation, and to convict their conscience of wrongdoing when they do sin.

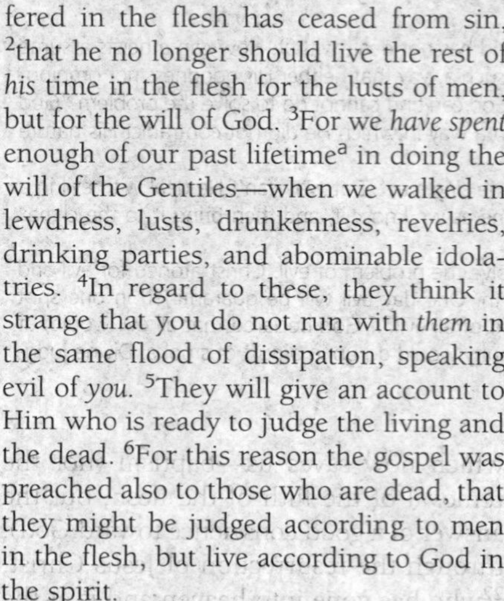

fered in the flesh has ceased from sin,
[2]that he no longer should live the rest of
his time in the flesh for the lusts of men,
but for the will of God. [3]For we *have spent*
enough of our past lifetime[a] in doing the
will of the Gentiles—when we walked in
lewdness, lusts, drunkenness, revelries,
drinking parties, and abominable idolatries. [4]In regard to these, they think it
strange that you do not run with *them* in
the same flood of dissipation, speaking
evil of *you.* [5]They will give an account to
Him who is ready to judge the living and
the dead. [6]For this reason the gospel was
preached also to those who are dead, that
they might be judged according to men
in the flesh, but live according to God in
the spirit.

Serving for God's Glory

[7]But the end of all things is at hand;
therefore be serious and watchful in your
prayers. [8]And above all things have fervent love for one another, for *"love will
cover a multitude of sins."*[a] [9]*Be* hospitable
to one another without grumbling. [10]As
each one has received a gift, minister it to
one another, as good stewards of the manifold grace of God. [11]If anyone speaks, *let
him speak* as the oracles of God. If anyone
ministers, *let him do it* as with the ability
which God supplies, that in all things God
may be glorified through Jesus Christ, to
whom belong the glory and the dominion
forever and ever. Amen.

Suffering for God's Glory

[12]Beloved, do not think it strange concerning the fiery trial which is to try you,
as though some strange thing happened
to you; [13]but rejoice to the extent that you
partake of Christ's sufferings, that when
His glory is revealed, you may also be
glad with exceeding joy. [14]If you are reproached for the name of Christ, blessed

4:3 [a]NU-Text reads *time.* 4:8 [a]Proverbs 10:12 4:14 [a]NU-Text omits the rest of this verse.

4:5 *Daniel Webster* (1782–1852), politician and diplomat, is considered one of the greatest orators in American history. When asked, "What is the greatest thought that ever passed through your mind?" Webster responded, "My accountability to God."

4:12 "The real problem is not why some pious, humble, believing people suffer, but why some do not." *C. S. Lewis*

4:13 "Joy in the Bible is the means by which we are sustained in suffering . . . and joy is that for which suffering is preparing us." *John Piper*

"For the Christian, joy is not the absence of suffering and adversity, but the nearness of God in our adversity." *Bob Deffinbaugh*

4:14 "There is a cost and a danger that come with being a follower of Jesus, with having the kind of close relationship that He calls us to. But, if we keep an eternal perspective, God's Word assures us that the reward that awaits is far greater than any risk we face. We are promised not only 'exceeding joy' [v. 13] when we suffer for Christ, but we will be blessed, God's glorious Spirit will rest on us, and most importantly, God will be glorified. As followers of Christ, that is the reason we exist." *Greg Musselman*

Science Confirms the Bible

THE BIBLE (2,000–3,500 years ago)	SCIENCE THEN	SCIENCE NOW
The earth is a sphere (Isa. 40:22).	The earth was a flat disk.	The earth is a sphere.
Innumerable stars (Jer. 33:22).	Only 1,100 stars.	Innumerable stars.
Free float of earth in space (Job 26:7).	Earth sat on a large animal.	Free float of earth in space.
Creation made of invisible elements (Heb. 11:3).	Science was ignorant on the subject.	Creation made of invisible elements (atoms).
Each star is different (1 Cor. 15:41).	All stars were the same.	Each star is different.
Light moves (Job 38:19,20).	Light was fixed in place.	Light moves.
Air has weight (Job 28:25).	Air was weightless.	Air has weight.
Winds blow in cyclones (Eccles. 1:6).	Winds blew straight.	Winds blow in cyclones.
Blood is the source of life and health (Lev. 17:11).	Sick people must be bled.	Blood is the source of life and health.
Ocean floor contains deep valleys and mountains (2 Sam. 22:16; Jon. 2:6).	The ocean floor was flat.	Ocean floor contains deep valleys and mountains.
Ocean contains springs (Job 38:16).	Ocean fed only by rivers and rain.	Ocean contains springs.
When dealing with disease, hands should be washed under running water (Lev. 15:13).	Hands washed in still water.	When dealing with disease, hands should be washed under running water.

(See Heb. 11:3 comment.)

RIDDLE:
Name nine people who were saved from drowning by an ark.

ANSWER:
Eight members of Noah's family were saved by an ark in the Flood (Gen. 7:13), and the infant Moses was also saved by an ark (Exod. 2:3).
(See 1 Pet. 3:20.)

are you, for the Spirit of glory and of God
rests upon you.[a] On their part He is blasphemed, but on your part He is glorified.
15But let none of you suffer as a murderer, a thief, an evildoer, or as a busybody in
other people's matters. 16Yet if *anyone suffers* as a Christian, let him not be ashamed,
but let him glorify God in this matter.[a]
17For the time *has come* for judgment
to begin at the house of God; and if *it begins* with us first, what will *be* the end of
those who do not obey the gospel of
God? 18Now

"If the righteous one is scarcely saved,
Where will the ungodly and the
sinner appear?"[a]

19Therefore let those who suffer according
to the will of God commit their souls *to
Him* in doing good, as to a faithful Creator.

Shepherd the Flock

5 The elders who are among you I exhort, I who am a fellow elder and a
witness of the sufferings of Christ, and also
a partaker of the glory that will be revealed:
2Shepherd the flock of God which is among
you, serving as overseers, not by compulsion but willingly,[a] not for dishonest gain
but eagerly; 3nor as being lords over those
entrusted to you, but being examples to
the flock; 4and when the Chief Shepherd
appears, you will receive the crown of
glory that does not fade away.

Submit to God, Resist the Devil

5Likewise you younger people, submit
yourselves to *your* elders. Yes, all of *you* be
submissive to one another, and be clothed
with humility, for

"God resists the proud,
But gives grace to the humble."[a]

6Therefore humble yourselves under
the mighty hand of God, that He may exalt
you in due time, 7casting all your care
upon Him, for He cares for you.
8Be sober, be vigilant; because[a] your
adversary the devil walks about like a
roaring lion, seeking whom he may devour. 9Resist him, steadfast in the faith,
knowing that the same sufferings are
experienced by your brotherhood in the
world. 10But may[a] the God of all grace,
who called us[b] to His eternal glory by
Christ Jesus, after you have suffered a
while, perfect, establish, strengthen, and
settle *you.* 11To Him *be* the glory and the
dominion forever and ever. Amen.

Farewell and Peace

12By Silvanus, our faithful brother as I
consider him, I have written to you briefly,
exhorting and testifying that this is the
true grace of God in which you stand.
13She who is in Babylon, elect together
with *you,* greets you; and *so does* Mark my
son. 14Greet one another with a kiss of
love.

Peace to you all who are in Christ Jesus.
Amen.

4:16 [a]NU-Text reads *name.* 4:18 [a]Proverbs 11:31 5:2 [a]NU-Text adds *according to God.* 5:5 [a]Proverbs 3:34 5:8 [a]NU-Text and M-Text omit *because.* 5:10 [a]NU-Text reads *But the God of all grace... will perfect, establish, strengthen, and settle you.* [b]NU-Text and M-Text read *you.*

5:3 "A message prepared in the mind reaches a mind; a message prepared in a life reaches a life." *Bill Gothard*

2 Peter

Greeting the Faithful

1 Simon Peter, a bondservant and apostle of Jesus Christ,

To those who have obtained like precious faith with us by the righteousness of our God and Savior Jesus Christ:

2Grace and peace be multiplied to you in the knowledge of God and of Jesus our Lord, 3as His divine power has given to us all things that *pertain* to life and godliness, through the knowledge of Him who called us by glory and virtue, 4by which have been given to us exceedingly great and precious promises, that through these you may be partakers of the divine nature, having escaped the corruption *that is* in the world through lust.

Fruitful Growth in the Faith

5But also for this very reason, giving all diligence, add to your faith virtue, to virtue knowledge, 6to knowledge self-control, to self-control perseverance, to perseverance godliness, 7to godliness brotherly kindness, and to brotherly kindness love. 8For if these things are yours and abound, *you will be* neither barren nor unfruitful in the knowledge of our Lord Jesus Christ. 9For he who lacks these things is shortsighted, even to blindness, and has forgotten that he was cleansed from his old sins.

10Therefore, brethren, be even more diligent to make your call and election sure, for if you do these things you will never stumble; 11for so an entrance will be supplied to you abundantly into the everlasting kingdom of our Lord and Savior Jesus Christ.

Peter's Approaching Death

12For this reason I will not be negligent to remind you always of these things, though you know and are established in the present truth. 13Yes, I think it is right, as long as I am in this tent, to stir you up by reminding *you,* 14knowing that shortly I *must* put off my tent, just as our Lord Jesus Christ showed me. 15Moreover I will be careful to ensure that you always have a reminder of these things after my decease.

The Trustworthy Prophetic Word

16For we did not follow cunningly devised fables when we made known to you the power and coming of our Lord Jesus Christ, but were eyewitnesses of His majesty. 17For He received from God the Father honor and glory when such a voice came to Him from the Excellent Glory: "This is My beloved Son, in whom I am well pleased." 18And we heard this voice which came from heaven when we were with Him on the holy mountain.

19And so we have the prophetic word confirmed,[a] which you do well to heed as a light that shines in a dark place, until the day dawns and the morning star rises

1:19 [a]Or *We also have the more sure prophetic word.*

QUESTIONS & OBJECTIONS

1:21 "Didn't men write the Bible?"

Absolutely. When you write a letter, do *you* write the letter, or does the pen? Obviously you do; the pen is merely the instrument you use. God used men as instruments to write His "letter" to humanity. They ranged from kings to common fishermen, but the 66 books of the Bible were all given by inspiration of God. Proof that this Book is supernatural can been seen with a quick study of its prophecies, among other things. See Psa. 119:105 comment.

in your hearts; [20]knowing this first, that
no prophecy of Scripture is of any private
interpretation,[a] [21]for prophecy never came
by the will of man, but holy men of God[a]
spoke *as they were* moved by the Holy
Spirit.

Destructive Doctrines

2 But there were also false prophets
among the people, even as there will
be false teachers among you, who will
secretly bring in destructive heresies, even
denying the Lord who bought them, *and*
bring on themselves swift destruction.
[2]And many will follow their destructive
ways, because of whom the way of truth
will be blasphemed. [3]By covetousness they
will exploit you with deceptive words;
for a long time their judgment has not
been idle, and their destruction does[a] not
slumber.

Doom of False Teachers

[4]For if God did not spare the angels
who sinned, but cast *them* down to hell
and delivered *them* into chains of darkness,
to be reserved for judgment; [5]and did not
spare the ancient world, but saved Noah,
one of eight *people*, a preacher of righteousness, bringing in the flood on the
world of the ungodly; [6]and turning the
cities of Sodom and Gomorrah into ashes,
condemned *them* to destruction, making

1:20 [a]Or *origin* 1:21 [a]NU-Text reads *but men spoke from God.* 2:3 [a]M-Text reads *will not.*

1:19 It is important to point out that it isn't the Bible that converts people. The first Christians didn't have the Bible as we know it. The New Testament hadn't been compiled, and there was no such thing as the printing press. Besides, many couldn't read. Rather, they were converted by the spoken message of the gospel. It is the gospel that is "the power of God to salvation" (Rom. 1:16). Until God gives light to His Word, it will remain a dry history book to its reader.

1:21 "The idea conveyed is that just as the wind controls the sails of a boat, so also the breath of God controlled the writers of the Bible. The end result was exactly what God intended." *Josh McDowell*

2:4,5,9 Judgment Day: For verses that warn of its reality, see 2 Pet. 3:7.

2:5 The Bible's fascinating facts. In Genesis 6, God gave Noah the dimensions of the 1.5 million cubic foot ark he was to build. In 1609 at Hoorn in Holland, a ship was built after that same pattern, revolutionizing shipbuilding. By 1900 every large ship on the high seas was inclined toward the proportions of the ark (as verified by "Lloyd's Register of Shipping" in the *World Almanac*).

2:6–8 Witnessing to homosexuals. I had an angry lesbian heckle me one Friday night while speaking in Santa Monica in front of a large crowd. I was so pleased to have the Law of God as a weapon. When she insisted that she was born with homosexual desires, I told her that I was too. I was born with a capacity to be a homosexual, a fornicator, adulterer, liar, and thief. I said that it was called 'sin,' and that we all had it in our nature. It diffused her intent on making me seem like a 'gay-basher.' I could see the frustration on her face when she wasn't able to take the discourse in the direction she wanted. Instead of seeming the poor victim, she found herself in the public hot-seat of having sinned against God.

The way to witness to a homosexual is simply to follow the biblical guidelines and use the Law. See Matt. 19:17–22 and 1 Tim. 1:9,10 comments.

QUESTIONS & OBJECTIONS

"How could a flood destroy every living thing?"

By Ken Ham, Answers in Genesis

Noah's Flood was much more destructive than any 40-day rainstorm ever could be. Scripture says that "all the fountains of the great deep" broke open (see Gen. 7:11). In other words, earthquakes, volcanoes, and geysers of molten lava and scalding water were squeezed out of the earth's crust in a violent, explosive upheaval. These fountains were not stopped until 150 days into the Flood—so the earth was literally churning underneath the waters for about five months! The duration of the Flood was extensive, and Noah and his family were aboard the Ark for over a year.

Relatively recent local floods, volcanoes, and earthquakes—though clearly devastating to life and land—are tiny in comparison to the worldwide catastrophe that destroyed "the world that then existed" (2 Pet. 3:6). All land animals and people not on board the Ark were destroyed in the floodwaters—billions of animals were preserved in the great fossil record we see today.

them an example to those who afterward
would live ungodly; 7and delivered righteous Lot, *who was* oppressed by the filthy
conduct of the wicked 8(for that righteous
man, dwelling among them, tormented
his righteous soul from day to day by seeing and hearing *their* lawless deeds)—
9*then* the Lord knows how to deliver the
godly out of temptations and to reserve
the unjust under punishment for the day
of judgment, 10and especially those who
walk according to the flesh in the lust of
uncleanness and despise authority. *They
are* presumptuous, self-willed. They are
not afraid to speak evil of dignitaries,
11whereas angels, who are greater in power
and might, do not bring a reviling accusation against them before the Lord.

Depravity of False Teachers

12But these, like natural brute beasts
made to be caught and destroyed, speak
evil of the things they do not understand,
and will utterly perish in their own corruption, 13*and* will receive the wages of
unrighteousness, *as* those who count it
pleasure to carouse in the daytime. *They
are* spots and blemishes, carousing in their
own deceptions while they feast with you,
14having eyes full of adultery and that
cannot cease from sin, enticing unstable
souls. *They have* a heart trained in covetous practices, *and are* accursed children.
15They have forsaken the right way and
gone astray, following the way of Balaam
the *son* of Beor, who loved the wages of
unrighteousness; 16but he was rebuked for
his iniquity: a dumb donkey speaking
with a man's voice restrained the madness of the prophet.

> I believe that the most damnable thing a man can do is to preach the gospel merely as an actor and turn the worship of God into a kind of theatrical performance.
>
> **CHARLES SPURGEON**

17These are wells without water, clouds[a]
carried by a tempest, for whom is reserved
the blackness of darkness forever.[b]

Deceptions of False Teachers

18For when they speak great swelling
words of emptiness, they allure through
the lusts of the flesh, through lewdness,
the ones who have actually escaped[a] from

2:17 [a]NU-Text reads *and mists.* [b]NU-Text omits *forever.*
2:18 [a]NU-Text reads *are barely escaping*

2:14 These workers of iniquity violate God's Law by transgressing the Seventh and Tenth Commandments.

those who live in error. 19While they
promise them liberty, they themselves
are slaves of corruption; for by whom a
person is overcome, by him also he is
brought into bondage. 20For if, after they
have escaped the pollutions of the world
through the knowledge of the Lord and
Savior Jesus Christ, they are again entangled in them and overcome, the latter end
is worse for them than the beginning.
21For it would have been better for them
not to have known the way of righteousness, than having known *it,* to turn from
the holy commandment delivered to them.
22But it has happened to them according
to the true proverb: *"A dog returns to his
own vomit,"*[a] and, "a sow, having washed,
to her wallowing in the mire."

God's Promise Is Not Slack

3 Beloved, I now write to you this second epistle (in *both of* which I stir up
your pure minds by way of reminder),
2that you may be mindful of the words
which were spoken before by the holy
prophets, and of the commandment of
us,[a] the apostles of the Lord and Savior,
3knowing this first: that scoffers will
come in the last days, walking according
to their own lusts, 4and saying, "Where
is the promise of His coming? For since
the fathers fell asleep, all things continue
as *they were* from the beginning of creation." 5For this they willfully forget:
that by the word of God the heavens
were of old, and the earth standing out
of water and in the water, 6by which the
world *that* then existed perished, being
flooded with water. 7But the heavens
and the earth *which* are now preserved
by the same word, are reserved for fire
until the day of judgment and perdition
of ungodly men.

2:22 [a]Proverbs 26:11 3:2 [a]NU-Text and M-Text read *commandment of the apostles of your Lord and Savior* or *commandment of your apostles of the Lord and Savior.*

2:21 When sinners make professions of faith and refuse to have any regard for God's moral Law, their latter end becomes worse than the first. They fall away and become hardened (inoculated) against the truth. It would have been better for them not to have known the way of righteousness (the gospel) than, after they have known it, to turn from the "holy commandment" (the moral Law).

The Law cannot condemn the Christian (Rom. 8:1), but those who are truly converted will not transgress its precepts. Those who do, prove to be "workers of iniquity" (lawlessness). See Matt. 7:21–23. This is why we must thunder out the precepts of God's Law before we offer sinners the pardon of the gospel. If they don't see the serious nature of sin, they will still toy with its pleasures after making a profession of faith.

2:22 Some argue that sins such as pornography are wrong because they are "harmful to society." However, you have more chance of convincing a pig that the mud in which he wallows is harmful to him. The reason he wallows is to cool his flesh. The only practical way to stop a pig wallowing in the mire is to kill him. That's the function of the Law: it nails the sin-loving sinner to the cross. It deals directly with the sinful nature. Sin is wrong not because it's harmful to society; it is wrong because God says that it's wrong.

3:3 Signs of the end times (combined from Matt. 24; Mark 13; Luke 21; 1 Tim. 4; and 2 Tim. 3): There will be false Christs; wars and rumors of wars; nation rising against nation; famines; disease (pestilence); false prophets who will deceive many; and lawlessness (forsaking of the Ten Commandments). The gospel will be preached in all the world. There will be earthquakes in various places; signs from heaven (in the sun, moon, and stars); and persecution against Christians in all nations. Men's hearts will fail them for fear of the future; they will be selfish, materialistic, arrogant, proud. Homosexuality will increase; there will be blasphemy; cold-heartedness; lack of self-control; brutality; rebellious youth; hatred of those who stand up for righteousness; ungodliness; pleasure-seeking; much hypocrisy. False Bible teachers will have many followers, be money-hungry, and slander the Christian faith (2 Pet. 2:1–3).

Men will scoff and say that there was no such thing as the flood of Noah and that these "signs" have always been around (see 2 Pet. 3:5,6 comment). Their motivation for hating the truth will be their love of lust (2 Pet. 3:1–7). The Scriptures tell us that they make one big mistake. Their understanding of God is erroneous. They don't understand that God's time frame is not the same as ours. They think (in their ignorance) that God's continued silence means that He doesn't see their sins. In truth, He is merely holding back His wrath, waiting for them to repent and escape the damnation of hell.

Jesus warned that the sign to look for was the repossession of Jerusalem by the Jews. That happened in 1967, after 2,000 years, bringing into culmination all the signs of the times.

3:5,6 *Rejecting a Global Flood*

By Bodie Hodge, Answers in Genesis

Did Noah experience a local flood which left only a few sediment layers, as floods do today? God's record is clear: the water covered the entire globe and killed all the animals on earth. Such unique conditions are the only way to explain worldwide fossil-bearing layers thousands of feet deep.

Scripture is clear about the historic reality of a global Flood in Noah's day. Genesis 7:19–22 specifically says that water covered all the high hills by 15 cubits (26 feet, or 8 m), and all air-breathing land animals and people that were outside the Ark died.

Today, many people unfortunately do not accept the biblical account of a worldwide Flood because they have been taught that most rocks and fossils were deposited over millions of years (and therefore not by a global Flood). Until the 1800s, most Westerners believed what the Bible records about the earth's recent creation and the global Flood. The secular idea of millions of years did not catch fire until the 1830s, under the influence of a man named Charles Lyell.

Based on how slowly rock layers usually form today, Lyell rejected the Bible's claims and declared that the earth's many rock layers must have been laid down slowly over millions of years. But he never witnessed the actual formation of the earlier rocks to see whether they could be laid by a unique, one-time global Flood unlike anything we observe today. Lyell's claim was based on his own preconceptions, not his observations.

Yet his idea took hold in Western universities and spread throughout the Western world. Sadly, many Christians simply tried to add this idea to the Bible. What these Christians should have done was stand on the authority of the Bible and defend the global Flood, which can easily account for the bulk of fossil-bearing rock layers we find all over the world.

Although there is tremendous physical evidence of a global flood (fossils in the rock layers all over the world), ultimately, it is a matter of trust in a perfect God who created everything (Gen. 1:1), knows everything (Col. 2:3), has always been there (Rev. 22:13), and cannot lie (Titus 1:2). The only alternative is to trust imperfect, fallible human beings who can only speculate on the past (see Rom. 3:4).

Some Christians have tried to put millions of years of rock formation before the global Flood to explain the bulk of the rock layers that contain fossils. But the problem is that the Flood waters could rip up many of the previous rock layers and redeposit them elsewhere! So this compromise not only fails to explain the rock layers but also dishonors the clear claims of Scripture.

A global Flood makes perfect sense, and it is wrong and foolish to stray from God's Word just because some men disagree.

8But, beloved, do not forget this one
thing, that with the Lord one day *is* as a
thousand years, and a thousand years as
one day. 9The Lord is not slack concerning *His* promise, as some count slackness,
but is longsuffering toward us,[a] not willing that any should perish but that all
should come to repentance.

The Day of the Lord

10But the day of the Lord will come as
a thief in the night, in which the heavens
will pass away with a great noise, and the
elements will melt with fervent heat; both
the earth and the works that are in it will
be burned up.[a] 11Therefore, since all these
things will be dissolved, what manner *of
persons* ought you to be in holy conduct
and godliness, 12looking for and hastening
the coming of the day of God, because of
which the heavens will be dissolved, being

3:9 [a]NU-Text reads *you.* 3:10 [a]NU-Text reads *laid bare* (literally *found*).

3:6 Peter believed the Genesis account of Noah's Flood.

3:7 Judgment Day: For verses that warn of its reality, see Jude 14,15.

3:8 Because God is eternal and dwells outside of the dimension of time, one day and a thousand years are the same to Him (see Psa. 90:4). In a similar way, a person who is in space, outside of the influence of gravity, will find that one ounce and a thousand pounds are the same. See also Gen. 1:31 comment.

3:9 Salvation is possible for every person. See John 3:16,17.

QUESTIONS & OBJECTIONS

3:9 ***"Why does God allow evil?"***

Why does God allow evil men and women to live? Should He instead kill them before they do evil deeds? Should He judge murderers and rapists now? What about thieves and liars, adulterers, fornicators, those who lust, and those who hate? If God judged evil today, all unconverted men and women would perish under His just wrath because of their sins. Thank God that He is patiently waiting for them to turn to the Savior and be saved from His terrible wrath.

on fire, and the elements will melt with
fervent heat? 13Nevertheless we, according to His promise, look for new heavens
and a new earth in which righteousness
dwells.

Be Steadfast

14Therefore, beloved, looking forward
to these things, be diligent to be found by
Him in peace, without spot and blameless; 15and consider *that* the longsuffering
of our Lord *is* salvation—as also our beloved brother Paul, according to the wisdom given to him, has written to you,
16as also in all his epistles, speaking in
them of these things, in which are some
things hard to understand, which untaught and unstable *people* twist to their
own destruction, as *they do* also the rest
of the Scriptures.
17You therefore, beloved, since you
know *this* beforehand, beware lest you
also fall from your own steadfastness, being led away with the error of the wicked;
18but grow in the grace and knowledge of
our Lord and Savior Jesus Christ.
To Him *be* the glory both now and forever. Amen.

"Bless O Lord
the whole race of
mankind, and let the
world be filled with the
knowledge of Thee
and Thy Son,
Jesus Christ."
GEORGE WASHINGTON

3:16 Never feel as though you have to be able to explain every Bible verse. Even Peter admits that some things Paul wrote are hard to understand. In doing so, he also puts his seal of approval on the fact that Paul's letters were not the mere writings of a man, but are "Scriptures."

"Try all things by the written Word, and let all bow down before it. You are in danger of [fanaticism] every hour, if you depart ever so little from Scripture; yea, or from the plain, literal meaning of a text, taken in connection with the context." *John Wesley*

1 John

What Was Heard, Seen, and Touched

1 That which was from the beginning, which we have heard, which we have seen with our eyes, which we have looked upon, and our hands have handled, concerning the Word of life— [2]the life was manifested, and we have seen, and bear witness, and declare to you that eternal life which was with the Father and was manifested to us— [3]that which we have seen and heard we declare to you, that you also may have fellowship with us; and truly our fellowship *is* with the Father and with His Son Jesus Christ. [4]And these things we write to you that your[a] joy may be full.

Fellowship with Him and One Another

[5]This is the message which we have heard from Him and declare to you, that God is light and in Him is no darkness at all. [6]If we say that we have fellowship with Him, and walk in darkness, we lie and do not practice the truth. [7]But if we walk in the light as He is in the light, we have fellowship with one another, and the blood of Jesus Christ His Son cleanses us from all sin.

[8]If we say that we have no sin, we deceive ourselves, and the truth is not in us. [9]If we confess our sins, He is faithful and just to forgive us *our* sins and to cleanse us from all unrighteousness. [10]If we say that we have not sinned, we make Him a liar, and His word is not in us.

2 My little children, these things I write to you, so that you may not sin. And if anyone sins, we have an Advocate with the Father, Jesus Christ the righteous. [2]And He Himself is the propitiation for our sins, and not for ours only but also for the whole world.

The Test of Knowing Him

[3]Now by this we know that we know Him, if we keep His commandments. [4]He who says, "I know Him," and does not keep His commandments, is a liar, and the truth is not in him. [5]But whoever keeps His word, truly the love of God is perfected in

1:4 [a]NU-Text and M-Text read *our*.

1:9 The Christian who sins. "The great foundational truth respecting the believer in relationship to his sins is the fact that his salvation comprehends the forgiveness of all his trespasses past, present and future so far as condemnation is concerned (see Rom. 8:1; Col. 2:13; John 3:18; 5:24). Since Christ has vicariously borne all sin and since the believer's standing in Christ is complete, he is perfected forever in Christ. When a believer sins, he is subjected to chastisement from the Father, but never to condemnation with the world (see 1 Cor. 11:31,32). By confession the Christian is forgiven and restored to fellowship (see 1 John 1:9). It needs to be remembered that were it not for Christ's finished work on the cross and His present intercession in heaven, the least sin would result in his banishment from God's presence and eternal ruin." *Unger's Bible Dictionary*

THE FUNCTION OF THE LAW

1:7 "The Law also shows us our great need—our need of cleansing, cleansing with the water and the blood. It discovers to us our filthiness, and this naturally leads us to feel that we must be washed from it if we are ever to draw near to God. So the Law drives us to accept Christ as the only Person who can cleanse us, and make us fit to stand within the veil in the presence of the Most High.

"The Law is the surgeon's knife that cuts out the proud flesh that the wound may heal. The Law by itself only sweeps and raises the dust, but the gospel sprinkles clean water upon the dust, and all is well in the chamber of the soul. The Law kills, the gospel makes alive; the Law strips, and then Jesus Christ comes in and robes the soul in beauty and glory. All the commandments, and all the types direct us to Christ, if we will but heed their evident intent." *Charles Spurgeon*

him. By this we know that we are in Him.
6He who says he abides in Him ought
himself also to walk just as He walked.

7Brethren,[a] I write no new commandment to you, but an old commandment
which you have had from the beginning.
The old commandment is the word which
you heard from the beginning.[b] 8Again, a
new commandment I write to you, which
thing is true in Him and in you, because
the darkness is passing away, and the true
light is already shining.

9He who says he is in the light, and
hates his brother, is in darkness until now.
10He who loves his brother abides in the
light, and there is no cause for stumbling
in him. 11But he who hates his brother is
in darkness and walks in darkness, and
does not know where he is going, because
the darkness has blinded his eyes.

Their Spiritual State

12I write to you, little children,
Because your sins are forgiven you
for His name's sake.
13I write to you, fathers,
Because you have known Him *who is*
from the beginning.
I write to you, young men,
Because you have overcome the
wicked one.
I write to you, little children,
Because you have known the Father.
14I have written to you, fathers,
Because you have known Him *who is*
from the beginning.
I have written to you, young men,
Because you are strong, and the
word of God abides in you,
And you have overcome the wicked
one.

Do Not Love the World

15Do not love the world or the things
in the world. If anyone loves the world,
the love of the Father is not in him. 16For
all that *is* in the world—the lust of the
flesh, the lust of the eyes, and the pride of
life—is not of the Father but is of the
world. 17And the world is passing away,
and the lust of it; but he who does the
will of God abides forever.

Deceptions of the Last Hour

18Little children, it is the last hour; and
as you have heard that the[a] Antichrist is
coming, even now many antichrists have
come, by which we know that it is the last
hour. 19They went out from us, but they

2:7 [a]NU-Text reads *Beloved.* [b]NU-Text omits *from the beginning.* 2:18 [a]NU-Text omits *the.*

2:11 "The Incarnation is the ultimate reason why the service of God cannot be divorced from the service of man. He who says he loves God and hates his brother is a liar." *Dietrich Bonhoeffer*

2:15 "Sense of sin and deep hatred to it, faith in Christ and love to him, delight in holiness and longing after more of it, love to God's people and distaste for the things of this world—these are the signs and evidences which always accompany true conversion." *J. C. Ryle*

2:16 See Heb. 4:15 comment.

2:19 "I have left my religious conversion behind and settled into a comfortable state of atheism. I have come to think that religion has caused more harm than any other idea since the beginning of time." *Larry Flynt* (publisher of *Hustler* magazine, in his autobiography *An Unseemly Man*)

QUESTIONS & OBJECTIONS

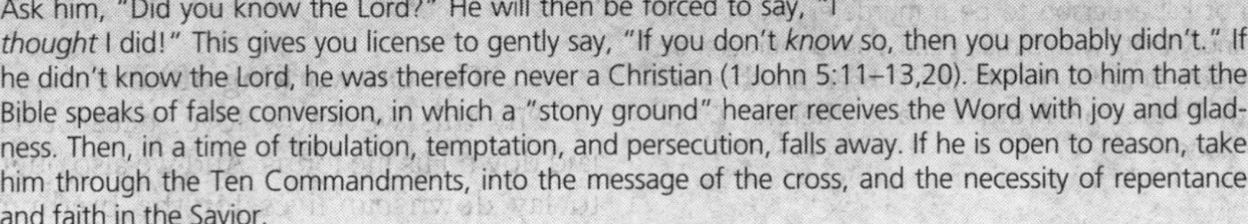

2:19 *"I was once a Christian. Now I believe it's all rubbish!"*

When a person maintains that he was once a Christian, but came to his senses, he is saying that he once knew the Lord (see John 17:3). Ask him, "Did you know the Lord?" He will then be forced to say, "I *thought* I did!" This gives you license to gently say, "If you don't *know* so, then you probably didn't." If he didn't know the Lord, he was therefore never a Christian (1 John 5:11–13,20). Explain to him that the Bible speaks of false conversion, in which a "stony ground" hearer receives the Word with joy and gladness. Then, in a time of tribulation, temptation, and persecution, falls away. If he is open to reason, take him through the Ten Commandments, into the message of the cross, and the necessity of repentance and faith in the Savior.

were not of us; for if they had been of us,
they would have continued with us; but
they went out that they might be made
manifest, that none of them were of us.
20But you have an anointing from the
Holy One, and you know all things.[a] 21I
have not written to you because you do
not know the truth, but because you
know it, and that no lie is of the truth.

> The most terrible warning to impenitent men in all the world is the death of Christ. For if God spared not His only Son, on whom was only laid imputed sin, will He spare sinners whose sins are their own?
>
> **CHARLES SPURGEON**

22Who is a liar but he who denies that
Jesus is the Christ? He is antichrist who
denies the Father and the Son. 23Who-
ever denies the Son does not have the
Father either; he who acknowledges the
Son has the Father also.

Let Truth Abide in You

24Therefore let that abide in you which
you heard from the beginning. If what you
heard from the beginning abides in you,
you also will abide in the Son and in the
Father. 25And this is the promise that He
has promised us—eternal life.
26These things I have written to you
concerning those who *try to* deceive you.
27But the anointing which you have received from Him abides in you, and you
do not need that anyone teach you; but
as the same anointing teaches you concerning all things, and is true, and is not
a lie, and just as it has taught you, you
will[a] abide in Him.

The Children of God

28And now, little children, abide in Him,
that when[a] He appears, we may have confidence and not be ashamed before Him
at His coming. 29If you know that He is
righteous, you know that everyone who
practices righteousness is born of Him.

3 Behold what manner of love the Father
has bestowed on us, that we should
be called children of God![a] Therefore the
world does not know us,[b] because it did
not know Him. 2Beloved, now we are
children of God; and it has not yet been
revealed what we shall be, but we know
that when He is revealed, we shall be
like Him, for we shall see Him as He is.
3And everyone who has this hope in Him
purifies himself, just as He is pure.

Sin and the Child of God

4Whoever commits sin also commits
lawlessness, and sin is lawlessness. 5And
you know that He was manifested to take
away our sins, and in Him there is no sin.
6Whoever abides in Him does not sin.

2:20 [a]NU-Text reads *you all know.* 2:27 [a]NU-Text reads *you abide.* 2:28 [a]NU-Text reads *if.* 3:1 [a]NU-Text adds *And we are.* [b]M-Text reads *you.*

The Function of the Law

3:15 "I used to say: 'What is the use of taking up a Law like this in an audience where, probably, there isn't a man who ever thought of, or ever will commit, murder?' But as one gets on in years, he sees many a murder that is not outright killing. I need not kill a person to be a murderer. If I get so angry that I wish a man dead, I am a murderer in God's sight. God looks at the heart and says he that hates his brother is a murderer." *D. L. Moody*

Whoever sins has neither seen Him nor known Him.

7Little children, let no one deceive you. He who practices righteousness is righteous, just as He is righteous. 8He who sins is of the devil, for the devil has sinned from the beginning. For this purpose the Son of God was manifested, that He might destroy the works of the devil. 9Whoever has been born of God does not sin, for His seed remains in him; and he cannot sin, because he has been born of God.

The Imperative of Love

10In this the children of God and the children of the devil are manifest: Whoever does not practice righteousness is not of God, nor *is* he who does not love his brother. 11For this is the message that you heard from the beginning, that we should love one another, 12not as Cain *who* was of the wicked one and murdered his brother. And why did he murder him? Because his works were evil and his brother's righteous.

13Do not marvel, my brethren, if the world hates you. 14We know that we have passed from death to life, because we love the brethren. He who does not love *his* brother[a] abides in death. 15Whoever hates his brother is a murderer, and you know that no murderer has eternal life abiding in him.

The Outworking of Love

16By this we know love, because He laid down His life for us. And we also ought to lay down *our* lives for the brethren. 17But whoever has this world's goods, and sees his brother in need, and shuts up his heart from him, how does the love of God abide in him?

18My little children, let us not love in word or in tongue, but in deed and in truth. 19And by this we know[a] that we are of the truth, and shall assure our hearts before Him. 20For if our heart condemns us, God is greater than our heart, and knows all things. 21Beloved, if our heart does not condemn us, we have confidence toward God. 22And whatever we ask we receive from Him, because we keep His commandments and do those things that are pleasing in His sight. 23And this is His commandment: that we should believe on the name of His Son Jesus Christ and love one another, as He gave us[a] commandment.

The Spirit of Truth and the Spirit of Error

24Now he who keeps His command-

3:14 [a]NU-Text omits *his brother*. 3:19 [a]NU-Text reads *we shall know*. 3:23 [a]M-Text omits *us*.

3:12 "The cool impudence of Cain is an indication of the state of heart which led up to his murdering his brother; and it was also a part of the result of his having committed that terrible crime. He would not have proceeded to the cruel deed of bloodshed if he had not first cast off the fear of God and been ready to defy his Maker." *Charles Spurgeon*

3:13 Hypocrisy in the Church. It is interesting to note that unbelievers hate hypocrisy in the Church. They detest the "pretender." Does that mean that they *want* the Christian to be genuine? Do they *want* us to be true and faithful in our witness and therefore speak of sin, righteousness, and judgment? Do they want us to live in holiness rather than in compromise? Does the world really want us to speak up against pornography, greed, adultery, abortion, homosexuality, fornication, and other sins they so love? In their eyes we are damned if we do, and damned if we don't.

3:16 "You are more sinful than you ever dared to believe, but you are more loved than you ever dared to hope." *Mark Liederbach*

QUESTIONS & OBJECTIONS

4:2 *"Jesus Christ never even existed."*

Surprisingly, some skeptics claim that Jesus didn't exist, though to do so they have to reject the entire New Testament historical record. The New Testament contains hundreds of references to Jesus Christ, and in terms of ancient manuscript evidence, this is extraordinarily strong proof of the existence of a man named Jesus of Nazareth in the early first century A.D.

While skeptics may choose to reject the Bible's moral message, they cannot deny its historical accuracy. Over 25,000 archaeological finds demonstrate that the people, places, and events mentioned in the Bible are real and are accurately described. No archaeological finding has ever refuted the Bible. In fact, the descriptions in the Bible have often led archaeologists to amazing discoveries. Non-Christian journalist Jeffery Sheler, author of the book *Is the Bible True?*, concluded, "In extraordinary ways, modern archaeology is affirming the historical core of the Old and New Testaments, supporting key portions of crucial biblical stories."

In addition, a surprising amount of information about Jesus can be drawn from secular historical sources. According to Richard M. Fales, "Writings confirming His birth, ministry, death, and resurrection include Flavius Josephus (A.D. 93), the Babylonian Talmud (A.D. 70–200), Pliny the Younger's letter to the Emperor Trajan (approx. A.D. 100), the Annals of Tacitus (A.D. 115–117), Mara Bar Serapion (sometime after A.D. 73), and Suetonius' Life of Claudius and Life of Nero (A.D. 120)."

The first-century Roman Tacitus, considered one of the more accurate historians of the ancient world, mentioned superstitious "Christians," named after Christus (Latin for Christ), who was executed by Pontius Pilate during the reign of Tiberius. Suetonius, chief secretary to Emperor Hadrian, wrote of a man named Chrestus (Christ) who lived during the first century (Roman Annals 15.44). Renowned Jewish historian Josephus wrote:

> Now, there was about this time Jesus, a wise man [if it be lawful to call him a man], for he was a doer of wonderful works, a teacher of such men as receive the truth with pleasure. He drew over to him both many of the Jews, and many of the Gentiles. [He was the Messiah.] And when Pilate, at the suggestion of the principal men amongst us, had condemned him to the cross, those that loved him at the first did not forsake him [for he appeared to them alive again at the third day; as the divine prophets had foretold these and ten thousand other wonderful things concerning him]. And the tribe of Christians, so named from him, are not extinct at this date.

ments abides in Him, and He in him. And by this we know that He abides in us, by the Spirit whom He has given us.

4 Beloved, do not believe every spirit, but test the spirits, whether they are of God; because many false prophets have gone out into the world. [2]By this you know the Spirit of God: Every spirit that confesses that Jesus Christ has come in the flesh is of God, [3]and every spirit that does not confess that[a] Jesus Christ has come in the flesh is not of God. And this is the *spirit* of the Antichrist, which you have heard was coming, and is now already in the world.

[4]You are of God, little children, and have overcome them, because He who is in you is greater than he who is in the world. [5]They are of the world. Therefore they speak *as* of the world, and the world

4:3 [a]NU-Text omits *that* and *Christ has come in the flesh.*

4:4 Confidence in witnessing. "When you represent the Lord Jesus Christ as His disciple, you can be assured that you are representing the One who possesses all power, wisdom, and authority. You have everything when you have Him. Jesus said: 'I tell you the truth, anyone who has faith in me will do what I have been doing. He will do even greater things than these, because I am going to the Father' (John 14:12). No power can resist you as you go in obedience and faith as His ambassador (2 Cor. 5:19,20). You have the promise, 'The one who is in you is greater than the one who is in the world' (1 John 4:4). Also, you are assured that even the gates of hell will not prevail against you (Matt. 16:18). The more you understand who Christ is and all that He has done and will do for you and through you, the more completely you will want to trust, obey, and serve Him." *Bill Bright*

4:8 *The Firefighters*

Imagine seeing a group of firefighters polishing their engine outside a burning building with people trapped at a top floor window. Obviously, there is nothing wrong with cleaning a fire engine—*but not while people are trapped in a burning building!* Instead of ignoring their cries, the firefighters should have an overwhelming sense of urgency to rescue them. That's the spirit that should be behind the task of evangelism. But according to *Bill Bright*, founder of Campus Crusade for Christ, "Only 2 percent of believers in America regularly share their faith with others." That means that 98 percent of the professing Body of Christ are "lukewarm" when it comes to obeying the Great Commission (Mark 16:15).

Oswald J. Smith said, "Oh my friends, we are loaded down with countless church activities, while the *real* work of the Church, that of evangelizing and winning the lost, is almost entirely neglected." We have polished the engines of worship, prayer, and praise and neglected the sober task given to us by God. A firefighter who ignores his responsibilities and allows people to perish in flames is not a firefighter; he is an impostor. How could we ignore our responsibility and allow the world to walk blindly into the fires of hell? If God's love dwells in us, we must warn them. The Bible tells us to "have compassion…save with fear, pulling them out of the fire, hating even the garment defiled by the flesh" (Jude 22,23). If we don't have love and compassion, then we don't know God; we are impostors (1 John 4:8).

Charles Spurgeon said, "Have you no wish for others to be saved? Then you are not saved yourself. Be sure of that." Please, examine yourself to see if you are in the faith (2 Cor. 13:5). See page 1630. Don't be part of the great multitude who called Jesus "Lord," but refused to obey Him. It is professing *believers* who will hear those fearful words, "I never knew you; depart from Me" (Matt. 7:21–23).

Backward Christian Soldiers

Backward Christian soldiers, fleeing from the fight
With the cross of Jesus nearly out of sight.
Christ, our rightful master, stands against the foe
But forward into battle, we are loathe to go.

Like a mighty tortoise moves the Church of God
Brothers, we are treading where we've always trod.
We are much divided, many bodies we,
Having many doctrines, not much charity.

Crowns and thorns may perish, kingdoms rise and wane,
But the Church of Jesus hidden does remain.
Gates of hell should never 'gainst the Church prevail.
We have Christ's own promise, but think that it will fail.

Sit here then ye people, join our useless throng,
Blend with ours your voices in a feeble song.
Blessings, ease and comfort, ask from Christ the King.
With our modern thinking, we don't do a thing.
(Anonymous)

If God is speaking to you about your lack of evangelistic concern, pray something like this now:

Father, please forgive me for my lack of love for this dying world. From this day forward I will strive to be a "true and faithful witness." Please give me the wisdom to know what to say to reach the lost. In Jesus' name I pray. Amen.

hears them. 6We are of God. He who
knows God hears us; he who is not of
God does not hear us. By this we know
the spirit of truth and the spirit of error.

Knowing God Through Love

7Beloved, let us love one another, for
love is of God; and everyone who loves is
born of God and knows God. 8He who
does not love does not know God, for God
is love. 9In this the love of God was manifested toward us, that God has sent His
only begotten Son into the world, that we
might live through Him. 10In this is love,
not that we loved God, but that He loved
us and sent His Son *to be* the propitiation
for our sins. 11Beloved, if God so loved us,
we also ought to love one another.

QUESTIONS & OBJECTIONS

5:10 ***"I find it difficult to have faith in God."***

The key that unlocks the door of salvation is faith. Without faith, we cannot please God (Heb. 11:6). Try establishing any sort of friendship without faith. Introduce yourself to someone, and when he tells you his name, say, "I don't believe you." Watch his reaction. When he tells you where he works, say you don't believe that either. Carry on like that, and before long you may be nursing a black eye. If you don't believe someone, it means you think that he is a liar.

If a mere mortal feels insulted by your lack of faith in his word, how much more do unbelievers insult Almighty God by refusing to believe His Word. Martin Luther said, "What greater insult... can there be to God, than to not believe His promises." In doing so, they are saying that God isn't worth trusting—that He is a liar and a deceiver. If a meaningful human relationship can't be established without faith, what sort of relationship could we expect to have with God, if by our unbelief we continue to call Him a liar? The Bible warns, "Beware, brethren, lest there be in any of you *an evil heart of unbelief*..." (Heb. 3:12, emphasis added). The Scriptures command us, "Have faith in God" (Mark 11:22).

Seeing God Through Love

12 No one has seen God at any time. If
we love one another, God abides in us,
and His love has been perfected in us.
13 By this we know that we abide in Him,
and He in us, because He has given us of
His Spirit. 14 And we have seen and testify
that the Father has sent the Son *as* Savior
of the world. 15 Whoever confesses that
Jesus is the Son of God, God abides in
him, and he in God. 16 And we have known
and believed the love that God has for us.
God is love, and he who abides in love
abides in God, and God in him.

The Consummation of Love

17 Love has been perfected among us
in this: that we may have boldness in the
day of judgment; because as He is, so are
we in this world. 18 There is no fear in
love; but perfect love casts out fear, because fear involves torment. But he who
fears has not been made perfect in love.
19 We love Him[a] because He first loved us.

Obedience by Faith

20 If someone says, "I love God," and
hates his brother, he is a liar; for he who
does not love his brother whom he has
seen, how can[a] he love God whom he has
not seen? 21 And this commandment we
have from Him: that he who loves God
must love his brother also.

5 Whoever believes that Jesus is the
Christ is born of God, and everyone
who loves Him who begot also loves him
who is begotten of Him. 2 By this we
know that we love the children of God,
when we love God and keep His commandments. 3 For this is the love of God,
that we keep His commandments. And
His commandments are not burdensome.
4 For whatever is born of God overcomes
the world. And this is the victory that
has overcome the world—our[a] faith.
5 Who is he who overcomes the world,
but he who believes that Jesus is the Son
of God?

The Certainty of God's Witness

6 This is He who came by water and
blood—Jesus Christ; not only by water,
but by water and blood. And it is the Spirit
who bears witness, because the Spirit is

4:19 [a]NU-Text omits *Him*. 4:20 [a]NU-Text reads *he cannot*. 5:4 [a]M-Text reads *your*.

4:20 "I really only love God as much as I love the person I love the least." *Dorothy Day*

"I shall allow no man to belittle my soul by making me hate him." *Booker T. Washington*

5:1 New birth—its necessity for salvation. See John 1:13.

QUESTIONS & OBJECTIONS

5:12,13

"I hope I'm going to heaven when I die."

Of all the things that you should be sure of, it's your eternal destiny. To say "I hope I'm going to heaven" is like standing at the open door of a plane 25,000 feet in the air and, when asked "Have you got your parachute on?" answering with "I hope so." You want to *know* so—and you can, simply by obeying the gospel. If you repent and place your faith in Jesus Christ, He will give you eternal life and you can *know* that your eternity is secure. These verses also make clear that those who refuse to trust in the Son of God can likewise *know* that they do not have eternal life—they will remain dead in their sins.

truth. 7For there are three that bear witness in heaven: the Father, the Word, and
the Holy Spirit; and these three are one.
8And there are three that bear witness on
earth:[a] the Spirit, the water, and the
blood; and these three agree as one.
9If we receive the witness of men, the
witness of God is greater; for this is the
witness of God which[a] He has testified of
His Son. 10He who believes in the Son of
God has the witness in himself; he who
does not believe God has made Him a
liar, because he has not believed the testimony that God has given of His Son.
11And this is the testimony: that God has
given us eternal life, and this life is in His
Son. 12He who has the Son has life; he who
does not have the Son of God does not
have life. 13These things I have written to
you who believe in the name of the Son
of God, that you may know that you have
eternal life,[a] and that you may *continue to*
believe in the name of the Son of God.

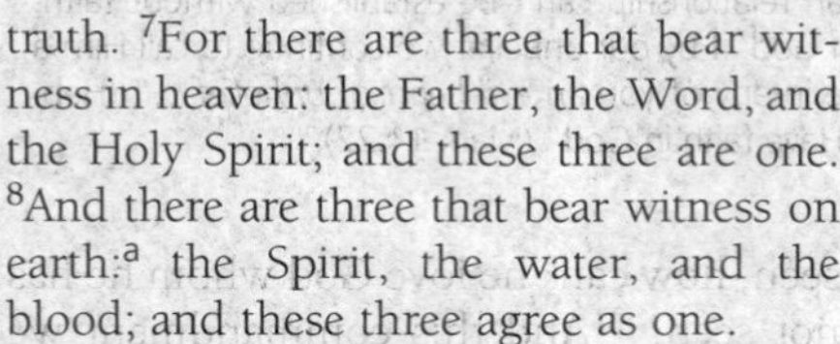

Confidence and Compassion in Prayer

14Now this is the confidence that we
have in Him, that if we ask anything according to His will, He hears us. 15And if
we know that He hears us, whatever we
ask, we know that we have the petitions
that we have asked of Him.
16If anyone sees his brother sinning a
sin *which does* not *lead* to death, he will
ask, and He will give him life for those who
commit sin not *leading* to death. There is
sin *leading* to death. I do not say that he
should pray about that. 17All unrighteousness is sin, and there is sin not *leading* to
death.

Knowing the True— Rejecting the False

18We know that whoever is born of
God does not sin; but he who has been
born of God keeps himself,[a] and the
wicked one does not touch him.
19We know that we are of God, and
the whole world lies *under the sway of* the
wicked one.
20And we know that the Son of God
has come and has given us an understanding, that we may know Him who is
true; and we are in Him who is true, in
His Son Jesus Christ. This is the true God
and eternal life.
21Little children, keep yourselves from
idols. Amen.

5:8 [a]NU-Text and M-Text omit the words from *in heaven* (verse 7) through *on earth* (verse 8). Only four or five very late manuscripts contain these words in Greek. 5:9 [a]NU-Text reads *God, that.* 5:13 [a]NU-Text omits the rest of this verse. 5:18 [a]NU-Text reads *him.*

5:14 "God prompts His people to pray and then acts in response to their prayers. Things happen or don't happen because of prayer. This does not mean God can be manipulated through prayer to do what we want if what we want is contrary to His will. Instead, God reveals His will to us by His Word and works in us by His Spirit so that we know His will and pray in accord with it. Then, in responding to our prayers, He accomplishes both His will and ours, and, in the process, involves us." *Alvin J. Vander Griend*

2 John

Greeting the Elect Lady

The Elder,

To the elect lady and her children, whom I love in truth, and not only I, but also all those who have known the truth, [2]because of the truth which abides in us and will be with us forever:

[3]Grace, mercy, *and* peace will be with you[a] from God the Father and from the Lord Jesus Christ, the Son of the Father, in truth and love.

Walk in Christ's Commandments

[4]I rejoiced greatly that I have found *some* of your children walking in truth, as we received commandment from the Father. [5]And now I plead with you, lady, not as though I wrote a new commandment to you, but that which we have had from the beginning: that we love one another. [6]This is love, that we walk according to His commandments. This is the commandment, that as you have heard from the beginning, you should walk in it.

Beware of Antichrist Deceivers

[7]For many deceivers have gone out into the world who do not confess Jesus Christ *as* coming in the flesh. This is a deceiver and an antichrist. [8]Look to yourselves, that we[a] do not lose those things we worked for, but *that* we[b] may receive a full reward.

> Humility and patience are the surest proofs of the increase of love.
>
> **JOHN WESLEY**

[9]Whoever transgresses[a] and does not abide in the doctrine of Christ does not have God. He who abides in the doctrine of Christ has both the Father and the Son. [10]If anyone comes to you and does not bring this doctrine, do not receive him into your house nor greet him; [11]for he who greets him shares in his evil deeds.

John's Farewell Greeting

[12]Having many things to write to you, I did not wish *to do so* with paper and ink; but I hope to come to you and speak face to face, that our joy may be full.

[13]The children of your elect sister greet you. Amen.

3 [a]NU-Text and M-Text read *us*. 8 [a]NU-Text reads *you*. [b]NU-Text reads *you*. 9 [a]NU-Text reads *goes ahead*.

7 Religions and "Christian" sects that deny the great truth that God was manifest in the flesh are deceivers and are antichrist in spirit. See 1 John 4:2; 1 Tim. 3:16.

9 Those who object to Christianity's claim that there is only one way to God usually argue that we should be tolerant of all religions. In that case, they should practice what they preach and be tolerant of the Christian claim. Jesus is *the* way, *the* truth, and *the* life. No one comes to the Father except through Him (John 14:6). See 1 John 2:23.

Roman Catholicism

The Roman Catholic church has always been identified with Christianity, mainly because it upholds the fundamentals of the Christian faith. It teaches the deity of Jesus Christ, the Trinity, the virgin birth, and the bodily resurrection and return of Christ to the earth.

However, most Roman Catholics when asked if they are Christians *will* make a distinction between New Testament Christianity and Roman Catholicism. If you ask, "Are you a Christian?" they will normally reply, "I'm a Catholic." They are right to do so, because there are clear and fundamental differences.

BACKGROUND

The Roman Catholic church is said to be the largest organized body of any world religion. According to the *Statistical Yearbook of the Church*, its worldwide membership is around 1.1 billion, or approximately one-sixth of the world's population.

The Catholic church traces its history back to the first century, and maintains that the true Church is built on Peter, whom they believe was the first "pope." However, Peter himself denied this fact, maintaining that Jesus Christ is the Rock and Chief Cornerstone of the Church (see 1 Pet. 2:6–8). The Protestant church asserts that Catholicism actually had a later beginning, in the fourth century, when Constantine unified the Roman Empire by merging paganism with Christianity. Declaring himself Vicar of Christ, he elevated "converts" to positions of influence and authority. These professing Christians brought their pagan rites and their gods and goddesses into the church. In time, church councils began to exalt their traditions above Scripture and condemn their opponents, and many devout men were labeled heretics and persecuted for defending the Bible's authority.

By the 12th century the Roman Catholic church had become the world's most powerful institution, using its power to set up and depose kings and queens. It also became the richest institution on earth by taxing people and confiscating property. Through the Crusades and later the Inquisition, the Catholic church put to death Muslims, heretics, and those who rejected papal supremacy.

SCRIPTURES

Roman Catholics use a version of the Bible that includes what is called the *Apocrypha*, a group of books found in their Old Testament. The Catholic Bible is based on a translation known as the Greek Septuagint, which included these books. Non-Catholics, however, do not accept them as inspired, primarily because the Apocrypha is not part of the official canon of Judaism. The excluded material is a group of fifteen late Jewish books, which were not found in Hebrew versions of the Jewish Scripture.

It is important to realize that the doctrinal differences between Catholics and non-Catholics are not fundamentally caused by the differences in their Scriptures. The problem comes rather with the Roman Catholic church's teachings. For example, it is puzzling why Roman Catholics bow down to and give homage to statues of "the saints," angels, images of Mary and Jesus, etc. Why do they do such a thing when bowing down to anything is a direct violation of the Ten Commandments, which they officially accept as God's Law?

If you look closely at the Catholic Catechism (the official teachings of the church), you will find that the Second Commandment has been completely removed. The Third Commandment then became the Second, the Fourth became the Third, and so on. The Roman Catholic church then took the Tenth Commandment (found in one verse and dealing with the one subject of covetousness; see Exod. 20:17), divided it in two, and made it into the Ninth and Tenth Commandments. Here are the Ten Commandments as listed on the official Vatican website:

1. I am the LORD your God: you shall not have strange Gods before me.
2. You shall not take the name of the LORD your God in vain.
3. Remember to keep holy the LORD's Day.
4. Honor your father and your mother.
5. You shall not kill.
6. You shall not commit adultery.
7. You shall not steal.
8. You shall not bear false witness against your neighbor.
9. You shall not covet your neighbor's wife.
10. You shall not covet your neighbor's goods.

You won't find a word of the Second Commandment in the Catholic Catechism. This is despite the fact that the Second Commandment is still listed in full in the Roman Catholic Bible. In fact, the Second Commandment against idolatry is cited seven times in the Old Testament and three times in the New Testament (Exod. 20:4; 20:23; 34:17; Lev. 19:4; 26:1; Deut. 4:23; 5:8; 1 Cor. 10:7; 10:14; and 1 John 5:21).

While Roman Catholics acknowledge Scripture as a source of authority and doctrine, they give equal weight to tradition: ". . . the Church, to whom the transmission and interpretation of Revelation is entrusted, does not derive her certainty about all revealed truths from the holy Scriptures alone. Both

(continued)

Roman Catholicism (continued)

Scripture and Tradition must be accepted and honored with equal sentiments of devotion and reverence" (Catechism of the Catholic Church, par. 82).

It is a tragedy that most Roman Catholics give as much credence to the teaching of the church (fallible men) as to the authority of inspired Scripture. This is why it is essential to move as quickly as possible from the intellect (arguing *about* Scripture) to the conscience (*using* Scripture, particularly God's Law). It is the Law that "stops every mouth" and brings "the knowledge of sin" (see Rom. 3:19,20). Remember, the work of the Law is written on the heart (see Rom. 2:15) and will therefore find a place of resonance in the conscience.

HEAVEN AND HELL

According to the Catholic Catechism, upon death each person will begin eternal life. After being judged by Christ each individual will gain "entrance into the happiness of heaven, immediately *or after an appropriate purification*, or entry into the eternal damnation of hell" (emphasis added). Heaven is described as "the state of supreme and definitive happiness [where] those who die in the grace of God and have no need of further purification are gathered around Jesus and Mary, the angels and the saints."

Catholics believe hell is a place of eternal damnation: "Immediately after death the souls of those who die in a state of mortal sin descend into hell, where they suffer the punishments of hell, 'eternal fire'" (Catechism, par. 1035). But Catholics also believe in a "holding place" called *purgatory*, for which there is no biblical basis. It is believed to be an intermediate stage that is used to purify souls that will eventually go to heaven, but that still have some temporal restitution they must make.

> The Church gives the name *Purgatory* to this final purification of the elect, which is entirely different from the punishment of the damned. The Church formulated her doctrine of faith on Purgatory especially at the Councils of Florence and Trent [in the 15th and 16th centuries]. The tradition of the Church, by reference to certain texts of Scripture, speaks of a cleansing fire: As for certain lesser faults, we must believe that, before the Final Judgment, there is a purifying fire. He who is truth says that whoever utters blasphemy against the Holy Spirit will be pardoned neither in this age nor in the age to come. From this sentence we understand that certain offenses can be forgiven in this age, but certain others in the age to come. (Catechism, par. 1031)

According to the church, Catholics can help get someone out of purgatory and into heaven by offering "prayers in suffrage for them, above all the Eucharistic sacrifice... The Church also commends almsgiving, indulgences, and works of penance" (Catechism, par. 1032): "An indulgence can be obtained through a good deed done, a Mass being offered on behalf of someone, prayer, abstinence, giving to the poor, or some other meritorious act performed in accordance with requirements set by a Pope or bishop having jurisdiction over that individual."

However, according to Scripture, none of our acts are "meritorious"—no amount of good deeds or money can buy eternal salvation: "But Peter said to him, 'Your money perish with you, because you thought that the gift of God could be purchased with money!'" (Acts 8:20). "None of them can by any means redeem his brother, nor give to God a ransom for him—for the redemption of their souls is costly..." (Psa. 49:7,8).

The doctrine of purgatory misleads people into thinking they can somehow be made right with God after this lifetime. Scripture clearly warns us: "It is appointed for men to die once, but after this the judgment" (Heb. 9:27). There are no second chances.

SIN AND SALVATION

Understandably, the greatest contention between the Catholic and the Protestant teachings is how a person can be made right with God. The Bible says that eternal life is not something we earn, but is a free gift from God to all who repent and trust the Savior. (See Eph. 2:8,9; Rom. 11:6; Titus 3:5.) The Vatican not only denies this doctrine, but actually condemns it, pronouncing the curse of God upon anyone who believes that eternal life is through "faith alone":

> If any one saith, that by faith alone the impious is justified; in such wise as to mean, that nothing else is required to co-operate in order to the obtaining the grace of Justification... let him be anathema. (Canon 9, Council of Trent)
>
> If any one saith, that man is truly absolved from his sins and justified... and that, by this faith alone, absolution and justification are effected; let him be anathema. (Canon 14, Council of Trent)

Like the Mormon church and others, the Roman Catholic church teaches that we can earn our salvation, calling heaven God's "reward for good works":

> We can therefore hope in the glory of heaven promised by God to those who love him and do his will. In every circumstance, each one of us should hope, with the grace of God, to persevere 'to the end' and *to obtain the joy of heaven, as God's eternal reward for the good works* accomplished with the grace of Christ. (Catechism, par. 1821, emphasis added)
>
> Moved by the Holy Spirit, *we can merit for ourselves and for others all the graces need-*

(continued)

Roman Catholicism (continued)

ed to attain eternal life. (Catechism, par. 2027, emphasis added)

The Vatican teaches that salvation comes only through the Roman Catholic church, and that salvation (because it is based on works) can be lost through sin and is never assured in this life. They believe the first step in salvation is to be baptized. Tragically, the Roman Catholic church maintains that in baptism (sprinkling) the new birth takes place. Jesus said that each one of us must be born again or we will not enter heaven (John 3:1–7), but Scripture teaches only what is called "believer's baptism," which occurs after a sinner repents and trusts in Jesus Christ. Because infants cannot repent, they are not saved by baptism—and therefore are not born again.

In Catholicism, baptism erases sins up to that point and merely begins a process of salvation that continues throughout life as one participates in the sacraments. The sacrament of penance is required to receive forgiveness of sins committed after baptism. Acts of penance vary but include prayer, saying the rosary, reading Scripture, saying a number of "Our Father" or "Hail Mary" prayers, doing good works, and fasting. In Catholic teaching, the sacraments "are necessary for salvation because they confer sacramental grace, forgiveness of sins, adoption as children of God, conformation to Christ the Lord and membership in the Church. The Holy Spirit heals and transforms those who receive the sacraments." God's "grace" that is conferred simply enables believers to perform works that *earn* them the right to heaven.

Because salvation does not depend on a person's repentance and faith in the saving work of Jesus Christ, according to the Catholic church even those who have never heard of Jesus can be saved —*even if they follow another religion*: "...thanks to Christ and to his Church, those who through no fault of their own do not know the Gospel of Christ and his Church but sincerely seek God and, moved by grace, try to do his will as it is known through the dictates of conscience can attain eternal salvation."

ROMAN CATHOLIC BELIEFS

In rejecting Scripture as the sole source of doctrine, the Roman Catholic church has justified several extrabiblical, and unbiblical, teachings. Some of these are discussed below.

Transubstantiation: Transubstantiation is the Roman Catholic doctrine of the Eucharist wafer turning into the literal body and blood of Jesus during Mass. This belief is based on John 6:53,54 where Jesus said, "Whoever eats My flesh and drinks My blood has eternal life..." However, when read in context the meaning becomes clear. Jesus went on to explain that He was speaking spiritually: "The words that I speak to you are spirit, and they are life" (John 6:63). He is speaking of the new birth (see John 3:1–5) when a sinner believes on Him, and it is then that he tastes of the Lord and Christ dwells in him by faith—"Taste and see that the Lord is good." This is extremely important because a sinner is saved not by taking the Eucharist, but only by repentance and faith in Christ.

Praying to saints: The Catholic church believes in praying to those, who, because of their good works, have been exulted to sainthood after their death: "They contemplate God, praise him and constantly care for those whom they have left on earth... Their intercession is their most exalted service to God's plan. We can and should ask them to intercede for us and for the whole world" (Catechism, par. 2683). But nowhere in Scripture is there any admonition for Christians to pray to someone who has died. Instead, Jesus Himself taught us to pray directly to the Father (Matt. 6:6–9). Through Christ, we can come boldly to the throne of grace (see Heb. 4:16).

Confession to a priest: The Roman Catholic church says that the priest is the only one who can forgive sins in the name of Christ. However, the good news of the gospel is that any sinner can go directly to God and have his sins washed away by the blood of Christ. The Bible tells us that Peter told sinners to go straight to God (not to a man) for forgiveness (see Acts 8:18–22).

Worship of Mary: For details on this, see Jer. 7:18 comment.

HOW TO REACH A ROMAN CATHOLIC

Again, the fact that salvation comes by grace through faith alone is wonderful news for both the Roman Catholic and traditional Protestant churches. Nothing we do can merit eternal life. We can only obey the command to repent and trust the Savior, and the moment we do so we will be born again and be granted the gift of God—eternal life through Jesus Christ our Lord.

Remember, the key is a right understanding of our state before God. If we think we are good people, then we simply have to do some good works to merit eternal life. But if we are confronted by God's Law, it shows us that we are desperate criminals in God's sight, and that the only way we could possibly be saved is through His mercy.

So how can we best relate this to Roman Catholics without offending them? When someone says, "I'm a Roman Catholic," don't panic and think you have to deal with papal infallibility, Mariology, confession to the priest, etc. Ignore all that, and simply aim for the conscience by doing what Jesus did and going through the Ten Commandments. The Law, in the hand of the Spirit, addresses the conscience and shows sinners that they are not good, and all the good works in the world cannot and will not bribe a holy God to pervert Eternal Justice. (See also Phil. 3:9 comment.)

(Adapted from *World Religions in a Nutshell*.)

3 John

Greeting to Gaius

The Elder,

To the beloved Gaius, whom I love in truth:

2Beloved, I pray that you may prosper in all things and be in health, just as your soul prospers. 3For I rejoiced greatly when brethren came and testified of the truth *that is* in you, just as you walk in the truth. 4I have no greater joy than to hear that my children walk in truth.[a]

Gaius Commended for Generosity

5Beloved, you do faithfully whatever you do for the brethren and[a] for strangers, 6who have borne witness of your love before the church. *If* you send them forward on their journey in a manner worthy of God, you will do well, 7because they went forth for His name's sake, taking nothing from the Gentiles. 8We therefore ought to receive[a] such, that we may become fellow workers for the truth.

Diotrephes and Demetrius

9I wrote to the church, but Diotrephes, who loves to have the preeminence among them, does not receive us. 10Therefore, if I come, I will call to mind his deeds which he does, prating against us with malicious words. And not content with that, he himself does not receive the brethren, and forbids those who wish to, putting *them* out of the church.

11Beloved, do not imitate what is evil, but what is good. He who does good is of God, but[a] he who does evil has not seen God.

> The Church has developed a theology that doesn't require much repentance. We have a theology that is uncomfortable with the very term 'Jesus is Lord.'
>
> **DR. PAUL A. CEDAR**

12Demetrius has a *good* testimony from all, and from the truth itself. And we also bear witness, and you know that our testimony is true.

Farewell Greeting

13I had many things to write, but I do not wish to write to you with pen and ink; 14but I hope to see you shortly, and we shall speak face to face.

Peace to you. Our friends greet you. Greet the friends by name.

4 [a]NU-Text reads *the truth.* 5 [a]NU-Text adds *especially.* 8 [a]NU-Text reads *support.* 11 [a]NU-Text and M-Text omit *but.*

9 Loving to have preeminence is not a fruit of godliness. Those who want it will manifest their unregenerate hearts with malicious words. They will divide the Body of Christ for their own ends, as did Diotrephes.

Test Your I.Q.

Read OUT LOUD the wording in the three triangles:

PARIS
IN THE
THE SPRING
BIRD
IN THE
THE HAND
ONCE
IN A
A LIFETIME

READ this sentence:

FINISHED FILES ARE THE RE-SULTS OF YEARS OF SCIEN-TIFIC STUDY COMBINED WITH THE EXPERIENCE OF YEARS

Now count aloud the F's in the box. Count them only ONCE; do not look back and count them again.

Answers: The words "the" and "a" are repeated. There are six F's.

Here is another I.Q. test:

This one is more important. Answer Yes or No OUT LOUD:

1. Is there a God?
2. Does God care about right and wrong?
3. Are God's standards the same as ours?
4. Will God punish sin?
5. Is there a hell?
6. Can you avoid hell by living a good life?

Answers:

1 Yes. **2** Yes. **3** No. **4** Yes. **5** Yes. **6** No.

Jude

Greeting to the Called

Jude, a bondservant of Jesus Christ, and brother of James,

To those who are called, sanctified[a] by God the Father, and preserved in Jesus Christ:

2Mercy, peace, and love be multiplied to you.

Contend for the Faith

3Beloved, while I was very diligent to write to you concerning our common salvation, I found it necessary to write to you exhorting you to contend earnestly for the faith which was once for all delivered to the saints. 4For certain men have crept in unnoticed, who long ago were marked out for this condemnation, ungodly men, who turn the grace of our God into lewdness and deny the only Lord God[a] and our Lord Jesus Christ.

Old and New Apostates

5But I want to remind you, though you once knew this, that the Lord, having saved the people out of the land of Egypt, afterward destroyed those who did not believe. 6And the angels who did not keep their proper domain, but left their own abode, He has reserved in everlasting chains under darkness for the judgment of the great day; 7as Sodom and Gomorrah, and the cities around them in a similar manner to these, having given themselves over to sexual immorality and gone after strange flesh, are set forth as an example, suffering the vengeance of eternal fire.

8Likewise also these dreamers defile the flesh, reject authority, and speak evil of

USING THE LAW IN EVANGELISM

3 Regarding the Law's use in evangelism, *Martin Luther* stated: "This now is the Christian teaching and preaching, which God be praised, we know and possess, and it is not necessary at present to develop it further, but only to offer the admonition that it be maintained in Christendom with all diligence. For Satan has attacked it hard and strong from the beginning until present, and gladly would he completely extinguish it and tread it under foot."

1 [a]NU-Text reads *beloved*. 4 [a]NU-Text omits *God*.

3 Never lose sight of the mandate of the Church: to contend earnestly for the faith. The battle in which we find ourselves is for the salvation of lost souls.

"When people inquire as to the relevance of our gospel, we must not be tricked into going on the defensive. We must immediately take the offensive, for our Lord Himself has promised that the gates of hell shall not withstand the assault of His Church." *Leighton Ford*

4 False converts have "crept in unnoticed" and sit among God's people. They think that salvation and sin are compatible. They are actually workers of iniquity. See Matt. 7:21–23.

QUESTIONS & OBJECTIONS

7

"God made me to be a homosexual, so He doesn't want me to change."

Homosexuals argue that they did not make a conscious decision to be that way, so it must be natural. They *are* "born that way"—just as all of us are born with a sin nature and sinful desires (Eph. 2:1–3). Tell them that it *is* natural for them, and for all of us, to be tempted to do things that God says are wrong. In the same way, pedophiles and adulterers (alcoholics, drug addicts, etc.) don't make a conscious decision to "choose" that self-destructive lifestyle, they simply give in to their sinful desires. However, although sin is natural for unbelievers, that does not mean God wants them to remain that way. God can set them free from their sinful nature (Rom. 7:23–8:2), give them a new heart with new desires (Eph. 4:22–24), and help them withstand temptations (1 Cor.10:13). See also 1 Cor. 6:9–11 comment.

dignitaries. 9Yet Michael the archangel, in
contending with the devil, when he disputed about the body of Moses, dared not
bring against him a reviling accusation,
but said, "The Lord rebuke you!" 10But
these speak evil of whatever they do not
know; and whatever they know naturally,
like brute beasts, in these things they corrupt themselves. 11Woe to them! For they
have gone in the way of Cain, have run
greedily in the error of Balaam for profit,
and perished in the rebellion of Korah.

Apostates Depraved and Doomed

12These are spots in your love feasts,
while they feast with you without fear,
serving *only* themselves. *They are* clouds
without water, carried about[a] by the winds;
late autumn trees without fruit, twice dead,
pulled up by the roots; 13raging waves of
the sea, foaming up their own shame;
wandering stars for whom is reserved the
blackness of darkness forever.
14Now Enoch, the seventh from Adam,
prophesied about these men also, saying,
"Behold, the Lord comes with ten thousands of His saints, 15to execute judgment
on all, to convict all who are ungodly
among them of all their ungodly deeds
which they have committed in an ungodly
way, and of all the harsh things which ungodly sinners have spoken against Him."

Preach with this object, that men may quit their sins and fly to Christ for pardon, that by His blessed Spirit they may be renovated and become as much in love with everything that is holy as they are now in love with everything that is sinful.

CHARLES SPURGEON

Apostates Predicted

16These are grumblers, complainers,
walking according to their own lusts; and
they mouth great swelling *words,* flattering
people to gain advantage. 17But you, beloved, remember the words which were
spoken before by the apostles of our Lord
Jesus Christ: 18how they told you that there
would be mockers in the last time who
would walk according to their own ungod-

12 [a]NU-Text and M-Text read *along.*

14 Second coming of Jesus: See Rev. 1:7.

"We talk of the Second Coming; half the world has never heard of the first." *Oswald J. Smith*

15 With the help of God, we are to convince the ungodly that their deeds and their speech are offensive to their Creator, and will bring swift judgment upon them.

ly lusts. 19These are sensual persons, who
cause divisions, not having the Spirit.

Maintain Your Life with God

20But you, beloved, building yourselves
up on your most holy faith, praying in
the Holy Spirit, 21keep yourselves in the
love of God, looking for the mercy of our
Lord Jesus Christ unto eternal life.
22And on some have compassion, making a distinction;[a] 23but others save with
fear, pulling *them* out of the fire,[a] hating
even the garment defiled by the flesh.

Glory to God

24Now to Him who is able to keep you[a]
from stumbling,
And to present *you* faultless
Before the presence of His glory with
exceeding joy,
25To God our Savior,[a]
Who alone is wise,[b]
Be glory and majesty,
Dominion and power,[c]
Both now and forever.
Amen.

"Before I can preach love, mercy, and grace, I must preach sin, Law, and judgment."

John Wesley

22 [a]NU-Text reads *who are doubting* (or *making distinctions*). 23 [a]NU-Text adds *and on some have mercy with fear* and omits *with fear* in first clause. 24 [a]M-Text reads *them.* 25 [a]NU-Text reads *To the only God our Savior.* [b]NU-Text omits *Who...is wise* and adds *Through Jesus Christ our Lord.* [c]NU-Text adds *Before all time.*

18,19 A failure to preach the Commandments of God has left an entire generation without the fear of God. They are mockers in these last days. Scripture sheds light on their secret sins: lust and sensuality.

20 "What is the reason that some believers are so much brighter and holier than others? I believe the difference, in nineteen cases out of twenty, arises from different habits about private prayer. I believe that those who are not eminently holy pray little, and those who are eminently holy pray much." *J. C. Ryle*

21 "For those who question their salvation, the best evidence is not the memory of having raised a hand or prayed a prayer. Nor is it having been baptized or christened. The true test of the authentic work of God in one's life is growth in Christlike character, increased love for God and other people, and the fruit of the Spirit (Gal. 5:22–25; James 2:18). A memorable conversion experience may serve as an important referent to God's saving work in one's life. But the ongoing work of the Holy Spirit in making a person more like Jesus is the clearest indicator that one has been made a new creation in Christ." *Erik Thoennes*

23 "The watchman who keeps silent when he sees a fire is guilty of gross neglect. The doctor who tells us we are getting well when we are dying is a false friend, and the minister who keeps back hell from his people in his sermons is neither a faithful nor a charitable man." *J. C. Ryle*

"Therefore, we should be like the prophet Ezekiel, the 'watchman on the wall,' telling our society, family, friends, and neighbors of the reality of heaven and hell. We are to be engaged in 'snatching them from the flames of judgment' (Jude 23). This act simply requires caring enough to warn of the very real danger of living without Christ. We need only tell people the truth: There is a hell to shun and a heaven to gain. We must join the apostle Paul who declared, 'It is because we know this solemn fear of the Lord that we work so hard to persuade others' (2 Cor. 5:11). It is our duty to share eternal truths with those we encounter." *Bill Bright*

"The world says you can't confront people with Jesus; you'll run them off. Where are you going to run them to? Hell number 2?" *Darrell Robinson*

Evolution: True Science Fiction

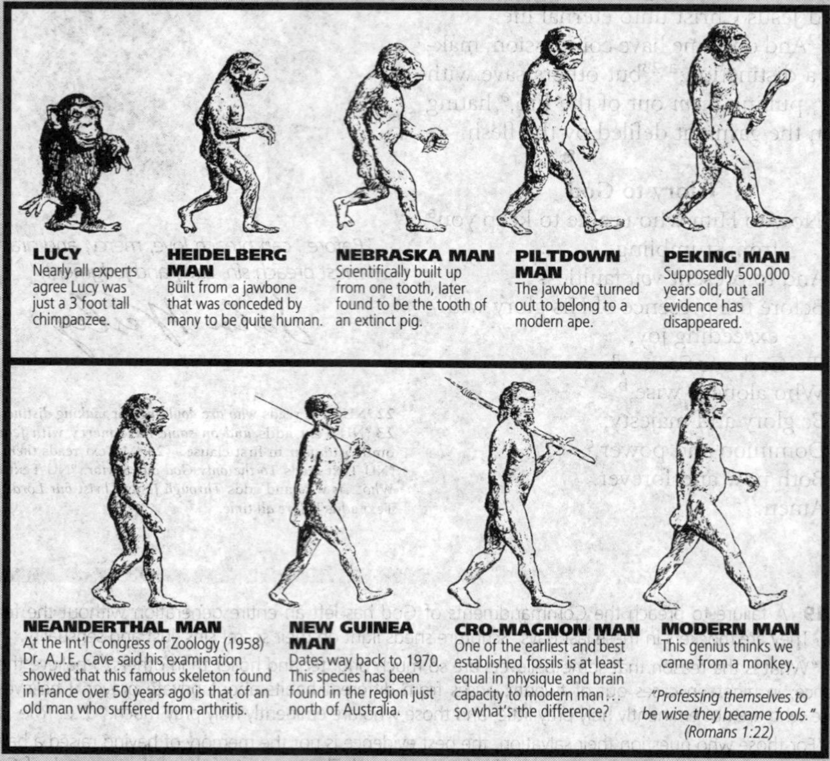

LUCY
Nearly all experts agree Lucy was just a 3 foot tall chimpanzee.
HEIDELBERG MAN
Built from a jawbone that was conceded by many to be quite human.
NEBRASKA MAN
Scientifically built up from one tooth, later found to be the tooth of an extinct pig.
PILTDOWN MAN
The jawbone turned out to belong to a modern ape.
PEKING MAN
Supposedly 500,000 years old, but all evidence has disappeared.
NEANDERTHAL MAN
At the Int'l Congress of Zoology (1958) Dr. A.J.E. Cave said his examination showed that this famous skeleton found in France over 50 years ago is that of an old man who suffered from arthritis.
NEW GUINEA MAN
Dates way back to 1970. This species has been found in the region just north of Australia.
CRO-MAGNON MAN
One of the earliest and best established fossils is at least equal in physique and brain capacity to modern man... so what's the difference?
MODERN MAN
This genius thinks we came from a monkey.
"Professing themselves to be wise they became fools." (Romans 1:22)

"In fact, evolution became in a sense a scientific religion; almost all scientists have accepted it and many are prepared to 'bend' their observations to fit in with it." *H. S. Lipson*, professor of physics, University of Manchester, UK

"We need not worry so much about what man descends from; it's what he descends to that shames the human race." *Mark Twain*

For details on the fallacy of evolution, see Isa. 42:5 comment.

Revelation

Introduction and Benediction

1 The Revelation of Jesus Christ, which
God gave Him to show His servants
—things which must shortly take place.
And He sent and signified *it* by His angel
to His servant John, 2who bore witness
to the word of God, and to the testimony
of Jesus Christ, to all things that he saw.
3Blessed *is* he who reads and those who
hear the words of this prophecy, and
keep those things which are written in it;
for the time *is* near.

Greeting the Seven Churches

4John, to the seven churches which
are in Asia:

Grace to you and peace from Him
who is and who was and who is to come,
and from the seven Spirits who are before
His throne, 5and from Jesus Christ, the
faithful witness, the firstborn from the
dead, and the ruler over the kings of the
earth.

To Him who loved us and washed[a] us
from our sins in His own blood, 6and has
made us kings[a] and priests to His God
and Father, to Him *be* glory and dominion forever and ever. Amen.

7Behold, He is coming with clouds,
and every eye will see Him, even they who
pierced Him. And all the tribes of the
earth will mourn because of Him. Even
so, Amen.

8"I am the Alpha and the Omega, *the*
Beginning and *the* End,"[a] says the Lord,[b]
"who is and who was and who is to come,
the Almighty."

Vision of the Son of Man

9I, John, both[a] your brother and companion in the tribulation and kingdom
and patience of Jesus Christ, was on the
island that is called Patmos for the word
of God and for the testimony of Jesus
Christ. 10I was in the Spirit on the Lord's
Day, and I heard behind me a loud voice,
as of a trumpet, 11saying, "I am the Alpha
and the Omega, the First and the Last,"[a]
and, "What you see, write in a book and
send *it* to the seven churches which are in
Asia:[b] to Ephesus, to Smyrna, to Pergamos,
to Thyatira, to Sardis, to Philadelphia,
and to Laodicea."

12Then I turned to see the voice that
spoke with me. And having turned I saw
seven golden lampstands, 13and in the
midst of the seven lampstands *One* like
the Son of Man, clothed with a garment
down to the feet and girded about the
chest with a golden band. 14His head and

1:5 [a]NU-Text reads *loves us and freed;* M-Text reads *loves us and washed.* 1:6 [a]NU-Text and M-Text read *a kingdom.* 1:8 [a]NU-Text and M-Text omit *the Beginning and the End.* [b]NU-Text and M-Text add *God.* 1:9 [a]NU-Text and M-Text omit *both.* 1:11 [a]NU-Text and M-Text omit *I am* through third *and.* [b]NU-Text and M-Text omit *which are in Asia.*

1:7 Second coming of Jesus: See Rev. 3:11.

QUESTIONS & OBJECTIONS

"The Bible teaches that the earth is flat."

This is often claimed because the Bible says that every eye will see Jesus at His Second Coming. However, it would seem that His coming will envelop the entire earth. The Bible actually tells us that the earth is round. For details, see Heb. 11:3 comment.

hair *were* white like wool, as white as
snow, and His eyes like a flame of fire;
[15]His feet *were* like fine brass, as if refined
in a furnace, and His voice as the sound
of many waters; [16]He had in His right hand
seven stars, out of His mouth went a
sharp two-edged sword, and His countenance *was* like the sun shining in its
strength. [17]And when I saw Him, I fell at
His feet as dead. But He laid His right hand
on me, saying to me,[a] "Do not be afraid;
I am the First and the Last. [18]I *am* He
who lives, and was dead, and behold, I
am alive forevermore. Amen. And I have
the keys of Hades and of Death. [19]Write[a]
the things which you have seen, and the
things which are, and the things which
will take place after this. [20]The mystery of
the seven stars which you saw in My right
hand, and the seven golden lampstands:
The seven stars are the angels of the seven
churches, and the seven lampstands which
you saw[a] are the seven churches.

The Loveless Church

2 "To the angel of the church of Ephesus write,

'These things says He who holds the
seven stars in His right hand, who walks
in the midst of the seven golden lampstands: [2]"I know your works, your labor,
your patience, and that you cannot bear
those who are evil. And you have tested
those who say they are apostles and are
not, and have found them liars; [3]and you
have persevered and have patience, and
have labored for My name's sake and
have not become weary. [4]Nevertheless I
have *this* against you, that you have left
your first love. [5]Remember therefore
from where you have fallen; repent and
do the first works, or else I will come to
you quickly and remove your lampstand
from its place—unless you repent. [6]But
this you have, that you hate the deeds of
the Nicolaitans, which I also hate.

[7]"He who has an ear, let him hear
what the Spirit says to the churches. To
him who overcomes I will give to eat
from the tree of life, which is in the midst
of the Paradise of God." '

The Persecuted Church

[8]"And to the angel of the church in
Smyrna write,

1:17 [a]NU-Text and M-Text omit *to me.* 1:19 [a]NU-Text and M-Text read *Therefore, write.* 1:20 [a]NU-Text and M-Text omit *which you saw.*

1:17 Perfection of mercy and love. "If you have studied the matchless purity of [Jesus'] character with adoring admiration, you must have been amazed at the absolute perfection of his manhood, and the glory of his moral and spiritual character. At such times, if you have had a true sense of your own position, you have been ready to sink into the dust, and you have exclaimed, 'Shall he wash my feet? Shall he give himself for me? Can it be that he could have loved one so stained and polluted, so mean and so beggarly, so altogether unworthy even to live, much less to be loved by such an altogether lovely one?'

"But I pray you always to remember, when you think of his perfection, that he has perfection of mercy as well as of holiness, and perfection of love to sinners as well as perfection of hatred of sin; and that, guilty as you are, you must never doubt his affection, for he has pledged you in his heart's blood, and proved his love by his death." *Charles Spurgeon*

2:4 "The nearer our souls draw to God the larger our love will grow, and the greater our love the more unselfish we shall become and the greater our care for the souls of others." *A. W. Tozer*

QUESTIONS & OBJECTIONS

"Hell is just a metaphor for the grave."

There are three words translated "hell" in Scripture:

Gehenna (Greek): The place of punishment (Matt. 5:22,29; 10:28; James 3:6)

Hades (Greek): The abode of the dead (Matt. 11:23; 16:18, Luke 16:23; Acts 2:27)

Sheol (Hebrew): The grave (Psa. 9:17; 16:10)

There are those who accept that hell is a place of punishment, but believe that the punishment is to be annihilated—to cease conscious existence. They cannot conceive that the punishment of the wicked will be conscious and *eternal*. If they are correct, then a man like Adolf Hitler, who was responsible for the deaths of millions, is being "punished" merely with eternal sleep. His fate is simply to return to the non-existent state he was in before he was born, where he is not even aware that he is being punished.

However, Scripture paints a different story. The rich man who found himself in hell (Luke 16:19–31) was conscious. He was able to feel pain, to thirst, and to experience remorse. He was not asleep in the grave; he was in a place of "torment."

If hell is a place of knowing nothing or a reference to the grave into which we go at death, Jesus' statements about hell make no sense. He said that if your hand, foot, or eye causes you to sin, it would be better to remove it than to go "into hell, into the fire that shall never be quenched—where 'Their worm does not die and the fire is not quenched'" (Mark 9:43–48).

The Bible refers to the fate of the unsaved with such fearful words as the following:

"Shame and everlasting contempt" (Dan. 12:2)

"Weeping and gnashing of teeth" (Matt. 24:51)

"Everlasting punishment" (Matt. 25:46)

"Unquenchable fire" (Luke 3:17)

"Indignation and wrath, tribulation and anguish" (Rom. 2:8,9)

"Everlasting destruction from the presence of the Lord" (2 Thess. 1:9)

"Eternal fire . . . the blackness of darkness forever" (Jude 7,13)

Revelation 14:10,11 tells us the final, eternal destiny of the sinner: "He shall be tormented with fire and brimstone . . . And the smoke of their torment ascends forever and ever; and they have no rest day or night." See also Amos 9:2 comment.

'These things says the First and the
Last, who was dead, and came to life: 9"I
know your works, tribulation, and poverty (but you are rich); and *I know* the
blasphemy of those who say they are Jews
and are not, but *are* a synagogue of Satan.
10Do not fear any of those things which
you are about to suffer. Indeed, the devil
is about to throw *some* of you into prison,
that you may be tested, and you will have
tribulation ten days. Be faithful until death,
and I will give you the crown of life.
11"He who has an ear, let him hear
what the Spirit says to the churches. He
who overcomes shall not be hurt by the
second death." '

The Compromising Church

12"And to the angel of the church in
Pergamos write,
'These things says He who has the sharp
two-edged sword: 13"I know your works,
and where you dwell, where Satan's throne
is. And you hold fast to My name, and
did not deny My faith even in the days in
which Antipas *was* My faithful martyr,
who was killed among you, where Satan
dwells. 14But I have a few things against

2:11 It has been well said that if we are born once, we will die twice (the first and the second death), but if we are born twice, we will only die once. See John chapter 3 for further details on the new birth. See Rev. 20:14 comment.

you, because you have there those who
hold the doctrine of Balaam, who taught
Balak to put a stumbling block before the
children of Israel, to eat things sacrificed
to idols, and to commit sexual immorality. 15 Thus you also have those who hold
the doctrine of the Nicolaitans, which thing
I hate.[a] 16 Repent, or else I will come to
you quickly and will fight against them
with the sword of My mouth.

17 "He who has an ear, let him hear
what the Spirit says to the churches. To
him who overcomes I will give some of
the hidden manna to eat. And I will give
him a white stone, and on the stone a
new name written which no one knows
except him who receives *it*." '

The Corrupt Church

18 "And to the angel of the church in
Thyatira write,

'These things says the Son of God,
who has eyes like a flame of fire, and His
feet like fine brass: 19 "I know your works,
love, service, faith,[a] and your patience;
and *as* for your works, the last *are* more
than the first. 20 Nevertheless I have a few
things against you, because you allow[a]
that woman[b] Jezebel, who calls herself a
prophetess, to teach and seduce[c] My servants to commit sexual immorality and
eat things sacrificed to idols. 21 And I gave
her time to repent of her sexual immorality, and she did not repent.[a] 22 Indeed I
will cast her into a sickbed, and those who
commit adultery with her into great tribulation, unless they repent of their[a] deeds.
23 I will kill her children with death, and
all the churches shall know that I am He
who searches the minds and hearts. And
I will give to each one of you according to
your works.

24 "Now to you I say, and[a] to the rest in
Thyatira, as many as do not have this doctrine, who have not known the depths of
Satan, as they say, I will[b] put on you no
other burden. 25 But hold fast what you
have till I come. 26 And he who overcomes,
and keeps My works until the end, to him
I will give power over the nations—

27 *'He shall rule them with a rod of iron;*
They shall be dashed to pieces like the
potter's vessels'[a]—

as I also have received from My Father;
28 and I will give him the morning star.
29 "He who has an ear, let him hear
what the Spirit says to the churches." '

The Dead Church

3 "And to the angel of the church in
Sardis write,

'These things says He who has the
seven Spirits of God and the seven stars:
"I know your works, that you have a
name that you are alive, but you are
dead. 2 Be watchful, and strengthen the
things which remain, that are ready to
die, for I have not found your works perfect before God.[a] 3 Remember therefore

2:15 [a]NU-Text and M-Text read *likewise* for *which thing I hate.* 2:19 [a]NU-Text and M-Text read *faith, service.* 2:20 [a]NU-Text and M-Text read *I have against you that you tolerate.* [b]M-Text reads *your wife Jezebel.* [c]NU-Text and M-Text read *and teaches and seduces.* 2:21 [a]NU-Text and M-Text read *time to repent, and she does not want to repent of her sexual immorality.* 2:22 [a]NU-Text and M-Text read *her.* 2:24 [a]NU-Text and M-Text omit *and.* [b]NU-Text and M-Text omit *will.* 2:27 [a]Psalm 2:9 3:2 [a]NU-Text and M-Text read *My God.*

2:16 "Some people do not like to hear much of repentance; but I think it is so necessary that if I should die in the pulpit, I would desire to die preaching repentance, and if out of the pulpit I would desire to die practicing it." *Matthew Henry*

2:20 "An unholy church! it is useless to the world, and of no esteem among men. It is an abomination, hell's laughter, heaven's abhorrence. The worst evils which have ever come upon the world have been brought upon her by an unholy church." *Charles Spurgeon*

3:1 "If the many activities engaged in by the average church led to the salvation of sinners or the perfecting of believers they would justify themselves easily and triumphantly; but they do not. My observations have led me to the belief that many, perhaps most, of the activities engaged in by the average church do not contribute in any way to the accomplishing of the true work of Christ on earth." *A. W. Tozer*

how you have received and heard; hold
fast and repent. Therefore if you will not
watch, I will come upon you as a thief,
and you will not know what hour I will
come upon you.
4"You[a] have a few names even in Sardis
who have not defiled their garments; and
they shall walk with Me in white, for they
are worthy. 5He who overcomes shall be
clothed in white garments, and I will not
blot out his name from the Book of Life;
but I will confess his name before My
Father and before His angels.
6"He who has an ear, let him hear what
the Spirit says to the churches." '

The Faithful Church

7"And to the angel of the church in
Philadelphia write,
'These things says He who is holy, He
who is true, *"He who has the key of David,
He who opens and no one shuts, and
shuts and no one opens"*:[a] 8"I know your
works. See, I have set before you an open
door, and no one can shut it;[a] for you
have a little strength, have kept My word,
and have not denied My name. 9Indeed I
will make *those* of the synagogue of Satan,

3:4 [a]NU-Text and M-Text read *Nevertheless you have a few names in Sardis.* 3:7 [a]Isaiah 22:22 3:8 [a]NU-Text and M-Text read *which no one can shut.*

3:8 ## *Knock, Knock! Door-to-door Evangelism*

By Emeal Zwayne

We have been commanded to *go* into all the world and share the gospel, but how exactly do we accomplish this? One approach is door-to-door evangelism—but it can be extremely nerve-racking. Just the thought of walking up to a stranger's door to share the gospel is enough to send the bravest of us into a panic attack. However, for those who are so inclined, this is a wonderful opportunity to present the soul-saving gospel of our Savior. If you are willing to be used by the Lord in this way, here are a few tips to help you in the process.

When going door-to-door, a great way to get people's attention is to begin by offering to do small handyman chores for free. This gesture is an effective way to demonstrate your care and concern for your neighbors.

To round up the necessary helpers, first set out two sign-up sheets at your church and make an announcement to the congregation. Explain that you are seeking people interested in using their handyman skills to freely serve the community when called on during an occasional weekend. Emphasize that their participation will be minimal and rarely required. (We have found that while most people sincerely appreciate the gesture to serve them, very few ever call to request assistance.) You are also looking for people interested in witnessing door to door. Once you have a reasonable number of people signed up (5 to 10, depending on your church size), specify a regular time and place that the witnessing team will meet each week (or however often you decide to go out).

Then map out the homes in your community. It is good to use a systematic approach and keep records of every address, jotting down the names of people you speak with and the responses you receive. This will come in handy for future visitations. If your church doesn't have a brochure or "calling cards," don't forget to print something containing the church contact information so people can respond to your offer. Once you create the questionnaire described below, you are ready to begin.

Always be sure to send people out in teams of two. No less (for their safety), and preferably no more (you don't want to intimidate people by appearing in a "gang" at their door!).

As you approach each door, I would recommend that you begin by saying the following:

> "Hi, how are you today? I'm sorry to bother you at your home. I'll make this really quick. My name is ____________ and this is my friend, ____________. We're from ______________, a local Christian church. We're not here to sell you anything or to get you to come to our church. We just wanted to let you know that we have a ministry set up to freely serve the community.
>
> "So, if you are ever doing any handyman work around your home—like painting, major gardening, putting up a fence, etc.—we have a team of people from our church who are eager to come out and help you. There is no charge, and absolutely no donations accepted. And let me assure you that there are no strings attached. We just want to be a blessing to you. Here is a card with our contact information. Please don't ever hesitate to call us. It would be our pleasure to serve you in any way we can.

(continued)

(3:8 continued)

"We're also conducting a really quick questionnaire today. It's only three short questions and will take only two to three minutes. Would that be okay?"

At this point, the majority of the people are overwhelmed and blessed by your offer to freely serve them, and are very open to participate in the questionnaire. The questionnaire should contain the following questions:

1. "Do you believe in the existence of any type of god or higher power?"
2. "I'm sure you've heard of something called Judgment Day. This is said to be the day when everyone will be judged by God, and receive either heaven or hell for all eternity. If there truly was a coming Day of Judgment, do you think it would be important for people to know what they would need to do in order to go to heaven and avoid hell?"
3. Depending on how they answered question 2, phrase the first part of this question in one of the following two ways:
   a. "Being that you believe this to be important,..."
   or
   b. "If you happen to be wrong and there is indeed a coming Judgment Day,..."
   "...do you think you would know what a person would need to do in order to go to heaven and avoid hell? If so, what would you say that is?"

You may want to summarize these questions on a printed questionnaire. However, it's important for members of the witnessing team to memorize these questions if possible, rather than read them. They should glance down at the questionnaire only for a second, just to remember the gist of each question, and then look the person in the eye when communicating.

On the questionnaire, place two columns beside each question where the team member can mark a yes or no. It's not necessary to write down the person's answer about how someone can go to heaven and avoid hell. If anyone asks why you're conducting the questionnaire, the honest answer should be: "We are conducting this questionnaire to familiarize ourselves with the overall spiritual perspective of our community."

Once the questions have been asked, most people will begin to open up and share their opinions. It is very important that you listen attentively and closely at this point. After they have finished sharing, transition by saying the following:

"Thank you so much. That concludes the questionnaire, but I had a couple of quick questions on a personal level: Would you consider yourself to be an open-minded person?"

Let them answer this. Then ask:

"And do you respect other people's beliefs?"

The overwhelming majority of people will answer yes to these two questions. From that point, you can springboard into the gospel by saying:

"I'm glad to hear that. Before we go, let me quickly tell you what we believe about the coming Day of Judgment, and what you can do to go to heaven and avoid hell, since this is the most important matter in the world."

During the conversation, you can refer back to the fact that they said they were open-minded and respectful of other people's beliefs, in order to reinforce what you are saying. We've found this to be quite effective. Make sure, if you are able to witness to the person, that you use the Law to bring the knowledge of sin (see 2 Sam. 12:1–14 and John 4:7 comments for details).

who say they are Jews and are not, but
lie—indeed I will make them come and
worship before your feet, and to know
that I have loved you. 10Because you have
kept My command to persevere, I also will
keep you from the hour of trial which
shall come upon the whole world, to test
those who dwell on the earth. 11Behold,[a]
I am coming quickly! Hold fast what you
have, that no one may take your crown.
12He who overcomes, I will make him a
pillar in the temple of My God, and he
shall go out no more. I will write on him
the name of My God and the name of the

3:11 [a]NU-Text and M-Text omit *Behold.*

3:11 Second coming of Jesus: See Rev. 16:15.

city of My God, the New Jerusalem, which
comes down out of heaven from My God.
And *I will write on him* My new name.
13"He who has an ear, let him hear
what the Spirit says to the churches." '

The Lukewarm Church

14"And to the angel of the church of
the Laodiceans[a] write,
'These things says the Amen, the Faithful and True Witness, the Beginning of the
creation of God: 15"I know your works,
that you are neither cold nor hot. I could
wish you were cold or hot. 16So then, because you are lukewarm, and neither
cold nor hot,[a] I will vomit you out of My
mouth. 17Because you say, 'I am rich,
have become wealthy, and have need of
nothing'—and do not know that you are
wretched, miserable, poor, blind, and
naked— 18I counsel you to buy from Me
gold refined in the fire, that you may be
rich; and white garments, that you may
be clothed, *that* the shame of your nakedness may not be revealed; and anoint your
eyes with eye salve, that you may see.
19As many as I love, I rebuke and chasten. Therefore be zealous and repent.
20Behold, I stand at the door and knock.
If anyone hears My voice and opens the
door, I will come in to him and dine with
him, and he with Me. 21To him who
overcomes I will grant to sit with Me on
My throne, as I also overcame and sat
down with My Father on His throne.
22"He who has an ear, let him hear
what the Spirit says to the churches." ' "

The Throne Room of Heaven

4 After these things I looked, and behold, a door *standing* open in heaven.
And the first voice which I heard *was*
like a trumpet speaking with me, saying,
"Come up here, and I will show you
things which must take place after this."

> The Bible in its totality ascribes only one intention to God: to save mankind. Every task of the Church makes sense and has a purpose only as it leads to the mission.
>
> **GEORG F. VICEDOM**

2Immediately I was in the Spirit; and
behold, a throne set in heaven, and *One*
sat on the throne. 3And He who sat there
was[a] like a jasper and a sardius stone in
appearance; and *there was* a rainbow
around the throne, in appearance like an
emerald. 4Around the throne *were* twenty-
four thrones, and on the thrones I saw
twenty-four elders sitting, clothed in
white robes; and they had crowns[a] of
gold on their heads. 5And from the throne

3:14 [a]NU-Text and M-Text read *in Laodicea.* 3:16 [a]NU-Text and M-Text read *hot nor cold.* 4:3 [a]M-Text omits *And He who sat there was* (which makes the description in verse 3 modify the throne rather than God). 4:4 [a]NU-Text and M-Text read *robes, with crowns.*

3:15 "The Christian world is in a deep sleep; nothing but a loud shout can awaken them out of it!" *George Whitefield*

"We are not a generation marked by passion. Passion can be lost in programs and progress reports and institutions and calendars. In doing what is good, we may fail to do what is best." *R. Albert Mohler Jr.*

"Why does the Church stay indoors? They have a theology that has dwindled into a philosophy, in which there is no thrill of faith, no terror of doom and no concern for souls. Unbelief has put out the fires of passion, and worldliness garlands the altar of sacrifice with the tawdry glitter of unreality." *Samuel Chadwick*

3:16,17 Here is a perfect description of the contemporary Church, especially in America, with its beautiful facilities, the finest music, and state-of-the-art technology. It has busied itself in everything but the will of God—to seek and save the lost. The word "evangelism" has as much attraction for the modern Church as the word "righteousness" has for the world.

3:18 See Gen. 3:7 comment.

3:20 "I want you to know that the greatest heresy in the American evangelical and Protestant Church is that 'If you pray and ask Jesus to come into your heart, He will definitely come in.' You will not find that in any place in Scripture." *Paul Washer*

proceeded lightnings, thunderings, and
voices.[a] Seven lamps of fire *were* burning
before the throne, which are the[b] seven
Spirits of God.

6Before the throne *there was*[a] a sea of
glass, like crystal. And in the midst of the
throne, and around the throne, *were* four
living creatures full of eyes in front and in
back. 7The first living creature *was* like a
lion, the second living creature like a calf,
the third living creature had a face like a
man, and the fourth living creature *was*
like a flying eagle. 8*The* four living creatures, each having six wings, were full of
eyes around and within. And they do not
rest day or night, saying:

"Holy, holy, holy,[a]
Lord God Almighty,
Who was and is and is to come!"

9Whenever the living creatures give
glory and honor and thanks to Him who
sits on the throne, who lives forever and
ever, 10the twenty-four elders fall down
before Him who sits on the throne and
worship Him who lives forever and ever,
and cast their crowns before the throne,
saying:

11"You are worthy, O Lord,[a]
To receive glory and honor and
power;
For You created all things,
And by Your will they exist[b] and were
created."

The Lamb Takes the Scroll

5 And I saw in the right *hand* of Him
who sat on the throne a scroll written
inside and on the back, sealed with seven
seals. 2Then I saw a strong angel proclaiming with a loud voice, "Who is worthy to open the scroll and to loose its
seals?" 3And no one in heaven or on the
earth or under the earth was able to
open the scroll, or to look at it.

4So I wept much, because no one was
found worthy to open and read[a] the scroll,
or to look at it. 5But one of the elders said
to me, "Do not weep. Behold, the Lion of
the tribe of Judah, the Root of David, has
prevailed to open the scroll and to loose[a]
its seven seals."

6And I looked, and behold,[a] in the
midst of the throne and of the four living
creatures, and in the midst of the elders,
stood a Lamb as though it had been slain,
having seven horns and seven eyes, which
are the seven Spirits of God sent out into
all the earth. 7Then He came and took the

"Evangelism must start with the holiness of God, the sinfulness of man, the demands of the law, and the eternal consequences of evil."

Martyn Lloyd-Jones

4:5 [a]NU-Text and M-Text read *voices, and thunderings.* [b]M-Text omits *the.* 4:6 [a]NU-Text and M-Text add *something like.* 4:8 [a]M-Text has *holy* nine times. 4:11 [a]NU-Text and M-Text read *our Lord and God.* [b]NU-Text and M-Text read *existed.* 5:4 [a]NU-Text and M-Text omit *and read.* 5:5 [a]NU-Text and M-Text omit *to loose.* 5:6 [a]NU-Text and M-Text read *I saw in the midst . . . a Lamb standing.*

4:11 This is the reason for our existence on earth. The entire creation was made for the pleasure of God. That doesn't mean that we are "God's toys" as some would suggest. Just as a father is pleased when he sees that his children have pleasure, so our pleasure is God's pleasure. Those who love God will have "pleasures forevermore" (Psa. 16:11).

scroll out of the right hand of Him who
sat on the throne.

Worthy Is the Lamb

8Now when He had taken the scroll,
the four living creatures and the twenty-
four elders fell down before the Lamb,
each having a harp, and golden bowls full
of incense, which are the prayers of the
saints. 9And they sang a new song, saying:

"You are worthy to take the scroll,
And to open its seals;
For You were slain,
And have redeemed us to God by
Your blood
Out of every tribe and tongue and
people and nation,
10And have made us[a] kings[b] and
priests to our God;
And we[c] shall reign on the earth."

. . . . . .

Why not preach that Jesus gives happiness? See 2 Cor. 2:17 comment.

. . . . . .

11Then I looked, and I heard the voice
of many angels around the throne, the
living creatures, and the elders; and the
number of them was ten thousand times
ten thousand, and thousands of thousands,
12saying with a loud voice:

"Worthy is the Lamb who was slain
To receive power and riches and
wisdom,
And strength and honor and glory
and blessing!"

13And every creature which is in heaven
and on the earth and under the earth and
such as are in the sea, and all that are in
them, I heard saying:

"Blessing and honor and glory and
power
Be to Him who sits on the throne,
And to the Lamb, forever and ever!"[a]

14Then the four living creatures said,
"Amen!" And the twenty-four[a] elders fell
down and worshiped Him who lives forever and ever.[b]

First Seal: The Conqueror

6 Now I saw when the Lamb opened
one of the seals;[a] and I heard one of
the four living creatures saying with a
voice like thunder, "Come and see." 2And
I looked, and behold, a white horse. He
who sat on it had a bow; and a crown
was given to him, and he went out conquering and to conquer.

Second Seal: Conflict on Earth

3When He opened the second seal, I
heard the second living creature saying,
"Come and see."[a] 4Another horse, fiery
red, went out. And it was granted to the
one who sat on it to take peace from the
earth, and that *people* should kill one another; and there was given to him a great
sword.

Third Seal: Scarcity on Earth

5When He opened the third seal, I
heard the third living creature say, "Come
and see." So I looked, and behold, a black
horse, and he who sat on it had a pair of
scales in his hand. 6And I heard a voice in
the midst of the four living creatures saying, "A quart[a] of wheat for a denarius,[b]

5:10 [a]NU-Text and M-Text read *them.* [b]NU-Text reads *a kingdom.* [c]NU-Text and M-Text read *they.* 5:13 [a]M-Text adds *Amen.* 5:14 [a]NU-Text and M-Text omit *twenty-four.* [b]NU-Text and M-Text omit *Him who lives forever and ever.* 6:1 [a]NU-Text and M-Text read *seven seals.* 6:3 [a]NU-Text and M-Text omit *and see.* 6:6 [a]Greek *choinix;* that is, approximately one quart [b]This was approximately one day's wage for a worker.

5:14 "Every glimpse that is given us of heaven and of God's created beings is always a glimpse of worship and rejoicing and praise because God is who He is...Any man or woman on this earth who is bored and turned off by worship is not ready for heaven." *A. W. Tozer*

and three quarts of barley for a denarius; and do not harm the oil and the wine."

Fourth Seal: Widespread Death on Earth

7When He opened the fourth seal, I heard the voice of the fourth living creature saying, "Come and see." 8So I looked, and behold, a pale horse. And the name of him who sat on it was Death, and Hades followed with him. And power was given to them over a fourth of the earth, to kill with sword, with hunger, with death, and by the beasts of the earth.

Fifth Seal: The Cry of the Martyrs

9When He opened the fifth seal, I saw under the altar the souls of those who had been slain for the word of God and for the testimony which they held. 10And they cried with a loud voice, saying, "How long, O Lord, holy and true, until You judge and avenge our blood on those who dwell on the earth?" 11Then a white robe was given to each of them; and it was said to them that they should rest a little while longer, until both *the number of* their fellow servants and their brethren, who would be killed as they *were,* was completed.

Sixth Seal: Cosmic Disturbances

12I looked when He opened the sixth seal, and behold,[a] there was a great earthquake; and the sun became black as sackcloth of hair, and the moon[b] became like blood. 13And the stars of heaven fell to the earth, as a fig tree drops its late figs when it is shaken by a mighty wind. 14Then the sky receded as a scroll when it is rolled up, and every mountain and island was moved out of its place. 15And the kings of the earth, the great men, the rich men, the commanders,[a] the mighty men, every slave and every free man, hid themselves in the caves and in the rocks of the mountains, 16and said to the mountains and rocks, "Fall on us and hide us from the face of Him who sits on the throne and from the wrath of the Lamb! 17For the great day of His wrath has come, and who is able to stand?"

> Unless we believe in a future judgment, the cutting edge of evangelism is blunted.
>
> **BILLY GRAHAM**

The Sealed of Israel

7 After these things I saw four angels standing at the four corners of the earth, holding the four winds of the earth, that the wind should not blow on the earth, on the sea, or on any tree. 2Then I saw another angel ascending from the east, having the seal of the living God. And he cried with a loud voice to the four angels to whom it was granted to

6:12 [a]NU-Text and M-Text omit *behold.* [b]NU-Text and M-Text read *the whole moon.* 6:15 [a]NU-Text and M-Text read *the commanders, the rich men.*

6:10,11 Never fear the thought that you are causing sinners to fear by referring to the Judgment. Judgment Day is the climax of the ages. It is an event for which the very creation cries out (Rom. 8:21,22). It has done so from the blood of Abel to the last injustice of this age.

With God, justice delayed is not justice denied. Every transgression against the moral Law will receive just recompense—in His time. God loves justice . . . and He will have it.

6:15 Note the truth of Prov. 11:4: "Riches do not profit in the day of wrath, but righteousness delivers from death." Those who are unrighteous—no matter how wealthy or prominent, great or mighty—all will be cowering in fear of a holy God's wrath.

6:16,17 Concern for the lost. The very thought of this terrible day should motivate the hardest heart into urgent evangelism.

"You blame me for weeping; but how can I help it when you will not weep for yourselves, although your own immortal souls are on the verge of destruction, and ought I know, you are hearing your last sermon, and may never have opportunity to have Christ offered to you." *George Whitefield*

"If you haven't got tears in your eyes, let them hear tears in your voice!" *Catherine Booth*

harm the earth and the sea, [3]saying, "Do not harm the earth, the sea, or the trees till we have sealed the servants of our God on their foreheads." [4]And I heard the number of those who were sealed. One hundred *and* forty-four thousand of all the tribes of the children of Israel *were* sealed:

[5]of the tribe of Judah twelve thousand
were sealed;[a]
of the tribe of Reuben twelve
thousand *were* sealed;
of the tribe of Gad twelve thousand
were sealed;
[6]of the tribe of Asher twelve thousand
were sealed;
of the tribe of Naphtali twelve
thousand *were* sealed;
of the tribe of Manasseh twelve
thousand *were* sealed;
[7]of the tribe of Simeon twelve
thousand *were* sealed;
of the tribe of Levi twelve thousand
were sealed;
of the tribe of Issachar twelve
thousand *were* sealed;
[8]of the tribe of Zebulun twelve
thousand *were* sealed;
of the tribe of Joseph twelve thousand
were sealed;
of the tribe of Benjamin twelve
thousand *were* sealed.

A Multitude from the Great Tribulation

[9]After these things I looked, and behold, a great multitude which no one could number, of all nations, tribes, peoples, and tongues, standing before the throne and before the Lamb, clothed with white robes, with palm branches in their hands, [10]and crying out with a loud voice, saying, "Salvation *belongs* to our God who sits on the throne, and to the Lamb!" [11]All the angels stood around the throne and the elders and the four living creatures, and fell on their faces before the throne and worshiped God, [12]saying:

"Amen! Blessing and glory and wisdom,
Thanksgiving and honor and power
and might,
Be to our God forever and ever.
Amen."

[13]Then one of the elders answered, saying to me, "Who are these arrayed in white robes, and where did they come from?"

[14]And I said to him, "Sir,[a] you know."

So he said to me, "These are the ones who come out of the great tribulation, and washed their robes and made them white in the blood of the Lamb. [15]Therefore they are before the throne of God, and serve Him day and night in His temple. And He who sits on the throne will dwell among them. [16]They shall neither hunger anymore nor thirst anymore; the sun shall not strike them, nor any heat; [17]for the Lamb who is in the midst of the throne will shepherd them and lead them to living fountains of waters.[a] And God will wipe away every tear from their eyes."

Seventh Seal: Prelude to the Seven Trumpets

8 When He opened the seventh seal, there was silence in heaven for about half an hour. [2]And I saw the seven angels who stand before God, and to them were given seven trumpets. [3]Then another angel, having a golden censer, came and stood at the altar. He was given much in-

7:5 [a]In NU-Text and M-Text *were sealed* is stated only in verses 5a and 8c; the words are understood in the remainder of the passage. 7:14 [a]NU-Text and M-Text read *My lord.* 7:17 [a]NU-Text and M-Text read *to fountains of the waters of life.*

7:4–8 These are not Jehovah's Witnesses who have been born again, as the Jehovah's Witnesses claim. (See page 1698.) The 144,000 are from the twelve tribes of Israel.

7:17 How we long for this day, and how the world will eternally regret beyond words its rejection of the gospel.

QUESTIONS & OBJECTIONS

8:11 ***"God kills masses of people in Revelation. If that's your 'God of love,' I want nothing to do with Him!"***

God does not confine His wrath to those mentioned in Revelation, or those killed in the flood of Noah's day, or the Canaanites of Joshua's day. He has proclaimed the death sentence upon the *whole* of humanity. We will all die because we have broken God's Law. Every one of us is waiting on death row. Instead of standing in moral judgment over Almighty God, we need to judge ourselves according to the Law of God. We will find that we have a multitude of sins and therefore are deserving of punishment. Yet God, out of love, paid the penalty for our sin so we would not have to. He offers everlasting life to all who repent and trust in Jesus.

cense, that he should offer *it* with the prayers of all the saints upon the golden altar which was before the throne. 4And the smoke of the incense, with the prayers of the saints, ascended before God from the angel's hand. 5Then the angel took the censer, filled it with fire from the altar, and threw *it* to the earth. And there were noises, thunderings, lightnings, and an earthquake.

6So the seven angels who had the seven trumpets prepared themselves to sound.

> Some want to live within the sound of church or chapel bell; I want to run a rescue shop within a yard of hell.
>
> C. T. STUDD

First Trumpet: Vegetation Struck

7The first angel sounded: And hail and fire followed, mingled with blood, and they were thrown to the earth.[a] And a third of the trees were burned up, and all green grass was burned up.

Second Trumpet: The Seas Struck

8Then the second angel sounded: And *something* like a great mountain burning with fire was thrown into the sea, and a third of the sea became blood. 9And a third of the living creatures in the sea died, and a third of the ships were destroyed.

Third Trumpet: The Waters Struck

10Then the third angel sounded: And a great star fell from heaven, burning like a torch, and it fell on a third of the rivers and on the springs of water. 11The name of the star is Wormwood. A third of the waters became wormwood, and many men died from the water, because it was made bitter.

Fourth Trumpet: The Heavens Struck

12Then the fourth angel sounded: And a third of the sun was struck, a third of the moon, and a third of the stars, so that a third of them were darkened. A third of the day did not shine, and likewise the night.

13And I looked, and I heard an angel[a] flying through the midst of heaven, saying with a loud voice, "Woe, woe, woe to the inhabitants of the earth, because of the remaining blasts of the trumpet of the three angels who are about to sound!"

Fifth Trumpet: The Locusts from the Bottomless Pit

9 Then the fifth angel sounded: And I saw a star fallen from heaven to the earth. To him was given the key to the bottomless pit. 2And he opened the bottomless pit, and smoke arose out of the pit like the smoke of a great furnace. So the sun and the air were darkened because of the smoke of the pit. 3Then out of the smoke locusts came upon the earth. And to them was given power, as the scorpions of the earth have power. 4They

8:7 [a]NU-Text and M-Text add *and a third of the earth was burned up.* 8:13 [a]NU-Text and M-Text read *eagle.*

were commanded not to harm the grass of the earth, or any green thing, or any tree, but only those men who do not have the seal of God on their foreheads. [5]And they were not given *authority* to kill them, but to torment them *for* five months. Their torment *was* like the torment of a scorpion when it strikes a man. [6]In those days men will seek death and will not find it; they will desire to die, and death will flee from them.

[7]The shape of the locusts was like horses prepared for battle. On their heads were crowns of something like gold, and their faces *were* like the faces of men. [8]They had hair like women's hair, and their teeth were like lions' *teeth.* [9]And they had breastplates like breastplates of iron, and the sound of their wings *was* like the sound of chariots with many horses running into battle. [10]They had tails like scorpions, and there were stings in their tails. Their power *was* to hurt men five months. [11]And they had as king over them the angel of the bottomless pit, whose name in Hebrew *is* Abaddon, but in Greek he has the name Apollyon.

[12]One woe is past. Behold, still two more woes are coming after these things.

Sixth Trumpet: The Angels from the Euphrates

[13]Then the sixth angel sounded: And I heard a voice from the four horns of the golden altar which is before God, [14]saying to the sixth angel who had the trumpet, "Release the four angels who are bound at the great river Euphrates." [15]So the four angels, who had been prepared for the hour and day and month and year, were released to kill a third of mankind. [16]Now the number of the army of the horsemen *was* two hundred million; I heard the number of them. [17]And thus I saw the horses in the vision: those who sat on them had breastplates of fiery red, hyacinth blue, and sulfur yellow; and the heads of the horses *were* like the heads of lions; and out of their mouths came fire, smoke, and brimstone. [18]By these three *plagues* a third of mankind was killed—by the fire and the smoke and the brimstone which came out of their mouths. [19]For their power[a] is in their mouth and in their tails; for their tails *are* like serpents, having heads; and with them they do harm.

[20]But the rest of mankind, who were not killed by these plagues, did not repent of the works of their hands, that they should not worship demons, and idols of gold, silver, brass, stone, and wood, which can neither see nor hear nor walk. [21]And they did not repent of their murders or their sorceries[a] or their sexual immorality or their thefts.

The Mighty Angel with the Little Book

10 I saw still another mighty angel coming down from heaven, clothed with a cloud. And a rainbow *was* on his head, his face *was* like the sun, and his

9:19 [a]NU-Text and M-Text read *the power of the horses.*
9:21 [a]NU-Text and M-Text read *drugs.*

9:9 Joel 2:1–10 relates a striking account of the coming Battle of Armageddon, the greatest of all battles. As this vision (which seems to entail flame-throwing tank warfare) was given to him approximately 2,800 years ago, the prophet relates it to the only thing he has seen in battle—horse-drawn chariots. Think of modern warfare and compare: fire goes before them (v. 3); they burn what is behind them (v. 3); they destroy everything in their path (v. 3); they move at the speed of a horse (30–40 mph, v. 4); their rumbling sounds like the noise of many chariots and the roar of a fire (v. 5); they climb over walls (v. 7); they don't break ranks (v. 7); the sword can't stop them (v. 8); they climb into houses (v. 9); they make the earth quake (v. 10).

9:21 "It is not your business to preach so many times, and to take care of this or that society; but to save as many souls as you can; to bring as many sinners as you possibly can to repentance." *John Wesley*

"Teach this post-Christian culture about God and then command repentance. That's the only message we have; without it, no one would be saved." *John MacArthur*

RIDDLE:
What is 750,000 miles long, reaches around the earth 30 times, and grows 20 miles longer each day?

ANSWER:
The line of people who are without Christ.
(For how to reach them, see 2 Sam. 12:1–14 comment.)

feet like pillars of fire. 2He had a little
book open in his hand. And he set his
right foot on the sea and *his* left *foot* on
the land, 3and cried with a loud voice, as
when a lion roars. When he cried out,
seven thunders uttered their voices. 4Now
when the seven thunders uttered their
voices,[a] I was about to write; but I heard
a voice from heaven saying to me,[b] "Seal
up the things which the seven thunders
uttered, and do not write them."
5The angel whom I saw standing on
the sea and on the land raised up his
hand[a] to heaven 6and swore by Him who
lives forever and ever, who created heaven
and the things that are in it, the earth and
the things that are in it, and the sea and
the things that are in it, that there should
be delay no longer, 7but in the days of the
sounding of the seventh angel, when he
is about to sound, the mystery of God
would be finished, as He declared to His
servants the prophets.

John Eats the Little Book

8Then the voice which I heard from
heaven spoke to me again and said, "Go,
take the little book which is open in the
hand of the angel who stands on the sea
and on the earth."
9So I went to the angel and said to
him, "Give me the little book."
And he said to me, "Take and eat it;
and it will make your stomach bitter, but
it will be as sweet as honey in your mouth."
10Then I took the little book out of the
angel's hand and ate it, and it was as sweet
as honey in my mouth. But when I had
eaten it, my stomach became bitter. 11And
he[a] said to me, "You must prophesy again
about many peoples, nations, tongues, and
kings."

The Two Witnesses

11 Then I was given a reed like a measuring rod. And the angel stood,[a]
saying, "Rise and measure the temple of
God, the altar, and those who worship
there. 2But leave out the court which is
outside the temple, and do not measure
it, for it has been given to the Gentiles.
And they will tread the holy city underfoot *for* forty-two months. 3And I will
give *power* to my two witnesses, and they
will prophesy one thousand two hundred
and sixty days, clothed in sackcloth."
4These are the two olive trees and the
two lampstands standing before the God[a]
of the earth. 5And if anyone wants to
harm them, fire proceeds from their
mouth and devours their enemies. And if
anyone wants to harm them, he must be
killed in this manner. 6These have power
to shut heaven, so that no rain falls in the
days of their prophecy; and they have
power over waters to turn them to blood,
and to strike the earth with all plagues, as
often as they desire.

The Witnesses Killed

7When they finish their testimony, the
beast that ascends out of the bottomless
pit will make war against them, overcome
them, and kill them. 8And their dead bodies *will lie* in the street of the great city
which spiritually is called Sodom and
Egypt, where also our[a] Lord was crucified. 9Then *those* from the peoples, tribes,
tongues, and nations will see their dead
bodies three-and-a-half days, and not allow[a] their dead bodies to be put into
graves. 10And those who dwell on the earth
will rejoice over them, make merry, and

10:4 [a]NU-Text and M-Text read *sounded.* [b]NU-Text and M-Text omit *to me.* 10:5 [a]NU-Text and M-Text read *right hand.* 10:11 [a]NU-Text and M-Text read *they.* 11:1 [a]NU-Text and M-Text omit *And the angel stood.* 11:4 [a]NU-Text and M-Text read *Lord.* 11:8 [a]NU-Text and M-Text read *their.* 11:9 [a]NU-Text and M-Text read *nations see . . . and will not allow.*

send gifts to one another, because these two prophets tormented those who dwell on the earth.

The Witnesses Resurrected

11Now after the three-and-a-half days the breath of life from God entered them, and they stood on their feet, and great fear fell on those who saw them. 12And they[a] heard a loud voice from heaven saying to them, "Come up here." And they ascended to heaven in a cloud, and their enemies saw them. 13In the same hour there was a great earthquake, and a tenth of the city fell. In the earthquake seven thousand people were killed, and the rest were afraid and gave glory to the God of heaven.

14The second woe is past. Behold, the third woe is coming quickly.

Seventh Trumpet: The Kingdom Proclaimed

15Then the seventh angel sounded: And there were loud voices in heaven, saying, "The kingdoms[a] of this world have become *the kingdoms* of our Lord and of His Christ, and He shall reign forever and ever!" 16And the twenty-four elders who sat before God on their thrones fell on their faces and worshiped God, 17saying:

"We give You thanks, O Lord God
Almighty,
The One who is and who was and
who is to come,[a]
Because You have taken Your great
power and reigned.
18The nations were angry, and Your
wrath has come,
And the time of the dead, that they
should be judged,
And that You should reward Your
servants the prophets and the
saints,
And those who fear Your name, small
and great,
And should destroy those who
destroy the earth."

19Then the temple of God was opened in heaven, and the ark of His covenant[a] was seen in His temple. And there were lightnings, noises, thunderings, an earthquake, and great hail.

The Woman, the Child, and the Dragon

12 Now a great sign appeared in heaven: a woman clothed with the sun, with the moon under her feet, and on her head a garland of twelve stars. 2Then being with child, she cried out in labor and in pain to give birth.

3And another sign appeared in heaven: behold, a great, fiery red dragon having seven heads and ten horns, and seven diadems on his heads. 4His tail drew a third of the stars of heaven and threw them to the earth. And the dragon stood before the woman who was ready to give birth, to devour her Child as soon as it was born. 5She bore a male Child who was to rule all nations with a rod of iron. And her Child was caught up to God and His throne. 6Then the woman fled into the wilderness, where she has a place prepared by God, that they should feed her there one thousand two hundred and sixty days.

Satan Thrown Out of Heaven

7And war broke out in heaven: Michael and his angels fought with the dragon; and the dragon and his angels fought, 8but they did not prevail, nor was a place

11:12 [a]M-Text reads *I.* 11:15 [a]NU-Text and M-Text read *kingdom... has become.* 11:17 [a]NU-Text and M-Text omit *and who is to come.* 11:19 [a]M-Text reads *the covenant of the Lord.*

11:18 These days, some would have us believe that those who "destroy the earth" are people who are not environmentally conscious. There are many who worship "Mother Earth" and think that those who harvest forests, utilize fossil fuels, and don't recycle should be punished. God has made us stewards of His creation, but we are to worship only Him, the Creator. Sinners who refuse to acknowledge Almighty God are the objects of wrath spoken of here.

They did not love their lives to the death:

"Now I have given up on everything else. I have found it to be the only way to really know Christ and to experience the mighty power that brought Him back to life again, and to find out what it means to suffer and to die with Him. So, whatever it takes, I will be one who lives in the fresh newness of life of those who are alive from the dead."

Cassie Bernall, *Columbine martyr (age 17)*

"I have no more personal friends at school. But you know what? I am not going to apologize for speaking the name of Jesus. I am not going to justify my faith to them, and I am not going to hide the light that God has put into me. If I have to sacrifice everything, I will. I will take it. If my friends have to become my enemies for me to be with my best friend, Jesus, then that's fine with me."

Rachel Scott, *Columbine martyr (age 17)*

"Father take my life, yes, my blood if Thou wilt, and consume it with Thine enveloping fire. I would not save it, for it is not mine to save. Have it Lord, have it all. Pour out my life as in oblation for the world. Blood is the only value as it flows before Thine altar."

Jim Elliot, *martyr (written at age 21)*

found for them[a] in heaven any longer.
9So the great dragon was cast out, that
serpent of old, called the Devil and Satan,
who deceives the whole world; he was
cast to the earth, and his angels were cast
out with him.
10Then I heard a loud voice saying in
heaven, "Now salvation, and strength, and
the kingdom of our God, and the power
of His Christ have come, for the accuser
of our brethren, who accused them before our God day and night, has been cast
down. 11And they overcame him by the
blood of the Lamb and by the word of
their testimony, and they did not love
their lives to the death. 12Therefore rejoice,
O heavens, and you who dwell in them!
Woe to the inhabitants of the earth and
the sea! For the devil has come down to
you, having great wrath, because he knows
that he has a short time."

The Woman Persecuted

13Now when the dragon saw that he

12:8 [a]M-Text reads *him.*

12:9 The god of this age blinds the minds of those who do not believe (2 Cor. 4:4). If they would *believe*, they would see their danger, and therefore obey the command to repent and be saved.

12:11 Here are the keys to victory in the Christian life:

1) Trust in the blood of Jesus. If sin enters our heart, we must confess it and the blood of Jesus Christ will cleanse us from all sin (1 John 1:7–9). If we do that, then the accuser will have nothing for which to accuse us before the throne of God (v. 10).
2) Our testimony is that Jesus Christ died for our sins and rose again, defeating the grave. Satan has been stripped of the power of death (Heb. 2:14).
3) We don't live to ourselves, but for the will of God. We love Jesus more than our life (Luke 14:26).

"The cross is laid on every Christian. As we embark upon discipleship we surrender ourselves to Christ in union with his death—we give over our lives to death. The cross is not the terrible end to an otherwise god-fearing and happy life, but it meets us at the beginning of our communion with Christ. When Christ calls a man, he bids him come and die." *Dietrich Bonhoeffer*

had been cast to the earth, he persecuted
the woman who gave birth to the male
Child. 14But the woman was given two
wings of a great eagle, that she might fly
into the wilderness to her place, where
she is nourished for a time and times and
half a time, from the presence of the serpent. 15So the serpent spewed water out
of his mouth like a flood after the woman,
that he might cause her to be carried
away by the flood. 16But the earth helped
the woman, and the earth opened its
mouth and swallowed up the flood which
the dragon had spewed out of his mouth.

> If persecution should arise, you should be willing to part with all that you possess—with your liberty, with your life itself, for Christ—or you cannot be His disciple.
>
> **CHARLES SPURGEON**

17And the dragon was enraged with the
woman, and he went to make war with
the rest of her offspring, who keep the
commandments of God and have the testimony of Jesus Christ.[a]

The Beast from the Sea

13 Then I[a] stood on the sand of the
sea. And I saw a beast rising up
out of the sea, having seven heads and
ten horns,[b] and on his horns ten crowns,
and on his heads a blasphemous name.
2Now the beast which I saw was like a
leopard, his feet were like *the feet of* a
bear, and his mouth like the mouth of a
lion. The dragon gave him his power, his
throne, and great authority. 3And I saw
one of his heads as if it had been mortally
wounded, and his deadly wound was
healed. And all the world marveled and
followed the beast. 4So they worshiped
the dragon who gave authority to the
beast; and they worshiped the beast, saying, "Who *is* like the beast? Who is able
to make war with him?"
5And he was given a mouth speaking
great things and blasphemies, and he was
given authority to continue[a] for forty-two
months. 6Then he opened his mouth in
blasphemy against God, to blaspheme
His name, His tabernacle, and those who
dwell in heaven. 7It was granted to him
to make war with the saints and to overcome them. And authority was given him
over every tribe,[a] tongue, and nation. 8All
who dwell on the earth will worship him,
whose names have not been written in
the Book of Life of the Lamb slain from
the foundation of the world.
9If anyone has an ear, let him hear.
10He who leads into captivity shall go into
captivity; he who kills with the sword
must be killed with the sword. Here is
the patience and the faith of the saints.

The Beast from the Earth

11Then I saw another beast coming up
out of the earth, and he had two horns
like a lamb and spoke like a dragon.
12And he exercises all the authority of the
first beast in his presence, and causes the
earth and those who dwell in it to worship the first beast, whose deadly wound
was healed. 13He performs great signs, so
that he even makes fire come down from
heaven on the earth in the sight of men.
14And he deceives those[a] who dwell on
the earth by those signs which he was
granted to do in the sight of the beast,
telling those who dwell on the earth to
make an image to the beast who was
wounded by the sword and lived. 15He
was granted *power* to give breath to the
image of the beast, that the image of the
beast should both speak and cause as
many as would not worship the image of
the beast to be killed. 16He causes all,
both small and great, rich and poor, free
and slave, to receive a mark on their right
hand or on their foreheads, 17and that no
one may buy or sell except one who has
the mark or[a] the name of the beast, or the

12:17 [a]NU-Text and M-Text omit *Christ.* 13:1 [a]NU-Text reads *he.* [b]NU-Text and M-Text read *ten horns and seven heads.* 13:5 [a]M-Text reads *make war.* 13:7 [a]NU-Text and M-Text add *and people.* 13:14 [a]M-Text reads *my own people.* 13:17 [a]NU-Text and M-Text omit *or.*

Did the Church persecute Galileo?
See 1 Tim. 6:20 comment.

Galileo

number of his name.
18Here is wisdom. Let him who has
understanding calculate the number of
the beast, for it is the number of a man:
His number *is* 666.

The Lamb and the 144,000

14 Then I looked, and behold, a[a] Lamb
standing on Mount Zion, and with
Him one hundred *and* forty-four thousand, having[b] His Father's name written
on their foreheads. 2And I heard a voice
from heaven, like the voice of many waters, and like the voice of loud thunder.
And I heard the sound of harpists playing
their harps. 3They sang as it were a new
song before the throne, before the four
living creatures, and the elders; and no
one could learn that song except the hundred *and* forty-four thousand who were
redeemed from the earth. 4These are the
ones who were not defiled with women,
for they are virgins. These are the ones
who follow the Lamb wherever He goes.
These were redeemed[a] from *among* men,
being firstfruits to God and to the Lamb.
5And in their mouth was found no deceit,[a] for they are without fault before the
throne of God.[b]

The Proclamations of Three Angels

6Then I saw another angel flying in the
midst of heaven, having the everlasting
gospel to preach to those who dwell on
the earth—to every nation, tribe, tongue,
and people— 7saying with a loud voice,
"Fear God and give glory to Him, for the
hour of His judgment has come; and worship Him who made heaven and earth,
the sea and springs of water."

14:1 [a]NU-Text and M-Text read *the.* [b]NU-Text and M-Text add *His name and.* 14:4 [a]M-Text adds *by Jesus.* 14:5 [a]NU-Text and M-Text read *falsehood.* [b]NU-Text and M-Text omit *before the throne of God.*

14:6 We have the great honor of preaching "the everlasting gospel," which is for *all* who dwell on the earth.

14:7 Law of probabilities refutes evolution. "The chance that higher life forms might have emerged in this way is comparable to the chance that a tornado sweeping through a junkyard might assemble a Boeing 747 from the materials therein." *Sir Fred Hoyle*, professor of astronomy, Cambridge University

"The likelihood of the formation of life from inanimate matter is one out of $10^{40,000}$... It is big enough to bury Darwin and the whole theory of evolution. There was no primeval soup, neither on this planet nor on any other, and if the beginnings of life were not random, they must therefore have been the product of purposeful intelligence." *Sir Fred Hoyle, Evolution from Space*

"I believe that Darwin's mechanism for evolution doesn't explain much of what is seen under a microscope. Cells are simply too complex to have evolved randomly. Intelligence was required to produce them." *Michael J. Behe*

"Contrary to the popular notion that only creationism relies on the supernatural, evolutionism must as well, since the probabilities of random formation of life are so tiny as to require a 'miracle' for spontaneous generation tantamount to a theological argument." *Chandra Wickramasinghe*

George Gallup, the famous statistician, said, "I could prove God statistically. Take the human body alone—the chance that all the functions of the individual would just happen is just a statistical monstrosity."

8And another angel followed, saying,
"Babylon[a] is fallen, is fallen, that great city,
because she has made all nations drink of
the wine of the wrath of her fornication."
9Then a third angel followed them,
saying with a loud voice, "If anyone worships the beast and his image, and receives *his* mark on his forehead or on his
hand, 10he himself shall also drink of the
wine of the wrath of God, which is poured
out full strength into the cup of His indignation. He shall be tormented with
fire and brimstone in the presence of the
holy angels and in the presence of the
Lamb. 11And the smoke of their torment
ascends forever and ever; and they have
no rest day or night, who worship the beast
and his image, and whoever receives the
mark of his name."
12Here is the patience of the saints;
here *are* those[a] who keep the commandments of God and the faith of Jesus.
13Then I heard a voice from heaven saying to me,[a] "Write: 'Blessed *are* the dead
who die in the Lord from now on.' "

"Yes," says the Spirit, "that they may rest from their labors, and their works follow them."

Reaping the Earth's Harvest

14Then I looked, and behold, a white
cloud, and on the cloud sat *One* like the
Son of Man, having on His head a golden
crown, and in His hand a sharp sickle.
15And another angel came out of the temple, crying with a loud voice to Him who
sat on the cloud, "Thrust in Your sickle
and reap, for the time has come for You[a]
to reap, for the harvest of the earth is
ripe." 16So He who sat on the cloud thrust
in His sickle on the earth, and the earth
was reaped.

Reaping the Grapes of Wrath

17Then another angel came out of the
temple which is in heaven, he also having
a sharp sickle.
18And another angel came out from the
altar, who had power over fire, and he
cried with a loud cry to him who had the
sharp sickle, saying, "Thrust in your sharp
sickle and gather the clusters of the vine
of the earth, for her grapes are fully ripe."
19So the angel thrust his sickle into the
earth and gathered the vine of the earth,
and threw *it* into the great winepress of
the wrath of God. 20And the winepress
was trampled outside the city, and blood
came out of the winepress, up to the
horses' bridles, for one thousand six hundred furlongs.

Prelude to the Bowl Judgments

15 Then I saw another sign in heaven, great and marvelous: seven angels having the seven last plagues, for in them the wrath of God is complete.

14:8 [a]NU-Text reads *Babylon the great is fallen,* is fallen, which has made; M-Text reads *Babylon the great is fallen. She has made.* 14:12 [a]NU-Text and M-Text omit *here are those.* 14:13 [a]NU-Text and M-Text omit *to me.* 14:15 [a]NU-Text and M-Text omit *for You.*

14:10 Warning of hell. "In His approximately 42 months of public ministry, there are 33 recorded instances of Jesus speaking about hell. No doubt He warned of hell thousands of times. The Bible refers to hell a total of 167 times.

"I wonder with what frequency this eternal subject is found in today's pulpits. I confess I have failed in my ministry to declare the reality of hell as often as I have the love of God and the benefits of a personal relationship with Christ. But Jesus spent more of His time warning His listeners of the impending judgment of hell than speaking of the joys of heaven...

"I have never felt the need to focus on telling people about hell. However, as a result of a steady decline in morals and spiritual vitality in today's culture and a growing indifference to the afterlife, I have come to realize the need for a greater discussion of hell... I have thus come to see that silence, or even benign neglect on these subjects, is disobedience on my part. To be silent on the eternal destinations of souls is to be like a sentry failing to warn his fellow soldiers of impending attack. It is like knowing calamity is coming and not sounding the alarm." *Bill Bright*

14:13 If we die in the Lord, our works follow us. No good deed will be forgotten by God.

2And I saw *something* like a sea of glass mingled with fire, and those who have the victory over the beast, over his image and over his mark[a] *and* over the number of his name, standing on the sea of glass, having harps of God. 3They sing the song of Moses, the servant of God, and the song of the Lamb, saying:

"Great and marvelous *are* Your works,
Lord God Almighty!
Just and true *are* Your ways,
O King of the saints![a]
4Who shall not fear You, O Lord, and
glorify Your name?
For *You* alone *are* holy.
For all nations shall come and
worship before You,
For Your judgments have been
manifested."

5After these things I looked, and behold,[a] the temple of the tabernacle of the testimony in heaven was opened. 6And out of the temple came the seven angels having the seven plagues, clothed in pure bright linen, and having their chests girded with golden bands. 7Then one of the four living creatures gave to the seven angels seven golden bowls full of the wrath of God who lives forever and ever. 8The temple was filled with smoke from the glory of God and from His power, and no one was able to enter the temple till the seven plagues of the seven angels were completed.

. . . . . .

Could the amazing seeing eye have come about purely by blind chance? *See Prov. 20:12 comment.*

. . . . . .

16 Then I heard a loud voice from the temple saying to the seven angels, "Go and pour out the bowls[a] of the wrath of God on the earth."

First Bowl: Loathsome Sores

2So the first went and poured out his bowl upon the earth, and a foul and loathsome sore came upon the men who had the mark of the beast and those who worshiped his image.

Second Bowl: The Sea Turns to Blood

3Then the second angel poured out his bowl on the sea, and it became blood as of a dead *man;* and every living creature in the sea died.

Third Bowl: The Waters Turn to Blood

4Then the third angel poured out his bowl on the rivers and springs of water, and they became blood. 5And I heard the angel of the waters saying:

"You are righteous, O Lord,[a]
The One who is and who was and
who is to be,[b]
Because You have judged these
things.
6For they have shed the blood of
saints and prophets,
And You have given them blood to
drink.
For[a] it is their just due."

7And I heard another from[a] the altar saying, "Even so, Lord God Almighty, true and righteous *are* Your judgments."

Fourth Bowl: Men Are Scorched

8Then the fourth angel poured out his bowl on the sun, and power was given to him to scorch men with fire. 9And men were scorched with great heat, and they blasphemed the name of God who has power over these plagues; and they did not repent and give Him glory.

Fifth Bowl: Darkness and Pain

10Then the fifth angel poured out his bowl on the throne of the beast, and his

15:2 [a]NU-Text and M-Text omit *over his mark.* 15:3 [a]NU-Text and M-Text read *nations.* 15:5 [a]NU-Text and M-Text omit *behold.* 16:1 [a]NU-Text and M-Text read *seven bowls.* 16:5 [a]NU-Text and M-Text omit *O Lord.* [b]NU-Text and M-Text read *who was, the Holy One.* 16:6 [a]NU-Text and M-Text omit *For.* 16:7 [a]NU-Text and M-Text omit *another from.*

kingdom became full of darkness; and they gnawed their tongues because of the pain. [11]They blasphemed the God of heaven because of their pains and their sores, and did not repent of their deeds.

Sixth Bowl: Euphrates Dried Up

[12]Then the sixth angel poured out his bowl on the great river Euphrates, and its water was dried up, so that the way of the kings from the east might be prepared. [13]And I saw three unclean spirits like frogs *coming* out of the mouth of the dragon, out of the mouth of the beast, and out of the mouth of the false prophet. [14]For they are spirits of demons, performing signs, *which* go out to the kings of the earth and[a] of the whole world, to gather them to the battle of that great day of God Almighty.

[15]"Behold, I am coming as a thief. Blessed *is* he who watches, and keeps his garments, lest he walk naked and they see his shame."

[16]And they gathered them together to the place called in Hebrew, Armageddon.[a]

Seventh Bowl: The Earth Utterly Shaken

[17]Then the seventh angel poured out his bowl into the air, and a loud voice came out of the temple of heaven, from the throne, saying, "It is done!" [18]And there were noises and thunderings and lightnings; and there was a great earthquake, such a mighty and great earthquake as had not occurred since men were on the earth. [19]Now the great city was divided into three parts, and the cities of the nations fell. And great Babylon was remembered before God, to give her the cup of the wine of the fierceness of His wrath. [20]Then every island fled away, and the mountains were not found. [21]And great hail from heaven fell upon men, *each hailstone* about the weight of a talent. Men blasphemed God because of the plague of the hail, since that plague was exceedingly great.

The Scarlet Woman and the Scarlet Beast

17 Then one of the seven angels who had the seven bowls came and talked with me, saying to me,[a] "Come, I will show you the judgment of the great harlot who sits on many waters, [2]with whom the kings of the earth committed fornication, and the inhabitants of the earth were made drunk with the wine of her fornication."

[3]So he carried me away in the Spirit into the wilderness. And I saw a woman sitting on a scarlet beast *which was* full of

16:14 [a]NU-Text and M-Text omit *of the earth and.* 16:16 [a]M-Text reads *Megiddo.* 17:1 [a]NU-Text and M-Text omit *to me.*

16:15 Second coming of Jesus: See Rev. 22:20.

16:16 Ezekiel 39, written over 2,500 years ago, speaks of God's judgment upon the enemies of Israel. Verses 12–15 describe what will happen after what many see as the Battle of Armageddon:

> For seven months the house of Israel will be burying them, in order to cleanse the land. Indeed all the people of the land will be burying . . . They will set apart men regularly employed, with the help of a search party, to pass through the land and bury those bodies remaining on the ground, in order to cleanse it. At the end of seven months they will make a search. The search party will pass through the land; and when anyone sees a man's bone, he shall set up a marker by it, till the buriers have buried it in the Valley of Hamon Gog.

Before the days of nuclear warfare, this portion of the Bible would have made no sense to the reader. We are told that even the weapons left by the enemy will have to be burned (Ezek. 39:9). So many will die that it will take those specially employed for the purpose seven months to bury the dead (v. 14). The Scriptures are very specific about the method of burial. When even a bone is found by searchers, a special marker is to be placed near the bone until the buriers have buried it. This would seem to be a clear reference to radioactive contamination after nuclear war. This thought is confirmed in Joel 2:30, which speaks of "pillars of smoke."

names of blasphemy, having seven heads
and ten horns. [4]The woman was arrayed
in purple and scarlet, and adorned with
gold and precious stones and pearls, having
in her hand a golden cup full of abominations and the filthiness of her fornication.[a] [5]And on her forehead a name *was*
written:

MYSTERY, BABYLON THE GREAT,
THE MOTHER OF HARLOTS AND
OF THE ABOMINATIONS
OF THE EARTH.

[6]I saw the woman, drunk with the blood
of the saints and with the blood of the
martyrs of Jesus. And when I saw her, I
marveled with great amazement.

The Meaning of the Woman and the Beast

[7]But the angel said to me, "Why did
you marvel? I will tell you the mystery of
the woman and of the beast that carries
her, which has the seven heads and the
ten horns. [8]The beast that you saw was,
and is not, and will ascend out of the bottomless pit and go to perdition. And those
who dwell on the earth will marvel, whose
names are not written in the Book of Life
from the foundation of the world, when
they see the beast that was, and is not,
and yet is.[a]

[9]"Here *is* the mind which has wisdom:
The seven heads are seven mountains on
which the woman sits. [10]There are also
seven kings. Five have fallen, one is, *and*
the other has not yet come. And when he
comes, he must continue a short time.
[11]The beast that was, and is not, is himself also the eighth, and is of the seven,
and is going to perdition.

[12]"The ten horns which you saw are
ten kings who have received no kingdom
as yet, but they receive authority for one
hour as kings with the beast. [13]These are
of one mind, and they will give their
power and authority to the beast. [14]These
will make war with the Lamb, and the
Lamb will overcome them, for He is Lord
of lords and King of kings; and those *who*
are with Him *are* called, chosen, and
faithful."

[15]Then he said to me, "The waters
which you saw, where the harlot sits, are
peoples, multitudes, nations, and tongues.
[16]And the ten horns which you saw on[a]
the beast, these will hate the harlot, make
her desolate and naked, eat her flesh and
burn her with fire. [17]For God has put it
into their hearts to fulfill His purpose, to
be of one mind, and to give their kingdom to the beast, until the words of God
are fulfilled. [18]And the woman whom you
saw is that great city which reigns over
the kings of the earth."

The Fall of Babylon the Great

18 After these things I saw another
angel coming down from heaven,
having great authority, and the earth was
illuminated with his glory. [2]And he cried
mightily[a] with a loud voice, saying, "Babylon the great is fallen, is fallen, and has
become a dwelling place of demons, a
prison for every foul spirit, and a cage for
every unclean and hated bird! [3]For all the
nations have drunk of the wine of the
wrath of her fornication, the kings of the
earth have committed fornication with
her, and the merchants of the earth have
become rich through the abundance of
her luxury."

[4]And I heard another voice from heaven
saying, "Come out of her, my people, lest
you share in her sins, and lest you receive
of her plagues. [5]For her sins have reached[a]
to heaven, and God has remembered her
iniquities. [6]Render to her just as she rendered to you,[a] and repay her double according to her works; in the cup which
she has mixed, mix double for her. [7]In
the measure that she glorified herself and
lived luxuriously, in the same measure
give her torment and sorrow; for she says
in her heart, 'I sit *as* queen, and am no

17:4 [a]M-Text reads *the filthiness of the fornication of the earth.* 17:8 [a]NU-Text and M-Text read *and shall be present.* 17:16 [a]NU-Text and M-Text read *saw, and the beast.* 18:2 [a]NU-Text and M-Text omit *mightily.* 18:5 [a]NU-Text and M-Text read *have been heaped up.* 18:6 [a]NU-Text and M-Text omit *to you.*

widow, and will not see sorrow.' 8Therefore her plagues will come in one day—death and mourning and famine. And she will be utterly burned with fire, for strong *is* the Lord God who judges[a] her.

The World Mourns Babylon's Fall

9"The kings of the earth who committed fornication and lived luxuriously with her will weep and lament for her, when they see the smoke of her burning, 10standing at a distance for fear of her torment, saying, 'Alas, alas, that great city Babylon, that mighty city! For in one hour your judgment has come.'

> Let us save men by all means under heaven; let us prevent men going down to hell. We are not half as earnest as we ought to be.
>
> **CHARLES SPURGEON**

11"And the merchants of the earth will weep and mourn over her, for no one buys their merchandise anymore: 12merchandise of gold and silver, precious stones and pearls, fine linen and purple, silk and scarlet, every kind of citron wood, every kind of object of ivory, every kind of object of most precious wood, bronze, iron, and marble; 13and cinnamon and incense, fragrant oil and frankincense, wine and oil, fine flour and wheat, cattle and sheep, horses and chariots, and bodies and souls of men. 14The fruit that your soul longed for has gone from you, and all the things which are rich and splendid have gone from you,[a] and you shall find them no more at all. 15The merchants of these things, who became rich by her, will stand at a distance for fear of her torment, weeping and wailing, 16and saying, 'Alas, alas, that great city that was clothed in fine linen, purple, and scarlet, and adorned with gold and precious stones and pearls! 17For in one hour such great riches came to nothing.' Every shipmaster, all who travel by ship, sailors, and as many as trade on the sea, stood at a distance 18and cried out when they saw the smoke of her burning, saying, 'What *is* like this great city?'

19"They threw dust on their heads and cried out, weeping and wailing, and saying, 'Alas, alas, that great city, in which all who had ships on the sea became rich by her wealth! For in one hour she is made desolate.'

20"Rejoice over her, O heaven, and *you* holy apostles[a] and prophets, for God has avenged you on her!"

Finality of Babylon's Fall

21Then a mighty angel took up a stone like a great millstone and threw *it* into the sea, saying, "Thus with violence the great city Babylon shall be thrown down, and shall not be found anymore. 22The sound of harpists, musicians, flutists, and trumpeters shall not be heard in you anymore. No craftsman of any craft shall be found in you anymore, and the sound of a millstone shall not be heard in you anymore. 23The light of a lamp shall not shine in you anymore, and the voice of bridegroom and bride shall not be heard in you anymore. For your merchants were the great men of the earth, for by your sorcery all the nations were deceived. 24And in her was found the blood of prophets and saints, and of all who were slain on the earth."

Heaven Exults over Babylon

19 After these things I heard[a] a loud voice of a great multitude in heaven, saying, "Alleluia! Salvation and glory and honor and power *belong* to the Lord[b] our God! 2For true and righteous *are* His judgments, because He has judged the great harlot who corrupted the earth with her fornication; and He has avenged on her the blood of His servants *shed* by her." 3Again they said, "Alleluia! Her smoke rises up forever and ever!" 4And the twenty-four elders and the four living creatures

18:8 [a]NU-Text and M-Text read *has judged.* 18:14 [a]NU-Text and M-Text read *been lost to you.* 18:20 [a]NU-Text and M-Text read *saints and apostles.* 19:1 [a]NU-Text and M-Text add *something like.* [b]NU-Text and M-Text omit *the Lord.*

fell down and worshiped God who sat on the throne, saying, "Amen! Alleluia!" 5Then a voice came from the throne, saying, "Praise our God, all you His servants and those who fear Him, both[a] small and great!"

6And I heard, as it were, the voice of a great multitude, as the sound of many waters and as the sound of mighty thunderings, saying, "Alleluia! For the[a] Lord God Omnipotent reigns! 7Let us be glad and rejoice and give Him glory, for the marriage of the Lamb has come, and His wife has made herself ready." 8And to her it was granted to be arrayed in fine linen, clean and bright, for the fine linen is the righteous acts of the saints.

9Then he said to me, "Write: 'Blessed *are* those who are called to the marriage supper of the Lamb!' " And he said to me, "These are the true sayings of God." 10And I fell at his feet to worship him. But he said to me, "See *that you do* not *do that!* I am your fellow servant, and of your brethren who have the testimony of Jesus. Worship God! For the testimony of Jesus is the spirit of prophecy."

Christ on a White Horse

11Now I saw heaven opened, and behold, a white horse. And He who sat on him *was* called Faithful and True, and in righteousness He judges and makes war. 12His eyes *were* like a flame of fire, and on His head *were* many crowns. He had[a] a name written that no one knew except Himself. 13He *was* clothed with a robe dipped in blood, and His name is called The Word of God. 14And the armies in heaven, clothed in fine linen, white and clean,[a] followed Him on white horses. 15Now out of His mouth goes a sharp[a] sword, that with it He should strike the nations. And He Himself will rule them with a rod of iron. He Himself treads the winepress of the fierceness and wrath of Almighty God. 16And He has on *His* robe and on His thigh a name written:

KING OF KINGS AND
LORD OF LORDS.

The Beast and His Armies Defeated

17Then I saw an angel standing in the sun; and he cried with a loud voice, saying to all the birds that fly in the midst of heaven, "Come and gather together for the supper of the great God,[a] 18that you may eat the flesh of kings, the flesh of captains, the flesh of mighty men, the flesh of horses and of those who sit on them, and the flesh of all *people,* free[a] and slave, both small and great."

19And I saw the beast, the kings of the earth, and their armies, gathered together to make war against Him who sat on the horse and against His army. 20Then the beast was captured, and with him the false prophet who worked signs in his presence, by which he deceived those who received the mark of the beast and those who worshiped his image. These two were cast alive into the lake of fire burning with brimstone. 21And the rest were killed with the sword which proceeded from the mouth of Him who sat on the horse. And all the birds were filled with their flesh.

Satan Bound 1000 Years

20 Then I saw an angel coming down from heaven, having the key to the bottomless pit and a great chain in his hand. 2He laid hold of the dragon, that serpent of old, who is *the* Devil and Satan, and bound him for a thousand years; 3and he cast him into the bottomless pit, and shut him up, and set a seal on him,

19:5 [a]NU-Text and M-Text omit *both.* 19:6 [a]NU-Text and M-Text read *our.* 19:12 [a]M-Text adds *names written, and.* 19:14 [a]NU-Text and M-Text read *pure white linen.* 19:15 [a]M-Text adds *two-edged.* 19:17 [a]NU-Text and M-Text read *the great supper of God.* 19:18 [a]NU-Text and M-Text read *both free.*

19:5 "Step into the average church these days and you will likely see that the services are designed more to remove the fear of God than to promote it." *Steven J. Lawson*

so that he should deceive the nations no
more till the thousand years were finished. But after these things he must be
released for a little while.

The Saints Reign with Christ 1000 Years

4And I saw thrones, and they sat on
them, and judgment was committed to
them. Then *I saw* the souls of those who
had been beheaded for their witness to
Jesus and for the word of God, who had
not worshiped the beast or his image,
and had not received *his* mark on their
foreheads or on their hands. And they
lived and reigned with Christ for a[a] thousand years. 5But the rest of the dead did
not live again until the thousand years
were finished. This *is* the first resurrection. 6Blessed and holy *is* he who has part
in the first resurrection. Over such the
second death has no power, but they
shall be priests of God and of Christ, and
shall reign with Him a thousand years.

Satanic Rebellion Crushed

7Now when the thousand years have
expired, Satan will be released from his
prison 8and will go out to deceive the nations which are in the four corners of the
earth, Gog and Magog, to gather them together to battle, whose number *is* as the
sand of the sea. 9They went up on the
breadth of the earth and surrounded the
camp of the saints and the beloved city.
And fire came down from God out of
heaven and devoured them. 10The devil,
who deceived them, was cast into the
lake of fire and brimstone where[a] the
beast and the false prophet *are*. And they
will be tormented day and night forever
and ever.

The Great White Throne Judgment

11Then I saw a great white throne and
Him who sat on it, from whose face the
earth and the heaven fled away. And
there was found no place for them. 12And
I saw the dead, small and great, standing
before God,[a] and books were opened.

> All roads lead to the judgment seat of Christ.
>
> **KEITH GREEN**

And another book was opened, which is
the Book of Life. And the dead were judged
according to their works, by the things
which were written in the books. 13The
sea gave up the dead who were in it, and
Death and Hades delivered up the dead
who were in them. And they were judged,
each one according to his works. 14Then
Death and Hades were cast into the lake

20:4 [a]M-Text reads *the*. 20:10 [a]NU-Text and M-Text add *also*. 20:12 [a]NU-Text and M-Text read *the throne*.

20:11 No hiding from God. "Whither can the enemies of God flee? If up to heaven their high-flown impudence could carry them, His right hand of holiness would hurl them thence, or, if under hell's profoundest wave they dive, to seek a sheltering grave, His left hand would pluck them out of the fire, to expose them to the fiercer light of His countenance. Nowhere is there a refuge from the Most High. The morning beams cannot convey the fugitive so swiftly as the almighty Pursuer would follow him; neither can the mysterious lightning flash, which annihilates time and space, journey so rapidly as to escape His far-reaching hand. 'If I mount up to heaven, thou art there; if I make my bed in hell, thou art there.'

"It was said of the Roman Empire under the Caesars that the whole world was only one great prison for Caesar, for if any man offended the emperor it was impossible for him to escape. If he crossed the Alps, could not Caesar find him out in Gaul? If he sought to hide himself in the Indies, even the swarthy monarchs there knew the power of the Roman arms, so that they would give no shelter to a man who had incurred imperial vengeance. And yet, perhaps, a fugitive from Rome might have prolonged his miserable life by hiding in the dens and caves of the earth.

"But oh! sinner, there is no hiding from God. The mountains cannot cover you from Him, even if they would, neither can the rocks conceal you. See, then, at the very outset how this throne should awe our minds with terror. Founded in right, sustained by might, and universal in its dominion, look ye and see the throne which John of old beheld." *Charles Spurgeon*

QUESTIONS & OBJECTIONS

20:14

"Since the wages of sin is death, I'll be okay because when I die I will have paid for my sins."

It is true that the Bible says, "The wages of sin is death" (Rom. 6:23). Those who say such things are gambling the whole of their eternity on the meaning of one word: "death." They assume it means the "termination of existence," but their assumption is erroneous, as a little reasoning should reveal.

For instance, Hitler was responsible for the cruel deaths of six million Jews, many of whom were children. Was his death the "wages" of his unspeakably terrible sins? If death is the end, then God will give you the exact same wages as Hitler. That would mean that God is unjust, which is unthinkable.

The person who believes that our demise is the end is in for the shock of their death. Their physical death (separation from their body) is just the beginning. There is going to be a resurrection of every human being, both "the just and the unjust" (see Acts 24:15). This is not referring to the good and the bad, because the Scriptures tell us that there are no "good" people (see Psa. 14:1–3; Mark 10:18). There are only those who have been made "just" before God, by the shed blood of Jesus Christ.

Through the gospel, God freely justifies all those who come in childlike faith to the Savior. That means He proclaims us innocent—as though we had never sinned in the first place—and we become part of the "just." However, those who die in their sins, the "unjust," will "fall into the hands of the living God" (Heb. 10:31). That is a very fearful thing, because He will give them justice—their exact wages due to them—and if that happens, there will be hell to pay. They will be thrown into the lake of fire, "which is the second death" (Rev. 20:14; 21:8). See also Gen. 2:17 comment.

of fire. This is the second death.[a] 15And
anyone not found written in the Book of
Life was cast into the lake of fire.

All Things Made New

21 Now I saw a new heaven and a new
earth, for the first heaven and the
first earth had passed away. Also there
was no more sea. 2Then I, John,[a] saw the
holy city, New Jerusalem, coming down
out of heaven from God, prepared as a
bride adorned for her husband. 3And I
heard a loud voice from heaven saying,
"Behold, the tabernacle of God *is* with men,
and He will dwell with them, and they
shall be His people. God Himself will be
with them *and be* their God. 4And God
will wipe away every tear from their eyes;
there shall be no more death, nor sorrow,
nor crying. There shall be no more pain,
for the former things have passed away."
5Then He who sat on the throne said,
"Behold, I make all things new." And He
said to me,[a] "Write, for these words are
true and faithful."

20:14 [a]NU-Text and M-Text add *the lake of fire.* 21:2 [a]NU-Text and M-Text omit *John.* 21:5 [a]NU-Text and M-Text omit *to me.*

20:13 "God predicts judgment for the ungodly: 'It is mine to avenge; I will repay. In due time their foot will slip; their day of disaster is near and their doom rushes upon them.' Yet many live as though they will never be judged. They scoff at the idea of an eternal hell. The final judgment has, however, been part of the biblical message for thousands of years. The Holy Spirit inspired Paul to write this ominous warning: 'Because of your stubbornness and your unrepentant heart, you are storing up wrath against yourself for the day of God's wrath, when His righteous judgment will be revealed.'" *Bill Bright*

20:15 Hell: For verses warning of its reality, see Rev. 21:8.

It should be grievous for any Christian to make light of or joke about hell. This verse should break our hearts, drive us to weep for the unsaved, and then motivate us to put legs to our prayers and plead with sinners to turn to the Savior.

21:1 "Aim at heaven and you will get earth thrown in. Aim at earth and you get neither." *C. S. Lewis*

Questions & Objections

21:4 "Death has always been part of life."

By Tommy Mitchell, Answers in Genesis

If creatures lived millions of years before God made the Garden of Eden, then suffering and death arose before sin ruined creation. In fact, their fossil remains would be buried under Adam's feet. But that's not the case!

In Gen. 1—3 we are told of the beginning of things. God created everything in six ordinary days—a perfect creation in which there was no death. God looked at His creation and called it "very good" (Gen. 1:31). So where did death come from?

Death came as a direct result of Adam's disobedience. Genesis 2:17 tells us, "But of the tree of the knowledge of good and evil you shall not eat, for in the day that you eat of it you shall surely die." So Adam knew there was a consequence to his actions. When he took of the fruit and ate, his rebellion brought a curse and death: "For since by man came death, by Man also came the resurrection of the dead" (1 Cor. 15:21). The disease and death in the fossil record reflect this curse upon all of creation.

We must understand that our sin is what broke God's perfect creation. We are all sinners because we are descended from sinners and we, too, rebel against God's command (Rom. 5:12). Not one is innocent. As a result of sin "the whole creation groans and labors with birth pangs together until now" (Rom. 8:22).

The good news is that the Last Adam, Jesus Christ, came to earth to bear the penalty of our sins and be nailed to the cross. He defeated death by His resurrection. By His atoning blood sacrifice for us, He has made a way for us to spend eternity with Him in heaven. Further, He promised to those who place their faith in Him that in the future there will be no more death, tears, or suffering. The perfect world will then be restored. See 2 Kings 2:1 comment.

6And He said to me, "It is done![a] I am
the Alpha and the Omega, the Beginning
and the End. I will give of the fountain of
the water of life freely to him who thirsts.
7He who overcomes shall inherit all
things,[a] and I will be his God and he shall
be My son. 8But the cowardly, unbelieving,[a] abominable, murderers, sexually immoral, sorcerers, idolaters, and all liars

21:6 [a]M-Text omits *It is done.* 21:7 [a]M-Text reads *overcomes, I shall give him these things.* 21:8 [a]M-Text adds *and sinners.*

21:8 Hell: For verses warning of its reality, see Matt. 5:22.

Leading sinners to Jesus: *God isn't willing that any perish.* "Behold, the LORD's hand is not shortened, that it cannot save; nor His ear heavy, that it cannot hear. But your iniquities have separated you from your God; and your sins have hidden His face from you, so that He will not hear" (Isa. 59:1,2). See Heb. 9:22 comment.

shall have their part in the lake which burns with fire and brimstone, which is the second death."

The New Jerusalem

[9]Then one of the seven angels who had the seven bowls filled with the seven last plagues came to me[a] and talked with me, saying, "Come, I will show you the bride, the Lamb's wife."[b] [10]And he carried me away in the Spirit to a great and high mountain, and showed me the great city, the holy[a] Jerusalem, descending out of heaven from God, [11]having the glory of God. Her light *was* like a most precious stone, like a jasper stone, clear as crystal. [12]Also she had a great and high wall with twelve gates, and twelve angels at the gates, and names written on them, which are *the names* of the twelve tribes of the children of Israel: [13]three gates on the east, three gates on the north, three gates on the south, and three gates on the west.

> When I enter that beautiful city
> And the saints all around me appear,
> I hope that someone will tell me:
> 'It was you who invited me here.'
>
> **CORRIE TEN BOOM**

[14]Now the wall of the city had twelve foundations, and on them were the names[a] of the twelve apostles of the Lamb. [15]And he who talked with me had a gold reed to measure the city, its gates, and its wall. [16]The city is laid out as a square; its length is as great as its breadth. And he measured the city with the reed: twelve thousand furlongs. Its length, breadth, and height are equal. [17]Then he measured its wall: one hundred *and* forty-four cubits, *according* to the measure of a man, that is, of an angel. [18]The construction of its wall was *of* jasper; and the city *was* pure gold, like clear glass. [19]The foundations of the wall of the city *were* adorned with all kinds of precious stones: the first foundation *was* jasper, the second sapphire, the third chalcedony, the fourth emerald, [20]the fifth sardonyx, the sixth sardius, the seventh chrysolite, the eighth beryl, the ninth topaz, the tenth chrysoprase, the eleventh jacinth, and the twelfth amethyst. [21]The twelve gates *were* twelve pearls: each individual gate was of one pearl. And the street of the city *was* pure gold, like transparent glass.

The Glory of the New Jerusalem

[22]But I saw no temple in it, for the Lord God Almighty and the Lamb are its temple. [23]The city had no need of the sun or of the moon to shine in it,[a] for the glory[b] of God illuminated it. The Lamb *is* its light. [24]And the nations of those who are saved[a] shall walk in its light, and the kings of the earth bring their glory and honor into it.[b] [25]Its gates shall not be shut at all by day (there shall be no night there). [26]And they shall bring the glory and the honor of the nations into it.[a] [27]But there shall by no means enter it anything that defiles, or causes[a] an abomination or a lie, but only those who are written in the Lamb's Book of Life.

The River of Life

22 And he showed me a pure[a] river of water of life, clear as crystal, proceeding from the throne of God and

21:9 [a]NU-Text and M-Text omit *to me.* [b]M-Text reads *I will show you the woman, the Lamb's bride.* **21:10** [a]NU-Text and M-Text omit *the great* and read *the holy city, Jerusalem.* **21:14** [a]NU-Text and M-Text read *twelve names.* **21:23** [a]NU-Text and M-Text omit *in it.* [b]M-Text reads *the very glory.* **21:24** [a]NU-Text and M-Text omit *of those who are saved.* [b]M-Text reads *the glory and honor of the nations to Him.* **21:26** [a]M-Text adds *that they may enter in.* **21:27** [a]NU-Text and M-Text read *anything profane, nor one who causes.* **22:1** [a]NU-Text and M-Text omit *pure.*

22:2 Charles Spurgeon on tracts. "I well remember distributing them in a town in England where tracts had never been distributed before, and going from house to house, and telling in humble language the things of the kingdom of God. I might have done nothing, if I had not been encouraged by finding myself able to do something . . . [Tracts are] adapted to those persons who have but little power and little ability, but nevertheless, wish to do something for Christ. They have not the tongue of the eloquent, *(continued)*

of the Lamb. [2]In the middle of its street,
and on either side of the river, *was* the
tree of life, which bore twelve fruits, each
tree yielding its fruit every month. The
leaves of the tree *were* for the healing of
the nations. [3]And there shall be no more
curse, but the throne of God and of the
Lamb shall be in it, and His servants shall
serve Him. [4]They shall see His face, and
His name *shall be* on their foreheads.
[5]There shall be no night there: They need
no lamp nor light of the sun, for the Lord
God gives them light. And they shall reign
forever and ever.

The Time Is Near

[6]Then he said to me, "These words *are*
faithful and true." And the Lord God of the
holy[a] prophets sent His angel to show His
servants the things which must shortly
take place.

[7]"Behold, I am coming quickly! Blessed
is he who keeps the words of the prophecy of this book."

[8]Now I, John, saw and heard[a] these
things. And when I heard and saw, I fell
down to worship before the feet of the
angel who showed me these things.

[9]Then he said to me, "See *that you do*
not *do that.* For[a] I am your fellow servant,
and of your brethren the prophets, and of
those who keep the words of this book.
Worship God." [10]And he said to me, "Do
not seal the words of the prophecy of this
book, for the time is at hand. [11]He who is
unjust, let him be unjust still; he who is
filthy, let him be filthy still; he who is
righteous, let him be righteous[a] still; he

22:6 [a]NU-Text and M-Text read *spirits of the prophets.* 22:8 [a]NU-Text and M-Text read *am the one who heard and saw.* 22:9 [a]NU-Text and M-Text omit *For.* 22:11 [a]NU-Text and M-Text read *do right.*

(22:2 continued) but they may have the hand of the diligent. They cannot stand and preach, but they can stand and distribute here and there these silent preachers... They may buy their thousand tracts, and these they can distribute broadcast.

"I look upon the giving away of a religious tract as only the first step for action not to be compared with many another deed done for Christ; but were it not for the first step we might never reach to the second, but that first attained, we are encouraged to take another, and so at the last... There is a real service of Christ in the distribution of the gospel in its printed form, a service the result of which heaven alone shall disclose, and the judgment day alone discover. How many thousands have been carried to heaven instrumentally upon the wings of these tracts, none can tell.

"I might say, if it were right to quote such a Scripture, 'The leaves were for the healing of the nations'—verily they are so. Scattered where the whole tree could scarcely be carried, the very leaves have had a medicinal and a healing virtue in them and the real word of truth, the simple statement of a Savior crucified and of a sinner who shall be saved by simply trusting in the Savior, has been greatly blessed, and many thousand souls have been led into the kingdom of heaven by this simple means. *Let each one of us, if we have done nothing for Christ, begin to do something now. The distribution of tracts is the first thing."*

See also Mark 4:14 and 1 Cor. 9:22 comments.

"You might have had a tract presented to you... That was the Son of God seeking for your soul. He has used a four-page tract—sometimes just one page—to seek to convert a man." *D. L. Moody*

22:3 A fallen creation. A magnificent doe stands with its fawn and drinks in the cool water from a mountain stream. The sun sparkles off the dew on deep green leaves of native tree branches. The mother gently caresses her offspring as it begins to also drink from the brook. The scene is one of incredible serenity ... the picture of innocence. What more could epitomize the beauty of God's creation?

Suddenly a mountain lion leaps from a tree and digs its sharp claws deeply into the mother's neck, dragging the helpless creature to the ground. As it holds its terrified prey in a death grip, its powerful jaws bite into the jugular vein, turning the mountain stream crimson with the creature's blood.

It is reassuring to know this is not the way God planned it in the beginning. Animals were not created to devour each other; they were created to be vegetarian (Gen. 1:29,30). The original creation was "good" and was not filled with violence and bloodshed. We live in a *fallen* creation (Rom. 8:20–23). As a result of Adam's sin, the perfect creation was cursed and death was introduced into the world (Rom. 5:12). The day will come when the entire creation will be delivered from the "bondage of corruption" and there will be no more curse. In the new heaven and earth, "the wolf and the lamb shall feed together, the lion shall eat straw like the ox... They shall not hurt nor destroy in all My holy mountain" (Isa. 65:25). See also Isa. 11:6–9.

who is holy, let him be holy still."

Jesus Testifies to the Churches

12"And behold, I am coming quickly,
and My reward *is* with Me, to give to
every one according to his work. 13I am
the Alpha and the Omega, *the* Beginning
and *the* End, the First and the Last."[a]
14Blessed *are* those who do His commandments,[a] that they may have the right
to the tree of life, and may enter through
the gates into the city. 15But[a] outside *are*
dogs and sorcerers and sexually immoral
and murderers and idolaters, and whoever
loves and practices a lie.

> If you see one hurrying on to destruction, use the utmost of your endeavor to stop him in his course.
>
> **A. W. TOZER**

16"I, Jesus, have sent My angel to testify to you these things in the churches. I
am the Root and the Offspring of David,
the Bright and Morning Star."
17And the Spirit and the bride say,
"Come!" And let him who hears say,
"Come!" And let him who thirsts come.
Whoever desires, let him take the water
of life freely.

A Warning

18For[a] I testify to everyone who hears
the words of the prophecy of this book: If
anyone adds to these things, God will
add[b] to him the plagues that are written
in this book; 19and if anyone takes away
from the words of the book of this prophecy, God shall take away[a] his part from
the Book[b] of Life, from the holy city, and
from the things which are written in this
book.

I Am Coming Quickly

20He who testifies to these things says,
"Surely I am coming quickly."
Amen. Even so, come, Lord Jesus!
21The grace of our Lord Jesus Christ *be*
with you all.[a] Amen.

22:13 [a]NU-Text and M-Text read *the First and the Last, the Beginning and the End.* 22:14 [a]NU-Text reads *wash their robes.* 22:15 [a]NU-Text and M-Text omit *But.* 22:18 [a]NU-Text and M-Text omit *For.* [b]M-Text reads *may God add.* 22:19 [a]M-Text reads *may God take away.* [b]NU-Text and M-Text read *tree of life.* 22:21 [a]NU-Text reads *with all;* M-Text reads *with all the saints.*

Just a Thought...

By Tony Miano

- Friendship evangelism is neither friendship nor evangelism without the verbal proclamation of the gospel.
- Don't worry about Satan. If you are not actively engaged in proclaiming the Law and the gospel to lost souls and praying for those who do, you pose no real threat to him. And if the enemy does not see you as a threat, then what kind of soldier are you, really?
- You can't be saved by a gospel you don't know. If you can't tell me biblically how I can get to heaven, then why should I believe you are going there?
- Remember, the same verse that says "all liars will have their part in the lake of fire" also says that the cowardly will meet the same fate. When did you last share the gospel with the lost? Can't remember? If you don't want to witness because you're scared, then you have a problem that may be more serious than you think.
- If you feed a lost person, give him something cool to drink, put a roof over his head and give him the shirt off your back, but you fail to share the gospel with him, know this. If he dies after you've lovingly served him, having never heard the gospel from your lips, he will be warmed and filled as he faces God's judgment and eternity in hell. Serve people? Yes. But please share the gospel.
- If you live by the extra-biblical adage, "Live your life in such a way that people ask you why," yet you dress like the world, talk like the world, act like the world, and enjoy the entertainment as the world, then what do you expect a spiritually dead and blind person to see in you? It won't be Jesus Christ. It will just be you. They won't ask what's different about you, because you look just like them.

Closing Words of Comfort

RARELY DO I become involved in counseling; I leave that to the expertise of the local pastor. However, I was awakened one morning by my wife, Sue. She said, "There is someone in the living room and he desperately wants to talk to you." I protested, "But it's not even 7 A.M. . . . and I don't do counseling!"

Nevertheless, I made my way into the living room and found a man whose eyes flashed with despair. I had met him a few months earlier when he purchased a series of our tapes, but this day he looked like a different man. It turned out that his whole life seemed to be falling to pieces. There were terrible problems at work, at home, and even in his church. Everything had suddenly gone wrong. I looked him in the eye and asked, "You didn't pray that God would 'break' you, did you?" He looked back at me and said, "I asked God to break me and grind me to powder . . ."

Make sure you realize what you are saying at church when you sing words like "Refiner's fire, my heart's one desire, is to be holy." I hum the song. Let me tell you why.

We may think that we are asking God for the "warm fuzzies," but the refining fire is what Job went through, and God may just give you your heart's one desire if you keep asking Him. After the service, you find that someone has just crashed into your new car. That week you discover that God has let the devil get at you and your house has burned to the ground, your spouse and children have been killed, and someone forgot to pay the insurance premium.

The loss of your family, car, and home and financial collapse give you a complete nervous breakdown. Well, rejoice—because you are getting your heart's one desire. Read the Book of Job. I've been through the Refiner's fire and I never want to go through it again. My prayer is, "If it is possible, let this cup pass from me." Jesus had to suffer; there was no alternative for Him. But there is an alternative for us. If we chasten ourselves, perhaps we will not be chastened by God. Instead of praying that God will break me, I say, "Please, Lord, be gentle on your servant. 'Do not chasten me in Your hot displeasure' [Psa. 38:1]. Help me to see the areas that I need to change."

If we discipline ourselves to pray and read the Word, we may avoid the Refiner's fire. If we draw close to Him, we won't need a lion's den to bring us to our knees. If we scatter abroad, preaching the Word everywhere, we may not need a Saul of Tarsus to breathe out slaughter against us. If we cut off unfruitful branches, we won't feel the pain of the Husbandman's sharp pruning sheers. Read the last chapters of Job and learn the lesson, so that you won't have to go through the earlier chapters. Scripture was written for our instruction. Lay your hand on your mouth and quickly bow to the sovereignty of God.

THE FIERY TRIAL

Let me share something very personal. In June 1985, I had just finished preaching in a small country church when a lean-looking young man approached me and said, "I wish I was like you." I managed a smile, but held onto the words that came to mind. *You don't know what you are saying.* Little did he know that at that moment I was going through sheer terror. I had been praying earlier that day when suddenly it seemed that all hell was let loose in my mind. It was as though God had removed every hedge of protection from me and a thousand spirits of terror invaded my thoughts. I fell upon the floor. I wept. I cried out to God. I exorcised myself, to no avail. There is no way I can describe the experience of the following months other than to say that it was like being held over a black pit of insanity by a spider's web.

When I arrived home from that series of meetings, Sue asked how they went. I said, "The meetings were fine," then broke down. I felt so crushed within my mind that I was unable to have family devotions, or even eat a meal at the table with my family for over twelve months.

I diagnosed myself as having a "wounded spirit." Before God could use me, I needed to have a broken spirit:

> But this is the man to whom I will look and have regard: he who is humble and of a broken or wounded spirit, and who trembles at My word and reveres My commands. (Isa. 66:2, *Amplified Bible*)

It was A. W. Tozer who said, "Before God uses a man, God will break the man."

It took years to overcome that experience. At one point, I couldn't even gather enough courage to go to my home church. I wanted to, but irrational fear was paralyzing me. The first Sunday after the initial experience, I was in my bedroom trying to gather strength to go with my family to church. The fear was so strong, I would actually lose my breath even while I lay in bed. My son, who was seven at the time, came into the bedroom and handed me a note. He had written out a few Scriptures he thought I should read, although he had no idea what I was going through. These were the verses:

> "The LORD is my helper; I will not fear. What can man do to me?" (Heb. 13:6)

> But the path of the just is like the shining sun, that shines ever brighter unto the perfect day. (Prov. 4:18)

> He who is in you is greater than he who is in the world. (1 John 4:4)

Then he had written the words, "I love you, Dad!"

HOW TO SPEED UP THE PROCESS

If there is a cry in your heart to be used by God, then you may go through a similar experience. I don't want to unnecessarily alarm you, but if you understand why it is happening and what you can do to speed up the process, it will help. If God in His great wisdom sees fit to use the Refiner's fire (if He takes you through a fiery trial), then it is only "if need be" (1 Pet. 1:6). Pray that you may avoid it, but this is often normal procedure in being prepared for ministry. A wild horse is no good to a rider. It can't be trusted. It needs its spirit broken so that it will willingly yield to the desire of the rider. So, let me share with you a few words of comfort, so that if you find yourself hanging over a dark chasm of insanity by the spider web of faith, you will know why, and realize that the web is unbreakable.

You are asleep in bed, when suddenly a creak of the floor causes you to open your eyes in the semi-dark room. Towering over you stands the ugly sight of a huge man, wearing a stocking over his face, with a gun pointed at your head.

Suddenly, your heart races with fear. Your mouth becomes dry. Terror paralyzes you. You can see his evil lips smile in delight at having another human being under his power. Time stands still. Your racing heart is taking too much blood into your brain, feeding it an oversupply of oxygen, making your mind go blank. This inability to respond, even mentally, brings a panic that causes your breathing to become erratic. The over-action of the heart has also speedily lifted your body temperature to a point where cold sweat is forming on your brow, back, and legs.

With malicious intent, the intruder slowly moves the gun to the temple of your moistened brow. You can feel its cold barrel against your warm skin. The reality of what is happening tells you that this is no mere nightmare.

Adrenaline is being pumped throughout your body. Your mind is instinctively screaming *Run!* and yet you know that if you move, you are dead. With both hands on the gun, the cruel intruder slowly cocks the weapon. You see his white teeth grit in perverted delight. *You are going to die!* Unspeakable terror grips your mind. Perspiration pours out of your flesh. Your mouth is totally dry. It's as though your heart is pounding through your chest. Your breath seems to have drained from your lungs and you can feel your eyes bulge with overwhelming dread…

That's what an attack of irrational fear feels like. There is no intruder, no gun, and no threat of death. Yet there are those same, very real, worse-than-nightmarish symptoms.

According to estimates, three million people in the U.S. have panic attacks. These are characterized by rapid heartbeat, dizziness, shortness of breath, and fear of losing control, going crazy, or dying.

The unsaved who experience panic attacks are often driven to drugs, alcohol, despair, or insanity. The Christian who suffers doesn't do so in vain, but there is a sense of guilt on top of the fear. The experience doesn't seem to match the Bible's description of a faith-filled Christian. He says, "I *will not* fear"…*and yet he still fears*. His will is incapacitated.

For those who have prayed, and prayed, and prayed for deliverance, and still find themselves in such a predicament, there are strong consolations.

The apostle Paul was no stranger to fear. He said, "For indeed, when we came to Macedonia, our bodies had no rest, but we were troubled on every side. Outside were conflicts, *inside were fears*" (2 Cor. 7:5, emphasis added).

Look at the following verses from 2 Cor. 12:7–9:

> And lest I should be exalted above measure by the abundance of the revelations, a thorn in the flesh was given to me, a messenger of Satan to buffet me, lest I be exalted above measure. Concerning this thing I pleaded with the Lord three times that it might depart from me. And He said to me, "My grace is sufficient for you, for My strength is made perfect in weakness." Therefore most gladly I will rather boast in my infirmities, that the power of Christ may rest upon me.

Paul asked for deliverance from this demonic attack three times. Yet God chose to leave him with it. Some say it was a sickness, but that doesn't seem to be what the Bible teaches. It says it was a "messenger of Satan" (a demon) that buffeted him.

Why then did God allow demonic oppression to come against His apostle? He wanted to use Paul, but He didn't want him to fall through pride and fail in his calling. The demonic oppression was to keep him humble as God gave him an abundance of revelations. He had to remain small in his own eyes. The Greek word for "buffet" is *kolaphizo*, which

means to "rap with the fist." Its root word is *kolos*, which means "dwarf."

Satan fires arrows only at those who have potential for the kingdom of God. You have great potential to be used by God in these last days. Instead of saying, "But God can't use me when I am paralyzed by fear," say, "Because His strength is made perfect in my weakness, God can use me for His glory *because the fear I am plagued by actually keeps me in weakness*."

EXAMINE YOURSELF

Today, there are many who name the name of Christ, but who never "depart from iniquity." They are false converts who "ask Jesus into their heart," but are actually unconverted because they have never truly repented. So it is important that you examine yourself to see if you are in the faith (2 Cor. 13:5). Those who allow sin in their lives are actually opening themselves up to demonic influence. The Bible instructs us not to "give place to the devil" (Eph. 4:27).

Afflictions only work together for our good, if we are "called according to [God's] purpose" (Rom. 8:28). Therefore, the following are questions each of us need to ask ourselves:

> Do I honor my parents? Do I value them implicitly? God commands that we honor our parents, then Scripture warns, "that it may be well with you and you may live long on the earth" (Eph. 6:3). In other words, if you don't value your parents, all will not be well with you. I have found that many people have demonic problems because they *hate* their parents.
>
> Is there any unconfessed sin in my life? Is there any bitterness, resentment, or jealousy? Have I been hurt by someone in the past whom I can't find it within my heart to forgive? Then I am giving place to the devil. If I won't forgive and forget, I'm like a man who is stung to death by one bee. You could understand someone being stung to death by a *swarm* of bees, but we can do something about one bee. The sad thing about someone who becomes bitter is that all they need to do to deal with their problem is to swat the thing through repentance. God says He will not forgive us if we will not forgive from our heart (Matt. 6:15).
>
> Has there been any occult activity in my life in the past? Do I have idols (even as souvenirs) in my home? Is there any pornography? I need to prayerfully walk around in the house and ask God if there is anything that is unpleasing to Him. Then I must consider the same thing within the temple of my own body. Am I a glutton? Do I feed filth into my mind through my eyes or through my ears? Do my hands touch only what is pleasing in His sight? Are my words kind and loving? Are the meditations of my mind pleasing to God?
>
> The only way to know if you are a Christian is by your fruit. There are a number of fruits in Scripture: the fruit of praise, the fruit of thanksgiving, the fruit of holiness, the fruit of repentance, the fruit of righteousness, and the fruit of the Spirit—love, joy, peace, patience, goodness, gentleness, faith, meekness, and temperance.

A key to overcoming trials is to understand that they are *relative*. The next time Satan tries to make you feel sorry for yourself in the midst of a trial, ask yourself, "Would I like to trade places with someone who has a horrible terminal disease? Would I like to trade places with a burn victim who has been burned over 90% of his body?" We can't imagine the agonies those in such a predicament go through. Have you ever burned your-

self on a toaster? Think what it must be like for those poor people. Such sober thoughts bring our problem into perspective, and should make us want to thank God for His many blessings. Not only for what we have, but also for those things we don't have—like unspeakable pain.

The fruit of thanksgiving should be evident in the Christian, not only for temporal blessings, but for the cross. Paul was persecuted beyond measure, merely for his faith in God, yet he said, "Thanks be to God for His indescribable gift!" (2 Cor. 9:15).

As Christians, we should have the fruit of holiness. We should be separated from this world, with all of its corruption, to God. We should have evidence of our repentance. If we have stolen, we will return what isn't ours. We will set right (where possible) that which we have wronged. Lastly, we will possess the fruit of the Spirit. If we are rooted and grounded in Him, we will have the fruits of His character hanging from the branches of our lives. Do we have love that cares for others? Do we care enough about the salvation of sinners to put feet to our prayers and take the gospel to them? Love is not passive. It will not be self-indulgent while others suffer. It is empathetic.

GOOD REASON

If we haven't given place to the devil, what is he doing in our lives? There must be good reason for him to be there. The only reasonable conclusion is that God has given permission. This happened in the Book of Job. God allowed Satan to buffet Job so that he would grow in his faith in God. As I have said before, God has given us the Book of Job for our admonition and instruction.

Study the following verse from the *Amplified Bible:*

> It is God who is all the while effectually at work in you [energizing and creating in you the power and desire], both to will and to work for His good pleasure and satisfaction and delight. (Phil. 2:13)

We have established that God is at work in you. You have this demonic "buffeting" from which God will not presently deliver you because He is doing a good work in you. Therefore, what should be your attitude to this good work He is doing? It should be one of joy—*because your joy is evidence of how much you trust God.* If you trust Him, then you will rejoice for His goodness, and that joy will be strength to you.

Take for instance a world champion boxer. His coach loves him to a point where he wants him above all things to be a winner. So what does the coach do—buy him a sofa, a TV, and potato chips? No. Instead, he places weights on his shoulders and resistance against his arms. He will even look around for the toughest sparring partner he can find. If the boxer doesn't understand what his trainer is doing, if he doesn't have faith in his methods, he will get depressed and lose heart. But if he knows what's going on, he will rejoice now in the trials because he sees, through the eyes of faith, the finished product.

That's why God is letting the devil loose on you: to make you strong. Paul says,

> For our light affliction, which is but for a moment [in the light of eternity], is working for us a far more exceeding and eternal weight of glory. (2 Cor. 4:17)

Afflictions work *for* us, not against us, if we are in God's will. How is your joy when the Trainer brings the resistance your way? How much faith do you have in Him? The joy you have will be your measuring rod.

> For You, O God, have tested us; You have refined us as silver is refined. You have caused men to ride over our heads; we went through

> fire and through water; but You brought us out to rich fulfillment. (Psa. 66:10,12)

God takes us through the fires of persecution, tribulation, and temptation to purify us, not to burn us. He takes us through water to cleanse us, not to drown us. Look at the reason God chastens His children, given in Heb. 12:9–15:

> Furthermore, we have had human fathers who corrected us, and we paid them respect. Shall we not much more readily be in subjection to the Father of spirits and live? For they indeed for a few days chastened us as seemed best to them, but He for our profit, that we may be partakers of His holiness. Now no chastening seems to be joyful for the present, but painful; nevertheless, afterward it yields the peaceable fruit of righteousness to those who have been trained by it.
>
> Therefore strengthen the hands which hang down, and the feeble knees, and make straight paths for your feet, so that what is lame may not be dislocated, but rather be healed. Pursue peace with all people, and holiness, without which no one will see the Lord: looking carefully lest anyone fall short of the grace of God; lest any root of bitterness springing up cause trouble, and by this many become defiled.

In other words, get it together. Don't fall into discouragement, which is essentially a lack of faith in God. If you let your arms hang down in depression instead of rejoicing that God is working all things out for your good, you are saying that God isn't faithful, that His promises aren't worth believing, that He is actually a liar. There is no greater insult to God than to not believe His promises. The result of unbelief will be depression, discouragement, self-pity, resentment, then bitterness, which you will end up spreading to others.

If you have never thanked God for His promises, for His faithfulness, for the fact that He is working with you, in you, and for you—if you have been joyless, or even despised what has been happening to you and moved into bitterness—then repent of the sin of mistrust. How insulted you would be if you were a faithful and loving trainer, and your boxer, for whose good you are laboring, began to despise you for what you were doing.

On the other hand, if you are "exercised thereby," the result will be the "peaceable fruit of righteousness." In other words, you will end up living a life that is in complete righteousness, and bring a smile to the heart of your heavenly Father.

Look at Heb. 12:11. Notice the word "afterward." That one word was my light in the dark tunnel. It meant there was an end to my terror, a light at the end of the tunnel that wasn't a train heading for me. Write down the word "afterward," and put it somewhere where you will be reminded that you have hope—and "hope never disappoints or deludes or shames us" (Rom. 5:5, *Amplified*).

Guard against condemnation. You are no "less spiritual" than those who seem to have complete victory. If you don't believe it, think of the experience of Oswald Chambers, author of the mega-bestselling devotional *My Utmost For His Highest*. Now there's a man whose life and words have been an inspiration to millions. He was "spiritual" in the truest sense of the word. However, the great author had four years in his life of which he said, "God used me during those years for the conversion of souls, but I had no conscious communion with Him. The Bible was the dullest, most uninteresting book in existence" (*Oswald Chambers: Abandoned to God*). He described those four years as "hell on earth." However, he found that there was an "afterward," saying,

> But those of you who know the experience know very well how God brings one to the point of utter despair, and I got to the place where I did not care whether everyone knew how bad I was, I cared not for another on earth, saving to get out of my present condition. (Ibid.)

If you have panic attacks or agoraphobia (fear of open spaces), don't fall into the deep pit of self-pity, because it has ugly bedfellows—discouragement, joylessness, condemnation, despair, and hopelessness. The sides of the pit of self-pity are very slippery, but there is one firm foothold. It is the uplifting stairs of thanksgiving. Let me explain how you can get your foot into it.

AN ATTITUDE OF THANKSGIVING

Sue and I were visiting an elderly lady named Helen, a 93-year-old who had broken her hip. She was unhappy because the food in the convalescent home wasn't very good. One day Mary walked into Helen's room. Mary was in her late seventies and had to be permanently fed through a tube that ran from a bottle directly into her stomach. Mary never tasted food or drink, and barring a miracle from God, she would never taste food or liquid again. Mary's condition made Helen thankful that at least she could have the pleasure of food and drink, even if it was not up to standard.

Then there was Robert. Robert had a good clear brain, but he had chronic emphysema. He couldn't breathe. Whenever she looked into his room, he was sitting on his bed, leaning over with his hand on his forehead. He gasped for every breath, twenty-four hours a day. Robert's problem made Mary thankful that at least she could breathe.

The point is that, despite your tormenting fears, you won't have to look too far for people who are suffering so badly that their problems dwarf yours. If you don't believe me, try being Robert for two minutes. Pinch your nose with one hand, then with the other one hold your lips together so that a meager amount of air gets into your mouth. Don't cheat. Do that for 120 long seconds. Feel the sweat break out on your forehead. Feel the panic. After two minutes of gasping for your breath, when you let go you will begin to thank God that you can breathe, and that will bring your problems into perspective. I'm not demeaning your fears. I'm offering you a way to lift yourself out of the pit of pity.

So next time you are attacked in some way, pull yourself together with a prayer of heartfelt thanksgiving, and say,

> Father I thank You that all things work together for my good; that it is You who are at work in me to will and do of Your good pleasure. Your strength is made perfect in my weakness. I will not let this attack discourage me because Your grace is sufficient for me. You will help me through it. When I think of the sufferings of many, many others, I feel ashamed for having any self-pity. I will therefore rejoice in the God of my salvation and give You thanks in and for everything. In Jesus' name I pray. Amen.

Your constant battle with trials will make you no stranger to them. Like a tree that is constantly beaten about by the wind, your roots will be deep. You will find, if you have an acquaintance with fear, etc., that you can live with it where others can't. You will be able to do things that others can't. The roots of your faith in God will be deeper than the roots of those who have never been ravaged by the winds of terror. Affliction works *for* us. God doesn't let the wind blow to destroy, but to strengthen. You will be able to go places and do things that others would fear to do, because those things that should (rationally) pro-

duce fear pale in significance compared to the average attack of irrational fear.

Again, do you believe God is at work in you to will and do of His good pleasure? Then rejoice, and let the joy of the Lord be your strength. There is a world weighed in the balance and found wanting. Don't fiddle while Rome burns. Your problems and fears are nothing compared to the terrible plight of the sinner. Eternal hell is his destiny. Lift up hands that hang down, lift up your heart through faith, then lift up your voice like a trumpet and show this people their transgression.

The Wordless Gospel

The following is a presentation of the gospel in picture form, so you can present it to someone who doesn't speak English. At the conclusion is John 3:16 in twenty-seven major languages.

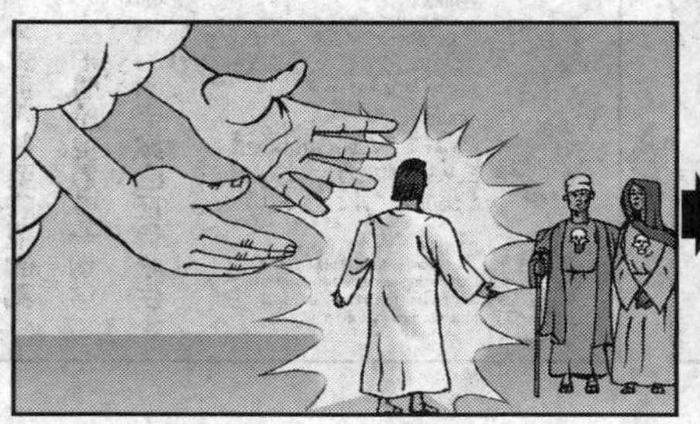

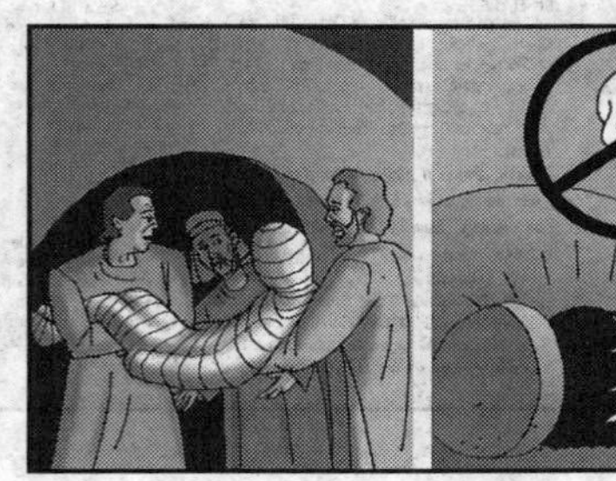

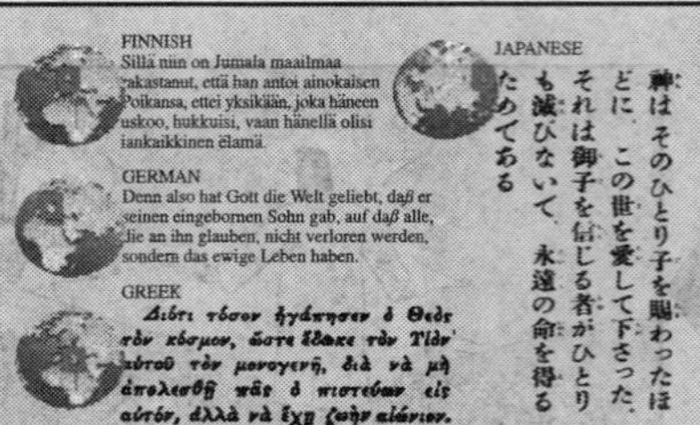
FINNISH
Sillä niin on Jumala maailmaa rakastanut, että hän antoi ainokaisen Poikansa, ettei yksikään, joka häneen uskoo, hukkuisi, vaan hänellä olisi iankaikkinen elämä.
GERMAN
Denn also hat Gott die Welt geliebt, daß er seinen eingebornen Sohn gab, auf daß alle, die an ihn glauben, nicht verloren werden, sondern das ewige Leben haben.
GREEK
Διότι τόσον ἠγάπησεν ὁ Θεὸς τὸν κόσμον, ὥστε ἔδωκε τὸν Υἱὸν αὐτοῦ τὸν μονογενῆ, διὰ νὰ μὴ ἀπολεσθῇ πᾶς ὁ πιστεύων εἰς αὐτόν, ἀλλὰ νὰ ἔχῃ ζωὴν αἰώνιον.
JAPANESE
神はそのひとり子を賜わったほどに、この世を愛して下さった。それは御子を信じる者がひとりも滅びないで、永遠の命を得るためである

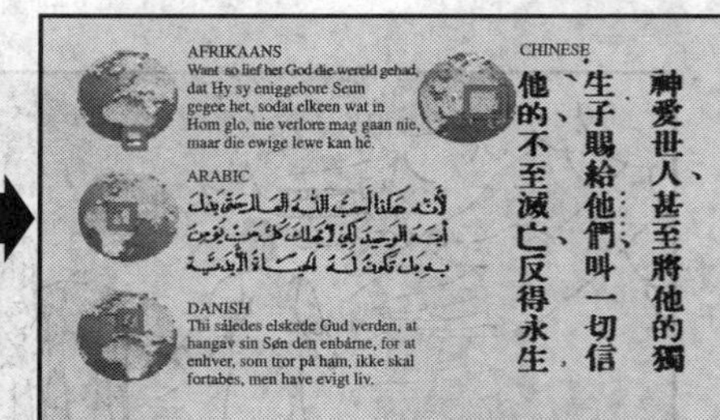
AFRIKAANS
Want so lief het God die wereld gehad, dat Hy sy eniggebore Seun gegee het, sodat elkeen wat in Hom glo, nie verlore mag gaan nie, maar die ewige lewe kan hê.
ARABIC
لأنه هكذا أحب الله العالم حتى بذل ابنه الوحيد لكي لا يهلك كل من يؤمن به بل تكون له الحياة الأبدية
DANISH
Thi således elskede Gud verden, at han gav sin Søn den enbårne, for at enhver, som tror på ham, ikke skal fortabes, men have evigt liv.
CHINESE
神爱世人、甚至將他的獨生子賜給他們、叫一切信他的、不至滅亡、反得永生。

DUTCH
Want alzo lief heeft God de wereld gehad, dat Hij zijn eniggeboren Zoon gegeven heeft, opdat een ieder, die in Hem gelooft, niet verloren ga, maar eeuwig leven hebbe.
ENGLISH
For God so loved the world, that He gave His only begotten Son, that whosoever believes in Him should not perish, but have everlasting life.
FRENCH
Car Dieu a tant aimé le monde qu'il a donné son Fils unique, afin que quiconque croit en lui ne périsse point, mais qu'il ait la vie éternelle.
KOREAN
하나님이 세상을 이처럼 사랑하사 독생자를 주셨으니 이는 저를 믿는 자마다 멸망치 않고 영생을 얻게 하려 하심이니라

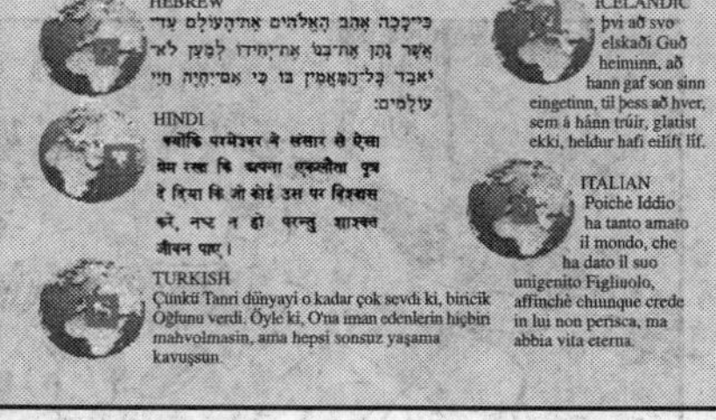
HEBREW
כי־ככה אהב האלהים את־העולם עד־אשר נתן את־בנו את־יחידו למען לא־יאבד כל־המאמין בו כי אם־יחיה חיי עולמים:
HINDI
क्योंकि परमेश्वर ने संसार से ऐसा प्रेम रखा कि अपना एकलौता पुत्र दे दिया कि जो कोई उस पर विश्वास करे, नष्ट न हो परन्तु शाश्वत जीवन पाए।
TURKISH
Çünkü Tanri dünyayi o kadar çok sevdi ki, biricik Oğlunu verdi. Öyle ki, O'na iman edenlerin hiçbiri mahvolmasin, ama hepsi sonsuz yaşama kavuşsun.
ICELANDIC
Því að svo elskaði Guð heiminn, að hann gaf son sinn eingetinn, til þess að hver, sem á hánn trúir, glatist ekki, heldur hafi eilíft líf.
ITALIAN
Poichè Iddio ha tanto amato il mondo, che ha dato il suo unigenito Figliuolo, affinchè chiunque crede in lui non perisca, ma abbia vita eterna.

NORWEGIAN
For så har Gud elsket verden at han gav siin Sønn, den enbårne, forat hver den som tror på ham, ikke skal fortapes, men ha evig liv.
POLISH
Ponieważ Bóg tak świat kochał, że dał swego syna jedynego, aby kto wierzy w Niego nie zginął, lecz żył wiecznie.
RUSSIAN
Ибо так возлюбил Бог мир, что отдал Сына Своего единородного, дабы всякий, верующий в Него, не погиб, но имел жизнь вечную.
PORTUGESE
Porque Deus amou o mundo de tal maneira, que deu o seu Filho unigênito, para que todo aquêle que nêle crê não pereça, mas tenha a vida eterna.
SPANISH
Porque de tal manera amó Dios al mundo, que ha dado á su Hijo unigénito, para que todo aquel que en él cree, no se pierda, mas tenga vida eterna.

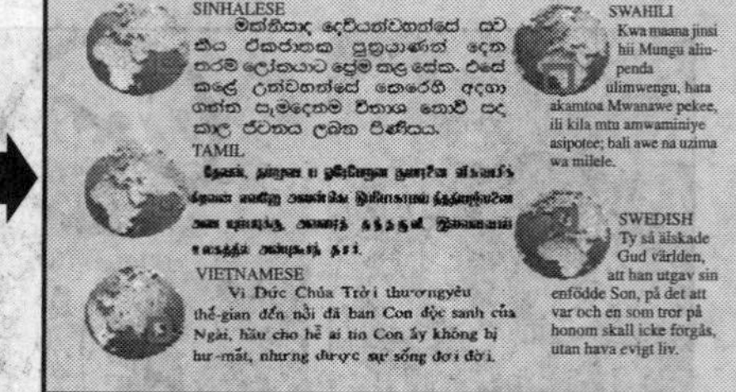
SINHALESE
TAMIL
VIETNAMESE
Vì Đức Chúa Trời thươngyêu thế-gian đến nỗi đã ban Con độc sanh của Ngài, hầu cho hễ ai tin Con ấy không bị hư-mất, nhưng được sự sống đời đời.
SWAHILI
Kwa maana jinsi hii Mungu aliupenda ulimwengu, hata akamtoa Mwanawe pekee, ili kila mtu amwaminiye asipotee; bali awe na uzima wa milele.
SWEDISH
Ty så älskade Gud världen, att han utgav sin enfödde Son, på det att var och en som tror på honom skall icke förgås, utan hava evigt liv.

One-Year Bible Reading Plan

By investing about fifteen minutes a day, reading an average of three chapters per sitting, you will be able to explore all the riches of God's Word in one year. Read the Bible every day without fail, and you have God's promise that you will "be like a tree planted by the rivers of water, that brings forth its fruit in its season, whose leaf also shall not wither; and whatever [you do] shall prosper" (see Psalm 1 for details).

	Date	Today's Scripture Reading
☐	Jan. 1	Genesis 1–3
☐	Jan. 2	Genesis 4–6
☐	Jan. 3	Genesis 7–9
☐	Jan. 4	Genesis 10–12
☐	Jan. 5	Genesis 13–15
☐	Jan. 6	Genesis 16–18
☐	Jan. 7	Genesis 19–21
☐	Jan. 8	Genesis 22–24
☐	Jan. 9	Genesis 25–27
☐	Jan. 10	Genesis 28–30
☐	Jan. 11	Genesis 31–33
☐	Jan. 12	Genesis 34–36
☐	Jan. 13	Genesis 37–39
☐	Jan. 14	Genesis 40–42
☐	Jan. 15	Genesis 43–46
☐	Jan. 16	Genesis 47–50
☐	Jan. 17	Exodus 1–3
☐	Jan. 18	Exodus 4–6
☐	Jan. 19	Exodus 7–9
☐	Jan. 20	Exodus 10–12
☐	Jan. 21	Exodus 13–15
☐	Jan. 22	Exodus 16–18
☐	Jan. 23	Exodus 19–21
☐	Jan. 24	Exodus 22–24

	Date	Today's Scripture Reading
☐	Jan. 25	Exodus 25–27
☐	Jan. 26	Exodus 28–30
☐	Jan. 27	Exodus 31–33
☐	Jan. 28	Exodus 34–36
☐	Jan. 29	Exodus 37–40
☐	Jan. 30	Leviticus 1–3
☐	Jan. 31	Leviticus 4–6
☐	Feb. 1	Leviticus 7–9
☐	Feb. 2	Leviticus 10–12
☐	Feb. 3	Leviticus 13–15
☐	Feb. 4	Leviticus 16–18
☐	Feb. 5	Leviticus 19–21
☐	Feb. 6	Leviticus 22–24
☐	Feb. 7	Leviticus 25–27
☐	Feb. 8	Numbers 1–3
☐	Feb. 9	Numbers 4–6
☐	Feb. 10	Numbers 7–9
☐	Feb. 11	Numbers 10–12
☐	Feb. 12	Numbers 13–15
☐	Feb. 13	Numbers 16–18
☐	Feb. 14	Numbers 19–21
☐	Feb. 15	Numbers 22–24
☐	Feb. 16	Numbers 25–27
☐	Feb. 17	Numbers 28–30

	Date	Today's Scripture Reading
☐	Feb. 18	Numbers 31–33
☐	Feb. 19	Numbers 34–36
☐	Feb. 20	Deuteronomy 1–3
☐	Feb. 21	Deuteronomy 4–6
☐	Feb. 22	Deuteronomy 7–9
☐	Feb. 23	Deuteronomy 10–12
☐	Feb. 24	Deuteronomy 13–15
☐	Feb. 25	Deuteronomy 16–18
☐	Feb. 26	Deuteronomy 19–21
☐	Feb. 27	Deuteronomy 22–24
☐	Feb. 28	Deuteronomy 25–27
☐	Mar. 1	Deuteronomy 28–30
☐	Mar. 2	Deuteronomy 31–34
☐	Mar. 3	Joshua 1–3
☐	Mar. 4	Joshua 4–6
☐	Mar. 5	Joshua 7–9
☐	Mar. 6	Joshua 10–12
☐	Mar. 7	Joshua 13–15
☐	Mar. 8	Joshua 16–18
☐	Mar. 9	Joshua 19–21
☐	Mar. 10	Joshua 22–24
☐	Mar. 11	Judges 1–3
☐	Mar. 12	Judges 4–6
☐	Mar. 13	Judges 7–9
☐	Mar. 14	Judges 10–12
☐	Mar. 15	Judges 13–15
☐	Mar. 16	Judges 16–18
☐	Mar. 17	Judges 19–21
☐	Mar. 18	Ruth 1–4
☐	Mar. 19	1 Samuel 1–3
☐	Mar. 20	1 Samuel 4–6
☐	Mar. 21	1 Samuel 7–9
☐	Mar. 22	1 Samuel 10–12
☐	Mar. 23	1 Samuel 13–15
☐	Mar. 24	1 Samuel 16–18
☐	Mar. 25	1 Samuel 19–21
☐	Mar. 26	1 Samuel 22–24
☐	Mar. 27	1 Samuel 25–27
☐	Mar. 28	1 Samuel 28–31
☐	Mar. 29	2 Samuel 1–3

	Date	Today's Scripture Reading
☐	Mar. 30	2 Samuel 4–6
☐	Mar. 31	2 Samuel 7–9
☐	Apr. 1	2 Samuel 10–12
☐	Apr. 2	2 Samuel 13–15
☐	Apr. 3	2 Samuel 16–18
☐	Apr. 4	2 Samuel 19–21
☐	Apr. 5	2 Samuel 22–24
☐	Apr. 6	1 Kings 1–3
☐	Apr. 7	1 Kings 4–6
☐	Apr. 8	1 Kings 7–9
☐	Apr. 9	1 Kings 10–12
☐	Apr. 10	1 Kings 13–15
☐	Apr. 11	1 Kings 16–18
☐	Apr. 12	1 Kings 19–22
☐	Apr. 13	2 Kings 1–3
☐	Apr. 14	2 Kings 4–6
☐	Apr. 15	2 Kings 7–9
☐	Apr. 16	2 Kings 10–12
☐	Apr. 17	2 Kings 13–15
☐	Apr. 18	2 Kings 16–18
☐	Apr. 19	2 Kings 19–21
☐	Apr. 20	2 Kings 22–25
☐	Apr. 21	1 Chronicles 1–6
☐	Apr. 22	1 Chronicles 7–9
☐	Apr. 23	1 Chronicles 10–12
☐	Apr. 24	1 Chronicles 13–15
☐	Apr. 25	1 Chronicles 16–18
☐	Apr. 26	1 Chronicles 19–21
☐	Apr. 27	1 Chronicles 22–25
☐	Apr. 28	1 Chronicles 26–29
☐	Apr. 29	2 Chronicles 1–3
☐	Apr. 30	2 Chronicles 4–6
☐	May 1	2 Chronicles 7–9
☐	May 2	2 Chronicles 10–12
☐	May 3	2 Chronicles 13–15
☐	May 4	2 Chronicles 16–18
☐	May 5	2 Chronicles 19–21
☐	May 6	2 Chronicles 22–24
☐	May 7	2 Chronicles 25–27
☐	May 8	2 Chronicles 28–30

	Date	Today's Scripture Reading
☐	May 9	2 Chronicles 31–33
☐	May 10	2 Chronicles 34–36
☐	May 11	Ezra 1–3
☐	May 12	Ezra 4–6
☐	May 13	Ezra 7–10
☐	May 14	Nehemiah 1–3
☐	May 15	Nehemiah 4–6
☐	May 16	Nehemiah 7–9
☐	May 17	Nehemiah 10–13
☐	May 18	Esther 1–3
☐	May 19	Esther 4–6
☐	May 20	Esther 7–10
☐	May 21	Job 1–3
☐	May 22	Job 4–6
☐	May 23	Job 7–9
☐	May 24	Job 10–12
☐	May 25	Job 13–15
☐	May 26	Job 16–18
☐	May 27	Job 19–21
☐	May 28	Job 22–24
☐	May 29	Job 25–27
☐	May 30	Job 28–30
☐	May 31	Job 31–33
☐	June 1	Job 34–36
☐	June 2	Job 37–39
☐	June 3	Job 40–42
☐	June 4	Psalms 1–5
☐	June 5	Psalms 6–10
☐	June 6	Psalms 11–15
☐	June 7	Psalms 16–20
☐	June 8	Psalms 21–25
☐	June 9	Psalms 26–30
☐	June 10	Psalms 31–35
☐	June 11	Psalms 36–40
☐	June 12	Psalms 41–45
☐	June 13	Psalms 46–50
☐	June 14	Psalms 51–55
☐	June 15	Psalms 56–60
☐	June 16	Psalms 61–65
☐	June 17	Psalms 66–70

	Date	Today's Scripture Reading
☐	June 18	Psalms 71–75
☐	June 19	Psalms 76–80
☐	June 20	Psalms 81–85
☐	June 21	Psalms 86–90
☐	June 22	Psalms 91–95
☐	June 23	Psalms 96–100
☐	June 24	Psalms 101–105
☐	June 25	Psalms 106–110
☐	June 26	Psalms 111–115
☐	June 27	Psalms 116–120
☐	June 28	Psalms 121–125
☐	June 29	Psalms 126–130
☐	June 30	Psalms 131–135
☐	July 1	Psalms 136–140
☐	July 2	Psalms 141–145
☐	July 3	Psalms 146–150
☐	July 4	Proverbs 1–3
☐	July 5	Proverbs 4–6
☐	July 6	Proverbs 7–9
☐	July 7	Proverbs 10–12
☐	July 8	Proverbs 13–15
☐	July 9	Proverbs 16–18
☐	July 10	Proverbs 19–21
☐	July 11	Proverbs 22–24
☐	July 12	Proverbs 25–27
☐	July 13	Proverbs 28–31
☐	July 14	Ecclesiastes 1–3
☐	July 15	Ecclesiastes 4–6
☐	July 16	Ecclesiastes 7–9
☐	July 17	Ecclesiastes 10–12
☐	July 18	Song of Songs 1–4
☐	July 19	Song of Songs 5–8
☐	July 20	Isaiah 1–3
☐	July 21	Isaiah 4–6
☐	July 22	Isaiah 7–9
☐	July 23	Isaiah 10–12
☐	July 24	Isaiah 13–15
☐	July 25	Isaiah 16–18
☐	July 26	Isaiah 19–21
☐	July 27	Isaiah 22–24

	Date	Today's Scripture Reading
☐	July 28	Isaiah 25–27
☐	July 29	Isaiah 28–30
☐	July 30	Isaiah 31–33
☐	July 31	Isaiah 34–36
☐	Aug. 1	Isaiah 37–39
☐	Aug. 2	Isaiah 40–42
☐	Aug. 3	Isaiah 43–45
☐	Aug. 4	Isaiah 46–48
☐	Aug. 5	Isaiah 49–51
☐	Aug. 6	Isaiah 52–54
☐	Aug. 7	Isaiah 55–57
☐	Aug. 8	Isaiah 58–60
☐	Aug. 9	Isaiah 61–63
☐	Aug. 10	Isaiah 64–66
☐	Aug. 11	Jeremiah 1–3
☐	Aug. 12	Jeremiah 4–6
☐	Aug. 13	Jeremiah 7–9
☐	Aug. 14	Jeremiah 10–12
☐	Aug. 15	Jeremiah 13–15
☐	Aug. 16	Jeremiah 16–18
☐	Aug. 17	Jeremiah 19–21
☐	Aug. 18	Jeremiah 22–24
☐	Aug. 19	Jeremiah 25–27
☐	Aug. 20	Jeremiah 28–30
☐	Aug. 21	Jeremiah 31–33
☐	Aug. 22	Jeremiah 34–36
☐	Aug. 23	Jeremiah 37–39
☐	Aug. 24	Jeremiah 40–42
☐	Aug. 25	Jeremiah 43–45
☐	Aug. 26	Jeremiah 46–48
☐	Aug. 27	Jeremiah 49–52
☐	Aug. 28	Lamentations 1–3
☐	Aug. 29	Lamentations 4–5
☐	Aug. 30	Ezekiel 1–3
☐	Aug. 31	Ezekiel 4–6
☐	Sept. 1	Ezekiel 7–9
☐	Sept. 2	Ezekiel 10–12
☐	Sept. 3	Ezekiel 13–15
☐	Sept. 4	Ezekiel 16–18
☐	Sept. 5	Ezekiel 19–21

	Date	Today's Scripture Reading
☐	Sept. 6	Ezekiel 22–24
☐	Sept. 7	Ezekiel 25–27
☐	Sept. 8	Ezekiel 28–30
☐	Sept. 9	Ezekiel 31–33
☐	Sept. 10	Ezekiel 34–36
☐	Sept. 11	Ezekiel 37–40
☐	Sept. 12	Ezekiel 41–44
☐	Sept. 13	Ezekiel 45–48
☐	Sept. 14	Daniel 1–3
☐	Sept. 15	Daniel 4–6
☐	Sept. 16	Daniel 7–9
☐	Sept. 17	Daniel 10–12
☐	Sept. 18	Hosea 1–3
☐	Sept. 19	Hosea 4–6
☐	Sept. 20	Hosea 7–10
☐	Sept. 21	Hosea 11–14
☐	Sept. 22	Joel 1–3
☐	Sept. 23	Amos 1–3
☐	Sept. 24	Amos 4–6
☐	Sept. 25	Amos 7–9
☐	Sept. 26	Obadiah
☐	Sept. 27	Jonah 1–4
☐	Sept. 28	Micah 1–3
☐	Sept. 29	Micah 4–7
☐	Sept. 30	Nahum 1–3
☐	Oct. 1	Habakkuk 1–3
☐	Oct. 2	Zephaniah 1–3
☐	Oct. 3	Haggai 1–2
☐	Oct. 4	Zechariah 1–3
☐	Oct. 5	Zechariah 4–6
☐	Oct. 6	Zechariah 7–10
☐	Oct. 7	Zechariah 11–14
☐	Oct. 8	Malachi 1–2
☐	Oct. 9	Malachi 3–4
☐	Oct. 10	Matthew 1–3
☐	Oct. 11	Matthew 4–6
☐	Oct. 12	Matthew 7–9
☐	Oct. 13	Matthew 10–12
☐	Oct. 14	Matthew 13–15
☐	Oct. 15	Matthew 16–18

	Date	Today's Scripture Reading
☐	Oct. 16	Matthew 19–21
☐	Oct. 17	Matthew 22–24
☐	Oct. 18	Matthew 25–28
☐	Oct. 19	Mark 1–3
☐	Oct. 20	Mark 4–6
☐	Oct. 21	Mark 7–9
☐	Oct. 22	Mark 10–12
☐	Oct. 23	Mark 13–16
☐	Oct. 24	Luke 1–3
☐	Oct. 25	Luke 4–6
☐	Oct. 26	Luke 7–9
☐	Oct. 27	Luke 10–12
☐	Oct. 28	Luke 13–15
☐	Oct. 29	Luke 16–18
☐	Oct. 30	Luke 19–21
☐	Oct. 31	Luke 22–24
☐	Nov. 1	John 1–3
☐	Nov. 2	John 4–6
☐	Nov. 3	John 7–9
☐	Nov. 4	John 10–12
☐	Nov. 5	John 13–15
☐	Nov. 6	John 16–18
☐	Nov. 7	John 19–21
☐	Nov. 8	Acts 1–3
☐	Nov. 9	Acts 4–6
☐	Nov. 10	Acts 7–9
☐	Nov. 11	Acts 10–12
☐	Nov. 12	Acts 13–15
☐	Nov. 13	Acts 16–18
☐	Nov. 14	Acts 19–21
☐	Nov. 15	Acts 22–24
☐	Nov. 16	Acts 25–28
☐	Nov. 17	Romans 1–3
☐	Nov. 18	Romans 4–6
☐	Nov. 19	Romans 7–9
☐	Nov. 20	Romans 10–12
☐	Nov. 21	Romans 13–16
☐	Nov. 22	1 Corinthians 1–3
☐	Nov. 23	1 Corinthians 4–6
☐	Nov. 24	1 Corinthians 7–9
☐	Nov. 25	1 Corinthians 10–12
☐	Nov. 26	1 Corinthians 13–16
☐	Nov. 27	2 Corinthians 1–3
☐	Nov. 28	2 Corinthians 4–6
☐	Nov. 29	2 Corinthians 7–9
☐	Nov. 30	2 Corinthians 10–13
☐	Dec. 1	Galatians 1–3
☐	Dec. 2	Galatians 4–6
☐	Dec. 3	Ephesians 1–3
☐	Dec. 4	Ephesians 4–6
☐	Dec. 5	Philippians 1–4
☐	Dec. 6	Colossians 1–4
☐	Dec. 7	1 Thessalonians 1–5
☐	Dec. 8	2 Thessalonians 1–3
☐	Dec. 9	1 Timothy 1–3
☐	Dec. 10	1 Timothy 4–6
☐	Dec. 11	2 Timothy 1–4
☐	Dec. 12	Titus 1–3
☐	Dec. 13	Philemon
☐	Dec. 14	Hebrews 1–3
☐	Dec. 15	Hebrews 4–6
☐	Dec. 16	Hebrews 7–9
☐	Dec. 17	Hebrews 10–13
☐	Dec. 18	James 1–3
☐	Dec. 19	James 4–5
☐	Dec. 20	1 Peter 1–5
☐	Dec. 21	2 Peter 1–3
☐	Dec. 22	1 John 1–3
☐	Dec. 23	1 John 4–5
☐	Dec. 24	2 John, 3 John, Jude
☐	Dec. 25	Revelation 1–3
☐	Dec. 26	Revelation 4–6
☐	Dec. 27	Revelation 7–9
☐	Dec. 28	Revelation 10–12
☐	Dec. 29	Revelation 13–15
☐	Dec. 30	Revelation 16–18
☐	Dec. 31	Revelation 19–22

Commentary Index

Concordance

A

ABASED
I know how to be *a* Phil 4:12

ABBA
And He said, "*A* Mark 14:36
whom we cry out, "*A* Rom 8:15

ABHOR
Therefore I *a* myself Job 42:6

ABHORRED
a His own inheritance Ps 106:40

ABIDE
the Most High Shall *a* Ps 91:1
Him, "If you *a* John 8:31
"If you *a* in Me John 15:7
a in My love John 15:9

ABIDES
He who *a* in Me John 15:5
will of God *a* forever 1 John 2:17

ABIDING
not have His word *a* John 5:38

ABILITY
to his own *a* Matt 25:15
a which God supplies 1 Pet 4:11

ABLE
shall give as he is *a* Deut 16:17
whom we serve is *a* Dan 3:17
God is *a* to raise up Matt 3:9
fear Him who is *a* Matt 10:28
you *a* to drink the Matt 20:22
that He is *a* 2 Tim 1:12
learning and never *a* 2 Tim 3:7
that God was *a* to Heb 11:19

ABOLISHED
having *a* in His flesh Eph 2:15
Christ, who has *a* 2 Tim 1:10

ABOMINABLE
deny Him, being *a* Titus 1:16
unbelieving, *a* Rev 21:8

ABOMINATION
Yes, seven are an *a* Prov 6:16
the scoffer is an *a* Prov 24:9
prayer is an *a* Prov 28:9
and place there the *a* Dan 11:31
the *a* of desolation Dan 12:11
the '*a* of desolation,' Matt 24:15

ABOMINATIONS
delights in their *a* Is 66:3
a golden cup full of *a* Rev 17:4

ABOUND
the offense might *a* Rom 5:20
sin that grace may *a* Rom 6:1
to make all grace *a* 2 Cor 9:8
and I know how to *a* Phil 4:12

ABOUNDED
But where sin *a* Rom 5:20

ABOUNDING
immovable, always *a* 1 Cor 15:58

ABOVE
that is in heaven *a* Ex 20:4
A it stood seraphim Is 6:2
"He who comes from *a* John 3:31
I am from *a* John 8:23
given you from *a* John 19:11
things which are *a* Col 3:1
perfect gift is from *a* James 1:17

ABSENT
in the body we are *a* 2 Cor 5:6

ABSTAIN
we write to them to *a* Acts 15:20
A from every form 1 Thess 5:22

ABUNDANCE
put in out of their *a* Mark 12:44
not consist in the *a* Luke 12:15

ABUNDANT
in labors more *a* 2 Cor 11:23

ABUNDANTLY
a satisfied with the Ps 36:8
may have it more *a* John 10:10
to do exceedingly *a* Eph 3:20

ACCEPT
offering, I will not *a* Jer 14:12
Should I *a* this from Mal 1:13

ACCEPTABLE
a time I have heard Is 49:8
proclaim the *a* year Is 61:2
proclaim the *a* year Luke 4:19
is that good and *a* Rom 12:2

ACCEPTABLY
we may serve God *a* Heb 12:28

ACCEPTED
Behold, now is the *a* 2 Cor 6:2
which He made us *a* Eph 1:6

ACCESS
whom also we have *a* Rom 5:2

ACCOMPLISHED
all things were now *a* John 19:28

ACCORD
continued with one *a* Acts 1:14

ACCOUNT
they will give *a* Matt 12:36
put that on my *a* Philem 18

ACCOUNTED
in the LORD, and He *a* Gen 15:6
his faith is *a* Rom 4:5
God, and it was *a* Gal 3:6
God, and it was *a* James 2:23

ACCURSED
not know the law is *a* John 7:49
of God calls Jesus *a* 1 Cor 12:3
to you, let him be *a* Gal 1:8

ACCUSATION
over His head the *a* Matt 27:37
they might find an *a* Luke 6:7

ACCUSE
they began to *a* Him Luke 23:2

ACCUSED
while He was being *a* Matt 27:12

ACCUSER
a of our brethren Rev 12:10

ACCUSING
their thoughts *a* Rom 2:15

ACKNOWLEDGE
a my transgressions Ps 51:3
In all your ways *a* Prov 3:6

ACKNOWLEDGES
a the Son has the 1 John 2:23

ACQUAINT
a yourself with Him Job 22:21

ACQUAINTED
A Man of sorrows and *a* Is 53:3

ACQUIT
at all *a* the wicked Nah 1:3

ACT
in the very *a* John 8:4

ACTIONS
by Him *a* are weighed 1 Sam 2:3

ACTS
of Your awesome *a* Ps 145:6

ADD
Do not *a* to His words Prov 30:6

ADDED
And the Lord *a* to the Acts 2:47
It was *a* because of Gal 3:19

ADMONISH
a him as a 2 Thess 3:15

ADMONITION
written for our *a* 1 Cor 10:11
in the training and *a* Eph 6:4

ADOPTION
the Spirit of *a* Rom 8:15
waiting for the *a* Rom 8:23
to whom pertain the *a* Rom 9:4

ADORN
also, that the women *a* 1 Tim 2:9

ADORNED
God also *a* themselves 1 Pet 3:5
prepared as a bride *a* Rev 21:2

ADRIFT
A among the dead Ps 88:5

ADULTERER
The eye of the *a* Job 24:15

ADULTERERS
nor idolaters, nor *a* 1 Cor 6:9
a God will judge Heb 13:4

ADULTEROUS
a generation Matt 12:39

ADULTERY
You shall not commit *a* Ex 20:14
already committed *a* Matt 5:28
is divorced commits *a* Matt 5:32
another commits *a* Mark 10:11
those who commit *a* Rev 2:22

ADVANTAGE
a that I go away John 16:7
Satan should take *a* 2 Cor 2:11

ADVERSARIES
and there are many *a* 1 Cor 16:9
terrified by your *a* Phil 1:28

ADVERSARY
"Agree with your *a* Matt 5:25
opportunity to the *a* 1 Tim 5:14
a the devil walks 1 Pet 5:8

ADVERSITY
I shall never be in *a* Ps 10:6
the day of *a* consider Eccl 7:14

ADVICE
in this I give my *a* 2 Cor 8:10

ADVOCATE
sins, we have an *A* 1 John 2:1

AFAR
and not a God *a* Jer 23:23
to you who were *a* Eph 2:17
having seen them *a* Heb 11:13

AFFAIRS
himself with the *a* 2 Tim 2:4

AFFECTION
to his wife the *a* 1 Cor 7:3

AFFECTIONATE
Be kindly *a* to one Rom 12:10

AFFIRM
you to *a* constantly Titus 3:8

AFFLICT
a Your heritage Ps 94:5
For He does not *a* Lam 3:33

AFFLICTED
To him who is *a* Job 6:14
hears the cry of the *a* Job 34:28
days of the *a* are evil Prov 15:15
Smitten by God, and *a* Is 53:4
"O you *a* one Is 54:11
being destitute, *a* Heb 11:37

AFFLICTING
A the just and taking Amos 5:12

AFFLICTION
is, the bread of *a* Deut 16:3
a take hold of me Job 30:16
and it is an evil *a* Eccl 6:2
For our light *a* 2 Cor 4:17
supposing to add *a* Phil 1:16

AFRAID
garden, and I was *a* Gen 3:10
saying, "Do not be *a* Gen 15:1
none will make you *a* Lev 26:6
ungodliness made me *a* Ps 18:4
Whenever I am *a* Ps 56:3
one will make them *a* Is 17:2
do not be *a* Matt 14:27
if you do evil, be *a* Rom 13:4
do good and are not *a* 1 Pet 3:6

AFTERWARD
a receive me to glory Ps 73:24
you shall follow Me *a* John 13:36

AGAIN
'You must be born *a* John 3:7
having been born *a* 1 Pet 1:23

AGAINST
come to 'set a man *a* Matt 10:35
or house divided *a* Matt 12:25
Me is *a* Me Matt 12:30
a the Spirit will not Matt 12:31
lifted up his heel *a* John 13:18
LORD and *a* His Christ Acts 4:26
to kick *a* the goads Acts 9:5
a the promises of God Gal 3:21
we do not wrestle *a* Eph 6:12
I have a few things *a* Rev 2:20

AGE
the grave at a full *a* Job 5:26
and in the *a* to come Mark 10:30

AGED
a one as Paul, the *a* Philem 9

AGES
ordained before the *a* 1 Cor 2:7

AGONY
And being in *a* Luke 22:44

AGREE
that if two of you *a* Matt 18:19

AGREED
unless they are *a* Amos 3:3

AGREEMENT
what *a* has the temple 2 Cor 6:16

AIR
the birds of the *a* Gen 1:26
of the *a* have nests Luke 9:58
of the power of the *a* Eph 2:2
the Lord in the *a* 1 Thess 4:17

ALIENATED
darkened, being *a* Eph 4:18
you, who once were *a* Col 1:21

ALIENS
A have devoured his Hos 7:9
Christ, being *a* Eph 2:12

ALIKE
esteems every day *a* Rom 14:5

ALIVE
I kill and I make *a* Deut 32:39
was dead and is *a* Luke 15:24
presented Himself *a* Acts 1:3
indeed to sin, but *a* Rom 6:11
all shall be made *a* 1 Cor 15:22
that we who are *a* 1 Thess 4:15
and behold, I am *a* Rev 1:18
These two were cast *a* Rev 19:20

ALLELUIA
Again they said, "*A* Rev 19:3

ALLOW
a Your Holy One Ps 16:10
a My faithfulness Ps 89:33
a Your Holy One Acts 2:27

ALLURE
of emptiness, they *a* 2 Pet 2:18

ALMOND
a tree blossoms Eccl 12:5

ALMOST
a persuade me to Acts 26:28

ALOES
of myrrh and *a* John 19:39

ALPHA
"I am the *A* and the Rev 1:8
"I am the *A* and the Rev 22:13

ALTAR
Then Noah built an *a* Gen 8:20
'An *a* of earth you Ex 20:24
it to you upon the *a* Lev 17:11
your gift to the *a* Matt 5:23
swears by the *a* Matt 23:18
I even found an *a* Acts 17:23
We have an *a* from Heb 13:10

ALTARS
Even Your *a*, O LORD Ps 84:3
and torn down Your *a* Rom 11:3

ALTERED
of His face was *a* Luke 9:29

ALWAYS
delight, Rejoicing *a* Prov 8:30
the poor with you *a* Matt 26:11
lo, I am with you *a* Matt 28:20

to them, that men *a* Luke 18:1
immovable, *a* 1 Cor 15:58
Rejoice in the Lord *a* Phil 4:4
thus we shall *a* 1 Thess 4:17
a be ready to give a 1 Pet 3:15

AM
to Moses, "I *A* WHO I Ex 3:14
First and I *a* the Last Is 44:6
in My name, I *a* Matt 18:20
a the bread of life John 6:35
a the light of the John 8:12
I *a* from above John 8:23
Abraham was, I *A* John 8:58
"I *a* the door John 10:9
a the good shepherd John 10:11
a the resurrection John 11:25
to him, "I *a* the way John 14:6
of God I *a* what I *a* 1 Cor 15:10

AMBASSADOR
for which I am an *a* Eph 6:20

AMBASSADORS
we are *a* for Christ 2 Cor 5:20

AMBITION
Christ from selfish *a* Phil 1:16

AMEN
are Yes, and in Him *A* 2 Cor 1:20
creatures said, "*A* Rev 5:14

ANCHOR
hope we have as an *a* Heb 6:19

ANCIENT
Do not remove the *a* Prov 23:10
"until the *A* of Days Dan 7:22

ANGEL
"Behold, I send an *A* Ex 23:20
Manoah said to the *A* Judg 13:17
the *A* of His Presence Is 63:9
things, behold, an *a* Matt 1:20
for an *a* of the Lord Matt 28:2
Then an *a* of the Lord Luke 1:11
And behold, an *a* Luke 2:9
a appeared to Him Luke 22:43
For an *a* went down at John 5:4
a has spoken to Him John 12:29
But at night an *a* Acts 5:19
A who appeared to him Acts 7:35
immediately an *a* Acts 12:23
himself into an *a* 2 Cor 11:14
even if we, or an *a* Gal 1:8
Then I saw a strong *a* Rev 5:2
Jesus, have sent My *a* Rev 22:16

ANGELS
If He charges His *a* Job 4:18
lower than the *a* Ps 8:5
He shall give His *a* Ps 91:11
He shall give His *a* Matt 4:6
not even the *a* Matt 24:36
and all the holy *a* Matt 25:31
twelve legions of *a* Matt 26:53
And she saw two *a* John 20:12
and worship of *a* Col 2:18
much better than the *a* Heb 1:4
entertained *a* Heb 13:2
things which *a* desire 1 Pet 1:12
did not spare the *a* 2 Pet 2:4
a who did not keep Jude 6

ANGER
For His *a* is but for a Ps 30:5
gracious, Slow to *a* Ps 103:8
Nor will He keep His *a* Ps 103:9
around at them with *a* Mark 3:5
bitterness, wrath, *a* Eph 4:31

ANGRY
Cain. "Why are you *a* Gen 4:6
"Let not the Lord be *a* Gen 18:30
the Son, lest He be *a* Ps 2:12
a man stirs up strife Prov 29:22
right for you to be *a* Jon 4:4
you that whoever is *a* Matt 5:22
"Be *a*, and do not Eph 4:26

ANGUISH
remembers the *a* John 16:21
tribulation and *a* Rom 2:9

ANIMAL
of every clean *a* Gen 7:2
set him on his own *a* Luke 10:34

ANIMALS
of *a* after their kind Gen 6:20
of four-footed *a* Acts 10:12

ANNUL
years later, cannot *a* Gal 3:17

ANNULS
is confirmed, no one *a* Gal 3:15

ANOINT
a my head with oil Ps 23:5
when you fast, *a* Matt 6:17
a My body for burial Mark 14:8
a your eyes with eye Rev 3:18

ANOINTED
"Surely the LORD's *a* 1 Sam 16:6
destroy the LORD's *a* 2 Sam 1:14
"Do not touch My *a* 1 Chr 16:22
Because He has *a* Luke 4:18
but this woman has *a* Luke 7:46
a the eyes of the John 9:6
that Mary who *a* John 11:2
Jesus, whom You *a* Acts 4:27
and has *a* us is God 2 Cor 1:21

ANOINTING
But you have an *a* 1 John 2:20

ANOTHER
that you love one *a* John 13:34

ANSWER
Call, and I will *a* Job 13:22
How shall I *a* Him Job 31:14
the day that I call, *a* Ps 102:2
In Your faithfulness *a* Ps 143:1
a turns away wrath Prov 15:1
a a fool according Prov 26:4
or what you should *a* Luke 12:11
you may have an *a* 2 Cor 5:12

ANT
Go to the *a* Prov 6:6

ANTICHRIST
heard that the *A* 1 John 2:18
a who denies the 1 John 2:22
is a deceiver and an *a* 2 John 7

ANTITYPE
a which now saves us 1 Pet 3:21

ANXIETIES
the multitude of my *a* Ps 94:19

ANXIETY
A in the heart of man Prov 12:25

ANXIOUS
Be *a* for nothing Phil 4:6

APART
justified by faith *a* Rom 3:28

APOSTLE
called to be an *a* Rom 1:1
consider the *A* Heb 3:1

APOSTLES
of the twelve *a* Matt 10:2
He also named *a* Luke 6:13
am the least of the *a* 1 Cor 15:9
none of the other *a* Gal 1:19
gave some to be *a* Eph 4:11

APOSTLESHIP
in this ministry and *a* Acts 1:25
are the seal of my *a* 1 Cor 9:2

APPAREL
gold rings, in fine *a* James 2:2
or putting on fine *a* 1 Pet 3:3

APPEAL
love's sake I rather *a* Philem 9

APPEAR
and let the dry land *a* Gen 1:9
also outwardly *a* Matt 23:28
God would *a* Luke 19:11
For we must all *a* 2 Cor 5:10

APPEARANCE
Do not look at his *a* 1 Sam 16:7
judge according to *a* John 7:24
those who boast in *a* 2 Cor 5:12
found in *a* as a man Phil 2:8

APPEARED
an angel of the Lord *a* Luke 1:11
who *a* in glory and Luke 9:31
brings salvation has *a* Titus 2:11
of the ages, He has *a* Heb 9:26

APPEARING
Lord Jesus Christ's *a* 1 Tim 6:14
and the dead at His *a* 2 Tim 4:1
who have loved His *a* 2 Tim 4:8

APPEARS
can stand when He *a* Mal 3:2
who is our life *a* Col 3:4
the Chief Shepherd *a* 1 Pet 5:4
that when He *a* 1 John 2:28

APPETITE
are a man given to *a* Prov 23:2

APPLE
And my law as the *a* Prov 7:2

APPLES
fitly spoken is like *a* Prov 25:11

APPLIED
a my heart to know Eccl 7:25

APPOINT
For God did not *a* 1 Thess 5:9

APPOINTED
And as it is *a* for men Heb 9:27

APPROACH
year, make those who *a* Heb 10:1

APPROACHING
as you see the Day *a* Heb 10:25

APPROVE
do the same but also *a* Rom 1:32

APPROVED
to God and *a* by men Rom 14:18
to present yourself *a* 2 Tim 2:15

ARBITRATOR
Me a judge or an *a* Luke 12:14

ARCHANGEL
the voice of an *a* 1 Thess 4:16

ARGUMENTS
casting down *a* and 2 Cor 10:5

ARISE
A, shine Is 60:1
But the LORD will *a* Is 60:2
you who sleep, *A* Eph 5:14

ARK
"Make yourself an *a* Gen 6:14
him, she took an *a* Ex 2:3
Bezalel made the *a* Ex 37:1
in heaven, and the *a* Rev 11:19

ARM
with an outstretched *a* Ex 6:6
Have you an *a* like God Job 40:9
strength with His *a* Luke 1:51
a yourselves also with 1 Pet 4:1

ARMED
a strong man, fully *a* Luke 11:21

ARMIES
And he sent out his *a* Matt 22:7
surrounded by *a* Luke 21:20
And the *a* in heaven Rev 19:14
the earth, and their *a* Rev 19:19

ARMOR
Put on the whole *a* Eph 6:11

ARMS
are the everlasting *a* Deut 33:27
took Him up in his *a* Luke 2:28

AROMA
the one we are the *a* 2 Cor 2:16
for a sweet-smelling *a* Eph 5:2

AROUSED
LORD was greatly *a* Num 11:10
Then Joseph, being *a* Matt 1:24

ARRAYED
his glory was not *a* Matt 6:29
"Who are these *a* Rev 7:13

ARROGANCE
Pride and *a* and the Prov 8:13

ARROW
a that flies by day Ps 91:5

ARROWS
a pierce me deeply Ps 38:2
Like *a* in the hand of Ps 127:4

ASCEND
Who may *a* into the Ps 24:3
If I *a* into heaven Ps 139:8
'I will *a* into heaven Is 14:13
see the Son of Man *a* John 6:62

ASCENDED
You have *a* on high Ps 68:18
"No one has *a* John 3:13
"When He *a* on high Eph 4:8

ASCENDING
the angels of God *a* John 1:51

ASCRIBE
A strength to God Ps 68:34

ASHAMED
Let me not be *a* Ps 25:2
And Israel shall be *a* Hos 10:6
For whoever is *a* Mark 8:38
am not *a* of the gospel Rom 1:16
Therefore God is not *a* Heb 11:16

ASHES
become like dust and *a* Job 30:19
in sackcloth and *a* Luke 10:13

ASIDE
lay something *a* 1 Cor 16:2
lay *a* all filthiness James 1:21
Therefore, laying *a* 1 Pet 2:1

ASK
when your children *a* Josh 4:6
"*A* a sign for yourself Is 7:11
whatever things you *a* Matt 21:22
a, and it will be Luke 11:9
that whatever You *a* John 11:22
a anything in My John 14:14
in that day you will *a* John 16:23
above all that we *a* Eph 3:20
wisdom, let him *a* James 1:5
But let him *a* in faith James 1:6
because you do not *a* James 4:2

ASKS
For everyone who *a* Matt 7:8
you who, if his son *a* Matt 7:9
Or if he *a* for a fish Luke 11:11

ASLEEP
But He was *a* Matt 8:24
some have fallen *a* 1 Cor 15:6
those who are *a* 1 Thess 4:15

ASSEMBLING
not forsaking the *a* Heb 10:25

ASSEMBLY
a I will praise You Ps 22:22
fast, Call a sacred *a* Joel 1:14
a I will sing praise Heb 2:12
to the general *a* Heb 12:23

ASSURANCE
riches of the full *a* Col 2:2
Spirit and in much *a* 1 Thess 1:5
to the full *a* of hope Heb 6:11

ASSURE
a our heats before 1 John 3:19

ASSURED
learned and been *a* 2 Tim 3:14

ASTONISHED
Just as many were *a* Is 52:14
who heard Him were *a* Luke 2:47

ASTRAY
one of them goes *a* Matt 18:12
like sheep going *a* 1 Pet 2:25

ATONEMENT
the blood that makes *a* Lev 17:11
for it is the Day of *A* Lev 23:28
there will be no *a* Is 22:14

ATTAIN
It is high, I cannot *a* Ps 139:6
worthy to *a* that age Luke 20:35
by any means, I may *a* Phil 3:11

ATTENTION
My son, give *a* to my Prov 4:20

ATTENTIVE
Let Your ears be *a* Ps 130:2

ATTESTED
a Man *a* by God to you Acts 2:22

AUSTERE
because you are an *a* Luke 19:21

AUTHOR
For God is not the *a* 1 Cor 14:33
unto Jesus, the *a* Heb 12:2

AUTHORITIES
a that exist are Rom 13:1

AUTHORITY
them as one having *a* Matt 7:29
"All *a* has been given Matt 28:18
a I will give You Luke 4:6
and has given Him *a* John 5:27
You have given Him *a* John 17:2
the flesh, reject *a* Jude 8

AUTUMN
a trees without fruit Jude 12

AVAILS
of a righteous man *a* James 5:16

AVENGE
Beloved, do not *a* Rom 12:19
a our blood on those Rev 6:10

AVENGER
the Lord is the *a* 1 Thess 4:6

AWAKE
be satisfied when I *a* Ps 17:15
it is high time to *a* Rom 13:11
A to righteousness 1 Cor 15:34

AWAY
the wind drives *a* Ps 1:4
Do not cast me *a* Ps 51:11
A time to cast *a* Eccl 3:5
fait one, And come *a* Song 2:10
minded to put her *a* Matt 1:19
and earth will pass *a* Matt 24:35
"I am going *a* John 8:21
they cried out, "*A* John 19:15
unless the falling *a* 2 Thess 2:3
in Asia have turned *a* 2 Tim 1:15

heard, lest we drift *a* Heb 2:1
if they fall *a* Heb 6:6
can never take *a* Heb 10:11
world is passing *a* 1 John 2:17
if anyone takes *a* Rev 22:19

AWESOME
a is this place Gen 28:17
God, the great and *a* Deut 7:21
By *a* deeds in Ps 65:5
O God, You are more *a* Ps 68:35
Your great and *a* name Ps 99:3

AWL
his ear with an *a* Ex 21:6

AX
If the *a* is dull Eccl 10:10
And even now the *a* Matt 3:10

B

BABBLER
"What does this *b* Acts 17:18

BABBLINGS
the profane and idle *b* 1 Tim 6:20

BABE
the *b* leaped in my Luke 1:44
You will find a *B* Luke 2:12
for he is a *b* Heb 5:13

BABES
Out of the mouth of *b* Ps 8:2
revealed them to *b* Matt 11:25
of the mouth of *b* Matt 21:16
as to carnal, as to *b* 1 Cor 3:1
as newborn *b* 1 Pet 2:2

BACK
for the fool's *b* Prov 26:3
I gave My *b* to those Is 50:6
plow, and looking *b* Luke 9:62
of those who draw *b* Heb 10:39
someone turns him *b* James 5:19

BACKBITERS
b, haters of God Rom 1:30

BACKBITING
b tongue an angry Prov 25:23

BACKSLIDER
The *b* in heart will be Prov 14:14

BACKSLIDINGS
And I will heal your *b* Jer 3:22

BACKWARD
ten degrees *b* 2 Kin 20:11

BAD
b trees bears *b* fruit Matt 7:17

BAG
"nor *b* for your Matt 10:10

BAKED
b unleavened cakes Ex 12:39

BAKER
the butler and the *b* Gen 40:1

BALANCES
Falsifying the *b* Amos 8:5

BALD
every head shall be *b* Jer 48:37

BALDHEAD
Go up, you *b* 2 Kin 2:23

BALM
no *b* in Gilead Jer 8:22

BANDAGED
and *b* his wounds Luke 10:34

BANKERS
my money with the *b* Matt 25:27

BANNERS
we will set up our *b* Ps 20:5
as an army with *b* Song 6:4

BANQUET
b that I have prepared Esth 5:4

BANQUETING
He brought me to the *b* Song 2:4

BAPTISM
coming to his *b* Matt 3:7
b that I am baptized Matt 20:22
"But I have a *b* Luke 12:50
said, "Into John's *b* Acts 19:3
Lord, one faith, one *b* Eph 4:5
buried with Him in *b* Col 2:12

BAPTISMS
of the doctrine of *b* Heb 6:2

BAPTIZE
"I indeed *b* you with Matt 3:11
Himself did not *b* John 4:2

BAPTIZED
b will be saved Mark 16:16
every one of you be *b* Acts 2:38
all his family were *b* Acts 16:33
Arise and be *b* Acts 22:16
were *b* into Christ Rom 6:3
I thank God that I *b* 1 Cor 1:14
Spirit we were all *b* 1 Cor 12:13

BAPTIZING
b them in the name of Matt 28:19

BARBARIAN
nor uncircumcised, *b* Col 3:11

BARLEY
here who has five *b* John 6:9

BARN
the wheat into my *b* Matt 13:30

BARNS
reap nor gather into *b* Matt 6:26
I will pull down my *b* Luke 12:18

BARREN
But Sarai was *b* Gen 11:30
"Sing, O *b* Is 54:1

BASE
and the *b* things of 1 Cor 1:28

BASIN
poured water into a *b* John 13:5

BASKET
and put it under a *b* Matt 5:15
I was let down in a *b* 2 Cor 11:33

BASKETS
they took up twelve *b* Matt 14:20

BATHED
to him, "He who is *b* John 13:10

BATS
To the moles and *b* Is 2:20

BATTLE
b is the LORD's 1 Sam 17:47
the *b* to the strong Eccl 9:11
became valiant in *b* Heb 11:34

BEAR
greater than I can *b* Gen 4:13
whom Sarah shall *b* Gen 17:21
not *b* false witness Ex 20:16
b their Iniquities Is 53:11
child, and *b* a Son Matt 1:23
A good tree cannot *b* Matt 7:18
how long shall I *b* Matt 17:17
by, to *b* His cross Mark 15:21
whoever does not *b* Luke 14:27
are strong ought to *b* Rom 15:1
B one another's Gal 6:2
b the sins of many Heb 9:28

BEARD
the edges of your *b* Lev 19:27
Running down on the *b* Ps 133:2

BEARING
goes forth weeping, *B* Ps 126:6
And He, *b* His cross John 19:17
b His reproach Heb 13:13

BEARS
Every branch that *b* John 15:2

BEAST
You preserve man and *b* Ps 36:6
And I saw a *b* rising Rev 13:1
the mark of the *b* Rev 19:20

BEASTS
like brute *b* Jude 10

BEAT
b their swords into Is 2:4
spat in His face and *b* Matt 26:67

BEATEN
Three times I was *b* 2 Cor 11:25

BEAUTIFUL
B in elevation Ps 48:2
has made everything *b* Eccl 3:11
my love, you are as *b* Song 6:4
How *b* upon the Is 52:7
indeed appear *b* Matt 23:27

BEAUTIFY
b the place of My Is 60:13

BEAUTY
"The *b* of Israel is 2 Sam 1:19
To behold the *b* Ps 27:4
see the King in His *b* Is 33:17
no *b* that we should Is 53:2

BECAME
b a living being Gen 2:7
to the Jews I *b* 1 Cor 9:20

BED
I remember You on my *b* Ps 63:6

if I make my *b* in hell Ps 139:8
"Arise; take up your *b* Matt 9:6
be two men in one *b* Luke 17:34
and the *b* undefiled Heb 13:4

BEDS
sing aloud on their *b* Ps 149:5

BEFOREHAND
up, do not worry *b* Mark 43:11
told you all things *b* Mark 13:23
when He testified *b* 1 Pet 1:11

BEG
b you as sojourners 1 Pet 2:11

BEGAN
since the world *b* Luke 1:70

BEGGAR
there was a certain *b* Luke 16:20

BEGGARLY
weak and *b* elements Gal 4:9

BEGINNING
b God created the Gen 1:1
In the *b* was the Word John 1:1
a murderer from the *b* John 8:44
True Witness, the *B* Rev 3:14
and the Omega, the *B* Rev 21:6

BEGOTTEN
I have *b* You Ps 2:7
glory as of the only *b* John 1:14
loves him who is *b* 1 John 5:1

BEGUILING
b unstable souls 2 Pet 2:14

BEGUN
Having *b* in the Spirit Gal 3:3

BEHALF
you on Christ's *b* 2 Cor 5:20

BEHAVE
does not *b* rudely 1 Cor 13:5

BEHAVED
blamelessly we *b* 1 Thess 2:10

BEHAVIOR
of good *b*, hospitable 1 Tim 3:2

BEHEADED
and had John *b* Matt 14:10

BEHOLD
B, the virgin shall Is 7:14
Judah, "*B* your God Is 40:9
* '*B* the Lamb of God John 1:36
to them, "*B* the Man John 19:5
B what manner of 1 John 3:1

BEHOLDING
with unveiled face, *b* 2 Cor 3:18

BEING
move and have our *b* Acts 17:28
who, *b* in the form of Phil 2:6

BELIEVE
tears, "Lord, I *b* Mark 9:24
have no root, who *b* Luke 8:13
slow of heart to *b* Luke 24:25
to those who *b* John 1:12
this, that they may *b* John 11:42
that you may *b* John 20:31
the Lord Jesus and *b* Rom 10:9
Christ, not only to *b* Phil 1:29
comes to God must *b* Heb 11:6
b that there is one James 2:19
Even the demons *b* James 2:19

BELIEVED
And he *b* in the LORD Gen 15:6
Who has *b* our report Is 53:1
seen Me, you have *b* John 20:29
"Abraham *b* God Rom 4:3
whom I have *b* 2 Tim 1:12

BELIEVERS
example to the *b* 1 Tim 4:12

BELIEVES
The simple *b* every Prov 14:15
that whoever *b* in Him John 3:16
"He who *b* in the Son John 3:36
with the heart one *b* Rom 10:10

BELIEVING
you ask in prayer, *b* Matt 21:22

BELLY
On your *b* you shall go Gen 3:14
and Jonah was in the *b* Jon 1:17
whose god is their *b* Phil 3:19

BELOVED
so He gives His *b* Ps 127:2
My *b* is mine Song 2:16
"This is My *b* Matt 3:17
us accepted in the *B* Eph 1:6
Luke the *b* physician Col 4:14
"This is My *b* 2 Pet 1:17

BELT
with a leather *b* Matt 3:4

BEND
The wicked *b* their bow Ps 11:2

BENEATH
"You are from *b* John 8:23

BENEFACTORS
them are called '*b* Luke 22:25

BENEFIT
have a second *b* 2 Cor 1:15

BESEECH
b you therefore Rom 12:1

BESIDE
He leads me *b* the Ps 23:2
"Paul, you are *b* Acts 26:24

BEST
desire the *b* 1 Cor 12:31

BESTOWED
love the Father has *b* 1 John 3:1

BETRAY
you, one of you will *b* Matt 26:21

BETRAYED
Man is about to be *b* Matt 17:22

BETRAYER
See, My *b* is at Matt 26:46

BETRAYING
"Judas, are you *b* Luke 22:48

BETRAYS
who is the one who *b* John 21:20

BETROTH
"I will *b* you to Me Hos 2:19

BETROTHED
to a virgin *b* to a man Luke 1:27

BETTER
b than sacrifice 1 Sam 15:22
It is *b* to trust in Ps 118:8
For it is *b* to marry 1 Cor 7:9
Christ, which is far *b* Phil 1:23
b than the angels Heb 1:4
b things concerning Heb 6:9

BEWARE
"*B* of false prophets Matt 7:15

BEWITCHED
b you that you should Gal 3:1

BEYOND
advanced in Judaism *b* Gal 1:14

BILLOWS
b have gone over me Ps 42:7

BIND
and whatever you *b* Matt 16:19
'*B* him hand and foot Matt 22:13

BIRD
soul, "Flee as a *b* Ps 11:1

BIRDS
b make their nests Ps 104:17
"Look at the *b* Matt 6:26
have holes and *b* Matt 8:20

BIRTH
the day of one's *b* Eccl 7:1
Now the *b* of Jesus Matt 1:18
will rejoice at his *b* Luke 1:14
conceived, it gives *b* James 1:15

BIRTHDAY
was Pharaoh's *b* Gen 40:20

BIRTHRIGHT
Esau despised his *b* Gen 25:34

BISHOP
the position of a *b* 1 Tim 3:1
b must be blameless Titus 1:7

BIT
and they *b* the people Num 21:6

BITE
A serpent may *b* Eccl 10:11
But if you *b* and Gal 5:15

BITTER
b herbs they Ex 12:8
and do not be *b* Col 3:19
But if you have *b* James 3:14

BITTERLY
And Hezekiah wept *b* 2 Kin 20:3
went out and wept *b* Matt 26:75

BITTERNESS
you are poisoned by *b* Acts 8:23
b springing up cause Heb 12:15

BLACK
one hair white or *b* Matt 5:36
a *b* horse Rev 6:5
and the sun became *b* Rev 6:12

BLACKNESS
whom is reserved the *b* Jude 13

BLACKSMITH
I have created the *b* Is 54:16

BLADE
first the *b* Mark 4:28

BLAME
be holy and without *b* Eph 1:4

BLAMELESS
and that man was *b* Job 1:1
body be preserved *b* 1 Thess 5:23

BLAMELESSLY
b we behaved 1 Thess 2:10

BLASPHEME
b Your name forever Ps 74:10
compelled them to *b* Acts 26:11
b that noble name James 2:7

BLASPHEMED
who passed by *b* Him Matt 27:39
great heat, and they *b* Rev 16:9

BLASPHEMER
I was formerly a *b* 1 Tim 1:13

BLASPHEMES
b the name of the Lev 24:16
"This Man *b* Matt 9:3

BLASPHEMIES
is this who speaks *b* Luke 5:21

BLASPHEMY
but the *b* against Matt 12:31
was full of names of *b* Rev 17:3

BLEATING
"What then is this *b* 1 Sam 15:14

BLEMISH
be holy and without *b* Eph 5:27
as of a lamb without *b* 1 Pet 1:19

BLEMISHED
to the Lord what is *b* Mal 1:14

BLESS
b those who *b* you Gen 12:3
You go unless You *b* Gen 32:26
"The LORD *b* you and Num 6:24
b the LORD at all Ps 34:1
b You while I live Ps 63:4
b His holy name Ps 103:1
b those who curse Luke 6:28
B those who Rom 12:14
Being reviled, we *b* 1 Cor 4:12

BLESSED
B is the man who walks Ps 1:1
B is the man to whom Ps 32:2
B is the nation whose Ps 33:12
B is he who comes Ps 118:26
rise up and call her *b* Prov 31:28
"*B* are the poor in Matt 5:3
B are those who mourn Matt 5:4
B are the meek Matt 5:5
B are those who hunger Matt 5:6
B are the merciful Matt 5:7
B are the pure in Matt 5:8
B are the peacemakers Matt 5:9
B are those who are Matt 5:10
B is He who comes Matt 21:9
'It is more *b* to give Acts 20:35
B be the God and Eph 1:3
"*B* are the dead who Rev 14:13

BLESSING
And you shall be a *b* Gen 12:2
before you today a *b* Deut 11:26
shall be showers of *b* Ezek 34:26
and you shall be a *b* Zech 8:13
that the *b* of Abraham Gal 3:14
with every spiritual *b* Eph 1:3

BLIND
To open *b* eyes Is 42:7
His watchmen are *b* Is 56:10
b leads the *b* Matt 15:14
to Him, "Are we *b* John 9:40
miserable, poor, *b* Rev 3:17

BLINDED
and the rest were *b* Rom 11:7

BLINDS
a bribe, for a bribe *b* Deut 16:19

BLOOD
of your brother's *b* Gen 4:10
b shall be shed Gen 9:6
b that makes atonement Lev 17:11
hands are full of *b* Is 1:15
And the moon into *b* Joel 2:31
For this is My *b* Matt 26:28
"His *b* be on us and Matt 27:25
covenant in My *b* Luke 22:20
were born, not of *b* John 1:13
b has eternal life John 6:54
with His own *b* Acts 20:28
propitiation by His *b* Rom 3:25
justified by His *b* Rom 5:9
through His *b* Eph 1:7
brought near by the *b* Eph 2:13
against flesh and *b* Eph 6:12
peace through the *b* Col 1:20
with the precious *b* 1 Pet 1:19
b of Jesus Christ His 1 John 1:7
our sins in His own *b* Rev 1:5
us to God by Your *b* Rev 5:9
them white in the *b* Rev 7:14
overcame him by the *b* Rev 12:11
a robe dipped in *b* Rev 19:13

BLOODSHED
me from the guilt of *b* Ps 51:14

BLOODTHIRSTY
The LORD abhors the *b* Ps 5:6

BLOSSOM
and *b* as the rose Is 35:1

BLOT
from my sins, and *b* Ps 51:9
and I will not *b* Rev 3:5

BLOTTED
your sins may be *b* Acts 3:19

BLOW
with a very severe *b* Jer 14:17

BLOWS
"The wind *b* where it John 3:8

BOAST
puts on his armor *b* 1 Kin 20:11
and make your *b* Rom 2:17
lest anyone should *b* Eph 2:9

BOASTERS
God, violent, proud, *b* Rom 1:30

BOASTING
Where is *b* then Rom 3:27

BODIES
b a living sacrifice Rom 12:1
not know that your *b* 1 Cor 6:15
wives as their own *b* Eph 5:28

BODILY
b form like a dove Luke 3:22
of the Godhead *b* Col 2:9

BODY
of the *b* is the eye Matt 6:22
those who kill the *b* Matt 10:28
this is My *b* Matt 26:26
of the temple of His *b* John 2:21
deliver me from this *b* Rom 7:24
redemption of our *b* Rom 8:23
members in one *b* Rom 12:4
But I discipline my *b* 1 Cor 9:27
b which is broken 1 Cor 11:24
baptized into one *b* 1 Cor 12:13
are the *b* of Christ 1 Cor 12:27
though I give my *b* 1 Cor 13:3
It is sown a natural *b* 1 Cor 15:44
in the *b* of His flesh Col 1:22
our sins in His own *b* 1 Pet 2:24

BOILS
Job with painful *b* Job 2:7

BOLDLY
therefore come *b* Heb 4:16

BOLDNESS
in whom we have *b* Eph 3:12
that we may have *b* 1 John 4:17

BOND
love, which is the *b* Col 3:14

BONDAGE
out of the house of *b* Ex 13:14
again with a yoke of *b* Gal 5:1

BONDS
"Let us break Their *b* Ps 2:3

BONDSERVANTS
B, be obedient to Eph 6:5
Masters, give your *b* Col 4:1

BONDWOMAN
the one by a *b* Gal 4:22

BONE
b clings to my skin Job 19:20

BONES
I can count all My *b* Ps 22:17
and my *b* waste away Ps 31:10
I kept silent, my *b* Ps 32:3
the wind, Or how the *b* Eccl 11:5
say to them, 'O dry *b* Ezek 37:4
of dead men's *b* Matt 23:27

b shall be broken John 19:36

BOOK
are written in the *b* Gal 3:10
in the Lamb's *B* Rev 21:27
the prophecy of this *b* Rev 22:18

BOOKS
b there is no end Eccl 12:12
not contain the *b* John 21:25
and *b* were opened Rev 20:12

BOOTH
of Zion is left as a *b* Is 1:8

BORDERS
and enlarge the *b* Matt 23:5

BORE
And to Sarah who *b* Is 51:2
b the sin of many Is 53:12
b our sicknesses Matt 8:17
Himself *b* our sins 1 Pet 2:24
b a male Child who was Rev 12:5

BORN
A time to be *b* Eccl 3:2
unto us a Child is *b* Is 9:6
b Jesus who is called Matt 1:16
unless one is *b* again John 3:3
"That which is *b* John 3:6
having been *b* again 1 Pet 1:23
who loves Is *b* of God 1 John 4:7

BORROWER
b is servant to the Prov 22:7

BORROWS
The wicked *b* and does Ps 37:21

BOSOM
to Abraham's *b* Luke 16:22
Son, who is in the *b* John 1:18

BOTTOMLESS
ascend out of the *b* Rev 17:8
the key to the *b* Rev 20:1

BOUGHT
b the threshing floor 2 Sam 24:24
all that he had and *b* Matt 13:46
For you were *b* at a 1 Cor 6:20
denying the Lord who *b* 2 Pet 2:1

BOUND
on earth will be *b* Matt 16:19
And see, now I go *b* Acts 20:22
who has a husband is *b* Rom 7:2
Are you *b* to a wife 1 Cor 7:27
Devil and Satan, and *b* Rev 20:2

BOUNTIFULLY
and he who sows *b* 2 Cor 9:6

BOW
"You shall not *b* Ex 23:24
let us worship and *b* Ps 95:6
who sat on it had a *b* Rev 6:2

BOWED
stood all around and *b* Gen 37:7
And they *b* the knee Matt 27:29

BOWL
and poured out his *b* Rev 16:2

BOWLS
Go and pour out the *b* Rev 16:1

BOX
had the money *b* John 13:29

BOYS
Shall be full of *b* Zech 8:5

BRAIDED
not with *b* hair or 1 Tim 2:9

BRANCH
raise to David a *B* Jer 23:5
forth My Servant the *B* Zech 3:8
b that bears fruit He John 15:2

BRANCHES
vine, you are the *b* John 15:5

BRASS
become sounding *b* 1 Cor 13:1

BRAVE
in the faith, be *b* 1 Cor 16:13

BREAD
brought out *b* Gen 14:18
shall eat unleavened *b* Ex 23:15
not live by *b* alone Deut 8:3
b eaten in secret is Prov 9:17
B gained by deceit is Prov 20:17
Cast your *b* upon the Eccl 11:1
for what is not *b* Is 55:2
these stones become *b* Matt 4:3
not live by *b* alone Matt 4:4
this day our daily *b* Matt 6:11
eating, Jesus took *b* Matt 26:26
"I am the *b* of life John 6:48
betrayed took *b* 1 Cor 11:23

BREADTH
is as great as its *b* Rev 21:16

BREAK
covenant I will not *b* Ps 89:34
together to *b* bread Acts 20:7

BREAKING
in the *b* of bread Acts 2:42
b bread from house to Acts 2:46

BREAKS
Until the day *b* Song 2:17

BREAST
back on Jesus' *b* John 13:25

BREASTPLATE
righteousness as a *b* Is 59:17
having put on the *b* Eph 6:14

BREASTS
Your two *b* are like Song 4:5
b which nursed You Luke 11:27

BREATH
nostrils the *b* of life Gen 2:7
that there was no *b* 1 Kin 17:17
Man is like a *b* Ps 144:4
everything that has *b* Ps 150:6
"Surely I will cause *b* Ezek 37:5
gives to all life, *b* Acts 17:25
power to give *b* Rev 13:15

BREATHES
indeed he *b* his last Job 14:10

BRETHREN
and you are all *b* Matt 23:8
least of these My *b* Matt 25:40
among many *b* Rom 8:29
thus sin against the *b* 1 Cor 8:12
over five hundred *b* 1 Cor 15:6
perils among false *b* 2 Cor 11:26
sincere love of the *b* 1 Pet 1:22
we love the *b* 1 John 3:14
our lives for the *b* 1 John 3:16

BRIBE
you shall take no *b* Ex 23:8
b blinds the eyes Deut 16:19

BRIBES
hand is full of *b* Ps 26:10

BRICK
people straw to make *b* Ex 5:7

BRICKS
"Come, let us make *b* Gen 11:3

BRIDE
I will show you the *b* Rev 21:9
the Spirit and the *b* Rev 22:17

BRIDEGROOM
And as the *b* rejoices Is 62:5
mourn as long as the *b* Matt 9:15
went out to meet the *b* Matt 25:1
the friend of the *b* John 3:29

BRIDLE
b the whole body James 3:2

BRIER
b shall come up the Is 55:13

BRIERS
there shall come up *b* Is 5:6

BRIGHTER
a light from heaven, *b* Acts 26:13

BRIGHTNESS
And kings to the *b* Is 60:3
who being the *b* Heb 1:3

BRIMSTONE
the lake of fire and *b* Rev 20:10

BRING
b back his soul Job 33:30
b My righteousness Is 46:13
Who shall *b* a charge Rom 8:33
b Christ down from Rom 10:6
even so God will *b* 1 Thess 4:14

BROAD
b is the way that Matt 7:13

BROKE
b them at the foot of Ex 32:19
He blessed and *b* Matt 14:19
b the legs of the John 19:32

BROKEN
this stone will be *b* Matt 21:44
Scripture cannot be *b* John 10:35
body which is *b* 1 Cor 11:24

BROKENHEARTED
He heals the *b* And Ps 147:3

BRONZE
So Moses made a *b* Num 21:9
b walls against the Jer 1:18
a third kingdom of *b* Dan 2:39

BROOD
"*B* of vipers Matt 12:34
hen gathers her *b* Luke 13:34

BROOK
disciples over the *B* John 18:1

BROOKS
for the water *b* Ps 42:1

BROTHER
"Where is Abel your *b* Gen 4:9
b offended is harder Prov 18:19
b will deliver up Matt 10:21
how often shall my *b* Matt 18:21
b will rise again John 11:23
b goes to law against 1 Cor 6:6
Whoever hates his *b* 1 John 3:15

BROTHERHOOD
Love the *b* 1 Pet 2:17

BROTHERLY
b love continue Heb 13:1

BROTHER'S
Am I my *b* keeper Gen 4:9
at the speck in your *b* Matt 7:3

BROTHERS
is My mother, or My *b* Mark 3:33
b are these who hear Luke 8:21

BRUISE
He shall *b* your head Gen 3:15
the LORD to *b* Him Is 53:10

BRUISED
He was *b* for our Is 53:5
b reed He will not Matt 12:20

BUCKLER
be your shield and *b* Ps 91:4

BUFFET
of Satan to *b* me 2 Cor 12:7

BUILD
b ourselves a city Gen 11:4
"Would you *b* a house 2 Sam 7:5
labor in vain who *b* Ps 127:1
down, And a time to *b* Eccl 3:3
'This man began to *b* Luke 14:30
What house will you *b* Acts 7:49
"For if I *b* again Gal 2:18

BUILDER
foundations, whose *b* Heb 11:10

BUILDING
in whom the whole *b* Eph 2:21

BUILDS
take heed how he *b* 1 Cor 3:10

BUILT
has *b* her house Prov 9:1
to a wise man who *b* Matt 7:24
having been *b* on the Eph 2:20

BULLS
For if the blood of *b* Heb 9:13

BULWARKS
Mark well her *b* Ps 48:13

BUNDLE
man's *b* of money Gen 42:35

BURDEN
Cast your *b* on the Ps 55:22
easy and My *b* is light Matt 11:30
we might not be a *b* 1 Thess 2:9
on you no other *b* Rev 2:24

BURDENS
"For they bind heavy *b* Matt 23:4
Bear one another's *b* Gal 6:2

BURDENSOME
I myself was not *b* 2 Cor 12:13
are not *b* 1 John 5:3

BURIAL
she did it for My *b* Matt 26:12
for the day of My *b* John 12:7

BURIED
Therefore we were *b* Rom 6:4
and that He was *b* 1 Cor 15:4
b with Him in baptism Col 2:12

BURN
the bush does not *b* Ex 3:3
"Did not our heart *b* Luke 24:32

BURNED
If anyone's work is *b* 1 Cor 3:15
my body to be *b* 1 Cor 13:3

BURNING
b torch that passed Gen 15:17
b fire shut up in my Jer 20:9
plucked from the *b* Amos 4:11

BURNT
lamb for a *b* offering Gen 22:7
delight in *b* offering Ps 51:16

BURST
the new wine will *b* Luke 5:37

BURY
and let the dead *b* Matt 8:22

BUSH
from the midst of a *b* Ex 3:2

BUSINESS
about My Father's *b* Luke 2:49

BUSYBODIES
at all, but are *b* 2 Thess 3:11

BUTLER
b did not remember Gen 40:23

BUTTER
were smoother than *b* Ps 55:21

BUY
Yes, come, *b* wine and Is 55:1
"I counsel you to *b* Rev 3:18
and that no one may *b* Rev 13:17

BUYS
has and *b* that field Matt 13:44

BYWORD
has made me a *b* Job 17:6

C

CAGE
foul spirit, and a *c* Rev 18:2

CAKE
Ephraim is a *c* Hos 7:8

CAKES
and love the raisin *c* Hos 3: I

CALAMITY
will laugh at your *c* Prov 1:26

CALCULATED
c the dust of the Is 40:12

CALDRON
this city is the *c* Ezek 11:3

CALF
and made a molded *c* Ex 32:4
bring the fatted *c* Luke 15:23

CALL
C upon Him while He Is 55:6
c His name JESUS Matt 1:21
c the righteous Matt 9:13
Lord our God will *c* Acts 2:39
c them My people Rom 9:25
c and election sure 2 Pet 1:10

CALLED
c the light Day Gen 1:5
c his wife's name Eve Gen 3:20
I have *c* you by your Is 43:1
"Out of Egypt I *c* Matt 2:15
city *c* Nazareth Matt 2:23
For many are *c* Matt 20:16
to those who are the *c* Rom 8:28
these He also *c* Rom 8:30
c children of God 1 John 3:1

CALLING
the gifts and the *c* Rom 11:29
For you see your *c* 1 Cor 1:26
remain in the same *c* 1 Cor 7:20

CALLS
c them all by name Ps 147:4
David himself *c* Mark 12:37
c his own sheep John 10:3

CALM
there was a great *c* Matt 8:26

CAMEL
it is easier for a *c* Matt 19:24

CAMP
to Him, outside the *c* Heb 13:13

CAN
I *c* do all things Phil 4:13

CANCER
will spread like *c* 2 Tim 2:17

CANOPY
His *c* around Him was Ps 18:11

CAPSTONE
bring forth the *c* Zech 4:7

CAPTAIN
Which, having no *c* Prov 6:7

CAPTIVE
and be led away *c* Luke 21:24
He led captivity *c* Eph 4:8

CAPTIVES
and make *c* 2 Tim 3:6

CAPTIVITY
every thought into *c* 2 Cor 10:5

CARCASS
"For wherever the *c* Matt 24:28

CARE
"Lord, do You not *c* Luke 10:40
how will he take *c* 1 Tim 3:5

CARED
he said, not that he *c* John 12:6

CAREFULLY
I shall walk *c* all my Is 38:15

CARELESS
But, he who is *c* Prov 19:16

CARES
No one *c* for my soul Ps 142:4
for He *c* for you 1 Pet 5:7

CARNAL
c mind is enmity Rom 8:7

CARNALLY
c minded is death Rom 8:6

CAROUSE
count it pleasure to *c* 2 Pet 2:13

CARPENTER
"Is this not the *c* Mark 6:3

CARRIED
And *c* our sorrows Is 53:4

CARRY
for you to *c* your bed John 5:10
it is certain we can *c* 1 Tim 6:7

CARRYING
will meet you *c* Mark 14:13

CASE
Festus laid Paul's *c* Acts 25:14

CASSIA
myrrh and aloes and *c* Ps 45:8

CAST
Why are you *c* down Ps 42:5
whole body to be *c* Matt 5:29
My name they will *c* Mark 16:17
by no means *c* out John 6:37
c their crowns before Rev 4:10
the great dragon was *c* Rev 12:9

CASTING
c down arguments 2 Cor 10:5
c all your care 1 Pet 5:7

CASTS
perfect love *c* out 1 John 4:18

CATCH
c Him in His words Mark 12:13
now on you will *c* Luke 5:10

CATCHES
and the wolf *c* the John 10:12
c the wise in their 1 Cor 3:19

CAUGHT
him was a ram *c* Gen 22:13
her Child was *c* up Rev 12:5

CAUSE
hated Me without a *c* John 15:25
For this *c* I was born John 18:37

CAVES
in dens and *c* of the Heb 11:38

CEASE
and night Shall not *c* Gen 8:22
He makes wars *c* Ps 46:9
tongues, they will *c* 1 Cor 13:8

CEASING
pray without *c* 1 Thess 5:17

CEDAR
dwell in a house of *c* 2 Sam 7:2

CEDARS
the LORD breaks the *c* Ps 29:5

CELESTIAL
but the glory of the *c* 1 Cor 15:40

CENSER
Aaron, each took his *c* Lev 10:1

CERTAINTY
you may know the *c* Luke 1:4

CERTIFICATE
a man to write a *c* Mark 10:4

CHAFF
be chased like the *c* Is 17:13
He will burn up the *c* Matt 3:12

CHAIN
pit and a great *c* Rev 20:1

CHAINED
of God is not *c* 2 Tim 2:9

CHAINS
And his *c* fell off Acts 12:7
am, except for these *c* Acts 26:29

CHAMBERS
brought me into his *c* Song 1:4

CHAMPION
And a *c* went out 1 Sam 17:4

CHANGE
now and to *c* my tone Gal 4:20
there is also a *c* Heb 7:12

CHANGED
c the glory of the Rom 1:23
but we shall all be *c* 1 Cor 15:51

CHANGERS'
and poured out the *c* John 2:15

CHANGES
c the times and the Dan 2:21

CHANNELS
c of the sea were seen Ps 18:15

CHARIOT
that suddenly a *c* 2 Kin 2:11

CHARIOTS
Some trust in *c* Ps 20:7

CHARITABLE
you do not do your *c* Matt 6:1
c deeds which she Acts 9:36

CHARM
C is deceitful and Prov 31:30

CHARMS
who sew magic *c* Ezek 13:18

CHASE
Five of you shall *c* Lev 26:8

CHASTE
present you as a *c* 2 Cor 11:2

CHASTEN
a father does not *c* Heb 12:7
I love, I rebuke and *c* Rev 3:19

CHASTENED
c us as seemed best Heb 12:10

CHASTENING
do not despise the *c* Job 5:17
Now no *c* seems to be Heb 12:11

CHASTENS
the LORD loves He *c* Heb 12:6

CHASTISEMENT
The *c* for our peace Is 53:5

CHATTER
c leads only to Prov 14:23

CHEAT
Beware lest anyone *c* Col 2:8

CHEATED
let yourselves be *c* 1 Cor 6:7

CHEEK
on your right *c* Matt 5:39

CHEEKBONE
my enemies on the *c* Ps 3:7

CHEEKS
His *c* are like a bed Song 5:13

CHEER
"Son, be of good *c* Matt 9:2

CHEERFUL
for God loves a *c* 2 Cor 9:7

CHEERFULNESS
shows mercy, with *c* Rom 12:8

CHEESE
And curdle me like *c* Job 10:10

CHERISHES
but nourishes and *c* Eph 5:29

CHERUBIM
above it were the *c* Heb 9:5

CHIEF
of whom I am *c* 1 Tim 1:15
Zion a *c* cornerstone 1 Pet 2:6

CHILD
Train up a *c* in the Prov 22:6
For unto us a *C* Is 9:6
virgin shall be with *c* Matt 1:23
of God as a little *c* Mark 10:15
So the *c* grew and Luke 1:80
When I was a *c* 1 Cor 13:11
She bore a male *C* Rev 12:5

CHILDBEARING
she will be saved in *c* 1 Tim 2:15

CHILDBIRTH
pain as a woman in *c* Is 13:8

CHILDHOOD
c you have known 2 Tim 3:15

CHILDLESS
give me, seeing I go *c* Gen 15:2
this man down as *c* Jer 22:30

CHILDREN
c are a heritage Ps 127:3
c rise up and call her Prov 31:28
and become as little *c* Matt 18:3
"Let the little *c* Matt 19:14
the right to become *c* John 1:12
now we are *c* of God 1 John 3:2

CHOOSE
therefore *c* life Deut 30:19
"You did not *c* John 15:16

CHOSE
Just as He *c* us in Him Eph 1:4

CHOSEN
servant whom I have *c* Is 43:10
whom I have *c* John 13:18
c the foolish things 1 Cor 1:27
Has God not *c* the James 2:5

CHRIST
Jesus who is called *C* Matt 1:16
"You are the *C* Matt 16:16
a Savior, who is *C* Luke 2:11
It is *C* who died Rom 8:34
to be justified by *C* Gal 2:17
been crucified with *C* Gal 2:20
C is head of the Eph 5:23
to me, to live is *C* Phil 1:21
which is *C* in you Col 1:27
C who is our Col 3:4
Jesus *C* is the same Heb 13:8
C His Son cleanses us 1 John 1:7
that Jesus is the *C* 1 John 5:1

CHRISTIAN
anyone suffers as a *C* 1 Pet 4:16

CHRISTIANS
were first called *C* Acts 11:26

CHRISTS
"For false *c* and Matt 24:24

CHURCH
rock I will build My *c* Matt 16:18
c daily those who were Acts 2:47
Himself a glorious *c* Eph 5:27
as the Lord does the *c* Eph 5:29
body, which is the *c* Col 1:24
assembly and *c* Heb 12:23

CHURCHES
these things in the *c* Rev 22:16

CIRCLE
who sits above the *c* Is 40:22

CIRCUMCISE
is necessary to *c* them Acts 15:5

CIRCUMCISED
among you shall be *c* Gen 17:10
who will justify the *c* Rom 3:30
if you become *c* Gal 5:2

CIRCUMCISION
c is that of the heart Rom 2:29
C is nothing and 1 Cor 7:19
Christ Jesus neither *c* Gal 5:6

CIRCUMSPECTLY
then that you walk *c* Eph 5:15

CISTERN
from your own *c* Prov 5:15

CITIES
He overthrew those *c* Gen 19:25
three parts, and the *c* Rev 16:19

CITIZEN
But I was born a *c* Acts 22:28

CITIZENS
but fellow *c* with the Eph 2:19

CITIZENSHIP
For our *c* is in heaven Phil 3:20

CITY
shall make glad the *c* Ps 46:4
c has become a harlot Is 1:21
How lonely sits the *c* Lam 1:1
c that is set on a Matt 5:14
He has prepared a *c* Heb 11:16
have no continuing *c* Heb 13:14
John, saw the holy *c* Rev 21:2

CLAP
of the field shall *c* Is 55:12

CLAY
pit, out of the miry *c* Ps 40:2
We are the *c* Is 64:8
blind man with the *c* John 9:6
have power over the *c* Rom 9:21

CLEAN
He who has *c* hands and Ps 24:4
make yourselves *c* Is 1:16
c out His threshing Matt 3:12
You can make me *c* Matt 8:2
"You are not all *c* John 13:11
"You are already *c* John 15:3

CLEANSE
C me from secret Ps 19:12
And *c* me from my sin Ps 51:2
How can a young man *c* Ps 119:9
might sanctify and *c* Eph 5:26
us our sins and to *c* 1 John 1:9

CLEANSED
"Were there not ten *c* Luke 17:17

CLEANSES
Christ His Son *c* 1 John 1:7

CLEAR
of life, *c* as crystal Rev 22:1

CLIFF
secret places of the *c* Song 2:14

CLIMBS
c up some other way John 10:1

CLING
C to what is good Rom 12:9

CLINGS
And My tongue *c* Ps 22:15

CLOAK
let him have your *c* Matt 5:40
using liberty as a *c* 1 Pet 2:16

CLODS
The *c* of the valley Job 21:33

CLOSE
c friends abhor me Job 19:19

CLOSED
The deep *c* around me Jon 2:5

CLOTH
a piece of unshrunk *c* Matt 9:16

CLOTHE
He not much more *c* Matt 6:30

CLOTHED
of skin, and *c* them Gen 3:21
A man *c* in soft Matt 11:8
naked and you *c* Matt 25:36
legion, sitting and *c* Mark 5:15
desiring to be *c* 2 Cor 5:2
that you may be *c* Rev 3:18

CLOTHES
c became shining Mark 9:3
many spread their *c* Luke 19:36
a poor man in filthy *c* James 2:2

CLOTHING
c they cast lots Ps 22:18
do you worry about *c* Matt 6:28
to you in sheep's *c* Matt 7:15
c they cast lots John 19:24

CLOTHS
in swaddling *c* Luke 2:12

CLOUD
My rainbow in the *c* Gen 9:13
day in a pillar of *c* Ex 13:21
He led them with the *c* Ps 78:14
behold, a bright *c* Matt 17:5
of Man coming in a *c* Luke 21:27
c received Him out of Acts 1:9
by so great a *c* Heb 12:1

CLOUDS
Man coming on the *c* Matt 24:30
with them in the *c* 1 Thess 4:17
are *c* without water Jude 12
He is coming with *c* Rev 1:7

CLOUDY
them by day with a *c* Neh 9:12

CLOVEN
chew the cud or have *c* Deut 14:7

CLUSTER
beloved is to me a *c* Song 1:14

COAL
in his hand a live *c* Is 6:6

COALS
doing you will heap *c* Rom 12:20

COBRA
the lion and the *c* Ps 91:13

COBRA'S
shall play by the *c* Is 11:8

COFFIN
and he was put in a *c* Gen 50:26
touched the open *c* Luke 7:14

COIN
if she loses one *c* Luke 15:8

COLD
and harvest, *C* and Gen 8:22
of many will grow *c* Matt 24:12
that you are neither *c* Rev 3:15

COLLECTION
concerning the *c* 1 Cor 16:1

COLT
on a donkey, A *c* Zech 9:9
on a donkey, A *c* Matt 21:5

COME
He will *c* and save you Is 35:4
who have no money, *C* Is 55:1
Your kingdom *c* Matt 6:10
"*C* to Me Matt 11:28
I have *c* in My John 5:43
thirsts, let him *c* John 7:37
c as a light into the John 12:46
O Lord, *c* 1 Cor 16:22
the door, I will *c* Rev 3:20

COMELINESS
He has no form or *c* Is 53:2

COMES
Lord's death till He *c* 1 Cor 11:26

COMFORT
and Your staff, they *c* Ps 23:4
yes, *c* My people Is 40:1
c each other 1 Thess 5:11

COMFORTED
So Isaac was *c* after Gen 24:67
Refusing to be *c* Jer 31:15

COMFORTER
She had no *c* Lam 1:9

COMFORTS
I, even I, am He who *c* Is 51:12

COMING
see the Son of Man *c* Mark 13:26
mightier than I is *c* Luke 3:16
are Christ's at His *c* 1 Cor 15:23
Behold, I am *c* Rev 3:11
"Surely I am *c* Rev 22:20

COMMAND
c I have received John 10:18
and I know that His *c* John 12:50
If you do whatever I *c* John 15:14

COMMANDED
not endure what was *c* Heb 12:20

COMMANDMENT
c of the LORD is pure Ps 19:8
which is the great *c* Matt 22:36
"A new *c* I give to John 13:34
which is the first *c* Eph 6:2
And this is His *c* 1 John 3:23

COMMANDMENTS
covenant, the Ten *C* Ex 34:28
as doctrines the *c* Matt 15:9
c hang all the Law Matt 22:40
He who has My *c* John 14:21

COMMANDS
with authority He *c* Mark 1:27

COMMEND
But food does not *c* 1 Cor 8:8

COMMENDABLE
patiently, this is *c* 1 Pet 2:20

COMMENDED
c the unjust steward Luke 16:8

COMMENDS
but whom the Lord *c* 2 Cor 10:18

COMMIT
"You shall not *c* Ex 20:14
into Your hands I *c* Luke 23:46

COMMITS
sin also *c* lawlessness 1 John 3:4

COMMITTED
c Himself to Him who 1 Pet 2:23

COMMON
c people heard Him Mark 12:37
had all things in *c* Acts 2:44
concerning our *c* Jude 3

COMMOTION
there arose a great *c* Acts 19:23

COMMUNED
I *c* with my heart Eccl 1:16

COMMUNION
c of the Holy Spirit 2 Cor 13:14

COMPANION
a man my equal, My *c* Ps 55:13

COMPANIONS
while you became *c* Heb 10:33

COMPANY
Great was the *c* Ps 68:11
to an innumerable *c* Heb 12:22

COMPARE
c ourselves with 2 Cor 10:12

COMPARED
are not worthy to be *c* Rom 8:18

COMPASSION
are a God full of *c* Ps 86:15
He was moved with *c* Man 9:36
whomever I will have *c* Rom 9:15
He can have *c* on those Heb 5:2

COMPASSIONATE
the Lord is very *c* James 5:11

COMPASSIONS
because His *c* fail not Lam 3:22

COMPEL
c them to come in Luke 14:23

COMPELS
the love of Christ *c* 2 Cor 5:14

COMPLAINED
some of them also *c* 1 Cor 10:10

COMPLAINERS
These are grumblers, *c* Jude 16

COMPLAINING
all things without *c* Phil 2:14

COMPLAINT
For the LORD has a *c* Mic 6:2

COMPLETE
work in you will *c* Phil 1:6
and you are *c* in Him Col 2:10
of God may be *c* 2 Tim 3:17

COMPLETELY
sanctify you *c* 1 Thess 5:23

COMPOSED
But God *c* the body 1 Cor 12:24

COMPREHEND
which we cannot *c* Job 37:5
the darkness did not *c* John 1:5

CONCEAL
of God to *c* a matter Prov 25:2

CONCEALED
Than love carefully *c* Prov 27:5

CONCEIT
selfish ambition or *c* Phil 2:3

CONCEITED
Let us not become *c* Gal 5:26

CONCEIVE
the virgin shall *c* Is 7:14
And behold, you will *c* Luke 1:31

CONCEIVED
in sin my mother *c* Ps 51:5

CONCERN
Neither do I *c* myself Ps 131:1

CONCERNED
Is it oxen God is *c* 1 Cor 9:9

CONCESSION
But I say this as a *c* 1 Cor 7:6

CONCLUSION
Let us hear the *c* Eccl 12:13

CONDEMN
world to *c* the world John 3:17

CONDEMNATION
can you escape the *c* Matt 23:33
"And this is the *c* John 3:19
Their *c* is just Rom 3:8
therefore now no *c* Rom 8:1

CORRODED
and silver are *c* James 5:3

CORRUPT
in these things they *c* Jude 10

CORRUPTED
for all flesh had *c* Gen 6:12
Your riches are *c* James 5:2

CORRUPTIBLE
redeemed with *c* 1 Pet 1:18

CORRUPTION
Your Holy One to see *c* Ps 16:10
c inherit incorruption 1 Cor 15:50
having escaped the *c* 2 Pet 1:4

COST
and count the *c* Luke 14:28

COULD
c remove mountains 1 Cor 13:2
which no one *c* number Rev 7:9

COUNCILS
deliver you up to *c* Mark 13:9

COUNSEL
Who walks not in the *c* Ps 1:1
We took sweet *c* Ps 55:14
guide me with Your *c* Ps 73:24
according to the *c* Eph 1:11
immutability of His *c* Heb 6:17
"I *c* you to buy from Rev 3:18

COUNSELOR
be called Wonderful, *C* Is 9:6

COUNSELORS
c there is safety Prov 11:14

COUNT
c my life dear to Acts 20:24
His promise, as some *c* 2 Pet 3:9

COUNTED
Even a fool is *c* Prov 17:28
who rule well be *c* 1 Tim 5:17

COUNTENANCE
The LORD lift up His *c* Num 6:26
with a sad *c* Matt 6:16
His *c* was like Matt 28:3
of the glory of his *c* 2 Cor 3:7

COUNTRY
"Get out of your *c* Gen 12:1
that is, a heavenly *c* Heb 11:16

COUNTRYMEN
for my brethren, my *c* Rom 9:3

COURAGE
strong and of good *c* Deut 31:6

COURT
They zealously *c* Gal 4:17

COURTEOUS
be tenderhearted, be *c* 1 Pet 3:8

COURTS
and into His *c* Ps 100:4

COVENANT
I will establish My *c* Gen 6:18
the LORD made a *c* Gen 15:18
will show them His *c* Ps 25:14
sons will keep My *c* Ps 132:12
I will make a new *c* Jer 31:31
the Messenger of the *c* Mal 3:1
cup is the new *c* Luke 22:20
He says, "A new *c* Heb 8:13
Mediator of the new *c* Heb 12:24
of the everlasting *c* Heb 13:20

COVENANTS
the glory, the *c* Rom 9:4

COVER
He shall *c* you with Ps 91:4
c a multitude of sins James 5:20

COVERED
Whose sin is *c* Ps 32:1
c all their sin Ps 85:2
For there is nothing *c* Matt 10:26

COVERING
spread a cloud for a *c* Ps 105:39

COVERINGS
and made themselves *c* Gen 3:7

COVET
"You shall not *c* Ex 20:17

COVETED
c no one's silver Acts 20:33

COVETOUS
nor thieves, nor *c* 1 Cor 6:10

COVETOUSNESS
heed and beware of *c* Luke 12:15

COWARDLY
the *c*, unbelieving Rev 21:8

CRAFTILY
His people, to deal *c* Ps 105:25

CRAFTINESS
deceived Eve by his *c* 2 Cor 11:3
in the cunning *c* Eph 4:14

CRAFTSMAN
instructor of every *c* Gen 4:22

CRAFTY
the devices of the *c* Job 5:12
Nevertheless, being *c* 2 Cor 12:16

CREAM
were bathed with *c* Job 29:6

CREATE
peace and *c* calamity Is 45:7

CREATED
So God *c* man in His Gen 1:27
Has not one God *c* Mal 2:10
c in Christ Jesus Eph 2:10
new man which was *c* Eph 4:24

CREATION
know that the whole *c* Rom 8:22
Christ, he is a new *c* 2 Cor 5:17
anything, but a new *c* Gal 6:15

CREATOR
Remember now your *C* Eccl 12:1
God, the LORD, The *C* Is 40:28
rather than the *C* Rom 1:25

CREATURE
the gospel to every *c* Mark 16:15

CREATURES
firstfruits of His *c* James 1:18

CREDIT
For what *c* is it if 1 Pet 2:20

CREDITOR
There was a certain *c* Luke 7:41

CREEP
sort are those who *c* 2 Tim 3:6

CREEPING
c thing and beast of Gen 1:24

CREPT
For certain men have *c* Jude 4

CRIB
donkey its master's *c* Is 1:3

CRIED
the poor who *c* out Job 29:12
of the depths I have *c* Ps 130:1

CRIES
your brother's blood *c* Gen 4:10

CRIMES
land is filled with *c* Ezek 7:23

CRIMINALS
also two others, *c* Luke 23:32

CROOKED
c places shall be made Is 40:4
in the midst of a *c* Phil 2:15

CROSS
does not take his *c* Matt 10:38
to bear His *c* Matt 27:32
down from the *c* Matt 27:40
lest the *c* of Christ 1 Cor 1:17
boast except in the *c* Gal 6:14
the enemies of the *c* Phil 3:18
Him endured the *c* Heb 12:2

CROWD
shall not follow a *c* Ex 23:2

CROWN
c the year with Your Ps 65:11
they had twisted a *c* Matt 27:29
obtain a perishable *c* 1 Cor 9:25
laid up for me the *c* 2 Tim 4:8
on his head a golden *c* Rev 14:14

CROWNED
angels, And You have *c* Ps 8:5
athletics, he is not *c* 2 Tim 2:5

CROWNS
His head were many *c* Rev 19:12

CRUCIFIED
"Let Him be *c* Matt 27:22
Calvary, there they *c* Luke 23:33
lawless hands, have *c* Acts 2:23
that our old man was *c* Rom 6:6
Jesus Christ and Him *c* 1 Cor 2:2
"I have been *c* Gal 2:20

CRUCIFY
out again, "*C* Him Mark 15:13

CRUEL
hate me with *c* hatred Ps 25:19

CRUELTY
the haunts of *c* Ps 74:20

CRUSH
of peace will *c* Rom 16:20

CRUSHED
every side, yet not *c* 2 Cor 4:8

CRUST
man is reduced to a *c* Prov 6:26

CRY
and their *c* came up to Ex 2:23
Does not wisdom *c* Prov 8:1
at midnight a *c* Matt 25:6
His own elect who *c* Luke 18:7

CRYING
nor sorrow, nor *c* Rev 21:4

CRYSTAL
a sea of glass, like *c* Rev 4:6

CUBIT
can add one *c* Matt 6:27

CUNNING
the serpent was more *c* Gen 3:1
c craftiness of deceitful Eph 4:14

CUP
My *c* runs over Ps 23:5
Then He took the *c* Matt 26:27
possible, let this *c* Matt 26:39
c is the new covenant Luke 22:20
cannot drink the *c* 1 Cor 10:21
c is the new 1 Cor 11:25

CURE
and to *c* diseases Luke 9:1

CURES
and perform *c* Luke 13:32

CURSE
c the ground for man's Gen 8:21
C God and die Job 2:9
"I will send a *c* Mal 2:2
law are under the *c* Gal 3:10

CURSED
c more than all cattle Gen 3:14
from Me, you *c* Man 25:41

CURSES
I will curse him who *c* Gen 12:3

CURTAIN
the heavens like a *c* Ps 104:2

CUSTOM
according to the *c* Acts 15:1

CUT
evildoers shall be *c* Ps 37:9
the wicked will be *c* Prov 2:22

CYMBAL
or a clanging *c* 1 Cor 13:1

D

DAILY
Give us this day our *d* Matt 6:11
take up his cross *d* Luke 9:23
the Scriptures *d* Acts 17:11

DANCE
mourn, And a time to *d* Eccl 3:4
And you did not *d* Matt 11:17

DANCED
Then David *d* before 2 Sam 6:14

DANCING
saw the calf and the *d* Ex 32:19
he heard music and *d* Luke 15:25

DARE
someone would even *d* Rom 5:7

DARK
I tell you in the *d* Matt 10:27
shines in a *d* place 2 Pet 1:19

DARKENED
their understanding *d* Eph 4:18

DARKNESS
d He called Night Gen 1:5
Those who sat in *d* Ps 107:10
d Have seen a Is 9:2
And deep *d* the people Is 60:2
body will be full of *d* Matt 6:23
cast out into outer *d* Matt 8:12
d rather than light John 3:19
For you were once *d* Eph 5:8
called you out of *d* 1 Pet 2:9
d is reserved 2 Pet 2:17
and in Him is no *d* 1 John 1:5
d is passing away 1 John 2:8

DARTS
quench all the fiery *d* Eph 6:16

DASH
You shall *d* them to Ps 2:9
Lest you *d* your foot Matt 4:6

DASHED
infants shall be *d* Hos 13:16

DAUGHTER
"Rejoice greatly, O *d* Zech 9:9
"Fear not, *d* of Zion John 12:15
the son of Pharaoh's *d* Heb 11:24

DAUGHTERS
of God saw the *d* Gen 6:2
d shall prophesy Acts 2:17

DAY
God called the light *D* Gen 1:5
And *d* and night Gen 8:22
the Sabbath *d* Ex 20:8
For a *d* in Your courts Ps 84:10
d the LORD has Ps 118:24
not strike you by *d* Ps 121:6
For the *d* of the LORD Joel 2:11
who can endure the *d* Mal 3:2
d our daily bread Matt 6:11
sent Me while it is *d* John 9:4
person esteems one *d* Rom 14:5
d will declare it 1 Cor 3:13
again the third *d* 1 Cor 15:4
with the Lord one *d* 2 Pet 3:8

DAYS
d are swifter than a Job 7:6
of woman is of few *d* Job 14;1
The *d* of our lives are Ps 90:10
Before the difficult *d* Eccl 12:1
shortened those *d* Mark 13:20
raise it up in three *d* John 2:20

DAYSPRING
With which the *D* Luke 1:78

DEACONS
with the bishops and *d* Phil 1:1
d must be reverent 1 Tim 3:8
d be the husbands 1 Tim 3:12

DEAD
But the *d* know nothing Eccl 9:5
d bury their own *d* Matt 8:22
not the God of the *d* Matt 22:32
this my son was *d* Luke 15:24
d will hear the voice John 5:25
was raised from the *d* Rom 6:4
yourselves to be *d* Rom 6:11
be Lord of both the *d* Rom 14:9
resurrection of the *d* 1 Cor 15:12
And the *d* in Christ 1 Thess 4:16
without works is *d* James 2:26
And the *d* were judged Rev 20:12

DEADLY
drink anything *d* Mark 16:18
evil, full of *d* poison James 3:8

DEADNESS
the *d* of Sarah's womb Rom 4:19

DEAF
d shall be unstopped Is 35:5
are cleansed and the *d* Matt 11:5

DEAL
My Servant shall *d* Is 52:13

DEATH
d parts you and me Ruth 1:17
and the shadow of *d* Job 10:21
I sleep the sleep of *d* Ps 13:3
of the shadow of *d* Ps 23:4
house leads down to *d* Prov 2:18
who hate me love *d* Prov 8:36
swallow up *d* forever Is 25:8
no pleasure in the *d* Ezek 18:32
who shall not taste *d* Matt 16:28
but has passed from *d* John 5:24
Nevertheless *d* reigned Rom 5:14
D no longer has Rom 6:9
the wages of sin is *d* Rom 6:23
the Lord's *d* 1 Cor 11:26
since by man came *d* 1 Cor 15:21
D is swallowed up in 1 Cor 15:54
The sting of *d* is sin 1 Cor 15:56
is sin leading to *d* 1 John 5:16
Be faithful until *d* Rev 2:10
shall be no more *d* Rev 21:4
which is the second *d* Rev 21:8

DEBTOR
I am a *d* both to Rom 1:14
that he is a *d* to keep Gal 5:3

DEBTORS
as we forgive our *d* Matt 6:12
of his master's *d* Luke 16:5
brethren, we are *d* Rom. 8:12

DISCIPLE
he cannot be My *d* Luke 14:26
d whom Jesus loved John 21:7

DISCIPLES
word, you are My *d* John 8:31
but we are Moses' *d* John 9:28

DISCIPLINES
he who loves him *d* Prov 13:24

DISCORD
And one who sows *d* Prov 6:19

DISCOURAGED
lest they became *d* Col 3:21
become weary and *d* Heb 12:3

DISCRETION
d will preserve you Prov 2:11

DISFIGURE
d their faces that Matt 6:16

DISGUISES
And he *d* his face Job 24:15

DISHONOR
Father, and you *d* Me John 8:49
d their bodies among Rom 1:24
It is sown in *d* 1 Cor 15:43

DISHONORED
But you have *d* the James 2:6

DISHONORS
For son *d* father Mic 7:6

DISOBEDIENT
out My hands To a *d* Rom 10:21

DISORDERLY
for this *d* gathering Acts 19:40

DISPENSATION
d of the fullness of Eph 1:10

DISPERSION
the pilgrims of the *D* 1 Pet 1:1

DISPLEASE
LORD see it, and it *d* Prov 24:18

DISPLEASED
they were greatly *d* Matt 20:24
it, He was greatly *d* Mark 10:14

DISPUTE
there was also a *d* Luke 22:24

DISPUTER
Where is the *d* of this 1 Cor 1:20

DISPUTES
But avoid foolish *d* Titus 3:9

DISQUALIFIED
should become *d* 1 Cor 9:27

DISQUIETED
And why are you *d* Ps 42:5

DISSENSION
had no small *d* and Acts 15:2

DISSIPATION
not accused of *d* Titus 1:6

DISSOLVED
the heavens will be *d* 2 Pet 3:12

DISTINCTION
compassion, making a *d* Jude 22

DISTRESS
d them in His deep Ps 2:5
tribulation, or *d* Rom 8:35

DISTRESSED
and deeply *d* Mark 14:33

DISTRESSES
Bring me out of my *d* Ps 25:17

DISTRIBUTED
and they *d* to each as Acts 4:35

DISTRIBUTING
d to the needs of the Rom 12:13

DITCH
will fall into a *d* Matt 15:14

DIVERSITIES
There are *d* 1 Cor 12:4

DIVIDE
d the spoil with the Prov 16:19
"Take this and *d* Luke 22:17

DIVIDED
and the waters were *d* Ex 14:21
they were not *d* 2 Sam 1:23
"Every kingdom *d* Matt 12:25
Is Christ *d* 1 Cor 1:13

DIVIDES
at home *d* the spoil Ps 68:12

DIVIDING
rightly *d* the word of 2 Tim 2:15

DIVINATION
shall you practice *d* Lev 19:26
a spirit of *d* met us Acts 16:16

DIVINE
d service and the Heb 9:1

DIVISION
So there was a *d* John 7:43

DIVISIONS
those who cause *d* Rom 16:17
persons, who cause *d* Jude 19

DIVISIVE
Reject a *d* man after Titus 3:10

DIVORCE
her a certificate of *d* Deut 24:1
a certificate of *d* Mark 10:4

DO
men to *d* to you, *d* Matt 7:12
He sees the Father *d* John 5:19
without Me you can *d* John 15:5
"Sirs, what must I *d* Acts 16:30
d evil that good may Rom 3:8
or whatever you *d*, *d* 1 Cor 10:31

DOCTRINE
What new *d* is this Mark 1:27
"My *d* is not Mine John 7:16
with every wind of *d* Eph 4:14
is contrary to sound *d* 1 Tim 1:10
is profitable for *d* 2 Tim 3:16
not endure sound *d* 2 Tim 4:3

DOCTRINES
commandments and *d* Col 2:22
various and strange *d* Heb 13:9

DOERS
But be *d* of the word James 1:22

DOG
d is better than a Eccl 9:4
d returns to his own 2 Pet 2:22

DOGS
what is holy to the *d* Matt 7:6
d eat the crumbs Matt 15:27
But outside are *d* Rev 22:15

DOMINION
let them have *d* Gen 1:26
d is an everlasting Dan 4:34
sin shall not have *d* Rom 6:14
glory and majesty, *D* Jude 25

DONKEY
d its master's crib Is 1:3
and riding on a *d* Zech 9:9
colt, the foal of a *d* Matt 21:5
d speaking with a 2 Pet 2:16

DOOM
for the day of *d* Prov 16:4

DOOR
stone against the *d* Matt 27:60
to you, I am the *d* John 10:7
before you an open *d* Rev 3:8
I stand at the *d* Rev 3:20

DOORKEEPER
I would rather be a *d* Ps 84:10

DOORPOSTS
write them on the *d* Deut 6:9

DOORS
up, you everlasting *d* Ps 24:7

DOUBLE
from the LORD's hand *D* Is 40:2
worthy of *d* honor 1 Tim 5:17

DOUBLE-MINDED
he is a *d* man James 1:8

DOUBT
faith, why did you *d* Matt 14:31

DOUBTING
in faith, with no *d* James 1:6

DOUBTS
why do *d* arise in Luke 24:38
for I have *d* about you Gal 4:20

DOVE
d found no resting Gen 8:9
descending like a *d* Matt 3:16

DOVES
and harmless as *d* Matt 10:16

DOWNCAST
who comforts the *d* 2 Cor 7:6

DRAGNET
d that was cast Matt 13:47

DRAGON
they worshiped the *d* Rev 13:4
He laid hold of the *d* Rev 20:2

DRAINED
All faces are *d* Joel 2:6

DRANK
them, and they all *d* Mark 14:23

DRAW
d honey from the Deut 32:13
me to *d* near to God Ps 73:28
And the years *d* Eccl 12:1
will *d* all peoples John 12:32
D near to God and He James 4:8

DRAWS
your redemption *d* Luke 21:28

DREAM
Now Joseph had a *d* Gen 37:5
Your old men shall *d* Joel 2:28
to Joseph in a *d* Matt 2:13
things today in a *d* Matt 27:19

DREAMERS
d defile the flesh Jude 8

DREAMS
Nebuchadnezzar had *d* Dan 2:1

DRIED
of her blood was *d* Mark 5:29
saw the fig tree *d* Mark 11:20

DRIFT
have heard, lest we *d* Heb 2:1

DRINK
gave me vinegar to *d* Ps 69:21
Lest they *d* and forget Prov 31:5
follow intoxicating *d* Is 5:11
d the milk of the Is 60:16
bosom, That you may *d* Is 66:11
"Bring wine, let us *d* Amos 4:1
that day when I *d* Matt 26:29
mingled with gall to *d* Matt 27:34
with myrrh to *d* Mark 15:23
to her, "Give Me a *d* John 4:7
him come to Me and *d* John 7:37
do, as often as you *d* 1 Cor 11:25
No longer *d* only 1 Tim 5:23

DRINKS
to her, "Whoever *d* John 4:13
d My blood has John 6:54
he who eats and *d* 1 Cor 11:29

DRIPPING
His lips are lilies, *D* Song 5:13

DROSS
purge away your *d* Is 1:25

DROUGHT
in the year of*d* Jer 17:8
"For I called for a *d* Hag 1:11

DROVE
So He *d* out the man Gen 3:24
temple of God and *d* Matt 21:12

DROWN
Nor can the floods *d* Song 8:7
harmful lusts which *d* 1 Tim 6:9

DROWSINESS
d will clothe a Prov 23:21

DRUNK
of the wine and was *d* Gen 9:21
the guests have well *d* John 2:10
"For these are not *d* Acts 2:15
and another is *d* 1 Cor 11:21
I saw the woman, *d* Rev 17:6

DRUNKARD
to and fro like a *d* Is 24:20
or a reviler, or a *d* 1 Cor 5:11

DRUNKEN
I am like a *d* man Jer 23:9

DRUNKENNESS
will be filled with *d* Ezek 23:33
not in revelry and *d* Rom 13:13
envy, murders, *d* Gal 5:21

DRY
place, and let the *d* Gen 1:9
made the sea into *d* Ex 14:21
It was *d* on the fleece Judg 6:40
will be done in the *d* Luke 23:31

DUE
pay all that was *d* Matt 18:34
d time Christ died Rom 5:6
d season we shall Gal 6:9
exalt you in *d* time 1 Pet 5:6

DULL
heart of this people *d* Is 6:10
people have grown *d* Matt 13:15

DUMB
the tongue of the *d* Is 35:6

DUST
formed man of the *d* Gen 2:7
d you shall return Gen 3:19
And repent in *d* Job 42:6
that we are *d* Ps 103:14
counted as the small *d* Is 40:15
city, shake off the *d* Matt 10:14
of the man of *d* 1 Cor 15:49

DUTY
done what was our *d* Luke 17:10

DWELL
Who may *d* in Your holy Ps 15:1
"I *d* in the high and Is 57:15
"I will *d* in them 2 Cor 6:16
that Christ may *d* Eph 3:17
men, and He will *d* Rev 21:3

DWELLING
built together for a *d* Eph 2:22
a foreign country, *d* Heb 11:9

DWELLS
He who *d* in the secret Ps 91:1
but the Father who *d* John 14:10
d all the fullness Col 2:9
which righteousness *d* 2 Pet 3:13
you, where Satan *d* Rev 2:13

DWELT
became flesh and *d* John 1:14
By faith he *d* in the Heb 11:9

DYING
in the body the *d* 2 Cor 4:10

E

EAGLE
fly away like an *e* Prov 23:5
The way of an *e* Prov 30:19
like a flying *e* Rev 4:7

EAGLES
up with wings like *e* Is 40:31
e will be gathered Matt 24:28

EAGLES'
how I bore you on *e* Ex 19:4

EAR
shall pierce his *e* Ex 21:6
And the *e* of the wise Prov 18:15
e is uncircumcised Jer 6:10
you hear in the *e* Matt 10:27
cut off his right *e* John 18:10
not seen, nor *e* heard 1 Cor 2:9
"He who has an *e* Rev 2:7

EARLY
Very *e* in the morning Mark 16:2
arrived at the tomb *e* Luke 24:22

EARNESTLY
He prayed more *e* Luke 22:44
e that it would not James 5:17
you to contend *e* Jude 3

EARS
And hear with their *e* Is 6:10
"He who has *e* Matt 11:15
they have itching *e* 2 Tim 4:3

EARTH
to judge the *e* 1 Chr 16:33
foundations of the *e* Job 3 8:4
e is the LORD's Ps 24:1
You had formed the *e* Ps 90:2
there was ever an *e* Prov 8:23
e abides forever Eccl 1:4
for the meek of the *e* Is 11:4
e is My footstool Is 66:1
I will darken the *e* Amos 8:9
shall inherit the *e* Matt 5:5
heaven and *e* pass Matt 5:18
e as it is in heaven Matt 6:10
treasures on *e* Matt 6:19
then shook the *e* Heb 12:26
heaven and a new *e* Rev 21:1

EARTHLY
"If I have told you *e* John 3:12
that if our *e* house 2 Cor 5:1
their mind on *e* things Phil 3:19
from above, but is *e* James 3:15

EARTHQUAKE
after the wind an *e* 1 Kin 19:11
there was a great *e* Matt 28:2

EARTHQUAKES
And there will be *e* Mark 13:8

EASIER
"Which is *e*, to say Mark 2:9
"It is *e* for a camel Mark 10:25

ERR
My people Israel to *e* Jer 23:13

ERROR
a sinner from the *e* James 5:20
led away with the *e* 2 Pet 3:17
run greedily in the *e* Jude 11

ERRORS
can understand his *e* Ps 19:12

ESCAPE
e all these things Luke 21:36
same, that you will *e* Rom 2:3
make the way of *e* 1 Cor 10:13
how shall we *e* if we Heb 2:3

ESCAPED
after they have *e* 2 Pet 2:20

ESTABLISH
seeking to *e* their own Rom 10:3
faithful, who will *e* 2 Thess 3:3
E your hearts James 5:8
a while, perfect, *e* 1 Pet 5:10

ESTABLISHED
Your throne is *e* Ps 93:2
built up In Him and *e* Col 2:7
covenant, which was *e* Heb 8:6

ESTEEM
and we did not *e* Is 53:3
e others better than Phil 2:3

ESTEEMED
For what is highly *e* Luke 16:15

ESTEEMS
One person *e* one day Rom 14:5

ETERNAL
e God is your refuge Deut 33:27
For man goes to his *e* Eccl 12:5
and inherit *e* life Matt 19:29
in the age to come. *e* Mark 10:30
not perish but have *e* John 3:15
you think you have *e* John 5:39
I give them *e* life John 10:28
"And this is *e* life John 17:3
the gift of God is *e* Rom 6:23
are not seen are *e* 2 Cor 4:18
lay hold on *e* life 1 Tim 6:12
e life which was 1 John 1:2

ETERNITY
Also He has put *e* Eccl 3:11
One who inhabits *e* Is 57:15

EUNUCH
of Ethiopia, a *e* Acts 8:27

EUNUCHS
made themselves *e* Matt 19:12

EVANGELIST
of Philip the *e* Acts 21:8
do the work of an *e* 2 Tim 4:5

EVANGELISTS
some prophets, some *e* Eph 4:11

EVERLASTING
from *E* is Your name Is 63:16
awake, Some to *e* life Dan 12:2
not perish but have *e* John 3:16
who sent Me has *e* John 5:24
endures to *e* life John 6:27
in Him may have *e* John 6:40
believes in Me has *e* John 6:47
e destruction from 2 Thess 1:9

EVIDENCE
e of things not seen Heb 11:1

EVIDENT
e that our Lord arose Heb 7:14

EVIL
of good and *e* Gen 2:9
knowing good and *e* Gen 3:5
his heart was only *e* Gen 6:5
I will fear no *e* Ps 23:4
e more than good Ps 52:3
To do *e* is like sport Prov 10:23
e will bow before the Prov 14:19
Keeping watch on the *e* Prov 15:3
e All the days of her Prov 31:12
to those who call *e* Is 5:20
of peace and not of *e* Jer 29:11
Seek good and not *e* Amos 5:14
deliver us from the *e* Matt 6:13
"If you then, being *e* Matt 7:11
e treasure brings Matt 12:35
everyone practicing *e* John 3:20
done any good or *e* Rom 9:11
Repay no one *e* for Rom 12:17
provoked, thinks no *e* 1 Cor 13:5

EVILDOER
"If He were not an *e* John 18:30
suffer trouble as an *e* 2 Tim 2:9

EVILDOERS
e shall be cut off Ps 37:9
from me, you *e* Ps 119:115
iniquity, A brood of *e* Is 1:4
against you as *e* 1 Pet 2:12

EXALT
e His name together Ps 34:3
E the humble Ezek 21:26
And he shall *e* himself Dan 8:25

EXALTATION
who rejoice in My *e* Is 13:3
brother glory in his *e* James 1:9

EXALTED
Let God be *e* 2 Sam 22:47
I will be *e* among the Ps 46:10
You are *e* far above Ps 97:9
His name alone is *e* Ps 148:13
valley shall be *e* Is 40:4
"Him God has *e* Acts 5:31
And lest I should be *e* 2 Cor 12:7
also has highly *e* Phil 2:9

EXALTS
Righteousness *e* Prov 14:34
high thing that *e* 2 Cor 10:5
e himself above all 2 Thess 2:4

EXAMINE
But let a man *e* 1 Cor 11:28
But let each one *e* Gal 6:4

EXAMPLE
to make her a public *e* Matt 1:19
I have given you an *e* John 13:15
youth, but be an *e* 1 Tim 4:12
us, leaving us an *e* 1 Pet 2:21
are set forth as an *e* Jude 7

EXAMPLES
to them as *e* 1 Cor 10:11
to you, but being *e* 1 Pet 5:3

EXCHANGE
give in *e* for his soul Matt 16:26

EXCHANGED
Nor can it be *e* Job 28:17
e the truth of God for Rom 1:25

EXCUSE
now they have no *e* John 15:22
they are without *e* Rom 1:20

EXCUSES
began to make *e* Luke 14:18

EXECUTE
e judgment also John 5:27
e wrath on him who Rom 13:4

EXECUTES
e justice for me Mic 7:9

EXERCISE
e yourself toward 1 Tim 4:7

EXHORT
e him as a father 1 Tim 5:1
Speak these things, *e* Titus 2:15
e one another Heb 3:13

EXHORTATION
he who exhorts, in *e* Rom 12:8
to reading, to *e* 1 Tim 4:13

EXHORTED
know how we *e* 1 Thess 2:11

EXIST
by Your will they *e* Rev 4:11

EXPECT
an hour you do not *e* Luke 12:40

EXPECTATION
the people were in *e* Luke 3:15
a certain fearful *e* Heb 10:27

EXPLAIN
no one who could *e* Gen 41:24
"*E* this parable to us Matt 15:15
to say, and hard to *e* Heb 5:11

EXPLAINED
He *e* all things to His Mark 4:34

EXPOSED
his deeds should be *e* John 3:20

EXPOUNDED
He *e* to them in all Luke 24:27

EXPRESS
of His glory and the *e* Heb 1:3

EXTORTION
they are full of *e* Matt 23:25

EXTORTIONERS
e will inherit 1 Cor 6:10

EYE
the ear, But now my *e* Job 42:5
guide you with My *e* Ps 32:8

e is not satisfied Eccl 1:8
the apple of His *e* Zech 2:8
if your right *e* Matt 5:29
it was said, 'An *e* Matt 5:38
plank in your own *e* Matt 7:3
e causes you to sin Matt 18:9
Or is your *e* evil Matt 20:15
the *e* of a needle Luke 18:25
the twinkling of an *e* 1 Cor 15:52
every *e* will see Him Rev 1:7
your eyes with *e* salve Rev 3:18

EYES
e will be opened Gen 3:5
And my *e* shall behold Job 19:27
e are ever toward the Ps 25:15
The *e* of the LORD are Ps 34:15
I will lift up my *e* Ps 121:1
but the *e* of a fool Prov 17:24
be wise in his own *e* Prov 26:5
You have dove's *e* Song 1:15
e have seen the King Is 6:5
Who have *e* and see Jer 5:21
rims were full of *e* Ezek 1:18
You are of purer *e* Hab 1:13
blessed are your *e* Matt 13:16
"He put clay on my *e* John 9:15
e they have closed Acts 28:27
E that they should not Rom 11:8
have seen with our *e* 1 John 1:1
the lust of the *e* 1 John 2:16
as snow, and His *e* Rev 1:14
creatures full of *e* Rev 4:6
horns and seven *e* Rev 5:6

EYESERVICE
not with *e* Eph 6:6

EYEWITNESSES
the beginning were *e* Luke 1:2
e of His majesty 2 Pet 1:16

F

FABLES
nor give heed to *f* 1 Tim 1:4
cunningly devised *f* 2 Pet 1:16

FACE
"For I have seen God *f* Gen 32:30
f shone while he Ex 34:29
sins have hidden His *f* Is 59:2
f shone like the sun Matt 17:2
dimly, but then *f* 1 Cor 13:12
with unveiled *f* 2 Cor 3:18
withstood him to his *f* Gal 2:11
They shall see His *f* Rev 22:4

FADE
We all *f* as a leaf Is 64:6
rich man also will *f* James 1:11
and that does not *f* 1 Pet 1:4

FADES
withers, the flower *f* Is 40:7

FAIL
title of the law to *f* Luke 16:17
faith should not *f* Luke 22:32
they will *f* 1 Cor 13:8
Your years will not *f* Heb 1:12

FAILING
"men's hearts *f* Luke 21:26

FAILS
Love never *f* 1 Cor 13:8

FAINT
shall walk and not *f* Is 40:31

FAINTS
My soul *f* for Your Ps 119:81
And the whole heart *f* Is 1:5
the earth, Neither *f* Is 40:28

FAITH
shall live by his *f* Hab 2:4
you, O you of little *f* Matt 6:30
not found such great *f* Matt 8:10
that you have no *f* Mark 4:40
"Increase our *f* Luke 17:5
will He really find *f* Luke 18:8
are sanctified by *f* Acts 26:18
God is revealed from *f* Rom 1:17
f apart from the deeds Rom 3:28
his *f* is accounted for Rom 4:5
those who are of the *f* Rom 4:16
f which we preach Rom 10:8
f comes by hearing Rom 10:17
and you stand by *f* Rom 11:20
in proportion to our *f* Rom 12:6
Do you have *f* Rom 14:22
though I have all *f* 1 Cor 13:2
And now abide *f* 1 Cor 13:13
For we walk by *f* 2 Cor 5:7
the flesh I live by *f* Gal 2:20
f are sons of Abraham Gal 3:7
But after *f* has come Gal 3:25
of the household of *f* Gal 6:10
been saved through *f* Eph 2:8
one Lord, one *f* Eph 4:5
taking the shield of *f* Eph 6:16
your work of *f* 1 Thess 1:3
for not all have *f* 2 Thess 3:2
the mystery of the *f* 1 Tim 3:9
I have kept the *f* 2 Tim 4:7
in our common *f* Titus 1:4
not being mixed with *f* Heb 4:2
f is the substance Heb 11:1
without *f* it is Heb 11:6
says he has *f* James 2:14
Show me your *f* James 2:18
and not by *f* only James 2:24
f will save the sick James 5:15
add to your *f* virtue 2 Pet 1:5
the patience and the *f* Rev 13:10

FAITHFUL
God, He Is God, the *f* Deut 7:9
LORD preserves the *f* Ps 31:23
eyes shall be on the *f* Ps 101:6
But who can find a *f* Prov 20:6
the Holy One who is *f* Hos 11:12
"Who then is a *f* Matt 24:45
good and *f* servant Matt 25:23
"He who is *f* in what Luke 16:10
Judged me to be *f* Acts 16:15
God is *f* 1 Cor 1:9
is my beloved and *f* 1 Cor 4:17
But as God is *f* 2 Cor 1:18
f brethren in Christ Col 1:2
who calls you is *f* 1 Thess 5:24
This is a *f* saying and 1 Tim 1:15
f High Priest in Heb 2:17
He who promised is *f* Heb 10:23
He is *f* and just to 1 John 1:9
Be *f* until death Rev 2:10

words are true and *f* Rev 21:5

FAITHFULNESS
I have declared Your *f* Ps 40:10
Your *f* also surrounds Ps 89:8
f endures to all Ps 119:90
Great is Your *f* Lam 3:23
unbelief make the *f* Rom 3:3

FAITHLESS
"O *f* generation Mark 9:19
If we are *f* 2 Tim 2:13

FALL
a deep sleep to *f* Gen 2:21
Let them *f* by their Ps 5:10
righteous man may *f* Prov 24:16
But the wicked shall *f* Prov 24:16
the blind, both will *f* Matt 15:14
the stars will *f* Matt 24:29
"I saw Satan *f* Luke 10:18
take heed lest he *f* 1 Cor 10:12
if they *f* away Heb 6:6
lest anyone *f* short of Heb 12:15
and rocks, "*F* on us Rev 6:16

FALLEN
"Babylon is *f* Is 21:9
you have *f* from grace Gal 5:4
"Babylon is *f* Rev 14:8

FALLING
great drops of blood *f* Luke 22:44
f away comes first 2 Thess 2:3

FALSE
"You shall not bear *f* Ex 20:16
I hate every *f* way Ps 119:104
f witness shall perish Prov 21:28
"Beware of *f* prophets Matt 7:15
f christs and *f* Matt 24:24
and we are found *f* 1 Cor 15:15
of *f* brethren Gal 2:4
f prophets have gone 1 John 4:1
mouth of the *f* prophet Rev 16:13

FALSEHOOD
For their deceit is *f* Ps 119:118
Offspring of *f* Is 57:4

FALSELY
of evil against you *f* Matt 5:11
f called knowledge 1 Tim 6:20

FAMILIES
in you all the *f* Gen 12:3
the God of all the *f* Jer 31:1
in your seed all the *f* Acts 3:25

FAMILY
shall mourn, every *f* Zech 12:12
f were baptized Acts 16:33

FAMINES
And there will be *f* Matt 24:7

FAMISH
righteous soul to *f* Prov 10:3

FAMISHED
honorable men are *f* Is 5:13

FAR
Your judgments are *f* Ps 10:5
Be not *f* from Me Ps 22:11
The LORD is *f* from Prov 15:29

their heart is *f* from Matt 15:8
going to a *f* country Mark 13:34
though He is not *f* Acts 17:27
you who once were *f* Eph 2:13

FARMER
The hard-working *f* 2 Tim 2:6
See how the *f* waits James 5:7

FASHIONED
have made me and *f* Job 10:8

FASHIONS
He *f* their hearts Ps 33:15

FAST
f as you do this day Is 58:4
f that I have chosen Is 58:5
"Moreover, when you *f* Matt 6:16
disciples do not *f* Matt 9:14
I *f* twice a week Luke 18:12

FASTED
'When you *f* and Zech 7:5
And when He had *f* Matt 4:2

FASTING
by prayer and *f* Matt 17:21
give yourselves to *f* 1 Cor 7:5

FASTINGS
in sleeplessness, in *f* 2 Cor 6:5

FAT
and you will eat the *f* Gen 45:18
f is the LORD's Lev 3:16

FATHER
man shall leave his *f* Gen 2:24
and you shall be a *f* Gen 17:4
I was a *f* to the poor Job 29:16
A *f* of the fatherless Ps 68:5
f pities his children Ps 103:13
God, Everlasting *F* Is 9:6
You, O LORD, are our *F* Is 63:16
time cry to Me, 'My *F* Jer 3:4
For I am a *F* to Israel Jer 31:9
"A son honors his *f* Mal 1:6
Have we not all one *F* Mal 2:10
Our *F* in heaven Matt 6:9
"He who loves *f* Matt 10:37
know the *F* Matt 11:27
'He who curses *f* Matt 15:4
for One is your *F* Matt 23:9
"*F* will be divided Luke 12:53
F loves the Son John 3:35
F raises the dead John 5:21
F judges no one John 5:22
He has seen the *F* John 6:46
F who sent Me bears John 8:18
we have one *F* John 8:41
of your *f* the devil John 8:44
"I and My *F* are one John 10:30
'I am going to the *F* John 14:28
came forth from the *F* John 16:28
that he might be the *f* Rom 4:11
one God and *F* of all Eph 4:6
"I will be to Him a *F* Heb 1:5
down from the *F* James 1:17
if you call on the *F* 1 Pet 1:17
and testify that the *F* 1 John 4:14

FATHERLESS
the helper of the *f* Ps 10:14
He relieves the *f* Ps 146:9

do not defend the *f* Is 1:23
they may rob the *f* Is 10:2
You the *f* finds mercy Hos 14:3

FATHER'S
you in My *F* kingdom Matt 26:29
I must be about My *F* Luke 2:49
F house are many John 14:2
that a man has his *f* 1 Cor 5:1

FATHERS
the LORD God of our *f* Ezra 7:27
f trusted in You Ps 22:4
our ears, O God, our *f* Ps 44:1
f ate the manna John 6:31
of whom are the *f* Rom 9:5
unaware that all our *f* 1 Cor 10:1

FATNESS
of the root and *f* Rom 11:17

FAULT
I have found no *f* Luke 23:14
does He still find *f* Rom 9:19
of God without *f* Phil 2:15

FAULTLESS
covenant had been *f* Heb 8:7
to present you *f* Jude 24

FAULTS
"I remember my *f* Gen 41:9
me from secret *f* Ps 19:12

FAVOR
granted me life and *f* Job 10:12
His *f* is for life Ps 30:5
A good man obtains *f* Prov 12:2
and stature, and in *f* Luke 2:52
God and having *f* Acts 2:47

FAVORED
"Rejoice, highly *f* Luke 1:28

FAVORITISM
not show personal *f* Luke 20:21
God shows personal *f* Gal 2:6

FEAR
live, for I *f* God Gen 42:18
to put the dread and *f* Deut 2:25
said, "Does Job *f* Job 1:9
Yes, you cast off *f* Job 15:4
The *f* of the LORD is Ps 19:9
of death, I will *f* Ps 23:4
Whom shall I *f* Ps 27:1
Oh, *f* the LORD Ps 34:9
There is no *f* of God Ps 36:1
The *f* of the LORD is Ps 111:10
The *f* of man brings a Prov 29:25
F God and keep His Eccl 12:13
Let Him be your *f* Is 8:13
"Be strong, do not *f* Is 35:4
who would not *f* Jer 10:7
f Him who is able Matt 10:28
"Do not *f* Luke 12:32
"Do you not even *f* Luke 23:40
And walking in the *f* Acts 9:31
given us a spirit of *f* 2 Tim 1:7
those who through *f* Heb 2:15
because of His godly *f* Heb 5:7
F God 1 Pet 2:17
love casts out *f* 1 John 4:18

FEARED
He is also to be *f* 1 Chr 16:25
f God more than Neh 7:2
Yourself, are to be *f* Ps 76:7
Then those who *f* Mal 3:16

FEARFUL
It is a *f* thing to Heb 10:31

FEARFULLY
f and wonderfully Ps 139:14

FEARING
sincerity of heart, *f* Col 3:22
forsook Egypt, not *f* Heb 11:27

FEARS
upright man, one who *f* Job 1:8
me from all my *f* Ps 34:4
nation whoever *f* Acts 10:35
f has not been made 1 John 4:18

FEAST
and you shall keep a *f* Num 29:12
hate, I despise your *f* Amos 5:21
every year at the *F* Luke 2:41
when you give a *f* Luke 14:13
Now the Passover, a *f* John 6:4
great day of the *f* John 7:37

FEASTING
go to the house of *f* Eccl 7:2

FEASTS
the best places at *f* Luke 20:46
spots in your love *f* Jude 12

FED
and *f* you with manna Deut 8:3
f you with milk and 1 Cor 3:2

FEEBLE
strengthened the *f* Job 4:4
And there was none *f* Ps 105:37
And my flesh is *f* Ps 109:24
hang down, and the *f* Heb 12:12

FEED
ravens to *f* you there 1 Kin 17:4
and *f* your flocks Is 61:5
to him, "*F* My lambs John 21:15
your enemy is hungry, *f* Rom 12:20
goods to *f* the poor 1 Cor 13:3

FEEDS
your heavenly Father *f* Matt 6:26

FEET
all things under his *f* Ps 8:6
He makes my *f* like the Ps 18:33
You have set my *f* Ps 31:8
For their *f* run to Prov 1:16
Her *f* go down to death Prov 5:5
mountains Are the *f* Is 52:7
place of My *f* glorious Is 60:13
in that day His *f* Zech 14:4
two hands or two *f* Matt 18:8
began to wash His *f* Luke 7:38
wash the disciples' *f* John 13:5
f are swift to shed Rom 3:15
beautiful are the *f* Rom 10:15
things under His *f* 1 Cor 15:27
and having shod your *f* Eph 6:15
fell at His *f* as dead Rev 1:17

FLEE
Or where can I *f* Ps 139:7
And the shadows *f* Song 2:17
who are in Judea *f* Matt 24:16
F sexual immorality 1 Cor 6:18
f these things and 1 Tim 6:11
devil and he will *f* James 4:7

FLESH
bone of my bones And *f* Gen 2:23
shall become one *f* Gen 2:24
f had corrupted their Gen 6:12
f I shall see God Job 19:26
My *f* also will rest in Ps 16:9
is wearisome to the *f* Eccl 12:12
And all *f* shall see it Is 40:5
"All *f* is grass Is 40:6
out My Spirit on all *f* Joel 2:28
two shall become one *f* Matt 19:5
were shortened, no *f* Matt 24:22
shall become one *f* Mark 10:8
the Word became *f* John 1:14
I shall give is My *f* John 6:51
f profits nothing John 6:63
of God, but with the *f* Rom 7:25
on the things of the *f* Rom 8:5
to the *f* you will die Rom 8:13
f should glory in His 1 Cor 1:29
"shall become one *f* 1 Cor 6:16
For the *f* lusts Gal 5:17
have crucified the *f* Gal 5:24
may boast in your *f* Gal 6:13
the lust of the *f* 1 John 2:16
has come in the *f* 1 John 4:2

FLESHLY
f wisdom but by the 2 Cor 1:12
f lusts which 1 Pet 2:11

FLIES
Dead *f* putrefy the Eccl 10:1

FLOAT
and he made the iron *f* 2 Kin 6:6

FLOCK
lead Joseph like a *f* Ps 80:1
He will feed His *f* Is 40:11
you do not feed the *f* Ezek 34:3
my God, "Feed the *f* Zech 11:4
sheep of the *f* Matt 26:31
"Do not fear, little *f* Luke 12:32
there will be one *f* John 10:16
Shepherd the *f* of God 1 Pet 5:2
examples to the *f* 1 Pet 5:3

FLOOD
the waters of the *f* Gen 7:10
them away like a *f* Ps 90:5
the days before the *f* Matt 24:38
bringing in the *f* 2 Pet 2:5
of his mouth like a *f* Rev 12:15

FLOODS
me, And the *f* of Ps 18:4
f on the dry ground Is 44:3
rain descended, the *f* Matt 7:25

FLOURISH
the righteous shall *f* Ps 72:7

FLOW
of his heart will *f* John 7:38

FLOWER
As a *f* of the field Ps 103:15
beauty is a fading *f* Is 28:4
grass withers, the *f* Is 40:7
of man as the *f* 1 Pet 1:24

FLOWERS
f appear on the earth Song 2:12

FLOWING
'a land *f* with milk Deut 6:3
the Gentiles like a *f* Is 66:12

FLUTE
play the harp and *f* Gen 4:21

FLUTES
instruments and *f* Ps 150:4

FLUTISTS
harpists, musicians, *f* Rev 18:22

FLY
soon cut off, and we *f* Ps 90:10

FOLLOW
f You wherever You go Matt 8:19
He said to him, "*F* Matt 9:9
up his cross, and *f* Mark 8:34
will by no means *f* John 10:5
serves Me, let him *f* John 12:26
that you should *f* 1 Pet 2:21
f the Lamb wherever Rev 14:4
and their works *f* Rev 14:13

FOLLOWED
f the LORD my God Josh 14:8
we have left all and *f* Mark 10:28

FOLLOWS
f Me shall not walk John 8:12

FOLLY
taken much notice of *f* Job 35:15
not turn back to *f* Ps 85:8
F is joy to him who is Prov 15:21
F is set in great Eccl 10:6

FOOD
you it shall be for *f* Gen 1:29
that lives shall be *f* Gen 9:3
f which you eat shall Ezek 4:10
the fields yield no *f* Hab 3:17
That there may be *f* Mal 3:10
to give them *f* Matt 24:45
and you gave Me *f* Matt 25:35
and he who has *f* Luke 3:11
have you any *f* John 21:5
they ate their *f* Acts 2:46
our hearts with *f* Acts 14:17
destroy with your *f* Rom 14:15
f makes my brother 1 Cor 8:13
the same spiritual *f* 1 Cor 10:3
sower, and bread for *f* 2 Cor 9:10
And having *f* and 1 Tim 6:8
and not solid *f* Heb 5:12
But solid *f* belongs to Heb 5:14
of *f* sold his Heb 12:16
destitute of daily *f* James 2:15

FOODS
f which God 1 Tim 4:3

FOOL
f has said in his Ps 14:1
is like sport to a *f* Prov 10:23
f is right in his own Prov 12:15
is too lofty for a *f* Prov 24:7
whoever says, 'You *f* Matt 5:22
I have become a *f* 2 Cor 12:11

FOOLISH
I was so *f* and Ps 73:22
f pulls it down with Prov 14:1
f man squanders it Prov 21:20
Has not God made *f* 1 Cor 1:20
O *f* Galatians Gal 3:1
were also once *f* Titus 3:3
But avoid *f* disputes Titus 3:9

FOOLISHLY
I speak *f* 2 Cor 11:21

FOOLISHNESS
F is bound up in the Prov 22:15
devising of *f* is sin Prov 24:9
of the cross is *f* 1 Cor 1:18
Because the *f* of God 1 Cor 1:25

FOOLS
f despise wisdom Prov 1:7
folly of *f* is deceit Prov 14:8
F mock at sin Prov 14:9
We are *f* for Christ's 1 Cor 4:10

FOOT
will not allow your *f* Ps 121:3
f will not stumble Prov 3:23
From the sole of the *f* Is 1:6
f causes you to sin Matt 18:8
you dash your *f* Luke 4:11
If the *f* should say 1 Cor 12:15

FOOTSTOOL
Your enemies Your *f* Ps 110:1
Your enemies Your *f* Matt 22:44

FORBID
said, "Do not *f* Mark 9:39
"Can anyone *f* Acts 10:47
f that I should boast Gal 6:14

FORBIDDING
f to marry 1 Tim 4:3

FOREFATHERS
conscience, as my *f* 2 Tim 1:3

FOREHEADS
put a mark on the *f* Ezek 9:4
seal of God on their *f* Rev 9:4
his mark on their *f* Rev 20:4

FOREIGNER
"I am a *f* and a Gen 23:4
of me, since I am a *f* Ruth 2:10
to God except this *f* Luke 17:18

FOREIGNERS
f who were there Acts 17:21
longer strangers and *f* Eph 2:19

FOREKNEW
For whom He *f* Rom 8:29
His people whom He *f* Rom 11:2

FOREKNOWLEDGE
purpose and *f* of God Acts 2:23

FOREORDAINED
He indeed was *f* 1 Pet 1:20

FORESAW
'I *f* the LORD Acts 2:25

FORESEEING
f that God would Gal 3:8

FORESEES
A prudent man *f* Prov 223

FORETOLD
have also *f* these days Acts 3:24
killed those who *f* Acts 7:52

FOREVER
and eat, and live *f* Gen 3:22
to our children *f* Deut 29:29
LORD sits as King *f* Ps 29:10
Do not cast us off *f* Ps 44:23
throne, O God, is *f* Ps 45:6
"You are a priest *f* Ps 110:4
His mercy endures *f* Ps 136:1
of our God stands *f* Is 40:8
My salvation will be *f* Is 51:6
will not cast off *f* Lam 3:31
Like the stars *f* Dan 12:3
and the glory *f* Matt 6:13
the Christ remains *f* John 12:34
who is blessed *f* 2 Cor 11:31
to whom be glory *f* Gal 1:5
generation, *f* and ever Eph 3:21
and Father be glory *f* Phil 4:20
throne, O God, is *f* Heb 1:8
lives and abides *f* 1 Pet 1:23
of darkness*f* Jude 13
power, Both now and *f* Jude 25
And they shall reign *f* Rev 22:5

FOREVERMORE
Blessed be the LORD *f* Ps 89:52
this time forth and *f* Ps 113:2
behold, I am alive *f* Rev 1:18

FORGAVE
to repay, he freely *f* Luke 7:42
God in Christ *f* Eph 4:32
even as Christ *f* Col 3:13

FORGET
f the LORD who Deut 6:12
I will not *f* Your word Ps 119:16
If I *f* you Ps 137:5
My son, do not *f* Prov 3:1
f the LORD your Maker Is 51:13
f your work and labor Heb 6:10

FORGETFULNESS
in the land of *f* Ps 88:12

FORGETS
and immediately *f* James 1:24

FORGETTING
f those things which Phil 3:13

FORGIVE
f their sin and heal 2 Chr 7:14
good, and ready to *f* Ps 86:5
And *f* us our debts Matt 6:12
Father will also *f* Matt 6:14
his heart, does not *f* Matt 18:35
Who can *f* sins but God Mark 2:7
f the sins of any John 20:23
you ought rather to *f* 2 Cor 2:7
F me this wrong 2 Cor 12:13
f us our sins and to 1 John 1:9

FORGIVEN
sins be *f* them Mark 4:12
to whom little is *f* Luke 7:47
f you all trespasses Col 2:13
your sins are *f* 1 John 2:12

FORGIVENESS
But there is *f* with Ps 130:4
preached to you the *f* Acts 13:38
they may receive *f* Acts 26:18
His blood, the *f* Eph 1:7

FORGIVES
f all your iniquities Ps 103:3
is this who even *f* Luke 7:49

FORGIVING
tenderhearted, *f* Eph 4:32
and *f* one another Col 3:13

FORGOT
Joseph, but *f* Gen 40:23
They soon *f* His works Ps 106:13

FORGOTTEN
f the God who Deut 32:18
not one of them is *f* Luke 12:6
f the exhortation Heb 12:5
f that he was 2 Pet 1:9

FORM
earth was without *f* Gen 1:2
Who would *f* a god or Is 44:10
f the light and create Is 45:7
descended in bodily *f* Luke 3:22
time, nor seen His *f* John 5:37
For the *f* of this 1 Cor 7:31
Who, being in the *f* Phil 2:6
having a *f* of 2 Tim 3:5

FORMED
And the LORD God *f* Gen 2:7
f my inward parts Ps 139:13
say of him who *f* Is 29:16
"Before I *f* you in Jer 1:5
Will the thing *f* Rom 9:20
until Christ is *f* Gal 4:19

FORMER
f days better than Eccl 7:10
f rain to the earth Hos 6:3
f prophets preached Zech 1:4
your *f* conduct Eph 4:22
f things have passed Rev 21:4

FORMS
clay say to him who *f* Is 45:9
f the spirit of man Zech 12:1

FORNICATION
"We were not born of *f* John 8:41
of the wrath of her *f* Rev 14:8

FORNICATOR
you know, that no *f* Eph 5:5
lest there be any *f* Heb 12:16

FORNICATORS
but *f* and adulterers Heb 13:4

FORSAKE
But I did not *f* Ps 119:87
father, And do not *f* Prov 1:8
of you does not *f* Luke 14:33
never leave you nor *f* Heb 13:5

FORSAKEN
My God, why have You *f* Ps 22:1
seen the righteous *f* Ps 37:25
a mere moment I have *f* Is 54:7
God, why have You *f* Matt 27:46
persecuted, but not *f* 2 Cor 4:9
for Demas has *f* 2 Tim 4:10

FORSAKING
f the assembling Heb 10:25

FORSOOK
f God who made him Deut 32:15
all the disciples *f* Matt 26:56
with me, but all *f* 2 Tim 4:16

FORTRESS
is my rock, my *f* 2 Sam 22:2
my rock of refuge, a *f* Ps 31:2

FOUND
f a helper comparable Gen 2:20
a thousand I have *f* Eccl 7:28
LORD while He may be *f* Is 55:6
fruit on it and *f* none Luke 13:6
he was lost and is *f* Luke 15:24
f the Messiah" (which John 1:41
and be *f* in Him Phil 3:9

FOUNDATION
Of old You laid the *f* Ps 102:25
the earth without a *f* Luke 6:49
loved Me before the *f* John 17:24
I have laid the *f* 1 Cor 3:10
f can anyone lay than 1 Cor 3:11
us in Him before the *f* Eph 1:4
not laying again the *f* Heb 6:1
Lamb slain from the *f* Rev 13:8

FOUNDATIONS
when I laid the *f* Job 3 8:4
And the *f* of the wall Rev 21:19

FOUNTAIN
will become in him a *f* John 4:14

FOUNTAINS
on that day all the *f* Gen 7:11
lead them to living *f* Rev 7:17

FRAGRANCE
was filled with the *f* John 12:3
we are to God the *f* 2 Cor 2:15

FREE
'You will be made *f* John 8:33
And having been set *f* Rom 6:18
Jesus has made me *f* Rom 8:2
is neither slave nor *f* Gal 3:28
Christ has made us *f* Gal 5:1
he is a slave or *f* Eph 6:8

FREED
has died has been *f* Rom 6:7

FREEDMAN
slave is the Lord's *f* 1 Cor 7:22

FREELY
the garden you may *f* Gen 2:16
F you have received Matt 10:8
f give us all Rom 8:32
the water of life *f* Rev 22:17

FRIEND
of Abraham Your *f* 2 Chr 20:7

only to the good and *g* 1 Pet 2:18
ornament of a *g* 1 Pet 3:4

GENTLENESS
love and a spirit of *g* 1 Cor 4:21
g, self-control Gal 5:23
all lowliness and *g* Eph 4:2
Let your *g* be known to Phil 4:5
love, patience, *g* 1 Tim 6:11

GHOST
supposed it was a *g* Mark 6:49

GIFT
it is the *g* of God Eccl 3:13
"If you knew the *g* John 4:10
but the *g* of God is Rom 6:23
each one has his own *g* 1 Cor 7:7
though I have the *g* 1 Cor 13:2
it is the *g* of God Eph 2:8
Do not neglect the *g* 1 Tim 4:14
you to stir up the *g* 2 Tim 1:6
tasted the heavenly *g* Heb 6:4
Every good *g* and James 1:17

GIFTS
You have received *g* Ps 68:18
and Seba Will offer *g* Ps 72:10
how to give good *g* Matt 7:11
rich putting their *g* Luke 21:1
g differing Rom 12:6
are diversities of *g* 1 Cor 12:4
and desire spiritual *g* 1 Cor 14:1
captive, And gave *g* Eph 4:8

GIRD
G Your sword upon Your Ps 45:3
and another will *g* John 21:18
Therefore *g* up the 1 Pet 1:13

GIRDED
a towel and *g* Himself John 13:4

GIVE
g you the desires Ps 37:4
Yes, the LORD will *g* Ps 85:12
G me understanding Ps 119:34
"*G* to him who asks Matt 5:42
G us this day our Matt 6:11
what you have and *g* Matt 19:21
authority I will *g* Luke 4:6
G them eternal life John 10:28
commandment I *g* John 13:34
but what I do have I *g* Acts 3:6
g us all things Rom 8:32
G no offense 1 Cor 10:32
g him who has need Eph 4:28
g thanks to God 2 Thess 2:13
g yourself entirely 1 Tim 4:15

GIVEN
to him more will be *g* Matt 13:12
has, more will be *g* Matt 25:29
to whom much is *g* Luke 12:48
g Me I should lose John 6:39
Spirit was not yet *g* John 7:39

GIVES
g life to the world John 6:33
"All that the Father *g* John 6:37
The good shepherd *g* John 10:11
not as the world *g* John 14:27
g us richly all things 1 Tim 6:17
who *g* to all liberally James 1:5

g grace to the humble James 4:6

GLAD
streams shall make *g* Ps 46:4
I was *g* when they said Ps 122:1
make merry and be *g* Luke 15:32
he saw it and was *g* John 8:56

GLADNESS
me hear joy and *g* Ps 51:8
Serve the LORD with *g* Ps 100:2

GLORIFIED
and they *g* the God of Matt 15:31
Jesus was not yet *g* John 7:39
when Jesus was *g* John 12:16
this My Father is *g* John 15:8
"I have *g* You on the John 17:4
g His Servant Jesus Acts 3:13
these He also *g* Rom 8:30
things God may be *g* 1 Pet 4:11

GLORIFY
g your Father in Matt 5:16
"Father, *g* Your name John 12:28
"He will *g* Me John 16:14
"And now, O Father, *g* John 17:5
death he would *g* John 21:19
therefore *g* God in 1 Cor 6:20
also Christ did not *g* Heb 5:5
ashamed, but let him *g* 1 Pet 4:16

GLORIOUS
G things are spoken Ps 87:3
g splendor of Your Ps 145:5
habitation, holy and *g* Is 63:15
it to Himself a *g* Eph 5:27
be conformed to His *g* Phil 3:21
g appearing of our Titus 2:13

GLORY
show me Your *g* Ex 33:18
g has departed from 1 Sam 4:21
Who is this King of *g* Ps 24:8
Your power and Your *g* Ps 63:2
wise shall inherit *g* Prov 3:35
It is the *g* of God to Prov 25:2
g I will not give Is 42:8
that they may have *g* Matt 6:2
the power and the *g* Matt 6:13
g was not arrayed Matt 6:29
will come in the *g* Matt 16:27
power and great *g* Matt 24:30
"*G* to God in the Luke 2:14
and we beheld His *g* John 1:14
and manifested His *g* John 2:11
not seek My own *g* John 8:50
"Give God the *g* John 9:24
g which I had with John 17:5
g which You gave Me John 17:22
he did not give *g* Acts 12:23
doing good seek for *g* Rom 2:7
fall short of the *g* Rom 3:23
in faith, giving *g* Rom 4:20
the adoption, the *g* Rom 9:4
the riches of His *g* Rom 9:23
God, alone wise, be *g* Rom 16:27
who glories, let him *g* 1 Cor 1:31
to His riches in *g* Phil 4:19
appear with Him in *g* Col 3:4
For you are our *g* 1 Thess 2:20
many sons to *g* Heb 2:10
grass, And all the *g* 1 Pet 1:24

to whom belong the *g* 1 Pet 4:11
for the Spirit of *g* 1 Pet 4:14
the presence of His *g* Jude 24
g Lord, to receive *g* Rev 4:11
g of God illuminated Rev 21:23

GLORYING
Your *g* is not good 1 Cor 5:6

GLUTTON
you say, 'Look, a *g* Luke 7:34

GLUTTONS
g shames his Prov 28:7
evil beasts, lazy *g* Titus 1:12

GNASHING
will be weeping and *g* Matt 8:12

GO
'Let My people *g* Ex 5:1
For wherever you *g* Ruth 1:16
Those who *g* down to Ps 107:23
Where can I *g* from Ps 139:7
to whom shall we *g* John 6:68
g you cannot come John 8:21
I *g* to prepare a place John 14:2
shall *g* out no more Rev 3:12

GOADS
to kick against the *g* Acts 9:5

GOAL
I press toward the *g* Phil 3:14

GOATS
his sheep from the *g* Matt 25:32
with the blood of *g* Heb 9:12
g could take away Heb 10:4

GOD
G created the heavens Gen 1:1
Abram of *G* Most Gen 14:19
and I will be their *G* Gen 17:8
"I am the LORD your *G* Ex 20:2
G is a consuming fire Deut 4:24
If the LORD is *G* 1 Kin 18:21
G is greater than all 2 Chr 2:5
You have been My *G* Ps 22:10
G is our refuge Ps 46:1
G is in the midst of Ps 46:5
me a clean heart, O *G* Ps 51:10
Our *G* is the *G* Ps 68:20
Who is so great a *G* Ps 77:13
Restore us, O *G* Ps 80:7
You alone are *G* Ps 86:10
Exalt the LORD our *G* Ps 99:9
Yes, our *G* is merciful Ps 116:5
For *G* is in heaven Eccl 5:2
Counselor, Mighty *G* Is 9:6
G is my salvation Is 12:2
stricken, Smitten by *G* Is 53:4
"*G* with us Matt 1:23
in *G* my Savior Luke 1:47
the Word was with *G* John 1:1
"For *G* so loved the John 3:16
"*G* is Spirit John 4:24
"My Lord and my *G* John 20:28
Christ Is the Son of *G* Acts 8:37
Indeed, let *G* be true Rom 3:4
If *G* is for us Rom 8:31
G is faithful 1 Cor 1:9
G shall supply all Phil 4:19
and I will be their *G* Heb 8:10

G is a consuming fire Heb 12:29
for *G* is love 1 John 4:8
No one has seen *G* 1 John 4:12
G Himself will be Rev 21:3
and I will be his *G* Rev 21:7

GODDESS
after Ashtoreth the *g* 1 Kin 11:5
of the great *g* Diana Acts 19:35

GODHEAD
eternal power and *G* Rom 1:20
the fullness of the *G* Col 2:9

GODLINESS
is the mystery of *g* 1 Tim 3:16
g with contentment 1 Tim 6:6
having a form of *g* 2 Tim 3:5
to perseverance *g* 2 Pet 1:6

GODLY
who desire to live *g* 2 Tim 3:12
reverence and *g* fear Heb 12:28
to deliver the *g* 2 Pet 2:9

GODS
God is God of *g* Deut 10:17
I said, "You are *g* Ps 82:6
yourselves with *g* Is 57:5
If He called them *g* John 10:35
g have come down to Acts 14:11

GOLD
g I do not have Acts 3:6
with braided hair or *g* 1 Tim 2:9
a man with *g* rings James 2:2
Your *g* and silver are James 5:3
more precious than *g* 1 Pet 1:7
like silver or *g* 1 Pet 1:18
of the city was pure *g* Rev 21:21

GONE
like sheep have *g* Is 53:6

GOOD
God saw that it was *g* Gen 1:10
but God meant it for *g* Gen 50:20
indeed accept *g* Job 2:10
is none who does *g* Ps 14:1
Truly God is *g* to Ps 73:1
g word makes it glad Prov 12:25
on the evil and the *g* Prov 15:3
A merry heart does *g* Prov 17:22
Learn to do *g* Is 1:17
talked to me, with *g* Zech 1:13
they may see your *g* Matt 5:16
"A *g* man out of the Matt 12:35
No one is *g* but One Matt 19:17
For she has done a *g* Matt 26:10
g works I have shown John 10:32
went about doing *g* Acts 10:3 8
g man someone would Rom 5:7
in my flesh) nothing *g* Rom 7:18
overcome evil with *g* Rom 12:21
Jesus for *g* works Eph 2:10
fruitful in every *g* Col 1:10
know that the law is *g* 1 Tim 1:8
For this is *g* and 1 Tim 2:3
bishop, he desires a *g* 1 Tim 3:1
for this is *g* and 1 Tim 5:4
prepared for every *g* 2 Tim 2:21
Every *g* gilt and James 1:17

GOODNESS
"I will make all My *g* Ex 33:19
and abounding in *g* Ex 34:6
"You are my Lord, My *g* Ps 16:2
Surely *g* and mercy Ps 23:6
That I would see the *g* Ps 27:13
the riches of His *g* Rom 2:4
consider the *g* and Rom 11:22
kindness, *g* Gal 5:22

GOSPEL
The beginning of the *g* Mark 1:1
and believe in the *g* Mark 1:15
g must first be Mark 13:10
separated to the *g* Rom 1:1
not ashamed of the *g* Rom 1:16
to a different *g* Gal 1:6
the everlasting *g* Rev 14:6

GOVERNMENT
And the *g* will be upon Is 9:6

GRACE
But Noah found *g* Gen 6:8
G is poured upon Your Ps 45:2
The LORD will give *g* Ps 84:11
the Spirit of *g* Zech 12:10
and the *g* of God was Luke 2:40
g and truth came John 1:17
And great *g* was upon Acts 4:33
receive abundance of *g* Rom 5:17
g is no longer *g* Rom 11:6
For you know the *g* 2 Cor 8:9
g is sufficient 2 Cor 12:9
The *g* of the Lord 2 Cor 13:14
you have fallen from *g* Gal 5:4
to the riches of His *g* Eph 1:7
g you have been Eph 2:8
g was given according Eph 4:7
G be with all those Eph 6:24
shaken, let us have *g* Heb 12:28
But He gives more *g* James 4:6
but grow in the *g* 2 Pet 3:18

GRACIOUS
he said, "God be *g* Gen 43:29
I will be *g* to whom I Ex 33:19
at the *g* words which Luke 4:22
that the Lord is *g* 1 Pet 2:3

GRAFTED
In unbelief, will be *g* Rom 11:23

GRAIN
it treads out the *g* Deut 25:4
be revived like *g* Hos 14:7
to pluck heads of *g* Matt 12:1
unless a *g* of wheat John 12:24

GRAPES
brought forth wild *g* Is 5:2
have eaten sour *g* Ezek 18:2
Do men gather *g* Matt 7:16
g are fully ripe Rev 14:18

GRASS
The *g* withers Is 40:7
so clothes the *g* Matt 6:30
"All Flesh is as *g* 1 Pet 1:24

GRAVE
my soul up from the *g* Ps 30:3
And they made His *g* Is 53:9
the power of the *g* Hos 13:14

GRAVES
g were opened Matt 27:52
g which are not Luke 11:44
g will hear His voice John 5:28

GRAY
the man of *g* hairs Deut 32:25

GREAT
and make your name *g* Gen 12:2
For the LORD is *g* 1 Chr 16:25
Who does *g* things Job 5:9
g is the Holy One Is 12:6
G is Your faithfulness Lam 3:23
he shall be called *g* Matt 5:19
one pearl of *g* price Matt 13:46
desires to become *g* Matt 20:26
g drops of blood Luke 22:44
appearing of our *g* Titus 2:13
g men, the rich men Rev 6:15
Mystery, Babylon the *G* Rev 17:5
the dead, small and *g* Rev 20:12

GREATER
of heaven is *g* Matt 11:11
place there is One *g* Matt 12:6
g than Jonah is here Matt 12:41
g than Solomon is Matt 12:42
a servant is not *g* John 13:16
"*G* love has no one John 15:13
'A servant is not *g* John 15:20
who prophesies is *g* 1 Cor 14:5
God is *g* 1 John 3:20
witness of God is *g* 1 John 5:9

GREATEST
little child is the *g* Matt 18:4
but the *g* of these is 1 Cor 13:13

GREATNESS
is the exceeding *g* Eph 1:19

GREED
part is full of *g* Luke 11:39

GREEDINESS
all uncleanness with *g* Eph 4:19

GREEDY
of everyone who is *g* Prov 1:19
not violent, not *g* 1 Tim 3:3

GREEK
written in Hebrew, *G* John 19:20
and also for the *G* Rom 1:16
is neither Jew not *G* Gal 3:28

GREEN
lie down in *g* pastures Ps 23:2

GRIEF
and acquainted with *g* Is 53:3
joy and not with *g* Heb 13:17

GRIEVE
g the Holy Spirit Eph 4:30

GRIEVED
earth, and He was *g* Gen 6:6
g His Holy Spirit Is 63:10
with anger, being *g* Mark 3:5

GROAN
even we ourselves *g* Rom 8:23
who are in this tent *g* 2 Cor 5:4

GROANING
I am weary with my *g* Ps 6:6
Then Jesus, again *g* John 11:38

GROANINGS
g which cannot Rom 8:26

GROUND
"Cursed is the *g* Gen 3:17
you stand is holy *g* Ex 3:5
up your fallow *g* Jer 4:3
others fell on good *g* Matt 13:8
bought a piece of *g* Luke 14:18
God, the pillar and *g* 1 Tim 3:15

GROUNDED
being rooted and *g* Eph 3:17

GROW
truth in love, may *g* Eph 4:15
but *g* in the grace and 2 Pet 3:18

GRUDGINGLY
in his heart, not *g* 2 Cor 9:7

GUARANTEE
in our hearts as a *g* 2 Cor 1:22
us the Spirit as a *g* 2 Cor 5:5
who is the *g* of our Eph 1:14

GUIDE
He will be our *g* Ps 48:14
g our feet into the Luke 1:79
has come, He will *g* John 16:13

GUIDES
to you, blind *g* Matt 23:16

GUILT
of your fathers' *g* Matt 23:32

GUILTLESS
g who takes His name Ex 20:7
have condemned the *g* Matt 12:7

GUILTY
"We are truly *g* Gen 42:21
world may become *g* Rom 3:19
in one point, he is *g* James 2:10

GULF
you there is a great *g* Luke 16:26

H

HABITATION
Is God in His holy *h* Ps 68:5
but He blesses the *h* Prov 3:33
Jerusalem, a quiet *h* Is 33:20
from His holy *h* Zech 2:13
be clothed with our *h* 2 Cor 5:2

HADES
be brought down to *H* Matt 11:23
H shall not Matt 16:18
in torments in *H* Luke 16:23
not leave my soul in *H* Acts 2:27
I have the keys of *H* Rev 1:18
H were cast into the Rev 20:14

HAIL
of the plague of the *h* Rev 16:21

HAIR
you cannot make one *h* Matt 5:36
"But not a *h* of your Luke 21:18
not with braided *h* 1 Tim 2:9
h like women's *h* Rev 9:8

HAIRS
"But the very *h* Matt 10:30

HALLOWED
the Sabbath day and *h* Ex 20:11
who is holy shall be *h* Is 5:16
heaven, *H* be Your name Matt 6:9

HAND
the *h* of God was 1 Sam 5:11
My times are in Your *h* Ps 31:15
"Sit at My right *h* Ps 110:1
heart is in the *h* Prov 2 1: 1
Whatever your *h* Eccl 9:10
is at his right *h* Eccl 10:2
do not withhold your *h* Eccl 11:6
My *h* has laid the Is 48:13
Behold, the LORD's *h* Is 59:1
are the work of Your *h* Is 64:8
"Am I a God near at *h* Jer 23:23
of heaven is at *h* Matt 3:2
if your right *h* Matt 5:30
do not let your left *h* Matt 6:3
h causes you to sin Mark 9:43
sitting at the right *h* Mark 14:62
at the right *h* of God Acts 7:55
The Lord is at *h* Phil 4:5
"Sit at My right *h* Heb 1:13
down at the right *h* Heb 10:12

HANDIWORK
firmament shows His *h* Ps 19:1

HANDLE
H Me and see Luke 24:39
do not taste, do not *h* Col 2:21

HANDLED
and our hands have *h* 1 John 1:1

HANDS
took his life in his *h* 1 Sam 19:5
but His *h* make whole Job 5:18
They pierced My *h* Ps 22:16
h formed the dry land Ps 95:5
than having two *h* Matt 18:8
"Behold My *h* and Luke 24:39
h the print of the John 20:25
his *h* what is good Eph 4:28
the laying on of the *h* 1 Tim 4:14
to fall into the *h* Heb 10:31

HANDWRITING
having wiped out the *h* Col 2:14

HANGED
went and *h* himself Matt 27:5

HANGS
h the earth on nothing Job 26:7
Is everyone who *h* Gal 3:13

HAPPY
H is the man who has Ps 127:5

HARD
I knew you to be a *h* Matt 25:24
"This is a *h* saying John 6:60
are some things *h* 2 Pet 3:16

HARDEN
But I will *h* his heart Ex 4:21
h your hearts as Heb 3:8

HARDENED
But Pharaoh *h* his Ex 8:32
their heart was *h* Mark 6:52
and *h* their hearts John 12:40
lest any of you be *h* Heb 3:13

HARDENS
whom He wills He *h* Rom 9:18

HARDSHIP
h as a good soldier 2 Tim 2:3

HARLOT
of a *h* named Rahab Josh 2:1
h is one body with 1 Cor 6:16
of the great *h* who Rev 17:1

HARLOTRIES
Let her put away her *h* Hos 2:2

HARLOTRY
are the children of *h* Hos 2:4
For the spirit of *h* Hos 5:4

HARLOTS
h enter the Matt 21:31
Great, The Mother of *H* Rev 17:5

HARP
Lamb, each having a *h* Rev 5:8

HARPS
We hung our *h* Upon the Ps 137:2

HARVEST
Seedtime and *h* Gen 8:22
"The *h* is past Jer 8:20
h truly is plentiful Matt 9:37
sickle, because the *h* Mark 4:29
already white for *h* John 4:35

HASTENS
and he sins who *h* Prov 19:2

HASTILY
utter anything *h* Eccl 5:2

HASTY
Do you see a man *h* Prov 29:20

HATE
love the LORD, *h* evil Ps 97:10
h every false way Ps 119:104
h the double-minded Ps 119:113
I *h* and abhor lying Ps 119:163
love, And a time to *h* Eccl 3:8
You who *h* good and Mic 3:2
either he will *h* Matt 6:24

HATED
But Esau I have *h* Mal 1:3
"And you will be *h* Matt 10:22
have seen and also *h* John 15:24
but Esau I have *h* Rom 9:13
For no one ever *h* Eph 5:29

HATEFUL
h woman when she is Prov 30:23
in malice and envy, *h* Titus 3:3

HATERS
backbiters, *h* of God Rom 1:30

HATES
six things the LORD *h* Prov 6:16
lose it, and he who *h* John 12:25
"If the world *h* John 15:18

h his brother is — 1 John 2:11

HAUGHTY
bring down *h* looks — Ps 18:27
my heart is not *h* — Ps 131:1
h spirit before a fall — Prov 16:18

HEAD
He shall bruise your *h* — Gen 3:15
and gave Him to be *h* — Eph 1:22
For the husband is *h* — Eph 5:23

HEAL
O LORD, *h* me — Ps 6:2
h your backslidings — Jer 3:22
torn, but He will *h* — Hos 6:1
"*H* the sick — Matt 10:8
So that I should *h* — Matt 13:15
sent Me to *h* the — Luke 4:18
Physician, *h* yourself — Luke 4:23

HEALED
And return and be *h* — Is 6:10
His stripes we are *h* — Is 53:5
"When I would have *h* — Hos 7:1
and He *h* them — Matt 4:24
that you may be *h* — James 5:16
his deadly wound was *h* — Rev 13:3

HEALING
shall arise With *h* — Mal 4:2
and *h* all kinds of — Matt 4:23
tree were for the *h* — Rev 22:2

HEALINGS
to another gifts of *h* — 1 Cor 12:9

HEALS
h all your diseases — Ps 103:3
Jesus the Christ *h* — Acts 9:34

HEALTH
all things and be in *h* — 3 John 2

HEAR
"*H*, O Israel — Deut 6:4
Him you shall *h* — Deut 18:15
H me when I call — Ps 4:1
O You who *h* prayer — Ps 65:2
ear, shall He not *h* — Ps 94:9
h rather than to give — Eccl 5:1
'Hearing you will *h* — Matt 13:14
heed what you *h* — Mark 4:24
that God does not *h* — John 9:31
And how shall they *h* — Rom 10:14
man be swift to *h* — James 1:19
h what the Spirit says — Rev 2:7

HEARD
h their cry because of — Ex 3:7
that they will be *h* — Matt 6:7
h the word believed — Acts 4:4
not seen, nor ear *h* — 1 Cor 2:9
things that you have *h* — 2 Tim 2:2
the word which they *h* — Heb 4:2
which we have *h* — 1 John 1:1
Lord's Day, and I *h* — Rev 1:10

HEARER
if anyone is a *h* — James 1:23

HEARERS
for not the *h* of the — Rom 2:13
the word, and not *h* — James 1:22

HEARING
'Keep on *h* — Is 6:9
h they do not — Matt 13:13
h they may hear — Mark 4:12
or by the *h* of faith — Gal 3:2

HEARS
out and the LORD *h* — Ps 34:17
of God *h* God's words — John 8:47
"And if anyone *h* — John 12:47
who is of the truth *h* — John 18:37
He who knows God *h* — 1 John 4:6
And let him who *h* — Rev 22:17

HEART
h was only evil — Gen 6:5
h rejoices in the LORD — 1 Sam 2:1
gave him another *h* — 1 Sam 10:9
LORD looks at the *h* — 1 Sam 16:7
his wives turned his *h* — 1 Kin 11:4
He pierces my *h* — Job 16:13
My *h* also instructs me — Ps 16:7
h is overflowing — Ps 45:1
h shall depart from me — Ps 101:4
look and a proud *h* — Ps 101:5
with my whole *h* — Ps 111:1
as he thinks in his *h* — Prov 23:7
h reveals the man — Prov 27:19
trusts in his own *h* — Prov 28:26
The *h* of the wise is — Eccl 7:4
And a wise man's *h* — Eccl 8:5
h yearned for him — Song 5:4
And the whole *h* — Is 1:5
The yearning of Your *h* — Is 63:15
h is deceitful above — Jer 17:9
I will give them a *h* — Jer 24:7
and take the stony *h* — Ezek 11:19
yourselves a new *h* — Ezek 18:31
are the pure in *h* — Matt 5:8
is, there your *h* — Matt 6:21
of the *h* proceed evil — Matt 15:19
h will flow rivers — John 7:38
"Let not your *h* — John 14:1
Satan filled your *h* — Acts 5:3
h that God has raised — Rom 10:9
refresh my *h* in the — Philem 20
and shuts up his *h* — 1 John 3:17

HEARTILY
you do, do it *h* — Col 3:23

HEARTS
God tests the *h* — Ps 7:9
And he will turn The *h* — Mal 4:6
h failing them from — Luke 21:26
will guard your *h* — Phil 4:7
of God rule in your *h* — Col 3:15

HEATHEN
repetitions as the *h* — Matt 6:7

HEAVEN
called the firmament *H* — Gen 1:8
LORD looks down from *h* — Ps 14:2
word is settled in *h* — Ps 119:89
For God is in *h* — Eccl 5:2
"*H* is My throne — Is 66:1
for the kingdom of *h* — Matt 3:2
your Father in *h* — Matt 5:16
On earth as it is in *h* — Matt 6:10
"*H* and earth will — Matt 24:35
Him a sign from *h* — Mark 8:11
have sinned against *h* — Luke 15:18
you shall see *h* — John 1:51
one has ascended to *h* — John 3:13
the true bread from *h* — John 6:32
a voice came from *h* — John 12:28
sheet, let down from *h* — Acts 11:5
laid up for you in *h* — Col 1:5
there was silence in *h* — Rev 8:1
Now I saw a new *h* — Rev 21:1

HEAVENLY
your *h* Father will — Matt 6:14
h host praising God — Luke 2:13
if I tell you *h* things — John 3:12
blessing in the *h* — Eph 1:3
a better, that is, a *h* — Heb 11:16
the living God, the *h* — Heb 12:22

HEAVENS
and the highest *h* — Deut 10:14
h cannot contain — 1 Kin 8:27
h declare the glory — Ps 19:1
For as the *h* are high — Ps 103:11
behold, I create new *h* — Is 65:17
and behold, the *h* — Matt 3:16
h will be shaken — Matt 24:29
h are the work of Your — Heb 1:10
h will pass away — 2 Pet 3:10

HEEDS
h counsel is wise — Prov 12:15

HEEL
you shall bruise His *h* — Gen 3:15
has lifted up his *h* — Ps 41:9
Me has lifted up his *h* — John 13:18

HEIGHT
nor *h* nor depth — Rom 8:39
length and depth and *h* — Eph 3:18

HEIR
He has appointed *h* — Heb 1:2
world and became *h* — Heb 11:7

HEIRS
if children, then *h* — Rom 8:17
should be fellow *h* — Eph 3:6

HELL
shall be turned into *h* — Ps 9:17
go down alive into *h* — Ps 55:15
H and Destruction are — Prov 27:20
be in danger of *h* fire — Matt 5:22
to be cast into *h* — Matt 18:9
condemnation of *h* — Matt 23:33
power to cast into *h* — Luke 12:5

HELMET
And take the *h* of — Eph 6:17
and love, and as a *h* — 1 Thess 5:8

HELP
May He send you *h* — Ps 20:2
A very present *h* — Ps 46:1
He is their *h* and — Ps 115:9
Our *h* is in the name — Ps 124:8
h my unbelief — Mark 9:24
and find grace to *h* — Heb 4:16

HELPED
fall, but the LORD *h* — Ps 118:13
of salvation I have *h* — Is 49:8
h His servant Israel — Luke 1:54

HELPER
I will make him a *h* Gen 2:18
Behold, God is my *h* Ps 54:4
give you another *H* John 14:16
"But when the *H* John 15:26
"The LORD is my *h* Heb 13:6

HELPFUL
all things are not *h* 1 Cor 6:12

HELPS
the Spirit also *h* Rom 8:26

HEM
and touched the *h* Matt 9:20

HERE
Then I said, "*H* am I Is 6:8

HERESIES
dissensions, *h* Gal 5:20

HERITAGE
for that is his *h* Eccl 3:22
This is the *h* of the Is 54:17
of My people, My *h* Joel 3:2
The flock of Your *h* Mic 7:14

HIDDEN
And my sins are not *h* Ps 69:5
Your word I have *h* Ps 119:11
h that will not Matt 10:26
the *h* wisdom which 1 Cor 2:7
bring to light the *h* 1 Cor 4:5
have renounced the *h* 2 Cor 4:2
rather let it be the *h* 1 Pet 3:4
give some of the *h* Rev 2:17

HIDE
H me under the shadow Ps 17:8
You shall *h* them in Ps 31:20
You *h* Your face Ps 104:29
darkness shall not *h* Ps 139:12
You are God, who *h* Is 45:15
"Fall on us and *h* Rev 6:16

HIDES
He *h* His face Ps 10:11

HIDING
You are my *h* place Ps 32:7

HIGH
priest of God Most *H* Gen 14:18
For the LORD Most *H* Ps 47:2
"I dwell in the *h* Is 57:15
know That the Most *H* Dan 4:17
up on a *h* mountain by Matt 17:1
your mind on *h* things Rom 12:16
h thing that exalts 2 Cor 10:5
and faithful *H* Priest Heb 2:17

HIGHER
you, 'Friend, go up *h* Luke 14:10

HIGHWAY
in the desert A *h* Is 40:3

HIGHWAYS
h shall be elevated Is 49:11
go into the *h* Matt 22:9

HILL
My King on My holy *h* Ps 2:6
h cannot be hidden Matt 5:14
and *h* brought low Luke 3:5

HILLS
of the everlasting *h* Gen 49:26
of the *h* are His also Ps 95:4
up my eyes to the *h* Ps 121:1

HINDER
all things lest we *h* 1 Cor 9:12

HINDERED
Who *h* you from obeying Gal 5:7
prayers may not be *h* 1 Pet 3:7

HOLD
right hand shall *h* Ps 139:10
h fast that word 1 Cor 15:2
h fast and repent Rev 3:3

HOLIER
near me, For I am *h* Is 65:5

HOLIEST
the way into the *H* Heb 9:8

HOLINESS
You, glorious in *h* Ex 15:11
I have sworn by My *h* Ps 89:35
the Highway of *H* Is 35:8
to the Spirit of *h* Rom 1:4
spirit, perfecting *h* 2 Cor 7:1
uncleanness, but in *h* 1 Thess 4:7
be partakers of His *h* Heb 12:10

HOLY
where you stand is *h* Ex 3:5
day, to keep it *h* Ex 20:8
LORD your God am *h* Lev 19:2
h seed is mixed Ezra 9:2
God sits on His *h* Ps 47:8
God, in His *h* mountain Ps 48:1
"*H*,*h*,*h* Is 6:3
child of the *H* Spirit Mark 1:18
baptize you with the *H* Mark 1:8
who speak, but the *H* Mark 13:11
H Spirit will come Luke 1:35
H Spirit descended Luke 3:22
Father give the *H* Luke 11:3
H Spirit will teach Luke 12:12
H Spirit was not John 7:39
H Spirit has come Acts 1:8
all filled with the *H* Acts 2:4
receive the *H* Spirit Acts 19:2
joy in the *H* Rom 14:17
H Spirit teaches 1 Cor 2:13
that we should be *h* Eph 1:4
were sealed with the *H* Eph 1:13
partakers of the *H* Heb 6:4
H Spirit sent from 1 Pet 1:12
it is written, "Be *h* 1 Pet 1:16
moved by the *H* Spirit 2 Pet 1:21
anointing from the *H* 1 John 2:20
says He who is *h* Rev 3:7
For You alone are *h* Rev 15:4
is *h*, let him be *h* Rev 22:11

HOME
sparrow has found a *h* Ps 84:3
to his eternal *h* Eccl 12:5
that while we are at *h* 2 Cor 5:6
to show piety at *h* 1 Tim 5:4

HOMEMAKERS
be discreet, chaste, *h* Titus 2:5

HONEY
and with *h* from the Ps 81:16
was locusts and wild *h* Matt 3:4

HONEYCOMB
than honey and the *h* Ps 19:10
fish and some *h* Luke 24:42

HONOR
"*H* your father and your Ex 20:12
will deliver him and *h* Ps 91:15
H and majesty are Ps 96:6
H the LORD with your Prov 3:9
before *h* is humility Prov 15:33
spirit will retain *h* Prov 29:23
Father, where is My *h* Mal 1:6
is not without *h* Matt 13:57
'*H* your father and Matt 15:4
h the Son Just as they John 5:23
"I do not receive *h* John 5:41
but I *h* My Father John 8:49
"If I *h* Myself John 8:54
him My Father will *h* John 12:26
to whom fear, *h* Rom 13:7
sanctification and *h* 1 Thess 4:4
alone is wise, be *h* 1 Tim 1:17
and clay, some for *h* 2 Tim 2:20
no man takes this *h* Heb 5:4
from God the Father *h* 2 Pet 1:17
give glory and *h* Rev 4:9

HONORABLE
His work is *h* and Ps 111:3
holy day of the LORD *h* Is 58:13
providing *h* things 2 Cor 8.21
Marriage is *h* among Heb 13:4
having your conduct *h* 1 Pet 2:12

HONORS
'This people *h* Me Mark 7:6
It is My Father who *h* John 8:54

HOPE
h He has uprooted Job 19:10
also will rest in *h* Ps 16:9
My *h* is in You Ps 39:7
For You are my *h* Ps 71:5
I *h* in Your word Ps 119:147
good that one should *h* Lam 3:26
to *h*, in *h* believed Rom 4:18
h does not disappoint Rom 5:5
were saved in this *h* Rom 8:24
now abide faith, *h* 1 Cor 13:13
life only we have *h* 1 Cor 15:19
may know what is the *h* Eph 1:18
were called in one *h* Eph 4:4
Christ in you, the *h* Col 1:27
Jesus Christ, our *h* 1 Tim 1:1
for the blessed *h* Titus 2:13
to lay hold of the *h* Heb 6:18
in of a better *h* Heb 7:19
who has this *h* in Him 1 John 3:3

HOPED
substance of things *h* Heb 11:1

HORSE
and behold, a white *h* Rev 6:2
and behold, a white *h* Rev 19:11

HOSANNA
H in the highest Matt 21:9

HOSPITABLE
Be *h* to one another 1 Pet 4:9

HOSTS
The LORD of *h* is with Ps 46:7
Praise Him, all His *h* Ps 148:2
against spiritual *h* Eph 6:12

HOUR
is coming at an *h* Matt 24:44
"But the *h* is coming John 4:23
save Me from this *h* John 12:27
keep you from the *h* Rev 3:10

HOUSE
as for me and my *h* Josh 24:15
Through wisdom a *h* Prov 24:3
better to go to the *h* Eccl 7:2
h was filled with Is 6:4
h divided against Matt 12:25
h shall be called a Matt 21:13
make My Father's *h* John 2:16
h are many mansions John 14:2
publicly and from *h* Acts 20:20
who rules his own *h* 1 Tim 3:4
the church in your *h* Philem 2
For every *h* is built Heb 3:4
His own *h*, whose *h* Heb 3:6

HOUSEHOLD
the ways of her *h* Prov 31:27
be those of his own *h* Matt 10:36
h were baptized Acts 16:15
saved, you and your *h* Acts 16:31
who are of Caesar's *h* Phil 4:22

HOUSEHOLDER
h who brings out of Matt 13:52

HOUSES
H and riches are an Prov 19:14
who has left *h* or Matt 19:29
you devour widows' *h* Matt 23:14

HOVERING
Spirit of God was *h* Gen 1:2

HUMBLE
man Moses was very *h* Num 12:3
the cry of the *h* Ps 9:12
h shall hear of it and Ps 34:2
contrite and *h* spirit Is 57:15
A meek and *h* people Zeph 3:12
associate with the *h* Rom 12:16
gives grace to the *h* James 4:6
H yourselves in the James 4:10
gives grace to the *h* 1 Pet 5:5
h yourselves under the 1 Pet 5:6

HUMBLED
as a man, He *h* Himself Phil 2:8

HUMBLES
h Himself to behold Ps 113:6

HUMILITY
the Lord with all *h* Acts 20:19
delight in false *h* Col 2:18
mercies, kindness, *h* Col 3:12
h correcting those 2 Tim 2:25
gentle, showing all *h* Titus 3:2
and be clothed with *h* 1 Pet 5:5

HUNGER
They shall neither *h* Is 49:10
are those who *h* Matt 5:6
for you shall *h* Luke 6:25
to Me shall never *h* John 6:35

hour we both *h* 1 Cor 4:11
"They shall neither *h* Rev 7:16

HUNGRY
and fills the *h* Ps 107:9
gives food to the *h* Ps 146:7
'for I was *h* and you Matt 25:35
did we see You *h* Matt 25:37
to be full and to be *h* Phil 4:12

HUNTER
Nimrod the mighty *h* Gen 10:9
Esau was a skillful *h* Gen 25:27

HURT
h a woman with child Ex 21:22
but I was not *h* Prov 23:35
another to his own *h* Eccl 8:9
They shall not *h* Is 11:9
it will by no means *h* Mark 16:18
shall not be *h* by the Rev 2:11

HUSBAND
She also gave to her *h* Gen 3:6
h safely trusts her Prov 31:11
your Maker is your *h* Is 54:5
now have is not your *h* John 4:18
you will save your *h* 1 Cor 7:16
the *h* of one wife 1 Tim 12

HUSBANDS
H, love your wives Eph 5:25
Let deacons be the *h* 1 Tim 3:2

HYMN
they had sung a *h* Matt 26:30

HYMNS
praying and singing *h* Acts 16:25
in psalms and *h* Eph 5:19

HYPOCRISY
you are full of *h* Matt 23:28
Pharisees, which is *h* Luke 12:1
Let love be without *h* Rom 12:9
away with their *h* Gal 2:13
and without *h* James 3:17
malice, all deceit, *h* 1 Pet 2:1

HYPOCRITE
and the joy of the *h* Job 20:5
For everyone is a *h* Is 9:17
also played the *h* Gal 2:13

HYPOCRITES
not be like the *h* Matt 6:5
do you test Me, you *h* Matt 22:18
and Pharisees, *h* Matt 23:13

I

IDLE
i Person will suffer Prov 19:15
i word men may Matt 12:36
saw others standing *i* Matt 20:3
they learn to be *i* 1 Tim 5:13

IDOL
thing offered to an *i* 1 Cor 8:7
That an *i* is anything 1 Cor 10:19

IDOLATER
or covetous, or an *i* 1 Cor 5:11

IDOLATERS
fornicators, nor *i* 1 Cor 6:9

and murderers and *i* Rev 22:15

IDOLATRIES
and abominable *i* 1 Pet 4:3

IDOLATRY
beloved, flee from *i* 1 Cor 10:14
i, sorcery Gal 5:20

IDOLS
land is also full of *i* Is 2:8
in the room of his *i* Ezek 8:12
who regard worthless *i* Jon 2:8
You who abhor *i* Rom 2:22
yourselves from *i* 1 John 5:21
worship demons, and *i* Rev 9:20

IGNORANCE
that you did it in *i* Acts 3:17
i God overlooked Acts 17:30
sins committed in *i* Heb 9:7

IGNORANTLY
because I did it *i* 1 Tim 1:13

ILLUMINATED
after you were *i* Heb 10:32
and the earth was *i* Rev 18:1
for the glory of God *i* Rev 21:23

IMAGE
Us make man in Our *i* Gen 1:26
since he is the *i* 1 Cor 11:7
He is the *i* of the Col 1:15
and not the very *i* Heb 10:1
the beast and his *i* Rev 14:9

IMAGINATION
the proud in the *i* Luke 1:51

IMITATE
as I also *i* Christ 1 Cor 11:1

IMMANUEL
shall call His name *I* Is 7:14
shall call His name *I* Matt 1:23

IMMORAL
murderers, sexually *i* Rev 21:8

IMMORALITY
except sexual *i* Matt 5:32
abstain from sexual *i* 1 Thess 4:3

IMMORTAL
to the King eternal, *i* 1 Tim 1:17

IMMORTALITY
mortal must put on *i* 1 Cor 15:53
who alone has *i* 1 Tim 6:16

IMMOVABLE
be steadfast, i 1 Cor 15:58

IMMUTABLE
that by two *i* things Heb 6:18

IMPART
that it may *i* grace Eph 4:29

IMPENITENT
i heart you are Rom 2:5

IMPOSSIBLE
God nothing will be *i* Luke 1:37
without faith it is *i* Heb 11:6

IMPUTE
the LORD does not *i* Ps 32:2

IMPUTED
might be *i* to them Rom 4:11
but sin is not *i* Rom 5:13

IMPUTES
i righteousness apart Rom 4:6

INCORRUPTIBLE
the glory of the *i* Rom 1:23
dead will be raised *i* 1 Cor 15:52
to an inheritance *i* 1 Pet 1:4

INCORRUPTION
corruption inherit *i* 1 Cor 15:50

INCREASE
Of the *i* of His Is 9:7
Lord, "*I* our faith Luke 17:5
"He must *i* John 3:30
but God gave the *i* 1 Cor 3:6

INCREASES
who have no might He *i* Is 40:29

INCURABLE
Your sorrow is *i* Jer 30:15

INDIGNATION
i which will devour Heb 10:27
into the cup of His *i* Rev 14:10

INEXCUSABLE
Therefore you are *i* Rom 2:1

INEXPRESSIBLE
Paradise and heard *i* 2 Cor 12:4
you rejoice with joy *i* 1 Pet 1:8

INFALLIBLE
suffering by many *i* Acts 1:3

INFIRMITIES
"He Himself took our *i* Matt 8:17

INHERIT
love me to *i* wealth Prov 8:21
i the kingdom Matt 25:34
unrighteous will not *i* 1 Cor 6:9
who overcomes shall *i* Rev 21:7

INHERITANCE
"You shall have no *i* Num 18:20
is the place of His *i* Deut 32:9
the portion of my *i* Ps 16:5
i shall be forever Ps 37:18
He will choose our *i* Ps 47:4
will arise to your *i* Dan 12:13
God gave him no *i* Acts 7:5
and give you an *i* Acts 20:32
For if the *i* is of the Gal 3:18
we have obtained an *i* Eph 1:11
be partakers of the *i* Col 1:12
receive as an *i* Heb 11:8
i incorruptible 1 Pet 1:4

INIQUITIES
i have overtaken me Ps 40:12
forgives all your *i* Ps 103:3
LORD, should mark *i* Ps 130:3
was bruised for our *i* Is 53:5
He shall bear their *i* Is 53:11
i have separated you Is 59:2

INIQUITY
God, visiting the *i* of the Ex 20:5
was brought forth in *i* Ps 51:5
If I regard *i* in my Ps 66:18
i have dominion Ps 119:133
i will reap sorrow Prov 22:8
A people laden with *i* Is 1:4
i is taken away Is 6:7
has laid on Him the *i* Is 53:6
will remember their *i* Hos 9:9
to those who devise *i* Mic 2:1
like You, Pardoning *i* Mic 7:18
all you workers of *i* Luke 13:27
a fire, a world of *i* James 3:6

INJUSTICE
i have your fathers Jer 2:5

INN
room for them in the *i* Luke 2:7
brought him to an *i* Luke 10:34

INNOCENCE
washed my hands in *i* Ps 73:13

INNOCENT
because I was found *i* Dan 6:22
saying, "I am *i* Matt 27:24
this day that I am *i* Acts 20:26

INQUIRED
Therefore David *i* 1 Sam 23:2
the prophets have *i* 1 Pet 1:10

INQUIRY
shall make careful *i* Deut 19:18

INSANE
images, And they are *i* Jer 50:38

INSPIRATION
is given by *i* of God 2 Tim 3:16

INSTRUCT
I will *i* you and teach Ps 32:8
LORD that he may *i* 1 Cor 2:16

INSTRUCTED
This man had been *i* Acts 18:25
are excellent, being *i* Rom 2:18
Moses was divinely *i* Heb 8:5

INSTRUCTION
seeing you hate *i* Ps 50:17
Hear *i* and be wise Prov 8:33
Give *i* to a wise man Prov 9:9
for correction, for *i* 2 Tim 3:16

INSTRUCTS
My heart also *i* Ps 16:7

INSTRUMENTS
your members as *i* Rom 6:13

INSUBORDINATE
for the lawless and *i* 1 Tim 1:9

INSUBORDINATION
of dissipation or *i* Titus 1:6

INSULTED
will be mocked and *i* Luke 18:32
i the Spirit of grace Heb 10:29

INSULTS
nor be afraid of their *i* Is 51:7

INTEGRITY
in the *i* of my heart Gen 20:5
in doctrine showing *i* Titus 2:7

INTERCEDE
the LORD, who will *i* 1 Sam 2:25

INTERCESSION
of many, And made *i* Is 53:12
Spirit Himself makes *i* Rom 8:26
always lives to make *i* Heb 7:25

INTERCESSOR
that there was no *i* Is 59:16

INTEREST
collected it with *i* Luke 19:23

INTERPRET
Do all *i*? 1 Cor 12:30
pray that he may *i* 1 Cor 14:13

INTERPRETATION
to another the *i* 1 Cor 12:10
of any private *i* 2 Pet 1:20

INTERPRETATIONS
"Do not *i* belong to Gen 40:8

INVISIBLE
of the world His *i* Rom 1:20
is the image of the *i* Col 1:15
eternal, immortal, *i* 1 Tim 1:17
as seeing Him who is *i* Heb 11:27

INWARD
You have formed my *i* Ps 139:13
God according to the *i* Rom 7:22
i man is being 2 Cor 4:16

INWARDLY
i they are Matt 7:15
is a Jew who is one *i* Rom 2:29

IRON
i sharpens *i* Prov 27:17
its feet partly of *i* Dan 2:33

ISRAEL
"Hear, O *I* Deut 6:4
For they are not all *I* Rom 9:6
and upon the *I* of God Gal 6:16

ITCHING
they have *i* ears 2 Tim 4:3

J

JEALOUS
God, am a *j* God Ex 20:5
a consuming fire, a *j* Deut 4:24
For I am *j* for you 2 Cor 11:2

JEALOUSY
provoked Him to *j* Deut 32:16
as strong as death, *j* Song 8:6
for you with godly *j* 2 Cor 11:2

JEOPARDY
stand in *j* every hour 1 Cor 15:30

JESTING
talking, nor coarse *j* Eph 5:4

JESUS
J Christ was as Matt 1:18
shall call His name *J* Matt 1:21

J was led up by the Matt 4:1
and laid hands on *J* Matt 26:50
and destroy *J* Matt 27:20
J withdrew with His Mark 3:7
J went into Mark 11:11
they were eating, *J* Mark 14:22
and he delivered *J* Mark 15:15
truth came through *J* John 1:17
J lifted up His eyes John 6:5
J wept John 11:35
J was crucified John 19:20
"This *J* God has raised Acts 2:32
of Your holy Servant *J* Acts 4:30
believed on the Lord *J* Acts 11:17
your mouth the Lord *J* Rom 10:9
among you except *J* 1 Cor 2:2
perfect in Christ *J* Col 1:28
But we see *J* Heb 2:9
looking unto *J* Heb 12:2
Revelation of *J* Christ Rev 1:1
so, come, Lord *J* Rev 22:20

JOIN
of the rest dared *j* Acts 5:13

JOINED
and mother and be *j* Gen 2:24
what God has *j* Matt 19:6
the whole body, *j* Eph 4:16

JOINT
j as He wrestled Gen 32:25
My bones are out of *j* Ps 22:14
j heirs with Christ Rom 8:17

JOINTS
and knit together by *j* Col 2:19
and spirit, and of *j* Heb 4:12

JOT
one *j* or one tittle Matt 5:18

JOY
is fullness of *j* Ps 16:11
j comes in the morning Ps 30:5
j you will draw Is 12:3
ashes, The oil of *j* Is 61:3
shall sing for *j* Is 65:14
receives it with *j* Matt 13:20
Enter into the *j* Matt 25:21
in my womb for *j* Luke 1:44
there will be more *j* Luke 15:7
did not believe for *j* Luke 24:41
My *j* may remain in John 15:11
they may have My *j* John 17:13
the Spirit is love, *j* Gal 5:22
are our glory and *j* 1 Thess 2:20
j that was set before Heb 12:2
count it all *j* James 1:2
with exceeding *j* 1 Pet 4:13

JOYFUL
Make a *j* shout to the Ps 100:1
And make them *j* Is 56:7

JUDGE
The LORD *j* between Gen 16:5
coming to *j* the earth 1 Chr 16:33
sword The LORD will *j* Is 66:16
deliver you to the *j* Matt 5:25
"*J* not Matt 7:1
who made Me a *j* Luke 12:14
j who did not fear God Luke 18:2
As I hear, I *j* John 5:30
"Do not *j* according John 7:24
I *j* no one John 8:15
j the world but to John 12:47
this, O man, you who *j* Rom 2:3
Therefore let us not *j* Rom 14:13
Christ, who will *j* 2 Tim 4:1
But if you *j* the law James 4:11

JUDGES
He makes the *j* of the Is 40:23
For the Father *j* John 5:22
he who is spiritual *j* 1 Cor 2:15
j me is the Lord 1 Cor 4:4
Him who *j* righteously 1 Pet 2:23

JUDGMENT
Teach me good *j* Ps 119:66
from prison and from *j* Is 53:8
be in danger of the *j* Matt 5:21
shall not come into *j* John 5:24
and My *j* is righteous John 5:30
if I do judge, My *j* John 8:16
"Now is the *j* John 12:31
the righteous *j* Rom 1:32
j which came from one Rom 5:16
appear before the *j* 2 Cor 5:10
after this the *j* Heb 9:27
time has come for *j* 1 Pet 4:17
a long time their *j* 2 Pet 2:3
darkness for the *j* Jude 6

JUDGMENTS
The *j* of the LORD are Ps 19:9
unsearchable are His *j* Rom 11:33

JUST
Noah was a *j* man Gen 6:9
j man who perishes Eccl 7:15
j shall live by his Hab 2:4
her husband, being a *j* Matt 1:19
resurrection of the *j* Luke 14:14
j persons who need no Luke 15:7
the Holy One and the *J* Acts 3:14
dead, both of the *j* Acts 24:15
j shall live by faith Rom 1:17
that He might be *j* Rom 3:26
j men made perfect Heb 12:23
have murdered the *j* James 5:6
He is faithful and *j* 1 John 1:9

JUSTICE
j as the noonday Ps 37:6
And Your poor with *j* Ps 72:2
j the measuring line Is 28:17
the LORD is a God of *j* Is 30:18
He will bring forth *j* Is 42:1
J is turned back Is 59:14
I, the LORD, love *j* Is 61:8
truth, and His ways *j* Dan 4:37
'Execute true *j* Zech 7:9
"Where is the God of *j* Mal 2:17
And He will declare *j* Matt 12:18
His humiliation His *j* Acts 8:33

JUSTIFICATION
because of our *j* Rom 4:25
offenses resulted in *j* Rom 5:16

JUSTIFIED
Me that you may be *j* Job 40:8
words you will be *j* Matt 12:37
"But wisdom is *j* Luke 7:35
j rather than the Luke 18:14
who believes is *j* Acts 13:39
"That You may be *j* Rom 3:4
law no flesh will be *j* Rom 3:20
j freely by His grace Rom 3:24
having been *j* by Rom 5:1
these He also *j* Rom 8:30
that we might be *j* Gal 2:16
no flesh shall be *j* Gal 2:16
the harlot also *j* James 2:25

JUSTIFIES
He who *j* the wicked Prov 17:15
It is God who *j* Rom 8:33

JUSTIFY
wanting to *j* himself Luke 10:29
"You are those who *j* Luke 16:15
is one God who will *j* Rom 3:30

K

KEEP
k you wherever you Gen 28:15
day, to *k* it holy Ex 20:8
Let all the earth *k* Hab 2:20
k the commandments Matt 19:17
"If you love Me, *k* John 14:15
k through Your name John 17:11
orderly and *k* the law Acts 21:24
k the unity of the Eph 4:3
k His commandments 1 John 2:3

KEEPER
Am I my brother's *k* Gen 4:9
The LORD is your *k* Ps 121:5

KEEPS
k truth forever Ps 146:6
k the commandment Prov 19:16
none of you *k* the law John 7:19
born of God *k* 1 John 5:18
and *k* his garments Rev 16:15

KEPT
For I have *k* the 2 Sam 22:22
these things I have *k* Matt 19:20
love, just as I have *k* John 15:10
k back part of the Acts 5:2
I have *k* the faith 2 Tim 4:7
who are *k* by the power 1 Pet 1:5

KEY
taken away the *k* Luke 11:52
"He who has the *k* Rev 3:7

KEYS
I will give you the *k* Matt 16:19
And I have the *k* Rev 1:18

KILL
k the Passover Ex 12:21
I *k* and I make alive Deut 32:39
"Am I God, to *k* 2 Kin 5:7
A time to *k* Eccl 3:3
of them they will *k* Luke 11:49
afraid of those who *k* Luke 12:4
Why do you seek to *k* John 7:19
k and eat Acts 10:13

KILLED
Abel his brother and *k* Gen 4:8
for Your sake we are *k* Ps 44:22
and scribes, and be *k* Matt 16:21
Siloam fell and *k* them Luke 13:4
k the Prince of life Acts 3:15

Your sake we are *k* Rom 8:36
k both the Lord 1 Thess 2:15

KILLS
the one who *k* the Matt 23:37
for the letter *k* 2 Cor 3:6

KIND
animals after their *k* Gen 6:20
k can come out by Mark 9:29
suffers long and is *k* 1 Cor 13:4
And be *k* to one Eph 4:32

KINDLY
Julius treated Paul *k* Acts 27:3
k affectionate to one Rom 12:10

KINDNESS
For His merciful *k* Ps 117:2
k shall not depart Is 54:10
I remember you, The *k* Jer 2:2
by longsuffering, by *k* 2 Cor 6:6
longsuffering, *k* Gal 5:22
and to brotherly *k* 2 Pet 1:7

KING
"Yet I have set My *K* Ps 2:6
The LORD is *K* forever Ps 10:16
And the *K* of glory Ps 24:7
For God is my *K* Ps 74:12
when your *k* is a child Eccl 10:16
and the everlasting *K* Jer 10:10
the LORD shall be *K* Zech 14:9
who has been born *K* Matt 2:2
This Is Jesus The *K* Matt 27:37
"Behold your *K* John 19:14
Now to the *K* eternal 1 Tim 1:17
only Potentate, the *K* 1 Tim 6:15
this Melchizedek, *k* Heb 7:1
K of Kings and Lord Rev 19:16

KINGDOM
Yours is the *k* 1 Chr 29:11
k is the LORD's Ps 22:28
the scepter of Your *k* Ps 45:6
is an everlasting *k* Ps 145:13
k which shall never be Dan 2:44
High rules in the *k* Dan 4:17
"Repent, for the *k* Matt 3:2
for Yours is the *k* Matt 6:13
"But seek first the *k* Matt 6:33
the mysteries of the *k* Matt 13:11
are the sons of the *k* Matt 13:38
of such is the *k* Matt 19:14
back, is fit for the *k* Luke 9:62
against nation, and *k* Luke 21:10
he cannot see the *k* John 3:3
he cannot enter the *k* John 3:5
If My *k* were of this John 18:36
for the *k* of God is Rom 14:17
will not inherit the *k* Gal 5:21
the scepter of Your *k* Heb 1:8
we are receiving a *k* Heb 12:28

KINGDOMS
the *k* were moved Ps 46:6
showed Him all the *k* Matt 4:8
have become the *k* Rev 11:15

KINGS
The *k* of the earth set Ps 2:2
By me *k* reign Prov 8:15
governors and *k* Matt 10:18
k have desired to see Luke 10:24

You have reigned as *k* 1 Cor 4:8
and has made us *k* Rev 1:6
that the way of the *k* Rev 16:12

KISS
K the Son Ps 2:12
"You gave Me no *k* Luke 7:45
one another with a *k* 1 Pet 5:14

KISSED
they *k* one another 1 Sam 20:41
and *k* Him Matt 26:49
and she *k* His feet and Luke 7:38

KNEE
That to Me every *k* Is 45:23
have not bowed the *k* Rom 11:4
of Jesus every *k* Phil 2:10

KNEES
make firm the feeble *k* Is 35:3
this reason I bow my *k* Eph 3:14
and the feeble *k* Heb 12:12

KNEW
in the womb I *k* Jer 1:5
to them, 'I never *k* Matt 7:23
k what was in man John 2:25
He made Him who *k* 2 Cor 5:21

KNIT
be encouraged, being *k* Col 2:2

KNOCK
k, and it will be Matt 7:7
at the door and *k* Rev 3:20

KNOW
k good and evil Gen 3:22
k that I am the LORD Ex 6:7
k that my Redeemer Job 19:25
make me to *k* wisdom Ps 51:6
Who can *k* it Jer 17:9
saying, '*K* the LORD Jer 31:34
k what hour your Matt 24:42
an oath, "I do not *k* Matt 26:72
the world did not *k* John 1:10
We speak what We *k* John 3:11
k that You are John 6:69
My voice, and I *k* John 10:27
If you *k* these things John 13:17
k whom I have John 13:18
are sure that You *k* John 16:30
k that I love You John 21:15
k times or seasons Acts 1:7
and said, "Jesus I *k* Acts 19:15
wisdom did not *k* 1 Cor 1:21
nor can he *k* them 1 Cor 2:14
For we *k* in part and 1 Cor 13:9
k the love of Christ Eph 3:19
k whom I have 2 Tim 1:12
we *k* that we *k* Him 1 John 2:3
and you *k* all things 1 John 2:20
By this we *k* love 1 John 3:16
k that He abides 1 John 3:24
k that we are of God 1 John 5:19
"I *k* your works Rev 2:2

KNOWLEDGE
and the tree of the *k* Gen 2:9
unto night reveals *k* Ps 19:2
k is too wonderful Ps 139:6
people store up *k* Prov 10:14
k spares his words Prov 17:27

and he who increases *k* Eccl 1:18
k is that wisdom Eccl 7:12
k shall increase Dan 12:4
more accurate *k* Acts 24:22
having the form of *k* Rom 2:20
law is the *k* of sin Rom 3:20
whether there is *k* 1 Cor 13:8
Christ which passes *k* Eph 3:19
is falsely called *k* 1 Tim 6:20
in the grace and *k* 2 Pet 3:18

KNOWN
If you had *k* Me John 8:19
My sheep, and am *k* John 10:14
The world has not *k* John 17:25
peace they have not *k* Rom 3:17
"For who has *k* Rom 11:34
after you have *k* Gal 4:9
requests be made *k* Phil 4:6
k the Holy Scriptures 2 Tim 3:15

KNOWS
"For God *k* that in Gen 3:5
k what is in the Dan 2:22
k the things you have Matt 6:8
and hour no one *k* Matt 24:36
God *k* your hearts Luke 16:15
searches the hearts *k* Rom 8:27
k the things of God 1 Cor 2:11
k those who are His 2 Tim 2:19
to him who *k* to do James 4:17
and *k* all things 1 John 3:20

L

LABOR
Six days you shall *l* Ex 20:9
things are full of *l* Eccl 1:8
has man for all his *l* Eccl 2:22
He shall see the *l* Is 53:11
to Me, all you who *l* Matt 11:28
"Do not *l* for the John 6:.27
knowing that your *l* 1 Cor 15:58
but rather let him *l* Eph 4:28
mean fruit from my *l* Phil 1:22
your work of faith, *l* 1 Thess; 1:3
forget your work and *l* Heb 6:10
your works, your *l* Rev 2:2

LABORED
l more abundantly 1 Cor 15:10
for you, lest I have *l* Gal 4:11

LABORERS
but the *l* are few Matt 9:37

LABORING
l night and day 1 Thess 2:9

LABORS
entered into their *l* John 4:38
creation groans and *l* Rom 8:22
l more abundant 2 Cor 11:23
may rest from their *l* Rev 14:13

LACK
What do I still *l* Matt 19:20
"One thing you *l* Mark 10:21

LADDER
and behold, a *l* Gen 28:12

LAID
the place where they *l* Mark 16:6

LIBERALITY
he who gives, with *l* Rom 12:8

LIBERALLY
who gives to all *l* James 1:5

LIBERTY
year, and proclaim *l* Lev 25:10
'To proclaim *l* to the Luke 4:18
into the glorious *l* Rom 8:21
Lord is, there is *l* 2 Cor 3:17
therefore in the *l* Gal 5:1

LIE
Do not *l* to one Col 3:9
God, who cannot *l* Titus 1:2
an abomination or a *l* Rev 21:27

LIED
You have not *l* to men Acts 5:4

LIES
sin *l* at the door Gen 4:7
speaking *l* in 1 Tim 4:2

LIFE
the breath of *l* Gen 2:7
'For the *l* of the Lev 17:11
before you today *l* Deut 30:15
He will redeem their *l* Ps 72:14
word has given me *l* Ps 119:50
She is a tree of *l* Prov 3:18
finds me finds *l* Prov 8:35
L is more than Luke 12:23
l was the light John 1:4
so the Son gives *l* John 5:21
spirit, and they are *l* John 6:63
have the light of *l* John 8:12
and I lay down My *l* John 10:15
resurrection and the *l* John 11:25
you lay down your *l* John 13:38
l which I now live Gal 2:20
l is hidden with Col 3:3
For what is your *l* James 4:14
l was manifested 1 John 1:2
and the pride of *l* 1 John 2:16
has given us eternal *l* 1 John 5:11
the Lamb's Book of *L* Rev 21:27
right to the tree of *l* Rev 22:14
the water of *l* freely Rev22:17
from the Book of *L* Rev 22:19

LIFT
I will *l* up my eyes to Ps 121:1
Lord, and He will *l* James 4:10

LIFTED
your heart is *l* Ezek 28:2
in Hades, he *l* up his Luke 16:23
the Son of Man be *l* John 3:14
"And I, if I am *l* John 12:32

LIGHT
"Let there be *l* Gen 1:3
The LORD is my *l* Ps 27:1
and a *l* to my path Ps 119:105
The *l* of the righteous Prov 13:9
The LORD gives *l* Prov 29:13
Truly the *l* is sweet Eccl 11:7
let us walk in the *l* Is 2:5
l shall break forth Is 58:8
"You are the *l* Matt 5:14
"Let your *l* so shine Matt 5:16
than the sons of *l* Luke 16:8
and the life was the *l* John 1:4
darkness rather than *l* John 3:19
saying, "I am the *l* John 8:12
God who commanded *l* 2 Cor 4:6
Walk as children of *l* Eph 5:8
You are all sons of *l* 1 Thess 5:5
into His marvelous *l* 1 Pet 2:9
to you, that God is *l* 1 John 1:5
l as He is in the 1 John 1:7
says he is in the *l* 1 John 2:9
The Lamb is its *l* Rev 21:23

LIGHTNING
"For as the *l* Matt 24:27
countenance was like *l* Matt 283

LIGHTNINGS
the throne proceeded *l* Rev 4:5

LIGHTS
"Let there be *l* Gen 1:14
whom you shine as *l* Phil 2:15

LIKENESS
according to Our *l* Gen 1:26
carved image—any *l* Ex 20:4
when I awake in Your *l* Ps 17:15
and coming in the *l* Phil 2:7

LILY
the *l* of the valleys Song 2:1

LIMIT
to the sea its *l* Prov 8:29

LINE
upon precept, *L* upon Is 28:10
I am setting a plumb *l* Amos 7:8

LINEN
wrapped Him in the *l* Mark 15:46

LINGER
salvation shall not *l* Is 46:13

LION
l shall eat straw Is 11:7

LIONS
the mouths of *l* Heb 11:33

LIPS
off all flattering *l* Ps 12:3
The *l* of the righteous Prov 10:21
But the *l* of Prov 20:15
am a man of unclean *l* Is 6:5
other *l* I will speak 1 Cor 14:21
from evil, And his *l* 1 Pet 3:10

LISTEN
you are not able to *l* John 8:43
you who fear God, *l* Acts 13:16

LISTENS
But whoever *l* to me Prov 1:33

LITTLE
Though you are *l* Mic 5:2
l ones only a cup Matt 10:42
"O you of *l* faith Matt 14:31
to whom *l* is forgiven Luke 7:47
faithful in a very *l* Luke 19:17

LIVE
eat, and *l* forever Gen 3:22
a man does, he shall *l* Lev 18:5
"Seek Me and *l* Amos 5:4
But the just shall *l* Hab 2:4
l by bread alone Matt 4:4
"for in Him we *l* Acts 17:28
l peaceably with all Rom 12:18
the life which I now *l* Gal 2:20
If we *l* in the Spirit Gal 5:25
to me, to *l* is Christ Phil 1:21

LIVED
died and rose and *l* Rom 14:9
And they *l* and reigned Rev 20:4

LIVES
but man *l* by every Deut 8:3
but Christ *l* in me Gal 2:20
to lay down our *l* 1 John 3:16
"I am He who *l* Rev 1:18

LIVING
and man became a *l* Gen 2:7
in the light of the *l* Ps 56:13
the dead, but of the *l* Matt 22:32
do you seek the *l* Luke 24;5
the word of God is *l* Heb 4:12
l creature was like a Rev 4:7

LOATHSOME
But a wicked man is *l* Prov 13:5

LOAVES
have here only five *l* Matt 14:17
you ate of the *l* John 6:26

LOCUST
What the chewing *l* Joel 1:4

LOCUSTS
and his food was *l* Matt 3:4

LOFTY
Wisdom is too *l* Prov 24:7

LONG
your days may be *l* Deut 5:16
Who *l* for death Job 3:21
I*l* for Your salvation Ps 119:174
go around in *l* robes Mark 12:38

LONGSUFFERING
is love, joy, peace, *l* Gal 5:22
and gentleness, with *l* Eph 4:2
for all patience and *l* Col 1:11
might show all *l* 1 Tim 1:16
once the Divine *l* 1 Pet 3:20
and consider that the *l* 2 Pet 3:15

LOOK
A proud *l* Prov 6:17
"*L* to Me Is 45:22
l on Me whom they Zech 12:10
say to you, '*L* here Luke 17:23
while we do not *l* 2 Cor 4:18

LOOKED
For He *l* down from Ps 102:19
He *l* for justice Is 5:7
the Lord turned and *l* Luke 22:61
for he *l* to the reward Heb 11:26

LOOKING
the plow, and *l* back Luke 9:62
l for the blessed hope Titus 2:13
l unto Jesus Heb 12:2
l carefully lest Heb 12:15
l for the mercy of Jude 21

LOOKS
The lofty *l* of man Is 2:11
to you that whoever *l* Matt 5:28

LOOSE
and whatever you *l* Matt 16:19
said to them, "*L* him John 11:44

LOOSED
the silver cord is *l* Eccl 12:6

LORD
L is my strength Ex 15:2
L our God, the *L* Deut 6:4
You alone are the *L* Neh 9:6
The *L* of hosts Ps 24:10
Gracious is the *L* Ps 116:5
L surrounds His people Ps 125:2
The *L* is righteous Ps 129:4
L is near to all who Ps 145:18
L is a God of justice Is 30:18
L Our Righteousness Jer 23:6
"The *L* is one Zech 14:9
shall not tempt the *L* Matt 4:7
shall worship the *L* Matt 4:10
Son of Man is also *L* Mark 2:28
who is Christ the *L* Luke 2:11
L is risen indeed Luke 24:34
Me Teacher and *L* John 13:13
He is *L* of all Acts 10:36
with your mouth the *L* Rom 10:9
say that Jesus is *L* 1 Cor 12:3
second Man is the *L* 1 Cor 15:47
the Spirit of the *L* 2 Cor 3:17
that Jesus Christ is *L* Phil 2:11
and deny the only *L* Jude 4
L God Omnipotent Rev 19:6

LORDS
for He is Lord of *l* Rev 17:14

LOSE
save his life will *l* Matt 16:25

LOSES
but if the salt *l* Matt 5:13
and *l* his own soul Matt 16:26

LOSS
count all things *l* Phil 3:8

LOST
save that which was *l* Matt 18:11
and none of them is *l* John 17:12
You gave Me I have *l* John 18:9

LOTS
garments, casting *l* Mark 15:24
And they cast their *l* Acts 1:26

LOUD
cried out with a *l* Matt 27:46
I heard behind me a *l* Rev 1:10

LOVE
l your neighbor as Lev 19:18
l the LORD your God Deut 6:5
Oh, *l* the LORD Ps 31:23
he has set his *l* Ps 91:14
Oh, how I *l* Your law Ps 119:97
l covers all sins Prov 10:12
A time to *l* Eccl 3:8
banner over me was *l* Song 2:4
l is as strong as Song 8:6
do justly, To *l* mercy Mic 6:8
to you, *l* your enemies Matt 5:44
which of them will *l* Luke 7:42
you do not have the *l* John 5:42
If you have *l* for one John 13:35
"If you *l* Me John 14:15
and My Father will *l* John 14:23
l one another as I John 15:12
l has no one than this John 15:13
because the *l* of God Rom 5:5
to *l* one another Rom 13:8
L suffers long and is 1 Cor 13:4
L never fails 1 Cor 13:8
greatest of these is *l* 1 Cor 13:13
For the *l* of Christ 2 Cor 5:14
of the Spirit is *l* Gal 5:22
Husbands, *l* your wives Eph 5:25
the commandment is *l* 1 Tim 1:5
For the *l* of money is 1 Tim 6:10
Let brotherly *l* Heb 13:1
having not seen you *l* 1 Pet 1:8
for "*l* will cover a 1 Pet 4:8
brotherly kindness *l* 2 Pet 1:7
By this we know *l* 1 John 3:16
Beloved, let us *l* 1 John 4:7
for God is *l* 1 John 4:8
There is no fear in *l* 1 John 4:18
l Him because He 1 John 4:19
loves God must *l* 1 John 4:21
For this is the *l* 1 John 5:3
have left your first *l* Rev 2:4

LOVED
L one and friend You Ps 88:18
Yet Jacob I have *l* Mal 1:2
forgiven, for she *l* Luke 7:47
so *l* the world that John 3:16
whom Jesus *l* John 13:23
"As the Father *l* John 15:9
l them as You have John 17:23
the Son of God, who *l* Gal 2:20
l the church and gave Eph 5:25
Beloved, if God so *l* 1 John 4:11
To Him who *l* us and Rev 1:5

LOVELY
he is altogether *l* Song 5:16
whatever things are *l* Phil 4:8

LOVES
"He who *l* father or Matt 10:37
l his life will lose John 12:25
l Me will be loved John 14:21
l a cheerful giver 2 Cor 9:7
If anyone *l* the world 1 John 2:15
l God must love his 1 John 4:21

LOVINGKINDNESS
To declare Your *l* Ps 92:2

LOWER
made him a little *l* Heb 2:7

LOWLINESS
with all *l* and Eph 4:2

LOWLY
for I am gentle and *l* Matt 11:29
in presence am *l* 2 Cor 10:1
l brother glory James 1:9

LUKEWARM
because you are *l* Rev 3:16

LUST
looks at a woman to *l* Matt 5:28
not fulfill the *l* Gal 5:16
You *l* and do not have James 4:2
the *l* of the flesh 1 John 2:16

LUSTS
to fulfill its *l* Rom 13:14
also youthful *l* 2 Tim 2:22
and worldly *l* Titus 2:12
to the former *l* 1 Pet 1:14
abstain from fleshly *l* 1 Pet 2:11
to their own ungodly *l* Jude 18

LUTE
Praise Him with the *l* Ps 150:3

LUXURY
in pleasure and *l* James 5:5
the abundance of her *l* Rev 18:3

LYING
I hate and abhor *l* Ps 119:163
righteous man hates *l* Prov 13:5
not trust in these *l* Jer 7:4
signs, and *l* wonders 2 Thess 2:9

M

MADE
m the stars also Gen 1:16
things My hand has *m* Is 66:2
All things were *m* John 1:3

MADNESS
m is in their hearts Eccl 9:3

MAGIC
m brought their books Acts 19:19

MAGNIFIED
let Your name be *m* 2 Sam 7:26
the Lord Jesus was *m* Acts 19:17
also Christ will be *m* Phil 1:20

MAGNIFIES
"My soul *m* the Lord Luke 1:46

MAGNIFY
m the LORD with me Ps 34:3

MAIDSERVANT
"Behold the *m* Luke 1:38

MAIDSERVANTS
m I will pour out My Acts 2:18

MAJESTY
right hand of the *M* Heb 1:3
eyewitnesses of His *m* 2 Pet 1:16
wise, Be glory and *m* Jude 25

MAKE
"Let Us *m* man in Our Gen 1:26
m you a great nation Gen 12:2
"You shall not *m* Ex 20:4
m Our home with John 14:23

MAKER
M is your husband Is 54:5
has forgotten his *M* Hos 8:14
builder and *m* is God Heb 11:10

MALICE
in *m* be babes 1 Cor 14:20
laying aside all *m* 1 Pet 2:1

MESSIAH
Until *M* the Prince Dan 9:25
"We have found the *M* John 1:41

MIDST
God is in the *m* Ps 46:5
I am there in the *m* Matt 18:20

MIGHT
'My power and the *m* Deut 8:17
'Not by *m* nor by Zech 4:6
in the power of His *m* Eph 6:10
honor and power and *m* Rev 7:12

MIGHTIER
coming after me is *m* Matt 3:11

MIGHTY
He was a *m* hunter Gen 10:9
m have fallen 2 Sam 1:19
The LORD *m* in battle Ps 24:8
their Redeemer is *m* Prov 23:11
m has done great Luke 1:49
the flesh, not many *m* 1 Cor 1:26
the working of His *m* Eph 1:19

MILK
come, buy wine and *m* Is 55:1
shall flow with *m* Joel 3:18
have come to need *m* Heb 5:12
desire the pure *m* 1 Pet 2:2

MILLSTONE
m were hung around Matt 18:6
a stone like a great *m* Rev 18:21

MIND
put wisdom in the *m* Job 38:36
perfect peace, Whose *m* Is 26:3
have an anxious *m* Luke 12:29
m I myself serve the Rom 7:25
who has known the *m* Rom 11:34
Be of the same *m* Rom 12:16
in his own *m* Rom 14:5
has known the *m* 1 Cor 2:16
are out of your *m* 1 Cor 14:23
Let this *m* be in you Phil 2:5
love and of a sound *m* 2 Tim 1:7

MINDFUL
is man that You are *m* Ps 8:4
for you are not *m* Matt 16:23
is man that You are *m* Heb 2:6

MINDS
put My law in their *m* Jer 31:33
I stir up your pure *m* 2 Pet 3:1

MINISTER
For he is God's *m* Rom 13:4
you will be a good *m* 1 Tim 4:6

MINISTERS
for they are God's *m* Rom 13:6
If anyone *m* 1 Pet 4:11

MINISTRIES
are differences of *m* 1 Cor 12:5

MINISTRY
But if the *m* of death 2 Cor 3:7
since we have this *m* 2 Cor 4:1
has given us the *m* 2 Cor 5:18
for the work of *m* Eph 4:12
fulfill your *m* 2 Tim 4:5
a more excellent *m* Heb 8:6

MIRACLE
one who works a *m* Mark 9:39

MIRACLES
worked unusual *m* Acts 19:11
the working of *m* 1 Cor 12:10

MISERY
And remember his *m* Prov 31:7

MITES
putting in two *m* Luke 21:2

MOCK
Fools *m* at sin Prov 14:9
to the Gentiles to *m* Matt 20:19

MOCKED
noon, that Elijah *m* 1 Kin 18:27
deceived, God is not *m* Gal 6:7

MOCKER
Wine is a *m* Prov 20:1

MOCKS
He who *m* the poor Prov 17:5

MODERATION
with propriety and *m* 1 Tim 2:9

MOMENT
in a *m* they die Job 34:20
in a *m*, in the 1 Cor 15:52

MONEY
be redeemed without *m* Is 52:3
And you who have no *m* Is 55:1
and hid his lord's *m* Matt 25:18
to give him *m* Mark 14:11
"Carry neither *m* Luke 10:4
I sent you without *m* Luke 22:35
be purchased with *m* Acts 8:20
not greedy for *m* 1 Tim 3:3
m is a root of all 1 Tim 6:10

MONEYCHANGERS
the tables of the *m* Matt 21:12

MOON
until the *m* is no more Ps 72:7
m will not give its Mark 13:24

MORNING
Evening and *m* and at Ps 55:17
Lucifer, son of the *m* Is 14:12
very early in the *m* Luke 24:1
the Bright and *M* Star Rev 22:16

MORTAL
sin reign in your *m* Rom 6:12
and this *m* must put 1 Cor 15:53

MORTALITY
m may be swallowed 2 Cor 5:4

MOTH
where *m* and rust Matt 6:19

MOTHER
because she was the *m* Gen 3:20
leave his father and *m* Matt 19:5
"Behold your *m* John 19:27
The *M* of Harlots Rev 17:5

MOUNT
come up to *M* Sinai Ex 19:23
They shall *m* up with Is 40:31

MOUNTAIN
to Horeb, the *m* Ex 3:1
let us go up to the *m* Is 2:3
became a great *m* Dan 2:35
are you, O great *m* Zech 4:7
you will say to this *m* Matt 17:20
Him on the holy *m* 2 Pet 1:18

MOUNTAINS
m were brought forth Ps 90:2
m shall depart And the Is 54:10
in Judea flee to the *m* Matt 24:16
that I could remove *m* 1 Cor 13:2

MOURN
A time to *m* Eccl 3:4
are those who *m* Matt 5:4
of the earth will *m* Rev 1:7

MOURNED
and have not rather *m* 1 Cor 5:2

MOURNING
shall be a great *m* Zech 12:11
be turned to *m* and James 4:9

MOUTH
"Who has made man's *m* Ex 4:11
Out of the *m* of babes Ps 8:2
knowledge, But the *m* Prov 10:14
The *m* of an immoral Prov 22:14
And a flattering *m* Prov 26:28
m speaking pompous Dan 7:8
m defiles a man Matt 15:11
m I will judge you Luke 19:22
I will give you a *m* Luke 21:15
m confession is made Rom 10:10
m great swelling words Jude 16
vomit you out of My *m* Rev 3:16

MOVED
she shall not be *m* Ps 46:5
spoke as they were *m* 2 Pet 1:21

MUCH
m study is Eccl 12:12
to whom *m* is given Luke 12:48

MULTIPLIED
of the disciples *m* Acts 6:7
of God grew and *m* Acts 12:24

MULTIPLY
"Be fruitful and *m* Gen 1:22
m the descendants Jer 33:22

MULTITUDE
stars of heaven in *m* Deut 1:10
In the *m* of words sin Prov 10:19
compassion on the *m* Matt 15:32
with the angel a *m* Luke 2:13
"love will cover a *m* 1 Pet 4:8
and behold, a great *m* Rev 7:9

MURDER
'You shall not *m* Ex 20:13
'You shall not *m* Matt 5:21
You *m* and covet and James 4:2

MURDERED
up Jesus whom you *m* Acts 5:30

MURDERER
He was a *m* from the John 8:44
his brother is a *m* 1 John 3:15

MURDERERS
and profane, for *m* 1 Tim 1:9
abominable, *m* Rev 21:8

MURDERS
evil thoughts, *m* Matt 15:19

MUSING
while I was *m* Ps 39:3

MUTILATION
beware of the *m* Phil 3:2

MUZZLE
"You shall not *m* 1 Tim 5:18

MYSTERIES
to you to know the *m* Matt 13:11
and understand all *m* 1 Cor 13:2

MYSTERY
given to know the *m* Mark 4:11
wisdom of God in a *m* 1 Cor 2:7
I tell you a *m* 1 Cor 15:51
made known to us the *m* Eph 1:9
the *m* of godliness 1 Tim 3:16

N

NAILED
n it to the cross Col 2:14

NAKED
And they were both *n* Gen 2:25
knew that they were *n* Gen 3:7
"*N* I came from my Job 1:21
'I was *n* and you Matt 25:36
but all things are *n* Heb 4:13
brother or sister is *n* James 2:15
poor, blind, and *n* Rev 3:17

NAKEDNESS
or famine, or *n* Rom 8:35
n may not be revealed Rev 3:18

NAME
Abram called on the *n* Gen 13:4
Israel shall be your *n* Gen 35:10
This is My *n* forever Ex 3:15
shall not take the *n* Ex 20:7
and awesome *n* Deut 28:58
excellent is Your *n* Ps 8:1
n will put their trust Ps 9:10
be His glorious *n* Ps 72:19
do not call on Your *n* Ps 79:6
to Your *n* give glory Ps 115:1
above all Your *n* Ps 138:2
A good *n* is to be Prov 22:1
what is His Son's *n* Prov 30:4
be called by a new *n* Is 62:2
Everlasting is Your *n* Is 63:16
They will call on My *n* Zech 13:9
to you who fear My *n* Mal 4:2
Hallowed be Your *n* Matt 6:9
prophesied in Your *n* Matt 7:22
n Gentiles will trust Matt 12:21
together in My *n* Matt 18:20
will come in My *n* Matt 24:5
who believe in His *n* John 1:12
comes in his own *n* John 5:43
his own sheep by *n* John 10:3
through faith in His *n* Acts 3:16
there is no other *n* Acts 4:12
which is above every *n* Phil 2:9
deed, do all in the *n* Col 3:17
a more excellent *n* Heb 1:4
you hold fast to My *n* Rev 2:13
n that you are alive Rev 3:1
having His Father's *n* Rev 14:1
and glorify Your *n* Rev 15:4
n written that no one Rev 19:12

NAMED
I have *n* you Is 45:4

NAME'S
saved them for His *n* Ps 106:8

NARROW
"Enter by the *n* gate Matt 7:13

NATION
make you a great *n* Gen 12:2
exalts a *n* Prov 14:34
n that was not called Is 65:1
make them one *n* Ezek 37:22
since there was a *n* Dan 12:1
n will rise against Matt 24:7
"for he loves our *n* Luke 7:5
those who are not a *n* Rom 10:19
tribe, tongue, and *n* Rev 13:7

NATIONS
Why do the *n* rage Ps 2:1
I will give You the *n* Ps 2:8
n shall serve Him Ps 72:11
disciples of all the *n* Matt 28:19
who was to rule all *n* Rev 12:5
the healing of the *n* Rev 22:2

NATURAL
exchanged the *n* Rom 1:26
the men, leaving the *n* Rom 1:27
did not spare the *n* Rom 11:21
n man does not 1 Cor 2:14
It is sown a *n* body 1 Cor 15:44

NATURE
"We who are Jews by *n* Gal 2:15
by *n* children of wrath Eph 2:3
of the divine *n* 2 Pet 1:4

NEAR
the word is very *n* Deut 30:14
upon Him while He is *n* Is 55:6
know that it is *n* Matt 24:33
kingdom of God is *n* Luke 21:31
"The word is *n* Rom 10:8
to those who were *n* Eph 2:17
for the time is *n* Rev 1:3

NEARER
now our salvation is *n* Rom 13:11

NEED
the things you have *n* Matt 6:8
supply all your *n* Phil 4:19
to help in time of *n* Heb 4:16

NEGLECT
if we *n* so great a Heb 2:3

NEGLECTED
n the weightier Matt 23:23

NEIGHBOR
'you shall love your *n* Lev 19:18
'You shall love your *n* Matt 5:43
"And who is my *n* Luke 10:29
"You shall love your *n* Rom 13:9

NEVER
in Me shall *n* thirst John 6:35
in Me shall *n* die John 11:26
Love *n* fails 1 Cor 13:8
n take away sins Heb 10:11
"I will *n* leave you Heb 13:5
prophecy *n* came by 2 Pet 1:21

NEW
And there is nothing *n* Eccl 1:9
"For behold, I create *n* Is 65:17
n every morning Lam 3:23
wine into *n* wineskins Matt 9:17
of the *n* covenant Matt 26:28
n commandment I John 13:34
he is a *n* creation 2 Cor 5:17
when I will make a *n* Heb 8:8
n heavens and a *n* 2 Pet 3:13
n name written which Rev 2:17
And they sang a *n* Rev 5:9
And I saw a *n* heaven Rev 21:1
I make all things *n* Rev 21:5

NEWNESS
also should walk in *n* Rom 6:4

NIGHT
darkness He called *N* Gen 1:5
It is a *n* of solemn Ex 12:42
pillar of fire by *n* Ex 13:22
gives songs in the *n* Job 35:10
and continued all *n* Luke 6:12
man came to Jesus by *n* John 3:2
n is coming when no John 9:4
came to Jesus by *n* John 19:39
as a thief in the *n* 1 Thess 5:2
there shall be no *n* Rev 21:25

NINETY-NINE
he not leave the *n* Matt 18:12

NOTHING
"I can of Myself do *n* John 5:30
Me you can do *n* John 15:5
men, it will come to *n* Acts 5:38
have not love, I am *n* 1 Cor 13:2
Be anxious for *n* Phil 4:6
For we brought *n* 1 Tim 6:7

NOURISHED
"I have *n* and Is 1:2

NOURISHES
n and cherishes it Eph 5:29

NUMBER
if a man could *n* Gen 13:16
teach us to *n* our days Ps 90:12
which no one could *n* Rev 7:9
His *n* is 666 Rev 13:18

O

OATH
for the sake of your *o* Eccl 8:2
he denied with an *o* Matt 26:72
o which He swore Luke 1:73

OATHS
shall perform your *o* Matt 5:33

OBEDIENCE
o many will be made Rom 5:19
captivity to the *o* 2 Cor 10:5
yet He learned *o* Heb 5:8

PIERCING
p even to the division Heb 4:12

PILGRIMAGE
heart is set on *p* Ps 84:5
In the house of my *p* Ps 119:54

PILGRIMS
we are aliens and *p* 1 Chr 29:15
were strangers and *p* Heb 11:13

PILLAR
and she became a *p* Gen 19:26
and by night in a *p* Ex 13:21
the living God, the *p* 1 Tim 3:15

PILLARS
break their sacred *p* Ex 34:13
Blood and fire and *p* Joel 2:30
and his feet like *p* Rev 10:1

PIT
who go down to the *p* Ps 28:1
a harlot is a deep *p* Prov 23:27
my life in the *p* Lam 3:53
up my life from the *p* Jon 2:6
into the bottomless *p* Rev 20:3

PITIABLE
of all men the most *p* 1 Cor 15:19

PITS
The proud have dug *p* Ps 119:85

PITY
for someone to take *p* Ps 69:20
p He redeemed them Is 63:9
just as I had *p* Matt 18:33

PLACE
Come, see the *p* Matt 28:6
My word has no *p* John 8:37
I go to prepare a *p* John 14:2
might go to his own *p* Acts 1:25

PLACES
And the rough *p* Is 40:4
They love the best *p* Matt 23:6
in the heavenly *p* Eph 1:3

PLAGUE
bring yet one more *p* Ex 11:1

PLAGUES
p that are written Rev 22:18

PLANK
First remove the *p* Matt 7:5

PLANS
He makes the *p* of the Ps 33:10
that devises wicked *p* Prov 6:18

PLANT
A time to *p* Eccl 3:2
Him as a tender *p* Is 53:2
p of an alien vine Jer 2:21
p which My heavenly Matt 15:13

PLANTED
shall be like a tree *p* Ps 1:3
by the roots and be *p* Luke 17:6
I *p*, Apollos watered 1 Cor 3:6

PLANTS
neither he who *p* 1 Cor 3:7

PLATTER
head here on a *p* Matt 14:8

PLEASANT
food, that it was *p* Gen 3:6
how good and how *p* Ps 133:1

PLEASANTNESS
ways are ways of *p* Prov 3:17

PLEASE
in the flesh cannot *p* Rom 8:8
p his neighbor for his Rom 15:2
he may *p* the Lord 1 Cor 7:32
is impossible to *p* Him Heb 11:6

PLEASED
Then You shall be *p* Ps 51:19
in whom I am well *p* Matt 3:17
God was not well *p* 1 Cor 10:5
testimony, that he *p* Heb 11:5

PLEASES
Whatever the LORD *p* Ps 135:6

PLEASING
sacrifice, well *p* Phil 4:18
for this is well *p* Col 3:20
in you what is well *p* Heb 13:21

PLEASURE
Do good in Your good *p* Ps 51:18
p will be a poor man Prov 21:17
shall perform all My *p* Is 44:28
your Father's good *p* Luke 12:32
to the good *p* of His Eph 1:5
for sin You had no *p* Heb 10:6
My soul has no *p* Heb 10:38
p that war in your James 4:1

PLEASURES
Your right hand are *p* Ps 16:11
cares, riches, and *p* Luke 8:14
to enjoy the passing *p* Heb 11:25

PLOW
put his hand to the *p* Luke 9:62

PLOWED
You have *p* Hos 10:13

PLOWMAN
p shall overtake the Amos 9:13

PLUCK
p the heads of grain Mark 2:23

PLUCKED
cheeks to those who *p* Is 50:6
And His disciples *p* Luke 6:1
you would have *p* Gal 4:15

PLUNDER
p the Egyptians Ex 3:22
The *p* of the poor is Is 3:14
house and *p* his goods Matt 12:29

PLUNDERED
a people robbed and *p* Is 42:22
"And when you are *p* Jer 4:30

PLUNDERING
me Because of the *p* Is 22:4
accepted the *p* of your Heb 10:34

POETS
some of your own *p* Acts 171:28

POISON
"The *p* of asps is Rom 3:13

POISONED
p by bitterness Acts 8:23

POLLUTIONS
have escaped the *p* 2 Pet 2:20

POMP
had come with great *p* Acts 25:23

POMPOUS
and a mouth speaking *p* Dan 7:8

PONDER
P the path of your Prov 4:26

PONDERED
p them in her heart Luke 2:19

PONDERS
p all his paths Prov 5:21

POOR
p will never cease Deut 15:11
So the *p* have hope Job 5:16
I delivered the *p* Job 29:12
p shall eat and be Ps 22:26
But I am *p* and needy Ps 40:17
Let the *p* and needy Ps 74:21
He raises the *p* Ps 113:7
slack hand becomes *p* Prov 10:4
p man is hated even Prov 14:20
has mercy on the *p* Prov 14:21
who oppresses the *p* Prov 14:31
p reproaches his Prov 17:5
Do not rob the *p* Prov 22:22
that same *p* man Eccl 9:15
The alien or the *p* Zech 7:10
"Blessed are the *p* Matt 5:3
p have the gospel Matt 11:5
"For you have the *p* Matt 26:11
sakes He became *p* 2 Cor 8:9
should remember the *p* Gal 2:10
God not chosen the *p* James 2:5
wretched, miserable, *p* Rev 3:17

PORTION
O LORD, You, are the *p* Ps 16:5
heart and my *p* forever Ps 73:26
You are my *p* Ps 119:57
I will divide Him a *p* Is 53:12
rejoice in their *p* Is 61:7
The *P* of Jacob is not Jer 10:16
"The LORD is my *p* Lam 3:24
and appoint him his *p* Matt 24:51
to give them their *p* Luke 12:42
give me the *p* Luke 15:12

POSSESS
descendants shall *p* Gen 22:17
p the land which Josh 1:11
"By your patience *p* Luke 21:19
p his own vessel 1 Thess 4:4

POSSESSED
"The LORD *p* me at Prov 8:22

POSSESSING
and yet *p* all things 2 Cor 6:10

POSSESSION
as an everlasting *p* Gen 17:8
and an enduring *p* Heb 10:34

POSSESSIONS
and sold their *p* Acts 2:45

POSSIBLE
God all things are *p* Matt 19:26
p that the blood Heb 10:4

POUR
p My Spirit on your Is 44:3
P out Your fury Jer 10:25
That I will *p* out My Joel 2:28
"And I will *p* Zech 12:10
angels, "Go and *p* Rev 16:1

POURED
I am *p* out like water Ps 22:14
grace is *p* upon Your Ps 45:2
strong, Because He *p* Is 53:12
and My fury will be *p* Jer 7:20
broke the flask and *p* Mark 14:3
I am already being *p* 2 Tim 4:6
whom He *p* out on us Titus 3:6

POVERTY
leads only to *p* Prov 14:23
p put in all the Luke 21:4
and their deep *p* 2 Cor 8:2
p might become rich 2 Cor 8:9
tribulation, and *p* Rev 2:9

POWER
that I may show My *p* Ex 9:16
him who is without *p* Job 26:2
p who can understand Job 26:14
p belongs to God Ps 62:11
p Your enemies shall Ps 66:3
gives strength and *p* Ps 68:35
a king is, there is *p* Eccl 8:4
No one has *p* over the Eccl 8:8
'Not by might nor by *p* Zech 4:6
the kingdom and the *p* Matt 6:13
the Son of Man has *p* Matt 9:6
Scriptures nor the *p* Matt 22:29
p went out from Him Luke 6:19
are endued with *p* Luke 24:49
I have *p* to lay it John 10:18
"You could have no *p* John 19:11
you shall receive *p* Acts 1:8
though by our own *p* Acts 3:12
man is the great *p* Acts 8:10
"Give me this *p* Acts 8:19
for it is the *p* Rom 1:16
saved it is the *p* 1 Cor 1:18
Greeks, Christ the *p* 1 Cor 1:24
that the *p* of Christ 2 Cor 12:9
greatness of His *p* Eph 1:19
the Lord and in the *p* Eph 6:10
to His glorious *p* Col 1:11
the glory of His *p* 2 Thess 1:9
of fear, but of *p* 2 Tim 1:7
by the word of His *p* Heb 1:3
p of death, that Heb 2:14
as His divine *p* 2 Pet 1:3
Dominion and *p* Jude 25
to him I will give *p* Rev 2:26
honor and glory and *p* Rev 5:13

POWERFUL
of the LORD is *p* Ps 29:4
of God is living and *p* Heb 4:12

POWERS
principalities and *p* Col 2:15
word of God and the *p* Heb 6:5

PRAISE
p shall be of You in Ps 22:25
the people shall *p* Ps 45:17
P is awaiting You Ps 65:1
Let all the peoples *p* Ps 67:3
p shall be continually Ps 71:6
And the heavens will *p* Ps 89:5
Seven times a day I *p* Ps 119:164
that has breath *p* Ps 150:6
Let another man *p* Prov 27:2
let her own works *p* Prov 31:31
And your gates *P* Is 60:18
He makes Jerusalem a *p* Is 62:7
For You are my *p* Jer 17:14
Me a name of joy, a *p* Jer 33:9
give you fame and *p* Zeph 3:20
You have perfected *p* Matt 21:16
men more than the *p* John 12:43
p is not from men but Rom 2:29
Then each one's *p* 1 Cor 4:5
should be to the *p* Eph 1:12
to the glory and *p* Phil 1:11
I will sing *p* to You Heb 2:12
the sacrifice of *p* Heb 13:15
and for the *p* of those 1 Pet 2:14
saying, "*P* our God Rev 19:5

PRAISED
daily He shall be *p* Ps 72:15
LORD's name is to be *p* Ps 113:3
and greatly to be *p* Ps 145:3
the Most High and *p* Dan 4:34

PRAISES
it is good to sing *p* Ps 147:1
and he *p* Prov 31:28

PRAISEWORTHY
If there is anything *p* Phil 4:8

PRAISING
They will still be *p* Ps 84:4
of the heavenly host *p* Luke 2:13
in the temple *p* Luke 24:53

PRAY
at noon I will *p* Ps 55:17
who hate you, and *p* Matt 5:44
"And when you *p* Matt 6:5
manner, therefore, *p* Matt 6:9
"Watch and *p* Matt 26:41
"Lord, teach us to *p* Luke 11:1
"And I will *p* John 14:16
I do not *p* for the John 17:9
"I do not *p* for John 17:20
p without ceasing 1 Thess 5:17
Brethren, *p* for us 1 Thess 5:25
Let him *p* James 5:13
to one another, and *p* James 5:16
say that he should *p* 1 John 5:16

PRAYED
p more earnestly Luke 22:44
p earnestly that it James 5:17

PRAYER
p made in this place 2 Chr 7:15
And my *p* is pure Job 16:17
A *p* to the God of my Ps 42:8
P also will be made Ps 72:15
He shall regard the *p* Ps 102:17
to the LORD, But the *p* Prov 15:8
go out except by *p* Matt 17:21
all night in *p* to God Luke 6:12
continually to *p* Acts 6:4
where *p* was Acts 16:13
steadfastly in *p* Rom 12:12
to fasting and *p* 1 Cor 7:5
always with all *p* Eph 6:18
but in everything by *p* Phil 4:6
the word of God and *p* 1 Tim 4:5
And the *p* of faith James 5:15

PRAYERS
though You make many *p* Is 1:15
pretense make long *p* Matt 23:14
fervently for you in *p* Col 4:12
p may not be hindered 1 Pet 3:7
which are the *p* Rev 5:8

PREACH
time Jesus began to *p* Matt 4:17
you hear in the ear, *p* Matt 10:27
P the gospel to the Luke 4:18
And how shall they *p* Rom 10:15
p Christ crucified 1 Cor 1:23
I or they, so we *p* 1 Cor 15:11
P the word 2 Tim 4:2

PREACHED
p that people Mark 6:12
out and *p* Mark 16:20
of sins should be *p* Luke 24:47
p Christ to them Acts 8:5
lest, when I have *p* 1 Cor 9:27
than what we have *p* Gal 1:8
the gospel was *p* Heb 4:2
also He went and *p* 1 Pet 3:19

PREACHER
they hear without a *p* Rom 10:14
I was appointed a *p* 1 Tim 2:7

PREACHES
the Jesus whom Paul *p* Acts 19:13
p another Jesus 2 Cor 11:4
p any other gospel Gal 1:9
p the faith which he Gal 1:23

PREACHING
p Jesus as the Acts 5:42
not risen, then our *p* 1 Cor 15:14

PRECEPTS
all His *p* are sure Ps 111:7
how I love Your *p* Ps 119:159

PRECIOUS
P in the sight of the Ps 116:15
She is more *p* than Prov 3:15
p things shall not Is 44:9
if you take out the *p* Jer 15:19
farmer waits for the *p* James 5:7
more *p* than gold 1 Pet 1:7
who believe, He is *p* 1 Pet 2:7
p in the sight of 1 Pet 3:4

PREDESTINED
foreknew, He also *p* Rom 8:29
having *p* us to Eph 1:5
inheritance, being *p* Eph 1:11

PREEMINENCE
He may have the *p* Col 1:18
loves to have the *p* 3 John 9

PREFERENCE
in honor giving *p* Rom 12:10

for God has *r* him Rom 14:3
For I *r* from the Lord 1 Cor 11:23
r Christ Col 2:6
R up in glory 1 Tim 3:16

RECEIVES
r you *r* Me Matt 10:40
and whoever *r* Me Mark 9:37

RECONCILE
and that He might *r* Eph 2:16

RECONCILED
First be *r* to your Matt 5:24
we were *r* Rom 5:10
Christ's behalf, be *r* 2 Cor 5:20

RECONCILIATION
now received the *r* Rom 5:11
to us the word of *r* 2 Cor 5:19

RECONCILING
cast away is the *r* Rom 11:15
God was in Christ *r* 2 Cor 5:19

REDEEM
But God will *r* my soul Ps 49:15
r their life from Ps 72:14
was going to *r* Israel Luke 24:21
r those who were Gal 4:5
us, that He might *r* Titus 2:14

REDEEMED
Let the *r* of the LORD Ps 107:2
r shall walk there Is 35:9
sea a road For the *r* Is 51:10
And you shall be *r* Is 52:3
and *r* His people Luke 1:68
Christ has *r* us from Gal 3:13
that you were not *r* 1 Pet 1:18
were slain, And have *r* Rev 5:9

REDEEMER
For I know that my *R* Job 19:25
Our *R* from Everlasting Is 63:16

REDEEMING
r the time Eph 5:16

REDEMPTION
those who looked for *r* Luke 2:38
your *r* draws near Luke 21:28
grace through the *r* Rom 3:24
the adoption, the *r* Rom 8:23
sanctification and *r* 1 Cor 1:30
In Him we have *r* Eph 1:7
for the day of *r* Eph 4:30
obtained eternal *r* Heb 9:12

REED
r He will not break Is 42:3
r shaken by the wind Matt 11:7

REFINED
us as silver is *r* Ps 66:10

REFINER
He will sit as a *r* Mal 3:3

REFORMATION
until the time of *r* Heb 9:10

REFRESH
r my heart in the Lord Philem 20

REFRESHED
his spirit has been *r* 2 Cor 7:13
for he often *r* 2 Tim 1:16

REFRESHES
r the soul of his Prov 25:13

REFRESHING
r may come from the Acts 3:19

REFUGE
eternal God is your *r* Deut 33:27
God is our *r* and Ps 46:1
who have fled for *r* Heb 6:18

REGARD
r iniquity in my heart Ps 66:18
did not fear God nor *r* Luke 18:2

REGARDED
my hand and no one *r* Prov 1:24
r the lowly state Luke 1:48

REGARDS
r a rebuke will be Prov 13:18

REGENERATION
to you, that in the *r* Matt 19:28
the washing of *r* Titus 3:5

REGISTERED
So all went to be *r* Luke 2:3

REGRETTED
but afterward he *r* Matt 21:29

REGULATIONS
yourselves to *r* Col 2:20

REIGN
"And He will *r* Luke 1:33
righteousness will *r* Rom 5:17
so grace might *r* Rom 5:21
do not let sin *r* Rom 6:12
For He must *r* till He 1 Cor 15:25
of Christ, and shall *r* Rev 20:6

REIGNED
so that as sin *r* Rom 5:21
You have *r* as kings 1 Cor 4:8
And they lived and *r* Rev 20:4

REIGNS
to Zion, "Your God *r* Is 52:7
Lord God Omnipotent *r* Rev 19:6

REJECT
"All too well you *r* Mark 7:9
R a divisive man Titus 3:10

REJECTED
He is despised and *r* Is 53:3
r Has become the Matt 21:42
many things and be *r* Luke 17:25
Moses whom they *r* Acts 7:35
to a living stone, *r* 1 Pet 2:4

REJECTION
you shall know My *r* Num 14:34

REJECTS
he who *r* Me *r* Luke 10:16

REJOICE
***R* in the LORD** Ps 33:1
of Your wings I will *r* Ps 63:7
Let them *r* before God Ps 68:3
Let the heavens *r* Ps 96:11
Let the earth *r* Ps 97:1
We will *r* and be glad Ps 118:24
She shall *r* in time to Prov 31:25
R, O young man Eccl 11:9
your heart shall *r* Is 66:14
Do not *r* over me Mic 7:8
do not *r* Luke 10:20
you would *r* John 14:28
but the world will *r* John 16:20
and your heart will *r* John 16:22
R with those who Rom 12:15
and in this I *r* Phil 1:18
faith, I am glad and *r* Phil 2:17
R in the Lord always Phil 4:4
R always 1 Thess 5:16
yet believing, you *r* 1 Pet 1:8

REJOICED
And my spirit has *r* Luke 1:47
In that hour Jesus *r* Luke 10:21
Abraham *r* John 8:56

REJOICES
glad, and my glory *r* Ps 16:9
but *r* in the truth 1 Cor 13:6

REJOICING
come again with *r* Ps 126:6
he went on his way *r* Acts 8:39
confidence and the *r* Heb 3:6

RELENT
sworn And will not *r* Ps 110:4
sworn And will not *r* Heb 7:21

RELENTED
and God *r* from the Jon 3:10

RELENTING
I am weary of *r* Jer 15:6

RELIGION
in self-imposed *r* Col 2:23
and undefiled *r* James 1:27

RELIGIOUS
things you are very *r* Acts 17:22

REMAIN
that My joy may *r* John 15:11
your fruit should *r* John 15:16
"If I will that he *r* John 21:22
the greater part *r* 1 Cor 15:6
are alive and *r* 1 Thess 4:15
the things which *r* Rev 3:2

REMAINS
"While the earth *r* Gen 8:22
Therefore your sin *r* John 9:41
There *r* therefore a Heb 4:9

REMEMBER
"*R* the Sabbath day Ex 20:8
But we will *r* the name Ps 20:7
r Your name in the Ps 119:55
R now your Creator Eccl 12:1
r the former things Is 43:18
and their sin I will *r* Jer 31:34
In wrath *r* mercy Hab 3:2
And to *r* His holy Luke 1:72
"*R* Lot's wife Luke 17:32
r the words of the Acts 20:35
R that Jesus Christ 2 Tim 2:8
R those who rule Heb 13:7

RETURNS
As a dog *r* to his own Prov 26:11
"A dog *r* to his own 2 Pet 2:22

REVEAL
the Son wills to *r* Him Matt 11:27
r His Son in me Gal 1:16

REVEALED
things which are *r* Deut 29:29
righteousness to be *r* Is 56:1
the Son of Man is *r* Luke 17:30
the wrath of God is *r* Rom 1:18
glory which shall be *r* Rom 8:18
the Lord Jesus is *r* 2 Thess 1:7
lawless one will be *r* 2 Thess 2:8
ready to be *r* in the 1 Pet 1:5
when His glory is *r* 1 Pet 4:13
r what we shall be 1 John 3:2

REVEALER
Lord of kings, and a *r* Dan 2:47

REVEALING
waits for the *r* Rom 8:19

REVEALS
as a talebearer *r* Prov 20:19
r His secret to His Amos 3:7

REVELATION
Where there is no *r* Prov 29:18
it came through the *r* Gal 1:12
spirit of wisdom and *r* Eph 1:17
r He made known to Eph 3:3
and glory at the *r* 1 Pet 1:7

REVERENCE
and *r* My sanctuary Lev 19:30
God acceptably with *r* Heb 12:28

REVERENT
man who is always *r* Prov 28:14
their wives must be *r* 1 Tim 3:11

REVILE
are you when they *r* Matt 5:11
r God's high priest Acts 23:4

REVILED
crucified with Him *r* Mark 15:32
who, when He was *r* 1 Pet 2:23

REVIVAL
give us a measure of *r* Ezra 9:8

REVIVE
Will You not *r* us Ps 85:6
two days He will *r* Hos 6:2

REVIVED
came, sin *r* and I died Rom 7:9

REWARD
exceedingly great *r* Gen 15:1
look, And see the *r* Ps 91:8
Behold, His *r* is with Is 40:10
for great is your *r* Matt 5:12
you, they have their *r* Matt 6:2
no means lose his *r* Matt 10:42
we receive the due *r* Luke 23:41
will receive his own *r* 1 Cor 3:8
cheat you of your *r* Col 2:18
for he looked to the *r* Heb 11:26
quickly, and My *r* Rev 22:12

REWARDS
Whoever *r* evil for Prov 17:13
And follows after *r* Is 1:23

RICH
Abram was very *r* Gen 13:2
The *r* and the poor Prov 22:2
r rules over the poor Prov 22:7
r man is wise in his Prov 28:11
Do not curse the *r* Eccl 10:20
it is hard for a *r* Matt 19:23
to you who are *r* Luke 6:24
the *r* man's table Luke 16:21
for he was very *r* Luke 18:23
You are already *r* 1 Cor 4:8
though He was *r* 2 Cor 8:9
who desire to be *r* 1 Tim 6:9
of this world to be *r* James 2:5
you say, 'I am *r* Rev 3:17

RICHES
R and honor are Prov 8:18
R do not profit Prov 11:4
in his *r* will fall Prov 11:28
of the wise is their *r* Prov 14:24
and *r* are an Prov 19:14
of the LORD Are *r* Prov 22:4
r are not forever Prov 27:24
do you despise the *r* Rom 2:4
make known the *r* Rom 9:23
what are the *r* Eph 1:18
show the exceeding *r* Eph 2:7
the unsearchable *r* Eph 3:8
r than the treasures Heb 11:26
To receive power and *r* Rev 5:12

RICHLY
Christ dwell in you *r* Col 3:16
God, who gives us *r* 1 Tim 6:17

RIGHT
the *r* of the firstborn Deut 21:17
"Is your heart *r* 2 Kin 10:15
Lord, "Sit at My *r* Ps 110:1
a way which seems *r* Prov 14:12
clothed and in his *r* Mark 5:15
to them He gave the *r* John 1:12
your heart is not *r* Acts 8:21
seven stars in His *r* Rev 2:1

RIGHTEOUS
also destroy the *r* Gen 18:23
and they justify the *r* Deut 25:1
that he could be *r* Job 15:14
"The *r* see it and Job 22:19
r shows mercy and Ps 37:21
I have not seen the *r* Ps 37:25
The LORD loves the *r* Ps 146:8
r is a well of life Prov 10:11
r will be gladness Prov 10:28
r will be delivered Prov 11:21
r will be recompensed Prov 11:31
the prayer of the *r* Prov 15:29
r are bold as a lion Prov 28:1
r considers the cause Prov 29:7
Do not be overly *r* Eccl 7:16
event happens to the *r* Eccl 9:2
with My *r* right hand Is 41:10
By His knowledge My *r* Is 53:11
The *r* perishes Is 57:1
they sell the *r* Amos 2:6
not come to call the *r* Matt 9:13
r men desired to see Matt 13:17
r will shine forth as Matt 13:43
that they were *r* Luke 18:9
this was a *r* Luke 23:47
"There is none *r* Rom 3:10
r man will one die Rom 5:7
Jesus Christ the *r* 1 John 2:1

RIGHTEOUSLY
should live soberly, *r* Titus 2:12
to Him who judges *r* 1 Pet 2:23

RIGHTEOUSNESS
it to him for *r* Gen 15:6
I put on *r* Job 29:14
I call, O God of my *r* Ps 4:1
from the LORD, And *r* Ps 24:5
shall speak of Your *r* Ps 35:28
the good news of *r* Ps 40:9
heavens declare His *r* Ps 50:6
R and peace have Ps 85:10
R will go before Him Ps 85:13
r endures forever Ps 111:3
r delivers from death Prov 10:2
The *r* of the blameless Prov 11:5
the way of *r* is life Prov 12:28
R exalts a nation Prov 14:34
He who follows *r* Prov 21:21
R lodged in it Is 1:21
in the LORD I have *r* Is 45:24
r will be forever Is 51:8
I will declare your *r* Is 57:12
r as a breastplate Is 59:17
r goes forth as Is 62:1
The Lord Our *R* Jer 23:6
to David A Branch of *r* Jer 33:15
The *r* of the righteous Ezek 18:20
who turn many to *r* Dan 12:3
to fulfill all *r* Matt 3:15
exceeds the *r* of the Matt 5:20
to you in the way of *r* Matt 21:32
For in it the *r* Rom 1:17
even the *r* of God Rom 3:22
accounted to him for *r* Rom 4:22
r will reign in life Rom 5:17
might reign through *r* Rom 5:21
ignorant of God's *r* Rom 10:3
might become the *r* 2 Cor 5:21
the breastplate of *r* Eph 6:14
not having my own *r* Phil 3:9
r which we have Titus 3:5
not produce the *r* James 1:20
a preacher of *r* 2 Pet 2:5
a new earth in which *r* 2 Pet 3:13
who practices *r* 1 John 2:29
He who practices *r* 1 John 3:7

RIGHTLY
wise uses knowledge *r* Prov 15:2
r dividing the word 2 Tim 2:15

RISE
for He makes His sun *r* Matt 5:45
third day He will *r* Matt 20:19
third day He will *r* Luke 18:33
be the first to *r* Acts 26:23
in Christ will *r* 1 Thess 4:16

RISEN
there has not *r* Matt 11:11
disciples that He is *r* Matt 28:7
"The Lord is *r* Luke 24:34
then Christ is not *r* 1 Cor 15:13
if Christ is not *r* 1 Cor 15:17

But now Christ is *r* 1 Cor 15:20

RIVER
peace to her like a *r* Is 66:12
he showed me a pure *r* Rev 22:1

RIVERS
By the *r* of Babylon Ps 137:1
All the *r* run into the Eccl 1:7
his heart will flow *r* John 7:38

ROAR
The LORD also will *r* Joel 3:16

ROARING
and the waves *r* Luke 21:25
walks about like a *r* 1 Pet 5:8

ROARS
"The LORD *r* from Amos 1:2
as when a lion *r* Rev 10:3

ROB
"Will a man *r* God Mal 3:8

ROBBED
r other churches 2 Cor 11:8

ROBBER
is a thief and a *r* John 10:1
Barabbas was a *r* John 18:40

ROBBERS
also crucified two *r* Mark 15:27
Me are thieves and *r* John 10:8

ROBBERY
did not consider it *r* Phil 2:6

ROBE
'Bring out the best *r* Luke 15:22
on Him a purple *r* John 19:2
Then a white *r* was Rev 6:11

ROBES
have stained all My *r* Is 63:3
go around in long *r* Luke 20:46
clothed with white *r* Rev 7:9

ROCK
you shall strike the *r* Ex 17:6
and struck the *r* Num 20:11
For their *r* is not Deut 32:31
"The LORD is my *r* 2 Sam 22:2
And who is a *r* 2 Sam 22:32
Blessed be my *R* 2 Sam 22:47
For You are my *r* Ps 31:3
r that is higher than Ps 61:2
been mindful of the *R* Is 17:10
shadow of a great *r* Is 32:2
his house on the *r* Matt 7:24
r I will build My Matt 16:18
stumbling stone and *r* Rom 9:33
R that followed them 1 Cor 10:4

ROD
Your *r* and Your staff Ps 23:4
shall come forth a *R* Is 11:1
rule them with a *r* Rev 2:27

ROOM
you a large upper *r* Mark 14:15
no *r* for them in the Luke 2:7
into the upper *r* Acts 1:13

ROOT
day there shall be a *R* Is 11:10
because they had no *r* Matt 13:6
of money is a *r* 1 Tim 6:10
lest any *r* of Heb 12:15
I am the *R* and the Rev 22:16

ROOTED
r and built up in Him Col 2:7

ROSE
end Christ died and *r* Rom 14:9
buried, and that He *r* 1 Cor 15:4
Jesus died and *r* 1 Thess 4:14

RULE
And he shall *r* Gen 3:16
puts an end to all *r* 1 Cor 15:24
let the peace of God *r* Col 3:15
Let the elders who *r* 1 Tim 5:17
Remember those who *r* Heb 13:7

RULER
to Me The One to be *r* Mic 5:2
by Beelzebub, the *r* Matt 12:24
the *r* of this world John 12:31
'Who made you a *r* Acts 7:27

RULERS
And the *r* take counsel Ps 2:2
"You know that the *r* Matt 20:25
which none of the *r* 1 Cor 2:8
powers, against the *r* Eph 6:12

RULES
That the Most High *r* Dan 4:17
that the Most High *r* Dan 4:32
r his own house well 1 Tim 3:4

RULING
r their children 1 Tim 3:12

RUMORS
hear of wars and *r* Matt 24:6

RUN
r and not be weary Is 40:31
us, and let us *r* Heb 12:1

S

SABAOTH
S had left us a Rom 9:29
ears of the Lord of *S* James 5:4

SABBATH
"Remember the *S* Ex 20:8
S was made for man Mark 2:27

SABBATHS
S you shall keep Ex 31:13

SACRIFICE
to the LORD than *s* Prov 21:3
For the LORD has a *s* Is 34:6
of My offerings they *s* Hos 8:13
LORD has prepared a *s* Zeph 1:7
desire mercy and not *s* Matt 9:13
an offering and a *s* Eph 5:2
put away sin by the *s* Heb 9:26
no longer remains a *s* Heb 10:26
offer the *s* of praise Heb 13:15

SACRIFICED
s their sons And their Ps 106:37

SACRIFICES
The *s* of God are a Ps 51:17
multitude of your *s* Is 1:11
priests, to offer up *s* Heb 7:27
s God is well pleased Heb 13:16

SAFE
he has received him *s* Luke 15:27

SAFELY
make them lie down *s* Hos 2:18

SAFETY
say, "Peace and *s* 1 Thess 5:3

SAINTS
s who are on the earth Ps 16:3
does not forsake His *s* Ps 37:28
Is the death of His *s* Ps 116:15
war against the *s* Dan 7:21
Jesus, called to be *s* 1 Cor 1:2
the least of all the *s* Eph 3:8
be glorified in His *s* 2 Thess 1:10
all delivered to the *s* Jude 3
shed the blood of *s* Rev 16:6

SALT
shall season with *s* Lev 2:13
"You are the *s* Matt 5:13
s loses its flavor Mark 9:50

SALVATION
still, and see the *s* Ex 14:13
S belongs to the LORD Ps 3:8
is my light and my *s* Ps 27:1
God is the God of *s* Ps 68:20
joy in the God of my *s* Hab 3:18
raised up a horn of *s* Luke 1:69
"Nor is there *s* Acts 4:12
the power of God to *s* Rom 1:16
now is the day of *s* 2 Cor 6:2
work out your own *s* Phil 2:12
chose you for *s* 2 Thess 2:13
neglect so great a *s* Heb 2:3

SAMARITAN
a drink from me, a *S* John 4:9

SANCTIFICATION
will of God, your *s* 1 Thess 4:3

SANCTIFIED
they also may be *s* John 17:19
but you were *s* 1 Cor 6:11
for it is *s* by the 1 Tim 4:5

SANCTIFIES
For both He who *s* Heb 2:11

SANCTIFY
s My great name Ezek 36:23
"*S* them by Your John 17:17
that He might *s* Eph 5:26

SANCTUARY
let them make Me a *s* Ex 25:8
and the earthly *s* Heb 9:1

SAND
descendants as the *s* Gen 32:12
innumerable as the *s* Heb 11:12

SAT
into heaven, and *S* Mark 16:19
And He who *s* there was Rev 4:3

SATAN
before the LORD, and *S* Job 1:6

"Away with you, *S* Matt 4:10
"Get behind Me, *S* Matt 16:23
"How can *S* cast out Mark 3:23
S has asked for you Luke 22:31
to the working of *S* 2 Thess 2:9
known the depths of *S* Rev 2:24
years have expired, *S* Rev 20:7

SATIATED
s the weary soul Jer 31:25

SATISFIED
I shall be *s* when I Ps 17:15
that are never *s* Prov 30:15
of His soul, and be *s* Is 53:11

SATISFIES
s the longing soul Ps 107:9

SATISFY
s us early with Your Ps 90:14
long life I will *s* Ps 91:16
for what does not *s* Is 55:2

SAVE
Oh, *s* me for Your Ps 6:4
s the children of the Ps 72:4
s the souls of the Ps 72:13
That it cannot *s* Is 59:1
s you And deliver you Jer 15:20
other, That he may *s* Hos 13:10
JESUS, for He will *s* Matt 1:21
s his life will Matt 16:25
s that which was Matt 18:11
let Him *s* Himself if Luke 23:35
but to *s* the world John 12:47
the world to *s* sinners 1 Tim 1:15

SAVED
"He *s* others Matt 27:42
That we should be *s* Luke 1:71
"Your faith has *s* Luke 7:50
might be *s* John 3:17
them, saying, "Be *s* Acts 2:40
what must I do to be *s* Acts 16:30
which also you are *s* 1 Cor 15:2
grace you have been *s* Eph 2:8
to His mercy He *s* Titus 3:5
of those who are *s* Rev 21:24

SAVES
antitype which now *s* 1 Pet 3:21

SAVIOR
I, the LORD, am your *S* Is 60:16
rejoiced in God my *S* Luke 1:47
the city of David a *S* Luke 2:11
up for Israel a *S* Acts 13:23
God, who is the *S* 1 Tim 4:10
and *S* Jesus Christ Titus 2:13

SAWN
stoned, they were *s* Heb 11:37

SAY
"But I *s* to you that Matt 5:22
"But who do you *s* Matt 16:15

SAYING
This is a faithful *s* 1 Tim 1:15

SAYINGS
whoever hears these *s* Matt 7:24

SCALES
on it had a pair of *s* Rev 6:5

SCARLET
your sins are like *s* Is 1:18

SCATTER
I will *s* you among the Lev 26:33

SCATTERED
"Israel is like *s* sheep Jer 50:17
the sheep will be *s* Mark 14:27

SCATTERS
not gather with Me *s* Matt 12:30

SCEPTER
s shall not depart Gen 49:10

SCHEMER
Will be called a *s* Prov 24:8

SCHEMES
sought out many *s* Eccl 7:29

SCHISM
there should be no *s* 1 Cor 12:25

SCHOOL
daily in the *s* of Acts 19:9

SCOFF
They *s* at kings Hab 1:10

SCOFFER
"He who corrects a *s* Prov 9:7
s is an abomination Prov 24:9

SCOFFERS
s will come in the 2 Pet 3:3

SCORCHED
And men were *s* with Rev 16:9

SCORN
My friends *s* me Job 16:20

SCORNS
He *s* the scornful Prov 3:34

SCORPIONS
on serpents and *s* Luke 10:19
They had tails like *s* Rev 9:10

SCOURGE
will mock Him, and *s* Mark 10:34

SCOURGES
s every son whom Heb 12:6

SCRIBES
"Beware of the *s* Mark 12:38

SCRIPTURE
S cannot be broken John 10:35
All *S* is given by 2 Tim 3:16

SCRIPTURES
S must be fulfilled Mark 14:49

SCROLL
eat this *s* Ezek 3:1
the sky receded as a *s* Rev 6:14

SEA
drowned in the Red *S* Ex 15:4
who go down to the *s* Ps 107:23
and the *s* obey Him Matt 8:27
throne there was a *s* Rev 4:6
there was no more *s* Rev 21:1

SEAL
stands, having this *s* 2 Tim 2:19

SEALED
by whom you were *s* Eph 4:30

SEAM
tunic was without *s* John 19:23

SE´ANCE
"Please conduct a *s* 1 Sam 28:8

SEARCH
glory of kings is to *s* Prov 25:2
s the Scriptures John 5:39

SEARCHED
s the Scriptures Acts 17:11

SEARCHES
For the Spirit *s* 1 Cor 2:10

SEASON
Be ready in *s* and out 2 Tim 4:2

SEASONED
how shall it be *s* Matt 5:13

SEASONS
the times and the *s* 1 Thess 5:1

SEAT
shall make a mercy *s* Ex 25:17
before the judgment *s* 2 Cor 5:10

SEATS
at feasts, the best *s* Matt 23:6

SECRET
s things belong Deut 29:29
In the *s* place of His Ps 27:5
Father who is in the *s* Matt 6:6

SECRETLY
He lies in wait *s* Ps 10:9

SECRETS
For He knows the *s* Ps 44:21
God will judge the *s* Rom 2:16

SECT
to the strictest *s* Acts 26:5

SECURELY
nation that dwells *s* Jer 49:31

SEDUCED
flattering lips she *s* Prov 7:21

SEE
in my flesh I shall *s* Job 19:26
For they shall *s* God Matt 5:8
seeing they do not *s* Matt 13:13
rejoiced to *s* My day John 8:56
They shall *s* His face Rev 22:4

SEED
He shall see His *s* Is 53:10
S were the promises Gal 3:16
you are Abraham's *s* Gal 3:29

SEEDS
the good *s* are the Matt 13:38

SEEK
pray and *s* My face 2 Chr 7:14
S the LORD while He Is 55:6
s, and you will find Matt 7:7

of Man has come to *s* Luke 19:10
"You will *s* Me and John 7:34
For all *s* their own Phil 2:21
s those things which Col 3:1

SEEKING
like a roaring lion, *s* 1 Pet 5:8

SEEKS
There is none who *s* Rom 3:11

SEEMS
is a way which *s* Prov 14:12

SEEN
s God face to face Gen 32:30
No one has *s* God at John 1:18
s Me has *s* the John 14:9
things which are not *s* 2 Cor 4:18

SEES
s his brother in need 1 John 3:17

SELF-CONFIDENT
a fool rages and is *s* Prov 14:16

SELF-CONTROL
gentleness, *s* Gal 5:23
to knowledge *s* 2 Pet 1:6

SELF-CONTROLLED
just, holy, *s* Titus 1:8

SELF-SEEKING
envy and *s* exist James 3:16

SELL
s whatever you have Mark 10:21

SEND
"Behold, I *s* you out Matt 10:16
has sent Me, I also *s* John 20:21

SENSES
of use have their *s* Heb 5:14

SENSIBLY
who can answer *s* Prov 26:16

SENSUAL
but is earthly, *s* James 3:15

SENT
unless they are *s* Rom 10:15

SEPARATED
it pleased God, who *s* Gal 1:15

SEPARATES
who repeats a matter *s* Prov 17:9

SEPARATION
the middle wall of *s* Eph 2:14

SERAPHIM
Above it stood *s* Is 6:2

SERIOUS
therefore be *s* and 1 Pet 4:7

SERPENT
s was more cunning Gen 3:1
"Make a fiery *s* Num 21:8
Moses lifted up the *s* John 3:14

SERPENTS
be wise as *s* Matt 10:16

SERVANT
s will rule over a son Prov 17:2
good and faithful *s* Matt 25:21

SERVANTS
are unprofitable *s* Luke 17:10

SERVE
to be served, but to *s* Matt 20:28
but through love *s* Gal 5:13

SERVES
"If anyone *s* Me John 12:26

SERVICE
is your reasonable *s* Rom 12:1
with good will doing *s* Eph 6:7

SERVING
fervent in spirit, *s* Rom 12:11

SET
"See, I have *s* Deut 30:15
s aside the grace Gal 2:21

SETTLE
"Therefore *s* it in Luke 21:14

SETTLED
O LORD, Your word is *s* Ps 119:89

SEVEN
s churches which are Rev 1:4

SEVENTY
"*S* weeks are Dan 9:24

SEVERE
not to be too *s* 2 Cor 2:5

SEVERITY
the goodness and *s* Rom 11:22

SHADE
may nest under its *s* Mark 4:32

SHADOW
In the *s* of His hand Is 49:2
the law, having a *s* Heb 10:1

SHAKE
s the earth Is 2:19
I will *s* all nations Hag 2:7

SHAKEN
not to be soon *s* 2 Thess 2:2

SHAKES
s the Wilderness Ps 29:8

SHAME
never be put to *s* Joel 2:26
to put to *s* the wise 1 Cor 1:27
glory is in their *s* Phil 3:19

SHAMEFUL
For it is *s* even to Eph 5:12

SHARE
to do good and to *s* Heb 13:16

SHARING
for your liberal *s* 2 Cor 9:13

SHARP
S as a two-edged sword Prov 5:4

SHARPEN
s their tongue like a Ps 64:3

SHARPENS
My adversary *s* His Job 16:9

SHARPNESS
I should use *s* 2 Cor 13:10

SHEATH
your sword into the *s* John 18:11

SHEAVES
Bringing his *s* Ps 126:6
gather them like *s* Mic 4:12

SHED
which is *s* for many Matt 26:28

SHEDDING
blood, and without *s* Heb 9:22

SHEEP
s will be scattered Zech 13:7
having a hundred *s* Luke 15:4
and I know My *s* John 10:14
"He was led as a *s* Acts 8:32

SHEEPFOLDS
lie down among the *s* Ps 68:13

SHEET
object like a great *s* Acts 10:11

SHELTER
the LORD will be a *s* Joel 3:16

SHELTERS
s him all the day long Deut 33:12

SHEOL
not leave my soul in *S* Ps 16:10
the belly of *S* I cried Jon 2:2

SHEPHERD
The LORD is my *s* Ps 23:1
His flock like a *s* Is 40:11
'I will strike the *S* Matt 26:31
"I am the good *s* John 10:11
the dead, that great *S* Heb 13:20
S the flock of God 1 Pet 5:2
when the Chief *S* 1 Pet 5:4

SHEPHERDS
"And I will give you *s* Jer 3:15
s have led them astray Jer 50:6

SHIELD
I am your *s* Gen 15:1
truth shall be your *s* Ps 91:4
all, taking the *s* Eph 6:16

SHINE
LORD make His face *s* Num 6:25
among whom you *s* Phil 2:15

SHINED
them a light has *s* Is 9:2

SHINES
heed as a light that *s* 2 Pet 1:19

SHINING
light is already *s* 1 John 2:8

SHIPS
down to the sea in *s* Ps 107:23

SLANDER
whoever spreads *s* Prov 10:18

SLANDERERS
be reverent, not *s* 1 Tim 3:11

SLANDEROUSLY
as we are *s* reported Rom 3:8

SLAUGHTER
led as a lamb to the *s* Is 53:7
as sheep for the *s* Rom 8:36

SLAVE
commits sin is a *s* John 8:34

SLAVES
should no longer be *s* Rom 6:6

SLAY
s the righteous Gen 18:25

SLEEP
God caused a deep *s* Gen 2:21
neither slumber nor *s* Ps 121:4
He gives His beloved *s* Ps 127:2
and many *s* 1 Cor 11:30
We shall not all *s* 1 Cor 15:51

SLEEPERS
gently the lips of *s* Song 7:9

SLEEPING
"Are you still *s* Matt 26:45

SLEEPLESSNESS
in labors, in *s* 2 Cor 6.5

SLEEPS
"Our friend Lazarus *s* John 11:11

SLEPT
I lay down and *s* Ps 3:5

SLIGHTED
is the one who is *s* Prov 12:9

SLING
he had, and his *s* 1 Sam 17:40

SLIP
Their foot shall *s* Deut 32:35

SLIPPERY
set them in *s* places Ps 73:18

SLOOPS
all the beautiful *s* Is 2:16

SLOW
hear, *s* to speak, *s* James 1:19

SLUGGARD
will you slumber, O *s* Prov 6:9

SLUMBERING
upon men, While *s* Job 33:15

SMALL
And I saw the dead, *s* Rev 20:12

SMELL
and he smelled the *s* Gen 27:27

SMELLS
s the battle from afar Job 39:25

SMITTEN
Him stricken, *S* Is 53:4

SMOKE
was filled with *s* Rev 15:8

SMOOTH
And the rough places *s* Is 40:4

SMOOTH-SKINNED
man, and I am a *s* Gen 27:11

SNAIL
s which melts away as Ps 58:8

SNARE
is a fowler's *s* Hos 9:8
it will come as a *s* Luke 21:35
and escape the *s* 2 Tim 2:26

SNARED
All of them are *s* Is 42:22

SNARES
who seek my life lay *s* Ps 38:12

SNATCH
neither shall anyone *s* John 10:28

SNATCHES
s away what was Matt 13:19

SNEER
And you *s* at it Mal 1:13

SNIFFED
They *s* at the wind Jer 14:6

SNORTING
s strikes terror Job 39:20

SNOW
shall be whiter than *s* Ps 51:7
shall be as white as *s* Is 1:18

SOAKED
Their land shall be *s* Is 34:7

SOAP
lye, and use much *s* Jer 2:22

SOBER
the older men be *s* Titus 2:2

SOBERLY
think, but to think *s* Rom 12:3

SODA
And like vinegar on *s* Prov 25:20

SODOMITES
nor homosexuals, nor *s* 1 Cor 6:9

SOJOURNER
no *s* had to lodge Job 31:32

SOJOURNERS
are strangers and *s* Lev 25:23

SOLD
s his birthright Gen 25:33
s all that he had Matt 13:46
but I am carnal, *s* Rom 7:14

SOLDIER
hardship as a good *s* 2 Tim 2:3

SOLDIERS
s twisted a crown John 19:2

SOLITARILY
heritage, Who dwell *s* Mic 7:14

SOLITARY
God sets the *s* in Ps 68:6

SOMEBODY
up, claiming to be *s* Acts 5:36

SOMETHING
thinks himself to be *s* Gal 6:3

SON
Me, 'You are My *S* Ps 2:7
is born, Unto us a *S* Is 9:6
fourth is like the *S* Dan 3:25
will bring forth a *S* Matt 1:21
"This is My beloved *S* Matt 3:17
Jesus, You *S* of God Matt 8:29
are the Christ, the *S* Matt 16:16
Whose *S* is He Matt 22:42
of the *S* of Man Matt 24:37
'I am the *S* of God Matt 27:43
of Jesus Christ, the *S* Mark 1:1
out, the only *s* Luke 7:12
The only begotten *S* John 1:18
that this is the *S* John 1:34
of the only begotten *S* John 3:18
S can do nothing John 5:19
s abides forever John 8:35
you believe in the *S* John 9:35
I said, 'I am the *S* John 10:36
behold your *s* John 19:26
Jesus Christ is the *S* Acts 8:37
by sending His own *S* Rom 8:3
not spare His own *S* Rom 8:32
live by faith in the *S* Gal 2:20
God sent forth His *S* Gal 4:4
the knowledge of the *S* Eph 4:13
"You are My *S* Heb 1:5
though He was a *S* Heb 5:8
but made like the *S* Heb 7:3
"This is My beloved *S* 2 Pet 1:17
denies the *S* 1 John 2:23
One like the *S* of Man Rev 1:13

SONG
Sing to Him a new *s* Ps 33:3
He has put a new *s* Ps 40:3
I will sing a new *s* Ps 144:9
they sang a new *s* Rev 5:9

SONGS
my Maker, Who gives *s* Job 35:10
and spiritual *s* Eph 5:19

SONS
s shall come from afar Is 60:4
He will purity the *s* Mal 3:3
you may become *s* John 12:36
who are of faith are *s* Gal 3:7
the adoption as *s* Gal 4:5
in bringing many *s* Heb 2:10
speaks to you as to *s* Heb 12:5

SOON
For it is *s* cut off Ps 90:10

SOOTHED
or bound up, Or *s* Is 1:6

SORCERER
But Elymas the *s* Acts 13:8

SORCERERS
outside are dogs and *s* Rev 22:15

SORCERESS
shall not permit a *s* Ex 22:18

SORCERY
idolatry, *s* Gal 5:20

SORES
and putrefying *s* Is 1:6

SORROW
multiply your *s* Gen 3:16
s is continually Ps 38:17
And He adds no *s* Prov 10:22
Your *s* is incurable Jer 30:15
them sleeping from *s* Luke 22:45
s will be turned John 16:20
s produces repentance 2 Cor 7:10
s as others who 1 Thess 4:13
no more death, nor *s* Rev 21:4

SORROWFUL
But I am poor and *s* Ps 69:29
he went away *s* Matt 19:22
soul is exceedingly *s* Matt 26:38
and I may be less *s* Phil 2:28

SORROWS
s shall be multiplied Ps 16:4
by men, A Man of *s* Is 53:3
are the beginning of *s* Matt 24:8

SORRY
s that He had made man Gen 6:6
For you were made *s* 2 Cor 7:9

SOUGHT
I *s* the LORD Ps 34:4
s what was lost Ezek 34:4

SOUL
with all your *s* Deut 6:5
"My *s* loathes my life Job 10:1
s draws near the Pit Job 33:22
will not leave my *s* Ps 16:10
converting the *s* Ps 19:7
He restores my *s* Ps 23:3
you cast down, O my *s* Ps 42:5
Let my *s* live Ps 119:175
No one cares for my *s* Ps 142:4
me wrongs his own *s* Prov 8:36
When You make His *s* Is 53:10
s delight itself Is 55:2
The *s* of the father As Ezek 18:4
able to destroy both *s* Matt 10:28
and loses his own *s* Matt 16:26
with all your *s* Matt 22:37
your whole spirit, *s* 1 Thess 5:23
to the saving of the *s* Heb 10:39
his way will save a *s* James 5:20
health, just as your *s* 3 John 2

SOULS
And will save the *s* Ps 72:13
And he who wins *s* Prov 11:30
unsettling your *s* Acts 15:24
is able to save your *s* James 1:21

SOUND
voice was like the *s* Ezek 43:2
do not *s* a trumpet Matt 6:2
s words which you 2 Tim 1:13

SOUNDNESS
him this perfect *s* Acts 3:16

SOUNDS
a distinction in the *s* 1 Cor 14:7

SOW
s trouble reap Job 4:8
Those who *s* in tears Ps 126:5
Blessed are you who *s* Is 32:20
"They *s* the wind Hos 8:7
s is not made alive 1 Cor 15:36

SOWER
"Behold. a *s* went Matt 13:3

SOWN
s spiritual things 1 Cor 9:11
of righteousness is *s* James 3:18

SOWS
s the good seed is the Matt 13:37
'One *s* and another John 4:37
for whatever a man *s* Gal 6:7

SPARE
He who did not *s* Rom 8:32
if God did not *s* 2 Pet 2:4

SPARES
s his rod hates his Prov 13:24

SPARK
the work of it as a *s* Is 1:31

SPARKLES
it is red, When it *s* Prov 23:31

SPARKS
to trouble, As the *s* Job 5:7

SPARROW
s has found a home Ps 84:3

SPARROWS
than many *s* Matt 10:31

SPAT
Then they *s* on Him Matt 27:30

SPEAK
only the word that I *s* Num 22:35
oh, that God would *s* Job 11:5
And a time to *s* Eccl 3:7
s anymore in His name Jer 20:9
or what you should *s* Matt 10:19
to you when all men *s* Luke 6:26
s what I have seen John 8:3 8
He hears He will *s* John 16:13
Spirit and began to *s* Acts 2:4

SPEAKING
envy, and all evil *s* 1 Pet 2:1

SPEAKS
to face, as a man *s* Ex 33:11
God has sent *s* John 3:34
When he *s* a lie John 8:44
he being dead still *s* Heb 11:4
of sprinkling that *s* Heb 12:24

SPEAR
His side with a *s* John 19:34

SPEARS
And their *s* into Is 2:4

SPECK
do you look at the *s* Matt 7:3

SPECTACLE
you were made a *s* Heb 10:33

SPEECH
one language and one *s* Gen 11:1
his *s* contemptible 2 Cor 10:10
s always be with grace Col 4:6

SPEECHLESS
your mouth for the *s* Prov 31:8

SPEED
they shall come with *s* Is 5:26

SPEEDILY
I call, answer me *s* Ps 102:2

SPEND
you *s* money for Is 55:2
amiss, that you may *s* James 4:3

SPENT
"But when he had *s* Luke 15:14

SPEW
nor hot, I will *s* Rev 3:16

SPIDER
s skillfully grasps Prov 30:28

SPIES
men who had been *s* Josh 6:23

SPIN
neither toil nor *s* Matt 6:28

SPINDLE
her hand holds the *s* Prov 31:19

SPIRIT
And the *S* of God was Gen 1:2
S shall not strive Gen 6:3
S that is upon you Num 11:17
portion of your *s* 2 Kin 2:9
Then a *s* passed Job 4:15
hand I commit my *s* Ps 31:5
The *s* of a man is the Prov 20:27
s will return to God Eccl 12:7
S has gathered them Is 34:16
I have put My *S* Is 42:1
"The *S* of the Lord Is 61:1
S entered me when He Ezek 2:2
and a new *s* Ezek 18:31
"I will put My *S* Ezek 36:27
walk in a false *s* Mic 2:11
and He saw the *S* Matt 3:16
I will put My *S* Matt 12:18
S descending upon Mark 1:10
s indeed is willing Mark 14:38
go before Him in the *s* Luke 1:17
manner of *s* you are of Luke 9:55
hands I commit My *s* Luke 23:46
they had seen a *s* Luke 24:37
"God is *S* John 4:24
I speak to you are *s* John 6:63
"the *S* of truth John 14:17
but if a *s* or an angel Acts 23:9
the flesh but in the *S* Rom 8:9
does not have the *S* Rom 8:9
s that we are children Rom 8:16
what the mind of the *S* Rom 8:27
to us through His *S* 1 Cor 2:10
gifts, but the same *S* 1 Cor 12:4
but the *S* gives life 2 Cor 3:6
Now the Lord is the *S* 2 Cor 3:17

Having begun in the *S* Gal 3:3
has sent forth the *S* Gal 4:6
with the Holy *S* Eph 1:13
the unity of the *S* Eph 4:3
stand fast in one *s* Phil 1:27
S expressly says that 1 Tim 4:1
S who dwells in us James 4:5
made alive by the *S* 1 Pet 3:18
do not believe every *s* 1 John 4:1
you know the *S* 1 John 4:2
has given us of His *S* 1 John 4:13
S who bears witness 1 John 5:6
not having the *S* Jude 19
I was in the *S* on the Rev 1:10
him hear what the *S* Rev 2:7
And the *S* and the Rev 22:17

SPIRITS
Who makes His angels *s* Ps 104:4
heed to deceiving *s* 1 Tim 4:1

SPIRITUAL
s judges all things 1 Cor 2:15
However, the *s* is not 1 Cor 15:46
s restore such a one Gal 6:1

SPIRITUALLY
s minded is life Rom 8:6

SPITEFULLY
for those who *s* Matt 5:44

SPITTING
face from shame and *s* Is 50:6

SPLENDOR
on the glorious *s* Ps 145:5

SPOIL
He shall divide the *s* Is 53:12

SPOILER
I have created the *s* Is 54:16

SPOKE
"No man ever *s* John 7:46
I was a child, I *s* 1 Cor 13:11
in various ways *s* Heb 1:1
s as they were moved 2 Pet 1:21

SPOKEN
I have not *s* in secret Is 45:19
why am I evil *s* 1 Cor 10:30

SPOKESMAN
"So he shall be your *s* Ex 4:16

SPONGE
them ran and took a *s* Matt 27:48

SPOT
church, not having *s* Eph 5:27
Himself without *s* Heb 9:14

SPOTS
These are *s* in your Jude 12

SPREAD
Then the word of God *s* Acts 6:7

SPREADS
s them out like a tent Is 40:22

SPRING
Truth shall *s* out of Ps 85:11
s send forth fresh James 3:11

SPRINGING
a fountain of water *s* John 4:14

SPRINGS
And the thirsty land *s* Is 35:7

SPRINKLE
"Then I will *s* Ezek 36:25

SPRINKLED
having our hearts *s* Heb 10:22

SPRINKLING
s that speaks Heb 12:24

SPROUT
and the seed should *s* Mark 4:27

SQUARES
voice in the open *s* Prov 1:20

STAFF
this Jordan with my *s* Gen 32:10
Your rod and Your *s* Ps 23:4
on the top of his *s* Heb 11:21

STAGGER
they will drink and *s* Jer 25:16

STAGGERS
As a drunken man *s* Is 19:14

STAKES
s will ever be removed Is 33:20

STALLS
be no herd in the *s* Hab 3:17

STAMMERERS
s will be ready Is 32:4

STAMMERING
s tongue that you Is 33:19

STAMPING
At the noise of the *s* Jer 47:3

STAND
one shall be able to *s* Deut 7:24
lives, And He shall *s* Job 19:25
ungodly shall not *s* Ps 1:5
not lack a man to *s* Jer 35:19
And who can *s* when He Mal 3:2
that kingdom cannot *s* Mark 3:24
he will be made to *s* Rom 14:4
Watch, *s* fast in the 1 Cor 16:13
for by faith you *s* 2 Cor 1:24
having done all, to *s* Eph 6:13
S therefore Eph 6:14
of God in which you *s* 1 Pet 5:12
"Behold, I *s* at the Rev 3:20

STANDARD
LORD will lift up a *s* Is 59:19

STANDING
they love to pray *s* Matt 6:5
and the Son of Man *s* Acts 7:56

STANDS
him who thinks he *s* 1 Cor 10:12

STAR
For we have seen His *s* Matt 2:2
Bright and Morning *S* Rev 22:16

STARS
He made the *s* also Gen 1:16

born as many as the *s* Heb 11:12

STATE
learned in whatever *s* Phil 4:11

STATURE
in wisdom and *s* Luke 2:52

STATUTE
shall be a perpetual *s* Lev 3:17

STATUTES
the *s* of the LORD are Ps 19:8
Teach me Your *s* Ps 119:12

STAY
S here and watch Matt 26:38

STEADFAST
brethren, be *s* 1 Cor 15:58
soul, both sure and *s* Heb 6:19
Resist him, *s* in the 1 Pet 5:9

STEADFASTLY
s set His face to go Luke 9:51
And they continued *s* Acts 2:42

STEADFASTNESS
good order and the *s* Col 2:5

STEADILY
could not look *s* 2 Cor 3:13

STEADY
and his hands were *s* Ex 17:12

STEAL
"You shall not *s* Ex 20:15
thieves break in and *s* Matt 6:19
night and *s* Him away Matt 27:64

STEM
forth a Rod from the *s* Is 11:1

STENCH
there will be a *s* Is 3:24
this time there is a *s* John 11:39

STEP
s has turned from the Job 31:7

STEPS
The *s* of a good man Ps 37:23
And established my *s* Ps 40:2
the LORD directs his *s* Prov 16:9
should follow His *s* 1 Pet 2:21

STEWARD
be blameless, as a *s* Titus 1:7

STEWARDS
of Christ and *s* 1 Cor 4:1

STEWARDSHIP
entrusted with a *s* 1 Cor 9:17

STICK
"For Joseph, the *s* Ezek 37:16

STICKS
a man gathering *s* Num 15:32

STIFF
rebellion and your *s* Deut 31:27

STIFF-NECKED
"You *s* and Acts 7:51

STILL
When I awake, I am *s* Ps 139:18
sea, "Peace, be *s* Mark 4:39

STILLBORN
burial, I say that a *s* Eccl 6:3

STINGS
like a serpent, And *s* Prov 23:32

STIR
I remind you to *s* 2 Tim 1:6

STIRRED
So the LORD *s* up the Hag 1:14

STIRS
It *s* up the dead for Is 14:9

STOCKS
s that were in the Jer 20:2

STOIC
and *S* philosophers Acts 17:18

STOMACH
Foods for the *s* 1 Cor 6:13

STOMACH'S
little wine for your *s* 1 Tim 5:23

STONE
him, a pillar of *s* Gen 35:14
s shall be a witness Josh 24:27
s which the builders Ps 118:22
I lay in Zion a *s* Is 28:16
take the heart of *s* Ezek 36:26
will give him a *s* Matt 7:9
s will be broken Matt 21:44
s which the builders Luke 20:17
those works do you *s* John 10:32
Him as to a living *s* 1 Pet 2:4

STONED
s Stephen as he was Acts 7:59
They were *s* Heb 11:37

STONES
Abraham from these *s* Matt 3:9
command that these *s* Matt 4:3

STONY
fell on *s* ground Mark 4:5

STOOPED
And again He *s* down John 8:8

STOPPED
her flow of blood *s* Luke 8:44

STORE
exist are kept in *s* 2 Pet 3:7

STORK
s has her home in the Ps 104:17

STORM
He calms the *s* Ps 107:29
for a shelter from *s* Is 4:6

STRAIGHT
Make *s* in the desert A Is 40:3
and make *s* paths for Heb 12:13

STRAIGHTFORWARD
that they were not *s* Gal 2:14

STRAIN
"Blind guides, who *s* Matt 23:24

STRAITS
and desperate *s* Deut 28:53

STRANGE
s thing happened 1 Pet 4:12

STRANGER
and loves the *s* Deut 10:18
I was a *s* and you Matt 25:35

STRANGERS
know the voice of *s* John 10:5
you are no longer *s* Eph 2:19

STRANGLING
that my soul chooses *s* Job 7:15

STRAP
than I, whose sandal *s* Mark 1:7

STRAW
stones, wood, hay, *s* 1 Cor 3:12

STRAY
Who make my people *s* Mic 3:5

STRAYED
Yet I have not *s* Ps 119:110
some have *s* 1 Tim 6:10

STREAM
like a flowing *s* Is 66:12

STREAMS
He also brought *s* Ps 78:16

STREET
In the middle of its *s* Rev 22:2

STREETS
You taught in our *s* Luke 13:26

STRENGTH
s no man shall 1 Sam 2:9
The LORD is the *s* Ps 27:1
is our refuge and *s* Ps 46:1
They go from *s* to Ps 84:7
S and honor are her Prov 31:25
might He increases *s* Is 40:29
O LORD, my *s* and my Jer 16:19
were still without *s* Rom 5:6
s is made perfect 2 Cor 12:9

STRENGTHEN
And He shall *s* Ps 27:14
S the weak hands Is 35:3
s your brethren Luke 22:32
s the things Rev 3:2

STRENGTHENED
unbelief, but was *s* Rom 4:20
stood with me and *s* 2 Tim 4:17

STRENGTHENING
s the souls of the Acts 14:22

STRENGTHENS
through Christ who *s* Phil 4:13

STRETCH
are old, you will *s* John 21:18

STRETCHED
I have *s* out my hands Ps 88:9
"All day long I have *s* Rom 10:21

STRETCHES
For he *s* out his hand Job 15:25

STRICKEN
of My people He was *s* Is 53:8

STRIFE
man stirs up *s* Prov 15:18
even from envy and *s* Phil 1:15
which come envy, *s* 1 Tim 6:4

STRIKE
The sun shall not *s* Ps 121:6
"*S* the Shepherd Zech 13:7
'I will *s* the Shepherd Matt 26:31

STRINGED
of your *s* instruments Amos 5:23

STRIP
S yourselves Is 32:11

STRIPES
s we are healed Is 53:5
s you were healed 1 Pet 2:24

STRIVE
"My Spirit shall not *s* Gen 6:3
"*S* to enter through Luke 13:24
the Lord not to *s* 2 Tim 2:14

STRIVING
for a man to stop *s* Prov 20:3

STROKE
with a mighty *s* Jer 14:17

STRONG
The LORD *s* and mighty Ps 24:8
S is Your hand Ps 89:13
"When a *s* man Luke 11:21
We then who are *s* Rom 15:1
weak, then I am *s* 2 Cor 12:10
my brethren, be *s* Eph 6:10
were made *s* Heb 11:34

STRONGHOLD
of my salvation, my *s* Ps 18:2

STRUCK
s the rock twice Num 20:11
the hand of God has *s* Job 19:21
Behold, He *s* the rock Ps 78:20
in My wrath I *s* Is 60:10
s the head from the Hab 3:13
took the reed and *s* Matt 27:30

STUBBLE
do wickedly will be *s* Mal 4:1

STUBBORN
"If a man has a *s* Deut 21:18

STUBBORN-HEARTED
"Listen to Me, you *s* Is 46:12

STUBBORNNESS
do not look on the *s* Deut 9:27

STUDIED
having never *s* John 7:15

STUMBLE
have caused many to *s* Mal 2:8
you will be made to *s* Matt 26:31
immediately they *s* Mark 4:17
who believe in Me to *s* Mark 9:42

For we all *s* in many James 3:2

STUMBLED
s that they should Rom 11:11

STUMBLES
immediately he *s* Matt 13:21

STUMBLING
the deaf, nor put a *s* Lev 19:14
But a stone of *s* Is 8:14
Behold, I will lay *s* Jer 6:21
I lay in Zion a *s* Rom 9:33
this, not to put a *s* Rom 14:13
of yours become a *s* 1 Cor 8:9
and "A stone of *s* 1 Pet 2:8
to keep you from *s* Jude 24

STUPID
hates correction is *s* Prov 12:1

SUBDUE
s all things to Phil 3:21

SUBJECT
for it is not *s* Rom 8:7
Let every soul be *s* Rom 13:1
all their lifetime *s* Heb 2:15

SUBJECTED
because of Him who *s* Rom 8:20

SUBJECTION
put all things in *s* Heb 2:8

SUBMISSION
his children in *s* 1 Tim 3:4

SUBMISSIVE
Yes, all of you be *s* 1 Pet 5:5

SUBMIT
Therefore *s* to God James 4:7
s yourselves to every 1 Pet 2:13

SUBSIDED
and the waters *s* Gen 8:1

SUBSTANCE
Bless his *s* Deut 33:11

SUCCESS
please give me *s* Gen 24:12
But wisdom brings *s* Eccl 10:10

SUCCESSFUL
Joseph, and he was a *s* Gen 39:2

SUDDENLY
s there was with the Luke 2:13

SUE
s you and take away Matt 5:40

SUFFER
for the Christ to *s* Luke 24:46
Christ, if indeed we *s* Rom 8:17
in Him, but also to *s* Phil 1:29

SUFFERED
s these things and to Luke 24:26
for whom I have *s* Phil 3:8
after you have *s* 1 Pet 5:10

SUFFERING
anyone among you *s* James 5:13

SUFFERINGS
I consider that the *s* Rom 8:18
perfect through *s* Heb 2:10

SUFFERS
Love *s* long and is 1 Cor 13:4

SUFFICIENCY
but our *s* is from God 2 Cor 3:5

SUFFICIENT
S for the day is Its Matt 6:34

SUM
How great is the *s* Ps 139:17

SUMMER
and heat, Winter and *s* Gen 8:22

SUMPTUOUSLY
fine linen and fared *s* Luke 16:19

SUN
So the *s* stood still Josh 10:13
s shall not strike you Ps 121:6
s returned ten degrees Is 38:8
The *s* and moon grow Joel 2:10
s shall go down on the Mic 3:6
for He makes His *s* Matt 5:45
the *s* was darkened Luke 23:45
do not let the *s* Eph 4:26
s became black as Rev 6:12
had no need of the *s* Rev 21:23

SUPPER
to eat the Lord's *S* 1 Cor 11:20
took the cup after *s* 1 Cor 11:25
together for the *s* Rev 19:17

SUPPLICATION
by prayer and *s* Phil 4:6

SUPPLIES
by what every joint *s* Eph 4:16

SUPPLY
And my God shall *s* Phil 4:19

SUPPORT
this, that you must *s* Acts 20:35

SUPREME
to the king as *s* 1 Pet 2:13

SURE
s your sin will find Num 32:23
call and elections 2 Pet 1:10

SURETY
Be *s* for Your servant Ps 119:122
Jesus has become a *s* Heb 7:22

SURROUND
LORD, mercy shall *s* Ps 32:10

SURROUNDED
also, since we are *s* Heb 12:1

SURVIVOR
was no refugee or *s* Lam 2:22

SUSPICIONS
reviling, evil *s* 1 Tim 6:4

SUSTAIN
S me with cakes of Song 2:5

SWADDLING
Him in *s* cloths Luke 2:7

SWALLOW
a gnat and *s* a camel Matt 23:24

SWEAR
'You shall not *s* Matt 5:33
began to curse and *s* Matt 26:74

SWEARING
By *s* and lying Hos 4:2

SWEARS
but whoever *s* by the Matt 23:18

SWEAT
His *s* became like Luke 22:44

SWEET
s are Your words Ps 119:103
but it will be as *s* Rev 10:9

SWEETNESS
mouth like honey in *s* Ezek 3:3

SWELLING
they speak great *s* 2 Pet 2:18

SWIFT
let every man be *s* James 1:19

SWIM
night I make my bed *s* Ps 6:6

SWOON
As they *s* like the Lam 2:12

SWORD
s which turned every Gen 3:24
The *s* of the LORD is Is 34:6
'A *s* is sharpened Ezek 21:9
Bow and *s* of battle I Hos 2:18
to bring peace but a *s* Matt 10:34
for all who take the *s* Matt 26:52
the *s* of the Spirit Eph 6:17
than any two-edged *s* Heb 4:12
mouth goes a sharp *s* Rev 19:15

SWORDS
shall beat their *s* Is 2:4

SWORE
So I *s* in My wrath Heb 3:11

SWORN
"By Myself I have *s* Gen 22:16
"The LORD has *s* Heb 7:21

SYMBOLIC
which things are *s* Gal 4:24

SYMPATHIZE
Priest who cannot *s* Heb 4:15

SYMPATHY
My *s* is stirred Hos 11:8

SYNAGOGUE
but are a *s* of Satan Rev 2:9

T

TABERNACLE
t He shall hide me Ps 27:5
I will abide in Your *t* Ps 61:4
And will rebuild the *t* Acts 15:16

t are my meditation Ps 119:99

TESTIMONY
two tablets of the *T* Ex 31:18
under your feet as a *t* Mark 6:11
no one receives His *t* John 3:32
not believed the *t* 1 John 5:10
For the *t* of Jesus is Rev 19:10

TESTING
came to Him, *t* Him Matt 19:3

TESTS
men, but God who *t* 1 Thess 2:4

THANK
"I *t* You, Father Matt 11:25
t You that I am not Luke 18:11

THANKFUL
as God, nor were *t* Rom 1:21

THANKFULNESS
Felix, with all *t* Acts 24:3

THANKS
the cup, and gave *t* Matt 26:27
T be to God for His 2 Cor 9:15

THANKSGIVING
His presence with *t* Ps 95:2
into His gates with *t* Ps 100:4
supplication. with *t* Phil 4:6

THEATER
and rushed into the *t* Acts 19:29

THIEF
do not despise a *t* Prov 6:30
because he was a *t* John 12:6
Lord will come as a *t* 2 Pet 3:10

THIEVES
And companions of *t* Is 1:23

THINGS
in heaven give good *t* Matt 7:11
kept all these *t* Luke 2:51
share in all good *t* Gal 6:6

THINK
t you have eternal John 5:39
not to *t* of himself Rom 12:3

THINKS
Yet the LORD *t* upon me Ps 40:17
For as he *t* in his Prov 23:7
t he stands take heed 1 Cor 10:12

THIRST
those who hunger and *t* Matt 5:6
in Me shall never *t* John 6:35
anymore nor *t* anymore Rev 7:16

THIRSTS
My soul *t* for God Ps 42:2
saying, "If anyone *t* John 7:37
freely to him who *t* Rev 21:6

THIRSTY
I was *t* and you gave Matt 25:35

THISTLES
or figs from *t* Matt 7:16

THORN
a *t* in the flesh was 2 Cor 12:7

THORNBUSHES
gather grapes from *t* Matt 7:16

THORNS
Both *t* and thistles it Gen 3:18
some fell among *t* Matt 13:7
wearing the crown of *t* John 19:5

THOUGHT
You understand my *t* Ps 139:2
I *t* as a child 1 Cor 13:11

THOUGHTS
The LORD knows the *t* Ps 94:11
unrighteous man his *t* Is 55:7
"For My *t* are not your Is 55:8
Jesus, knowing their *t* Matt 9:4
heart proceed evil *t* Matt 15:19
The LORD knows the *t* 1 Cor 3:20

THREAT
shall flee at the *t* Is 30:17

THREATEN
suffered, He did not *t* 1 Pet 2:23

THREATENING
to them, giving up *t* Eph 6:9

THREATS
still breathing *t* Acts 9:1

THREE
hope, love, these *t* 1 Cor 13:13

THRESH
It is time to *t* her Jer 51:33

THRESHING
t shall last till the Lev 26:5

THROAT
t is an open tomb Rom 3:13

THRONE
Your *t*, O God, is Ps 45:6
Lord sitting on a *t* Is 6:1
"Heaven is My *t* Is 66:1
for it is God's *t* Matt 5:34
will give Him the *t* Luke 1:32
"Your *t*, O God, is Heb 1:8
come boldly to the *t* Heb 4:16
My Father on His *t* Rev 3:21
I saw a great white *t* Rev 20:11

THRONES
invisible, whether *t* Col 1:16

THRONG
house of God in the *t* Ps 55:14

THROW
t Yourself down Matt 4:6

THROWN
neck, and he were *t* Mark 9:42

THRUST
and rose up and *t* Luke 4:29

THUNDER
The voice of Your *t* Ps 77:18
the voice of loud *t* Rev 14:2

THUNDERED
"The LORD *t* from 2 Sam 22:14

THUNDERINGS
the sound of mighty *t* Rev 19:6

THUNDERS
The God of glory *t* Ps 29:3

TIDINGS
I bring you good *t* Luke 2:10

TILL
no man to *t* the ground Gen 2:5

TILLER
but Cain was a *t* Gen 4:2

TILLS
t his land will have Prov 28:19

TIME
pray to You In a *t* Ps 32:6
for the *t* is near Rev 1:3

TIMES
the signs of the *t* Matt 16:3
not for you to know *t* Acts 1:7
last days perilous *t* 2 Tim 3:1

TITHE
And he gave him a *t* Gen 14:20
For you pay *t* of mint Matt 23:23

TITHES
and to bring the *t* Neh 10:37
Bring all the *t* Mal 3:10

TITHING
the year of *t* Deut 26:12

TITLE
Now Pilate wrote a *t* John 19:19

TITTLE
away, one jot or one *t* Matt 5:18

TODAY
T I have begotten You Ps 2:7
t you will be with Me Luke 23:43
"*T*, if you will hear Heb 3:7
the same yesterday, *t* Heb 13:8

TOIL
t you shall eat of Gen 3:17

TOILED
"Master, we have *t* Luke 5:5

TOLD
Behold I have *t* Matt 28:7
so, I would have *t* John 14:2

TOLERABLE
you, it will be more *t* Matt 10:15

TOMB
in the garden a new *t* John 19:41

TOMBS
like whitewashed *t* Matt 23:27

TOMORROW
drink, for *t* we die Is 22:13
do not worry about *t* Matt 6:34
what will happen *t* James 4:14

TONGUE
remember you, Let my *t* Ps 137:6
forever, But a lying *t* Prov 12:19
t breaks a bone Prov 25:15

t should confess that Phil 2:11
does not bridle his *t* James 1:26
no man can tame the *t* James 3:8
every nation, tribe, *t* Rev 14:6

TONGUES
From the strife of *t* Ps 31:20
speak with new *t* Mark 16:17
divided *t*, as of fire Acts 2:3
I speak with the *t* 1 Cor 13:1

TOOTH
eye for an eye and a *t* Matt 5:38

TOPHET
the high places of *T* Jer 7:31

TORCH
and like a fiery *t* Zech 12:6

TORCHES
When he had set the *t* Judg 15:5
come with flaming *t* Nah 2:3

TORMENT
You come here to *t* Matt 8:29
t ascends forever Rev 14:11

TORMENTED
And they will be *t* Rev 20:10

TORMENTS
"And being in *t* Luke 16:23

TORN
of the temple was *t* Matt 27:51

TORTURED
Others were *t* Heb 11:35

TOSSED
t to and fro and Eph 4:14

TOTTER
drunkard, And shall *t* Is 24:20

TOUCH
"If only I may *t* Matt 9:21

TOUCHED
t my mouth with it Is 6:7

TOUCHES
He *t* the hills Ps 104:32

TOWER
t whose top is in the Gen 11:4
a watchman in the *t* Is 21:5

TRACKED
t our steps So that we Lam 4:18

TRADERS
are princes, Whose *t* Is 23:8

TRADITION
transgress the *t* Matt 15:2
according to the *t* Col 2:8

TRAIN
T up a child in the Prov 22:6

TRAINED
those who have been *t* Heb 12:11

TRAINING
bring them up in the *t* Eph 6:4

TRAITOR
also became a *t* Luke 6:16

TRAITORS
t, headstrong 2 Tim 3:4

TRAMPLE
serpent you shall *t* Ps 91:13
swine, lest they *t* Matt 7:6

TRAMPLED
t the Son of God Heb 10:29
the winepress was *t* Rev 14:20

TRANCE
t I saw a vision Acts 11:5

TRANSFIGURED
and was *t* before them Matt 17:2

TRANSFORMED
this world, but be *t* Rom 12:2

TRANSGRESS
do Your disciples *t* Matt 15:2

TRANSGRESSED
"Yes, all Israel has *t* Dan 9:11
t your commandment Luke 15:29

TRANSGRESSES
Whoever *t* and does not 2 John 9

TRANSGRESSION
no law there is no *t* Rom 4:15
deceived, fell into *t* 1 Tim 2:14

TRANSGRESSIONS
mercies, Blot out my *t* Ps 51:1
For I acknowledge my *t* Ps 51:3
was wounded for our *t* Is 53:5
For the *t* of My people Is 53:8

TRANSGRESSOR
I make myself a *t* Gal 2:18

TRANSGRESSORS
Then I will teach *t* Ps 51:13
numbered with the *t* Is 53:12

TRAP
of Israel, As a *t* Is 8:14

TRAPS
for me, And from the *t* Ps 141:9

TRAVEL
You *t* land and sea Matt 23:15

TRAVELER
t who turns aside Jer 14:8

TRAVELING
lie waste, The *t* Is 33:8

TREACHEROUS
are insolent, *t* Zeph 3:4

TREACHEROUSLY
"This man dealt *t* Acts 7:19

TREAD
You shall *t* upon the Ps 91:13

TREADS
an ox while it *t* 1 Tim 5:18
t the winepress Rev 19:15

TREASURE
and you will have *t* Matt 19:21
he who lays up *t* Luke 12:21
But we have this *t* 2 Cor 4:7

TREASURED
t the words of His Job 23:12

TREASURER
Erastus, the *t* of the Rom 16:23

TREASURES
it more than hidden *t* Job 3:21
I will give you the *t* Is 45:3
for yourselves *t* Matt 6:19
are hidden all the *t* Col 2:3
riches than the *t* Heb 11:26

TREATY
Now Solomon made a *t* 1 Kin 3:1

TREE
you eaten from the *t* Gen 3:11
t Planted by the Ps 1:3
like a native green *t* Ps 37:35
t bears good fruit Matt 7:17
His own body on the *t* 1 Pet 2:24
the river, was the *t* Rev 22:2

TREES
late autumn *t* without Jude 12
the sea, or the *t* Rev 7:3

TREMBLE
That the nations may *t* Is 64:2
they shall fear and *t* Jer 33:9

TREMBLED
Then everyone who *t* Ezra 9:4
the earth shook and *t* Ps 18:7
and indeed they *t* Jer 4:24

TREMBLING
in fear, and in much *t* 1 Cor 2:3
t you received 2 Cor 7:15
flesh, with fear and *t* Eph 6:5

TRENCH
and he made a *t* 1 Kin 18:32

TRESPASSES
forgive men their *t* Matt 6:14
not imputing their *t* 2 Cor 5:19
who were dead in *t* Eph 2:1

TRIAL
concerning the fiery *t* 1 Pet 4:12

TRIBE
the Lion of the *t* Rev 5:5
blood Out of every *t* Rev 5:9

TRIBES
t which are scattered James 1:1

TRIBULATION
there will be great *t* Matt 24:21
world you will have *t* John 16:33
with her into great *t* Rev 2:22
out of the great *t* Rev 7:14

TRIBULATIONS
t enter the kingdom Acts 14:22
but we also glory in *t* Rom 5:3
t that you endure 2 Thess 1:4

TRIED
A *t* stone, a precious Is 28:16

TRIMMED
and *t* their lamps Matt 25:7

TRIUMPH
always leads us in *t* 2 Cor 2:14

TRIUMPHED
the LORD, For He has *t* Ex 15:1

TRODDEN
t the winepress alone Is 63:3

TROUBLE
few days and full of *t* Job 14:1
t He shall hide me Ps 27:5
not in *t* as other men Ps 73:5
will be with him in *t* Ps 91:15
Savior in time of *t* Jer 14:8
there are some who *t* Gal 1:7

TROUBLED
worried and *t* Luke 10:41
shaken in mind or *t* 2 Thess 2:2

TROUBLES
Out of all their *t* Ps 25:22
will be famines and *t* Mark 13:8
him out of all his *t* Acts 7:10

TROUBLING
wicked cease from *t* Job 3:17

TRUE
He who sent Me is *t* John 7:28
Indeed, let God be *t* Rom 3:4
whatever things are *t* Phil 4:8
Him who is *t* 1 John 5:20
for these words are *t* Rev 21:5

TRUMPET
deed, do not sound a *t* Matt 6:2
t makes an uncertain 1 Cor 14:8
For the *t* will sound 1 Cor 15:52

TRUST
T in the LORD Ps 37:3
T in the LORD with all Prov 3:5
Do not *t* in a friend Mic 7:5
who *t* in riches Mark 10:24

TRUSTED
"He *t* in the LORD Ps 22:8
"He *t* in God Matt 27:43

TRUSTS
But he who *t* in the Ps 32:10

TRUTH
led me in the way of *t* Gen 24:48
Behold, You desire *t* Ps 51:6
t shall be your shield Ps 91:4
And Your law is *t* Ps 119:142
t is fallen in the Is 59:14
called the City of *T* Zech 8:3
you shall know the *t* John 8:32
"I am the way, the *t* John 14:6
He, the Spirit of *t* John 16:13
to Him, "What is *t* John 18:38
who suppress the *t* Rom 1:18
but, speaking the *t* Eph 4:15
your waist with *t* Eph 6:14
I am speaking the *t* 1 Tim 2:7
they may know the *t* 2 Tim 2:25
the knowledge of the *t* 2 Tim 3:7
that we are of the *t* 1 John 3:19
the Spirit is *t* 1 John 5:6

TRY
which is to *t* you 1 Pet 4:12

TUMULT
Your enemies make a *t* Ps 83:2

TUNIC
Also he made him a *t* Gen 37:3

TUNICS
the LORD God made *t* Gen 3:21

TURBAN
"Remove the *t* Ezek 21:26

TURN
you shall not *t* Deut 17:11
"Repent, *t* away from Ezek 14:6
on your right cheek, *t* Matt 5:39
t them from darkness Acts 26:18

TURNED
The wicked shall be *t* Ps 9:17
of Israel, They have *t* Is 1:4
and how you *t* 1 Thess 1:9

TURNING
marvel that you are *t* Gal 1:6
or shadow of *t* James 1:17

TURNS
A soft answer *t* Prov 15:1
that he who *t* James 5:20

TURTLEDOVE
t Is heard in our land Song 2:12

TUTOR
the law was our *t* Gal 3:24

TWIST
unstable people *t* to 2 Pet 3:16

TWO
T are better than one Eccl 4:9
t shall become one Matt 19:5
new man from the *t* Eph 2:15

TYPE
of Adam, who is a *t* Rom 5:14

U

UNAFRAID
Do you want to be *u* Rom 13:3

UNBELIEF
because of their *u* Matt 13:58
help my *u* Mark 9:24
did it ignorantly in *u* 1 Tim 1:13
enter in because of *u* Heb 3:19

UNBELIEVERS
yoked together with *u* 2 Cor 6:14

UNBELIEVING
Do not be *u* John 20:27
u nothing is pure Titus 1:15
"But the cowardly, *u* Rev 21:8

UNCIRCUMCISED
not the physically *u* Rom 2:27

UNCLEAN
I am a man of *u* lips Is 6:5
man common or *u* Acts 10:28
there is nothing *u* Rom 14:14
that no fornicator, *u* Eph 5:5

UNCLEANNESS
men's bones and all *u* Matt 23:27
flesh in the lust of *u* 2 Pet 2:10

UNCLOTHED
we want tobe*u* 2Cor5:4

UNCOVERS
u deep things out of Job 12:22

UNDEFILED
incorruptible and *u* 1 Pet 1:4

UNDERMINE
And you *u* your friend Job 6:27

UNDERSTAND
if there are any who *u* Ps 14:2
hearing, but do not *u* Is 6:9
"Why do you not *u* John 8:43
lest they should *u* Acts 28:27
some things hard to *u* 2 Pet 3:16

UNDERSTANDING
His *u* is infinite Ps 147:5
lean not on your own *u* Prov 3:5
u will find good Prov 19:8
His *u* is unsearchable Is 40:28
also still without *u* Matt 15:16
also pray with the *u* 1 Cor 14:15
the Lord give you *u* 2 Tim 2:7
Who is wise and *u* James 3:13

UNDERSTANDS
There is none who *u* Rom 3:11

UNDERSTOOD
Then I *u* their end Ps 73:17
clearly seen, being *u* Rom 1:20

UNDESIRABLE
gather together, O *u* Zeph 2:1

UNDIGNIFIED
I will be even more *u* 2 Sam 6:22

UNDISCERNING
u, untrustworthy Rom 1:31

UNDONE
"Woe is me, for I am *u* Is 6:5

UNEDUCATED
that they were *u* Acts 4:13

UNFAITHFUL
way of the *u* is hard Prov 13:15

UNFAITHFULLY
back and acted *u* Ps 78:57

UNFORGIVING
unloving, *u* Rom 1:31

UNFORMED
substance, being yet *u* Ps 139:16

UNFRUITFUL
and it becomes *u* Mark 4:19

UNGODLINESS
heaven against all *u* Rom 1:18

UNGODLY
u shall not stand Ps 1:5
Christ died for the *u* Rom 5:6

UNHOLY
the holy and *u* Ezek 22:26

UNINFORMED
the place of the *u* 1 Cor 14:16

UNINTENTIONALLY
kills his neighbor *u* Deut 4:42

UNITE
U my heart to fear Ps 86:11

UNITY
to dwell together in *u* Ps 133:1
to keep the *u* of the Eph 4:3

UNJUST
commended the *u* Luke 16:8
of the just and the *u* Acts 24:15
For God is not *u* Heb 6:10

UNJUSTLY
long will you judge *u* Ps 82:2

UNKNOWN
To The *U* God Acts 17:23

UNLEAVENED
the Feast of *U* Bread Ex 12:17

UNLOVING
untrustworthy, *u* Rom 1:31

UNMERCIFUL
unforgiving, *u* Rom 1:31

UNPREPARED
with me and find you *u* 2 Cor 9:4

UNPRESENTABLE
u parts have greater 1 Cor 12:23

UNPROFITABLE
'We are *u* servants Luke 17:10
for that would be *u* Heb 13:17

UNPUNISHED
wicked will not go *u* Prov 11:21

UNQUENCHABLE
up the chaff with *u* Matt 3:12

UNRESTRAINED
that the people were *u* Ex 32:25

UNRIGHTEOUS
u man his thoughts Is 55:7
u will not inherit the 1 Cor 6:9

UNRIGHTEOUSNESS
all ungodliness and *u* Rom 1:18
cleanse us from all *u* 1 John 1:9
All *u* is sin 1 John 5:17

UNRULY
those who are *u* 1 Thess 5:14

UNSEARCHABLE
u are His judgments Rom 11:33

UNSKILLED
only of milk is *u* Heb 5:13

UNSPOTTED
to keep oneself *u* James 1:27

UNSTABLE
U as water Gen 49:4

UNSTOPPED
of the deaf shall be *u* Is 35:5

UNTAUGHT
which *u* and unstable 2 Pet 3:16

UNTRUSTWORTHY
undiscerning, *u* Rom 1:31

UNWASHED
eat bread with *u* hands Mark 7:5

UNWISE
Therefore do not be *u* Eph 5:17

UNWORTHY
u manner will be 1 Cor 11:27

UPHOLD
U me according to Ps 119:116

UPHOLDING
u all things by the Heb 1:3

UPHOLDS
LORD *u* all who fall Ps 145:14

UPPER
show you a large *u* Mark 14:15

UPRIGHT
u is His delight Prov 15:8

UPRIGHTNESS
princes for their *u* Prov 17:26

UPROOT
u the wheat with Matt 13:29

URIM
Thummim and Your *U* Deut 33:8

US
"God with *u* Matt 1:23
If God is for *u* Rom 8:31
of them were of *u* 1 John 2:19

USE
who spitefully *u* you Matt 5:44
u liberty as an Gal 5:13

USELESS
one's religion is *u* James 1:26

USES
if one *u* it lawfully 1 Tim 1:8

USING
u liberty as a 1 Pet 2:16

USURY
'Take no *u* or Lev 25:36

UTTER
u dark sayings of old Ps 78:2

UTTERANCE
the Spirit gave them *u* Acts 2:4

UTTERED
which cannot be *u* Rom 8:26

UTTERMOST
u those who come Heb 7:25

UTTERS
Day unto day *u* speech Ps 19:2

V

VAGABOND
v you shall be on the Gen 4:12

VAIN
the people plot a *v* Ps 2:1
you believed in *v* 1 Cor 15:2

VALIANT
They are not *v* for the Jer 9:3

VALIANTLY
God we will do *v* Ps 60:12

VALLEY
v shall be exalted Is 40:4

VALOR
a mighty man of *v* 1 Sam 16:18

VALUE
of more *v* than they Matt 6:26

VALUED
It cannot be *v* in the Job 28:16

VANISH
knowledge, it will *v* 1 Cor 13:8

VANISHED
and He *v* from their Luke 24:31

VANITY
of vanities, all is *v* Eccl 1:2

VAPOR
best state is but *v* Ps 39:5
It is even a *v* that James 4:14

VARIATION
whom there is no *v* James 1:17

VEGETABLES
and let them give us *v* Dan 1:12
is weak eats only *v* Rom 14:2

VEHEMENT
of fire, A most *v* Song 8:6

VEIL
v of the temple was Matt 27:51
Presence behind the *v* Heb 6:19

VENGEANCE
V is Mine Deut 32:35

VENOM
It becomes cobra *v* Job 20:14

VESSEL
like a potter's *v* Ps 2:9
for he is a chosen *v* Acts 9:15

VESSELS
treasure in earthen *v* 2 Cor 4:7

VEXED
grieved, and I was *v* Ps 73:21

VICE
as a cloak for *v* 1 Pet 2:16

VICTIM
And plucked the *v* Job 29:17

VICTORY
v that has overcome 1 John 5:4

VIEW
"Go, *v* the land Josh 2:1

VIGILANT
Be sober, be *v* 1 Pet 5:8

VIGOR
nor his natural *v* Deut 34:7

VILE
them up to *v* passions Rom 1:26

VINDICATED
know that I shall be *v* Job 13:18

VINDICATION
Let my *v* come from Ps 17:2

VINE
"I am the true *v* John 15:1

VINEDRESSER
and My Father is the *v* John 15:1

VINEGAR
As *v* to the teeth and Prov 10:26

VINES
foxes that spoil the *v* Song 2:15

VINEYARD
Who plants a *v* and 1 Cor 9:7

VIOLENCE
was filled with *v* Gen 6:11
of heaven suffers *v* Matt 11:12

VIOLENT
haters of God, *v* Rom 1:30

VIPER
And stings like a *v* Prov 23:32

VIPERS
to them, "Brood of *v* Matt 3:7

VIRGIN
v shall conceive Is 7:14
"Behold, the *v* shall Matt 1:23

VIRGINS
v who took their lamps Matt 25:1

VIRTUE
to your faith *v* 2 Pet 1:5

VISAGE
v was marred more than Is 52:14

VISIBLE
that are on earth, *v* Col 1:16

VISION
in a trance I saw a *v* Acts 11:5
to the heavenly *v* Acts 26:19

VISIONS
young men shall see *v* Joel 2:28

VISIT
v orphans and James 1:27

VISITATION
God in the day of *v* 1 Pet 2:12

VISITED
Israel, for He has *v* Luke 1:68

VISITING
v the iniquity of the Ex 20:5

VISITOR
am a foreigner and a *v* Gen 23:4

VITALITY
v was turned into the Ps 32:4

VOICE
fire a still small *v* 1 Kin 19:12
if you will hear His *v* Ps 95:7
"The *v* of one crying Matt 3:3
And suddenly a *v* Matt 3:17
for they know his *v* John 10:4
the truth hears My *v* John 18:37
If anyone hears My *v* Rev 3:20

VOICES
And there were loud *v* Rev 11:15

VOID
they are a nation *v* Deut 32:28
heirs, faith is made *v* Rom 4:14

VOLUME
In the *v* of the book Heb 10:7

VOLUNTEERS
Your people shall be *v* Ps 110:3

VOMIT
returns to his own *v* 2 Pet 2:22

VOW
for he had taken a *v* Acts 18:18

VOWS
to reconsider his *v* Prov 20:25

W

WAGE
w the good warfare 1 Tim 1:18

WAGES
For the *w* of sin is Rom 6:23
Indeed the *w* of the James 5:4

WAIL
"Son of man, *w* Ezek 32:18

WAILING
There will be *w* Matt 13:42

WAIT
w patiently for Him Ps 37:7
those who *w* on the Is 40:31
To those who eagerly *w* Heb 9:28

WAITED
w patiently for the Ps 40:1
Divine longsuffering *w* 1 Pet 3:20

WAITING
ourselves, eagerly *w* Rom 8:23
from that time *w* Heb 10:13

WAITS
the creation eagerly *w* Rom 8:19

WAKE
that whether we *w* 1 Thess 5:10

WALK
w before Me and be Gen 17:1
Yea, though I *w* Ps 23:4
W prudently when you Eccl 5:1
"This is the way, *w* Is 30:21
be weary, they shall *w* Is 40:31
w humbly with your God Mic 6:8
W while you have the John 12:35
so we also should *w* Rom 6:4
For we *w* by faith 2 Cor 5:7
W in the Spirit Gal 5:16
And *w* in love Eph 5:2
that you may *w* worthy Col 1:10
and they shall *w* Rev 3:4

WALKED
Methuselah, Enoch *w* Gen 5:22
The people who *w* Is 9:2
in which you once *w* Eph 2:2

WALKING
not *w* in craftiness 2 Cor 4:2

WALKS
the LORD your God *w* Deut 23:14
is the man Who *w* Ps 1:1
he who *w* in darkness John 12:35
adversary the devil *w* 1 Pet 5:8

WALL
then the *w* of the city Josh 6:5
you whitewashed *w* Acts 23:3
a window in the *w* 2 Cor 11:33
Now the *w* of the city Rev 21:14

WALLS
By faith the *w* of Heb 11:30

WANDER
they have loved to *w* Jer 14:10

WANDERED
They *w* in deserts and Heb 11:38

WANDERERS
And they shall be *w* Hos 9:17

WANDERING
w stars for whom is Jude 13

WANDERS
among you *w* James 5:19

WANT
I shall not *w* Ps 23:1

WANTING
balances, and found *w* Dan 5:27

WANTON
have begun to grow *w* 1 Tim 5:11

WAR
"There is a noise of *w* Ex 32:17
w may rise against Ps 27:3
shall they learn *w* Is 2:4
going to make *w* Luke 14:31
You fight and *w* James 4:2
fleshly lusts which *w* 1 Pet 2:11
judges and makes *w* Rev 19:11

WARFARE
to her, That her *w* Is 40:2
w entangles 2 Tim 2:4

WARMED
in peace, be *w* James 2:16

WARMING
she saw Peter *w* Mark 14:67

WARMS
w them in the dust Job 39:14

WARN
w those who are 1 Thess 5:14

WARNED
Then, being divinely *w* Matt 2:12
Who *w* you to flee Matt 3:7

WARNING
w every man and Col 1:28

WARPED
such a person is *w* Titus 3:11

WARRING
w against the law of Rom 7:23

WARRIOR
He runs at me like a *w* Job 16:14

WARS
you will hear of *w* Matt 24:6
Where do *w* and fights James 4:1

WASH
w myself with snow Job 9:30
W me thoroughly Ps 51:2
w His feet with her Luke 7:38
said to him, "Go, *w* John 9:7
w the disciples' John 13:5
w away your sins Acts 22:16

WASHED
w his hands before Matt 27:24
But you were *w* 1 Cor 6:11
Him who loved us and *w* Rev 1:5

WASHING
us, through the *w* Titus 3:5

WASHINGS
and drinks, various *w* Heb 9:10

WASTE
the cities are laid *w* Is 6:11
"Why this *w* Matt 26:8

WASTED
this fragrant oil *w* Mark 14:4

WASTELAND
w shall be glad Is 35:1

WASTING
that this man was *w* Luke 16:1

WATCH
is past, And like a *w* Ps 90:4
" *W* therefore Matt 24:42

WATCHED
he would have *w* Matt 24:43

WATCHES
Blessed is he who *w* Rev 16:15

WATCHFUL
But you be *w* in all 2 Tim 4:5

WATCHING
he comes, will find *w* Luke 12:37

WATCHMAN
I have made you a *w* Ezek 3:17

WATCHMEN
I have set *w* on your Is 62:6

WATER
Eden to *w* the garden Gen 2:10
I am poured out like *w* Ps 22:14
For I will pour *w* Is 44:3
given you living *w* John 4:10
rivers of living *w* John 7:38
can yield both salt *w* James 3:12
the Spirit, the *w* 1 John 5:8
are clouds without *w* Jude 12
let him take the *w* Rev 22:17

WATERED
I planted, Apollos *w* 1 Cor 3:6

WATERS
me beside the still *w* Ps 23:2
Though its *w* roar and Ps 46:3
your bread upon the *w* Eccl 11:1
thirsts, Come to the *w* Is 55:1
fountain of living *w* Jer 2:13
living fountains of *w* Rev 7:17

WAVE
Its fruit shall *w* Ps 72:16

WAVER
He did not *w* at the Rom 4:20

WAVERING
of our hope without *w* Heb 10:23

WAVES
sea, tossed by the *w* Matt 14:24

WAX
My heart is like *w* Ps 22:14

WAY
As for God, His *w* 2 Sam 22:31
the LORD knows the *w* Ps 1:6
Teach me Your *w* Ps 27:11
in the *w* everlasting Ps 139:24
w that seems right Prov 14:12
The *w* of the just is Is 26:7
wicked forsake his *w* Is 55:7
And pervert the *w* Amos 2:7
he will prepare the *w* Mal 3:1
and broad is the *w* Matt 7:13
will prepare Your *w* Matt 11:10
to him, "I am the *w* John 14:6
to him the *w* Acts 18:26
to have known the *w* 2 Pet 2:21

WAYS
For all His *w* are Deut 32:4
transgressors Your *w* Ps 51:13
w please the LORD Prov 16:7
"Stand in the *w* Jer 6:16
and owns all your *w* Dan 5:23
w are everlasting Hab 3:6
unstable in all his *w* James 1:8
and true are Your *w* Rev 15:3

WEAK
gives power to the *w* Is 40:29
knee will be as *w* Ezek 7:17
but the flesh is *w* Matt 26:41
Receive one who is *w* Rom 14:1
God has chosen the *w* 1 Cor 1:27
We are *w* 1 Cor 4:10
w I became as *w* 1 Cor 9:22
For when I am *w* 2 Cor 12:10

WEAKENED
w my strength in the Ps 102:23

WEAKENS
w the hands of the men Jer 38:4

WEAKER
the wife, as to the *w* 1 Pet 3:7

WEAKNESS
w were made strong Heb 11:34

WEAKNESSES
also helps in our *w* Rom 8:26

WEALTH
W gained by Prov 13:11

WEALTHY
rich, have become *w* Rev 3:17

WEANED
w child shall put his Is 11:8

WEAPON
w formed against you Is 54:17

WEAPONS
For the *w* of our 2 Cor 10:4

WEAR
'What shall we *w* Matt 6:31

WEARIED
You have *w* Me with Is 43:24
therefore, being *w* John 4:6

WEARINESS
say, 'Oh, what a *w* Mal 1:13

WEARISOME
and much study is *w* Eccl 12:12

WEARY
shall run and not be *w* Is 40:31
And let us not grow *w* Gal 6:9
do not grow *w* in 2 Thess 3:13

WEATHER
'It will be fair *w* Matt 16:2

WEDDING
day there was a *w* John 2:1

WEEK
the first day of the *w* Matt 28:1

WEEKS
w are determined Dan 9:24

WEEP
A time to *w* Eccl 3:4
You shall *w* no more Is 30:19
are you who *w* Luke 6:21
do not *w* Luke 23:28
w with those who *w* Rom 12:15

WEEPING
the noise of the *w* Ezra 3:13
They shall come with *w* Jer 31:9
There will be *w* Matt 8:12
by the tomb *w* John 20:11

WEIGH
O Most Upright, You *w* Is 26:7

WEIGHED
You have been *w* Dan 5:27

WEIGHS
eyes, But the LORD *w* Prov 16:2

WEIGHT
us lay aside every *w* Heb 12:1

WEIGHTIER
have neglected the *w* Matt 23:23

WELFARE
does not seek the *w* Jer 38:4

WELL
have done *w* Prov 31:29
wheel broken at the *w* Eccl 12:6
"Those who are *w* Matt 9:12
said to him, '*W* done Matt 25:21

WELLS
These are *w* without 2 Pet 2:17

WENT
They *w* out from us 1 John 2:19

WEPT
out and *w* bitterly Matt 26:75
saw the city and *w* Luke 19:41
Jesus *w* John 11:35

WET
his body was *w* with Dan 4:33

WHEAT
w falls into the John 12:24

WHEEL
in the middle of a *w* Ezek 1:16

WHEELS
noise of rattling *w* Nah 3:2

WHERE
not knowing *w* he was Heb 11:8

WHIP
A *w* for the horse Prov 26:3

WHIRLWIND
Job out of the *w* Job 38:1
has His way in the *w* Nah 1:3

WHISPER
my ear received a *w* Job 4:12

WHISPERER
w separates the best Prov 16:28

WHISPERERS
they are *w* Rom 1:29

WHISPERINGS
backbitings, *w* 2 Cor 12:20

WHITE
clothed in *w* garments Rev 3:5
behold, a *w* horse Rev 6:2
and made them *w* Rev 7:14

WHOLE
w body were an eye 1 Cor 12:17

WHOLESOME
not consent to *w* words 1 Tim 6:3

WHOLLY
w followed the LORD Deut 1:36

WICKED
w shall be silent 1 Sam 2:9
w shall be no more Ps 37:10
if there is any *w* Ps 139:24
w forsake his way Is 55:7
And desperately *w* Jer 17:9
the sway of the *w* 1 John 5:19

WICKEDLY
God will never do *w* Job 34:12

WICKEDNESS
LORD saw that the *w* Gen 6:5
in the tents of *w* Ps 84:10
man repented of his *w* Jer 8:6
is full of greed and *w* Luke 11:39
sexual immorality, *w* Rom 1:29
and overflow of *w* James 1:21

WIDE
open your hand *w* Deut 15:8
w is the gate and Matt 7:13
to you, our heart is *w* 2 Cor 6:11

WIDOW
the fatherless and *w* Ps 146:9
How like a *w* is she Lam 1:1
Then one poor *w* Mark 12:42
w has children or 1 Tim 5:4

WIDOW'S
And I caused the *w* Job 29:13

WIDOWS
w were neglected Acts 6:1
visit orphans and *w* James 1:27

WIFE
and be joined to his *w* Gen 2:24
w finds a good thing Prov 18:22
But a prudent *w* Prov 19:14
"Go, take yourself a *w* Hos 1:2
divorces his *w* Mark 10:11
'I have married a *w* Luke 14:20
"Remember Lot's *w* Luke 17:32
so love his own *w* Eph 5:33
the husband of one *w* Titus 1:6
bride, the Lamb's *w* Rev 21:9

WILD
olive tree which is *w* Rom 11:24

WILDERNESS
I will make the *w* Is 41:18
of one crying in the *w* Matt 3:3
the serpent in the *w* John 3:14

WILES
to stand against the *w* Eph 6:11

WILL
w be done On earth as Matt 6:10
but he who does the *w* Matt 7:21
not My *w* Luke 22:42
flesh, nor of the *w* John 1:13
not to do My own *w* John 6:38
w is present with me Rom 7:18
and perfect *w* of God Rom 12:2
works in you both to *w* Phil 2:13
according to His own *w* Heb 2:4
work to do His *w* Heb 13:21

WILLFULLY
For if we sin *w* Heb 10:26
For this they *w* 2 Pet 3:5

WILLING
If you are *w* and Is 1:19
The spirit indeed is *w* Matt 26:41
w that any should 2 Pet 3:9

WILLINGLY
by compulsion but *w* 1 Pet 5:2

WILLOWS
our harps Upon the *w* Ps 137:2

WILLS
to whom the Son *w* Matt 11:27
it is not of him who *w* Rom 9:16
say, "If the Lord *w* James 4:15

WIN
to all, that I might *w* 1 Cor 9:19

WIND
the chaff which the *w* Ps 1:4
reed shaken by the *w* Matt 11:7
"The *w* blows where John 3:8
of a rushing mighty *w* Acts 2:2

WINDOWS
not open for you the *w* Mal 3:10

WINDS
be, that even the *w* Matt 8:27

WINDSTORM
And a great *w* arose Mark 4:37

WINE
W is a mocker Prov 20:1
love is better than *w* Song 1:2
Yes, come, buy *w* Is 55:1
they gave Him sour *w* Matt 27:34
do not be drunk with *w* Eph 5:18
not given to much *w* Titus 2:3

WINEBIBBERS
Do not mix with *w* Prov 23:20

WINEPRESS
"I have trodden the *w* Is 63:3
into the great *w* Rev 14:19
Himself treads the *w* Rev 19:15

WINESKINS
new wine into old *w* Matt 9:17

WING
One *w* of the cherub 1 Kin 6:24

WINGS
the shadow of Your *w* Ps 36:7
With healing in His *w* Mal 4:2

WINNOW
You shall *w* them Is 41:16

WINS
w souls is wise Prov 11:30

WINTER
For lo, the *w* is past Song 2:11
flight may not be in *w* Matt 24:20

WIPE
w away every tear Rev 21:4

WORLD
"The field is the *w* Matt 13:38
He was in the *w* John 1:10
God so loved the *w* John 3:16
His Son into the *w* John 3:17
w cannot hate you John 7:7
You are of this *w* John 8:23
overcome the *w* John 16:33
w may become guilty Rom 3:19
be conformed to this *w* Rom 12:2
loved this present *w* 2 Tim 4:10
Do not love the *w* 1 John 2:15
w is passing away 1 John 2:17

WORLDS
also He made the *w* Heb 1:2

WORM
But I am a *w* Ps 22:6
w does not die Mark 9:44

WORMS
he was eaten by *w* Acts 12:23

WORMWOOD
of the star is *W* Rev 8:11

WORRY
to you, do not *w* Matt 6:25

WORRYING
w can add one Matt 6:27

WORSE
w than their fathers Jer 7:26

WORSHIP
come to *w* Him Matt 2:2
w what you do not John 4:22
the angels of God *w* Heb 1:6

WORSHIPED
on their faces and *w* Rev 11:16

WORSHIPER
if anyone is a *w* John 9:31

WORTH
make my speech *w* Job 24:25

WORTHLESS
Indeed they are all *w* Is 41:29

WORTHLESSNESS
long will you love *w* Ps 4:2

WORTHY
present time are not *w* Rom 8:18
to walk *w* Eph 4:1
the world was not *w* Heb 11:38
"*W* is the Lamb who Rev 5:12

WOUND
And my *w* incurable Jer 15:18
and his deadly *w* Rev 13:3

WOUNDED
But He was *w* for our Is 53:5

WOUNDING
killed a man for *w* Gen 4:23

WOUNDS
Faithful are the *w* Prov 27:6

WRANGLINGS
useless *w* of men of 1 Tim 6:5

WRATH
speak to them in His *w* Ps 2:5
Surely the *w* of man Ps 76:10
So I swore in My *w* Ps 95:11
W is cruel and anger a Prov 27:4
in My *w* I struck you Is 60:10
w remember mercy Hab 3:2
For the *w* of God is Rom 1:18
up for yourself *w* Rom 2:5
nature children of *w* Eph 2:3
sun go down on your *w* Eph 4:26
Let all bitterness, *w* Eph 4:31
holy hands, without *w* 1 Tim 2:8
So I swore in My *w* Heb 3:11
not fearing the *w* Heb 11:27
for the *w* of man James 1:20
of the wine of the *w* Rev 14:8
for in them the *w* Rev 15:1
fierceness of His *w* Rev 16:19

WRATHFUL
w man stirs up strife Prov 15:18

WRESTLE
For we do not *w* Eph 6:12

WRETCHED
w man that I am Rom 7:24
know that you are *w* Rev 3:17

WRETCHEDNESS
let me see my *w* Num 11:15

WRINGING
w the nose produces Prov 3 0:3 3

WRINKLE
not having spot or *w* Eph 5:27

WRITE
w them on their hearts Heb 8:10

WRITING
the *w* was the *w* Ex 32:16

WRITINGS
do not believe his *w* John 5:47

WRITTEN
tablets of stone, *w* Ex 31:18
your names are *w* Luke 10:20
"What I have *w* John 19:22

WRONG
done nothing *w* Luke 23:41
But he who does *w* Col 3:25

WRONGED
We have *w* no one 2 Cor 7:2

WRONGS
me *w* his own soul Prov 8:36

WROTE
stooped down and *w* John 8:6

WROUGHT
And skillfully *w* Ps 139:15

Y

YEAR
the acceptable *y* Is 61:2
of sins every *y* Heb 10:3

YEARS
and for days and *y* Gen 1:14
lives are seventy *y* Ps 90:10
when He was twelve *y* Luke 2:42
with Him a thousand *y* Rev 20:6

YES
let your *Y* be 'Y,' Matt 5:37

YESTERDAY
For we were born *y* Job 8:9

YOKE
"Take My *y* upon you Matt 11:29

YOKED
Do not be unequally *y* 2 Cor 6:14

YOUNG
I have been *y* Ps 37:25
she may lay her *y* Ps 84:3
I write to you, *y* 1 John 2:13

YOUNGER
Likewise you *y* people 1 Pet 5:5

YOURS
the battle is not *y* 2 Chr 20:15
Y is the kingdom Matt 6:13
all Mine are *Y* John 17:10
for I do not seek *y* 2 Cor 12:14

YOUTH
the sins of my *y* Ps 25:7
and *y* are vanity Eccl 11:10
I have kept from my *y* Matt 19:20

YOUTHFUL
Flee also *y* lusts 2 Tim 2:22

YOUTHS
y shall faint and be Is 40:30

Z

ZEAL
The *z* of the LORD of 2 Kin 19:31
"*Z* for Your house has John 2:17
that they have a *z* Rom 10:2

ZEALOUS
z for good works Titus 2:14